DISSOCIATION AND THE DISSOCIATIVE DISORDERS

DISSOCIATION AND THE DISSOCIATIVE DISORDERS

DSM-V AND BEYOND

EDITED BY
Paul F. Dell, PhD
John A. O'Neil, MD, FRCPC

Routledge
Taylor & Francis Group
270 Madison Avenue
New York, NY 10016

Routledge
Taylor & Francis Group
2 Park Square
Milton Park, Abingdon
Oxon OX14 4RN

Routledge is an imprint of Taylor & Francis Group, an Informa business

Printed in the United States of America on acid-free paper
10 9 8 7 6 5 4 3 2

International Standard Book Number-13: 978-0-415-95785-4 (Hardcover)

Library of Congress Cataloging-in-Publication Data

Dissociation and the dissociative disorders : DSM-V and beyond / Paul F. Dell, John A. O'Neil, editors.
p. ; cm.
Includes bibliographical references and index.
ISBN 978-0-415-95785-4 (hardbound : alk. paper)
1. Dissociative disorders. I. Dell, Paul F. II. O'Neil, John A.
[DNLM: 1. Dissociative Disorders. WM 173.6 D6108 2009]

RC553.D5D54 2009
616.85'23--dc22 2008038704

Visit the Taylor & Francis Web site at
http://www.taylorandfrancis.com

and the Routledge Web site at
http://www.routledge.com

To our wives, Sue & Su

Paul: Sue Crommelin has been my soul mate for three decades. We met in the family therapy world, and then each of us followed our own diverging, but intertwined, paths. Sue became a Jungian analyst, then a spiritual director, and is now an Episcopal priest. I directed a family therapy training institute, obtained a live consultation from Salvador Minuchin for a difficult marital therapy case, and watched the therapy explode into an overt case of MPD. That event sent me down the long road of trauma, dissociation, and eventually this book. Sue was initially attracted to me, in part, because I was a creative theorist and writer. Since then, she has discovered that writing and the creative process all too often produces a cranky spouse. I am deeply grateful for her generosity of spirit which has so steadily nourished and supported me, my work, and our marriage.

John: Su Baker has accompanied me though philosophy, high school teaching, medical school, psychiatry residency, psychoanalytic training, child rearing, and my earlier years as a staffperson, and then presented me with her first case of Dissociative Identity Disorder, after which nothing was quite the same. Our professional lives became closer as we found ourselves working increasingly with similar patients, undertaking hypnosis and EMDR training together, and teaching together in various contexts. I look forward to our sharing many more adventures in the decades to come.

Contents

PART III Normal and Exceptional Dissociation

PART IV Acute Dissociation

PART V Chronic Dissociation

PART VI Neurobiology of Dissociation

PART VII The DSM-IV Dissociative Disorders

PART VIII Dissociation in Posttraumatic Stress Disorder

Contributors

NB:	The principal professional organization devoted to dissociation has had the following names:
1983–93:	ISSMP&D International Society for the Study of Multiple Personality and Dissociation
1994–2005	ISSD International Society for the Study of Dissociation
2006–ongoing:	ISSTD International Society for the Study of Trauma & Dissociation

M. Rose Barlow, PhD
Assistant professor, Boise State University, Idaho. Dr. Barlow publishes in the areas of trauma and dissociation, with a special interest in memory functioning, integration, and the switch process.

Donald B. Beere, PhD
Professor Emeritus clinical psychology, Central Michigan University. Formerly with a part-time practice and concurrent full-time academic post as Director of Clinical Training, APA-accredited doctoral program. Has taught and trained students to research, assess, and treat trauma and dissociation for many years.

Ilaria Bianchi, PhD
Psychologist, PhD in developmental psychology from the Università Cattolica di Milano, Milan, Italy. Former International Research Scholar at Harvard Medical School. Research interests include the effect of the quality of mother-infant interactions on cognitive development.

Ruth A. Blizard, PhD
Psychologist in private practice in Boulder, Colorado. Vice President, Rocky Mountain Trauma and Dissociation Society. Past editor, *ISSTD News*. Presentations and published articles integrate psychoanalytic concepts, attachment theory, and trauma in the genesis and treatment of borderline personality, dissociation, and psychosis.

Robyn L. Bluhm, MA
Assistant professor, Department of Philosophy and Religious Studies, Old Dominion University, Norfolk, Virginia.

Stephen E. Braude, PhD
Professor and former chair of philosophy, University of Maryland Baltimore County. Recipient of numerous research grants, including a fellowship from the National Endowment for the Humanities, and author of *First Person Plural: Multiple Personality and the Philosophy of Mind*.

J. Douglas Bremner, MD
Professor of psychiatry and radiology, Emory University School of Medicine; Director of Mental Health Research, Atlanta VAMC. Performed the first neuroimaging studies in PTSD and DID measuring hippocampal volume, and mapped neural correlates of depression and PTSD using positron emission tomography.

Philip M. Bromberg, PhD
Training and Supervising Analyst, William Alanson White Institute; clinical professor of psychology, New York University Postdoctoral Program in Psychotherapy and Psychoanalysis. Editorial Board member, *Contemporary Psychoanalysis*, *Psychoanalytic Dialogues*, *Psychoanalytic Inquiry*, and *Journal of the American Academy of Psychoanalysis*. Author of *Standing in the Spaces: Essays on Clinical Process, Trauma, and Dissociation* (1998), and of *Awakening the Dreamer: Clinical Journeys* (2006).

Laura S. Brown
Psychologist, Fremont Community Therapy Project. Professor of psychology, Washington School of Professional Psychology, Argosy University, Seattle, Washington. Private practice of feminist psychotherapy, forensic psychology, and consultation. Extensive publication on feminist theory and practice, feminist forensic practice, ethics and boundary issues, psychotherapy with lesbians, trauma, and memory of abuse.

Richard A. Bryant, PhD
Scientia Professor of Psychology, School of Psychology, University of New South Wales; Director of the Traumatic Stress Clinic at Westmead Hospital, Sydney, Australia. His major interest is evaluating the nature of early psychological responses to trauma and evaluating early intervention programs for survivors of trauma.

Lisa D. Butler, PhD
Senior Research Scholar, Department of Psychiatry and Behavioral Sciences, Stanford University School of Medicine, Stanford, California. Her research examines traumatic experience, resilience, and thriving across a variety of populations, pathological and normative dissociation, affective and cognitive determinants of paranoia, and psychosocial interventions that include hypnosis.

Etzel Cardeña, PhD
Thorsen Professor of Psychology, Lund University, Sweden. Member of the DSM-IV Dissociative Disorders Task-Force; recipient of various awards from the ISSTD and Division 30 of the American Psychological Association (APA), among others.

Elizabeth A. Carlson, PhD
Researcher, instructor, and Codirector of the Infant and Early Childhood Mental Health Program, Institute of Child Development, University of Minnesota. Training, research, and clinical work relate to attachment relationships, early experience, and the development of psychopathology.

Eve Carlson, PhD
Clinical psychologist and a Research Health Science Specialist with the National Center for PTSD and the VA Palo Alto Health Care System, Department of Veterans Affairs. She conducts research on traumatic stress, focusing on measurement development, assessment methods, and the processes involved in the development of PTSD.

Constance J. Dalenberg, PhD
Professor, California School of Professional Psychology and Trauma Research Institute, Alliant International University, San Francisco, California. Board member, International Society for Traumatic Stress Studies. Author of *Countertransference and the Treatment of Trauma* (2000), for which she was the recipient of a 2002 ISSD award for outstanding clinical contribution.

Stephanie Dallam, RN, MSN
A doctoral candidate at the University of Kansas School of Nursing, and research associate for the Leadership Council. In the past, a nurse practitioner in pediatric trauma at University of Missouri Hospital and Clinics, and a nursing instructor at the University of Missouri–Columbia.

Paul F. Dell, PhD
Director of the Trauma Recovery Center in Norfolk, Virginia. Developer of the *Multidimensional Inventory of Dissociation* (MID) and the subjective-phenomenological model of dissociation. Research efforts have focused on the phenomenology of dissociation, diagnosis, DSM-V, and empirical delineation of the domain of dissociation.

Johan A. den Boer, MD, PhD
Professor of biological psychiatry, Department of Psychiatry, University Medical Centre Groningen, The Netherlands. His research program involves preclinical and clinical research into the neurobiology of stress and anxiety.

Martin J. Dorahy, PhD, DClinPsych
Senior lecturer, Department of Psychology, University of Canterbury, Christchurch, New Zealand. Cochair, David Caul Graduate Research Award, ISSTD.

Lissa Dutra, PhD
Researcher and clinician, National Center for Posttraumatic Stress Disorder. Research interests include parent-child attachment processes, personality development, posttraumatic stress disorder, and childhood trauma. Clinical work focuses on the treatment of complex posttraumatic stress disorder, dissociative disorders, and personality pathology.

Ceri Evans, MBChB, MRCPsych, PhD
Clinical Director & Consultant Forensic Psychiatrist, Canterbury Regional Forensic Psychiatry Service, Hillmorton Hospital, Christchurch, New Zealand. Research interests include the nature of memory for violent crime in perpetrators, including amnesia and intrusive memories.

John A. Fairbank, PhD
Professor of medical psychology, Department of Psychiatry and Behavioral Sciences, Duke University Medical Center; Codirector, National Center for Child Traumatic Stress; Director, Mid-Atlantic (VISN 6)

Mental Illness Research, Education, and Clinical Center (MIRECC), Duham VA Medical Center. A clinical psychologist with over 25 years of research and clinical experience in the field of traumatic stress in children and adults.

Susie Farrelly, MBChB
Adult community psychiatrist, Auckland District Health Board, Auckland, New Zealand. Has come to focus, conceptually, on the relationship between traumatic childhood experience and what we see as "mental illness," with an increasing clinical interest in the prevalence of dissociative phenomena in this population.

Julian D. Ford, PhD
Associate professor, Department of Psychiatry, University of Connecticut School of Medicine, Farmington, Connecticut. Senior academic fellow, Child Health and Development Institute. Clinical psychologist, University of Connecticut Health Center.

A. Steven Frankel, PhD, JD
Clinical and forensic psychologist and clinical professor of psychology, University of Southern California. Attorney at law and adjunct professor of law, Golden Gate University School of Law, San Francisco, California. President of the ISSTD for 2001–02. Author of many publications on healthcare policy, regulation of healthcare practice, and mental disorder and the law.

Jennifer J. Freyd, PhD
Professor of psychology, University of Oregon. Author of the book, *Betrayal Trauma: The logic of forgetting childhood abuse.* Author or coauthor of over 100 articles. Current editor of the *Journal of Trauma & Dissociation*, the official journal of the ISSTD.

Karni Ginzburg, PhD
Senior lecturer, Bob Shapell School of Social Work, Tel Aviv University, Israel. Her work is focused on the reciprocal relations between stress and somatic illness, and the dynamics of adaptation to various types of traumatic events.

Steven N. Gold, PhD
Professor, Center for Psychological Studies, Nova Southeastern University. Director, Trauma Resolution & Integration Program. President, American Psychological Association Division of Trauma Psychology. President of ISSD for 2003–04. Author, *Not Trauma Alone* (2000). Editor of the APA journal, *Psychological Trauma: Theory, Research, Practice and Policy.*

Elizabeth F. Howell, PhD
Adjunct associate professor, Department of Psychology, New York University. Faculty, Trauma Program, National Institute for the Psychotherapies (New York), and Dissociative Disorders Psychotherapy Training Program (ISSTD); private practice. Author of *The Dissociative Mind* (2005). Book review editor, *Journal of Trauma and Dissociation.*

Shari Jager-Hyman, MA
Doctoral student, Temple University Department of Psychology, Philadelphia, Pennsylvania. Previously worked with Dr. Mary Zanarini at McLean Hospital. Primary interests include the relations between borderline personality disorder, mood disorders, and trauma.

Mary Ellen Jessop, MBBS, FRANZCP
Child and adolescent psychiatrist, Child and Youth Mental Health Service, Royal Children's Hospital and Health Service District, Brisbane, Queensland, Australia.

Hilit Kletter, PhD
Postdoctoral fellow, Kaiser Permanente, Milpitas, California. Past experience as a project manager with the Stanford Early Life Stress Project on research examining brain function and posttraumatic stress in victims of interpersonal violence. Research interests include childhood trauma, PTSD, and resiliency.

Richard P. Kluft, MD
Clinical professor of psychiatry, Temple University School of Medicine. Faculty member, Psychoanalytic Center of Philadelphia, Philadelphia, Philadelphia. Private practice of psychiatry and psychoanalysis in Bala Cynwyd, Philadelphia. Founding member of ISSMP&D and President of ISSD for 1985–86. Editor-in-chief of *Dissociation* (1988–97). Past president of the American Society of Clinical Hypnosis. Current President of the Society for Clinical and Experimental Hypnosis.

Cheryl Koopman, PhD
Associate research professor of psychiatry and Behavioral Sciences, Stanford University. Research focuses predominantly on psychosocial reactions to political trauma, serious illness, and other stressful life events and evaluates interventions to help people cope with such events.

Ruth A. Lanius, MD, PhD, FRCPC
Associate professor and Harris-Woodman Chair in Psyche and Soma, Department of Psychiatry, Schulich School of Medicine & Dentistry, University of Western Ontario, London, Ontario, Canada. Traumatic stress service at University Hospital, London Health Sciences Centre. Research using fMRI on patients with PTSD, dissociative disorders, and related comorbidities.

Douglas Lawson, DC, MSc
Consultant in research design and psychometrics with a special interest in medical education. Recently withdrew from the PhD program in medical education at the University of Calgary, Faculty of Medicine due to health problems.

Giovanni Liotti, MD
Psychiatrist and psychotherapist. Pierre Janet Writing Award, ISSTD, 2005. Teaches developmental psychopathology at the postgraduate Scuola di Psicoterapia Cognitiva (School of Cognitive Psychotherapy), Rome, Italy.

Karlen Lyons-Ruth, PhD
Associate professor of psychology, Department of Psychiatry, Harvard Medical School. Director, Family Studies Lab, Cambridge Hospital. Research interests include longitudinal study of adaptation from infancy to adolescence; genetic and caregiving influences on young adult psychopathology; infant social development; maternal trauma and depression; and the parent-child attachment relationship.

Andrew Moskowitz, PhD
Clinical Senior Lecturer of Trauma Psychology, Department of Mental Health, University of Aberdeen, Scotland. Research interests include the impact of trauma, dissociation, and insecure attachment on subsequent psychopathology, particularly psychosis; historical perspectives on schizophrenia; and connections between dissociation and violence.

Ellert R.S. Nijenhuis, PhD
Psychologist, psychotherapist, supervisor, and researcher in the diagnosis and treatment of severely traumatized patients, Top Referent Trauma Center of Mental Health Care Drenthe, Assen, The Netherlands, at which hospital he conducts his research in collaboration with several European universities.

Barry Nurcombe, MD, FRANZCP, FRACP
Professor of child and adolescent psychiatry, The University of Western Australia, Perth, Western Australia, Australia. Emeritus Professor of child and adolescent psychiatry, Vanderbilt University and The University of Queensland; Vice President, International Association of Child and Adolescent Psychiatry and Psychology.

John A. O'Neil, MD, FRCPC
Assistant professor of psychiatry, McGill University and St. Mary's Hospital, Montréal, Québec, Canada. Psychoanalyst, Canadian and International Psychoanalytic Associations. Fellow of the ISSTD. Clinical work has focused on the psychotherapy, with adjunctive hypnosis, of dissociative disorders for the past 2 decades.

Erdinç Öztürk, PhD
Clinical psychologist, Clinical Psychotherapy Unit and Dissociative Disorders Program, Faculty of Medicine, Istanbul University, Turkey. Clinical work has focused on crisis intervention and long-term psychotherapy for trauma-related conditions and complex dissociative disorders over the past decade.

Clare Pain, MD, FRCPC
Assistant professor of psychiatry, University of Toronto. Director, Psychological Trauma Program, Mount Sinai Hospital. Co-project director, Toronto Addis Ababa Psychiatry Project. Recipient of the ISSD President's Award. Clinical and research focus is on the assessment and treatment of patients with psychological trauma and transcultural aspects of psychological trauma.

Kelsey L. Paulson, MA
Trauma Research Institute, Alliant International University, San Diego, California.

John Read, PhD
Psychology Department, University of Auckland, New Zealand. Coordinating editor of *Models of Madness: Psychological, Social and Biological Approaches to Schizophrenia* (2004). Editor of the forthcoming international journal, *Psychosis: Psychological, Social and Integrative Approaches*, the official journal of the International Society for the Psychological Treatment of Schizophrenia.

Colin A. Ross, MD, FRCPC
The Colin A. Ross Institute for Psychological Trauma, Richardson, Texas. President of ISSD for 1993–94. Author of *Dissociative Identity Disorder: Diagnosis, clinical features, and treatment of multiple personality (1997).*

Thomas Rudegeair, MD, PhD
Psychiatrist, Auckland District Health Board, Auckland, New Zealand. American-trained, emigrated to New Zealand to help design a trauma-informed inpatient service. Interested in how all severe mental illness, whether labeled "psychosis" or "dissociation," may be a manifestation of trauma-induced vulnerability.

Kasey Saltzman, PhD
Psychologist in private practice, Palo Alto, California, specializing in the assessment and treatment of trauma and PTSD. Former project manager of the Stanford Pediatric PTSD Program. Research focuses on the neurobiology of trauma, and developmental implications of traumatic events in children.

Vedat Şar, MD
Professor of psychiatry, Director, Clinical Psychotherapy Unit and Dissociative Disorders Program, Faculty of Medicine, Istanbul University, Turkey. President of ISSTD for 2007–08. Clinician, teacher, and researcher of dissociative disorders. Author of many articles and several book chapters devoted to the lifelong psychiatric consequences of childhood trauma and dissociative disorders.

Allan N. Schore, PhD
Department of Psychiatry and Biobehavioral Sciences, David Geffen School of Medicine, UCLA, Los Angeles, California. Editor, Norton Series on Interpersonal Neurobiology. Author of seminal articles and books with relevance to affective neuroscience, neuropsychiatry, trauma theory, developmental psychology, attachment theory, pediatrics, infant mental health, psychoanalysis, psychotherapy, and behavioral biology.

James Graham Scott, MBBS, FRANZCP
Hospital Kids in Mind Mater Hospital Child and Youth Mental Health Service, South Brisbane, Australia.

Stacey L. Seibel, PhD
Psychologist at Park Nicollet Clinic, Sexual Health Center, Saint Louis Park, Minnesota. Specializes in the treatment of sexual disorders and sexual trauma.

Daniel J. Siegel, MD
UCLA School of Medicine. Codirector, UCLA Mindful Awareness Research Center. Director, Mindsight Institute. Author of *The Developing Mind* (1999) and *The Mindful Brain* (2007). Coauthor of *Parenting from the Inside Out* (2003). Founding editor, Norton Series on Interpersonal Neurobiology.

Joyanna L. Silberg, PhD
Psychologist and forensic expert specializing in child sexual abuse and dissociative disorders. Coordinator of trauma disorder services for children and adolescents, Sheppard Pratt Health System. Executive Vice-President, Leadership Council on Child Abuse & Interpersonal Violence. President of ISSD for 2000–01. Recipient of the 1992 Walter P. Klopfer Award for research, and of the 1997 Cornelia Wilbur Award for clinical excellence. Editor of *The Dissociative Child.*

Louise Silvern, PhD
Clinical psychologist and associate professor, University of Colorado at Boulder. Research and clinical work focus on posttraumatic and dissociative psychological consequences of childhood parent loss and maltreatment.

Daphne Simeon, MD
Psychiatrist and psychoanalyst. Associate professor of psychiatry Director, Depersonalization and Dissociation Research Program, and Codirector of the Compulsive and Impulsive Disorders Research Program, Mount Sinai School of Medicine, New York. Faculty, Columbia Psychoanalytic Institute, New York.

Eli Somer, PhD
Associate professor, clinical psychology, University of Haifa, Israel. President of the ISSTD for 2005–06. Recipient of the ISSTD Cornelia Wilbur Award (2000). Director of the Boards of the European Society for Trauma and Dissociation, and of Trauma and Dissociation Israel.

L. Alan Sroufe, PhD
William Harris Professor of child psychology in the Institute of Child Development and adjunct professor in the Department of Psychiatry at the University of Minnesota. Internationally recognized expert on attachment relationships, emotional development, and psychopathology. Author of *Emotional development: The organization of emotional life in the early years* (1996).

Kathy Steele, MN, CS
Clinical director of Metropolitan Counseling Services, a nonprofit low-fee center for long-term psychotherapy, and private practice, Atlanta, Georgia. President of

ISSTD for 2008–09. Coauthor with Ellert Nijenhuis and Onno van der Hart, *The Haunted Self: Structural dissociation and the treatment of chronic traumatization* (2006).

Donnel B. Stern, PhD
Training and supervising analyst, William Alanson White Institute. Faculty and supervisor, NYU Postdoctoral Program in Psychoanalysis and Psychotherapy. Author of *Unformulated Experience: From Dissociation to Imagination in Psychoanalysis* (1997). Editor, *Psychoanalysis in a New Key* Book Series (Routledge). Former editor, *Contemporary Psychoanalysis.* Coeditor, *The Handbook of Interpersonal Psychoanalysis* (1995).

Devin B. Terhune, MSc
Doctoral student, Department of Psychology, Lund University, Malmö, Sweden. Research interests include hypnosis, dissociation, and hallucinations.

Onno van der Hart, PhD
Honorary professor of psychopathology of chronic traumatization, Utrecht University, The Netherlands. Psychotherapist and consultant, Sinai Centre for Mental Health, Amstelveen, The Netherlands. Coauthored with Ellert Nijenhuis and Kathy Steele, *The Haunted Self: Structural dissociation and the treatment of chronic traumatization* (2006).

Marjolein van Duijl, MD, PhD
Psychiatrist and head of the inpatient-clinic for refugees, "de Vonk," at Center '45, national expert center for the treatment of victims of persecution, war, and violence in Oegstgeest, The Netherlands. Formerly Head, Department of Psychiatry, Mbarara University, Uganda. PhD research was on dissociation in Uganda.

Lynn C. Waelde, PhD
Professor, Pacific Graduate School of Psychology, Palo Alto, California. Founder and director, Inner Resources Center, Kurt and Barbara Gronowski Psychology Clinic. Consulting associate professor, Department of Psychiatry and Behavioral Sciences, Stanford University School of Medicine. Her research and clinical work focus on the therapeutic uses of meditation and on trauma, dissociation, and PTSD.

Lupita A. Weiner, MA
Department of psychology, The University of Texas–Pan American.

Ondra Williams, MA
Psychotherapist-clinician in private practice specialized in the treatment of dissociative, affiliated with the New Zealand Association of Psychotherapists. Presenter of many workshops on dissociation to clinicians from various disciplines within New Zealand.

Tuppett M. Yates, PhD
Clinical and developmental psychologist, Department of Psychology, University of California, Riverside, studying the developmental sequelæ of childhood adversity. Active areas of research include self-injurious behavior, child maltreatment, resilience, representation, and regulation.

Mary C. Zanarini, EdD
Professor of psychology, Department of Psychiatry, Harvard Medical School, Boston Massachusetts. Director, Laboratory for the Study of Adult Development, McLean Hospital, Belmont, Massachusetts. Has studied the phenomenology, etiology, comorbidity, familiality, and long-term course of borderline personality disorder in large-scale, naturalistic studies, and the psychosocial and psychotropic treatments for BPD.

Preface

Paul F. Dell, PhD
John A. O'Neil, MD, FRCPC

Dissociation and the Dissociative Disorders: DSM-V and Beyond is a book that has no real predecessor in the dissociative disorders field. It

(1) reports the most recent scientific findings and conceptualizations about dissociation,
(2) defines and establishes the boundaries of current knowledge in the dissociative disorders field,
(3) identifies and carefully articulates the field's current points of confusion, gaps in knowledge, and conjectures,
(4) clarifies the different aspects and implications of dissociation, and
(5) sets forth a research agenda for the next decade. In many respects, *Dissociation and the Dissociative Disorders: DSM-V and Beyond* both defines and redefines the field.

In 2000 John Curtis,[1] the President of the International Society for the Study of Dissociation (ISSD),[2] appointed three people to a Scientific Consensus Task Force: Donald Beere, Paul Dell, and John O'Neil. Our first task was to write a consensus definition of dissociation. After months of email discussion, it became apparent that we simply could not accomplish this task. This was disconcerting to say the least. We had known at the outset that the term *dissociation* was often used in a vague, overly-broad fashion, but we never anticipated that we might be unable to agree upon a definition.

In the immediately ensuing years, we organized panel discussions at the Annual Fall Conferences of the ISSD, where our initial trio was ably complemented by Andreas Laddis.[3] Each year, we presented analyses and definitions of dissociation. These sessions were well-attended, even crowded. Enthusiastic discussions took place each year. There were, we think, meaningful advances in clarity. Consensus, however, rarely visited the room. Indeed, consensus receded when articulate debaters such as Lisa Butler, Constance Dalenberg, and Steven Gold insisted that we were over-pathologizing dissociation: "What about normal dissociation?" they asked. Unsatisfied with the answers they received, they began to organize their own panels (and write articles) on normal dissociation. In other words, the already-broad meaning of dissociation became broader still, rather than narrower. This edited volume is, in part, our latest response to these discussions and debates.

Strictly speaking, the present volume is designed with two goals in mind. Our first goal is to move the field forward in order to prepare for the writing of DSM-V. Accordingly, we picked specific authors to write about specific issues regarding dissociation and the dissociative disorders. Our hand-picked community of authors performed admirably and the primary goal of the book is already being realized. That is, as the book goes into production in late 2008, many of its ideas are already influencing the writing of the Dissociative Disorders Literature Review, the rawest initial blueprint for the American Psychiatric Association work group that will draft the Dissociative Disorders section of DSM-V.

Our second goal for the book is to clarify the concept, phenomena, and pathogenesis of dissociation. There remain significant differences of opinion regarding all these questions, but we are confident that the chapters of this book have made such differences clearer, and helped to separate out the substantive differences from the merely semantic ones.

[1] Dr. John Curtis, MD, FRCPC, psychiatrist in private practice, Halifax, Nova Scotia.
[2] Since 2006, the name has been expanded to the International Society for the Study of Trauma and Dissociation (ISSTD; www.isst-d.org).
[3] Dr. Andreas Laddis, MD, psychiatrist, Shrewsbury, MA.

Remaining differences of opinion about dissociation, at least as voiced within the chapters of this book, are typical of any academic, scientific, or clinical field.

Looking back on our unsuccessful effort in 2001 to provide a simple scientific definition of dissociation, and where we are now, it seems clear that our differences were the product of the inherent complexity of dissociation and of our own 'observer bias': while the original three of us are experienced clinicians in the field, we have quite different professional backgrounds, and, worse still, are all philosophically inclined. One of us is a psychologist-philosopher (DB) who is partial to Maurice Merleau-Ponty. Another is a psychiatrist-psychoanalyst-philosopher (JO'N) who is partial to Karl Popper and Gerald Edelman. And the last of us is an academically-oriented clinician (PD) who is partial to Martin Heidegger and the Chilean biologist, Humberto Maturana. In short, we suspect that our inability to define dissociation stemmed from the subject's longstanding tangled complexity and our competing preferences for approaching the topic from different angles.

Now, eight years later, it will be clear from this book that the complexity is real, with ever more possible viewing angles. At the same time, there is some emerging consensus about what is being viewed, a consensus prompted both by fierce conceptual debate and by empirical test. Remaining differences have become fewer and sharper.

Some summary statements about the controversies can be made, and these may prove illuminating in reading the book's various chapters. There are conditions, states or disorders that are commonly labeled as *dissociative*. Some prefer that the word *dissociation* apply to the condition's surface appearance (signs and symptoms, or phenomena), others to what putatively underlies the signs and symptoms (the "noumena"). Because this surface-deep distinction is not controversial, the choice as to which to label as 'dissociation' is largely semantic.

Of those who opt for what underlies the phenomena, some prefer that the word apply to putative actions of the subject (ability, propensity, motive, defense, flight, etc.), others to what the subject passively suffers (division, fragmentation, disintegration, etc.). These choices are not merely semantic, as they reflect competing hypotheses about the genesis of dissociation—hypotheses which invite empirical test, and which have indeed been tested empirically. The term *multiplicity* itself cuts across these preferences, as it may be viewed as a sign (switching) or symptom (with some degree of co-presence), or as the structural end-product of whatever event, actively enacted or passively suffered, underlies the appearance.

Normal-pathological is another polarity. While most agree that there is both normal and pathological dissociation, there is disagreement about whether the boundary between them is sharp or blurred, and whether the boundary is merely quantitative—a matter of degree—or qualitative—a question as to what kinds of dissociation fall to the normal or pathological side. These competing hypotheses have again invited and undergone empirical test, though, as in most other complex scientific fields, empirical results generally raise as many further questions as they answer.

Distinct from the normal-pathological axis, dissociation connotes two distinct sets of phenomena whose relationship remains uncertain—faculty dissociation and multiplicity—and which commonly co-occur. *Faculty dissociation* implies a disruption in the normal integration of the psychological faculties or functioning of a given consciousness with a sense of self. *Multiplicity* implies the presence of more than one centre of consciousness, more than one self. Autohypnotic analgesia-anesthesia and focused attention during the execution of a complex task illustrate normal faculty dissociation. Depersonalization and dissociative amnesia illustrate pathological faculty dissociation. The presence of ego states in an otherwise healthy individual, or culturally-sanctioned psychogenic altered states of consciousness, illustrate normal multiplicity. Dissociative Identity Disorder, DDNOS-1 and DDNOS-4 (Dissociative Trance Disorder) illustrate pathological multiplicity. The two-by-two grid generated by normal/pathological and faculty/multiplicity is not controversial, while the question as to whether to apply the word *dissociation* to all four boxes, or just to some, remains hotly debated.

True to the complexity of the subject matter, the book balances the exuberant fecundity of historical, conceptual, and clinical inspiration with the more sober pruning afforded by empirical test. The first six parts deal with dissociation in general, the next four parts focus on dissociation in various DSM-IV disorders, then a part each on forensic evaluation and clinical treatment, with a final part outlining the latest empirical delineation of pathological dissociation, the most pressing outstanding research that remains to be done, and an extended historical, conceptual, and empirical analysis of dissociation.

As for a consensus definition of dissociation, the viewpoints remain many. At the same time, it is worthwhile to start off in the clinic, where one encounters patients who, first and foremost, consciously experience pathological dissociative symptoms, for which the co-editors offer the following:

> The essential manifestation of pathological dissociation is a partial or complete disruption of the normal integration of a person's psychological functioning. Dissociative disruptions unexpectedly change the person's usual functioning in ways that the person cannot easily explain. Any aspect of a person's conscious, psychological functioning can be disrupted by dissociation. Specifically, dissociation can unexpectedly disrupt, alter, or intrude upon a person's consciousness and experience of body, world, self, mind, agency, intentionality, thinking, believing, knowing, recognizing, remembering, feeling, wanting, speaking, acting, seeing, hearing, smelling, tasting, touching, and so on.
>
> Although some dissociative disruptions involve amnesia (which is only detected later by the person—and sometimes not detected at all), the vast majority of dissociative experiences do *not* involve amnesia. Instead, *the vast majority of dissociative intrusions into functioning are consciously experienced at the moment of their occurrence.* And, because these disruptions of normal functioning are utterly unanticipated, they are typically experienced by the person as startling, autonomous intrusions into this or her usual ways of responding or functioning.
>
> The most common dissociative intrusions include hearing voices, depersonalization, derealization, 'made' thoughts, 'made' urges, 'made' desires, 'made' emotions, and 'made' actions. Although some dissociative disruptions of normal functioning are visible to an observer (e.g., conversion symptoms such as blindness or paralysis), most dissociative symptoms are entirely subjective (with minimal or no external signs); thus, they are 'invisible' to others.

It is with this clinical starting point in mind that we invite you to delve further into the fascinating world of dissociation.

Acknowledgments

Many people contributed to the crafting of this book. We wish to thank the Board of Directors of ISSD of 2001 whose discussions about DSM-V evoked the idea to produce this book.

We are grateful to the ISSMP&D, and then the ISSD, and now the ISSTD for being a professional 'home' to us for the past two decades. We thank and congratulate the 68 contributing authors of the book's 46 chapters, many of whom are ISSTD members (and whom you may briefly meet in the list of Contributors). We have been learning from them to varying degrees over varying time spans and are delighted to be able to collect some of their recently-developed wisdom in this book.

We are especially grateful to George Zimmar of Routledge who was instrumental in accepting this book for publication, and to Fred Coopersmith, Marta Moldvai, Jennifer Smith, Marc Johnston, and Ruth Einstein for their patience, encouragement and guidance in shepherding this book into production.

P.F.D.
J.A.O'N.

When John Curtis, president of ISSD, appointed me to chair a Scientific Consensus Task Force in 2000, he also appointed a person of fearsome intellect to the Task Force—John O'Neil. Although John was always affable, I found his mind to be downright intimidating. Still, when I decided to edit this book, I had no doubt whom I wanted as a co-editor. Working with John has been, and continues to be, a delightful intellectual voyage.

Over the years, my thinking has been enriched by the entire body of literature on dissociation, hypnosis, and trauma. My primary guide and mentor, however, has always been Rick Kluft.

P.F.D.

I thank Paul Dell for inviting me to join him as co-editor of this important book. Our back and forth emailing and text editing has been my major intellectual stimulation for the past few years. Paul's keen intellect and clear mode of expression permitted us to have agreements and disagreements which were substantive and not merely semantic.

In addition to many of the contributing authors, I wish to thank a few more colleagues who have been most instrumental in contributing to my own interest, knowledge and competence in the dissociative disorders: James Chu, Catherine Fine, George Fraser, Richard Loewenstein, Frank Putnam, and Jack and Helen Watkins.

J.A.O'N.

Introduction

Paul F. Dell, PhD
John A. O'Neil, MD, FRCPC

In this book, dissociation is introduced historically and conceptually (Part I); its origins in the early developmental phases of childhood are explored (Part II); its normal and exceptional expression is delineated (Part III); the circumstances of its acute manifestation are debated (Part IV); its manifestation, structure, and mechanisms, both acute (Part IV) and chronic (Part V) are discussed; and its neurobiology is explored (Part VI). The core DSM-IV Dissociative Disorders are finally dealt with in Part VII, followed by explorations of dissociation in other diagnostic groups, such as PTSD (Part VIII), Borderline Personality Disorder and Substance Dependence (Part IX), and psychosis (Part X). The forensic assessment of dissociation is updated (Part XI). Cutting across all diagnostic categories, various treatment approaches to dissociation are outlined (Part XII). Part XIII concludes by moving from the latest empirical delineation of pathological dissociation to the most pressing outstanding research that remains to be done, and culminates in an extended historical, conceptual, and empirical analysis of dissociation.

PART I. AN OVERVIEW

We begin with historical and philosophical introductions to the field, both of which make strong arguments in favor of particular points of view.

In chapter 1, "History of the Concept of Dissociation," Onno van der Hart and Martin Dorahy analyze the various definitions and understandings of dissociation—from its origins in the eighteenth century to the current discussions of dissociation in the twenty-first century. Literature from the early years yields twenty-eight different terms or expressions that refer to what we now call dissociation. The story begins with the pioneer theorists, both French (Puységur, Moreau de Tours, Gros Jean, Taine, Charcot, Janet, Binet) and Anglo-American (F. Myers, James, Sidis, Prince), then moves on to discuss the era of World War I (C. S. Myers, Mitchell, McDougall). A step back is then taken to review the dissociative origins of Freud's thinking, and his break with that tradition, as well as subsequent psychoanalysts who tried to heal the rift (Ferenczi, Fainbairn). The story then jumps forward to the 1970s (Tart, Ludwig, Ellenberger, Wilbur, Hilgard), after which the names become increasingly numerous and familiar. In conclusion, Drs. Van der Hart and Doherty argue that dissociation has tended to be conceptualized narrowly and broadly. They argue forcefully in favor of the narrow conceptualization: dissociation as a division of consciousness, which may be normal (hypnotically-induced) or pathological (trauma-induced). They argue forcefully against the broad conceptualization: dissociation as any breakdown in integrative functioning, regardless of origin.

In chapter 2, "The Conceptual Unity of Dissociation: A Philosophical Argument," philosopher Stephen Braude extends the philosophical analysis of dissociation that he has been elaborating in his books and articles over the past many years. He opens with a welcome clarification about certain assumptions we make about dissociation, and distinguishes it from certain other phenomena (repression, suppression, denial). Dr. Braude concludes with a plea for an inclusive view of dissociation: to regard dissociation, "in all its richness and variety, as a legitimate and single object of psychological and theoretical inquiry."

PART II. DEVELOPMENTAL APPROACHES TO DISSOCIATION

The roots of dissociation in the psychological development of the child are explored from both relational and neurodevelopmental perspectives.

In chapter 3, "Dissociation and Development of the Self," Elizabeth Carlson, Tuppett Yates, and Alan Sroufe describe how both developmental adaptation and deviation give rise to dissociative processes especially with regard to the development of the self. They review the history of etiological theories of dissociation as an introduction to their organizational developmental framework integrating developmental psychopathology, normal development of the self, and normal dissociation. The authors then discuss various developmental pathways of dissociation resulting from various combinations of these elements, and mutual influences of dissociation and self functioning on each other. They detail the effects of dissociation on a number of core levels of self experience: motivational, attitudinal, emotional, instrumental and relational. Drs. Carlson, Yates, and Sroufe conclude by underscoring the multitude of variables which enter into self development and how dissociation, initially protective of self integrity, may become pathological.

In chapter 4, "Attachment and Dissociation," Giovanni Liotti applies John Bowlby's Attachment Theory to dissociation and throughout the chapter cites research which supports his views. He explains how the parents' attachment style, especially as related to their own unresolved relational loss and trauma, gives rise to disorganized attachment patterns in the child, and discusses why this should be the case. Dr. Liotti argues that the current best hypothesis involves the simultaneous activation of conflicting motivational systems: defense and attachment, with respect to caregivers who are either vulnerable, or confused, or both frightened and frightening to the child. He proposes that the IWM (Internal Working Model) of infant disorganized attachment is the single common basis for all subsequent dissociation: dissociative amnesia, depersonalization and derealization, dissociative voices, and typical ego states (persecutor, rescuer, victim), and explains defensive dissociation as a secondary phenomenon. Dr. Liotti concludes with a variety of competing theoretical predictions of etiology, pathogenesis, and treatment response which call for further empirical test.

In chapter 5, "Dissociation in Childhood and Adolescence: At the Crossroads," Joyanna Silberg and Stephanie Dallam review the history of the field and the current woeful state of misdiagnosis of dissociation in children. They then clarify the nature of childhood dissociative symptomatology as it evolves from the preschooler to the grade-schooler to the adolescent, approximating that of the adult in step-wise fashion, and underscoring the high prevalence of adolescent DID in the juvenile probation population. The ISSD (2004) *Guidelines for the Evaluation and Treatment of Dissociative Symptoms in Children and Adolescents* is summarized and updated. Dr. Silberg and Ms. Dallam conclude with a lengthy discussion of theoretical disputes that remain to be resolved, in the course of which they critically examine the work of Fonagy, Liotti, Lyons-Ruth, Freyd, Putnam, LeDoux, Siegel, Schore, and Nijenhuis with respect to dissociation in childhood and adolescence.

In chapter 6, "The Relational Context of Dissociative Phenomena," Lissa Dutra, Ilaria Bianchi, Daniel Siegel and Karlen Lyons-Ruth examine dissociation from the developmental perspectives of Dr. Siegel's consilient approach to neurobiology and the developing mind, and Dr. Lyons-Ruth's theory and research about the developmental relationship between attachment and dissociation. The authors begin with the classic view of dissociation as an intrapsychic defense, then broaden this view to dissociation as an interpersonal developmental process, drawing especially on attachment theory as discussed in chapter 4. This view is backed up by extraordinary prospective studies indicating that the quality of mother-infant interaction in the first year and a half of life accounts for fully half of subsequent dissociative pathology in early adulthood, independent of trauma, and that lack of positive maternal involvement overrides negative-intrusive involvement in predicting subsequent dissociative pathology. Illuminating clinical illustrations are provided. Dr. Dutra and colleagues conclude with important clinical implications which bear especially on the time course of treatment: resolving discrete traumatic events is quicker and easier than resolving long-standing internalized patterns of distorted interpersonal relationships.

In chapter 7, "Adaptive Dissociation: Information Processing and Response to Betrayal," Jennifer Freyd and Rose Barlow use research on Freyd's betrayal theory of dissociation to demonstrate the adaptive cognitive nature of dissociative functioning in the face of betrayal by loved ones: how traumatized individuals can be unaware of information that would otherwise threaten an important relationship. Trauma and attachment are again the major etiological players, but interpreted here as interfering with certain mechanisms of information processing to produce a specific information processing style aimed more at preserving attachment than at warding off trauma. Drs. Freyd and Barlow complement theory with research findings which test each component of their overall theory, and recommend specific future research to answer outstanding questions.

In chapter 8, "Origins of Pathological Dissociation: Attachment Trauma and the Developing Right Brain," Allan Schore takes familiar elements—early trauma and attachment pathology, declarative and procedural memory, and sense of self and body image—and traces the neural pathways that mediate their translation into dissociative pathology. The locus of the discussion is the limbic system, whose daunting complexity Dr. Schore clearly explains: the right limbic system, and its primary components, both deep gray (the amygdala) and mesocortical (hippocampus, anterior cingulate, insula), their reciprocal interactions; their primary forward links to the neocortex through the right orbitofrontal cortex, and to the body through the hypothalamus and the descending right vagal system. Dr. Schore's anatomically-specific neurodevelopmental discussion explains the where and the how of many clinically familiar phenomena.

PART III. NORMAL AND EXCEPTIONAL DISSOCIATION

Normal or nonpathological dissociation is debated from two contrasting points of view (chapters 9 and 10), complemented by a discussion of cross-cultural expressions of dissociation, both normal and pathological.

In Chapter 9, "The Case for the Study of "Normal" Dissociation Processes," Constance Dalenberg and Kelsey Paulson argue against the hypothesis that some kinds of dissociation (e.g. amnesia, depersonalization) are pathological and others (e.g., absorption, detachment) are normal or not even properly dissociative at all. They interpret empirical research indicating that dissociation is normal or pathological depending on context, and that this cuts across the qualitatively different kinds of dissociation. Thus, absorption, amnesia and depersonalization may each be adaptive or pathological, normal or abnormal, depending on context or purpose, and all these kinds of dissociation correlate with each other. Dr. Dalenberg and Ms. Paulson conclude that absorption is indeed a form of dissociation, and that dissociation in general cannot be understood in its absence.

In chapter 10, "Dissociation versus Alterations in Consciousness: Related but Different Concepts," Kathy Steele, Martin Dorahy, Onno van der Hart and Ellert Nijenhuis present their arguments in support of the view that dissociation is essentially the trauma-related structural dissociation of the personality, while altered states of consciousness are not essentially dissociative. This is consistent with the history advanced in chapter 1. Altered states result in a varying but consistent sense of self, while dissociation proper results in inconsistent alternating senses of self. The authors cite empirical research consistent with this thesis. Their view is grounded in their overall 'deep' hypothesis that all trauma-related pathology is consequent to a psychobiological division of the personality, and that it is uniquely the symptoms of such a division that are properly dissociative. Thus, *alterations* of consciousness are not dissociative, whereas *alternations* of consciousness are.

In chapter 11, "Possession/Trance Phenomena," Etzel Cardeña, Marjolein van Duijl, Lupita Weiner and Devin Terhune delineate their most recent research into possession/trance phenomena in various cultures. They show that possession/trance phenomena are normal in many cultures (including some Western subcultures), but that there are also abnormal forms of possession/trance in those same cultures. The authors argue that pathological forms of possession/trance phenomena have two features. First, they cause dysfunction or distress and are associated with maladjustment. Second, they occur in a way that is not part of a culturally-accepted practice. The authors propose that both normal and pathological forms of possession/trance phenomena are rooted in a predisposition, probably biological, to dissociate, be suggestible, and/or have unusual experiences. Finally, Dr. Cardeña and colleagues emphasize the very important fact that, in non-Western cultures, the most common dissociative disorders involve trance and/or possession.

PART IV. ACUTE DISSOCIATION

The focus is on dissociation which is acutely precipitated and of relatively brief duration. This pertains especially to peritraumatic dissociation and the question as to whether it is necessarily pathological. A phenomenological theory about acute dissociative experience follows.

In chapter 12, "Is Peritraumatic Dissociation Always Pathological?," Richard Bryant presents evidence that refutes a popular hypothesis: that peritraumatic dissociation is pathological and leads to PTSD. This evidence casts significant doubt on DSM-IV Acute Stress Disorder as a construct: while ASD predicts PTSD, PTSD fails to retrodict ASD. Dr. Bryant discusses a number of hypotheses which could account for this complex relationship, including the idea that nondissociative pretrauma factors predict eventual PTSD, while dissociative pretrauma factors predict peritraumatic dissociation and dissociative PTSD. Most peritraumatic dissociation, moreover, is adaptive: only persistent dissociation is pathological. Dr. Bryant discusses the difference between the mechanisms and 'purposes' of nonpersisting peritraumatic dissociation as opposed to persisting peritraumatic dissociation, and calls for further research into nondissociative pretrauma determinants of PTSD.

In chapter 13, "Peritraumatic Dissociation and Amnesia in Violent Offenders," Andrew Moskowitz and Ceri Evans analyze and explain the remarkably common phenomenon of criminals who report dissociating during the commission of a violent crime. They cite research which indicates significant dissociation around the violent act itself, possibly identical to peritraumatic dissociation in trauma victims, and comprising variable depersonalization, derealization, and amnesia. Such dissociation seems to arise in three different contexts: with subsequent nondissociative PTSD to the trauma of their own violent act; as the expression of a criminal alter in true DID; most controversially, as a structurally dissociative state arising specifically for the violent act, not present either before or after the act, and possibly akin to Amok. Drs. Moskowitz and Evans conclude with forensic and clinical implications that may be drawn from this research.

In chapter 14, "Dissociative Perceptual Reactions: The Perceptual Theory of Dissociation," Donald Beere explains dissociative reactions from the point of view of Gestalt psychology (figure-ground) and its elaboration by Maurice Merleau-Ponty in his *Phenomenology of Perception.* The perceptual standpoint allows for a number of reformulations: distinctions among dissociative experiences, reactions and symptoms; extending figure-ground to figure-ground-background; appending detemporalization to depersonalization and derealization; in trauma, focusing on figure at the expense of ground and background. Dr. Beere's perceptual theory predicts dissociative reactions in trauma but also in certain positive nontraumatic contexts, and he reports the results of his empirical tests of these predictions, underscoring the importance of experiences with high personal significance. Dr. Beere concludes with theoretical implications, strengths, and weaknesses of his theory, and outlines additional needed research. He develops these themes further in chapter 18.

PART V. CHRONIC DISSOCIATION

Chronic and pathological dissociation is discussed with chapters on its phenomenology, its underlying structure, and its somatoform manifestations. The phenomenological theory of chapter 14 is extended. The central meaning of dissociation is clarified with regard to psychoanalytic conceptualizations which fail to grasp it.

In chapter 15, "The Phenomenology of Pathological Dissociation," Paul Dell provides a rich, clinical description of 23 manifestations of pathological dissociation. Drawing on his subjective/phenomenological model of dissociation, he asserts that that the overwhelming majority of dissociative symptoms are consciously experienced by the person, but essentially 'invisible' to observers. Dr. Dell defines pathological dissociation as "*recurrent, jarring, involuntary intrusions into executive functioning and sense of self.*" This model of dissociation underlies his Multidimensional Inventory of Dissociation (MID), a comprehensive assessment measure of dissociation that is shedding new light on the breadth of the domain of dissociation (also see Chapter 44 of this volume).

In chapter 16, "The Theory of Trauma-Related Structural Dissociation of the Personality," Kathy Steele, Onno van der Hart and Ellert Nijenhuis clearly present their model of the etiology, mechanisms, and dynamics of dissociative functioning. In keeping with the history of dissociation argued in chapter 1, the authors contend that trauma-related dissociation is prompted by trauma which overwhelms one's integrative capacity resulting in the coexistence of two or more self-organizing systems of psychobiological states: a structural dissociation of the personality. Their theory derives in part from Myers' World War II description of the split between the *emotional personality* (EP) and the *apparently normal personality* (ANP). To this the authors add current evolutionary psychobiology: inborn action tendencies (including motive, emotion, perceptual bias, and behavior) that exist in two major clusters: non-threat, concerned with daily life and survival of the species (for the ANP), and threat, concerned with defense and individual survival (for the EP). Having outlined the groundwork, Ms. Steele and colleagues then discuss the genesis, maintenance, severity levels, and symptoms of structural dissociation. They cite psychobiological research compatible with their theory, and conclude with how their theory restructures the entire trauma field.

In chapter 17, "Somatoform Dissociation and Somatoform Dissociative Disorders," Ellert Nijenhuis explores in more depth this neglected manifestation of dissociation that arises out of the theory outlined in chapter 16. The symptoms of both EP and ANP are cross-classified into positive and negative (Pierre Janet's mental *stigmata* and *accidents*), psychoform and somatoform. The Somatoform Dissociation Questionnaire is described, as is its replication and correlation with the Dissociative Experiences Scale (which primarily measures psychoform dissociation) in various countries. Its presence in various diagnostic groups and consequent relevance in screening and in nosology (especially regarding DSM-IV's somatoform disorder) are underscored. Dr. Nijenhuis accounts for somatoform dissociation in line with his general theory: as a manifestation of inborn psychobiological animal defensive reactions, and refutes the contention that it may be due either to general psychopathology or suggestion.

In chapter 18, "The Self-System as Mechanism for the Dissociative Disorders: An Extension of the Perceptual Theory of Dissociation," Donald Beere adds Harry Stack Sullivan's self system to the perceptual theory of dissociation he derived from Merleau-Ponty (see chapter 14). This allows him to extend his discussion to alter formation, depersonalization, amnesia, posttraumatic flashbacks, fugue, and DID, which he illustrates with clinical vignettes and backs up with empirical research.

In chapter 19, "Dissociative Multiplicity and Psychoanalysis," John O'Neil briefly presents his philosophy of the DSM, of psychologies in general, and of psychoanalysis, and then presents dissociative multiplicity as a major challenge for psychoanalysis. He focuses on relatively 'classical' psychoanalytic themes, distinguishing dissociation from various kinds of splitting and from repression, and clarifies the varieties of somatoform expression. He argues how the explanatory models of most psychoanalytic schools, such as ego psychology, object relations theory, and self psychology, are inadequate to explain multiplicity. Dr. O'Neil outlines likely paths for the further evolution of psychoanalytic theory and practice as they may come to accommodate dissociation.

PART VI. NEUROBIOLOGY OF DISSOCIATION

Extraordinary advances in neurobiology have illuminated the dissociation field, and promise to remain in the vanguard for the foreseeable future.

In chapter 20, "Neurobiology of Dissociation: A View From the Trauma Field," Douglas Bremner discusses his research on PTSD and on the dissociative disorders, concluding that there may be two types of acute trauma response: (1) primarily intrusive/hyperaroused and (2) primarily dissociative. Dr. Bremner summarizes the neurobiological research on dissociation and concludes that future neurobiological research should not focus on specific dissociative disorders (i.e., DID, Depersonalization Disorder), but should rather examine dissociation in the context of traumatization in general and the hyperarousal profile of classic PTSD in particular.

In chapter 21, "Psychobiology of Traumatization and Trauma-Related Structural Dissociation of the Personality," Ellert Nijenhuis and Johan den Boer explain how dissociation reflects a lack of integration among psychobiological emotional systems (e.g., reproduction, attachment, defense). They argue that primary structural dissociation (see chapter 16) is a failed integration between systems dedicated to daily life (ANP) and systems dedicated to defense in the face of severe threat (EP). The neurobiology (including gene-environment interactions, neuroendocrinology and psychophysiology) explains different reaction patterns in different survivors overall, and in their different dissociative parts. Drs. Nijenhuis and Den Boer's research recognizes that psychobiological reactivity to threat cues depends on the type of dissociative psychobiological system that dominates a subject's functioning at the time of measurement.

In chapter 22, "Neurobiology of Depersonalization Disorder," Daphne Simeon summarizes her and others' research on the biology and unique neurobiology of this enigmatic and little-studied area of the dissociative disorders. This includes its neurochemistry and alterations in autonomic and neuroendocrine functioning, as well as sensory association cortex dysfunction, and limbic inhibition of prefrontal cortical areas. This chapter functions as a conceptual prologue to chapter 27, which concerns Depersonalization Disorder proper.

In chapter 23, "Dissociation in Patients With Chronic PTSD: Hyperactivation and Hypoactivation Patterns, Clinical and Neuroimaging Perspectives," Clare Pain, Robyn Bluhm, and Ruth Lanius present data from functional magnetic resonance imaging (fMRI) compatible with Bremner's thesis of two subtypes of acute trauma response. They report that about 30% of persons with PTSD respond to symptom-provocation with hypoarousal and dissociative distancing; the remaining 70% manifest hyperarousal, flashbacks, and other intrusive symptoms. Moreover, the authors demonstrate that PTSD patients with a dissociative response to traumatic script-driven imagery activate neuronal circuitry *different* from PTSD patients with a hyperarousal response. They also note that some PTSD patients manifest mixed presentations, with hyperarousal and secondary dissociative distancing. Combining this point with the finding that some PTSD patients report subjective emotional arousal in the absence of objective autonomic reactivity, Dr. Pain and colleagues conclude that even the common dichotomy (of hyperarousal vs. dissociation) does not adequately portray the range of symptomatic reactions in PTSD.

PART VII. THE DSM-IV DISSOCIATIVE DISORDERS

Each of the four specific Dissociative Disorders of DSM-IV are dealt with, as well as the all-important 'DDNOS-1'.

In chapter 24, "The Long Struggle to Diagnose Multiple Personality Disorder (MPD): I. MPD," Paul Dell provides a historical analysis of the deliberations and debates within the American Psychiatric Association work groups that constructed the diagnostic criteria for MPD in DSM-III, -III-R, and -IV. He shows that these successive sets of diagnostic criteria for MPD have consistently presented only a structural criterion for its diagnosis (i.e., "the presence of two or more distinct identities or personality states"), rather than a more typical set of clinical signs and symptoms. Drawing on the science of nosology that informed the construction of successive editions of the modern DSM, Dr. Dell shows that DSM-IV continues to use a primitive monothetic set of diagnostic criteria that are distinctly 'user-unfriendly' and which ensure underdiagnosis of DID. He argues that DSM-V should employ polythetic criteria (as does almost the entirety of DSM-IV) to diagnose DID. Using data based on his Multidimensional Inventory of Dissociation (MID), he shows that research-based polythetic diagnostic criteria for DID have excellent sensitivity and specificity. Moreover, Dr. Dell provocatively notes that, since these diagnostic studies were performed with a self-administered instrument (MID), they show that DID can be efficiently diagnosed solely on the basis of its characteristic pattern of dissociative symptoms, without the need for a clinician to independently determine "the presence of two or more distinct identities or personality states."

In chapter 25, "The Long Struggle to Diagnose Multiple Personality Disorder (MPD): II. Partial MPD," Paul Dell takes up from where he left off in the previous chapter. He provides a historical analysis of the deliberations and debates within the American Psychiatric Association work groups that constructed the diagnostic criteria for Atypical Dissociative Disorder and Dissociative Disorder Not Otherwise Specified, Example 1(DDNOS-1) in DSM-III-R and DSM-IV. Dr. Dell shows that these successive sets of diagnostic criteria are directly derived from the problematic monothetic, structural criterion for MPD (i.e., "Clinical presentations similar to Dissociative Identity Disorder … in which … there are not two or more distinct identities or personality states"). He reviews the literature on DDNOS and shows that the extensive overdiagnosis of DDNOS (a nosology- straining 40% of dissociative diagnoses) is directly due to the poor utility of the "distinct identities or personalities states" criterion that is embedded in the diagnostic criteria for both DID and DDNOS-1. He argues that both DID and DDNOS-1 should have polythetic diagnostic criteria and that DDNOS-1 should be 'promoted' to a specific dissociative disorder. In fact, Dr. Dell suggests that DID and DDNOS-1 should be combined within a single diagnostic entity, "Complex Dissociative Disorder," a disorder with two subtypes: With Overt Switching (DID) and Without Overt Switching (DSM-IV's DDNOS-1).

In chapter 26, "Dissociative Amnesia and Dissociative Fugue," Colin Ross draws upon his experience with over 3000 dissociative cases to conclude that Dissociative Amnesia and Dissociative Fugue are not only rare, but of questionable separability. He concludes that amnesia (especially generalized amnesia) is the common core of these cases, and that travel and the development of a new identity are secondary (optional) phenomena. He also raises the question of whether Dissociative Fugue might be an adult-onset variant of DID. Given the rarity of Dissociative Amnesia and Dissociative Fugue, Dr. Ross recommends that special methodology be developed in order to identify, and study with modern assessment instruments, a sizable sample of such cases.

In chapter 27, "Depersonalization Disorder," Daphne Simeon, North America's leading researcher on the subject, discusses the symptoms, onset, course, comorbidity, prevalence, antecedents, and cognitive profile of Depersonalization Disorder. She notes that persons with Depersonalization Disorder are remarkably unresponsive to medications that have routinely proved efficacious in the treatment of mood and anxiety disorders, a finding which implies that Depersonalization Disorder is neither a mood spectrum nor anxiety spectrum disorder. Dr. Simeon concludes by summarizing what we presently know and don't know about Depersonalization Disorder.

PART VIII. DISSOCIATION IN POSTTRAUMATIC STRESS DISORDER

We move on to discussing dissociation in disorders beyond the Dissociative Disorders, with a focus on PTSD. It is clear that there are conflicting views regarding to what extent trauma and dissociation can account for each other, leaving the question about true comorbidity unresolved.

In chapter 28, "Dissociation in PTSD," Lynn Waelde, Louise Silvern, Eve Carlson, John Fairbank and Hilit Kletter examine the relationship between dissociation and PTSD. They conclude that manifestations of dissociation in PTSD depend on (1) the nature of a trauma, (2) its severity, and (3) the person's developmental level at the time of the trauma. They also highlight the existence of a distinct subgroup of persons with chronic PTSD that is characterized by the presence of severe dissociation and severe symptoms of PTSD. They distinguish three positions in the debate about dissociation in the PTSD diagnosis: (1) dissociation is an associated feature of PTSD; (2) dissociation is a central feature of PTSD; and (3) dissociation is a central feature only of Complex PTSD. Dr. Waelde and colleagues conclude that further research and additional nosological development will probably be necessary to resolve this debate.

In chapter 29, "Dissociative Reactions in PTSD," Karni Ginzburg, Lisa Butler, Kasey Saltzman and Cheryl Koopman also discuss the relationship between dissociation and PTSD. They believe that each type of dissociation is related to PTSD and that each form is successively more pathological. The authors consider chronic posttraumatic dissociation to be a marker for dissociative hypersensitivity to even ordinary daily stressors. They contend that severe PTSD is especially associated with dissociative hypersensitivity. They identify three models of the relationship between dissociation and PTSD: (1) PTSD and dissociation are different facets of a single phenomenon (thereby making PTSD a dissociative disorder); (2) PTSD has a dissociative subtype; and (3) PTSD and dissociation are distinct, but frequently comorbid, phenomena. After carefully discussing the evidence for each model, Dr. Ginzburg and colleagues conclude that extant research is still insufficient to definitively opt for one of the three models.

In chapter 30, "Dissociation in Complex PTSD or Disorders of Extreme Stress not Otherwise Specified (DESNOS)," Julian Ford describes the role of dissociation in Complex PTSD as a natural, spontaneous response to extreme emotional reactivity and disorganized attachment. He believes that, when this occurs, the body automatically shifts from operations of self-regulation to operations of self-preservation. The role of dissociation in Complex PTSD has been muddled by the fact that most of the relevant research is based upon the Structured Interview for Disorders of Extreme Stress (SIDES); the psychometric properties of the SIDES' dissociation scale are questionable. Keeping that in mind, SIDES research shows that dissociation, as currently measured by the SIDES, does not constitute a distinct factor in Complex PTSD. Dr. Ford argues that dissociation may still be central to Complex PTSD, but that better research instruments are needed to resolve this question.

PART IX. DISSOCIATION IN BORDERLINE PERSONALITY DISORDER AND SUBSTANCE DEPENDENCE

Continuing to explore dissociation beyond the Dissociative Disorders, the discussion moves to other common 'comorbidities': Borderline Personality Disorder and substance abuse.

In chapter 31, "Dissociation in Borderline Personality Disorder," Mary Zanarini and Shari Jager-Hyman carefully examine the entire literature on dissociation and Borderline Personality Disorder (BPD), dividing that literature into two phases or generations. The first generation of research consistently showed that about half of BPD patients reported depersonalization and derealization. This research led to the implementation in DSM-IV of Criterion 9 (i.e., transient paranoid ideation or dissociative symptoms). The second generation of research on dissociation in BPD patients is marked by the use of the DES. This research shows that samples of BPD patients show considerable variability in DES scores (i.e., from very low to very high scores) with a mean of 18–25. Studies that examined the diagnostic comorbidity of BPD and dissociative disorders showed substantial levels of comorbidity (31–64%). Despite these findings, Drs. Zanarini and Jager-Hyman contend that a relatively small minority of BPD patients meet the diagnostic criteria for DID or for another dissociative disorder. They also question the clinical utility of a dissociative diagnosis in a BPD patient if the diagnostic criteria of that disorder overlap with the diagnostic criteria of BPD itself (e.g., Depersonalization Disorder, DDNOS).

In chapter 32, "Chronic Relational Trauma Disorder: A New Diagnostic Scheme for Borderline Personality and the Spectrum of Dissociative Disorders," Elizabeth Howell and Ruth Blizard argue that BPD is a form of dissociative disorder, and that the hallmarks of BPD (i.e., affect dysregulation, fear of abandonment, idealization and devaluation, explosive rage, and self-mutilation) are manifestations of dissociative fragmentation resulting from neurobiological state changes, disorganized attachment, traumatic reenactment, and avoidance of overwhelming memories.

In chapter 33, "Opioid Use Disorder and Dissociation," Eli Somer argues that some traumatized individuals use the "chemical dissociation" of substance abuse as a second stage of defense against emotional pain (when psychological dissociation is insufficient). He shows that a trauma history is extremely common in those with Opioid Use Disorder.

Dr. Somer reports that heroin users seek four experiences in particular: (1) chemical amnesia, (2) chemical suppression of the arousal symptoms of PTSD, (3) chemical numbing, depersonalization, and derealization, and (4) soothing and gratifying pleasure.

PART X. DISSOCIATION AND PSYCHOSIS

The relationship between dissociation and psychosis is a most underdeveloped and controversial question. Four chapters examine, from very different perspectives, the interface (or overlap) between them.

In chapter 34, "Are Psychotic Symptoms Traumatic in Origin and Dissociative in Kind?," Andrew Moskowitz, John Read, Susie Farrelly, Thomas Rudegeair and Ondra Williams suggest that most, if not all, psychotic symptoms may be viewed as dissociative in nature. In keeping with this idea, they present a traumagenic neurodevelopmental model of dissociation and psychosis. Specifically, they contend that dissociative symptoms mediate the pathway between early trauma and later psychotic symptoms. Dr. Moskowitz and colleagues review the literature on trauma and psychosis and demonstrate that there is, in fact, a startlingly consistent positive relationship between trauma and the positive symptoms of psychosis. They further argue that the four positive symptoms of schizophrenia (delusions, hallucinations, disorganized speech, and grossly disorganized behavior or catatonia) are consistent with dissociative processes.

In chapter 35, "Psychotic Presentations of Dissociative Identity Disorder," Vedat Şar and Erdinç Öztürk describe and explain psychotic presentations of DID in Turkey. They note that there are two forms of psychotic presentation in DID: (1) full-blown Dissociative Psychosis (formerly hysterical psychosis), and (2) dissociative presentations which mimic psychosis. They provide a rich conceptual and clinical account of these dissociative/psychotic presentations. Drs. Şar and Öztürk argue that Dissociative Psychosis would fill a gap in the nosology of the DSM (i.e., dissociation-laden psychoses with a relatively benign outcome), and discuss the issues involved in diagnosing Dissociative Psychosis in different settings.

In chapter 36, "Dissociative Hallucinosis," Barry Nurcombe, James Graham Scott and Mary Ellen Jessop present their latest thinking about dissociative hallucinosis and interfaces among posttraumatic, dissociative, and psychotic symptoms. They describe dissociative hallucinosis in adolescents: a florid, psychotic-like disorder that is especially characterized by derogatory and commanding voices, and that appears to be equally related to PTSD and to the dissociative disorders. Dr. Nurcombe and colleagues suggest that Dissociative Hallucinosis might appropriately be placed within a section of Trauma-Spectrum Disorders in the DSM.

In chapter 37, "The Theory of a Dissociative Subtype of Schizophrenia," Colin Ross argues in favor of this construct, which would be characterized by three essential features: (1) childhood trauma, (2) dissociative symptoms, and (3) extensive comorbidity. Ross draws on the work of Eugen Bleuler (who coined the word *schizophrenia*) and more contemporary autobiographical accounts in the schizophrenia literature to provide evidence for his contention that there are dissociative cases of schizophrenia. Dr. Ross reviews the phenomenological overlap between the symptoms of psychosis, PTSD, and severe dissociation, and concludes by outlining the research that is necessary to empirically test 'Schizophrenia, Dissociative Subtype.'

PART XI. ASSESSMENT AND MEASUREMENT OF DISSOCIATION

Two gifted clinicians of assessment explain formal testing procedures and the intricacies of forensic expertise.

In chapter 38, "Clinical and Forensic Assessment of Dissociation," Steven Frankel provides a superb outline for assessing potentially dissociative patients in clinical settings and forensic settings. The chapter is structured by ten assessment questions, many of which are often neglected (and, hence, unevaluated) by both front-line clinicians and by those who work in forensic settings. Because Dr. Frankel is both a clinical psychologist and a lawyer, his recommendations for forensic evaluation are especially well-informed and insightful, but also illuminating and sobering to almost all frontline clinicians who tend to be underprepared for encounters with the courts. Every clinician can benefit from what Dr. Frankel has to offer in this chapter.

In chapter 39, "Forensic Trauma Assessment and Detecting Malingering," Laura Brown builds her chapter about forensic trauma assessment on a crucial foundational fact: persons with valid posttraumatic and dissociative symptoms routinely produce elevated validity scales (e.g., MMPI-2 F Scale). In most instances, these elevations do not indicate either faking or exaggeration. Because most clinicians do not know this basic fact about trauma patients, they incorrectly draw pejorative conclusions about them. These issues are especially problematic when traumatized individuals are assessed in a forensic setting. Moreover, as Dr. Brown correctly notes, since the late 1800s, forensic evaluators have often been distinguished by a particularly jaundiced attitude toward psychological trauma and its aftereffects. Thus, in forensic settings, traumatized individuals are at considerable risk for being incorrectly labeled as malingerers. Dr. Brown provides a detailed guide to the differential diagnosis of malingering and nonmalingering in persons who report trauma in a forensic setting.

PART XII. TREATMENT OF DISSOCIATION

Various approaches to the treatment of dissociative disorders are presented—from initial clinical assessment, to containing strategies, to general dissociative approaches that can apply more widely to a broad spectrum of patients.

Chapter 40, "A Clinician's Understanding of Dissociation: Fragments of an Acquaintance," by Richard Kluft, is a gift to clinicians and scholars alike. Justly regarded as *the* leading clinical expert in the dissociative disorders, Dr. Kluft presents some extraordinarily detailed clinical vignettes from the treatment of a DID patient. These clinical vignettes, in turn, serve as springboards for a wide variety of illuminating phenomenological, theoretical, and technical asides. This is the close process account of the treatment of a dissociative patient for which clinicians have long yearned.

In chapter 41, "Treating Dissociation: A Contextual Approach," Steven Gold and Stacy Seibel describe a non-trauma-focused treatment approach to dissociation. Their contextual perspective considers dissociation to be a basic aspect of human functioning which has wide range of manifestations, both adaptive and pathological. They assert that one can learn to recognize, anticipate, decondition, and modulate dissociative responses so as to reduce maladaptive functioning and enhance effective responding. Drs. Gold and Seibel provide an overview of how treatment is structured and guided by this model.

In chapter 42, "Multiple Self-States, the Relational Mind, and Dissociation: A Psychoanalytic Perspective," Phillip Bromberg reinterprets much that is centrally psychoanalytic from a dissociative and relational point of view: the normal self as a multiplicity of discontinuous self states, and object relations as configurations of different selves matching similarly multiple perceptions of others. The psychoanalytic theory is bolstered by research in cognition, neuroscience, attachment theory, and Putnam's theories about mental states. As a general psychotherapeutic approach, Dr. Bromberg does not limit his dissociative relational interpretation to manifestly dissociative disorders. Indeed, in what for the DSM would be his most daring proposal, he reinterprets all personality disorders as covert dissociative disorders: the proactive defensive dissociation of self-other schemata against the repetition of early trauma. Transference and countertransference are interpreted as products of dissociated enactments where the analyst's self states reverberate with the patient's own dissociated self states. The chapter concludes with a discussion of that most central affect, shame.

In chapter 43, "Dissociation and Unformulated Experience: A Psychoanalytic Model of Mind," Donnel Stern critiques Freud's repression model of mind and articulates a new model around the idea of unformulated experience. Dr. Stern draws from Harry Stack Sullivan in replacing repression with dissociation. This involves a rejection of what Stern interprets as Freud's naïve realism and correspondence theory of truth. It is not so much that one formulates experience and then represses it, but rather that one declines to formulate it in the first place. Dr. Stern draws from the hermeneutic philosopher Hans-Georg Gadamer to better articulate this understanding that fails to occur, and in so doing sheds new light on the central role of curiosity: dissociation is the refusal to be curious, the refusal to formulate or understand experience. A consequence of this lack of curiosity is the unconscious enactment of what remains unformulated.

PART XIII. TOWARD A CLARIFIED UNDERSTANDING OF DISSOCIATION

The book culminates with a major empirical delineation of the domain of dissociation, a chapter on research remaining to be done, and a concluding encyclopedic analysis of dissociation.

In chapter 44, "An Empirical Delineation of the Domain of Pathological Dissociation," Paul Dell and Douglas Lawson report landmark findings about the domain of pathological dissociation. They assert that the comprehensiveness of the Multidimensional Inventory of Dissociation (MID) makes possible an empirical delineation of the domain of pathological dissociation. Analyzing MID item-data from two large international samples (each of 1,300+ subjects), Drs. Dell and Lawson replicate a Confirmatory Factor Analysis which shows that pathological dissociation has 12 first-order factors and a single second-order factor (i.e., Pathological Dissociation). Several of their first-order factors of dissociation represent dissociative phenomena that are well-known to clinicians, but which had not been found by any previous factor analysis of dissociation data—because all previous factor analytic studies had been conducted with data from brief screening instruments such as the DES. Thus, Drs. Dell and Lawson find, for the first time, empirical factors of Self-Confusion, Angry Intrusions, Dissociative Disorientation, Trance, and Persecutory Intrusions.

In chapter 45, "A Research Agenda for the Dissociative Disorders Field," Vedat Şar and Colin Ross contribute a truly momentous 'first'; they set forth a research agenda for the dissociative disorders field. Drs. Şar and Ross analyze the extant research and specify the 'logical next steps' for a wide variety of research issues in the dissociative disorders field. The editors of this book think that this chapter is a landmark achievement. We recommend that ISSTD use this chapter as a starting point for an ISSTD Research Task Force that would publish a revised research agenda every three years.

Chapter 46, "Understanding Dissociation," is almost a small book in itself. In this concluding chapter, Paul Dell delivers an encyclopedic analysis of the concept of dissociation. He addresses almost every major issue about dissociation and draws several critical distinctions, the lack of which has bred vagueness and confusion in many previous accounts of dissociation. Beginning with a rich history of the nineteenth century, Dr. Dell shows that the concept of dissociation arose from hypnotic phenomena, rather than from posttraumatic phenomena. Drawing extensively upon the writings of Janet, Freud, and their contemporaries, Dr. Dell carefully distinguishes between dissociation and repression. He then analyzes the current relationships between dissociation and hypnosis, and argues that more hypnosis-related research on dissociation is needed. Dr. Dell attributes much of the longstanding vagueness about the meaning and scope of dissociation to the fact that there are so many dissociation-like phenomena, only some of which entail genuine dissociation. He demonstrates persuasively that there are both normal and pathological kinds of dissociation. Finally, Dr. Dell identifies five kinds of dissociation, each of which he defines and describes in considerable depth.

The editors believe that all the chapters in this book, and especially the final three chapters, provide a sound platform for major advances in our understanding of dissociation and the dissociative disorders. We also hope, as was our original goal, that the American Psychiatric Association work group, which will write the Dissociative Disorders section of DSM-V, will find ample guidance within these pages.

Part I

Dissociation: An Overview

1 History of the Concept of Dissociation

Onno van der Hart, PhD
Martin J. Dorahy, PhD, DClinPsych

OUTLINE

The study of dissociation in the scientific literature has a long and diverse theoretical and clinical history. Initial observations by the early proponents of animal magnetism and hypnosis led to dissociation being associated with divisions or splits in consciousness. The term *consciousness* at that time, and ever since, has been used interchangeably with terms like *personality, mind, psyche,* and *ego*.[1] The division of consciousness (to which the concept of dissociation referred) was then used to explain specific dissociative phenomena, such as post-hypnotic amnesia.

Clinicians working in the mid to late 19th century utilized a similar understanding of dissociation (i.e., divisions in consciousness) to explain hysteria and hysterical symptoms. Although the dominant conception at the time limited dissociation to the psychiatric arena, theoreticians working in other areas began to describe various nonclinical psychological phenomena in terms of dissociation. In addition, with the beginning of the 20th century, psychoanalytic thinking began to produce a change in clinical language and theory. Over time these psychoanalytic innovations brought about a commensurate change in the conceptualization of dissociation.

At the same time theoretical speculation was producing changes in previous views of dissociation, the original clinical observations that related dissociation to divisions in the personality were being replicated during and after World War I and World War II. As a result, army psychiatrists and other clinicians began to rediscover and elaborate on earlier theoretical ideas about traumatic dissociation and its treatment. The late 1960s saw an increased academic interest in altered states of consciousness, which eventually became synonymous with dissociation. During the early 1970s, empirical and theoretical work in cognitive psychology recaptured the initial conceptualization of dissociation (i.e., as divisions in consciousness). Shortly thereafter, clinical interest in psychiatric dissociation reignited; this led to the proliferation of ideas, models, and empirical directions that are evident today. Despite this highly beneficial renaissance of clinical and (nonclinical) interest in dissociation, there continues to be a very large conceptual problem: Namely, there is little agreement about (1) the definition or meaning of dissociation, and (2) the specific psychological phenomena to which the construct refers.

In this chapter, we will provide a detailed history of dissociation. In doing so, we will focus on two conceptual issues that have been recurrently debated: (1) whether dissociation refers to a division in the personality (psyche, consciousness, etc.), as was originally claimed by Janet (1889), or simply alterations in consciousness (e.g., a retraction and/or lowering of the field of consciousness), and (2) whether dissociation can be both pathological *and* nonpathological. The second issue addresses whether dissociation is best understood as (1) a continuum of phenomena that ranges from the normal to the pathological or (2) limited to the pathological (i.e., psychiatric symptoms and pathological divisions in the personality).

[1] For example, Hacking (1991) notes that during various periods different terms were favored (e.g., *personality*, rather than *consciousness* was dominant in late 1800's psychiatric discourse on dissociation). Throughout this chapter we will tend to use the dominant term in the literature being discussed.

1.1 ORIGINS OF DISSOCIATION IN THE SCIENTIFIC LITERATURE

1.1.1 Dissociation as Division of the Personality/Consciousness/Psyche

In Germany, Eberhardt Gmelin (1791) published the first treatise on a case of double personality, and in the same year the Reverend Joseph Lathrop described another case in a letter to Ezra Stiles, the president of Yale University (Carlson, 1981; Crabtree, 1993). In the early 19th century, S. L. Mitchill (1816) presented Mary Reynolds, who was to become a famous American case of multiple personality disorder (Ellenberger, 1970; Goodwin, 1987). Before this time, other such cases were reported but were regarded as individuals possessed by devils and demons (e.g., the 16th-century case of Jeanne Fery; Bourneville, 1886; cf., Van der Hart, Lierens, & Goodwin, 1996).

The initial observations and investigations of dissociation, however, did not begin with these cases of "split" personality. Instead, the initial reports of dissociation came from the French pioneers and early investigators of animal magnetism and hypnosis.

1.1.1.1 Puységur

Franz-Anton Mesmer was the father of animal magnetism. In Vienna, he developed his treatment approach of inducing a so-called magnetic (convulsive) crisis. One of his students, Amand-Marie-Jacques de Chastenet, Marquis de Puységur (1751–1825), discovered that some subjects entered a remarkable state of consciousness. In this state, subjects were aware of no one except the magnetizer whose commands they executed; when they emerged from this state, the subjects were amnesic for all that had occurred during the state. Because of its resemblance to natural somnambulism, this induced state was called *artificial somnambulism* (much later Braid [1843] was to call this condition *hypnosis*).

Puységur and colleagues quickly became aware that the essence of both somnambulism and artificial somnambulism was a dissociation or division of consciousness (Van der Hart, 1997). This led Puységur to assert that "the line of demarcation [in the personality during artificial somnambulism] is so complete that these two states may almost be described as two different existences" (cited in Forrest, 1999, p. 95). Puységur observed that an individual in a somnambulistic state (either natural or artificially induced) displayed two separate streams of thought and memory, in which, at any particular moment, one stream operated outside conscious awareness (Crabtree, 1993).

In conjunction with this division of consciousness, Puységur and colleagues also observed and explained certain discrete dissociative phenomena, especially the psychogenic amnesia that followed lucid (i.e., hypnotic) states (Crabtree, 1993; Ellenberger, 1970). Puységur stated, "I have noticed that in the magnetic state the patients have a clear recollection of all their doings in the normal state, but in the normal state, they can recall nothing of what has taken place in the magnetic condition" (cited in Forrest, 1999, p. 95). Similarly, Deleuze (1819) noted that

> when [the subject] enters the natural state, he loses the memory of all sensations, all ideas which he had in the state of somnambulism, in such a way that these two states seem so foreign to each other as if the somnambule and the awakened individual were two different beings. (p. 176)

1.1.1.2 Moreau de Tours

Initially, this division of consciousness was not referred to as dissociation. The French psychiatrist Moreau de Tours (1845) was probably the first to use the term *dissociation* in a manner that is consistent with contemporary understanding of the concept[2] (Crabtree, 1993; Van der Hart & Horst, 1989). In his experimental studies of the psychological effects of hashish, Moreau de Tours concluded that

> the action of hashish weakens the will—the mental power that rules ideas and associations and connects them together. Memory and imagination become dominant; present things become foreign to us, and we are concerned entirely with things of the past and the future. (1845/1973, p. 33).

According to Moreau de Tours, dissociation—or disaggregation (*désagrégation*)—was the splitting off or isolation of ideas, a division of the personality. If ideas had been aggregated, or integrated, they would have become part of the normal harmonious whole. Moreau de Tours's work preceded fictional representations of chemically induced dissociative states, such as that depicted in the psychological battle between good and evil in Robert Louis Stevenson's *Dr. Jekyll and Mr. Hyde.* Although Moreau de Tours first dealt with chemically induced dissociation, he subsequently studied purely psychological phenomena such as hysterical psychosis (Moreau de Tours, 1865, 1869; Van der Hart, Witztum, & Friedman, 1993).

1.1.1.3 Gros Jean

Gros Jean (1855), a pseudonym for Paul Tascher (Crabtree, 1993), posited the concept of a secondary personality. Tascher broke new psychological ground with his speculation that certain nervous disorders—specifically, possession states, magnetism, and automatic writing—involved a division of the personality. Tascher argued that these phenomena derived from the existence of a second personality—capable of "romantic fabrications" and "digressions"—which *concurrently* existed with the ordinary personality. This notion was new; it went well beyond the idea of a division in the personality that was induced by hypnosis or chemicals. Tascher's theory presented a novel means of understanding behaviors that originated outside the conscious awareness of the primary personality.

1.1.1.4 Taine

Like Tascher, the French philosopher, critic, and historian Hippolyte Taine (1828–1893), in a major work on psychology, *De l'intelligence*, described automatic writing as involving a profound division of consciousness (Taine, 1878):

> In spiritistic manifestations themselves we have shown the coexistence in the same individual of two thoughts, of two wills, of two distinctive actions, of one of which the subject is conscious, but the other of which he has no consciousness and which he attributes to invisible beings. The human brain is thus a theatre where at the same time several different pieces are played, on different stages of which one is in the spotlight. Nothing is more worthy of study than this fundamental plurality

[2] Despite the fact that dissociative phenomena were recognized well before 1812 (e.g., in the 1791 cases of multiple personality, Crabtree, 1993; or Mary Reynolds, the first American case of "double personality," S.L. Mitchell, 1816; S.W. Mitchell, 1888; see also Van der Hart, Lierens, & Goodwin, 1996, for a retrospective 16th century case of DID), the American physician, Benjamin Rush, devoted a chapter of his 1812 psychiatric text to what he named "Dissociation." This may be the earliest medical use of the term (Carlson, 1986). Rush used the term to refer to patients who were "flighty," "hairbrained," or "a little cracked." According to Rush, dissociation came from "an association of unrelated perceptions, or ideas, from the inability of the mind to perform the operations of judgment and reason." Such dissociation was seen in patients with "great volubility of speech" and "rapid bodily movements."

> of the ego; it goes much farther than one can imagine. I have seen a person who, while chatting and singing, wrote complete sentences without looking at the paper, without being conscious of what she wrote. I thoroughly believed in her sincerity. She declares that from the beginning to the end of the page she has no idea of what she had written on the paper. When she reads it she is astonished and sometimes alarmed. The handwriting is quite different from her usual style. The movement of the fingers and pencil is stiff and seems automatic.... We certainly find here a doubling of the ego [*dédoublement du moi*], the simultaneous presence of two parallel and independent series, of two centers of action, or, if you wish, two moral persons side by side in the same brain, each having its work and each a different work—one on the stage and the other behind the scenes. (pp. 16–17)

Taine made an important addition to this account, noting that these two "lives" are neither clearly nor completely separated: "Some images of the one always or almost never enter the other" (p. 160).

Thus, the initial study of dissociative phenomena such as amnesia following artificial somnambulism and automatic writing explained dissociation in terms of a doubling of consciousness (or a division in the personality or ego). Many 19th-century clinicians used this same explanatory mechanism to account for hysteria and hysterical symptoms.

1.1.2 Division or Doubling of Consciousness and Clinical Dissociation: Hysteria and Hysterical Symptoms

By the mid-1800s clinicians were detecting a link between the splitting of consciousness in hypnosis and the clinical phenomena of hysteria.[3] In the same work in which he presented his famous patient with dissociative identity disorder (DID), Estelle, Charles Despine (1840) argued that hypnosis was clearly connected to hysteria (Fine, 1988; Kluft, 1986). Similarly, Briquet (1859) reported that most people who were called magnetic somnambules [hypnotics] were hysterical women. Charcot (1887) further developed these ideas when he theorized that hysterical symptoms (e.g., paralyses, contractures) were based on subconscious ideas that had become separated from consciousness. Finally, Pierre Janet came to view somnambulism as paradigmatic for the dissociative nature of hysteria (Van der Hart, 1997; Van der Hart & Friedman, 1989). In other words, Janet considered both somnambulism and hysteria to be based upon a division of the personality.

In the late 1800s, many clinicians and theorists advanced two theses: (1) dissociation is a division or splitting of consciousness or the personality, and (2) dissociation underlies hysterical symptoms and hysterical phenomena (Binet, 1890, 1892; Legrand du Saule, 1883; Myers, 1887; Ribot, 1885; Richet, 1884). For example, Gilles de la Tourette (1887) described the abolition of certain senses in hysterical patients in terms of dissociation—the absent senses had become dissociated from the patients' normal mental state.

In 1888, Jules Janet used the model of double personality to explain dissociated psychological phenomena. Although his model of the double personality left no room for the notion of *multiple* personalities, it offered a succinct model of hysteria. Jules Janet claimed that each person has two personalities, one conscious and one unconscious (*inconçue* = unconceived). In normal individuals, the two personalities are equal and in harmony with each other; in hysterical patients, the two personalities are unequal and unbalanced. In hysterics, the first personality is incomplete (i.e., exhibits hysterical *losses*, negative dissociative symptoms; cf. Nijenhuis & Van der Hart, 1999) and the second personality is "perfect."

In 1893, Feinkind, a student of Charcot at the Salpêtrière in Paris, published a treatise on "natural somnambulism" and hysterical attacks in the form of somnambulism. Feinkind argued that both kinds of somnambulism are characterized by "doubling (*dédoublement de la personnalité*) or rather *dissociation of the personality*, in the psychological sense of the word" (p. 139). In both instances, the individual's return from the somnambulistic episode is almost always characterized by forgetfulness (*l'oublie*). That forgetfulness, Feinkind insisted, was "previously explained [*dit*] by the dissociation between two personalities, more or less completely ignorant of each other" (p. 140).

1.1.2.1 Janet

Of the many theorists of dissociation, Pierre Janet (1859–1947) unquestionably presented the most detailed and articulate account of the connection between division of the personality or consciousness (i.e., dissociation) and hysteria (cf., Perry & Laurence, 1984; Putnam,

[3] In the clinical domain, dissociation was also linked to other disorders. For example, James (1995) has noted that in the early 1860s, both Maury's (1861) famous study on dreams and Baillarger's (1862) review of this study proposed that certain psychotic patients were characterized by a doubling of the personality (*dédoublement de la personnalité*). Not long after, Littré's (1875) article on *double conscience* used the concept of dissociation to describe depersonalization.

1989a; Van der Hart & Friedman, 1989; Van der Kolk & Van der Hart, 1989). Originally a philosopher and experimental psychologist, in his position as psychiatrist at the Salpêtrière Janet became the leading scientist in the study of hysteria. His thesis for the *doctorat ès-lettres*, *L'automatisme psychologique: Essai de psychologie expérimentale sur les formes inféreures de l'activité humaine* (1889), can be regarded as history's most important work on dissociation. In his editorial of the *American Journal of Psychiatry* celebrating its centenary, John C. Nemiah (1989) wrote:

> The recent festivities celebrating the bicentennial of the French Revolution have overshadowed the remembrance of another occurrence in French history that, from a scientific point of view at least, is perhaps of equal magnitude. (p. 1527)

Janet considered hysteria to be "an illness of the *personal synthesis*" (1907, p. 332). By this, he meant "a form of mental depression [i.e., lowered integrative capacity] characterized by the retraction of the field of consciousness and a tendency to the dissociation and emancipation of the systems of ideas and functions that constitute personality" (p. 332). Although Janet was not always explicit about this, he thought that these dissociative "systems of ideas and functions" had their own sense of self, as well as their own range of affect and behavior. Janet's definition of hysteria makes it clear that he distinguished between retraction of the field of consciousness and dissociation. For him, retraction of consciousness merely implied that individuals have "in their conscious thought a very limited number of facts" (p. 307). Now, many students of dissociation subsume phenomena related to retraction of the field of consciousness, such as absorption and imaginative involvement, under the label of dissociation.

Janet acknowledged a role for constitutional vulnerability in illnesses of personal synthesis, but he regarded physical illness, exhaustion, and, especially, the vehement emotions inherent in traumatic experiences as the primary causes of this integrative failure (1889, 1909, 1911). In keeping with this formulation, the most obvious of these dissociative systems contain traumatic memories, which he originally described as *primary idées fixes* (1894b, 1898). These systems consisted of "psychological and physiological phenomena, of images and movements of a multiform character" (1919/25, p. 597). When these systems are reactivated, patients are "continuing the action, or rather the attempt at action, which began when the [trauma] happened; and they exhaust themselves in these everlasting recommencements" (p. 663).

Janet actually observed that dissociative patients alternate between experiencing too little and experiencing too much of their trauma:

> Two apparently contrasting phenomena constitute a syndrome: They are linked together, and the illness consists of two simultaneous things: 1) the inability of the subject to consciously and voluntarily recall the memories, and 2) the automatic, irresistible and inopportune reproduction of the same memories. (1904/11, p. 528)

Janet (1889, 1904, 1928) observed that traumatic memories/fixed ideas not only may alternate with the habitual personality, but also may intrude upon it, especially when the individual encounters salient reminders of the trauma.

Janet also drew upon traumatic memories to explain the distinction between the *mental stigmata* and the *mental accidents* that characterize hysteria (1893, 1894a, 1907, 1911; cf., Nijenhuis & Van der Hart, 1999). He did not make any distinction between dissociation of the mind and dissociation of the body in mental stigmata and accidents. And, like his contemporaries, he regarded symptoms pertaining to movements and sensations as dissociative in nature. The mental stigmata are negative dissociative symptoms that reflect functional losses, such as losses of memory (amnesia), sensation (anæsthesia), and motor control (e.g., paralysis). The mental accidents are positive dissociative symptoms that involve acute, often transient, intrusions, such as additional sensations (e.g., pain), movements (e.g., tics) and perceptions, up to the extremes of complete interruptions of the habitual part of the personality. These complete interruptions were due to a different part of the patient's personality that was completely immersed in reexperiencing trauma.

Related to primary *idées fixes*, that is, traumatic memories, were *secondary idées fixes*, or fixed ideas not based on actual events, but nevertheless related to them, such as fantasies or dreams. For example, a patient might develop hallucinations of being in hell secondarily related to an extreme sense of guilt during or following a traumatic experience. Such dissociative episodes were called hysterical psychosis, more recently relabelled as (reactive) dissociative psychosis (Van der Hart, Witztum, & Friedman, 1993).

According to Janet, the more an individual is traumatized, the greater is the fragmentation of that individual's personality: "[Traumas] produce their disintegrative effects in proportion to their intensity, duration, and repetition" (1909, p. 1556). Janet regarded multiple personality disorder as the most complex form of dissociation and he noted the differences in character, intellectual functioning, and memory among dissociative parts of the personality (1907). He observed that certain dissociative parts had access only to their own past experience, while other parts could access a more complete range of the individual's history. Dissociative parts could be present side by side or alternate with each other, or both.

In general, Janet believed that dissociation pertains to the division of the personality into dissociative "systems of ideas and functions," each with its own sense of self. For Janet, the division of the personality into dissociative "systems of ideas and functions" was not restricted to DID, but occurred in many forms of hysteria. It has been suggested that in his later life Janet became dismissive of dissociation and DID as psychological concepts (Hacking, 1995). As testified in one of Janet's later books, published a year before his death (1946), this belief is unfounded. His conclusion on double and multiple personalities in this treatise leaves no space for misunderstanding the value he attached to the phenomenon of dissociation, in even a wider range of mental disorders:

> These divisions of the personality offer us a good example of dissociations which can be formed in the mind when the laboriously constructed syntheses are destroyed. The personal unity, identity, and initiative are not primitive characteristics of psychological life. They are incomplete results acquired with difficulty after long work, and they remain very fragile. All constructions built by the work of thought belong to the same genre: Scientific ideas, beliefs, memories, languages can be dissociated in the same way, and the end of illnesses of the mind is the dissociation of tendencies as one observes in the most profound insanities. (p. 146)

Janet (1898, 1911, 1919/25) developed a phase-oriented three-stage treatment approach *avant la lettre*: (1) *stabilization and symptom reduction*, aimed at raising the patient's integrative capacity; (2) *treatment of traumatic memories*, aimed at the resolution or completion of the unfinished mental and behavioral actions inherent in these traumatic memories; and (3) *personality (re)integration and rehabilitation*, which is the resolution of dissociation of the personality and fostering of further personality development (Van der Hart, Brown, & Van der Kolk, 1989).

1.1.2.2 Binet

The experimental psychologist Alfred Binet (1857–1911), a contemporary of Janet, was the director of the Laboratory of Physiological Psychology at the Sorbonne, Paris. Although most recognized as the creator of the first formal test of intellectual ability, Binet is a wrongly forgotten pioneer in the field of dissociation. Ross (1989) has pointed out that his experimental studies on hypnosis addressed what Hilgard (e.g., 1977) later described as the "hidden observer" phenomenon.

Initially Binet emphasized the doubling of consciousness, as demonstrated in his 1887 statement (cited by Ellenberger, 1970, p. 143):

> I believe it satisfactorily established, in a general way, that two states of consciousness, not known to each other, can co-exist in the mind of a hysterical patient.

However, in 1891, Binet had clearly broadened his view:

> In general, observers have only noted two different conditions of existence in their subjects; but this number two is neither fixed nor prophetic. It is not perhaps, even usual, as is believed; on looking closely we find three personalities in the case of Félida, and still a greater number in that of Louis V. That is sufficient to make the expression "double personality" inexact as applied to these phenomena. There may be duplication, as there may be division in three, four, etc., personalities. (1891/96, p. 38)

In his excellent experimental studies, Binet confirmed many of the findings established by Janet. He also established that even when "states of consciousness" are unknown to each other, there may take place between them an exchange of information. The nature and extent of the information exchanged is still the focus of experimental investigation by contemporary researchers (e.g., Elzinga, Phaf, Ardon, &Van Dyck, 2003; Huntjens et al., 2002; see Dorahy, 2001).

1.1.3 Society for Psychical Research in Britain

At the same time that the French were investigating the dissociative basis of hysteria, the British were studying dissociative phenomena under the auspices of the Society for Psychical Research (SPR). In his analysis of the SPR between 1882 and 1900, Alvarado (2002) noted that the study of dissociative phenomena in Britain was largely (though not exclusively) dominated by nonclinical subjects and nonclinical dissociative experiences. In contrast, clinical participants and clinical phenomena constituted the bulk of dissociation studies in France.[4]

[4] However, some cases of clinical dissociation were reported by British physicians, such as the extreme case of H.P. (Bruce, 1895). Bruce attributed the radically different behaviors observed in two distinct states to alterations in the dominance of left and right hemispheres. Around this time, the British physician John Hughlings Jackson was developing his understanding of dissociation (see Meares, 1999). Hacking (1991) has presented several clinical cases of dissociation in Britain from the period of 1815–1875.

SPR members vigorously studied hypnosis, mediumship, automatic speaking and writing, telepathy, double and multiple personality, fugue, trance states, creativity, and secondary and subconscious consciousness. These diverse psychological phenomena were believed to be based upon divisions in consciousness (i.e., dissociation). For example, Frederic Myers (1887) initially proposed the concept of *multiplex personality* to explain how multiple personalities and hypnosis derived from divisions in the personality. He then proposed that the psychic structure was made up of a supraliminal self that operated at a consciousness level and a subliminal self that operated outside conscious and volitional awareness. Hysteria, and various other phenomena, were explained by one self impinging on the other. In further developing his theoretical ideas, Myers (1903) sought to bring together under his concept of the subliminal mind various phenomena that he believed were characterized by divisions of the personality, such as hypnotic trance, telepathy, hysteria, and creativity (Alvarado, 2002).

In their studies of hysterical patients, many French clinicians, such as Janet, viewed the division of consciousness or the personality as a pathological process. However, for British SPR members, dissociation had both pathological and nonpathological expressions. Alvarado (2002) pointed out that SPR literature also placed less emphasis on the connection between dissociation and trauma. As a consequence, it is unclear what proportion of their participants, especially those with profound mediumship ability, acquired their dissociative "skills" courtesy of trauma-induced splits in their personality.

1.1.4 19th-Century Conceptualizations of Dissociation

It is interesting to note that 19th-century literature did not commonly use the term *dissociation*. Still, there existed a strong interest in dissociative phenomena (especially in France, but also Britain), of which somnambulism was often considered to be the paradigmatic manifestation. Nineteenth-century students of dissociation included the old magnetizers, psychiatrists, and philosophers, among others. In addition to somnambulism, dissociative phenomena of interest included possession phenomena, automatic writing, talking tables, mediumship, and various manifestations of hysteria. Multiple personality disorder, which was regarded as the most complex form of hysteria, received special attention. Famous cases such as Félida X (Azam, 1876a, 1876b, 1887; cf., Hacking, 1995; Van der Hart, Faure, Van Gerven, & Goodwin, 1991) and Louis Vivet (Bourru & Burot, 1888; Camuset, 1882; cf., Faure et al., 1997; Hacking, 1995) were the subjects of intense scientific discussion.

Other terms were often used in lieu of *dissociation*. Beginning with Gmelin's (1791) terminology, Table 1.1 provides a comprehensive but not exhaustive list of alternative terms. Many of these concepts are directly related to the division of consciousness or the personality (which defined dissociation at that time). However, in his comments on some of these concepts, O'Neil (1997) argued that they basically refer to two metaphors, one pertaining to a division or splitting, and the other to a doubling or multiplication of consciousness or the personality. Both metaphors are ultimately complementary. As Binet (1890) concluded and modern views have confirmed (e.g., Braude, 1995; Ross, 1989), dissociative parts of the personality may appear separate and even display no awareness of one another. But together these *divided* or *doubled* parts of the personality make up the individual's complete psychological experience, and they may influence each other more than is commonly assumed.

1.1.5 Dissociation in North America Following Developments in Europe

1.1.5.1 James

William James was a diligent and eager student of dissociation. He was influenced and richly inspired by the writings of Janet[5] and other French investigators (e.g., Binet, Charcot), as well as by the ideas of SPR members such as Gurney and Frederic Myers. James was the first to convey European ideas about dissociation to American scholars and clinicians.

Although James gave some coverage to dissociation in his magnum opus, *The Principles of Psychology* (1890), his 1896 Lowell lectures on *Exceptional Mental States* (Taylor, 1983) were the culmination of his ideas about the various normal and abnormal manifestations of dissociation. Like many others at the time, James spoke of dissociation in terms of a division of consciousness. For example, in Lecture 3 of this series, James began by presenting F. Myers's notion of the subliminal self. According to Myers, the psyche is represented by double (or multiple) consciousness, one operating above the threshold of awareness and the other (or others) operating simultaneously outside awareness. Drawing on observations from French clinicians, James used splits in consciousness to account for various hysterical symptoms, including visual

[5] James's admiration for Janet's work is explicit in his 1894 review of Janet's ideas in which he suggested that "every psychologist should make their acquaintance" (p. 198).

TABLE 1.1

Terms Used to Describe Dissociation in the 18th and 19th Centuries and the Author/s Who Used Them

	Authors	Alternative Terms for Dissociation
1	Gmelin, 1791	Exchanged personality (Umgetauschte Persönlichkeit)
2	Dwight, 1818	Two souls
3	Baillarger, 1845	Intellectual duality (*dualité intellectuelle*)
	Tascher, 1855	
4	Lemoine, 1855	Schism of the personality (*scission de la personnalité*)
5	Tascher, 1855	Intellectual doubling (*dédoublement intellectuelle*)
	Richet, 1884	Doubling of the intelligence (*dédoublement de l'intelligence*)
6	Tascher, 1855	Intellectual division (*division intellectuelle*)
7	Tascher, 1855	Intellectual schism (*scission intellectuelle*)
8	Tascher, 1855	Schism between the will and the overactive organism (*scission entre la volonté et l'organisme suractif*)
9	Gautier, 1858	Doubling of the personality (*dédoublement de la personnalité*)
	Baillarger, 1861, 1862	
	Azam, 1876b	
	Boeteau, 1892	
	Bourneville, 1892	
10	Littré, 1875	Double consciousness *(double conscience)*
	Azam, 1887	
	Binet, 1890	
	Breuer & Freud, 1893	
	Hyslop, 1899	
11	Azam, 1876a	Doubling of life (*dédoublement de la vie*)
12	Taine, 1878	Doubling of the ego (*dédoublement du moi*) (also translated as "dual ego" or "doubling of the self")
	Delboeuf, 1879	
13	Ribot, 1885	Double personality *(double personnalité)*
	J. Janet, 1888	
14	Ribot, 1885	Dissolution of the personality
15	Bérillon, 1886	Dissolution of indissoluble phenomena
16	Beaunis, 1887	Doubling of memory and consciousness (*dédoublement de la mémoire et de la conscience*)
17	Myers, 1887	Multiplex personality
	Osgood Mason, 1895	
18	Bourru & Burot, 1888	Multiple personality
19	Bourru & Burot, 1888	Variations of the personality
	Binet, 1892	Alterations of the personality
	Laurent, 1892	
20	P. Janet, 1889	Psychological disaggregation (*désagrégation psychologique*)
	Binet, 1892	Disaggregation of psychological elements
21	Binet, 1890	Duplication of personality
22	Dessoir, 1890	Double ego (*Doppel-Ich*)
23	Binet, 1892/1896	Division of personality
24	Laurent, 1892	The existence of secondary states (*états seconds*)
25	Myers, 1893	Subliminal consciousness
26	Bruce, 1895	Dual brain action
27	Osgood Mason, 1895	Duplex personality
28	James, 1896 (in Taylor, 1983)	Alternating personality

anæsthesia and its resultant negative hallucinations (i.e., failing to perceive a sensation). James described a case of hysterical blindness in the left eye: "[t]he mind is split in two. One part agrees not to see anything with the left eye alone, while the other sees with the right eye perfectly well" (Taylor, 1983, p. 59). In describing this and other cases of anæsthesia, James concluded that "[s]omething sees and feels in the person, but the waking self of the person does not" (p. 60).

Having covered dreams, hypnotism, automatism, and hysteria, James began his fourth lecture by stating: "we are by this time familiar with the notion that a man's consciousness need not be a fully integrated thing.... But we must pass now to cases where the division of personality is more obvious" (Taylor, 1983, p. 73). This lecture addressed the topic of multiple personality; in such individuals, there exist intelligent and seemingly independent dissociative personalities. James favored Myers's model of subliminal consciousness because, he argued, it could explain both Janet's pathological fragmentations from the primary personality as well as the nonpathological cases of mediumship.

Following James's interest in dissociation, especially its clinical manifestations, Boris Sidis and Morton Prince were probably the most important American clinicians who studied dissociation at the beginning of the 20th century.

1.1.5.2 Sidis

Sidis provided a developmental perspective on the ætiology of simultaneous, discontinuous streams of consciousness (Sidis & Goodhart, 1904). In his book, *Multiple Personality: An Experimental Investigation into the Nature of Human Individuality*, Sidis argued that "under the influence of hurtful stimuli, be they toxic or traumatic in nature, the first stage of functional degeneration may give rise to functional dissociations" (Sidis & Goodhart, 1904, p. 53). For Sidis, loss of memory was the essential indicator of the dissociative effects of "hurtful stimuli":

> The breaks and gaps in the continuity of personal consciousness are gauged by loss of memory. Mental systems not bridged over by memory are so many independent individualities, and if started on their career with a good supply of mental material, they form so many independent personalities. For, after all, where memory is gone the dissociation is complete. (p. 44)

Sidis relied on case studies to exemplify his ideas about multiple personality, including a famous case that had been described by his New England contemporary, Morton Prince.

1.1.5.3 Prince

A keen clinical observer and researcher of dissociation, Prince (1854–1929) is probably best known for his celebrated multiple personality case, Miss Beauchamp (1906a). Actually, however, Prince was probably more interested in the unconscious than dissociation. He spent most of his career using the many manifestations of dissociation (e.g., *induced*, such as hypnosis; *spontaneous*, such as dissociative disorders) to undercover and understand the unconscious (Hales, 1975). Although his ideas about dissociation were primarily influenced by the French theories of Pierre Janet and others (e.g., Charcot), Prince did not uniformly accept all French ideas about dissociation. For example, he was critical of the formulations of dissociation that were offered by J. Janet and Azam. Prince (1906b) argued that these individuals misunderstood the structural nature of the psyche in patients with hysteria, especially in terms of what constituted the "first" and "second" personalities. Prince's view was the reverse of that offered by J. Janet and Azam. They considered the "hysteric" personality to be the original or first state, and the "normal" personality to be the dissociated secondary state. Prince (1906b), on the other hand, claimed that the "hysteric" state was the secondary, dissociative, or disintegrated state that was characterized by both positive and negative "physiological" (i.e., somatic) and psychological symptoms (i.e., "stigmata"). The first or normal personality, according to Prince, displayed no symptoms. In a prescient anticipation of modern thinking, Prince (1906b) argued that these "personalities" (especially the hysteric personality state) were able to split further, thus moving from double to multiple personality. In the case of multiple personality, the personalities of "hysterics" may alternate with one another or with the "normal" personality: "Where there are more than two personalities, we may have two hysteric states successively changing with each other, and it may be, with the complete healthy person [normal personality]" (p. 172).

Like many of his contemporaries (e.g., Janet, 1907; Sidis, 1902; Sidis & Goodhart, 1904), Prince was interested in the structure of the personality and the divisions or splits that it manifested. He devoted a great deal of his academic writing to the development of a structural model of personality. This structural model accounted for both the integrated functioning that is evident in the normal population and the disintegrated (dissociated) functioning that he observed in his dissociative patients, such as Miss Beauchamp and B.C.A. (e.g., Prince, 1921, 1924). Prince was one of the first to conceive of dissociation as a mechanism that was not solely pathological, but which could operate as a part of normal psychological functioning (1909). However, unlike contemporary ideas of a continuum of dissociative experience that emphasize dissociative phenomenology, Prince remained firmly focused on the structural elements of psychic functioning and how psychological systems and complexes (associated ideas) become disconnected and synthesized.

Prince seemed to have a greater interest in the structure and dynamics of the personality than in the etiological factors that gave rise to dissociations in the otherwise integrated organization of "unitary complexes and systems" (1921, p. 408). According to Prince (1906b), different structural elements of the psyche (i.e., the "hysteric" and "normal" personality states) in double or multiple personality could be evoked (or caused to alternate) by "the hypnotizing process ... or as a result of emotional shock ... or it may be without demonstrable cause" (p. 174). Prince's greater concern for (1) the structure/dynamics of personality than (2) the ætiology of dissociation is the reverse of what we see in the contemporary study of dissociation and dissociative disorders. Today, etiological factors have probably attracted more attention than the dissociated structure and organization of the personality.

1.1.6 Dissociation in British Psychiatry During and After World War I

As noted above, dissociation received much attention in the early 20th century through the work of F. Myers, Sidis, Prince (e.g., F. Myers, 1903; Prince, 1906a; Sidis, 1902), and others (e.g., W.F. Prince, 1917). Less well known is the interest of several British Army psychiatrists, especially Charles Samuel Myers (1916, 1920–21, 1940; cf., Van der Hart, Van Dijke, Van Son, & Steele, 2000; Van der Hart, Nijenhuis, & Steele, 2006).

1.1.6.1 Myers

Myers (1873–1946) found Janet's dissociation theory to be of great clinical value for the diagnosis and treatment of traumatized combat soldiers (cf., Van der Hart & Brown, 1992). In reflecting on his clinical experiences with acutely traumatized WWI combat soldiers, Myers (1940) found that the mental condition in which his patients (re)experienced their trauma could best be described as a (dissociated) personality, that is, an "emotional" personality. The failure to integrate the various sensory and psychological aspects of horrific experiences had led to a division of the personality into an "apparently normal personality" and an "emotional personality."

Myers's conceptual formulation (i.e., of the apparently normal personality and the emotional personality) can be regarded as an important precursor to modern claims that acute stress disorder and posttraumatic stress disorder are actually dissociative disorders (cf., Chu, 1998; Spiegel & Cardeña, 1991; Nijenhuis, Van der Hart, & Steele, 2002; Van der Hart et al., 2006; Van der Hart, Van der Kolk, & Boon, 1998). Myers described an acutely traumatized patient in a stuperous state as follows:

> At this stage, the normal personality is in abeyance. Even if it is capable of receiving impressions, it shows no signs of responding to them. The recent emotional [i.e., traumatic] experiences of the individual have the upper hand and determine his conduct: the normal has been replaced by what we call the "emotional" personality. Gradually or suddenly an "apparently normal" personality usually returns—normal save for the lack of all memory of events directly connected with the shock, normal save for the manifestation of other ("somatic") hysterical disorders indicative of mental dissociation. Now and again there occur alterations of the "emotional" and the "apparently normal" personalities, the return of the former being often heralded by severe headache, dizziness or by a hysteric convulsion. On its return, the "apparently normal" personality may recall, as in a dream, the distressing experiences revived during the temporary intrusion of the "emotional" personality. The "emotional" personality may also return during sleep, the "functional" disorders of mutism, paralysis, contracture, etc., being then usually in abeyance. On waking, however, the "apparently normal" personality may have no recollection of the dream state and will at once resume his mutism, paralysis, etc. (p. 66–67)

Following the therapeutic lead of Janet, Myers (1920–21; cf., Van der Hart & Brown, 1992) emphasized the integration of traumatic memories rather than abreaction. This approach implies the integration of both parts of the personality (Myers, 1940). In keeping with the French tradition, Myers was also very aware of the dissociative phenomena that have in recent times been subsumed under the name *somatoform dissociation* (Nijenhuis, 1999; Nijenhuis, Spinhoven, Van Dyck, Van der Hart, & Vanderlinden, 1996).

1.1.6.2 Mitchell and McDougall

Several post–World War I British psychiatrists and psychologists were also very interested in dissociation (e.g., W. McDougall, T.W. Mitchell, and B. Hart). Mitchell (1922) summarized the then current state of knowledge regarding dissociation:

> It is now very generally admitted by psychologists that in some persons consciousness may become split up into two or more parts. The split-off or dissociated portion may be but a fragment of the whole self, or it may be so extensive, so complex, and so self-sufficient as to be capable of all the functions of a personal consciousness. In hysteria we find isolated paralyses or localized anæsthesias which are due to the dissociation of relatively simple ideas, or we may find a splitting so deep, a dissociation of so many kinds of mental activity, that it leads to a complex change of the personality. (p. 105)

Both Mitchell (1921, 1922) and McDougall (1926) took issue with what they perceived as Janet's mechanistic view of the construct; they thought that Janet was describing separate mental systems that had no sense of self. We believe that Mitchell and McDougall's (inaccurate) understanding of Janet was due to reading only *The Major Symptoms of Hysteria* (1907), which was available in English. In many of his original French publications, Janet had emphasized the sense of self as a basic characteristic of dissociative mental states (e.g., 1889). Nevertheless, Mitchell and McDougall shone light on an issue that is still difficult to grasp for many contemporary clinicians. For Mitchell (1922), that which is dissociated always resides in another part of the personality. Discussing Janet's dissociation theory, he wrote:

> [I]t cannot be too often repeated and insisted on that we have absolutely no knowledge of any such isolated mental material. If normally an experience that passes out of consciousness is conserved as a psychical disposition, it is as a psychical disposition of *some* personality. If it is not dissociated, it remains part of the normal personality and retains the privilege of being able to reappear above the normal threshold. But if its passage out of consciousness is accompanied by dissociation, it may continue to exist as an unconscious psychical disposition or as a coconscious experience, and *forms an integral part of some personality which may or may not be wider than that which manifests in waking life.* (p. 113/4, emphasis added)

In his major work on abnormal psychology, McDougall (1871–1938) concurred with Mitchell:

> [W]e must interpret the minor phenomena of dissociation in the light of the major cases, the extreme cases in which the phenomena lend themselves better to investigation. In all such major cases, we find the dissociated activity to be not something that can be adequately described as an idea or a group or train of ideas, but rather the self-conscious purposive thinking of a personality; and, when we study the minor cases in the light of the major cases, we see that the same is true of them. (1926, pp. 543/4)

For McDougall, Mitchell, and many others (e.g., Janet, Prince, C. Myers), dissociated material was not simply an isolated psychological element of an experience (e.g., the memory of the event) that failed to integrate in the personality as a whole. Rather, dissociated material formed another part of the personality within the individual. Why? Because the dissociated material (1) was made up of multiple elements of psychological experience (e.g., memories, emotions, conations, sensations), (2) had a sense of self (e.g., the ability to introspect and the capacity to remember autobiographical experiences knowing that they are one's own) and, (3) operated more or less independently of the dominant part of the personality (or, in the case of DID, operated more or less independently of other parts of the personality). In short, the parts of the personality that were developed by the failure to integrate information into a unified personality were more or less independent psychobiological organizations that had a sense of self.

1.2 DISSOCIATION IN THE PSYCHOANALYTIC LITERATURE

1.2.1 Breuer and Freud

Although it may often be understated, downplayed, or ignored, dissociation takes pride of place as the first identified mechanism of ego defense in psychoanalysis (Vaillant, 1992). In 1893, Breuer and Freud wrote:

> [W]e have become convinced that *the splitting of consciousness which is so striking in the well known classical cases under the form of* "double conscience" [fn: the French term ("dual consciousness")] *is present in a rudimentary degree in every hysteria, and that a tendency to such a dissociation, and with it the emergence of abnormal states of consciousness (which we shall bring together under the term "hypnoid"), is the basic phenomena of this neurosis.* In these views we concur with Binet and the two Janets.... These hypnoid states share with one another and with hypnosis ... one common feature: the ideas which emerge in them are very intense but are cut off from the associative communication with the rest of the content of consciousness. (p. 12, italics and footnote in original)

Breuer's concept of hypnoid states (see quotation above) was his adaptation of the French expression for somnambulistic states. Yet despite their general agreement with French observations and thoughts, Breuer and Freud (1893) claimed that "splitting of the mind" or "splitting of consciousness" was not related to a constitutional predisposition to mental weakness; but rather that mental weakness was brought about by dissociation. This idea contradicted what was believed to be Pierre Janet's formulation that psychological weakness (manifesting in low integrative capacity) was a biological predisposing factor for the splitting of consciousness (i.e., dissociation) that gave rise to hysteria. In passing, it should be noted that it would be an oversimplification of Janet's ideas to concentrate on biological predisposition. As outlined above, Janet was very aware of factors other than biological predisposition that contributed to a lowering of integrative capacity (e.g., physical ill-health). Furthermore, like Breuer and Freud, Janet emphasized the disintegrative effect of the vehement emotions experienced during and after trauma.

Freud himself initially perceived dissociation as an ego defense against the intense affect that manifested in hysterical paralysis (1893). He also initially gave childhood trauma, especially abuse, a core etiological role in hysteria (1896). However, his focal interest in dissociation and abuse were short-lived. Two years later he began to work on his repression model (e.g., 1895) and turned his attention away from dissociative phenomena in general and multiple nuclei of consciousness in particular.[6] In addition, he quickly came to place great emphasis on the etiological role of instinctual drives and intrapsychic conflict in the development of hysteria and other neurotic forms.

Discussion of dissociation was largely absent from early 20th-century psychoanalytic literature (Hart, 1926). However, neither dissociation nor trauma vanished from the rise and evolution of psychoanalytic ideas (e.g., Alexander, 1956); over time conceptualizations of dissociation were developed from psychoanalytic frameworks. Perhaps Erdelyi (1994) said it best when he stated that "dissociationism itself was not abandoned or absorbed, but rather a dissociationism different from Janet's was pursued" (p. 9).

In the psychoanalytic literature, dissociation is often referred to as a defense,[7] be it immature or neurotic (see Vaillant, 1992). From this perspective, integrated functioning temporarily (and defensively) gives way in order to minimize the impact of internal and external stressors.

The core of the difference between this psychoanalytic view of dissociation and the nonpsychoanalytic views that were prevalent in the late 19th and early 20th centuries is the following. Nonpsychoanalytic investigators conceptualized dissociation in terms of two aspects: (1) integrated functioning that temporarily gave way in the face of stressors, and (2) the concomitant development of a separate, split off, psychic organization, personality, or stream of consciousness. This separate organization was made up of the unintegrated perceptual and psychological elements of the traumatic event. This personality organization operated outside of the individual's conscious awareness and could be accessed by various means including hypnosis and automatic writing. It was the division (dissociation) of consciousness (or the personality) that caused such hysterical (dissociative) symptoms as amnesia and contractures. For nonpsychoanalysts, dissociation referred not only to the process of failed integration, but also to a psychical organization or structure (i.e., a dissociative psychic organization). Early Freudians, on the other hand, limited their view of dissociation solely to the first aspect (i.e., the process of failed integration, which, for the analysts, was motivated by the ego in the service of defense).

The nonpsychoanalytic understanding of dissociation differed substantially from Freud's general framework and guiding principles.[8] This made direct application from one model to another conceptually difficult (Hart, 1926). A clearer conceptualization of dissociation as a psychical or structural organization remained a task for later psychoanalytic writers, such as Ferenczi and several object relations theorists (Tarnopolsky, 2003).

1.2.2 Ferenczi

Being schooled in the psychological effects of trauma during his time as a World War I army psychiatrist, Ferenczi was probably the earliest psychoanalytic writer to give serious attention to the phenomena of divided personality states. In 1933, Ferenczi noted that dissociation or "splits in the personality," reflected the structure of the psyche. He stated explicitly that such splits in the personality were related to childhood trauma:

[6] Erdelyi (1985) has argued that Freud used the terms *repression* and *dissociation* interchangeably.

[7] Dissociation as a *defense* in psychoanalytic thinking can be distinguished from dissociation as *insufficient psychological capacity for integrated functioning*. In the latter Janetian sense, dissociation may come to have a secondary defensive value. However, unlike the psychoanalytic understanding, Janet's dissociation does not occur for the primary purpose of psychic defense (i.e., ego-derived expulsion or splitting off of noxious internal or external material).

[8] Hart (1926) points out that Freud's psychoanalytic theory focused on the dynamic principles that gave rise to the observable phenomena, whereas the observable dissociative phenomena were the focal point (and objects of analysis) for Janetian dissociative theory.

> If the shocks increase in number during the development of the child, the number and the various kinds of splits in the personality increase too, and soon it becomes extremely difficult to maintain contact without confusion with all the fragments, each of which behaves as a separate personality yet does not know of even the existence of the others. (p. 229)

Although he probably overstated the degree of separateness of these dissociative personalities, Ferenczi provided in the early 1930s a rudimentary prototype of the contemporary posttraumatic model of dissociation and DID (e.g., Kluft, 1985; Putnam, 1989b, 1997b; Ross, 1989, 1997).

1.2.3 Fairbairn

The object relations theorist Fairbairn (1944/1992) argued that dissociation was the basis of hysteria:

> Here it may be added that my own investigations of patients with hysterical symptoms leaves me in no doubt whatever that the dissociation phenomena of "hysteria" involves a split of the ego fundamentally identical with that which confers upon the term "schizoid" its etymological significance. (p. 92)

Thus, for Fairbairn, "dissociation," "schizoid," and "splitting of the ego" were interchangeable terms that referred to a specific type of division in psychic organization.

1.2.4 Bridging Psychoanalysis and Hypnosis: Spiegel

In 1963, Herbert Spiegel (1963) took up the term *dissociation* and used it in two related, but quite different ways: (1) dissociation as a defensive process, and (2) dissociation as a conceptual framework (i.e., the dissociation-association continuum). In reference to defense, Spiegel (1963) viewed dissociation as a "fragmentation process that serves to defend against anxiety and fear (or instinctual demands)" (p. 375). With reference to conceptual framework, Spiegel offered dissociation as one pole on a dissociation-association continuum that subsumed the phenomena explained by repression. The dissociation-association continuum provided a dynamic model of psychological experience that was not constrained by continual references to instinctual conflict. Spiegel's dissociation-association continuum stretches from (1) evasive defense strategies that minimize anxiety and are associated with constricted awareness, through (2) strategies designed to sustain an adaptive level of awareness, to (3) the resurfacing and (re)integration of dissociated fragments, which leads to a more expanded level of awareness, and creativity and growth. Thus, for Spiegel, dissociation referred to (1) the dis-integration of otherwise associated ideas and (2) the constriction of awareness. Clearly, Spiegel emphasized the defensive rather than the organizational aspects of dissociation.

Psychoanalytic studies of dissociation proliferated in the 1970s (e.g., Gruenewald, 1977; Lasky, 1978) and early 1980s (e.g., Berman, 1981; Marmar, 1980). The psychoanalytic understanding and treatment of dissociation continues to evolve (e.g., Blizard, 2001; Brenner, 2001; Bromberg, 1998; Chefetz, 1997; Davies & Frawley, 1994; Howell, 2003; Kluft, 2000; Loewenstein & Ross, 1992; O'Neil, 1997; Stern, 1997).

1.3 THE RENAISSANCE OF DISSOCIATION: NONPATHOLOGICAL AND PATHOLOGICAL MANIFESTATIONS

Dissociation attracted only minimal attention in the 1940s and 1950s (e.g., Lipton, 1943; Maddison, 1953; Taylor & Martin, 1944), but did produce the famous DID case of "Eve" (Osgood & Luria, 1954; Thigpen & Cleckley, 1954, 1957). The general dearth of interest in dissociation continued during the 1960s even though one clinical paper argued that multiple personality was far more prevalent than generally assumed (Morton & Thoma, 1964). The end of the 1960s, however, was marked by a rise in academic, nonclinical interest in dissociation (or, at least, dissociation-like experiences). Unlike previous work, this new interest led to a broadening of the concept of dissociation; the concept of dissociation began to be applied to experiences that were unrelated to divisions of consciousness (or what, at times, had been referred to as splits in the personality).

At that time, dissociation was increasingly described in two ways: (1) as a continuum of phenomena that stretched from normal experiences (e.g., daydreaming, hypnotic trance) to clearly pathological experiences (e.g., multiple personality), and (2) as being synonymous with alterations in consciousness. Experiences that fell at the lower end of the dissociation continuum (e.g., daydreaming, trance) exemplified the emerging tendency to equate dissociation with alterations of consciousness. This new view of dissociation paid particular attention to *phenomenal* changes in conscious experience from a normal waking state (as opposed to the earlier focus on structural splits or divisions in the personality or ego—which, of course, also have phenomenal correlates).

Some alterations of consciousness may still entail a "breakdown" in integrated functioning,[9] the *sine qua non* of the American Psychiatric Association's (2000) definition of dissociation. For example, during a daydream, the person may not integrate stimuli from the outside world into his or her conscious experience. The crucial point, however, regarding dissociation-as-alterations-of-consciousness is that the origin of the phenomenal experience is *not* a division in consciousness or the personality, but rather a failure to encode information. That is, a division in the personality is not necessary to have this type of "dissociative" experience. Echoing the thoughts of F. Myers in the 19th century, this view of dissociation holds that dissociative experiences are neither the exclusive domain of the clinical world, nor are they restricted to symptoms. However, unlike F. Myers, and others (e.g., M. Prince), this modern view focuses solely on phenomenal expressions rather than underlying psychic organization.

1.3.1 Tart and Ludwig

In 1969, Charles Tart published his monumental edited volume, *Altered States of Consciousness.* This work outlined the alterations in consciousness that were induced by psychedelic drugs, hypnosis, and meditation. In addition, the volume examined specific altered states of consciousness (ASC) such as depersonalization, derealization, trance states, absorption, and some of the residual effects of such states (e.g., subsequent amnesia). Of most interest to the current discussion is the opening chapter by Arnold Ludwig, a reprinting of his 1966 paper, "Altered States of Consciousness." The importance of this chapter lies in Ludwig's definition of ASC. He does not view ASC as analogous to dissociation, but his definition of ASC is clearly comparable to contemporary understandings of the dissociative continuum. Ludwig defined ASC

> as any mental state(s), induced by various physiological, psychological or pharmacological maneuvers or agents, which can be recognized subjectively by the individual himself (or by an objective observer of that individual) as representing a sufficient deviation in subjective experience or psychological functioning from certain general norms for that individual during alert, waking consciousness. This sufficient deviation may be represented by a greater preoccupation than usual with internal sensations or mental processes, changes in the formal characteristics of thought, and impairments of reality testing to various degrees. (p. 11)

In advance of, but consistent with, contemporary continuum ideas, Ludwig (1969) argued "that ASC might be regarded ... as a 'final common pathway' for many different forms of human expression and experience, both adaptive and maladaptive" (p. 20). The year after Ludwig published this idea (1966), West (1967) made similar assertions: Dissociation could be *experienced* in both pathological and nonpathological forms.

In later work, Ludwig (1983) clearly implied a continuum of dissociative experience when he suggested that both daydreams and multiple personality are examples of dissociation. Still, he grappled with two questions: (1) What should fall under the banner of "dissociation?" and (2) Is "dissociation" analogous to ASC?

> [I]t is difficult to know the extent to which many other altered states of consciousness, such as transcendental meditative states, Yoga, alpha rhythm and peak experiences, should be regarded as examples of dissociation or whether dissociative states should be regarded as a subcategory of altered states of consciousness. (p. 94)

The question of what does and what does not constitute dissociation continues to be a source of disagreement; this, in turn, has serious consequences for the definition, theoretical utility, and descriptive value of the concept (e.g., Cardeña, 1994).

Recently, Nijenhuis, Van der Hart, and Steele (2002; cf., Van der Hart et al., 2006) have drawn upon both clinical and basic research to argue that, for the sake of clarity and clinical accurateness, dissociation should revert to its original Janetian understanding. By this they mean that dissociation pertains to the development of two or more parts of the personality that are insufficiently integrated with each other; most of these dissociative parts are characterized by a significant retraction of the field of consciousness. If this view were adopted, dissociative episodes and ASC would be distinct psychological phenomena (though they may occur together).

A remarkably rich and fertile volume that regenerated clinical interest in dissociation was published in 1970—Henri Ellenberger's monumental monograph, *The Discovery of the Unconscious.* In a highly detailed and stunning piece of scholarship, Ellenberger reintroduced the modern reader to Pierre Janet and his dissociative model of hysteria. Ellenberger demonstrated the

[9] In the contemporary dissociation literature the term *breakdown* is used synonymously with the term *disruption.* It remains unclear exactly what these terms actually mean. For example, is a state of absorption in a book or television program accurately categorized as a *breakdown* or *disruption* in integrated processing in the same way as a failure to integrate traumatic elements of an event? On account of their ambiguity these terms are often loosely applied and utilized.

importance of Janet's ideas not only to his contemporaries, but also to the evolution of dynamic psychiatry. *The Discovery of the Unconscious* has influenced both clinical and nonclinical scholars and researchers; it continues to be a valuable source of historical information today.

At least four significant developments occurred in the early 1970s: (1) the publication of Sybil (Schreiber, 1973); (2) the publication of several papers that outlined treatment approaches for multiple personality disorder (MPD; e.g., Allison, 1974a; Bowers et al., 1971; Gruenewald, 1971; Howland, 1975); (3) the publication of one of the first modern controlled attempts to examine the transfer of cognitive information across so-called dissociative barriers in MPD (Ludwig, Brandsma, Wilbur, Benfeldt, & Jameson, 1972); and (4) with the publication of Hilgard's neo-dissociation theory, mainstream cognitive psychology became seriously interested in dissociation.

1.3.2 Hilgard

Coming from a long background in hypnosis research (Hilgard, 1973), and being captivated by the secular interests in altered states of consciousness that were occurring at that time, Hilgard became deeply interested in dissociation. In 1974, he outlined what he called a "reference experiment" (p. 307) that laid the foundation for a dissociative theory of simultaneous or near-simultaneous mental operations. In the "reference experiment," Hilgard induced in highly hypnotizable students analgesia for cold-pressor pain (i.e., from immersion of an arm in ice-cold water). To his initial surprise, Hilgard discovered that he could use automatic writing or talking to communicate with a "subconscious" part of the individual that reported feeling the pain and discomfort that the hypnotized person did not feel. Hilgard (1977) later referred to this "subconscious" part as the "hidden observer" (see also Hilgard, 1992).

From this and further experiments with hypnosis, Hilgard developed his neo-dissociation theory, which was most extensively outlined in his 1977 monograph (expanded and reprinted in 1986), *Divided Consciousness: Multiple Controls in Human Thought and Action* and subsequent papers (e.g., 1994). Hilgard's theory explicitly acknowledged the influence of Janet in particular, and other early investigators of dissociation who had identified "vertical splits" in consciousness that seemed to account for various psychiatric and psychological phenomena.

Neo-dissociation theory differed from classic dissociation theory in its *goals* and the *phenomena* that it emphasized. Unlike classic models of dissociation that emphasized (1) structural divisions in the personality or ego (2) in order to understand the phenomena of hypnosis, somnambulism, and hysteria, neo-dissociation theory emphasized (1) mental activities or structures (2) in order to explain the simultaneous or near-simultaneous performance of different activities such as automatic writing and monitoring unfelt pain. Janet called such consciously undirected activities as automatic writing *psychological automatisms*.

Neo-dissociation theory was utilized to explain the observation that seemingly "separate controls operate within a common nervous system" (Hilgard, 1973, p. 215). Thus, for neo-dissociation theory, mental structures and their ostensibly concurrent yet somewhat independent functioning (rather than personality structures) were the focus of attention. It should be noted, however, that both neo-dissociation theory and classic dissociation theory addressed the misapprehension that consciousness is unitary. Otherwise, their respective concentration on cognitive structures and personality structures were in keeping with the dominant discourse of their times.

Unlike previous models of dissociation, neo-dissociation theory brought into the domain of dissociation the simultaneous performance of two cognitive activities (e.g., driving a car while simultaneously being deeply absorbed in a daydream or conversation). Turning to more clinical phenomena, Hilgard (1973) argued that because neo-dissociation theory was focused on the splitting and simultaneous operation of control processes it might provide a framework for understanding multiple personality, which he called an example of "dissociation *par excellence*" (p. 216, italics in original). Following Hilgard's lead, Kihlstrom has used neo-dissociation theory to understand various manifestations of clinical dissociation (e.g., Kihlstrom, 1992a, 1992b; Kihlstrom, Tataryn, & Hoyt, 1993).

During the 1970s, academic and nonclinical interest in dissociation gave way to a significant rejuvenation of clinical interest in dissociation. Like much of the 19th-century *fin-de-siècle* interest in dissociation, the study of clinical dissociation in the late 1970s focused primarily on multiple personality. A rapidly growing number of cases of multiple personality were identified in North America. In the absence of suitable outlets for exchange (i.e., dedicated conferences and journals on dissociation), clinicians communicated their ideas, thoughts, and experiences informally, in what Ross (1997) and others have called an oral tradition (e.g., letters, telephone correspondence, generic conferences). Kluft (2003) has provided a personalized account of the clinical developments and enthusiasm that characterized that time. Greaves (1993), in turn, has described the skepticism in mainstream psychiatry evoked by the rejuvenation of clinical interest in multiple personality.

1.4 1980 AND BEYOND

Without doubt, 1980 was a watershed year for the study of dissociation. Not only did that single year see the publication of several articles on MPD (e.g., Bliss, 1980; Coons, 1980; Rosenbaum & Weaver, 1980), including Greaves' (1980) classic review, but the DSM moved to a phenomenological classification of psychiatric illness in which the dissociative types of hysterical neurosis were grouped with depersonalization under a new major heading: Dissociative Disorders.

The consolidation of the Dissociative Disorders in DSM-III, however, came at a cost; the conversion type of hysterical neurosis, which represented somatoform expressions of dissociation, so central to earlier conceptualizations of dissociation, was regrouped under another new major heading, Somatoform Disorders, together with somatoform conditions not classically considered as dissociative. In addition, DSM-III's focus on phenomenology shifted attention (1) away from the structure or organization of the personality/psyche, and (2) onto observable or reported symptoms (i.e., phenomena).

Despite the sidelining of somatoform expressions of dissociation and the shift of emphasis away from the structure of the personality/psyche, DSM-III had an immense and salutary impact on the study of dissociation. Because the phenomenal view is not tied to an underlying personality structure/organization, dissociation became understood more broadly as a psychologically derived "breakdown" in normal integrated functioning. This focus on phenomenology reinforced the growing trend to conceptualize dissociation along a continuum that stretched from (1) phenomena that represented basic everyday breakdowns in integrated functioning like daydreams to (2) severe pathological breakdowns in integrated functioning, such as symptoms and disorders (e.g., Braun, 1988).

Based on discrete phenomenological experiences, self-report dissociation questionnaires began to be developed during the mid-1980s.[10] These measures have tended to focus on a wide range of phenomena that are regarded as dissociative in contemporary thinking. As one of the authors of the Dissociative Experiences Scale (DES) notes: "The definition of dissociation incorporated into the DES was intentionally broad. The authors attempted to include as wide a range of items as possible in the DES.... Consequently, the authors included many different kinds of *experiences* that had been previously *associated* with dissociation" (Carlson, 2005, p. 42, italics added). Most measures of dissociation have not been restricted to assessing phenomena that originate from a dissociative personality structure (which was the focus of attention for scholars of dissociation until contemporary times). The Somatoform Dissociation Questionnaire (SDQ-20) is probably an exception in this regard, because its authors derived the scale directly from symptoms that manifest from one or more dissociative parts of the personality (Nijenhuis et al., 1996).

Measures of *peritraumatic dissociation* (e.g., Peritraumatic Dissociative Experiences Questionnaire; Marmar, Weiss, & Metzler, 1997) are even further removed from the historical understanding of dissociation as divisions in the personality. Trait dissociation measures like the DES have items that tap the influence of one division of the personality on another (e.g., identity alteration; flashbacks), for example. Peritraumatic measures, however, tend to focus primarily on narrowing of the field of consciousness, alterations in sensory perception, and the activation of multiple streams of consciousness. Peritraumatic dissociation researchers do not deny dissociative divisions in the personality, which may be derived from dissociative episodes at the time of a trauma (see Marmar, Weiss, & Metzler, 1997). However, such instruments assess phenomenological experiences that occur around the time of a trauma (i.e., during or immediately after). As such (1) they do not fully capture the phenomena that are associated with dissociative divisions in the personality (because such phenomena may not start until *after* the trauma, *once* the personality has been divided), and (2) peritraumatic phenomena may be unrelated to the development of dissociative parts of the personality and may represent mere alterations of consciousness.

The development and use of dissociation questionnaires provided a basis for the empirical examination of clinically observed developmental, affective, experiential, and environmental correlates of dissociation (e.g., Coons & Milstein, 1986; Putnam, Guroff, Silberman, Barban, & Post, 1986). Moreover, because many self-report questionnaire measures of dissociation are based on the continuum model of dissociation, hypotheses that were drawn from clinical cases of dissociation could be legitimately tested in large, nonclinical samples. In

[10] Self-report measures of dissociation include the Dissociative Experiences Scale (Bernstein & Putnam, 1986; Carlson & Putnam, 1993); the Perceptual Alterations Scale (PAS; Sanders, 1986); the Questionnaire of Experiences of Dissociation (QED; Riley, 1988); Dissociation Questionnaire (DIS-Q; Vanderlinden et al., 1993); North Carolina Dissociation Index (NCDI; Mann, 1995); the Multidimensional Inventory of Dissociation (MID; Dell, 2000); Multiscale Dissociation Inventory (MDI; Briere, 2002); the Somatoform Dissociation Questionnaire (Nijenhuis, Spinhoven, Van Dyck, Van der Hart, & Vanderlinden, 1996). Measures are also available to assess dissociation in children and adolescents (Armstrong, Putnam, & Carlson, 1998; Putnam, 1997b).

addition, the continuum model suggests that the findings from nonclinical studies of dissociation could enlighten clinical understanding. In short, the combination of (1) dissociation questionnaires and (2) the recent dominance of the continuum model have allowed an integration of clinical and nonclinical research and theory.

We would argue, however, that both (1) the continuum model and (2) the questionnaires that are based upon that model are obstacles to a clear understanding of the concept of dissociation.[11] The forefathers of the study of dissociation employed a much narrower domain of dissociative phenomena that was limited to those experiences that resulted from a division (dissociation) of consciousness or the personality. The many phenomena that are considered to be "dissociative" by the continuum model (and which are assessed by most dissociation questionnaires) have many different psychological origins. The original domain of dissociative phenomena had just one psychological origin—divisions in personality or consciousness.

1.5 CHANGES IN THE CONCEPT OF DISSOCIATION: PROGRESS IN UNDERSTANDING OR CONCEPTUAL DRIFT?

The concept of dissociation in the 18th, 19th and early 20th centuries related to a division or dissociation in the personality/consciousness. This division was best illustrated by actions that were performed outside the awareness of the individual. Initially, the division of the personality was thought to be due to artificial somnambulism (e.g., the Marquis de Puységur). As the psychological phenomena resulting from a division in consciousness began to be appreciated, clinicians came to understand hysterical symptoms and hysterical neurosis in terms of dissociation (i.e., division of consciousness, or the personality). Janet was the first to recognize the connection between hysterical divisions of the personality and exposure to traumatic stress (see Dorahy & Van der Hart, 2007 for an historical analysis of the link between trauma and dissociation). In the case of traumatic stress, Janet believed that an alternate part of the personality was created. This alternate part of the personality was composed of the unintegrated psychological and behavioral elements of the trauma. In these instances, dissociation described a trauma-induced personality organization.

According to Janet, dissociation (division of the personality/consciousness), could be induced in two ways: (1) via artificial somnambulism or (2) as a result of stress (e.g., trauma). Yet, dissociation still ultimately referred to the division of the personality. Psychological experiences that derived from such a divided personality organization were understood as dissociative phenomena. Janet viewed dissociation and dissociative phenomena as representing psychological pathology. Several of his contemporaries (e.g., F. Myers, M. Prince) did not restrict dissociative phenomena to clinical symptoms and expressions. Yet, they still conceptualized dissociation in structural terms.

The latter half of the 20th century increasingly presented a much broader version of dissociation. As noted previously, several sources contributed to this change: (1) the study of altered states of consciousness (e.g., Ludwig, 1966; Tart, 1969) and the subsequent acceptance of a dissociative continuum, which came to equate almost any altered state of consciousness with dissociation; (2) DSM-III's strict adherence to nonconceptual, phenomenological descriptions of mental disorders; and (3) dissociation questionnaires that used *phenomena* rather than *structure* as their starting point. Those phenomena encompassed a broad range of clinical and nonclinical experiences that were believed to exemplify a breakdown in integrated functioning.

Despite being ill-defined, almost any psychologically derived breakdown in integrated functioning was considered to exemplify dissociation. Everyday nonclinical breakdowns in integrated functioning were conceptualized as operating on the same psychological continuum as the most pathological expressions of dissociation. This massively heterogeneous version of dissociation led to a fairly inevitable result—the implicit hypothesis that different dissociative phenomena had different causes. Some nonpathological alterations in perceptual experience were considered to have many possible causes. Other dissociative phenomena were believed to be due to the operation of simultaneous independent streams of consciousness. Finally, pathological phenomena such

[11] The problem of conceptual ambiguity in the contemporary understanding of dissociation has been identified before and one solution was sought with the DES-Taxon (DES-T). The DES-T is a subset of DES items which emerged statistically from studies on patients with dissociative and nondissociative disorders. Taxon items represent a statistically derived cluster of symptoms experienced by those with a dissociative illness but not by individuals with a nondissociative illness. The DES-T offered a measure of pathological dissociation as opposed to nonpathological dissociation. However, some pathological symptoms in the taxon model are not per se related to an underlying dissociative personality structure and may have their foundation in other psychological sources; for example, some episodes of severe derealization (e.g., DES item 12: "some people have the experience of feeling that their body does not seem to belong to them") and depersonalization (e.g., feeling the body as alien). With its basis in phenomena and not underlying psychological structure, the taxon model does not provide an effective resolution to conceptual ambiguity in the modern understanding of dissociation.

as amnesia or dissociative identities were explained as being due to trauma-induced divisions in the personality. So-called breakdowns in integrated functioning were the basis from which dissociative phenomena were derived and understood. Historically, structural divisions of consciousness or the personality were the basis from which dissociative phenomena were derived and understood.

We contend that this broader understanding of dissociation brought with it a variety of disadvantages, the most serious being a fuzzy, all-encompassing meaning (Frankel, 1994; Marshall, Spitzer, & Liebowitz, 1999) and a concomitant lack of clearly definable phenomenological boundaries (Cardeña, 1994).

1.6 CONCLUSION

This review and analysis of the history of the concept of dissociation has identified at least five important portrayals of dissociation: (1) dissociation was first utilized to describe a personality organization (i.e., a division in the personality, consciousness, or ego); (2) dissociation was reinterpreted by Freud and others as a defense (and is often subsumed under the concept of repression by psychoanalytic thinkers); (3) dissociation has been viewed as a process, which, for example, characterizes the initial dissociative division of the personality following trauma and also the switching between dissociative parts of the personality; (4) dissociation came to be seen as a very broad set of experiences and symptoms that are characterized by a so-called breakdown in integrated psychological functioning; and (5) today, dissociation is widely believed to lie on a continuum that stretches from normal experiences to pathological symptoms.[12]

From our analysis of the historical and contemporary literatures, we conclude that dissociation has two major conceptualizations: narrow and broad. These two conceptualizations relate directly to the *hypothesized origins of* what are described as *dissociative phenomena.*

The narrow conceptualization of dissociation was dominant from the birth of the study of dissociation until the later part of the 20th century. This conceptualization defines dissociation as a division of consciousness or a division of the personality. From this perspective, unless phenomena derive from a division of consciousness or the personality, they are *not dissociative.* Said differently, dissociative phenomena have a single origin (i.e., the division of consciousness or personality).

There are at least two important versions of the narrow conceptualization of dissociation: (1) hypnotically induced divisions of consciousness, and (2) trauma-induced divisions of consciousness.

The hypnotic version of the narrow conceptualization of dissociation applies to divisions of consciousness that are (1) hypnotically induced by either self or other, and (2) transient in nature. The leading examples of the narrow conception where dissociation is induced by another are (1) the 18th and 19th century studies of artificial somnambulism[13] and hypnosis, and (2) Hilgard's studies of the hidden observer phenomenon.

Self-induced (hypnotic) divisions of consciousness are probably best exemplified by some mediums who were studied by members of the Society of Psychical Research in Britain. Following the hypnotic-induction procedure, the consciousness of these mediums divided into multiple streams. In mediums who acquired their skills through the use of auto-hypnosis, at least one stream of consciousness operated outside of his or her awareness. This divided psychic organization or structure was transient. That is, when the hypnotic state was terminated, the structural organization of the psyche also changed (i.e., the separate streams of consciousness were no longer easily accessible). It is essential to note that hypnotically induced divisions of consciousness (and their accompanying hypnotic phenomena) are not the exclusive domain of the clinical world; such hypnotically-induced divisions of consciousness reflect a capacity that is possessed by many normal and healthy individuals.

The trauma-induced narrow conceptualization of dissociation applies to a posttraumatic division of the personality into dissociated parts that are either (1) trauma-avoidant or (2) trauma-fixated. Prominent historical scholars of clinical dissociation (e.g., Janet and C.S. Myers) espoused this view. This posttraumatic dissociative personality structure generates dissociative symptoms; these dissociative symptoms are both positive and negative, psychoform and somatoform. Thus, in contrast to the hypnotic narrow version of dissociation, the posttraumatic narrow version of dissociation refers only to psychopathology. The divisions of the personality that characterize dissociative psychopathology are relatively fixed and stable. That is, the memory composition, emotional range, and behavioral patterns of dissociative parts

[12] Recognizing the lack of a single coherent meaning, Cardeña (1994) has clustered the many uses of the term *dissociation* under the banner, *the domain of dissociation.*

[13] We would hold that not all cases of artificial somnambulism displayed the induction of a transient division in the personality that is evident in hypnosis. In several classic cases of artificial somnambulism (e.g., Puységur's case of Victor Race) it seems that more stable dissociative parts of the personality were evoked. Cases such as this are consistent with trauma-induced divisions of the personality.

of the personality remain highly organized and divided. In the absence of effective treatment, the dissociated functioning of the personality will continue.

The two versions of the narrow conceptualization of dissociation are not mutually exclusive and both share the same cornerstone: They both define dissociation as a division of consciousness or a division of the personality. Both apply the term *dissociative* only to the phenomena produced by divided consciousness or a divided personality.

Since the 1980s the narrow conceptualization of dissociation has been overshadowed and largely ignored in favor of a phenomenologically-based broad conceptualization of dissociation. As noted above, the broad conceptualization of dissociation is rooted in a continuum model of phenomenological experiences that puts much less emphasis on the putative origin/s of dissociative phenomena. It focuses on the *phenomena* themselves (rather than on their putative underlying ætiology, or the personality structure that gives rise to them). This broad conceptualization defines dissociation as a breakdown in integrated function. Thus, any psychological experience characterized by a breakdown in integrated function is considered dissociative. The broad conceptualization of dissociation is quite eclectic with regard to the ætiology of these phenomena. They may be due to (1) parallel streams of consciousness, (2) a narrowing of the field of consciousness, (3) alterations in conscious experience, (4) a posttraumatic, divided personality structure, and so on.

In our opinion, the broad conceptualization of dissociation impedes conceptual clarity (cf., Holmes et al., 2005). Moreover, the broad conceptualization's focus on phenomena *per se* (without consideration for the personality organization that gives rise to them), has led to some important dissociative symptoms being overlooked (e.g., somatoform dissociative symptoms).

Although the broad conceptualization has generated an immense body of important clinical and experimental research, it appears too broad and too vague to support and sustain the future study of dissociation. Worse, the fuzziness of the broad conceptualization of dissociation is directly responsible for triggering criticism on the grounds that it is simply too broad to be useful (e.g., Marshall, Spitzer, & Liebowitz, 1999).

In conclusion, we contend that the dissociation field is in need of some conceptual housecleaning. The following terms must be clarified and unambiguously related to one another: *dissociation, personality, consciousness, identity, state* (i.e., mental state, state of consciousness, ego state, identity state, self-state), *alter personality,* and *dissociative parts of the personality.* Because many of these terms are effectively synonymous, it would probably be helpful to decide which terms are to be preferred.

The specific goals of the current volume are to clarify the concept of dissociation and to specify the phenomena that should be considered *dissociative.*

The authors want to thank Paul Dell, PhD, Julian Ford, PhD, Warwick Middleton, MD, Ellert Nijenhuis, PhD, John O'Neil, MD, and Kathy Steele, MN, CS, for their helpful comments on earlier drafts of this chapter.

REFERENCES

Alexander, V. K. (1956). A case of a multiple personality. *Journal of Abnormal and Social Psychology, 52,* 272–276.

Allison, R. B. (1974). A new treatment approach for multiple personalities. *American Journal of Clinical Hypnosis, 17,* 15–32.

Alvarado, C. S. (2002). Dissociation in Britain during the late nineteenth century: The Society for Psychical Research, 1882–1900. *Journal of Trauma and Dissociation, 3,* 9–33.

American Psychiatric Association (1980). *DSM-III—Diagnostic and statistical manual of mental disorders* (3rd ed.). Washington, DC: Author.

American Psychiatric Association (2000). *DSM-IV-TR—Diagnostic and statistical manual of mental disorders* (4th ed., text rev.). Washington, DC: Author.

Armstrong, J. G., Putnam, F. W., Carlson, E. B., Libero, D. Z., & Smith, S. R. (1997). Development and validation of a measure of adolescent dissociation: The Adolescent Dissociative Experiences Scale (A-DES). *Journal of Nervous and Mental Disease, 185,* 491–497.

Azam, A. A. (1887). *Hypnotisme, double conscience et altérations de la personnalité.* Paris: J.-B. Baillière & Fils.

Azam, E. (1876a). Amnésie périodique ou dédoublement de la vie. *Annales Médico-Psychologiques, 16,* 5–35.

Azam, E. (1876b). Le dédoublement de la personnalité, suite de l'histoire de Félida X. *Revue Scientifique, 2,* 265–269.

Baillarger, J. (1845). De l'influence de l'état intermédiaire à la veille et au sommeil sur la production et la marche des hallucinations. *Annales Médico-Psychologiques, 6,* 1–29; 168–195.

Baillarger, J. (1861). Case history on spiritism. *Annales Médico-Psychologiques, 1,* 92–93.

Baillarger, J. (1862). Review of Maury's *Le sommeil et les rêves. Annales Médico-Psvchologiques, 8,* 357.

Beaunis, H. (1887). *Le somnambulisme provoqué* (2nd., enlarged ed.). Paris: J.-B. Baillière & Fils.

Bérillon, E. (1886). Dissociation, dans l'état d'hypnotisme et à l'état de veille, des phénomènes psycho-moteurs. *Revue de l'Hypnotisme, ii*, 79–81.

Berman, E. (1981). Multiple personality: Psychoanalytic perspectives. *International Journal of Psychoanalysis, 62*, 283–300.

Bernstein, E. M., & Putnam, F. W. (1986). Development, reliability, and validity of a dissociation scale. *Journal of Nervous and Mental Disease, 174*, 727–735.

Binet, A. (1890). *On double consciousness: Experimental psychological studies.* Chicago: Open Court, 1890. Reprint: Washington, DC: University Publications of America, 1977.

Binet, A. (1892/1896/1977). *Les altérations de la personnalité.* Paris: F. Alcan. English edition: *Alterations of personality.* New York: D. Appleton and Company, 1896. Reprint: Washington, DC: University Publications of America, 1977.

Bliss, E. L. (1980). Multiple personalities: A report of 14 cases with implications for schizophrenia. *Archives of General Psychiatry, 37*, 1388–1397.

Blizard, R. A. (2001). Masochistic and sadistic ego states: Dissociative solutions to the dilemma of attachment to an abusive caretaker. *Journal of Trauma and Dissociation, 2*, 37–58.

Bœteau, M. (1892). Automatisme somnambulique avec dédoublement de la personnalité. *Annales Médico-Psycholoqiques, 50*, 63–79.

Bourneville, D. (1886). Preface. In D. Bourneville (Ed.), *La possession de Jeanne Fery, religieuse professe du couvent des sœurs noires de la ville de Mons (1584).* Paris: Progrès Médical en A. Delahaye & E. Lecrosnie.

Bourru, H., & Burot, P. (1888). *Les variations de la personnalité.* Paris: J.-B. Baillière & Fils.

Bowers, M. K., Brecher-Marer, S., Newton, B. W., Piotrowski, Z., Spyer, T. C., Taylor, W. S., & Watkins, J. G. (1971). Therapy of multiple personality. *International Journal of Clinical and Experimental Hypnosis, 19*, 57–65.

Braid, J. (1843). *Neurypnology or the rationale of nervous sleep considered in relation to animal magnetism.* London: J. Churchill.

Braude, S. E. (1995). *First person plural: Multiple personality and the philosophy of mind. Rev.* Lanham, MD: Rowman & Littlefield.

Braun, B. G. (1988). The BASK model of dissociation. *Dissociation, 1*, 4–23.

Brenner, I. (2001). *Dissociation of trauma: Theory, phenomenology, and technique.* Madison, CT: International Universities Press.

Breuer, J., & Freud, S. (1893/2001). On the psychical mechanism of hysterical phenomena. In J. Strachey (Ed.), *Standard edition of the complete psychological works of Sigmund Freud, 2* (pp. 1–17). London: Hogarth.

Briere, J. (2002). *Multiscale Dissociation Inventory.* Odessa, FL: Psychological Assessment Resources.

Briquet, P. (1859). *Traité clinique et thérapeutique de l'hystérie.* Paris: J.-P. Baillière & Fils.

Bromberg, P. M. (1998). *Standing in the spaces: Essays on clinical process, trauma, and dissociation.* Hillsdale, NJ: The Analytic Press.

Bruce, L. C. (1895). Notes of a case of dual brain action. *Brain, 18*, 54–65.

Camuset, L. (1882). Un cas de dédoublement de la personnalité: Période amnésique d'une année chez un jeune homme. *Annales Médico-Psychologiques, 40*, 75–86.

Cardeña, E. (1994). The domain of dissociation. In S. J. Lynn & J. W. Rhue (Eds.), *Dissociation: Clinical and theoretical perspectives* (pp. 15–31). New York: Guilford.

Carlson, E. B. (2005). Studying the interaction between physical and psychological states with the Dissociative Experiences Scale. In D. Spiegel (Ed.), *Dissociation: Culture, mind, and body* (pp. 41–58). Washington, DC: American Psychiatric Press.

Carlson, E. B., & Putnam, F. W. (1993). An update on the Dissociative Experiences Scale. *Dissociation, 6*, 16–27.

Carlson, E. T. (1981). The history of multiple personality in the United States: I. The beginnings. *American Journal of Psychiatry, 138*, 666–668.

Carlson, E. T. (1986). The history of dissociation until 1880. In J. M. Quen (Ed.), *Split minds/Split brains: Historical and current perspectives* (pp. 7–30). New York: New York University Press.

Charcot, J.-M. (1887). *Leçons sur les maladies du système nerveux faites à la Salpêtrière.* Paris: Progrès Médical, Delahaye & Lecrosnie.

Chefetz, R. A. (1997). Special case transferences and countertransferences in the treatment of dissociative disorders. *Dissociation, 10*, 255–265.

Chu, J. A. (1998). *Rebuilding shattered lives: The responsible treatment of complex posttraumatic stress and dissociative disorders.* New York: Guilford Press.

Coons, P. M. (1980). Multiple personality: Diagnostic considerations. *Journal of Clinical Psychiatry, 41*, 330–336.

Coons, P. M., & Milstein, V. (1986). Psychosexual disturbances in multiple personality: Characteristics, etiology and treatment. *Journal of Clinical Psychiatry, 47*, 106–110.

Crabtree, A. (1993). *From Mesmer to Freud: Magnetic sleep and the roots of psychological healing.* New Haven: Yale University Press.

Davies, J., & Frawley, M. (1994). *Treating the adult survivor of childhood sexual abuse.* New York: Basic Books.

Delbœuf, J. (1879). Sur le dédoublement du moi dans les rêves. *Revue Philosophique, 8*, 616–618.

Deleuze, J. P. F. (1819). *Histoire critique du magnétisme animal,* Vol. 1. Paris: Mame.

Dell, P. F. (2000). *MID: Multidimensional Inventory of Dissociation.* Unpublished Assessment Battery.

Despine, C. (1840). *De l'emploi du magnétisme animal et des eaux minérales, dans le traitement des maladies nerveuses.* Paris: Germer Baillière.

Dessoir, M. (1890). *Das doppel-Ich.* Leipzig: Günther.

Dorahy, M. J. (2001). Dissociative Identity Disorder and memory dysfunction: The current state of experimental research, and its future directions. *Clinical Psychology Review, 21*, 771–795.

Dorahy, M. J., & Van der Hart, O. (2007). Trauma and Dissociation: An historical perspective. In E. Vermetten, M. J. Dorahy, & D. Spiegel (Eds.), *Traumatic Dissociation:*

Neurobiology and Treatment (pp. 3–30). Arlington, VA: American Psychiatric Publishing, Inc.

Dwight, B. W. (1818). Facts illustrative of the powers and operations of the human mind in a diseased state. *American Journal of Science, 1*, 431–433.

Ellenberger, H. F. (1970). *The discovery of the unconscious.* New York: Basic Books.

Elzinga, B. M., Phaf, R. H., Ardon, A. M., & Van Dyck, R. (2003). Directed forgetting between, but not within, dissociative personality states. *Journal of Abnormal Psychology, 112*, 237–243.

Erdelyi, M. H. (1985). *Psychoanalysis: Freud's cognitive psychology*. New York: W. H. Freedman.

Erdelyi, M. H. (1994). Dissociation, defense, and the unconscious. In D. Spiegel (Ed.), *Dissociation: Culture, mind and body* (pp. 3–20). Washington, DC: American Psychiatric Press.

Fairbairn, W. R. D. (1944). Endopsychic structure considered in terms of object-relationship. In D. E. Scharff & E. F. Birtle (Eds.), *W. R. D. Fairbairn: Psychoanalytic studies of the personality* (pp. 82–132). London: Routledge, 1992.

Faure, H., Kersten, J., Koopman, D., & Van der Hart, O. (1997). The 19th century DID case of Louis Vivet: New findings and re-evaluation. *Dissociation, 10*, 104–113.

Feinkind, S. (1893). *Du somnambulisme dit naturel (somnambulisme): Ses rapports avec l'hystérie et l'attaque hystérique à forme somnambulique.* Paris: Oilier-Henry.

Ferenczi, S. (1933/1949). Confusion of tongues between the adult and the child. *International Journal of Psychoanalysis, 30*, 225–230.

Fine, C. G. (1988). The work of Antoine Despine: The first scientific report on the diagnosis and treatment of a child with multiple personality disorder. *American Journal of Clinical Hypnosis, 31*, 33–39.

Forrest, D. (1999). *The evolution of hypnotism*. Forfar, Scotland: Black Ace Books.

Frankel, F. H. (1994). Dissociation in hysteria and hypnosis: A concept aggrandized. In S. J. Lynn & J. W. Rhue (Eds.), *Dissociation: Clinical and theoretical perspectives* (pp. 80–93). New York: Guilford Press.

Freud, S. (1893/2001). Some points for a comparative study of organic and hysterical paralyses. In J. Strachey & A. Strachey (Eds.), *Standard edition of the complete psychological works of Sigmund Freud, 1*. London: Hogarth. [hereinafter, *S. E.*]

Freud, S. (1895/1950/1966). Project for a scientific psychology. *S. E., 1*, 283–388.

Freud, S. (1896/2001). The ætiology of hysteria. *S. E., 3*.

Gautier, T. (1858). Honoré de Balzac. *Le Moniteur,* 23 and 31 March, pp. 371, 407. (Quoted by James, 1995)

Gilles de la Tourette, G. (1887). *L'Hypnotisme et les états analogues au point de vue médico-légal*. Paris: Librairie Plon.

Gmelin, E. (1791). *Materialen für die Anthropologie,* Vol. 1. Tübingen: Cotta.

Goodwin, J. (1987). Mary Reynolds: A post-traumatic reinterpretation of a classic case of multiple personality disorder. *Hillside Journal of Clinical Psychiatry, 9*, 89–99.

Greaves, G. B. (1980). Multiple personality: 165 years after Mary Reynolds. *Journal of Nervous and Mental Disease, 168*, 577–596.

Greaves, G. B. (1993). A history of multiple personality disorder. In R. P. Kluft & C. G. Fine (Eds.), *Clinical perspectives on multiple personality disorder* (pp. 355–380). Washington, DC: American Psychiatric Press.

Gros-Jean (1855). *Seconde lettre de Gros-Jean à son évêque au sujet des tables parlantes, des possessions, des Sybilles, du magnétisme et autres diableries.* Paris: Ledoyen.

Gruenewald, D. (1971). Hypnotic techniques without hypnosis in the treatment of dual personality. *Journal of Nervous and Mental Disease, 153*, 41–46.

Gruenewald, D. (1977). Multiple personality and splitting phenomena: A reconceptualization. *Journal of Nervous and Mental Disease, 164*, 385–393.

Hacking, I. (1991). Double personality in Britain, 1815–1875. *Dissociation, 4*, 134–146.

Hacking, I. (1995). *Rewriting the soul: Multiple personality and the sciences of memory.* New Haven: Princeton University Press.

Hales, N. G. (1975). *Morton Prince. Psychotherapy and multiple personality: Selected essays.* Cambridge, MA: Harvard University Press.

Hart, B. (1926). The conception of dissociation. *British Journal of Medical Psychology, 6*, 241–257.

Hart, B. (1927). *Psychopathology: Its development and its place in medicine.* New York: Macmillan.

Hilgard, E. R. (1973). Dissociation revisited. In M. Henle, J. Jaynes & J. J. Sullivan (Eds.), *Historical conceptions of psychology* (pp. 205–219). New York: Springer Publishing.

Hilgard, E. R. (1974). Toward a neo-dissociation theory: Multiple cognitive controls in human functioning. *Perspectives in Biology and Medicine, 17*, 301–316.

Hilgard, E. R. (1977). *Divided consciousness: Multiple controls in human thought and action.* New York: Wiley.

Hilgard, E. R. (1986). *Divided consciousness: Multiple controls in human thought and action* (2nd ed., rev'd.) New York: Wiley.

Hilgard, E. R. (1992). Divided consciousness and dissociation. *Consciousness and Cognition, 1*, 16–31.

Hilgard, E. R. (1994). Neodissociation theory. In S. J. Lynn & J. W. Rhue (Eds.), *Dissociation: Clinical and theoretical perspectives* (pp. 32–51). New York: Guilford Press.

Holmes, E. A., Brown, R. J., Mansell, W., Fearon, R. P., Hunter, E. C. M., Frasquilho, F., & Oakley, D. A. (2005). Are there two qualitatively distinct forms of dissociation? A review and some clinical implications. *Clinical Psychology Review, 25*, 1–23.

Howell, E. F. (2003). Narcissism, a relational aspect of dissociation. *Journal of Trauma and Dissociation, 4*, 51–71.

Howland, J. S. (1975). The use of hypnosis in the treatment of a case of multiple personality. *Journal of Nervous and Mental Disease, 161*, 138–142.

Huntjens, R. J. C., Postma, A., Hamaker, E. L., Peters, M., Woertman, L., & Van der Hart, O. (2002). Perceptual and conceptual priming in patients with dissociative identity disorder. *Memory and Cognition, 30*, 1033–1043.

Hyslop, T. B. (1899). On "double consciousness." *British Medical Journal, ii*, September 23, 782–786.

James, T. (1995). *Dreams, creativity, and madness in nineteenth-century France.* Oxford: Clarendon Press.

James, W. (1890). *The principles of psychology*. New York: Henri Holt.

James, W. (1894). Book Review. *Psychological Review, 1*, 195–199.

Janet, J. (1888). L'hystérie et l'hypnotisme d'après la théorie de la double personnalité. *Revue Scientifique, 1*, 616–623.

Janet, P. (1889). *L'automatisme psychologique: Essai de psychologie expérimentale sur les formes inférieures de l'activité humaine*. Paris: Félix Alcan. Reprint: Paris: Société Pierre Janet, 1973.

Janet, P. (1893). *L'état mental des hystériques: Les stigmates mentaux.* Paris: Rueff & Cie.

Janet, P. (1894a). *L'état mental des hystériques: Les accidents mentaux.* Paris: Rueff & Cie.

Janet P. (1894b). Histoire d'une idée fixe. *Revue Philosophique, 37*, 121–163.

Janet, P. (1898). *Névroses et idées fixes*, Vol. 1. Paris: F. Alcan.

Janet, P. (1904). L'amnésie et la dissociation des souvenirs par l'émotion. *Journal de Psychologie, 3*, 417–453. Also in P. Janet (1911). *L'État mental des hystériques* (pp. 506–544). Paris: F. Alcan.

Janet, P. (1907). *The major symptoms of hysteria.* London/New York: Macmillan. Reprint of 1920 edition: New York: Hafner, 1965.

Janet, P. (1909). Problèmes psychologiques de l'émotion. *Revue de neurologie, 17*, 1551–1687.

Janet, P. (1911). *L'état mental des hystériques* (2nd. ed.). Paris: F. Alcan. Reprint: Marseille: Lafitte Reprints, 1983.

Janet, P. (1919). *Les médications psycholoqiques.* Paris: F. Alcan. Reprint: Paris: Société Pierre Janet, 1986. English edition: *Psychological healing.* New York: Macmillan, 1925. Reprint: New York: Arno Press, 1976.

Janet, P. (1928). *L'évolution de la mémoire et de la notion du temps* [The evolution of memory and of the notion of time]. Paris: A. Chahine.

Janet, P., with the collaboration of H. Piéron and C. Lalo (1946). *Manuel du baccalauréat,* seconde partie, *Philosophie: Questions complémentaires* (7th ed.). Paris: Librairie Vuibert.

Kihlstrom, J. F. (1992a). Dissociative and conversion disorders. In D. J. Stein & J. E. Young (Eds.), *Cognitive science and clinical disorders* (pp. 248–270). San Diego: Academic Press.

Kihlstrom, J. F. (1992b). Dissociation and dissociations: A comment on consciousness and cognition. *Consciousness and Cognition, 1*, 47–53.

Kihlstrom, J. F., Tataryn, D. J., & Hoyt, I. P. (1993). Dissociative disorders. In P. B. Sutker & H. E. Adams (Eds.), *Comprehensive handbook of psychopathology* (2nd ed.; pp. 203–234). New York: Plenum Press.

Kluft, R. P. (Ed). (1985). *Childhood antecedents of multiple personality*. Washington, DC: American Psychiatric Press.

Kluft, R. P. (1986). Treating children who have multiple personality disorder. In B. G. Braun (Ed.), *Treatment of Multiple Personality Disorder* (pp. 79–105). Washington, DC: American Psychiatric Press.

Kluft, R. P. (2000). The psychoanalytic psychotherapy of dissociative identity disorder in the context of trauma therapy. *Psychoanalytic Inquiry, 20*, 259–286.

Kluft, R. P. (2003). The founding of the ISSD. In J. A. O'Neil (Ed.), *From organizational infancy to early adulthood, 1983–2003.* Booklet published by the International Society for the Study of Dissociation.

Lasky, R. (1978). The psychoanalytic treatment of a case of multiple personality. *Psychoanalytic Review, 65*, 355–380.

Laurent, L. (1892). *Des états seconds: Variations pathologiques du champs de la conscience.* Bordeaux: V. Cardoret/Paris: Octave Doin.

Legrand du Saulle (1883). *Les hystériques: État physique et état mental.* Paris: J. B. Baillière & Fils.

Lemoine, A. (1855). *Du sommeil du point de vue physiologique et psychologique*. Paris: J.-B. Baillière & Fils.

Lipton, S. D. (1943). Dissociated personality: A case report. *Psychiatric Quarterly, 17*, 33–56.

Littré, E. (1875). La double conscience: Fragments de physiologie physique. *Revue de Philosophie Positive, 14*, 321–336.

Loewenstein, R. J., & Ross, D. R. (1992). Multiple personality and psychoanalysis: An introduction. *Psychoanalytic Inquiry, 12*, 3–48.

Ludwig, A. M. (1966). Altered states of consciousness. *Archives of General Psychiatry, 15*, 225–234.

Ludwig, A. M. (1969). Altered states of consciousness. In C. T. Tart (Ed.), *Altered states of consciousness* (pp. 11–24). New York: Anchor Books.

Ludwig, A. M. (1983). The psychobiological functions of dissociation. *American Journal of Clinical Hypnosis, 26*, 93–99.

Ludwig, A. M., Brandsma, J. M., Wilbur, C. B., Bendfeldt, F., & Jameson, D. H. (1972). The objective study of a multiple personality. *Archives of General Psychiatry, 26*, 298–310.

Maddison, D. C. (1953). A case of double personality. *The Medical Journal of Australia, 6*, 814–816.

Mann, B. J. (1995). The North Carolina dissociation index: A measure of dissociation using items from the MMPI-2. *Journal of Personality Assessment, 64*, 349–359.

Marmar, S. S. (1980). Psychoanalysis of multiple personality. *International Journal of Psychoanalysis, 61*, 439–459.

Marmar, C. R., Weiss, D. S., & Metzler, T. (1997). The peritraumatic dissociative experiences questionnaire. In J. P. Wilson & T. M. Keane (Eds.), *Assessing psychological trauma and PTSD* (pp. 412–428). New York: Guilford Press.

Marshall, R. D., Spitzer, R., & Liebowitz, M. R. (1999). Review and critique of the new DSM-IV diagnosis of acute stress disorder. *American Journal of Psychiatry, 156*, 1677–1685.

Maury, L. F. A. (1861). *Le sommeil et les rêves.* Paris: Didier.

McDougall, W. (1926). *An outline of abnormal psychology.* London: Methuen & Co.

Meares, R. (1999). The contribution of Hughlings Jackson to an understanding of dissociation. *American Journal of Psychiatry, 156,* 1850–1855.

Mitchill, S. L. (1816). A double consciousness, or a duality of persons in the same individual. *Medical Repository, 3,* 185–186.

Mitchell, S. W. (1888). Mary Reynolds: A case of double consciousness. *Transactions of the College of Physicians of Philadelphia, 10,* 366–389.

Mitchell, T. W. (1921). *The psychology of medicine.* London: Methuen & Co.

Mitchell, T. W. (1922). *Medical psychology and psychical research.* London: Methuen & Co.

Moreau de Tours, J. J. (1845). *Du hachisch et de l'aliénation mentale: Études psychologiques.* Paris: Fortin, Masson & Cie. English edition: *Hashish and mental illness.* New York: Raven Press, 1973.

Moreau de Tours, J. J. (1865). *De la folie hystérique et de quelques phénomènes nerveux propres à l'hystérie convulsive, à l'hystéro-épilepsie et à l'épilepsie.* Paris: Masson.

Moreau de Tours, J. J. (1869). *Traité pratique de la folie névropathique (yulgo hystérique).* Paris: Germer Baillière.

Morton, J. H., & Thoma, E. (1964). A case of multiple personality. *American Journal of Clinical Hypnosis, 6,* 216–225.

Myers, C. S. (1916). Contributions to the study of shell shock. *The Lancet,* January 8, 65–69.

Myers, C. S. (1920–21). The revival of emotional memories and its therapeutic value (II). *British Journal of Medical Psychology, 1,* 20–22.

Myers, C. S. (1940). *Shell shock in France 1914–18.* Cambridge: Cambridge University Press.

Myers, F. W. H. (1887). Multiplex personality. *Proceedings of the Society of Psychical Research, 4,* 496–514.

Myers, F. W. H. (1893). The subliminal consciousness: The mechanism of hysteria. *Proceedings of the Society for Psychical Research, 9,* 2–25.

Myers, F. W. H. (1903). *Human personality and its survival of bodily death* (2 vols.). London: Longmans, Green.

Nemiah, J. C. (1989). Editorial: Janet redivivus: The centenary of *L'automatisme psychologique. American Journal of Psychiatry, 146,* 1527–1529.

Nijenhuis, E. R. S. (1999). *Somatoform dissociation: Phenomena, measurement and theoretical issues.* Assen: Van Gorcum. Reprint: New York: Norton, 2004.

Nijenhuis, E. R. S., Spinhoven, P., Van Dyck, R., Van der Hart, O., & Vanderlinden, J. (1996). The development and psychometric characteristics of the somatoform dissociation questionnaire (SDQ-20). *Journal of Nervous and Mental Disease, 184,* 688–694.

Nijenhuis, E. R. S., & Van der Hart, O. (1999). Somatoform dissociative phenomena: A Janetian perspective. In J. M. Goodwin & R. Attias (Eds.), *Splintered reflections: Images of the body in trauma* (pp. 89–127). New York: Basic Books.

O'Neil, J. A. (1997). Expanding the psychoanalytic view of the intrapsychic: Psychic conflict in the inscape. *Dissociation, 10,* 192–202.

Osgood, C. E., & Luria, Z. (1954). A blind analysis of a case of multiple personality disorder using semantic differential. *Journal of Abnormal and Social Psychology, 49,* 579–591.

Osgood Mason, R. (1895). Duplex personality—Its relation to hypnotism and to lucidity. *Journal of the American Medical Association, 25,* 928–933.

Perry, C., & Laurence, J.-R. (1984). Mental processing outside of awareness: The contributions of Freud and Janet. In K. S. Bowers & D. Meichenbaum (Eds.), *The unconscious reconsidered* (pp. 9–48). New York: Wiley.

Prince, M. (1906a). *The dissociation of a personality.* New York: Longmans, Green. Reprint: New York: Greenwood Press, 1969.

Prince, M. (1906b). Hysteria from the point of view of dissociated personality. *Journal of Abnormal Psychology, 1,* 170–187.

Prince, M. (1909). The psychological principles and field of psychotherapy. *Journal of Abnormal Psychology, 4,* 72–98.

Prince, M. (1921). The structure and dynamic elements of human personality. *Journal of Abnormal Psychology, 15,* 403–413.

Prince, M. (1924). The problem of personality: How many selves have we? *Pedagogical Seminary and Journal of Genetic Psychology, 32,* 266–292.

Prince, W. F. (1917). The Doris case of quintuple personality. *Journal of Abnormal Psychology, 11,* 73–122.

Putnam, F. W. (1989a). Pierre Janet and modern views of dissociation. *Journal of Traumatic Stress, 2,* 413–429.

Putnam, F. W. (1989b). *Diagnosis and treatment of multiple personality disorder.* New York: Guilford.

Putnam, F. W. (1997a). *Dissociation in children and adolescents: A developmental perspective.* New York: Guilford Press.

Putnam, F. W. (1997b). Child Dissociative Checklist—Version 3. In F. W. Putnam, *Dissociation in children and adolescents: A developmental perspective* (pp. 354–356). New York: Guilford Press.

Putnam, F. W., Guroff, J. J., Silberman, E. K., Barban, L., & Post, R. M. (1986). The clinical phenomenology of multiple personality disorder: Review of 100 recent cases. *Journal of Clinical Psychiatry, 47,* 285–293.

Ribot, T. (1885). *Les maladies de la personnalité.* Paris: F. Alcan.

Richet, C. (1884). *L'homme et l'intelligence: Fragments de physiologie et de psychologie.* Paris: F. Alcan.

Riley, K. C. (1988). Measurement of dissociation. *Journal of Nervous and Mental Disease, 176,* 449–450.

Rosenbaum, M., & Weaver, G. M. (1980). Dissociated state: Status of a case after 38 years. *Journal of Nervous and Mental Disease, 168,* 597–603.

Ross, C. A. (1989). *Multiple Personality Disorder: Diagnosis, clinical features, and treatment.* New York: Wiley.

Ross, C. A. (1997). *Dissociative identity disorder: Diagnosis, clinical features, and treatment of multiple personality.* New York: Wiley and Sons.

Rush, B. (1812). *Medical inquiries upon the diseases of mind.* Philadelphia: Kimber & Richardson.

Sanders, S. (1986). The perceptual alteration scale: A scale measuring dissociation. *American Journal of Clinical Hypnosis, 29*, 95–102.

Schreiber, F. R. (1973). *Sybil.* New York: Warner Books.

Sidis, B. (1902). *Psychopathological researches: Studies in mental dissociation.* New York: G. E. Stechert.

Sidis, B., & Goodhart, S. P. (1904). *Multiple personality: An experimental investigation into the nature of human individuality.* New York: D. Appleton & Co.

Spiegel, D., & Cardeña, E. (1991). Disintegrated experience: The dissociative disorders revisited. *Journal of Abnormal Psychology, 100*, 366–378.

Spiegel, H. (1963). The dissociation-association continuum. *Journal of Nervous and Mental Disease, 136*, 374–378.

Stern, D. (1997). *Unformulated experience: From dissociation to imagination in psychoanalysis*. Hillsdale, NJ: Analytic Press.

Taine, H. (1878). *De l'intelligence* (3rd. ed.). Paris: Librairie Hachette & Cie.

Tascher: See Gros-Jean.

Tarnopolsky, A. (2003). The concept of dissociation in early psychoanalytic writers. *Journal of Trauma and Dissociation, 4*, 7–25.

Tart, C. T. (Ed.) (1969). *Altered states of consciousness*. New York: Anchor Books.

Taylor, E. (1983). *William James on exceptional mental states: The 1896 Lowell lectures*. Amherst, MA: The University of Massachusetts Press.

Taylor, W. S., & Martin, M. F. (1944). Multiple personality. *Journal of Abnormal and Social Psychology, 29*, 281–300.

Thigpen, C. H., & Cleckley, H. (1954). A case of multiple personality. *Journal of Abnormal and Social Psychology, 49*, 135–151.

Thigpen, C. H., & Cleckley, H. (1957). *The three faces of Eve.* New York: McGraw-Hill.

Tourette: *See* Gilles de la Tourette.

Vaillant, G. E. (1992). The historical origins of Sigmund Freud's concept of the mechanisms of defense. In G. E. Vaillant (Ed.), *Ego mechanisms of defense: A guide for clinicians and researchers* (pp. 3–28). Washington, DC: American Psychiatric Press, Inc.

Van der Hart, O. (1997, June). *Dissociation: Past developments.* Keynote address presented at the 14th International Congress of Hypnosis. San Diego, CA.

Van der Hart, O., & Brown, P. (1992). Abreaction re-evaluated. *Dissociation, 5*, 127–140.

Van der Hart, O., Brown, P., & Van der Kolk, B. A. (1989). Pierre Janet's psychological treatment of posttraumatic stress. *Journal of Traumatic Stress, 2*, 379–395.

Van der Hart, O., Faure, H., Van Gerven, M. , & Goodwin, J. (1991). Unawareness and denial of pregnancy in patients with multiple personality disorder. *Dissociation, 4,* 65–73.

Van der Hart, O., & Friedman, B. (1989). A reader's guide to Pierre Janet on dissociation: A neglected intellectual heritage. *Dissociation, 2*, 3–16.

Van der Hart, O., & Horst, R. (1989). The dissociation theory of Pierre Janet. *Journal of Traumatic Stress, 2*, 397–412.

Van der Hart, O., Lierens, R., & Goodwin, J. (1996). Jeanne Fery: A 16th century case of dissociative identity disorder. *Journal of Psychohistory, 24,* 18–35.

Van der Hart, O., Nijenhuis, E. R. S., & Steele, K (2006). *The haunted self: Structural dissociation and the treatment of chronic traumatization*. New York/London: Norton.

Van der Hart, O., Van Dijke, A., Van Son, M., & Steele, K. (2000). Somatoform dissociation in traumatized World War I combat soldiers: A neglected clinical heritage. *Journal of Trauma & Dissociation, 1*, 33–66.

Van der Hart, O., Van der Kolk, B. A., & Boon, S. (1998). Treatment of dissociative disorders. In J. D. Bremner & C. R. Marmar (Eds.), *Trauma, memory and dissociation* (pp. 253–283). Washington, DC: American Psychiatric Press.

Van der Hart, O., Witztum, E., & Friedman, B. (1993). From hysterical psychosis to reactive dissociative psychosis. *Journal of Traumatic Stress, 6,* 43–64.

Van der Kolk, B. A., & Van der Hart, O. (1989). Pierre Janet and the breakdown of adaptation in psychological trauma. *American Journal of Psychiatry, 146*, 1530–1540.

Vanderlinden, J., Van Dyck, R., Vandererycken, W., Vertommen, H., & Verkes, R. J. (1993). The Dissociation Questionnaire (DIS-Q): Development and characteristics of a new self-report questionnaire. *Clinical Psychology and Psychotherapy, 1*, 1–7.

West, L. J. (1967). Dissociative reaction. In A. M. Freedman & H. I. Kaplan (Eds.), *Comprehensive Textbook of Psychiatry* (pp. 885–899). Baltimore: Williams and Wilkins.

2 The Conceptual Unity of Dissociation: A Philosophical Argument

Stephen E. Braude, PhD

OUTLINE

2.1 INTRODUCTION

Psychologists and psychiatrists have studied dissociative phenomena for a long time. However, they demonstrate surprisingly little agreement about what dissociation is and about which things exemplify it. Of course, many agree that certain florid phenomena count as dissociative—for example, fugue states and DID. But when mental health professionals tackle the topic of dissociation theoretically and attempt to define it, they do so in ways that often conflict with one another, and (perhaps most surprising of all) they tend to overlook a large and important class of phenomena. Historically—and contrary to what the recent clinical literature would lead one to believe—most (if not all) hypnotic phenomena have been regarded as dissociative (see, e.g., Gauld, 1992; Van der Hart and Dorahy, 2009). In the late 19th and early 20th centuries, researchers into hypnosis were trying to study systematically the same sorts of subconscious mental divisions they believed occurred spontaneously in hysteria and to some extent in somnambulism. Indeed, some considered hypnotically induced systematized anesthesia or negative hallucination to be *paradigm* instances of dissociation. Yet when clinicians now try to analyze dissociation, hypnotic phenomena are largely ignored.

Despite evidence to the contrary (e.g., Crabtree, 1993; Braude, 1995; Van der Hart & Dorahy, 2009), historians of psychology usually credit Pierre Janet with having originated the concept of dissociation, although he regularly used the term *désagrégation* instead. Janet focused on a distinctive and relatively limited type of trauma-induced psychopathology. He considered dissociation to be a kind of weakness, a failure (in the face of disturbing events) to integrate parts of consciousness and maintain conscious unity.

However, the concept has evolved in the hundred years since Janet tackled the subject. Subsequent researchers (e.g., James, Binet, Myers, Liègeois, Sidis) also recognized an apparent causal link between trauma and dissociative pathology. But they tended to agree that the processes Janet was describing from cases of hysteria (which included conversion disorder and double consciousness) were also at work in a wider variety of phenomena, drawn not just from psychopathology but also from experimental psychology and even everyday life (see, e.g., Binet, 1896; Myers, 1903; Sidis, 1902). And along with that, they tended to view dissociation not as a weakness, but as a kind of capacity (not necessarily maladaptive) to sever familiar links with one's own mental states.

Significantly, this evolution of the concept of dissociation happened quite rapidly. Other turn-of-the-century researchers, interested at least as much in hypnosis as in psychopathology, were eager to explore the ways in which hypnotic states seemed to produce a kind of division or doubling of consciousness, or creation of seemingly autonomous sets of mental processes (for a quick history of these developments, see Braude, 1995, and Van der Hart & Dorahy, 2009. For a more detailed account, see Gauld, 1992). As Messerschmidt (1927) eventually made clear, these apparent divisions weren't as fully autonomous as they seemed. But that didn't undermine the view that the phenomena in question could arise either experimentally or spontaneously or, for that matter, pathologically or nonpathologically.

These nonpathological (including hypnotic) contexts, in which the concept of dissociation has historically played an important role, tend to be neglected by most clinicians. Given their pressing clinical concerns, perhaps that is not surprising. Nevertheless, keeping in mind what pathological and nonpathological dissociative phenomena have in common may bring clarity to other issues, such as the difference (if any) between dissociation and apparently similar or related concepts—in particular, repression.

In a fairly recent development, some clinicians have examined the concept of dissociation by using diagnostic surveys (e.g., the Dissociative Experiences Scale (DES) and the Multiscale Dissociation Inventory (MDI)) to consider how dissociative symptoms cluster. These survey instruments were initially designed as screening devices, to assess the presence or absence of phenomena already believed by the test designers to be dissociative. However, subsequent research on thousands of survey results has a more ambitious goal—namely, to determine more precisely *what dissociation is*. But data of the sort elicited by these surveys can't tell us what the *concept* of dissociation is. To reiterate, the surveys look only for symptoms antecedently judged as relevant by their designers, who are limited by their selective grasp of the history of the concept. What they most clearly tend to neglect are the many nonpathological hypnotic phenomena that have been considered dissociative, but simply fall outside the purview of the surveys.

In some cases, the studies in question are even more problematical than these remarks might suggest. For example, Briere et al. (2005) apply the MDI to determine whether dissociation is a multidimensional construct, and they conclude that it is, and that "the notion of 'dissociation' as a general trait was not supported" (p. 221). Apparently, then, the authors see themselves as trying to settle the issue of what sort of thing dissociation is. Indeed, on the basis of their survey they claim that "the term dissociation may be a misnomer to the extent that it implies a single underlying phenomenon" (p. 230). We'll consider shortly whether dissociation can in fact be regarded as a single underlying phenomenon. But for now, I want only to observe that Briere et al. can't possibly have shown that it isn't (quite apart from concerns about using survey instruments for conceptual analysis). Briere et al. purport to uncover what dissociation is on the basis of a survey that tracks relationships among a handful of factors—of course, factors they antecedently determined to be relevant. Moreover, one of those factors is identity dissociation and, obviously, one can't analyze the concept of dissociation by appealing to that very concept. So if Briere et al. are (as it seems) trying to analyze the concept of dissociation, their attempt is blatantly circular.

So I believe we need to do some conceptual and methodological housecleaning. I agree with Cardeña (1994; Prince, 1905) that when clinicians attempt to characterize dissociation, they tend either to exclude too much or include too much. However (and apparently unlike Cardeña), I think it may be possible to pull together many of the varied intuitions about and approaches to dissociation and come up with a single, general, and useful characterization of dissociation that covers both its pathological and nonpathological forms, including many of those once deemed important but largely ignored today. I shall attempt to define a single inclusive concept of dissociation that rests only on reasonable and recurrent assumptions distilled from more than a century's literature on the subject. I start by identifying specific assumptions underlying typical uses of the term *dissociation*, then see if they can be stated plausibly, and then see whether we can extract from them a definition that has both generality and utility.[1]

2.2 ASSUMPTIONS

We can begin with an observation about terminology. The term *dissociation* can be used in a number of different ways, but in the present context two in particular

[1] Much of what follows draws from, and to some extent improves upon, a more expansive discussion of the concept of dissociation in Braude, 1995.

deserve our attention. First, *dissociation* can pick out an occurrent state (i.e., the state of being dissociated), and second, it can pick out a disposition or ability to dissociate (i.e., a capacity to experience dissociative states). As we will see again shortly, in this respect the term *dissociation* parallels many other psychological-kind terms. For example, the term *empathy* has both occurrent and dispositional senses. In the former, it picks out the occurrent state of experiencing empathy; in the latter it picks out the disposition or capacity to experience such states.

This observation leads to the first assumption underlying the concept of dissociation: that dissociation is not simply an occurrent psychological condition or state, but also something for which we may have a capacity—in fact, a capacity that may have both positive and negative personal consequences. This seems to be a sensible move away from Janet's view of dissociation as a failure of integration, and it's continuous with the way we treat a great many other areas of human cognition and performance. It's also why we can sensibly ask whether everyone can dissociate, and to what degree. So the first assumption may be stated as follows.

2.2.1 Capability Assumption

Dissociation is one of many capacities people have—that is, it's one of many things that (at least some) people are able to do. So, in that respect, dissociation is analogous to, for example, irony, patience, indignation, dishonesty, kindness, sarcasm, self-deception, empathy, and sensuality.

Although my list of other capacities here was restricted to psychological attributes that people express in varying degrees and with respect to which some people are clearly either impaired or gifted, notice that the issue here isn't whether the capacity to dissociate must be cognitive or even whether it's subject to voluntary control. As far as we need to suppose, talk of dissociation might be analogous to talk of various noncognitive organic capacities that are typically not subject to voluntary control. For example, yogis can control many organic functions that most of us affect only to a very limited degree or only involuntarily (e.g., breathing, vasoconstriction, and vasodilation). Yet it's still proper to speak about our capacity for pulmonary functioning, vasoconstriction, and so on. In fact, those capacities are things that can change after a period of study on a Tibetan mountaintop, and also with (say) disease and old age.

The capability assumption leads smoothly to the next.

2.2.2 Nonuniqueness Assumption

Although dissociation has distinctive features, insofar as it's a capacity, it will be similar in broad outline to most other human capacities, that is, it will share features found generally in human (or just cognitive) capacities.

In other words, failing evidence to the contrary, we should not assume that dissociation is completely unprecedented in the realm of human cognition and performance, however distinctive it may be in certain of its details.

The third assumption is particularly important, and we will see later how it figures in a prominent contemporary debate. We begin by observing that capacities generally are things that people express in different ways and to varying degrees. For example, the capacities for self-deception, intimidation, malice, neatness, self-criticism, and generosity can range from extreme to very moderate forms, and they can be expressed in highly idiosyncratic ways. So it seems reasonable to assume the following.

2.2.3 Diversification Assumption

Like other capacities, dissociation (1) assumes a variety of (possibly idiosyncratic) forms, (2) affects a broad range of states (both occurrent and dispositional), and (3) spreads out along various continua—for example, of pervasiveness, frequency, severity, completeness, reversibility, degree of functional isolation, and importance to the subject.

Another important assumption allows us to distinguish dissociation from what we might call cognitive or sensory filtering. Of course, the term *filtering* also has many meanings, and to appreciate the distinction in question we must use the term more carefully and narrowly than we might ordinarily. In the sense of *filtering* that matters here, the term picks out a total blocking of information from a subject. Examples of this sort of filtering would be blindfolding, audio band-pass filtering, or local chemical anesthesia. Compare those states of affairs to the rather different situations we find in (say) hypnotic anesthesia or negative hallucination, where subjects merely fail to experience consciously what they are nevertheless aware of subconsciously or unconsciously. So the relevant difference between filtering (as the term is used here) and dissociation is that in filtering, information never reaches the subject (consciously or otherwise), whereas dissociation merely blocks the subject's conscious awareness of information or sensations that had otherwise registered. So, the next important assumption follows.

2.2.4 Ownership Assumption

The things dissociated from a person are always the person's own states—for example, sensory, cognitive, volitional, and physical states.

Granted, it's common to say that information or data are dissociated. But I believe that's a careless way of speaking. Strictly speaking, what is dissociated are the subjects' states—for example, volitions, knowledge (e.g., the knowledge *that* …, or the knowledge *how* to …), beliefs, memories, dispositions and, sometimes, behavior (as in automatic writing).

The ownership assumption connects with a fifth and very important assumption. At least since the early detailed accounts of multiple personality (e.g., Prince, 1905), researchers have noted that when a state is dissociated, it is not totally obliterated or isolated completely from the subject, although retrieving the state might be quite difficult in both experimental and real-life contexts. That is, dissociated states may be subjectively hidden or psychologically remote, but they are always potentially knowable, recoverable, or capable of re-association. So our final assumption is accessibility.

2.2.5 Accessibility Assumption

Dissociation is a theoretically (but perhaps not practically) reversible functional isolation of a state from conscious awareness.

Before moving on, we should also note that the relation "*x* is dissociated from *y*" is nonsymmetrical, like "*x* loves *y*" (even though *x* loves *y*, *y* may not love *x*). We see this nonsymmetry clearly in cases of one-way amnesia in DID or in hidden observer experiments, where states of a hypnotically hidden observer may be dissociated from those of the hypnotized subject, even though the subject's states may not be dissociated from those of the hidden observer (see Braude, 1995; Braun, 1988; Cardeña, 1994; Hilgard, 1986).

2.3 DISSOCIATION RELATIVE TO OTHER NAMED PHENOMENA

2.3.1 Repression

With these assumptions in mind, we can now examine their utility. First, we can see how they help us distinguish dissociation from at least superficially similar phenomena, and then we can see to what extent they enable us to specify what both pathological and nonpathological forms of dissociation have in common.

Repression may be the concept most often and most easily confused with that of dissociation. Granted, neither concept is precise, and so we shouldn't expect the distinction between dissociation and repression to be sharp. Nevertheless, there seems to be a distinction worth making. While repression and dissociation both concern psychological barriers that prevent one's states from reaching conscious awareness, the two concepts rest on different presuppositions. The barriers differ clearly in scope, function and vulnerability, and so may be distinguished clearly enough to show that they mark off different (if occasionally overlapping) classes of phenomena.

Writers often describe repression as a barrier preventing only certain *mental* states from becoming conscious, whereas the dissociative barrier can hide both mental and physical states from conscious awareness. For example, during hypnotically induced anesthesia one can dissociate bodily sensations and permit radical surgery, but that sort of phenomenon has never been offered as an instance of repression. Moreover, as Hilgard (1986) has noted, writers tend to employ different metaphors when describing the psychological barriers of repression and dissociation. Typically, they characterize repressive barriers as horizontal, whereas dissociated barriers are described as vertical. As a result, repressed material is usually considered to be psychologically deeper than what we can access consciously. By contrast, dissociated states are not necessarily deeper than consciously accessible states. For example, in hypnosis very trivial states can be dissociated (e.g., the ability to say the letter "r," tactile sensitivity in a band around the arm, or the perception of a chair in one's visual field).

This alleged difference connects with the different roles repression and dissociation ostensibly play in a person's psychological economy. Ordinarily, repression is linked to dynamic psychological forces and active mental defenses that inhibit recall. Granted, some writers likewise describe dissociation as a defense or avoidance mechanism (primarily, one producing amnesia), but that view seems needlessly restrictive. In fact, paradigm cases of dissociation needn't involve any impairment of memory, and dissociation may have nothing to do with the urgent needs of psychological survival—that is, it needn't be defensive. For example, systematized anesthesia does not affect memory, and posthypnotic amnesia can concern virtually any kind of state or material, important or unimportant. (For more on shortcomings with particular definitions of "dissociation," see Braude, 1995 and Cardeña, 1994.)

Historically, the concept of repression is bound up with the psychoanalytic concept of a dynamic unconscious, which (according to the standard view) acts as the repository for repressed material. But most important, on that view we gain access to repressed material only by indirect methods, or at least methods more circuitous than those by which we identify dissociated states. Thus, according to the traditional and still standard view of repression, we learn about the unconscious through its by-products (e.g., dreams, or slips of the tongue), and expressions of unconscious material tend to be distorted, either symbolically or by means of more primitive primary-process thinking. So one important difference between repression and dissociation is that repressed mental activities can only be inferred from their behavioral or phenomenological by-products, whereas dissociated states can be accessed relatively directly, as in automatic writing, hypnosis, and interactions with alter identities in cases of DID.

Another way of putting this point would be to say that third- and first-person knowledge of dissociated—but not unconscious—states can be as direct as (respectively) third- and first-person knowledge of nondissociated states. So for example, I can (at least in principle) have direct access to some of my own dissociated states (e.g., beliefs, memories), because they can eventually be retrieved with the help of hypnosis or other interventions. And others can have third-person access to my dissociated states even when I don't. For instance, we have evidence (i.e., third-person access to the fact) that in hidden observer studies, the hypnotized subject feels pain even when that person's non-hidden-observer state does not. And that third-person access is as direct as it would be to ordinary nondissociated states. In both cases, we learn about the other person's sensations or other internal states through that person's behavior. In both hidden observer studies and ordinary cases, we learn that a person feels pain through their pain behavior (e.g., wincing, limping, saying "ouch").

So we can say that if *x* is repressed for *S* (in this sense of "repressed"), then (1) *S* is not consciously aware of (or has amnesia for) *x*, and (2) third- and first-person knowledge of *x* is indirect as compared (respectively) with third- and first-person knowledge of both conscious and dissociated states (i.e., it must be inferred from its possibly distorted or primitive cognitive, phenomenological, or behavioral by-products).

Of course, the directness of third-person access to another's mental states is a matter of degree, and that access requires both inferences and interpretation no matter whether the other person's states are conscious, dissociated, or repressed. For example, you may be directly aware of your anger, but I can be aware of your anger only by virtue of drawing an inference from your behavior and assuming you're not feigning anger.[2] When you dissociate your anger and I elicit a hypnotically induced report of your angry feelings, my knowledge of your anger again requires me to infer that your behavior is a reliable guide to what's happening to you subjectively. In these two cases, I would say that third-person access to your anger is comparably direct, requiring little more than assumptions about behavior-reliability. But when you repress your anger, I don't have at my disposal anything as straightforward as a report from you that you're feeling angry or other relatively transparent outbursts of angry behavior. I might have suggestive word-associations, slips of the tongue, or intriguing constrictions of behavior (e.g., obsessive behavior, sexual frigidity), but usually nothing as blunt as reports of angry feelings, overtly hostile remarks, or punches in the nose.

Not surprisingly, many cases are not this clear-cut. So not surprisingly (and not alarmingly), this way of characterizing repression allows for an appropriate range of borderline cases. Consider, for example, behavior that reveals hidden feelings but whose interpretation is clear even to the person exhibiting it (e.g., forgetting an appointment you prefer to avoid). In fact, in some cases the only difference between a repressed and a dissociated state may be the conceptual framework in terms of which it is treated clinically. For example, obsessional or compulsive behavior might be approached psychoanalytically, using indirect methods (e.g., free association) to uncover the reasons for the behavior. Or, it might be treated as a dissociative disorder, using hypnosis to reveal hidden memories lying at the root of the problem. So, which diagnosis we choose could easily (and appropriately) depend on whether the clinician treated the patient by means of hypnosis, EMDR, free association, or something else. Therefore, in some cases at least, there may be no preferred or privileged answer to the question, "Is this state dissociated or repressed?" The world may not have a sharp cleavage here, and there is no need for our concepts to do so.

[2] Some might think instead that we are immediately aware of another person's anger or pain (say), and then only later, upon reflection, wonder whether the anger or pain is feigned. That is certainly a respectable alternative view, and one whose viability can't be adequately addressed here. For now, our concern is with the relative directness or indirectness of first- and third-person knowledge of mental states. To that end I believe it's sufficient to say that we need to focus on what we might call the "logical" as opposed to the "historical" order of ideas. No matter how instinctively and reliably we might accept uncritically various behaviors as indicators of another person's mental states, our third-person knowledge of those states can be analyzed plausibly as involving interpretations and assumptions not required for first-person knowledge of our own states.

We might even want to say that, for borderline cases at least, there is but one psychological condition, which is simply identified and treated according to different criteria and methods. And presumably, the indeterminacy of our description is no more unusual or objectionable than it would be in many ordinary cases where we can describe the same state from different perspectives, each of them revealing and valuable in its own way. For example, from one perspective it might be useful to view a person's actions as shy, and from another perspective as cowardly. Similarly, it might be illuminating to see a person's behavior as exemplifying both arrogance and insecurity. Each of those descriptive categories allows us to systematize the person's behavior in a different way, neither of which is inherently preferable to the other, and both of which may give us genuine and distinctive insights into the person's behavioral regularities.

2.3.2 Suppression

The concept of suppression is also a bit difficult to pin down, and certainly the term *suppression* gets used in various ways (often as a synonym for *repression*). To the extent that there is a standard view of the difference between suppression and repression, there seem to be two distinguishing features. First, suppression is always a conscious activity, and second, "amnesia is absent in suppression, present in repression" (Hilgard, 1986, p. 251). So suppression seems to be "a conscious putting-out-of-mind of something we don't want to think about" (Braun, 1988, p. 5). Thus, if we agree to use "suppression" in this fairly narrow technical sense, we can say that when *x* is suppressed for *S*, (1) *S* consciously diverts attention from *x* (i.e., puts *x* "out of mind"), and (2) *S* does not have amnesia for *x*.

2.3.3 Denial

Although Braun regards denial as yet another distinct point on a continuum of awareness, I submit that if we define the relevant terms as I suggest here, a distinct category of denial is gratuitous. I propose instead that we consider analyzing the term *denial* in terms of repression, suppression, and dissociation. For example, one handy (if slightly oversimplified) approach would be the following. Let's suppose first that the difference between unconscious and subconscious mental states is that the former can only be accessed relatively indirectly (as previously explained), whereas the latter can be accessed relatively directly. Then we can regard repression as unconscious denial, dissociation as subconscious denial, and suppression as conscious denial.

2.4 WHAT DISSOCIATION IS

With these considerations in mind, I offer the following provisional analysis of dissociation—in particular, the general expression-form "*x* is dissociated from *y*." We can then see how this analysis bears on current debates about dissociation. So let's say "*x* is dissociated from *y*" if and only if:

(1) *x* is an occurrent or dispositional state, or else a system of states (as in traits, skills, and alter identities) of a subject *S*; and *y* is either a state or system of states of *S*, or else the subject *S*.[3]
(2) *y* may or may not be dissociated from *x* (i.e., dissociation is a nonsymmetrical relation).
(3) *x* and *y* are separated by a phenomenological or epistemological barrier (e.g., amnesia, anesthesia) erected by *S*.
(4) *S* is not consciously aware of erecting the barrier between *x* and *y*.
(5) The barrier between *x* and *y* can be broken down, at least in principle.
(6) Third- and first-person knowledge of *x* may be as direct as (respectively) third- and first-person knowledge of *S*'s nondissociated states.

Condition (1) takes the capability, ownership, and diversification assumptions into account, and condition (5) acknowledges the accessibility assumption. Since condition (4) requires *S* to erect the dissociative barrier either subconsciously or unconsciously, it provides a way of ruling out cases of suppression. Similarly, condition (6) rules out a large set of cases ordinarily classified as instances of repression.

Condition (3) is designed to rule out a large class of cases we would presumably not count as dissociative, but in which *S*'s states seem to lie behind an epistemological barrier. In particular, this condition rules out many examples of conceptual naïveté and inevitable forms of self-ignorance. For example, *S* might desire or dislike something but lack the introspective or conceptual sophistication, or the relevant information, needed to recognize those states. So condition (3) will rule out cases

[3] The syntactic complexity of this condition reflects the fact that we assert the presence of dissociation under a great variety of conditions. For example, we can say that a subject has dissociated a memory, trait, or alter identity. But we also sometimes say that one memory or skill is dissociated from another.

where infants, small children, or naïve or mentally challenged adults lack the conceptual categories to identify their own mental states. The epistemological barrier in these cases is not something they erect. Similarly, many conceptually sophisticated adults may fail to recognize they have certain mental states, either because they are insufficiently introspective or because they lack relevant information. For example, *S* might be unaware he detests the sound of a fortepiano, because he has not yet heard enough examples for that disposition (or regularity in his preferences) to become clear. He might mistakenly think he dislikes only the one or two fortepianos he has heard. That is clearly not a case of dissociation, and condition (3) rules it out as well.

Moreover, my proposed criteria of dissociation countenance a large range of phenomena as instances. Naturally (and predictably), classic forms of pathological dissociation satisfy the criteria, including DID and dissociative fugue. Moreover, other familiar impressive phenomena likewise satisfy the criteria—for example, hypnotic amnesia, anesthesia or analgesia, and automatic writing. Perhaps more interesting, the criteria are apparently satisfied by a range of normal phenomena many want to regard as dissociative. These include, for example, blocking out the sound of ongoing conversation while reading (but being able to respond when your name is mentioned), and shifting gears and obeying traffic lights while driving but consciously focusing only on your conversation with your passenger. I consider it a virtue of these criteria that they undergird a variety of disparate intuitions about which phenomena are instances of dissociation.

Furthermore, I believe this account of dissociation is sufficiently abstract and general to support and unify the various analyses or definitions of dissociation scattered throughout the clinical and experimental literature. Also, I believe (or at least hope) that it corrects prevailing approaches, which are either needlessly restrictive or overinclusive.

2.5 WHAT DISSOCIATION IS NOT

Among prevailing approaches to dissociation, some (1) characterize dissociation as a defensive response to trauma or stress. But as we've noted, that can't be the whole story, because it rules out the vast majority of hypnotic phenomena and also many widely accepted examples of dissociation in everyday life.

Some have said (2) that dissociation is the absence of conscious awareness of impinging stimuli or ongoing behaviors. But if that were the case, then sleep, chemical anesthesia, and subliminal perception would count—incorrectly—as dissociative.

Others take dissociation to be (3) ongoing behaviors or perceptions that are inconsistent with a person's introspective verbal reports. But if that were true, dissociation would encompass far too much—for example, cases of self-deception, cognitive dissonance or confusion, or outright ignorance or stupidity. For instance, it would include a person's simply failing to grasp that simultaneously held beliefs are inconsistent. And incredibly, it would also include Cartesian or Humean skepticism about the external world—that is, the philosophical position implied by someone who, while leaning against a wall, says (in a state of philosophical seriousness) that he can't be certain the wall exists.

Still others say (4) that dissociation is an alteration of consciousness in which one feels disconnected from the self or from the environment. But first of all, that rules out what many have taken to be a paradigm instance of dissociation—namely, negative hallucination. In classic cases of this phenomenon, the subject doesn't feel disconnected from the self or environment, merely consciously unaware of certain items in the vicinity. Second, it too seems overinclusive, because it apparently includes as dissociative the experience of paralysis, sleep, and sensory deprivation.

Finally, some say (5) that dissociation is the coexistence of separate mental systems or identities that are ordinarily integrated in the person's consciousness, memory, or identity. But this approach is either empty or also too inclusive. Consider: what does it mean to refer to *separate* mental systems? In the absence of a description of what the separateness amounts to (e.g., of the sort I've provided), that term either has no clear meaning or else it seems merely to be a synonym for *dissociated*, in which case the definition would be circular. The likely alternative to this would be to let *separate* stand for something like *distinguishable*. But in that case the definition would, after all, be too inclusive, because it would then cover ordinary (retrievable) forgetting and the common (though perhaps only occasional) failure to juggle disparate roles in life (e.g., the person who sometimes has trouble coordinating the different mind-sets required for being both a loving parent and mob assassin, or—to keep it personal—philosopher and musician).

Some proposed definitions of *dissociation* commit more than one of the errors already noted. For example, Marlene Steinberg claims that dissociation is "an adaptive defense in response to high stress or trauma characterized by memory loss and a sense of disconnection from oneself or one's surroundings" (Steinberg & Schnall, 2001, p. 3).

As we have seen, this definition errs in several respects. First, dissociation is not just a defensive response, and (as we noted earlier) it doesn't always involve an impairment of memory. Second, this definition excludes most (if not all) hypnotic phenomena.

2.6 INCLUSIVITY VERSUS EXCLUSIVITY

Earlier, when I surveyed assumptions underlying the concept of dissociation, I described what I called the diversification assumption. According to that assumption, dissociation manifests in many different forms, affects a wide variety of states, and spreads out along a number of different continua. I argued that this is one of several ways in which dissociation resembles many other human capacities. For example, courage, sensuality, and wit are human capacities that likewise vary greatly in their range of manifestations and in the degree to which they are expressed along a number of different dimensions. People are not simply more or less courageous, sensual, or funny. They manifest these capacities in different ways and in different styles, and to different degrees with respect to them. Human behavior generally is so complex and varied that it would be incredible if dissociation failed to exhibit a similar range and diversity of expression.

However, a recent development in the study of dissociation has apparently led some to challenge the diversification assumption. Officially, what's at issue is whether normal, experimental, and pathological dissociation are all forms of a single phenomenon (let's call this the inclusivity position), or whether pathological and nonpathological dissociation are radically distinct, lacking any significant unifying features (the exclusivity position). Perhaps curiously, this has become one of the most hotly debated and even polarizing topics in that field of research. Although in my view the issue has never been stated very clearly, until recently most clinicians and experimenters seemed to embrace the inclusivity position. But on the basis of some recent taxonometric analyses by Waller, Putnam, and Carlson, and several subsequent studies by other investigators, some now claim that pathological and nonpathological dissociation are sharply distinct categories. Accordingly, they argue that dissociation is not a single phenomenon and that it's a mistake to regard normal and pathological dissociation as continuous (see, e.g., Boon & Draijer, 1993; Briere et al., 2005; Ogawa et al., 1997; Putnam, 1997; Waller et al., 1996).

However, the underlying reasoning here is questionable. First, even if pathological and nonpathological forms of dissociation differ consistently and dramatically (so that many properties of one are never properties of the other), that could not by itself show that dissociation is not a unitary or single phenomenon embracing both pathological and nonpathological forms. That conclusion would follow only in conjunction with an apparently unjustified assumption about the distribution of dissociative phenomena—namely, that if pathological and nonpathological dissociation were instances of the same class of phenomena, we would expect to find a fairly even distribution of dissociative phenomena along a dissociative continuum. And because according to some diagnostic surveys dissociative phenomena seem instead to cluster into two distinct groups—not the relatively smooth distribution to which the inclusivity view (or diversification assumption) is allegedly committed—some believe that the inclusivity view has been disconfirmed. That is, they believe that there is no longer justification for treating dissociation as a concept unifying the varied occurrences that have been considered dissociative.

But in fact there is no reason to insist that the distribution between normal and pathological dissociation has to be smooth. On the contrary, uneven distributions are clearly compatible with treating dissociation as a single concept unifying a quite motley range of manifestations. At least some leading researchers recognize this (Nijenhuis, 1999, pp. 175f). For example, pathological lying and ordinary lying may indeed be dramatically different in degree, enough so to warrant treating cases of the former (but not the latter) as a special class deserving of clinical attention. But both are still types of lying, and to ignore what they have in common is to miss an important theoretical or conceptual unity. Similar observations can be made about the differences between normal orderliness and pathological or compulsive orderliness, and between ordinary anxiety and panic attacks.

The situation is the same with regard to pathological and nonpathological dissociation. The former seems clearly to be distinguishable from the latter in several respects (as one would expect). But both remain forms of dissociation, as our convention of using the term *dissociation* in connection with each tacitly acknowledges.

Interestingly, Waller et al. seem not to make the error of concluding on the basis of their data that there is no viable general concept of dissociation uniting the phenomenon's various manifestations. In fact, although they criticize the DES for not capturing certain observed and significant regularities in the data, they concede that pathological and nonpathological dissociation are nevertheless "related" (p. 301) and are both forms of dissociation. They even state explicitly that there are "nonpathological or healthy forms of dissociation" (p. 302).

It's less clear whether Briere et al. avoid the error. Like some others, they claim to have shown (in their case with the MDI) that the "notion of 'dissociation' as a *general trait* was not supported" (p. 221, emphasis added). Instead, they claim that "dissociation may represent a variety of phenomenologically distinct and only moderately related symptom clusters whose ultimate commonality is more theoretical than empirical" (ibid). More specifically, they claim that the "finding of discrete dissociation factors supports a view of dissociation as a multifaceted collection of distinct, but overlapping, dimensions, as opposed to a unitary trait" (p. 228). Of course, what's at issue in this paper is precisely the theoretical question of whether the variety of dissociative phenomena can be plausibly construed as falling under a general concept. And although it's unclear what exactly Briere et al. mean by "unitary trait" and "general trait," they seem to deny this. Indeed, they seem to be arguing for a certain analysis of the general concept of dissociation, and they state explicitly that on the basis of their survey, "the term dissociation may be a misnomer to the extent that it implies a single underlying phenomenon" (p. 230).

We should also note that the appearance of sharply distinct classes or taxons of dissociative phenomena may simply be an artifact of the categories and form of questions used in the surveys from which the data were gathered. Questions and their embedded descriptive categories are like conceptual grids. To put the matter picturesquely, depending on the shape and size (e.g., fineness or coarseness) of the grids, objects of only certain sizes and shapes will pass through. That means that items on questionnaires will, from the start, allow only certain kinds of responses and thereby permit only certain kinds of results or types of discriminations. The appearance of dissociative taxons might therefore reveal little more than the inevitably theory-laden biases or grossness of the distinctions permitted by the questionnaire. For example, from Briere's et al. use of the MDI, we can't conclude anything more than that dissociative phenomena can be parsed nonarbitrarily in a way that reveals no underlying connectedness. And of course that's no more revelatory or theoretically interesting than the observation that the things in this room can be divided nonarbitrarily into nomologically anomalous classes each one of which exhibits its own distinctive regularities—for example, when insurance agents, household movers, or interior decorators classify them into wet things, heavy things, green things, valuable things, fragile things, and things that even a mother couldn't love. But in that case, if my foregoing conceptual analysis shows that the concept can be made to unify and cover the broad range of phenomena that have been considered dissociative, and if application of the MDI (or another survey instrument) fails to capture that unity and systematicity, there's little reason to think it captures or helps analyze the concept of dissociation.

Moreover, we've already noted one reason to doubt the ability of current diagnostic surveys to illuminate the concept of dissociation—namely, their neglect of hypnotic phenomena. Even when the surveys were administered both to clinical and nonclinical populations, their questions were not designed to distinguish, say, those who are good hypnotic subjects from those who are not, much less those who are hypnotizable to varying degrees. So right from the start, they won't identify one clear group of dissociators or tease out what they have in common. But then they can't be expected to reveal what ordinarily hypnotizable persons have in common with those experiencing clinically interesting forms of dissociation, much less whether there's a smooth transition from the former class of subjects to those suffering from pathological dissociation—or failing that smooth transition, something theoretically relevant that they have in common.

So it appears that proponents of the exclusivity position have set up a straw man when they state the inclusivity view. In fact, there are two signs of this. We've just considered the first: assuming that the distribution of dissociative phenomena must be smooth if the inclusivity view is correct. The second apparent instance of strawman reasoning is this. Contrary to what proponents of the exclusivity view seem to suggest, to say that normal and pathological dissociative phenomena are continuous is not to say that there is a *single* dissociative continuum along which those forms of dissociation spread (unevenly or evenly). That's a needlessly simple and antecedently incredible formulation of the inclusivity position, and it's all too easy to overturn. Presumably, one can always select a list of allegedly relevant properties in such a way that the classes of normal and pathological dissociation appear to be profoundly separate. But on different characterizations of dissociation, or using different lists of relevant properties, the two forms of dissociation might turn out to overlap or distribute quite evenly. In fact, we saw that the criteria of dissociation I listed previously countenance both normal and pathological forms of dissociation. So we know already that dissociation can in fact be characterized in a way that embraces the phenomenon in all of its widely recognized forms and which still allows dissociation to be distinguished from repression, and so on. Moreover, it's clear that dissociative phenomena satisfying those criteria spread out (smoothly or otherwise) along the several continua mentioned when I stated the diversification assumption: pervasiveness, frequency, severity, degree of functional isolation, and degree of personal importance to the subject.

So it seems to me that the current debate over taxons is really a nonissue, at least so far as it purports to be a debate over the concept of dissociation. However, none of this is to deny the importance—and perhaps the clinical necessity—of recognizing and focusing on the manifest disparities between pathological and nonpathological forms of dissociation. (But notice, I refer to both—as one should—as forms of dissociation.) For the clinician, the differences are what matter, and perhaps the distinctive aspects of pathological dissociation are the only features that deserve their attention. In that sense, it's pragmatically defensible to regard pathological dissociation as a phenomenon distinct from nonpathological dissociation Similarly, it's defensible for clinicians to focus on pathological lying as a phenomenon of interest, but not the everyday lies we tell to protect another's feelings, to avoid embarrassment, and to avert countless other mini conflicts. But it's still confused to think that warrants rejection of the inclusivity view. And as I believe we can now see, to reject that view is to lose sight of the interesting properties that seem to link all forms of dissociation and which justify, for the time being, treating dissociation, in all its richness and variety, as a legitimate and single object of psychological and theoretical inquiry.

I am grateful to Paul Dell and John O'Neil for very helpful criticisms of an ancestor of this chapter.

REFERENCES

Binet, A. (1892/1896/1977). *Les altérations de la personnalité*. Paris: F. Alcan. English edition: Alterations of personality. New York: D. Appleton & Company, 1896. Reprint: Washington, DC: University Publications of America, 1977.

Boon, S., & Draijer, N. (1993). *Multiple personality disorder in the Netherlands*. Amsterdam: Swets & Zeitlinger.

Braude, S. E. (1995). *First person plural: Multiple personality and the philosophy of mind*. Rev. Lanham, MD: Rowman & Littlefield.

Braun, B. G. (1988). The BASK (Behavior, Affect, Sensation, Knowledge) model of dissociation. *Dissociation, 1,* 4–23.

Briere, J., Weathers, F. W., & Runtz, M. (2005). Is dissociation a multidimensional construct? Data from the Multiscale Dissociation Inventory. *Journal of Traumatic Stress, 18,* 221–231.

Cardeña, E. (1994). The domain of dissociation. In S. J. Lynn & J. W. Rhue (Eds.), *Dissociation: Clinical and theoretical perspectives* (pp. 15–31). New York: Guilford.

Crabtree, A. (1993). *From Mesmer to Freud: Magnetic sleep and the roots of psychological healing*. New Haven: Yale University Press.

Gauld, A. (1992). *A history of hypnotism*. Cambridge: Cambridge University Press.

Hilgard, E. R. (1986). *Divided consciousness: Multiple controls in human thought and action* (Expanded Edition). New York: Wiley-Interscience.

Messerschmidt, R. A. (1927). Quantitative investigation of the alleged independent operation of conscious and subconscious processes. *Journal of Abnormal & Social Psychology, 22,* 325–340.

Myers, F. W. H. (1903). *Human personality and its survival of bodily death*. London: Longmans, Green & Co.

Nijenhuis, E. R. S. (1999). *Somatoform dissociation*. Assen: Van Gorcum.

Ogawa, J. R., Sroufe, L. A., Weinfeld, N. C., Carlson, E. A., & Egeland, B. (1997). Development and the fragmented self: longitudinal study of dissociative symptomatology in a nonclinical sample. *Development & Psychopathology, 9,* 855–879.

Prince, M. (1905). *Dissociation of a personality*. Oxford: Oxford University Press.

Putnam, F. W. (1997). *Dissociation in children and adolescents: a developmental perspective*. New York: The Guilford Press.

Sidis, B. (1902). *Psychopathological researches: studies in mental dissociation*. Boston: Richard G. Badger.

Steinberg, M., & Schnall, M. (2001). *The stranger in the mirror: Dissociation—the hidden epidemic*. New York: Harper Collins.

Van der Hart, O., & Dorahy, M. J. (2009). Dissociation: History of a concept. In P. F. Dell & J. A. O'Neil (Eds.), *Dissociation & the Dissociative Disorders: DSM-V & Beyond* (pp. 3–26). New York: Routledge.

Waller, N. G., Putnam, F. W., & Carlson, E. B. (1996). Types of dissociation and dissociative types: a taxometric analysis of dissociative experiences. *Psychological Methods, 1,* 300–321.

Part II

Developmental Approaches to Dissociation

3 Dissociation and Development of the Self

Elizabeth A. Carlson, PhD
Tuppett M. Yates, PhD
L. Alan Sroufe, PhD

OUTLINE

Dissociation is a complex psychophysiological process that alters the accessibility of memory and knowledge, integration of behavior, and sense of self (Putnam, 1994). The etiologic role of traumatic experience in dissociative processes has long been posited (Breuer & Freud, 1986/1895; Janet 1889), but relatively little attention has aimed to understand the developmental processes that underlie observed associations between trauma and dissociation. Recently, scholars have suggested that the developing self (or disruptions in self processes) may account for this association (Bowlby, 1969/1982; Kohut, 1971). In this chapter, we employ an organizational developmental framework to understand dissociative processes with respect to both developmental adaptation and deviation. We argue that dissociation is integrally related to the developing self, and that pathological dissociation disrupts the development of the self (Putnam, 1994, 1995) and/or results from disturbances in the self (Liotti, 1992). Thus, dissociative processes both affect and are affected by organization of the self.

3.1 DISSOCIATION: DESCRIPTION AND DIAGNOSIS

Across the developmental spectrum, dissociative processes may manifest as disturbances of affect regulation (e.g., depression, mood swings, feelings of isolation), identity disruptions (e.g., splitting, fragmentation), autohypnotic phenomena (e.g., trances, time distortions, psychogenic numbing), memory dysfunction (e.g., psychogenic amnesia, fugue), revivification of traumatic experience (e.g., flashbacks, hallucinations), and behavioral disturbance (e.g., inattention, poor impulse control, self-harm) (Hornstein & Putnam, 1992). Efforts to define dissociation emphasize deficits in integrative memory, disturbances of identity, passive influence experiences, and trance-absorption phenomena that are not better accounted for by organic pathology (American Psychiatric Association, 1994; Putnam, 1997). Memory dysfunctions include the inability to recall autobiographical information or complex behavior and disruptive intrusions of traumatic memories. Disturbances of identity consist of experiences of discrete behavioral states (each associated with a subjective sense of individuality) as well as depersonalization, and psychogenic amnesia. Passive influence experiences involve feelings of mind-body disconnection (e.g., being controlled by an outside force). Experiences of intense absorption or enthrallment may take the form of spontaneous trance states (e.g., lack of awareness of immediate surroundings).

As in adults, dissociative processes in children and adolescents are characterized by disturbances of memory, identity, and perception; however, developmental considerations are paramount in understanding early forms of dissociation (Putnam, 1997). Identification of pathological dissociation in childhood may be confounded by normative dissociative tendencies, particularly in young children (Cole & Putnam, 1992; Fischer & Ayoub, 1994). Dissociative behaviors may not have the same meaning across development, and a number of normative processes may underlie dissociative states in early childhood (e.g., fantasy proneness, hypnotizability, behavioral state regulation) (Hornstein & Putnam, 1992; Putnam, 2000). Moreover, children, adolescents, and adults differ in their cognitive capacity to recognize discontinuities in their behavior or sense of awareness, and in their subjective distress about any perceived inconsistencies. The assignment of dissociative diagnoses, particularly in childhood, requires familiarity with spectrums of both normal (e.g., imaginative behavior, fantasy/reality boundaries) and disordered behavior (e.g., pathological dissociation) (Putnam, 1997). Pathological dissociation may reflect an absence of the normative decline of dissociative processes across development and/or an increase in individual (idiosyncratic) dissociation.

Dissociation has been characterized both as a continuum of behavior and as an extreme deviation from normality (i.e., a taxon of psychopathology separate from the normative continuum). At the level of process, dissociative experiences range along a continuum of severity from short, often situation-dependent, normative episodes such as daydreaming to prolonged or frequent episodes that interfere with individual functioning to profound disturbances in the organization and integration of self, cognitive, and behavioral processes (Putnam, 1991). At the level of diagnosis, dissociation has been conceptualized as a marked deviation from normality. The current *Diagnostic and Statistical Manual of Mental Disorders* (DSM-IV-TR; American Psychiatric Association, 2000) recognizes five types of dissociative disorder: Dissociative Amnesia, Dissociative Fugue, Depersonalization Disorder, Dissociative Identity Disorder (DID), and Dissociative Disorder Not Otherwise Specified (DDNOS). Child and adolescent diagnoses include only DDNOS and DID. Contemporary diagnostic paradigms are consistent with a taxonic interpretation of dissociation.

The taxonic claim is supported by research in which taxon-related items from the Dissociative Experiences Scale (DES; Bernstein & Putnam, 1986), measuring amnesia for dissociative experiences, identity confusion, and depersonalization/derealization, distinguish dissociative individuals (i.e., DID) from both normals and patients with other forms of psychopathology (Waller, Putnam, & Carlson, 1996). In longitudinal study, the consistent strength with which discriminant functions distinguish clinical and normal subgroups provides support for the position that pathological dissociation is distinct from normative dissociation (Ogawa, Sroufe, Weinfield, Carlson, & Egeland, 1997). Available data suggest that clinical dissociation represents more than the high end of a distribution of scores; it reflects a deviation from normative development that results in maladaptive behavior that can be differentiated from normal behavior. From the perspective of development, dissociation may be viewed as a continuum process; at the level of diagnosis, dissociative phenomena may be categorical (Putnam, 1995). However, critical questions concerning environmental and biological factors that influence the developmental processes toward or away from pathological dissociation remain.

3.2 ETIOLOGY OF DISSOCIATION

First noted by 20th-century psychologists, dissociation and its developmental underpinnings have been a central focus of psychological inquiry. On the periphery of the psychoanalytic tradition, Janet (1889) proposed that constitutional vulnerability interacts with extreme experience to foster cognitive-affective disintegration. In later works, Freud (1926) placed greater emphasis on environmental influences and their interaction with psychological processes. He suggested that trauma (i.e., extreme experiences of helplessness) precipitates defense mechanisms, such as dissociation, in an effort to manage environmentally and psychologically induced anxiety and avoid retraumatization. Contemporary theories have integrated these early notions to suggest that the combined influence of experience (i.e., repeated trauma) and biological reorganization as a function of experience contribute to pathological dissociation. These theories propose that dissociation begins as an individual defense against unexpected overwhelming negative experience. The defensive pattern becomes entrenched as an automatic and uncontrollable response to stress with repetition and anticipation of probable attack (Perry, Pollard, Blakley, Baker, & Vigilante, 1995; Putnam, 1997; Terr, 1990, 1991, 1994).

Object-relations perspectives conceptualize the psychological phenomenon of dissociation in terms of internal dynamics whereby trauma necessitates the premature maturation of a "false" self that rigidifies and obscures more spontaneous authentic experience (the "true" self) (Winnicott, 1965, 1971). The false self is viewed as predominantly a mental construction in which secondary (primarily cognitive) processes are enlisted to ensure survival in unpredictable overwhelming conditions. From a Jungian perspective, Kalsched (1996) describes this dissociative dynamic as a "dyadic self-care structure" that consists of both precocious caretaking and regressed infantile aspects of the self. Similar to Winnicott's "false" self, the caretaking aspect of the self-care system strives to protect the regressed self, even becoming persecutory in the service of self-preservation and the avoidance of retraumatization. In this view, experience becomes traumatic when existing regulatory capacities are overwhelmed (due to developmental immaturity, structural rigidity, and/or lack of supportive emotional relationships), yet evolving systems strive to maintain or preserve existing organization. Thus, trauma in and of itself does not shatter self-organization; internal processes shatter the organization in an effort to protect or maintain a sense of coherence that is the self.

Empirical research has demonstrated consistent associations between traumatic experience and biological and behavioral manifestations of dissociation. Moreover, these relations appear to be moderated by the frequency of the trauma and the developmental status of the individual at the time of traumatic exposure. Level of dissociation has been related to chronicity and severity of trauma in retrospective self-report studies (Chu & Dill, 1990; Kirby, Chu, & Dill, 1993; Waldinger, Swett, Frank, & Miller, 1994) and in a recent prospective study (Ogawa et al., 1997). Links between dissociation and child sexual, physical abuse, and neglect have been demonstrated in adult nonclinical (e.g., Briere & Runtz, 1988; Irwin, 1996; Ross, Joshi, & Currie, 1990; Sanders & Becker-Lausen, 1995), clinical (e.g., Briere & Zaidi, 1989; Chu & Dill, 1990; Kirby et al., 1993; Lipschitz, Kaplan, Sorkeen, & Chorney, 1996; Putnam et al., 1996), and dissociative disordered (e.g., Putnam, Guroff, Silberman, Barban, & Post, 1986; Ross et al., 1991) samples. Dissociation in adulthood has also been related to experiences of loss in childhood (Irwin, 1994) and to witnessing violence (Zlotnick, Shea, Pearlstein et al., 1996).

Much of the research concerning trauma and dissociation has been retrospective, focusing on relations between self-reported abuse in childhood and high levels of dissociation in adulthood. Several retrospective studies have found severity of dissociation in adulthood to be related to age of onset of trauma, suggesting a particular vulnerability to the dissociative effects of negative experience in early childhood (e.g., Kirby et al., 1993; Van IJzendoorn & Schuengel, 1996; Zlotnick, Shea, Zakriski, et al., 1995). Recent studies suggest that trauma may lead to elevated levels of contemporaneous dissociation in childhood. Dissociative processes in childhood have been related to multiple forms of maltreatment, including sexual abuse, physical abuse, and neglect (Coons, 1996; Hornstein & Putnam, 1992; Macfie, Cicchetti, & Toth, 2001; Malinosky-Rummel & Hoier, 1991; Ogawa et al., 1997; Putnam, Helmers, & Trickett, 1993; Sanders & Giolas, 1991).

Despite considerable evidence connecting pathological dissociation with prior trauma, little is known about the normative trajectory of dissociation or processes linking maltreatment and dissociation across development (Putnam, 1995). Our own view of the developmental relation between trauma and dissociation is grounded within the integrative framework of developmental psychopathology which encompasses ideas from a range of theoretical perspectives (Cicchetti, 1984; Rutter, 1996a; Sroufe & Rutter, 1984). The remainder of the chapter provides an overview of: (1) the organizational developmental perspective derived from the domain of developmental psychopathology, (2) normative processes in self development, (3) normative dissociative processes, (4) dissociative developmental trajectories, (5) effects of dissociation on self functioning, and finally, (6) diagnostic implications of a developmental approach to the study of dissociation.

3.2.1 Dissociation Within the Framework of Developmental Psychopathology

As the study of the origins and course of individual patterns of behavioral adaptation, developmental psychopathology provides a useful framework for integrating diverse theoretical accounts of dissociative processes and the developing self (e.g., Cicchetti & Toth, 1997; Rutter, 1996a; Sameroff, 2000; Sroufe & Rutter, 1984). Beyond descriptive psychopathology and risk identification paradigms, developmental psychopathology encourages process-level analyses of experiences that probabilistically lead to disturbance, that modify the expression of disorder, and that contribute to the maintenance or desistance of developmental pathways and patterns (see Cicchetti & Tucker, 1994; Gottlieb, 1991; Rutter, 1996b; Sameroff & Emde, 1989). These dynamic processes include both internal and external influences and biological and psychological transformations and reorganizations that occur over time (Cicchetti, 2006).

An organizational perspective of development incorporates core principles of developmental psychopathology within a theoretical framework that yields testable hypotheses about the nature of both typical and atypical development (Cicchetti, 2006; Sroufe, 1979; Sroufe & Rutter, 1984). A central tenet of developmental psychopathology is that normal and atypical developmental patterns are mutually informing (Cicchetti, 1990, 1993; Cicchetti, 2006; Sroufe, 1990b; Sroufe & Rutter, 1984). The organizational perspective conceptualizes development as a series of qualitative reorganizations whereby earlier patterns of adaptation provide a framework for, and are transformed by, later adaptations. In this way, development is cumulative, and early experience is uniquely influential. Each successive adaptation represents the combined influence of contemporaneous experience and development up to that point (Bowlby, 1980). Across developmental patterns and pathways, whether normal or disordered, relations among successive adaptations are probabilistic and multidetermined (Thelen, 1992). Thus, a single developmental starting point may yield divergent outcomes (i.e., multifinality), while different patterns of early adaptation may converge on a single developmental endpoint (i.e., equifinality; Cicchetti & Rogosch, 1996). For example, harsh parental treatment may lead to both conduct problems and depression; yet, neither form of pathology stems solely from parental harshness.

Within the organizational model, adaptation is defined with respect to the quality of integration among domains of functioning related to salient developmental issues and later adaptation (Cicchetti, 1989; Waters & Sroufe, 1983). Positive adaptation is enabled by integrations of biological, socioemotional, cognitive, and representational capacities that promote the flexible negotiation of concurrent and future developmental issues (Cicchetti, 1993; Egeland, Carlson, & Sroufe, 1993; Sroufe, 1989; Waters & Sroufe, 1983). Maladaptation (i.e., psychopathology) reflects developmental deviation(s) from normal patterns of adaptation, rigid patterns of functioning that compromise subsequent development (Cicchetti, 1993; Sroufe, 1989). From a developmental perspective, individuals actively participate in constructing and perpetuating experience, whether adaptive or maladaptive, by interpreting and selecting experiences that are consistent with their developmental history (Sroufe & Fleeson, 1986).

As suggested by an emphasis on developmental challenges, the organizational model focuses on patterns of adaptation, rather than continuities in manifest discrete behaviors (Sroufe & Waters, 1977). Thus, developmental coherence occurs at the level of the meaning and function of behavior (Sameroff & Chandler, 1975; Waddington, 1940). The same observable behavior (e.g., the child's dependence on caregivers) may be viewed as adaptive at one point and maladaptive at another depending upon the individual's developing capacities and environmental resources and demands. Just as equivalent levels of adaptation may appear dissimilar across developmental periods, manifestations of psychopathology may change across development (Cicchetti & Schneider-Rosen, 1986; Sroufe & Rutter, 1984). Herein lies the contribution of a developmental perspective to the study of psychopathology. Whereas early models of psychopathology were largely downward extensions of adult manifestations of psychopathology to child and adolescent populations, a developmental approach is informed by the study of both normative and disordered processes in the developing child. This chapter aims to further our understanding of dissociation from such a perspective, wherein dissociative processes are inextricably linked to normative processes of self development.

3.2.2 Normative Self Processes

From a developmental perspective, the self is conceived as an inner *organization* of attitudes, feelings, expectations, and meanings (Sroufe, 1990a). The self arises from an organized caregiving matrix (an organization that exists prior to the emergence of self) and has organizational significance for adaptation and experience (Sroufe, 1990a, 1996; Sroufe & Waters, 1977). Organization of the self evolves from dyadic experience through recursive patterns of differentiation and integration, providing a framework for subsequent individual experience (Sander, 1975; Sroufe, 1996). Recognition of others as part of regulation, of one's actions as effective or ineffective in eliciting care, and of the self as the origin of experience are all part of the self system.

Within an organizational developmental framework, core levels of self-competence derive from the quality of early experience in the caregiving milieu and contribute to the negotiation of developmental issues at multiple, interactive levels (Sroufe, Egeland, & Carlson, 1999). At the *motivational* level, the child who has experienced responsive care holds positive expectations about relationships with others that motivate her/him to seek out, derive pleasure from, and rely on interpersonal connections. *Attitudes* formed in the caregiving relationship lay the foundation for views of the self as worthy of, and effective in, eliciting care and responsiveness from others. A strong *emotional* base, derived from a supportive caregiving relationship, provides a solid foundation for flexible and effective arousal modulation, impulse control, and adaptation to the demands of the environment. At the *instrumental* level, relationship experience shapes the development of specific skills that enable the successful negotiation of salient developmental issues. Finally, at the *relational* level, the child with a history of responsive care possesses capacities to apprehend the rules of social reciprocity and to establish and maintain genuine empathic connections with others.

The regulation of emotion lies at the core of early socioemotional experience (Thompson, 2006). Such regulation entails processes responsible for monitoring, evaluating, and modifying arousal that enable individuals to function adaptively in the environment (Cicchetti, Ganiban, & Barnett, 1991). Moreover, core affective dimensions endow individuals with a sense of continuity of self throughout development and across relationships with others (Emde, 1983). Longitudinal research supports the link between well-functioning affective attunement in early childhood and adaptive functioning in motivational, attitudinal, instrumental, emotional, and relational domains across development (Thompson, 2006; Sroufe, Egeland, Carlson, & Collins, 2005; Weinfield, Sroufe, Egeland, & Carlson, 2008).

The foundations of emotional regulation are laid in early physiological and affective experience within the primary caregiving relationship (i.e., emotional synchrony and distress modulation) (Cicchetti et al., 1991; Sroufe, 1996). Examining the quality of these early affective exchanges is critical to understanding compensatory regulatory processes, such as dissociation. Infants enter the world with a biologically based propensity for interaction (Bowlby, 1969/1982), initiating, maintaining, and terminating interactions reflexively and without intention (Ainsworth, Bell, & Stayton, 1974). Within the caregiving environment, the infant's fluctuating states are incorporated into increasingly varied and complex behavioral and affective caregiver-orchestrated exchanges. With the emergence of motoric and intentional capabilities, the child assumes an increasingly active role in regulation, and dyadic regulatory patterns based on differences in caregiving history and infant expectations regarding caregiver availability become apparent (Sroufe, 1996). The range of emotional experience, including both positive (e.g., joy, love) and negative (e.g., anger, fear, grief) affects, plays a vital role in human adaptation by promoting closeness in relationships. Relational distortions result when emotions repeatedly fail to achieve their purpose, when they are persistently activated, or when their expression is blocked or punished. Distortions in emotional regulation (and associated defensive distortions of behavior) reflect distortions in care (Bowlby, 1969/1982) that manifest as dysynchronies between caregiving behavior and child emotional experience and needs (Sameroff & Emde, 1989).

During the toddler and preschool years, emotional challenges involve the expression of affect and the control and modulation of affective experience (Sroufe, 1996). Direct affective expression requires access to feelings and positive expectations regarding one's safety in expressing emotion. Emotional control and modulation require the capacity to maintain organization in the face of high arousal and the belief that one can reorganize following strong affective experience. In the preschool years, increasingly stable patterns of self-regulation or enduring aspects of the emerging personality emerge, and broad differences in developmental trajectories become apparent (Kopp, 1982; Kopp, Krakow, & Vaughn, 1983; Schore, 1994; Sroufe, 1996). Interpersonal exchanges in the caregiving milieu become internalized as part of the child's repertoire of affect and behavior (Sroufe, 1996), neurological organization (Cicchetti & Lynch, 1995; Schore, 1994), and relationship expectations and beliefs (Carlson & Sroufe, 1995; Sroufe, Carlson, Levy, & Egeland, 1999).

Developing representational processes (i.e., internalized expectations of self, other, and self in relation to others) and their regulatory functions also develop in the context of the early caregiving relationship (Sander, 1975; Schore, 1994, Sroufe, 1996; Stern, 1985, 1995). Expectations and attitudes regarding the self and other in relationship emerge in coordination with emotional regulatory patterns (Sameroff & Emde, 1989; Sander, 1975) and bias infant reactions to subsequent experience (Sroufe, 1996; Stern, 1995). This early network of emotional, behavioral, and representational associations evolves interactively with development (Thompson, 2006). Because interactive experiences are occurring in the context of maturing biological systems, transactional experience in the caregiving environment may entrain excitatory and inhibitory neurological processes that underlie the child's capacity for arousal modulation and socioemotional regulation (Kraemer, 1992; Schore, 1994). With development, dynamic changes in emerging cognitive and neurological capabilities, caregiver scaffolding (e.g., parental modeling, reinforcing, structuring, redirecting, and altering interpretations), and interactions with the social world contribute to the child's evolving repertoire of self-regulatory strategies (Buchsbaum & Emde, 1990; Carlson, Sroufe, & Egeland, 2004; Maccoby, 1992; Nelson, 1999; Sroufe, 1983; Vygotsky, 1978).

3.2.3 Normative Dissociative Processes

From the beginning, development is defined by advances in complexity, integration, and differentiation. Typically, self-organization progresses towards more flexible levels of complexity and integration with respect to diverse aspects of experience (Sroufe, 1996). Pathological dissociation represents a profound distortion of core self processes such that development progresses toward greater complexity without complementary integration. Integration and dissociation are viewed as antagonistic options of self-development in the face of salient experience (Breger, 1974). When experience is acknowledged and accepted, integration follows; to the extent that dissociation prevails, there is fragmentation of the self.

To some degree, dissociative processes, or the fractionation of experience, are characteristic of early childhood functioning. Young children may be prone to dissociative processes as basic skills are acquired and prior to transitions to new levels of integrative organization (Cole & Putnam, 1992; Fischer & Ayoub, 1994; Harter, 1983). Thus, dissociative processes may represent typical manifestations of childhood cognitive structures and a normative regulatory strategy through early childhood (Breger, 1974; Cole & Putnam, 1992). The mind of the young child naturally fractionates prior to the development of the ability to process complex or contradictory experiences (e.g., compartmentalizing content into positive versus negative, good versus bad) (Harter, 1998; Putnam, 1991). Moreover, early self-representations are highly differentiated and isolated from one another. Fischer and colleagues refer to this natural tendency toward fractionation as "passive" dissociation (Fischer & Ayoub, 1994; Fischer & Pipp, 1984). Although uncoordinated initially, a potential for subsequent integration exists. "Active" dissociation, a motivated response to extreme or traumatic experience, capitalizes on the child's natural proclivity for compartmentalizing affect and experience (e.g., Fischer & Ayoub, 1994; Fischer & Pipp, 1984; Putnam, 1995). Because a significant level of cognitive and perceptual fluidity is developmentally normative during this period, it remains unclear whether pathological dissociation can be diagnosed in early childhood.

From a developmental perspective, organization, or the formation of links between isolated repeated experiences and the extraction of invariants in relationship interactions, is forged in caregiving relationship experiences. Responsive caregiving enables the infant to maintain organization in the context of internal arousal and/or external threat (Bowlby, 1969/1982; Winnicott, 1965). From a history of responsive care, children gain access to both affectively and cognitively generated information, and over time integrate these dimensions with increasing complexity and flexibility to meet intra- and interpersonal demands. Thus, cognition moderates affect, and affect informs cognition (Crittenden, 1992; Sroufe, 1996). Within the caregiving environment, normative processes may be shaped by experience to serve adaptive or maladaptive functions (Bowlby, 1973). Because core self-regulatory processes are formed in the context of the caregiving relationship, experiences of insensitive care may be particularly powerful, promoting distortions in patterns of adaptation.

Overwhelming emotional experience (i.e., trauma) in childhood may consolidate normative dissociative propensities into rigid patterns of pathological dissociation. Based on a developmental perspective, the process by which dissociative phenomena in childhood become crystallized into pathological dissociation depends in part upon the caregiving environment (i.e., qualities of the caregiving relationship independent of trauma) and upon the developmental capacities of the child (e.g., capacities to self-soothe, symbolize experience through play or language). Vulnerability to dissociative coping mechanisms is more likely in the absence of experiences of reliable support and self efficacy.

Insensitive care compromises infants' beliefs in their own worthiness and efficacy and, in turn, the formation of normal levels of defenses and integration that such beliefs afford. In the context of malevolent caregiving relationships, extreme emotionally arousing experience evokes simultaneous conflicting needs to flee toward and away from the parent. Contradictory and dramatically fluctuating cues may overwhelm immature cognitive processing, resulting in multiple, incompatible emotional cues, behavioral patterns, and expectations of self and other (Liotti, 1992). Repeated experiences of "fright without solution" contribute to a collapse in attentional and behavioral strategies for coping with distress (Hesse & Main, 2000; Main & Solomon, 1990). The collapse in regulatory strategies may allow multiple cues to determine action simultaneously, giving rise to dissociative regulatory patterns.

As the child assumes a more active role in the regulation of emotion and behavior, these patterns become evident as disorganization in the attachment relationship. Behavioral manifestations of the breakdown in dyadic attachment organization include stilling, freezing, contradictory, or incomplete behaviors. These behaviors bare a phenotypic resemblance to later manifestations of dissociative defensive patterns (Liotti, 1999; Main & Morgan, 1996) and to conflict behaviors resulting from the simultaneous activation of incompatible behavioral systems (see Hinde, 1979). Up to 80% of maltreated infants (vs. 20% to 40% of controls) exhibit such behaviors, or attachment disorganization (Carlson, Cicchetti, Barnett, & Braunwald, 1989).

Attachment disorganization may be one mechanism by which traumatic experience in the caregiving environment is translated into adaptational vulnerabilities, such as dissociation (Liotti, 1992, 1999). Preliminary support for this hypothesis has been demonstrated in correlations between attachment disorganization measured in infancy and dissociative behaviors and experiences from middle childhood through adulthood (Carlson, 1998; Ogawa et al., 1997). However, the data reflect an asymmetrical relation between disorganization and dissociation such that, prospectively, most infant disorganization is not related to manifest pathological dissociation, but, retrospectively, most dissociation in later development can be traced to attachment disorganization in infancy. These data are consistent with a biological/evolutionary perspective on dissociation, which suggests that dissociative behaviors are more normative early in life and become increasingly indicative of psychopathology with age (Perry et al., 1995).

With increasing capacities and changing social environments, development provides opportunities for adaptive integration of experience as well as for the consolidation of maladaptive regulatory patterns. Typically, as the self develops, increasing capacities for representation and symbolization through language, play, and fantasy provide new avenues for managing affective experience (Carlson & Sroufe, 1995; Sroufe, 1990a; Stern, 1985). In particular, language and interpersonal interaction enable the formation of a personal narrative and verbal exchange that connects experience with the self and enables the integration of affect, cognition, and sensory information. Symbolic capacities (especially language) allow children to talk about feeling states, to share interpretations regarding the motivations, effects, and affects associated with behavior, and to clarify misinterpretations (Bretherton, Fritz, Zahn-Waxler, & Ridgeway, 1986). Thus, within the context of emotional support, adaptive capacities or functions of the mind concern not so much the conscious organization of experience as tolerance (and thereby integration) of disparate feelings, attitudes, and experiences (Winnicott, 1965). In trauma, the individual encounters a "speechless terror" processed largely in nonverbal or preverbal domains of experience (Kafka, 1969; Van der Kolk, 1994). Dissociative processes interfere with the formation of a personal narrative and verbal exchange, undermining the integration of traumatic events with other experience (Mollon, 1996; Van der Hart & Horst, 1989). When capacities to verbalize affect have been compromised by intolerable experience and lack of relationship support, important avenues for affective differentiation and integration may be restricted, and development proceeds along alternate pathways (Cicchetti & Toth, 1995). In the absence of supportive relationships (shared experience), secondary or compensatory psychological processes, such as dissociation, substitute to organize experience.

Cognitive development in middle childhood and adolescence may enable adaptive integration across splits and dissociations or the pathological construction of more advanced and varied types of splitting and dissociation. In this way, dissociative processes reflect normative developmental phenomena, becoming increasingly complex and paralleling ongoing cognitive development in adolescence and adulthood. For example, normative (largely conscious) experiences of multiplicity of self in adolescence (e.g., friend and employee) are thought to allow for higher order thinking and moral deliberation (Fischer & Ayoub, 1994; Wolf, 1990). As a result, transient experiences of depersonalization and derealization may be more common during adolescence (Putnam, 1995). In contrast, a history of trauma and experiential fragmentation may instantiate a maladaptive pathway in which advanced and sophisticated ways of dissociating evolve with developing capacities. Dissociative behaviors may be more natural (and prevalent) in early childhood; however, with the appearance of more advanced modes of thought, the significance and complexity of dissociative behavior as an indicator of psychopathology may increase with age (Breger, 1974; Putnam, 1997; Waller et al., 1996).

3.2.4 Developmental Pathways of Dissociation

Thus far, we have described how disorganization in the attachment relationship may undermine effective adaptation, rendering the child vulnerable to pathological dissociative processes, particularly in the face of subsequent trauma. In accordance with organizational principles, however, initiating conditions are shaped by subsequent experience and may yield divergent outcomes. For example, early experiences of attachment disorganization followed by normative life experience may yield elevated, but subclinical dissociative levels. Such individuals may harbor a latent predisposition toward dissociative behavior that surfaces only infrequently under stress (see Figure 3.1, pattern A) (Liotti, 1992). In contrast, severe and chronic trauma following disorganized dyadic relational experience may reinforce a pathological dissociative trajectory (see Figure 3.1, pattern B). Within this pattern, oscillating or disruptive caregiving interactions in infancy interfere with emerging dyadic integrative processes, and elaborated dissociative mechanisms become established later in development in response to experiences of severe or

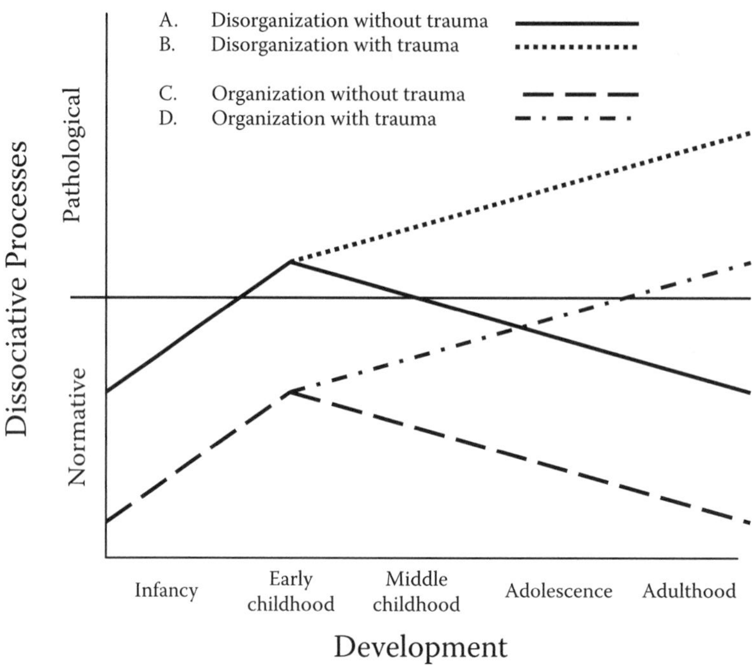

FIGURE 3.1 Developmental pathways of dissociation.

chronic trauma and the pervasive absence of emotional support. Empirical support for these pathways can be found in negative relations between the strength of the self (e.g., esteem, ego control, ego resilience) and dissociation (Ogawa et al., 1997; Waller et al., 1996).

A healthy self may imbue the child with a greater capacity for subsequent integration of disturbing experience (i.e., a return to nondissociative functioning), but it does not confer immunity to dissociative reactions in the face of overwhelming experience (Liotti, 1992). A history of dyadic organization and supportive relationship experience may initiate a normative developmental trajectory of dissociative processes (see Figure 3.1, pattern C). Within the context of stable self-organization, defensive responses such as dissociation are employed adaptively (i.e., flexibly and temporarily) in service of the self, postponing the impact of overwhelming experience until environmental support becomes available and integration possible. However, in the event of severe or chronic trauma (i.e., experiences that overwhelm normal defenses) following early self-organization, a trajectory of dissociative processes may result despite early organization (see Figure 3.1, pattern D). Consistent with developmental theory (i.e., developmental bias toward integration and positive adaptation), the threshold of caregiving quality required to facilitate the development of cohesive self-organization may be fairly low, whereas the severity and repetition of empathic failures required to induce fragmentation may be relatively high.

3.2.5 Dissociation and Self Functioning

Sustained and pervasive dissociation in early childhood distorts or disrupts the development of basic self processes, including experiences of self-agency (i.e., authorship of one's own experience and behavior), expectations of specific consequences from one's actions, and capacities for self-observation and -reflection (Herman, 1992; Mollon, 1996; Putnam, 1994, 1995). As development proceeds under typical conditions (i.e., average expectable environment), children develop increasing capacities for cognitive and emotional coordination and organization, which enables the progressive integration of contradictory expectations and beliefs (e.g., Carlson & Sroufe, 1995; Cicchetti & Lynch, 1995) and the development of an enduring core view of self with a positive bias (Sroufe, 1996). Traumatic experience (especially related to caregiving relationships) may begin to channel experience via active dissociative mechanisms and the reversal of a normative positive bias (Calvery, Fischer, & Ayoub, 1994; Westen & Cohen, 1992).

Disruptions and distortions in self processes occur at core levels of experience (i.e., motivational, attitudinal, instrumental, emotional, and/or relational). At the motivational level, dissociative processes (and intrusive thoughts and actions) interfere with the development of consistent positive expectations regarding self experience and relationships, and sense of safety and security. Dissociative processes instill a sense of passivity whereby events are perceived as happening *to* the individual or controlled outside of the self (i.e., without volition) (e.g., Breger, 1974; Bowlby, 1969/1982). Children become hypervigilant to the attitudes and intentions of others, further compromising emergent self-awareness and the child's ability to attend to her/his own needs and thoughts (Briere, 1988; Calvery et al., 1994; Putnam, 1997; Westen, 1994). A lack of sense of authorship, in turn, undermines (provides basis for fragmentation of) temporal, physical, emotional, and autobiographical aspects of self continuity.

Dissociative processes related to compartmentalization and passivity of experience in conjunction with the developmental need to view the caregiving relationship as a source of safety support a distorted sense of self and negativity bias (attitudinal base). In order to preserve a semblance of safety and adult protection within a harsh caregiving relationship, the child may internalize a sense of self-criticism and hostility to protect an idealized image of the caregiver (Westen, 1994). Over time, the child may come to regard the self as defective, unlovable, and loathsome (Fischer & Ayoub, 1994; Westen & Cohen, 1992). Empirical research supports a relation between traumatic experience (i.e., maltreatment) and low self-regard across development (e.g., Armsworth, Stronck, & Carlson, 1999; Egeland, Sroufe, & Erickson, 1983; Schneider-Rosen & Cicchetti, 1984; 1991).

By definition, dissociation is related to deficits in flexible and effective arousal modulation, impulse control, and/or adaptation to environmental demands (emotional base). Early traumatic experience may instantiate developmental deviation in emotional regulation (Cicchetti & Toth, 1995), compromising emerging regulatory strategies and fostering maladaptive compensatory strategies. Dissociative experience may include intrusive thoughts and behaviors, unpredictable state changes, and marked shifts in arousal levels disproportionate to environmental context. The child may develop a propensity for hyper- or hypo-aroused responses to emotional stimuli, especially those related to signals of threat or danger.

Dissociative experience is associated with deficits in the capacity to symbolize and mentalize affective experience (i.e., to integrate affective experience into higher order cognition) at the instrumental level. Trauma "overwhelms and defeats one's capacity to organize it" (Laub & Auerhahn, 1993, p. 288). Deficits in affective processing may include the inability to describe internal states (i.e., alexithymia; Krystal, 1988) and restrictions in attributional focus (i.e., negative bias; Beeghly & Cicchetti, 1994). Similar deficits in symbolic capacities have been observed in the play behavior of maltreated children (Allessandri, 1991) and in their ability to recognize a range of emotional displays (Barahal, Waterman, & Martin, 1981; Camras, Grow, & Ribordy, 1983). In general, these children appear to have difficulty reflecting upon affective states of others, and by extension, of the self (Fonagy & Target, 1997).

Finally, dissociative experiences may lead to poor relational competence due to the misreading of interpersonal cues and lack of access to inner emotional experience. In this way, self functioning in social relationships may mirror individual experience. Social behavior may be characterized by intrusiveness, aggression, and insensitivity to interpersonal cues and rules.

3.3 CONCLUSIONS AND DIAGNOSTIC IMPLICATIONS

From a developmental perspective, organization and integration of experience defines the self (Breger, 1974; Loevinger, 1976). Failure to integrate salient experience represents a profound distortion or fragmentation in the self system. When experience is unnoticed, disallowed, unacknowledged, or forgotten, connections among experiences are thwarted, and the resulting gaps in personal history compromise the integrity of the self and subsequent adaptation. In infancy, the "self" consists of discrete behavioral states of consciousness. Early on, these states are modulated by the caregiver and her/his daily routines. Over time, however, the capacity for self-regulation is internalized. Through repeated exchanges with a sensitive caregiver, the child comes to experience the self as a cohesive, unitary entity (Emde, 1983; Sroufe, 1996). Consistent responsive caregiving enables the recognition of consistency in the self and affective experience across time and context. In contrast, in the context of extreme hypo- or hyperarousal (i.e., due to parent neglect or abuse, respectively), the child's emergent capacity for regulation may be overwhelmed and the developing organization of the self may be fragmented (see Van der Kolk, 1987, 1988).

Within an organizational framework, the study of dissociation is also a study of the self. The process of dissociation, which begins as a protective mechanism to promote the integrity of the self in the face of trauma, may directly threaten optimal functioning when employed routinely or pervasively as a response to real or anticipated environmental threat. The study of developmental mechanisms and processes underlying the origin and evolution of dissociative behavior is integrally related to the study of the organization of behavior, representation, and environmental influences on the developing self.

The diagnostic and clinical implications of complementary studies of integration and dissociation of self processes are manifold. First, early experiences of trauma (especially within caregiving relationships) may be particularly influential in instantiating dissociative developmental trajectories. Second, the meaning and significance of dissociative behaviors may change across development. Moreover, normally developing behavior (e.g., polarized evaluations, emerging discrete behavioral states) must be differentiated from pathological dissociative processes. Finally, the transactional processes by which normative dissociative phenomena in childhood become crystallized into pathological dissociation depend upon multiple influences, including the quality of the caregiving environment (i.e., parent-child relationship) and developmental capacities of the child (e.g., language). We believe the organizational theory of development provides a useful framework within which these issues and future investigations of dissociation and development may be effectively conceptualized.

REFERENCES

Ainsworth, M., Bell, S., & Stayton, D. (1974). Infant-mother attachment and social development: Socialization as a product of reciprocal responsiveness to signals. In M. Richards (ed.), *The integration of the child into the social world* (pp. 99–135). Cambridge, U.K.: Cambridge University Press.

Allessandri, S. M. (1991). Play and social behaviors in maltreated preschoolers. *Developmental Psychopathology, 3*, 191–206.

American Psychiatric Association. (2000). *Diagnostic and statistical manual of mental disorders* (4th ed., Text Revision). Washington, DC: Author.

Armsworth, M. T., Stronck, K., & Carlson, C. D. (1999). Body image and self perception in women with histories of incest. In J. Goodwin & R. Attias (eds.), *Splintered reflections: Images of the body in trauma* (pp. 137–153). New York: Basic Books.

Barahal, R. M., Waterman, J., & Martin, H. P. (1981). The social cognitive development of abused children. *Journal of Consulting and Clinical Psychology, 49*, 508–516.

Beeghly, M., & Cicchetti, D. (1994). Child maltreatment, attachment, and the self system: Emergence of an internal state lexicon in toddlers at high social risk. *Development and Psychopathology, 6*, 5–30.

Bernstein, E. M., & Putnam, F. W. (1986). Development, reliability, and validity of a dissociation scale. *Journal of Nervous and Mental Disease, 174(12)*, 727–735.

Bowlby, J. (1969/1982). *Attachment and loss, Vol. 1, Attachment.* New York: Basic Books.

Bowlby, J. (1973). *Attachment and loss, Vol. 2, Separation.* New York: Basic Books.

Bowlby, J. (1980). *Attachment and loss, Vol. 3, Loss, sadness and depression.* New York: Basic Books.

Breger, L. (1974). *From instinct to identity.* Englewood Cliffs, NJ: Prentice-Hall.

Bretherton, I. J., Fritz, C., Zahn-Waxler, C., & Ridgeway, D. (1986). Learning to talk about emotions: A functionalist perspective. *Child Development, 57*, 529–548.

Breuer, J., & Freud, S. (1955). Studies on hysteria (J. Strachey, trans.). In J. Strachey (ed.), *The standard edition of the complete psychological works of Sigmund Freud* (Vol. 2). London: Hogarth Press. (original work published 1893–1895).

Briere, J. (1988). The long-term clinical correlates of childhood sexual victimization. *Annals of the New York Academy of Sciences, 528*, 327–334.

Briere, J., & Runtz, M. (1988). Multivariate correlates of childhood psychological and physical maltreatment among university women. *Child Abuse and Neglect, 12*, 331–341.

Briere, J., & Zaidi, L. (1989). Sexual abuse histories and sequelae in female psychiatric emergency room patients. *American Journal of Psychiatry, 146*, 1602–1606.

Buchsbaum, H. K., & Emde, R. (1990). Play narratives in 36-month-old children: Early moral development and family relationships. *Psychoanalytic Study of the Child, 45*, 129–155.

Calvery, R., Fischer, K. W., & Ayoub, C. (1994). Complex splitting of self-representation in sexually abused adolescent girls. *Development and Psychopathology, 6*, 195–213.

Camras, L., Grow, G., & Ribordy, S. (1983). Recognition of emotional expressions by abused children. *Journal of Clinical Child Psychology, 12*(3), 325–328.

Carlson, E. A. (1998). A prospective longitudinal study of attachment disorganization/disorientation. *Child Development, 69*(4), 1107–1128.

Carlson, E. A., & Sroufe, L. A. (1995). The contribution of attachment theory to developmental psychopathology. In D. Cicchetti & D.J. Cohen (eds.), *Developmental processes and psychopathology: Vol. 1. Theoretical perspectives and methodological approaches* (pp. 581–617). New York: Wiley & Sons.

Carlson, V., Cicchetti, D., Barnett, D., & Braunwald, K. (1989). Disorganized/disoriented attachment relationships in maltreated infants. *Developmental Psychology, 25*, 525–531.

Carlson, E. A., Sroufe, L. A., & Egeland, B. (2004). The construction of experience: A longitudinal study of representation and behavior. *Child Development, 75*(1), 66–83.

Chu, J. A., & Dill, D. L. (1990). Dissociative symptoms in relation to childhood physical and sexual abuse. *American Journal of Psychiatry, 147*, 887–892.

Cicchetti, D. (1984). The emergence of developmental psychopathology. *Child Development, 55*, 1–7.

Cicchetti, D. (1989). How research on child maltreatment has informed the study of child development: Perspectives from developmental psychology. In D. Cicchetti & V. Carlson (eds.), *Child maltreatment* (pp. 377–431). Cambridge: Cambridge University Press.

Cicchetti, D. (1990). Perspectives on the interface between normal and atypical development. *Development and Psychopathology, 2*, 329–333.

Cicchetti, D. (1993). Developmental psychopathology: Reactions, reflections, projection. *Developmental Review, 13*, 471–502.

Cicchetti, D., & Cohen, D. J. (2006). Development and psychopathology. In D. Cicchetti & D. J. Cohen (eds.), *Developmental psychopathology (2nd ed.), Vol. 1: Theory and methods* (pp. 1–23). New York: Wiley.

Cicchetti, D., Ganiban, J., & Barnett, D. (1991). Contributions from the study of high risk populations to understanding the development of emotion regulation. In J. Garber & K. Dodge (eds.), *The development of emotion regulation and dysregulation* (Vol. 15–49). New York: Cambridge University Press.

Cicchetti, D., & Lynch, M. (1995). Failures in the expectable environment and their impact on child development: The case of child maltreatment. In D. Cicchetti & D. Cohen (eds.), *Developmental psychopathology: Vol. 2. Risk, disorder, and adaptation* (pp. 32–71). New York: Wiley.

Cicchetti, D., & Rogosch, F. A. (1996). Equifinality and multifinality in developmental psychopathology. *Development and Psychopathology, 8*, 597–600.

Cicchetti, D., & Schneider-Rosen, K. (1986). An organizational approach to childhood depression. In M. Rutter, C.E. Izard, & P.B. Read (eds.), *Depression in young people: Developmental and clinical perspectives* (pp. 71–134). New York: Guilford.

Cicchetti, D., & Toth, S. L. (1995). Developmental psychopathology and disorders of affect. In D. Cicchetti & D. J. Cohen (eds.), *Developmental psychopathology: Vol. 2. Risk, disorder, and adaptation* (pp. 369–420). New York: Wiley.

Cicchetti, D., & Toth, S. L. (1997). Transactional ecological systems in developmental psychopathology. In S. S. Luthar, J. A. Burack, D. Cicchetti, & J. R. Weisz (eds.), *Developmental psychopathology: Perspectives on adjustment, risk, and disorder* (pp. 317–349). New York: Cambridge University Press.

Cicchetti, D., & Tucker, D. (1994). Development and self-regulatory structures of the mind. *Development and Psychopathology, 6*, 533–549.

Cicchetti, D., & Beeghly, M. (1987). Symbolic development in maltreated youngsters: An organizational perspective. In D. Cicchetti & M. Beeghly (ed.), *Atypical symbolic development. New Directions for Child Development, 36*, 5–29. San Francisco: Jossey-Bass.

Cole, P. M., & Putnam, F. W. (1992). Effects of incest on self and social functioning: A developmental psychopathology perspective. *Journal of Consulting and Clinical Psychology, 60*, 174–184.

Coons, P. M. (1996). Clinical phenomenology of 25 children and adolescents with dissociative disorders. *Child and Adolescent Psychiatric Clinics of North America, 5*, 361–373.

Crittenden, P. M. (1992). Children's strategies for coping with adverse home environments: An interpretation using attachment theory. *Child Abuse & Neglect, 16*, 329–343.

Egeland, B., Carlson, E., & Sroufe, L. A. (1993). Resilience as process. *Development and Psychopathology, 5*(4), 517–528.

Egeland, B., Sroufe, L. A., & Erikson, M. (1983). The developmental consequences of different patterns of maltreatment. *Child Abuse and Neglect, 7*, 155–157.

Emde, R. N. (1983). The prerepresentational self. *Psychoanalytic Study of the Child, 38*, 165–192.

Fischer, K. W., & Pipp, S. L. (1984). Development and the structures of unconscious thought. In K. Bowers & D. Meichenbaum (ed.), *The unconscious reconsidered* (pp. 88–148). New York: Wiley.

Fischer, K. W., & Ayoub, C. (1994). Affective splitting and dissociation in normal and maltreated children: Developmental pathways for self in relationships. In D. Cicchetti & S.L. Toth (eds.), *Rochester symposium on developmental psychopathology: Vol. 5. Disorders and dysfunctions of the self* (pp. 149–222). Rochester, NY: University of Rochester Press.

Fonagy, P., & Target, M. (1997). Attachment and reflective function: Their role in self-organization. *Development and Psychopathology, 9*, 679–700.

Freud, S. (1926/1959). Inhibitions, symptoms, and anxiety (J. Strachey, trans.). In J. Strachey (ed.), *The standard edition of the complete psychological works of Sigmund Freud.* London: Hogarth.

Gottlieb, G. (1991). Experiential canalization of behavioral development: Theory. *Developmental Psychology, 27*, 4–13.

Harter, S. (1983). Developmental perspectives on the self-system. In E. M. Hetherington (ed.), *Handbook of child psychology (4th ed.). Socialization, personality, and social development* (pp. 275–386). New York: Wiley.

Harter, S. (1998). The development of self-representations. In W. Damon & N. Eisenberg (eds.), *Handbook of child psychology, Vol. 3. Social, emotional, and personality development* (5th ed., pp. 553–617). New York: Wiley & Sons, Inc.

Herman, J. L. (1992). *Trauma and recovery*. New York: Basic Books.

Hesse, E., & Main, M. (2000). Disorganized infant, child, and adult attachment: Collapse in behavioral and attentional strategies. *Journal of the American Psychoanalytic Association, 48*, 1097–1127.

Hinde, R. (1979). *Toward understanding relationships*. London: Academic Press.

Hornstein, N. L., & Putnam, F. W. (1992). Clinical phenomenology of child and adolescent dissociative disorders. *Journal of the American Academy of Child and Adolescent Psychiatry, 31*, 1077–1085.

Irwin, H. J. (1994). Proneness to dissociation and traumatic childhood events. *Journal of Nervous and Mental Diseases, 182*, 456–460.

Irwin, H. J. (1996). Traumatic childhood events, perceived availability of emotional support, and the development of dissociative tendencies. *Child Abuse & Neglect, 20*, 701–707.

Janet, P. (1889). *L'automatisme psychologique: Essai de psychologie expérimentale sur les formes inférieures de l'activité humaine*. Paris: Félix Alcan.

Kafka, J. S. (1969). The body as transitional object: A psychoanalytic study of a self-mutilating patient. *British Journal of Medical Psychology, 42*, 207–212.

Kalsched, D. (1996). *The inner world of trauma: Archetypal defenses of the personal spirit.* New York: Routledge.

Kirby, J. S., Chu, J. A., & Dill, D. L. (1993). Correlates of dissociative symptomatology in patients with physical and sexual abuse histories. *Comprehensive Psychiatry, 34*, 258–263.

Kohut, H. (1971). *The analysis of the self.* Madison, CT: International Universities Press, Inc.

Kopp, C. B. (1982). Antecedents of self-regulation: A developmental perspective. *Developmental Psychology, 18*, 199–214.

Kopp, C., Krakow, J., & Vaughn, B. (1983). The antecedents of self-regulation in young handicapped children. In M. Perlmutter (ed.), *Minnesota Symposia on Child Psychology* (Vol. 17, pp. 93–128). Hillsdale, NJ: Erlbaum.

Kraemer, G. W. (1992). A psychobiological theory of attachment. *Behavioral and Brain Sciences, 15*, 493–511.

Krystal, J. H. (1988). *Integration and self-healing: Affect, trauma, and alexithymia.* NJ: The Analytic Press.

Laub, D., & Auerhahn, N. C. (1993). Knowing and not knowing massive psychic trauma: Forms of traumatic memory. *International Journal of Psycho-Analysis, 74*, 287–302.

Liotti, G. (1992). Disorganized/disoriented attachment in the etiology of the dissociative disorders. *Dissociation, 4*, 196–204.

Liotti, G. (1999). Disorganization of attachment as a model for understanding dissociative psychopathology. In J. Solomon & C. George (eds.), *Attachment disorganization* (pp. 39–70). New York: Guilford Press.

Lipschitz, D. S., Kaplan, M. L., Sorkenn, J., & Chorney, P. (1996). Childhood abuse, adult assault, and dissociation. *Comprehensive Psychiatry, 37*(4), 261–266.

Loevinger, J. (1976). *Ego development.* San Francisco: Jossey-Bass.

Maccoby, E. E. (1992). The role of parents in the socialization of children: An historical overview. *Developmental Psychology, 28*, 1006–1017.

Macfie, J., Cicchetti, D., & Toth, S. L. (2001). The development of disssociation in maltreated preschool-aged children. *Development and Psychopathology, 13*, 233–254.

Main, M., & Morgan, H. (1996). Disorganization and disorientation in infant Strange Situation behavior: Phenotypic resemblance to dissociative states? In L. Michelson & W. Ray (eds.), *Handbook of dissociation* (pp. 107–137). New York: Plenum.

Main, M., & Solomon, J. (1990). Procedures for identifying infants as disorganized/disoriented in the Ainsworth Strange Situation. In M. Greenberg, D. Cicchetti, & E. M. Cummings (eds.), *Attachment during the preschool years* (pp. 121–160). Chicago, IL: University of Chicago Press.

Malinosky-Rummel, R. R., & Hoier, T. S. (1991). Validating measures of dissociation in sexually abused and non-abused children. *Behavioral Assessment, 13,* 341–357.

Mollon, P. (1996). *Multiple selves, multiple voices: Working with trauma, violation, and dissociation.* Chichester, England: Wiley.

Nelson, K. (1999). Levels and modes of representation: Issues for the theory of conceptual change and development. In E. K. Scholnick, K. Nelson, S. Gelman, & P. H. Miller (eds.), *Conceptual development: Piaget's legacy. The Jean Piaget Series* (pp. 269–291). Mahwah, NJ: Lawrence Erlbaum Assoc.

Ogawa, J. R., Sroufe, L. A., Weinfield, N. S., Carlson, E. A., & Egeland, B. (1997). Development and the fragmented self: A longitudinal study of dissociative symptomatology in a non-clinical sample. *Development and Psychopathology, 9*, 855–879.

Perry, B. D., Pollard, R. A., Blakely, T. L., Baker, W. L., & Vigilante, D. (1995). Childhood trauma, the neurobiology of adaptation, and "use dependent" development of the brain: How "states" become "traits." *Infant Mental Health Journal, 16*, 271–291.

Perry, B. D. (1999). The memories of states: How the brain stores and retrieves traumatic memories. In J. Goodwin & R. Attias (eds.), *Splintered reflections: Images of the body in trauma* (pp. 9–38). New York: Basic Books.

Putnam, F. W. (1991). Dissociative disorders in children and adolescents: A developmental perspective. *Psychiatric Clinics of North America, 14*, 519–532.

Putnam, F. W. (1994). Dissociation and disturbances of self. In D. Cicchetti & S.L. Toth (eds.), *Rochester symposium on developmental psychopathology: Vol. 5. Disorders and dysfunctions of the self* (pp. 251–265). New York: University of Rochester Press.

Putnam, F. W. (1995). Development of dissociative disorders. In D. Cicchetti & J. D. Coatsworth (eds.), *Developmental psychopathology: Vol.2. Risk, disorder, and adaptation* (pp. 581–608). New York: Wiley-Interscience.

Putnam, F. W. (1997). *Dissociation in children and adolescents: A developmental approach.* New York: Guilford Press.

Putnam, F. W. (2000). Dissociative disorders. In A.J. Sameroff, M. Lewis, & S. Miller (eds.), *Handbook of developmental psychopathology* (2nd ed.; pp. 739–754). New York: Kluwer Academic/Plenum Publishers.

Putnam, F. W., Carlson, E. B., Ross, C. A., Anderson, G., Clark, D. C., Torem, M., Bowman, E., Coons, P. M., Chu, J. A., & Dill, D. L. (1996). Patterns of dissociation in clinical and nonclinical samples. *Journal of Nervous and Mental Diseases, 184*, 673–679.

Putnam, F. W., Guroff, J. J., Silberman, E. K., Barban, L., & Post, R. M. (1986). The clinical phenomenology of multiple personality disorder: Review of 100 recent cases. *Journal of Clinical Psychiatry, 47*, 285–293.

Putnam, F. W., Helmers, K., & Trickett, P. K. (1993). Development, reliability, and validity of a child dissociation scale. *Child Abuse & Neglect, 17*, 731–741.

Ross, C. A., Joshi, S., & Currie, R. (1990). Dissociative experiences in the general population. *American Journal of Psychiatry, 147*, 1547–1552.

Ross, C. A., Miller, S. D., Bjornson, L., Reagor, P., Fraser, G., & Anderson, G. (1991). Abuse histories in 102 cases of multiple personality disorder. *Canadian Journal of Psychiatry, 36*, 97–101.

Rutter, M. (1996a). Developmental psychopathology: Concepts and prospects. In M. Lenzenweger & J. Havgaard (eds.), *Frontiers of developmental psychopathology* (pp. 209–237). New York: Oxford University Press.

Rutter, M. (1996b). Transitions and turning points in developmental psychopathology: As applied to the age span between childhood and mid-adulthood. *International Journal of Behavioral Development, 19*, 603–626.

Sameroff, A. (2000). Dialectical processes in developmental psychopathology. In A. Sameroff, M. Lewis, & S. Miller (eds.), *Handbook of developmental psychopathology* (2nd ed., pp. 23–40). New York: Kluwer Academic/Plenum.

Sameroff, A. J., & Chandler, M. J. (1975). Reproductive risk and the continuum of caretaking casualty. In F. D. Horowitz, M. Hetherington, S. Scarr-Salapatek, & G. Siegel (eds.), *Review of child development research* (Vol. 4, pp. 187–243). Chicago: Chicago University Press.

Sameroff, A., & Emde, R. (1989). *Relationship disturbances in early childhood*. New York: Basic Books.

Sander, L. (1975). Infant and caretaking environment. In E. J. Anthony (ed.), *Explorations in child psychiatry* (pp. 129–165). New York: Plenum Press.

Sanders, B., & Giolas, M. H. (1991). Dissociation and childhood trauma in psychologically disturbed adolescents. *American Journal of Psychiatry, 148*, 50–54.

Sanders, B., & Becker-Lausen, E. (1995). The measurement of psychological maltreatment: Early data on the Child Abuse and Trauma Scale. *Child Abuse & Neglect, 19* (3), 315–323.

Schneider-Rosen, K., & Cicchetti, D. (1984). The relationship between affect and cognition in maltreated infants: Quality of attachment and the development of visual self-recognition. *Child Development, 55*, 648–658.

Schneider-Rosen, K., & Cicchetti, D. (1991). Early self-knowledge and emotional development: Visual self-recognition and affective reactions to mirror self-images in maltreated and nonmaltreated toddlers. *Developmental Psychology, 27*, 471–478.

Schore, A. N. (1994). *Affect regulation and the origin of the self: The neurobiology of emotional development*. Hillsdale, NJ: Erlbaum.

Sroufe, L. A. (1979). The coherence of individual development: Early care, attachment, and subsequent developmental issues. *American Psychologist, 34*, 834–841.

Sroufe, L. A. (1983). Infant-caregiver attachment and patterns of adaptation in preschool: The roots of maladaptation and competence. In M. Perlmutter (ed.), *Minnesota symposium in child psychology* (Vol. 16, pp. 129–135). Hillsdale, NJ: Erlbaum.

Sroufe, L. A. (1989). Pathways to adaptation and maladaptation: Psychopathology as developmental deviation. In D. Cicchetti (ed.), *Rochester symposium on developmental psychopathology: Vol. 1. The emergence of a discipline* (pp. 13–40). Hillsdale, NJ: Erlbaum.

Sroufe, L. A. (1990a). An organizational perspective on the self. In D. Cicchetti & M. Beeghly (eds.), *The self in transition* (pp. 281–308). Chicago, IL: The University of Chicago Press.

Sroufe, L. A. (1990b). Considering normal and abnormal together: The essence of developmental psychopathology. *Development and Psychopathology, 2*, 335–347.

Sroufe, L. A. (1996). *Emotional development: The organization of emotional life in the early years*. New York: Cambridge University Press.

Sroufe, L. A., Carlson, E. A., Levy, A. K., & Egeland, B. (1999). Implications of attachment theory for developmental psychopathology. *Development and Psychopathology, 11*, 1–13.

Sroufe, L. A., Egeland, B., & Carlson, E. (1999). One social world: The integrated development of parent-child and peer relationships. In W. A. Collins & B. Laursen (eds.), *Relationships as developmental context: The 30th Minnesota symposium on child psychology* (pp. 241–262). Hillsdale, NJ: Erlbaum.

Sroufe, L. A., Egeland, B., Carlson, E. A., & Collins, W. (2005). *The development of the person: The Minnesota study of risk and adaptation from birth to adulthood.* New York: Guilford Press.

Sroufe, L. A., & Fleeson, J. (1986). Attachment and the construction of relationships. In W. Hartup & Z. Rubin (eds.), *Relationships and development*. Hillsdale, NJ: Erlbaum.

Sroufe, L. A., & Rutter, M. (1984). The domain of developmental psychopathology. *Child Development, 55*, 17–29.

Sroufe, L. A., & Waters, E. (1977). Attachment as an organizational construct. *Child Development, 48*, 1184–1199.

Stern, D. N. (1985). *The interpersonal world of the infant*. New York: Basic Books.

Stern, D. (1995). *The motherhood constellation: A unified view of parent-infant psychotherapy.* New York: Basic Books.

Terr, L. (1990). *Too scared to cry: Psychic trauma in childhood.* New York: Harper & Row Publishers.

Terr, L. (1991). Childhood traumas: An outline and overview. *American Journal of Psychiatry, 148*, 10–20.

Terr, L. (1994). *Unchained memories: True stories of traumatic memories, lost and found*. New York: Basic Books.

Thelen, E. (1992). Development as a dynamic system. *Current Directions, 1*, 189–193.

Thompson, R. A. (2006). The development of the person: Social understanding, relationships, conscience, self. In N. Eisenberg, W. Damon, & R. Lerner (Eds.), *Handbook of child psychology: Vol. 3. Social, emotional, and personality development* (6th ed., pp. 24–98). New York: Wiley.

Van der Hart, O., & Horst, R. (1989). The dissociation theory of Pierre Janet. *Journal of Traumatic Stress, 2*, 397–412.

Van der Kolk, B. A. (1987). *Psychological trauma*. Washington, DC: American Psychiatric Press.

Van der Kolk, B. A. (1988). The trauma spectrum: The interaction of biological and social events in the genesis of the trauma response. *Journal of Traumatic Stress, 1*(3), 278.

Van der Kolk, B. A. (1994). The behavioral and psychobiological effects of developmental trauma. In A. Stoudemire (ed.), *Human behavior: An introduction for medical students* (pp. 328–343). New York: Lippincott.

Van IJzendoorn, M. H., & Schuengel, C. (1996). The measurement of dissociation in normal and clinical populations: Meta-analytic validation of the Dissociative Experiences Scale (DES). *Clinical Psychology Review, 16*, 365–382.

Vygotsky, L. S. (1978). *Mind in society: The development of higher psychological processes.* Cambridge, MA: Harvard University Press.

Waddington, C. H. (1940). *Organizers and genes*. Cambridge: Cambridge University Press.

Waldinger, R. J., Swett, C., Frank, A., & Miller, K. (1994). Levels of dissociation and histories of abuse among women outpatients. *Journal of Nervous and Mental Disease, 182*, 625–630.

Waller, N., Putnam, F. W., & Carlson, E. B. (1996). Types of dissociation and dissociative types: A taxometric analysis of dissociative experiences. *Psychological Methods, 1*, 300–321.

Waters, E., & Sroufe, L. A. (1983). Social competence as a developmental construct. *Developmental Review, 3*, 79–97.

Weinfield, N. S., Sroufe, L. A., Egeland, B., & Carlson, E. A. (2008). Individual differences in infant-caregiver attachment: Conceptual and empirical aspects of security. In J. Cassidy & P. Shaver (eds.), *Handbook of Attachment: Theory, research and clinical applications, 2nd ed.* (pp. 73–95). New York: Guilford.

Westen, D. (1994). The impact of sexual abuse on self structure. In D. Cicchetti & S. L. Toth (eds.), *Rochester symposium on developmental psychopathology: Vol. 5. Disorders and dysfunctions of the self* (pp. 78–101). New York: University of Rochester Press.

Westen, D., & Cohen, R. (1992). The self in borderline personality disorder: A psychodynamic perspective. In Z. Segal & S. Blatt (eds.), *Self-representation and emotional disorder: Cognitive and psychodynamic perspectives*. New York: Guilford.

Winnicott, D. W. (1965). *The maturational process and the facilitating environment*. New York: International Universities Press.

Winnicott, D. W. (1971). *Playing and reality*. New York: Basic Books.

Wolf, D. (1990). Being of several minds: Voices and versions of the self in early childhood. In D. Cicchetti & M. Beeghly (eds.), *The self in transition: Infancy to childhood* (pp. 183–212). Chicago: University of Chicago Press.

Zlotnick, C., Shea, M. T., Zakriski, A., Costello, E., Begin, A., Pearlstein, T., & Simpson, E. (1995). Stressors and close relationships during childhood and dissociative experiences in survivors of sexual abuse among inpatient psychiatric women. *Comprehensive Psychiatry, 36*, 207–212.

Zlotnick, C., Shea, M. C., Pearlstein, T., Begin, A., Simpson, E., & Costello, E. (1996). Differences in dissociative experiences between survivors of childhood incest and survivors of assault in adulthood. *Journal of Nervous and Mental Diseases, 184*, 52–54.

4 Attachment and Dissociation

Giovanni Liotti, MD

OUTLINE

Attachment theory (Bowlby, 1969/1982; 1973; 1980) holds that human beings are endowed with a strong, inborn, evolved disposition to seek help, care, and comfort from a familiar member of their social group. This disposition is activated whenever human beings experience physical or emotional pain, and whenever they, through the emotion of fear, perceive themselves vulnerable in the face of danger. It is also activated by separation from, and loss of, attachment figures. Past interactions with caregivers give rise to specific structures of memory and expectation (i.e., Internal Working Models, IWM: Bretherton & Munholland, 1999) which shape and individualize the expression of this inborn disposition. The inborn disposition and the IWM constitute the attachment behavioral-motivational system.

The attachment system is one of a number of inborn motivational systems (Cassidy, 1999, p. 7–11; Gilbert, 1989; Lichtenberg, 1989; Liotti & Intreccialagli, 2003; Panksepp, 1998). When activated, the attachment system coordinates not only specific feelings and goal-directed behaviors, but also memories—both conscious (explicit) and unconscious (implicit)—and thoughts about self and attachment figures.

The attachment system mediates individual responses to trauma. Research has identified a particular attachment style, disorganized attachment (DA), that may be the earliest instance of a dissociative mental process in personality development.

4.1 DISORGANIZATION OF INFANT ATTACHMENT AND DISSOCIATION

Early attachment patterns are assessed with the Strange Situation (SS; Ainsworth, Blehar, Waters, & Wall, 1978), a structured procedure whereby one-year-old infants are exposed to two brief episodes of separation from, and reunion with, the parent in an unfamiliar laboratory environment. Three main *organized* patterns of infant attachment behavior have been observed in the SS. The *secure pattern* comprises clear-cut protest (separation cry) when the parent leaves, and quick comfort on reunion. The *insecure-avoidant* pattern is characterized by a lack of protest when the parent leaves, and by ignoring or actively avoiding the parent upon reunion. Infants with an *insecure-ambivalent* pattern protest during separation, resist their parents' efforts to calm them upon reunion, and seem distressed by, and/or angry with, the presence of the parent throughout the procedure.

Some infants fail to organize their attachment behavior according to any of these coherent patterns. Instead, they manifest *disorganized* attachment (DA) (Main & Solomon, 1990); disorganized infants are found in 13% of low-risk families and as many as 82% of high-risk families (Lyons-Ruth & Jacobvitz, 1999). The infants' organizing functions of consciousness, memory, and identity (see, e.g., Stern, 1985) appear to have failed. Because pathological dissociation is a disruption in the organizing and usually integrated functions of consciousness, memory, identity, and perception of the environment (American Psychiatric Association, 1994), DA can be understood as a very early dissociative process (Main & Morgan, 1996). DA is different from normal dissociation (see Dalenberg, this volume) because it implies (1) a deviation from the optimal, functional, and statistical norms of attachment behavior, and (2) a disruption of the usually integrated workings of memory and consciousness.

In low-risk samples, the IWMs of past interactions with each parent are usually sufficiently unitary, coherent, and integrated to be expressed in an organized pattern of attachment behavior. In DA, however, infants display contradictory behavior patterns (e.g., approaching the parent while averting the head so as to avoid meeting his/her gaze; calling loudly for the parent at the closed door, followed by avoidance of the parent on entrance). This suggests an obstacle to the construction and operation of the normally unitary IWM representing the self and the parent. Some behaviors that are often observed in DA suggest a disruption in the functions of consciousness. For instance, infants with DA may show an abrupt interruption of movements that previously seemed to be meaningful and aimed at interacting with the caregiver. Such interruptions may last for 30 seconds or longer. The interruption may be accompanied by a dazed, trance-like expression that indicates a sudden disruption of the previously intact perception of the environment. After the interruption, the original movement is resumed—as if nothing had happened.[1] The similarities between DA behavior, as observed in the SS, and behavioral predictors of dissociative disorders in childhood are impressive:

> the single best predictor of a dissociative disorder is frequent *trance-like behavior*. … The child … on termination of the trance state may resume an *interrupted task* as if nothing had happened (Putnam, 1993, p. 42, italics added).

Infant DA behavior suggests that altered strategies of attention are a crucial feature of early dissociative processes; this is reminiscent of speculations about the role of modified attentional strategies in hypnosis and dissociation (see, e.g., Bliss, 1986). A coherent attentional strategy is easily identified in the organized patterns of infant attachment (Main, 2000): (1) secure infants manifest a flexible attentional strategy that can easily shift from the caregiver to the toys scattered in the room of the SS; (2) avoidant infants inflexibly shift their attention away from the caregiver (to focus on the toys); and (3) resistant infants inflexibly attend to their caregiver. In DA, there are no consistent attentional strategies toward either the caregiver or the surrounding environment (Hesse & Main, 2000).

Attention deficit (that suggests abrupt, unwitting absorption in the inner world of feelings and memories) and disruption of at least some functions of consciousness (metacognitive monitoring of thought and discourse, reflective functions) may also be observed in the study of *adult* attachments. These phenomena may be subsumed, together with infant DA, under the rubric of attachment-related dissociation.

4.2 DISSOCIATIVE PHENOMENA IN THE STUDY OF ADULT ATTACHMENT

The most reliable method for studying adult attachment is based on the *Adult Attachment Interview* (AAI: Main & Goldwyn, 1998; see also Hesse, 1999). The AAI is a semi-structured interview aimed at assessing the attachment state of mind through an analysis of the individual's autobiographical narratives of attachment-related memories. The emergence of memories of traumatic losses of attachment figures, or of physical and sexual abuse suffered at the hands of attachment figures, is not a rare occurrence during administration of the AAI. In about 15% of nonclinical interviews (Lyons-Ruth & Jacobvitz, 1999, p. 523), lapses, poor metacognitive monitoring, and notable incoherence in the narratives suggest that these traumatic experiences have not been resolved and still hamper the organizing functions of attention and consciousness ("unresolved" classification of the AAI). In these cases, to think that dissociative processes related to traumatic memories interfere with the report of one's attachment history is, at the very least, an educated guess (Hesse & Main, 2000, p. 1115; Main & Morgan, 1996). An empirical finding supporting this conjecture has been provided by Hesse and Van IJzendoorn (1999): people who describe unresolved traumatic memories during the AAI also rate high in a scale measuring the propensity toward absorption in daydreaming and self-hypnotic states of consciousness.

A major finding of attachment research is the collection of robust statistical evidence linking unresolved AAI classifications to infant DA. Unresolved memories of past attachment-related traumas and losses in the parent strongly predict DA in the child (see Van IJzendoorn, 1995, for a meta-analysis of early studies on this topic; for overviews of later research see Hesse et al., 2003,

[1] Main has provided detailed descriptions of DA behaviors (Main & Morgan, 1996; Main & Solomon, 1990). For theoretical interpretations of DA, see Solomon and George (1999).

or Lyons-Ruth & Jacobvitz, 1999). It is noteworthy that the reporting of *resolved* memories of past traumas and losses in the parent's AAI does *not* predict DA in the child. Thus, there is evidence supporting the following statement: dissociative processes in the infant, produced during the activation of the attachment system, are linked to mental processes in the parent that are also related to the attachment system and can also be considered dissociative (or micro-dissociative, if one wishes to stress that they appear only during the reporting of autobiographical memories of attachment and are not symptoms of clinically evident disorders).

This statement calls attention to aspects of dissociation that are intersubjective—rather than merely intrapsychic and defensive—and invites inquiry into the particular role the attachment system plays in the genesis of pathological dissociation. This role emerges from three main areas of theoretical reflection and empirical research: (1) mechanisms underpinning the link between infant DA and the parental "unresolved" AAI classification; (2) the nature of the disorganized IWM of early attachment; (3) the increased vulnerability to pathological dissociation as a sequel to early DA.

4.3 HOW DOES THE CAREGIVER'S UNRESOLVED TRAUMA GIVE RISE TO THE INFANT'S ATTACHMENT DISORGANIZATION?

Genetic factors may be part of the explanation of the link between infant DA to the unresolved mental states of the caregivers. An allele of the DRD4 gene (a gene regulating postsynaptic dopamine receptors) increases vulnerability to infant DA in the presence of an unresolved caregiver (Lakatos et al., 2000, 2002).[2] While behavioral genetic studies suggest that genetic influences play a minor role in determining the infant attachment pattern (Bockhorst et al., 2003; O'Connor & Croft, 2001), it is possible that genes have relatively stronger effects in DA than in the organized patterns. However, regardless of the strength of genetic factors in DA, environmental factors would remain crucial in determining whether the infant's attachment behavior becomes disorganized. Infants who are disorganized in their attachment to an unresolved parent have been observed displaying organized attachment behavior toward other caregivers, whose AAI is not unresolved. Moreover, in the previously quoted studies (Lakatos et al., 2000, 2002), the majority of infants carrying the DRD4 allele were *not* disorganized, arguing for environmental factors—the attachment relationship between infant and caregiver—as playing the major role in the genesis of DA.

To explain why unresolved memories of losses and traumas in the caregiver's past attachment relationships are linked to DA in the infant, Main and Hesse (1990) suggested that the caregiver's behavior, in such circumstances, is likely to become frightening to the infant. The intrusion, in the caregiver's consciousness, of painful, unresolved memories of traumatic interactions with attachment figures may lead to parental behaviors that are either directly (e.g., violent) or indirectly (e.g., frightened, confused, or eerie) frightening to the infant. These parental frightening behaviors produce a paradox in parent-child communication: fear is induced by the very person who cares for the infant's fear and distress. This condition has been properly called "fright without solution," since the caregiver is at the same time "the source and the solution of the infant's alarm" (Main & Hesse, 1990, p. 163).

Main and Hesse's hypothesis can be formulated in terms of current theories of multiple inborn motivational systems. Any human being is endowed with two systems that have evolved to deal with environmental threat: the defense system (fight/flight responses to the threat) and the attachment system (seeking the protective closeness to a member of the social group that may help against the threat). In DA both systems become simultaneously active in a conflicting manner: they motivate both flight from and approach to the caregiver (Liotti, 2000, 2002). Such an *insoluble* conflict between two inborn motivational systems, both necessary for survival, exceeds the limited capacity of the infant's mind for organizing coherent conscious experiences or unitary memory structures, and reflects itself in the collapse of any attempt at developing an organized strategy of attention and behavior.

Empirical support to Main and Hesse's hypothesis is accumulating. Videotaping home interactions between mothers and infants, Schuengel, Van IJzendoorn, and Bakermans-Kranenburg (1999) demonstrated an association between mothers' overtly aggressive, frightened, or dissociated behavior toward the baby and their AAI "unresolved" classification. Other studies that confirm such an association have been reviewed by Lyons-Ruth and Jacobvitz (1999), Hesse and Main (2000), and Hesse et al. (2003). On reviewing these studies, Lyons-Ruth, Bronfman, and Atwood (1999) suggested that parental frightening behaviors are embedded in a broader context of disrupted affective communication. Exchanges of

[2] Brain dopaminergic function is very likely related to the mechanism of attention (see, e.g., Panksepp, 1998). This is a further hint at the important contribution of disordered attention to DA and to dissociation.

contradictory affect cues between parent and infant, of a more subtle quality than the typical frightening parental behaviors, may be involved in mediating parents' unresolved states of mind and infants' DA: "Attachment disorganization … is a function both of the intensity of fear-producing experience and of the adequacy of the attachment relationship to help resolve the fearful affect" (Lyons-Ruth & Jacobvitz, 1999, p. 547).

The study, in daily home settings, of parental behaviors that may be frightening to the infant involves complex coding systems. One of these comprises six categories, all suggestive of dissociative mental states in the parent: (1) direct indices of entrance into a dissociative state, (2) threatening behavior inexplicable in origin and/or anomalous in form, (3) frightened behavior inexplicable in origin and/or anomalous in form, (4) deferential (role-inverting) behavior, (5) sexualized behavior, and (6) disorganized/disoriented behavior (Hesse et al., 2003). Such anomalous types of parental behavior only rarely are violent, overtly abusive, or frankly related to psychopathology (nonclinical, low-risk samples of parents and children are typically involved in these researches). This is particularly noteworthy for the theory of dissociation, insofar as it hints at the possibility that a type of pathological dissociation emerges in the context of attachment relationships where the priming, by the infant's requests for soothing and care, of caregiver's unresolved traumatic memories brings on dissociation in both members of the dyad, without necessarily implying an overt repetition of frankly traumatic interactions.

In other words, pathological dissociation is not necessarily always the outcome of violent, abusive, or humiliating interactions between an adult and a child. *Provided that activation of the attachment system is involved*, parental communications that are frightened or confused, but not obviously maltreatment of the infant, may set dissociative mental processes into motion. Such a theoretical explanation of DA suggests that pathological dissociation, in infancy, is a primary failure in organizing unitary mental states and coherent behavioral strategies—a failure taking place in an interpersonal context of defective caregiving—rather than an intrapsychic defense against the unbearable mental pain of severely traumatic experiences.

4.4 THE INTERNAL WORKING MODEL OF INFANT DA: MULTIPLICITY OF EGO STATES?

One feature of pathological dissociation from childhood to adult age is the coexistence of reciprocally segregated, contradictory ego states. These may alternate in controlling the patient's feelings, attitudes, and behavior along reciprocally incompatible patterns, as may be observed, in an extreme form, in Dissociative Identity Disorder (DID). Attachment theory and research suggest that a subclinical parallel to this feature of dissociation exists in the IWM of infant DA.

The IWMs corresponding to the early patterns of attachment are usually inferred from the statistical links between such patterns, as observed in the SS, and the corresponding states of mind of the caregivers, as assessed in the AAI (for an overview see Main, 1995).[3] The caregiver's "free" AAI classification, that predicts secure infant attachment in the SS, is characterized by a positive, defense-free attitude toward attachment needs and their expression in human life. Therefore, it can be inferred that secure infants construct a unitary and coherent IWM, in which representations of the subjective experience and of the expression of attachment emotions are accompanied by memories of positive, validating responses from the caregiver. The caregiver's "dismissing" AAI classification, which predicts avoidant infant attachment, is characterized by a consistently negative evaluation of attachment emotions: the IWM of avoidant attachment therefore portrays such a negative mirroring, by the caregiver, of one's attachment needs. The AAI "entangled" classification, which is predictive of resistant infant attachment, is characterized by a continuing preoccupation about the meaning and value of attachment experiences, that very likely corresponds, in the infant's IWM, to uncertain evaluation of the meaning of one's attachment emotions. Each of these three types of IWM is quite compatible with the corresponding type of attachment behavior observed in the SS.

Although they are very different in content, all three IWMs of organized attachments are sufficiently unitary and coherent: each of them portrays a "singular" representation of self-with-other. The nature of the IWM corresponding to DA is quite different: as Main (1991) hypothesized, it is very likely incoherent and multiple, portraying a "plural," nonintegrated self-representation. The line of reasoning that leads to such a conclusion may be summarized as follows.

The emotional information conveyed to the infant by the frightening, dissociated parental behavior is dramatic, multiple, and contradictory: in a quick sequence, during many of daily episodes of care-seeking, the disorganized

[3] Infant IWM should be considered as a structure of implicit memory, constructed on the basis of actual experience of attachment interaction with the caregiver (Amini et al., 1996). In later phases of development, aspects of this implicit structure may become explicit and enter into autobiographical narratives.

infant, *while receiving help* from the unresolved caregiver (otherwise the infant would not survive), is frightened by him/her, witnesses his/her fear and impotence, and experiences the extreme tension of an insolvable conflict (fright without solution) that may be accompanied by an extreme degree of impotent rage. Multiple, simultaneous, reciprocally incompatible information is sufficient to induce altered states of consciousness even in normal adults (some techniques for inducing a hypnotic trance are based on this possibility: Erickson, 1964). On the basis of this line of reasoning, Liotti (1992) suggested that disruption of the infant's consciousness, resembling a trance-like state, may take place during interactions with frightening caregivers. The early IWM, that is continuously constructed and remodelled during such altered states of consciousness, will tend to remain at least partially disconnected from the organizing functions of memory and consciousness for the same reason the memories of hypnotic trances are usually at least partially inaccessible to conscious recall (state dependent memory and learning). The implicit representations of self and the caregiver (IWM) constructed during DA will therefore be multiple, contradictory, and reciprocally disassociated.

The metaphor of the drama triangle—according to which the characters of drama theatre shift between the reciprocal roles of rescuer, persecutor, and victim (Karpman, 1968)—may be instrumental in capturing the intrinsically multiple and disassociated feature of the disorganized IWM (Liotti, 1999a, 1999b, 2000, 2002). The parent is represented negatively in the child's IWM, that is, as the cause of the ever-growing fear experienced by the self (self as victim of a persecutor). However, the parent is also and simultaneously represented positively, as a rescuer: the parent, although frightened by unresolved traumatic memories, is nevertheless usually willing to offer comfort to the child, and the child may feel such comforting availability in conjunction with the fear. Together with these two opposed representations of the attachment figure (persecutor and rescuer) meeting a vulnerable and helpless (victim) self, the disorganized IWM also conveys a negative representation of a powerful, evil self meeting a fragile or even devitalized attachment figure (persecutor self, held responsible for the fear expressed by the attachment figure). Moreover, there is the possibility, for the child, of representing both the self and the parent as the helpless victims of a mysterious, invisible source of danger. And finally, since the frightened parent may be comforted by the tender feelings evoked by contact with the child, the implicit memories of DA may also convey the possibility of construing the self as the powerful rescuer of a fragile attachment figure (i.e., the little child perceives the self as able to comfort a frightened adult).

The hypothesized three main types of self-representation in the disorganized IWM bear generic formal resemblance with the three main types of ego states that alternate in DID: persecutor, rescuer and victim ego states (Liotti, 1995, 1999a, 1999b). Is it possible that such a generic similarity reflects a particular psychopathological pathway, leading from infant DA to adult DID? Liotti (1992) advanced the hypothesis that, starting from infant DA, three main developmental pathways may follow. The first, leading to progressive integration of the initially multiple representations of the IWM, is contingent upon the progressive integration of the caregiver's traumatic memories (e.g., thanks to psychotherapy), and/or the lack of further risk factors during development (i.e., lack of traumas during childhood and adolescence). This developmental pathway is compatible with either full mental health, or with a mildly increased vulnerability to react to adult life stressors with dissociation or anxiety (see also Hesse & Main, 1999). The second developmental pathway laid open by infant DA, thanks to an only moderate exposure to other specific risk factors (childhood traumas or adverse genetic influences), may lead to relatively mild types of dissociative disorder (DD). The third pathway leads from early DA to DID, or to other serious types of pathological dissociation, mainly because of the repeated exposure to sexual, physical, or emotional traumas during childhood and adolescence. The repeated exposure to traumas is expected to have deep and long-lasting dissociative effects if the perpetrators are attachment figures (thereby reenacting in later developmental phases the experience of interaction with a frightening attachment figure that lies at the basis of infant DA), or if the attachment figures do not offer support and comfort. According to Liotti's (1992) hypothesis, then, early DA constitutes a sort of template for responding with pathological dissociation to later traumas. In other words, there is an additive, cumulative, or interactive effect between traumas and the disorganized quality of previous attachments in producing clinically significant dissociative symptoms (cf. Lyons-Ruth & Jacobvitz, 1999, p. 547, and Liotti, 2004).

4.5 VULNERABILITY TO DISSOCIATION AS A SEQUEL OF EARLY ATTACHMENT DISORGANIZATION

An increased tendency toward dissociative experiences in adolescents and young adults who had been disorganized in their infant attachments has been clearly demonstrated by two longitudinal studies (Carlson,

1998; Ogawa et al., 1997). Increased vulnerability to dissociation as a sequel of early DA is also suggested by the results of a correlational study (Hesse & Van IJzendoorn, 1998). In particular, Ogawa's et al. (1997) study lends support to Liotti's hypothesis that there is a cumulative effect between infant DA and later traumas in yielding clinically significant levels of dissociation. Also noteworthy is the anecdotal evidence collected during Carlson's (1998) longitudinal study: three adolescents in her sample suffered from a DD, and all three had been disorganized in their infant attachments (for a discussion of these findings, see also Dozier, Stovall, & Albus, 1999, p. 507). These longitudinal studies provide strong support for the contention that pathological dissociation should not be viewed as the top end of a continuum of dissociative experiences ranging from normality to psychopathology, "but as a separate taxon that represents an extreme deviation from normal development" (Ogawa et al., 1997, p. 855).

Other evidence supporting Liotti's hypothesis comes from retrospective studies of a particular type of risk factor for mental disorders: the anamnestic datum of having had a mother who suffered from attachment-related losses and traumas in the two years before or the two years after the patient's birth. This factor significantly increases, with respect to other mental disorders, the risk of developing a DD (Pasquini et al., 2002) or BPD (Liotti, Pasquini, & the Italian Group for the Study of Dissociation, 2000) in adulthood.[4] Since traumatic events and serious losses in the mothers' lives that take place close to the patients' births are likely to remain unresolved during the period in which the patients developed their infant attachments, and since unresolved losses and traumas in the mothers are strong predictors of DA in the infants, these findings are compatible with the hypothesis that early DA is a risk factor in the development of adult disorders implying dissociation, such as a DD and BPD.

The increased vulnerability to pathological dissociation brought on by early DA, that the previously quoted studies demonstrate, may be readily explained by attachment theory. Whenever, from infancy to old age, human beings are called upon to cope with a traumatic stressor, their attachment system is activated (i.e., they experience a strong wish to seek help and comfort). When the operations of the system are guided by a secure IWM, help and comfort will be expected and actively sought by the traumatized person, while efficient self-soothing will take place while waiting for outside support. This situation will greatly reduce the likelihood of PTSD or long-lasting pathological dissociation after the traumatic experience. When, on the contrary, the operations of the attachment system are guided by an insecure IWM, emotional reactions to distressing experiences may be made even more painful by the automatic inner evaluation that one's wishes for comfort are either illegitimate (avoidant attachment) or produce distressing interactions with the attachment figures (resistant attachment). Attachment theory suggests, on these grounds, that all types of insecure IWM may generically increase the vulnerability to trauma-related *emotional* disorders (while, in contrast, the IWM of secure attachment is a protective factor: Adam, Keller, & West, 1995; Dozier, Stovall, & Albus, 1999). The IWM of early DA likely adds specificity to this generic vulnerability, in the direction of greatly facilitating *dissociative* reactions to later traumas throughout the life span. The activation of the attachment system contingent upon trauma, insofar as it implies a dramatic, multiple, and nonintegrated representation of self-with-other, hampers the organizing functions of consciousness and identity, and brings on by itself a dissociative state of mind that cumulates with the dissociating effects of trauma (Liotti, 1999a, 1999b, 2004).

These studies of AAI unresolved interviews lend empirical support to the theory that the activation of the attachment system is particularly apt to prime traumatic memories that may have remained in a dissociated state for years (and that are not sufficiently troublesome to produce mental disorders). Many of these studies involve parents who do not suffer from any clinically evident mental disorder, and whose children are being simultaneously observed in the SS. These parents' attachment systems are activated, one can reasonably hypothesize, by their experience of taking care of their children. In such a context, unresolved traumatic memories that have been dormant for years are brought to consciousness and exert their dissociating power both on the parent's state of mind and on the child's developing IWM of attachment.

Even more impressive illustrations of the implication of the attachment system in yielding dissociative responses are offered by those rare types of AAI that are coded "Cannot Classify" (CC: Hesse, 1999; Hesse et al., 2003). These interviews are typically split in two parts, one of which would lead to a "dismissing" classification, while the other should be coded "entangled." Often, the responder is totally unaware of such a marked change of attitude in the evaluation of attachment-related

[4] A recent review of studies on DA and BPD (Levy, 2005) suggests that DA may be related to a wide range of psychiatric disorders, rather than specifically to BPD. A neodissociationist view of psychopathology may interpret this hypothesis in keeping with the idea that dissociative processes lie at the base of a wide range of mental disorders.

autobiographical memories, showing a disruption of the monitoring functions of attention and consciousness that can be considered an instance of dissociation. Moreover, the shift in attitudes during CC interviews is sometimes quite similar—insofar as it implies, for instance, a change in the tone of voice while reporting traumas that had been forgotten—to the switch between different ego states clinically observable in DID. Not surprisingly, the AAI of patients suffering from a DD receive, rather typically, the CC code together with the "unresolved" code (Steele, 2002; Steele & Steele, 2003, p. 115–117).

4.6 DISSOCIATION IN THE LIGHT OF ATTACHMENT THEORY: TWO ALTERNATIVE HYPOTHESES

The study of attachment, in summary, suggests that dissociation during personality development concerns primarily a failure in the integration, into a unitary meaning structure, of memories concerning attachment interactions with a particular caregiver. Such a failure should be ascribed to a type of intersubjective experience that appears exceedingly complex besides being frightening. The frightening aspect of this experience, moreover, is not always due to overt maltreatment or aggression: it can be the consequence of the infant's need for protection being met by a frightened or dissociated response from the caregiver, who is not otherwise maltreating. Once established, the intrinsically dissociated IWM of such an attachment relationship fosters further dissociative responses to later traumatic experiences. Moreover, every time a life stressor activates the attachment system (and therefore the intrinsically dissociated IWM), a painful experience of disorientation, disorganization, and fear, linked to implicit memories of past frightening attachment interactions and to usually unconscious expectations of their repetition, may follow. Such a dissociative experience, contingent upon the activation of the attachment system and to the state of "fright without solution," should not be considered as a defense against, but rather as a straightforward cause of, mental pain (Liotti, 1999b).

The theory that dissociation is *primarily* a defense mechanism whose function is to compartmentalize perceptions and memories related to trauma, and to allow the victims to detach themselves from the full impact of trauma, therefore, is not supported by this interpretation of attachment theory and research. Other interpretations of attachment research are more compatible with the theory that views dissociation as a defense. The type of experience leading to infant DA, even when it does not imply violence or obvious maltreatment, may be equated to a life-threatening trauma (cf. the concept of early relational trauma in Schore, 2001, 2002). The main consequence of this early relational trauma may be held to be a defensive inhibition of one of the organizing functions of consciousness: the capacity to reflect on one's own and on other people's mental states (a capacity that may be related to such constructs as "theory of mind," "metacognition," and "mentalizing ability": Fonagy et al., 1995). Such a defense would operate by dissociating from the child's consciousness any beginning representation of the *mind* of the attachment figure as harbouring aggressive, even murderous intentions toward the child (Fonagy, 2002; Fonagy et al., 1995, p. 263).

In the perspective this chapter holds, the metacognitive deficit that is a well-known developmental sequel of insecure and DA (Fonagy, Target, & Gergely, 2000; Fonagy et al., 2003; Meins, 1997) is interpreted as the direct result of hindered intersubjective processes of reciprocal mind-reading rather than as the child's defensive disabling, to guard against mental pain, of emerging mentalizing capacities. It is impossible, for the time being, to devise empirical studies that could falsify one or the other hypothesis. In search of a preliminary evaluation of the two competing hypotheses we could reflect, however, on what is known about the developmental sequelæ of DA in middle childhood.

4.7 DISSOCIATION IN THE CHILDHOOD SEQUELÆ OF INFANT DA

Longitudinal studies from infancy to age 6 show that most (i.e., over 80%) children, whose attachments had been classified disorganized in the SS, progressively organize their behavior toward the unresolved caregivers around the apparent, unitary goal of controlling the interaction with them (Main, Kaplan, & Cassidy, 1985; NICHD Early Childcare Research Study, 2001; Wartner et al., 1994). This observation may simply reflect the natural, spontaneous tendency of the human mind toward the construction of unitary meaning structures concerning self-with-others (a tendency that Pierre Janet termed "personal synthesis": Janet, 1907). An alternative interpretation is that the controlling strategy expresses, on a behavioral level, the defensive disruption of mentalization (Fonagy, Target, & Gergely, 2000; Fonagy et al., 2003). A third interpretation views the controlling strategy as an attempt to *repair, or at least to compensate for,* the painful failure of the organizing functions of consciousness, memory, and identity.

It is noteworthy, in trying to choose among the three hypotheses, that a strong activation of the attachment motivational system leads to a collapse of the controlling strategy, and to the re-emerging of disorganization. When 6-year-old disorganized-controlling children are asked to respond to imagined child-parent separations (a technique for activating attachment motivations and attachment-related representations), states of disorganization and disorientation resembling dissociation reappear (Jacobsen & Hoffman, 1997; Solomon, George, & DeJong, 1995). In these test situations, disorganized-controlling children may use nonsense language, make contradictory statements without acknowledging the contradiction, engage in chaotic fantasies often of a catastrophic content, or may suddenly fall silent and appear disoriented, as if they had entered a trance-like state (see Hesse et al., 2003, p. 61–63, for an overview of research studies, comments, and illustrative examples).

The reappearance of dissociative processes *contingent upon the activation of the attachment system* suggest that the more unitary controlling strategies had been based on a relative inhibition of this specific motivational system, rather than on a defensive disabling of the more general mental capacity for mentalization. An inhibition of the attachment system, aimed at protecting from the painful experience of dissociation linked to it (which is quite different from a defense against traumatic representations based on dissociation of the mentalizing function of consciousness), may obtain through the activation of different, equally inborn motivational systems mediating different aspects of human relatedness. One such system mediates caregiving behavior (George & Solomon, 1999). Another mediates competitive, ranking behavior (Gilbert, 1989) aimed at establishing the reciprocal roles of dominance and submission in relationships (see also Panksepp, 1998). Either one or the other inborn motivational system, caregiving or ranking, is implied in each of two different controlling strategies that formerly disorganized infants may gradually come to employ.

When they reach their sixth year of age, formerly disorganized infants use either a controlling-caregiving or a controlling-punitive strategy toward their unresolved caregivers (for reviews of research on this topic, see Lyons-Ruth & Jacobvitz, 1999, or Hesse et al., 2003). The controlling-caregiving strategy is characterized by an exaggerated sense of responsibility, inhibition of aggression, role-reversal, and concern for the well-being of the parent. The controlling-punitive strategy is characterized by anger and dominant attitudes toward the parent. Controlling-caregiving children take control by entertaining, directing, comforting, and giving approval to the parent. Controlling-punitive children take control of the relationship with the parent through coercive, hostile, or humiliating behavior. Controlling-caregiving strategies may be based on those representations of the multiple IWM of DA that portray the self as a rescuer, and the parent as a helpless victim. Controlling-punitive strategies may emerge from selecting the persecutor-victim theme of the drama triangle characterizing this IWM. Although controlled research findings are still lacking in this respect, it can be hypothesized that controlling-caregiving children resort to this strategy as a response to the interaction with vulnerable, frightened, confused "unresolved" parents who nevertheless are not directly maltreating or neglecting. Controlling-punitive children may more likely be the offspring of parents who display neglecting, hostile, or straightforwardly maltreating parental behavior.[5] Parents of both controlling-caregiving and -punitive children would be expected to have suffered from unresolved traumas or losses.

Thus, reflections on the developmental sequelæ of infant DA in middle childhood corroborate the theory that pathological dissociation is in itself such a painful experience that the mind tries to defend against it through an inhibition of the motivational system upon which dissociation is based—more than they corroborate the theory viewing dissociation as a defense against painful experiences. A strong activation of the attachment system leads to a collapse of defenses based on its attempted inhibition and to reemerging dissociative experiences, rather than such an activation bringing on painful attachment-related memories against which disruption of consciousness is employed as a defense. Dissociation may subsequently become a defense against trauma in phases of personality development that follow early DA, in the form of absorption of attention to aspects of the inner world different from traumatic memories. The activation of the IWM of DA, moreover, plays an important role, throughout development, in increasing the risk of reacting to traumas with chronic dissociation. Attachment theory and research suggest that this role remains more important,

[5] It is likely that in middle childhood, in order to control the relationship with an abusing caregiver, some formerly disorganized infants are forced to use the sexual system (besides the caregiving and the ranking systems) instead of the attachment system. This possibility, of great clinical relevance given the role attributed to incest in the genesis of pathological dissociation, may be more easily observed in studies involving high-risk samples. High-risk samples have been studied in a minority of research on childhood attachment. In this context, the hypothesized power of secure and organized attachments normally inhibiting the sexual system within family interactions, and the likelihood that such an inhibition is less efficient in DA, should be mentioned (Erickson, 1993, 2000).

in the genesis of dissociative and complex posttraumatic disorders across the life cycle, than the secondary use of dissociation as a defense against trauma.

4.8 DA AND THE DOMAIN OF DISSOCIATION

The study of early DA and its developmental sequelæ suggests that three intertwined phenomena constitute the core of pathological dissociation throughout the life span:

(1) Disruption of attention and consciousness (expressed in episodes of abnormal, unwitting absorption of attention and in trance-like states);
(2) Nonintegrated multiplicity of self-representations (expressed, in its simpler form, in the IWM of DA and, in its extreme form, in the disruption of identity and the alternate ego states of DID);
(3) Erratic difficulties in accessing some attachment-related autobiographic memories, linked to controlling strategies aimed at inhibiting the attachment system (these difficulties may take the extreme form of dissociative amnesia and fugue).

The dynamics of the attachment system (activation and deactivation) play a major role, together with traumatic experiences and related defensive strategies, in shaping the vicissitudes of this dissociative core through the life span. Severe traumatic experiences may exert an immediate dissociating effect from childhood to adulthood (e.g., they may exert a disruptive effect on attentional strategies, and hinder the encoding in semantic memory of implicit memories related to traumas: Allen, 2001; Allen, Console, & Lewis, 1999; Van der Kolk, 1996). They may also lead to defensive dissociation of traumatic memories and therefore to reversible amnesia. However, traumas can lead to full-fledged, chronic disorders implying the aforementioned core of pathological dissociation only through the activation of a disorganized IWM, and/or through the prolonged and complete absence of response to the attachment needs activated by mental pain.

Other symptoms that are commonly observed in patients suffering from a DD should be explained starting from this dissociative core. For instance, blank spells may be the result of episodic failure of conscious processing when contradictory representations of self-with-other surface simultaneously during attachment interactions. The unwitting absorption of attention on the body schema, or on the outside environment, during the activation of a DA system may yield depersonalization and derealization. Dissociated mental states that are regulated by one or the other part of the disorganized IWM may be experienced as "voices" expressing the persecutory, rescuer, or victim (i.e., child voices) aspects of the drama triangle that characterizes such an IWM. Metacognitive (mentalization) and self-regulatory deficits stemming from DA (Fonagy et al., 2003; Schore, 2001, 2002) may explain other symptoms (notably, dysregulation of emotions and aggressive impulses: cf. Lyons-Ruth, 1996; Lyons-Ruth & Jacobvitz, 1999).

If the core of pathological dissociation is as described, then boundaries between the different categories of DD listed by the DSM-IV could not be expected to be neat (a contention that is in keeping with some proposals of nosological revision: Dell, 2001). Considerable overlap would be also expected between different types of mental disorders for which early DA may be a common risk factor and that may share important aspects of their developmental pathways, such as the DDs, the complex forms of chronic PTSD (Liotti, 2004), and BPD (Fonagy et al., 2003; Liotti, 1999a, 2002, 2004; Liotti et al., 2000).

4.9 DIRECTIONS FOR FUTURE RESEARCH

Models of dissociation based on DA have been applied to the treatment of a few published clinical cases (Fonagy, 1999; Gold et al., 2001; Liotti, 1993, 1995; Liotti & Intreccialagli, 2003), with particular advantages for dealing successfully with the multiple transferences so typical in the psychotherapy of DDs (Davies & Frawley, 1994). Three new approaches to the psychotherapy of DDs are based on the concept of DA as a key for understanding pathological dissociation (Blizard, 2001; Gold, 2000; Steele, Van der Hart & Nijenhuis, 2001). These clinical applications may become manualized and allow for outcome research testing the fruitfulness of this approach.

Research on therapeutic process could test some predictions of the theory of dissociation presented in this chapter. The theory predicts that dissociative patients would manifest, in their behavior toward the psychotherapist, multiple representations of self-with-other that shift among the poles of the drama triangle (Liotti, 1995; Fonagy, 1999). The theory also predicts a marked decrease of metacognitive capacity when multiple transferences emerge. Controlled studies on the therapeutic process that test these predictions are feasible: problematic mental states, such as the nonintegrated representations of the drama triangle, and transient changes in metacognitive capacity can be reliably assessed in transcripts of therapeutic sessions (Semerari et al., 2003a, 2003b). Unfortunately, methods for reliably assessing the activation of any given motivational system within the therapeutic relationship are still lacking. The crucial prediction of the model here expounded—that dissociative experiences of clinical relevance (such as those observed in the DDs) are contingent upon the activation of the attachment system—cannot therefore be empirically tested within the therapeutic relationship, for the time being, in any systematic way. Careful analyses, in sufficiently large clinical samples, of the interpersonal contexts in which the dissociative symptoms make their first appearance in the patient's adult life could, however, provide support for this prediction. The theory would predict that such interpersonal contexts are characterized by actual or expected separations from attachment figures, by losses, and/or by the making of new affectional bonds implying attachment (besides lack of appropriate soothing responses to traumatic stressors intervening in the patient's life).

Available data strongly support the hypothesis that, *in adulthood*, unresolved traumatic memories of attachment-related experiences are a risk factor for many types of mental disorder (Dozier et al., 1999; Lyons-Ruth & Jacobvitz, 1999). There is only preliminary support for the hypothesis that *infant* DA predisposes to disorders implying dissociation (Carlson, 1998; Ogawa et al., 1997)—such as a DD (Pasquini et al., 2002) or BPD (Liotti et al., 2000). Queries regarding parental loss experiences—employed in studies by Hesse and Van IJzendoorn (1998), Liotti et al. (2000), and Pasquini et al. (2002)—provide "rough and ready" estimates of early DA that can be useful for large-scale studies, but cannot reliably assess the frequency of early DA in adult clinical samples. The unresolved classifications of the AAI, on the other hand, have other limitations; they exclude cases of early DA that have not faced attachment-related trauma or loss during later years, and include some cases of early non-DA with subsequent attachment-related traumas and losses. Further evidence that infant DA is a specific risk factor for the DDs, and for other disorders implying pathological dissociation, will therefore depend either on replication of large-scale longitudinal studies (e.g., Carlson, 1998; Ogawa et al., 1997) or on the identification of methods for estimating early DA in adult populations.

REFERENCES

Adam, K. S., Keller, A. E., & West, M. (1995). Attachment organization and vulnerability to loss, separation and abuse in disturbed adolescents. In S. Goldberg, R. Muir, & J. Kerr (Eds.), *Attachment theory: Social, developmental and clinical perspectives* (pp. 309–41). Hillsdale, NJ: Analytic Press.

Ainsworth, M. D. S., Blehar, M., Waters, E., & Wall, S. (1978). *Patterns of attachment: A psychological study of the Strange Situation*. Hillsdale, NJ: Erlbaum.

Allen, J. G. (2001). *Interpersonal trauma and serious mental disorders*. Chichester, UK: Wiley.

Allen, J. G., Console, D. A., & Lewis, L. (1999). Dissociative detachment and memory impairment: reversible amnesia or encoding failure? *Comprehensive Psychiatry, 40*, 160–71.

American Psychiatric Association (1994). *Diagnostic and Statistical Manual Of Mental Disorders, 4th ed: DSM-IV.* Washington, DC: American Psychiatric Association.

Amini, F., Lewis, T., Lannon, R., Louie, A., Baumbacher, G., McGuinnes, T., & Zirker, E. (1996). Affect, attachment, memory: Contributions toward psychobiologic integration. *Psychiatry, 59*, 213–39.

Bliss, E. L. (1986). *Multiple personality, allied disorders, and hypnosis*. New York: Oxford University Press.

Blizard, R. A. (2001). Masochistic and sadistic ego states: Dissociative solutions to the dilemma of attachment to an abusive caregiver. *Journal of Trauma & Dissociation, 2*, 37–58.

Bockhorst, C. L., Bakermans-Kranenburg, M. J., Pascofearson R. M., Van IJzendoorn, M. H., Fonagy, P., & Schuengel, C. (2003). The importance of shared environment in mother-infant attachment security: A behavioral-genetic study. *Child Development, 74*, 1769–82.

Bowlby, J. (1969/1982). *Attachment and loss: Vol. 1. Attachment*. London: Hogarth Press.

Bowlby, J. (1973). *Attachment and loss: Vol. 2. Separation*. London: Hogarth Press.

Bowlby, J. (1980). *Attachment and loss: Vol. 3. Loss*. London: Hogarth Press.

Bretherton, I., & Munholland, K. A. (1999). Internal working models in attachment relationships: A construct revisited. In J. Cassidy & P. R. Shaver (Eds.), *Handbook of attachment* (pp. 89–111). New York: Guilford.

Carlson, E. A. (1998). A prospective longitudinal study of attachment disorganization/disorientation. *Child Development, 69*, 1107–28.

Cassidy, J. (1999). The nature of the child's ties. In J. Cassidy & P. R. Shaver (Eds.), *Handbook of attachment* (pp. 3–20). New York: Guilford.

Davies, J. M., & Frawley, M. G. (1994). *Treating the adult survivor of childhood sexual abuse: A psychoanalytic perspective*. New York: Basic Books.

Dell, P. F. (2001). Why the diagnostic criteria for Dissociative Identity Disorder should be changed. *Journal of Trauma & Dissociation, 2*, 7–37.

Dozier, M., Stovall, K. C., & Albus, K. E. (1999). Attachment and psychopathology in adulthood. In J. Cassidy & P. R. Shaver (Eds.), *Handbook of attachment* (pp. 497–519). New York: Guilford.

Erickson, M. H. (1964). The confusion technique in hypnosis. *American Journal of Clinical Hypnosis, 6*, 183–207.

Erickson, M. T. (1993). Rethinking Oedipus: An evolutionary perspective of incest avoidance. *American Journal of Psychiatry, 150*, 411–6.

Erickson, M. T. (2000). The evolution of incest avoidance: Oedipus and the psychopathologies of kinship. In J. Gilbert & K. Bailey (Eds.), *Genes on the couch: Essays in evolutionary psychotherapy* (pp. 211–31). Hove: Psychology Press.

Fonagy, P. (1999). The transgenerational transmission of holocaust trauma: Lessons learned from the analysis of an adolescent with obsessive-compulsive disorder. *Attachment and Human Development, 1*, 92–114.

Fonagy, P. (2002). Multiple voices versus meta-cognition: An attachment theory perspective. In V. Sinason (Ed.), *Attachment, trauma and multiplicity* (pp. 71–85). London: Brunner/Routledge.

Fonagy, P., Steele, M., Steele, H., Leigh, T., Kennedy, R., Mattoon, G., & Target, M. (1995). The predictive validity of Mary Main's Adult Attachment Interview: A psychoanalytic and developmental perspective on transgenerational transmission of attachment and borderline states. In S. Goldberg, R. Muir, & J. Kerr (Eds.), *Attachment theory: Social, developmental and clinical perspectives* (pp. 233–78). Hillsdale, NJ: Analytic Press.

Fonagy, P., Target, M., & Gergely, G. (2000). Attachment and borderline personality disorder: A theory and some evidence. *Psychiatric Clinics of North America, 23*, 103–22.

Fonagy, P., Target, M., Gergely, G., Allen, J. G., & Bateman, A. W. (2003). The developmental roots of borderline personality disorder in early attachment relationships: A theory and some evidence. *Psychoanalytic Inquiry, 23*, 412–59.

George, C., & Solomon, J. (1999). Attachment and caregiving: The caregiving behavioral system. In J. Cassidy & P. R. Shaver (Eds.), *Handbook of attachment* (pp. 649–71). New York: Guilford.

Gilbert, P. (1989). *Human nature and suffering*. London: LEA.

Gold, S. N. (2000). *Not trauma alone: Therapy for child abuse survivors in family and social context*. Philadelphia: Brunner/Routledge.

Gold, S. N., Elhai, J. D., Rea, B. D., Weiss, D., Masino, T., Morris, S. L., & McInich, J. (2001). Contextual treatment of dissociative identity disorder: Three case studies. *Journal of Trauma & Dissociation, 2*, 5–35.

Hesse, E. (1999). The Adult Attachment Interview: Historical and current perspectives. In J. Cassidy & P. R. Shaver (Eds.), *Handbook of attachment* (pp. 395–433). New York: Guilford.

Hesse, E., & Main, M. (2000). Disorganized infant, child and adult attachment: Collapse in behavioral and attentional strategies. *Journal of the American Psychoanalytic Association, 48*, 1097–127.

Hesse, E., Main, M., Abrams, K. Y., & Rifkin, A. (2003). Unresolved states regarding loss or abuse can have "second-generation" effects: Disorganized, role-inversion and frightening ideation in the offspring of traumatized non-maltreating parents. In D. J. Siegel & M. F. Solomon (Eds.), *Healing trauma: Attachment, mind, body and brain* (pp. 57–106). New York: Norton.

Hesse, E., & Van IJzendoorn, M. H. (1998). Parental loss of close family members and propensities toward absorption in offspring. *Developmental Science, 1*, 299–305.

Hesse, E., & Van IJzendoorn, M. H. (1999). Propensities toward absorption are related to lapses in the monitoring of reasoning or discourse during the Adult Attachment Interview: A preliminary investigation. *Attachment and Human Development, 1*, 67–91.

Jacobsen, T., & Hoffman, V. (1997). Child attachment representations: Longitudinal relations to school behavior and academic competency in middle childhood and adolescence. *Developmental Psychology, 33*, 703–10.

Janet, P. (1907). *The major symptoms of hysteria*. New York: MacMillan (reprinted by Hafner, New York, 1965).

Karpman, S. (1968). Fairy tales and script drama analysis. *Transactional Analysis Bulletin, 7*, 39–43.

Lakatos, K., Nemoda, Z., Toth, I., Ronai, Z., Ney, K., Sasvari, M., & Gervai, J. (2002). Further evidence for the role of the dopamine D4 receptor (DRD4). gene in attachment disorganization. *Molecular Psychiatry, 7*, 27–31.

Lakatos, K., Toth, I., Nemoda, Z., Ney, K., Sasvari, M., & Gervai, J. (2000). Dopamine D4 receptor gene polymorphism as associated with attachment disorganization in infants. *Molecular Psychiatry, 5*, 633–7.

Levy, K. N. (2005). The implications of attachment theory and research for understanding borderline personality disorder. *Development and Psychopathology, 17*, 959–86.

Lichtenberg, J. D. (1989). *Psychoanalysis and motivation*. Hillsdale, NJ: The Analytic Press.

Liotti, G. (1992). Disorganized/disoriented attachment in the etiology of the dissociative disorders. *Dissociation, 5*, 196–204.

Liotti, G. (1993). Disorganized attachment and dissociative experiences: An illustration of the developmental-ethological approach to cognitive therapy. In K. T. Kuehlvein & H. Rosen (Eds.), *Cognitive therapies in action* (pp. 213–39). San Francisco: Jossey-Bass.

Liotti, G. (1995). Disorganized/disoriented attachment in the psychotherapy of the dissociative disorders. In S. Goldberg, R. Muir, & J. Kerr (Eds.), *Attachment theory: Social, developmental and clinical perspectives* (pp. 343–63). Hillsdale, NJ: Analytic Press.

Liotti, G. (1999a). Disorganized attachment as a model for the understanding of dissociative psychopathology. In J. Solomon & C. George (Eds.), *Attachment disorganization* (pp. 291–317). New York: Guilford Press.

Liotti, G. (1999b). Understanding the dissociative processes: The contribution of attachment theory. *Psychoanalytic Inquiry, 19*, 757–83.

Liotti, G. (2000). Disorganized attachment, models of borderline states, and evolutionary psychotherapy. In J. Gilbert & K. Bailey (Eds.), *Genes on the couch: Essays in evolutionary psychotherapy* (pp. 232–56). Hove: Psychology Press.

Liotti, G. (2002). The inner schema of borderline states and its correction during psychotherapy: A cognitive-evolutionary approach. *Journal of Cognitive Psychotherapy, 16*, 310–25.

Liotti, G. (2004). Trauma, dissociation and disorganized attachment: three strands of a single braid. *Psychotherapy, 41*, 472–86.

Liotti, G., & Intreccialagli, B. (2003). Disorganized attachment, motivational systems and metacognitive monitoring in the treatment of a patient with borderline syndrome. In M. Cortina & M. Marrone (Eds.), *Attachment theory and the psychoanalytic process* (pp. 356–81). London: Whurr.

Liotti, G., Pasquini, P., & The Italian Group for the Study of Dissociation (2000). Predictive factors for borderline personality disorder: Patients' early traumatic experiences and losses suffered by the attachment figure. *Acta Psychiatrica Scandinavica, 102*, 282–9.

Lyons-Ruth, K. (1996). Attachment relationship among children with aggressive behavior problems: The role of disorganized early attachment patterns. *Journal of Consulting and Clinical Psychology, 64*, 64–73.

Lyons-Ruth, K., Bronfman, E., & Atwood, G. (1999). A relational-diathesis model of hostile-helpless states of mind: Expressions in mother-infant interaction. In J. Solomon & C. George (Eds.), *Attachment disorganization* (pp. 33–70). New York: Guilford Press.

Lyons-Ruth, K., & Jacobvitz, D. (1999). Attachment disorganization: Unresolved loss, relational violence and lapses in behavioral and attentional strategies. In J. Cassidy & P. R. Shaver (Eds.), *Handbook of attachment* (pp. 520–54). New York: Guilford Press.

Main, M. (1991). Metacognitive knowledge, metacognitive monitoring, and singular (coherent) vs. multiple (incoherent) model of attachment. In C. M. Parkes, J. Stevenson-Hinde, & J. Marris (Eds.), *Attachment across the life cycle* (pp. 127–60). London: Routledge.

Main, M. (1995). Recent studies in attachment: Overview, with selected implications for clinical work. In S. Goldberg, R. Muir, & J. Kerr (Eds.), *Attachment theory: Social, developmental and clinical perspectives* (pp. 407–74). Hillsdale, NJ: Analytic Press.

Main, M. (2000). The organized categories of infant, child, and adult attachment: Flexible vs. inflexible attention under attachment-related stress. *Journal of the American Psychoanalytic Association, 48*, 1055–95.

Main, M., & Goldwyn, R. (1998). *Adult Attachment Scoring and Classification System. Version 6.* Unpublished manuscript. University of California at Berkeley.

Main, M., & Hesse, E. (1990). Parents' unresolved traumatic experiences are related to infant disorganized attachment status: Is frightened and/or frightening parental behavior the linking mechanism? In M. T. Greenberg, D. Cicchetti, & E. M. Cummings (Eds.), *Attachment in the preschool years* (pp. 161–82). Chicago: Chicago University Press.

Main, M., Kaplan, N., & Cassidy, J. (1985). Security in infancy, childhood and adulthood: A move to the level of representation. *Monographs of the Society for Research in Child Development, 50*, 66–104.

Main, M., & Morgan, H. (1996). Disorganization and disorientation in infant Strange Situation behavior: Phenotypic resemblance to dissociative states? In L. Michelson & W. Ray (Eds.), *Handbook of dissociation* (pp. 107–37). New York: Plenum Press.

Main, M., & Solomon, J. (1990). Procedures for identifying infants as disorganized/disoriented during the Ainsworth Strange Situation. In M. T. Greenberg, D. Cicchetti, & E. M. Cummings (Eds.), *Attachment in the preschool years* (pp. 121–60). Chicago: Chicago University Press.

NICHD Early Childcare Research Network (2001). Childcare and family predictors of preschool attachment and stability from infancy. *Developmental Psychology, 37*, 847–62.

O'Connor, T. G., & Croft, C. M. (2001). A twin study of attachment in preschool children. *Child Development, 72*, 1501–11.

Ogawa, J. R., Sroufe, L. A., Weinfield, N. S., Carlson, E. A., & Egeland, B. (1997). Development and the fragmented self: Longitudinal study of dissociative symptomatology in a nonclinical sample. *Development and Psychopathology, 9*, 855–79.

Panksepp, J. (1998). *Affective neuroscience: The foundations of human and animal emotions.* Oxford: Oxford University Press.

Pasquini, P., Liotti, G., Mazzotti, E., Fassone, G., & The Italian Group for the Study of Dissociation (2002). Risk factors in the early family life of patients suffering from dissociative disorders. *Acta Psychiatrica Scandinavica, 105*, 110–6.

Putnam, F. W. (1993). Dissociative disorders in children: Behavioral profiles and problems. *Child Abuse and Neglect, 17*, 39–45.

Schore, A. N. (2001). The effects of early relational trauma on right brain development, affect regulation and infant mental health. *Infant Mental Health Journal, 22*, 201–69.

Schore, A. N. (2002). Dysregulation of the right brain: A fundamental mechanism of traumatic attachment and the psychopathogenesis of posttraumatic stress disorder. *Australian and New Zealand Journal of Psychiatry, 36*, 9–30.

Schuengel, C., Van IJzendoorn, M. H., & Bakermans-Kranenburg, M. J. (1999). Frightening maternal behavior linking unresolved loss and disorganized infant attachment. *Journal of Consulting and Clinical Psychology, 67*, 54–63.

Semerari, A., Carcione, A., Dimaggio, G., Falcone, M., Nicolò, G., Procacci, M., & Alleva, G. (2003a). The evaluation of metacognitive functioning in psychotherapy: The Metacognition Assessment Scale and its applications. *Clinical Psychology and Psychotherapy, 10*, 238–61.

Semerari, A., Carcione, A., Dimaggio, G., Falcone, M., Nicolò, G., Procacci, M., Alleva, G., & Mergenthaler, E. (2003b). Assessing problematic states inside patient's narratives: The grid of problematic conditions. *Psychotherapy Research, 13*, 337–53.

Solomon, J., & George, C. (1999). The place of disorganization in attachment theory. In J. Solomon & C. George (Eds.), *Attachment disorganization* (pp. 3–32). New York: Guilford Press.

Solomon, J., George, C., & DeJong, A. (1995). Children classified as controlling at age six: Evidence for disorganized representational strategies and aggression at home and at school. *Development and Psychopathology, 7*, 447–63.

Steele, H. (2002). Multiple dissociation in the context of the Adult Attachment Interview: Observations from interviewing individuals with dissociative identity disorder. In V. Sinason (Ed.), *Attachment, trauma and multiplicity* (pp. 107–21). London: Brunner/Routledge.

Steele, H., & Steele, M. (2003). Clinical uses of the Adult Attachment Interview. In M. Cortina & M. Marrone (Eds.), *Attachment theory and the psychoanalytic process* (pp. 107–26). London: Whurr.

Steele, K., Van der Hart, O., & Nijenhuis, E. R. (2001). Dependency in the treatment of complex posttraumatic stress disorder and dissociative disorders. *Journal of Trauma & Dissociation, 2*, 79–115.

Stern, D. N. (1985). *The interpersonal world of the infant*. New York: Basic Books.

Van der Kolk, B. A. (1996). The body keeps the score: approaches to the psychobiology of posttraumatic stress disorder. In B. A. van der Kolk, A. C. MacFarlane, & L. Weisaeth (Eds.), *The effects of overwhelming experiences on mind, body and society* (pp. 214–41). New York: Guilford.

Van IJzendoorn, M. H. (1995). Adult attachment representations, parental responsiveness and infant attachment: A meta-analysis of the predictive validity of the Adult Attachment Interview. *Psychological Bulletin, 117*, 387–403.

Van IJzendoorn, M. H., Schuengel, C., & Bakermans-Kranenburg, M. J. (1999). Disorganized attachment in early childhood: Meta-analysis of precursors, concomitants and sequelæ. *Development and Psychopathology, 11*, 225–49.

Wartner, U. G., Grossmann, K., Fremmer-Bombick, E., & Suess, G. (1994). Attachment patterns at age six in South Germany: Predictability from infancy and implications for preschool behavior. *Child Development, 65*, 1014–27.

5 Dissociation in Children and Adolescents: At the Crossroads

Joyanna L. Silberg, PhD
Stephanie Dallam, RN, MSN

OUTLINE

It is an important historical moment in the emerging field of child and adolescent dissociation. Streams of research and theoretical writings from the fields of neurobiology (Damasio, 1999; LeDoux, 1996; Schore, 1994, 2001), developmental psychology (Carlson, 2009; Liotti, 1999, 2009; Lyons-Ruth, Bronfman, & Atwood, 1999; 2009; Stien & Kendall, 2004), interpersonal neurobiology (Siegel, 1999), and dissociation theory (Putnam, 1997; Nijenhuis, Steele, & Van der Hart, 2002) have converged in provocative ways to shed light on our theoretical understanding of dissociation. Meanwhile, clinicians and researchers from a variety of disciplines have begun to describe symptom patterns in children with dissociative pathology (Haugaard, 2004; Silberg, 2001a; Şar, Öztürk, & Kundakçı, 2002; Waters, 2005a; Yehuda, 2005).

This accumulating body of information about dissociation in children and adolescents has established that there are predictable dissociative symptom patterns in children and adolescents that lend support to the theorized developmental origins of these disorders.

5.1 A BRIEF HISTORY OF THE FIELD

Although there is strong consensus that DID begins in childhood (Putnam, 1997), the documentation of dissociative disorders in children and adolescents during the last two decades has lagged behind that of adults (Putnam, 1991).

5.1.1 1980s

The contemporary literature on child and adolescent dissociative disorders began in 1984 with coincidental articles by Fagan and McMahan (1984) and Kluft (1984). Fagan and McMahon reported four cases in which children presented with identity alterations, apparent amnesia, and a constellation of self-destructive behaviors. Each of these children had a clear history of trauma, including sexual and physical abuse. Their clinical presentations differed from those of dissociative adults, and family interventions and play therapy proved effective (Fagan & McMahon, 1984; McMahon & Fagan, 1989). Fagan and McMahon concluded that, when recognized this early in life, dissociation may respond to treatment fairly rapidly. Kluft (1985) reported five childhood cases of DID (then called multiple personality disorder: MPD), some of whom had parents with DID. Kluft noted both similarities and differences between child and adult cases. Like McMahon and Fagan, he reported greater ease and shorter lengths of treatment with children.

These early descriptions of child dissociative cases were soon followed by more fully described cases, including a 10-year-old victim of severe sexual and physical abuse (Weiss, Sutton, & Utecht, 1985), a 14-year-old incest victim (Bowman, Blix, & Coons, 1985), and several mother-child pairs (Braun, 1985; Coons, 1985; Malenbaum & Russell, 1987). Preschool children with dissociative pathology were reported—a 4-year-old with dissociative pathology (Jones, 1986) and a 3-year-old with similar symptoms (Riley & Mead, 1988). Vincent and Pickering (1988) developed a symptom list from the extant case descriptions in the literature and recommended that clinicians use screening questionnaires to detect dissociative cases in high-risk populations of children.

5.1.2 1990s

In 1991, Peterson reviewed the 25 dissociative cases in the literature and noted that fully elaborated alter personalities were uncommon in dissociative children. Peterson proposed diagnostic criteria for a childhood dissociative disorder that does not meet adult criteria for MPD. In 1992, Hornstein and Putnam pooled data from two centers to describe 64 dissociative children whose symptoms included amnesia, trance states, hallucinations, self-destructive behavior, and profound identity fluctuations or a sense of divided identity. They noted that dissociative children typically manifest an array of posttraumatic and other comorbid symptoms. In the 1990s, larger case series of dissociative children began to appear in the literature—25 children (Coons, 1996), 11 MPD adolescents (Dell & Eisenhower, 1990), 17 dissociative inpatient children (Hornstein & Tyson, 1991), and 5 dissociative child and adolescent males (Klein, Mann, & Goodwin, 1994). Individual cases were also reported (Jacobsen, 1995; Laporta, 1992; McElroy, 1992; Peterson, 1991; Snow, White, Pilkington, & Beckman, 1995; Zoroğlu, Yargıç, Tutkun, Öztürk, & Şar, 1996).

The publication of large case series prompted researchers to develop diagnostic assessment tools. In 1994, Peterson and Putnam offered the *Child Dissociation Checklist* (CDC), which has become the mostly widely used assessment tool for dissociation in children. The CDC contains 20 questions that ask parents (or other adult observers) to rate on a 3-point scale how often a child evidences such behaviors as rapid regressions, fluctuating identity states, vivid imaginary friends, disavowed behaviors, sleep disruptions, and sexual precocity. The CDC has good reliability and validity (Peterson & Putnam, 1994; Putnam, Helmers, & Trickett, 1993); it correlates well with children's histories of family disruption and sexual abuse (Malinosky-Rummell & Hoier, 1991). The *Child's Perceptual Alteration Scale* (CPAS; Evers-Szostak & Sanders, 1992) was also developed during this time period. The CPAS assesses children's cognitive, behavioral, affective, and perceptual experiences on a continuum that ranges from pathologically restricted dissociative responses to normal ones. The CPAS correlates significantly with parental inconsistency or rejection (Mann & Sanders, 1994) and fantasy proneness (Rhue, Lynn, & Sandberg, 1995).

Several assessment tools were modeled after the *Dissociative Experiences Scale* (DES; Bernstein & Putnam, 1986), a measure of dissociation in adults. Stolbach (1997) developed the *Children's Dissociative Experience Scale* and *Traumatic Stress Inventory*. This innovative tool asks latency-age children to rate how alike or different they are to children with described dissociative traits. This measure has been used to identify dissociation in burn patients (Stolbach, Silvern, Williams, Reyes, & Kaersvang, 1997). The *Adolescent Dissociative Experiences Scale* (A-DES; Armstrong, Putnam, Carlson, Libero, & Smith, 1997; Smith & Carlson, 1996) measures dissociative amnesia, absorption and imaginative involvement, depersonalization and derealization, and passive influence. The A-DES has been shown to be a reliable and valid instrument for measuring dissociation in adolescents (Smith & Carlson, 1996). Briere's (1996) *Trauma Symptom Checklist for Children* (TSC-C) includes a dissociation subscale. The TSC-C correlated with a history of sexual abuse in adolescents (Friedrich, Jaworski, Huxsahl, & Bengston, 1997). Silberg (1998) identified indicators of dissociation in children that could be found with standard psychological testing. These indicators included images of multiplicity, malevolent religiosity, dissociative coping, depersonalized imagery, emotional confusion, extreme dichotomization, images of mutilation and torture, and magical transformation. A combination of these indicators and behaviors was able to discriminate 93% of the dissociative sample from a non-dissociative sample of psychiatric inpatient children.

The 1990s saw much research into the etiology of dissociative disorders and their presumed origins in traumatic events in childhood. Retrospective investigations demonstrated that adult dissociative symptoms were associated with childhood abuse, neglect, and other traumatic experiences (Chu & Dill, 1990; Coons, 1994; Waldinger, Swett, Frank, & Miller, 1994; Zlotnick et al., 1996). Prospective investigations found that attachment disorganization in infancy may mediate the relationship between early traumatic experiences and later psychopathology and dissociation. Longitudinal investigations demonstrated that disorganized and avoidant attachment in early childhood (along with age of onset, chronicity, and severity of abuse) predicted dissociative symptoms at age 19 (Carlson, 1998; Ogawa, Sroufe, Weinfeld, Carlson, & Egeland, 1997).

Four books on childhood dissociative disorders were published during the 1990s. Shirar's (1996) *Dissociative Children* described the in-depth treatment of dissociative children with play therapy and Gestalt therapy techniques. Volume 5 of *Child and Adolescent Psychiatric Clinics of North America* (1996) was devoted to the epidemiology, assessment, and treatment of dissociative disorders in children. Silberg (1996, 1998) published an edited volume, *The Dissociative Child: Diagnosis, Treatment and Management*. Finally, in 1997, Frank Putnam's *Dissociation in Children and Adolescents: A Developmental Approach* contributed an important theoretical advance by integrating the literature on childhood dissociative disorders with findings from developmental psychopathology.

5.1.3 2000s

Since the turn of the millennium, dissociative psychopathology has been increasingly accepted in journals that focus on maltreatment (e.g., Silberg, 2000; Haugaard, 2004: *Child Maltreatment*), textbooks on child psychopathology (e.g., Orvashel, Faust, & Hersen, 2001: *Handbook of Conceptualization and Treatment of Child Psychopathology*; Netherton, Holmes, & Walker, 1999: *Child and Adolescent Psychological Disorders*), and a book on childhood trauma and neurobiology (Stien & Kendall, 2004: *Psychological Trauma and the Developing Brain*). New diagnostic tools have continued to be developed. The *Multidimensional Inventory for Dissociation* (MID; Dell, 2006) has an adolescent version (A-MID) that has undergone preliminary testing in the United States (Ruths, Silberg, Dell, & Jenkins, 2002) and Belgium (Goffinet, 2005). The A-MID found that symptoms in dissociative adolescents closely mirror the pattern found in dissociative adults. Macfie, Cicchetti, and Toth (2001) used children's narrative story-stem completions on a storytelling task to investigate dissociation in preschoolers. Their findings suggest that the self becomes increasingly fragmented during the preschool period for some maltreated children. New trauma instruments for children, such as Briere's (2005) *Trauma Symptom Checklist for Young Children*, increasingly include dissociation scales. In addition, researchers have developed a posttraumatic stress disorder and dissociation scale (Sim et al., 2005) from a composite of items in the *Child Behavior Checklist* (Achenbach, 1991).

Well-established diagnostic measures, such as the A-DES and the CDC, are increasingly being integrated into research; they are generating new findings about perceptual, traumatic, and symptom-related factors associated with dissociation. Using the A-DES, Kisiel and Lyons (2001) found that dissociation may be a critical mediator of psychiatric symptoms and risk-taking behavior among sexually abused children. Using the CDC, Collin-Vézina and Hébert (2005) found a relationship between dissociation and sexual abuse history of school-age girls independent of posttraumatic stress symptoms. Bonanno, Noll, Putnam, O'Neill, & Trickett (2003) used the A-DES with children with documented abuse to examine their abuse disclosures in relation to dissociation and repressive coping. They found that dissociative experiences and repressive coping were inversely related and showed opposite patterns of adjustment. Repressors (i.e., those who show high autonomic arousal despite verbal denial of discomfort) were less likely to disclose their abuse, expressed greater negative and positive emotion, and were relatively better adjusted. Dissociators, on the other hand, were more likely to disclose their abuse, but expressed little emotion and had relatively poorer adjustment. Using the A-DES, Diseth (2006) found that medical trauma (i.e., a painful anal-dilation procedure during infancy) predicted dissociation in adolescents. Friedrich et al. (2001) successfully used the A-DES to diagnose dissociative pathology in adolescent sex offenders.

Both the A-DES and the CDC have been translated into Spanish; they are reliable and valid for identifying dissociation in Puerto Rican children with abuse histories (Martinez-Toboas et al., 2004; Reyes-Perez, Martinez-Toboas, & Ledesma-Amador, 2005). Similarly, the Turkish version of the A-DES has exhibited good reliability and validity in Turkish adolescents (Zoroğlu, Şar, Tüzün, Tutkun, & Savaş, 2002).

Heightened awareness of the implications of dissociation in children has led to a resurgence of interest in therapeutic approaches with dissociative children and adolescents. In 2000, a special issue of *Psychoanalytic Inquiry* was devoted exclusively to the treatment of an adolescent girl with DID. The issue provided perspectives from a variety of different theoretical and therapy frameworks (Bartholomew, 2000; Chefetz, 2000; Kluft, 2000; Lewin, 2000; Saakvitne, 2000). A special issue of *Psychotherapy* devoted to trauma included an article on treating dissociative symptoms in sexually abused children from a family perspective (Silberg, 2004a). Other scholarly articles have addressed the treatment of special populations. For instance, Johnson (2002) delineated a continuum of sexual behaviors in children who engage in problematic sexual behavior and described the treatment of dissociative children with sexual behavior problems. Stolbach (2005) described the treatment of a young burn patient with dissociative manifestations. Chapters on treatment of dissociative pathology were included in two psychopathology textbooks (Wallach & Dollinger, 1999: *Child and Adolescent Psychological Disorders*; Silberg, 2001a: *Handbook of Conceptualization and Treatment of Child Psychopathology*). Dissociation was addressed in the guidelines for the treatment of child abuse that was released by the National Crime Victims Research and Treatment Center (Saunders, Berliner, & Hanson, 2004). The International Society for the Study of Dissociation (ISSD, 2004) released updated guidelines for the assessment and treatment of dissociative symptoms on children.

Finally, reliable and validated measures are now providing information about the prevalence and correlates of dissociation in diverse populations of children.

5.2 DIAGNOSTIC CONSIDERATIONS IN CHILDREN AND ADOLESCENTS

Early recognition of dissociation can avert a trajectory of maladaptive mental processes and behavior that can continue throughout the life span (Silberg, 2001b). Unfortunately, few children receive the early treatment that they need. Children with dissociative disorders are frequently misdiagnosed because of their comorbid symptomatology: attention deficit and hyperactivity disorder, conversion and other somatoform disorders, conduct disorder, oppositional defiant disorder, schizophrenia, various forms of epilepsy, and affective disorders (Zoroğlu et al., 1996). Kluft (1985) described reasons for the nonrecognition of dissociative conditions by child clinicians. These reasons include lack of familiarity with dissociative phenomena, differences in the presentation of dissociation in children as compared to adults, the availability of more familiar diagnoses (e.g., ADHD, psychosis, seizure disorders), and the normative nature of fluctuating behaviors in children. In particular, the normative dissociative experiences of children can make it hard to differentiate between a pathological process and imaginative involvement in play (Haugaard, 2004). Finally, lacking a point of comparison, children and adolescents may not report dissociative symptoms; they may consider them to be normal.

Lack of recognition of dissociative disorders in children is enabled by several factors: few clinicians receive adequate training in the diagnosis of dissociative disorders; child-specific categories of dissociation do not exist in DSM-IV (American Psychiatric Association [APA], 1994); and childhood dissociative disorders are not adequately represented by adult criteria (Fagan & McMahon, 1985; Peterson, 1991; Putnam, 1997). In our opinion, the lack of consensus on diagnostic criteria is the greatest barrier to identifying dissociative pathology in children and adolescents.

The need for accurate diagnostic descriptors of chronically traumatized children has prompted clinicians, organized through the National Traumatic Stress Network, to propose that a category of Developmental Trauma Disorder (DTD) be added to the DSM. DTD includes dissociative symptoms, and the attachment difficulties and problems with impulse control, cognition, attention, and self-concept that are typical of chronically traumatized children (Putnam, 2005).

Dell (2009) has advocated revising the diagnostic criteria for DID in a way that is more descriptive and data-driven than the current criteria. Although these proposed criteria are not aimed at a child population, they could facilitate identifying dissociative adolescents, whose symptom picture tends to parallel that of adults (Ruths et al., 2002).

In summary, diagnostic categories that efficiently describe the symptom profile of dissociative children would greatly assist in their early identification. Until such time, however, clinicians must rely on the symptom profiles of dissociative children and adolescents that appear in the literature.

5.3 DISSOCIATIVE SYMPTOMATOLOGY

Research shows that adult-like presentations of dissociation are uncommon in young children. In early childhood, dissociated aspects of the self do not tend to have a well-elaborated sense of autonomy. Instead, feelings, thoughts, and impulses that the child experiences as foreign may be projected onto transitional objects such as dolls or fantasy playmates. Fagan & McMahon (1984) coined the term *incipient MPD* to describe their observation that the presumed precursors to fully fledged DID initially appear in less crystallized forms during childhood.

Young children from traumatic backgrounds may present with a variety of dissociative symptoms, such as trance-like states, perplexing forgetfulness, and behavioral and emotional fluctuations. Dissociative-state phenomena may be observed in young children, such as hearing internal voices, referring to self in the third person, and involvement with imaginary playmates that seem real to the child (Waters, 2005a). Young children may use their own body parts as transitional objects, having imaginary self-states, called "handy" or "footy," that appear to the child to be autonomous. Similarly, stuffed animals, dolls, or other toys may have a perceived reality far beyond the fantasy involvement of normal preschool children. The dissociative child may talk to these toys, hear their answers, consult them for advice, insist that the toy be given a place at the dinner table, and resist when the fantasy element is suggested to them. These dissociation-specific symptoms are differentiated from normal fantasy play because they are usually accompanied by intense posttraumatic symptomatology (e.g., fearfulness, night terrors, intrusive traumatic thoughts, etc.). Imaginary friends may be in internal warfare, with splits between pretend playmates who advocate cooperation and those that advocate destructiveness and rage (Frost, Silberg, & McIntee, 1996). The child may hear internal voices, sometimes of abusive caregivers, who internally criticize and command the child. Some children loudly talk to themselves in different voices and appear impervious to interruption, or angered by disruption (Waters, 2005a). Terr (1988) described trance-like states in traumatized children during which they rigidly and compulsively reenact traumatic scenarios.

In young children, fluctuating behavior may include unpredictable eruptions into tantrums of surprising intensity that appear out of context to what is going on around them. Although regressive behavior is frequently present, it may be hard to detect unless the child is assessed over time. An attuned caregiver or clinician will often report episodes in which the child's use of language is suddenly developmentally less sophisticated, or in which verbal children suddenly speak in monosyllabic "baby talk." Premeditated self-destructive and self-injurious masturbatory behavior may also be observed (Albini & Pease, 1989; Fagan & McMahon, 1984; Haugaard, 2004; Riley & Mead, 1988; Waters, 2005a).

Amnesia may be present but may be viewed by the child's caregivers as lying or forgetfulness. Amnesia is often difficult to distinguish from denial; however, some dissociative children deny knowledge of clearly witnessed behavior when there is little incentive for denial. In some cases the denials involve personal accomplishments that are praiseworthy (Hornstein, 1998). The rigid amnestic barriers of dissociative adolescents or adults generally do not occur in young children; and gentle focusing of attention can usually promote access to previously dissociated memory. While clear-cut childhood DID is uncommon, it does occur. In a well-documented case of DID (Riley & Mead, 1988), a 3-year-old presented with two personalities that represented adaptive reactions to two discrete environments. One was an adaptation to a profoundly abusive birth home, and the other was an adaptation to the home of a nonabusive guardian.

The frequency of DID-like symptoms increases with age (Putnam, Hornstein, & Peterson, 1996). During school age, children may present with more differentiated dissociated identities; however, these identities may continue to be projected onto stuffed animals or toys (McElroy, 1992). Identity fluctuations may become more discernible as children age because the regressive states become more developmentally aberrant. Amnestic symptoms become more pronounced and easier to discern; children may deny observed behavior and forget autobiographical information. Trance-like behavior may become more intense and may span the range from vacant staring and blanking-out to profound states of dissociative disconnection, where children seem unresponsive to their external surroundings (Perry, Pollard, Blakely, Baker, & Vigilante, 1995). The literature documents a 10-year-old presenting with an apparently dissociative "coma" who responded only after two years of intensive trauma-oriented psychotherapy and hypnotic intervention (Cagiada, Camaido, & Pennan, 1997).

In adolescence, symptom patterns become more similar to those of adults (Ruths et al., 2002). Identity consolidation is a developmental task of adolescence and it appears that dissociative identities may consolidate as well (Silberg, 2001b). Dissociative states tend to become more rigid, displaying gender symptoms and a gender prevalence that is more comparable to that of adults (Putnam et al., 1996). The normal developmental tasks of adolescence make it a challenging time for treatment (Kluft, 2000). These challenges include the frequency of self-destructive acting out and unstable relationships, often in shifting environments (e.g., residential placements, foster homes, etc.). Even when they live in a stable home, their shifting patterns of relatedness (e.g., alternating between regression and mistrust) often produce chaos anyway. For instance, Ruths et al. (2002) described 19 severely dissociative adolescents (11 DID and 8 DDNOS) whose symptom profiles closely mirrored those of severely dissociative adults. Most of these teenagers had been referred for evaluation due to assaultive behavior or recent amnesia. They had many comorbid symptoms and stormy courses of treatment, including hospitalizations, runaway attempts, and involvements with the law.

Comorbid, nondissociative symptoms also increase during adolescence and may constitute the presenting complaint. Typical comorbid disorders and symptoms include conduct problems, sexual behavior problems, mood disorders, eating disorders, self-mutilation, substance abuse, and suicidal ideation/attempts (Silberg,

Stipic, & Taghizadeh, 1997). The associated symptoms are frequently so intense that it is easy to miss the dissociative phenomena. Dissociative adolescents are also at risk for being misdiagnosed as psychotic; auditory hallucinations may have an especially strong relation with dissociative processes (Altman, Collins, & Mundy, 1997).

The A-DES has improved our ability to recognize adolescent dissociation. Moreover, it has documented a high prevalence of dissociative symptoms across a wide range of clinical populations. In a study of 198 consecutively admitted inpatients, Carrion and Steiner (2000) found that 28% of 64 delinquent adolescents in juvenile probation met criteria for a dissociative disorder. Dissociative symptoms have also been identified in adolescent psychiatric inpatients (Brunner, Parzer, Schuld, & Resch, 2000), and are associated with overall symptomatology in nonclinical and clinical groups of adolescent girls (Farrington, Niederman, Sutton, Chopping, & Lask, 2002). Despite these striking associations between dissociation and psychiatric problems in adolescence, descriptive studies of adolescents in treatment for dissociation remain rare. This hole in the literature likely indicates nonrecognition of dissociation and discomfort in the general psychiatric community with diagnosing dissociation in adolescents who qualify for a variety of more commonly described comorbid disorders.

Recent literature on depersonalization disorder, fugue states, and dissociative amnesia in children and adolescents is sparse. There is, however, an older literature that describes dissociative states in children following stressful events; for example, fugue states (Keller & Shaywitz, 1986; Venn, 1984), depersonalization (Dollinger, 1983; McKellar, 1978), and amnesia (Coons, 1996). Waters (2005b) suggested that undiagnosed DID accounted for autobiographical amnesia in a teenage girl. Adolescents may experience depersonalization more often than the current literature suggests. As noted above, Carrion and Steiner (2000) found that 28% of delinquents in juvenile probation met criteria for a dissociative disorder. These teens endorsed all kinds of dissociative symptoms, but they most frequently endorsed depersonalization.

In summary, dissociation in childhood and adolescence may best be viewed as a malleable developmental phenomenon that may result in a wide range of severe symptoms (ISSD, 2004). Careful assessment is needed in order to prevent dissociative children and adolescents from progressing along a developmental trajectory that leads, with age, to much higher levels of morbidity and resistance to treatment.

5.4 TREATMENT CONSIDERATIONS

The ISSD (2004) *Guidelines for the Evaluation and Treatment of Dissociative Symptoms in Children and Adolescents* constitutes a major advance in the therapeutic management of dissociative disorders in children. Written by the ISSD Child and Adolescent Task Force, the *Guidelines* are available on the ISSD Website (www.issd.org). These guidelines reflect the consensus of the field regarding the treatment of children and adolescents with dissociative symptoms and disorders.

The *Guidelines* delineate seven therapeutic goals for working with dissociative children (see Table 5.1) and they recommend a careful psychoeducational approach. Foremost, the *Guidelines* emphasize safety; dissociative youngsters cannot be successfully treated unless they are in a safe environment that is free of all forms of abuse and violence. In cases of unstable families, the therapy may have more limited goals (e.g., crisis intervention, promoting stability). Clinicians are cautioned to avoid reinforcing dissociative splits in young children. Clinicians are encouraged to take a gentle yet firm approach, which helps young people to take responsibility for their behavior even though the behavior may seem to be out of their control. At the same time, the clinician should continuously emphasize unity and wholeness of the self.

TABLE 5.1
Therapeutic Goals When Working with Dissociative Children and Adolescents

1. Help the child achieve a sense of cohesiveness about his affects, cognitions, and associated behavior.
2. Enhance motivation for growth and future success.
3. Promote self-acceptance of behavior and self-knowledge about feelings viewed as unacceptable.
4. Help the child resolve conflicting feelings, wishes, loyalties, identifications, or contrasting expectations.
5. Desensitize traumatic memories, and correct learned attitudes towards life resulting from traumatic events.
6. Promote autonomy and encourage the child to independently regulate and express affects and to self-regulate state changes.
7. Promote healthy attachments and relationships through direct expression of feelings.

Source: From the Guidelines for the evaluation and treatment of dissociative symptoms in children and adolescents by the International Society for the Study of Dissociation, 2004, *Journal of Trauma and Dissociation, 5,* pp. 119–150. Copyright 2004 by The Haworth Press. Adapted with permission.

A major goal of treatment involves helping the child learn to regulate affect and to improve self-soothing skills. The clinician should help these young people acknowledge how dissociation has helped them deal with overwhelming trauma, while also recognizing that its usefulness has passed. Dissociative avoidance that occurs during the therapy should be become a focus of treatment so that the situations or interactions that precede these moments can be identified and their traumatic associations desensitized (Allers, White, & Mullis, 1997; Haugaard, 2004; Wallach & Dollinger, 1999). Children can also be taught to practice using focused attention to interrupt dissociation (Johnson, 2002).

The relational impairments of dissociative children make the reciprocal relationship with a trustworthy adult a key component in the healing process. The therapist can help the child work through feelings about issues of safety and betrayal to help establish trust. Cognitive behavioral techniques can be used to desensitize the child to traumatic memories and to correct dysfunctional belief systems resulting from traumatic events. Learning to communicate directly about frustrations, anger, and fear can help serve as a substitute for dissociative coping. The therapist can help break down dissociative barriers by modeling acceptance of all of the child's contrasting feelings. Therapists should also remind the child of these feelings when they are not immediately accessible. Throughout this process, the therapist should work to encourage in the child a sense of efficacy and mastery (ISSD, 2004).

A number of adjunctive therapeutic techniques may prove helpful. Gestalt-like techniques and play therapy can help the child to dramatize conflicting emotions and dissociated feeling states (Friedrich, 1991; Gil, 1991; Shirar, 1996; Waters & Silberg, 1998). Art therapy (Sobol & Schneider, 1998) and guided imagery (Wieland, 1997) may be useful for this purpose as well. Hypnotic techniques may be useful when dealing with traumatic flashbacks (Wieland, 1998) or to guide the child toward mastery experiences (Friedrich, 1991; Williams & Velazquez, 1996).

Family work is extremely important because patterns in the family often unwittingly reinforce dissociative coping (Silberg, 2004a). Enhancing parent-child attachment and communication is particularly important, especially in light of research showing that children with disorganized or avoidant attachment styles might be particularly at risk for developing dissociative symptomatology (e.g., Ogawa et al., 1997). The ISSD (2004) *Guidelines* advocate family interventions that enhance reciprocity in communication, encourage direct expression of feeling, and avoid the reinforcement of regressive coping. Parental education is needed to help caregivers gain tolerance for the expression of the child's feelings and to help them reframe the child's problematic behavior. Caregivers should be helped to see dissociation as a form of communication and as a coping tool that helped the child to survive. The therapist also seeks to model an interactive style with the child and caregiver that promotes responsibility. For instance, clinicians should debunk any tendency for caregivers to interact with the child's dissociative states as if they are literally separate from the child and out of his or her control (ISSD, 2004).

Although there are no controlled studies on the use of medications with dissociative children, some clinicians have found medications to be a helpful adjunct to psychotherapy. Pharmacological treatment tends to focus on managing symptoms such as anxiety, inattention, depression, insomnia, or behavioral dyscontrol (Nemzer, 1998; Putnam, 1991; Putnam, 1997; Silberg et al., 1997). When medications are used, communication and teamwork between the therapist and the prescribing physician is essential (ISSD, 2004).

Sometimes more restrictive levels of care become necessary when the behavior of the child or adolescent is dangerous, self-injurious, or destructive. Unfortunately, there is a dearth of appropriate inpatient services available for these children. Of those that are available, time and reimbursement constraints promote reliance on medications to control symptoms (as opposed to addressing the underlying traumatogenic roots of the child's behavioral problems). Even long-term inpatient stays are not without their problems. Extended stays in residential or hospital settings make it difficult to address the child's ongoing attachment dilemmas with their caregivers (ISSD, 2004).

In summary, a variety of therapy techniques may be efficacious. The current literature suggests that dissociative children and adolescents respond well to appropriate care. Case reports (e.g., Cagiada et al., 1997; Kluft, 1985; Şar et al., 2002; Silberg, 2004a) and a follow-up case series (e.g., Silberg, 2004b) have documented positive treatment outcomes. In one study, positive treatment outcomes were correlated with parental involvement and the length of time in treatment (Waters & Silberg, 1998).

5.5 THEORETICAL CONSIDERATIONS

We have yet to fully understand how traumatic events contribute to dissociative processes. Research suggests that the effects of childhood trauma vary due to a complex interaction between abuse-related characteristics, individual factors, and interactions with others (Barker-Collo & Read, 2003). A comprehensive theory of dissociation is needed to integrate these domains. Research findings are contradictory regarding which traumatic events best predict dissociation. Part of this problem may be the difference between instruments. The CDC and A-DES may tap different aspects of dissociation; research with sexually abused children and adolescents raises the question of whether these two instruments measure the same construct. Kisiel and Lyons (2001) reported that scores on the A-DES and CDC were not strongly correlated with each other ($r = 0.28$) in a group of sexually abused children and adolescents. Whereas the CDC correlated with both physical abuse and sexual abuse, the A-DES only correlated with sexual abuse. However, contradictory findings emerge in a study by Brunner et al. (2000), which found that the A-DES correlated with all forms of childhood maltreatment in a study of consecutively admitted psychiatric adolescent inpatients, but correlated most strongly with emotional neglect.

We need to understand the cognitive, attentional, and affective processes that underlie dissociative states. Silberg (2001a) has speculated that children at risk for dissociative symptomatology may have a unique composite of traits and abilities, including symbolic skills, fantasy proneness, empathic perceptiveness, and social traits, such as social compliance or high attachment needs, which may be related to the capacity for trance induction.

A particular focus of interest is the child's recognition of, and reaction to, another's affective state. Based on her work with maltreated sibling groups in which only one of the children is dissociative, Silberg has proposed that dissociation is more likely to occur in the child who is particularly sensitive and attuned to conflicting messages from alternately nurturing and abusive caregivers. Such sensitive children may adapt to conflicting messages via dissociative disavowal and disconnection, perhaps facilitated by fantasy and trance-induction skills that allow the child to escape. This hypothesis, however, contrasts markedly with the views of Fonagy and Target (1997) and Carlson et al. (this volume) who note that maltreated children have social learning deficits. They hypothesize that dissociation is driven by the fact that some traumatized children have an impaired ability to mentally extrapolate the minds of others.

Research suggests that both viewpoints may be valid. Pollak, Cicchetti, Hornung, and Reed (2000) examined the emotion-recognition abilities of preschool children. When asked to match facial expressions to emotional situations, neglected preschool children had more difficulty discriminating facial expressions than did physically abused and control preschool children. Physically abused and nonmaltreated school-aged children were equally accurate in identifying facial displays of emotions—with one important exception: anger (Pollak & Sinha, 2002). Physically abused children overidentified anger, whereas normal children underidentified anger. These studies suggest that physical abuse exaggerates one's immediate perception of another's anger. On the other hand, Pine et al. (2005), using a visual-probe task, found that abused children were more likely to shift their attention away from threatening faces, suggesting that immediate perception may be accurate, but compromised by a subsequent attentional shift, which was itself associated with severity of physical abuse and diagnosis of PTSD. It is not yet clear whether such attentional bias correlates with dissociation, but preliminary research on dissociation in abused preschoolers suggests that high dissociators may use divided attention to keep perceived threat out of awareness (Becker-Blease, Freyd, & Pears, 2004).

Because these findings are open to different interpretations, we need research that directly addresses how dissociative children process emotion. Investigation of the attentional and emotional processing skills of diagnosed dissociative children could help resolve some of these complex theoretical questions about the interaction of individual differences, maltreatment histories, and information-processing skills and deficits.

Attachment theorists have advanced our understanding of childhood dissociation. Several scholars have explored the relationship between early attachment patterns and dissociative responding (Barach, 1991; Carlson et al., 2009; Liotti, 1999, 2009; Lyons-Ruth et al., 1999). Theorists have noted some resemblances between infant behavior in the Strange Situation and adult dissociative behavior (e.g., Main & Morgan, 1996). Longitudinal research indicates that disorganized attachment in infancy is an important predictor of dissociative symptoms in late adolescence (Lyons-Ruth, 2003). To date, however, the actual attachment patterns of pathologically dissociative children have yet to be described. Thus, despite the evocative nature of the commonalities between disorganized attachment and dissociative states, theory cannot advance until research actually documents that these attachment patterns distinguish pathologically dissociative children from maltreated children who are not dissociative.

Attachment and developmental perspectives have informed several new theories that seek to explain why children may dissociate in response to traumatic events. Freyd (1996) offers Betrayal Trauma Theory (BTT) to explain the development of dissociative amnesia after traumatic events. Drawing from the child abuse literature, evolutionary psychology, and attachment theorists, Freyd proposes that abused children maintain attachment to caregivers who have betrayed them by forgetting what happened (Freyd, 1999). Research has confirmed several of the predictions of BBT. For instance, the presence of betrayal trauma before the age of 18 predicts pathological dissociation after age 18 (DePrince, 2005). Similarly, exposure to traumas with high betrayal positively and significantly correlates with increased dissociative symptoms (Freyd, Klest, & Allard, 2005).

Putnam's (1997) *Discrete Behavioral States* (DBS) model has advanced our theoretical understanding of dissociative processes. The DBS model proposes that dissociative states derive from the basic states of infants (e.g., crying, alert, fussy, etc.). According to Putnam, during the process of maturation, new discrete behavioral states are added, earlier behavioral states are refined or replaced, and new connections and behavioral pathways between states are developed. Appropriate nurturing facilitates behavioral flexibility and the capacity to navigate state changes with increasing autonomy. Conversely, abusive parenting can prompt the development of discrete traumatic states and disrupt the integration of pathways to these traumatic states, thereby compromising the overall integration of the child's states. Instead of learning to modulate appropriate changes of state with a modicum of voluntary control, mistreated children may, instead, abruptly vary their behavioral states in relation to the requirements of the abusive parent. Putnam views the eventual integration of self as a developmental phenomenon that he regards as metacognitive, in that it involves the generalization of state-specific cognitions (knowledge, memories, feelings) from one's discrete states of mind to a general state of mind, the "authorial I." This authorial self, which allows the growing child to begin to view himself as consistent across changes of state and context (Putnam, 1997, p. 164), emerges during the preschool years together with other metacognitive abilities, such as source monitoring, visual perspective taking, and the awareness of others' minds.

In our view, however, Putnam's emphasis on such putatively metacognitive abilities as the key developmental achievement that integrates state changes is overstated. Research on the neurobiology of emotions (e.g., Damasio, 1999; LeDoux, 1996; Siegel, 1999) indicates that integrative neurophysiological functioning is often unconscious and not a process that would typically be labeled as cognitive, *per se*. First of all, research shows that conscious awareness often follows, rather than precedes, action. Cognitive events, such as attempts to explain or make sense of our own actions, are generally after the fact, and thus user illusions (Norretranders, 1998) that should not be mistaken for real explanations of our behavior (Gazzaniga, 1998). As these scholars point out, conscious thoughts about ourselves, or metacognitive processes involving reflection and awareness, can be a source of insight that helps us to correct our actions, but should not be confused with the cause of consistent behavior. In fact, enhancing metacognitive processes is a common therapeutic strategy to promote awareness in dissociative individuals.

We believe that dissociative children's deficits in integrative functioning are rooted in complex neurophysiological processes, including conditioned emotional reactions that precede conscious awareness and persist despite metacognitive achievements. In fact, one could argue that a child's theory of self involving multiple identities is a very sophisticated metacognitive achievement that provides a coherent formulation to account for self-observed discrepancies in behavior across states. Clinical work with dissociative children demonstrates that, unlike their adult counterparts with DID, they often have coconsciousness and are able to self-observe the changes in behavior that they attribute to imaginary friends or other selves, a seemingly rather sophisticated metacognitive achievement. Conditioned changes in affective responses and associated state-dependent behaviors in dissociative children in response to caregiver cues are clearly powerful enough to sustain dissociative changes even after sophisticated metacognitive skills develop. Certainly adults with DID show superior metacognitive abilities, and are capable of highly abstract and sophisticated self-schemas once they become open enough to describe the intricacies of their internal world and the dissociative barriers begin to erode. Experience with early forms of dissociative disorders in children suggest that DID adults who do not have coconsciousness and demonstrate primitive and segregated self states may have evolved into this extreme form of complex pathology over time through a complex interplay of interpersonal, emotional, and cognitive factors. It is possible that metacognitive development may be independent of the pathological processes that lead children to severe dissociative symptomatology. Careful studies of well-defined metacognitive, perceptual and emotional processing skills with populations of dissociative and nondissociative maltreated children may help answer some of these complex theoretical questions.

The emotional valences that we unconsciously ascribe to people and objects can organize action patterns in preconscious ways (LeDoux, 1996). There can be little doubt that such preconscious emotional processing plays an important role in shaping the attachment behavior of dissociative children. A child may react with fear and avoidance when confronted with subtle cues that a parent is about to become abusive, but respond more openly to the same parent when subtle cues indicate that the parent is entering a more receptive state. These patterns of relating to caregivers are rehearsed and overlearned in the chaotic family environment. Such overlearned patterns of behavior may evolve into automatic disconnections between thought and action and the fluctuating behavior observed in dissociative children. In their studies of interpersonal neurobiology, Siegel (1999) and Schore (1991) show that early interpersonal relationships play an important role in organizing the development of brain structures that coordinate social and emotional information. Their insights also imply that metacognitive processes are only one part of the complex puzzle of how healthy minds organize and integrate experiences in flexible ways.

Brain imaging and neuroendocrine studies are contributing important information about maltreated children. Magnetic resonance imaging (MRI) has shown that maltreated children and adolescents with PTSD have significantly smaller intracranial and cerebral volumes than matched controls with no history of maltreatment (De Bellis et al., 1999). Brain volume inversely correlated with age of onset of abuse, duration of abuse, and severity of dissociative and PTSD symptoms. Children with histories of severe maltreatment have deficits in left cortical differentiation (Ito, Teicher, Glod, & Ackerman, 1998). Studies of both adults and children suggest that trauma produces permanent neurochemical, functional, and structural abnormalities in brain areas associated with the integrative process of cognition and memory (Bremner, 2005; Diseth, 2005). Patients with DID have smaller hippocampal and amygdalar volumes than do healthy subjects (Vermetten, Schmahl, Lindner, Loewenstein, & Bremner, 2006).

Neurobiological research has informed Nijenhuis's et al. (2002) theory of structural dissociation. This theory predicts that dissociative fragmentation develops along predictable evolutionary lines. Specifically, it predicts that dissociative children would first show splits in the emotional area, and experience further splits along the dimension of the apparently normal personality (ANP) as the child develops. The theory of structural dissociation is promising; however, its advancement depends on testing children with dissociative pathology. For example, dissociative children from different developmental periods could be studied to determine whether structural splits occur along lines predicted by the model.

In summary, the comprehensive model that we seek must not only explain the processes by which maltreated children become pathologically dissociative; it also must identify the individual, environmental, and interpersonal factors that drive these processes. Our current understanding suggests that dissociative symptoms can be viewed as the effects of failed processing of emotional information, from both oneself and others, consequent to the overwhelming nature of traumatic events that occur in a chaotic and deficient caregiving environment. These integrative failures generate compartmentalized traumatic memories and unprocessed traumatic emotions, both of which may manifest as fluctuations in consciousness and behavior. We have become increasingly familiar with the behavioral aspects of dissociation in children, but we have yet to fully explore the interpersonal, emotional, and cognitive processes that underlie the development of dissociative processes. Investigations of clinical populations of dissociative children may provide the next big advances in the theory of dissociation. Integrating new neurobiological findings with our psychological models will no doubt enrich our understanding, recognition, and treatment of dissociative patients across the entire developmental continuum.

REFERENCES

Achenbach, T. M. (1991). *Manual for the Child Behavior Checklist*. Burlington: University of Vermont Department of Psychiatry.

Albini, T. K., & Pease, T. E. (1989). Normal and pathological dissociations of early childhood. *Dissociation, 2*, 144–150.

Allers, C. T., White, J. F., & Mullis, F. (1997). The treatment of dissociation in an HIV-infected sexually abused adolescent male. *Psychotherapy, 34*, 201–206.

Altman, H., Collins, M., & Mundy, P. (1997). Subclinical hallucinations and delusions in nonpsychotic adolescents. *Journal of Child Psychology & Psychiatry, 38*, 413–420.

American Psychiatric Association (1994). *DSM-IV – Diagnostic and statistical manual of mental disorders* (4th ed.). Washington, DC: Author.

Armstrong, J. G., Putnam, F. W., Carlson, E. B., Libero, D. Z., & Smith, S. R. (1997). Development and validation of a measure of adolescent dissociation: The Adolescent Dissociative Experiences Scale (A-DES). *Journal of Nervous & Mental Disease, 185*, 491–497.

Barach, P. M. (1991). Multiple Personality Disorder as an attachment disorder. *Dissociation, 4*, 117–123.

Barker-Collo, S., & Read, J. (2003). Models of response to childhood sexual abuse: Their implications for treatment. *Trauma, Violence & Abuse, 4*, 95–111.

Bartholomew, K. (2000). Clinical protocol. *Psychoanalytic Inquiry, 20*, 227–248.

Becker-Blease, K. A., Freyd, J. J, & Pears, K. C. (2004). Preschoolers' memory for threatening information depends on trauma history and attentional context: Implications for the development of dissociation. *Journal of Trauma & Dissociation, 5*(1), 113–131.

Bernstein, E. M., & Putnam, F. W. (1986). Development, reliability, and validity of a dissociation scale. *Journal of Nervous & Mental Disease, 174,* 727–735.

Bonanno, G. A., Noll, J. G., Putnam, F. W., O'Neill, M., & Trickett, P. K. (2003). Predicting the willingness to disclose childhood sexual abuse from measures of repressive coping and dissociative tendencies. *Child Maltreatment, 8,* 302–318.

Bowman, E. S., Blix, S. F., & Coons, P. M. (1985). Multiple personality in adolescence: Relationship to incestual experience. *Journal of the American Academy of Child & Adolescent Psychiatry, 24,* 109–114.

Braun, B. G. (1985). The transgenerational incidence of dissociation and multiple personality disorder In R. P. Kluft (Ed.), *Childhood antecedents of Multiple Personality Disorder* (pp. 127–150). Washington, DC: American Psychiatric Press.

Bremner, J. D. (2005). Effects of traumatic stress on brain structure and function: Relevance to early responses to trauma. *Journal of Trauma & Dissociation, 6*(2), 51–68.

Briere, J. (1996). *The Trauma Symptom Checklist for Children.* Odessa, FL: Psychological Assessment Resources.

Briere, J. (2005). *The Trauma Symptom Checklist for Young Children.* Odessa, FL: Psychological Assessment Resources.

Brunner, R., Parzer, P., Schuld, V., & Resch, F. (2000). Dissociative symptomatology and traumatogenic factors in adolescent psychiatric patients. *Journal of Nervous & Mental Disease, 188,* 71–77.

Cagiada, S., Camaido, L., & Pennan, A. (1997). Successful integrated hypnotic and psychopharmacological treatment of a war-related post-traumatic psychological and somatoform dissociative disorder of two years duration (psychogenic coma). *Dissociation, 10,* 182–189.

Carlson, E. A. (1998). A prospective longitudinal study of attachment disorganization/disorientation. *Child Development, 69,* 1107–1128.

Carrion, V. G., & Steiner, H. (2000). Trauma and dissociation in delinquent adolescents. *Journal of the American Academy of Child & Adolescent Psychiatry, 39,* 353–359.

Chefetz, R. A. (2000). Disorder in the therapist's view of the self: Working with the person with dissociative identity disorder. *Psychoanalytic Inquiry, 20,* 305–329.

Chu, J. A., & Dill, D. L. (1990). Dissociative symptoms in relation to childhood physical and sexual abuse. *American Journal of Psychiatry, 147,* 887–892.

Collin-Vezina, D., & Herbert, M. (2005). Comparing Dissociation and PTSD in sexually abused school-aged girls. *Journal of Nervous & Mental Disease,* 93, 47–52.

Coons, P. M. (1985). Children of parents with multiple personality disorder. In R. P. Kluft (Ed.), *Childhood antecedents of Multiple Personality Disorder* (pp. 151–165). Washington, DC: American Psychiatric Press.

Coons, P. M. (1994). Confirmation of childhood abuse in child and adolescent cases of multiple personality disorder and dissociative disorder not otherwise specified. *Journal of Nervous & Mental Disease, 182,* 461–464.

Coons, P. M. (1996). Clinical phenomenology of 25 children and adolescents with dissociative disorders. *Child and Adolescent Psychiatric Clinics of North America, 5,* 361–374.

Damasio, A. R. (1999). *The feeling of what happens: Body and emotion in the making of consciousness.* New York: Harcourt.

De Bellis, M. D., Keshavan, M. S., Clark, D. B., Casey, B. J., Giedd, J. N., Boring, A. M., Frustaci, K., & Ryan, N. D. (1999). A. E. Bennett Research Award. Developmental traumatology. Part II: Brain development. *Biological Psychiatry, 45,* 1271–1284.

Dell, P. F. (2006). The Multidimensional Inventory of Dissociation (MID): A comprehensive measure of pathological dissociation. *Journal of Trauma & Dissociation, 7*(2), 77–106.

Dell, P. F. (2009). The long struggle to diagnose Multiple Personality Disorder (MPD) I. MPD. In P. F. Dell & J. A. O'Neil (Eds.), *Dissociation and the dissociative disorders: DSM-V and beyond* (pp. 383–402). New York: Routledge.

Dell, P. F., & Eisenhower, J. W. (1990). Adolescent Multiple Personality Disorder: A preliminary study of eleven cases. *Journal of the American Academy of Child & Adolescent Psychiatry, 29,* 359–366.

DePrince, A. P. (2005). Social cognition and revictimization risk. *Journal of Trauma and Dissociation, 6*(1), 125–141.

Diseth, T. H. (2005). Dissociation in children and adolescents as reaction to trauma–An overview of conceptual issues and neurobiological factors. *Nordic Journal of Psychiatry, 59,* 79–91.

Diseth, T. (2006). Dissociation following traumatic medical procedures in childhood: A longitudinal Follow-up. *Development and Psychopathology, 18,* 233–251.

Dollinger, S. J. (1983). A case report of dissociative neurosis (depersonalization disorder) in an adolescent treated with family therapy and behavior modification. *Journal of Consulting & Clinical Psychology, 51,* 479–484.

Evers-Szostak, M., & Sanders, S. (1992). The Children's Perceptual Alteration Scale (CAPS): A measure of children's dissociation. *Dissociation, 5,* 91–97.

Fagan, J., & McMahon, P. P. (1984). Incipient multiple personality in children. *Journal of Nervous & Mental Disease, 172,* 26–36.

Farrington, A., Waller, G., Neiderman, M., Sutton, V., Chopping, J., & Lask, B. (2002). Dissociation in adolescent girls with anorexia: Relationship to comorbid psychopathology. *Journal of Nervous & Mental Disease, 190,* 746–751.

Fonagy, P., & Target (1997). Attachment and reflective function: Their role in self-organization. *Development and Psychopathology, 9,* 679–700.

Freyd, J. J. (1996). *Betrayal trauma: The logic of forgetting childhood abuse.* Cambridge, MA: Harvard University Press.

Freyd, J. J. (1999). Blind to betrayal: New perspectives on memory for trauma. *Harvard Mental Health Letter, 15*(12), 4–6.

Freyd, J. J., Klest, B., & Allard, C. B. (2005). Betrayal trauma: Relationship to physical health, psychological distress, and a written disclosure intervention. *Journal of Trauma & Dissociation, 6*(3), 83–104.

Friedrich, W. (1991). Hypnotherapy with traumatized children. *The International Journal of Clinical & Experimental Hypnosis, 39*, 67–81.

Friedrich, W. N., Gerber, P. N., Koplin, B., Davis, M., Giese, J., Mykelbust, C., & Franckowiak, D. (2001). Multimodal assessment of dissociation in adolescents: Inpatients and juvenile sex offenders. *Sexual Abuse, 13*, 167–177.

Friedrich, W. N., Jaworski, T. M., Huxsahl, J. E., & Bengston, B. S. (1997). Dissociative and sexual behaviors in children and adolescents with sexual abuse and psychiatric histories, *Journal of Interpersonal Violence, 12*(2), 155–171.

Frost, J., Silberg, J. L., & McIntee, J. (1996, November). *Imaginary friends in normal and traumatized children.* Paper presented at the 13th meeting of the International Society for the Study of Dissociation, San Francisco, CA.

Gazzaniga, M. S. (1998). *The mind's past.* Los Angeles, CA: University of California Press.

Gil, E. (1991). *The healing power of play*. New York: Guilford Press.

Goffinet, S. (2005, November). *The prevalence of dissociative disorders in adolescent inpatients.* Paper presented at 22nd meeting of the International Society for the Study of Dissociation, Toronto, Canada.

Haugaard, J. J. (2004). Recognizing and treating uncommon behavioral and emotional disorders in children and adolescent who have been severely maltreated: Dissociative disorders. *Child Maltreatment, 9*, 2,146–153.

Hornstein, N. L. (1998). Complexities of psychiatric differential diagnosis in children with dissociative symptoms and disorders. In J. Silberg (Ed.), *The dissociative child: Diagnosis, treatment and management* (2nd ed.) (pp. 27–45). Lutherville, MD: The Sidran Press.

Hornstein, N. L., & Putnam, F. W. (1992). Clinical phenomenology of child and adolescent dissociative disorders. *Journal of the American Academy of Child & Adolescent Psychiatry, 31*, 1077–1085.

Hornstein, N. L., & Tyson, S. (1991). Inpatient treatment of children with multiple personality/dissociation and their families. *Psychiatric Clinics of North America, 4*, 631–648.

International Society for the Study of Dissociation. (2004). Guidelines for the evaluation and treatment of dissociative symptoms in children and adolescents. *Journal of Trauma and Dissociation, 5*(3), 119–150. (also available for download at http://www.issd.org/indexpage/ChildGuidelinesFinal.pdf)

Ito, Y., Teicher, M. H., Glod, C. A., & Ackerman, E. (1998). Preliminary evidence for aberrant cortical development in abused children: A quantitative EEG study. *Journal of Neuropsychiatry & Clinical Neurosciences, 10*, 298–307.

Jacobsen, T. (1995). Case study: Is selective mutism a manifestation of dissociative identity disorder? *Journal of American Academy of Child & Adolescent Psychiatry, 31*, 1077–1085.

James, B. (1989). *Treating traumatized children.* New York: Free Press/Simon & Schuster.

James, B. (1994). *Handbook for treatment of attachment-trauma problems in children.* New York: Free Press/Simon & Schuster.

Johnson, T. C. (2002). Some considerations about sexual abuse and children with sexual behavior problems. *Journal of Trauma and Dissociation, 3*(4), 83–105.

Jones, D. P. (1986). Individual psychotherapy for the sexually abused child. *Child Abuse & Neglect, 10*, 377–385.

Keller, R., & Shaywitz, B. A. (1986). Amnesia or fugue states: A diagnostic dilemma. *Journal of Developmental & Behavioral Pediatrics, 7*, 131–132.

Kisiel, C., & Lyons, J. S. (2001). Dissociation as a mediator of psychopathology among sexually abused children & adolescents. *American Journal of Psychiatry, 158*, 1034–1039.

Klein, H., Mann, D. R., & Goodwin, J. M. (1994). Obstacles to the recognition of sexual abuse and dissociative disorders in child and adolescent males. *Dissociation, 7*, 138–144.

Kluft, R. P. (1984). MPD in childhood. *Psychiatric Clinics of North America, 7*, 9–29.

Kluft, R. P. (1985). Hypnotherapy of childhood multiple personality disorder. *American Journal of Clinical Hypnosis, 27*, 201–210.

Kluft, R. P. (2000). The psychoanalytic psychotherapy of dissociative identity disorder in the context of trauma therapy. *Psychoanalytic Inquiry, 20*, 259–286.

Laporta, L. D. (1992). Childhood trauma and multiple personality disorder: The case of a 9-year-old girl. *Child Abuse & Neglect, 16*, 615–620.

LeDoux, J. (1996). *The emotional brain.* New York: Touchstone.

Lewin, R. A. (2000). Uncertainty, mammalian fundamentals, ambivalence, effort: Commentary on Bartholomew. *Psychoanalytic Inquiry, 20*, 287–300.

Liotti, G. (1999). Disorganization of attachment as a model of understanding dissociative psychopathology. In J. Solomon & C. George (Eds.), *Attachment disorganization* (pp. 291–317). New York: Guilford.

Lyons-Ruth, K. (2003). Dissociation and the parent-infant dialogue: A longitudinal perspective from attachment research. *Journal of the American Psychoanalytic Association, 51*, 883–911.

Lyons-Ruth, K., Bronfman, E., & Atwood, G. (1999). A relational diathesis model of hostile-helpless states of mind. Expressions in mother-infant interaction. In J. Solomon & C. George (Eds.), *Attachment disorganization* (pp. 33–70). New York: Guilford.

Macfie, J., Cicchetti, D., & Toth, S. L. (2001). The development of dissociation in maltreated preschool-aged children. *Development and Psychopathology, 13*, 233–254.

Main, M., & Morgan, H. (1996). Disorganization and disorientation in infant Strange Situation behavior: Phenotypic resemblance to dissociative states? In L. Michelson & W. Ray (Eds.), *Handbook of dissociation* (pp. 107–137). New York: Plenum.

Malenbaum, R., & Russell, A. T. (1987). Multiple personality disorder in an eleven-year-old boy and his mother. *Journal of the American Academy of Child & Adolescent Psychiatry, 26*, 436–439.

Malinosky-Rummell, R. R., & Hoier, T. S. (1991). Validating measures of dissociation. *Behavior Assessment, 13*, 341–357.

Mann, B. J., & Sanders, S. (1994). Child dissociation and the family context. *Journal of Abnormal Child Psychology, 22*, 373–388.

Martinez-Taboas, A., Shrout, P. E., Canino, G., Chavez, L. M., Ramirez, R., Bravo, M., Bauermeister, J. J., Ribera, J., & Ribera, J. C. (2004). The psychometric properties of a shortened version of the Spanish Adolescent Dissociative Experiences Scale. *Journal of Trauma and Dissociation, 5*(4), 33–54.

McElroy, L. P. (1992). Early indicators of pathological dissociation in sexually abused children, *Child Abuse & Neglect, 16*, 833–846.

McKellar, A. (1978). Depersonalization in a 16 year old boy. *Southern Medical Journal, 71*, 1580–1581.

McMahon, P. P., & Fagan, J. (1993). Play therapy with children with multiple personality disorder. In R. P. Kluft and C. G. Fine (Eds.), *Clinical perspectives on multiple personality disorder* (pp. 253–276). Washington, DC: American Psychiatric Press.

Nemzer, E. (1998). Psychopharmacological interventions for children and adolescents with dissociative disorders. In J. Silberg (Ed.), *The dissociative child: Diagnosis, treatment and management* (2nd ed., pp. 231–272). Lutherville, MD: The Sidran Press.

Netherton, S., Holmes, D., & Walker, C., eds. (1999). *Child and adolescent psychological disorders*. New York: Oxford University Press.

Nijenhuis, E. R. S., Van der Hart, O., & Steele, K. (2002). The emerging psychobiology of trauma-related dissociation and dissociative disorders. In H. D'Haenen, H. den Boer, & P. Willner (Eds.), *Biological psychiatry* (pp. 1079–1098). London: Wiley.

Norretranders, T. (1998). *The user illusion*. New York: Viking.

Ogawa, J. R., Sroufe, L. A., Weinfield, N. S., Carlson, E. A., & Egeland, B. (1997). Development and the fragmented self: Longitudinal study of dissociative symptomatology in a nonclinical sample. *Development and Psychopathology, 9*, 855–979.

Orvashel, H., Faust, J., & Hersen, M. (Eds.) (2001). *Handbook of conceptualization and treatment of child psychopathology*. Oxford, UK: Elsevier Science Ltd.

Perry, B. D., Pollard, R., Blakely, T., Baker, W., & Vigilante, D. (1995). Childhood trauma, the neurobiology of adaptation and use-dependent development of the brain: How states become traits. *Infant Mental Health Journal, 16*, 271–291.

Peterson, G. (1991). Children coping with trauma: Diagnosis of Dissociation Identity Disorder. *Dissociation, 4*, 152–164.

Peterson, G., & Putnam, F. W. (1994). Further validation of the Child Dissociation Checklist. *Dissociation, 7*, 204–211.

Pine, D. S., Mogg, K., Bradley, B. P., Montgomery, L., et al. (2005). Attention bias to threat in maltreated children: Implications for vulnerability to stress-related psychopathology. *American Journal of Psychiatry, 162*, 291–296.

Pollak, S. D., Cicchetti, D., Hornung, K., & Reed, A. (2000). Recognizing emotion in faces: Developmental effects of child abuse and neglect. *Developmental Psychology, 36*, 679–688.

Pollak, S. D., & Sinha, P. (2002). Effects of early experience on children's recognition of facial displays of emotion. *Developmental Psychology, 38*, 784–791.

Putnam, F. W. (1991). Dissociative disorders in children and adolescents. *Psychiatric Clinics of North America, 14*, 519–531.

Putnam, F. W. (1997). *Dissociation in children and adolescents: A developmental approach*. New York: Guilford.

Putnam, F. (2005, November). *Developmental trauma disorder*. Paper presented at the 22nd meeting of the International Society for the Study of Dissociation Conference, Toronto, Canada.

Putnam, F. W., Helmers, K., & Trickett, P. K. (1993). Development, reliability, and validity of a child dissociation scale. *Child Abuse & Neglect, 17*, 731–741.

Putnam, F. W., Hornstein, N. L., & Peterson, G. (1996). Clinical phenomenology of child and adolescent dissociative disorders: Gender and age effects. *Child and Adolescent Psychiatric Clinics of North America, 5*, 303–442.

Reyes-Perez, C. D., Martinez-Taboas, A., & Ledesma-Amador, D. (2005). Dissociative experiences in children with abuse histories: A replication in Puerto Rico. *Journal of Trauma and Dissociation, 6*(1), 99–112.

Riley, R. L., & Mead, J. (1988). The development of symptoms of multiple personality in a child of three. *Dissociation, 1*, 41–46.

Rhue, J. W., Lynn, S. J., & Sandberg, D. (1995). Dissociation, fantasy and imagination in childhood: A comparison of physically abused, sexually abused, and non-abused children. *Contemporary Hypnosis, 12*, 131–136.

Ruths, S., Silberg, J. L., Dell, P. F., & Jenkins, C. (2002, November). *Adolescent DID: An elucidation of symptomatology and validation of the MID*. Paper presented at the 19th meeting of the International Society for the Study of Dissociation, Baltimore, MD.

Saakvitne, K. (2000). Some thoughts about dissociative identity disorder as a disorder of attachment. *Psychoanalytic Inquiry, 20*, 249–258.

Şar, V., Öztürk, E., & Kundakçı, T. (2002). Psychotherapy of an adolescent with dissociative identity disorder: Change in Rorschach patterns. *Journal of Trauma & Dissociation, 3*(2), 81–96.

Saunders, B. E., Berliner, L., & Hanson, R. F., eds. (2004). *Child physical and sexual abuse: Guidelines for treatment*. Charleston, SC: National Crime Victims Research and Treatment Center. Retrieved on March 31, 2006, from http://www.musc.edu/cvc/guidelinesfinal.pdf

Schore, A. (1994). *Affect regulation and the origins of self.* Hillsdale, NJ: Lawrence Erlbaum.

Schore, A. (2001). The effects of early relational trauma on right brain development, affect regulation, and infant mental health. *Infant Mental Health Journal. 22*, 201–269.

Shirar, L. (1996). *Dissociative children.* New York: W. W. Norton.

Siegel, D. J. (1999). *The developing mind.* New York: Guilford.

Silberg, J. L. (Ed). (1996/1998). *The dissociative child: Diagnosis, treatment and management.* Lutherville, MD: Sidran Press.

Silberg, J. L. (1998). Dissociative symptomatology in children and adolescents as displayed of psychological testing. *Journal of Personality Assessment, 71*, 421–439.

Silberg, J. L. (2000). Fifteen years of dissociation in maltreated children: Where do we go from here? *Child Maltreatment, 5*, 119–136.

Silberg, J. L. (2001a). Treating maladaptive dissociation in a young teenage girl. In H. Orvaschel, J. Faust, & M. Hersen (Eds.), *Handbook of conceptualization and treatment of child psychopathology* (pp. 449–474). Oxford, UK: Elsevier Science.

Silberg, J. (2001b). An optimistic look at childhood dissociation, *ISSD NEWS, 19*(2), 1.

Silberg, J. L. (2004a). The treatment of dissociation in sexually abused children from a family/attachment perspective. *Psychotherapy: Theory, Research, Practice & Training, 41*, 487–496.

Silberg, J. L. (2004b, November). *Longitudinal observations on children and adolescents with dissociative disorders.* Paper presented at the 21st meeting of the International Society for the Study of Dissociation, New Orleans, LA.

Silberg, J. L., Stipic, D., & Tagizadeh, F. (1997). Dissociative disorders in children and adolescents. In J. Noshpitz (Ed.), *The handbook of child and adolescent psychiatry* (Vol. III, pp. 329–355). New York: Wiley.

Silberg, J. L., & Waters, F. S. (1998). Factors associated with positive therapeutic outcome. In J. L. Silberg (Ed.), *The dissociative child: Diagnosis, treatment & management* (2nd ed., pp. 105–112). Lutherville, MD: Sidran Press.

Sim, L., Friedrich, W. N., Davies, W. H., Trentaham, B., Lengua, L., & Pithers, W. (2005). The child behavior checklist as an indicator of posttraumatic stress disorder and dissociation in normative, psychiatric, and sexually abused children. *Journal of Traumatic Stress 18*(6), 697–705.

Smith, S. R., & Carlson, E. B. (1996). Reliability and validity of the Adolescent Dissociative Experiences Scale. *Dissociation 9*, 125–129.

Snow, M. S., White, J., Pilkington, L., & Beckman, D. (1995). Dissociative Identity Disorder revealed through play therapy: A case study of a four year old. *Dissociation, 8*, 120–123.

Sobol, B., & Schneider, K. (1998). Art as an adjunctive therapy in the treatment of children who dissociate. In J. L. Silberg, *The dissociative child: Diagnosis, treatment and management* (2nd ed., pp. 219–230). Lutherville, MD: Sidran Press.

Stien, P., & Kendall, J. (2004). *Psychological trauma and the developing brain: Neurologically based interventions for troubled children.* Binghamton, NY: Haworth.

Stolbach, B. C. (1997). The Children's Dissociative Experiences Scale and Posttraumatic Symptom Inventory: Rationale, development, and validation of a self-report measure. *Dissertation Abstracts International, 58*(03), 1548B.

Stolbach, B. C. (2005). Psychotherapy of a dissociative 8-year-old boy burned at age 3. *Psychiatric Annals, 35*, 685–694.

Stolbach, B. C., Silvern, L., Williams, W., Reyes, G., & Kaersvang, L. (1997, November). *The Children's Dissociative Experiences Scale and Posttraumatic Symptom Inventory.* Poster session presented at the 13th meeting of the International Society for Traumatic Stress Studies, Montreal, Canada.

Terr, L. (1988). What happens to early memories of trauma: A study of 20 children under age 5 at the time of documented traumatic events. *Journal of the American Academy of Child & Adolescent Psychiatry, 27,* 1, 96–104.

Venn, J. (1984). Family etiology and remission in a case of psychogenic fugue. *Family Process, 23*, 429–435.

Vermetten, E., Schmahl, C., Lindner, S., Loewenstein, R. J., & Bremner, J. D. (2006). Hippocampal and amygdala volume in dissociative identity disorder. *American Journal of Psychiatry, 163*, 630–636.

Vincent, M., & Pickering M. R. (1988). Multiple personality disorder in childhood. *Canadian Journal of Psychiatry, 33*, 524–529.

Waldinger, R. J., Swett, C., Frank, A., & Miller, K. (1994). Levels of dissociation and histories of reported abuse among women outpatients. *Journal of Nervous & Mental Disease, 182*, 625–630.

Wallach, H., & Dollinger, S. (1999). Dissociative disorders in childhood and adolescence. In S. Netherton, D. Holmes, & C. Walker (Eds.), *Child and adolescent psychological disorders* (pp. 344–366). New York: Oxford University Press.

Waters, F. S. (2005a). Recognizing dissociation in preschool children, *ISSD NEWS, 23*(4), 1–5.

Waters, F. S. (2005b). Atypical DID adolescent case. *ISSD News, 23*(3), 1–2, 4–5.

Waters, F. W., & Silberg, J. L. (1998). Therapeutic phases in the treatment of dissociative children. In J. L. Silberg (Ed.), *The dissociative child: Diagnosis, treatment & management* (2nd ed., pp. 135–156). Lutherville, MD: Sidran Press.

Weiss, M., Sutton, P. J., & Utecht, A. J. (1985). Multiple personality in a 10-year-old girl. *Journal of the American Academy of Child & Adolescent Psychiatry, 24*, 495–501.

Wieland, S. (1997). *Hearing the internal trauma.* Thousand Oaks, CA: Sage.

Wieland, S. (1998). *Techniques and issues in abuse-focused therapy.* Thousand Oaks, CA: Sage.

Williams, D. T., & Velazquez, L. (1996). The use of hypnosis in children with dissociative disorders. *Child and Adolescent Psychiatric Clinics of North America, 5,* 495–508.

Yehuda, N. (2005). The language of dissociation. *Journal of Trauma and Dissociation, 6*(1), 9–30.

Zlotnick, C., Shea, M. T., Zakriski, A., Costello, E., Begin, A., Pearlstein, T., & Simpson, E. (1996). Stressors and close relationships during childhood and dissociative experiences in survivors of sexual abuse among inpatient psychiatric women. *Comprehensive Psychiatry, 36,* 207–212.

Zoroğlu, S. S., Şar, V., Tüzün, Ü., Tutkun, H., & Savaş, H. A. (2002). Reliability and validity of the Turkish version of the adolescent dissociative experiences scale. *Psychiatry & Clinical Neurosciences, 56*, 551–556.

Zoroğlu, S., Yargıç, L. M., Tutkun, H., Öztürk, M., & Şar, V. (1996). Dissociative identity disorder in childhood: Five cases. *Dissociation, 11*, 253–260.

6 The Relational Context of Dissociative Phenomena

Lissa Dutra, PhD
Ilaria Bianchi, PhD
Daniel J. Siegel, MD
Karlen Lyons-Ruth, PhD

OUTLINE

6.1 DISSOCIATION AS AN INTRAPSYCHIC DEFENSE

Clinical literature has described dissociation as an intrapsychic defensive process. Putnam (1997) describes the defensive functions of dissociation as falling into three categories, including behavioral automatization, affective and informational compartmentalization, and identity alteration/depersonalization. According to Putnam (1997), behavioral automatization refers to one's ability to "automatically" engage in a behavior, while simultaneously attending to another task, such as driving while participating in a conversation with another person. Affective and informational compartmentalization refers to a lack of integration of affect and/or knowledge, which may be demonstrated via the forgetting of such affect or knowledge. Lastly, identity alteration and depersonalization refer to ways in which the individual may be unable to access a part of his identity and/or feels "detached" from himself and his cognitions and/or affect. Continuum models of dissociation describe these processes as ranging from normal/adaptive to pathological/maladaptive, the most pathological extreme of the spectrum being represented by dissociative identity disorder. In general, each of these defensive functions of dissociation may be conceptualized as relating to one's ability to integrate and compartmentalize behavioral, cognitive, and/or affective mental processes. In fact, Van der Kolk, Van der Hart, and Marmar (1996, p. 306) simply define dissociation as a "compartmentalization of experience."

On the extreme end of the dissociative continuum, severe compartmentalization and lack of integration of experiences may result in a sense of altered reality. Trauma researchers suggest that when dissociation is employed, it is often in the service of altering a reality that may be unbearable to endure, as in the case of trauma. For example, Herman (1992) describes how tortured prisoners become very skilled at altering consciousness such that they enable themselves to temporarily cognitively escape the torture that they are involuntarily subjected to. It is not surprising, then, that the vast majority of literature and research pertaining to dissociation has been presented in the context of trauma. Terr's (1991) classic article on childhood trauma postulates that children are forced to employ dissociation as a common defense against recurrent, long-standing abuse in order to "mentally escape" their reality while being subjected to the abuse. Since the child comes to expect abuse on an unpredictable basis, he eventually begins to employ dissociation as a defense during times of extreme stress, even when the threat of abuse does not exist. Dissociation, in this case, becomes a defense that is triggered by stress, anxiety, and fear, which may be frequently experienced by a child with a severe trauma history. In accordance with this theory that implicates trauma in the etiology of dissociation, there have been numerous studies demonstrating a significant association between dissociation and trauma (Putnam, 1997). In essence, trauma theory suggests that dissociation originates when an individual may be unable to integrate the entirety of his reality in the face of an overwhelming threat of danger (Van der Kolk, 1996). This intrapsychic defense allows the individual to endure his reality, as malignant as it may be, without feeling annihilated as a result of having to endure it.

Van der Kolk, Van der Hart, and Marmar (1996) distinguish between three associated, but separate, categories of dissociative phenomena, including primary, secondary, and tertiary dissociation. They define primary dissociation as an inability to integrate sensory and emotional aspects of trauma into consciousness, such that the individual may be unaware of the reality of their trauma. Secondary dissociation, on the other hand, is described as a dissociation between the observing versus experiencing egos, such that the individual may remain conscious of the trauma itself, but dissociates, or pushes out of conscious awareness, the overwhelming negative affect connected to the trauma. Lastly, tertiary dissociation, as reflected by dissociative identity disorder, represents a dissociation of separate "ego states" consisting of organized cognitive, affective, and behavioral patterns, in which the individual is believed to experience distinct "identities" or ego states.

Tertiary dissociation is most often demonstrated by individuals with a long-lasting history of severe abuse (Van der Kolk, Van der Hart, & Marmar, 1996) and can be considered the most pathological extreme of dissociative processes. The concept of dissociating aspects of the self is especially relevant to individuals who have been abused by their parents. Spiegel (1986) describes the chaos that a child experiences when he becomes aware that his caregiver, who is responsible for his protection, safety, and survival, is the same individual who threatens his very existence. The child, faced with the impossible notion that his parent is both his protector and his annihilator, is thought to conceptualize the abusing parent as separate entities of "good" versus "bad," often dissociating and pushing the "bad" out of conscious awareness. These representations of the parent may then become intertwined with the child's internalized representations of the self. Thus, it is not surprising that children who have experienced extreme abuse at the hands of their parents are also likely to dissociate aspects of their own identity, which, at the extreme, may result in the presentation of different "ego states" or distinct selves. As such, while clinicians and researchers have primarily focused on understanding dissociation as an intrapsychic phenomenon, it is important to investigate whether dissociation might be interpersonally generated and/or originate in interpersonal phenomena. An exploration of dissociation in light of developmental theory may lead to a better understanding of the interpersonal aspects of dissociation.

6.2 DISSOCIATION AS A DEVELOPMENTAL PROCESS

Other than the etiological role of trauma in dissociation, Putnam (1997) points out that relatively little is known about the etiology and development of dissociation. The fact that nontraumatized individuals sometimes demonstrate dissociation and that not all trauma survivors dissociate suggests that there may be more to the etiology and development of dissociation than trauma alone. Putnam (1997) explored the role of various potential moderating variables, including age, gender, culture, genetic factors, and education/intelligence, in the development of dissociation, and although moderating trends were found for some of these variables, existing research has not convincingly demonstrated that any of them significantly influence dissociation. Family environmental factors, however, are one set of factors that has been shown to be significantly related to dissociation, above and beyond trauma alone. More specifically, factors such as inconsistent parenting or disciplining (Braun & Sachs, 1985; Kluft, 1984; Mann & Sanders, 1994), level of family risk (Malinosky-Rummel & Hoier, 1991), lack of parental care and warmth (Mann & Sanders, 1994; Modestin, Lotscher, & Thomas, 2002), parental control (Modestin et al., 2002), as well as poor parental relationship (Maaranen et al., 2004) have been demonstrated to be significantly associated with higher levels of dissociation in adulthood. In general, however, the bulk of available research on dissociation has focused on trauma, leaving many unanswered questions regarding the developmental trajectory of dissociation throughout the life span.

Barach (1991) was one of the first theorists to connect dissociation with attachment theory when he suggested that multiple personality disorder (now known as dissociative identity disorder) may actually be a variant of an "attachment disorder." He pointed out that individuals with this disorder tend to demonstrate the "extreme detachment" experienced by children faced with a loss of their primary caretaker, as described by Bowlby (1973). Barach further suggested that children of unresponsive caretakers are also very likely to engage in dissociative or "detached" behaviors. As an offshoot of this work, developmental theorists and researchers have begun to explore the role of early childhood attachment and parenting in the etiology and development of dissociation.

In this book, Liotti's chapter presents an excellent overview of attachment theory that will provide the basis for the subsequent sections of this chapter. Liotti's (1992) work has been instrumental in pointing to the role of disorganized infant attachment as a potential precursor to the development of dissociation later in life. He has pointed out that there are striking parallels between infant disorganization and dissociation in that both phenomena reflect a pervasive lack of mental integration and that this primary failure of integration in infancy, as is believed to occur with infant disorganization, may result in vulnerability to dissociation later in life. His view might be best conceptualized as a vulnerability model in which early dyadic processes lead to a "primary breakdown" or disintegration of a coherent sense of self. Liotti's model challenges the theory that the primary function and etiology of dissociation is as a defense against trauma. Although he has not suggested that disorganized attachment is the only etiological factor in dissociation, he has hypothesized that disorganized attachment is an initial step in the variety of developmental trajectories that may eventually lead an individual to be predisposed and vulnerable to developing dissociation in response to later experiences of trauma.

Bowlby (1973) first suggested that infants may internalize dissociated or unintegrated internal working models of their primary caretakers, as well as of themselves. Main and Hesse (1990) have hypothesized that parents of disorganized infants are likely to engage in frightened or frightening interactions with their children, which presents the infant with the paradox that the parent is both a source of threat and his primary source of comfort, simultaneously. Under these conditions, during times of stress when the attachment system is activated, contradictory internalized working models of the self and other may develop. These seemingly incompatible models of the parent and the self are similar to Barach's model of an abusive parent causing a child to be faced with the incompatible notion that his parent is both his protector and his annihilator.

Main and Hesse further theorize that when the parent appears frightened in her interactions with the infant, the infant may be led to believe that there is something threatening in the environment that should be feared. Although such a perceived environmental threat would lead a securely attached infant to approach his parent for protection, the parent's frightened stance may cause the child to wonder if his parent is helpless in the face of this threat and, if so, the infant may feel conflicted about approaching her for protection and show disorganized approach-avoidance behaviors. Alternatively, the parent's frightened stance may cause the child to wonder if he, himself, is frightening the parent, potentially resulting in a sense of self as threatening. Thus, the infant's internalization of multiple models of the self and other can be conceptualized in terms of contradictory approach-avoidance stances, as well as contradictory views of the parent as both hostile and helpless when the infant is engaged in interaction with his parent. This primary lack of integration with respect to one's sense of self or other is that which Liotti (1992) suggests may lay the groundwork for dissociative processes later in life.

Liotti (1992) further hypothesized that there exist three theoretical pathways that disorganized infants might take toward (or against) the development of dissociative symptomatology. The first pathway, in which interactions with the parent become more consistent in childhood, regardless of whether this consistency is positive or negative in nature, is believed to result in the child eventually choosing one of the incompatible models of the self and other and developing in accordance with that pathway. The second pathway, in which parent-child interactions continue to be inconsistent and contradictory, but in which the child does not encounter severe trauma, is likely to result in the experience of infrequent dissociation during times of extreme stress. In this case, although the child is predisposed to the development of dissociative symptoms, there are not sufficient environmental stressors (e.g., trauma) to result in the realization of this disposition, so the child is asymptomatic or only displays mild dissociation. In the third pathway, however, in which the disorganized infant is predisposed to dissociation and subsequently experiences severe and/or chronic stressors/trauma, the vulnerability is likely to be realized, resulting in the frequent employment of dissociation during times of stress. The more disintegrated the child's model of self and other and the more severe and/or chronic the trauma, the more dissociation the child is likely to experience, potentially moving toward the extreme of developing dissociative identity disorder. Thus, while Liotti's (1992) model sets forth the notion that infant disorganization lays the groundwork and acts as a key precursor for the development of dissociation, the experience of significant environmental stressors, or traumas, remains an important and necessary factor in this diathesis-stress model.

6.3. DISSOCIATION AS AN INTERPERSONAL PROCESS IN THE CONTEXT OF NEW DATA

Aspects of Liotti's model have recently been empirically supported by longitudinal research. Ogawa, Sroufe, Weinfield, Carlson, and Egeland (1997) carried out a prospective longitudinal study of 126 high-risk children, following this sample from birth to age 19, in an attempt to test Liotti's model. According to models of dissociation based in trauma theory, one might expect trauma to be the strongest independent predictor of adult dissociation. Ogawa's et al. (1997) multiple regression analyses indicated, however, that disorganized attachment and psychological unavailability of the caregiver during infancy were the strongest predictors of clinical levels of dissociation, to the extent that these variables alone accounted for approximately one-quarter of the variance in dissociation at age 19. Surprisingly, trauma history did not significantly add to the predictive value of this equation. Trauma did serve to predict a more notable portion of the variance in dissociative behaviors as measured during the elementary and high school years, but even in this equation, the effects of early attachment continued to be independent predictors of dissociation and were not mediated by the occurrence of trauma. The strength with which infant disorganization independently predicted dissociation across the age span in Ogawa's et al. (1997) study was a surprising and notable finding that lends support to the conceptualization of disorganized attachment as a key precursor in the development of dissociation. These findings lead to the question of whether disorganized attachment may be as central to the development of dissociation as trauma itself.

It is also notable that Ogawa's et al. (1997) study demonstrated that some nondisorganized infants in the sample developed dissociative symptomatology in young adulthood. This finding suggests that there may be factors above and beyond disorganized attachment that serve to predispose children to the development of dissociation. Liotti's model of infant disorganization serving as a precursor to dissociation facilitates a better understanding of why it is that some people exposed to trauma develop dissociation, while others do not. His model suggests that disorganized attachment negatively impacts the onset of early individually based processes of mental segregation that will become the basis for later dissociation. The pathways from infant disorganization to adult dissociation may be more dynamic and complex than it seems at first glance, however. Liotti's "first pathway" of development represents disorganized infants who experience more stability with their parent later in life and manage to "escape" becoming vulnerable to dissociation by settling on one of their contradictory models of the self and other. This pathway speaks to why it may be that not all disorganized infants develop dissociative tendencies or pathological dissociative symptomatology later in life. Disorganized infants who later dissociate may be on a different pathway, however, in that the continuation of unstable and inconsistent interactions with their parent may serve to reinforce or crystallize their vulnerability to developing dissociation in the face of trauma. In fact, one might question whether prolonged and chronic exposure to such inconsistent parenting may, in and of itself, lead to the experience of dissociation even when there is a lack of traumatic stressors. There are, in fact, individuals without any known history of trauma who dissociate in times of stress, although this population is often underrepresented in inpatient settings and neglected in dissociation research. Thus, a more nuanced exploration of enduring patterns of contradictory parent-child communication processes that may act to continually reinforce the child's segregated and contradictory mental processes is warranted. Such exploration might facilitate a better understanding of this population of nontraumatized dissociating individuals, as well as help fill in some of the theoretical gaps inherent in the models of dissociation that have been reviewed thus far.

Dutra, Bureau, Holmes, Lyubchik, and Lyons-Ruth (in press) further investigated the association between infant attachment and dissociation in a prospective longitudinal study of a high-risk sample followed from birth to age 19. This study examined the impact of social risk factors on child development throughout the infant, preschool, school-age, and adolescent periods. Participants were low socioeconomic status, at-risk families and, as in the Ogawa et al. (1997) study, adolescent dissociative symptoms were measured by the Dissociative Experiences Scale (DES) at age 19. Disorganized attachment status at 18 months of age was assessed via the Strange Situation; mother-infant interaction at home at 12 months was assessed with the Home Observation of Maternal Interaction Rating Scales

(HOMIRS); maternal disrupted affective communication was assessed at 18 months using the Atypical Maternal Behavior Instrument for Assessment and Classification (AMBIANCE) coding system; and mothers were assessed for psychopathology with the Diagnostic Interview Schedule, the DES, and the Center for Epidemiologic Studies Depression Scale (CES-D).

Our results partially confirm and extend Ogawa's et al. (1997) findings. The occurrence of early childhood maltreatment did not predict adolescent dissociative symptoms ($r = 0.16$). Additionally, maternal psychiatric symptoms, including dissociative, PTSD, depressive, and anxiety symptoms assessed through child age 9, also failed to predict adolescent dissociative symptoms ($-0.17 < r < 0.17$). In contrast, quality of maternal communication during infancy significantly contributed to the prediction of dissociative symptoms at age 19. The quality of mother-infant interaction in the first 18 months of life accounted for half of the variance in dissociative symptoms, ($R^2 = 0.50$), consistent with Ogawa's et al. (1997) findings that psychological unavailability of the caregiver and infant disorganization accounted for nearly one-quarter of the variance in DES scores at age 19. Infant disorganization in itself, however, was not a strong predictor of later dissociation in our data.

While these data do not imply that traumatic experiences are not influential in the development of dissociation, they do suggest that early attachment and relational experiences may also be important in accounting for this phenomenon. Additional factors in adolescence are yet to be examined in this study and, thus, it is possible that experiences during adolescence, such as adolescent trauma and parent-adolescent interaction, may play a mediating role in the association between early caregiver-infant interaction and future dissociation. Such mediators in later life were not found in the Ogawa et al. (1997) study, however, and even the existence of such mediators would not discount the importance of the strong association between the quality of parent-infant interaction and the development of dissociation over the course of 19 years.

6.4 THE PARENT-INFANT DIALOGUE: A MORE NUANCED UNDERSTANDING OF THE RELATIONSHIP BETWEEN DISORGANIZATION AND DISSOCIATION

As previously described, Main and Hesse (1990) have theorized that maternal frightened or frightening behaviors in infancy may be the etiologic factors that produce infant disorganized attachment behaviors. For our study, we measured various dimensions of disrupted maternal affective communication that we expected to be related to disorganization, including the following: affective errors (e.g., giving contradictory cues; not responding to infant), disorientation (e.g., being confused or frightened by infant; exhibiting disoriented behavior), negative-intrusive behavior (e.g., mocking or teasing infant; pulling infant by the wrist), role confusion (e.g., role reversal, such as eliciting reassurance from infant; sexualization, such as speaking in hushed intimate tone to infant), and withdrawal (e.g., creating physical or verbal distance in relation to the infant, such as interacting silently, or backing away from the infant). Each of these aspects of disrupted maternal affective communication has been theorized to be associated with disorganized attachment and, in a final set of analyses, we looked at the predictive power of each of these dimensions with respect to dissociation in young adulthood.

Trauma theory dictates that maternal hostile (negative-intrusive) and/or disoriented behaviors would likely be the strongest predictors of dissociation in young adulthood, but, surprisingly, this is not what was found. Maternal hostile or intrusive behavior was not significantly related to later dissociation. Instead, lack of positive maternal affective involvement, maternal flatness of affect, and overall disrupted maternal communication were the strongest predictors of dissociation in young adulthood. What is notable about these types of maternal interactions is that they all serve to subtly override or ignore the infant's needs and attachment signals, but without overt hostility.

Both Ogawa's and our findings indicate that something in the parent-infant dialogue itself appears to independently influence the development of dissociation, above and beyond any effects of infant disorganization. We use the word *dialogue* here in the broadest sense, encompassing all meaningful communications between the child and parent. Early in life these communications occur at the level of affective exchanges and signals. These data may begin to shed light on the specific aspects of the parent-infant dialogue that are linked to later dissociation. Although Ogawa et al. (1997) did not investigate particular aspects of this early dialogue, their study did touch on one aspect of this dialogue that they termed *psychological unavailability*. This dimension may be akin to lack of positive maternal affective involvement and maternal flatness of affect, in that it represents the mother's unavailability to respond to the infant's attachment cues. As previously discussed, this psychological unavailability variable, together with infant disorganization, accounted for approximately one-quarter of the variance in DES scores at age 19 in Ogawa's et al. (1997) sample. What is notable is that a hefty 19% of this variance was carried by the psychological unavailability variable.

These parent-infant dialogue dimensions that carry so much weight in the studies of the prediction of dissociation might also help to explain why some nondisorganized infants eventually develop dissociative symptomatology. It is possible that, even though these infants do not meet criteria for disorganized attachment, they may be exposed to elements of the parent-infant dialogue that are particularly influential in the development of dissociation. Such distortions of the parent-infant dialogue are likely experienced less frequently between nondisorganized infants and their caregivers, which may account for the lower levels of dissociation in nondisorganized populations.

6.5 ILLUSTRATIONS OF PARENT-INFANT INTERACTIONS

6.5.1 A Research Case Illustration

To illustrate the types of early disrupted mother-infant communication patterns observed in our research, one of the videotaped mother-infant interactions from our study will be described as an example of what such disrupted communication may look like in infancy. The manner in which such disrupted communication may be connected to the future development of dissociative symptoms will also be discussed. The mother and child to be described were taped during a Strange Situation session, an experimental procedure developed by Ainsworth and colleagues (1978) to assess infant attachment patterns. Mother and child are observed in a room equipped with a bidirectional mirror and undergo a sequence of eight interactive episodes, involving two mother-infant separations; first leaving the child with a stranger and then leaving the child alone. The child's reactions to separation and reunion with the mother are used as indices of his/her security of attachment with the mother and serve as the basis for classifying the infant into one of four attachment categories: secure, avoidant, ambivalent, or disorganized.

The boy to be described was classified as disorganized in infancy and reported high levels of dissociation at age 19. We will focus this case study on the peculiar features of this dyad's communication style when the boy was 18 months old.

Throughout the Strange Situation session, affective unavailability, withdrawal, and disrupted communication characterize the manner in which the mother relates to her child, while the child displays disorientation and aimlessness. When alone with the mother, the child wanders around the room without being able to focus on a single toy or initiate focused activity. Watching the video in slow motion, the child's movements appear lost, confused, and aimless—he walks around, turning and turning, briefly touching and then leaving a few objects. The frequency of this behavior increases after his mother's lack of response to his attempt to initiate an interaction by showing her a toy. The child's disoriented behavior and the depressing feel of the environment dissipates, however, upon the mother's departure, when the child is given the opportunity to interact with the stranger. His attempt to engage the stranger in a game with the ball is successful and he seems to enjoy this interaction. This game is an example of a bidirectional and well-functioning interaction, where the "other" is available and responds to the child's initiative, in contrast to the mother who failed to respond to such initiatives.

Examples of maternal affective unavailability and withdrawal are also demonstrated in this observational material. Upon the first reunion, the mother enters the room but neither approaches nor greets her child. Rather than attempt to attune to her child's mood and engage him after the separation, she stands on one leg, the other leg relaxed, with her right hand in her pocket and leans back a bit, without interacting. In the meantime, the child lowers his gaze and moves toward the door. This segment demonstrates the poverty of the mother's initiative with respect to interacting with her child and subsequent attempts from the mother to interest him with the toys are not successful. Rather, he attempts to keep his distance by refusing any shared activity with his mother and proceeds to engage in a new sequence of disoriented behaviors. In the second reunion, the mother, after some hesitation, does not try to comfort her distressed child, but asks for a kiss and wants him to tell her about his activities while she was out of the room. This may be interpreted as her asking her child to respond to *her* needs, rather than displaying an interest in or recognition of his internal state.

These examples of parent-infant dialogue involve subtle movements and slight affective cues that are unlikely to be described as traumatizing or openly conflictual; yet they very likely have a strong effect on the quality of the interactants' exchange and on the child's subsequent behavioral organization. We stress the "dialogic" quality of such disrupted communication because through the small movements and affective cues that occur, the two parties may reciprocally influence one another and impact the course of the interaction's development.

As previously mentioned, the child presented in this vignette endorsed significant dissociation at the age of 19. On the DES, for example, he endorsed often "finding [himself] someplace and not remembering how [he] got there" and "getting confused about whether [he] has done something or only thought about doing it" as a young adult. The connection between these experiences and his observed experience of disorientation and aimlessness following withdrawal in his early interactions with his mother is noteworthy.

In addition, when administered the Adult Attachment Interview (AAI), a semi-structured interview that evaluates attachment in adulthood, this young man verbally describes a sense of disorientation and of being pulled in several directions in his first years of life, which is reminiscent of the disorientation and aimless qualities of the taped interaction. He describes early childhood as follows: "Bounce here, bounce there. Go to court one week for my parents and have to go talk to judges and all this....I really didn't have many friends at the time because I was always ... moving from here to there." His disappointment with the lack of stability that characterizes his relationship with his mother is also addressed in the AAI: "Each time I get bounced around it takes me six months to get settled back down and then resentment builds for another while. Every time I try to ... finally open up I get moved around and just basically shut down again." Not surprisingly, this young man expresses hope that his relationship with his parents will move toward stability in his adulthood, "and then I can reach a sort of equilibrium around here."

In addition, this man describes his role-reversed, caregiving stance during the AAI: "From the age of twelve on ... I kind of brought myself up. I started becoming an adult at the age of twelve, I think ... I consider my mom more of a friend right now than a mom ... someone I can go and talk to and hang out with....And I know she's my mother and everything, but I just have this weird feeling about—she's so young." When his mother would cry in front of him after fighting with his father, this man reports, "I used to stay by her side ... and help her out. I'd give her a hug or something ... tried to make her laugh." He also describes trying to think of ways to solve his parents' conflicts when he was six years old: "[When I heard them fighting] it just made me start thinking—think and think. Think of ways of trying to fix—but could never."

His mother, separately questioned about her experiences of being a parent to her son, describes herself as "too easy," having difficulty setting rules, and as a "friend" for her child; she reports wishing that her children would show more appreciation for her and that the best moments with them are when she feels "wanted." In brief, she demonstrates a tendency to abdicate her parental role and ask for love and attention, rather than attending to her children's needs. Accordingly, in this vignette, it is notable that the affectively unavailable and withdrawn nature of the parent's involvement with the child was evident in the second-to-second interactive dialogue between mother and infant, after which the child eventually begins to focus on his mother's needs, as per her request, rather than attend to his own needs.

6.5.2 Clinical Vignette 1

The dimensions of the parent-infant dialogue that seem most relevant to the later development of dissociation, then, appear to be the quieter behaviors of maternal affective unavailability and disrupted maternal communication, which result in an overriding or ignoring of the infant's attachment cues. In such instances, the mother behaves in ways that have the effect of "shutting out" the child from the process of dialogue. This "shutting out" appears to characterize a relational context that results in the child's inability to internalize the resources necessary to self-soothe and/or experience a sense of safety and care, particularly at times of distress.

In the case of an abusive parent, it is clear how the child's attempts to participate in the parent-child dialogue may be shut out. To give one clinical example, a patient with a dissociative identity disorder who was in treatment over a 10-year period had experienced severely sadistic physical and sexual abuse at the hands of her father from the age of 4 (and possibly earlier). After a few years of treatment, she recalled that as a child she often felt that there was something she urgently needed to tell her mother at bedtime and, accordingly, she would often call her mother into the bedroom. When her mother came in, however, she could never remember what it was that she wanted to tell her. Only later in the treatment did the patient recall that her mother had also participated in her sexual abuse from an early age. Her mother remained closed to any acknowledgment of the abuse both during her childhood and later when confronted during the patient's adulthood. This case material illustrates both the contradictory approach-avoidance attempts at dialogue of the disorganized child, as well as the inability of the abusive mother to help the child integrate the contradictory aspects of her experiences through a collaborative dialogue. In the case of abusive behavior, then, it is clear how the child is "shut out" from collaborative dialogue with the parent.

6.5.3 Clinical Vignette 2

It is notable, however, that this process of shutting out the child does not only occur in the context of abuse. In fact, this shutting out can be conceived of as a more fundamental process, a process that provides the relational context in which abuse becomes possible. In another clinical example, a young man described his mother as very emotionally distant during his childhood: "I have no memories of her being around even though she must have been there." As he grew older and demanded more interaction from his mother, he found her to be quite childlike, emotionally labile, and self-focused. In his late teens, he disclosed to his mother that he thought he had been sexually abused by his father. His mother fell to the floor sobbing, ignored her son, and ultimately decided that he had to be mistaken. Only much later was the father revealed to be engaging in a variety of sexually deviant practices that involved children. This information came to light after the son had refused to have contact with the family for several years and, upon being informed of this, he felt incredible relief and validation. At the end of the same session, however, he commented thoughtfully, "To be sexually abused was terrible, but it is my relationship with my mother that has affected me all these years and that I've struggled most to overcome." While this does not excuse the abuse or minimize this father's criminal behavior, it does speak eloquently to the equal importance of the qualities of the ongoing relational dialogue in central attachment relationships for the eventual integration of one's experiences into a coherent sense of self. This hypothesis has important implications for treatment that are quite compatible with trauma theory in that it highlights the importance of trauma survivors being "heard" in their journey to recovery. Herman (1997) describes dissociation as the "internal mechanism by which terrorized people are silenced," which may parallel the manner in which infants vulnerable to developing dissociation are silenced, or shut out of collaborative dialogue with their parent, perhaps setting the stage for the later silencing associated with dissociative processes.

However, this invalidation of the child's input can also occur without the degree of deviation represented by abusive parenting. Whitmer (2001) describes dissociation as a process of simultaneously knowing and not knowing and relates this process to the difficulty dissociative individuals experience when engaging in interpretation or meaning-making of their sensations and perceptions. He postulates that one cannot truly "know" his own experience until he is seen, recognized, and reflected upon by the other. In essence, then, dissociated experiences are not really experienced and then lost, but may instead be "unthinkable" in that they have gone unrecognized by the other. This model suggests that the etiology of dissociation does not lie in an individual intrapsychic process, but rather represents a dynamic, interactive dialogic process that originates in the space between the self and other. That which occurs in this dyadic space may then become intrapsychic via internalization. In the case of primary failure of the parent-infant dialogue, the child is faced with a lack of integrated affective, symbolic, or interactive dialogue with the parent, such that this lack of integration, in the form of dissociation, is eventually internalized by the child. Thus, this model postulates that for an individual to be able to experience fully integrated mental states, a collaborative dialogue between the parent and child must be constructed. This dialogue must be constructed with the collaboration of the child, such that the parent elicits the child's contributions and actively considers his experience, and an expression of this consideration on the part of the parent is demonstrated back to the child in developmentally appropriate ways that will be understood by the child. Conversely, the parent's inability to acknowledge the child's experiences or needs while in dialogue (in other words, "shutting out" the child) may result in the child's failure to understand and/or integrate these same self-experiences and eventually lead to the development of dissociative symptoms.

6.5.4 Clinical Vignette 3

Another clinical example, in which there was a frightening childhood experience in the context of a nonabusive family, provides a vivid illustration of the pivotal role of parental containment in the processes leading to dissociative phenomena. A man in his mid-forties, whom we'll call John, presented for treatment with a severe generalized anxiety disorder, as well as intense fears of abandonment in his short and unstable romantic relationships. As the treatment relationship progressed over a 3-year period, he began to comment on the therapist's reliability and also began to have increasingly frightening nightmares of being killed, tortured, or mutilated. These increasingly fearful images finally culminated in a fugue state one evening that lasted several hours and was accompanied by chills, nausea, and diarrhea. In this state, which he said was like "dreaming while he was awake," he became increasingly frantic as he experienced himself being in a refugee camp desperately trying to match up young children with their mothers, only to find that they kept getting separated again.

He called the therapist and she scheduled an extra session to meet the next day. When he arrived at the session, he sat down and said that he had had trouble taking off his coat as he came into the office. It was difficult, he said, because there were two of him in the coat. One persona was a young boy named Buddy, who was the one who loved people and had feelings. Buddy's name was the same as the name of the boy in the movie *Fried Green Tomatoes* who was killed by a train when his foot became stuck in the railroad tracks. The other person in his coat was a hostile and distrustful man named Max, whose job it was to protect Buddy and drive away anyone who tried to get close to him. As he left the session, he said to his therapist of three years, "I just want you to know that if I left treatment now, I wouldn't remember who you are."

In the sessions after that eventful day, John alternated between being enraged at the therapist and beginning to recall images of being hospitalized for several weeks unexpectedly at age 4½ for a life-threatening infection. As he recalled this experience, which he only remembered in a fragmentary way, several pivotal scenes emerged. He remembered that he was told by his family that they were going for a drive and then he found himself in the hospital with no warning or discussion. After he had been admitted, his parents told him they were going to park the car and would be back in a minute, but they didn't return. His mother had never learned how to drive, so his parents only visited him once a week on Sundays. In one particularly poignant session, he remembered his parents coming to visit and seeing his mother looking at him very upset and frightened. He said, "I knew that she needed someone to help her and a part of me slipped out through a crack in the floor." Later in the same session he said, "I think I forgot my mother when I was in the hospital." His tendency to dissociate at moments of neediness continued into his adult life.

At the time that these images of his hospitalization were being explored in treatment, the extended separation from his parents was viewed as traumatic by definition and as fully accounting for the severity of his symptoms. It was not until much later in the treatment that both he and his therapist more fully appreciated how role-reversed his relationship with his mother always had been and continued to be. Accordingly, both the research results previously reviewed and John's account of his early hospitalization point to the relational context of this event as critical to whether or not a dissociative solution occurred. If his parents had been able to tolerate his sadness and rage and remain in a collaborative and psychologically containing dialogue with him throughout that experience, would the dissociative outcome have been the same?

6.6 CLINICAL IMPLICATIONS

The first clinical implication of the new data from developmental research is that the capacity of attachment figures for modulating fearful arousal in a responsive dialogue with the child may have a major impact on the development of dissociative symptoms over time. The second clinical implication of these data is that traumatic events are often discrete occurrences, while maternal affective unavailability and disrupted maternal communication are frequently enduring day-in-day-out features of the childhood years. In contrast to a more discrete traumatic event, the child's fear of remaining unseen and unheard by his caregiver, resulting in unmet needs, is worked into the fabric of identity from a very early age. Therefore, the resolution of traumatic events and dissociative symptoms in treatment may come about more quickly than the resolution of long-standing patterns of affective unavailability, disrupted communication, and role reversal in the transference. The imbalance in the relationship is so constant and implicit from a very early age that it can be extremely difficult for the patient to articulate or the therapist to identify and may take a very long time to work out in the therapeutic engagement.

What is unique about this model of the parent-child dialogue is that it may help to address current gaps in the dissociation literature. This model may lend itself to providing a better understanding of nontraumatized individuals who dissociate, as well as of individuals traumatized by war or other nonfamilial experiences who do not develop dissociation. It offers a framework for understanding why individuals vary so greatly in the development of dissociation in response to trauma. This model may also provide a more nuanced understanding of Liotti's work regarding the relationship between infant disorganization and dissociation, by adding to the model a finer description of the particular relational transactions that underlie both disorganization in infancy and dissociation in early adulthood.

It is important to note, however, that while the studies reviewed in this chapter provide empirical evidence regarding the influential role of infant disorganization and the parent-infant dialogue in the development of dissociation, it is not our intent to advance the view that these variables are the only, or even the most important, factors in this development. Clearly, such development occurs within a complex web of environmental, societal, familial, and genetic factors that are all likely to interact in ways that we have only begun to understand.

Accordingly, more research is needed in this field in an attempt to expand our current understanding of the role of relational factors in the phenomenology, etiology, and development of dissociation throughout the life span.

Portions of this chapter have been reprinted from *Psychiatric Clinics of North America*, Volume 29, Lyons-Ruth, K., Dutra, L., Schuder, M., & Bianchi, I., From infant attachment disorganization to adult dissociation: Relational adaptations or traumatic experiences?, pp. 63-86, Copyright (2006), with permission from Elsevier.

REFERENCES

Ainsworth, M. D. S., Blehar, M., Waters, E., & Wall, S. (1978). *Patterns of attachment: A psychological study of the Strange Situation*. Hillsdale, NJ: Erlbaum.

Barach, P. M. (1991). Multiple Personality Disorder as an attachment disorder. *Dissociation, 4*, 117–123.

Bowlby, J. (1973). *Attachment and Loss, Vol. 2, Separation*. New York: Basic Books.

Braun, B. G., & Sachs, R. G. (1985). The development of multiple personality disorder: Predisposing, precipitating, and perpetuating factors. In R. P. Kluft (Ed.), *Childhood antecedents of multiple personality* (pp. 37–64). Washington, DC: American Psychiatric Press.

Dutra, L., Bureau, J. F., Homes, B., Lyubchik, A., & Lyons-Ruth, K. (in press). Quality of early care and childhood trauma: A prospective study of developmental pathways to dissociation. *Journal of Nervous and Mental Disease.*

Egeland, B., & Susman-Stillman, A. (1996). Dissociation and abuse across generations. *Child Abuse and Neglect, 20 (11)*, 1123–1132.

Herman, J. L. (1992). Complex PTSD: A syndrome in survivors of prolonged and repeated trauma. *Journal of Traumatic Stress, 5*, 377–391.

Herman, J. L. (1997). Trauma and recovery: The aftermath of violence from domestic abuse to political terror. New York: Basic Books.

Kluft, R. P. (1984). Multiple personality in childhood. *Psychiatric Clinics of North America, 7 (1)*, 121–134.

Liotti, G. (1992). Disorganized/disoriented attachment in the etiology of the dissociative disorders. *Dissociation, 5(4)*, 196–204.

Maaranen, P., Tanskanen, A., Haatainen, K., Koivumaa-Honkanen, H., Hintikka, J., & Viinamaki, H. (2004). Somatoform dissociation and adverse childhood experiences in the general population. *Journal of Nervous and Mental Disease, 192*, 337–342.

Main, M., & Hesse, E. (1990). Parents' unresolved traumatic experiences are related to infant disorganized attachment status: Is frightened and/or frightening parental behavior the linking mechanism? In M. Greenberg, D. Cicchetti, & E. M. Cummings (Eds.), *Attachment in the preschool years: Theory, research and intervention* (pp. 161–184). Chicago: University of Chicago Press.

Malinosky-Rummell, R. R., & Hoier, T. S. (1991). Validating measures of dissociation in sexually abused and non-abused children. *Behavioral Assessment, 13*, 341–357.

Mann, B. J., & Sanders, S. (1994). Child dissociation and the family context. *Journal of Abnormal Child Psychology, 22*, 373–388.

Modestin, J., Lotscher, K., & Thomas, E. (2002). Dissociative experience and their correlates in young non-patients. *Psychology and Psychotherapy, 75*, 53–64.

Ogawa, J., Sroufe, L. A., Weinfield, N. S., Carlson, E., & Egeland, B. (1997). Development and the fragmented self: A longitudinal study of dissociative symptomatology in a non-clinical sample. *Development and Psychopathology, 4*, 855–879.

Putnam, F. W. (1997). *Dissociation in children and adolescents*. New York: Guilford.

Spiegel, D. (1986). Dissociation, double binds, and posttraumatic stress in Multiple Personality Disorder. In B. G. Braun (Ed.), *Treatment of Multiple Personality Disorder* (pp. 61–77). Washington, DC: American Psychiatric Press.

Terr, L. A. (1991). Childhood traumas: An outline and overview. *American Journal of Psychiatry, 148*, 1–20.

Van der Kolk, B. A. (1996). The complexity of adaptation to trauma: self-regulation, stimulus discrimination, and characterological development. In B. A. van der Kolk, A. C. McFarlane, & L. Weisaeth (Eds.), *Traumatic stress: The effects of overwhelming experience on mind, body, and society* (pp. 182–213). New York: The Guilford Press.

Van der Kolk, B. A., Van der Hart, O., & Marmar, C. R. (1996). Dissociation and information processing in posttraumatic stress disorder. In B. A. van der Kolk, A. C. McFarlane, & L. Weisaeth, (Eds.), *Traumatic stress: The effects of overwhelming experience on mind, body, and society* (pp. 303–327). New York: The Guilford Press.

Whitmer, G. (2001). On the nature of dissociation. *Psychoanalytic Quarterly, 70*, 807–837.

7 Adaptive Dissociation: Information Processing and Response to Betrayal

M. Rose Barlow, PhD
Jennifer J. Freyd, PhD

OUTLINE

7.1 ABSTRACT

Betrayal trauma theory (Freyd, 1996) proposes that dissociation is one mechanism by which traumatized individuals can be unaware of information that could threaten an important relationship. This chapter proposes a view of dissociation as a set of characteristics, including information processing tendencies, that can be organized into two separate but connected branches of symptoms. One branch consists of more transient, normative dissociative experiences without a trauma-based etiology, and the other consists of trauma-based dissociation that is less transient and more severe. Dissociative information processing includes differences in dividing and directing attention, as well as deficits in memory and metacognition. Suggestions are discussed for future research regarding dissociation as an adaptive information processing style.

Severe dissociation involves a profound fragmentation of the self. It affects and is affected by physiological responses, cognitions, and social interactions. As part of this fragmentation of self, dissociation can also be seen as a fragmented style of information processing, whether the information to be processed consists of stimuli in a laboratory or emotions in everyday life. In this chapter we present the viewpoint that the dissociative information processing style is developed as an adaptation to trauma, and is a way to not know about potentially threatening information. A primary type of threatening information is that which threatens a necessary attachment relationship. Using betrayal trauma theory (Freyd, 1996, 2001), we explain in this chapter why it may be advantageous for a trauma victim's survival to dissociate information that threatens the attachment relationship. First we offer a framework for understanding the phenomenology of dissociation based on the idea of two branches.

7.2 A PROPOSED FRAMEWORK: TWO BRANCHES OF DISSOCIATION

How should dissociation be understood? Van der Hart and Dorahy (this volume) discuss "broad" and "narrow" conceptualizations of dissociation. Carlson, Yates, and Sroufe (this volume) also discuss the debate between the "continuum" and "taxon" views of dissociation. In defining the realm of dissociation and in resolving the seeming contradictions among these views, it may be helpful to view dissociation as a set of characteristics, including information processing, that consists of two separate but connected branches. One branch, called Branch A dissociation for convenience, consists mainly of "normative" types of dissociative activity that are not caused by trauma. Examples include highway hypnosis, absorption, fantasy, and voluntary identity alteration (e.g., in religious rituals). These examples are more transient states of dissociation. The other branch, Branch B, has a trauma-based etiology. Examples of this type of dissociation include less transient occurrences such as depersonalization, identity confusion, and involuntary identity alteration. Branch B dissociation may itself consist of several sub-branches, and empirical research can help clarify the relationships among these concepts. For example, how are depersonalization symptoms related to amnesia symptoms? They have in common that they are more persistent than are Branch A symptoms and are regarded as more pathological. To what degree do they covary? Do they function in parallel or synergistically?

Dividing dissociation into branches in this manner is consistent with factor analyses of the Dissociative Experiences Scale (DES; Bernstein & Putnam, 1986) conducted by Ross and colleagues (Ross, Ellason, & Anderson, 1995; Ross, Joshi, & Currie, 1991). The analyses revealed three factors measured by the DES: absorption-imagination, activities of dissociated states, and depersonalization-derealization (Ross, et al., 1991; Ross, et al., 1995). Three similar factors emerged from a modified version of the DES (Goldberg, 1999). (For a review of factor analysis studies, see Holmes, Brown, Mansell, Fearon, Hunter, Frasquilho, et al., 2005.) In the current chapter's framework, Branch A dissociation is measured by the first factor, absorption-imagination. The other two factors make up Branch B dissociation, and the existence of these differing factors argues for a possible further division of the Branch B symptoms.

The two classes of symptoms are not unrelated. For example, it is possible that the presence of Branch A symptoms may facilitate the development of Branch B symptoms in the face of sufficient trauma and betrayal. In general, dissociation is high in children and declines with age, in part due to the high percentage of time children spend in fantasy play and imaginary worlds. Macfie, Cicchetti, and Toth (2001) found that, during the preschool years, dissociation increased for maltreated children but did not increase for nonmaltreated children. Becker-Blease, Deater-Deckard, Eley, Freyd, Stevenson, and Plomin (2004) examined genetic and environmental effects on individual differences in dissociation in children and adolescents. This study was unique in that it allowed analysis of how influences may change over time, because in one of their samples the children were reevaluated every year for four years. Their results showed that amount of dissociation was relatively stable from middle childhood through mid-adolescence. Although there is some support for the assertion that dissociation declines with age, this decline is probably driven largely by the presence or absence of abuse, and by whether hypnotizability is used as a measure of dissociation (see Putnam, 1997, for a review; cf. Macfie, Cicchetti, & Toth, 2001). The authors hypothesized that environmental factors reinforce sibling differentiation rather than sibling similarity, and that the normative dissociation measured in this study may constitute an underlying diathesis that affects how children respond to later trauma (Becker-Blease, Deater-Deckard, et al., 2004). They pointed out, however, that their methods were based on the assumption that all the siblings of the same family (full siblings, adopted siblings, MZ and DZ twins) had the same environment, an assumption that may be faulty in some circumstances. For normative dissociation at least, genetic factors may play a role in the development of dissociation. This theory is bolstered by the findings of Ogawa and colleagues (1997) that temperament measured at the age of three months was one of the best predictors of dissociation in adolescence.

It is possible that characteristics such as fantasy-proneness and absorption (Branch A symptoms) facilitate the development of dissociation later in life (Pekala, Angelini, & Kumar, 2001). Indeed, some early theorists in the field of dissociation proposed that multiple personalities cannot develop without a higher-than-usual inborn capacity to dissociate (see Braun & Sachs, 1985). However, very little research has assessed different types of dissociative experiences in young children and compared them longitudinally to types of symptoms experienced in adulthood. Future research should address the relationships between Branch A and Branch B symptoms.

It is currently unclear how somatoform dissociation fits into this classification system. Somatoform dissociation (see Nijenhuis, this volume) consists of physical symptoms, such as sensory losses, perceptual alterations, and pain, which are not well measured by the DES or similar instruments. However, somatoform dissociation has been shown to have a strong association with the psychological symptoms measured on the DES (Nijenhuis, Van Dyck, Spinhoven, Van der Hart, Chatrou, Vanderlinden, et al., 1999). The current measure of somatoform dissociation, the Somatoform Dissociation Questionnaire (Nijenhuis, Spinhoven, Van Dyck, Van der Hart, & Vanderlinden, 1996, 1997), was developed specifically on patients with dissociative disorders, in order to measure the symptoms of those disorders. Therefore, it seems plausible that somatoform dissociation should be considered a branch of the Branch B symptoms, which are less transient and more disruptive than are the Branch A symptoms.

Brown (2002) also divided dissociation into two categories, which he called Type 1 and Type 2 dissociation. Brown's Type 2 dissociation is in some ways related to the Branch A symptoms discussed in this chapter, but Brown included certain kinds of more serious, trauma-based dissociation in this category. According to Brown (2002), Type 2 dissociation involves altered states of consciousness including derealization and out-of-body experiences, similar to the symptoms described as Branch A. However, Brown's Type 2 dissociation also involves peritraumatic dissociation. In keeping with the proposed Branch A definition, these dissociative symptoms are relatively transient. Similar to the framework of this chapter, Brown (2002) also combined somatoform symptoms with dissociative symptoms that are long-lasting and severe, including most of the dissociative disorders. Again, this classification is similar to the current description of Branch B symptoms. One difference is that Brown defined this category of dissociation by the presence of physical symptoms, in essence stating that the defining characteristic of dissociative disorders is physical, rather than psychological, symptoms. Although this focus is somewhat at odds with the conceptualization of dissociation outlined in this chapter, it is nevertheless interesting to note that Brown (2002) related dissociative disorders specifically to information processing.

The current conceptualization of dissociation as two branches of symptoms allows a place for both the broad and narrow views, and combines the continuum and the taxon views of dissociation. It also allows the field to study both severe dissociation, which is caused by trauma, and less severe dissociation, which can be either trauma-based or merely an altered state of consciousness. Further, it allows these two conceptualizations of dissociation to be separated from each other, so that researchers and clinicians can decide more easily where to focus their efforts.

7.3 DISSOCIATION AS AN INFORMATION PROCESSING STYLE

Dissociation has been defined as a jump between behavioral states, or as a special and distinct state of profound disconnection (Putnam, 1997). The American Psychiatric Association (2000) defines it as a separation between processes that are normally integrated, such as events, emotions, and memories. What these definitions have in common is a separation of information. Whether dissociation is seen as a jump between states, as a special state, or as a functional (rather than physiological) separation, all definitions agree that dissociation allows memories, skills, affects, and other knowledge to be sectioned off and stored in less easily accessible ways. The state-dependent nature of dissociated memories is not disputed, although the motivations assumed to underlie this segmentation can vary by theory. Whereas psychoanalytic theory views dissociation as a primitive defense against being overwhelmed by unacceptable or unmanageable emotions, other theories (such as attachment theories, including betrayal trauma theory, discussed later) emphasize that the most salient danger is not that of being threatened by one's own emotions, but rather the very real danger of losing an essential attachment relationship and with it the physical and emotional care necessary for survival.

The phenomenon of state-dependent memory is well documented and does appear to play a role in memory functioning in dissociative identity disorder (DID). Context exerts a definite influence on what is remembered. For example, people in a depressed state tend to disproportionately report negative memories, while people in a manic episode inflate their recall of personal successes (Putnam, 1997). An intriguing application of this effect is Sahakyan and Kelley's (2002) theory of contextual change and amnesia in directed forgetting tasks. Sahakyan and Kelley proposed that memory performance in directed forgetting tasks can be explained by the participants in the "forget" group changing their internal context in between the lists. For participants in the "forget" group, they are told to forget List 1 but not List 2, so therefore the testing situation is different from the context of List 1, and more closely matches the context in which they saw List 2. For the "remember" group, there is no difference between the two lists and therefore the testing context is similar to the context of both lists, essentially creating one long list with a break in the middle.

Solid cognitive experimental evidence supports this theory, but Sahakyan and Kelley (2002) have not extended their results to the realm of memory for trauma. The conditions of child abuse that lead to dissociation are very similar to a directed forgetting task. It is easy to see how this situation, in conjunction with the contextual hypothesis of forgetting, can explain the dissociation of traumatic memory. In most of everyday life, the context is radically different from the context in which abuse occurs. Abuse usually happens only in private, in secret, often at night. Therefore the context mismatch makes it less likely that the victim will recall the abuse until placed in a similar situation. The more effectively the encoding context is reinstated, the easier it is to recall the memories (Sahakyan & Kelley, 2002).

As compelling as this account is, however, state-dependent memory is not likely to be the main explanation for the patterns of amnesia seen in DID. Amnesia in DID tends to be more robust under recognition conditions than is forgetting caused by state-dependent memory, which usually only manifests under conditions of free recall (e.g., Bower, 1994). The amnesia seen in DID also tends to be much more severe than is state-dependent forgetting (Bower, 1994; Peters, Uyterlinde, Consemulder, & Van der Hart, 1998; Silberman, Putnam, Weingartner, Braun, & Post, 1985; Szostak, Lister, Eckardt, & Weingartner, 1994).

Studies conducted with nondiagnosed college student participants have shown some interesting results regarding the interactions of attention, memory, and dissociation. While it is debatable how well their results would generalize to actual memories and experiences of abuse, these studies provide an intriguing look at the advantages and cognitive processes of dissociation. Freyd, Martorello, Alvarado, Hayes, and Christman (1998) found that high dissociators showed greater Stroop interference but not overall reaction time slowing in a standard, selective attention Stroop task. The stimuli were all neutral words; the use of kinship terms had no effect on results. DePrince and Freyd (1999) found that performance on the Stroop task was related to the attentional demands of the task, such that high dissociators (DES > 20) performed worse in a selective attention task and better in a divided attention task relative to low dissociators (DES < 10). The high dissociators also recalled fewer sexual trauma words and more neutral words compared to the low dissociators. These results may indicate that at least nonpathological dissociation is a distinct style of information processing.

The results of DePrince and Freyd (1999) were partially replicated in a sample of four- and five-year-olds (Becker-Blease, Freyd, & Pears, 2004). The sample included 48 children with no reported abuse and 20 children with parent-reported abuse histories. In contrast to the findings of DePrince and Freyd, Becker-Blease and colleagues found that dissociation levels alone did not predict memory scores under either selective or divided attention conditions. However, the combination of abuse history and dissociation scores did predict memory performance. Eight children had both high dissociation scores and reported abuse, while 30 children had low dissociation scores and no reported abuse. Comparing these two groups, the same effect as was shown by DePrince and Freyd (1999) appeared: under divided attention conditions, the high dissociators with abuse remembered fewer charged pictures than did the low dissociation/no abuse group (Becker-Blease, Freyd, & Pears, 2004). These findings provide further support for the idea that abuse may lead to a distinctive attention style that includes dissociation and memory differences.

Another study of 105 female college students also assessed dissociation and attentional direction (Waller, Quinton, & Watson, 1995). Participants were split at the median DES score into high and low dissociator groups. In a selective attention task with neutral and threatening words, the high dissociation group responded more slowly to the presence of threatening words than did the low dissociation group, although they perceived the words equally well (Waller, et al., 1995). This effect was mostly the result of high levels of absorption in the high dissociators, not of the presence of "pathological" dissociation, which is not surprising because participants with present or past DSM diagnoses of any kind were excluded from analysis.

Supporting the findings of DePrince and Freyd (1999), De Ruiter and colleagues (2003) found that high dissociators in a college population had an advantage in both selecting *and* dividing attention relative to low dissociators. In this study, nonspecific threat words, but not neutral words, helped only the high dissociators reduce reaction time in detecting a relevant characteristic of the words. Low dissociators did not show a reaction time benefit with negative emotional valence and overall performed worse than the high dissociators (De Ruiter, Phaf, Veltman, Kok, & Van Dyck, 2003). Like DePrince and Freyd, this study supports the assertion that divided attention is a situation in which high levels of dissociation are differentially adaptive.

High dissociators also showed slightly longer verbal working memory than low dissociators in another college sample (De Ruiter, Phaf, Elzinga, & Van Dyck, 2004). A difference of about half a word may be attributable to the effects of having a few very high or "pathological" dissociators in the high dissociation group; this advantage was more associated with identity confusion/amnesia than it was with absorption. In a smaller follow-up study, Veltman, De Ruiter, Rombouts, Lazeron, Barkhof, Van Dyck, and colleagues (2005) found that high dissociators performed better than low dissociators on two different working memory tasks. In addition, the high dissociators recruited relevant brain networks more highly during the tasks than did the low dissociators.

Further evidence of a distinct information processing style in clinical samples of DID participants comes from the work of Dorahy and colleagues, who assessed cognitive inhibition. Cognitive inhibition is the extent to which distracting or irrelevant stimuli can be inhibited or ignored in order to free up attentional resources to focus on relevant stimuli. In an initial study assessing inhibitory functioning in DID with the use of neutral words as distracters, the participants with DID had slower reaction times compared to general population and psychiatric samples. The DID participants also showed weakened inhibitory functioning compared to the general population (Dorahy, Irwin, & Middleton, 2002). In contrast, two subsequent studies found that, when single numbers rather than words were used as distracters, the DID participants did *not* have lower inhibitory functioning than other groups. All the DID participants in these studies completed the experiments while in their host alters, which were disconnected from the emotions of traumatic memories. Unfortunately, neither of these two studies could determine whether the findings were affected by gender differences among the groups (Dorahy, Irwin, & Middleton, 2004; Dorahy, Middleton, & Irwin, 2004).

A final study did use comparison groups matched for gender, and attempted to explain the discrepancy in these three studies with regard to the presence or absence of deficits in cognitive inhibition in DID (Dorahy, Middleton, & Irwin, 2005). The authors hypothesized that the initial study using words as stimuli was a more anxiety-producing context for the DID participants than for the other groups, because some participants had reported that they were constantly on alert for triggering associations from the seemingly neutral words. This anxiety therefore reduced the DID participants' abilities to effectively filter distracting stimuli, but the single digits used in the other two studies did not present this problem. Therefore, the final study used a manipulation of numbers and words in order to vary the experimental context from neutral to negative. DID participants reported more anxiety in the negative context than did the depressed and general population control groups. DID participants showed reduced cognitive inhibition in the negative but not the neutral context, while for the other two groups the neutral and negative contexts did not affect performance. Furthermore, the DID participants also displayed an attentional bias that slowed their reactions to negative but not neutral words, and this result did not occur in the other two groups (Dorahy, et al., 2005). This experiment provided support for the theory that anxiety differentially affects high dissociators' abilities to process information.

A related line of research using different methodology also examined information processing in dissociation. In a directed forgetting paradigm, again using a college student sample, DePrince and Freyd (2001) found the same pattern of memory results that they had found before, namely, high dissociators recalled fewer trauma and more neutral words when divided attention was required, compared with low dissociators. This pattern was true of the to-be-remembered (TBR) words that had been presented using the item method; there was no difference between high and low dissociators on memory for to-be-forgotten (TBF) words. The authors concluded that high levels of dissociation were helpful in blocking out traumatic information only in situations where participants could not ignore it. The same pattern of results regarding divided attention and dissociation was later replicated using the list method of directed forgetting (DePrince & Freyd, 2004). This interaction effect has also been analyzed elsewhere (see DePrince, Freyd, & Malle, 2007).

Results that seem to contradict this pattern came from two other directed forgetting experiments using the item method (Elzinga, De Beurs, Sergeant, Van Dyck, & Phaf, 2000). In the first experiment, 35 college students were split at the median DIS-Q score into two groups, labeled high and low dissociative groups. When presented with neutral words, the two groups had no significant difference in directed forgetting performance. In fact, using only the performance of the 15 lowest and highest dissociators, the high dissociators appeared to have a decrease in directed forgetting ability, being less able to forget the TBF words. A follow-up experiment included 43 college students, again split into high and low dissociators, as well as 14 patients with dissociative disorders. In this experiment, sexual words and anxiety words were added to the neutral words. Again, the patient group showed a decreased ability to forget the TBF words, especially words related to sex. The overall results showed that the high-dissociating students and the diagnosed patients outperformed the low-dissociating students on memory tests (Elzinga, et al., 2000). These experiments were performed under selective attention demands. Therefore the lack of benefit in high levels of dissociation from the first experiment is not surprising, as DePrince and Freyd only find these benefits under divided attention conditions. The other results are slightly more puzzling, however, and more careful control over and analysis of experimental conditions is needed in future research.

In a further examination of these effects, Elzinga and colleagues conducted a directed forgetting experiment within and across the alters of 12 patients with DID who could switch on demand (Elzinga, Phaf, Ardon, & Van Dyck, 2003). Stimuli were neutral and sexual trauma words. Consistent with participants' reports of inter-identity amnesia, they recalled more words when tested in the same alter who had read the words than when tested across alters. Overall, the participants recalled more trauma words than neutral words, which is the normal finding under selective attention conditions. Also consistent with their previous research, the authors found that, when tested within an alter, there was a lack of forgetting for the TBF words. However, when tested across alters, directed forgetting functioned so that TBF words were recalled less frequently than TBR words. The authors suggested that switching alters is a major strategy that DID patients can use to block out unwanted information (Elzinga, et al., 2003).

Additional investigation into dissociation and memory processing has revealed that there may be fundamental differences in the way memory is organized in participants with DID. In one study (Barlow, under review), DID participants showed a decreased ability to answer detailed questions about a story containing fear, compared with a neutral story. This decrease did not appear in a student comparison group. The DID participants' ability to answer questions about the gist of the stories was unaffected by emotional valence. This pattern of results is consistent with the DID participants' verbal reports. They reported being more distracted during the fearful story and giving less attention to the details because they were either "spaced out," trying not to switch, actively switching, or having internal dialogue (Barlow, under review). Putnam (1994) suggested that during the switch process, participants' abilities to observe stimuli, to learn, and to form new memories are impaired.

Differences between implicit and explicit access systems have also been hypothesized to play a role in dissociation (Siegel, 1996; Van der Kolk & Fisler, 1995). Van der Kolk has proposed that a narrowing of awareness and the disabling of Broca's area are partially responsible for the difficulty of retrieving memories of trauma. As a result, traumatic memories are encoded without words and are difficult to access.

In a study with 30 DID participants, one-third of the participants reported some amnesia for childhood events that were nontraumatic but emotionally significant (Van der Hart, Bolt, & Van der Kolk, 2005). The DID participants not only reported the common finding of fragmented and sensory recall of traumatic memories, but, unexpectedly, they also reported having the same kind of fragmented and somatosensory memories for nontraumatic significant events. The authors suggested that a key feature of dissociation is a reduced integration of sensory information with autobiographical memory, possibly due to impaired hippocampal functioning (Van der Hart, et al., 2005).

7.4 THE DOMAIN OF DISSOCIATION: METACOGNITION

Dissociation includes many kinds of disruptions of the self (see Dell, this volume). Even common, voluntary forms of dissociation, such as fantasy, absorption, or meditation, involve a temporary removal of or change in the self. In the case of DID, the self is most highly fragmented. People with DID often exhibit a wide variety of confusing and seemingly bizarre physical, mental, and emotional symptoms (Putnam, 1989, provides an excellent overview of DID phenomenology). The five most prominent symptoms of DID are amnesia, depersonalization, derealization, alterations in identity, and identity confusion (APA, 2000; Gleaves, May, & Cardeña, 2001; ISSD, 1997; Steinberg, 2001). Patients with DID are highly polysymptomatic, presenting with almost every other disorder in the DSM. Because of this factor, they are often misdiagnosed and can spend years in unproductive treatment before receiving the correct diagnosis (e.g., Maldonado, Butler, & Spiegel, 1998).

Severe dissociation also involves deficits in metacognition, and these deficits complicate the assessment of amnesia. In addition to having absolute memory loss, people with DID also have a reduced ability to access or utilize the information they do have. Therefore, they honestly report amnesia for information that can be recalled by other parts of themselves than the one being tested, or information that is accessible by other testing methods than the one being used. One of the most frequently cited studies was conducted by Nissen, Ross, Willingham, MacKenzie, and Schacter (1988). In one participant with DID, mutually amnesic alters reported no transfer of information on explicit memory tests, although some of the implicit tests showed some "leakage" of information. The authors hypothesized that this pattern of results was due to differences in the stimuli. Material most likely to leak was stimuli that were interpretable without knowledge-based processing; material that did not leak required interpretation and gist for understanding.

In two studies, Eich, Macaulay, Loewenstein, and Dihle (1997a, 1997b) again found that, while there was no explicit transfer of knowledge between amnesic alters, there was some leakage of information when measured on tests that used priming, such as picture-fragment completion. Peters and colleagues (1998) examined the transfer of neutral information between amnesic alters in four participants with DID. Word list memory was assessed both explicitly, using free recall and recognition, and implicitly, using word stem completion. Contrary to the authors' hypothesis, but in line with the findings of Nissen and colleagues (1988), there was no leakage of information between alters on the word stem completion task. On the explicit memory tests, evidence supported participants' reports of one-way amnesia, though one participant showed mixed results (Peters, et al., 1998).

A more recent study of information transfer in DID used a one-week delay to test memory for word lists in 21 DID participants that reported the presence of one-way amnesia between two of their alters (Huntjens, Postma, Peters, Woertman, & Van der Hart, 2003). The stimuli used in this experiment were all emotionally neutral. Overall, the performance of the DID participants was equivalent to that of control participants. When exposed to lists of words that shared categories and therefore caused interference, the DID participants were no better than other participants at resisting the memory interference or at discriminating lists. On explicit memory tests of recall and recognition, however, the DID participants did not perform as well as the controls (Huntjens, et al., 2003).

A similar pattern of results was found in a study of 40 nondiagnosed college students (Kindt & Van den Hout, 2003). The more participants dissociated while watching an aversive film, the more fragmented were their reported memories of the film. However, on cued recall and recognition tests, the high-dissociating participants performed no worse than those participants who did not dissociate while watching the film. The authors suggested that amnesia related to dissociation is largely a phenomenon of meta-memory, rather than of "objective" memory performance (Kindt & Van den Hout, 2003).

7.5 WHAT LEADS TO HIGH TRAIT DISSOCIATION?

Models of dissociation continue to be revised as researchers become increasingly aware of the prevalence of trauma and of its effects. This section discusses the pathway to high dissociation according to betrayal trauma theory: trauma and the importance of human attachment. Though there is some evidence that other factors, such as genetics, may play a role in the development of dissociation (e.g., Becker-Blease, Deater-Deckard, et al., 2004), this section will focus on interpersonal betrayal.

7.6 TRAUMA

Severe dissociative disorders are almost always the result of childhood trauma (e.g., Maldonado, et al., 1998; Putnam, 1995, 1996). Numerous correlational studies have confirmed a high incidence of childhood trauma—sexual, physical, and probably emotional abuse—in adults and children with dissociative disorders or very high levels of dissociation (e.g., Bowman, Blix, & Coons, 1985; Chu & Dill, 1990; Draijer & Langeland, 1999; Kisiel & Lyons, 2001; Loewenstein, 1994; Nijenhuis, Spinhoven, Van Dyck, Van der Hart, & Vanderlinden, 1998; Zlotnick, Begin, Shea, Pearlstein, Simpson, & Costello, 1994; Zlotnick, Shea, Pearlstein, Begin, Simpson, & Costello, 1996). Many of these studies further find that an earlier age of trauma, more severe trauma, and more perpetrators also increase the risk of developing a dissociative disorder. It is difficult to know which aspect of trauma leads most specifically to dissociation, because many of the risk factors are confounded—for example, more severe and frequent trauma may begin at a younger age, involve more perpetrators and more force, and occur in a general atmosphere of family dysfunction (e.g., Putnam, 1996). It is probably the combination of several of these factors, rather than trauma alone, that causes impaired information processing and high levels of state dissociation (Briere, 2006).

7.7 DEVELOPMENT OF TRAUMATIC DISSOCIATION

7.7.1 MECHANISMS

The mechanisms by which trauma disrupts information processing and leads to dissociation are still under debate. High levels of trauma may result in an increased facility with divided attention (e.g., DePrince & Freyd, 1999). Intense psychological trauma may also constrain the functioning of neural networks by "cementing" just a few connections into a schema, which is a rigid pattern of connection strengths. This process leads to an inability to respond flexibly to situations, even when the trauma is no longer present (Li & Spiegel, 1992). Disorganized attachment also increases vulnerability to dissociative disorders, but is not in itself sufficient without additional trauma (Hesse & Main, 2000). Dissociative disorders emerge when defense mechanisms break down and attachment to a caregiver is massively activated, causing rapid switching of internal working models (IWMs) to occur. These incoherent and multiple IWMs only increase the feelings of fear and anxiety in the face of a new trauma, and ensure that further dissociation will occur (Liotti, 1999).

In a thorough examination of the effects of trauma on infants' brain development, Schore (2001) explained that abusive caregivers not only do not help infants learn to regulate their arousal, but they actively induce dysregulation without repair capabilities. This situation results in wild alterations of the infant's biochemistry, with resulting damage to the developing brain. The orbitalfrontal cortex (OFC) develops substantially during the same years that attachment to a caregiver is being formed and emphasized, approximately age 10 to 12 months, with another period of rapid maturation between the ages of 6 and 9 years. This development aids in regulating emotions and their related states so that the individual experiences inner continuity across contexts, which is critical for the development of a coherent sense of self. Interactions with the caregiver are the primary input used to shape the development and abilities of the OFC. Relational trauma during this early period results in drastic pruning in the OFC and subsequent information processing that relies on the amygdala instead, leading to fearful states without cortical input. Infants therefore cannot learn to regulate their states effectively and soothe themselves. Because of damaged connections from the right orbitofrontal area to the left language areas, affective information is not effectively transferred into language for processing, leading to difficulty expressing emotions (Schore, 2001). In this case, the OFC prohibits the integration of different representations of the self into one coherent self. When different contexts arise, the OFC responds on the basis of the immediate environment, which triggers different conceptions of the self to be active, without taking into account all the other senses of self from other contexts (Forrest, 2001). Therefore, the child grows up practicing dissociation.

7.7.2 Attachment and Betrayal Trauma Theory

Freyd's (1996) betrayal trauma theory is based largely on attachment models. It starts from two basic premises: infants need attachment, and the social human species needs to avoid cheaters. As infants, humans are dependent on their caregivers not only for basic physical needs of food, warmth, and so on, but also for emotional needs of love and care. In most circumstances, this attachment is what enables infants to survive. In situations of distress, such as hunger or loneliness, infants will seek the parents to whom they are attached, for example by crying or motioning to be picked up. Parents become attached to their offspring and take care of them; in return, babies give back love and affection.

Like other social primates, humans also have a strong motivation to avoid being cheated or betrayed (see Freyd, 1996, for further discussion of "cheater detectors"). The most adaptive responses to being cheated are either to confront the cheater or withdraw from further contact. Empowered individuals may do both.

When a young child is abused by a parent or caregiver, these two needs come into direct conflict. Withdrawing from or confronting the betrayer threatens survival in direct and indirect ways. Losing basic care may result in physical starvation, while losing or damaging the emotional care of the attachment relationship may result in emotional starvation. In this situation, it is more adaptive to not know about the trauma that is occurring. Therefore, the theory proposes, people become blind to betrayal to the extent that being aware of it would threaten a relationship in which they are dependent (Freyd, 1996).

Under this theory, the purpose of dissociation is not escape from pain, but the maintenance of the attachment relationship by not-knowing about information that would threaten it (Goldsmith, Barlow, & Freyd, 2004). The more important the relationship, the stronger the motivation to preserve it. Thus, abuse by a parent or other trusted caregiver is more likely to lead to amnesia and/or dissociation than is abuse by a stranger. Dissociation is therefore conceptualized as an adaptive survival response to a bad situation. Simultaneously, it may also be a maladaptive deficit in information processing that can make future revictimization more likely (DePrince & Freyd, 2007).

Betrayal trauma theory is supported by empirical evidence that relationship to the perpetrator is related to rates of forgetting (e.g., Freyd, DePrince, & Zurbriggen, 2001), as well as by reports from people with DID that the betrayal by trusted family and caregivers was the part of the trauma that most disrupted their internal organization of self (Steele, 2002). This basis of dissociation is consistent with Liotti's (1999) conceptualization of how disorganized attachment leads to dissociative disorders. Further support for this theory can be found in Freyd's (1996) reanalysis of previous data, as well as in many recent studies of sexual abuse that assess closeness and betrayal (e.g., Chu & Dill, 1990; Schultz, Passmore, & Yoder, 2003). Sheiman (1999) reported that sexually abused participants who had memory loss for the abuse were more likely to dissociate and to have been abused by someone close to them, compared to sexually abused participants without memory loss.

7.8 ALTERNATE CONCEPTUALIZATIONS OF DISSOCIATION

Nijenhuis's theory of structural dissociation has gained prominence in recent years, partly because it provides testable hypotheses about dissociative responses to various situations. Nijenhuis and colleagues distinguish between two possible kinds of states: the emotional personality, or EP, and the apparently normal personality, or ANP. EPs hold traumatic memory, often being stuck in the sensory experience of the memory and unaware of the passage of time (Nijenhuis, Van der Hart, & Steele, 2002). ANPs, in contrast, manage the tasks of daily life, such as working, and the functions of attachment and caretaking. They may be emotionally unconnected to, or amnesic for, past traumatic events (Nijenhuis & Van der Hart, 1999).

One benefit of this theory is that it can explain what appear to be opposite responses to threatening stimuli, depending on whether the personality being tested is an EP or an ANP. For example, ANPs seem to deal with threatening stimuli by averting their gaze, while EPs pay close attention to any potential threat; simulators cannot reproduce this pattern of results (cited in Nijenhuis, et al., 2002). The two types of systems evaluate memories and stimuli differently and may even become afraid of each other. Because these two systems are so different, it is difficult for integration to occur across them, particularly under conditions of neuroendocrine instability that are produced by chronic childhood stress and arousal. In fact, the activation of traumatic memories in an EP state can actually inhibit access to other kinds of memories (Nijenhuis & Van der Hart, 1999).

This theory explains the perpetuation and increase of dissociation, as the ANP is not equipped to deal with the emotional trauma held by the EP, and must therefore redissociate the traumatic memories and avoid anything that will trigger the emergence of the EP (Nijenhuis, et al., 2002). Further dissociation leads to even more deficits in integration. Nijenhuis and colleagues have also argued that structural dissociation is the key element that distinguishes true dissociation from related variations in consciousness that should not be considered in the taxonomy of dissociation (Van der Hart, Nijenhuis, Steele, & Brown, 2004).

Putnam's (1997) theory of discrete behavioral states is another theory that has been very influential. In brief, humans are born with the capacity for a few basic states (resting, dreaming, awake and alert, fussing, crying). These discrete states can be distinguished by patterns of affect, motor activity, spontaneous verbalization, heart rate, respiratory patterns, and attention. Later, development and experience contribute to the formation of more numerous and complex states. The infant's main task in the first few years of life is to acquire the ability to control his or her own behavioral state transitions. Parents play a crucial role in this process, teaching children to recognize and control their own emotional states, and how to reestablish them if they are disrupted. Parents also help children to know which state is appropriate for various situations, and to integrate these various states across contexts so that a unified sense of self develops (Putnam, 1997).

Abuse disrupts these processes. It leads to the necessity of children having different senses of self for different situations, which they use in an attempt to control the state of their caregivers and not get hurt. The vital importance of attachment prevents children from disconnecting entirely from abusive caregivers, but at the same time children are left reliant on parents who are actively undermining their growth. When the caregiver does not help regulate transitions between states, metacognition is impaired and the child does not develop a unitary self (Forrest, 2001; Putnam, 1997); in fact, abusive, dissociative, or inconsistent parents force the child to alternate rapidly between various behavioral states. Under these circumstances, the child's development takes a serious departure from the usual route. Dissociative states arise in response to social and environmental cues, and the child's knowledge and skills are isolated into mutually inaccessible states that are not always available (Putnam, 1997).

7.9 STRENGTHS AND WEAKNESSES OF THE CURRENT TWO-BRANCH THEORY

This chapter's conceptualization of dissociation as two branches of symptoms allows a place for both the broad and narrow views, and combines the continuum and the taxon views of dissociation. It also allows the field to study both severe dissociation, which is caused by trauma, and less severe dissociation, which can be either trauma-based or merely an altered state of consciousness. Furthermore, it is consistent with existing factor analyses and with other theorists who have viewed dissociation as an alteration in information processing abilities. A potential weakness of this theory is that it may be overinclusive and may rest (implicitly or explicitly) on perceived etiology in order to separate symptoms. Much of the experimental evidence that supports dissociation as an adaptive style of information processing is based on measurements of dissociation that are one-dimensional. Most laboratory research has measured as a unitary construct, which may have affected the specificity, applicability, and generalizability of the results.

7.10 DIRECTIONS FOR FUTURE RESEARCH

Further research is necessary in order to determine how the various Branch A and Branch B symptoms fit together as branches of a tree, much like the cladograms used in biology to represent how closely organisms are related to each other. Researchers should not only analyze results based on different dimensions of dissociation, but should include a dimensional approach in experimental design. Tasks should be designed to access and differentiate among various components of dissociation. For example, can laboratory tasks be constructed that induce depersonalization in participants, independent of derealization? Do results differ within participants depending on whether depersonalization or absorption is induced? Other studies should take a longitudinal approach in order to examine possible developmental relationships between Branch A and Branch B symptoms. Additional trauma symptoms, such as alexithymia and impaired social decision-making, may turn out to have strong connections to dissociative information processing styles, but these areas have typically not been studied in relation to dissociation (see DePrince & Freyd, 2007). Factor analysis and meta-analysis are useful techniques that have been infrequently applied in this domain. Such methods could help researchers create a clearer understanding of the multifaceted construct of dissociation.

Portions of this chapter are based on the first author's doctoral dissertation. The writing of this chapter was facilitated by funds from the Trauma and Oppression Research Fund of the University of Oregon Foundation. Address for correspondence: M. Rose Barlow, Department of Psychology, 1910 University Dr., Boise ID 83725-1715, U.S.A. E-mail: rosebarlow@boisestate.edu

REFERENCES

American Psychiatric Association (2000). DSM-IV-TR – *Diagnostic and statistical manual of mental disorders* (4th ed., text rev.). Washington, DC: Author.

Barlow, M. R. (under review). Memory for complex material in dissociative identity disorder.

Becker-Blease, K. A., Deater-Deckard, K., Eley, T., Freyd, J. J., Stevenson, J., & Plomin, R. (2004). A genetic analysis of individual differences in dissociative behaviors in childhood and adolescence. *Journal of Child Psychology and Psychiatry, 45*, 522–532.

Becker-Blease, K. A., Freyd, J. J, & Pears, K. C. (2004). Preschoolers' memory for threatening information depends on trauma history and attentional context: Implications for the development of dissociation. *Journal of Trauma & Dissociation*, *5*(1), 113–131.

Bernstein, E. M., & Putnam, F. W. (1986). Development, reliability, and validity of a dissociation scale. *Journal of Nervous and Mental Disease*, *174*, 727–735.

Bower, G. (1994). Temporary emotional states act like multiple personalities. In R. M. Klein & B. K. Doane (Eds.), *Psychological concepts and dissociative disorders* (pp. 207–234). Hillsdale, NJ: Lawrence Erlbaum Associates.

Bowman, E. S., Blix, S. F., & Coons, P. M. (1985). Multiple personality in adolescence: Relationship to incestual experience. *Journal of the American Academy of Child and Adolescent Psychiatry, 24,* 109–114.

Braun, B. G., & Sachs, R. G. (1985). The development of multiple personality disorder: Predisposing, precipitating, and perpetuating factors. In R. P. Kluft (Ed.), *Childhood antecedents of multiple personality* (pp. 37–64). Washington, DC: American Psychiatric Press.

Briere, J. (2006). Dissociative symptoms and trauma exposure: Specificity, affect dysregulation, and posttraumatic stress. *Journal of Nervous and Mental Disease, 194*, 78–82.

Brown, R. J. (2002). The cognitive psychology of dissociative states. *Cognitive Neuropsychiatry, 7*, 221–235.

Chu, J. A., & Dill, D. L. (1990). Dissociative symptoms in relation to childhood physical and sexual abuse. *American Journal of Psychiatry, 147*, 887–892.

DePrince, A. P., & Freyd, J. J. (1999). Dissociative tendencies, attention, and memory. *Psychological Science, 10*, 449–452.

DePrince, A. P., & Freyd, J. J. (2001). Memory and dissociative tendencies: The roles of attentional context and word meaning in a directed forgetting task. *Journal of Trauma & Dissociation, 2*, 67–82.

DePrince, A. P., & Freyd, J. J. (2004). Forgetting trauma stimuli. *Psychological Science, 15*, 488–492.

DePrince, A. P., & Freyd, J. J. (2007). Trauma-induced dissociation. In M. J. Freidman, T. M. Keane, & P. A. Resick (Eds.), *Handbook of PTSD: Science & practice* (pp. 135–150). New York: Guilford Press.

DePrince, A. P., Freyd, J. J., & Malle, B. F. (2007). A replication by another name: A response to Devilly et al. (2007). *Psychological Science, 18*, 218–219.

De Ruiter, M. B., Phaf, R. H., Veltman, D. J., Kok, A., & Van Dyck, R. (2003). Attention as a characteristic of nonclinical dissociation: An event-related potential study. *NeuroImage, 19*, 376–390.

De Ruiter, M. B., Phaf, R. H., Elzinga, B. M., & Van Dyck, R. (2004). Dissociative style and individual differences in verbal working memory span. *Consciousness and Cognition, 13*, 821–828.

Dorahy, M. J., Irwin, H. J., & Middleton, W. (2002). Cognitive inhibition in dissociative identity disorder (DID): Developing an understanding of working memory function in DID. *Journal of Trauma & Dissociation, 3*, 111–132.

Dorahy, M. J., Irwin, H. J., & Middleton, W. (2004). Assessing markers of working memory function in dissociative identity disorder using neutral stimuli: A comparison with clinical and general population samples. *Australian and New Zealand Journal of Psychiatry, 38*, 47–55.

Dorahy, M. J., Middleton, W., & Irwin, H. J. (2004). Investigating cognitive inhibition in dissociative identity disorder compared to depression, posttraumatic stress disorder and psychosis. *Journal of Trauma & Dissociation, 5*, 93–110.

Dorahy, M. J., Middleton, W., & Irwin, H. J. (2005). The effect of emotional context on cognitive inhibition and attentional processing in dissociative identity disorder. *Behaviour Research and Therapy, 43*, 555–568.

Draijer, N., & Langeland, W. (1999). Childhood trauma and perceived parental dysfunction in the etiology of dissociative symptoms in psychiatric inpatients. *American Journal of Psychiatry, 156*, 379–385.

Eich, E., Macaulay, D., Loewenstein, R. J., & Dihle, P. H. (1997a). Implicit memory, interpersonality amnesia, and dissociative identity disorder: Comparing patients with simulators. In J. D. Read & D. S. Lindsay (Eds.), *Recollections of trauma: Scientific evidence and clinical practice* (pp. 469–474). New York: Plenum.

Eich, E., Macaulay, D., Loewenstein, R. J., & Dihle, P. H. (1997b). Memory, amnesia, and dissociative identity disorder. *Psychological Science, 8*, 417–422.

Elzinga, B. M., De Beurs, E., Sergeant, J. A., Van Dyck, R., & Phaf, R. H. (2000). Dissociative style and directed forgetting. *Cognitive Therapy and Research, 24*, 279–295.

Elzinga, B. M., Phaf, R. H., Ardon, A. M., & Van Dyck, R. (2003). Directed forgetting between, but not within, dissociative personality states. *Journal of Abnormal Psychology, 112*, 237–243.

Forrest, K. A. (2001). Toward an etiology of dissociative identity disorder: A neurodevelopmental approach. *Consciousness & Cognition, 10*, 259–293.

Freyd, J. J. (1996). *Betrayal trauma: The logic of forgetting childhood abuse*. Cambridge, MA: Harvard University Press.

Freyd, J. J. (2001). Memory and dimensions of trauma: Terror may be 'all-too-well remembered' and betrayal buried. In J. R. Conte (Ed.), *Critical issues in child sexual abuse: Historical, legal, and psychological perspectives* (pp. 139–173). Thousand Oaks, CA: Sage Publications.

Freyd, J. J., DePrince, A. P., & Zurbriggen, E. L. (2001). Self-reported memory for abuse depends upon victim-perpetrator relationship. *Journal of Trauma & Dissociation, 2*, 5–16.

Freyd, J. J., Martorello, S. R., Alvarado, J. S., Hayes, A. E., & Christman, J. C. (1998). Cognitive environments and dissociative tendencies: Performance on the Standard Stroop Task for high vs. low dissociators. *Applied Cognitive Psychology, 12*, S91–S103.

Gleaves, D. H., May, M. C., & Cardeña, E. (2001). An examination of the diagnostic validity of dissociative identity disorder. *Clinical Psychology Review, 21*, 577–608.

Goldberg, L. R. (1999). The Curious Experiences Survey, a revised version of the Dissociative Experiences Scale: Factor structure, reliability, and relations to demographic and personality variables. *Psychological Assessment, 11*, 134–145.

Goldsmith, R. E., Barlow, M. R., & Freyd, J. J. (2004). Knowing and not knowing about trauma: Implications for therapy. *Psychotherapy: Theory, Research, Practice, Training, 41*, 448–463.

Hesse, E., & Main, M. (2000). Disorganized infant, child, and adult attachment: Collapse in behavioral and attentional strategies. *Journal of the American Psychoanalytic Association, 48*, 1097–1127.

Holmes, E. A., Brown, R. J., Mansell, W., Fearon, R. P., Hunter, E. C. M., Frasquilho, F., & Oakley, D. A. (2005). Are there two qualitatively distinct forms of dissociation? A review and some clinical implications. *Clinical Psychology Review, 25*, 1–23.

Huntjens, R. J. C., Postma, A., Peters, M., Woertman, L., & Van der Hart, O. (2003). Interidentity amnesia for neutral, episodic information in dissociative identity disorder. *Journal of Abnormal Psychology, 112*, 290–297.

International Society for the Study of Dissociation (ISSD; 1997). Guidelines for treating dissociative identity disorder (multiple personality disorder) in adults. Chicago: Author.

Kindt, M., & Van den Hout, M. (2003). Dissociation and memory fragmentation: Experimental effects on meta-memory but not on actual memory performance. *Behaviour Research and Therapy, 41*, 167–178.

Kisiel, C. L., & Lyons, J. S. (2001). Dissociation as a mediator of psychopathology among sexually abused children and adolescents. *American Journal of Psychiatry, 158*, 1034–1039.

Li, D., & Spiegel, D. (1992). A neural network model of dissociative disorders. *Psychiatric Annals, 22*, 144–147.

Liotti, G. (1999). Understanding the dissociative processes: The contribution of attachment theory. *Psychoanalytic Inquiry, 19*, 757–783.

Loewenstein, R. J. (1994). Diagnosis, epidemiology, clinical course, treatment, and cost effectiveness of treatment for dissociative disorders and MPD: Report submitted to the Clinton Administration Task Force on Health Care Financing Reform. *Dissociation, 7*, 3–11.

Macfie, J., Cicchetti, D., & Toth, S. L. (2001). The development of dissociation in maltreated preschool-aged children. *Development & Psychopathology, 13*, 233–254.

Maldonado, J. R., Butler, L. D., & Spiegel, D. (1998). Treatments for dissociative disorders. In P. E. Nathan & J. M. Gordon (Eds.), *A guide to treatments that work* (pp. 423–446). New York: Oxford University Press.

Nijenhuis, E. R. S., Spinhoven, P., Van Dyck, R., Van der Hart, O., & Vanderlinden, J. (1996). The development and psychometric characteristics of the Somatoform Dissociation Questionnaire (SDQ-20). *Journal of Nervous and Mental Disease, 184*, 688–694.

Nijenhuis, E. R. S., Spinhoven, P., Van Dyck, R., Van der Hart, O., & Vanderlinden, J. (1997). The development of the Somatoform Dissociation Questionnaire (SDQ-5) in the screening for dissociative disorders. *Acta Psychiatrica Scandinavica, 96*, 311–318.

Nijenhuis, E. R. S., Spinhoven, P., Van Dyck, R., Van der Hart, O., & Vanderlinden, J. (1998). Degree of somatoform and psychological dissociation in dissociative disorder is correlated with reported trauma. *Journal of Traumatic Stress, 11*, 711–730.

Nijenhuis, E. R. S., Van Dyck, R., Spinhoven, P., Van der Hart, O., Chatrou, M., Vanderlinden, J., & Moene, F. (1999). Somatoform dissociation discriminates among diagnostic categories over and above general psychopathology. *Australian and New Zealand Journal of Psychiatry, 33*, 511–520.

Nijenhuis, E. R. S., & Van der Hart, O. (1999). Forgetting and reexperiencing trauma: From anesthesia to pain. In J. Goodwin & R. Attias (Eds.), *Splintered reflections: Images of the body in trauma* (pp. 39–65). New York: Basic Books.

Nijenhuis, E. R. S., Van der Hart, O., & Steele, K. (2002). The emerging psychobiology of trauma-related dissociation and dissociative disorders. In H. D'Haenen, J. A. den Boer, & P. Pillner (Eds.), *Biological psychiatry* (pp. 1079–1098). New York: John Wiley & Sons, Ltd.

Nissen, M. J., Ross, J. L., Willingham, D. B., MacKenzie, T. B., & Schacter, D. L. (1988). Memory and awareness in a patient with multiple personality disorder. *Brain and Cognition, 8*, 117–134.

Ogawa, J. R., Sroufe, L. A., Weinfield, N. S., Carlson, E. A., & Egeland, B. (1997). Development and the fragmented self: Longitudinal study of dissociative symptomatology in a nonclinical sample. *Development & Psychopathology, 9*, 855–879.

Pekala, R. J., Angelini, F., & Kumar, V. K. (2001). The importance of fantasy-proneness in dissociation: A replication. *Contemporary Hypnosis, 18*, 204–214.

Peters, M. L., Uyterlinde, S. A., Consemulder, J., & Van der Hart, O. (1998). Apparent amnesia on experimental memory tests in dissociative identity disorder: An exploratory study. *Consciousness and Cognition, 7*, 27–41.

Putnam, F. W. (1989). *Diagnosis and treatment of multiple personality disorder*. New York: The Guilford Press.

Putnam, F. W. (1994). The switch process in multiple personality disorder and other state-change disorders. In R. M. Klein & B. K. Doane (Eds.), *Psychological concepts and dissociative disorders* (pp. 283–304). Hillsdale, NJ: Lawrence Erlbaum Associates.

Putnam, F. W. (1995). Development of dissociative disorders. In D. Cicchetti & D. J. Cohen (Eds.), *Developmental psychopathology, Volume 2: Risk, disorder, and adaptation* (pp. 581–608). New York: Wiley.

Putnam, F. W. (1996). Child development and dissociation. *Child & Adolescent Psychiatric Clinics of North America, 5*, 285–301.

Putnam, F. W. (1997). *Dissociation in children and adolescents: A developmental perspective.* New York: The Guilford Press.

Ross, C. A., Ellason, J. W., & Anderson, G. (1995). A factor analysis of the Dissociative Experiences Scale (DES) in dissociative identity disorder. *Dissociation, 8*, 229–235.

Ross, C. A., Joshi, S., & Currie, R. (1991). Dissociative experiences in the general population: A factor analysis. *Hospital & Community Psychiatry, 42*, 297–301.

Sahakyan, L., & Kelley, C. M. (2002). A contextual change account of the directed forgetting effect. *Journal of experimental psychology: Learning, memory, and cognition, 28*, 1064–1072.

Schore, A. N. (2001). The effects of early relational trauma on right brain development, affect regulation, and infant mental health. *Infant Mental Health Journal, 22*, 201–269.

Schultz, T. M., Passmore, J., & Yoder, C. Y. (2003). Emotional closeness with perpetrators and amnesia for child sexual abuse. *Journal of Child Sexual Abuse, 12*, 67–88.

Sheiman, J. A. (1999). Sexual abuse history with and without self-report of memory loss: Differences in psychopathology, personality, and dissociation. In L. M. Williams & V. L. Banyard (Eds.), *Trauma & memory* (pp. 139–148). Thousand Oaks, CA: Sage Press.

Siegel, D. J. (1996). Cognition, memory, and dissociation. *Child and Adolescent Psychiatric Clinics of North America, 5*, 509–536.

Silberman, E. K., Putnam, F. W., Weingartner, H., Braun, B. G., & Post, R. M. (1985). Dissociative states in multiple personality disorder: A quantitative study. *Psychiatry Research, 15*, 253–260.

Steele, H. (2002). Multiple dissociation in the context of the Adult Attachment Interview. In V. Sinason (Ed.), *Attachment, trauma and multiplicity: working with dissociative identity disorder* (pp. 107–122). New York: Taylor & Francis Inc.

Steinberg, M. (2001). Updating diagnostic criteria for dissociative disorders: Learning from scientific advances. *Journal of Trauma & Dissociation, 2*, 59–64.

Szostak, C., Lister, R., Eckardt, M., & Weingartner, H. (1994). Dissociative effects of mood on memory. In R. M. Klein & B. K. Doane (Eds.), *Psychological concepts and dissociative disorders* (pp. 187–206). Hillsdale, NJ: Lawrence Erlbaum Associates.

Van der Hart, O., Bolt, H., & Van der Kolk, B. A. (2005). Memory fragmentation in dissociative identity disorder. *Journal of Trauma & Dissociation, 6*, 55–70.

Van der Hart, O., Nijenhuis, E., Steele, K., & Brown, D. (2004). Trauma-related dissociation: Conceptual clarity lost and found. *Australian and New Zealand Journal of Psychiatry, 38*, 906–914.

Van der Kolk, B. A., & Fisler, R. (1995). Dissociation and the fragmentary nature of traumatic memories: Overview and exploratory study. *Journal of Traumatic Stress, 8*, 505–525.

Veltman, D. J., De Ruiter, M. B., Rombouts, S. A. R. B., Lazeron, R. H. C., Barkhof, F., Van Dyck, R., et al. (2005). Neurophysiological correlates of increased verbal working memory in high-dissociative participants: A functional MRI study. *Psychological Medicine, 35*, 175–185.

Waller, G., Quinton, S., & Watson, D. (1995). Dissociation and the processing of threat-related information. *Dissociation, 8*, 84–90.

Zlotnick, C., Begin, A., Shea, M. T., Pearlstein, T., Simpson, E., & Costello, E. (1994). The relationship between characteristics of sexual abuse and dissociative experiences. *Comprehensive Psychiatry, 35*, 465–470.

Zlotnick, C., Shea, M. T., Pearlstein, T., Begin, A., Simpson, E., & Costello, E. (1996). Differences in dissociative experiences between survivors of childhood incest and survivors of assault in adulthood. *Journal of Nervous and Mental Disease, 184*, 52–54.

8 Attachment Trauma and the Developing Right Brain: Origins of Pathological Dissociation

Allan N. Schore, PhD

OUTLINE

The concept of dissociation has a long history of bridging psychiatry, psychology, and neurology. Because dissociation is inextricably linked to trauma, theoretical and clinical models of dissociation have spanned the psychological and biological realms. Although the relationship between childhood trauma and dissociation was noted at the end of the 19th century, only recently has a developmental perspective been used to understand dissociation's etiological mechanisms. Dissociative phenomena are now being viewed through an interdisciplinary lens.

There is a growing appreciation of the unique contributions that developmental models can make to psychopathogenesis. As Putnam (1995) noted, a developmental view of dissociation offers "potentially very rich models for understanding the ontogeny of environmentally produced psychiatric conditions" (p. 582). In particular, I will suggest that regulation theory (Schore, 1994, 2003a, 2003b) can provide such models. Towards that end I will draw upon (1) recent findings about infant behavior from developmental psychology, (2) current data on brain development from neuroscience, (3) updated basic research in biological psychiatry on stress mechanisms, and (4) new information from developmental psychobiology on the essential functions of the autonomic nervous system in order to construct a model of the etiology and underlying psychoneurobiological mechanisms of pathological dissociation. I will use posttraumatic stress disorder as a paradigm for dissociative disorder. I will discuss the earliest expression of dissociation in human infancy—pediatric posttraumatic stress disorder—and its enduring impact on the experience-dependent maturation of the right brain, including the characterological use of dissociation at later points of interpersonal stress.

8.1 INTRODUCTION

This chapter will focus on pathological dissociation (Waller, Putnam, & Carlson, 1996). Dissociation is defined by DSM-IV as "a disruption in the usually integrated functions of consciousness, memory, identity, or perception of the environment" (American Psychiatric Association, 1994) and by the 10th edition of the International Classification of Diseases (ICD-10) as "a partial or complete loss of the normal integration between memories of the past, awareness of identity and immediate sensations, and control of body movements" (World Health Organization, 1992). Although both stress a deficit in integration, only ICD-10 includes an alteration of bodily processes. Finally, Spiegel and Cardeña (1991) characterized dissociation as "a structured separation of mental processes (e.g., thoughts, emotions, conation, memory, and identity) that are ordinarily integrated" (p. 367). Note that Spiegel and Cardeña include emotion in their definition of dissociation, whereas DSM-IV and ICD-10 did not.

The concept of dissociation can be directly traced to the work of Pierre Janet. Janet (1887, 1889) considered (pathological) dissociation to be a phobia of memories that was expressed as excessive or inappropriate physical responses to thought or memories of old traumas (see Van der Hart & Dorahy, 2009). This dissociation of cognitive, sensory, and motor processes is adaptive in the context of overwhelming traumatic experience, and yet such unbearable emotional reactions result in an altered state of consciousness. Janet described an *abaissement du niveau mental*, a lowering of the mental level, a regression to a state that is constricted and disunified. Furthermore, Janet speculated that dissociation was the result of a deficiency of psychological energy. Due to early developmental factors, the quantity of psychological energy is lowered below a critical point, and thus individuals with pathological dissociation are deficient in binding together all their mental functions into an organized unity under the control of the self.

Following Charcot (1887), Janet also posited that early trauma is a fundamental psychopathogenic factor in the etiology of hysteria. Freud (1893/1955), who cited Janet in his early pre-psychoanalytic work, defined dissociation as a splitting of consciousness, frequently associated with bizarre physical symptoms. Although Freud initially considered developmental trauma to be essential to hysteria, he soon rejected this idea and posited that repression—not dissociation—was the primary psychopathogenic mechanism.

Summarizing the essentials of Janet's model, Van der Kolk, Weisaeth, and Van der Hart stated:

> Janet proposed that when people experience *"vehement emotions,"* their minds may become incapable of matching their *frightening experiences* with existing cognitive schemes. As a result the memories of the experience cannot be integrated into personal awareness; instead, they are split off [dissociated] from consciousness and voluntary control ... extreme *emotional arousal* results in failure to integrate traumatic memories.... The memory traces of the trauma linger as unconscious "fixed ideas" that cannot be "liquidated" ... they continue to intrude as terrifying perceptions, obsessional preoccupations, and *somatic reexperiences.* (1996, p. 52, my italics)

In Janet's view, traumatized individuals

> seem to have lost their capacity to assimilate new experiences as well. It is ... as if their personality development has stopped at a certain point, and cannot enlarge any more by the addition of new elements. (1911, p. 532)

Translating Janet's concept of personality into contemporary terms, Van der Kolk, Van der Hart, and Marmar concluded that "*Dissociation* refers to a compartmentalization of experience: Elements of a trauma are not integrated into a unitary whole or an integrated sense of *self*" (1996, p. 306, my italics).

At the dawn of modern psychiatry, many major pioneers (e.g., Charcot, Janet, Freud, Hughlings Jackson) were interested in the neurology of dissociation (i.e., its structure-function relationships). Devinsky (2000) has noted that late 19th-century clinicians linked the right hemisphere with emotion (Luys, 1881) and dissociative phenomena (Myers, 1885; Richer, 1881); he cited Hughlings Jackson's (1874/1915) work on the duality of the brain, and the role of the right hemisphere in "emotional" speech, as opposed to the left hemisphere's "voluntary expression and conscious awareness of propositional speech." Dissociative psychopathology continues to be a focus of the epilepsy literature. Patients with intractable epilepsy show high rates of "dissociative convulsions" (De Wet et al., 2003), and "dissociative pseudoseizures" are common sequelae of traumatic experiences (Harden, 1997), especially in patients with histories of sexual and physical abuse (Alper et al., 1993) and diagnoses of personality disorders and depression (Bowman & Markand, 1996).

Recently, Brown and Trimble (2000) have argued that we must move beyond a purely descriptive approach: "The first goal must be to provide a precise definition of dissociation based on a conceptually coherent and empirically justified account of the processes underlying these phenomena" (p. 288). Other investigators have made similar assertions:

> A precise definition of the term "dissociation" must be established, based on a coherent and empirically checkable concept. Furthermore, it is important to discover the primary pathophysiologic mechanism that leads to the dissociative symptoms, using neurobiological research mechanisms. (Prueter, Schultz-Venrath, & Rimpau, 2002, p. 191)

Over the last few decades a few authors have proposed neurobiological models of dissociation in adults. Whitlock (1967) and Ludwig (1972) suggested that the primary pathophysiological mechanism of dissociative symptoms is an attentional dysfunction that results from an increase in the corticofugal inhibition of afferent stimulation. This inhibition impairs the processing of essential information, which subsequently fails to be integrated into awareness, and thereby generates dissociative symptoms. More recently J. Krystal et al. (1998), Scaer (2001), and Nijenhuis, Van der Hart, and Steele (2002) have made contributions to the psychobiology of dissociation (see also Nijenhuis & Den Boer, 2009). Current neuroimaging research is also contributing new information about the structure-function relationships of dissociation in mature brain systems.

Several important observations about dissociation have been advanced. In psychological studies of adults, Loewenstein noted that "Dissociation is conceptualized as a basic part of the psychobiology of the human trauma response: a protective activation of altered states of consciousness in reaction to overwhelming psychological trauma" (1996, p. 312). In neuropsychiatric studies of adult trauma patients, Bremner and colleagues demonstrated that (1) there are two subtypes of acute trauma response, hyperarousal and dissociation (1999), (2) dissociation represents an effective short-term strategy that is detrimental to long-term functioning (Bremner & Brett, 1997), and (3) extreme stress invokes neural mechanisms that produce long-term alterations of brain functioning (Krystal et al., 1998). Finally, Meares concluded that "dissociation, at its first occurrence, is a consequence of a 'psychological shock' or high arousal" (1999, p. 1853).

I will offer evidence that each of the above observations about dissociation in adults applies to infants as well. I will argue that developmental studies offer specific models of the process whereby early trauma alters the human ontogenetic trajectory and creates a predisposition for later pathological dissociation. These models, in turn, afford a deeper understanding of the neurobiological mechanisms of dissociation. I believe that attachment theory, "the dominant approach to understanding early socioemotional and personality development during the past quarter-century of research" (Thompson, 1990, p. 145), best describes the interactions among development, trauma, and dissociation. Disorganized-disoriented insecure attachment, a primary risk factor for the development of psychiatric disorders (Main, 1996), has been specifically implicated in the etiology of the dissociative disorders (Chefetz, 2004; Liotti, 2004; Schore, 1997). Longitudinal attachment studies have demonstrated an association between traumatic childhood events and proneness to dissociation (Ogawa et al., 1997).

Current neurobiological models of attachment focus on the formation of the implicit self system, located in the early maturing right brain (Schore, 1994, 2001a). Researchers now assert that fearful arousal and the relational modulation of that arousal lie at the heart of attachment theory, and that relational trauma triggers states of hyperarousal and dissociation in the developing brain. I will show that abuse and neglect elicit dissociative defenses in the developing infant. As such, they represent a deleterious influence during the critical growth period of cortical, limbic, brainstem, and autonomic centers in the early maturing right brain.

Janet's ideas about early trauma and dissociation are strongly supported by recent developmental studies. A traumatizing caregiver negatively impacts the child's attachment security, strategies for coping with stress, and sense of self (Crittenden & Ainsworth, 1989; Erickson, Egeland, & Pianta, 1989). There is substantial and convincing evidence that childhood trauma arrests affective development; conversely, trauma in adulthood produces a regression in affective development (H. Krystal, 1988). The most significant consequence of early relational trauma is the child's failure to develop the capacity for emotional self-regulation (Toth & Cicchetti, 1998); the child (and subsequent adult) cannot adequately regulate affective intensity and duration (Van der Kolk & Fisler, 1994). This chapter contends that these established principles of early emotional development must be incorporated into an overarching model of dissociation.

8.2 THE NEUROBIOLOGY OF SECURE ATTACHMENT

The essential task of the first year of human life is the creation of a secure attachment bond between the infant and his/her primary caregiver. Secure attachment depends upon the mother's psychobiological attunement with the infant's internal states of arousal. Through visual-facial, tactile-gestural, and auditory-prosodic communication, caregiver and infant learn the rhythmic structure of the other and modify their behavior to fit that structure, thereby cocreating a specifically fitted interaction. During the bodily based affective communications of mutual gaze, the attuned mother synchronizes the spatiotemporal patterning of her exogenous sensory stimulation with the infant's spontaneous expressions of endogenous organismic rhythms. Via this contingent responsivity, the mother appraises the nonverbal expressions of her infant's internal arousal and affective states, regulates them, and communicates them to the infant. To accomplish this, the mother must successfully modulate nonoptimal high *or* nonoptimal low levels of stimulation which would induce supra-heightened or extremely low levels of arousal in the infant.

If attachment is the regulation of interactive synchrony, then attachment *stress* is an asynchrony in that interactional synchrony. In optimal interpersonal contexts, following such stress, a period of reestablished synchrony allows the child to recover his/her regulatory equilibrium. Resilience in the face of stress is an ultimate indicator of attachment security. In secure attachments, the regulatory processes of affect synchrony amplify positive arousal, and interactive repair alters states of negative arousal. Thus, attachment represents biological regulation between and within organisms.

Research supports the proposal (Schore, 1994) that the long-enduring regulatory effects of attachment are due to their impact on brain development. According to Ziabreva et al. (2003):

> [T]he mother functions as a regulator of the socio-emotional environment during early stages of postnatal development … subtle emotional regulatory interactions, which obviously can transiently or permanently alter brain activity levels … may play a critical role during the establishment and maintenance of limbic system circuits. (p. 5334)

I have suggested that the attachment mechanism is embedded in infant-caregiver right-hemisphere-to-right-hemisphere affective transactions (Schore, 1994, 2000, 2003a, 2003b). Because (1) the human limbic system myelinates in the first year and a half (Kinney et al., 1988) and (2) the early-maturing right hemisphere (Allman et al., 2005; Bogolepova & Malofeeva, 2001; Chiron et al., 1997; Geschwind & Galaburda, 1987)—which is deeply connected into the limbic system (Tucker, 1992)—is undergoing a growth spurt at this time, attachment experiences specifically impact limbic and cortical areas of the developing right cerebral hemisphere (Henry, 1993; Schore, 1994, 2005b; Siegel, 1999; Wang, 1997).

This model accounts for a body of recent developmental neurobiological research. At two months of age, the onset of a critical period during which synaptic connections in the developing occipital cortex are modified by visual experience (Yamada et al., 1997, 2000), infants show right hemispheric activation when exposed to a woman's face (Tzourio-Mazoyer, 2002). The development of the capacity to efficiently process information from faces requires visual input to the right (and not left) hemisphere during infancy (Le Grand et al., 2003), and mutual gaze activates face-processing areas of the right hemisphere (Pelphrey, Viola, & McCarthy, 2004; Watanabe, Miki, & Kakigi, 2002). Spontaneous gestures that express feeling states communicated within a dyad also activate right hemispheric structures (Gallagher & Frith, 2004). With respect to prosody, the tendency of mothers to cradle infants on their left side "facilitates the flow of affective information from the infant via the left ear and eye to the center for emotional decoding, that is, the right hemisphere of the mother" (Manning et al., 1997, p. 327). Finally, the human maternal response to an infant's cry is accompanied by activation of the mother's right brain (Lorberbaum et al., 2002).

8.3 THE NEUROBIOLOGY OF RELATIONAL TRAUMA

Optimal attachment communications directly affect the maturation of (1) the central nervous system (CNS) limbic system that processes and regulates social-emotional stimuli and (2) the autonomic nervous system (ANS) that generates the somatic aspects of emotion. It is important to stress that a growth-facilitating emotional environment is required for a child to develop an internal system that can adaptively regulate arousal and other psychobiological states (and thereby affect, cognition, and behavior), The good-enough mother offers her securely attached infant access to her after a separation; she tends to respond appropriately and promptly to his/her emotional expressions. She also allows high levels of positive affect to be generated during co-shared play states. Such events as these support an expansion of the child's coping capacities and illustrate why secure attachment is the primary defense against trauma-induced psychopathology.

In contrast to caregivers who foster secure attachment, abusive caregivers not only play less, but also induce enduring negative affect in the child. Such caregivers provide little protection against other environmental impingements, including that of an abusive father. This caregiver is emotionally inaccessible, given to inappropriate and/or rejecting responses to her infant's expressions of emotions and stress, and provides minimal or unpredictable regulation of the infant's states of overarousal. Instead, she induces extreme levels of stimulation and arousal (i.e., the very high stimulation of abuse and/or the very low stimulation of neglect). And finally, because she provides no interactive repair, she leaves the infant to endure intense negative states for long periods of time.

The infant has two psychobiological response patterns to trauma: hyperarousal and dissociation (Perry et al., 1995; Schore, 1997). Beebe describes the "mutually escalating overarousal" of a disorganized attachment pair:

> Each one escalates the ante, as the infant builds to a frantic distress, may scream, and, in this example, finally throws up. In an escalating overarousal pattern, even after extreme distress signals from the infant, such as ninety-degree head aversion, arching away … or screaming, the mother keeps going. (2000, p. 436)

In this initial stage of threat, the child's alarm or startle reaction indicates activation of the infant's right hemisphere (Bradley, Cuthbert, & Lang, 1996). This, in turn, evokes a sudden increase of ANS sympathetic activity, resulting in significantly elevated heart rate, blood pressure, and respiration. Distress is expressed in crying and then screaming. Crying represents an autonomic response to stress, whereby the nucleus ambiguus of the right vagus excites both the right side of the larynx and the sinoatrial node of the heart (Porges et al., 1994).

The infant's state of frantic distress, or what Perry terms *fear-terror*, is mediated by sympathetic hyperarousal that is expressed in increased secretion of corticotropin releasing factor (CRF)—the brain's major stress hormone. CRF regulates sympathetic catecholamine activity (Brown et al., 1982). Thus, brain adrenaline, noradrenaline, and dopamine levels are significantly elevated, creating a hypermetabolic state within the developing brain. In addition, there is increased secretion of vasopressin, a hypothalamic neuropeptide that is released when the environment is perceived to be unsafe and challenging (Kvetnansky et al., 1989, 1990).

Hyperarousal is the infant's first reaction to stress. Dissociation is a later reaction to trauma, wherein the child disengages from the stimuli of the external world. Traumatized infants are observed to be "staring off into space with a glazed look":

> [W]hen infants' attempts fail to repair the interaction infants often lose postural control, withdraw, and self-comfort. The disengagement is profound even with this short disruption of the mutual regulatory process and break in intersubjectivity. The infant's reaction is reminiscent of the withdrawal of Harlow's isolated monkey or of the infants in institutions observed by Bowlby and Spitz. (Tronick & Weinberg, 1997, p. 66)

Winnicott (1958) holds that a particular failure of the maternal holding environment causes a discontinuity in the baby's need for "going-on-being." Kestenberg (1985) refers to dead spots in the infant's subjective experience, an operational definition of dissociation's restriction of consciousness.

The child's dissociation in the midst of terror involves numbing, avoidance, compliance, and restricted affect (the same pattern as adult PTSD). This parasympathetic-dominant state of conservation-withdrawal occurs in helpless and hopeless stressful situations in which the individual becomes inhibited and strives to avoid attention in order to become "unseen" (Schore, 1994, 2001b). This state of metabolic shutdown is a primary regulatory process that is used throughout the life span. In conservation-withdrawal, the stressed individual passively disengages in order "to conserve energies … to foster survival by the risky posture of feigning death, to allow healing of wounds and restitution of depleted resources by immobility" (Powles, 1992, p. 213). This parasympathetic mechanism mediates the "profound detachment" (Barach, 1991) of dissociation. If early trauma is experienced as "psychic catastrophe" (Bion, 1962), then dissociation is a "detachment from an unbearable situation" (Mollon, 1996), "the escape when there is no escape" (Putnam, 1997), "a last resort defensive strategy" (Dixon, 1998).

The neurobiology of dissociative hypoarousal is different from that of hyperarousal. In this passive state of pain-numbing and pain-blunting, endogenous opiates (Fanselow, 1986) are elevated. The dorsal vagal complex in the brainstem medulla is activated, which decreases blood pressure, metabolic activity, and heart rate—despite increases in circulating adrenaline. This elevated parasympathetic arousal is a survival strategy (Porges, 1997) that allows the infant to maintain homeostasis in the face of the internal state of sympathetic hyperarousal. It is seldom acknowledged that (1) parasympathetic energy-conserving hypoarousal and (2) sympathetic energy-expending hyperarousal are both Janetian states of "extreme emotional arousal."

Although vagal tone is defined as "the amount of inhibitory influence on the heart by the parasympathetic nervous system" (Field et al., 1995), it is now known that there are two parasympathetic vagal systems. The late-developing "mammalian" or "smart" ventral vagal system in the nucleus ambiguus enables contingent social interactions via the ability to communicate with facial expressions, vocalizations, and gestures. The early developing "reptilian" or "vegetative" system in the dorsal motor nucleus of the vagus shuts down metabolic activity during immobilization, death feigning, and hiding behaviors (Porges, 1997). As opposed to the mammalian ventral vagal complex that can rapidly regulate cardiac output to foster engagement and disengagement with the social environment, the reptilian dorsal vagal complex "contributes to severe emotional states and may be related to emotional states of 'immobilization' such as extreme terror" (Porges, 1997, p. 75).

There is now agreement that sympathetic nervous system activity manifests in tight engagement with the external environment and high level of energy mobilization and utilization, while the parasympathetic component drives disengagement from the external environment and utilizes low levels of internal energy (Recordati, 2003). Perry's description of the traumatized infant's sudden switch from high-energy sympathetic hyperarousal to low-energy parasympathetic dissociation is reflected in Porges's characterization of

> the sudden and rapid transition from an unsuccessful strategy of struggling requiring massive sympathetic activation to the metabolically conservative immobilized state mimicking death associated with the dorsal vagal complex. (1997, p. 75)

Similarly, H. Krystal has described the switch from sympathetic hyperaroused terror to parasympathetic hypoaroused hopelessness and helplessness:

> The switch from anxiety to the catatonoid response is the subjective evaluation of the impending danger as one that cannot be avoided or modified. With the perception of fatal helplessness in the face of destructive danger, one surrenders to it. (1988, p. 114–115)

Whereas the nucleus ambiguus exhibits rapid and transitory patterns (associated with perceptive pain and unpleasantness), the dorsal vagal nucleus exhibits an involuntary and prolonged pattern of vagal outflow. This prolonged dorsal vagal parasympathetic activation explains the lengthy "void" states that are associated with pathological dissociative detachment (Allen, Console, & Lewis, 1998).

8.4 DEVELOPMENTAL NEUROPSYCHOLOGY OF DISSOCIATION

How are the trauma-induced alterations of the developing right brain expressed in the socioemotional behavior of a traumatized toddler? Main and Solomon's (1986) classic study of attachment in traumatized infants revealed a new attachment category, Type D, an insecure-disorganized/disoriented pattern that occurs in 80% of maltreated infants (Carlson et al., 1989). Type D attachment is also associated with pre- and/or postnatal maternal alcohol or cocaine use (Espinosa et al., 2001; O'Connor, Sigman, & Brill, 1987). Hesse and Main (1999) noted that Type D disorganization and disorientation is phenotypically similar to dissociative states. Main and Solomon (1986) concluded that Type D infants have low stress tolerance and that their disorganization and disorientation indicate that the infant is alarmed by the parent. Because infants inevitably seek the parent when alarmed, Main and Solomon concluded that frightening parents placed infants in an irresolvable bind wherein they could neither approach their parents, shift their attention, nor flee. These infants are utterly unable to generate a coherent way to cope with their frightening parents.

Main and Solomon detailed the uniquely bizarre behaviors of 12-month-old Type D infants in the Strange Situation procedure. These infants displayed brief (frequently only 10 to 30 seconds) but significant interruptions of organized behavior. At such times, Type D infants may exhibit a contradictory behavior pattern such as "backing" toward the parent rather than approaching face-to-face.

The impression in each case was that approach movements were continually being inhibited and held back through simultaneous activation of avoidant tendencies. In most cases, however, proximity-seeking sufficiently overrode avoidance to permit the increase in physical proximity. Thus, contradictory patterns were activated but were not mutually inhibited (Main & Solomon, 1986, p. 117).

Notice the simultaneous activation of the energy-expending sympathetic and energy-conserving parasympathetic components of the ANS.

Maltreated infants exhibit apprehension, confusion, and very rapid shifts of state during the Strange Situation. Main and Solomon describe the child's entrance into a dissociated state:

> One infant hunched her upper body and shoulders at hearing her mother's call, then broke into extravagant laugh-like screeches with an excited forward movement. Her braying laughter became a cry and distress-face without a new intake of breath as the infant hunched forward. Then suddenly she became silent, blank and dazed. (1986, p. 119)

These behaviors are not restricted to the infant's interactions with the mother; the intensity of the baby's dysregulated affective state is often heightened when the infant is exposed to the added stress of an unfamiliar person. At a stranger's entrance, two infants moved away from both mother and stranger to face the wall; another

FIGURE 8.1 An infant losing postural control and self-comforting in response to the mother being still-faced. From *Emotional development*, by Tronick, E. Z, 2004, New York: Oxford University Press. Copyright 2004 Oxford University Press. Reprinted with permission.

"leaned forehead against the wall for several seconds, looking back in apparent terror." These infants exhibit "behavioral stilling," that is, "dazed" behavior and depressed affect. These are behavioral manifestations of dissociation. One infant "became for a moment excessively still, staring into space as though completely out of contact with self, environment, and parent." Another showed "a dazed facial appearance ... accompanied by a stilling of all body movement, and sometimes a *freezing* of limbs which had been in motion." Yet another "fell face-down on the floor in a depressed posture prior to separation, stilling all body movements." Guedeney and Fermanian (2001) have developed an alarm distress scale that appraises the sustained withdrawal that is associated with disorganized attachment. It assesses frozen, absent facial expression; total avoidance of eye contact; immobility; absence of vocalization; absence of relating to others; and the impression that the child is beyond reach.

Dissociation in infants has also been studied with the *still-face procedure*, an experimental paradigm of traumatic neglect (see Figure 8.1). In the still-face procedure, the infant is exposed to a severe relational stressor; the mother maintains eye contact with the infant, but she suddenly inhibits all vocalization and suspends all emotionally expressive facial expressions and gestures. This triggers an initial increase of interactive behavior and arousal in the infant. According to Tronick (2004), the infant's confusion and fearfulness at the break in connection is accompanied by the idea that "this is threatening." This is rapidly followed by bodily collapse, loss of postural control, withdrawal, gaze aversion, sad facial expression, and self-comforting behavior.

Most interestingly, this behavior is accompanied by a "dissipation of the infant's state of consciousness" and a diminishment of self-organizing abilities that reflect "disorganization of many of the lower level psychobiological states, such as metabolic systems." Recall that dissociation, a hypometabolic state, has been defined in the DSM as "a disruption in the usually integrated functions of consciousness" and described as "a protective activation of altered states of consciousness in reaction to overwhelming psychological trauma" (Loewenstein, 1996). Tronick (2004) suggests that infants who have a history of chronic breaks of connections exhibit an "extremely pathological state" of emotional apathy; he equates this state with Spitz's concept of hospitalism and Romanian orphans who fail to grow and develop. Such infants ultimately adopt a communication style of "stay away, don't connect." This defensive stance is a very early forming, yet already chronic, pathological dissociation that is associated with loss of ventral vagal activation and dominance of dorsal vagal parasympathetic states.

The still-face induction of hyperarousal and dissociation occurs face-to-face with the mother. The mother's face is the most potent visual stimulus in the child's world; it is well known that direct gaze can mediate not only loving, but aggressive messages. Hesse and Main (1999, p. 511) described a mother's frightening behavior: "in non-play contexts, stiff-legged 'stalking' of infant on all fours in a hunting posture; exposure of canine tooth accompanied by hissing; deep growls directed at infant." Thus, during the trauma, the infant is presented with an aggressive expression on the mother's face. Both the image of this aggressive face and the associated alterations in the infant's bodily state are indelibly imprinted into limbic circuits; they are stored in the imagistic procedural memory of the visuospatial right hemisphere, the locus of implicit (Hugdahl, 1995) and autobiographical (Fink et al., 1996; Greenberg et al., 2005; Markowitsch et al., 2000) memory.

Main and Solomon (1986) noted that Type D infants often encounter a second kind of disturbing maternal behavior: a maternal expression of fear-terror. This occurs when the mother withdraws from the infant as though the *infant* were frightening; such mothers of Type D infants exhibit dissociated, trancelike, and fearful behavior. Current studies have shown a link between frightening maternal behavior, dissociation, and disorganized infant attachment (Schuengel, Bakersmans-Kranenburg, & Van IJzendoorn, 1999). In recent work, Hesse and Main observe that when the mother enters a dissociative state, a fear alarm state is triggered in the infant. The caregiver's entrance into the dissociative state is expressed as "parent suddenly completely 'freezes' with eyes unmoving, half-lidded, despite nearby movement; parent addresses infant in an 'altered' tone with simultaneous voicing and devoicing" (2006, p. 320). In describing the mother as she submits to the freeze state, they note:

> Here the parent appears to have become completely unresponsive to, or even aware of, the external surround, including the physical and verbal behavior of their infant.... [W]e observed one mother who remained seated in an immobilized and uncomfortable position with her hand in the air, blankly staring into space for 50 sec. (p. 321)

During these episodes, I suggest that the infant is matching the rhythmic structures of the mother's dysregulated states, and that this synchronization is registered in the firing patterns of the stress-sensitive corticolimbic regions of the infant's brain, especially in the right brain, which is in a critical period of growth. It has been established that maternal care influences both the infant's reactivity (Menard et al., 2004) and the infant's defensive responses to threat; these "serve as the basis for the transmission of individual differences in stress responses from mother to offspring" (Weaver et al., 2004, p. 847). Because many of these mothers suffer from unresolved trauma, their chaotic and dysregulated alterations of state become imprinted into the developing brain and self-system of the child. This is the psychopathogenetic mechanism for the intergenerational transmission of (1) trauma and (2) dissociative defenses against overwhelming and dysregulating affective states.

8.5 RIGHT BRAIN PROCESSES AND DISSOCIATION THROUGHOUT THE LIFE SPAN

Early traumatic attachment takes place when infants and toddlers repeatedly encounter massive misattunement from caregivers who trigger (and do not repair) long-lasting intensely dysregulated states in the child. The growth-inhibiting environment of relational trauma generates dense and prolonged levels of negative affect associated with extremely stressful states of hyper- and hypoarousal. In self-defense the child severely restricts overt expression of the attachment need and significantly reduces the output of the emotion-processing, limbic-centered, attachment system. When the child is stressed, defensive functions are rapidly initiated that quickly shift the brain from interactive regulatory modes into long-enduring, less complex autoregulatory modes. These patterns are primitive strategies for survival that remain online for long intervals of time, periods in which the developing brain is in a hypometabolic state that is detrimental to the substantial amounts of energy required for critical period biosynthetic processes. This hypometabolic brain state (Janetian deficiency of psychological energy) causes dissociative "encoding failures" (Allen et al., 1998) in the autobiographical memory of the developing self.

Attachment trauma thus sets the stage for characterological use of primitive autoregulation—that is, pathological dissociation during subsequent stages of development. In accord with this model, (1) severe early maternal dysfunction is associated with high dissociation in psychiatric patients (Draijer & Langeland, 1999); (2) physical abuse and parental dysfunction by the mother—not the father—is associated with somatoform dissociative symptoms (Roelofs et al., 2002); and (3) individuals with Type D attachment utilize dissociative behaviors in later stages of life (Van IJzendoorn et al., 1999). Allen and Coyne describe the characterological use of dissociation:

> Although initially they may have used dissociation to cope with traumatic events, they subsequently dissociate to defend against a broad range of daily stressors, including their own posttraumatic symptoms, pervasively undermining the continuity of their experience. (1995, p. 620)

This psychic-deadening defense is maladaptive not only because the individual resorts to dissociation at low levels of stress, but also finds it difficult to exit this state of conservation-withdrawal. During these episodes, the person is impermeable to attachment communications and interactive regulation. This deprives the person of input that is vital to emotional development. Dissociative detachment (Allen et al., 1998) thus becomes an attractor state whereby social intimacy is habitually deemed to be dangerous (because such intimacy is always a potential trigger of "vehement emotions"). The avoidance of emotional connections, especially those that contain novel and complex affective information, prevents emotional learning; this, in turn, precludes advances in right brain emotional intelligence (Schore, 2001a) or what Janet (1889) called "enlargement" of personality development.

A fundamental question that must be addressed in any developmental model of dissociation is: What is the precise mechanism by which the early psychological events of "maltreatment-related" (Beer & De Bellis, 2002) or "pediatric" (Carrion et al., 2001) posttraumatic stress disorder affect the later behavior of the self system as it develops at further stages of the life cycle? I maintain that a purely psychological conception cannot answer this question; a psychoneurobiological perspective that integrates both biological structure and psychological function is required. Research clearly indicates that "the overwhelming stress of maltreatment in childhood is associated with adverse influences on brain development" (1999, p. 1281).

During the first years of life when the right brain is growing (Trevarthen, 1996) and dominant (Chiron et al., 1997), adverse influences on brain development particularly impact the right brain (Allman et al., 2005). During this time, states of the infant brain become traits (Perry et al., 1995); thus, early relational trauma and dissociation will be imprinted and embedded into the core structure of the developing right brain. Indeed, evidence shows that early relational trauma is particularly expressed in right hemisphere deficits. Recent studies reveal that maltreated children diagnosed with PTSD manifest right-lateralized metabolic limbic abnormalities (De Bellis et al., 2000), and that adults severely abused in childhood (Raine et al., 2001) and diagnosed with PTSD (Galletly et al., 2001) show reduced right hemisphere activation during a working memory task. This research supports earlier assertions that (1) the symptoms of PTSD fundamentally reflect an impairment of the right brain (Schore, 1997; Van de Kolk, 1996) and (2) the right hemisphere is paramount in the perceptual and cognitive processing and the regulation of biological responses in PTSD patients (Spivak et al., 1998).

Thus, neurobiological research suggests that there is continuity over the life span in the expression of the coping deficits of PTSD and the use of pathological dissociation in persons who have a childhood history of relational trauma. The principle that severe attachment pathology frequently copes with Janetian "vehement emotions" via primitive modes of autoregulation can be translated into the clinical tenet that in PTSD (and other early forming severe pathologies of the self), the individual is cut off (disassociated) from experiencing intense affective states: "traumatic stress in childhood could lead to self-modulation of painful affect by directing attention away from internal emotional states" (Lane et al., 1997, p. 840). The right hemisphere is dominant not only for attachment regulation of affects, but also for attention (Raz, 2004) and pain processing (Symonds et al., 2006). Thus, the right brain strategy of dissociation represents the ultimate defense for blocking emotional pain.

This affective deficit ensues when attachment trauma produces an enduring impairment of the "affective core" (Emde, 1983), the primordial central integrating structure of the nascent self. Joseph (1992) describes this as the "childlike central core" that maintains the self-image and all associated emotions, cognitions, and memories that are formed during childhood. Joseph localizes this core system in the right brain and limbic system. Recall (1) Devinsky's (2000) assertion that optimal right hemispheric functions allow for "a coherent, continuous, and unified sense of self," and (2) Devinsky's citation of 19th century authors who postulated a connection between right hemispheric dysfunction and dissociation.

Both developmental (Perry et al., 1995; Schore, 1997) and adult (Bremner, 1999) studies support the proposition that there are two subtypes of acute trauma response in PTSD, hyperarousal and dissociative. I suggest that, in all stages of life, dissociation is a consequence of a psychological shock or high arousal (Meares, 1999) and that "at extremely high levels of arousal, coherent integration of sensory information breaks down and dissociative symptoms emerge" (J. Krystal et al., 1995). According to Gadea et al. (2005) mild to moderate negative affective experiences activate the right hemisphere, but an intense experience "might interfere with right hemisphere processing, with eventual damage if some critical point is reached" (p. 136). This damage is specifically hyperarousal-induced apoptotic cell death in the hypermetabolic right brain. Thus, via a switch into a hypoarousal, a hypometabolic state allows for cell survival at times of intense stress (Schore, 2003a).

8.5.1 Hyperarousal

Current research indicates that both hyperarousal and dissociative responses are essentially driven by right brain processes. Metzger et al. (2004) report "PTSD arousal symptoms are associated with increased right-sided parietal activation" (p. 324). Bonne et al. (2003) note that "regional blood flow in right precentral, superior temporal, and fusiform gyri in posttraumatic stress disorder was higher than in healthy controls" (p. 1077), a finding that "may represent continuous preparatory motor activation, reflecting an increased basal level of anxiety and arousal." They suggest that "this may reflect a component common to all survivors of trauma" (p. 1081). Similarly, Rabe et al. find that PTSD patients show a pattern of right hemisphere activation that is associated with anxious arousal during processing of trauma-specific information. In perhaps the most extensive investigation, Lanius et al. (2004) observe that PTSD patients (as opposed to traumatized patients without PTSD) who experience traumatic memories with heart rate increases (i.e., hyperarousal) show a pattern of right brain connectivity: activation of the right posterior cingulate, right caudate, right occipital, and right parietal lobe. They deduced that this right-lateralized pattern "may account for the nonverbal nature of traumatic memory in PTSD subjects" and cited other studies showing that "subjects who had experienced early trauma displayed … right dominance during memory recall."

8.5.2 Hypoarousal

Dissociation in PTSD is also centered in right brain processes. fMRI research of PTSD patients while they were in a dissociative state (as reflected in a lack of increase in heart rate when exposed to their traumatic script) revealed:

> activation effects in the superior and middle temporal gyrus, anterior cingulate, medial parietal lobe, and medial frontal gyres in the dissociated PTSD subjects were lateralized to the right side. The possibility that childhood trauma sets the stage for lateralized responses is given credence by report from Schiffer et al. (1995) who showed right hemisphere activation … during recall of unpleasant memories in adults with a history of childhood abuse. (Lanius et al., 2002, p. 309)

These authors concluded that "prefrontal and limbic structures underlie dissociative responses in PTSD" and stated that activation of the right superior and middle temporal gyri in dissociated PTSD patients is consistent with a corticolimbic model of dissociation. In a more recent study, Lanius et al. (2005) observe predominantly right-hemispheric frontal and insula activation in PTSD patients while they are dissociating, and concluded that patients dissociate in order to escape from the overwhelming emotions associated with the traumatic memory, and that dissociation can be interpreted as representing a nonverbal response to the traumatic memory.

Gundel et al. (2004) note that dissociating (and alexithymic) patients "have difficulties in integrating aspects of certain neuropsychological functions, namely memories and feelings, into current awareness" and proposed that the right anterior cingulate "may represent the structural, neuroanatomical correlate of an active inhibitory system causing a down regulation of emotional processing during the … expressive aspects of emotion" (p. 138). Very similar findings were reported by Spitzer et al. (2004) in a transcranial magnetic stimulation study; they argue that their data show that dissociation may involve

> a lack of integration in the right hemisphere. This corresponds with the idea that the right hemisphere has a distinct role in establishing, maintaining, and processing personally relevant aspects of an individual's world. Thus a right hemispheric dysfunction might result in an altered sense of personally relevant familiarity, which resembles phenomenologically the dissociative symptoms of depersonalization and derealization … trauma-related conditions, which themselves are closely-associated with dissociative psychopathology, lack right hemispheric integration. (p. 167)

Citing the DSM-IV, they conclude, "In dissociation-prone individuals, a trauma that is perceived and processed by the right hemisphere will lead to a 'disruption in the usually integrated functions of consciousness'" (p. 168).

8.6 DYSREGULATION OF RIGHT-LATERALIZED LIMBIC-AUTONOMIC CIRCUITS AND DISSOCIATION

These studies reflect the ontogenetic development of an early-dysregulated system, and provide further evidence that prefrontal cortical and limbic areas, particularly of the right hemisphere, are central to dissociative response. More so than the left, the right hemisphere is densely interconnected with limbic regions and subcortical areas that generate the physiological aspect of emotions, including fear-terror (Adamec, 1999; Adolphs, Tranel, & Damasio, 2001; Borod, 2000; Gainotti, 2000; Tucker, 1992). Hecaen and Albert (1978) have described the much overlooked importance of hierarchical vertical corticosubcortical functional systems:

> Cortical neural mechanisms of one hemisphere would be responsible for a particular performance, and subcortical structures connected to these cortical zones would participate in the realization of the performance, creating a complex, corticosubcortical functional system specific to each hemisphere. (p. 414)

This "vertical" model of cortical-subcortical circuits directly applies to the right hemisphere, "the emotional brain":

> Neural processing of emotions engages diverse structures from the highest to the lowest levels of the neuraxis. On the one hand, high-order association areas are necessary to understand the significance of an emotional situation, and on the other hand, low level structures must be activated to express the emotion through changes in the rhythm of peripheral organs. (Barbas et al., 2003)

These vertical circuits also account for the fact that the right hemisphere contains the major circuitry of emotion regulation (Brake et al., 2000; Porges, Doussard-Roosevelt, & Maiti, 1994; Schore, 1994; Sullivan & Dufresne, 2006).

I suggest that dissociation, a primitive coping strategy of affect regulation, is best understood as a loss of vertical connectivity between cortical and subcortical limbic areas within the right hemisphere. In contrast, J. Krystal et al. (1998) emphasize "shifts in interhemispheric processing" and "cortical disconnectivity" between higher frontal and limbic structures. Ontogenetically, however, dissociation appears well before the frontal areas of the cerebral cortex are myelinated and before callosal connections are functional (Bergman, Linley, & Fawcus, 2004; Schore, 2001a). Thus, models of early dissociative defense against organismic threat must move down the neuraxis into the brain stem that generates states of arousal.

In a congruent model, Scaer postulates that dissociation

> is elicited by internal and external cue-specific stimuli, but because the threat itself has not been resolved, internal cues persist without inhibition from external messages of safety, and kindling is triggered in the *cortical, limbic, and brainstem centers.* (2001, p. 84, my italics)

Notice that Scaer's reference to brain stem centers and *external and internal* cues clearly implies both top-down and bottom-up processing. Pathological dissociative detachment is a defensive state, driven by fear, in which the stressed individual copes by pervasively and diffusely disengaging attention "from both the *outer and inner* worlds" (Allen et al., 1998, p. 164, my italics). In a similar conceptualization, Putnam (1997) describes dissociation between "*an observing and experiencing ego.*" Such terms (i.e., "inner world," "experiencing ego"), however, have not been clearly defined by the dissociation literature.

I have suggested that what is "experienced" are bodily states, and that the "inner world," the source of "internal cues," is more so than cognitions, the realm of bodily processes, central components of emotional states (Schore, 1994). According to Allen and his colleagues, "dissociatively-detached individuals are not only detached from the environment, but also from the self—their body, their own actions, and their sense of identity" (p. 165). This is reminiscent of the ICD-10 definition of dissociation: "a partial or complete loss of the normal integration between memories of the past, awareness of identity and immediate sensations, and control of body movements."

Specifically, recent findings about the autonomic nervous system, or what Hughlings Jackson (see Taylor, 1958) called the "physiological bottom of the mind," are vital to understanding the mind-body alterations of trauma and the mechanism of dissociation (Schore, 2001b, 2002). Indeed, the higher regulatory systems of the right hemisphere form extensive reciprocal connections with the limbic, sympathetic, and parasympathetic branches of the ANS (Aftanas et al., 2005; Critchley et al., 2000; Erciyas et al., 1999; Spence, Shapiro, & Zaidel, 1996; Tucker, 1992; Yoon et al., 1997). These control the somatic components of many emotional responses, especially autonomic physiological responses to social stimuli. Adaptive right-brain emotion processing depends upon an integration of the activities of the CNS and the ANS (Hagemann, Waldstein, & Thayer, 2003).

According to Porges et al. (1994), the lower right side of the brain stem that controls the ANS is innervated by the amygdala and unnamed higher limbic structures; this "vagal circuit of emotion regulation" provides the primary central regulation of homeostasis and physiological reactivity. Porges's model emphasizes the lower structures of a vertical system. Although he details the brain stem components, he refers to the higher structures as the "cortex" that processes information from the social environment. And yet, his model clearly implies a bidirectional system in which both top-down and bottom-up processes are responsible for generating adaptive regulatory functioning.

Benarroch (1997) describes such CNS-ANS limbic-autonomic circuits in his model of a central autonomic network (CAN)—an internal regulation system through which the brain controls visceromotor, neuroendocrine, and behavioral responses. Like Porges's model, Benarroch's CAN is a bidirectional hierarchical system. Benarroch, however, focuses more on higher limbic structures than lower brain stem structures. The CAN is composed of (1) limbic areas in the ventromedial (orbital) prefrontal cortex, anterior cingulate, insula, and amygdala, (2) diencephalic areas in the hypothalamus, (3) brain stem structures in the periaqueductal grey matter, and (4) the nucleus of the solitary tract and nucleus ambiguus in the medulla. Hagemann, Waldstein, and Thayer (2003) characterize the CAN as

> a network of neural structures that generate, receive, and integrate internal and external information in the service of goal-directed behavior and organism adaptability.... These structures are reciprocally interconnected such that information flows in both directions—top-down and bottom-up. The primary output of the CAN is mediated through the preganglionic sympathetic and parasympathetic neurons. These neurons innervate the heart via the stellate ganglia and the vagus nerve. (pp. 83–84)

When this network is either completely uncoupled or rigidly coupled, the individual is less able to dynamically and adaptively assemble the components of the network to meet an environmental challenge, thereby displaying deficits in emotional expression and affect regulation (Demaree et al., 2004). This finding leads back to the problem of psychopathogenesis—what events could be responsible for such deficits?

Authors are now describing the developmental process of "cerebral maturation in the vertical dimension" (Luu & Tucker, 1996). Both the ANS and the CNS continue to develop postnatally; importantly, the assembly of these limbic-autonomic circuits (Rinaman, Levitt, & Card, 2000) is experience dependent (Schore, 1994, 2001a). These experiences are provided by attachment transactions of the first and second year, during which the primary caregiver provides complex interpersonal stimuli and interactive regulation of the infant's core systems of central and autonomic arousal. Optimal environments promote secure attachments that facilitate the organization of limbic-autonomic circuits and a right hemispheric limbic-modulated ventral vagal parasympathetic circuit of emotion regulation that mediates both emotion and communication processes (Porges et al., 1994).

Under stress, this complex system manifests itself as a flexible coping pattern in which homeostatic increases in the activity in one ANS division are associated with decreases in the other. An autonomic mode of coupled reciprocal sympathetic-parasympathetic control is evident when an organism responds alertly and adaptively to a personally meaningful (especially social) stressor, yet promptly returns to the relaxed state of autonomic balance as soon as the context is appraised as safe. Thus, the ANS is not only sensitive to environmental demands and perceived stresses and threats, but will also, in a predictable order, rapidly reorganize to different neural-mediated states (Porges, 2001).

In contrast to this healthy developmental scenario, traumatizing primary caregivers amplify the infant's states of hyperarousal and/or dissociative hypoarousal. This relational intersubjective context inhibits the experience-dependent maturation of CNS-ANS links (which are more extensive on the right side of the brain). In this manner, dysregulation of the developing right brain is associated in the short term with traumatic attachment and in the long term with the psychopathogenesis of dissociation. An extensive apoptotic parcellation of vertical circuits in the developing right brain would lead to an inefficient regulation of the ANS by higher centers in the CNS, functionally expressed as a dissociation of central regulation of sympathetic and hypothalamic-pituitary-adrenal systems (Young, Ross, & Landsberg, 1984).

This model of dissociation as a stress-induced disconnect between right brain CNS and ANS systems directly applies to the etiology and psychobiological mechanism of "somatoform dissociation," which is an outcome of early onset traumatization, often involving physical abuse and threat to life by another person. In somatoform dissociation there is a lack of integration of sensorimotor experiences, reactions, and functions of the individual and his/her self-representation (Nijenhuis, 2000). Recall Devinsky's (2000) assertion: optimal right hemispheric functions allow for the operations of "a coherent, continuous, and unified sense of self."

Psychopathological regulatory systems thus contain poorly evolved CNS-ANS limbic-autonomic switching mechanisms that are inefficient or incapable of uncoupling and recoupling the sympathetic and parasympathetic components of the ANS in response to changing environmental circumstances. This "nonreciprocal mode of autonomic control" (Berntson et al., 1991) is unable to adapt to stress; in fact, the coping limitations of pathological dissociation are essentially defined by these systems' overly rigid and continuing inhibition of certain internal systems. In other words, dissociation reflects the inability of the right brain cortical-subcortical system to (1) recognize and co-process exteroceptive information from the relational environment and (2) on a moment-to-moment basis integrate this information from moment to moment with interoceptive information from the body. Neuroscience writers now refer to "a dissociation between the emotional evaluation of an event and the physiological reaction to that event, with the process being dependent on intact right hemisphere function" (Crucian et al., 2000, p. 643).

An immature right brain circuit of emotion regulation would show deficits in "intense emotional-homeostatic processes" (Porges et al., 1994), that is, it would too easily default from fast-acting ventral vagal to slow-acting dorsal vagal systems in moments of "vehement emotions" and, thereby, be unable to flexibly shift internal states and overt behavior in response to stressful external demands. Indeed, the ventral vagal complex is known to be defective in PTSD patients (Sahar, Shalev, & Porges, 2001); this may account for the basal hyperarousal and high heart rates of these patients (Sack, Hopper, & Lamprecht, 2004). I suggest that under high stress an unstable ventral vagal system could be rapidly displaced by a dorsal vagal system; this would account for the low heart rate of dissociative hypoarousal.

The disassociation of higher corticolimbic areas of the CAN internal regulation system and Porges's right brain circuit of emotion regulation precludes (1) top-down control of lower brain stem and autonomic functions and (2) adaptive integration of CNS exteroceptive and ANS interoceptive information processing. This disinhibition releases lower control structures in the right amygdala via a mechanism that Hughlings Jackson (1884) called *dissolution*:

> The higher nervous arrangements inhibit (or control) the lower, and thus, when the higher are suddenly rendered functionless, the lower rise in activity.

What do we know about higher control systems? Current neuroimaging research indicates that the highest level of regulatory control structures in the human brain are located in frontolimbic systems of the right hemisphere.

8.6.1 The Essential Role of Right Frontolimbic Structures in the Regulation of Dissociation

Note that the neuroanatomy of the right brain allows for a reciprocal connection between the highest level of the limbic system (the orbitofrontal and medial frontal cortices) and the brain stem medullary vagal systems that regulate parasympathetic hypoarousal and dissociation. A similar model is proposed by Phillips et al. (2003), who described a "ventral" regulation system, including orbitofrontal cortex, insula, anterior cingulate, and amygdala. As opposed to a nonlimbic "dorsal" effortful regulation system in the dorsolateral cortex, hippocampus, and other structures involved in explicit processing of the "verbal components of emotional stimuli," this ventral system is important for the implicit identification of the emotional significance of environmental stimuli, and is central to the "automatic regulation and mediation of autonomic responses to emotional stimuli and contexts that accompany the production of affective states" (p. 510).

I have described a model of dual limbic-autonomic circuits, a hierarchical sequence of interconnected limbic areas in the orbitofrontal cortex, insular cortex, anterior cingulate, and amygdala (Schore, 1994, 1996). Each component of this "rostral limbic system" interconnects with the other and with brain stem bioaminergic arousal and neuromodulatory systems, including vagal nuclei in the medulla and hypothalamic neuroendocrine nuclei that regulate the sympathetic and parasympathetic nervous systems (Schore, 1994, 2003a, 2003b). Of particular importance are the highest levels of this vertical cortical-subcortical system, especially the orbitofrontal cortex, which monitors and controls responses initiated by other brain regions and is involved in the selection and active inhibition of neural circuits associated with emotional responses (Rule, Shimamura, & Knight, 2002). This prefrontal system performs a "hot" executive function—regulating affect and motivation via control of basic limbic system functions (Zelazo & Muller, 2002).

According to Barbas and her colleagues (2003),

> Axons from orbitofrontal and medial prefrontal cortices converge in the hypothalamus with neurons projecting to brainstem and spinal autonomic centers, linking the highest with the lowest levels of the neuraxis....

> Descending pathways from orbitofrontal and medial prefrontal cortices [anterior cingulate], which are linked with the amygdala, provide the means for speedy influence of the prefrontal cortex on the autonomic system, in processes underlying appreciation and expression of emotions.... Repetitive activation of the remarkably specific and bidirectional pathways linking the amygdala with the orbitofrontal cortex may be necessary for conscious appreciation of the emotional significance of events.

This top-down influence can either be excitatory or inhibitory; the latter expressed in the documented activation of the orbitofrontal cortex during defensive responses (Roberts et al., 2001). Recall Lanius's et al. (2002) conclusion that prefrontal and limbic structures underlie dissociative responses in PTSD, and Gundel's et al. (2004) proposal that the right anterior cingulate can act as an inhibitory system that down-regulates emotional processing, resulting in dissociation (i.e., an inability to integrate feelings into conscious awareness).

Indeed, this limbic-autonomic circuit is right-lateralized. The right orbitofrontal cortex, the hierarchical apex of the limbic system, exercises executive control over the entire right brain. Right orbitofrontal areas are more critical to emotional functions than left orbitofrontal areas (Tranel, Bechara, & Denburg, 2002). Within the orbitofrontal cortex, the lateral orbital prefrontal areas are specialized for regulating positive emotional states, while medial orbitofrontal areas are specialized for processing negative emotional states (Northoff et al., 2000; Schore, 2001a). The functioning of these two limbic-autonomic circuits, one capped by the lateral orbitofrontal cortex and the other by the medial orbitofrontal cortex (which in earlier writings I termed the excitatory ventral tegmental limbic forebrain-midbrain circuit and the inhibitory lateral tegmental limbic forebrain-midbrain circuits, respectively; Schore, 1994) are organized by the attachment experiences of the first and second year.

Optimal maturation of this prefrontolimbic system allows for the highest level of integration of exteroceptive and interoceptive information. The right orbitofrontal cortex, in conjunction with the right anterior insula, supports a representation of visceral responses accessible to awareness, and provides a substrate for subjective feeling states and emotional depth and awareness (Craig, 2004; Critchley et al., 2004). In contrast, recall that pathological dissociation is defined in ICD-10 as a loss of "awareness of identity and immediate sensations, and control of body movements." Just as secure attachment constrains trauma and dissociation, so does optimal functioning of the orbitofrontal system oppose somatoform dissociation.

Furthermore, the right prefrontal cortex, the "senior executive of limbic arousal" (Joseph, 1996), is most directly linked to stress-regulatory systems (Brake et al., 2000) and, therefore, is essential for the regulation of the hyperaroused and hypoaroused states that accompany traumatic stress. During the acquisition of conditioned fear (Fischer et al., 2002), the right prefrontal brain is activated. This cortical-subcortical regulatory mechanism allows for orbitofrontal modulation of the right amygdala that is specialized for fear conditioning (Baker & Kim, 2004; Moses et al., 2007) and processing frightening faces (Adolphs, Tranel, & Damasio, 2001; Whalen et al., 1998). The right amygdala directly projects to the brain stem startle center (Bradley, Cuthbert, & Lang, 1996; Davis, 1989) and to the dorsal motor vagal nucleus (Schwaber et al., 1982), and the amygdala's connections with the dorsolateral periaqueductal gray in the brain stem mediate the defensive freeze response (Oliveira et al., 2004; Vianna et al., 2001). In this manner, the right orbitofrontal cortex "organizes the appropriate cortical and autonomic response based on the implications of ... sensory information for survival. The orbitofrontal cortex therefore functions as a master regulator for organization of the brain's response to threat" (Scaer, 2001, p. 78).

These data strongly suggest that an individual with an impaired or developmentally immature orbitofrontal system resulting from early relational trauma will be vulnerable to pathological dissociation under stress. Without orbital prefrontal feedback regarding the level of threat, the organism remains in an amygdala-driven defensive response state longer than necessary (Morgan & LeDoux, 1995). In humans, conditioned fear acquisition and extinction are associated with right-hemisphere-dominant amygdala function (La Bar et al., 1998). Such amygdala-driven startle and fear-freeze responses are intense because they are totally unregulated by the orbitofrontal (and medial frontal) cortex. Indeed, dysfunction of the right frontal lobe is involved in PTSD symptomatology (Freeman & Kimbrell, 2001) and dissociative flashbacks (Berthier et al., 2001).

In classic neurological primate research, Ruch and Shenkin (1943) lesioned the orbitofrontal cortex (Brodman area 13) and observed a "definite reduction in emotional expression" and an elimination of fear and aggressive behaviors (that were replaced by "gazing into the distance with a blank expression"). Neurological patients with orbitofrontal damage show a "dissociation among autonomic measures" and an altered response to a startle. Such patients show a *decrease* in heart rate in anticipation of, or in response to, an aversive stimulus (Roberts et al., 2004). This is reminiscent of the deceleration of heart rate that has been observed in traumatized dissociating infants and dissociating adult psychiatric patients.

In support of earlier proposals (Schore, 1994), it is now well established that orbitofrontal maturation is experience dependent (Neddens et al., 2001; Poeggel, Nowicki, & Braun, 2003), that human prefrontal functions emerge around the end of the first year (Happeney, Zelazo, & Stuss, 2004), and that conditions that modify early maternal variability in infancy produce "significant differences in right but not left adult prefrontal volumes, with experience-dependent asymmetric variation most clearly expressed in ventral medial cortex" (Lyons et al., 2002, p. 51). During these critical periods extensive hypometabolic states preclude complex organization and complex functional capacity of the highest frontolimbic levels of the right brain. Pathological dissociation reflects an impairment of the affect regulatory functions of the higher centers in the orbitofrontal cortex. Through its connections with the ANS the orbitofrontal system is implicated in "the representation of emotional information and the regulation of emotional processes" (Roberts et al., 2004, p. 307) and "the conscious appreciation of the emotional significance of events" (Barbas et al., 2003). In the dorsal vagal parasympathetic-dominant state of dissociation, however, the individual is cut off (dis-associated) from both the external and the internal environment and, therefore, specific emotions are not consciously experienced.

Although triggered by subcortical mechanisms, dissociation is regulated by higher corticolimbic centers. Pathological dissociation is the product of an inefficient frontolimbic system that cannot regulate the onset and offset of the dissociative response. Instead, for long periods of time, disinhibited lower subcortical centers (especially the right amygdala) drive the dissociative response; this reflects a Janetian regression to a constricted and disunified state. Adequate orbitofrontal activity is needed to integrate information from the external world and the internal world (especially "messages of safety"); "such integration might provide a way whereby incoming information may be associated with motivational and emotional states to subserve processes such as selective attention and memory formation and retrieval" (Pandya & Yeterian, 1985, p. 51). Loss of orbitofrontal functions that maintain "the integration of past, present, and future experiences, enabling adequate performance in behavioral tasks, social situation, or situations involving survival (Lipton et al., 1999, p. 356) is reflected in pathological dissociation: "a disruption in the usually integrated functions of consciousness, memory, identity, or perception of the environment" (APA, 1994). Indeed, patients using pathological dissociation who experience severe alterations of consciousness and loss of identity—dissociative identity disorder—show significant reduction of blood flow and therefore hypoactivation of the orbitofrontal cortices (Şar et al., 2007).

8.7 FURTHER SPECULATIONS ON THE BIOLOGICAL MECHANISM OF DISSOCIATION

As previously noted, Prueter (2002) has called for an understanding of the "primary pathophysiologic mechanism that leads to the dissociative symptoms, using neurobiological research mechanisms." Towards that end, I have used regulation theory to offer a model of the earliest psychobiological expression of dissociation in human infancy. I argued that dissociation is a basic survival mechanism for coping with intense states of energy-expending hyperarousal by shifting into an energy-conserving hypometabolic state. This regulation strategy of hypoarousal, which is reflected in heart rate deceleration in response to stress, remains unchanged over the life span. This model is based in part on (1) Main's observations (Main & Solomon, 1986; Main & Hesse, 1999, 2006; i.e., that the disorganization and disorientation of type D attachment phenotypically resembles dissociative states), and (2) Tronick's (Tronick & Weinberg, 1997; Tronick, 2004) still-face procedure—a threatening interpersonal context that triggers "massive disengagement."

I have suggested that these paradigms describe the same state of dissociation that clinicians have described as "profound detachment" (Barach, 1991), "detachment from an unbearable situation" (Mollon, 1996), and "dissociative detachment" (Allen et al., 1998). At all points in the life span, the functional aspects of Janetian "extreme emotional arousal" and dissociation reflect a structural alteration in arousal systems in the brain stem associated with a loss of ventral vagal, and dominance of dorsal vagal, parasympathetic states. In this section I will offer further speculations about the basic biological mechanisms that underlie dissociation.

Under stress, Type D infants show "a dazed facial appearance … accompanied by a stilling of all body movement, and sometimes a *freezing* of limbs which had been in motion" (Main & Solomon, 1986). Experiences of traumatic freezing are encoded in enduring implicit-procedural memory, representing what Janet termed unconscious "fixed ideas" that cannot be "liquidated." Indeed, the relationship between freeze behavior and dissociation has been noted by authors from various disciplines. In psychophysiological research, Porges (1997) observes a trauma-induced "immobilized state" associated with the dorsal vagal complex. In one of the most important psychiatric texts on trauma written in the last century, Henry Krystal (1988) characterizes a traumatic "catatonoid" affective reaction to "the perception of fatal helplessness in the face of destructive danger," and equates this "pattern of surrender" with the "cataleptic immobility" of animals. In the trauma literature, I have described (1) the "frozen watchfulness" of the abused child who waits warily for parental demands, responds quickly and compliantly, and then returns to her previous vigilant state, and (2) the "frozen state" of speechless terror seen in adult PTSD patients (Schore, 2001a).

In neurological writings, Scaer (2001) postulates that dissociation "is initiated by a failed attempt at defensive/escape efforts at the moment of a life threat, and is perpetuated if spontaneous recovery of the resulting *freeze response* is blocked or truncated" (p. 84, my italics):

> If deterrence of the threat through defense or fight fails, the animal enters a state of helplessness, associated by a marked increase in dorsal vagal complex tone, initiating the freeze/immobility response.... The extremes of vagal parasympathetic tone as manifested in the state of dorsal vagal activation, therefore, contribute greatly to the generation of severe emotions, especially those of terror and helplessness. Although freeze/immobility states ... may be useful for short-term survival, prolongation or repeated activation of that state clearly has serious implications for health and long-term survival. (Scaer, 2001, p. 81)

Several studies indicate that the freeze response is right lateralized. Freezing in primate infants, which is elicited by eye contact, correlates with extreme right frontal EEG activity and high basal cortisol levels (Kalin et al., 1998). Right parietal lesions in rats are associated with a conditioned freezing deficit (Hogg, Sanger, & Moser, 1998). In human catatonia, a basic somatic defense mechanism associated with "immobilization of anxieties," there is a right lower prefronto-parietal cortical dysfunction (Northoff et al., 2000).

But other studies in the developmental literature, those of Tronick, describe not freeze behavior but a collapsed state of "profound disengagement" (see Figure 8.2). Tronick (2004) observes both a suspension of spontaneous emotional expression and gesture, and a "dissipation of the infant's state of consciousness" that is associated with "the disorganization of many of the lower level psychobiological states, such as metabolic systems." How does this relate to freezing? Keep in mind that the full manifestation of the fear-freeze response is a late-occurring behavior; in human infants, it occurs in the second half of the first year. But dissociation is seen in the hypoxic human fetus (Reed et al., 1999) and soon after birth (Bergman et al., 2004).

Again, clues come from studies in basic biology and neuroscience. Citing this literature, Scaer states that freeze behavior is a state of alert immobility in the presence of a predator. He points out that a freeze may be succeeded by flight or, if attacked and captured by a predator, by a "*deeper state of freeze*—one associated with apparent unresponsiveness and with marked changes in basal autonomic state" (2001, p. 76, my italics). This state of helplessness lasts for up to 30 minutes, and is accompanied by marked bradycardia (heart rate deceleration) and a pronounced state of "deep" parasympathetic vagal tone. Recall that Porges' (1995) description of an "involuntary and often prolonged characteristic pattern of vagal outflow from the dorsal vagal nucleus" (1995, p. 228). I equate this with a deep dissociative state which, if prolonged, is the psychobiological engine of pathological dissociation.

Studies in basic biology offer further information about the psychobiological mechanism of this deeper state of freeze. Gabrielsen and Smith (1985) have explored the physiological responses that underlie basic defenses (i.e., "threat-induced behavior") in all animals. In reaction to an environmental threat (a predator), an organism can respond in various ways: the organism may fight or flee in fear. Both responses are associated with tachycardia and increased activity, reflective of sympathetic hyperarousal.

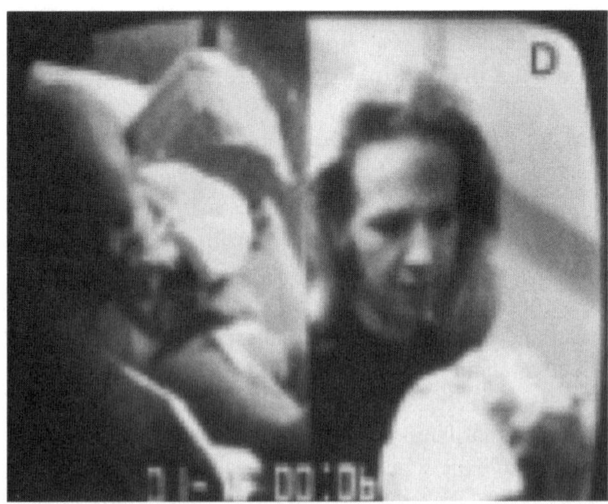

FIGURE 8.2 Close-up of the still-face induced collapse. From *Emotional development*, by Tronick, E. Z, 2004, New York: Oxford University Press. Copyright 2004 Oxford University Press. Reprinted with permission.

Gabrielson and Smith delineate two *active* defenses (i.e., fight or flight) and two passive defenses (i.e., freezing and paralysis). The passive, immobile defenses differ; freezing occurs in response to visual or auditory stimuli of a predator's approach, whereas paralysis occurs in response to strong tactile stimulation by the predator.

Intriguingly, the organism is alert during a freeze, but "unconscious" during paralysis; parasympathetic heart-rate deceleration, which they term *emotional bradycardia*, occurs in both. Biologists call this *fear bradycardia* or *alarm bradycardia* (Jacobsen, 1979). I suggest that the differentiation of freeze versus paralysis is the same difference as (1) Scaer's freeze versus deeper state of freeze, and (2) Main's type D freezing when the infant is "alarmed by the parent" versus Tronick's still-face collapse, loss of postural control, and "dissipation of consciousness." Because high levels of dorsal vagal activation are associated with dangerous bradycardia, these data strongly suggest that the mother's failure to repair infant dissociative states of deep freeze would be a potent generator of psychopathogenesis. Recall Bremner and Brett's (1997) caution: "dissociation represents an effective short-term strategy that is detrimental to long-term functioning."

Gabrielsen and Smith (1985) refer to another term for the deep freeze state—*feigned death*—a defense mechanism that is utilized by a number of vertebrates, amphibians, reptiles, birds, and mammals (including humans). A mild threat (the face of a human in this study) to the American opossum elicited freezing and a 12% decrease in heart rate. A more severe threat (vigorous tactile shaking), however, induced death feigning and a stunning 46% decrease of heart rate deceleration. In a conception that is congruent with the neurobiological model of dissociation outlined in this chapter, Gabrielsen and Smith (1985) postulate that (1) the sudden depression in heart rate and respiration strongly indicates that higher CNS structures are directly controlling the parasympathetic cardiovascular "centres" in the medulla and (2) this alteration reflects a severe decrease in oxygen consumption and body temperature.

I propose: (1) the freeze response is a dorsal vagal parasympathetic energy-conserving state that is coupled with, but dominant over, a weaker state of energy-expending sympathetic arousal; and (2) during the collapsed state of death feigning, the two ANS components are uncoupled. Thus, in the deep freeze there is no sympathetic activity (low levels of vasopressin, catecholamines, cortisol) and pure dorsal vagal activation that produces massive bradycardia (Cheng et al., 1999) and a hypometabolic state. This decrease in oxygen consumption during dissociative death feigning is congruent with the role of the dorsal vagal system in hypoxic responses (Porges, 2001; Potter & McCloskey, 1986) and with the reptilian diving reflex, an energy conservation strategy of heart rate deceleration that acts as a "metabolic defense" (Boutiler, 2001; Guppy & Withers, 1999).

Parasympathetic vagal tone also increases "during entrance in hibernation, a long lasting disengagement from the external environment characterized by decreases in heart rate, breathing frequency, and metabolic rate" (Recordati, 2003, p. 4). The hypometabolic changes in brain plasticity (Von der Ohe et al., 2006) and in mitochondrial energy generation (Eddy et al., 2006) during the hibernation state of torpor (apathy, low responsiveness) may thus be directly related to the neurobiological mechanism of dissociation. This shift into hypoxia also mediates "suspended animation" in developing systems (Padilla & Roth, 2001; Teodoro & O'Farrell, 2003). These data support my model of dissociation as a hypometabolic state (Schore, 2001b), a Janetian deficiency of psychological energy.

Note the similarity of this "emotional bradycardia" to (1) the earlier psychoneurobiological portraits of the infant's parasympathetic-driven heart rate deceleration and dissociative response to attachment trauma, (2) Kestenberg's (1985) dead spots in the infant's subjective experience, and (3) Powles's (1992) state of conservation-withdrawal in which the stressed individual passively disengages by "the risky posture of feigning death." The clinical literature refers to dissociation as "a last resort defensive strategy" (Dixon, 1998) and "a submission and resignation to the inevitability of overwhelming, even psychically deadening danger" (Davies & Frawley, 1994, p. 65).

8.8 CONCLUSIONS AND IMPLICATIONS FOR DSM–V

We are currently experiencing a period of rapid change within, and perhaps more importantly between, the theoretical and applied sciences. The DSM-V conception of dissociation should be substantially impacted by the advances in basic science and clinical knowledge that have occurred during "the decade of the brain."

With what we now understand about development and brain behavior (structure-function) relationships, can we now more precisely characterize the classic statement of Classen, Koopman, and Spiegel?:

> Trauma victims who lack the cognitive and emotional structures to immediately assimilate the experience use the state of consciousness known as dissociation to escape from the full psychological impact of the event. (1993, p. 29)

In other words, how do cognition and emotion relate to dissociation? Can we now locate these cognitive and emotional structures in known brain systems?

8.8.1 Cognitive Structures and Dissociation

DSM-IV defines dissociation as a disruption in the usually integrated functions of consciousness, perception, and memory. It is now well established that memory is not a single process; DSM-V's definition of dissociation should reflect this fact. In fact studies on trauma and dissociation have made important contributions to the distinction between declarative-explicit-semantic memory (i.e., conscious recall of traumatic experiences) and procedural-implicit-nonverbal memory (i.e., unconscious organization of emotional memories and storage of conditioned sensorimotor traumatic responses). According to Scaer, "Although declarative memory may account for much of the arousal-based cognitive symptoms of PTSD, procedural memory provides the seemingly unbreakable conditioned link that perpetuates the neural cycle of trauma and dissociation" (2001, p. 76).

Recent data from developmental and affective neuroscience reflect the importance of implicit-procedural memory in dissociation. Kandel (1999) notes that "the infant relies primarily on its procedural memory systems" during "the first 2–3 years of life," a period of right hemispheric dominance (Chiron et al., 1997). Relational trauma can be stored at an early age: "The clinical data, reinforced by research findings, indicate that preverbal children, even in the first year of life, can establish and retain some form of internal representation of a traumatic event over significant periods of time" (Gaensbauer, 2002, p. 259). This early representation is encoded in nonverbal implicit-procedural memory that matures well before verbal explicit-declarative memory does. Such representations of attachment trauma are encoded as a "frozen whole" (Gendlin, 1970); they include "nonverbal presymbolic forms of relating" that "protect the infant from trauma and continue to be used by patients to avoid retraumatization" (Kiersky & Beebe, 1994, p. 389), that is, the right brain defensive regulatory strategy of dissociation.

A growing body of studies show that "the right hemisphere has been linked to implicit information processing, as opposed to the more explicit and more conscious processing tied to the left hemisphere" (Happaney et al., 2004, p. 7). Recall, pathological dissociative detachment "escapes conscious control and is often experienced passively, as automatic or reflexive" (Allen et al., 1998, p. 163). Although trauma seriously impairs left-lateralized declarative memory and hippocampal function, dissociative mechanisms are efficiently encoded in right-lateralized amygdala-driven implicit memory that is primarily regulatory, automatized, and unconscious. Research on the memory mechanisms of PTSD has recently focused on deficits in hippocampal function and impairments of conscious explicit memory. Stress-induced elevations of cortisol impair declarative memory (Kirschbaum et al., 1996). Hippocampal dysfunction in PTSD is more lateralized to the left hemisphere (Mohanakrishnan Menon et al., 2003).

PTSD models are now shifting from the hippocampus to the amygdala, from explicit memory of places to implicit memory of faces. Chronic stress induces contrasting patterns of dendritic remodeling in hippocampal and amygdaloid neurons, leading to (1) a loss of hippocampal inhibitory control, (2) a gain of excitatory control by the amygdala, and (3) a resulting imbalance in HPA functioning (Vyas, Mitra, Shankaranarayana Rao, & Chattarji, 2002). Recent clinical models of PTSD suggest that the amygdala inhibits hippocampal functioning during high levels of arousal, thereby mediating a diminution of explicit memory for peritraumatic events (Layton & Krikorian, 2002). McNally and Amir (1996) argue that the amygdala is centrally involved in the consolidation of the traumatic experience and in the storage of perceptual implicit memory for trauma-related information.

It is important to note that dissociation not only impairs explicit memory, but also impairs higher levels of implicit memory. J. Krystal and his colleagues are describing the disconnection that occurs under extremes of arousal between the explicit dorsal regulation system involved in the "verbal components of emotional stimuli" and the implicit ventral regulation system involved in the automatic regulation of emotional stimuli (Phillips et al., 2003). This disconnection produces cognitive dissociation. On the other hand, somatoform dissociation—indeed the fundamental mechanism of pathological dissociation itself—reflects an impairment in the ventral regulation system and, thus, a deficit in the implicit identification and regulation of autonomic responses and the production of affective states.

Two common misunderstandings have confounded the dissociation literature. The first common misunderstanding is to define consciousness narrowly as (1) reflective consciousness and (2) correlated with left hemispheric verbal functions. In fact, another form of consciousness exists; primary consciousness relates emotional and visceral information about the biological self to information about outside reality. Edelman (1989) claims that primary consciousness is lateralized to the right brain. Thus, *somatoform dissociation represents a disruption of primary consciousness.* The second common misunderstanding is to equate cognition with conscious verbal mentation and to view the left hemisphere as the sole domain of cognition. This is untrue. Cognition is the faculty of knowledge, but knowing can be both conscious and nonconscious. Information about external and internal environments is appraised via nonconscious as well as conscious mechanisms.

In fact, right brain appraisal of threat in the social environment is performed implicitly and very quickly, below conscious awareness (see Schore, 2003b, 2004, 2005a). Thus, cognition includes right-lateralized social cognition of faces; this allows for the appraisal of exteroceptive social cues in a relational intersubjective context. Interoceptive sensitivity (Barrett et al., 2004), the tracking of somatovisceral information coming up from the body, is also a cognitive process. Both exteroceptive processing of social cues and interoceptive sensitivity to the body are cognitive operations of the right hemisphere, the locus of implicit learning (Hugdahl, 1995).

Pathological dissociation impairs implicit cognitive appraisal of the external world and the internal world. New models of dissociation must reflect these findings that shift the emphasis from explicit to implicit memory and from left hemisphere to right hemisphere.

8.8.2 Right Brain Emotional Structures and Dissociation

In DSM-IV, the clinical manifestations of dissociation include derealization and amnesia for autobiographical information and derealization, phenomena that reflect a heavy emphasis on cognition. However, psychiatry, psychology, and neuroscience are now emphasizing the primacy of affect and affect regulation. This convergence suggests that DSM-V should (re)incorporate emotion into the definition of dissociation. The contemporary revitalization of the work of Janet (Nemiah, 1989; Putnam, 1989; Van der Hart, Nijenhuis, & Steele, 2006) clearly implies a return to a model of dissociation in which "vehement emotions" and "extreme emotional arousal" are central, rather than secondary, to cognition. A large body of converging clinical and experimental research suggests that *severe affect dysregulation lies at the core of the disintegration that occurs in the dissociative response to overwhelming traumatic experience.*

The original Janetian concept of dissociation implies that the trigger for disintegration is an unbearable emotional reaction and an appraisal that the experience is overwhelming. What is disassociated is a structural system that rapidly detects, processes, and copes with unbearable emotional information and overwhelming survival threat. This characterization applies to the right brain, which is dominant for the reception (Adolphs et al., 1996; Anderson & Phelps, 2000; Borod et al., 1998; George et al., 1996; Lucas et al., 2003; Nakamura et al., 1999) and expression (Borod, Haywood, & Koff, 1997; Mandal & Ambady, 2004) of emotion, as well as responding to preattentive negative emotional stimuli (Kimura et al., 2004), coping with negative affects (Davidson et al., 1990; Silberman & Weingartner, 1986), and controlling vital functions that support survival and enable the organism to cope with stressors (Wittling & Schweiger, 1993).

The human threat detection system is located in the subcortical areas of the right brain, especially in the right amygdala, which is specialized for detecting "unseen fear" (Morris et al., 1999), for fear conditioning (Fischer et al., 2002), for stress and emotionally related processes (Scicli et al., 2004), and for the expression of memory of aversively motivated experiences (Coleman-Mesches & McGaugh, 1995). In a study of predator-related stress-activation of the right amygdala and periaqueductal gray, Adamaec, Blundell, and Burton (2003) reported findings that "implicate neuroplasticity in right hemispheric limbic circuitry in mediating long-lasting changes in negative affect following brief but severe stress" (p. 1264). The right amygdala is regulated by the right insula, right anterior cingulate, and right orbitofrontal cortex; this prefrontal hierarchical apex of the limbic system is activated in "situations involving survival" (Lipton et al., 1999) and functions as "a master regulator for organization of the brain's response to threat" (Scaer, 2001). Indeed, "the right ventral medial prefrontal cortex plays a primary role in optimizing cautious and adaptive behavior in potentially threatening situations" (Sullivan & Gratton, 2002, p. 69).

Earlier in this chapter, I described how secure attachment experiences allow for optimal maturation of the right orbitofrontal cortex. Accordingly, the psychological principle that secure attachment is the primary defense against trauma-induced psychopathology is directly related to the developmental neurobiological tenet that healthy attachment experiences facilitate the experience-dependent maturation of a right-lateralized affect regulatory system that can efficiently modulate the extreme emotional arousal and vehement emotions of trauma. The capacity to consciously experience regulated negative (and positive) emotional states is profoundly adaptive. Affects provide an internal evaluation of our encounters with the environment (Lazarus, 1991), and allow for actual or expected changes in events that are important to the individual (Frijda, 1988).

In contrast, the relational context of a disorganized-disoriented insecure attachment acts as a growth-inhibiting environment that generates immature and inefficient orbitofrontal systems, thereby precluding higher complex forms of affect regulation. Under stress, these immature prefrontal corticolimbic systems rapidly disorganize, disinhibiting lower subcortical systems that activate either states of hyperarousal or the primitive defense of dissociation that counterbalances these states. When dissociated from top-down orbitofrontal influences, an "exaggerated amygdala" response to masked facially expressed fearful reminders of traumatic events occurs in PTSD patients (Rauch et al., 2000). Characterological use of this "last-resort defensive strategy" precludes the capacity to consciously experience affective states, thereby forfeiting their adaptive use in interpersonal and intraorganismic functioning and further emotional development.

The symptomatology of dissociation reflects a structural impairment of a right brain regulatory system and its accompanying deficiencies of affect regulation. The clinical principle that dissociation is detrimental to long-term functioning (Bremner & Brett, 1997) is directly related to the developmental observation that early-forming yet enduring disorganized insecure attachment associated with dissociative states is a primary risk factor for the development of mental disorders (Hesse & Main, 1999; Main, 1996), and to the neuropsychiatric observation that affect dysregulation and right hemisphere dysfunction play a prominent role in all psychiatric disorders (Cutting, 1992; Taylor et al., 1997).

Returning to Classen's dictum (i.e., that individuals who lack the cognitive and emotional structures to assimilate trauma are predisposed to dissociation), it is important to note that efficient orbitofrontal function is essential for "the conscious appreciation of the emotional significance of events" (Barbas et al., 2003). In normal subjects, the right orbitofrontal cortex shows "an enhanced response to consciously perceived, as opposed to neglected fearful faces" (Winston, Vuillemer, & Dolan, 2003, p. 1827). In contrast, PTSD patients with dissociative flashbacks exhibit dysfunctional right frontal activity (Berthier et al., 2001).

The orbitofrontal system is also critical for processing cognitive-emotional interactions (Barbas, 1995). This "thinking part of the emotional brain" (Goleman, 1995) functions as an "internal reflecting and organizing agency" (Kaplan-Solms & Solms, 1996) that is involved in "emotion-related learning" (Rolls, Hornak, Wade, & McGrath, 1994). It acts to "integrate and assign emotional-motivational significance to cognitive impressions; the association of emotion with ideas and thoughts" (Joseph, 1996) and "presents an important site of contact between emotional or affective information and mechanisms of action selection" (Rogers et al., 1999). These data suggest that dissociating trauma victims' deficient cognitive and emotional structures are located in the right orbitofrontal structure and its cortical and subcortical connections.

The DSM and ICD definitions of dissociation both refer to a dis-association of a normally integrated system, but neither the DSM nor the ICD identify this system. In 1994, I described the unique neuroanatomical interconnectivity of the right hemisphere:

> This hemisphere, with dense reciprocal interconnections with limbic and subcortical structures (Tucker, 1981), is specialized to regulate arousal (Levy, Heller, Banich, & Burton, 1983) and to *integrate perceptual processes* (Semmes, 1968).... It contains larger cortical areas than the left of intermodal associative zones that *integrate* processing of the three main sensory modalities (Goldberg & Costa, 1981).... This right hemisphere, more so than the left, is structurally specialized for greater cross-modal *integration* (Chapanis, 1977; Tucker, 1992), perhaps due to the facts that it contains more myelinated fibers that optimize transfer across regions than the left (Gur et al., 1980), and that it is specialized to represent multiple information channels in parallel (Bradshaw & Nettleton, 1981). (Schore, 1994, p. 308, my italics)

Recent studies demonstrate that when the intracortical connections within this hemisphere are functioning in an optimal manner, the hemisphere adaptively coordinates cross-sensory information and thereby subserves the integration of different representational information systems (Calvert et al., 2001; Raij et al., 2000). However, under the extreme stress of both hyperarousal and hypoarousal, the right cortical hemisphere loses its capacity to integrate posterior cortical sensory processing, thus causing the disruption in the integration of perceptual information depicted in the current DSM-IV. Moreover, under these intensely stressful periods, the right brain also loses its capacity to act as an integrated vertical cortical-subcortical system.

When this happens, limbic-autonomic information is processed only at the lowest right amygdala level and blocked from access to higher right anterior cingulate and orbitofrontal areas. Such "partially processed" information (Ludwig, 1972; Whitlock, 1967) cannot be integrated into awareness as a conscious, subjectively experienced emotion. Instead, such "partially processed" somatic information is expressed as what Janet termed "excessive or inappropriate physical responses" and Freud described as "bizarre physical symptoms." In short, *dissociation* refers to the loss of the integrative capacity of the vertically organized emotional right brain.

8.8.3 The Right Brain Emotional-Corporeal Self and Somatoform Dissociation

DSM-IV uses the term *identity* in its definition of dissociation. The contemporary traumatology literature prefers to use the term *self* (Schore, 1994, 2003a, 2003b). For example, "Dissociation refers to a compartmentalization of experience: Elements of a trauma are not integrated into a unitary whole or an integrated sense of self" (Van der Kolk, 1996). Similarly, in the psychoanalytic literature Kohut (1971) postulates that trauma survivors have a shattered self, and Krystal (1988) states that the focus of treatment for trauma survivors is integration of the self. Developmentalists contend that traumatizing caregivers negatively impact the child's attachment security, stress coping strategies, and sense of self (Crittenden & Ainsworth, 1989; Erickson, Egeland, & Pianta, 1989).

The concept of self has also been absorbed into developmental neuroscience. Indeed, the self-organization of the right brain and the origin of the self have been an essential theme of my own writings (Schore, 1994, 2003a, 2003b). A central principle of my work dictates that "The self-organization of the developing brain occurs in the context of a relationship with another self, another brain" (Schore, 1996). Decety and Chaminade (2003) echo this: "The sense of self emerges from the activity of the brain in interaction with other selves." They conclude that "self-awareness, empathy, identification with others, and more generally intersubjective processes, are largely dependent upon ... right hemisphere resources, which are the first to develop" (p. 591). Indeed, the neuroscience literature is also very interested in the self. There is a growing consensus that "The self and personality, rather than consciousness, is the outstanding issue in neuroscience" (Davidson, 2002). Note the relevance of this statement to DSM-IV's overemphasis on consciousness in its definition of dissociation.

It is currently thought that there are dual representations of self, one in each hemisphere. Verbal self-description is mainly a linguistic process associated with a left hemisphere advantage, while self-description in terms of affective tone is associated with a right hemisphere advantage (Faust, Kravetz, & Nativ-Safrai, 2004). This dual model is echoed in LeDoux's statement, "That explicit and implicit aspects of the self exist is not a particularly novel idea. It is closely related to Freud's partition of the mind into conscious, preconscious (accessible but not currently accessed), and unconscious (inaccessible) levels" (2002, p. 28). This dichotomy reflects the aforementioned link between the right hemisphere and nonconscious implicit processing, and the left with conscious explicit processing (Happaney et al., 2004). In support of earlier theoretical proposals on the relationship between right hemispheric operations and the implicit self (Schore, 1994), a substantial amount of current research indicates that the right hemisphere is specialized for generating self-awareness and self-recognition, and for the processing of "self-related material" (Craik et al., 1999; Decety & Chaminade, 2003; Decety & Sommerville, 2003; Feinberg & Keenan, 2005; Fossati et al., 2004; Keenan et al., 2000, 2001; Kircher et al., 2001; Miller et al., 2001; Molnar-Szakacs et al., 2005; Perrin et al., 2005; Platek, Thomson, & Gallup, 2004; Ruby & Decety, 2001).

According to Miller and his colleagues, "a nondominant frontal lobe process, one that connects the individual to emotionally salient experiences and memories underlying self-schema, is the glue holding together a sense of self" (2001, p. 821). Traumatic emotional experiences dissolve the right frontal "glue" that integrates the self. Similarly, Stuss and Alexander state that the right prefrontal cortex plays a central role in "the appreciation, integration, and modulation of affective and cognitive information" and serves as "a specific convergence site for all of the neural processes essential to affectively personalize higher order experience of self and to represent awareness of that experience" (1999, p. 223). The major debilitating impact of trauma is clearly on this right-lateralized implicit system—*not* the language functions of the left hemisphere.

Devinsky (2000) argues that the right hemisphere plays an ontogenetic role in "maintaining a coherent, continuous, and unified sense of self" and in "identifying a corporeal image of self." This concept of self is not just a mental one; it is a psychobiological, right-lateralized bodily-based process. Lou et al. (2004) report "a role for the right lateral parietal region in representation of the physical Self" (p. 6831). Decety and Chaminade (2003) show that the right inferior parietal cortex is involved in somatic experience that is related to awareness and, therefore, participates in the sense of self. The rostral part of the posterior parietal cortex sends efferents to the insular cortex (Cavada & Goldman-Rakic, 1989). As noted above, the right anterior insula and the right orbitofrontal cortex jointly generate a representation of visceral responses that is accessible to awareness; this provides a somatosensory substrate for subjective emotional states that are experienced by the corporeal self (Critchley et al., 2004). This right limbic structure is centrally involved in visceral and autonomic functions that mediate the generation of an image of one's physiological state (Craig et al., 2000).

These neurobiological data mirror the ICD-10 description of dissociation—as a partial or complete loss of control of body movements. Recall Crucian's (2000) description of a right hemisphere-dependent dissociation between the emotional evaluation of an event and the physiological reaction to that event, and Spitzer's (2004) observation that the dissociative symptoms of depersonalization reflect a lack of right hemispheric integration. In a study of "out-of-body" experiences (i.e., episodes in which "a person's consciousness seems to become detached from the body and take up a remote viewing position"), Blanke et al. (2002) report that "the experience of dissociation of self from the body is a result of failure to integrate complex somatosensory and vestibular function" (p. 269). Importantly, right medial temporal lobe activation is seen during the patient's dissociative episode (see Figure 8.3).

Thus, the assertion that "impaired self-awareness seems to be associated predominantly with right hemisphere dysfunction" (Andelman et al., 2004, p. 831) refers to a deficit in the right brain corporeal self during

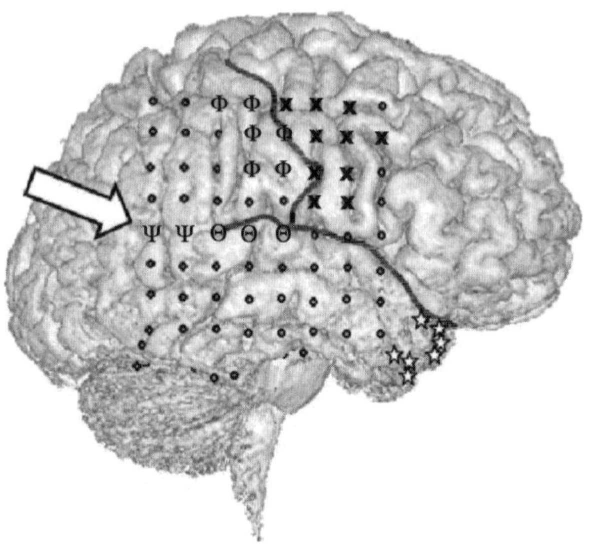

FIGURE 8.3 Electrodes stimulated at right hemispheric sites trigger depersonalization reactions in a 43-year-old woman with right temporal lobe (starred) epilepsy. Locations: X = motor; Φ = somatosensory cortex; Θ = auditory cortex; Ψ = site at which out-of-body experience, body-part illusions and vestibular responses were induced (arrow). During these dissociative states the patient states "I see myself lying on the bed, from above, but I only see my legs and lower trunk." From Stimulating illusory own-body perceptions, by O. Blanke, S. Ortigue, T. Landis, and M. Seeck, 2002, *Nature, 419*, pp. 269–270. Copyright 2002 by Macmillan Publishers Ltd. Adapted and reprinted with permission.

dissociative disruptions of identity. Scaer (2001) contends that the least appreciated manifestations of traumatic dissociation are perceptual alterations and somatic symptoms. In earlier work, I have offered a model by which attachment trauma alters the development of right-lateralized limbic-autonomic circuits that process visceral-somatic information and set the stage for the characterological predisposition to somatoform dissociation (Schore, 2001b, 2002). This chapter elaborates this model and strongly indicates that somatoform dissociation should be incorporated into DSM-V.

This model also gives important clues for identifying psychobiological markers of somatoform dissociation. I have described the hypoarousal and heart rate deceleration of dissociating human infants and adults. In addition I have also presented biological data to show that this passive defense mechanism is common to all vertebrates. In this "last resort defensive strategy," bradycardia occurs in response to survival threat. This rapid shift from a hypermetabolic state of hyperarousal into a hypometabolic state of hypoarousal reflects a significant homeostatic alteration of brain-cardiovascular interactions through higher CNS adjustments of the sympathetic and especially the medullary dorsal vagal parasympathetic energy-conserving branches of the ANS. The activation of "the escape when there is no escape" represents a reorganization of vertical circuits in the right hemisphere, which is dominant for cardiovascular (Erciyas et al., 1999; Yoon et al., 1997) and survival (Wittling & Schweiger, 1993) functions.

In traumatizing contexts where active coping mechanisms are blocked or irrelevant, lateralized limbic-autonomic structures of the central autonomic network (ventromedial prefrontal cortex, anterior cingulate, insula, and amygdala) trigger an instantaneous reorganization of the vagal circuit of emotion regulation on the right side of the brain (Porges et al., 1994)—specifically, a shift in dominance from ventral vagal to dorsal vagal parasympathetic systems. Bradycardia is controlled by orbitofrontal, cingulate, and insula cortices (Buchanan, Powell, & Valentine, 1984; Hardy & Holmes, 1988; Kaada, 1960). Tracing down this limbic-autonomic vertical circuit, each of these cortical structures, like the central nucleus of the amygdala and the periaqueductal gray, regulates the lateral hypothalamus (Loewy, 1991); the lateral hypothalamus modulates dorsal vagal complex neurons (Jiang, Fogel, & Zhang, 2003); cardiac vagal motoneurons lateralized on the right side of the medulla, down the right vagus, regulate the heart (Rentero et al., 2002); and ultimately. parasympathetic efferent neurons that are primarily located in the right atrial ganglionated plexus (Stauss, 2003) trigger a hypometabolic response of "emotional bradycardia."

This pattern of dis-organization, which also occurs in "posttraumatic stress disorders and the consequences of child abuse," is described by Porges (2000):

> [W]hen mobilization strategies (fight-flight behaviors) are ineffective in removing the individual from the stressor and modulating stress, then the nervous system may degrade to a phylogenetically earlier level of organization ... (This) may reflect a neural strategy associated with immobilization (e.g. passive avoidance, death feigning, *dissociative states*) that would require a reduction of energy resources. (p. 15, my italics)

I have cited several clinical studies that indicate that parasympathetic emotional bradycardia is a psychobiological marker of pathological dissociation. Peritraumatic dissociation associated with low heart rate has been reported by Griffin, Resick, and Mechanic (1997), Lanius et al. (2002), Koopman et al. (2004), and Williams, Haines, and Sale (2003). In a clinical study, Schmahl and colleagues (2002) documented a heart rate decline while a PTSD patient with a history of childhood abuse was dissociating (Figure 8.4).

Very recent studies have shown that the human right insula is activated by perceptual awareness of threat (Critchley, Mathias, & Dolan, 2002), anticipation of emotionally aversive visual stimuli (Simmons et al., 2004) and harm avoidance (Paulus et al., 2003). In normal functioning, the right insula supports a representation of visceral responses accessible to awareness (Critchley et al., 2004). On the other hand, neurological damage of the right insula in infancy is associated with abnormal bradycardia (Seeck et al., 2003). Increased right insula activity is also found in adult subjects with bradycardia (Volkow et al., 2000). These studies suggest that the right insula may play a key role in somatoform dissociation.

In short, developmental and neurobiological data suggest that DSM-V can specify a neuropsychobiological marker for somatoform dissociation—namely, heart rate deceleration in response to intersubjective contexts that are associated with nonconsciously perceived survival threat.

8.8.4 Early Attachment Trauma and the Psychopathogenesis of Dissociation

In the final part of this work, I would like to return to the problem of psychopathogenesis. Over 15 years ago, Van der Kolk and Van der Hart (1989), and Spiegel and Cardeña (1991) returned to the work of Janet, proposing that dissociation is a response to "overwhelming" emotional experience, particularly in childhood. At the end of the last decade, several major theoreticians in traumatology echoed this conclusion. Putnam et al. asserted that "numerous clinical studies have established that elevated levels of dissociation are significantly associated with histories of antecedent trauma" (1996, p. 673). Van der Kolk and colleagues stated that "numerous studies have demonstrated a strong relation between trauma and dissociative symptoms" (1996, p. 85). Indeed, a large body of research in the psychiatric and psychological (e.g., Bowman & Markand, 1996; Chu & Dill, 1990; Coons et al., 1989; Draijer & Langeland, 1999; Gershuny

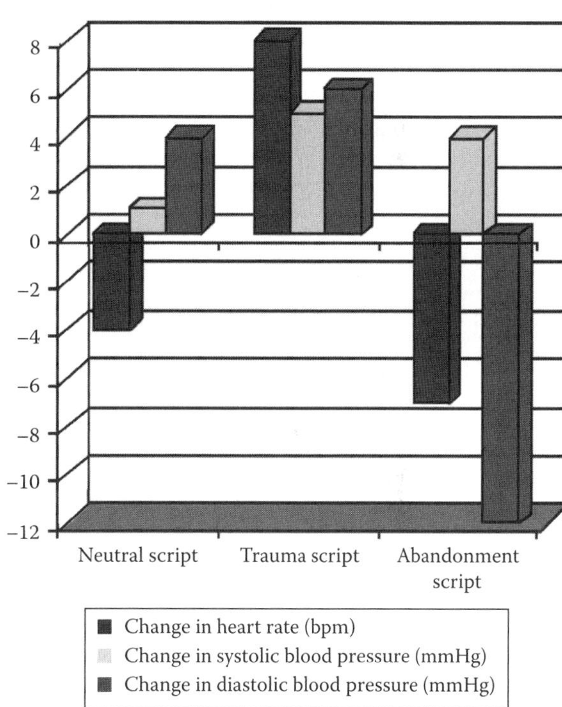

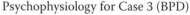

FIGURE 8.4 As this patient diagnosed with PTSD and borderline personality disorder heard her trauma script, she displayed an intense emotional reaction and her heart rate rose by 11 bpm. While listening to an abandonment script she dissociated. She had the impression that things were moving in slow motion, that things seemed unreal, and that she was watching the situtation as an observer. She felt disconnected from her own body and the sense of her body felt changed. Duing this period her heart rate fell by 14 bpm. After the interview the dissociative state lasted for a few more minutes. From Individual differences in psychophysiological reactivity in adults with childhood abuse, by C.G. Schmahl, B.M. Elzinga, and J.D. Bremner, 2002, *Clinical Psychology and Psychotherapy, 9,* pp. 271–276. Copyright 2002 by John Wiley & Sons, Ltd. Reprinted with permission.

& Thayer, 1999; Irwin, 1994; Lipschitz et al., 1996; Merckelbach & Muris, 2001; Mulder et al., 1998; Nash et al., 1993; Sanders, McRoberts, & Tollefsin, 1989) and neurological (Alper et al., 1993; Kuyk et al., 1999) literatures now supports the link between childhood trauma and pathological dissociation.

Although these studies are convincing, the precise psychopathogenetic mechanism by which early trauma produces a later predisposition to pathological dissociation has not been identified. The more general developmental question of how early traumatic psychological experience generates deficits of later adaptive functioning is, in fact, the central issue of psychopathogenesis. Here, an interdisciplinary perspective can provide more detailed and complex models. Developmental psychopathology provides a theoretical perspective for "understanding the causes, determinants, course, sequelae, and treatment of psychopathological disorders by integrating knowledge from multiple disciplines within an ontogenetic framework" (Cicchetti, 1994, p. 286). Developmental psychologists have demonstrated a strong link between early attachment trauma and dissociation (Carlson, Yates, & Sroufe, 2009; Dutra, Bianchi, Lyons-Ruth, & Siegel, 2009; Ogawa et al., 1997). Neuropsychiatrists have established that "the overwhelming stress of maltreatment in childhood is associated with adverse influences on brain development" (De Bellis, 1999, p. 1281).

My work in developmental psychopathology integrates attachment theory, psychiatry, and developmental affective neuroscience in order to explore how attachment trauma alters the developmental trajectory of the right brain (Schore, 1994, 2003a, 2003b). From a developmental viewpoint, early abuse and neglect generates disorganized-disoriented attachment which endures into adolescence and adulthood, and acts as a risk factor for later psychiatric disorders (Schore, 2001b). From a psychiatry viewpoint, "maltreatment-related" (Beer & De Bellis, 2002) or "pediatric" (Carrion et al., 2001) PTSD is the short-term negative effect; a predisposition to later psychiatric disorders is the negative long-term effect. From a developmental neuroscience viewpoint, early abuse and neglect have immediate impact on the developing right brain during a critical growth period; this produces an immature right brain that has a limited capacity to regulate intense affective states. These perspectives converge on a basic developmental principle: early trauma is critical to the genesis of an enduring predisposition to pathological dissociation.

I have offered extensive evidence to show that relational traumatic attachment experiences are "affectively burnt in" (Stuss & Alexander, 1999) limbic-autonomic circuits of the cortical and subcortical components of the right brain during its critical period of growth. Basic research in neuroscience and neuropsychiatry firmly supports the following principles: (1) "early adverse developmental experiences may leave behind a permanent physiological reactivity in limbic areas of the brain" (Post, Weiss, & Leverich, 1994); (2) emotional and social deprivation interfere with the normal development of the synaptic architecture and lead to "neurological scars" which underlie "subsequent behavioral and cognitive deficits" (Poeggel & Braun, 1996; Poeggel et al., 1999); and (3) "early adverse experiences result in an increased sensitivity to the effects of stress later in life and render an individual vulnerable to stress-related psychiatric disorders" (Graham et al., 1999). Although I have focused here on PTSD, in other works I have shown that this same developmental neurobiological description applies to the ontogeny of pathological dissociation in borderline personality disorder (Schore, 2003b, 2003c).

In the introduction, I cited Brown and Trimble's (2000) call for a more "precise definition of dissociation based on a conceptually coherent and empirically justified account of the processes underlying these phenomena." This chapter suggests that such a definition must include a developmental model of dissociative phenomena. In total, the interdisciplinary data cited here indicate that the developing brain imprints not only the overwhelming affective states that are at the core of attachment trauma, but also the early appearing primitive defense used against these affects—the regulatory strategy of dissociation. The developmental principle, that maltreatment in childhood is associated with adverse influences on brain development, specifically refers to an impairment of higher corticolimbic modulation of the vagal circuit of emotion regulation on the right side of the brain that generates the psychobiological state of dissociation. This model accounts for the findings that somatoform dissociation is specifically associated with maternal dysfunction, and that early onset traumatization via emotional neglect and abuse and interpersonal threat to the body predict somatoform dissociation. The model also strongly supports Putnam's (1995) assertion that dissociation offers "very rich models for understanding the ontogeny of environmentally produced psychiatric conditions."

Although dissociation has been quite controversial, there is now solid convergent evidence from different disciplines that there is a direct relationship between early trauma and pathological dissociation. The next DSM should reflect this advance in our knowledge.

REFERENCES

Adamec, R. E. (1999). Evidence that limbic neural plasticity in the right hemisphere mediates partial kindling induced lasting increases in anxiety-like behavior: effects of low frequency stimulation (Quenching?) on long-term potentiation of amygdala efferents and behavior following kindling. *Brain Research, 839*, 133–152.

Adamec, R. E., Blundell, J., & Burton, P. (2003). Phosphorylated cyclic AMP response element bonding protein expression induced in the periaqueductal gray by predator stress; its relationship to the stress experience, behavior, and limbic neural plasticity. *Progress in Neuro-Pharmacology & Biological Psychiatry, 27*, 1243–1267.

Adolphs, R., Damasio, H., Tranel, D., & Damasio, A. R. (1996). Cortical systems for the recognition of emotion in facial expressions. *Journal of Neuroscience, 23*, 7678–7687.

Adolphs, R., Tranel, D., & Damasio, H. (2001). Emotion recognition from faces and prosody following temporal lobectomy. *Neuropsychology, 15*, 396–404.

Aftanas, L. I., Savotina, N., Makhnev, V. P., & Reva, N. V. (2005). Analysis of evoked EEG synchronization and desynchronization during perception of emotiogenic stimuli: association with automatic activation process. *Neuroscience and Behavioral Physiology, 35*, 951–957.

Allen, J. G., Console, D. A., & Lewis, L. (1999). Dissociative detachment and memory impairment: reversible amnesia or encoding failure? *Comprehensive Psychiatry, 40*, 160–171.

Allen, J. G., & Coyne, L. (1995). Dissociation and vulnerability to psychotic experience. The Dissociative Experiences Scale and the MMPI-2. *Journal of Nervous and Mental Disease, 183*, 615–622.

Allman, J. M., Watson, K. K., Tetreault, N. A., & Hakeem, A. (2005). Intuition and autism: a possible role for Von Economo neurons. *Trends in Cognitive Sciences, 9*, 367–373.

Alper, K., Devinsky, O., Perrine, K., Luciano, D., Vazquez, B., Pacia, S., & Rhee, E. (1997). Dissociation in epilepsy and conversion nonepileptic seizures. *Epilepsia, 38*, 991–997.

American Psychiatric Association. (1994). *Diagnostic and statistical manual of mental disorders (DSM III-R) (4th ed. rev)*. Washington, DC: American Psychiatric Press.

Andelman, F., Zuckerman-Feldhay, E., Hoffien, D., Fried, I., & Neufeld, M. Y. (2004). Lateralization of deficit in self-awareness of memory in patients with intractable epilepsy. *Epilepsia, 45*, 826–833.

Anderson, A. K., & Phelps, E. A. (2000). Perceiving emotion: There's more than meets the eye. *Current Biology, 10*, R551–R554.

Baker, K. B., & Kim, J. J. (2004). Amygdalar lateralization in fear conditioning: Evidence for greater involvement of the right amygdala. *Behavioral Neuroscience, 118*, 15–23.

Barach, P. M. M. (1991). Multiple personality disorder as an attachment disorder. *Dissociation, 4*, 117–123.

Barbas, H., Saha, S., Rempel-Clower, N., & Ghashghaei, T. (2003). Serial pathways from primate prefrontal cortex to autonomic areas may influence emotional expression. *BMC Neuroscience, 2003*, 4.

Barrett, L. F., Quigley, K. S., Moreau, E. B., & Aronson, K. R. (2004). Interoceptive sensitivity and self-reports of emotional experience. *Journal of Personality and Social Psychology, 87*, 684–697.

Beebe, B. (2000). Coconstructing mother-infant distress: the microsynchrony of maternal impingement and infant avoidance in the face-to-face encounter. *Psychoanalytic Inquiry, 20*, 412–440.

Beer, S. R., De Bellis, M. D. (2002). Neuropsychological function in children with maltreatment-related posttraumatic stress disorder. *American Journal of Psychiatry, 159*, 483–486.

Benarroch, E. E. (1997). *Central autonomic network: Functional organization and clinical correlations*. Armonk, NY: Futura Publishing Company.

Bergman, N. J., Linley, L. L., & Fawcus, S. R. (2004). Randomized controlled trial of skin-to-skin contact from birth versus conventional incubator for physiological stabilization in 1200 to 2199 gram newborns. *Acta Paediatrica, 93*, 779–785.

Berntson, G. G., Cacioppo, J. T., & Quigley, K. S. (1991). Autonomic determinism: The modes of autonomic control, the doctrine of autonomic space, and the laws of autonomic constraint. *Psychological Review, 98*, 459–487.

Berthier, M. L., Posada, A., & Puentes, C. (2001). Dissociative flashbacks after right frontal injury in a Vietnam veteran with combat-related posttraumatic stress disorder. *Journal of Neuropsychiatry and Clinical Neuroscience, 13*, 101–105.

Bion, W. R. (1962). *Learning from experience*. London: Heinemann.

Blanke, O., Ortigue, S., Landis, T., & Seeck, M. (2002). Stimulating illusory own-body perceptions. *Nature, 419*, 269–270.

Bogolepova, I. N., & Malofeeva, L. I. (2001). Characteristics of the development of speech areas 44 and 45 in the left and right hemisphere of the human brain in early post-natal ontogenesis. *Neuroscience and Behavioral Physiology*, 31, 349–354.

Bonne, O., Gilboa, A., Louzoun, Y., Brandes, D., Yona, I., Lester, H., Barkai, G., Freedman, N., Chisin, R., & Shalev, A. Y. (2003). Resting regional cerebral perfusion in recent posttraumatic stress disorder. *Biological Psychiatry, 54*, 1077–1086.

Borod, J., Cicero, B. A., Obler, L. K., Welkowitz, J., Erhan, H. M., Santschi, C., Grunwald, I. S., Agosti, R. M., & Whalen, J. R. (1998). Right hemisphere emotional perception: Evidence across multiple channels. *Neuropsychology, 12*, 446–458.

Borod, J., Haywood, C. S., & Koff, E. (1997). Neuropsychological aspects of facial asymmetry during emotional expression: A review of the adult literature. *Neuropsychology Review, 7*, 41–60.

Borod, J. (2000). *The neuropsychology of emotion*. New York: Oxford University Press.

Boutilier, R. G., & St-Pierre, J. (2000). Surviving hypoxia without really dying. *Comparative Biochemistry and Physiology A, 126*, 481–490.

Bowman, E. S., & Markand, O. N. (1996). Psychodynamics and psychiatric diagnoses of pseudoseizure subjects. *American Journal of Psychiatry, 153*, 57–63.

Bradley, M., Cuthbert, B. N., & Lang, P. J. (1996). Lateralized startle probes in the study of emotion. *Psychophysiology, 33*, 156–161.

Bradshaw, J. L., & Nettleton, N. C. (1981). The nature of hemispheric specialization in man. *Behavioral and Brain Sciences, 4*, 51–91.

Brake, W. G., Sullivan, R. M., & Gratton, A. (2000). Perinatal distress leads to lateralized medial prefrontal cortical dopamine hypofunction in adult rats. *Journal of Neuroscience, 20*, 5538–5543.

Bremner, J. D., & Brett, E. (1997). Trauma-related dissociative states and long-term psychopathology in posttraumatic stress disorder. *Journal of Traumatic Stress, 10*, 37–49.

Bremner, J. D., Staib, L. H., Kaloupek, D., Southwick, S. M., Soufer, R., & Charney, D. S. (1999). Neural correlates of exposure to traumatic pictures and sound in combat veterans with and without posttraumatic stress disorder: A positron emission tomography study. *Biological Psychiatry, 45*, 806–818.

Brown, M. R., Fisher, L. A., Spiess, J., Rivier, C., Rivier, J., & Vale, W. (1982). Corticotropin-releasing factor: actions on the sympathetic nervous system and metabolism. *Endocrinology, 111*, 928–931.

Brown, R. J., & Trimble, M. R. (2000). Dissociative psychopathology, non-epileptic seizures, and neurology. *Journal of Neurology, Neurosurgery, & Psychiatry, 69*, 285–291.

Buchanan, S. L., Powell, D. A., & Valentine, J. (1984). Cardiovascular adjustments elicited by electrical stimulation of frontal cortex in conscious rabbits. *Neuroscience Abstracts, 10*, 614.

Calvert, G. A., Hanses, P. C., Iversen, S. D., & Brammer, M. J. (2001). Detection of audio-visual integration sites in humans by application of electrophysiological criteria to the BOLD effect. *NeuroImage, 14*, 427–438.

Carlson, E., Yates, T. M., & Sroufe, L. A. (2009). Development of dissociation and development of the self. In P. F. Dell & J. A. O'Neil (Eds.), *Dissociation and the dissociative disorders: DSM-V and beyond* (pp. 39–52). New York: Routledge.

Carlson, V., Cicchetti, D., Barnett, D., & Braunwald, K. (1989). Disorganized/disoriented attachment relationships in maltreated infants. *Developmental Psychology, 25*, 525–531.

Carrion, V. G., Weems, C. F., Eliez, S., Patwardhan, A., Brown, W., & Ray, R. D. (2001). Attenuation of frontal asymmetry in pediatric posttraumatic stress disorder. *Biological Psychiatry, 50*, 943–951.

Cavada, C., & Goldman-Rakic, P. S. (1989). Posterior parietal cortex in rhesus monkey. I. Parcellation of areas based on distinctive limbic and sensory corticocortical connections. *Journal of Comparative Neurology, 287*, 393–421.

Chapanis, L. (1977). Language deficits and cross-modal sensory perception. In S. J. Segalowitz & F. A. Gruber (Eds.), *Language development and neurological theory* (pp. 107–120). New York: Academic Press.

Charcot, J.-M. (1887). *Leçons sur les maladies du système nerveux faites à la Salpêtrière* [Lessons on the illnesses of the nervous system held at the Salpêtrière] (Vol. 3). Paris: Progrès Médical en A. Delahaye & E. Lecrosie.

Chefetz, R. A. (2004). The paradox of "detachment disorders": binding-disruptions of dissociative process. *Psychiatry, 67*, 246–255.

Cheng, Z., Powley, T. L., Schwaber, J. S., & Doye, F. J. (1999). Projections of the dorsal motor nucleus of the vagus to cardiac ganglia of rat atria: an anterograde tracing study. *Journal of Comparative Neurology, 410*, 320–341.

Chiron, C., Jambaque, I., Nabbout, R., Lounes, R., Syrota, A., & Dulac, O. (1997). The right brain hemisphere is dominant in human infants. *Brain, 120*, 1057–1065.

Chu, J. A., & Dill, D. L. (1990). Dissociative symptoms in relation to childhood physical and sexual abuse. *American Journal of Psychiatry, 147*, 887–892.

Cicchetti, D. (1994). Integrating developmental risk factors: Perspectives from developmental psychopathology. In C. A. Nelson (Ed.), *Minnesota symposium on child psychology. Vol. 27, Threats to optimal development* (pp. 285–325). Mahweh, NJ: Erlbaum.

Classen, C., Koopman, C., & Spiegel, D. (1993). Trauma and dissociation. *Bulletin of the Menninger Clinic, 57*, 178–194.

Coleman-Mensches, K., & McGaugh, J. L. (1995). Differential involvement of the right and left amygdalae in expression of memory for aversively motivated training. *Brain Research, 670*, 75–81.

Coons, P. M., Bowman, E. S., Pellow, T. A., & Schneider, P. (1989). Post-traumatic aspects of the treatment of victims of sexual abuse and incest. *Psychiatric Clinics of North America, 12*, 325–335.

Craig, A. D. (2004). Human feelings: why are some more aware than others? *Nature Neuroscience, 7*, 239–241.

Craik, F. I. M., Moroz, T. M., Moscovitch, M., Stuss, D. T., Winocur, G., Tulving, E., & Kapur, S. (1999). In search of self: a positron emission tomography study. *Psychological Science, 10*, 26–34.

Critchley, H. D., Elliott, R., Mathias, C. J., & Dolan, R. J. (2000). Neural activity relating to generation and representation of galvanic skin responses: a functional magnetic resonance imaging study. *Journal of Neuroscience, 20*, 3033–3040.

Critchley, H. D., Mathias, C. J., & Dolan, R. J. (2002). Fear conditioning in humans: the influence of awareness and autonomic arousal on functional neuroanatomy. *Neuron, 33*, 653–663.

Critchley, H. D., Wiens, S., Rothstein, P., Ohman, A., & Dolan, R. J. (2004). Neural systems supporting interoceptive awareness. *Nature Neuroscience, 7*, 189–195.

Crittenden, P. M, & Ainsworth, M. D. S. (1989). Child maltreatment and attachment theory. In D. Cicchetti & V. Carlson (Eds.), *Child maltreatment: Theory and research on the causes and consequences of child abuse and neglect* (pp. 432–463). New York: Cambridge University Press.

Crucian, G. P., Hughes, J. D., Barrett, A. M., Williamson, D. J. G., Bauer, R. M., Bowres, D., & Heilman, K. M. (2000). Emotional and physiological responses to false feedback. *Cortex, 36*, 623–647.

Cutting, J. (1992). The role of right hemisphere dysfunction in psychiatric disorders. *British Journal of Psychiatry, 160*, 583–588.

Davidson, R. J. (2002). Synaptic substrates of the implicit and explicit self. *Science, 296*, 268.

Davidson, R. J., Ekman, P., Saron, C., Senulis, J., & Friesen, W. V. (1990). Approach/withdrawal and cerebral asymmetry: 1. Emotional expression and brain physiology. *Journal of Personality and Social Psychology, 58*, 330–341.

Davis M. (1989). The role of the amygdala and its efferent projections in fear and anxiety. In P. Tyrer (Ed.), *Psychopharmacology of anxiety* (pp. 52–79). Oxford: Oxford University Press.

De Bellis, M. D., Casey, B. J., Dahl, R. E., Birmaher, B., Williamson, D. E., Thomas, K. M., Axelson, D. A., Frustaci, K., Boring, A. M., Hall, J., & Ryan, N. D. (2000). A pilot study of amygdala volume in pediatric generalized anxiety disorder. *Biological Psychiatry, 48*, 51–57.

Decety, J., & Chaminade, T. (2003). When the self represents the other: A new cognitive neuroscience view on psychological identification. *Consciousness and Cognition, 12*, 577–596.

Decety, J., & Sommerville, J. A. (2003). Shared representations between self and other: a social cognitive neuroscience view. *Trends in Cognitive Science, 7*, 527–533.

Devinsky, O. (2000). Right cerebral hemisphere dominance for a sense of corporeal and emotional self. *Epilepsy & Behavior, 1*, 60–73.

De Wet, C. J., Mellers, J. D. C., Gardner, W. N., & Toone, B. K. (2003). Pseudoseizures and asthma. *Journal of Neurology, Neurosurgery, & Psychiatry, 74*, 639–641.

Dixon, A. K. (1998). Ethological strategies for defense in animals and humans: Their role in some psychiatric disorders. *British Journal of Medical Psychology, 71*, 417–445.

Draijer, N., & Langeland, W. (1999). Childhood trauma and perceived parental dysfunction in the etiology of dissociative symptoms in psychiatric inpatients. *American Journal of Psychiatry, 156*, 379–385.

Dutra, L., Bianchi, I., Lyons-Ruth, C., & Siegel, D. (2009). The relational context of dissociative phenomena. In P. F. Dell & J. A. O'Neil (Eds.), *Dissociation and the dissociative disorders: DSM-V and beyond* (pp. 83–92). New York: Routledge.

Eddy, S. F., Morin, P. Jr., & Storey, K. B. (2006). Differential expression of selected mitochondrial genes in hibernating little brown bats, *Myotis lucifugus*. *Journal of Experimental Zoology, 305A*, 620–630.

Edelman, G. (1989). *The remembered present: A biological theory of consciousness*. New York: Basic Books.

Emde, R. N. (1983). The pre-representational self and its affective core. *Psychoanalytic Study of the Child, 38*, 165–192.

Erciyas, A. H., Topaktas, S., Akyuz, A., & Dener, S. (1999). Suppression of cardiac parasympathetic functions in patients with right hemispheric stroke. *European Journal of Neurology, 6*, 685–690.

Erickson, M. F., Egeland, B., & Pianta, R. (1989). The effects of maltreatment on the development of young children. In D. Cicchetti & V. Carlson (Eds.), *Child maltreatment: Theory and research on the causes and consequences of child abuse and neglect* (pp. 647–684). New York: Cambridge University Press.

Espinosa, M., Beckwith, L., Howard, J., Tyler, R., & Swanson, K. (2001). Maternal psychopathology and attachment in toddlers of heavy cocaine-using mothers. *Infant Mental Health Journal, 22*, 316–333.

Fanselow, M. S. (1986). Conditioned fear-induced opiate analgesia: A compelling motivational state theory of stress analgesia. In D. D. Kelly (Ed.), *Stress-induced analgesia* (pp. 40–54). New York: The New York Academy of Sciences.

Faust, M., Kravetz, S., & Nativ-Safrai, O. (2004). The representation of aspects of the self in the two hemispheres. *Personality and Individual Differences, 37*, 607–619.

Field, T., Pickens, J., Fox, N. A., Nawrocki, T., & Gonzalez, J. (1995). Vagal tone in infants of depressed mothers. *Development and Psychopathology, 7*, 227–231.

Fink, G. R., Markowitsch H. J., Reinkemeier, M., Bruckbauer, T., Kessler, J., & Heiss, W-D. (1996). Cerebral representation of one's own past: Neural networks involved in autobiographical memory. *Journal of Neuroscience, 16*, 4275–4282.

Fischer, H., Andersson, J. L. R., Furmark, T., Wik, G., & Fredrickson, M. (2002). Right-sided human prefrontal brain activation during acquisition of conditioned fear. *Emotion, 2*, 233–241.

Fossati, P., Hevenor, S. J., Lepage, M., Graham, S. J., Grady, C., Keightley, M. L., Craik, F., & Mayberg, H. (2004). Distributed self in episodic memory: neural correlates of successful retrieval of self-centered positive and negative personality traits. *NeuroImage, 22*, 1596–1604.

Freeman, T. W., & Kimbrell, T. (2001). A "cure" for chronic combat-related posttraumatic stress disorder secondary to a right frontal lobe infarct: a case report. *Journal of Neuropsychiatry and Clinical Neuroscience, 13*, 106–109.

Freud, S. (1893/1955). The etiology of hysteria. In J. Strachey (Ed.), *The standard edition of the complete psychological works of Sigmund Freud, Vol. 3* (pp. 189–221). London: Hogarth Press.

Frijda, N. H. (1988). The laws of emotion. *American Psychologist, 43*, 349–358.

Gabrielson, S. W., & Smith, E. N. (1985). Physiological responses associated with feigned death in the American opossum. *Acta Physiologica Scandinavica, 123*, 393–398.

Gabrielsen, G. W., Steen, J. B., & Kanwisher, J. W. (1977). Emotional bradycardia: A telemetry study of incubating willow grouse. *Acta Physiologica Scandinavica, 100*, 255–257.

Gadea, M., Gomez, C., Gonzalez-Bono, E., Espert, R., & Salvador, A. (2005). Increased cortisol and decreased right ear advantage (REA) in dichotic listening following a negative mood induction. *Psychoneuroendocrinology, 30*, 129–138.

Gaensbauer, T. J. (2002). Representations of trauma in infancy: clinical and theoretical implications for the understanding of early memory. *Infant Mental Health Journal, 23*, 259–277.

Gainotti, G. (2000). Neuropsychological theories of emotion. In J. Borod (Ed.), *The neuropsychology of emotion*. New York: Oxford University Press.

Gallagher, H. L., & Frith, C. D. (2004). Dissociable neural pathways for the perception and recognition of expressive and instrumental gestures. *Neuropsychologia, 42*, 1725–1736.

Galletly, C., Clark, C. R., McFarlane, A. C., & Weber, D. L. (2001). Working memory in posttraumatic stress disorder—An event-related potential study. *Journal of Traumatic Stress, 14*, 295–309.

Gendlin, E. T. (1970). A theory of personality change. In J. T. Hart & T. H. Tomlinson (Eds.), *New directions in client-centered therapy* (pp. 129–174). Boston: Houghton Mifflin.

George, M. S., Parekh, P. I., Rosinsky, N., Ketter, T. A., Kimbrell, T. A., Heilman, K. M., Herscovitch, P., & Post, R. M. (1996). Understanding emotional prosody activates right hemispheric regions. *Archives of Neurology, 53*, 665–670.

Gershuny, B., & Thayer, J. (1999). Relations among psychological trauma, dissociative phenomena, and trauma-related distress: a review and integration. *Clinical Psychology Review, 19*, 651–657.

Geschwind, N., & Galaburda, A. M. (1987). *Cerebral lateralization: Biological mechanisms, associations, and pathology.* Boston: MIT Press.

Goldberg, E., & Costa, L. D. (1981). Hemisphere differences in the acquisition and use of descriptive systems. *Brain and Language, 14*, 144–173.

Goleman, D. (1995). *Emotional intelligence*. New York: Bantam Books.

Graham, Y. P., Heim, C., Goodman, S. H., Miller, A. H., & Nemeroff, C. B. (1999). The effects of neonatal stress on brain development: implications for psychopathology. *Development and Psychopathology, 11*, 545–565.

Greenberg, D. L., Rice, H. J., Cooper, J. J., Cabeza, R., Rubin, D. C., & LaBar, K. S. (2005). Co-activation of the amygdala, hippocampus and inferior frontal gyrus during autobiographical memory retrieval. *Neuropsychologia, 43*, 659–674.

Griffin, M. G., Resick, P. A., & Mechanic, M. B. (1997). Objective assessment of posttraumatic dissociation: Psychophysiological indicators. *American Journal of Psychiatry, 154*, 1081–1088.

Guedeney, A., & Fermanian, J. (2001). A validity and reliability study of assessment and screening for sustained withdrawal in infancy: the alarm distress scale. *Infant Mental Health Journal, 22*, 559–575.

Gundel, H., Lopez-Sala, A., Ceballos-Baumann, A. O., Deus, J., Cardoner, N., Marten-Mittag, B., Soriano-Mas, C., & Pujol, J. (2004). Alexithymia correlates with the size of the right anterior cingulate. *Psychosomatic Medicine, 66*, 132–140.

Guppy, M., & Withers, P. (1999). Metabolic depression in animals: physiological perspectives and biochemical generalizations. *Biological Review, 74*, 1–40.

Gur, R. C., Packer, I. K., Hungerbuhler, J. P., Reivich, M., Obrist, W. D., Amarnek, W. S., & Sackeim, H. A. (1980). Differences in the distribution of gray and white matter in human cerebral hemispheres. *Science, 207*, 1226–1228.

Hagemann, D., Waldstein, S. R., & Thayer, J. F. (2003). Central and autonomic nervous system integration in emotion. *Brain and Cognition, 52*, 79–87.

Happaney, K., Zelazo, P. D., & Stuss, D. T. (2004). Development of orbitofrontal function: Current themes and future directions. *Brain and Cognition, 55*, 1–10.

Harden, C. L. (1997). Pseudoseizures and dissociative disorders: a common mechanism involving traumatic experiences. *Seizures, 6*, 151–155.

Hardy, S. G. P., & Holmes, D. E. (1988). Prefrontal stimulus-produced hypotension in the rat. *Experimental Brain Research, 73*, 249–255.

Hecaen, H., & Albert, M. L. (1978). *Human neuropsychology*. New York: Wiley.

Henry, J. P. (1993). Psychological and physiological responses to stress: The right hemisphere and the hypothalamo-pituitary-adrenal axis, an inquiry into problems of human bonding. *Integrative Physiological and Behavioral Science, 28*, 369–387.

Hesse, E., & Main, M. M. (1999). Second-generation effects of unresolved trauma in nonmaltreating parents: dissociated, frightened, and threatening parental behavior. *Psychoanalytic Inquiry, 19*, 481–540.

Hesse, E., & Main, M. (2006). Frightened, threatening, and dissociative parental behavior in low-risk samples: Description, discussion, and interpretations. *Development and Psychopathology, 18*, 309–343.

Hogg, S., Sanger, D. J., & Moser, P. C. (1998). Mild traumatic lesion of the right parietal cortex in the rat: characterisation of a conditioned freezing deficit and its reversal by dizocilpine. *Behavioural Brain Research, 93*, 157–165.

Hugdahl, K. (1995). Classical conditioning and implicit learning: The right hemisphere hypothesis. In R. J. Davidson & K. Hugdahl (Eds.), *Brain asymmetry* (pp. 235–267). Cambridge, MA: MIT Press.

Hughlings Jackson, J. (1874). On the nature of the duality of the brain. *Brain, 38,* 80–86. See also J. Taylor (Ed.), *Selected writing of John Hughlings Jackson*. New York: Basic Books, 1958.

Hughlings Jackson, J. (1884). Evolution and dissolution of the nervous system. Croonian Lectures delivered at the Royal College of Physicians, March 1884. *Lancet 1884(i)*, 739–44. See also J. Taylor (Ed.), *Selected writings of John Hughlings Jackson* (pp. 45–118). 1958, New York: Basic Books.

Irwin, H. J. (1994). Proneness to dissociation and traumatic childhood events. *Journal of Nervous and Mental Disease, 182,* 456–460.

Jacobsen, N. K. (1979). Alarm bradycardia in white-tailed deer fawns. *Odocoileus virginianus*. *Journal of Mammalogy, 60,* 343–349.

Janet, P. (1887). L'anesthésie systematiée et la dissociation des phénomènes psychologiques. *Revue Philosophique, 23*, 449–472.

Janet, P. (1889). *L'automatisme psychologique.* Paris: Alcan.

Janet, P. (1911). *L'état mental des hystériques* (2nd ed.). Paris: Alcan.

Jiang, C., Fogel, R., & Zhang, X. (2003). Lateral hypothalamus modulates gut-sensitive neurons in the dorsal vagal complex. *Brain Research, 980*, 31–47.

Joseph, R. (1992). *The right brain and the unconscious: Discovering the stranger within.* New York: Plenum Press.

Joseph, R. (1996). *Neuropsychiatry, neuropsychology, and clinical neuroscience, Second ed.* Baltimore: Williams & Wilkins.

Kaada, B. R. (1960). Cingulate, posterior orbital, anterior insular and temporal pole cortex. In H. W. Magoun (Ed.), *Neurophysiology* (pp. 1345–1372). Baltimore: Waverly Press.

Kalin, N. H., Larson, C., Shelton, C. E., & Davidson, R. J. (1998). Asymmetric frontal brain activity, cortisol, and behavior associated with fearful temperament in rhesus monkeys. *Behavioral Neuroscience, 112*, 286–292.

Kandel, E. R. (1999). Biology and the future of psychoanalysis: A new intellectual framework for psychiatry revisited. *American Journal of Psychiatry, 156*, 505–524.

Kaplan-Solms, K., & Solms, M. (1996). Psychoanalytic observations on a case of frontal-limbic disease. *Journal of Clinical Psychoanalysis, 5*, 405–438.

Keenan, J. P., Nelson, A., O'Connor M., & Pascual-Leone, A. (2001). Self-recognition and the right hemisphere. *Nature, 409*, 305.

Keenan, J. P, Wheeler, M. A., Gallup, G. G. Jr., & Pascual-Leone, A. (2000). Self-recognition and the right prefrontal cortex. *Trends in Cognitive Science, 4*, 338–344.

Kestenberg, J. (1985). The flow of empathy and trust between mother and child. In E. J. Anthony & G. H. Pollack (Eds.), *Parental influences in health and disease* (pp. 137–163). Boston, MA: Little Brown.

Kiersky, S., & Beebe, B. (1994). The reconstruction of early nonverbal relatedness in the treatment of difficult patients. A special form of empathy. *Psychoanalytic Dialogues, 4*, 389–408.

Kimura, Y., Yoshino, A., Takahashi, Y., & Nomura, S. (2004). Interhemispheric difference in emotional response without awareness. *Physiology & Behavior, 82*, 727–731.

Kinney, H. C., Brody, B. A., Kloman, A. S., & Gilles, F. H. (1988). Sequence of central nervous system myelination in human infancy. II. Patterns of myelination in autopsied infants. *Journal of Neuropathology and Experimental Neurology, 47*, 217–234.

Kircher, T. T. J., Senior, C., Phillips, M. L., Rabe-Hesketh, S., Benson, P. J., Bullmore, E. T., Brammer, M., Simmons, A., Bartels, M., & David, A. S. (2001). Recognizing one's own face. *Cognition, 78*, B1–B5.

Kirschbaum, C., Wolf, O. T., May, M., Wippich, W., & Hellhammer, D. H. (1996). Stress- and treatment-induced elevations of cortisol levels associated with impaired declarative memory in healthy adults. *Life Sciences, 58*, 1475–1483.

Kohut, H. (1971). *The analysis of the self.* New York: International Universities Press.

Koopman, C., Carrion, V., Butler, L. D., Sudhakar, S., Palmer, L., & Steiner, H. (2004). Relationships of dissociation and childhood abuse and neglect with heart rate in delinquent adolescents. *Journal of Traumatic Stress, 17*, 47–54.

Krystal, H. (1988). *Integration and self-healing: Affect-trauma-alexithymia.* Hillsdale, NJ: Analytic Press.

Krystal, J. H., Bremner, J. D., Southwick, S. M., & Charney, D. S. (1998). The emerging neurobiology of dissociation: implications for treatment of posttraumatic stress disorder. In J. D. Bremner & C. R. Marmar (Eds.), *Trauma, memory, and dissociation* (pp. 321–363). Washington, DC: American Psychiatric Press.

Kuyk, J., Spinhoven, P., Emde Boas, W., & Van Dyck, R. (1999). Dissociation in temporal lobe and pseudoepileptic seizure patients. *Journal of Nervous and Mental Disease, 187*, 713–720.

Kvetnansky, R., Dobrakovova, M., Jezova, D., Oprsalova, Z., Lichardus, B., & Makara, G. (1989). Hypothalamic regulation of plasma catecholamine levels during stress: Effect of vasopressin and CRF. In G. R. Van Loon, R. Kvetnansky, R. McCarty, & J. Axelrod (Eds.), *Stress: neurochemical and humoral mechanisms* (pp. 549–570). New York: Gordon and Breach Science Publishers.

Kvetnansky, R., Jezova, D., Oprsalova, Z., Foldes, O., Michjlovskij, N., Dobrakovova, M., Lichardus, B., & Makara, G. B. (1990). Regulation of the sympathetic nervous system by circulating vasopressin. In J. C. Porter & D. Jezova (Eds.), *Circulating regulatory factors and neuroendocrine function* (pp. 113-134). New York: Plenum Press.

La Bar, K. S., Gatenby, J. C., Gore, J. C., LeDoux, J. E., & Phelps, E. A. (1998). Human amygdala activation during conditioned fear acquisition and extinction: A mixed-trial fMRI study. *Neuron, 20*, 937–945.

Lane, R. D., Ahern, G. L., Schwartz, G. E., & Kaszniak, A. W. (1997). Is alexithymia the emotional equivalent of blindsight? *Biological Psychiatry, 42*, 834–844.

Lanius, R. A., Williamson, P. C., Boksman, K., Densmore, M., Gupta, M., Neufeld, R. W. J., Gati, J. S., & Menon, R. S. (2002). Brain activation during script-driven imagery induced dissociative responses in PTSD: a functional magnetic resonance imaging investigation. *Biological Psychiatry, 52*, 305–311.

Lanius, R. A., Williamson, P. C., Bluhm, R. L., Densmore, M., Boksman, K., Neufeld, R. W. J., Gati, J. S., & Menon, R. S. (2005). Functional connectivity of dissociative responses in posttraumatic stress disorder: A functional magnetic resonance imaging investigation. *Biological Psychiatry, 57*, 873–884.

Lanius, R. A., Williamson, P. C., Densmore, M., Boksman, K., Neufeld, R. W., Gati, J. S., & Menon, R. S. (2004). The nature of traumatic memories: A 4-T fMRI functional connectivity analysis. *American Journal of Psychiatry, 161*, 36–44.

Layton, B., & Krikorian, R. (2002). Memory mechanisms in posttraumatic stress disorder. *Journal of Neuropsychiatry and Clinical Neuroscience, 14*, 254–261.

Lazarus, R. S. (1991). Progress on a cognitive-motivational-relational theory of emotion. *American Psychologist, 46*, 819–834.

LeDoux, J. (2002). *Synaptic self: How our brains become who we are.* New York: Viking.

Le Grand, R., Mondloch, C., Maurer, D., & Brent, H. P. (2003). Expert face processing requires visual input to the right hemisphere during infancy. *Nature Neuroscience, 6*, 1108–1112.

Levy, J., Heller, W., Banich, M. T., & Burton, L. A. (1983). Are variations among right-handed individuals in perceptual asymmetries caused by characteristic arousal differences between hemispheres? *Journal of Experimental Psychology: Human Perception and Performance, 9*, 329–359.

Liotti, G. (2004). Trauma, dissociation, and disorganized attachment: Three strands of a single braid. *Psychotherapy: Theory, Research, Training, 41*, 472–486.

Lipschitz, D., Kaplan, M., Sorkenn, J., Chorney, P., & Asnis, G. (1996). Childhood abuse, adult assault, and dissociation. *Comprehensive Psychiatry, 37*, 261–266.

Lipton, P. A., Alvarez, P., & Eichenbaum, H. (1999). Crossmodal associative memory representations in rodent orbitofrontal cortex. *Neuron, 22*, 349–359.

Loewenstein, R. J. (1996). Dissociative amnesia and dissociative fugue. In L. K. Michaelson & W. J. Ray (Eds.), *Handbook of dissociation: Theoretical, empirical, and clinical perspectives* (pp. 307–336). New York, NY: Plenum.

Loewy, A. D. (1991). Forebrain nuclei involved in autonomic control (review). *Progress in Brain Research, 87*, 253–268.

Lorberbaum, J. P., Newman, J. D., Horwitz, A. R., Dubno, J. R., Lydiard, R. B., Hamner, M. B., Bohning, D. E., & George, M. S. (2002). A potential role for thalamocingulate circuitry in human maternal behavior. *Biological Psychiatry, 51*, 431–445.

Lou, H. C., Luber, B., Crupain, M., Keenan, J. P., Nowak, M., Kjaer, T. W., Sackeim, H. A., & Lisanby, S. H. (2004). Parietal cortex and representation of the mental self. *Proceedings of the National Academy of Sciences USA, 17*, 6827–6832.

Lucas, T. H., Schoenfield-McNeill, J., Weber, P. B., & Ojemann, G. A. (2003). A direct measure of human lateral temporal lobe neurons responsive to face matching. *Cognitive Brain Research, 18*, 15–25.

Ludwig, A. M. (1972). Hysteria: a neurobiological theory. *Archives of General Psychiatry, 27*, 771–777.

Luu, P., & Tucker, D. M. (1996). Self-regulation and cortical development: Implications for functional studies of the brain. In R. W. Thatcher, G. Reid Lyon, J. Rumsey, & N. Krasnegor (Eds.), *Developmental neuroimaging: Mapping the development of brain and behavior* (pp. 297–305). San Diego: Academic Press.

Luys, J. (1881). Recherches nouvelles sur les hemiplégies émotives. *Encéphale, 1*, 378–398.

Lyons, D., Afarian, H., Schatzberg, A., Sawyer-Glover, A., & Moseley, M. (2002). Experience-dependent asymmetric variation in primate prefrontal morphology. *Behavioral Brain Research, 136*, 51–59.

Main, M. (1996). Introduction to the special section on attachment and psychopathology: 2. Overview of the field of attachment. *Journal of Consulting and Clinical Psychology, 64*, 237–243.

Main, M., & Solomon, J. (1986). Discovery of an insecure-disorganized / disoriented attachment pattern: Procedures, findings and implications for the classification of behavior. In T. B. Brazelton & M. W. Yogman (Eds.), *Affective development in infancy* (pp. 95–124). Norwood, NJ: Ablex.

Mandal, M. K., & Ambady, N. (2004). Laterality of facial expressions of emotion: universal and culture-specific influences. *Behavioural Neurology, 15*, 23–34.

Manning, J. T., Trivers, R. L., Thornhill, R., Singh, D., Denman, J., Eklo, M. H., & Anderton, R. H. (1997). Ear asymmetry and left-side cradling. *Evolution and Human Behavior, 18*, 327–340.

Markowitsch, H. J., Thiel, A., Reinkemeier, M., Kessler, J., Koyuncu, A., & Heiss, W. -D. (2000). Right amygdalar and temporofrontal activation during autobiographic, but not during fictitious memory retrieval. *Behavioral Neurology, 12*, 181–190.

McNally, R. J., & Amir, N. (1996). Perceptual implicit stimuli for trauma-related information in post-traumatic stress disorder. *Cognition and emotion, 10*, 551–556.

Meares, R. (1999). The contribution of Hughlings Jackson to an understanding of dissociation. *American Journal of Psychiatry, 156*, 850–1855.

Menard, J. L., Champagne, D. L., & Meaney, M. J. P. (2004). Variations of maternal care differentially influence 'fear' reactivity in response to the shock-probe burying test. *Neuroscience, 129*, 297–308.

Merckelbach, H., & Muris, P. (2001). The causal link between self-reported trauma and dissociation: a critical review. *Behavior Research and Therapy, 39*, 245–254.

Metzger, L. J., Paige, S. R., Carson, M. A., Lasko, N. B., Paulus, L. A., Pitman, R. K., & Orr, S. P. (2004). PTSD arousal and depression symptoms associated with increased right-sided parietal EEG asymmetry. *Journal of Abnormal Psychology, 113*, 324–329.

Miller, B. L., Seeley, W. W., Mychack, P., Rosen, H. J., Mena, I., & Boone, K. (2001). Neuroanatomy of the self. Evidence from patients with frontotemporal dementia. *Neurology, 57*, 817–821.

Mohanakrishnan Menon, P., Nasrallah, H. A., Lyons, J. A., Scott, M. F., & Liberto, V. (2003). Single-voxel proton MR spectroscopy of right versus left hippocampi in PTSD. *Psychiatry Research: Neuroimaging, 123*, 101–108.

Mollon, P. (1996). *Multiple selves, multiple voices: working with trauma, violation and dissociation*. Chichester: John Wiley & Sons.

Molnar-Szakacs, I., Uddin, L. Q., & Iacoboni, M. (2005). Right-hemisphere motor facilitation by self-descriptive personality-trait words. *European Journal of Neuroscience, 21*, 2000–2006.

Morgan, M. A., & LeDoux, J. E. (1995). Differential acquisition of dorsal and ventral medial prefrontal cortex to the acquisition and extinction of conditioned fear in rats. *Behavioral Neuroscience, 109*, 681–688.

Morris, J. S., Ohman, A., & Dolan, R. J. (1999). A subcortical pathway to the right amygdala mediating 'unseen' fear. *Proceedings of the National Academy of Sciences of the United States of America, 96*, 1680–1685.

Moses, S. N., Houck, J. M., Martin, T., Hanlon, F. M., Ryan, J. D., Thoma, R. J., Weisend, M. P., Jackson, E. M., Pekkonen, E., & Tesche, C. D. (2007). Dynamic neural activity recorded from human amygdala during fear conditioning using magnetoencephalography. *Brain Research Bulletin, 71*, 452–460.

Mulder, R. T., Beautrais, A. L., Joyce, P. R., Fergusson, D. M. (1998). Relationship between dissociation, childhood sexual abuse, childhood physical abuse, and mental illness in a general population sample. *American Journal of Psychiatry, 155*, 806–811.

Myers, F. (1885). Automatic writing. *Proceedings of the Society of Psychical Research,* 1, 1–63.

Nakamura, K., Kawashima, R., Ito, K., Sugiura, M., Kato, T., Nakamura, A., Hatano, K., Nagumo, S., Kubota, K., Fukuda, H., & Kojima, S. (1999). Activation of the right inferior frontal cortex during assessment of facial emotion. *Journal of Neurophysiology, 82*, 1610–1614.

Nash, M. R., Hulsey, T. L., Sexton, M. C., Harralson, T. L., & Lambert, W. (1993). Long-term sequelæ of childhood sexual abuse: Perceived family environment, psychopathology, and dissociation. *Journal of Consulting and Clinical Psychology, 61*, 276–283.

Neddens, J., Brandenburg, K., Teuchert-Noodt, G., & Dawirs, R. (2001). Differential environment alters ontogeny of dopamine innervation of the orbital prefrontal cortex in gerbils. *Journal of Neuroscience Research, 63*, 209–213.

Nemiah, J. C. (1989). Janet redivivus: The centenary of l'automatisme psychologique. *American Journal of Psychiatry, 146*, 1527–1530.

Nijenhuis, E. R. S. (2000). Somatoform dissociation: major symptoms of dissociative disorders. *Journal of Trauma & Dissociation, 1(1)*, 7–32.

Nijenhuis, E. R. S., & Den Boer, J. A. (2009). Psychobiology of traumatization and trauma-related structural dissociation of the personality. In P. F. Dell & J. A. O'Neil (Eds.), *Dissociation and the dissociative disorders: DSM-V and beyond* (pp. 337–365). New York: Routledge.

Nijenhuis, E. R. S., Van der Hart, O., & Steele, K. (2002). The emerging psychobiology of trauma-related dissociation and dissociative disorders. In H. D'Haenen, J. A. den Boer, & P. Willner, P. (Eds.), *Biological Psychiatry* (pp. 1079–1098). London: Wiley.

Northoff, G., Steinke, R., Nagel, D., Czerwenka, C., Grosser, O., Danos, P., Genz, A., Krause, R., Boker, H., Otto, H. J., & Bogerts, B. (2000). Right lower prefronto-parietal cortical dysfunction in akinetic catatonia; a combined study of neuropsychology and regional blood flow, *Psychological Medicine, 30*, 583–596.

O'Connor, M. J., Sigman, M., & Brill, N. (1987). Disorganization of attachment in relation to maternal alcohol consumption. *Journal of Consulting and Clinical Psychology, 55*, 831–836.

Ogawa, J. R., Sroufe, L. A., Weinfield, N. S., Carlson, E. A., & Egeland, B. (1997). Development and the fragmented self: Longitudinal study of dissociative symptomatology in a nonclinical sample. *Development and Psychopathology, 9*, 855–879.

Olivera, L. C., Nobre, M. J., Brandao, M. L., & Landeira-Fernandez, J. (2004). Role of the amygdala in conditioned and unconditioned fear generated in the periaqueductal gray. *NeuroReport, 15*, 2281–2285.

Padilla, P. A., & Roth, M. B. (2001). Oxygen deprivation causes suspended animation in the zebrafish embryo. *Proceedings of the National Academy of Sciences USA, 98*, 7331–7335.

Pandya, D. N., & Yeterian, E. H. (1985). Architecture and connections of cortical association areas. In A. Peters & E. G. Jones (Eds.), *Cerebral cortex. Vol. 4. Association and auditory cortices* (pp. 3–61). New York: Plenum Press.

Paulus, M. P., Rogalsky, C., Simmons, A., Feinstein, J. S., & Stein, M. B. (2003). Increased activation in the right insula during risk-taking decision making is related to harm avoidance and neuroticism. *NeuroImage, 19*, 1439–1448.

Pelphrey, K. A., Viola, R. J., & McCarthy, G. (2004). When strangers pass. Processing of mutual and averted social gaze in the superior temporal sulcus. *Psychological Science, 15*, 598–603.

Perrin, F., Maqut, P., Peigneux, P., Ruby, P., Degueldre, C., Balteau, E., Del Fiore, G., Moonen, G., Luxen, A., & Laureys, S. (2005). Neural mechanisms involved in the detection of our first name: a combined ERPs and PET study. *Neuropsychologia, 43*, 12–19.

Perry, B. D., Pollard, R. A., Blakley, T. L., Baker, W. L., & Vigilante, D. (1995). Childhood trauma, the neurobiology of adaptation, and 'use-dependent' development of the brain: How states become traits. *Infant Mental Health Journal, 16*, 271–291.

Phillips, M. L., Drevets, W. C., Rauch, S. L., & Lane, R. (2003). Neurobiology of emotion perception I: The neural basis of normal emotion perception. *Biological Psychiatry, 54*, 504–514.

Platek, S. M., Keenan, J. P., Gallup, G. G. Jr., & Mohammed, F. B. (2004). Where am I? The neurological correlates of self and other. *Cognitive Brain Research, 19*, 114–122.

Poeggel, G., & Braun, K. (1996). Early auditory filial learning in degus *(Octodon degus)*: Behavioral and autoradiographic studies. *Brain Research, 743*, 162–170.

Poeggel, G., Lange, E., Haase, C., Metzger, M., Gulyaeva, N. V., & Braun, K. (1999). Maternal separation and early social deprivation in *Octodon degus*: quantitative changes of

NADPH-diaphorase reactive neurons in the prefrontal cortex and nucleus accumbens. *Neuroscience, 94*, 497–504.

Poeggel, G., Nowicki, L., & Braun, K. (2003). Early social deprivation alters monoaminergic afferents in the orbital prefrontal cortex of *Octodon degus*. *Neuroscience, 116*, 617–620.

Porges, S. W. (1997). Emotion: an evolutionary by-product of the neural regulation of the autonomic nervous system. *Annals of the New York Academy of Sciences, 807*, 62–77.

Porges, S. W. The polyvagal theory: phylogenetic substrates of a social nervous system. *International Journal of Psychophysiology, 42,* 123–146.

Porges, S. W., Doussard-Roosevelt, J. A., & Maiti, A. K. (1994). Vagal tone and the physiological regulation of emotion. *Monographs of the Society for Research in Child Development, 59*, 167–186.

Post, R. M., Weiss, S. R. B., & Leverich, G. S. (1994). Recurrent affective disorder: Roots in developmental neurobiology and illness progression based on changes in gene expression. *Development and Psychopathology, 6*, 781–813.

Potter, E. K., & McCluskey, D. I. (1986). Effects of hypoxia on cardiac vagal efferent activity and on the action of the vagus nerve at the heart in the dog. *Journal of the Autonomic Nervous System, 17*, 325–329.

Powles, W. E. (1992). *Human development and homeostasis*. Madison, CT: International Universities Press.

Prueter, C., Schultz-Venrath, U., & Rimpau, W. (2002). Dissociative and associated psychopathological symptoms in patients with epilepsy, pseudoseizures, and both seizure forms. *Epilepsia, 43*, 188–192.

Putnam, F. W. (1989). Pierre Janet and modern views of dissociation. *Journal of Traumatic Stress, 2*, 413–429.

Putnam, F. W. (1995). Development of dissociative disorders. In D. Cicchetti & D.J. Cohen (Eds.), *Developmental psychopathology: Vol. 2 Risk, disorder, and adaptation* (pp. 581–608). New York: Wiley.

Putnam, F. W. (1997). *Dissociation in children and adolescents: a developmental perspective.* New York: Guilford Press.

Putnam, F. W., Carlson, E. B., Ross, C. A., Anderson, G., Clark, P. Torem, M., Bowman, E. S., Coons, P. H., Chu, J. A., Dill, D. L., Loewenstein, R. J., & Braun, B. G. (1996). Patterns of dissociation in clinical and nonclinical samples. *Journal of Nervous and Mental Disease, 184*, 673–679.

Rabe, S., Beauducel, A., Zollner, T., Maercker, A., & Karl, A. (2006). Regional brain electrical activity in posttraumatic stress disorder after motor vehicle accident. *Journal of Abnormal Psychology*, 115, 687–698.

Raij, T., Utela, K., & Riita, R. (2000). Audio-visual integration of letters in the human brain. *Neuron, 28*, 617–625.

Raine, A., Park, S., Lencz, T., Bihrle, S., Lacasse, L., Widom, C. S., Louai, A. -D., Singh, M. (2001). Reduced right hemisphere activation in severely abused violent offenders during a working memory task: An fMRI study. *Aggressive Behavior, 27*, 111–129.

Rauch, S. L., Whalen, P. J., Shin, L. M., McInerney, S. C., Macklin, M. L., Lasko, N. B., Orr, S. P., & Pitman, R. K. (2000). Exaggerated amygdala response to masked facial stimuli in posttraumatic stress disorder: A functional MRI study. *Biological Psychiatry, 47*, 769–776.

Raz, A. (2004). Anatomy of attentional networks. *Anatomical Records, 281B*, 21–36.

Recordati, G. (2003). A thermodynamic model of the sympathetic and parasympathetic nervous systems. *Autonomic Neuroscience: Basic and Clinical, 103*, 1–12.

Reed, S. F., Ohel, G., David, R., & Porges, S. W. (1999). A neural explanation of fetal heart rate patterns: a test of the polyvagal theory. *Developmental Psychobiology, 35*, 108–118.

Rentero, N., Cividjian, A., Trevaks, D., Poquignot, J. M., Quintin, L., & McAllen, R. M. (2002). Activity patterns of cardiac vagal motoneurons in rat nucleus ambiguus. *American Journal of Physiology: Regulatory, Integrative and Comparative Physiology, 283*, R1327–R1334.

Richer, P. (1881). *Études cliniques sur l'hystéro-épilepsie ou grande hystérie.* Paris: Delahaye & Lecrosnier.

Rinaman, L., Levitt, P., & Card, J. P. (2000). Progressive postnatal assembly of limbic-autonomic circuits revealed by central transneuronal transport of pseudorabies virus. *Journal of Neuroscience, 20*, 2731–2741.

Roberts, N. A., Beer, J. S., Werner, K. H., Scabini, D., Levens, S. M., Knight, R. T., & Levenson, R. W. (2004). The impact of orbital prefrontal cortex damage on emotional activation to unanticipated and anticipated acoustic startle stimuli. *Cognitive, Affective, and Behavioral Neuroscience, 4*, 307–316.

Roberts, N. A., Levens, S. M., McCoy, K., Werner, K., Beer, J. S., Scabini, D., & Knight, R. T. (2001). Orbitofrontal cortex and activation of defensive responses. *Society for Neuroscience Abstracts, 27*, 1705.

Roelofs, K., Keijers, G. P. J., Hoogduin, K. A. L., Naring, G. W. B., & Moene, F. C. (2002). Childhood abuse in patients with conversion disorder. *American Journal of Psychiatry, 159*, 1908–1913.

Rogers, R. D., Owen, A. M., Middleton, H. C., Williams, E. J., Pickard, J. D., Sahakian, B. J., & Robbins, T. W. (1999). Choosing between small, likely rewards and large, unlikely rewards activates inferior and orbital prefrontal cortex. *Journal of Neuroscience, 20*, 9029–9038.

Rolls, E. T., Hornak, J., Wade, D., & McGrath, J. (1994). Emotion-related learning in patients with social and emotional changes associated with frontal lobe damage. *Journal of Neurology, Neurosurgery, and Psychiatry, 57*, 1518–1524.

Ruby, P., & Decety, J. (2001). Effect of subjective perspective taking during stimulation of action: a PET investigation of agency. *Nature Neuroscience, 4*, 546–550.

Ruch, T. C., & Shenkin, H. A. (1943). The relation of area 13 on orbital surface of frontal lobes to hyperactivity and hyperphagia in monkeys. *Journal of Neurophysiology, 6*, 349–360.

Rule, R. R., Shimamura, A. P., & Knight, R. T. (2002). Orbitofrontal cortex and dynamic filtering of emotional stimuli. *Cognitive, Affective, and Behavioral Neuroscience, 2*, 264–270.

Sack, M., Hopper, J. W., & Lamprecht, F. (2004). Low respiratory sinus arrhythmia and prolonged psychophysiological arousal in posttraumatic stress disorder: heart rate dynamics and individual differences in arousal regulation. *Biological Psychiatry, 55*, 284–290.

Sahar, T., Shalev, A. Y., & Porges, S. W. (2001). Vagal modulation of responses to mental challenge in posttraumatic stress disorder. *Biological Psychiatry, 49*, 637–643.

Sanders, B., McRoberts, G., & Tollefson, C. (1989). Childhood stress and dissociation in a college population. *Dissociation, 2*, 17–23.

Şar, V., Ünal, S. N., & Öztürk, E. (2007). Frontal and occipital perfusion changes in dissociatve identity disorder. *Psychiatry Research: Neuroimaging, 156*, 217–223.

Scaer, R. C. (2001). The neurophysiology of dissociation and chronic disease. *Applied Psychophysiology and Biofeedback, 26*, 73–91.

Schiffer, F., Teicher, M. H., & Papanicolaou, A. C. (1995). Evoked potential evidence for right brain activity during the recall of traumatic memories. *Journal of Neuropsychiatry and Clinical Neurosciences, 7*, 169–175.

Schmahl, C. G., Elzinga, B. M., & Bremner, J. D. (2002). Individual differences in psychophysiological reactivity in adults with childhood abuse. *Clinical Psychology and Psychotherapy, 9*, 271–276.

Schore, A. N. (1994). *Affect regulation and the origin of the self: The neurobiology of emotional development.* Mahwah, NJ: Erlbaum.

Schore, A. N. (1996). The experience-dependent maturation of a regulatory system in the orbital prefrontal cortex and the origin of developmental psychopathology. *Development and Psychopathology, 8*, 59–87.

Schore, A. N. (1997). Early organization of the nonlinear right brain and development of a predisposition to psychiatric disorders. *Development and Psychopathology, 9*, 595–631.

Schore, A. N. (2000). Attachment and the regulation of the right brain. *Attachment & Human Development, 2*, 23–47.

Schore, A. N. (2001a). The effects of a secure attachment relationship on right brain development, affect regulation, and infant mental health. *Infant Mental Health Journal, 22*, 7–66.

Schore, A. N. (2001b). The effects of relational trauma on right brain development, affect regulation, and infant mental health. *Infant Mental Health Journal, 22*, 201–269.

Schore, A. N. (2002). Dysregulation of the right brain: a fundamental mechanism of traumatic attachment and the psychopathogenesis of posttraumatic stress disorder. *Australian & New Zealand Journal of Psychiatry, 36*, 9–30.

Schore, A. N. (2003a). *Affect dysregulation and disorders of the self.* New York: Norton.

Schore, A. N. (2003b). *Affect regulation and the repair of the self.* New York: Norton.

Schore, A. N. (2003c). Early relational trauma, disorganized attachment, and the development of a predisposition to violence. In D. Siegel & M. Solomon (Eds.), *Healing Trauma: Attachment, Mind, Body, and Brain* (pp. 101–167). New York: Norton.

Schore, A. N. (2004). Commentary on "Dissociation: a developmental psychobiological perspective" by A. Panzer and M. Viljoen. *South African Psychiatry Review, 7*, 16–17.

Schore, A. N. (2005a). Developmental affective neuroscience describes mechanisms at the core of dynamic systems theory. *Behavioral and Brain Science*, 15, 829–854.

Schore, A. N. (2005b). Attachment, affect regulation and the developing right brain: linking developmental neuroscience to pediatrics. *Pediatrics in Review, 26*, 204–211.

Schuengel, C., Bakersmans-Kranenburg, M. J., & Van IJzendoorn, M. H. (1999). Frightening maternal behavior linking unresolved loss and disorganized infant attachment. *Journal of Consulting and Clinical Psychology, 67*, 54–63.

Schwaber, J. S., Kapp, B. S., Higgins, G. A., & Rapp, P. R. (1982). Amygdaloid and basal forebrain direct connections with the nucleus of the solitary tract and the dorsal motor nucleus. *Journal of Neuroscience, 2*, 1424–1438.

Scicli, A. P., Petrovich, G. D., Swanson, L. W., & Thompson, R. F. (2004). Contextual fear conditioning is associated with lateralized expression of the immediate early gene *c-fos* in the central and basolateral amygdalar nuclei. *Behavioral Neuroscience, 118*, 5–14.

Seeck, M., Zaim, S., Chaves-Vischer, V., Blanke, O., Maeder-Ingvar, M., Weissert, M., & Roulet, E. (2003). Ictal bradycardia in a young child with focal cortical dysplasia in the right insular cortex. *European Journal of Paediatric Neurology, 7*, 177–181.

Semmes, J. (1968). Hemispheric specialization: A possible clue to mechanism. *Neuropsychologia, 6*, 11–26.

Siegel, D. J. (1999). *The developing mind: Toward a neurobiology of interpersonal experience.* New York: Guilford Press.

Silberman, E. K., & Weingartner, H. (1986). Hemispheric lateralization of functions related to emotion. *Brain and Cognition, 5*, 322–353.

Simmons, A., Matthews, S. C., Stein, M. B., & Paulus, M. P. (2004). Anticipation of emotionally aversive visual stimuli activates right amygdala. *NeuroReport, 15*, 2261–2265.

Spence, S., Shapiro, D., & Zaidel, E. (1996). The role of the right hemisphere in the physiological and cognitive components of emotional processing. *Psychophysiology, 33*, 112–122.

Spiegel, D., & Cardena, E. (1991). Disintegrated experience: the dissociative disorders revisited. *Journal of Abnormal Psychology, 100*, 366–378.

Spitzer, C., Wilert, C., Grabe, H. -J., Rizos, T., & Freyberger, H. J. (2004). Dissociation, hemispheric asymmetry, and dysfunction of hemispheric interaction: a transcranial magnetic approach. *Journal of Neuropsychiatry and Clinical Neurosciences, 16*, 163–169.

Spivak, B., Segal, M., Mester, R., & Weizman, A. (1998). Lateral preference in post-traumatic stress disorder. *Psychological Medicine, 28*, 229–232.

Stauss, H. M. (2003). Heart rate variability. *American Journal of Physiology: Regulatory, Integrative and Comparative Physiology,* 285, R927–R931.

Stuss, D. T., & Alexander M. P. (1999). Affectively burnt in: one role of the right frontal lobe? In E. Tulving (Ed.), *Memory, consciousness, and the brain: the Talin conference* (pp. 215–227). Philadelphia: Psychology Press.

Sullivan, R. M., & Dufresne, M. M. (2006). Mesocortical dopamine and HPA axis regulation: Role of laterality and early environment. *Brain Research, 1076*, 49–59.

Sullivan, R. M., & Gratton, A. (2002). Prefrontal cortical regulation of hypothalamic-pituitary-adrenal function in the rat and implications for psychopathology: side matters. *Psychoneuroendocrinology, 27*, 99–114.

Symonds, L. L., Gordon, N. S., Bixby, J. C., & Mande, M. M. (2006). Right-lateralized pain processing in the human cortex: An fMRI study. *Journal of Neurophysiology, 95*, 3823–3830.

Taylor, G. J., Bagby, R. M., & Parker, J. D. A. (1997). *Disorders of affect regulation: Alexithymia in medical and psychiatric illness.* Cambridge, UK: Cambridge University Press.

Taylor, J. (Ed.) (1958). *Selected Writings of J. Hughlings Jackson. Vol. I.* New York: Basic Books.

Teodoro, R. O., & O'Farrell, P. H. (2003). Nitric-oxide-induced suspended animation promotes survival during hypoxia. *EMBO Journal, 22*, 580–587.

Thompson, R. A. (1990). Emotion and self-regulation. *Nebraska Symposium on Motivation* (pp. 367–467). Lincoln: University of Nebraska Press.

Toth, S. C., & Cicchetti, D. (1998). Remembering, forgetting, and the effects of trauma on memory: a developmental psychopathologic perspective. *Developmental and Psychopathology, 10*, 580–605.

Tranel, D., Bechara, A., & Denburg, N. L. (2002). Asymmetric functional roles of right and left ventromedial prefrontal cortices in social conduct, decision-making, and emotional processing. *Cortex, 38*, 589–612.

Trevarthen, C. (1996). Lateral asymmetries in infancy: implications for the development of the hemispheres. *Neuroscience and Biobehavioral Reviews, 20*, 571–586.

Tronick, E. Z. (2004). Why is connection with others so critical? Dyadic meaning making, messiness and complexity governed selective processes which co-create and expand individuals' states of consciousness. In J. Nadel & D. Muir (Eds.), *Emotional development.* New York: Oxford University Press.

Tronick, E. Z., & Weinberg, M. K. (1997). Depressed mothers and infants: failure to form dyadic states of consciousness. In L. Murray & P. J. Cooper (Eds.), *Postpartum depression in child development* (pp. 54–81). New York: Guilford Press.

Tucker, D. M. (1981). Lateral brain function, emotion, and conceptualization. *Psychological Bulletin, 89*, 19–46.

Tucker, D. M. (1992), Developing emotions and cortical networks. In M. R. Gunnar & C. A. Nelson (Eds.), *Minnesota symposium on child psychology. Vol. 24, Developmental behavioral neuroscience* (pp. 75–128). Mahwah, NJ: Erlbaum.

Tzourio-Mazoyer, N., De Schonen, S., Crivello, F., Reutter, B., Aujard, Y., & Mazoyer, B. (2002). Neural correlates of woman face processing by 2-month-old infants. *Neuroimage, 15*, 454–461.

Van der Hart, O., & Dorahy, M. (2009). Dissociation: History of a concept. In P. F. Dell & J. A. O'Neil (Eds.), *Dissociation and the dissociative disorders: DSM-V and beyond* (pp. 3–26). New York: Routledge.

Van der Hart, O., Nijenhuis, E. R. S., & Steele, K. (2006). *The haunted self. Structural dissociation and the treatment of chronic traumatization.* New York: Norton.

Van der Kolk, B. A. (1996). The body keeps the score. Approaches to the psychobiology of posttraumatic stress disorder. In B. A. van der Kolk, A. C. McFarlane, & L. Weisaeth (Eds.), *Traumatic stress: the effects of overwhelming experience on mind, body, and society* (pp. 214–241). New York: Guilford Press.

Van der Kolk, B. A., & Fisler, R. E. (1994). Childhood abuse and neglect and loss of self-regulation. *Bulletin of the Menninger Clinic, 58*, 145–168.

Van der Kolk, B. A., Pelcovitz, D., Roth, S., Mandel, F. S., McFarlane, A., & Herman, J. L. (1996). Dissociation, somatization, and affect dysregulation: The complexity of adaptation to trauma. *American Journal of Psychiatry, 153*, 83–93.

Van der Kolk, B., & Van der Hart, O. (1989). Pierre Janet and the breakdown of adaptation in psychological trauma. *American Journal of Psychiatry, 146*, 1530–1540.

Van der Kolk, B., Van der Hart, O., & Marmar, C. R. (1996). Dissociation and information processing in posttraumatic stress disorder. In B. A. van der Kolk, A. C. McFarlane, & L. Weisaeth (Eds.), *Traumatic stress: The effects of overwhelming experience of mind, body, and society* (pp. 303–327). New York: Guilford Press.

Van der Kolk, B. A., Weisaeth, L., & Van der Hart, O. (1996). History of trauma in psychiatry. In B. A. van der Kolk, A. C. McFarlane, & L. Weisaeth (Eds.), *Traumatic stress: The effects of overwhelming experience of mind, body, and society* (pp. 47–74). New York: Guilford Press.

Van der Ohe, C. G., Darian-Smith, C., Garner, C. C., & Heller, H. C. (2006). Ubiquitous and temperature-dependent neural plasticity in hibernators. *Journal of Neuroscience, 26*, 10590–10598.

Van IJzendoorn, M. H., Schuengel, C., & Bakermans-Kranenburg, M. J. (1999). Disorganized attachment in early childhood: Meta-analysis of precursors, concomitants, and sequelae. *Development and Psychopathology, 11*, 225–249.

Vianna, D. M. L., Graeff, F. G., Brandao, M. L., & Landeira-Fernandez, J. (2001). Defensive freezing evoked by electrical stimulation of the periaqueductal gray: comparison between dorsolateral and ventrolateral regions. *NeuroReport, 12*, 4109–4112.

Volkow, N. D., Wang, G.-J., Fowler, J. S., Logan, J., Gatley, J. S., Pappas, N. R., Wong, C. T., & Felder, C. (2000). Increased activity of the temporal insula in subjects with bradycardia. *Life Sciences, 67*, 2213–2220.

Vyas, A., Mitra, R., Shankaranarayyana, Rao, B. S., & Chattarjai, S. (2002). Chronic stress induces contrasting pattern of dendritic remodeling in hippocampal and amygdaloid neurons. *Journal of Neuroscience, 22*, 6810–6818.

Wang, S. (1997). Traumatic stress and attachment. *Acta Physiologica Scandinavica, Supplement, 640*, 164–169.

Watanabe, S., Miki, K., & Kakigi, R. (2002). Gaze direction affect face perception in humans. *Neuroscience Letters, 325*, 163–166.

Weaver, I. C. G., Cervoni, N., Champagne, F. A., D'Alessio, A. C., Sharma, S., Seckl, J. R., Dymov, S., Szyf, M., & Meaney, M. J. (2004). Epigenetic programming by maternal behavior. *Nature Neuroscience, 7*, 847–854.

Whalen, P. J., Rauch, S. L., Etcoff, N., McInerney, S. C., Lee, M. B., & Jenike, M. A. (1998). Masked presentations of emotional facial expressions modulate amygdala activity without explicit knowledge. *Journal of Neuroscience, 18*, 411–418.

Whitlock, F. A. (1967). The ætiology of hysteria. *Acta Psychiatrica Scandinavica, 43*, 144–162.

Williams, C. L., Haines, J., & Sale, I. M. (2003). Psychophysiological and psychological correlates of dissociation in a case of dissociative identity disorder. *Journal of Trauma & Dissociation, 4(1)*, 101–118.

Winnicott, D. W. (1958). The capacity to be alone. *International Journal of Psycho-Analysis, 39*, 416–420.

Winston, J. S., Vuilleumier, P., & Dolan, R. J. (2003). Effects of low-spatial frequency components of fearful faces on fusiform cortex activity. *Current Biology, 13*, 1824–1829.

Wittling, W., & Schweiger, E. (1993). Neuroendocrine brain asymmetry and physical complaints. *Neuropsychologia, 31*, 591–608.

World Health Organization. (1992). *The ICD-10 classification of mental and behavioural disorders: Clinical descriptions and diagnostic guidelines*. Geneva: WHO.

Yamada, H., Sadato, N., Konishi, Y., Kimura, K., Tanaka, M., Yonekura, Y., & Ishii, Y. (1997). A rapid brain metabolic change in infants detected by fMRI. *NeuroReport, 8*, 3775–3778.

Yamada, H., Sadato, N., Konishi, Y., Muramoto, S., Kimura, K., Tanaka, M., Yonekura, Y., Ishii, Y., & Itoh, H. (2000). A milestone for normal development of the infantile brain detected by functional MRI. *Neurology, 55*, 218–223.

Yoon, B-W., Morillo, C. A., Cechetto, D. F., & Hachinski, V. (1997). Cerebral hemispheric lateralization in cardiac autonomic control. *Archives of Neurology, 54*, 741–744.

Young, J. B., Rosa, R. M., & Landsberg, L. (1984). Dissociation of sympathetic nervous system and adrenal medullary responses. *American Journal of Physiology, 247*, E35–E40.

Zelazo, P. D., & Muller, U. (2002). Executive function in typical and atypical development. In U. Goswami (Ed.), *Handbook of childhood cognitive development* (pp. 445–469). Oxford: Blackwell.

Ziabreva, I., Poeggel, G., Schnabel, R., & Braun, K. (2003). Separation-induced receptor changes in the hippocampus and amygdala of *Octodon degus*: Influence of maternal vocalizations. *Journal of Neuroscience, 23*, 5329–5336.

Part III

Normal and Exceptional Dissociation

9 The Case for the Study of "Normal" Dissociation Processes

Constance J. Dalenberg, PhD
Kelsey Paulson, BS

OUTLINE

The concept of dissociation has exploded into the awareness of scientists over the last 30 years. Exploring the PILOTS database, a search engine devoted entirely to trauma-related scientific research, the key word *dissociation* returns 64 studies published in 1985 to 1989; 236 articles published in 1990 to 1994; 426 publications in 1995 to 1999; and 477 publications in the last 5-year block available (2000 to 2004). A clear turning point for this increase in attention was the 1986 publication of Bernstein and Putnam's *Dissociative Experiences Scale (DES)*, the first validated instrument available to screen for dissociative disorders. Since then, a variety of instruments have come into use, including the Phillips Dissociation Scale (Phillips, 1994), the North Carolina Dissociation Index (Mann, 1995), the Dissociation Questionnaire (Bernstein, Ellason, & Ross, 2001), the Child Dissociative Checklist (Putnam, Helmers, & Trickett, 1993), the Somatoform Dissociation Questionnaire (Nijenhuis, Spinhoven, & Van Dyck, 1997), and more recently, the presentation by Professional Assessment Resources of the first normed and T-scaled dissociation measure available for clinical use (Briere's [2006] Multiscale Dissociation Inventory).

The available literature now includes dozens of articles that relate dissociation to trauma with increasing sophistication in design. The many correlational and quasi-experimental studies (e.g., Berg, Grieger, & Spira, 2005; Briere, 2006; Narang & Nijenhuis, 2005) have been augmented by prospective studies in which dissociation is measured before and after known high-level stressors and/or followed over time (e.g., Diseth, 2006; Morgan, Southwick, & Hazlett, 2004). Most recently, scientists have been drawn into the study of dissociation by the findings that dissociative episodes may have characteristic physiology (Ebner-Priemer, Badeck, Beckmann, Wagner, Feige, Weiss et al., 2005), that those with dissociative disorders may have characteristic fMRI results (Lanius & Williamson, 2002), and that dissociativity is highly comorbid with a number of prevalent nondissociative psychiatric conditions, such as borderline personality disorder (Şar, Kundackçı, Kızıltan, Yargıç, Tutkun, Bakım, Bozkurt et al., 2003), major depression (Fullerton, Ursano, Epstein, Crowley, Vance, Kao, & Braun, 2000) and chemical dependency (Ellason, Ross, & Sainton, 1996).

As dissociation has entered more frequently into scientific discussion, and has passed as a concept into the hands of those who are not centrally focused on the study of dissociative disorders, complaints about the muddiness of the definition of dissociation have grown. Marshall, Spitzer, and Liebowitz (1999), for instance, describe dissociation as a "vague term used to describe a broad range of phenomena" (p. 1681). Certainly the breadth of application of the term cannot be denied. Table 9.1 includes a partial list of terms that have been associated with dissociation.

TABLE 9.1
Concepts Related to Dissociation

Depersonalization	Disengagement
Perceptual Alteration	Emotional constriction
Derealization	Isolation
Absorption	Dissociative Stupor
Hypnotizibility	Conversion Disorders
Imaginative Involvement	Flashbacks
Cognitive Avoidance	Compartmentalization
Fugue State	Out-of-Body Experiences
Dissociative Amnesia	Spacing Out
Hypnotic Analgesia	Freezing
Dissociative Detachment	Numbing

Within the dissociation field, scientists thus were spurred to refine their terms. The most common results of this effort were various dichotomies that attempted to sort dissociative phenomena into two unlike categories. Most commonly, the dichotomy rests (or teeters) on a distinction between "pathological" dissociation and "normal" dissociation. Very rarely, "normal" dissociation is argued not to be dissociation at all (cf. Briere, 2006).

9.1 WHAT DO WE MEAN BY NORMAL AND PATHOLOGICAL DISSOCIATION?

Although the distinction between normal and pathological dissociation is woven throughout the literature, the nature of the distinction has not itself been well articulated. As different writers attempt to make use of the dichotomy, they appear to be using different dimensions to distinguish "normal" from "pathological."

1. *Type.* Some theoreticians argue that certain "types" of dissociation are normal while others are not. Thus, pathological dissociation might include amnesia (Waller, Putnam, & Carlson, 1996), depersonalization (Simeon, Knutelska, & Nelson, 2003), and identity diffusion (e.g., DID: Waller et al., 1996), while normal dissociation might include absorption (Banos, Botella, Garcia-Palacios, Villa, Perpina, & Gallardo, 1999), grade 5 hypnotizability (Spiegel, 1974), or detachment/numbing (Briere, 2006). Alternatively, the type distinction is based on the purported existence of a dissociative "taxon" (see the following) that allegedly mathematically differentiates between qualitatively distinct groups of people who do or do not experience pathological dissociation. Type theorists then argue that the "normal" in normal dissociation refers to the lack of relationship to psychopathology. More specifically, taxon-positive individuals are likely to have a dissociative "disorder," while taxon-negative individuals are not necessarily at risk.
2. *Level.* Other authors refer to a continuum of dissociation, a view championed by Steven Gold. In a plenary address at the annual meeting of the *International Society for the Study of Dissociation*, Gold (2004) proposed that structural dissociation (DID) represents one end of a dissociative continuum, whereas more common dissociative experiences (such as absorption) represent the other extreme. This view has also been expressed by Ross (1996), Ray, June, Turaj, and Lundy (1992) and Eisen and Carlson (1998), who refer to absorption as "a mild form of dissociation" (p. 49).
3. *Timing.* Recent years have seen the emergence of the terms *peritraumatic* and *posttraumatic* dissociation (cf. Marmer, Weiss, & Schlenger, 1994). Peritraumatic dissociation, defined as dissociation occurring at the time of the event, may predispose an individual to PTSD (Ozer, Best, & Lipsey, 2003). On the other hand, it is generally regarded as normal to experience (1) fleeting "out of body" experiences immediately after trauma, (2) temporary dampening of awareness of pain during crisis, or (3) "shock" accompanied by perceptual distortion and amnestic phenomena in a period immediately after receipt of unexpected horrifying news. Butler (2006) argues that dissociative disorders are "disorders" due "not to the fact that dissociation *per se* is present, nor that it was deployed in the face of trauma as a tactic (or reflex) of immediate survival, but rather that severe dissociation and its fallout continue in the absence of such conditions" (p. 54).
4. *Relationship to defense.* Hilgard (1986), Leavitt (2001), and Putnam (1997) have spoken of normal dissociation as a process operating through the allocation of attention. In absorption, for example, normal dissociation focuses attention on one aspect of experience, thereby avoiding or blocking other aspects. The neglected material, poorly elaborated and lacking integration into various neural networks, sits at the outskirts of consciousness or attention, and may be poorly

recalled at a later time. In pathological dissociation, the material is allegedly more fully encoded, but actively blocked in a defensive process.

5. *Frequency.* The "normal" in normal dissociation at times refers to frequency or base rate. The base rates of the absorption items on the DES, for instance, are higher than the base rates of the amnesia or depersonalization items (Waller, Putnam, & Carlson, 1996).
6. *Purpose.* Related to the concepts of timing and defense is the issue of the purpose of dissociation in the given case. Numbing may be judged as "normal" for the individual who must ignore the pain of a combat wound to get to safety, but may be diagnosed as "pathological" when it appears in the distressed spouse of the soldier (who injures herself due to failure to notice initial physical pain). Such distinctions are made by Ludwig (1983) in his argument for the positive evolutionary functions of dissociation—protection of experience through isolation or compartmentalization of catastrophic experience, conservation of energy through efficiency of effort during dissociative flow states, or resolution (through avoidance) of irreconcilable conflicts. Each of these functions has its place in healthy life experience; pathological dissociation thus might be the hijacking of a normative process to serve an unhealthy purpose.

The concepts of normal and pathological dissociation thus have been operationalized in several ways. Most commonly, pathological dissociation is defined through use of the dissociative taxon (Waller, Putnam, & Carlson, 1996). Thus, those who are positive on the taxon are diagnosed with pathological dissociation; taxon-negative individuals are not so diagnosed. Positive taxon status is determined by certain levels of elevation on certain DES items. According to this perspective, persons who obtain high scores on the DES, but are not taxon-positive, must be considered to be "normal" dissociators.

Taxon studies of dissociation have typically found that taxon-positive participants are more likely to have a dissociative disorder, and that the eight taxon items are a better screen for dissociative disorder than is the full 28-item DES. Waller, Putnam, and Carlson's original mixed sample (228 normal controls and 228 patients with diagnosed dissociative identity disorder) did provide evidence for a noncontinuous distribution of "pathological dissociation." However, it is likely that Waller's et al. decision to combine a sample with an extreme form of dissociation and a normal control group (rather than to compose a sample of participants from the entire continuum of DES scores) may have contributed to their taxonic results. Similar findings on smaller samples have subsequently been reported. Seven of Modestin and Erni's (2004) 10 dissociative disorder patients had a higher DES-Taxon score than DES score.

Unfortunately, it is not at all clear that the DES-Taxon is itself a stable measure. Watson (2003) replicated Waller's et al. (1996) analysis with 465 undergraduates at the University of Iowa. Watson calculated four indices of pathological dissociation: the sum of the eight DES-T items, the Baysian probability of taxon membership calculated by the SAS scoring program developed by Waller and Ross (1997), a dichotomous measure of taxon membership using a 0.50 probability cutoff, and a dichotomous measure of taxon membership using a 0.90 cutoff. Watson found that the four indices had two-month stability coefficients of 0.62, 0.34, 0.29, and 0.27. The Big Five Inventory, a measure of basic personality traits that Watson administered concurrently with the DES, yielded stability coefficients between 0.79 and 0.89. The "unimpressive short-term stability" of the taxon as shown by Watson raises concerns about the ultimate appropriateness of the taxon model. This is particularly true given the large body of evidence and mathematical theory that note that artificial dichotomization of continuous measures produces loss of reliability and validity (cf., Cohen, 1983; Widiger, 1992, 2001).

In other research, normal dissociation and pathological dissociation are defined more continuously, either by use of different scales or factors within the DES and other instruments, or by contrasting scales across measures. For example, normal dissociation has been defined as the score on the Absorption factor of the DES or as the overall score on the Tellegen Absorption Scale (Tellegen & Atkinson, 1974). Pathological dissociation then is defined as the score on the Amnesia or Depersonalization/Derealization factor of the DES, as Identity Impairment/Diffusion on the MDI, and so on. When this methodology is used, the researcher is conceding that pathological dissociation may be measured continuously, but implicitly or explicitly arguing that certain "types" of dissociation (e.g., absorption) are benign (i.e., normal) at any level.

9.1.1 Is Normal Dissociation Normal?

Taken as a whole, the discussion above seems to indicate that normal dissociation is a common but temporary response to trauma, mild or even positive in its effects, and minimally related to pathology. It is distributed in a continuous form, probably has a genetic base (Jang, Paris, Zweig-Frank, & Livesley, 1998; Waller & Ross, 1997) and is not necessarily trauma-related. Conversely, pathological dissociation is taxonic, negative in its effects, and highly related to trauma and pathology. In the more extreme version of the argument for pathological dissociation (wherein "normal" dissociation is not dissociation at all), one would also expect that absorption would not relate well to dissociative (or even nondissociative) psychopathology. So, how does the scientific evidence speak to these hypotheses?

Absorption does appear as a separate factor in several factor analyses of the DES (Ray, June, Turaj, & Lundy, 1992; Ross, Ellason, & Anderson, 1995; Stockdale, Gridley, Balogh, & Holtgraves, 2002), and the Dissociative Continuum Scale (Coe, Dalenberg, & Aransky, 1995; Dalenberg & Palesh, 2004). Thus, amnesia-related items correlate at least marginally better with other amnesia-related items than they do with absorption-related items, and the item content largely dictates the factor loadings. This is hardly surprising. More interesting is the fact that these factors are highly correlated with each other, enough so to seriously question the notion that they depend on entirely separate processes. Levin and Spei (2004), for instance, found a correlation of 0.80 between the taxon and the absorption factor. Leavitt (2001) found that 75% of individuals with a diagnosed dissociative disorder had high absorption scores (30 or higher). Further, pathological dissociation (as defined by the amnesia factor, the depersonalization factor, or the taxon) rarely correlates more highly with other predictors of dissociation than does absorption.

Leavitt (2001) provided a telling example of the comparative relationships of normal and pathological dissociation to other psychological symptoms. Leavitt broke a large psychiatric sample into two groups based on their scores on normal dissociation (a median split on the absorption factor). The same group was divided based on the presence or absence of a dissociative disorder (dissociative diagnosis or other psychiatric diagnosis comparison). Large and significant differences appeared between high and low absorption groups on 8 of the 10 MMPI scales; a third of the variance was accounted for by absorption in Schizophrenia and Psychasthenia scales. When Leavitt separated his sample by the presence or absence of a dissociative disorder, few differences emerged. Thus, absorption was highly related to psychiatric pathology in general (just as it has been shown to relate to dissociative pathology in particular). In support of the latter point, Leavitt (1999) also found incrementally higher numbers of absorption cases in groups of increasing pathological dissociation severity. He concluded that the case frequency of high normal dissociation rises in a linear fashion with successive levels of abnormal dissociation.

Levin and Spei (2004) present findings that support Leavitt's results. Pathological and normal dissociation were equally related to depression (r = 0.38 and 0.36, respectively) and equally related to anxiety (r = 0.32 and 0.30, respectively). A set of pathology measures accounted for 36% of the variance in the taxon and 33% of the variance in absorption, while a set of imagination and fantasy immersion variables (fantasy proneness, poor attentional control, daydreaming) accounted for 24% of the variance in the taxon and 24% of the variance in absorption. Levin and Spei noted that positive-constructive daydreaming correlated significantly with absorption, but not with the taxon, a finding in keeping with the abnormal/normal dichotomy. However, the significant and nonsignificant correlations fall only slightly on either side of the revered 0.05 probability line, and are not significantly different from each other.

In a series of studies from the Menninger Clinic, Jon Allen and colleagues began their research with the assumption that absorption represented the "mild, normal, and benign" form of dissociation and that amnesia represented the most pathological form. They were surprised to find that absorption correlated more strongly with psychotic symptomatology (Allen & Coyne, 1995) and general distress (Allen, Coyne, & Console, 1996) than did amnesia. Allen, Coyne, and Console (1997) concluded that dissociative absorption is decidedly not benign in psychiatric or traumatized populations, noting that "to be absorbed in one facet of experience is to be detached from every other" (p. 332). The detachment, they believe, suspends the higher-order reflection and reappraisal that would, in Butler, Duran, Jasiukaitis, Koopman, and Spiegel's (1996) view, normally "control or constrain thoughts and actions" (p. 44).

9.1.2 The Relationship of Normal and Pathological Dissociation to Memory Disturbance

The process of repeatedly turning away from a thought by means of absorption in a competing thought has known negative effects on memory (cf. Levy & Anderson, 2002). Thus, the absorption in trauma-related cognitions that is characteristic of one subset of traumatized survivors may undermine memory of positive facets of the experience (such as the offers of help from friends). This cognitive strategy or mechanism may explain Harvey, Bryant, and

Dang's (1998) finding that highly dissociative survivors often lose memories for positive aspects of their experience. Conversely, absorption in a positive distracter (arguably more difficult, given the pull of an immediate negative event) may lead to disturbance of memory of the trauma.

A similar process lies at the heart of "unformulated experience" (Stern, 1997). Describing patients who have come to a point in therapy when they feel able to turn toward a negative experience that they have previously avoided, Stern writes:

> The refusal to formulate—to think—is a different solution to the problem of defense than repression, which is a matter of keeping unconscious thoughts that already exist. Instead of positing the intentional removal and continuing exclusion of content from awareness, as the repression hypothesis does, lack of formulation as defense means never allowing ourselves to interpret our experience in the first place. The refusal to formulate is quite simple; one just restricts one's freedom of thought, and the "offending" experience is never created. (Stern, 1997, p. 63)

Unlike repression, then, where the repressed memories are alleged to be "forever leaning against the door of consciousness, just waiting for a chance to overcome resistance and tumble into the room" (Stern, 1997, p. 69), unformulated experiences are sitting rather quietly in isolated corners of our memories. Absorption and repeated inattention may create unformulated experiences, such that the unrehearsed and poorly conceptualized experience could become irretrievable. Certainly such lack of formulation and attention leads to a limiting of the number of available (neural) connections to the memory, so that there are fewer associated thoughts and events that call the memory to mind. The direct relationship between rehearsal of a memory and latter recall is one of the most replicable findings in the memory literature (cf. Levy & Anderson, 2002). Butler (2006) appears to be making a related point in arguing that normal and pathological dissociation have in common the "telescoping of the attentional field to concentrate on a narrow range of experience and the concomitant exclusion of other material (internal or external) from awareness, and, to some degree, from accessibility" (p. 45).

At this juncture, it is reasonable to conclude that normal dissociation (e.g., absorption) is highly related to psychopathology. Therefore, at high levels, normal dissociation is not always benign. There is also evidence that normal dissociation may be related to the loss of memory for traumatic or negative experience, a phenomenon that is more typically associated with pathological dissociation. Furthermore, absorption is clearly related to pathological dissociation itself. Accordingly, we contend that it is unreasonable to argue that absorption is not a form of dissociation given that we know that absorption (1) relates strongly to other dimensions of dissociation and (2) relates as predicted by dissociation theory to other general phenomena (e.g., amnesia) typically understood as dissociative.

9.1.3 The Relationship Between Normal and Pathological Dissociation

While we know that taxon-positive individuals, or those high on pathological dissociation, almost always have high absorption scores, the reverse is not true. Researchers studying both forms of dissociation find large numbers of high absorption individuals who do not receive high DES-Taxon scores. For example, Table 9.2 shows the results from the Trauma Research Institute data bank on 828 adults who completed the Dissociative Continuum Scale (DCS). The DCS contains the identical stems from the original DES for the first 28 items, but the response format is changed to a frequency scale (never, no more than once a year, etc.), rather than the original percentile scale (occurs x% of the time). The DCS includes 13 additional items that were intended to enhance and strengthen the normative dissociation factor. Ten of the new items do correlate more strongly with the absorption scale than with the taxon scale. The DCS taxon scale correlates over 0.90 with the original DES taxon scale in several of our studies, while the new absorption scale (adding the 10 items to the original 9) correlates from 0.84 to 0.92 with the original absorption scale (if the two are given simultaneously). In test-retest sample, however, the new

TABLE 9.2
Relationship Between Taxon Membership and Absorption Level

	Nontaxon member	Taxon Member
Low Absorption	n = 455	n = 2
	99.6 %[1]	0.4 %
	56.9 %[2]	4.3 %
High Absorption	n = 337	n = 44
	88.5 %	11.5 %
	43.1 %	95.7 %

[1]*Percentage of n with absorption category;*
[2]*Percentage within taxon category*

absorption scale outperformed the original in terms of reliability. The 6-month temporal stability coefficient for the new absorption scale was 0.84, while the same figure for the original version was 0.67 (with a college sample).

Using the sample cutoff shown to be most similar to taxon results for the original DES scores (a mean item score of 1.75 on the Taxon items), 5.6% of our sample were taxon-positive. As can be seen in Table 9.2, 44 of these 46 individuals also scored positively on the absorption scale. Of the two individuals who were taxon-positive and not high-absorption, it should be noted that one individual missed the cutoff by one hundredth of a point. This one remaining exception may plausibly be attributed to measurement error.

9.1.4 Absorption and Taxon Performance in the Trauma Research Institute Data Set

Table 9.3 shows the correlations of the DCS-Taxon and DCS-Absorption scales with various measures that are often associated with dissociation—the Violence History Questionnaire (VHQ, which measures frequency of physical discipline in childhood), fearful attachment, the Beck Depression Inventory (BDI), self-report of sexual abuse, and four scales from the Trauma Symptom Inventory (TSI). Note that in each case, the correlations of the dissociative subscales with the associated measures are relatively similar. Further, when the taxon scores and absorption scores are used to predict the report of failure to remember an important event, both scales are similarly predictive (r = 0.28 and 0.25, $p < 0.001$, for the taxon and absorption scales respectively). Finally, in conducting regressions using absorption and the taxon to predict Trauma Symptom Inventory scales, it is the shared variance in absorption and the taxon that best predicts most TSI values, rather than the unique variance of either the "pathological" or "normal" scales.

With the possible exception of TSI Dissociation, the variables in Table 9.3 are not dissociative disorder variables. Yet they do provide a foundation for the argument that the skills, talents, or vulnerabilities that are possessed by high absorption individuals are either necessary to the development of a dissociative disorder (in this case, indicated by taxon score) or highly facilitative of that development. To say that the "structural" dissociator, to use Steele, Van der Hart, and Nijenhuis's (2005) term, is doing something different and more than showing extreme absorption is by definition true, given that most high absorption participants in our study, and in other research, are not taxon-positive (see Table 9.2). We contend, however, that extending the argument to a conclusion that high absorption is unrelated to pathological dissociation, or not a form of dissociation at all, may destroy a very precious link in a causal chain. It is possible that "normal" dissociation plays a crucial role in the development and/or maintenance of pathological dissociation, and that normal dissociative processes should be assessed as part of the general trauma battery in the service of the construction of more useful preventive and early treatment plans.

By way of analogy, consider that absorption is to pathological dissociation as diabetes mellitus is to diabetic retinopathy. Retinopathy (a deterioration of the retina) occurs in only 10.2% of diabetic persons older than 50 (Saaddine et al., 2004). Yet if we were to uncouple

TABLE 9.3
Relationship of Taxon and Absorption to Trauma Related Variables

	Taxon	Absorption
VHQ	0.199**	0.199**
	0.001	0.001
	n = 816	n = 816
Sexual Abuse	0.313**	0.314**
	0.001	0.001
	n = 127	n = 127
BDI	0.258*	0.246*
	0.028	0.036
	n = 73	n = 73
Fearful Attachment	0.213**	0.218**
	0.001	0.001
	n = 473	n = 473
TSI Anxious Arousal	0.338**	0.392**
	0.001	0.001
	n = 245	n = 245
TSI Re-experiencing	0.395**	0.453**
	0.001	0.001
	n = 245	n = 245
TSI Defensive Avoidance	0.359**	0.421**
	0.001	0.001
	n = 245	n = 245
TSI Dissociation	0.565**	0.571**
	0.001	0.001
	n = 245	n = 245
TSI Dysfunctional Sexual Behaviors	0.280**	0.409**
	0.001	0.001
	n = 245	n = 245

Note: VHQ: Violence History Questionnaire; BDI: Beck Depression Inventory; TSI: Trauma Symptom Inventory diabetic retinopathy and diabetes (arguing that each is distinct from the other), we would be less likely to conduct a yearly dilated eye examination as part of diabetes management. Our knowledge that diabetes is a risk factor for retinopathy and our knowledge that retinopathy is part of the diabetic syndrome, guide our management of the disease.

If absorption is a precursor, facilitator, or foundation for structural dissociation (i.e., DID, DDNOS, Dissociative Amnesia), then this could occur in a number of ways. In a diathesis-stress model, absorption would be the underlying vulnerability; additional stress (or in this case, additional trauma) would be necessary to produce structural dissociation. Gold (2004) proposes a "phase shift" at a given level of the dissociative continuum, where a set of dissociative strategies (including reliance on absorption), perhaps in interaction with trauma (of variable intensity), might take on a different appearance or set of functions (as water might appear as gas, liquid, or solid in different conditions). Thus relatively more minor trauma in someone with high constitutional absorption could trigger a cascade into a severe dissociative disorder, provoking structural change, whereas relatively severe trauma may be required to produce the same result in someone with low constitutional absorption. If the narrowing of attention typically cited as a characteristic mechanism of absorption succeeds in cutting back the number of associations to the memory, the result could be an individual with extreme state-dependence who lacks ready access to various trauma-related memories.

In one study conducted in our lab (Duvenage, 1993) and recently replicated, we measured the degree to which college students were state-dependent for fear and sadness. In the sadness manipulation, the students were induced into mood states (happy/sad) by reading a set of mood induction cards. Mood states induced in this manner are usually maintained for 20 to 30 minutes (Ellis & Ashbrook, 1989). Participants learned the material in one state, and recalled it in the same or a different state. An interference task, with more material to learn, occurred between the two testings. In the fear induction, frightening movie clips were used.

The results were quite interesting. First, sadness state-dependency and fear state-dependency were poorly related. In debriefing, some subjects reported that fear states were more difficult to tolerate; others claimed that sadness and loss states were more noxious. Second, we found two groups of high dissociators who responded quite differently to the paradigm. One group, high on absorption, became immersed in the movie, reporting above average fear scores. This group was highly state-dependent for fear. Another group with high absorption scores used their talents to distance themselves from the movie; they absorbed themselves in the thought that this was "just an experiment." This group reported low fear, and evidenced less state-dependency than the average nondissociative participant. Finally, participants with a serious physical abuse history were more state-dependent for fear, but not for sadness.

Scholars have connected state-dependent learning to dissociative multiplicity (i.e., DID) for many years. Braun (1984) wrote that "repeated dissociation under similar circumstances (for instance, child abuse) facilitates the formation of personalities via state dependent encoding of information" (p. 172). Spiegel, Hunt, and Dondershine (1988) described nonintegrated memories and emotions that developed into personalities through the process of state-dependent learning. The "amnestic barriers" of DID patients may not always be defensively erected walls; instead, they may be winding, obstacle-laden pathways between memories, produced by repeated narrowing of attention (absorption) in the presence of intolerable affect.

9.2 NORMAL USES FOR NORMAL AND PATHOLOGICAL DISSOCIATION PROCESSES

As we implied earlier, the distinction between normal and pathological dissociation need not be a difference in types (i.e., amnesia vs. absorption or taxon vs. continuum). Instead, it is possible that the difference between normal and pathological dissociation depends upon *how* the dissociative mechanisms are used. The use of amnesia to temporarily (or permanently) forget an incident of mistreatment by a valued other may be quite practical, as long as it does not damage the person's ability to function and assess risk. A process such as absorption, implemented to avoid negative affect, may be an effective emotion-regulation tool in the short term. Processes that sever the connection between body and self (i.e., depersonalization) are reported by individuals with chronic pain (Duckworth, Lezzi, & Archibald, 2000), and may allow temporary or even permanent relief of some unbearable physical experiences. Acute elevations in general dissociation, across subtypes, have been noted in skydivers, who are engaging in a behavior that is at once exciting and frightening (Sterlini & Bryant, 2002). In each case, the individual is using dissociation as a form of temporary self-protection—to ward off physical pain until it is safe to experience it and/or to ward off mental pain until it is potentially resolvable or until the resolution of the situation is bearable.

Through a constellation of dissociative strategies, the individual under attack cuts the ties between ongoing mental processes. If overused, this strategy leaves the person lacking internal anchors, bereft of coherent self-understandings, and without the basic data that could allow reappraisal of action rather than suppression of affect (John & Gross, 2004). Such internal incoherency places the individual at risk for a wide variety of psychiatric disorders, dissociative and nondissociative. Finally, dissociative processes, working as they do to free the individual from the constraints of reality, also have been associated by several authors with positive feelings (Butler & Palesh, 2004). Thus, absorption may not only protect the individual from the negative, but may also immerse the individual in a contrasting positive state. To be "absorbed" in a novel or movie is typically a positive experience, independent of whether one consciously chose to absorb in order to avoid or reject a traumatic memory.

9.3 CONCLUSIONS

In conclusion, we argue that:

1. Empirical evidence, the evidence that should ultimately guide us, suggests that "normal" dissociation, or absorption, is a form of dissociation.
2. Cutting the linkages between the more common dissociative strategies, such as absorption, and the rarer forms, such as dissociative amnesia and dissociative identity disorder, may lead us to ignore precursors and vulnerability factors that are essential to the development of these disorders.
3. The dissociative processes themselves may have evolutionary significance and biological markers. "Normal" and "pathological" dissociation may have positive and negative functions, depending on nature and chronicity of use. As such, they deserve the intense interest that they are generating in the greater scientific community.

REFERENCES

Allen, J., & Coyne, L. (1995). Dissociation and vulnerability to psychotic experience: The Dissociative Experiences Scale and the MMPI-2. *Journal of Nervous and Mental Disease, 183*, 615–622.

Allen, J., Coyne, L., & Console, D. (1996). Dissociation contributes to anxiety and psychoticism on the Brief Symptom Inventory. *Journal of Nervous and Mental Disease, 184*, 639–644.

Allen, J., Coyne, L., & Console, D. (1997). Dissociative detachment relates to psychotic symptoms and personality decompensation. *Comprehensive Psychiatry, 38*, 327–334.

Banos, R., Botella, C., & Garcia-Palacios, A. (1999). Psychological variables and reality judgment in virtual environments: The roles of absorption and dissociation. *CyberPsychology and Behavior, 2,* 143–148.

Berg, J., Grieger, T., & Spira, J. (2005). Psychiatric symptoms and cognitive appraisal following the near sinking of a research submarine. *Military Medicine, 170,* 22–47.

Bernstein, I., Ellason, J., & Ross, C. (2001). On the dimensionalities of the Dissociative Experiences Scale (DES) and the Dissociation Questionnaire (DIS-Q). *Journal of Trauma and Dissociation, 2,* 103–123.

Bernstein-Carlson, E., & Putnam, F. (1986). Development, reliability, and validity of a dissociation scale. *Journal of Nervous and Mental Disease, 174*, 727–735.

Braun, B. (1984). Towards a theory of multiple personality and other dissociative phenomena. *Psychiatric Clinics of North America, 7,* 171–193.

Briere, J. (2006). Dissociative symptoms and trauma exposure: Specificity, affect dysregulation, and posttraumatic stress. *Journal of Nervous and Mental Disease, 194,* 78–82.

Butler, L. (2006). Normative dissociation. *Psychiatric Clinics of North America, 29*, 45–62.

Butler, L., Duran, R., Jasiukaitis, P., Koopman, C., & Spiegel, D. (1996). Hypnotizability and traumatic experience: a diathesis-stress model of dissociative symptomatology. *American Journal of Psychiatry, 153*, 42–63.

Butler, L., & Palesh, O. (2004). Spellbound: Dissociation in the movies. *Journal of Trauma & Dissociation, 5*, 61–87.

Coe, M., Dalenberg, C., & Aransky, K. (1995). Adult attachment style, reported in childhood violence history and types of dissociative experiences. *Dissociation, 8,* 142–154.

Cohen, J. (1983). The cost of dichotomization. *Applied Psychological Measurement, 7*, 249–253.

Dalenberg, C., & Palesh, O. (2004). Relationship between child abuse history, trauma, and dissociation in Russian college students. *Child Abuse and Neglect, 28,* 461–474.

Diseth, T. (2006). Dissociation following traumatic medical treatment procedures in childhood: A longitudinal follow-up. *Development and Psychopathology, 18,* 233–251.

Duckworth, M., Lezzi, T., Archibald, Y., & Haertlein, P. (2000). Dissociation and posttraumatic stress symptoms in patients with chronic pain. *International Journal of Rehabilitation & Health, 5*, 129–139.

Duvenage, C. (1992). *Dissociation, child abuse history, and amnesiac barrier strength in a non-clinical population.* Unpublished doctoral dissertation, California School of Professional Psychology, San Diego.

Ebner-Priemer, U., Badeck, S., & Beckmann, C. (2005). Affective dysregulation and dissociative experience in female patients with borderline personality disorder: A startle response study. *Journal of Psychiatric Research, 39,* 85–92.

Ebner-Priemer, U. W., Badeck, S., Beckmann, C., Wagner, A., Feige, B., Weiss, I., Lieb, K., & Bohus, M. (2005). Affective dysregulation and dissociative experience in female patients with borderline personality disorder: A startle response study. *Journal of Psychiatric Research, 39*, 85-92.

Eisen, M., & Carlson, E. (1998). Individual differences in suggestibility: Examining the influence of dissociation, absorption, and a history of childhood abuse. *Applied Cognitive Psychology, 12,* 47–61.

Ellason, J., Ross, C., & Sainton, K. (1996). Axis I and II comorbidity and childhood trauma history in chemical dependency. *Bulletin of the Menninger Clinic, 60,* 39–51.

Ellis, H., & Ashbrook, P. (1989). The 'state' of mood and memory research: A selective review. *Journal of Social Behavior & Personality, 4,* 1–21.

Fullerton, C., Ursano, R., & Epstein, R. (2000). Peritraumatic dissociation following motor vehicle accidents: Relationship to prior trauma and prior major depression. *Journal of Nervous and Mental Disease, 188,* 267–272.

Gold, S. (2004, November). On dissociation, mainstream psychology, and the nature of human being. Plenary presentation at the 21st Annual International Society for the Study of Dissociation, New Orleans, LA.

Harvey, A., Bryant, R., & Dang, S. (1998). Autobiographical memory in acute stress disorder. *Journal of Consulting and Clinical Psychology, 66*, 500–506.

Hilgard, E. (1986). *Divided consciousness: Multiple consciousness in human thought and action*. New York: Wiley.

Jang, K., Paris, J., Zweig-Frank, H., & Livesley, W. (1998). Twin study of dissociative experience. *Journal of Nervous and Mental Disease, 186*, 345–351.

John, O., & Gross, J. (2004). Healthy and unhealthy emotion regulation: Personality processes, individual differences, and life span development. *Journal of Personality, 72,* 1301–1333.

Lanius, R., Williamson, P., & Boksman, K. (2002). Brain activation during script-driven imagery induced dissociative responses in PTSD: A functional magnetic resonance imaging investigation. *Biological Psychiatry, 52,* 305–311.

Laor, N., Wolmer, L., & Kora, M. (2002). Posttraumatic, dissociative and grief symptoms in Turkish children exposed to the 1999 earthquakes. *Journal of Nervous and Mental Disease, 190,* 824–832.

Leavitt, F. (1999). Dissociative experiences scale taxon and measurement of dissociative pathology: Does the taxon add to an understanding of dissociation and its associated pathologies. *Journal of Clinical Psychology in Medical Settings, 6*, 427–440.

Leavitt, F. (2001). MMPI profile characteristics of women with varying levels of normal dissociation. *Journal of Clinical Psychology, 57,* 1469–1477.

Levin, R., & Spei, E. (2004). Relationship of purported measures of pathological and nonpathological dissociation to self-reported psychological distress and fantasy immersion. *Assessment, 11,* 160–168.

Levy, B., & Anderson, M. (2002). Inhibitory processes and the control of memory retrieval. *Trends in Cognitive Sciences, 6*, 299–305.

Ludwig, A. (1983). The psychobiological functions of dissociation. *American Journal of Clinical Hypnosis, 26,* 93–99.

Mann, B. (1995). The North Carolina Dissociation Index: A measure of dissociation using items from the MMPI-2. *Journal of Personality Assessment, 64,* 349–359.

Marmar, C., Weiss, D., & Schlenger, W. (1994). Peritraumatic dissociation and posttraumatic stress in male Vietnam theater veterans. *American Journal of Psychiatry, 151,* 902–907.

Marshall, R., Spitzer, R., & Liebowitz, M. (1999). Review and critique of the new DSM-IV diagnosis of acute stress disorder. *American Journal of Psychiatry, 156,* 1677–1685.

Modestin, J., & Erni, T. (2004). Testing the dissociative taxon. *Psychiatry Research, 126,* 77–82.

Morgan, C., Hazlett, G., & Wang, S. (2001). Symptoms of dissociation in humans experiencing acute, uncontrollable stress: A prospective investigation. *American Journal of Psychiatry, 158,* 1239–1247.

Narang, G., & Nijenhuis, E. (2005). Relationships between self-reported potentially traumatizing events, psychoform and somatoform dissociation, and absorption, in two nonclinical populations. *Australian and New Zealand Journal of Psychiatry, 39,* 982–988.

Nijenhuis, E., Spinhoven, P., & Van Dyck, R. (1997). The development of the Somatoform Dissociation Questionnaire (SDQ-5) as a screening instrument for dissociative disorders. *Acta Psychiatrica Scandinavica, 96,* 311–318.

Ozer, E., Best, S., & Lipsey, T. (2003). Predictors of posttraumatic stress disorder and symptoms in adults: A meta-analysis. *Psychological Bulletin, 129,* 52–73.

Paulsen, S. (1995). Eye movement desensitization and reprocessing: Its cautious use in the dissociative disorders. *Progress in the Dissociative Disorders, 8,* 32–44.

Phillips, D. (1994). Initial development and validation of the Phillips Dissociation Scale (PDS) of the MMPI. *Dissociation, 7*, 92–100.

Putnam, F. (1997). *Dissociation in children and adolescence: A developmental perspective*. New York: Guilford Press.

Putnam, F., Helmers, K., & Trickett, P. (1993). Development, reliability, and validity of a child dissociation scale. *Child Abuse and Neglect, 17,* 731–741.

Ray, W., June, K., Turaj, K., & Lundy, R. (1992). Dissociative experiences in a college age population: A factor analytic study of two dissociation scales. *Personality and Individual Differences, 13*, 417–424.

Ross, C. (1996). History, phenomenology, and epidemiology of dissociation. In L. K. Michelson & W.J. Ray (Eds.), *Handbook of dissociation*. New York: Plenum Press.

Ross, C., Ellason, J., & Anderson, G. (1995). A factor analysis of the Dissociative Experiences Scale (DES) in dissociative identity disorder. *Dissociation: Progress in the Dissociative Disorders, 8,* 229–235.

Saaddine, J., Benjamin, S., Pan, L., Narayan, K., Tierney, E., Kanjilal, S., & Geiss, L. (2004). Prevalence of visual impairment and selected eye diseases among persons aged >50 years with and without diabetes – United States, 2002. *MMWR Weekly, 53*, 1069–1071.

Şar, V., Kundakçı, T., Kızıtan, E., Yargıç, I., Tutkun, H., Bakım, B, Bozkurt, O., Özpulat, T., Keser, V., & Özdemir, Ö. (2003). The Axis-I dissociative disorder comorbidity of borderline personality disorder among psychiatric outpatients. *Journal of Trauma and Dissociation, 4,* 119–136.

Simeon, D., Knutelska, M., & Nelson, D. (2003). Examination of the Pathological Dissociation Taxon in depersonalization disorder. *Journal of Nervous and Mental Disease, 191,* 738–744.

Spiegel, H. (1974). The grade 5 syndrome: The highly hypnotizable person. *International Journal of Clinical and Experimental Hypnosis, 22,* 303–319.

Spiegel, D., Hunt, T., & Dondershire, H. (1988). Dissociation and hypnotizability in post-traumatic stress disorder. *American Journal of Psychiatry, 145*, 301–305.

Steele, K., Van der Hart, O., & Nijenhuis, E. (2005). Phase-oriented treatment of structural dissociation in complex traumatization: Overcoming trauma-related phobias. *Journal of Trauma & Dissociation, 6*, 11–53.

Sterlini, G., & Bryant, R. (2002). Hyperarousal and dissociation: A study of novice skydivers. *Behaviour Research and Therapy, 40*, 431–437.

Stern, D. (1997) *Unformulated experience: From dissociation to imagination in psychoanalysis*. Hillsdale, NJ: Analytic Press.

Stockdale, G., Gridley, B., & Balogh, D. (2002). Confirmatory factor analysis of single- and multiple-factor competing models of the Dissociative Experiences Scale in a non-clinical sample. *Assessment, 9,* 94–106.

Tellegen, A., & Atkinson, G. (1974). Openness to absorbing and self-altering experiences ('absorption'), a trait related to hypnotic susceptibility. *Journal of Abnormal Psychology, 83,* 268–277.

Vanderlinden, J., Van Dyck, R., & Vanderreycken, W. (1991). Dissociative experiences in the general population in the Netherlands and Belgium: A study with the Dissociative Questionnaire (DIS-Q). *Progress in the Dissociative Disorders, 4,* 180–184.

Waller, N., Putnam, F., & Carlson, E. (1996). Types of dissociation and dissociative types: A taxometric analysis of dissociative experiences. *Psychological Methods, 1,* 300–321.

Waller, N., & Ross, C. (1997). The prevalence and biometric structure of pathological dissociation in the general population: Taxometric and behavior genetic findings. *Journal of Abnormal Psychology, 106,* 499–510.

Watson, D. (2003). Investigating the construct validity of the dissociative taxon: Stability analyses of normal and pathological dissociation. *Journal of Abnormal Psychology, 112,* 298–305.

Widiger, T. (1992). Categorical versus dimensional classification: Implications from and for research. *Journal of Personality Disorders, 6*, 287–300.

Widiger, T. (2001). What can be learned from taxometric analyses? *Clinical Psychology: Science and Practice, 8*, 528–533.

10 Dissociation versus Alterations in Consciousness: Related but Different Concepts

Kathy Steele, MN, CS
Martin J. Dorahy, PhD, DClinPsych
Onno van der Hart, PhD
Ellert R. S. Nijenhuis, PhD

OUTLINE

In the 19th and early 20th centuries, mental dissociation denoted an organized *division of the personality* (Janet, 1889, 1907; Myers, 1940; Prince, 1905; Van der Hart & Dorahy, 2009). This division involves insufficient integration among two or more "systems of ideas and functions that constitute personality" (Janet, 1907, p. 332). Each of these psychobiological systems has its own unique combination of perception, cognition, affect, and behavior; each has its own sense of self, no matter how rudimentary (e.g., Mitchell, 1922; Prince, 1905). In our terms, dissociation was originally conceptualized as a *structural dissociation of the personality* (Nijenhuis, Van der Hart, & Steele, 2004; Steele, Van der Hart, & Nijenhuis, 2004, 2005, Chapter 16, this volume; Van der Hart, Nijenhuis, Steele, & Brown, 2004). Dissociative phenomena are manifestations of this temporary (e.g., as in dissociative hypnotic phenomena) or chronic (e.g., as in trauma-related disorders) division of the personality organization.

Since the 1980s, the definition of dissociation has been broadened. It has been vaguely defined as a *breakdown or disruption in usually integrated functioning* (APA,

2000). Subsequently, alterations in consciousness such as absorption, altered time sense, spaciness, daydreaming, imaginative involvement, and trance-like behavior, none of which necessarily derive from a dissociative organization of the personality, have been considered to be dissociative phenomena (e.g., Bernstein & Putnam, 1986; Bowins, 2004; Butler, 2004; Ray, 1996; Ray & Faith, 1995; Ross, Joshi, & Currie, 1991; see Van der Hart & Dorahy, Chapter 1, this volume). Consequently, there is serious conceptual confusion about dissociation (Brunet, Holowka, & Laurence, 2001; Cardeña, 1994; Dell, Chapter 15, this volume; Frankel, 1996; Holmes et al., 2005; Marshall, Spitzer, & Liebowitz, 1999; Nijenhuis, Van der Hart, & Steele, 2004; Steele, Van der Hart, & Nijenhuis, Chapter 16, this volume; Van der Hart & Dorahy, Chapter 1, this volume; Van der Hart et al., 2004). These alterations in consciousness are typically labeled as *normal dissociation* and are conceptualized as residing on a continuum with normal dissociation at one end and pathological dissociation (i.e., symptoms that typically manifest from a division of the personality; e.g., identity alteration, dissociative amnesia) at the other end. However, several authors have strongly challenged this continuum model of dissociation (Boon & Draijer, 1993; Holmes et al., 2005; Ogawa et al., 1997; Putnam, 1997; Waller, Putnam, & Carlson, 1996; Watson, 2003).

This chapter addresses two essential questions. First, can alterations in consciousness reach pathological proportions? Second, are alterations in consciousness actually dissociative? For example, does absorption in work fall within the same domain of psychological experience as one dissociative part of the personality hearing the voice of another dissociative part?

We propose that disruptions in integrative functioning involve at least two different but related phenomena: (1) structural dissociation (i.e., a division of the personality) and (2) alterations in consciousness. The manifestations of these phenomena are different, but may coexist. Below, we will focus on the similarities and differences between (1) trauma-related structural dissociation of the personality, and (2) normal and pathological alterations in consciousness. We believe that the distinction between structural dissociation of the personality and alterations in consciousness has several important implications. If they are truly different categories of phenomena, then clinicians should *not* conclude that patients with a severe alteration of consciousness have a dissociative disorder. Similarly, if these phenomena are truly different, then we must distinguish between empirical findings about alterations in consciousness and empirical findings about the manifestations of structural dissociation. Finally, research instruments should clearly distinguish between structural dissociation of the personality and alterations in consciousness.

10.1 TRAUMA-RELATED STRUCTURAL DISSOCIATION OF THE PERSONALITY

Janet (1889, 1907) believed that structural dissociation of the personality results from an inability to successfully engage in integrative mental and physical actions (due to physical illness, exhaustion, or exposure to highly stressful events). He proposed that a chronic or temporary *low integrative capacity* promotes trauma-related structural dissociation whereby some experiential memories are not integrated into the personality as a whole. According to Janet (1907), such deficits in integrative capacity could cause other psychological disruptions (e.g., pathological alterations in consciousness, greater emotivity, and reactive behaviors and beliefs). Janet distinguished these phenomena from structural dissociation.

Research (cf. Nijenhuis & Den Boer, Chapter 21, and Steele, Van der Hart, & Nijenhuis, Chapter 16, this volume) supports Janet's thesis that structural dissociation can emerge from insufficient integrative capacity to manage stressful events; thus, the likelihood of traumatization significantly depends on the individual's integrative capacity. For example, children have lower integrative capacity than adults, due in part to immaturity of integrative brain structures. This implies that children are more prone to dissociate under stress. Research supports this; age at the time of trauma is associated with structural dissociation (Boon & Draijer, 1993; Fullerton et al., 2000; Nijenhuis, Spinhoven, Van Dyck, Van der Hart, & Vanderlinden, 1998; Ogawa et al., 1997).

10.1.1 Action Systems as the Foundation for Trauma-Related Structural Dissociation of the Personality

Janet's conception of dissociation involves psychobiological "systems of ideas and functions that constitute personality." An obvious question then is which systems are involved in structural dissociation? Personality involves a range of psychobiological motivational (Toates, 1986), behavioral (Cassidy, 1999), or emotional operating systems (Panksepp, 1998)—also known as *action systems* (Nijenhuis et al., 2002, 2004; Steele et al., Chapter 16, this volume). Two major categories of action systems (Carver, Sutton, & Scheier, 2000; Lang, Bradley, & Cuthbert,

1998) shape our personalities. One category guides activities of daily living (e.g., work, play, learning, maintaining relationships, energy regulation [eating and sleep], and sexual behavior/reproduction). The second category mediates physical defense under threat (e.g., attachment cry, fight, freeze, submit). Social defense against abandonment and rejection and interoreceptive defense against one's own mental contents (e.g., thoughts, feelings, beliefs, sensations, memories) can involve both categories of action systems. Such defenses range from the primitive (e.g., projection and splitting) to the relatively sophisticated (e.g., rationalization, passive-aggressiveness, obstinacy, "codependent" behaviors, etc.).

10.1.1.1 Dissociative Parts of the Personality

There are two prototypical dissociative parts of the personality, each mediated by different action systems or constellations of action systems (Nijenhuis et al., 2002, 2004; Steele et al., Chapter 16, this volume; Van der Hart et al., 2004).

We call parts that are mediated by action systems of daily life the *Apparently Normal Parts of the Personality* (ANP), and those mediated by the action systems of defense the *Emotional Parts of the Personality* (EP). These terms derive from the writings of British psychologist and psychiatrist, Charles S. Myers. Myers noted the presence of ANPs and EPs in acutely traumatized World War I combat soldiers (Myers, 1940). Dissociative parts that exert functions in daily life (ANPs) fear the retrieval or integration of traumatic memories; they prevent this via mental avoidance and escape strategies. We hypothesize that these phobic mental actions involve the natural tendency of different action systems to inhibit one another to a varying degree. For example, the action systems of (physical) defense and play tend to completely inhibit one another. This implies that dissociative parts that focus on daily life (ANP) would be impaired in their ability to play and socialize whenever they are intruded upon by dissociative parts that are rooted in defensive action systems (EP). ANPs and EPs have at least a rudimentary sense of self; each retrieves memories that other parts do not (or do not retrieve in the same manner).

Dissociative parts vary in their *degree of structural division* from one another, in their *autonomy*, and in their *sense of self* (which may or may not include secondary elaborations such as ages, gender, names, etc.). The *number* of dissociative parts also varies. The individual's *subjective experience* and the *overt manifestations* of structural dissociation vary. In all cases, however, structural dissociation is a division of the personality.

10.1.1.2 Dissociative Symptoms

Dissociative symptoms are manifestations of structural dissociation (Nijenhuis & Van der Hart, 1999; Nijenhuis, Van der Hart, & Steele, 2004; Steele, Van der Hart, & Nijenhuis, 2004; Van der Hart et al., 2004). *Negative dissociative symptoms* (e.g., dissociative amnesia) occur when a part is unable to retrieve mental contents (e.g., memories) or unable to execute normal functions (e.g., movement of an arm) that are still available to another part, at least in principle. *Positive dissociative symptoms* occur when the mental contents (e.g., a traumatic memory) or functions (e.g., movement of an arm) of one part intrude into the functioning or consciousness of another part. Negative and positive symptoms can be classified as either psychoform or somatoform. *Psychoform dissociative symptoms* are typically associated with episodic memory or other mental functions or contents that do not involve the body *per se* (e.g., hearing voices of other parts). *Somatoform dissociative symptoms* manifest in the body: anesthesia, analgesia, inability to move some part of the body, inability to inhibit particular movements, and so on.

10.2 ALTERATIONS IN THE FIELD AND LEVEL OF CONSCIOUSNESS

We use the term *consciousness* to mean conscious awareness of internal and external stimuli. Two aspects of alterations in consciousness are often considered, incorrectly in our opinion, to be manifestations of dissociation: (1) the quantity of material that is conscious and (2) the quality of consciousness. We maintain that the quantity and quality of consciousness are essentially different from the manifestations of structural dissociation.

10.2.1 Quantity: The Field of Consciousness

The quantity of internal and external stimuli held in conscious awareness at a given time is referred to as *the field of consciousness*. The field of consciousness can be very wide, extremely narrow (retracted), or anything in between (Janet, 1907). The breadth of our field of consciousness fluctuates; that is, the extent to which we perceive internal and external events varies. This is generally adaptive. Sometimes it is most adaptive to focus narrowly on specific stimuli. At other times, it is most adaptive to attend to a broad range of stimuli. We are limited, however, in the number of stimuli to which we can attend at a given time. We simply cannot perceive (and remember, i.e., encode, store, consolidate and retrieve) everything. Even if we could, the task would rapidly become overwhelming; the demands on our energy would be just too great, and we would not be able to focus (Luria, 1968). Some changes in our field of consciousness are voluntary (e.g., intentional concentration, guided imagery, meditation); other changes are involuntary (e.g., inability to concentrate or selectively attend when we are tired or stressed).

10.2.2 Quality: The Level of Consciousness

The quality of our mental functioning is largely dependent on the *level of consciousness*. With a few exceptions such as sleep and deep relaxation, a lowering of consciousness impairs mental functioning. Common forms of lowered consciousness include temporary mental relaxation, inattentiveness, daydreaming, and concentration problems due to fatigue, anxiety, stress, or illness. Less common forms of lowered consciousness include depersonalization and derealization (e.g., feeling unreal, staring down a tunnel, feeling foggy or detached, pathological trance states, time distortion, degrees of unresponsiveness, Allen, Consolo, & Lewis, 1999; Van der Hart & Steele, 1997). Low levels of conscious awareness can cause disorganization, forgetfulness, spaciness, and undue drowsiness. Extreme forms of lowered consciousness include the loss of consciousness in pseudoseizures (Bowman, 1998; Kuyk, 1999), stupor, and coma. These phenomena, however, do not exclude engagement in some inner experiences. The latter two phenomena may have an organic basis.

Field and level are inherent features of consciousness; they coexist in numerous combinations and may fluctuate voluntarily or involuntarily. Low levels of consciousness can coincide with either a wide or narrow field of consciousness.

10.3 NORMAL VERSUS PATHOLOGICAL ALTERATIONS IN CONSCIOUSNESS

Not all alterations in consciousness are normal. Alterations in field and level of consciousness can be described in terms of intensity, frequency, duration, appropriateness (to a given situation), and degree to which they can be controlled voluntarily.

In healthy individuals, field and level of consciousness wax and wane in moderated oscillations throughout the day. Periods of alertness and concentration are interspersed with periods of drowsiness, fatigue, or distraction. *Alterations in consciousness are pathological when they are excessive, frequent, inflexible, and cannot be consciously controlled.* For example, some people need to "stare at the wall" for a few minutes before they can get going in the morning. It is normal to have a rather low level of consciousness and a retracted field of consciousness just before and after sleep. But, if "staring at the wall" continues for hours, recurs frequently, or cannot be voluntarily interrupted, then it is pathological. Similarly, daydreaming is not healthy or normal if the person is lost in fantasy for hours at a time when he/she should be dealing with daily life (Janet, 1903; Somer, 2002). It is not unusual for a person who is preoccupied to miss an exit while driving or to be unaware of a brief passage of time. It is pathological, however, if the person is regularly and intensely absorbed in daydreams, constantly misses exits, gets lost, and drives dangerously.

Lowering of the level of consciousness is adaptive when we relax or sleep. On the other hand, our field of consciousness is maladaptive if we fail to perceive and remember significant facts and experiences. Even high levels of consciousness can be maladaptive if a person invests too much mental effort in matters that should be of little concern. For example, a patient tried to avoid flashbacks by cleaning obsessively—to the extent that she was chronically late to therapy and work: "If only I could be aware of needing to get someplace on time, but I can only think of what I must clean in the moment!"

A particular field and level of consciousness can be appropriate for one situation, but not for another. A high level of conscious awareness and a retracted field of consciousness to threat cues are adaptive when one is in danger. On the other hand, it is maladaptive and exhausting to maintain this high level and small field during daily life; it would foster intense fear and chronic hypervigilance. It is adaptive to enter trance states intentionally for healthy relaxation (low level), whereas spaciness (low level) and lack of focus (unduly wide field and low level) in therapy sessions or at work are maladaptive.

Maladaptive fields and levels of consciousness occur in both traumatized and nontraumatized populations. For example, preoccupation with trauma-related issues may cause poor concentration and severe inattentiveness while driving (e.g., resulting in 19 car accidents over a 10-year period for one patient); it may even contribute to revictimization ("After he beats me and I heal, somehow I am only able to think of the good times; the bad stuff is very fuzzy in my mind.").

Etty, a patient with dissociative identity disorder (DID), dealt with dissociative intrusions by intentionally retracting her field of consciousness to an extreme degree. When plagued by persecutory voices, she tried to ignore them or drown them out by turning on the TV, radio, and CD player at the same time; she then focused on the sounds of one instrument on the CD recording. Sally, a patient with DID, often felt spacey and had tunnel vision; this low level and retracted field of consciousness usually preceded intrusions from a dissociative part (in the form of a flashback). Andy, a patient with PTSD, often felt like he was a player on a stage, merely acting out a script in a state of derealization. Andy also had symptoms of structural dissociation, such as watching himself from a distance and feeling sorry for "that man who seems so empty."

In short, *we disagree with the idea that normal and pathological dissociation lie on a single dimension, with alterations in consciousness representing the "normal" end of that dissociative continuum.* Alterations in field and level of consciousness can be quite pathological in and of themselves.

10.4 ALTERATIONS IN CONSCIOUSNESS VERSUS STRUCTURAL DISSOCIATION

Alterations in consciousness are distinct from but related to manifestations of structural dissociation. In the following, we will articulate three similarities and differences between alterations in consciousness and structural dissociation.

10.4.1 Failures of Perception and Memory

A retracted field and low level of consciousness that is accompanied by failure to perceive and remember experiences has been called "dissociation of context" (Butler, Duran, Jasiukaitis, Koopman, & Spiegel, 1996), "dissociative detachment" (Allen, Console, & Lewis, 1999), or simply, "detachment" (Holmes et al., 2005). During this so-called dissociation, the individual is too overwhelmed, preoccupied, or spacey to perceive and remember. Clearly, such alterations in consciousness can occur in the absence of a division of the personality. In fact, such alterations of consciousness are ubiquitous in both normal and clinical populations (Giesbrecht, Merckelbach, Geraerts, & Smeets, 2004; Hunter, Sierra, & David, 2004). They occur in traumatized individuals (Darves-Bornoz, Degiovanni, & Gaillard, 1999), but are not limited to them. In a word, structural dissociation does not need to exist for failures of perception and memory to occur.

Low levels and retracted fields of consciousness can impair the creation of episodic and semantic memories (Janet, 1889, 1907; Myers, 1940; Van der Hart, Van Dijke, Van Son, & Steele, 2000). When we are very tired or spacey we may remember our experiences poorly, if at all. When we are absorbed in a particular experience, our field of consciousness is retracted and we only remember the absorbing experience. Such limitations of episodic memory do not require the existence of dissociative parts of the personality.

Ted, a business executive, left stressful meetings with little conscious awareness of what had been discussed. Ted had no dissociative parts of his personality, but during these stressful meetings he was unable to concentrate and had recurring experiences of daydreaming and absentmindedness (i.e., "blank mind"). Mary, a woman with a history of child abuse and neglect, had very large gaps in her memory of childhood. She had dissociative parts, but continued to have many memory gaps after she had completely integrated her parts. When she described the unrelenting stress of her daily life as a child, it was clear that none of her parts perceived and remembered much of her childhood:

> People thought I was a space cadet. I kept my nose in a book. I tried not to pay attention, but just to stay focused on what was in front of me. I could never remember the details of things. Sometimes I can remember when I watched TV or read a book, I could almost feel this wall coming between me and the rest of the world. I didn't have to know about certain things that way.

Structural dissociation is *not* characterized by this failure to encode that occurs in many alterations in consciousness. Instead, some of the experience is always perceived and remembered by at least one part of the personality.

More than a century of clinical observations (e.g., Culpin, 1931; Janet, 1889, 1907; Kardiner, 1941; Myers, 1940; Putnam, 1989) and research (e.g., Lanius, et al., 2002; Van der Kolk, Burbridge, & Suzuki, 1997) have confirmed that patients with dissociative disorders retrieve memory differently. Dissociative parts may (1) share episodic and semantic memories (Elzinga, Phaf, Ardon, & Van Dyck, 2003; Huntjens, Postma, Peters, Woertman, & Van der Hart, 2003), (2) retrieve particular memories that are not retrieved by other dissociative parts (Dorahy, 2001), or (3) have different patterns of psychobiologic reaction to descriptions of traumatizing events (e.g., Reinders et al., 2003; see Nijenhuis & Den Boer, 2008).

10.4.2 Sense of Self

The sense of self of mentally healthy individuals alternates within relatively fixed limits. We are parents with our children, children in relation to our parents, professionals at work, and lovers of sports, books, arts, collecting, gardening, and writing. We are not always exactly the same, but our sense of self is *consistent.*

When nondissociative individuals experience alterations in consciousness, their sense of self remains relatively stable and consistent over time and experience. On the other hand, the sense of self in dissociative individuals *alternates* and is *inconsistent* across time and experience (cf., Braude, 2004). Laura had DDNOS; one part of her personality felt that she did not exist. That part said, "I'm not real. I don't feel anything. I'm not a person. I'm nothing." This outlook was related to a fixed idea: "If I'm not real, then those traumatic experiences didn't happen to me." This is a structurally dissociated person with a part that manifests a pathologically low level of consciousness regarding sense of self—a part that has a very different sense of self from Laura. Laura experienced herself as existing and being in the present; she experienced the other part as "not me."

10.4.3 Alterations in Consciousness in Dissociative Parts of the Personality

Because fluctuating fields and levels of consciousness are inherent features of consciousness, they are necessarily features of the consciousness of dissociative parts of the personality as well. It should be noted, however, that the field of consciousness of dissociative parts is usually much more retracted than that of healthy individuals. The attentional focus of dissociative parts is typically restricted by the limited range of the action systems on which they are based. For example, ANPs generally focus exclusively on daily life activities; they avoid traumatic reminders. EPs, on the other hand, focus almost exclusively on physical defense against perceived threat to life—and are unable to deal appropriately with normal life.

Different dissociative parts of the personality often have different fields and levels of consciousness in the same moment in time. While one part has a very low level of consciousness, a second part may be completely deactivated, a third part may be alert and responsive, and a fourth part may be narrowly focused on threat cues. Similarly, while one part's entire consciousness is focused on a traumatic memory, feeling, or sensation, another part may be focused on a wide variety of activities of daily life. Finally, although dissociative parts may share some conscious awareness, they may assiduously retract their fields of consciousness in order to avoid any reminders of each other.

Lowering of the level of consciousness often, but by no means always, accompanies a switch. The patient may become unfocused, drowsy, not present, and even close his or her eyes as if going to sleep. Janet (1907) described this lowering of the level of consciousness that can precede a switch:

> When the change is sudden, there is, as it seems, a loss of consciousness, a half faint. When the change is slow, one may easily observe the abasement of mental activity; the patient pays no more attention to exterior events; he understands less and less what you tell him, and he answers with difficulty, is absent-minded, works more slowly, or interrupts his work. (p. 32)

10.4.4 Complexities of Distinguishing Between Structural Dissociation and Alterations in Consciousness

In theory, it is simple to distinguish between the symptoms of structural dissociation and pathological fields and levels of conscious awareness: the former involves a division of the personality and the latter does not. In reality, these phenomena are easily confused because they tend to occur simultaneously in dissociative individuals. A person with DID often experiences alterations in consciousness (e.g., spaciness, absorption) and dissociative phenomena (e.g., intruding images or voices) at the same time.

In addition, some pathological forms of conscious awareness are phenomenologically similar to dissociative symptoms. When patients become completely unresponsive in therapy, there are at least two possible explanations: (1) they do not perceive the current situation because they are experiencing a very low level of consciousness (i.e., a pathological alteration in consciousness) or (2) their personality is, indeed, divided and a defensive part is engaged in total submission (collapse). In the latter case, another part may be listening to the therapist, but be unable to respond directly.

It often takes time, careful clinical observation, and open-ended questioning to discern the difference between an alteration of consciousness and the manifestations of structural dissociation. Nevertheless, it is imperative to discern whether these phenomena are alterations in consciousness, structural dissociation, or both. Correct treatment depends upon this distinction (e.g., Allen et al., 1999; Butler et al., 1996).

10.5 PERITRAUMATIC ALTERATIONS IN CONSCIOUSNESS VERSUS STRUCTURAL DISSOCIATION

Diverse symptoms can occur during and immediately after a traumatic event. We contend that some of these symptoms of "peritraumatic dissociation" are alterations in consciousness; other symptoms are manifestations of structural dissociation. Severe, involuntary alterations in consciousness usually occur during a traumatic experience. These phenomena may or may not be related to the development of structural dissociation.

During threat, it is adaptive to retract one's field of consciousness to focus solely on what really matters; this requires a high level of consciousness. There is also a place for low levels of consciousness during threat: total submission is adaptive when escape is impossible and physical resistance would only evoke (further) violence. The submission action system is characterized by a very low level of awareness, which inhibits movement and protects against pain and suffering. Still, retraction and lowering of consciousness during threat can be maladaptive; if a previously raped individual becomes submissive whenever she feels sexually threatened, she will severely compromise her ability to cope, resist, or escape.

Hyperalertness and hyperarousal during a traumatic experience may exhaust the individual and bring about a significant drop in the level of consciousness. This was frequently observed in "shell-shocked" soldiers during World War I (e.g., Culpin, 1931; Léri, 1918). Myers (1940) described this phenomenon in soldiers who were structurally dissociated. Immediately after the traumatizing event, there is

> a certain loss of consciousness. But this may vary from a very slight, momentary, almost imperceptible dizziness or "clouding" to profound and lasting unconsciousness. (p. 66)

Even an extremely low level of consciousness (i.e., to the point of unconsciousness) may be actually an extreme retraction of the field of consciousness—so that it includes nothing but the traumatic experience (Culpin, 1931; Léri, 1918): "the mimicry of unconsciousness was complete, but more often the man was still in contact with his environment and capable of being roused" (Culpin, 1931, p. 26). When roused, he seemed to be reliving the trauma. In the words of Léri (1918), his "whole field of attention is occupied by the haunting memory of the traumatic event itself" (p. 78; cf. Culpin, 1931; Myers, 1940). In short, the retraction of the field of consciousness was so extreme that the soldier was perceived to be unconscious.

Similarly, many survivors of chronic child abuse report that they experienced a severe drop of consciousness in the immediate wake of abuse episodes. They report hiding in closets, under blankets, or other "safe places"; there, they described themselves as "zoning out," being "unable to think," unable to concentrate, getting "lost in my head," "sinking into darkness," "closing off from my body," and feeling spacey. These experiences can occur with or without structural dissociation.

We believe that current measures of peritraumatic dissociation assess an indiscriminate mixture of alterations of consciousness and manifestations of structural dissociation. For example, Item 3 of the Peritraumatic Dissociative Experiences Questionnaire (PDEQ; Marmar, Weiss, & Metzler, 1997) states, "My sense of time changed—things seemed to be happening in slow motion." Time sense can be altered in the absence of structural dissociation.

Other measures of dissociation also assess a mixture of alterations in consciousness and manifestations of structural dissociation. For example, the Dissociative Experiences Scale (DES; Bernstein and Putnam, 1986) assesses absorption: "Some people find that when they are watching television or a movie they become so absorbed in the story that they are unaware of other events happening around them." In the absence of structural dissociation, an individual likely retains a consistent sense of self during such an experience; she simply does not perceive and remember what was happening: "I just lay there (during a rape) and focused on a song in my head. I don't remember what the man said to me." This survivor experienced *herself* as being raped, but did not recall much about the rape because her attentional focus was turned inward in an attempt to avoid a terrible experience. A patient such as this will never remember much about the event because she did not perceive the entire event in the first place.

Ideally, measures of peritraumatic dissociation should distinguish between manifestations of structural dissociation and alterations in consciousness. Still, it can be quite difficult to determine whether certain items tap structural dissociation or an alteration in consciousness.

Despite these psychometric problems, measures of peritraumatic dissociation have shown clinical and empirical value. Numerous retrospective and prospective studies indicate that peritraumatic dissociation—however imperfectly it may be measured—is experienced by a substantial number of individuals who are exposed to severe stressors (e.g., Goenjian et al., 2000; Koopman, Classen, & Spiegel, 1994; Marmar et al., 1994; Morgan et al., 2001; Nijenhuis, Van Engen, Kusters, & Van der Hart, 2001; Olde et al., 2005; Shalev, Peri, Canetti, & Schreiber, 1996; Tichenor, Marmar, Weiss, Metzler, & Ronfeldt, 1996). Moreover, many studies have shown that peritraumatic dissociation predicts the development of PTSD (e.g., Benotsch et al., 2000; Dunsmore, Clark, & Ehlers, 1998; Epstein, Fullerton, & Ursano,

1998; Griffin, Resick, & Mechanic, 1997; Roemer, Orsillo, Borkovec, & Litz, 1998). These findings show a strong association between alterations in consciousness and manifestations of structural dissociation in trauma survivors.

10.6 SYMPTOMS OF DEPERSONALIZATION AND DEREALIZATION AS ALTERATIONS IN CONSCIOUSNESS AND STRUCTURAL DISSOCIATION

Although depersonalization and derealization have long been held to be dissociative symptoms, we believe that many (but not all) manifestations of depersonalization and derealization are alterations in consciousness.

Depersonalization has been described as (1) the existence of an observing and experiencing ego or part of the personality (Fromm, 1965); (2) detachment of consciousness from the self or body (i.e., feelings of strangeness or unfamiliarity with self, out-of-body experiences); (3) detachment from affect (i.e., numbness); (4) a sense of unreality such as being in a dream; and (5) perceptual alterations or hallucinations regarding the body (Noyes & Kletti, 1977). *Derealization* involves a sense of unreality or unfamiliarity with one's environment, and distortions of space and time (Steinberg, 1995). The primary difficulty in depersonalization may be a disruption in the focus of attention (i.e., alterations in consciousness; Guralnik, Schmeidler, & Simeon, 2000).

Both depersonalization and derealization occur with intact reality testing (Steinberg, 1993). Although neither necessarily involves a division of the personality, we believe that the presence of an "observing ego," observing part of the personality, or out-of-body experience is a hallmark of structural dissociation. Most other symptoms of depersonalization, however, reflect alterations in consciousness. According to Steinberg (1995), "pathological" depersonalization is distinguished by a dissociation between an observing ego and an experiencing ego; this is a structural dissociation of the personality. In a similar vein, Putnam (1997) has proposed that dissociation between an observing and an experiencing ego or part is different from other symptoms of depersonalization (i.e., hose that are characterized by alterations in consciousness). Such divisions between an observing part and an experiencing part have been described by victims of childhood sexual abuse (Gelinas, 1983; Putnam, 1997), victims of motor vehicle accidents (Noyes & Kletti, 1977), and soldiers in combat (Cloet, 1972). Schwartz (2000) illustrates structural dissociation in describing an observing part of the personality in a survivor of chronic, organized sexual abuse:

> When they made me dance … in front of all those men I just took three steps backwards, and then there was some girl there and she was dancing for them, and I watched her do it from far away … she was not me, but I could see her. I didn't like her and I didn't like what she was doing. Even though I know she is me, she is not really me. (p. 40)

When a person exhibits depersonalization, it is often difficult to determine whether structural dissociation is present (Van der Hart & Steele, 1997). In part, this difficulty is often due to the joint presence of structural dissociation and alterations in consciousness. This interpretation is consistent with the finding that high scores on the DES-Taxon are obtained by only a subset of persons with depersonalization disorder (Simeon et al., 1998). In fact, it seems likely that many individuals who have symptoms of depersonalization and derealization do *not* have structural dissociation. Why? Because these symptoms are reported by a substantial proportion of the general population (Aderibigbe, Bloch, & Walker, 2001), while symptoms of structural dissociation are not.

Symptoms of depersonalization and derealization are so prevalent that Cattell and Cattell (1974) found them to be the third most common complaint in psychiatric patients (following anxiety and depression). Mild to severe forms of depersonalization and derealization are found in anxiety disorders, depression, schizophrenia, substance abuse disorders, borderline personality disorder (BPD), seizure disorders, and dissociative disorders (Boon & Draijer, 1993; Dell, 2002; Steinberg, 1995). In normal individuals, these symptoms may be related to stress, hypnagogic states, fatigue, illness, medication, or intoxication. Note that these latter instances of depersonalization typically reflect only an alteration in consciousness. We still know too little, however, about which symptoms of depersonalization occur under which conditions.

Symptoms of depersonalization and derealization are commonly reported in trauma victims (e.g., Cardeña & Spiegel, 1993; Carrion & Steiner, 2000; Darves-Bornoz, Degiovanni, & Gaillard, 1999; Harvey & Bryant, 1998) and persons with trauma-related disorders such as acute stress disorder (ASD; Harvey & Bryant, 1998, 1999), PTSD (Bremner et al., 1993), BPD (Şar et al., 2003; Zanarini, Ruser, Frankenburg, & Hennen, 2000), and complex dissociative disorders (Boon & Draijer, 1993; Dell, 2002; Steinberg, 1995).

Although persons with depersonalization disorder (DPD) have a high rate of childhood traumatization, especially of emotional maltreatment (Simeon et al., 2001), Simeon (2004) contends that DPD does not involve the disturbances of memory or identity that would be consistent with structural dissociation. Persons with DPD and persons with structural dissociation share some neurobiological correlates: HPA axis dysregulation and disturbances of serotonergic, endogenous opioid, and glutamatergic NMDA pathways (e.g., Nijenhuis, Van der Hart, & Steele, 2002; Simeon et al., 2000). But there are differences as well. We believe that these facts support our clinical observation: *structural dissociation and alterations in consciousness are closely related, but they are, nevertheless, different concepts.*

10.7 ALTERATIONS IN CONSCIOUSNESS AND DISSOCIATIVE SYMPTOMS: RESEARCH FINDINGS

Research supports the idea that retraction and lowering of consciousness may accompany, but are different from, structural dissociation. The absorption factor of the Dissociation Questionnaire (DIS-Q; Vanderlinden, Van Dyck, Vandereycken, Vertommen, & Verkes, 1993) only correlates modestly with the DIS-Q's other three factors; conversely, the amnesia factor, identity fragmentation factor, and loss of control factor—which indicate structural dissociation—correlate highly with one another. Similarly, scores on the Somatoform Dissociation Questionnaire (SDQ-20; Nijenhuis et al., 1996)—a strong measure of structural dissociation (Nijenhuis et al., 1997, 1998)—correlate more weakly with the DIS-Q absorption factor than they do with the DIS-Q's other three factors (Nijenhuis, Spinhoven, Van Dyck, Van der Hart, & Vanderlinden, 1996). Finally, we believe that the DES's "nonpathological" items (see Waller, Putnam, & Carlson, 1996) do not tap structural dissociation; conversely, at least five of the DES-T's eight "pathological" items (see Waller, Putnam, & Carlson, 1996) *do* suggest structural dissociation (e.g., being commanded by voices, observing one's body from a distance, and the experience of being two or more different "people").

Research suggests two interesting facts: (1) most persons who experience alterations in consciousness do not have structural dissociation, and (2) most persons with structural dissociation do have alterations in consciousness. Leavitt (2001) found that alterations in consciousness were prominent among patients with all kinds of mental disorders, not just trauma-related disorders. He reported that the severity of alterations in consciousness was associated with general psychopathology (in both dissociative and nondissociative patients). These findings reiterate two points: (1) alterations in consciousness are not unique to dissociative individuals and (2) some alterations of consciousness fall outside the normal range (cf. Carlson, 1994).

These findings show that alterations in consciousness are *sensitive but not specific* indicators of structural dissociation. That is, structurally dissociated persons typically display alterations in consciousness, but few persons with alterations in consciousness are structurally dissociated. Irwin (1999) reported that "pathological" dissociation (i.e., structural dissociation) is associated with exposure to highly stressful events, but that "nonpathological" dissociation (i.e., alterations in consciousness) is not.

In a recent important paper, Holmes and colleagues (2005) marshaled evidence that "detachment" (a form of altered consciousness) and "compartmentalization" (structural dissociation) are qualitatively distinct phenomena. They asserted that the evidence of a qualitative distinction between detachment and compartmentalization "directly contrasts with the common notion that these experiences lie on the same continuum … somewhere between 'daydreaming' and 'Dissociative Identity Disorder'" (p. 12). They contend that detachment and compartmentalizaton are different in kind, rather than degree. Although we disagree with Holmes and colleagues' proposal to abandon the term *dissociation*, as it has a clear historical definition that reflects the symptoms of traumatized individuals, we fully agree with their assessment of the differences between compartmentalization (their substitute for *dissociation*) and detachment, which they do not regard as dissociative in nature. We prefer to call compartmentalization *structural dissociation* and detachment *alterations in consciousness.*

10.8 THE RELEGATION OF STRUCTURAL DISSOCIATION TO COMPLEX DISSOCIATIVE DISORDERS

The confusion between alterations in consciousness and dissociation seems to derive from two related diagnostic problems. First, an overly vague notion of a breakdown or disruption in usually integrated functioning (APA, 2000) has been used to define dissociation. In the absence of a detailed specification of the effects or symptoms of a *breakdown of integrated functioning*, the symptoms of breakdown have been defined overinclusively to include alterations in level and field of consciousness. Second, structural dissociation has been relegated to the severe dissociative disorders (i.e., DID and some forms of Dissociative Disorders Not Otherwise Specified; DDNOS) while its role in other trauma-related disorders has been neglected.

There is general agreement in the literature that (1) DID is the most extreme form of PTSD (e.g., Chu, 1998; Dell, 1998; Spiegel, 1993) and (2) the core pathology of DID is dissociation (e.g., Boon & Draijer, 1993; Kluft, 1996; Putnam, 1989; Ross, 1989). At the same time, however, the traumatic stress field seems to have avoided thinking of PTSD as a dissociative disorder (that might be conceptually linked to DID).

There is agreement that peritraumatic dissociation is a common precursor to PTSD, and that ongoing "dissociation" (which in most publications includes abnormal shifts in field and level of consciousness) occurs in ASD, PTSD, and trauma-related BPD. Typically, however, dissociation is only listed as one of many symptoms; it is not considered to be an underlying psychobiological organization or structure (e.g., Bremner, 2003; Brodsky, Cloitre, & Dulit, 1995; Davidson, Kudler, Saunders, & Smith, 1989; Feeny, Zoellner, Fitzgibbons, & Foa, 2000; Harvey & Bryant, 1999; see Gershuny & Thayer, 1999, for a review). Even when the dissociative nature of trauma-related disorders is noted, as in ASD (e.g., Spiegel, Koopman, Cardeña, & Classen, 1996), it is not acknowledged that dissociation is *an underlying structure* (that manifests itself in the form of dissociative symptoms).

The theory of structural dissociation of the personality proposes that all trauma-related disorders are linked by a common psychobiological division of the personality. The nature and severity of dissociative symptoms are related to the extent of that psychobiological division—the number of divisions and their degree of mutual impermeability. Some authors have noted the dissociative underpinnings of PTSD (e.g., Braun, 1993; Chu, 1998; Nijenhuis et al., 2004; Van der Hart et al., 2004); there has even been a debate about whether to classify PTSD as a dissociative disorder (Brett, 1996). Brett cited the vagueness of the definition of dissociation as a primary reason for continuing to classify PTSD as an anxiety disorder. Others have noted that trauma-related cases of BPD and complex PTSD are fundamentally dissociative (Blizard, 2003; Golynkina & Ryle, 1999; Howell, 2002; Van der Hart, Nijenhuis, & Steele, 2005).

The reluctance of the trauma field to recognize structural dissociation as an underlying psychobiological organization has contributed to clinicians' tendency to dismiss dissociation as "irrelevant" to clinical conceptualization and treatment. By limiting their acknowledgment of dissociation to the status of "a few irrelevant symptoms," clinicians too easily fail to recognize that structural dissociation may underlie complex behaviors and symptoms such as recurrent substance use, affect dysregulation, or chronic difficulties in relationships. Remember, a hallmark of structural dissociation is that many symptoms are not immediately obvious; they may even be intentionally hidden by a frightened or ashamed individual (Kluft, 1987, 1996; Loewenstein, 1991; Steinberg, 1995). Dissociative parts of the personality seldom present as clear-cut "dissociative identities"; rather, they tend to present as symptom-complexes that seem unrelated to dissociation.

10.9 DISCUSSION

There is major conceptual confusion regarding the term *dissociation.* We believe that this confusion has at least four sources: (1) alterations in consciousness have been incorrectly added to the concept of dissociation (which originally meant a division of the personality); (2) structural dissociation and alterations in consciousness typically co-occur in traumatized persons; (3) some alterations in consciousness and most forms of structural dissociation involve a temporary or chronic integrative deficit; and (4) structural dissociation has been relegated solely to psychiatric conditions where it is clearly observable (e.g., DID), rather than to all trauma-related disorders.

These factors have produced a lack of consensus about what is and what is not *dissociative.* Some suggest that the term *dissociation* should be abandoned (e.g., Holmes et al., 2005). Others have proposed that dissociation is a multidimensional concept that involves such diverse experiences as disengagement, depersonalization, emotional constriction, multiplicity, amnestic experiences, gaps in awareness, absorption, and imaginative involvement (e.g., Bernstein & Putnam, 1986; Briere, 2002). We think that such a multidimensional concept of dissociation is too vague and too broad.

The distinction between structural dissociation and alterations in consciousness has major implications for identifying truly discriminating indicators of dissociative pathology. This is critical because dissociative disorders are so often misdiagnosed. Because the clinical distinction between dissociation and alterations in consciousness is often difficult to discern, we need to identify additional distinctions between structural dissociation and alterations in consciousness.

Even though retraction of the field and lowering of the level of consciousness can occur in the absence of structural dissociation, they may typically accompany it in trauma survivors. Consequently, the presence of these alterations, especially in chronic pathological forms, should alert the clinician to the possibility of structural dissociation.

Peritraumatic dissociation and depersonalization disorder are two logical targets for further study of the differences between alterations in consciousness and structural dissociation. We should also compare dissociative and nondissociative individuals who experience pathological states of absorption and fantasy proneness. Somer (2002) noted that when pathological daydreamers do not have a dissociative disorder, their DES scores were much lower than those of daydreamers with a dissociative disorder. Moreover, unlike the dissociative group, the nondissociative maladaptive daydreamers reported no history of childhood physical, sexual, or emotional abuse, despite having other adverse childhood experiences.

Much research remains to be done. We must study (1) the extent to which structural dissociation can exist in normal individuals; (2) the neurobiological and psychological underpinnings of pathological alterations in consciousness; and (3) the differential correlates (e.g., trauma history, other psychopathology, cognition, brain activity, etc.) of structural dissociation and alterations of consciousness.

In summary, we have delineated a theoretical framework that differentiates alterations in consciousness from trauma-related dissociative manifestations of a division of the personality. Future research will assess the clinical utility and empirical accuracy of our theory.

REFERENCES

Aderibigbe, Y. A., Bloch, R. M., & Walker, W. R. (2001). Prevalence of depersonalization and derealization experiences in a rural population. *Social Psychiatry & Psychiatric Epidemiology, 36*, 63–69.

Allen, J. G., Console, D. A., & Lewis, L. (1999). Dissociative detachment and memory impairment: Reversible amnesia or encoding failure? *Comprehensive Psychiatry, 40*, 160–171.

American Psychiatric Association (2000). *DSM-IV-TR–Diagnostic and statistical manual of mental disorders* (4th ed., text rev.). Washington, DC: Author.

Benotsch, E. G., Brailey, K., Vasterling, J. J., Uddo, M., Constans, J. I., & Sutker, P. B. (2000). War zone stress, personal and environmental resources, and PTSD in Gulf War veterans. *Journal of Abnormal Psychology, 109*, 205–213.

Bernstein, E. M., & Putnam, F. W. (1986). Development, reliability, and validity of a dissociation scale. *Journal of Nervous and Mental Disease, 174*, 727–735.

Blizard, R. (2003). Disorganized attachment: Development of dissociated self states & a relational approach to treatment. *Journal of Trauma & Dissociation, 4*(3), 27–50.

Boon, S., & Draijer, N. (1993). *Multiple personality disorder in the Netherlands*. Amsterdam: Swets & Zeitlinger.

Bowins, B. (2004). Psychological defense mechanisms: A new perspective. *American Journal of Psychoanalysis, 64*, 1–26.

Bowman, E. S. (1998). Pseudoseizures. *Psychiatric Clinics of North America, 21*, 649–657.

Braude, S. E. (2004). Memory: The nature and significance of dissociation. In J. Radden (Ed.), *The philosophy of psychiatry: A companion* (pp. 106–117). Oxford: Oxford University Press.

Braun, B. G. (1993). Multiple personality disorder and posttraumatic stress disorder: Similarities and differences. In J. P. Wilson & B. Raphael (Eds.), *International handbook of traumatic stress syndromes* (pp. 35–47). New York: Plenum Press.

Bremner, J. D. (2003). Long-term effects of childhood abuse on brain and neurobiology. *Child & Adolescent Psychiatric Clinics of North America, 12*, 271–292.

Bremner, J. D., Southwick, S. M., Johnson, D. R., Yehuda, R., & Charney, D. S. (1993). Childhood physical abuse in combat-related posttraumatic stress disorder in Vietnam veterans. *American Journal of Psychiatry, 150*, 235–239.

Brett, E. A. (1996). The classification of posttraumatic stress disorder. In B. A. Van der Kolk, A. C. McFarlane, & L. Weisaeth (Eds.), *Traumatic stress* (pp. 117–128). New York: Guilford Press.

Briere, J. (2002). *Multiscale Dissociation Inventory*. Odessa, FL: Psychological Assessment Resources.

Brodsky, B. S., Cloitre, M., & Dulit, R. A. (1995). Relationship of dissociation to self-mutilation and childhood abuse in borderline personality disorder. *American Journal of Psychiatry, 152*, 1788–1792.

Brunet, A., Holowka D., & Laurence, J. R. (2002). Dissociative phenomena. In M. J. Aminoff & R. B. Daroff (Eds.), *Encyclopedia of the neurological sciences* (pp. 25–27). San Diego: Academic Press.

Butler, L. D. (2004). Editorial: The dissociation of everyday life. *Journal of Trauma & Dissociation, 5*(1), 1–11.

Butler, L. D., Duran, R. E. F., Jasiukaitis, P., Koopman, C., & Spiegel, D. (1996). Hypnotizability and traumatic experience: A diathesis-stress model of dissociative symptomatology. *American Journal of Psychiatry, 153 (Suppl. 7S)*, 42–63.

Cardeña, E. (1994). The domain of dissociation. In S. J. Lynn & J. W. Rhue (Eds.), *Dissociation: Clinical and theoretical perspectives* (pp. 15–31). New York: Guilford.

Cardeña, E., & Spiegel, D. (1993). Dissociative reactions to the San Francisco Bay Area earthquake of 1989. *American Journal of Psychiatry, 150*, 474–478.

Carlson, E. B. (1994). Studying the interaction between physical and psychological states with the Dissociative Experiences Scale. In D. Spiegel (Ed.), *Dissociation: Culture, mind and body* (pp. 41–58). Washington, DC: American Psychiatric Press.

Carrion, V. G., & Steiner, H. (2000). Trauma and dissociation in delinquent adolescents. *Journal of the American Academy of Child and Adolescent Psychiatry, 39*, 353–359.

Carver, C. S., Sutton, S. K., & Scheier, M. F. (2000). Action, emotion, and personality: Emerging conceptual integration. *Personality and Social Psychology Bulletin, 26*, 741–751.

Cassidy, J. (1999). The nature of the child's ties. In J. Cassidy & P. R. Shaver (Eds.), *Handbook of attachment* (pp. 3–20). New York: Guilford.

Cattell, J. P., & Cattell, J. S. (1974). Depersonalization: Psychological and social perspectives. In S. Arieti (Ed.), *American handbook of psychiatry* (2nd ed., pp. 766–799). New York: Basic Books.

Chu, J. A. (1998). *Rebuilding shattered lives: The responsible treatment of complex posttraumatic stress and dissociative disorders.* New York: Wiley.

Cloete, S. (1972). *A Victorian son: An autobiography*. London: Collins.

Culpin, M. (1931). *Recent advances in the study of the psychoneuroses*. Philadelphia: P. Blakiston's Son & Co.

Darves-Bornoz, J.-M., Degiovanni, A., & Gaillard, P. (1999). Validation of a French version of the Dissociative Experiences Scale in a rape-victim population. *Canadian Journal of Psychiatry, 44*, 271–275.

Davidson, J., Kudler, H., Saunders, W. B., & Smith, R. D. (1989). Symptom and comorbidity patterns in World War II and Vietnam veterans with PTSD. *Comprehensive Psychiatry, 31*, 162–170.

Dell, P. F. (1998). Axis II pathology in outpatients with dissociative identity disorder. *Journal of Nervous and Mental Disease, 186*, 352–356.

Dell, P. F. (2002). Dissociative phenomenology of dissociative identity disorder. *Journal of Nervous and Mental Disease, 190*, 10–15.

Dell, P. F. (2009). The phenomena of chronic pathological dissociation. In P. F. Dell & J. A. O'Neil (Eds.), *Dissociation and the dissociative disorders: DSM-V and beyond* (pp. 225–237). New York: Routledge.

Dorahy, M. J. (2001). Dissociative identity disorder and memory dysfunction: The current state of experimental research, and its future directions. *Clinical Psychology Review, 21*, 771–795.

Dunsmore, E., Clark, D. M., & Ehlers, A. (1999). Cognitive factors involved in the onset and maintenance of posttraumatic stress disorder (PTSD) after physical and sexual assault. *Behaviour, Research, and Therapy, 37*, 808–829.

Elzinga, B. M., Phaf, R. H., Ardon, A. M., & Van Dyck, R. (2003). Directed forgetting between, but not within, dissociative personality states. *Journal of Abnormal Psychology, 112*, 237–243.

Epstein, R. S., Fullerton, C. S., & Ursano, R. J. (1998). Posttraumatic stress disorder following an air disaster: A prospective study. *American Journal of Psychiatry, 155*, 934–938.

Feeny, N. C., Zoellner, L. A., Fitzgibbons, L. A., & Foa, E. B. (2000). Exploring the roles of emotional numbing, depression and dissociation in PTSD. *Journal of Traumatic Stress, 13*, 489–498.

Frankel, F. H. (1996). Dissociation: The clinical realities. *American Journal of Psychiatry, 153*, 64–70.

Fromm, E. (1965). Hypnoanalysis: Theory and two case excerpts. *Psychotherapy: Theory, Research, and Practice, 2*, 127–133.

Fullerton, C. S., Ursano, R. J., Epstein, R. S., Crowley, B., Vance, K. L., Kao, T. C., & Baum, A. (2000). Peritraumatic dissociation following motor vehicle accidents: Relationship to prior trauma and prior major depression. *Journal of Nervous and Mental Disease, 188*, 267–272.

Gelinas, D. J. (1983). The persisting negative effects of incest. *Psychiatry, 46*, 312–332.

Gershuny, B. S., & Thayer, J. F. (1999). Relations among psychological trauma, dissociative phenomena, and trauma-related distress: A review and integration. *Clinical Psychology Review, 19*, 631–657.

Giesbrecht, T., Merckelbach, H., Geraerts, E., & Smeets, E. (2004). Dissociation in undergraduate students: Disruptions in executive functioning. *Journal of Nervous and Mental Disease, 192*, 567–569.

Goenjian, A. K., Steinberg, A. M., Najarian, L. M., Fairbanks, L. A., Tashjian, M., & Pynoos, R. S. (2000). Prospective study of posttraumatic stress, anxiety, and depressive reactions after earthquake and political violence. *American Journal of Psychiatry, 157*, 911–1491.

Golynkina, K., & Ryle, A. (1999). The identification and characteristics of the partially dissociated states of patients with borderline personality disorder. *British Journal of Medical Psychology, 77*, 429–445.

Griffin, M. G., Resick, P. A., & Mechanic, M. B. (1997). Objective assessment of peritraumatic dissociation: Psychophysiological indicators. *American Journal of Psychiatry, 154*, 1081–1088.

Guralnik, O., Schmeidler, J., & Simeon, D. (2000) Feeling unreal: Cognitive processes in depersonalization. *American Journal of Psychiatry, 157*, 103–109.

Harvey, A. G., & Bryant, R. A. (1998). The relationship between acute stress disorder and posttraumatic stress disorder: A prospective evaluation of motor vehicle accident survivors. *Journal of Consulting and Clinical Psychology, 66*, 507–512.

Harvey, A. G., & Bryant, R. A. (1999). Dissociative symptoms in acute stress disorder. *Journal of Traumatic Stress, 12*, 673–680.

Holmes, E. A., Brown, R. J., Mansell, W., Fearon, R. P., Hunter, E. C. M., Frasquilho, F., & Oakley, D. A. (2005). Are there two qualitatively distinct forms of dissociation? A review and some clinical implications. *Clinical Psychology Review, 25*, 1–23.

Howell, E. F. (2002). Back to the "states": Victim and abuser states in borderline personality disorder. *Psychoanalytic Dialogues, 12*, 921–958.

Hunter, E. C., Sierra, M., & David, A. S. (2004). The epidemiology of depersonalisation and derealisation: A systematic review. *Social Psychiatry and Psychiatric Epidemiology, 39*, 9–18.

Huntjens, R. J. C., Postma, A., Peters, M. L., Woertman, L., & Van der Hart, O. (2003). Interidentity amnesia for neutral, episodic information in dissociative identity disorder. *Journal of Abnormal Psychology, 112*, 290–297.

Irwin, H. J. (1999). Pathological and nonpathological dissociation: The relevance of childhood trauma. *Journal of Psychology, 133*, 157–164.

Janet, P. (1889). *L'automatisme psychologique: Essai de psychologie expérimentale sur les formes inférieures de l'activité humaine* [Psychological automatism: Essays from experimental psychology on the inferior forms of human activity] Paris: Félix Alcan. Reprint: Paris: Société Pierre Janet, 1973.

Janet, P. (1903). *Les obsessions et la psychasthénie* [Obsessions and psychasthenia] Vol. 1. Paris: Félix Alcan.

Janet, P. (1907). *The major symptoms of hysteria*. London/New York: Macmillan. Reprint of 1920 edition: New York: Hafner, 1965.

Kardiner, A. (1941). *The traumatic neuroses of war*. New York: Paul B. Hoeber.

Kluft, R. P. (1987). The simulation and dissimulation of multiple personality disorder. *American Journal of Clinical Hypnosis, 30*, 104–118.

Kluft, R. P. (1996). Dissociative identity disorder. In L. K. Michelson & W. J. Ray (Eds.), *Handbook of dissociation* (pp. 337–366). New York: Plenum.

Koopman, C., Classen, C., & Spiegel, D. (1994). Predictors of posttraumatic stress symptoms among survivors of the Oakland/Berkeley, California firestorm. *American Journal of Psychiatry, 151*, 888–894.

Kuyk, J. (1999). *Pseudo-epileptic seizures: Differential diagnosis and psychological characteristics*. Amsterdam: Vrije Universiteit.

Lang, P. J., Bradley, M. M., & Cuthbert, B. N. (1998). Emotion, motivation, and anxiety: Brain mechanisms and psychophysiology. *Biological Psychiatry, 44*, 1248–1263.

Lanius, R. A., Williamson, P. C., Boksman, K., Densmore, M., Gupta, M., Neufeld, R. W., Gati, J. S., & Menon, R. S. (2002). Brain activation during script-driven imagery induced dissociative responses in PTSD: A functional magnetic resonance imaging investigation. *Biological Psychiatry, 52*, 305–311.

Leavitt, F. (2001). MMPI profile characteristics of women with varying levels of normal dissociation. *Journal of Clinical Psychology, 57*, 1469–1477.

Léri, A. (1918). *Commotions et émotions de guerre*. [Shocks and emotions of war] Paris: Masson & Cie.

Loewenstein, R. J. (1991). An office mental status examination for complex chronic dissociative symptoms and multiple personality disorder. *Psychiatric Clinics of North America, 14*, 567–604.

Luria, A. R. (1968). *The mind of a mnemonist*. New York: Avon Books.

Marmar, C. R., Weiss, D. S., & Metzler, T. (1997). The peritraumatic dissociative experiences questionnaire. In J. P. Wilson & T. M. Keane (Eds.), *Assessing psychological trauma and PTSD* (pp. 412–428). New York: Guilford Press.

Marmar, C. R., Weiss, D. S., Schlenger, W. F., Fairbank, J. A., Jordon, K., Kulka, R. A., & Hough, R. L. (1994). Peritraumatic dissociation and posttraumatic stress in male Vietnam theater veterans. *American Journal of Psychiatry, 151*, 902–907.

Marshall, R. D., Spitzer, R., & Liebowitz, M. R. (1999). Review and critique of the new DSM-IV diagnosis of acute stress disorder. *American Journal of Psychiatry, 156*, 1677–1685.

Mitchell, T. W. (1922). *Medical psychology and psychical research*. London: Methuen & Co.

Morgan, C. A., Hazlett, G., Wang, S., Richardson, E. G., Schnurr, P., & Southwick, S. M. (2001). Symptoms of dissociation in humans experiencing acute, uncontrollable stress: A prospective investigation. *American Journal of Psychiatry, 158*, 1239–1247.

Myers, C. S. (1940). *Shell shock in France 1914-18*. Cambridge: Cambridge University Press.

Nijenhuis, E. R. S., & Den Boer, J. A. (2009). Psychobiology of traumatization and structural dissociation of the personality. In P. F. Dell & J. A. O'Neil (Eds.), *Dissociation and the dissociative disorders: DSM-V and beyond* (pp. 337–365). New York: Routledge.

Nijenhuis, E. R. S., Spinhoven, P., Van Dyck, R., Van der Hart, O., & Vanderlinden, J. (1996). The development and psychometric characteristics of the somatoform dissociation questionnaire (SDQ-20). *Journal of Nervous and Mental Disease, 184*, 688–694.

Nijenhuis, E. R., Spinhoven, P., Van Dyck, R., Van der Hart, O., & Vanderlinden, J. (1997). The development of the somatoform dissociation questionnaire (SDQ-5) as a screening instrument for dissociative disorders. *Acta Psychiatrica Scandinavia, 96*, 311–318.

Nijenhuis, E. R., Spinhoven, P., Van Dyck, R., Van der Hart, O., & Vanderlinden, J. (1998). Degree of somatoform and psychological dissociation in dissociative disorder is correlated with reported trauma. *Journal of Traumatic Stress, 11*, 711–730.

Nijenhuis, E. R. S., & Van der Hart, O. (1999). Somatoform dissociative phenomena: A Janetian perspective. In J. M. Goodwin & R. Attias (Eds.), *Splintered reflections: Images of the body in trauma* (pp. 89–127). New York: Basic Books.

Nijenhuis, E. R. S., Van der Hart, O., & Steele, K. (2002). The emerging psychobiology of trauma-related dissociation and dissociative disorders. In H. D'haenen, J. A. Den Boer, & P. Willner (Eds.), *Biological Psychiatry* (pp. 1079–1098). New York: Wiley and Sons.

Nijenhuis, E. R. S., Van der Hart, O., & Steele, K. (2004). Strukturelle Dissoziation der Persönlichkeitsstruktur: traumatischer Upsprung, phobische Residuen [Structural dissociation of the personality: Traumatic origins, phobic maintenance]. In A. Hofmann, L. Reddemann, & U. Gast (Eds.), *Psychotherapie der dissoziativen Störungen* [Psychotherapy of dissociative disorders] (pp. 47–69). Stuttgart/New York: Georg Thieme Verlag.

Nijenhuis, E. R. S., Van Engen, A., Kusters, I., & Van der Hart, O. (2001). Peritraumatic somatoform and psychological dissociation in relation to recall of childhood sexual abuse. *Journal of Trauma & Dissociation, 2*(3), 49–68.

Noyes, R., & Kletti, R. (1979). Depersonalization in response to life-threatening danger. *Psychiatry, 18*, 375–384.

Ogawa, J. R., Sroufe, L. A., Weinfield, N. S., Carlson, E. A., & Egeland, B. (1997). Development and the fragmented self: A longitudinal study of dissociative symptomatology in a normative sample. *Development and Psychopathology, 9*, 855–879.

Olde, E., Van der Hart, O., Kleber, R., Van Son, M., Wijnen, H., & Pop, V. (2005). Peritraumatic dissociation and emotions as predictors of PTSD symptoms following childbirth. *Journal of Trauma & Dissociation, 6(3)*, 125–142.

Panksepp, J. (1998). *Affective neuroscience: The foundations of human and animal emotions.* New York: Oxford University Press.

Prince, M. (1905). *The dissociation of a personality.* London: Longmans, Green & Co.

Putnam, F. W. (1989). *Diagnosis and treatment of multiple personality disorder.* New York: Guilford.

Putnam, F. W. (1997). *Dissociation in children and adolescents: A developmental perspective.* New York: Guilford.

Ray, W. J. (1996). Dissociation in normal populations. In L. K. Michelson & W. J. Ray (Eds.), *Handbook of dissociation: Theoretical, empirical, and clinical perspectives* (pp. 51–66). New York: Plenum Press.

Ray, W. J., & Faith, M. (1995). Dissociative experiences in a college age population: Follow-up with 1190 subjects. *Personality and Individual Differences, 18*, 223–230.

Reinders, A. A. T. S., Nijenhuis, E. R. S., Paans, A. M. J., Korf, J., Willemsen, A. T. M., & Den Boer, J. A. (2003). One brain, two selves. *NeuroImage, 20*, 2119–2125.

Roemer, L., Orsillo, S. M., Borkovec, T. D., & Litz, B. T. (1998). Emotional response at the time of a potentially traumatizing event and PTSD symptomatology: A preliminary retrospective analysis of the DSM-IV Criterion A-2. *Journal of Behavioral Therapy and Experimental Psychiatry, 29*, 123–113.

Ross, C. A. (1989). *Multiple personality disorder: Diagnosis, clinical features and treatment.* New York: Wiley.

Ross, C. A., Joshi, S., & Currie, R. (1991). Dissociative experiences in the general population: A factor analysis. *Hospital and Community Psychiatry, 42*, 297–301.

Şar, V., Kundakçı, T., Kızıltan, E., Yargıç, I. L., Tutkun, H., Bakım, B., Bozkurt, O., Özpulat, T., Keser, V., & Özdemir, Ö. (2003). The axis-I dissociative disorder comorbidity of borderline personality disorder patients among psychiatric outpatients. *Journal of Trauma & Dissociation, 4*(1), 119–116.

Schwartz, H. L. (2000). *Dialogues with forgotten voices: Relational perspectives on child abuse trauma and treatment of dissociative disorders.* New York: Basic Behavioral Science.

Shalev, A. Y., Peri, T., Canetti, L., & Screiber, S. (1996). Predictors of PTSD in injured trauma survivors: A prospective study. *American Journal of Psychiatry, 153*, 219–225.

Simeon, D. (2004). Depersonalisation disorder: A contemporary overview. *CNS Drugs, 18*, 343–354.

Simeon, D., Guralnik, O., Gross, S., Stein, D. J., Schmeidler, J., & Hollander, E. (1998). The detection and measurement of depersonalization disorder. *Journal of Nervous and Mental Disease, 186*, 536–542.

Simeon, D., Guralnik, O., Hazlett, E. A., Spiegel-Cohen, J., Hollander, E., & Buchsbaum, M. S. (2000). Feeling unreal: A PET study of depersonalization disorder. *American Journal of Psychiatry, 157*, 1782–1788.

Simeon, D., Guralnik, O., Schmeidler, J., Sirof, B., & Knutelska, M. (2001). The role of childhood interpersonal trauma in depersonalization disorder. *American Journal of Psychiatry, 158*, 1027–1528.

Somer, E. (2002). Maladaptive daydreaming: A qualitative study. *Journal of Contemporary Psychotherapy, 32*, 197–212.

Spiegel, D. (1993). Multiple posttraumatic personality disorder. In R. P. Kluft & C. G. Fine (Eds.), *Clinical perspectives on multiple personality disorder* (pp. 87–99). Washington, DC: American Psychiatric Press.

Spiegel, D., Koopman, C., Cardeña, E., & Classen, C. (1996). Dissociative symptoms in the diagnosis of acute stress disorder. In L. K. Michelson & W. J. Ray (Eds.), *Handbook of dissociation* (pp. 367–380). New York: Plenum.

Steele, K., Van der Hart, O., & Nijenhuis, E. R. S. (2004). Allgemeine Behandlungsstrategien komplexer dissoziativer Störungen [General treatment strategies for complex dissociative disorders]. In A. Eckhart-Henn & S. O. Hoffman (Eds.), *Dissoziative Störungen des Bewußtseins* [Dissociative disorders of consciousness] (pp. 357–394). Stuttgart: Schatterauer-Verlag.

Steele, K., Van der Hart, O., & Nijenhuis, E. R. S. (2005). Phase-oriented treatment of structural dissociation in complex traumatization: Overcoming trauma-related phobias. *Journal of Trauma & Dissociation, 6*(3), 11–53.

Steele, K., Van der Hart, O., & Nijenhuis, E. R. S. (2009). The theory of trauma-related structural dissociation of the personality. In P. F. Dell & J. A. O'Neil (Eds.), *Dissociation and the dissociative disorders: DSM-V and beyond* (pp. 239–258). New York: Routledge.

Steinberg, M. (1993). The spectrum of depersonalization: Assessment and treatment. In D. Spiegel (Ed.), *Dissociative disorders: A clinical review* (pp. 79–103). Lutherville, MD: Sidran Press.

Steinberg, M. (1995). *Handbook for the assessment of dissociation: A clinical guide.* Washington, DC: American Psychiatric Press.

Tichenor, V., Marmar, C. R., Weiss, D. S., Metzler, T. J., & Ronfeldt, H. M. (1996). The relationship between peritraumatic dissociation and posttraumatic stress: Findings in female Vietnam Theater Veterans. *Journal of Consulting and Clinical Psychology, 64*, 1054–1059.

Toates, F. M. (1986). *Motivational systems.* Cambridge: Cambridge University Press.

Van der Hart, O., & Dorahy, M. (2009). Dissociation: History of a concept. In P. F. Dell & J. A. O'Neil (Eds.), *Dissociation and the dissociative disorders: DSM-V and beyond* (pp. 3–26). New York: Routledge.

Van der Hart, O., Nijenhuis, E. R. S., & Steele, K. (2005). Dissociation: An under-recognized major feature of Complex PTSD. *Journal of Traumatic Stress, 18*, 413–424.

Van der Hart, O., Nijenhuis, E. R. S., Steele, K., & Brown, D. (2004). Trauma-related dissociation: Conceptual clarity lost and found. *Australian and New Zealand Journal of Psychiatry, 38*, 906–914.

Van der Hart, O., & Steele, K. (1997). Time distortions in dissociative identity disorder: Janetian concepts and treatments. *Dissociation, 10*, 91–103.

Van der Hart, O., Van Dijke, A., Van Son, M., & Steele, K. (2000). Somatoform dissociation in traumatized World War I combat soldiers: A neglected clinical heritage. *Journal of Trauma & Dissociation, 1*(4), 33–66.

Van der Kolk, B. A., Burbridge, J. A., & Suzuki, J. (1997). The psychobiology of traumatic memory: Clinical implications of neuroimaging studies. *Annals of the New York Academy of Science, 821*, 99–113.

Vanderlinden, J., Van Dyck, R., Vandereycken, W., Vertommen, H., & Verkes, R. J. (1993). The Dissociation Questionnaire (DIS-Q): Development and characteristics of a new self-report questionnaire. *Clinical Psychology and Psychotherapy, 1*, 1–7.

Waller, N. G., Putnam, F. W., & Carlson, E. B. (1996). Types of dissociation and dissociative types. *Psychological Methods, 1*, 300–321.

Zanarini, M. C., Ruser, T., Frankenburg, F. R., & Hennen, J. (2000). The dissociative experiences of borderline patients. *Comprehensive Psychiatry, 41*, 223–227.

11 Possession/Trance Phenomena

Etzel Cardeña, PhD
Marjolein van Duijl, MD, PhD
Lupita A. Weiner, MA
Devin B. Terhune, MSc

OUTLINE

> I felt an almost electrical interaction between myself and the spectators. Their mounting excitement had the effect of heightening my physical strength until I was dancing with a sustained force that seemed far beyond my reach at other times. For one moment it seemed as if some other person within me was performing the dance.
>
> Leonid Massine,
> in his memoirs for the performance of
> *The Three Cornered Hat*

11.1 PREAMBLE

As this recollection from the brilliant Russian dancer Massine illustrates, experiences in which "something" or "someone" else takes control over one's actions are not necessarily bizarre or pathological. Even those of us who are not star performers or athletes may find at times that a rhythm or an action appears to "take over" our self for a moment, whether in the midst of dancing or while "being inspired." Depending on the time and the place, this "otherness" has been called or attributed to the Id, the muses, Platonic manias, unconscious forces, Apollo or enthusiasm (literally "being filled with the gods"), Jungian complexes, right hemisphere processes, or various types of spiritual forces. From this angle, it should not be surprising that in a review of 488 societies Erika Bourguignon found that 74% believed that spiritual forces can affect the personality and well-being of individuals, and 52% maintained that the individual's personality can be replaced by that of another being (Bourguignon, 1973, p. 31).

In contrast to Massine's account, the experience of an alternate identity is sometimes associated with distress and serious conflict. Consider a case seen by MvD in Uganda. For many years, a 33-year-old woman had experienced regular attacks during which she exhibited aggressive, unusual behaviors and spoke with other voices. These attacks occurred when the family prepared to go to church or pray. During the intake interview, the client held her hands like claws, made animal-like noises, and spoke in a strange language and voice. Her sister explained that this was the voice of an uncle who had died many years ago. Because the attacks often occurred when religious activities were about to be performed, the clinicians suspected that they expressed her suppressed anger against her rigid Christian father who had ruined her life because of his unyielding principles. The client agreed to attend counseling to learn to control her attacks and understand and deal with the underlying experience; she now uses medication to control her anxiety when she feels that an attack is coming. In short, it is crucial to differentiate between instances of possession that may benefit from clinical intervention and possession experiences that are neutral or may even be beneficial to the individual and his/her community, especially considering the proposal for a Trance Dissociative Disorder (APA, 2000; Cardeña, 1992).

The experience of being taken over by some entity from within (e.g., DID) or from without (e.g., spirit possession) challenges basic Western premises about the self. One of them, questioned by Buddhism and other philosophies, is that we have a *single,* discrete identity or self that cannot be replaced by external influences, spiritual or otherwise. A related premise is that our conscious self *owns* and controls our bodies and mental life. A myriad of perspectives can be brought to bear on this issue—from philosophical analyses of selfhood and identity to neurocognitive explanations of agency. Here, we will limit our analysis to the domain of possession/trance phenomena (PTP) and to whether they can be characterized as dissociative. In doing so, we will propose features that distinguish pathological from nonpathological PTP and we will review the various explanations for it.

11.2 POSSESSION/TRANCE PHENOMENA (PTP) AND DISSOCIATION

In psychology, the term *dissociation* originated as the opposite of the "association" of psychological processes. Cardeña (1994) proposed two main descriptive senses for the term *dissociation* (see also Holmes et al., 2005). First, *experiential detachment* describes dissociation as an alteration in consciousness wherein disconnection/disengagement from the self or the environment is experienced (e.g., out-of-body experiences, depersonalization, derealization; Alvarado, 2000).

Second, *psychological compartmentalization* refers to dissociated or nonintegrated psychological processes or systems that should ordinarily be integrated. This sense of the term is most germane to the present chapter. This sense of *dissociation* can be further divided into three categories of phenomena: (1) lack of awareness of current or previous information that should ordinarily be integrated; (2) the coexistence of separate mental systems that should ordinarily be integrated in consciousness, memory, or identity; and (3) ongoing behavior or perception that contradicts a sincere introspective verbal report. PTP mostly involves the first two categories: absence of reflective awareness of stimuli and behavior (trance), and lack of integration of different identities and memories (spirit possession). Like all types of dissociative phenomena, PTP has nonpathological and pathological expressions (Cardeña, 1994).

It is important to distinguish spirit possession from Eliade's (1964) paradigmatic shamanic experience of "magical flight." This distinction is similar to (1) Rouget's (1985) classification of "ecstasy" (immobility, silence, recollection, imaginal events, etc.) and "trance" (movements, noise, crisis, amnesia, etc.), and (2) proposed typologies of hypnotic virtuosos (Barrett, 1990; Barber, 1999; Cardeña, 1996). The shamanic magical flight is a mostly imaginal experience in which the soul of the healer is purported to fly to other worlds or realities to seek spirit assistance, retrieve the sick person's soul, and so on. In contrast with this "disembodied" imaginal journey, spirit possession is characterized by a "radical alteration of embodied identity" (Cardeña, 1989, p. 2), in which the identity of the individual is replaced—typically by a spirit or an ancestor, but sometimes by an animal (Van Duijl, Cardeña, & de Jong, 2005). When the person recovers the original identity, she or he usually claims amnesia for what transpired during the possession.

Although we focus in this chapter on PTP, it should be borne in mind that "spirit possession" and "magical flight" experiences can coexist in the same person or culture. For instance, the Chukchees engage in both types of religious practices (Lewis, 1989).

11.3 THE DOMAIN OF PTP

Academic discourse about possession has shifted from singling it out as an exotic event to immersing it within personal and cultural notions of identity, relationships, and reality (Boddy, 1994; Swartz, 1998). In this chapter, we will focus on psychological and psychiatric perspectives.

There is an important preliminary distinction to be made between two senses of spirit possession: (1) possession as an attribution or explanation of events (e.g., illness), and (2) possession as an experience of one's identity being replaced by that of an ancestor, spirit, or other entity (Bourguignon, 1976). *Spirit possession as attribution* connotes the belief that the person's condition is caused by a spiritual influence. Note, however, that attributions of this type of influence often occur when the patient evidences no alteration of consciousness. In both Western and non-Western societies, individuals may explain their psychiatric or medical condition as being caused by some type of spiritual interference (Kua, 1993; Pfeifer, 1999), but *without* any accompanying alterations of consciousness (such as narrowing of awareness, stereotyped movements, substitution of identities, amnesia for the event, etc.). From a psychiatric point of view, depending on the observed symptoms, these patients may be diagnosed as suffering from a medical, psychotic, mood, somatoform, anxiety, or neurological disorder. In some cases, the illness attributed to spirit possession may be a communal one that is medically unexplained, such as epidemics of psychogenic fainting among a group of Bhutanese refugees (Van Ommeren et al., 2001). Such attributions have parallels in the common practice of assigning causal agency for ambiguous or inexplicable events to discarnate entities (Lange & Houran, 2001). This chapter does not address spirit possession as attribution but concentrates on spirit possession as the experience of substitution of one's identity by another.

Bourguignon (1976) also drew a distinction between trance and possession trance. According to her, possession trance is an altered state of consciousness during which the individual's identity is replaced by another. Trance, on the other hand, is an alteration of consciousness that is not accompanied by the belief that the change is caused by a spirit or entity. We find Bourguignon's distinction to be problematic because the term *trance* is polysemantic and vague. Moreover, there is no hard evidence that conditions called trance are homogeneous or that they vary from "possession trance" only in their causal attribution (Cardeña, 1990). An alternative to Bourguignon's classification is to delineate specific features of trance and possession trance. Cardeña (1992) distinguished trance and possession trance as follows:

Trance is a temporary alteration of consciousness, identity, and/or behavior evidenced by at least two of the following:

(1) Marked alteration of consciousness or loss of the usual sense of identity without replacement by an alternate identity
(2) Narrowing of awareness of immediate surroundings, or unusually narrow and selective focusing on environmental stimuli
(3) Stereotyped behaviors or movements experienced as being beyond one's control

Possession trance is a temporary alteration of consciousness, identity, and/or behavior, attributed to possession by a spiritual force or another person, and evidenced by at least two of the following:

(1) Single or episodic replacement of the usual sense of identity by that attributed to the possessing force
(2) Stereotyped and culturally determined behaviors or movements attributed to the possessing identity
(3) Full or partial amnesia for the event

This classification has two arguable merits: First, it seeks to define what trance is, rather than just using the term as a synonym for any alteration of consciousness. For instance, there are mystical experiences in which awareness is expanded rather than narrowed. Second, it provides a distinction between trance and possession trance besides the causal attribution to spiritual forces. For instance, possession trance requires replacement by a new identity, whereas trance does not. This distinction would seem to be useful in classifying such culture-bound syndromes as amok and latah, which include narrowing of attention and hypersuggestibility but without the adoption of a new identity (e.g., Rhoades, 2005a), and seems to be consistent with the neuroscientific research that differentiates between the feeling of being in control and the feeling of being the agent of an action (Hohwy & Frith, 2004). If empirically valid, this distinction may help guide research on the etiology and, if necessary, treatment of both conditions.

There is some empirical support for the construct validity of PTP. Gaw, Ding, Levine, and Gaw (1998) studied a Chinese sample of possession inpatients; they observed loss of control of actions, of awareness of surroundings, and of personal identity, perceived insensitivity to pain, changes in tone of voice, and problems with distinguishing reality from fantasy. In a sample of Singaporean inpatients, Ng (2000) encountered similar manifestations: unusual vocalizations and movements including shaking, apparent immunity from pain, unfocused or fixed gaze, and assumption of a different identity. Kianpoor and Rhoades (2005) described a possession state in Iran, Djinnati, that involved unresponsiveness to external stimuli, glossolalia, identity alteration, and subsequent amnesia. Case descriptions from India and other places are very similar (Cardeña, Lewis-Fernández, Beahr, Pakianathan, & Spiegel, 1996). Among 119 spirit-possessed patients who had visited traditional healers in Uganda, MvD observed involuntary shaking of the head or parts of the body attributed to spirits, talking in a different voice (which others recognized as the voice of a specific spirit), and feeling influenced by unidentified forces that caused unusual behavior. Nearly half of the possessed patients mentioned something holding the body such that they were unable to move or speak.

Finer distinctions can be made. Cardeña (1989) has proposed three major types of PTP: (1) transitional states (e.g., saoulé or inebriation in Haitian Vodou, irradiación in Afro-Brazilian religions; Frigerio, 1989) where individuals are in a cognitively disorganized state as they move from their usual state of consciousness to an alternate state or identity (a phenomenon observed in other transitions between states of consciousness; Tart, 1975); (2) in the prototypical type of PTP, the person adopts an alternative identity (e.g., a culturally recognized spirit or an ancestor); and (3) spirit possession involving a transcendent, non-ego state in which the person experiences a union with everything or a Godhead rather than a different, discrete identity (Cardeña, 1989; see also Wulff, 2000). Most authors use the term *spirit possession* to refer to the second, prototypical type of PTP; we will follow that practice in the rest of this chapter.

Possession practitioners differentiate between levels of the experience (Frigerio, 1989), and the extent of the accompanying amnesia varies from time to time and according to the context (Friedson, 1994). There are also PTP variations as to whether the usual identity of the individual is completely absent while possessed, or whether some coconsciousness between identities occur.

Even if we restrict our focus to the "alternate identity" type of possession, we find that its domain is quite large: it also includes related phenomena such as mediumship and channeling, glossolalia ("speaking in tongues," typically in the midst of certain religious ceremonies), and dissociative identity disorder (Cardeña, in press). In this regard, it should be noted that surveys report that practitioners of channeling/mediumship and speaking in tongues are typically normal, psychologically healthy individuals (Hastings, 1991, p. 25; Samarin, 1972).

11.4 WHAT DISTINGUISHES NONPATHOLOGICAL FROM PATHOLOGICAL PTP?

When PTP causes dysfunction and/or distress, and is not part of a culturally accepted practice, it can be considered a disorder. The fourth edition of the Diagnostic and Statistical Manual of Mental Disorders-IV-TR (APA, 2000, pp. 785–786; Cardeña et al., 1996) lists Dissociative Trance Disorder, following the criteria for trance and possession described earlier, as a disorder that merits further study. DSM-IV presently classifies Dissociative Trance Disorder as a Dissociative Disorder Not Otherwise Specified. The ICD-10 (WHO, 1992) includes Trance and Possession Disorders as a separate entity. If the DSM taxonomy is not to be considered ethnocentric, there is a need to consider seriously the criteria for Dissociative Trance Disorder; research in non-Western cultures suggests that the most common dissociative disorders involve trance and/or possession. For instance, when asked to provide examples of previously defined dissociative identity disorder, Ugandan informants described local examples of spirit possession (Van Duijl, Cardeña, & de Jong, 2005), a similar presentation to that in India (Saxena & Prasad, 1989). In an era of increased multiculturalism, it is important to recognize the interaction of different cultural narratives in both the expression and resolution of individual possession cases (Gingrich, 2005; Rhoades, 2005b). Some criticisms of the diagnostic validity of PTP (e.g., Onchev, 1998) can be reduced if we clearly differentiate Dissociative Trance Disorder from pathological states where spirit possession is just a belief or one among various symptoms.

Most Westerners view spirit possession as malignant or demoniacal (from a religious perspective) or psychopathological (from a secular perspective). Most cross-cultural data, however, show a very different picture. For many non-Christian religious traditions (e.g., African, Afro-American, Asian), spirit possession is a central liturgical event. In Haiti the faithful interact with the Vodou lwas (spirits, universal forces) by inviting them to take over their identity and "ride" them (Desmangles & Cardeña, 1996). In the Philippines, the widespread occurrence of spirit possession renders it a bona fide social institution (Gingrich, 2005), whereas in Tibet, the religious figure of the oracle becomes possessed only when requested and for religious purposes (Crook, 1997). Within the Christian tradition, there is a long history among many groups (e.g., Pentecostalists, Shakers, and members of the Charismatic Church) of being taken over by the Holy Ghost, receiving the "gifts," and so on (Garrett, 1987).

The fact that spiritual possession is culturally widespread does not mean, however, that it is never psychopathological. Before confronting this problem directly, we need to make some clarifications. First, we must distinguish between (1) "spirit possession" as an altered state with the replacement of identity, from (2) psychopathological conditions that include the person's belief that the disorder is caused by a spirit, or in which thoughts about spirits may be just part of a larger condition. A certain percentage of psychotic and less severely disturbed individuals attribute their condition to the devil (Goff, Grotman, Kindlon, Waites, & Amico, 1991; Pfeifer, 1999). In these cases, spirit belief or possession is merely incidental to the pathology, as opposed to being a cardinal symptom.

Second, Lewis (1989) distinguished between central and peripheral possession. Central possession is culturally sanctioned and typically occurs only during a religious ritual that follows cultural prescriptions for when possessions occur (perhaps following a certain rhythmic pattern), what is acceptable from the possessing entity, and so on. This type of possession is episodic, sought-after, time-limited, generally organized, and its practice follows culturally established parameters. The general criteria for psychopathology (i.e., disabling distress and/or dysfunction) does not justify classifying central possession as pathological.

Not all followers of ecstatic religions become possessed, so what distinguishes those who become possessed from those who do not? There have been a few studies on this issue, some of them using sampling or assessment techniques of questionable validity and reliability. An early study (Ward & Beaubrun, 1981) examined possession in a religion that considers possession to be a disorder (i.e., Pentecostalists from Trinidad). Those who experienced possession obtained higher scores on the Eysenck Personality Inventory and MMPI measures of neuroticism and hysteria than did a control group. These findings agreed with case studies that showed a higher degree of somatization among the possessed. The authors cautioned, however, against arguing "that possession per se is pathological" (p. 296). Seligman (2005) proposed, in a study with a sample of Brazilian Candomblé practitioners, that the tendency to somatize predicts who will become possessed, although it bears mentioning that her statistical analyses are unclear and difficult to interpret.

Several recent studies provide a clearer picture. In a Filipino sample, Gingrich (2005) found no relationship between a DID diagnosis and reports of being spirit possessed. Similarly, there is evidence that spiritist mediums in Brazil, as compared with patients with DID, show significantly better health and psychological adjustment, and less early trauma, as indexed by a structured interview (Moreira de Almeida, Lotufo Neto, & Cardeña, 2000). Also in Brazil, Negro (2002) studied 110 Spiritists and found that controlled dissociation was positively related to training in mediumship, and that mediums reported good socialization and adaptation. In contrast, pathological forms of dissociation were associated with younger age, less control of mediumship activity, poorer social support, and previous psychiatric history. Newberg, Wintering, Morgan, and Waldman (2006) found that a sample of Christian women who regularly experienced glossolalia did not have neurological, medical, or psychiatric conditions. Laria (1998) compared three groups of Cubans: spirit mediums, mental health patients, and a control group of nonmediums/nonpatients. He concluded that mediums reported higher levels of normal dissociative experiences, lower levels of psychopathology, fewer traumatic experiences (including sexual abuse), and exhibited less subjective distress than mental health patients, despite having endured more stressful events than the controls. Reinsel (2003) reported that a sample of North American mediums exhibited more depersonalization and absorption than controls, but that the two groups did not differ in self-reported well-being or psychological distress.

Some of the studies mentioned earlier suggest overall that participants in central possession groups are psychologically healthy and that training/socialization into mediumship may provide an organizing-therapeutic function. Similarly, Boddy (1988) studied the Zar cult in Sudan and concluded that possession, which was exhibited by almost 50% of women over 15 years of age, provides a form of communal bonding and insight therapy.

Lewis's (1989) second type of possession, peripheral possession, occurs outside of a ritual setting, seems uncontrollable, is often chronic, and involves conflict between the individual and the surrounding social or work milieu. In this type of possession, a traditional healer may conduct an exorcism and/or introduce the person to a possession group where the afflicted may learn how to better control and organize their experience (a good strategy, it would seem, judging by Negro's results). Rhoades (2005b) noted that Hawaiian possession cases are often interpreted as being instances of "spiritual help" for a troubled person, and that lack of beneficence on the part of the possessing agent was often interpreted as indicating its falsity. Individuals with chronic conditions may become hospitalized (Gaw et al., 1998).

Peripheral possessions may best be considered as a culturally shaped "idiom of distress" (Nichter, 1981) for a gamut of interpersonal conflicts, stressors, and chronic personal maladjustment (Gaw et al., 1998; Ward & Beabrun, 1981). In a sophisticated study using logistic regression analyses, Ng and Chan (2004) found that conflicts over religious and cultural issues, prior exposure to "trance" states, and being a spiritual healer or his/her assistant were significant predictors of a diagnosis of dissociative trance disorder in Singapore. Unfortunately the authors did not distinguish between being an actual healer or only an assistant.

In summary, the primary distinguishing characteristics of pathological possession seem to be: (1) the possession is not related to a culturally accepted practice, and (2) the possession is associated with individual, idiosyncratic events, distress and maladjustment, a psychiatric history, and, perhaps, less training in ritual practices. Process variables, such as (1) the ability to induce the onset of the possession where it is contextually appropriate, suggesting control over it, and (2) the capacity to organize the experience in a personal and socially meaningful way, may distinguish nonpathological from pathological expressions, and they have been discussed under the general concept of "regression in the service of the ego" (Walker, 1972).

11.5 EXPLANATORY FRAMEWORKS OF PTP

Because the domain of spirit possession is vast and complex, we can expect a variety of explanations, from different disciplines and at different levels of analysis. The reader should be aware, however, that comparing our Western diagnostic categories with local concepts risks making a category fallacy. That is, we may impose a Western construct on a different culture without knowing whether our Western construct is valid in that culture (Kleinman, 1988). Anthropology makes a similar distinction between emic (i.e., indigenous) and etic (universalizing, typically Western-based) explanations. Bearing this in mind, we now turn to different explanatory theories of PTP, but mention should be made that both field studies of spirit possession (e.g., Stoller, 1989) and of "reincarnation" experiences (Mills & Lynn, 2000) suggest that the indigenous explanation of some type of unexplained influence on someone's personality cannot be dismissed offhand.

11.5.1 Biological Theories of PTP

Biological explanations have been offered for specific findings such as the observation that, throughout the world, possession tends to occur more often among women and those of low socioeconomic status (SES). Kehoe and Giletti (1981) proposed that the effect on the CNS of deficiencies of thiamine, tryptophan-niacin, calcium, and vitamin D may be culturally interpreted and shaped as a manifestation of spirit possession. Although nutritional deficiencies may play a part in such cases, this theory obviously cannot account for possession among well-fed, middle-class individuals.

A recent study sheds light on some unusual physical feats of possessed individuals. Kawai and collaborators (2001) compared Balinese dancers who exhibited trance behaviors (e.g., unfocused gaze, tremors, lack of facial expression) with those who did not. Trance-dancers had significantly higher concentrations of noradrenaline, dopamine, and beta-endorphin (a neuropeptide associated with analgesia). This study did not determine whether these neurochemical phenomena preceded or followed the trance behavior. It is relevant to note, however, that lack of reaction to painful or burning stimuli is sometimes used to test whether an individual is possessed (Broch, 1985). The literature on hypnotic analgesia may be apposite in this regard (Cardeña, 2004).

The putative *genetic* basis of dissociation as a trait is currently in some dispute. Two studies have found evidence for genetic and nonshared environmental contributions (Becker-Blease et al., 2004; Jang, Paris, Zweig-Frank, & Livesley, 1998), whereas an earlier one did not (Waller & Ross, 1997). Absorption, the ability to fully deploy one's attention toward internal or external stimuli, is a construct related to dissociation and hypnotizability, and it shows substantial heritability (Tellegen et al., 1988). Individuals with high levels of absorption, dissociation, and/or hypnotizability tend to report unusual experiences, including reputed psychic phenomena and an openness to experiencing altered states (Cardeña, Lynn, & Krippner, 2000). This is consistent with Laria's (1998) finding that mediums had "thinner mental boundaries" (e.g., greater fluidity between states of consciousness).

There has also been some brain research on spirit possession and related phenomena. A clear neuropsychological profile of PTP has yet to emerge, but some evidence points to frontal cortical structures. A SPECT study of Christian glossolalists (Newberg et al., 2006) found decreased cerebral blood flow in the dorsolateral prefrontal cortices after glossolalia, in contrast with regular singing, consistent with participants' reported experience of involuntariness while singing in tongues. The frontal lobes may also be implicated in the performance of stereotyped, culturally appropriate behaviors outside of awareness, as is evident from case studies of frontal lobe lesion patients (Lhermitte, 1986). This does not suggest that spirit possession is associated with frontal lobe dysfunction, but that these experiences may be related to a propensity for the decoupling of frontal lobe structures under particular conditions, as has been found with highly hypnotizable individuals (Egner, Jamieson, & Gruzelier, 2005; Gruzelier, 2006; Jamieson & Woody, 2007). Research on the experience of not feeling in control also suggests that attenuation of activity in the inferior parietal cortex, modulated by the anterior cingulate and the dorsolateral prefrontal cortex, may also be relevant to the experience of possession (Hohwy & Frith, 2004).

11.5.2 Cultural and Sociopolitical Theories of PTP

Probably the most influential theory in anthropology proposes that spirit possession provides women and other underprivileged groups with a vehicle for expressing their complaints in a context where they may be heard (Lewis, 1989). Silverman's (2005) data clearly show that distress and perhaps pathology is related to a low SES status in Brazil, but do not clearly indicate that these factors affect who gets possessed by the spirits. On the other hand, in some cultures, it is the elite rather than the underprivileged who become possessed (Behrend & Luig, 1999).

Anthropologists have also described the emergence of new types of spirit possession and the shaping of their specific features by changing sociopolitical circumstances, either to support or oppose them (Behrend & Luig, 1999). For instance, Masquelier (1999) notes that new emerging Dodo spirits in Southern Niger remind people of traditional moral and social values, in contrast with the pollution and decline of values of modernity. Igreya (2003) describes how the Gamba spirits and healers who emerged after the war in Mozambique seemed to support the recovery process of war survivors from their psychosocial hurts. Boddy (1994) has especially emphasized the bonding and therapeutic aspects of group support for those who are possessed by the spirits.

There is also, to be sure, a dramaturgical component to ritual spirit possession (Métraux, 1955). Not only are the characteristics of the possessing agent enacted, but full representations of historical and political dynamics take place. Witness, for instance, Jean Rouch's film *Les Maîtres Fous*, in which the African colonial order was simultaneously represented and mocked by the possessed Hauka group. For a sophisticated analysis of perhaps the most famous case of possession in the West that included aspects of performance, suggestibility, and sociocultural tensions see De Certeau (1996).

11.5.3 Psychological Theories of PTP

Any analysis of possession phenomena must address the unusual relationship of the conscious self toward its body. Even if we disagree with Cartesian dualism, we still experience ourselves as a core of consciousness, somewhere inside the center of the head, which controls its "vehicle," the body—in Ryle's terms "the ghost in the machine." Our ownership of our bodily and mental events is, however, frequently compromised. Unbidden and sometimes surprising images, memories, and impulses are everyday occurrences (Klinger, 1978): our bodies obey us only so far, a limb may become "restless," pains and other sensations may show up surprisingly. And, of course, there are our nightly dreams in which we may act atypically and seem to be characters in a play created by someone else.

Psychology has documented how we are greatly affected by a myriad of biological, cognitive, social, and environmental variables. Indeed, our judgments of the probable causes of our behavior tend to be quite inaccurate (Nisbett & Wilson, 1977; Wegner, 2002). So, perhaps the question should not be why some people experience being taken over by a foreign identity, but why we do not have that experience more often. One answer proposes that different aspects of the self cohere in a unified sense of self only after a number of developmental stages (Stern, 1985). During development, children in Western technological societies are led to cover experiential gaps and incomprehensible actions through a narrative of a single, impermeable subjective self (Kirmayer, 1994). Other cultures, however, provide different "theories of the mind," including the influence of unseen, spiritual forces which may become fully manifested as "spirit possession" (Cardeña, 1991). Swartz (1999) describes how some social scientists in our current postmodern times have moved from the idea of a single "unitary" subject to the idea that identity is fragmented and that reality is negotiable and questionable. This latter point of view has fostered an increasing interest in dissociation and an acknowledgment of voices and expressions of dissociated realities, including experiences of spiritual forces.

Spirit possession has been analyzed according to the functionality it may have to express individual (e.g., Mischel & Mischel, 1958), cultural (e.g., Lewis, 1989), and sociopolitical conflicts (e.g., Behrend & Luig, 1999; Laguerre, 1980). There is little explanation, however, of why some believers become possessed easily and others become possessed only with difficulty, or not at all. The earlier assumption of individual psychopathology (typically "neurosis" or "hysteria") clashes with more recent data on the psychological health of many if not most ritual practitioners (Laria, 1998; Negro, 2002). Seligman (2005) proposes that Candomblé mediums tend to somatize, but the statistical analyses presented are suspect and only clearly show lower reports of emotionality, somatization, and dissociation among persons of a high-SES status as compared with individuals of a lower SES status, whether mediums or not. Psychological variables may yet bridge some of this explanatory gap. Still, possession has so many cultural variations that it is improbable that any single theory or set of variables will explain them all. Nonetheless, following a model on the development of dissociation in general, we can propose two paths to possession.

Central possession might be explained by a predisposition, probably biological, to dissociate/be suggestible/have unusual experiences. These predispositions, in turn, are interpreted and shaped by sociocultural factors into the experience of controlled ritual possession and mediumship. Through these practices, individuals may "let themselves follow" their impulses and intuitions, and acquire a more authoritative voice in their community than they would have otherwise. Once the experience is over, they can go back to their usual sense of an identity. The process of socialization into these practices starts very early. For example, EC witnessed little children in Haiti dance and imitate the possessed adults during Vodou ceremonies.

Peripheral, dysfunctional possession might be explained by a second path. Here, a predisposition to dissociate is accompanied by a very distressing, idiosyncratic development that would make alterations of identity difficult to control or organize. The literature on pathological dissociation posits two similar risk factors: (1) early, severe trauma/neglect that may interact with a disturbed form of attachment with the main caretaker ("disorganized attachment") (for a review see Cardeña & Gleaves, 2007) and (2) an inherited diathesis to dissociate and be highly suggestible (Butler, Duran, Jasiukaitis, Koopman, & Spiegel, 1996).

It is still an open question whether a history of chronic, severe trauma helps to distinguish central from peripheral possession. An American study did find a relationship between childhood trauma, dissociation, and delusions of possession among chronically psychotic patients (Goff et al., 1991). There is also evidence that Bhutanese refugees who exhibited mass psychogenic illness (explained as spirit possession) had more recent and more early trauma than a comparison group (Van Ommeren et al., 2001). Spirit-possessed patients of traditional healers in Uganda reported more potentially traumatic events than did the nonpossessed control group; they also obtained higher scores on measures of somatoform and psychoform dissociation (Van Duijl, Nijenhuis, Komproe, Gernaat, & de Jong, under review). The extent to which this finding can be generalized to other individuals exhibiting peripheral possession remains unknown. Regrettably, no study has yet compared the history and possession phenomenology of individuals with "healthy" and "dysfunctional" possession.

11.6 CONCLUSIONS AND FURTHER RESEARCH

Despite the PTP criteria that were "provided for further study" in DSM-IV (Cardeña, 1992; APA, 1994), we are unaware of a single published research project that has systematically applied them. We believe that this reflects the paucity of psychological research in this area, rather than the criteria's usefulness when actually applied in the field (Van Duijl & Cardeña, under review). Considering that pathological PTP may be the most common dissociative presentation in non-Western cultures, diagnostic criteria for PTP would seem to be a nosological must for DSM-V. Well-defined PTP can (1) facilitate recognition of these disorders by mental health care personnel, (2) encourage programmatic research on them, and (3) help devise suitable, culturally sensitive ways to assist the afflicted (e.g., through referral to healers, churches, or, if available, well-trained therapists). It is also not trivial that inclusion of PTP would bring DSM-V into greater agreement with the ICD.

Above all else, this review underscores the need for systematic research on PTP and its relationship to other psychological variables. Several lines of study are worth pursuing. Foremost, the validity and reliability of the proposed criteria must be evaluated. If needed, the criteria should be revised, while avoiding the category fallacy mentioned earlier. Second, investigation should determine whether there are indigenous classifications that resemble the two-path developmental model described here. Third, research should evaluate if persons with dysfunctional possession have experienced more trauma and attachment dysfunction than persons with controlled, organized possession. A number of the studies reviewed suggest that greater control over one's possession abilities, perhaps gained in part by a more extensive or rigorous training regimen, may characterize nonpathological possession. Research is needed to show whether this is indeed the case. Fourth, since people with dysfunctional possessions often go to ritual centers to be treated, it would be useful to have an estimate of the efficacy of such treatment, as compared with the Western psychiatric one.

The paucity of systematic psychological and psychiatric study of possession—a phenomenon that has been described though the ages in most cultures—shows how far we are from having a basic understanding of human experience.

REFERENCES

Alvarado, C. (2000). Out-of-body experiences. In E. Cardeña, S. J. Lynn, & S. Krippner (Eds.), *Varieties of anomalous experience* (pp. 183–218). Washington, DC: American Psychological Association.

American Psychiatric Association (2000). *DSM-IV-TR–Diagnostic and statistical manual of mental disorders* (4th ed., text rev.). Washington, DC: Author.

Barber, T. X. (1999). A comprehensive three-dimensional theory of hypnosis. In I. Kirsch, A. Capafons, E. Cardeña, & S. Amigó (Eds.), *Clinical hypnosis and self-regulation* (pp. 21–48). Washington, DC: American Psychological Association.

Barrett, D. (1990). Deep trance subjects: A schema of two distinct subgroups. In R. G. Kunzendorf (Ed.), *Mental imagery* (pp. 101–112). New York: Plenum Press.

Becker-Blease, K. A., Deater-Deckard, K., Eley, T., Freyd, J. J., Stevenson, J., & Plomin, R. (2004). A genetic analysis of individual differences in dissociative behaviors in childhood and adolescence. *Journal of Child Psychology and Psychiatry, 45,* 522–532.

Behrend, H., & Luig, U. (Eds.). (1999). *Spirit possession, modernity and power in Africa.* Oxford: James Currey.

Boddy, J. (1988). Spirits and selves in Northern Sudan: The cultural therapeutics of possession and trance. *Medical Anthropology, 15,* 4–27.

Boddy, J. (1994). Spirit possession revisited: Beyond instrumentality. *Annual Reviews of Anthropology, 23,* 407–434.

Bourguignon, E. (1973). *Religion, altered states of consciousness and social change.* Columbus: Ohio State University.

Bourguignon, E. (1976). *Possession.* San Francisco: Chandler & Sharp.

Broch, H. B. (1985). Crazy women are performing in Sombali. *Ethos, 13,* 262–281.

Butler, L. D., Duran, R. E. F., Jasiukaitis, P., Koopman, C., & Spiegel, D. (1996). Hypnotizability and traumatic experience: A diathesis-stress model of dissociative symptomatology. *American Journal of Psychiatry, 153 (Suppl. 7S),* 42–63.

Cardeña, E. (1989). The varieties of possession experience. *Association for the Anthropological Study of Consciousness Quarterly, 5* (2–3), 1–17.

Cardeña, E. (1990). *The concept(s) of trance.* Annual Conference of the Society for the Anthropology of Consciousness, Spring 1990, Pacific Palisades, CA.

Cardeña, E. (1991). Max Beauvoir. An island in an ocean of spirits. In R. I. Heinze (Ed.), *Shamans of the XXth century.* New York: Irvington, 27–32.

Cardeña, E. (1992). Trance and possession as dissociative disorders. *Transcultural Psychiatric Research Review, 29,* 287–300.

Cardeña, E. (1994). The domain of dissociation. In S. J. Lynn & J. W. Rhue (Eds.), *Dissociation: Clinical and theoretical perspectives* (pp. 15–31). New York: Guilford.

Cardeña, E. (1996). "Just floating on the sky." A comparison of shamanic and hypnotic phenomenology. In R. Quekelbherge & D. Eigner (Eds.), *6th Jahrbuch für transkulturelle medizin und psychotherapie* (6th Yearbook of cross-cultural medicine and psychotherapy) (pp. 367–380). Berlin: Verlag für Wissenschaft und Bildung.

Cardeña, E. (2004). Hypnosis for the relief and control of pain. Contribution to Psychology matters: www.psychologymatters.org/hypnosis_pain.html.

Cardeña, E. (in press). Anomalous identity experiences: Mediumship, spirit possession, and dissociative identity disorder (DID, MPD). In C. S. Alvarado, L. Coly, & N. L. Zingrone (Eds.), *The study of mediumship: Interdisciplinary perspectives.* New York: Parapsychology Foundation.

Cardeña, E., Fernández, R., Beahr, D., Pakianathan, I., & Spiegel, D. (1996). Dissociative disorders. In T. A. Widiger, A. J. Frances, et al. (Eds.) *Sourcebook for the DSM-IV. Vol. II.* Washington, DC: American Psychiatric Press (pp. 973–1005).

Cardeña, E., & Gleaves, D. (2007) Dissociative disorders. In M. Hersen, S. M. Turner, & D. Beidel (Eds.), *Adult psychopathology & diagnosis.* Fifth edition (pp. 473–503). New York: Wiley.

Cardeña, E., Lynn, S. J., & Krippner, S. (Eds.). (2000). *Varieties of anomalous experience: Examining the scientific evidence.* Washington, DC: American Psychological Association.

Crook, J. H. (1997). The indigenous psychiatry of Ladakh, part I: Practice theory approaches to trance possession in the Himalayas. *Anthropology & Medicine*, 4, 289–307.

De Certeau, M. (1996). *The possession at Loudun.* Chicago: University of Chicago Press.

Desmangles, L., & Cardeña, E. (1996). Trance possession and Vodou ritual in Haiti. In R. Quekelbherge & D. Eigner (Eds.), 6th Jahrbuch für transkulturelle medizin und psychotherapie (6th Yearbook of cross-cultural medicine and psychotherapy) (pp. 297–309). Berlin: Verlag für Wissenschaft und Bildung.

Egner, T., Jamieson, G. A., & Gruzelier, J. (2005). Hypnosis decouples cognitive control from conflict monitoring processes of the frontal lobe. *Neuroimage, 27,* 969–978.

Eliade, M. (1964). *Shamanism: Archaic techniques of ecstasy.* Princeton: Princeton University Press.

Friedson, S. (1994). *Consciousness-doubling: Trance technology in Tumbuka healing.* Presented at the 102nd Annual Meeting of the American Psychological Association, Los Angeles.

Frigerio, A. (1989). Levels of possession awareness in Afro-Brazilian religions. *AASC Quarterly, 5,* 5–11.

Garrett, C. (1987). *Spirit possession and popular religion.* Baltimore, MD: Johns Hopkins University Press.

Gaw, A. C., Ding, Q. Levine, R. E., & Gaw, H. (1998). The clinical characteristics of possession disorder among 20 Chinese patients in the Hebei Province of China. *Psychiatric Services, 49,* 360–365.

Goff, D. C., Grotman, A. W., Kindlon, D., Waites, M., & Amico, E. (1991). The delusion of possession in chronically psychotic patients. *Journal of Nervous and Mental Disease,* 179, 567–571.

Gruzelier, J. H. (2006). Frontal functions, connectivity and neural efficiency underpinning hypnosis and hypnotic susceptibility. *Contemporary Hypnosis, 23,* 15–32.

Hastings, A. (1991). *With the tongues of men and angels. A study of channeling.* Fort Worth, TX: Holt, Rinehart and Winston.

Hohwy, J., & Frith, C. (2004). Can neuroscience explain consciousness. In A. Jack & A. Roepstorff (Eds.), *Trusting the subject? V. 2* (pp. 180–198). Exeter, UK: Imprint Academic.

Holmes, E. A., Brown, R. J., Mansell, W., Fearon, R. P., Hunter, E. C., Frasquilho, F., & Oakley, D. A. (2005). Are there two qualitatively distinct forms of dissociation? A review and some clinical implications. *Clinical Psychological Review, 25,* 1–23.

Igreja, V. (2003). "Why are there so many drums playing until dawn?" Exploring the role of Gamba spirits and healers in the post-war recovery period in Gorongosa, Central Mozambique. *Transcultural Psychiatry, 40,* 459–487.

Jamieson, G. A., & Woody, E. (2007). Dissociated control as a paradigm for cognitive neuroscience research and theorizing in hypnosis. In G. A. Jamieson (Ed.), *Hypnosis and conscious states: The cognitive neuroscience perspective* (pp. 111–129). Oxford: Oxford University Press.

Jang, K. L., Paris, J., Zweig-Frank, H., & Livesley, W. J. (1998). Twin study of dissociative experience. *Journal of Nervous and Mental Diseases, 186,* 345–351.

Kawai, N., Honda, M., Nakamura, S., Samatra, P., Sukardika, K., Nakatani, Y., Shimojo, N., & Oohashi, T. (2001). Catecholamines and opioid peptides increase in plasma in humans during possession trances. *Cognitive Neurosciences and Neuropsychology, 12,* 3419–3423.

Kehoe, A. B., & Giletti, D. H. (1981). Women's preponderance in possession cults: The calcium-deficiency hypothesis extended. *American Anthropologist, 83,* 549–561.

Kianpoor, M., & Rhoades, G. F., Jr. (2005). "Djinnati," a possession state in Baloochistan, Iran. *Journal of Trauma Practice, 4,* 147–155.

Kirmayer, L. J. (1994). Pacing the void: Social and cultural dimensions of dissociation. In D. Spiegel (Ed.), *Dissociation: Culture, mind, and body* (pp. 91–122). Washington, DC: American Psychiatric Press.

Kleinman, A. (1988). *Rethinking psychiatry: From cultural category to personal experience.* New York: Free Press.

Klinger, E. (1978). Modes of normal conscious flow. In K. S. Pope & J. L. Singer (Eds.), *The stream of consciousness* (pp. 226–258). New York: Plenum.

Kua, E.H., Chew, P. H., & Ko, S.M. (1993). Spirit possession and healing among Chinese psychiatric patients. *Acta Psychiatrica Scandinavica, 88,* 447–450.

Laguerre, M. (1980). *Voodoo heritage.* California: Sage.

Lange, R., & Houran, J. (2001). Ambiguous stimuli brought to life: The psychological dynamics of hauntings and poltergeists. In J. Houran & R. Lange (Eds.), *Hauntings and poltergeists: Multidisciplinary perspectives* (pp. 280–306). Jefferson, NC: McFarland.

Laria, A. J. (1998). *Dissociative experiences among Cuban mental health patients and spiritist mediums.* Typescript. University of Massachusetts, Boston: Harvard Medical School.

Lewis, I. M. (1989). *Ecstatic religion.* Second edition. London: Routledge.

Lhermitte, F. (1986). Human autonomy and the frontal lobes. Part II: Patient behavior in complex and social situations: The "environmental dependency syndrome". *Annals of Neurology, 19,* 335–343.

Masquelier A. (1999). The invention of anti-tradition, Dodo spirits in Southern Niger. In H. Behrend & U. Luig (Eds.), *Spirit possession, modernity and power in Africa.* Oxford: James Currey Ltd.

Métraux, A. (1955). Dramatic elements in ritual possession. *Diogenes, 11,* 18–36.

Mills, A., & Lynn, S. J. (2000). Past-life experiences. In E. Cardeña, S. J. Lynn, & S. Krippner (Eds.), *Variety of anomalous experience* (pp. 283–313). Washington, DC: American Psychological Association.

Mischel, W., & Mischel, F. (1958). Psychological aspects of spirit possession. *American Anthropologist, 60,* 249–260.

Moreira-Almeida, A., Lotufo Neto, F., & Cardeña, E. (2008). Comparison between Brazilian Spiritist mediumship and dissociative identity disorder. *Journal of Nervous and Mental Disease, 196,* 420–424.

Negro, P. J. (2002). Do religious mediumship dissociative experiences conform to the sociocognitive theory of dissociation? *Journal of Trauma and Dissociation, 3,* 51–73.

Newberg, A. B., Wintering, N. A., Morgan, D., & Waldman, M. R. (2006). The measurement of regional cerebral blood flow during glossolalia: A preliminary SPECT study. *Psychiatry Research: Neuroimaging, 148,* 67–71.

Ng, B. Y. (2000). Phenomenology of trance states seen at a psychiatric hospital in Singapore: A cross-cultural perspective. *Transcultural Psychiatry,* 37, 560–579.

Ng, B. Y., & Chan, Y. H. (2004). Psychosocial stressors that precipitate dissociative trance disorder in Singapore. *Australian and New Zealand Journal of Psychiatry, 38,* 426–432.

Nichter, M. (1981). Idioms of distress: Alternatives in the expression of psychosocial distress. *Culture, Medicine and Psychiatry, 5,* 379–408.

Nisbett, R. E., & Wilson, T. D. (1977). Telling more than we can know: Verbal reports on mental processes. *Psychological Review, 84,* 231–259.

Onchev, G. (1998). Heterogeneity of the "possession states": A case study from Pemba. *European Psychiatry, 13, Supplement 4,* 254s.

Pfeifer, S. (1999). Demonic attributions in nondelusional disorders. *Psychopathology, 32,* 252–259.

Reinsel, R. (2003). Dissociation and mental health in mediums and sensitives: A pilot survey. *Parapsychological Association 46th Annual Convention Proceedings of Presented Papers* (pp. 200–221).

Rhoades, G. F., Jr. (2005a). Cross-cultural aspects of trauma and dissociation. *Journal of Trauma Practice, 4,* 21–33.

Rhoades, G. F., Jr. (2005b). Trauma and dissociation in paradise (Hawaii). *Journal of Trauma Practice, 4,* 133–145.

Rouget, G. (1985). *Music and trance: A theory of the relations between music and possession.* Chicago: University of Chicago Press.

Samarin, W. J. (1972). *Tongues of men and angels.* New York: Macmillan.

Saxena, S., & Prasad, K. V. (1989). DSM-III subclassification of dissociative disorders applied to psychiatric outpatients in India. *American Journal of Psychiatry, 146,* 261–262.

Seligman, R. (2005). Distress, dissociation, and embodied experience: Reconsidering the pathways to mediumship and mental health. *Ethos, 33,* 71–99.

Stern, D. N. (1985). *The interpersonal world of the infant.* New York: Basic Books.

Stoller, P. (1989). *Fusion of the worlds. An ethnography of possession among the Songhay of Nigeria.* Chicago: University of Chicago Press.

Swartz, L. (1998). *Culture and mental health: A Southern African view.* Oxford: Oxford University Press.

Tart, C. T. (1975). *States of consciousness.* New York: E. P. Dutton.

Tellegen, A., Lykken, D. T., Bouchard, T. J., Wilcox, K. J., Segal, N. L., & Rich, S. (1988). Personality similarity in twins reared apart and together. *Journal of Personality and Social Psychology, 54,* 1031–1039.

Van Duijl, M., Cardeña, E., & de Jong, J. (2005). The validity of DSM-IV dissociative disorders categories in SW Uganda. *Transcultural Psychiatry, 42,* 219–241.

Van Duijl, M., & Cardeña, E. (under review). Characteristics of spirit possession in Uganda.

Van Duijl, M.., Nijenhuis, E., Komproe, I., Gernaat, H., & de Jong, J. (under review) Dissociative symptoms and reported trauma among patients with spirit possession and matched healthy controls in Uganda.

Van Ommeren, M. V., Sharma, B., Komproe, I., Sharma, G. K., Cardeña, E., de Jong, J. T., Poudyal, B., & Makaju, R. (2001) Trauma and loss as determinants of medically unexplained epidemic illness in a Bhutanese refugee camp. *Psychological Medicine, 31,* 1259–1267.

Walker, S. S. (1972). *Ceremonial spirit possession in Africa and Afro-America.* Leiden, The Netherlands: E. J. Brill.

Waller, N. G., & Ross, C. A. (1997). The prevalence and biometric structure of pathological dissociation in the general population: Taxometric and behavior genetic findings. *Journal of Abnormal Psychology, 106,* 499–510.

Ward, C.A., & Beaubrun, M. H. (1981). Spirit possession and neuroticism in a West Indian Pentecostal community. *British Journal of Clinical Psychology,* 20, 295–296.

Wegner, D.M. (2002). *The illusion of conscious will.* Cambridge, MA: MIT Press.

World Health Organization (WHO) (1992). *International statistical classification of diseases and related health problems.* Geneva: Switzerland: Author.

Wulff, D. M. (2000). Mystical experiences. In E. Cardeña, S. J. Lynn, & S. Krippner (Eds.), *Varieties of anomalous experience* (pp. 397–440). Washington, DC: American Psychological Association.

Part IV

Acute Dissociation

12 Is Peritraumatic Dissociation Always Pathological?

Richard A. Bryant, PhD

OUTLINE

12.1 DISSOCIATION

Peritraumatic dissociation may be understood as a collection of strategies used to reduce awareness of aversive emotions and control of cognition, which cause "disruption in the usually integrated functions of consciousness, memory, identity, or perception of the environment" (American Psychological Association, 1994, p. 766). Dissociative responses may be evident in perceptual alterations, memory impairment, or emotional detachment from one's environment (Cardeña & Spiegel, 1993).

12.2 THE DOMAIN OF DISSOCIATION

Dissociative responses that may be reported in the context of acute stress include an array of reactions that purportedly minimize negative emotional states. A sense of emotional numbing or detachment may include the absence of normal emotional responses to stimuli that typically elicit emotional reactions. Reduced awareness of one's surroundings may involve limited encoding of events that are occurring during a traumatic experience. Derealization involves a distorted perception of reality, and may include time distortion or seeing events as if they are in a dream. Depersonalization may involve a fragmented sense of the self, such as perceiving the self being attacked from the third-person perspective. Finally, dissociative amnesia may involve an inability to recall a particular aspect (usually a very distressing aspect) of a traumatic experience.

Dissociative symptoms during the acute trauma phase are reportedly common. A sense of numbing (Feinstein, 1989; Noyes et al., 1977) and reduction in awareness of one's environment (Berah, Jones, & Valent, 1984; Hillman, 1981; Titchener & Kapp, 1976) are reportedly common during a traumatic experience. This reaction has been reported in 40% of earthquake survivors (Cardeña & Spiegel, 1993), 30% of accident survivors (Noyes & Kletti, 1977), and 53% of witnesses of an execution (Freinkel, Koopman, & Spiegel, 1994). Depersonalization has been reported in 25% of earthquake survivors (Cardeña & Spiegel, 1993), 31% of accident survivors (Noyes et al., 1977), 54% of airline disaster survivors (Sloan, 1988), 26% of prisoners of war (Siegel, 1984), and 40% of execution witnesses (Freinkel et al., 1994). Finally, dissociative amnesia has been reported in 57% of ambush victims (Feinstein, 1989), 61% of tornado survivors (Madakasira & O'Brien, 1987), and 5% of World War II combatants (Torrie, 1944). These reports suggest that dissociative responses may be common in the acute phase of a traumatic experience.

One needs to be cautious in interpreting these rates of dissociative reactions. These rates of dissociation are obtained from questionnaire studies or completion of checklists. Positive responses on checklists of dissociative responses do not necessarily allow us to infer that these responses actually reflect distinct alterations of awareness. For example, studies of dissociative amnesia have typically asked people if there is some aspect of their traumatic experience that they cannot recall. Positive endorsement of this question is often interpreted as evidence of dissociative amnesia. This approach is problematic because these studies do not recognize the potential roles of normal forgetting or intentional attempts to not recall or to not report recalling unpleasant events. Many studies ask respondents if they can recall everything that occurred or whether they cannot recall some aspect of the experience. This approach fails to disentangle dissociative amnesia, forgetting, and intentional avoidance (for a review, see McNally, 2003). Reflecting this confusion, Brown, Scheflin, and Whitfield's (1999) review of memory and trauma cite studies purportedly indicating amnesia after trauma, despite the apparent lack of evidence that these studies were directly indexing amnesia. For example, Brown et al. (1999) misinterpret studies that indexed "difficulties with everyday memory" (Cardeña & Spiegel, 1993) as evidence of amnesia. Memory and attentional deficits are reportedly common after trauma (Dalton, Pederson, & Ryan, 1989) but this problem in ongoing attentional focus does not reflect functional amnesia. Further, Brown et al. (1999) confuse studies where individuals do not initially report an event with amnesia. For example, they cite the study of Pynoos and Nader (1989), which interviewed 133 children after sniper attack, and found that five children who did not recall their own gunshot wounds; when these children were asked to recall the experience in slow motion, however, they correctly recalled the previously omitted details. In this context, it is important to note the distinction between amnesia and cognitive avoidance of trauma memories. For example, although Terr (1983) reported that children who suffered a kidnapping tried effortfully to avoid thinking about the experience, none were amnesic of the experience. In summary, it appears that many reports of so-called dissociative amnesia do not really reflect an inability to retrieve memories of trauma.

We should recognize that so-called dissociative symptoms may reflect a common shift in awareness rather than multiple forms of dissociation. Psychiatric disorders are operationally defined in terms of the number of distinct symptoms. For example, the ASD criteria specify that five different dissociative symptoms may be present: emotional numbing, reduced awareness of surroundings, derealization, depersonalization, and dissociative amnesia (APA, 1994). A number of these symptoms appear to overlap. It would be repetitive to consider that a traumatized individual is suffering amnesia of an event if they did not adequately encode it because of reduced awareness during the trauma. Regarding these two symptoms as separate responses artificially reifies two aspects of the same response. Reinforcing this possibility is evidence that 85% of individuals who reported lack of awareness of their surroundings also reported derealization (Harvey & Bryant, 1999c). One possible explanation for this overlap is that the constructs of derealization and reduced awareness are conceptually similar, and these allegedly distinct symptoms may be indexing a similar response to trauma.

It should be recognized that although this chapter focuses on peritraumatic dissociation, there is considerable confusion in operationally defining the time frame of the peritraumatic period. *Peritraumatic* typically refers to the period during or immediately after a traumatic period. This chapter will focus on dissociative responses during the traumatic incident and also during the initial month after trauma exposure. This time frame is adopted because (1) many studies use variable time frames within the initial month for assessing peritraumatic dissociation, (2) formal diagnostic systems use this time frame, and (3) there are potentially important theoretical reasons for distinguishing dissociative responses at variable points during the initial month after trauma exposure (see the following).

12.3 EXPLANATORY MECHANISMS OF PERITRAUMATIC DISSOCIATION

Perhaps the most influential theory, and undoubtedly the earliest proposal, involves the notion that dissociative reactions to trauma contribute to ongoing psychopathology. Current notions of dissociation trace their historical roots to the work of Janet (1907), Prince (1905/1978), and Breuer and Freud (1895/1986). This perspective proposes that people who have been exposed to a traumatic event may minimize the adverse emotional consequences of the trauma by restricting their awareness of the traumatic experience (Putnam, 1989; Spiegel, 1991; Van der Kolk & Van der Hart, 1989). This perspective originated in work conducted at the Salpêtrière in Paris over 100 years ago. Charcot (1987) proposed that traumatic shock could evoke responses that were phenomenologically similar to hypnotic states, and in this sense Charcot believed that traumatic experiences resulted in dissociative states that are evident in hysteria and during hypnosis. Extending this argument, Janet (1907) proposed that traumatic experiences that were incongruent with existing cognitive schema led to dissociated awareness. He argued that although this splitting of traumatic memories from awareness led to a reduction in distress, there was a loss of mental functioning because mental resources were not available for other processes. Janet proposes that adaptation following trauma required integrating the fragmented memories of the trauma into awareness. These views have enjoyed renewed attention in recent times, and represent the basis for the current notion that trauma-induced dissociation is a pivotal trauma response (Van der Kolk & Van der Hart, 1989; Nemiah, 1989). In terms of peritraumatic dissociation, this perspective posits that dissociating trauma memories and associated affect leads to ongoing psychopathology because the critical memories cannot be accessed and emotional processing is impaired (Marmar et al., 1994). Indirect support for this view has come from evidence that people diagnosed with PTSD report higher levels of hypnotizability (Spiegel, Hunt, & Dondershine, 1988; Stutman & Bliss, 1985) and dissociation (Bernstein & Putnam, 1986; Branscomb, 1991; Bremner et al., 1992; Carlson & Rosser-Hogan, 1991; Coons, Bowman, Pellow, & Schneider, 1989) than other psychiatric patient groups and the general community. Clearly, these correlational data do not support a causal link between traumatic events and dissociative responses.

12.3.1 Does Peritraumatic Dissociation Predict PTSD?

Although acute stress reactions are very common, there is also strong evidence that the majority of these stress responses are transient. That is, the majority of people who initially display distress naturally adapt to their experience in the following months. For example, whereas 94% of rape victims displayed sufficient PTSD symptoms two weeks posttrauma to meet criteria (excluding the 1-month time requirement), this rate dropped to 47% 11 weeks later (Rothbaum, Foa, Riggs, Murdock, & Walsh, 1992). In another study 70% of women and 50% of men were diagnosed with PTSD at an average of 19 days after an assault; the rate of PTSD at 4-month follow-up dropped to 21% for women and zero for men (Riggs, Rothbaum, & Foa, 1995). Similarly, half of a sample meeting criteria for PTSD shortly after a motor vehicle accident had remitted by 6 months and two-thirds had remitted by 1-year posttrauma (Blanchard et al., 1996). There is also evidence that most stress responses after the terrorist attacks of September 11, 2001, were temporary reactions. Galea et al. (2002) surveyed residents of New York City to gauge their response to the terrorist attacks. Five to 8 weeks after the attacks, 7.5% of a random sample of adults living south of 110th Street in Manhattan had developed PTSD, and of those living south of Canal Street, 20% had PTSD. In February 2002, Galea's group did a follow-up study on another group of adults living south of 110th Street, and found that only 1.7% of the sample had PTSD related to the attacks (Galea et al., 2003). This convergent evidence indicates that the normative response to trauma is to initially experience transient stress reactions, and that the majority of these reactions will remit in the following months. The proposal that dissociation is causally related to psychopathology has led commentators to suggest that those individuals who display peritraumatic dissociation are more likely to suffer chronic PTSD rather than a transient stress reaction (Spiegel, 1996).

Although many reports have indicated a relationship between peritraumatic dissociation and subsequent PTSD, a proportion of these earlier reports need to be discounted because they relied on retrospective accounts of acute dissociation that were obtained months after trauma exposure (e.g., Barton, Blanchard, & Hickling, 1996; Holen, 1993; Marmar et al., 1994; McFarlane, 1986). This design is inherently flawed because of evidence that recollections of acute reactions to trauma are often inaccurate and are influenced by the psychological state of the individual at the time of the recollection (Harvey & Bryant, 2000b; Marshall & Schell, 2002; Southwick, Morgan, Nicolaou, & Charney, 1997). Stronger support for the relationship between peritraumatic dissociation and PTSD comes from a series of prospective studies that have assessed trauma survivors shortly after trauma exposure and reassessed them months or years later. These studies have typically used measures of peritraumatic dissociation, such as the Peritraumatic Dissociative Experiences Questionnaire (Marmar, 1997; Marmar et al., 1997), or measures of acute stress reaction that include dissociative reactions, such as the Stanford Acute Stress Reaction Questionnaire (SASRQ; Cardeña, Koopman, Classen, Waelde, & Spiegel, 2000) or the Acute Stress Disorder Interview (Bryant, Harvey, Dang, & Sackville, 1998). A range of prospective studies have found that peritraumatic dissociation is a strong predictor of PTSD (Ehlers et al., 1998; Koopman, Classen, & Spiegel, 1994; Murray et al., 2002; Shalev, Freedman, et al., 1997; for a review, see a meta-analysis by Ozer et al., 2003).

In 1994 the fourth edition of the Diagnostic and Statistical Manual of Mental Disorders (DSM-IV; American Psychiatric Association, 1994) introduced the acute stress disorder (ASD) diagnosis to describe stress reactions in the initial month after a trauma. A major goal of this diagnosis was to identify people who shortly after trauma exposure would subsequently develop PTSD (Koopman, Classen, Cardeña, & Spiegel, 1995). DSM-IV stipulates that ASD can occur after a fearful response to experiencing or witnessing a threatening event (Cluster A). The requisite symptoms to meet criteria for ASD include three dissociative symptoms (Cluster B), one reexperiencing symptom (Cluster C), marked avoidance (Cluster D), marked anxiety or increased arousal (Cluster E), and evidence of significant distress or impairment (Cluster F). The disturbance must last for a minimum of 2 days and a maximum of 4 weeks (Cluster G) after which time a diagnosis of PTSD should be considered. The primary difference between the criteria for ASD and PTSD is the time frame and the former's emphasis on dissociative reactions to the trauma. ASD refers to symptoms manifested during the period from 2 days to 4 weeks posttrauma, whereas PTSD can only be diagnosed from 4 weeks. The diagnosis of ASD requires that the individual has at least three of the following: (1) a subjective sense of numbing or detachment, (2) reduced awareness of one's surroundings, (3) derealization, (4) depersonalization, or (5) dissociative amnesia.

There are now 12 prospective studies that have assessed the relationship between ASD in the initial month after trauma, and development of subsequent PTSD (Brewin et al., 1999; Bryant & Harvey, 1998; Creamer, O'Donnell, & Pattison, 2004; Difede et al., 2002; Harvey & Bryant, 1998a, 1999b, 2000a; Holeva et al., 2001; Kangas, Henry, & Bryant, 2005; Murray et al., 2002; Schnyder et al., 2001; Staab et al., 1996; for a review, see Bryant, 2003). In terms of people who meet criteria for ASD, a number of studies have found that approximately three-quarters of trauma survivors who display ASD subsequently develop PTSD (Brewin et al., 1999; Bryant & Harvey, 1998; Difede et al., 2002; Harvey & Bryant, 1998a, 1999b, 2000a; Holeva et al., 2001; Kangas et al., 2005; Murray et al., 2002). Compared to the expected remission of most people who display initial posttraumatic stress reactions, these studies indicate that the ASD diagnosis is performing reasonably well in predicting people who will develop PTSD. However, the utility of the ASD diagnosis is less encouraging when one considers the proportion of people who eventually developed PTSD and who initially displayed ASD. In most studies, the minority of people who eventually developed PTSD initially met criteria for ASD. That is, whereas the majority of people who develop ASD are high risk for developing subsequent PTSD, there are many other people who will develop PTSD who do not initially meet ASD criteria. It appears that a major reason for people who are high risk for PTSD not meeting ASD criteria is the requirement that three dissociative symptoms be displayed. In one study, 60% of people who met all ASD criteria except for the dissociation cluster met PTSD criteria 6 months later (Harvey & Bryant, 1998a), and 75% of these people still had PTSD 2 years later (Harvey & Bryant, 1999b). This pattern suggests that emphasizing dissociation as a critical factor in predicting subsequent PTSD leads to a neglect of other acute stress reactions that also represent a risk for development of chronic PTSD.

There is also evidence suggesting that dissociation is not necessary for subsequent development of PTSD and that the reported relationship between acute or peritraumatic dissociation and subsequent PTSD is more complex than has been assumed. For example, one retrospective investigation of ASD following road trauma found that early dissociation was not associated with PTSD 6 months posttrauma (Barton, Blanchard, & Hickling, 1996). Holen (1993) reported that whereas peritraumatic reactions were predictive of short-term outcome, they were less important in contributing to longer-term adjustment. Dancu, Riggs, Hearst-Ikeda, Shoyer, & Foa (1996) found that whereas acute dissociative reactions were linked to persistent PTSD in nonsexual assault victims, this relationship was not observed in rape victims. Other prospective studies have also found that peritraumatic dissociation is not a predictor of subsequent PTSD (Marshall & Schell, 2002). There is also evidence that dissociation is not necessarily present in PTSD, and it has been shown to decrease over time in those who display it initially (Davidson, Kudler, Saunders, & Smith, 1989). Further, prospective studies of ASD indicate that significant proportions of acutely traumatized individuals who do not display acute dissociation develop PTSD (Bryant & Harvey, 1998; Harvey & Bryant, 1998a, 1999b, 2000a). Overall, it appears that the presence of dissociative responses in the initial period after trauma may play some role in subsequent PTSD development, but the relationship between peritraumatic dissociation and subsequent disorder remains unclear.

12.3.2 Alternative Views of Peritraumatic Dissociation

There are several possible mechanisms that may account for the mixed findings about peritraumatic dissociation and subsequent PTSD. One possibility is that dissociation plays a role in PTSD development in some individuals but not others. Diathesis-stress models of dissociative disorders suggest that only people who possess dissociative tendencies respond to trauma with dissociative reactions (Butler, Duran, Jasiukaitis, Koopman, & Spiegel, 1996; Kihlstrom, Glisky, & Angiulo, 1994). Consistent with this view, Davidson and Foa (1991) suggest that dissociative responses are coping mechanisms that are used by individuals who can utilize these skills. Accordingly, only people who possess dissociative tendencies prior to the traumatic experience will display acute dissociation in response to a trauma (Atchison & McFarlane, 1994). This notion is supported by evidence that higher levels of hypnotizability have been reported in people with ASD compared to those who report a comparable acute stress reaction but lack dissociative symptoms (Bryant, Moulds, & Guthrie, 2001). Although both groups may have high risk for developing PTSD, only the subset of people who possess dissociative tendencies appear to respond with acute dissociative symptoms.

Another possibility is that peritraumatic dissociation is associated with subsequent PTSD because it is associated with other known risk factors for PTSD development. For example, there is a documented relationship between a history of childhood trauma and subsequent dissociation tendencies (Spiegel & Cardeña, 1991). Moreover, childhood trauma is a known risk factor for adult PTSD (Brewin, Andrews, & Valentine, 2000). It is possible that peritraumatic dissociation may be linked to PTSD because of its association with childhood trauma (Keane et al., 2001). This view suggests that proper understanding of the role of dissociation in PTSD development requires analysis of childhood trauma, prior dissociation, and peritraumatic dissociation in models that recognize the relative influences of pretrauma, peritraumatic, and posttrauma factors (Keane et al., 2001).

Another potential role of dissociation is its association with hyperarousal in the acute phase after trauma exposure. Peritraumatic dissociation may be a consequence of elevated arousal that occurs during trauma. Many of the reactions that are observed during peritraumatic dissociation overlap with panic experiences. Indirect support for this proposal comes from evidence that dissociative phenomenon (e.g., flashbacks) occur in PTSD individuals with yohimbine-induced arousal (Southwick et al., 1993). Further, dissociative reactions are commonly reported during panic attacks (Krystal, Woods, Hill, & Charney, 1991). Panic attacks are very common during trauma, with more than half of trauma survivors experiencing panic attacks during the trauma itself (Bryant & Panasetis, 2001; Resick, Falsetti, Kilpatrick, & Foy, 1994). Moreover, dissociative responses can be induced in recently trauma-exposed individuals with hyperventilation (Nixon & Bryant, 2005a). There is also evidence that panic during trauma is associated with ongoing panic in trauma survivors (Nixon & Bryant, 2003). Further, hyperarousal in the acute phase following trauma has been associated with subsequent PTSD (Shalev, 1992). It is possible that peritraumatic dissociation may be associated with later PTSD because it is linked to hyperarousal, which contributes directly to PTSD development.

Another possibility is that appraisals of peritraumatic dissociation, rather than peritraumatic dissociation itself, may influence subsequent PTSD. Cognitive theories of PTSD play much emphasis on the role of appraisals of the trauma and resulting symptoms in the development and maintenance of PTSD (Ehlers & Clark, 2000). There is much evidence that psychopathological responses to trauma are characterized by catastrophic interpretations of events. Individuals with ASD exaggerate the probability of various stimuli, including internal and somatic cues (Smith & Bryant, 2000). Catastrophic appraisals of peritraumatic dissociation may predict subsequent PTSD more than actual dissociative reactions. For example, a woman who interprets her emotional numbing toward her child as a normal response to an assault may be much less distressed than a woman who interprets emotional numbing as an indication of an uncaring mother. This interpretation accords with findings that appraisal of symptoms shortly after trauma exposure as indications of madness or impending deterioration predict subsequent PTSD (e.g., Dunmore et al., 2001; Ehlers et al., 1998).

12.4 NOSOLOGY

A major issue that will need to be addressed in DSM-V is whether ASD diagnosis should be retained in DSM-V. Similarly, should peritraumatic dissociation retain its central role in the ASD diagnosis? There have been many criticisms of the ASD diagnosis (see Koopman, 2000; Simeon & Guralnik, 2000; Butler, 2000; Bryant & Harvey, 2000; Harvey & Bryant, 2002; Keane, Kaufman, & Kimble, 2001; Marshall, Spitzer, & Liebowitz, 2000; Spiegel, Classen, & Cardena, 2000). First, the emphasis on dissociation as a necessary response to trauma has been criticized on the grounds that there is insufficient evidence to warrant this construct playing such a pivotal role in acute trauma response (Bryant & Harvey, 1997; Keane et al., 2001; Marshall et al., 2000). Second, some commentators have objected to the notion that the primary role of the ASD diagnosis is to predict another diagnosis (McNally, 2003). Third, there is concern that the diagnosis may pathologize transient reactions (Wakefield, 1996). Fourth, distinguishing between two diagnoses (ASD and PTSD) that have comparable symptoms on the basis of the duration of these symptoms is not well justified (Marshall et al., 1999).

It is apparent from the available evidence that the ASD diagnosis does not accurately identify the majority of people who will eventually develop PTSD. Although peritraumatic dissociation is often related to psychopathological responses, the apparently complex role that dissociation plays argues against dissociation being given the important role that it holds in the current ASD diagnosis. It is possible that embodying risk factors for chronic PTSD into a diagnostic category limits the potential for accurately identifying people who will develop PTSD. There is evidence that there are many other factors that can predict PTSD. Developing formulae that involve pretrauma factors, acute symptoms, biological responses, and cognitive styles may be more effective in identifying people who will develop PTSD. To this end, the ASD diagnosis may not be needed to perform this predictive function. It has been suggested that an important role of the ASD diagnosis is to also describe people who are currently experiencing severe stress reactions in the initial month after trauma. Describing people who are suffering stress reactions could be achieved by (1) applying the PTSD diagnosis in the initial period, or (2) describing acute stress reactions as responses that require clinical attention but are not conceptualized as a mental disorder. The DSM-IV Task Force considered using a V code to describe acute stress reactions in this way but decided against this option (Blank, 1993). A sensible alternative may be to use existing categories to describe acute reactions, and to identify people who will develop PTSD by using a range of empirically supported indicators rather than relying on a diagnostic label.

12.5 EVIDENCE FOR THE NATURE OF PERITRAUMATIC DISSOCIATION

In contrast to views that peritraumatic dissociation lead to psychopathology, another perspective holds that this reaction may actually assist adaptation. For example, Horowitz (1986) posits that dissociative responses to trauma may serve a protective function because they limit awareness of threatening experiences. This position holds that the less one encodes a threatening experience, the less aversive memories that one needs to manage. There is some evidence that acute dissociative reactions have been found to reduce subjective levels of fear (Moleman, Van der Hart, & Van der Kolk, 1992). At this point in time, however, we do not have strong evidence that limiting awareness of a traumatic experience is protective. There is indirect evidence that this possibility may exist. It appears that younger children may be protected to some degree from the adverse effects of trauma because they are unaware of the threat involved. For example, Handford et al. (1986) reported that children under 8 years did not become distressed by the Three Mile Island nuclear incident, possibly because they did not understand the risk posed to them. Similarly, Kazak et al. (1998) proposed that the preschool and school-aged children in their study of PTSD in cancer survivors might have been protected from the impact of the trauma by their limited ability to perceive the threat posed by their illness. There is also evidence that people who sustain a severe traumatic brain injury are largely spared from intrusive memories because they are unconscious during much of the traumatic experience (Bryant, Marosszeky, Crooks, & Gurka, 2000). It appears that losing consciousness during a traumatic experience lessens the likelihood of that experience being encoded and reduces the opportunity for subsequent aversive memories (Bryant, 2001).

One possible confusion in determining whether peritraumatic dissociation is protective or harmful is the duration of the dissociation. The time frame of peritraumatic dissociation is typically defined in very ambiguous terms. For example, DSM-IV defines dissociation in ASD as occurring "either during or after experiencing the distressing event." The ambiguity concerning the time frame for dissociation is potentially problematic because transient dissociation (peritraumatic dissociation) and persistent dissociation can lead to contrary predictions concerning outcome. Cognitive models of trauma would predict that persistent dissociation would be maladaptive and would be associated with subsequent PTSD. Network models posit that following a trauma fear structures develop that contain mental representations of the traumatic experience and are characterized by excessive threat-related beliefs (Foa & Kozak, 1986). The model suggests that adaptive recovery from a trauma requires, in part, activation of the fear structures so that the cognitive schema may be modified. Accordingly, excessive avoidance and dissociation following trauma can impede activation of the fear network and preclude adequate resolution of the fear-related material (Foa & Hearst-Ikeda, 1996). This view would predict that persistent, but not peritraumatic, dissociation would lead to psychopathology. Understanding the role of peritraumatic dissociation may be enhanced by discriminating between cognitive processes that limit encoding of traumatic experiences (which may serve a protective function) and those processes that impede retrieval of traumatic memories (which may be maladaptive). Initial support for the differential roles of transient and persistent dissociation comes from a study that compared the relationship between dissociative responses reported to occur at the time of a trauma and those that persisted after the trauma (Panasetis & Bryant, 2003). This study found that whereas persistent dissociation was a significant predictor of the severity of ASD, peritraumatic dissociation was not. Similarly, a recent prospective study found that persistent dissociation was a stronger predictor of subsequent PTSD than dissociation occurring immediately after the trauma (Murray et al., 2002). This pattern accords with evidence that much peritraumatic dissociation is transient. For example, Noyes and Kletti (1977) found that the vast majority of trauma survivors who experienced dissociative reactions at the time of the trauma did not develop pathology, and their dissociative symptoms did not persist beyond the trauma.

The available evidence suggests that not all dissociative responses are pathological. Alterations in awareness appear to occur under many circumstances in which there is increased arousal or perceived threat; many of these dissociative responses do not develop into pathological states. For example, weapon focus studies involve a research participant being approached by a stranger (who is actually an experimental confederate) and the stranger holds either a pen or a knife. These studies have found that when a knife is present, people have better recall of the knife and surrounding detail (such as wristwatch, rings) and poorer recall of the person's face; in contrast, there is better recall of the person's face and poorer recall of the hand when there is a benign object being held (Kramer, Buckhout, & Eugenio, 1990; Maas & Kohnken, 1989). These studies indicate that there are marked alterations in attentional focus toward the narrow source of threat, and reduced awareness of peripheral events during mildly stressful experiences. Similarly, there is evidence of elevated levels of dissociation in people who experience stress but do not develop subsequent disorder. Novice skydivers display elevated levels of dissociative reactions during their skydives, even though they do not develop subsequent problems (Sterlini & Bryant, 2002).

Part of the consideration of the potential role that peritraumatic dissociation may play in posttraumatic stress is its potential relationship with psychophysiological activity. A popular theory in recent years has been that dissociation reduces physiological arousal. This view has arisen, in part, from extrapolating from animal studies that have found that shocked animals display freezing responses. Parallels have been drawn between these observations in animals and dissociative responses in trauma-exposed humans (Van der Kolk, Greenberg, Boyd, & Krystal, 1985). In an influential study, Griffin, Resick, and Mechanic (1997) reported in a sample of recent rape victims (2 weeks posttrauma) that individuals who reported high levels of peritraumatic dissociation demonstrated suppressed autonomic reactivity (heart rate, skin conductance) when recounting their trauma compared with low dissociators. Bryant et al. (2000) observed resting heart rate was significantly lower in acutely stressed motor vehicle accident survivors with dissociation compared to survivors without dissociation. Although the latter study did not allow causal inferences to be drawn, one possibility is that dissociative responses after trauma suppressed sympathetic activation. In contrast, recent studies have challenged the proposal that dissociation is associated with suppressed autonomic functioning. In a study of domestic violence victims that replicated the Griffin et al. (1997) design, Griffin, Nishith, and Resick (2002) did not find suppressed reactivity in dissociative individuals. Similarly, PTSD combat veterans who retrospectively reported high levels of peritraumatic dissociation showed similar levels of autonomic response to both neutral and combat-related stimuli as their PTSD counterparts characterized by low dissociation (Kaufman et al., 2002). Finally, a study that indexed psychophysiological responses during recounting of trauma narratives shortly after trauma found no differences in reactivity in high and low dissociators (Nixon & Bryant, 2005b).

12.6 RESEARCH DIRECTIONS

The mixed evidence about the role of peritraumatic dissociation points to the need for more sophisticated research into the mechanisms and correlates of these alterations in awareness. The well-documented tendency for peritraumatic dissociation to be associated with subsequent psychopathology has been countered by repeated evidence that this relationship is not linear. Accordingly, research is needed that delineates the specific roles of all potential factors that may account for the association between dissociation and psychopathology. These factors may include panic, prior trauma, catastrophic appraisals, or other variables. We will not advance our knowledge about peritraumatic dissociation until we move beyond descriptive level research that merely correlates scores on measures of dissociation with psychopathology responses in the absence of other potentially relevant variables. This form of research needs to adopt structural modeling procedures that can account for the interacting influences of multiple variables rather than simplistically assuming linear relationships between dissociative responses and key psychopathology outcomes. Similarly, the construct of peritraumatic dissociation needs to be deconstructed into more specific factors, such as time distortion, reduced awareness, amnesia, and derealization. The exact mechanisms of these responses and their role in posttraumatic perception and response need to be experimentally studied. Finally, future research needs to be more careful in determining the time frame of dissociative responses, and special attention should be given to the distinction between transient alterations in awareness during a traumatic experience and more persistent dissociative reactions.

Understanding the mechanisms that underpin successful and unsuccessful responses to trauma is essential if optimal prevention and treatment strategies are to be developed. Effective advances in our knowledge about trauma response will only be achieved through research that moves beyond descriptive research that shows a tendency for dissociation to be associated with psychopathology. The study of peritraumatic dissociation has stalled at this point for many years. We need a fresh approach that is not limited by adherence to Janet's (1907) early views but instead is willing to investigate the broad array of possible roles that dissociative responses may play in the aftermath of trauma.

REFERENCES

American Psychiatric Association (1994). *DSM-IV – Diagnostic and statistical manual of mental disorders* (4th ed.). Washington, DC: Author.

Atchison, M., & McFarlane, A. C. (1994). A review of dissociation and dissociative disorders. *Australian and New Zealand Journal of Psychiatry, 28*, 591–599.

Barton, K. A., Blanchard, E. B., & Hickling, E. J. (1996). Antecedents and consequences of acute stress disorder among motor vehicle accident victims. *Behaviour Research and Therapy, 34,* 805–813.

Berah, E. F., Jones, H. J., & Valent, P. (1984). The experience of a mental health team involved in the early phase of a disaster. *Australian and New Zealand Journal of Psychiatry, 18,* 354–358.

Bernstein, E. M., & Putnam, F. W. (1986). Development, reliability, and validity of a dissociation scale. *Journal of Nervous and Mental Disease, 174*, 727–735.

Blanchard, E. B., Hickling, E. J., Barton, K. A., Taylor, A. E., Loos, W. R., & Jones Alexander, J. (1996). One-year prospective follow-up of motor vehicle accident victims. *Behaviour Research and Therapy, 34,* 775–786.

Blank, A. S. (1993). Suggested recommendations for DSM-IV on course and subtypes. In J. R. Davidson & E. B. Foa (Eds.), *Posttraumatic stress disorder in review: Recent research and future developments* (pp. 237–240). Washington, DC: American Psychiatric Press.

Branscomb, L. (1991). Dissociation in combat-related posttraumatic stress disorder. *Dissociation, 4*, 13–30.

Bremner, J. D., Southwick, S., Brett, E., Fontana, A., Rosenheck, R., & Charney, D. S. (1992). Dissociation and posttraumatic stress disorder in Vietnam combat veterans. *American Journal of Psychiatry, 149*, 328–332.

Breuer, J., & Freud, S. (1895/1986). *Studies on hysteria.* New York: Basic Books (Original work published in 1895).

Brewin, C. R., Andrews, B., Rose, S., & Kirk, M. (1999). Acute stress disorder and posttraumatic stress disorder in victims of violent crime. *American Journal of Psychiatry, 156*, 360–366.

Brewin, C. R., Andrews, B., & Valentine, J. D. (2000). Meta-analysis of risk factors for posttraumatic stress disorder in trauma-exposed adults. *Journal of Consulting and Clinical Psychology, 68*, 748–766.

Brown, L. S., Scheflin, A. W., & Whitfielkd, C. L. (1999). Recovered memories: The current weight of the evidence in science and in the courts. *Journal of Psychiatry and Law, 27*, 5–156.

Bryant, R. A. (2001). Posttraumatic stress disorder and traumatic brain injury: Can they co-exist? *Clinical Psychology Review, 21*, 931–945.

Bryant, R. A. (2003). Early predictors of posttraumatic stress disorder. *Biological Psychiatry, 53*, 789–795.

Bryant, R. A., & Harvey, A. G. (1997). Acute stress disorder: a critical review of diagnostic issues. *Clinical Psychology Review, 17*, 757–773.

Bryant, R. A., & Harvey, A. G. (1998). Relationship of acute stress disorder and posttraumatic stress disorder following mild traumatic brain injury. *American Journal of Psychiatry, 155*, 625–629.

Bryant, R. A., & Harvey, A. G. (2000). New DSM-IV diagnosis of acute stress disorder. *American Journal of Psychiatry, 157*, 1889–1890.

Bryant R. A., Harvey A. G., Guthrie, R. M., & Moulds, M. L. (2000). A prospective study of psychophysiological arousal, acute stress disorder, and posttraumatic stress disorder. *Journal of Abnormal Psychology, 109,* 341–344.

Bryant, R. A., Harvey, A. G., Dang, S., & Sackville, T. (1998). Assessing acute stress disorder: Psychometric properties of a structured clinical interview. *Psychological Assessment, 10,* 215–220.

Bryant, R. A., Marosszeky, J. E., Crooks, J., & Gurka, J. A. (2000). Posttraumatic stress disorder following severe traumatic brain injury. *American Journal of Psychiatry, 157*, 629–631.

Bryant, R. A., Moulds, M., & Guthrie, R. M. (2001). Hypnotizability in acute stress disorder. *American Journal of Psychiatry, 158*, 600–604.

Bryant, R. A., & Panasetis, P. (2001). Panic symptoms during trauma and acute stress disorder. *Behaviour Research and Therapy, 39*, 961–966.

Butler, L. D. (2000). New DSM-IV diagnosis of acute stress disorder. Letter to the Editor. *American Journal of Psychiatry, 157*, 1889.

Butler, L. D., Duran, R. E. F., Jasiukaitis, P., Koopman, C., Spiegel, D. (1996). Hypnotizability and traumatic experience: A diathesis-stress model of dissociative symptomatology. *American Journal of Psychiatry, 153 (Suppl. 7S)*, 42–63.

Cardeña, E., Koopman, C., Classen, C., Waelde, L. C., & Spiegel, D. (2000). Psychometric properties of the Stanford Acute Stress Reaction Questionnaire (SASRQ):

A valid and reliable measure of acute stress. *Journal of Traumatic Stress, 13*, 719–734.

Cardeña, E., & Spiegel, D. (1993). Dissociative reactions to the San Francisco Bay Area earthquake of 1989. *American Journal of Psychiatry, 150*, 474–478.

Carlson, E. B., & Rosser-Hogan, R. (1991). Trauma experiences, posttraumatic stress, dissociation, and depression in Cambodian refugees. *American Journal of Psychiatry, 148*, 1548–1551.

Charcot, J.-M. (1987). *Leçons sur les maladies du système nerveux faites à la Salpêtrière* (Vol. 3). Paris: Progrès Médical en A. Delahaye & E. Lecrosnie.

Coons, P. M., Bowman, E. S., Pellow, T. A., & Schneider, P. (1989). Post-traumatic aspects of the treatment of victims of sexual abuse and incest. *Psychiatric Clinics of North America, 12*, 325–335.

Creamer, M. C., O'Donnell, M. L., & Pattison, P. (2004). The relationship between acute stress disorder and posttraumatic stress disorder in severely injured trauma survivors. *Behaviour Research and Therapy, 42*, 315–328.

Dalton, J. E., Pederson, S. L., & Ryan, J. J. (1989). Effects of post-traumatic stress disorder on neuropsychological test performance. *International Journal of Clinical Neuropsychology, 11*, 121–124.

Dancu, C. V., Riggs, D. S., Hearst-Ikeda, D., Shoyer, B. G., & Foa, E. B. (1996). Dissociative experiences and posttraumatic stress disorder among female victims of criminal assault and rape. *Journal of Traumatic Stress, 9*, 253–267.

Davidson, J., & Foa, E. B. (1991). Diagnostic issues in posttraumatic stress disorder: Considerations for DSM-IV. *Journal of Abnormal Psychology, 100*, 346–355.

Davidson, J., Kudler, H., Saunders, W. B., & Smith, R. D. (1989). Symptom and comorbidity patterns in World War II and Vietnam veterans with PTSD. *Comprehensive Psychiatry, 31*, 162–170.

Difede, J., Ptacek, J. T., Roberts, J. G., Barocas, D., Rives, W., Apfeldorf, W. J., & Yurt, R. (2002). Acute stress disorder after burn injury: A predictor of posttraumatic stress disorder. *Psychosomatic Medicine, 64*, 826–834.

Dunmore, E., Clark, D. M., & Ehlers, A. (2001). A prospective investigation of the role of cognitive factors in persistent Posttraumatic Stress Disorder (PTSD) after physical and sexual assault. *Behaviour Research and Therapy, 39*, 1063–1084.

Ehlers, A., & Clark, D. (2000). A cognitive model of posttraumatic stress disorder. *Behaviour Research and Therapy, 38*, 319–345.

Ehlers, A., Mayou, R. A., & Bryant, B. (1998). Psychological predictors of chronic PTSD after motor vehicle accidents. *Journal of Abnormal Psychology, 107*, 508–519.

Feinstein, A. (1989). Posttraumatic stress disorder: A descriptive study supporting DSM III-R criteria. *American Journal of Psychiatry, 146*, 665–666.

Foa, E. B., & Hearst-Ikeda, D. (1996). Emotional dissociation in response to trauma: An information-processing approach. In L. K. Michelson & W. J. Ray (Eds.), *Handbook of dissociation: Theoretical and clinical perspectives* (pp. 207–222). New York: Plenum Press.

Foa, E. B., & Kozak, M. J. (1986). Emotional processing of fear: Exposure to corrective information. *Psychological Bulletin, 99*, 20–35.

Freinkel, A., Koopman, C., & Spiegel, D. (1994). Dissociative symptoms in media witnesses of an execution. *American Journal of Psychiatry, 151*, 1335–1339.

Galea, S., Vlahov, D., Resnick, H., Ahern, J., Susser, E., Gold, J., Bucuvalas, M., & Kilpatrick, D. (2003). Trends of probable post-traumatic stress disorder in New York City after the September 11 terrorist attacks. *American Journal of Epidemiology, 158*, 514–524.

Galea, S., Resnick, H., Kilpatrick, D., Bucuvalas, M., Gold, J., & Vlahov, D. (2002). Psychological sequelae of the September 11 terrorist attacks in New York City. *New England Journal of Medicine, 346*, 982–987.

Griffin, M. G., Nishith, P., & Resick, P. A. (2002, November). *Peritraumatic dissociation in domestic violence victims*. Paper presented at the 18th Annual Meeting of the International Society of Traumatic Stress Studies, Baltimore, USA.

Griffin, M. G., Resick, P. A., & Mechanic, M. B. (1997). Objective assessment of peritraumatic dissociation: Psychophysiological indicators. *American Journal of Psychiatry, 154*, 1081–1088.

Handford, H. A., Mayes, S. D., Matterson, R. E., Humphrey, F. J., Bagnato, S., Bixler, E. O., & Kales, J. K. (1986). Child and parent reaction to the Three Mile Island nuclear accident. *Journal of the American Academy of Child Psychiatry, 25*, 346–356.

Harvey, A. G., & Bryant, R. A. (1998a). Relationship of acute stress disorder and posttraumatic stress disorder following motor vehicle accidents. *Journal of Consulting and Clinical Psychology, 66*, 507–512.

Harvey, A. G., & Bryant, R. A. (1999b). A two-year prospective evaluation of the relationship between acute stress disorder and posttraumatic stress disorder. *Journal of Consulting and Clinical Psychology, 67*, 985–988.

Harvey, A. G., & Bryant, R. A. (1999c). Dissociative symptoms in acute stress disorder. *Journal of Traumatic Stress, 12*, 673–680.

Harvey, A. G., & Bryant, R. A. (2000a). A two-year prospective evaluation of the relationship between acute stress disorder and posttraumatic stress disorder following mild traumatic brain injury. *American Journal of Psychiatry, 157*, 626–628.

Harvey, A. G., & Bryant, R. A. (2000b). Memory for acute stress disorder symptoms: A two-year prospective study. *Journal of Nervous and Mental Disease, 188*, 602–607.

Harvey, A. G., & Bryant, R. A. (2002). Acute stress disorder: a synthesis and critique. *Psychological Bulletin, 128*, 892–906.

Hillman, R. G. (1981). The psychopathology of being held hostage. *American Journal of Psychiatry, 138*, 1193–1197.

Holen, A. (1993). The North Sea oil rig disaster. In J. P. Wilson & B. Raphael (Eds.), *International handbook of traumatic stress syndromes* (pp. 471–478). New York: Plenum.

Holeva, V., Tarrier, N., & Wells, A. (2001). Prevalence and predictors of acute stress disorder and PTSD following road traffic accidents: thought control strategies and social support. *Behavior Therapy, 32*, 65–83.

Horowitz, M. J. (1986). *Stress response syndromes* (2nd ed.). New York: Jason Aronson.

Janet, P. (1907). *The major symptoms of hysteria*. New York: McMillan.

Kangas, M., Henry, J. L., & Bryant, R. A. (2005). The relationship between acute stress disorder and posttraumatic stress disorder following cancer. *Journal of Consulting and Clinical Psychology*, *73*, 360–364.

Kaufman, M. L., Kimble, M. O., Kaloupek, D. G., McTeague, L. M., Bachrach, P., Forti, A. M., & Keane, T. M. (2002). Peritraumatic dissociation and physiological response to trauma-relevant stimuli in Vietnam combat veterans with posttraumatic stress disorder. *Journal of Nervous and Mental Disease, 190*, 167–174.

Kazak, A. E., Barakat, L. P., Meeske, K., Chrstiakis, D., Meadows, A. T., Casey, R., Penati, B., & Stuber, M. (1998). Posttraumatic stress, family functioning, and social support in survivors of childhood cancer and their mothers and fathers. *Journal of Consulting and Clinical Psychology, 65,* 120–129.

Keane, T. M., Kaufman, M. L., & Kimble, M. O. (2001). Peritraumatic dissociative symptoms, acute stress disorder, and the development of posttraumatic stress disorder: Causation, correlation or epiphenomena. In L. Sanchez-Planell & C. Diez-Quevedo (Eds.), *Dissociative states* (pp. 21–43). Barcelona, Spain: Springer-Verlag.

Kihlstrom, J. F., Glisky, M. L., & Angiulo, M. J. (1994). Dissociative tendencies and dissociative disorders. *Journal of Abnormal Psychology, 103*, 117–124.

Koopman, C. (2000). New DSM-IV diagnosis of acute stress disorder. Letter to the Editor. *American Journal of Psychiatry, 157*, 1888.

Koopman, C., Classen, C., & Spiegel, D. (1994). Predictors of posttraumatic stress symptoms among survivors of the Oakland/Berkeley, Calif., firestorm. *American Journal of Psychiatry, 151,* 888–894.

Koopman, C., Classen, C., Cardeña, E., & Spiegel, D. (1995). When disaster strikes, acute stress disorder may follow. *Journal of Traumatic Stress, 8*, 29–46.

Kramer, T., Buckhout, R., & Eugenio, P. (1990). Weapon focus, arousal, and eyewitness memory: Attention must be paid. *Law and Human Behavior, 14*, 167–184.

Krystal, J., Woods, S., Hill, C. L., & Charney, D. S. (1991). Characteristics of panic attack subtypes: assessment of spontaneous panic, situational panic, sleep panic, and limited symptom attacks. *Comprehensive Psychiatry, 32*, 4474–4480.

Maas, A., & Kohnken, G. (1989). Eyewitness identification. *Law and Human Behavior, 11*, 397–408.

Madakasira, S., & O'Brien, K. F. (1987). Acute posttraumatic stress disorder in victims of a natural disaster. *Journal of Nervous and Mental Disease, 175,* 286–290.

Marmar, C. R. (1997). Trauma and dissociation. *PTSD Research Quarterly, 8*, 1–8.

Marmar, C. R., Weiss, D. S., Schlenger, W. E., Fairbank, J. A., Jordan, K., Kulka, R. A., & Hough, R. L. (1994). Peritraumatic dissociation and posttraumatic stress in male Vietnam theater veterans. *American Journal of Psychiatry, 151,* 902–907.

Marshall, G. N., & Schell, T. L. (2002). Reappraising the link between peritraumatic dissociation and PTSD symptom severity: Evidence from a longitudinal study of community violence survivors. *Journal of Abnormal Psychology, 111*, 626–636.

Marshall, R. D., Spitzer, R., & Liebowitz, M. R. (1999). Review and critique of the new DSM-IV diagnosis of acute stress disorder. *American Journal of Psychiatry, 156*, 1677–1685.

Marshall, R. D., Spitzer, R., & Liebowitz, M. R. (2000). New DSM-IV diagnosis of acute stress disorder. *American Journal of Psychiatry, 157*, 1890–1891.

McFarlane, A. C. (1986). Posttraumatic morbidity of a disaster. *Journal of Nervous and Mental Disease, 174,* 4–14.

McNally, R. J. (2003). *Remembering trauma*. Cambridge, MA: Belknap Press.

Moleman, N., Van der Hart, O., & Van der Kolk, B. A. (1992). Dissociation and hypnotizability in posttraumatic stress disorder. *Journal of Nervous and Mental Disease 180*, 271–272.

Murray, J., Ehlers, A., & Mayou, R. A. (2002). Dissociation and post-traumatic stress disorder: Two prospective studies of road traffic accident survivors. *British Journal of Psychiatry*, *180*, 363–368.

Nemiah, J. C. (1989). Janet redivivus [Editorial]. *American Journal of Psychiatry, 146*, 1527–1529.

Nixon, R., & Bryant, R. A. (2003). Peritraumatic and persistent panic attacks in acute stress disorder. *Behaviour Research and Therapy, 41*, 1237–1242.

Nixon, R., & Bryant, R. A. (2005a). Induced arousal and reexperiencing in acute stress disorder. *Journal of Anxiety Disorders, 19*, 587–594.

Nixon, R. D. V., & Bryant, R. A. (2005b). Physiological arousal and dissociation in acute trauma victims during trauma narratives. *Journal of Traumatic Stress, 18,* 107–114.

Noyes, R., Hoenk, P. R., Kuperman, S., & Slymen, D. J. (1977). Depersonalization in accident victims and psychiatric patients. *Journal of Nervous and Mental Disease, 164*, 401–407.

Noyes, R., & Kletti, R. (1977). Depersonalizaton in response to life-threatening danger. *Comprehensive Psychiatry, 18*, 375–384.

Ozer, E. J., Best, S. R., Lipsey, T. L., & Weiss, D. S. (2003). Predictors of posttraumatic stress disorder and symptoms in adults: A meta-analysis. *Psychological Bulletin, 129,* 52–73.

Panasetis, P., & Bryant, R. A. (2003). Peritraumatic versus persistent dissociation in acute stress disorder. *Journal of Traumatic Stress*, *16*, 563–566.

Prince, M. (1905/1978). *The dissociation of a personality*. New York: Oxford University Press (Original work published in 1905).

Putnam, F. W. (1989). Pierre Janet and modern views of dissociation. *Journal of Traumatic Stress, 2*, 413–429.

Pynoos, R. S., & Nader, K. (1989). Children's memory and proximity to violence. *Journal of the American Academy of Child and Adolescent Psychiatry, 28*, 236–241.

Resnick, H. S., Falsetti, S. A., Kilpatrick, D. G., & Foy, D. W. (1994). Associations between panic attacks during rape assaults and follow-up PTSD or panic-attack outcomes. Presented at the 10th Annual Meeting of the International Society of Traumatic Stress Studies, Chicago, IL, November 1994.

Riggs, D. S., Rothbaum, B. O., & Foa, E. B. (1995). A prospective examination of symptoms of posttraumatic stress disorder in victims of non-sexual assault. *Journal of Interpersonal Violence, 10,* 201–214.

Rothbaum, B. O., Foa, E. B., Riggs, D. S., Murdock, T., & Walsh, W. (1992). A prospective examination of posttraumatic stress disorder in rape victims. *Journal of Traumatic Stress, 5*, 455–475.

Schnyder, U., Moergeli, H., Klaghofer, R., & Buddeberg, C. (2001). Incidence and prediction of posttraumatic stress disorder symptoms in severely injured accident victims. *American Journal of Psychiatry, 158*, 594–599.

Shalev, A. Y. (1992). Posttraumatic stress disorder among injured survivors of a terrorist attack. *Journal of Nervous and Mental Disease, 180,* 505–509.

Shalev, A. Y., Freedman, S., Peri, T., Brandes, D., & Sahar, T. (1997). Predicting PTSD in trauma survivors: Prospective evaluation of self-report and clinician-administered instruments. *British Journal of Psychiatry, 170,* 558–564.

Siegel, R. K. (1984). Hostage hallucinations: Visual imagery induced by isolation and life-threatening stress. *Journal of Nervous and Mental Disease, 172*, 264–272.

Simeon, D., & Guralnik, O. (2000). New DSM-IV diagnosis of acute stress disorder. Letter to the Editor. *American Journal of Psychiatry, 157*, 1888–1889.

Smith, K., & Bryant, R. A. (2000). The generality of cognitive bias in acute stress disorder. *Behaviour Research and Therapy, 38*, 709–715.

Sloan, P. (1988). Post-traumatic stress in survivors of an airplane crash-landing: A clinical and exploratory research intervention. *Journal of Traumatic Stress, 1*, 211–229.

Southwick, S. M., Krystal, J. H., Morgan, C. A., Johnson, D. R., Nagy, L. M., Nicolaou, A. L., Heninger, G. R., & Charney, D. S. (1993). Abnormal noradrenergic function in posttraumatic stress disorder. *Archives of General Psychiatry, 50*, 266–274.

Southwick, S. M., Morgan, C. A., Nicolaou, A. L., & Charney, D. S. (1997). Consistency of memory for combat-related traumatic events in veterans of Operation Desert Storm. *American Journal of Psychiatry, 154*, 173–177.

Spiegel, D. (1991). Dissociation and trauma. In A. Tasman & S. M. Goldfinger (Eds.), *American Psychiatric Press review of psychiatry, 10* (pp. 261–275). Washington, DC: American Psychiatric Press.

Spiegel, D. (1996). Dissociative disorders. In R. E. Hales & S. C. Yudofsky (Eds.), *Synopsis of psychiatry* (pp. 583–604). Washington, DC: American Psychiatric Press.

Spiegel, D., & Cardeña, E. (1991). Disintegrated experience: The dissociative disorders revisited. *Journal of Abnormal Psychology, 100*, 366–378.

Spiegel, D., Classen, C., & Cardeña, E. (2000). New DSM-IV diagnosis of acute stress disorder. Letter to the Editor. *American Journal of Psychiatry, 157*, 1890–1891.

Spiegel, D., Hunt, T., & Dondershine, H. E. (1988). Dissociation and hypnotizability in posttraumatic stress disorder. *American Journal of Psychiatry, 145*, 301–314.

Staab, J. P., Grieger, T. A., Fullerton, C. S., & Ursano, R. J. (1996). Acute stress disorder, subsequent posttraumatic stress disorder and depression after a series of typhoons. *Anxiety, 2*, 219–225.

Sterlini, G., & Bryant, R. A. (2002). Hyperarousal and dissociation: A study of novice skydivers. *Behaviour Research and Therapy, 40*, 431–437.

Stutman, R. K., & Bliss, E. L. (1985). Posttraumatic stress disorder, hypnotizability, and imagery. *American Journal of Psychiatry, 142*, 741–743.

Terr, L. C. (1983). Chowchilla revisited: The effects of psychic trauma four years after a school-bus kidnapping. *American Journal of Psychiatry, 140*, 1543–1550.

Titchener, J. T., & Kapp, F. T. (1976). Family and character change at Buffalo Creek. *American Journal of Psychiatry, 133*, 295–299.

Torrie, A. (1944). Psychosomatic casualties in the Middle East. *Lancet, 29*, 139–143.

Van der Kolk, B. A., Greenberg, M., Boyd, H., & Krystal, J. (1985). Inescapable shock, neurotransmitters, and addiction to trauma: Towards a psychobiology of post traumatic stress. *Biological Psychiatry, 20*, 314–325.

Van der Kolk, B. A., & Van der Hart, O. (1989). Pierre Janet and the breakdown of adaptation in psychological data. *American Journal of Psychiatry, 146*, 1530–1540.

Wakefield, J. C. (1996). DSM-IV: Are we making diagnostic progress? *Contemporary Psychology, 41*, 646–652.

13 Peritraumatic Dissociation and Amnesia in Violent Offenders

Andrew Moskowitz, PhD
Ceri Evans, MBChB, MRCPsych, PhD

OUTLINE

13.1 INTRODUCTION

The validity of reports of peritraumatic dissociation and amnesia in violent offenders are often, and understandably, questioned. Violent crimes trigger powerful emotional reactions not only in the relatives and friends of those affected, but also in the citizens at large of any civilized society. Such shocking actions as rape and murder threaten cherished notions of the world as a safe place, and of other people as trustworthy and reliable. Partly to maintain these beliefs, violent individuals are often viewed as inherently evil or all bad, incapable of producing anything but lies and manipulation. Thus, when someone who has committed a terrible crime claims not to recall the event, or reports feeling "outside of himself" during its commission, such claims are often viewed with skepticism or outright hostility.

However, if we hope to better understand and prevent violent episodes, it is in the interests of society, as well as science, to further explore such claims. Is it possible that some individuals who commit violent crimes do, in fact, experience depersonalization or derealization during the commission of the act, or not recall some or all of the event afterward? If so, are these experiences simply epiphenomena, or do they point to a causal role for dissociation in the expression of some forms of violent behavior? What do such experiences tell us about the psychological mechanisms underlying violent behavior and the individuals who engage in such behavior? It is to these questions that this chapter is dedicated.

In the first section, we review the concept of peritraumatic dissociation (PTD), including its relationship with amnesia and posttraumatic stress disorder (PTSD). In so doing, we note that PTD does not fall within the definition of dissociation that Dorahy and Van der Hart put forth in Chapter 1, and explain our reasons for retaining the concept here. In the second section, we review the limited literature on PTD in violent offenders, primarily focusing on experiences of depersonalization and derealization, and the more extensive but problematic literature on amnesia in violent offenders. Emphasis will be placed on a recent series of studies (Evans, Ehlers, Mezey, & Clark, 2007a, 2007b; Evans, Mezey, Ehlers, & Clark, in press), covering both PTD and amnesia in violent young offenders, which challenges previous findings. Finally, we address the significance of these findings, suggesting that such experiences may indicate any of three possible scenarios: (1) a traumatic reaction to one's own violent actions, possibly predictive of PTSD but unrelated to any dissociative disorder, (2) the presence of a preexisting dissociative disorder, and (3) the emergence of a dissociative disorder through the act of violence, for which there is limited or no evidence afterward. Case illustrations for each of these three scenarios will be provided.

13.2 THE DOMAIN OF DISSOCIATION

Van der Hart and Dorahy (Chapter 1) explicitly criticize the notion of PTD, noting that such alterations in consciousness do not necessarily require the fissure in personality they see as fundamental to the concept of dissociation. They are, of course, correct: while PTD may arise in individuals who are "structurally dissociated" (to use their terminology), it also occurs in individuals who are not. However, for the purposes of this chapter, we use the term PTD to describe a set of experiences that *may*, we suggest, indicate prior or incipient structural dissociation, as in dissociative disorders. We also suggest that PTD may simply indicate a traumatic reaction, potentially related to the subsequent development of PTSD, but unrelated to any (other) dissociative disorder.

Peritraumatic dissociation refers to dissociative symptoms experienced by individuals during traumatic events. Most commonly, these experiences consist of some form of depersonalization (such as feelings of being "beside" oneself or "watching" oneself) and/or derealization (such as feeling as though one were in a dream or watching a movie). PTD became of interest to trauma specialists when research suggested that it robustly predicted the later development of PTSD (Marmar et al., 1994; Shalev, Peri, Canetti, & Schreiber, 1996). While some recent results have questioned this assertion (for example, Panasetis & Bryant, 2003, emphasize the importance of ongoing dissociation over peritraumatic dissociation), a recent meta-analysis found PTD to be the best predictor of subsequent PTSD, with an average effect size of r = 0.35 (Ozer, Best, Lipsey, & Weiss, 2003). There is also some preliminary evidence that PTD may predict subsequent amnesia (Yates & Nasby, 1995).

13.3 PERITRAUMATIC DISSOCIATION[1] AND AMNESIA IN VIOLENT OFFENDERS

There has been a recent upsurge of interest in the relationship between dissociation and violence, with several studies exploring the prevalence of dissociation and dissociative disorders amongst offenders (e.g., Carrion & Steiner, 2000; Simoneti, Scott, & Murphy, 2000; Snow, Beckman, & Brack, 1996), and two recent review/integrations of the area (Moskowitz, 2004a, 2004b). However, there has been relatively little research conducted on PTD in violent offenders. While there is a more extensive literature on amnesia in violent offenders, none of these studies addresses the issue of dissociation empirically. Further, there are significant methodological limitations to this body of research, outlined in the following, encouraging caution in interpreting the data from these studies. Some of these methodological challenges have been addressed in a recent study of convicted violent offenders that included a measure of dissociation (Evans, Mezey et al., in press).

13.4 DEPERSONALIZATION AND DEREALIZATION EXPERIENCES DURING THE COMMISSION OF VIOLENT CRIMES

While there have been occasional anecdotal accounts of depersonalization/derealization experiences during violent crime (Dutton, Fehr, & McEwen, 1982; Meloy, 1988; Tanay, 1969), only two studies have systematically assessed such experiences in violent offenders (Evans, Ehlers et al., 2007b; Evans, Mezey et al., in press; Simoneti et al., 2000).

Simonetti et al. (2000) examined dissociative experiences in 47 domestic violence male offenders participating in a community-based treatment program. Dissociative experiences were assessed with the Dissociative Experiences Scale (DES; Bernstein & Putnam, 1986) and Dissociative Disorders Interview Schedule (DDIS; Ross, Heber, Norton, Anderson, & Barchet, 1989). Dissociation

[1] Technically speaking, the term used here should be peri-violence dissociation (PVD) rather than peritraumatic dissociation (PTD), as the possibility that such experiences occur because the individual responds to his or her own violent actions as a trauma has yet to be presented. However, for ease of use, we will continue to use the term PTD. In this context, however, it does not necessarily mean that the individual was traumatized by the event, only that this was potentially the case; alternatively, such experiences may indicate the presence of a dissociative disorder (both may, of course, be true in some individuals).

during the violent assault was examined with an instrument constructed for the study, entitled the Dissociation Violence Interview (DVI). The DVI consists of 21 questions about various possible dissociative experiences during violent episodes, rated on a 5-point Likert-type scale, ranging from never to all the time. The items were rated as positive only if they occurred when the individual was not under the influence of a substance. Included among the 21 questions were 8 considered indicative of severe dissociation, which made up a DVI Severe subscale (Simonetti et al., 2000).

While symptoms of dissociative disorders were assessed with the DDIS, whether any men actually met criteria for a dissociative disorder was not reported. However, 11% of the men scored above 30 on the DES, indicating pathological levels of dissociation. In addition, 33% of the sample endorsed at least one of the DVI Severe items. Three of these items relate to the concept of depersonalization; the items and percentage endorsing such experiences are as follows (Simonetti et al., 2000, p. 1273):

Have there been times that, while being physically aggressive with a female partner, you:

- Felt as if someone else was being aggressive with her and not you? (15%)
- Felt that you could actually see yourself from a distance aggressing against this female partner? (9%)
- Felt that you were changed, that you were somehow bigger or smaller, or something about you was different from before? (24%)

In addition, one item related to derealization—feeling as though the victim was "not actually real"—was endorsed by 6% of the sample.

Simonetti et al. (2000) also found that endorsement of these eight items was significantly correlated with both the *frequency* and *severity* of perpetrated violence, as assessed via structured interview with a modified version of the Conflict Tactics Scale (Straus, 1979). In other words, men who reported dissociative experiences were more violent than men who did not.

Evans and colleagues (Evans, Ehlers et al., 2007a, 2007b; Evans, Mezey et al., in press) examined peritraumatic experiences and disorders of memory in 105 young offenders convicted of violent crimes, using the Peritraumatic Dissociative Experiences Questionnaire-Rater version, (PDEQ-R). The PDEQ-R is a 10-item interviewer-administered questionnaire that assesses the degree of dissociative experiences during and immediately after a traumatic event. Possible scores for each item include 1 for "absent or false," 2 for "subthreshold," and 3 for "threshold"; subjects who are unsure about an item or can't recall are not given a score. In this study, total scores on the PDEQ-R ranged from 9 to 27 with a mean score of 16.5, indicating widespread endorsement of items on the scale by offenders in relation to their violent crime. Each of the items on the scale reached threshold for some violent offenders. Classic derealization, captured most clearly by item 4 ("Did what was happening seem unreal to you, as though you were in a dream or watching a movie or a play"), was rated 3 (i.e., meeting threshold) for 30.5% of the offenders, while classic depersonalization, item 5 ("Were there moments when you felt as though you were a spectator watching what was happening to you—for example, did you feel as if you were floating above the scene or observing it as an outsider?"), was rated 3 for 14.3% of the cases. Another item, capturing other aspects of depersonalization ("Were there moments when your sense of your own body seemed distorted or changed—that is, did you feel yourself to be unusually large or small, or did you feel disconnected from your body?") was endorsed for 11.4% of the subjects. In addition, higher PDEQ-R mean scores were associated with symptoms of PTSD ($F_{1,804} = 1.9$, $p < 0.05$), amnesia for part or all of the assault ($F_{1,103} = 2.35$, $p < 0.05$),[2] and, most powerfully, intrusive memories of the violence ($F_{1,103} = 18.5$, $p < 0.0005$).

Taken together, the studies of Simonetti et al. (2000) and Evans and colleagues (Evans, Ehlers et al., 2007a, 2007b; Evans, Mezey et al., in press) suggest that experiences of depersonalization and derealization are not uncommon in violent offenders. Of note, while the reported levels of depersonalization experiences were similar between the two studies, far more derealization (30% vs. 6%) was reported by Evans and colleagues' participants (Evans, Ehlers et al., 2007a, 2005b; Evans, Mezey et al., in press). As the two samples differed in the degree of their violence—this can be presumed as Simonetti's subjects received a community sentence while Evans and colleagues' subjects were incarcerated (and over a third had committed homicide)—it is possible that derealization experiences, in particular, may be more common in extreme forms of violence. This is one of many hypotheses remaining to be tested.

From one perspective, the frequency of dissociative experiences during violent episodes is not that unexpected. Experiences of depersonalization and derealization appear to be partly a reflection of how frequently

[2] T-test for unequal variances used. Item 8 (memory gaps) was excluded from the analysis.

we find ourselves engaging in a particular behavior. As most individuals are only rarely violent—for some, only once or twice in their life—it is not that unexpected that someone would not "recognize himself" (or herself) while engaging in a highly emotionally arousing but very low frequency behavior such as violence. After all, this is essentially what depersonalization is: "I seem like a stranger to myself." The same argument could be made for derealization. Nonetheless, as suggested below, such experiences sometimes herald the onset of PTSD, and can also be associated with dissociative disorders.

13.5 AMNESIA SUBSEQUENT TO VIOLENT ACTS

In contrast to the limited studies of PTD in violent offenders, there have been several studies assessing the prevalence and nature of amnesia in violent offenders. These have been reviewed by Moskowitz (2004a), who found rates of amnesia ranging from 20% in a sample of 206 men convicted of homicide (Holcomb & Daniel, 1988) to 87% (partial) amnesia in a sample of women accused of infanticide (Spinelli, 2001). Based on 10 studies published since 1948, Moskowitz (2004a) concluded that approximately 30% of persons convicted of homicide experienced amnesia for some aspect of the crime. Compared to persons who did not experience amnesia, these homicides tended to lack planning, involved persons the perpetrator knew, and were associated with alcohol use (Moskowitz, 2004a).[3]

However, Evans, Mezey et al. (in press) have highlighted several methodological issues for this body of research. First, there is concern about the veracity of the reports of unconvicted offenders because of the confounding influence of the legal process. The majority of studies in this field either used unconvicted samples or data that were collected retrospectively.[4] Second, previous studies have generally used inconsistent and inadequate measurement of the dependent variable, amnesia. Measurement problems have included: (1) a lack of operational definitions of amnesia, (2) limited differentiation between complete and partial amnesia,[5] (3) reliance on self-report data (sometimes amounting to a simple statement that the individual could not remember what happened), (4) absence of written transcripts of accounts of offending behavior, (5) the use of retrospective case note descriptions, and (6) the absence of interrater reliability testing. Third, several study designs did not incorporate a meaningful comparison group, for example, similar offenders (in background and offense type) who did not report amnesia. Fourth, research has focused mainly on offenders who have killed; few studies have used populations who have committed nonlethal violence, raising questions about the extent to which conclusions drawn from homicide studies are generalizable. Fifth, despite dissociation being proposed as a potential mechanism for amnesia in several studies, there is a lack of data from attempts to measure peritraumatic dissociation. Overall, the body of research on amnesia in relation to violent crime is relatively small and, from a scientific perspective, subject to significant limitations.

An attempt to address some of these methodological challenges was carried out in a study involving 105 young offenders convicted of a violent crime (36% of which was murder or manslaughter) by rigorously delimiting the boundaries of what was and was not remembered, using transcripts, a semi-structured interview, and interrater reliability testing (Evans, Mezey et al., in press). Among the significant findings was that while 20% (n = 21) of participants in the study reported amnesia for at least some significant aspect of their violent crime, only one individual reported complete amnesia. In some cases, however, the amnesia was substantial; just over half of these 21 men estimated (supported by detailed questioning and information from legal and medical sources) that they could not recall at least 50% of the salient events surrounding their violence. Of those convicted of murder or manslaughter, 24% reported some degree of amnesia, a figure that was not significantly higher than that for those who committed nonlethal (but still serious) forms of violent crime.

13.6 EXPLANATIONS FOR PERITRAUMATIC DISSOCIATION AND AMNESIA IN VIOLENT OFFENDERS

Thus, a significant proportion of violent offenders experience PTD and amnesia, and there is some preliminary

[3] The relation between alcohol, dissociation, and amnesia in violent populations is a complex matter, one beyond the purview of this chapter. For our purposes here, however, it is sufficient to note that: (1) alcohol blackouts do not appear to be an adequate explanation for most cases of amnesia for violent crime, and (2) alcohol use may trigger dissociative states in some cases (Moskowitz, 2004a).

[4] This concern is mitigated somewhat for two studies in which all of the offenders claiming amnesia nonetheless accepted responsibility for their violent crimes (Gudjonsson, Hannesdottir, & Petursson, 1999; Parwatikar, Holcomb, & Menninger, 1985).

[5] A notable exception is Bradford and Smith (1979).

evidence that the more substantial the violence, the greater the likelihood of these dissociative experiences. What is the significance of this? As previously indicated, we theorize that these experiences can arise from one of (at least) three scenarios, differing with regard to the causal significance of the dissociative experiences and the presence of dissociative pathology before the crime. They may indicate (1) a traumatic reaction to one's violent actions, in the absence of a preexisting dissociative disorder, (2) a preexisting dissociative disorder, or (3) the emergence of a dissociative disorder through the act of violence, for which there is limited or no evidence afterward. These three possibilities, illustrated with clinical vignettes, will be explored in the following.

13.6.1 Traumatic Reactions to Violent Acts

Peritraumatic dissociative experiences have been strongly linked to the development of PTSD in a wide range of populations (Birmes et al., 2001; Marmar et al., 1994; Shalev et al., 1996). Indeed, dissociative symptoms make up the bulk of the diagnostic criteria for Acute Stress Disorder (DSM-IV-TR, American Psychiatric Association, 2000), the precursor to PTSD. While some have questioned this accepted view (particularly Richard Bryant and colleagues: Harvey & Bryant, 1998; Panasetis & Bryant, 2003), a recent meta-analysis found peritraumatic dissociative experiences to be the most powerful predictor of PTSD (with an effect size of r = 0.35), more so than perceived threat to life (r = 0.26) or prior trauma (r = 0.17; Ozer et al., 2003). Is it possible that the presence of dissociative experiences during the commission of violent acts may be similar to the peritraumatic dissociative experiences associated with traumatic events? In other words, does the presence of these experiences indicate that some individuals are traumatized by their own violent actions and may develop PTSD in response to them? The evidence suggests that this may be so.

While dissociative experiences during the commission of a violent act have not yet been directly linked to subsequent PTSD (though Evans's et al. research links them to symptoms of PTSD), it is now becoming clear that a portion of violent offenders do develop PTSD in response to their own actions. One study of juvenile offenders found 5% of those with trauma histories to report PTSD symptoms to their own violence (Steiner, Garcia, & Matthews, 1997). Another study of forensic inpatients found 20% of those with PTSD to have been traumatized by their own violent act(s); strikingly, *all* of the murder cases in this study had developed PTSD to their crime (Spitzer et al., 2001). More recently, evidence that a significant proportion of violent offenders find their behavior traumatic is reported in Evans, Ehlers et al. (2007b), who found that 46% of convicted violent young offenders reported intrusive memories of their offending, with 5.7% meeting diagnostic criteria for PTSD to their crime.

Finally, working with a noncriminal population, police officers involved in shooting incidents, Rivard, Dietz, Martell, and Widawski (2002) found that over 90% of the officers had experienced dissociative symptoms at the time of the incident, and 20% experienced partial amnesia. Extrapolating from their findings, Rivard et al. (2002) argued that similar dissociative experiences reported by criminals should not be taken as indications of a dissociative disorder, but were best seen as "a response … to the traumatic events they create" (p. 6).

Thus, it is becoming recognized that the traumatic events underpinning PTSD can be of an individual's own doing. An individual developing PTSD in response to stabbing someone is perhaps not so different from someone developing PTSD in response to a car accident he caused. As noted above, the likelihood of PTSD developing under these circumstances may be increased in the presence of peritraumatic dissociative symptoms.

Likewise, the presence of amnesia in these cases likely serves the same purpose as amnesia in response to more common traumas—that of protecting the individual from becoming overwhelmed with the most distressing aspects of the trauma before he or she is equipped to deal with it.

As an illustration, the following individual, evaluated by the second author, presented with pronounced peritraumatic symptoms and amnesia, but did not appear to suffer from a dissociative disorder either before or after the crime.[6]

13.6.1.1 Case Study

A 22-year-old male with no previous offending history was convicted of wounding with intent following an assault on another male outside a public bar at night, in which he stabbed the victim across the head and face with a bottle, causing extensive lacerations. The precipitant for the attack was a disrespectful look by the victim toward the perpetrator. He denied any planning or forethought for the assault. The offender was under the influence of moderate amounts of alcohol and illicit stimulant drugs at the time of the offense. The offender reported being very emotional prior to the assault, with

[6] Details of these cases have been modified to protect the anonymity of the offenders and their victims.

elements of anger and depression. There had been preceding conflict between the two parties and the victim had tried to bait and taunt the offender. The perpetrator described losing control at the time of the assault and subsequently having memory gaps for salient features of the assault, including stabbing the victim in the face and the screaming of the crowd. In his narrative of the assault, he said,

> "I was really disoriented, I didn't know where I was, what I was doing, anything. It was just really … surreal."

He scored 20 on the PDEQ-R, and reported shutting off, being on automatic pilot, events going unusually fast, feeling as if he was watching a film, significant memory gaps, and not knowing where he was. The memory gaps continued for the subsequent year. While he was not formally assessed for a dissociative disorder, screening questions included in the study did not identify any evidence that he suffered from a dissociative disorder either before or after the assault.

13.6.2 Preexisting Dissociative Pathology

Despite Rivard's et al. (2002) pronouncement stated previously, there appears to be little doubt that some violent individuals who report peritraumatic dissociative symptoms or amnesia do in fact have a dissociative disorder. The dissociation literature contains several clinical reviews and anecdotal reports in this regard (Dell & Eisenhower, 1990; Loewenstein & Putnam, 1990; Nijenhuis, 1996). Loewenstein and Putnam (1990) report that 20% of their male Dissociative Identity Disorder (DID) patients claim to have been incarcerated for homicide; however, it is not clear that such claims were validated from other sources. It is generally believed that violent or homicidal alters or personality states are among those most commonly found in persons diagnosed with DID (Dell & Eisenhower, 1990; Putnam, Guroff, Silberman, Barban, & Post, 1986), perhaps resulting from identification with the perpetrator or abuser (Putnam, 1989). While no study has yet to rigorously assess for the presence of DID in a prison population, Stein (2000) found just over 6% DID in a sample of inmates sent for psychiatric or medical evaluation, and Lewis et al. (1997) estimated that over 9% of the approximately 150 homicide defendants she had evaluated suffered from DID. In addition, there are several well-known cases of individuals found Not Guilty by Reason of Insanity with DID (Keyes, 1981; Nijenhuis, 1996). In these cases, the most common dissociative symptom reported is amnesia. Such occurred in a case reported by Dorothy Otnow Lewis (1998) of an individual convicted of a murder and diagnosed with schizophrenia, whom she later became convinced was actually suffering from DID.

13.6.2.1 Case Study

Sixty pages of Dorothy Otnow Lewis's book, *Guilty by Reason of Insanity* (1998), is dedicated to the case of Johnny Frank Garrett, a 17-year-old male convicted of raping and murdering an elderly nun in Texas, and sentenced to die for that crime. Despite confessing (in a peculiar about-face), Johnny Garrett subsequently consistently denied having committed the crime, insisting that he had been framed (as had frequently occurred previously, he believed, in his life). When first evaluated by Dr. Lewis and her colleagues, Johnny Garrett was viewed as suffering from schizophrenia, demonstrating a range of delusions, bizarre behavior, and auditory hallucinations. With a childhood full of extremely sadistic physical and sexual abuse, and substantial head trauma, he was one of the most disturbed adolescents Dr. Lewis had ever examined. The prison authorities agreed, and he was treated for years with antipsychotic medications, with only marginal success.

However, after a gap of several years, during which time Dr. Lewis became familiar with the sequelæ of DID, she reexamined Johnny Garrett. Now, his auditory hallucinations and delusions appeared differently—as the voices of alternate personalities and their belief systems. Changes of voice, demeanor, and facial expression several times during their videotaped interview heralded the arrival of other personalities such as Aaron Shockman and Aunt Barbara. Further, Dr. Lewis discovered that Johnny Garrett's grandmother, who raised him through much of his childhood, had been sadistically physically abusive to him (including placing him, naked, on a lit stove), and would provide him to his grandfather, dressed in women's clothing, for his sexual satisfaction. She argued that extreme experiences such as these triggered the development of his alternate personalities. Dr. Lewis became convinced that Johnny Garrett should not have been diagnosed with schizophrenia, but instead with DID; with this realization, a new theory of the murder (which Johnny never recalled) took form.

> Whatever happened that night at his grandparents' place and at his mother's trailer had kindled in Johnny an old, excruciating, sexual arousal; it also ignited in him an old, murderous, uncontrollable rage. When Johnny could no longer tolerate these feelings, as in childhood, his alternate personalities took over. Aaron sent Johnny creepy

crawling. Together they made their way to the convent. Then Johnny entered the void and Aaron raped Sister Catherine. To that Aaron willingly confessed. We shall never know for sure who among Johnny's alters actually murdered the aged nun.... We can be fairly certain, however, that whoever committed the murder, whoever slashed the throat of the innocent nun, did not see Sister Catherine's face when he did it. He saw instead the face of Granny. (pp. 235–236)

13.6.3 Emergent Dissociative Disorders

Finally, and most speculatively, we contend that a dissociative disorder may develop over time, emerging fully during a violent episode, but then fading back into the underlying personality structure afterward. Thus, some individuals may not meet criteria for a dissociative disorder prior to and subsequent to an act of violence, but would have met criteria at the time.

This is consistent with the fact that a certain percentage of violent individuals who are mentally ill only come to the attention of clinicians after they become violent. For example, recent comprehensive homicide studies in New Zealand and the United Kingdom both found approximately 30% of persons with substantial symptoms of mental illness at the time of the crime (most of whom were psychotic) had not previously had contact with a mental health facility (Shaw et al., 1999; Simpson, McKenna, Moskowitz, Skipworth, & Barry-Walsh, 2004). Thus, in most of these cases, the first psychotic episode resulted in a homicide. We suggest that a similar pattern may hold for some individuals with a dissociative disorder.

Carlisle (1993) describes a process by which an individual may turn to violence through dissociative identity changes spawned by intense fantasies. Such fantasies always include an imagined self quite different from the self as perceived by others:

> As the person shifts back and forth between the two identities in his attempt to meet his various needs, they both become an equal part of him, the opposing force being suppressed when he is attempting to have his needs met through the one. Over time, the dark side (representing the identity or entity the person has created to satisfy his deepest hunger) becomes stronger than the "good" side, and the person begins to experience being possessed, or controlled by this dark side of him. This is partly because the dark side is the part anticipated to meet the person's strongest needs, and partly because the good side is the part that experiences the guilt over the "evil" thoughts, and therefore out of necessity is routinely suppressed. Thus, the monster is created. (p. 27)

We would suggest that individuals with a certain personality structure (e.g., an inability to tolerate even minor forms of frustration or anger, akin to Megargee's (1966) "overcontrolled" offenders) may be particularly susceptible to this process. Thus, the culturally bound syndrome Amok, offered as an example of Dissociative Disorder NOS in the DSM-IV-TR (American Psychiatric Association, 2000), is most common in Southeast Asian countries such as Malaysia, in which, traditionally, the public expression of negative emotions is not socially sanctioned (Gaw & Bernstein, 1992; Hatta, 1996). Pent-up feelings of frustration or anger may be expressed explosively in some individuals if there is no acceptable outlet for such feelings. This is particularly the case if the "overcontrolled hostility" is combined with an intense fantasy life, as in the individual described in the following (assessed by the first author).

13.6.3.1 Case Study

A 19-year-old male, raised in a strict religious family, stabbed his father to death. He had no history of mental illness or psychiatric treatment, but was found not guilty by reason of insanity with the diagnosis of Dissociative Disorder NOS. As a child, he was described as shy and introverted, but also "exceptionally" nice; "no one disliked him," his mother said. However, as a teenager, he found himself increasingly at odds with his family's attitudes and life plans for him. He questioned his religious beliefs as well, but found it impossible to talk to his parents about his conflicts or disagreements with their vision of his future.

About 6 months before the murder, he became increasingly immersed in a fantasy world, articulated in his imaginings and in his diary, peopled by characters from fantasy/science fiction movies and comic books. During this time, he began to hear the voice of a comic book villain with whom he particularly identified, because he was "everything that I was not." The villain would chastise him, and tell him to let him take control of his actions. He resisted the voice, though he increasingly felt its presence inside of him, and did not allow it to take control.

After a while, partly because his concentration was impaired and partly because of a lack of interest, he left school entirely, and spent almost all his days going to movies, reading comic books, or writing in his diary—which increasingly included intense, disruptive fantasies and powerful dysphoric emotions. The money his parents gave him was spent on various distractions and items. He was tremendously guilty about this, and felt his life spiraling out of control, but knew he couldn't talk to his parents, as he couldn't bear the disappointment he imagined they'd express. Much as Carlisle describes previously, to cope with the stress and the guilt about his actions and fantasies, he paradoxically immersed himself more and more in his fantasy world.

It all came to a head when his mother opened a bank statement and found that he had been spending far more money than his courses should have cost him. Confronted with their disapproval, he went up to his room and turned on the radio. He realized that they would soon discover that he had also left university, shattering their future plans for him. Filled with guilt and despair, he considered suicide but decided not to; with his life at what felt like a dead end, he felt impossible to resist the villain's exhortations, who promised to get him out of the mess he was in. Under the influence of the villain (though unclear as to whether he became this character), he found himself stabbing his father. Much of the assault is not recalled; those parts he can recall are described as though he was in a dream, watching himself. The voice and the felt presence of the comic book villain dissipated almost immediately after the killing, when he came to and realized what he had done. Through the trial and afterward, he remained subdued but was cooperative with the requisite evaluations. He never received any psychiatric medication while awaiting trial, nor while hospitalized subsequent to the finding of not guilty by reason of insanity. Further, he did not appear to meet criteria for a dissociative disorder, or any other mental disorder, subsequent to the crime. Within a few years, he left the hospital where he had been confined since the homicide, reconciled with his remaining family members, and returned to university. His basic personality structure appeared largely unchanged.

As in this case, there may be no evidence of dissociative symptoms subsequent to the violent episode. What does this mean? Has the dissociative disorder, present at the time of the crime, disappeared? We would contend, at least in some cases, this is precisely what happens. Ironically and tragically, through the expression of the violent act, these individuals may have expiated the forces that drove them to the violence, and to such powerful dissociation, in the first place. Of course, without any change in the underlying personality structure, it is conceivable that significant dissociation could emerge again, under similar substantial pressures. However, in the absence of any clear dissociative pathology in the meantime, the diagnosis of a dissociative disorder subsequent to the event does not appear to be justified.

13.7 SUMMARY AND CONCLUSIONS

The prevalence and nature of dissociative experiences during the commission of violent crime is just beginning to be explored, with only two sets of studies addressing these issues systematically (Evans, Ehlers et al., 2007a, 2005b; Evans, Mezey et al., in press; Simoneti et al., 2000). Amnesia has a longer history of investigation, but the methodological concerns outlined in this chapter limit strong conclusions. Given the dearth of reliable studies, the provisional nature of any generalizations must be acknowledged. Nevertheless, there is empirical evidence to support the following positions.

- **The validity of claims of PTD.** To assume that all claims of peritraumatic dissociation and/or amnesia made by violent offenders are malingered would be a mistake. While malingering no doubt occurs, the frequency with which such reports are made by convicted offenders, who would appear to have nothing to gain by such claims (for example, postconviction samples), suggests that such experiences may not be uncommon.
- **Prevalence of PTD in violent offenders.** The extent to which offenders experience depersonalization and/or derealization during the commission of violent crime is an area in dire need of further research. Thirty percent of Evans and colleagues' (Evans, Ehlers et al., 2007b; Evans, Mezey et al., in press) violent young offenders reported significant derealization during the assault, while almost 15% reported classic depersonalization. PTD in general was associated with symptoms of PTSD, amnesia, and, most strongly, intrusive memories for the assault.
- **PTSD in violent offenders.** Evans and colleagues' (2007) findings confirm prior studies' claims that offenders can develop PTSD in response to their own violent actions (Spitzer et al., 2001; Steiner, Garcia, & Matthews, 1997). Almost 10% of the young violent offenders in his study met criteria for PTSD to their crime. The magnitude of the violence was significantly related to the development of PTSD, with over 18% of those who killed their victim developing PTSD, compared to less than 5% whose assault did not result in death.
- **Prevalence of amnesia in violent offenders.** On the basis of a study with several methodological strengths (Evans, Mezey et al., in press), it appears that about a fifth of young violent

offenders in general, and about a quarter of homicide offenders, claim amnesia for part of their violent assault, in some cases a considerable part. This figure is lower than the 30% of homicide offenders suggested by Moskowitz's (2004a) review of prior studies, but still constitutes a significant minority.

- **The extent of amnesia in violent offenders.** Importantly, there is strong evidence that amnesia for violent offending is common, but only rarely complete. By carefully exploring the extent of inmates' memories for their violence, Evans, Mezey et al. (in press) established that almost all inmates recalled some aspects of their crimes. Thus, claims of complete amnesia for violence should be treated with skepticism. Future researchers must be careful to use methodology that assesses the extent of memory gaps in a reliable and detailed manner.

13.7.1 Theoretical, Clinical, and Forensic Implications

- **The significance of PTD and amnesia in violent offenders.** PTD and amnesia reported by violent offenders is not inconsistent with the presence of a dissociative disorder, Rivard's et al. (2002) position notwithstanding. Three different theoretical possibilities were explored. First, some individuals who report such experiences appear to have been traumatized by their violent actions and, while potentially suffering from PTSD, do not show evidence of a dissociative disorder. Second, some individuals suffering from a dissociative disorder, particularly DID, who engage in violent crime, may do so as an expression of a violent or homicidal alternative personality. Finally, and more speculatively, some vulnerable individuals, with limited capacity to express frustration or irritation, an intense immersion in aggressive or violent fantasies or—especially—both, may meet criteria for a dissociative disorder at the time of the crime, but not previously or subsequently. These two final categories of explanation for violent offending would be more consistent with Van der Hart and Dorahy's (Chapter 1) conception of structural dissociation. Theoretically, individuals with either preexisting or emerging dissociative disorders can also develop PTSD in response to their actions.
- **Forensic implications.** In light of the above, claims of PTD and/or amnesia by a violent offender should encourage a systematic clinical evaluation, which takes into account not only malingering but also the possibility of peritraumatic dissociation or more fundamental structural dissociation. The different scenarios have potentially important legal implications including criminal responsibility and competence to stand trial, and should be carefully considered.
- **Clinical implications.** The empirical and theoretical evidence reviewed here and elsewhere identifying dissociation as a risk factor for violence (Evans, Ehlers et al., 2007a, 2007b; Evans, Mezey et al., in press; Moskowitz, 2004a, 2004b), strongly calls for the careful assessment of dissociative tendencies when engaging in risk assessments of violent individuals, and when planning clinical interventions. For example, in individuals who are structurally dissociated (Van der Hart and Dorahy, Chapter 1) and for whom dissociation is linked with violence, treatment designed to ameliorate the structural dissociation may decrease their risk for future violence.

REFERENCES

American Psychiatric Association (2000). *DSM-IV-TR – Diagnostic and statistical manual of mental disorders* (4th ed., text rev.). Washington, DC: Author.

Bernstein, E. M., & Putnam, F. W. (1986). Development, reliability, and validity of a dissociation scale. *Journal of Nervous and Mental Disease, 174,* 727–735.

Birmes, P., Carreras, D., Charlet, J. P., Warner, B. A., Lauque, D., & Schmitt, L. (2001). Peritraumatic dissociation and posttraumatic stress disorder in victims of violent assault. *Journal of Nervous and Mental Disease, 189(11),* 796–798.

Bradford, J. W., & Smith, S. M. (1979). Amnesia and homicide: The Padola case and a study of thirty cases. *Bulletin of the American Academy of Psychiatry & the Law, 7(3),* 219–231.

Carlisle, A. L. (1993). The divided self: Toward an understanding of the dark side of the serial killer. *American Journal of Criminal Justice, 17(2),* 23–36.

Carrion, V. G., & Steiner, H. (2000). Trauma and dissociation in delinquent adolescents. *Journal of the American Academy of Child & Adolescent Psychiatry, 39(3),* 353–359.

Dell, P. F., & Eisenhower, J. W. (1990). Adolescent multiple personality disorder. *Journal of the American Academy of Child & Adolescent Psychiatry, 29,* 359–366.

Dutton, D. G., Fehr, B., & McEwen, H. (1982). Severe wife battering as deindividuated violence. *Victimology: An International Journal, 7(1-4),* 13–23.

Evans, C., Ehlers, A., Mezey, G., & Clark, D. (2007a). Intrusive memories and ruminations related to violent crime among young offenders: Phenomenological characteristics. *Journal of Traumatic Stress, 20(2),* 183–196.

Evans, C., Ehlers, A., Mezey, G., & Clark, D. (2007b). Intrusive memories in memories of violent crime: emotions and cognitions. *Journal of Consulting and Clinical Psychology, 75(1),* 134–144.

Evans, C., Mezey, G., Ehlers, A., & Clark, D. (in press). Amnesia for violent crime in young offenders. *The Journal of Forensic Psychiatry and Psychology.*

Gaw, A. C., & Bernstein, R. L. (1992). Classification of amok in DSM-IV. *Hospital & Community Psychiatry, 43(8),* 789–793.

Gudjonsson, G. H., Hannesdottir, K., & Petursson, H. (1999). The relationship between amnesia and crime: The role of personality. *Personality & Individual Differences, 26(3),* 505–510.

Harvey, A. G., & Bryant, R. A. (1998). The relationship between acute stress disorder and posttraumatic stress disorder following motor vehicle accidents. *Journal of Consulting & Clinical Psychology, 66,* 507–512.

Hatta, S. M. (1996). A Malay crosscultural worldview and forensic review of amok. *Australian & New Zealand Journal of Psychiatry, 30(4),* 505–510.

Holcomb, W. R., & Daniel, A. E. (1988). Homicide without an apparent motive. *Behavioral Sciences and the Law, 6(3),* 429–437.

Keyes, D. (1981). *The Minds of Billy Milligan.* New York: Random House.

Lewis, D. O. (1998). *Guilty by reason of insanity: A psychiatrist explores the minds of killers.* New York: Ballantine.

Lewis, D. O., Yeager, C. A., Swica, Y., Pincus, J. H., & Lewis, M. (1997). Objective documentation of child abuse and dissociation in 12 murderers with dissociative identity disorder. *American Journal of Psychiatry, 154(12),* 1703–1710.

Loewenstein, R. J., & Putnam, F. W. (1990). The clinical phenomenology of males with MPD: A report of 21 cases. *Dissociation: Progress in the Dissociative Disorders, 3(3),* 135–143.

Marmar, C. R., Weiss, D. S., Schlenger, W. E., Fairbank, J. A., Jordan, B. K., Kulka, R. A., & Hough, R. L. (1994). Peritraumatic dissociation and posttraumatic stress in male Vietnam theater veterans. *American Journal of Psychiatry, 151,* 902–907.

Megargee, E. I. (1966). Undercontrolled and overcontrolled personality types in extreme antisocial aggression. *Psychological Monographs, 80(611),* 1–29.

Meloy, J. R. (1988). *The psychopathic mind: Origins, dynamics, and treatment.* Northvale, NJ: Jason Aronson, Inc.

Moskowitz, A. (2004a). Dissociation and violence: A review of the literature. *Trauma, Violence, and Abuse: A Review Journal, 5(1),* 21–46.

Moskowitz, A. (2004b). Dissociative pathways to homicide: Clinical and forensic implications. *The Journal of Trauma and Dissociation, 5(3),* 5–32.

Nijenhuis, E. R. S. (1996). Dissociative identity disorder in a forensic psychiatric patient: A case report. *Dissociation: Progress in the Dissociative Disorders, 9(4),* 282–288.

Ozer, E. J., Best, S. R., Lipsey, T. L., & Weiss, D. S. (2003). Predictors of posttraumatic stress disorder and symptoms in adults: A meta-analysis. *Psychological Bulletin, 129(1),* 52–73.

Panasetis, P., & Bryant, R. A. (2003). Peritraumatic versus persistent dissociation in acute stress disorder. *Journal of Traumatic Stress, 16(6),* 563–566.

Parwatikar, S. D., Holcomb, W. R., & Menninger, K. A. (1985). The detection of malingered amnesia in accused murderers. *Bulletin of the American Academy of Psychiatry & the Law, 13(1),* 97–103.

Putnam, F. W. (1989). *Diagnosis and treatment of Multiple Personality Disorder.* New York: Guilford Press.

Putnam, F. W., Guroff, J. J., Silberman, E. K., Barban, L., & Post, R. K. (1986). The clinical phenomenology of multiple personality disorder: Review of 100 recent cases. *Journal of Clinical Psychiatry, 47(6),* 285–293.

Rivard, J. M., Dietz, P., Martell, D., & Widawski, M. (2002). Acute dissociative responses in law enforcement officers involved in critical shooting incidents: the clinical and forensic implications. *Journal of Forensic Sciences, 47(5),* 1093–1100.

Ross, C. A., Heber, S., Norton, C. A., Anderson, G., & Barchet, P. (1989). The Dissociative Disorders Interview Schedule: A structured interview. *Dissociation: Progress in the Dissociative Disorders, 2,* 169–189.

Shalev, A. Y., Peri, T., Canetti, L., & Schreiber, S. (1996). Predictors of PTSD in injured trauma survivors: A prospective study. *American Journal of Psychiatry, 153(2),* 219–225.

Shaw, J., Appleby, L., Amos, T., McDonnell, R., Harris, C., McCann, K., Kiernan, K., Davies, S., Bickley, H., & Parsons, R. (1999). Mental disorder and clinical care in people convicted of homicide: national clinical survey. *BMJ, 318(7193),* 1240–1244.

Simoneti, S., Scott, E. C., & Murphy, C. M. (2000). Dissociative experiences in partner-assaultive men. *Journal of Interpersonal Violence, 15(12),* 1262–1283.

Simpson, A. I. F., McKenna, B., Moskowitz, A. K., Skipworth, J., & Barry-Walsh, J. (2004). Mental illness and homicide in New Zealand: 1970–2000. *British Journal of Psychiatry, 185,* 394–398.

Snow, M. S., Beckman, D., & Brack, G. (1996). Results of the Dissociative Experiences Scale in a jail population. *Dissociation: Progress in the Dissociative Disorders, 9(2),* 98–103.

Spinelli, M. G. (2001). A systematic investigation of 16 cases of neonaticide. *American Journal of Psychiatry, 158(5),* 811–813.

Spitzer, C., Dudeck, M., Liss, H., Orlob, S., Gillner, M., & Freyberger, H. J. (2001). Post-traumatic stress disorder in forensic inpatients. *Journal of Forensic Psychiatry, 12(1),* 63–77.

Stein, A. (2000). Dissociation and crime: Abuse, mental illness, and violence in the lives of incarcerated men. Dissertation Abstracts International, A (Humanities and Social Sciences), 61(4-A), 1626, US: Univ Microfilms International.

Steiner, H., Garcia, I. G., & Matthews, Z. (1997). Posttraumatic stress disorder in incarcerated juvenile delinquents. *Journal of the American Academy of Child & Adolescent Psychiatry, 36,* 357–365.

Straus, M. A. (1979). Measuring intrafamily conflict and violence: The Conflict Tactics Scales. *Journal of Marriage and the Family, 41*, 75–88.

Tanay, E. (1969). Psychiatric study of homicide. *American Journal of Psychiatry, 125(9),* 146–153.

Yates, J. L., & Nasby, W. (1995). Dissociation, affect and network models of memory: An integrative proposal. *Journal of Traumatic Stress, 8,* 649–673.

14 Dissociative Perceptual Reactions: The Perceptual Theory of Dissociation

Donald B. Beere, PhD, ABPP

OUTLINE

A theory has merit if it explains known patterns of data; it has even more merit if it correctly predicts phenomena that were previously unreported. Research data will show that the perceptual theory of dissociation (Beere, 1995a) not only has merit, but that it may help us to understand both dissociation and dissociative pathology. The perceptual theory also identifies a blind spot in current approaches to personality, psychopathology, and psychotherapy. Namely, the process of perception has been ignored. Even more important, the perceptual theory reveals that current theory and research on perception has ignored the background context.

14.1 DISSOCIATION AND ITS DOMAIN

The perceptual theory of dissociation was derived from efforts to understand the genesis of an initial perceptual, dissociative experience (as opposed to recurrent, dissociative symptoms). In the mid-1980s, the author accepted two basic assertions about dissociation: (1) dissociation was evoked by overwhelming trauma, and (2) dissociation was a defense mechanism or a coping strategy. Eventually, the author realized that intermediary processes must mediate the relationship between trauma and dissociative reaction. It also seemed likely that an explanation of initial dissociative reactions would apply to chronic dissociative symptoms. Using phenomenological methods (Husserl, 1931/1962; Giorgi, 1985), the author educed the sequence of events whereby trauma engenders a dissociative response. That analysis (1) yielded a theory of how initial dissociative perceptual reactions occur; (2) showed those reactions to be perceptual in nature; and (3) generated deductive predictions that were discrepant from currently accepted ideas about dissociation.

Some basic distinctions need to be drawn. *Dissociative experiences* are any dissociation-like experiences [such as those described in the DSM-IV-TR (American Psychiatric Association, 2000); or the SCID-D (Steinberg, 1993)]. For example, experiencing one's body as unreal is a dissociative experience. *Dissociative reactions* are dissociative experiences that arise during, and in response to, a specific situation. Thus, experiencing one's body as unreal during an earthquake is a dissociative reaction. *Dissociative symptoms* are enduring or repeated dissociative experiences that continue when no apparent external trauma is occurring. So, recurrent experience of one's body as unreal (when there are no current external traumas) is a dissociative symptom.

14.2 THE EXPLANATORY MECHANISMS OF DISSOCIATION: THE PERCEPTUAL THEORY

Beere (1995a) formulated the perceptual theory to explain how an initial dissociative reaction arises during a traumatic experience. Fine (1988) asserted that the cognitions of persons with dissociative identity disorder (DID) stem from a dysfunctional perceptual organization:

> I propose that a dysfunctional perceptual organization underlies their often disjointed cognitions and affects and is, therefore, at the origin of their distorted perceptions of reality.... [S]ome Gestalt perceptual organizing principle subtends initially cognition and then affect. (p. 5)

The most elemental Gestalt principle is the organizing of perception into figure and ground: The figure is *what* is perceived, and the ground surrounds yet recedes "behind" the figure.

The perception of figure/ground can be considered to be both dissociative and associative. That is, the figure is dissociated from the ground and the figure becomes the figure via association. Although this conceptualization does not explain dissociative reactions, Beere (1995a) has convincingly shown that dissociative symptoms are perceptual experiences. Accordingly, perception *should* be a central construct in understanding dissociation.

Phenomenology of Perception (Merleau-Ponty, 1962) proposed five essential components of experience. First, there is always an "I" or "identity" who "perceives" the "figure" in a "ground." Second, the I is always located in a "mind." And wherever there is a mind, there is an associated "body"; and wherever there is an embodied person, there is an associated mind. Third, I is in a body. Fourth, my embodiment is in the "world." The world is not an objective reality; it is a subjective one that is meaning-filled. Phenomenologically, it is called the *lived-world*. Fifth, all perception occurs in and over time: the present moment comes from a past that leads to a future. These five components comprise a background framework for all perceptual experience; we take this underlying organization of perceptual experience (i.e., figure-ground-background) for granted. The term *background*, as distinct from ground, defines these ever-present and essential components of the perceptual framework. Experience generally presents itself whole and has this basic perceptual structure: *I*, having this *mind*, in this *body*, in this *world*, all of which are in *time*, perceive this figure in this ground.

Everyday experience involves a constant flow of different figure/ground perceptions. Time, world, body, mind, and identity are usually present in the background. Recognizing the presence of the background in perception clarifies what happens during dissociation. *During dissociation, the background is lost or loses constancy.* The lived-integration of figure-ground-background constitutes meaningful lived-experience; in dissociation, this meaningful lived-integration is ruptured—and is felt to be weird.

Dissociative symptoms map isomorphically onto changes in the perception of the background components of experience (see Table 14.1); conversely, the perceptual background maps isomorphically onto dissociative reactions and dissociative symptoms. Amnesia, a post-hoc "symptom," cannot yet be explained by the perceptual theory because amnesia occurs subsequent to the trauma. As such, amnesia is *not* a perceptual phenomenon.

14.2.1 The Experiential Structure of Dissociation

During trauma, a person focuses on the threat so completely that perception of the background components are blocked, thereby evoking a dissociative experience.

TABLE 14.1
Relationship Between Loss of or Change in the Specific Component of the Perceptual Background and Dissociative Diagnosis

Component lost or changed	Dissociative Disorder
"I" or Identity	Fugue; Multiple Personality Disorder
Mind	Depersonalization; Amnesia
Body	Depersonalization (Disembodiment)
World	Derealization
Time	Changes in experienced time (Detemporalization)

Dissociation occurs because the figure becomes the exclusive focus of attention; when this occurs, the background fades, changes, or is lost.

14.2.2 General Principles Involved in Dissociation

Traumatic situations that evoke dissociation need not be physically painful, "objectively" intense, or sudden. *To elicit a dissociative reaction, a threat merely needs to be of sufficient importance that it so focuses perception that background components are lost. In a traumatic situation, when the locus of threat is in one domain of the background, that domain is not perceived dissociatively. Conversely, in a traumatic situation, the background domains that do not contain threats are likely to manifest dissociative reactions.*

14.2.3 A Continuum of Dissociative Complexity

Dissociative phenomena vary in their complexity. For example, an alter personality is a very complex dissociative phenomenon that probably does not result from a single trauma; alter personalities probably require substantial preparatory experience and psychological mediation. An alteration in time, on the other hand, involves changes in the perception of sequences of events as they occur; this immediate response would seem to require less complex psychological processing than that required to create an alter personality. These two kinds of dissociative reaction lie at opposite extremes of a continuum of psychological complexity. Creating an alter demands more psychologically from the individual than do changes in the experience of time. The author hypothesizes that severe and repeated trauma will evoke the most complex dissociative reactions.

14.3 Empirical Data That Support the Theory

14.3.1 Frequency of Dissociative Reaction

The author hypothesized that symptoms that are more psychologically complex will occur less frequently, and that symptoms that are less psychologically complex will occur more frequently (Beere, 1995a).

My investigation of the frequency of different dissociative reactions (Beere, 1992) is preliminary, but the percentages of subjects that reported 15 specific dissociative reactions during trauma (Table 14.2) are consistent with the perceptual theory. The frequency of reports of trauma-evoked changes in perception of the *world* (24%) ranked between changes in perception of the *body* (12%) and changes in the experience of the *mind* (36%). Changes in body-experience during trauma were reported least frequently. This makes theoretical sense because the body is a stable and consistent source of perceptual input; as a perceptual "constant," the body is resistant to change. To experience a change in the size or shape of the body requires a marked alteration in perceptual processing. Greater force is needed to alter perception of the body than to alter perception of the mind or world.

In contrast, world-linked perception involves continuous processing of incongruities (for example, inconstancies of size and color). Distant objects, which stimulate small areas of the retina, are perceived as being equal in size to closer objects, which stimulate larger areas. The world as a percept is less constant or stable relative to the body and, as a result, should require less force for alteration and demonstrate, as found, a higher frequency of dissociative perception. Finally, the experience of "mind" has no external stimuli that could provide stability, constancy, or consistency. Accordingly, mind-related perception should be easiest to alter and should show (as demonstrated in Table 14.2) the highest frequency of

TABLE 14.2
Percentage of Subjects Reporting Perceptual Domain-Specific Dissociative Experiences During Trauma (N = 189)

Domain-specific dissociations	Percent reporting
Disembodiment: changes in the experience of the **body**	12%
Derealization: changes in perception of the **world**	24%
Depersonalization: changes in the experience of the **mind**	36%

dissociative experience. In short, the relative frequencies of dissociative reactions in different domains of the background (i.e., body, world, mind; see Table 14.2) do, indeed, make sense.

In reality, of course, traumatic situations seldom affect just the body, or just the world, or just the mind. Traumatic situations and their evoked dissociative reactions usually affect several domains of the background simultaneously.

14.3.2 The Relationship of Dissociative Reactions to the Focus of Perception

Beere (1995b) tested three *general hypotheses* and seven *specific hypotheses* about the relationships between the perceptual focus of the traumatic event and the ensuing dissociative reaction (see Table 14.3).

Two-hundred and ninety college students reported (1) how often they had been traumatized, (2) whether they had experienced specific dissociative reactions during those traumas (e.g., time slowing, objects appearing far away, changes in body size, feeling as if in a dream), and (3) reported the characteristics of the traumas. They also indicated whether they had ever experienced the same list of dissociative reactions at a time when they were *not* undergoing a trauma. Reports of dissociative reactions by subjects who experienced only one trauma (N = 82) were compared with the reports of subjects who reported no traumas (N = 90). The data from these nontraumatized subjects are important; they provide a baseline for the frequency of *nontraumatic dissociative reactions*.

Conclusion. Seven of the 10 hypotheses received significant support. Briefly addressing Table 14.3, some hypotheses predicted nonsignificant differences and support the theory. Probabilities were calculated with different statistical tests leading to apparent discrepancies in the reporting of their values. See Beere (1995b) for explanation. Although two hypotheses received inconsistent support, the results were still explainable by the theory. The 10th hypothesis received no support. Two post-hoc hypotheses were advanced; these were (1) pertinent to the 10th hypothesis, and (2) based on the theory. These post-hoc hypotheses received strong support, thereby suggesting that the 10th hypothesis had been a misapplication of the theory. Overall, the findings support the perceptual theory and warrant three conclusions: (1) as predicted, perception of the background is lost or altered during trauma and a dissociative reaction occurs; (2) specific dissociative reactions are unique to perceptually specific traumatic conditions; and (3) some trauma-evoked dissociative reactions do *not* appear to be defensive in nature; instead, they simply reflect a perceptual hyperfocus on the traumatic threat.

14.3.3 Temperamental Traits and Blocking Out the Background

Beere and Pica (1995) tested the hypothesis that specific temperamental traits are associated with blocking out the background. Four hypotheses about temperament were proposed: (1) distractibility correlates with dissociativity; (2) the ability to pay attention does not correlate with dissociativity; (3) flexibility/rigidity correlates with dissociativity; and (4) no other temperamental variable correlates with dissociativity.

College students completed the DES (Bernstein & Putnam, 1986) and two measures of temperament: the Dimensions of Temperament-Revised (DOTS-R; Windle & Lerner, 1992) and the Structure of Temperament Questionnaire (STQ; Rusalov, 1989). The DES correlated significantly with Flexibility/Rigidity ($r = -0.2250$, $p < 0.05$), Rhythmicity-Daily Habits ($r = -0.1876$, $p < 0.05$), Emotionality ($r = -0.2154$, $p < 0.05$), Social Emotionality ($r = -0.1782$, $p < 0.05$), and Social Tempo ($r = 0.1984$, $p < 0.05$). There were no other significant correlations between temperament and the DES.

Conclusions. These results support the basic hypothesis: Dissociators block out background stimuli. The correlation between Flexibility/Rigidity and the DES shows that high dissociators tend to be unresponsive to changes in the environment; they persist in their prior mode of response. In this regard, they are less adaptive and less flexible than non-dissociators. In addition, high dissociators do not have regular daily habits (i.e., responses to tiredness, hunger, need to toilet, etc.). This might be due to blocking out bodily cues. The findings on two emotionality scales that tap dysphoric emotional reactions may imply that high dissociators (1) do not perceive (bodily) emotional reactions; or (2) do not connect failure, conflict, or difficulty to their self-concept or self-esteem. Finally, distractibility and attention are closely related, but *blocking out the background* is a different perceptual process than *inhibiting distractions*.

14.3.4 Dissociation in Significant Situations

Beere, Cooper, Pica, and Maurer (1997) tested the hypothesis that dissociation occurs in situations that are personally significant; they tested the hypothesis that individuals will hyperfocus in situations that are personally significant to them, thereby making dissociation more likely.

TABLE 14.3
Were Hypotheses Derived from the Perceptual Theory Supported?

Hypothesis	Significance	Predicted by theory?
1 Restricting perception is associated with dissociation.	$p < .01$	Yes
	n.s.	Yes
2 Different traumas lead to different dissociative reactions.	$p < .0001$	Yes
3 Dissociative reactions rank-order by complexity and demand.	Supported	Yes
4 Time slowing relates to anticipation of trauma, not suddenness.	$p \sim .04$	Yes
	$p \sim .211$	Yes
5 Time stopping relates to startling trauma.	$p = .003$	Yes
	$p = .264$	Yes
	$p \sim .802$	Yes
	$p \sim .604$	Yes
	$p \sim .007$	No
6 Depersonalization pertains to unacceptable thoughts or emotions. (Assessed as: Depersonalization pertains to emotionality and not calm during trauma.)	$p \sim .131$	Yes
	$p = .0007$	Yes
	$p < .0001$	Yes
	$p \sim .002$	Yes
	$p < .0001$	Yes
	$p \sim .032$	No
	$p < .0001$	Yes
	$p = .004$	Yes
7 Depersonalization pertains to anticipated trauma.	$p = .0003$	Yes
	$p = .047$	No
	$p = .022$	Yes
	$p = .024$	No
	$p = .323$	No
8 Derealization pertains to startling trauma.	$p < .0001$	Yes
	$p = .019$	Yes
	$p < .0001$	Yes
	$p = .062$	No
	$p \sim .44$	Yes
	$p = .032$	Yes
9 Disembodiment pertains to anticipated, not actual bodily injury.	$p = .11$	No
	$p = .22$	No
	$p = .022$	Yes
	$p = .165$	No
10 Derealization pertains to bodily pain.	$p = .568$	No
	$p = .003$	Yes
	$p = .268$	No
	$p = .281$	Yes
Post hoc 1	$p = .131$	Yes
Pain does not pertain to disembodiment.	$p = .009$	Inconclusive
	$p = .009$	Inconclusive
	$p \sim .275$	No
	$p = .003$	Yes*
Post hoc 2	$p = .009$	Yes*
Pain pertains to depersonalization.	$p = .009$	Yes*
	$p < .0001$	Yes
	$p = .09$	No

* Listed twice since the reaction is also interpretable as a depersonalization reaction.

College students (N = 115) were administered a prayer/dissociation questionnaire, the DES, the Dissociation Questionnaire (DIS-Q; Vanderlinden, Van Dyck, Vandereycken, & Vertommen, 1993), and the Religious Orientation Scale (ROS; Allport & Ross, 1967). Subjects were assigned to the intrinsically religious group or the extrinsically religious group based on Hood's (1970) median-split scoring method. Subjects who scored above the median on the intrinsic scale and below the median on the extrinsic scale were categorized as intrinsically religious. Subjects who scored above the median on the extrinsic scale and below the median on the intrinsic scale were categorized as extrinsically religious. The study excluded subjects who did not fall into either category. This reduced the sample size to 44 subjects: 25 intrinsically religious persons and 19 extrinsically religious persons.

Results. Consistent with other research, 32% of the sample reported dissociative experiences during prayer. These subjects did not differ on the DES or DIS-Q from subjects who did not report prayer-related dissociative experiences (t-test for equal variances = 1.2822, $df = 113.0$, $p = 0.2024$; t-test for equal variances = 1.5360, $df = 113.0$, $p = 0.1273$). As predicted, intrinsically religious persons reported a greater percentage of prayer-related dissociative episodes (56%) than did extrinsically religious persons (11%; Yates corrected $\chi^2 = 7.78$, $df = 1$, $p = 0.005$).

Conclusions. As hypothesized, a significantly higher percentage of intrinsically religious individuals (i.e., those who experience their religion as personally meaningful) reported prayer-related dissociative experiences than did extrinsically religious individuals (i.e., those who engage in religious activities for ulterior motives). Subjects who did and did not report prayer-related dissociative experiences did not differ on their dissociation scores.

14.3.5 Dissociation During Positive Situations

Beere (1995a) theorized that dissociation would occur during positive and nontraumatic situations. Three studies have substantiated this.

14.3.5.1 Study 1

Thirty-seven percent of 90 randomly selected undergraduate students reported dissociation during positive situations (Pica & Beere, 1995). Nine percent of these 33 subjects reported more than one of these experiences ($\chi^2 = 71.1$, $df = 1$, $p < .0001$). This is an important finding: If dissociation is solely a traumatically induced experience, then no subject should have reported dissociation in positive situations.

Table 14.4 summarizes the frequency of dissociative experiences that were associated with positive events. Both low dissociators and high dissociators reported dissociating during positive situations. The distribution of DES scores of those who dissociated during positive situations was similar to that of subjects who did not (2.3 to 56.6, $M = 16.7$, $SD = 12.6$); the mean DES scores of the two groups did not differ. This implies that high DES scores are not required for positive dissociation. Subjects who did not report positive dissociation had a more extreme range of DES scores; this suggests that, in some who did not report positive dissociation, the absence of positive dissociation may be related to the presence of traumatic dissociation.

Subjects who dissociated during a positive experience wrote a description of that experience. Phenomenological methods (Giorgi, 1985) were then used to educe the experiential structure of the dissociative experience; the experiential structure was precisely as Beere (1995a) had theorized.

The experiential structure of a positive dissociative experience. Positive dissociative experiences occur during an intensely lived situation of considerable personal significance. At this time, perception narrows to just those aspects of the lived situation that carry its meaning for the person—and the person dissociates.

14.3.5.2 Study 2

Beere, Pica, and Greba (1996) replicated and extended the prior study because Pica and Beere had concluded that their subjects' reports of dissociation were artifactually limited by (1) the definition of dissociation that was provided to them and (2) the open-ended response format: "it is likely that the frequency of dissociative experience in positive situations is greater than that reported here" (p. 244). The findings of Beere, Pica, and Greba (1996) suggest that Pica and Beere were correct in their conclusion because a significantly higher percentage of subjects (76% vs. 37%, $\chi^2 = 20.82$, $df = 1$, $p < .0001$) in their replication study reported at least one positive dissociative experience. Approximately six times as many subjects (52%) reported two or more positive dissociative experiences. These findings strongly support (1) the occurrence of positive dissociative experiences (Table 14.4) and (2) Pica and Beere's (1995) assertion that dissociation is "a more widely occurring phenomenon than an adaptive or defensive response to trauma" (p. 244).

As in Study 1, the mean DES scores of subjects who did and did not report a positive dissociative experience did not differ ($t = 1.21$, $df = 52$, $p = 0.233$). Mean DIS-Q scores also did not differ ($t = 1.97$, $df = 52$, $p = 0.054$), but

TABLE 14.4
Percent of Total Subjects Reporting Dissociative Experiences in Specific Positive Situations

Positive Situation	Study 1	Study 2	Study 3
N =	90	54	130
Sports	15	43	42
Nature	3	31	37
Theatrical/musical performance	3	26	23
Sex	3	26	33
Prayer	3	22	25
Anticipating extremely positive news	2	20	27
Upon hearing extremely positive news	2	19	30
Hobbies	1	15	16
Percent reporting dissociation in positive situations	37	76	81
Percent reporting dissociation in two or more situations	8.8	52	63

Study 1 – Pica & Beere (1995);
Study 2 – Beere, Pica & Greba (1996);
Study 3 – Beere, Pica, Mallory, Durfee, Baldys & Cooper (1997)

mean Perceptual Alteration Scale scores (PAS; Sanders, 1986) did differ (t = 2.59, df = 52, p = 0.012). Perhaps the PAS measures a different construct from what the DES and DIS-Q measure. Some authors have suggested that the PAS measures hypnotizability (Frischholz et al., 1991; Rosen & Petty, 1994).

14.3.5.3 Study 3

Beere, Pica, Mallory, Durfee, Baldys, and Cooper (1997) sought to clarify the role of hypnotizability in positive dissociative experiences. Four hypotheses were advanced: (1) at least three-quarters of the subjects would report a positive dissociative experience; (2) subjects who did and did not report a positive dissociative experience would not differ on the DES; but (3) would differ on the PAS and DIS-Q; and (4) hypnotizability would be unrelated to dissociation during positive situations.

One-hundred and thirty undergraduate students were administered a survey of positive dissociative experiences (SPDE), the DES, the DIS-Q, the PAS, and the True Response Index of the Multidimensional Personality Questionnaire (MPQ-TRIN score; Council, Grant, & Mertz, 1995). According to Council et al. (1995), the MPQ-TRIN scale assesses hypnotic suggestibility, but does not correlate with dissociativity. The MPQ-TRIN scale was chosen for this study because of its ease of administration.

The three measures of dissociativity correlated significantly with one another ($p < 0.0001$ for all). However, the MPQ-TRIN also correlated significantly with the three measures of dissociativity; this contradicts the findings of Council et al. (1995). Men and women did not differ in their reported frequencies of positive dissociative experiences. Consistent with Hypothesis 2, the DES scores, of subjects who did and did not report a positive dissociative experience, did not differ (t = 1.1650, df = 128.0, p = 0.2462). Consistent with Hypothesis 3, subjects who reported a positive dissociative experience obtained higher scores on both the DIS-Q (t = 3.6574, df = 51.7, p = 0.0006) and the PAS (t = 3.2281, df = 50.0, p = 0.0022). Hypothesis 4 was disconfirmed; subjects who reported a positive dissociative experience scored higher on the MPQ-TRIN scale (t = 2.0844, df = 128.0, p = 0.019), thereby indicating that hypnotic suggestibility (or the tendency to give a Yes response) plays a role in dissociation during positive situations. Social desirability probably did not influence these results as the Marlowe-Crowne Social Desirability Scale (Crowne & Marlowe, 1960) has no relationship with the DES (Beere, Pica, & Maurer, 1996).

Some subjects with low scores on the PAS, DIS-Q, and MPQ-TRIN reported positive dissociative experiences. Thus, although dissociativity and hypnotic suggestibility differentiate between those who do and do not report positive dissociative experiences, one does not need to be dissociative or suggestible in order to dissociate during a positive situation.

14.3.6 Perceptual Experiments

Beere, Pica, Maurer, and Fuller (1996) conducted four experiments with 92 subjects in order to test the fundamental assumption of the perceptual theory of dissociation: dissociators block out the background. The theory posits that high dissociators more readily block out background influences than do low dissociators.

The total number of subjects in each experiment differed: Minnesota Percepto Diagnostic (MPD; N = 65), Stroop Color Word Test (SCWT; N = 92), Embedded Figures Test (EFT; N = 69), and Necker Cube (NC; N = 45). Subjects completed the experimental tasks in the order listed, ending with the DES (N = 92).

A DES score of 17.5 was used to dichotomize the sample into high and low dissociators (high dissociators' mean DES = 27.04, *SD* = 6.75, N = 30; low dissociators' mean DES = 9.22, *SD* = 4.65, N = 79). A cutoff score of 17.5 was selected for two reasons. First, "considering both sensitivity and specificity, the use of a DES cutoff of 15 or 20 would seem most suitable for screening purposes, since these dividing points result in the highest sensitivity and specificity" (Steinberg, Rounsaville, & Cicchetti, 1991, p. 1053). Second, "the mean total Dissociative Experiences Scale score for the subjects without multiple personality disorder from all seven centers (N = 823) was 17.7 (*SD* = 16.6)" (Carlson et al., 1993, p. 1033).

14.3.6.1 The Minnesota Percepto Diagnostic (MPD)

The MPD (Fuller, 1982) uses Bender-Gestalt-like designs to assess dysfunction by evaluating rotation, separations, and distortions in the drawings of six designs. The experimental manipulation did not provide the expected outcome. Accordingly, the results could not be used to test the hypothesis.

14.3.6.2 The Stroop Color Word Test (SCWT)

The SCWT is a robust test of attention and interference (MacLeod, 1991). A "color word name" (i.e., the word) is printed in various "colors" (i.e., the color). Subjects are instructed to respond to the color, not the word. Control words are printed as "xxxx." The reaction times for correct responses are measured. When the color and word are incongruent in the SCWT, reaction times are significantly slower than when the color and word are congruent (MacLeod, 1991). The congruent condition is also slightly, but not significantly, faster than the control condition (MacLeod, 1991). Words (both color words and control words) and colors are presented randomly in the center of the screen on a computer monitor.

Background conditions. Consistent with the hypothesis being tested, the computer presented three different background conditions: no background (regular, black screen), static colored border, and flashing colored border (rate of flashing = three times per second). The border consisted of eight colored, nested line-rectangles that parallel the edges of the screen. In both the static and blinking conditions, the background was presented on the screen 2 seconds prior to the target word. The display disappeared as soon as the subject responded; following a half-second delay, the next trial began. Subjects received 20 practice trials to establish familiarity and competency with the task. Two hundred random trials, in groups of 50, presented all possible combinations of word-name, word-color, and background conditions (i.e., no background, static-colored background, flashing-colored background), separated by a 20-second rest period. Only correct responses were used for data analysis.

Hypotheses. Six hypotheses were advanced: (1) the background will potentiate the Stroop effect; (2) when the background is congruent with the color, response times will be faster; (3) when the background is incongruent with the color, response times will be slower; (4) when the background is congruent with the word, response times will be slowest; (5) in the no background condition, there will be no difference in reaction times between high and low dissociators; and (6) high dissociators will be less influenced by the background condition (i.e., will have shorter reaction times) than will low dissociators.

Results. Did the computer-generated SCWT demonstrate the typical interference phenomenon? Yes. Figure 14.1 shows the typical Stroop response pattern: reaction times to the Incongruent Condition were longer than reaction times to the Neutral ($t = 1.96$, $df = 182$, $p = 0.026$) and Congruent Conditions situations ($t = 2.23$, $df = 182$, $p = 0.014$). Our conjecture about the effect of the background was not supported. When the background color was congruent with the word color, the response times were faster only in the static condition. In the flashing condition, however, the congruent background color created interference and produced longer reaction times. Our conjecture, that an incongruent background color would create more interference, was not supported. In the static condition, all response times were faster; in the flashing condition, the congruent and incongruent conditions were faster, while the neutral condition was slightly slower. In short, contradictory to our hypothesis, incongruent background color generally evoked *faster*

TABLE 14.5
Reaction Times for Correct Responses to the Stroop Color Word Test by High and Low Dissociators in Various Background Conditions

Conditions				Mean Reaction Time			
				High Dissociators		Low Dissociators	
B-C	B-W	W-C	B	*M*	*SD*	*M*	*SD*
--	--	I	--	871.9	211.4	881.4	188.8
--	--	N	--	779.3	251.7	831.1	204.7
--	--	C	--	775.3	253.7	825.1	188.4
C	I	I	S	843.2	219.4	879.3	141.9
C	N	N	S	790.3	196.6	814.0	145.5
C	C	C	S	752.5	200.5	817.6	139.3
C	I	I	F	856.3	229.9	905.6	130.4
C	N	N	F	922.1	147.7	870.5	199.9
C	C	C	F	840.9	158.4	845.0	164.6
I	I	I	S	810.1	190.8	843.8	150.3
I	C	I	S	806.5	204.2	841.8	154.2
I	N	N	S	750.3	171.6	809.1	168.9
I	I	C	S	771.0	193.3	780.3	153.1
I	I	I	F	839.0	204.0	868.5	149.2
I	C	I	F	853.3	223.2	870.8	155.3
I	N	N	F	798.0	199.0	831.7	172.9
I	I	C	F	792.9	207.1	815.2	139.9
			DES	27.0	6.7	9.2	4.7

M = mean reaction times (thousandths of a second)
SD = standard deviations
High dissociators: N = 22
Low dissociators: N = 69
NB: B-C = background/word color relationship,
B-W = background/word relationship,
W-C = word/word color relationship,
B = background condition,
C = congruent,
N = neutral (either "XXX" or no background),
I = incongruent,
S = static,
F = flashing

response times. This is surprising because there is more information to process in order to respond accurately.

Although the mean reaction times of high and low dissociators were sizably different, the difference was not statistically significant due to large variances. All but one of the high dissociators' mean reaction times were faster than those of the low dissociators (see Table 14.5), but is the frequency of this pattern (i.e., highs faster than lows) statistically *significant*? If there were no difference between high and low dissociators, then an equal number of conditions would be faster (and slower) for each group. Given this assumption, the probability that high dissociators would have faster reaction times in all three no-background conditions was 0.07 (according to the binomial probability test). Similarly, the probability that high dissociators would demonstrate faster reaction times in 13 out of 14 comparisons (in all background conditions) was less than 0.001; this shows that high dissociators

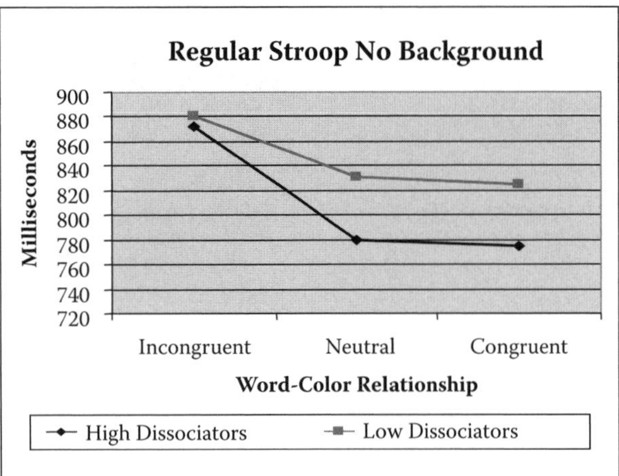

FIGURE 14.1 Typical Stroop response pattern

did have significantly faster reaction times. In the No Background Condition (i.e., the traditional SCWT), high dissociators were consistently quicker than low dissociators (Figure 14.1).

14.3.6.3 The Embedded Figures Test (EFT)

The EFT (Witkin, Oltman, Raskin, & Karp, 1971) measures psychological differentiation. In Witkin's perceptual experiment, the subject sat in a chair that was tilted to the right or to the left in a darkened room. The subject's task was to align a lighted rod with the gravitational vertical. The rod was in the center of a lighted frame, which was also tilted. In other words, the subject had kinesthetic (the chair) and visual (the frame) "tilt," which were not aligned with the vertical, and needed to align the rod with the gravitational vertical by using his or her vestibular sense. This task samples the variables tested here (figure [rod], ground [frame], and background [vestibular sense]). The EFT was designed to be a more easily administered task than Witkin's tilted chair/rod and frame; the EFT should accurately measure a subject's capacity to block out irrelevant and confounding cues. Subjects who can do this task well should also be able to block out the background.

The EFT involves 12 "tasks"—namely, finding geometric figures (e.g., rectangles, polygons, diamonds) in 12 different complex designs. Each trial lasts no more than 180 seconds; the time recorded is the individual's score for that task. Average time per task is the subject's EFT score. The faster the subject performs, the more field-independent he or she is; the slower the subject performs, the more field-dependent he or she is.

Hypothesis. Low scorers (i.e., fast responders) should be high dissociators; high scorers (i.e., slow responders) should be low dissociators.

Results. As hypothesized, high dissociators were significantly faster than low dissociators (Table 14.6).

14.3.6.4 The Necker Cube (NC)

The NC is a reversible figure that shows the outer edges of a cube. As an individual looks at the figure, it periodically reverses perspective so that different faces are in front. Necker cubes with 3/4 inch sides were drawn in the center of two 5-inch-square cards with the sides of the cube parallel to the edges of the card. In the diamond or *perceptually unstable condition*, the card was rotated 90 degrees. The task matches the theory being tested: the cube face is the figure, the rest of the cube is the ground, and the card outline is the background.

Counterbalancing for order effects. Half of the subjects viewed the NC first in the diamond condition and half viewed it first in the square condition. In 30-second viewings, subjects tapped a pencil on the tabletop each time their perception of the cube reversed.

Hypothesis. Relative to the stable condition, the unstable condition will show fewer reversals by high dissociators than by low dissociators.

Results. Order of administration did not affect reversal rate. The number of reversals in the diamond (unstable) condition ($M = 6.533$, $SD = 4.310$) was greater than in the square (stable) condition ($M = 5.222$, $SD = 3.483$; paired samples $t = 3.284$, $df = 44$, $p = .002$). This result supported the experimental manipulation.

High dissociators reported significantly fewer reversals in both the stable (square) and the unstable (diamond)

TABLE 14.6
Means (M) and Standard Deviations (SD) for High and Low Dissociators on the EFT

	High dissociators		Low dissociators				
	M	*SD*	*M*	*SD*	*t*	*df*	*p*
EFT Score	36.7	17.4	51.3	32.9	2.39	66	.0198

TABLE 14.7
Necker Cube Reversals Reported by High (N = 14) vs. Low (N = 31) Dissociators in the Square (Stable) and Diamond (Unstable) Background Conditions

	Number of Reversals						
Back-ground	**High dissociators**		**Low dissociators**				
	M	*SD*	*M*	*SD*	t^b	*df*	*p*
Stable	3.6	1.87	5.94	3.82	2.70	42.6	.0049
Unstable	4.1	1.77	7.65	4.67	3.71	42.6	.0003
t^a	1.472		3.092				
df	13		30				
p	.165		.004				

[a] *t*-test for paired samples
[b] *t*-test for independent groups

conditions (Table 14.7). High dissociators did not significantly change their number of reversals from the square to the diamond conditions, but the low dissociators did (see Figure 14.2).

Discussion. Three of the four experiments yielded significant differences between high and low dissociators that were predicted by the theory. The only experiment that failed to support the theory (i.e., MPD) did not demonstrate a background effect at all; hence, this was an inadequate test of the theory. Overall, these results strongly support the basic assumption of the perceptual theory of dissociation: dissociators tend to block out background stimuli.

14.4 THEORETICAL IMPLICATIONS

Although it has garnered support, the perceptual theory's conceptualization of dissociation requires further substantiation and elaboration, especially with regard to the dissociative disorders. The author believes that the perceptual theory of dissociation is the only theory of dissociation that has been subjected to empirical testing and qualitative analysis. Still, the author does *not* claim that the perceptual theory explains all dissociative phenomena. The theory began by explaining dissociative reactions during trauma. Then, the hypothesized mechanism (i.e., hyperfocus that influences perception of the background) was used to explain dissociation during significant and positive situations. The theory is assumed to be applicable to dissociative symptomatology. Dissociative patients should possess some of the same characteristics as nonpathological high dissociators. Undoubtedly, the perceptual theory will need to be modified, clarified, and extended as further evidence is gathered.

The present theory does not explain alterations in identity. Identity alteration involves a different order of psychological processes than do the immediate perceptual reactions that were discussed in this chapter. Nonetheless, perception is an underlying construct that links both of these dissociative phenomena.

The perceptual theory and its associated research warrant several conclusions. First, *dissociation is not always a defense, a coping mechanism, or a marker of overwhelming or unmanageable experience.* Second, because life is multifaceted, dissociative reactions *seem* to be global—but they rarely are. Instead, dissociative perceptual reactions are differentiated and linked to specific personally significant perceptual experiences via background domains. Third, dissociativity and hypnotizability need to be more clearly distinguished. Fourth, "blocking out the background" is a different perceptual

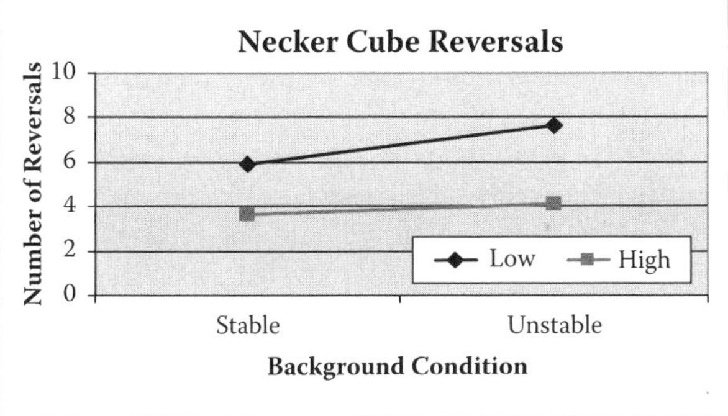

FIGURE 14.2 Necker Cube Reversals

process than inhibiting distractions. High dissociation is not associated with paying attention *per se*. Thus, blocking out the background is a different psychological process than paying attention (i.e., not being distracted).

The research reported in this chapter shows that dissociators have several unique characteristics. First, high dissociators tend to be unresponsive to changes in their environment; they persist in their prior mode of response. Thus, high dissociators are less adaptive and less flexible than low dissociators.

Second, high dissociators do not have regular daily habits (i.e., responses to tiredness, hunger, need to toilet, etc.), perhaps because they block out bodily cues. Third, high dissociators either (1) do not perceive emotional reactions or bodily experience, or (2) do not connect failure, conflict, or difficulty with their self-concept or self-esteem.

Fourth, high dissociators are less affected by interference and confounding cues than are low dissociators; their focal perception is quite stable. High dissociators do not change how they "see things" as readily as do low dissociators and are less influenced by the environment.

These research findings highlight the vagueness of our current understanding of the relationships among dissociativity, hypnotizability, "trance," peak experience, and mystic experiences. Hopefully, some of these phenomena (and their relationships to hypnosis) can be "explained" by the processes whereby dissociative perception arises.

Two processes have been described as contributing to hypnotizability: suggestibility and absorption (Braffman & Kirsch, 1999; Lynn & Rhue, 1988). Inhibiting the Generalized Reality Orientation (GRO; Shore, 1959) can be construed as part of an "as if" state of mind linked to both of these processes. In absorption, an individual becomes so engrossed that he or she loses track of present reality; at its extreme, absorption blocks out all other sensory inputs. The research reported above distinguished between (1) focused attention (i.e., absorption) and (2) blocking out the background. Paying attention and inhibiting distractions are two aspects of a single process that is distinct from blocking out the background.

The perceptual background subsumes the GRO. In other words, reality (i.e., the world and how it works over time) needs to be perceived in order to engage the GRO. If the world is blocked out (so that one ceases to perceive the world in its usual or everyday form), then the GRO is inhibited. Thus, *the processes that evoke dissociative experience (i.e., blocking out the background) may be essential to hypnosis.*

Suggestible persons respond to hypnotic intimations while remaining unaware of the limitations or constraints that would otherwise inhibit them from accepting those intimations. Conversely, logical persons who analyze hypnotic inductions are difficult to hypnotize; they maintain an active mind that rejects suggestions. Thus, hypnosis requires blocking out (1) the usual functioning of the mind and (2) the usual perception of the world.

The sharpest distinction between hypnosis and dissociative reactions is spontaneity. Dissociation emerges spontaneously and without induction, but hypnosis does not; in hypnosis, the operator must conduct a set of activities that induce the subject to shift into a hypnotic state. Reactive dissociation comes and goes as a function of the situation. How might one understand dissociation-inducing activities, such as drumming, chanting, dancing, or whirling? These activities require the individual to remain focused on particular repetitive stimuli and actions. For example, drumming requires the drummer to follow a detailed rhythm over a long period of time. The continuous focus (auditory, behavioral, and mental) totally engages perception: the background then becomes flexible, allowing it to change and transform. This process is similar to "highway hypnosis." Clearly, there are important questions about the relationship between hypnosis and dissociation that still need to be answered.

Dissociativity as measured by the DES did not differentiate subjects who did and did not report positive dissociative experiences. On the other hand, the DIS-Q and the PAS did. Thus, despite their significant intercorrelations, these three instruments seem to measure different constructs.

Because both low and high dissociators reported dissociation in positive situations, the author infers that dissociative reactions may be facilitated by certain traits (e.g., hypnotizability), but that those traits are not necessary. As well, might it be that, once a person dissociates in a traumatic situation, that the person *learns* how to dissociate? Furthermore, can one learn to be dissociative?

The perceptual theory also explains peritraumatic dissociation (Marmar, Weiss, Fairbank, Jordan, Kulka, & Hough, 1994). On this view, peritraumatic dissociation indicates that the situation is of determining significance for the individual; moreover, these same individuals will most likely develop PTSD later. Conversely, individuals who do not dissociate during a trauma probably do not find the situation to be significant. This suggests that it is the significance of the trauma that predicts later PTSD, not the peritraumatic dissociation *per se*. This leads to another important question: what distinguishes peritraumatic dissociators who develop subsequent PTSD from those who do not?

14.4.1 Strengths of the Perceptual Theory of Dissociation

The experiential structure of dissociation was developed from Merleau-Ponty's phenomenological view of perception; this structure has been empirically validated in positive situations. The perceptual theory of dissociation (1) explains previous data and (2) has made possible the prediction and subsequent discovery of new phenomena (e.g., dissociation in positive and significant situations, perception-specific dissociative reactions, etc.).

The perceptual theory of dissociation is conceptually catholic; it allows neurological, biochemical, structural, and behavioral explanations of dissociation. These other viewpoints can mutually inform and enrich one another.

14.4.2 Weaknesses of the Theory and Its Empirical Foundation

Because no data have yet been gathered from individuals with a dissociative disorder, the perceptual theory has not yet been generalized to the dissociative disorders.

The theory does not include strong negative emotion (e.g., terror and pain) as particular theoretical foci. We do not yet know how perceptual dissociative reactions relate to (1) the damping of emotions or (2) alterations in physiological functioning.

The theory does not account for either amnesia or the formation of alter personalities.

14.5 ADDITIONAL NEEDED RESEARCH

The field of dissociation needs exploratory studies that determine (1) the complete domain of dissociative reactions; (2) the kinds of trauma that precipitate each specific kind of dissociative reaction; and (3) the kinds of dissociative reactions that cluster together. Research also needs to determine (4) how a dissociative reaction becomes a dissociative style of functioning; (5) how dissociation becomes a defense; (6) the circumstances of the trauma or the individual that are associated with a dissociative reaction becoming a persistent dissociative symptom; and (7) how this kind of perceptual learning comes about. Research also needs to determine (8) the interrelationships among dissociative reactions, emotion, and amnesia; (9) the conditions associated with learning (or not learning) a dissociative style of perceiving; and (10) the relationship between pathological dissociation and the dissociogenic mechanisms that have been identified by the perceptual theory of dissociation.

Finally, research on positive dissociation has unearthed a knotty theoretical issue. At some point, positive dissociative experiences seem to be potentiated by hypnotizability, rather than dissociativity. Is this also true of trauma-induced dissociation? More broadly, what is the link between dissociativity and hypnotizability? Clearly, there are similarities between hypnotizability and dissociativity, but *how do they differ?*

The author thanks Central Michigan University and the department of psychology for its financial and other kinds of help in carrying out many of the experiments reported here.

REFERENCES

Allport, G. W., & Ross, M. (1967). Personal religious orientation and prejudice. *Journal of Personality and Social Psychology*, *5*, 432–443.

American Psychiatric Association (2000). *DSM-IV-TR. Diagnostic and statistical manual of mental disorders* (4th ed., text rev.). Washington, DC: Author.

Beere, D. B. (1992). Dissociative symptoms and characteristics of trauma: A test of hypotheses derived from a perceptual theory of dissociation. Paper presented at the Ninth International Conference on Multiple Personality and Dissociative States, Chicago.

Beere, D. B. (1995a). Loss of "Background": A perceptual theory of dissociation. *Dissociation*, *8*, 166–174.

Beere, D. B. (1995b). Dissociative reactions and characteristics of the trauma: Preliminary tests of a perceptual theory of dissociation. *Dissociation*, *8*, 175–202.

Beere, D. B., Cooper, N., Pica, M., & Maurer, L. (1997). Prayer and the perceptual theory of dissociation. In D. Beere (Chair), The perceptual theory of dissociation: An overview and discussion. Symposium conducted at the meeting of the American Psychological Association, Aug. 1997, Chicago IL.

Beere, D. B., & Pica, M. (1995). The predisposition to dissociate: The temperamental traits of flexibility/rigidity, daily rhythm, emotionality and interactional speed. *Dissociation*, *8*, 236–240.

Beere, D. B., Pica, M., & Greba, J. (1996). Dissociation in positive situations: A replication and extension. Presented at the 104th Annual Convention of the American Psychological Association, Aug. 1996, Toronto, ON.

Beere, D. B., Pica, M., Mallory, T., Durfee, J., Baldys, A, & Cooper, N. (1997). Dissociation during positive situations: A third look. Presented at the meeting of the American Psychological Association, Aug. 1997, Chicago IL.

Beere, D. B., Pica, M., & Maurer, L. (1996). Social desirability and the Dissociative Experiences Scale. *Dissociation, 9*, 130–133.

Beere, D. B., Pica, M., Maurer, L, & Fuller, G. (1996). Dissociation and loss of background: A test of the perceptual theory of dissociation. In D. Beere (Chair), Psychological research on dissociation. Symposium conducted at the meeting of the International Society for the Study of Dissociation, Nov. 1996, San Francisco, CA.

Bernstein, E. M., & Putnam, F. W. (1986). Development, reliability, and validity of a dissociation scale. *Journal of Nervous and Mental Disease, 174*, 727–735.

Braffman, W., Kirsch, I. (1999.) Imaginative suggestibility and hypnotizability: An empirical analysis. *Journal of Personality & Social Psychology*, *77*, 578–587.

Carlson, E. B., Putnam, F. W., Ross, C. A., Torem, M., Coons, P., Dill, D. L., Lœwenstein, R. J., & Braun, B. G. (1993). Validity of the Dissociative Experiences Scale in screening for multiple personality disorder: A multicenter study. *American Journal of Psychiatry*, *150*, 1030–1036.

Council, J., Grant, D., & Mertz, H. (1995). Hypnotizability and the MPQ: Absorption, context, and acquiescence. Paper presented at the 103rd Annual Convention of the American Psychological Association, New York, August 14.

Crowne, D. P., & Marlowe, D. (1960). A new scale of social desirability independent of psychopathology. *Journal of Consulting Psychology, 24,* 349–354.

Fine, C. (1988). Thoughts on the cognitive perceptual substrate of multiple personality disorder. *Dissociation*, *1*, 5–10.

Frischholz, E. J., Braun, B. J., Sachs, R. G., Schwartz, D. R., Lewis, J., Shaeffer, D., Westergaard, C., & Pasquotto, J. (1991). Construct validity of the Dissociative Experiences Scale (DES): The relationship between the DES and other self-report measures of DES. *Dissociation*, *4*, 185–188.

Fuller, G. B. (1982). *The Minnesota Percepto-Diagnostic Test* (1982 revision). Vermont: Clinical Psychology Publishing.

Giorgi, A. (Ed.). (1985). *Phenomenology and psychological research*. Pittsburgh: Duquesne University Press.

Hood, R. W. (1970). Religious orientation and the report of religious experience. *Journal for the Scientific Study of Religion, 9*, 285–291.

Husserl, E. (1931/1962). *Ideas: General introduction to pure phenomenology*. (W. R. Boyce Gibson, trans.) New York: Collier Books (Macmillan Publishing Co.).

Lynn, S. J., & Rhue, J. W. (1988.) Fantasy proneness: Hypnosis, developmental antecedents, and psychopathology. *American Psychologist*, *43*, 35–44.

MacLeod, C. M. (1991). Half a century of research on the Stroop Effect: An integrative review. *Psychological Bulletin, 109(2),* 163–203.

Marmar, C. R., Weiss, D. S., Schlenger, W. E., Fairbank, J. A., Jordan, B. K., Kulka, R. A., & Hough, R. L. (1994). Peritraumatic dissociation and posttraumatic stress in male Vietnam theater veterans. *American Journal of Psychiatry*, *151(6),* 902–907.

Merleau-Ponty, M. (1962). *Phenomenology of perception*. (Trans. C. Smith). New York: The Humanities Press, Routledge & Kegan Paul.

Pica, M., & Beere, D. B. (1995). Dissociation during positive situations. *Dissociation*, *8*, 241–246.

Rosen, E. F., & Petty, L. C. (1994). Dissociative states and disordered eating. *American Journal of Clinical Hypnosis*, 36, 266–275.

Rusalov, V. A. (1989). Object-related and communicative aspects of human temperament: A new questionnaire of the structure of temperament. *Personality and Individual Differences, 10*, 817–827.

Sanders, S. (1986). The perceptual alteration scale: A scale measuring dissociation. *American Journal of Clinical Hypnosis*, *29*, 95–102.

Shore, R. E. (1959). Hypnosis and the concept of the generalized reality-orientation. *American Journal of Psychotherapy, 13*, 582–602, Reprinted in C. E. Tart (Ed.), *Altered states of consciousness*. New York: John Wiley and Sons, 1969, 233–250.

Steinberg, M. (1993). I*nterviewer's guide to the Structured Clinical Interview for DSM-IV Dissociative Disorders* (SCID-D). Washington, DC: American Psychiatric Press, Inc.

Steinberg, M., Rounsaville, B., & Cicchetti, D. (1991). Detection of Dissociative Disorders in psychiatric patients by a screening instrument and a structured diagnostic interview. *American Journal of Psychiatry*, *148*, 1050–1054.

Vanderlinden, J., Van Dyck, R., Vandereycken, W., & Vertommen, H. (1993). The Dissociation Questionnaire: Development and characteristics of a new self-report questionnaire. In J. Vanderlinden (Ed.), *Dissociative experiences, trauma, and hypnosis* (pp. 19–32). Netherlands: Delft.

Windle, M., & Lerner, R. M. (1992). *Revised Dimensions of Temperament Survey–Adult*. Unpublished manuscript.

Witkin, H. A., Oltman, P. K., Raskin, E., & Karp, S. A. (1971). *A manual for the Embedded Figures Tests*. Palo Alto, CA: Consulting Psychologists Press, Inc.

Part V

Chronic Dissociation

15 The Phenomena of Pathological Dissociation

Paul F. Dell, PhD

OUTLINE

Dissociation has been a remarkably elusive concept. Despite intense investigation during the final decades of the 19th century and the final decades of the 20th century, the concept of dissociation continues to be vague, confusing, and even controversial (Braude, 1995; Brunet, Holowka, & Laurence, 2003; Cardeña, 1994; Frankel, 1990, 1994; Marshall, Spitzer, & Liebowitz, 1999; Van der Hart & Dorahy, 2009). In the absence of consensus, many investigators have simply adopted the American Psychiatric Association's (2000) 'definition' of dissociation and the dissociative disorders: "a disruption in the usually integrated functions of consciousness, memory, identity, or perception" (p. 519). This characterization, however, is both limited and parochial (see Dell, 2006b). It is limited to, and defined by, the symptoms of the four dissociative disorders that are recognized by the American Psychiatric Association (2000). Similarly, the World Health Organization (WHO; 1992) has its own parochial characterization of dissociation and the dissociative disorders that is limited to, and defined by, the symptoms of the dissociative disorders that are recognized by the WHO: "partial or complete loss of the normal integration between memories of the past, awareness of memory and immediate sensations, and control of bodily movements" (p. 151).

Part of the difficulty with dissociation is that explanations and descriptions of dissociation have often failed to clearly identify the level(s) or domain(s) of explanation/description that are being employed. *There are at least three important levels or domains of explanation and description for dissociation: (1) neuroanatomical-neurophysiological explanation; (2) psychological explanation; and (3) phenomenological description.*

Beginning with the familiar example of depression, a *neuroanatomical-neurophysiological explanation* might involve serotonin and serotonin receptors. A *psychological explanation* might explain depression in terms of aggression turned against the self. Finally, a *phenomenological description* of depression would depict the syndrome of depression in terms of *signs* that are observable (e.g., sad facies, psychomotor retardation) and *symptoms* that are subjectively experienced by the patient (e.g., feeling sad, having no concentration, early morning awakening).

Phenomenological description and the two kinds of explanation listed previously each have their own domain; they are separate and distinct from one another. When scientific discussion unreflectively mixes these separate domains, a muddled and confusing account is inevitable.

Neuroanatomical-neurophysiological explanations of dissociation are in their infancy (e.g., Reinders et al., 2003). Most accounts of dissociation to date have been psychological explanations. Even the DSM provides a descriptive account of dissociation at the psychological level. Similarly, most of the recent controversy about DID has involved competing psychological explanations of the disorder (e.g., Lilienfeld, Kirsch, Sarbin, Lynn, Chaves, Ganaway, et al., 1999; McHugh, 1995; Merskey, 1992).

The subjective-phenomenological[1] model of dissociation, however, is *not* another psychological explanation of dissociation. Instead, it is a phenomenological explication of dissociation. I do have a psychological explanation of dissociation, but it is not part of this subjective/phenomenological model. In brief, my psychological explanation is that chronic dissociative symptoms are manifestations of posttraumatic self-states or alter personalities (for a more detailed explanation, see the following). The subjective-phenomenological model of dissociation focuses on the person's *experience* of dissociative symptoms. This, in turn, leads to the following phenomenological definition of dissociation. *The phenomena of pathological dissociation are recurrent, jarring, involuntary intrusions into executive functioning and sense of self.*[2] Thus, dissociative symptoms are startling, alien invasions of one's mind and one's experience.

The subjective/phenomenological approach centers our attention on the subjective *symptoms* of pathological dissociation (rather than the observable *signs* of pathological dissociation). I believe that this is an essential investigational and clinical/diagnostic strategy for at least three reasons. First, a comprehensive account of the subjective phenomenology of pathological dissociation is the necessary foundation for any theoretical explanation of a dissociative disorder (Jaspers, 1963/1997). Second, *the phenomenology of pathological dissociation is disproportionately subjective, rather than objective.* Although observable manifestations of pathological dissociation certainly exist (e.g., nonresponsive states of trance, intrasession amnesias, patients named John who assert that their name is Mary, etc.), observable signs of pathological dissociation are often few and far between. In contrast, careful assessment typically reveals that a dissociative individual is experiencing a multitude of "invisible" dissociative symptoms. Third, the ability of raters to reliably assess dissociative signs has yet to be demonstrated. Bremner, Krystal, Putnam, Southwick, Marmar, Charney, et al. (1998) reported that, despite careful training in rating objective signs of dissociation with the Clinician-Administered Dissociative States Scale (CADSS), raters achieved only a modest intraclass correlation coefficient (ICC = 0.34). When analyzing this finding, Bremner et al. (1998) were led to a striking conclusion: it "may be possible that observable dissociative behaviors do not represent a viable construct, and that *dissociation is essentially a subjective phenomenon*" (p. 134, emphasis added).

I believe that diagnosis of dissociative disorders is, and must necessarily be, heavily dependent upon the patient's report of dissociative *symptoms* (as opposed to the clinician's observation of dissociative *signs*). This point of view is implicitly affirmed by the diagnostic criteria for three of the four dissociative disorders in the DSM. Depersonalization disorder can only be diagnosed by means of the patient's report of depersonalization symptoms. Similarly, the diagnosis of dissociative amnesia and dissociative fugue are almost invariably based on the patient's report of his or her symptoms of amnesia. There are rather few circumstances that afford visible diagnostic signs of either amnesia or fugue.

Unlike the diagnostic criteria for the other three DSM dissociative disorders (i.e., depersonalization disorder, dissociative amnesia, and dissociative fugue), however, the diagnostic criteria for Dissociative Identity Disorder (DID) are largely based on observable signs of the disorder (American Psychiatric Association, 2000): the clinician must observe multiple personalities and switching.[3] But there is a problem here. Just as Bremner et al. (1998) noted that other signs of pathological dissociation are very difficult to reliably assess, so, too, switching from one personality to another is extremely difficult to reliably detect (see Dell, 2009a). Moreover, switching is a relatively infrequent event.

It is a central thesis of this paper that *the phenomenology of DID is overwhelmingly internal and subjective, not external and observable.* If this is so, then the

[1] Psychiatry has used the term *phenomenology* to refer to both the subjective symptoms and the objective signs of a disorder. Jaspers (1963), psychiatry's original phenomenologist, used the term *phenomenology* to refer only to subjective experiences. I have "split the difference" between these two conventions by using the term *subjective/phenomenological* to refer to subjective symptoms.

[2] Some pathological dissociative phenomena are more mild than jarring; others are only realized after the fact (at which point they become jarring). My point, however, is that the essential experience of pathological dissociation is one of unanticipated, involuntary, and inexplicable intrusion or disruption.

[3] Strictly speaking, the wording of the DSM-IV-TR criteria (i.e., "the presence of two or more distinct identities or personality states") can be interpreted to mean that "the clinician was not even required to witness the alter personality states" (Putnam, 2001, p. 48). Although some clinicians may proceed in that fashion, my consultation experience and the controversy surrounding DID suggest that most clinicians interpret the DSM to require that they *observe* multiple personalities and switching.

diagnosis of DID is made immeasurably more difficult when (1) the *symptoms* of pathological dissociation that occur in DID are ignored or considered irrelevant to the diagnostic process (as they are in DSM-IV-TR), and (2) the diagnosis depends upon an infrequently occurring, and difficult to detect, diagnostic *sign* (i.e., visible switching from one personality to another).

A subjective/phenomenological portrayal of the symptoms of pathological dissociation not only assists diagnosis of the dissociative disorders, it also has profound implications for *understanding* DID. A subjective/phenomenological approach to pathological dissociation places the subjective experience of DID squarely in the foreground. Thus, persons with DID experience the 23 symptoms of pathological dissociation (see the following) as jarring intrusions into their sense of who they are. They experience the 23 symptoms as unexpected and startling disruptions of their executive functioning.

Consider one of the most replicated empirical findings about DID. Research with the Dissociative Experiences Scale (DES; Bernstein & Putnam, 1986)—which measures the "percentage of the time" that a person has 28 different dissociative experiences—has repeatedly shown that DID patients report undergoing dissociative intrusions about 40% to 50% of the time (Van IJzendoorn & Schuengel, 1996). These findings corroborate my claim: *highly frequent intrusions into executive functioning and sense of self are the experiential core of DID* (Dell, 2006b).

Braude's (1995) analysis of dissociation and DID sheds additional light on the experiential core of DID. Braude has argued that our understanding of DID can be meaningfully furthered by attending to the indexical and autobiographical aspects of human experience. "A state is *indexical* when an individual *believes* it to be his own (i.e., assignable to himself)" (p. 72). On the other hand, a state is *autobiographical* "when an individual *experiences* [that] state as his own" (p. 72).[4] Braude's distinction between indexical and autobiographical, between believing and experiencing, clarifies why dissociative intrusions are so jarring. DID patients undergo recurrent experiences that are distinctly involuntary and ego-alien (i.e., nonautobiographical)—but which they believe to be their own (i.e., indexical)! This, then, is the unresolvable tension at the heart of their daily experience: "This doesn't feel like me, but it must be. Is this how I really feel? I don't know. I guess I do. Am I losing my mind?"

The subjective/phenomenological description of DID and a Braudian analysis of these patients' dissociative intrusions provide a strikingly different understanding of identity confusion from the one that is implied by the classic picture of DID. Specifically, persons with DID are not confused because they switch from one personality to another; they often are unaware of switching. Rather, they are confused by what they are experiencing when they do *not* switch. Namely, about 40% to 50% of the time, they are undergoing (1) pathological dissociative, nonautobiographical invasions of their executive functioning and (2) pathological dissociative, nonautobiographical intrusions into their sense of self. These constant intrusions leave them with two unappetizing alternatives: (1) "I must not be who I think I am," or (2) "I do not make any sense (to me); I must be going crazy." This experiential situation is underlined by the fact that self-confusion is the first factor of pathological dissociation (see Dell & Lawson, 2009).

Dissociative intrusions also have important clinical utility. In DID, dissociative intrusions occur much more frequently than do switches from one personality to another. I do not know the ratio of intrusions to switches, but I have estimated that it is probably on the order of 100:1. If this estimate is correct, it means that the modern DSM has (1) overlooked the experiential core of DID (i.e., extremely frequent intrusions into the person's executive functioning and sense of self) and (2) made the diagnosis of DID dependent on an infrequently occurring diagnostic sign (i.e., visible switching from one personality to another).

So, if the general culture and the modern DSM have overlooked the experiential core of DID, has the dissociative disorders field overlooked it as well? No. As early as the 1970s, Richard Kluft was teaching the diagnostic importance of "passive-influence" experiences during his workshops on DID. Eight of Kurt Schneider's (1959) 11 first-rank symptoms of schizophrenia are passive-influence experiences: voices arguing or discussing, voices commenting, "made" feelings, "made" impulses, "made" actions, influences playing on the body, thought withdrawal, and thought insertion. *These eight Schneiderian passive-influence experiences are, in fact, pathological, ego-alien intrusions into executive functioning and sense of self. The subjective/phenomenological concept of pathological dissociation is the generalized version of these eight Schneiderian passive-influence experiences.*[5]

[4] The autobiographical quality of a state or an experience has also been referred to as a "sense of me-ness" (or, conversely, the nonautobiographical quality of a state has been referred to as a "sense of not me-ness") by Sullivan (1953), his followers (e.g., Beere, 2009; Bromberg, 1998), and others.

[5] Kurt Schneider was a colleague of Karl Jaspers and a leading member of the German school of phenomenological psychiatry. It is, perhaps, fitting that Schneider's phenomenologically derived first-rank symptoms of schizophrenia should provide a "jumping off place" for a phenomenologically derived conceptualization of DID.

15.1 THE SUBJECTIVE/PHENOMENOLOGICAL CONCEPT OF PATHOLOGICAL DISSOCIATION

What is the domain of pathological dissociation? DSM-IV-TR says that the domain of dissociative psychopathology is bounded by consciousness, memory, identity, and perception (p. 519). ICD-10 says that the domain of dissociative phenomena is bounded by memory, identity, sensation, and bodily movements (p. 151). The eight Schneiderian passive-influence experiences imply that the domain of dissociative experiences must include sensation, feelings, impulses, actions, and thinking. The subjective/phenomenological concept of pathological dissociation generalizes the eight Schneiderian passive-influence experiences and asserts that *the domain of dissociative psychopathology is all of human experience*. There is no human experience that is immune to invasion by the symptoms of pathological dissociation. Pathological dissociation can (and often does) affect seeing, hearing, smelling, tasting, touching, emoting, wanting, dreaming, intending, expecting, knowing, believing, recognizing, remembering, and so on.

The subjective/phenomenological concept of pathological dissociation has immediate relevance to DID: the domain of symptoms of DID is directly specified by the subjective/phenomenological domain of pathological dissociative intrusions into executive functioning and sense of self—all of human experience. In other words, the symptoms of DID occur in every domain of human experience. This view of the domain of pathological dissociation is reflected in proposed diagnostic criteria for DID (Dell, 2001) that have received corroboration from three studies (Dell, 2001b, 2006b; Gast et al., 2003; see also Gast, 2002). The subjective/phenomenological domain of pathological dissociation is also reflected in the 23 dissociative symptoms that are listed below, each of which is rigorously assessed by the Multidimensional Inventory of Dissociation (MID). Said differently, these 23 symptoms of pathological dissociation represent my effort to outline the entire domain of human experience (and the corresponding dissociative intrusions to which that domain is subject).

15.1.1 Partial and Full Pathological Dissociation

Pathological dissociative intrusions take two forms: (1) intrusions that are only partially excluded from consciousness and (2) intrusions that are fully excluded from consciousness. This dichotomization of dissociative phenomena is not new. Janet (1889) drew a similar distinction when he spoke of partial automatisms and total automatisms.

The essential difference between partial pathological dissociation and full pathological dissociation is the person's contemporaneous awareness of "his" or "her" actions. *Full* pathological dissociation entails frank amnesia (i.e., actions of which the individual is consciously unaware). The individual had no conscious awareness (contemporaneous or otherwise) of what he or she did during the amnestic period.[6] In sharp contradistinction, during *partial* pathological dissociation, the individual is contemporaneously (and disturbingly) aware of the involuntary, ego-alien intrusions into his or her executive functioning and sense of self.

In DID, not only does the host personality undergo full and partial dissociative experiences; alter personalities do, too. This is most dramatically seen in angry alters who typically undergo both partial and full pathological dissociation due to the intrusions of an even angrier alter from "behind" them. In Braude's (1995) terms, during therapy, the angry alter often initially considers consciously dissociated intrusions from "behind" to be both *indexical* (i.e., believes them to be his/her own impulses) and *autobiographical* (i.e., experiences them as being his/her own actions). However, when the therapist calls the angry one's attention to the experiential quality of those impulses, the angry one realizes that he/she had been ignoring or reframing the distinctly nonautobiographical quality of these intrusions. The angry alter then begins to redefine these impulses and actions as being nonindexical and nonautobiographical (i.e., "They are not mine; they come from an *other*.").

15.1.2 The Relative Frequency of Partial Pathological Dissociation versus Full Pathological Dissociation

With the exception of amnesia, dissociative individuals have contemporary, conscious awareness of all other

[6] In DID, of course, other personalities are fully aware of what they did when they assumed executive control of the body (and left the host personality with an amnestic lacuna). The subjective/phenomenological perspective on pathological dissociation, however, is always based on the point of view of the individual (i.e., self, personality, alter, identity, etc.) whose self and executive functioning have just been disrupted—in this case, the host personality.

dissociative intrusions.[7] Thus, in a person with DID, the overwhelming majority of pathological dissociative events are consciously experienced. This insight highlights an important shortcoming of the DSM's portrayal of DID. The DSM is wed to the classic picture of DID that focuses solely on amnesia (i.e., symptoms of full pathological dissociation). Incidents of amnesia, however, are much less frequent (1:100?) than incidents of partial pathological dissociation. Yet, the modern DSM (and the general culture) imply that the essential core of DID is full pathological dissociation—switching and amnesia. If the DSM (and the general culture) are wrong about this—that is, if full pathological dissociation is *not* the central phenomenon of DID—then the DSM's portrayal of DID is so skewed that it constitutes a serious misrepresentation of the disorder (Dell, 2006b).

15.2 THE SUBJECTIVE/PHENOMENOLOGICAL DOMAIN OF PATHOLOGICAL DISSOCIATION

15.2.1 Consciously Experienced Intrusions into Executive Functioning and Sense of Self

15.2.1.1 General Symptoms of Pathological Dissociation

General symptoms of pathological dissociation not only occur in persons with a dissociative disorder, but also in persons with certain nondissociative diagnoses (e.g., posttraumatic stress disorder, borderline personality disorder, somatization disorder, psychotic disorders, panic disorder, epilepsy, etc.). I consider the following six symptom clusters to be general symptoms of pathological dissociation:

1. *General memory problems.* General memory problems are nonspecific shortcomings in recollection: poor day-to-day memory, ongoing forgetfulness, the subjective sense that important events have been forgotten, feeling that poor memory is a source of difficulty in daily life, and distress about poor memory. Such memory problems are different from recurrent recent episodes of frank amnesia. The trauma literature has documented the objective presence of memory problems in persons with PTSD (Bremner, Scott, Delaney, Southwick, Mason, Johnson, et al., 1993; Golier et al., 2002; Jenkins, Langlais, Delis, & Cohen, 1998; Vasterling, Brailey, Constans, & Sutker, 1998; Yehuda, Keefe, Harvey, Levengood, Gerber, & Siever, 1995). I believe that general memory problems have been overlooked as a *dissociative* phenomenon. Some of these memory problems are assessed by the amnesia section of the Structured Clinical Interview for DSM-IV Dissociative Disorders-Revised (SCID-D-R; Steinberg, 1994). Amnesia is the first of the five core dissociative symptoms that are measured by the SCID-D-R. Circumscribed Loss of Autobiographical Memory is one of the 12 factors of pathological dissociation (Dell & Lawson, 2009); that factor taps many of these general memory problems.
2. *Depersonalization.* Depersonalization includes a variety of forms of felt disconnection from one's body, self, or actions: feeling disconnected, distant, or detached from one's body and one's actions; feeling that one's body is strange, unreal, alien, mechanical, different, changed, or not one's own; feeling that one's body and one's actions operate independently or autonomously, as if they were not directed by the self, and so on. Depersonalization is the second of the five core dissociative symptoms measured by the SCID-D-R. Depersonalization/Derealization is one of the 12 factors of pathological dissociation (Dell & Lawson, 2009).
3. *Derealization.* Derealization entails perceived alterations of the relationship between self and environment: feeling that the world is distant, far away, foggy, or disappearing; feeling that the world has become different, strange, foreign, or unreal; feeling that time slows down or stops. Derealization is the third of the five core symptoms that are measured by the SCID-D-R. The Dissociative Disorders Interview Schedule (DDIS; Ross et al., 1989) also inquires about derealization. Depersonalization/Derealization is one of the 12 factors of pathological dissociation (Dell & Lawson, 2009).
4. *Posttraumatic flashbacks.* Flashbacks are the core intrusive symptom of posttraumatic stress disorder (PTSD). Every clinician who treats DID

[7] There is a form of amnesia that entails only partial dissociation: temporarily dissociated knowledge or skills (see No. 15 below). Unlike the fully dissociated amnesia that typically accompanies the actions of alter personalities, temporary amnesia for knowledge or skills is accompanied by a jarring contemporaneous awareness on the part of the person. The person is acutely and uncomfortably aware of what he or she cannot remember (e.g., how to read, how to drive, who one is, etc.).

learns to dread the power and destabilizing effects of flashbacks. Flashbacks can occur on every channel of sensory and affective experience. They cause intrusive, autonomous experiences of sight, sound, touch, hearing, smell, and affect.[8] Their affective intensity even causes behavioral compulsions to reenact the trauma (Blank, 1985). At their strongest, flashbacks cause the individual to lose contact with current circumstances and to become completely re-immersed in a past traumatic reality. Uncontrolled flashbacks are probably the primary source of anguish, pain, and desperation that drive dissociative individuals to self-medicate, self-injure, attempt suicide, and require hospitalization. Both the DDIS and the SCID-D-R inquire about flashbacks. Flashbacks is one of the 12 factors of pathological dissociation (Dell & Lawson, 2009).

5. *Somatoform symptoms.* Somatoform symptoms entail peculiar alterations of bodily functioning that have no physical or medical basis. Most commonly, somatoform dissociative phenomena affect movement (e.g., paralysis, difficulty walking, difficulty urinating, difficulty swallowing) or sensory experience (e.g., unexplainable pain, not feeling pain, tunnel vision, blindness, auditory distancing, deafness, loss of physical sensation). Some of these symptoms subsequently prove to be partial posttraumatic flashbacks: reexperiencing or reenacting some specific interval in a past experience. Other symptoms, like conversion disorder, classically understood, may derive from a particular intent or wish. Conversion and somatoform dissociative symptoms are measured by a major section of the DDIS and some are assessed within the depersonalization section of the SCID-D-R. Body Symptoms is one of the 12 factors of pathological dissociation (Dell & Lawson, 2009).
6. *Trance.* Episodes of *absence*-like staring and unresponsiveness have been reported in severely dissociative individuals for well over 100 years. This longstanding appreciation of the occurrence of trance in dissociative conditions probably springs from the fact that trance is easily noticed by an observer; trance has very visible signs. Both the DDIS and the SCID-D-R inquire about trance. Trance is one of the 12 factors of pathological dissociation (Dell & Lawson, 2009).

15.2.1.2 Consciously Experienced Intrusions of Another Self-State

7. *Child voices.* Dissociative individuals almost always hear the voice of a child. Child voices may be happy, sad, crying, or angry. Frequently, but not always, dissociative individuals also see (i.e., have a visual image of) the child that they are hearing; this seeing may range from a strictly imaginative picturing to a frank visual hallucination. Both the DDIS and the SCID-D-R inquire about voices. The SCID-D-R explicitly asks how old the voices are.
8. *Two or more voices or parts that converse, argue, or struggle.* Voices that converse, argue, or struggle constitute the person's awareness that different parts of the mind are autonomously conversing or contending for control: hearing two or more voices that discuss or argue about what should be done; feeling a *force* or an *other* that tries to control or change what one does; feeling or hearing an angry *other* that tries to control one, and so on. This symptom has much in common with two of Schneider's first-rank symptoms: voices arguing and voices commenting. The SCID-D-R carefully inquires about the presence of internal dialogue or internal struggle.
9. *Persecutory voices that comment harshly, make threats, or command self-destructive acts.* Persecutory voices are routine in persons with DID. Such persecutory voices contemptuously degrade the individual via repeated name-calling (e.g., stupid, worthless, failure, wimp, no good, whore, slut, bitch, etc.). Such voices often threaten to harm the person or demand that the person commit acts of self-harm or suicide. Persecutory voices have much in common with Schneider's first-rank symptom of voices commenting (Kluft, 1987). Both the DDIS and the SCID-D-R ask about the presence of voices, but they do not specifically inquire about persecutory voices. Persecutory Intrusions is one of the 12 factors of pathological dissociation (Dell & Lawson, 2009).
10. *Speech insertion (unintentional or disowned utterances).* In speech insertion, words are

[8] Sensory flashbacks, often called *body memories*, are distinctly somatoform and could also be classified as manifestations of somatoform dissociation. I would argue that sensory flashbacks are more meaningfully considered to be flashbacks than somatoform symptoms.

experienced as autonomously issuing from one's mouth. Most commonly, such eruptions of partially dissociated words come from an angry alter. Patients occasionally describe this phenomenon as, "I didn't say those words; somebody else did." Although the SCID-D-R asks about partially dissociated speech, no SCID-D-R publication has reported data regarding this phenomenon.

11. *Thought insertion or withdrawal.* Partially dissociated thoughts have two basic forms: thought insertion and thought withdrawal. Thought withdrawal is experienced as thoughts being suddenly taken away or the mind going blank. More noticeable (and more distressing) to the patient is thought insertion. When this occurs, strong thoughts seem to come from out of nowhere. Such thoughts may be distinctly ego-alien; they often feel like they do not belong to the person. The intrusive thoughts of PTSD patients could also be classified as partially dissociated thoughts. The DDIS assesses the presence of thought insertion and thought withdrawal.
12. *Made or intrusive feelings and emotions.* "Made" or intrusive feelings and emotions are unexpected surges of feeling—pain, hurt, anger, fear, shame, and so on. Often, these surges of feeling are inexplicable and frankly puzzling to the individual. Made or intrusive feelings and emotions tend to be the leading edge of partially dissociated intrusions from another self-state. That is, a person who has only a few kinds of partially dissociated intrusions (i.e., 2 to 4 kinds of intrusion) is still likely to have made or intrusive feelings and emotions. Such partially dissociated emotions are also fairly common in patients who have only a modest score on the DES. Not surprisingly, made or intrusive feelings and emotions are fairly common in certain nondissociative disorders that are characterized by affective instability (e.g., PTSD, borderline personality disorder, bipolar disorder, panic disorder, ADHD). The SCID-D-R inquires about partially dissociated emotions and the DDIS assesses made feelings.
13. *Made or intrusive impulses.* "Made" or intrusive impulses are described as coming from somewhere else or someone else. Such partially dissociated impulses often feel like they do not belong to the person. Often, such impulses are experienced as part of a struggle wherein some *other part* is trying to overrule the host personality. Hostile impulses may surge from a dissociated angry part; sexual impulses may surge from a highly sexualized part, and so on. The DDIS assesses made impulses. Angry Intrusions is one of the 12 factors of pathological dissociation (Dell & Lawson, 2009).
14. *Made or intrusive actions.* "Made" or intrusive actions are highly frequent in persons with DID. These partially dissociated actions tend to be experienced in one of three ways: (1) from a depersonalized stance thought of as inside or outside of the body wherein the person just passively watches or observes the self do things on its own; or (2) from an experiential standpoint of being suddenly overpowered, taken over, controlled, or even possessed; or (3) despite an intact sensorium, the person observes that a particular part of the body suddenly has a mind of its own, and performs an unintended act. In all three cases, the person tends to feel that the behavior is not his (or not hers). The degree of the person's awareness of the source of these acts varies considerably—from having "no idea at all" to actually "seeing" another part take control of the body. The SCID-D-R inquires about partially dissociated actions. Angry Intrusions is one of the 12 factors of pathological dissociation (Dell & Lawson, 2009). Angry intrusions typically involve (1) sudden unexpected surges of anger into one's conscious mind and/or (2) *partially dissociated seizures of executive control* wherein the person has conscious awareness of being invaded and/or taken over by an autonomous *other*.
15. *Temporary loss of well-rehearsed knowledge or skills.* Temporary loss of well-rehearsed knowledge or skills refers to a circumscribed amnesia for information that the person knows well and would never just forget (e.g., how to drive, how to read, how to do one's job, etc.). Distress about Severe Memory Problems is one of the 12 factors of pathological dissociation (Dell & Lawson, 2009); this factor is centered on temporary loss of well-rehearsed skills.
16. *Disconcerting experiences of self-alteration.* DID experiences of self-alteration include the acute sensation that one's body has become small like a young child; switching back and

forth between feeling like a man and feeling like a woman; seeing someone other than oneself in the mirror; feeling that one's emotions, thoughts, behavior, or body are not one's own; discovering that one has changed one's appearance (e.g., hair length, hair color, cosmetics, apparel, etc.) with no memory of having done so, and so on. Identity alteration is the fifth of the five core symptoms assessed by the SCID-D-R. Subjective Experience of the Presence of Alter Personalities and/or Self-States is one of the 12 factors of pathological dissociation (Dell & Lawson, 2009).

17. *Profound and chronic self-puzzlement.* Self-puzzlement is not itself a partially dissociated intrusion. Rather, self-puzzlement is the unavoidable *consequence* of repeated encounters with the 16 preceding partially dissociated intrusions into executive functioning and sense of self. Individuals who undergo recurrent pathological dissociative intrusions are seriously puzzled and confused about themselves. They don't understand why they feel and behave as they do; they are frankly confused about who they really are. Persons with DID even have greater identity confusion than persons with borderline personality disorder (Laddis & Dell, 2002)! Identity confusion is the fourth of the five core symptoms assessed by the SCID-D-R. Self-Confusion is the first of the 12 factors of pathological dissociation (Dell & Lawson, 2009).

15.2.2 Fully Dissociated Intrusions into Executive Functioning and Self

15.2.2.1 Amnesia

Amnesia (i.e., fully dissociated actions of another self-state) is the sole point of overlap between (1) DSM-IV's diagnostic criteria for DID and (2) the subjective/phenomenological view of DID. Even so, the DSM criteria address only the clinician's judgment of the presence of both switching and amnesia, whereas the subjective/phenomenological criteria address the patient's detection of the evidence of such phenomena. A person with DID can only discover, learn, or deduce the fully dissociated actions of another personality. There are at least six ways that this can happen.

18. *Time loss.* The fact that a chunk of time has vanished can be discovered in one of three ways: (1) a sudden, acute realization that "something (i.e., a chunk of time) is missing"; (2) noticing by the clock or newspaper that it is *much* later than one thought (e.g., hours or days later) and that one cannot account for the missing period of time; and (3) being asked or told something that calls one's attention to the hitherto unappreciated fact that one has lost time. Both the DDIS and the SCID-D-R assess time loss. Amnesia is one of the 12 factors of pathological dissociation (Dell & Lawson, 2009); this factor taps time loss and the other five forms of amnesia listed in the following (#19 to #23).
19. *Coming to.* "Coming to" is characterized by suddenly discovering oneself in the midst of circumstances of which one had no awareness even 5 seconds before. Coming to may or may not be accompanied by an acute sense of having lost time. Dramatic examples of coming to include finding oneself standing amidst the wreckage of one's room or home; or discovering that there are cuts all over one's arms and finding a blood-covered razorblade in one's hand. Other examples include finding oneself in the midst of a set of actions (e.g., vacuuming, cooking, spanking a child, sitting at the breakfast table with a newspaper and coffee) that one does not remember initiating; and discovering oneself in mid-conversation with someone (when one was previously unaware of talking to that person), and so on.
20. *Fugues.* The classic definition of a fugue involves purposeful travel that is fully dissociated. That is, fuguing individuals discover themselves somewhere else with no knowledge of how they came to be in that place (i.e., in their car, at the beach, at a nightclub, at their place of work, in another city or state). Persons with DID not only have classic fugues, but they also have at-home mini-fugues: waking up on a bed or a sofa with no memory of having lain down there in the first place; discovering themselves in an odd place in their home (e.g., inside the closet, under the bed, curled up on the floor) with no memory of how they got there; awakening from a nightmare to find themselves elsewhere than in bed (with no idea how they came to be in that place). Both the DDIS and the SCID-D-R inquire about fugues.
21. *Being told of disremembered actions.* DID patients are often told by others about actions of which they have no memory. Unremembered

actions may include incidents of not recognizing their spouse or children, angry words and actions, highly atypical sexualized behavior, and so on. The DDIS inquires about incidents of being told about disremembered actions.

22. *Finding objects among their possessions.* It is quite common for DID individuals to discover objects among their possessions (e.g., clothes, toys, toilet articles, etc.) that they do not remember acquiring. Similarly, they may discover writings or drawings that they cannot account for, or they may find articles in their shopping bags that they do not remember buying. Both the DDIS and the SCID-D-R inquire about incidents of finding objects among one's possessions.
23. *Finding evidence of one's recent actions.* DID patients often discover evidence of recent actions that only they could have done (e.g., a task completed at work, a room painted, the lawn mowed, objects moved from room to room, etc.). They may also belatedly discover the presence of serious injuries and even suicide attempts that they do not remember.

Currently, the Multidimensional Inventory of Dissociation (MID) is the only instrument that measures all 23 of these dissociative symptoms (Dell, 2006a).

15.3 DISCUSSION

15.3.1 Pathological Dissociation and the Self

The experiential locus of pathological dissociation is the self—specifically, the conscious self. *Only the conscious self can experience and notice dissociative intrusions into executive functioning and sense of self.* No self, no intrusions. This assertion is integral to the phenomenological method: "We confine [phenomenological] description solely to the things that are present to the patients' consciousness. Anything which is not a conscious datum is for the present non-existent" (Jaspers, 1963/1997, p. 56). No human consciousness, no intrusions. No intrusions, no dissociation.

In short, pathological dissociative symptoms are ontologically grounded in a conscious self that feels, recognizes, and knows its own experiences. Only the self can sense the involuntary, ego-alien quality and inherent weirdness of pathological dissociative experiences. And only the self can be bothered and confused by those experiences.

I think that the failure to consider the conscious self's experience of dissociative intrusion has led many theorists astray in their efforts to comprehend dissociation. Or, as Jaspers (1963/1997) would put it, too many investigators of dissociation did not (1) complete the preparatory work of phenomenological investigation of dissociation and (2) did not thematize the features of those phenomena in descriptive concepts before attempting to theorize about dissociation. In this chapter, *I am proposing a descriptive/phenomenological concept of pathological dissociation; namely, that the subjective experience of pathological dissociation consists of recurrent, involuntary, nonautobiographical intrusions into one's executive functioning and sense of self.*

I believe that many theorists of dissociation have made two interlinked errors. First, they have ignored the fact that it is probably meaningless to speak of pathological dissociation in the absence of a conscious, experiencing human self. Second, by ignoring the conscious, experiencing self, they have inevitably given too little attention to the inherently intrusive and disruptive nature of pathological dissociation.

Although theorists have sensed that consciousness and unconsciousness are central to dissociation, they have typically ignored the conscious self and focused, instead, on the unconscious. I agree with Cardeña (1994) who argued that theorists and researchers have too often, and wrongly, equated two types of unconsciousness with clinical dissociation: (1) phenomena that can never be made conscious (e.g., the dissociated functioning of the modular human brain, the dissociated functioning of implicit learning and implicit knowledge, etc.), and (2) phenomena that are temporarily unconscious, but that can be made conscious at will (e.g., Freud's preconscious, the ignored ear in dichotic listening experiments, etc.).

I am saying that, from a subjective/phenomenological perspective, whenever dissociation occurs outside of human conscious experience, such dissociation is not a dissociative symptom. It does not exist in the domain of experience; its existence lies somewhere else. Most commonly, when dissociation occurs outside of human conscious experience, it exists in one of three domains: (1) the domain of explanation, (2) the domain of psychological structures or dynamics, or (3) the domain of neuroanatomy or neurophysiology.

15.3.2 An Explanatory Mechanism for Pathological Dissociation

Over a century of clinicians—especially those who have treated seriously traumatized patients—have described independent parts of the mind or splits in the psyche that appear to be directly related to trauma (Breuer & Freud, 1895/1954; Charcot, 1889/1991; Fairbairn, 1981; Ferenczi,

1933/1980; Freud, 1896, 1933, 1940a; Janet, 1889; Jung, 1934; Myers, 1940; Steele, Van der Hart, & Nijenhuis, 2001; Van der Hart, Nijenhuis, & Steele, 2006; Watkins & Watkins, 1997; Winnicott, 1960).

Earlier clinical theorists tended to speak of *ego-states* and *splits in the ego* (e.g., Fairbairn, 1981; Federn, 1952; Freud, 1940a, 1940b; Guntrip, 1969; Watkins & Watkins, 1997), whereas modern trauma theorists increasingly speak of *self-states* (Beere, 2009; Blizard, 1997; Bromberg, 1998, 2001; Dell, 2001a, 2003; Davies & Frawley, 1994; Howell, 1997a, 1997b; Kluft, 1988; Peterson, 1996a, 1996b; Siegel, 1999) and a self that is split into different parts (Kalsched, 1996; Putnam, 1997; Spiegel, 1986).

These separate parts of the psyche, ego, or self seem to have arisen as posttraumatic reactions or adaptations. Unable to be managed, metabolized, or even thought about, traumatic experiences are sequestered elsewhere in the psyche—in one or more traumatized parts of the self that have become separate from the everyday self that deals with daily life.

There is a growing consensus that the traumatized self often becomes split into radically different parts or states. In fact, Kluft (1988) claimed that multiple personality could best be described as a "disaggregate self-state disorder." I believe that Kluft is exactly and precisely correct about this. *DID is a disaggregate self-state disorder. Moreover, the existence (and subsequent activity) of traumatized self-states are the* sine qua non *of chronic, pathological dissociative experiences.*[9]

These self-states contain raw, unmetabolized, traumatic, sensory experience and affects such as fear, shame, rage, and so on. Many self-states are dominated by overvalued ideas, needs, attitudes, and reactions, which are driven by trauma (e.g., neediness, lack of trust, feelings of worthlessness, the belief that one is contaminated, a fear-driven compulsion to appease others, attention-seeking behavior, guilt, rigid counterdependence, needs for control, wishes to humiliate another, etc.). When activated, these trauma-shaped self-states *intrude* into the functioning and experience of the everyday self. In doing so, they bring about "the consciously-experienced intrusions of another self-state" (see previous discussion). In short, whether they are full-blown alter personalities or just (what used to be called) strong ego-states, these self-states cause consciously experienced dissociative intrusions (see #1 to #16). And *some* self-states, when strong enough relative to the everyday self, are the source of the fully dissociated intrusions known as amnesia (see #18 to #23).

[9] With the possible exception of Depersonalization Disorder.

For the most part, clinical ideas about trauma and the self (i.e., split or multiple selves and other descriptions of the fragmented psyche) have not been taken up by mainstream psychology or psychiatry. This is unfortunate because these ideas are not just "weird clinical concepts" or "strange clinical theories." These concepts refer to very real clinical phenomena that have been repeatedly observed in traumatized patients for more than a century. Independently of one another, clinicians who worked with traumatized patients have repeatedly discovered startlingly powerful *parts* of the mind that appear to function quite autonomously from the rest of the mind.

Only rarely have clinicians (who observed these phenomena) resorted to the concept of multiple personality in their theorizing. Instead, they attempted to theoretically articulate, via an elaboration of their preexisting concepts, the autonomous parts of the psyche that they were repeatedly observing.

Their conceptualizations of autonomous parts of the psyche include psychological automatisms (Janet, 1889), successive existences (Janet, 1889), hypnoid states (Breuer & Freud, 1893, 1895), a second psychical group (Freud, 1894), traumatic progression (Ferenczi, 1933), complexes (Jung, 1934), an animated foreign body in the sphere of consciousness (Jung, 1934), a State within a State (Freud, 1939), splitting of the ego (Freud, 1940b), splitting and part-objects (Klein, 1946), the apparently normal personality (Myers, 1940), the emotional personality (Myers, 1940), internal saboteur (Fairbairn, 1981), antilibidinal ego (Guntrip, 1969), split-off destructive omnipotent parts of the self (Rosenfeld, 1971), the psychotic narcissistic structure (Rosenfeld, 1971), ego states (Watkins, 1978), addiction to near-death (Joseph, 1982), the pathological organization (Steiner, 1987), a separate entity inside the personality (Spillius, 1988), the cocoon (Goldberg, 1995), the archetypal self-care system (Kalsched, 1996), and defensively unlinked islands of self-experience (Bromberg, 1998).

I fear that academic psychology and psychiatry have been so put off by these "weird" ideas that little thought has been given to the possibility that these ideas refer to phenomena that are quite real.

REFERENCES

American Psychiatric Association (2000). *DSM-IV-TR – Diagnostic and statistical manual of mental disorders* (4th ed., text rev.). Washington, DC: Author.

Beere, D. (2009). The self-system as mechanism for the dissociative disorders: An extension of the perceptual theory of dissociation. In P. F. Dell & J. A. O'Neil (Eds.), *Dissociation and the dissociative disorders: DSM-V and beyond* (pp. 277–285). New York: Routledge.

Bernstein, E. M., & Putnam, F. W. (1986). Development, reliability, and validity of a dissociation scale. *Journal of Nervous and Mental Disease, 174*, 727–735.

Blank, A. S. (1985). The unconscious flashback to the war in Vietnam veterans: Clinical mystery, legal defense, and community problem. In S. M. Sonnenberg, A. S. Blank, & J. A. Talbot (Eds.), *The trauma of war: Stress and recovery in Vietnam veterans* (pp. 239–308). Washington, DC: American Psychiatric Press.

Blizard, R. A. (1997). The origins of dissociative identity disorder from an object relations and attachment theory perspective. *Dissociation, 10*, 223–229.

Braude, S. E. (1995). *First person plural: Multiple personality and the philosophy of mind. Rev*. Lanham, MD: Rowman & Littlefield.

Bremner, J. D., Krystal, J. H., Putnam, F. W., Southwick, S. M., Marmar, C., Charney, D. S., et al. (1998). Measurement of dissociative states with the Clinician-Administered Dissociative States Scale (CADSS). *Journal of Traumatic Stress, 11*, 125–136.

Bremner, J. D., Scott, T. M., Delaney, R. C., Southwick, S. M., Mason, J. W., Johnson, D. R., et al. (1993). Deficits in short-term memory in posttraumatic stress disorder. *American Journal of Psychiatry, 150*, 1015–1019.

Breuer, J., & Freud, S. (1893). On the psychical mechanism of hysterical phenomena. *Standard Edition, 2*, 1–17.

Breuer, J., & Freud, S. (1895). Studies on hysteria. In J. Strachey (Ed. & Trans.), *Standard Edition, 2*.

Briere, J. (2002). Treating adult survivors of severe childhood abuse and neglect: Further development of an integrative model. In J. E. B. Myers, L. Berliner, J. Briere, C. T. Hendrix, T. Reid, & C. Jenny (Eds.), *The APSAC handbook on child maltreatment* (2nd ed., pp. 175–202). Newbury Park, CA: Sage Publications.

Bromberg, P. M. (1998). *Standing in the spaces: Essays on clinical process, trauma, and dissociation*. Hillsdale, NJ: Analytic Press.

Bromberg, P. M. (2001). Treating patients with symptoms, and symptoms with patience: Reflections on shame, dissociation, and eating. *Psychoanalytic Dialogues, 11*, 891–912.

Brunet, A., Holowka D. W., & Laurence, J. R. (2002). Dissociative phenomena. In M. J. Aminoff, & R. B. Daroff (Eds.), *Encyclopedia of the neurological sciences* (pp. 25–27). San Diego: Academic Press.

Cardeña, E. (1994). The domain of dissociation. In S. J. Lynn & J. W. Rhue (Eds.), *Dissociation: Clinical and theoretical perspectives* (pp. 15–31). New York: Guilford.

Charcot, J.-M. (1887/1991). *Clinical lectures on diseases of the nervous system*, Volume, III. London: Tavistock/ Routledge.

Davies, J. M., & Frawley, M. G. (1994). *Treating the adult survivor of childhood sexual abuse: A psychoanalytic perspective*. New York: Basic Books.

Dell, P. F. (2001a). Why the diagnostic criteria for dissociative identity disorder should be changed. *Journal of Trauma & Dissociation, 2(1)*, 7–37.

Dell, P. F. (2001b). Should the dissociative disorders field choose its own diagnostic criteria? Reply to Cardeña, Coons, Putnam, Spiegel, and Steinberg. *Journal of Trauma & Dissociation, 2(1)*, 65–72.

Dell, P. F. (2006a). Multidimensional Inventory of Dissociation (MID): A comprehensive measure of pathological dissociation. *Journal of Trauma & Dissociation, 7(2)*, 77–106.

Dell, P. F. (2006b). A new model of dissociative identity disorder. *Psychiatric Clinics of North America, 29(1)*, 1–26.

Dell, P. F. (2009a). The long struggle to diagnose multiple personality disorder (MPD): II Partial MPD. Empirically In P. F. Dell & J. A. O'Neil (Eds.), *Dissociation and the dissociative disorders: DSM-V and beyond* (pp. 403–428). New York: Routledge.

Dell, P. F. (2009b). Understanding dissociation. In P. F. Dell & J. A. O'Neil (Eds.), *Dissociation and the dissociative disorders: DSM-V and beyond* (pp. 709–825). New York: Routledge.

Dell, P. F., & Lawson, D. (2009). Delineating the domain of pathological dissociation. In P. F. Dell & J. A. O'Neil (Eds.), *Dissociation and the dissociative disorders: DSM-V and beyond* (pp. 667–692). New York: Routledge.

Fairbairn, R. (1981). *Psychoanalytic studies of the personality*. London: Routledge and Kegan Paul.

Federn, P. (1952). E. Weiss (Ed.), *Ego psychology and the psychoses*. New York: Basic Books.

Ferenczi, S. (1980). Confusion of tongues between adults and the child. In M. Balint (Ed.), *Final contributions to the problems and methods of psycho-analysis* (pp. 156–167). New York: Brunner/Mazel. (Original work published 1933.)

Frankel, F. H. (1990). Hypnotizability and dissociation. *American Journal of Psychiatry, 147*, 823–829.

Frankel, F. H. (1994). Dissociation in hysteria and hypnosis: A concept aggrandized. In S. J. Lynn & J. W. Rhue (Eds.), *Dissociation: Clinical and theoretical perspectives* (pp. 80–93). New York: Guilford Press.

Freud, S. (1894). The neuro-psychoses of defence. *Standard Edition, 3*, 3–66.

Freud, S. (1896). Heredity and the ætiology of the neuroses. *Standard Edition, 3*, 141–156.

Freud, S. (1933). Moses and monotheism. *Standard Edition, 23*, 7–137.

Freud, S. (1940a). An outline of psycho-analysis. *Standard Edition, 23*, 139–207.

Freud, S. (1940b). Splitting of the ego in the process of defence. *Standard Edition, 23*, 271–278.

Gast, U. (2002). *Komplexe dissoziative Störungen. Konzeptionelle Untersuchung zur Diagnostik und Behandlung der Dissoziativen Identitätsstörung und ähnlicher Erkrankungen*. Habilitationsschrift, Medizinische Hochschule Hannover.

Goldberg, P. (1995). "Successful" dissociation, pseudovitality, and inauthentic use of the senses. *Psychoanalytic Dialogues, 5*, 493–510.

Golier, J. A., Yehuda, R., Lupien, S. J., Harvey, P. D., Grossman, R., & Elkin, A. (2002). Memory performance in holocaust survivors with posttraumatic stress disorder. *American Journal of Psychiatry, 159*, 1682–1688.

Guntrip, H. (1969). *Schizoid phenomena, object relations and the self*. New York: International Universities Press.

Howell, E. F. (1997a). Desperately seeking attachment: A psychoanalytic reframing of the harsh ego. *Dissociation, 10*, 230–239.

Howell, E. F. (1997b). Masochism: A bridge to the other side of abuse. *Dissociation, 10*, 240–245.

Janet, P. (1889). *L'automatisme psychologique: Essai de psychologie expérimentale sur les formes inférieures de l'activité humaine* [Psychological automatism: Essay of experimental psychology on the lower forms of human activity]. Paris: Félix Alcan.

Janet, P. (1965). *The major symptoms of hysteria*. New York: Hafner [reprint]. (Original work published 1907)

Jaspers, K. (1997). *General psychopathology* (7th ed., Volume I, J. Hoenig & M. W. Hamilton, Trans.). Baltimore: Johns Hopkins University Press. (Original work published 1963.)

Jenkins, M. A., Langlais, P. J., Delis, D., & Cohen, R. (1998). Learning and memory in rape victims with posttraumatic stress disorder. *American Journal of Psychiatry, 155*, 278–279.

Joseph, B. (1982). Addiction to near-death. *International Journal of Psycho-Analysis, 63*, 449–456.

Jung, C. G. (1969). A review of the complex theory. *Collected works of C. G. Jung, Volume 8* [R. F. C. Hull, Trans.] (pp. 92–104). Princeton NJ: Princeton University Press. (Original work published 1934.)

Kalsched, D. (1996). *The inner world of trauma: Archetypal defenses of the personal spirit*. London: Routledge.

Klein, M. (1946). Notes on some schizoid mechanisms. *International Journal of Psycho-Analysis, 27*, 99–110.

Kluft, R. P. (1987). First-rank symptoms as a diagnostic clue to multiple personality disorder. *American Journal of Psychiatry, 144*, 293–298.

Kluft, R. P. (1988). The phenomenology and treatment of extremely complex multiple personality disorder. *Dissociation, 1*, 47–58.

Laddis, A., & Dell, P. F. (2002, November). *A comparison of borderline personality disorder and dissociative identity disorder with the Multidimensional Inventory of Dissociation*. Paper presented at the conference of the International Society for the Study of Dissociation, Baltimore, Maryland.

Lilienfeld, S. O., Kirsch, I., Sarbin, T. R., Lynn, S. J., Chaves, J. F., Ganaway, G. K., et al. (1999). Dissociative identity disorder and the sociocognitive model: Recalling the lessons of the past. *Psychological Bulletin, 125*, 507–523.

Marshall, R. D., Spitzer, R., & Liebowitz, M. R. (1999). Review and critique of the DSM-IV diagnosis of acute stress disorder. *American Journal of Psychiatry, 156*, 1677–1685.

McHugh, P. R. (1995). Resolved: Multiple personality disorder is an individually and socially created artifact. Affirmative. *Journal of the American Academy of Child and Adolescent Psychiatry, 34*, 957–959.

Merskey, H. (1992). The manufacture of personalities: The production of multiple personality disorder. *British Journal of Psychiatry, 160*, 327–340.

Myers, C. S. (1940). *Shell shock in France 1914-1918*. Cambridge: Cambridge University Press.

Peterson, G. (1996a). Diagnostic taxonomy: past to future. In J. L. Silberg (Ed.), *The dissociative child: Diagnosis, treatment and management* (pp. 3–26). Lutherville, Maryland: Sidran Press.

Peterson, G. (1996b). Treatment of early onset. In J. L. Spira (Ed.), *Treating dissociative identity disorder* (pp. 135–181). San Francisco: Jossey-Bass.

Putnam, F. W. (1997). *Dissociation in children and adolescents*. New York: Guilford Press.

Putnam, F. W. (2001). Reclaiming dissociative diagnoses. *Journal of Trauma & Dissociation, 2(1)*, 47–49.

Reinders, A. A. T. S., Nijenhuis, E. R. S., Paans, A. M. J., Korf, J., Willemsen, A. T. M., & Den Boer, J. A. (2003). One brain, two selves. *NeuroImage, 20*, 2119–2125.

Rosenfeld, H. (1971). A clinical approach to the psychoanalytic theory of the life and death instincts: An investigation into the aggressive aspects of narcissism. *International Journal of Psycho-Analysis, 52*, 169–178.

Ross, C. A., Heber, S., Norton, G. R., Anderson, D., Anderson, G., & Barchet, B. (1989). The Dissociative Disorders Interview Schedule: A structured interview. *Dissociation, 2*, 169–189.

Schneider, K. (1959). *Clinical psychopathology*. New York: Grune & Stratton.

Siegel, D. J. (1999). *The developing mind: Toward a neurobiology of interpersonal experience*. New York: Guilford Press.

Spiegel, D. (1986). Dissociating damage. *American Journal of Clinical Hypnosis, 29*, 123–131.

Spillius, E. B. (1988). Pathological organizations: Introduction. In E. B. Spillius (Ed.), *Melanie Klein today: Developments in theory and practice. Volume 1: Mainly theory* (pp. 193–202). London: Routledge.

Steele, K., van der Hart, O., & Nijenhuis, E. R. S. (2001). Dependency in the treatment of complex PTSD and dissociative disorder patients. *Journal of Trauma & Dissociation, 2(4)*, 79–116.

Steinberg, M. (1994). *Structured Clinical Interview for DSM-IV Dissociative Disorders (SCID-D), Revised*. Washington, DC: American Psychiatric Press.

Steiner, J. (1987). The interplay between pathological organizations and the paranoid-schizoid and depressive positions. *International Journal of Psycho-Analysis, 68*, 69–80.

Van der Hart, O., & Dorahy, M. (2009). Dissociation: History of a concept. In P. F. Dell & J. A. O'Neil (Eds.), *Dissociation and the dissociative disorders: DSM-V and beyond* (pp. 3–26). New York: Routledge.

Van der Hart, O., Nijenhuis, E. R. S., & Steele, K. (2006). *The haunted self: Structural dissociation and treatment of chronic traumatization*. London: W. W. Norton & Company.

Van IJzendoorn, M., & Schuengel, C. (1996). The measurement of dissociation in normal and clinical populations: Meta-analytic validation of the Dissociative Experiences Scale (DES). *Clinical Psychology Review, 16*, 365–382.

Watkins, J. G. (1978). *The therapeutic self: Developing resonance—Key to effective relationships*. New York: Human Sciences Press.

Watkins, J. G., & Watkins, H. H. (1997). *Ego states: Theory and therapy*. New York: Norton.

Winnicott, D. W. (1965). Ego distortion in terms of true and false self. In D. W. Winnicott (Ed.), *The maturational processes and the facilitating environment* (pp. 140–152). London: Hogarth Press. (Original work published 1960.)

World Health Organization (1992). *The ICD-10 classification of mental and behavioural disorders: Clinical descriptions and diagnostic guidelines*. Geneva: Author.

Yehuda, R., Keefe, R. S. E., Harvey, P. D., Levengood, R. A., Gerber, D. K., Geni, J., & Siever, L. J. (1995). Learning and memory in combat veterans with posttraumatic stress disorder. *American Journal of Psychiatry, 152*, 137–139.

16 The Theory of Trauma-Related Structural Dissociation of the Personality

Kathy Steele, MN, CS
Onno van der Hart, PhD
Ellert R. S. Nijenhuis, PhD

OUTLINE

The 150-year history of dissociation began with a fundamental idea: components of the personality or consciousness may become divided from each other under conditions of extreme stress and may manifest as different psychobiological conditions (e.g., Butler et al., 1996; Crabtree, 1993; Janet, 1889, 1907, 1909a; cf. Van der Hart & Dorahy, 2009). The recently developed theory of structural dissociation of the personality is founded upon this original definition of dissociation and integrates it with research and contemporary theories about responses to overwhelming events (Nijenhuis, Van der Hart, & Steele, 2002, 2004; Nijenhuis, Spinhoven, Vanderlinden, Van Dyck, & Van der Hart 1998; Van der Hart, Nijenhuis, & Steele, 2005, 2006; Van der Hart, Nijenhuis, Steele, & Brown, 2004). We propose that trauma-related dissociation refers to the existence of at least two self-organizing *systems of psychobiological states*. These dissociative systems are parts of the personality, each with its own sense of self that is insufficiently integrated with the other. However, they share some underlying implicit and explicit functions and mental contents.

We maintain that trauma-related dissociation is primarily an ongoing integrative *deficit* that results in a *structural dissociation* of the personality. Only secondarily is dissociation a psychological *defense*. Chronic dissociative *processes* are maintained by specific factors. Structural dissociation manifests in dissociative *symptoms* that can be categorized as positive or negative, psychoform or somatoform. We differentiate structural dissociation from the alterations in consciousness that are often referred to as *normal dissociation*. Normal dissociation occurs in both normal and clinical populations. We contend that normal dissociation does not require the existence of a divided personality.

16.1 THE ORIGINS OF STRUCTURAL DISSOCIATION

We developed the theory of trauma-related structural dissociation in response to several issues. First, our clinical work repeatedly showed us that different dissociative parts handle different functions in defense and daily life. We sought an explanation for those differences. Second, we observed much confusion in the literature regarding the construct of dissociation; we sought to formulate a clearer theory of trauma-related dissociation. Third, most current theories do not do justice to the complexity and breadth of dissociative symptoms; we sought a theory that could explain *all* dissociative symptoms. Fourth, we found both help and confusion in the research literature on trauma and dissociation; we sought a theory that would explain discrepant findings in that literature. Finally, we sought a language and a theory that would be readily applicable to both research and clinical practice.

The theory of structural dissociation integrates (1) the authors' collective clinical experience with trauma and dissociation and (2) the clinical literature of the late 19th and early 20th centuries (e.g., Jackson, 1931/32; Janet, 1889, 1907, 1919/25; McDougall, 1926; Mitchell, 1922; Myers, 1940), and more recent literature (e.g., Chu, 1998; Herman, 1992; Kluft & Fine, 1993; Lœwenstein, 1991; Putnam, 1997; Ross, 1997; Van der Hart, Van der Kolk, & Boon, 1998). The theory also seeks to integrate neurobiology (e.g., Bremner, 2003; Carrion, Weems, & Reiss, 2007; Damasio, 1999; Frewen & Lanius, 2006; Krystal et al., 1996; LeDoux, 1996; Nijenhuis & Den Boer, 2007; Nijenhuis et al., 2002; Panksepp, 1998; Schore, 2002, 2003; Siegel, 1999; Teicher, Andersen, Polcari, Anderson, & Navalta, 2002; Van der Kolk, 2003); learning theory, ethology (Gould, 1982; Toates, 1986; cf. Nijenhuis, 1999/2004), attachment theory (e.g., Bowlby, 1969/1982; Cassidy & Shaver, 1999; Liotti, 1995; Main & Morgan, 1996), and developmental psychopathology (Fonagy, Gergely, Jurist, & Target, 2002; Schore, 2003).

16.1.1 Deficits in Integrative Capacity

Mental health is characterized by the capacity to integrate ongoing events into a coherent personality that allows for adaptive functioning (Jackson, 1931/32; Janet, 1889; Meares, 1999; Nijenhuis et al., 2002; Van der Hart et al., 2006). Integration is grounded in two essential mental actions: (1) synthesis and (2) realization. *Synthesis* meaningfully associates experiences and functions into more complex experiences and functions; this process generates the ever-evolving personality. *Realization* analyzes and digests facts and personal experiences; it is the process by which one becomes fully aware of the implications of facts and experiences for one's life (Van der Hart et al., 2006; Van der Hart, Steele, Boon, & Brown, 1993).

Integration is based on two aspects of synthesis: (1) synthesis of components of experiences (sensations, perceptions, including sense of self and behavioral actions) *within a given episode of time* into meaningful and coherent mental structures (Braude, 1995; Ciompi, 1991; Siegel, 1999) and (2) synthesis of experiences, knowledge, and functions *across time* (Braude, 1995; Ciompi, 1991; Siegel, 1999) into a coherent personality. Janet maintained that adaptive behavior depends upon one's synthetic capacity to create meaningful combinations of sensations, affects, behaviors, and perceptions of the environment within a given moment and across time. Thus, adaptive response to extremely stressful events requires the capacity to synthesize one's sensory, emotional, cognitive, and behavioral reactions within a coherent mental structure.

Realization consists of two complex mental actions: personification and presentification (Van der Hart et al., 2006). *Personification* is the mental action by which one endows experience with one's personal sense of ownership (Janet, 1903): "That happened to me, and I think and feel thus and so about it." *Presentification* is the mental action of integrating one's past, present, and future and brings that integration to bear on one's actions in the moment (Janet, 1928; Van der Hart & Steele, 1977). In presentification, the individual accords the present with the highest degree of reality. At the same time, the proximate past and future (e.g., yesterday and last week, or tomorrow and next week) are considered to be more real than the distant past and future (e.g., 30 years ago or

30 years in the future). Thus, although the person realizes that past events affect who one is and how one acts, the present is accorded a higher reality. Presentification allows one to address the present in a reflective, mindful manner.

When personification fails, one's knowledge of the synthesized event is merely factual. The experience does not become personalized. Thus, a traumatized individual may say: "I know my life was threatened, but it feels as if it happened to somebody else." The memory is semantic, rather than episodic (Tulving, 1972). Semantic memory involves declarative knowledge. One knows something to be a fact, but that fact has no link to one's autobiographical sense of self. Thus, when personification fails and memories remain semantic, one's coherent sense of personal existence is compromised. Episodic memories involve a double awareness: (1) memories of experiences and (2) knowledge that the experiences are part of one's personal history. Successful personification produces episodic memories that are integrated into a relatively context-independent sense of self. Adaptive functioning requires that a person's current experiences be personified and integrated with his or her entire past history.

Sustained, high levels of integrative capacity are needed to integrate extremely stressful events. If a person's integrative capacity is too low, it may drop further during stressful events, falling below a critical level. Such stress-related integrative failure may be mediated neurobiologically via stress hormones and stress-related alterations of the hippocampus and the prefrontal cortex (e.g., Bremner et al., 1995; Ehling, Nijenhuis, & Krikke, 2003; Frewen & Lanius, 2006; Nijenhuis & Den Boer, 2007; Nijenhuis et al., 2002; Tsai, Condie, Wu, & Chang, 1999). There is mounting evidence that the brain and body are changed by traumatic experiences, such that preexisting integrative capacity is reduced (Carrion et al., 2007; Perry, 1999; Van der Kolk, 1994, 2003).

16.1.2 Prototypes of Structural Dissociation

Traumatized individuals reexperience traumatic memories and undergo affective numbing or avoid reminders of trauma. Reexperiencing and avoidance/numbing may coexist or alternate. This pattern, which has been observed for over a century (e.g., Breuer & Freud, 1893; Brewin, Dalgleish, & Joseph, 1996; Brewin, 2001, 2003; Janet, 1889, 1904; Kardiner, 1941; Myers, 1940; Nijenhuis & Van der Hart, 1999; Van der Kolk & Van der Hart, 1989, 1991), is the foundation for the diagnosis of posttraumatic stress disorder (PTSD). In fact, the parallel activation of, or the alternation between, experiencing "too much" and "too little" seems to be a hallmark of trauma-related disorders.

We propose that the psychobiological differences between experiencing too much (i.e., intrusion) and experiencing too little (i.e., avoidance, numbing and detachment) respectively characterize the structurally dissociated parts of the personality (Van der Hart et al., 2006). One or more dissociative parts become fixated on traumatic memory and experience too much of the past and not enough of the present. Another type of dissociative part focuses on daily life, compulsively avoiding traumatic memories. This kind of part experiences too little of the past. Dissociative *process* is a stable integrative failure in which the personality is divided into two or more psychobiological systems. Normally, these psychobiological systems are relatively integrated with one another. In patients with trauma-related disorders, however, these psychobiological structures are poorly integrated with one another.

The idea that traumatized individuals are divided is not new. Many theorists have proposed their own terminology for such divisions. We have adopted the terminology of British army psychiatrist and psychologist, Charles Samuel Myers (1916a, 1916b, 1940). Myers's observations of World War I "shell-shocked" combat soldiers are the cornerstone of our understanding of trauma-related structural dissociation of the personality (cf. Nijenhuis & Van der Hart, 1999; Nijenhuis et al., 2002; Van der Hart et al., 1998; Van der Hart et al., 2006; Van der Hart, Van Dijke, Van Son, & Steele, 2000). Myers (1940) postulated that a structural dissociation occurred between a so-called *emotional* personality (EP) and an *apparently normal* personality (ANP) in acutely traumatized World War I combat soldiers. The EPs of these soldiers recurrently suffered from vivid sensorimotor experiences and painful affects that subjectively mirrored the original trauma. EPs are stuck in traumatic reexperiencing that persistently fails to resolve into a narrative memory. On the other hand, the ANP in these soldiers used avoidance, detachment, numbing, and partial or complete amnesia to escape the traumatic memories.

16.1.2.1 The Concept of "Parts of the Personality"

We made a small but significant change in Myers's terminology. In our opinion, he overstated his case when he used the term *personality*, particularly in relation to acutely traumatized individuals. We believe that dissociative mental structures, no matter how autonomous and elaborated they might be, are still components of a single personality. Thus, we prefer the term dissociative *parts* of the personality. Depending on how much division has occurred, a traumatized person may have anywhere from (1) a single EP and a single ANP to (2) numerous EPs and several ANPs. Each part includes at least a rudimentary sense of an experiencing "I." Although we use the terms *ANP* and *EP*, it is important to note that ANPs and EPs often do not present as clear-cut "alternate identities" or "personality states" (American Psychiatric Association, 1994, p. 484). In fact, the theory of structural dissociation opposes undue reification of separate "identities" or "personality states," even in cases of DID.

The theory of structural dissociation holds that there is insufficient psychobiological integration among dissociative parts of the personality. ANPs and EPs routinely differ from one another on a large variety of variables: intrusion and avoidance of trauma-related cues, affect regulation, psychological defenses, capacity for insight, response to stimuli, body movements, behavior, cognitive schemas, attention, attachment styles, sense of self, self-destructiveness, suicidality, and flexibility and adaptability in daily life (Figley, 1978; Tauber, 1996; Wang, Wilson, & Mason, 1996; Wilson, 1989). ANPs and EPs also have many similar features. They lack full realization of the trauma; they have deficits that hinder the individual's ability to adapt to the present. Both display significant dissociative symptoms. They tend to be reciprocally dissociated from one another.

It should be noted that structural dissociation is a chronic condition that exists until fusion among all parts occurs. This means that there is *not* one part of the personality that is dissociated and another that is not. Similarly, there are *not* times when an individual is dissociated and times when he or she is not. In most cases, structural dissociation has overt manifestations that can be assessed with instruments such as the Structured Interview for DSM-IV Dissociative Disorders (Steinberg, 1994) or the Multidimensional Inventory of Dissociation (Dell, 2004).

When a well-functioning ANP is dominant, the patient may appear to be *normal* as the term ANP suggests. This apparent normality may be due to the fact that dissociative symptoms are latent prior to the emergence of delayed PTSD (Schnurr, Lunney, Sengupta, & Waelde, 2003). Interestingly, survivors who develop delayed PTSD function more poorly prior to the onset of PTSD than do survivors who do not develop PTSD (e.g., Bryant & Harvey, 2002; Buckley, Blanchard, & Hickling, 1996). Those who develop delayed PTSD have a higher resting heart rate during the first month posttrauma and more psychopathological symptoms during the first 6 months (Bryant & Harvey, 2002). Thus, the normality of survivors with delayed onset PTSD is limited, even prior to the onset of definitive symptoms.

But nevertheless, there are likely negative symptoms present, though they may not be recognized or reported as such; they may be dissimulated (e.g., Kluft 1987b); or simply neither mentioned nor labeled as symptoms by the patient because they have been an integral part of the survivor's experience for such a long time.

16.1.2.2 The "Emotional" Part of the Personality (EP)

EPs remain fixed in the traumatic experience, with vivid, terrifying sensorimotor memories of the traumatizing event. Despite their name, EPs are not emotional in the sense of having a normal range of affects. Instead, many experience "vehement" emotions (e.g., intense fear, helplessness, horror, anger, and shame) that are overwhelming and disorganizing (Janet, 1909b). We understand these vehement emotions and their resulting impulsive and reactive behaviors to be ineffective substitutes for adaptive mental and behavioral actions (Janet, 1909b). Some EPs may not display such vehemence; rather they seem to be in utter collapse, listless or unresponsive, a condition related to the animal defense of total submission (see the following). Other EPs may be almost entirely devoid of feeling (i.e., EPs with out-of-body experiences wherein they observed traumatizing events from a distance).

EPs and their corresponding traumatic memories are usually associated with a specific image of the body and a separate sense of self (McDougall, 1926). EPs vary in complexity. EPs in PTSD are relatively simple; they are primarily manifest in symptoms of reexperiencing. EPs in severe dissociative disorders tend to be more elaborated, more autonomous, and more numerous. EPs are found in all trauma-related disorders, from PTSD to DID. They are analogous to: Laufer's (1988) "war self"; Wang et al.'s (1996) "survivor mode"; the child part of the Holocaust survivor's "compound" personality (Tauber, 1996); the dissociative parts that embody abuser rage, victim rage, and passivity; zombie parts in trauma-related borderline personality disorder (BPD, Golynkina & Ryle, 1999); certain alter identities in DID, such as the "frozen in time" child and persecutors (Kluft, 1984a; Kluft & Fine, 1993; Putnam, 1989; Putnam et al., 1986); and identities associated with situationally accessible memories related to trauma (SAM; Brewin et al., 1996; Brewin, 2001, 2003). Because they are so fixed in reactions to the dreadful past, EPs are not very functional in present-day circumstances.

The traumatic "memories" of EPs are very different from normal memories (i.e., integrated narratives of traumatic experiences; Brewin, 2003; Janet, 1889, 1904, 1919/25, 1928; Van der Hart, Bolt, & Van der Kolk, 2005;

Van der Kolk & Van der Hart, 1991). Normal memories convey a narrative to the listener, stories told and retold, changeable over time, and adapted to an audience. Whereas narrative memories are verbal, time-condensed, social, and reconstructive in nature, traumatic memories are often experienced as if the overwhelming event were happening *right now*. Hallucinatory and involuntary experiences, that consist of visual images, sensations, and motor actions, pervade the entire perceptual field. This traumatic reexperiencing is subjectively characterized by a sense of timelessness and immutability (Modell, 1990; Spiegel, Frischholz, & Spira, 1993; Van der Hart & Steele, 1997). This traumatic memory has no social function (Janet, 1928).

Traumatic memories have a very distinctive feature. When reactivated, they tend to simultaneously block access to many other memories. Thus, when the EP is activated, the patient typically loses access to many memories that are readily available to the ANP. These unavailable memories are typically episodes of personal experience; in some cases, however, semantic memories (i.e., factual knowledge) and procedural memories (e.g., memories for skills and associations due to classical conditioning; Van der Hart & Nijenhuis, 2001) may also be unavailable.

16.1.2.3 The "Apparently Normal" Part of the Personality (ANP)

The ANP, the part of the personality that strives for normal life, is only apparently normal. The ANP phobically avoids reminders of traumatic experience. If the survivor as ANP speaks of the traumatic experience, he or she speaks of it distantly, without a sense of personal ownership (i.e., with insufficient personification). The ANP has integrated neither the traumatic memory, nor the mental system (EP) that is associated with that memory. As noted above, ANPs often manifest a range of negative dissociative symptoms (Nijenhuis & Van der Hart, 1999; Van der Hart et al., 2006; Van der Hart et al., 2000) such as partial or complete amnesia for the traumatizing event, sensory anesthesias, restricted emotion, numbness, and depersonalization.

The ANP is generally the "major shareholder" (Fraser, 1987) of the personality and is in evidence most of the time. ANPs are analogous to: Laufer's (1988) "adaptive self"; Wang et al.'s (1996) "normal personality functioning mode"; the adult part of the Holocaust survivor's "compound" personality (Tauber, 1996); the dissociative "coping part" in BPD (Golynkina & Ryle, 1999); the "host personality" and other alter identities that function in daily life in DID (Kluft, 1984a; Putnam, 1989); and identities associated with verbally accessible memories of general autobiographical experience and of some elements of traumatic events (VAM; Brewin et al., 1996; Brewin, 2001, 2003). ANPs vary widely in their degree of adaptive functioning. An individual generally functions at a higher level as ANP than as EP.

16.1.3 Action Systems Mediate ANP and EP

Although the personality can become divided in countless ways, some forms of trauma-related structural dissociation seem far more likely than others. In our view, the fault lines between dissociative parts are substantially mediated by evolutionary prepared, psychobiological systems (Gould, 1982; Panksepp, 1998; Toates, 1986). These systems have been referred to as motivational (e.g., Gould, 1982; Toates, 1986), behavioral (e.g., Bowlby, 1969/1982; Cassidy, 1999), functional (Fanselow & Lester, 1988), and emotional operating systems (Panksepp, 1998). Their purpose is to generate affective feelings that help animals and humans to (1) determine whether an event is biologically useful or harmful, and (2) evoke adaptive responses to current life circumstances. We call them *action* systems (Van der Hart et al., 2006), because they involve a readiness or tendency to act (Arnold, 1960; Frijda, 1986). They do not compel an individual to act in a fixed way; rather, they influence and shape action through action tendencies. Each of these action systems seems to inhere in its own neural network. Action systems manifest as patterns of activation in sensory awareness, perceptual bias, emotional tone, emotional regulation, memory processes, mental models, behavioral response patterns (Siegel, 1999), and in humans, a sense of self. There are two broad categories of action systems: (1) those that promote functioning in daily life and survival of the species, and (2) those that serve survival of the individual by promoting defense in the face of threat.

Ideally, development involves synthesis among action systems. Action systems that are functionally related (e.g., attachment and sociability) may be synthesized more readily than those that involve quite different functions. Metaphorically speaking, there are natural fault lines between action systems of daily life and those of defense. Under threat, action systems of daily life will be inhibited; in the absence of threat, defense systems will be inhibited.

If our hypothesis is correct, that is, if psychobiological action systems largely mediate the functioning of ANPs and EPs, then those psychobiological systems must have characteristics that are congruent with the known features of ANPs and EPs.

First, the psychobiological action systems must be self-organizing and self-stabilizing, as demonstrated in the prototypes of ANP and EP. Second, because structural dissociation can occur early in life, the psychobiological action systems must be available early in life. Third, these systems should have certain universal characteristics, but also allow for individual differences. For example, ANPs universally avoid traumatic memories and deal with daily life and survival of the species (e.g., sexuality, attachment, caretaking, and social interaction). EPs are universally fixated on trauma; they focus on traumatic memories and readily display defensive and emotional reactions to threat. ANPs and EPs also have individual differences that have been shaped by life history and innate psychobiological characteristics. Fourth, because both ANPs and EPs have survival functions, their mediating psychobiological systems must be (1) functional systems that have been developed in the course of evolution, and (2) similar to analogous animal systems. Fifth, because ANPs and EPs have relatively cohesive complexes of sensation, perception, cognition, behavior, and probably (neuro)physiology, the evolutionarily prepared action systems must integrate and control each of these psychobiological phenomena. Sixth, because ANPs and EPs both react strongly to cues that could reactivate traumatic memories, their underlying psychobiological systems must be very open to classical conditioning.

Action systems meet the six criteria that we have just described. Panksepp (1998) argued that the action systems are inborn, self-organizing, self-stabilizing, and homeostatic: "Many of the ancient, evolutionary derived brain systems all mammals share still serve as the foundations for the deeply experienced affective proclivities of the human mind" (p. 4).

When there is trauma-related structural dissociation of the personality, the coordination and coherence of action systems seem to be disrupted. Because action systems of daily life and action systems of defense naturally inhibit one another, traumatic stress will more readily derail their mutual *integration*. Conversely, we hypothesize traumatic stress less often disrupts the integration of the action systems of daily life with one another (or the action systems of defense with one another). We thus propose that a threat-driven dissociative division between action systems of daily life and action systems of defense substantially accounts for the prototypical organizations of ANPs and EPs.

Action systems that mediate functions in daily life belong to the ANP; the ANP manages life, in part, by avoiding traumatic memories. The functions of the ANP include exploration of the environment (including work and study), play, energy management (sleeping and eating), attachment, sociability, reproduction/sexuality, and caretaking (especially rearing of children) (e.g., Cassidy, 1999; Panksepp, 1998).

The EP is focused on traumatic memories, and is grounded in the action systems of defense (which include subsystems that are based on the imminence of threat). First, there is the separation cry, the young animal's or child's distressed vocalization when separated from a caretaker. Because this cry is an attempt to regain attachment, we call it the attachment cry. Other defensive subsystems include hypervigilance, flight, freeze with analgesia, fight, total submission with anesthesia (collapse), and recuperative states of rest, wound care, isolation from the group, and gradual return to daily activities (i.e., to the action systems of daily life) (Fanselow & Lester, 1988; Nijenhuis, 1999/2004). Each EP is typically grounded in one or more of these subsystems of *physical defense*; EPs that are more elaborated may engage in *psychological defense* as well. These animal defensive reactions are linked to the physical manifestations of dissociation in humans such as analgesia, anesthesia, motor inhibitions, and motor paralysis (Nijenhuis, Spinhoven, & Vanderlinden, 1998; Nijenhuis et al., 1998, 2004).

16.1.3.1 Dissociation as Psychological Defense

Dissociation is often understood as a psychological defense (as defined in psychodynamic terms) against the intolerable effects and experiences of trauma (e.g., Briere, 1992; Cardeña, 1994; Chu, 1990; Freyd, 1994; Putnam, 1985; Spiegel, 1990). Psychological defense is compatible with our proposal that dissociation is grounded in specific action systems, including those of physical defense. We are sentient, social beings with psychological needs, especially in the realms of attachment and sociability. Extremely complex, and sometimes contradictory, social behaviors and attitudes are required to maintain an acceptable social status within the family and within society. Accordingly, we need psychological defenses as well as physical ones. Both ANPs and EPs wield psychological defenses that serve their specific action tendencies. For example, various parts of the personality may disown affect or project, devalue, and deny. ANPs effectively "use" EPs for psychological protection; EPs contain the emotions, thoughts, sensations, and so on that the ANPs deem unbearable. Other mental contents that are unacceptable to ANPs, such as thoughts, ideas, fantasies, wishes, and needs are usually found in the EPs. For example, EPs that have dependency needs and extreme attachment insecurity are quite common; they are fixed in the defensive subsystem of attachment cry, whereas the

ANP remains detached and phobic of dependence (Steele, Van der Hart, & Nijenhuis, 2001). Although dissociation is viewed as a primary psychological defense, we contend that that psychological defense occurs secondarily to the deficit in integrative capacity (at least initially).

16.1.4 Developmental Pathways to Structural Dissociation

So far, we have discussed the pretraumatized personality as if it were a reasonably well-integrated mental system. With young children, this is simply not the case. Young children are still developing a coherent personality organization. Thus, the earliest developmental pathways to structural dissociation of the personality probably involve hindering the natural integration of action systems and "discrete behavioral states" (Putnam, 1997; Siegel, 1999). In the infant, the sense of self is still highly state-dependent (Putnam, 1997; Wolf, 1990; Wolff, 1987). Because young children have not yet developed a coherent personality structure, they are especially susceptible to trauma. Abuse and neglect can alter the mind and the brain of young children in ways that promote state-dependent or personality-dependent functioning. Their rudimentary behavioral states (that are shaped by different action systems) can become easily dissociated.

Secure interactions with caretakers allow young children to slowly acquire skills to sustain, modulate, and integrate states (Putnam, 1997; Siegel, 1999). "Good enough" parenting (secure attachment) critically enhances integration of states in the child (Putnam, 1997). The child's ability to modulate his or her behavioral states can be strongly promoted by the caretaker's sharing of parallel or complementary states with the child. This social sharing is associated with a powerful synchronization of physiological processes between the child and the adult that assists the child to regulate states. Conversely, lack of synchronization has disruptive effects (Field, 1985). A "good enough" parent adapts to the child's states, tolerates the child's states within nurturing limits, soothes, and plans cycles of activity and rest for the child. Such caretaking activities enhance the integration of states in the child (Putnam, 1997). In short, children are vitally dependent on their attachment figures for initial regulation of inborn action tendencies; without such support, children are prone to integrative failure and psychobiological dysregulation.

The neurobiological changes that are attendant upon trauma and disruptions of attachment contribute significantly to dissociation (e.g., Glaser, 2000; Nijenhuis et al., 2002; Perry & Pollard, 1998; Perry, Blakely, Baker, & Vigilante, 1995; Schore, 2002, 2003; Siegel, 1999). Disrupted attachment in traumatized children appears to be a significant cause of chronic dissociation (Carlson, 1998; Draijer, & Langeland, 1999; Ogawa, Sroufe, Weinfield, Carlson, & Egeland, 1997; Van IJzendoorn, Schuengel, & Bakersman-Kranenberg, 1999). Early, chronic trauma and neglect often induce disorganized/disoriented attachment (D-attachment; Liotti, 1992, 1995, 1999a, 1999b, 2006; Lyons-Ruth, 2003; Main, 1991; Main & Hesse, 1990; Main & Morgan, 1996; Schore, 2002). In our view, D-attachment is not actually disorganized, nor does it necessarily involve disorientation. Instead, we propose that Type D attachment involves concurrent or rapid successive activations of the attachment action system and the defense action system in a child who simultaneously approaches and defends against a scary caregiver. This insoluble approach-avoidance dilemma can promote a structural dissociation of the attachment system and the defensive system that generates an ANP and an EP.

In primary structural dissociation, the ANP is attached to the dangerous caretaker(s), but is dissociated from, or avoidant of, the EP that holds memories of abuse/neglect and represents the defensive system. An EP may divide into a second EP that represents the attachment system. Attachment-related EPs have two common forms: (1) a childlike part of the personality that loves the perpetrating parent, and (2) the part of the personality that seeks attachment to a "stronger and wiser" therapist or other perceived "caregiver." The dissociative parts of the personality that avoid awareness of attachment needs display a phobia of attachment: avoidance of contact, pseudo-independence, and disconnection from basic self needs. Parts of the personality that are dedicated to attachment display a phobia of emotional loss: fear of abandonment, emotional clinging, intolerance of aloneness, and maladaptive dependency (Steele et al., 2001).

Overwhelming events may precipitate an integrative failure, even in children who are securely attached. This is so for at least three reasons. First, brain regions that have major integrative functions, such as the prefrontal cortices and the hippocampus, have not yet fully matured in children (e.g., Benes, 1998), making more complex integration extremely difficult. Second, extremely stressful events compromise integrative functioning of the brain in general, but particularly in children (for reviews see Bremner, 1999a, 2003; Glaser, 2000; Siegel, 1999). Finally, the integrative capacity of children is limited due to a relative absence of experience-derived templates that serve as "attractors" (Siegel, 1999) to integrate new and/or emotionally charged experiences.

16.2 MAINTENANCE OF STRUCTURAL DISSOCIATION

Trauma-related disorders are characterized by persisting structural dissociation of the personality. Although many factors help to perpetuate structural dissociation, most of these factors are beyond the scope of this chapter. Here, we will limit our discussion to the effects of intrapersonal and interpersonal learning.

In trauma-related classical conditioning, survivors create associations between (1) the traumatizing, unconditioned stimuli and (2) previously neutral stimuli that saliently precede or refer to these unconditioned stimuli. As a result, the previously neutral, now conditioned stimuli evoke a memory of the traumatizing event. Classical conditioning plays an essential role in all trauma-related mental disorders (Coupland, 2000; Nijenhuis et al., 2002; Van der Hart et al., 2005, 2006). For example, once children learn that the caretaker's anger signals the likelihood of physical abuse, that anger serves as a conditioned stimulus that reactivates the memory of the abuse. This memory will subsequently tend to activate the child's defensive system whether or not the caretaker becomes abusive. As a result of generalization learning, *anyone's* anger will tend to activate the child's defensive system. In children who are structurally dissociated, this defensive response will include a reactivation of the EP and an inhibition of the ANP. Intermittent success in preventing anger by being excessively obedient and pleasing will lead to appeasement-based, insecure attachment. This is then likely to be the predominant attachment style of one or more dissociative parts of the personality.

Complex cases of structural dissociation often involve more than one EP. For example, anger and abuse causes one EP to freeze and submit, whereas another EP tries to prevent the anger and abuse by being pleasing. When threat is chronic, pleasing EPs sometimes develop the features of an ANP because appeasement is felt to be a necessity. That kind of pleasing may be understood to be a function of (1) the caretaking system and (2) evolutionary tendencies toward social submission that can avert perceived physical threat.

Dissociative parts are not totally separate; they maintain certain dynamic interrelationships. For example, when the EP's traumatic memories are triggered, they tend to intrude into the ANP. When the integrative capacity of the ANP is insufficient to integrate these intruding traumatic memories, the ANP will exhibit avoidance reactions: retraction of the field of consciousness, lowering of the level of consciousness, and efforts to mentally avoid the EP and its intruding traumatic memories. Because the EP represents the traumatizing event, the ANP develops a classically conditioned fear of the EP. Through generalization, the ANP also fears and avoids internal and external stimuli that saliently relate to the EP. Over time, the range of conditioned stimuli and phobic contexts steadily widens. The fundamental *phobia of traumatic memory* (Janet, 1904) leads to (or is accompanied by) a growing range of phobias: *of mental actions, of dissociative parts of the personality, of attachment and intimacy, attachment loss*, and *of normal life and change* (Nijenhuis et al., 2004; Steele, Van der Hart, & Nijenhuis, 2001, 2004).

Evaluative conditioning (Bayens, Hermans, & Eelen, 1993) of external and internal stimuli may also occur. In evaluative conditioning, the conjoint presentation of a stimulus that an individual evaluates as neutral and stimulus he or she evaluates as negative (or positive), leads him or her to subsequently evaluate the previously neutral as negative (or positive). For example, when a traumatic experience was experienced as shameful and disgusting, the ANP may become ashamed of, and disgusted with, the EP. In short, like fear conditioning, evaluative conditioning interferes with integration.

Active behavioral avoidance of external and internal conditioned fear stimuli includes distancing from places, people, objects, emotions, and inner voices. It can include physical distancing, workaholism, compulsive busyness, (ab)using substances, and self-mutilation (Joseph, Yule, Williams, & Andrews, 1993; King, King, Fairbank, Keane, & Adams, 1998; Solomon, Mikulincer, & Avitzur, 1988). Dissociative patients may use drugs or self-mutilation to temporarily silence inner voices of EPs. *Passive behavioral avoidance* prevents exposure to perceived threat (e.g., refraining from actions that involve physical or emotional arousal, avoiding social interaction). For example, sexually abused individuals often avoid looking at or touching their bodies. One parent could not set limits on her children because their crying evoked terrible anxiety in her and caused an EP to start crying in her head.

Active mental actions to avoid conditioned fear stimuli include thought suppression, diversion of attention, and engagement in incompatible mental activities. A patient with depersonalization disorder engaged in involuntary subvocal singing and switched off almost all emotions and body sensations when reactivation of a traumatized state was imminent. A patient with complex PTSD "switched" from ANP to EP when exposed to traumatic memories in therapy. After he learned to prevent this involuntary transition, he could only perceive the trauma from a third-person perspective. Most patients experience this dissociation as involuntary and automatic. However, data suggest that mental avoidance of trauma and the EP may involve a *preconscious* mental effort (Van Honk, Nijenhuis, & Van der Hart, 1999). *Passive mental avoidance* prevents encounters with cues of threat via mental withdrawal from the world. For example, a PTSD patient sat for hours on end with an extremely retracted field of consciousness (i.e., a blank mind).

Structural dissociation can be partially maintained by poor social support and lack of restorative experiences following trauma. Social support buffers negative effects in the aftermath of trauma (Joseph, Yule, Williams, & Andrews, 1993; Runtz & Schallow, 1997; Solomon, Mikulincer, & Avitzur, 1988). Lack of support enhances dissociative tendencies (Freyd, 1996) because it deprives the person of the relational sustenance and regulation that are necessary for integration of extremely difficult experiences (Freyd, DePrince, & Zurbriggen, 2001; King, King, Fairbank, Keane, & Adams, 1998; Kluft, 1984a, 1984b; Laub & Auerhahn, 1989; Vanderlinden, Van Dyck, Vandereycken, & Vertommen, 1993). In therapy, structural dissociation can be reinforced by (1) reification of parts, (2) undue attention to differences among dissociative parts (Janet, 1889; Kluft, 1993), and (3) premature focus on traumatic memories.

16.3 LEVELS OF STRUCTURAL DISSOCIATION AND DIAGNOSTIC IMPLICATIONS

Symptoms of traumatization can be categorized in many ways; there is no inherently preferable system of classification. The value of a given taxonomy of mental disorders lies in its practical utility—how well it describes a patient's core difficulties, how well it serves research interests, and how well it informs treatment. Some experts in the trauma field have criticized the classification of trauma-related disorders in DSM-IV and ICD-10; they have proposed a spectrum of trauma-related symptoms (e.g., Allen, 2001; Van der Kolk et al., 1996) and trauma-related disorders (Bremner, 1999b; Bremner, Vermetten, Southwick, Krystal, & Charney, 1998; Moreau & Zisook, 2002). It has been noted that the "one central element that all these [posttraumatic] conditions have in common is the high prevalence of dissociation" (McFarlane & Van der Kolk, 1996, p. 570).

Although DSM-IV separates the dissociative disorders from the classic trauma-related disorders (ASD, PTSD, Complex PTSD), many authors have noted that DID is the most complex form of PTSD (e.g., Dell, 1998; Loewenstein, 1991; Spiegel, 1984, 1986, 1993), and that PTSD should be considered to be a dissociative disorder (e.g., Chu, 1998; Chu, Frey, Ganzel, & Matthews, 1998; Spiegel & Cardeña, 1991; Van der Hart et al., 1998). *We suggest that complexity of structural dissociation provides an important organizing principle for classifying posttraumatic disorders.* In fact, much research already supports the idea that the severity and extent of dissociative symptoms increases with the complexity of trauma-related disorders (e.g., Bremner et al., 1992; Bremner, Steinberg, Southwick, Johnson, & Charney, 1993; El-Hage, Darves-Bornoz, Allilaire, & Gaillard, 2002; Van IJzendoorn & Schuengel, 1996). Whether levels of structural dissociation are directly related to various diagnoses remains to be seen. In the meantime, our clinical experience suggests that it is a strong possibility.

16.3.1 Primary Structural Dissociation

Structural dissociation of the personality into *two* psychobiological systems has been termed *primary* structural dissociation (Nijenhuis & Van der Hart, 1999; Nijenhuis et al., 2004; Van der Hart et al., 1998; Van der Hart et al., 2006). In primary structural dissociation, there is a single EP (associated with reexperiencing the trauma) and a single ANP (that has failed to integrate the traumatic experience, and that handles daily life).

ASD may involve and simple PTSD always involves primary structural dissociation. ASD is strongly related to peritraumatic dissociation; its diagnosis requires the presence of dissociative symptoms. Simple cases of ASD probably include a rudimentary EP and an ANP that encompasses the individual's personality prior to the trauma. In the weeks following a trauma that produced ASD, some people resolve the disorder by spontaneously integrating their EP and ANP. On the other hand, a significant number of ASD cases do not resolve; these traumatized persons develop PTSD, which is the quintessential disorder of trauma. PTSD is characterized by an ANP and an EP that produce the classic alternation between numbing/detachment/avoidance, and intrusion. Cases of pure dissociative amnesia or fugue may also involve a single ANP and a single EP.

16.3.2 Secondary Structural Dissociation

When the severity and/or duration of traumatization is great, or when the individual has a fairly limited integrative capacity to begin with, further division of the EP may occur, with a single ANP remaining intact. We have called this secondary structural dissociation. It is usually based on a lack of integration of different animal-defense-like subsystems. Thus, one EP may be mediated by flight (as in dissociative fugue), another EP in freeze, and still others in fight or in total submission. The division among two or more EPs can also involve a lack of integration of psychological or physical components of traumatic experiences. For example, one EP may be associated with sexual arousal during rape, another with an extremely physically painful phase of the experience, and still another with the moment of near death.

Each EP experiences different aspects of a traumatizing event, or of that which occurred in different places or with different perpetrators (abuse at home by father versus abuse at a neighbor's). Each EP may be mediated by particular defensive subsystems (e.g., flight, fight, freeze, total submission); each EP may also be bound to a particularly unbearable aspect of the trauma.

We hypothesize that an ANP and two or more EPs are found in three diagnostic groups: (1) DID-like cases of DDNOS, (2) Complex PTSD, also known as Disorders of Extreme Stress Not Otherwise Specified (DESNOS) (Van der Hart et al., 2005, 2006), and (3) many, but not all, cases of BPD (Blizard, 2003; Howell, 2006; Ross, 2006; Van der Hart et al., 2006). The clinical presentation of dissociative parts in secondary structural dissociation tends to be more subtle than that of DID. We suggest that this subtlety reflects a lesser degree of elaboration and autonomy of parts in secondary structural dissociation. When parts present less subtly than they do in DID, clinicians are less likely to identify the person's symptoms as being dissociative.

Despite being rejected for inclusion in DSM-IV, DESNOS or Complex PTSD (Herman, 1992b, 1993; Pelcovitz et al., 1997; Roth et al., 1997) has gained respect as a clinical entity. Most individuals with Complex PTSD experienced chronic interpersonal traumatization as children (Bremner et al., 1993; Breslau et al., 1999; Donovan et al., 1996; Ford, 1999; Roth et al., 1997; Zlotnick et al., 1996a). Thus, Complex PTSD is associated with more severe and more prolonged traumatization than is simple PTSD. Finally, consistent with the theory of structural dissociation, patients with Complex PTSD have severe dissociative symptoms (Dickinson, DeGruy, Dickinson, & Candib, 1998; Pelcovitz et al., 1997; Zlotnick et al., 1996b).

Research has found that BPD is strongly associated with early trauma and neglect (e.g., Yen et al., 2002); BPD also has a strong association with ongoing dissociation (e.g., Anderson, Yasenik, & Ross, 1993; Chu & Dill, 1991; Gershuny & Thayer, 1999; Stiglmayr, 2001; Zanarini, Ruser, Frankenburg, & Hennen, 2000). Some have suggested that many cases of BPD could be better conceptualized as Complex PTSD (Driessen et al. 2002; Herman, 1992b; McLean & Gallop, 2003).

16.3.3 Tertiary Structural Dissociation

Tertiary structural dissociation—more than one ANP and more than one EP—seems to best characterize DID. DID has long been associated with severe childhood trauma (e.g., Boon & Draijer, 1993; Chu, Frey, Ganzel, & Matthews, 1999; Coons, 1994; Draijer & Boon, 1993; Kluft, 1984a; Nijenhuis, 1999; Nijenhuis, Spinhoven, Van Dyck, Van der Hart, & Vanderlinden, 1998; Ogawa et al., 1997; Putnam, Guroff, Silberman, Barban, & Post, 1986).

In tertiary structural dissociation, the EP is fragmented as a result of trauma and the ANP is fragmented along the lines of daily life actions systems (e.g., the worker, the mother, the student). ANPs divide when aspects of daily life are inescapably associated with trauma. In other words, these aspects of daily life become conditioned stimuli that reactivate traumatic memories. ANPs may also divide if their functioning becomes too low to cope with daily life.

In patients with secondary and tertiary dissociation, especially those with lower functioning, we have observed dissociative parts that show characteristics of *both* ANPs and EPs. Thus, ANPs and EPs are prototypes that have innumerable variations. For example, a part attempts to function at work (ANP daily life action system), but is highly aggressive (fight defense action system). We postulate that this "mixture" of ANP and EP is most likely to occur in persons with secondary or tertiary structural dissociation who experienced chronic abuse in daily life. Such abuse activates both daily life action systems and defense action systems in close approximation so that they are more likely to be present in a single part of the personality, albeit in dysfunctional ways.

16.4 THE DOMAIN OF DISSOCIATION

There is confusion in the literature about which symptoms are dissociative (cf. Brunet et al., 2001; Cardeña, 1994; Marshall, Spitzer, & Leibowitz, 1999; Van der Hart & Dorahy, 2009). Alterations in consciousness (i.e., absorption, daydreaming, imaginative involvement, etc.) should be distinguished from trauma-related structural dissociation (Steele, Dorahy, Van der Hart, & Nijenhuis, this volume, Ch. 10). Even though these two categories of symptoms generally occur together (Janet, 1907), they have different underlying processes.

The quantity of stimuli held in conscious awareness at a given time is referred to as the *field of consciousness*; this field can range from very wide to extremely narrow or retracted. Thus, an individual can be aware of a lot in a given moment, or very little. Alterations in consciousness affect the quantity and quality of experiences that are memorized.

The quality of information processing is largely dependent on the level of consciousness. Lowered levels of consciousness impair the perception and memorization of important information, regardless of how wide or narrow the field of consciousness. Lowering of consciousness takes many forms: concentration problems due to fatigue, anxiety, or illness; symptoms of depersonalization, such as feeling unreal, spacey, foggy, detached or strange; derealization; sleepiness unrelated to fatigue; complete unresponsiveness; and time distortion (Allen, Consolo, & Lewis, 1999; Van der Hart & Steele, 1997). Again, none of these experiences require structural dissociation (though they often accompany it).

Alterations in consciousness have been described as "normal dissociation," "nonpathological dissociation," "mild dissociation," and "minor dissociation" (Bernstein & Putnam, 1986; Carlson, 1994; Prince, 1927; Putnam, 1991; see Dalenberg & Paulson, 2009; Steele et al., 2009). Similarly, "spacing out" and absorption are described as dissociative, even though they are nearly universal, perfectly normal when transient and mild, and need not involve structural dissociation. It should also be noted that absorption, daydreaming, and the like can be thoroughly involuntary and quite pathological (rather than normal, mild, or minor). The continuum view of dissociation (i.e., that dissociative experiences lie upon a continuum that stretches from normal to pathological) has been challenged (e.g., Waller, Putnam, & Carlson, 1996). This continuum view of dissociation must be distinguished from the dimensional view of structural dissociation that we propose. Primary, secondary, and tertiary structural dissociation are prototypes on this dimension.

We have proposed a distinction between structural dissociation and alterations in consciousness because these two categories of phenomena appear to have different underlying mechanisms (Steele et al., this volume; Van der Hart et al., 2004, Van der Hart et al., 2005, 2006). In structural dissociation, different parts of the personality *do not completely share* the same episodic and semantic memories. Alterations in consciousness may involve a *failure to create* episodic and semantic memories in any part of the personality (Allen et al., 1999; Brown, 2006; Butler et al., 1996; Holmes et al., 2005; Janet, 1907; Myers, 1940; Steele et al., 2009; Van der Hart et al., 2000; Van der Hart et al., 2006). Thus, *many individuals who experience alterations in consciousness do not have structural dissociation, but all individuals who have developed structural dissociation also have alterations in consciousness.* Both ANPs and EPs exhibit alterations in consciousness that can range from mild to extremely pathological at different moments.

16.5 SYMPTOMS OF STRUCTURAL DISSOCIATION

Structural dissociation of the personality generates a spectrum of mental and physical symptoms whose diversity is more apparent than real. Dissociative symptoms may be understood as positive (i.e., intrusions) or negative (i.e., losses); they also may be understood as mental (i.e., psychoform dissociative symptoms) or somatic (i.e., somatoform dissociative symptoms; Nijenhuis, 1999/2004; Nijenhuis et al., 1996; Van der Hart et al., 2000). Psychoform and somatoform dissociation are highly correlated phenomena (Dell, 2002; El-Hage et al., 2002; Nijenhuis & Van Duyl, 2001; Nijenhuis et al., 1996; Şar et al., 2000; Waller et al., 2000).

Theory clearly discerns dissociative symptoms from nondissociative ones, but it is often quite difficult to do so in practice. There are numerous symptoms, which are not considered to be dissociative, that we claim are often dissociative. For example, trauma-related symptoms of general psychopathology (e.g., suicidality, substance use, self-harm, and promiscuity) may be dissociative whenever they are manifestations of a particular dissociative part of the personality (Van der Hart et al., 2006). This is in keeping with our definition of dissociative symptoms: *a symptom can be said to be dissociative only if (1) there is clear evidence of dissociative parts of the personality, and (2) the symptom is found in one or some parts of the personality, but not in others.* This definition implies that responses to self-report questionnaires should not be used as the sole indication of structural dissociation. Structural dissociation cannot adequately be diagnosed in the absence of careful clinical questioning and observation. This same diagnostic process is needed to determine whether apparently dissociative symptoms are due to (1) structural dissociation or (2) nondissociative alterations in consciousness.

16.5.1 Negative Psychoform Dissociative Symptoms

Negative psychoform dissociative symptoms include loss of memory (i.e., amnesia); loss of affect (i.e., numbing); loss of critical function (i.e., impaired thinking); loss of needs, wishes, and fantasies; and loss of previously existing skills (Van der Hart et al., 2006). Negative symptoms are characteristic of ANPs, but some occur in

EPs (e.g., the emotional anesthesia that accompanies the defensive reaction of total submission or collapse).

16.5.2 Negative Somatoform Dissociative Symptoms

Early clinical sources (e.g., Charcot, 1887; Janet, 1889; McDougall, 1926; Myers, 1940; Nemiah, 1991; Van der Hart et al., 2000) and modern empirical studies (El-Hage et al., 2002; Nijenhuis et al., 1996, 1999; Nijenhuis & Van Duyl, 2001; Şar et al., 2001; Waller et al., 2001) both indicate that structural dissociation generates somatic symptoms such as loss of motor functions, loss of motor skills, and loss of sensations that should be present or available (i.e., anesthesia, analgesia, and loss of vision, smell, taste, or hearing). Negative somatoform symptoms mostly occur in ANPs, but freezing and total submission occur in some EPs.

16.5.3 Positive Psychoform Dissociative Symptoms

Positive psychoform dissociative symptoms are intrusive symptoms. They occur in all posttraumatic disorders. They reflect the intrusions of EPs into ANPs, and full alternations among ANPs and EPs (i.e., switching). Mental intrusions of one dissociative part into another part are often interpreted as Schneiderian first-rank symptoms (FRS) of schizophrenia (Boon & Draijer, 1993; Ellason & Ross, 1995; Kluft, 1987b; Lœwenstein, 1991; Ross & Joshi, 1992). The voices arguing, voices commenting, thought insertion, thought withdrawal, and so on that occur in dissociative patients should be distinguished from the FRS that occur in psychotic patients.

16.5.4 Positive Somatoform Dissociative Symptoms

Positive somatoform dissociative symptoms are the behaviors and physical experiences of *specific* dissociative parts of the personality; they occur in some parts, but not in others (Janet, 1907; Butler et al., 1996; Van der Hart et al., 2000). These symptoms include pain without organic cause; nonvolitional behavior; repetitive, uncontrollable movements such as tics, tremors, and palsy; and sensory perceptions (i.e., vision, physical sensation, hearing, taste, and smell) that may or may not be distorted. Some positive somatoform symptoms have been described as an FRS: influences playing on the body.

16.6 RESEARCH IN SUPPORT OF STRUCTURAL DISSOCIATION

The theory of structural dissociation of the personality predicts psychobiological differences between the dissociative parts of the personality (i.e., ANP and EP). Preliminary research supports this prediction (Hermans et al., 2006; Reinders et al., 2003; Reinders et al., 2006). The psychophysiological reactions of ANPs and EPs in DID patients were assessed using audiotaped descriptions of traumatic memories that only EPs experienced as personal, and of shared neutral autobiographical memories (Reinders et al., 2003). EPs were "responders" to trauma memory scripts; EPs demonstrated significant changes in heart rate and heart rate variability, systolic blood pressure, and had a wide range of sensorimotor and affective reactions. ANPs were basically "nonresponders." Neither ANPs nor EPs displayed significant psychophysiological differences in response to scripts of shared neutral autobiographical memories.

In the same experiment, patterns of neural activity were studied using PET (Reinders et al., 2003). There were no differences in regional cerebral blood flow (rCBF) for ANPs and EPs when patients listened to the shared neutral autobiographical memories. On the other hand, ANPs and EPs showed large differences in rCBF when they listened to trauma memory scripts that were regarded as personal memories by EPs, but not by ANPs. These findings (Nijenhuis & Den Boer, 2007) demonstrate that ANP and EP engage different neural networks when exposed to reminders of traumatizing events.

Much empirical work remains to be done. Future studies need to establish whether the different types of dissociative parts of the personality have the same underlying process and structure in all posttraumatic disorders. The distinction between ANP and EP will continue to serve a heuristic function in the study of trauma-related mental disorders.

16.7 CONCLUSION

The problems associated with an overly broad view of dissociation, and the need for conceptual housecleaning in regards to dissociation were emphasized in Chapter 1 (Van der Hart & Dorahy, 2009). The theory of structural dissociation of the personality is an attempt to define dissociation more rigorously. The theory offers a unifying perspective on the symptoms and processes that occur in trauma-related disorders. Our overview of dissociative symptoms is precise; it includes some dissociative symptoms (e.g., positive and somatoform dissociative symptoms) that other recent views of dissociation have omitted. We distinguish alterations in consciousness from structural dissociation, but recognize that traumatized individuals display both. This suggests that they are probably closely related phenomena, albeit with different underlying processes. We have highlighted the pattern of avoidance and fixation in trauma that we consider to be a *sine qua non* of trauma-related disorders. Because this pattern has often been set aside by nosologists, the fundamental commonality among the trauma-related disorders has been obscured or lost. The dichotomy of ANP and EP may appear to be unduly reductionistic, but we wish to emphasize five points: (1) ANPs and EPs are prototypes of the phenomena of structural dissociation; (2) disssociative structures take somewhat different forms across different levels of dissociative complexity; (3) we distinguish many different, occasionally overlapping, functions of ANPs and EPs; (4) we recognize that more complex dissociative structures may have parts that manifest a mixture of the characteristics of ANPs and EPs; and (5) the sum of these dissociated structures do not comprise the personality entire: it is a superordinate system within which these parts function with limited integration and coordination. Finally, the theory of the structural dissociation of the personality is more complex than could be detailed in this chapter. A more complete account is offered elsewhere (Van der Hart et al., 2006).

Much research from other perspectives is consistent with our theory. It is not easy, however, to extrapolate the findings of that research to structural dissociation because most of that research has not taken into account the theory of structural dissociation. We anticipate that our theory may offer a plausible explanation for previously confounding findings, such as the presence of physiological responders and nonresponders within PTSD groups (Nijenhuis & Den Boer, Ch. 21, this volume).

Treatment applications of the theory of structural dissociation are vast and practical (cf. Steele et al., 2001, 2004, 2005; Van der Hart et al., 2006). The theory provides both an integrative understanding of the maladaptive mental and behavioral actions of traumatized individuals and a blueprint for more adaptive ones. For example, the theory guides treatment by specifying which parts of the personality should first be strengthened (ANP) and which should first be contained (EP). The theory provides interventions and a specific rationale for gradually raising the integrative level of the patient. Integration is defined in detail.

We have attempted to integrate 150 years of clinical observation, research, and theory on posttraumatic and dissociative symptoms. We believe that we have developed a basic theory that is useful to clinicians and researchers alike.

REFERENCES

Allen, J. G. (2001). *Traumatic relationships and serious mental disorders.* Chichester/New York: John Wiley & Sons.

Allen, J. G., Console, D. A., & Lewis, L. (1999). Dissociative detachment and memory impairment: Reversible amnesia or encoding failure? *Comprehensive Psychiatry, 40,* 160–171.

American Psychiatric Association. (1994). DSM-IV – *Diagnostic and statistical manual of mental disorders* (4th ed.). Washington, DC: Author.

Anderson, G., Yasenik, L., & Ross, C. A. (1993). Dissociative experiences and disorders among women who identify themselves as sexual abuse survivors. *Child Abuse & Neglect, 17,* 677–686.

Arnold, M. B. (1960). *Emotion and personality* (Two parts). New York: Columbia University Press.

Baeyens, F., Hermans, D., & Eelen, P. (1993). The role of CS-UCS contingency in human evaluative conditioning. *Behavior Research and Therapy, 31,* 731–737.

Benes, F. M. (1998). Human brain growth spans decades. *American Journal of Psychiatry, 155,* 1489.

Bernstein, E. M., & Putnam, F. (1986). Development, reliability, and validity of a dissociation scale. *Journal of Nervous and Mental Disease, 174,* 727–735.

Blizard, R. (2003). Disorganized attachment: Development of dissociated self states and a relational approach to treatment. *Journal of Trauma & Dissociation, 4*(3), 27–50.

Boon, S., & Draijer, N. (1993). *Multiple personality disorder in the Netherlands.* Lisse: Swets & Zeitlinger.

Bowlby, J. (1969/1982). *Attachment* (2nd ed., Vol. I). New York: Basic Books.

Braude, S. E. (1995). *First person plural: Multiple personality and the philosophy of mind* (Rev. ed.). London: Routledge.

Braun, B. G., & Sachs, R. G. (1985). The development of multiple personality disorder: Predisposing, precipitating, and perpetuating factors. In R. P. Kluft (Ed.), *Childhood antecedents of multiple personality* (pp. 37–64). Washington, DC: American Psychiatric Press.

Bremner, J. D. (1999a). Does stress damage the brain? *Biological Psychiatry, 45,* 797–805.

Bremner, J. D. (1999b). Acute and chronic responses to psychological trauma: Where do we go from here? *American Journal of Psychiatry, 156,* 349–351.

Bremner, J. D. (2003). Long-term effects of childhood abuse on brain and neurobiology. *Child & Adolescent Psychiatric Clinics of North America, 12,* 271–292.

Bremner, J. D., Randall, P., Scott, T. M., Bronen, R. A., Seibyl, J. P., Southwick, S. M., *et al.* (1995). MRI-based measures of hippocampal volume in patients with PTSD. *American Journal of Psychiatry, 152,* 973–981.

Bremner, J., Southwick, S., Brett, E., Fontana, A., Rosenheck, R., & Charney, D. (1992). Dissociation and posttraumatic stress disorder in Vietnam combat veterans. *American Journal of Psychiatry, 149*, 328–363.

Bremner, J. D., Southwick, S. M., Johnson, D. R., Yehuda, R., & Charney, D. S. (1993). Childhood physical abuse and combat-related posttraumatic stress disorder in Vietnam veterans. *American Journal of Psychiatry, 150*, 235–239.

Bremner, J. D., Vermetten, E., Southwick, S. M., Krystal, J. H., & Charney, D. S. (1998). Trauma, memory, and dissociation: An integrative formulation. In J. D. Bremner & C. R Marmar (Eds.), *Trauma, memory, and dissociation* (pp. 365–402). Washington, DC: American Psychiatric Press.

Breslau, N., Chilcoat, H. D., Kessler, R. C., & Davis, G. C. (1999). Previous exposure to trauma and PTSD effects of subsequent trauma: Results from the Detroit Area Survey of Trauma. *American Journal of Psychiatry, 156*, 902–1491.

Breuer, J., & Freud, S. (1893–1895/1955). *Studies on hysteria.* London: Hogarth Press.

Brewin, C. R. (2001). A cognitive neuroscience account of posttraumatic stress disorder and its treatment. *Behaviour Research and Therapy, 39*, 373–393.

Brewin, C. R. (2003). *Posttraumatic stress disorder: Malady or myth?* New Haven: Yale University Press.

Brewin, C. R., Dalgleish, T., & Joseph, S. (1996). A dual representation theory of posttraumatic stress disorder. *Psychology Review, 103*, 670–686.

Briere, J. N. (1992). *Child abuse trauma: Theory and treatment of the lasting effects.* Newbury Park, CA: Sage Publications.

Briere, J. N. (2002). *Multiscale Dissociation Inventory*. Odessa, FL: Psychological Assessment Resources.

Brown, R. J. (2006). Different types of "dissociation" have different psychological mechanisms. *Journal of Trauma and Dissociation, 7*(4), 7–28.

Brown, W. (1919) War neuroses: A comparison of early cases seen in the field with those seen at the base. *Lancet, ii*, 833–836.

Brunet, A., Weiss, D. S., Metzler, T. J., Best, S. R., Neylan, T. C., Rogers, C., Fagan, J., & Marmar, C. R. (2001). The peritraumatic distress inventory: A proposed measure of PTSD criterion A. *American Journal of Psychiatry, 158*, 1480–1485.

Bryant, R. A., & Harvey, A. G. (2002). Delayed-onset posttraumatic stress disorder: a prospective evaluation. *Australian & New Zealand Journal of Psychiatry, 36*, 205–209.

Buckley, T. C., Blanchard, E. B., & Hickling, E. J. (1996). A prospective examination of delayed onset PTSD secondary to motor vehicle accidents. *Journal of Abnormal Psycholology, 105*, 617–625.

Butler, L., Duran, R., Jasiukaitis, P., Koopman, C., & Spiegel, D. (1996). Hypnotizability and traumatic experience: A diathesis-stress model of dissociative symptomatology. *American Journal of Psychiatry, 153*(Festschrift), 42–63.

Cardeña, E. (1994). The domain of dissociation. In S. J. Lynn & J. W. Rhue (Eds.), *Dissociation: Clinical and theoretical perspectives* (pp. 15–31). New York: Guilford.

Carlson, E. A. (1998). A prospective longitudinal study of disorganized/disoriented attachment. *Child Development, 69*, 1107–1128.

Carlson, E. B. (1994). Studying the interaction between physical and psychological states with the Dissociative Experiences Scale. In D. Spiegel (Ed.), *Dissociation: Culture, mind, and body* (pp. 41–58). Washington, DC: American Psychiatric Press.

Carrion, V. G., Weems, C. F., & Reiss, A. L. (2007). Stress predicts brain changes in children: A pilot longitudinal study on youth stress, posttraumatic stress disorder, and the hippocampus. *Pediatrics, 119*, 509–516.

Cassidy, J. (1999). The nature of the child's ties. In J. Cassidy & P. R. Shaver (Eds.), *Handbook of attachment: Theory, research, and clinical applications* (pp. 3–20). New York: Guilford.

Cassidy, J., & Shaver, P. R. (Eds.) (1999). *Handbook of attachment: Theory, research and clinical applications.* New York: Guilford.

Charcot, J. M. (1887). *Clinical lectures on diseases of the nervous system.* London: New Sydenham Society.

Chu, J. A. (1998). *Rebuilding shattered lives: The responsible treatment of complex posttraumatic and dissociative disorders.* New York: Wiley.

Chu, J. A., & Dill, D. L. (1991). Dissociation, borderline personality disorder, and childhood trauma. *American Journal of Psychiatry, 148*, 812–813.

Chu, J. A., Frey, L. M., Ganzel, B. L., & Matthews, J. A. (1999). Memories of childhood abuse: Dissociation, amnesia and corroboration. *American Journal of Psychiatry, 156*, 749–755.

Ciompi, L. (1991). Affects as central organizing and integrating factors: A new psychosocial/biological model of the psyche. *British Journal of Psychiatry, 159*, 97–105.

Coons, P. M. (1994). Confirmation of childhood abuse in child and adolescent cases of multiple personality disorder and dissociation not otherwise specified. *Journal of Nervous and Mental Disease, 182*, 461–464.

Coupland, N. J. (2000). Brain mechanisms and neurotransmitters. In D. Nutt, J. R. T. Davidson, & J. Zohar (Eds.), *Posttraumatic stress disorder: Diagnosis, management, and treatment* (pp. 69–100). London: Dunitz.

Crabtree, A. (1993). *From Mesmer to Freud: Magnetic sleep and the roots of psychological healing.* New Haven: Yale University Press.

Dalenberg, C., & Paulson, K. (2009). The case for the study of "normal" dissociation processes. In P. F. Dell & J. A. O'Neil (Eds.), *Dissociation and the dissociative disorders: DSM-V and beyond* (pp. 145–154). New York: Routledge.

Damasio, A. R. (1999). *The feeling of what happens: Body and emotion in the making of consciousness.* New York: Harcourt, Brace.

Dell, P. F. (1998). Axis II pathology in outpatients with dissociative identity disorder. *Journal of Nervous and Mental Disease, 186*, 352–356.

Dell, P. F. (2002). Dissociative phenomenology of dissociative identity disorder. *Journal of Nervous and Mental Disease, 190*, 10–15.

Dell, P. F. (2004). The Multidimensional Inventory of Dissociation (MID): A comprehensive measure of the subjective/phenomenological domain of dissociation. Unpublished manuscript.

Dickinson, L. M., deGruy, F. V., 3rd, Dickinson, W. P., & Candib, L. M. (1998). Complex posttraumatic stress disorder: evidence from the primary care setting. *General Hospital Psychiatry, 20*, 214–224.

Donovan, B. S., Padin-Rivera, E., Dowd, T., & Blake, D. D. (1996). Childhood factors and war zone stress in chronic PTSD. *Journal of Traumatic Stress, 9*, 361–368.

Draijer, N., & Boon, S. (1993). Trauma, dissocation, and dissociative disorders. In S. Boon & N. Draijer (Eds.), *Multiple personality disorder in the Netherlands: A study on reliability and validity of the diagnosis* (pp. 177–193). Amsterdam/Lisse: Swets & Zeitlinger.

Draijer, N., & Langeland, W. (1999). Childhood trauma and perceived parental dysfunction in the etiology of dissociative symptoms in psychiatric inpatients. *American Journal of Psychiatry, 156*, 379–385.

Driessen, M., Beblo, T., Reddemann, L., Rau, H., Lange, W., Silva, A., Berea, R. C., Wulff, H., & Radzka, S. (2002). Ist die Borderline-Persönlichkeitsstörung eine komplexe posttraumatische Störung? *Nervenartz, 73*, 820–829.

Ehling, T., Nijenhuis, E. R. S., & Krikke, A. (2003). Volume of discrete brain structures in florid and recovered DID, DDNOS, and healthy controls. *Proceedings of the 20th International Fall Conference of the International Society for the Study of Dissociation*. Chicago, November 2–4.

El-Hage, W., Darves-Bornoz, J.-M., Allilaire, J.-F., & Gaillard, P. (2002). Posttraumatic somatoform dissociation in French psychiatric outpatients. *Journal of Trauma and Dissociation, 3*(3), 59–73.

Ellason, J. W., & Ross, C. A. (1995). Positive and negative symptoms in dissociative identity disorder and schizophrenia: A comparative analysis. *Journal of Nervous and Mental Disease, 183*, 236–241.

Fanselow, M. S., & Lester, L. S. (1988). A functional behavioristic approach to aversively motivated behavior: Predatory imminence as a determinant of the topography of defensive behavior. In R. C. Bolles & M. D. Beecher (Eds.), *Evolution and learning* (pp. 185–212). Hillsdale, NJ: Erlbaum.

Field, T. M. (1985). Attachment as psychobiological attunement: Being on the same wavelength. In M. Reite & T. M. Fields (Eds.), *The psychobiology of attachment and separation* (pp. 415–454). Orlando, FL: Academic Press.

Figley, C. R. (1978). *Stress disorders among Vietnam veterans*. New York: Brunner/Mazel.

Fonagy, P., Gergely, G., Jurist, E. L., & Target, M. (2002). *Affect regulation, mentalization, and the development of the self*. New York: Other Press.

Ford, J. (1999). Disorder of extreme stress following war-zone military trauma: Associated features of posttraumatic stress disorder or comorbid but distinct syndromes? *Journal of Consulting and Clinical Psychology, 67*, 3–12.

Fraser, S. (1987). *My father's house: A memoir of incest and of healing*. Toronto: Doubleday Canada.

Frewen, P. A., & Lanius, R. A. (2006). Neurobiology of dissociation: Unity and disunity in mind-body-brain. *Psychiatric Clinics of North America, 29*, 113–128.

Freyd, J. J. (1996). *Betrayal trauma: The logic of forgetting childhood trauma*. Cambridge, MA: Harvard University Press.

Frijda, N. (1986). *The emotions*. Cambridge, UK: Cambridge University Press.

Gershuny, B. S., & Thayer, J. F. (1999). Relations among psychological trauma, dissociative phenomena, and trauma-related distress: A review and integration. *Clinical Psychology Review, 19*, 631–657.

Glaser, D. (2000). Child abuse and neglect and the brain: A review. *Journal of Child Psychology and Psychiatry, 41*, 97–116.

Golynkina, K., & Ryle, A. (1999). The identification and characteristics of the partially dissociated states of patients with borderline personality disorder. *British Journal of Medical Psychology, 72*(Pt 4), 429–445.

Gould, J. L. (1982). *Ethology: The mechanisms and evolution of behavior*. New York: Norton.

Herman, J. L. (1992a). Complex PTSD: A syndrome in survivors of prolonged and repeated trauma. *Journal of Traumatic Stress, 5*, 377–392.

Herman, J. L. (1992b). *Trauma and recovery*. New York: Basic Books.

Herman, J. L. (1993). Sequelae of prolonged and repeated trauma: evidence for a complex posttraumatic syndrome (DESNOS). In J. R. T. Davidson & E. B. Foa (Eds.), *Posttraumatic stress disorder: DSM-IV and beyond* (pp. 213–228). Washington, DC: American Psychiatric Press.

Hermans, E. J., Nijenhuis, E. R., Van Honk, J., Huntjens, R. J., & Van der Hart, O. (2006). Identity state-dependent attentional bias for facial threat in dissociative identity disorder. *Psychiatry Research, 141*, 233–236.

Holmes, E., Brown, R. J., Mansell, W., Fearon, R. P., Hunter, E., Frasquillho, F., & Oakley, D. A. (2005). Are there two qualitatively distinct forms of dissociation? A review and some clinical implications. *Clinical Psychology Review, 25*, 1–23.

Howell, E. F. (2006). *The dissociative mind*. Mahwah, NJ: Analytic Press.

Jackson, J. H. (1931/32). *Selected writings of John Hughlings Jackson* (Vol. 1 & 2). London: Milford.

Janet, P. (1889). *L'Automatisme psychologique*. Paris: Félix Alcan.

Janet, P. (1901). *The mental state of hysterica: A study of mental stigmata and mental accidents*. New York: G. P. Putnam's Sons.

Janet, P. (1903). *Les obsessions et la psychasthénie* (2 vols.). Paris: F. Alcan.

Janet, P. (1904). L'amnésie et la dissociation des souvenirs par l'émotion. *Journal de Psychologie, 1*, 417–453.

Janet, P. (1907). *The major symptoms of hysteria*. London & New York: Macmillan.

Janet, P. (1909a). *Les névroses*. Paris: E. Flammarion.

Janet, P. (1909b). Problèmes psychologiques de l'émotion. *Revue Neurologique, 17*, 1551–1687.

Janet, P. (1919). *Les médications psychologiques*. Paris: Félix Alcan. English edition: *Psychological healing*. New York: Macmillan, 1925.

Janet, P. (1928). *L'évolution de la mémoire et de la notion du temps*. Paris: A Chahine.

Joseph, S., Yule, W., Williams, R., & Andrews, B. (1993). Crisis support in the aftermath of a disaster: A longitudinal perspective. *British Journal of Clinical Psychology, 32*, 177–185.

Kardiner, A. (1941). *The traumatic neuroses of war*. New York: Paul Hoeber.

King, L. A., King, D. W., Fairbank, J. A., Keane, T. M., & Adams, G. A. (1998). Resilience-recovery factors in post-traumatic stress disorder among female and male Vietnam veterans: Hardiness, postwar social support, and additional stressful life events. *Journal of Personality and Social Psychology, 74*, 420–434.

Kluft, R. P. (1984a). An introduction to multiple personality disorder. *Psychiatric Annals, 14*, 19–24.

Kluft, R. P. (1984b). Multiple personality in childhood. *Psychiatric Clinics of North America, 7*, 121–134.

Kluft, R. P. (1987a). The simulation and dissimulation of multiple personality disorder. *American Journal of Clinical Hypnosis, 30*, 104–118.

Kluft, R. P. (1987b). First-rank symptoms as a diagnostic clue to multiple personality disorder. *American Journal of Psychiatry, 144*, 293–298.

Kluft, R. P. (1993). The initial stages of psychotherapy in the treatment of multiple personality disorder patients. *Dissociation, 6*, 145–161.

Kluft, R. P., & Fine, C. G. (Eds.) (1993). *Clinical perspectives on multiple personality disorder*. Washington, DC: American Psychiatric Press.

Krystal, J. H., Bannett, A., Bremner, J. D., Southwick, S. M., & Charney, D. S. (1996). Recent developments in the neurobiology of dissociation: Implications for posttraumatic stress disorder. In L. Michelson & W. J. Ray (Eds.), *Handbook of dissociation: Theoretical, empirical, and clinical perspectives* (pp. 163–190). New York: Plenum Press.

Krystal, J. H., Bremner, J. D., Southwick, S. M., & Charney, D. S. (1998). The emerging neurobiology of dissociation: Implications for the treatment of posttraumatic stress disorder. In J. D. Bremner & C. R. Marmar (Eds.), *Trauma, memory, and dissociation* (pp. 321–363). Washington, DC: American Psychiatric Press.

Laub, D., & Auerhahn, N. C. (1989). Failed empathy: A central theme in the survivor's Holocaust experiences. *Psychoanalytic Psychology, 6*(4), 377–400.

Laufer, R. S. (1988). The serial self: War trauma, identity and adult development. In J. P. Wilson, Z. Harel, & B. Kahana (Eds.), *Human adaptation to extreme stress: From the Holocaust to Vietnam* (pp. 33–53). New York: Plenum.

LeDoux, J. E. (1996). *The emotional brain: The mysterious underpinning of emotional life*. New York: Simon & Schuster.

Liotti, G. (1992). Disorganized/disoriented attachment in the etiology of dissociative disorders. *Dissociation, 5*, 196–204.

Liotti, G. (1995). Disorganized/disoriented attachment in the psychotherapy of the dissociative disorders. In S. Goldberg, R. Muir, & J. Kerr (Eds.), *Attachment theory: Social, developmental and clinical perspectives* (pp. 343–363). Hillsdale, NJ: The Analytic Press.

Liotti, G. (1999a). Disorganization of attachment as a model for understanding dissociative psychopathology. In J. Solomon & C. George (Eds.), *Attachment disorganization* (pp. 297–317). New York: Guilford.

Liotti, G. (1999b). Understanding the dissociative process: The contributions of attachment theory. *Psychoanalytic Inquiry, 19*, 757–783.

Liotti, G. (2006). A model of dissociation based on attachment theory and research. *Journal of Trauma & Dissociation, 7(4)*, 55–74.

Lœwenstein, R. J. (1991). An office mental status examination for complex chronic dissociative symptoms and multiple personality disorder. *Psychiatric Clinics of North America, 14*, 567–604.

Lyons-Ruth, K. (2003). Dissociation and the parent-infant dialogue: A longitudinal perspective from attachment research. *Journal of the American Psychoanalytic Association, 51*, 883–911.

Main, M. (1991). Metacognitive knowledge, metacognitive monitoring, and singular (coherent) versus multiple (incoherent) models of attachment. In C. M. Parkes, J. Stevenson-Hinde, & P. Marris (Eds.), *Attachment across the life cycle* (pp. 127–159). London: Routledge.

Main, M., & Hesse, E. (1990). Parent's unresolved traumatic experiences are related to infant disorganized attachment status: Is frightened and/or frightening parental behavior the linking mechanism? In M. T. Greenberg, D. Cicchetti, & E. M. Cummings (Eds.), *Attachment in the preschool years* (pp. 161–182). Chicago, IL: University of Chicago Press.

Main, M., & Morgan, H. (1996). Disorganization and disorientation in infant Strange Situation behavior: Phenotypic resemblance to dissociative states? In L. Michelson & W. Ray (Eds.), *Handbook of dissociation* (pp. 107–137). New York: Plenum.

Marmar, C. R., Weiss, D. S., & Metzler, T. J. (1998). Peritraumatic dissociation and posttraumatic stress disorder. In J. D. Bremner & C. R. Marmar (Eds.), *Trauma, memory, and dissociation* (pp. 229–252). Washington, DC: American Psychiatric Press.

Marshall, R. D., Spitzer, R., & Liebowitz, M. R. (1999). Review and critique of the new DSM-IV diagnosis of acute stress disorder. *American Journal of Psychiatry, 156*, 1677–1685.

McDougall, W. (1926). *An outline of abnormal psychology*. London: Methuen.

McFarlane, A. (1996). Resilience, vulnerability, and the course of posttraumatic reactions. In B. A. van der Kolk, A. McFarlane, & L. Weisaeth (Eds.), *Traumatic Stress: The effects of overwhelming experiences on mind, body, and society* (pp. 155–181). New York: Guilford.

McLean, L. M., & Gallop, R. (2003). Implications of childhood sexual abuse for adult borderline personality disorder and complex posttraumatic stress disorder. *American Journal of Psychiatry, 160*, 369–371.

Meares, R. (1999). The contribution of Hughlings Jackson to an understanding of dissociation. *American Journal of Psychiatry, 156*, 1850–1855.

Modell, A. (1990). *Other times, other realities: Towards a theory of psychoanalytic treatment*. Cambridge, MA: Harvard University Press.

Moreau, C., & Zisook, S. (2002). Rationale for a posttraumatic stress spectrum disorder. *Psychiatric Clinics of North America, 25*, 775–790.

Myers, C. S. (1916a). Contributions to the study of shell shock. *The Lancet, March 18*, 608–613.

Myers, C. S. (1916b). Contributions to the study of shell shock. *The Lancet, September 9*, 461–467.

Myers, C. S. (1940). *Shell shock in France 1914–1918*. Cambridge: Cambridge University Press.

Nemiah, J. C. (1991). Dissociation, conversion, and somatization. In A. Tasman & S. M. Goldfinger (Eds.), *American Psychiatric Press Review of Psychiatry*, Vol. 10 (pp. 248–260). Washington, DC: American Psychiatric Press.

Nijenhuis, E. R. S. (1999). *Somatoform dissociation: Phenomena, measurement, and theoretical issues*. Assen, The Netherlands: Van Gorcum. Reprint: Norton, New York, 2004.

Nijenhuis, E. R. S., & Den Boer, J. A. (2007). Psychobiology of traumatization and structural dissociation of the personality. In E. Vermetten, M. J. Dorahy, & D. Spiegel (Eds.), *Traumatic dissociation: Neurobiology and treatment* (pp. 219–236). Washington, DC: American Psychiatric Publishing.

Nijenhuis, E. R. S., Spinhoven, P., & Vanderlinden, J. (1998). Animal defensive reactions as a model for dissociative reactions. *Journal of Traumatic Stress, 11*, 243–260.

Nijenhuis, E. R. S., Spinhoven, P., Van Dyck, R., & Van der Hart, O. (1996). The development and psychometric characteristics of the Somatoform Dissociation Questionnaire (SDQ-20). *Journal of Nervous and Mental Disease, 184*, 688–694.

Nijenhuis, E. R. S., Spinhoven, P., Vanderlinden, J., Van Dyck, R., & Van der Hart, O. (1998). Somatoform dissociative symptoms as related to animal defense reactions to predatory imminence and injury. *Journal of Abnormal Psychology, 107*, 63–73.

Nijenhuis, E. R. S., Spinhoven, P., Van Dyck, R., Van der Hart, O., & Vanderlinden, J. (1998). Degree of somatoform and psychological dissociation in dissociative disorders is correlated with reported trauma. *Journal of Traumatic Stress, 11*, 711–730.

Nijenhuis, E. R. S., & Van der Hart, O. (1999). Forgetting and reexperiencing trauma. In J. Goodwin & R. Attias (Eds.), *Splintered reflections: Images of the body in treatment* (pp. 39–65). New York: Basic Books.

Nijenhuis, E. R. S., Van der Hart, O., Kruger, K., & Steele, K. (2004). Somatoform dissociation, reported abuse, and animal defence-like reactions. *Australian and New Zealand Journal of Psychiatry, 38*, 678–686.

Nijenhuis, E. R. S., Van der Hart, O., & Steele, K. (2002). The emerging psychobiology of trauma-related dissociation and dissociative disorders. In H. D'Haenen, J. A. Den Boer, & P. Willner (Eds.), *Biological Psychiatry* (pp. 1079–1098). London: Wiley.

Nijenhuis, E. R. S., Van der Hart, O., & Steele, K. (2004). Strukturelle Dissoziation der Persönlichkeitsstruktur: traumatischer Upsprung, phobische Residuen [Structural dissociation of the personality: Traumatic origins, phobic maintenance]. In A. Hofmann, L. Reddemann, & U. Gast (Eds.), *Psychotherapie der dissoziativen Störungen [Psychotherapy of dissociative disorders]* (pp. 47–69). Stuttgart/New York: Georg Thieme Verlag.

Nijenhuis, E. R. S., & Van Duyl, M. (2001). Dissociative symptoms and reported trauma among Ugandan patients with possessive trance disorder. *Proceedings of the 18th International Fall Conference of the International Society for the Study of Dissociation*. New Orleans, December 2–4.

Ogawa, J. R., Sroufe, L. A., Weinfield, N. S., Carlson, E. A., & Egeland, B. (1997). Development and the fragmented self: Longitudinal study of dissociative symptomatology in a nonclinical sample. *Development and Psychopathology, 9*, 855–879.

Panksepp, J. (1998). *Affective neuroscience: The foundations of human and animal emotions*. New York: Oxford University Press.

Pelcovitz, D., Van der Kolk, B. A., Roth, S., Mandel, F., Kaplan, S., & Resick, P. (1997). Development of a criteria set and a structured interview for the disorders of extreme stress (SIDES). *Journal of Traumatic Stress, 10*, 3–16.

Perry, B. D. (1999). The memory of states: How the brain stores and retrieves traumatic experience. In J. Goodwin & R. Attias (Eds.), *Splintered Reflections: Images of the body in treatment* (pp. 9–38). New York: Basic Books.

Perry, B. D., & Pollard, R. (1998). Homeostasis, stress, trauma, and adaptation. A neurodevelopmental view of childhood trauma. *Child & Adolescent Psychiatric Clinics of North America, 7*, 33–51, viii.

Perry, B. D., Pollard, R. A., Blakely, T. L., Baker, W. L., & Vigilante, D. (1995). Childhood trauma, the neurobiology of adaptation, and "use dependent" development of the brain: How "states" become "traits." *Infant Mental Health Journal, 16*, 271–291.

Prince, M. (1927). Suggestive repersonalization. *Archives of Neurology and Psychiatry, 21*, 159–189.

Putnam, F. W. (1985). Dissociation as a response to extreme trauma. In R. P. Kluft (Ed.), *Childhood antecedents of multiple personality* (pp. 65–97). Washington, DC: American Psychiatric Press.

Putnam, F. W. (1989). *Diagnosis and treatment of multiple personality disorder.* New York: Guilford.

Putnam, F. W. (1991). Recent research on multiple personality disorder. *Psychiatric Clinics of North America, 14*, 489–502.

Putnam, F. W. (1997). *Dissociation in children and adolescents: A developmental perspective.* New York: Guilford.

Putnam, F. W., Guroff, J. J., Silberman, E. K., Barban, L., & Post, R. M. (1986). The clinical phenomenology of multiple personality disorder: Review of 100 recent cases. *Journal of Clinical Psychiatry, 47*, 285–293.

Reinders, A. A., Nijenhuis, E. R., Paans, A. M., Korf, J., Willemsen, A. T., & Den Boer, J. A. (2003). One brain, two selves. *NeuroImage, 20*, 2119–2125.

Reinders, A. A., Nijenhuis, E. R., S., Quak, J., Korf, J., Haaksma, J., Paans, A. M. J., Willemsen, A. T. M., & Den Boer, J. A. (2006). Psychobiological characteristics of Dissociative Identity Disorder: A symptom provocation study. *Biological Psychiatry, 60*, 730–740.

Ross, C. A. (1997). *Dissociative identity disorder: Diagnosis, clinical features and treatment of multiple personality* (2nd ed.). New York: Wiley.

Ross, C. A. (2007). Borderline personality disorder and dissociation. *Journal of Trauma & Dissociation, 8*(1), 71–80.

Ross, C. A., & Joshi, S. (1992). Schneiderian symptoms and childhood trauma in the general population. *Comprehensive Psychiatry, 33*, 269–273.

Ross, C. A., Miller, S. D., Reagor, P., Bjornson, L., Fraser, G. A., & Anderson, G. (1990). Schneiderian symptoms in multiple personality disorder and schizophrenia. *Comprehensive Psychiatry, 31*, 111–118.

Roth, S., Newman, E., Pelcovitz, D., Van der Kolk, B. A., & Mandel, F. S. (1997). Complex PTSD in victims exposed to sexual and physical abuse: Results from the DSM-IV Field Trial for Posttraumatic Stress Disorder. *Journal of Traumatic Stress, 10*, 539–556.

Runtz, M. G., & Schallow, J. R. (1997). Social support and coping strategies as mediators of adult adjustment following childhood maltreatment. *Child Abuse & Neglect, 21*, 211–226.

Şar, V., Kundakçı, T., Kızıltan, E., Bakım, B., & Bozkurt, O. (2000). Differentiating dissociative disorders from other diagnostic groups through somatoform dissociation in Turkey. *Journal of Trauma and Dissociation, 1*(4), 67–80.

Schnurr, P. P., Lunney, C. A., Sengupta, A., & Waelde, L. C. (2003). A descriptive analysis of PTSD chronicity in Vietnam veterans. *Journal of Traumatic Stress, 16*, 545–553.

Schore, A. N. (2002). Dysregulation of the right brain: A fundamental mechanism of traumatic attachment and the psychopathogenesis of posttraumatic stress disorder. *Australian & New Zealand Journal of Psychiatry, 36*, 9–30.

Schore, A. N. (2003). *Affect dysregulation and disorders of the self.* New York: Norton.

Schuengel, C., Bakermans-Kranenburg, M. J., & Van, IJzendoorn. M. H. (1999). Frightening maternal behavior linking unresolved loss and disorganized infant attachment. *Journal of Consulting and Clinical Psychology, 67*, 54–63.

Siegel, D. J. (1999). *The developing mind: Toward a neurobiology of interpersonal experience.* New York: Guilford.

Solomon, Z., Mikulincer, M., & Avitzur, E. (1988). Coping, locus of control, social support, and combat-related posttraumatic stress disorder: A prospective study. *Journal of Personality and Social Psychology, 55*, 279–285.

Spiegel, D. (1984). Multiple personality as a post-traumatic stress disorder. *Psychiatric Clinics of North America, 7*, 101–110.

Spiegel, D. (1986). Dissociating damage. *American Journal of Clinical Hypnosis, 29*, 123–131.

Spiegel, D. (1990). Hypnosis, dissociation, and trauma: Hidden and overt observers. In J. Singer (Ed.), *Repression and dissociation: Implications for personality theory, psychopathology, and health* (pp. 121–142). Chicago: The University of Chicago Press.

Spiegel, D. (1993). Multiple posttraumatic personality disorder. In R. P. Kluft & C. G. Fine (Eds.), *Clinical perspectives on multiple personality disorder* (pp. 87–99). Washington, DC: American Psychiatric Press.

Spiegel, D., & Cardeña, E. (1991). Disintegrated experience: The dissociative disorders revisited. *Journal of Abnormal Psychology, 100*, 366–378.

Spiegel, D., Frischholz, E. J., & Spira, J. (1993). Functional disorders of memory. In A. Tasman & S. M. Goldfinger (Eds.), *American Psychiatric Press Review of Psychiatry*, Vol. 12 (pp. 747–782). Washington, DC: American Psychiatric Press.

Steele, K., Dorahy, M. J., Van der Hart, O., & Nijenhuis, E. R. S. (2009). Dissociation versus alterations in consciousness: Related but different concepts. In P. F. Dell & J. A. O'Neil (Eds.), *Dissociation and the dissociative disorders: DSM-V and beyond* (pp. 155–169). New York: Routledge.

Steele, K., Van der Hart, O., & Nijenhuis, E. R. S. (2001). Dependency in the treatment of complex posttraumatic stress disorder and dissociative disorders. *Journal of Trauma and Dissociation*, 2(4), 79–116.

Steele, K., Van der Hart, O., & Nijenhuis, E. R. S. (2004). Allgemeine Behandlungsstrategien komplexer dissoziativer Störungen [General treatment strategies for complex dissociative disorders]. In A. Eckhart-Henn & S. O. Hoffman (Eds.), *Dissoziative Störungen des Bewußtseins [Dissociative disorders of consciousness]* (pp. 357–394). Stuttgart: Schatterauer-Verlag.

Steele, K., Van der Hart, O., & Nijenhuis, E. R. S. (2005). Phase-oriented treatment of structural dissociation in complex traumatization: Overcoming trauma-related phobias. *Journal of Trauma & Dissociation*, 6(3),11–53.

Steinberg, M. (1994). *Structured clinical interview for DSM-IV dissociative disorders, revised.* Washington, DC: American Psychiatric Press.

Stiglmayr, C. E., Shapiro, D. A., Stieglitz, R. D., Limberger, M. F., & Bohus, M. (2001). Experience of aversive tension and dissociation in female patients with borderline personality disorder: A controlled study. *Journal of Psychiatric Research, 35*, 111–118.

Tauber, Y. (1996). The traumatized child and the adult: Compound personality in child survivors of the Holocaust. *Israel Journal of Psychiatry & Related Sciences, 33*, 228–237.

Teicher, M. H., Andersen, S. L., Polcari, A., Anderson, C. M., & Navalta, C. P. (2002). Developmental neurobiology of childhood stress and trauma. *Psychiatric Clinics of North America, 25*, 397–426.

Toates, F. M. (1986). *Motivational systems.* Cambridge: Cambridge University Press.

Tsai, G. E., Condie, D., Wu, M. T., & Chang, I. W. (1999). Functional magnetic resonance imaging of personality switches in a woman with dissociative identity disorder. *Harvard Review of Psychiatry, 7,* 119–122.

Tulving, E. (1972). Episodic and semantic memory. In E. Tulving & W. Donaldson (Eds.), *Organization of Memory* (pp. 381–403). New York: Plenum.

Van der Hart, O., Bolt, H., & Van der Kolk, B. A. (2005). Memory fragmentation in DID. *Journal of Trauma & Dissociation, 6*(1), 55–70.

Van der Hart, O., & Dorahy, M. (2009) History of the concept of dissociation. In P. F. Dell & J. A. O'Neil (Eds.), *Dissociation and the dissociative disorders: DSM-V and beyond* (pp. 3–26). New York: Routledge.

Van der Hart, O., & Nijenhuis, E. R. S. (2001). Loss and recovery of different memory types in generalized dissociative amnesia. *Australian and New Zealand Journal of Psychiatry, 35,* 589–600.

Van der Hart, O., Nijenhuis, E. R. S., & Steele, K. (2005). Dissociation: An under-recognized feature of complex PTSD. *Journal of Traumatic Stress, 18,* 413–424.

Van der Hart, O., Nijenhuis, E. R. S., & Steele, K. (2006). *The haunted self: Chronic traumatization and the theory of structural dissociation of the personality.* New York: Norton.

Van der Hart, O., Nijenhuis, E. R. S., Steele, K., & Brown, D. (2004). Trauma-related dissociation: Conceptual clarity lost and found. *Australian and New Zealand Journal of Psychiatry, 38,* 906–914.

Van der Hart, O., & Steele, K. (1997). Time distortions in dissociative identity disorder: Janetian concepts and treatment. *Dissociation, 10,* 91–103.

Van der Hart, O., Steele, K., Boon, S., & Brown, P. (1993). The treatment of traumatic memories: Synthesis, realization and integration. *Dissociation, 6,* 162–180.

Van der Hart, O., Van der Kolk, B. A., & Boon, S. (1998). Treatment of dissociative disorders. In J. D. Bremner & C. R. Marmar (Eds.), *Trauma, memory, and dissociation* (pp. 253–283). Washington, DC: American Psychiatric Press.

Van der Hart, O., Van Dijke, A., Van Son, M., & Steele, K. (2000). Somatoform dissociation in traumatized World War I combat soldiers: A neglected clinical heritage. *Journal of Trauma and Dissociation, 1*(4), 33–66.

Van der Kolk, B. A. (1994). The body keeps the score: memory and the evolving psychobiology of posttraumatic stress. *Harvard Review of Psychiatry, 1,* 253–265.

Van der Kolk, B. A. (2003). The neurobiology of childhood trauma and abuse. *Child & Adolescent Psychiatric Clinics of North America, 12,* 293–317.

Van der Kolk, B. A., Pelcovitz, D., Roth, S., Mandel, F. S., McFarlane, A., & Herman, J. L. (1996). Dissociation, somatization, and affect dysregulation: The complexity of adaptation of trauma. *American Journal of Psychiatry, 153*(Festschrift Suppl), 83–93.

Van der Kolk, B. A., & Van der Hart, O. (1989). Pierre Janet and the breakdown of adaptation in psychological trauma. *American Journal of Psychiatry, 146,* 1530–1560.

Van der Kolk, B. A., & Van der Hart, O. (1991). The intrusive past: The flexibility of memory and the engraving of trauma. *American Imago, 48,* 425–454.

Van Honk, J., Nijenhuis, E. R. S., & Van der Hart, O. (1999). Identity-dependent psychophysiological responses to subliminal threat cues in DID patients. Paper presented at the 15th Annual Meeting of the International Society for Traumatic Stress Studies, Miami, FL.

Van IJzendoorn, M. H., & Bakermans-Kranenburg, M. J. (1996). Attachment representations in mothers, fathers, adolescents, and clinical groups: A meta-analytic search for normative data. *Journal of Consulting and Clinical Psychology, 64,* 8–21.

Van IJzendoorn, M. H., Schuengel, C., & J., Bakersman-Kranenberg, M. (1999). Disorganized attachment in early childhood: Meta-analysis of precursors, concomitants, and sequelae. *Development & Psychopathology, 11,* 225–249.

Vanderlinden, J., Van Dyck, R., Vandereycken, W., & Vertommen, H. (1993). Dissociation and traumatic experiences in the general population of The Netherlands. *Hospital & Community Psychiatry, 44,* 786–788.

Waller, G., Hamilton, K., Elliott, P., Lewendon, J., Stopa, L., Waters, A., Kennedy, F., Lee, G., Pearson, D., Kennerley, H., Hargreaves, I., Bashford, V., Chalkley, J. (2000). Somatoform dissociation, psychological dissociation and specific forms of trauma. *Journal of Trauma and Dissociation, 1*(4), 81–98.

Waller, N. G., Putnam, F. W., & Carslon, E. B. (1996). Types of dissociation and dissociative types: A taxometric analysis of dissociative experiences. *Journal of Abnormal Psychology, 106,* 499–510.

Wang, S., Wilson, J. P., & Mason, J. W. (1996). Stages of decompensation in combat-related posttraumatic stress disorder: a new conceptual model. *Integrative Physiolology & Behavioral Science, 31,* 237–253.

Wilson, J. P. (1989). *Trauma, transformation, and healing: An integrative approach to theory, research, and posttraumatic therapy.* New York: Burnner/Mazel.

Wolf, D. P. (1990). Being of several minds: Voices and versions of the self in early childhood. In D. Cicchetti & M. Beeghly (Eds.), *The self in transition: Infancy to childhood* (pp. 183–212). Chicago, IL: The Chicago University Press.

Wolff, P. H. (1987). *The development of behavioral states and the expression of emotions in early childhood.* Chicago: University of Chicago Press.

Yen, S., Shea, M. T., Battle, C. L., Johnson, D. M., Zlotnick, C., Dolan-Sewell, R., *et al.* (2002). Traumatic exposure and posttraumatic stress disorder in borderline, schizotypal, avoidant, and obsessive-compulsive personality disorders: findings from the collaborative longitudinal personality disorders study. *Journal of Nervous and Mental Disease, 190,* 510–518.

Zanarini, M. C., Ruser, T., Frankenburg, F. R., & Hennen, J. (2000). The dissociative experiences of borderline patients. *Comprehensive Psychiatry, 41,* 223–227.

Zlotnick, C., Shea, M. T., Pearlstein, T., Begin, A., Simpson, E., & Costello, E. (1996a). Differences in dissociative experiences between survivors of childhood incest and survivors of assault in adulthood. *Journal of Nervous and Mental Disease, 184*, 52–54.

Zlotnick, C., Zakriski, A. L., Shea, M. T., Costello, E., Begin, A., Pearlstein, T., & Simpson, E. (1996b). The long-term sequelae of sexual abuse: Support for a complex post-traumatic stress disorder. *Journal of Traumatic Stress, 9*, 195–220.

17 Somatoform Dissociation and Somatoform Dissociative Disorders

Ellert R. S. Nijenhuis, PhD

OUTLINE

Mental dissociation can be described from three major perspectives: symptoms, structure, and process. To avoid conceptual confusion, a definition of dissociation must clearly specify which of these three domains is being addressed.

17.1 THE DOMAIN OF DISSOCIATIVE SYMPTOMS

According to the *Diagnostic and Statistical Manual for Mental Disorders*, fourth edition (DSM-IV; American Psychiatric Association, 1994), the essential feature of dissociation is a disruption of the normal integrative functions of consciousness, memory, identity, and perception of the environment. Thus the current standard for the assessment of dissociative disorders, the *Structural Clinical Interview for DSM-IV Dissociative Disorders* (SCID-D; Steinberg, 1994), involves four symptom clusters: dissociative amnesia, depersonalization, derealization, and identity confusion/identity fragmentation. Well-known self-report measures of dissociation, such as the *Dissociative Experiences Scale* (DES; Bernstein & Putnam, 1986) and the *Dissociation Questionnaire* (DIS-Q; Vanderlinden, 1993), predominantly focus on symptoms that reflect dissociative amnesia, depersonalization, derealization, identity confusion, and identity fragmentation. These phenomena have been collectively labeled *psychological dissociation* (Nijenhuis, Spinhoven, Van Dyck, Van der Hart, & Vanderlinden, 1996) and, more recently, *psychoform dissociation* (Van der Hart, Van Dijke, Van Son, & Steele, 2000; Van der Hart, Nijenhuis, & Steele, 2006).

But does dissociation not affect the body? DSM-IV's descriptive definition of dissociation and the contents of the SCID-D, DES, and DIS-Q give the impression that dissociation is only a psychoform phenomenon. This impression is strengthened by the DSM-IV criteria for the dissociative disorders, which seldom mention the body. Only the diagnostic criterion for depersonalization disorder refers to the body—detachment from one's body or from parts of one's body. The diagnostic features of depersonalization disorder include various types of perceptual (i.e., sensory) anesthesia. Yet patients with DSM-IV dissociative disorders often report somatoform symptoms. In fact, many dissociative disordered patients meet the DSM-IV criteria for conversion disorder, or even somatization disorder (Pribor, Yutzy, Dean, & Wetzel, 1993; Ross, Heber, Norton, & Anderson, 1989; Saxe et al., 1994). Conversely, many patients with somatization disorder report episodes of amnesia (Othmer & De Souza, 1985). The strong correlation between dissociative disorders and somatoform disorders (see also Darves-Bornoz, 1997) suggests that dissociative symptoms, conversion symptoms, and certain somatization symptoms may be manifestations of a single underlying principle.

The major somatoform symptoms of hysteria provide another indication of the existence of *somatoform* dissociation (Nijenhuis, 2004). During the heyday of hysteria in the 19th century, many authors focused almost exclusively on the somatoform manifestations of hysteria (e.g., Briquet, 1859). Somatoform dissociation characterized many traumatized World War I soldiers as well; an important historical fact that Van der Hart and colleagues (2000) were able to retrieve from near oblivion. Recent clinical observations also indicate that dissociation can manifest in somatoform ways (Cardeña, 1994; Kihlstrom, 1994; Nemiah, 1991; Van der Hart & Op den Velde, 1995).

The labels "psychoform dissociation" and "somatoform dissociation" should *not* be taken to mean that only psychoform dissociation is of a mental nature. Both adjectives refer to *manifestations* of the existence of a structural dissociation of the personality as a whole dynamic biopsychosocial system into two or more insufficiently integrated subsystems (Van der Hart et al., 2006). Dissociative symptoms that phenomenologically involve the body are called somatoform; dissociative symptoms that phenomenologically involve the mind are called psychoform. The adjective *somatoform* refers to physical symptoms that suggest, but cannot be explained by, a medical condition or the direct effects of a substance.

Dissociative symptoms, whether somatoform or psychoform, must be distinguished from two other phenomena: (1) manifestations of low levels of consciousness (e.g., general inattention as in daydreaming or drowsiness), and (2) retractions of the field of consciousness during which fewer phenomena are consciously processed (i.e., absorption and other forms of selective attention). This distinction is often overlooked (Van der Hart, Nijenhuis, Steele, & Brown, 2004), as is argued by Steele et al. (2009a) in this book.

17.2 THE DOMAIN OF DISSOCIATIVE DISORDERS

DSM-IV recognizes four dissociative disorders (i.e., dissociative amnesia, dissociative fugue, depersonalization disorder, disssociative identity disorder; DID), and several atypical dissociative disorders (i.e., dissociative disorder not otherwise specified; DDNOS). In this chapter, I argue that somatoform dissociation routinely occurs in the DSM-IV dissociative disorders. In particular, I seek to show that (1) somatoform dissociation is as characteristic of DID and DDNOS as is psychoform dissociation; and (2) somatoform dissociation is *the* major feature of DSM-IV conversion disorder, and that conversion disorders are better understood as somatoform dissociative disorders (see also Brown, Cardeña, Nijenhuis, Şar, & Van der Hart, 2007). In contrast to DSM-IV, the *International Classification of Diseases, tenth edition* (ICD-10; World Health Organization, 1992) recognizes somatoform dissociation. ICD-10 classifies conversion disorders as *dissociative disorders of movement and sensation.* I will propose a briefer label for these disorders: *somatoform dissociative disorders.*

Both DSM-IV and ICD-10 omit significant somatoform dissociative symptoms. For example, neither DSM-IV nor ICD-10 acknowledge that pain and sexual dysfunctions can be dissociative. Localized pain may reflect a traumatic memory of physical pain that has been reactivated in a dissociative part of the personality. In fact, *traumatic memories*—experiential phenomena that must be distinguished from memories of trauma that have been integrated into autobiographical memory—primarily consist of sensorimotor and emotional reactions (Nijenhuis, Van Engen, Kusters, & Van der Hart, 2001; Van der Hart et al., 2000; Van der Kolk & Fisler, 1995).

17.3 THE DOMAIN OF DISSOCIATIVE PROCESSES AND ACTIONS

Dissociative symptoms presumably result from psychobiological processes and actions (Van der Hart et al., 2006). These processes and actions involve a postulated defense mechanism (Cardeña, 1994), a lack of integrative capacity (Nijenhuis, Van der Hart, & Steele, 2004; Van der Hart et al., 2006), and human capacities such as the hypnotic talents or dissociative talents that are displayed by mediums (Braude, 1995). Dissociative symptoms can also be induced by substances such as drugs. These different processes are not mutually exclusive. Whatever their nature, all of these processes entail a lack of integration of psychobiological phenomena and functions. In somatoform dissociation, there is a lack of integration of somatoform experiences, reactions, and functions.

17.4 A CLASSIFICATION OF DISSOCIATIVE SYMPTOMS

Janet's (1889/1973, 1893, 1901/1977) clinical observations indicated that hysteria involves psychoform and somatoform functions and reactions. Because Janet saw mind and body as inseparable, his classification of the symptoms of hysteria does not follow a mind-body distinction. According to Janet, two kinds of symptoms occurred in hysteria: (1) permanent symptoms that occur in all hysterics (i.e., the "mental stigmata"), and (2) intermittent and variable symptoms whose nature differs from case to case (i.e., "mental accidents"; Nijenhuis, 2004; Van der Hart & Friedman, 1989).

The *mental stigmata* are partial or complete functional losses—of knowledge (i.e., amnesia), of sensations (i.e., anesthesia), of sensory abilities (i.e., touch, kinesthesia, smell, taste, hearing, vision), of sensitivity to pain (i.e., analgesia), and of motor control (i.e., loss of the ability to move or speak). We have referred to mental stigmata as losses or negative symptoms (Nijenhuis & Van der Hart, 1999).

Mental accidents are intrusions or positive symptoms. These relate to mental actions and contents that should have been integrated into the personality, but were not (Van der Hart et al., 2006). At times, dissociated mental actions and contents associated with one dissociative part of the personality intrude into the domain of consciousness of one or more other dissociative parts of the personality. These mental actions and contents can pertain to sensations, emotions, thoughts, memories (e.g., traumatic memories), motor actions, and the voice of one dissociative part that intrude another dissociative part.

According to Janet, the simplest form of mental accidents are *ideés fixes* (i.e., fixed ideas) that often generate intrusions of dissociated emotion, thought, sensory perception, or movement. These intrusions may take the form of "hysterical attacks," currently known as reactivated traumatic memories. Janet observed that some dissociative patients are subject to "somnambulisms"; today, many authors think of this as reactivations of dissociative "identities." Since *ideés fixes* involve much more than a different sense of self, we feel that they should be considered to be dissociative parts of the personality (Nijenhuis, Van der Hart, & Steele, 2004; Van der Hart et al., 2006). When patients lose all touch with reality during dissociative episodes, they experience a "delirium," a reactive dissociative psychosis (Van der Hart, Witztum, & Friedman, 1993; see Şar & Öztürk, 2009, this volume).

Janet (1889/1973, 1893, 1901/1977, 1907/1965) gave many clinical examples of dissociated sensory, motor, and other bodily (re)actions and functions. For example, in one dissociative part of the personality, the patient may be insensitive to pain or touch, but in another, these mental stigmata can be absent, or exchanged for mental accidents, such as localized pain. Whatever has not been integrated into one dissociative part of the personality (i.e., not-knowing; not-sensing; not-perceiving) is likely to be prominent in another part, and may be manifested in "hysterical attacks."

17.5 JANET'S DISSOCIATION THEORY

Janet's dissociation theory (1889/1973, 1893, 1901/1977, 1911/1983) postulates that both somatoform and psychoform components of experience, (re)actions, and functions can be associated with dissociative parts of the personality. He used the construct "personality" to denote the complex, but relatively-integrated, psychobiological system that encompasses consciousness, memory, identity, and other personal characteristics such as habits, motivations, psychophysiological features, somatic markers (e.g., gait and posture), and so on. Janet observed that dissociative psychobiological systems are also characterized by a retracted field of consciousness (i.e., mental functioning during which there is a significant reduction in the number of psychological phenomena that are consciously processed and integrated at the same time).

In Janet's conceptualization, mental accidents are reactivations of dissociated "systems of ideas and functions." As time goes by, due to recurrent dissociation and imagery, these systems may "emancipate" (i.e., synthesize and assimilate additional sensations, feelings, emotions, thoughts, behaviors, etc.). When this happens, dissociated systems may become associated with a range of experiences, a name, age, and other personality-like characteristics. Today, these emancipated systems are described as dissociative parts of the personality. The personality-like features of these dissociative parts may result from, or be enhanced by, secondary elaborations (Nijenhuis, Spinhoven, Vanderlinden, Van Dyck, & Van der Hart, 1998a). These elaborations are probably promoted by hypnotic-like imagination, restricted fields of consciousness, and the needs of specific dissociative parts of the personality. Secondary shaping of dissociative psychobiological systems may also be due to sociocultural influences (Gleaves, 1996; Janet, 1929/1984; Laria & Lewis-Fernández, 2001).

TABLE 17.1
A Phenomenological Categorization of Dissociative Symptoms: The Continuity Between 19th Century and Contemporary Observations

	Psychoform Dissociation	Somatoform Dissociation
Mental stigmata or *negative* dissociative symptoms	Amnesia: loss of knowledge, memory Abulia: loss of will Modifications of character: loss of character traits, predominantly affects Suggestibility: loss of control over ideas	Anesthesia: loss of sensory awareness; all sensory modalities Analgesia: loss of sensitivity for pain Loss of motor control (movements, voice, swallowing, etc.)
Mental accidents or *positive* dissociative symptoms	Psychoform components of subconscious acts, hysterical accidents, and fixed ideas	Somatoform components of subconscious acts, hysterical accidents, and fixed ideas: singular somatoform symptoms associated with one dissociative part which intrude another part's functioning
	Psychoform components of hysterical attacks and reactivated traumatic memories	Somatoform components of hysterical attacks and reactivated traumatic memories
	Somnambulism: psychoform aspects of dissociative parts of the personality, notably but not exclusively EPs	Somnambulism: somatoform aspects of dissociative parts, notably EPs, that take executive control
	Deliriums: dissociative psychosis, i.e., psychoform manifestations of dissociative psychotic parts. These parts display enduring failures of reality testing.	Deliriums: dissociative psychosis, i.e., somatoform manifestations of dissociative psychotic parts: grotesque somatoform alterations

17.6 THE "APPARENTLY NORMAL" PART OF THE PERSONALITY AND THE "EMOTIONAL" PART OF THE PERSONALITY

Many cases of dissociative disorder remain predominantly in a condition that has been metaphorically described as an *apparently normal part of the personality* (ANP; Myers, 1940; Nijenhuis & Van der Hart, 1999; Van der Hart et al., 2000, 2006). This observation lies at the root of the theory of structural dissociation of the personality (Van der Hart et al., 2006; Steele et al., 2009b). As ANP, the patient appears to be mentally normal. On closer scrutiny, however, he or she has negative dissociative symptoms (Nijenhuis & Van der Hart, 1999), for example, partial amnesia and anesthesia. The ANP is structurally dissociated from one or more *emotional parts of the personality* (EP; Nijenhuis & Van der Hart, 1999; Van der Hart et al., 2000, 2006). In our view, dissociative psychobiological systems that involve EPs[1] often encompass traumatic memories and defensive reactions to major threat (Nijenhuis, Vanderlinden, & Spinhoven, 1998d; Nijenhuis et al., 1998a). Because dissociative barriers are not impenetrable, EPs may influence ANPs and *vice versa*. Thus, intrusions of EPs—whatever their degree of complexity and emancipation—into ANPs or other EPs, and intrusions of ANPs into EPs or other ANPs constitute positive symptoms. However, as to *phenomenal content*, these intrusions, hence positive symptoms, can contain functional losses. For example, EPs can include functional losses—hence negative symptoms—such as analgesia and motor inhibitions; these are expressions of defensive freezing. Examples of positive phenomenal content include pain and particular trauma-related movements. Alternations between ANPs and EPs and intrusions of dissociative parts into each other's domains occur in mental disorders that range from posttraumatic stress disorder to DID (Nijenhuis & Van der Hart, 1999; Nijenhuis et al., 2004; Van der Hart et al., 2006).

Table 17.1 summarizes dissociative symptoms in terms of two dichotomies: (1) mental stigmata/negative symptoms versus mental accidents/positive symptoms, and (2) psychoform symptoms versus somatoform symptoms.

17.7 THE SOMATOFORM DISSOCIATION QUESTIONNAIRE

The *Somatoform Dissociation Questionnaire* (SDQ-20) is a self-report instrument with excellent psychometric characteristics that measures the severity of somatoform

[1] EPs may range from Janetian fixed ideas to somnambulism.

dissociation (Nijenhuis et al., 1996, 1998b, 1999). The original SDQ-20 findings in Dutch/Flemish samples have been largely replicated in Turkey (Şar, Kundakçı, Kızıltan, Bakım, & Bozkurt, 2000), France (El-Hage, Darves-Bornoz, Allilaire, & Gaillard, 2002), and Portugal (Espirito Santo & Pio-Abreu, 2007). SDQ-20 items reflect negative and positive somatoform dissociative symptoms, and converge with the major symptoms of hysteria as formulated by Janet. The SDQ-20 assesses such *negative* symptoms as analgesia ("Sometimes my body, or a part of it, is insensitive to pain"), kinesthetic anesthesia ("Sometimes it is as if my body, or a part of it, has disappeared"), motor inhibitions ("Sometimes I am paralyzed for a while"; "Sometimes I cannot speak, or only whisper"), blindness ("Sometimes I cannot see for a while"), and alterations of auditory perception ("Sometimes I hear sounds from nearby as if they were coming from far away"). The SDQ-20 assesses such *positive* somatoform dissociative symptoms as pain ("Sometimes I have pain while urinating," and "Sometimes I feel pain in my genitals—at times other than sexual intercourse").

In most SDQ-20 studies performed to date, somatoform dissociation was not affected by age or gender. In samples of French and Dutch psychiatric outpatients, women had slightly higher scores than men (El-Hage et al., 2002; Nijenhuis, Van der Hart, & Kruger, 2002), and in Turkey, a weak but statistically significant correlation with age was found (Şar et al., 2000).

17.8 SOMATOFORM DISSOCIATION AND PSYCHOFORM DISSOCIATION: MANIFESTATIONS OF A COMMON PROCESS

Somatoform dissociation is strongly and consistently associated with psychoform dissociation as measured by the DES and DIS-Q in both clinical and nonclinical samples, ranging from $r = 0.58$ (Nijenhuis et al., 2003) to $r = 0.85$ (Nijenhuis et al., 1999). Dell (1997), El-Hage et al. (2002), Maaranen et al. (2005), Şar, Kundakçı, Kızıltan, Bahadır, and Aydıner (1998), Şar et al. (2000), and Nijenhuis and Van Duyl (2001) documented strong correlations between the SDQ-20 and DES in the United States, France, Finland, Turkey, and Uganda, respectively. Waller et al. (2000) found a somewhat lower, but still considerable correlation between somatoform and psychoform dissociative symptoms in psychiatric outpatients in the United Kingdom ($r = 0.51$).

A close link between somatoform and psychoform dissociation is also suggested by the finding that the 14 dimensions of the Multidimensional Inventory of Dissociation (Dell, 2002), including the somatoform dissociation dimension, loaded on one factor that accounted for 84% of the variance. Similarly, somatoform dissociation as measured with the Hebrew version of the MID was strongly correlated with different measures of psychoform dissociation ($r = 0.58$, $r = 0.73$, and $r = 0.77$) in two Israeli studies (Somer & Dell, 2005).

These results suggest that somatoform and psychoform dissociation are overlapping, but not identical, manifestations of a common process. *Peritraumatic* somatoform and psychoform dissociation (i.e., dissociation that occurs during or *immediately* after a potentially traumatizing event) were correlated as well (Nijenhuis et al., 2001).

17.9 SOMATOFORM DISSOCIATION IN VARIOUS DIAGNOSTIC GROUPS

Somatoform dissociation is a unique construct. As Table 17.2 indicates, it is a major feature of DSM-IV dissociative disorders (Nijenhuis et al., 1996, 1998b, 1999; Şar et al., 2000). Patients with DSM-IV dissociative disorders had significantly higher SDQ-20 scores than psychiatric outpatients with other DSM-IV diagnoses, and DID patients had higher SDQ-20 scores than patients with DDNOS or depersonalization disorder (Nijenhuis et al., 1996, 1998b; Şar et al., 2000). Nijenhuis and Van Duyl (2001) found that Ugandan patients with spirit possession disorder—a culture-related dissociative disorder—had much higher SDQ-20 scores than mentally healthy controls. PTSD can also be seen as a dissociative disorder because it involves a continuing failure to integrate traumatic memories. Compared to healthy controls, patients with current or past PTSD reported higher levels of somatoform and psychoform dissociation, which were both strongly correlated with scores on the Clinician-Administered PTSD Scale (CAPS; El-Hage et al., 2002; see also Espirito Santo & Pio-Abreu, 2007).

The SDQ-20 discriminates among various diagnostic categories (Espirito Santo & Pio-Abreu, 2007; Nijenhuis et al., 1999; Şar et al., 2000). Compared to patients with DDNOS or depersonalization disorder, DID patients had significantly higher scores. Patients with DDNOS had significantly higher scores than patients with somatoform disorders or eating disorders, and the latter two diagnostic categories had significantly higher scores than did patients with anxiety disorder, depression, adjustment disorders, and bipolar mood disorders. Bipolar mood disorder was associated with extremely low somatoform dissociation (see also Nijenhuis et al., 1997a). The above group differences on the SDQ-20 remained after controlling for the influence of general psychopathology (Nijenhuis et al., 1999). Thus, the severity of somatoform dissociation across diagnostic groups is not explained by general psychopathology.

Waller et al. (2003) reported that somatoform dissociation was strongly linked to bulimic attitudes and certain bulimic features (i.e., excessive exercise, laxative abuse, diet pill abuse, diuretic abuse). In contrast, Nijenhuis et al. (1999) found that eating disorders were not associated with high somatoform dissociation scores, but that eating disorder patients who reported substantial exposure to potentially traumatizing events had higher scores.

TABLE 17.2
Somatoform Dissociation in Different Diagnostic Categories

		SDQ-20	
		M	SD
Dissociative Disorders			
Dissociative Identity Disorder	Nijenhuis et al., 1996	51.8	12.6
	Nijenhuis et al., 1998b	57.3	14.9
	Şar et al., 2000	58.7	17.9
DDNOS (+ some with depersonalization disorder)	Nijenhuis et al., 1996	43.8	7.1
DDNOS	Nijenhuis et al., 1998b	44.6	11.9
	Şar et al., 2000	46.3	16.2
Mixed group of dissociative disorders, including depersonalization disorder and DDNOS	Espirito Santo & Pio-Abreu, 2007	39.3	12.0
Spirit possession disorder	Nijenhuis & Van Duyl, 2001	39.4	7.4
Somatoform Dissociative Disorders			
Mixed somatoform dissociative disorders	Roelofs et al., 2002a	30.5	8.5
	Nijenhuis et al., 1999	31.9	9.4
Pseudo-epilepsy	Kuyk et al., 1999	29.8	7.5
Conversion disorder	Şar et al., 2004	81.6% of sample: M >35	
	Espirito Santo & Pio-Abreu, 2007	39.8	14.1
Somatoform and Somatic Disorders			
Somatoform pain disorder			
Chronic headache	Yücel et al., 2002	32.6	10.4
Chronic low back pain	Yücel et al., 2002	30.6	10.9
Temporal lobe epilepsy	Kuyk et al., 1999	24.3	6.8
Non-temporal lobe epilepsy	Kuyk et al., 1999	25.6	7.3
General Psychiatric Patients, With and Without Trauma			
	El-Hage et al., 2002		
1. Reporting potentially traumatizing events		29.5	–
2. No trauma reporting		21	–
	Nijenhuis et al., 2002		
1. No trauma reporting		1	5.3
2. Emotional neglect and abuse only		22.5	2.6
3. One criterion A event		22.6	3.8
4. Up to 4 different criterion A events		25.4	5.0
5. More than 4 different criterion A events		31.7	10.5
(According to ANOVA and post-hoc Tukey HSD, group 5 had higher SDQ-20 scores than the other four groups)			

TABLE 17.2
Somatoform Dissociation in Different Diagnostic Categories *(Continued)*

Other DSM-IV Axis I Diagnoses			
PTSD	Espirito Santo & Pio-Abreu, 2007	38.7	11.7
Schizophrenia	Şar et al., 2000	27.1	9.5
Eating disorders	Nijenhuis et al., 1999	27.7	8.8
Mixed types			
Anorexia nervosa, restricive	Waller et al., 2003	27.0	7.6
Anorexia nervosa, binge purge	Waller et al., 2003	38.2	14.8
Bulimia nervosa	Waller et al., 2003	32.6	–
Anxiety disorders	Şar et al., 2000	26.8	6.4
Anxiety disorders and depression	Espirito Santo & Pio-Abreu, 2007	29.2	6.7
Affective disorders	Roelofs et al., 2002a	23.0	3.8
Major depressive episode	Şar et al., 2000	28.7	8.3
Bipolar mood disorder	Nijenhuis et al., 1999	21.6	1.9
	Sar et al., 2000	22.7	3.5
Mixed psychiatric disorders, notably anxiety disorder and major depressive episode	Nijenhuis et al., 1996	23.5	4.0
	Nijenhuis et al., 1999	22.9	3.9
Nonclinical Groups			
Adults in Turkey	Şar et al., 2000	27.4	8.2
Adults in Uganda	Nijenhuis & Van Duyl, 2001	27.0	4.7
Adults	Nähring & Nijenhuis, 2005	23.2	5.0
Students	Nähring & Nijenhuis, 2005	24.4	4.4

17.10 SOMATOFORM DISSOCIATION IN DSM-IV AND ICD-10 SOMATOFORM DISSOCIATIVE DISORDERS

The SDQ-20 discriminated between bipolar mood disorder and DSM-IV somatoform disorders, whereas the DES did not (Nijenhuis et al., 1999). This research sample primarily included cases of conversion and pain disorder, but not hypochondriasis. Another study also documented that psychiatric patients with DSM-IV somatoform disorders (i.e., ICD-10 dissociative disorders of movement, sensation, convulsions, or combinations of these symptoms) had more somatoform dissociation compared to patients with affective disorders (Roelofs et al., 2002a; see also Espirito Santo & Pio-Abreu, 2007).

Only those somatoform disordered patients with a comorbid DSM-IV dissociative disorder had more psychoform dissociation. Whereas Moene, Spinhoven, Hoogduin, Sandijck, and Roelofs (2001) found that patients with somatoform dissociative disorders had higher DIS-Q scores compared to healthy controls, their sample's level of psychoform dissociation was quite modest; in fact, their somatoform sample had lower DIS-Q scores than the psychiatric controls. A contrasting finding emerged from a German study (Spitzer, Spelsberg, Grabe, Mundt, & Freyberger, 1999). In this study, patients with conversion disorder had more dissociative symptoms as measured by the German version of the DES than gender- and age-matched psychiatric patients with various mental disorders. However, this version of the DES includes items assessing somatoform dissociation. Nonetheless, conversion disorder, hence somatoform dissociation, can be associated with psychoform dissociation (Şar, Akyüz, Kundakçı, Kızıltan, & Doğan, 2004). In this study, half of the sample of conversion disorder patients also met the criteria of a DSM-IV dissociative disorder and still other DSM-IV diagnoses. This comorbidity is common in complex dissociative disorders.

From these findings, it can be concluded that somatoform dissociation is a stable characteristic of somatoform dissociative disorders, whereas psychoform dissociation is not. Clinical data suggest that hypochondriasis does not involve substantial somatoform dissociation, but the issue awaits systematic study. Patients with pseudoseizures had higher psychoform dissociation scores than individuals with epilepsy (Fleisher et al., 2002), but this difference could be attributed to the influence of general psychopathology. Kuyk, Spinhoven, Van Emde Boas, and Van Dyck (1999; see Table 17.2) documented higher SDQ-20 and DIS-Q scores for patients with pseudo-epileptic seizures than for patients with temporal lobe epilepsy and non temporal lobe epilepsy. However, when statistically corrected for general psychopathology, only the SDQ-20 difference remained.

In a sample of patients with somatoform pain disorders (i.e., chronic headache and low back pain), Yücel et al. (2002) reported mean SDQ-20 scores that were quite similar to the mean SDQ-20 scores of patients with somatoform dissociative disorders in other studies. As Table 17.2 shows, SDQ-20 scores differ little across different somatoform disorders.

17.11 SOMATOFORM DISSOCIATION IN SCREENING FOR DSM-IV DISSOCIATIVE DISORDERS

The data discussed previously have shown that somatoform dissociation is very characteristic of patients with DDNOS and DID. The question remains, however, whether somatoform dissociation is as characteristic of these disorders as is psychoform dissociation. This issue can be examined by contrasting the relative abilities of somatoform and psychoform dissociation screening instruments to discriminate between patients with and without a DSM-IV dissociative disorder.

The SDQ-5 was developed as a screening instrument for DSM-IV dissociative disorders (Nijenhuis, Spinhoven, Van Dyck, Van der Hart, & Vanderlinden, 1997b; Nijenhuis et al., 1998b). The *sensitivity* (i.e., the proportion of true positives selected by the test) of the SDQ-5 among SCID-D assessed patients with dissociative disorders in various Dutch/Flemish samples (n = 50, n = 33, n = 31, respectively) ranged from 82% to 94%. The *specificity* (i.e., the proportion of the comparison patients that was correctly identified by the test) of the SDQ-5 ranged from 93% to 98% (n = 50, n = 42, n = 45, respectively). The *positive predictive value* (i.e., the proportion of cases with scores above the chosen cut-off value of the test that were true positives) among these samples ranged from 90% to 98%, and the *negative predictive value* (i.e., the proportion of cases with scores below this cut-off value that were true negatives) from 87% to 96%. The corresponding values of the SDQ-20 were slightly lower (Nijenhuis et al., 1997b).

High sensitivity and specificity of a test do not imply a high predictive value when the prevalence of the disorder in the population of concern is low (Rey, Morris-Yates, & Stanislaw, 1992). The prevalence of dissociative disorders among psychiatric patients has been estimated at approximately 8% to 18% (Friedl & Draijer, 2000; Horen, Leichner, & Lawson, 1995; Johnson, Cohen, Kasen, & Brook, 2006; Şar, Akyüz, & Doğan, 2007; Şar et al., 1999; Saxe et al., 1993). Corrected for a prevalence rate of 10%, the positive predictive values among the indicated samples ranged from 57% to 84%, and the negative predictive values from 98% to 99%. Averaged over three samples, the positive predictive value of the SDQ-5 was 66%. Hence, it can be predicted that among Dutch/Flemish samples two of three patients with scores at or above the cut-off will have a DSM-IV dissociative disorder.

Among Dutch dissociative disorder patients and psychiatric comparison patients, Draijer and Boon (1993) found that the sensitivity of the DES was 93%, the specificity 86%, the corrected positive predictive value 42%, and the corrected negative predicted value 99%. It thus seems that somatoform dissociation is at least as characteristic of complex dissociative disorders as is psychoform dissociation (in Dutch samples).

The SDQ-5 performed less well as a screening instrument for DSM-IV disorders in Turkey compared to the SDQ-20 (Şar et al., 2000). The positive and negative predictive value of the SDQ-20 were 45% and 99%, respectively, when corrected for an estimated prevalence rate of 10%. It is interesting to note that the SDQ-20 performed almost as well as the SDQ-5 in the Netherlands at a cutoff score of > 28. Clinicians are recommended to administer the SDQ-20 (that includes the SDQ-5 items), and to calculate and interpret the scores of both scales.

17.12 IS SOMATOFORM DISSOCIATION A UNIVERSAL PHENOMENON?

There are no empirical indications to date that somatoform dissociation is a culturally dependent phenomenon. Studies of somatoform dissociation from the Netherlands/Flanders, Finland, France, Portugal, the United Kingdom, Turkey, the United States, and Uganda have produced findings that are quite similar. Future research will be needed to explore the phenomenon in the Middle East, South America, and in Asia. A study from Nepal has reported that lifetime and 12-month ICD-10 dissociative disorders of movement and sensation, dissociative amnesia, persistent somatoform pain disorder, and PTSD were more likely among tortured Bhutanese refugees than among refugees who had not been tortured (Van Ommeren et al., 2001).

17.13 SOMATOFORM DISSOCIATION AND PSYCHOBIOLOGICAL FEATURES

Several studies have found associations between somatoform dissociation and structural and functional brain features of patients with dissociative disorders. These studies are reviewed in this book (Nijenhuis & den Boer, 2009).

17.14 SUGGESTION AND ROLE-PLAYING

Hypnotic suggestion can elicit somatoform dissociative reactions (e.g., analgesia, motor inhibitions) in susceptible and motivated individuals. Hypnotic reactions are time-limited and can be altered by countersuggestions. Somatoform dissociative symptoms of psychiatric patients usually have a tendency to be chronic and often resist hypnotic or other therapeutic suggestions. Some authors postulate that suggestion and role-playing affects dissociation scores. For example, Merskey (1992, 1997) maintained that dissociative disorder patients are extremely suggestible, and therefore vulnerable to indoctrination by therapists who mistake the symptoms of bipolar mood disorder for dissociative symptoms.

Empirical data do not support Merskey's position. The correlation between hypnotizability and dissociativity is remarkably low, both in the normal population and in traumatized individuals (Putnam & Carlson, 1998). Groups of traumatized individuals did not have higher hypnotizability scores than nontrauma groups in most studies (Putnam & Carlson, 1998). A few studies found that patients with PTSD were more hypnotizable than other psychiatric patients and healthy controls (Spiegel, Hunt, & Dondershine, 1988) or combat veterans without PTSD (Stutmann & Bliss, 1985). However, it should be noted that patients with anxiety disorders, impulse control behaviors, and personality disorders also had higher hypnotizability scores (see Maldonado & Spiegel, 1998), suggesting that high hypnotizability is not specific for traumatized individuals. Patients with dissociative disorders had high scores on hypnotic suggestibility scales, but their mean scores were not "off the scale" (Putnam & Carlson, 1998). If dissociative symptoms were the result of hypnotic suggestibility, one would expect that dissociative patients would be extremely hypnotizable.

Furthermore, the weight of the current data suggests that traumatization does not increase suggestibility in most individuals. Only a subset of sexually abused girls had high scores on hypnotic suggestibility scales and dissociation scales (Putnam, Helmers, Horowitz, & Trickett, 1995). In a single case study that used positron emission tomography (PET) functional imaging, hypnotic paralysis activated similar brain areas to those that are activated in DSM-IV conversion disorder, suggesting that hypnosis and somatoform dissociation may share common neurophysiological mechanisms (Halligan, Athwal, Oakley, & Frackowiak, 2000). This study requires replication among a group of patients with somatoform dissociative disorders. The observed correlation does not prove a causal relationship.

There are noteworthy reasons to believe that suggestion and indoctrination do *not* explain the somatoform dissociation of psychiatric patients. Dissociative patients who completed the SDQ-20 in the assessment phase, and prior to the SCID-D interview, had higher SDQ-20 scores than dissociative patients who completed the instrument during the course of their therapy (Nijenhuis, Van Dyck, Van der Hart, & Spinhoven, 1998e; Nijenhuis et al., 1999). Moreover, prior to our research, the symptoms described by the SDQ-20 were not known as major symptoms of dissociative disorders among diagnosticians and therapists, let alone patients. It was also found that my dissociative patients did not exceed the SDQ-20 scores of other therapists' dissociative patients. Given my theoretical orientation and expectations, I was the most likely person to suggest somatoform dissociative symptoms. Roelofs et al. (2002a) found that patients with somatoform dissociative disorders were significantly more responsive to hypnotic suggestions than patients with affective disorders, and that they showed a significant correlation between hypnotic susceptibility and the number of "conversion complaints." Still, their hypnotic susceptibility scores were only moderate and their SDQ-20 scores did not correlate with hypnotizability. Another study of somatoform dissociative disorders also reported moderate hypnotizability in somatoform dissociative disorders (Moene et al., 2001). Thus, patients with somatoform dissociative disorders do not seem to be hypnotic virtuosos.

In summary, the available empirical data run contrary to the hypothesis that somatoform dissociation results from suggestion. Even if somatoform dissociation were strongly related to suggestibility and related factors such as absorption and fantasy proneness, this in itself would not prove that somatoform dissociation is *caused* by suggestibility. It may well be that traumatization prompts individuals to practice and elaborate their potential for absorption and fantasy as a means of coping with events that they cannot integrate. The finding of Roelofs et al. (2002a), that physical abuse fully mediated the association between hypnotic susceptibility and the number of conversion symptoms in their study of somatoform disorders, is consistent with this possibility. Research in progress (Nijenhuis, in progress) suggests that women with DID or DDNOS are more fantasy prone than normal women, but most were not extremely fantasy prone. All of these patients used fantasy of positive experiences to cope with abuse and neglect.

17.15 CUMULATIVE TRAUMATIZATION

Given the link between psychoform dissociation and traumatization, and the link between psychoform and somatoform dissociation, somatoform dissociation may relate to traumatization. There are also theoretical reasons (see the following) for postulating such a link.

SDQ-20 scores are generally predicted best by cumulative exposure to potentially traumatizing events (e.g., Nijenhuis et al., 1998c, 1999, 2001, 2002; Nijenhuis & Van Duyl, 2001; Waller et al., 2000). Maaranen et al. (2004) documented a strong graded between an increasing number of adverse childhood experiences and high somatoform dissociation in a large sample of the general population. The finding that somatoform dissociation in dissociative disorders is strongly associated with multiple types of reported traumatization (see Table 17.3) converges with findings about the incidence of verified multiple and chronic traumatization in DID patients (Coons, 1994; Hornstein & Putnam, 1992; Kluft, 1995; Lewis, Yeager, Swica, Pincus, & Lewis, 1997).

The association between somatoform dissociation and reported traumatization may be nonlinear, that is,

TABLE 17.3
Somatoform Dissociation and (Reported) Cumulative Potentially Traumatizing Events

Correlations between reporting potentially traumatizing events and:	1. SDQ-20		2. DES	
	r	*p*	*R*	*p*
Students (n=73; Näring & Nijenhuis, 2005)	0.27*	<0.01	0.32*	<0.001
Normal adults (n=147; Näring & Nijenhuis, 2005)	0.20*	<0.05	0.10*	ns
Women with chronic pelvic pain (n=52; Nijenhuis et al., 2003)	0.69	<0.0001	0.44	<0.001
Substance use disorder (n = 229; Baars et al., 2001)	0.41	<0.0001	0.29	<0.0001
General psychiatric patients (n =155; Nijenhuis et al., 2002)	0.57	<0.0001	0.43	<0.0001
General psychiatric patients (n=72; Waller et al., 2000)	0.32	<0.01	0.27	<0.05
Eating disorders (Waller et al., 2003)				
Nonclinical controls (n=75)	0.35	<0.01	0.13	ns
Restrictive anorexia nervosa (n=21)	0.40	<0.01	0.22	ns
Binge-purge anorexia nervosa (n=40)	0.32	<0.05	0.25	ns
Bulimia nervosa (n=70)	0.09	ns	0.06	ns
Spirit possession disorder (n=112) vs. mentally healthy controls (n=73; Nijenhuis & Van Duyl, 2001)	0.65	<0.0001	0.61	<0.0001
General psychiatric patients (n=140; El-Hage et al., 2002)	0.41	<0.0001		
Dissociative disorders (n = 47) and psychiatric controls (n = 43; Nijenhuis, 1999)	0.69	<0.0001		
Somatoform dissociative disorders				
Different types (n=54) and controls with affective disorders (n=50; Roelofs et al., 2002b)	More childhood trauma in somatoform disorders (67.9% correct classification)			
Pseudo-seizures (n=27) and true epilepsy (n=72; Kuyk et al., 1999)	More severe traumatization in pseudo-epilepsy			

Note: * Correlations after partialling out absorption as a measure of fantasy proneness considerable somatoform dissociation may only emerge after very substantial traumatization. Thus, studying general psychiatric outpatients, Nijenhuis et al. (2004) found that only patients who reported four or more different types of potentially traumatizing events had high somatoform dissociation scores (see Table 17.3). This finding was essentially replicated in substance abuse patients (Baars, Nijenhuis, & Van der Hart, 2001).

When administered a structured trauma interview, patients with somatoform disorders reported more potentially traumatizing events than did affective disorder patients (Roelofs, Keijsers, Hoogduin, Näring, & Moene, 2002b). Futhermore, patients with DSM-IV conversion disorder who reported histories of *multiple* traumatization had more pseudoneurological symptoms and higher SDQ-20 scores, but not higher DES scores, than did conversion disorder patients who reported only *one* type of traumatization. Thus, somatoform dissociation seems to be a better predictor of cumulative traumatization in these patients than does psychoform dissociation.

Table 17.3 shows that the association between somatoform dissociation and cumulative traumatization is generally stronger than the association between psychoform dissociation and cumulative traumatization. Reported traumatization was predicted by somatoform dissociation over and above the influence of gender, psychoform dissociation, and posttraumatic stress symptoms in psychiatric patients (Nijenhuis et al., 2004). This predictive superiority of somatoform dissociation may be due to the inclusion of nondissociative items in psychoform dissociation instruments such as the DES and DIS-Q (i.e., items that assess selective attention and lowering of consciousness; see Chapter 11).

Although somatoform dissociation is associated with cumulative traumatization, and sometimes quite strongly, it must be noted that traumatization does *not* explain all of the variance in somatoform dissociation. It seems likely that exposure to potentially traumatizing events is only one of the factors that account for somatoform dissociation. Other known explanatory factors include age at onset of exposure to these events and lack of support (Nijenhuis et al., 1998c).

Some authors have suggested that the personality characteristic of fantasy proneness may mediate the correlation between reported potentially traumatizing events and dissociative symptoms. However, taking absorption as a measure of fantasy proneness, the correlation between reported potentially traumatizing events and somatoform dissociation remained significant after partialling out absorption in nonclinical students and nonclinical adults (Näring & Nijenhuis, 2005).

Studies of somatization symptoms and somatoform disorders have also reported a link to reported traumatization. For example, undifferentiated somatoform disorder was one of the three DSM-IV axis I diagnoses that characterized Gulf War veterans who were referred for medical and psychiatric syndromes (Labbate, Cardeña, Dimitreva, Roy, & Engel, 1998). More specifically, reports of potentially traumatizing events were correlated with both PTSD and somatoform diagnoses, and veterans who handled dead bodies had a three-fold risk of receiving a somatoform diagnosis. In addition, several studies found associations among reported traumatization, psychoform dissociation, and somatization symptoms or somatoform disorders (e.g., Atlas, Wolfson, & Lipschitz, 1995; Darves-Bornoz, 1997; Van der Kolk et al., 1996).

17.16 SOMATOFORM DISSOCIATION AND ANIMAL DEFENSIVE REACTIONS

DID and related types of DDNOS manifest alternating dissociative parts of the personality. These parts are relatively discrete, discontinuous, and resistant to integration; they vary in the degree of complexity. These alternating parts are ANPs and EPs that have particular somatoform dissociative symptoms. Exploring the roots of dissociative psychobiological systems and symptoms, Nijenhuis, Vanderlinden, and Spinhoven (1998d) drew a parallel between (1) animal defensive and recuperative states that are evoked in the face of predatory imminence and injury, and (2) the somatoform dissociative responses of patients with dissociative disorders who report trauma. Their review of animal and human research data, and clinical observations, suggested that there are cross-species similarities of disturbances of normal eating patterns and normal behavioral patterns in the face of diffuse threat. Freezing and stilling (i.e., forms of motor inhibition) occur when serious threat materializes. Analgesia occurs when a predator is about to strike. And anesthesia with total submission occurs when the attack is proceeding and escape is impossible. Finally, acute pain occurs after the threat has subsided; actions that promote recuperation then occur. In the theory of structural dissociation of the personality (Nijenhuis et al., 2004; Van der Hart et al., 2006; Steele et al., 2009b), EPs are mediated—but not exclusively so—by animal defense-like systems; ANPs are mediated by action systems for daily functioning and survival of the species. ANPs exhibit behavioral and mental avoidance reactions to EPs and the traumatic memories that are associated with EPs.

Consistent with this model, several studies have suggested that threat to life may induce analgesia and numbness (Cardeña et al., 1998; Cardeña & Spiegel, 1993; Pitman, Van der Kolk, Orr, & Greenberg, 1990; Van der Kolk, Greenberg, Orr, & Pitman, 1989). Nijenhuis et al. (1998a) conducted the first empirical test of the hypothesized similarity between animal defensive reactions and certain somatoform dissociative symptoms of dissociative disorder patients who reported trauma. Twelve clusters of clinically observed somatoform dissociative phenomena were constructed. Each cluster discriminated between patients with dissociative disorders and patients with other psychiatric diagnoses. The clusters that were hypothesized to be most similar to animal defensive reactions—motor inhibitions, anesthesia/analgesia, and disturbed eating—ranked among the four most characteristic symptom-clusters of dissociative disorder patients. Anesthesia/analgesia, urogenital pain, and freezing independently contributed to predicted caseness of dissociative disorder. The three symptom clusters anesthesia/analgesia, urogenital pain, and motor inhibitions correctly classified 93% of cases from the original sample. The symptom clusters anesthesia/analgesia and urogenital pain correctly classified 96% of cases from an independent sample. After statistically controlling for the effect of general psychopathology, the anesthesia/analgesia symptom cluster still proved to be highly predictive of dissociative disorder. These results are largely consistent with the hypothesized similarity between somatoform dissociative phenomena and animal defensive reactions.

Anesthesia symptoms characterize EPs that are fixated in total submission. Anesthesia may also occur in ANPs that are motivated to avoid aversive affective feelings and body sensations. ANPs are phobic of traumatic memories and phobic of the associated EPs (Nijenhuis & Van der Hart, 1999; Nijenhuis et al., 2004; Van der Hart et al., 2006). These phobias tend to manifest in a number of negative dissociative symptoms: amnesia, depersonalization, and sensory and emotional anesthesia. Recent data from psychobiological experimental research with EPs and ANPs support this interpretation (Hermans, Nijenhuis, Van Honk, Huntjens, & Van der Hart, 2006; Reinders et al., 2003, 2006; see also Nijenhuis & Den Boer, this volume).

Consistent with a hypothesized link between somatoform dissociation and animal defense-like reactions, somatoform dissociation (1) was predicted best by bodily threat or bodily contact from a person, or (2) was most severe in patients that reported these types of traumatization. These findings were reported in a variety of different populations: general psychiatric patients (Nijenhuis et al., 2004; Waller et al., 2000); substance abuse patients (Baars et al., 2001); somatoform patients (Roelofs et al., 2002b); women who reported childhood sexual abuse and other forms of abuse (Nijenhuis et al., 2003); and spirit disorder patients (Nijenhuis & Van Duyl, 2001). These data suggest that bodily threat may evoke an enduring activation of animal defense-like psychobiological systems, especially when the threat is recurrent and occurs in a context of emotional neglect.

In Roelof et al.'s (2002a) study of patients with somatoform dissociative disorders, physical abuse fully mediated the relationship between hypnotic susceptibility and the number of somatoform dissociative symptoms. In this study, maternal parental dysfunction (but not paternal parental dysfunction) was associated with higher SDQ-20 scores. Emotional neglect, emotional abuse, and family pathology often constitute the context in which physical and sexual abuse occur (Nijenhuis et al., 1998c). We found that emotional neglect and abuse, sexual abuse, and sexual harassment independently contributed to the prediction of somatoform dissociation. Recognizing that retrospective studies restrict causal inference (Briere & Elliott, 1993; Tabachnick & Fidell, 1989), Nijenhuis et al. noted that only prospective studies can determine whether childhood events such as sexual and physical abuse actually cause somatoform dissociation.

To date, one longitudinal study of traumatization and somatoform dissociation has been performed (Diseth, 2006). At first admission, adolescents with anorectal anomalies or Hirschsprung disease, and hospitalized controls were assessed for treatment procedures, somatic function, mental health, and dissociative experiences as measured by the Adolescent-DES. At 10-year follow-up, the patients completed the DES and SDQ-20. Anal dilatation, a painful invasive medical treatment procedure performed on daily by the parents the first 4 years, was correlated with the frequency and severity of persisting psychoform and somatoform dissociation. The procedure was the only significant predictor of A-DES and SDQ-20 scores, and one of two significant predictors of DES scores. These findings strongly suggest a causal relationship between traumatizing events in early childhood involving the body and the parents as (forced) agents of anal dilatation, and somatoform and psychoform dissociation in early adolescence.

17.17 DISCUSSION

The items of the SDQ are based on Janet's (1893, 1907/1965) symptoms of hysteria. Modern empirical data have shown that Janet's symptoms of hysteria are characteristic of 20th century dissociative disorders. Recent studies have confirmed that these symptoms involve both mental stigmata (i.e., the negative symptoms of anesthesia, analgesia, and motor inhibitions) and mental accidents (i.e., the positive symptoms of localized pain, and alternation of taste and smell preferences/aversions). Although I firmly believe that the so-called body-mind split is incorrect, I insist that the phenomenological distinction between psychoform and somatoform manifestations of dissociation is a clarifying one. It highlights a largely forgotten clinical observation—that dissociation affects the body. Moreover, modern research has affirmed that this is so.

There are no indications that somatoform dissociative symptoms are due to (1) general psychopathology or (2) suggestion. Although this is far from saying that dissociative disorder patients are immune to suggestion, or that factitious dissociative disorder cases (Draijer & Boon, 1999) do not exist, it seems reasonable to assert that suggestion does not explain somatoform dissociation.

Somatoform dissociation is a major manifestation of DSM-IV dissociative disorders, but it also characterizes many patients with DSM-IV somatoform disorders, and a subgroup of eating disordered patients. Like the dissociative disorders, somatization disorder (i.e., Briquet's syndrome) has its roots in hysteria. Briquet's pioneering research revealed that many patients with hysteria had both amnesia and a plethora of somatoform symptoms (Briquet, 1859). Contemporary research has shown that psychoform dissociation and somatization are related. For example, Saxe et al. (1994) found that two-thirds of dissociative disordered inpatients met the DSM-IV criteria for somatization disorder. Still, somatization may not be a distinct clinical entity, nor even the result of a single pathological process (Kellner, 1995). It seems likely that somatoform dissociative symptoms constitute a subgroup of somatoform symptoms.

The research to date on somatoform dissociation is more consistent with the nosology of ICD-10 (which includes dissociative disorders of movement and sensation) than the nosology of DSM-IV (which restricts dissociation to psychoform manifestations and regards somatoform manifestations of dissociation as "conversion symptoms"). The SDQ-5 in the Netherlands and the SDQ-20 in Turkey were at least as effective as the DES in screening for DSM-IV dissociative disorders. The consistent finding that psychoform and somatoform dissociation are strongly associated suggests that they are manifestations of a common process. Finally, as previously noted, somatoform dissociation is characteristic of DSM-IV conversion disorder. Patients with pseudoepileptic seizures exhibit somatoform dissociation, but not psychoform dissociation.

In conclusion, research indicates that (1) conversion symptoms should be relabeled as somatoform dissociation, and (2) the DSM-IV conversion disorders should be reclassified as somatoform dissociative disorders. The same relabeling and reclassification should probably apply to those cases of somatization disorder that are predominantly characterized by somatoform dissociation, but this is an issue that awaits further research. If research does support this thesis, it would promote a reinstitution of the 19th century category of hysteria under the general label of dissociative disorders. Such a nosological regrouping of the dissociative disorders would include the current DSM-IV dissociative disorders, DSM-IV conversion disorder (c.q., ICD-10 dissociative disorders of movement and sensation), and DSM-IV somatization disorder. Alternately, future studies of DSM-IV somatization disorder may reveal the presence of meaningful subgroups; for example, one subgroup might show severe somatoform dissociation, whereas another subgroup might show low or modest somatoform dissociation. It also seems doubtful that conversion disorder and hypochondriasis share a similar pathology. Further study of somatoform dissociation in the various DSM-IV somatoform disorders is urgently needed.

REFERENCES

American Psychiatric Association (1994). *DSM-IV: Diagnostic and statistical manual of mental disorders*, fourth edition. Washington, DC: American Psychiatric Association.

Atlas, J. A., Wolfson, M. A., & Lipschitz, D. S. (1995). Dissociation and somatization in adolescent inpatients. *Psychological Reports, 76,* 1101–1102.

Baars, E., Van der Hart, O., & Nijenhuis, E. R. S. (2001). Trauma, dissociation, and the maintenance of substance abuse. *Proceedings of the 18th International Fall Conference of the International Society for the Study of Dissociation.* New Orleans, December 2–4.

Bernstein, E., & Putnam, F. W. (1986). Development, reliability, and validity of a dissociation scale. *Journal of Nervous Mental Disease, 102*, 280–286.

Braude, S. E. (1995). *First person plural: Multiple personality and the philosophy of mind.* Lanham: Rowman and Littlefield.

Briere, J., & Elliott, D. M. (1993). Sexual abuse, family environment, and psychological symptoms: On the validity of statistical control. *Journal of Consulting and Clinical Psychology, 61*, 284–288.

Briquet, P. (1859). *Traité clinique et thérapeutique de l'hystérie* (2 vols.) [Clinical and therapeutic treatise on hysteria]. Paris: J.-P. Baillière & Fils.

Brown, R. J., Cardeña, E., Nijenhuis, E. R. S., Şar. V., & Van der Hart, O. (2007). Should DSM-IV conversion disorder be re-classified as a dissociative disorder in DSM-V? *Psychosomatics, 48,* 369–378.

Cardeña, E. (1994). The domain of dissociation. In S. J. Lynn & J. W. Rhue (Eds.), *Dissociation: Clinical and theoretical perspectives* (pp. 15–31). New York: Guilford.

Cardeña, E., Holen, A., McFarlane, A., Solomon, Z., Wilkinson, C., & Spiegel, D. (1998). A multisite study of acute stress reaction to a disaster. In *Sourcebook for the DSM-IV, Vol. IV*. Washington, DC: American Psychiatric Association.

Cardeña, E., & Spiegel, D. (1993). Dissociative reactions to the San Francisco Bay area earthquake of 1989. *American Journal of Psychiatry, 150,* 474–478.

Coons, P. M. (1994). Confirmation of childhood abuse in child and adolescent cases of multiple personality disorder and dissociative disorder not otherwise specified. *Journal of Nervous and Mental Disease, 182,* 461–464.

Darves-Bornoz, J.-M. (1997). Rape-related psychotraumatic syndromes. *European Journal of Obstetrics & Gynecology, 71,* 59–65.

Dell, P. F. (1997). Somatoform dissociation in DID, DDNOS, chronic pain, and eating disorders in a North American sample. *Proceedings of the 14th International Conference of the International Society for the Study of Dissociation,* November 8–11, p. 130.

Dell, P. F. (2002). Dissociative phenomenology of dissociative identity disorder. *Journal of Nervous and Mental Disease, 190,* 10–15.

Diseth, T. H. (2006). Dissociation following traumatic medical treatment procedures in childhood: A longitudinal follow-up. *Developmental Psychopathology, 18,* 233–251.

Draijer, N., & Boon, S. (1993). Trauma, dissociation, and dissociative disorders. In S. Boon & N. Draijer (Eds.), *Multiple personality disorder in the Netherlands: A study on reliability and validity of the diagnosis* (pp. 177–193). Amsterdam/Lisse: Swets & Zeitlinger.

Draijer, N., & Boon, S. (1999). The imitation of dissociative identity disorder: Patients at risk; therapists at risk. *Journal of Psychiatry & Law, 27,* 423–458.

El-Hage, W., Darves-Bornoz, J.-M., Allilaire, J.-F., & Gaillard, P. (2002). Posttraumatic somatoform dissociation in French psychiatric outpatients. *Journal of Trauma & Dissociation, 3*(3), 59–73.

Espirito Santo, H. M. A., & Pio-Abreu, J. L. (2007) Dissociative disorders and other psychopathological groups: exploring the differences through the Somatoform Dissociation Questionnaire (SDQ-20). *Revista Brasileira de Psiquiatria, 29*(4), 354–358.

Fleisher, W., Staley, D., Krawetz, P., Pillay, N., Arnett, J. L., & Maher, J. (2002). Comparative study of trauma-related phenomena in subjects with pseudoseizures and subjects with epilepsy. *American Journal of Psychiatry, 159,* 660–663.

Friedl, M. C., & Draijer, N. (2000). Dissociative disorders in Dutch psychiatric inpatients. *American Journal of Psychiatry, 157,* 1012–1013.

Gleaves, D. H. (1996). The sociocognitive model of dissociative identity disorder: A reexamination of the evidence. *Psychological Bulletin, 120,* 42–59.

Halligan, P. W., Athwal, B. S., Oakley, D. A., & Frackowiak, R. S. (2000). Imaging hypnotic paralysis: Implications for conversion hysteria [letter]. *Lancet, 355,* 986–987.

Hermans, E. J., Nijenhuis, E. R. S., van Honk, J., Huntjens, R., & Van der Hart, O. (2006). State dependent attentional bias for facial threat in dissociative identity disorder. *Psychiatry Research, 141,* 233–236.

Horen, S. A., Leichner, P. P., & Lawson, J. S. (1995). Prevalence of dissociative symptoms and disorders in an adult psychiatric inpatient population in Canada. *Canadian Journal of Psychiatry, 40,* 185–191.

Hornstein, N. L., & Putnam, F. W. (1992). Clinical phenomenology of child and adolescent disorders. *Journal of the American Academy of Child and Adolescent Psychiatry, 31,* 1077–1085.

Janet, P. (1889/1973). *L'automatisme psychologique*. Paris: Félix Alcan. Reprint: Société Pierre Janet, Paris.

Janet, P. (1893). *L'état mental des hystériques: Les stigmates mentaux* [The mental state of hysterics: Mental stigmata]. Paris: Rueff & Cie.

Janet, P. (1901/1977). *The mental state of hystericals*. New York: Putnam & Sons. Reprint: University Publications of America, Washington DC.

Janet, P. (1907/1965). *Major symptoms of hysteria*. London: Macmillan. Reprint: Hafner, New York.

Janet, P. (1911/1983). *L'état mental des hystériques*. Paris: Félix Alcan. Second extended edition. Reprint: Lafitte Reprints, Marseille.

Janet, P. (1929/1984). *L'évolution psychologique de la personnalité*. Paris: Chahine. Reprint: Société Pierre Janet, Paris.

Johnson, J. G., Cohen, P., Kasen, S., & Brook, J. S. (2006). Dissociative disorders among adults in the community, impaired functioning, and axis I and II comorbidity. *Journal of Psychiatric Research., 40,* 131–140.

Kellner, R. (1995). Psychosomatic syndromes, somatization, and somatoform disorders. *Psychotherapy and Psychosomatics, 61,* 4–24.

Kihlstrom, J. F. (1994). One hundred years of hysteria. In S. J. Lynn & J. W. Rhue (Eds.), *Dissociation: Clinical and theoretical perspectives* (pp. 365–395). New York: Guilford.

Kluft, R. P. (1995). The confirmation and disconfirmation of memories of abuse in DID patients: A naturalistic clinical study. *Dissociation, 8,* 251–258.

Kuyk, J., Spinhoven, P., Van Emde Boas, M. D., & Van Dyck, R. (1999). Dissociation in temporal lobe epilepsy and pseudo-epileptic seizure patients. *The Journal of Nervous and Mental Disease, 187,* 713–720.

Labatte, L. A., Cardeña, E., Dimitreva, J., Roy, M. J., & Engel, C. (1998). Psychiatric syndromes in Persian Gulf War veterans: An association of handling dead bodies with somatoform disorders. *Psychotherapy and Psychosomatics, 67,* 275–279.

Laria, A. J., & Lewis-Fernández, R. (2001). The Professional fragmentation of experience in the study of dissociation, somatization, and culture. *Journal of Trauma & Dissociation, 2*(3), 17–47.

Lewis, D. O., Yeager, C. A., Swica, Y., Pincus, J. H., & Lewis, M. (1997). Objective documentation of child abuse and dissociation in 12 murderers with dissociative identity disorder. *American Journal of Psychiatry, 154*, 1703–1710.

Maaranen, P., Tanskanen, A., Haatainen, K., Honkalampi, K., Koivumaa-Honkanen, H., Hintikka, J. et al. (2005). The relationship between psychological and somatoform dissociation in the general population. *Journal of Nervous and Mental Disease, 193,* 690–692.

Maaranen, P., Tanskanen, A., Haatainen, K., Koivumaa-Honkanen, H., Hintikka, J., & Viinamaki, H. (2004). Somatoform dissociation and adverse childhood experiences in the general population. *Journal of Nervous and Mental Disease, 192,* 337–342.

Maldonado, J. R., & Spiegel, D. (1998). Trauma, dissociation and hypnotizability. In J. D. Bremner & C. A. Marmar (Eds.), *Trauma, memory and dissociation* (pp. 57–106). Washington, DC: American Psychiatric Press.

Merskey, H. (1992). The manufacture of personalities: The production of multiple personality disorder. *British Journal of Psychiatry, 160*, 327–340.

Merskey, H. (1997). Tests of "dissociation" and mood disorder (letter). *British Journal of Psychiatry, 171*, 487.

Moene, F. C., Spinhoven, P., Hoogduin, C. A. L., Sandijck, P., & Roelofs, K. (2001). Hypnotizability, dissociation, and trauma in patients with a conversion disorder: An exploratory study. *Clinical Psychology and Psychoptherapy, 8*, 400–410.

Myers, C. S. (1940). *Shell shock in France 1914-18*. Cambridge: Cambridge Unversity Press.

Nähring, G., & Nijenhuis, E. R. S. (2005). Relationships between self-reported potentially traumatizing events, psychoform and somatoform dissociation, and absorption, in two non-clinical populations. *Australian and New Zealand Journal of Psychiatry, 39*, 982–988.

Nemiah, J. C. (1991). Dissociation, conversion, and somatization. In A. Tasman & S. M. Goldfinger (Eds.), *American Psychiatric Press Annual Review of Psychiatry* (Vol. 10) pp. 248–260. Washington, DC: American Psychiatric Press.

Nijenhuis, E. R. S. (2004). *Somatoform dissociation: Phenomena, measurement, and theoretical issues*. New York: W. W. Norton.

Nijenhuis, E. R. S., & Den Boer, J. A. (2009) Psychobiology of traumatization and structural dissociation of the personality. In P. F. Dell & J. A. O'Neil (Eds.), *Dissociation and the dissociative disorders: DSM-V and beyond* (pp. 337–365). New York: Routledge.

Nijenhuis, E. R. S., Spinhoven, P., Van Dyck, R., Van der Hart, O., De Graaf, A. M. J., & Knoppert, E. A. M. (1997a). Dissociative pathology discriminates between bipolar mood disorder and dissociative disorder. *British Journal of Psychiatry, 170,* 581.

Nijenhuis, E. R. S., Spinhoven P., Van Dyck R., Van der Hart, O., & Vanderlinden, J. (1996). The development and the psychometric characteristics of the Somatoform Dissociation Questionnaire (SDQ-20). *Journal of Nervous and Mental Disease, 184,* 688–694.

Nijenhuis, E. R. S., Spinhoven, P., Van Dyck, R., Van der Hart, O., & Vanderlinden J. (1997b). The development of the Somatoform Dissociation Questionnaire (SDQ-5) as a screening instrument for dissociative disorders. *Acta Psychiatrica Scandinavica, 96*, 311–318.

Nijenhuis, E. R. S., Spinhoven, P., Vanderlinden, J., Van Dyck, R., & Van der Hart, O. (1998a). Somatoform dissociative symptoms as related to animal defensive reactions to predatory threat and injury. *Journal of Abnormal Psychology, 107*, 63–73.

Nijenhuis, E. R. S., Spinhoven, P., Van Dyck, R., Van der Hart, O., & Vanderlinden J. (1998b). Psychometric characteristics of the Somatoform Dissociation Questionnaire: A replication study. *Psychotherapy and Psychosomatics, 67*, 17–23.

Nijenhuis, E. R. S., Spinhoven, P., Van Dyck, R., Van der Hart, O., & Vanderlinden J. (1998c). Degree of somatoform and psychological dissociation in dissociative disorders is correlated with reported trauma. *Journal of Traumatic Stress, 11*, 711–730.

Nijenhuis, E. R. S., & Van der Hart, O. (1999). Somatoform dissociative phenomena: A Janetian Perspective. In J. M. Goodwin & R. Attias (Eds.), *Splintered reflections: Images of the body in trauma* (pp. 89–127). New York: Basic Books.

Nijenhuis, E. R. S., Van der Hart, O., & Kruger, K. (2002). The psychometric characteristics of the Traumatic Experiences Questionnaire (TEC): First findings among psychiatric outpatients. *Clinical Psychology and Psychotherapy, 9*(3), 200–210.

Nijenhuis, E. R. S., Van der Hart, O., Kruger, K., & Steele, K. (2004). Somatoform dissociation, reported abuse, and animal defence-like reactions. *Australian and New Zealand Journal of Psychiatry, 38*, 678–686.

Nijenhuis, E. R. S., Van der Hart, O., & Steele, K. (2004). Strukturelle Dissoziation der Persönlichkeitsstruktur, traumatischer Ursprung, phobische Residuen [Structural dissociation of the personality: Traumatic origins, phobic maintenance]. In L. Reddemann, A. Hofmann, & U. Gast, *Psychotherapie der dissoziativen Störungen* (pp. 47–69). Stuttgart: Thieme.

Nijenhuis, E. R. S., Vanderlinden, J., & Spinhoven, P. (1998d). Animal defensive reactions as a model for trauma-induced dissociative reactions. *Journal of Traumatic Stress, 11*, 243–260.

Nijenhuis, E. R. S., & Van Duyl, M. (2001). Dissociative symptoms and reported trauma among Ugandan patients with possessive trance disorder. *Proceedings of the 18th International Fall Conference of the International Society for the Study of Dissociation.* New Orleans, December 2–4.

Nijenhuis, E. R. S., Van Dyck, R., Spinhoven, P., Van der Hart, O., Chatrou, M., Vanderlinden, J., & Moene, F. (1999). Somatoform dissociation discriminates among diagnostic categories over and above general psychopathology. *Australian and New Zealand Journal of Psychiatry, 33,* 512–520.

Nijenhuis, E. R. S., Van Dyck, R., Ter Kuile, M. M., Mourits, M. J. E., Spinhoven, P., & Van der Hart, O. (2003). Evidence for associations among somatoform dissociation, psychological dissociation and reported trauma in patients with chronic pelvic pain. *Journal of Psychosomatic Obstetrics and Gynecology, 24,* 87–98.

Nijenhuis, E. R. S., Van Dyck, R., Van der Hart, O., & Spinhoven, P. (1998e). Somatoform dissociation is unlikely to be a result of indoctrination by therapists (letter). *British Journal of Psychiatry, 172,* 452.

Nijenhuis, E. R. S., Van Engen, A., Kusters, I., & Van der Hart, O. (2001). Peritraumatic somatoform and psychological dissociation in relation to recall of childhood sexual abuse. *Journal of Trauma & Dissociation, 2*(3), 49–68.

Othmer, E., & DeSouza, C. (1985). A screening test for somatization disorder (hysteria). *American Journal of Psychiatry, 142*, 1146–1149.

Pitman, R. K., Van der Kolk, B. A., Orr, S. P., & Greenberg, M. S. (1990). Naloxone reversible stress induced analgesia in post traumatic stress disorder. *Archives of General Psychiatry, 47,* 541–547.

Pribor, E. F., Yutzy, S. H., Dean, J. T., & Wetzel, R. D. (1993). Briquet's syndrome, dissociation and abuse. *American Journal of Psychiatry, 150,* 1507–1511.

Putnam, F. W., & Carlson, E. B. (1998). Hypnosis, dissociation, and trauma: Myths, metaphors, and mechanisms. In J. D. Bremner & C. A. Marmar (Eds.), *Trauma, memory, and dissociation* (pp. 27–56). Washington, DC: American Psychiatric Press.

Putnam, F. W., Helmers, K., Horowitz, L. A., & Trickett, P. K. (1995). Hypnotizability and dissociativity in sexually abused girls. *Child Abuse and Neglect, 19,* 645–655.

Reinders, A. A. T. S., Nijenhuis, E. R. S., Paans, A. M. J., Korf, J., Willemsen, A. T. M., & Den Boer, J. A. (2003). One brain, two selves. *NeuroImage, 20,* 2119–2125.

Reinders, A. A. T. S., Nijenhuis, E. R. S., Quak, J., Korf, J., Paans, A. M. J., Haaksma, J., Willemsen, A. T. M., & Den Boer, J. (2006). Psychobiological characteristics of dissociative identity disorder: A symptom provocation study. *Biological Psychiatry, 60,* 730–740.

Rey, J. M., Morris-Yates, A., & Stanislaw, H. Measuring the accuracy of diagnostic tests using Receiver Operating Characteristics (ROC) analysis. *International Journal of Methods in Psychiatric Research, 2,* 39–50.

Roelofs, K., Hoogduin, K. A., Keijsers, G. P., Naring, G. W., Moene, F. C., & Sandijck, P. (2002a). Hypnotic susceptibility in patients with conversion disorder. *Journal of Abnormal Psychology, 111,* 390–395.

Roelofs, K., Keijsers, G. P., Hoogduin, K. A., Naring, G. W., & Moene, F. C. (2002b). Childhood abuse in patients with conversion disorder. *American Journal of Psychiatry, 159,* 1908–1913.

Ross, C. A., Heber, S., Norton, G. R., & Anderson, G. (1989). Somatic symptoms in multiple personality disorder. *Psychosomatics, 30,* 154–160.

Şar, V., Akyüz, G., & Doğan, O. (2007). Prevalence of dissociative disorders among women in the general population. *Psychiatry Research, 149,* 169–176.

Şar, V., Akyüz, G., Kundakçı, T., Kızıltan, E., & Doğan, O. (2004). Childhood trauma, dissociation, and psychiatric comorbidity in patients with conversion disorder. *American Journal of Psychiatry, 161,* 2271–2276.

Şar, V., Kundakçı, T., Kızıltan, E., Bahadır, B., & Aydıner, O. (1998). Reliability and validity of the Turkish version of the Somatoform Dissociation Questionnaire (SDQ-20). *Proceeding of the International Society of Dissociation 15th International Fall Conference.* Seattle, November 14–17.

Şar, V., Kundakçı, T., Kızıltan, E., Yargıç, I. L., Tutkun, H., Bakım, B., Aydıner, O., Özpulat, T., Keser, V., & Özdemir, Ö. (1999). Frequency of dissociative disorders among psychiatric outpatients with borderline personality disorder. *Proceedings of the 6th European Conference on Traumatic Stress: Psychotraumatology, clinical practice, and human rights.* Istanbul, Turkey, June 5–8, p. 115.

Şar, V., Kundakçı, T., Kızıltan, E., Bakım, B., & Bozkurt, O. (2000). Differentiating dissociative disorders from other diagnostic groups through somatoform dissociation in Turkey. *Journal of Trauma & Dissociation, 1*(4), 67–80.

Şar, V., & Öztürk, E. (2009) Psychotic presentations of Dissociative Identity Disorder. In P. F. Dell & J. A. O'Neil (Eds.), *Dissociation and the dissociative disorders: DSM-V and beyond* (pp. 535–545). New York: Routledge.

Saxe, G. N., Chinman, G., Berkowitz, M. D., Hall, K., Lieberg, G., Schwartz J., & Van der Kolk, B. A. (1994). Somatization in patients with dissociative disorders. *American Journal of Psychiatry, 151,* 1329–1334.

Saxe, G. N., Van der Kolk, B. A., Berkowitz, R., Chinman, G., Hall, K., & Lieberg, G. (1993). Dissociative disorders in psychiatric inpatients. *American Journal of Psychiatry, 150,* 1037–1042.

Somer, E., & Dell, P. F. (2005). Development of the Hebrew-Multidimensional Inventory of Dissociation (H-MID): a valid and reliable measure of pathological dissociation. *Journal of Trauma & Dissociation, 6,* 31–53.

Spiegel, D., Hunt, T., & Dondershine, H. E. (1988). Dissociation and hypnotizability in posttraumatic stress disorder. *American Journal of Psychiatry, 145,* 301–305.

Spitzer, C., Spelsberg, B., Grabe, H.-J., Mundt, B., & Freiberger, H. (1999). Dissociative experiences and psychopathology in conversion disorders. *Journal of Psychosomatic Research, 46,* 291–294.

Steele, K., Dorahy, M. J., van der Hart, O., & Nijenhuis, E. R. S. (2009a). Dissociation versus alterations in consciousness. In P. F. Dell & J. A. O'Neil (Eds.), *Dissociation and the dissociative disorders: DSM-V and beyond* (pp. 155–169). New York: Routledge.

Steele, K., Dorahy, M. J., van der Hart, O., & Nijenhuis, E. R. S. (2009b). The theory of trauma-related structural dissociation of the personality. In P. F. Dell & J. A. O'Neil (Eds.), *Dissociation and the dissociative disorders: DSM-V and beyond* (pp. 239–258). New York: Routledge.

Steinberg, M. (1994). *Interviewer's guide to the structured clinical interview for DSM-IV dissociative disorders (revised ed.).* Washington, DC: American Psychiatric Press.

Stutman, R. K., & Bliss, E. L. (1985). Posttraumatic stress disorder, hypnotizability, and imagery. *American Journal of Psychiatry, 142,* 741–743.

Tabachnick, B. G., & Fidell, L. S. (1989). *Using multivariate statistics,* Second edition. Northridge: Harper Collins Publishers.

Van der Hart, O., & Friedman, B. (1989). A reader's guide to Pierre Janet on dissociation: A neglected intellectual heritage. *Dissociation, 2,* 3–16.

Van der Hart, O., Nijenhuis, E. R. S., & Steele, K. (2006). *The haunted self: Structural dissociation and the treatment of chronic traumatization.* New York/London: W. W. Norton.

Van der Hart, O., Nijenhuis, E. R. S, Steele, K., & Brown, D. (2004). Trauma-related dissociation: Conceptual clarity lost and found. *Australian and New Zealand Journal of Psychiatry, 38,* 906–914.

Van der Hart, O., & Op den Velde, W. (1995). Traumatische herinneringen [Traumatic memories]. In O. van der Hart (Ed.), *Trauma, dissociatie en hypnose* [Trauma, dissociation and hypnosis], 3rd edition (pp. 79–101). Lisse, The Netherlands: Swets & Zeitlinger.

Van der Hart, O., Van Dijke, A., Van Son, M. J. M., & Steele, K. (2000). Somatoform dissociation in traumatized World War I combat soldiers: A neglected clinical heritage. *Journal of Trauma & Dissociation, 1*(4), 33–66.

Van der Hart, O., Witztum, E., & Friedman, B. (1993). From hysterical psychosis to reactive dissociative psychosis. *Journal of Traumatic Stress, 6,* 43–64.

Van der Kolk, B. A., & Fisler, R. (1995). Dissociation and the fragmentary nature of traumatic memories: Overview and exploratory study. *Journal of Traumatic Stress, 8,* 505–525.

Van der Kolk, B. A., Greenberg, M. S., Orr, S. P., & Pitman, R. K. (1989). Endogenous opioids, stress induced analgesia, and posttraumatic stress disorder. *Psychopharmacalogy Bulletin, 25,* 417–422.

Van der Kolk, B. A., Pelcovitz, D., Roth, S., Mandel, F. C., McFarlane, A. C., & Herman, J. L. (1996). Dissociation, somatization, and affect dysregulation: The complexity of adaptation to trauma. *American Journal of Psychiatry, 153* (Festschrift Supplement), 83–93.

Vanderlinden, J. (1993). *Dissociative experiences, trauma, and hypnosis: Research findings and clinical applications in eating disorders.* Delft: Eburon.

Van Ommeren, M., de Jong, J. T., Sharma, B., Komproe, I., Thapa, S. B., & Cardena, E. (2001). Psychiatric disorders among tortured Bhutanese refugees in Nepal. *Archives of General Psychiatry, 58,* 475–482.

Yücel, B., Özyalçın, S., Sertel, H. O., Çamlıca, H., Ketenci, A., & Talu, G. K. (2002). Childhood traumatic events and dissociative experiences in patients with chronic headache and low back pain. *Clinical Journal of Pain, 18,* 394–401.

Waller, G., Hamilton, K., Elliott, P., Lewendon, J., Stopa, L. Waters, A., Kennedy, F., Chalkley, J., F., Lee, G., Pearson, D., Kennerley, H., Hargreaves, I., & Bashford, V. (2000). Somatoform dissociation, psychological dissociation and specific forms of trauma. *Journal of Trauma & Dissociation, 1*(4), 81–98.

Waller, G., Babbs, M., Wright, F., Potterton, C., Meyer, C., & Leung, N. (2003). Somatoform dissociation in eating-disordered patients. *Behavior Research & Therapy, 41,* 619–627.

World Health Organization (1992). *The ICD-10 classification of mental and behavioral disorders. Clinical description and diagnostic guidelines.* Geneva: Author.

18 The Self-System as Mechanism for the Dissociative Disorders: An Extension of the Perceptual Theory of Dissociation

Donald B. Beere, PhD, ABPP

OUTLINE

Alter personalities are complex; they probably do not develop from a single trauma or without substantial preparatory experience and psychological mediation. Derealization, on the other hand, is a less complex psychological process; this alteration in how the world is perceived is a more immediate response to current sensory input. These two observations about alters and derealization reflect the fact that dissociation is characterized by two quite different phenomena: (1) alters and (2) perceptual alterations. Based on his perceptual theory of dissociation, Beere (1995) asserted that the creation of an alter identity is an order of phenomenon different from dissociative perceptual experience (though, in the process of living, these two phenomena often occur together). Amnesia is a third type of dissociative phenomenon that stands on its own (as well as being strongly linked to alter identities).

In short, the domain of dissociation has three conceptual foci: dissociative perception, alters, and amnesia. This chapter will present a theoretical explanation of these phenomena: the first theoretical explanation pertains to dissociative perception; the second has to do with the functioning of the self-system and how that leads to depersonalization, amnesia, and alter identities in fugue and Dissociative Identity Disorder (DID).

18.1 DISSOCIATIVE PERCEPTION

Beere's (1995) perceptual theory of dissociation asserts that dissociative perception stems from a blocking-out of the perceptual background. Experience generally presents itself whole, but it has the following structure: (1) I, (2) having this mind, (3) in this body, (4) in this world, (5) all of which are in time, perceive this figure in this ground (Figure 18.1). These five components comprise the background framework for all perceptual experience; each of us takes this figure-ground-background organization of perceptual experience for granted. The term *background* defines these five ever-present components of the perceptual framework. Everyday experience involves a constant flow of different figure/ground perceptions; time, world, body, mind, and identity usually reside in the background. *During dissociation, however, the background is lost or loses its constancy. Because*

Inherent action of consciousness	Essential structures of perception	
CONSCIOUSNESS constitutes	Identity Mind Body World	in and over TIME

FIGURE 18.1 The essential structures of all perception according to the perceptual theory of dissociation (see Merleau-Ponty, 1962).

the lived-integration of figure-ground-background constitutes meaningful lived-experience, the rupture of this lived-integration makes dissociative experience weird, bizarre, or uncanny.

All of these aspects of experience—identity, the world, and its constituents (i.e., inanimate objects and living beings), my body, my mind, even the experience of time—are created in consciousness, from consciousness, and through consciousness (Merleau-Ponty, 1962). To emphasize this point, my identity—who I am—is *not* created by me. Rather, I, as I know myself, am the creation of consciousness. Two alternative perspectives might be helpful in clarifying these ideas. Harry Stack Sullivan's (1956) self-system approximates the creation of self in consciousness because the self-system creates the "I," the "other," and the relationship between them. Alternatively, from a neuropsychological perspective, everything we experience must be "created" in the brain. All neurological input must be integrated into the various particulars we experience, whether external objects, our bodies, our minds, or our identities.

In a situation that leads to dissociative perception, the individual blocks out the background by focusing solely on one critical aspect of the situation. That aspect is of such importance that perception focuses on it exclusively—and blocks out the background. Those blocked inputs from the background become dissociative perceptual experiences.

Can dissociative perception occur in the absence of environmental situations of determining significance? Yes, but such dissociative perception has an earlier origin in trauma. That is, at an earlier moment of trauma, reactive perceptual dissociation occurred. Those particular perceptual dissociative experiences (i.e., the world looking foggy; objects appearing larger or smaller; time speeding up or slowing down; experiencing one's body as distant, not mine, or mechanical) became conditioned to specific cues in that traumatic situation. Subsequent encounters with those cues evoke the related dissociative perceptual experiences. When dissociative perceptual experiences occur in this kind of context, they are appropriately considered to be dissociative *symptoms* (rather than dissociative *experiences*). So, specific dissociative perceptions are often learned responses to specific cues. This conclusion is based on the author's clinical experience as well as his attempt to explain the relationship between non-trauma-associated dissociative perceptual experiences and dissociative symptoms.

This explanation of dissociative symptoms requires empirical validation. Several related questions also need empirical answers. Under what conditions does a dissociative perceptual experience later become a dissociative symptom? When and when not? What seems to make the difference?

In addition to the above *cue-linked explanation* of dissociative perception, there is also a *state-linked explanation*: when an individual experiences a state in which a dissociative experience previously occurred, the state evokes the same dissociative experience—which is now properly considered to be a dissociative symptom. Said differently, when the state in question re-presents itself, it also re-presents the dissociative experience as a *symptom* (because the dissociative experience was originally a component of that state).

For example, as a client discussed losing his job, he felt more and more derealized. This sense of personal distance and unreality was part of the original experience of being fired. Discussing the experience in session re-presented the dissociation-linked state which, in turn, evoked the original experience of distance and unreality.

Although clients often say that they chronically feel depersonalized or derealized, in the author's clinical experience these dissociative symptoms come and go; they wax and wane in strength. Dissociative clients notice the dissociative symptoms, but often they do not notice the symptoms' variations. When given an assignment to track their symptoms, clients begin to realize that specific stimuli or contexts precede the dissociation. These stimuli need not be external. Thinking about the car accident, hearing news about traffic problems, or hearing sirens might evoke the dissociative symptom. Similarly, physical states, such as anxiety, over-caffeination, or a startle might evoke the symptom. Some clients have such extensive trauma histories that they seem to encounter almost continual triggers of dissociation.

Finally, there are nonpathological dissociative experiences related to meditation and other practices. Practitioners can learn to restrict perception such that dissociative experiences arise.

18.2 DEPERSONALIZATION DISORDER AND THE SELF-SYSTEM

Depersonalization can also be caused by a self-system that rigidly excludes specific experiences. Harry Stack Sullivan (1956) developed the concept of the self-system in order to explain the functioning of the individual. According to Sullivan, the self-system is the inner structuring of awareness that maintains me-you relationships. There are good and bad aspects of the "me" that reciprocally interrelate with good and bad "yous." Thus, there are various me-you relationships. Certain experiences fall outside the range established by the self-system and are deemed to be "not-me." When an experience is "not-me," I am likely to say "That just wasn't me" and I would feel what Sullivan called "uncanny emotion"—for example, awe or horror. *Dissociative symptoms are not-me.* When dissociative symptoms occur, they are experienced as being bizarre or weird. Using Sullivanian terminology, I would say that these are experiences that I cannot integrate into my self-system.

The phenomenological notion of the constituting character of consciousness is superordinate to Sullivan's concept of the self-system. From the phenomenological viewpoint, the background (Beere, 1995; Merleau-Ponty, 1962) is the result of the constituting character of consciousness. In other words, identity, mind, body, world, and time are all constituted in consciousness. Sullivan's self-system conceptualizes how the individual creates a sense of "me" in relation to "others." These Sullivanian concepts are subsumed by Merleau-Ponty's more comprehensive model of experience (i.e., I, having this mind, in this body, in this world, all of which are in time, perceive this other). The self-system structures how I view myself and others, my body, world events, and what will and can happen over time. Stated differently, my beliefs about who I am, how others are, the nature of reality, my religious beliefs, what is possible for me individually, in relationships, or in my work are all subtended by, and constituted within, this self-system. At this juncture, it is essential to note that, within consciousness, there can be multiple self-systems.

The self-system limits what can be experienced. This limitation allows for the establishment of this particular individual who relates in these particular ways to others, has these specific beliefs and attitudes, engages in these particular actions, and feels these particular emotions. Being born at a particular time in history or to a specific ethnic group also limits or defines who and how an individual will become. This limiting defines an individual's existence as this and not that. Consciousness is more inclusive than what becomes limited as a particular individual; yet, consciousness has its own boundaries and limitations. For example, sight and hearing work only within certain limits. *The self-system establishes what is of determining significance for the individual.* Experiences of determining significance are those that are most likely to evoke dissociative perceptual experiences (see Figure 18.2). The limits of consciousness are drawn in an amoeba-like fashion in order to indicate its boundaries (e.g., range of perceivable light, sound, or kinds of tactile input). This, then, represents the range of what is possible for, in, and through consciousness.

Now let us consider what happens when an individual begins to have experiences that lie outside the limits of his or her *self-system.* Unlike consciousness that limits what can be experienced, the self-system only limits what *ought* to be experienced. When experiences lie outside the boundaries of the self-system, depersonalization ensues. From the point of view of the self-system, such experiences are not-me; as such, they elicit uncanny emotion.

Example. My client was an accountant. He was logical, organized, and hard-working. From his point of view, he had done everything required to get promoted. He referred himself for treatment because of depersonalization. I discovered that he did everything asked of him, even if it seemed unfair or, to my ears, hostile and undercutting. He tried to be unflaggingly upbeat. When an action by his supervisor would have evoked anger from almost anyone, he felt no anger. As homework, I asked him to track his experience of dissociation. When did it occur? Where and how did it come and go? What was the dissociative experience? Before doing this assignment, he claimed that the depersonalization was constant. Several weeks later, however, he reported that he had discovered that his experience of dissociation varied from situation to situation. He said that he had become less dissociated at home. He noted that his depersonalization tended to be associated with conflictual situations at the office. In successive weeks, he began to report feelings of

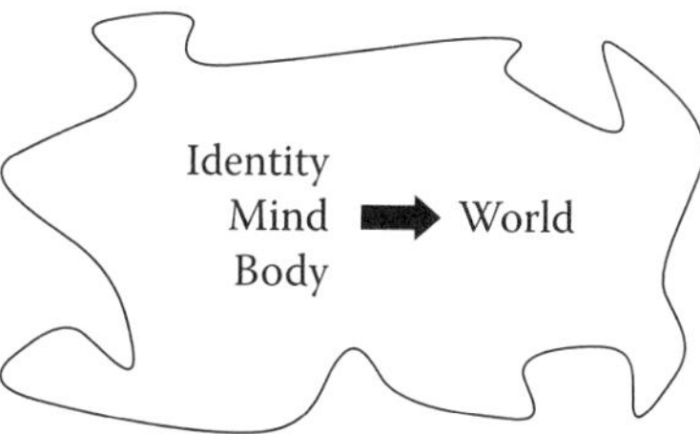

FIGURE 18.2 Existence as constituted within the limits of consciousness.

irritation and anger; concomitantly, the intensity of his depersonalization diminished and, at times, remitted.

He was then passed over for promotion, an event that exacerbated his depersonalization. At this point, the boundaries of his self-system quickly became apparent. This logical, "good," and fair-minded man was confronted by rage, an emotion discrepant from how he constituted himself. At the same time, he was confronted by his lived-belief in fair and equitable treatment, his lived-belief that hard and good work has a just reward, and his lived-belief that being assertive and angry are counterproductive. He reported that he did not like having emotions; they were not only disconcerting, but difficult to experience. As he integrated these experiences into his understanding of himself, others, and the world, his depersonalization diminished and he began to feel consistently real.

18.3 AMNESTIC DISORDER

A theoretical understanding of amnesia can be developed by examining what happens when the amnesia lifts, especially during the reliving of previously amnestic trauma.

The following clinical example is an introduction to several concepts that I will present below. Early in therapy my client relived a particularly violent rape, perceiving my office as a field and seeing the rapists as present. Though she responded to my words during the reliving, I later discovered that my words had become "included" as part of the reexperienced rape. After the reliving ended, she had no memory for the reliving and the rape from her past. On later occasions, she again relived the rape following recollection of specific rape-preceding details. Still later, after working through the rape in therapy, she recalled the rape as a past event and did not relive it.

Based on such clinical evidence as the preceding example, I draw the following conclusions about relived traumas. Relived traumas change present-time perception, repeat identically as a series of past events experienced as taking place "now," do not lead to change unless recalled as past events, occur without conscious choice, and are triggered by trauma-linked stimuli occurring in a precipitating context. Finally, traumas that are relived remain amnestic until they are psychologically metabolized and resolved. These conclusions are not new; they closely track conclusions that were first drawn by Janet (van der Hart & Friedman, 1989) over a century ago.

As a prelude to examining the mechanisms of traumatic reliving, let us first examine some basic mechanisms of perception. In perception, a stimulus-array impinges on the sensory system. To be perceived, the array must be integrated as a meaningful, perceptual figure (see Burton, 1990a, 1990b). To accomplish this, the received sensory array is automatically compared, outside of conscious awareness, to other arrays stored in memory, until a match is found. When that match is found, the array is then "perceived" as "that particular percept." Context guides this automatic, nonconscious matching process. An example may shed light on this abstruse process.

Some individuals, when viewing modern art, ask "What is it?" The individual might even be subjectively aware of the inner search for known or familiar percepts. "Oh, it's like the side of a building" might suddenly bloom in awareness and the abstract painting becomes transformed into the side of a building. Thenceforth, returning to the previous, confusing way of viewing the piece of art is almost impossible; it will almost always be seen as the side of a building. In other words, the unconscious, automatic search for matching percepts brings up "side of a building."

Using this model of perception as a guide, I have argued that traumatic reliving is precipitated by exactly the same mechanism (Beere, 2001, 2002). That is, a stimulus initiates an automatic, nonconscious search to find a match and retrieves, not a present-time percept, but a nonconscious memory of an amnestic trauma. Traumas are amnestic because they were subjectively overwhelming and unmanageable. When an amnestic trauma is elicited via the mechanisms just described, it completely floods conscious awareness with the overwhelming, unmanageable emotions and sensations that occurred at that prior time. Awareness apprehends the present environment as if it were the past. Once activated, the relived trauma unfolds, as if it were a present-time experience, eventually stopping on its own.

One might critique the use of perception as an explanatory paradigm by saying that the relived trauma is simply a learned response to triggering cues. A learned response, however, cannot explain what happens when a trauma is relived. How can one explain as a "learned response" the temporal unfolding of a long series of past events, as if they are being experienced right now? A learning paradigm can explain neither the fullness of the reexperiencing nor its power to change the person's perception of the current environment.

Exposure is the treatment of choice for PTSD. Specifically, the client needs to repeatedly experience the traumatic emotion with no negative consequences. According to this treatment rationale, the fear response will eventually extinguish. The reliving experience seems to be precisely what exposure attempts to activate—the full sensory and emotional experience. When reliving occurs spontaneously, however, this exposure to the trauma usually does not lead to resolution. Why? Because *conscious recall of the trauma continues to be unavailable.* The individual clearly remembers the trauma, but as a reexperiencing rather than as a conscious memory. Again, why? Why an intense reexperiencing, rather than a memory? One explanation is that the trauma has not been filed in a way that allows for its resolution and for its being remembered as a normal memory. Clinical experience has shown that a trauma is not resolved until it (1) is available to conscious awareness and memory, and (2) does not evoke overwhelming emotions when remembered.

This explanation posits that there are different memory systems (i.e., conscious and nonconscious) and different retrieval processes (i.e., conscious memory retrieval and automatic, nonconscious search). In the psychological literature, there is a distinction between narrative and procedural memory and between explicit and implicit memory. Narrative and explicit memory are available to conscious recall, but procedural and implicit memory are not. Memory for relived trauma, however, seems to be different from the foregoing. Brewin (2003) draws a similar distinction, positing a situationally accessible memory system.

Perhaps there is a different dichotomy among memory systems than is reflected by dichotomies such as implicit/explicit, and so on: (1) memory that preserves an event as an ongoing first-person experience; (2) memory that is nonimmediate, psychologically distant, and accompanied by a conviction that the experience is over (even if emotionally distressing). Although one can remember and become upset by experiences that one knows are over, reliving of trauma that was previously amnestic seems to evoke an overwhelmingly intense and painful emotion. I am suggesting that relived memories have been filed as ongoing or unfinished. Successful treatment allows that experience to be stored as the second kind of memory (i.e., a memory of experience that is known to be over). Then, the individual can remember without being pulled back into the experience; the person can remember and know that the trauma is a past experience.

In short, a trauma is amnestic because it cannot be integrated into the person's existence or self-system. Using Sullivanian language, these traumatic experiences remain not-me. Using more phenomenological language, these traumatic experiences are excluded by the me-you-world structure (i.e., existence-as-constituted). Strong, overwhelming emotion is associated with the experience being outside the bounds of "my reality."

Thus, the crucial characteristic of traumas that become amnestic is that they cannot be integrated into the individual's existence-as-constituted. These traumas may involve (1) intolerable distress, (2) an unacceptable emotion, or (3) a mortifying conclusion about one's self or the world. These aspects of the situation lie outside the scope of existence-as-constituted.

18.4 FLASHBACKS AND INTRUSIONS

Flashbacks are important clinical phenomena.

Based on more than 20 years of clinical experience, I have concluded that most DID individuals are beset by flashbacks that are fragmented reexperiencings of trauma. As the therapy process deepens, these intrusions increase in both frequency and intensity. Life events, especially crises, also exacerbate flashbacks. The contextual significance of events and crises determines whether they will trigger intrusions. In my clinical experience, (1) specific life events and (2) context work together to trigger (or not trigger) flashbacks. According to what I have learned from my DID clients, *traumatic intrusions flash in and out of awareness, but are frequently, consciously ignored.* Emotional and sensory components of the trauma frequently intrude as well. Thus, a client might report anxiety, fear, dread, or some kind of somatic complaint such as a stomachache, shortness of breath, or muscle pain. Most of the DID clients that I have worked with, even if they have clear switching between alters, report frequently the intrusion of traumatic flashbacks. This is similar to Dell's (2002, 2006) conclusion that clear and explicit switching between DID alters, as presented in the DSM-IV-TR (American Psychiatric Association, 2000), is less frequent than the intrusions of alter states.

When fragmentary intrusions have been occurring (or are increasing), they typically signify an upwelling of turmoil linked to a reactivated trauma. Note that a complete reexperiencing of the trauma is not occurring; instead, fragments are surfacing during daily activities (and possibly during the session). The fragmentation is similar to what Braun (1988a, 1988b) describes in his BASK model. If the client opens up that traumatic experience, the alter who managed this particular trauma frequently comes out. Switching, then, is often reliving-linked. *When questioned persistently, the host personality may admit that she has been ignoring frequent intrusions of traumatic scenes or perceptual fragments such as smells, sensations, or visual flashes.* This DID phenomenon of ignoring traumatic intrusions is similar to what occurs in PTSD where individuals avoid traumatic reminders and vacillate between numbing and hyperarousal. In my experience, the host personality typically notices that the intrusion is uncomfortable, but she neither thinks about the intrusion, nor what it implies. The host personality might also experience a cognitive fragment of the trauma. He might say that his job situation is "like living in hell. You never know when you'll be thrown in the pit."

18.5 AMNESIA AND DISSOCIATIVE PATHOLOGY

Beere (1997) developed *The Memory Line*, an instrument that measures continuity of memory. He reported that, as dissociative pathology increased, reports of amnesia first increased and then dropped to zero. This is displayed in Table 18.1 and Figure 18.3. Notice that individuals with moderate levels of dissociativity report being amnestic. As dissociativity increases to the DID range, reports of amnesia disappear. They have amnesia for their (episodes of) amnesia. The author has heard Rick Kluft describe DID individuals as having "amnesia for amnesia." The data reported here are consistent with his description. The data indicate that individuals who are dissociative, but not DID, report more amnesia than nondissociative individuals. As the dissociative pathology enters the DID range, reports of amnesia appear to decrease, although we know clinically that there is even more amnesia. This phenomenon is similar to a host being unaware of alters. Once DID individuals become involved in psychotherapy, they become more aware of their amnesias (e.g., time losses during the day or amnesia for earlier life events).

18.6 FUGUE AND DISSOCIATIVE IDENTITY DISORDER

Amnesia is consistently associated with alter identity. In a qualitative study of switching from one alter to another, Beere (1996a, 1996b) concluded that the rigidity of the self-system generates the rigid amnestic barriers between alters.

18.6.1 The General Structure of the Experience of Externally Precipitated Switching

Externally precipitated switching from one personality to another has three contexts: (1) DID, (2) energizing lived-situations that can lead to action for a non-host-alter, and (3) energized needs, impulses, and actions that are not included in the host's self-system.

First, within this person's experienced-totality, there are at least two personalities who can assume control of the body. They are characterized by coherent and self-referential thoughts, memories, traits, emotions, and behaviors. Second, the lived-world presents a lived-situation that energizes an alter who is not currently in control of

TABLE 18.1
Memory Line Measures and Different Levels of Dissociative Pathology

	Normal Late Adolescence	Other Psychiatric Disorders	DDNOS	PTSD DID
DES-T	< 5.17	5.18–23.22	23.23–41.57	> 41.58
N	96	77	12	3
	Percent Reporting Number of Memory Breaks			
0	75	70.1	91.7	100
1+	25	29.9	8.3	0
	Age of Earliest Memory			
M	3.42	3.26	3.62	3.00
SD	1.24	1.28	1.75	0.00
	Age of First Continuous Memory			
M	6.08	5.87	7.40	4.33
SD	2.64	2.93	4.21	1.16
	Total Length of Amnesia (Years)			
M	0.445	0.766	0.292	0.0
SD	0.964	1.54	1.01	0.0

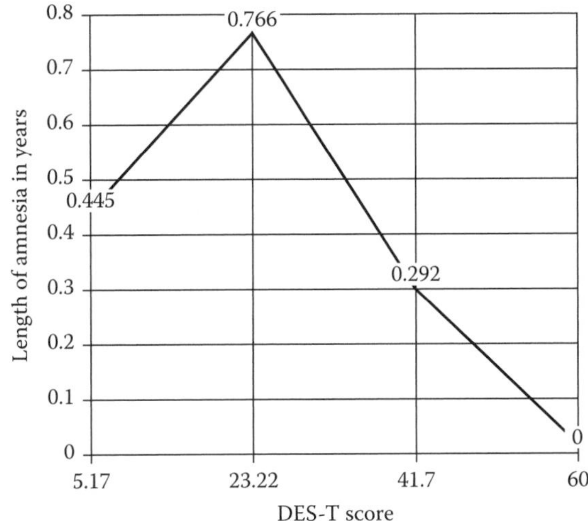

FIGURE 18.3 Length of amnesia versus dissociative pathology (DES-T).

the body. This lived-situation can lead to the enactment of the energized need, impulse or emotion. If the alter has already been energized prior to the person's entering the lived-situation, the alter will be predisposed to react even more strongly. Third, the host alter constitutes itself so as to exclude the energized need, impulse, or emotion in the lived-situation that is activating the second alter. Conversely, the self-system of the alter who is not currently in control does include the expression of these specific needs, impulses, or actions; these needs and impulses possess significance for this second alter's being-in-the-world.

The lived-world presents situations that may elicit increasingly intense responses in the noncontrolling alter. Actual switching seems to be predicated on the alter's belief that events will proceed toward a specific outcome—often, but not necessarily, one that is feared—to which the alter reacts in characteristic ways. The alter for whom these possibilities are energizing engages in psychological activities that are designed to minimize feared realities and to actualize desired lived-realities. The noncontrolling alter (whose self-system includes accepting, expressing, or enacting these particular, energized needs, impulses, or emotions) assumes control of the body after the intensity of the energized needs have overwhelmed the host alter. The switch to the second alter is evoked because a lived-possibility could, in fact, become a reality. Said differently, as the experience intensifies and becomes less distant, the host alter's ability to maintain executive control lessens until the energized alter takes over. The new alter's being-in-the-world re-presents itself as a unique lived-body in a unique lived-world. When the host alter later resumes executive control, she frequently is distressed about having switched (Beere, 1996a; Beere, 1996b).

In the preceding paragraphs, *self-system* refers to the process whereby identity-mind-body-world-time are constituted into a meaningful whole. One might also use the term *existence-as-constituted* since the entire scope of self-in-the-world is included. In this description of switching, one sees that multiple existences-as-constituted coexist within a single consciousness (see Figure 18.4).

Beere's (1996a, 1996b) study of switching did *not* support the following hypotheses: switching is (1) a coping mechanism, (2) a defense mechanism, (3) elicited by triggers, (4) a form of state-dependent learning, or (5) a change in state of consciousness. The results clearly indicated that intensity of state was a necessary precondition for externally precipitated switching—not fear, pain, or stress. Moreover, switching required that the alter currently in control (e.g., the host) have a rigid self-system that *excluded* that particular, intense state. Switching always involved taking control of the body; bodily control makes action in the world possible. The assumption of bodily control follows intensification associated with a realizable possibility. In switching, the "new" alter seeks to actualize a potential and significant lived-possibility. This analysis yields the following conclusion: self-control is bounded by the way that identity is constituted in consciousness; a self can control only those experiences that occur within its boundaries. Importantly, however, *nonexecutive alters can, without the awareness or choice of the currently executive alter, perceive worldly events, anticipate possibilities, plan future actions, and even influence the executive alter.*

One might conceptualize alters as younger self-systems (ego states) that are "trapped" in a past trauma.

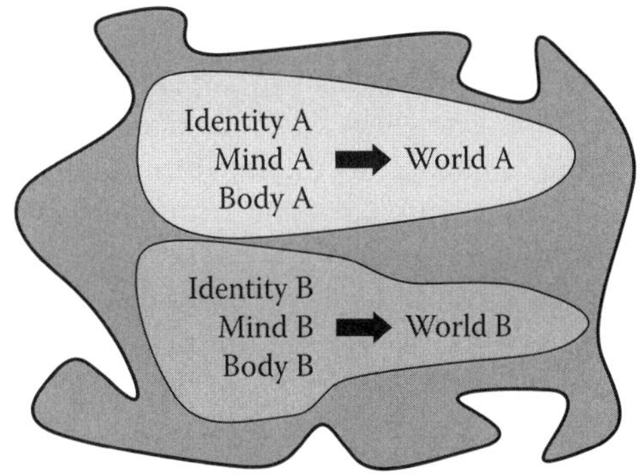

FIGURE 18.4 Illustration of alters amnestic for each other: Existence-as-constituted for each alter excludes the other.

When a current context resonates with one of those traumas, the associated ego states can readily be activated by trauma-associated perceptions. *Interestingly, in most trauma-cue-elicited switches, an alter comes out, but the associated trauma does not surface as a full reexperiencing. This clinical datum suggests that such switching somehow continues to insulate the "system" from the complete reliving of the trauma.*

From the point of view of a rigid alter, experiences outside its scope simply do not exist; if the alter experienced such alter-discrepant experiences, it could no longer be as it is. Such experiences are not-me; they are outside the scope of the self-system. When identity-discrepant experiences become too likely, there will be a switch to another alter whose scope includes those experiences.

In situations such as this, the avoided experience is of determining significance to the alter who "goes away"; an encounter with that experience would undermine that alter's existence-as-constituted. In short, because that experience would undo the alter's existence (as he or she knows it), the potential for that experience evokes a constriction of the alter's perception to what is already known. Thus, the experience is excluded, avoided, or denied. This is an example of what Sullivan called *selective inattention.*

18.7 CONCLUSION AND SUMMARY

There are several theoretical issues worth emphasizing. First, the paradigm of perception is a powerful tool for understanding dissociation and the dissociative disorders. Second, the concept of the self-system sheds still more light on dissociative perception, depersonalization, and amnesia in both DID and simpler dissociative disorders.

Dissociation is a consequence of unique ways of perceiving. One might argue that this assertion adds nothing to our understanding of dissociation because dissociative symptoms are obviously perceptual. But, if this is so, why has perception never been emphasized in previous discussions of dissociation? A perceptual analysis of dissociation distinguishes two kinds of dissociation: (1) perceptual alteration, and (2) the formation of alters. Amnesia and alters are qualitatively different from dissociative reactions.

Perceptual organization, first noted by Fine (1988), "explains" all three dissociative phenomena. This simplicity of explanation is a virtue, not a vice. Remember the principle of Occam's razor: the simplest theory that explains the largest number of phenomena is the best theory ("It is in vain to do with more what can be done with fewer"—William of Occam).

The determining significance of an experience cuts across dissociative reactions, switching, and abreactions. In other words, dissociation only occurs in situations of great import to the individual. *In a dissociative reaction*, perception narrows to a focus on what is of determining significance. *In switching*, perception narrows in order to restrict what can be experienced. That is, existence-as-constituted narrows so as to exclude certain experiences. When those experiences arise nonetheless, existence-as-constituted reorganizes itself so as to include these new experiences; this reorganization excludes the previous one. In reliving, the hitherto amnestic trauma is one that cannot be included in current existence-as-constituted; it remains unintegrated.

The model explains the involuntariness of dissociative experiences. Within the experiential structure that I have called "existence-as-constituted," identity has choice and will. Dissociative experiences occur because experiences arise spontaneously and the underlying structure of consciousness reorganizes perception outside of the purview of the identity, in other words, involuntarily.

REFERENCES

American Psychiatric Association (2000). *DSM-IV-TR. Diagnostic and statistical manual of mental disorders* (4th ed., text rev.). Washington, DC: Author.

Beere, D. B. (1995). Loss of "Background": A perceptual theory of dissociation. *Dissociation, 8*, 166–174.

Beere, D. B. (1996a). Switching: Part I – An investigation using experimental phenomenology. *Dissociation, 9*, 49–60.

Beere, D. B. (1996b). Switching: Part II – Theoretical implications of an investigation using experimental phenomenology. *Dissociation, 9*, 61–68.

Beere, D. B. (1997). The Memory Line: A measure of amnesia and continuity of memory. In L. VandeCreek (Ed.), *Innovations in clinical practice: A source book* (Vol. 15, pp. 83–95). Sarasota, FL: Professional Resource Exchange, Inc.

Beere, D. B. (2001). Abreaction: Internal context, theoretical implications, and treatment options. 18th Annual Meeting of the International Society for the Study of Dissociation, New Orleans, LA. Dec. 2001.

Beere, D. B. (2002). A perceptual view of dissociation. In P. Dell (chair), What the heck is dissociation anyway? 19th Annual International Conference of the International Society for the Study of Dissociation, Baltimore, MD, Nov. 2002.

Braun, B. G. (1988a). BASK model of dissociation: Part I. *Dissociation, 1*, 4–23.

Braun, B. G. (1988b). The BASK model of dissociation: Part II-Treatment. *Dissociation, 1*, 16–23.

Brewin, C. R. (2003). *Posttraumatic Stress Disorder: Malady or Myth?* New Haven, CT: Yale University Press.

Burton, P. (1990a). A search for explanation of the brain and learning: Elements of the psychonomic interface between psychology and neurophysiology. I. A cognitive approach to early learning. *Psychobiology, 18:2*, 119–161.

Burton, P. (1990b). A search for explanation of the brain and learning: Elements of the psychonomic interface between psychology and neurophysiology. II. Early behavior and its control, the origin of consciousness, and the rise of symbolic thought. *Psychobiology, 18:2*, 162–194.

Dell, P. F. (2002). Is dissociation fundamentally a phenomenon of the self? In P. Dell (chair), Symposium: What the heck is dissociation, anyway? 19th Annual Conference of the International Society for the Study of Dissociation, Baltimore, MD, Nov. 2002.

Dell, P. F. (2006). A new model of Dissociative Identity Disorder. *Psychiatric Clinics of North America, 29*, 1–26.

Fine, C. (1988). Thoughts on the cognitive perceptual substrate of multiple personality disorder. *Dissociation, 1*, 5–10.

Merleau-Ponty, M. (1962). *Phenomenology of perception* (trans. C. Smith). London: Routledge & Kegan Paul.

Sullivan, H. S. (1956). *The collected works of Harry Stack Sullivan*, Vols. I & II. New York: Norton.

Van der Hart, O., & Friedman, B. (1989). A reader's guide to Pierre Janet on dissociation: A neglected intellectual heritage. *Dissociation, 2*, 3–1.

19 Dissociative Multiplicity and Psychoanalysis

John A. O'Neil, MD, FRCPC

OUTLINE

19.1 INTRODUCTION: BEYOND THE DSM

"DSM-V and Beyond": this chapter clearly belongs to the "Beyond." The clinician (of whatever expertise) selects a DSM diagnosis on the basis of history and mental state exam (signs and symptoms), and then prescribes investigations and treatment. These steps needn't involve psychoanalysis, nor any other clinical interpretive discipline. But once the patient is in treatment, it becomes useful to have a systematic way not only to characterize the patient descriptively, but also to interpret the essentially unobservable: what the patient is up to—his/her intentionality or conation (wishes, drives, appetites, desires, beliefs, motives); what s/he does to cope with these and with the human and nonhuman environment (defense mechanisms and other coping strategies), including how he/she interacts with the clinician (transference/countertransference, etc.). So clinicians all engage in various issues that are of central concern to psychoanalysis, whether they intend to or not.

The complex interface of dissociation, psychoanalysis, psychiatry, and the DSM calls for some reflection on each, and on their interrelations. This may prove to be a rather lengthy foreword, but may also help put my views in context.

Psychoanalysis has been singled out as having a questionable scientific basis, with the implication that the alternatives, such as the methodology of the DSM or the basic assumptions of academic psychology, are beyond such a critique. I begin, therefore, with a reflection on the scientificity of the DSM and on psychologies and psychotherapies in general to level the playing field and sharpen the nature of the critique.

In an effort to do justice to what others have contributed and to say something original within the confines of a chapter, I have elected to address more traditional psychoanalytic concepts in greater depth, and cover more recent perspectives more summarily, as these are already well discussed by others.[1] I reverse history somewhat in discussing dissociation versus splitting prior to discussing dissociation versus repression, as this makes more conceptual sense to me. Having dealt with these "two-body problems," I then discuss "three-body problems" as reflected in various psychoanalytic triads, followed by a briefer discussion of theories that allow for "many-bodies": object relations theory, attachment theory, and ego state theory.

I conclude with a summary view and reflection on what needs to occur for dissociation to once again become part and parcel of psychoanalysis.

19.2 PUTTING THE DSM IN CONTEXT: A CRITICAL LOOK

19.2.1 Hempel, Positivism, and Operational Definitions

According to a recent editorial in the *British Journal of Psychiatry* (Turner, 2003) the paper that crucially influenced the development of the DSM-III was Carl Gustav Hempel's *Fundamentals of Taxonomy* (1959), which specifically dealt with the taxonomy of mental disorders. Hempel quotes the description of only one DSM-II diagnosis, and it is, extraordinarily, conversion reaction, in order to demonstrate that some of the terms are not "directly observable phenomena," but rather invoke theoretically assumed psychodynamic factors having meaning only in the context of psychodynamic theory, in parallel with "gravitational field," which only has meaning in the context of a theory of gravity. The DSM committee interpreted Hempel more narrowly, electing to promote criteria based on "theory-independent observables" but rejecting criteria based on theory-dependent interpretables.

Hempel's paper introduces the now-familiar idea of an operational definition, originally proposed by a physicist, Percy W. Bridgman (1927), and soon after incorporated into the logical positivist philosophy of science. The idea was that instead of defining something semantically, in terms of what it means, one ought to define it by the operation of measurement. Thereby the sciences would be exact and certain, and all else would be meaningless babble.

Did the DSM become more scientific in following Hempel? No. Medicine, psychiatry, and psychology unwittingly jumped on the positivist bandwagon just as the "harder" sciences were jumping off. Operationalism never took hold in physics, chemistry, or biology, because those subjects are basic enough that its limitations became obvious early on. Operationalism was imported into the social sciences in an effort to be more "scientific," and has lingered there because the subject matter is so complex that it isn't obvious that operationalism is conceptually flawed.

19.2.2 Popper: The Unsung Death of Positivism and Operational Definition

> Before, and even after the Second World War, books and papers went on appearing.... But by then logical positivism had really been dead some years.... Everybody knows nowadays that logical positivism is dead.... Who has done it?... I fear that I must admit responsibility. (Popper, 1972/1992)

Methodologically, Hempel's 1959 paper was one of those that "went on appearing," even though Popper's *Logik der Forschung* (1935/1968) predated it by 24 years, and Hempel would have read it in the original German. Hempel implies pre-Popperian logical inductivism throughout, that is, that we start with observation and proceed to make empirical generalizations from them, moving up from there in a kind of summary fashion to theory, and so on. Popper (1935/1968) had also demonstrated the

[1] See especially Elizabeth Howell's recent book (2005), which is the first full text devoted to dissociation and psychoanalysis.

definitional circularity of operational definitions early on[2] but this was insufficient to quash the positivist craving for certainty, nor the wholesale adoption of operational criteria into psychiatric nosology.

Popper's preemptive critique of the DSM may be less familiar to readers than his oft-quoted critique of psychoanalysis.[3] Being a Popperian psychoanalyst is not an oxymoron: J. O. Wisdom, a philosopher, was analyzed and considered becoming a psychoanalyst, but elected to work with Popper at the London School of Economics instead, while continuing to contribute significantly to the psychoanalytic literature (e.g., see Wisdom, 1961, 1984, 1987). Popper's critique remains valid and superior to some of the critiques that have appeared since then (O'Neil, 1993).

The resuscitated corpse of positivism is not limited to psychiatry. A vestige of the mistaken tradition can be found in Evidence-Based Medicine (EBM) or its subset, Evidence-Based Psychiatry (EBP), whose actual logic is admirably intact, but whose derivative rhetoric continues to imply the erroneous belief that theories and treatments can be "based on evidence." When originally and properly defined, "Evidence-based medicine is the conscientious, explicit, and judicious use of current best evidence in making decisions about the care of individual patients" (Sackett, Rosenberg, Gray, Haynes, & Richardson, 1996). The definition is excellent and precise: it applies to one's clinical judgment—not to the truth or validity of theories or treatments themselves. In practice, the methods of EBP are soundly hypothetico-deductive, convincingly separating out worthy hypotheses from mistaken ones on the basis of evidence, but also tempting one into the false conclusion that the surviving psychiatric "truths" are themselves based on evidence, as invited by the moniker, Evidence-Based Psychiatry. The specific logical error involved is the Fallacy of Affirming the Consequent[4] (O'Neil, 2001). Regardless of the current ubiquity of adducing so-called evidence-based theories and treatments (including a number in the present volume), if one wishes to avoid manifesting mild formal thought disorder, one ought to try neither to invoke, nor imply, the Fallacy of Affirming the Consequent: one ought not to claim that any theory or treatment is itself "based on evidence."

Following Popper, it is well to recall that attribution of scientific truth is based on two *inabilities:*

1. The inability to refute the hypothesis on the basis of evidence (no matter how hard we try), while its competing hypotheses have all been so refuted, and
2. The inability to conceive of another hypothesis against which to test it.

Scientific truth is thus always relative to refuted alternatives, and never relative to evidence *per se*. The one additional criterion of scientific truth is positive, but esthetic rather than logical: given two competing hypotheses, neither of which is refuted, the more elegant is preferred. Elegance is simplicity. Occam's razor[5] is an early invocation of this. And so scientific truth is based not on evidence, but rather on two particular inabilities, with a dash of elegance.

19.2.3 How the DSM-III-IV May Work in Practice, Even if It Doesn't Work in Theory

Positivism could well echo Mark Twain: "Reports of my death are greatly exaggerated." What accounts for positivism's postmortem vitality? The answer, I believe, lies in its practical side effects. Wishful thinking about theory-free observations and operational definitions may inspire authors of diagnostic criteria to craft formulations that subsequently prove to yield higher interrater reliability. The downside is to tempt us with the fantasy that high interrater reliability demonstrates the criteria to be theory-free. I am persuaded, in any case, that the positivist esthetic has indeed reaped some methodological rewards. But reports of its vitality remain greatly exaggerated.

19.3 PUTTING PSYCHOLOGIES AND PSYCHOTHERAPIES IN CONTEXT

Psychologies and psychotherapies have certain peculiarities beyond the general limits of scientific methodology, as previously circumscribed.

[2] Even for such basic measurements as length and temperature, you need to specify temperature to reliably measure length, and specify length to measure temperature. So theories (e.g., about length and temperature) always predate measurement; and semantics (what we intend by the concepts) always trumps method.

[3] Roughly 25 pages worth over a number of his books and papers.

[4] Very briefly, the *Fallacy of Affirming the Consequent*: $[(H \supset P).P] \supset H$. Hypothesis H implies prediction P, the consequent, and P is affirmed (found to be true), which we mistakenly take to imply the truth of H. The language has eroded over time. Logical positivists invoked "verification," which connoted implication of truth, and since this never occurs, it was serially downgraded to "confirmation," then to "corroboration," and now to "support," which still means nothing at all, except "not refuted when it might have been." The FAC is obtained by tampering with one of two tautologies: *Modus* Ponens (tautology of affirming the antecedent) or *Modus Tollens* (tautology of denying the consequent).

[5] William of Ockham, 1285–1349: "Entia non sunt multiplicanda præter necessitatem" = "Entities should not be multiplied beyond necessity."

19.3.1 Talking About Ourselves as if Talking About Something Else

Psychology manifests a number of self-referential knots. This is owing to the fact that the subject matter is ourselves, including ourselves as the source of all accounts of the psyche. I may have an account of your psyche, but if you hear about it, you may give me an argument. Psychology is the only discipline whose subject matter talks back. Behaviorism is one refuge: dealing only with observed behavior shields one against back talk.

There is no escape from back talk in any psychotherapy, or any psychology with a derivative psychotherapy, where one is in dialogic relation with a patient-client-analysand. In practice, underlying any manifest psychotherapeutic theory is a latent statement I can make to my client that may foster her universe of freedom (by liberating islands of growth from restraint by loss, impossibility, inability, neglect, prohibition, punishment, transience, poverty, weakness, mortality, etc.). To that extent, method and treatment ought to trump theory.

The mind-set of the therapist engaging with the client/patient is different from the mind-set of the therapist theorizing, though ideally we can achieve a mixed mode when communicating to peers, trying to be theoretically clear, though motivated by an ideal of caring for and individually addressing the audience. We are aware of this implicitly when reading any clinical or theoretical paper, where the theory counts, but the extent to which it is therapeutic to the reader as a therapist counts for more. If the writer seems not to care about being understood, nor to care about how one might care for another, nothing rings true.

An important implication of the discontinuity between theory and therapy is that in the hands of a therapist, what most counts is whether an interpretive schema works. For example, Kohut's theory may be true, or not; and it may be convincing, or not, to someone reading it. Applying Kohutian theory and technique to a given case may prove to be therapeutic, or not, regardless both of its truth and of whether it is convincing to the therapist. Still, it is more likely to be therapeutic if it is convincing to the therapist. And when all is said and done, Kohut's technique may never seem to work quite as well as it did in Kohut's own hands.

19.3.2 Biology versus Analogies from Artefacts

Another way around the problem of self-reference is to translate the psyche into something we understand already: something we have made on purpose and whose operating is thus transparent to us. This inevitably trips up and turns what tries too hard to be scientific into something that is scientistic.[6]

Aristotle's (383–321 BCE) psychology derives from his metaphysics (1941b), which in turn is inspired by ceramics: the efficient cause (potter) turns a material cause (clay) into a formal cause (bowl) for a final cause (to contain). The metaphysics works very well for bowls, but less well for natural things, such as dogs: the material, efficient and formal causes are all dog, while the final cause is to be a dog. This ontological redundancy indicates how Aristotle was barking up the wrong tree. In any case, his psychology (1941a) was an application of this metaphysics: the thing's formal cause (dogness) would somehow enter into the mind through the organs of sense, leaving the material cause (dog flesh) behind, and be inscribed on the mind, the *form of forms*, like chalk traces on an erased slate or tablet (*tabula rasa*), and one would then perceive DOG. This was the process of perceptual induction, which provided content for the logical induction that the positivists would continue to resurrect (O'Neil, 2001). We still manifest a certain Aristotelian nostalgia when we talk about "starting with a clean slate," and about "memory traces," and about sensation as if it involved the input of information (formal causes) through the organs of sense, that gets stored in our memory banks, like an archive of tracings. And so we find Aristotelian vestiges both in Freud's *Project* and in cognitivism (see following).

Thomas Hobbes (1588–1679) moved from ceramics to mechanics, interpreting the workings of the brain as a mechanical array of microscopic levers and pulleys:

> The external body … presseth the organ … which pressure, by the mediation of the nerves and other strings and membranes of the body … causeth there a resistance … to deliver itself which, … because outward, seemeth to be some matter without. And this seeming, or fancy, is that which men call sense.… Neither in us that are pressed, are they any thing else, but divers motions. (Hobbes, 1651/1962)

This charmingly mechanical passage anticipates some of Freud's ideas in the *Project* (see ff.) and some of his theories about hallucinations in dreaming.

Descartes (1596–1650) knew some anatomy and practiced some dissection, and so moved the discussion from sense organs and peripheral nerves to the central nervous system. He proposed (1649/1961) that thinking happens in the flow of animal spirits (cerebrospinal fluid),

---

[6] From *scientism* = excessive belief in the power of scientific knowledge and techniques.

especially as it bathes the centrally located pineal body hanging from the brain into the CSF.[7]

Mesmer (1734–1815) arrived when magnets had become objects of fascination, and referred to hypnotic phenomena as evidence of so-called animal magnetism. He mistook magnetism as a kind of fluid, and so had magnetized baths (his *baquets*) and trees that contained this fluid (Ellenberger, 1970). These analogies worked as long as magnets remained mysterious. Once they were better understood, the analogies dissolved and could be maintained only by those obstinately ignorant of magnets.

Freud (1856–1939) had more to work with: 19th-century physical and neurological theories. The equations for direct-current circuits were almost identical to those for hydraulics (as for steam engines), and so electric current could be interpreted as a fluid.[8] Neurons had been identified, and Emil Heinrich du Bois-Reymond had discovered the resting membrane potential across a neuron (positive outside, negative inside). The idea was that in signal transmission (as in a spinal reflex such as the knee jerk) the positive charge on the outside could flow along the axon to account for nervous conductivity, just like direct current.

Freud applied the theories of the day to his posthumously published *Project for a Scientific Psychology* (1895). What emerged was a mental apparatus that functioned like a cross between a hydraulic system and a direct current circuit. The fluid or electric current, which Freud designated as Q (for quantity), was measurable and conserved, as it would be for total charge or volume of fluid. Since magnetism wasn't a fluid, but electric charge behaved as if it were, this seemed an advance over the *baquets* of Mesmer.

Of course, we know now (as neurophysiologist Julius Bernstein had hypothesized certainly by 1902—see Seyfarth, 2006) that an action potential involves no conduction of electricity nor of any other conserved quantity: there is no Q. In any case, an enormous literature testifies to Q derivatives influencing important aspects of Freud's thought right to the end, as the quantitative or economic point of view (Strachey, 1966), including cathexis, abreaction, and quota of affect. These concepts persist, as do Q derivatives in some aspects of dissociation theory, such as ego-state therapy. Freud, just like Hobbes and Descartes, in trying so hard to be scientific, ended up being scientistic.[9]

More recently, the digital computer has been invented, and psychologists can describe how the mind (and/or brain) works as if it were a digital computer. This approach is more sophisticated than psychoanalysis to the extent that digital computers are more sophisticated than steam engines. But as an extended projection of an artefact onto oneself, it commits the same ultimate error.

The idea that the brain *processes* things—such as information, sensation, input, emotion, trauma, memory, whatever—is a cybernetic metaphor, and has become so general that alternatives seem inconceivable. What on earth would the brain do if it didn't process information? The metaphor is astonishingly recent. The OED (1991) finds that computers were first said to process information in 1960, and brains in 1968. My own brain, consequently, began to process information when I was 19 years old. If you wonder what my brain could have been doing other than processing information testifies to the uncritical generalization of the cybernetic metaphor.

But the drift from biology, the study of real life, to cybernetics, the study of human computational artefacts, has its limits. Gerald Edelman, Nobel Prize Laureate and neuroscientist, claims:

> The brain in this view is a kind of computer.... The acceptance of this view or version of it is widespread in psychology, linguistics, computer science, and artificial intelligence. It is one of the most remarkable misunderstandings in the history of science. Indeed, not only is it not in accord with the known facts of human biology and brain science, but it constitutes a major category error as well.... [T]he majority of those working in cognitive psychology hold to the views I attack here.... [S]omeday the more vocal practitioners of cognitive psychology and the frequently smug empiricists of neuroscience will understand that they have unknowingly subjected themselves to an intellectual swindle. (Edelman, 1992)

The leap from ceramics to cybernetics, from Aristotle to cognitivism, is enormous. Because computers help us with mental tasks, and are better at many than we are

[7] He is better known, and more maligned, for originating the "mind-body" dichotomy, between *res extensa* and *res cogitans*, but he was merely giving clearer expression to what had been present since antiquity.

[8] At the time, the fluid was thought to be positive charges flowing in a given direction. Later, when the electron was discovered, the idea was changed to electrons flowing in the opposite direction. The math works fine in either direction.

[9] Meissner (1995) attempts to salvage the economic point of view, but the resulting product is quite meager, as it is distinct from energy and involves no conservation of quantity.

(though hilariously inept at others), they are the first artefacts that seem to think, and so we have projected psychological categories into computer systems, such as memory and cognition, then forgotten the projection, and then reintrojected the meaning back into ourselves, so that we now talk about brains functioning as if they were computers. Edelman's point is that brains don't function that way, don't mediate behavior the way computers process information. The metaphor is what Popper would call a metaphysical research program: a useful heuristic for prompting scientific research.

Of course, metaphors from any familiar artefact (bowl, pressure cooker, automobile, filing cabinet, computer) may be useful in therapy. I often find computer metaphors helpful with patients even if I am persuaded by Edelman that brains don't process information *per se*.

19.4 DEFINING PSYCHOANALYSIS AS A PSYCHOLOGY (ACCOUNT OF THE PSYCHE)

The special peculiarities of translating an interpersonal encounter into theory are more evident in psychoanalysis than in other psychotherapies.

19.4.1 Freud's Definition

> Psychoanalysis is the name (1) of a procedure for the investigation of mental processes which are almost inaccessible in any other way, (2) of a method (based upon that investigation) for the treatment of neurotic disorders and (3) of a collection of psychological information obtained along those lines, which is gradually being accumulated into a new scientific discipline. (S. Freud, 1923b)

Freud's definition may be shorthanded by saying that psychoanalysis is (1) a *method* of psychological investigation, (2) a *psychotherapy*, or treatment of some, but not all, mental disorders, and (3) a scientific *theory* (though worded in mistaken inductivist-empiricist terms). The sequence, method-psychotherapy-psychology, implies that method instructs the treatment, and the results of treatment inform the theory. By this reading, psychoanalytic treatment is not an application of psychoanalytic theory, but rather the theory is derived from the treatment. This claim is in keeping with Freud's wrongheaded inductivist-empiricist aspirations, and sidesteps the enormous importation of nonclinical theory into therapy as first heralded by his *Project*. In any case, dynamic tension among these three facets has been the motor of change and differentiation in psychoanalysis over the years.

19.4.2 Method, Treatment, Theory

In any psychoanalytic debate, the method and treatment generally take precedence over the theory, in theory. The idea is that within the boundaries of regular timed encounters (sessions), and other understandings that constitute the therapeutic frame (confidentiality, a nonjudgmental attitude, etc.), two people encounter each other with the understanding that one, the analysand, is there to understand himself, and be understood, and another, the analyst, is there to assist in this understanding. The analysand talks about what he doesn't know, until he knows what he is talking about. One human being gradually reveals himself to another in communications that are equivocal, ambiguous, or analogical; they will be motivated, and affect-laden. The therapeutic relationship is enfolded within motive, affect, and communication, what we call transference and countertransference. The radical asymmetry of the encounter replays the original mother-infant dyad. The analysand is not an infant, however, and so the work is inescapably collaborative: diagnosis and cure occur simultaneously, in a way, because a diagnosis or interpretation is legitimated by the analysand accepting it, and by this acceptance making a difference in the analysand's psyche.

19.4.3 Freedom and Determinism in the Method

In practice, method, treatment, and theory do not so much lead from one to the other as contend with each other. Freedom is the essence of the method: free association for the analysand, and freely hovering attention for the analyst. Constraint is the essence of the theory: psychic determinism. Freedom transcending constraint is the essence of the treatment: "Where id was, there ego shall be" (1933). The method of investigation, free association, and freely hovering attention, informs the treatment, and these theoretically yield psychic truth.

Theory describes what renders people *unfree*, and therapy directs *how* to free them. Thus freedom figures prominently in the method and barely appears in the theory. True psychic freedom doesn't warrant analysis, and attaining it is a signal to terminate. So freedom tends to act as a *telos*, goal or ideal, but is rarely directly talked about. Psychoanalytic theory rather focuses on the psychic determinism[10] that blocks freedom: unconscious memories and wishes and feelings; mechanisms of defense that operate to keep things unconscious, which are themselves unconscious; unconscious repetitive patterns of perception and behavior and interpersonal relationship; psychic deficits that impoverish, and so on.

When we invite analysands to freely associate, we are inviting them to act as if already cured. Analysts interpret how the associations are not free: they dwell on a single theme at the expense of everything else, or else that range over everything except for some missing theme. Failing to freely associate is thus always a doing: concerning oneself with something, or avoiding doing so, and enacting this doing in what one does, including but not limited to what one says, to the analyst. In this way, failing to free associate, acting out, and transference are all different facets of the same phenomenon.

Unbiased listening is an unnatural ability that needs cultivation. The analyst's self-instruction, to engage in "freely hovering attention," means paying even attention to everything the patient says. You can't tell how a patient's associations are unfree unless you have a *telos* of freedom of which these associations fall short. One way to formulate this *telos* is with a few handy lists. Speaking freely ought to result in a mix of past, present, and future; of love and hate; of love and work and play; of creation and judgment; of daydreams and nightdreams and resignation to necessity; of hopes and fears; of mother, father, siblings, superiors, peers, and inferiors; and so on.

Just as for empirical science, however, nothing works in practice the way it is supposed to in theory. There is no freely hovering attention, really. Every item of theory (i.e., everything that one believes to be the case) constrains freely hovering attention, which is why technique recommends the foregoing lists. Such lists are somewhat contrived, however, compared to the ideal: unbiased listening is something of a not-doing rather than a doing, akin to what Keats called negative capability (Leavy, 1970). Similarly, Bion (1970) recommends approaching each session without memory or desire. The reader can judge whether what's being recommended are technical rules of thumb, or altered states of consciousness in the analyst. In any case, the method is designed to allow everything to come to light, and to be put into words: to be narrated. When all is consciously utterable, the sphere of conscious control and mastery—the realm of freedom—expands.

Dissociative multiplicity is an illustration of how the method backfires. Following the evidence, let us assume it to be a real phenomenon with a significant prevalence worldwide (Ross, 1991). The psychoanalytic method of investigation ought to permit it to come to light at some regular frequency wherever it is practiced. This hasn't been the case. Therefore, either multiples never seek psychoanalysis, or multiples in psychoanalysis are undetected. Assuming the latter, multiples could be undetected because (1) the analyst is blind to multiplicity and interprets it otherwise, or (2) the analysand conforms to the analyst's expectations by concealing multiplicity, or (3) the multiplicity is misinterpreted as psychosis and the analysand judged to be unanalyzable, or something to that effect. In short, method and treatment may be compromised by theory. We only see what we have been trained to see. Bias-free methods don't exist, nor can they.

19.4.4 Clean and Dirty Starts: Abandoning Hypnosis

Freud was not alone in seeking a method free of bias. The natural sciences still seek such a method. The mythical clean start was one reason Freud abandoned hypnosis as a method of investigation and treatment. The psychoanalytic couch remains as a concrete vestige of Freud's early use of hypnosis, which was in two brief phases.

The first brief hypnotic phase (S. Freud, 1914a) was inspired by the Nancy school of Liébault and Bernheim, with a focus on treatment—the elimination of symptoms through mendacious hypnotic suggestion (suggesting that some traumatic event didn't in fact happen, for example). Freud also bemoaned the therapeutic futility of his hypnotic suggestions. So not only did this practice require lying to patients—it didn't work.

The second brief hypnotic phase derives from Breuer's celebrated treatment of Anna O (Breuer & Freud, 1895), which eschews therapeutic suggestion and uses hypnosis to investigate the origins of symptoms in the so-called cathartic method. This preserves truth and permits treatment. But Freud abandoned the hypnosis, and retained the catharsis first through the pressure technique (which, to my mind, he misinterpreted as being nonhypnotic) and eventually through free association. Why?

> I soon came to dislike hypnosis.... When I found that ... I could not succeed in bringing more than a fraction of my patients into a hypnotic state, I determined to give up hypnosis. (S. Freud, 1910)

[10] Strictly speaking, the doctrine of psychic determinism is self-refuting. If all mental phenomena are causally determined, then so are all mental products, including all doctrines, such as the doctrine of psychic determinism, at which point no doctrine can maintain any claim to truth but rather reduces to just another bit of behavior warranting a causal explanation in the psychic determinism governing the one making the claim.

Thus both hypnotic approaches were abandoned, though for different reasons: the first, to preserve truth, and the second, because Freud was not very good at it. Since Freud abandoned hypnosis, psychoanalytic conceptualizations of it have been consistently wrongheaded, primarily, no doubt, due to lack of exposure to it and to how it has evolved over the past century.[11]

19.4.5 Scientific Hypotheses versus Interpretive Schemata: Hermeneutics

The irreducible dialectic of freedom and determinism invites interpreting psychoanalysis as other than a natural science. The question of clean starts and dirty starts mirrors the passage from Husserl's "clean" phenomenology to "dirty" hermeneutics. Husserl tried to do philosophy in the manner of his fellow mathematician, Descartes, from a clean start, and spent his life having to start over and over again. The futility of his phenomenology spurred the ascent of hermeneutics, which makes no pretense to a clean start, but contents itself with whatever dirt is already around.[12] Paul Ricœur (1970) interprets Freud from a hermeneutic viewpoint. This starts from the idea that Descartes' *Cogito ergo sum* is a "certitude devoid of truth," to use Ricœur's provocative phrase: in effect, true, but so what?—a truth with no issue. For Ricœur, there is no privileged beginning, no best way, no clean way, to begin. Meanings are always already there in every culture, and the task is to interpret them—a messy, ambiguous task with no sterile procedure.

This agrees with and complements Popper's contention that all scientific theories derive from prior theories, and ultimately from myths, rather than from data, so that meaning comes from prior meaning, and data can only refute (surprise, disappoint). In brief, hermeneutics may be interpreted as "the hypothetico-deductive method applied to meaningful material" (Føllesdal, 2001).

It is also clear to Ricœur that psychoanalysis must be more than a hermeneutics: a discourse that mixes meaning and force into a "semantics of desire." The meaning part is the hermeneutics; the force part recognizes that what is to be interpreted is a real living human being, and not just a text, requiring recourse to explanatory (rather than interpretive) models such as those used in natural science—thus, the need for something like Hobbes's strings, or Freud's Q, or the cybernetic metaphors of cognitivism. The point here is that while these force dimensions are mistaken, they may need to be replaced, tinkered with, or updated, rather than dumped. Nor does this rule out, of course, explanations that are not artefactual metaphors: the ongoing promise of theories anchored in biology, neurosciences, and ethology. Human beings remain terrestrial biological organisms, after all.[13]

Hermeneutics, curiously, is closer than phenomenology to biology. The baby is not born with a *tabula rasa*, but with an enormous array of expectations and quirks that have arisen by chance (random mutation) and that have not yet proven to be lethal over hundreds of millions of years (natural selection). I word it this way so as to avoid the overvaluation of survival and adaptation, which are not causes in the drama, but results. Survival is a nonevent: the nonoccurrence of premature death. The baby starts dirty rather than clean, unlike a virgin hard drive. Some of the baby's earliest and seemingly most primitive behaviors, ontogenetically, are structurally late and sophisticated phylogenetically. We might like to think that relating is primary, whether it be object relating or attachment or interpersonal rapport, just as Freud thought that sucking at the breast was primary and earlier than biting. But teeth have been around since the fish, and breasts only since the mammals. We bit and copulated long before we sucked.

19.4.6 The Theory—A Psychology: The Necessary Drift Away from Its Primary Subject Matter

Psychoanalysis is inevitably self-referential in that we talk about ourselves. Self-reference is logically fatal for any scientific theory, however, so it is interesting to reflect on how psychoanalysis evades the issue.

19.4.6.1 The Reification of Freud's Ich

There are two senses of I in Freud. Freud's *das Ich,* while deriving from the common pronoun, is from the outset a technical one: the subject or agent of any verb that might follow, which he then promoted to a central position in his structural theory to be the ego of that celebrated trio, *das Es, das Ich, das Über-Ich:* the Id, the I, the Over-I; the id, the ego, the superego (S. Freud, 1923a).

I judge myself to speak directly in uttering "I," whereas others describe my thinking and speaking as acts of my "the I," and different from what I might judge myself. Of course, "the I" arrived in the English-speaking world in Latin as "the ego," facilitating its divorce from "I."

[11] Notable past exceptions are Lawrence Kubie (Silverstein & Silverstein, 1990) and Merton Gill (Hoffman, 1985).

[12] My shamelessly free interpretation of the essential difference between phenomenology and hermeneutics.

[13] Merton Gill (1988) succinctly summarizes various sides to this conundrum up to 1988.

What happens when "we" enter the scene? Faced with somebody serially manifesting more than one "I," or self-proclaiming as "we," Freud is faced with a conundrum: either he must rupture the semantic link between "I" and "the I," or he must disbelieve the patient; or he may do both. The first option involves subordinating "I" to a superficial conscious manifestation of "the I," such that "the I" is the special structure that, among other things, gives rise to a conscious "I." So the submerged (unconscious) iceberg, "the I," may have more than one tip, more than one "I," breaking the (conscious) surface—an attractive possibility that is further developed in the following.

A deeper problem in Freud's later theory is his reduction of consciousness to a "sense-organ of the entire apparatus" (S. Freud, 1933). This formulation seems wrongheaded, because most of what we sense is unconscious, and consciousness can't be restricted to sense, but must retain motor as well, at least in the general sense of doing: independence of judgment and act needs to be retained, or else we once again founder in footnote 10. Somebody with DID, moreover, would require a multiplicity of such sense-organs, further straining the metaphor.

In any case, the idea of a common unconscious ego having more than one conscious "outcropping" does fulfill Braude's (1991) idea of a unity beneath multiplicity, a "Kantian transcendental synthesizing self."

Another inescapable source of self-reference is psychoanalytic training. Analysts in training undergo analysis as part of the training, just as clinicians training in hypnosis undergo hypnosis. The extent of the treatment is very large, however (e.g., 800 sessions minimum for the IPA). To the extent that analysts may judge the theory and technique of their analyst to be inadequate to themselves, they may then, consciously or unconsciously, reformulate theory for the purpose of self-cure and, having done so, selectively recognize similar patterns in analysands they treat, and then publish their new ideas in the literature. It is likely that this happens unconsciously all the time. One reason for the paucity of psychoanalytic interest in dissociation may be the relative lack of psychoanalysts who are integrated multiples.

19.4.6.2 Subject and Object in External, Inner, and Internal Worlds

As summarized by Meissner (1972), Hartmann and Rapaport distinguished between the *inner world*, a map or schema of one's external world (including oneself in it), and the *internal world*, "the organization and integration of intrapsychic structures that compose the psychic apparatus," such as the id, the ego, the superego. He concludes that the inner world is representational, whereas the internal world is structural. This provides a stage for the psychoanalytic concept of *object*. Objects are so called because they were originally regarded as objects of a given drive (e.g., the breast as the object of hunger). While objects eventually expand into whole others, the term is retained, so that 'object relations' means one's relations with others. More precisely, one's perception of others (or aspects of others) is represented in inner or internal objects, and it is the relation of oneself to such an object that is intended by "object relation." Curiously, the word *subject* hardly appears in any psychoanalytic text, whereas *object* is ubiquitous.[14]

The inner-internal distinction bears on a major difference between Ego psychology and the Kleinian school. Ego psychology regards one's objects as representations of objects in the inner world, whereas Kleinians regard one's objects as structural entities in the internal world, akin to Freud's superego, about which one may then have secondary representations in one's inner world (Hinshelwood, 1991). More discussion follows in the sections on splitting and schemata.

19.4.6.3 Psychoanalysis and Memory

The question of memory and psychoanalysis has been recently reviewed (Pugh, 2002) chronologically: (1) Freud's attempt to explain memory in his unpublished *Project*; (2) his elucidation of screen memories as revealing and concealing and his resigning himself to merely assigning memory a place in the topography (*Cs, Pcs, Ucs*) in Chapter 7 of *The Interpretation of Dreams*; (3) the hypothesis that all perceptions are preserved, as well as all their further developments; (4) the structural model (Id, Ego, Superego) to solve the problem of memory trace theory and the problem of having identified the perceptual system with the Conscious.

Pugh notes that Freud was aware of procedural memory in his *Remembering, Repeating and Working Through* (1914b): "Something is 'remembered' which could never have been 'forgotten' because it was … never conscious." This theme is ably developed by Stern (1997, 2009) in his theory of unformulated experience, and is revisited in the following.

How do memories "get in"? The wrong answer is through some process of induction (e.g., engrams, memory traces, information input, or whatever). In short, strictly speaking, nothing gets in from the outside (O'Neil, 2001). Pugh points out how Freud's process of *Identification*

[14] Jessica Benjamin exploits this lack in her book, *Like Subjects, Love Objects* (1995).

avoided memory trace difficulties. An identification is one's creation that mimics one's perception of another.

19.4.7 Political Currents in Psychoanalysis

Psychoanalysis is sometimes depicted from the outside as a seamless orthodoxy. This is far from the case. There were the early expulsions of Jung and Adler; the exclusion of nonmedical psychoanalysts from the American Psychoanalytic Association (APA) in the United States, against Freud's (1926b) very clear preferences, and the consequent burgeoning of heterodox non-APA societies; the British split between the Anna Freudians and the Kleinians, with the independents occupying the middle, and subsequently spawning object relations theory; the conversion of Latin America to Klein and Bion; the development of attachment theory largely alongside rather than within psychoanalysis; the expulsion of Lacan, his spawning of further French splits, and his recent espousal by the Latin Americans; the autonomous development of Kohut's self psychology in the United States and beyond; the interweaving of object relations and attachment theory with interpersonal and relational psychoanalysis; and so on.

So this is the psychoanalysis that is to contend with dissociation. The interpersonal-relational school is currently ahead of the pack, in quality and volume of psychoanalytic literature. It will be interesting to see the effect on other schools, and whether it helps bring them closer together or drives them further apart.

19.5 DEFINING DISSOCIATION

Having defined some of the peculiarities of science, psychology, and psychoanalysis, we now move to our central concern, dissociation. *Dissociation* has come to mean a number of things that are not necessarily related. The meanings are often confused or conflated.

19.5.1 Dissociation as Symptom versus Defense

Dissociative signs and symptoms, like those of schizophrenia or PTSD, may be divided into positive and negative. Negative phenomena are characterized by something missing that ought to be there (e.g., amnesia, depersonalization, anesthesia, blindness, deafness, etc.), whereas positive phenomena are characterized by something present that ought not to be there (e.g., hallucinations of any sensory modality, including voices, made or withdrawn affects, thoughts, impulses and actions, pseudoseizures, etc.).

If one interprets *dissociation* as denoting all the signs and symptoms arising from dissociation, then the severity of positive and negative phenomena will be directly proportional to the severity of the dissociation. If one interprets *dissociation* as denoting a defense mechanism or aptitude (my preferred interpretation), then negative symptoms will be directly proportional, and positive symptoms inversely proportional, to the strength of the dissociation. From this point of view, negative symptoms are dissociative, as something is kept away, whereas positive symptoms are indicative of failing dissociation, as that which dissociation tries to keep away succeeds in coming back. Thus, failing dissociation is generally more clinically evident than intact dissociation.

19.5.2 Dissociation of Faculties versus Multiplicity

Either interpretation (symptom or defense) cuts across another primary distinction between the dissociation of mental faculties and dissociative multiplicity. The two kinds of dissociation often coexist in somebody, but they are conceptually, and possibly ontologically, distinct. Psychoanalysis, in my view, is somewhat challenged by faculty dissociation, but far more challenged by dissociative multiplicity, which accounts for its being singled out in the title of this chapter.

19.5.2.1 Dissociation of Faculties

Dissociation of mental faculties is exemplified in the classic BASK model (Braun, 1988). This view distinguishes separate mental faculties, specifically Behavior, Affect, Sensation, and Knowledge, which may then be dissociated from each other synchronically. Diachronically, what is dissociated are the behavioral, affective, sensory, and narrative components of a given event.

The dissociation of faculties may also cover a variety of phenomena, such as absorption, suggestibility, hypnotizability, and so on. In this regard, the question as to whether there is a sharp or blurred boundary between the normal and pathological is an ongoing debate. If one regards the dissociation of mental faculties as primary, which may subsequently be personified into an alter, then multiplicity is necessarily a more severe grade of dissociation than the dissociation of faculties.

19.5.2.2 Dissociative Multiplicity

Dissociative multiplicity, by contrast, implies more than one consciousness. Van der Hart and Dorahy (2009) opt for restricting the term *dissociation* to a structural division of the mind, implying some degree of multiplicity, and recommend withholding the term entirely from functional dissociation in a single consciousness. Again, the question as to whether there is a sharp or blurred boundary between normal and pathological multiplicity is an ongoing debate.

If one regards dissociative multiplicity as primary, then any apparent dissociation of mental faculties is viewed as epiphenomenal to the alternating or simultaneous presence of oneself and another (i.e., another self, or another of one's selves).

Combinations of the two are most common: multiple subjects with different samplings of B, A, S, and K. We generally find that any presumption of clean divisions among B, A, S, and K are dashed, as alters are rarely entirely devoid of any three of the four. Some symptoms, depersonalization in particular, are hard to place with the one or the other kind of dissociation.

19.5.2.3 Multiplication and Division

Is dissociation multiplicative or divisive? Where Van der Hart and Dorahy (2009) invoke the *division* of consciousness, I prefer the *multiplication* of consciousness, as multiplication better describes dissociative multiplicity, while division better describes functional dissociation. It is not difficult to find sources of the confusion.

Multiplication and division are present in the double meanings of both *split* and *double*. German *Spaltung* becomes English *splitting* and French *clivage* (Laplanche & Pontalis, 1967/1973). *Cleave* is equivocal, meaning both "hew, cut asunder, split" and "stick fast, adhere" (Onions, 1966). When something is halved, we tend to say cleft, as in cleft palate, but when doubled, we tend to say cloven, as in cloven hoof or clove of garlic. Cleavage, need it be said, occurs between two whole breasts in close proximity.

Similarly, the common French-English word *double* (Robert, 1994) means two-fold, from Latin *duplus*, which itself has two roots, *duos* (two) and *plicare* (fold). When you fold something in two, you double the layers and halve the size. So *double* has a double meaning: both division and multiplication. Multiplication prevailed, as *double* generally connotes twice as much, and a second layer of clothing became a *doublure* or jacket lining, or doublet (Larousse, 1990). The French verb *dédoubler* and its cognate noun *dédoublement* reverse the process: you *dedouble* a cloth when you unfold it or open it up, thereby doubling the size; you *dedouble* a jacket when you remove its *doublure* or lining, in other words, when the *doublure* emerges from within. But a *doublure* is also one's double in the sense of understudy, stand-in, or stuntman. So *dédoublement de la personnalité* may be taken to connote both alter creation and switching, when one's understudy comes out in one's place. Repeated *dédoublements* in the creative sense would produce multiplicity: a multiplicity of wholes, or whole others, or *alters* (*alter* is Latin for *other*). This sense invites one to think of the human being as a group, "myself and my others," of somebody (literally) as a vehicle for a number of someones. There are some psychoanalytic concepts that hint at this view: the superego, introjective identification, the false self, internal objects that seem to act, and so on.

The language of division is more restrictive. *Désagrégation*, *splitting* (*Spaltung*), and *dissociation* itself all connote a fragmenting process whose sum adds up to one whole at most. Dissociation is a verbal contraction of dis-association, and derives from the wrongheaded associationist psychology of the 19th century. The idea of a psychic division in somebody is at odds with *individual*, which means indivisible, just as *atom* means unsplittable. But while we now know that atoms can be split, and individuals as well, neither atoms nor individuals split into parts. Whole atoms don't split into parts of atoms, but rather into different whole atoms. Similarly, when somebody divides into parts, what results is a plurality of someones, not of parts of a someone. So there is wisdom in continuing to invoke atoms and individuals rather than toms and dividuals.

19.5.3 Dissociative Multiplicity: How Many of What?

Faculty dissociation presents no numerical or ontological difficulties, as any number of faculties, functions, states, or behaviors can be predicated of a single I, ego, self, subject, person, personality, whatever. Dissociative multiplicity, on the other hand, opens the question: how many of what? Various terms are used, such as *persons, personalities, selves, self-states, self representations, I's, egos, ego-states, identities, agents, subjects, parts,* and so on, according to the observer's metaphysical taste. *Psyche* and *mind* would seem to be in a special position, as words that are impersonal enough that they are generally never used in the plural.

Again, our language has evolved to conspire against any simple answer to the question. What exactly are there more than one of, and of what does there remain one, despite the multiplicity?

19.5.3.1 Personality

Personality connotes the predicates or characteristics of a person: what someone is like ("She has quite a personality!"). Personality disorders were originally called *character* disorders, both terms emphasizing the presence of certain exaggerated personal characteristics. Multiple *Personality* Disorder originally underscored this difference in *character* between one alter and another. From this point of view, there is little difficulty in someone having more than one personality. Actors make their living doing it, and DSM-IV allows for somebody to have more than one personality disorder. Personality, consequently, is a term whose meaning remains superficial—remote from someone's core. On the other hand, the word has taken on depth in the dissociation literature through its widespread use.

19.5.3.2 Person

Person has come to mean what is most core in someone. But its original meaning is quite the opposite: *mask*, especially dramatic mask (*dramatis personæ*). The Greek equivalent *prósopon* (πρόσωπον) intends pros (on or towards) + ops (eye), the act of putting on the mask so as to see through it with the eyes, and the Latin *persona* intends per (through) + sonare (to sound) as one would speak through the mask. "I prosopon my mask, and then I person it" = "I put on my mask, and then I speak through it," an eerie evocation of some of the patients we treat. To that extent, the original *person* necessarily implied as-if, guile, disguise, inauthenticity, assumed identity, put-on façade, while *personality* would reduce to the character of the mask (e.g., its expression, decoration, paint job, etc.). If *person* is our phenomenon, our public mask, then something else must serve as our noumenon (as we really are behind the mask).

19.5.3.3 Self Representation; Self

Representations are clearly objects (thoughts) rather than subjects (thinkers); and this goes for self representations. Representations don't act. The self "itself," of which one might have a representation, has an ambiguous status as an element of intrapsychic structure. Self as one of my objects is clearly privileged by me (or ought to be), and so is vaguely both subjective and objective, or reflexive.[15] This ambiguity permits some authors to prefer *self* over *ego* (with the bonus of preferring Anglo-Saxon to Latin), and similarly prefer *self-state* over *ego-state.* The ambiguity permits such a shift, although *self* remains in the objective case whereas *I* (ego) am in the subjective. *Self* is what I appropriate as myself (literally, *my* self). But self is not the I that does the appropriating. Self isn't the subject of the verb. Self is not agency.

[15] French *verbes pronominaux* (pronominal verbs) are a good example of self-reflexivity, where the object is the subject, as in *je me lave les mains* = I wash me the hands, rather than I wash my hands.

19.5.3.4 I, Ego

And so by elimination we are left with *the I*, the ego. I (ego) am clearly in the subjective case (nothing else is). Only I can act, only I am an agent in this sense. And in interacting with the *I* of another, I am inescapably in an interpersonal relationship. That is our predicament in therapy, in any lived relationship, even as we inevitably distort the lived relationship into some theoretical schema.

19.5.3.5 I as Subject; Subjectivity

The *I* as subject warrants some reflection. When attempting to study something, we invoke subjects and objects (e.g., calling the *object* of study the *subject* matter). The relationship between these two throwns or jects (*ject* being the Latin root past participle of "to throw") is that one is thrown under (sub) and the other is thrown in the way (ob). So we stumble over the object thrown in our way, and wonder about the underlying subject. The relationship between surface object and underlying subject has animated millennia of philosophical and scientific debate. It is formulated in our grammar: a sentence is a subject followed by a predicate, which itself is often a verb-object combination. Predication itself (i.e., predicating something of a subject, of somebody) cannot be taken for granted. Donald Davidson's (2005) last book, published posthumously, is 163 pages about that very subject.

Subject has traditionally been granted priority of place over *object*, as deeper, more real, truer, and fewer. Fewer is key: a subject is a unity underlying some diversity of objects. Plato's deep forms are what things really are, underlying all their surface details or predications or appearances or phainomena. One could have true knowledge (epistémé) of the subject, but only opinion (doxa) about the object, where the most one can hope for is to come up with an account (logos) which "saves the appearances," that is, isn't contradicted by them. His doctrine of the eternal forms would seem to have been abandoned by science, and yet science has evolved with a neat compromise between knowledge and opinion: it routinely hypothesizes deep structures to save the appearances, and these structures are routinely more unitary, and carry more conviction of reality, than the appearances they purport to save or explain. Science remains covertly Platonic.

It is not a coincidence that *subject* connotes the actor or agent of a sentence; and the human being as agent, conscious or unconscious; and the unity underlying surface multiplicity. The conscious human being takes itself as a model for what it thinks of whatever. Projection is ubiquitous. I am conscious of the unity of my consciousness. This is *my body*, all that I perceive are *my perceptions*, all that I do are *my acts*, and so on. Consciousness itself is the model of a unitary subject underlying surface multiplicity. I project this subjectivity onto all other entities. The universe becomes alive or, as Thales (ca. 600–545 BCE) said, "everything is full of gods." So the world starts pantheist and polytheist.

Thales is remembered, however, for that other thing he said: "The One is Water," a projection of subjectivity to the cosmos as a whole. This was the inaugural proposition of western philosophy: an answer to the question of the One and the Many (Copleston, 1946/1962), for which Thales has been deemed the first philosopher. So the central problem of dissociative multiplicity is very ancient: how can what seems to be many really be one? How can what is one manifest as many? Just what is it that there are many of, and what is it that remains one throughout?

Thales's *One* bounced from opinion to opinion, from water to air to fire to earth, settling into these four elements of the ancients, but at another extreme becoming the One-Good-Truth-Beauty which unified ontology, ethics, cognition, and esthetics. We have whittled consciousness down over time and eliminated the gods (soul, psyche, spirit) from almost everything except ourselves and kindred metazoa, possibly; and demoted soul to mind or intentional agency. We have also turned the tables on subject and object by reinterpreting subjectivity as something arising from that very complex organization of objects known as a brain.

And so subject (the mind) is reduced to object (the brain) even if the latter is an intentional object of the former (to the extent that it is knowable). While human subjectivity may not be as unitary as we once thought, its unity remains the source of that very concept of unity of which we subsequently deem it to fall short. Consequently, claims that the unity of consciousness is *merely* an illusion are greatly exaggerated.

19.5.3.6 Of What There Remains Only One: Psyche, Mind, Body

These terms escape the controversy. The Greek *psyche* is sufficiently remote and impersonal that it is not difficult to conceive of an *ego* or *self* being some subset of *psyche*, and the Anglo-Saxon *mind* is not far behind. But even *psyche* has an experience-near, concrete origin. As Julian Jaynes points out from the language of Homer's *Iliad*:

> The word *psyche*, which later means soul or conscious mind, is in most instances life-substances, such as blood or breath: a dying warrior bleeds out his *psyche* onto the ground or breathes it out in his last gasp. (Jaynes, 1976)

So Mesmer's magnetic fluid and Freud's Q error, thought of as a conservable fluid quantity, is a presupposition present from the dawn of history. Some ideas, old enough, become cultural *idées fixes*.

Another Anglo-Saxon word is *body*. We all know what it generally connotes, but its original meaning was broader, connoting a whole somebody, a meaning obviously implicit in *somebody,* as well as in *anybody, everybody,* and *nobody*. If we are wondering of what there remains one, despite any multiplicity, we may at least count on the body, even if our patients don't agree with us.

19.5.4 Depersonalization

Depersonalization warrants its own heading as it is not clearly an aspect of faculty dissociation nor of multiplicity. Historically, it was distinct from Hysterical Neurosis (dissociative or conversion) up to DSM-II/ICD-9, and remains *sui generis* in ICD-10. Depersonalization seems to be of a particular mental faculty, namely of sensation and perhaps affect as well, to the extent that the body doesn't seem real. But such sensory change is whole body, very close to whole-person, as a sort of out-of-body experience "prior to takeoff."

Frank out-of-body experiences are sometimes considered a kind of depersonalization. Clinically, however, an out-of-body experience prompts the differential diagnosis of depersonalization and multiplicity: for example, self-A may report having had an out-of-body experience; but in a subsequent experience, self-A may be perceived by self-B, currently in the body, as the (hallucinated) copresence of self-A off to one side. I have had moments in a session where it is clear only to me which self is "in" the real body. We are fortunate that others have made depersonalization their primary research interest (see Simeon, 2009a, 2009b).

19.5.5 Full-Blown Dissociative Multiplicity: What Needs To Be Accounted For

A theory is as robust as the empirical tests it can survive. Dissociative disorders constitute severe tests for any psychological theory, such as psychoanalytic theory, and full-blown DID constitutes the most severe test. So it is worth rehearsing the general features of a worst case. There are many classic texts regarding the basic facts of DID, about which there can be little debate (Dell, 2009a;

Kluft, 1987, 1988; Loewenstein & Ross, 1992; Putnam, 1989; Ross, 1997). These are admirably updated in this book (Beere, 2009; Dell, 2009a; Steele, Van der Hart, & Nijenhuis, 2009).

The alters may be few or many, of various ages, including older than the body, same- or cross-gendered, hetero- or homosexual, alive or dead, with either or both coconsciousness and copresence to varying degrees, which may not be commutative (i.e., may be one-way), communicating not at all, or through hallucinations, or through direct thought transfer, manifesting different physiological signs in the body when out, clustered in various arrays of dyads, subgrouping, layers, purposes, and so on. Subhuman, animal, or imaginary alters are not uncommon, with likely links to children's fantasy. When out, a given host or alter may appear globally to be mentally and behaviorally whole and normal or an exaggerated caricature or a single-function agent, and so on, but not necessarily congruent with the age and gender of the body.

The alters' realities are similarly varied. Kluft (1991) introduced the felicitous term *Multiple Reality Disorder* as each alter has its own take on current reality, its own inner reality (mis)interpreting outer reality, greatly complicating the transference. But there is often a common internal reality or landscape or inscape[16] inhabited by the distinct phantom bodies[17] of host and alters (O'Neil, 1997), which is likely group autohypnotic, as a common inscape may be prompted on purpose through clinical hypnosis (see Fraser, 1991, 2003). Even if no one agrees with another on the external world, all generally agree on the inscape itself and on their respective appearances in it. The inscape is experienced by whoever is out as distinct from external reality, dream, fantasy, or posttraumatic hallucinatory flashback, and is thus clearly distinct from both the inner and internal worlds as cited by Meissner previously. Each alter has a distinct phantom body in a common phantom landscape that demonstrates continuity over time, and in which historical events can take place with repercussions, just as for real reality.[18]

Despite this multiplicity of the ego, however, and of corresponding internal bodies, the inscape also constitutes a single psychic context of unity underlying the multiplicity. The inscape does for the internal world what the single physical body does for the external.

An interesting question is whether this common inscape is simply epiphenomenal to having arisen from a single brain, or rather is created and managed by some underlying common agency (e.g., a Kantian transcendental ego).

19.6 DISSOCIATION AND PSYCHOANALYSIS: THE LITERATURE

Dissociative multiplicity is a *persona non grata* in the psychoanalytic mainstream. As various histories relate (Dell, 2009b; Ellenberger, 1970; Van der Hart & Dorahy, 2009), dissociation is present in the very early Freud, but then he abandoned it soon after. It came to be dismissed as prepsychoanalytic, and was relegated to the status of a historical curiosity or mistake. Freud went on to elaborate his entire œuvre, followed by Klein and the postkleinians, Bowlby and attachment theory, the various Lacanian schools, Kohut and self psychology, and the interpersonal school. Psychoanalysis has managed to do all this while leaving dissociation out of the picture. When dissociation has been invoked, it is usually in the context of a prepsychoanalytic historical note or in the informal sense of something that isn't associated, making for little difference in theory, and none in practice. Faced with such a history, the reincorporation of dissociation within psychoanalysis is a major challenge. There have been more attempts to explain it away than attempts to come to terms with it.

The psychoanalyst who has made the most substantial general contribution to the dissociation literature is Richard Kluft (2000, 2009), an IPA member who has the unique distinction of having served as president of the ISSTD, of ASCH, and of SCEH.[19] There have been other contributions from IPA analysts (Brenner, 2001, 2002; Tarnopolsky, 2003), but in the past decade or more the most significant and voluminous contributions have come from non-IPA analysts, such as Philip Bromberg (1998, 2009), Donnel Stern (2009), Elizabeth Howell (2005), and others, and from psychoanalytic psychotherapists inspired especially by non-IPA schools of psychoanalysis, such as Ruth Blizard (2001) and Richard Chefetz (2000). My explanation for this is that proximity to the

[16] The oral tradition seems to have borrowed "inscape" directly from the visual arts as intending an "internal landscape," rather than from Gerard Manley Hopkins who independently coined the term earlier, but gave it an unrelated meaning.

[17] These bodies may be considered the body schemata of the respective alters, akin to virtual bodies in virtual reality. I prefer "phantom" body to relate it to the older concept of phantom limb.

[18] An excellent published autobiographic example is detailed by Robert Oxnam (2005).

[19] The International Society for the Study of Trauma & Dissociation; The American Society of Clinical Hypnosis; The Society for Clinical and Experimental Hypnosis.

IPA is inversely proportional to the ability to think about, or recognize, hypnoid defenses and dissociation.

19.7 DISSOCIATION AND SPLITTING

The usual discussion would be chronological, beginning with Freud's replacement of hypnoid hysteria with defensive repression, and then proceed onto other psychoanalytic concepts. There is conceptual merit, however, in first dealing with splitting in its various meanings, as splitting in its most common sense, the one developed by Klein, is generally understood to occur before the onset of repression ontogenetically, and to be central to borderline character structure—the differential diagnosis of DID and Borderline Personality Disorder (BPD) is an ongoing debate. DSM-IV Criterion 9 for BPD allows for transient dissociative symptoms, which invites borderline partisans to interpret all dissociatives as borderline, and dissociative partisans to interpret all borderlines as dissociative.

19.7.1 Kinds of Splitting

Splitting is a common word, and so has taken on a variety of meanings. Brook (1992) identifies three meanings in Freud that emerged in sequence: the dissociative splitting of consciousness into hypnoid states; the splitting of representations of self, object (other), and affect into good and bad; and the splitting of one's attitude to some aspect of reality. Early on, Freud rejected the first sense, dissociative splitting, in favor of repression. Melanie Klein and the British object relations school developed and deepened the second sense, and this has become the default meaning of splitting today, nosologically associated especially with BPD. Brook interprets Kohutian splitting as another application of this second kind of splitting, though I will deal with it separately under triads. The third kind is best exemplified by Freud's "Splitting of the ego in the process of defense" (1940), which Freud applied to sexual perversion and psychosis (see "Perverse-Psychotic Splitting" below).

19.7.2 Good-Bad Splitting of Representations

Freud briefly discussed the polar (good-bad) splitting of representations of self and object only three times (Brook, 1992). In fact, this kind of representational splitting in the inner world Klein would later regard as a later and more superficial sort of splitting than the structural splitting in the internal world that she had in mind. An early example of polar splitting shows up in Aristotle's account of the Pythagoreans:

> There are ten principles which they arrange in two columns of cognates—limit and unlimited, odd and even, one and plurality, right and left, male and female, resting and moving, straight and curved, light and darkness, good and bad, square and oblong. (Aristotle, 1941, Metaphysics A, 986a, p. 698)

This splitting consists of (1) a multitude of polar opposites, (2) all grouped into a single overarching polarity, a single table of opposites. The Pythagoreans could comfortably conceive of one good limited right light resting straight square male. This grouping would effectively defend them against the alarming alternative: the many bad dark unlimited moving curved oblong females. The Pythagorean table of opposites is, *inter alia*, a misogynist defense against irrational lust. This early attempt at systematizing the world is preambivalent: everything is simply good or bad, light or dark. This is not to say that all Pythagoreans were borderlines functioning in the paranoid-schizoid position. It may just be that their theory hadn't caught up with their practice (hardly a surprise, as neither has ours). They likely showed relative stability and adherence to the male pole in their waking hours (though perhaps exploring the other pole in their dreams).

Can the splitting of representations explain multiplicity? Not at all, for two reasons.[20] First, a split is into two, not many. The splitting of self and object representations manifest polarity: self-object, good-bad, male-female, friend-foe, and so on, whereas alters generally don't (though they may). Second, hosts and alters are intentional subjects or agents, entities capable of uttering "I." Indeed, one may profitably regard *alter* as short for *alter ego*, literally "other I." A given "I" has intentional objects that are its respective self and object representations. In other words, a split representation, even of the self, is an object of thought, not a thinker, not a subject or agent or "I." Split representations are the basis of virtually all categorical thinking about anything.

The contribution of polar opposites to categorical thinking is enormous: good-bad, white-black, day-night, edible-inedible, love-hate, friend-foe, birth-death, male-female, truth-lie, beauty-ugliness, hot-cold, wet-dry, high-low, over-under, in-out, tall-short, young-old, near-far, deep-shallow, consonance-dissonance, positive-negative, rational-irrational, real-imaginary, past-future, sacred-profane, infinite-finite, faithful-infidel, etc.

The advance from splitting to ambivalence happened when one set of contraries and another were made into an orthogonal grid, for example when Empedocles played

[20] This argument borrows from Young (1988).

dry-wet against hot-cold, giving rise to the 2x2 grid that explained the four elements: earth (cold dry), air (hot wet), fire (hot dry), and water (cold wet).

Philosophically, this grid thinking largely supplanted Pythagorean splitting. It was now possible to conceive of the odd good enlightened curved female, about whom one might feel so-so, at least. And to recognize that men could be dark and crooked. But ambivalence can't do away with splitting. Splitting remains necessary to resolve ambivalence. Once all the pros and cons are evaluated, one must make a choice, and this choice is necessarily unreasonable because it collapses one's ambivalence back into white or black, yes or no. The alternative is obsessive paralysis. We move from low-level splitting to ambivalence, and resolve ambivalence with a higher-level splitting. And so echoes of Pythagorean splitting remain with us today, not only in various religions, philosophies, and ethical systems, but in mathematics and the sciences, and in all effective decision making.

19.7.3 Kleinian Splitting Proper

19.7.3.1 Good-Bad Structural Splitting

As noted previously, Klein would interpret Pythagorean splitting of representations as the surface result in the adult of a prior and deeper splitting of more concrete internal objects in the child. Complementing Laplance and Pontalis's (1967/1973) exegesis of the Freudian œuvre, Hinshelwood's *Dictionary of Kleinian Thought* (1991) is a convenient digest of Kleinian thinking. *Dissociation* is not an entry; nor is *multiplicity. Internal object* "denotes an unconscious experience or phantasy of a concrete object physically located internal to the ego (body) which has is own motives and intentions towards the ego and to other objects."

In this conceptualization, such internal objects are introjected from experience with real objects; some are identified with, and become ego nuclei; selves and objects inhabit a phantasied internal world and may be creatively visualized; in acting out, such introjects are externalized. Freud's punishing superego becomes just another introjected and internal object, while the ego ideal would be another. This underscores how Kleinian metapsychology reduces Freud's structural theory to a special case. Instead of everybody having a Freud-prescribed id-ego-superego, somebody might now have an idiosyncratic internal structure that reflects one's own psychic history. To the punishing superego Klein adds helpful internal objects or "good objects," which may be "in various degrees of synthesis and separateness in different contexts and at different times" (ibid., p. 71). Such internal objects are experienced (consciously or unconsciously) as real, rather than as representations; they may be experienced as "mine" or "not mine," as ego syntonic or ego alien.

Can Kleinian splitting explain multiplicity? Certainly far better than the splitting of representations. It appears that the internal others (objects) are experienced as real, and with their own intentions; the set of split selves and objects in a fantasied internal landscape constitutes psychic structure; there is ambiguity as to what is more self-like and what is more object-like, as both are constituted by identification; helper alters are there; different degrees of proximity and difference are there. And so internal objects (and split parts of self) look like dissociative alters. None of this is possible in a psychic structure where id, ego, and superego hold a monopoly.

19.7.3.2 Splitting Leading to Fragmentation

Klein also used the term *splitting* to refer to what she took to be a more pathological grade of splitting, the nonpolar splitting of the internal object into multiple fragments (Hinshelwood, 1991), which would imply a concomitant fragmentation of the self. This conceptualization, while multiple, does not serve our purposes, however, as Klein applied it to the mind of the schizophrenic, the psychotic.

19.7.4 Can Splitting Explain Dissociation?

That Kleinian splitting enables one to comprehend dissociative multiplicity predicts that London and Latin America would be dissociative hotbeds. Instead, they are dissociative deserts. Why? Hinshelwood's definition is precise and tricky. While it invokes a fairly concrete internal object with motives and intentions located within somebody, this remains a *fantasy* of a concrete internal object with motives and intentions rather than an internal object which *in fact has* motives and intentions. There remains a single Kleinian ego, however concrete may be that ego's fantasies of its own splits. Imagine a patient manifesting apparent borderline pathology. It is interesting to wonder whether a given manifestation of splitting is the appearance of a single ego's transient identification with one of its fantasied part-selves or part-objects as it enacts the appropriate script of the object relation implied or, on the other hand, the appearance of a dissociative switch from ego-1 to ego-2, perhaps complicated by the fact that ego-2 is similar to one of ego-1's internal objects, as both are identifications with the same real person. The crucial difference is that ego-2 is independently endowed with its own subjectivity.

Klein's conceptualization of the splitting of internal objects thus brings us to the doorstep of frank dissociative multiplicity, but doesn't quite cross the threshold. Does this suggest what happens in fact? If somebody reacts to trauma through Kleinian splitting, might he react to further or worse trauma by crossing that threshold into frank dissociative multiplicity? In brief, can an internal object or introject somehow become secondarily imbued with agency, with subjectivity?

My own view is that at this juncture, Kleinian splitting encounters the same obstacle as the splitting of representations. There are good reasons for assuming that primary proliferative dissociation predates Kleinian splitting. The *dédoublement* occurs because the baby or child is not yet capable of effective splitting, and the resulting multiplicity preempts the need to split. Alternatively, if somebody has achieved a certain level of mental maturity, relative to the trauma suffered, then splitting without *dédoublement* becomes an option. The first child will grow up with DID. The second will grow up with BPD. Combinations of the two are common, of course, as once splitting becomes an option, the host or any of the alters may then, individually, split defensively. Multiples whose hosts are characterologically borderline are more challenging to treat than those who aren't. But certainly the hosts of many multiples are not borderline in any diagnostic sense. And many borderlines, including the very severe ones, may split without switching.

So I would conclude that the Kleinians and British object-relations theorists interpret preambivalent splitting in everybody, which is appropriate to the extent that it is present, and this enables them to treat analysands at the sicker end of the spectrum who engage primarily in preambivalent structural splitting. Their analysands include some who have DID, and who also split, of course, but not all of whom may primarily split, whose multiplicity remains unseen, whose internal subjects (alters) are misinterpreted as internal objects. We only find what we are looking for.

There are British object-relations theorists who are not dissociation-blind. Alex Tarnopolsky[21] (2003) has no difficulty crossing the threshold, but does so through a general recategorization. He regroups dissociative multiplicity, borderline splitting, perverse splitting, and neurotic repression under a single catchphrase of Freud: "keeping things apart." But while Freud's user-friendly expression may well capture what these various mechanisms have in common, it fails to adequately explain how they are different. Indeed, if they are all aspects of the same thing, then the choice of primary entity—dissociation, repression, or splitting—becomes a matter of taste, and able to guide effective therapy in a given therapist.

19.7.5 Can Dissociation Explain Splitting?

If, as I suggest, *dédoublement* predates splitting, then perhaps we ought to cross the threshold in the other direction, beginning with dissociative multiplicity and having it explain the structural splitting of internal objects. Certainly, an alter created by *dédoublement* may have the character of a victim, in conformity with Ferenczi's (1933/1949) concept of identification with the aggressor,[22] or with the concept of the EP, the Emotional Personality (Steele et al., 2009; Van der Hart, Nijenhuis, & Steele, 2006); or, less commonly, identify with an admired or envied figure. My view is that patients who appear to have BPD, where their defensive style and apparent psychic structure are dominated by splitting, may well be covertly multiple. Howell and Blizard (2009) advance strong arguments in support of the view that splitting and projective identification are both manifestations of dissociation. They interpret the spectrum of (1) frank DID, (2) BPD with dissociative symptoms, and (3) BPD without dissociative symptoms as indicating that splitting is fundamentally dissociative. But the spectrum may equally be interpreted as indicating the opposite: that the two are distinct. Of course, if dissociative multiplicity predates Kleinian splitting, then perhaps the dédoublement occurs first, and then partial integration reunites the ego but leaves traces of its history as fantasies of concrete internal part-selves and part-objects. This is theoretically possible, though perhaps not possible to test empirically, as the research subjects would need to be traumatized babies and toddlers; and retrospective constructions from adults are open to all the usual methodological hazards.

I have certainly assessed patients identified as having BPD who prove to have DID; and others where I do not detect DID, which may be a reflection of my diagnostic limitations. But the interpretation of all splitting as dissociative in the same sense leads to a conceptual conundrum. Imagine a patient with DID who has an alter who splits (e.g., a borderline alter), alongside others who may be obsessional, or histrionic, say. The apparently borderline alter would really be a pair of alters (or some multiple of two) that are in close but polar reverberation with

[21] Alex Tarnopolsky trained in London and is now an IPA training analyst in the Canadian Institute of Psychoanalysis.

[22] Identification with the aggressor is most often associated with Anna Freud (1966), but the concept originates with Sándor Ferenczi (Frankel, 2002).

each other. But this pair clearly wouldn't be alters in the same sense as the other alters were alters. And if either of the pair seemed to split, this would entail a possible infinite regress that could only be avoided by rejecting splitting as necessarily dissociative—at least in the sense of *dédoublement*. Of course, it may remain descriptively dissociative, according to taste.

19.7.6 Perverse-Psychotic Splitting

We now turn to Freud's "Splitting of the Ego in the Process of Defence" (1940), which he applied to sexual perversion and psychosis. While this work was very late in Freud's life, perversion had long occupied an important position in his thought as "neuroses are, so to say, the negative of perversions" (1905). This is because what is hidden or repressed in the neurotic is manifest in the pervert.

For "classical" psychoanalysts or Ego Psychologists of the USA, the repertoire of available concepts to explain dissociative multiplicity is quite limited: dissociation itself is dismissed as prepsychoanalytic, the topography is eclipsed by the structural theory, and the splitting of representations is tarnished by its Kleinian elaboration. That leaves perverse splitting as a remaining recourse. Perverse splitting of the ego is of the fetishist's *attitude to reality as a whole* (Brook, 1992; de Mijolla-Mellor, 2005). One attitude is realistic: women have no penises, castration has taken place, and so one's penis is in danger. The other attitude is based on wishful thinking: women have penises, so castration has not taken place, and thus one's penis is safe; and, in any case, even if women don't have penises, at least they have high-heeled shoes—thus, the fetish. Displacing the penis onto the high heel (or the whole shoe) allows for a perversion that saves the man from psychosis: the outright denial of the reality of woman without a penis. Such attitudinal splitting has cleavage, in the sense of just two contradictory attitudes in close juxtaposition: the real and the perverse. Such splitting, therefore, begins as a splitting of reality, of one's attitude to reality, engendering a splitting of the ego, which results in perversion or, if sufficiently extreme, in psychosis.

19.7.6.1 Brenner: Reducing Dissociative Multiplicity to Perverse Splitting

In the recent *Freud Encyclopedia* (Erwin, 2002), Ira Brenner's entry, *Dissociation* (2002), summarizes views he states elsewhere (2001). He interprets the Janet/Freud dispute as one over passive/active, with dissociation being passive, and repression being active. In such standoffs, activity always prevails. He clarifies that dissociation can be interpreted as active defense as well, and so rescues Janet's stance to some degree. He describes psychoanalysis as having developed into ego psychology, self-psychology, and object relations theory, and lumps these together under splitting. Repression and splitting are given explanatory precedence, so that dissociation "augments repression or primitive splitting of ego," a view echoed by Dell (2009b). Finally, Brenner reduces multiple personality to a "dissociative character," and, with another bow to orthodoxy, claims that the respective ego states are "aggressively and libidinally derived self and object representations"; there is no mention of alter creation precipitated by external trauma.

I agree that dissociation can be interpreted as an active defense, and this will be discussed under "Repression" (in the following). Otherwise, there are serious difficulties with Brenner's formulation. First of all, lumping together ego psychology, self-psychology, and object relations theory under *splitting* confuses perverse, narcissistic, and preambivalent (Kleinian) splitting. Second, does dissociation really augment repression or primitive splitting of ego? Or does this put the cart before the horse? Dissociation, clinically, tends to be prerepressive, and certainly prior to perverse splitting, which is itself subsequent to Kleinian splitting. In my view, it is early major defensive dissociation, which may subsequently be augmented by splitting and then by either repression or its negative (perverse splitting). Third, the reduction of multiple personality to a "dissociative character" suffers from the weakness of the "character" construct (see previous discussion), as well as confusing DSM's Axes I and II. Finally, the attempt to promote self or object representations, whether these be aggressively or libidinally derived or not, to the status of alternate *subjects* is certainly more of a stretch than promoting Kleinian internal objects to subjects. Ultimately, I read Brenner's formulation as a defensive maneuver, a compromise formation, between ego psychological orthodoxy and dissociative multiplicity. One category mistake in this conceptualization is that alters are necessarily aggressive or libidinal, whereas clinically we confront alters that are neither. The second category mistake is that alters derive from representations. With respect to *dédoublement* of the ego, representations are beside the point.

On the other hand, a host or alter might be perverse, and in fact perverse dynamics are commonly found in multiples. One may be curious about whether the perversion is simply an activation of innate perversion, especially of sado-masochism, along "classical" lines, or whether it is rather an identification with, or introjection of, the perversion of the perpetrator, or whatever, but in any case to that extent this sort of perverse ego splitting remains a serviceable concept in the treatment of dissociative patients, and helps me explain and deal with the special perverse characteristics of a given alter, or perverse dynamics in the transference-countertransference. This sort of splitting can apply to a given alter, but cloven attitudes can hardly explain the genesis of alters each of whom utters a distinct "I."

19.7.6.2 Fostering Attitudinal Splitting in Therapy

At the healthy end of this spectrum, splitting of one's attitude to reality, so as to hold, concurrently, two incompatible versions of reality, may be understood as a therapeutic goal that one hopes to achieve with each alter. Take the example of an alter exhibiting so-called Rip van Winkle Syndrome.[23] She insists that she is 5 years old, and that this is 1983. We hope to induce "splitting of the ego in the process of defense" so that she can know, at one and the same time, that she is now 5 years old in 1983, and that she is also now "really" 30 years old in 2008. Another example would be for a host or alter to know, at one and the same time, that she is sitting in a chair in trance in her therapist's office, and also sitting in a special chair in a workroom in the presence of her alters projecting images on a screen that all can see (except for her therapist).

19.8 DISSOCIATION AND REPRESSION

So much for polar splitting. We now return to Freud's first use of the word *splitting*, the splitting of hypnoid hysteria, as that historically led directly to his *repression*, even if the latter was subsequently interpreted to be developmentally later than other sorts of splitting (of internal objects and of attitudes) discussed previously. So it is of interest to understand a little about what allows for the progression from Kleinian splitting to repression.

19.8.1 The Shift from Splitting to Repression: Klein's Positions, Bowlby's Phases, Kübler-Ross's Stages

Klein distinguished her model of development from Freud's by replacing his term, *phase* (e.g., oral phase), with *position*: "a constellation of anxieties, defenses, object-relations and impulses" (Hinshelwood, 1991). She settled on two major positions, the paranoid-schizoid and the depressive, as representing the major move from borderline pathology, dominated by persecutory anxiety, splitting and projective identification, to normal-neurotic pathology, dominated by ambivalence and repression. The hoped-for goal of mental health is rarely advertised as *repression, depression, and ambivalence*, however. Clifford Scott (1964) added a position of postdepressive *zest* to the picture. This is perhaps best anticipated by Klein's concept of *reparation* (Hinshelwood, 1991).

John Bowlby (1980) expanded Klein's positions to four phases of mourning: (1) numbness, (2) yearning & protest, (3) disorganization and despair, (4) reorganization. The first is roughly schizoid, the second roughly paranoid, the third depressive, and his fourth can be construed as somewhat less optimistic *zest*.

A parallel has also been drawn between Klein's positions and Kübler-Ross's five stages of death and dying (Burch, 1989), a parallel which many find more user-friendly. Kübler-Ross's (1969) first two stages, denial and anger, would correspond to Klein's paranoid-schizoid and to Bowlby's first two phases; her last two, despair and acceptance, would correspond to Klein's depressive position and to Bowlby's last two phases. Kübler-Ross adds her third stage, bargaining, between paranoia-protest-anger and depression-despair. This would correspond to an obsessive-compulsive interlude between Klein's positions. Earlier on, Klein referred to an "obsessional position," but later on folded this into her manic defenses against the depressive position (Hinshelwood, 1991).

These parallels underscore the general applicability of this progression to somebody's reaction not just to loss or death, but to any dysphoric event, and also to different concurrent time frames: child development; an entire lifetime; a response to and recovery from a major loss, trauma, or life challenge; the response of a patient to a therapist's vacation or other frame distortion; the overall course of a therapy; the sequence within a single therapeutic session, and so on. And so our discussion moves on to repression.

19.8.2 Freud's Inaugural Category Mistake: Rejecting Hypnoid Hysteria in Favor of Defense

Dissociative multiplicity predated psychoanalysis, under various names such as grand hysteria, hypnoid hysteria, *dédoublement de la personnalité, désagrégation mentale, état second, existences successives,* and so on. The early Freud often references Jean-Martin Charcot and Pierre Janet. At the time, dissociation and hypnosis were complementary concerns, and overt trauma was considered the primary etiology. These items all figure centrally and undisguised in what has been dubbed the *primal book of*

[23] Named after a short story by Washington Irving published in 1819.

psychoanalysis (Grubrich-Simitis, 1997), the *Studies on Hysteria* (Breuer & Freud, 1895):

> The splitting[24] of consciousness which is so striking in the well-known classical cases under the form of *"double conscience"* [fn: The French term ("dual consciousness")] is present to a rudimentary degree in every hysteria, and … a tendency to such a dissociation, and with it the emergence of abnormal states of consciousness (which we shall bring together under the term "hypnoid") is the basic phenomenon of this neurosis. In these views we concur with Binet and the two Janets [fn: Pierre and Jules]. (p. 12)

The passage is striking in a number of respects: there is confusion between division (splitting) and multiplication (doubling); multiplicity is regarded as primary, and functional dissociation as secondary, so that any somatoform symptoms are subsumed under more global altered states of consciousness.[25] Another telling citation is from Freud's *Neuro-Psychoses of Defense*[26] (1894). Freud distinguished four accounts of hysteria, which I have labelled 0-1-2-3 so as to accord with Freud's naming of them, as he immediately discarded the first [0]:

> [T]he syndrome of hysteria … justifies the assumption of there being a splitting of consciousness.… [0] According to Janet … it is based on an innate weakness of the capacity for psychical synthesis,… evidence of the degeneracy of hysterical individuals.…
>
> [1] According to [Breuer], "the basis and *sine qua non* of hysteria" is the occurrence of peculiar dream-like states of consciousness with a restricted capacity for association, for which he proposes the name "hypnoid states." In that case, the splitting of consciousness is secondary and acquired.…
>
> [There are] two other extreme forms of hysteria in which it is impossible to regard the splitting of consciousness as primary in Janet's sense.… [2] the splitting of consciousness is the result of an act of will on the part of the patient; … initiated by an effort of will whose motive can be specified.…
>
> [3] the splitting of consciousness plays an insignificant part, or perhaps none at all.… [T]he reaction to traumatic stimuli has failed to occur.… [T]hese are the pure "retention hysterias." (pp. 45–47)

Again, hysterical symptoms imply an underlying splitting of consciousness. Then apples and oranges muddy the waters. Is Janetian splitting of consciousness different from Breuerian oneiric or hypnoid states? Are Janetian "weakness of the capacity for psychical synthesis" and Breuerian "restricted capacity for association" essentially different? Are Janetian splits in consciousness congenital rather than acquired? Would an act of the will necessarily induce a splitting of consciousness distinguishable from a Breuerian hypnoid state? Does the presence of motive preclude certain altered states of consciousness? The implied Freudian answer to all these questions would be "Yes"; in my view, the correct answer to all of them is "No." In any case, Freud discards Janet's sense and calls the three remaining kinds (1) hypnoid, (2) defense, and (3) retention hysteria (which he subsequently abandoned).[27] His dismissing of Janet may have been polemically mutual, as any text referencing Janet in Freud is more noise than signal, and ascribes more noise than signal to what Janet has to say about psychoanalysis (Dell, 2009b). For example, Freud criticized Janet for blaming genetic or innate predisposition, while he was concurrently (1896) attributing "choice of neurosis" to constitutional (hereditary) liability—a theme that persisted throughout his life (Grubrich-Simitis, 1988). And in the quote, Freud neglects to mention traumatic stimulus as an ætiological agent for either hypnoid or defense hysteria, as if it were not central to all authors concerned (Janet, Breuer, and Freud).

My reading of the original texts and of various excellent treatments on this complex topic (Bromberg, 1998; Dell, 2009b; Grubrich-Simitis, 1997; Howell, 2005; Van der Hart & Dorahy, 2009) is that Janet, Breuer, and the early Freud had views that were essentially equivalent: both constitution and trauma were necessary etiological factors; splitting of consciousness, or oneiric or hypnoid states, resulted; which then manifest themselves through various hysterical symptoms. Freud exaggerated the differences as he was associated with Breuer [hysteria-1] and wished to distance himself from Janet [hysteria-0]. Freud then adds the interpretation that the subject's reaction to

[24] *Spaltung*, Freud's first sense of the word, the vertical splitting of consciousness, dissociative multiplicity.

[25] In agreement with Steele, Van der Hart, and Nijenhuis (2009).

[26] A *neuro-psychosis* is now generally called a *psychoneurosis* or just plain *neurosis*. To some extent the senses of the two words have switched, in that a neurosis was originally thought to be strictly neurological, calling for a general physician, whereas a psychosis was thought to be a mental, or higher-level, disorder, and so needing an alienist (psychiatrist). Freud's first use of "neurosis" was for neurasthenia and anxiety neurosis, which later became his so-called actual neuroses, having no roots in the past and only direct physical causes in the present (e.g., excessive masturbation for neurasthenia), as *opposed* to the psychoneuroses, having meaningful roots in childhood.

[27] The pervasiveness of "hysteria" is in sharp contrast to the general hysterectomy undergone by DSM-III, which carried over into DSM-IV.

trauma is on purpose: for defense. This occasions what, for the purposes of this chapter, I have dubbed his inaugural category mistake: the confounding of defense and repression. This comes through *in statu nascendi* later in the text: "I willingly adhere to this hypothesis of there being a hypnoid hysteria" (Breuer & Freud, 1895). But the import of this is immediately undercut:

> Strangely enough, I have never in my own experience met with a genuine hypnoid hysteria. Any that I took in hand has turned into a defence hysteria.... I was able to show afterwards that the so-called hypnoid state owed its separation to the fact that in it a psychical group had come into effect which had previously been split off by defence.... I am unable to suppress a suspicion that somewhere or other the roots of hypnoid and defence hysteria come together, and that there the primary factor is defence. But I can say nothing about this....
>
> [A]t the basis of retention hysteria, too, an element of defence is to be found.... It is to be hoped that fresh observations will soon decide whether I am running the risk of falling into one-sidedness and error in thus favouring an extension of the concept of defence to the whole of hysteria. (ibid.)

The tension is palpable. Freud "willingly adheres" to hypnoid hysteria, but is "unable to suppress a suspicion"; he says a great deal about how he "can say nothing"; he wonders if he is falling into error by making a risky hypothesis: defense characterizes the whole of hysteria. We can agree with Freud that the primary factor is defense, and we can disagree with him that only repression can defend.

The mistake persisted, and emerges again roughly 30 years later:

> Breuer supposed that the pathogenic ideas produced their traumatic effect because they arose during *"hypnoid states,"* in which mental functioning was subject to special limitations. [I] rejected this explanation and inclined to the belief that an idea became pathogenic if its content was in opposition to the predominant trend of the subject's mental life so that it provoked him into *"defence."* (Janet had attributed to hysterical patients a constitutional incapacity for holding together the contents of their minds; and it was at this point that his path diverged from that of Breuer and Freud.) (S. Freud, 1923b)

Freud again dismisses Janet parenthetically in the last sentence. The initial two sentences confuse resultant state (hypnoid state) with rationale or purpose (defense). In between are mechanisms, such as dissociation or repression. Why can the rationale for dissociation not be defense? The autohypnotic nature of hypnoid states was clear from the beginning to all concerned. Why was Freud unable to conceive of such an act of autohypnosis as unconsciously motivated or intended? The solution staring him in the face was that (imperfect) dissociation results in hypnoid states, and (imperfect) repression results in conversion. By 1923, Freud is still so muddled that he cites trauma as an effect rather than a cause: pathogenic ideas in the presence of hypnoid states produces trauma as an effect.

Freud was trapped in his own Pythagorean table of opposites. One side of the table would be bad, Janet/Breuer, heredity, degeneracy, trauma, splitting of consciousness, hypnoid hysteria, dissociation. The other side would be good, Freud, drive, defense, repression, conversion. He was unable to advance to an Empedoclean grid, which would have allowed for defensive dissociative induction of hypnoid states, a move which would have allowed him to distinguish dissociation from repression without dismissing it, and forego the subsequent general psychoanalytic marginalization and abandonment of that significant patient population represented by a number of cases in his own *Studies on Hysteria* (Breuer & Freud, 1895). And so the latter is not only the primal book of psychoanalysis, but also the primal book of the psychoanalytic misinterpretation of major posttraumatic pathology. In this regard, I have some sympathy for Josef Breuer, who stated:

> Freud is a man given to absolute and exclusive formulations: this is a psychical need which, in my opinion, leads to excessive generalization. There may in addition be a desire *d'épater le bourgeois* [to shock middle-class attitudes]....
>
> The case of Anna O., which was the germ-cell of the whole of psycho-analysis, proves that a fairly severe case of hysteria can develop, flourish, and be resolved without having a sexual basis. I confess that the plunging into sexuality in theory and practice is not to my taste. But what have my taste and my feeling about what is seemly and what is unseemly to do with the question of what is true?
>
> ... I still regard Freud's work as magnificent: built up on the most laborious study in his private practice and of the greatest importance—even though no small part of its structure will doubtless crumble away again. (Cranefield, 1958)

The quotation is poignant: Breuer accurately identifies Freud's excessive generalization, then denies the very significant sexuality in the case, then admits to a distaste for the sexuality that he just claimed wasn't there, then grants magnificent truth to Freud, then predicts that science will no doubt refute that magnificence.

Freud's absolute and exclusive formulation was to confound repression and defense. This underscores the two meanings of repression in the literature. The early meaning is equivalent to defense, a blanket term for all conceivable defense mechanisms. The late meaning is just one of the potential set of defense mechanisms. His daughter Anna Freud (1966), for example, listed 10, the other nine being: regression, reaction formation, isolation, undoing, projection, introjection, turning against the self, reversal, and sublimation. This doesn't include Freud's own perverse splitting, nor the Kleinian defenses, such as splitting, introjection, assimilation, disparagement, control, idealization, identification, and projective identification.

Freud clarified this in 1926:

> *(c) Repression and Defence*
>
> I have revived a ... term, of which I made exclusive use thirty years ago ... "defensive process." I afterwards replaced it by the word "repression"... It will be an undoubted advantage ... to revert to ... "defence," provided we employ it explicitly as a general designation for all the techniques which the ego makes use of in conflicts which may lead to a neurosis, while we retain the word "repression" for the special method of defence which the line of approach taken by our investigations made us better acquainted with in the first instance. (S. Freud, 1926a)

Alas, despite disentangling defense and repression, Freud was still unable to recognize that his early cases included different kinds of resultant psychopathology, and thus invited the hypothesis that more than one kind of defense was involved. While *undoing* was now in the wider defensive repertoire, Freud was unable to undo his break with Breuer.

In any case, Breuer's comments focus more on sex, Freud's second major shift in excessive generalization: in place of all psychopathology based on childhood sexual trauma, all psychopathology was now based on repressed sexual wishes.

Freud's "dissociative period" was thus short-lived (coming to an end even prior to the publication of the *Studies*), and clearly designated as prepsychoanalytic by Freud himself, and most psychoanalysts have dutifully followed his path.

The abandonment of major dissociative hysteria was not just psychoanalytic, of course. By the early 20th century, hysteria had slipped from fashion as a diagnosis, and Eugen Bleuler (1911/1950) lumped some hysterics (i.e., patients with multiple personality) in with Kraepelin's Dementia Præcox, which he renamed Schizophrenia [schizo = split; phren = mind], a misnomer which has fostered a century of diagnostic obfuscation and popular confusion. While hysteria continued on the books (e.g., DSM-II, the ICDs) as both dissociative and conversion types, the diagnosis still fell into disuse.

The shift from hypnoid to defense hysteria was thus a shift from dissociation to repression, from trauma to drive, from hypnosis to free association. There were obviously positive by-products of such a shift: psychoanalysis went on to clarify the understanding of normal-neurotic psychopathology and its treatment. The Kleinians went on to develop a convincing understanding of (Pythagorean) splitting, and gave birth to the object relations tradition in psychoanalysis (though not independently). And Kohut went on to clarify narcissistic pathology, and so on. But psychoanalysis has had to venture into the more serious psychopathologies burdened with an obstinate and even sanctimonious ignorance of trauma, dissociation, and hypnosis. And so hysteria underwent a split in meaning when Freud shifted from dissociation to repression, and one needs to distinguish the original dissociative hysteria and conversion, which continued to develop in clinical psychiatry outside of psychoanalysis, from the repressive hysteria and conversion that developed within psychoanalysis.

19.8.3 Dissociation, Repression, and Conversion

19.8.3.1 Conversion in Psychiatric Nosology

This is the simplest definition. In essence, a conversion symptom is pseudoneurological and psychogenic. ICD-9 and DSM-II specified *hysterical neurosis*, which could then be *dissociative type* or *conversion type*. DSM-III-IV relabelled conversion hysteria as *Conversion Disorder* and moved it to its new category of *Somatoform Disorders*. ICD-10 dropped the word *hysterical* but maintained the grouping of the two types under the heading, *Dissociative (Conversion) Disorders*, despite having its own somatoform disorders category. And despite DSM's move, it admits that "Conversion Disorder shares features with Dissociative Disorders. Both disorders involve symptoms that suggest neurological dysfunction and may also have shared antecedents. If both conversion and dissociative symptoms occur in the same individual (which is common), both diagnoses should be made." This statement virtually guarantees that a certain degree of artefactual comorbidity, in Michael First's (2005) sense, is built into the diagnostic criteria.

19.8.3.2 Within Psychoanalysis: Conversion and Repression

> In hysteria, the incompatible idea is rendered innocuous by its sum of excitation being transformed into something somatic. For this I should like to propose the name of conversion. (S. Freud, 1894)

This early quote coined the word. Note that it is directly tied to Freud's Q (sum of excitation) and thus part of his wrongheaded economic point of view, and for that reason *frankly* neurological at the time (though as the neurology in question was refuted, it became pseudoneurological). Originally, the "sum of excitation" was due to external trauma; then to both external trauma and internal drive; and finally, primarily (though not exclusively) to internal drive. It rapidly became the paradigmatic compromise formation between drive (urge, intent, wish, motive) and defense (repression), and only secondarily between trauma and defense; and a paradigmatic example of primary gain: better to suffer the symptom than to be conscious of the wish or impulse. The psychiatric sense of conversion—pseudoneurological—would then be considered as a surface phenomenon of a more specific underlying dynamic—repressed drive.

19.8.3.3 Conversion in Dissociative Disorders

In the dissociative disorders realm, conversion slips to subset status. Van der Hart et al. (2006) reflect psychiatric tradition by promoting *dissociation* to replace the umbrella term *hysteria*, and then by qualifying the two types as *psychoform* and *somatoform* dissociation, a persistent pairing that is also in keeping with that high comorbidity which even the DSM-IV grants. But somatoform dissociation is broader than repressed drive, and thus broader than psychoanalytic conversion. Indeed, the most common somatoform symptoms in dissociative disorders are partial posttraumatic revivifications, rather than repressed wishes, and so it is not entirely clear whether psychoanalytic conversion warrants being considered as dissociative at all.

When faced with a somatoform symptom, then, one first rules out a neurological condition. One may then wonder whether it is a partial posttraumatic revivification (or the blunting of same), a repressed wish, or neither.

So if somebody wakes up with pain and stiffness in the neck and shoulders, one wants to figure out, say, whether this is a tactile flashback of having struggled against being pinned down and strangled 30 years ago; or, on the other hand, whether while visiting mother last night she said something grossly unempathic and demeaning, and the immediate reaction was the impulse to strangle her. If the latter, then better to have pain and stiffness in the muscle groups needed to strangle mother than to recall what she said or, indeed, that one wanted to strangle her. If somebody presents with blindness, one wants to clarify whether this is, say, a posttraumatic revivification of having been imprisoned in the pitch-black cellar at 3 years old or, rather, the somatic expression of the wish not to see oneself in the mirror, motivated by self-loathing, having recently discovered that one's alter had sexually abused a child last autumn. If the latter, then better to be blind than to look at the face of a child molester, oneself, in the mirror.

Revivifications may also be of one's dissociative state at the time of the trauma, and so have the quality of negative PTSD symptoms (e.g., local anesthesia or analgesia, oneiric state, etc.). For example, while working in an eating disorders in-patient unit, I had a patient who was anesthetic from umbilicus to mid-thigh. She manifested curious surprise when I informed her that most women had sensation "down there" (*la belle indifférence* is not *passée*).

The distinction between revivification and conversion proper is independent of the question of source of the symptom. In general, the source needs to be ascertained before such a distinction can be clarified. Is the symptom coming from the one before me in the office, or is it an intrusion from one of her/his alters? In the case of multiplicity, the most common somatoform symptoms are intrusions from an alter, and so that is where one must go to determine whether they are partial posttraumatic revivifications or conversion symptoms. In such cases, true conversion symptoms (as incompletely repressed impulses) are rare enough that they come as a surprise. Intrusion phenomena are more commonly partial and undisguised revivifications from a traumatized child alter (e.g., oneself being strangled 30 years ago, or oneself in the cellar at 3), so that psychoanalytic interpretation of symbolic significance may then be in the service of denial rather than insight—a "fallacy of misplaced abstraction."[28] For example, if a patient feels "as if I'm being fucked in the head" this may be interpreted as symbolic of some sophisticated interpersonal manipulation enacted through verbal communications from a mate or boss, obscuring the more concrete possibility of having endured forced fellatio as a child. Combinations may also occur. A partial somatic (primarily posttraumatic)

[28] As the negative of Alfred North Whitehead's oft-cited "fallacy of misplaced concreteness": misinterpreting an abstract belief, opinion or concept as physically or "concretely" real.

symptom may have secondary symbolic elaboration, as a compromise formation expressive of a wish-defense conflict.

It is also important not to needlessly multiply entities. If my neck and shoulders are stiff because I want to strangle my mother, I don't need to have an alter of whose stiffness I am the recipient. Where my alter is the child being strangled, and whose struggle I experience as an intrusion, that child alter may well have *repressed* the experience *as well*, and have the symptom instead of the memory. An infinite regress looms if that alter requires a subalter to hold the experience. And so my dissociated traumatized child alter may herself engage in the repression of the trauma. And if this is called dissociation, then it has nothing whatever to do with the dissociation that leads to that alter having the experience in place of myself. So better to retain the concept, repression.

Developmentally, I assume that *dissociation of trauma predates its repression*. In other words, one's defensive elaboration of an alter who suffers the overt trauma, in order for oneself to avoid such an experience, predates the subsequent repression of that trauma in the alter concerned. That alter may no longer experience the trauma, and have no memory of it, but may alternate between periods of blissful ignorance and excruciating flashbacks, on the pattern of an alternation between the criterion sets B and C for PTSD. And such criterion B symptoms may not manifest in the host for decades, until some untoward event in later adulthood overwhelms the fragile dissociative defenses and the alter's revivification intrudes into the host's sensorium and occasions a trip to the clinic.

So then classic Freudian repression remains a serviceable concept *especially* in the most flagrant cases of DID. Without it, two entirely separate kinds of dissociation need to be invoked: the dissociation into an alter of a given trauma; and the dissociation (= repression) of that trauma in a given alter.

In practice, I accept the classic Freudian concept of repression not only as the repression of a wish that gains somatic expression in a compromise formation (conversion proper), but also as the repression of a trauma, in a given host or alter, that gains somatic expression in a partial posttraumatic flashback (body memory). It is worth noting that this second sort of conversion is what gave Freud the idea that the first sort might exist in the first place. Historically, trauma preceded wish. And then wish replaced trauma. And now we have the return of the repressed: trauma trumps wish. But both survive.

This is not to imply that partial posttraumatic revivification and repressed wishes exhaust the somatoform dissociative repertoire. Depersonalization, that perplexing whole-body somatoform symptom, is previously discussed. And then there are complex enactments that involve the simultaneous play of real reality and the inscape, and conflict between the phantom realities of different alters. Examples follow.

A patient walks through the toy section of a department store heading for adult female clothing; her left hand reaches out and grabs a little doll in the bin and shoves it into her left pocket; the patient can't budge her left hand, and has to reach over and remove the doll with her right hand to put it back. It is hardly pertinent to label the inability to move the left hand as pseudoneurological paralysis. It does make sense to assume that her 5-year-old alter was copresent in the eyes (she had to see the doll), and intruded her executive control into the left hand.

A patient is talking and relating to me normally, except that her fingers are clawed at the interphalangeal joints. I point this out. She denies it, and says they are normal. I hold a pencil by both ends, and sweep it down her palm. It catches on the clawed fingers and pulls her hand. "How did you do that?!" she responds in amazement. Her legs are crossed but she thinks they aren't. She perceives her left foot as somewhere it isn't. With her permission, I hold her left foot as, from her point of view, I'm holding nothing. I pull, and she is pulled in her chair. She looks around to see who pushed her. She wonders if she's on Candid Camera. Later, I 'speak through' and ask who is in the hands and foot. More astonishment. She says a male child is in the hands, and he's laughing; an adolescent is in the foot, and he's more surly. So in this case, we have a pseudoneurological symptom that most resembles phantom limb, except that no limb has been amputated. Rather, the patient's phantom body has overridden the real one so that she can't perceive the local presence of her alters in the hands and foot. This is clearly neither posttraumatic revivification (though the claws *per se* would be for the child alter) nor conversion.

19.8.4 Repression Reinterpreted: Unformulated Experience

Stern (1997, 2009) advances an interesting alternative to repression that bridges repression and dissociation. He defines dissociation as the refusal to formulate experience so that it never enters consciousness. Thus, instead of there being something conscious that needs to be rendered unconscious by repression, dissociation blocks it from becoming conscious in the first place. By this view, dissociation is earlier than and more basic than repression. It involves a refusal to be curious, to engage in imagination. Becoming conscious requires curious, imaginative, effortful formulation, and refusing to do so is dissociation.

This hypothesis adds another dimension to the difference between partial posttraumatic revivification and repressed wish (conversion). Returning to our posttraumatic example of somebody waking up with pain and stiffness in the neck and shoulders, having struggled against being pinned down and strangled 30 years ago, is this because the event was formulated in consciousness and then repressed, only to be dis-covered later in therapy; or, on the other hand, was it never fully formulated, and thus not fully conscious, at the time, and instead was registered as a somatic memory, until finally formulated in therapy for the first time? If the pain and stiffness reflects the wish to strangle mother last night, was the wish conscious last night and then repressed? Or was it never conscious, but rather unformulated from the outset, and made conscious for the first time in therapy through an unconscious decision to belatedly formulate it? These are interesting alternatives, and difficult to test. It strikes me as very likely that unformulated experience results especially when the trauma is in excess of somebody's ability to formulate, and thus more likely for more severe trauma, and younger victims. It would also better explain those amorphous symptoms and vague interpersonal conundra for which there seems to be no words. It also matches the demographics of DID. And so if we grant an *early inability* to formulate, it is hardly a stretch to suppose a *subsequent refusal* to formulate. The former would be closer to Janet; the latter would be a bridge between Janet and Freud.

But that is not to say that all repression is really unformulated experience. It is common for DID patients to suddenly remember something, consciously, and then to remember that they once remembered it, and that they forgot it for an interval, during which time they both forgot it and forgot they forgot, prior to remembering it today. This is more in keeping with classic dissociation or repression of previously formulated experience.[29] A middle-aged patient complains of an itchy torso. She switches to a 4-year-old child alter, who tearfully explains: "Daddy's peepee is hurting him; he tries to make it feel better by rubbing it, but that only makes it worse; you can see it in his face; then his peepee gets really sick and suddenly throws up; daddy is sorry it threw up on me, and he tries to clean me off, but instead just seems to spread the throw-up all over me; poor daddy." Switch to a disdainful teen: "The idiot kid can't figure out he was just jerking off over her! She makes excuses for him all the time! What a loser." Switch to the sobbing adult: feeling betrayed and outraged—but the itch is gone. So in the same patient we have two formulations, at different ages, expressed on the same day, but they seem to have a prior history. And while the formulation is faulty, there is no lack of imagination, and includes mentalization: what the 4-year-old thought was going through daddy's head at the time.

[29] And see Williams (1994) for a study reflecting just this pattern.

19.9 DISSOCIATION AND ASSORTED TRIADS

Dédoublement produces two from one, but we wish to know if there is a route to multiplicity other than through successive *dédoublements*. Obvious alternatives consist in various triadic conceptualizations that begin with Freud and have continued with other authors.

19.9.1 Dissociation and the Oedipal Triangle

Returning to Breuer's comments previously cited, which focus more on sex, the switch from dissociation to repression was also the switch from the so-called seduction theory to the Œdipus Complex. Freud came to doubt some of the trauma stories that emerged, and wondered if they were due to suggestion. There is some irony in this, as the kind of hypnosis he engaged in at the time was essentially suggestive. In any case, this major shift in his thinking (Laplanche & Pontalis, 1967/1973) has been, at one extreme, hailed as the founding moment of psychoanalysis, the discovery of the Unconscious and, at the other extreme, condemned as a defensive, conformist fabrication (Masson, 1984). More recent scholarship (Blum, 1996) clarifies the mythic character of both extremes, finding some fault with Freud, but finding more fault with selective misreadings of him.

The core œdipal triangle is the child faced with the parents, wishing for an exclusive relationship with one, jealous and wishing to be rid of the other for that reason. Variations on œdipal dynamics accommodate age, gender, hetero- and homosexuality, identification, love and hate, and libido and aggression, and so the œdipal core may be viewed as a general schema underlying all triadic conflicts, as opposed to dyadic ones. Two's company, three's a crowd. Jealousy requires a trio. The first triad in a child's life is with the parents. Leaving etiology aside, dissociative patients, host and alters, have triadic conflicts, and thus manifest œdipal dynamics. By the same token, such a universal dynamic is unable to account for the genesis of alters *per se*.

In the manifestly traumatized, the œdipal triangle may be richly and ably complemented by a traumatic triangle. Davies and Frawley (1994) define eight relational positions within four relational matrices typically enacted in the transference and countertransference with adult survivors of childhood sexual abuse. While these positions are dyadic (e.g., uninvolved nonabusing parent and neglected child; sadistic abuser and helpless enraged victim), they invite a triadic interpretation that for certain patients may replace or supersede the œdipal triangle (e.g., neglected victim confronting sadistic abuser under the blindly indifferent gaze of the uninvolved nonabusing parent). This reconfiguration implies not only the bad things that shouldn't have happened (sadistic abuser), but the lack of good things that should have happened (uninvolved parent).

19.9.2 Dissociation and the Topography: Cs, Pcs, and Ucs

When Freud replaces dissociation with repression, the vertical dissociative split rotates by a right angle to become the horizontal repressive split of the topography between the Preconscious (*Pcs*) and the Unconscious (*Ucs*) (S. Freud, 1915a). There is also the minor horizontal split between *Pcs* and Conscious (*Cs*), caused by inattention.[30] The idea is that repression is a dynamic forgetting, and so needs work (working-through) to be undone (S. Freud, 1914b), whereas inattention just needs a reminder. This all remains clinically useful. The connection to multiplicity is complicated. Freud does claim that "The content of the *Ucs* may be compared to an aboriginal population in the mind" (S. Freud, 1915b), but this proves to be strictly metaphoric. No actual population is intended. The remark rather anticipates his later theory of the Id, apart from whatever mental contents are rendered unconscious by repression. As noted above, the difficulty with this triad is that a given alter will commonly have its own repressed contents, but Freud would be unlikely to condone a plurality of *Unconsciouses*. This puzzle carries over to the structural theory.

19.9.3 Dissociation and the Structural Theory: Id, Ego, and Superego

The classic sense of structural splitting is the split between the Id, Ego, and Superego (S. Freud, 1923a). In the prior topography, the ego (small "e") is in the *Pcs-Cs* and, among other things, was responsible for defense mechanisms. But defenses are also dynamically unconscious. That is to say, one needs to work to get people to recognize not only *what* they repress, but *that* and *how* they repress. So ego defenses seem to belong in the *Ucs*, not the *Pcs-Cs*. Freud also interpreted dynamically unconscious guilt in some of his analysands, and so needed to put some of the conscience into the *Ucs*. Freud solves this problem by giving the *Ucs* two levels. The sub-basement he calls the Id, which remains the source of impulses (the "aboriginal population"). Above that he partitions the *Ucs* into unconscious Ego (defenses and repressed contents) and unconscious Superego (the source of unconscious guilt), then allows this new division to carry up through the old systems *Pcs-Cs*, so that Ego and Superego are side by side at each level (despite the name "superego," which literally means "above the ego").

This division is mostly functional: various mental faculties are allocated to various structures. But it is personal as well: "the Ego," of course, must remain "I"—the subject of the verb, as opposed to "me" or "self" or "myself" or any object of the verb; what Braude (1991), after Immanuel Kant, would call an "apperceptive centre." The Superego, in turn, is something like the little angel telling the Ego to be good, over one shoulder, while the devilish (aboriginal) Id tells the Ego to be bad, over the other, much like Plato's charioteer with the rational white and lusty black horses.

What happens when such a conceptual structure encounters multiplicity? The division might indeed seem to apply if the alters of a given patient happened to be exactly two and functionally distinct in just the right way (e.g., pure impulse vs. pure intellect, morality, guilt, etc.). Just as stopped clocks tell the right time exactly twice every 24 hours. As we noted previously, however, working even with the average alter generally requires dealing with different apperceptive centers, different I's, each of whom requires working through of her own unconscious defenses against unconscious mental contents, her own impulses, defensive style, cognitive ability, and moral code. In general, in other words, a given alter has its own Id, Ego, and Superego, regardless of how muted, exaggerated, or perverse these might be. This suffices to reject structural splitting as a viable explanation for alter generation or for relations between alters.

Freud's double layering of the *Ucs* invites a third layering between the Id and the unconscious ego of the one facing you in the clinic: a deeper and singular unconscious ego, above which would be the various unconscious egos (and superegos) of the host and alters. Some clinicians insist that such an ego can be met in every patient. That hasn't been my experience. But there are reasons to assume this underlying commonality. There is some agency that seems to decide who is to be out when. There

[30] Freud used the letters rather than the words when intending to denote parts of the psychic system.

is also the remarkable internal reality or inscape inhabited by the distinct phantom bodies of host and alters, and even if no one agrees with another on anything else, they generally agree on the inscape itself and on the respective appearances of their phantom bodies. All the same, whether this is simply epiphenomenal to having arisen from the same brain, or rather directed by some underlying common agency, the therapeutic goal is to achieve integration, such that Freud's structural theory can play a teleological role: we intend that the patient eventually become such that the id-ego-superego model applies.

Furthermore, the enormous psychoanalytic structural literature on the Superego may apply to intra-alter, alter-alter, and alter-therapist dynamics that feature conflict among impulses, defenses, prohibition, punishment, and guilt. More particularly, just as is the case for internal object representations, a "harsh superego" may indicate the presence of an alter defensively identifying with an aggressor, or authority figure, in which case psychoanalytic literature on the harsh superego may be found to apply (Howell, 1997), even if it does not suffice.

19.9.4 Fairbairn's Triad

The theorizing of Ronald Fairbairn promises more to the clinician of dissociation than the work of any other classic author. Some of the headings of his (1944) paper on endopsychic structure hint at a return to 19th-century multiplicity: "Back to hysteria," "A multiplicity of egos," "... the central ego and the subsidiary egos," and so on. There are a number of excellent summary discussions of this challenging author (Greenberg & Mitchell, 1983; Howell, 2005; Rubens, 1994, 1996).

Freud is "corrected." The economic theory is jettisoned: no psychic energy comes from the Id—psychic structures have their own energies. The topographic theory is jettisoned: repression is a mere subset of dissociation: the dissociation of the unpleasant; and a rather late arrival, requiring some degree of higher mental functioning. Drive theory is jettisoned: libido is object-seeking, not pleasure-seeking, and pleasure is a by-product of successful object-seeking. Hedonism, or the seeking for pure pleasure, is reinterpreted as the result of a failure of object-relatedness. As a damning corollary, classical drive theory is reinterpreted as a symptom of conversion hysteria in the theorist, focusing on erotogenic zones and missing how they are somatic displacements from interpersonal longing. Classical narcissism is jettisoned: newborn infants are not narcissistic but primordially object-seeking, a view which anticipates attachment theory and interpersonal/relational psychoanalysis.

Klein is also "corrected." The good breast and bad breast are not inborn templates, but the result of internalization of a real disappointing mother-breast, and the split reinterpreted as the exciting and rejecting aspects of an ungratifying real mother. Splitting is not so much into good-bad self-object relations, as into a primary triad. The "original" ego confronts the ungratifying mother, and becomes the "central ego" by maintaining her as an ideal object. This it does by introjecting her ungratifying aspect as a split into the exciting and rejecting mother. The split mother has comparable split-off parts of the ego: the two "subsidiary" egos, libidinal and antilibidinal. Then the libidinal ego with its exciting mother and the antilibidinal ego with its rejecting mother are all repressed (or dissociated) into unconsciousness. This leaves the central ego free to have an "ideal" relationship with an "ideal" mother and to carry on "normally" with the real world, similar to the clinical reality of a host with its alters, and unlike Kleinian splitting, which produces polar opposites but has no remaining center or core. The repressed (or dissociated) ego-object pairs fight it out with each other, and intrude into the real world. Indeed, Fairbairn had previously called the antilibidinal ego the "internal saboteur"—a wording that resonates clearly with troublesome alters in therapy. For Fairbairn, this is universal psychopathology—"normal" psychopathology.

From the perspective of a clinician treating DID, Fairbairn seems to be engaged in three separate lines of thought that he confounds. One is the introjection of a real object and the concomitant dissociation of a related part of the self into an unconscious subsidiary ego. This could be understood as his interpretation of the genesis of a dissociated alter personality, and it works quite well, but only to a point. It stops working when the patient switches and we discover that the subsidiary ego is quite conscious and has been conscious of the central ego (host) all along, even if the central ego has not been conscious of it.

The second line of thought is that the introjected object is necessarily split in a Kleinian sense (i.e., into polar opposites) into exciting and rejecting internal objects, related to which are the unconscious subsidiary libidinal and antilibidinal egos. This formulation requires that all alters show up in polar pairs. In practice, a significant portion of DID alters may be paired, such as contrasting child alters of the same age, or twins, or child-adult combinations such that the traumatized child is disguised as the traumatizing adult, and so on, but certainly not all alters arrive in pairs. This difficulty was addressed long ago by Young (1988).

The third line of thought is that all patients may be understood through this triadic schema. If so, then the triad would indeed apply to a host, but would also apply to each of the alters as they showed in therapy. We arrive at the same conundrum as we did with Freud's structural theory. So the extent that such triadic dynamics are universally applicable, they can't at the same time explain the genesis of DID and how it is different from universal normal neurosis. At the same time, a Fairbairnian analyst who "gets" dissociative multiplicity would likely be able to profitably reinterpret Fairbairn's approach for the successful treatment of a given patient, just as Brenner does with Freud, or Tarnopolsky with Klein.

19.9.5 Kohut's Triad: Dissociation and Self Psychology

Another tempting conceptualization is Kohut's self psychology. Kohut contrasted Freud's horizontal split between preconscious above and unconscious below with his own vertical split between different aspects of self, which would then be side-by-side rather than at different depths. Can Kohutian vertical splitting accommodate dissociation? The limiting feature, as with Fairbairn, is that Kohut delimits three specific kinds of self defect, reflected in the three typical self-object transferences that would emerge in analysis: the mirroring, alter-ego, and idealizing self-object deficits (Kohut, 1984). Self-object mirroring is the earliest, and happens between mother and baby, wherein baby looks into mother's eyes to discover what mother thinks of baby, and thus what baby thinks of itself—the relational origin of basic self-esteem, good, bad, or indifferent. Self-object idealizing happens later, as child contemplates parent in the world beyond the home, serving as a concrete example of what the child might hope to become in life—the relational origin of hope, admiration, emulation, optimism, idealism, and so on. The alter-ego dynamic mediates between mirroring (how wonderful I am) and idealizing (how much more wonderful I can hope to be) by showing how: having a peer just a little more advanced than oneself who can show you the ropes, who can help you realize your raw talent, your potential, in the real world.[31]

So Kohut is to some extent more old wine in new skins. Mirroring recycles the oral phase and the id: primarily with mother, focusing on the eyes instead of the mouth, needing the satisfaction of an adoring, benevolent, tolerant gaze. The alter-ego dynamic recycles the anal phase, latency and the ego: concerned with how-to, competence, sibling relationships, group identity, mediating between the mirror and the ideal, just as the ego mediates between id and superego. Idealizing recycles the phallic phase, and the superego: concerned with wanting to become like another (instead of wanting another), and emphasizing the parental imago as ideal more than punishing. So Kohut makes a break from Freud, emphasizing the narcissistic side of both conflict and structure, but then dresses up the result in refitted Freudian clothing so that in succeeding to fit universally, it fails to fit dissociation in particular.

[31] Such as is summed up in the medical training adage: "See one, do one, teach one."

19.9.6 Triadic Conclusion

The fact that the structural theories of Freud (id/ego/superego), Fairbairn (central, libidinal, and antilibidinal egos) and Kohut (mirror/alter-ego/ideal) are all triadic may well reveal important ways to conceptualize the human psyche, and variations on a theme, serving to complement each other, and so on, and engendering debate as to which is primary and which derivative, or whether they are all derivative of some psychic core. But that such triads are by definition universally applicable to any given self means that they are applicable to any given self state, ego state, alter personality, or what have you, and this means that they cannot accommodate dissociation itself, though dissociation has no trouble accommodating them.

19.10 Dissociation and Schemata in General

19.10.1 Object Relations Theory

This topic has been implicit in the discussions involving splitting, the structural theory, and especially Fairbairn. As noted, ego psychology regards one's objects as representations of objects in the *inner* world, while the superego and Klein's internal objects are structural entities in the *internal* world, about which one may then have secondary representations in one's inner world. In this regard, object relations theorists (e.g., Fairbairn, Winnicott, Balint, Guntrip, Bion) reflect Klein's interpretation (Hinshelwood, 1991).

An object relations theory that abandons forced dyads and triads and embraces a general multiplicity of internal objects gets around one problem of accounting for multiplicity, but is left with another: since object relations theory help us understand the interpersonal schemata operative in any patient, underlying her attitude to others in the world, and especially to us in the transference, the theory helps us understand the interpersonal schemata operative in *any given* host or alter, underlying her attitude to others in the world *and to her alters*, and especially to us in the transference. I've never met a host or alter in whom I was unable to interpret an internal world of object relations distinct from the world that would represent the host and alters as a whole, concretely manifest in the inscape. So in the true multiple, there are two very distinct levels of internal object relations, and the theory itself would need to explain that difference.

19.10.2 Attachment Theory

Attachment theory also invokes internalized object relations schemata under the label of Internal Working Models (IWMs). John Bowlby's conceptualizations derive from a number of different sources (Sigmund and Anna Freud, Klein, ethology, systems theory, direct observation of parents and children, etc.), and so the resultant system has not been assimilated by any one psychoanalytic school without difficulty. Bowlby's work has been interpreted as enriching many areas of psychoanalysis (Fonagy, 2001), and, to the contrary, of being essentially nonpsychoanalytic (Zepf, 2006). At one extreme, it may be seen as rescuing psychoanalysis from scientific error by bringing in elements of an updated natural science (ethology), and at the other extreme of being irrelevant because it doesn't all derive "from the couch."

Barach (1991) first proposed interpreting MPD as an attachment disorder. Liotti (1999, 2004, 2009) has most developed the theme since. A multi-authored book has been published on the topic (Sinason, 2002). The emphasis shifts from trauma to neglect, from the abuser to the uninvolved parent: not so much the bad things that happened to the child, but the good things the child did not get from the nonabusing parent—the absence of a secure base. The literature on attachment and dissociation is enormously bolstered by the very large literature on attachment and allied concerns (e.g., child development, mental state theory, early trauma and deprivation, PTSD, personality disorders, especially borderline, the interface with the neurosciences, etc.).

There seems little doubt that psychoanalysts who are able to incorporate attachment theory in all its complexity would be better able not only to critically evaluate a host of psychoanalytic theories, but also to reincorporate hypnoid hysteria: dissociative multiplicity. Hypnoid hysteria now tends to be called ego state theory or self state theory, and these theories have cross-fertilized with attachment theory for a number of years. For further reading on this topic, please refer to the excellent chapters that discuss attachment and dissociation elsewhere in this book (Carlson, Yates, & Sroufe, 2009; Howell & Blizard, 2009; Liotti, 2009; Nijenhuis & Den Boer, 2009; Schore, 2009; Steele et al., 2009).

19.11 DISSOCIATION AND STATES OF MIND

19.11.1 Back to Breuer's Hypnoid Hysteria

We are returned to Breuer's hypnoid hysteria as the earliest psychoanalytic example of a state of mind. The concept hasn't really recovered since Freud made his inaugural category mistake. The recently translated *International Dictionary of Psychoanalysis* (de Mijolla, 2005), an encyclopedic work of 1,600 pages in 3 volumes with about 1,430 separate entries, is woefully deficient when it comes to dissociation. Indeed, *dissociation* and *multiple personality* are not even among the entries. The entries *Hysteria* and *Conversion* manage not to mention dissociation, despite their decades-long joint coding under hysterical neurosis in the ICDs and DSM-II. *Depersonalization* is an entry, as a withdrawal of libidinal cathexis from the body image, but similarly with no reference to dissociation. Dissociation is finally mentioned under *Hypnoid states* (Perron, 2005), as Breuer's mistaken interpretation, while Freud "correctly" interpreted such states in terms of repression. The entry concludes that "the notion of hypnoid states is so contrary to metapsychology as a whole that it cannot be accepted as being a part of psychoanalysis." So much the worse for psychoanalysis.

It is interesting to wonder how psychoanalysis may have evolved if Freud had retained a conception of defensive dissociative induction of hypnoid states, and then added defensive repression as well. In my view, the best current exemplar of how psychoanalysis might have evolved is represented by Richard Kluft, an IPA psychoanalyst who has been a leading figure in the dissociation field for the past 35 years in all its aspects (Kluft, 2003): diagnosis, treatment, teaching, research, publication, editing, and so on. While remaining a psychoanalyst, he also mastered hypnosis to the point of rising to the forefront of that field,[32] a trajectory that has led him to publish very widely outside the psychoanalytic literature with just two notable exceptions (Kluft, 1999, 2000). Kluft's eclectic theoretical origins and his seamless incorporation of formal and informal hypnosis into the process of treatment

[32] He has been president of the American Society of Clinical Hypnosis, and is current president of the Society for Clinical and Experimental Hypnosis.

makes it difficult to discuss Kluft's psychoanalysis of dissociation, but then his work (e.g. see Kluft, 2009, in this book) clearly speaks for itself.

19.11.2 Federn's Ego States and the Watkins' Ego State Therapy

It is curious that Paul Federn was dubbed "Apostle Paul" by his colleagues for his religious devotion to Freud and the psychoanalytic movement (Accerboni, 2005). Federn analyzed Edoardo Weiss, who founded the Italian psychoanalytic society before emigrating to the United States. Weiss analyzed John G. (Jack) Watkins in Chicago. It was through this route that Federn's (1952) seminal "heresy" regarding ego states took root, sprouted, and flowered into "ego state therapy" (Watkins & Watkins, 1997),[33] familiar to virtually everyone in the dissociation world. Watkins, a psychologist nonphysician, was not permitted to join the American Psychoanalytic Association (APA). This is perhaps fortuitous, as close affiliation with the APA may have precluded his subsequent theorizing and hypnoanalytic innovations, and constrained him to ego psychological orthodoxy. Given the Watkins' preeminence in dissociative circles, it is interesting to follow what has become of Federn's ego states within psychoanalysis.

The *International Dictionary of Psychoanalysis* (de Mijolla, 2005) has entries that discuss Federn's contributions, by Hurvich under *Ego states* (2005a), *Ego feeling* (2005b), and *Ego boundaries* (2005c), and by Ernst Federn (Paul's son) under *Alteration of the ego* (2005a) and *Damage inflicted on the ego* (2005b) with reference to repression (neurosis) and splitting (psychosis), as well as to fatigue, sleep, and illness, but manage somehow to avoid any reference to dissociation, despite Ernst Federn's introduction to the Watkins' book. *Hypnosis* (Carroy, 2005) is largely 19th-century, brief, and skeptical, betraying gross ignorance of developments in hypnosis over the past century.

The Watkins' book (1997) is a welcome summary of their contributions over the previous four decades, and elevates Federn's ego state construct to a general interpretive schema. This schema well describes and instructs the therapy of the most severe dissociative patients. But it is also an interpretation of normal-neurotic patients generally as suffering from symptoms understood as dissociative. That is to say, in patients who are not manifestly dissociative in the diagnostic sense, the Watkins, in using hypnosis as a general therapeutic adjunct, are able to have patients encounter the ego states that "hold" whatever symptom, affect, conflict, deficit, whatever, is in question, or in relation to whom the "host" is in conflict. This amounts to interpreting all psychopathology as subclinical multiplicity. Like Fairbairn's theorizing, it eclipses Freud's drive theory, topography, and structural theory in favor of an expanded interpretation of Federn's concept of ego state, and accords very well with Fairbairn's idea of subsidiary egos, though without being hamstrung by his libidinal-antilibidinal splitting. This general applicability exemplifies what they call the differentiation-dissociation continuum. There is little question about the approach being faster than traditional psychoanalysis. Jack Watkins' perennial complaint about psychoanalysis is how slow and time-consuming it is (personal communications).

The approach invites a variety of questions. Assuming that DID is real, there is no question about the reality of alters. But in those who don't have DID, and in whom ego states may be discovered under hypnosis, an interesting research question is whether these ego states are preexistent, or rather hypnotically created at the time of discovery. Truth and therapeutic efficacy are independent, of course, so positive therapeutic outcome can't decide the matter. Nor would the creation be a contrived artefact of the treatment, to the extent that it appropriately packaged the pathology into a subjective ego structure and rendered it capable of speedy resolution. The issue is one that will likely be debated for years.

And while ego state theory may best *describe* multiplicity, that is not to say that it *explains* it. The Watkins retain a number of classic psychoanalytic constructs in their explanations: energy economics of the self, self and object cathexis and decathexis, object relation, abreaction, adaptation, and so on. As with Klein, the problem has to do with explaining the difference between subjects and objects. Federn conceived of there being a variety of mental objects, comparable to Kleinian self and object representations, and these could then be invested with more or less ego energy or cathexis.[34] But "energy" is also a mental object, in the mind of the theorist, and calling it "ego energy" (in whatever language) hardly explains its

[33] A work he coauthored with his late wife, equally celebrated, Helen Watkins (née Helyanthe Maria Wagner), 1921–2002.

[34] When translating Freud's plain German "besetzung" into English, Strachey instead picked an obscure Greek term meaning "a holding in" or "that which is held fast." The nearest English cognate is "beset," so "that with which one is beset"; the French chose to translate the plain German into plain French, and came up with "investissement," roughly, "investment," or that with which something is invested.

character as subjective agency. We don't generally converse with energy.

Ego state theory thus tries to recycle Freud's Q: his energic or economic viewpoint, his pseudoscientific fairy tale. Updated versions of the metaphor invoke information-processing, but also miss the point: while information can be thought, it cannot think. Information can, however, be duplicated or proliferated, so that information-processing at least provides a metaphor for alter genesis other than splitting.

19.11.3 Putnam: Discrete Behavioral States

Independent of psychoanalysis, Frank Putnam, who authored the original classic text on MPD (1989), has since drawn on research into infant behavioral states especially as described by Wolff (1987), and proposes a Discrete Behavioural States (DBS) model to describe and explain the derivation of normality, ego or self state disorders, and frank DID from infant behavioral states (Putnam, 1997).

This approach promises to clarify the Breuer-Freud split by beginning at the heart of the matter. The DBS model has already yielded a very detailed elaboration even for the perfectly normally developing child, an elaboration that clearly sets the stage for speculating about pathological development. Howell (2002, 2005) has introduced Putnam's contribution into the psychoanalytic literature.

In explaining multiplicity, it is clearly an advantage to begin with a multiplicity of states, and especially of different kinds or hierarchies of states. There would seem to be no conceptual difficulty with any degree of proliferation of *my* states of mind (asleep, dreaming, sleepy, alert, studious, enthusiastic, triumphant, disappointed, mortified, depressed, bored, irritable, demanding, childish, comforted, sleepy, asleep, etc.). With regard to multiplicity, there is the question as to whether some quantum leap is required to explain how *I* can have a whole set of states of mind, but apparently can manifest another whole set of states of mind that seem to be as if *another's* whole set of states of mind.

Another question has to do with genesis. Putnam assumes an early failure to achieve the core developmental task of integrating self states, much along the lines of Janet's explanation. My preference is closer to Freud's: that *dédoublement* is a creative defense in response to trauma that may subsequently become the person's default defense even after other defenses eventually mature (e.g., splitting, repression, etc.). Another interesting research question.

19.11.4 Interpersonal and Relational Psychoanalysis

As I previously noted, the interpersonal and relational schools of psychoanalysis have produced the most significant and voluminous contributions to dissociation in the psychoanalytic literature, and so I refer the reader to the appropriate chapters (see Bromberg, 2009; Stern, 2009). Especially significant in this development is the smooth incorporation of attachment theory that has proven to be not only a link between psychoanalysis and empirical research in general, but a link between "heretics" in the United States and the United Kingdom as well.

19.12 NEEDED RESEARCH

Researchers have little time to spend in prolonged empathic immersion with a given patient. And depth psychotherapists of whatever stripe have little time to spend in prolonged research design and data analysis. I am a psychotherapist and so my comments are more conceptual and clinical than research-oriented.

Hypotheses need to be formulated before they can be tested. There is no privileged source of scientific hypotheses, which is why both psychiatry, concerned with the diagnosis and treatment of the mentally ill, and psychoanalysis, concerned with the psychotherapeutic through open-ended regular empathic immersion in the mind of another, after being filtered through colleagues and after arriving at some degree of consensus, can be so fertile for the generation of various hypotheses and even of elaborate diagnostic and explanatory systems about the human mind. But while such clinical experience can give rise to bumper cash crops, it can also result in a luxuriant overgrowth of weeds. The primary vocation of research is to do the weeding. Clinical experience comes up with bright ideas, and research shoots down the faulty ones. This relationship is irreducibly dialectical, and there is no way around it. "True" theories are not so much evidence-based as evidence-vulnerable.

There is also no way around the self-reference implicit in any psychology, and especially in any psychotherapy. This self-reference is intrinsic to the problem of consciousness, and to any interpretive discipline regarding human intentionality. Psychoanalytic theories need to be tested against evidence, of course, but psychoanalysis also needs to be able to analyze the proponent of evidence-based medicine who hides behind methodology in order to protect himself from real encounters with life. Guile is core in the behavior of all metazoans, and raised to an exquisite art form in the human species, and psychoanalysis must remain free to circumvent it.

That being said, it also seems to me that psychoanalysis has suffered from a century-old selective blindness inherited from Sigmund Freud with regard to severe repetitive trauma happening during early development and the kind of psychopathology that results in the adult. The blindness includes willful ignorance about hypnosis.

Solving the theoretical issues among the various camps requires first and foremost communication. Technical jargons differ. Resolution of interpretative questions would be helped by the following:

1. Dissociative disorders should be considered part of the routine differential diagnosis in psychiatric, psychoanalytic, and psychotherapeutic clinics.
2. Psychoanalysts should include "hypnoid hysteria," states of consciousness, dissociation, multiplicity, body memories, the inscape, and so on, in what they routinely look for in treating analysands.

These modest recommendations are asking a great deal from some traditions. But until multiplicity is widely recognized and treated with eyes open, its psychotherapeutic treatment will be unpredictably compromised by selection bias in the patient sample and those inevitable blinders that all therapists wear, whether they know it or not.

19.13 A SUMMARY VIEW

19.13.1 Dédoublement

One of the most primitive defenses available to the child is the hypnoid (hypnosis-like) defense of auto-duplication. I say auto-duplication rather than self-duplication so as not to imply that it is the child's self, as one of its intentional objects, that is duplicated. The duplication is rather of subjective agency: of the "I" rather than the "me" or the "self"; of the *Ich* or Ego. From among various historical designations, *dédoublement* (doubling) would be closest to what I intend, as the action is essentially multiplicative rather than divisive.

Dédoublement may occur if (1) the child has the capacity to do so; (2) the trauma is some combination of sufficiently early, severe and repeated; (3) there is no one available to appropriately rescue, soothe, and comfort the child. Naturally, 2 and 3 are related, as if there were someone available to appropriately soothe the child, then the trauma would tend not to be repeated. Thus both trauma and disordered attachment are prerequisites for *dédoublement.*

19.13.2 Weakness versus Defense

In this formulation, I opt, structurally, for Breuer's hypnoid hysteria over Freud's repression and, dynamically, for Freud's active defense over Janet's fragmentation due to weakness. This circumvents what I dubbed as Freud's "inaugural category mistake" of assuming that the hypnoid state could not be the result of an active defense. At the same time, the formulation does allow for a little of Janet's weakness in the age of onset—early childhood—with the implication that the elements of multiplicity in the adult must have been there from early childhood. This weakness does not reflect constitutional deficit. If anything, it may reflect constitutional propensity to dissociate as a specific ability.

The active and creative aspect of the defense of *dédoublement* is consonant with a remorselessly Darwinian view of mentation, to the extent that all mental contents and structures can be interpreted as being internally generated and acted upon selectively (never instructively) by environmental signals. To that extent, metaphors that connote instruction, such as induction, internalization, incorporation, introjection, intromission, alien haunting, and so on, mislead, to the extent that they imply that something literally gets in from the outside. Other metaphors such as imitation and identification do not mislead in that sense.

19.13.3 Full Adult DID

The paradigm case of *dédoublement* is somebody with full DID or MPD (both of which are misnomers, more or less), in whom the creative defense has been used repeatedly and become something of the default defense. Such a patient will have amnesia or lost time due to switching without coconsciousness. She may or may not experience herself as having distinct identities, to the extent that she honestly denies experiencing herself that way, though the clinician may be convinced that she (in the larger sense) has multiple identities, having met them.

This is the "hard case" to which psychoanalysis needs to accommodate.

19.13.4 Repression as a Defense

In opting for hypnoid states as the result of an active defense, I do not replace or supplant Freud's repression as a defense. Indeed, the attempt to reduce repression to dissociation leads to an infinite regress. In any frank multiple, it is common for distinct alters to have body memories of a repressed traumatic event (or series of events), and, less commonly, classic conversion symptoms (somatized wishes). When a host has amnesia for an event, it may well be that repression is not in play, because the event is located in a dissociated alter. In that circumstance, explaining the amnesia by repression is an error. But the alter may likewise have amnesia for the event because it is repressed in the alter itself. Thus, defensive dissociation and defensive repression both operate and can be distinguished. They can most clearly be distinguished when they co-occur in the same patient.

The question of whether one is dealing with a traumatic event or a forbidden wish is distinct from whether repression or dissociation is involved. A somatic symptom is commonly dissociated from the host (say) and repressed in the alter concerned. What is repressed is commonly a traumatic event, so that the symptom is not, technically speaking, a conversion symptom at all, but rather a partial posttraumatic revivification of the event, or what are succinctly called body memories in the dissociation and trauma fields. It may be a classic conversion symptom, however: not a body memory, but rather a somatoform compromise formation between a wish and a defense.

19.13.5 Polar Splitting of Self and Object Representations

In opting for a multiplicative rather than divisive concept, *dédoublement*, I do not supplant the classic Freudian or Kleinian polar splitting of self and object. Splitting and dissociation cannot account for each other. Splitting is a primitive style of mental categorization that predates ambivalence. No adult is entirely incapable of either splitting or ambivalence, and no measure of dissociative multiplicity is required for either. Anyone may have a greater propensity to split or to be ambivalent; the former tend to be labelled borderline and the latter normal neurotic. Dissociative multiplicity predates polar splitting, and the child who can effectively split needn't engage in *dédoublement*. Similarly, both splitting and ambivalence are available as defensive styles to host and alters.

19.13.6 Id, Ego, Superego, and Other Triads

Freud's most concrete evocation of a variety of multiplicity is his structural theory of Id, Ego, and Superego. Of the three, only the Ego is really a subject, however, a role betrayed by its name, Ego, I, the subject of the verb (or defense mechanism). The Id is on the border of biology and mentation; and the Superego is the personification of one's conscience. There is merit in considering whether someone's Superego is rather a dissociated self-state or alter personality. This ought to enter routinely into the differential diagnosis of anyone with a Superego which seems to go beyond the norm, such as being too harsh, or arbitrary, or idiosyncratic in one way or another. But the Superego, in general, cannot be reduced to a dissociated self-state. That is because any patient with DID will have alters who themselves are not devoid of a conscience, and some who will have relatively well-delineated and personified consciences (i.e., Superegos). And so then to avoid the infinite regress, we would have to postulate two levels of Superego: that which gives rise to an alter who poses as the host's conscience, and a set of subordinate Superegos variably personifying the individual consciences of the host and alters, including of the alter posing as the Superego.

19.13.7 Internal Object Relations, Attachment, IWMs, Templates, Schemas

These approaches get beyond the triadic limit. The absence of someone to soothe the child can best be understood in terms of attachment pathology, and lends credence to the claim that dissociative multiplicity is essentially a result of disturbed attachment. The attachment paradigm works primarily from the stance of the external observer. This is what renders it so amenable to empirical tests. The internal working model (IWM) of attachment theory has a counterpart in object relations theory: the internal object relation, which is a representation of the relation between a self representation and an object representation. What all such schemata have in common is a patterning of self-other relationships.

A case can always be made that one's alters are simply one's internal objects that have somehow become subjects, using such ideas as cathexis by ego energy, or whatever. But all such explanations are a way of hypothesizing subjectivity as a kind of conservable fluid that can flow into this or that internal object to endow it with subjectivity: covert translations of the mistaken hydraulics of Freud's Project.

The internal-object-become-subject poses another conundrum. Alters function as relatively full psychological subjects. Consequently, their mentation is similarly interpretable in terms of their own repertoires of internal object relations, or IWMs, or templates, or schemata, some of which may overlap or coincide with those of the host or other alters, and some of which may prove to be unique. So we would then need two levels of object relation, a supraordinate one constituting the field of host and alters, and a set of subordinates variably characterizing the individual repertoires of the host and alters.

19.13.8 States

Multiplicity is unquestionably a disorder of mental states, as has been conceptualized from the beginning. Two challenges facing any mental state theory are: (1) to account for the difference between self states that define the alters of somebody with DID and the various self states of any given alter; (2) to answer the original Janet-Freud question: to what extent is the appearance of an alter due to a failure to integrate self states, and to what extent is it a purposive creative act of defense?

19.13.9 Technique

There is no consensus about altering "classical" technique for DID analysands. There is variable use of the couch, variable use of adjunctive techniques, such as hypnosis and EMDR, variable mixing of paradigms, with approaches borrowed from CBT, a tendency toward fewer but longer sessions per week, variable use of techniques from child analysis (especially for child alters), and so on.

19.14 PSYCHOANALYSIS AND MULTIPLICITY: FUTURE PROSPECTS

Psychoanalysts are better at interpreting the past than predicting the future. But I can hazard to extrapolate certain possibilities from current trends. There are theoretical-technical issues, and then there are those governed by fashion, politics, and serendipity.

A major obstacle to the smooth re-adoption of multiplicity by psychoanalysis has been, and will likely continue to be, Freud's personal rejection of hypnoid hysteria and hypnosis at the dawn of psychoanalysis itself. Pointing out how this rejection manifests a category mistake on his part, an overgeneralization with suspect motives, or whatever, will likely have little effect on the religiously Freudian.

Theoretically, since interpretive disciplines (e.g., any psychotherapy) are formulated so as to be able to interpret anything and everything, they are rendered immune to refutation to some extent. The various psychoanalyses have this characteristic, and so does the general construct of dissociative multiplicity, as is clear from the ego state therapy tradition.

Nothing happens without critical mass. Dissociation won't really return to mainstream psychoanalysis until there are a sufficient number of IPA analysts who will be prepared to look for it, recognize it, and undertake to treat it. As psychoanalytic treatments (with and without so-called parameters) of dissociative multiplicity approach the "average expectable" range of case reports, and so on, it will become clear how "hypnoid hysteria" will be reincorporated into psychoanalysis.

Classic ego psychology would seem to have the least room to maneuver in accommodating multiplicity, as the structural theory would need replacing. The most direct line of approach is exemplified by Kluft, who corrects Freud's inaugural category mistake by accepting hypnoid hysteria as an entity and adding hypnosis as a practice, both updated by the past century, of course. Following his lead, one would then allow treatment to unfold as it will and allow one's mind to change in the process. Hypnosis remains a formidable stumbling block, however, given its spurning by Freud, and dated misconceptions, which construe it as necessarily judgmental, suggestive, authoritarian, seductive, and iatrogenic, and put it at odds with the central ethos of psychoanalytic practice. Of course, psychoanalysts have always been free to be all of the foregoing even in the absence of hypnosis (Kahr, 2003).

Declining to correct Freud's inaugural error leads to solutions that are more contrived. Following Brenner, one would define a deeper level of perverse splitting of the ego that allows for any of the split egos to themselves engage in more conventional perverse splitting. Following in the Kleinian and object relations tradition, one would define a deeper kind of splitting and a deeper kind of internal world of object relations, which would allow for each of the deeper selves and objects to split in the conventional way, and to each have their own conventional internal worlds of object relations. Following in the Kohutian tradition, one would define a more severe kind of vertical split that would produce side-by-side selves, each of which would be free to have its own conventional mirroring, idealizing, and alter ego splits.

The more recent paradigms are a welcome side effect of the exclusion of nonphysicians from the American Psychoanalytic Association (APA),[35] which gave rise to a variety of societies with otherwise perfectly orthodox roots but which, by virtue of that very exclusion, were freed from the constraints of ongoing IPA oversight, and able to evolve toward what are now loosely called

[35] A policy authored by A. A. Brill, against Freud's (1926b) very clear preferences to the contrary. Canada and Latin America, in contrast, followed the international model.

interpersonal and relational psychoanalysis. The medical exclusion clause likewise allowed for Jack Watkins to develop ego state therapy. Lacanians have barely ventured into the dissociation field, and I am unable to hazard a guess as to what their contribution might be.

An important source of ongoing research will likely continue to be attachment theory, given its interdisciplinary roots, which links psychoanalysis to biology, animal behavior and neuroscience.

The key to further psychoanalytic progress in this field is thus the same as in the psychiatric field: the need for dissociation to become generally recognized as a predictable portion of the average expectable psychopathology one would encounter in any clinic.

REFERENCES

Accerboni, A. M. (2005). Paul Federn (The Gale Group: http://www.answers.com/topic/federn-paul?cat=health)

Aristotle (1941a). De anima (On the soul) (J. A. Smith, Trans.). In R. McKeon (Ed.), *The basic works of Aristotle* (pp. 533–603). New York: Random House.

Aristotle (1941b). Metaphysics (Metaphysics) (W. D. Ross, Trans.). In R. McKeon (Ed.), *The basic works of Aristotle* (pp. 681–926). New York: Random House.

Barach, P. M. M. (1991). Multiple personality disorder as an attachment disorder. *Dissociation, 4*, 117–123.

Beere, D. B. (2009). The self-system as mechanism for the dissociative disorders. In P. F. Dell & J. A. O'Neil (Eds.), *Dissociation and the dissociative disorders: DSM-V and beyond* (pp. 277–285). New York: Routledge.

Benjamin, J. (1995). *Like subjects, love objects.* New Haven, CT: Yale University Press.

Bion, W. R. (1970). *Attention and interpretation.* London: Tavistock.

Bleuler, E. (1911/1950). *Dementia præcox or the group of schizophrenias* (J. Zinkin, Trans.). New York: International Universities Press.

Blizard, R. A. (2001). Masochistic and sadistic ego states: Dissociative solutions to the dilemma of attachment to an abusive caretaker. *Journal of Trauma and Dissociation, 2*(4), 37–58.

Blum, H. P. (1996). Seduction trauma: Representation, deferred action, and pathogenic development. *Journal of the American Psychoanalytic Association, 44*, 1147–1164.

Bowlby, J. (1980). *Loss: Sadness and depression* (Vol. 3). Penguin Books.

Braude, S. E. (1991). *First person plural: Multiple personality and the philosophy of mind.* New York: Routledge.

Braun, B. G. (1988). The BASK model of dissociation. *Dissociation, 1*, 4–23.

Brenner, I. (2001). *Dissociation of trauma: Theory, phenomenology, and technique.* Madison, CT: International Universities Press.

Brenner, I. (2002). Dissociation. In E. Erwin (Ed.), *The Freud encyclopedia* (pp. 153–154). New York: Routledge.

Breuer, J., & Freud, S. (1895). Studies on hysteria. *Standard Edition, 2*, 1–319.

Bridgman, P. W. (1927). *The logic of modern physics.* New York: Macmillan.

Bromberg, P. M. (1998). *Standing in the spaces.* Hillsdale NJ: The Analytic Press.

Bromberg, P. M. (2009). The relational mind and dissociation. In P. F. Dell & J. A. O'Neil (Eds.), *Dissociation and the dissociative disorders: DSM-V and beyond* (pp. 637–652). New York: Routledge.

Brook, A. (1992). Freud and splitting. *International Review of Psycho-Analysis, 19*, 335–350.

Burch, B. (1989). Mourning and failure to mourn – An object-relations view. *Contemporary Psychoanalysis, 25*, 608–623.

Carlson, E., Yates, T. M., & Sroufe, L. A. (2009). Development of dissociation and development of the self. In P. F. Dell & J. A. O'Neil (Eds.), *Dissociation and the dissociative disorders: DSM-V and beyond* (pp. 39–52). New York: Routledge.

Carroy, J. (2005). Hypnosis. In A. de Mijolla (Ed.), *International dictionary of psychoanalysis* (pp. 1647–1648). Farmington Hills, MI: Thomson Gale.

Chefetz, R. A. (2000). Disorder in the therapist's view of the self: Working with the person with Dissociative Identity Disorder. *Psychoanalytic Inquiry, 20*, 305–329.

Copleston, F. (1946/1962). *A history of philosophy. Volume 1: Greece & Rome. New revised edition.* Garden City, NY: Image Books.

Cranefield, P. F. (1958). Josef Breuer's evaluation of this contribution to psycho-analysis. *International Journal of Psycho-Analysis, 39*, 319–322.

Davidson, D. (2005). *Truth and predication.* Cambridge, MA: Harvard University Press.

Davies, J. M., & Frawley, M. G. (1994). *Treating the adult survivor of childhood sexual abuse: A psychoanalytic perspective* (Vol. 2). New York: Basic Books.

de Mijolla, A. (Ed.). (2005). *International dictionary of psychoanalysis.* Farmington Hills, MI: Thomson Gale.

De Mijolla-Mellor, S. (2005). Splitting of the ego; "Splitting of the ego in the process of defence." In A. de Mijolla (Ed.), *International dictionary of psychoanalysis* (pp. 1647–1648). Farmington Hills, MI: Thomson Gale.

Dell, P. F. (2009a). The phenomenology of chronic pathological dissociation. In P. F. Dell & J. A. O'Neil (Eds.), *Dissociation and the dissociative disorders: DSM-V and beyond* (pp. 225–237). New York: Routledge.

Dell, P. F. (2009b). Understanding dissociation. In P. F. Dell & J. A. O'Neil (Eds.), *Dissociation and the dissociative disorders: DSM-V and beyond* (pp. 709–825). New York: Routledge.

Descartes, R. (1649/1961). The passions of the soul (L. Bair, Trans.). In *Essential works of Descartes* (pp. 108–210). Toronto: Bantam Books.

Edelman, G. M. (1987). *Neural Darwinism: The theory of neuronal group selection.* New York: Basic Books.

Edelman, G. M. (1992). *Bright air, brilliant fire: On the matter of the mind.* New York: Basic Books.

Ellenberger, H. F. (1970). *The discovery of the unconscious; The history and evolution of dynamic psychiatry*. New York: Basic Books.

Erwin, E. (Ed.). (2002). *The Freud encyclopedia: theory, therapy, and culture*. New York: Routledge.

Fairbairn, W. R. D. (1944). Endopsychic structure considered in terms of object-relationships. *International Journal of Psycho-Analysis, 25*, 70–92.

Federn, E. (2005a). Ego, alteration of the. In A. de Mijolla (Ed.), *International dictionary of psychoanalysis* (pp. 468–469). Farmington Hills, MI: Thomson Gale.

Federn, E. (2005b). Ego, damage inflicted on the. In A. de Mijolla (Ed.), *International dictionary of psychoanalysis* (pp. 475). Farmington Hills, MI: Thomson Gale.

Federn, P. (1952). *Ego psychology and the psychoses*. New York: Basic Books.

Ferenczi, S. (1933/1949). Confusion of tongues between the adult and the child. *International Journal of Psycho-Analysis, 30*, 225–230.

First, M. B. (2005). Mutually exclusive versus co-occurring diagnostic categories: the challenge of diagnostic comorbidity. *Psychopathology, 38*, 206–210.

Fonagy, P. (2001). *Attachment theory and psychoanalysis*. New York: Other Press.

Føllesdal, D. (2001). Hermeneutics. *International Journal of Psycho-Analysis, 82*, 375–379.

Frankel, J. (2002). Exploring Ferenczi's concept of identification with the aggressor: Its role in trauma, everyday life, and the therapeutic relationship. *Psychoanalytic Dialogues, 12*(1), 101–139.

Fraser, G. A. (1991). The dissociative table technique: A strategy for working with ego states in dissociative disorders and ego state therapy. *Dissociation, 4*, 205–213.

Fraser, G. A. (2003). Fraser's "Dissociative table technique" revisited, revised: A strategy for working with ego states in dissociative disorders and ego-state therapy. *Journal of Trauma and Dissociation, 4*(4), 5–28.

Freud, A. (1966). *The ego and the mechanisms of defense. Revised edition.* New York, NY: International Universities Press.

Freud, S. (1894). The neuro-psychoses of defence (I). *Standard Edition, 3*, 41–61.

Freud, S. (1895). Project for a scientific psychology. *Standard Edition, 1*, 281–397.

Freud, S. (1896). Heredity and the ætiology of the neuroses. *Standard Edition, 3*, 141–156.

Freud, S. (1905). Three essays on the theory of sexuality. *Standard Edition, 7*, 121–245.

Freud, S. (1910). Five lectures on psycho-analysis. *Standard Edition, 11*, 1–55.

Freud, S. (1914a). On the history of the psycho-analytic movement. *Standard Edition, 14*, 1–66.

Freud, S. (1914b). Remembering, repeating and working through (Further recommendations in the technique of psychoanalysis II). *Standard Edition, 12*, 145–156.

Freud, S. (1915a). Repression. *Standard Edition, 14*, 141–158.

Freud, S. (1915b). The unconscious. *Standard Edition, 14*, 159–215.

Freud, S. (1923a). The ego and the id. *Standard Edition, 19*, 1–66.

Freud, S. (1923b). Two encyclopædia articles. *Standard Edition, 18*, 231–259.

Freud, S. (1926a). Inhibitions, symptoms and anxiety. *Standard Edition, 20*, 77–175.

Freud, S. (1926b). The question of lay analysis. *Standard Edition, 20*, 183–258.

Freud, S. (1933). New introductory lectures on psycho-analysis. *Standard Edition, 22*, 3–182.

Freud, S. (1940). Splitting of the ego in the process of defence. *Standard Edition, 23*, 271–278.

Gill, M. M. (1988). Metapsychology revisited. *Annual of Psychoanalysis, 16*, 35–48.

Greenberg, J. R., & Mitchell, S. A. (1983). W. R. D. Fairbairn. In *Object relations in psychoanalytic theory*. Cambridge MA: Harvard University Press.

Grubrich-Simitis, I. (1988). Trauma or drive—Drive and trauma—A reading of Sigmund Freud's phylogenetic fantasy of 1915. *Psychoanalytic Study of the Child, 43*, 3–32.

Grubrich-Simitis, I. (1997). *Early Freud and late Freud*. New York: Routledge.

Hempel, C. G. (1959). Fundamentals of taxonomy. In C. G. Hempel (Ed.), *Aspects of scientific explanation & other essays in the philosophy of science* (pp. 137–154). New York: The Free Press.

Hinshelwood, R. D. (1991). *A dictionary of Kleinian thought, 2nd ed.* Northvale, NJ: Jason Aronson.

Hobbes, T. (1651/1962). *Leviathan*. London: Collier-Macmillan.

Hoffman, I. Z. (1985). Merton M. Gill: A study in theory development in psychoanalysis. In J. Reppen (Ed.), *Beyond Freud: A study of modern psychoanalytic theorists*. Hillsdale, JN: The Analytic Press.

Howell, E. F. (1997). Desperately seeking attachment: A psychoanalytic reframing of harsh superego. *Dissociation, 10*, 230–239.

Howell, E. F. (2002). Back to the "States". *Psychoanalytic Dialogues* (12), 921–957.

Howell, E. F. (2005). *The dissociative mind*. Hillsdale, NJ: The Analytic Press.

Howell, E. F., & Blizard, R. A. (2009). Chronic relational trauma and Borderline Personality Disorder. In P. F. Dell & J. A. O'Neil (Eds.), *Dissociation and the dissociative disorders: DSM-V and beyond* (pp. 495–509). New York: Routledge.

Hurvich, M. S. (2005a). Ego states. In A. de Mijolla (Ed.), *International dictionary of psychoanalysis* (pp. 488–489). Farmington Hills, MI: Thomson Gale.

Hurvich, M. S. (2005b). Ego feeling. In A. de Mijolla (Ed.), *International dictionary of psychoanalysis* (pp. 477–478). Farmington Hills, MI: Thomson Gale.

Hurvich, M. S. (2005c). Ego boundaries. In A. de Mijolla (Ed.), *International dictionary of psychoanalysis* (p. 474). Farmington Hills, MI: Thomson Gale.

Jaynes, J. (1976). *The origin of consciousness in the breakdown of the bicameral mind.* Toronto, ON: University of Toronto Press.

Kahr, B. (2003). Masud Khan's Analysis with Donald Winnicott. *Free Associations, 10B*, 190–222.

Kluft, R. P. (1987). First-rank symptoms as a diagnostic clue to multiple personality disorder. *American Journal of Psychiatry, 144*, 293–298.

Kluft, R. P. (1988). The phenomenology and treatment of extremely complex multiple personality disorder. *Dissociation, 1*, 47–58.

Kluft, R. P. (1991). Multiple personality disorder. In A. Tasman & G. S. M. (Eds.), *In Annual Review of Psychiatry* (Vol. 10, pp. 161–188). Washington, DC: American Psychiatric Press.

Kluft, R. P. (1999). Memory. *Journal of the American Psychoanalytic Association*, 47, 227–236.

Kluft, R. P. (2000). The psychoanalytic psychotherapy of Dissociative Identity Disorder in the context of trauma therapy. *Psychoanalytic Inquiry, 20*, 259–286.

Kluft, R. P. (2003). The founding of the ISSD. In J. A. O'Neil (Ed.), *From organization infancy to early adulthood—1983–2003—Celebrating our 20th anniversary* (pp. 9–17). Montreal, QC: International Society for the Study of Dissociation.

Kluft, R. P. (2009). A clinician's understanding of dissociation. In P. F. Dell & J. A. O'Neil (Eds.), *Dissociation and the dissociative disorders: DSM-V and beyond* (pp. 599–623). New York: Routledge.

Kohut, H. (1984). *How does analysis cure?* Chicago, IL: University of Chicago Press.

Kübler-Ross, E. (1969). *On death and dying*. New York: Macmillan.

Laplanche, J., & Pontalis, J.-B. (1967/1973). *The language of psychoanalysis*. New York: Norton.

Larousse. (1990). *Petit Larousse illustré*. Paris: Librairie Larousse.

Leavy, S. A. (1970). John Keats's psychology of creative imagination. *Psychoanalytic Quarterly, 39*, 173–197.

Liotti, G. (1999). Understanding the dissociative processes: The contribution of attachment theory. *Psychoanalytic Inquiry, 19*, 757–783.

Liotti, G. (2004). Trauma, dissociation and disorganized attachment: Three strands of a single braid. *Psychotherapy, 41*, 472–486.

Liotti, G. (2009). Attachment and dissociation. In P. F. Dell & J. A. O'Neil (Eds.), *Dissociation and the dissociative disorders: DSM-V and beyond* (pp. 53–65). New York: Routledge.

Loewenstein, R. J., & Ross, D. R. (1992). Multiple personality and psychoanalysis: An introduction. *Psychoanalytic Inquiry, 12*, 3–48.

Masson, J. M. (1984). *The assault on truth: Freud's suppression of the seduction theory*. New York: Farrar, Straus & Giroux.

Meissner, W. W. (1972). Notes on Identification—III. The Concept of Identification. *Psychoanalytic Quarterly, 41*, 224–260.

Meissner, W. W. (1995). The Economic Principle in Psychoanalysis: I. Economics and Energetics; II. Regulatory Principles; III. Motivational Principles. *Psychoanalysis and Contemporary Thought, 18*, 197–292.

Nijenhuis, E. R. S., & Den Boer, J. A. (2009). Psychobiology of traumatization and trauma-related structural dissociation of the personality. In P. F. Dell & J. A. O'Neil (Eds.), *Dissociation and the dissociative disorders: DSM-V and beyond* (pp. 337–365). New York: Routledge.

O'Neil, J. A. (1993). Popper, Grünbaum, and induction. *Canadian Journal of Psychoanalysis, 1*(2), 105–130.

O'Neil, J. A. (1997). Expanding the psychoanalytic view of the intrapsychic: Psychic conflict in the inscape. *Dissociation, 10*, 192–202.

O'Neil, J. A. (2001). Épistémologie. In P. Lalonde, J. Aubut & F. Grunberg (Eds.), *Psychiatrie clinique* (Vol. 2, pp. 1468–1483). Boucherville, QC: Gaëtan Morin Éditeur.

OED (Ed.) (1991). *The compact Oxford English dictionary* (Second Edition). Oxford, UK: Oxford University Press.

Onions, C. T., Ed. (1966). *The Oxford dictionary of English etymology*. Oxford, UK: Oxford University Press.

Oxnam, R. B. (2005). *A fractured mind: My life with multiple personality disorder*. New York: Hyperion.

Perron, R. (2005). Hypnoid states. In A. de Mijolla (Ed.), *International dictionary of psychoanalysis* (pp. 768). Farmington Hills, MI: Thomson Gale.

Popper, K. R. (1935/1968). *The logic of scientific discovery, 2nd ed.* New York: Harper & Row.

Popper, K. R. (1972/1992). *Unended quest: An intellectual autobiography*. London & New York: Routledge.

Pugh, G. (2002). Freud's 'Problem': Cognitive neuroscience and psychoanalysis working together on memory. *International Journal of Psychoanalysis, 83*, 1375–1394.

Putnam, F. W. (1989). *Diagnosis and treatment of Multiple Personality Disorder*. New York: Guilford.

Putnam, F. W. (1997). The "Discrete Behavioral States" model. In *Dissociation in children and adolescents: A developmental perspective* (pp. 151–179). New York: Guilford.

Ricœur, P. (1970). *Freud & philosophy: An essay on interpretation* (D. Savage, Trans.). New Haven: Yale University Press.

Robert. (1994). *Dictionnaire étymologique du français*. Paris: Dictionnaires le Robert.

Ross, C. A. (1991). Epidemiology of multiple personality disorder and dissociation. *Psychiatric Clinics of North America, 14*, 503–517.

Ross, C. A. (1997). *Dissociative Identity Disorder: Diagnosis, clinical features, and treatment of multiple personality*. New York: Wiley.

Rubens, R. L. (1994). Fairbairn's structual theory. In J. S. Grotstein & D. B. Rinsley (Eds.), *Fairbarin and the origins of object relations*. New York: Guilford.

Rubens, R. L. (1996). The unique origins of Fairbairn's theories: From instinct to self: Selected papers of W. R. D. Fairbairn, Vols. I and II, edited by David Scharff and Ellinor Fairbairn Birtles. *Psychoanalytic Dialogues, 6*, 413–435.

Sackett, D. L., Rosenberg, W. M., Gray, J. A., Haynes, R. B., & Richardson, W. S. (1996). Evidence based medicine: what it is and what it isn't. *British Medical Journal, 312*, 71–72.

Schore, A. N. (2009). Attachment trauma and the developing right brain: Origins of pathological dissociation. In P. F. Dell & J. A. O'Neil (Eds.), *Dissociation and the dissociative disorders: DSM-V and beyond* (pp. 107–141). New York: Routledge.

Scott, W. C. M. (1964). Mania and mourning. *International Journal of Psycho-Analysis, 45,* 373–377.

Seyfarth, E. A. (2006). Julius Bernstein (1829–1917): pioneer neurobiologist and biophysicist. *Biological Cybernetics, 94*, 2–8.

Silverstein, S. M., & Silverstein, B. R. (1990). Post-Freudian developments in psychoanalytic views of hypnosis from libido theory to ego psychology. *Annual of Psychoanalysis, 18*, 195–211.

Simeon, D. (2009a). Neurobiology of depersonalization disorder. In P. F. Dell & J. A. O'Neil (Eds.), *Dissociation and the dissociative disorders: DSM-V and beyond* (pp. 367–372). New York: Routledge.

Simeon, D. (2009b). Depersonalization disorder. In P. F. Dell & J. A. O'Neil (Eds.), *Dissociation and the dissociative disorders: DSM-V and beyond* (pp. 435–444). New York: Routledge.

Sinason, V. (Ed.). (2002). *Attachment, trauma and multiplicity*. London: Brunner/Routledge.

Steele, K. S., Van der Hart, O., & Nijenhuis, E. R. S. (2009). The theory of trauma-related structural dissociation of the personality. In P. F. Dell & J. A. O'Neil (Eds.), *Dissociation and the dissociative disorders: DSM-V and beyond* (pp. 239–258). New York: Routledge.

Stern, D. B. (1997). Unformulated experience: From dissociation to imagination in psychoanalysis. Hillsdale, NJ: The Analytic Press.

Stern, D. B. (2009). Dissociation and unformulated experience. In P. F. Dell & J. A. O'Neil (Eds.), *Dissociation and the dissociative disorders: DSM-V and beyond* (pp. 653–663). New York: Routledge.

Strachey, J. (1966). Appendix C: the nature of Q. *Standard Edition (of the complete psychological works of Sigmund Freud)*, 1, 392–397.

Tarnopolsky, A. (2003). The concept of dissociation in early psychoanalytic writers. *Journal of Trauma and Dissociation, 4*, 7–25.

Turner, M. A. (2003). Psychiatry and the human sciences. *British Journal of Psychiatry, 182*, 472–474.

Van der Hart, O., & Dorahy, M. J. (2009). History of the concept of dissociation. In P. Dell & J. A. O'Neil (Eds.), *Dissociation and the Dissociative Disorders: DSM-V and Beyond* (pp. 3–26). New York: Routledge.

Van der Hart, O., Nijenhuis, E. R. S., & Steele, K. (2006). *The haunted self: Structural dissociation and the treatment of chronic traumatization*. New York, NY: Norton.

Watkins, J. G., & Watkins, H. H. (1997). *Ego states: Theory and therapy*. New York: Norton.

Williams, L. M. (1994). Recall of childhood trauma: A prospective study of women's memories of child sexual abuse. *Journal of Consulting and Clinical Psychology, 62*, 1167–1176.

Wisdom, J. O. (1961). A methodological approach to the problem of hysteria. *International Journal of Psycho-Analysis, 42*, 224–237.

Wisdom, J. O. (1984). What is left of psychoanalytic theory? *International Review of Psycho-Analysis, 11*, 313–326.

Wisdom, J. O. (1987). *Challengeability in modern science*. Aldershot UK: Gower Publishing.

Wolff, P. H. (1987). *The development of behavioral states and the expression of emotions in early infancy*. Chicago: University of Chicago Press.

Young, W. C. (1988). All that switches is not split. *Dissociation, 1*, 31–41.

Zepf, S. (2006). Attachment theory and psychoanalysis: Some remarks from an epistemological and from a Freudian viewpoint. *International Journal of Psycho-Analysis, 87*, 1526–1548.

Part VI

Neurobiology of Dissociation

20 Neurobiology of Dissociation: A View From the Trauma Field

J. Douglas Bremner, MD

OUTLINE

20.1 INTRODUCTION

The dissociative disorders are associated with considerable morbidity and loss of productivity. On a clinical level the presence of dissociative symptoms in a number of traumatized patients is impossible to deny. However, a clear consensus regarding the diagnostic formulation of the dissociative disorders has been slow to develop. Controversies about the validity of the dissociative disorders, both within the mental health field and the popular culture, have hindered development in this area. The absence of consensus regarding diagnosis has slowed the advance of neurobiological research in the dissociative disorders. This is unfortunate, as evidence for biological abnormalities can add confidence in the validity of psychiatric diagnoses, as has been seen in the past decade for the other trauma-related disorders, posttraumatic stress disorder (PTSD), and more recently borderline personality disorder (BPD). This chapter reviews the diagnostic formulation of the dissociative disorders and preliminary work in the area of neurobiology, with suggestions for future research.

20.2 DIAGNOSTIC DEVELOPMENT OF THE DISSOCIATIVE DISORDERS

Dissociation is currently defined as a breakdown in memory, identity, and consciousness. Dissociative symptoms include amnesia: gaps in memory not due to ordinary forgetting; depersonalization: out-of-body experiences and other distortions of the sense of one's own body, such as feelings that your arms are like toothpicks or your body is very large; derealization: distortions in visual perception, such as seeing things as if they are in a tunnel, things are in black and white or colors are very bright, and distortions in time, like the feeling that time stands still or is moving very fast, and; identity disturbance: fragmentation of the sense of the self. Current DSM-IV dissociative disorders include Dissociative Identity Disorder (DID), depersonalization disorder, dissociative amnesia, and dissociative disorder not otherwise specified (DDNOS) (which includes fugue states and derealization disorders).

The diagnostic development of the dissociative disorders has evolved in a strange and parallel fashion to posttraumatic stress disorder (PTSD). Our current psychiatric nosological approach to trauma-related psychiatric diagnosis has its roots in 19th-century England, Germany, and France. Victims of railroad accidents who had no physical injury but had a range of symptoms including somatic complaints, confusion, anxiety, and memory loss, were given diagnoses such as "railway spine," "traumatic neurosis," or "traumatic hysteria." These disorders were typically conceived as related to physical injury to the spine or other bodily functions that were below the limits of detection with the technology of the time. Although some doctors felt that the traumatic event itself could contribute to the observed symptoms, they were quickly drowned out by a medical establishment bent on preventing a feared wave of pensioners from draining the national treasuries, or maintaining large numbers of soldiers on the battlefield during the First World War. The antagonism toward the idea that psychological trauma could result in a real disorder (as opposed to weaknesses in personality or other factors) culminated in Germany when some people claimed that they developed a traumatic neurosis from the process of seeking pension compensation. This was cited as evidence that the traumatic neuroses were created by the existence of the compensation system itself, and that there were no true trauma-related disorders.

Hidden within these disorders are the rudimentary elements of PTSD and the dissociative disorders. The anxiety and fear responses evolved into PTSD, while the confusion and amnesia are probably an incompletely described formulation of dissociation. In the First World War the diagnosis of "shell shock" was closer to a pure dissociative disorder. Soldiers were described as forgetting their names or who they were, and wandering off of the battlefield with no memory of what had happened to them. Because of the close proximity of exploding shells, this disorder was originally conceived of as being secondary to the physical impact of the explosions, although this idea was later revised.

The psychiatric approach to the dissociative disorders, however, had an oddly parallel existence that had no relationship to psychological trauma. In the early part of the 20th century, American psychiatrists published case reports of individuals who wandered away from their homes, forgot about their past identities, and developed new lives in another city. This became known as fugue states. Depersonalization disorder was similarly developed with a focus on the symptoms, rather than the etiology. Dissociative amnesia (originally psychogenic amnesia) had a psychoanalytical bent that emphasized repressed conflicts in the etiology. At some times in the mid 20th century it was grouped with the old remnant of hysteria, conversion disorder, and called "dissociative hysteria." Due to this the dissociative disorders had difficulty shaking the suspicion that they were not true disorders, or that they were a disguise for secondary gain, malingering, or criminality. Also, a psychoanalytic emphasis on unconscious conflicts in the etiology of psychiatric disorders led to a deemphasis on the pathogenic role of psychological trauma. When DID (originally multiple personality disorder) emerged from the dissociative disorders spectrum, it was initially fueled by interest in the fascinating phenomena of seemingly multiple personalities emanating out of the same individual. In all of this, there was no appreciation for the critical role that psychological trauma routinely played in these disorders.

Psychological trauma was co-opted by clinicians who originally were advocates for Holocaust survivors, and later Vietnam veterans. An alliance between these groups led to the formulation of PTSD in the DSM-III in 1980. PTSD then became the sine qua non of a trauma-related psychiatric disorder. PTSD and the dissociative disorders then developed in odd parallel, with two separate scientific/clinical societies, the International Society for Traumatic Stress Studies (ISTSS) for PTSD, and the International Society for Dissociative Disorders (ISDD) for the dissociative disorders. Two groups of researchers developed in each society, focused on their own particular disorder. Only in the mid-1990s did it start to gradually occur to these two separate groups that they may have something in common, which led to a move to have the two societies meet in the same city with an adjacent calendar to allow people to attend both meetings. The advocates of PTSD and the dissociative disorders were plagued from the beginning by a large body of doubting Thomases who carried over old suspicions like those related to the pension neuroses. These advocates had to fight for their respective diagnoses, which promoted the tendency of investigators to ignore the obvious overlap between the two disorders, and to emphasize the uniqueness and specificity of their particular disorder.

An overemphasis on the spectacle of multiple personalities by some clinicians and the controversy over "false memories" led to a backlash against the diagnosis of multiple personality disorder (MPD), which led to its being renamed Dissociative Identity Disorder (DID). The controversy over MPD has contributed to the fact that most psychiatrists do not make diagnoses of dissociative disorders. For instance, we conducted a chart review of admitting diagnoses in a psychiatric hospital in The Netherlands, and could find only two cases of the diagnosis of dissociative amnesia out of thousands of admissions. This is in spite of the fact that 86% of PTSD patients have a diagnosis of a dissociative disorder (most commonly amnesia) when they are formally assessed (Bremner et al., 1998). I have been dismayed to encounter psychiatry residents who have not even heard of dissociative amnesia. The fact the patients with dissociative symptoms often "suffer in silence" with their symptoms, because they are so strange as to be difficult to even put into words, also contributes to the fact that dissociative disorders are vastly under-recognized.

In spite of this, the existence of dissociative symptoms in a substantial number of individuals in the general population, and the strong relationship between dissociative disorders and psychological trauma is indisputable (Bremner et al., 1992; Bremner, Steinberg, Southwick, Johnson, & Charney, 1993; Cardena & Spiegel, 1993; Chu & Dill, 1990; Lewis & Putnam, 1996; Loewenstein & Putnam, 1988; Marmar et al., 1994; Putnam, Guroff, Silberman, Barban, & Post, 1986; Sanders & Giolas, 1991; Spiegel, 1984; Spiegel, 1994; Spiegel & Cardena,

1991; Spiegel, Hunt, & Dondershine, 1988; Stutman & Bliss, 1985). Furthermore, dissociative symptoms always cluster together. In our own studies, we were not able to find any evidence for the distinctness of amnesia, depersonalization, derealization, and identity diffusion as separate constructs (Bremner et al., 1998; Bremner et al., 1993). In fact these symptoms are highly correlated. For instance, following a car accident, many individuals report looking down on the scene from above (depersonalization); however, when they are doing this things look strange or unreal (derealization) and they may have gaps of memory for the event (amnesia). The identity disturbance of DID is really related to a series of amnestic episodes, which when extreme can lead the patient to feel like there are multiple unconnected facets of themselves that are imperfectly connected with one another. Again, the different personality states are often experienced in a dreamy, dissociative state.

The past decade has seen a rapid expansion of research in the field of dissociation. The development of instruments, including the Dissociative Experiences Scale (DES) (Bernstein & Putnam, 1986), Structured Clinical Interview for DSMIIIR-Dissociative Disorders (SCID-D) (Steinberg, Rounsaville, & Cicchetti, 1990), Dissociative Disorders Interview Schedule (DDIS) (Ross, Joshi, & Currie, 1990), Peritraumatic Dissociation Questionnaire (Marmar et al., 1994), and Clinician Administered Dissociative States Scale (CADSS) (Bremner et al., 1998), has facilitated research in this field.

Acute stress disorder (ASD) was introduced as part of DSM-IV in 1994. This reversed the trend of DSM-IIIR, which did not include acute PTSD or any acute stress response diagnosis, and harkened back to the acute PTSD in DSM-III. ASD is of duration of less than 1 month, and (like PTSD) requires exposure to an acute threat to life with accompanying fear, helplessness, or horror. In addition, a diagnosis of ASD requires three to five dissociative symptoms (numbing, derealization, depersonalization, amnesia, or being "in a daze"); one or more of each of the PTSD reexperiencing, avoidance, and hyperarousal symptoms; and functional disturbance (as in DSM-IV PTSD). Studies have shown that ASD diagnosis predicts 83% of cases at 1 year (Brewin, Andrews, Rose, & Kirk, 1999). Reexperiencing and hyperarousal (but not avoidance) were equally adept at predicting development of chronic PTSD. These findings indicate that perhaps there are two subtypes of acute trauma response—one primarily dissociative and the other intrusive/hyperarousal—that both can lead to chronic PTSD.

There has been some controversy about whether dissociation is a normal psychological response or a pathological symptom seen only in trauma survivors (Bremner & Marmar, 1998; Kluft, 1990; Lewis & Putnam, 1996). Part of this controversy relates to overlap of dissociation with other constructs, like hypnotizability and absorption. Both hypnotizability and absorption (e.g., the capacity to become absorbed in a movie) are normal personality features that vary in the general population. Some of the questions asked on scales to measure dissociation include absorption-type questions, which may identify a normal personality trait instead of a pathological response. In my opinion, dissociative symptoms, such as repeatedly seeing things as if you were in a tunnel, are indicators of psychopathology and are primarily found in patients with pathological responses to trauma.

My colleagues and I asked Vietnam veterans about dissociative symptoms at the time of combat trauma. We found that Vietnam veterans who dissociated at the time of combat trauma were more likely to later develop PTSD and continued to have dissociative responses to subsequent stressors (Bremner & Brett, 1997; Bremner et al., 1992). We found that Vietnam combat veterans with PTSD had increased dissociative symptom levels compared to combat veterans without PTSD (Bremner et al., 1992; Bremner et al., 1993), and that individuals with dissociative responses to trauma are at increased risk for PTSD (Bremner et al., 1992) and continue to have dissociative responses to subsequent stressors (Bremner & Brett, 1997). These studies showed a close relationship between the diagnosis of PTSD and dissociative disorders. For example, 86% of a PTSD sample met criteria for a comorbid dissociative disorder (Bremner & Brett, 1997), whereas essentially 100% of patients with dissociative identity disorder (DID) meet criteria for PTSD. Marmar and colleagues found that dissociative responses to trauma predict long-term PTSD in emergency personnel (Marmar et al., 1994), whereas more recent prospective studies have documented the association between dissociative states at the time of trauma and the development of chronic PTSD (Koopman, Classen, & Spiegel, 1994; Shalev, Peri, Canetti, & Schreiber, 1996). One recent study showed that dissociative symptoms in the first 24 hours after a trauma were not predictive, rather dissociative symptoms at about 1 week after trauma were predictive of long-term outcome (McFarlane, 2000). It may be that immediate dissociative responses are nonspecific responses to trauma, and that continued dissociation in a situation of chronic stress is the best predictor of pathology. These findings have led to the argument for inclusion of PTSD and dissociative disorders in a common "trauma spectrum disorders" cluster of psychiatric diagnoses (Bremner, 2002; Ross, 2000).

In order to conduct studies of treatment and neurobiology of dissociation, we developed a scale for use as a repeated measure of dissociative states (previously mentioned), the Clinician Administered Dissociative States Scale (CADSS) (Bremner et al., 1998). The CADSS is a 27-item scale with 19 subject-rated items and 8 items scored by an observer. The subjective component consists of 19 items that are administered by a clinician who begins each question with the phrase "at this time" and then reads the item to the subject. The subject then endorses one of a range of possible responses: 0 not at all, 1 slightly, 2 moderately, 3 considerably, 4 extremely. The subject's response on this 0 to 4 scale is recorded, and the clinician moves on to the next item. Some of the dissociative symptoms measured with the CADSS that were most commonly endorsed in traumatized patients included "Did things seem to be moving in slow motion?" "Did sounds change, so that that they became very soft or very loud?" and "Did it seem as if you were looking at things as an observer or a spectator?" We found that these symptoms increased when PTSD patients were reexposed to reminders of their original trauma during a traumatic memories group I conducted at the inpatient PTSD program at the VA hospital.

Tests of reliability and validity of the CADSS were performed in both normal individuals and patients with psychiatric disorders. The CADSS was found to be a reliable and valid measure for the assessment of childhood trauma. PTSD patients with high dissociative disorder comorbidity were compared to other patient groups and control subjects. Scores on the CADSS were significantly different for patients with PTSD versus patients with schizophrenia, depression, normal individuals, and Vietnam combat veterans without PTSD (Bremner et al., 1998). A group of patients with PTSD were assessed before and after exposure to a traumatic memories group. They showed a significant increase in dissociative symptomatology in comparison to baseline, during exposure to a traumatic memories group.

Sometimes dissociative symptoms can resemble symptoms of psychosis. Paying attention to some specific clinical characteristics can aid in differentiating dissociative from psychotic symptomatology. First of all, dissociative symptomatology is invariably related to a traumatic event, whereas psychotic symptomatology does not show such a specific connection with trauma. Second, auditory hallucinations are a recognized clinical feature of dissociative disorders that many patients experience, and should not be considered to be indicative only of psychosis. Auditory hallucinations in dissociative disorders are related to the traumatic event, and often consist of a dead buddy talking to the patient, voices crying out in pain, or other actual traumatic memories. Psychotic auditory hallucinations, on the other hand, commonly consist of an unrecognized foreign voice with specific types of content, such as making disparaging comments about the individual. Finally, visual hallucinations in dissociative disorders are related to the traumatic memory and involve the perception of normal "intact" scenes, whereas psychotic visual hallucinations have bizarre content and often involve a breakdown of the scenario of the scene.

A particularly troubling dissociative disorder that has received extensive media attention (e.g., the movies *The Three Faces of Eve* and *Sybil*) is DID. This disorder was previously termed *multiple personality disorder* but the name was changed by the American Psychiatric Association in order to emphasize the identity fragmentation that occurs with the disorder. The name change is also in response to extensive media attention, which has focused on the "either/or" aspect of whether an individual has one personality or more than one. In my clinical work, I have not found this type of dichotomous thinking to be helpful in traumatized patients with identity disturbances. Typically, patients describe identity fragments to which they may have attached a name label, and which may have different levels of development but are not completely formed into distinct personalities in the same way that we would think of normal personality. Some of the identity fragments may be associated with painful memories (e.g., a 6-year-old fragment who was sexually abused, is very angry, and carries the feelings of fear and shame), whereas others are protected from these painful memories (a 10-year-old "good girl" who is happy and polite). However, these identity fragments are all part of the same person, and ultimately it is not possible to have "multiple personalities"; rather, it is the perception of traumatized patients that they have distinct identity fragments within themselves. These identity fragments may play a role in avoiding painful memories of trauma that can incapacitate the individual in his or her daily life. However, ultimately patients need to come to terms with their painful memories and realize that all of the identity fragments are part of just one person.

In order to understand dissociative identity disorder, it is important to have an understanding of normal personality development. Almost all cases of DID are related to early childhood abuse (Putnam et al., 1986). Childhood abuse can have lasting effects on the sense of self. Our sense of self does not exist from the time of birth; rather, it is the result of an accumulation of a lifetime's experiences and positive relationships with others. For example, a particularly positive experience with a math teacher will allow the individual to "take away" an aspect of that role model's personality, incorporate it into the sense of self, and lead to a strengthening of the personality. A more fundamental example of this phenomenon is the interaction between infant and mother. This is what Winnicott and others who wrote about object relations theory called the phenomenon of the "good enough mother." In abusive families, the mother may not only be not "good enough," but may actually be a source of threat. This has an important impact on the child's development of the sense of self, leading to a fragmentation of identity and a walling-off of aspects of memory and the self. Childhood abuse can also be associated with lasting feelings of shame (related to a common process of self-blame) and rage against the perpetrator and others in the family who did not provide protection. A sense of powerlessness in the face of the aggressor can put abuse victims at risk for becoming perpetrators themselves when they become adults, in an attempt to have the feeling of power over another that they could not have as children.

The current diagnostic schema does not appropriately address the experiences of clinicians who take care of patients with stress-related psychiatric disorders on a daily basis. In my opinion, this is an artifact of the continuing drive to create categories and classifications of psychiatric diagnoses that contain discrete disorders that are unrelated to one another and not based on any particular theoretical foundation or view of etiology. This is largely a by-product of the domination of psychiatric diagnosis by the field of psychoanalysis for the better part of the 20th century and the subsequent reaction to this domination. For psychoanalysis, theories of etiology were central to diagnosis; for example, anxiety neurosis was related to repressed conflicts that were made manifest only in symptoms where the relationship to the disorder was not immediately obvious. The development of the Diagnostic and Statistical Manual represented a gradual removal of psychiatric diagnosis from the psychoanalysts under the mantel of "science" and "objective diagnosis." A major objective of the move to make psychiatric diagnosis empirical was to remove any etiological underpinning for these diagnoses. However, what is not appreciated is that there often was little or no empirical basis for these new psychiatric diagnoses.

Based on the close relationship among dissociation, PTSD and trauma, I have argued for a reorganization of the current diagnostic criteria for the anxiety disorders (which currently includes PTSD) and dissociative disorders (Bremner, 1999a). Currently in the diagnostic criteria of the American Psychiatric Association, there is the diagnosis acute stress disorder (ASD), which describes dissociative and PTSD symptoms in the first month after psychological trauma. Recent research indicates that ASD and PTSD are closely related disorders (Brewin et al., 1999). Their criteria should therefore be made to be consistent with one another.

20.3 NEUROBIOLOGICAL STUDIES IN DISSOCIATION

Because of the delay in achieving a consensus regarding the diagnostic formulation of the dissociative disorders, there have been few studies in the area of the neurobiology of dissociative disorders. In one early study, patients with DID were found to have changes in autonomic indexes and reaction times when voluntarily moving between alter personality states (Putnam, Zahn, & Post, 1990). Hypnotizability, which has been associated with dissociation, was found to correlate with cerebrospinal fluid (CSF) levels of the dopamine metabolite, homovanillic acid (HVA) in a mixed group of psychiatric patients (Spiegel & King, 1992). Kappa opioid receptor agonists can induce depersonalization, derealization and perceptual alterations (Pfeiffer, Brantl, Herz, & Emrich, 1986). In patients with eating disorders, dissociative symptoms as measured by the DES were positively correlated with CSF HVA and negatively correlated with CSF beta-endorphin (Demitrack et al., 1993).

The hypothalamic-pituitary-adrenal HPA axis is known to play a central role in the stress response, which is critical in the development of dissociative disorders. The role of the HPA axis in mediating dissociation is still unclear. Cortisol levels were found to fall during hypnosis (Sachar, Cobb, & Shor, 1966). One study in depersonalization disorder (DPD) found nonsignificantly lower basal salivary cortisol in DPD patients compared to healthy controls (Stanton et al., 2001), while another study showed a tendency for elevated basal urinary and plasma cortisol and a resistance to low-dose dexamethasone suppression in DPD compared to controls (Simeon, Guralnik, Knutelska, Hollander, & Schmeidler, 2001).

Apart from single case reports, brain imaging studies of dissociative disorders published in the literature are few. In one study, patients with depersonalization disorder (DPD) had higher activity in somatosensory association areas (Simeon et al., 2000). One brain imaging study used functional MRI in PTSD patients in a dissociative state while reexperiencing traumatic memories and found more activation in the temporal, inferior and medial frontal, occipital, parietal, anterior cingulated, and medial prefrontal cortical regions (Lanius et al., 2002).

Brain regions such as the hippocampus that are sensitive to stress may mediate symptoms of dissociation. Two studies have found a negative correlation between dissociative symptom level as measured by the DES and hippocampal volume as measured with MRI in women with early childhood sexual-abuse-related PTSD (Bremner et al., 2003; Stein, Koverola, Hanna, Torchia, & McClarty, 1997). One study of women with early abuse and DID found smaller hippocampal volume relative to healthy subjects (Vermetten et al., 2006). Electrical stimulation of the hippocampus and adjacent regions in patients with epilepsy resulted in a number of dissociative-like symptoms, including feelings of déjà vu, depersonalization, derealization, and memory alterations (Halgren, Walter, Cherlow, & Crandall, 1978; Penfield & Perot, 1963). Administration of the NMDA receptor antagonist, ketamine, resulted in dissociative symptoms in healthy subjects, including feeling out of body, time standing still, body distortions, and amnesia (Krystal et al., 1994). NMDA receptors are highly concentrated in the hippocampus and play a role in memory on a molecular level. Stress inhibits long-term potentiation (LTP), which is the molecular model for memory (Diamond, Branch, Fleshner, & Rose, 1995; Diamond, Fleshner, Ingersoll, & Rose, 1996). Based on these findings we have hypothesized that stress, acting through the NMDA receptor in the hippocampus, may mediate symptoms of dissociation (Bremner, 2002; Bremner & Marmar, 1998). Because of trance-like states seen in some individuals with thalamic lesions, and given the role of the thalamus as a gateway of sensory information from the outside world to the brain, we have also hypothesized that thalamic dysfunction may play a role in dissociation (Krystal, Bennett, Bremner, Southwick, & Charney, 1996).

Medication trials in dissociative disorders have been similarly limited. The serotonin reuptake inhibitor (SSRI) fluoxetine was shown to reduce symptoms of depersonalization (Fichtner, Horevitz, & Braun, 1992; Hollander et al., 1990; Ratliff & Kerski, 1995). The anticonvulsant lamotrigine, which inhibits glutamate release, was found to attenuate ketamine-induced dissociation in healthy subjects (Anand et al., 2000). It has been hypothesized that NMDA antagonists such as ketamine may induce depersonalization via increased glutamate neurotransmission at non-NMDA glutamate receptors. Along these lines, there was a promising preliminary open-label-trial of lamotrigine in chronic depersonalization (Sierra et al., 2001). Opioid receptor antagonists have been reported to reduce dissociation, including naltrexone in patients with borderline personality disorder (Bohus et al., 1999), and IV naloxone in chronic depersonalization (Nuller, Morozova, Kushnir, & Hamper, 2001).

20.4 SUMMARY AND FUTURE DIRECTIONS

In summary there are few studies of the neurobiology of dissociative disorders. Much of this delay has been related to the historical development of dissociative disorders being connected with the idea of hysteria, and therefore not a worthy topic for investigations using biological parameters. However, the past decade of research in PTSD, and more recent studies in other trauma-related psychiatric disorders like borderline personality disorder, have demonstrated the utility of applying imaging, genetics, neuroendocrinology, and other research tools to trauma-related psychiatric disorders. Given the high correlation between the diverse symptom areas of dissociation, including amnesia, depersonalization, derealization, and identity disturbance, future studies should not be delayed by uncertainty about the specific diagnosis within the dissociative disorders. Rather than perform research to prove that multiple personalities can exist, or to establish a specific biological fingerprint for depersonalization disorder, or dissociative amnesia, future approaches should examine the neurobiological underpinnings of dissociation conceptualized in a broader sense, and establish the similarities and differences with the hyperarousal profile of classic PTSD.

REFERENCES

Anand, A., Charney, D., Oren, D. A., Berman, R. M., Hu, X. S., Cappiello, A., & Krystal, J. H. (2000). Attenuation of the neuropsychiatric effects of ketamine with lamotrigine: Suport for hyperglutamatergic effects of N-methyl-D-aspartate receptor antagonists. *Archives of General Psychiatry, 57,* 270–276.

Bernstein, E. M., & Putnam, F. W. (1986). Development, reliability, and validity of a dissociation scale. *Journal of Nervous and Mental Disease, 174,* 727–735.

Bohus, M. J., Landwehrmeyer, G. B., Stiglmayr, C. E., Limberger, M. F., Boehme, R., & Schmahl, C. G. (1999). Naltrexone in the treatment of dissociative symptoms in patients with borderline personality disorder: An open-label trial. *Journal of Clinical Psychiatry, 60,* 598–603.

Bremner, J. D. (2002). *Does stress damage the brain? Understanding trauma-related disorders from a mind-body perspective.* New York: W. W. Norton.

Bremner, J. D., & Brett, E. (1997). Trauma-related dissociative states and long-term psychopathology in posttraumatic stress disorder. *Journal of Traumatic Stress, 10,* 37–49.

Bremner, J. D., Krystal, J. H., Putnam, F. W., Southwick, S. M., Marmar, C., Charney, D. S., et al. (1998). Measurement of dissociative states with the Clinician-Administered Dissociative States Scale (CADSS). *Journal of Traumatic Stress, 11,* 125–136.

Bremner, J. D., & Marmar, C. (1998). *Trauma, memory, and dissociation.* Washington, DC: American Psychiatric Press.

Bremner, J. D., Southwick, S. M., Brett, E., Fontana, A., Rosenheck, A., & Charney, D. S. (1992). Dissociation and posttraumatic stress disorder in Vietnam combat veterans. *American Journal of Psychiatry, 149,* 328–332.

Bremner, J. D., Steinberg, M., Southwick, S. M., Johnson, D. R., & Charney, D. S. (1993). Use of the Structured Clinical Interview for DSMIV-Dissociative Disorders for systematic assessment of dissociative symptoms in posttraumatic stress disorder. *American Journal of Psychiatry, 150,* 1011–1014.

Bremner, J. D., Vythilingam, M., Vermetten, E., Southwick, S. M., McGlashan, T., Nazeer, A., Khan, S., Vaccarino, L. V., Soufer, R., Garg, P., Ng, C. K., Staib, L. H., Duncan, J. S., & Charney, D. S. (2003). MRI and PET study of deficits in hippocampal structure and function in women with childhood sexual abuse and posttraumatic stress disorder (PTSD). *American Journal of Psychiatry, 160,* 924–932.

Brewin, C. R., Andrews, B., Rose, S., & Kirk, M. (1999). Acute stress disorder and posttraumatic stress disorder in victims of violent crime. *American Journal of Psychiatry, 156,* 360–366.

Cardeña, E., & Spiegel, D. (1993). Dissociative reactions to the San Francisco Bay Area earthquake of 1989. *American Journal of Psychiatry, 150,* 474–478.

Chu, J. A., & Dill, D. L. (1990). Dissociative symptoms in relation to childhood physical and sexual abuse. *American Journal of Psychiatry, 147,* 887–892.

Demitrack, M. A., Putnam, F. W., Rubinow, D. R., Pigott, T. A., Altemus, M., Krahn, D. D., & Gold, P. W. (1993). Relationship of dissociative phenomena to levels of cerebrospinal fluid monoamine metabolites and beta-endorphin in patients with eating disorders: A pilot study. *Psychiatry Research, 49,* 1–10.

Diamond, D. M., Branch, B. J., Fleshner, M., & Rose, G. M. (1995). Effects of dehydroepiandosterone and stress on hippocampal electrophysiological plasticity. *Annals of the New York Academy of Sciences, 774,* 304–307.

Diamond, D. M., Fleshner, M., Ingersoll, N., & Rose, G. M. (1996). Psychological stress impairs spatial working memory: Relevance to electrophysiological studies of hippocampal function. *Behavioral Neuroscience, 110,* 661–672.

Fichtner, C. G., Horevitz, R. P., & Braun, B. G. (1992). Fluoxetine in depersonalization disorder. *American Journal of Psychiatry, 149,* 1750–1751.

Halgren, E., Walter, R. D., Cherlow, D. G., & Crandall, P. H. (1978). Mental phenomena evoked by electrical stimulation of the hippocampal formation and amygdala. *Brain, 101,* 83–117.

Hollander, E., Liebowitz, M. R., DeCaria, C. M., Fairbanks, J., Fallon, B., & Klein, D. F. (1990). Treatment of depersonalization with serotonin reuptake blockers. *Journal of Clinical Psychopharmacology, 10,* 200–203.

Kluft, R. P. (1990). *Childhood antecedents of Multiple Personality Disorder.* Washington, DC: American Psychiatric Press.

Koopman, C., Classen, C., & Spiegel, D. (1994). Predictors of posttraumatic stress symptoms among survivors of the Oakland/Berkeley, Calif., firestorm. *American Journal of Psychiatry, 151,* 888–894.

Krystal, J. H., Bennett, A., Bremner, J. D., Southwick, S. M., & Charney, D. S. (1996). Recent developments in the neurobiology of dissociation: Implications for Posttraumatic Stress Disorder. In Michelson, L. K., & Ray, W. J. (Eds.), *Handbook of dissociation: Theoretical, empirical, and clinical perspectives.* New York: Plenum Press, pp. 163–190.

Krystal, J. H., Karper, L. P., Seibyl, J. P., Freeman, G. K., Delaney, R., Bremner, J. D., Heninger, G. R., Bowers, M. B., & Charney, D. S. (1994). Subanesthetic effects of the non-competitive NMDA antagonist, ketamine, in humans: Psychotomimetic, perceptual, cognitive, and neuroendocrine responses. *Archives of General Psychiatry, 51,* 199–214.

Lanius, R. A., Williamson, P. C., Boksman, K., Densmore, M., Gupta, M. A., Neufeld, R. W. J., Gati, J. S., & Menon, R. S. (2002). Brain activation during script-driven imagery induced dissociative responses in PTSD: A functional magnetic resonance imaging investigation. *Biological Psychiatry, 52,* 305–311.

Lewis, D. O., & Putnam, F. W. (1996). *Dissociative Identity Disorder/Multiple Personality Disorder: Child and adolescent psychiatric clinics of North America.* Philadelphia: Saunders.

Lœwenstein, R. J., & Putnam, F. W. (1988). A comparison study of dissociative symptoms in patients with complex partial seizures, MPD, and posttraumatic stress disorder. *Dissociation, 1,* 17–23.

Marmar, C. R., Weiss, D. S., Schlenger, D. S., Fairbank, J. A., Jordan, B. K., Kulka, R. A., & Hough, R. L. (1994). Peritraumatic dissociation and posttraumatic stress in male Vietnam theater veterans. *American Journal of Psychiatry, 151,* 902–907.

McFarlane, A. C. (2000). Posttraumatic stress disorder: A model of the longitudinal course and the role of risk factors. *Journal of Clinical Psychiatry, 61,* 15–20.

Nuller, Y. L., Morozova, M. G., Kushnir, O. N., & Hamper, N. (2001). Effect of naloxone therapy on depersonalization. *Journal of Psychopharmacology, 15,* 93–95.

Penfield, W., & Perot, P. (1963). The brain's record of auditory and visual experience: A final summary and discussion. *Brain, 86,* 595–696.

Pfeiffer, A., Brantl, V., Herz, A., & Emrich, H. E. (1986). Psychotomimesis mediated by opiate receptors. *Science, 233,* 774–776.

Putnam, F. W., Guroff, J. J., Silberman, E. K., Barban, L., & Post, R. M. (1986). The clinical phenomenology of multiple personality disorder: A review of 100 recent cases. *Journal of Clinical Psychiatry, 47,* 285–293.

Putnam, F. W., Zahn, T. P., & Post, R. M. (1990). Differential autonomic nervous system activity in multiple personality disorder. *Psychiatry Research, 31,* 251–260.

Ratliff, N. B., & Kerski, D. (1995). Depersonalization treated with fluoxetine. *American Journal of Psychiatry, 152,* 1689–1690.

Ross, C. A. (2000). *The trauma model: A solution to the problem of comorbidity in psychiatry.* Richardson, TX: Manitou Publications.

Ross, C. A., Joshi, S., & Currie, R. (1990). Dissociative experiences in the general population. *American Journal of Psychiatry, 147,* 1547–1552.

Sachar, E. J., Cobb, J. C., & Shor, R. E. (1966). Plasma cortisol changes during hypnotic trance. *Archives of General Psychiatry, 14,* 482–490.

Sanders, B., & Giolas, M. H. (1991). Dissociation and childhood trauma in psychologically disturbed adolescents. *American Journal of Psychiatry, 148,* 50–54.

Shalev, A. Y., Peri, T., Canetti, L., & Schreiber, S. (1996). Predictors of PTSD in injured trauma survivors: A prospective study. *American Journal of Psychiatry, 153,* 219–225.

Simeon, D., Guralnik, O., Hazlett, S., Spiegel-Cohen, J., Hollander, E., & Buchsbaum, M. S. (2000). Feeling unreal: A PET study of depersonalization disorder. *American Journal of Psychiatry, 157,* 1782–1788.

Simeon, D., Guralnik, O., Knutelska, M., Hollander, E., & Schmeidler, J. (2001). Hypothalamic-pituitary-adrenal axis dysregulation in depersonalization disorder. *Neuropsychopharmacology, 25,* 793–795.

Spiegel, D. (1984). Multiple personality as a posttraumatic stress disorder. *Psychiatric Clinics of North America, 7,* 101–110.

Spiegel, D. (1994). *Dissociation: Culture, mind, and body.* Washington, DC: American Psychiatric Press.

Spiegel, D., & Cardena, E. (1991). Disintegrated experience: The dissociative disorders revisited. *Journal of Abnormal Psychology, 100,* 366–378.

Spiegel, D., Hunt, T., & Dondershine, H. E. (1988). Dissociation and hypnotizability in posttraumatic stress disorder. *American Journal of Psychiatry, 145,* 301–305.

Spiegel, D., & King, R. (1992). Hypnotizability and CSF HVA levels among psychiatric patients. *Biological Psychiatry, 31,* 95–98.

Stanton, B. R., David, A. S., Cleare, A. J., Sierra, M., Lambert, M. V., Phillips, M. L., Porter, R. J., Gallagher, P., & Young, A. H. (2001). Basal activity of the hypothalamic-pituitary-adrenal axis in patients with depersonalization disorder. *Psychiatry Research, 104,* 85–89.

Stein, M. B., Koverola, C., Hanna, C., Torchia, M. G., & McClarty, B. (1997). Hippocampal volume in women victimized by childhood sexual abuse. *Psychological Medicine, 27,* 951–959.

Steinberg, M. J., Rounsaville, B., & Cicchetti, D. V. (1990). The structured clinical interview for DSM-III-R dissociative disorders: Preliminary report on a new diagnostic instrument. *American Journal of Psychiatry, 147,* 76–82.

Stutman, R. K., & Bliss, E. L. (1985). Posttraumatic stress disorder, hypnotizability, and imagery. *American Journal of Psychiatry, 142,* 741–743.

Vermetten, E., Schmahl, C., Lindner, S., Loewenstein, R. J., & Bremner, J. D. (2006). Hippocampal and amygdalar volumes in Dissociative Identity Disorder. *American Journal of Psychiatry, 163,* 1–8.

21 Psychobiology of Traumatization and Trauma-Related Structural Dissociation of the Personality

Ellert R. S. Nijenhuis, PhD
Johan A. den Boer, MD, PhD

OUTLINE

About one in five individuals who are exposed to a highly stressful event, such as an event that involves major threat to the integrity of the body, will not integrate the experience into their personality (i.e., will develop a trauma-related disorder) (Brewin, Andrews, & Rose, 2003; Elklit & Brink, 2003). How traumatizing an event will be depends on factors such as the nature of the event(s), the degree of exposure to the event (Fullerton, Ursano, & Wang, 2004), the degree of exposure to prior stressful events (Daviss et al., 2000), and the individual's integrative capacity. For example, particular events such as severe and chronic physical and sexual abuse are traumatizing for most people, and adults with premorbid psychiatric disorders and children will generally be more vulnerable to become traumatized than mentally healthy adults given their lower integrative capacity (Fuglsang, Moergeli, Hepp-Beg, & Schnyder, 2002; Fullerton et al., 2004). Some studies suggest that younger children are even more vulnerable than older children (Vizek-Vidovic, Kuterovac-Jagodic, & Arambasic, 2000).

Nonintegrated, traumatizing experiences do not tend to vanish from a survivor's mind, but remain in a dissociated form. One common form in which survivors memorize these experiences are as traumatic memories (Nijenhuis & Van der Hart, 1999; Nijenhuis, Van Engen, Kusters, & Van der Hart, 2001; Van der Kolk & Fisler, 1995; Van der Kolk & Van der Hart, 1991). Traumatic memories are recurrent, involuntary, and mostly nonverbal, sensorimotor experiences, often charged with intense affects such as fear, sadness, or disgust, that survivors have not integrated. These positive dissociative symptoms include daytime flashbacks, somatic symptoms, panic attacks, or in even more complete reexperiencings of the traumatizing event. Unintegrated traumatic memories can also manifest as nightmares and night terrors. Traumatic memories thus usually go along with hyperarousal, intense bodily reactions, and strong emotionality. However, they can also involve hypoarousal, degrees of bodily anesthesia, and little affect. Sometimes, survivors shift between states of hyperarousal and states of hypoarousal when they reexperience traumatizing events. For example, they may first become hypervigilant, next they may freeze while being hyperaroused, and then they engage in flight or ward-off (the image) of a perpetrator. Finally, they may totally submit and become bodily and affectively numbed.

Another form in which survivors memorize their traumatic experiences is as a more or less complete and coherent narrative that they have not sufficiently realized (Simeon, Guralnik, Schmeidler, Sirof, & Knutelska, 2001). That is, they have not developed full conscious awareness that the event really happened or that it happened to them, and they do not sufficiently appreciate the personal consequences of the experience. In addition to this lack of realization, some survivors block the retrieval of traumatic memories to the extent that they seem to have forgotten them more or less completely for a time. This partial or complete dissociative amnesia—a *negative* dissociative symptom—can be interrupted by phases in which survivors recollect what happened as traumatic memories.

These different ways of remembering traumatizing events thus coexist in traumatized individuals (Nijenhuis & Van der Hart, 1999). That is, they tend to alternate between reexperiencing traumatizing events in one of more forms and being more or less detached from these painful memories. At one point in time, survivors engage in defensive physical actions in response to perceived threat or real threat (e.g., when traumatization is ongoing) to the integrity of the body. In the next moment, they engage in tasks of daily life, such as taking care of children, earning money, or playing a game, while being depersonalized and partially amnestic for their traumatic experiences.

The survivor's sense of self typically changes with these alternations. They reflect that the personality of traumatized individuals is divided into different dissociative parts, each of which can dominate consciousness and behavior for some time (Nijenhuis & Van der Hart, 1999). These different ways of being-in-the-world are sometimes activated in parallel. In this case, one dissociative part of the personality may intrude the domain of another dissociative part. For example, one part may hear the voice of this other part, and can be intruded by this other part's affects, thoughts, and bodily feelings and movements.

These essential features of trauma-related disorders have met insufficient recognition in psychobiological studies of traumatization. The bulk of the studies to date seem to rest on the implicit assumption that reminders of traumatic experiences will typically evoke reaction patterns that are mediated by the sympathetic nervous system. For example, it is usually hypothesized that trauma survivors will have fear reactions to these reminders that include elevated heart rate frequency (HR) and blood pressure, and that they will commonly activate the "emotional brain" (LeDoux, 2003), including the amygdala. This perspective goes back to Walter Cannon's classic idea of the flight or fight response to major stress, which involves dominance of the sympathetic nervous system. In this chapter, we maintain that this perspective may be overly simplistic as it seems to ignore that survivors may respond with a range of very different response patterns to salient reminders of traumatic experiences. As indicated, these patterns include (apart from defensive reactions such as flight or fight) very different defensive reactions such as total submission to (perceived) major threat. They also include being detached (Holmes et al., 2005) while focusing on tasks in daily life.

This chapter addresses this psychobiological complexity in reactions to (potentially) traumatizing events. It first presents an introduction into the theory of trauma-related structural dissociation of the personality. A range of psychobiological hypotheses can be derived from this theory. Some of these will be subsequently examined using some recent research findings. (Note: for space, we will not discuss emerging structural neuroimaging research of structural dissociation in this chapter.) The basic idea of the theory is that the personality of trauma survivors is divided in two or more different but interacting dissociative parts, that the functioning of these parts is mediated by different (constellations of) action systems, and that these different action systems relate to different aspects of the central nervous system. The theory thus holds that survivors' reaction patterns to stressors and reminders of stressors depend on the part(s) of the personality that is (are) dominant during the exposure to the stressor. Some conclusions complete the chapter.

21.1 THE THEORY OF TRAUMA-RELATED STRUCTURAL DISSOCIATION OF THE PERSONALITY

Many individuals with PTSD or more complex trauma-related disorders alternate between being fixated on traumatic experiences and being detached from them (Nijenhuis & Van der Hart, 1999). As Janet (1907, p. 332) proposed, they alternate between two or more dissociative "systems of ideas and functions that constitute personality." According to the theory of structural dissociation (Nijenhuis, Van der Hart, & Steele, 2002, 2004b; Steele, Van der Hart, & Nijenhuis, 2005; Van der Hart, Nijenhuis, Steele, & Brown, 2004; Van der Hart, Nijenhuis, & Steele, 2006), this alternating pattern reflects failed integration between different parts of the personality. The "emotional" part of the personality (EP; cf. Myers, 1940) is largely stuck in defense from major threat, in particular, threat to the integrity of the body. The "apparently normal" part of the personality (ANP; cf. Myers, 1940) is fixated on fulfilling functions in daily life. As ANP, survivors are more or less detached from traumatic experiences, experience some degree of amnesia, or are depersonalized regarding the traumatic experience and their affects more generally. Using the metaphor of dissociative parts of the personality, it should not be overlooked that they range from very simple to highly complex. Some dissociative parts encompass just one psychobiological state, whereas others are complex assemblies of such states.

Structural dissociation of the personality may involve constellations of one ANP and one EP, as in PTSD; one ANP and more than one EP, as in complex PTSD (Herman, 1992), also known as disorders of extreme stress (Pelcovitz et al., 1997), and more than one ANP and more than one EP, as seen only in DID. According to the theory of structural dissociation, the extent to which the personality becomes divided depends on factors such as the severity of the traumatization in terms of developmental age at trauma onset, chronicity and intensity of the traumatization, the relationship to the perpetrator(s), and lack of support and social recognition of the traumatic experience(s).

ANP and EP constitute two different psychobiological systems, each endowed with its own sense of self, however rudimentary. According to Damasio (1999, p. 26), consciousness and sense of self are essentially grounded in "a feeling that accompanies the making of any kind of image—visual, auditory, tactile, visceral—within our living systems" and may involve several integrative levels: (1) the proto-self that emerges from the activity of brain devices that continuously and nonconsciously maintain the body state within the narrow range and relative stability required for survival; (2) the core self that relates to core consciousness defined as conscious awareness of the here and now based on the mental representation of how our own state is affected by our processing of an object; and (3) the autobiographical self that involves extended consciousness (i.e., conscious awareness of our personal existence across subjective time).

The existence of the EP can be limited to reexperiencing traumatic memories (i.e., sensorimotor experiences that hardly involve narrative components, if at all) (Nijenhuis et al., 2001; Van der Kolk & Fisler, 1995; Van der Kolk & Van der Hart, 1991). In this case, the EP may involve little more than core consciousness and core self. Yet clinical observations suggest that with recurrent reactivations of traumatic memories and chronic traumatization (and treatment), the EP may develop a degree of extended consciousness and autobiographical self. Even in these cases, however, extended consciousness and the sense of autobiographical self tend to remain quite limited. EPs are typically fixed in past traumatic experiences with absent or only partial awareness of the present or the passage of time. ANPs typically have developed a more substantial degree of extended consciousness, yet lack personification and realization of the traumatic past and the associated EPs. EPs and ANPs have a narrowed field of consciousness focused on issues relevant to the functions they exert. Dissociative parts involve a sense of self that is different from the pretraumatic sense of self. However, because young children encompass psychobiological systems that are still relatively unintegrated, their pretraumatic sense of self is rather inconsistent and changeable. That is, their sense of self may not be stable even prior to early traumatization.

What psychobiological "systems of ideas and functions that constitute personality" are involved in EP and ANP? These systems should meet a range of shared criteria:

(1) They must be self-organizing and self-stabilizing within windows of homeostasis, time, and context to control and integrate all the rather coherent complexes of psychobiological phenomena exhibited by ANP and EP;
(2) They should be basic, functional systems that have been developed in the course of evolution, and should be rather analogous to animal biological systems. These two criteria are derived from clinical observations that ANPs typically engage in essential tasks of daily life such as reproduction, attachment, caretaking, and socialization, and avoidance of traumatic memories that support focus on daily life issues. In contrast, EPs primarily display basic defensive and emotional reactions to the (perceived) threat on which they seem to be fixated;
(3) They should be very susceptible to classical conditioning, because, as we discuss below, EP and ANP strongly respond to conditioned threat cues;
(4) They should involve stable characteristics, but also allow for case-dependent variation, because ANP and EP exhibit both invariant and idiosyncratic variations; and
(5) They should be available early in life, since dissociative disorders can manifest from a very early age.

To address the question of what systems mediate the functioning of ANP and EP, we discuss the concept of personality and explore whether personality entails certain systems that meet these five criteria.

21.1.1 Personality

The hypothesis that structural dissociation of the personality marks an abnormal personality structure requires a definition of personality. Allport (1961) proposes that personality is "the dynamic organization within the individual of those psychophysical systems that determine his characteristic behavior and thought" (p. 28). His definition raises the question, What "psychophysical systems" would be involved?

Many authors have proposed that an individual's personality involves a set of distinctive psychological traits, that is, psychological characteristics relatively invariant across contexts such as mental states and environmental situations. More specifically, these traits concern features known as an individual's temperament. Temperament indicates affective qualities of an individual's functioning and denotes, for example, to what extent an individual is generally cheerful, optimistic, sad, fearful, or angry, his common interest in exploring his social and material environment, and how responsible he usually feels for his actions.

The study of personality aims to assess the range of psychological traits that distinguish among different individuals. As Davis, Panksepp, and Normansell (2003, p. 57) note, "there is no agreement whether personality should be studied without any theoretical preconceptions or whether theoretical views of human nature are essential to identify the most important psychological dimensions that need to be evaluated." For example, the currently popular five-factor model that includes Neuroticism—also described as Emotional Stability—Extraversion, Openness to Experience, Agreeableness, and Conscientiousness, was derived empirically without a priori theorizing (Hofstee, Raad, & Goldberg, 1992). This radical positivistic approach has its drawbacks. Thus, in a meta-analytic study of the five-factor model and personality disorder empirical literature, Saulsman and Page (2004, p. 1080) conclude that "a chief factor limiting the progress of [research of the nature of trait maladaptivity] is that the five-factor model is a descriptive account of personality structure, and it does not reveal how personality traits are related to specific behaviors (Benjamin, 1994)." Progress in the study of personality, Saulsman and Page suggest, "requires seeking guidance from existing theories and hypotheses of personality dynamics that complement the five-factor model" (p. 1081).

What theories seem particularly worthwhile to extend our understanding of personality and, more specifically, what psychophysical systems personality would entail? McCrae and Costa (1996) have suggested that the five-factor model represents "genotypic" personality traits. Consistent with this position, various authors have demonstrated a genetic basis for these factors (Cattell, 1986; Eysenck, 1990; Loehlin, 1992; Pedersen, Plomin,

McClearn, & Friberg, 1988; Viken, Rose, Kaprio, & Kowkenvuo, 1994). According to Cattell (1986), the "source" traits of personality have physiological roots, and other studies also suggest that personality traits are predominantly determined by biological factors rather than social ones (Bouchard & Loehlin, 2001; Lucas, Diener, Suh, Shao, & Grob, 2000). However, important as it is, the role of biology for personality must not be overstated. First, phenotypic attributes are produced jointly by genetic and developmental processes (Heyes, 2003; Mayr, 1974). As Heyes (2003) notes

> The information obtained through natural selection and stored in the genotype cannot produce a phenotype without developmental [i.e., ontogenetic] processes of some kind, and development is not always tightly genetically constrained or canalized (Waddington, 1959) such that it does all and only what natural selection "desires." Development can produce outcomes, some of them adaptive, that were not anticipated (not specifically favored) by natural selection, and these outcomes may be said to have an ontogenetic source (D.T. Campbell, 1974; Karmiloff-Smith, 1992).

Animal studies have demonstrated that major stress can completely and permanently alter the phenotypic expression of an animal's genotype (Cools & Ellenbroek, 2002). Thus, an animal of a breed that is extraverted by nature can become introverted for life after major traumatization. On a more general plane, there is mounting evidence that emotional neglect and abuse can significantly or even dramatically affect neurobiological (neurogenesis, neuron migration and differentiation, apoptosis, arborization, synaptogenesis, synaptic sculpting, and myelination) and psychological development, relative to age/developmental windows (Perry, 2002). Genes are required for this development, as well as macro- and micro-environmental stimulation. Thus, development is gene-dependent and user-dependent.

21.1.1.1 Genetic Factors in Personality

The heritable component of personality is associated with variations in multiple alleles and cannot be attributed to a single gene (Livesley & Jang, 2000). It is nonetheless striking that almost every personality dimension studied has been found to have a heritable component, with genetic factors accounting for nearly half the variance on every trait (Plomin, DeVries, McClearn, & Rutter, 1997). Especially adoption studies and twin research have contributed to this conclusion (Kendler, Neale, Kessler, Heath, & Eaves, 1993). Adoption studies (Plomin et al., 1997), as well as studies of twins separated at birth (Tellegen et al., 1988), confirm the heritability of personality traits. It therefore seems justified to conclude that individual differences in personality and temperament have a strong basis in heredity.

Associations between personality traits and genetic variations derive from many different genes, and are therefore measurable as quantitative trait loci. But, thus far, this line of investigation has been disappointing. Promising earlier reports (e.g., Lesch et al., 1996) have not been consistently replicated (Gelertner, Kranzler, & Lacobelle, 1998). The main reason is that single alleles account for only a small percentage of the variance on any trait. These studies also suffer from the lack of a precise phenotype for personality traits.

The presence of a genetic component in personality also implies that traits should be linked to biological markers. Research in this area is at an early stage. Thus far, the strongest finding has been a strong relationship, established in clinical populations, between low levels of central serotonin activity and impulsivity.

21.1.1.2 Gene-Environment Interaction

The other half of the variance in personality derives from the environment. As recent studies show, environmental factors do not occur in isolation; there exists a gene-environment interaction. Genetic factors may also contribute to the vulnerability for environmental events, and genetic factors also appear to contribute to personality characteristics, which may influence the person's risk for entering into potentially hazardous situations (Jang, Stein, Taylor, Asmundson, & Livesley, 2003). Maltreatment at a young age, although causally involved in predicting either PTSD, DID, or antisocial behavior increases the likelihood different subtypes of psychopathology even more when a certain genetic or biological predisposition is present (Raine, 2002a, 2002b).

In a prospective study of male children it was found that a functional polymorphism of the gene encoding for monoamine-oxidase-A (MAO-A plays a role in the enzymatic degradation of noradrenalin and serotonin) predicted the occurrence of antisocial behavior only if the children were maltreated (Caspi et al., 2002). This study shows that a specific genotype (low activity of the MAO-A gene) can influence children's sensitivity and behavioral response toward environmental events. In addition, a polymorphism of the gene for the 5-HT transporter, which determines the availability of serotonin in the synaptic cleft (e.g., in the amygdala) influences the activity of the amygdala (leading to greater activity of the amygdala) when confronted with fearful faces (Hariri et al., 2002). In short, subjects with the short allele (leading to more serotonin in the amygdala) are more prone to anxiety and to feeling threatened even in nonthreatening situations, which may lead to a tendency toward dysfunctional sociability.

The implication of these findings is that our sensitivity for, and interpretation of, environmental events do not occur in a cognitive/emotional vacuum but can be modified by genetic and biological factors. There is a paucity of knowledge about the relative contribution of genetic and environmental influences on biological risk factors for the development of specific personality traits. This issue needs urgent study in the future.

21.1.1.3 Personality and Action Systems

People's personality manifests in, and can only be inferred from, their predominant affectively charged mental and behavioral actions. Hence, their personality is theoretically perhaps best analyzed in terms of the (constellation of) psychobiological systems that essentially mediate their actions. Many human mental and behavioral actions constitute manifestations of innate, but experience-dependent and in many cases maturation-dependent action systems that are founded in primitive subcortical neural systems that we share with many other creatures, and that in us have become linked with higher cortical functions (Damasio et al., 2000; Lang, 1995; Lang, Davis, & Ohman, 2000; Panksepp, 1998, 2003). Defense, attachment of offspring to parents, parental attachment to and care for offspring, procreation, sociability, energy management, exploration, and play constitute the major action systems (Panksepp, 1998), and each of these may encompass a range of subsystems (e.g., Fanselow & Lester, 1988). Panksepp argued that basic emotional processes arise from distinct psychobiological systems that reflect coherent integrative processes of the nervous system (cf. Ciompi, 1991). In his view, the essence of emotionality is organized on subcortical and precognitive levels, and each of the action systems involves specific patterns of activation of neural networks and associated neurochemical activity in the brain. Lang (1995) suggests that emotions are driven by two major evolutionary derived action systems (i.e., appetitive and aversive subcortical circuits that mediate reactions to primary reinforcers). Carver, Sutton, and Scheier (2000) similarly propose that personality involves approach of rewarding social and material resources, and escape from and avoidance of threat.

Our position concurs with the view of Panksepp and colleagues (Davis et al., 2003, p. 58) that "optimal personality evaluation should be based on empirically based viewpoints that attempt to carve personality along the lines of emerging brain systems that help generate the relevant psychological attributes." In an original study, Davis et al. (2003) hypothesized that a great deal of variability of personality relates to strengths and weaknesses found in six major action systems. Three of these involve appetitive, approach action systems: Play (playing games with physical contact, making jokes, laughing, expressing joy and happiness), Seek (feeling curious, feeling like exploring, seeking solutions for problems and puzzles, positively anticipating new experiences), and Care (nurturing, being drawn to young children and pets, feeling softhearted toward people and animals in need, feeling empathy, liking to care for the sick, feeling affection for and liking to care for others, liking to be needed by others). Three other action systems pertain to aversion-related, avoidance/escape action tendencies: Fear (feeling anxious or tense, worrying, struggling with decisions, ruminating about past decisions and statements, losing sleep, not typically being courageous), Anger (feeling hotheaded, being easily irritated and frustrated leading to anger, expressing anger verbally or physically, and remaining angry for long periods), and Sadness (feeling lonely, crying frequently, thinking about loved ones and past relationships, and feeling distress when not with loved ones). Sadness thus denotes frustrated attachment needs.

Davis et al. added a seventh category that they described as Spirituality, because of their interest in the highest human emotions. We are not aware of psychobiological evidence for Spirituality (feeling "connected" to humanity and creation as a whole, feeling a sense of "oneness" with creation, striving for inner peace and harmony, searching for meaning in life) as an action system. The essential qualities of religious experience include a direct sensory awareness of a higher power, but also a feeling of having touched the ultimate ground of reality and the sense of the incommunicability of the experience of unity. As all human experience is brain-based the same should be true for these experiences. Available evidence indicates that the dorsolateral prefrontal, dorsomedial frontal, and medial parietal cortices play a role in religious experiences (Azari et al., 2001). Others have suggested that the limbic system including the temporal lobe constitutes the neural substrate for religious experience (for review see Saver & Rabin, 1997).

Davis et al. found strong relationships between scales measuring approach and avoidance/escape action systems and the Big Five. The most robust correlations were Extraversion with Play, Agreeableness with Care and inversely with Anger, Openness to Experience with Seek, and Emotional Stability inversely with the three aversive emotions. Conscientiousness was more weakly associated with these emotions. Spirituality only correlated (positively) with Caring and Seeking scales. They concluded that each of the six action systems is closely related to at least one of the Big Five personality factors, and that each of the action systems may form a substantial part of the adult five-factor personality structure.

The avoidance/escape action systems (Fear, Sadness, and Anger) were moderately to strongly correlated, and loaded on one factor "low emotional stability." In regard of these findings, Davis et al. suggested that "negative affect" may emerge as a superordinate personality factor. We speculate that this factor could represent a complex defense system grounded in primitive subcortical brain structures, which we share with many other species. It would include hypervigilance, startle, flight, freeze, total submission (Fear), fight (Anger), and attachment cry (Sadness).

Davis et al. do not claim that the action systems they studied provide a comprehensive representation of human personality. They rather argue that these ancient psychobiological action systems involve defensible core elements of emotional experience and may serve as a foundation for many "higher" mental attributes and faculties. They also point out that there may be other action systems in the human brain and in some other mammals, such as those for dominance, guilt, greed, disgust, and shame. Davis et al. feel that current neurobiological evidence is insufficient for inclusion of these potential factors, and consider that many of those feelings are derived largely through social learning.

However, it is questionable that the emotion of disgust is solely acquired through social learning. The most direct experience of disgust is related to taste aversion, which immediately leads to a characteristic facial expression and sometimes a vomiting response. The second type relates to our animal origin and is disgust of bodily products such as saliva and excretions. Finally, disgust may play a role in moral and legal judgments (Nussbaum, 2004). The emotion of disgust (literal meaning of disgust is: bad taste) is based on the role that objects or events can be potential sources of contamination and transmission of disease (Rozin, Lowey, & Ebert, 1994). Fear and disgust may serve different evolutionary purposes: fear as part of the appraisal of danger (LeDoux, 1995), and disgust to deal with the risk of contamination and disease (Rozin et al., 1994). Moreover, the importance of basic emotions such as disgust in psychiatry prompted some authors to speak of disgust as the "forgotten emotion" (Phillips, Senior, Fahy, & David, 1998).

Using fMRI and electrophysiological techniques, several studies showed that facial expressions of fear activated the amygdala, whereas expressed disgust specifically activated the anterior insula, together with the medial frontal cortex, thalamus, and putamen (Phillips et al., 1997; Schienle et al., 2002; Krolak-Salmon et al., 2003, Wicker et al., 2003). Another study showed that facial expressions of disgust activated the anterior insula (and caudate and putamen), whereas vocal expression of disgust did not (Phillips et al., 1998). This latter finding differs from studies of other groups who found that the neural system for the recognition of disgust can recognize signals of disgust from different sensory modalities (Lavenu, Pasquier, Lebert, Petit, & Van der Linden, 1999). Finally, it appears that it is indeed the same sectors of the insula responding to the recognition of disgust in others and in the participants' own experience of disgust (Wicker et al., 2003), supporting the idea that our brain transforms the sight of someone else's facial expression of disgust into our own experience of disgust (Gallese, Keysers, & Rizolatti, 2004). It is conceivable, but at present unknown, that DID patients who have been sexually abused during childhood show greater signs of disgust and insula activation compared to DID patients who suffered from physical abuse. We will present evidence later in this chapter that DID patients tend to experience disgust when they listen to a personal trauma script as EP, but not as ANP, and that this emotion is associated with potent insula and caudate activation. The scripts pertained to a range of traumatic experiences, including sexual and physical abuse.

Davis et al. did not include other ancient action systems in their study, notably Reproduction/Lust, Energy Management, and Safety Seeking. We speculate that greed for food and other resources could relate to extremes of energy management and safety seeking (e.g., collecting too much food, overeating; collecting/buying/possessing too many objects [e.g., for shelter, i.e., a house too big]). Sexual predation could involve a mixture of action tendencies of dominance and sexual lust, and oftentimes anger. It seems worthwhile to include these tendencies in future research of personality.

In sum, personality crucially involves two major groups of evolutionary derived but maturation-dependent action systems (i.e., those for approach of rewarding social and material resources, and those for escape/avoidance of perceived threat). More specifically, there is an approach regarding positive social and environmental rewards (Play, Seek, Care), and a fear-related approach of safety cues (Care in the form of seeking reunion with a caretaker when feeling threatened). And there is active physical withdrawal from real or perceived threat or resistance (Anger/Fight), as well as physically passive defense in the form of total submission, which is characterized by mental escape and avoidance.

21.1.2 Dissociative Parts and Action Systems

The theory of structural dissociation holds that ANP and EP are essentially mediated by (constellations of) these two basic groups of action systems. Action systems closely meet the five criteria of dissociative parts of the personality previously described. They are organizational, evolutionary derived, functional, flexible within limits, and inborn but epigenetic. Action systems are functional in that they activate various types of affective feelings, which help identify events in the world that are either biologically useful or harmful, and generate adaptive responses to many life-challenging circumstances. Although the resulting behavior is unconditionally summoned by the appropriate cues, approach and avoidance are adaptable to prevailing environmental conditions within limits, rather than being mere inflexible responses. For example, flight involves not just running away from threat, but running that is adapted to the current situation in form, direction, and duration. Thus, threat as an unconditional stimulus does not evoke a single unconditional response, but an integrated series of psychobiological responses that can be adapted to prevailing external and internal conditions within limits.

Action systems are epigenetic, that is, the result of influences by nature and nurture. Experiences, especially early ones, can change the fine details of the brain forever. These experiences include learning associations between events. Action systems are susceptible to classical conditioning: for instance, learning that some previously neutral events predict or refer to unconditioned stimuli. These conditioned stimuli tend to reactivate a memory of the unconditioned stimuli, and this association generates action tendencies described as conditioned responses. The conditioned response that an individual develops when perceiving a conditioned stimulus may but need not be identical or even similar to the original unconditioned response to the unconditioned stimulus. For example, the original, unconditioned response may have been flight, whereas the conditioned response may be freeze. However, the emitted response still belongs to a particular category of action systems, in the example, defense. Classical conditioning allows in many cases for some flexibility of response, which allows for adaptation to changeable internal and external conditions.

Subsystems of defense are of particular interest in trauma-related dissociation because of exposure to threat. Each defensive subsystem controls a pattern of psychobiological reactions that is adapted to meet a particular degree of threat imminence (Fanselow & Lester, 1988). This degree of imminence can be expressed in terms of the time and space that separate the subject from the threat (i.e., the distance between predator and prey), as well as in terms of an evaluation of the defensive abilities of the subject (e.g., the subject's psychosocial influence and physical force). *Pre-encounter defense* involves an apprehensive state with increased arousal, potentiated startle response, interruption of "normal life" behaviors, and nearly exclusive attentional focus on the potential threat. *Post-encounter defense* includes several subsystems: flight, freeze with associated analgesia, and fight. *Post-strike defense* involves total submission and bodily as well as emotional anesthesia. Upon survival, a recuperative subsystem is activated that allows for a return of affective awareness and body sensations (e.g., pain, fatigue), and that drives wound care and rest through social isolation, as well as sleep. Upon recovery, there will be a reactivation of (sub)systems that control daily life interests such as consumption of food, reproduction, and taking care of offspring.

21.1.2.1 EP is Primarily Fixated on Survival under Threat

According to the theory of structural dissociation, EPs are primarily, not exclusively, manifestations of the action system that mediates defense in the face of threat—particularly threat to the integrity of the body by a person—and potentially also of the action system that controls separation panic in relation to caretakers. Both systems serve survival interests and strongly influence the mental and physical experiences and actions of the EP. While EPs essentially rely on evolutionary derived action systems, their manifest form will be shaped by environmental conditions, especially traumatic experiences that evoke threat, in particular those that occurred in early childhood, and subsequent external and internal conditions. These conditions include the degree and quality of social support in the aftermath of trauma, repetition of traumatization, and the degree of structural dissociation between EP and ANP.

21.1.2.2 ANP Primarily Involves Action Systems That Manage Daily Life

Clinical observations suggest that action systems of the ANP primarily function to direct performance of daily tasks necessary to living (work, social interaction, energy control), and some of the tasks related to survival of the species (caretaking of children). ANPs approach attractive stimuli and mentally avoid EPs and their aversive mental contents. ANPs' escapism from reminders of traumatic experiences can perhaps involve an extreme of the normative and adaptive tendency of action systems to inhibit each other (e.g., we do not tend to eat, sleep, fight, or totally submit simultaneously). Some ANPs may execute daily life action systems with passion, while others do so in more or less depersonalized and automatic ways (e.g., caretaking). This depersonalization probably relates to ANPs' avoidance of emotional and bodily feelings that have become conditioned stimuli for reexperiencing traumatic memories, a hypothesis that will be explored in more detail later. We note in passing that detached, depersonalized functioning in caretaking and attachment may interfere with synchronizations of physiological processes between adult and child that assist the child in regulating states (Field, 1985), potentially leading to structural dissociation in the offspring of dissociative parents (Schore, 2003).

21.1.2.3 A Dimension of Trauma-Related Structural Dissociation

In cases of primary structural dissociation, which would characterize simple PTSD, and simple cases of somatoform dissociative disorders (i.e., the ICD-10 dissociative disorders of sensation and movement, described in DSM-IV as conversion disorder), a single EP can include all defensive subsystems. Secondary structural dissociation is a manifestation of a range of defensive subsystems that have not, or not sufficiently, been integrated among each other. Thus the EP may become divided into several EPs that serve different defensive functions. In secondary structural dissociation, some EPs typically display freezing and are analgesic, others are inclined to physically resist threat and experience anger, or totally submit to threat while being severely anesthetic. This threat often consists of reexperiencing (traumatic) memories of severe and chronic childhood abuse and neglect, or in responding to cues that are salient reminders of these events. Insecure attachment to caretakers can also become associated with one or more EPs in secondary structural dissociation. This level of integrative failure is mediated by traumatization that is more severe than that associated with simple PTSD. Secondary dissociation is characteristic of complex acute stress disorder, complex PTSD, complex cases of somatoform dissociative disorders, many cases of dissociative disorder not otherwise specified (APA, 1994), and perhaps borderline personality disorder (APA, 1994) as well.

Many authors refer to states of hypoarousal, as in submission, as dissociative, but exclude sympathetic hyperarousal states from this category (Perry, Pollard, Blakely, Baker, & Vigilante, 1995; Schore, 2003). However, defining dissociation as a lack of integration among dissociative parts mediated by action systems that may include single or clusters of states implies that hyperarousal states can also be dissociative. But these, as well as states involving analgesia and motor inhibition (freezing), bodily and emotional anesthesia, detachment from environmental cues, and submission (total submission, regulated by the parasympathetic nervous system; Porges, 2001, 2003; Schore, 2003) may all be manifestations of unintegrated subsystems of defense.

In addition to secondary structural dissociation (division of the defensive system, thus of the EP), division of the ANP may also occur. Thus, this *tertiary structural dissociation* (Nijenhuis et al., 2004b; Steele, Van der Hart, & Nijenhuis, 2005; Van der Hart, Nijenhuis, Steele, & Brown, 2004; Van der Hart, Nijenhuis, & Steele, 2006), characteristic only of DID, involves a division among two or more action systems that serve functions in daily life and in survival of the species. For example, one ANP regarded herself as the mother of her children, and another ANP engaged in a job. Remaining as the mother, the patient did not appreciate or understand the interests that she had as a worker, and vice versa. Tertiary structural dissociation does not occur during traumatization, but rather emerges when certain inescapable aspects of daily life become associated with past traumatization, such that systems of daily life become dissociated. Apart from extreme generalization of stimuli that reactivate traumatic memories, tertiary dissociation can also result from traumatization that started before the individual had been able to create a cohesive personality. Early and chronic traumatization may lead to some unclear mix of ANP/EP, where neither can be clearly distinguished. Such complexes are clinically observed in more dysfunctional DID patients.

21.1.2.4 Structural Dissociation and Disorganized Attachment

When traumatization by caretakers begins early in the life of the child, a particular style of attachment often develops in the child, termed *disorganized/disoriented* (Liotti, 1999; Main & Morgan, 1996). In normal, middle-class families, about 15% of the infants develop this attachment style, but in cases of maltreatment its prevalence may be up to three times higher (Van IJzendoorn, Schuengel, & Bakermans-Kranenburg, 1999). Thus frightened or frightening parental behavior predicted infant disorganized attachment (Schuengel, Bakermans-Kranenburg, & Van IJzendoorn, 1999). Prospective longitudinal research has demonstrated that disorganized and avoidant attachment in early childhood, along with age of onset, chronicity, and severity of abuse, predicted dissociation in various developmental stages, up to late adolescence (Ogawa, Sroufe, Weinfield, Carlson, & Egeland, 1997). Both ANP and EP may be insecurely attached to original abusive caretakers or to (positive or negative) substitute caretakers.

Disorganized attachment may neither be disorganized nor disoriented. Instead, it involves concurrent or rapid successive activation of the attachment system and the defense system when primary attachment figures are both the source of protection from threat and the threat itself for the traumatized child. Separation from attachment figures activates the innate attachment system, which evokes mental and behavioral approach to the caregiver. However, approach yields an increasing degree of imminence of threat, and therefore evokes a succession of defensive subsystems (flight, freeze, fight, submission). This approach and avoidance conflict cannot be resolved by the child and promotes a structural dissociation of the attachment and the defensive system.

21.2 SIMILARITIES BETWEEN THE HUMAN AND ANIMAL DEFENSIVE SYSTEM

At a general level, Nijenhuis, Vanderlinden, and Spinhoven (1998c) drew a parallel between animal defensive/recuperative systems and characteristic somatoform dissociative responses of trauma-reporting patients with dissociative disorders. Their review suggested that there are similarities between animal and human disturbances of normal eating patterns and other normal behavioral patterns in the face of diffuse threat; freezing and stilling when serious threat materializes; analgesia and anesthesia when strike is about to occur; and acute pain when threat has subsided and recuperation is at stake.

Nijenhuis, Spinhoven, Vanderlinden, Van Dyck, and Van der Hart (1998a) performed a first empirical test of the hypothesized similarity between animal defensive reactions and certain somatoform dissociative symptoms of dissociative disorder patients who reported traumatization. All 12 somatoform dissociative symptom clusters tested were found to discriminate between patients with dissociative disorders and patients with other psychiatric diagnoses. Those clusters expressive of the hypothesized similarity between animal and human models—freezing, anesthesia-analgesia, and disturbed eating—belonged to the five most characteristic symptom clusters of dissociative disorder patients. Anesthesia-analgesia, urogenital pain and freezing symptom clusters independently predicted the presence of dissociative disorder. Using an independent sample, it appeared that anesthesia-analgesia best predicted the presence of dissociative disorder after controlling for symptom severity. The indicated symptom clusters correctly classified 94% of cases that constituted the original sample, and 96% of an independent second sample. These results were largely consistent with the hypothesized similarity to animal defense systems.

Among Dutch and Flemish dissociative disorders patients, the severity of somatoform dissociation—as measured by the Somatoform Dissociation Questionnaire (SDQ-20; Nijenhuis, Spinhoven, Van Dyck, Van der Hart, & Vanderlinden, 1996; Nijenhuis et al., 1999)—was best predicted by threat to the integrity of the body in the form of childhood physical abuse and childhood sexual trauma (Nijenhuis et al., 1998b). The particularly strong association between the SDQ-20—which includes many items that assess anesthesia, analgesia, and motor inhibitions—and physical abuse has also been found in a range of other populations: nonclinical subjects (Waller et al., 2000), gynecology patients with chronic pelvic pain (Nijenhuis et al., 2003), women reporting childhood sexual abuse (Nijenhuis et al., 2001), psychiatric outpatients (Nijenhuis, Van der Hart, Kruger, & Steele, 2004a), as well as North American (Dell, 1997) and Ugandan patients with dissociative disorders (Nijenhuis & Van Duyl, 2001). Bodily threat from a person and threat to life somatoform disorders also predicted somatoform dissociation in patients with somatoform disorders (Roelofs, Keijsers, Hoogduin, Naring, & Moene, 2002) and nonclinical subjects (Maraanen et al., 2004).

We will discuss in the following recent experimental research suggesting that (1) animal defense-like reactions particularly characterize the EP, and that (2) EPs and ANPs have different psychophysiological stress responses to threat-related stimuli, even if these stimuli are presented preconsciously. Future research will need to decipher whether various EP-subtypes have the hypothesized features of animal defensive subsystems.

21.3 PSYCHOBIOLOGICAL INTERFERENCE WITH INTEGRATION OF ANP AND EP

21.3.1 Peritraumatic Integrative Failure

Evocation of the defense system or any other psychobiological system is not dissociative in itself, rather the lack of integration between various systems and subsystems is what constitutes dissociation. Extremely high levels of arousal may interfere with the execution of normal integrative mental and behavioral actions (Ludwig, Brandsma, Wilbur, Bendtfeldt, & Jameson, 1972; Krystal, Woods, Hill, & Charney, 1991; Siegel, 1999), and integrative functions may be compromised by long-lasting neuroendocrine instability induced by severe stress in early childhood. It is likely that some action systems can be integrated more readily than others. As Panksepp (1998) argued, multiple feedbacks within and across action systems promote synthesis of components of a system (e.g., perceptions, feelings, thoughts, behaviors, sense of self) and integration across action systems. However, integration across action systems that involve quite different and sometimes conflicting functions may be far more demanding than synthesizing components of a particular action system or integrating functionally related systems. If this is correct, the integration of systems dedicated to daily life and survival of the species (ANP), and systems dedicated to survival of the individual in the face of that threat (EP) will fail more readily than integration across subsystems of these two complex systems. Structural dissociation between the ANP and the EP will thus be the basic type of integrative failure, for instance, primary structural dissociation, when overwhelming experiences occur. When stress levels rise, integration of subsystems of defense may be compromised as well, yielding secondary dissociation (i.e., division of the EP).

21.3.2 Posttraumatic Integrative Failure

Since living organisms have a natural tendency toward integration (Siegel, 1999), what maintains structural dissociation when trauma has ceased and stress-induced monoaminergic reactivity has returned to baseline? According to the theory of structural dissociation, apart from integrative deficiency that relates to enduring neuroendocrine changes induced by stress in early life, integrative failure in the aftermath of trauma also involves fear conditioning.

21.3.2.1 Traumatization and Classical Conditioning

Trauma-related classical conditioning involves association of stimuli that saliently signaled or accompanied the overwhelming event. As a result, these previously neutral cues will thereafter reactivate a representation of the traumatic experience. Thus the essence of classical conditioning is the development of an anticipatory (conditioned stimulus signals unconditioned stimulus) or referential response (conditioned stimulus refers to unconditioned stimulus). For example, the specific mood (e.g., anger) of the caretaker when abusive, as well as the stimuli that apparently tended to elicit this mood, will tend to become conditioned stimuli.

21.3.2.2 Phobias of Traumatic Memories and Dissociative Personalities

Classical trauma conditioning can also generate effects that support continued structural dissociation (Nijenhuis et al., 2002, 2004b). First of all, structural dissociation is less than perfect. When the EP's traumatic memories are reactivated by potent external (e.g., certain smells, sounds, sights) or internal (e.g., feelings or body sensations) conditioned stimuli, they can intrude into the experiential domain of the ANP. Since traumatic memories represent the traumatic experience, they are formally conditioned stimuli. But the sensorimotor and highly affectively charged properties of these unintegrated experiences are inherently aversive for the ANP and *will therefore act as unconditioned stimuli*. Indeed, when traumatized patients reexperience their terror, it is as if the traumatizing event happens "here and now." When the integrative capacity of the ANP does not suffice for integration of the intruding traumatic memory, the ANP will respond to intrusions (unconditioned stimuli) with typical behavioral and mental defensive action tendencies (unconditioned reactions). The ANP cannot escape from the highly stressful intrusions by behavioral means, but mental escape can be effective, as applies to factual (inescapable) traumatizing events. Thus, typical mental (re)actions of the ANP include retracting the field of consciousness, lowering the level of consciousness (with pseudo-epileptic loss of consciousness as an extreme) manifesting as detachment (cf. the introduction to this chapter), and (re)dissociating the EP and the traumatic memories. At the same time, the ANP learns to fear and avoid internal and external conditioned stimuli that signal or refer to the EP. As time progresses and the dissociative condition continues, there is an ever widening range of conditioned stimuli that the ANP will physically and mentally avoid due to stimulus generalization.

21.3.2.3 Evaluative Conditioning

In addition to classical fear conditioning, evaluative conditioning (Baeyens, Hermans, & Eelen, 1993) of external and internal stimuli may occur. This type of associative learning produces robust effects and involves the presentation of two stimuli conjointly: a neutral stimulus and a stimulus that the individual evaluates in a negative (or positive) manner. As a result of this simple procedure, the previously neutral stimulus adopts a similar negative (or positive) tone. The ANP and EP evaluate traumatic memories differently, and clinical observations strongly suggest that evaluative conditioning applies to trauma-related structural dissociation. For example, when the traumatic experience pertained to a shameful event, the ANP may learn to be ashamed of the EP, and to despise it, and the EP may learn to despise itself.

In cases of secondary and tertiary dissociation, EPs and ANPs may learn to fear, reject, and avoid each other along similar pathways of evaluative and classical conditioning. In tertiary structural dissociation, avoidance of different ANPs may be based on similar trauma-related issues and conflicts. In summary, many dissociative personalities become phobic of each other. These conditioned effects interfere with normal integrative action tendencies. Hence, structural dissociation involves a strong tendency toward chronicity when the survivor's integrative capacity is low.

In some individuals, alternations between the ANP and EP manifest from the acute phase onward, but other individuals function apparently well for extended periods of time before displaying posttraumatic stress symptoms. However, upon close scrutiny it often appears that the latency period was marked by avoidance of the traumatic memories and associated internal and external cues, yielding a condition of chronic depersonalization. In cases of trauma-related dissociative amnesia as a disorder (APA, 1994), access to the memory of the trauma and to other parts of one's previous nontraumatic life seem to be inhibited (Markowitsch, 1999; Markowitsch et al., 2000; Van der Hart & Brom, 2000; Van der Hart, Nijenhuis, & Brown, 2001; Van der Hart, Brown, & Graafland, 1999).

21.3.2.4 Relational Factors that Maintain Structural Dissociation

When significant others deny trauma instead of assisting in the integration of the painful experience, or prohibit talking about it, dissociative tendencies are enhanced. These adverse social influences prevail in intrafamilial childhood sexual abuse (Freyd, 1996), and seem to promote dissociative amnesia (Vanderlinden, Van Dyck, Vandereycken, & Vertommen, 1993). PTSD has been associated with lack of support in the aftermath of traumatizing events (King, King, Fairbank, Keane, & Adams, 1998), and in another study, patients with complex dissociative disorders reported total absence of support and consolation when abused (Nijenhuis et al., 1998b). As the structural dissociation theory predicts, social support can buffer negative effects of exposure to (potentially) traumatizing events (Elklit, 1997; Runtz & Schallow, 1997). It might be that social support provides safety cues, assists the individual in modulating the affective state and biological stress levels, and thus promotes the integration of the EP and ANP.

21.4 DIFFERENT SURVIVORS, DIFFERENT PSYCHOBIOLOGICAL REACTIONS TO THREAT

Most traumatic stress researchers assume that different survivors have in principle similar (abnormal) reactions to natural and experimental cues and that their functioning is relatively stable over time. These assumptions are convenient because they allow for straightforward group comparisons between survivor and controls. However, these points of departure are at odds with 150 years of clinical observations and associated theoretical analyses suggesting that the psychobiological condition of traumatized people can be different for different individuals, and are inherently changeable per individual. The theory of structural dissociation holds that this changeability is systematic. That is, the psychobiological functioning of survivors would alternate with the part(s) of the personality that is (are) activated at the time of measurement. The functioning of each of these parts would also alternate to an extent or change with temporary or chronic changes of available mental energy and integrative capacity. For example, ANPs would generally have more integrative capacity than EPs. Some survivors may predominantly display ANPs during measurement, others EPs, and still others may alternate among these different parts, or have parallel activation of different parts.

An increasing number of studies indeed suggest that different survivors can display different, sometimes even opposite, psychobiological features. Such differences also appear in animals (Cohen, Zohar, & Matar, 2003; Cools & Ellenbroek, 2002). They include contrasting cortisol levels and autonomic nervous system reactions, as well as different patterns of cerebral blood flow.

21.5 AROUSAL, POLYVAGAL THEORY, AND STRUCTURAL DISSOCIATION

Most psychobiological trauma research is based on the assumption that "arousal," hence traumatic stress, is regulated by the sympathetic branch of the autonomic nervous system. This view, originally proposed by Cannon (1927, 1932), predicts that stress reactions involve fight and flight behaviors and concomitant increases in HR, blood pressure, sweat gland activity, and circulating catecholamines. However, researchers of the animal defensive responses (e.g., Fanselow & Lester, 1988) and several authors on trauma-related dissociation have observed that defense is not limited to increases of "arousal" and active defensive motor actions but also involves passivity and losses (e.g., immobilization, bodily and emotional anesthesia, and physiological deactivation). As Porges (2003) notes, the rather exclusive focus on the sympathetic nervous system neglects the role of the parasympathetic branch of the nervous system in survival.

Porges's polyvagal theory is more differentiated and details essential neural structures and neurobehavioral systems we share with, or have adapted from, our phylogenetic ancestry (Porges, 2001, 2003). His theory proposes three response systems that relate to different branches of the autonomic nervous system (i.e., the ventral and dorsal vagal branches of the parasympathetic nervous system and the sympathetic-catecholaminergic branch). These systems are related to their own adaptive strategies. In this paradigm, state can be changed in a predictable manner and specific state changes are associated with potentiating or limiting the range of specific behaviors.

The functions of the phylogenetically most recent system is social communication, self-soothing and calming (i.e., a major component of self-regulation and affect-regulation) and inhibition of sympathetic-catecholaminergic influences. This mammalian signaling system for motion, emotion, and communication involves cranial nerve regulation of the striated facial muscles coordinated with a myelinated vagus that inhibits sympathetic activity at the level of the heart. Porges has described this ventral vagal control as the vagal brake. This brake regulates the heart and allows the individual to stay calm in safe environments. The lower motor neurons of this social engagement system are situated in the nucleus ambiguous. This system involves pathways that originate in the frontal cortex. Hence, there is cortical control of these medullary motor neurons.

The second, phylogenetically older system serves active defense from threat, and is dependent on the sympathetic nervous system. This adaptive system innervates the heart to provide the energy required to focus on threat cues, to run, or to fight. The lower neurons are found in the spinal cord. However, individuals can achieve mobilization in two ways. The quickest way is to release the vagal brake. This action instantly activates the heart and thus provides energy for active defense. Individuals can rapidly calm themselves by reengaging the ventral vagal system that decreases metabolic output. The sympathetic system can assist in energy mobilization under prolonged challenge.

The third and phylogenetically oldest system is the dorsal vagal system that serves major immobilization under threat. It provides inhibitory input to the sinoatrial node of the heart (i.e., the heart's pacemaker) via unmyelinated fibers and also provides low tonic influences on the bronchi. Massive bradycardia (i.e., low HR) may thus be determined by the unmyelinated dorsal vagal fibers. We hold that this system serves total submission rather than mere immobilization.

It seems that Porges does not distinguish between freezing and total submission. However, freezing is very different from dorsal vagal immobilization. Freezing marks being immobile and silent, but ready to explode into motor action. It occurs in close proximity to hypervigilance, flight, and fight, and is probably under ventral vagal and sympathetic control (Nijsen et al., 2000; Nijsen, Croiset, Diamant, De Wied, & Wiegant, 2001). However, the autonomic nervous system is differentially involved in heart rate regulation in fear-conditioned rats and in nonshocked controls (Nijsen et al., 1998). In nonshocked controls a predominant sympathetic nervous system activation results in an increase in heart rate, whereas in fear-conditioned rats the tachycardic response is attenuated by a simultaneous activation of sympathetic nervous system and parasympathetic nervous system. Freezing involves rapid, shallow breathing, high HR, increase of norepinephrine and epinephrine, and high muscle tone. Total submission is associated with low HR and blood pressure, and slow breathing. Freezing is associated with analgesia (i.e., insensitivity for painful stimulation), whereas total submission goes along with bodily and emotional anesthesia (Nijenhuis et al., 1998a). While freezing consumes much energy, total submission involves conservation of energy.

Porges proposes a hierarchical response strategy to environmental challenges with the most recently developed system employed first and the most primitive last. This idea is consistent with Jackson's dissolution theory (Jackson, 1958), and with Janet's ideas on vehement emotions (Janet, 1928). Jackson proposes that "[t]he higher nervous arrangements inhibit (or control) the lower, and thus, when the higher are suddenly rendered functionless, the lower rise in activity" (Jackson, 1958, quoted in Porges, 2001, p. 132). However, Porges adds that "the neurophysiological substrate of specific behavioral states and coping strategies may incorporate activation of a sequence of response systems representing more than one phylogenetic stage" (p. 132). Thus, the response strategies may include transitional blends between the boundaries of the different stages. These may be determined by visceral feedback and higher brain structures, including the HPA axis, and vasopressin and oxytocinergic pathways that communicate between the hypothalamus and the dorsal vagal system.

Porges (2001) maintains that these three systems are not per se activated as a result of dissolution. They would involve adaptive biobehavioral response strategies to different environmental challenges. When the tone of the ventral vagal complex is high, individuals are able to communicate via facial expressions, vocalizations, and gestures (i.e., via verbal and nonverbal motor actions). When the tone of this system is low, the sympathetic-catecholaminergic system is unopposed and easily expressed to support defensive mobilization or freezing. Finally, when the tone of the dorsal vagal complex is high, there is immobilization in the sense of total submission.

We agree that these systems involve adaptation but also suggest that integration of the three systems is required for adaptive behavior beyond threat exposure (i.e., for adaptation when threat has passed). Thus we hypothesize that structural dissociation involves a lack of integration of the three systems and their blends (see Table 21.1). ANP would be predominantly mediated by the ventral vagal complex, as well as EPs that can engage in attachment behaviors, play, and some exploration when they feel safe. However, ANPs also encompass the sympathetic system to a degree in that they engage in defensive actions when they feel threatened, for example, by threatening internal experiences that relate to EPs such as intrusions of traumatic memories that EP retrieves. EPs' active defensive actions would be predominantly mediated by the sympathetic-catecholamine system and their passive defensive actions by the dorsal vagal complex. Primary structural dissociation involves lack of integration of the ventral vagal complex and the two older phylogenetic systems, secondary structural dissociation lack of integration of the sympathetic-catecholamine system and the dorsal vagal complex, or even lack of integration within the sympathetic-catecholamine system. Tertiary structural dissociation additionally involves lack of integration among different subsystems of the ventral vagal complex. Vehement emotions denote the individual's failure to engage in efficacious, goal-directed mental and motor actions within or across any of these three psychophysiological complexes. To the extent that these emotions dominate, the individual does not manage to use energy supplies, such as mental and physical energy, for adaptive, creative actions within any psychophysiological system.

Porges (2001) argues that mobilization is associated with increases in cortisol, whereas immobilization (i.e., total submission) involves reduced cortisol secretion because the dorsal vagal complex has an inhibitory influence on the HPA axis. Furthermore, oxytocin is associated with vagal processes, and vasopressin with sympathetic processes. Vasopressin stimulates the HPA axis during chronic stress (Aguilera & Rabadan-Diehl, 2000) and is involved in active behavioral strategies aimed at coping with threat (Ebner, Wotjak, Holsboer, Landgraf, & Engelmann, 1999). Release of oxytocin would be associated with perceiving the environment as safe (e.g., with recognition of familiar individuals, and attachment), hence would promote the ventral vagal system. Release of vasopressin may be a component of a response profile related to the perception that the environment is unsafe, and that active behavioral defense is required. Interactions among cortisol, oxytocin, vasopressin, and norepinephrine occur (Haller, Albert, & Makara, 1997).

In this context, it can be hypothesized that ANPs and EPs have different psychobiological, including neuroendocrine and psychophysiological profiles. EPs would theoretically have different neuroendocrine profiles compared to ANPs and healthy controls, and some types of EPs would have different neuroendocrine profiles than other EPs. For example, notably when they perceive threat, EPs that typically engage in freeze, flight, or fight would have increased cortisol and catecholamine levels, and totally submissive EPs decreased cortisol (cf. Porges, 2001). ANPs that feel safe would have higher levels of oxytocin, as would EPs that are essentially mediated by attachment (cf. Uvnas-Moberg, 1997), whereas most EPs would have higher levels of vasopressin (Teicher, Andersen, Polcari, Anderson, & Navalta, 2002; cf. Porges, 2001). ANPs would likely have low basal levels of norepinephrine, as

TABLE 21.1
Dissociative Parts and the Polyvagal Theory: Some Hypotheses

Ventral vagal parasympathetic system	Social communication, exploration of the environment attachment, play	ANP; EPs when feeling safe
Sympathetic-catecholaminergic system	Behavioral defensive actions (e.g., taking care in traffic)	ANP
Sympathetic-catecholaminergic system	Hypervigilance, freeze, flight, fight	EPs when threatened
Dorsal vagal parasympathetic system	Total submission	EPs when threatened

is suggested by low basal norepinephrine in depersonalization disorder (Simeon, Guralnik, Knutelska, Yehuda, & Schmeidler, 2003).

The theory suggests that EPs that engage in active defense when they feel threatened have increased HR, blood pressure, and decreased skin conductance response compared to ANPs. It also maintains that totally submissive EPs have decreased HR and blood pressure when exposed to (perceived) threat. Furthermore, "sympathetically mediated" EPs, "parasympathetically mediated" EPs, and ANPs would all have different patterns of cerebral metabolism. For example, EPs would have more activity in amygdala, insula, and somatosensory cortex. These brain structures are known to be involved in emotional reactions to perceived threat. ANPs would have more activity in the anterior cingulate and the medial prefrontal cortex (mPFC) when exposed to major reminders of traumatizing events (i.e., brain structures that exert inhibitory influences on the "emotional brain"). ANPs would also have more activity in parietal multimodal sensory association areas in this situation. However, all dissociative parts would have less frontal activity compared to mentally healthy controls because dissociative patients involve lower integrative capacity than mentally healthy individuals. The theory proposes that ANPs will tend to become depersonalized and feel detached when exposed to reminders of traumatizing events, and depersonalization is associated with surplus metabolism in the parietal multisensory association areas. This detachment/depersonalization could relate to conscious as well as preconscious mental actions—conscious and subconscious inhibition of emotional reactions, including perception of trauma-related internal (e.g., sensations) and external stimuli. As clinical observations suggest, many ANPs display efforts to evade reminders of traumatizing events and other trauma-related stimuli. Their mental escapism prominently include the narrowing of attention of these parts to concerns of daily life, which might include, we speculate, conscious or unconscious effort to keep the ventral vagal system online. We will now explore some recent findings in the light of these hypotheses.

21.6 DIFFERENT REACTION PATTERNS IN DIFFERENT SURVIVORS

21.6.1 Different Neuroendocrinological Features in Different Survivors: Cortisol

Some scientists maintain that survivors have elevated cortisol levels compared to controls, and others hold that survivors have depressed cortisol. Very few of them have hypothesized that different survivors can have different cortisol levels. However, this possibility is suggested by early and more recent neuroendocrine studies. Price, Thaler, and Mason (1957) found that most patients anticipating high-risk elective cardiac surgery had relatively low preoperative cortisol levels. These patients were those who used disengagement coping strategies such as emotional avoidance, denial, and withdrawal in the face of the impending surgery. Parents of fatally ill children with low cortisol levels also used disengagement as a coping style (Friedman, Mason, & Hamburg, 1963; Wolff, Friedman, Hofer, & Mason, 1964). In 1967, Bourne, Rose and Mason, documented that special forces soldiers

> who used disengagement coping had lower cortisol levels on the day they expected a massive overrunning by the Vietcong than on the days before and after the expected attack, whereas men who were forced to remain engaged with the life-threatening situation because of the nature of their duties (the officer and the radio operator) showed increased cortisol levels. (Mason et al., 2001, p. 388)

Vietnam veterans with PTSD who felt guilt over their military actions in Vietnam (i.e., who were emotionally engaged in their trauma history at the time of measurement) had elevated cortisol, whereas veterans with PTSD who were emotionally numb, avoidant, and generally disengaged had low cortisol levels (Mason et al., 2001).

Mason et al. suggested that emotional engagement and disengagement may represent primary (i.e., immediate) and secondary (i.e., subsequent avoidant) emotional responses to traumatizing events. In our terms, the immediate reactions could denote EP engaging in flight, freeze, or fight, and the avoidant reactions ANP or EPs under dorsal vagal control. We are not aware of direct studies of cortisol levels in ANPs and EPs.

Recent studies have shown that genetic factors influence HPA axis functioning. There is accumulating evidence that variants of the glucocorticoid (GR) receptor affect the cell's sensitivity for glucocorticoids and thus contribute to the large intraindividual variability of HPA axis reactivity in nonclinical samples (DeRijk, Schaaf, & de Kloet, 2002). However, it is questionable whether different GR polymorphisms also contribute to the cortisol-response in PTSD and DID. There is only one study in PTSD in which it was found that subtypes of GR polymorphisms were not more frequent in PTSD compared to controls. The only positive association was a reduced cortisol baseline level in a subset of PTSD patients that was associated with the presence a GR polymorphism (Bachmann et al., 2005). Whether this relationship also holds for DID is at present not known.

21.6.2 Different Psychophysiological Features in Different Survivors

Several studies have found that survivors tend to have elevated HR and blood pressure in the acute stage of the disorder (Bryant, Harvey, Guthrie, & Moulds, 2000; Shalev et al., 1998), and when exposed to perceived threat cues such as script-driven imagery (Kinzie et al., 1998; Orr, 1997; Orr et al., 1997; Shalev, Peri, Gelpin, Orr, & Pitman, 1997) or loud tones (Orr et al., 2003). These effects could be due to sympathetic control, but also to release of the vagal brake. Some preliminary findings indeed suggest that elevated sympathetic tone in survivors in response to mild cognitive challenge can relate to a dysfunctional parasympathetic system (Sahar, Shalev, & Porges, 2001).

Kinzie et al. (1998) and Osuch et al. (2001) found that only a proportion of survivors had increased psychophysiological responses to general emotional challenge and to trauma cue exposure. These subgroups have been labeled physiologic responders and physiological nonresponders. Lack of HR increases to challenge in a substantial proportion of PTSD patients may suggest not a flight or fight, but a "giving up response" that involves inhibition (i.e., total submission). This inhibition could be related to dorsal vagal parasympathetic control in these survivors. In our terms, absent HR increases or rather HR decreases to emotional challenge mark EPs that engage in total submission, whereas absent HR changes to such challenge would be characteristic for ANPs. Flight, freeze, and fight EPs would have increased HR.

HR reflects both sympathetic and parasympathetic nervous system activity and can be measured both tonically (i.e., beats per minute at rest) or phasically (i.e., change in response to a stimulus). Accelerations in HR to a stimulus are thought to reflect sensory rejection or "tuning out" of noxious environmental events, while decelerations are thought to reflect sensory intake or an environmental openness (Lacey & Lacey, 1974). Emotionally, HR has been associated with the experience of anxiety. As such, high-tonic HR is thought to reflect fear, while low-tonic HR may reflect fearlessness.

One of the most consistent findings is the reduced resting HR in antisocial behavior in children and adolescents with externalizing behavior (Ortiz & Raine, 2004). Raine (1993) noted that of 14 relevant studies, all replicated the finding of reduced resting HR in the antisocial groups. Low HR is a robust marker independent of cultural context, with the relationship having been established in the United Kingdom (e.g., Farrington, 1997), Germany (Schmeck & Poustka, 1993), New Zealand (Moffit & Caspi, 2001), the United States (e.g., Rogeness, Cepeda, Macedo, Fisher, & Harris. 1990), Mauritius (Raine, Venables, & Mednick, 1997), and Canada (Mezzacappa et al., 1997).

Lack of HR changes to emotional challenge may relate to negative dissociative symptoms, suggesting parasympathetic dominance. Thus, adult raped women with high degrees of negative dissociative symptoms had lower HR when talking about their rape compared to survivors with low degrees of negative dissociation (Griffin, Resick, & Mechanic, 1997). In general, there was a suppression of autonomic physiological responses in the high dissociation group. Delinquent, traumatized adolescents with many negative dissociative symptoms also had lower HR compared to those with few negative dissociative symptoms (Koopman, Carion, Sudhakar, Palmer, & Steiner, 2000). This effect was more pronounced when the survivors spoke in a free association task, compared to talking about their most stressful life experience. However, higher mean HR was found among youths reporting greater frequency and intensity of adverse childhood experiences. We suggest that these differences could relate to the activation of different types of dissociative parts.

Schmahl, Elzinga, and Bremner (2002) also reported that survivors of childhood abuse can have very different subjective psychological and physiological reactions to trauma scripts. A woman with PTSD and a woman with histrionic personality disorder had elevated HR and blood pressure during the experiment. However, a woman with borderline personality disorder and a "dissociative" reaction in response to an abandonment script (i.e., negative dissociative symptoms) had an extreme decline in physiological reactivity.

21.6.3 Different Neural Activity in Different Survivors

Lanius et al. (2002) studied the neural circuitry underlying the response patterns of sexual-abuse-related PTSD patients to trauma scripts using fMRI. They found that the reactivity depended on whether the patients tended to reexperience the traumatizing event or become detached. They did not describe reexperiencing the traumatizing event as a positive dissociative response, and described detachment as a dissociative response, although this might rather involve some different kind of alteration of consciousness (see Steele, Van der Hart, Dorahy, & Nijenhuis, 2009).

Compared to controls, the PTSD patients who became detached showed more activation in the superior and middle temporal gyri (Brodmann area [BA] 38), the inferior frontal gyrus, the occipital lobe (BA 19), the mPFC (BA 10), the parietal lobe (BA 7), the medial cortex (BA

9), and the anterior cingulate gyrus (BA 24 and 32). However, the PTSD patients who reexperienced traumatizing events showed significantly less activation of the thalamus, the anterior cingulate gyrus (BA 32), and the medial frontal gyrus (BA 10/11) than did the comparison subjects. In terms of the theory of structural dissociation, reexperiencing constitutes a positive dissociative response and probably an EP engaging in active defense, whereas what Lanius et al. called a dissociative response pertains to negative dissociative symptoms, and possibly a detached ANP or EP.

Similarly, Lanius, Hopper, and Menon (2003) described a husband and wife who had developed PTSD in the context of a very serious motor vehicle accident in which they saw a child burn to death and in which they feared they too would die. Whereas both reported peritraumatic dissociative symptoms, they exhibited very different subjective, psychophysiological, and neurobiological responses to trauma-script-driven imagery that caused them to reexperience the accident. The husband successfully had managed to rescue himself and his wife by breaking the window shield while feeling extremely aroused. She could hardly move because she was frozen. When reexperiencing the accident, he was very psychologically and physically aroused, and she felt numb and frozen. Thus, they reengaged in their original response patterns. His HR increased 13 bpm from baseline, and had increased activity in his anterior frontal, anterior cingulate, superior and medial temporal, thalamic, parietal, and occipital brain regions. She had no HR change from baseline and had only increased activity in occipital regions. Lanius et al. (2002) concluded that their "fMRI results demonstrate that PTSD patients can have very different responses, both subjectively and biologically, while reexperiencing traumatic events" (p. 668).

21.7 DIFFERENT PSYCHOBIOLOGICAL REACTIONS FOR DIFFERENT DISSOCIATIVE PARTS

The studies discussed so far demonstrate that different survivors can have very different psychobiological profiles. A range of studies of DID patients suggest that different dissociative parts of the personality can have different psychobiological profiles that are not reproduced by DID-simulating controls. Differences have been reported in electrodermal activity (skin conductance; Ludwig et al., 1972; Larmore, Ludwig, & Cain, 1977), EEG—in particular in the beta 2 band (Coons, Milstein, & Marley, 1982; Hughes, Kuhlman, Fichtner, & Gruenfeld, 1990; Ludwig et al., 1972; Putnam, Buchsbaum, & Post, 1993), visual evoked potentials (Putnam et al., 1992), regional cerebral blood flow (Mathew et al., 1985; Saxe et al., 1992), autonomic nervous system variables (Putnam et al., 1993), optical variables (Birnbaum & Thomann, 1996; Miller, 1989; Miller & Triggiano, 1992; Miller, Blackburn, Scholes, White, & Mammalis, 1991), and arousal (Putnam, Zahn, & Post, 1990).

While these studies are valuable, it is difficult to say what the data actually tell beyond suggesting that these physiological data sets "are most parsimoniously explained by regarding the alter personalities [i.e., dissociative parts of the personality] as discrete states of consciousness" (Putnam, 1997, p. 138). Advances in the field critically depend on theoretical predictions with respect to the *kind* of differences that exist among different *types* of dissociative parts of the personality. As indicated, the theory of structural dissociation offers such predictions.

21.7.1 Psychophysiological Reactivity

Reinders et al. (2006) studied the psychophysiological reactions of DID patients to auditory scripts while functioning as ANP and as fearful EP. In this first and only study to date of ANP and EP dependent psychophysiological functioning, each participant listened to two scripts. One script involved a neutral personal memory that the ANPs and fearful, thus emotionally engaged EPs, experienced as a personal narrative memory, and the other script described a traumatic experience that EPs but not ANPs regarded as a personal experience. Reinders et al. hypothesized that EPs, compared to controls, would only have increased physiological activity, and subjective emotional and sensorimotor reactions to the trauma scripts.

These hypotheses were strongly supported by the results. ANPs and EPs did not have increased HR and blood pressure in response to neutral memories, compared to each other and compared to baseline. However, EPs but not ANPs had highly significant increases of HR and systolic blood pressure compared to baseline and neutral script exposure when listening to the trauma scripts. As was also hypothesized, EPs had significantly less HR variability compared to ANPs when these dissociative parts listened to the trauma scripts. EPs but not the ANPs had strong subjective emotional and sensorimotor reactions to the trauma scripts. Only EPs reported a spectrum of primary emotions, including fear, anger, and disgust, and experienced many positive and negative somatoform dissociative symptoms such as being physically touched, having visual images of the traumatic experience, smelling smells, and bodily paralysis.

To exclude that the participants in this study responded to demand characteristics of the experiment, Reinders et al. (2008) explored whether DID simulating controls would replicate the findings for DID patients (Reinders et al., 2006). They hypothesized that neither low nor high fantasy prone healthy controls who were instructed and highly motivated to simulate ANP and EP would have increased HR or blood pressure and decreased HR variability when they simulated EP and listened to audiotaped descriptions of painful memories. It is difficult for non-PTSD patients to simulate physiological responses marking traumatized patients (Gerardi, Keane, & Penk, 1989; Orr & Pitman, 1993). Moreover, previous studies demonstrated that simulating controls generally were not able to produce psychophysiological state-changes equivalent to those in DID patients (Putnam, 1997). Reinders et al. (2008) found that low and high suggestible, fantasy prone healthy individuals had similar levels of HR and blood pressure whether they simulated ANP or EP, and whether they listened to audiotapes with descriptions of neutral personal memories and of painful personal memories. These findings strongly suggest that the performance of authentic ANPs and EPs in DID cannot be explained as effects of fantasy proneness and motivated role-playing.

Nijenhuis (2004) documented HR and bodily movements in response to perceived threat cues of ANPs and EPs of patients with complex dissociative disorders. This exposure constituted a clinical exercise designed to help the patients develop assertive reactions, notably to stop ongoing abuse or threats of further traumatization. As ANPs, the patients did not have HR changes, looked composed, and reported that they had felt at ease during the exposure. As EPs that engaged in freezing or in inclinations to ward off the "threat" cue (a small, insignificant object that the therapist moved in the direction of the patient's face), the patients had sharp increases of HR. These EPs had very fearful facial expressions, were totally fixated on the moving object, and reported intense fear, inability to move (freeze), or a strong impulse to run (flight). Some tended to assume a fetal body posture. Sometimes "fight" EPs became activated during the exposure, but these parts did not dare to execute their impulses to ward off the object. Finally, as EPs that engaged in total submission, patients had decreasing HR, averted their gaze, and reported that they mentally left their body. Some report amnesia for the experience after the exposure. Figures 21.1 to 21.4 provide some examples of HR responsivity of ANPs and EPs to the test. Nijenhuis, Matthess, and Sack currently study DID patients as ANP and as "sympathetic" and "parasympathetic" EP, as well as mentally healthy controls who simulate ANP and EP, to stimuli that are likely conditioned threat stimuli for survivors of chronic interpersonal traumatization. They move objects (i.e., a piece of plastic, and picture of an angry face) in 10 steps from 100 cm to 5 cm in the direction of the participant's face, and assess a range of variables, including continuous HR and HR variability, breathing patterns, eye movements, facial and body movements, and galvanic skin conductance, as well as blood pressure, and subjective emotional and sensorimotor reactivity.

Emotional support during "threat" exposure in the form of a hand of a trusted person on the back prevents extreme increases and decreases of psychophysiological activity (Nijenhuis, 2004; see fig. 21.4). This support likely activates the ventral vagal nervous system, more specifically, the attachment action system. The ventral vagal system implies the vagal brake, and inhibits full activation of defensive system in response to potent reminders of traumatic experience (i.e., conditioned stimuli). In other words, emotional support raises the survivors' integrative capacity.

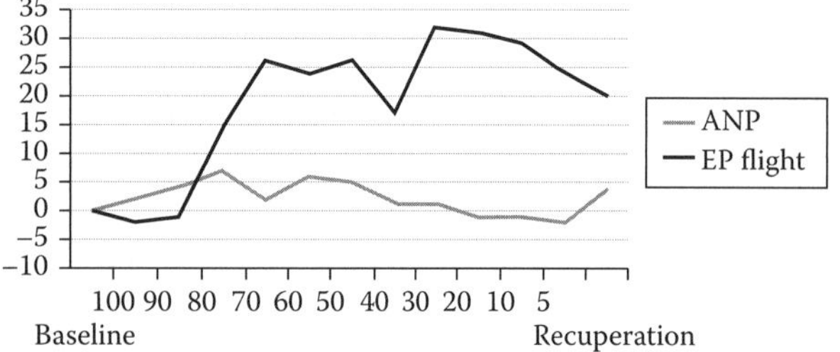

FIGURE 21.1 Heart rate changes compared to baseline for different dissociative parts in a DID patient upon exposure to approaching picture of a man with an angry facial expression.

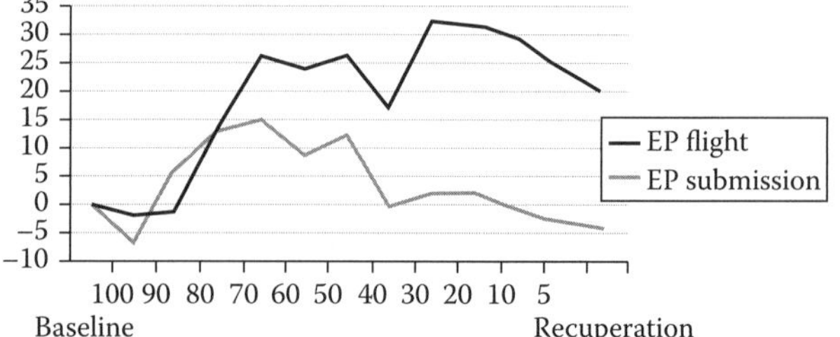

FIGURE 21.2 Heart rate changes compared to baseline for different dissociative parts in a DID patient upon exposure to approaching picture of a man with an angry facial expression.

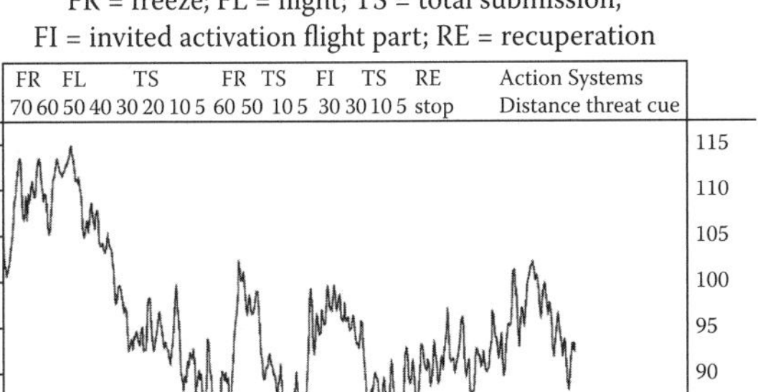

FIGURE 21.3 Heart rate frequency in a patient with Dissociative Disorder NOS-1 during exposure to approaching perceived threat cue.

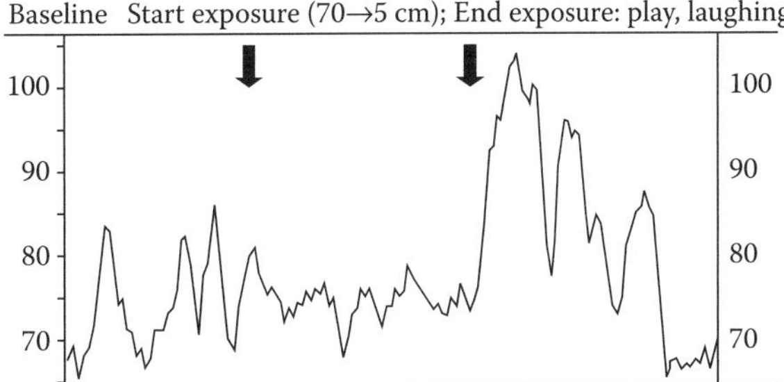

FIGURE 21.4 Heart rate frequency of DID patient involved in Figure 1 and 2 in response to a picture of a male with an angry facial expression that is moved from 70 cm to 5 cm in the direction of the patient's face in a therapy session. This time, the hand of the co-therapist whom the patient has learned to trust is on the patient's back. The activated parts are the EPs that otherwise engage in flight and freeze. The experienced support is associated with a stable HR, which effect may reflect dominance of the ventral vagal system.

21.7.2 ANP and EP Dependent Neural Activity

21.7.2.1 Supraliminal Exposure to Perceived Threat

The study in which psychophysiological reactions of ANP and EP in DID patients to neutral and trauma scripts were examined, also included assessment of rCBF patterns to these challenges using positron emission tomography (PET; Reinders et al., 2003, 2006). As hypothesized, exposure to neutral memories that the patients regarded both as ANP and EP as a personal memory did not yield any difference in regional cerebral blood flow patterns but major differences emerged between ANP's and EP's psychobiological responses to trauma scripts that only the EP regarded as a personal memory.

Compared to ANPs, EPs had more increased activity (or rCBF) in the amygdala, insular cortex, the somatosensory areas I and II in the parietal cortex, and the basal ganglia. This activity may reflect that EPs receive major somotosensory information that these parts interpreted in alarming and painful ways (amygdala and insular cortex), and that urged them to generate defensive motor plans (basal ganglia). EPs also reported disgust when listening to the trauma scripts. This disgust may relate to the observed increase of activation in the insula and caudate (see page 343). Compared to ANPs, EPs had more brain metabolism in the occipital cortex (BA 19: visual perception), the parietal cortex (BA 7/40: somatosensory integration), the anterior cingulate (BA 24 and 32: inhibition of emotional reactions), and several other frontal areas, including BA 10 (planning, self-awareness). Many of these areas were also involved in the detachment that some PTSD patients displayed in Lanius's study.

As suggested, the major activity for ANPs in BA 7, BA 40, and BA 19 may be linked with depersonalization. Depersonalization is related to several negative somatoform dissociative symptoms, for example, experiencing the body as a foreign object. Simeon et al. (2000) reported that the disorder was associated with functional abnormalities along sequential hierarchical areas, secondary and cross-modal areas of the sensory cortex (visual, auditory, and somatosensory), as well as areas responsible for an integrated body schema. More specifically, they found less blood flow in right temporal cortex (auditory association area), and more metabolism in parietal somatosensory association area and multimodal association area. Dissociation and depersonalization scores among the sample were strongly correlated with activation patterns in the posterior parietal association area (BA 7).

It thus seems that integrative failure with respect to bodily cues—which may be at the heart of basic forms of consciousness (Damasio, 1999)—is related to dysfunctioning of the temporal, parietal, and occipital association areas. Indeed, "[t]here is a hierarchy of sensory processing in the brain, from primary sensory areas to unimodal and then polymodal association areas and finally to the PFC" (Simeon et al., 2000, p. 1786). Depersonalization and negative somatoform dissociative symptoms may thus relate to dysfunction of the posterior association areas, which negatively affects the input into the prefrontal cortex. ANPs indeed report low body awareness, and feel generally more or less detached from their body.

To return to Reinders et al.'s symptom provocation study of DID, reduced activity in the PFC for EPs suggests lack of inhibition regarding emotional reactivity. Stress hormones also interfere with the activation of the mPFC. Thus, elevated levels of norepinephrine were associated with dysfunction of the PFC (Arnsten, 1999). Interestingly, the reverse is also true. Reduced activity in neural networks in the PFC has been shown to increase c-FOS (one of the immediate early genes responding to environmental stimuli) expression in the paraventricular nucleus, thus leading to increased stress-vulnerability (Gerrits et al., 2003).

Stress hormones related to interference of the mPFC presents a major problem of affect regulation in that hippocampal (McCormick & Thompson, 1982) and medial prefrontal (Armony & LeDoux, 1997) information processing are crucially involved in inhibiting the amygdala. Bremner et al. (1999) documented mPFC and anterior cingulate dysfunction in women with and without PTSD who reported childhood sexual abuse (CSA). The participants were exposed to neutral personal memories and to descriptions of personalized CSA events. CSA scripts were associated with greater increases in rCBF in portions of the PFC, posterior cingulate, and motor cortex in women with PTSD than in those women without PTSD. These scripts also induced alterations in rCBF in the mPFC (i.e., decreased blood flow in subcallosal gyrus and the anterior cingulate. Compared with women who had not developed PTSD, those with PTSD also had decreased blood flow in the right hippocampus, fusiform/inferior temporal gyrus, supramarginal gyrus, and visual association cortex.

Reinders et al. (2008) recently reported that healthy controls who were instructed and motivated to simulate an ANP and an EP were unable to generate neural network patterns that marked genuine ANPs and EPs in DID patients. This failure pertained to low fantasy-prone individuals, as well as to high fantasy-prone controls. These findings are at odds with the sociocognitive theory of DID, but corroborate the theory of trauma-related structural dissociation of the personality.

"Host" parts of the personality in patients with DID (i.e., ANPs) had less cerebral blood flow in the orbitofrontal cortex bilaterally than did healthy controls (Şar, Ünal, & Öztürk, 2007). They also had more blood flow in median and superior frontal regions and occipital regions. These findings also generally corroborate the theory of structural dissociation.

21.7.2.2 Subliminal Exposure to Perceived Threat

Preconscious information processing plays a key role in responding to unconditioned and conditioned threat cues and in fear-related learning (Davies, 2000; Dolan, 2000; LeDoux, 1996; Morris, Ohman, & Dolan, 1998). The theory of structural dissociation considers that ANPs aim to avoid this threat, and that EPs will selectively attend to these cues. Thus in an original study, Hermans, Nijenhuis, van Honk, Huntjens, and Van der Hart (2006) hypothesized that dissociative personality-dependent reactivity to (un)conditioned threat will be evident following exposure to cues that are presented very briefly in order to preclude conscious perception. More specifically, the effects of exposing the ANP and EP in DID patients to masked neutral, fearful, and angry facial expressions were tested.

Whereas ANPs named the color of the mask that immediately followed the experimental stimuli more quickly when this stimulus involved angry facial expressions compared to exposure to neutral facial expressions, EPs did not show differential responses to these cues. DID-simulating controls showed the reverse pattern: a tendency toward longer response latencies after exposure to angry faces when enacting ANPs, and a tendency toward shorter reaction times after exposure to angry faces when enacting EPs. The interaction "group (genuine DID vs. DID-simulators) x condition (angry vs. neutral faces)" was statistically significant. Because this effect was absent when comparing fearful and neutral faces, it was specific for cues that signal an increased possibility of attack.

The results are consistent with the hypothesis that ANPs avoid subliminal threat cues by means of gaze aversion, and that EPs particularly attend to bodily threat from a person, with increased sympathetic tone. The response of the EP is pathological in that angry faces represent social threat that can be reduced by gaze aversion: a social cue that signals submission to a dominant individual. On the other hand, the results of the study are at odds with the theory that DID involves effects of suggestion and role-playing.

If ANPs can preconsciously avoid externally presented (un)conditioned threat cues, it is reasonable to assume that they can also preconsciously avoid internal (un)conditioned threatening stimuli. Hence, it seems possible that the ANP preconsciously avoids the EP and its memories, as the theory of structural dissociation holds. Some neurobiological data are consistent with the interpretation that dissociative amnesia involves inhibited access to episodic memory. Markowitsch and his colleagues have demonstrated that trauma-related dissociative amnesia as a disorder (APA, 1994) can be associated with reduced blood flow in parts of the brain that are normally activated during retrieval of autobiographical memories (Markowitsch, 1999; Markowitsch, 1997; Fink, Thone, Kessler, & Heiss, 1997; Markowitsch et al., 1997, 1998, 2000). Moreover, partial regaining of these memories was correlated with a return to normal blood flow in these brain areas (Markowitsch et al., 2000).

21.7.2.3 Limitation

The experimental DID research of Reinders et al. and Hermans et al. is limited to women, which may have affected the results. Preclinical studies have suggested large gender differences with respect to responsivity to identical stressors (e.g., c-fos expression in the PFC and other brain regions) (Trentani et al., 2003). Hence, the degree of activation of various brain structures may be dependent on gender. Next, enhanced activity of the right (but not the left) amygdala in men, and enhanced activity of the left (but not the right) amygdala is related to enhanced memory for emotional films (Cahill et al., 2001). For the time being, we disregarded this complexity, but remark that future research should control for gender.

21.8 POSITIVE FEEDFORWARD EXCITATION (EP) AND NEGATIVE FEEDBACK INHIBITION (ANP)

Based on the findings presented, we now give an overview of how EP and ANP seem to have different psychobiological reactions to stimuli these parts consciously and unconsciously perceive as threat.

21.8.1 EP-Dependent Responsivity to Threat

Exposure to major external threat causes rapid activation of the defensive system by the amygdala and related structures. This is mandatory for survival, as is learning and memorizing by means of classical conditioning that which signals or refers to threat. The range of threat-related responses orchestrated by the amygdala includes activation of the sympathetic nervous system and the HPA-axis, defensive behavior (through the central grey), startle response, and stress-induced hypoalgesia (Aggleton, 2000). The lateral amygdala receives sensory inputs directly from the sensory thalamus and indirectly from the sensory cortex. The lateral amygdala projects to the central nucleus of the amygdala, which projects to structures controlling defensive behavior (flight, freeze, fight, total submission), autonomic arousal, hypoalgesia, stress hormones, and potentiated startle. Thus, the amygdala will be hyperactivated in the face of threat (unconditioned stimuli), will encode and store associations between conditioned and unconditioned stimuli (e.g., conditioned stimulus signals unconditioned stimulus), and will modulate trauma memories more generally. When conditioned stimuli (re)appear, the amygdala and other aspects of the emotional brain and the defensive systems tend to become reactivated.

Hyperactivation of the defensive system during traumatic stress may produce hypermnesia through mediation of the basolateral nucleus of the amygdala. The basolateral amygdala has a major role in stress-mediated neuromodulatory influences on memory storage (Cahill, 2000; McGaugh, Ferry, Vazdarjanova, & Roozendaal, 2000). Post-event memory consolidation for emotional experiences involves not only the basolateral amygdala, but the stria terminalis as well. This is a major afferent/efferent amygdala pathway, which interacts with peripheral stress hormone feedback locally in the amygdala, and with emotional memory storage elsewhere in the brain (Cahill, 2000).

Reactivated traumatic memories represent internal threat and aversion (disgust) in that these memories are not narratives but somatosensory and emotionally charged experiences. Findings of Reiman, Lane, Ahern, Schwartz, and Davidson (2000) suggest that internal threat cues (including body signals) are associated with activity of the insula. We already noted a correlation between activation of the insula and disgust. Because the insula have afferent/efferent connections with the amygdala, internal threat cues may activate the amygdala through this path.

Hyperactivation of the amygdala in the EPs exposed to external and internal threat cues (angry faces) may be related to failed inhibition of the amygdala and insula by the hippocampus and the mPFC due to excessive release of stress hormones: uninhibited positive feedforward loops would seem to stabilize the defensive system, and impede the integration of EP and ANP. In this context, reactivation of traumatic memories and the defensive system (the EP) by conditioned stimuli implies sensitization rather than modulation of associations between conditioned and unconditioned stimuli. Finally, hyperactivation of the defensive system/limbic structures and potent somatosensory activity combined with relatively low levels of prefrontal cortical activity could perhaps explain why in most cases EPs have only developed a quite limited degree of extended consciousness.

Thus it seems that exposure of the EP to (perceived) threat cues (re)activates defensive responses with concomitant lack of contextual information processing, uninhibited conditioned emotional responding within limits of homeostasis, and hampered integration of traumatic memories. Hypermnesia, sensitization, and maintenance of structural dissociation between ANP and EP can co-occur.

21.8.2 ANP-Dependent Responsivity to Threat

Because ANPs displayed reactivity to masked angry faces, it seems unlikely that the amygdala and related brain structures were not activated at all when ANPs were exposed to these threat cues. However, in the EP, the emotional brain is strongly activated. While the EP selectively attends to threat cues, the ANP averts its gaze from threat and selectively attends to cues that matter to daily life functioning. It seems possible that there is transient activation of the lateral amygdala by means of input from the sensory thalamus when the ANP is exposed to threat. However, due to ANP's mental avoidance of threat cues and retraction of the field of consciousness to matters of daily life, the lateral amygdala could become readily subject to a form of negative feedback inhibition. When emotional systems that regulate daily life are in executive control, the amygdala—which has a role in selective attention (Gallagher, 2000)—and related structures may operate in a mode that is different from the mode associated with the defensive system.

It is known that activation of the PFC inhibits the amygdala. Therefore, another explanation could be that as the ANP has to rely more on executive functions in order to function in daily life, more frontal networks are activated. Thus the ANP recruits more neural networks such as the dorsolateral PFC and other PFC-related areas, thus leading to inhibition of the amygdala.

Because ANPs are often depersonalized, studies of DID could help understand ANP reactivity to threat in various trauma-related disorders. Depersonalization is related to several negative somatoform dissociative symptoms (e.g., experiencing the body as a foreign object), and involves functional abnormalities along sequential hierarchical areas, secondary and cross-modal areas of the sensory cortex (visual, auditory, and somatosensory), as well as areas responsible for an integrated body schema (Simeon et al., 2000). Perhaps the ANP's lack of sensory perception, including bodily and peripheral stress hormone feedback, could be instrumental in inhibiting the defensive system, hence, the insula and amygdala, and the responsivity it orchestrates. One way to study the presumed negative feedback and positive feedforward loops would be to apply functional MRI while ANPs and EPs are exposed to external and internal threat cues.

21.9 CONCLUSION

The integrative functions of the human mind can be hampered by overwhelming events, especially when these events begin early in life, are recurrent, involve threat to the body and to life itself, and are accompanied by compromised attachment, and lack of social recognition and support. Trauma-related structural dissociation does not involve an accidental division of the personality. Clinical, empirical, and experimental evidence rather suggests that trauma-related structural dissociation of the personality reflects a lack of integration among specific psychobiological action systems, and this lack of integration may also pertain to different aspects of the human central nervous system. The primary form of this structural dissociation involves failed integration between systems dedicated to daily life and survival of the species, and systems dedicated to the survival of the individual in the face of severe threat. Positive and negative dissociative symptoms are manifestations of structural dissociation of the personality. They are different from alterations of consciousness that do not imply a division of personality (for a review of the psychobiology of these alterations see Vaitl et al., 2005). However, traumatization can also involve phenomena such as lowering and retraction of consciousness. For example, many EPs have a lower level and smaller field of consciousness than ANPs.

The evidence to date suggests that in PTSD and the dissociative disorders, (re)activation of the defensive system—metaphorically addressed as the "emotional" part of the personality, EP—by trauma-related cues implies increased activation of the amygdala, insula, and related structures, and decreased activation of the hippocampus, anterior cingulate gyrus, mPFC, and perhaps other prefrontal areas as well. The amygdala orchestrates a range of unconditioned and conditioned reactions to threat, including sympathetic and parasympathetic nervous system activity, analgesia, defensive motor reaction patterns, subjective emotional feelings such as fear, and retraction of the field of consciousness to threat cues in the immediate, subjective present. These reactions seem to lack modulation by the PFC. However, when the psychobiological systems that involve daily life functioning (i.e., the "apparently normal" part of the personality, ANP) are dominant, threat cues are avoided (gaze aversion, mental inhibition), and attention is directed to cues that have a bearing on daily life. The depersonalization and negative somatoform dissociative symptoms that characterize the ANP may be related to disturbed metabolism in the somatosensory association areas. While structural dissociation may be adaptive when the integrative level is not sufficient to integrate both systems, continued structural dissociation is maladaptive when integration of traumatic experiences would be feasible.

To date, research of PTSD and most research of dissociative disorders have largely overlooked that findings may depend on the type of dissociative parts of the personality that dominates the functioning of the patient at the time of measurement. In this regard, at a minimum, the theory of structural dissociation can serve as a heuristic for future research of trauma-related dissociation. More specifically, the theory may be of help (1) in selecting minimal sets of variables needed to assess the different types of dissociative parts that patients with trauma-related dissociative disorders encompass; (2) in conceptualizing and studying the features of these different types of parts in terms of these essential variables; and (3) in conceptualizing dynamics of transitions between these different dissociative parts that constitute these patients' personality (cf. Vaitl et al., 2005).

REFERENCES

Aggleton, J. P. (2000). *The amygdala: A functional analysis.* New York: Oxford University Press.

Aguilera, G., & Rabadan-Diehl, C. (2000). Vasopressinergic regulation of the hypothalamic-pituitary-adrenal axis: implications for stress adaptation. *Regulatory Peptides, 96,* 23–29.

Allport, G. W. (1961). *Pattern and growth in personality.* New York: Holt, Rinehart, and Winston.

American Psychiatric Association (1994). *DSM-IV – Diagnostic and statistical manual of mental disorders* (4th ed.). Washington, DC: Author.

Armony, J. G., & LeDoux, J. E. (1997). How the brain processes emotional information. *Annals of the New York Academy of Sciences, 821,* 259–270.

Arnsten, A., 1999. Development of the prefrontal cortex: XIV. Stress impairs prefrontal cortical function. *Journal of the American Academy of Child and Adolescent Psychiatry, 38,* 220–222.

Azari, N. P., Nickel, J., Wunderich, G., Niedeggen, M., Hefter, H., Tellman, L., Herzog, H., Stoerig, P., Birnbacher, D., & Seitz, R. J. (1997). Neural correlates of religious experience. *European Journal of Neuroscience, 13,* 1649–1652.

Bachmann, A. W., Sedgley, T. L., Jackson, R. V., Gibson, J. N., Young, R. M., & Torpy, D. J. (2005). Glucocorticoid receptor polymorphisms and posttraumatic stress disorder. *Psychoneuroendocrinology, 30,* 297–306.

Baeyens, F., Hermans, D., & Eelen, P. (1993). The role of CS-UCS contingency in human evaluative conditioning. *Behavior Research* and *Therapy, 31,* 731–737.

Benjamin, L. S. (1994). SASB: A bridge between personality theory and clinical psychology. *Psychological Inquiry, 5,* 273–316.

Birnbaum, M. H., & Thomann, K. (1996). Visual function in multiple personality disorder. *Journal of American Optom Assoc, 67,* 327–334.

Bouchard, T. J. Jr., & Loehlin, J. C. (2001). Genes, evolution, and personality. *Behavior Genetics, 31,* 243–273.

Bourne, P. G., Rose, R. M., & Mason, J. W. (1967). 17-OHCS levels in combat: Special Forces "A" Team under threat of attack. *Archives of General Psychiatry, 19,* 135–140.

Bremner, J. D., Narayan, M., Staib, L. H., Southwick, S. M., McGlashan, T., & Charney, D. S. (1999). Neural correlates of memories of childhood sexual abuse in women with and without posttraumatic stress disorder. *American Journal of Psychiatry, 156,* 1787–1795.

Brewin, C. R., Andrews, B., & Rose, S. (2003). Diagnostic overlap between acute stress disorder and PTSD in victims of violent crime. *American Journal of Psychiatry, 160,* 783–785.

Bryant, R. A., Harvey, A. G., Guthrie, R. M., & Moulds, M. L. (2000). A prospective study of psychophysiological arousal, acute stress disorder, and posttraumatic stress disorder. *Journal of Abnormal Psychology, 109,* 341–344.

Cahill, L. (2000). Modulation of long-term memory in humans by emotional arousal: Adrenergic activation and the amygdala. In J. P. Aggleton (Ed.), *The amygdala* (pp. 425–446). New York: Oxford University Press.

Cahill, L., Haier, R. J., White, N. S., Fallon, J., Kilpatrick, L., Lawrence, C. et al. (2001). Sex-related difference in amygdala activity during emotionally influenced memory storage. *Neurobiology of Learning and Memory, 75,* 1–9.

Campbell, D. T. (1974). Evolutionary epistemology. In P. A. Schlipp (Ed.), *The philosophy of Karl Popper* (pp. 413–463). LaSalle, IL: Open Court.

Cannon, W. B. (1927). The James-Lange theory of emotions. *American Journal of Psychology, 39,* 115–124.

Cannon, W. B. (1932). *The wisdom of the body.* 2nd Ed., 1939. New York: Norton.

Carver, C. S., Sutton, S. K., & Scheier, M. F. (2000). Action, emotion, and personality: Emerging conceptual integration. *Personality and Social Psychology Bulletin, 26,* 741–751.

Caspi, A., McClay, J., Moffitt, T. E., Mill, J., Martin, J., Craig, I. W., Taylor, A., & Poulton, R. (2002). Role of genotype in the cycle of violence in maltreated children. *Science 297,* 851–854.

Cattell, R. B. (1986). Structured tests and functional diagnoses. In R. B. Cattell & R. C. Johnson (Eds.), *Functional psychological testing: Principles and instruments,* pp. 3–14. New York: Brunner/Mazel.

Ciompi, L. (1991). Affects as central organizing and integrating factors: A new psychosocial/biological model of the psyche. *British Journal of Psychiatry, 159,* 97–105.

Cohen, H., Zohar, J., & Matar, M. (2003). The relevance of differential response to trauma in an animal model of posttraumatic stress disorder. *Biological Psychiatry, 53,* 463–473.

Cools, A. R., & Ellenbroek, B. A. (2002). Animal models of personality. In H. D'Haenen, J. A. den Boer, & P. Willner (Eds.), *Biological psychiatry* (pp. 1333–1344). London: Wiley.

Coons, P. M., Milstein, V., & Marley, C. (1982). EEG studies of two multiple personalities and a control. *Archives of General Psychiatry, 39,* 823–825.

Damasio, A. R. (1999). *The feeling of what happens: Body and emotion in the making of consciousness*. New York: Harcourt Brace.

Damasio, A. R., Grabowski, T. J., Bechara, A., Damasio, H., Ponto, L. L., Parvizi, J. et al. (2000). Subcortical and cortical brain activity during the feeling of self-generated emotions. *Nature Neuroscience, 3,* 1049–1056.

Davies, M. (2000). The role of the amygdala in conditioned and unconditioned fear and anxiety. In J. P. Aggleton (Ed.), *The amygdala* (pp. 213–288). New York: Oxford University Press.

Davis, K. L., Panksepp, J., & Normansell, L. (2003). The affective neuroscience personality scales: Normative data and implications. *Neuro-Psychoanalysis, 5,* 57–69.

Daviss, W. B., Mooney, D., Racusin, R., Ford, J. D., Fleischer, A., & McHugo, G. J. (2000). Predicting posttraumatic stress after hospitalization for pediatric injury. *Journal of the American Academy of Child and Adolescent Psychiatry, 39,* 576–583.

Dell, P. F. (1997). Somatoform dissociation and reported trauma in DID and DDNOS. Proceedings of the 14th International Conference of the International Society for the Study of Dissociation, November 8–11, p. 130.

DeRijk, R. H., Schaaf, M., & de Kloet, E. R. (2002). Glucocorticoid receptor variants: Clinical implications. *Journal of Steroid Biochemistry and Molecular Biology, 81,* 103–122.

Dolan, R. J. (2000). Functional neuroimaging of the amygdala during emotional processing and learning. In J. P. Aggleton (Ed.), *The amygdala* (pp. 631–655). New York: Oxford University Press.

Ebner, K., Wotjak, C. T., Holsboer, F., Landgraf, R., & Engelmann, M. (1999). Vasopressin released within the septal brain area during swim stress modulates the behavioural stress response in rats. *European Journal of Neuroscience, 11,* 997–1002.

Elklit, A. (1997). The aftermath of an industrial disaster. *Acta Psychiatrica Scandinavica, 96,* 1–25.

Elklit, A., & Brink, O. (2003). Acute Stress Disorder in physical assault victims visiting a Danish emergency ward. *Violence and Victims, 18,* 461–472.

Eysenck, H. J. (1990). Genetic and environmental contributions to individual differences: The three major dimensions of personality. *Journal of Personality, 58I,* 245–261.

Fanselow, M. S., & Lester, L. S. (1988). A functional behavioristic approach to aversively motivated behavior: Predatory imminence as a determinant of the topography of defensive behavior. In R. C. Bolles & M. D. Beecher (Eds.), *Evolution and learning* (pp. 185–212). Hillsdale, NJ: Erlbaum.

Farrington, D. P. (1997). The relationship between low resting heart rate and violence. In A. Raine, P. A. Brennan, D. P. Farrington, & S. A. Mednick (Eds.), *Biosocial bases of violence* (3rd ed., pp. 89–106). New York: Plenum Press.

Field, T. M. (1985). Attachment as psychobiological attunement: Being on the same wavelength. In M. Reite & T. M. Fields (Eds.), *The psychobiology of attachment and separation* (pp. 415–454). Orlando, FL: Academic Press.

Freyd, J. J. (1996). *Betrayal trauma: The logic of forgetting Childhood Trauma*. Cambridge, MA: Harvard University Press.

Friedman, S. B., Mason, J. W., & Hamburg, D. A. (1963). Urinary 17-hydroxycorticoisteroid levls in parents of children with neoplastic disease. *Osychosomatic Medicine, 25,* 364–376.

Fuglsang, A. K., Moergeli, H., Hepp-Beg, S., & Schnyder, U. (2002). Who develops acute stress disorder after accidental injuries? *Psychotherapy and Psychosomatics, 71,* 214–222.

Fullerton, C. S., Ursano, R. J., & Wang, L. (2004). Acute stress disorder, posttraumatic stress disorder, and depression in disaster or rescue workers. *American Journal of Psychiatry, 161,* 1370–1376.

Gallagher, M. (2000). The amygdala and associative learning. In J. P. Aggleton (Ed.), *The amygdala: A functional analysis* (pp. 311–329). New York: Oxford University Press.

Gallese, V., Keysers, C., & Rizzolatti, G. (2004). A unifying view of the basis of social cognition. *Trends in Cognitive Sciences, 8,* 396–403.

Gelernter, J., Kranzler, H., & Lacobelle, J. (1998). Population studies of polymorphisms at loci of neuropsychiatric interest (tryptophan hydroxylase (TPH), dopamine transporter protein (SLC6A3), D3 dopamine receptor (DRD3), apolipoprotein E (APOE), mu opioid receptor (OPRM1), and ciliary neurotrophic factor (CNTF)). *Genomics, 52,* 289–297.

Gerardi, R., Keane, T. M., & Penk, W. (1989). Utility: Sensitivity and specificity in developing diagnostic tests of combat-related post-traumatic stress disorder (PTSD). *Journal of Clinical Psychology, 45,* 691–703.

Gerrits, M., Westenbroek, C., Fokkema, D. S., Jongsma, M. E., Den Boer, J. A., & Ter Horst, G. (2003). Increased stress vulnerability after a prefrontal cortex lesion in female rats. *Brain Research Bulletin, 61,* 627–635.

Griffin, M. G., Resick, P. A., & Mechanic, M. B. (1997). Objective assessment of peritraumatic dissociation: Psychophysiological indicators. *American Journal of Psychiatry, 154,* 1081–1088.

Haller, J., Albert, I., & Makara, G. B. (1997). The effects of the alpha 2 adrenoceptor blocker idazoxan on defeat-induced immobility and plasma corticosterone in rats is antagonized by administration of adrenocorticotrophin-antiserum. *Behavioural Pharmacology, 8,* 269–273.

Hariri, A. R., Mattay, V. S., Tessitore, A., Kolachana, B., Fera, F., Goldman, D., Egan, M. F., & Weinberger, D. R. (2002). Serotonin transporter genetic variation and the response of the human amygdala. *Science, 297,* 400–403.

Herman, J. L. (1992). Complex PTSD: A syndrome in survivors of prolonged and repeated trauma. *Journal of Traumatic Stress, 5,* 377–392.

Hermans, E. J., Nijenhuis, E. R. S., van Honk, J., Huntjens, R., & Van der Hart, O. (2006). State-dependent attentional bias for facial threat in dissociative identity disorder. *Psychiatry Research, 141,* 233–236.

Heyes, C. (2003). Four routes to cognitive evolution. *Psychological Review, 110,* 713–727.

Hofstee, W. K. B., Raad, B., & Goldberg, L. R. (1992). Integration of the Big Five and circumplex approaches to trait structure. *Journal of Personality and Social Psychology, 63*, 146–163.

Holmes, E. A., Brown, R. J., Mansell, W., Fearon, R. P., Hunter, E. C., Frasquilho, F. et al. (2005). Are there two qualitatively distinct forms of dissociation? A review and some clinical implications. *Clinical Psychology Review, 25*, 1–23.

Hughes, J. R., Kuhlman, D. T., Fichtner, C. G., & Gruenfeld, M. J. (1990). Brain mapping in a case of multiple personality. *Clinical Electroencephalography, 21*, 200–209.

Jackson, J. H. (1958). Evolution and dissolution of the nervous system. In J. Taylor (Ed.), *Selected writings of John Hughlings Jackson* (pp. 45–118). London: Stapes Press.

Janet, P. (1907). *The major symptoms of hysteria*. London and New York: Macmillan.

Janet, P. (1928). *De l'angoisse à l'extase, Vol 2: Les sentiments fondamentaux*. Paris: Félix Alcan. New edition: Société Pierre Janet, Paris, 1975.

Jang, K. L., Stein, M. B., Taylor, S., Asmundson, G. J., & Livesley, W. J. (2003). Exposure to traumatic events and experiences: Aetiological relationships with personality function. *Psychiatry Research, 120*, 61–69.

Karmiloff-Smith, A. (1998). Development itself is the key to understading developmental disorders. *Trends in Cognitive Sciences, 2*, 389–398.

Kendler, K. S., Neale, M. C., Kessler, R. C., Heath, A. C., & Eaves, L. J. (1993). A test of the equal-environment assumption in twin studies of psychiatric illness. *Behavioral Genetics, 23*, 21–27.

King, L. A., King, D. W., Fairbank, J. A., Keane, T. M., & Adams, G. A. (1998). Resilience-recovery factors in posttraumatic stress disorder among female and male Vietnam veterans: Hardiness, postwar social support study of reactivation of posttraumatic stress disorder symptoms; American and Cambodian psychophysiological response to viewing traumatic video scenes. *Journal of Nervous and Mental Disease, 186*, 670–676.

Kinzie, J. D., Denney, D., Riley, C., Boehnlein, J., McFarland, B., & Leung, P. (1998). A cross-cultural study of reactivation of posttraumatic stress disorder symptoms: American and Cambodian psychophysiological response to viewing traumatic video scenes. *Journal of Nervous and Mental Disease, 186*, 670–676.

Koopman, C., Carion, V., Sudhakar, S., Palmer, L., & Steiner, H. (2000). Dissociation, childhood abuse and heart rate during a stressful speech. Poster presented at the 16th Conference of the International Society for Traumatic Stress Studies, San Antonio, November 18.

Krolak-Salmon, P., Henaff, M. A., Isnard, J., Tallon-Baudry, C., Guenot, M., Vighetto, A., Bertrand, O., & Mauguiere, F. (2003). An attention modulated response to disgust in human ventral anterior insula. *Annals of Neurology, 53*, 446–453.

Krystal, J. H., Woods, S. W., Hill, C. L., & Charney, D. S. (1991). Characteristics of panic attack subtypes: Assessment of spontaneous panic, situational panic, sleep panic, and limited symptom attacks. *Comprehensive Psychiatry, 32*, 474–478.

Lacey, B. C., & Lacey, J. I. (1974). Studies of heart rate and other bodily processes in sensorimotor behavior. In P. A. Orbist, A. H. Black, J. Brener, & L. DiCara (Eds.), *Cardiovascular psychophysiology: Current issues in response mechanisms, biofeedback, and methodology* (pp. 538–564). Chicago: Aldine.

Lang, P. J. (1995). The emotion probe. Studies of motivation and attention. *American Psychologist, 50*, 372–385.

Lang, P. J., Davis, M., & Ohman, A. (2000). Fear and anxiety: animal models and human cognitive psychophysiology. *Journal of Affective Disorders, 61*, 137–159.

Lanius, R. A., Hopper, J. W., & Menon, R. S. (2003). Individual differences in a husband and wife who developed PTSD after a motor vehicle accident: A functional MRI case study. *American Journal of Psychiatry, 160*, 667–669.

Lanius, R. A., Williamson, P. C., Boksman, K., Densmore, M., Gupta, M., Neufeld, R. W. et al. (2002). Brain activation during script-driven imagery induced dissociative responses in PTSD: A functional magnetic resonance imaging investigation. *Biological Psychiatry, 52*, 305–311.

Larmore, K., Ludwig, A. M., & Cain, R. L. (1977). Multiple personality: An objective case study. *British Journal of Psychiatry, 131*, 35–40.

Lavenu, I., Pasquier, F., Lebert, F., Petit, H., & Van der Linden, M. (1999). Perception of emotion in frontotemporal dementia and Alzheimer disease. *Alzheimer Disease and Associated Disorders, 13*, 96–101.

LeDoux, J. E. (1995). Emotion: Clues from the brain. *Annual Review of Psychology, 46*, 209–235.

LeDoux, J. E. (1996). *The emotional brain: The mysterious underpinning of emotional life*. New York: Simon and Schuster.

LeDoux, J. E. (2003). The emotional brain, fear, and the amygdala. *Cellular and Molecular Neurobiology, 23*, 727–738.

Lesch, K. P., Bengel, D., Heils, A., Sabol, S. Z., Greenberg, B. D., Petri, S., Benjamin, J., Muller, C. R., Hamer, D. H., & Murphy, D. L. (1996). Association of anxiety-related traits with a polymorphism in the serotonin transporter gene regulatory region. *Science, 274*, 1527–1531.

Liotti, G. (1992). Disorganized/disoriented attachment in the etiology of dissociative disorders. *Dissociation, 5*, 196–204.

Livesley, W. J., & Jang, K. L. (2000). Toward an empirically based classification of personality disorder. *Journal of Personality Disorders, 14*, 137–151.

Loehlin, J. C. (1992). *Genes and environment in personality*. Newbury Park, CA: Sage.

Lucas, R. E., Diener, E., Suh, E. M., Shao, L., & Grob., A. (2000). Crosss cultural evidence for the fundamental features of extraversion. *Journal of Personality and Social Psychology, 79*, 452–468.

Ludwig, A. M., Brandsma, J. M., Wilbur, C. B., Bendtfeldt, F., & Jameson, D. H. (1972). The objective study of a multiple personality. *Archives of General Psychiatry, 26*, 298–310.

Maaranen, P., Tanskanen, A., Haatainen, K., Koivumaa-Honkanen, H., Hintikka, J., & Viinamaki, H. (2004). Somatoform dissociation and adverse childhood experiences in the general population. *Journal of Nervous and Mental Disease, 192,* 337–342.

Main, M., & Morgan, H. (1996). Disorganization and disorientation in infant Strange Situation behavior: Phenotypic resemblance to dissociative states? In L. Michelson & W. Ray (Eds.), *Handbook of dissociation* (pp. 107–137). New York: Plenum.

Markowitsch, H. J. (1999). Functional neuroimaging correlates of functional amnesia. *Memory, 7,* 561–583.

Markowitsch, H. J., Calabrese, P., Fink, G. R., Durwen, H. F., Kessler, J., Harting, C., Konig, M., Mirzaian, E. B., Heiss, W. -D., Heuser, L., & Gehlen, W. (1997). Impaired episodic memory retrieval in a case of probably psychogenic amnesia. *Psychiatry Research: Neuroimaging Section, 74,* 119–126.

Markowitsch, H. J., Fink, G. R., Thone, A., Kessler, J., & Heiss, W. -D. (1997). A PET study of persistent psychogenic amnesia covering the whole life span. *Cognitive Neuropsychiatry, 2,* 135–158.

Markowitsch, H. J., Kessler, J., Van der Ven, C., Weber-Luxenburger, G., Albers, M., & Heiss, W.-D. (1998). Psychic trauma causing grossly reduced brain metabolism and cognitive deterioration. *Neuropsychologica, 36,* 77–82.

Markowitsch, H. J., Kessler, J., Weber-Luxenburger, G., Van der Ven, C., Albers, M., & Heiss, W. -D. (2000). Neuroimaging and behavioral correlates of recovery from mnestic block syndrome and other cognitive deteriorations. *Neuropsychiatry, Neuropsychology, and Behavioral Neurology, 13,* 60–66.

Mason, J. W., Wang, S., Yehuda, R., Riney, S., Charney, D. S., & Southwick, S. M. (2001). Psychogenic lowering of urinary cortisol levels linked to increased emotional numbing and a shame-depressive syndrome in combat-related posttraumatic stress disorder. *Psychosomatic Medicine, 63,* 387–401.

Mathew, R. J., Jack, R. A., & West, W. S. (1985). Regional cerebral blood flow in a patient with multiple personality. *American Journal of Psychiatry, 142,* 504–505.

Mayr, E. (1974). Behavior programs and evolutionary strategies. *American Scientist, 62,* 650–659.

McCormick, D. D., & Thompson, R. F. (1982). Locus coeruleus lesions and resistance to extinction of a classically conditioned response: Involvement of the neocortex and hippocampus. *Brain Research, 245,* 239–249.

McCrae, R. R., & Costa, P. T. (1996). Toward a new generation of personality theories: Theoretical contexts for the five-factor model. In J. S. Wiggins (Ed.), *The five-factor model of personality: Theoretical perspectives* (pp. 51–87). New York: Guilford Press.

McGaugh, J., Ferry, B., Vazdarjanova, A., & Roozendaal, B. (2000). Amygdala: Role in modulation of memory storage. In J. P. Aggleton (Ed.), *The amygdala* (pp. 391–424). New York: Oxford University Press.

Mezzacappa, E., Tremblay, R. E., Kindlon, D., Saul, J. P., Arseneault, L., Seguin, J., Pihl, R. O., & Earls, F. (1997). Anxiety, antisocial behavior, and heart rate regulation in adolescent males. *Journal of Child Psychology and Psychiatry, 38,* 457–469.

Miller, S. D. (1989). Optical differences in cases of multiple personality disorder. *Journal of Nervous and Mental Disease, 177,* 480–486.

Miller, S. D., Blackburn, T., Scholes, G., White, G. L., & Mammalis, N. (1991). Optical differences in multiple personality disorder: A second look. *Journal of Nervous and Mental Disease, 179,* 132–135.

Miller, S. D., & Triggiano, P. J. (1992). The psychophysiological investigation of multiple personality disorder: Review and update. *American Journal of Clinical Hypnosis, 35,* 47–61.

Moffitt, T. E., & Caspi, A. (2001). Childhood predictors differentiate life-course persistent and adolescence-limited antisocial pathways among males and females. *Development and Psychopathology, 13,* 355–375.

Morris, J. S., Ohman, A., & Dolan, R. J. (1998). Conscious and unconscious emotional learning in the human amygdala. *Nature, 393,* 467–470.

Myers, C. S. (1940). *Shell shock in France 1914-1918.* Cambridge: Cambridge University Press.

Nijenhuis, E. R. S. (2004). Structural dissociation of the personality: Phenomena, theory, and psychobiological research. Keynote address. The Fifth European EMDR Conference. Stockholm, June 11–13.

Nijenhuis, E. R. S., Spinhoven, P., Van Dyck, R., Van der Hart, O., & Vanderlinden, J. (1996). The development and the psychometric characteristics of the Somatoform Dissociation Questionnaire (SDQ-20). *Journal of Nervous and Mental Disease, 184,* 688–694.

Nijenhuis, E. R. S., Spinhoven, P., Vanderlinden, J., Van Dyck, R., & Van der Hart, O. (1998a). Somatoform dissociative symptoms as related to animal defensive reactions to predatory threat and injury. *Journal of Abnormal Psychology, 107,* 63–73.

Nijenhuis, E. R. S., Spinhoven, P., Van Dyck, R., Van der Hart, O., & Vanderlinden, J. (1998b). Degree of somatoform and psychological dissociation in dissociative disorders is correlated with reported trauma. *Journal of Traumatic Stress, 11,* 711–730.

Nijenhuis, E. R. S., & Van der Hart, O. (1999). Forgetting and reexperiencing trauma: From anesthesia to pain. In J. M. Goodwin & R. Attias (Eds.), *Splintered reflections: Images of the body in trauma* (pp. 39–65). New York: Basic Books.

Nijenhuis, E. R. S., Van der Hart, O., Kruger, K., & Steele, K. (2004a). Somatoform dissociation, reported abuse, and animal defence-like reactions. *Australian and New Zealand Journal of Psychiatry, 38,* 678–686.

Nijenhuis, E. R. S., Van der Hart, O., & Steele, K. (2002). The emerging psychobiology of trauma-related dissociation and dissociative disorders. In H. D'Haenen, J. A. den Boer, & P. Willner (Eds.), *Biological psychiatry* (pp. 1079–1098). London: Wiley.

Nijenhuis, E. R. S., Van der Hart, O., & Steele, K. (2004b). Strukturelle Dissoziation der Persönlichkeitsstruktur, traumatischer Ursprung, phobische Residuen. In L. Reddemann, A. Hofmann, & U. Gast, *Psychotherapie der dissoziativen Störungen* (pp. 47–69). Stuttgart: Thieme.

Nijenhuis, E. R. S., Vanderlinden, J., & Spinhoven, P. (1998c). Animal defensive reactions as a model for trauma-induced dissociative reactions. *Journal of Traumatic Stress, 11,* 243–260.

Nijenhuis, E. R. S., & Van Duyl, M. (2001). Dissociative symptoms and reported trauma among Ugandan patients with possessive trance disorder. Proceedings of the 18th International Fall Conference of the International Society for the Study of Dissociation. New Orleans, December 2–4.

Nijenhuis, E. R. S., Van Dyck, R., Spinhoven, P., Van der Hart, O., Chatrou, M., Vanderlinden, J., & Moene, F. (1999). Somatoform dissociation discriminates between diagnostic categories over and above general psychopathology. *Australian and New Zealand Journal of Psychiatry, 33,* 512–520.

Nijenhuis, E. R. S., Van Dyck, R., Ter Kuile, M. M., Mourits, M. J. E., Spinhoven, P., & Van der Hart, O. (2003). Evidence for associations among somatoform dissociation, psychological dissociation and reported trauma in patients with chronic pelvic pain. *Journal of Psychosomatic Obstetrics and Gynecology, 24,* 87–98.

Nijenhuis, E. R. S., Van Engen, A., Kusters, I., & Van der Hart, O. (2001). Peritraumatic somatoform and psychological dissociation in relation to recall of childhood sexual abuse. *Journal of Trauma and Dissociation, 2,* 49–68.

Nijsen, M. J., Croiset, G., Diamant, M., De Wied, D., & Wiegant, V. M. (2001). CRH signalling in the bed nucleus of the stria terminalis is involved in stress-induced cardiac vagal activation in conscious rats. *Neuropsychopharmacology, 24,* 1–10.

Nijsen, M. J., Croiset, G., Diamant, M., Stam, R., Delsing, D., De Wied, D., & Wiegant, V. M. (1998). Conditioned fear-induced tachycardia in the rat: Vagal involvement. *European Journal of Pharmacology, 350,* 211–222.

Nijsen, M. J., Croiset, G., Diamant, M., Stam, R., Kamphuis, P. J., Bruijnzeel, A. et al. (2000). Endogenous corticotropin-releasing hormone inhibits conditioned-fear-induced vagal activation in the rat. *European Journal of Pharmacology, 389,* 89–98.

Nussbaum, M. C. (2004). *Hiding from humanity. Disgust, shame and the law*. Princeton/Oxford: Princeton University Press.

Ogawa, J. R., Sroufe, L. A., Weinfield, N. S., Carlson, E. A., & Egeland, B. (1997). Development and the fragmented self: Longitudinal study of dissociative symptomatology in a nonclinical sample. *Development and Psychopathology, 9,* 855–879.

Orr, S. P. (1997). Psychophysiologic reactivity to trauma-related imagery in PTSD. Diagnostic and theoretical implications of recent findings. *Annals of the New York Academy of Sciences, 821,* 114–124.

Orr, S. P., Lasko, N. B., Metzger, L. J., Berry, N. J., Ahern, C. E., & Pitman, R. K. (1997). Psychophysiologic assessment of PTSD in adult females sexually abused during childhood. *Annals of the New York Academy of Sciences, 821,* 491–493.

Orr, S. P., Metzger, L. J., Lasko, N. B., Macklin, M. L., Hu, F. B., Shalev, A. Y. et al. (2003). Physiologic responses to sudden, loud tones in monozygotic twins discordant for combat exposure: association with posttraumatic stress disorder. *Archives of General Psychiatry, 60,* 283–288.

Orr, S. P., & Pitman, R. K. (1993). Psychophysiologic assessment of attempts to simulate posttraumatic stress disorder. *Biological Psychiatry, 33,* 127–129.

Ortiz, J., & Raine, A. (2004). Heart rate level and antisocial behavior in children and adolescents: A meta-analysis. *Journal of the American Academy of Child and Adolescent Psychiatry, 43,* 154–162.

Osuch, E. A., Benson, B., Geraci, M., Podell, D., Herscovitch, P., McCann, U. D., & Post. R. M. (2001). Regional cerebral blood flow correlated with flashback intensity in patients with posttraumatic stress disorder. *Biological Psychiatry, 50,* 246–253.

Panksepp, J. (1998). *Affective neuroscience: The foundations of human and animal emotions*. New York: Oxford University Press.

Panksepp. J. (2003). At the interface of affective, behavioral, and cognitive neurosciences: Decoding the emotional feelings of the brain. *Current Directions in Psychological Sciences, 7,* 91–98.

Pedersen, N. L., Plomin, R., McClearn, G. E., & Friberg, L. (1988). Neuroticism, extraversion, and related traits in adult twins reared apart and reared together. *Journal of Personality and Social Psychology, 55,* 950–957.

Pelcovitz, D., van der, K. B., Roth, S., Mandel, F., Kaplan, S., & Resick, P. (1997). Development of a criteria set and a structured interview for disorders of extreme stress (SIDES). *Journal of Traumatic Stress., 10,* 3–16.

Perry, B. D. (2002). Childhood experience and the expression of genetic potential: What childhood neglect tells us about nature and nurture. *Brain and Mind, 3,* 79–100.

Perry, B. D., Pollard, R. A., Blakely, T. L., Baker, W. L., & Vigilante, D. (1995). Childhood trauma, the neurobiology of adaptation, and "use dependent" development of the brain: How "states" become "traits." *Infant Mental Health Journal, 16,* 271–291.

Phillips, M. L., Senior, C., Fahy, T., & David, A. S. (1998). Disgust—the forgotten emotion of psychiatry. *British Journal of Psychiatry, 172,* 373–375.

Phillips, M. L., Young, A. W., Senior, C., Brammer, M., Andrew, C., Calder, A. J., Bullmore, E. T., Perrett, D. I., Rowland, D., Williams, S. C., Gray, J. A., & David, A. S. (1997). A specific neural substrate for perceiving facial expressions of disgust. *Nature, 389,* 495–498.

Plomin, R., DeFries, J. C., McClearn, G. E., & Rutter, M. (1997). *Behavioral genetics* (3rd ed.). New York: Freeman.

Porges, S. W. (2001). The polyvagal theory: Phylogenetic substrates of a social nervous system. *International Journal of Psychophysiology, 42,* 123–146.

Porges, S. W. (2003). The polyvagal theory: Phylogenetic contributions to social behavior. *Physiology of Behavior, 79,* 503–513.

Price, D. B., Thaler, M., & Mason, J. W. (1957). Preoperative emotional states and adrenal contrical activity. *Archives of General Psychiatry, 77,* 646–656.

Putnam, F. W. (1997). *Dissociation in children and adolescents: A developmental perspective*. New York: Guilford.

Putnam, F. W., Buchsbaum, M. S., Howland, F., & Post, R. M. (1992, May). Evoked potentials in multiple personality disorder: New Research Abstract #137. Presented at the Annual Meeting of the American Psychiatric Association, New Orleans.

Putnam, F. W., Buchsbaum, M. S., & Post, R. M. (1993). Differential brain electrical activity in multiple personality disorder. Unpublished manuscript.

Putnam, F. W., Zahn, T. P., & Post, R. M. (1990). Differential autonomic nervous system activity in multiple personality disorder. *Psychiatry Research, 31*, 251–260.

Raine, A. (1993). *The psychopathology of crime: Criminal behavior as a clinical disorder.* San Diego, CA: Academic Press.

Raine, A. (2002a). Annotation: the role of prefrontal deficits, low autonomic arousal, and early health factors in the development of antisocial and aggressive behavior in children. *Journal of Child Psychology and Psychiatry, 43,* 417–434.

Raine, A. (2002b). Biosocial studies of antisocial and violent behavior in children and adults: A review. *Journal of Abnormal Child Psychology, 30*, 311–326.

Raine, A., Venables, P. H., Mednick, S. A. (1997). Low resting heart rate at age 3 years predisposes to aggression at age 11 years: Evidence from the Mauritius Child Health Project. *Journal of the American Academy of Child and Adolescent Psychiatry, 36*, 1457–1464.

Reiman, E. M., Lane, R. D., Ahern, G. L., Schwartz, G. E., & Davidson, R. J. (2000). Positron emission tomography in the study of emotion, anxiety, and anxiety disorders. In R. D. Lane & L. Nadel (Eds.), *Cognitive neuroscience of emotion* (pp. 389–406). New York: Oxford University Press.

Reinders, A. A., Nijenhuis, E. R., Paans, A. M., Korf, J., Willemsen, A. T., & den Boer, J. A. (2003). One brain, two selves. *Neuroimage, 20,* 2119–2125.

Reinders, A. A. T. S., Nijenhuis, E. R. S., Quak, J., Korf, J., Paans, A. M. J., Haaksma, J., Willemsen, A. T. M., & Den Boer, J. (2006). Psychobiological characteristics of dissociative identity disorder: A symptom provocation study. *Biological Psychiatry, 60,* 730–740.

Reinders, A. A. T. S., Van Ekeren, M., Vos, H., Haaksma, J., Willemsen, A., Den Boer, J. A., & Nijenhuis, E. R. S. (2008). The dissociative brain: Feature or ruled by fantasy? In *Proceedings of the First Conference of the European Society of Trauma & Dissociation* (p. 30). Amsterdam, April 17–19.

Roelofs, K., Keijsers, G. P., Hoogduin, K. A., Naring, G. W., & Moene, F. C. (2002). Childhood abuse in patients with conversion disorder. *American Journal of Psychiatry, 159,* 1908–1913.

Rogeness, G. A., Cepeda, C., Macedo, C. A., Fischer, C., & Harris, W. R. (1990) Differences in heart rate and blood pressure in children with conduct disorder, major depression, and separation anxiety. *Psychiatry Research, 33,* 199–206.

Rozin, P., Lowery, L., & Ebert, R. (1994). Varieties of disgust faces and the structure of disgust. *Journal of Personality and Social Psychology, 66,* 870–881.

Runtz, M. G., & Schallow, J. R. (1997). Social support and coping strategies as mediators of adult adjustment following childhood maltreatment. *Child Abuse and Neglect, 21*, 211–226.

Sahar, T., Shalev, A. Y., & Porges, S. W. (2001). Vagal modulation of responses to mental challenge in posttraumatic stress disorder. *Biological Psychiatry, 49,* 637–643.

Saulsman, L. M., & Page, A. C. (2004). The five-factor model and personality disorder empirical literature: A meta-analytic review. *Clinical Psychology Review, 23*, 1055–1085.

Şar, V., Ünal, S. N., & Öztürk, E. (2007). Frontal and occipital perfusion changes in dissociative identity disorder. *Psychiatry Research, 156,* 217–223.

Saver, J. L., & Rabin, J. (1997). The neural substrates of religious experience. In S. Salloway, P. Malloy, & J. L. Cummings (Eds.), *The neuropsychiatry of limbic and subcortical disorders* (pp. 195–207). American Psychiatric Press.

Saxe, G. N., Vasile, R. G., Hill, T. C., Bloomingdale, K., & Van der Kolk, B. A. (1992). SPECT imaging and multiple personality disorder. *Journal of Nervous and Mental Disease, 180*, 662–663.

Schienle, A., Stark, R., Walter, B., Blecker, C., Ott, U., Kirsch, P., Sammer, G., & Vaitl, D. (2002) The insula is not specifically involved in disgust processing: An fMRI study. *Neuroreport, 13*, 2023–2026.

Schmahl, C. G., Elzinga, B. M., & Bremner, J. D. (2002). Individual diffrences in psychophysiological reactivity in adults with childhood abuse. *Clinical Psychology and Psychotherapy, 9,* 271–276.

Schmeck, K., & Poustka F. (1993). Psychophysiologische Reacktionsmuster und psychische Auffälligkeiten in Kindesalter. In P. Baumann (Ed.), *Biologische Psychiatrie der Gegenwart*. Vienna: Springer-Verlag.

Schore, A. N. (2003). *Affect dysregulation and disorders of the self.* New York: Norton.

Schuengel, C., Bakermans-Kranenburg, M. J., & Van IJzendoorn, M. H. (1999). Frightening maternal behavior linking unresolved loss and disorganized infant attachment. *Journal of Consulting and Clinical Psychology, 67*, 54–63.

Shalev, A. Y., Peri, T., Gelpin, E., Orr, S. P., & Pitman, R. K. (1997). Psychophysiologic assessment of mental imagery of stressful events in Israeli civilian posttraumatic stress disorder patients. *Comprehensive Psychiatry, 38,* 269–273.

Shalev, A. Y., Sahar, T., Freedman, S., Peri, T., Glick, N., Brandes, D. et al. (1998). A prospective study of heart rate response following trauma and the subsequent development of posttraumatic stress disorder. *Archives of General Psychiatry, 55,* 553–559.

Siegel, D. J. (1999). *The developing mind: Toward a neurobiology of interpersonal experience*. New York: Guilford.

Simeon, D., Guralnik, O., Hazlett, E. A., Spiegel-Cohen, J., Hollander, E., & Buchsbaum, M. S. (2000). Feeling unreal: A PET study of depersonalization disorder. *American Journal of Psychiatry, 157*, 1782–1788.

Simeon, D., Guralnik, O., Knutelska, M., Yehuda, R., & Schmeidler, J. (2003). Basal norepinephrine in depersonalization disorder. *Psychiatry Research, 121,* 93–97.

Simeon, D., Guralnik, O., Schmeidler, J., Sirof, B., & Knutelska, M. (2001). The role of childhood interpersonal trauma in depersonalization disorder. *American Journal of Psychiatry, 158,* 1027–1033.

Steele, K., Dorahy, M. J., Van der Hart, O., & Nijenhuis, E. R. S. (2009). Dissociation versus alterations in consciousness. In P. F. Dell & J. A. O'Neil (Eds.), *Dissociation and the dissociative disorders: DSM-V and beyond* (pp. 155–169). New York: Routledge.

Taylor, J. (1959). *Selected writings of John Hughlings Jackson.* Volumes 2. London: Staples Press.

Teicher, M. H., Andersen, S. L., Polcari, A., Anderson, C. M., & Navalta, C. P. (2002). Developmental neurobiology of childhood stress and trauma. *Psychiatric Clinics of North America, 25,* 397-viii.

Tellegen, A., Lykken, D. T., Bouchard, T. J., Jr., Wilcox, K. J., Segal, N. L., Rich, S. (1988). Personality similarity in twins reared apart and together. *Journal of Personality and Social Psychology*, 54, 1031–1039.

Trentani, A., Kuipers, S., Ter Horst, G. J., & Den Boer, J. A., (2003). Intracellular signaling transduction dysregulation in depression and possible future targets for antidepressant therapy. In S. Kasper, J. A. den Boer, & J. M. A. Sitsen (Eds.), *Handbook of depression and anxiety* (pp. 349–386). New York: Marcel Dekker.

Uvnas-Moberg, K. (1997). Physiological and endocrime effects of social contact. *Annals of the New York Academy of Sciences, 807,* 146–163.

Vailt, D., Birbaumer, N., Gruzelier, J., Jamieson, G. A., Kotoubey, B., Kübler, A., Lehmann, D., Miltner, W. H. R., Ott, U., Pütz, P., Sammer, G., Strauch, I., Strehl, U., Wackermann, J., & Weiss, T. (205). Psychobiology of altered states of consciousness. *Psychological Bulletin, 131,* 98–127.

Van der Hart, O., & Brom, D. (2000). When the victim forgets: Trauma-induced amnesia and its assessment in Holocaust survivors. In A. Y. Shalev, R. Yehuda, & A. C. McFarlane (Eds.), *International handbook of human response to trauma* (pp. 223–248). New York: Kluwer Academic/ Plenum Publishers.

Van der Hart, O., Brown, P., & Graafland, M. (1999). Trauma-induced dissociative amnesia in World War I combat soldiers. *Australian and New Zealand Journal of Psychiatry, 33,* 37–46.

Van der Hart, O., Nijenhuis, E. R. S., & Brown, P. (2001). Loss and recovery of different memory types in generalized dissociative amnesia. *Australian and New Zealand Journal of Psychiatry, 35,* 589–600.

Van der Hart, O., Nijenhuis, E. R. S., & Steele, K. (2006). *The haunted self: Structural dissociation and the treatment of chronic traumatization.* New York: Norton.

Van der Hart, O., Nijenhuis, E. R. S., Steele, K., & Brown, D. (2004). Trauma-related dissociation: Conceptual clarity lost and found. *Australian and New Zealand Journal of Psychiatry, 38,* 906–914.

Van der Kolk, B. A., & Fisler, R. (1995). Dissociation and the fragmentary nature of traumatic memories: Overview and exploratory study. *Journal of Traumatic Stress, 8,* 505–525.

Van der Kolk, B. A., & Van der Hart, O. (1991). The intrusive past: The flexibility of memory and the engraving of trauma. *American Imago, 48,* 425–454.

Vanderlinden, J., Van Dyck, R., Vandereycken, W., & Vertommen, H. (1993). Dissociation and traumatic experiences in the general population of The Netherlands. *Hospital and Community Psychiatry, 44,* 786–788.

Van IJzendoorn, M. H., Schuengel, C., & Bakersman-Kranenburg, M. (1999). Disorganized attachment in early childhood: Meta-analysis of precursors, concomitants, and sequelae. *Development & Psychopathology, 11,* 225–249.

Viken, R. J., Rose, R. J., Kaprio, J., & Kowkenvuo, M. (1994). A developmental genetic analysis of adult personality extraversion and neuroticism from 18 to 59 years of age. *Journal of Personality and Social Psychology, 47,* 127–144.

Vizek-Vidovic, V., Kuterovac-Jagodic, G., & Arambasic, L. (2000). Posttraumatic symptomatology in children exposed to war. *Scandinavian Journal of Psychology, 41,* 297–306.

Waddington, C. H. (1959). Canalization of development and the inheritance of acquired characters. *Nature, 183,* 1654–1655.

Waller, G., Hamilton, K., Elliott, P., Lewendon, J., Stopa, L. Waters, A., Kennedy, F., Chalkley, J., F., Lee, G., Pearson, D., Kennerley, H., Hargreaves, I., & Bashford, V. (2000). Somatoform dissociation, psychological dissociation and specific forms of trauma. *Journal of Trauma and Dissociation, 1,* 81–98.

Wicker, B., Keysers, C., Plailly, J., Royet, J. P., Gallese, V., & Rizzolatti, G. (2003). Both of us disgusted in My insula: the common neural basis of seeing and feeling disgust. *Neuron 40,* 655–664.

Wolff, C. T., Friedman, S. B., Hofer, M. A., & Mason, J. W. (1964). Relationship between psychological defenses and mean urinary 17-OHCS excretion rates: A predictive study of parents of fatally ill children. *Psychosomatic Medicine, 26,* 576–591.

22 Neurobiology of Depersonalization Disorder

Daphne Simeon, MD

OUTLINE

This chapter presents a critical review of what is currently known about the neurobiology of depersonalization disorder. We will present all relevant studies in organized subsections, and conclude with a discussion of what the neurobiological findings to date tell us about the taxonomy of Depersonalization Disorder (DPD) as a dissociative disorder. This chapter is partly based on an article entitled "Depersonalization disorder: a contemporary overview" (Simeon, 2004).

22.1 NEUROCHEMISTRY OF DEPERSONALIZATION

Several neurotransmitter systems have been implicated in DPD, although evidence for each is scant and partly indirect. The four classes of chemicals consistently implicated in inducing depersonalization in healthy subjects are NMDA antagonists, cannabinoids, hallucinogens, and opioid agonists. Below we examine each of these:

1. The NMDA antagonist ketamine, also known as the "dissociative anesthetic" and as the street drug, "Special K," induces a profound dissociative state in healthy subjects that has been likened to the negative symptoms of schizophrenia (Curran & Morgan, 2000). The dissociative, but not the psychotogenic, effects of ketamine can be blocked in normal subjects by pretreatment with the medication lamotrigine (Anand et al., 2000). Lamotrigine has been speculated to attenuate ketamine-induced dissociation by inhibiting the release of the excitatory neurotransmitter glutamate (glutamate is an agonist at NMDA and non-NMDA glutamate receptors). NMDA receptors are widely distributed in the cortex, and well as in the hippocampus and the amygdala, and are thought to mediate associative functioning and long-term potentiation of memory, facilitating new learning. It is thus plausible to imagine how diminished NMDA-related neurotransmission may be related to dissociative states.
2. Cannabinoids, such as marijuana, have been consistently shown to induce depersonalization, with a pronounced component of temporal disintegration, in both naturalistic and experimental paradigms in healthy subjects. In addition to their action at the cannabinoid CB receptors, whose natural function is largely unknown, cannabinoids have been shown to block NMDA receptors at sites distinct from other noncompetitive NMDA antagonists (Feigenbaum et al., 1989). Thus, their dissociative effect might in fact be mediated via the NMDA receptor. There are case reports in the literature of the inducement of chronic depersonalization by sporadic cannabis ingestion (Szymanski, 1981; Keshaven & Lishman, 1986). In our series of 117 DPD subjects studied to date, about 13% reported the acute triggering of chronic depersonalization by marijuana smoking (Simeon et al., 2003).

3. Depersonalization states in normal subjects are also transiently induced by the use of hallucinogens, such as LSD, psilocybin, and DMT, in both naturalistic and experimental settings. In our series of 117 DPD subjects, 6% reported the induction of chronic depersonalization by acute hallucinogen use (Simeon et al., 2003). These substances are believed to act as agonists of serotonin 5HT2A and 5HT2C receptors, suggesting a possible mediating role for serotonin in depersonalization. Such a relationship is indirectly and anecdotally supported by the prominent obsessional phenomenology in at least a subgroup of DPD patients. Neurochemical challenge studies with the 5HT2C agonist m-CPP have demonstrated the induction of depersonalization in subjects of various diagnoses such as social phobia, borderline personality disorder, and obsessive compulsive disorder (Simeon et al., 1995), as well as the induction of flashbacks and dissociative symptoms in a subgroup of patients with PTSD (Southwick et al., 1997).
4. Stress-induced analgesia is known to be mediated by the endogenous opioid system (EOS) (Madden et al., 1977), and the PTSD analgesic response to combat stimuli can be blocked by pretreatment with the opioid antagonist naloxone (Pitman et al., 1990). The kappa opioid agonist, enadoline, induces a depersonalization-like syndrome in healthy subjects compared to placebo, with perceptual disturbances and a sense of detachment (Walsh et al., 2001). Along these lines, opiate antagonists have been reported to reduce dissociation, such as high-dose naltrexone in borderline personality disorder (Bohus et al., 1999), and intravenous naloxone in chronic depersonalization (Nuller et al., 2001). The opioid antagonist nalmefene has been reported to decrease emotional numbing in veterans with PTSD (Glover, 1993). Selective kappa opioid antagonists have not yet been developed for human use.

22.2 AUTONOMIC SYSTEM AND NOREPINEPHRINE IN DEPERSONALIZATION

The autonomic system is also of particular interest in dissociation. While there is extensive evidence for autonomic hyperreactivity in PTSD, there is some evidence for autonomic blunting in dissociation, such as the finding of decreased heart rate and galvanic skin response in women who were raped with high dissociation (Griffin et al., 1997). Specifically in DPD, there is compelling evidence for autonomic blunting. Sierra et al. (2002) showed that compared to subjects with anxiety disorders and healthy controls, DPD subjects exhibited reduced magnitude and increased latency of skin conductance response to unpleasant emotional stimuli, but not to nonspecific startle stimuli, suggesting a selective inhibition of emotional processing in the presence of intact arousal. Similarly, Giesbrecht and Simeon (personal communication) found that in response to a highly emotionally frightening video, SCR in DPD participants peaked faster than normals and subsequently flattened out.

Norepinephrine is a neurotransmitter central to facilitating alertness, selective attention, and enhanced memory encoding under stress (Southwick et al., 1999). In a preliminary report, 24-hour urine norepinephrine was found to be strongly inversely correlated ($r = -0.88$) to depersonalization severity in nine subjects with DPD (Simeon et al., 2001). Supporting this latter finding is a similar one in a study of peritraumatic dissociation after motor vehicle accidents, in which urinary norepinephrine in the immediate aftermath of the trauma was found to be significantly inversely correlated to dissociation severity (Delahanty et al., 2003).

22.3 THE HYPOTHALAMIC-PITUITARY-ADRENAL AXIS IN DEPERSONALIZATION

The hypothalamic-pituitary-adrenal (HPA) axis is known to play a central role in mediating the stress response, and there is extensive evidence for its sensitization in PTSD (Yehuda, 1997). The HPA axis has been preliminarily investigated in DPD, and the results of the two studies reported to date are conflicting. One study reported nonsignificantly lower basal salivary cortisol in DPD patients compared to healthy controls and significantly lower basal salivary cortisol in DPD patients compared to those with major depression—however, conditions of sleep, eating, and activity were not controlled in this study (Stanton et al., 2001). In contrast, another study of the HPA axis in DPD compared to healthy controls under highly standardized inpatient conditions found a tendency for elevated basal urinary and plasma cortisol in DPD compared to controls, with a highly statistically significant resistance to low-dose dexamethasone suppression, suggesting diminished HPA axis sensitivity (Simeon et al., 2001). In a recent replication in a much larger sample, Simeon and colleagues (2007) demonstrated a unique cortisol profile in DPD, compared to PTSD and healthy volunteers. The DPD group had higher cortisol levels at baseline, and increased resistance to low-dose dexamethasone challenge; in both the PTSD and DPD group, dissociation severity was significantly inversely correlated with cortisol reactivity to psychosocial stress. Of importance, individuals with comorbid current major depression were excluded from the study, and the findings in the DPD group persisted irrespective of lifetime major depression.

22.4 BRAIN CIRCUITRY IN DEPERSONALIZATION

The brain circuitry that underlies depersonalization is also of great interest, and a few hypotheses figure most prominently in the literature. As far back as 1950, Penfield and Rasmussen (1950) described "queer sensations of not being present and floating away, … far off and out of this world" with stimulation of the superior and middle temporal gyrus. They postulated that these "illusions of unfamiliarity, strangeness and remoteness" involved an "alteration in the usual mechanism of comparison of immediate sensory perceptions with memory records," and claimed that these perceptual illusions could be produced by cortical stimulation "only in the temporal region, perhaps extending somewhat into the occipital cortex."

Sierra and Berrios (1998) put forth the "corticolimbic disconnection hypothesis." This model was theoretically extrapolated from experiential narratives of depersonalized subjects, the neurologic literature, and cognitive neuroscience. It proposed bilateral corticolimbic disconnection with prefrontal activation and limbic inhibition, resulting in hypoemotionality (via amygdalar inhibition) as well as attentional difficulties (via cingulate inhibition). Along the same lines, Sierra et al. (2002) proposed two distinct components of the depersonalization experience subsumed by distinct neurocircuitry: "visual derealization" associated with occipito-temporal dysfunction, and "body alienation" associated with parietal dysfunction. Lambert et al. (2002) highlighted the organic etiologies that sometimes underlie chronic depersonalization and proposed consideration of an "organic" subtype of the condition.

John Krystal (1998) has proposed that the integration of various cortical areas may be necessary for cohesive conscious experience, and that this corticocortical connectivity may be NMDA-receptor-mediated and therefore blocked by ketamine. Therefore, dissociation may involve disruption of corticocortical, thalamocortical, amygdalocortical, and hippocampocortical connectivity.

These models are clearly not mutually exclusive, but rather build on and expand upon one another in offering brain function models for conceptualizing depersonalization. From an evolutionary perspective, acute depersonalization precipitated by severe or life-threatening stress may be viewed as adaptive, allowing the individual emotional distance and detachment from circumstances that might otherwise be overwhelming, so that steps appropriate to survival can be taken. However, chronic depersonalization symptoms that become autonomous of the original stressful triggers are clearly maladaptive, and suggest dysregulated brain functioning that has failed to reestablish homeostasis.

The actual evidence for the above brain circuitry models in DPD is limited but definitely present. Certainly the neurological literature, when reviewed, is helpful in providing evidence for brain areas that may mediate neurologic syndromes that are at least phenomenologically similar to depersonalization, such as neglect and asomatognosia[1] syndromes. These all coalesce in suggesting a unique role for the inferior parietal lobule and other transmodal sensory cortical areas in mediating depersonalization-like experiences:

1. Depersonalization is common in seizure patients, especially in temporal lobe epilepsy with left-sided foci (Devinsky et al., 1989).
2. Inferior parietal and angular gyrus tumors can manifest with depersonalization symptoms (Ackner, 1954).
3. Structural lesions underlying "neglect" syndromes have been found to be concentrated in the right inferior parietal lobule (Vallar & Perani, 1986).
4. In 82 patients with parietal lobe epilepsy, frequent somatosensory aurae, disturbances of body image, vertiginous sensations, and visual illusions were reported (Salanova et al., 1988).
5. In a study of the visual recognition of emotion of 108 subjects with focal brain lesions, the right somatosensory-related cortex was found to play a critical role, especially the supramarginal gyrus and somatosensory cortex S1 (Adolphs et al., 2000).

[1] Lack of awareness of all or part of one's own body (a = not; soma = body; gnosis = knowledge).

6. Studies of visual familiarity have found that unfamiliar faces activate unimodal visual association areas, whereas familiar (famous) faces activate transmodal areas, specifically the middle temporal gyrus BA21 and angular gyrus BA39 (Tempini et al., 1998).
7. Out-of-body experiences in one patient with refractory epilepsy were induced, for the first time, by direct focal stimulation of the right angular gyrus (Blanke et al., 2002).

A very limited number of studies in healthy volunteers have addressed the induction of depersonalization symptoms. A PET study using IV tetrahydrocannabinol (marijuana) found that cerebral blood flow increase in the right frontal and anterior cingulate correlated with depersonalization severity, while there was subcortical CBF decrease in amygdala, hippocampus, basal ganglia, and thalamus (Mathew et al., 1999). A PET imaging study with the hallucinogenic 5HT1A/2A agonist psilocybin resulted in increased dopamine in striatum that correlated with depersonalization severity, but there was also prominent mood and psychotic symptom induction (Vollenweider et al., 1999). Finally, an FDG-PET study using high-dose amphetamine found increased metabolism in the anterior cingulate, striatum, and thalamus; however, mania was more prominent than depersonalization in these subjects (Vollenweider et al., 1998). It can readily be seen that the findings of these three studies are partly in accord and partly contradictory of the three models previously outlined.

In thinking then about the neurobiological underpinnings of depersonalization, identifying its core feature is a helpful approach. The subjective sense of unfamiliarity is central to the depersonalization experience. That is, if an incoming perception is not processed as familiar, it will be experienced as unreal, strange, detached, or unemotional. Therefore depersonalization may be characterized by key disturbances in areas of the brain responsible for matching incoming sensory information to preexisting memory networks of these percepts, involving both limbic structures and sensory association cortical areas.

There are a few recent imaging studies in subjects suffering from dissociation. Lanius et al. (2002) studied women with PTSD secondary to childhood sexual abuse, using fMRI with traumatic script-driven imagery. Of the PTSD subjects, about 70% responded to the scripts with reliving, arousal and increased heart rate, while 30% dissociated in response to the scripts. In the latter group, compared to a normal control group, the dissociative state was associated with increased activation in the medial prefrontal cortex (BA 9,10) and inferior frontal gyrus (BA 47), the anterior cingulate (BA 24 and 32), the superior and middle temporal gyri (BA 38), the parietal lobe (BA 7), and the occipital lobe (BA 19). Interestingly, this pattern of activation was distinctly different from that found in the PTSD with reliving subgroup, but similar to that of two imaging studies in DPD described in the following.

In an fMRI study by Phillips et al. (2001), three groups were compared (DPD, OCD, and normals) in their responses to neutral and aversive visual stimuli. DPD patients rated the aversive pictures as less emotive than OCD and NC patients. Also, DPD patients, in response to the aversive pictures, did not activate the insula (part of the limbic system that is the center for disgust) and showed heightened activation in the right ventral prefrontal cortex. These findings suggested a neural mechanism for emotional detachment that is mediated by prefrontal activation and limbic inhibition.

In a PET study of DPD, 8 DPD patients and 24 age- and sex-matched healthy controls were compared, using a semantic memory task (CVLT) during the 18F-deoxyglucose uptake as a control for mental activity (Simeon et al., 2000). PET scans were coregistered with MRI scans, and there were no differences between the two groups on a brief baseline neuropsychological battery and on the CVLT. The DPD group exhibited stronger left-sided laterality. Analyses by individual Brodmann areas were performed for six brain regions: prefrontal, precentral, cingulate, temporal, parietal, and occipital. The DPD group had significantly different overall patterns of activity in the posterior cortex (temporal, parietal, and occipital lobes). Post-hoc analyses of these areas revealed that the DPD group had significantly lower activity in right temporal BA 22 and 21, higher activity in parietal BA 7B and 39, and higher activity in left occipital BA 19. Dissociation scores were very strongly correlated with BA 7B activity ($r = 0.84$, $df = 6$, $p = 0.008$). Interestingly, all of these areas of dysfunction are components of the sensory cortex. Brodmann area 22 is an auditory association area, area 19 is a visual association area responsible for visual integration and depth perception, and area 7B is a somatosensory association area responsible for somatosensory integration. Finally, Area 39 (the angular gyrus) is a multimodal associative area in the inferior parietal lobule, strategically situated to receive sensory input from the parietal, temporal, and occipital cortex, and is central to a well-integrated body schema. This study then suggests that depersonalization may be related to disruptions in functioning along hierarchical sensory association areas, unimodal and cross-modal, responsible for the processing of incoming perceptions against preexisting brain templates. Interestingly, work in healthy volunteers as well has implicated the inferior parietal lobule (BA39 and 40) as the "seat" of out-of-body experiences (Blanke et al., 2005).

22.5 SUMMARY OF NEUROBIOLOGICAL FINDINGS IN DEPERSONALIZATION

In summary then, the following preliminary statements can be made about the still largely unknown neurobiology of DPD:

- NMDA, 5-HT2A/5HT2C, and endogenous opioid receptors may be implicated.
- *Autonomic blunting* may be present, as evidenced by psychophysiologic and noradrenergic measures.
- *HPA axis dysregulation* may be present, characterized by baseline heightened activity yet blunted reactivity to stress.
- *Disruptions in sensory cortex associative functioning* may mediate the perceptual disturbances (somatosensory, visual, auditory) and sense of "unfamiliarity" characteristic of DPD.
- *Frontal inhibition of limbic structures* may mediate the hypoemotionality characteristic of DPD.

22.6 CONCLUSIONS REGARDING THE NEUROBIOLOGY OF DEPERSONALIZATION

The findings presented in this chapter, although still not as extensive as those reported in other psychiatric disorders, still delineate a unique neurobiological profile for chronic depersonalization, supporting its conceptualization as a unique psychiatric disorder. Neurochemically, there is evidence for NMDA system dysregulation, possibly central to the disorder, also modulated by serotonergic, endogenous opioid, and cannabinoid dysfunction. There is also evidence of association sensory cortex dysfunction, prefrontal hyperactivity, and limbic inhibition. These patterns are clearly unique from those elaborated, to date, for major depression, posttraumatic stress disorder, and for anxiety disorders such as panic disorder, generalized anxiety disorder, or OCD. They support a unique emerging neurobiology of DPD that will hopefully remain the subject of fruitful investigation.

REFERENCES

Ackner, B. (1954). Depersonalization. I: Etiology and phenomenology. II. Clinical syndromes. *Journal of Mental Science, 100,* 838–872.

Adolphs, R., Damasio, H., Tranel, D., et al. (2000). A role for somatosensory cortices in the visual recognition of emotion as revealed by three-dimensional lesion mapping. *Journal of Neuroscience, 20,* 2683–2690.

Anand, A., Charney, D., Oren, D., et al. (2000). Attenuation of the neuropsychiatric effects of ketamine with lamotrigine: support for hyperglutamatergic effects of N-methyl-D-aspartate receptor antagonists. *Archives of General Psychiatry, 57,* 270–276.

Blanke, O., Ortigue, S., Landis, T., & Seeck, M. (2002). Stimulating illusory own-body perceptions. *Nature, 419,* 269–270.

Blanke, O., Mohr, C., Michel, C. M., et al. (2005). Linking out-of-body experience to mental own-body imagery and the temporoparietal junction. *Journal of Neuroscience, 25,* 550–557.

Bohus, M. J., Landwehrmeyer, G. B., Stiglmayr, C. E., Limberger, M. F., Boehme, R., & Schmahl, C. G. (1999). Naltrexone in the treatment of dissociative symptoms in patients with borderline personality disorder: An open-label trial. *Journal of Clinical Psychiatry, 60,* 598–603.

Curran, H. V., & Morgan, C. (2000). Cognitive, dissociative, and psychotogenic effects of ketamine in recreational users on the night of drug use and 3 days later. *Addiction, 95,* 575–590.

Delahanty, D. L., Royer, D. K., Raimonde, A. J., & Spoonster, E. (2003). Peritraumatic dissociation is inversely related to catecholamine levels in initial urine samples of motor vehicle accident victims. *Journal of Trauma and Dissociation, 4(1),* 65–79.

Devinsky, O., Putnam, F., Grafman, J., et al. (1989). Dissociative states and epilepsy. *Neurology, 39,* 835–840.

Feigenbaum, J. J., Bergmann, F., Richmond, S. A., et al. (1989). Nonpsychotropic cannabinoid acts as a functional N-methyl-D-aspartate receptor blocker. *Proceedings of the National Academy of Sciences USA, 63,* 9584–9587.

Glover, H. (1993). A preliminary trial of nalmefene for the treatment of emotional numbing in combat veterans with posttraumatic stress disorder. *Israel Journal of Psychiatry & Related Sciences, 30,* 255–263.

Griffin, M. G., Resick, P. A., & Mechanic, M. B. (1997). Objective assessment of peritraumatic dissociation: Psychophysiological indicators. *American Journal of Psychiatry, 154,* 1081–1088.

Keshaven, M. S., & Lishman, W. A. (1986). Prolonged depersonalization following cannabis abuse. *British Journal of Addiction, 81,* 140–142.

Krystal, J., Bremner, D., Southwick, S. M., & Charney, D. S. (1998). The emerging neurobiology of dissociation: implications for the treatment of posttraumatic stress disorder. In J. D. Bremner, C. R. Marmar (Eds.), *Trauma, memory, and dissociation.* Washington, DC: American Psychiatric Press Inc.

Lambert, M. V., Sierra, M., Phillips, M. L., & David, A. S. (2002). The spectrum of organic depersonalization. A review plus four new cases. *Journal of Neuropsychiatry and Clinical Neuroscience, 14*, 141–154.

Lanius, R. A., Williamson, P. C., Boksman, K., et al. (2002). Brain activation during script-driven imagery induced dissociative responses in PTSD: A functional magnetic resonance imaging investigation. *Biological Psychiatry, 52*, 305–311.

Madden, J., Akil, H., Patrick, R. L., et al. (1977). Stress-induced parallel changes in central opioid levels and pain responsiveness in the rat. *Nature, 265*, 358–360.

Mathew, R. J., Wilson, W. H., Chiu, N. Y., et al. (1999). Regional cerebral blood flow and depersonalization after tetrahydrocannibol administration. *Acta Psychiatrica Scandinavica, 100*, 67–75.

Nuller, Y. L., Morozova, M. G., Kushnir, O. N., et al. (2001). Effect of naloxone therapy on depersonalization: A pilot study. *Journal of Psychopharmacology, 15*, 93–95.

Penfield, W., & Rasmussen, T. (1950). *The cerebral cortex of man: A clinical study of localization of function*. New York: MacMillan Company, 157–181.

Phillips, M. L., Medford, N., Senior, C., et al. (2001). Depersonalization disorder: Thinking without feeling. *Psychiatry Research: Neuroimaging, 108*, 145–160.

Pitman, R. K., Van der Kolk, B. A., Orr, S. P., et al. (1990). Naloxone-reversible analgesic response to combat-related stimuli in posttraumatic stress disorder: A pilot study. *Archives of General Psychiatry, 47*, 541–544.

Salanova, V., Andermann, F., Rasmussen, T., et al. (1995). Parietal lobe epilepsy: Clinical manifestations and outcome in 82 patients treated surgically between 1929 and 1988. *Brain, 118*, 607–627.

Sierra, M., Senior, C., Dalton, J., et al. (2002). Autonomic response in depersonalization disorder. *Archives of General Psychiatry, 59*, 833–838.

Sierra, M., & Berrios, G. E. (1998). Depersonalization: neurobiological perspectives. *Biological Psychiatry, 44*, 898–908.

Sierra, M., Lopera, F., Lambert, M. V., Phillips, M. L., & David, A. S. (2002). Separating depersonalization and derealisation: the relevance of the "lesion" method. *Journal of Neurology, Neurosurgery and Psychiatry, 72*, 530–532.

Simeon, D., Guralnik, O., Hazlett, E. A., et al. (2000). Feeling Unreal: A PET Study of Depersonalization Disorder. *American Journal of Psychiatry, 157*, 1782–1788.

Simeon, D. (2004). Depersonalization disorder: a contemporary overview. *CNS Drugs, 18*, 343–354.

Simeon, D., Knutelska, M., Nelson, D., & Guralnik, O. (2003). Feeling unreal: a depersonalization disorder update of 117 cases. *Journal of Clinical Psychiatry, 64*, 990–997.

Simeon, D., Guralnik, O., Knutelska, M., et al. (2001). Hypothalamic-pituitary-adrenal axis dysregulation in depersonalization disorder. *Neuropsychopharmacology, 25*, 793–795.

Simeon, D., Knutelska, M., Yehuda, R., et al. (2007). Hypothalamic-pituitary-adrenal axis function in dissociative disorders, PTSD, and healthy volunteers. *Biological Psychiatry, 61*, 966–973.

Simeon, D., Hollander, E., Stein, D. J., et al. (1995). Induction of depersonalization by the serotonin agonist meta-chlorophenylpiperazine. *Psychiatry Research, 58*, 161–164.

Southwick, S. M., Krystal, J. H., Bremner, J. D., et al. (1997). Noradrenergic and serotonergic function in posttraumatic stress disorder. *Archives of General Psychiatry, 54*, 749–758.

Southwick, S. M., Bremner, J. D., Rasmusson, A., et al. (1999). Role of norepinephrine in the pathophysiology and treatment of posttraumatic stress disorder. *Biological Psychiatry, 46*, 1192–1204.

Stanton, B. R., David, A. S., Cleare, A. J., et al. (2001). Basal activity of the hypothalamic-pituitary-adrenal axis in patients with depersonalization disorder. *Psychiatry Research, 104*, 85–89.

Szymanski, H. V. (1981). Prolonged depersonalization after marijuana use. *American Journal of Psychiatry, 138*, 231–233.

Tempini, M. L., Gorno Price, C. J., Josephs, O., et al. (1998). The neural systems sustaining face and proper-name processing. *Brain, 121*, 2103–2118.

Vallar, G., & Perani, D. (1986). The anatomy of unilateral neglect after right-hemisphere stroke lesions: A clinical/CT-scan correlation study in man. *Neuropsychologia, 24*, 609–622.

Vollenweider, F. X., Vontobek, P., Hell, D., et al. (1999). 5-HT modulation of dopamine release in basal ganglia in psilocybin-induced psychosis in man – a PET study with [11C] raclopride. *Neuropsychopharmacology, 20*, 424–433.

Vollenweider, F. X., Maguire, R. P., Leenders, K. L., et al. (1998). Effects of high amphetamine dose on mood and cerebral glucose metabolism in normal volunteers using positron emission tomography (PET). *Psychiatry Res Neuroimaging, 83*, 149–162.

Walsh, S. L., Geter-Douglas, B., Strain, E. C., et al. (2001). Enadoline and butorphanol: Evaluation of kappa-agonists on cocaine pharmacodynamics and cocaine self-administration in humans. *Journal of Pharmacology & Experimental Therapeutics, 299*, 147–158.

Yehuda, R. (1997). Sensitization of the hypothalamic-pituitary-adrenal axis in posttraumatic stress disorder. *Annals of the NY Academy of Science, 821*, 57–75.

23 Dissociation in Patients With Chronic PTSD: Hyperactivation and Hypoactivation Patterns, Clinical and Neuroimaging Perspectives

Clare Pain, MD, FRCPC
Robyn L. Bluhm, PhD
Ruth A. Lanius, MD, PhD, FRCPC

OUTLINE

23.1 DISSOCIATION AND TRAUMATIC MEMORIES

The immutability of traumatic memories has been discussed in the literature from the time of Janet, as has their tendency to consist of emotional and perceptual, rather than declarative or narrative components. Bessel van der Kolk has emphasized that "the imprints of traumatic experiences seem to be qualitatively different from memories of ordinary events" (Van der Kolk et al., 1996). These clinical observations have prompted speculation that the encoding of experiences of traumatic events into memory may be different from that of nontraumatic events, possibly due to stress-induced alterations in hippocampal memory functions (Pitman et al., 1993; Van der Kolk, 1994). Only recently, however, have neuroimaging techniques been developed that allow investigators to see the functional alterations that are associated with the memory of traumatic events. There is now a substantial literature on the neural pathways associated with the recall of traumatic memories in patients with Posttraumatic Stress Disorder (PTSD). This chapter examines the nature of dissociative reactions to traumatic memory in chronic PTSD (i.e., PTSD that has existed for 3 months or more), a topic that has been underemphasized in both the clinical and neuroimaging literature. Until recently, research has focused on the particularly vivid sensory qualities of traumatic memories and their capacity to provoke emotional arousal and subjective distress. In the trauma literature, discussion of dissociative reactions has largely been confined to articles on peritraumatic phenomena.

Classical views of dissociation tend to conflate (1) the dissociation of hyperarousal with reexperiencing phenomena and the accompanying highly distressed emotional experience and (2) the hypoarousal states of dissociation where the self is subjectively experienced as separate or distanced from the emotional distress. The latter is more commonly associated with the term *dissociation*; while the former (although also a dissociative phenomenon) is more commonly associated with PTSD.

This chapter will begin by exploring the concept of dissociation more thoroughly. We differentiate two major patterns of dissociation within PTSD: hyperarousal and hypoarousal states. Following the nomenclature of Van der Kolk et al. (1996) we consider hyperarousal states to be primary and hypoarousal states to be secondary dissociation. We propose that these two dissociative states can be distinguished not only subjectively, but also physiologically and in terms of neural activation patterns. While most work in neuroimaging has been focused on hyperarousal states in PTSD in response to symptom provocation studies, some recent literature supports and extends clinical reports of hypoarousal or secondary dissociative responses in PTSD patients.

In addition to these two major patterns, the word *dissociation* has been used to convey a number of different meanings over the past few decades. Dissociation has been described as a process, as a variety of symptom, as a mental structure, as a psychological defense, and as a deficit in integrative capacity (Nijenhuis et al., 2002). The DSM-IV defines dissociation as "a disruption in the usual integrated functions of consciousness, memory, identity or perception of the environment; the disturbance may be sudden or gradual, transient or chronic" (APA, 1994). Dissociation has been shown to be etiologically connected to psychological trauma (Boon & Draijer, 1993; Coons, 1994; Kluft, 1995; Lewis et al., 1997; Nijenhuis et al., 1998). It has been suggested (Allen, 2001; Van der Kolk et al., 1996) that trauma elicits dissociation, promoting a discontinuity between conscious experience and memory. In this context, the word *dissociation* refers to secondary dissociation or hypoarousal states. We distinguish two broad components of dissociative hypoarousal: (1) subjective detachment from the overwhelming emotional content of the experience, and (2) compartmentalization or separation of the experience from general awareness (Allen, 2001). As a result, the traumatic experience does not become part of a unitary whole or of an integrated sense of self. Several authors (see Bremner & Southwick, 1992; Butler et al., 1996; Nijenhuis et al., 2002; Spiegel, 1997) see this disruption as serving a protective function in the face of an acute stressor (i.e., in peritraumatic dissociation) or as a routine mode of coping with a predictably chronically traumatic environment or the memory of this.

As a defensive splitting of consciousness, dissociation results in alterations in perception, emotion, cognition, and behavior. Because these alterations give rise to multiple subjective experiences or symptoms, it is difficult to see how such a disparate group of symptoms can be usefully conceptualized as protective defenses. It is also difficult to see how important differences between these phenomena can be identified. For instance, perceptual alterations may occur in the experience of time (e.g., flashbacks), in self-experience (e.g., depersonalization), and in the perception of reality (e.g., derealization). Similarly, cognitive abnormalities can include amnesia, fugue states, confusional states, and deficits in attention. Somatic changes, sensory, motor, and behavioral, can involve sensory distortions, motor weakness, paralysis, ataxia, tremors, shaking, and convulsions.

Nevertheless, our clinical observations and those of others (Sierra & Berrios, 1998; Van der Hart et al., 1998; Van der Kolk et al., 1996) support the idea that secondary dissociation reduces acute emotional distress by promoting a subjective sense of distance from present events. This effect is most evident when patients with PTSD suddenly shift from states of overwhelming emotional and physiological hyperarousal to states of hypoarousal, characterized by numbness, detachment, resignation, and distance from their emotions. Although significant suffering is still connected with the state of hypoarousal, it may support the psychological capacity to endure inescapable danger by alleviating the overwhelming emotional experience and the concurrent high physiological responses of the sympathetic nervous system. However, it is more difficult to find the defensive or protective function of hyperarousal (i.e., reexperiencing and flashbacks). Somewhat paradoxically primary dissociative experiences like reexperiencing and flashbacks may fail to be desensitized or accommodated to if secondary dissociation is pervasive. This is because secondary dissociation seems to interfere with integration of the traumatic information; and therefore the highly arousing states of somatosensory experience remain unintegrated. Accordingly, they are susceptible to being triggered by environmental reminders.

Secondary dissociation has not been featured prominently in the PTSD literature; when mentioned, secondary dissociation tends to be described as *peritraumatic dissociation* (Marmar et al., 1994). The diagnostic criteria for acute stress disorder (ASD) include dissociative symptoms at or around the time of the traumatic event. Some contend that peritraumatic dissociation predicts the development of PTSD (Birmes et al., 2003; Ozer et al., 2003; Spiegel 1997), but this is controversial (Panasetis & Bryant, 2003). Although dissociative symptoms at the time of a car accident do not predict PTSD, their persistence for 10 days does (McFarlane, 1997). This implies that persisting dissociation may prevent resolution of the effects of the traumatic event.

The three symptom-clusters of PTSD (American Psychiatric Association, 1994) are characterized by two distinct states: (1) hyperarousal and (2) hypoarousal.

The hyperaroused state is typified by the fragmentation of perceptual experience into emotional or sensory elements: "the most dramatic symptoms are expressions of dissociated traumatic memories—intensely upsetting intrusive recollections, nightmares, and flashbacks" (Van der Kolk et al., 1996, p. 307). Flashbacks are often described as being "dissociative" because the person is estranged from present reality, believing and acting as if the past event were happening again. Flashbacks are associated with high-arousal states, rapid heart rate, elevated blood pressure, altered skin conductance, and subjective reports of fear and panic (Lanius et al., 2006). Van der Kolk et al. (1996) calls this hyperarousal *primary dissociation*, noting that it can occur both at the time of the initial traumatic event, which is not experienced as a cohesive whole, and also when the memory of that experience is triggered subsequently in patients with PTSD. For these patients, the traumatic memory is "timeless"; it retains its fragmented, sensory character and does not undergo conversion to a narrative, declarative form. PTSD patients are often unable to give a coherent narrative account of their traumatic experience; the memory retains its initial intensity as well as its intrusive and uncontrollable nature. Spiegel (1997) argues that PTSD involves a reduction in the ability of specific brain systems to facilitate integration, modulate affect, and synthesize information (across sensory modalities and between images and lexical processing). In the next section we will review the neuroimaging literature in chronic PTSD that may provide support for Spiegel's view.

23.2 SYMPTOM PROVOCATION NEUROIMAGING STUDIES IN PTSD

Over the past half-dozen years, a number of neuroimaging symptom-provocation studies of PTSD have been published. Most of these studies focused on patients who experienced a hyperarousal/reliving response to symptom-provocation. In these patients, the response to reminders of a traumatic experience included emotional and autonomic arousal: the memories were often more vivid, with stronger sensory features than ordinary memories. This response resembles primary dissociation. In its most extreme form, this response includes full-blown flashbacks, during which the subject feels she or he is fully reexperiencing the event (at the cost of not being fully grounded in the present).

A small but significant percentage of patients, however, respond to exposure to relevant traumatic cues in ways that are characteristic of *secondary* dissociation (Lanius et al., 2002). These patients report feelings of leaving their body or of experiencing their traumatic memory "at a distance." This subjective response to script-driven imagery is also associated with patterns of neural activity that are distinct from those associated with the "hyperarousal" response.

As mentioned, most symptom-provocation studies have concentrated on patients who exhibited a hyperarousal response to trauma cues. In fact, some of these studies (Bremner et al., 1999b; Pissiota et al., 2002; Rauch et al., 1996; Shin et al., 1999) included *only* those patients that demonstrated physiological reactivity (e.g., increased heart rate) and subjective arousal in response to the proposed traumatic stimulus; this presumably means that patients who had secondary dissociation responses to their trauma script (i.e., who responded with the same or lowered heart rates) were excluded from these studies. In other studies, subjects were assigned to the "hyperarousal" group or the "hypoarousal group" on the basis of their reactivity during the scanning procedure (Lanius et al., 2001; Lanius et al., 2004b).

Symptom-provocation studies have used visual or auditory cues as reminders of the trauma. These cues may be "impersonal" pictures or sounds, or personalized scripts of a particular traumatic memory. A neutral condition (pictures/sounds/script) is usually included as well. It is not clear whether the differences in trauma-related cues account for any of the differences in activation patterns across studies. Other sources of variation include imaging technique (PET, SPECT, fMRI) and subject variables such as comorbidity, chronicity of illness, and so on.

Despite these variations, the following studies reported changes in neural activation that are associated with the hyperarousal response in PTSD.

23.2.1 Trauma Pictures and Sounds

The following three studies used trauma pictures and sounds to elicit a hyperarousal response in chronic PTSD subjects.

In a Positron Emission Tomography (PET) study, Bremner et al. (1999b) compared the responses of 10 Vietnam veterans with PTSD to combat-related pictures and sounds with those of 10 veterans with combat exposure, but no PTSD. All subjects had previously been screened to ensure their physiological and emotional reactivity. During the PET scanning session, PTSD patients reported significantly more fear, anxiety, and subjective distress than did controls in response to the trauma stimuli. On the other hand, neither group manifested a significant difference in heart rate in response to the traumatic stimuli (compared to baseline rates). Significant differences in PET blood flow were observed between groups. PTSD patients showed a significant decrease in blood flow to the medial prefrontal cortex (Broadman Area [BA] 25) and the medial temporal gyrus. Controls showed greater activation of the right anterior cingulate gyrus (BA 24) than did the PTSD group.

Pissiota et al. (2002) conducted a similar but uncontrolled PET study with patients who had combat-related PTSD. They were previously screened for heart-rate and emotional reactivity to the trauma-related stimuli. Increases in regional cerebral blood flow (rCBF) were seen in the right sensorimotor cortex (BA 4, 6), right somatosensory cortex (BA 1, 2, 3), the cerebellar vermis, and the periaqueductal grey. Decreased blood flow was observed in the right retrosplenial cortex (BA 26, 29, 30, and parts of BA 23). Significant increases in rCBF were also seen in the right amygdala; these increases correlated significantly with subjects' self-reports of anxiety.

Liberzon et al. (1999) used single photon emission computerized tomography (SPECT) with [^{99m}Tc] HMPAO[1] to measure changes in rCBF in three groups: Vietnam veterans with PTSD (n = 11), veterans without PTSD (n = 11), and noncombat controls (n = 14). SPECT scanning took place in two separate sessions. In one session, subjects were exposed to white noise; in the other session, they were exposed to combat sounds. All three groups showed increases in rCBF in the anterior cingulate and medial prefrontal cortex during exposure to the traumatic sounds, but not during the white noise condition. The PTSD group also showed increased blood flow to the amygdala.

23.2.2 Script-Driven Imagery

The script-driven imagery paradigm was originally used in studies that examined the psychophysiological correlates of symptomatic states; it was later adapted for use in neuroimaging studies. This paradigm involves having each subject complete a personalized script of a traumatic memory (and usually a neutral memory as well) that is rich in sensory description. The script is read to the subject during the scan.

The following four studies identified areas in the brain that were associated with the hyperarousal/reexperiencing state in chronic PTSD.

Rauch et al. (1996) conducted a PET study using script-driven imagery in eight patients with PTSD. Alterations in rCBF were seen during exposure to the traumatic script: increased blood flow to the right hemispheric limbic, paralimbic, and visual areas, and decreased blood flow to the left inferior frontal cortex and left middle temporal cortex. It is of note that the subjects in this study described their experiences during the trauma script as being similar to their usual symptomatic states (i.e., intense reexperiencing of the incident).

Shin et al. (1999) reported phenomenological and PET findings during script-driven, imagery-induced symptomatic states. Participants in this study included eight women with sexual-abuse-related PTSD and eight women with histories of sexual abuse, but without PTSD. During the traumatic script, PTSD patients reported higher average ratings of guilt and disgust than did the control group. PET findings for the trauma condition were significantly different from those for the two control conditions (i.e., exposure to a neutral script and teeth clenching) combined. Significant increases in rCBF were seen in controls, but not in PTSD subjects, in the anterior cingulate gyrus and insular cortex. PTSD subjects, but not controls, showed increases in rCBF in the left inferior frontal gyrus.

Bremner et al. (1999a) conducted a PET study in 10 women with childhood sexual abuse (CSA) and PTSD and 12 control subjects with CSA, but without PTSD. In response to the trauma script, PTSD subjects reported higher levels of fear and anxiety than did controls. All subjects reported higher levels of subjective distress for the trauma script (compared to a neutral script), but PTSD subjects reported higher levels of distress than did controls. PTSD patients showed greater rCBF than controls in the posterior cingulate (BA 31) and anterolateral prefrontal cortex (BA 9, 10), decreased blood flow in the medial prefrontal cortex (BA 25), and no activation in the anterior cingulate gyrus (BA 32). Relative rCBF decreases were also seen in the PTSD group in parts of the parietal cortex (BA 40), right hippocampus, visual association cortex (BA 19), fusiform gyrus/inferior temporal gyrus (BA 20), and dorsolateral prefrontal cortex (BA 6, 8).

In an fMRI investigation of the neural correlates of script-driven imagery, Lanius et al. (2001) included only those PTSD subjects who experienced subjective and autonomic hyperarousal during recall of their traumatic memory. The response patterns observed in these hyperaroused PTSD subjects are consistent with previous PET studies of PTSD in combat veterans and victims of sexual abuse (Bremner et al., 1999b; Liberzon et al.,

[1] Technitium-99m HexaMethylPropyleneAmineOxime, or hexametazime, a gamma-emitting radionuclide imaging agent used in the evaluation of regional cerebral blood flow.

1996; Liberzon et al., 1999; Shin et al., 1997; Shin et al., 1999; Zubieta et al., 1999). Compared to control subjects, individuals with PTSD who exhibited hyperarousal and "reliving" of the memory showed significantly less activation of the thalamus, anterior cingulate gyrus (BA 32), medial prefrontal gyrus (BA 10, 11), occipital lobe, and inferior frontal gyrus (BA 47).

The brain areas implicated in PTSD subjects' high-arousal/reexperiencing response have also been implicated in nonpathological emotional responses (e.g., amygdala, insula, and anterior cingulate cortex). Chronic PTSD subjects, however, manifested greater activation in these areas than did healthy controls. The increased activity in sensory cortices in the parietal and occipital lobes that was observed in several studies may account for PTSD patients' vividness of memories. This possibility is explored in the following.

23.3 FUNCTIONAL CONNECTIVITY IN THE HYPERAROUSAL RESPONSE IN PTSD PATIENTS

The previously mentioned studies utilized the "subtraction analysis" paradigm. In this type of study, rCBF (for PET) or BOLD[2] signal (for fMRI) is measured during the task of interest and during a control task or resting state. The activity during the latter is "subtracted from" activity during the target task in order to determine which areas of the brain are specifically recruited during the activity of interest.

Functional connectivity analyses provide different information from subtraction analysis. In functional connectivity analyses, a brain region is selected that is activated in both control subjects and in subjects with PTSD, and then the brain areas whose activity *correlates with* the activity of this reference point (or reference voxel) can be identified. Using this technique, Lanius et al. (2004b) found dramatically different patterns of functional connectivity in controls and in PTSD patients who experienced a hyperarousal/flashback response to exposure to a traumatic script. A reference point in the right anterior cingulate gyrus (that activated equally in both groups of subjects) was selected. In control subjects, there was greater covariation between this point and the left superior frontal gyrus (BA 9), left anterior cingulate gyrus (BA 32), left striatum (caudate), left parietal lobe (BA 40 and 43), and left insula (BA 13). This pattern of memory retrieval is consistent with retrieval of *verbal episodic memory*, and with the fact that this group of subjects tended to experience the memory as a narrative of an event.

The PTSD group showed a very different pattern of covariation with the reference voxel in the right anterior cingulate. In the PTSD group, co-activation was seen in the right posterior cingulate gyrus (BA 29), right caudate, right parietal lobe (BA 7, 40), and right occipital lobe (BA 19). This pattern of connectivity is consistent with recall of *nonverbal memory*, and so with the sensory-based nature of traumatic memories in PTSD patients. Thus, the functional connectivity of traumatic memories in PTSD supports the description of traumatic memories given by patients (that Van der Kolk et al. have described as primary dissociation). We are currently analyzing functional connectivity data from the group of PTSD patients who responded to their traumatic script with hypoarousal or secondary dissociative responses.

23.4 FLASHBACKS

Although flashbacks are a paradigmatic symptom of PTSD, we still do not know how flashbacks fit into the overall picture of altered neural functioning in PTSD patients in a symptomatic state. Generally, the literature has considered flashbacks to constitute one end of a spectrum of "reliving" phenomena. Nevertheless, as Osuch et al. (2001) have noted, studies have not assessed (1) reexperiencing subjects' locations on this continuum, or (2) how their subjective experience is related to neural activation patterns. In part, this is because there has been no explicit discussion of the relationship between full-blown flashbacks and secondary dissociative phenomena in the neuroimaging literature.

Liberzon et al. (1996) report a case study of a PTSD patient who experienced a significant flashback in response to trauma sounds. Alterations in rCBF as measured by SPECT showed a dramatically altered ratio of cortical to subcortical perfusion during the flashback. It could not be determined, however, whether this was due to (1) an increase in subcortical activity or (2) a decrease in cortical activity (because only relative perfusion was measured). In this same subject, perfusion relative to the thalamus was below the group mean by more than two standard deviations for 11 of the 13 measured regions. There were no qualitative differences in activation patterns between this subject and other subjects who "reexperienced" their trauma, but did not have a flashback. This suggests that flashbacks are an extreme form of reliving/reexperiencing (i.e., primary dissociation), rather than being a qualitatively different kind of phenomenon.

[2] Blood-Oxygen-Level-Dependent.

This view is further supported by a PET study of 11 subjects with PTSD (Osuch et al., 2001). Three reported flashback experiences in response to the script, but not during control (resting) scan. Five reported flashbacks early in the procedure; these flashbacks were exacerbated upon hearing the script. Three reported no flashbacks at all. The eight subjects who experienced flashbacks were included in an analysis that correlated rCBF with the reported intensity of flashbacks. Intensity of flashbacks was positively correlated with rCBF in the left inferior frontal gyrus, left insula, left perihippocampal region, left somatosensory cortex, left cerebellum, right insula, right putamen, lingula, and brainstem. Intensity of flashbacks was negatively correlated with rCBF in the left superior frontal gyrus, right superior frontal gyrus, right fusiform gyrus, and right medial temporal gyrus.

Intensity of flashbacks was also related to heart rate. Of the 11 PTSD subjects, 7 were heart-rate responders and 4 were heart-rate nonresponders. On average, responders increased their heart rate by approximately 20 beats per minute. One subject, who did not report a subjective response to the script, did have an increase in heart rate. Two subjects, who did experience flashbacks, showed no increase in heart rate. This study did not address the possibility that physiological or emotional nonresponse might be linked to secondary dissociative phenomena.

23.5 SECONDARY DISSOCIATION IN RESPONSE TO SYMPTOM PROVOCATION IN PTSD PATIENTS

As noted earlier, Lanius et al. (2002) found a distinct pattern of neural activation in subjects that experienced hypoarousal (i.e., secondary dissociation) in response to script-driven imagery. In PTSD patients who exhibited a primary dissociative response (i.e., flashbacks) to script-driven recall of their traumatic memory, higher levels of brain activation (compared to baseline) were seen in the superior and middle temporal gyrus (BA 38), inferior frontal gyrus (BA 7), occipital lobe (BA 19), parietal lobe (BA 7), medial frontal gyrus (BA 10), medial prefrontal cortex (BA 9), and anterior cingulate gyrus (BA 24, 32). Activation was predominately right hemispheric. The control group in this study showed higher activation levels than the hypoaroused PTSD subjects in the left parahippocampal gyrus (BA 35), right middle frontal gyrus (BA 8, 9) and left superior temporal gyrus (BA 41, 13). By contrast, PTSD subjects who exhibited secondary dissociation (i.e., hypoarousal) showed no differences in activation in the thalamus compared to controls. In addition, hypoaroused subjects did not have an increase in heart rate while remembering their traumatic memory. Instead, they reported feeling distanced from their experience of the memory; some said that they were "zoned out," or "out of their body."

These findings about PTSD patients with a response of hypoarousal to symptom-provocation are congruent with studies of dissociation in other patient populations. In a study of eight patients with depersonalization disorder, Simeon et al. (2000) found increased brain glucose metabolism in BA 7B and BA 19, similar to our patients. On the other hand, these patients with depersonalization disorder exhibited decreased metabolic activity in the superior and middle temporal gyri, whereas the secondary dissociation PTSD patients in our study showed increased activation in these areas. It is unclear what factors may account for these differences, but our findings of activation in the superior and middle temporal gyri are consistent with the hypothesis that secondary dissociation is mediated largely by alterations of activity in the temporal lobe. The temporal lobe is important in the dissociative phenomena associated with epilepsy (Blumer & Walker, 1969; Devinsky et al., 1989; Kenna & Sedman, 1965). In short, preliminary results in PTSD patients appear to indicate a role for the temporal lobes in both primary and secondary dissociative phenomena.

Sierra and Berrios (1998) have proposed a model of depersonalization that emphasizes the relationship between the cerebral cortex and limbic regions. They suggest that concurrent left medial prefrontal activation and amygdala inhibition causes decreases in emotionality and arousal. By contrast, concurrent activation of the right dorsolateral prefrontal cortex and inhibition of the anterior cingulate gyrus underlie hypervigilance and attentional difficulties. These findings overlap with the neural activation patterns of hypoaroused PTSD subjects: alterations in activation of the dorsolateral prefrontal cortex (BA9), medial prefrontal cortex, and anterior cingulate gyrus (Lanius et al., 2002). It should be noted that the model proposed by Sierra and Berrios (1998) goes further than our data allow; their model sorts dissociative symptoms into subtypes and proposes specific causal mechanisms that mediate each subtype.

In conclusion, the results of Lanius et al. (2002) have similarities to depersonalization disorder and the dissociative phenomena of temporal lobe epilepsy. Further research may clarify the similarities and differences between the dissociation of epilepsy patients (which appears to involve the temporal lobes) and the dissociation of patients with chronic PTSD (which also involves frontal lobe structures).

23.6 SUMMARY

Neuroimaging studies suggest that PTSD patients have two contrasting response patterns to symptom provocation. First, in the more thoroughly studied pattern of hyperarousal or primary dissociation, patients show an increased heart rate and report feeling emotionally overwhelmed by their traumatic memories. This pattern of responses is associated with alterations in activation of the anterior cingulate cortex, medial prefrontal cortex, and thalamus (compared to control subjects). Second, the pattern of hypoarousal or secondary dissociation involves the temporal, occipital, and parietal cortices, frontal regions, and anterior cingulate. In the PTSD literature, hypoarousal has primarily been investigated in terms of peritraumatic responses to a traumatic event, especially in ASD. Our finding suggests that hypoarousal is also seen in chronic PTSD.

Although hypoarousal and hyperarousal can be seen as paradigmatic, it would be a mistake to conclude at this point that they are completely discrete. There is evidence that secondary dissociation can co-occur with hyperarousal. Bremner administered the Clinician-Administered Dissociative States Scale (CADSS) at baseline and after each of the two neutral and two trauma scripts to PTSD patients who experienced a "reliving" response to trauma cues (Bremner et al., 1999a, 1999b). CADSS scores were higher, indicating greater secondary dissociation symptoms, in PTSD patients after exposure to the trauma script. Bremner's data suggest the existence of mixed dissociative states where fear/anxiety and secondary dissociative distancing co-occur.

Autonomic response to symptom provocation can also vary. Of their subjects who experienced flashbacks, Osuch et al. (2001) found that some showed an increase in heart rate while others had no autonomic reactivity despite *subjective* emotional arousal. Thus, symptom provocation can elicit a range of possible responses, not just hyperarousal or hypoarousal.

The symptom-provocation neuroimaging literature suggests that we must seriously consider the relationships among subjective experience, autonomic arousal, and neural activation in order to better understand patients with chronic PTSD. Although the responses of these patients most often fall into two patterns (i.e., primary or secondary dissociation), these two patterns of response do not appear to be always mutually exclusive. Future research should place a high priority on further elucidating these patterns and variations and the relationships among them.

REFERENCES

Allen, J. G. (2001). *Traumatic relationships and serious mental disorders*. New York: Wiley.

American Psychiatric Association (1994). *Diagnostic criteria from DSM-IV*. Washington, DC: Author.

Birmes, P., Brunet, A., Carreras, D., Ducasse, J. L., Charlet, J. P., Lauque, D. et al. (2003). The predictive power of peritraumatic dissociation and acute stress symptoms for posttraumatic stress symptoms: a three-month prospective study. *American Journal of Psychiatry, 160*, 1337–1339.

Blumer, D., Walker, A. E. (1969). Memory in temporal lobe epileptics. In G. A. Tallan & N. C. Waugh (Eds.), *The pathology of memory*. New York: Academic Press. pp. 65–73.

Boon, S. & Draijer, N. (1993). Multiple personality disorder in The Netherlands: A clinical investigation of 71 patients. *American Journal of Psychiatry, 150*, 489–494.

Bremner, J. D., Narayan, M., Staib, L. H., Southwick, S. M., McGlashan, T., & Charney, D. S. (1999a). Neural correlates of memories of childhood sexual abuse in women with and without posttraumatic stress disorder. *American Journal of Psychiatry, 156*, 1787–1795.

Bremner, J. D., Southwick, S., Brett, E., Fontana, A., Rosenheck, R., & Charney, D. S. (1992). Dissociation and posttraumatic stress disorder in Vietnam combat veterans. *American Journal of Psychiatry, 149*, 328–332.

Bremner, J. D., Staib, L. H., Kaloupek, D., Southwick, S. M., Soufer, R., & Charney, D. S. (1999b). Neural correlates of exposure to traumatic pictures and sound in Vietnam combat veterans with and without posttraumatic stress disorder: a positron emission tomography study. *Biological Psychiatry, 45*, 806–816.

Butler, L. D., Duran, R. E. F., Jasiukaitis, P., Koopman, C., Spiegel, D. (1996). Hypnotizability and traumatic experience: A diathesis-stress model of dissociative symptomatology. *American Journal of Psychiatry, 153 (Suppl. 7S)*, 42–63.

Coons, P. M. (1994). Confirmation of childhood abuse in child and adolescent cases of multiple personality disorder and dissociative disorder not otherwise specified. *Journal of Nervous and Mental Diseases, 182*, 461–464.

Devinsky, O., Putnam, F., Grafman, J., Bromfield, E., & Theodore, W. H. (1989). Dissociative states and epilepsy. *Neurology, 39*, 835–840.

Kenna J. C. & Sedman G. (1965). Depersonalization in temporal lobe epilepsy and the organic psychoses. *British Journal of Psychiatry, 111*, 293–299.

Kluft, R. P. (1995). The confirmation and disconfirmation of memories of abuse in dissociative identity disorder patients. *Dissociation, 8*, 235–258.

Lader, M. H. (1975). *The psychophysiology of mental illness*. London: Routledge and Kegan Paul.

Lanius, R. A., Bluhm, R., Lanius, U., & Pain, C. (2006). A review of neuroimaging studies in PTSD: Heterogeneity of response to symptom provocation. *Journal of Psychiatric Research, 40*, 709–729.

Lanius, R. A., Williamson, P. C., Boksman, K., Densmore, M., Gupta, M., Neufeld, R. W. et al. (2002). Brain activation during script-driven imagery induced dissociative responses in PTSD: A functional magnetic resonance imaging investigation. *Biological Psychiatry, 52,* 305–311.

Lanius, R. A., Williamson, P. C., Densmore, M., Boksman, K., Gupta, M. A., Neufeld, R. W. et al. (2001). Neural correlates of traumatic memories in posttraumatic stress disorder: a functional MRI investigation. *American Journal of Psychiatry, 158,* 1920–1922.

Lanius, R. A., Williamson, P. C., Densmore, M., Boksman, K., Neufeld, R. W., Gati, J. S. et al. (2004b). The nature of traumatic memories: a 4-T fMRI functional connectivity analysis. *American Journal of Psychiatry, 161*, 36–44.

Lewis, D. O., Yeager, C. A., Swica, Y., Pincus, J. H., & Lewis, M. (1997). Objective documentation of child abuse and dissociation in 12 murderers with Dissociative Identity Disorder. *American Journal of Psychiatry, 154*, 1703–1710.

Liberzon, I., Taylor, S. F., Amdur, R., Jung, T. D., Chamberlain, K. R., Minoshima, S. et al. (1999). Brain activation in PTSD in response to trauma-related stimuli. *Biological Psychiatry, 45*, 817–826.

Liberzon, I., Taylor, S. F., Fig, L. M., & Koeppe, R. A. (1996). Alteration of corticothalamic perfusion ratios during a PTSD flashback. *Depression and Anxiety, 4*, 146–150.

Marmar, C. R., Weiss, D. S., Schlenger, W. E., Faribank, J. A., Jordan, K., Kulka, R. A., & Hough, R. L. (1994). Peritraumatic dissociation and posttraumatic stress in male Vietnam theatre veterans. *American Journal of Psychiatry, 151*, 902–907.

McFarlane, A. C. (1997). The prevalence and longitudinal course of PTSD. Implications for the neurobiological models of PTSD. *Annals of the New York Academy of Sciences, 821*, 10–23.

Nijenhuis, E. R. S., Spinhoven, P., Van Dyck, R., Van der Hart, O., & Vanderlinden, J. (1998). Degree of somatoform and psychological dissociation in dissociative disorder is correlated with reported trauma. *Journal of Traumatic Stress, 11,* 711–730.

Nijenhuis, E. R. S., Van der Hart, O., & Steele, K. (2002). The emerging psychobiology of trauma-related dissociation and dissociative disorders. In H. D'Haenen, J. A. Den Boer, H. Westenberg & P. Willner (Eds.), *Textbook of biological psychiatry* (pp. 1079–1098). London: Wiley.

Osuch, E. A., Benson, B., Geraci, M., Podell, D., Herscovitch, P., McCann, U. D. et al. (2001). Regional cerebral blood flow correlated with flashback intensity in patients with posttraumatic stress disorder. *Biological Psychiatry, 50,* 246–253.

Ozer, E. J., Best, S. R., Lipsey, T. L., & Weiss, D. S. (2003). Predictors of posttraumatic stress disorder and symptoms in adults: a meta-analysis. *Psychological Bulletin, 129*, 52–73.

Panasetis, P. & Bryant, R. A. (2003). Peritraumatic versus persistent dissociation in acute stress disorder. *Journal of Traumatic Stress, 16,* 563–566.

Pissiota, A., Frans, O., Fernandez, M., von Knorring, L., Fischer, H., & Fredrikson, M. (2002). Neurofunctional correlates of posttraumatic stress disorder: A PET symptom provocation study. *European Archives of Psychiatry and Clinical Neuroscience, 252*, 68–75.

Pitman, R. K., Orr, S. P., & Shalev, A. Y. (1993). Once bitten, twice shy: beyond the conditioning model of PTSD. *Biological Psychiatry, 33*, 145–146.

Rauch, S. L., Van der Kolk, B. A., Fisler, R. E., Alpert, N. M., Orr, S. P., Savage, C. R. et al. (1996). A symptom provocation study of posttraumatic stress disorder using positron emission tomography and script-driven imagery. *Archives of General Psychiatry, 53*, 380–387.

Shin, L. M., Kosslyn, S. M., McNally, R. J., Alpert, N. M., Thompson, W. L., Rauch, S. L. et al. (1997). Visual imagery and perception in posttraumatic stress disorder. A positron emission tomographic investigation. *Archives of General Psychiatry, 54,* 233–241.

Shin, L. M., McNally, R. J., Kosslyn, S. M., Thompson, W. L., Rauch, S. L., Alpert, N. M. et al. (1999). Regional cerebral blood flow during script-driven imagery in childhood sexual abuse-related PTSD: A PET investigation. *American Journal of Psychiatry, 156*, 575–584.

Sierra, M. & Berrios, G. E. (1998). Depersonalization: Neurobiological perspectives. *Biological Psychiatry, 44,* 898–908.

Simeon, D., Guralnik, O., Hazlett, E. A., Spiegel-Cohen, J., Hollander, E., & Buchsbaum, M. S. (2000). Feeling unreal: a PET study of depersonalization disorder. *American Journal of Psychiatry, 157*, 1782–1788.

Spiegel, D. (1997). Trauma, dissociation and memory. In R. Yehuda & A. C. McFarlane (Eds.), *Psychobiology of posttraumatic stress disorder*. Annals of the New York Academy of Sciences, *821*, 225–237.

Van der Hart, O., Van der Kolk, B. A., Boon, S. (1998). Treatment of dissociative disorders. In J. D. Bremner & D. R. Marmar (Eds.), *Trauma, memory and dissociation*. Washington, DC: American Psychiatric Press.

Van der Kolk, B. A. (1994). The body keeps the score: Memory and the evolving psychobiology of posttraumatic stress. *Harvard Review of Psychiatry, 1,* 253–265.

Van der Kolk, B. A. (1996). Trauma and memory. In B. van der Kolk, A. McFarlane, & L. Weisaeth (Eds.), *Traumatic stress: The effects of overwhelming experience on mind, body, and society* (pp. 279–302). New York: Guilford Press.

Van der Kolk, B. A., Van der Hart, O., & Marmar, C. (1996). Dissociation and information processing in Posttraumatic Stress Disorder. In B. van der Kolk, A. McFarlane, & L. Weisaeth (Eds.), *Traumatic stress: The effects of overwhelming experience on mind, body, and society* (pp. 303–330). New York: Guilford Press.

Zubieta, J. K., Chinitz, J. A., Lombardi, U., Fig, L. M., Cameron, O. G., & Liberzon, I. (1999). Medial frontal cortex involvement in PTSD symptoms: a SPECT study. *Journal of Psychiatric Research, 33*, 259–264.

Part VII

The DSM-IV Dissociative Disorders

24 The Long Struggle to Diagnose Multiple Personality Disorder (MPD): MPD

Paul F. Dell, PhD

OUTLINE

What is multiple personality disorder (MPD) and how do we diagnose it? The modern dissociative disorders field has struggled with these questions for the past 25 years. This chapter brings together the different strands of this effort and argues that the literature on MPD contains robust answers to these questions that are not contained in the modern Diagnostic and Statistical Manual of Mental Disorders (DSM; American Psychiatric Association, 1980, 1987, 1994, 2000).

MPD received considerable scientific attention in the late 1800s, but scientific interest in MPD underwent a lengthy interregnum from about 1910 to 1980 (Rosenbaum, 1980). MPD was "rediscovered" by clinicians in the 1970s, many of whom gathered careful data on their cases. Curiously, there is a notable difference between what these clinicians learned about MPD and what has been portrayed in the DSM (e.g., Coons, 2001; Kluft, 1985a; Peterson & Putnam, 1994; Ross, 1997).

Similarly, there is a large gap between what the scientific research literature says about MPD and what is portrayed in the DSM (Dell, 2006b).

24.1 MPD AND THE DSM

MPD was formally returned to scientific attention in 1980 when several significant papers on MPD were published (Bliss, 1980; Coons, 1980; Greaves, 1980; Marmar, 1980; Rosenbaum, 1980). That same year, MPD received the imprimatur of the American Psychiatric Association. Whereas DSM-II (APA, 1968) had listed multiple personality as a symptom of Hysterical Neurosis, Dissociative Type, DSM-III (APA, 1980) "elevated [MPD] from the position of symptom to disorder" (Coons, 1989, p. 1).

24.1.1 MPD AND DSM-III

The DSM-III Dissociative Disorders Work Group was dominated by clinical experts on MPD. These experts devised a set of diagnostic criteria for MPD that set the DSM on a path from which it has never deviated. Specifically, the DSM presents a definition of MPD rather than a typical set of diagnostic criteria (i.e., signs and symptoms).

24.1.1.1 DSM-III Criteria for MPD

A. The existence within the individual of two or more distinct personalities, each of which is dominant at a particular time.
B. The personality that is dominant at any particular time determines the individual's behavior.
C. Each individual personality is complex and integrated with its own unique behavior patterns and social relationships. (DSM-III, p. 259)

The DSM-III diagnostic criteria for MPD are oddly at variance with the core mission of DSM-III. Because DSM-II had generated such poor levels of diagnostic reliability, the raison d'être of DSM-III was to devise criteria that would improve diagnostic reliability (Spitzer, Williams, & Skodol, 1980). The diagnostic criteria in DSM-III were mandated to consist of (1) well-defined, unambiguous clinical phenomena, and (2) specific inclusion and exclusion criteria (Spitzer, Endicott, & Robins, 1975). If the subsequent controversy about MPD has shown anything, it is that the criteria for MPD are neither well-defined nor unambiguous.[1] I consider the DSM criteria for MPD to be lethally abstract. Subsequent revisions of the DSM have made some adjustments to these criteria, but the 1980 diagnostic criteria for MPD remain fundamentally unchanged. Even the 1994 amnesia criterion for MPD is just another abstract definition: "Inability to recall important personal information that is too extensive to be explained by ordinary forgetfulness" (DSM-IV, p. 487).

The issue that I am raising here is not the correctness or accuracy of the criteria, but their ambiguity, their high level of abstraction, and worst, their lack of usefulness to the average clinician. The criteria for other disorders in DSM-IV are often models of detail, specificity, and concreteness: (1) Major Depressive Disorder: "depressed mood most of the day, nearly every day, as indicated by either subjective report (e.g., feels sad or empty) or observation made by others (e.g., appears tearful)..." (DSM-IV, p. 327); (2) Panic Attack: "A discrete period of intense fear or discomfort, in which four (or more) of the following symptoms developed abruptly and reached a peak within 10 minutes: palpitations, pounding heart, or accelerated heart rate; sweating, trembling or shaking; sensations of shortness of breath or smothering; feeling of choking; chest pain or discomfort; nausea or abdominal distress; feeling dizzy, unsteady, lightheaded, or faint; derealization (feelings of unreality) or depersonalization (being detached from oneself); fear of losing control or going crazy; fear of dying; paresthesias (numbness or tingling situations); chills or hot flushes" (DSM-IV, p. 395); (3) Posttraumatic Stress Disorder (PTSD): "The traumatic event is persistently reexperienced in one (or more) of the following ways: ..." (DSM-IV, p. 428).[2]

24.1.2 MPD AND DSM-III-R

The DSM-III-R Dissociative Disorders Work Group wrestled with at least six issues regarding MPD: (1) clinical inaccuracies in the DSM-III diagnostic criteria, (2) whether to make the criteria more restrictive, (3) whether to add an amnesia criterion, (4) whether to totally revise the

[1] One reviewer hoped that I meant this statement to refer only to DSM-III—because, otherwise, I might be understood to be claiming that "MPD is not a clearly defined condition." Unfortunately, with regard to the DSM diagnostic criteria for MPD/DID, that is precisely what I mean. The criteria in DSM-III, DSM-III-R, DSM-IV, and DSM-IV-TR are unremittingly vague. They have left the average clinician to view MPD only as "through a glass, darkly."

[2] To be fair, it should be noted that the criteria for PTSD have suffered from ambiguous (and shifting) definitions of trauma/traumatization.

criteria, (5) putative cross-cultural forms of MPD, and (6) the boundary between MPD and partial forms of MPD.

24.1.2.1 DSM-III-R Criteria for MPD

A. The existence within the person of two or more distinct personalities or personality states (each with its own relatively enduring pattern of perceiving, relating to, and thinking about the environment and self).
B. At least two of these personalities or personality states recurrently take full control of the person's behavior. (DSM-III-R, p. 273)

24.1.2.1.1 Clinical Inaccuracies in the DSM-III Criteria

In a landmark paper on the natural history of MPD, Kluft (1985b) convincingly argued that the DSM-III criteria for MPD were inaccurate in several ways. His arguments appear to have convinced the DSM-III-R Dissociative Disorders Work Group; the Work Group incorporated into the revised criteria several of his recommended changes (Kluft, 1987a; Kluft, Steinberg, & Spitzer, 1988). In recognition of the phenomena of passive influence and copresence, DSM-III-R's criteria for MPD no longer required one personality to be dominant at any given time.[3] Recognizing that (1) alters vary in their complexity and elaboration, and (2) different persons' systems or complexes of alters have different styles of operation, DSM-III-R no longer required each personality to be "complex and integrated with its own unique behavior patterns and social relationships" (DSM-III, p. 259).[4]

24.1.2.1.2 Should the Criteria for MPD Be More Specific?

At the time of the deliberations of the DSM-III-R Dissociative Disorders Work Group (i.e., 1986–1987), there were significant differences of opinion in the dissociative disorders field about whether the diagnostic criteria for MPD should be more specific and, hence, more diagnostically restrictive. Kluft (1982, 1985) and Bliss (1980) advocated less restrictive criteria; Braun (1985), Coons (1984), Loewenstein (Loewenstein & Putnam 1990), and Putnam (2001) advocated more restrictive criteria. The subcommittee chose to make the DSM-III-R criteria for MPD less specific and less diagnostically restrictive than the DSM-III criteria that they replaced:

> The argument that carried the day was that DID was seriously underdiagnosed and that having a few, very general criteria would encourage its diagnosis. It was also argued (primarily on the basis of experience with a few atypical/questionable cases) that there were variants of the disorder, who would be inappropriately excluded if the diagnostic criteria were made more specific. (Putnam, 2001, p. 48)

I think that this reasoning (i.e., that diagnostic recognition of persons with MPD would be increased if the diagnostic criteria were made less specific) was substantially incorrect. In my opinion, the primary diagnostic problem regarding persons with MPD is *not* that clinicians rule out a diagnosis of MPD on the basis of the (restrictive) clinical inaccuracies in the DSM-III diagnostic criteria for MPD (or on the basis of clinicians' incorrect stereotypes of MPD/DID). Yes, both of these frequently happen, but I think that the primary problem is that the average clinician simply does not know what MPD patients really look like (i.e., their typical signs and symptoms)—and DSM-III and DSM-III-R failed (and DSM-IV continues to fail) to delineate the typical signs and symptoms of MPD patients.

24.1.2.1.3 Should Amnesia Be a Diagnostic Criterion for MPD?

The amnesia issue has been a bone of contention for every Dissociative Disorders Work Group (i.e., DSM-III, DSM-III-R, and DSM-IV). Coons, Loewenstein, and Putnam have been longstanding advocates of the need for an amnesia criterion (Coons, 1980, 1984; Loewenstein & Putnam, 1990). Kluft has been an equally longstanding opponent of the amnesia criterion (Kluft, 1985b; Putnam, 2001; Spiegel & Cardeña, 1991). Kluft argued that amnesia was difficult to detect because it fluctuated and because the patient often defensively denied it or truly did not remember it (i.e., the patient has amnesia for his/her amnesia). In the DSM-III-R Dissociative Disorders Work Group,

[3] "Criterion B is potentially confusing. The personality that appears to be dominant and may represent itself as dominant may in fact be strongly influenced by another, of whose influence it may or may not be aware … [T]he personalities' experiences of one another's impact may take the form of hallucinations, illusions, and passive influence experiences…" (Kluft et al., 1988, p. 40).

[4] "Criterion C is problematic. The degree of elaboration and complexity of the separate entities has proven to be an expression of the interaction style of the personalities, the structure of the dissociative defenses, overall adaptive patterns, and character style of the individual patient rather than a core criterion of the illness" (Kluft et al., 1988, p. 40).

an amnesia criterion for MPD was voted down; the argument in favor of less restrictive criteria held sway:

> … the inclusion of an amnesia criterion, notwithstanding substantial considerations to the contrary, was considered likely to contribute to the underdiagnosis of such cases. (Kluft, Steinberg, & Spitzer, 1988, p. 41)

Kluft's arguments against adding an amnesia criterion stemmed from his strong concern that MPD was underdiagnosed because clinicians ruled out MPD on the basis of misguided reasons (e.g., an absence of apparent amnesia) and incorrect rules-of-thumb (e.g., if the person remembers what a supposed alter personality did or said, then that person does not have MPD).[5] As stated above, I think that Kluft's concern was correct, but that his concern also amounted to a *de facto* underemphasizing of the average clinician's profound lack of education about the typical presentations of MPD. The DSM should provide that education, but, in my opinion, it has substantially foregone that responsibility by failing to provide the typical diagnostic signs and symptoms of MPD.

24.1.2.1.4 The Boundary Between MPD and Partial Forms of MPD

The boundary between MPD and partial MPD is the crucial exclusionary criterion for MPD.[6] This boundary separates DID from its nearest nosological neighbor (see DDNOS-1[7] in DSM-IV). This nosological boundary was not addressed by DSM-III, perhaps because the existence of partial MPD and other forms of ego state disorder (see Dell, 2009a and Watkins & Watkins, 1997) were little recognized or understood at the time DSM-III was written. In DSM-III, Atypical Dissociative Disorder included trance states, states of derealization, and the effects of brainwashing, but Atypical Dissociative Disorder did not explicitly acknowledge the likely existence of partial forms of MPD. Thus, DSM-III-R was the first DSM to explicitly mention partial forms of MPD. Still, DSM-III-R's handling of partial MPD was, at best, ambivalent. The DSM-III-R Work Group members clearly disagreed about the nosological status of these cases:

> Proposals were received to create separate classifications for patients who have syndromes that have the same structure as Multiple Personality Disorder, but with less overt manifestations, and for children with such a condition in its incipient phase (e.g., Fagan & McMahon, 1984) or in the process of evolving toward the adult form (e.g., Kluft, 1984c, 1985b). The committee acknowledged that these conditions exist and have been documented, but that at this time the evidence remains too preliminary to serve as the basis of new classifications. *Longitudinal data suggests that they may all prove to be phases of the same disorder* (Kluft, 1985a). A decision was made to refer to the differences between adult and childhood cases in the descriptive text for Multiple Personality Disorder, and to include examples under Dissociative Disorder NOS that explicitly acknowledged less overtly manifested conditions. (Kluft, Steinberg, & Spitzer, 1988, p. 44. italics added)

A careful reading of this quotation shows that it does not acknowledge that partial forms of DID actually exist: "they may all prove to be phases of the same disorder." In other words, these new examples of DDNOS may only be "less overtly manifested" cases of MPD.

My sense is that the DSM-III-R Work Group harbored significant differences of opinion about what is and what is not MPD, but that the extant empirical data were too sparse to support any one point of view regarding the boundaries of MPD and partial MPD. So, the Work Group tentatively acceded to the strongly articulated views of the group's *de facto* leader on "matters multiple"—Richard Kluft. Although I think that Kluft was substantially correct, the nosological status of the relationship between MPD and DDNOS-1 (i.e., DDNOS-1-as-a-variant/subtype-of-MPD vs. DDNOS-1-as-a-different-disorder-than-MPD) is still an open question. That nosological question is the topic of Part II of this chapter (Dell, 2008a).

24.1.2.1.5 What Should Be Done About Culture-Bound Dissociative Syndromes?

The committee took note of the large number of culture-bound dissociative syndromes that have no corresponding diagnosis in DSM-III. Some argued that a diagnosis of trance/possession disorder should be added to DSM-III-R so that it would provide a home for many of the

[5] One reviewer of this chapter averred that Kluft's implicit hypothesis (i.e., that increasing the specificity of the diagnostic criteria would increase the underdiagnosis of DID) has received little support; that is, MPD was underdiagnosed both when the DSM included an amnesia criterion (i.e., DSM-IV and DSM-IV-TR) and when the DSM did not include an amnesia criterion (i.e., DSM-III and DSM-III-R).

[6] The concept of partial MPD is highly important, but it cannot be adequately addressed in the present chapter. Partial MPD (as well as MPD, itself) is inseparable from Watkins's concept of ego state disorders (Watkins & Watkins, 1997). Both ego state disorders and the concept of partial MPD are addressed in detail in the sequel to this chapter: "The long struggle to diagnose multiple personality disorder (MPD): II. Partial MPD" (Dell, 2009a).

[7] DDNOS-1 refers to the first example of dissociative disorder not otherwise specified (DDNOS) in DSM-IV: "1. Clinical presentations similar to Dissociative Identity Disorder that fail to meet full criteria for this disorder. Examples include presentations in which a) there are not two or more distinct personality states, or b) amnesia for important personal information does not occur" (p. 490).

culture-bound dissociative syndromes. Ultimately, the Work Group decided not to add such a disorder on the grounds that the culture-bound syndromes closely resembled MPD:

> the close resemblance of many of these syndromes to MPD (Kenny, 1981) argues against such a revision, pending further study. (Kluft, 1987a, p. 423)

24.1.2.1.6 Should the Diagnostic Criteria for MPD Be Totally Revised?

The disposition of this question during the writing of DSM-III-R was, in my view, a fateful one for the dissociative disorders field. With apologies to Robert Frost, this is "the road not taken."

> By the time of the drafting of DSM-III-R, however, a fair amount had been learned about the clinical features of DID. An extensive set of specific criteria based on several, independent, relatively large sample, studies could have been generated. After considerable debate, the committee chose instead to continue with the very general (monothetic) DSM-III profile. (Putnam, 2001, pp. 47–48)

And that has made all the difference. Shortly following the publication of DSM-III-R, all hell broke loose. MPD, the diagnostic criteria for MPD, and the concept of dissociation were subjected to torrents of criticism. Although I think that this backlash had a variety of determinants, I believe that MPD's vague diagnostic criteria in DSM-III and, especially, DSM-III-R helped to fuel the backlash (see Dell, 2001c).

24.1.3 DID[8] and DSM-IV

24.1.3.1 DSM-IV Criteria for DID

A. The presence of two or more distinct identities or personality states (each with its own relatively enduring pattern of perceiving, relating to, and thinking about the environment and self).
B. At least two of these identities or personality states recurrently take control of the person's behavior.
C. Inability to recall important personal information that is too extensive to be explained by ordinary forgetfulness. (DSM-IV, p. 529)

[8] DSM-IV changed the name of MPD to Dissociative Identity Disorder (DID), as described in the following.

The DSM-IV Dissociative Disorders Work Group wrestled with at least four issues regarding DID: (1) whether to change the name of the disorder, (2) whether to add an amnesia criterion, (3) whether to totally revise the diagnostic criteria, and (4) the nature of the boundary between DID and partial forms of DID. First and foremost, however, it is essential to recognize that the DSM-IV Dissociative Disorders Work Group was deeply divided:

> By the time that the DSM-IV was being drafted, DID was deeply mired in controversy—which continues to this day. The political need to "balance" the committee with proponents and critics, who were then forced to conduct meetings by conference call, insured virtual paralysis. (Putnam, 2001, p. 48)

24.1.3.1.1 Should the Name of the Disorder Be Changed?

Many subcommittee discussions wrestled with the question of whether to change the name of the disorder:

> The issue that almost exclusively dominated the discussion was whether or not to change the name of multiple personality disorder to something else—with many alternatives being proposed and rejected. Although the committee consistently voted against name changes, one was imposed anyway.[9] (Putnam, 2001, p. 48)

Ultimately, three of the four specific dissociative disorders underwent a name change (i.e., Dissociative Amnesia, Dissociative Fugue, and Dissociative Identity Disorder), thereby bringing the names of the first two into closer accord with the International Classification of Disease-10 (ICD-10), but, ironically, distancing Dissociative Identity Disorder from the ICD-10, which continues to use the term *multiple personality disorder.*

24.1.3.1.2 Should DID Have an Amnesia Criterion?

The debate about an amnesia criterion for MPD was taken up again by the DSM-IV Dissociative Disorders Work Group. As before, Kluft argued that such a criterion would lead to underdiagnosis of DID. This time, he was outvoted: an amnesia criterion was adopted for DID:

> On the basis of ... research [Ross et al., 1989; Putnam et al., 1986; Bliss, 1984] that shows the very high incidence of amnesic symptoms among MPD patients, the risk of making false negative diagnoses seems remote,

[9] By the chair of the Work Group.

> particularly when the professional is sensitized to the association between amnesia and dissociation. (Spiegel & Cardeña, 1991, p. 372)

Perhaps as a result of the strained conditions of the Work Group's functioning, something odd occurred: the Work Group developed a false memory. The Work Group's debate about an amnesia criterion somehow became a debate about whether to *reinstate* DSM-III's amnesia criterion for MPD. There never was an amnesia criterion for MPD in DSM-III. Still, DSM-IV's Appendix D (Annotated Listing of Changes in DSM-IV) incorrectly states: "The DSM-III requirement that there be an inability to recall important personal information has been reinstated" (p. 784).

24.1.3.1.3 Should the Diagnostic Criteria for DID Be Totally Revised?

Here, once again, is "the road not taken." The DSM-III-R Work Group had voted to retain MPD's broad, abstract diagnostic criteria. Now, 7 years later, more research data on MPD had accumulated. The data easily could have enabled the development of a polythetic[10] set of diagnostic criteria for MPD. But that did not happen. The opportunity to develop specific, polythetic criteria was lost again, apparently a casualty of the Work Group's stormy functioning:

> The "amnesia" criterion was added, but other attempts to increase criterion specificity stalled amid the contention, confusion, and inertia of the group. (Putnam, 2001, p. 48)

24.1.3.1.4 The Boundary Between DID and Partial Forms of DID

As noted, the boundary between DID and partial DID is the crucial exclusionary criterion for DID; it defines what is, and what is not, DID. DSM-IV suggested that two features distinguish between DID and partial DID: (1) amnesia, and (2) the distinctness of the parts or alters (see Footnote 8 for DSM-IV's description of DDNOS-1).

Despite the vagueness of its characterization, DSM-IV's DDNOS-1 is an important advance; the DSM is starting to delineate the boundary between DID and its nearest nosological neighbor.

Curiously, the DSM-IV Work Group did not address a major nosological problem that affects DSM-III's classification of the dissociative disorders. Three epidemiological investigations of the dissociative disorders (Mezzich et al., 1989; Saxe et al., 1993; Saxena & Prasad, 1986) had reported a disproportionate number of DDNOS cases; that is, 57% to 90% of the dissociative disorders in those three epidemiological investigations were diagnosed as DDNOS. The DSM-IV Work Group bequeathed this nosological problem to the next (i.e., DSM-V) Dissociative Disorders Work Group:

> One of the greatest challenges for editors of future editions of the DSM will be to obtain greater taxonomical clarity, considering that the majority of diagnosed dissociative disorders do not fit the established criteria. (Spiegel & Cardeña, 1996, p. 235)

24.2 WHY THE MODERN DSM HAS PROVIDED ONLY A STRUCTURAL DEFINITION OF DID

For 28 years, the modern DSM has given clinicians only a structural definition of DID (Dell, 2001a, 2001c). This definition of DID is tautological: "If multiple personalities/identities are present, then the person has DID." The DSM provides no guidance about *how* to identify persons with DID—just the preceding tautological guideline: "When multiple personalities are present, make a diagnosis of DID." Efforts within the Work Group to increase the specificity of the diagnostic criteria by adding signs and symptoms have been consistently voted down—on the grounds that those additional criteria would be too restrictive and lead to false negative diagnoses of MPD/DID. Thus, since 1980, Criterion A for DID has remained essentially unchanged: "The presence of two or more distinct identities or personality states…" (DSM-IV, p. 487). From the perspective of such a structural definition of DID, it does not matter which dissociative symptoms are present (or not present). It only matters that multiple personalities/identities be present:

> what is essential to multiple personality disorder across its many presentations is no more than the presence, within an individual, of more than one structured entity with a sense of its own existence. (Kluft, 1985b, p. 231)

Richard Kluft has been to DID what Kraepelin and Bleuler were to schizophrenia. Many of his papers are

[10] The concept of polythetic classes was first advanced by a biologist, Michael Beckner, in 1959. Polythetic classes are defined by a large number of characteristics, none of which is considered to be necessary. Polythetic diagnostic criteria are widely considered to be more accurate than monothetic diagnostic criteria (i.e., a small number of characteristics, all of which are necessary). Polythetic and monothetic diagnostic criteria are described in detail in the next section of this chapter.

monuments of descriptive psychiatry, especially his chapter on the natural history of MPD (from which the above quotation is drawn). In that chapter, Kluft documented why he believes that efforts to increase the specificity of the diagnostic criteria for MPD would undermine the diagnosis of MPD. He argued that the symptoms of persons with MPD vary widely—across persons with MPD and across time in each person with MPD. Accordingly, Kluft (1985b) opposed DSM criteria that were more specific or more behavioral. He insisted that "definitions and criteria based on behavioral evidence may misrepresent multiple personality disorder as it actually occurs" (p. 231). Most important, however, Kluft reported in that same article that most cases of MPD were hidden, rather than overt. He argued convincingly that *overt display of alter personalities is neither essential nor typical of MPD*:

> Approximately 15 percent of adult patients are diagnosed when they dissociate spontaneously during assessment or therapy. Another 40 percent show some subtle form of classic signs that could alert the clinician to multiple personality disorder if he or she has an index of suspicion for the condition, and has seen the subtle signs of switching that one observes during the treatment of such patients. The remaining 40 percent show no classic signs of multiple personality disorder and are diagnosed either serendipitously, when the clinician makes a strong effort to pursue diagnostic clarity, when ancillary information raises the issue, or when personalities suppressed in session try to get the clinician to see what is going on. (Kluft, 1985b, pp. 218–219)

Why is overt display of alter personalities not basic to MPD? Kluft (1985a, 1985b) provided a plethora of reasons. Kluft (1985b) noted (1) that alters "often passed for one another" (p. 205), (2) that alters often come and go so quickly "that the only trace they left was a brief fluctuation in facial expression" (p. 205), and (3) that the emergence of personalities (i.e., switching) is often quite infrequent: "Often several months passed during which personalities did not emerge fully" (p. 205). He also noted that the alter personalities of child cases were often indistinct, "muted or attenuated" (p. 213), and that the alter personalities of adult cases were often relatively invisible because they were "uninvested and unmotivated in being conspicuously separate" (p. 213). Finally, Kluft deftly reminded the reader that MPD exists for certain reasons, and that those reasons seldom include a need to display their presence:

> The *raison d'être* of multiple personality disorder is to provide a structured dissociative defense against overwhelming traumata. The emitted observable manifestations of multiple personality disorder are epiphenomena and tools of the defensive purpose. In terms of the patients needs, the personalities need only be as distinct, public, and elaborate as becomes necessary in the handling of stressful situations. (Kluft, 1985b, p. 231)

No wonder DID can be so difficult to diagnose. No wonder many clinicians do not notice that some of their patients have other personalities. No wonder that so many clinicians and scholars are skeptical or unaware of the existence of this disorder. Kluft's take-home message in this regard is incisive (and profoundly important for the diagnosis of MPD/DID):

> the mental health disciplines have come to expect as normative what in fact is a relatively unusual presentation: florid, overt, and unconcealed multiple personality disorder. (Kluft, 1985b, p. 211)

In my opinion, this observation is so true that clinicians who routinely treat DID hardly notice it anymore; the hiddenness of MPD patients is as noticeable to them as the air that they breathe. In fact, I believe that complete switching (from one personality to another) is actually one of the least frequent phenomena of DID (Dell, 2006b, 2009a, 2009b).[11]

So, how does this bear upon "the long struggle to diagnose MPD"? Here, I think, Kluft's solution to the problem of MPD hiddenness has taken us astray. As noted, he has counseled that the DSM diagnostic criteria should cleave to what is essential about MPD: "the presence, within an individual, of more than one structured entity with a sense of its own existence" (Kluft, 1985b, p. 231). From Kluft's point of view, even the DSM-IV criteria are too restrictive: the diagnostic criteria for DID should be *just* Criterion A and Criterion B:

> A. The presence of two or more distinct identities or personality states (each with its own relatively enduring pattern of perceiving, relating to, and thinking about the environment and self).

[11] For a potentially different point of view, see Loewenstein, Hamilton, Alagna, Reid, and deVries (1987). Their experiential sampling study with a single DID patient during a 3-month hospitalization at NIMH found switching to be frequent during the first month (11 switches per day) and less frequent during the third month (3 per day). It is not known whether these findings (based on a single patient who was undergoing intensive, long-term, inpatient treatment for DID) are typical of the day-to-day functioning of persons with DID who are not being treated for DID.

> B. At least two of these identities or personality states recurrently take control of the person's behavior. (DSM-IV, p. 487)

As a characterization of the essence of our classical concept of DID, I think that criteria A and B are fine. As diagnostic criteria, I think they are a disaster. Criteria A and B are largely useless to the average clinician; they provide no signs or symptoms of DID. They leave the average clinician almost groping in the dark. As Brenner (2001) has quietly observed, "the revised diagnostic criteria of the DSM-IV do not greatly help the average clinician" (p. 38).

24.3 DISADVANTAGES OF THE CURRENT DIAGNOSTIC CRITERIA FOR DID

There is a science of classification that has guided zoologists (Beckner, 1959; Sneath, 1962; Sneath & Sokal, 1973), philosophers (Wittgenstein, 1953), and psychiatric nosologists (Blashfield, 1986; Cantor, French, Smith, & Mezzich, 1980; Frances & Widiger, 1986; Livesley, 1985; Spitzer, Endicott, & Robins, 1978). This science of classification was brought to bear on the writing and rewriting of most of the diagnostic criteria in the modern DSM—but not the diagnostic criteria for DID (Dell, 2001a, 2001c).

The distinction between monothetic and polythetic classes has been particularly influential on the modern DSM.

> Monothetic classification is based on a simple conceptual strategy; it organizes data according to (what are considered to be) the predominant or compelling features of the members of the class.... In a monothetic class, *every defining feature is essential.* Each member of a monothetic class must possess *all* of the class's defining characteristics. (Dell, 2001a, pp. 10–11)

Monothetic classification belongs mostly to "the early days" (Sokal, 1966, p. 107) of an area of investigation. In keeping with this view, Blashfield contends that monothetic diagnoses are poorly formulated and rarely used:

> Generally the categories that are given monothetic definitions are those that have poorly formulated diagnostic criteria (e.g., depersonalization disorder) and/or those categories that are rarely used in applied clinical practice (e.g., pyromania). (Blashfield, 1986, p. 374)

Monothetic classes have many disadvantages—not least of which is the annoying inconvenience that the natural world is rarely monothetic (Bailey, 1973; Kendell, 1975). For psychiatric nosologists, there are three major disadvantages of monothetic classification: (1) monothetic classification ignores many other features of the category or class in question, (2) monothetic classes produce a high rate of false-negative diagnoses (Widiger, Frances, Spitzer, & Williams, 1988), and (3) monothetic classes generate an artifactually low base-rate of the disorder (Clark, Watson, & Reynolds, 1995). DID is one of the few disorders in DSM-IV that still uses monothetic diagnostic criteria.

The justification for the unadorned simplicity of DID's Criterion A and Criterion B was that greater specificity would lead to false-negative diagnoses of DID. Yet, critics of monothetic classification note that monothetic classes *always* increase false negative diagnoses (Eysenck, 1986; Frances, Pincus, Widiger, Davis, & First, 1994; Livesley, 1985; Sneath & Sokal, 1973; Wittgenstein, 1953). From one perspective, both are correct. If more behavioral criteria are added to a *monothetic* class, the class will become still narrower and false negative diagnoses will increase. But from another perspective, only one side is correct. If more behavioral and symptom criteria are added *and* the class is changed from a monothetic one to a polythetic one, then the class will become broader and false negative diagnoses will decrease. The current monothetic criteria for DID are a genuine problem. The critics of monothetic classes are correct. Monothetic classes increase false-negative diagnoses and produce an artifactually low base-rate of the disorder.

The bottom line is that DID needs polythetic diagnostic criteria. Polythetic classes afford behavioral specificity *without* increasing false-negative diagnoses.

Most disorders in DSM-IV have polythetic criteria (or monothetic/polythetic hybrids wherein monothetic criteria are specified polythetically). Borderline personality disorder (BPD), for example, has polythetic criteria. A person can be diagnosed with BPD when any five of BPD's nine criteria are present. PTSD, on the other hand, has three monothetic criteria (i.e., reexperiencing, avoidance/numbing, and hyperarousal) each of which is specified polythetically. Thus, in PTSD, any one of five types of reexperiencing must be present; *and* any three of seven types of avoidance/numbing must be present; *and* any two of five kinds of hyperarousal must be present.[12]

[12] Strictly speaking, this paragraph is an oversimplification because it addresses only the core clinical diagnostic criteria for BPD and PTSD. In fact, BPD has six monothetic criteria, and its first criterion has nine polythetic items. BPD's other five monothetic criteria are those that must be satisfied by each personality disorder in the DSM. Similarly, PTSD has six monothetic criteria, of which reexperiencing, avoidance/numbing, and hyperarousal are the second, third, and fourth.

As noted, the mandate of the modern DSM (i.e., DSM-III and later) was to increase diagnostic reliability by (1) eliminating abstract criteria that are too susceptible to idiosyncratic interpretations by different clinicians, and (2) increasing the behavioral and symptomatic specificity of the diagnostic criteria. Polythetic elaboration of monothetic criteria has been a frequent vehicle for achieving behavioral and symptomatic specificity in the modern DSM. The larger number of features that are typical of polythetic criteria (e.g., 9 criteria for BPD, 17 criteria for PTSD) are scientifically important. Within limits, the more features that a polythetic class is based upon, the more predictive that class will be—both of external correlates of the class and of internal correlates of the class (Sneath & Sokal, 1973; Sokal, 1966).

Although the purpose of the DSM is to provide "guidelines for making diagnoses" (DSM-IV-TR, p. xxxvii), *the DSM does not provide guidelines for diagnosing DID.* Even researchers despair about the criteria for diagnosing DID:

> What is the gold standard for the diagnosis of multiple personality disorder? There has been a change of diagnostic criteria for multiple personality disorder over time from DSM-III to DSM-III-R and now to DSM-IV. We are still uncertain as to what specific clinical criteria should be used to make the diagnosis, not to mention research diagnostic criteria for multiple personality disorder. (Latz, Kramer, & Hughes, 1995, p. 1348)

Instead, it provides definitions—of DID, of switching, and of amnesia. Thus, for 25 years, the DSM has provided almost no signs or symptoms for diagnosing DID. As such, the DSM's criteria for DID cannot be considered to be user-friendly:

> The DSM-IV criteria for DID are *profoundly* unfriendly to the average clinician. Criteria A, B, and C (especially Criterion C) for DID are so abstract as to be almost indecipherable, and hence, substantially unusable. (Dell, 2001a, p. 20)

The most convincing evidence that the DSM provides little guidance for diagnosing DID may be the fact that experts on DID have universally composed longer lists of diagnostic symptoms of DID (Bliss, 1986; Boon & Draijer, 1993b; Braun, 1988; Coons, Bowman, & Milstein, 1988; Dell, 2006b; Fraser, 1994; Horevitz, 1994; Kluft, 1985a, 1987, 1999; Loewenstein, 1991; Loewenstein, Hornstein, & Farber, 1988; Putnam, 1989, 1993, 1997; Ross, 1997; Spira, 1996; Steinberg, 1995). In contrast, experts on depression or anxiety do not construct their own personal lists of diagnostic symptoms for DSM-IV disorders; the DSM provides excellent explications of major depressive episodes, panic attacks, and so on.

The fact that experts on DID have routinely compiled their own lists of DID symptoms is an indication that the DSM-IV diagnostic criteria for DID have *poor content validity.* When applied to diagnostic criteria, "content validity refers to the extent that the criteria of a disorder represent the domain of symptoms associated with that disorder" (Blashfield & Livesley, 1991, p. 266). The DSM-IV diagnostic criteria for DID poorly represent the domain of symptoms of DID (Dell, 2006b; see also Table 24.1).

TABLE 24.1
Thirteen Well-Documented Dissociative Symptoms of Dissociative Identity Disorder

Symptom	Empirical Studies
Straightforward dissociative symptoms	
1. Amnesia	32
2. Conversion	28
3. Voices	22
4. Depersonalization	20
5. Trances	17
6. Self-alteration	16
7. Derealization	14
8. Awareness of the presence of alters	10
9. Identity confusion	10
10. Flashbacks	8
Psychotic-like dissociative symptoms	
11. Auditory hallucinations	13
12. Visual hallucinations	11
13. Some Schneiderian first-rank symptoms*	14
'Made' actions	6
Voices arguing	5
Voices commenting	4
'Made' feelings	3
Thought withdrawal	2
Thought insertion	2
'Made' impulses	1

Note: Empirical studies = the number of empirical studies that have reported the occurrence of that dissociative symptom in persons with Dissociative Identity Disorder. This Table has been adapted from A new model of dissociative identity disorder, by P.F. Dell, 2006, *Psychiatric Clinics of North America, 29,* pp. 1–26. Copyright 2006 by Elsevier B. V. Adapted with permission.

* These passive-influence Schneiderian symptoms are correlated with DID. Three remaining Schneiderian symptoms (i.e., audible thoughts, thought broadcasting, and delusional perceptions) are not correlated with DID.

As noted, monothetic diagnostic criteria are founded upon "the predominant or compelling features of the members of the class" (Dell, 2001a, p. 10). In the case of DID, the predominant or compelling feature is "the presence of two or more distinct identities or personality states … that recurrently take control of the person's behavior" (DSM-IV, p. 529). This monothetic focus on distinct identities and switching has a very serious disadvantage; namely, *distinct-identities-who-switch (i.e., florid DID) is an uncommon event in the lives of persons with DID* (Dell, 2006b; Kluft, 1985b). In fact, visible switching from one alter to another probably ranks among the least frequent phenomena of DID (Dell, 2006b, 2008a, 2008b; Kluft, 1985b). So, why base the diagnosis of DID solely upon an infrequent and difficult-to-discern sign of the disorder?[13] No wonder so many clinicians have been skeptical that DID really exists.[14]

The problems with diagnosing DID also reside in the names of the disorder: *multiple personality disorder, dissociative identity disorder.* Other names have been proposed. Kluft (1988) once suggested calling the disorder "disaggregate self-state disorder," which I actually think is quite accurate. My own favorite name for DID is "dissociative self-state disorder." Still, there is a problem with all of these names; they focus *solely* on personalities, identities, self-states, and so on.

Over the past few decades, it has become increasingly clear that DID is characterized by much more than alter personalities. Persons with DID routinely exhibit a vast array of dissociative symptoms. In other words, DID is more than an alter disorder; it is a chronic complex dissociative disorder. Coons (2001), for example, has argued that DID needs a name that "truly reflects the polysymptomatic nature of DID" (p. 44). In keeping with this understanding, Dell (2001a) has suggested renaming DID *major dissociative disorder* and Coons (2001) has suggested *pervasive dissociative disorder.* Perhaps the most common referent or label for DID (other than MPD or DID) is "complex dissociative disorder." To my knowledge, no one has actually proposed that DID be renamed *Complex Dissociative Disorder,*[15] but variations of this term have been cropping up in the literature with increasing frequency: "chronic complex dissociative disorders" (Ross, 1990), "complex chronic dissociative symptoms" (Loewenstein, 1991), "complex posttraumatic and dissociative disorders" (Chu, 1998), "chronic, complex dissociative disorder" (Tutkun et al., 1998, p. 804), "complex dissociative disorders" (Coons, 2001), and "the taxon of chronic complex dissociative disorder" (Ross, Duffy, & Ellason, 2002, p. 15). Clearly, the authors cited in this paragraph understand DID to be much more than just "an alter disorder." They understand DID to be a major, pervasive, complex, chronic, dissociative disorder. Perhaps the DSM should call DID *Complex Dissociative Disorder.*

Finally, it should be noted that many DID scholars have expressed dissatisfaction with the DSM-IV diagnostic criteria for DID (Coons, 2001; Coons & Chu, 2000; Dell, 2001a, 2001c, 2006b; Nakdimen, 1992, 2006; Putnam, 1997; Ross, 1997; Steinberg, 2001). These critics have been quite explicit in faulting the DSM criteria for (1) their vagueness, (2) their failure to cover the polysymptomatic presentation of DID, (3) their failure to reflect the empirical literature on DID, and (4) their contribution to the controversiality that has surrounded DID, and (5) their obstruction of research. For example:

> Focusing on the polysymptomatic nature of DID and DDNOS with other ego states would do what the name change from "multiple personality disorder" to "dissociative identity disorder" was only mildly successful in doing—emphasizing the cross-cultural aspects of complex dissociative disorders and de-emphasizing the fascination of clinicians, patients, and the lay public and press for the sensational aspects of alternate personality states. (Coons, 2001, p. 44)

> I believe that the portrayal of … DID in The Diagnostic and Statistical Manual of Mental Disorders has been (1) an unnoticed obstacle to progress in the dissociative

[13] I am *not* asserting that some people with DID do not switch. Although I actually believe that the frequency, context, and visibility of switching is a matter of individual style—including the possibility of a style of not switching at all (see, for example, the case described by Fraser, 1994)—I am not making that case here. I am simply stating that infrequent and hidden switching is characteristic of the vast majority of persons with DID. And that this (1) typically has negative consequences for diagnosis, and (2) has helped to provoke skepticism about DID.

[14] I do not claim that skepticism about the existence of DID is solely due to putative inadequacies or deficiencies in the DSM's diagnostic criteria for the disorder. There are many other reasons for skepticism, including starkly countertransferential ones. In any case, the present chapter is not an analysis of skepticism about DID. Instead, this chapter is an analysis of the history and, I believe, the deficiencies of the modern DSM's diagnostic criteria for DID. I address skepticism regarding DID only in so far as it may relate to clinicians' encounters with the interface between (1) typical clinical presentations of DID, and (2) the DSM's diagnostic criteria for DID.

[15] In the interim between when this chapter was written and its final proofreading, Richard Lowenstein has proposed using the term Complex Dissociative Disorder.

disorders field, and (2) an indirect contributor to the field's loss of credibility. (Dell, 2001c, p. 4)

Although I served on both the DSM-III-R and DSM-IV dissociative disorder work groups, I have strong reservations about the diagnostic criteria specified by the DSM for MPD/DID. More stringent, better-operationalized criteria for MPD can readily be devised. (Putnam, 2001, p. 94).

First, Pincus, Levine, Williams, Ustun, and Peele (2004) have suggested that DSM-III, DSM-III-R, and DSM-IV collectively addressed the issue of diagnostic reliability and validity. First et al. believe that DSM-V should continue to focus on validity, but that it should give priority to clinical utility.

As the time for DSM-V approaches, the DSM-IV criteria for DID still portray a 1980-vintage disorder; the diagnostic criteria for DID have not progressed beyond what was barely acceptable in DSM-III. Consequently, the diagnostic criteria for DID are now badly out of step with the rest of DSM-IV. Worse, the DSM's abstract monothetic criteria for DID have done the opposite of what was intended; *the DSM's diagnostic criteria have undermined the diagnostic reliability of DID*:

DID has not been lifted by the rising tide of diagnostic reliability; the everyday reliability of the diagnosis of DID is abysmal. It is true that, when used by trained researchers and clinicians, the Structured Clinical Interview for DSM-IV Dissociative Disorders-Revised (SCID-D-R) and the Dissociative Disorders Interview Schedule (DDIS) have excellent reliability for the diagnosis of DID.... There is little evidence, however, that the diagnosis of DID is reliable when it is made (or not made) by the average clinician who uses (only) DSM-IV or DSM-IV-TR. (Dell, 2001a, p. 9)

I think that researchers in the dissociative disorders field have been almost reluctant to report data that compare the diagnoses of average clinicians with the diagnoses of dissociative disorder experts. Comparative reports provoke the skeptics of DID who consider such data to be further evidence of the "outrageous" and "dubious" diagnostic practices of those who "believe in" DID.

Still, there is considerable *sotto voce*[16] evidence that the diagnostic practices of the average clinician differ considerably from those of dissociative disorder researchers. First, the comparative difference in diagnostic practices is part of the daily experience of clinicians who treat DID (and interact with other clinicians). Second, although no study has rigorously compared and reported the diagnostic practices of the average clinician versus those of experts on DID, the essential study has actually been conducted many times. Studies of the prevalence of DID in inpatient settings implicitly compare the diagnoses of average clinicians with those of DID experts, but those data are seldom reported in a focal way. For example, a review of 12 inpatient prevalence studies shows that one article clearly reported and discussed comparative diagnostic data, four tangentially provided comparative data but did not discuss it, and seven reported no comparative data at all. In many of these papers, however, the authors implied (or the reader was left to infer) that the unit's regular psychiatrists seldom diagnosed DID.

I contend that the time has come for the DSM-V Dissociative Disorders Work Group to develop well-specified, polythetic diagnostic criteria for DID (and the other dissociative disorders). Such criteria would accomplish two essential goals: (1) they would make it much easier for the average clinician to correctly identify cases of DID; and (2) they would greatly increase the everyday diagnostic reliability of the disorder.

24.4 DEVELOPING POLYTHETIC DIAGNOSTIC CRITERIA FOR DID

At the present time, there seem to be two alternative paths for developing polythetic criteria for DID: (1) develop polythetic criteria for DSM-IV DID, or (2) develop polythetic criteria for DID-as-a-complex-dissociative-disorder.

24.4.1 Polythetic Criteria for DSM-IV DID

Table 24.2 delineates a polythetic elaboration of (1) "two or more distinct identities or personality states," that (2) "recurrently take control of the person's behavior," and (3) are accompanied by an "inability to remember important personal information."

Because I disagree with DSM-IV's concept of DID, I did not make an extensive effort to elaborate and refine Criterion A and Criterion B (Table 24.2). On the other hand, I consider Criterion C to be a *sine qua non* for DID (and most of the dissociative disorders). Accordingly, I have invested much time and thought in Criterion C's polythetic elaboration of amnesia. This polythetic elaboration of Criterion C not only illustrates the amnesia of persons with DID; it also provides the clinician with a set of implicit diagnostic inquiries about amnesia.

[16] *Sotto voce*. Italian. "Spoken softly or in an undertone so as not to be overheard."

TABLE 24.2
A Polythetic Elaboration of DSM-IV's Diagnostic Criteria for DID

A. At least one additional distinct personality or personality state is present, as evidenced by three (or more) of the following:
 (1) the personality or personality state has its own relatively enduring pattern of perceiving, relating to, and thinking about the environment and self as manifested by affect, opinions, and/or attitudes
 (2) the personality or personality state appears to be noticeably different from the person's customary self as manifested by two (or more) of the following:
  (i) facial expression
  (ii) body posture
  (iii) tone of voice
  (iv) mannerisms
  (v) affect
  (vi) opinions
  (vii) attitudes
 (3) the personality or personality state claims/perceives itself to be a different part or a different person from another part of the person
 (4) the individual perceives/claims that the personality or personality state is "not me"
 (5) the individual is subjectively aware of the existence of separate parts 'inside'

B. At least two identities or personality states recurrently take control of the person's behavior, as evidenced by one (or more) of the following:
 (1) the individual is witnessed (by the clinician or a collateral informant) to undergo a transition (i.e., a 'switch') from one distinct personality or personality state to another as evidenced by one (or more) of the following:
  (i) an announced change of identity (e.g., "I'm not *her*, I'm Janice.")
  (ii) a relatively sudden change of self-presentation as manifested by two (or more) of the following:
   (a) facial expression
   (b) body posture
   (c) tone of voice
   (d) mannerisms
   (e) affect
   (f) opinions
   (g) attitudes
 (2) the individual exhibits dissociative amnesia for the activities of another personality or personality state (as witnessed by the clinician or described by a collateral informant)

C. Incidents of dissociative amnesia that are reported by the person or a collateral informant, as evidenced by at least three (or more) incidents of the following:
 (1) discovering that one has 'lost' a chunk of time; being completely unable to account for a period of time—hours or longer—including the loss of memory for up to years of his/her life
 (2) "coming to": suddenly discovering that he/she was in the middle of doing something that he/she did not remember initiating (e.g., conversing with someone, disciplining the children, cooking dinner, etc.) or suddenly discovering that he/she had done something he/she does not remember doing (e.g., smashed something, cut self, cleaned the whole house)
 (3) fugues: suddenly discovering that he/she was somewhere with no memory of having gone there in the first place (e.g., finding self at the mall, at the beach, in one's car, under the bed, in a closet, etc.)
 (4) being told of things that he/she had recently done, but having no memory of doing those things
 (5) finding objects among his/her possessions or in his/her shopping bags—that he/she does not remember acquiring, purchasing, or producing (e.g., shoes, clothes, toys, toilet articles, drawings, handwritten materials, etc.)
 (6) finding evidence of his/her recent actions, but with no memory of having done those things (e.g., mowed the lawn, completed a task at work, cleaned the house, changed one's apparel or hairstyle or cosmetics, having a significant injury—a cut, a burn, many bruises, having attempted suicide)
 (7) not remembering who he/she is or what her or his name is
 (8) being unable to remember well-established skills (e.g., how to read, how to drive, how to play the piano, how to do his/her job, etc.)
 (9) other incidents of being unable to recall personal information that is so unlikely or so extensive that it cannot be explained by ordinary forgetfulness

A well-described amnesia criterion is absolutely crucial to the diagnosis of DID and other dissociative disorders (Friedl, Draijer, & de Jonge, 2000).

Before presenting an alternative path to developing diagnostic criteria for DID, I want to review four reasons why I do *not* recommend that the DSM-V Dissociative Disorders Work Group pursue a polythetic elaboration of the DSM-IV criteria for DID (as in Table 24.2). First, the DSM-IV criteria are completely centered on alter identities/personalities. Alter personalities are immersed in a pervasive cloud of dissociative symptoms, but the diagnostic criteria completely ignore this cloud of symptoms (Dell, 2001a, 2006b). Second, the modern DSM's alter-centric approach to DID fuels controversy about the disorder (Dell, 2001c).

Third, the DSM-IV criteria focus on switching, but switching is infrequent and difficult-to-discern (Dell, 2006b; Kluft, 1985b). As Kluft (1985b) has noted, 94% of MPD patients try to hide or dissimulate their pathology. It simply does not make sense to make the diagnosis of DID completely dependent upon such an infrequent and elusive phenomenon.

Fourth, the DSM-IV criteria omit the most common symptoms of DID: ongoing intrusions into the executive functioning and sense of self of the person (Dell, 2006b, 2009a, 2009b). These intrusions have previously been described in terms of first-rank symptoms (Kluft, 1985a, 1987b), passive influence phenomena (Kluft, 1985a, 1987b), process symptoms of DID (Loewenstein, 1991; Putnam, 1993, 1997; Putnam & Loewenstein, 2000), and secondary features of DID (Ross, 1997). If I were to use the "control-language" of the modern DSM, then I would characterize these intrusions as incidents of partial control of the host by another personality (who influences the host "from within" rather than completely emerging or switching).

These intrusions and influences are especially important for diagnosis. They are vastly more frequent than switching and they answer a question that Kluft (1985b, p. 203) asked (and answered) 20 years ago: "What does multiple personality disorder look like when it does not look like multiple personality disorder as one expects to see it?" In other words, what does MPD look like when the personalities are not switching? What does MPD look like most of the time?

> Well-disguised adult patients often present with nothing more to suggest multiple personality disorder than affirmative answers to inquiry about passive influence or special hallucination experiences, the Schneiderian first rank symptoms. (Kluft, 1985b, p. 222)

Elizabeth Bowman (personal communication, 8-15-05) notes that intrusions are characteristic of both DID and DDNOS-1 (and other ego state disorders), but that switching has special diagnostic significance because only persons with DID switch. I completely agree. Yet, I do not agree that the diagnosis of DID should always wait upon an observed incident of switching. Why? Because switching is so often hidden, so often limited to private contexts (e.g., home alone), so infrequent, and so difficult-to-discern that many (most?) DID patients are unreasonably penalized because their undetectable switching deprives them of the correct diagnosis and the correct treatment.

I completely agree that the diagnostic criteria for DID should include switching, but I contend that those diagnostic criteria should also include an alternative diagnostic criterion to switching: recurrent incidents of amnesia. Recurrent incidents of amnesia are a potent indicator of switching. Accordingly, I contend that recurrent incidents of recent amnesia is a valid alternative to switching as an indicator of DID.

24.4.2 DSM-IV DID Is a Culturally Biased Portrayal of Complex Dissociative Disorders

The incidence of Western-style DID in non-Western cultures is low, especially in Asian cultures (Adityanjee, Raju, & Khandelwal, 1989; Alexander, Joseph, & Das, 1997; Takahashi, 1990; Umesue, Matsuo, Iwata, & Tashiro, 1996). Such cultures breed a different kind of self and foster different expressions of dissociative psychopathology (Martínez-Taboas, 1991; Takahashi, 1990; Umesue et al., 1996). There is little doubt that the DSM's nosology of the dissociative disorders is biased toward the dissociative disorders that are familiar to American psychiatrists (i.e., dissociative presentations that are common to North America and Western Europe; Das & Saxena, 1989; Saxena & Prasad, 1989; Wig, 1983). If the DSM is ever to achieve accordance with the ICD, then it will probably be necessary for the American Psychiatric Association to present a version of DID that is much less culturally biased. As Ross (1990) has noted, "There are probably cultures in which chronic, complex dissociative disorders take forms other than MPD" (p. 64).[17]

[17] I further contend that the names, *dissociative identity disorder* and *multiple personality disorder*, are themselves culturally biased because they reflect the Western concept of self. DID should have a name that is culturally neutral.

24.4.3 Polythetic Criteria for Complex Dissociative Disorder

Table 24.1 summarizes the empirical literature on the dissociative symptoms of DID. There are 13 well-documented dissociative symptoms of DID (Table 24.1; see Dell, 2006b).[18] The DSM-IV diagnostic criteria for DID contain only 2 of these 13 dissociative symptoms: (1) amnesia, and (2) awareness of the presence of alters. DSM-IV, of course, does not actually require that the patient be *aware* of the presence of alters—only that alters be present. The other 11 well-documented dissociative symptoms of DID in Table 24.1 are absent from the DSM-IV diagnostic criteria. In contrast, Table 24.3's proposed criteria for Complex Dissociative Disorder include all 13 of these well-documented symptoms.[19]

The diagnostic criteria for Complex Dissociative Disorder[20] have three monothetic elements[21] that are elaborated polythetically: (A) classic dissociative symptoms, (B) conscious awareness of influences-from-within, and (C) recurrent amnesia.

[18] Table 24.1 has a major shortcoming; it does not indicate how common these symptoms are in DID. Instead, Table 24.1 indicates how often these symptoms have been reported in the scientific literature on DID. Thus, a symptom could be noted in numerous studies, but be found in only 5% to 10% of patients in the literature that is summarized by Table 24.1. Similarly, a symptom could be noted in a small number of studies, but be present in more than 90% of patients in those studies. Part of the problem is that, prior to the development of the Multidimensional Inventory of Dissociation (MID; Dell, 2006a), no instrument could simultaneously assess and compare the incidence of the 13 dissociative phenomena in Table 24.1. Table 24.4, however, reports the MID-assessed incidence of Table 24.1's dissociative phenomena (and other dissociative phenomena) in 41 SCID-D-diagnosed persons with DID.

[19] The criteria for Complex Dissociative Disorder incorporate the literature's reports of "auditory hallucinations" and "visual hallucinations" under the headings of child voices, persecutory voices, internal struggle, and posttraumatic flashbacks. Visual images of alter personalities are not directly reflected in the criteria for Complex Dissociative Disorder, but they are assessed by the MID.

[20] I proposed an earlier version of these diagnostic criteria under the name of *Major Dissociative Disorder* (Dell, 2001a).

[21] The three monothetic elements of Complex Dissociative Disorder were chosen for two reasons: (1) they provide comprehensive coverage of the dissociative symptoms of DID/Complex Dissociative Disorder; and (2) they provide a template that encompasses every kind of dissociative presentation. Persons with DID manifest classic dissociative symptoms, intrusions, and amnesia. Persons with DDNOS-1 manifest primarily classic dissociative symptoms and intrusions. Finally, persons with nondissociative disorders manifest primarily classic dissociative symptoms. The complete dissociative profiles of many disorders are still substantially unknown (e.g., depersonalization disorder, dissociative amnesia, dissociative fugue, posttraumatic stress disorder, borderline personality disorder, etc.).

24.5 EMPIRICAL TESTS OF TABLE 24.3'S POLYTHETIC CRITERIA FOR COMPLEX DISSOCIATIVE DISORDER

Three studies have tested slightly different versions of the diagnostic criteria in Table 24.3. In a pilot study of the Multidimensional Inventory of Dissociation (MID; Dell, 2006a), which assesses all but two of the above diagnostic criteria (i.e., B1 and C1), 91% of 34 persons with DSM-IV DID met the above diagnostic criteria (Dell, 2001b). The remaining 9% of the 34 DID cases (N = 3) were diagnosed as DDNOS-1b.[22] Persons were diagnosed as DDNOS-1b if they met Criterion A and Criterion B, but not Criterion C. Of the 34 persons with DSM-IV DID, 97% met Criterion A, 100% met Criterion B, and 91% met Criterion C.[23] The internal consistency of scores on the above diagnostic symptoms was calculated for 203 research participants (i.e., nonclinical adults, patients with no dissociative disorder, DDNOS-1b patients, and DID patients). Scores on the above diagnostic symptoms had a Cronbach alpha coefficient of 0.99 (Dell, 2001b).

In a much larger MID study of 220 DSM-IV cases of DID, 87% met the above criteria: 93% met Criterion A, 93% met Criterion B, and 94% met Criterion C (Dell, 2006b). In this study, the MID assessed 23 of the above symptoms; the 220 DID cases had a mean of 20.2 of the 23 symptoms. Table 24.4 shows the incidence of 24 of the proposed dissociative symptoms of Complex Dissociative Disorder in 41 SCID-D-diagnosed persons with DID (Dell, 2006b). The Cronbach alpha coefficient of scores on these symptoms was 0.98.

Finally, Gast, Rodewald, Dehner-Rau, Kowalewsky, Engl, Reddemann, and Emrich (2003) used the German translation of the MID to compare SCID-D diagnoses with MID diagnoses. In their research sample (of DID patients, DDNOS-1 patients, nondissociative psychiatric patients, and nonclinical adults), Gast and colleagues reported that a slightly different version of the diagnostic criteria in Table 24.3 had a positive predictive power of 0.93, a negative predictive power of 0.84, and an overall

[22] DDNOS-1b refers to a subset of the cases that DSM-IV describes in the first example of DDNOS: "1. Clinical presentations similar to Dissociative Identity Disorder that fail to meet full criteria for this disorder. Examples include presentations in which…b) amnesia for important personal information does not occur" (p. 490).

[23] Nine percent of these DSM-IV DID cases did not meet the MID criterion for the presence of amnesia. Two possible explanations for this occurrence are (1) a genuine, reduced incidence of amnesia due to psychotherapy or (2) a false denial of amnesia (which reflects some DID patients' denial of the reality or extent of their clinical condition).

TABLE 24.3
Diagnostic Criteria for Complex Dissociative Disorder*

A. Classic dissociative symptoms, as indicated by three (or more) of the following:
  (1) Circumscribed amnesia for autobiographical memory (e.g., cannot remember childhood before age 12; no memory of age 9-11; no memory of an important life event such as getting married, giving birth, or grandmother's funeral)
  (2) Depersonalization (e.g., feeling detached/distant from self; body feeling unreal or not all there; feeling separate from self and/or watching self from outside one's body)
  (3) Derealization (e.g., feeling disconnected/distant from everything; surroundings feel strange, unreal, oddly different; not recognizing familiar people or places)
  (4) Posttraumatic flashbacks (e.g., re-experiencing some or all of the sensory elements of a past trauma)
  (5) Somatoform symptoms (e.g., motor symptoms, sensory alterations, genital pain without physical explanation)
  (6) Trance (e.g., recurrent involuntary episodes of staring off into space, being 'gone' from conscious awareness, and unresponsive to environmental stimuli)

B. The person has conscious awareness of the intrusions/influences from another self-state, as indicated by either (1) or (2):
  (1) Switching without concomitant amnesia: The clinician or a collateral informant witnesses a self-state that claims (or appears) to be someone other than the person in question, as indicated by a, b, and c:
    (a) The visible presence of a different self-state, as evidenced by one (or more) of the following:
      (i) an announced change of identity (e.g., "I'm not her; I'm Janice.")
      (ii) a relatively sudden change of self-presentation as manifested by changes in two (or more) of the following:
        (1) facial expression
        (2) body posture
        (3) tone of voice
        (4) mannerisms
        (5) affect
        (6) opinions
        (7) attitudes
    (b) the person's conscious awareness of that self-state, as evidenced by both of the following three features: the person's
      (i) reported co-conscious awareness of the activities of that other self-state
      (ii) subsequent remembering of what the other self-state said and did
    (c) the person reports experiencing that self-state as "other," "not me," or not self
  (2) The person has conscious awareness of intrusions/influences from another self-state, as indicated by five (or more) of the following:
    (a) hearing the voice of a child in his/her head
    (b) noticing an internal struggle (that may or may not involve voices that argue). Note: internal struggle goes well beyond ambivalence; it involves a sense of the presence of different parts that are strongly opposing one another.
    (c) hearing a persecutory voice (usually in the head) that comments harshly, makes threats, or commands self-destructive acts
    (d) speech insertion (unintentional or disowned utterances)
    (e) thought insertion or withdrawal
    (f) 'made' or intrusive feelings and emotions (or sudden withdrawal/absence of feelings and emotions)
    (g) 'made' or intrusive impulses
    (h) 'made' or intrusive actions (i.e., actions that are perceived/experienced as depersonalized) or actions or behaviors that are blocked actions
    (i) atypical experiences of self-alteration (e.g., feeling very physically small or mentally young like a young child; having emotions, thoughts, or feelings that don't feel like they belong to oneself; seeing someone else instead of oneself in the mirror, etc.)
    (j) self-puzzlement secondary to 2a–2i

C. Recurring incidents of amnesia secondary to intrusions by another self-state, as indicated by either (1) or (2):
  (1) Switching that is accompanied by amnesia: The clinician or a collateral informant witnesses a self-state that claims (or appears) to be someone other than the person being interviewed, followed by the person's subsequent amnesia for what the other self-state was witnessed to do or say, as evidenced by a and b.
    (a) the visible presence of a different self-state, as evidenced by one (or more) of the following:
      (i) an announced change of identity (e.g., "I'm not her; I'm Janice.")

(Continued)

TABLE 24.3
Diagnostic Criteria for Complex Dissociative Disorder* *(Continued)*

(ii) a relatively sudden change of self-presentation as manifested by changes in two (or more) of the following:
(1) facial expression
(2) body posture
(3) tone of voice
(4) mannerisms
(5) affect
(6) opinions
(7) attitudes

(b) amnesia: the person is subsequently unable to recall what the other self-state said and did

(2) Recurring incidents of amnesia, as indicated by the person's report of two (or more) incidents of two (or more) of the following:
(a) discovering that he/she has amnesia for a discrete interval of time ('lost time'): being completely unable to account for a period of time—an hour or longer—including the loss of memory for up to years of one's life)
(b) "coming to": discovering that he/she was in the middle of doing something that he/she did not remember initiating (e.g., conversing with someone, disciplining the children, cooking dinner, performing occupational tasks, etc.) or suddenly discovering that he/she had done something he/she does not remember doing (e.g., smashed something, cut self, cleaned the whole house, etc.)
(c) fugues: suddenly discovering that he/she was somewhere with no memory of having gone there in the first place (e.g., finding self at the mall, at the beach, in one's car, under the bed, in a closet, etc.)
(d) being told of things that he/she had recently done, but with no memory of having done those things
(e) finding objects among his/her possessions or in his/her shopping bags—that he/she does not remember acquiring, purchasing, or producing (e.g., shoes, clothes, toys, toilet articles, drawings, handwritten materials, etc.)
(f) finding evidence of his/her recent actions, but with no memory of having done those things (e.g., mowed the lawn, produced written work, completed a task at work, cleaned the house, changed one's apparel or personal appearance, having a significant injury—a cut, a burn, many bruises, having attempted suicide, etc.)
(g) not remembering who he/she is or what her/his name is
(h) being unable to remember well-established skills (e.g., how to read, how to drive, how to play the piano, how to do his/her job, etc.)
(i) other incidents of being unable to recall personal information that is so unlikely or so extensive that it cannot be explained by ordinary forgetfulness.

D. The disturbance is not better accounted for by Schizophrenia, Schizoaffective Disorder, Brief Psychotic Disorder, Mood Disorder With Psychotic Features, or Borderline Personality Disorder and is not due to the direct physiological effects of a substance (e.g., a drug or substance of abuse, a medication) or a general medical condition (e.g., temporal lobe epilepsy).

E. The symptoms cause clinically significant distress or impairment in social, occupational, or other important areas of functioning.

* Although all of these diagnostic criteria are assessed by the MID (see Dell, 2006a, 2006b, and 2009b), they are obviously too extensive and too complex to function as diagnostic criteria for DSM-V. Possible new diagnostic criteria for DID are currently being contemplated by the Dissociative Disorders Research Planning Conferences and the American Psychiatric Association's DSM-V Task Force.

predictive power of 0.89 for diagnosing major dissociative disorder (i.e., DID or DDNOS-1).

In Gast's et al. sample, the Cronbach alpha coefficient for scores on the MID's 23 diagnostic symptoms was 0.98. Thus, the diagnostic symptoms in Table 24.4 cluster together almost perfectly (Cronbach alpha values of 0.98 to 0.99). A self-report instrument that is based on these criteria (i.e., the MID) was able to do an excellent job of diagnosing DID in two studies (Dell, 2001b, 2006b) and major dissociative disorder (i.e., DID or DDNOS-1) in another study (Gast et al., 2003). These findings suggest that the criteria listed previously have much to recommend them.

Finally, the findings of these three MID studies have a provocative implication. When I originally proposed the diagnostic criteria for DID, I predicted that these criteria would make it possible to diagnose DID "*before* unambiguous contact with alters has been established" (Dell, 2001a, p. 26). Two studies have now shown that this is, indeed, possible (Dell, 2001b, 2006b). In other words, *if the diagnostic criteria for DID are based on the full range of dissociative symptoms that occur in DID, it is possible to reliably and validly diagnose DID before unambiguous contact has been made with alter personalities.* It is possible to do this because, in addition to switching, DID has a pathognomonically distinctive pattern of dissociative symptoms.

TABLE 24.4
Incidence of 24 Dissociative Symptoms of Complex Dissociative Disorder in 41 SCID-D DID Cases

A. Classic dissociative symptoms	
1. Circumscribed autobiographical amnesia	83%
2. Depersonalization	95%
3. Derealization	93%
4. Posttraumatic flashbacks	93%
5. Somatoform symptoms	83%
6. Trance	88%
B. Intrusions/influences from another self-state	
1. Child voices	95%
2. Internal struggle	100%
3. Persecutory voice	88%
4. Speech insertion	85%
5. Thought insertion/withdrawal	93%
6. 'Made' feelings	95%
7. 'Made' impulses	85%
8. 'Made' actions	98%
9. Experiences of self-alteration	98%
10. Self-puzzlement	98%
C. Amnesia	
1. Time loss	88%
2. Coming to	78%
3. Fugues	83%
4. Being told of things done/said	85%
5. Finding objects among possessions	61%
6. Evidence of one's recent actions	71%
7. Not remembering name/identity	68%
8. Forgetting a well-rehearsed skill	93%

I would like to thank John O'Neil and Vedat Şar for their very helpful comments. I would especially like to thank Elizabeth Bowman; this chapter has benefited immeasurably from her wise and detailed critique.

REFERENCES

Adityanjee, G. S., Raju, G. S., & Khandelwal, S. K. (1989). Current status of multiple personality disorder in India. *American Journal of Psychiatry, 146,* 1607–1610.

Alexander, P. J., Joseph, S., & Das, A. (1997). Limited utility of ICD-10 and DSM-IV classification of dissociative and conversion disorders in India. *Acta Psychiatrica Scandinavica, 95,* 177–182.

American Psychiatric Association (1968). DSM-II – *Diagnostic and statistical manual of mental disorders* (2nd ed.). Washington, DC: Author.

American Psychiatric Association (1980). DSM-III – *Diagnostic and statistical manual of mental disorders* (3rd ed.). Washington, DC: Author.

American Psychiatric Association (1987). DSM-III-R–*Diagnostic and statistical manual of mental disorders* (3rd ed., revised). Washington, DC: Author.

American Psychiatric Association (1994). DSM-IV – *Diagnostic and Statistical Manual of Mental Disorders* (4th ed.). Washington, DC: Author.

Bailey, K. D. (1973). Monothetic and polythetic typologies and their relation to conceptualization, measurement and scaling. *American Sociological Review, 38,* 18–33.

Beckner, M. (1959). *The biological way of thought.* New York: Columbia University Press.

Blashfield, R. K. (1986). Structural approaches to classification. In T. Millon & G. L. Klerman (Eds.), *Contemporary directions in psychopathology: Toward the DSM-IV* (pp. 363–380). New York: Guilford Press.

Blashfield, R. K., & Livesley, W. J. (1991). Metaphorical analysis of psychiatric classification as a psychological test. *Journal of Abnormal Psychology, 100,* 262–270.

Bliss, E. L. (1980). Multiple personalities: A report of 14 cases with implications for schizophrenia. *Archives of General Psychiatry, 37,* 1388–1397.

Bliss, E. L. (1986). *Multiple personality, allied disorders, and hypnosis.* New York: Oxford University Press.

Boon, S., & Draijer, N. (1993). *Multiple personality disorder in The Netherlands: A study on reliability and validity of the diagnosis.* Amsterdam/Lisse: Swets & Zeitlinger.

Braun, B. G. (1985). The transgenerational incidence of dissociation and multiple personality disorder: A preliminary report. In R. P. Kluft (Ed.), *Childhood antecedents of multiple personality* (pp. 127–150). Washington, DC: American Psychiatric Press.

Braun, B. G. (1988). The BASK model of dissociation. *Dissociation, 1*(1), 4–23.

Brenner, I. (2001). *Dissociation of trauma: Theory, phenomenology, and technique.* Madison, CT: International Universities Press.

Cantor, N., Smith, E. E., French, R. S., & Mezzich, J. (1980). Psychiatric diagnosis as prototype categorization. *Journal of Abnormal Psychology, 89,* 181–193.

Cardeña, E., & Spiegel, D. (1996). Diagnostic issues, criteria, and comorbidity of dissociative disorders. In L. K. Michelson & W. J. Ray (Eds.), *Handbook of dissociation: Theoretical, empirical, and clinical perspectives* (pp. 227–250). New York: Plenum Press.

Chu, J. A. (1998). *Rebuilding shattered lives: The responsible treatment of complex posttraumatic and dissociative disorders.* New York: Wiley.

Clark, L. A., Watson, D., & Reynolds, S. (1995). Diagnosis and classification of psychopathology: Challenges to the current system and future directions. *Annual Review of Psychology, 46,* 121–153.

Coons, P. M. (1980). Multiple personality: Diagnostic considerations. *Journal of Clinical Psychiatry, 41*, 330–336.

Coons, P. M. (1984). The differential diagnosis of multiple personality. *Psychiatric Clinics of North America, 7*, 51–67.

Coons, P. M. (1989). The importance of nosology for MPD/dissociative states. *Newsletter of the International Society for the Study of Multiple Personality and Dissociation, 7*(2), 1–2.

Coons, P. M. (2001). On changing the diagnostic criteria for dissociative identity disorder. *Journal of Trauma & Dissociation, 2*(1), 43–46.

Coons, P. M., Bowman, E. S., & Milstein, V. (1988). Multiple personality disorder: A clinical investigation of 50 cases. *Journal of Nervous and Mental Disease, 176*, 519–527.

Coons, P. M., & Chu, J. (2000). Psychiatrists' attitudes toward dissociative disorder diagnoses. *American Journal of Psychiatry, 157*, 1179–1180.

Das, P. S., & Saxena, S. (1991). Classification of dissociative states in DSM-III-R and ICD-10 (1989 Draft): A study of Indian outpatients. *British Journal of Psychiatry, 159*, 425–427.

Dell, P. F. (2001a). Why the diagnostic criteria for dissociative identity disorder should be changed. *Journal of Trauma & Dissociation, 2*(1), 7–37.

Dell, P. F. (2001b). Should the dissociative disorders field choose its own diagnostic criteria for dissociative identity disorder? Reply to Cardeña, Coons, Putnam, Spiegel, and Steinberg. *Journal of Trauma & Dissociation, 2*(1), 65–72.

Dell, P. F. (2001c). Why DSM-IV's portrayal of DID is a problem. *ISSD News, 19*(2), 4–7.

Dell, P. F. (2006a). The Multidimensional Inventory of Dissociation (MID): A comprehensive measure of pathological dissociation. *Journal of Trauma & Dissociation, 7*(2), 77–106.

Dell, P. F. (2006b). A new model of dissociative identity disorder. *Psychiatric Clinics of North America, 29*(1), 1–26.

Dell, P. F. (2009a). The long struggle to diagnose multiple personality disorder (MPD). II Partial MPD. In P. F. Dell & J. A. O'Neil (Eds.), *Dissociation and the dissociative disorders: DSM-V and beyond* (pp. 403–428). New York: Routledge.

Dell, P. F. (2009b). The phenomena of pathological dissociation. In P. F. Dell & J. A. O'Neil (Eds.), *Dissociation and the dissociative disorders: DSM-V and beyond* (pp. 225–238). New York: Routledge.

Eysenck, H. J. (1986). A critique of contemporary classification and diagnosis. In T. Millon & G. L. Klerman (Eds.), *Contemporary directions in psychopathology: Toward the DSM-IV* (pp. 73–98). New York: Guilford Press.

Frances, A. J., Pincus, H. A., Widiger, T. A., Davis, W. W., & First, W. (1994). DSM-IV: Work in Progress. In J. E. Mezzich, M. R. Jorge, & I. M. Saloum (Eds.), *Psychiatric epidemiology: Assessment concepts and methods* (pp. 116–135). Baltimore: Johns Hopkins University Press.

Friedl, M. C., Draijer, N., & de Jonge, P. (2000). Prevalence of dissociative disorders in psychiatric in-patients: The impact of study characteristics. *Acta Psychiatrica Scandinavica, 102,* 423–428.

Gast, U., Rodewald, F., Dehner-Rau, C., Kowalewsky, E., Engl, V., Reddemann, L., & Emrich, H. M. (2003, November). *Validation of the German version of the Multidimensional Inventory of Dissociation (MID-d).* Paper presented at annual meeting of the International Society for the Study of Dissociation. Chicago, IL.

First, M. B., Pincus, H. A., Levine, J. B., Williams, J. B. W., Ustun, B., & Peele, R. (2004). Clinical utility as a criterion for revising psychiatric diagnoses. *American Journal of Psychiatry, 161*, 946–954.

Frances, A., & Widiger, T. A. (1986). Methodological issues in personality disorder diagnosis. In T. Millon & G. L. Klerman (Eds.), *Contemporary directions in psychopathology: Toward the DSM-IV* (pp. 381–400). New York: Guilford Press.

Fraser, G. A. (1994). Dissociative phenomena and disorders: Clinical presentations. In R. M. Klein & B. K. Doane (Eds.), *Psychological concepts and dissociative disorders* (pp. 131–151). Hillsdale, NJ: Lawrence Erlbaum Associates.

Greaves, G.B. (1980). Multiple personality: 165 years after Mary Reynolds. *Journal of Nervous and Mental Disease, 168*, 577–596.

Horevitz, R. (1994). Dissociation and multiple personality: Conflicts and controversies. In S. J. Lynn & J. W. Rhue (Eds.), *Dissociation: Clinical and theoretical perspectives* (pp. 434–461). New York: Plenum Press.

Kendell, R. E. (1975). *The role of diagnosis in psychiatry.* Oxford: Blackwell Scientific Publications.

Kenny, M. G. (1981). Multiple personality and spirit possession. *Psychiatry, 44*, 337–358.

Kluft, R. P. (1982). Varieties of hypnotic interventions in the treatment of multiple personality. *American Journal of Clinical Hypnosis, 24*, 230–240.

Kluft, R. P. (1985a). Making the diagnosis of multiple personality disorder (MPD). In F. F. Flach (Ed.), *Directions in Psychiatry, 5*(23), 1–10.

Kluft, R. P. (1985b). The natural history of multiple personality disorder. In R. P. Kluft (Ed.), *Childhood antecedents of multiple personality* (pp. 197–238). Washington, DC: American Psychiatric Press.

Kluft, R. P. (1987a). Dissociative disorders. In A. E. Skodol & R. L. Spitzer (Eds.), *An annotated bibliography of DSM-III* (pp. 119–124). Washington, DC: American Psychiatric Press.

Kluft, R. P. (1987b). First-rank symptoms as a diagnostic clue to multiple personality disorder. *American Journal of Psychiatry, 144*, 293–298.

Kluft, R. P. (1988). The phenomenology and treatment of extremely complex multiple personality disorder. *Dissociation, 1*, 47–58.

Kluft, R. P. (1999). Current issues in dissociative identity disorder. *Journal of Practice of Psychiatry and Behavioral Health, 7*, 3–19.

Kluft, R. P., Steinberg, M., & Spitzer, R. L. (1988). DSM-III-R revisions in the dissociative disorders: An exploration of their derivation and rationale. *Dissociation, 1*, 39–46.

Livesley, W. J. (1985). The classification of personality disorder: I. The choice of category concept. *Canadian Journal of Psychiatry, 30*, 353–358.

Loewenstein, R. J. (1991). An office mental status examination for complex chronic dissociative symptoms and multiple personality disorder. *Psychiatric Clinics of North America, 14*, 567–604.

Loewenstein, R. J., Hamilton, J., Alagna, S., Reid, N., & deVries, M. (1987). Experiential sampling in the study of multiple personality disorder. *American Journal of Psychiatry, 144*(1), 19–24.

Loewenstein, R. J., Hornstein, N., & Farber, B. (1988). Open trial of clonazepam in the treatment of posttraumatic stress symptoms of multiple personality disorder. *Dissociation, 1*, 3–12.

Loewenstein, R. J., & Putnam, F. W. (1990). The clinical phenomenology of males with multiple personality disorder: A report of 21 cases. *Dissociation, 3*, 135–143.

Marmer, S.S. (1980). Psychoanalysis of multiple personality. *International Journal of Psycho-Analysis, 61*, 439–459.

Martínez-Taboas, A. (1991). Multiple personality disorder as seen from a social constructionist viewpoint. *Dissociation, 4*, 129–133.

Mezzich, J. E., Fabrega, H., Coffman, G. A., & Haley, R. (1989). DSM-III disorders in a large sample of psychiatric patients: Frequency and specificity of diagnoses. *American Journal of Psychiatry, 146*, 212–219.

Nakdimen, K. A. (1992). Diagnostic criteria for multiple personality disorder. *American Journal of Psychiatry, 149*, 576–577.

Nakdimen, K. A. (2006). Dissociative disorder undiagnosed due to undescriptive criteria? *American Journal of Psychiatry, 163*(9), 1645.

Peterson, G., & Putnam, F. W. (1994). Preliminary results of the field trial of proposed criteria for dissociative disorder of childhood. *Dissociation, 7*, 212–220.

Putnam, F. W. (1997). *Dissociation in children and adolescents: A developmental perspective.* New York: Guilford Press.

Putnam, F. W. (1989). *Diagnosis and treatment of multiple personality disorder.* New York: Guilford Press.

Putnam, F. W. (1993). Diagnosis and clinical phenomenology of multiple personality disorder: A North American perspective. *Dissociation, 6*, 80–86.

Putnam, F. W. (2001). Reclaiming dissociative disorders. *Journal of Trauma & Dissociation, 2*(1), 47–49.

Putnam, F. W., & Loewenstein, R. J. (2000). Dissociative identity disorder. In B. J. Sadock & V. A. Kaplan (Eds.), *Comprehensive Textbook of Psychiatry* (7th ed., pp. 1552–1564). Baltimore, MD: Lippincott Williams & Wilkins.

Rosenbaum, M. (1980). The role of the term schizophrenia in the decline of diagnoses of multiple personality. *Archives of General Psychiatry, 37*, 1383–1385.

Ross, C. A. (1990). Comments on Takahashi's "Is MPD really rare in Japan?" *Dissociation, 3*, 64–65.

Ross, C. A. (1991). Epidemiology of multiple personality disorder and dissociation. *Psychiatric Clinics of North America, 14*(3), 503–517.

Ross, C. A. (1997). *Dissociative Identity Disorder: Diagnosis, clinical features, and treatment of multiple personality.* New York: Wiley.

Ross, C. A., Duffy, C. M. M., & Ellason, J. W. (2002). Prevalence, reliability and validity of dissociative disorders in an inpatient setting. *Journal of Trauma & Dissociation, 3*(1), 7–17.

Ross, C. A., Miller, S. D., Reagor, P., Bjornson, L., Fraser, G. A., & Anderson, G. (1990b). Schneiderian symptoms in multiple personality disorder and schizophrenia. *Comprehensive Psychiatry, 31*(2), 111–118.

Saxe, G. N., Van der Kolk, B. A., Berkowitz, R., Chinman, G., Hall, K., Lieberg, G., & Schwartz, J. (1993). Dissociative disorders in psychiatric inpatients. *American Journal of Psychiatry, 150*, 1037–1042.

Saxena, S., & Prasad, K. V. S. R. (1989). DSM-III subclassification of dissociative disorders applied to psychiatric outpatients in India. *American Journal of Psychiatry, 146*, 261–262.

Schneider, K. (1959). *Clinical psychopathology.* New York: Grune & Stratton.

Sneath, P. H. A. (1962). The construction of taxonomic groups. In G. C. Ainsworth & P. H. A. Sneath (Eds.), *Microbiological classification. 12th symposium of the Society for general Microbiology* (pp. 289–332). Cambridge: Cambridge University Press.

Sneath, P. H. A., & Sokal, R. R. (1973). *Numerical taxonomy: The principles and practice of numerical classification.* San Francisco: Freeman.

Sokal, R. R. (1966). Numerical taxonomy. *Scientific American, 215*, 106–117.

Spiegel, D., & Cardeña, E. (1991). Disintegrated experience: The dissociative disorders revisited. *Journal of Abnormal Psychology, 100*, 366–378.

Spira, J. L. (1996). Introduction: Understanding and treating dissociative identity disorder. In J. L. Spira (Ed.), *Treating dissociative identity disorder* (pp. xvii–lv). San Francisco: Jossey-Bass Publishers.

Spitzer, R. L., Endicott, J., & Robins, E. (1975). Clinical criteria for psychiatric diagnosis and DSM-III. *American Journal of Psychiatry, 132*, 1187–1192.

Spitzer, R. L., Endicott, J., & Robins, E. (1978). Research diagnostic criteria: Rationale and reliability. *Archives of General Psychiatry, 35*, 773–782.

Spitzer, R. L., Williams, J. B. W., & Skodol, A. E. (1980). DSM-III: The major achievements and an overview. *American Journal of Psychiatry, 137*, 151–164.

Steinberg, M. (1995). *Handbook for the assessment of dissociation: A clinical guide.* Washington, DC: American Psychiatric Press.

Steinberg, M. (2001). Updating diagnostic criteria for dissociative disorders: Learning from scientific advances. *Journal of Trauma & Dissociation, 2*(1), 59–63.

Takahashi, Y. (1990). Is multiple personality disorder really rare in Japan? *Dissociation, 3*, 57–59.

Tutkun, H., Şar, V., Yargıç, L. I., Özpulat, T., Yanık, M., & Kızıltan, E. (1998). Frequency of dissociative disorders among psychiatric inpatients in a Turkish University Clinic. *American Journal of Psychiatry, 155*, 800–805.

Umesue, M., Matsuo, T., Iwata, N., & Tashiro, N. (1996). Dissociative disorders in Japan: A pilot study with the Dissociative Experience Scale and a semi-structured interview. *Dissociation, 9*, 182–189.

Widiger, T. A., Frances, A., Spitzer, R. L., & Williams, J. B. W. (1988). The DSM-III-R personality disorders: An overview. *American Journal of Psychiatry, 145*, 786–795.

Wig, N. N. (1983). DSM-III: A perspective from the Third World. In R. L. Spitzer, J. B. W. Williams, & A. E. Skodol (Eds.), *International perspectives on DSM-III*. Washington, DC: American Psychiatric Press.

Wittgenstein, L. (1953). *Philosophical investigations*. New York: Macmillan Publishers.

25 The Long Struggle to Diagnose Multiple Personality Disorder (MPD): Partial MPD

Paul F. Dell, PhD

OUTLINE

In the fourth edition of the Diagnostic and Statistical Manual of Mental Disorders (DSM-IV; American Psychiatric Association), the first example of Dissociative Disorder Not Otherwise Specified (i.e., DDNOS-1) is "clinical presentations similar to Dissociative Identity Disorder that fail to meet full criteria for this disorder" (p. 490). This definition of DDNOS-1 has a necessary implication. As the criteria for DID change, so, too, must the nature of DDNOS-1 change.

Before discussing DDNOS-1, a few prefatory comments are necessary regarding the Not Otherwise Specified (NOS) category of the modern DSM (American Psychiatric Association, 1980, 1987, 1994). The examples that are listed in an NOS category do not have the same DSM-status as do the specific disorders. In fact, NOS *examples* have no diagnostic status whatsoever, except as almost a footnote in the NOS category. NOS examples simply identify *some clinical presentations that the DSM does not recognize as specific disorders*. So, even though the DSM lists some NOS examples, they are not official disorders. That is why NOS examples do not have their own numerical ICD-9 codes. Only the NOS category as a whole (e.g., DDNOS) has a numerical ICD-9 code (i.e., 300.15). Note also that NOS examples do not have a set of framed "Diagnostic Criteria," as do all of the specific disorders in the DSM.

So, what does this mean for DDNOS-1? It means that partial DID (i.e., DDNOS-1) exists in the minds of clinicians, but that it has no diagnostic status in the DSM. It means that partial DID exists in the empirical literature (which diagnoses it as DDNOS and reports its prevalence and dissociative characteristics), but partial DID has no official existence in the DSM.[1] This is a significant problem because, in studies of clinical populations, DDNOS-1 is the most common diagnosis (see the following). In fact, partial forms of DID are so common that the term *DDNOS* has come to mean "DDNOS-1" in the dissociative disorders field. The bottom line is that clinicians and researchers in the dissociative disorders field

[1] It is my impression that many clinicians incorrectly believe the NOS examples to be either (1) officially recognized disorders, or (2) disorders that, by virtue of being listed as NOS examples, are being considered for promotion to a specific disorder. Clinical presentations that are being evaluated for possible promotion to specific disorders are not listed as NOS examples; they are listed in Appendix B, Criteria Sets and Axes Provided for Further Study.

treat DDNOS as if it were a specific disorder (see the following), but it is not.[2]

25.1 DSM-III

25.1.1 The Official Birth of MPD—But Not of Partial MPD

DSM-III (American Psychiatric Association, 1980) set forth the first diagnostic criteria for MPD:

A. The existence within the individual of two or more distinct personalities, each of which is dominant at a particular time.
B. The personality that is dominant at any particular time determines the individual's behavior.
C. Each individual personality is complex and integrated with its own unique behavior patterns and social relationships. (DSM-III, p. 259)

On the other hand, DSM-III did not provide diagnostic criteria for partial MPD. In fact, DSM-III did not even acknowledge the possibility that partial MPD might exist. Clinicians, however, promptly overcame this nosological lacuna by using the Atypical category to diagnose what they witnessed in some of their patients.

25.1.2 Immediate Clinical Usage of Atypical Dissociative Disorder

Almost immediately, clinicians in the dissociative disorders field adopted the DSM-III's residual dissociative category (i.e., Atypical Dissociative Disorder) as a rule-out for MPD. That is, patients who were strongly suspected to have MPD were routinely issued a diagnosis of atypical dissociative disorder (ADD). This usage of the term *ADD* became a form of "diagnostic shorthand." That is, "ADD" generally *meant* "ADD, rule out MPD" (Boon & Draijer, 1993; Coons, 1992; Franklin, 1988; see also Ross et al., 1992;). A second usage of the diagnostic label soon evolved: ADD was used to refer to true partial MPD (Coons, 1992; Ross et al., 1992). By the time that the Dissociative Disorders Work Group for DSM-III-R was appointed, the dual usage of the diagnosis ADD was well-established: (1) ADD as a rule-out place-holder for MPD, and (2) ADD as a diagnostic label for partial forms of MPD.

Meanwhile, another nosological difficulty was brewing; all three of MPD's diagnostic criteria were misleading (Kluft, 1985b, 1987; Kluft, Steinberg, & Spitzer, 1988). In the following pages, I hope to show that revising the DSM-III diagnostic criteria for MPD was just the first step in a long struggle to clarify (1) the phenomena of MPD, and (2) the diagnostic criteria that would reflect those phenomena.

25.2 DSM-III-R

25.2.1 A Minimalist Version of MPD

DSM-III-R removed three glaring inaccuracies from the DSM-III diagnostic criteria for MPD: (1) Criterion A: at any given time, one of the personalities is dominant or in control[3]; (2) Criterion B: the personality that is dominant, determines the individual's behavior[4]; and (3) Criterion C: all personalities are complex and have their own behavior patterns and social relationships.[5] These DSM-III criteria were erroneous overgeneralizations from a small, atypical subset of people with MPD. The DSM-III-R Work Group then produced a stripped-down, minimalist description of MPD:

A. The existence within the person of two or more distinct personalities or personality states (each with its own relatively enduring pattern of perceiving, relating to, and thinking about the environment and self).
B. At least two of these personalities or personality states recurrently take full control of the person's behavior. (DSM-III-R, p. 273)

---

[2] What kind of existence does partial MPD have in the DSM? Put simply (and informally), DDNOS-1 is not even in the same ballpark as the specific dissociative disorders. Not even close. To quote my colleague, John O'Neil, "DSM's partial MPD ballpark is really just a little vacant space between the stands and the parking lot where 6-year-olds toss a ball back and forth and pretend they're ballplayers."

[3] "Criterion A mistakenly implies that at any given time, one person is dominant. In fact, periods of mixed, shared, contested, or rapid and unstable alternating dominance are commonly seen in many cases." (Kluft et al., 1988, p. 40)

[4] "Criterion B is potentially confusing. The personality that appears to be dominant and may represent itself as dominant may in fact be strongly influenced by another, of whose influence it may or may not be aware." (Kluft et al., 1988, p. 40)

[5] "Criterion C is problematic. The degree of elaboration and complexity of the separate entities has proven to be an expression of the interaction style of the personalities, the structure of the dissociative defenses, overall adaptive patterns, and character style of the individual patient rather than a core criterion of the illness." (Kluft et al., 1988, p. 40)

DSM-III-R defined MPD as multiple-personalities-that-switch. That's it. Nothing else. This was Kluft's view of MPD:

> what is essential to multiple personality disorder ... is no more than the presence ... of more than one structured entity with a sense of its own existence. (Kluft, 1985b, p. 231)

25.2.2 The Unofficial Birth of Atypical/Partial MPD: DDNOS

DSM-III-R acknowledged the existence of atypical or partial MPD—but minimally, by listing it as an example of DDNOS:

> *DSM-III-R's Example 2 of DDNOS:*
>
> cases in which there is more than one personality state capable of assuming executive control of the individual, but not more than one personality is sufficiently distinct to meet the full criteria for Multiple Personality Disorder, or cases in which a second personality never assumes complete executive control. (DSM-III-R, p. 277)

The addition of this new type of DDNOS was anything but whole-hearted on the part of the DSM-III-R Work Group (Dell, 2009a). The Work Group was divided about whether these cases were a different disorder (i.e., different from MPD), or whether they were just a less symptomatic form of MPD. This division of opinion can be seen in the article that described the decisions of the DSM-III-R Dissociative Disorders Work Group:

> Proposals were received to create separate classifications for patients who have syndromes that have the same structure as Multiple Personality Disorder, but with less overt manifestations.... The committee acknowledged that these conditions exist and have been documented, but that at this time the evidence remains too preliminary to serve as the basis of new classifications. *Longitudinal data suggests that they may all prove to be phases of the same disorder* (Kluft, 1985b). A decision was made to ... include examples under Dissociative Disorder NOS that explicitly acknowledged less overtly manifested conditions. (Kluft et al., 1988, p. 44. italics added)

So, how did DSM-III-R differentiate these new examples of DDNOS from MPD? DSM-III-R suggested two differences between MPD and MPD-like forms of DDNOS: (1) whether a second personality is *sufficiently distinct*, and (2) whether a second personality ever *assumes complete control*. I believe that these boundary-defining criteria are not as transparent as they may seem. In particular, I contend that the MPD criterion of "distinct personalities" is a quagmire of vagueness that has impaired research, burdened clinical assessment, and undermined our understanding of both DID[6] and partial forms of DID.

25.2.3 The Distinct Personalities Criterion

The *distinct personalities* criterion resides in every edition of the DSM since 1980; it is, arguably, *the* central diagnostic criterion of MPD/DID. That is, both Criterion A (personalities) and Criterion B (complete switches of control) depend upon the second personality being "sufficiently distinct" to actually *be* a second personality. Thus, the distinctness of a second personality is the DSM's foundation for the diagnosis of MPD. The "distinct personalities" criterion lies at the heart of (1) the criteria for MPD and (2) the descriptions of partial/atypical MPD in (3) all three editions of the modern DSM (American Psychiatric Association, 1980, 1987, 1994).

And yet, despite its foundational importance, the "distinct personalities" criterion has never been defined! The DSM has never specified the clinical phenomena or the diagnostic rules for determining whether a personality is "sufficiently distinct." The DSM hasn't even clarified which meaning of the word *distinct* is intended (i.e., "different from" vs. "clearly perceivable").[7]

What, exactly, is a *personality*? DSM-III-R tells us that a personality has "its own relatively enduring pattern of perceiving, relating to, and thinking about the environment and self" (p. 273). That's all that DSM-III-R tells us about alter personalities. How well does this prepare the average clinician to diagnose MPD? Fortunately, there is some more sophisticated help. As is true of so much that pertains to MPD, Kluft has offered the literature's best description of an alter personality:

> I have tended to define a personality, alter, or disaggregate self state in a manner that stresses what such an entity does and how it behaves and functions rather than by emphasizing quantitative dimensions: A disaggregate self state (i.e., personality) is the mental address of a relatively stable and enduring particular pattern of selective mobilization of mental contents and functions, which may be behaviorally enacted with noteworthy role-taking and role-playing dimensions and sensitive to intrapsychic, interpersonal, and environmental stimuli.... It has

---

[6] DSM-IV renamed multiple personality disorder as *Dissociative Identity Disorder* (DID).

[7] "**distinct** *a*. [1] Not identical, separate, individual, different in quality or kind, unlike (*from*, or abs.); [2] clearly perceptive, plain, definite." (Oxford, 1976)

> a sense of its own identity and ideation, and a capacity for initiating thought processes and actions. (Kluft, 1988, p. 51)

In MPD, there are two or more of these that are "distinct." In DDNOS-1a, there are two or more of these, but only one of them is "sufficiently distinct" (DSM-III-R, p. 277). Clear? My question is, "Why haven't the clinicians and researchers in the dissociative disorders field complained loudly about this situation?"

25.2.4 Two Basic Facts About MPD

So, how can clinicians discern the presence of alter personalities? What do alter personalities look like? The best answers to these questions can be found in Kluft's (1985b) superb clinical description of MPD: "The natural history of multiple personality disorder." This 20-year-old clinical-descriptive essay is still the single best account of the appearance and behavior of alter personalities. Upon re-reading this remarkable piece of clinical-descriptive psychiatry, we (re)discover two basic facts about MPD.

First, *although the DSM requires the presence of distinct personalities, naturally occurring DID does not.* Quite the contrary. DID is a defensive adaptation that protects the person from a chronically dangerous environment. DID's first priority is defense—not the conspicuous display of distinct personalities:

> The *raison d'être* of multiple personality disorder is to provide a structured dissociative defense against overwhelming traumata. The emitted observable manifestations of multiple personality disorder are epiphenomena and tools of the defensive purpose. In terms of the patient's needs, the personalities need only be as distinct, public, and elaborate as becomes necessary in the handling of stressful situations. (Kluft, 1985b, p. 231)

In fact, most multiples self-protectively *hide* their multiplicity from others (Kluft, 1985b). Second, visible switches from one distinct personality to another are infrequent: "visible switching from one alter to another probably ranks among the least frequent phenomena of DID" (Dell, 2009a).

In short, "overtness is not a basic ingredient of MPD" (Kluft, 1985a, p. 6)—even if the DSM implies that it is (or that it should be). Remember, the DSM *requires* overt DID; if the clinician cannot discern the presence of two or more distinct identities who switch (i.e., overt DID), then the patient cannot receive a diagnosis of DID.

Now, obviously, many cases of DID have been successfully diagnosed on the basis of the "distinct personalities" criterion. What about them? Kluft (1985b) has discussed five factors that render the personalities distinctly visible (and, thus, susceptible to being diagnosed as MPD): (1) lack of psychological resilience, (2) significant stress, (3) contention and conflict among the alters, (4) certain styles of exerting influence over the host personality (e.g., inner verbalized threats and seizure of executive control), and (5) alters who have a narcissistic investment in appearing visibly different. These five clinical factors unmistakably facilitate the diagnosis of MPD on the basis of the "distinct personalities" criterion. The problem is that these factors pertain to a small minority of MPD patients at the sicker end of the scale or during episodic decompensations. The overwhelming majority of MPD patients do not manifest "distinct personalities" (or, they do so very infrequently).

I do not believe that it is possible to operationalize the "distinct personalities" criterion in a way that will allow clinicians to successfully diagnose those MPD patients who are currently undetectable (according to the "distinct personalities" criterion). Kluft cut to the heart of this matter when he urged the dissociative disorders field to ask the following question:

> How can one discover the presence of multiple personality disorder in the absence of its classical manifestations [i.e., distinct personalities and switching]? (Kluft, 1985b, p. 203)

In my opinion, *this* is the question that we must ask (and answer) in order to devise diagnostic criteria for DID (and DDNOS-1) that are both efficacious and user-friendly.[8]

25.2.5 Too Little Awareness of the Impediments to Diagnosing DID?

Let us summarize the situation that clinicians faced between 1987 and 1994 when they sought to diagnose DID with DSM-III-R: (1) DSM-III-R says that the diagnosis of DID requires the presence of two or more "distinct personalities" that switch; (2) in contrast, DID itself

[8] Some would assert that there is a more important question: "*Can* we diagnose DID in the absence of switching?" That is, if identity alteration does not occur, then how can we say that there is an *identity* disorder? How can we say that there are multiple personalities? From the perspective of the modern DSM, it would seem that the answer to these latter two questions must be: "We can't." And yet, I believe that this prohibitory answer stems from the DSM's *definition* of the disorder, rather than from *the nature of the disorder itself.*

does not require that personalities be overtly visible;[9] (3) in fact, persons with DID typically hide and dissemble any evidence of their alters (Kluft, 1985b); (4) visible switching from one distinct alter to another is one of the most infrequent phenomena of DID (Dell, 2009a; Kluft, 1985b); and (5) the DSM provides no guidance whatsoever (i.e., signs and symptoms) about how to discern the presence of alter personalities.

These facts were known to the DSM-III-R Dissociative Disorders Work Group back in 1985. Nevertheless, efforts to base the diagnostic criteria for MPD upon signs and symptoms were voted down, thereby reaffirming the "distinct personalities" criterion. Accordingly, it would seem that the Work Group was unresponsive to, or did not seem to appreciate, the almost untenable position of the average clinician when faced with the task of diagnosing DID.

This was also the context for the unofficial birth of partial MPD. True to its commitment to the "distinct personalities" criterion of MPD, the Work Group described the personalities of partial MPD as being "not ... sufficiently distinct." Thus, DSM-III-R described partial MPD as:

> cases in which there is more than one personality state capable of assuming executive control of the individual, *but not more than one personality is sufficiently distinct* to meet the full criteria for Multiple Personality Disorder. (p. 277, italics added)

In my opinion, the DSM-III-R Work Group made a fateful error when they described this example of DDNOS with the phrase, "not ... sufficiently distinct." This phrase has profoundly influenced the diagnostic practices of both clinicians and researchers. Specifically, given the hiddenness of alter personalities and the infrequency of visible switching, it was inevitable that many persons with DID would be diagnosed as having DDNOS (because their alter personalities were "not ... sufficiently distinct" to the diagnostician). In short, I contend that the Work Group built into DSM-III-R[10] a slippery diagnostic slope that relegates many persons with DID to the DDNOS category.[11]

25.3 DSM-IV

25.3.1 A Work Group Riven by Dissent

Has any psychiatric disorder evoked as much controversy as MPD? Have disagreements about a psychiatric disorder ever produced such intense skepticism, contempt, and *ad hominem* arguments? Was the DSM-IV Work Group assisted in its endeavors by the inclusion of representatives from both sides of this vitriolic debate? The answer to these three questions is, "No." As Putnam (2001) has declared, "The political need to 'balance' the committee with proponents and critics ... insured virtual paralysis" (p. 48).

At that point in history, MPD was surrounded by a firestorm of attack and controversy. Challenges to the scientific literature on MPD more closely resembled the emotional rhetoric of courtroom prosecutors than the reasoned analysis of scientific debate. If ever there was a time when a Work Group needed to put its scientific house in order, this was it. Unfortunately, the controversy about DID afflicted the DSM-IV Work Group itself; this circumstance made it impossible for the Work Group to remedy the DSM's problematic adherence to the criterion of "distinct personalities" (see the following).

25.3.2 Finally—An Amnesia Criterion for DID

Following years of debate (since 1980 or earlier; see Dell, 2009a), the DSM-IV Work Group voted to add an amnesia criterion to DID:

> Inability to recall important personal information that is too extensive to be explained by ordinary forgetfulness. (DSM-IV, p. 529)

[9] Strictly speaking, the DSM does not say that personalities must be overtly visible—just that they exist. The bottom line, of course, is that the DSM should, but does not, enumerate a set of signs and/or symptoms whereby the clinician can determine the presence or existence of other distinct personalities. This issue is further complicated by the fact that this determination is more easily and reliably based on the patient's subjective report of symptoms (rather than the clinician's observation of the signs of a distinct personality). The gold standard for assessing DID (i.e., the SCID-D-R), for example, makes this determination on the basis of the patient's reports of symptoms rather than the clinician's observation of signs (see footnote 16).

[10] To be precise, this slippery slope originated with DSM-III (which was the first DSM to place the "distinct personalities" criterion in the diagnostic criteria for Multiple Personality Disorder). DSM-III-R retained DSM-III's distinct personalities criterion and imposed it upon DDNOS (i.e., partial MPD) as well.

[11] The pragmatic clinical view may be that the incorrect DDNOS diagnosis "doesn't really matter." This view correctly notes that DID and partial DID are treated similarly; therefore, either diagnosis will lead (or should lead) to appropriate treatment for the patient. As a clinician, I am quite sympathetic to this point of view. As a nosologist and a researcher, however, I am not. The pragmatic clinical perspective may be quite appropriate to the arena of clinical care (although we really don't know for sure because we still know so little about the differences between DID and DDNOS-1), but this pragmatic clinical perspective has no place in the arena of nosology and nosological research.

Although defined in a vague and unhelpful manner, this amnesia criterion is important for at least two reasons. First, it redrew the boundaries of DID. Second, it finally placed an actual diagnostic sign or symptom within the diagnostic criteria for DID—DID's first true diagnostic criterion (in the usual DSM sense of the term).

25.3.3 The Continued Reign of the "Distinct Personalities" Criterion

On the other hand, the Work Group did not enumerate any other signs or symptoms of DID that could explicate (or replace) the "distinct personalities" criterion:

> The "amnesia" criterion was added, but other attempts to increase criterion specificity stalled amid the contention, confusion, and inertia of the group. (Putnam, 2001, p. 48)

And so, the reign of the criterion of "distinct personalities" would continue—in both DID and DDNOS-1a—for at least another 18 years (i.e., 1994–2012):

> **Criterion A for DID:** The presence of two or more *distinct identities or personality states* (each with its own relatively enduring pattern of perceiving, relating to, and thinking about the environment and self). (DSM-IV, p. 529, italics added)
>
> **Description of DDNOS-1a:** Clinical presentations similar to Dissociative Identity Disorder ... in which a) there are not two or more *distinct personality states* ... (DSM-IV, p. 532, italics added)

25.3.4 DDNOS-1: Hostage to the Diagnostic Criteria for DID

As I noted above, partial DID (i.e., DDNOS-1) is defined in reference to DID. As DID changes, so, too, must DDNOS-1 change. In DSM-IV, DID's Criterion A and B did not change (except that the "distinct personalities" criterion became the "distinct identities or personality states" criterion). Criterion C, however, was completely new. This necessitated a change in the DSM's characterization of DDNOS-1. Whereas DSM-III-R allowed for cases of MPD without amnesia, DSM-IV labeled these cases, *DDNOS-1b*:

> Clinical presentations similar to Dissociative Identity Disorder ... in which ... amnesia for personal information does not occur. (DSM-IV, p. 532)[12]

DSM-IV made one additional change to DDNOS. Whereas DSM-III-R DDNOS had included "cases in which a second personality never assumes complete executive control" (DSM-III-R, p. 277), the DSM-IV Work Group elected to remove these cases from DDNOS-1. According to Spiegel and Cardeña (1991), these cases were left out "because of the changes in the criteria for MPD" (p. 374). The reasoning for this, however, is not readily apparent. Are Spiegel and Cardeña claiming that amnesia is the defining marker of complete assumption of executive control by a second personality?

In closing, I contend that the 28-year reign of the "distinct personalities" criterion has seriously undermined the quality of research data on both DID and DDNOS. For the last 29 years, and for the next 3 years (until the publication of DSM-V), the slippery diagnostic slope in the DSM will continue to label many persons with DID as "DDNOS" (-1a). This means that most of the published data on DID may be based on biased samples that contain only the obvious cases of DID (i.e., those with sufficiently "distinct personalities"). If so, it necessarily follows that the reported prevalence-rates of DID are artifactually low. Finally, most of the research data on DDNOS may be contaminated with cases of covert DID (see the following). If so, it necessarily follows that the reported prevalence rates of DDNOS are artifactually high.

25.4 THE PREVALENCE OF DDNOS

In 1991, the chair of the DSM-IV Dissociative Disorders Work Group stated that something was seriously amiss with the DSM-III-R nosology of the dissociative disorders (Spiegel & Cardeña, 1991). Namely, epidemiological studies had shown that DDNOS was the most common dissociative disorder diagnosis. A high rate of any NOS diagnosis indicates a faulty nosology. When a nosology is accurate, NOS disorders should *never* be more common than the specific disorders. Cardeña and Spiegel recommended that the developers of DSM-V should solve this nosological problem:

> One of the greatest challenges for editors of future editions of the DSM will be to obtain greater taxonomical clarity, considering that the majority of diagnosed dissociative disorders do not fit the established criteria [for the specific dissociative disorders]. (Cardeña & Spiegel, 1996, p. 235)

Table 25.1 lists the published data on the prevalence of DDNOS and DID. Table 25.2 condenses and summarizes the findings in Table 25.1.

The most striking aspect of the data in Table 25.2 is the wide range of estimates of prevalence for each setting. Inspection of Table 25.1 reveals that the variance *within*

[12] Thus, a subset of DSM-III MPD patients and DSM-III-R MPD patients (i.e., those with no amnesia) would be classified as DDNOS-1b under DSM-IV.

TABLE 25.1
The Prevalence of Dissociative Disorders, DDNOS, and DID in 33 Samples

			N			Prevalence (%)			Proportion	
Study	**Research Population**	**Country**	**DD**	**NOS**	**DID**	**DD**	**NOS**	**DID**	**NOS**	**DID**
				Non-clinical						
Ross 1991	454 adults[a]	Canada	51	1	14	11.2%	0.2%	3.1%	2.0%	27.5%
	14 DDIS DID[b]				6			1.3%[a]		11.8%[a]
Akyüz et al. 1999	994 adults	Turkey								
	17 (of 62 w DES > 17)[a]		17	6	0	1.7%	0.6%	0%	35.3%	0%
	8 (of 17 w DDIS DD)[c]		7	1	4	0.7%	0.1%	0.4%	14.3%	57.1%
Xiao et al. 2006	618 factory workers[a]	China	2	0	0	0.3%	0%	0%	0%	0%
Şar et al. 1998	648 adult women[a]	Turkey	115	52	7	18.3%	8.3%	1.1%	45.2%	6.1%
				26[d]			4.1%[b]		22.6%[b]	
Ross, et al. 1991	345 college students	USA	14	2	8	4.1%	0.6%	2.3%	10.0%	40.0%
	20 w DES > 22.6[a]									
Murphy 1994	415 college students	USA	16	5	4	3.9%	1.2%	1.0%	31.3%	25.0%
	20 (of 37 w DES > 30)[a]									
				Outpatient series						
Mezzich et al. 1989	11,292 OPs[f]	USA	13	4	0	0.1%	0.04%	0%	30.8%	0%
			7[g]	4	0	0.06%	0.04%	0%	57.1%	0%
Graves 1989	125 CMHC OPs[c]	USA	11	8	3	8.8%	6.4%	2.4%	72.7%	27.3%
Dell 1998	58 consec. DD OPs[c]	USA	58	16	42				27.6%	72.4%
Sar et al. 2000b	150 Ops	Turkey								
	20 (of 23 w DES > 30)[a]		18	12	6	12.0%	8.0%	4.0%	67.7%	33.3%
	12 (of 18 w DDIS DD)		12	9	3	8.0%	6.0%	2.0%	75%	25%
Dell 2002	57 consec. DD OPs[c]	USA	57	23	34				40.4%	59.6%
Coons 1992	50 consec. DDNOS OPs[c]	USA		50						
				27[h]					54.0%	
Şar et al. 2003	240 OPs	Turkey								
	129 of 153 hi DES/ BPD[a]		33	23	6	13.8%	9.6%	2.5%	69.7%	18.2%
	44 w BPD or DDID DD[e]									
Somer & Dell 2005	16 DD OPs[e]	Israel	16	6	4				37.5%	25.0%
Lussier et al. 1997	70 day hosp. pts[i]	USA	6	1	5	8.6%	1.4%	7.1%	16.7%	83.3%
Foote et al. 2006	82 82 OPs[a]	USA	24	7	5	29.0%	9.0%	6.0%	29.0%	21.0%
				Inpatient series						
Horen et al. 1995	48 IPs	Canada								
	11 (of 14 w DES ≥ 25)[a]		8	0	4	16.7%	0%	8.3%	0%	50.0%
	9 (of 14 w DES ≥ 25)[e]		8	1	3	16.7%	2.1%	6.3%	12.5%	37.5%
Modestin et al. 1996	207 IPs	Switzerland								
	37 (of 41 w DES ≥ 20)[a]		10	4	1	4.8%	1.9%	0.5%	40.0%	10.0%
Gast et al. 2001	115 IPs	Germany								
	15 (of 25 w FDS > 20)[e]		5	3	0	4.3%	2.6%	0%	60.0%	0%
Tutkun et al. 1998	166 IPs	Turkey								
	21 of 24 w DES > 30)[a]		17	6	11	10.2%	3.6%	6.6%	35.3%	64.7%
	17 (of 17 w DDIS DD)[c]		17	8	9	10.2%	4.8%	5.4%	47.1%	52.9%
Friedl & Draijer 2000	122 IPs	NL								
	34 (of 36 w DES ≥ 25)[e]		10	8	2	8.2%	6.6%	1.6%	80.0%	20.0%

TABLE 25.1
The Prevalence of Dissociative Disorders, DDNOS, and DID in 33 Samples *(Continued)*

Lipsanen et al. 2004	34 IPs[a]	Finland	17	7	4	15.5%	9.9%	5.6%	41.2%	23.5%
	37 OPs									
Saxe et al. 1993	110 state hosp. IPs	USA								
	15 (of 17 w DES > 25)[a]		15	9	4	13.6%	8.2%	3.6%	60.0%	25.0%
Latz et al. 1995	176 state hosp. IPs[a]	USA	102	34	21	58.0%	19.3%	11.9%	33.3%	20.6%
			Specialty series							
Bowman et al. 1996	45 pseudoseizure OPs[c,e]	USA	41	28	7	91.1%	62.2%	15.6%	68.3%	17.1%
Frischholz et al. 1990	62 DD Unit IPs[c]	USA	62	29	33	100.0%	46.8%	53.2%	46.8%	53.2%
Ross et al. 2002	201 Trauma Unit IPs[a]	USA				40.8%	15.4%	7.5%	37.7%	18.4%
	110 of 201[e]					44.5%	20.0%	9.1%	44.9%	20.4%
	52 of 201[c]					26.9%	5.8%	9.6%	21.6%	35.7%
Şar et al. 2003	108 male prisoners	Turkey	17	10	0	15.7%	9.3%	0%	58.8%	0%
			Multisite research series							
Ensink et al.1989	20 recruited DD pts[c]	NL	20	13	7				65.0%	35.0%
Carlson & Putnam 1993	327 accum. DD pts[c]	USA		99	228				30.3%	69.7%
Dell 2005	73 accum. DD OPs[c]	USA	73	19	47				26.0%	64.4%
			Non-Western series							
Saxena & Prasad 1989	2,651 OPs[j]	India	62	56	0	2.3%	0.02%	0%	90.3%	0%
Das & Saxena 1991	1,517 OPs[j]	India	78			5.1%				
			42[k]	40	0	2.8%	2.6%	0%	95.2%	0%
Umesue et al. 1996	19 consec. DD OPs[e]	Japan	19	8	1				43.1%	5.3%
Alexander et al. 1997	720 IPs[j]	India	36	20	0	5.0%	2.8%	0%	55.6%	0%
Chand et al. 2000	1,294 IPs[j]	Oman	111	0	0	8.6%	0.0%	0%	0%	0%
Xiao et al. 2006	423 IPs[a]	China	7	3	2	1.7%	0.7%	0.5%	42.9%	28.6%
	304 OPs[a]		15	6	1	5.0%	2.0%	0.3%	40.0%	7.7%

Notes:
[a] Diagnoses in this row are based on the Dissociative Disorder Interview Schedule (DDIS)
[b] Diagnoses in this row require a history of trauma in addition to a DDIS diagnosis of DID
[c] Diagnoses in this row are based on clinical interview
[d] "DID-like conditions" (i.e., DDNOS-1)
[e] Diagnoses in this row are based on the Structured Clinical Interview for DSM-IV Dissociative Disorders (SCID-D)
[f] Diagnoses in this study were based on the Initial Evaluation Form
[g] Data in this row consist solely of patients with a primary diagnosis of dissociative disorder
[h] Data in this row consist solely of DDNOS patients with ego states
[i] Diagnoses in this row are based on the Mini-SCID-D
[j] Diagnoses in this row are based on chart review
[k] Data in this row consist of patients whose only diagnosis was a dissociative disorder

settings is due to the countries in which the studies were conducted. China, Germany, and Switzerland have low prevalences; the Netherlands has a moderate prevalence; and Canada, United States, Turkey, and Finland have high prevalences. For the most part (with the exception of DDNOS outpatients), the settings show a linear relationship between level of care and prevalence of DID and DDNOS.

25.4.1 Is DDNOS the Most Common Dissociative Diagnosis?

Scholars in the dissociation field have been divided about this matter. Some have argued that DDNOS is the most common dissociative diagnosis (Chu, 1996; Dell, 2001a; Fraser, 1994; Ross, 1997). Others have argued

TABLE 25.2
Prevalence of DDNOS and DID

	DDNOS		DID	
	Median (%)	**Range (%)**	**Median (%)**	**Range (%)**
Nonclinical	0.6	0–8.3	1.1	0–2.3
Outpatient	6.4	1.4–9.6	2.5	2.0–7.1
Inpatient	3.1	0–9.9	3.5	0–6.3
State Hospital	13.8	8.2–19.3	7.8	3.6–11.9

that diagnoses of Dissociative Amnesia are (or should be) most common (Coons & Milstein, 1992; Nemiah, 1985; Steinberg, 1993, 1995).

The relative prevalences of Dissociative Amnesia and DDNOS in the studies listed in Table 25.1[13] are as follows: (1) DDNOS tended to be the most prevalent dissociative diagnosis in psychiatric settings (Ensink et al., 1989; Friedl & Draijer, 2000; Frischholz et al., 1990; Gast et al., 2001; Graves, 1989; Mezzich et al., 1989; Modestin et al., 1996; Ross et al., 2002; Şar et al. 2000b, 2003; Saxe et al., 1993; Somer & Dell, 2005), but (2) Dissociative Amnesia was usually the most prevalent dissociative diagnosis in the general population (Akyüz et al., 1999; Ross, 1991; Xiao et al., 2006). In epidemiological samples of the general population, Dissociative Amnesia had an overall prevalence of 0.2% in China, 0.9% and 7.3% in Turkey, and 3.0% in Canada (versus 0%, 0.6%, 8.3%, and 0.09%, respectively for DDNOS).

25.4.2 What Proportion of Dissociative Diagnoses Are DDNOS?

Of all persons who are diagnosed with a dissociative disorder, what proportion has Dissociative Amnesia? What proportion has DDNOS? In China, the proportion of dissociative-disordered persons in the general population with Dissociative Amnesia was 50.0%; in Turkey, 52.9% and 40%; in Canada, 59.3%; and in the United States, 33% (versus 0%, 35.3%, 45.2%, and 2.0%, respectively for DDNOS).

In short, Dissociative Amnesia tends to be the most frequent dissociative diagnosis in the general population, whereas DDNOS is the most common dissociative diagnosis in psychiatric clinics and psychiatric hospitals. This difference may be due to (1) the particular patient population that inhabits psychiatric settings, or (2) the different diagnostic criteria and diagnostic habits of epidemiological researchers versus practicing clinicians.

25.4.3 Proportion of DDNOS Cases Among All Patients With a Dissociative Diagnosis[14]

In eight outpatient prevalence studies that specifically assessed the presence of dissociative disorders, the median proportion of DDNOS cases was 39.0% (range = 16.7% to 72.7%); the median proportion of DID cases was 26.1% (range = 18.2% to 83.3%). In six inpatient prevalence studies that specifically assessed for the presence of dissociative disorders, the median proportion of DDNOS cases was 40.6% (range = 12.5% to 80.0); the median proportion of DID cases was 21.8% (range = 0% to 52.9%). Finally, in two state hospital prevalence studies that specifically assessed for the presence of dissociative disorders, the median proportion of DDNOS cases was 46.7% (range = 33.3% to 60.0%); the median proportion of DID cases was 22.8% (range = 20.6% to 25.0%). Thus, the median proportion of DDNOS cases (compared to all DD

[13] Note: data on the prevalence of Dissociative Amnesia are *not* included in Table 25.1.

[14] Although Table 25.1 contains data from six non-Western clinical studies, none of the discussion in this chapter addresses these studies. DSM-IV is extremely ill-suited to non-Western dissociative disorders (Wig, 1983), but the reasons for that are quite different from the DSM's shortcomings vis-à-vis DID and DDNOS-1 in Western settings. In brief, many non-Western countries are characterized by a very different kind of self from that of Western countries (Martínez-Taboas, 1991; Takahashi, 1990; Umesue et al., 1996). Thus, from a Western perspective, most non-Western dissociative disorders are considered to be strongly culture-bound. Similarly, from a non-Western perspective, many DSM-IV dissociative disorders (especially DID and DDNOS-1) appear to be strongly culture-bound (Adityanjee, 1990). In short, DSM-IV is inadequate for non-Western settings because it is very culturally biased in its coverage of the dissociative disorders (Alexander et al., 1997; Das & Saxena, 1991; Saxena & Prasad, 1989; Wig, 1983). Hopefully, this bias will be rectified by DSM-V.

cases) is 39.0%, 40.6%, and 46.7% in outpatient, general inpatient, and state hospital settings, respectively.

This consistent finding (i.e., that 39% or more of dissociative cases are DDNOS) is *prima facie* evidence of nosological strain; too many NOS cases are being diagnosed.

But what *kind* of DDNOS cases are these? Are they almost-DID cases with insufficiently distinct personalities (i.e., DDNOS-1a) or are they almost-DID cases with no amnesia (i.e., DDNOS-1b)? Or some other type of almost-DID? Or are they examples of derealization, brainwashing, trance, stupor/coma, or Ganser's syndrome (as DDNOS also invites)? Or are they instances of DDNOS that the DSM hasn't mentioned at all? Tacit knowledge, based on formal and informal gossip among researchers and clinicians worldwide, provides one answer to these questions; namely, that DDNOS generally means DDNOS-1. Tacit knowledge indicates that other forms of DDNOS (i.e., DDNOS-2 to DDNOS-6) are exceedingly rare in comparison.[15]

Citing her database for the Structured Clinical Interview for the DSM-IV Dissociative Disorders-Revised (SCID-D-R), Steinberg has made two relevant observations: (1) that the DSM nosology produces too many diagnoses of DDNOS (Steinberg, 2001), and (2) that the most common form of DDNOS is DDNOS-1a:

> SCID-D research indicates that the most common forms of DDNOS appear to be variants of DID in which personality states may take over consciousness and behavior but are not sufficiently distinct to qualify as full personalities. (Steinberg, 1995, p. 288)

Still, Steinberg's data about DDNOS-1a may not be as definitive as they appear. That is, the existence of her finding about DDNOS-1a is only possible because the SCID-D has specified its own standard for "sufficiently distinct," a standard that is lacking in the DSM (and, consequently, in general clinical practice as well). Thus, Steinberg's finding about the prevalence of DDNOS-1a is necessarily dependent on her particular standard for "sufficiently distinct." If that standard is lax, the SCID-D will generate relatively more diagnoses of DID and relatively fewer diagnoses of DDNOS-1a. Conversely, if that standard is strict, the SCID-D will generate relatively fewer diagnoses of DID and relatively more diagnoses of DDNOS-1a. In fact, the SCID-D-R standard for "distinct personalities" is reasonably strict.[16] Accordingly, the SCID-D-R would be expected to generate a substantial number of DDNOS-1a diagnoses.

25.4.4 There Is a High Incidence of Recurring Amnesia in DDNOS Cases

Table 25.3 summarizes the psychometric literature on dissociation in persons with DDNOS; these data imply that only a minority of these DDNOS cases have DDNOS-1b (i.e., almost-DID but without amnesia). In 12 of 16 studies, the DDNOS samples' mean scores on dissociation instruments *indicate the presence of substantial amnesia* (i.e., DES scores > 25, MID scores > 25, SCID-D total scores > 15, and DIS-Q scores > 2.5). Accordingly, these DDNOS cases cannot have DDNOS-1b (i.e., "Clinical presentations similar to Dissociative Identity Disorder ... in which ... *amnesia for personal information does not occur*"; italics added). Instead, they may have DDNOS-1a (i.e., "Clinical presentations similar to Dissociative Identity Disorder ... in which ... there are not two or more distinct personalities").[17] Indeed, one group of investigators considered the DSM-III-R criteria for DDNOS to be so vague that they created their own diagnostic criteria for DDNOS. Their criteria *required* the presence of amnesia (and at least four features associated with DID; Saxe et al., 1993), thereby excluding DDNOS-1b.

Only two studies have reported data on subtypes of DDNOS (see also Boon & Draijer, 1993). Coons (1992) reported that nearly half of his series of 50 clinic patients

[15] When reviewing this paper, Elizabeth Bowman commented that the disproportionate number of DDNOS cases in psychiatric settings is probably accurate, but that the relative proportion of DDNOS cases may be lower in other settings. For example, she noted that, in neurology clinics, the most frequent dissociative symptom, by far, is amnesia.

[16] The SCID-D-R's standard for "distinct identities or personality states" (DSM-IV, p. 487) is: "Persistent manifestations of the presence of different personalities, as indicated by at least four of the following: a) ongoing dialogues between different people; b) acting or feeling that the different people inside of him/her take control of his/her behavior or speech; c) characteristic visual image that is associated with the other person, distinct from the subject; d) characteristic age associated with the different people inside of him/her; e) feeling that the different people inside of him/her have different memories, behaviors, and feelings; f) feeling that the different people inside of him/her are separate from his/her personality and have lives of their own" (Steinberg, 1994, p. 106). [The author believes that it is of considerable importance that *none* of the SCID-D-R's six criteria for "distinct personalities or personality states" are observable signs; each of the six is a subjective symptom or experience that must be reported to the test administrator. This striking fact supports the contention that assessment of dissociation should be based on subjective symptoms rather than signs (Dell, 2006b, 2009b).] Finally, those who do not meet the SCID-D-R standard for "distinct identities or personality states," but who do meet the SCID-D-R's other four standards (for DSM-IV's Criterion A and Criterion B) for DID, receive a SCID-D-R diagnosis of DDNOS-1a.

[17] They may also have other types of DDNOS (e.g., a dissociative presentation of amnesia, depersonalization, and derealization, but without parts or ego states).

TABLE 25.3
Psychometric Measurement of Dissociation in 16 Samples of DDNOS and DID

			N		DES		SCID-D		DIS-Q		SDQ-20		MID	
Study	**Research Population**	**Country**	**NOS**	**DD**	**NOS**	**DID**	**NOS**	**DID**	**NOS**	**DID**	**NOS**	**DID**	**NOS**	**DID**
					Outpatient series									
Dell 1998	58 consec. DD OPs	USA	16	42	25.9	54.9								
Dell 2002	57 consec. DD OPs	USA	23	34	18.4	46.2								
Coons 1992	50 consec. DDNOS	USA	50	50	32.0	41.0								
Somer & Dell 2005	16 DD Ops	Israel	6	4	22.0	51.9	15.0	18.8					29.2	54.8
					Inpatient series									
Latz et al. 1995	176 state hosp. Ips	USA	34	21	38.3	59.5								
Frischholz et al. 1990	62 DD Unit Ips	USA	29	33	40.8	55.0								
Multisite research series														
Ensink et al. 1989	20 recruited DD pts	NL	13	7	36.4	53.4								
Boon & Draijer 1991	23 accum. DD pts	NL	11	12			14.9	18.2						
Ross et al. 1992	223 multisite DID/ NOS pts	USA/ Can.	57	166	21.7	39.7								
Carlson & Putnam 1993	327 accum. DD pts	USA	99	226	29.8	42.8								
Boon & Draijer 1993	•• accum. DD pts	NL	24	49			18.2	18.9						
Vanderlinden 1993	•• accum. DD pts	NL	23	30					2.9	3.5				
Nijenhuis et al. 1999	44 DD pts	NL	21	23	43.0	55.1								
Şar et al. 2000a	50 accum. DD pts	Turkey	25	25							46.3	58.7		
Dell 2005	73 accum. DD OPs	USA	19	47			15.0	19.0					27.9	49.2
					Non-Western series									
Umesue et al. 1996	19 consec. DD OPs	Japan	8	1	49.0	32.2								

with DDNOS had no apparent ego states. Şar, Akyüz, and Doğan (2007) reported that 50% of their general population DDNOS cases had DDNOS-1 and that another 29% of their DDNOS cases had a variation of DDNOS-1a (i.e., internal voices, passive influences symptoms, and amnesias). These two studies imply that half or more of the empirical literature on DDNOS may be based on DDNOS-1a.

25.4.5 When DDNOS Patients Encounter the DSM

DSM-IV-TR states that there are "four situations in which an NOS diagnosis may be appropriate" (p. 4): (1) cases that seem to fall within a given diagnostic class, but where the symptomatic presentation does not meet the criteria for a specific disorder (due to the symptoms being either atypical or below the diagnostic threshold); (2) cases with a symptom pattern that is not a specific disorder, but the symptoms cause clinically significant distress or impairment; (3) cases with an uncertain etiology—that is, cases where it is unclear "whether the disorder is due to a general medical condition, is substance induced, or is primary" (p. 4); and (4) cases where the data collected by the clinician are incomplete or inconsistent, but there is still sufficient information to place the case within a particular diagnostic class. From this, it can be seen that some NOS diagnoses are only temporary (because they are due to insufficient information). On the other hand, when clinicians have finally gathered sufficient information, they may still judge some patients to have an NOS diagnosis (because the patient's symptomatic picture is either atypical of any specific disorder, or subthreshold for one of the specific diagnoses). Such NOS diagnoses are assumed to be *final*. They are also supposed to be rare. As Ross has noted, however, DDNOS is neither atypical nor rare:

> DDNOS currently encompasses partial forms of DID which in fact are not at all atypical, and are probably more common than full DID. (Ross, 1997, pp. 98–99)

Precisely because partial forms of DID are so common, they should not be assigned to the NOS category.

There is another reason why partial forms of DID should not be assigned to the NOS category. The DSM often forbids it; a diagnosis of DDNOS-1 often conflicts with the diagnostic rules of the DSM. Despite providing a description of partial DID (i.e., DDNOS-1), DSM-IV often *prohibits* the clinician from issuing a diagnosis of DDNOS to patients who fit that description (Dell, 2001a; Ross, 1985, 1997; Ross et al., 2002):

> By DSM-IV rules [these persons] should receive a diagnosis of dissociative disorder not otherwise specified because they meet the DDNOS description of partial forms of DID. They cannot, however, because they often meet criteria for dissociative amnesia and/or depersonalization disorder: *DSM-IV states that a DDNOS diagnosis is to be made only when the person does not meet criteria for one of the other [specific] dissociative disorders*. (Ross et al., 2002, p. 15, italics added)

Thus, if the patient has amnesia, the DSM tells clinicians not to diagnose DDNOS. Since most cases of partial DID have amnesia, this is a problem. Worse, a diagnosis of Dissociative Amnesia is an inadequate and unhelpful characterization of a person with partial DID (Ross et al., 2002).

Given this clash between clinical reality and the diagnostic rules of the DSM, it is not surprising that three teams of investigators have chosen to override the DSM in their research on DDNOS (Şar et al., 2000b; Saxe et al., 1993; Tutkun et al., 1998). Each of these research teams redefined DDNOS as a supraordinate disorder with respect to amnesia, fugue, and depersonalization. For example:

> Any patient who met criteria for dissociative amnesia, dissociative fugue, or depersonalization disorder and also met criteria for dissociative identity disorder or dissociative disorder not otherwise specified received the overall diagnosis of either dissociative identity disorder or dissociative disorder not otherwise specified. Thus, dissociative identity disorder and dissociative disorder not otherwise specified were considered supraordinate diagnoses. (Şar et al., 2000b, p. 21)

I believe that these three research teams have described a routine diagnostic practice of dissociation experts; when it comes to patients with partial forms of DID, dissociation experts routinely violate the diagnostic rules of DSM-IV. I contend that this diagnostic practice should be ratified by removing partial DID from the DDNOS category and reclassifying it as a specific dissociative disorder.

25.4.6 Many Cases That Are Diagnosed as DDNOS-1a Really Have DID

I argued above that the "distinct personalities" criterion for DID relegated many persons with DID to the DDNOS category. Is there evidence that this is actually occurring? Is there evidence that DDNOS samples are contaminated with DID cases? Yes.

The authors of six studies in Table 25.2 have stated in print that many of their DDNOS cases probably had DID

(Akyüz et al., 1999; Boon & Draijer, 1993; Gast et al., 2001; Graves, 1989; Saxe et al., 1993; Tutkun et al., 1998). Here are three examples from three different continents:

> Of the nine patients who received a diagnosis of dissociative disorder not otherwise specified, three met all three criteria for multiple personality disorder, and four responded affirmatively to two of the three criteria and "unsure" to the third. This suggests that a number of patients [as many as 7 out of 9] who were given a diagnosis of dissociative disorder not otherwise specified may, upon further examination, meet diagnostic criteria for multiple personality. (Saxe et al., 1993, pp. 1040–1041)

> In six of these [8 DDNOS] patients, some personality states were observed repeatedly, but they were not considered sufficiently distinct and separate to diagnose a dissociative identity disorder at this stage of the evaluation. (Tutkun et al., 1998, p. 802)

> Finally we would like to comment on the patients in this study with the diagnosis DDNOS. In a majority of these cases the diagnosis MPD was strongly suspected during the research interview. This diagnosis could not be made because the patient was unaware of the existence of alter personalities or unable to talk about this subject. In those cases we assigned the diagnosis DDNOS, although it might be better to speak of "covert MPD" to differentiate these cases from true atypical cases. From a follow-up one year later, we obtained information on 20 of the 24 patients with DDNOS; 19 of the 20 patients were given the diagnosis MPD, instead of DDNOS, by the treating clinician and a description of distinct alter personalities could be given. (Boon & Draijer, 1993, pp. 120–121)

This has significant consequences. *If "DDNOS" samples routinely contain persons with DID, then the research literature on both DID and DDNOS is skewed.* Thus, in Table 25.3, the dissociation scores for DDNOS may be artifactually high and the dissociation scores for DID may be artifactually high as well (because covert DID cases, which have lower dissociation scores than do overt DID cases [Boon & Draijer, 1993], have been excluded from the DID samples).

25.4.7 Pause for Reflection

So, where does this leave us? It leaves us with remarkably little clarity about "clinical presentations similar to Dissociative Identity Disorder that fail to meet full criteria for this disorder" (DSM-IV, p. 532).

The struggle to understand and diagnose what is presently called *DDNOS-1* began with a basic question. Are cases of so-called "partial DID" truly atypical (and, therefore, deserving of NOS status) or are they just covert cases of DID? A quarter-century of struggle with the nosology of the dissociative disorders and their diagnostic criteria has not provided an easy answer to this question.

At this juncture, I believe that our thinking about DDNOS-1 can be enriched by revisiting Watkins' concept of *ego state disorders*—an important clinical-conceptual precursor of modern DID and DDNOS-1.

25.5 A Continuum of Ego State Disorders

Modern study of dissociation was founded upon a continuum model of dissociation (e.g., Bernstein & Putnam, 1986; Braun, 1988; Hilgard, 1977). According to this model, dissociation stretches from normal phenomena (e.g., absorption, dreams, highway hypnosis) to increasingly pathological phenomena (e.g., episodes of amnesia, fugues, and DID). This original continuum model of dissociation has been called into question, however, by data suggesting that pathological dissociation is a discontinuous process (rather than a continuum that stretches smoothly from low dissociation to high dissociation; Putnam et al., 1996; Waller, Putnam, & Carlson, 1996). Putnam et al. (1996) have interpreted their data as suggesting "the possible existence of two or three [discrete] dissociative types (e.g., low, moderate, and high)" (p. 677).

Watkins has proposed a different continuum of dissociation that is consistent with Putnam's et al. putative dissociative types—whereas the original continuum model of dissociation (see previous paragraph) is not.

Watkins has described a continuum of ego states or "covertly segmented personality structures" (Watkins & Watkins, 1997, p. ix) that extend from flexible and adaptive ego states to rigid *ego state disorders.* From Watkins's perspective, DDNOS-1 and DID are both ego state disorders.

25.5.1 Features of All Ego States

All ego states have seven important characteristics (Watkins & Watkins, 1997). First, most arise when the person is young. Many ego states are fixated in development and think like a child (i.e., concretely) or an adolescent (i.e., rebelliously). Second, ego states come into being to deal with specific situations or problems:

> Thus, one ego state may have taken over the overt, executive position when dealing with parents, another on the playground, another during athletic contests, etc. (Watkins & Watkins, 1997, p. 29)

Third, ego states *want to exist*:

> Once created, ego states are highly motivated to protect and continue their existence.... Part-persons seek to protect their existence as do whole persons. (Watkins & Watkins, 1997, p. 29)

Fourth, the initial purpose of each ego state is to "protect and facilitate the adaptation of the primary person" (Watkins & Watkins, 1997, p. 29). Fifth, ego states have a sense of separateness and a sense of their own selfhood. Sixth, ego states influence one another covertly. *Covert influence is the primary means by which ego states accomplish their goals (and generate symptoms).* The seventh characteristic of ego states is the bridge to the ego state disorders: ego states may become engaged in conflict with one another or with the primary person. These conflicts generate symptoms.

25.5.2 Four Points on the Continuum of Ego States

25.5.2.1 Ego States of Normal, Well-Adjusted Persons

Most normal people have ego states that are separated from one another by very permeable boundaries. These ego states share much content in common and they are quite aware of each other:

> The general principle is that these more normal ego states come about through adaptive segmentation by the personality in the solving of fairly normal problems of living. (Watkins & Watkins, p. 78)

These ego states originate mostly from adaptive processes of differentiation, seldom from trauma.

25.5.2.2 Ego State Disorders That Generate Neurotic Symptoms and Maladaptive Behaviors

25.5.2.2.1 The Ego States

These ego states conflict with one another and generate neurotic symptoms and maladjusted behavior:

> In this region [of the dissociative continuum] we find that a conflict between states may be manifested by headaches, anxiety, and maladaptive behaviors, such as found in the neuroses and psychophysiologic conditions. (Watkins & Watkins, p. 33)

Despite their conflict, these ego states have much in common. They are quite aware of one another; they retain communication, they interact, and they share content. They influence the person, but they never assume full executive control. They can be "activated into executive position by hypnosis" (p. 33). These ego states have semipermeable boundaries; they see themselves as parts of the whole self. These ego states do not undergo further elaboration during adulthood; they do not become more fully developed or more separate from one another.

Ego states at this point on the continuum originated in an effort to solve recurrent problems in childhood (e.g., critical parents). Typically, these recurrent childhood problems fall short of being frankly abusive; nevertheless, these problems may be quite psychologically significant (e.g., chronic difficulties with one's parents' caretaking and attachment behavior).

25.5.2.2.2 The Person

The person is aware that he/she is unable to control certain behaviors or symptoms, but is generally unaware of the presence of well-defined parts. When persons with this kind of ego state disorder do become aware of the presence of distinct parts, they experience them as being part of them. There is no amnesia, little disturbance of consciousness, and very little identity disturbance; these persons have continuity in their experience of self.

25.5.2.3 Ego State Disorders That Are "Almost MPD"

25.5.2.3.1 The Ego States

These ego states have strong reactions and conflicts, often because they have trauma-driven priorities and sensitivities. They have substantial awareness of each other. For the most part, they retain communication, interact, share much content, and consider themselves to be part of the whole self. Still, they consider themselves to be very separate from what Watkins calls *the primary person.* These ego states do not assume full executive control, but they exert profound, and often frequent, influence on the person's experience and behavior. They can be activated into the executive position by hypnosis. Their boundaries are fairly impermeable, but less so than those of MPD alters. These ego states typically originated in an effort to deal with recurrent harsh problems in early life, including trauma and abuse. They generally do not become more fully developed or more separate from one another during adulthood.

25.5.2.3.2 The Person

These persons are intensely aware of, and discomfited by, the ego-alien intrusions that they undergo. They hear voices and/or experience strong, ego-alien thoughts, feelings, and urges. They are uncomfortably aware of the presence and activities of well-defined parts. Although they experience these parts as very separate from them, they still own them as "parts of me" (Beahrs, 1982; Bloch, 1991; Chu, 1996):

> Each subpart or "personality," no matter how discrete and different, is still experienced as an aspect of an overall cohesive selfhood, not *as if* it were a separate self as is the case in true multiples. (Beahrs, 1982, p. 96)

Persons with this kind of ego state disorder experience so many peculiar intrusions and inexplicable influences that they are puzzled, apprehensive, and somewhat estranged from themselves. They have frequent disturbances of consciousness and substantial identity disturbance. They have only moderate continuity in their experience of self. Although mostly nonamnestic, these persons may experience some contemporary incidents of amnesia (Bloch, 1991; Watkins & Watkins, 1997).

25.5.2.4 The Most Severe Ego State Disorder: MPD

25.5.2.4.1 The Ego State

MPD alter personalities are starkly dissociated from one another. They have rigid, impermeable, amnestic barriers. They often have little interaction or communication; many alter personalities are unaware that other parts exist. Their sense of separateness is complete or nearly complete; they even may consider themselves to be different persons with different bodies. Their trauma-driven priorities and sensitivities are so strong that, when activated, these ego states easily seize full executive control or interfere so powerfully from within that they completely disempower the primary personality. Some MPD alters continue to develop; they become more complex, more active, and come to occupy a larger proportion of the person's life-space. Unlike persons with less severe ego state disorders, persons with MPD may develop additional ego states (i.e., alter personalities) during adolescence and adulthood.

25.5.2.4.2 The Person

Persons with MPD experience peculiar intrusions and inexplicable influences with great frequency—they hear voices; undergo "made" feelings, thoughts, urges, and actions; experience weird bodily changes and influences, and so on. They know that they are being affected by autonomous centers of functioning within them. Their understanding of (or admissions about) these internal parts is often strongly limited by denial. They experience frequent disturbances of consciousness and severe identity disturbance. They have little continuity in their experience of self. They have recurring, contemporary episodes of time loss and amnesia, and often have little memory of their childhood.

25.5.3 Four Features of Ego State Disorders That Are Relevant to DDNOS-1

We revisited Watkins's concept of ego state disorders in order to assist our analysis of DDNOS-1. Watkins was not very interested in diagnoses or the diagnostic signs and symptoms of ego state disorders. Bloch (1991) was more interested in these matters. When I study ego state disorders with DDNOS-1 in mind, four points stand out.

25.5.3.1 DID and DDNOS-1 Lie Upon a Dissociative Continuum of Ego State Disorders

Ego state disorders lie upon a dimension of increasing dissociation. Nevertheless, to draw diagnostic boundaries at certain places on that continuum is an arbitrary act about which no agreement has yet been reached:

> no firm consensus has been achieved to date to guide the categorical diagnosis of the essentially dimensional phenomena of dissociation … (Bloch, 1991, p. 25)

Proposals for such diagnostic boundaries need to be clearly articulated and justified.

Watkins seems to distinguish MPD from almost-MPD on the basis of two clinical phenomena: (1) ego states that spontaneously assume full executive control, and (2) recurring incidents of amnesia. Beahrs (1982) and Bloch (1991) agree with Watkins that MPD is characterized by recurring incidents of amnesia. Bloch (1991) agrees with Watkins that only persons with MPD spontaneously assume full executive control; Beahrs (1982) is ambiguous about this issue.

25.5.3.2 DID Patients Have Recurring Incidents of Amnesia

DSM-IV requires the presence of amnesia in DID, but does not specify (1) what kind of amnesia must be present (i.e., contemporary incidents of amnesia vs. amnesia for part of one's childhood) or (2) how frequent or extensive that amnesia must be. The role of amnesia in almost-DID (i.e., DDNOS-1) is not completely clear. According to DSM-IV, persons who have alters that switch and assume full executive control have DDNOS-1b *if they do not have amnesia*. On the other hand, DSM-IV is silent about the role of amnesia in DDNOS-1a; DDNOS-1a is solely defined by failure to meet the "distinct personalities" criterion. Nevertheless, analysis of the DDNOS literature (see previous discussion) argues that many (most?) persons diagnosed with DDNOS could fall under DDNOS-1a by default, owing to their recurring incidents of amnesia.

25.5.3.3 DID Patients Exhibit Spontaneous Switching

Watkins and DSM-IV implicitly agree that spontaneous switching[18] must occur in DID. On the other hand, Watkins and DSM-IV implicitly disagree about the role of spontaneous switching in DDNOS-1. Watkins insists that almost-DID cases cannot switch spontaneously; they require hypnotic facilitation to assume full executive control. DSM-IV, on the other hand, implies spontaneous switching in both DDNOS-1a and DDNOS-1b.[19] This means that Watkins would diagnose many DDNOS-1 cases as DID.

Still, the text for DDNOS-1 remains very sketchy; DSM-IV actually says nothing about spontaneous switching in DDNOS-1. In DSM-III-R, DDNOS explicitly included "cases in which a second personality never assumes complete executive control" (DSM-III-R, p. 277). As noted earlier in this chapter, the DSM-IV Work Group deleted this issue from DDNOS-1, leaving some ambiguity in its wake.

Although the DSM-IV Work Group discarded it as irrelevant, the spontaneous assumption of full executive control may be of major diagnostic import. Watkins and Bloch have asserted that spontaneous switching defines the boundary between MPD and almost-MPD. If Watkins and Bloch are correct—and I think that they are—then persons with DDNOS-1a who exhibit spontaneous switching actually have DID.

This notion, that many DDNOS cases really have DID, is not new. Kluft, in particular, has long taken this position (Kluft et al., 1988).

25.5.3.4 Influencing-From-Within Is the Central Clinical Phenomenon of All Ego State Disorders—Including DID and DDNOS-1

The central clinical phenomenon of ego state disorders is influencing-from-within. The primary means by which ego states assert their interests and pursue their goals is by influencing, intruding into, and interfering with the primary personality (or the ego state that is currently in executive control). The most extreme form of influencing, intruding, and interfering is the spontaneous, complete switch that occurs in DID. Even in DID, the most common form of influencing and intruding is done from within, not by switching and coming out (Dell, 2006a, 2009a, 2009b; Kluft, 1985b).

If influencing-from-within (rather than switching) is the primary clinical phenomenon of DID and DDNOS-1, then the DSM has completely overlooked (1) the core dynamic of DID and (2) the core dynamic of DDNOS-1. Three studies have shown that rigorous assessment of (1) influences-from-within and (2) incidents of contemporary amnesia allows accurate assessment of DID (Dell, 2001b, 2006b; Gast et al., 2003). I believe that rigorous assessment of (1) influences-from-within and (2) incidents of contemporary amnesia will afford accurate assessment of DDNOS-1 (i.e., less symptomatic forms of DID).

25.6 IN SUMMARY

What has the foregoing examination of DDNOS-1 shown us so far? I consider eight points to be important.

First, the proportion of diagnosed dissociative persons that are diagnosed with DDNOS (40%) is too high. This undue proportion of NOS diagnoses indicates that something is seriously amiss with the nosology of the dissociative disorders and/or with the diagnostic criteria for the dissociative disorders.

Second, assignment of DDNOS-1 to the NOS category makes neither clinical nor nosological sense; several authors have recommended that DDNOS-1 be reclassified as a subtype of DID (Coons, 2001; Dell, 2001; Ross et al., 2002). If this were done, then DDNOS-1, that most diagnosed of dissociative disorders, would finally have its own diagnostic criteria.

Third, the debate about whether a portion of DDNOS cases really have DID (Boon & Draijer, 1993; Dell, 2001a; Franklin, 1988; Kluft, 1985b; Ross et al., 2002) has not been resolved, but the evidence suggests that many DDNOS-1a cases are actually false-negative cases of DID (because many DDNOS cases in the literature were later found to be unambiguous cases of DID).

[18] Throughout this chapter, the term *switching* refers to the phenomenon of an ego state (i.e., alter personality) spontaneously assuming full executive control.

[19] Strictly, this discussion about DDNOS-1 cannot be resolved solely on the basis of DDNOS-1a and DDNOS-1b. DSM-IV declines to suggest (but does not preclude) that other forms of DDNOS-1 may exist. Thus, for example, a putative DDNOS-1c might have highly distinct personalities with no switching but, with amnesia. Similarly, DDNOS-1d might have highly distinct personalities with neither switching nor amnesia.

Fourth, the "distinct personalities" criterion for DID has been very counterproductive; it is probably responsible for most DDNOS diagnoses. The "distinct personalities" criterion for diagnosis is phenomenologically indefensible because DID is a disorder of hiddenness. Switching is relatively infrequent and most persons with DID routinely hide their alter personalities. In short, *the "distinct personalities" criterion guarantees that only a subset of persons with DID will be correctly diagnosed as DID. Conversely, given the average clinician's lack of knowledge about DID, the "distinct personalities" criterion guarantees that the majority of persons with DID will be misdiagnosed.*

In retrospect, it can also be seen that the diagnostic practice, which uses DDNOS as place-holder or rule-out for patients who are suspected of DID, is yet another undesirable side effect of the "distinct personalities" criterion.

Fifth, DDNOS-1 and DID lie on a continuum of increasingly dissociated ego states (see also Van der Hart, Nijenhuis, & Steele, 2006). Diagnostic criteria for DID should reflect this continuum of dissociation by specifying two (or more) subtypes of DID.

Sixth and seventh, Watkins used two clinical features of DID to draw the boundary between DID and almost-DID: (1) spontaneous switching, and (2) recurring incidents of contemporary amnesia. There are clear similarities between Watkins' criteria for DID and DSM-IV's criteria for DID, but (1) Watkins does a better job of specifying amnesia (i.e., recurring incidents of contemporary amnesia) and, most important, (2) Watkins does not burden his criteria for DID with the "distinct personalities" criterion.

Eighth, Watkins demonstrates that the central clinical phenomenon of all ego state disorders is influencing-from-within. Influencing-from-within has long been recognized by authorities in the dissociative disorders field (i.e., Janet's *idée fixe* and subconscious acts, Kluft's passive influence phenomena, Loewenstein and Putnam's process symptoms of dissociation, and Ross's secondary features of DID), but the full significance of influencing-from-within does not seem to have been recognized or acknowledged.[20] Influencing-from-within goes unmentioned by the modern DSM, but, in my view, it should play a central organizing role in the diagnosis of both DID and DDNOS-1.

At this juncture in our analysis, we should briefly revisit an important historical example of failure to understand the meaning and significance of influencing-from-within. In the first half of the 20th century, skeptical researchers of dissociation claimed (incorrectly) that the activities of a dissociated part of the mind should *not* interfere with the functioning of the rest of the mind (e.g., Messerschmidt, 1927–1928). Janet never claimed that dissociation entailed noninterference (Hilgard, 1977; Kihlstrom, 1992; Perry & Laurence, 1984). The original version of dissociative influencing-from-within (i.e., Janet's subconscious acts) had clearly stated the opposite (Janet, 1889). Nevertheless, these debunkers of dissociation (1) demonstrated that the activity of a dissociated part of the mind *did* interfere with the operation of the rest of the mind, and (2) claimed that this disproved the construct of dissociation![21] In reality, of course, these debunkers were demonstrating a core phenomenon of dissociation—influencing, intruding into, or interfering with the functioning of the rest of the mind. The early 20th century debunkers of dissociation had it backwards. *The hallmark of dissociated functioning is the occurrence of influencing-from-within* (rather than the absence of such influencing).[22]

25.7 TOWARD A RECONCEPTUALIZATION OF DID AND ALMOST-DID

From all of the preceding, I draw two clinical-conceptual conclusions, two diagnostic conclusions, and one nosological conclusion.

[20] Exceptions to this generalization include Loewenstein (1991) who said that the process symptoms of dissociation "reflect the core aspects of the patient's multiplicity" (p. 593) and Ross (1997) who said that the secondary features of DID are "most valuable to the clinician … [because] usually, in most cases, DID does not present in an obvious overt fashion" (p. 101).

[21] Kihlstrom discussed this same issue in reference to White and Shevach (1942), who followed Messerschmidt in rejecting dissociation due to the phenomenon of interference: "White and Shevach expected that dissociated mental processes would be so isolated from other ongoing mental life that the one stream of consciousness would not interfere with the other. It is not at all clear where they got this idea, since it has no basis in the classic statements of dissociation by Janet. For Janet, a dissociated stream of thought is isolated from conscious awareness and from the phenomenal experience of agency and control, but he never suggested that the dissociation will extend to the matter of interference. Quite the contrary: from Janet's point of view, one of the hallmarks of hysteria was the manner in which *dissociated mental contents intruded on conscious experience, thought, and action. These intrusions are a form of interference*" (p. 307).

[22] Matters may be different, however, with simple Dissociative Amnesia—which raises an interesting question. How does simple Dissociative Amnesia differ from complex dissociative disorders such as DID and DDNOS-1? And how different are they?

25.7.1 Two Clinical-Conceptual Conclusions About Dissociation in Ego State Disorders

The most important marker of dissociation in ego state disorders (including DDNOS-1 and DID) is influencing-from-within. The most important marker of *severity* of dissociation in ego state disorders is recurring incidents of contemporary amnesia.[23]

25.7.2 Two Diagnostic Conclusions About DID and Almost-DID

The best diagnostic indicators of DID are (1) pervasive and frequent symptoms of influencing-from-within, and (2) frequent incidents of contemporary amnesia. Similarly, the best diagnostic indicators of DDNOS-1 are (1) frequent symptoms of influencing-from-within (but less frequent than in DID), and (2) recurring incidents of contemporary amnesia (but less frequent than in DID). From this perspective, DID and DDNOS-1 differ only in the frequency and severity of their dissociative symptoms.[24]

25.7.3 One Nosological Conclusion About DDNOS-1

DDNOS-1, as redefined in the previous paragraph, should be reclassified as a *specific* dissociative disorder, probably as a less symptomatic subtype of DID.

25.7.4 New Diagnostic Criteria for DDNOS-1 and DID

The diagnostic criteria for DID ought to be based on the two most powerful indicators of dissociation in ego state disorders—influences-from-within and recurring incidents of contemporary amnesia. These two indicators of dissociation answer Kluft's (1985b, p. 203) question, "How can one discover the presence of multiple personality disorder in the absence of its classical manifestations [i.e., distinct personalities that switch]?" One can discover the presence of MPD by assessing the frequency of influences-from-within and the frequency and duration of incidents of contemporary amnesia. Of course, one can also discover the presence of (some cases of) MPD by observing distinct personalities that switch. The diagnostic criteria in Table 25.4 allow MPD to be diagnosed via either route—that is, (1) by observing distinct personalities that switch, or (2) by documenting the presence of classic dissociative symptoms[25] plus pervasive influences-from-within plus recurring incidents of amnesia.

25.7.5 Reconceptualizing DID as a Complex Dissociative Disorder

Whereas the modern DSM portrays DID as an Alter Personality Disorder, the diagnostic criteria that are proposed in Table 25.4 portray the disorder as a complex dissociative disorder. I contend that complex dissociative disorder is more accurate, less controversial, has greater face validity, and is much easier for the average clinician to diagnose than DSM-IV DID (see also Dell, 2009a).

The criteria in Table 25.4 provide two ways to satisfy Criterion B and two ways to satisfy Criterion C. The first way requires witnessing a switch. Criterion B1 requires witnessing a switch that is *not* followed by amnesia, whereas Criterion C1 requires witnessing a switch that *is* followed by amnesia.

The second way to satisfy Criterion B is to document the presence of five or more kinds of influence-from-within. Similarly, the second way to satisfy Criterion C is to document the occurrence of four or more incidents of amnesia.

25.7.6 Complex Dissociative Disorder I and II

Complex Dissociative Disorder II (i.e., DDNOS-1) is a less symptomatic variant of Complex Dissociative Disorder I (i.e., DID). The diagnosis of Complex Dissociative

[23] I have limited my assertions about dissociation to dissociation in ego state disorders. I know rather little about dissociation in simple dissociative disorders such as Dissociative Amnesia, Dissociative Fugue, Depersonalization Disorders, and Conversion Disorders. Elizabeth Bowman (personal communication, 9-23-05) suggests that the most important marker of dissociation in simple dissociative disorders is the unavailability of mental content (e.g., lack of awareness of emotions that are obvious in facial expressions, lack of memory for events during conversion seizures in patients who show no evidence of altered identity, lack of awareness of physical sensations or movements [i.e., conversion sensory deficits or motor symptoms], and recurrent involuntary entrance into trance states with subsequent amnesia for conversations that were held during the trance.).

[24] Persons with DDNOS-1 also manifest fewer kinds of dissociative symptoms (i.e., fewer of the symptoms in Table 25.4) than do persons with DID.

[25] The classic dissociative symptoms (i.e., circumscribed amnesia for autobiographical memory, depersonalization, derealization, flashbacks, somatoform dissociation, and trance) are common influences-from-within that routinely occur in major ego state disorders (i.e., DID and DDNOS-1). These classical dissociative symptoms may also occur in simpler dissociative disorders (i.e., disorders that are not driven by clinically important ego states).

TABLE 25.4
Diagnostic Criteria for Complex Dissociative Disorder I

A. Classic dissociative symptoms, as indicated by three (or more) of the following:
   - (1) Circumscribed amnesia for autobiographical memory (e.g., cannot remember childhood before age 12; no memory of age 9–11; no memory of an important life event such as getting married, giving birth, grandmother's funeral)
   - (2) Depersonalization (e.g., feeling detached/distant from self; body feeling unreal or not all there; feeling separate from self and/or watching self from outside one's body)
   - (3) Derealization (e.g., feeling disconnected/distant from everything; surroundings feel strange, unreal, oddly different; not recognizing familiar people or places)
   - (4) Posttraumatic flashbacks (e.g., reexperiencing some or all of the sensory elements of a past trauma)
   - (5) Somatoform symptoms (e.g., motor symptoms, sensory alterations, genital pain without physical explanation)
   - (6) Trance (e.g., recurrent involuntary episodes of staring off into space, being "gone" from conscious awareness, and unresponsive to environmental stimuli)

B. The person has conscious awareness of the intrusions/influences from another self-state, as indicated by *either* (1) or (2):
   - (1) Switching without concomitant amnesia: The clinician or a collateral informant witnesses a self-state that claims (or appears) to be someone other than the person in question, as indicated by a, b, and c:
     - (a) The visible presence of a different self-state, as evidenced by one (or more) of the following:
       - (i) An announced change of identity (e.g., "I'm not her; I'm Janice.")
       - (ii) A relatively sudden change of self-presentation as manifested by changes in two (or more) of the following;
         - (1) Facial expression
         - (2) Body posture
         - (3) Tone of voice
         - (4) Mannerisms
         - (5) Affect
         - (6) Opinions
         - (7) Attitudes
     - (b) The person's conscious awareness of that self-state, as evidenced by both of the following features: the person's
       - (i) Reported coconscious awareness of the activities of that other self-state
       - (ii) Subsequent remembering of what the other self-state said and did
     - (c) The person reports experiencing that self-state as "other," "not me," or not self
   - (2) The person has conscious awareness of intrusions/influences from another self-state, as indicated by five (or more) of the following (in the absence of a delusional or psychotic explanation for these intrusions/influences):
     - (a) Hearing the voice of a child in his/her head
     - (b) Noticing an internal struggle (that may or may not involve voices that argue). Note: internal struggle goes well beyond ambivalence; it involves a sense of the presence of different parts that are strongly opposing one another.
     - (c) Hearing a persecutory voice (usually in the head) that comments harshly, makes threats, or commands self-destructive acts (in the absence of formal thought disorder or delusions)
     - (d) Speech insertion (unintentional or disowned utterances)
     - (e) Thought insertion or withdrawal
     - (f) "Made" or intrusive feelings and emotions (or sudden withdrawal/absence of feelings and emotions)
     - (g) "Made" or intrusive impulses
     - (h) "Made" or intrusive actions (i.e., actions that are perceived/experienced as depersonalized) or actions or behaviors that are blocked
     - (i) Atypical experiences of self-alteration (e.g., feeling very physically small or mentally young like a young child; having emotions, thoughts, or feelings that don't feel like they belong to oneself; seeing someone else instead of oneself in the mirror, etc.)
     - (j) Self-puzzlement secondary to 2a-2i

C. Recurring incidents of amnesia secondary to intrusions by another self-state, as indicated by *either* (1) or (2):
   - (1) Switching that is accompanied by amnesia: The clinician or a collateral informant witnesses a self-state that claims (or appears) to be someone other than the person being interviewed, *followed by the person's subsequent amnesia for what the other self-state was witnessed to do or say, as evidenced by a and b.*
     - (a) The visible presence of a different self-state, as evidenced by one (or more) of the following:
       - (i) An announced change of identity (e.g., "I'm not *her*; I'm Janice.")
       - (ii) A relatively sudden change of self-presentation as manifested by changes in two (or more) of the following;
         - (1) Facial expression

TABLE 25.4
Diagnostic Criteria for Complex Dissociative Disorder I *(Continued)*

(2) Body posture
(3) Tone of voice
(4) Mannerisms
(5) Affect
(6) Opinions
(7) Attitudes

(b) Amnesia: the person is subsequently unable to recall what the other self-state said and did.

(2) Recurring incidents of amnesia, as indicated by the person's report of two (or more) incidents of two (or more) of the following:

(a) Discovering that he/she has amnesia for a discrete interval of time ("lost time"): being completely unable to account for a period of time—an hour or longer—including the loss of memory for up to years of one's life)

(b) "Coming to": discovering that he/she was in the middle of doing something that he/she did not remember initiating (e.g., conversing with someone, disciplining the children, cooking dinner, performing occupational tasks, etc.) or suddenly discovering that he/she had done something he/she does not remember doing (e.g., smashed something, cut self, cleaned the whole house, etc.)

(c) Fugues: suddenly discovering that he/she was somewhere with no memory of having gone there in the first place (e.g., finding self at the mall, at the beach, in one's car, under the bed, in a closet, etc.)

(d) Being told of things that he/she had recently done, but with no memory of having done those things

(e) Finding objects among his/her possessions or in his/her shopping bags—that he/she does not remember acquiring, purchasing, or producing (e.g., shoes, clothes, toys, toilet articles, drawings, handwritten materials, etc.)

(f) Finding evidence of his/her recent actions, but with no memory of having done those things (e.g., mowed the lawn, produced written work, completed a task at work, cleaned the house, changed one's apparel or personal appearance, having a significant injury—a cut, a burn, many bruises, having attempted suicide, etc.)

(g) Not remembering who he/she is or what her/his name is

(h) Being unable to remember well-established skills (e.g., how to read, how to drive, how to play the piano, how to do his/her job, etc.)

(i) Other incidents of being unable to recall personal information that is so unlikely or so extensive that it cannot be explained by ordinary forgetfulness

D. The disturbance is not better accounted for by Schizophrenia, Schizoaffective Disorder, Brief Psychotic Disorder, Mood Disorder With Psychotic Features, or Borderline Personality Disorder and is not due to the direct physiological effects of a substance (e.g., a drug or substance of abuse, a medication) or a general medical condition (e.g., temporal lobe epilepsy).

E. The symptoms cause clinically significant distress or impairment in social, occupational, or other important areas of functioning.

Disorder II requires that the person meet only two of the three criteria for Complex Dissociative Disorder I.[26]

[26] DSM-IV DDNOS-1a would be diagnosed by meeting Criterion A and Criterion C, but not Criterion B. Readers who are following closely will notice that this assertion *adds* an amnesia requirement to DDNOS-1a. DSM-IV is silent about whether DDNOS-1a must have amnesia. I have required that amnesia be present (because I do not know how a clinical presentation could be similar to DID (i.e., DDNOS-1) if it has neither distinct personality states nor recurring amnesia). DSM-IV DDNOS-1b would be diagnosed by meeting Criterion A and Criterion B, but not Criterion C. Finally, a third kind of DDNOS-1 that is not described in DSM-IV would be diagnosed by meeting Criterion B and Criterion C, but not Criterion A. Please note that I am *not* suggesting that Complex Dissociative Disorder II has three subtypes or that these subtypes should be diagnosed. The description above of DDNOS-1a, -1b, and so on is offered merely to illustrate the relationships between the DSM-IV description of DDNOS-1 and the criteria in Table 25.4.

25.7.7 Three Clinical Presentations of DID

Most scholars and researchers in the dissociative disorders field agree upon the existence of a less symptomatic variant of DID (e.g., Beahrs, 1982; Bloch, 1991; Boon & Draijer, 1993; Coons, 1992; Dell, 2001a; Franklin, 1988; Kluft, 1985b; Ross et al., 1992, 2002; Şar et al., 2007; Watkins & Watkins, 1997). A review of the literature, however, shows that scholars have identified *two kinds of less symptomatic DID.*

Boon and Draijer have discussed one kind of less symptomatic DID: *covert DID.* They showed that many difficult-to-diagnose cases of MPD were defensive:

> these patients showed more defensive reactions—such as amnesia or blank spells, strong interference of voices—and denial during the SCID-D interview. (Boon & Draijer, 1993, p. 121)

Although they classified these patients as having DDNOS on the basis of SCID-D interviews, Boon and Draijer considered these patients to have "covert MPD" (p. 120). They noted that these patients had lower DES scores than patients with overt MPD. Franklin (1988) has described the differences between covert DID and a second kind of less symptomatic DID: *subtle DID*. According to Franklin, covert MPD patients are especially skilled at hiding their distinct personalities, whereas subtle MPD patients have subdued symptoms because their dissociation is truly less frequent and less severe than that of covert MPD patients:

> Patients with subtle forms of MPD have less dissociation among many of their alters, which have more permeable boundaries and share more memories and behavior patterns. Their alters are, in general, less distinct and substantial. (Franklin, 1988, p. 29)

Franklin's distinctions among overt, covert, and subtle MPD provide a phenomenological typology of three major presentations of MPD; this tripartite typology sheds some additional light on DID and DDNOS-1.

25.7.7.1 Overt DID

Persons with overt DID are diagnosable by means of the "distinct personalities" criterion in the DSM. They have higher DES scores than do persons with covert DID (Boon & Draijer, 1993). The empirical literature on DID is largely based on overt DID.

25.7.7.2 Covert DID

The overwhelming majority of persons with DID have covert DID (Kluft, 1985b). It is uncommon for a person with covert DID to be diagnosed as DID by means of the DSM's "distinct personalities" criterion. Consequently, many cases of covert DID are diagnosed as DDNOS-1a. Because of this, much of the empirical literature on DDNOS may actually be based on cases of covert DID.

Although patients with covert DID have lower DES scores than patients with overt DID (i.e., mean DES = 39.6 vs. 57.8, respectively), these two groups of DID patients obtain almost identical scores on the SCID-D (i.e., SCID-D total = 18.5 vs. 19.3, respectively; Boon & Draijer, 1993). Thus, overt DID and covert DID differ dramatically in the *visibility* of their alter personalities, but differ minimally in their other dissociative symptoms (i.e., amnesia, depersonalization, derealization, identity confusion, and identity alteration; see Boon & Draijer; Steinberg, 1995). Because the criteria for Complex Dissociative Disorder I can diagnose DID without an observed switch between personalities (i.e., the diagnosis is based solely on classic dissociative symptoms, influences-from-within, and amnesia; see Dell, 2001b, 2006b; Gast et al., 1993), I predict that Table 25.4's diagnostic criteria will readily diagnose covert DID as DID (i.e., as Complex Dissociative Disorder I) rather than as DDNOS-1. Said differently, the criteria in Table 25.4 would classify both overt DID and covert DID as Complex Dissociative Disorder I.

25.7.7.3 Subtle DID

We know rather little about subtle DID other than the fact that such cases exist (Coons, 1992; Franklin, 1988: Kluft, 1985b; Ross et al., 1992) and that their dissociation is less frequent and less severe than that of overt and covert DID:

> The data also clearly show that a subcategory of a dissociative disorder exists with less identity disturbance and less amnesia than are seen with MPD. (Coons, 1992, p. 193)

I believe that the original purpose of DDNOS-1 was to detect and diagnose subtle DID. Unfortunately, the current empirical literature on DDNOS-1 can tell us little about subtle DID because the data on DDNOS-1 have probably been contaminated by numerous cases of covert DID. Under the criteria in Table 25.4, I would classify subtle DID as Complex Dissociative Disorder II. Unpublished MID data show that persons who meet the criteria for Complex Dissociative Disorder II have significantly fewer dissociative symptoms than persons with Complex Dissociative Disorder I (i.e., 10–13 vs. 19–20 of the 23 dissociative symptoms that are assessed by the MID).

25.8 A FEW RESEARCH PREDICTIONS

The proposed diagnostic criteria for DID and DDNOS-1 (i.e., for Complex Dissociative Disorder I and Complex Dissociative Disorder II) need to be empirically evaluated. Three studies have already shown that the criteria in Table 25.4, as measured by the Multidimensional Inventory of Dissociation (MID; Dell, 2006a), can successfully diagnose DID cases. The results of these three studies are interesting because they demonstrate two points: (1) the criteria for Complex Dissociative Disorder I are diagnostically effective (i.e., they readily identify persons with a SCID-D diagnosis of DID), and (2) DID/Complex Dissociative Disorder I cases can be diagnosed solely on the basis of classical dissociative symptoms, influences-from-within, and amnesia—in other words, *without* observing distinct personalities that switch.

As noted above, we know very little about subtle cases of Complex Dissociative Disorder II (i.e., true DDNOS-1).

I predict that these cases will prove to have (1) lower DES, MID, and SCID-D scores than persons who meet Criteria A, B, and C (i.e., cases of Complex Dissociative Disorder I), (2) higher DES, MID, and SCID-D scores than all other dissociative diagnoses (except Complex Dissociative Disorder I), (3) some amnesia (rather than "no amnesia" as per DDNOS-1b in DSM-IV), (4) alters that spontaneously switch less frequently than do alters in Complex Dissociative Disorder I, (5) alters that sometimes (often?) require trance-facilitated emergence, and (6) lower levels of depression, anxiety, general psychopathology, and functional impairment than persons with Complex Dissociative Disorder I.

25.8.1 Prevalence of Complex Dissociative Disorder I

The criteria for Complex Dissociative Disorder I should prevent cases of covert DID from being misclassified as DDNOS-1; therefore, the prevalence of Complex Dissociative Disorder I should be higher than existent reports of the prevalence of DID. In other words, the prevalence of Complex Dissociative Disorder I is probably the sum of the prevalence of overt DID *plus* the prevalence of covert DID. I estimate that the prevalence of Complex Dissociative Disorder (see Table 25.5) will approximate the current reported prevalence of DID (i.e., overt DID) *plus* one-third to two-thirds the current reported prevalence of DDNOS (i.e., covert DID).

TABLE 25.5
Estimated Prevalence of Complex Dissociative Disorder I in Various Settings

		Estimated Range of Prevalence (%)
Nonclinical	China	0
	Canada	1.36–1.42
	USA	3.30–5.10
	Turkey	3.80–6.60
Outpatient	USA	7.9–10.7
	Turkey	4.8–7.4
Inpatient	Canada	7.0–7.7
	Switzerland	1.1–1.7
	Germany	0.9–1.7
	Turkey	7.0–8.9
	Netherlands	3.8–6.0
	Finland	8.9–12.1
State Hospital	USA	12.3–16.8

Note: Because these estimates are based on the studies listed in Table 25.1, they are also "based on" the defining characteristics of those particular research settings.

25.8.2 What Is the Most Common Dissociative Disorder?

The most common dissociative disorder should be reconsidered in light of Complex Dissociative Disorder I. Given that 40.6% of diagnosed dissociative disorders have DDNOS and 22.8% have DID, I estimate that 36.3% to 49.5% of dissociative cases diagnosed in clinical settings will have Complex Dissociative Disorder I.

25.8.3 Prevalence of Complex Dissociative Disorder II

We know so little about subtle MPD (i.e., Complex Dissociative Disorder II) that we can make no predictions regarding its prevalence. What we *can* predict is the likelihood that over 50% of dissociative presentations in psychiatric settings will be diagnosed as complex dissociative disorders (i.e., either Complex Dissociative Disorder I or Complex Dissociative Disorder II). Said differently, at least half of the dissociative cases encountered by present-day clinicians have chronic, complex dissociative disorders. Both their clinical diagnoses and the diagnostic nosology of DSM-V should reflect that fact: *50% or more of DD patients have a chronic complex dissociative disorder.*

I want to thank Vedat Şar and John O'Neil for their very helpful comments on earlier drafts. John's consistently incisive editorial comments have been invaluable. I especially want to thank Elizabeth Bowman; this chapter has benefited immeasurably from her wise and detailed critique.

REFERENCES

Adityanjee, G. S. (1990). Multiple personality in India: Dr. Adityanjee replies. *American Journal of Psychiatry, 147*, 1260–1261.

Akyüz, G., Doğan, O., Şar, V., Yargıç, I. L., & Tutkun, H. (1999). Frequency of dissociative identity disorder in the general population in Turkey. *Comprehensive Psychiatry, 40*, 151–159.

Alexander, P. J., Joseph, S., & Das, A. (1997). Limited utility of ICD-10 and DSM-IV classification of dissociative and conversion disorders in India. *Acta Psychiatrica Scandinavica, 95*, 177–182.

American Psychiatric Association (1980). *DSM-III – Diagnostic and statistical manual of mental disorders* (3rd ed.). Washington, DC: Author.

American Psychiatric Association (1987). *DSM-III-R– Diagnostic and statistical manual of mental disorders* (3rd ed., revised). Washington, DC: Author.

American Psychiatric Association (1994). *DSM-IV – Diagnostic and statistical manual of mental disorders* (4th ed.). Washington, DC: Author.

Beahrs, J. O. (1982). *Unity and multiplicity: Multilevel consciousness of self in hypnosis, psychiatric disorder and mental health.* New York: Brunner/Mazel.

Bernstein, E. M., & Putnam, F. W. (1986). Development, reliability, and validity of a dissociation scale. *Journal of Nervous and Mental Disease, 174*, 727–735.

Bloch, J. P. (1991). *Assessment and treatment of multiple personality and dissociative disorders.* Sarasota, FL: Practitioner's Resource Series.

Boon, S., & Draijer, N. (1991). Diagnosing dissociative disorders in The Netherlands: A pilot study with the Structured Clinical Interview for DSM-III-R Dissociative Disorders. *American Journal of Psychiatry, 148*, 458–462.

Boon, S., & Draijer, N. (1993). *Multiple personality disorder in The Netherlands: A study on reliability and validity of the diagnosis.* Amsterdam/Lisse: Swets & Zeitlinger.

Braun, B. G. (1988). The BASK (behavior, affect, sensation, knowledge) model of dissociation. *Dissociation, 1*(1), 4–23.

Cardeña, E., & Spiegel, D. (1996). Diagnostic issues, criteria, and comorbidity of dissociative disorders. In L. K. Michelson & W. J. Ray (Eds.), *Handbook of dissociation: Theoretical, empirical, and clinical perspectives* (pp. 227–250). New York: Plenum Press.

Carlson, E. B., & Putnam, F. W. (1993). An update on the Dissociative Experiences Scale. *Dissociation, 6*, 16–27.

Chand, S. P., Al Hussaini, A. A., Martin, R., Mustapha, S., Zaidan, Z., Viernes, N., & Al-Adawi, S. (2000). Dissociative disorders in the Sultanate of Oman. *Acta Psychiatrica Scandinavica, 102*, 185–187.

Chu, J. A. (1996). Posttraumatic responses to childhood abuse and implications for treatment. In L. K. Michelson & W. J. Ray (Eds.), *Handbook of dissociation: Theoretical, empirical, and clinical perspectives* (pp. 381–397). New York: Plenum Press.

Coons, P. M. (1992). Dissociative disorder not otherwise specified: A clinical investigation of 50 cases with suggestions for typology and treatment. *Dissociation, 5*(4), 187–195.

Coons, P. M. (2001). On changing the diagnostic criteria for dissociative identity disorder. *Journal of Trauma & Dissociation, 2*(1), 43–46.

Coons, P. M., & Milstein, V. (1992) Psychogenic amnesia: A clinical investigation of 25 cases. *Dissociation*, 5, 73–79.

Das, P. S., & Saxena, S. (1991). Classification of dissociative states in DSM-III-R and ICD-10 (1989 Draft): A study of Indian outpatients. *British Journal of Psychiatry, 159*, 425–427.

Dell, P. F. (1998). Axis II pathology in outpatients with dissociative identity disorder. *Journal of Nervous and Mental Disease, 186*, 352–356.

Dell, P. F. (2001a). Why the diagnostic criteria for dissociative identity disorder should be changed. *Journal of Trauma & Dissociation, 2*(1), 7–37.

Dell, P. F. (2001b). Should the dissociative disorders field choose its own diagnostic criteria for dissociative identity disorder? Reply to Cardeña, Coons, Putnam, Spiegel, and Steinberg. *Journal of Trauma & Dissociation, 2*(1), 65–72.

Dell, P. F. (2001c). Why DSM-III's portrayal of DID is a problem. *ISSD News, 19(2)*, 4–7.

Dell, P. F. (2002). Dissociative phenomenology of dissociative identity disorder. *Journal of Nervous and Mental Disease, 190*, 10–15.

Dell, P. F. (2006a). The Multidimensional Inventory of Dissociation (MID): A comprehensive measure of pathological dissociation. *Journal of Trauma & Dissociation, 7*(2), 77–106.

Dell, P. F. (2006b). A new model of dissociative identity disorder. *Psychiatric Clinics of North America, 29*(1), 1–26.

Dell, P. F. (2009a). The long struggle to diagnose multiple personality disorder (MPD) I. Multiple Personality Disorder. In P F. Dell & J. A. O'Neil (Eds.), *Dissociation and the dissociative disorders: DSM-V and beyond* (pp. 383–402). New York: Routledge.

Dell, P. F. (2009b). The phenomena of pathological dissociation. In P. F. Dell & J. A. O'Neil (Eds.), *Dissociation and the dissociative disorders: DSM-V and beyond* (pp. 225–238). New York: Routledge.

Ensink, B. J., & van Otterloo, D. (1989). A validation study of the DES in The Netherlands. *Dissociation, 2*(4), 221–223.

Foote, B., Smolin, Y., Kaplan, M., Legatt, M. E., & Lipschitz, D. (2006). Prevalence of dissociative disorders in psychiatric outpatients. *American Journal of Psychiatry, 163*(4), 623–629.

Franklin, J. (1988). Diagnosis of covert and subtle forms of multiple personality disorder. *Dissociation, 1*(2), 27–33.

Fraser, G. A. (1994). Dissociative phenomena and disorders: Clinical presentations. In R. M. Klein & B. K. Doane (Eds.), *Psychological concepts and dissociative disorders* (pp. 131–151). Hillsdale, NJ: Lawrence Erlbaum Associates.

Friedl, M. C., & Draijer, N. (2000). Dissociative disorders in Dutch psychiatric inpatients. *American Journal of Psychiatry, 157*, 1012–1013.

Frischholz, E. J., Braun, B. G., Sachs, R. G., Hopkins, L., Schaeffer, D. M., Lewis, J., Leavitt, F., Pasquotto, M. A., & Schwartz, D. R. (1990). The Dissociative Experiences Scale: Further replication and validation. *Dissociation, 3*(3), 151–153.

Gast, U., Rodewald, F., Nickel, V., & Emrich, H. M. (2001). Prevalence of dissociative disorders among psychiatric inpatients in a German university clinic. *Journal of Nervous and Mental Disease, 189*, 249–257.

Graves, S. M. (1989). Dissociative disorders and dissociative symptoms at a community mental health center. *Dissociation, 2*(3), 119–127.

Hilgard, E. R. (1977). *Divided consciousness: Multiple controls in human thought and action.* New York: Wiley.

Horen, S. A., Leichner, P. P., & Lawson, J. S. (1995). Prevalence of dissociative symptoms and disorders in an adult psychiatric inpatient population in Canada. *Canadian Journal of Psychiatry, 40*(5), 185–191.

Janet, P. (1889). *L'automatisme psychologique: Essai de psychologie expérimentale sur les formes inférieures de l'activité humaine* [Psychological automatism: Essay of experimental psychology on the lower forms of human activity]. Paris: Félix Alcan.

Kihlstrom, J. F. (1992). Hypnosis: A sesquicentennial essay. *International Journal of Clinical and Experimental Hypnosis, 40*, 301–314.

Kluft, R. P. (1985a). Making the diagnosis of multiple personality disorder (MPD). In F. F. Flach (Ed.), *Directions in Psychiatry, 5*(23), 1–10.

Kluft, R. P. (1985b). The natural history of multiple personality disorder. In R. P. Kluft (Ed.), *Childhood antecedents of multiple personality* (pp. 197–238). Washington, DC: American Psychiatric Press.

Kluft, R. P. (1987). Dissociative disorders. In A. E. Skodol & R. L. Spitzer (Eds.), *An annotated bibliography of DSM-III* (pp. 119–124). Washington, DC: American Psychiatric Press.

Kluft, R. P. (1988). The phenomenology and treatment of extremely complex multiple personality disorder. *Dissociation, 1*(4), 47–58.

Kluft, R. P., Steinberg, M., & Spitzer, R. L. (1988). DSM-III-R revisions in the dissociative disorders: An exploration of their derivation and rationale. *Dissociation, 1*(1), 39–46.

Latz, T. T., Kramer, S. I., & Hughes, D. L. (1995). Multiple personality disorder among female inpatients in a state hospital. *American Journal of Psychiatry, 152*(9), 1343–1348.

Lipsanen, T., Korkeila, J., Peltola, P., Järvinen, J., Langen, K., & Lauerma, H. (2004). Dissociative disorders among psychiatric patients: Comparison with a nonclinical sample. *European Psychiatry, 19*, 53–55.

Loewenstein, R. J. (1991). An office mental status examination for complex chronic dissociative symptoms and multiple personality disorder. *Psychiatric Clinics of North America, 14*(3), 567–604.

Lussier, R. G., Steiner, J., Grey, A., & Hansen, C. (1997). Prevalence of dissociative disorders in an acute care day hospital population. *Psychiatric Services, 48*(2), 244–246.

Martínez-Taboas, A. (1991). Multiple personality disorder as seen from a social constructionist viewpoint. *Dissociation, 4*(3), 129–133.

Messerschmidt, R. (1927–1928). A quantitative investigation of the alleged independent operation of conscious and subconscious processes. *Journal of Abnormal and Social Psychology, 22*, 325–340.

Mezzich, J. E., Fabrega, H., Coffman, G. A., & Haley, R. (1989). DSM-III disorders in a large sample of psychiatric patients: Frequency and specificity of diagnoses. *American Journal of Psychiatry, 146*, 212–219.

Modestin, J., Ebner, G., Junghan, M., & Erni, T. (1996). Dissociative experiences and dissociative disorders in acute psychiatric inpatients. *Comprehensive Psychiatry, 37*(5), 355–361.

Murphy, P. E. (1994). Dissociative experiences and dissociative disorders in a non-clinical university group. *Dissociation, 7*(1), 28–34.

Nemiah, J. (1985). Dissociative disorders. In H. Kaplan & B. Sadock (Eds.), *Comprehensive textbook of psychiatry* (4th ed., pp. 942–957). Baltimore: Williams & Wilkins.

Nijenhuis, E. R. S., Van Dyck, R., Spinhoven, P., van der Hart, O., Chatrou, M., Vanderlinden, J., & Moene, F. (1999). Somatoform dissociation discriminates among diagnostic categories over and above general psychopathology. *Australian and New Zealand Journal of Psychiatry, 33*, 511–520.

Perry, C., & Laurence, J.-R. (1984). Mental processing outside of awareness: The contributions of Freud and Janet. In K. S. Bowers & D. Meichenbaum (Eds.), *The unconscious reconsidered* (pp. 9–48). New York: Wiley.

Putnam, F. W. (2001). Reclaiming dissociative disorders. *Journal of Trauma & Dissociation, 2*(1), 47–49.

Putnam, F. W., Carlson, E. B., Ross, C. A., Anderson, G., Clark, P., Torem, M., Bowman, E. S., Coons, P., Chu, J. A., Dill, D. L., Loewenstein, R. J., & Braun, B. G. (1996). Patterns of dissociation in clinical and nonclinical samples. *Journal of Nervous and Mental Disease, 184*, 673–679.

Ross, C. A. (1985). DSM-III: Problems in diagnosing partial forms of multiple personality disorder: discussion paper. *Journal of the Royal Society of Medicine, 78*, 933–936.

Ross, C. A. (1991). Epidemiology of multiple personality disorder and dissociation. *Psychiatric Clinics of North America, 14*(3), 503–517.

Ross, C. A. (1997). *Dissociative Identity Disorder: Diagnosis, clinical features, and treatment of multiple personality.* New York: Wiley.

Ross, C. A., Anderson, G., Fraser, G. A., Reagor, P., Bjornson, L., & Miller, S. D. (1992). Differentiating multiple personality disorder and dissociative disorder not otherwise specified. *Dissociation, 5*(2), 87–90.

Ross, C. A., Duffy, C. M. M., & Ellason, J. W. (2002). Prevalence, reliability and validity of dissociative disorders in an inpatient setting. *Journal of Trauma & Dissociation, 3*(1), 7–17.

Ross, C. A., Ryan, L., Voigt, H., & Eide, L. (1991). High and low dissociators in a college population. *Dissociation, 4*(3), 147–151.

Şar, V., & Akyüz, G. (2003, November). *Trauma and dissociation among prisoners*. Paper presented at the 20th annual conference of the International Society for the Study of Dissociation. Baltimore, MD.

Şar, V., Akyüz, G., & Doğan, O. (2007). Prevalence of dissociative disorders among women in the general population. *Psychiatry Research, 149*(1–3), 169–176.

Şar, V., Kundakçı, T., Kızıltan, E., Bakım, B., & Bozkurt, O. (2000a). Differentiating dissociative disorders from other diagnostic groups through somatoform dissociation in Turkey. *Journal of Trauma & Dissociation, 1*(4), 67–80.

Şar, V.,Tutkun, H., Alyanak, B., Bakım, B., & Baral, I. (2000b). Frequency of dissociative disorders among psychiatric outpatients in Turkey. *Comprehensive Psychiatry, 41*, 216–222.

Şar, V., Kundakçı, T., Kızıltan, E., Yargıç, I. L., Tutkun, H., Bakım, B., Bozkurt, O., Özpulat, T., Keser, V., & Özdemir, Ö. (2003). The Axis-I dissociative disorder comorbidity of borderline personality disorder among psychiatric patients. *Journal of Trauma & Dissociation, 4*(1), 119–136.

Saxe, G. N., van der Kolk, B. A., Berkowitz, R., Chinman, G., Hall, K., Lieberg, G., & Schwartz, J. (1993). Dissociative disorders in psychiatric inpatients. *American Journal of Psychiatry, 150*, 1037–1042.

Saxena, S., & Prasad, K. V. S. R. (1989). DSM-III subclassification of dissociative disorders applied to psychiatric outpatients in India. *American Journal of Psychiatry, 146*, 261–262.

Somer, E., & Dell, P. F. (2005). Development of the Hebrew-Multidimensional Inventory of Dissociation (H-MID): A valid and reliable measure of pathological dissociation. *Journal of Trauma & Dissociation, 6*(1), 31–53.

Spiegel, D., & Cardeña, E. (1991). Disintegrated experience: The dissociative disorders revisited. *Journal of Abnormal Psychology, 100*(3), 366–378.

Steinberg, M. (1993*). Interviewer's guide to the Structured Clinical Interview for DSM-IV Dissociative Disorders (SCID-D).* Washington, DC: American Psychiatric Press.

Steinberg, M. (1994). *Interviewer's guide to the Structured Clinical Interview for DSM-IV Dissociative Disorders (SCID-D)-Revised.* Washington, DC: American Psychiatric Press.

Steinberg, M. (1995). *Handbook for the assessment of dissociation: A clinical guide.* Washington, DC: American Psychiatric Press.

Steinberg, M. (2001). Updating diagnostic criteria for dissociative disorders: Learning from scientific advances. *Journal of Trauma & Dissociation, 2*(1), 59–63.

Takahashi, Y. (1990). Is multiple personality disorder really rare in Japan? *Dissociation, 3*, 57–59.

Tutkun, H., Şar, V., Yargıç, L. I., Özpulat, T., Yanık, M., & Kızıltan, E. (1998). Frequency of dissociative disorders among psychiatric inpatients in a Turkish University Clinic. *American Journal of Psychiatry, 155*, 800–805.

Umesue, M., Matsuo, T., Iwata, N., & Tashiro, N. (1996). Dissociative disorders in Japan: A pilot study with the Dissociative Experience Scale and a semi-structured interview. *Dissociation, 9*(3), 182–189.

Van der Hart, O., Nijenhuis, E., & Steele, K. (2006). *The haunted self: Structural dissociation and the treatment of chronic dissociation.* New York: W. W. Norton.

Vanderlinden, J. (1993). *Dissociative experiences, trauma and hypnosis: research findings & clinical applications in eating disorders.* Delft, The Netherlands: Uitgeverij Eburon.

Waller, N. G., Putnam, F. W., & Carlson, E. B. (1996). Types of dissociation and dissociative types: A taxometric analysis of dissociative experiences. *Psychological Methods, 1*(3), 300–321.

Watkins, J. G., & Watkins, H. H. (1997). *Ego states: Theory and therapy*. New York: W. W. Norton and Company.

White, R. W., & Shevach, B. J. (1942). Hypnosis and the concept of dissociation. *Journal of Abnormal and Social Psychology*, 37, 309–328.

Wig, N. N. (1983). DSM-III: A perspective from the Third World. In R. L. Spitzer, J. B. W. Williams & A. E. Skodol (Eds.), *International perspectives on DSM-III.* Washington, DC: American Psychiatric Press.

Xiao, Z., Yan, H., Wang, Z., Zou, Z., Xu, Y., Chen, J., Zang, H., Ross, C. A., & Keyes, B. B. (2006). Trauma and dissociation in China. *American Journal of Psychiatry, 163*, 1388–1391.

26 Dissociative Amnesia and Dissociative Fugue

Colin A. Ross, MD

OUTLINE

The literature on dissociative amnesia and dissociative fugue has been reviewed by Coons (1999, 2000), Ford (1989), Kenny (1986), Kilhstrom, Tataryn, and Hoyt (1984) and Loewenstein (1991, 1993, 1995, 1996). A case of dissociative fugue with further discussion of the literature was published by Howley and Ross (2003) subsequent to these reviews. An additional modern fugue case is available in Ross (1994).

Compared to the large literature on dissociative identity disorder (DID), the literature on dissociative amnesia and dissociative fugue is sparse. The clinical case literatures on dissociative amnesia and dissociative fugue overlap and are comprised mostly of papers that are half century old (Abeles & Schilder, 1935; Akhtar & Brenner, 1979; Berrington, Liddell, & Foulds, 1956; Fisher, 1945, 1947; Fisher & Joseph, 1949; Stengel & Vienna, 1941).

Given the small volume and slow evolution of these literatures, there are no data-based reasons to modify the DSM-IV-TR diagnostic criteria for amnesia and fugue (American Psychiatric Association, 2000). There are some problematic issues, however, that may warrant modification of the next DSM *text* about dissociative amnesia and dissociative fugue.

26.1 DEFINITIONS OF DISSOCIATION, DISSOCIATIVE AMNESIA, AND DISSOCIATIVE FUGUE

There are four meanings of the word *dissociation* (Ross, 1999, 2007). First, there is a general systems meaning of dissociation: *the opposite of association, a disconnection, or lack of interaction between two variables.* There are dissociation constants in physical chemistry, for instance.

Second, dissociation is a technical term in experimental cognitive psychology. In cognitive psychology, dissociation is often *a normal property of cognitive functioning.* For example, countless studies have demonstrated the dissociation between procedural and declarative memory (Cohen & Eichenbaum, 1993). Such dissociation is normal; it does not entail any special operations or exceptional properties of the mind.

Third, dissociation is *a phenomenological term in clinical psychology and psychiatry that has been operationalized by various measures.* In this sense, dissociation is what is measured by the items of the Dissociative Experiences Scale (DES) (Bernstein & Putnam, 1986; Carlson et al.,

1993), Dissociative Disorders Interview Schedule (DDIS) (Ross, 1997), Structured Clinical Interview for DSM-IV Dissociative Disorders (SCID-D) (Steinberg, 1995; Steinberg, Cicchetti, Buchanan, Rakfeldt, & Rounsaville, 1994; Steinberg, Rounsaville, & Cicchetti, 1990), the Multidimensional Inventory of Dissociation (MID) (Dell, 2002, 2004), and so on.

Fourth, dissociation is an intrapsychic defense mechanism.

Confusion arises when these different meanings of the word *dissociation* have not been specified. For instance, lack of experimental evidence for dissociation as an intrapsychic defense mechanism is not relevant to (1) the scientific status of dissociation in cognitive psychology, or (2) the psychometric properties of measures of dissociation.

In this chapter, I will deal primarily with the phenomena of dissociation as operationalized by structured interviews and self-report measures of dissociation (Pincus, Rush, First, & McQueen, 2000).

Approximately 3000 individuals with dissociative disorders have been admitted to my Trauma Program in Dallas, Texas, in the last 12 years. During this time, to the best of my recollection, I have encountered fewer than 10 individuals with pure dissociative amnesia or pure dissociative fugue. On the other hand, *symptoms* of amnesia and fugue were common in those 3000 dissociative patients.

26.2 PROBLEMS WITH THE DSM-IV-TR RULES FOR DISSOCIATIVE DISORDER NOT OTHERWISE SPECIFIED

In my opinion, there is a problem with either the DSM-IV-TR rules or the DSM-IV-TR nosology for the dissociative disorders. The problem is occasioned by the high epidemiological frequency of partial DID. In DSM-IV-TR, partial DID is classified as Dissociative Disorder Not Otherwise Specified (DDNOS-1). The diagnostic rules of DSM-IV-TR only allow the diagnosis of NOS if the individual does not meet criteria for a specified disorder (Ross, 1985). Thus, in the case of DDNOS-1 (i.e., partial DID), DSM-IV-TR forces the clinician to issue a diagnosis of dissociative fugue or dissociative amnesia (or both). Unfortunately, neither dissociative fugue nor dissociative amnesia provides an accurate portrayal of the symptomatology of partial DID.

In earlier versions of the DSM, DDNOS was called *atypical dissociative disorder*. The NOS diagnosis in DSM-IV-TR still carries that connotation—atypical. Yet, DDNOS-1 is definitely not atypical. In fact, DDNOS-1 is probably the most common dissociative disorder (Akyüz, Doğan, Şar, Yargıç, & Tutkun, 1999; Ross, 1991, 1997). Conversely, given their rarity, pure Dissociative Amnesia and Dissociative Fugue are atypical.

DSM-V should find a better way to diagnose cases of partial DID.

26.3 PERSONS WITH DISSOCIATIVE AMNESIA DO NOT APPEAR TO BE MEMBERS OF THE DISSOCIATIVE TAXON

I have carefully interviewed individuals with previously undiagnosed dissociative amnesia (Ross, Duffy, & Ellason, 2002). These are the only cases of pure dissociative amnesia that I have encountered in recent years. Unlike persons with DDNOS and DID, these individuals did not seem to be members of the dissociative taxon (Waller, Putnam, & Carlson, 1996; Waller & Ross, 1997). They had low scores on the Dissociative Experiences Scale and were not experiencing part-self intrusions (i.e., ongoing Schneiderian symptoms, amnesias, or depersonalization).

These individuals had experienced one to three past episodes of amnesia in response to specific events; the durations of these episodes of amnesia ranged from hours to a few days. These individuals constitute a type of dissociative disorder that is quite different from members of the dissociative taxon (such as persons with DDNOS-1 or DID). The DSM-V Dissociative Disorders Committee should consider whether the issue of taxon membership deserves comment in the DSM-V texts about dissociative amnesia and dissociative fugue.

26.4 PROBLEMS WITH THE SEPARATENESS AND DISTINCTNESS OF DISSOCIATIVE AMNESIA AND DISSOCIATIVE FUGUE

Despite the fact that dissociative amnesia and dissociative fugue are both based upon amnesia, DSM-IV-TR considers them to be separate disorders. My clinical experience with 3000 dissociative cases, however, does not suggest that this nosological distinction really exists in nature. For instance, my diagnosis of a recent case was "fugue without travel." In response to an accumulation of noncatastrophic stressors, the patient awoke one morning with complete amnesia for his past life. Subsequently, he gradually developed a new identity, *but did not travel away from home*.

Since DSM-IV-TR does not allow the diagnosis of "fugue without travel," I might have issued a diagnosis of dissociative amnesia. If I had done so, I could then have described him as a case of *generalized amnesia*. However, the man had created a new identity, therefore he had more than a simple amnesia. I might have diagnosed dissociative fugue but, since he had not traveled, I could not do so. Given the options afforded by DSM-IV-TR, I was forced to render a diagnosis of DDNOS, even though he was, in fact, a classical case of fugue (albeit without the travel).

While thinking about this case, I was struck by a clarifying idea: in dissociative fugue both the travel and the development of a new identity are *secondary* phenomena. The primary dissociative process is one of generalized amnesia. This viewpoint receives implicit support from DSM-IV. DSM-IV weakened the identity criterion for fugue from DSM-III-R's "assumption of a new identity (partial or complete)" to DSM-IV's "confusion about personal identity or assumption of a new identity (partial or complete)."

DSM-IV's revision of Criterion B for dissociative fugue has a very interesting implication. If fugue can occur *without* the person assuming a new identity, then identity change is a secondary process that need not occur. As DSM-IV specifies, there may be only "confusion" about personal identity. DSM-IV-TR says that travel is the "predominant disturbance" in dissociative fugue. *I suggest that generalized amnesia is the predominant disturbance in fugue*. From this perspective, we could distinguish two forms of dissociative amnesia: generalized dissociative amnesia (i.e., fugue) and selective dissociative amnesia. For generalized dissociative amnesia (i.e., fugue) the criteria would be:

A. Sudden inability to recall one's past.
B. Confusion about personal identity or assumption of a new identity (partial or complete).
C. Sudden, unexpected travel away from home or one's place of work may or may not occur.

DSM-IV-TR's Criteria C and D for dissociative fugue would be retained, but would become D and E.

Still, I do not recommend that these revised diagnostic criteria be implemented in DSM-V; there is insufficient research to support such a change. I do recommend, however, that the previously stated issues be addressed in the *text* of the next DSM.

Clinically, it seems likely that there are cases of sudden, unexpected travel that occur in a depersonalized state (i.e., without amnesia). How should such cases be classified?

I have also seen a case of pure continuous dissociative amnesia. According to DSM-IV-TR, this is a case of dissociative amnesia. The amnesia in this case, however, was far more disabling than simple, limited selective amnesia. This patient's amnesia was much more incapacitating than that of most people with DID.

There is another problem with DSM-IV-TR's distinction between dissociative amnesia and dissociative fugue. Dissociative fugues typically resolve into dissociative amnesias; that is, these persons emerge from the fugue and regain both their memory and their identity—but then they have amnesia for the period of fugue. For this reason, dissociative fugue could be conceptualized as a variant of dissociative amnesia (with a more complex structure and a sequence of stages). Here again, the travel would be considered to be a secondary feature.

To further complicate matters, it is also possible to conceptualize dissociative fugue as a variant of DID. I interviewed the case of "fugue without travel" (see previous discussion) *during* the fugue episode. In other words, I was able to interview the person's new identity. This identity did not differ from the alter personalities that occur in DID—except that the identity had been created quite recently. The new "person" was like an alter personality that was characterized by (1) complete two-way amnesia for the host personality and (2) a full-blown delusion of separateness. He believed that the prefugue identity had a separate physical body. He was prepared to become physically violent with the prefugue identity if it tried to come back and take over. Thus, the new identity exhibited the trance logic that is so typical of alter personalities in DID.

From this perspective, dissociative fugue is an adult-onset form of dual personality in which the "host personality" is suppressed (during the period of fugue), and then reemerges. If an "alter personality" was created during the period of fugue, it is suppressed after the host emerges from the fugue and resumes executive control. Clinicians and researchers have not yet addressed the question of whether a fugue "alter personality" *continues to exist* after the return of the host.

Viewed in this way, amnesia for the period of fugue occurs because the original identity and the fugue identity have not been integrated. Integration would produce continuity of memory—and also an integration of the hopes, dreams, attitudes, and feelings that were not possessed by (i.e., were unavailable to) the original prefugue personality (but which are part of the larger self). Clinicians tend not to think this way because cases of fugue are rare and because they seldom encounter the case until the fugue is over. Consequently, clinicians very rarely have an opportunity to speak with the alter personality that existed during the fugue.

26.5 DSM-V ISSUES

The DSM-V Dissociative Disorders Committee should discuss (1) the degree of separateness between dissociative amnesia and dissociative fugue, (2) the possibility that fugue is a variant of DID, and (3) whether the core feature of fugue is travel or amnesia.

The DSM-V text for dissociative fugue should also include some discussion of the frequency with which fugue is characterized by antecedent depression and a history of childhood trauma. In addition, the complex internal structure of fugue episodes should be more clearly delineated (Howley & Ross, 2003). A fugue is not an undifferentiated period of time; a fugue is divided into two sub-stages, each with its own form of amnesia: (1) the stage of flight, and (2) the stage in the new location (that is characterized by amnesia for the period of flight).

Finally, as noted, I do not recommend that DSM-V incorporate any substantial changes in the diagnostic criteria for dissociative amnesia or dissociative fugue. There is insufficient empirical evidence for any changes at this time.

26.6 THE DOMAINS OF DISSOCIATION, DISSOCIATIVE AMNESIA, AND DISSOCIATIVE FUGUE

Dissociative symptoms occur across the entire domain of psychopathology. In particular, dissociative symptoms may occur during psychosis, mood disorder, anxiety disorder, somatoform disorder, eating disorder, and substance abuse disorder. Dissociative symptoms are included among the diagnostic criteria for acute stress disorder, posttraumatic stress disorder, somatization disorder, borderline personality disorder, schizotypal disorder, and, of course, dissociative disorder.

Dissociative amnesia and dissociative fugue can occur as a circumscribed disorder or as a part of a more complex disorder, especially DID and DDNOS.

26.7 INCONSISTENCIES BETWEEN DSM-IV-TR AND ICD-10

There are several important differences between DSM-IV-TR's understanding of the dissociative disorders and that of *The International Classification of Diseases-10* (ICD-10) (World Health Organization, 1992).

First, in contrast to DSM-IV-TR, ICD-10 classifies the dissociative and the conversion disorders in a single subsection (F44) entitled "dissociative [conversion] disorders." This section indicates that the World Health Organization (WHO) conceptualizes dissociation as occurring in parts of the brain responsible for sensation and motor function (while DSM-IV-TR limits dissociation to disturbances of consciousness, memory, identity, or perception of the environment).

Second, WHO considers dissociative disorders to be transient: "All types of dissociative state tend to remit after a few weeks or months, particularly if their onset was associated with a traumatic life event" (WHO, 1992, p. 152). Finally, there are several other major differences between ICD-10 and DSM-IV-TR that affect dissociative disorders, but they lie outside the scope of the present article (i.e., DID and depersonalization disorder).

26.8 EXPLANATORY MECHANISMS OF DISSOCIATION, DISSOCIATIVE AMNESIA, AND DISSOCIATIVE FUGUE

How the brain and mind carry out the operation of dissociation is unknown. Cardeña (1994) has argued that any and all mental contents can be dissociated from each other in any and all possible combinations. If this is so, then dissociation cannot be localized to one neuroanatomical structure or one neurotransmitter. I assume that there are numerous mechanisms for the phenomenon of dissociation.

That said, I endorse the trauma model of pathological dissociation (Ross, 1994, 1997, 1999, 2004, 2007). Trauma, however, is not the *mechanism* of dissociation. Instead, it is a stressor that evokes different reactions in different individuals. In any given instance, the nature of that reaction is determined by a complex interactional field of meaning, memory, affect, cognition, and biological events in the hippocampus, adrenal cortex and many other locations.

Typically, the stressors that precede dissociative fugue and dissociative amnesia are milder, simpler, briefer, and less numerous than those that precede DID and DDNOS. This conclusion, however, is based on limited clinical experience with dissociative amnesia and dissociative fugue; there are no large published case series of amnesia and fugue that comprehensively enumerate their trauma histories. The empirical literature on dissociative fugue emphasizes trauma during adulthood, especially military combat, but also frequently mentions traumatic and abusive childhoods (Howley & Ross, 2004). Similarly, the literature on dissociative amnesia emphasizes a single, antecedent event (or set of stressful circumstances).

26.9 EMPIRICAL STRENGTHS AND WEAKNESSES OF DISSOCIATIVE FUGUE AND DISSOCIATIVE AMNESIA

The clinical literature on dissociative amnesia and dissociative fugue dates back to the 19th century (Ross, 1997; Ross & Howley, 2004). Curiously, that literature is better accepted by the mental health field than is the literature on DID (Lalonde, Hudson, Gigante, & Pope, 2001; Pope, Oliva, Hudson, Bodkin, & Gruber, 1999). Amnesia and fugue have not engendered great controversy. This is almost odd because dissociative fugue often involves a more abrupt and radical dissociation of memory and identity than is typically the case in DID.

Dissociative amnesia is a rigorously demonstrated phenomenon in cognitive psychology and is validated by the common experience of having something on the tip of your tongue for a period of time before remembering it. Everyone has had the experience of not being able to remember a name, details of an encounter, or other information without repeated recall effort or a triggering cue.

The major weakness of the empirical literature on fugue and amnesia is the lack of large modern case series that report psychometric data.

26.10 NEEDED RESEARCH

The reliability and validity of dissociative amnesia and dissociative fugue need to be demonstrated with modern measures of dissociation. Because cases of dissociative fugue are rare in the clinical and research caseloads of experts in dissociation, a registry of some sort would be beneficial. A central bank could accumulate data on a sizable series of fugue cases by sending self-report measures to reporting clinicians. The central bank could also assist clinicians to administer structured diagnostic interviews to these cases.

The International Society for the Study of Trauma and Dissociation (ISSTD) would be the logical candidate to set up and administer this data bank. ISSTD members could be requested to report fugue cases that they encounter in their practices, as well as cases reported in their local media.

A sizable series of dissociative amnesia cases could be identified by screening clinical populations with the 12-item Memory Problems Scale of the MID. Respondents who scored above a cutoff would then be administered the DDIS, SCID-D, or a specially designed structured interview for dissociative amnesia. Such research should also assess comorbid disorders and antecedent stressors.

REFERENCES

Abeles, M., & Schilder, P. (1935). Psychogenic loss of personal identity: Amnesia. *Archives of Neurology and Psychiatry, 34*, 587–604.

Akhtar, S., & Brenner, I. (1979). Differential diagnoses of fugue-like states. *Journal of Clinical Psychology, 40*, 381–385.

Akyüz, G., Doğan, O., Şar, V., Yargıç, I. L., & Tutkun, H. (1999). Frequency of dissociative identity disorder in the general population in Turkey. *Comprehensive Psychiatry, 40*, 151–159.

American Psychiatric Association (2000). *DSM-IV-TR–Diagnostic and statistical manual of mental disorders* (4th ed., text rev.). Washington, DC: Author.

Bernstein, E. M., & Putnam, F. W. (1986). Development, reliability, and validity of a dissociation scale. *Journal of Nervous and Mental Disease, 174*, 727–735.

Berrington, W. P., Liddell, D. W., & Foulds, G. A. (1956). A re-evaluation of the fugue. *Journal of Mental Science, 102*, 280–286.

Cardeña, E. (1994). The domain of dissociation. In S. J. Lynn & J. W. Rhue (Eds.), *Dissociation: Clinical and theoretical perspectives* (pp. 15–31). New York: Guilford.

Carlson, E. B., Putnam, F. W., Ross, C. A., Torem, M., Coons, P., Dill, D. L., Loewenstein, R. J., & Braun, B. G. (1993). Validity of the Dissociative Experiences Scale in screening for multiple personality disorder: A multicenter study. *American Journal of Psychiatry, 150*, 1030–1036.

Cohen, N. J., & Eichenbaum, H. (1993). *Memory, amnesia, and the hippocampal system*. Cambridge: MIT Press.

Coons, P. M. (1999). Psychogenic or dissociative fugue: A clinical investigation of five cases. *Psychological Reports, 84*, 881–886.

Coons, P. M. (2000). Dissociative fugue. In B. J. Sadock & V. Sadock (Eds.), *Comprehensive textbook of psychiatry* (7th ed., pp. 1549–1552). New York: Lippincott, Williams, & Wilkins.

Dell, P. F. (2002). Dissociative phenomenology of dissociative identity disorder. *Journal of Nervous and Mental Disease, 190*, 10–15.

Dell, P. F. (2004). *The Multidimensional Inventory of Dissociation (MID): A comprehensive measure of the subjective/phenomenological domain of dissociation.* Submitted for publication.

Fisher, C. (1945). Amnestic states in war neuroses: The psychogenesis of fugues. *Psychoanalytic Quarterly, 14*, 437–468.

Fisher, C. (1947). The psychogenesis of fugue states. *American Journal of Psychotherapy, 1*, 211–221.

Fisher, C., & Joseph, E. D. (1949). Fugue with loss of personal identity. *Psychoanalytic Quarterly, 18*, 480–493.

Ford, C. V. (1989). Psychogenic fugue. In T. B. Karasu (Ed.), *Treatments of psychiatric disorders* (vol. 3, pp. 2190–2196). Washington, DC: American Psychiatric Press.

Howley, J., & Ross, C. A. (2003). The structure of dissociative fugue: A case report. *Journal of Trauma and Dissociation, 4*, 109–124.

Kenny, M. G. (1986). *The passion of Ansel Bourne*. Washington, DC: Smithsonian Institution Press.

Kihlstrom, J. F., Tataryn, D. J., & Hoyt, I. (1984). Dissociative disorders. In P. B. Sutker & H. E. Adams (Eds.), *Comprehensive handbook of psychopathology* (pp. 203–234). New York: Plenum Press.

Lalonde, J. K., Hudson, J. L., Gigante, R. A., & Pope, H. G. (2001). Canadian and American psychiatrist's attitudes toward dissociative disorder diagnoses. *Canadian Journal of Psychiatry*, *46*, 407–412.

Loewenstein, R. J. (1991). Psychogenic amnesia and psychogenic fugue: a comprehensive review. In A. Tasman & S. M. Goldfinger (Eds.), *American psychiatric press review of psychiatry* (pp. 189–221). Washington, DC: American Psychiatric Press.

Loewenstein, R. J. (1993). Psychogenic amnesia and psychogenic fugue: A comprehensive review. In D. Spiegel (Ed.), *Dissociative disorders, a clinical review* (pp. 45–77). Lutherville, MD: Sidran Press.

Loewenstein, R. J. (1995). Dissociative amnesia and dissociative fugue. In G. O. Gabbard (Ed.), *Treatments of psychiatric disorders* (vol. 2, pp. 1569–1597). Washington, DC: American Psychiatric Press.

Loewenstein, R. J. (1996). Dissociative amnesia and dissociative fugue. In L. K. Michelson & W. J. Ray (Eds.), *Handbook of dissociation: Theoretical, empirical and clinical perspectives* (pp. 307–336). New York: Plenum Press.

Pincus, H. A., Rush, A. J., First, M. B., & McQueen, L. E. (2000). *Handbook of psychiatric measures*. Washington, DC: American Psychiatric Association.

Pope, H. G., Oliva, P. S., Hudson, J. I., Bodkin, J. A., & Gruber, A. J. (1999). Attitudes towards DSM-IV dissociative disorders diagnoses among Board-certified American psychiatrists. *American Journal of Psychiatry*, *156*, 321–232.

Ross, C. A. (1985). DSM-III: Problems in diagnosing partial forms of multiple personality disorder. *Journal of the Royal Society of Medicine*, *75*, 933–936.

Ross, C. A. (1991). Epidemiology of multiple personality disorder and dissociation. *Psychiatric Clinics of North America*, *14*, 503–517.

Ross, C. A. (1994). *The Osiris Complex: Case studies in multiple personality disorder.* Toronto: University of Toronto Press.

Ross, C. A. (1997). *Dissociative identity disorder. Diagnosis, clinical features, and treatment of multiple personality* (2nd ed.). New York: John Wiley & Sons.

Ross, C. A. (1999). The dissociative disorders. In T. Million, P. P. Blaney, & R. Davis (Eds.), *Oxford textbook of psychopathology* (pp. 466–481). New York: Oxford University Press.

Ross, C. A. (2007). *The trauma model: A solution to the problem of comorbidity in psychiatry*. Richardson, TX: Manitou Communications.

Ross, C. A., Duffy, C. M. M., & Ellason, J. W. (2002). Prevalence, reliability and validity of dissociative disorders in an inpatient setting. *Journal of Trauma and Dissociation, 3,* 7–17.

Steinberg, M. (1995). *Handbook for the assessment of dissociation. A clinical guide*. Washington, DC: American Psychiatric Press.

Steinberg, M., Cicchetti, D., Buchanan, J., Rakfeldt, J., & Rounsaville, B. (1994). Distinguishing between multiple personality disorder (dissociative identity disorder) and schizophrenia using the structured clinical interview for DSM-IV dissociative disorders. *Journal of Nervous and Mental Disease*, *182*, 495–502.

Steinberg, M., Rounsaville, B. J., & Cicchetti, D. V. (1990). The Structured Clinical Interview for DSM-III-R Dissociative Disorders: Preliminary report on a new diagnostic instrument. *American Journal of Psychiatry*, *147*, 76–82.

Stengel, E., & Vienna, M. D. (1941). On the aetiology of the fugue states. *Journal of Mental Science,* 87, 572–599.

Takahashi, Y. (1988). Suicide and amnesia in Mt. Fuji's Black Forest. *Suicide and Life-Threatening Behavior*, *18*, 164–175.

Waller, N. G., Putnam, F. W., & Carlson, E. B. (1996). The types of dissociation and dissociative types: A taxometric analysis of dissociative experiences. *Psychological Methods*, *1*, 300–321.

Waller, N. G., & Ross, C. A. (1997). The prevalence and taxometric structure of pathological dissociation in the general population: Taxometric structure and behavior genetic findings. *Journal of Abnormal and Social Psychology*, *106*, 499–510.

World Health Organization (1992). ICD-10: The ICD-10 classification of mental and behavioral disorders. Clinical descriptions and diagnostic guidelines. Geneva: Author.

27 Depersonalization Disorder

Daphne Simeon, MD

OUTLINE

The goal of this chapter is to present an overview of depersonalization disorder and to explore its relationship to the construct of dissociation, highlighting questions that to date appear adequately addressed, as well as issues that need future investigation. The case will be made that various lines of evidence support the conceptualization of chronic depersonalization as a primary dissociative disorder. The chapter begins with an overview of the phenomenology of depersonalization disorder (DPD), its relationship to trauma and stress, the cognitive profile of DPD, and DPD response to pharmacological treatments. Throughout these sections, reference will be made to what the data tell us about DPD as a primary dissociative disorder. Next, we will pose some further important questions regarding the relationship of depersonalization and depersonalization disorder to other dissociative symptoms and disorders. We will conclude with a summary of what we definitively know about DPD, and what needs to be addressed in future research.

27.1 DPD: OVERVIEW OF PHENOMENOLOGY

Research into the phenomenology of DPD has now advanced to the point that we now have two large cohorts, one from the United States of 117 consecutively recruited individuals (Simeon et al., 2003) and one from the United Kingdom of 204 individuals (Baker et al., 2003) suffering from chronic depersonalization. The two studies differed in some respects, both in their assessment methodology and in the nature of the cases included. The U.S. cohort only included subjects with primary DPD, whereas of the U.K. sample only 71% were deemed to have primary DPD. Furthermore only 61% of the U.K. sample underwent a full psychiatric interview; the remainder was evaluated by phone or mail-in questionnaires. Still, the two studies yielded strikingly similar phenomenological findings in most respects.

27.1.1 Symptom Description

Depersonalization is a particular type of dissociation involving a disrupted integration of self-perceptions with the sense of self, so that individuals experiencing depersonalization are in a subjective state of feeling estranged, detached, or disconnected from their own being. The following are common descriptions of depersonalization experiences: watching oneself from a distance like looking at a movie; candid out-of-body experiences; a sense of just going through the motions; one part acting/participating while the other part observing; feeling in a dream or fog; looking in the mirror and feeling detached from one's image; feeling detached from body parts or the whole body; not feeling in control of one's speech or physical movements; feeling disconnected from one's own thoughts; feeling detached from one's emotions, numbed, or blunted. Depersonalization is frequently accompanied by derealization, that is, a sense of unfamiliarity or detachment from one's own surroundings, people, and objects.

In summary, the subjective experience of depersonalization involves two core phenomenological features: a subjective sense of hypoemotionality and a subjective sense of unreality/unfamiliarity. An interesting question, then, which we will be again discussing later in the chapter, is whether both core features are, or need to be, present to make the determination of depersonalization. Can a person who is experiencing hypoemotionality alone (i.e., emotional blunting or numbing) be said to suffer from depersonalization, or is the second core feature of "unreality" usually referring to the perceptual experience of an unfamiliar self and world, a necessary feature of the condition?

Shedding some light on the issue of core symptom domains in DPD, a recent factor-analytic study in 394 affected adults revealed phenomenological complexity with five emerging symptom domains: numbing, unreality of self, perceptual alterations, unreality of surroundings, and temporal disintegration (Simeon et al., 2009).

27.1.2 Prevalence

Short-lived experiences of depersonalization are common in the general population, with an estimated 23% annual prevalence (Aderibigbe et al., 2001). Transient depersonalization is a common experience under severe or life-threatening stress, so that depersonalization and derealization comprise two of the five dissociative diagnostic criteria for acute stress disorder, a condition that can occur in the first month after a traumatic event and is frequently the prelude to PTSD. When depersonalization occurs persistently or recurrently, and is associated with significant distress and/or impairment, the diagnosis of depersonalization disorder (DPD) must be entertained. According to the DSM-IV, arriving at this diagnosis requires the presence of intact reality testing (i.e., an awareness on behalf of the individual that the depersonalization is an "as-if" experience). Second, comorbid psychiatric and medical conditions need to be identified in order to assess in what context the depersonalization is occurring. For example, depersonalization occurring simply in the context of a major depressive episode, a panic attack, or another dissociative disorder (e.g., dissociative identity disorder) should be diagnosed as such. Similarly, depersonalization due to a medical condition, neurological condition, or ongoing substance use should not be diagnosed as DPD.

The prevalence of DPD in the general population is unknown, but it is probably more common than its typical label as a "rare" disorder that most clinicians have never encountered. Indirect estimates suggest a 1% to 2% prevalence (Ross, 1991), yet DPD is rarely diagnosed. There are several factors likely to figure into the infrequent diagnosis of DPD: limited familiarity on the part of many clinicians regarding the entity and its typical presentation; reluctance on the part of many patients to disclose their symptoms because of an expectation that they will not be understood, that they may sound "crazy," or are unable to describe their depersonalization experiences; and a tendency to diagnose depersonalization as simply a variant of depression or anxiety, even when the diagnosis of a distinct condition is clearly warranted.

27.1.3 Onset and Course

Average age of onset is in adolescence, although some may have suffered from depersonalization as far back as they can remember, and others may have had onset in their 20s, 30s, or even 40s. Simeon et al. (2003) found a mean age of onset of 16 years of age, while Baker et al. (2003) reported a mean onset age of 22. Both cohorts are holding up to the initial impression, as described in the DSM-IV, of a 1:1 gender ratio. Of note, this gender distribution is different from that found in more "severe" dissociative disorders such as dissociative identity disorder (DID), and needs to be accounted for in viewing DPD as a dissociative spectrum disorder—this matter is further discussed in the "Trauma and Stress Antecedents" section. Furthermore, it is important to note that this gender distribution differs from the one that is well established in depression and anxiety disorders in which there is an overall predominance of females in a roughly 2:1 ratio to males—this finding then argues against conceptualizing DPD as a mood or anxiety spectrum condition.

The onset of DPD is sometimes acute and sometimes insidious. With acute onset, individuals may recall the exact moment, setting, and circumstance when they had their first depersonalization experience. This can be after a prolonged period of severe stress and adjustment efforts; after a traumatic event such as death of a loved one; with the initial episode of another mental condition such as panic disorder or depression (however, when these resolve, the depersonalization continues); with acute marijuana, hallucinogen, MDMA[1] or ketamine ingestion; or seemingly out-of-the-blue onset with no identifiable triggers. When the onset is insidious, it may either be so far back in time that there is no clear memory, or it may begin with limited episodes of lesser severity and frequency that gradually become more pronounced and lasting. The nature of the onset of DPD therefore differs, in some ways, from the more predictable onset of severe dissociative disorders such as DID, namely extreme childhood trauma. DPD can be triggered by various extreme emotional states, specific drugs, or seemingly nothing at all—this is another feature of the disorder that needs to be explicated within the construct of a dissociative spectrum, and we again discuss this later on.

The course of DPD over the years is continuous in about two-thirds of sufferers, for instance, the depersonalization is always present, either at constant intensity or with varying intensity, according to various environmental or emotional factors that alleviate or exacerbate symptoms. The course is episodic in about one-third of individuals, and each episode may last hours, days, weeks, or months at a time. In a sizable proportion of people, the depersonalization may start episodically for months or even years, and subsequently set in continuously. The continuous nature of chronic depersonalization, at its extreme represented by those individuals who have suffered from the same depersonalization intensity every moment for decades, is another "puzzling" feature of the disorder that raises questions about its relationship to other dissociative disorders such as DID. In the latter disorders, the nature of the dissociation is typically fluctuant, as individuals go in and out of various self states. In contrast to those fluctuant states, DPD often is better conceptualized as a trait, possibly an endophenotype, which at some point in time in an individual's life becomes manifest rather than latent.

[1] Methylenedioxymethamphetamine, popularly known as Ecstasy.

The distress associated with DPD can be profound. Many sufferers find the robotic, detached state analogous to the "walking dead," and deeply question the meaning of being alive if they do not feel alive and real. Fears of going crazy, losing control, and having permanent brain damage are also common. Cognitive complaints are frequent, specifically a decline in ability to focus on tasks, especially complex ones, increased forgetfulness in their daily lives, and difficulty in vividly evoking past memories. Accordingly, specific attention and memory deficits have been demonstrated with neuropsychiatric testing (Guralnik et al., 2000). Complaints of occupational impairment are very common, and many individuals feel they are working at well below their previous capacity; some are even unable to work. Interpersonally as well, sufferers are often deeply troubled by the intense sense of emotional disconnection from those close to them, which can greatly impede their sense of spontaneous interpersonal connectedness.

27.1.4 Comorbidity

There is frequent comorbidity with Axis I mood and anxiety disorders in DPD. Specifically, lifetime depressive disorders have been reported at 73% and lifetime anxiety disorders at 64% (Simeon et al., 2003). However, none of these disorders have been found to have an onset prior to DPD, and none predict the severity of symptoms. Similarly, there is extensive comorbidity with Axis II personality disorders, found in about 60% of subjects. The most common are borderline, avoidant, and obsessive-compulsive personality disorders; however, all personality disorders are represented. As with Axis I, no Axis II disorder emerges as uniquely related to the presence or severity of DPD, and no Axis II disorder has been found to significantly predate, by history, the onset of DPD (Simeon et al., 1997, 2003). Both panic disorder and depression were found, on average, to start significantly later than DPD (Simeon et al., 2003). These comorbidity findings support the conceptualization of DPD as a distinct disorder rather than a depressive or anxiety spectrum condition.

27.2 TRAUMA AND STRESS ANTECEDENTS

The relation of trauma to DPD is also a very interesting one, especially when compared to the relation of trauma to other dissociative disorders. While hundreds of studies to date have confirmed the relationship between traumatic stress and dissociation in dissociative identity disorder (DID) and in peritraumatic dissociation, the relationship of trauma to DPD has only recently been clarified. In the only study systematically investigating the relationship of DPD to childhood trauma, Simeon et al. (2001) showed that, compared to normal controls, DPD subjects suffered significantly more childhood trauma, including physical and sexual abuse, but especially emotional abuse. This was not a mere nonspecific finding, as the total emotional abuse score uniquely predicted depersonalization severity, measured by the DES-depersonalization factor. On the other hand, combined emotional and sexual abuse best predicted total dissociation severity, measured by the total DES score. We thus speculate that there exists a severity spectrum for dissociative disorders, represented at the "milder" end by DPD and mediated in part by chronic and moderate emotional abuse or neglect, whereas more "severe" dissociative disorders, such as DID, are mediated by more extreme forms of early abuse, such as severe sexual and physical abuse.

Furthermore, later-life traumatic stressors, such as the traumatic death or suicide of a close family friend or relative, can trigger DPD, as can prolonged subacute stress involving severe interpersonal or role adjustment conflicts (25% of all cases, Simeon et al., 2003). These typically occur around adolescence or early adulthood and involve romantic, educational, or occupational struggles. DPD is also frequently triggered by a severe episode of depression (9% of cases, Simeon et al., 2003) or extreme anxiety/panic (12% of cases, Simeon et al., 2003). This is a fact that has commonly led researchers and clinicians alike to misinterpret chronic depersonalization as a depression or anxiety equivalent. This conceptualization would seem to be reflected in the classification of DPD in the ICD-10 as a miscellaneous neurotic disorder, though this may simply be a unreflective remnant of DSM-II/ICD-9, where depersonalization and hysteria were distinct neuroses. In any case, such a conceptualization clearly fails to explain why depersonalization would continue unabated months, years, or decades after the initial episode of depressive or anxiety disorder subsides. Rather, a more plausible explanation is that an overwhelming emotional state such as that induced by a depressive or anxiety episode might, in predisposed individuals, trigger a dissociative response which subsequently becomes autonomous. Such overwhelming emotional states are probably not limited to anxiety or depression—these may just be the better documented ones. In a similar fashion, it appears that psychosis such as schizophrenia or the disturbingly intense and fluctuant states of bipolar disorder might similarly be associated with depersonalization in vulnerable individuals.

In summary, then, we can safely say that chronic depersonalization can occur in the context of widely varying traumatic stressors, mainly chronic childhood trauma, later severe life stress, and overwhelming states of other emotional illness. What all these have in common might be an overwhelming challenge to one's sense of self which, in individuals genetically predisposed, might trigger a chronic depersonalization state. In those less vulnerable, a more transient depersonalization state might be triggered that spontaneously resolves, thus the phenomena of transient depersonalization, acute stress disorder, depersonalization occurring only during a panic attack or during a major depression, and so on. This model of depersonalization is one that needs empirical testing.

If broadened, this interpretation of depersonalization could even account for individuals presenting with drug-induced depersonalization, sometimes in the absence of significant traumatic stressors. One explanation is that these drugs, in depersonalization-susceptible individuals, may induce a profound alteration in self-state that is experienced as highly destabilizing, in effect traumatic, thus triggering a depersonalization reaction. The other explanation is that these drugs act as highly specific chemical triggers that dysregulate already vulnerable neurochemical systems that may underlie the neurobiology of DPD, even in the absence of a subjectively stressful experience. Indeed, histories obtained from DPD sufferers with drug-induced onset lend support to both scenarios. The two models are, of course, not mutually exclusive. It may be that, in certain individuals, a strong genetic loading renders a chemical insult, even if a one-time event, sufficient for the expression of chronic depersonalization in the absence of other insults. In others, additional emotional insults might be necessary to induce a chronic depersonalized state that otherwise would have quickly resolved after the initial drug ingestion.

This discussion leads to the question of a dissociative diathesis, genetically determined and expressed phenotypically in the face of environmental or chemical adversity. Such stress-diathesis models of dissociation have been put forth, although not specifically for depersonalization. It has been proposed that certain heritable traits such as suggestibility, hypnotizability, or absorption may lead to more pathological forms of dissociation if notable environmental stressors occur over the course of a lifetime, childhood or adult (Butler et al., 1996). With regard to genetic predisposition, the only research to date consists of two twin studies with conflicting findings, and not specifically examining depersonalization. One study found no evidence for a genetic component (Waller & Ross, 1997), while another study found 48% genetic influence (Jang et al., 1998).

27.3 COGNITIVE PROFILE

As noted earlier, individuals with DPD typically report difficulties with focusing, processing of perceptual complexity, attention, and memory. The only reported neuropsychological studies to date have been conducted by Simeon and colleagues, and have begun to delineate a cognitive profile in DPD. Rather than present an exhaustive review, we focus here on some of the highlights of this research, and in particular on their implications on the taxonomic conceptualization of depersonalization. In short, the studies have shown that DPD is not associated with an overall cognitive deficit—intelligence scores are intact.

We have conducted three consecutive cognitive studies in DPD (Guralnik et al., 2000; Guralnik et al., 2007; Simeon et al., unpublished). With respect to memory for neutral material, such as is measured by the widely used Wechsler Memory Scale, DPD subjects have mild impairments in short-term memory, possibly partially mediated by attentional deficits, but intact delayed memory for material already encoded.

We have also studied attention in DPD. We have found selective attention, as traditionally measured by the Standard Stroop task, to be intact in our three successive studies (see previous discussion). Selective attention (i.e., freedom from cognitive interference) is preserved even when emotional word stimuli are used, in all three studies. Furthermore, divided attention, tested via a PASAT task and a modified Stroop task, respectively, is also preserved (Guralnik et al., 2007; Simeon et al., unpublished). These Stroop findings can be referenced to the general literature in two important ways. First, DePrince and Freyd have proposed a "cognitive environment" betrayal trauma theory of cognition in dissociation, suggesting that traumatized individuals adapt to trauma by developing a cognitive style with enhanced divided attention, or multitasking, capacities (DePrince & Freyd, 2004). Our DPD data only lend partial support to this model for DPD. Second, the classic cognitive finding in the Stroop task for both the anxiety and the mood disorders, replicated in numerous studies, is heightened interference by disorder-specific, threatening stimuli (i.e., a cognitive bias towards such stimuli which slows down targeted attention). Our findings in DPD have refuted this model. Thus, attention findings to date distinguish DPD both from anxiety disorders, as well as from posttraumatic dissociation. In addition, our studies suggest that the particular attentional deficits of DPD may have more to do with highly demanding attentional conditions involving high "noise" levels (Guralnik et al., 2000).

Finally, we turn to emotional memory and related findings in DPD. In our latest cognitive study (Simeon et al., unpublished), DPD individuals, compared to healthy controls, had better memory for neutral than negative word stimuli under rest conditions, but showed better memory for negative material after psychosocial stress. Thus DPD individuals manifest a memory pattern that is the reverse of that of healthy controls. These limited emotional memory findings, to date, support the classification of DPD as a dissociative disorder: emotionally negative material is dissociated at baseline, and becomes less dissociated with exposure to stress. This is an area of research that merits more study.

27.4 PHARMACOLOGICAL TREATMENT RESPONSE

The intent of this brief section is not to present in any depth what we know about pharmacological treatment response in DPD, but rather to discuss what these data might be telling us about the taxonomy of the disorder. In their 1997 and 2003 reviews, Simeon et al. presented extensive retrospective treatment history data essentially showing the failure of chronic depersonalization to markedly respond to any of our standard pharmacological interventions. Indeed, no dissociative disorder does, and we can safely say that we have not yet discovered an "anti-dissociative" medication. Some individuals with DPD showed partial responses to serotonin reuptake inhibitors or benzodiazepines, yet the proportions of responders were quite low and the responses were partial. Some also benefited from stimulants, although tending to say that the stimulant helped their focus without essentially modifying their depersonalization. The few controlled treatment trials in DPD have confirmed the negative clinical impressions. A controlled trial of both fluoxetine (Simeon et al., 2004) and lamotrigine (Sierra et al., 2003) did not find efficacy superior to placebo.

What do these findings tell us about the taxonomy of depersonalization? In this author's opinion, they strongly support the thesis that primary chronic depersonalization in not a mood or anxiety spectrum disorder, despite being often triggered by, or co-occurring with, the latter. A mood or anxiety spectrum condition would be expected to show a notable response to antidepressants, anxiolytics, or mood stabilizers, yet DPD does not. We can safely state this based both on the research data accrued to date, as well as the so frequently reported treatment experiences of countless patients.

27.5 RELATIONSHIP TO OTHER DISSOCIATIVE CONSTRUCTS AND TAXONOMY: ABSORPTION, AMNESIA, DEREALIZATION, NUMBING

27.5.1 General Psychometrics of DPD

Both the U.S. and U.K. cohort reported a virtually identical mean DES score of around 24. As this author has previously cautioned (Simeon et al., 1998), the DES is not an ideal instrument for the detection of primary depersonalization and is weighted more heavily towards more severe types of dissociation. In an initial psychometric study of 50 DPD subjects, Simeon et al. (1998) reported that a DES total cutoff score of 13 yielded 80% sensitivity and 95% specificity, and a DES-Taxon cutoff score of 12 yielded 80% sensitivity and 100% specificity against a healthy control sample. The large U.K. cohort (2003) precisely confirmed the proposed DES-Taxon cutoff of 13 as detecting 80% of all its participants.

When screening for DPD and employing the DES alone, it is very useful to "eyeball" or average the depersonalization/derealization related items in relation to the remaining items. Although the latent structure of the DES has been extensively debated and is beyond the realm of our discussion here, from a practical standpoint a "depersonalization" factor of the DES can be employed to more accurately detect DPD. As originally proposed by Carlson et al. (1991), in a large sample of normal and dissociative disorder subjects, the DES-DP/DR consisted of items 7, 11, 12, 13, 27, 28. A factor analysis in a much smaller sample consisting only of DPD participants (Simeon et al., 1998) yielded a somewhat different item content: 7, 12, 13, 24, 28. This discrepancy clearly reflects, in my view, the nature of depersonalization experiences in DPD which in some ways differ from those of DID. For example, DES item 11 inquires about not "recognizing" oneself in the mirror, a phrase often endorsed in DID but typically denied in DPD: "I always recognize myself." If slightly rephrased from "nonrecognition" to reflect "disconnection" from one's mirror image, as it appears in the Depersonalization Severity Scale (Simeon et al.), the item is much more highly endorsed. Along the same lines, DES item 27, hearing internal voices, is rarely endorsed by DPD individuals, and thus did not significantly load on to the depersonalization factor derived in DPD subjects by Simeon et al. (1998). Instead, DES item 24, which refers to cognitive errors ("uncertain if just did something or thought of doing it") was highly endorsed in DPD; more about the cognitive profile of the disorder is described in the following.

27.5.2 Absorption

The presence and degree of absorption as a feature of DPD have not been particularly addressed. In general, absorption is viewed as a "nonpathological" form of dissociation (Waller & Ross, 1997) that is commonly encountered in varying degrees in individuals without dissociative disorders. Although some view and describe the nonpathological capacity for absorption as a "diathesis," rendering individuals at higher risk of pathological dissociation (Butler et al., 1996), this issue remains an unresolved one. Table 27.1 presents absorption scores in the U.S. cohort, according to both the Carlson et al. (1991) and the Simeon et al. (1998) factor analyses. A distribution skewed to the left was evident for absorption, with most DPD individuals scoring relatively low in absorption yet few manifesting very high scores. Absorption and depersonalization factor scores were strongly intercorrelated in the U.S. cohort, whether the DES factor defined by Carlson (1991) or by Simeon (1998) was employed ($r = 0.55$, $p < 0.001$, and $r = 0.49$, $p < 0.001$ respectively). Absorption measured by either factor was marginally negatively correlated with age of onset ($r = -0.18$, $p = 0.05$) indicating that individuals with younger onset of depersonalization disorder demonstrated higher absorption. Clinically, in some DPD individuals with very high absorption, the "quality" of the depersonalized state can be also strongly reminiscent of a "trance" state. In this author's view, then, the relationship between depersonalization and absorption requires further explication. Several possibilities merit more research: (1) greater capacity for absorption could comprise an underlying diathesis for chronic depersonalization under certain conditions, accounting for the earlier onset of DPD in individuals with greater absorption; (2) greater absorption could be a consequence of greater depersonalization in individuals with DPD, for instance the depersonalized state could somehow result in a stronger cognitive bias to absorption states (however, such an explanation would not be able to account for the association between earlier onset of DPD and greater absorption, since age of DPD onset is not significantly associated with depersonalization severity); (3) depersonalization and absorption may be discrete phenotypes with an underlying shared vulnerability, so that they commonly co-occur, something analogous to anxiety and depression, for example.

27.5.3 Amnesia

Findings for amnesia are somewhat similar to those for absorption. By definition, individuals diagnosed with

TABLE 27.1
DES Scores in 17 Individuals with Prominent Derealization but Not Depersonalization, Compared to the Remainder 100 DPD Individuals

DES	Derealization	Remaining	t (df = 115)	p
DES total score	14.7 ± 8.2	26.7 ± 14.8	4.81	<0.001
DES taxon	11.2 ± 5.5	27.8 ± 12.8	8.98	<0.001
DES absorption*	18.8 ± 12.9	31.5 ± 20.7	3.39	0.002
	13.7 ± 9.6	26.7 ± 19.3	4.30	<0.001
DES amnesia*	2.7 ± 4.7	9.1 ± 10.9	4.02	<0.001
	6.7 ± 9.4	13.1 ± 13.3	1.89	0.06
DES depersonalization/	22.6 ± 10.3	42.3 ± 17.7	6.46	<0.001
derealization*	31.8 ± 15.0	50.2 ± 20.3	3.56	0.001
DES-7	0.6 ± 2.0	32.6 ± 33.0	9.61	<0.001
DES-11	2.1 ± 3.6	26.3 ± 31.8	7.35	<0.001
DES-12	64.3 ± 30.6	67.9 ± 29.5	0.47	NS
DES-13	3.3 ± 4.4	58.6 ± 31.0	16.88	<0.001
DES-28	63.5 ± 32.5	59.4 ± 38.1	0.42	NS

Cohort of N = 117

Note: *Top row is DES factors as per Carlson et al., 1991; bottom row is DES factors as per Simeon et al., 1998

DPD cannot manifest clinically significant amnesia such as losing time. Still, a wide range of amnesia scores were observed in individuals with DPD in the U.S. cohort (DES amnesia subscore 8.2 ± 10.5). A skewed-to-the-left distribution was evident for amnesia, with most individuals scoring low in amnesia yet few manifesting higher scores in the range of 30–60 on the DES-amnesia factor. Furthermore, amnesia and depersonalization factor scores were strongly intercorrelated in the U.S. cohort, whether the DES amnesia factor defined by Carlson (1991) or by Simeon (1998) was examined ($r = 0.49$, $p < 0.001$ and $r = 0.39$, $p < 0.001$ respectively). Amnesia severity as measured by the Simeon et al. (1998) factor was marginally negatively correlated with DPD age of onset ($r = -0.17$, $p = 0.06$), although amnesia measured by the Carlson et al. factor (1991) was not ($r = -0.14$, $p = 0.13$). Similarly in the U.K. cohort, both absorption and amnesia were found to be significantly higher in DPD subjects with a younger age of onset of the disorder. Clinically, some DPD individuals complain of "poor memory" in a very persistent fashion that is hard to disregard, despite not "losing time." Our cognitive data (presented previously in this chapter) substantiate this subjective complaint.

In their 2003 U.K. series, the eminent British group studying depersonalization concluded that in DPD, "links with anxiety and depression appear to be stronger than dissociation, given the low scores on amnesia items in the DES." They then argued that amnesia comprises the true hallmark symptom of pathological dissociation, and argue that its absence in DPD, along with the "relatively low level of childhood abuse" in their cohort "favour placing Depersonalization Disorder with anxiety and mood disorders rather than with dissociative disorders." Yet, this is a circular argument. If, by definition, patients with clinically notable amnesia cannot be labeled as having DPD, but rather must be classified as DDNOS, then DPD by definition will have relatively low amnesia scores. A more pertinent question therefore might be whether depersonalization and amnesia categorically parcel out as entities, or occur on a continuum of memory impairment that we arbitrarily divide into separate disorders in our current DSM taxonomy. In other words, is the distribution of "amnesia" bimodal in the dissociative population, so that some individuals have DPD with no amnestic symptoms, while others have an amnestic disorder that can be classified as Dissociative Amnesia, DID, or DDNOS; or do individuals with DPD have varying degrees of amnesia that lie on a continuum that is secondarily taxonomized by our current diagnostic system into either DPD or DDNOS? This matter is clearly not resolved and needs further open-minded study.

27.5.4 Derealization

In the U.K. cohort, 73% reported derealization along with depersonalization while derealization alone was "rare," and the authors argued that the two do belong together in a classification system. Still, they noted that pure derealization alone can occur, and might have a distinct neurobiological basis from depersonalization (Sierra et al., 2002), involving visual occipitotemporal rather than parietal brain pathways (for further discussion, see Simeon, this volume).

From a phenomenological viewpoint, we chose to explore the issue of prominent derealization without depersonalization by going back to our original cohort of 117 subjects (Simeon et al., 2003), and comparing those with prominent derealization only (DR) to the remainder (DP). We defined derealization alone using DES item scores, as occurring in those individuals with very low (≤ 10) DES scores on the three major items signifying depersonalization (#7, #11, #13) while having DES scores of at least 30 on one or both of the DES items signifying derealization (#12, #28). Seventeen subjects with pure "derealization" were thus identified and compared to the remaining sample of 100. The comparison of the two groups is presented in Table 27.1. Not surprisingly because of the absence of depersonalization, DR subjects had lower total DES and DES depersonalization/derealization factor scores than the DP subjects. Interestingly, however, they did not differ in the severity of the two derealization items (#7: unreal surroundings, and #28: looking through a fog). Of note, DR subjects had lower absorption and amnesia scores than the remaining sample. There were no significant differences between the two groups in gender distribution, age of onset, duration, type of onset, course type, or comorbidity. There were also no differences between the two groups in the acute precipitants of the disorder, including various drugs, stress, anxiety, depression, or no identifiable stressors. These analyses suggest that derealization alone is similar in all respects to depersonalization (± derealization) except for having less coexistent absorption and amnesia. This is an intriguing finding that must be further investigated. It may suggest that, in some way, the rare occurrence of derealization alone may be less closely related to the remaining dissociative spectrum of symptoms.

27.5.5 Numbing

The issue of numbing is an even more obscure one, as this is a phenomenological entity that has been more poorly quantified and studied. Numbing refers to some kind of inability to feel, and in particular to feel positive feelings. Numbing does figure diagnostically in the DSM-IV criteria for PTSD, comprising one of the seven diagnostic criteria under the "avoidance" cluster. In a sense, by definition numbing comprises a form of dissociation, since it alludes to an inability to be connected to one's feelings. By extension, this might be thought of as a manifestation of depersonalization, since depersonalization implicates a detachment from various aspects of the self. However, the DSM makes no reference to numbing in its description of depersonalization, rather emphasizing the sense of perceptual unfamiliarity and unreality. It is conceivable then that a person might feel numb but not "unreal." The DES does not contain items referring to numbing, and thus it is difficult to go back to large databases and conduct retrospective analyses of numbing. The U.K. depersonalization research group has, from early on, emphasized "hypoemotionality" as a core feature of depersonalization disorder. The Cambridge Depersonalization Scale (Sierra & Berrios, 2000) contains several items that assess numbing. It could well be worth investigating the relationship of these items to the remainder of depersonalization experiences. Are the phenomena of "numbing" and "hypoemotionality" one and the same? What is the relationship of physical numbing, or analgesia, to emotional numbing? Do the two often co-occur, or not? The DES does contain one item assessing analgesia (#19: sometimes able to ignore pain). It is well-known that some individuals with PTSD, borderline personality disorder associated with childhood trauma, or various severe dissociative disorders, such as DID, manifest clear analgesia. What about DPD? We investigated this question by returning to our cohort of 117 and examining DES item 19. Mean score was a modest 21.4 (range 0–95), which is not suggestive of markedly heightened analgesia, as a whole, in this population. Indeed, clinically, DPD subjects very rarely offer this as a symptom, although on occasion it is encountered in those with profound sensory disconnection (i.e., those who do not feel hunger, taste, smell, etc.). Of interest, in our cohort, DES item 19 correlated much more strongly with absorption ($r = 0.68$) and with amnesia ($r = 0.56$) than with depersonalization ($r = 0.29$), suggesting that it may be more closely related to those entities.

Finally, it is important to mention that in a recent factor-analytic study (Simeon et al., 2009), all symptoms relating to hypoemotionality, physical and emotional numbing, and blunted sensations, factored out together into a single factor.

27.6 CONCLUSIONS: WHAT WE KNOW AND WHAT WE NEED TO LEARN ABOUT DEPERSONALIZATION

27.6.1 What We Know

1. DPD has a distinct nosologic presentation, which merits its independent classification.
2. Despite the frequent comorbidity or acute precipitation of DPD by mood or anxiety disorders, several lines of evidence, including nonresponse to any conventional pharmacological treatments, suggest that it is a distinct disorder that does not lie on a mood or anxiety spectrum.
3. DPD is commonly triggered by severe stress, whether this be childhood trauma, later life environmental stress, internal stress (such as a severe episode of mental illness) or chemical stress (such as tetrahydrocannabinol, hallucinogens, MDMA ("Ecstasy") or ketamine). Subsequently, DPD typically becomes autonomous of these stressors over time.
4. DPD has a cognitive profile suggestive of immediate memory deficits, intact selective and divided attention, attentional deficits under highly demanding perceptual conditions, and a dissociation of emotional memory at baseline, which breaks through with stress.

27.6.2 What We Don't Know

1. DPD is accompanied by varying degrees of absorption. The relationship of absorption to chronic depersonalization, and three explicatory models presented, need further investigation.
2. DPD is accompanied by varying degrees of amnesia. The relationship of amnesia to depersonalization needs further investigation, hampered by our current automatic classification of disorders into DPD versus DDNOS. Is the distribution of amnesia in the presence of chronic depersonalization bimodal or continuous?
3. Derealization is present in the large majority of DPD cases. Individuals who have prominent derealization alone, a small minority, appear to differ from the rest only with respect to lesser amnesia and absorption, but not otherwise in the characteristics, precipitants, and course of the disorder. What does this mean?
4. Numbing is a dissociative entity that is poorly investigated. Is emotional numbing such as that noted in PTSD the same or different from the hypoemotionality of DPD? Analgesia does not appear as elevated in DPD as in more "severe" dissociative disorders such as DID.
5. The precise symptomatology of depersonalization in DPD appears to differ in some respects from that of DID. Is that because the depersonalization of DID is intimately linked to identity shifts? Do these differences have taxonomic implications?

REFERENCES

Aderibigbe, Y. A., Bloch, R. M., & Walker, W. R. (2001). Prevalence of depersonalization and derealizaiton experiences in a rural population. Social *Psychiatry & Psychiatric Epidemiology, 36*, 63–69.

Baker, D., Hunter, E., Lawrence, E., et al. (2003). Depersonalisation disorder: clinical features of 204 cases. *British Journal of Psychiatry, 182*, 428–433.

Butler, L. D., Duran, R. E. F., Jasiukaitis, P., Koopman, C., & Spiegel, D. (1996). Hypnotizability and traumatic experience: A diathesis-stress model of dissociative symptomatology. *American Journal of Psychiatry, 153* (Suppl. 7S), 42–63.

Carlson, E. B., Putnam, F. W., Ross, C. A., et al. (1991). Factor analysis on the Dissociative Experiences Scale: a multicenter study. In: B. G. Braun & E. B. Carlson (Eds.), *Proceedings of the Eighth International Conference on Multiple Personality and Dissociative States*. Chicago: Rush.

DePrince, A. P., & Freyd, J. J. (2004). Forgetting trauma stimuli. *Psychological Science, 15*, 488–492.

Guralnik, O., Giesbrecht, T., Knutelska, M., Siroff, B., & Simeon, D. (2007). Cognitive functioning in depersonalization disorder. *Journal of Nervous & Mental Disease, 195*, 983–988.

Guralnik, O., Schmeidler, J., & Simeon, D. (2000). Feeling unreal: cognitive processes in depersonalization. *American Journal of Psychiatry, 157*, 103–109.

Jang, K. L., Paris, J., Zweig-Frank, H., et al. (1998). Twin study of dissociative experience. *Journal of Nervous & Mental Disease, 186*, 345–351.

Ross, C. A. (1991). Epidemiology of multiple personality disorder and dissociation. *Psychiatric Clinics of North America, 14*, 503–517.

Sierra, M., & Berrios, G. E. (1998). Depersonalization: neurobiological perspectives. *Biological Psychiatry, 44*, 898–908.

Sierra, M., & Berrios, G. E. (2000). The Cambridge Depersonalisation Scale: a new instrument for the measurement of depersonalisation. *Psychiatric Research, 93*, 163–164.

Sierra, M., Lopera, F., Lambert, M. V., Phillips, M. L., & David, A. S. (2002). Separating depersonalization and derealisation: the relevance of the "lesion" method. *Journal of Neurology, Neurosurgery and Psychiatry, 72*, 530–532.

Sierra, M., Phillips, M. L., Krystal, J., & David, A. S. (2003). A placebo-controlled, crossover trial of lamotrigine in depersonalization disorder. *Journal of Psychopharmacology, 17*, 103–105.

Simeon, D. (2009). Neurobiology of depersonalization disorder. In P. F. Dell & J. A. O'Neil (Eds.), *Dissociation and the dissociative disorders: DSM-V and beyond* (pp. 367–372). New York: Routledge.

Simeon, D., Gross, S., Guralnik, O., Stein, D. J., Schmeidler, J., & Hollander, E. (1997). Feeling unreal: 30 cases of DSM-III-R depersonalization disorder. *American Journal of Psychiatry, 154*, 1107–1113.

Simeon, D., Guralnik, O., Gross, S., Stein, D. J., Schmeidler, J., & Hollander, E. (1998). The detection and measurement of depersonalization disorder. *Journal of Nervous & Mental Disease, 186*, 536–542.

Simeon, D., Guralnik, O., Schmeidler, J., & Knutelska, M. (2004). Fluoxetine therapy in depersonalization disorder: randomized controlled trial. *British Journal of Psychiatry, 185*, 31–36.

Simeon, D., Guralnik, O., Schmeidler, J., Sirof, B., & Knutelska, M. (2001). The role of childhood interpersonal trauma in depersonalization disorder. *American Journal of Psychiatry, 158*, 1027–1033.

Simeon, D., Knutelska, M., Nelson, D., & Guralnik, O. (2003). Feeling unreal: a depersonalization disorder update of 117 cases. *Journal of Clinical Psychiatry, 64*, 990–997.

Simeon, D., Kozin, D. S., Segal, K., Lerch, B., Dujour, R., & Giesbrecht, T. (2008). De-constructing depersonalization: further evidence for symptom clusters. *Psychiatric Research, 157*, 303–306.

Waller, N. G., & Ross, C. A. (1997). The prevalence and biometric structure of pathological dissociation in the general population: taxometric and behavior genetic findings. *Journal of Abnormal Psychology, 106*, 499–510.

Part VIII

Dissociation in Posttraumatic Stress Disorder

28 Dissociation in PTSD

Lynn C. Waelde, PhD
Louise Silvern, PhD
Eve Carlson, PhD
John A. Fairbank, PhD
Hilit Kletter

OUTLINE

There has been considerable debate about the relationship of dissociation to posttraumatic stress disorder (PTSD). Some have argued that dissociation is a central feature of posttraumatic pathology and, therefore, PTSD should be classified as a dissociative disorder. Others have emphasized the fact that many persons who develop PTSD do not experience acute dissociative symptoms; this suggests there might be distinct subgroups of PTSD, namely PTSD with and PTSD without clinically significant dissociation. Discrepant findings about whether peritraumatic dissociation predicts the development of PTSD have added to the uncertainty about the role of dissociation in the development and maintenance of PTSD. Taxometric analyses have been used to examine whether different diagnostic groups include a subtype of persons with clinically significant dissociation (Waller, Putnam, & Carlson, 1996). For example, a recent taxometric analysis of dissociation among Vietnam veterans concluded there is a categorical subtype of severe PTSD characterized by elevated dissociation (Waelde, Silvern, & Fairbank, 2005). Research and scholarship has also explored whether different types of trauma exposure produce different posttraumatic consequences. For example, repeated interpersonal trauma may engender greater ongoing dissociation than do single or impersonal traumas. In particular, we speculate that (1) the nature of a trauma, (2) its severity, and (3) the person's developmental level at the time of the trauma may each influence manifestations of dissociation in PTSD.

28.1 DEFINITIONS OF DISSOCIATION

Numerous definitions of dissociation address a spectrum that extends from normative experiences of dissociation to the pathological dissociation that occurs in severe PTSD and in dissociative disorders. Bernstein and Putnam (1986) defined dissociation as an impairment in the normal integration of thoughts, feelings, and experiences into the stream of consciousness and memory. Within the concept of dissociation, they included: gaps in awareness, absorption, imaginal involvement, identity alteration, derealization, depersonalization, and amnesia. Dissociation, thus, refers to heterogeneous symptoms and reactions, representing alterations in emotions, perceptions, and cognitions (Gray & Lombardo, 2001; Scaer, 2001).

There is some confusion in the current Diagnostic and Statistical Manual (DSM-IV; APA, 1994) about which symptoms correspond to manifestations of dissociation in PTSD. Van der Hart, Nijenhuis, and Steele (2005) noted that the DSM-IV considers some PTSD intrusive symptoms to be "dissociative flashback episodes" but does not consider acute stress disorder (ASD) flashbacks to be dissociative. Similarly, Van der Hart and colleagues noted that the DSM-IV does not identify the avoidance or numbing symptoms of PTSD as being dissociative, but does identify the avoidance and numbing symptoms of ASD as dissociative.

Despite these inconsistencies, some studies sought to identify specific dissociative symptoms that distinguish persons with versus those without PTSD. Waller and colleagues (1996) found that amnesia and derealization/depersonalization, but not absorption, distinguished participants with PTSD from normal controls and from those in eight other diagnostic groups. Vietnam combat veterans with PTSD had higher scores on identity confusion, identity alteration, depersonalization, derealization, and amnesia than did combat veterans without PTSD (Bremner, Steinberg, Southwick, & Johnson, 1993). Both of these studies found that veterans with PTSD had similarly severe levels of dissociation compared to those with a dissociative disorder. Some authors consider flashbacks and other reexperiencing symptoms to be PTSD-related dissociative symptoms. For example, Holmes and colleagues (2005) noted that flashbacks and other PTSD reexperiencing symptoms involve features of detachment (e.g., a sense of separation from reality) that are essentially dissociative. Laboratory analog experiments with nonclinical subjects reported that trauma-related dissociation and reexperiencing symptoms were interrelated (Holmes, Brewin, & Hennessey, 2004), although it is unclear whether this finding can be generalized to persons with PTSD.

The time frame when dissociative experiences occur relative to the traumatic event may be crucially important. Given that there are inconsistencies in use of terms, we suggest that the following definitions of dissociation be used: *peritraumatic dissociation* occurs *during or immediately following* a high magnitude stressor (Marmar et al., 1994). *Acute posttraumatic dissociation* occurs during the *week or two following* a high magnitude stressor. Persistent dissociation begins after the event and persists more than 2 weeks after a high magnitude stressor (Briere, Scott, & Weathers, 2005). *Chronic dissociation continues for years* after a stressor. Chronic dissociation may become a habitual response to relatively lower magnitude stressors in daily life.

Dissociative phenomena that emerge at these varied times after a traumatizing event may each emerge through different causal pathways and each might have different psychological functions. Indeed, there might be more than one cause or function for dissociation that emerges at a particular time after the traumatizing event.

For example, peritraumatic dissociation may be caused or influenced by the emotional stress and physiological arousal inherent in the event. In a clever demonstration, Sterlini and Bryant (2002) found that diverse dissociative experiences were reported at rates as elevated as the rates of peritraumatic dissociation among first-time skydivers. These skydivers apparently dissociated during a highly arousing activity, but apparently without aversive emotional stress. In clear contrast, most events considered to trigger peritraumatic dissociation involve both arousal and distress. Nonetheless, the skydiving example demonstrates that physiological arousal may cause dissociation independently, that is, even without emotional distress. In contrast to dissociation, traumatization might require only severe emotional distress; severe arousal or distress alone might be insufficient to cause traumatization. If arousal or emotional stress during a stressor independently cause peritraumatic dissociation, then such dissociation would be observed in (1) individuals who are both aroused and emotionally stressed, and (2) those who are only aroused (but not emotionally distressed). Thus, PTSD might not occur in the latter group (because the event was arousing, but not distressing). Conversely, some who are emotionally distressed, but not highly aroused, by an event would not report peritraumatic dissociation, but might develop PTSD due to their emotional distress (and perhaps other factors as well). This formulation may help explain why peritraumatic dissociation does not consistently predict subsequent PTSD.

On the other hand, persistent dissociation after a traumatic event might be influenced by different, overlapping factors. Persistent dissociation might reflect the degree to which individuals are emotionally overwhelmed by traumatizing events. Being emotionally overwhelmed by an event is thought to be influenced by the event's suddenness and negative valence, by the individual's pretrauma characteristics (e.g., previous trauma, expectancies, habitual affective dysregulation), and by postevent experiences (e.g., social support, social constraints, and posttrauma life stressors) (Carlson & Dalenberg, 2000). We propose that only those who are emotionally overwhelmed by an event would experience persistent dissociation and would, thereby, be at risk for PTSD. If persistent dissociation is, indeed, influenced by the distinctive factors just listed, then those factors would, in turn, predict that both peritraumatic and persistent dissociation predict the severity of subsequent PTSD (see the following).

Are dissociative phenomena ever a form of cognitive avoidance? We think so. Dissociative experiences are distinctive from other forms of cognitive avoidance: (1) dissociative phenomena are experienced as nonvolitional (as opposed to intentional); and (2) dissociative phenomena involve more distortions of perception or memory than do other forms of cognitive avoidance. Most dissociative phenomena, including depersonalization, derealization, gaps in awareness, and amnesia, seem to serve the function of distancing a person from his or her surroundings. At the time of a trauma, dissociation may occur in response to extreme physiological arousal. After the event has passed, dissociative experiences serve to protect the person psychologically by providing emotional distance from distress triggered by reminders of the event. Gaps in awareness and amnesia are relatively direct ways to exclude distress from awareness. Depersonalization and derealization appear to achieve emotional distance by distorting perceptions of self in relationships to surroundings (i.e., "this isn't me this is happening to" or "what is happening isn't really happening to me").

There are a variety of ways to test these theoretical formulations. If some dissociative phenomena function as forms of cognitive avoidance, one would expect to see more severe dissociative symptoms in response to traumas that are more emotionally threatening. Traumatizing events might be relatively more threatening insofar as they have more severe consequences, for example, the death of a loved one could have pervasive effects on one's life.

We expect dissociative symptoms to be related in a conceptually meaningful way to the other symptoms of PTSD. For example, we think that persistent dissociative symptoms should relate to arousal and reexperiencing in the same way that other symptoms of cognitive-avoidance, for example, trying to not think about the traumatizing event, or forgetting aspects of the event. Lastly, studies could examine the impact of factors that are expected to either mitigate or exacerbate the need for cognitive avoidance. If dissociative phenomena are, indeed, a form of cognitive avoidance, then we would expect persistent dissociation to be related to variables such as posttraumatic social support in ways that are consistent with cognitive avoidance. Social support would be expected to mitigate the need for cognitive avoidance because the presence and reassurance of a supportive person would help reduce distressing feelings of anxiety, helplessness, loss, guilt, or shame associated with the event. Therefore, persistent dissociation should be negatively related to social support.

28.2 IS DISSOCIATION A CENTRAL FEATURE OF PTSD?

Dissociation may be found to be more or less integral to the diagnosis of PTSD, depending on the definition of dissociation and the type of traumatizing event studied. Research has tended to address the presence and predictive value of dissociative symptoms, such as those assessed by the DES (Bernstein & Putnam, 1986) in acute and chronic forms of PTSD. Divergent findings have led to varied conclusions about the role of dissociation in PTSD.

Many writers argue that dissociation is central to the development and maintenance of PTSD, and that dissociative symptoms are important to both the diagnosis and the conceptualization of PTSD (Brett, 1992; Putnam, 1993; Spiegel, 1986; Spiegel & Cardeña, 1991; Van der Kolk, Van der Hart, & Marmar, 1996). Dissociation has repeatedly been found to be related to the severity of chronic PTSD (Branscomb, 1991; Bremner, Southwick, Brett, & Fontana, 1992; Bremner, Steinberg, Southwick, & Johnson, 1993; Carlson, 2001; Bernstein & Putnam, 1993; Carlson & Rosser-Hogan, 1991; Hyer, Albrecht, Boudewyns, & Woods, 1993; O'Toole, Marshall, Schureck, & Dobson, 1999; Putnam, Carlson, Ross, & Anderson, 1996). Similarly, acute dissociation is related to the development and severity of later PTSD, independent of other influences, such as anxiety and subjective loss (Koopman, Classen, & Spiegel, 1994), and severity of trauma exposure (Waelde, Koopman, Rierdan, & Spiegel, 2001). Finally, two recent meta-analyses concluded that peritraumatic dissociation was a stronger predictor of PTSD among individuals exposed to potentially traumatizing events, compared to many other relevant variables, such as prior trauma exposure, perceived threat during the trauma, and socioeconomic variables. Ozer, Best, Lipsey, and Weiss's (2003) meta-analysis found peritraumatic dissociation to be the strongest predictor of many potential predictors of PTSD among exposed individuals, and Brewin, Andrews, and Valentine (2000) found that peritraumatic dissociation, weak social support, and the context of life stress virtually "tied" as predictors.

Although Ozer and colleagues (2003) concluded that among many people, peritraumatic responses to stressors play an important role in the development of PTSD, they noted that findings of relationships of peritraumatic dissociation to subsequent PTSD are inconsistent. Moreover, although peritraumatic dissociation has proven to be important in meta-analyses of PTSD, the absolute power of its statistical effect on PTSD is modest. Layne, Warren, Watson, and Shalev (2007) and Ozer et al. implied that such findings cannot be employed as evidence that dissociative phenomena are integral to posttraumatic psychopathology. In a prospective study of motor vehicle accident victims, Harvey and Bryant (1998) found that although some acute dissociative symptoms significantly predicted later PTSD, a substantial proportion of individuals who developed PTSD did not manifest peritraumatic dissociation. Harvey and Bryant (2002) suggested that although they are correlated, dissociation is not necessarily inherent in PTSD, given that there are substantial individual differences in dissociation among persons with PTSD.

Conceptualizations that can account for these seemingly contradictory viewpoints have been offered by Harvey and Bryant (2002) and by Briere and colleagues (2005). These authors proposed that peritraumatic dissociation may reflect the severity of the stressor as experienced. This would explain, at least in part, the observed association between peritraumatic dissociation and PTSD.

Recent research has attempted to resolve discrepant findings about the predictive role of peritraumatic dissociative symptoms by examining the relative contributions of peritraumatic versus persistent dissociation to the prediction of later stress disorders. Briere et al. (2005) studied peritraumatic dissociation in one community sample and one general population sample. In multivariate analyses, when persistent dissociation was statistically controlled, peritraumatic dissociation was not related to PTSD among trauma-exposed community residents. Similarly, a prospective study of peritraumatic versus persistent dissociation among motor vehicle accident survivors concluded that persistent dissociation was a stronger predictor of chronic PTSD than dissociation during the accident, although the authors did not report statistical comparisons of the magnitude of the two correlations (Murray, Ehlers, & Mayou, 2002). In a study of civilian trauma survivors with ASD, subclinical ASD, or no-ASD, peritraumatic dissociation was higher for the two ASD groups compared to the no-ASD group, but persistent dissociation was more strongly associated with ASD severity than was peritraumatic dissociation (Panasetis & Bryant, 2003). Lastly, a prospective study of Dutch fireworks disaster victims found that, after controlling for initial PTSD symptoms, peritraumatic dissociation did not predict PTSD severity at 18 months or 4 years postdisaster (Van der Velden et al., 2006). Taken together, these studies suggest that persistent or ongoing dissociation is more strongly related to current ASD and PTSD symptoms than is dissociation that occurred during the traumatic event.

Moreover, several of these studies suggest that initial findings of associations between peritraumatic dissociation and subsequent PTSD have emerged as a function of relationships of peritraumatic to persistent dissociation. Thus, the focus in recent literature on relationships of peritraumatic dissociation to PTSD to decide the question of whether dissociation is central to PTSD may be misplaced. Possibly persistent dissociation is a more important focus. In any case, studies cited previously do not address the question of whether dissociation is inherent to PTSD, that is, whether clinically significant dissociation is common to all cases of PTSD or only characterizes a distinct subgroup among persons with PTSD.

Alternative studies that relay on taxometric analyses more directly approach the question of whether or not dissociation is inherent in PTSD, testing whether elevated posttraumatic or persistent dissociation characterizes only a distinct subgroup among individuals with PTSD. Taxometric analyses can detect the presence of distinctive subgroups. Meehl and colleagues developed methods to identify a taxon or subgroup by scores that are discontinuous with a dimensional distribution; thus a taxon points to a typology among participants, in contrast to those who simply obtain relatively low or high scores on a continuous dimension (Meehl, 1995; Meehl & Yonce, 1994; Waller & Meehl, 1998).

In a study of trauma-exposed Vietnam veterans, Waelde and colleagues (2005) found that elevated dissociative symptoms characterized a distinctive subgroup or taxon of individuals. These dissociative taxon members had significantly higher posttraumatic symptoms than did nontaxon members. Eighty percent of these dissociative taxon members had current PTSD, but only 18.2% of nontaxon members had current PTSD. Nonetheless, only one-third (32%) of PTSD cases were members of the dissociative taxon. In sum, this study demonstrated that most veterans with PTSD did not manifest elevated levels of dissociation. These findings are consistent with proposals that there may be two distinct subtypes of PTSD, with and without prominent dissociation (Bremner, 1999; Briere, 2003; Guralnik, Schmeidler, & Simeon, 2000; Pearlman, 2001; Silvern et al., 1995; Van der Hart et al., 2005).

It may be that there are different pathways to the development of PTSD that result in symptom presentations with and without elevated dissociation. Research and scholarship about DESNOS/Complex PTSD as well as Developmental Trauma Disorder have called attention to the hypothesis of greater dissociation and other distinctive symptom manifestations among those who have been repeatedly exposed to traumatizing events in interpersonal contexts, in contrast to those persons who have experienced single or impersonal traumatic experiences (e.g., Herman, 1995; Van der Kolk, 2005).

28.3 DISSOCIATION AND TRAUMA HISTORY

Dissociation is considered especially likely if PTSD follows repeated mistreatment by a person on whom the victim is dependent for material and attachment-related needs, as is the case in child or spouse abuse. A number of authors have argued that new diagnostic categories are needed to capture the full symptom complex that attends these stressors, such as Complex PTSD (Chu, 1991; Herman, 1995; Pearlman, 2001), Disorders of Extreme Stress Not Otherwise Specified (DESNOS; Pearlman, 2001; Pelcovitz et al., 1997; Van der Hart et al., 2005), and Developmental Trauma Disorder for Complex PTSD with childhood onset (DTD; Cook et al., 2005; Stolbach, 2005). Van der Hart and colleagues (2005) were probably correct when they asserted that the differences among these proposed diagnostic entities are less important than the fact that each is characterized by prominent dissociation, whereas DSM-IV's "simple PTSD" is not.

We can now distinguish three positions in the debate about the role of dissociation in PTSD. First, dissociation has traditionally been considered to be an associated feature of PTSD (APA, 1994); PTSD can be diagnosed in the absence of dissociation, but dissociation is expected to occur at elevated rates in PTSD, compared to its rates among most individuals (except those with dissociative disorders). Second, some have argued that dissociation is a central feature of PTSD, with a linear relationship to all other defining characteristics of the disorder (for review, see Waelde et al., 2005). If dissociation were a central feature, an argument could be made that the diagnosis of PTSD should require dissociation (e.g., Brett, 1992; Putnam, 1993). Third, if the ideas of Complex PTSD/ DESNOS and of DTD were adopted, and distinguished from DSM-IV's simple PTSD, then dissociation would be hypothesized to be a central feature of complex PTSD or DTD, but would continue to be an associated feature of simple PTSD. The distinction would be hypothesized to be associated with features of traumatic events in these proposed disorders, including but not limited to early age of occurrence.

There are potentially several ways to test these positions. If dissociation is an associated feature of PTSD, then only a subset of individuals with PTSD would manifest elevated dissociation. As described previously, Waelde's et al. (2005) finding of a qualitatively distinct taxon of high dissociators among combat veterans with diagnosed PTSD was consistent with considering dissociation an associated feature. That is, the dissociative taxon was significantly more likely to occur among individuals with PTSD than among those without, but most PTSD patients did not belong to the taxon, and those that did belong to the taxon could be distinguished by having relatively severe posttraumatic symptoms.

On the other hand, the central feature position predicts that such a dissociative taxon will not be found. Insofar as dissociation were integral to posttraumatic symptoms, dissociation should be uniformly elevated in PTSD; high dissociation should be found fairly evenly among those with PTSD, not only among a qualitatively distinct taxon of "high dissociators."

Testing the third position requires distinguishing Complex PTSD /DESNOS from simple PTSD. To do so requires gathering information about the nature of traumatic events that is usually ignored in the studies about the relationship between dissociative and posttraumatic symptoms, as reviewed previously. The third position described rests on the distinction of repeated, interpersonal events, especially those imposed at the hands of caregivers, in contrast to single impersonal traumatic events.

If the third position is valid, ignoring this distinction between types of traumatic stressors would be sure to create the inconsistencies that have previously emerged from studies about relationships between PTSD and dissociation. Traditional PTSD symptoms, as described in the DSM-IV, are expected from both types of events, but dissociation is expected only from the repeated interpersonal traumatic events. When the two patterns of events are mixed together in studies, it is expected that the manifestation of dissociation along with the traditional symptoms would be inconsistent. If information about the type of events is not even collected, there is no way to test whether the inconsistency is due to the hypothesized variation in events.

Recently, a new distinction in types of trauma disorders has been added to Complex PTSD and DESNOS, Developmental Trauma Disorder (DTD). DTD is very like Complex PTSD/ DESNOS in that it is caused by traumatic events that are recurring events at the hands of caregivers, but in addition, DTD is explicitly defined as having its onset only during childhood, when victims are especially vulnerable to dissociative reactions to severe interpersonal stressors (Putnam, 1995, 2000; Valentino, Cicchetti, Rogosch, & Toth, 2008). Indeed, like the other controversial diagnoses, the presence of interpersonal childhood stressors predicts that dissociative symptoms are central to PTSD. Specifically, dissociation will correlate highly with all traditional PTSD symptoms. Moreover, if samples consist of only individuals with Complex PTSD/DESNOS or Developmental Trauma Disorder, with their putative central role for dissociation, then dissociation should not appear as a taxon among those PTSD patients. That is, a dissociative taxon ought not to emerge among such samples, because dissociation should be too homogeneous and high to allow a distinct subtype of dissociators to emerge. In order for a taxon of dissociators to be identified, there must be substantial variation in dissociation in the sample, including individuals who have low dissociation and do not fall into the taxon.

The concepts of Complex/DESNOS or DTD suggest that dissociation should covary with additional criteria of these proposed disorders. These other criteria include, as examples: (1) very diverse symptoms such as, affect dysregulation, impulsive aggression, dramatically shifting relationships, substance abuse, disorders of self-image, suicidality, and learning problems; (2) the development of those symptoms through pathways involving child maltreatment or other disruptions to secure child-caregiver attachment; and (3) the presence of developmental deficits (e.g., Herman, 1995; Pearlman, 2001; Stolbach & Waters, 2006; Stolbach, 2005; Van der Kolk, 1996, 2005). Empirically testing hypotheses about relationships of these new criteria to posttraumatic dissociation raises new questions and problems that were previously ignored when simple PTSD was conceptualized as the only form of posttraumatic pathology. For example, until recently, there has been little interest in studying the relationship between dissociation and secure attachment or delinquency, but such questions are now flourishing (Dutra, 2008; Harari, Bakermans-Kranenburg, Van IJzendoorn, & Marinus, 2007; Van IJzendoorn, Schuengel, & Barkermans-Kranenburg, 1999; Silvern, McClintic, Schulz-Heik, & Stolbach, 2008).

Contemporary emphasis on recurrent, early maltreatment by caregivers as the cause of the new forms of traumatic pathology has been especially connected to the diversity of proposed symptoms, including dissociation and its many proposed correlates. For example, Van der Hart et al.'s (2005) model proposes that, in the presence of Complex PTSD that is subsequent to early, chronic interpersonal trauma, structural dissociation has a more pervasive impact on personality (dis)integration than structural dissociation in the context of simple PTSD. That is, Van der Hart and colleagues propose that posttraumatic dissociation occurs following both singular and chronic interpersonal traumatic events, but the latter dissociation has much more pervasive implications for development and personality.

Consistent with Van der Hart's model, Stolbach and colleagues (Stolbach, 2005; Stolbach & Waters, 2006) argued that early, recurrent, interpersonal stressors (e.g., intrafamilial maltreatment) affect many aspects of developmental abilities. Thus, such stressors naturally have pervasive effects on children and strongly increase the risks of dissociation and other developmental disruptions (compared to the consequences of single, impersonal traumas). Such chronic stressors disrupt diverse aspects of development and foster overwhelming dysregulation and dissociation. Complex, early stressors may result in greater number of subsequent triggers for dissociation (and other avoidant defenses) compared to a single stressor. Daily life events recurrently trigger dissociative reactions that disrupt affect regulation, cognitive and academic functioning, attachment security, behavioral inhibition, continuity of self, and other difficulties, as reflected in the symptoms of Complex PTSD. To date, however, there is no consensus about how, precisely, to conceptualize the relationship between dissociation and the other symptoms of Complex PTSD.

On the other hand, the diverse symptoms of Complex PTSD or DTD, including dissociative defenses and reactions, may develop from the same underlying interpersonal trauma without dissociation being the explanatory "force," as strongly implied by Van der Hart and others. To begin, however, it is important to empirically test the increasingly popular assumption that under certain stressor conditions, dissociation is highly intercorrelated not only with traditional PTSD symptoms, but also with other serious problems, including disruptions in relationship or attachment capacities.

The literature about disorganized attachment also raises questions about the correlates of dissociation among PTSD patients. It is by now well established that maltreated children typically have disorganized attachment (rather than insecure attachment) (Carlson, 1998; Cicchetti, Toth, & Lynch, 1995; Van IJzendoorn et al., 1999). Dissociation plays a profound role in attachment disorganization (Main & Morgan, 1996; Ogawa, Sroufe, Weinfield, Carlson, & Egeland, 1997). Research indicates that the child's disorganized attachment typically occurs within a context of the mother's own problematic attachment status. Specifically, these mothers have unresolved childhood traumas which make it possible (and inevitable) for their children to trigger "disorganized/disoriented" (dissociated?) reactions in their mothers. Thus, research has shown that the mother's unresolved childhood traumas predict their children's disorganized attachment (Main & Hesse, 1990).

Conversely, Van der Kolk (1996) has suggested that securely attached children are better able to soothe themselves when confronted with otherwise overwhelming distress, and are less likely to dissociate or develop PTSD. Here, again, dissociation is hypothesized to be more prominent whenever a person with DSM-IV PTSD has attachment deficits or whenever that person's childhood was characterized by conditions that were antithetical to the development of secure attachment.

There is no consensus yet regarding the stressors that foster Complex PTSD. Research does not yet tell us whether Complex PTSD is a sequela of child maltreatment, specifically, or whether the etiology of Complex PTSD lies in many types of child or adult interpersonal stress. Most authors are vague about this point. To this end, it would be fruitful to clearly identify the stressors that are most likely to induce PTSD-cum-dissociation. Herman (1995) suggested that any stressor of long duration (not just child maltreatment), which involved extreme material and emotional dependence on the perpetrator creates a risk of Complex PTSD. On the other hand, there is strong evidence that early maltreatment is a risk factor for dissociation, disrupted affect regulation, and disrupted attachment; thus, child maltreatment may be a uniquely powerful predictor of Complex PTSD.

If childrearing factors other than maltreatment predict prominent dissociation in trauma disorders, then it becomes crucial to identify those factors. Recent literature about DTD, for example, points to a pathogenic role for adverse childhood experiences (such as loss of a parent) that do not involve frank mistreatment (Van der Kolk, 2005). Similarly, Moor and Silvern (2006) found that parental narcissism/low empathy, compared to other aspects of parenting, was a powerful mediator of the relationships between abuse (sexual and physical) and posttraumatic outcome.

At present, much work remains to be done in the effort to specify and validate the early life stressors that predict prominent dissociation in PTSD patients. Moreover, multivariate research will be crucial to this endeavor. That is, it has become insufficient to study the development of dissociation in isolation; it must be studied, "at one go," in the context of various stressors, other posttraumatic symptoms, and other maladaptive reactions.

28.4 CLINICAL IMPLICATIONS AND DIRECTIONS FOR FUTURE RESEARCH

Further exploration of the relationships among various stressors, contextual factors, and their associated levels of dissociation may significantly increase our understanding of PTSD and how to treat and prevent it.

28.4.1 Effects of Secrecy versus Disclosure of Maltreatment

If chronic maltreatment produces prominent dissociation, then it is crucial to identify the factors that underlie this outcome. One such factor may be secrecy about the abuse and violence (Zellman & Fair, 2002). Conversely, disclosure of child maltreatment appears to reduce the incidence of subsequent PTSD (Ruggiero et al., 2004). Perhaps child maltreatment is an especially powerful risk factor for PTSD precisely because it is usually kept secret. Disclosure may provide both social support and assistance for victims to weave together into a coherent narrative their often fragmented, peritraumatically dissociated impressions of the traumatic events (Pennebaker & Seagal, 1999; Roth, Lebowitz, & DeRosa, 1997; Smyth, True, & Souto, 2001). Only with that coherence can the peritraumatically dissociated, fragmented impressions become integrated into stable schemata of self and others (Silvern et al., 1995). Relatedly, disclosure and narrative repair may be needed in order to transform into verbally accessible memory the nonverbal, confused material that is stored in situationally accessible memory (Brewin & Sanders, 2001).

Further investigation into the efficacy and the buffering properties of disclosure is needed, because the effects of disclosure on dissociation are likely to be complex. It may be necessary to carefully (and comparatively) study the role of dissociation in traumatic reactions to varied categories of stressors and then seek to identify the particular dimensions that render those categories psychologically different from one another. For example, when both the traumatic stressor in question and the context in which it occurs permits or facilitates disclosure, dissociation might only be peripheral, with prominent dissociation being restricted to a subtype of severe PTSD patients (Waelde et al., 2005). In contrast, when stressors are severe and chronic, and occur in a manner (such as child or spouse abuse) that impedes disclosure or renders it inconceivable, prominent dissociation might be universal among those PTSD patients. In that case, the person's fragmented impressions of the stressor would not be integrated into long-term memory (Van der Hart et al., 2005).

The symptoms of Complex PTSD that reflect disrupted interpersonal relationships fit with the disorder's pathogenic source: overwhelming interpersonal violence or abuse that interrupted the continuity of the survivors' sense of self and others (Pearlman, 2001). If our speculations are correct, then the role of dissociation may be quite different in survivors of chronic maltreatment who were forced into silence versus single-trauma survivors who were able to disclose what happened in a supportive setting.

28.4.2 Greater Specificity in Dissociation Research

It would be helpful if future researchers, clinicians, and theoreticians could be more specific about what they mean when they refer to *dissociation*. In particular, the type of dissociative experience (e.g., depersonalization, derealization, gaps in awareness, amnesia, etc.) and the time of its occurrence relative to a traumatic stressor (peritraumatic, acute posttraumatic, persistent posttraumatic, or chronic) should be specified. These phenomena need to be defined and studied, both separately and in combination with one another. It would also be helpful to study the relationship between these dissociative phenomena and the other symptoms of PTSD. Lastly, it would be useful to examine individual differences in dissociative symptoms and other posttraumatic symptoms so that we can discover if there are different patterns across individuals.

REFERENCES

American Psychiatric Association (1994). *Diagnostic and statistical manual of mental disorders (4th ed.)*. Washington, DC: Author.

Bernstein, E. M., & Putnam, F. W. (1986). Development, reliability, and validity of a dissociation scale. *Journal of Nervous and Mental Disease, 174*, 727–735.

Branscomb, L. P. (1991). Dissociation in combat-related posttraumatic stress disorder. *Dissociation, 4*, 13–20.

Bremner, J. D. (1999). Does stress damage the brain? *Biological Psychiatry, 45*, 797–805.

Bremner, J. D., Southwick, S., Brett, E., & Fontana, A. (1992). Dissociation and posttraumatic stress disorder in Vietnam combat veterans. *American Journal of Psychiatry, 149*, 328–332.

Bremner, J. D., Steinberg, M., Southwick, S. M., & Johnson, D. R. (1993). Use of the Structured Clinical Interview for DSM-IV Dissociative Disorders for systematic assessment of dissociative symptoms in posttraumatic stress disorder. *American Journal of Psychiatry, 150*, 1011–1014.

Brett, E. A. (1992). Classifications of posttraumatic stress disorder in DSM-IV: Anxiety disorder, dissociative disorder, or stress disorder? In J. R. T. Davidson & E. B. Foa (Eds.), *Posttraumatic stress disorder: DSM-IV and beyond* (pp. 191–204). Washington, DC: American Psychiatric Press.

Brewin, C., Andrews, B., & Valentine, J. (2000). Meta-analysis of risk factors for posttraumatic stress disorder in trauma-exposed adults. *Journal of Consulting and Clinical Psychology*, *68*, 748–766.

Brewin, C. R., & Sanders, J. (2001). The effect of dissociation at encoding on intrusive memories for a stressful film. *British Journal of Medical Psychology, 74*, 467–472.

Briere, J. (2003). Integrating HIV/AIDS prevention activities into psychotherapy for child sexual abuse survivors. In L. J. Koenig, L. S. Doll, A. O'Leary, & W. Pequegnat (Eds.), *From child sexual abuse to adult sexual risk: Trauma, revictimization, and intervention* (pp. 219–232). Washington, DC: American Psychological Association.

Briere, J., Scott, C., & Weathers, F. (2005). Peritraumatic and persistent dissociation in the presumed etiology of PTSD. *American Journal of Psychiatry, 162*, 2295–2301.

Carlson, E. A. (1998). A prospective longitudinal study of attachment disorganization/disorientation. *Child Development, 69*, 1107–1128.

Carlson, E. B. (2001). Psychometric study of a brief screen for PTSD: Assessing the impact of multiple traumatic events. *Assessment, 8*, 431–441.

Carlson, E. B., & Dalenberg, C. (2000). A conceptual framework for the impact of traumatic experiences. *Trauma, Violence, and Abuse, 1*, 4–28.

Carlson, E. B., & Rosser-Hogan, R. (1991). Trauma experiences, posttraumatic stress, dissociation, and depression in Cambodian refugees. *American Journal of Psychiatry, 148*, 1548–1551.

Chu, J. A. (1991). On the misdiagnosis of multiple personality disorder. *Dissociation, 4*, 200–204.

Cicchetti, D., Toth, S. L., & Lynch, M. (1995). Bowlby's dream comes full circle: The application of attachment theory to risk and psychopathology. *Advances in Clinical Child Psychology, 17*, 1–75.

Cook, A., Spinazzola, J., Ford, J., Lanktree, C., Blaustein, M., Cloitre, M., et al. (2005). Complex trauma in children and adolescents. *Psychiatric Annals, 35*, 390–398.

Dutra, L. (2008). Quality of early care and childhood trauma: Developmental pathways to dissociation. *Dissertation Abstracts International: Section B: The Sciences and Engineering, 68(9-B)*, 6299.

Gray, M. J., & Lombardo, T. W. (2001). Complexity of trauma narratives as an index of fragmented memory in PTSD: a critical analysis. *Applied Cognitive Psychology, 15*, S171–S186.

Guralnik, O., Schmeidler, J., & Simeon, D. (2000). Feeling unreal: Cognitive processes in depersonalization. *American Journal of Psychiatry, 157*, 103–109.

Harari, D., Bakermans-Kranenburg, M. J., Van IJzendoorn, M. H., & Marinus, J. (2007). In E. Vermetten, M. Dorahy, & D. Spiegel (Eds.), *Traumatic dissociation: Neurobiology and treatment* (pp. 31–54). Washington, DC: American Psychiatric Publishing.

Harvey, A. G., & Bryant, R. A. (1998). The relationship between acute stress disorder and posttraumatic stress disorder: A prospective evaluation of motor vehicle accident survivors. *Journal of Consulting and Clinical Psychology, 66*, 507–512.

Harvey, A. G., & Bryant, R. A. (2002). Acute stress disorder: A synthesis and critique. *Psychological Bulletin, 128*, 886–902.

Herman, J. L. (1995). Complex PTSD: A syndrome in survivors of prolonged and repeated trauma. In G. S. Everly, Jr., & J. M. Lating (Eds.), *Psychotraumatology: Key papers and core concepts in post-traumatic stress* (pp. 87–100). New York: Plenum Press.

Holmes, E. A., Brewin, C. R., & Hennessey, R. G. (2004). Trauma films, information processing, and intrusive memory development. *Journal of Experimental Psychology: General, 133*, 3–22.

Holmes, E. A., Brown, R. J., Mansell, W., Fearon, R. P., Hunter, E. C. M., Frasquilho, F., et al. (2005). Are there two qualitatively distinct forms of dissociation? A review and some clinical implications. *Clinical Psychology Review, 25*, 1–23.

Hyer, L. A., Albrecht, J. W., Boudewyns, P. A., & Woods, M. G. (1993). Dissociative experiences of Vietnam veterans with chronic posttraumatic stress disorder. *Psychological Reports, 73*, 519–530.

Koopman, C., Classen, C., & Spiegel, D. A. (1994). Predictors of posttraumatic stress symptoms among survivors of the Oakland/Berkeley, Calif., firestorm. *American Journal of Psychiatry, 151*, 888–894.

Main, M., & Hesse, E. (1990). Parents' unresolved traumatic experiences are related to infant disorganized attachment status: Is frightened and/or frightening parental behavior the linking mechanism? In M. T. Greenberg, D. Cicchetti, & E. M. Cummings (Eds.), *Attachment in the preschool years: Theory, research, and intervention* (pp. 161–182). Chicago, IL: University of Chicago Press.

Main, M., & Morgan, H. (1996). Disorganization and disorientation in infant strange situation behavior: Phenotypic resemblance to dissociative states. In L. K. Michelson & W. J. Ray (Eds.), *Handbook of dissociation: Theoretical, empirical, and clinical perspective* (pp. 107–138). New York: Plenum Press.

Marmar, C. R., Weiss, D. S., Schlenger, W. E., Fairbank, J. A., Jordan, B. K., Kulka, R. A., & Hough, R. L. (1994). Peritraumatic dissociation and posttraumatic stress in male Vietnam theater veterans. *American Journal of Psychiatry, 151,* 902–907.

Meehl, P. (1995). Bootstraps taxometrics: Solving the classification problem in psychopathology. *The American Psychologist, 50*, 266–275.

Meehl, P. E., & Yonce, L. J. (1994). Taxometric analysis: I. Detecting taxonicity with two quantitative indicators using means above and means below a sliding cut (MAMBAC procedure). *Psychological Reports, 74,* 1059–1274.

Moor, A., & Silvern, L. (2006). Identifying pathways linking child abuse to psychological outcome: The mediating role of perceived parental failure of empathy. *Journal of Emotional Abuse, 6*, 91–114.

Murray, J., Ehlers, A., & Mayou, R. A. (2002). Dissociation and post-traumatic stress disorder: Two prospective studies of road traffic accident survivors. *British Journal of Psychiatry, 180*, 363–368.

Ogawa, J. R., Sroufe, L. A., Weinfield, N. S., Carlson, E. A., & Egeland, B. (1997). Development and the fragmented self: Longitudinal study of dissociative symptomatology in a nonclinical sample. *Development and Psychopathology, 9*, 855–879.

O'Toole, B. I., Marshall, R. P., Schureck, R. J., & Dobson, M. (1999). Combat, dissociation, and posttraumatic stress disorder in Australian Vietnam veterans. *Journal of Traumatic Stress, 12*, 625–640.

Ozer, E. J., Best, S. R., Lipsey, T. L., & Weiss, D. S. (2003). Predictors of posttraumatic stress disorder and symptoms in adults: A meta-analysis. *Psychological Bulletin, 129*, 52–73.

Panasetis, P., & Bryant, R. A. (2003). Peritraumatic versus persistent dissociation in acute stress disorder. *Journal of Traumatic Stress, 16*, 563–566.

Pearlman, L. A. (2001). Treatment of persons with complex PTSD and other trauma-related disruptions of the self. In J. P. Wilson, M. J. Friedman, & J. Lindy (Eds.), *Treating psychological trauma and PTSD* (pp. 205–236). New York: Guilford Press.

Pelcovitz, D., Van der Kolk, B., Roth, S., Mandel, F., Kaplan, S., & Resick, P. (1997). Development of a criteria set and a structured interview for disorders of extreme stress (SIDES). *Journal of Traumatic Stress, 10*, 3–16.

Pennebaker, J. W., & Seagal, J. D. (1999). Forming a story: The health benefits of narrative. *Journal of Clinical Psychology, 55*, 1243–1254.

Putnam, F. W. (1993). Dissociative disorders in children: Behavioral problems and profiles. *Child Abuse & Neglect, 17*, 39–45.

Putnam, F. W. (1995). Development of dissociative disorders. In D. Cicchetti & D. Cohen (Eds.), *Developmental psychopathology: Risk, disorder, and adaptation* (Vol. 2, pp. 581–608). New York: Wiley.

Putnam, F. W. (2000). Dissociative disorders. In A. Sameroff, M. Lewis, & S. Miller (Eds.), *Handbook of developmental psychopathology* (Vol. 771, pp. 708–715). New York: Kluwer Academic/Plenum Press.

Putnam, F. W., Carlson, E. B., Ross, C. A., & Anderson, G. (1996). Patterns of dissociation in clinical and nonclinical samples. *Journal of Nervous and Mental Disease, 184*, 673–679.

Roth, S., Lebowitz, L., & DeRosa, R. R. (1997). Thematic assessment of posttraumatic stress reactions. In J. P. Wilson & T. M. Keane (Eds.), *Assessing psychological trauma and PTSD* (pp. 512–528). New York: Guilford Press.

Ruggiero, K. J., Smith, D. W., Hanson, R. F., Resnick, H. S., Saunders, B. E., Kilpatrick, D. G., et al. (2004). Is disclosure of childhood rape associated with mental health outcome? Results from the National Women's Study. *Child Maltreatment, 9*, 62–77.

Scaer, R. C. (2001). The neurophysiology of dissociation and chronic disease. *Applied Psychophysiology & Biofeedback, 26*, 73–91.

Silvern, L., Karyl, J., & Landis, T. Y. (1995). Individual psychotherapy for the traumatized children of abused women. In E. Peled, P. G. Jaffe, & J. L. Edleson (Eds.), *Ending the cycle of violence: Community responses to children of battered women* (pp. 43–76). Thousand Oaks, CA: Sage Publications.

Silvern, L., McClintic, B., Schulz-Heik, J., & Stolbach, B. (2008, November). Correlates of high dissociation in child and adolescent samples: Implications for Development Trauma Disorder. In Bradley Stolbach (Chair), *Correlates of high dissociation in child and adolescent samples: Implications for Development Trauma Disorder*. Symposium conducted at the 25th Annual Conference of the International Society for the Study of Trauma and Dissociation, Chicago, IL.

Smyth, J., True, N., & Souto, J. (2001). Effects of writing about traumatic experiences: The necessity for narrative structuring. *Journal of Social & Clinical Psychology, 20*, 161–172.

Spiegel, D. (1986). Dissociating damage. *American Journal of Clinical Hypnosis, 29*, 123–131.

Spiegel, D., & Cardeña, E. (1991). Disintegrated experience: The dissociative disorders revisited. *Journal of Abnormal Psychology, 100*, 366–378.

Sterlini, G. L., & Bryant, R. A. (2002). Hyperarousal and dissociation: a study of novice skydivers. *Behavior Research and Therapy, 40*, 431–437.

Stolbach, B. C. (2005). Psychotherapy of a dissociative 8-year-old boy burned at age 3. *Psychiatric Annals, 35*, 685–694.

Stolbach, B. C., & Waters, F. (2006). Assessment of dissociative symptoms in children and adolescents. Workshop presented at the 23rd Annual Meeting of the International Society for the Study of Dissociation, Los Angeles, CA.

Valentino, K., Cicchetti, D., Rogosch, F. A., & Toth, S. L. (2008). True and false recall and dissociation among maltreated children: The role of self-schema. *Development and Psychopathology*, *20*, 213–232.

Van der Hart, O., Nijenhuis, E. R. S., & Steele, K. (2005). Dissociation: An insufficiently recognized major feature of complex posttraumatic stress disorder. *Journal of Traumatic Stress, 18*, 413–423.

Van der Kolk, B. A. (1996). The complexity of adaptation to trauma: Self-regulation, stimulus discrimination, and characterological development. In B. A. van der Kolk, A. C. McFarlane, & L. Weisaeth (Eds.), *Traumatic stress: The effects of overwhelming experience on mind, body, and society* (pp. 182–213). New York: Guilford Press.

Van der Kolk, B. A. (2005). Developmental Trauma Disorder: Toward a rational diagnosis for children with complex trauma histories. *Psychiatric Annals, 35*, 401–408.

Van der Kolk, B. A., Van der Hart, O., & Marmar, C. R. (1996). Dissociation and information processing in posttraumatic stress disorder. In B. A. Van der Kolk, A. C. McFarlane, & L. Weisaeth (Eds.), *Traumatic stress: The effects of overwhelming experience on mind, body, and society* (pp. 303–327). New York: Guilford Press.

Van der Velden, P. G., Kleber, R. J., Christiaanse, B., Gersons, B. P. R., Marcelissen, F. G. H., Drogendijk, A. N., et al. (2006). The independent predictive value of peritraumatic dissociation for postdisaster intrusions, avoidance reactions, and PTSD symptom severity: A 4-year prospective study. *Journal of Traumatic Stress, 19*, 493–506.

Van IJzendoorn, M. H., Schuengel, C., & Barkermans-Kranenburg, M. J. (1999). Disorganized attachment in early childhood: Meta-analysis of precursors, concomitants, and sequelae. *Development & Psychopathology, 11*, 225–249.

Waelde, L. C., Koopman, C., Rierdan, J., & Spiegel, D. (2001). Symptoms of acute stress disorder and posttraumatic stress disorder following exposure to disastrous flooding. *Journal of Trauma & Dissociation, 2*, 37–52.

Waelde, L. C., Silvern, L., & Fairbank, J. A. (2005). A taxometric investigation of dissociation in Vietnam veterans. *Journal of Traumatic Stress, 18*, 359–369.

Waller, N. G., & Meehl, P. E. (1998). *Multivariate taxometric procedures: Distinguishing types from continua.* Thousand Oaks, CA: Sage.

Waller, N. G., Putnam, F., & Carlson, E. (1996). Types of dissociation and dissociative types: A taxometric analysis of dissociative experiences. *Psychological Methods, 1*, 300–321.

Zellman, G. L., & Fair, C. C. (2002). Preventing and reporting abuse. In J. E. B. Myers, L. Berliner, J. Briere, C. T. Hendrix, & C. Jenny (Eds.), *The APSAC handbook on child maltreatment* (2nd ed., pp. 449–475). Thousand Oaks, CA: Sage Publications.

29 Dissociative Reactions in PTSD

Karni Ginzburg, PhD
Lisa D. Butler, PhD
Kasey Saltzman, PhD
Cheryl Koopman, PhD

OUTLINE

Dissociative experiences often occur in reaction to exposure to traumatic life events or reminders of them (Koopman, Classen, Cardeña, & Spiegel, 1995; Koopman, Drescher et al., 2001; Spiegel, Koopman, & Classen, 1994). Dissociative reactions can also occur in response to stressful everyday life experiences (Koopman, Gore-Felton, Classen, Kim, & Spiegel, 2001; Koopman et al., 2002). Such dissociative *reactions* can manifest as a disruption in perception of time, physical sensations, memory, sense of self and personal identity, and/or sense of reality; these experiences are captured, for the most part, by the terms *derealization* and *depersonalization* (American Psychiatric Association, 1994). Dissociation occurs when aspects or discrete components of experience fail to integrate, thereby remaining cut off or inaccessible from each other (Butler, Duran, Jasiukaitis, Koopman, & Spiegel, 1996; Spiegel & Cardeña, 1991).

Although other types of dissociative experiences (e.g., daydreaming, fantasizing, becoming absorbed in activity or entertainment, and flow experiences) are normal aspects of the waking state for many individuals (Butler, 2004a; Butler & Kaufman, unpublished data, cited in Butler, 2004b, 2006), evidence suggests that dissociative *reactions* to everyday life stressors are more likely to be reported by individuals with posttraumatic stress disorder (PTSD; Koopman, Gore-Felton, et al., 2001; Koopman et al., 2002). We will discuss several aspects of the relationship between dissociation and PTSD, including the proneness of persons with PTSD to dissociative reactions under stressful conditions, and three possible conceptualizations of the PTSD-dissociation link.

It is important to differentiate clinically significant dissociation from normal dissociation. The term *dissociation* refers to a wide collection of symptoms and experiences. Some of these (e.g., identity confusion, derealization, depersonalization, amnesia) are relatively uncommon in nonclinical samples under normal conditions (Waller, Putnam, & Carlson, 1996; Seedat, Stein, & Forde, 2003); other dissociative phenomena (e.g., fantasy proneness, imaginative involvement, absorption) are normally distributed in the general population (Ray, 1996; Vanderlinden, Van Dyck, Vandereycken, & Vertommen, 1993).

Some authors contend that a single underlying capacity (such as absorption) may underlie the seeming continuum from nonpathological to pathological dissociation (e.g., Butler, 2006; Dalenberg, 2004), and that dissociative pathology represents perturbations of normative dissociative functions (Butler, 2004a, 2006). However, others believe that pathological and nonpathological dissociation are two distinct constructs (e.g., Waller et al., 1996). Butler and Palesh (2004; see also Butler, 2004a, 2006) distinguish three kinds of dissociation that map onto the three major factors typically identified by factor analytic studies of dissociation instruments (e.g., Ray, 1996): (1) everyday dissociative experiences (that exemplify intense absorption); (2) dissociative reactions to highly stressful experiences (that exemplify transient derealization and depersonalization); and (3) full-blown dissociative disorders (that exemplify chronic disruptions of memory and identity as well as other dissociative experiences). While everyday dissociative experiences may be used to escape stress or dysphoria, they are not associated with PTSD (Butler, 2004a, 2006), whereas the latter two factors seem to be pathological, necessarily related to stress and to the development of PTSD (Butler et al., 1996; Irwin, 1999). Most studies, unfortunately, do not make these distinctions, and treat dissociation as a single category.

29.1 TRAUMA, DISSOCIATION, AND PTSD

Dissociation is associated with traumatic events in several ways. The terms *peritraumatic*, *acute*, and *posttraumatic* indicate the temporal relationship between dissociation and the precipitating trauma. Trauma-driven dissociative symptoms can also be conceptualized in terms of outcome complexity (e.g., isolated symptoms versus a relatively distinct coherent syndrome).

29.1.1 Peritraumatic Dissociation

Peritraumatic dissociation refers to dissociative symptoms that are experienced during and immediately after a traumatic or highly stressful experience (Marmar et al., 1994; Marmar et al., 1996; Marmar et al., 1997; Spiegel & Cardeña, 1991). Peritraumatic symptoms are extremely common (Morgan et al., 2001; Noyes & Kletti, 1977); they include alterations in one's experience of the world (i.e., derealization experiences such as time distortion) and one's self or body (i.e., depersonalization experiences such as feeling separate from what is happening, feeling like an automaton, feelings of floating outside one's body, feeling that one's body or one's relationship to it has changed in some way; American Psychiatric Association, 1994; Noyes & Kletti, 1977). Individuals who were interviewed about their subjective experiences "during moments of life threatening danger" reported feelings of unreality and altered passage of time (70%), increased speed of thoughts, unusually vivid thoughts, and automatic movements (60%), and detachment and lack of emotion (50%; Noyes & Kletti, 1977). Two-thirds reported five or more manifestations of dissociation.

A prospective study of military trainees found a striking increase in dissociative reactions after exposure to high-stress training (Morgan et al., 2001). Prior to the training, less than a quarter of the trainees reported symptoms of derealization and depersonalization; after the training, more than two-thirds of the sample reported such experiences. Some symptoms (i.e., changes in time perception and a sense of looking at the world through a fog) were endorsed by more than 90% of the sample. Similarly, almost 80% of survivors of a sinking car-ferry (Eriksson & Lundin, 1996) and of a motor vehicle accident (MVA; Ursano et al., 1999) reported at least one peritraumatic dissociative symptom. Changes in time perception was the most prevalent symptom in the MVA group.

Several studies indicate that dissociative reactions during and immediately after an event are dose-related; that is, the more severe the *level of exposure* to traumatic stress, the more intense the dissociation (Koopman et al., 1996; Tichenor et al., 1996).

29.1.2 Peritraumatic Dissociation and PTSD

A body of evidence suggests that peri-event dissociative symptoms may predict later posttraumatic states. Specifically, although peri-event symptoms are common, they may predict or even precipitate the development of various psychopathologies if they are extremely intense or persistent. Retrospectively recalled peritraumatic dissociation is more common among Vietnam combatants (Bremner & Brett, 1997; Kaufman et al., 2002; Marmar et al., 1994; O'Toole et al., 1999) and female Vietnam theater veterans (Tichenor et al., 1996) *with* chronic PTSD than among veterans without PTSD. Similar findings were made among survivors of a sinking car-ferry (Eriksson & Lundin, 1996), MVA victims (Ursano et al., 1999), and emergency services personnel (Marmar et al., 1999).

Prospective studies have also found that intense and persistent peri-event dissociation predicted subsequent PTSD. Dissociation during the 4 weeks after an MVA predicted PTSD 6 months later (Murray, Ehlers, & Mayou, 2002). Similarly, of the four acute stress disorder (ASD) symptom-clusters (i.e., dissociation, intrusion, avoidance, and hyperarousal) that were assessed 1 month post-MVA, dissociative symptoms best predicted PTSD at 6 months post-MVA (Bryant & Harvey, 1998; Harvey & Bryant, 1998) and 2 years post-MVA (Harvey & Bryant, 1999a). The same pattern was observed among people who were exposed to a firestorm (Koopman et al., 1994), witnessed a mass shooting (Classen et al., 1998), experienced pregnancy loss (Engelhard et al., 2003), or were victims of assault (Birmes et al., 2001; 2003) or other traumas that caused injuries (Michaels et al., 1999; Shalev et al., 1996, 1998).

Indeed, a meta-analysis of pre- and peritraumatic risk factors for PTSD (i.e., trauma history, family history of psychopathology, perceived life threat, peritraumatic emotionality, and peritraumatic dissociation) concluded that peritraumatic dissociation was the strongest predictor of PTSD (Ozer et al., 2003).

29.1.3 Acute Dissociation

Dissociative experiences that occur during the immediate aftermath and the first four weeks following a trauma are referred to as *acute*. Journalists who had witnessed an execution reported an average of five event-related dissociative symptoms in the weeks after the event, with detachment or estrangement from others being the most common (Freinkel, Koopman, & Spiegel, 1994). When these reactions are severe and last for at least 2 days, they are considered to be pathological. A diagnosis of ASD (APA, 1994) requires the presence of at least three of five dissociative symptoms: a sense of numbing, detachment or absence of emotional responsiveness; reduction in the awareness of the surroundings; derealization; depersonalization; and psychogenic amnesia.

29.1.4 Posttraumatic Dissociation

Trauma may also breed chronic dissociative symptoms. A history of trauma, especially during childhood, is prevalent among adults who dissociate (Dancu, Riggs, Hearst-Ikeda, Shoyer, & Foa, 1996; Saxe et al., 1993; Irwin, 1996). Even decades after the event, individuals with a trauma history dissociate more than persons who were not exposed to such events (Chu & Dill, 1990; Maercker & Schutzwohl, 1997; Vanderlinden et al., 1993; Van den Bosch, Verheul, Langeland, & Van den Brink, 2003). Again, the tendency to dissociate increases with the intensity of the traumatic event to which the victim was exposed (Maercker, Beauducel, & Schutzwohl, 2000; Marshall & Orlando, 2002; Zatzick, Marmar, Weiss, & Metzler, 1994).

29.1.5 Chronic Dissociative Tendencies and Reactivity in Individuals with PTSD

In some individuals who develop PTSD, trauma-driven dissociative symptoms may solidify into a trait-like tendency to dissociate (Marmar et al., 1994): disengagement from the cognitive and/or emotional environment, depersonalization, derealization, emotional constriction, memory disturbances, and identity confusion (Briere, 2002). These dissociative tendencies are greater among trauma survivors with PTSD than among those who did not develop PTSD; furthermore, the intensity of the dissociative symptoms is positively associated with the intensity of the PTSD symptoms. This pattern is true of war veterans (Bremner et al., 1992; Bremner & Brett, 1997; Hyer, Albrecht, Boudewyns, Woods, & Brndsma, 1993), refugees (Carlson & Rosser-Hogan, 1991), victims of assault (Halligan, Michael, Clark, & Ehlers, 2003), police officers (Carlier, Lamberts, Fouwels, & Gersons, 1996), Holocaust survivors (Yehuda et al., 1996), offspring of Holocaust survivors (Halligan & Yehuda, 2002), and individuals with various histories of trauma (Warshaw et al., 1993). Interestingly, the association between dissociation and PTSD remains significant even after controlling for severity of trauma (Yehuda et al., 1996; O'Toole et al., 1999).

There is also evidence of a heightened dissociative reactivity among individuals suffering from PTSD. Some individuals with PTSD react with intense dissociative symptoms to reminders of previous traumatic experiences, new traumatic stressors, and even minor life stresses. Some of these reactions fall under the purview of PTSD diagnostic criteria (e.g., psychological reactivity to the threat of exposure to cues reminiscent of their previous experience). For example, trauma symptoms worsened among veterans with PTSD when they were faced with the prospect of more combat (McCarroll, Fagan, Hermsen, & Ursano, 1997; Solomon, Mikulincer, & Jakob, 1987). Similarly, combat veterans reported symptom-exacerbation when they were exposed to war-related media coverage (e.g., Vietnam veterans and the 1991 Gulf War coverage, Long, Chamberlain, & Vincent, 1994; Vietnam veterans and the Sept. 11, 2001, terrorist attacks coverage, Niles, Wolf, & Kutter, 2003). In many cases, this psychological reactivity takes the form of dissociative symptoms.

Traumatized individuals, especially those with PTSD, may exhibit dissociative sensitivity to everyday stressful events that would not be experienced as traumatizing to others. In a study of 64 women and men living with HIV/AIDS, participants were asked to (1) describe the most stressful event that they had experienced within the past month and (2) rate the frequency of their dissociative reactions to that event (Koopman et al., 2002). Thirty-nine percent of the sample reported having *at least three* dissociative symptoms in reaction to that event. Forty-two percent of the events involved personal relations (e.g., "trying to communicate with my husband"), 37% referred to health-related events (e.g., a toothache). Other stressful events related to legal, financial, or work issues. Fewer than 10% described a life-threatening event that met the DSM-IV stressor criterion for a diagnosis of ASD.

Dissociative hypersensitivity is especially prevalent among individuals with PTSD. Among a sample of 54 women with PTSD for childhood sexual abuse (CSA), 59% reported having *at least three* dissociative symptoms in reaction to a stressful event during the last month (Koopman, Gore-Felton, et al., 2001). Again, the vast majority of these women described minor stressful events, such as an interpersonal problem (50%), a health problem (20%), or a financial problem (17%). Even stronger dissociative reactivity was observed among PTSD combat veterans. Koopman, Drescher et al. (2001) examined the prevalence of five dissociative reactions to daily stresses in Vietnam veterans with PTSD (i.e., emotional numbing, derealization, depersonalization, amnesia for everyday events, and lack of awareness of surroundings). Eighty percent had experienced all five symptoms in response to a recent stressor; only 1% reported none of the symptoms. Dissociative symptoms were particularly likely to occur *in response to combat-related intrusive symptoms* such as flashbacks, nightmares, intrusive thoughts, or intrusive memories of combat. Half (51%) of the participants reported that intrusive symptoms were their most stressful life event in the previous 4 weeks; an additional 25% reported that seeking help from the Veterans Administration was their most stressful event in the previous 4 weeks. Thus, despite an absence of new traumas during the previous month, nearly all of these PTSD veterans were dissociating in response to lesser stressors, especially intrusive symptoms of PTSD.

Evidence suggests that severe PTSD is associated with even greater dissociative reactivity. Vietnam veterans with PTSD who retrospectively reported substantial peritraumatic dissociation during their combat experiences tended to react with dissociative symptoms to post-military traumatic events, when compared to veterans without PTSD (Bremner & Brett, 1997). Similarly, adult female survivors of CSA who reported higher levels of dissociative symptoms in response to recent stressors had higher cortisol levels in the 24 hours after a trauma-related interview (Koopman et al., 2003). These findings are consistent with the possibility that highly dissociative women used this defense successfully when they recounted their sexual abuse experiences (to manage their distress about the abuse), but experienced a breakthrough of intrusive thoughts during the subsequent 24 hours (thus leading to a rise in cortisol). Finally, Koopman et al. (1997) found that the intensity of dissociative reactions to everyday stresses in CSA survivors with PTSD was positively related to severity of PTSD and intensity of trait anxiety.

To summarize, there is considerable evidence of persistent and reactive dissociation following exposure to trauma, especially in persons with PTSD. There is little agreement, however, regarding the nature of the relationships among trauma, dissociation, and PTSD (Marshall, Spitzer, & Liebowitz, 1999). The relationship between dissociative experience and PTSD can be conceptualized in three ways: (1) PTSD and dissociation are different facets of the same phenomenon, thereby making PTSD a dissociative disorder (Butler et al., 1996; Nijenhuis, Van der Hart, & Steele, 2004; Putnam, 1989; Spiegel, 1988; Van der Kolk & Fisler, 1995); (2) there is a dissociative subtype of PTSD (Bremner, 1999; Ginzburg et al., 2006; Griffin, Resick, & Mechanic, 1997); and (3) PTSD and dissociation are distinct, but often comorbid, phenomena (APA, 1994).

29.2 THEORETICAL PERSPECTIVES

29.2.1 PTSD as a Dissociative Disorder

If dissociation and PTSD are different facets of the same phenomenon, then PTSD is a dissociative disorder—it has dissociative processes as its core (Butler et al., 1996; Nijenhuis et al., 2004; Putnam, 1989; Spiegel, 1988; Van der Kolk & Fisler, 1995). This perspective was first explicitly formulated by Pierre Janet at the end of the 19th century. Following close observations of hysterical patients, Janet described dissociation as a defensive response to acute trauma (Putnam, 1989). According to this view, dissociation is a failure of the memory system due to intense emotional and physiological arousal. Some individuals are unable to process and integrate traumatic events into memory; these experiences become isolated from the memory system (Van der Kolk, Brown, & Van der Hart, 1989; Van der Kolk & Van der Hart, 1989). This failure of integration occurs when there is insufficient psychic energy to incorporate these mental operations into a unified synthesis under the control of the self (Nemiah, 1998).

According to Janet, the memory traces of the unintegrated horrifying experiences remain as *fixed ideas* in a parallel stream of consciousness. Fixed ideas incorporate various sensory, cognitive, and affective elements of the trauma (Van der Hart & Horst, 1989; Van der Kolk & Van der Hart, 1989) and may later manifest themselves in dreams, under hypnosis, or in uncontrolled situations (Van der Hart & Horst, 1989). Subsequently, when the individual feels stressed, he or she may be controlled by automatic patterns of behavior that reflect the fixed ideas (Van der Kolk et al., 1989). Dissociation may provide an effective defense during trauma by screening out some of the threatening stimuli, reducing pain, helplessness, and anxiety, and maintaining some sense of control and security (Balson, Dempster, & Brooks, 1984; Spiegel, 1988); nevertheless, dissociation does so at the cost of a persistently fragmented state of mind (Spiegel, 1988).

Janet's ideas have received some empirical support. Several studies have documented a positive relationship between the level of dissociation during the first days posttrauma and symptoms of anxiety (e.g., Freinkel et al., 1994) and symptoms of hyperarousal (e.g., Griffin et al., 1997). These findings support the proposal that the initial inability to process and integrate the traumatic event into the memory system arises from the intense emotional and physiological arousal that was evoked by the trauma.

Janet's view that traumatic memories are fixated fragments of traumatic events has received support. In a study of PTSD individuals with troubling persistent memories, Van der Kolk and Fisler (1995) found that traumatic memories are stored as disconnected sensory fragments. When retrieved, they tend to present as dissociated mental imprints of sensory and affective elements of the original traumatic experience (i.e., without semantic representation). In contrast, nontraumatic memories were less vivid and were not accompanied by sensory experiences or amnesic elements. Similarly, the flashback memories of PTSD individuals differed from their ordinary memories: flashback memories had more sensory contents, were characterized by verbs in the present tense, and were more detailed (Hellwaell & Brewin, 2004).

Further support for Janet's concept of traumatic memory is provided by a study that examined dissociation and traumatic memories 2 to 12 days following an MVA. Accident survivors with higher levels of dissociation tended to present disorganized and dissociated memories. Their memories were characterized by confusion, repetitions, lack of awareness, depersonalization, derealization, time distortion, numbing, and withdrawal (Harvey & Bryant, 1999b).

29.2.1.1 PTSD Symptoms as Dissociative Phenomena

Fragmented memories may manifest themselves intensely and vividly in the daily life of trauma survivors. DSM-IV describes the phenomena of fragmented memories via the intrusive symptoms of PTSD. Several of these intrusive symptoms can be considered to be dissociative: unbidden and distressing recollections, perceptions, and images; reexperiencing of the traumatic event in dreams and daydreams; flashbacks or reliving experiences; and psychological or physiological reactivity upon exposure to internal or external cues that symbolize the traumatic event (Butler et al., 1996; Van der Hart & Horst, 1989). From the perspective of dissociation, intrusive symptoms are sensations, emotions, and memory fragments of the traumatic experience that break into consciousness (Van der Hart et al., 2004).

During these dissociative states, the individual may be so profoundly absorbed in the reexperiencing that other contextual cues lose their accessibility; the individual may temporarily lose the ability to distinguish between memory and reality (Butler et al., 1996). Such episodes may be brief or lengthy (i.e., hours or days) and may be accompanied by alternations in the perception of the self and the surrounding. The individual may appear confused and detached (American Psychiatric Association, 1994; Spiegel, 1988).

Four of the avoidance symptoms of PTSD can be classified as dissociative: amnesia for an important aspect of the trauma; diminished interest in significant activities; detachment from others; and a restricted range of affect. In each instance, the narrowed range (of memory access, interest, or affect) may signal a dissociative barrier or a compartmentalization of experience.

In addition to the possible defensive function of such memory disturbance (e.g., Ludwig, 1983; Putnam, 1989), the inability to recall some or all details of the event and the vivid and detailed recollections of other elements of the event may be accounted for by (1) absorption in one aspect of the event coupled with (2) the dissociation of other external or internal contextual stimuli during the trauma (Butler et al., 1996).

According to Janet, amnesia prevents the trauma survivor from telling what happened; this absence of a complete narrative prevents synthesis and helps to maintain the dissociation (Van der Kolk et al., 1989). Indeed, there is evidence that amnesia immediately after a traumatic event strongly predicts PTSD 6 months later (Harvey, Bryant, & Dang, 1998). Lack of narrative memory for the event is associated with the severity of dissociative tendencies (Van der Kolk & Fisler, 1995). A cognitivist perspective predicts that severe and chronic traumatic exposure would be more memorable than a single trauma because of severity and the repeated trials of experience (Butler & Spiegel, 1997). Evidence, however, indicates that those exposed to severe and chronic trauma are at greater risk of developing amnesia than are those exposed to a single trauma (Briere & Conte, 1993; Terr, 1991).

The numbing symptoms of PTSD (i.e., diminished interest, detachment, and restricted affect) may be viewed as a continuing defense against the pain that is aroused by painful memories (Butler et al., 1996) or as a manifestation of the profound fragmentation that can follow trauma. It is proposed that trauma induces a disaggregation of experience, including a fragmented perception of the self, characterized by inauthenticity, and that this is what constitutes depersonalization. Such individuals would numbly continue to perform their daily activities, but be unable to perceive them as interesting, enjoyable, or even relevant to their inner self (Spiegel, Hunt, & Dondershine, 1988).

Finally, PTSD hyperarousal symptoms (i.e., hypervigilance, exaggerated startle, sleep disturbance, concentration difficulties, and anger) may be viewed as manifestations of dissociative processes. Hyperarousal symptoms may reflect the anxiety attached to the dissociated fixed ideas. Moreover, when reminded of their traumatic experiences, PTSD individuals often anticipate vulnerability and a loss of control, which may activate tendencies toward hypersensitivity and overreactivity (Carlson, Armstrong, Lœwenstein, & Roth, 1998).

Those who argue that the symptoms of PTSD are dissociative in nature tend to view PTSD as part of a wider posttraumatic spectrum that includes ASD, some somatoform disorders, borderline personality disorder, and the dissociative disorders (Braun, 1988; Butler et al., 1996; Nijenhuis et al., 2004; Putnam, 1989; Spiegel, 1988; Van der Hart et al., 2004; Van der Kolk & Fisler, 1995). All of these disorders have traumatic elements in their etiology and dissociation in their phenomenology. Some would argue, however, that this dissociative concept of PTSD is inconsistent with the fact that a considerable proportion of individuals with PTSD do not present with dissociative symptoms (e.g., Yehuda et al., 1996).

29.2.2 A Dissociative Subtype of PTSD

In contrast to those who regard dissociative processes to be the core of PTSD, others have suggested a multitrack model of PTSD. Bremner (1999) has suggested that there are two subtypes of PTSD, one that is primarily dissociative and another that is based upon intrusion and hyperarousal. Bremner has argued in favor of a new nosological category: trauma spectrum disorders. This category would include (1) acute and chronic forms of PTSD that emphasize intrusion and hyperarousal, and (2) a posttraumatic dissociative disorder that emphasizes dissociative amnesia and depersonalization. Similarly, Jung (2004) has proposed a posttraumatic spectrum disorder that includes six subtypes of PTSD (including PTSD with dissociative features). In short, it may be quite fruitful to distinguish among individuals with PTSD according to the severity of certain symptom clusters, such as dissociative symptoms.

Previous studies provide some support for a dissociative subtype of PTSD. Yehuda et al. (1996) found that the mean level of dissociation is higher among aging Holocaust survivors with PTSD than among those without PTSD. Only about one-third of the PTSD subjects had high levels of dissociation. The level of dissociation among the rest of the PTSD sample was similar to that of the Holocaust survivors without PTSD. Similar findings have been reported for PTSD Vietnam veterans (Bremner et al., 1992). In a large clinical sample, Putnam et al. (1996) differentiated two PTSD subgroups: high dissociators and moderate dissociators. Finally, a recent study of adult women survivors of CSA (Ginzburg et al., 2006) found that a dissociative subtype of PTSD can be distinguished from a relatively nondissociative subtype of PTSD. Specifically, a constellation of high hypervigilance, sense of a foreshortened future, and sleep difficulties characterized the dissociative PTSD subgroup (OR = 8.15).

Additional support for a dissociative subtype of PTSD comes from two laboratory studies that reported physiological differences between PTSD participants with high versus low dissociation. Griffin et al. (1997) studied rape survivors within 2 weeks of their assault. Among the survivors with severe PTSD symptoms, those who reported high levels of peritraumatic dissociation during their rape experience were characterized by suppression of autonomic response during later exposure to trauma-related memories; survivors with high levels of PTSD symptoms who reported lower levels of dissociation responded to these memories with autonomic arousal (i.e., increased skin conductance and heart rate). Koopman et al. (2003) found that female CSA survivors with PTSD and higher levels of acute dissociative symptoms following stressful life events in the previous month had higher levels of salivary cortisol 24 hours following a stressful interview in which they discussed their worst sexual abuse experiences.

Delinquent adolescents with higher levels of dissociative symptoms, compared to those with lower levels, had lower mean heart rates in response to a stressful interview (Carrion & Steiner, 2000; Koopman et al., 2004). Similarly, adult CSA survivors with PTSD, who reacted with depersonalization and derealization upon exposure to a traumatic script, showed no increase in heart rate when recalling a traumatic memory (Lanius et al., 2002). These physiological findings suggest that dissociative symptoms may be related to blunted autonomic responses. This is striking because research has generally found PTSD to be associated with increased autonomic responses to stress, such as increases of heart rate responses to sudden, loud tones (Orr et al., 2003), exposure to trauma-related material (e.g., Elsesser, Sartory, & Tackenberg, 2004), or a self-chosen anger memory (Beckham et al., 2002). Thus, evidence suggests that there are notable physiological differences between PTSD individuals with dissociative symptoms and those without such symptoms.

What determines a person's subtype of PTSD? Perhaps it is the nature of the traumatic event (e.g., Bremner, 1999; Putnam et al., 1996). For example, exposure to repeated chronic traumatic events (Terr, 1991), particularly human-perpetrated abuse and/or trauma that involved protracted control and captivity (Herman, 1992), is considered to be a powerful risk factor for PTSD involving heightened dissociative-symptoms (e.g., Bremner, 1999; Putnam et al., 1996).

Developmental stage may also be a crucial determinant of dissociative PTSD. Severe traumatic events during childhood tend to evoke persistent dissociative tendencies (Chu & Dill, 1990; Dancu et al., 1996; Saxe et al., 1993). Traumatic experiences during this preadolescent developmental period when normal dissociation is at its peak (Morgan & Hilgard, 1973; Steiner et al., 2003) may prompt the persistent use of dissociation to deflect or ward off aversive traumatic experiences. A chaotic, violent, or neglectful childhood environment may cause dissociation to become an overlearned, relatively automatic, response to difficult situations.

There is evidence that dissociative symptoms in PTSD are associated with the severity of childhood trauma (Van der Kolk & Fisler, 1995). Women CSA survivors with PTSD exhibited a nonlinear relationship between the severity of their abuse and the level of their dissociative symptoms (Ginzburg et al., 2006). The median childhood maltreatment score was used to divide the sample into two groups. Dissociation and maltreatment were unrelated in the low maltreatment group, but positively related in the high maltreatment group.

Childhood trauma may be a risk factor for dissociative symptoms if the person encounters trauma later in life. Simeon et al.'s study (2004) of 21 people who were exposed to the World Trade Center attack found that they had not experienced dissociative symptoms prior to the attack. At 9 months postattack, however, their level of dissociation was associated with the extent of their childhood trauma, rather than their level of exposure to the attack. Pathological dissociation in delinquent adolescents was associated with intrafamilial (but not extrafamilial) trauma (Plattner et al., 2003); this suggests that familial traumata are particularly likely to promote dissociative symptoms. This finding is consistent with Freyd's (1996) argument that traumas involving familial betrayal are especially likely to induce dissociative (in particular, amnestic) symptoms.

Hypnotizability or the capacity to dissociate is another possible risk factor for dissociative PTSD (Butler et al., 1996). A disposition to dissociate may be composed of hypnotic susceptibility (hypnotizability), absorptive capacity, fantasy proneness, and imaginative involvement—experiences that are often referred to as normal (Irwin, 1999; Waller et al., 1996; Waller & Ross, 1997), nonpathological, or normative dissociation (Butler, 2006).

Bryant, Guthrie, and Moulds (2001) tested the hypothesis that hypnotizability is a diathesis for dissociative symptoms under conditions of traumatic stress (Butler et al., 1996). They found that acutely traumatized MVA and nonsexual assault survivors who developed ASD had higher levels of hypnotizability than (1) those with subthreshold ASD (who met all ASD criteria except for the dissociative symptom-cluster) and (2) those without ASD. Butler et al. (1996; see also Bryant et al., 2001) suggest that hypnotizability is not a general risk factor for stress disorders; instead, it is a predisposition that can shape the *form* of the stress response. In short, persons with high hypnotizability tend to develop conditions that are characterized by high levels of dissociation, whereas persons with low hypnotizability tend to develop nondissociative posttraumatic conditions.

Although a putative dissociative subtype of PTSD has received some empirical support, additional validation studies must be conducted (Robins & Guze, 1989): laboratory studies that permit refined classification and specification of exclusion criteria, follow-up studies of the clinical course of the condition, research on treatment outcomes, study of subtype prognoses, and family studies.

29.2.3 PTSD and Dissociation as Comorbid Phenomena

Some consider PTSD and dissociation to be distinct phenomena that are often comorbid (Marshall et al., 1999). PTSD is known to be strongly comorbid with affective disorders, anxiety disorders, and substance abuse (Kessler et al., 1995). From this perspective, dissociation is just another aspect of PTSD's comorbidity.

The view that PTSD and dissociation are separate phenomena is consistent with evidence that dissociation is not associated exclusively with PTSD; it is also linked with other pathologies. For example, their association may be due to a third factor (such as traumatic experience) that is also common to psychiatric conditions that are comorbid with dissociation. In a study of adult offspring of Holocaust survivors, Halligan and Yehuda (2002) found that dissociation was not only associated with PTSD, but also with mood disorders, anxiety disorders, eating disorders, substance abuse, and somatoform disorders. Interestingly, the number of lifetime psychiatric diagnoses was positively associated with level of dissociation (regardless of PTSD status).

In a community sample, dissociative symptoms were associated with a number of psychiatric disorders, including mood disorders, anxiety disorders, substance use disorders, as well as PTSD (Mulder et al., 1998). Saxe et al. (1993) found high levels of dissociative tendencies among psychiatric inpatients with a variety of diagnoses. Noyes et al. (1977) found similar levels of depersonalization among trauma survivors (accident victims) and psychiatric inpatients. Some dissociative symptoms (e.g., disconnected thoughts, slowed thoughts, dreaminess) were even more prevalent among the psychiatric patients.

Although these studies show that dissociative symptoms occur in psychiatric disorders other than PTSD, these same studies often demonstrated that the dissociation was related to traumatic stress. Psychiatric inpatients with high levels of dissociation reported higher rates of childhood trauma, than those with low levels of dissociation (Saxe et al., 1993). Mulder et al. (1998) found similar results in a community sample.

A positive correlation between trauma and dissociative symptoms has also been reported in dissociative disorders (Nijenhuis et al., 1998; Putnam et al., 1996), eating disorders (Waller et al., 2001), and borderline personality disorder (Heffernan & Cloitre, 2000). Each of these latter disorders has trauma as part of its reputed etiology (reviewed in Butler et al., 1996).

Although research robustly links early trauma to dissociation, and PTSD to dissociation, the crucial question is whether any of these relationships are *causal*. Marshall et al. (1999) suggest that the link between PTSD and dissociation is an artifact that reflects common risk factors (e.g., early abuse). This hypothesis needs to be investigated. Some evidence for a causal relationship between PTSD and dissociation comes from the finding that the relationship between CSA and dissociation diminishes when the association between CSA and adult mental disorder is taken into account (Mulder et al., 1998). This suggests that the influence of CSA on dissociation is indirect—mediated by more general linkages between CSA and PTSD.

29.3 SUMMARY

The three theoretical perspectives generate different positions and competing hypotheses about traumatogenic processes. For example, the theory that PTSD symptoms are dissociative leads to the nosological view that PTSD should be classified as a dissociative disorder (e.g., Braun, 1988). Similarly, analysis of the relationship between dissociation and PTSD has spurred the proposal of a new category: stress-induced disorders (Bremner, 1999; Jung, 2004; Moreau & Zisook, 2002). This category would be similar to that of ICD-10 (1992); it would not imply any theoretical assumptions about PTSD (i.e., whether it is an anxiety or dissociative disorder). Indeed, a recent report suggests that this issue is being examined for DSM-V (see McNamara, 2004).

The hypothesis of a dissociative subtype of PTSD challenges researchers to differentiate between this subtype and other potential subtypes. If the hypothesis of a dissociative subtype were to garner strong support, then PTSD would become similar to schizophrenia and depression—a disorder with subtypes—which might improve diagnosis, treatment, and identification of physiological substrates and/or correlates (e.g., McGinn, Asnis, & Rubinson, 1996). Distinct subtypes of PTSD might indicate important differences in the type, intensity, and dosage of treatment, thereby improving treatment outcomes. Finally, the perspective that PTSD and dissociation are distinct, though often comorbid, phenomena is the regnant nosological view in American psychiatry (American Psychiatric Association, 1994). While this position avoids jumping to etiological conclusions, it also compartmentalizes the development of theory, basic research, and treatments with respect to PTSD on the one hand and dissociation on the other, thus potentially neglecting an examination of their possible relatedness.

Future research on the relationship between dissociation and PTSD should use large samples, be prospective, and use measures that are valid and reliable. Clarification of the relationship between dissociation and PTSD would improve our understanding and treatment of severe dissociative reactions to everyday life stressors among persons who have PTSD. For example, if a dissociative subtype of PTSD could be distinguished from a non-dissociative subtype, then persons with dissociative PTSD could receive treatment that (1) helps them to manage their dissociative reactivity to everyday events and (2) ameliorates their posttraumatic symptoms as well.

Researchers who distinguish between normal and pathological dissociation generally consider pathological dissociation to be related to PTSD. Most researchers, however, do not differentiate between normal and pathological dissociation in their study designs, assessment instruments, and analyses. In fact, the most frequently used measure of dissociation, the Dissociative Experiences Scale (Bernstein & Putnam, 1986), does not distinguish between the two phenomena. Fortunately, many recent instruments focus solely on pathological dissociation: Posttraumatic Dissociation Scale (Carlson & Waelde, 2000), Multiscale Dissociation Inventory (Briere, 2002), and Multidimensional Inventory of Dissociation (Dell, 2002). These pure measures of pathological dissociation may help future studies to resolve the controversy about the relationship between dissociation and PTSD.

REFERENCES

American Psychiatric Association (1994). *DSM-IV – Diagnostic and statistical manual of mental disorders* (4th ed.). Washington, DC: Author.

Balson, P. M., Dempster, C. R., & Brooks, F. R. (1984). Auto-hypnosis as a defense against coercive persuasion. *American Journal of Clinical Hypnosis, 26*, 252–260.

Beckham, J. C., Vrana, S. R., Barefoot, J. C., Feldman, M. E., Fairbank, J., & Moore, S. D. (2002). Magnitude and duration of cardiovascular responses to anger in Vietnam veterans with and without posttraumatic stress disorder. *Journal of Consulting Clinical Psychology, 70*, 228–234.

Bernstein, E. M., & Putnam, F. W. (1986). Development, reliability, and validity of a dissociation scale. *Journal of Nervous and Mental Disease, 174*, 727–735.

Birmes, P., Brunet, A., Carreras, D., Ducasse, J., Lauque, D., Sztulman, H., & Schmitt, L. (2003). The predictive power of peritraumatic dissociation and acute stress symptoms for posttraumatic stress symptoms: A three-month prospective study. *American Journal of Psychiatry, 160*, 1337–1339.

Birmes, P., Carreras, D., Charlet, J. P., Warner, B. A., Lauque, D., & Schmitt, L. (2001). Peritraumatic dissociation and posttraumatic stress disorder in victims of violent assault. *Journal of Nervous and Mental Disease, 189*, 796–798.

Braun, B. G. (1988). The BASK model of dissociation. *Dissociation, 1*, 4–23.

Bremner, J. D. (1999). Acute and chronic responses to psychological trauma: Where do we go from here? *American Journal of Psychiatry, 156*, 349–351.

Bremner, J. D., & Brett, E. (1997). Trauma-related dissociative states and long-term psychopathology in posttraumatic stress disorder. *Journal of Traumatic Stress, 10*, 37–49.

Bremner, J. D., Southwick, S. M., Brett, E., Fontana, A., Rosenheck, R., & Charney, D. S. (1992). Dissociation and posttraumatic stress disorder in Vietnam veterans. *American Journal of Psychiatry, 149*, 328–332.

Briere, J. (2002). *Multiscale Dissociation Inventory*. Odessa, FL: Psychological Assessment Resources.

Briere, J., & Conte, J. R. (1993). Self-reported amnesia for abuse in adults molested as children. *Journal of Traumatic Stress, 6*, 21–31.

Bryant, R. A., Guthrie, R. M., & Moulds, M. L. (2001). Hypnotizability in acute stress disorder. *American Journal of Psychiatry, 158*, 600–604.

Bryant, R. A., & Harvey, A. G. (1998). Relationship between acute stress disorder and posttraumatic stress disorder following mild traumatic brain injury. *American Journal of Psychiatry, 155*, 625–629.

Butler, L. D. (2004a). The dissociations of everyday life (editorial). *Journal of Trauma and Dissociation, 5(2)*, 1–11.

Butler, L. D. (2004b). *Dissociation in everyday life – A theory of adaptive functions and some preliminary findings.* Paper presented at the annual meeting of the International Society for the Study of Dissociation, November 2004, New Orleans, LA.

Butler, L. D. (2006). Normative dissociation. *Psychiatric Clinics of North America, 29*, 45–62.

Butler, L. D., Duran, R. E. F., Jasiukaitis, P., Koopman, C., & Spiegel, D. (1996). Hypnotizability and traumatic experience: A diathesis-stress model of dissociative symptomatology. *American Journal of Psychiatry, 153 (Suppl. 7S)*, 42–63.

Butler, L. D., & Palesh, O. (2004). Spellbound: Dissociation in the movies. *Journal of Trauma and Dissociation, 5(2)*, 61–87.

Butler, L. D., & Spiegel, D. (1997). Trauma and memory. In L. J. Dickstein, M. B. Riba & J. O. Oldham (Eds.), *Review of psychiatry, 16* (pp. 1113–1153). Washington, DC: American Psychiatric Press.

Carlier, I. V. E., Lamberts, R. D., Fouwels, A. J., & Gersons, B. P. R. (1996). PTSD in relation to dissociation in traumatized police officers. *American Journal of Psychiatry, 153*, 1325–1328.

Carlson, E. B., Armstrong, J., Loewenstein, R., & Roth, D. (1998). Relationships between traumatic experiences and symptoms of posttraumatic stress, dissociation, and amnesia. In J. D Bremner & C. R. Marmar (Eds.), *Trauma, memory, and dissociation* (pp. 205–227). Washington, DC: American Psychiatric Press.

Carlson, E. B., & Rosser-Hogan, R. (1991). Trauma experiences, posttraumatic stress, dissociation, and depression in Cambodian refugees. *American Journal of Psychiatry, 148*, 1548–1551.

Carlson, E. B., & Waelde, L. (2000, November). *Preliminary psychometric properties of the Trauma-Related Dissociation Scale (TRDS).* Paper presented at the annual meeting of the International Society for Traumatic Stress Studies, San Antonio, TX.

Carrion, V., & Steiner, H. (2000). Trauma and dissociation in delinquent adolescents. *Journal of the American Academy of Child and Adolescent Psychiatry, 39*, 353–359.

Chu, J. A., & Dill, D. L. (1990). Dissociative symptoms in relation to childhood physical and sexual abuse. *American Journal of Psychiatry, 147*, 887–892.

Classen, C., Koopman, C., Hales, R., & Spigel, D. (1998). Acute stress disorder as a predictor of posttraumatic stress symptoms. *American Journal of Psychiatry, 155*, 620–624.

Dalenberg, C. J. (2004, November). *What is normal about normal and pathological dissociation?* Paper presented at the annual meeting of the International Society for the Study of Dissociation, New Orleans, LA.

Dancu, C. V., Riggs, D. S., Hearst-Ikeda, D., Shoyer, B. G., & Foa, E. B. (1996). Dissociative experiences and posttraumatic stress disorder among female victims of criminal assault and rape. *Journal of Traumatic Stress, 9*, 253–267.

Dell, P. F. (2002). Dissociative phenomenology of dissociative identity disorder. *Journal of Nervous and Mental Disorders, 190*, 10–15.

Elsesser, K., Sartory, G., & Tackenberg, A. (2004). Attention, heart rate, and startle response during exposure to trauma-relevant pictures: A comparison of recent trauma victims and patients with posttraumatic stress disorder. *Journal of Abnormal Psychology, 113*, 289–301.

Eriksson, N. G., & Lundin, T. (1996). Early traumatic stress reactions among Swedish survivors of the m/s Estonia disaster. *British Journal of Psychiatry, 169*, 713–716.

Engelhard, I. M., Van den Hout, M. A., Kindt, M., Arntz, A., & Schouten, E. (2003). Peritraumatic dissociation and posttraumatic stress after pregnancy loss: A prospective study. *Behaviour Research ad Therapy, 41*, 67–78.

Freinkel, A., Koopman, C., & Spiegel, D. (1994). Dissociative symptoms in media execution witnesses. *American Journal of Psychiatry, 151*, 1335–1339.

Freyd, J. J. (1996). *Betrayal trauma: The logic of forgetting childhood abuse*. Cambridge, MA: Harvard University.

Ginzburg, K., Koopman, C., Butler, L. D., Palesh, O., Kraemer, H. C., Classen, C., & Spiegel, D. (2006). Evidence for a dissociative subtype of posttraumatic stress disorder among help-seeking childhood sexual abuse survivors. *Journal of Trauma and Dissociation, 7(2)*, 7–27.

Griffin, M., Resick, P., & Mechanic, M. (1997). Objective assessment of peritraumatic dissociation: Psychophysiological indicators. *American Journal of Psychiatry, 154*, 1081–1088.

Halligan, S. L., Michael, T., Clark, D., & Ehlers, A. (2003). Posttraumatic stress disorder following assault: The role of cognitive processing, trauma memory, and appraisals. *Journal of Consulting and clinical Psychology, 71*, 419–431.

Halligan, S. L., & Yehuda, R. (2002). Assessing dissociation as a risk factor for posttraumatic stress disorder: A study of adult offspring of holocaust survivors. *Journal of Nervous and Mental Disease, 190*, 429–436.

Harvey, A. G., & Bryant, R. A. (1998). Relationship of acute stress disorder and posttraumatic stress disorder following motor vehicle accidents. *Journal of Consulting and Clinical Psychology, 66*, 507–512.

Harvey, A. G., & Bryant, R. A. (1999a). The relationship between acute stress disorder and posttraumatic stress disorder: A 2-year prospective evaluation. *Journal of Consulting and Clinical Psychology, 67*, 985–988.

Harvey, A. G., & Bryant, R. A. (1999b). A qualitative investigation of the organization of traumatic memories. *British Journal of Clinical Psychology, 38*, 401–405.

Harvey, A. G., Bryant, R., & Dang, S. T. (1998). Autobiographical memory in acute stress disorder. *Journal of Consulting and Clinical Psychology, 66*, 500–506.

Heffernan, K., & Cloitre, M. (2000). A comparison of posttraumatic stress disorder with and without borderline personality disorder among women with a history of childhood sexual abuse: Etiological and clinical characteristics. *Journal of Nervous and Mental Disease, 188*, 589–595.

Hellwaell, S. J., & Brewin, C. R. (2004). A comparison of flashbacks and ordinary autobiographical memories of trauma: Content and language. *Behaviour Research and Therapy, 42*, 1–12.

Herman, J. L. (1992). *Trauma and recovery*. New York: Basic Books.

Hyer, L. A., Albrecht, J. W, Boudewyns, P. A., Woods, M. G., & Brndsma, J. (1993). Dissociative experiences of Vietnam veterans with chronic posttraumatic stress disorder. *Psychological Reports, 73*, 519–530.

Irwin, H. J. (1996). Traumatic childhood events, perceived availability of emotional support, and the development of dissociative tendencies. *Child Abuse and Neglect, 20*, 701–707.

Irwin, H. J. (1999). Pathological and nonpathological dissociation: The relevance of childhood trauma. *Journal of Psychology, 133*, 157–164.

Jung, K. E. (2004). Posttraumatic spectrum disorder: A radical revision. *Psychiatric Times,* XVIII.

Kaufman, M. L., Kimble, M. O., Kaloupek, D. G., McTeague, L. M., Bachrach, P., Forti, A. M., & Keane, T. M. (2002). Peritraumatic dissociation and physiological response to trauma-relevant stimuli in Vietnam combat veterans with posttraumatic stress disorder. *Journal of Nervous and Mental Disease, 190*, 167–174.

Kessler, R. C., Sonnega, A., Bromet, E., Hughes, M., & Nelson, C. B. (1995). Posttraumatic stress disorder in the national comorbidity survey. *Archives of General Psychiatry, 52*, 1048–1063.

Koopman, C., Carrion, V., Butler, L. D., Sudhaker, S., Palmer, L., & Steiner, H. (2004). Relationships of dissociation and childhood abuse and neglect with heart rate in delinquent adolescents. *Journal of Traumatic Stress, 17*, 47–54.

Koopman, C., Classen, C., Cardeña, E., & Spiegel, D. (1995). When disaster strikes, acute stress disorder may follow. *Journal of Traumatic Stress, 8*, 29–46.

Koopman, C., Classen, C., & Spiegel, D. (1994). Predictors of posttraumatic stress symptoms among survivors of the Oakland/Berkeley, Calif. firestorm. *American Journal of Psychiatry, 151*, 888–894.

Koopman, C., Classen, C., & Spiegel, D. (1996). Dissociative responses in the immediate aftermath of the Oakland/Berkeley firestorm. *Journal of Traumatic Stress, 9*, 521–540.

Koopman, C., Drescher, K., Bowles, S., Gusman, F., Blake, D., Dondershine, H., Chang, V., Butler, L. D., & Spiegel, D. (2001). Acute dissociative symptoms in veterans with PTSD. *Journal of Trauma and Dissociation, 2*, 91–111.

Koopman, C., Gore-Felton, C., Azimi, N., O'Shea, K., Ashton, E., Power, R., DeMaria, S., Israelski, D., & Spiegel, D. (2002). Acute stress reactions to recent life events among women and men living with HIV/AIDS. *The International Journal of Psychiatry in Medicine, 32*, 361–378.

Koopman, C., Gore-Felton, C., Classen, C., Kim, P., & Spiegel, D. (2001). Acute stress reactions to everyday stressful life events among sexual abuse survivors with PTSD. *Journal of Child Sexual Abuse, 10*, 83–99.

Koopman, C., Gore-Felton, C., & Spiegel, D. (1997). Acute stress disorder symptoms among sex abuse survivors seeking treatment. *Journal of Child Sexual Abuse, 6*, 65–85.

Koopman, C., Sephton, S., Abercrombie, H. C., Classen, C., Butler, L. D., Gore-Felton, C., Borggrefe, A., & Spiegel, D. (2003). Dissociative symptoms and cortisol responses to recounting traumatic experiences among childhood sexual abuse survivors with PTSD. *Journal of Trauma & Dissociation, 4(4)*, 29–46.

Lanius, R. A., Williamson, P. C., Boksman, K., Densmore, M., Gupta, M., Neufeld, R. W. J. et al. (2002). Brain activation during script-driven imagery induced dissociative responses in PTSD: A functional magnetic resonance imaging investigation. *Biological Psychiatry, 52*, 305–311.

Long, N., Chamberlain, K., & Vincent, C. (1994). Effect of the Gulf War on reactivation of adverse combat-related memories in Vietnam veterans. *Journal of Clinical Psychology, 50*, 138–144.

Ludwig, A. M. (1983). The psychobiological functions of dissociation. *American Journal of Clinical Hypnosis, 26*, 93–99.

Maercker, A., Beauducel, A., & Schutzwohl, M. (2000). Trauma severity and initial reactions as precipitating factors for posttraumatic stress symptoms and chronic dissociation in former political prisoners. *Journal of Traumatic Stress, 13*, 651–660.

Maercker, A., & Schutzwohl, M. (1997). Long term effects of political imprisonment: A group comparison study. *Social Psychiatry and Psychiatric Epidemiology, 32*, 435–442.

Marmar, C. R., Weiss, D. S., & Metzler, T. J. (1997). The peritraumatic dissociative experiences questionnaire. In J. P. Wilson & T. M. Keane (Eds.), *Assessing psychological trauma and PTSD* (pp. 412–428). New York: The Guilford Press.

Marmar, C. R., Weiss, D. S., Metzler, T. J., Delucchi, K. L., Best, S. R., & Wentworth, K. A. (1999). Longitudinal course and predictors of continuing distress following critical incident exposure in emergency services personnel. *Journal of Nervous and Mental Disease, 187*, 15–22.

Marmar, C. R., Weiss, D. S., Metzler, T. J., Ronfeldt, H. M., & Foreman, C. (1996). Stress responses of emergency services personnel to the Loma Prieta earthquake Interstate 880 freeway collapse and control traumatic incidents. *Journal of Traumatic Stress, 9*, 63–85.

Marmar, C. R., Weiss, D. S., Schlenger, W. E., Fairbank, J. A., Jordan, B. K., Kulka, R. A., & Hough, R. L. (1994). Posttraumatic dissociation and posttraumatic stress in male Vietnam theater veterans. *American Journal of Psychiatry, 151*, 902–907.

Marshall, G. N., & Orlando, M. (2002). Acculturation and peritraumatic dissociation in young adult Latino survivors of community violence. *Journal of Abnormal Psychology, 111*, 166–174.

Marshall, R. D., Spitzer, R., & Liebowitz, M. R. (1999). Review and critique of the new DSM-IV diagnosis of Acute Stress Disorder. *American Journal of Psychiatry, 156*, 1677–1685.

McCarroll, J. E., Fagan, J. G., Hermsen, J. M., & Ursano, R. J. (1997). Posttraumatic stress disorder in U. S. Army Vietnam veterans who served in the Persian Gulf War. *Journal of Nervous and Mental Disease, 185*, 682–685.

McGinn, L. K., Asnis, G. M., & Rubinson, E. (1996). Biological and clinical validation of atypical depression. *Psychiatric Research, 60*, 191–198.

McNamara, D. (2004, April). Proposals for DSM-V need high evidence threshold. Diagnostic research conferences planned. *Clinical Psychiatry News, 32*, 1, 8.

Michaels, A. J., Michaels, C. E., Zimmerman, M. A., Smith, J. S., Moon, C. H., & Peterson, C. (1999). Posttraumatic stress disorder in injured adults: Etiology by path analysis, *Journal of Trauma, 47*, 867–873.

Moreau, C., & Zisook, S. (2002). Rationale for posttraumatic stress spectrum disorder. *Psychiatric Clinics of North America, 25*, 775–790.

Morgan, A. H., & Hilgard, E. R. (1973). Age differences in susceptibility to hypnosis. *International Journal of Clinical and Experimental Hypnosis, 21*, 78–85.

Morgan, C. A., Hazlett, G., Wang, S., Richardson, E. G., Schnurr, P., & Southwick, S. M. (2001). Symptoms of dissociation in humans experiencing acute, uncontrollable stress: A prospective investigation. *American Journal of Psychiatry, 158*, 1239–1247.

Mulder, R. T., Beautrais, A. L., Joyce, P. R., & Fergusson, D. M. (1998). Relationship between dissociation, childhood sexual abuse, childhood physical abuse, and mental illness in a general population sample. *American Journal of Psychiatry, 155*, 806–811.

Murray, J., Ehlers, A., & Mayou. R. A. (2002). Dissociation and post-traumatic stress disorder: two prospective studies of road traffic accident survivors. *British Journal of Psychiatry, 180*, 363–368.

Nemiah, J. C. (1998). Early concepts of trauma, dissociation, and the unconscious: Their history and current implications. In J. D Bremner & C. R. Marmar (Eds.), *Trauma, memory, and dissociation.* (pp. 1–26). Washington, DC: American Psychiatric Press.

Nijenhuis, E. R., Spinhoven, P., Van Dyck, R., Van der Hart, O., & Vanderlinden, J. (1998). Degree of somatoform and psychological dissociation in dissociative disorder is correlated with reported trauma. *Journal of Traumatic Stress, 11*, 711–730.

Nijenhuis, E., Van der Hart, O., & Streele, K. (2004, January). *Trauma related structural dissociation of the personality*. Trauma Information Pages website. Web URL: http://www.trauma-pages.com/nijenhuis-2004.htm.

Niles, B. L., Wolf, E. J., & Kutter, C. J. (2003). Posttraumatic stress disorder symptomatology in Vietnam veterans before and after September 11. *Journal of Nervous and Mental Disease, 191*, 682–684.

Noyes, R., Hoenk, P. R., Kuperman, S., & Sylmen, D. J. (1977). Depersonalization in accident victims and psychiatric patients. *Journal of Nervous and Mental Disease, 164*, 401–407.

Noyes, R., & Kletti, R. (1977). Depersonalization in response to life-threatening danger. *Comprehensive Psychiatry, 18*, 375–384.

Orr, S. P., Metzger, L. J., Lasko, N. B., Macklin, M. L., Hu, F. B., Shalev, A. Y., & Pitman, R. K. (2003). Physiologic responses to sudden, loud tones in monozygotic twins discordant for combat exposure: association with posttraumatic stress disorder. *Archives of General Psychiatry, 60*, 283–288.

O'Toole, B. I., Marshall, R. P., Schureck, R. J., & Dobson, M. (1999). Combat, dissociation, and posttraumatic stress disorder in Australian Vietnam veterans. *Journal of Traumatic Stress, 12*, 625–640.

Ozer, E. J., Best, S. R., Lipsey, T. L., & Weiss, D. S. (2003). Predictors of posttraumatic stress disorder and symptoms in adults: A meta-analysis. *Psychological Bulletin, 129*, 52–73.

Plattner, B., Silvermann, M. A., Redlich, A. D., Carrion, V. G., Feucht, M., Friedrich, M. H., & Steiner, H. (2003). Pathways to dissociation: Intrafamilial versus extrafamilial trauma in juvenile delinquents. *The Journal of Nervous and Mental Disease, 191*, 781–788.

Putnam, F. W. (1989). Pierre Janet and modern views of dissociation. *Journal of Traumatic Stress, 2*, 413–429.

Putnam, F. W., Carlson, E. B., Ross, C. A., Anderson, G., Clark, P., Torem, M., Bowman, E. S., Coons, P., Chu, J. A., Dill, D. L., Lœwenstein, R. J., & Braun, B. G. (1996). Patterns of dissociation in clinical and nonclinical samples. *Journal of Nervous and Mental Disease, 184*, 673–679.

Ray, W. J. (1996). Dissociation in normal populations. In L. K. Michelson & W. J. Ray (Eds.), *Handbook of dissociation: Theoretical, empirical, and clinical perspectives* (pp. 51–66). New York: Plenum Press.

Robins, E., & Guze, S. B. (1989). Establishment of diagnostic validity in psychiatric illness: Its application to schizophrenia. In L. N. Bobins & J. E. Barrett (Eds.), *The validity of psychiatric diagnosis* (pp. 1–7). New York: Raven Press.

Saxe, G. N., Van der Kolk, B. A., Berkowitz, R., Chinman, G., Hall, K., Lieberg, G., & Schwartz, J. (1993). Dissociative disorders in psychiatric patients. *American Journal of Psychiatry, 150*, 1037–1042.

Seedat, S., Stein, M. B., & Forde, D. R. (2003). Prevalence of dissociative experiences in a community sample: Relationship to gender, ethnicity, and substance use. *Journal of Nervous and Mental Diseases, 191*, 115–120.

Shalev, A. Y., Freedman, S., Peri, T., Brandes, D., Sahar, T., Orr, S. P., & Pitman, K. R. (1998). Prospective study of posttraumatic stress disorder and depression following trauma. *American Journal of Psychiatry, 155*, 630–637.

Shalev, A. Y., Peri, T., Canetti, L., & Schreiber, S. (1996). Predictors of PTSD in injured trauma survivors: A prospective study. *American Journal of Psychiatry, 153*, 219–225.

Simeon, D., Yehuda, R., Knutelska, M., Nelson, D., & Schmeidler, J. (2004, November). *Biological, psychological and cognitive outcomes nine months after the World Trade Center disaster*. Paper presented at the annual meeting of the International Society for the Study of Dissociation, New Orleans, LA.

Solomon, Z., Mikulincer, M., & Jakob, B. R. (1987). Exposure to recurrent combat stress: Combat stress reactions among Israeli soldiers in the Lebanon War. *Psychological Medicine, 17*, 433–440.

Spiegel, D. (1988). Dissociation and hypnosis in posttraumatic stress disorder. *Journal of Traumatic Stress, 1*, 17–34.

Spiegel, D., & Cardeña, E. (1991). Disintegrated experience: The dissociative disorders revisited. *Journal of Abnormal Psychology, 100*, 366–378.

Spiegel, D., Hunt, T., & Dondershine, H. E. (1988). Dissociation and hypnotizability in posttraumatic stress disorder. *American Journal of Psychiatry, 145*, 301–305.

Spiegel, D., Koopman, C., & Classen, C. (1994). Acute stress disorder and dissociation. *Australian Journal of Clinical and Experimental Hypnosis, 22(1)*, 11–23.

Steiner, H., Carrion, V., Plattner, B., & Koopman, C. (2003). Dissociative symptoms in posttraumatic stress disorder; Diagnosis and treatment. *Child and Adolescent Psychiatric Clinics in North America, 12*, 231–249.

Terr, L. C. (1991). Acute responses to external events and posttraumatic stress disorders. In M. Lewis (Ed.), *Child and adolescent psychiatry: A comprehensive textbook* (pp. 755–763). Baltimore, MD: Williams & Wilkins.

Tichenor, V., Marmar, C. R., Weiss, D. S., Metzler, T. J., & Ronfeldt, H. M. (1996). The relationship of peritraumatic dissociation and posttraumatic stress: Findings in female Vietnam theater veterans. *Journal of Consulting and Clinical Psychology, 64*, 1054–1059.

Ursano, R. J., Fullerton, C. S., Epstein, R. S., Crowley, B., Vance, K., Kao, T. C., & Baum, A. (1999). Peritraumatic dissociation and posttraumatic stress disorder following motor vehicle accidents. *American Journal of Psychiatry, 156*, 1808–1810.

Van den Bosch, L. M. C., Verheul, R., Langeland, W., & Van den Brink, W. (2003). Trauma, dissociation, and osttraumatic stress disorder in female borderline patients with and without substance abuse problems. *Australian and New Zealand Journal of Psychiatry, 37*, 549–555.

Van der Hart, O., & Horst, R. (1989). The dissociation theory of Pierre Janet. *Journal of Traumatic Stress, 2*, 397–412.

Van der Hart, O., Nijenhuis, E., Steele, K., & Brown, D. (2004). Trauma-related dissociation: Conceptual clarity lost and found. *Australian and New Zealand Journal of Psychiatry, 38*, 906–914.

Van der Kolk, B. A., Brown, P., & Van der Hart, O. (1989). Pierre Janet on post-traumatic stress. *Journal of Traumatic Stress, 2*, 365–378.

Van der Kolk, B. A., & Fisler, R. (1995). Dissociation and the fragmentary nature of traumatic memories: Overview and exploratory study. *Journal of Traumatic Stress, 8*, 505–525.

Van der Kolk, B. A., & Van der Hart, O. (1989). Pierre Jane and the breakdown of adaptation in psychological trauma. *American Journal of Psychiatry, 146*, 1530–1540.

Vanderlinden, J., Van Dyck, R., Vandereycken, W., & Vertommen, H. (1993). Dissociation and traumatic experiences in the general population of the Netherlands. *Hospital and Community Psychiatry, 44*, 786–788.

Waller, G., Ohanian, V., Meyer, C., Everill, J., & Rouse, H. (2001). The utility of dimensional and categorical approaches to understanding dissociation in the eating disorders. *British Journal of Clinical Psychology, 40*, 387–397.

Waller, N. G., Putnam, F. W., & Carlson, E. B. (1996). Types of dissociation and dissociative types: A taxometric analysis of dissociative experiences. *Psychological Methods, 1*, 300–321.

Waller, N. G., & Ross, C. A. (1997). The prevalence and biometric structure of pathological dissociation in the general population: Taxometric and behavior genetic findings. *Journal of Abnormal Psychology, 106*, 499–510.

Warshaw, M. G., Fierman, E., Pratt, L., Hunt, M., Yonkers, K. A., Massion, A. O., & Keller, M. B. (1993). Quality of life and dissociation in anxiety disorder patients with histories of trauma or PTSD. *American Journal of Psychiatry, 150*, 1512–1516.

World Health Organization (1992). International Statistical Classification of Diseases and Related Health Problems (ICD-10). Authors.

Yehuda, R., Elkin, A., Binder-Brynes, K., Kahana, B., Southwick, S. M., Schmeidler, J., & Giller, E. L. (1996). Dissociation in aging Holocaust survivors. *American Journal of Psychiatry, 153*, 935–940.

Zatzick, D. F., Marmar, C. R., Weiss, D. S., & Metzler, T. (1994). Does trauma-linked dissociation vary across ethnic groups? *Journal of Nervous and Mental Disease, 182*, 576–582.

30 Dissociation in Complex Posttraumatic Stress Disorder or Disorders of Extreme Stress not Otherwise Specified (DESNOS)

Julian D. Ford, PhD

OUTLINE

Exposure to psychological trauma in early life is associated with adverse, complex, and enduring sequelae that include, but extend beyond, posttraumatic stress disorder (PTSD) (Bremner & Vermetten, 2001; Cicchetti & Rogosch, 2001; Heim & Nemeroff, 2001; Kaufman, Plotsky, Nemeroff, & Charney, 2000; Nijenhuis, Van der Hart, & Steele, 2002, 2005). A common theme in the sequelæ of early life trauma is dysregulation of the psychobiological processes that underlie (1) the development of a coherent sense of self and (2) the capacity for relational engagement (Lyons-Ruth & Jacobvitz, 1999; Schore, 2001a, 2001b; Simpson & Miller, 2002). Childhood maltreatment (including neglect) is associated with severe, early-onset self- and relational dysregulation that is often accompanied by chronic Axis I and Axis II disorders (Leverich et al., 2002; Lysaker, Meyer, Evans, Clements, & Marks, 2001; Zanarini, Ruser, Frankenburg, Hennen, & Gunderson, 2000).

Clinically, these self-regulatory impairments have been called *complex PTSD*, or *Disorders of Extreme Stress Not Otherwise Specified (DESNOS)* (Herman, 1992; Roth et al., 1997; Van der Kolk et al., 1996). DESNOS comprises seven aspects of self-regulation and psychosocial functioning that have been altered by traumatic stress: (1) affect and impulse regulation (e.g., difficulty modulating anger, fear, shame, risky behavior, or self-harming behavior); (2) somatic self-regulation (e.g., pain or physical symptoms that exceed medically explainable pathology); (3) consciousness (i.e., dissociation); (4) perceptions of perpetrator(s) (e.g., idealization of the perpetrator or preoccupation with revenge); (5) self-perception (e.g., shame, guilt, or seeing the self as damaged or ineffective); (6) relationships (e.g., being unable to trust, being revictimized, avoiding sexuality); and (7) systems of meaning (e.g., hopelessness, loss of faith).

In this chapter, I will discuss empirical findings and clinical observations that suggest dissociation ought to be reconceptualized and methodologically rethought *vis-à-vis* DESNOS. Specifically, dissociation appears to contribute to each of the other six features of DESNOS, rather than standing apart as a separate feature itself.

30.1 DISSOCIATION: DEFINITION, DOMAIN, AND EXPLANATORY MECHANISMS

As traditionally described, dissociative symptoms include alterations in consciousness (e.g., derealization, depersonalization) and memory (e.g., amnesia, flashbacks) as well as the fragmentation and reorganization of the self (e.g., dissociated identities). Van der Hart, Nijenhuis, Steele, and Brown (2004) assert that alterations in consciousness do *not* provide an adequate basis for defining or measuring dissociation. They propose that dissociation is more than a diminution of consciousness (e.g., confusion, absorption, disorientation, detachment), but instead is a "division of consciousness or personality" (Van der Hart & Dorahy, this volume, Chapter 1). They view structural dissociation as the result of fragmentation of the personality into "emotional" (i.e., defensive) and "apparently normal" (i.e., daily life) parts, each of which is a distinct "apperceptive center" (Braude, 1995), for instance, organized by a reproducible, self-stabilizing, and distinct sense of self (Nijenhuis, personal communication).

Dissociation can be understood phenomenologically as a splitting of self-awareness such that an individual experiences perceptions, feelings, thoughts, motives, and action as organized by a self that either is transiently absent (e.g., fugue states), alien (e.g., depersonalization), altered (e.g., derealization), or so fundamentally altered as to seem to be distinct other selves (e.g., DID). What can account psychobiologically for this dissociative breakdown of apperceptive (i.e., self-aware autobiographical) *information processing* (Braude, 1995)?

Van der Hart et al. (2004) postulate that exposure to trauma, when the personality is still forming, causes structural dissociation. They assert that dissociation is then maintained by classically conditioned defensive or evaluative responses and insufficient immediate or long-term social support. Although childhood exposure to psychological trauma is associated with increased risk of complex PTSD in adulthood (Ford, 1999), it is important to note that many survivors of childhood trauma do *not* develop dissociative disorders or PTSD (Yehuda, Spertus, & Golier, 2001). Certainly, it is unlikely that the psychobiological effects of early interpersonal trauma are nil, but the effects may take forms other than dissociation (e.g., depression, generalized or social anxiety).

I believe that *extreme emotional reactivity* and *disorganized attachment* alter the interaction between working memory and episodic/autobiographical memory (Baddeley, 2002); this alteration manifests itself as structural dissociation. Extreme emotional reactivity may result from significant stressors and/or certain personality dispositions (e.g., irritability, inhibition, or anxiety sensitivity; Kagan, 2001). Emotional reactivity alone does not lead to dissociation; and it may, instead, lead to suicidality, emotional numbing, rage without fugue, depersonalization, or a sense of being quite different from one's usual self. Similarly, confusion about or difficulty in sustaining trust, intimacy, and mutuality in close relationships can occur as the result of major disruptions in primary relationships (Lyons-Ruth & Jacobvitz, 1999), but severe relational problems do not, alone, lead to dissociation. For example, divorce, social avoidance, or negative psychotic symptoms often occur without a dissociative loss of consistent, integrated self-awareness and autobiographical memory.

On the other hand, when a person experiences emotions and primary relationships as extreme, unpredictable, and unmanageable, then this individual is likely to have great difficulty in sustaining a consistent organized sense of self. Extreme emotions can cause a person to feel so changeably different from moment to moment that it may seem that there is no consistent "me." Or, there might be several "me's" whose emotions are so different that they seem not to be the same person. Persons with disorganized attachment may perceive others as constantly and unpredictably changing. When this happens, relationships become a source of conflict and distress, rather than security or succorance. This leaves the person with no external framework to help regulate affect (e.g., to feel soothed by contact with others). Similarly, disorganized attachment makes it very difficult to develop or sustain a consistent sense of self because the person does not engage in relationships in a way that enables others to dependably and accurately respond to and mirror his or her identity.

When extreme emotional reactivity and disorganized attachment occur, *I postulate that dissociation develops as an automatic (versus consciously instigated and controlled) attempt to reinstate bodily integrity by shifting the body's dominant mode of operation from self-regulation to self-preservation.*

Primitive and largely automatic processes of *self-preservation* ordinarily assist the development of integrative self-regulation capacities and a coherent sense of self—that is, sensorimotor bodily awareness (Ogden & Fisher, in press) and metacognitive monitoring (by which the person observes and revises her or his own thoughts and modes of thinking; Sheppard & Teasdale, 2004). These processes of self-preservation are both somatic (e.g., "sucking, swallowing, breathing, thermoregulating, vocalizing," Doussard-Roosevelt, Porges, Scanlon, Alemi,

& Scanlon, 1997, p. 174) and mental (e.g., expectancies, appraisals, drives). When extreme affect dysregulation and attachment disorganization make self-regulatory processes insufficient to restore bodily integrity, dissociation will occur in a defensive attempt to prevent further psychobiological disintegration. At this moment, the integrated functioning of self-preservation and self-regulation is abandoned in the interest of bodily integrity. Thus, in the service of psychobiological survival, the dissociative split separates the preconscious/automatic modes of self-preservation from the conscious/modes of self-regulation.

This conceptualization is consistent with and informed by several theoretical models of stress and adaptation, including Bowlby's (1969) "working models," McEwen's (2002) "allostatic load," Hobfoll and colleagues' (2003) "conservation of resources," Brewin's (2001) "verbally versus situationally accessible memory," Allen and Badcock's (2003) "social risk hypothesis of depressed mood," and Van der Hart and colleagues' (2004) disconnection of "defensive action systems" (i.e., self-preservation) from "daily life action systems" (i.e., self-regulation). The consistent theme in these models is that *self-regulation shifts from controlled integrative modes to automatic self-preservation modes when bodily integrity cannot be sustained in the face of extreme stressors.*

When the split is transient or occurs subsequent to the development of solid self-regulatory capacities, the primacy of self-preservation tends to be temporary. It is succeeded by a restoration of self-regulation. This is not dissociation; but rather something more like anxiety or depression. On the other hand, when self-preservation becomes necessary prior to the attainment of solid self-regulatory capacities, then self-preservation may retain its primacy at the cost of more integrative modes of self-regulation (see Ford, 2005).

A lasting split between self-preservation and integrative self-regulation leads to a vicious cycle. *Extreme affective states become infused into* the person's self- and other-representations ("bad objects," Benatar, 2003), producing *disorganized and unstable mental representations*, which further destabilize and fragment affect, perception, and behavior. Thus, dissociation results when extreme stressors necessitate a lasting split of the integrated relationship between self-preservation and self-regulation. The resultant subjugation of self-regulation to self-preservation during psychological development is likely to prevent the attainment of the consistent, integrated, and personified self- and relational (Blizard, 1997) representations that are necessary in order to respond to subsequent stressors with a unified and coherent sense of self. This shift places a potentially severe strain on the person's biological as well as relational resources (Maunder & Hunter, 2001).

In contrast to the normal, ongoing, coherent sense of self ("me"), *dissociation is characterized by a fluctuating and fragmented sense of self and others' selves.* When individuals attempt to access mental representations of self (e.g., "what am I feeling and what do I want to do in this situation?") or others (e.g., "what do I know about this person that can help me decide how to deal with her?"), these representations are inaccessible or experienced as confusing and alien (e.g., "I have no idea who I am or who she is") when dissociation occurs.

Neurobiologically, both extreme affect dysregulation and disorganized attachment are associated with altered brain and bodily patterns of stress reactivity that can compromise working and autobiographical memory (Collette & Van der Linden, 2002; Ford, 2005; Nijenhuis et al., 2002). The findings about the neurobiology of affect regulation and attachment are consistent with the hypothesis that dissociation is associated with affect dysregulation and disorganized attachment.

For example, a 40-year-old female patient with generalized anxiety disorder described alternately feeling flooded with "thought soup" and feeling paralyzed or frozen mentally when trapped in a position of conflict and dependency in her family and at work, but she was fully aware of (1) her own constant presence and (2) even the most threatening or withholding persons in her life. She felt terrified that she might be losing her finely honed mental faculties. She felt despondent and helpless when overwhelmed by anxiety, but she did not lose track of a constant unitary internal self, nor did she experience others as shifting amongst split identities in relation to her. On the other hand, a 47-year-old female patient experienced a similar sense of overwhelming panic due to episodes of "losing time" that were precipitated not by anxiety relative to external stressors, but by disorientation about her own identity ("My feelings and thoughts, and even my body, feel completely strange") or about other people ("I know I should know who you are, but you seem like a complete stranger"). This depersonalized state tended to occur when the patient attempted to resolve internal or external conflicts by considering perspectives that differed from the highly scripted formulations that she had developed to survive childhood abuse. At such times, she first shifted into a state of frozen watchfulness, followed by adopting a position of either icy detachment and thinly concealed disdain (e.g., "you're just another stupid therapist, you should stay out of things you don't understand") or developmental regression and speechlessness. Over time, she was able to recognize and articulate (rather than simply reenact) her fear of catastrophic failure and punishment—at best, shame and loss; at worst, death.

Therapy for both patients involved a reexamination of how they viewed themselves, other persons, and the nature of their relationship to others. The therapeutic goal for the former patient was to enhance her ability to recognize and modulate stress-related anxiety (i.e., Freud's "actual" neurosis). The therapeutic goal for the latter patient was for her to gain the psychic capacity to retain a consistent sense of self-in-relation to others; this was accomplished by enhancing her ability to recognize and modulate intense abuse-related terror and shame while simultaneously holding a stable integrated sense of herself. The therapy for the first patient bolstered and drew upon the patient's ability to retain and utilize a view of herself and others that was consistent with, and functional in relation to, her personality and relationships. The therapy for the second patient addressed her self-loathing, helplessness in the face of her inner experiences, and relational detachment; the therapy accomplished this by focusing first on recognizing and organizing perceptions of self and others, and emotions and goals congruent with those perceptions. The first patient described therapy as "helping me get out of the soup of anxiety when I feel I'm drowning, by remembering ways of coping that work for me." The second patient described therapy as "helping me to come back from feeling lost and overwhelmed, without getting me or anyone else killed or making something terrible happen."

In contrast to the structural model (Van der Hart et al., 2004), I believe that dissociation does *not* necessarily entail the formation of separate part-selves. Phenomenologically, dissociation involves what Dell (this volume, Chapter 15) describes as: *"recurrent, jarring intrusions into executive functioning and sense of self."* To paraphrase Yeats, the dissociated person has "a center that cannot hold"—the "center" in this case is a coherent mental representation of self. A dissociative sense of "not being myself" or of "not being present," or even of "being someone else," does not require that the personality be fractionated into part selves (that supersede or replace a unitary self). Instead, dissociation results when *self-representations* are fractionated by extreme affect dysregulation and disorganized attachment.

A 32-year-old patient was referred for substance abuse treatment while the State Child Protective Services agency was determining whether to terminate her parental rights. She had been diagnosed with Antisocial Personality Disorder (ASPD) and PTSD (secondary to sexual molestation as a child and repeated rapes and domestic violence in adulthood). She had no remorse for killing a woman whom she had caught having sex with her boyfriend, saying that after having seen her mother gang-raped and left to die when she was 7 years old, and having had her home burn down at age 13 as a result of an explosion of the methamphetamine lab being run by her foster father (who at that time was pimping her), she didn't care what happened to anyone—"just leave me alone." She showed affect only when talking about her children, primarily expressing rage that they were being "kidnapped by the Man," leaving her feeling no purpose for living. She could not describe how she would like to interact with or care for her children, only that she wanted them back. Her sense of self-in-relation to others paralleled that of the profoundly damaged internal representations of Kosovar women (Almqvist & Broberg, 2003) and the "absence of attachment relations" in "catastrophically traumatized Holocaust child survivors" (Koren-Karie, Sagi-Schwartz, & Joels, 2003).

This woman did not show evidence of stable self-organizing part-selves. Instead, she consistently presented with a monolithic and impenetrable bastion of rage and indifference, within which she kept (what seemed to her to be) an endless and untouchable supply of unresolved grief and grievance. When given the opportunity to watch herself and therapeutic role models interact with her children on videotape, she very gradually and tentatively (with periodic retreats behind a wall of ruthlessness and entitlement) became able to observe, comment upon, and experiment with increasingly responsive and intimate ways of making sense of her children's states of mind. She began to play with, set limits for, and teach them. The dyadic psychotherapy (Van Horn & Lieberman, in press) helped her to recognize and understand intrusive reexperiencing and hypervigilance symptoms as automatic efforts by her body and mind to protect herself and her child. Reframing the symptoms as attempts at self-preservation provided a basis for therapeutic exploration of ways that she could choose to attend to and preserve her own and her child's safety, rather than having this occur reactively.

30.2 RESEARCH ON DISSOCIATION AND DESNOS

DESNOS has been assessed by the Structured Interview for Disorders of Extreme Stress (SIDES; Pelcovitz et al., 1997) in midlife and older adult community samples (Roth et al., 1997; Van der Kolk et al., 1996), and in inpatient (Ford, 1999) and outpatient (Roth et al., 1997; Van der Kolk et al., 1996) mental health samples. The SIDES is reliable and has shown convergent and discriminant validity in clinical (e.g., substance abuse, Scoboria, Ford, Lin, & Frisman, in press), high-risk (e.g., incarcerated men and women, Scorboria et al., in press; homeless women, Ford & Frisman, 2002), and community samples (e.g., college women; Ford, Stockton, Kaltman, & Green, 2006). Nevertheless, psychometric analyses of the data from these studies have called into question both the structure of DESNOS and the conceptualization and operationalization of dissociation within DESNOS (or within the SIDES).

The SIDES measures dissociation with five items (e.g., losing time, fugue states, and life as unreal and dreamlike) that tap: (1) total amnesia for important past experiences, (2) derealization, and (3) depersonalization. The amnesia and derealization items do not necessarily involve a loss or fragmentation of self- and other-representations. The depersonalization item includes only an extreme form of this phenomenon: "Having separate parts within oneself that are in competition or take control." Other than this component of the depersonalization item, I contend that endorsement of SIDES dissociation items could reflect problems with attention, orientation, and motivation rather than true dissociation. To constitute dissociation, the symptoms must reflect a loss or fragmentation of self- and other representations (that was caused by impaired attachment, affect regulation, and information processing).

The difference between true dissociation and intentional or transient diminutions in self-relevant and autobiographical memory is illustrated by a patient with a posttraumatic fugue disorder. This patient had intact implicit memory, but denied explicit memory of his primary language (German) and of autobiographical events (Glisky, Ryan, & Reminger, 2004). Compared to (1) healthy controls and (2) bilingual English-German subjects who simulated an inability to understand German, the fugue patient had *reduced* prefrontal activation on fMRI neuroimaging scans. In contrast, prefrontal activation was *exaggerated* by the simulators (consistent with a conscious attempt to "forget") and *active* for healthy controls (consistent with autobiographical memory retrieval). The fugue patient had greater parietal lobe activity than the simulators or healthy controls; this suggests heightened reliance on preconscious utilization of lexical rules for word recognition. Although the study did not formally assess self- or other-representations, the patient's history and clinical presentation suggested significant fragmentation of self-representations (e.g., simultaneously self-reliant and responsible vs. avoidant and dependent) and relational representations (e.g., trusting vs. betrayed and betraying). The patient not only had a history of trauma, but described substantial emotional distress that had "disappeared" on two occasions when he ran away from mounting stressors and then entrusted his well-being to a virtual stranger (who inflicted further trauma). The patient's autobiographical memory and sense of realness (of his life, himself, and his relationships) appeared to have been fundamentally compromised by a psychological and physical trauma that overwhelmed his capacity to regulate his emotions and to sustain stable "working models" that represented himself and other persons.

Although the SIDES dissociation subscale showed fair internal consistency in the DSM-IV field trial (Alpha = 0.76; Pelcovitz et al., 1997), it shared 20% to 33% variance with each of the other SIDES subscales (except Perceptions of Perpetrators). By comparison, the remaining subscales shared no more than 5% to 10% of their variance with one another. In subsequent studies with samples of men and women in substance abuse treatment (N = 236), community mental health treatment for chronic mental illness (N = 52), prison (N = 301), and homeless families (N = 163), the dissociation scale manifested poor internal consistency (Alpha = 0.27–0.35) and low inter-item correlations ($r = 0.08–0.33$).

The SIDES dissociation scale clearly did not capture a methodologically sound construct in these three studies. Perhaps the dissociation subscale is ill-suited to these populations of persons who face multiple ongoing psychosocial adversities. Perhaps the interviewers failed to administer and score the items correctly, but this seems unlikely because interrater reliability was adequate (i.e., intraclass correlations > 0.80). All interviewers had been extensively trained and supervised on the SIDES. Also, the psychometrics of the SIDES in those studies compared favorably to those reported by Pelcovitz et al. (1997): total SIDES Alpha = 0.80–0.82, versus 0.96 in the field trial. The dissociation subscale had the weakest correlations with the total SIDES score: 0.36–0.44 versus 0.60–0.80 for all other subscales. All things considered, the data suggest that the SIDES dissociation subscale needs to be revised (perhaps based on a better definition of dissociation). The utility of the structural or A/S/O models as a basis for such a revision warrants testing.

Bearing in mind our finding that the SIDES dissociation scale does not adequately measure dissociation (at least in these three studies), we examined the structure of DESNOS, based on our SIDES data. In a series of exploratory principal components factor analyses with varimax rotations, variables producing anti-image correlations below 0.5 were removed and variables that loaded above 0.45 on factors were retained. In the substance abuse sample, a 5-factor solution was obtained that accounted for 42% of the common variance: affect dysregulation (12% variance, *Alpha* = 0.71), somatization (10% variance, *Alpha* = 0.72), self-harm (8.5% variance, *Alpha* = 0.66), damage/despair (7.5% variance, *Alpha* = 0.66), and sexual violation (5.5% variance, *Alpha* = 0.67). The dissociation items did not load on any factor. When the community mental health sample was included (Total N = 256), the same factor analytic procedure produced a similar 5-factor solution (with somewhat stronger internal consistencies; *Alphas* ranged from 0.73–0.77) that accounted for 49% of the common variance. In this analysis, the depersonalization item loaded on the Impulsive Aggression Toward Self or Others Factor. The amnesia and derealization items loaded on the Somatization Factor.

A 5-factor solution of the prison sample (N = 301) accounted for 50% and 47% of the common variance in lifetime and current DESNOS symptoms, respectively. The largest factor in each analysis reflected affect dysregulation (13%–17% variance), followed by factors for impulsive aggression/self-harm, externalized anger, somatization, and sexual violation. The amnesia item did not load on any factor. The depersonalization and derealization items loaded moderately on the affect dysregulation factor. Structural equation modeling tested the fit of three different models in the prison sample: (1) the SIDES structure with all items included, (2) the SIDES structure minus the items that did not contribute to the 5-factor solution, and (3) the 5-factor structure obtained from the substance abuse sample. Both SIDES models fit the data poorly; but the 5-factor structure from the substance abuse sample yielded a good fit with the data.

These findings (reported in more detail by Scoboria et al., 2008) raise questions about the structure of DESNOS and the role of dissociation in complex PTSD. *As currently measured by the SIDES, dissociative symptoms do not constitute a distinct factor; dissociative symptoms either do not contribute to, or are inconsistently involved in, the other factor analytically derived components of DESNOS.* Specifically, *apparent* dissociative dysregulation of memory (amnesia), *apparent* dissociative perceptions of the environment and events (derealization), or *apparent* dissociative perceptions of the body, identity, and relationships (depersonalization), may be due to other psychogenic factors (e.g., anxiety, depression, confusion) that do *not* intrinsically involve a dis-association between these forms of experiencing and the individual's sense of being the source and owner of them as a coherent personified self (i.e., a stable "me"). The significant loading of dissociation items on two of the SIDES' five factors (i.e., somatic distress, affect dysregulation) suggests that dissociation may not be an independent feature within DESNOS but may instead contribute to two primary DESNOS components (which represent the breakdown of bodily and affective self-regulation).

30.3 CLINICAL AND NEUROBIOLOGICAL FINDINGS ABOUT DISSOCIATION IN COMPLEX TRAUMA DISORDERS

The SIDES measures *affect dysregulation* by asking about intense emotions that seem unmanageable, particularly anger. The SIDES assesses *impulsive aggression* by asking about excessive risk-taking and self-harm. The SIDES assesses *somatoform distress* by asking about symptoms that may reflect somatization. The SIDES assesses *sexual violation* by asking about aversion to being touched or avoidance of sexual contact. The items of two factors, *externalized anger* and *self as damaged,* often load on the Affect Dysregulation and Impulsive Aggression factors, so I will not discuss them separately. Let us consider the role of dissociation in the remaining four factors.

30.3.1 Dissociation and Affect Dysregulation

Buck (1999) has proposed a metamodel that conceptualizes emotions in terms of an ascending hierarchy of regulatory capacities. This metamodel of emotions provides a frame of reference for examining the relationship between dissociation and affect dysregulation.

Emotion I maximizes hedonic tone and deals with potential threats by managing arousal. Emotion I is largely automatic (i.e., preconscious); it involves the sensory organs, brainstem, and midbrain—CNS areas that have been linked to dissociative flashbacks in PTSD (Osuch et al., 2001). Structural dissociation of Emotion I is a breakdown of biological self-regulation; this, in turn, disrupts self-representations and relational schemas. Nijenhuis (1999) calls this *somatoform dissociation.*

Dissociative dysregulation of Emotion I may manifest as extreme states of rage, helpless pain, impulsive rage, emotionless freezing, or hysterical sensorimotor loss (Vuillemier et al., 2001). Although somatoform dissociation serves adaptive functions via primitive "animal defenses" (Nijenhuis, 1999), it renders the individual's emotions, self-representations, and relational schemas too inaccessible or too chaotic to modulate the flood of interoceptive feedback (Craig, 2002). When dysregulation of Emotion I occurs *without* dissociation, the person feels "frazzled" (Arnsten, 1998), but can still observe and influence bodily states via mood or relational self-management strategies that reflect and enhance self-awareness, personality integration, and self-efficacy.

A person is not aware of Emotion I, except for nonverbally "felt" emotion that results from automatic optimization of bodily integrity and effective interaction with the external environment. When dysregulation involves somatoform structural dissociation (Nijenhuis, 1999), Emotion I systems operate in a rigid and overdetermined manner (based on "animal defense" schemas). For example, a patient with panic disorder might be incapacitated by impulsive aggression, acute suicidality, or regressive dependency if dissociation blocks access to affect management capacities and supportive representations of self and others (that previously have made panic seem survivable and even curable). Vianna, Graeff, Landeira-Fernandez, and Brandão (2001) have provided an example of Emotion I structural dissociation in rats: when there is a lesion to the rat's ventral periaqueductal gray area, the rat freezes when threatened (i.e., a primitive somataform defense), but does not learn avoidance responses (i.e., adaptive, self-regulated protective responses).

Emotion II expresses felt affect through automatic and purposeful "expressive displays" that coordinate social interactions (Buck, 1999, p. 305). Emotion II is based on CNS systems (DeBellis, 2001; Northoff et al., 2000; Patterson & Schmidt, 2003; Winston, Strange, & O'Doherty, 2002) that underlie the capacity to experience emotions consciously and to use emotions as a guide in relationships. These complex emotions require (1) that one be aware of oneself as being distinct from, but related to, others, (2) the capacity to identify trustworthy people (which is associated with the anterior cingulate), and (3) competent empathy and attachment in primary relationships (which are associated with the orbital and dorsolateral prefrontal cortices). Emotion II affords introspective reflection on emotions and relationships (i.e., "what I feel and how this makes sense in my life").

Dysregulation of Emotion II is evident when an individual recognizes emotions, but is unable to (1) organize them, (2) express them, and (3) respond to them with an appropriate level of intensity. Mood and anxiety disorders, including PTSD, involve *nondissociative* dysregulation of Emotion II. When dissociation occurs, there is an additional breakdown; the person is unable to relate his or her felt emotions to an integrated self (Horowitz, 2002) in secure relationships. Felt emotions are no longer experienced as belonging to, and being expressed by, a coherent known self.

For example, a 54-year-old Latina patient said she had *ataques de nervios* (i.e., comorbid anxiety and dysphoria) when she heard her husband use a tone of voice that she associated with childhood beatings and sexual molestation by her father. She was able to identify and (with prayer, breathing skills, and distracting social activities) manage similarly severe flashbacks that were triggered by sudden noises that reminded her of an earthquake (that had destroyed her family home and sent her to the hospital for several months). Reminders of abuse, however, evoked an unmanageable state of terrified alienation from herself which she described as "becoming someone who can only feel hatred, which is still me, but not the real me—*I* get angry, but I don't hate."

Thus, dissociative dysregulation of Emotion II differs qualitatively from severe PTSD. The individual is unable to retain her sense of being the person that she knows herself to be (i.e., with emotions that she can identify, express, and recognize as her own). Dissociation of Emotion II does *not* involve the crystallization of alternate or part selves; instead, it means that the self is no longer experienced as being the source of one's emotions.

Emotion III is "self-regulation through subjectively experienced feelings and desires, or affects" (Buck, 1999, pp. 305–306). Emotion III integrates felt emotions into a coherent sense of self-with-body-and-personality that have continuity across the lifespan in sustaining relationships. Emotion III requires the following developmental achievements and functional corticolimbic areas (Adolphs, 2001, 2002; Davidson, 2002; Frith & Frith, 2003; Hariri, Bookheimer, & Mazziotta, 2000; Young, 2002): (1) the capacity to sustain a coherent image of the body in space and in time (the insula and right inferior parietal cortices), (2) the capacity for self-relevant short-term memory (hippocampus and parahippocampal limbic areas), (3) the ability to distinguish mental from physical states, and to initiate actions (medial prefrontal cortex), (4) acquisition of social knowledge scripts that are infused with a sense of personal agency (temporal prefrontal cortex and posterior superior temporal sulcus), and (5) the development of self-reflective executive functions (anterior cingulate, dorsolateral prefrontal cortex). These CNS areas are implicated in dissociation (Nijenhuis et al., 2002). In extreme cases of structural dissociation such as dissociative identity disorder, these functions and their brain substrates may be fundamentally split (Reinders et al., 2003), with fundamentally impaired ability to locate emotions within a unitary self (orbitofrontal cortex) and an increased demand upon basic perceptual processing and inhibitory brain areas (frontal, parietal, occipital cortices) due to self-fragmentation (Şar, Ünal, & Öztürk, 2007).

Although severe nondissociative psychiatric disorders (e.g., schizophrenia, bipolar disorder, or substance dependency) can dysregulate Emotion III, they do not fundamentally alter self- and object-relatedness or emotional self-regulation. Dissociation of Emotion III does not just destabilize the continuity, integrity, and controllability of Emotion I and II schemas (i.e., felt emotions and associated beliefs, intentions, and action plans). *Dissociation of Emotion III disrupts the individual's ability to locate these schemas within meaningful relationships and a known cohesive self.* This is consistent with disorders involving "neurotic" conflicts and defenses that are the focus of psychoanalytic theory (O'Neil, 1997), as well as those involving more primitive self-fragmentation and self-object defenses.

For example, two African American Vietnam veterans had similar symptoms of PTSD. One had served as a rifleman. He had difficulty with intense rage that was triggered by perceived injustice or disrespect. He had a history of periodically "seeing red and losing it" (i.e., aggressive outbursts that had led to loss of jobs, loss of relationships, and incarceration). The other man was a former medic who had suppressed the rage that he felt when he witnessed intentional exploitation or harm of vulnerable persons. He had a history of severe depression, suicidality, stress-related medical illness, aborted education degrees, and homelessness "on the streets and in the woods."

Both veterans had chronic PTSD and recurrent affect dysregulation associated with impulsive aggression (see the following), but only the second veteran had structural dissociation. The second veteran was unable to maintain a stable sense of self or relatedness to others due to alternating states of mind that were dominated by mixtures of rage, emptiness, altruistic concern, and terror. He was able to observe and reflect on the disparity among these affect/self states, but he could not integrate them when he felt emotionally overwhelmed. He compared himself to a "shattered ... mirror that breaks into pieces whenever I try to look at me and hold myself together." The first veteran overcame his strong distrust and developed a committed attachment to his therapy group; the second veteran showed a more disorganized attachment to the therapy group—at times insightful and committed, yet periodically alternating between detachment and crisis.

30.3.2 Dissociation and Impulsive Aggression

Davidson (2000, p. 593) hypothesizes that affect dysregulation can precipitate impulsive aggression when serotonergic pathways in ventral and orbital areas of the prefrontal cortex fail to inhibit the amygdala and anterior cingulate (Churchland & Churchland, 2002; Eisenberger, Lieberman, & Williams, 2003; Schnider, 2001; Van Veen & Carter, 2002). Impulsive aggression involves a failure to: (1) modulate stress responses involving the hypothalamus, brainstem, and autonomic nervous system, (2) modulate negative emotions by incorporating information about the social context, (3) accurately monitor the source of perceptions and impulses, and (4) shift from emotion-driven impulsivity or aggression to planful goal-directed decisions and actions.

Dissociation is not necessarily involved in impulsive aggression. However, breakdown in self- and relational-representations (that otherwise sustain judgment and self-protection even in the face of intense negative affects and impulses) may escalate distress into aggressive risk-taking or self-harm due to #1). Thus, if one loses contact with the self- and relational-representations that support affect regulation and behavioral control, even transient experiences of anger or desperation, confusion, and impulsivity may escalate into chronic impulsive aggression.

Posttraumatic dissociative symptoms involve dysregulation in several biological systems that contribute directly or indirectly to impulsive aggression: (1) glutamate release (Chambers et al., 1999); (2) brainstem, midbrain, and limbic (hippocampal) areas (specifically related to the intensity of flashbacks (Osuch et al., 2001); and (3) prefrontal, anterior cingulate, hippocampus, and midbrain structures that are responsible for pain tolerance (Price, 2000), impulse control, problem solving, focused attention, and appetitive behavior (specifically related to self-harm; Bohus et al., 1999).

30.3.3 Dissociation and Somatoform Distress

In DESNOS, somataform distress reflects a sense of being dissociated from, and trapped in, a body that is profoundly damaged, frozen, empty, tortured, malformed, or falling apart. The former medic with complex PTSD believed that other person's bodies were sacred ("a temple for which I was trained to be the healer"), but he experienced his own body as an irreparably damaged foreign object. The woman who had complex PTSD following childhood sexual abuse was medically healthy. Nevertheless, she often felt that her body would not let her rest; she experienced her PTSD hyperarousal symptoms as a struggle between her mind and her body.

Somatoform dissociation involves dysregulation (Nijenhuis et al., 2002) of CNS areas that handle sensory processing (e.g., thalamus, midbrain, sensory association cortices; Simeon et al., 2000; Vuillemier et al.,

2001) and that infuse perceptions with self-awareness (e.g., anterior cingulate; Adolphs, 2002; Hariri et al., 2000). Neuroimaging studies have linked acute dissociation, chronic posttraumatic dissociation (Lanius et al., 2002, 2003), and alexithymia (Henry et al., 1992; Lane, Ahern, Schwartz, & Kazniak, 1997) to these same corticolimbic brain areas. Thus, neuroimaging findings are consistent with a binary model of the somatic component of DESNOS. That is, somatic symptoms in DESNOS involve both somatization and the preconscious "animal defenses" of somatoform dissociation (Nijenhuis, 1999).

30.3.4 Dissociation and Sexual Violation

Sexual trauma, particularly childhood sexual trauma, is strongly related to dissociative symptoms in adult clinical samples. Sexual trauma predicts both somatoform and psychoform dissociation; physical abuse predicts somatoform (but not psychoform) dissociation (Nijenhuis, Spinhoven, Van Dyck, Van der Hart, & Vanderlinden, 1998). Zanarini and colleagues (2000) identified five risk factors for dissociation in personality-disordered psychiatric patients, three involving sexual trauma (i.e., sexual abuse by a caretaker, witnessing sexual violence as a child, and rape in adulthood). The other two risk factors that predicted association were borderline personality disorder and remembering their primary caregivers as being emotionally inconsistent or neglectful. Similarly, Draijer and Langeland (1999) reported that childhood sexual abuse, physical abuse, and maternal dysfunction were risk factors for dissociative symptoms among adult psychiatric patients—even after controlling for the effects of gender, age, witnessing domestic violence, and separation from primary caregivers. *Severe* sexual abuse was associated with the highest levels of dissociative symptoms. Thus, the relationship between childhood sexual abuse and dissociation appears to be robust.

The SIDES assesses sexual violation by asking about aversion to, avoidance of, or preoccupation with, physical touch or sexual contact. These attitudes and behaviors reflect an attempt to prevent memories and experiences of sexual violation from intruding into consciousness. The SIDES does *not* assess two other key aspects of sexual violation, namely feelings of: (1) having been violated or damaged by physical or sexual contact; and (2) being starved for touch and sexual contact.

The unique feature of sexual violation symptoms in complex PTSD is their dissociative quality. Sex and physical contact elicit fragmented and unstable self-representations and relational schemas that are infused with alternately intense and empty affect. Patients describe being unable to reconcile, or even live with, a split between (1) their nurturant self-awareness (e.g., "I need and deserve physical and psychological privacy, safety, comfort, intimacy, and pleasure") and (2) their intense disgust or terror in response to thoughts of, or desires for, touch or sexual contact. One patient said, "Being touched makes me long to be held forever. Then I feel disgusted with myself for being weak and I remember that it's my job to take care of other people and I don't deserve anything. That makes me determined to hurt anyone who tries to touch me—just like they're going to hurt me."

30.4 IMPLICATIONS FOR DIAGNOSTIC CLASSIFICATION

Both the construct of DESNOS and its operationalization are controversial. DESNOS was not included as a diagnostic category in the fourth edition of *The Diagnostic and Statistical Manual of Mental Disorders* (DSM-IV; American Psychiatric Association, 1994), but its symptoms were listed as associated features of PTSD. These decisions with regard to DSM-IV were based, in part, on the finding that most persons who met the criteria for DESNOS also met the criteria for PTSD (Van der Kolk et al., 1996).

Data from the DSM-IV PTSD Field Trial showed that dissociation, affect dysregulation, and somatization were each problematic for 70% to 90% of community or clinical research participants who were diagnosed with lifetime PTSD. Van der Kolk and colleagues (1996, pp. 89–90) concluded that the symptoms of DESNOS are best conceptualized as "associated features of PTSD [that are] not likely to constitute separate 'double diagnoses' but represent the complex somatic, cognitive, affective, and behavioral effects of psychological trauma." The Field Trial data, however, did *not* show dissociation, somatization, and affect dysregulation to be isomorphic with PTSD; each of these symptoms shared only 26% to 28% of its variance with PTSD (Van der Kolk et al., 1996, Table 30.1). Thus, despite DESNOS's strong correlation with PTSD, features of DESNOS may still occur independently of PTSD; many trauma survivors, who had *not* suffered from PTSD, nevertheless met the DESNOS criteria for dissociation (61%), somatization (47%), and affect dysregulation (34% to 37%). Because a diagnosis of DESNOS requires the simultaneous presence of all seven features, many non-DESNOS field trial participants still displayed several DESNOS symptoms.

Subsequently, Ford (1999) replicated the Field Trial's findings of (1) an association between PTSD and DESNOS, and (2) the etiologic distinction between the two syndromes.

Ford reported that DESNOS (but not PTSD) was associated with interpersonal trauma in early childhood; and PTSD (but not DESNOS) was associated with war zone trauma and witnessing war atrocities. DESNOS (but not PTSD) was related to *participation* in war zone atrocities. Finally, DESNOS (but not PTSD) was associated with extreme levels of intrusive symptoms, impaired characterological functioning (i.e., compromised object relations), and high utilization of psychiatric acute care (Ford, 1999).

Both PTSD and DESNOS occurred in 60% of the veterans in this study. PTSD and DESNOS were highly comorbid, but were not isomorphic. Almost 50% of those with DESNOS did *not* meet the diagnostic criteria for PTSD; this finding was quite different from the DSM-IV PTSD Field Trial in which only 8% of persons with DESNOS did not have PTSD (Roth et al., 1997; Van der Kolk et al., 1996). DESNOS was often accompanied by depression and ASPD or borderline personality disorder. This comorbidity is consistent with the view that DESNOS is a complex variant of PTSD that is comorbid with, but distinct from, PTSD itself. Further evidence of the singularity of DESNOS comes from treatment outcome data. DESNOS patients from Ford's sample had poorer outcomes than PTSD patients (i.e., higher rates of dropout from inpatient treatment), even after controlling for child abuse, depression, and personality disorder (Ford & Kidd, 1998).

Two of the 17 symptoms of traditional PTSD often are considered dissociative (i.e., flashbacks and amnesia for important parts of traumatic experiences). Yet, neither of these symptoms necessarily is dissociative. Flashbacks are dissociative only if they involve a loss of self-representations due to affect dysregulation and disorganized attachment. For example, a flashback of childhood abuse is not dissociative *unless* the person loses awareness of being (1) the adult in whom the childlike feelings reside and (2) the adult who can recall these experiences without actually reliving them. In this case, dissociation is evident because the person's self-representations do not include: (1) being the same person as the child, (2) having an accessible store of experiential knowledge that was not yet formed or psychically unavailable to himself as a child, (3) knowing how this experiential knowledge base evolved as the result of trustworthy and facilitative relationships and effective self-assertion, and (4) an ability to translate this knowledge of self and others into an empathic connection to himself as a child that is affectively soothing and that would have been reassuring and protective to him as a child. Similarly, posttraumatic amnesia is dissociative *only* if the person not only cannot recall events or experiences, but also *cannot recognize the self who had those experiences and the relationships that formed the context for those experiences.*

Borderline personality disorder (BPD) shares a number of features with DESNOS and was the impetus for the development of DESNOS as a nosological entity (Herman, 1992). BPD may involve structural dissociation (Zanarini et al., 2000). Three BPD features parallel core aspects of structural dissociation: marked reactivity of mood, unstable relationships characterized by alternating idealization and devaluation, and markedly unstable sense of self. In addition, terror of abandonment may elicit a fugue-like trance state that is accompanied by an absent or fluctuating (1) sense of self, (2) security in and sense of connectedness to stable relationships, and (3) ability to tolerate separation and self-soothe (i.e., affect regulation). Similarly, rage, self-harm, or impulsivity can occur in an altered state of consciousness that includes emotional flooding or detachment and a profound sense of alienation in which the self or other persons are seen as damaged and damaging (Adler, 1985) or utterly empty and absent (Balint, 1963). Thus, *BPD often, but not always, involves structural dissociation.*

30.5 CONCLUSION

Dissociation may offer an organizing construct for research and clinical treatment of DESNOS. Nevertheless, advances in the conceptualization and measurement of dissociation are greatly needed (Van der Hart & Dorahy, this volume, Chapter 1). Research on the impact of developmentally adverse interpersonal trauma provides two clinically and scientifically relevant observations: (1) affect regulation, core self-representations, and object relations are profoundly altered by developmentally adverse trauma; and (2) our current nosology poorly accounts for these effects of early trauma. For DESNOS to become an accepted clinical syndrome, an organizing paradigm and biopsychosocial mechanism will be needed—and dissociation could play an instrumental role in that paradigm.

I would like to thank Paul Dell, Ellert Nijenhuis, Kathy Steele, Onno van der Hart, and Bessel van der Kolk for their substantive and editorial comments on earlier drafts of this chapter. Writing of the chapter was supported by a K23 career development grant from the National Institute of Mental Health, *MH01889-01A1* (J. Ford, PI).

REFERENCES

Adler, (1985). *Borderline psychopathology and its treatment.* San Francisco: Jason Aronson.

Adolphs, R. (2001). The neurobiology of social cognition. *Current Opinion in Neurobiology, 11,* 231–239.

Adolphs, R. (2002). Neural systems for recognizing emotion. *Current Opinion in Neurobiology, 12,* 169–177.

Allen, N., & Badcock, P. (2003). The social risk hypothesis of depressed mood. *Psychological Bulletin, 129,* 887–913.

Almqvist, K., & Broberg, A. G. (2003). Young children traumatized by organized violence together with their mothers—The critical effects of damaged internal representations. *Attachment & Human Development, 5,* 367–380.

Arnsten, A. F. T. (1998). The biology of being frazzled. *Science, 280,* 1711–1712.

Baddeley, A. (2002). The concept of episodic memory. In A. Baddeley & J. Aggleton (Eds.), *Episodic memory* (pp. 1–10). London: Oxford University Press.

Balint, E. (1963). On being empty of oneself. *International Journal of Psycho-Analysis, 44,* 470–480.

Benatar, M. (2003). Surviving the bad object. *Journal of Trauma and Dissociation, 4*(2), 11–25.

Blizard, R. A. (1997). The origins of dissociative identity disorder from an object relations and attachment theory perspective. *Dissociation, 10,* 223–229.

Bohus, M. J., Landwehrmeyer, G. B., Stiglmayr, C. E., Limberger, M. F., Boehme, R., & Schmahl, C. G. (1999). Naltrexone in the treatment of dissociative symptoms in patients with borderline personality disorder: An open-label trial. *Journal of Clinical Psychiatry, 60,* 598–603.

Bowlby, J. (1969). *Attachment and loss,* Volume I. New York: Basic Books.

Braude, S. E. (1995). *First person plural: Multiple personality and the philosophy of mind* (revised ed.). Lanham, England: Rowman & Littlefield.

Bremner, J. D., & Vermetten, E. (2001). Stress and development: behavioral and biological consequences. *Development and Psychopathology, 13,* 473–489.

Brewin, C. R. (2001). A cognitive neuroscience account of posttraumatic stress disorder and its treatment. *Behaviour Research and Therapy, 39,* 373–393.

Buck, R. (1999). The biological affects: a typology. *Psychological Review, 106,* 301–336.

Chambers, R., Bremner, J. D., Moghaddam, B., Southwick, S., Charney, D., & Krystal, J. (1999). Glutamate and PTSD: A psychobiology of dissociation. *Seminars in Clinical Neuropsychiatry, 4,* 274–284.

Churchland, P. S., & Churchland, P. M. (2002). Neural worlds and real worlds. *Nature Reviews Neuroscience, 3,* 903–907.

Cicchetti, D., & Rogosch, F. (2001). The impact of child maltreatment and psychopathology on neuroendocrine function. *Development and Psychopathology, 13,* 783–804.

Collette, F., & Van der Linden, M. (2002). Brain imaging of the central executive component of working memory. *Neuroscience & Biobehavioral Reviews, 26,* 105–125.

Craig, A. D. (2002). How do you feel? Interoception: the sense of the physiological condition of the body. *Nature Reviews Neuroscience, 3*(8), 655–666.

Davidson, R. (2002). Anxiety and affective style: role of prefrontal cortex and amygdala. *Biological Psychiatry, 51,* 68–80.

DeBellis, M. (2001). Developmental traumatology. *Psychoneuroendocrinology, 27,* 155–170.

Dell, P. F. (2009). The phenomenology of chronic pathological dissociation. In P. F. Dell & J. A. O'Neil (Eds.), *Dissociation and the dissociative disorders: DSM-V and beyond* (pp. 225–237). New York: Routledge.

Doussard-Roosevelt, J., Porges, S., Scanlon, J., Alemi, B., & Scanlon, K. (1997). Vagal regulation of heart rate in the prediction of developmental outcome for very low birth weight preterm infants. *Child Development, 68,* 173–186.

Draijer, N., & Langeland, W. (1999). Childhood trauma and perceived parental dysfunction in the etiology of dissociative symptoms in psychiatric inpatients. *American Journal of Psychiatry, 156,* 379–385.

Eisenberger, N., Lieberman, M., & Williams, K. (2003). Does rejection hurt? An FMRI study of social exclusion. *Science, 302*(5643), 237–239.

Felitti, V., Anda, R., Nordenberg, D., Williamson, D., Spitz, A., Edwards, V., Koss, M., & Marks, J. (1998). Relationship of childhood abuse and household dysfunction to many of the leading causes of death in adults: the Adverse Childhood Experiences (ACE) study. *American Journal of Preventive Medicine, 14,* 245–258.

Ford, J. D. (1999). PTSD and disorders of extreme stress following warzone military trauma. *Journal of Consulting and Clinical Psychology, 67,* 3–12.

Ford, J. D. (2005). Treatment implications of altered neurobiology, affect regulation and information processing following child maltreatment. *Psychiatric Annals, 35,* 410–419.

Ford, J. D., & Frisman, L. (2002, December). *Complex PTSD among Homeless and Addicted Women.* Paper presented at the Annual Meeting of the International Society for Traumatic Stress Studies.

Ford, J. D., & Kidd, P. (1998). Early childhood trauma and disorders of extreme stress as predictors of treatment outcome with chronic PTSD. *Journal of Traumatic Stress, 11,* 743–761.

Ford, J. D., Stockton, P., Kaltman, S., & Green, B. L. (2006). Disorders of Extreme Stress (DESNOS) symptoms are associated with interpersonal trauma exposure in a sample of healthy young women. *Journal of Interpersonal Violence, 21,* 1399–1416.

Frith, U., & Frith, C. D. (2003). Development and neurophysiology of mentalizing. *Philosophical Transactions of the Royal Society of London, 358* (1431), 459–473.

Glisky, E., Ryan, L., & Reminger, S. (2004). A case of psychogenic fugue: I understand, aber ich verstehe nichts. *Neuropsychologia, 42,* 1132–1147.

Hariri, A. R., Bookheimer, S. Y., & Mazziotta, J. C. (2000). Modulating emotional responses: effects of a neocortical network on the limbic system. *Neuroreport, 11,* 43–48.

Heim, C., & Nemeroff, C. (2001). The role of childhood trauma in the neurobiology of mood and anxiety disorders. *Biological Psychiatry, 49,* 1023–1039.

Henry, J. P., Haviland, M. G., Cummings, M. A., Anderson, D. L., Nelson, J. C., MacMurray, J. P., McGhee, W. H., & Hubbard, R. W. (1992). Shared neuroendocrine patterns of post-traumatic-stress disorder and alexithymia. *Psychosomatic Medicine, 54,* 407–415.

Herman, J. (1992). *Trauma and recovery.* New York: Basic Books.

Hobfoll, S. E., Johnson, R. J., Ennis, N. E., & Jackson, A. P. (2003). Resource loss, resource gain, and emotional outcomes among inner-city women. *Journal of Personality and Social Psychology, 84,* 632–643.

Horowitz, M. (2002). Defining character integrity. *Journal of the American Psychoanalytic Association, 50,* 551–573.

Kagan, J. (2001). Emotional development and psychiatry. *Biological Psychiatry, 49,* 973–979.

Kaufman, J., Plotsky, P., Nemeroff, C., & Charney, D. (2000). Effects of early adverse experiences on brain structure and function: clinical implications. *Biological Psychiatry, 48,* 778–790.

Koren-Karie, N., Sagi-Schwartz, A., & Joels, T. (2003). Absence of attachment representations (AAR) in the adult years: The emergence of a new AAI classification in catastrophically traumatized Holocaust child survivors. *Attachment & Human Development, 5,* 381–397.

Lane, R., Ahern, G., Schwartz, G., & Kaszniak, A. (1997). Is alexithymia the emotional equivalent of blindsight? *Biological Psychiatry, 42,* 832–844.

Lanius, R., Hopper, J., & Menon, R. (2003). Individual differences in a husband and wife who developed PTSD after a motor vehicle accident. *American Journal of Psychiatry, 160,* 667–669.

Lanius, R., Williamson, P., Boksman, K., Densmore, M., Gupta, M., Neufeld, R., Gati, J., & Menon, R. (2002). Brain activation during script-driven imagery induced dissociative responses in PTSD: a functional magnetic resonance imaging investigation. *Biological Psychiatry, 52,* 305–311.

Leverich, G., McElroy, S., Suppes, T., Keck, P., Denicoff, K., Nolen, W., Altshuler, L., Rush, A. J., Hapka, R., Frye, M., Autio, K., & Post, R. (2002). Early physical and sexual abuse associated with an adverse course of bipolar illness. *Biological Psychiatry, 51,* 288–297.

Lyons-Ruth, K., & Jacobvitz, D. (1999). Attachment Disorganization: Unresolved loss, relational violence, and lapses in behavioral and attentional strategies. In J. Cassidy & P. Shaver (Eds.), *Handbook of attachment: Theory, research, and clinical implications* (pp. 520–554). New York: Guildford.

Lysaker, P., Meyer, P., Evans J., Clements, C., & Marks, K. (2001). Childhood sexual trauma and psychosocial functioning in adults with schizophrenia. *Psychiatric Services, 52,* 1485–1488.

Maunder, R., & Hunter, J. (2001). Attachment and psychosomatic medicine; developmental contributions to stress and disease. *Psychosomatic Medicine, 63,* 556–567.

McEwen, B. (2002). The neurobiology and neuroendocrinology of stress. *Psychiatric Clinics of North America, 25,* 469–494.

Nijenhuis, E. R. S. (1999). *Somatoform dissociation: Phenomena, measurement, and theoretical issues.* Assen, the Netherlands: Van Gorcum.

Nijenhuis, E. R. S., Spinhoven, P., Van Dyck, R., Van der Hart, O., & Vanderlinden, J. (1998). Degree of somatoform and psychological dissociation in dissociative disorder is correlated with reported trauma. *Journal of Traumatic Stress, 11,* 711–730.

Nijenhuis, E. R. S., Van der Hart, O., & Steele, K. (2002). The emerging psychobiology of trauma-related dissociation and dissociative disorders. In H. D'haenen, J. den Boer, & P. Wilner (Eds.), *Biological Psychiatry* (pp. 1079–1098). London: John Wiley & Sons.

Nijenhuis, E. R. S., Van der Hart, O., & Steele, K. (2005). Dissociation: An insufficiently recognized feature of complex PTSD. *Journal of Traumatic Stress, 18,* 413–423.

Northoff, G., Richter, A., Gessner, M., Schlagenhauf, F., Fell, J., Baumgart, F., Kaulisch, T., Kotter, R., Stephan, K., Leschinger, A., Tilman-Hagner, T., Bargel, B., Witzel, T., Hinrichs, H., Bogerts, B., Scheich, H., & Heinze, H. (2000). Functional dissociation between medial and lateral prefrontal cortical spatiotemporal activation in negative and positive emotions: a combined fMRI/MEG study. *Cerebral Cortex, 10,* 93–107.

Ogden, P., & Fisher, J. (in press). Sensorimotor psychotherapy for complex traumatic stress disorders. In C A. Courtois & J. D. Ford (Eds.), *Complex psychological trauma disorders: An evidence-based clinician's guide.* New York: Guilford.

O'Neil, J. (1997). Expanding the psychoanalytic view of the intrapsychic: Psychic conflict in the inscape. *Dissociation, 10,* 192–202.

Osuch, E., Benson, B., Geraci, M., Podell, D., Herscovitch, P., McCann, U., & Post, R. (2001). Regional cerebral blood flow correlated with flashback intensity in patients with posttraumatic stress disorder. *Biological Psychiatry, 50,* 246–253.

Patterson, D., & Schmidt, L. (2003). Neuroanatomy of the human affective system. *Brain and Cognition, 52,* 24–26.

Pelcovitz, D., Van der Kolk, B., Roth, S., Mandel, F., Kaplan, S., & Resick, P. (1997). Development of a criteria set and a structured interview for disorders of extreme stress (DESNOS). *Journal of Traumatic Stress, 10,* 3–16.

Price, D. (2000). Psychological and neural mechanisms of the affective dimension of pain. *Science, 288,* 1769–1772.

Reinders, A. A., Nijenhuis, E. R., Paans, A. M., Korf, J., Willemsen, A. T., & Den Boer, J. A. (2003). One brain, two selves. *Neuroimage, 20,* 2119–2125.

Roth, S., Newman, E., Pelcovitz, D., Van der Kolk, B., & Mandel, F. (1997). Complex PTSD in victims exposed to sexual and physical abuse. *Journal of Traumatic Stress, 10,* 539–555.

Şar, V., Ünal, S. N., & Öztürk, E. (2007). Frontal and occipital perfusion changes in dissociative identity disorder. *Psychiatry Research: Neuroimaging, 156,* 217–223.

Schnider, A. (2001). Spontaneous confabulation, reality monitoring, and the limbic system: a review. *Brain Research Reviews, 36*, 150–160.

Schore, A. (2001a). Effects of a secure attachment relationship on right brain development, affect regulation, and infant mental health. *Infant Mental Health Journal, 22*, 7–66.

Schore, A. (2001b). The effects of early relational trauma on right brain development, affect regulation, and infant mental health. *Infant Mental Health Journal, 22*, 201–269.

Scoboria, A., Ford, J. D., Lin, H., & Frisman, L. (2008). Exploratory and confirmatory factor analyses of the Structured Interview for Disorders of Extreme Stress. *Assessment*, http://asm.sagepub.com/cgi/rapidpdf/1073191108319005v1<http://asm.sagepub.com/cgi/rapidpdf/1073191108319005v1> (Accessed November 17, 2008).

Sheppard, L., & Teasdale, J. (2004). How does dysfunctional thinking decrease during recovery from major depression? *Journal of Abnormal Psychology, 113*, 64–71.

Simeon, D., Guralnik, O., Hazlett, E. A., Spiegel-Cohen, J., Hollander, E., & Buchsbaum, M. S. (2000). Feeling unreal: a PET study of depersonalization disorder. *American Journal of Psychiatry, 157*, 1782–1788.

Van der Kolk, B., Pelcovitz, D., Roth, S., Mandel, F., McFarlane, A., & Herman, J. (1996). Dissociation, somatization, and affect dysregulation: Complexity of adaptation to trauma. *American Journal of Psychiatry, 153* (7 Festschrift Supplement), 83–93.

Van der Hart, O., & Dorahy, M. (2009). Dissociation: History of a concept. In P. F. Dell & J. A. O'Neil (Eds.), *Dissociation and the dissociative disorders: DSM-V and beyond* (pp. 3–26). New York: Routledge.

Van der Hart, O., Nijenhuis, E., Steele, K., & Brown, D. (2004). Trauma-related dissociation: Conceptual clarity lost and found. *Australian & New Zealand Journal of Psychiatry, 38*, 906–914.

Van Horn, P., & Lieberman, A. (in press). Using dyadic therapies to treat traumatized children. In D. Brom, R. Pat-Horenzcyk, & J. D. Ford (Eds.), *Traumatized children: Risk, resilience and recovery.* London: Routledge.

Van Veen, V., & Carter, C. S. (2002). The anterior cingulate as a conflict monitor: fMRI and ERP studies. *Physiology & Behavior, 77*, 477–482.

Vianna, D., Graeff, F., Landeira-Fernandez, J., & Brandão, M. (2001). Lesion of the ventral periaqueductal gray reduces conditioned fear but does not change freezing induced by stimulation of the dorsal periaqueductal gray. *Learning & Memory, 8*, 164–169.

Vuillemier, P., Chicerio, C., Asal, F., Schwartz, S., Slosmen, D., & Landis, T. (2001). Functional neuroanatomical correlates of hysterical sensorimotor loss. *Brain, 124*, 1077–1090.

Winston, J., Strange, B., & O'Doherty, J. (2002). Automatic and intentional brain responses during evaluation of trustworthiness of faces. *Nature Neuroscience, 5*, 277–283.

Yehuda, R., Spertus, I., & Golier, J. (2001). Relationship between childhood traumatic experiences and PTSD in adults. In S. Eth (Ed.), *PTSD in children and adolescents* (pp. 117–158). Washington: American Psychiatric Press.

Young, L. (2002). The neurobiology of social recognition, approach, and avoidance. *Biological Psychiatry, 51*, 18–26.

Zanarini, M., Ruser, T., Frankenburg, F., Hennen, J., & Gunderson, J. (2000). Risk factors associated with the dissociative experiences of borderline patients. *Journal of Nervous and Mental Disease, 188*, 26–30.

Part IX

Dissociation in Borderline Personality Disorder and Substance Dependence

31 Dissociation in Borderline Personality Disorder

Mary C. Zanarini, EdD
Shari Jager-Hyman, MA

OUTLINE

The relationship in the psychiatric literature between borderline personality disorder (BPD) and dissociation is long and complicated. In early phenomenological studies, dissociation (i.e., depersonalization and/or derealization) was assessed categorically and described as a psychotic or psychotic-like symptom. The main goals of these phenomenological studies were to assess the prevalence of dissociative symptoms in patients meeting criteria for BPD and to determine if these rates were significantly different in borderline and comparison subjects. In other words, these studies were addressing the question: "Are depersonalization and derealization both characteristic of, and discriminating for, the borderline diagnosis?"

More recent studies have assessed dissociation dimensionally. The main goal of these studies was to determine the severity of the dissociative symptoms of BPD, which were conceptualized as experiences ranging from the normality of absorption, through depersonalization, to the extreme of amnesia and identity fragmentation.

All of these more recent studies also investigated the etiology or the putative etiology of these dissociative experiences. Some of these studies have characterized dissociation as a serious symptom intrinsic to BPD, while others have conceptualized dissociation as a trauma-related symptom.

Each of these waves of phenomenological studies will be reviewed in detail. Studies of the etiology of dissociation in borderline patients will then be reviewed. Finally, the small literature on the overlap of BPD and dissociative disorders will be presented and their implications for DSM-V discussed.

31.1 EARLY STUDIES OF DISSOCIATION AND BPD

Between 1968 and 1990, 28 studies were published that described some aspect of the cognition of borderline patients (Carpenter & Gunderson, 1977; Carpenter, Gunderson, & Strauss, 1977; Conte, Plutchik, Karasu, & Jerrett, 1980; Chopra & Beatson, 1986; Frances, Clarkin, Gilmore, Hurt, & Brown, 1984; George & Soloff, 1986; Grinker, Werble, & Drye, 1968; Gunderson, 1977; Gunderson, Carpenter, & Strauss, 1975; Gunderson & Kolb, 1978; Jacobsberg, Hymowitz, Barasch, & Frances, 1986; Koenigsberg, 1982; Links, Steiner, & Mitton, 1989; McGlashan, 1987; Nurnberg, Hurt, Feldman, & Suh, 1988; Perry & Klerman, 1980; Pope, Jonas, Hudson, Cohen, & Tohen, 1985; Sheehy, Goldsmith, & Charles, 1980; Silk, Lohr, Western, & Goodrich, 1989; Snyder & Pitts, 1986; Soloff, 1981a, 1981b; Soloff & Ulrich, 1981; Spitzer, Endicott, & Gibbon, 1979; Tarnopolsky & Berelowitz, 1984; Werble, 1970; Widiger, Frances, Warner, & Bluhm, 1986; Zanarini, Gunderson, & Frankenburg, 1990). Of these, only 12 actually studied dissociative symptoms in some way. While all of these

12 studies assessed the presence of dissociation categorically, seven relied on clinically diagnosed samples of borderline patients and five used a semistructured interview to diagnose BPD.

31.1.1 Studies of Clinically Diagnosed Borderline Patients

In the first of these studies, Gunderson, Carpenter, and Strauss (1975) studied matched samples of 24 borderline and 29 schizophrenic inpatients. They found that 57% of the borderline patients and 79% of the schizophrenic patients reported dissociative symptoms. They also found that these symptoms were significantly less common among borderline than schizophrenic patients.

Gunderson (1977) later conducted another cross-sectional study of borderline phenomenology. He studied three groups of inpatients: 31 borderline patients, 22 schizophrenic patients, and 11 neurotic depressives. He found that depersonalization was more common than derealization among borderline patients. He also found that severe and/or continuous dissociative experiences were rare. However, the derealization (but not the depersonalization) experiences of borderline patients were significantly less common than those reported by schizophrenic comparison subjects. This was the first study to use Gunderson's Diagnostic Interview for Borderlines (DIB) (Gunderson, Kolb, & Austin, 1981) to assess the phenomenology of BPD.

Soloff (1981b) replicated Gunderson's study. Thirty-six borderline and/or schizotypal inpatients (all of whom were at that time thought to be in the borderline realm), 31 inpatients with schizophrenia, and 27 unipolar depressed inpatients were interviewed with the DIB. No significant differences between borderline and schizophrenic patients were found on items measuring depersonalization and derealization. However, depersonalization was significantly more common among borderline than depressed comparison subjects.

Koenigsberg (1982) also conducted a replication study of Gunderson's (1977) assessment of borderline phenomenology. Fourteen borderline inpatients, 24 borderline outpatients, and 24 inpatients with schizophrenia were studied. No significant differences in dissociative phenomena were found between inpatient and outpatient borderline subjects. While both depersonalization and derealization were more common among borderline inpatients than schizophrenic inpatients, these differences were not significant.

Conte and colleagues (1980) used a 52-item self-report questionnaire, the Borderline Symptom Index (BSI), to study three groups of clinically diagnosed patients: 35 borderline outpatients, 36 outpatients with nonpsychotic depression, and 20 inpatients meeting DSM-III criteria for schizophrenia. Fifty normal subjects who had never been hospitalized for psychiatric reasons were also studied. Two of the BSI items pertain to depersonalization ("I feel as if I am watching myself in a play," "I seem to live in a fog"), while none pertain to derealization. The first depersonalization item was endorsed by a significantly higher percentage of borderline patients (52%) than depressed patients (19%) or normal comparison subjects (6%). However, the second depersonalization item only successfully discriminated the borderline patients from the normal comparison subjects (57% vs. 4%).

Perry and Klerman (1980) studied the performance of 120 outpatients on the Borderline Ego Functions Inventory (EFI), a measure developed by Perry to diagnose BPD and to assess borderline psychopathology. They compared the ratings of 18 clinically diagnosed borderline patients to those of 102 comparison subjects with a variety of psychotic and nonpsychotic clinical diagnoses. Borderline patients were significantly more likely than comparison subjects to report experiencing episodic and chronic depersonalization as well as episodic (but not chronic) derealization.

Sheehy, Goldsmith, and Charles (1980) studied the phenomenology of four clinically diagnosed groups of outpatients on a 16-item checklist, which they had devised. These groups were: (1) 45 borderline patients, (2) 30 schizophrenic patients, (3) 30 patients with other forms of personality disorder, and (4) 30 patients with neurotic disorders. They found that borderline patients were significantly more likely than neurotic comparison subjects to have had episodes of dissociation.

31.1.2 Studies Using Semi-Structured Interviews to Diagnose BPD

Chopra and Beatson (1986) studied the cognitive symptoms of 13 DIB-diagnosed borderline inpatients. They found that dissociative experiences were almost ubiquitous. More specifically, they found that derealization was present in 92% and depersonalization in 85%.

Nurnberg and associates (1988) assessed the overall phenomenology of BPD in 17 inpatients meeting DIB criteria for BPD and 20 normal comparison subjects. Forty-seven percent of the borderline patients, but only 5% of the comparison subjects, reported being depersonalized and/or derealized.

Links, Steiner, and Mitton (1989) studied the cognitive functioning of 88 DIB-diagnosed borderline inpatients and compared their cognitive experiences to those of 42 inpatients with borderline traits (and a variety of Axis I diagnoses). They found that experiences of depersonalization and/or derealization were significantly more common among those with definite BPD than those with borderline traits.

Silk and his associates (1989) studied the cognitive performance of 20 DIB-diagnosed borderline inpatients with concurrent major depression and compared it to that of 20 depressed inpatients. Definite or possible depersonalization was significantly more common among borderline patients than depressed comparison subjects (46% vs. 10%). Definite or possible derealization was also more common among borderline patients (42% vs. 15%), but not significantly so. In addition, definite depersonalization and/or derealization were significantly more common among borderline patients than depressed comparison subjects (37% vs. 10%).

Zanarini, Gunderson, and Frankenburg (1990) studied the cognition of four groups of subjects: 50 outpatients meeting both the Revised Diagnostic Interview for Borderlines (DIB-R) (Zanarini, Gunderson, Frankenburg, & Chauncey, 1989) and DSM-III criteria for BPD, 55 outpatients meeting DSM-III criteria for another Axis II disorder, 32 schizophrenic patients, and 46 normal comparison subjects. Thirty-six percent of borderline patients reported depersonalization experiences during the past two years and 30% reported feeling derealized. The rate of depersonalization was significantly higher among borderline patients than among those in all three of the other groups studied. The rate of derealization was significantly higher among borderline patients than those with other Axis II disorders and normal comparison subjects (but not patients with schizophrenia).

Taken together, two main findings have emerged from the results of these studies. First, both depersonalization and derealization are relatively common among borderline patients. Depersonalization was reported by 36% to 85% of borderline patients, with a median of 52%. Derealization was reported by 30% to 92%, with a median of 42%. Second, dissociative experiences, particularly depersonalization, are significantly more common among borderline patients than among all comparison groups studied except for patients with schizophrenia. The inconsistent findings with regard to schizophrenia might be due to the changing definition of schizophrenia over the years; the pre-DSM-III studies of Gunderson (1975, 1977) diagnosed a broader range of patients as having schizophrenia than more recent studies.

31.2 SECOND-GENERATION STUDIES

Second-generation studies used the Dissociative Experiences Scale or DES (Bernstein & Putnam, 1986) to measure dissociation in borderline patients and comparison subjects. The DES is a 28-item self-report questionnaire that yields an overall mean score and three sector scores: absorption, depersonalization, and amnesia. Each item is rated by the patient according to the percentage of time that he or she has had that experience within a specified time period.

Shearer (1994) studied dissociative symptoms in 62 female inpatients with DSM-III-R BPD. These patients had a mean DES score of 25.0 (SD = 21.2), with a range of 0–76. The 48 borderline patients without a clinical diagnosis of a dissociative disorder (mean = 20.9; SD = 19.3) and the eight borderline patients with a concurrent clinical diagnosis of dissociative disorder not otherwise specified (mean = 32.4; SD = 23.3) each had a mean DES score that was significantly lower than that of the six borderline patients with a concurrent clinical diagnosis of dissociative identity disorder (mean = 48.5; SD = 17.8).

Brodsky, Cloitre, and Dulit (1995) assessed the dissociative experiences of 60 female borderline inpatients. They found a mean DES score of 19.6 (SD = 16.4). They also found that half of these borderline subjects had a DES score of 15 or above.

Zweig-Frank, Paris, and Guzder (1994a, 1994b) conducted two studies of dissociation in DIB-R borderlines. In the first of these studies (Zweig-Frank, Paris, & Guzder, 1994a), they compared the DES scores of 78 borderline women to the DES scores of 72 women with other Axis II disorders. They found that the overall DES score of women with BPD was significantly higher than the overall mean score of the women with other personality disorders (mean = 24.8 and SD = 15.2 vs. mean = 13.2 and SD = 10.2). They also found that the absorption, depersonalization, and amnesia factor scores of the borderline subjects were significantly higher than the factor scores of the comparison women.

In their second study, Zweig-Frank, Paris, and Guzder (1994b) compared the DES scores of 32 male borderline clinic patients and 29 male borderline symptomatic volunteers (who had responded to an ad describing borderline symptoms) to those of 60 men with other Axis II disorders. The borderline patients who had responded to the newspaper ad had a significantly higher mean DES score than the borderline patients who were clinic patients. In addition, both borderline groups were found to have significantly higher mean DES scores than the comparison subjects (clinic mean = 17.8 and SD = 11.2;

advertisement mean = 27.4 and SD = 20.9; comparison subject mean = 12.5 and SD = 11.7).

Zanarini and associates (2000) used the DES to study dissociation in 290 borderline inpatients and 72 Axis II comparison subjects. They found that the mean DES score as well as the three mean factor scores of the DES (i.e., absorption, depersonalization, and amnesia) were all significantly higher than those found for Axis II comparison subjects. The overall mean DES score of the borderline subjects was 21.8 (SD = 18.6). This score suggests that, on average, borderline subjects felt dissociated about 20% of the time. However, relying on the average score of a sample of borderline patients may be misleading. In fact, 32% of the borderline patients in this study had a low level of dissociation (even when hospitalized for psychiatric reasons) (DES score of less than 10), 42% had a moderate level (DES score between 10 and 29.9), and 26% had a high level of dissociation (DES score of 30 or higher) similar to that reported by patients meeting criteria for posttraumatic stress disorder or dissociative disorders. In contrast, the comparison subjects had a significantly different distribution of overall DES scores: 71% reported a low level of dissociation, 26% reported a moderate level, and only 3% reported a high level of dissociation. As previously noted, borderline patients scored significantly higher on the three factor scores contained in the DES. In addition, they had a significantly higher score than comparison subjects on all 28 of the items that comprise the DES. Taken together, these results suggest that the severity of the dissociation experienced by borderline inpatients is more heterogeneous than previously reported. They also suggest that borderline patients have a wider range of dissociative experiences than is commonly recognized (i.e., they have experiences of absorption and amnesia as well as the more commonly studied, depersonalization). In addition, male and female borderline patients reported comparable levels of dissociation.

31.3 RISK FACTORS FOR DISSOCIATION AMONG BORDERLINE PATIENTS

Some clinicians believe that the dissociative experiences of borderline patients are linked to or caused by their adverse childhood experiences, particularly being sexually abused. This is so because numerous studies have found high rates of reported abuse (and neglect) among borderline inpatients and outpatients (Herman, Perry, & van der Kolk, 1989; Links, Steiner, Offord, & Eppe, 1988; Ogata et al., 1990; Paris, Zweig-Frank, & Guzder, 1994a, 1994b; Salzman et al., 1993; Shearer, Peters, Quaytman, & Ogden, 1990; Westen, Ludolph, Misle, Ruffins, & Block, 1990; Zanarini, Gunderson, Marino, Schwartz, & Frankenburg, 1989; Zanarini et al., 1997).

Other clinicians believe that dissociation is part of the temperamental endowment of borderline patients. In this view, dissociation is a biologically determined vulnerability or symptom.

The available empirical evidence supports both positions to some extent. Both Shearer (1994) and Brodsky and associates (1995) studied the relationship of adverse events or experiences to dissociation in uncontrolled studies of inpatient borderline subjects who were all female. (See previous discussion for more details.) Shearer found that childhood experiences of both physical and sexual abuse as well as adult experiences of sexual assault were all significant predictors of adult DES scores. Brodsky and her colleagues found that severity of childhood abuse was a significant predictor of adult DES scores.

Zweig-Frank, Paris, and Guzder (1994a, 1994b) studied dissociation, as previously noted, in two separate samples of borderline patients and Axis II comparison subjects—one female and the other male. In both samples, the borderline diagnosis was a significant predictor of severity of dissociation, but adverse childhood experiences were not, when both diagnosis and childhood adversity were studied together.

Zanarini and colleagues (2000) studied the risk factors associated with severity of dissociation in the inpatient sample of 290 borderline patients and 72 Axis II comparison subjects described previously. In the entire sample of 362 patients, the borderline diagnosis as well as four types of adverse experience were found to be predictive of the severity of dissociation: caretaker inconsistent treatment, caretaker sexual abuse, witness to sexual violence, and adult rape history. Thus, a more complicated predictive model was found in this study.

This difference between the McGill group led by Paris and the McLean group may be due to the severity of childhood abuse reported in each sample. In the McGill samples, ongoing abuse involving penetration was relatively rare (Paris el al., 1994a, 1994b). In contrast, severe abuse was the rule in the McLean sample (Zanarini et al., 2002).

31.4 NOSOLOGICAL ISSUES

The results of first-generation studies of dissociation among borderline patients led to the inclusion of an additional symptom-cluster (i.e., Criterion 9) in the DSM-IV criteria set for BPD. Criterion 9 refers to experiences of paranoia and severe dissociation. It is important to note that transient, stress-related paranoia is reported by more than 90% of borderline patients (Zanarini, Gunderson, & Frankenburg, 1990), but that severe dissociative experiences tend to be substantially less common. In practice, Criterion 9 tends to be understood as assessing stress-related, nondelusional paranoia and stress-related depersonalization and derealization. The associated text of DSM-IV states that these experiences typically are too short-lived and too mild in intensity to warrant another diagnosis.

Several studies have looked at the overlap between dissociative identity disorder (DID) and BPD. Ross and his associates (1990) studied the comorbidity of 102 cases of clinically diagnosed DID and found that 64% of these patients met DSM-III-R criteria for BPD. Şar and colleagues (1996) studied the comorbidity of 35 cases of clinically diagnosed DID and found that 31% of these patients met DSM-IV criteria for BPD. Şar and associates (2003) also conducted a study of DID and BPD in a sample of 240 consecutive patients at a university outpatient department in Turkey. They found that 25 subjects met DSM-III-R criteria for BPD and that 16 (64%) of these subjects met criteria for a dissociative disorder. One (4%) of these subjects met criteria for dissociative amnesia, 6 (24%) for DID, and 9 (36%) for dissociative disorder NOS (DDNOS).

The results of these studies are interesting and potentially clinically important. They suggest that BPD is quite common among those meeting criteria for DID, although the percentage reporting overlapping disorders ranged from 31% to 64%. However, the finding, in a third study, that 64% of borderline patients met criteria for a dissociative disorder seems problematic in two ways. First, based on our clinical and research experience, the percentage of borderline patients meeting criteria for a well-defined and severe dissociative disorder (i.e., DID or dissociative amnesia) seems high (30%), particularly as this was an outpatient sample. Second, the clinical utility of another 36% being diagnosed with DDNOS seems particularly questionable. It is important to note that the DSM-III-R criteria for BPD were used in this study. Thus, the DDNOS diagnosis may simply have captured the dissociative symptoms that are now part of DSM-IV's cognitive criterion (i.e., Criterion 9) for BPD.

In general, it would seem that only a relatively small minority of borderline patients would meet criteria for DID (and other severe dissociative disorders); these borderline patients would be expected to have a history of hospitalization. Additionally, it seems unwise to give borderline patients a comorbid dissociative diagnosis if the diagnostic criteria of that dissociative disorder overlap with the diagnostic criteria for BPD itself (e.g., depersonalization disorder, DDNOS).

This contention or series of contentions is supported by the fact that most treatment studies, whether they are of psychotropic medications (Zanarini, 2004) or psychotherapy (Gunderson, 2001), focus on the affective dysregulation, impulsivity, and troubled relationships of borderline patients. Dissociative symptoms, while common among borderline patients, do not seem to be as pressing an issue to most clinicians or treatment researchers as affective dysregulation, impulsivity, and troubled relationships.

In any case, further research needs to be conducted to determine the overlap between BPD and dissociative disorders. Large-scale studies using established interviews for both BPD and dissociative disorders are needed. Until and unless such studies find high rates of dissociative disorders among criteria-defined borderline patients, it would seem unwise to issue a comorbid dissociative diagnosis to BPD patients.

31.5 SUMMARY FINDINGS

- Depersonalization and derealization are common among borderline patients, and are reported in most studies by about a third to one-half of patients.
- Severe dissociative symptoms are found in about a third of borderline inpatients and presumably, a smaller percentage of borderline outpatients who have never been hospitalized.
- The etiology of dissociative *symptoms* (as opposed to disorders) among borderline patients is complex, with both adverse events and some type of temperamental vulnerability seemingly involved.
- The research on the overlap between borderline personality disorder and dissociative disorders is quite preliminary in nature. Additional studies, particularly large-scale studies that simultaneously use well-established interviews for diagnosing BPD and the dissociative disorders, are needed.

REFERENCES

Bernstein, E. M., & Putnam, F. W. (1986). Development, reliability, and validity of a dissociation scale. *Journal of Nervous and Mental Disease, 174*, 727–735.

Brodsky, B. S., Cloitre, M., & Dulit, R. A. (1995). Relationship of dissociation to self-mutilation and childhood abuse in borderline personality disorder. *American Journal of Psychiatry, 152,* 1788–1792.

Carpenter, W. T. Jr., & Gunderson, J. G. (1977). Five year follow-up comparison of borderline and schizophrenic patients. *Comprehensive Psychiatry, 18,* 567–571.

Carpenter, W. T. Jr., Gunderson, J. G., & Strauss, J. S. (1977). Considerations of the borderline syndrome: A longitudinal comparative study of borderline and schizophrenic patients. In P. Hartocollis (Ed.), *Borderline personality disorder*. New York: International Universities Press.

Chopra, H. D., & Beatson, J. A. (1986) Psychotic symptoms in borderline personality disorder. *American Journal of Psychiatry, 143,* 1605–1607.

Conte, H. R., Plutchik, R., Karasu, T. B., & Jerrett, L. (1980) A self-report borderline scale: Discriminative validity and preliminary norms. *Journal of Nervous and Mental Disease, 168,* 428–435.

Frances, A., Clarkin, J. F., Gilmore, M., Hurt, S. W., & Brown, R. (1984). Reliability of criteria for borderline personality disorder: A comparison of DSM-III and the Diagnostic Interview for Borderline Patients. *American Journal of Psychiatry, 141,* 1080–1084.

George, A., & Soloff, P. H. (1986). Schizotypal symptoms in patients with borderline personality disorder. *American Journal of Psychiatry, 143,* 212–215.

Grinker, R. R., Werble, B., & Drye, R. C. (1968). *The borderline syndrome*. New York: Basic Books.

Gunderson, J. G. (1977). Characteristics of borderlines. In P. Hartocollis (Ed.), *Borderline personality disorder*. New York: International University Press.

Gunderson, J. G. (2001). *Borderline personality disorder: A clinical guide.* Washington, DC: American Psychiatric Association.

Gunderson, J. G., Carpenter, W. T. Jr, & Strauss, J. S. (1975). Borderline and schizophrenic patients: A comparative study. *American Journal of Psychiatry, 132,* 1257–1264.

Gunderson, J. G., & Kolb, J. E. (1978). Discriminating features of borderline patients. *American Journal of Psychiatry, 135,* 792–796.

Gunderson, J. G., Kolb J. E., & Austin, V. (1981). The diagnostic interview for borderline patients. *American Journal of Psychiatry, 138,* 896–903.

Herman, J. L., Perry, J. C., & van der Kolk, B. A. (1989). Childhood trauma in borderline personality disorder. *American Journal of Psychiatry, 146,* 490–495.

Jacobsberg, L. B., Hymowitz, P., Barasch, A., & Frances, A. J. (1986). Symptoms of schizotypal personality disorder. *American Journal of Psychiatry, 143,* 1222–1227.

Koenigsberg, H. W. (1982). A comparison of hospitalized and nonhospitalized borderline patients. *American Journal of Psychiatry, 139,* 1292–1297.

Links, P. S., Steiner, M., & Mitton, J. (1989). Characteristics of psychosis in borderline personality disorder. *Psychopathology, 22,* 188–193.

Links, P. S., Steiner, M., Offord, D. R., & Eppe, A. (1988). Characteristics of borderline personality disorder: A Canadian study. *Canadian Journal of Psychiatry, 33,* 336–340.

McGlashan, T. H. (1987). Testing DSM-III symptom criteria for schizotypal and borderline personality disorder. *Archives of General Psychiatry, 44,* 143–148.

Nurnberg, H. G., Hurt, S. W., Feldman, A., & Suh, R. (1988). Evaluation of diagnostic criteria for borderline personality disorder. *American Journal of Psychiatry, 145,* 1280–1284.

Ogata, S. N., Silk, K. R., Goodrich, S., Lohr, N. E., Westen, D., & Hill, E. M. (1990). Childhood sexual and physical abuse in adult patients with borderline personality disorder. *American Journal of Psychiatry, 147,* 1008–1013.

Paris, J., Zweig-Frank, H., & Guzder, J. (1994a). Psychological risk factors for borderline personality disorder in female patients. *Comprehensive Psychiatry, 35,* 301–305.

Paris, J., Zweig-Frank, H., & Guzder, J. (1994b). Risk factors for borderline personality in male outpatients. *Journal of Nervous and Mental Disease, 182,* 375–380.

Perry, J. C., & Klerman, G. L. (1980). Clinical features of the borderline personality disorder. *American Journal of Psychiatry, 137,* 165–173.

Pope, H. G. Jr, Jonas, J. M., Hudson, J. I., Cohen, B. M., & Tohen, M. (1985). An empirical study of psychosis in borderline personality disorder. *American Journal of Psychiatry, 142,* 1285–1290.

Ross, C. A., Miller, S. D., Reagor, P., Bjornson, L., Fraser, G. A., & Anderson, G. (1990). Structured interview data on 102 cases of multiple personality disorder from four centers. *American Journal of Psychiatry, 147,* 596–601.

Salzman, J. P., Salzman, C., Wolfson, A. N., Albanese, M., Looper, J., Ostacher, M., Schwartz, J., Chinman, G., Land, W., & Miyawaki, E. (1993). Association between borderline personality structure and history of childhood abuse in adult volunteers. *Comprehensive Psychiatry, 34,* 254–257.

Şar, V., Kundakçı, T., Kızıltan, E., Yargıç, I. L., Tutkun, H., Bakım, B., Bozkurt, O., Özpulat, T., Keser, V., & Özdemir, Ö. (2003). The Axis-I dissociative disorder of comorbidity of borderline personality disorder among psychiatric outpatients. *Journal of Trauma and Dissociation, 4,* 119–136.

Şar, V., Yargıç, L. I., & Tutkun, H. (1996). Structured interview data on 35 cases of dissociative identity disorder in Turkey. *American Journal of Psychiatry, 153,* 1329–1333.

Shearer, S. L. (1994). Dissociative phenomena in women with borderline personality disorder. *American Journal of Psychiatry, 151,* 1324–1328.

Shearer, S. L., Peters, C. P., Quaytman, M. S., & Ogden, R. L. (1990). Frequency and correlates of childhood sexual and physical abuse histories in adult female borderline inpatients. *American Journal of Psychiatry, 147,* 214–216.

Sheehy, M., Goldsmith, L., & Charles, R. (1980). A comparative study of borderline patients in a psychiatric outpatient clinic. *American Journal of Psychiatry, 137,* 1374–1379.

Silk, K. S., Lohr, N. E., Western, D., & Goodrich, S. (1989). Psychosis in borderline patients with depression. *Journal of Personality Disorders, 3,* 92–100.

Snyder, S., & Pitts, W. M. (1986). Characterizing paranoia in the DSM-III borderline personality disorder. *Acta Psychiatrica Scandinavica, 73,* 500–505.

Soloff, P. H. (1981a). Affect, impulse, and psychosis in borderline disorders: a validation study. *Comprehensive Psychiatry, 22,* 337–350.

Soloff, P. H. (1981b). A comparison of borderline with depressed and schizophrenic patients on a new diagnostic interview. *Comprehensive Psychiatry, 22,* 291–300.

Soloff, P. H., & Ulrich, R. F. (1981). Diagnostic Interview for Borderline Patients: A replication study. *Archives of General Psychiatry, 38,* 686–692.

Spitzer, R. L., Endicott, J., & Gibbon, M. (1979). Crossing the border into borderline personality and borderline schizophrenia. *Archives of General Psychiatry, 36,*17–24.

Tarnopolsky, A., & Berelowitz, M. (1984). Borderline personality: Diagnostic attitudes at the Maudsley Hospital. *British Journal of Psychiatry, 144*, 364–369.

Werble, B. (1970). Second follow-up study of borderline patients. *Archives of General Psychiatry, 23,* 3–7.

Westen, D., Ludolph, P., Misle, B., Ruffins, S., & Block, J. (1990). Physical and sexual abuse in adolescent girls with borderline personality disorder. *American Journal of Orthopsychiatry, 60,* 55–66.

Widiger, T. A., Frances, A., Warner, L., & Bluhm, C. (1986). Diagnostic criteria for borderline and schizotypal personality disorder. *Journal of Abnormal Psychology, 95,* 43–51.

Zanarini, M. C. (2004). Update of pharmacotherapy of borderline personality disorder. *Current Psychiatry Report, 6,* 66–70.

Zanarini, M. C., Gunderson, J. G., & Frankenburg, F. R. (1990). Cognitive features of borderline personality disorder. *American Journal of Psychiatry, 147,* 57–63.

Zanarini, M. C., Gunderson, J. G., Frankenburg, F. R., & Chauncey, D. L. (1989). The Revised Diagnostic Interview for Borderlines: Discriminating BPD from other axis II disorders. *Journal of Personality Disorders, 3*, 10–18.

Zanarini, M. C., Gunderson, J. G., Marino, M. F., Schwartz, E. O., & Frankenburg, F. R. (1989). Childhood experiences of borderline patients. *Comprehensive Psychiatry, 30,* 18–25.

Zanarini, M. C., Ruser, T., Frankenburg, F. R., & Hennen, J. H. (2000). The dissociative experiences of borderline patients. *Comprehensive Psychiatry, 41,* 223–227.

Zanarini, M. C., Ruser, T., Frankenburg, F. R., Hennen, J. H., & Gunderson, J. G. (2000). Risk factors associated with the dissociative experiences of borderline patients. *Journal of Nervous and Mental Disease, 188,* 26–30.

Zanarini, M. C., Williams, A. A., Lewis, R. E., Reich, D. B., Vera, S. C., Marino, M. F., Levin, A., Yong, L., & Frankenburg, F. R. (1997). Reported pathological childhood experiences associated with the development of borderline personality disorder. *American Journal of Psychiatry, 154,* 1101–1106.

Zanarini, M. C., Yong, L., Frankenburg, F. R., Hennen, J., Reich, D. B., & Marino, M. F. (2002). Severity of reported childhood sexual abuse and its relationship to severity of borderline psychopathology and psychosocial impairment. *Journal of Nervous and Mental Disease, 190*, 381–387.

Zweig-Frank, H., Paris, J., & Guzder, J. (1994a). Dissociation in female patients with borderline and non-borderline personality disorders. *Journal of Personality Disorders, 8,* 203–209.

Zweig-Frank, H., Paris, J., & Guzder, J. (1994b). Dissociation in male patients with borderline and non-borderline personality disorders. *Journal of Personality Disorders, 8,* 210–218.

32 Chronic Relational Trauma Disorder: A New Diagnostic Scheme for Borderline Personality and the Spectrum of Dissociative Disorders

Elizabeth F. Howell, PhD
Ruth A. Blizard, PhD

OUTLINE

Borderline personality may be best understood, and its etiology most accurately described, as a disorder of trauma, attachment, and dissociation. Dissociated self-states underlie the stable instability (i.e., the affect dysregulation), unstable identity, and sudden changes in relationships, that characterize BPD.

The dissociative disorders literature describes highly conspicuous dissociative symptoms and florid manifestations of fully dissociated self-states (i.e., alter personalities). The dissociative symptoms of BPD may often be overshadowed by problematic behavior. More important, the alternating self-states in BPD are often partially, rather than fully, dissociated, thus their dissociative nature is easily missed.

State changes in BPD may be more subtle than in dissociative identity disorder (DID). In milder cases of BPD, these shifts are often characterized by changes in perception of self and other, usually fluctuating between idealizing and devaluing. In DID, self-state switches involve the more obvious alterations of identity, often with amnesia. In contrast, state changes in BPD may be missed, because they may not involve such obvious changes in demeanor as are often seen in DID. Splitting is often considered to be the hallmark characteristic of borderline personality. However, this specific formulation may often deflect attention away from the significant shifts among dissociated self-states in BPD, which may be sequelæ of relational trauma. We will demonstrate (1) how splitting can be better understood as the dissociation of self-states pursuant to relational trauma, and (2) that this dissociative process explains the stable instability of BPD. We propose that BPD be replaced by a new diagnostic formulation: Chronic Relational Trauma Disorder. This formulation is based on (1) the evidence that the symptoms of BPD tend to follow from a history of repeated trauma within significant childhood relationships, (2) the quality of the relationship with the primary caregiver was contradictory or frightening to the young child, and (3) many of the symptoms, and notably the alternation between self-states, are dissociative. To support this new conceptualization, in this chapter we will (1) show why BPD should be placed on the continuum of the dissociative spectrum, (2) differentiate the effects of discrete-incident posttraumatic stress from those of relational trauma, and (3) propose etiological pathways that lead to Chronic Relational Trauma Disorder.

32.1 INTRODUCTION: WHO IS THE BORDERLINE PATIENT?

Borderline personality disorder (BPD) has traditionally been characterized by splitting, affect dysregulation, identity disturbance, impulsive behavior, and brief, psychotic-like episodes. It is this "stable instability" (Schmideberg, 1959), rather than any particular cluster of personality characteristics, that has been the heart of the syndrome through its many incarnations (Millon, 1981). The term *stable instability* captures the enduring pattern of frequent and unpredictable shifts in affect, cognition, behavior, self-image, roles, perceptions of others, relationships, values, and even sexual identity described in the DSM-IV narrative (American Psychiatric Association, 1994). According to DSM-IV, personality disorders are enduring, inflexible, and pervasive patterns of perceiving, relating to, and thinking about the environment and oneself, across a broad range of personal and social situations that lead to significant distress or impairment in important areas of functioning. Onset can be traced back at least to adolescence or early adulthood. *The dramatic shifts in the various aspects of personality seen in BPD are more suggestive of a dissociative disorder than a personality disorder.*

In its diagnostic history *borderline personality disorder* often became a "wastebasket" category for patients of uncertain diagnosis (Millon, 1981). The term *borderline* originally referred to patients who were considered to be on the border between neurosis and psychosis (Stern, 1938), or who were considered to be borderline schizophrenic (Kreisman & Straus, 1989; Stone, 1990). The placement of BPD within the schizophrenia spectrum was ultimately not supported by research (Lerner, Sugarman, & Barbour, 1985; Stone, 1992). This early conceptualization of BPD was later followed by its transient inclusion within the affective spectrum (Stone, 1992), and more recently on the trauma spectrum (Kroll, 1993). Millon (1981) has lamented the use of the term *borderline personality disorder* as a formal syndrome. He protested that *borderline* was meant to convey a level of severity of pathology that could be applied to a number of personality disorders. This pathology included a tendency to be *labile*, *cycloid*, or *unstable*.

32.2 OVERINCLUSIVENESS OF THE CURRENT DSM-IV DEFINITION OF BPD

One reason BPD is so misunderstood is that the DSM-IV criteria combine a potpourri of symptoms that cover a wide range of severity. The BPD criteria cast such a broad net that, like tuna fishermen, diagnosticians also catch dolphins and sharks. In keeping with Millon's position, a recent review argued that, because BPD in DSM-III-R (APA, 1987) encompassed such a heterogeneity of traits and levels of severity, BPD would be better regarded as severe personality dysfunction than as a discrete diagnostic entity (Berelowitz & Tarnopolsky, 1993). Most patients with BPD also meet criteria for antisocial, histrionic, or narcissistic personality disorders (Dolan, Evans, & Norton, 1995), as well as depression, anxiety, substance abuse, or eating disorders. Various combinations of BPD criteria describe varying degrees of impairment, impulsivity, self-destructive behavior, and dissociation that might be better categorized under dissociative disorders, posttraumatic stress disorder (PTSD), or antisocial personality.

32.2.1 Example 1: Dissociative Disorder

A person with dissociative symptoms and disorganized attachment subsequent to an abusive or neglectful childhood might be described by these five BPD criteria: (1) frantically avoiding abandonment; (2) unstable, intense relationships, with idealizing and devaluing; (3) unstable sense of self; (6) affective instability; and (9) transient, severe, dissociative symptoms. As we will explain, these criteria can be understood as the manifestations of partially or fully dissociated self-states, and thus such a symptom picture might be more meaningfully classified as dissociative disorder not otherwise specified (DDNOS).

One of the drawbacks of the DSM-IV is that different diagnostic categories may describe what appear to be distinct sets of signs and symptoms when they are actually manifestations of the same phenomena. Our point is that dissociative phenomena underlie most of the criteria for BPD. Two large studies using standardized diagnostic interviews showed that 72% of subjects qualifying for a diagnosis of BPD also had a dissociative disorder (Şar, Akyüz, Kuğu, Öztürk, & Ertem-Vehid, 2006), and DDNOS is the most prevalent diagnosis for women with a history of trauma (Şar, Akyüz, & Doğan, 2007, provide some evidence for this). In diagnosing patients, the training and theoretical orientation of clinicians may color the way in which they view symptoms, what aspects of psychopathology they determine to be predominant, and even which diagnostic tests they choose.

32.2.2 Example 2: PTSD

A survivor of adult rape who is suffering from PTSD-related dissociative symptoms might be described by six BPD criteria: (1) frantically avoiding abandonment; (4) compulsive reenactment of sexual abuse; (5) self-mutilation to achieve emotional numbing; (6) affective instability, with traumatic memories being frequently triggered, alternating with (7) chronic feelings of emptiness due to emotional numbing; and (9) transient, dissociative symptoms such as blanking out and intrusive images. A clinician who loses sight of the onset of this pathology in adulthood might easily misdiagnose this subject with BPD because she satisfies these criteria.

32.2.3 Example 3: Antisocial Personality Disorder

An abusive spouse might be described by another combination of BPD criteria: (4) impulsivity in sexual activity, substance abuse, and reckless driving; (5) recurrent, manipulative, suicidal threats, such as, "If you leave me, I'll kill myself"; (6) affective instability, becoming unpredictably upset by minor incidents; (8) inappropriate, intense anger, and recurrent physical fights, including spouse-battering; and (9) transient, stress-related paranoid ideation, manifested in excessive suspicion about a partner being unfaithful. This constellation might be better conceptualized as a sociopathic character.

It is important to note that while these diverse individuals satisfy several of the same criteria, the quality of the behavior in question is very different (e.g., emotional numbing vs. manipulative threats). The individual in the second example (i.e., PTSD) may have alternating self-states that are based on fearfulness and avoidance. However, these self-states probably would not manifest contradictory models of attachment or the accompanying instability of identity and relationships distinctive of BPD. The person in the antisocial personality disorder example resembles patients whom clinicians often describe as being "very borderline." Significant correlations between BPD and histrionic, narcissistic or antisocial traits (Dolan et al., 1995; Golier et al., 2003; Laddis & Dell, 2003) may be due more to overlap among personality disorder symptom clusters in the current DSM-IV diagnostic scheme than a naturally occurring personality syndrome. In some studies, these correlations may be an artifact of particular populations of subjects, which are restricted by gender, SES, inpatient or outpatient status. Westen and Shedler (1999a) have questioned the empirical and conceptual foundation of the current DSM-IV system on a number of counts: (1) patients often meet the criteria for several personality disorders; (2) assessment instruments are circularly based on current diagnostic criteria; thus, these instruments will diagnose patients who meet those criteria, but new criteria will not be found; (3) because these diagnostic criteria were not empirically derived, diagnostic instruments are being asked to assess personality syndromes that may not actually exist in nature.

Analysis of experienced clinicians' descriptions of their patients with personality disorders led Westen and Shedler to report that the following syndromes occurred naturally: dysphoric, antisocial, schizoid, paranoid, obsessional, histrionic, and narcissistic. A borderline group did not naturally occur. Patients that had been *diagnosed* as borderline tended to fall into either the dysphoric or histrionic groups. Additionally, two personality subfactors, *emotionally dysregulated* and *dependent-masochistic*, characterized many members of the dysphoric group. Interestingly, the correlations between borderline and antisocial traits were very small.

These experienced clinicians' descriptions of their borderline patients were quite different from the DSM-IV picture. Their borderline patients were distinguished by (1) intense, poorly modulated affect, (2) omnipresent dysphoria, and (3) desperate efforts at affect regulation.

Westen and Shedler (1999a, 1999b) suggested that these are defining features of BPD. Their research is consistent with the contention of other clinicians that affect dysregulation is the central feature of BPD (Linehan & Koerner, 1993; Zanarini, 1997).

Although much literature attributes affect dysregulation in BPD patients to posttraumatic sequelæ (Herman & Van der Kolk, 1987; Kernberg, 1988; Schore, 2003a, 2003b), difficulties with affect regulation are also characteristic of dissociative disorders. Moreover, dissociation can be both a cause and an effect of affect dysregulation.

How is dissociation related to personality disorder, especially borderline personality disorder? Kernberg (1975) has suggested that splitting, which he views as a primitive form of dissociation, underlies the larger category of Borderline Personality Organization that includes borderline, narcissistic, antisocial, and addictive character disorders. Kernberg described these patients as having, "Contradictory characteristics ... without real ... awareness of the conflictual nature of the material ... lack of clear identity ... and mutual dissociation of contradictory ego states reflecting ... early, pathological internalized object relationships" (1975, pp. 161–162).

Kernberg's (1975) conceptualization clearly portrays a disorder of dissociated ego states. Similarly, Bromberg (1998) views all personality disorders as based in dissociation. The underlying structure of dissociated self-states in narcissistic, psychopathic, schizoid, sadistic, and masochistic personality has been discussed elsewhere (Blizard, 2001, 2003a; Howell, 1996, 1997, 2003a, 2003b, 2005). Rather than focus on broader conceptions of personality or borderline organization, we will focus on the more narrowly defined borderline personality, because, (1) borderline patients present more frequently for treatment, (2) they have become the *bête noir* of many clinicians, and (3) the configuration of dissociated self-states in BPD differs from the dissociative patterns characteristic of other personality disorders and PTSD.

While the term *borderline* has been applied to many different patients, we propose that the core group of people generally designated by this vexing term are those stably unstable people whose sudden alterations in mood, sense of self, and relationship to others are manifestations of partially or fully dissociated self-states. When dissociation is partial, there is usually (1) continuity of identity, (2) superficial awareness of abrupt changes in affect or behavior, (3) minimal ability to link these states in consciousness, and (4) little acknowledgment of the significance of these shifting states. Often conceptualized as "splitting," these shifts are *not* assessed by tests of dissociation such as the Dissociative Experiences Scale (DES; Carlson & Putnam, 1992) or the Multidimensional Inventory of Dissociation (MID; Dell, 2001, 2006a).

Ultimately, an understanding of BPD depends on how we understand the process of dissociation in personality disorders in general and its role in specific personality patterns. Perhaps it is better not to rely on diagnostic categories that have significant overlap in criteria and questionable validity. Behavior that is impulsive, attention-seeking, manipulative, or mendacious might be better described for what it actually is. The current formulation for BPD conflates histrionic and antisocial traits with posttraumatic and dissociative symptoms. This may confound therapeutic efforts by implying a common etiology and course of treatment for diverse disorders. Nor does it make sense to confuse the symptoms of simple PTSD with the severe relationship disturbances that derive from attachment to an abusive caregiver. Borderline personality, as defined by DSM-IV, refers to a variety of problematic behaviors and a broad range of impairment, none of which are clearly specified simply by assigning the diagnosis of BPD. It makes more sense to focus on the characteristic alternation of dissociated self-states in BPD, and to conceptualize these shifts in terms of a spectrum of dissociated self-states, rather than an assortment of symptoms that are often, but not necessarily, associated with this core feature.

We consider the key process in BPD to be the shifting of dissociated self-states, rather than an assortment of symptoms that are often, but not necessarily, associated with this core feature. These shifts generate the affect dysregulation, identity disturbance, and unstable relationships that have characterized BPD in both the traditional and contemporary literature. Accordingly, we recommend that BPD be defined as the presence of dissociated, alternating self-states with contradictory patterns of attachment. The manifestations of the disorder in the particular individual should be described by specifying (1) the presence and severity of the full range of dissociative symptoms, and (2) personality traits. Co-occurring pathology such as substance abuse, eating disorders, or antisocial behavior should be separately diagnosed. This would avoid forcing patients into the Procrustean bed of a single category that currently has such pejorative implications.

32.3 DISSOCIATION IN BORDERLINE PERSONALITY DISORDER

Dissociation refers to a broad range of phenomena, both observable signs and subjective symptoms (Dell, 2006b, 2009). Dissociative phenomena involve striking discontinuities (i.e., lack of integration, in consciousness, affect, mood, perception, memory, or sense of identity). The dissociative phenomena in persons with BPD are qualitatively the same as those manifested by persons with dissociative disorders, for example, identity confusion, thought intrusion, sudden affect changes, full and partial dissociation between self-states, and *splitting*.

In *partial* dissociation (Dell, 2006a), there is a subjectively experienced or objectively observable discontinuity in thought, affect, or behavior, but no amnesia for behavior or identity. Dell notes that most dissociative symptoms in severely dissociative patients are subjectively experienced, "made" thoughts, emotions, or behaviors that seem to come from "out of nowhere." The phenomena of partial dissociation are quite different from the relatively rare switches between fully dissociated self-states (alter personalities) that are accompanied by amnesia for identity and behavior. Even though partial dissociation may have dramatic impact, leaving both patient and clinician confused and disoriented, it often is not recognized as dissociation. Splitting has often been understood to be BPD's cardinal characteristic (Kernberg, 1975). Although many authors have not emphasized its broader categorization as dissociation, or do not consider it dissociative, most of the British object-relations theorists consider splitting and dissociation to be synonymous (Tarnopolsky, 2003). Splitting involves the dissociation of representations of self and other into "black" and "white," or "good" and "bad." Split self-states show clear affective, and often behavioral, discontinuity. Although it may involve full dissociation, splitting entails at least a partial dissociation of self-states incorporating incompatible models of attachment. The transient psychotic symptoms of BPD, historically viewed as borderline schizophrenia, can be understood as dissociative. Posttraumatic flashbacks, perceptual distortions, and illusions (Ellenson, 1986; Terr, 1990) are dissociative in nature rather than psychotic. They may be triggered by reminders of a traumatic event, for example, (1) excessive fearfulness and paranoid ideation, (2) seeing a shadowy figure from the corner of the eye, or (3) perceiving that someone resembling an abuser actually is that person.

Clinicians often do not recognize that partial dissociation, splitting, and transient, psychotic symptoms are manifestations of dissociation; this usually leads to a diagnosis of BPD because the patient's behavior otherwise fits the DSM-IV criteria for BPD. Depending upon the type of treatment and the therapist's style, dissociation may be more or less evident in the session. In general, dissociative events are responsive to their current context; dissociation most frequently occurs in situations that are unstructured, threatening, or evocative of past traumatic memories.

32.3.1 DSM-IV BPD and Dissociated Self-States

Although DSM-IV considers BPD and DID to be separate disorders, the shifts between dissociated self-states in BPD and DID are very similar. Perhaps it makes better sense to think of BPD and DID in terms of their commonality (i.e., dissociated self-states), than as distinct disorders that may be comorbid. Our formulation of BPD as a disorder of alternating, dissociated, self-states is consistent with the DSM-IV description of BPD:

> Profound changes in self-image, affect, cognition, and behavior ... sudden and dramatic shifts in their view of others, who may alternately be seen as beneficent supporters or as cruelly punitive ... There may be an identity disturbance characterized by ... unstable ... sense of self ... and dramatic shifts in self-image ... goals, values ... sexual identity ... and friends. (American Psychiatric Association, 1994, pp. 650–651)

This DSM-IV description of BPD closely mirrors the identity shifts that occur in DID (Putnam, 1989); it is also similar to DSM-IV's description of DID: "The presence of two or more distinct identities or personality states (each with its own relatively enduring pattern of perceiving, relating to, and thinking about the environment and self)" (American Psychiatric Association, 1994, p. 487). Although "inability to recall personal information" is required for DID, the definition of BPD neither includes nor excludes this criterion.

32.3.1.1 The Signs of BPD Can Be Understood as Signs of Dissociated Self-States

1. Unstable relationships, identity disturbance, and affective instability can be viewed as the direct consequences of shifts among partially dissociated self-states.
2. Fear of abandonment, difficulty controlling anger, and transient psychotic symptoms may all arise when traumatic memories are triggered and distinct self-states are activated.
3. Substance abuse may serve to facilitate a shift to an emotionally numb self-state in an attempt to self-medicate overwhelming affect.
4. Sexual impulsivity may be the manifestation of a dissociated self-state reenacting earlier abuse.

32.3.2 The Place of BPD in the Spectrum of Dissociative Disorders

Our view of BPD as a disorder of dissociated self-states is compatible with Kernberg's (1975) conception of contradictory ego states wherein introjections and identifications of opposite quality are kept apart, as well as with Masterson's (1976) model of split self- and object-representation units. Our conceptualization of BPD as a disorder of dissociated self-states emphasizes its placement on the dissociative spectrum. On one end of this spectrum, dissociation is briefer, more attenuated, and more accessible to consciousness, and on the other end of the spectrum, personified self-states occur and there is the amnesia for behavior and identity typically observed in DID. This conceptualization is consistent with the findings that a significant proportion of BPD patients also meet the criteria for a dissociative disorder (Dell, 1998; Putnam, 1997; Ross, 1997; Şar, et al., 2003; Şar, et al., 2006).

BPD encompasses a broad range of the dissociative spectrum. On one end are BPD patients, without severe dissociative symptoms, who nevertheless manifest alternating self-states with corresponding shifts in affect, perception, and behavior. These BPD patients have continuity of memory and constancy of identity, but minimal recognition of the emotional and behavioral discrepancies between states, and minimal appreciation of the significance of these emotional and behavioral contradictions (Howell, 2002).

In the middle of the dissociative spectrum, there are BPD patients who hear voices and who undergo "made" actions and other subjective experiences that are caused by partially dissociated self-states. These BPD patients have little or no amnesia. Patients in the intermediate range of the dissociative spectrum are often currently diagnosed as DDNOS, Type 1.

At the other extreme of the dissociative spectrum are persons with DID. These patients could be conceptualized as suffering from BPD with personification of self-states and amnesia for behavior and identity. The major difference between DID and classic BPD is the degree of dissociation between self-states.

The model of BPD that we propose, that is, partial or full dissociation of two or more alternating self-states that harbor incompatible relational models, is conceptually similar to Ryle's (1997a, 1997b) multiple self-states model of BPD. In Ryle's model, BPD exists on a continuum of dissociation:

> From normal, state-dependent memory ... to the elaboration of distinct identities with mutual amnesia described in DID.... In patients with BPD two or more distinct states are found, each with a different pattern of reciprocal role relationships and differences in the dominant modes of feeling and behavior. Between these states there may be impaired memory but complete amnesia is rare, and some capacity for self-observation across all, or nearly all states is present. (Golynkina & Ryle, 1999, pp. 430–431)

Ryle's (1999a, 1999b) model of reciprocal role patterns closely parallels Lyons-Ruth's (1999, 2001) view that dissociation can result from disconnections among various systems of dyadic, relational, procedural enactments, especially in families with hostile/helpless relational patterns. Both Ryle and Lyons-Ruth present a two-person model of cognition, affect, and behavior. Both models are based on procedural learning of dyadic roles. The patterns of dissociated, internalized, dyadic role relationships provide templates for rigid reenactments of old experience.

32.3.3 Research on the Diagnostic Convergence of BPD and DID

Not surprisingly, given the similarities in etiology and dissociative structure, studies have found there is significant diagnostic overlap between BPD and DID (Dell, 1998; Putnam, 1997; Ross, 1997; Şar et al., 2003, 2006). Childhood abuse occurs in 50% to 81% of BPD patients and 85% to 100% of DID patients (Putnam, 1997). Of those diagnosed with DID, 30% to 70% also meet criteria for BPD (Putnam, 1997). Among DID outpatients, 53% were borderline, 68% self-defeating, 76% avoidant, and 45% passive-aggressive; many qualified for two or more personality disorders (Dell, 1998). In two studies, Şar et al. (2003, 2006) found that 64% and 72%, respectively, of subjects with BPD had a dissociative disorder. Given (1) the twin difficulties of measuring personality disorders and dissociative disorders, and (2) the controversy regarding the status of BPD as a naturally occurring syndrome (Westen & Shedler, 1999a, 1999b), it is remarkable that there is so much concordance between BPD and DID.

In a study of patients who were grouped according to the severity of their dissociative symptoms—(1) mild BPD and related personality disorders, (2) BPD with dissociative symptoms, and (3) DID—dissociation was positively correlated with severity of PTSD, self-injurious symptoms, and the severity and age of onset of childhood abuse (Boon & Draijer, 1993). By using the Structured Clinical Interview for DSM-IV Dissociative Disorders (SCID-D; Steinberg, et al., 1993), Boon and Draijer were able to carefully assess both the presence and the quality of dissociative experiences. They found that most patients reported an ongoing internal struggle, but that BPD patients described a struggle between *two ideas or internal parts*, while dissociative disorder patients described a struggle between *several parts,* which they often heard as voices. Interestingly, in a brilliant description of what he refers to as "covert MPD," Kluft (1991) describes its most important form, "phenocopy MPD." In phenocopy MPD, the organization of the alters' influences results in behavioral manifestations similar to those of other disorders. One of those is BPD: "those [alters] in contention may create the chaotic appearance of a BPD" (p. 624).

One question on the SCID-D assesses identity alteration by asking if the person had ever "behaved like a different person." The affirmative responses of most BPD patients described very polarized behavior. In contrast, the affirmative responses of most DID patients described (1) the unexpected exhibition of previously unknown capabilities, and (2) actions for which they had amnesia (Boon & Draijer, 1993). The BPD patients' description of an internal struggle between polarized attitudes or behavioral dispositions is congruent with our portrayal of BPD: partially dissociated and incompatible self-states that have opposing attitudes and temperament (accompanied by a substantial lack of ability to integrate these opposing dispositions). These findings point to a continuum of dissociative processes that is characterized by increasing severity and increasing prevalence of dissociative symptoms.

32.4 THE ORIGINS OF DISSOCIATED SELF-STATES

32.4.1 Posttraumatic Affect Dysregulation

Affect dysregulation has long been considered to be a core feature of BPD (Linehan & Koerner, 1993; Masterson, 1976; Stone, 1990). Affect dysregulation and dissociation appear to be closely interconnected. Although some have speculated that affect dysregulation in BPD has its roots in constitutional factors (Kernberg, 1976; Goodman et al., 2003), and others have suggested that affect dysregulation is due to a genetically based affective disorder (e.g., Stone, 1990), there is no convincing empirical evidence for either of these positions. On the other hand, there *is* increasing evidence that affective instability is due to a combination of (1) the neurobiological sequelae of extreme traumatic stress, (2) the intrusion of dissociated memories, and (3) accompanying changes in self-states (Van der Kolk, 1996).

Trauma survivors may experience sudden state transitions from normal consciousness to hypoarousal or hyperarousal; such state changes can engender abrupt alterations of behavior, affect, sensitivity to pain, and awareness of self and environment (Perry, 1999; Nijenhuis, 1999). These state changes may also be understood in terms of the animal defensive states of freeze, flight/fight, and total submission observed by Nijenhuis (1999). When dissociated memories of trauma are triggered or activated, there may be accompanying changes of biological state (Perry, 1999), affect, and self-state (Nijenhuis, 1999).

State-dependent memory and learning involves the decreased ability to remember what was experienced during a different physiological state, and the correspondingly increased ability to recall it when one returns to the original state. Braun (1984, 1988) has suggested that state-dependent learning is the basis of much dissociation. Thus, when a person perceives a threat and suddenly enters a state of freeze or flight/fight, and then just as precipitously returns to a normal state, she may have difficulty remembering what she thought, felt, or did during the hypoaroused or hyperaroused state. Such state-dependent functioning may partially account for BPD patients' difficulties explaining their sudden reactions; it may also contribute to their apparent lack of awareness that these states are contrary to their normal demeanor.

In short, sudden changes of neurophysiological state may explain many of the disjunctions of behavior, sensation, cognition, and affect that are observed in BPD. Conversely, extremes of emotion may precipitate a shift from a highly charged self-state to an emotionally constricted one as a dissociative means of affect regulation (Chefetz, 2003).

Thus, in BPD, each self-state tends to have a predominant affect (e.g., cheerful, calm, fearful, angry, etc.) that depends on the quality of the relationship with the object represented by that state (Kernberg, 1975; Ryle, 1997). Accordingly, shifts from one dissociated self-state to another may precipitate sudden mood changes. Finally, Lansky (2003) has noted that shame, an affect that is usually evoked by relational trauma, can be a powerful precipitant of dissociation (Lansky, 2003).

32.4.2 Relational Trauma

In borderline personality, dissociated self-states appear to be the product of disorganized attachment and repeated relational trauma, especially intrafamilial abuse or neglect that is of early onset. Disorganized attachment is caused by bizarre or frightening parental behavior, including maltreatment, as well as role-reversals, and contradictory, double-bind relationships in the family of origin (Fonagy et al., 1996; Fonagy, Gergely, Jurist, & Target,

2002; Fonagy, Target, Gergely, Allen, & Bateman, 2003; Lyons-Ruth, Bronfman, & Atwood, 1999; Lyons-Ruth, Bronfman, & Parsons, 1999; Main & Hesse, 1990, 1992–1998). Such severely misattuned, caretaking behavior can be viewed as "hidden trauma" (Lyons-Ruth, 2003). These conditions are often co-occurrent, and may even contribute to one another. Thus, the cause of dissociation in BPD is relational trauma, whether due to overt intrafamilial abuse or to disorganized attachment relationships. There appears to be a complex interplay among relational patterns, disorganized attachment, trauma, and dissociation, each in turn interacting with the others (Ogawa, Sroufe, Weinfeld, Carlson, & Egeland, 1997).

There is increasing evidence that disorganized attachment predisposes to dissociation, particularly as a response to trauma (Carlson, 1998; Lyons-Ruth, 2003; Ogawa et al. 1997). An internal working model of attachment is a mental representation of the self, the attachment figure, and the relationship between them (Bowlby, 1969/1982; Solomon & George, 1999). Internal working models are essential to the organization of self-states. Disorganized attachment develops when the attachment figure is frightening or abusive. Thus, the person on whom the child depends for comfort and protection is the very person who threatens her safety (Hesse & Main, 1999; Main & Hesse, 1990, 1992). As a result, the child experiences cognitive and behavioral collapse, and a breakdown of the attachment system, leading to apparent dissociative symptoms, including disorientation, trance-like states or contradictory behavioral responses. The child may alternate rapidly between approach and avoidance strategies, which, in turn, may develop into incompatible, segregated models of attachment. If frightening parental behavior continues, these models of attachment may evolve into dissociated self-states (Blizard, 1997, 2001, 2003; Hesse & Main, 1999; Liotti, 1992, 1999a, 1999b; Lyons-Ruth, 1996, 1999; Main & Hesse, 1990, 1992).

Fonagy and colleagues (2002) cite evidence that maltreatment and severe misattunement inhibit the child's reflective capacity. Our proposal, that BPD develops via disorganized attachment, shares Fonagy's emphasis upon the disorganizing role of maltreatment. Our conceptualization, however, is based on dissociated self-states, while Fonagy's conceptualization emphasizes deficient reflective functioning.

Dissociation among self-states in BPD may be reinforced via two routes: (1) continued relational trauma, which heightens the child's need to segregate favorable and abusive representations of the caregiver (Blizard, 1997, 2001, 2003; Liotti, 1992, 1999a, 1999b); and (2) lack of opportunity to integrate fragmented self- and object-representations. This latter may be due to lack of parental validation of feelings and too little opportunity for articulation or modulation of affect during interpersonal interaction (Fischer & Ayoub, 1995; Lyons-Ruth, 2001; Putnam, 1997; Silk, Nigg, Westen, & Lohr, 1997). While attachment patterns are typically stable throughout development, negative life events, including loss, severe illness or dysfunction of parents, and child abuse, can change attachment classification (Waters, Merrick, Treboux, Crowell, & Albersheim, 2000). Severe loss or trauma later in childhood could conceivably precipitate a disorganization of previously healthy attachment paradigms and predispose to the development of dissociated self-states, even if a child began life with a relatively coherent attachment.

In BPD, the oscillation between dissociated self-states continually reenacts the traumatic violation of the attachment relationship (Howell, 2002). The child's traumatic experiences of an abusive caregiver are likely to be encoded in procedural repertoires and somatosensory modalities, rather than in declarative, explicit memories (Van der Kolk, 1996). Often these experiences are learned in terms of abuser/victim relational positions, which are then enacted as separate self-states, unlinked to the rest of conscious experience.

These self-states may be based in biological state changes that were caused by childhood trauma. When trauma is early, severe, and chronic, it induces neurophysiological hypoarousal and hyperarousal reactions that become use dependent (Perry, 1999). The substrates for the passive, victim state are hypoarousal and the animal defense reactions of total submission and freezing as described by Nijenhuis (1999). These are defeat responses, similar to learned helplessness, which are adaptive to situations of inescapable pain and immobilization. This pattern, which Perry calls "dissociative," includes depersonalization, numbing, decreased heart rate, analgesia, catatonia, and robotic compliance. The hyperarousal pattern involves "fight/flight" reactions that are characterized by elevated heart rate, behavioral irritability, increased locomotion, startle response, and a hypervigilant tendency to overread cues as being threatening. This increases the probability of violent behavior. Most severely traumatized persons use a combination of both patterns.

In the victim-identified position, the child may be passive, helpless, robotic, and experience herself as dependent upon the aggressor/caregiver. She may idealize the aggressor to protect the good internal and external objects from being overwhelmed by badness (Kernberg, 1975) and to promote a conflict-free interpersonal way of engaging with the aggressor. Nevertheless, the victimized child learns both roles—victim and abuser. She may imitatively play the aggressor role; she knows this role quite intimately because she had to focus so intently on her abuser's needs (Blizard, 2001; Ferenczi, 1949; Frankel, 2001; Howell, 2002, 2003).

In chaotic, neglectful, and abusive family environments, the child closely studies her abuser's postures, facial expressions, words, and feelings. She hopes to prevent harm by calming or pleasing her abuser. Because of her intense traumatic attachment to her abuser, the child mimics the abuser's behavior; this is a form of enactive, procedural, dyadic learning. The abuser's goals and behaviors may appear to have replaced the child's own agency, initiative, and rage, but the abuser's identity has not literally become part of the child. Rather, the child mimics the abuser due to intense attachment and dissociates due to sheer terror.

The rage that the child displays is her own, as are the contempt and omnipotence which are often labeled identification with the aggressor. Some borderline defenses that Kernberg connects to splitting can be understood as the dissociation of victim and aggressor states. Primitive idealization, for example, is only felt from the victim/masochistic state. Similarly, omnipotence and devaluation may be experienced ego syntonically when the person is in an aggressor-identified state, even though they may have been imitatively learned from the perspective of an attached victim state (Howell, 2002, 2005).

32.4.3 Splitting

BPD patients' unstable affect, shifts in identity, and alternation between idealizing and devaluing can be best explained etiologically by the construct of *dissociated self-states* as organized around relational trauma. The conventional understanding of the etiology of splitting (i.e., the very young child's failure to integrate good and bad self- and object-representations) (1) is not consistent with the capabilities of children of this age (Lyons-Ruth, 1991; Stern, 1985), and (2) does not acknowledge the actual, contradictory behavior of the caregiver that generates disorganized attachment.

32.5 BPD Is a Disorder of Relational Trauma

32.5.1 Differentiating BPD from PTSD

The evidence suggests that BPD is a disorder of *relational* trauma. Although many contemporary thinkers conceptualize BPD simply as a trauma disorder, its origins in relational trauma distinguish it from PTSD. Trauma caused by natural disasters, war, or stranger violence may result in dissociated self-states based around terrifying experiences, which alternate with affectively constricted states based on everyday coping (Steele, Van der Hart, & Nijenhuis, 2003; Nijenhuis, Van der Hart, & Steele, 2004b). But, BPD is characterized by more than just unstable affect that alternates between fearful and constricted. Several authors have noted that BPD may be better understood as a complex form of PTSD. They have proposed new diagnostic terms: complex trauma disorder (Herman, 1992; Herman & Van der Kolk, 1987; Kroll, 1993), chronic trauma disorder (Ross, 1989), and Type II trauma (Terr, 1994) that clearly have a significant overlap with BPD (McLean & Gallop, 2002).

Both BPD and dissociative disorders are highly correlated with a history of chronic trauma and neglect (Golier et al., 2003; Gunderson & Sabo, 1993a, 1993b; Herman & Van der Kolk, 1987; Linehan & Koerner, 1993; Perry & Herman, 1993; Silk et al. 1997; Yen et al., 2002; Zanarini, 1997). The history of trauma in BPD patients suggests that dissociative symptoms and experiences should be common. On the other hand, concepts such as complex PTSD and chronic trauma disorder do not fully address the victim/perpetrator fluctuations in self-image and relationships that characterize BPD. An understanding of BPD as a posttraumatic disorder does not, by itself, provide a conceptual framework for treating the contradictory relational strategies of dissociated self-states in BPD (Blizard, 2001, 2003; Howell, 2002, 2003).

Relational trauma is generated by frightening behavior or abuse in significant relationships. It is likely to result in the alternating, dissociated self-states with contradictory, idealizing, and devaluing relational patterns, distinctive of BPD, as conceptualized by Kernberg (1975), Masterson (1976), and other psychoanalytically oriented theorists. This oscillation between dissociated relational paradigms underlies BPD patients' enigmatic switches between "the role of needy supplicant for help and righteous avenger of past mistreatment" (APA, 1994, p. 651). Depending on the qualities of relationships, the severity of abuse, and caregivers' use of withdrawal versus intimidation, these dissociated, victim and perpetrator self-states may predispose to development of borderline personality disorder (Blizard, 2001; Howell, 2002; Lyons-Ruth, 1996, 1999, 2001).

32.5.2 Empirical Evidence for Relational Trauma in the Etiology of BPD

A number of studies show that relational trauma, including child sexual abuse (McLean & Gallop, 2003; Ogata et al., 1990), severe emotional, verbal, and physical abuse, neglect, lack of parental protection (Zanarini, Ruser,

Frankenburg, Hennen, & Gunderson, 2000) and lack of secure attachment (Simeon, Nelson, Elias, Greenberg, & Hollander, 2003) are important factors in the development of both dissociation and BPD. Compared to other personality disorders, depressed subjects, and controls, borderline patients appear to have suffered more severe sexual abuse (Silk et al., 1997), with earlier onset (McLean & Gallop, 2003; Yen et al., 2002). Disorganized attachment may be a childhood precursor of BPD (Lyons-Ruth, 1996, 1999, 2001). Silk et al. (1997) reported that borderline patients often come from families that do not provide empathic support of children's feelings, thus undermining the development of healthy attachment to caregivers. Silk and colleagues concluded that when abuse occurred in this environment, children had no avenue to work through emotional pain. Accordingly, they had little opportunity to develop independence and self-esteem, and tended to dissociate.

Recent studies have demonstrated the importance of relational trauma in the development of dissociation and the development of affective instability in BPD. Simeon et al. (2003) found that subjects with BPD had significantly greater childhood trauma and more dissociation than healthy controls; furthermore, dissociation was significantly correlated with emotional neglect and fearful (disorganized) attachment. This is consistent with other studies showing that emotional neglect is a significant risk factor for dissociation. It is not easy to tease apart the many confounding and often interacting factors (Kroll, 1993; Zanarini, Dubo, Lewis, & Williams, 1997). What is important here is that relational trauma (e.g., child abuse and neglect), as opposed to extrafamilial trauma such as accidents or natural disasters, is correlated with development of BPD.

32.6 A NEW DIAGNOSTIC MODEL: CHRONIC RELATIONAL TRAUMA DISORDER

We propose that BPD is a dissociative spectrum disorder whose clinical phenomena are caused by shifts among dissociated self-states that have contradictory working models of relationships. BPD should be diagnosed on the basis of identity confusion, affect dysregulation, unstable relationships, and rapid shifts in attitudes, values, and goals, as described in the current DSM-IV criteria. Because there is considerable symptom-overlap among BPD, PTSD, and the dissociative disorders, a diagnostic model should also describe the patient with BPD in terms of: (1) type and severity of posttraumatic and dissociative symptoms, (2) specific personality characteristics.

Rather than separating BPD from the dissociative disorders and PTSD, this model would center around the core feature of dissociated self-states with incompatible relational patterns. Differences in the presence, frequency, and severity of the full range of dissociative and posttraumatic symptoms would be specified. This would allow discrimination among cases with (1) mild identity confusion, (2) identity alteration without amnesia, and (3) fully dissociated self-states. It would also permit specification of other posttraumatic, dissociative symptoms, such as trance states, intrusive thoughts and images, and somatoform disturbances. Personality traits could be described using the current diagnostic categories or a dimensional model, if that is adopted. This would avoid categorizing patients who qualify for diverse personality disorders within a single diagnosis, as often happens with the current BPD model.

Since substance abuse, eating disorders, and difficulty controlling anger are not specific to BPD, they should be diagnosed separately. An underlying medical or neurological disorder may exacerbate symptoms and degree of impairment in BPD or any disorder, and likewise should be diagnosed separately.

32.6.1 Diagnostic Criteria for Chronic Relational Trauma Disorder

A. Identity disturbance characterized by profound changes in self-image, affect, cognition, and behavior, including dramatic shifts in goals, values, and sexual identity
B. Affect dysregulation: intense fear, anger, depression, or emotional numbness not apparently appropriate to the situation
C. Unstable and intense relationships, characterized by sudden and dramatic shifts between idealizing and devaluing others (adapted from APA, 1994)
D. The presence of significant dissociative symptoms, as indicated by symptoms from four or more of the following eight dissociative symptom clusters:
   1. Memory problems as indicated by one or both of the following:
      a. Significant gaps in memory for one's past, recent events, or significant life events,
      b. Recurrent amnesia for one's immediate past behavior
   2. Depersonalization or derealization
   3. Intrusive thoughts, images, or sensations that appear to derive from a past traumatic event, as indicated by one or both of the following:

   a. Recurrent thoughts, images, or bodily sensations related to traumatic events while aware of present surroundings
   b. Reliving traumatic experiences with concomitant loss of contact with the present time, place, and/or persons
4. Somatic or neurological symptoms without medical cause, as indicated by the presence of one or more of the following:
   a. Motor symptoms (e.g., paralysis, difficulty swallowing or urinating)
   b. Sensory deficits or alterations (e.g., blindness, deafness, anesthesia, tunnel vision, alterations of taste, smell)
   c. Neurological symptoms (e.g., seizures, pain)
5. Trance states
6. Hearing voices in the head
7. Partially dissociated thoughts, emotions, or behavior, as evidenced by three or more of the following:
   a. Thoughts or feelings that seem to come out of nowhere or suddenly go away
   b. Experiencing one's actions as not being in one's control
   c. Temporarily dissociated knowledge or skills (e.g., forgetting one's age, address, or name; or forgetting how to drive, use the computer, etc.)
   d. Inability to perceive experiences within a relevant emotional, cognitive, or social context
   e. Dissociation of the social or emotional significance of one's behaviors and verbalizations
8. Identity confusion or alteration, as indicated by three or more of the following:
   a. Feeling or acting like a different person (e.g., opposite gender, a young child, uncharacteristic attitudes or values)
   b. Puzzlement about oneself due to recurrent, discrepant shifts in thought, attitude, emotions, ability, and behavior
   c. Partially dissociated self-state, experienced as "other" but with conscious awareness of its thoughts, feelings, and behavior
   d. Partially dissociated self-state, experienced as "self," but without conscious recognition of the discrepancy of its thoughts, feelings, and behavior from one's usual state
   e. Fully dissociated self-state, who claims to be a different individual, with full amnesia for the thoughts, feelings, and behavior of that state (adapted from Dell, in 2006b, 2009)

E. These symptoms lead to significant distress or impairment in social, occupational, or other important functioning
F. There is evidence of this pattern of symptoms going back at least to adolescence, with signs of affect dysregulation or impairment of social or academic functioning in childhood

Depending on the diagnostic nosology in use—whether personality disorders or one of the proposed dimensional models—an additional specification may be made to indicate personality traits (e.g., paranoid, schizoid, schizotypal, antisocial, histrionic, narcissistic, avoidant, dependent, obsessive-compulsive, self-defeating) or dimensions (e.g., positive/negative affectivity, introversion/extraversion, conscientiousness/nonconscientiousness, agreeableness/nonagreeableness).

32.7 STRENGTHS AND LIMITATIONS OF OUR POSITION

Currently, there are four major, alternative interpretations of the data on BPD:

1. BPD is due to a genetic vulnerability to affect dysregulation.
2. BPD is caused by a constitutional defect.
3. BPD is based on *splitting*, traditionally understood as a developmental failure to integrate split, self- and object-representations.
4. BPD may be caused by chronic, complex trauma that is not relational.

Our formulation, that BPD is based in chronic, relational trauma, is more strongly supported by the research on trauma, child development, and dissociation than are the first three, alternative conceptualizations listed previously. Some have suggested that affect dysregulation stems from a constitutional defect or genetic vulnerability, but research has not supported this position. On the other hand, abundant research supports an etiology of relational trauma. Affect dysregulation and dissociation are inextricably intertwined; both may result from trauma. The concepts of dissociation and trauma are directly related to affect and are more accessible to observation and discussion than are hypotheses regarding constitutional defect. Current theories of infant development do not support the traditional etiology of splitting, but there *is* convergent evidence that relational trauma and disorganized attachment foster the development of dissociated (i.e., *split*) representations of self and other. The question of whether chronic trauma, not inflicted within significant relationships, can engender BPD remains to be determined. This effort may be confounded by the difficulty in gaining an accurate trauma history outside of a long-term therapeutic relationship. Self-report methods may not be valid, since memory for abuse inflicted by persons in close relationship to the victim is more likely to be dissociated than if inflicted by strangers (Freyd, 1996; Williams, 1994).

Finally, given the overinclusiveness of the current DSM-IV criteria, all of these interpretations, including our own, run the risk of overstatement of applicability to all of the currently recognized manifestations of BPD. Some of these cases may, in fact, have at their root neurological pathology or some unknown genetic disorder yet to be discovered. It is our hope that by permitting greater specificity, the proposed diagnostic scheme will contribute to a solution to this problem.

32.8 NEEDED RESEARCH

Meaningful research on BPD and dissociation requires (1) that meaningful questions be asked, (2) that BPD be clearly and accurately defined, (3) that the populations studied be clearly defined, and (4) that measurement instruments be adequate to the task. As noted earlier, the heterogeneity of borderline patients permits a wide variety of distinct populations with that diagnosis to be studied, depending upon, among other things: (1) gender, (2) exclusion criteria such as legal involvement, substance abuse, or use of psychiatric medication, (3) whether inpatient or outpatient, and, naturally, (4) the clusters of diagnostic criteria satisfied. To avoid confounding these variables, diagnostic instruments need to be refined to separate items that assess for substance abuse, self-destructive behavior, and angry acting-out from those that tap what has traditionally been understood as splitting. Meaningful conclusions can only be drawn when the specific characteristics of persons who have been collectively classified as BPD can be related to specific forms of dissociation.

The measurement of the kind of dissociation traditionally referred to as *splitting* is problematic. Current tests measure dissociative symptoms such as amnesia, identity alteration, hearing voices, but do not assess sudden changes in manner of relating to others. Neither the DES nor the MID were designed to assess sudden changes in self-image and perceptions of others. Because dissociation involves lack of awareness of shifts in mood, perception, attitude, or behavior, patients may neither recognize nor be able to indicate the presence of self-state changes on self-report questionnaires like the DES and MID (Pollock, Broadbent, Clarke, Dorrian, & Ryle, 2001).

The SCID-D assesses identity confusion, sudden mood changes, internal struggle, and conflict about one's identity. It allows the interviewer to observe state changes and assess the *quality* of dissociative symptoms. None of these dissociation instruments, however, adequately assesses the kind of dissociation encompassed in *splitting* (i.e., the polarized representations of self and others), and the contradictory relational schemas that comprise dissociated self-states. Yet, these are the kinds of dissociation that generate the *stable instability* of BPD. Only when we have an adequate measure of these phenomena can we investigate their relationship with other forms of dissociation and other phenomena typical of BPD (see Pollock et al., 2001, for new instruments that appear to measure splitting).

REFERENCES

American Psychiatric Association (1994). *DSM-IV – Diagnostic and statistical manual of mental disorders* (4th ed.). Washington, DC: Author.

Berelowitz, M., & Tarnopolsky, A. (1993). The validity of borderline personality disorder: An updated review of recent research. In P. Tyrer & G. Stein (Eds.), *Personality disorder reviewed*. London: Gaskell. pp. 90–112.

Blizard, R. A. (2001). Masochistic and sadistic ego states: Dissociative solutions to the dilemma of attachment to an abusive caretaker. *Journal of Trauma and Dissociation, 2(4)*, 37–58.

Blizard, R. A. (2003). Disorganized attachment, development of dissociated self-states, and a relational approach to treatment. *Journal of Trauma and Dissociation, 4(3)*, 27–50.

Boon, S., & Draijer, N. (1993). The differentiation of patients with MPD or DDNOS from patients with a cluster B personality disorder. *Dissociation, 6*, 126–135.

Bowlby, J. (1969/1982). *Attachment and loss, Vol. 1: Attachment.* New York: Basic Books.

Braun, B. G. (1984). Towards a theory of multiple personality and other dissociative phenomena. *Psychiatric Clinics of North America, 7(4)*, 171–193.

Braun, B. G. (1988). The BASK model of dissociation. *Dissociation, 1*, 4–23.

Bromberg, P. M. (1998). *Standing in the spaces: Essays on clinical process, trauma and dissociation.* Hillsdale, NJ: The Analytic Press.

Carlson, E. A. (1998). A prospective longitudinal study of attachment disorganization/disorientation. *Child Development, 69*, 1107–1128.

Carlson, E. B., & Putnam, F. W. (1992). *Manual for the dissociative experiences scale*. Beloit, WI: Author.

Chefetz, R. A. (2000). Affect dysregulation as a way of life. *Journal of the American Academy of Psychoanalysis, 28*, 289–303.

Chu, J. A. (2001). A decline in the abuse of children? *Journal of Trauma and Dissociation, 2(2),* 1–4.

Davies, J., & Frawley, M. G. (1994). *Treating the adult survivor of childhood sexual abuse: A psychoanalytic perspective*. New York: Basic Books.

Dell, P. F. (1998). Axis II pathology in outpatients with Dissociative Identity Disorder. *Journal of Nervous and Mental Disease, 186*, 352–356.

Dell, P. F. (2001). Why the diagnostic criteria for dissociative identity disorder should be changed. *Journal of Trauma and Dissociation, 2(1)*, 7–37.

Dell, P. F. (2006a). The Multidimensional Inventory of Dissociation (MID): A comprehensive measure of pathological dissociation. *Journal of Trauma & Dissociation, 7(2)*, 77–106.

Dell, P. F. (2006b). A new model of dissociative identity disorder. *Psychiatric Clinics of North America, 29(1)*, 1–26

Dell, P. F. (2009). The phenomena of pathological dissociation. In P. F. Dell & J. A. O'Neil (Eds.), *Dissociation and the dissociative disorders: DSM-V and beyond* (pp. 225–237). New York: Routledge.

Dolan, B., Evans, C., & Norton, K. (1995). Multiple axis II diagnoses of personality disorder. *British Journal of Psychiatry, 166*, 107–112.

Ellenson, G. S. (1986). Disturbances of perception in adult female incest survivors. *Social Casework, 67*, 149–159.

Ferenczi, S. (1949). Confusion of tongues between the adult and the child. *International Journal of Psycho-Analysis, 30*, 225–231.

Fine, C. G. (1991). Treatment stabilization and crisis prevention: Pacing the therapy of the multiple personality disorder patient. *Psychiatric Clinics of North America, 14*, 661–676.

Fischer, K. W., & Ayoub, C. (1994). Affective splitting and dissociation in normal and maltreated children: Developmental pathways for self in relationships. In D. Cicchetti & S. L. Toth (Eds.), *Rochester Symposium on Developmental Psychopathology, 5*, 149–222.

Fonagy, P., Gergely, G., Jurist, E. L., & Target, M. (2002). *Affect regulation, mentalization, and the development of the self.* New York: Other Press.

Fonagy, P., Steele, M., Steele, H., et al. (1996). Attachment, the reflective self and borderline states: The predictive specificity of the Adult Attachment Interview and pathological emotional development. In S. Goldberg, R. Muir, & J. Kerr (Eds.), *Attachment Theory: Social Developmental and Clinical Perspectives* (pp. 233–278). Hillsdale, NJ: The Analytic Press.

Fonagy, P., Target, M., Gergely, G., et al. (2003). The developmental roots of borderline personality disorder in early attachment relationships: A theory and some evidence. *Psychoanalytic Inquiry, 23*, 412–459.

Frankel, J. (2002). Exploring Ferenczi's concept of identification with the aggressor: Its role in everyday life and the therapeutic relationship. *Psychoanalytic Dialogues, 12*, 101–140.

Freyd, J. J. (1996). *Betrayal trauma: The logic of forgetting childhood abuse.* Cambridge, MA: Harvard University Press.

Golier, J. A., Yehuda, R., Bierer, L. M., et al. (2003). The relationship of borderline personality disorder to posttraumatic stress disorder and traumatic events. *American Journal of Psychiatry, 160*, 2018–2024.

Golynkina, K., & Ryle, A. (1999). The identification and characteristics of the partially dissociated states of patients with borderline personality disorder. *British Journal of Medical Psychology, 72*, 429–445.

Goodman, M., Weiss, D. S., Koenigsberg, H., et al. (2000). The role of childhood trauma in differences in affective instability in those with personality disorders. *CNS Spectrums, 8(10)*, 763–770.

Gunderson, J. G., & Sabo, A. N. (1993). The phenomenological and conceptual interface between borderline personality disorder and PTSD. *American Journal of Psychiatry, 150*, 19–27.

Herman, J. L. (1992). *Trauma and recovery.* New York: Basic Books.

Herman, J. L., & Van der Kolk, B. A. (1987). Traumatic antecedents of borderline personality disorder. In B. A. van der Kolk (Ed.), *Psychological trauma.* Washington, DC: American Psychiatric Press, pp. 111–126.

Hesse, E., & Main, M. (1999). Second generation effects of unresolved trauma in non-maltreating parents: Dissociated, frightened and threatening parental behavior. *Psychoanalytic Inquiry, 19*, 481–540.

Howell, E. F. (1996). Dissociation in masochism and psychopathic sadism. *Contemporary Psychoanalysis, 32*, 427–452.

Howell, E. F. (1997a). Desperately seeking attachment: A psychoanalytic reframing of the harsh superego. *Dissociation, 10*, 230–239.

Howell, E. F. (1997b). Masochism: A bridge to the other side of abuse. *Dissociation, 10*, 240–245.

Howell, E. F. (2002). Back to the "states": Victim and abuser states in borderline personality disorder. *Psychoanalytic Dialogues, 12(6)*, 921–957.

Howell, E. F. (2003). Narcissism, a relational aspect of dissociation. *Journal of Trauma and Dissociation, 4(3)*, 51–72.

Kernberg, O. F. (1975). *Borderline conditions and pathological narcissism.* Northvale, NJ: Jason Aronson.

Kernberg, O. F. (1998). Object relations theory in clinical practice. *Psychoanalytic Quarterly, 57*, 481–504.

Kluft, R. P. (1991). Clinical presentations of multiple personality disorder. *Psychiatric Clinics of North America, 14*, 605–630.

Kreisman, J., & Straus, H. (1989). *I hate you—don't leave me: Understanding the borderline personality.* New York: Avon.

Kroll, J. (1993). *PTSD/Borderlines in therapy.* New York: Norton.

Laddis, A., & Dell, P. F. (2003). Dissociation and personality traits in 100 persons with borderline personality disorder. *International Society for the Study of Personality Disorders*, Florence, Italy.

Lansky, M. R. (2003). Discussion of Peter Fonagy et al.: The developmental roots of borderline personality disorder in early attachment relationships: A theory and some evidence. *Psychoanalytic Inquiry*, *23*, 461–473.

Lerner, H., Sugarman, A., & Barbour, C. G. (1985). Patterns of ego boundary disturbance in neurotic, borderline, and schizophrenic patients. *Psychoanalytic Psychology*, *2*, 47–66.

Linehan, M., & Koerner, K. (1993). A behavioral theory of borderline personality disorder. In J. Paris (Ed.), *Borderline Personality Disorder: Etiology and treatment*. Washington, DC: American Psychiatric Press.

Liotti, G. (1992). Disorganized/disoriented attachment in the etiology of the dissociative disorders. *Dissociation*, *5*, 196–204.

Liotti, G. (1999a). Disorganization of attachment as a model for understanding dissociative pathology. In J. Solomon & C. George, *Attachment Disorganization*. New York: Guilford.

Liotti, G. (1999b). Understanding the dissociative processes: The contribution of attachment theory. *Psychoanalytic Inquiry*, *19*, 757–783.

Lyons-Ruth, K. (1991). Rapprochement or Approchement: Mahler's Theory reconsidered from the vantage point of recent research on early attachment relationships. *Psychoanalytic Psychology*, *8*, 1–23.

Lyons-Ruth, K. (1996). Attachment relationships among children with aggressive behavior problems: The role of disorganized early attachment patterns. *Journal of Consulting and Clinical Psychology*, *64*, 64–73.

Lyons-Ruth, K. (1999). Two person unconscious: Intersubjective dialogue, enactive relational representation, and the emergence of new forms of relational organization. *Psychoanalytic Inquiry*, *19*, 576–617.

Lyons-Ruth, K. (2001). The two person construction of defenses: Disorganized attachment strategies, unintegrated mental states and hostile/helpless relational processes. *Psychologist Psychoanalyst*, *21*, 40–45.

Lyons-Ruth, K. (2003). Disorganized attachment and the relational context of dissociation. Paper presented in the symposium, 'Complex sequellae of disorganized attachment and unresolved trauma,' at the *International society for Traumatic Stress Studies*, Chicago.

Lyons-Ruth, K., Bronfman, E., & Atwood, G. (1999). A relational diathesis model of hostile-helpless states of mind. In J. Solomon & C. George (Eds.), *Attachment disorganization*. New York: Guilford.

Lyons-Ruth, K., Bronfman, E., & Parsons, E. (1999). Maternal disrupted affective communication, maternal frightened or frightening behavior, and disorganized infant attachment strategies. In J. Vondra & D. Barnett (Eds.), Atypical patterns of infant attachment: Theory, research and current directions. *Monographs of the Society for Research in Child Development*, *64*, serial No. 258.

Main, M., & Hesse, E. (1990). Parents' unresolved traumatic experiences are related to infant disorganized attachment status: Is frightened and/or frightening behavior the linking mechanism? In M. T. Greenberg, D. Cicchetti & E. M. Cummings (Eds.), *Attachment in the preschool years*. Chicago: U. Chicago Press, pp. 161–182.

Main, M., & Hesse, E. (1992). Disorganized/disoriented infant behavior in the strange situation, lapses in the monitoring of reasoning and discourse during the parent's Adult Attachment Interview, and dissociative states. In M. Ammaniti & D. Stern (Eds.), *Attachment and psychoanalysis* (translated from the Italian). pp. 86–140.

Masterson, J. F. (1976). *Psychotherapy of the borderline adult: A developmental approach*. New York: Brunner/Mazel.

McLean, L. M., & Gallop, R. (2003). Implications of childhood sexual abuse for adult borderline personality disorder and complex posttraumatic stress disorder. *American Journal of Psychiatry*, *160*, 369–371.

Millon, T. (1981). *Disorders of personality, DSM-III, Axis II*. New York: Wiley.

Nijenhuis, E. R. S. (1999). *Somatoform dissociation: Phenomena, measurement, and theoretical issues*. The Netherlands: Van Gorcum.

Nijenhuis, E. R. S., Vanderlinden, J., & Spinhoven, P. (1998). Animal defensive reactions as a model for trauma-induced dissociative reaction. *Journal of Traumatic Stress*, *11*, 243–260.

Nijenhuis, E. R. S., Van der Hart, O., & Steele, K. (2004a). Strukturelle Dissoziation der Persönlichkeitsstruktur, traumatischer Ursprung, phobische Residuen. In L. Reddemann, A. Hofmann, & U. Gast, *Psychotherapie der dissoziativen Störungen* (pp. 47–69). Stuttgart: Thieme.

Nijenhuis, E. R. S., Van der Hart, O., & Steele, K. (2004b). Trauma-related structural dissociation of the personality. Trauma Information Pages website, January 2004. Web URL: http://www.trauma-pages.com/nijenhuis-2004.htm

Ogata, S. N., Silk, K. R. Goodrich, S., Lohr, N. E., Westen, D., & Hill, E. M. (1990). Childhood sexual and physical abuse in adult patients with borderline personality disorder. *American Journal of Psychiatry*, *147*, 1008–1012.

Ogawa, J. R., Sroufe, L. A., Weinfeld, N. S., Carlson, E. A., & Egeland, B. (1997). Development and the fragmented self: Longitudinal study of dissociative symptomatology in a nonclinical sample. *Development and Psychopathology*, *9*, 855–879.

Perry, B. D. (1999). The memory of states: How the brain stores and retrieves traumatic experience. In J. Goodwin & R. Attias (Eds.), *Splintered reflections: Images of the body in treatment*. New York: Basic Books, pp. 9–38.

Perry, J. C., & Herman, J. L. (1993). Trauma and defense in the etiology of borderline personality disorder. In J. Paris (Ed.), *Borderline personality disorder: Etiology and treatment*. Washington, DC: American Psychiatric Press, pp. 123–139.

Pollock, P. H., Broadbent, M., Clarke, S., Dorrian, A., & Ryle, A. (2001). The personality structure questionnaire (PSQ): A measure of the multiple self states model of

identity disturbance in cognitive analytic therapy. *Clinical Psychology and Psychotherapy*, 8, 59–72.
Putnam, F. W. (1989). *Diagnosis and treatment of multiple personality disorder*. New York: Guilford.
Putnam, F. W. (1997). *Dissociative disorders in children and adolescents: A developmental perspective*. New York: Guilford.
Putnam, F. W., Guroff, J. J., Silberman, E. K., Barban, L., & Post, R. M. (1986). The clinical phenomenology of multiple personality disorder: Review of 100 recent cases. *Journal of Clinical Psychiatry*, *47*, 285–293.
Ross, C. A. (1989). *Multiple personality disorder: Diagnosis, clinical features and treatment*. New York: Wiley.
Ross, C. A. (1997). Histrionic and borderline comorbidity in DID. Paper presented at the *14th International Conference of the International Society for the Study of Dissociation*. Montreal, QC.
Ryle, A. (1997a). The structure and development of borderline personality disorder: a proposed model. *British Journal of Psychiatry*, *170*, 82–87.
Ryle, A. (1997b). *Cognitive analytic therapy and borderline personality disorder: The model and the method*. New York: Wiley.
Şar, V., Akyüz, G., & Doğan, O. (2007). Prevalence of dissociative disorders among women in the general population. *Psychiatry Research, 149(1–3)*, 169–176.
Şar, V., Akyüz, G., Kuğu, N., Öztürk, E., & Ertem-Vehid, H. (2006). Axis-I dissociative disorder comorbidity in borderline personality disorder and reports of childhood trauma. *Journal of Clinical Psychiatry*, *67(10)*, 1583–1590.
Şar, V., Kundakçı, T., Kızıltan, E., Yargıç, I. L., Tutkun, H., Bakım, B., Bozkurt, O., Özpulat, T., Keser, V., & Özdemir, O. (2003). The axis-I dissociative disorder comorbidity of borderline personality disorder among psychiatric outpatients. *Journal of Trauma and Dissociation*, *4(1)*, 119–136.
Schmideberg, M. (1959). The borderline patient. In S. Arieti (Ed.), *American Handbook of Psychiatry, Vol. 1*. New York: Basic Books, pp. 398–416.
Schore, A. N. (2003a). *Affect dysregulation and disorders of the self*. New York: W.W. Norton.
Schore, A. N. (2003b). *Affect regulation and the repair of the self*. New York: W.W. Norton.
Silk, K., Nigg, J., Westen, D., & Lohr, N. (1997). Severity of childhood sexual abuse, borderline symptoms, and familial environment. In M. Zanarini (Ed.), *Role of sexual abuse in the etiology of borderline personality disorder*. Washington, DC: American Psychiatric Press, pp. 131–164.
Simeon, D., Nelson, D., Elias, R., Greenberg, J., & Hollander, E. (2003). Relationship of personality to dissociation and childhood trauma in borderline personality disorder. *CNS Spectrums*, *8*, 755–762.
Solomon, J., & George, C. (1999). The place of disorganization in attachment theory: Linking classic observations with contemporary findings, In J. Solomon & C. George (Eds.), *Attachment disorganization*. New York: Guilford.
Steele, K., Van der Hart, O., & Nijenhuis, E. R. S. (2003). A structural model of dissociation. Retrieved November 23, 2003, from http://www.atlantapsychotherapy.com/articles/steele1.htm.
Steinberg, M., Cicchetti, D., Buchanan, J., Hall, P., & Rounsaville, B. (1993). Clinical assessment of dissociative symptoms and disorders: The Structured Clinical Interview for DSM-IV Dissociative Disorders (SCID-D). *Dissociation*, *6*, 3–15.
Stern, A. (1938). Psychoanalytic investigation of and therapy in the border line group of neuroses. *Psychoanalytic Quarterly*, *7*, 467–489.
Stern, D. N. (1985). *The interpersonal world of the infant: A view from psychoanalysis and developmental psychology*. New York: Basic Books.
Stone, M. H. (1990). Incest in the borderline patient, In R. P. Kluft (Ed.), *Incest-related syndromes of adult psychopathology*. Washington, DC: American Psychiatric Press.
Stone, M. H. (1992). *The fate of borderline patients*. New York: Guilford.
Terr, L. C. (1990). *Too scared to cry: How trauma affects children and ultimately us all*. New York: Basic Books.
Terr, L. C. (1994). *Unchained memories*. New York: Basic Books.
Van der Kolk, B. (1996). The complexity of adaptation to trauma: Self-regulation, stimulus discrimination, and characterological development. In B. A. van der Kolk, A. C. McFarlane & L. Weisaeth (Eds.), *Traumatic stress: The effects of overwhelming experience on mind, body and society*. New York: Guilford Press.
Waters, E., Merrick, S., Treboux, D., Crowell, J., & Albersheim, L. (2000). Attachment security in infancy and early adulthood: A twenty-year longitudinal study. *Child Development*, *71*, 684–689.
Westen, D., & Shedler, J. (1999a). Revising and assessing axis II, part I: Developing a clinically and empirically valid assessment method. *American Journal of Psychiatry*, *156*, 258–272.
Westen, D., & Shedler, J. (1999b). Revising and assessing axis II, part II: Toward an empirically based and clinically useful classification of personality disorders. *American Journal of Psychiatry*, *156*, 273–285.
Williams, L. M. (1994). Recall of childhood trauma: A prospective study of women's memories of child sexual abuse. *Journal of Consulting and Clinical Psychology*, *62(6)*, 1167–1176.
Yen, S., Shea, M. T., Battle, C. L., et al. (2002). Traumatic exposure and posttraumatic stress disorder in borderline, schizotypal, avoidant, and obsessive-compulsive personality disorders: Findings from the collaborative longitudinal personality disorders study. *Journal of Nervous and Mental Disease*, *190*, 510–518.
Zanarini, M. C. (1997). Evolving perspectives on the etiology of borderline personality disorder. In M. C. Zanarini (Ed.), *The role of sexual abuse in the etiology of borderline personality disorder*. Washington: American Psychiatric Press, pp. 1–14.

Zanarini, M. C., Dubo, E. D., Lewis, R. E., & Williams, A. A. (1997). Childhood factors associated with the development of borderline personality disorder. In M. C. Zanarini (Ed.), *The role of sexual abuse in the etiology of borderline personality disorder*. Washington: American Psychiatric Press, pp. 29–44.

Zanarini, M. C., Ruser, T. F., Frankenburg, F. R., Hennen, J., & Gunderson, J. G. (2000). Risk factors associated with the dissociative experiences of borderline patients. *Journal of Nervous and Mental Disease*, *188*, 26–30.

33 Opioid Use Disorder and Dissociation

Eli Somer, PhD

OUTLINE

This chapter explores the interrelationship between addiction to narcotics and dissociation. The focal premise is that drug use disorder, particularly Opioid Use Disorder (OUD), is a condition driven by the need to chemically induce a state that mimics psychogenic dissociation. In other words, some individuals suffering from OUD are motivated to chemically induce a dissociative state to defend themselves against the memories of childhood abuse and the related pain experience. Consequently, I call this *chemical dissociation.*

For the purposes of this chapter, dissociation is assumed to be a psychological defense mechanism developed in the face of extreme, or prolonged and inescapable, physical, sexual, and emotional traumata. It works as a shield against the conscious experience of overwhelming stress by producing psychological and/or physical analgesia, emotional calming, and a breakdown of the normally integrated experiential components of behavior, affect, sensation, knowledge, and identity. The main thesis in this essay is that for many individuals suffering from OUD, chemical dissociation serves similar purposes by inducing powerful tranquilizing and numbing effects.

It is posited that in a certain subgroup of people, OUD constitutes the second stage of a strategy developed for coping with intolerable experiences and their memories. When psychological dissociation is ineffective, or when substances that are able to produce rapid and efficient relief are available, some traumatized persons look beyond their own mental resources for relief. When these victims get access to consciousness-altering substances, they discover the immediate advantages of chemical dissociation, and its rapid effect on both the body and the mind. This is when chemical dissociation can become a self-medicating alternative. In such persons, the first-stage psychogenic dissociation may manifest itself in the usual way, but it is more often masked by second-stage chemical dissociation in the intoxicated state.

To substantiate this thesis I present data on common etiological roots of posttraumatic stress, dissociative disorders, and OUD; common neurobiological mechanisms of these disorders; their comorbidity, and their similarities in the dimension of subjective experience (phenomenology).

33.1 COMMON ETIOLOGICAL ROOTS

People with a childhood trauma history constitute a significant proportion of opioid users (Van Hassselt, Ammerman, Glancy, & Bukstein, 1992). An overview of several epidemiological studies of comorbid posttraumatic stress disorder (PTSD) and substance use disorders (SUD) reveals that the odds of drug use disorders are three times greater in individuals with PTSD than in those without it (Chilcoat & Menard, 2003). Gianconia et al. (2000), for example, reported that the data for comorbid cases of SUD and PTSD in which PTSD was the primary disorder was 66.7%. Four predominant hypotheses have been proposed to explain the consistent findings around PTSD-SUD comorbidity:

1. High-risk hypothesis: Drug use is a high-risk behavior that increases the risk for trauma exposure (Brown & Wolfe, 1994).
2. Susceptibility hypothesis: Drug users are more susceptible to PTSD following exposure to threatening events (Brown & Wolfe, 1994).
3. No direct relationship hypothesis: The association appears because both conditions derive from a third common factor (e.g., genetics).
4. Self-medication hypothesis: Individuals with PTSD use substances to control their emotional pain (Khantzian, 1985).

Using reports about the date of onset of the disorder, Kessler et al. (1995) estimated that among comorbid PTSD-SUD subjects, PTSD occurred first in 53% to 65% of the men, and in 65% to 84% of the women, arguing that PTSD generally predates SUD in those who experience both disorders. Based on their prospective study, Chilcoat and Menard (2003) concluded that preexisting SUD does not significantly increase the risk for PTSD among adults relative to those without SUD. On the other hand, adults with a history of PTSD had a fourfold increase in the risk of SUD compared with those without PTSD. Hypotheses 1 to 3 do not predict such findings, while hypothesis 4 does, lending relative support for the self-medication hypothesis. Further evidence for a possible casual relationship between PTSD and SUD has been provided by Stewart, Conrod, Pihl, and Dongier (1999). They show that the severity of alcohol disorder symptoms correlates with the severity of PTSD arousal symptoms and that the severity of anxiolytic and analgesic dependence correlates with the severity of PTSD numbing and arousal symptoms. They also show how analgesic dependence severity correlates with PTSD intrusion symptoms. Other researchers (Liebschutz et al., 2002; Malinkovsky-Rummel & Hansen, 1993) have demonstrated that adult SUD is the most prominent consequence of childhood abuse.

The prominence of childhood trauma in the lives of recovering OUD patients has been demonstrated in three separate studies conducted in Israel. Data consistently showed higher traumatization history scores (typically reflecting childhood abuse and neglect) among patients recovering from OUD compared to those measured in consecutive admissions to outpatient stress clinics (Somer, 2004; Somer, Soref, & Lawental, 2004; Somer & Avni, 2003).

In sum, trauma history, particularly childhood trauma, would seem to be an etiological factor in both dissociative disorders and OUD. Significant statistical relationships exist among trauma history, severity of PTSD symptoms, and SUD, especially the use of tranquilizing drugs.

33.2 TRAUMA AND THE NEUROBIOLOGICAL BASIS FOR OUD

How does trauma influence the biochemistry of the brain? Is there a possible connection between posttraumatic neurochemical changes in the brain and the proclivity to self-medicate with opiates? In the locus ceruleus, hippocampus, amygdala, and anterior hypothalamus, the areas of the brain most concerned with emotions and stress, there is a high density of both norepinephrine and opioid receptors (Langer, 1978). People with PTSD responding to cues associated with noxious stimuli trigger the firing of the locus ceruleus, releasing abnormal levels of key hormones involved in response to stress, such as norepinephrine (NE) (Cohen & Servan-Schreiber, 1992). Van der Kolk, Greenberg, Boyd et al. (1985) suggested that physiological aspects of both opiate withdrawal and PTSD are related to central noradrenergic hyperactivity associated with a relative decrease in opioid receptor binding; such endogenous opioid release may result in a temporary sense of control. When people are in danger, they produce high levels of natural opioids, which can also temporarily mask physical pain. Scientists have found that people with PTSD continue to produce much higher levels even after the danger has passed; this may be associated with the blunted emotions associated with the condition (Yehuda, 1998). The relationship between peri- and posttraumatic secretion of natural opioids and dissociation has not yet been explored, but the role of dissociation in shielding individuals from the full impact of trauma has been discussed extensively in the literature (e.g., Chu & Dill, 1990; Irwin, 1994; Herman, Perry, & Van der Kolk, 1989; Putnam, 1995).

The animal model of inescapable shock parallels the equivalent of learned helplessness in humans and could shed further light on neurochemical mechanisms likely to be operating. Animals exposed to inescapable shock develop analgesia when exposed to another stressor shortly thereafter; this response is mediated by endogenous opioids and is reversed by naloxone (Van der Kolk & Greenberg, 1987). Subsequent studies suggest that serious physical threats may induce analgesia and numbness in human victims as well (Cardeña et al., 1998; Cardeña & Spiegel, 1993) and that anesthesia-analgesia were the symptoms that best predicted cases of posttraumatic dissociative disorders (Nijenhuis, Spinhoven, Vanderlinden et al., 1998). In animal models of PTSD, numbness is likened to a conditioned analgesia in response to inescapable shock (Foa, Zinbarg, & Rothbaum, 1992; Pitman, Van der Kolk, Orr, & Greenberg, 1990). Schiele (1992) even argued that chronic stress induces a physiological state that resembles dependency on high levels of exogenous opiates; and that when severely stressed, subsequent fear and the accompanying endogenous opioid secretion attenuates the perceived intensity of subsequent shocks.

All told, preliminary evidence shows that traumatized people produce elevated levels of natural opioids, which can temporarily mask emotional and physical pain. It is, therefore, conceivable that traumatized individuals would find the effect of exogenous opiates to be a gratifying shield between posttraumatic torment and conscious awareness.

33.3 COMORBIDITY OF DISSOCIATIVE DISORDERS AND OUD

If OUD and dissociative disorders have common etiological roots and if opioids (either endogenous or exogenous) are a natural recourse in the face of traumatic duress, it is only natural that OUD and dissociative disorders would co-occur. Most of the literature on dissociative disorders (DD), trauma, and addictions reveal a probabilistic concurrence of the phenomena. Ross, Kronson, Koensen et al. (1992) reported that individuals who abuse alcohol and drugs have four times the incidence of child sexual abuse and three times the incidence of DD compared to nonclinical controls. In a survey of 185 individuals with severe dissociative disorders, 57% had problems with drug abuse (Rivera, 1991). Dunn, Paolo, Ryan, and Van Fleet (1995) showed that 41.5% of chemically dependent veterans received an average DES score of 15 or higher (DES range 0–100), which is considered to be rather elevated. In comparison, Israeli patients with DD scored 29.45 on the DES (Somer, Dolgin, & Saadon, 2001). The average total score on the Hebrew-Dissociative Experiences Scale (H-DES) for detoxified heroin users was 21.27 (SD = 15.02) (Somer & Avni, 2003). In comparison, Somer, Dolgin, and Saadon (2001) reported mean H-DES scores for two relevant groups as follows: Post-traumatic Stress Disorder and Acute Stress Disorder: 20.36; Dissociative Disorders: 29.45.

A newly developed tool for the assessment of pathological dissociation, the Hebrew version of the Multidimensional Inventory of Dissociation (H-MID; Somer & Dell, 2005) has a range of 0 to 100, with scores of 21 or higher indicative of possible dissociative psychopathology. A study was conducted in Israel comparing a recovering heroin users group, to respondents sampled from stress and trauma clinics. One in three of the ex-heroin users scored 21 or higher on the H-MID, compared to only one in 10 for the stress and trauma clinic controls (Somer, Soref, & Lawental, 2004). The same study similarly indicated that ex-heroin users showed significantly higher scores on posttraumatic measures of avoidance, intrusion, and hyperarousal than the stress and trauma clinic controls. The same ex-heroin users sample was also statistically more disturbed than stress and trauma clinic controls on the following H-MID clinical scales: memory problems, flashbacks, somatoform dissociation, identity confusion, ego-alien experiences, self-alteration, self-states and alters, and Schneiderian first-rank symptoms.

To recapitulate, a history of childhood trauma and dissociative psychopathology seem to be risk factors for OUD. The insufficiency of psychogenic dissociation in the protection of the conscious mind could be a pathway to OUD. Deficiencies in dissociative defenses may be the consequence of great posttraumatic suffering that cannot be effectively contained, or of meager dissociative capacities. Thus, we hypothesize that some survivors of child abuse self-medicate with opiates to mimic chemicals endogenously released to attenuate traumatic distress. This hypothesis predicts that individuals with OUD would actually seek out and go through dissociative experiences during opiate use, a testable prediction.

33.4 SIMILAR PHENOMENOLOGY

The similarity between chemically induced and psychologically induced symptoms of dissociation required special underscoring of the disclaimers to the instructions on scales measuring dissociation, which ask respondents to endorse items only if the described experiences did NOT occur under the influence of alcohol or drugs (e.g., DES: Carlson & Putnam, 1993; H-MID: Somer & Dell, 2005; MID: Dell, 2006).

To study the meaning and function of opioid use among a group of Israelis recovering from a heroin use disorder, we conducted five focus groups comprised of 10 to 15 individuals each. In total, we met 66 consenting persons receiving outpatient treatment in private and government drug rehabilitation clinics.[1] These individuals had abused alcohol, cannabis, amphetamines, and opiates, but for 60 (91%) participants, heroin was the preferred drug. Fifty-nine participants (89%) had a history of child

[1] The author wishes to thank Ronit Avni, MSW, for contributing the idea for this study.

abuse. I asked them to describe their experience with the drugs. Specifically, I asked them to tell me what effects and sensations of the drugs had been most meaningful or important to them. In other words, what functions had the drugs fulfilled? What role had they fulfilled? Their discussions were audiotaped and transcribed verbatim. Analysis of the text was conducted in two main steps. In the first phase, I read the transcribed discussions of the five groups and systematically coded and sorted the material into key themes by means of cross-case analyses with a constant-comparison method. Core themes were identified and compared, and analytical categories were later illustrated/exemplified by specific quotations (Krueger, 1994).

Four main themes emerged from the focus groups in regard to their experience with drugs: (1) chemical amnesia, (2) chemical suppression of posttraumatic arousal symptoms, (3) chemical numbing, depersonalization, and derealization, and (4) soothing, gratifying pleasure. The themes will be presented with illustrative, representative quotes.

33.4.1 Chemical Amnesia

One recovering heroin user described how the substance has helped him not to remember current and past feelings and thoughts:

> Heroin helps me forget the pain in my life. Soon after the injection I feel I can stop thinking about the troubles … the horrible memories … without heroin I couldn't leave home. I was simply too overwhelmed.

He had experienced the drug as a means of distancing himself from incapacitating memories and of reducing conscious awareness of current troubling issues.

Here is how another recovering user described the amnestic function of her drug habit:

> When I am high I don't care about the horrors of my childhood. I manage to ignore my fears as if they had never been there. I can't remember my nightmares … geez, I hate those nightmares … they keep haunting me for years. Only when I'm on heroin I get not to think about them … It is as if I never dreamt them in the first place … and my daily problems with bills and my family become so small I could hardly care about them. They just fade away.

This individual uses the substance to induce a memory disorder that shields her against chronic nightmares concerning childhood traumata. It seems that she also finds the amnestic agent useful in helping her forget about current life problems and challenges. A habit that was conceivably developed to deal with posttraumatic distress has evolved into an apparently maladaptive means to cope with daily stressors.

33.4.2 Chemical Suppression of Posttraumatic Arousal Symptoms

Several respondents described heroin as their preferred calming agent and as an effective course toward controlling a variety of posttraumatic symptoms, representing both sympathetic and affective arousal. Here is what one 35-year-old participant, a survivor of child abuse and a convicted wife beater, said when he talked about the role that heroin played in the management of his explosive anger:

> I have always been a very angry person. Often I can't control my temper. I feel that the anger consumes me…. I feel like I want to get even. It's like I constantly want to beat the s**t out of someone. Anyone. I have so much hate in me, it consumes me. After I shoot up, the anger doesn't bother me anymore. It's like I disconnect it. I turn it off. Maybe it is still there, but I am elsewhere, unbothered by it.

This man describes lifelong problems with violent anger. He portrays heroin use as a process of self-medication. The burning and distressful drive for violence ("It consumes me") only subsides following the use of narcotics. This man eloquently portrays a dissociative experience when he acknowledges the existence of the dissociated anger during the consciousness-altered state.

A 28-year-old woman, an abandoned child that lived her entire childhood in foster homes, portrayed her heroin intoxication in terms of its role in controlling fears, anxieties, and an overall tense condition:

> I suffer from many fears. Men scare me, I can't trust women, and children make me feel uneasy, I hate the night, I can't stand crowds, and I dread doctors and dentists. I am constantly on edge. On guard. As soon as I get high I, umm … nothing bothers me anymore. I can calm down and it's like I am able to deal with many of those fears much better … sometimes I also get a feeling that nothing scares me anymore. It's such a relief to be able to unwind from all my stresses and get a real break from my tensions … it sure beats sleep.

This woman describes many fears triggered by others. In a world crowded by human beings her fears seem to be constantly triggered. Simple interactions, even with ostensibly innocuous figures (e.g., children) produce distress to a point where she cannot receive proper medical care without the experience of considerable discomfort. Her only gratifying respite from her steady state of hypervigilance and hyperarousal is opiate intoxication.

33.4.3 Chemical Numbing, Depersonalization, and Derealization

Most comments on the experience sought in or felt during heroin use were also characteristic of classical dissociative experiences. One 50-year-old recovering user, an incest survivor, described how a variety of somatic problems had been temporarily eased by the drug use:

> I always walk around with a splitting headache. No pain medication has ever helped me. I also have this other problem, it is as if I have extensive burn wounds, my skin is sore, I can't be touched.... I think I might be arthritic, too. I have been roughed up pretty badly throughout my life. I think that my joints are a total mess.... Heroin lets me not feel these pains and aches. For a few hours I am fairly well. I can rest.
>
> I hate my sexuality, my sex drive makes me sick.... When I'm high I am not in touch with my real sexual drive. I prefer it that way.

Heroin is described here as a preferred analgesic and as an effective depressing agent for her conflicted sexual drive. Several participants talked about depersonalizing and derealizing effects that they derived from heroin use. Here is what a 37-year-old former prostitute had to say:

> I can disregard my emotions when I am on the drug. I couldn't care less about myself because I hardly felt myself. It is pretty awful to be myself you know.... I'd rather not feel the stuff that makes me feel so bad, the sadness and the emptiness, those endless internal quarrels. This white stuff helps me not to feel my depression, I can ignore all the threats and the dangers in this f**king world they don't even seem real anymore, I couldn't give a s**t about nothing. This world is full of all sorts of creeps who always want to f**k you or hurt you. When I was on the drug, they could take my body and do what they f**king pleased with it. I wasn't home.

This individual convincingly tells the interviewer how she yearned to distance herself from her emotional pain by the disconnecting effect of the opiate. Ironically, this survivor of child abuse is being continuously revictimized in her sex trade profession. Chemical depersonalization helps her tolerate the unsavory experiences involved in providing sexual services to her customers.

33.4.4 Soothing, Gratifying Pleasure

Heroin did not only help our respondents in numbing their pain and in distancing them from their painful memories, but also helped generate pleasurable feelings that were ordinarily so scarce in their lives. Here is what a 40-year-old man who grew up in an extremely neglectful and emotionally abusive family said:

> I always feel cold. I am cold from the inside ... I feel so empty. When I shoot up, I have this great rush of warmth building up at the pit of my stomach. It radiates inside as if I have an internal fireplace. It's so comforting.

His description of the appealing warmth of the drug can only be appreciated when contrasted with the portrayed coldness inside him. This same man also talked about how he had yearned to be hugged and comforted by his mother whom he also depicted as a "cold bitch."

It seemed that some participants had anthropomorphized the heroin and had perceived it as having benevolent traits. One recovering heroin user shared the following observations about his unresolved craving for the substance:

> Nothing beats the feeling I got from heroin ... just found this good stuff irresistible ... like a gentle blanket that was lovingly wrapped around my shoulders it covered my entire body, it calmed me down, sometimes it glowed from me within.
>
> There was something sweet about the seduction of the stuff. I am not sure I can describe it to you but imagine being caressed from inside.

This man described the substance as a "loving" protective entity that is capable of radiating soothing warmth. His account of the opiate also portrays a "being" that is quite sensual, almost erotic.

The results of this qualitative inquiry render credible preliminary support to the idea that some survivors of childhood abuse or neglect utilize heroin defensively as a dissociating agent, specifically seeking the numbing, depersonalizing, and amnestic capacities of the drug. Moreover, a few survivors that were recovering from their addiction assigned benevolent nurturing human qualities to the drug. This was a sad testimonial to the emotional emaciation of these individuals.

Preliminary controlled research provided some quantitative support for these qualitative findings. Somer and Avni (2003) demonstrated that respondents with higher trauma scores were more likely to report dissociative experiences during their drug use (chemical dissociation).

That is to say, traumatized users tended to experience heroin as producing more dissociative experiences than users with a milder trauma history. Specifically, these drug-free high dissociators were more likely to report, retrospectively, depersonalizing and derealizing experiences when they had been using drugs. Furthermore, stronger dissociative experiences during drug use were found to be related to greater psychological distress during interuse craving (nonwithdrawal-related). This datum demonstrates the possible shielding function of the narcotic for users who are survivors of child abuse. For respondents who tended to experience higher levels of chemical dissociation during heroin use, being off the drug was more distressful than for users who had experienced lower levels of chemically induced dissociation. Interestingly, a statistical relationship was also discovered between retrospectively reported psychological distress, experienced during interuse craving, and current psychological dissociation, which was measured in a detoxified state. This may imply that when these individuals attempt to relinquish their chemical dissociation by detoxification, they may experience an increase in distress that is predictive of their likelihood to employ psychological dissociation later on during their recovery. That is, the two dissociative mechanisms, exogenous and endogenous, are more likely to be measured in survivors of childhood trauma and they are interchangeable. If specific treatment for posttraumatic dissociation is not provided, detoxifying survivors may tend to substitute one type of dissociative defense with another.

The employment of psychological dissociation by survivors of child abuse who are recuperating from OUD may compromise the stability of their recovery. Dissociation has been found to be an independent predictor of abstinence from heroin use (Somer, 2003). The two variables appear to be inversely related: recovering heroin-dependent persons who were high dissociators are less likely to enjoy favorable treatment outcomes as reflected in extended periods of abstinence. Dissociative psychopathology may be conducive to relapse by compromising the awareness of rehabilitating opiate users to high-risk situations. It may also impair the quality of control over their behavior. Alternatively, and as posited earlier, persons who had only recently become abstinent could be more likely to compensate for the missing chemical dissociation by evoking their psychogenic trauma-related dissociative defenses.

Further support to the interchangeability of psychogenic and chemical dissociation in the lives of recovering opiate users was provided by Somer, Soref, and Lawental (2004). The investigators compared dissociative psychopathology across three groups of recovering heroin users: (1) individuals on an agonist treatment; these respondents received Methadone, a synthetic, less addictive form of heroin, to keep them from uncontrolled use of street drugs; (2) individuals in early full remission who were treated in a controlled environment (inpatient detoxification and rehabilitation) and; (3) people in early full remission who were drug-free for more than 6 months. The first two groups had enjoyed some form of support and containment, either through the ingestion of heroin-mimicking substances prescribed by the clinics that were treating them or through the professional boundaries and support that were provided in the total environment of the detoxifying agency. The third group had to rely more profoundly on their own internally developed coping mechanisms. Compared to the first two research groups, these respondents reported the highest levels of psychoticism, hostility, anxiety (both general and phobic), posttraumatic intrusions, avoidance, and hyperarousal. They also scored highest on the following clinical scales of the H-MID: memory problems, flashbacks, somatoform dissociation, identity confusion, ego-alien experiences, self-alteration, self-states and alters, and Schneiderian first-rank symptoms, revealing significant dissociative psychopathology. Given that the three groups did not differ significantly on biographic indices, length of treatment, severity of drug use disorder, or trauma history, I conclude that the elevated general, posttraumatic and dissociative psychopathology was best accounted for by the want of critical sustaining factors: the strong boundaries of a treatment milieu or (synthetic) chemical dissociation. This dearth of external coping resources probably played a significant part in the exacerbation of their preexisting dissociative and related psychopathology.

The implications of the material presented in this chapter are important for the design of effective clinical practice with OUD patients. It is sensible to screen candidates for substance abuse treatment for posttraumatic and dissociative pathology. Before clinicians encourage recovering traumatized patients with drug use disorders to give up their chemical dissociation, they should vigorously address their underlying posttraumatic problems. Clearly, without a thorough resolution of trauma-related dissociation, a timely solution for the underlying psychopathology and the successful treatment outcome are less likely.

Part of the data presented in this essay are a result of a study supported by the Israel Anti-Drug Authority

REFERENCES

Cardeña, E., Holen, A., McFarlane, A., Solomon, Z., Wilkinson, C., & Spiegel, D. (1998). A multisite study of acute stress reaction to a disaster. In *Sourcebook for the DSM-IV, Vol. IV*. Washington, DC: American Psychiatric Association.

Cardeña, E., & Spiegel, D. (1993). Dissociative reactions to the San Francisco Bay area earthquake of 1989. *American Journal of Psychiatry, 150,* 474–478.

Carlson, E. B., & Putnam, F. W. (1993). An update on the Dissociative Experiences Scale. *Dissociation, 6*, 16–27.

Chilcoat, H. D., & Menard, C. (2003). Epidemiological investigations: Co-morbidity of post-traumatic stress disorder and substance use disorder. In P. Ouinmette and P. J. Brown (Eds.) *Trauma and substance abuse: Causes, consequences, and treatment of co-morbid disorders*. Washington: American Psychological Association, pp 9–28.

Cohen J. D., & Servan-Schreiber, D, (1992). A neural network model of disturbances in the processing of context in schizophrenia. *Psychiatric Annals, 22*, 131–136.

Chu, J. A., & Dill, D. L. (1990). Dissociative symptoms in relation to childhood physical and sexual abuse. *American Journal of Psychiatry, 147*, 887–892.

Dell, P. F. (2006) Multidimensional Inventory of Dissociation (MID): A comprehensive measure of pathological dissociation. *Journal of Trauma & Dissociation, 7(2),* 77–106.

Dunn, G. E., Paolo, A. M., Ryann, J. J., & Van Fleet, J. (1995). Co-morbidity of dissociative disorders among patients with substance use disorders. *Psychiatric Services, 46*(2), 153–156.

Foa, E. B., Zinbarg, R., & Rothbaum, B. (1992). Uncontrollability and unpredictability in post-traumatic stress disorder: An animal model. *Psychological Bulletin, 112*, 218–238.

Gianconia, R. M., Reinherz, H. Z., Hauf, A. C., Paradis, A. D., Wasserman, M. S., & Langhammer, D. M. (2000). Co-morbidity of substance use and post-traumatic stress disorders in a community sample of adolescents. *American Journal of Orthopsychiatry, 70,* 253–262.

Herman, J. L., Perry, J. C., & Van der Kolk, B. A. (1989). Childhood trauma in borderline personality disorder. *American Journal of Psychiatry, 146*, 490–495.

Irwin, H. J. (1994). Proneness to dissociation and traumatic childhood events. *Journal of Nervous and Mental Disease, 182*, 456–460.

Krueger, R. A., (1994*). Focus groups: A practical guide for applied research* (2nd ed.). Thousand Oaks, CA: Sage.

Langer, S. Z. (1978). Morphine and beta endorphin inhibit release of noradrenaline from cerebral cortex but not of dopamine from rat striatum. *Nature, 271*, 559–560.

Liebschutz, J., Savetsky, J. B., Saitz, R., Horton, N. J., Lloyd-Travaglini, C., & Samet, J. H. (2002). The relationship between sexual and physical abuse and substance abuse consequences. *Journal of Substance Abuse Treatment, 22,* 121–12.

Malinovsky-Rummel, R., & Hansen, D. J. (1993). Long-term consequences of childhood physical abuse. *Psychological Bulletin, 14*(10), 68–79.

Nijenhuis, E. R. S., Spinhoven, P., Vanderlinden, J., Van Dyck, R., & Van der Hart, O. (1998a). Somatoform dissociative symptoms as related to animal defensive reactions to predatory threat and injury. *Journal of Abnormal Psychology, 107,* 63–73.

Pitman, R. K., Orr, S. P., Van der Kolk, B. A., Greenberg, M. S., Meyerhof, J. L., & Mougey, E. H. (1990). Analgesia: A new dependent variable for the biological study of post-traumatic stress disorder. In M. E. Wolf, & E. D. Mosnaim, (Eds), *Post-traumatic stress disorder: Etiology, phenomenology, and treatment* (pp. 141–147). Washington: American Psychiatric Publishing.

Putnam, F. W. (1995). Development of dissociative disorders. In D. Ciccheti & D. J. Cohen (Eds.). *Development psychopathology, Vol. 2. Risk, disorder, and adaptation.* (pp. 581–608). New York: Wiley.

Rivera, M. (1991). Multiple personality disorder and the social systems: 185 cases. *Dissociation, 4(2),* 79–82.

Ross, C. R., Kronson, J., Koensen, S., Barkman, K., Clark, P., & Rockman, G. (1992). Dissociative co-morbidity in 100 chemically dependent patients. *Hospital and Community Psychiatry, 43(8),* 840–842.

Schiele, D. R. (1992). The neuropsychobiology of addication, trauma and dissociation. Paper presented at the 5th Annual Western Clinical Conference on Multiple Personality and Dissociation, Costa Mesa, CA, April 10–12.

Somer, E. (2003). Prediction of abstinence from heroin addiction by childhood trauma, dissociation, and extent of psychosocial treatment. *Addiction Research and Theory, 11*(5), 339–348.

Somer, E., & Avni, R. (2003). Dissociative phenomena among recovering heroin users and their relationship to duration of abstinence. *Journal of Social Work Practice in the Addictions, 3(1),* 25–38.

Somer, E., & Dell, P. F. (2005). The development and psychometric characteristics of the Hebrew version of the Multidimensional Inventory of Dissociation (H-MID): A valid and reliable measure of pathological dissociation. *Journal of Trauma and Dissociation, 6(1),* 31–53.

Somer, E., Dolgin, M., & Saadon, M (2001). Validation of the Hebrew version of the Dissociation Experiences Scale (H-DES) in Israel. *Journal of Trauma and Dissociation, 2(2),* 53–66.

Somer, E., Soref, E., & Lowental, E. (2004). Dissociative disorders among individuals with opiate use disorder: A research report. Jerusalem: The Israel Anti-drug Authority (In Hebrew).

Stewart, S. H., Conrod, P. J., Pihl, R. O., & Dongier, M. (1999). Relationship between post-traumatic stress symptom dimensions and substance dependence in a community-recruited sample of substance-abusing women. *Psychology of Addictive Behaviors, 13*, 78–88.

Van der Kolk, B. A., & Greenberg, M. S. (1987). Psychobiology of the trauma response: Hyperarousal, constriction and addiction to trauma, traumatic reexposure. In B. A. Van der Kolk (Ed.), *Psychological trauma.* Washington, DC: American Psychiatric Press, pp 63–87.

Van der Kolk B. A., Greenberg M. S., Boyd H., et al. (1985). Inescapable shock, neurotransmitters and addiction to trauma: Towards a psychobiology of post traumatic stress. *Biological Psychiatry 20*, 314–325.

Van Hasselt, V. B., Ammerman, R. T., Glancy, L. G., & Bukstein, O. G. (1992). Maltreatment in psychiatrically hospitalized dually diagnosed adolescent substance abusers. *Journal of the American Academy of Child and Adolescent Psychiatry, 31(5),* 868–874.

Yehuda R. (1998). Psychoneuroendocrinology of post-traumatic stress disorder. *Psychiatric Clinics of North America, 21(2),* 359–379.

Part X

Dissociation and Psychosis

34 Are Psychotic Symptoms Traumatic in Origin and Dissociative in Kind?

Andrew Moskowitz, PhD
John Read, PhD
Susie Farrelly, MBChB
Thomas Rudegeair, MD, PhD
Ondra Williams, MA

OUTLINE

34.1 INTRODUCTION

The relationship between dissociation and psychosis has been a subject of controversy since at least the time of Eugen Bleuler. Bleuler renamed Kraepelin's Dementia præcox with the term *schizophrenia* (i.e., "split mind"), reminiscent of contemporary definitions of dissociation. Rosenbaum (1980) noted that the introduction of the construct of schizophrenia was followed by a dramatic decrease in reports of, and interest in, multiple personality. It is easy to see how this could have occurred. Bleuler insisted that the "splitting of psychic functions" was central to schizophrenia. Indeed, Bleuler (1950/1911) claimed that there was a loss of the "unity" of the personality:[1]

> Different psychic complexes … dominate the personality for a time, while other groups of ideas or drives are "split off" and seem either partly or completely impotent.[2] (p. 9)

[1] Interestingly, so did Kraepelin. He claimed that dementia præcox led to "a loss of the inner unity of the activities of intellect, emotion and volition, in themselves and among one another" (Kraepelin, 1919, pp. 74–75).

[2] The notion of "complexes," which was adopted by Bleuler from Jung—his close associate at the Burghölzli Hospital— (continued)

Although current views of schizophrenia no longer emphasize these Bleulerian notions, the current concept of dissociation does. For example, the Oxford English Dictionary (1989) defines dissociated as "characterized by the disjunction of associated mental connections or the disaggregation of consciousness" (p. 843).

Was Bleuler entirely misguided, or did he have good reason to describe schizophrenia in these terms? What is the relationship between schizophrenia and the dissociative disorders or, more broadly, between psychosis and dissociation? This question has been addressed in various ways, such as by examining the comorbidity of psychotic disorders and dissociative disorders (Ross, Miller, Reagor, Bjornson et al., 1990; Steinberg, Cicchetti, Buchanan, Rakfeldt et al., 1994), or by assessing the correlation between measures of dissociation and measures of psychosis or psychoticism (Allen, Coyne, & Console, 1997; Bauer & Power, 1995; Moskowitz, Barker-Collo, & Ellson, 2005). We will take a different approach.

We will explore whether psychotic symptoms (i.e., the "positive" symptoms of schizophrenia) can be explained in terms of dissociation. In taking this course, we are going beyond the position that individuals with dissociative disorders may be misdiagnosed as psychotic (Bliss, Larson, & Nakashima, 1983; Ross, 2004; Ross & Norton, 1988), or that dissociative symptoms can, under some circumstances, mimic psychotic symptoms (Steingard & Frankel, 1985; Tutkun, Yargıç, & Şar, 1996), both of which we believe to be true. Rather, we will argue that dissociative processes mediate between early trauma and later psychotic symptoms. In short, we believe that some or all psychotic symptoms may be dissociative in their very essence.

The notion that traumatic experiences are related to psychotic symptoms is not new. It has long been known that some individuals become psychotic after an acute trauma (Eitenger, 1964; Hollender & Hirsch, 1964; Kardiner, 1941). This clinical phenomenon is reflected in the diagnostic categories of hysterical psychosis (popular at the turn of the 20th century) and brief reactive psychosis (now called "brief psychotic disorder," American Psychiatric Association, 2000). On the other hand, evidence that psychotic symptoms are related to childhood trauma has been less well received (until recently, see Janssen et al., 2004; Morrison et al., 2003; Read et al., 2004).

Perhaps the most famous proposed linkage between childhood trauma and psychosis was advanced by Schatzman (1973). In *Soul Murder: Persecution in the Family*, Schatzman connected the bizarre delusions of Judge Daniel Schreber (Schreber, 1955) to his father's extreme and bizarre methods of child rearing. Schatzman (1973) documented a series of remarkable similarities between Schreber's delusions and his father's use of extreme discipline and abuse (including bizarre mechanical contraptions that were designed to improve a child's posture, etc.). Schatzman convincingly argued that Schreber's delusions were a reexperiencing of his childhood "torture" at the hands of his father.

The circumstances under which such childhood experiences can become transformed into delusions are discussed in the following, and are a centerpiece of our argument.

34.2 DEFINITION OF TERMS

34.2.1 Dissociation

DSM-IV-TR defined dissociation as "a disruption in the usually integrated functions of consciousness, memory, identity, or perception of the environment," which may be "sudden or gradual, transient or chronic" (American Psychiatric Association, 2000, p. 822). Braun (1988) proposed that dissociation may affect some or all of the following: Behavior, Affect, Sensation, and Knowledge (i.e., the BASK model). Although dissociation has typically been viewed as a continuum, some have recently argued that "pathological dissociation" is better viewed as a qualitatively distinct taxon (Waller, Putnam, & Carlson, 1996; Waller & Ross, 1997).

For our purposes, Steinberg's five dissociative symptoms are more useful than the definition of dissociation. Steinberg, the developer of the Structured Clinical Interview for DSM-IV Dissociative Disorders-Revised (SCID-D-R), considered five symptoms to underlie the dissociative disorders: amnesia, identity confusion, identity alteration, depersonalization, and derealization (Steinberg, 1994, 1995). We believe that the latter three symptoms and dissociative flashbacks play crucial roles in the genesis of psychotic symptoms.

Steinberg (1995) defined identity alteration as a shift in role or identity that produces changes in the person's behavior. We prefer to use the term *dissociated identity*

(continued) also provides another important link between dissociation and schizophrenia. Jung, who briefly studied with Janet in the early 1900s, drew his concept of complex from Janet's "fixed ideas" (Ellenberger, 1970). He viewed complexes as affectively charged clusters of ideas, accompanied by somatic innervations (Jung, 1960a/1907), and, in terms strikingly reminiscent of Janet, described them as "splinter psyches" possessing a "remarkable degree of autonomy" typically engendered by traumatic experiences (Jung, 1960b/1948).

because it does not limit itself to observable behavior. We will argue that a rudimentary form of dissociated identity underlies most auditory hallucinations.

Steinberg (1995) defined depersonalization as: "feeling detached from the self, feeling that the self is strange or unreal, feeling detached from ... emotions, or feeling ... [like] an automaton or robot" (p. 10). We believe that depersonalization is important to some forms of delusion.

DSM-IV-TR defined derealization as "an alteration in the perception or experience of the external world so that it seems strange or unreal (i.e., people may seem unfamiliar or mechanical)" (American Psychiatric Association, 2000, p. 822). We will argue that derealization underlies many forms of delusion, including delusions of misidentification such as Capgras Syndrome. Derealization may also play a role in thought disorder.

Steinberg (1995) emphasizes that derealization often occurs in conjunction with flashbacks, because the present environment may "fade away" while the past reasserts itself. A core symptom of PTSD, flashbacks are dissociative states that may last from seconds to hours. During a flashback, an individual is "acting or feeling as if the traumatic event were recurring" (American Psychiatric Association, 2000, p. 468). It is important to note that a person may have flashbacks that they do not recognize as such (Blank, 1985; Krikorian & Layton, 1998). We believe that flashback-like experiences, outside of conscious awareness, may cause some psychotic symptoms.

34.2.2 Psychosis

The term *psychosis* has a long and troubled history. Even DSM-IV-TR (American Psychiatric Association, 2000) hedges its bets when it comes to defining psychosis; it provides three definitions, each broader than the previous: (1) delusions and prominent hallucinations that are experienced without insight, (2) delusions and prominent hallucinations (regardless of whether the person realizes that the hallucinations are, in fact, hallucinations), and (3) the four Criterion A positive symptoms of schizophrenia (i.e., delusions, hallucinations, disorganized speech, and grossly disorganized behavior or catatonic behavior).

We will use the third definition of psychotic (i.e., the four Criterion A positive symptoms of schizophrenia) because we want to determine whether the positive symptoms of schizophrenia can be viewed as dissociative. Criterion A for schizophrenia requires the presence of (1) two of the following five symptoms: delusions; hallucinations; disorganized speech; grossly disorganized behavior or catatonic behavior; negative symptoms such as affective flattening, alogia, or avolition; or (2) one of the following three symptoms: bizarre delusions; a voice making a running commentary on a person's thoughts or behavior; two or more voices conversing with one another.

34.3 THE DISSOCIATIVE NATURE OF MEMORY

Human memory consists of a number of divergent systems (Tulving, 1972). The distinction between explicit memory (which includes episodic, autobiographical, or contextual memory) and implicit memory (i.e., outside of awareness) is well accepted, as is the association of explicit memory with the hippocampus (Baddeley, Conway, & Aggleton, 2001). Individuals also have procedural memories for how things are done (i.e., riding a bike, playing tennis, etc.), which are implicit in nature, and semantic memories for words or concepts, which may be either implicit or explicit.

Additional systems of memory have been proposed by University of Arizona psychologists Lynn Nadel and W. Jake Jacobs who, over the past 20 years, have applied O'Keefe and Nadel's (1978) cognitive map theory of memory and the hippocampus to understand anxiety disorders; they contend that humans have five separate memory systems. In addition to the systems described previously, they also describe: (1) valence memory (or emotional memory) that encodes, via the amygdala, the "goodness" or "badness" of things, and (2) feature memory that is associated with the frontal lobes and encodes the sensory features of objects (Nadel & Jacobs, 1996).

In our view, Nadel and Jacob's most important innovations are their analyses of: (1) the differing responses of these memory systems to stress and trauma, and (2) the implications of that differential response for anxiety disorders such as phobias (Jacobs & Nadel, 1985), panic disorder (Jacobs & Nadel, 1999), and PTSD (Nadel & Jacobs, 1996). We believe that Nadel and Jacob's model can help to explain psychotic symptoms (with the exception of auditory hallucinations).

Nadel and Jacobs contend that the hippocampus normally "re-aggregates" the different components of memory, stored separately in the brain at encoding, into a seamless autobiographical memory (Nadel & Jacobs, 1996). High levels of stress, however, may impair the functioning of the hippocampus. When this happens, the hippocampus fails to encode the spatial and temporal aspects of memory; it also fails to re-aggregate the memory at retrieval (this disaggregation of memory can itself be seen as dissociative in nature).[3] The implications of this may be profound:

> When memories are formed under intense stress, a critical component of normal memory formation—the hippocampus—is disabled, and memories without spatiotemporal content are created. At the same time, another component of normal memory function—the amygdala—can be potentiated, leading to stronger-than-usual memory for highly charged emotional events. When a person retrieves a traumatic event memory, the retrieved information is bereft of spatiotemporal context. Instead of being bound firmly to the past, this "disembodied" event memory is conflated with the ongoing spatio/temporal frame. (Nadel & Jacobs, 1996, p. 459)

Jacobs and Nadel (1985) claim that the first few years of life, before the hippocampus comes "online," have a special importance. During that time, strong emotional memories may be laid down without any space-time context. Jacobs and Nadel argue that these disembodied memories can surface as overwhelming affective experiences. This may happen when the person encounters: (1) an object that is linked to the early memory (in the case of phobias and PTSD; Jacobs & Nadel, 1985; Nadel & Jacobs, 1996) or (2) perceptual features of an object that was linked to the early memory (in the case of panic attacks), in which case the proximal trigger is unrecognizable (Nadel & Jacobs, 1996; Jacobs & Nadel, 1999). We suggest that similar processes may generate delusions and other psychotic symptoms.

34.4 RELEVANT RESEARCH FINDINGS IN SCHIZOPHRENIA

34.4.1 Childhood Trauma

Studies of the prevalence of childhood trauma in persons with psychotic disorders have reported that childhood trauma is consistently more prevalent in psychotic individuals than in: (1) members of the general population and (2) nonpsychotic psychiatric patients (Morrison et al., 2003; Mueser et al., 1998; Read, 1997). A recent comprehensive review (Read, Fink, Rudegeair, Felitti, & Whitfield, 2008) found that child maltreatment reliably predicted psychotic symptoms in adulthood (even after controlling for factors such as a family history of psychosis) in 10 of 11 large-scale general population studies; in addition, 8 of the 11 studies looked for and found a dose-response relationship (that is, greater levels of childhood trauma or neglect were associated with greater levels of psychotic symptoms or pathology). For example, a prospective community-based study of 4045 individuals found that those who had experienced severe childhood abuse were 48 times more likely to develop pathology level psychosis than those not abused (Janssen et al., 2004). Of all psychotic symptoms, the evidence suggests that hallucinations are most strongly associated with childhood trauma (Nurcombe et al., 1996; Read, Agar, Argyle, & Aderhold, 2003; Ross, Anderson, & Clark, 1994).

34.4.2 Hippocampal Abnormalities

Hippocampal structural abnormalities have been reported in schizophrenia patients[4] for over 20 years (Bogerts, Meertz, & Schonfeldt-Bausch, 1985; Scheibel & Kovelman, 1981). Frontal abnormalities and hippocampal abnormalities are the most frequent brain abnormalities in schizophrenia (Harrison, 1999; Shenton, Dickey, Frumin, & McCarley, 2001). Reductions in hippocampal volume (1) have been demonstrated repeatedly (reviewed in Nelson, Saykin, Flashman, & Riordan, 1998; Vita, De Peri, Silenzi, & Dieci, 2006), (2) appear to be present at the onset of symptoms (Velakoulis et al., 1999), and (3) are matched by abnormal hippocampal functioning at baseline and during memory tasks (Heckers, 2001).

The hippocampus has long been associated with memory (e.g., O'Keefe & Nadel, 1978), and hippocampal abnormalities are associated with memory disturbances in schizophrenia (Heckers, 2001; Heckers et al., 1998). Importantly, there is strong animal evidence and presumptive human evidence that chronic stress can produce hippocampal and memory abnormities that are similar to those found in schizophrenia (McEwen, 2000; O'Brien, 1997; Sapolsky, 2000). Indeed, Read, Perry, Moskowitz, and Connolly (2001) have argued that there is a causal link between childhood trauma and the characteristic biological and cognitive deficits of schizophrenia.

34.4.3 Memory Impairment

Deficits in explicit or autobiographical memory, in conjunction with intact or even exaggerated (Linscott & Knight, 2001) implicit memory, is a well-documented

[3] Of note, Janet's first term for dissociation was *disaggregation* ("désagrégation"; Kihlstrom, Tataryn, & Hoyt, 1993).

[4] For the sake of brevity, *patient* is used in place of the more cumbersome, but correct, "persons diagnosed with Schizophrenia (or DID)." This use does not imply an endorsement of a medical perspective of these disorders.

pattern in schizophrenia (Achim & Lepage, 2003; Bazin & Perruchet, 1996; Corcoran & Frith, 2003; Marie et al., 2001; Schwartz, Rosse, & Deutsch, 1993), and is particularly associated with: (1) acute psychotic states (Hofer et al., 2003), (2) the positive symptoms of schizophrenia (Brebion et al., 1999; McDermid, Vaz, & Heinrichs, 2002; Servan-Schreiber, Cohen, & Steingard, 1996), and (3) delusions and thought disorder (but not hallucinations; Brebion et al., 1999).

Memory deficits in schizophrenia are associated with decreased limbic activation and increased frontal activation. This pattern may reflect a compensatory overemphasis on implicit assessments of familiarity when adequate conscious recollection of events is lacking (Heckers, 2001; Hofer et al., 2003; Tendolkar, Ruhrmann, Brockhaus, Pukrop, & Klosterkotter, 2002). Danion, Rizzo, and Bruant (1999) have argued that the autobiographical/spatiotemporal component of the memory may not be lost, but is rather "misplaced"—due to the impaired ability of patients with schizophrenia to "bind the separate components of events into a coherent, relational memory representation" (p. 643). This fragmentation is believed to be central to the memory deficits of schizophrenia (Danion et al., 1999; Huron et al., 1995), considered one of the most common deficits of the disorder (Heinrichs & Zakzanis, 1998).

34.5 DISSOCIATIVE PROCESSES IN PSYCHOTIC SYMPTOMS

34.5.1 Hallucinations

DSM-IV-TR defines hallucination as "a sensory perception that has the compelling sense of reality of a true perception but that occurs without external stimulation of the relevant sensory organ" (p. 823). The most common hallucinations in schizophrenia are auditory ones (usually voices).

Dissociative persons also hear voices. Bliss argued that voices were a primary cause for misdiagnosing DID patients as schizophrenic (Bliss et al., 1983). In DID, the voices belong to different personality states or alters. DID voices supposedly differ from those that occur in schizophrenia. DID voices are said to be: (1) less circumscribed in content, (2) longer in duration, and (3) mostly heard inside the head rather than outside the head (Steinberg, 1995; Van der Zwaard & Polak, 2001).

However, little research has been conducted in this area. The few studies that have been conducted have not supported the above distinctions. Specifically, 50% to 69% of persons with schizophrenia hear internal voices, 27% to 33% exclusively so (Honig et al., 1998; Judkins & Slade, 1981; Mott, Small, & Anderson, 1965). The one study that compared the auditory hallucinations of DID patients with those of patients with schizophrenia found no significant difference in the perceived location of voices (Honig, et al., 1998). Many DID patients hear both internal and external voices. Similarly, Judkins and Slade (1981) found no support for the claim that external voices are more hostile and punitive than internal voices. Still, it is premature to dismiss the possibility that the voices of DID patients will yet be found to differ from those of schizophrenia patients.

On the other hand, there are some important similarities between patient with schizophrenia or those with DID. For example, the most common voices in schizophrenia and the most common alters in DID are hostile or punitive (Honig et al., 1998; Judkins & Slade, 1981; Putnam, 1989). These voices and alters often have characteristics that are identifiably those of their abusers (Putnam, 1989; Read et al., 2003). Thus, the question arises: "Might all voices, regardless of diagnostic group, be essentially dissociative in nature?" That is, when a person perceives voices to be different from his or her own thoughts and speech, are such voices best characterized as being split-off components of his or her personality—and, therefore, dissociative (Moskowitz & Corstens, 2007)?

We believe that the DSM-IV criteria for schizophrenia contain a psychotic/dissociative conundrum. DSM-IV's three pathognomic symptoms for schizophrenia include two forms of auditory hallucination—voices commenting and voices conversing—that are among the first-rank symptoms of schizophrenia (Schneider, 1959), but also occur in 30% to 80% of DID patients (Kluft, 1987; Ross, Heber, Norton, & Anderson, 1989; Ross et al., 1990), where they are viewed as arising from alter personalities.

Sensory hallucinations in modalities other than auditory are often best characterized as flashbacks. Flashbacks are a cardinal symptom of PTSD; they are intrusions of sensory/perceptual aspects of a previous trauma. Consistent with the views of Nadel and Jacobs (1996), a person may undergo sensory flashbacks without being aware of their connection to the past.

34.5.2 Grossly Disorganized or Catatonic Behavior

Neither grossly disorganized behavior nor catatonic behavior is defined in DSM-IV-TR, but examples are provided. Grossly disorganized behavior includes child-like silliness, unpredictable agitation, and inappropriate sexual behavior (p. 300). Catatonic behavior includes catatonic stupor and excitement.

Behavior is typically considered to be disorganized if its organization is not understood. However, that does not necessarily mean that no organization exists. Thus, behavior may appear to be irrational if the reasons for that behavior are not obvious to an observer; that is, if the observer is ignorant of the context within which that behavior makes sense. This can occur because the person in question is unwilling or unable to communicate that information, or because that person is actually unaware of the behavior's original spatial and temporal context. Evidence for this latter hypothesis comes from several sources.

During flashbacks, a person acts or feels as though the traumatic event were recurring (American Psychiatric Association, 2000). Importantly, flashbacks may lead persons with PTSD to behave as though they were experiencing the traumatic event again, but without conscious recollection of the trauma (Blank, 1985; Krikorian & Layton, 1998; Shiloh, Schwartz, Weizman, & Radwan, 1995). A clinician who connects such disorganized behavior to the earlier trauma is unlikely to make a diagnosis of psychosis. Conversely, a clinician who does not connect the patient's behavior to the earlier trauma—as occurred in the case of an elderly Israeli Holocaust survivor (Shiloh et al., 1995)—may consider the person to be psychotic.

Further evidence for this proposition comes from recent research on catatonia. In a recent review, Moskowitz (2004) proposed that catatonic stupor and catatonic excitement are clinical parallels of the freeze response and the fight/flight response in animals, and, as such, are best understood as fear responses. If this is so, then some catatonic symptoms may reflect: (1) nonconscious flashbacks to past trauma (Moskowitz, 2004; Shiloh et al., 1995), (2) implicit memory of events that occurred under the veil of infantile amnesia (Nadel & Jacobs, 1996), or (3) the reactions of a terrified, but dissociated, personality state in a DID patient (e.g., a child).

34.5.3 Disorganized Speech or Thought Disorder

The editors of DSM-IV-TR prefer the term *disorganized speech* to the traditional term *thought disorder* because thought disorder is difficult to define and because inferences about thought are based primarily on speech. While DSM-IV-TR does not define disorganized speech *per se*, it provides two examples of disorganized speech—derailment and incoherence. Derailment (i.e., loosening of associations) is defined as "a pattern of speech in which a person's ideas slip off one track onto another that is completely unrelated or only obliquely related" (p. 822). Incoherence is defined as "speech or thinking that is essentially incomprehensible to others" (p. 824). In short, disorganized speech is speech that is difficult or impossible to understand. Can such phenomena be related to dissociation?

Some cases of thought disorder arise, like disorganized behavior, simply because the speaker has failed to provide the listener with adequate contextual information. This idea was first suggested by Martin Harrow, one of the foremost researchers in the thought disorder field. Harrow discovered that many instances of thought disorder arose because the person had "intermingled" associations from past events with the current context, but had failed to explain this to listeners (Harrow & Prosen, 1979). Thus, apparent thought disorder may occur if the speaker does not disclose to the listener the nature of his or her personal associations (Harrow & Prosen, 1978, 1979). More recently, Harrow has suggested that the "intermingling" of past and present is due to the intrusion of emotionally charged historical material (Harrow, Lanin-Kettering, & Miller, 1989), and hypothesized that the amygdala is involved in this process (Harrow et al., 2000). Given the amygdala's role in emotional memory, Harrow's hypothesis fits nicely with Nadel and Jacobs' model.

Harrow's view, that disorganized speech reflects an intermingling of past and present experiences, is also reminiscent of Steinberg's (1995) assertion that derealization may involve the intrusion of the past upon the present. In keeping with Steinberg's position that flashbacks are a form of derealization, it is possible that some instances of thought disorder may occur because the person is undergoing a flashback. When the listener does not know this, the person's comments may appear to be disorganized or thought disordered.

In support of this, there is empirical evidence that thought disorder is related to dissociation on the one hand, and memory disturbances on the other. Allen, Coyne, and Console (1997) found thought disorder, as measured on the Millon Clinical Multiaxial Inventory, to be highly correlated (r = 0.69) with DES scores in psychiatric inpatients. Thought disorder is also related to explicit memory impairment in schizophrenia (Brebion et al., 1999; Linscott & Knight, 2001). Thus, thought disorder may result from flashback-type experiences that are not recognized as such, because of impaired explicit memory.

Thought disorder may also result from a struggle for control or dominance between personality states or alters. This may explain why thought disorder was recorded in 50% to 60% of children and adolescents with DDNOS or DID (Hornstein & Putnam, 1992) and 20% of adults with DID (Putnam, Guroff, Silberman, Barban, & Post, 1986).

34.5.4 Delusions

Delusions are the only symptom included in all three of DSM-IV-TR's definitions of psychosis, and as such, are central to the concept of psychosis. They are also strongly emphasized in the diagnosis of schizophrenia. DSM-IV-TR defines a delusion as a culturally or subculturally inappropriate "false belief based on incorrect inference about external reality that is firmly sustained despite what almost everyone else believes and despite what constitutes incontrovertible and obvious proof or evidence to the contrary" (p. 821).

"Bizarre" delusions, one of three pathognomic symptoms of schizophrenia, are beliefs that the person's culture would regard as "totally implausible"—in contrast to nonbizarre delusions, which are not inherently impossible (e.g., believing that one is being poisoned, spied on by the government, or worth billions of dollars). DSM-IV-TR notes that beliefs of loss of control of mind or body "are generally considered to be bizarre" (p. 299). These delusions include "a person's belief that his or her thoughts have been taken away by some outside force ('thought withdrawal'), that alien thoughts have been put into his or her mind ('thought insertion'), or that his or her body or actions are being acted on or manipulated by some outside force ('delusions of control')" (p. 299).[5]

At least one of DSM-IV-TR's bizarre delusions (i.e., thought withdrawal, thought insertion, or delusions of control) occur in one-third to two-thirds of DID patients (Kluft, 1987; Ross et al., 1989; Ross et al., 1990). In DID, these symptoms are due to the effects of alter personalities on the consciousness or behavior of the host personality. Could schizophrenia patients' symptoms of thought withdrawal, thought insertion, "made" actions, and influences on the body indicate an underlying dissociative process? This possibility is supported by Goff's finding that delusions of possession (which overlaps with delusions of control) in patients with chronic psychosis were associated with significantly elevated DES scores (Goff, Brotman, Kindlon, Waites, & Amico, 1991).

What about nonbizarre delusions, such as paranoia or grandiosity? Could dissociative processes underlie their formation, too? These questions are best addressed by consideration of Jaspers' (1913/1963) concepts of primary and secondary delusions.

Jaspers (1963/1913) considered secondary delusions to be (delusional) interpretations of preceding stimuli. In contrast, primary delusions have no apparent precursors; he considered them to be "psychologically irreducible" (p. 96). The clinical distinction between primary and secondary delusions requires careful inquiry. For example, a psychotic individual may report that there are snakes in his bed. Absent inquiry, one might conclude that this is a primary delusion, arising *de novo*. Inquiry, however, might reveal that, while no snakes were seen, the delusional idea of snakes was preceded by a sensation of something slithering over his skin as he lay in bed. Further inquiry might reveal a history of childhood sexual abuse by an older sibling who regularly crawled into his bed. Given this information, the clinician might deduce that the patient's delusion was a secondary one that arose from a tactile hallucination. The tactile hallucination could be understood as a decontextualized somatic memory of the patient's abuse experiences—triggered by bedtime stimuli. Indeed, tactile hallucinations have also been linked to experiences of childhood abuse (Read et al., 2003). Lacking awareness that this tactile experience was, in fact, a memory, the patient generated a delusional explanation for it. Parenthetically, note that the delusion of snakes not only corresponds to the patient's physical sensations; it also matches the disgust, revulsion, and fear he likely felt at the time of his abuse.

In this example and in similar situations, the spatiotemporal context of the memory would be either: (1) lost, following Nadel and Jacobs (1996), or (2) split off from the emotional and perceptual aspects of the experience. As decontextualization is typical of both traumatic memories (Nadel & Jacobs, 1996) and schizophrenia (Danion et al., 1999), secondary delusions, such as this one, may derive from sensory and emotional flashbacks that are so dissociated from their spatiotemporal context as to be unknowable as memories.

The validity of the concept of primary delusions has been challenged by Roberts (1992) who accurately noted that Jaspers did describe an antecedent to primary delusions, namely a particular anxiety state he called *delusional atmosphere* (or *delusional mood*). Roberts's position is consistent with Freeman and Garety's (2003) assertion that essentially all delusions arise from preexisting mood states. The question then becomes, where do these affective states come from?

Nadel and Jacobs (1996) have argued that "disembodied event memories are conflated with the ongoing spatio/temporal frame" (p. 459) in anxiety disorders. We wonder if delusions may have a similar genesis. That is, do delusions, which are often preceded by intense anxiety states

[5] Some would claim that these are not delusions *per se* because they do not refer to "external reality," as required by the DSM-IV definition, but rather unusual internal experiences (Spitzer, 1990). In this view, such delusions should be referred to instead as disorders of experience (Spitzer, 1990), or anomalous experiences (World Health Organization, 1992).

(Cutting & Dunne, 1989; Jaspers, 1963/1913; Yung & McGorry, 1996), arise in an effort to make sense out of overwhelming affective experiences? If so, then perhaps persecutory delusions, for example, might involve feelings of danger that intrude without the patient recalling the original source of those feelings (Moskowitz, Nadel, Watts, & Jacobs, 2008).

34.6 DOES THE DOMAIN OF DISSOCIATION DIFFER IN PERSONS DIAGNOSED WITH PSYCHOTIC AND DISSOCIATIVE DISORDERS?

We believe that a person's diagnosis is partly dependent on whether the clinician knows the context in which the patient's signs and symptoms make sense (Morrison et al., 2003). If clinicians know the traumatic context, then they are likely to issue a posttraumatic diagnosis; if not, they will probably issue a psychotic diagnosis. Indeed, the same patient's diagnosis may be changed from schizophrenia to PTSD when symptoms are linked to trauma, with major clinical implications (Read, 1997; Shiloh et al., 1995).

Nonetheless, there may be important differences between persons with dissociative and psychotic diagnoses that are best explored by considering the symptom of delusions. Steinberg (1995) contends that reality testing is maintained in dissociative disorders. Should this position be correct (which remains to be seen), and assuming, as outlined previously, that delusions relate to powerful affective experiences, not necessarily unique to psychosis, several questions arise. Why do some individuals develop delusions and others not? Can some individuals tolerate powerful affective experiences without resorting to delusions, whereas others cannot? Does this explain why some individuals develop hypervigilance or derealization, whereas others become paranoid and develop delusions? Highly dissociative individuals are very good at distancing themselves from uncomfortable experiences—via depersonalization, derealization, amnesia, or switching to another personality state. Perhaps persons with psychosis are simply less capable dissociators.

If so, this may also explain why the voices of schizophrenia patients are described as more rudimentary and circumscribed than those of DID patients (Steinberg, 1995). Is it possible that a limited capacity to dissociate might constrain the ability to "cultivate" a voice, leading to less differentiated, personified voices?

Possible differences between the diagnostic groups are best illustrated by contrasting derealization with a delusion of misidentification, the Capgras delusion (Capgras & Reboul-Lachaux, 1923). Steinberg (1995) has claimed that derealization often involves people close to the individual (e.g., parents, individuals who remind them of their parents) who suddenly seem strange or alien to them. She proposed that some derealization experiences are a reemergence of negative feelings (i.e., what we would call decontextualized affective memories) toward people who are typically seen in a positive way. Steinberg suggests that derealization is secondary to a process of splitting-off negative affect in an effort to "integrate the experiences of the parent as caretaker and at the same time as a source of severe pain, neglect, or deprivation" (Steinberg, 1995, p. 156).

Derealization may also underlie delusions of misidentification (Christodoulou, 1986, 1991; Todd, Dewhurst, & Wallis, 1981) such as the Capgras delusion (Capgras & Reboul-Lachaux, 1923), in which an individual believes that someone close to him has been replaced by an imposter. Perhaps individuals with depersonalization disorder are better able to tolerate their experiences of derealization than those who go on to develop Capgras delusions because they are better at separating themselves from their distressing experiences. Schizophrenia patients may be less able to distance themselves from their aversive experiences or inhibit their distressing emotions. Interestingly, impaired frontal lobe activity in schizophrenia (e.g., Goldman-Rakic & Selemon, 1997), consistent with these deficits, can be contrasted with intact (or even hyperactive) frontal lobe activity in depersonalization disorder (Phillips et al., 2001; Sierra & Berrios, 1998).[6]

34.7 SUMMARY

The four positive symptoms of schizophrenia appear to be consistent with dissociative processes. Hallucinations, which are more strongly linked to trauma than are other psychotic symptoms, may be fundamentally dissociative in nature—regardless of whether the person's diagnosis is schizophrenia, DID, or PTSD (Moskowitz & Corstens, 2007). We suggest that voices are a form of dissociated identity. Other modalities of hallucination may be considered to be decontextualized sensory/perceptual flashbacks.

Grossly disorganized behavior, catatonic behavior, and thought disorder/disorganized speech can also be linked to dissociative processes. We suggest that speech

[6] Of course, there may be other differences between persons with derealization experiences and those with Capgras delusions. The development of Capgras delusions could be related to: (1) more intense or more lengthy affective experiences, or (2) different types of traumatic experiences. Such possibilities should be explored in future investigations.

or behavior often appears disorganized because information about its traumatic or affectively charged context is not conveyed to the listener/observer. This may occur when the individual is unaware of the context or chooses not to disclose it. Disorganized speech or behavior can also result from slippage between personality states or alters.

Finally, we suggest that delusions may be driven by dissociative flashbacks. That is, most delusions are attempts to explain decontextualized emotional flashbacks (triggered by some feature of the environment). Because delusions are more strongly linked to memory deficits than to remembered trauma, we suggest that delusions may derive from early intense affective experiences that are hidden under the veil of infantile amnesia—akin to the manner in which Jacobs and Nadel (1999) conceptualize panic attacks.

34.8 FUTURE RESEARCH

There are at least four crucial research questions that arise from this overview. First, are delusions uncommon in dissociative disorders, as Steinberg (1995) contends? Is intact reality testing really a "line in the sand" between the disorders? Second, are there qualitative and quantitative differences between the auditory hallucinations of DID patients and those of schizophrenia patients? Third, what is the nature of dissociation in schizophrenia? How frequently do persons diagnosed with schizophrenia have dissociative experiences? Are their dissociative experiences differentially related to specific psychotic symptoms? Is amnesia relatively uncommon? Fourth, do delusional patients and nondelusional dissociative patients differ in their frontal lobe functioning? This last question might be assessed by comparing persons who experience frequent derealization and persons with Capgras delusions on a neuropsychological test that is sensitive to frontal lobe functioning, such as the Wisconsin Card Sorting Test (Heaton, Chelune, Talley, Kay, & Curtiss, 1993).

34.9 IMPLICATIONS FOR SCHIZOPHRENIA

It can no longer be tacitly assumed that the content of psychotic symptoms is unrelated to an individual's life. Although psychotic persons are often unable to connect their symptoms to earlier trauma, that connection may still exist. This disconnection (or dissociation) may be maintained by the ability of psychotic symptoms to keep memories of trauma or components of those memories out of awareness. Ironically, however, when psychotic symptoms are linked to trauma, those same symptoms may facilitate the retrieval of additional traumatic memories. The potential therapeutic impact of retrieving memories of psychosis-linked trauma have been little investigated but may be quite beneficial (see Harris & Landis, 1997; Heins, Gray, & Tennant, 1990). We exhort clinicians who work with apparently psychotic individuals to consider the possibility that psychotic symptoms may represent real life events worthy of exploration.

The validity of schizophrenia has been questioned by many authors in recent years (Bentall, 1993; Boyle, 1990; Read, 2004). We, too, challenge the validity of this diagnosis. Strong links to dissociation and dissociative disorders have been found in Kraepelin, Bleuler, and Schneider's conceptions of schizophrenia. Here, we argue that dissociative processes may underlie the four positive symptoms of schizophrenia, and that schizophrenia's pathognomonic symptoms are strongly linked to DID. This latter finding strikes at the heart of schizophrenia's diagnostic validity.

Our analysis does not necessarily mean that schizophrenia is best conceptualized as a dissociative disorder. Rather, we hypothesize that some persons develop psychotic symptoms precisely because their capacity to handle traumatic or highly emotional experiences via dissociative mechanisms is limited. In other words, the level of dissociation in schizophrenia, while still high, may be lower than that of the dissociative disorders. It is notable in this regard that patients with schizophrenia have lower dissociation scores than those with DID or PTSD, but higher dissociation scores than all other psychiatric conditions (Bernstein & Putnam, 1986; Ross et al., 1989). Perhaps only those meeting criteria for a dissociative disorder would qualify as members of the dissociative taxon.

Alternatively, the possibility of conceptualizing schizophrenia as a dissociative disorder should not be dismissed. Ross has repeatedly argued, most recently in Ross (2004), for a dissociative subtype of schizophrenia. Moreover, Steinberg's (1995) position notwithstanding, the prevalence of psychotic symptoms in adults and children with DID (Hornstein & Putnam, 1992; Putnam et al., 1986), and dissociative symptoms in persons diagnosed schizophrenic (Moise & Leichner, 1996; Steinberg et al., 1994), as well as the strong family history of schizophrenia in relatives of DID patients (Putnam et al., 1986), suggest that these two disorders may be more closely related than previously thought. Some of the research projects proposed in this chapter should help to shed light on this area.

Finally, we return to the question posed by our title: Are psychotic symptoms traumatic in origin and dissociative in kind? Overall, we think that the answer is a qualified yes. On a symptom-by-symptom basis, we say *yes* with regard to hallucinations, *quite likely* with regard to disorganized behavior, catatonia, and disorganized speech, and *possibly* with regard to delusions. This does not mean, of course, that psychotic symptoms can *only* arise through dissociative means. Still, as we have demonstrated that they may, we believe that a "re-think" of the concept of schizophrenia may be in order, as well as a review of the treatment accorded those with this diagnosis.

REFERENCES

Achim, A. M., & Lepage, M. (2003). Is associative recognition more impaired than item recognition memory in Schizophrenia? A meta-analysis. *Brain & Cognition, 53(2),* 121–124.

Allen, J. G., Coyne, L., & Console, D. A. (1997). Dissociative detachment relates to psychotic symptoms and personality decompensation. *Comprehensive Psychiatry, 38,* 327–334.

American Psychiatric Association (2000). *DSM-IV-TR–Diagnostic and statistical manual of mental disorders* (4th ed., text rev.). Washington, DC: Author.

Baddeley, A., Conway, M., & Aggleton, J. (Eds.). (2001). *Episodic memory: New directions in research.* Oxford: Oxford University Press.

Bauer, A. M., & Power, K. G. (1995). Dissociative experiences and psychopathological symptomatology in a Scottish sample. *Dissociation, 8(4),* 209–219.

Bazin, N., & Perruchet, P. (1996). Implicit and explicit associative memory in patients with Schizophrenia. *Schizophrenia Research, 22,* 241–248.

Bentall, R. P. (1993). Deconstructing the concept of "Schizophrenia." *Journal of Mental Health, 2(3),* 223–238.

Bernstein, E. M., & Putnam, F. W. (1986). Development, reliability, and validity of a dissociation scale. *Journal of Nervous and Mental Disease, 174,* 727–735.

Blank, A. S. (1985). The unconscious flashback to the war in Vietnam veterans: Clinical mystery, legal defense, and community problem. In S. M. Sonnenberg, A. S. Blank, & J. A. Talbot (Eds.), *The trauma of war: Stress and recovery in Vietnam veterans* (pp. 239–308). Washington, DC: American Psychiatric Press.

Bleuler, E. (1911/1950). *Dementia præcox oder die Gruppe der Schizophrenien.* Leipzig: Deuticke. Trans. J. Zinkin, Dementia præcox or the group of Schizophrenias. New York: International Universities Press.

Bliss, E. L., Larson, E. M., & Nakashima, S. R. (1983). Auditory hallucinations and Schizophrenia. *Journal of Nervous & Mental Disease, 171(1),* 30–33.

Bogerts, B., Meertz, E., & Schonfeldt-Bausch, R. (1985). Basal ganglia and limbic system pathology in Schizophrenia. A morphometric study of brain volume and shrinkage. *Archives of General Psychiatry, 42(8),* 784–791.

Boyle, M. (1990). *Schizophrenia: A scientific delusion?* London: Routledge.

Brebion, G., Amador, X., Smith, M. J., Malaspina, D., Sharif, Z., & Gorman, J. M. (1999). Opposite links of positive and negative symptomatology with memory errors in Schizophrenia. *Psychiatry Research, 88(1),* 15–24.

Capgras, J., & Reboul-Lachaux, J. (1923). Illusion des sosies dans un délire systématisé chronique. *Bulletin de la Société clinique de médecine mentale, 2,* 6–16.

Christodoulou, G. N. (1986). Role of depersonalization-derealization phenomena in the delusional misidentification syndromes. In G. N. Christodoulou (Ed.), *The delusional misidentification syndromes.* Basel: Karger.

Christodoulou, G. N. (1991). The Delusional Misidentification Syndromes. *British Journal of Psychiatry, 159,* 65–69.

Corcoran, R., & Frith, C. D. (2003). Autobiographical memory and theory of mind: Evidence of a relationship in Schizophrenia. *Psychological Medicine, 33(5),* 897–905.

Cutting, J., & Dunne, F. (1989). Subjective experience of Schizophrenia. *Schizophrenia Bulletin, 15(2),* 217–231.

Danion, J. M., Rizzo, L., & Bruant, A. (1999). Functional mechanisms underlying impaired recognition memory and conscious awareness in patients with Schizophrenia. *Archives of General Psychiatry, 56,* 639–644.

Eitenger, L. (1964). *Concentration camp survivors in Norway and Israel.* Oslo: Universitetforlaget.

Ellenberger, H. F. (1970). *The discovery of the unconscious: The history and evolution of dynamic psychiatry.* New York: Basic Books.

Freeman, D., & Garety, P. A. (2003). Connecting neurosis and psychosis: the direct influence of emotion on delusions and hallucinations. *Behavior Research and Therapy, 41(8),* 923–947.

Goff, D. C., Brotman, A. W., Kindlon, D., Waites, M., & Amico, E. (1991). The delusion of possession in chronically psychotic patients. *The Journal of Nervous and Mental Disease, 179(9),* 567–571.

Goldman-Rakic, P. S., & Selemon, L. D. (1997). Functional and anatomical aspects of prefrontal pathology in Schizophrenia. *Schizophrenia Bulletin, 23(3),* 437–458.

Harris, M., & Landis, C. (1997). *Sexual abuse in the lives of women diagnosed with serious mental illness.* London: Harwood.

Harrison, P. J. (1999). The neuropathology of Schizophrenia—A critical review of the data and their interpretation. *Brain, 122,* 593–624.

Harrow, M., Green, K. E., Sands, J. R., Jobe, T. H., Goldberg, J. F., Kaplan, K. J., & Martin, E. M. (2000). Thought disorder in Schizophrenia and mania: impaired context. *Schizophrenia Bulletin, 26(4),* 879–891.

Harrow, M., Lanin-Kettering, I., & Miller, J. G. (1989). Impaired perspective and thought pathology in schizophrenic and psychotic disorders. *Schizophrenia Bulletin, 15(4),* 605–623.

Harrow, M., & Prosen, M. (1978). Intermingling and disordered logic as influences on schizophrenic 'thought disorders.' *Archives of General Psychiatry, 35(10),* 1213–1218.

Harrow, M., & Prosen, M. (1979). Schizophrenic thought disorders: bizarre associations and intermingling. *American Journal of Psychiatry, 136(3),* 293–296.

Heaton, R., Chelune, G., Talley, J., Kay, G., & Curtiss, G. (1993). *Wisconsin Card Sorting Test Manual, Revised.* Odessa, FL: Psychological Assessment Resources.

Heckers, S. (2001). Neuroimaging studies of the hippocampus in Schizophrenia. *Hippocampus, 11(5),* 520–528.

Heckers, S., Rauch, S. L., Goff, D., Savage, C. R., Schacter, D. L., Fischman, A. J., & Alpert, N. M. (1998). Impaired recruitment of the hippocampus during conscious recollection in Schizophrenia. *Nature Neuroscience, 1(4),* 318–323.

Heinrichs, R. W., & Zakzanis, K. K. (1998). Neurocognitive deficit in Schizophrenia: a quantitative review of the evidence. *Neuropsychology, 12(3),* 426–445.

Heins, T., Gray, A., & Tennant, M. (1990). Persisting hallucinations following childhood sexual abuse. *Australian & New Zealand Journal of Psychiatry, 24,* 561–565.

Hofer, A., Weiss, E. M., Golaszewski, S. M., Siedentopf, C. M., Brinkhoff, C., Kremser, C., Felber, S., & Fleischhacker, W. W. (2003). Neural correlates of episodic encoding and recognition of words in unmedicated patients during an acute episode of Schizophrenia: a functional MRI study. *American Journal of Psychiatry, 160(10),* 1802–1808.

Hollender, M., & Hirsch, S. (1964). Hysterical psychosis. *American Journal of Psychiatry, 120,* 1066–1074.

Honig, A., Romme, M. A. J., Ensink, B. J., Escher, S. D. M. A. C., Pennings, M. H. A., & deVries, M. W. (1998). Auditory hallucinations: A comparison between patients and nonpatients. *Journal of Nervous & Mental Disease, 186(10),* 646–651.

Hornstein, N., & Putnam, F. W. (1992). Clinical phenomenology of child and adolescent dissociative disorders. *Journal of the American Academy of Child & Adolescent Psychiatry, 31(6),* 1077–1085.

Huron, C., Danion, J.-M., Giacomoni, F., Grange, D., Robert, P., & Rizzo, L. (1995). Impairment of recognition memory with, but not without, conscious recollection in Schizophrenia. *American Journal of Psychiatry, 152(12),* 1737–1742.

Jacobs, W. J., & Nadel, L. (1985). Stress-induced recovery of fears and phobias. *Psychological Review, 92(4),* 512–531.

Jacobs, W. J., & Nadel, L. (1999). The first panic attack: A neurobiological theory. *Canadian Journal of Experimental Psychology, 53(1),* 92–107.

Janssen, I., Krabbendam, L., Bak, M., Hanssen, M., Vollebergh, W., De Graaf, R., & Van Os, J. (2004). Childhood abuse as a risk factor for psychotic experiences. Acta *Psychiatrica Scandinavica, 109(1),* 38–45.

Jaspers, K. (1963). *General Psychopathology* (J. Hoenig & M. Hamilton, Trans.). Manchester, UK: Manchester University Press.

Judkins, M., & Slade, P. D. (1981). A questionnaire study of hostility in persistent auditory hallucinators. *British Journal of Medical Psychology, 54(3),* 243–250.

Jung, C. G. (1960a). *The psychology of Dementia præcox* (R. F. C. Hull, Trans.), The psychogenesis of mental disease (pp. 3–151). London: Routledge & Kegan Paul.

Jung, C. G. (1960b). A review of the complex theory (R. F. C. Hull, Trans.), The structure and dynamics of the psyche (pp. 92–104). London: Routledge & Kegan Paul.

Kardiner, A. (1941). *The traumatic neuroses of war.* New York: Hoeber.

Kihlstrom, J. F., Tataryn, D. J., & Hoyt, I. P. (1993). Dissociative disorders. In P. B. Sutker & H. E. Adams (Eds.), *Comprehensive handbook of psychopathology* (2nd ed., pp. 203–234). New York: Plenum Press.

Kluft, R. P. (1987). First-rank symptoms as a diagnostic clue to multiple personality disorder. *American Journal of Psychiatry, 144,* 293–298.

Kraepelin, E. (1919). *Dementia præcox and paraphrenia* (R. M. Barclay, Trans.). Edinburgh: E. & S. Livingstone.

Krikorian, R., & Layton, B. S. (1998). Implicit memory in posttraumatic stress disorder with amnesia for the traumatic event. *Journal of Neuropsychiatry and Clinical Neurosciences, 10(3),* 359–362.

Linscott, R. J., & Knight, R. G. (2001). Automatic hypermnesia and impaired recollection in Schizophrenia. *Neuropsychology, 15(4),* 576–585.

Marie, A., Gabrieli, J. D. E., Vaidya, C., Brown, B., Pratto, F., Zajonc, R. B., & Shaw, R. J. (2001). The mere exposure effect in patients with Schizophrenia. *Schizophrenia Bulletin, 27(2),* 297–303.

McDermid Vaz, S. A., & Heinrichs, R. W. (2002). Schizophrenia and memory impairment: evidence for a neurocognitive subtype. *Psychiatry Research, 113(1–2),* 93–105.

McEwen, B. S. (2000). Effects of adverse experiences for brain structure and function. *Biological Psychiatry, 48(8),* 721–731.

Moise, J., & Leichner, P. (1996). Prevalence of dissociative symptoms and disorders within an adult outpatient population with Schizophrenia. *Dissociation, 9(3),* 190–196.

Morrison, A. P., Frame, L., & Larkin, W. (2003). Relationships between trauma and psychosis: A review and integration. *British Journal of Clinical Psychology, 42(4),* 331–353.

Moskowitz, A. (2004). "Scared stiff": Catatonia as an evolutionary-based fear response. *Psychological Review, 111(4),* 984–1002.

Moskowitz, A., Barker-Collo, S., & Ellson, L. (2005). Replication of dissociation-psychosis link in New Zealand students and inmates. *Journal of Nervous and Mental Disease, 193,* 722–727.

Moskowitz, A., & Corstens, D. (2007). Auditory hallucinations: Psychotic symptom or dissociative experience? *The Journal of Psychological Trauma, 6 (2–3), 35–63.*

Moskowitz, A., Nadel, L., Watts, P., & Jacobs, W. J. (2008). Delusional atmosphere, the psychotic prodrome and decontexualized memories. In A. Moskowitz, I. Schäfer, & M. J. Dorahy (Eds.), Psychosis, trauma and dissociation: Emerging perspectives on severe psychopathology (pp. 65–78). London: Wiley.

Mott, R. H., Small, I. F., & Anderson, J. M. (1965). A comparative study of hallucinations. *Archives of General Psychiatry, 12(6),* 595–601.

Mueser, K. T., Trumbetta, S., Rosenberg, S., Vivader, R., Goodman, L., Osher, F., Auciello, P., & Foy, D. (1998).

Trauma and post-traumatic stress disorder in severe mental illness. *Journal of Consulting and Clinical Psychology, 66,* 493–499.

Nadel, L., & Jacobs, W. J. (1996). The role of the hippocampus in PTSD, panic, and phobia. In N. Kato (Ed.), *The hippocampus: Functions and clinical relevance* (pp. 455–463). Amsterdam: Elsevier Science.

Nadel, L., & Moscovitch, M. (1997). Memory consolidation, retrograde amnesia and the hippocampal complex. *Current Opinion in Neurobiology, 7(2),* 217–227.

Nelson, M. D., Saykin, A. J., Flashman, L. A., & Riordan, H. J. (1998). Hippocampal volume reduction in Schizophrenia as assessed by magnetic resonance imaging: a meta-analytic study. *Archives of General Psychiatry, 55(5),* 433–440.

Nurcombe, B., Mitchell, W., Begtrup, R., Tramontana, M., LaBarbera, J., & Pruitt, J. (1996). Dissociative hallucinosis and allied conditions. In F. Volkmar (Ed.), *Psychoses and pervasive developmental disorders in childhood and adolescence*. Washington, DC: American Psychiatric Press.

O'Brien, J. (1997). The "glucocorticoid cascade" hypothesis in man: Prolonged stress may cause permanent damage. *British Journal of Psychiatry, 170,* 199–201.

O'Keefe, J., & Nadel, L. (1978). *The hippocampus as a cognitive map*. Oxford: Oxford University Press.

Oxford University Press (1989). *The Oxford English Dictionary* (2nd ed.). Oxford: Oxford University Press.

Phillips, M. L., Medford, N., Senior, C., Bullmore, E. T., Suckling, J., Brammer, M. J., Andrew, C., Sierra, M., Williams, S. C. R., & David, A. S. (2001). Depersonalization disorder: Thinking without feeling. *Psychiatry Research: Neuroimaging, 108(3),* 145–160.

Putnam, F. W. (1989). *Diagnosis and treatment of Multiple Personality Disorder*. New York: Guilford Pres.

Putnam, F. W., Guroff, J. J., Silberman, E. K., Barban, L., & Post, R. K. (1986). The clinical phenomenology of multiple personality disorder: Review of 100 recent cases. *Journal of Clinical Psychiatry, 47(6),* 285–293.

Read, J. (1997). Child abuse and psychosis: A literature review and implications for professional practice. *Professional Psychology Research & Practice, 28(5),* 448–456.

Read, J. (2004). Does 'Schizophrenia' exist? Reliability and validity. In J. Read, L. R. Mosher & R. P. Bentall (Eds.), *Models of madness: Psychological, social and biological approaches to Schizophrenia* (pp. 43–56). London: Brunner-Routledge.

Read, J., Agar, K., Argyle, N., & Aderhold, V. (2003). Sexual and physical abuse during childhood and adulthood as predictors of hallucinations, delusions and thought disorder. *Psychology & Psychotherapy: Theory, Research & Practice, 76(1),* 1–22.

Read, J., Fink, P. J., Rudegeair, T., Felitti, V., & Whitfield, C. L. (2008). Child maltreatment and psychosis: A return to a genuinely integrated bio-psycho-social model. *Clinical Schizophrenia & Related Psychoses, 2(3),* 235–254.

Read, J., Goodman, L., Morrison, A. P., Ross, C. A., & Aderhold, V. (2004). Childhood trauma, loss and stress. In J. Read, L. Mosher & R. Bentall (Eds.), *Models of madness: Psychological, social and biological approaches to Schizophrenia.* Brunner-Routledge: London.

Read, J., Perry, B. D., Moskowitz, A., & Connolly, J. (2001). The contribution of early traumatic events to Schizophrenia in some patients: A traumagenic neurodevelopmental model. *Psychiatry, 64(4),* 319–345.

Roberts, G. (1992). The origins of delusion. *British Journal of Psychiatry, 161,* 298–308.

Rosenbaum, M. (1980). The role of the term Schizophrenia in the decline of the diagnosis of multiple personality. *Archives of General Psychiatry, 37,* 1383–1385.

Ross, C. A. (2004). *Schizophrenia: Innovations in diagnosis and treatment*. New York: Haworth Press.

Ross, C. A., Anderson, G., & Clark, P. (1994). Childhood abuse and the positive symptoms of Schizophrenia. *Hospital & Community Psychiatry, 45(5),* 489–491.

Ross, C. A., Heber, S., Norton, G. R., & Anderson, G. (1989). Differences between multiple personality disorder and other diagnostic groups on structured interview. *Journal of Nervous & Mental Disease, 177(8),* 487–491.

Ross, C. A., Miller, S. D., Reagor, P., Bjornson, L., & et al. (1990). Schneiderian symptoms in multiple personality disorder and Schizophrenia. *Comprehensive Psychiatry, 31(2),* 111–118.

Ross, C. A., & Norton, G. R. (1988). Multiple personality disorder patients with a prior diagnosis of Schizophrenia. *Dissociation, 1(2),* 39–42.

Sapolsky, R. M. (2000). Glucocorticoids and hippocampal atrophy in neuropsychiatric disorders. *Archives of General Psychiatry, 57(10),* 925–935.

Schatzman, M. (1973). *Soul murder: Persecution in the family.* London: Allan Lane.

Scheibel, A., & Kovelman, J. (1981). Disorientation of the hippocampal pyramid cell and its processes in the schizophrenic patient. *Biological Psychiatry, 16,* 101–102.

Schreber, D. P. (1955). *Memoirs of my mental illness* (R. A. Hunter, Trans.). London: W. Dawson.

Schwartz, B., Rosse, R., & Deutsch, S. (1993). Limits of the processing view in accounting for dissociations among memory measures in a clinical population. *Memory & Cognition, 21(1),* 63–72.

Servan-Schreiber, D., Cohen, J. D., & Steingard, S. (1996). Schizophrenic deficits in the processing of context. A test of a theoretical model. *Archives of General Psychiatry, 53(12),* 1105–1112.

Shenton, M. E., Dickey, C. C., Frumin, M., & McCarley, R. W. (2001). A review of MRI findings in Schizophrenia. *Schizophrenia Research, 49(1–2),* 1–52.

Shiloh, R., Schwartz, B., Weizman, A., & Radwan, M. (1995). Catatonia as an unusual presentation of posttraumatic stress disorder. *Psychopathology, 28(6),* 285–290.

Sierra, M., & Berrios, G. E. (1998). Depersonalization: neurobiological perspectives. *Biological Psychiatry, 44(9),* 898–908.

Spitzer, M. (1990). On defining delusions. *Comprehensive Psychiatry, 31(5),* 377–397.

Steinberg, M. (1994). *Structured Clinical Interview for DSM-IV Dissociative Disorders* (SCID-D), Revised. Washington, DC: American Psychiatric Press.

Steinberg, M. (1995). *Handbook for the assessment of dissociation: A clinical guide.* Washington, DC: American Psychiatric Press.

Steinberg, M., Cicchetti, D., Buchanan, J., Rakfeldt, J., & et al. (1994). Distinguishing between multiple personality disorder (Dissociative Identity Disorder) and Schizophrenia using the structured clinical interview for DSM-IV dissociative disorders. *Journal of Nervous & Mental Disease, 182(9),* 495–502.

Steingard, S., & Frankel, F. H. (1985). Dissociation and psychotic symptoms. *American Journal of Psychiatry, 142(8),* 953–955.

Tendolkar, I., Ruhrmann, S., Brockhaus, A., Pukrop, R., & Klosterkotter, J. (2002). Remembering or knowing: electrophysiological evidence for an episodic memory deficit in Schizophrenia. *Psychological Medicine, 32(7),* 1261–1271.

Todd, J., Dewhurst, K., & Wallis, G. (1981). The syndrome of Capgras. *British Journal of Psychiatry, 139,* 319–327.

Tulving, E. (1972). Episodic and semantic memory. In E. Tulving & W. Donaldson (Eds.), *Organization of memory* (pp. 381–403). New York: Academic Press.

Tutkun, J., Yargıç, L. I., & Sar, V. (1996). Dissociative identity disorder presenting as hysterical psychosis. *Dissociation, 9(4),* 244–252.

Van der Kolk, B. A., & Fisler, R. (1995). Dissociation and the fragmentary nature of traumatic memories: Overview and exploratory study. *Journal of Traumatic Stress, 8(4),* 23–43.

Van der Zwaard, R., & Polak, M. A. (2001). Pseudohallucinations: a pseudoconcept? A review of the validity of the concept, related to associate symptomatology. *Comprehensive Psychiatry, 42(1),* 42–50.

Velakoulis, D., Pantelis, C., McGorry, P. D., Dudgeon, P., Brewer, W., Cook, M., Desmond, P., Bridle, N., Tierney, P., Murrie, V., Singh, B., & Copolov, D. (1999). Hippocampal volume in first-episode psychoses and chronic Schizophrenia: a high-resolution magnetic resonance imaging study. *Archives of General Psychiatry, 56(2),* 133–141.

Vita, A., De Peri, L., Silenzi, C., & Dieci, M. (2006). Brain morphology in first-episode Schizophrenia: A meta-analysis of quantitative magnetic resonance imaging studies. Schizophrenia Research, 82, 75–88.

Waller, N. G., Putnam, F. W., & Carlson, E. B. (1996). Types of dissociation and dissociative types: A taxometric analysis of dissociative experiences. *Psychological Methods, 1(3),* 300–321.

Waller, N. G., & Ross, C. A. (1997). The prevalence and biometric structure of pathological dissociation in the general population: Taxometric and behavior genetic findings. *Journal of Abnormal Psychology, 106(4),* 499–510.

World Health Organization (1992). *SCAN: Schedules for clinical assessment in neuropsychiatry.* Geneva: World Health Organization.

Yung, A. R., & McGorry, P. D. (1996). The prodromal phase of first-episode psychosis: Past and current conceptualizations. *Schizophrenia Bulletin, 22*, 353–370.

35 Psychotic Presentations of Dissociative Identity Disorder

Vedat Şar, MD
Erdinç Öztürk, PhD

OUTLINE

35.1 DISSOCIATION AND PSYCHOSIS

The *American Psychiatric Glossary* (Stone, 1988) defines psychosis as a major mental disorder of organic or emotional origin in which a person's ability to think, respond emotionally, remember, communicate, interpret reality, and behave appropriately is sufficiently impaired so as to interfere grossly with the capacity to meet the ordinary demands of life. This term is applicable to conditions having a wide range of severity and duration, including schizophrenia, bipolar disorder, depression, and organic mental disorder.

Dissociative identity disorder (DID) and related forms of dissociative disorder not otherwise specified (DDNOS) are thought to be the most severe and complex types of dissociative disorders (American Psychiatric Association, 1994). Many clinicians, however, also accept the existence of a dissociative psychosis (DP) which was formerly called hysterical psychosis (Cavenar, Sullivan, & Maltbie, 1979; Gift, Strauss, & Young, 1985; Hirsch

& Hollender, 1969; Hollender & Hirsch, 1964; Maleval, 1981; Öztürk & Göğüş, 1973; Spiegel & Fink, 1979; Van der Hart, Witztum, & Friedman, 1993). Although never included in the standard nomenclature, the concept of DP lives on without official sanction (Libbrecht, 1995; Modestin & Bachman, 1992).

In fact, the construct of dissociation was not applied only to "hysteria" originally. Bleuler (1911) also linked it with the typical schizophrenic symptoms, such as disruption of thinking and emotions, thought to be the primary psychopathogenic mechanism in schizophrenia. Unfortunately, this approach led to the neglect of major dissociative disorders in mainstream psychiatry for many decades, rather than contributing to better understanding of human suffering due to chronic traumatization. Recently, there has been a renewed interest in the relationship between dissociation and schizophrenia. For example, Ross (1997, 2000) has proposed a dissociative subtype of schizophrenia. Notwithstanding the importance of this new stance, we will focus solely on psychotic presentations of major dissociative disorders (DID and related types of DDNOS). First, however, we will elaborate six domains of clinical psychopathology that will help to elaborate a concept of dissociation that is relevant to this debate.

35.1.1 Psychogenic Psychosis

The concept of a psychogenic psychosis distinct from schizophrenia has persisted throughout the 20th century (Faergeman, 1963; Strömgren, 1974). Psychogenic psychosis is usually considered reactive, in contrast to schizophrenia and manic depressive illness, which have been considered endogenous, that is, conditions with an unknown, but supposedly biological, origin (Strömgren, 1986).

European psychiatry has retained psychogenic psychosis in its tradition. Scandinavian psychiatrists adopted Jasper's distinction between process schizophrenia and reactive psychoses, with a better prognosis for the latter (Gelder, Gath, Mayou, & Cowen, 1996). In Denmark and Norway, the terms *reactive psychosis* or *psychogenic psychosis* are commonly applied to conditions that appear to be precipitated by stress, are to some extent understandable in their symptoms, and have a good prognosis (Strömgren, 1974, 1986). In France, the term *Bouffée délirante polymorphe aigüe* (literally, "acute polymorphous delusional puff") is used for a sudden-onset syndrome of good prognosis (Pichot, 1982, 1984). In Germany, Leonhard (1957/1979) published a classification that distinguishes schizophrenia from the cycloid psychoses, a group of non-affective psychoses with a good outcome.

In North American psychiatry, many concepts that purported to explain the psychopathogenesis of schizophrenia may be applicable to the etiology of dissociation: for example, double bind (Bateson, Jackson, Haley, & Weakland, 1956), schizophrenogenic parent (Fromm-Reichmann, 1950), marital schism (Lidz, Fleck, & Cornelison, 1965), and pseudomutuality (Wynne, 1958). These models had collapsed in the face of evidence that supported a biogenetic etiology for schizophrenia during the so-called neo-Kraepelinian period. While the models may apply to schizophrenia only to a modest degree, they may, nevertheless, more accurately apply to dissociative disorders, especially to DID (Spiegel, 1986), which tends to arise not only in overtly disturbed families but also in the context of an "apparently normal" but dysfunctional (i.e., dissociative) family type (Öztürk & Şar, 2005). In fact, many famous patients who were previously thought to have had schizophrenia are now considered to have had a dissociative disorder (Greenberg, 1964).

Geographic trajectories are interesting. European psychiatry and the Kraepelinian tradition provided a niche for DP and DID cases in the psychogenic psychosis category. The mainstream of North American psychiatry and the Bleulerian tradition put them at the psychogenic pole of a broad schizophrenic spectrum. Turkish psychiatry has recognized the existence of a DP distinct from schizophrenia or any other "endogenous" psychosis for many decades, though this recognition did not lead to the discovery of DID until the 1990s (Şar, Yargıç, & Tutkun, 1996). Nevertheless, the long-standing recognition of DP has provided a firm basis for the effective introduction of DID as a valid diagnostic category in mainstream Turkish psychiatry.

35.1.2 Reality Testing

The *American Psychiatric Glossary* (Stone, 1988) defines reality testing as the ability to evaluate the external world objectively and to differentiate adequately between it and the internal world. Impaired reality testing is one of the major hallmarks of psychosis. Patients with DID or related types of DDNOS usually have insight into their illness. Their reality testing is intact except during DP episodes.

The dissociative patient's reported claim of containing another person's existence, or of having more than one personality, cannot be considered a delusion. Such claims do not originate from a primary thought disorder, but rather from experience itself—the actual experience of the other as "not me" (Sullivan, 1953). In contrast, the delusions of a schizophrenic patient are thought to be the result of a primary disturbance of thought content.

Dissociation allows for the existence of several different (subjective) versions of reality within one person's internal world. Thus, Kluft (1993) once called DID "multiple reality disorder" and referred to "alternating reality states" (Kluft, 2003); Chefetz (2003) referred to identity alteration in DID as "isolated subjectivities"; Şar and Öztürk (2003) proposed a dissociation model based on "fragmented sociological and psychological realities." However, among dissociative subjects, external reality and the internal world are confused neither permanently nor pervasively. When it happens, it does so only in a time-limited and circumscribed fashion (i.e., restricted to distinct alter personality states and the limited information accessible to them).

35.1.3 Borderline Personality Disorder

The prodromal manifestations of schizophrenia may mimic obsessive compulsive disorder, an affective disorder, or a dissociative disorder. Some authors labeled prodromal cases or cases suggestive of schizophrenia pseudoneurotic schizophrenia or borderline schizophrenia (Hoch & Polatin, 1949). After a period of debate about its relationship to schizophrenic and affective disorders (Akiskal, 1981; McGlashan, 1983), the borderline syndrome was formally classified as borderline personality disorder, on Axis-II in DSM-III (American Psychiatric Association, 1980). While BPD was formally classified as a personality disorder, BPD cases are still considered psychosis-prone (Volkan, 1987), for instance, as living "on the borderline between psychosis and neurosis."

Research concerning paranoid ideation and depersonalization/derealization among patients with BPD (Zanarini, Gunderson, Frankenburg, & Chauncey, 1990) led to the introduction of the ninth diagnostic criterion of BPD in DSM-IV. This diagnostic criterion states: "during periods of extreme stress, transient paranoid ideation or dissociative symptoms may occur, but these are generally of insufficient severity or duration to warrant an additional diagnosis" (American Psychiatric Association, 1994). This criterion unfortunately confounded dissociative phenomena with the psychosis-proneness that had traditionally been considered a characteristic feature of "borderlines" by clinicians and theoreticians, even the core meaning of the still popular term.

Studies report a high frequency of dissociative symptoms among patients with BPD (Brodsky, Cloitre, & Dulit, 1995; Shearer, 1994; Zanarini, Ruser, Frankenburg, & Hennen, 2000). However, recent research (Şar et al., 2003; Şar et al., 2006) demonstrates that roughly two-thirds of patients with DSM-III-R BPD and three-fourths of patients with DSM-IV BPD have symptoms that are not simply stress-related or transient, and which call for a separate DSM-IV Axis-I diagnosis. Among the most frequently observed dissociative symptoms are chronic or repeated depersonalization, dissociative amnesia and other symptoms of DID. Consequently, the dissociative psychopathology seen in these putative BPD patients extends far beyond the boundaries of BPD's ninth diagnostic criterion.

High rates of childhood abuse and/or neglect have also been reported as central to both BPD (Herman, Perry, & Van der Kolk, 1989; Ogata, Silk, Goodrich, Lohr, Westen, & Hill, 1990) and dissociative disorders (Chu & Dill, 1990; Lewis, Yeager, Swica, Pincus, & Lewis, 1997; Nijenhuis, Spinhoven, Van Dyck, Van der Hart, & Vanderlinden, 1998; Ogawa, Sroufe, Weinfield, Carlson, & Egeland, 1997) Chu and Dill (1990) argued that BPD is a type of posttraumatic syndrome involving the mechanism of dissociation. Although Kernberg's psychoanalytic concept of BPD is not identical to DSM-III BPD (American Psychiatric Association, 1980), it played a major role in the conceptualization of this syndrome as a personality disorder. Kernberg regarded "splitting" (after Melanie Klein) as the main defense mechanism in BPD, whereas some current authors (e.g., Bromberg, 1998; Ross, 1997, 2000) would reinterpret splitting as dissociation. Alternation between dissociated self-states may account for the identity disturbance, affective instability, and idealizing and devaluing relationships that are characteristic of BPD (Blizard, 2003). We hypothesize BPD is a heterogeneous diagnostic category: that trauma-related BPD is a dissociative disorder, while other BPD cases may be prodromal, subsyndromal, or attenuated forms of mood disorders, organic mental disorders, or schizophrenic disorders (Gunderson, 1984).

Such a view allows us to reinterpret those highly communicative and benign crises of BPD sufferers, their so-called transient psychotic reactions and transference psychoses, as episodes of DP.

35.1.4 Crisis and Process

Crisis is a state of psychological disequilibrium (Stone, 1988). Although DID is a chronic condition, its course is largely determined by crises. DID may remain dormant for a long time (Kluft, 1985). Most subjects with DID enter the mental health system during a crisis that they are unable to resolve using their own psychological resources. We define three types of crisis situations in this context.

We define a *primary crisis* as any overt dissociative condition that causes subjective distress or interferes with daily functioning to a certain extent, but does not lead to a collapse of overall adjustment. For example, dissociative symptoms may be recognizable in a psychiatric examination; there may also be some occupational and intimacy problems, difficulties in school, fluctuating suicidal tendencies, or depressive mood.

We define a *secondary crisis* as any grossly inappropriate behavior leading to overt instability. For example, a patient with DID or DDNOS may enter an unstable phase characterized by rapid switching of personality states, severe anxiety and depression, fear due to hallucinations, and the like. Such a condition may lead to hospitalization.

We define a *tertiary crisis* as any transient condition (lasting no longer than a few hours) that interferes with the normal activities of daily living. These episodic behavioral disturbances include acute somatoform dissociative symptoms (e.g., pseudoseizures), flashbacks, self-mutilation, suicide attempts, or micropsychotic episodes.

Any acute dissociative condition (including somatoform dissociation, such as conversion disorder) should raise suspicion about an underlying chronic dissociative condition that may have been present since childhood (Şar, Akyüz, Kundakçı, Kızıltan, & Doğan, 2004; Tutkun, Yargıç, & Şar, 1996). DP would then apply to the most severe forms of crisis.

35.1.5 Culture-Bound ("Exotic") Syndromes

Psychiatry is the medical specialty most influenced by cultural issues. This is due not only to cultural differences in the phenomenology of psychiatric disorders, but also to differences in psychiatrists' attitudes and varying mental health delivery systems of different countries.

The thesis that DID is merely a North American phenomenon has been refuted in the past decade by research reports based on standardized assessment from diverse countries, such as from The Netherlands, Turkey, and Germany (Boon & Draijer, 1993; Gast, Rodewald, Nickel, & Emrich, 2001; Şar et al, 1996). Clinicians and researchers should be careful to avoid categorizing a universal human condition as culture-bound. Far from being culture-sensitive, such a mistake impedes scientific bridge-building among scientists from diverse cultures. Conversely, the identification of universal psychopathological conditions, regardless of cultural differences, would lead to significant clarifications about what is, in fact, cultural. The ongoing story of the "discovery" of DID in various cultures has underscored the importance of this stance.

With regard to dissociative psychosis, what is universal and what is culture-bound have also to be clarified.

Many conditions listed under DSM-IV's DDNOS, example 4, Dissociative Trance Disorder in the DDNOS section of the DSM-IV (with suggested research criteria in Appendix B), were previously categorized as culture-bound or exotic syndromes (Meth, 1974; American Psychiatric Association, 1994): for example, amok (Indonesia), bebainan (Indonesia), latah (Malaysia), pibloktoq (Arctic), ataque de nervios (Latin America), and possession (India). DSM-IV defines dissociative trance disorder as "single or episodic disturbances in the state of consciousness, identity or memory that are indigenous to particular locations and cultures … [but] not a normal part of a broadly accepted collective cultural or religious practice." Langness (1965) considers the *bena bena* syndrome in the New Guinea highlands as a DP.

DP is not limited to certain cultures (Langness, 1967); precipitating factors, however, may differ. From a general clinical perspective, DP is an urgent medico-psychiatric-legal condition. Within general clinical psychiatry, we regard DP as a trauma-related psychopathology ranking with other traditional severe conditions such as schizophrenia, manic depressive illness, and organic mental disorders. We believe that psychotherapy might prevent such severe crises by allowing other ways to express dissociative psychopathology, and consequently that limited availability of psychotherapy ought to predict a high prevalence of DP. Such limited availability might be due to diverse reasons: insufficient mental health delivery, ignorance of dissociative disorders by professionals prompting inappropriate interventions, or the pervasive presence of unbearable and inescapable realities, such as a restrictive cultural environment or outright war.

35.1.6 Hypnosis

Steingard and Frankel (1985) proposed that certain highly hypnotizable persons are prone to experience transient but severe psychotic states. Spiegel and Fink (1979) stated that DP patients are highly hypnotizable and curable with psychotherapy, in contrast to schizophrenics. Hypnotizability has a bearing on the differential diagnosis between schizophrenia and DP (Van der Hart & Spiegel, 1993). Hypnosis can be used productively in psychotherapy with patients with DP (Van der Hart & Spiegel, 1993; Van der Hart & Van der Velden, 1987; Van der Hart et al., 1993).

35.1.7 A Definition of Dissociation

Dissociation is defined in DSM-IV (American Psychiatric Association, 1994) as a disruption in the usually integrated functions of consciousness, memory, identity, or perception of the environment. We would propose a reexplanation of the term *dissociation*. In our view, the construct *dissociation*, as defined in DSM-IV, is merely a reflection of *depersonalization*. We consider *depersonalization* to be a mental mechanism rather than merely a symptom. Depersonalization is the only concept that covers all dissociative phenomena. While the construct *dissociation* connotes a loss of integrity in at least one of various psychological faculties, *depersonalization* connotes an impairment of a single faculty, which Jaspers (1913) called *personalization*—the experience that all psychological faculties (perception, body perception, memory retrieval, imagination, thought, feeling, etc.) belong to oneself.

All traumatic events (interpersonal or impersonal) have the inherent character of a double bind, creating multiple perceptions of reality (Şar & Öztürk, 2005). These multiple and simultaneous perceptions of reality destroy personalization. To cope with this, the traumatic fact (person, idea, situation, etc.) may be kept at a distance or, alternatively, the subject may remain in an oscillating relationship with the various perceptions. Intact personalization is possible only if there is just one perception of reality concerning a given fact (person, idea, situation, etc.) over a given time period. Metapsychologically, dissociation is based on a chronic developmental detachment of the sociological and psychological selves from each other, leading to overall psychological disharmony and to a hypertrophy of the sociological self (for a more complete treatment of this discussion, see Şar & Öztürk, 2007).

35.2 THE DOMAIN OF DISSOCIATION

Psychotic phenomena observed among patients with DID can be subsumed under two headings: dissociative psychosis (DP) proper and conditions that mimic psychosis. DP fits most psychosis definitions in general psychiatry, whereas the latter merely resemble psychosis, such that a psychotic diagnosis would be considered a misdiagnosis due to ignorance of an underlying dissociative disorder.

35.2.1 Dissociative Psychosis (Formerly Hysterical Psychosis)

While the term *hysterical psychosis* has a long history, we prefer the term *dissociative psychosis* in this study, in keeping with the modern nosology of dissociative disorders, even in referring to earlier works; for instance, we use the terms *DP* and *hysterical psychosis* interchangeably.

Hollender and Hirsch (1964) gave a clinical phenomenological description of DP. Van der Hart et al. (1993), reviewing Hoek, Breukink, and Janet, emphasized the dissociative foundation and traumatic etiology of DP. Hollender and Hirsch's definition requires a brief duration (three weeks or less) and emphasizes amnesia for the episode. Van der Hart et al. (1993) argue against the criterion of brief duration. Integrating both approaches, and agreeing with a traumatic etiology, Tutkun et al. (1996) underscored the link between DP and DID.

35.2.1.1 Four Perspectives

35.2.1.1.1 Descriptive Perspective

Hollender and Hirsch (1964) provided a clinical description of DP that has been considered useful by most psychiatrists in the second half of the 20th century. From the descriptive standpoint, DP begins suddenly and dramatically. The onset is temporally related to an event or circumstance that has been profoundly upsetting. The manifestations may take the form of hallucinations, delusions, depersonalization, or grossly unusual behavior. Affectivity is usually not altered. If altered, it is in the direction of volatility rather than flatness. Thought disorders, when they do occur, are generally circumscribed and transient. The acute episode in DP usually lasts 1 to 3 weeks. The process recedes as suddenly and dramatically as it began, leaving practically no residue, and, occasionally, with amnesia for the episode.

35.2.1.1.2 Dissociative Nature

Van der Hart and Friedman (1989), on the basis of Janet and Breukink's forgotten works on DP, and on their own experiences, have a different perspective on DP from Hollender and Hirsch. They emphasize the essential role of traumatically induced dissociation in the genesis of reactive psychosis. Based on case reports of DP (in the literature and their own), they conclude that a dissociative foundation is essential to DP, while brief duration is not (Van der Hart & Spiegel, 1993; Van der Hart et al., 1993).

Van der Hart et al. (1993) quote Janet, who said that the criteria for a dissociative psychosis would be: (1) the psychosis is embedded in dissociative phenomena; (2) the psychosis itself is seen as a dissociated state; (3) a splitting or doubling of the mind has occurred; (4) subconscious phenomena are observed; and (5) altered states of consciousness occur.

35.2.1.1.3 Common Traumatic Ground

Some authors who try to explain the psychodynamics and precipitating environmental stresses accompanying DP suggest intrafamilial relationships and environmental stress (Richman & White, 1970), disturbed marriages (Martin, 1971), an unwelcome or wished-for but not forthcoming sexual advance (Cavenar, Sullivan, & Maltbie,

1979), and complacent overadjustment to a restrictive environment (Öztürk & Göğüş, 1973) as etiological factors. Şar (1983) underscores maternal rejection among female patients in particular. Van der Hart and Spiegel (1993) consider both DP and DID as trauma-induced severe dissociative disorders; however, they do not mention a possible overlap between the two.

35.2.1.1.4 Overlap of DID and DP

Studies on DP and DID have had little overlap in the 20th century. One exception is the study by Tutkun et al. (1996); they evaluated Turkish patients for both conditions over a period of time, demonstrating the link between DP and DID. They conclude that DP might be a manifestation of a more chronic and complex dissociative disorder (DID or DDNOS). The initial clinical presentation of these cases fits most of the criteria for DP proposed by Hollender and Hirsch (1964). In patients with recurrent DP episodes, other long-lasting dissociative experiences and symptoms, not spontaneously reported, could easily be detected if evaluated. Large-scale surveys about this thesis are still lacking. A similar observation, however, was reported in a case presentation from Canada (Ghadirian, Lehmann, Dongier, & Kolivakis, 1985). In our experience, besides spontaneous incidences, DP may also develop during long-term psychotherapy of DID and related types of DDNOS.

Although DP may be superimposed on a chronic dissociative condition, it may also occur on its own in the face of severe trauma or for unknown reasons. This point needs further study.

35.2.1.2 Symptomatology of Dissociative Psychosis

The clinical symptomatology of DP is not uniform. Overall, it may resemble a schizophrenic, manic, and/or organic mental disorder (Table 35.1). Dissociative symptoms may be difficult to identify in the mixture of positive symptoms. Lack of affective flatness, a good premorbid psychosocial functionality, and an unexpected and sudden onset (often leading to emergency psychiatric admission) are very helpful clues for a diagnosis.

Organic mental disorder (delirium) ought to be ruled out immediately, as this might imply a medical emergency. Suicidal and homicidal tendencies should be carefully evaluated, as any dissociative patient is more likely to act on these impulses during a DP. Admission to a closed unit is advised until the accurate diagnosis is established. Hospitalization itself may have a therapeutic effect, as patients may need to remain at a distance from their environments for a certain time prior to returning to their premorbid levels of functioning.

TABLE 35.1
Symptoms of Acute Dissociative Psychosis

A. Core dissociative symptoms
   1. Dissociative amnesia and fugue
   2. Depersonalization, derealization
   3. Identity confusion or alteration, possession
B. Schizophrenia-like symptoms
   1. Hallucinations (visual, auditory, tactile, olfactory, gustatory)
   2. Schneiderian first rank symptoms, persecutory delusions
   3. Apparent discontinuity in thought flow (due to rapid switching between personality states)
   4. Impaired reality testing
   5. Flashbacks
C. Disorganized behavior
   1. Childlike movements and speech
      Urination and defecation in inappropriate places, childlike speech etc.
   2. Animal-like behavior
      Freezing or submission: stupor, catatonia, mutism, dissociative trance, suggestibility
      Fight-flight: violence, trying to escape
      Movements and voices: unorganized movements ("movement storm"), singing like a bird, etc.
   3. Flashback-related behavior: undressing, stereotypical movements and speech, self-mutilation, etc.
D. Organic-like symptoms
   1. Disorientation to person, place, and time
   2. Pseudoseizures and other somatoform symptoms
E. Affective symptoms
   1. Suicidal ideation and gestures
   2. Anxiety, euphoria, fear, anger, sadness
F. Autohypnotic symptoms
   1. Trance states, altered consciousness
   2. Altered time perception
   3. Suggestibility
G. Symptoms that exclude schizophrenia:
   1. Rapid fluctuation in mood and overall symptomatology
   2. No affective flatness
   3. Sudden onset, abrupt and dramatic improvement

Visual and auditory hallucinations and disorganized or grossly unusual behavior are predominant symptoms. Thought form may appear discontinuous, and reality testing may be impaired. Childlike behavior, trying to escape, catatonia, unorganized, or animal-like, behavior may be observed. There may also be flashback experiences. The patient's overall behavior and level of cooperation may change. The patient may appear quite improved and transiently cooperative. The patient may have total or partial amnesia for the episode.

Spiegel and Spiegel (1978) mention that patients with a previously good level of functioning may respond to severe environmental stress with rapid psychotic decompensation. They may be delusional and have ideas of reference, loose associations, and affect disturbance that may range from bland indifference or flatness to intense agitation. They frequently mobilize tremendous attention and anxiety from their social network. These patients often recompensate rapidly, especially when an appropriate intervention is made in their environment. The differential diagnosis between DP and bipolar mood disorder can be difficult as well.

35.2.2 Conditions That Mimic a Psychotic Disorder

Symptoms that can be explained simply by a diagnosis of DID do not warrant an additional diagnosis of DP.

35.2.2.1 Persecutory Personality State Deriving from a Real Person in the Environment of the Patient

Most DID patients have so-called persecutory personality states with hostile tendencies toward the host personality. In some cases, such a personality state derives from a person in the environment of the patient, for example, a family member, spouse, close friend, neighbor. The patient may temporarily confuse the alter personality state (in the internal world) with the corresponding person in the external world. For example, the threats of a persecutory personality state may be attributed to the person in the real world. In this case, the confused patient perceives the real person as the origin of threat and reports her experience correspondingly. It is not possible to distinguish this situation on a phenomenological basis from a paranoid psychosis unless the clinician suspects the presence of a dissociative disorder and explores this link. The observation of switching to the persecutory personality state and resolving of the persecutory delusions following the fusion of this personality state with the host personality makes the distinction possible.

35.2.2.2 Psychotic Personality State

Some patients have personality states with psychotic features such as delusions or hallucinations. These features are usually observed when the relevant personality state has executive control. These patients do not warrant any diagnosis beyond dissociative disorder, as these symptoms do not generalize to the rest of the personality system. The relevant personality state might take executive control only episodically during a tertiary crisis. For some patients, their only psychiatric symptomatology might be limited to tertiary crises throughout their lives. A sudden onset and abrupt improvement, and the dramatic nature of the hallucinations (visually hallucinated figures speaking as the origin of acoustic hallucinations) differentiate such dissociative episodes from psychotic disorders.

35.2.2.3 Imaginary Companionship by a Persecutory Personality State

The existence of a distinct personality state is usually felt by the patient as the presence of another person in the environment, a presence that may be very real for some, quite vague for others. In its mildest form, the subject complaints of a feeling as if "somebody is behind me," accompanied by anxious expectation and worrying, particularly if the accompanying personality state is a persecutory one. This situation may mimic an idea of reference, and thus a paranoid psychosis.

35.2.2.4 Features of DID Traditionally Known as Schizophrenic Symptoms

DID and schizophrenia share a number of psychopathological similarities such as auditory hallucinations, paranoid ideas, and Schneiderian first-rank symptoms, such as "made" feelings (Kluft, 1987; Ross et al., 1990). The differential diagnosis between schizophrenia and DID is an important clinical task. Two clinical conditions provide especially difficult challenges for differential diagnosis: (1) incipient schizophrenia in adolescence and (2) a dissociative subtype of schizophrenic disorder, as proposed by Ross (2000).

35.3 EXPLANATORY MECHANISMS

DP is thought to be produced in a patient with DID as follows: an acute stressful life event leads to a struggle for control and influence between alter identities who have frightening, fearful, aggressive, or delusional features, and some of whom may have been long dormant (Tutkun et al., 1996). This may take the form of Putnam's (1989) "revolving door crisis" or Kluft's (personal communication, 1995) "co-consciousness crisis." In a DID patient who is controlled by the host personality most of the time (with the alters being suppressed), diagnosing DID may be impossible. However, if a triggering stressful event occurs, this equilibrium may disappear and forceful activities of many alters (including the formation of new alters) may ensue, and severe dissociative symptoms and flashbacks may cause DP. So, DP may also be a "diagnostic window" (Kluft, 1987) for DID. On the other hand, DP can also occur separately as a diagnostic category on its own; that is, we do not consider DP to be simply an epiphenomenon of DID.

35.4 NOSOLOGY OF DISSOCIATIVE DISORDERS

From a general psychiatric perspective, brief psychoses are poorly understood; they probably are a heterogeneous group of psychotic disorders that have long created diagnostic dilemmas for psychiatry (Susser, Fennig, Jandorf, Amador, & Bromet, 1995). The relationship of these cases to schizophrenic disorder and the mood disorders remains uncertain (Susser & Wanderling, 1994; Susser, Varma, Malhotra, Conover, & Amador, 1995). The ICD-10 provides a special category for acute and transient psychotic conditions that is restricted to brief psychoses of acute onset; there is no equivalent to this group in the DSM-IV (World Health Organization, 1991; American Psychiatric Association, 1994).

Neither the DSM-IV nor the ICD-10 acknowledges that dissociative states can appear as a transient psychotic disorder. DSM-IV has no category appropriate for DP. Accordingly, one must resort to the diagnosis of psychotic disorder not otherwise specified.

We propose the introduction of a new category, Dissociative Psychosis (formerly Hysterical Psychosis), within the dissociative disorders grouping, with an accurate account of its etiology and phenomenology. An alternative to this option would be creation of a new category, Acute Dissociative Disorder with Psychotic Features (as opposed to without psychotic features).

Some famous cases of hysteria (e.g., Anna O. and Emmy von N.), who also manifested DP (Hollender & Hirsch, 1964), are now considered to be examples of chronic complex dissociative disorders (Ross, 1997). In the historical cases section of the DSM-IV casebook, Breuer's famous patient, Anna O., has been discussed (Spitzer, Gibbon, Skodol, Williams, & First, 1994). Anna O. had many symptoms that suggest a psychotic disorder, such as disorganized speech (e.g., "her language was devoid of all grammar, all syntax, to the extent that the whole conjugation of verbs was wrong"), hallucinations (e.g., of black snakes and death's heads), and possible delusions (e.g., she complained that she "had two egos, her real and an evil one, which force her to evil things"). Because of these seemingly psychotic symptoms, rigid use of the DSM-IV criteria might lead to a diagnosis of schizophrenia. The authors added that this diagnosis fails to capture the essence of Anna O.'s illness. They suggested that the problem is that DSM-IV does not recognize hysterical psychotic symptoms, with the exception of the category Factitious Disorder with Psychological Symptoms. Neither the authors, nor Breuer, nor Freud think that Anna O. intentionally produced her symptoms (i.e., factitious disorder).

35.5 DISCUSSION

Epidemiological data about DP are rather scarce. These patients are usually admitted to psychiatric emergency wards and require hospitalization. A retrospective investigation of inpatient admissions to a university psychiatry clinic in Turkey between 1970 and 1980 reported that 0.5% of the patients were diagnosed as having DP (Şar, 1983).

DP may occur in the presence or absence of a preexisting dissociative disorder; this raises the issue of inclusion and exclusion criteria. One approach would be exclusionary: where patients have preexisting DID, DP would be considered merely as an unstable presentation, rather than an additional diagnosis. Indeed, in clinics where DID is recognized as an appropriate diagnostic category, the number of subjects diagnosed as having DP diminishes. This is due to the increased expertise of clinicians who can accurately interpret rapid switching, the appearance of alter personalities, and flashback experiences. However, despite the common dissociative pathogenesis, this approach complicates the phenomenological description of DID as a homogeneous diagnostic category. Moreover, psychosocial functioning in DP is generally much more impaired than in regular DID. The DP category has many useful implications and consequences concerning hospitalization, forensic assessment, and research.

An alternative approach would recognize the diagnosis of DP whereas a concurrent DID might be an exclusion criterion. But this approach would likely further increase the difficulties of differential diagnosis. Moreover, (1) the overall approach of the DSM is basically phenomenological, and (2) a common dissociative pathogenesis should not necessarily lead to a single diagnosis.

The category of DP is typically used by clinicians who are aware of the difference between an acute schizophrenic episode and psychotic dissociative syndromes with a rather benign prognosis, but who are not familiar with DID and its incomplete forms (some of the DDNOS examples). The concept of DP would be one of the starting points for the recognition of DID in countries where professionals are more familiar with the concept of acute psychogenic psychosis.

35.6 NEEDED RESEARCH

The introduction of DP (or Acute Dissociative Disorder with Psychotic Features) as an official diagnostic category may fill the gap that was created by the current narrow definition of schizophrenic disorder. A diagnostic category of DP may provide a basis for research and theoretical studies on nonschizophrenic psychotic phenomena. This strategy seems to be more in accordance with the historical development of psychiatry than would a reintroduction of a broader (Bleulerian) concept of schizophrenia. Here are suggestions for further research:

1. There is a need for diagnostic tools and reliable diagnostic criteria for DP. The differential diagnosis from schizophrenic disorder, bipolar disorder, major depression, and other dissociative disorders should be considered.
2. The relationship between DP, DID, the various DDNOSs, Brief Psychotic Disorder, and Acute Stress Disorder should be clarified. Are all acute, transient psychotic disorders dissociative in nature?
3. Considering their episodic nature, relatively benign prognosis, and phenomenological overlap, a relationship between DP and mood disorders (i.e., manic episode, psychotic depression) should be investigated.
4. Patients with DP, but without an underlying chronic dissociative disorder, need to be researched separately.
5. Comparison of DP with the (proposed) dissociative subtype of schizophrenia might provide important insights for clinicians and researchers.
6. If there are subacute or chronic forms of DP, then how would they differ from schizophrenia?
7. The consideration of DID in forensic settings is controversial (Ross, 1997). The new category of DP would likely have important implications for forensic psychiatry, a point that needs further clarification.
8. Much social-psychological research is needed, especially regarding the role given to the dissociative subject by the family. Many concepts that animated theory and (failed) research into a psychosocial etiology of schizophrenia (e.g., schizophrenogenic mother, double bind, marital schism, pseudomutuality, etc.) may prove to be relevant for dissociative psychopathology (Spiegel, 1986).

REFERENCES

Akiskal, H. S. (1981). Subaffective disorders: Dysthymic, cyclothymic and bipolar II disorders in the "borderline" realm. *Psychiatric Clinics of North America, 4*, 25–46.

American Psychiatric Association (1980). *DSM-III – Diagnostic and statistical manual of mental disorders* (3rd ed.). Washington, DC: Author.

American Psychiatric Association (1987). *DSM-III-R– Diagnostic and statistical manual of mental disorders* (3rd ed., revised). Washington, DC: Author.

American Psychiatric Association (1994). *DSM-IV – Diagnostic and statistical manual of mental disorders* (4th ed.). Washington, DC: Author.

Bateson, G., Jackson, D. D., Haley, J., & Weakland, J. H. (1956). Toward a theory of schizophrenia. *Behavioral Science, 1*, 251–64.

Bleuler, E. (1911/1950). *Dementia Præcox oder die Gruppe der Schizophrenien.* Leipzig: Deuticke. Trans. J. Zinkin, *Dementia Præcox or the Group of Schizophrenias.* New York: International Universities Press.

Blizard, R. A. (2003). Disorganized attachment, development of dissociated self-states, and a relational approach to treatment. *Journal of Trauma & Dissociation, 4(3)*, 27–50.

Boon, S., & Draijer, N. (1993). Multiple personality disorder in the Netherlands: a clinical investigation of 71 patients. *American Journal of Psychiatry, 150*, 489–94.

Brodsky, B. S., Cloitre, M., & Dulit, R. A. (1995). Relationship of dissociation to self-mutilation and childhood abuse in borderline personality disorder. *American Journal of Psychiatry, 152*, 1788–92.

Bromberg, P. M. (1998). *Standing in the spaces. Essays on clinical process, trauma, and dissociation.* London: The Analytic Press.

Cavenar, J. O. Jr., Sullivan, J. L., & Maltbie, A. A. (1979). A clinical note on hysterical psychosis. *American Journal of Psychiatry, 136*, 830–2.

Chefetz, R. A. (2003). Fishing in dissociative waters: Subjectivity, power, and relatedness in the therapeutic dyad. *Plenary speech, 20th Annual Conference of the ISSD,* Chicago.

Chu, J. A., & Dill, D. L. (1990). Dissociative symptoms in relation to childhood physical and sexual abuse. *American Journal of Psychiatry, 147*, 887–92.

Faergeman, P. M. (1963). *Psychogenic psychoses.* London: Butterwords.

Fromm-Reichmann, F. (1950). *Principles of intensive psychotherapy.* Chicago: University of Chicago Press.

Gast, U., Rodewald, F., Nickel, V., & Emrich, H. M. (2001). Prevalence of dissociative disorders among psychiatric inpatients in a German university clinic. *Journal of Nervous and Mental Disease, 189*, 249–57.

Gelder, M., Gath, D., Mayou, R., & Cowen, P. (1996). *Oxford textbook of psychiatry* (3rd ed., pp. 246–93). New York: Oxford University Press.

Ghadirian, A. M., Lehmann, H. E., Dongier, M., & Kolivakis, T. (1985). Multiple personality in a case of functional psychosis. *Comprehensive Psychiatry, 26*, 22–8.

Gift, T. E., Strauss, J. S., & Young, Y. (1985). Hysterical psychosis: an empirical approach. *American Journal of Psychiatry, 142*, 345–7.

Goldman, S. J., D'Angelo, E. J., DeMaso, D. R., & Mezzacappa, E. (1992). Physical and sexual abuse histories among children with borderline personality disorder. *American Journal of Psychiatry, 149*, 1723–6.

Greenberg, J. (1964). *I never promised you a rose garden*. New York: New American Library.

Gunderson, J. G. (1984). *Borderline personality disorder.* Washington: American Psychiatric Press.

Herman, J. L., Perry, J. C., & Van der Kolk, B. A. (1989). Childhood trauma in borderline personality disorder. *American Journal of Psychiatry, 14*, 490–5.

Hirsch, S. J., & Hollender, M. H. (1969). Hysterical psychosis: clarification of the concept. *American Journal of Psychiatry, 125*, 909–15.

Hoch, P., & Polatin, P. (1949). Pseudo-neurotic forms of schizophrenia. *Psychiatric Quarterly, 23*, 248–76.

Hollender, M. H., & Hirsch, S. J. (1964). Hysterical psychosis. *American Journal of Psychiatry, 120*, 1066–74.

Jaspers, K. (1913). *Allgemeine psychopathologie (General psychopathology)*. Berlin: Springer/Verlag.

Kernberg, O. (1967). Borderline personality organization. *Journal of the American Psychoanalytic Association, 15*, 641–85.

Kluft, R. P. (1985). The natural history of multiple personality disorder. In R. P. Kluft (Ed.), *Childhood antecedents of multiple personality* (pp. 197–238). Washington, DC: American Psychiatric Press.

Kluft, R. P. (1987). First rank symptoms as a diagnostic clue to multiple personality disorder. *American Journal of Psychiatry, 144*, 293–8.

Kluft, R. P. (1993). Basic principles in conducting the psychotherapy of multiple personality disorder. In: R. P. Kluft, C. G. Fine (Eds.), *Clinical perspectives on multiple personality disorder*. Washington, DC: American Psychiatric Press.

Kluft, R. P. (2003). Workshop. *20th Annual Conference of the ISSD,* Chicago.

Langness, L. L. (1965). Hysterical psychosis in the New Guinea highlands: a *bena bena* example. *Psychiatry, 28*, 258–77.

Langness, L. L. (1967). Hysterical psychosis: the cross-cultural evidence. *American Journal of* Psychiatry, 124, 143–52.

Leonhard, K. (1957/1979). *The classification of endogenous psychoses.* New York: Irvington.

Lewis, D. O., Yeager, C. A., Swica, Y., Pincus, J. H., & Lewis, M. (1997). Objective documentation of child abuse and dissociation in 12 murderers with Dissociative Identity Disorder. *American Journal of Psychiatry, 154*, 1703–10.

Libbrecht, K. (1995). *Hysterical psychosis: A historical survey.* New Brunswick/London: Transaction Publishers.

Lidz, T., Fleck, S., & Cornelison, A. R. (1965). *Schizophrenia and the family.* New York: International Universities Press.

Maleval, J. C. (1981). *Folies hystériques et psychoses dissociatives.* Paris: Payot.

Martin, P. A. (1971). Dynamic considerations of the hysterical psychosis. *American Journal of Psychiatry, 128*, 745–8.

McGlashan, T. H. (1983). The borderline syndrome: II. Is it a variant of schizophrenia or affective disorder? *Archives of General Psychiatry, 40*, 1319–23.

Meth, J. M. (1974). Exotic psychiatric syndromes. In S. Arieti (Ed.), *American Handbook of Psychiatry* (vol. 3, pp. 723–39). New York: Basic Books.

Modestin, J., & Bachman, K. M. (1992). Is the diagnosis of the hysterical psychosis justified? Clinical study of hysterical psychosis, reactive/psychogenic psychosis, and schizophrenia. *Comprehensive Psychiatry, 33*, 17–24.

Nijenhuis, E. R. S., Spinhoven, P., Van Dyck, R., Van der Hart, O., & Vanderlinden, J. (1998). Degree of somatoform dissociation in dissociative disorder is correlated with reported trauma. *Journal of Traumatic Stress, 11*, 711–30.

Ogata, S. N., Silk, K. R., Goodrich, S., Lohr, N. E., Westen, D., & Hill, E. M. (1990). Childhood sexual and physical abuse in adult patients with borderline personality disorder. *American Journal of Psychiatry, 147*, 1008–13.

Ogawa, J. R., Sroufe, L. A., Weinfield, N. S., Carlson, E. A., & Egeland, B. (1997). Development and the fragmented self: longitudinal study of dissociative symptomatology in a nonclinical sample. *Development and Psychopathology, 4*, 855–79.

Öztürk, E., & Şar, V. (2005). "Apparently normal" family. A contemporary agent of transgenerational trauma and dissociation. *Journal of Trauma Practice, 4(3–4)*, 287–303.

Öztürk, O. M., & Göğüş, A. (1973). Ağır regressif belirtiler gösteren histerik psikozlar (Hysterical psychoses presenting with severe regressive symptoms). In: 9. *Ulusal Psikiyatri ve Nörolojik Bilimler Kongresi Calismalari* (Proceedings of the 9th National Congress of Psychiatry and Neurology, Turkey), pp. 155–64. Ankara: Meteksan.

Pichot, P. (1982). The diagnosis and classification of mental disorders in French speaking countries: background, current view, and comparison with other nomenclature. *Psychological Medicine, 12*, 475–92.

Pichot, P. (1984). The French approach to classification. *British Journal of Psychiatry, 144*, 113–8.

Putnam, F. W. (1989). *Diagnosis and treatment of multiple personality disorder*. New York: Guilford Press.

Richman, J., & White, H. (1970). A family view of hysterical psychosis. *American Journal of Psychiatry, 127*, 280–5.

Ross, C. A. (1997). *Dissociative Identity Disorder. Diagnosis, clinical features, and treatment of multiple personality.* New York: Wiley.

Ross, C. A. (2000). *The trauma model*. Richardson: Manitou Communications Inc.

Ross, C. A., Miller, S. D., Reagor, P., Bjronson, L., Fraser, G., & Anderson, G. (1990). Schneiderian symptoms in multiple personality disorder and schizophrenia. *Comprehensive Psychiatry, 31*, 111–8.

Şar, İ. (1983). *1970–1980 yılları arasında Hacettepe Üniversitesi Psikiyatri Kliniklerine yatarak tedavi gören hastalardan "histeri" tanısı alanların değerlendirilmesi.* (Dissertation: A retrospective investigation on inpatients diagnosed as having "hysteria" in Hacettepe University Psychiatry Clinic between 1970–1980). Ankara: Hacettepe University.

Şar, V., Akyüz, G., Kuğu, N., Öztürk, E., & Ertem-Vehid, H. (2006). Axis-I dissociative disorder comorbidity of borderline personality disorder and reports of childhood trauma. *Journal of Clinical Psychiatry, 67(10),* 1583–90.

Şar, V., Akyüz, G., Kundakçı, T., Kızıltan, E., & Doğan, O. (2004) Childhood trauma, dissociation, and psychiatric comorbidity in patients with conversion disorder. *American Journal of Psychiatry, 161,* 2271–6.

Şar, V., Kundakçı, T., Kızıltan, E., Yargıç, L. İ., Tutkun, H., Bakım, B., Aydıner, O., Özpulat, T., Keser, V., & Özdemir, O. (2003). Axis-I dissociative disorder comorbidity of borderline personality disorder among psychiatric outpatients. *Journal of Trauma & Dissociation, 4(1),* 119–36.

Şar, V., & Öztürk, E. (2005). What is trauma and dissociation? *Journal of Trauma Practice, 4(1–2),* 7–20.

Şar, V., & Öztürk, E. (2007). Functional dissociation of the self: a sociocognitive approach to trauma and dissociation. *Journal of Trauma & Dissociation, 8(4),* 69–89.

Şar, V., & Tutkun, H. (1997). The treatment of Dissociative Identity Disorder in Turkey: A case presentation. *Dissociation, 10,* 146–52.

Şar, V., Yargıç, L. İ., & Tutkun, H. (1995). Current status of Dissociative Identity Disorder in Turkey. Proceedings of the 5th Spring Conference of the International Society for the Study of Dissociation, Amsterdam.

Şar, V., Yargıç, L. İ., & Tutkun, H. (1996). Structured interview data on 35 cases of Dissociative Identity Disorder in Turkey. *American Journal of Psychiatry, 153,* 1329–33.

Schneider, K. (1946/1976). *Klinische Psychopathologie* (Clinical psychopathology). Stuttgart: Georg Thieme Verlag.

Shearer, S. L. (1994). Dissociative phenomena in women with borderline personality disorder. *American Journal of Psychiatry, 151,* 1324–8.

Shearer, S. L., Peters, C. P., Quaytman, M. S., & Ogden, R. L. (1990). Frequency and correlates of childhood sexual and physical abuse histories in adult female borderline inpatients. *American Journal of Psychiatry, 14,* 214–6.

Spiegel, D. (1986). Dissociation, double binds, and posttraumatic stress in multiple personality disorder. In: B. G. Braun (Ed.), *Treatment of multiple personality disorder* (pp. 62–77). Washington, DC: American Psychiatric Press.

Spiegel, D., & Fink, D. (1979). Hysterical psychosis and hypnotizability. *American Journal of Psychiatry, 136,* 777–81.

Spiegel, H., & Spiegel, D. (1978). *Trance and treatment.* Washington, DC: American Psychiatric Press.

Spitzer, C., Haug, H. J., & Freyberger, H. J. (1997). Dissociative symptoms in schizophrenic patients with positive and negative symptoms. *Psychopathology, 30,* 67–75.

Spitzer, R. L., Gibbon, M., Skodol, A. E., Williams, J. B. W., & First, M. B. (1994). *DSM-IV Case Book. A learning companion to the diagnostic and statistical manual of mental disorders, fourth edition.* Washington, DC: American Psychiatric Press.

Steingard, S., & Frankel, F. H. (1985). Dissociation and psychotic symptoms. *American Journal of Psychiatry, 142,* 953–5.

Stone, E. M. (1988). *American psychiatric glossary.* Washington, DC: American Psychiatric Press.

Strömgren, E. (1974). Psychogenic psychoses. In: S. R. Hirsch, M. Shepherd (Eds.), *Themes and variations in European psychiatry* (pp. 97–120). Bristol: Wright.

Strömgren, E. (1986). The development of the concept of reactive psychoses. *Psychopathology, 20,* 62–7.

Sullivan, H. S. (1953). *The interpersonal theory of psychiatry.* New York: Norton.

Susser, E., Fennig, S., Jandorf, L., Amador, X., & Bromet, E. (1995). Epidemiology, diagnosis, and course of brief psychoses. *American Journal of Psychiatry, 152,* 1743–8.

Susser, E., & Wanderling, J. (1994). Epidemiology of nonaffective acute remitting psychosis vs. schizophrenia. *Archives of General Psychiatry, 51,* 294–301.

Susser, E., Varma, V. K., Malhotra, S., Conover, S., & Amador, X. F. (1995). Delineation of acute and transient psychotic disorders in a developing country setting. *British Journal of Psychiatry, 167,* 216–9.

Tutkun, H., Yargıç, L., & Şar, V. (1996). Dissociative Identity Disorder presenting as hysterical psychosis. *Dissociation, 9,* 241–9.

Van der Hart, O., & Friedman, B. (1989). A reader's guide to Pierre Janet on dissociation: a neglected intellectual heritage. *Dissociation, 2,* 3–16.

Van der Hart, O., & Spiegel, D. (1993). Hypnotic assessment and treatment of trauma induced psychosis: the early psychotherapy of H. Breukink and modern views. *International Journal of Clinical and Experimental Hypnosis, 41,* 191–209.

Van der Hart, O., & Van der Velden, K. (1987). The hypnotherapy of Dr. Andries Hoek: uncovering hypnotherapy before Janet, Breuer, and Freud. *American Journal of Clinical Hypnosis, 29,* 264–71.

Van der Hart, O., Witztum, E., & Friedman, B. (1993). From hysterical psychosis to reactive dissociative psychosis. *Journal of Traumatic Stress,* 6, 43–64.

Volkan, V. D. (1987). *Six steps in the treatment of borderline personality organization.* Northwale, NJ: Jason Aronson.

World Health Organization (1991). *Tenth Revision of the International Classification of Diseases (ICD-10) Chapter V (F): Mental and behavioral disorders (including disorders of psychological development). Clinical descriptions and diagnostic guidelines.* Geneva: World Health Organization.

Wynne, L. C., Ryckoff, I. M., Day, J., & Hirsch S. (1958). Pseudomutuality in the family relations of schizophrenics. *Psychiatry, 21,* 204–19.

Zanarini, M. C., Gunderson, J. G., Frankenburg, F. R., & Chauncey, D. L. (1990). Discriminating borderline personality disorder from other axis II disorders. *American Journal of Psychiatry, 147,* 161–7.

Zanarini, M. C., Ruser, T., Frankenburg, F. R., & Hennen, J. (2000). The dissociative experiences of borderline patients. *Comprehensive Psychiatry, 41,* 223–7.

Zanarini, M. C., Williams, A. A., Lewis, R. E., Reich, R. B., Vera, S. C., Marino, M. F., Levin, A., Yong, L., & Frankenburg, F. R. (1997). Reported pathological childhood experiences associated with the development of borderline personality disorder. *American Journal of Psychiatry, 154,* 1101–6.

36 Dissociative Hallucinosis

Barry Nurcombe, MD, FRANZCP, FRACP
James Graham Scott, MBBS, FRANZCP
Mary Ellen Jessop, MBBS, FRANZCP

OUTLINE

36.1 THE DEFINITION OF DISSOCIATION

In its narrow definition, *dissociation* refers to an unconscious defense mechanism that protects the individual from unregulated affect by restricting the field of consciousness.

In normal conditions, thought, emotion, volition, action, identity, and memory are integrated.

The concept of dissociation has been extended to the separation of emotion from thought, the dislocation of volition from action, and pathological alterations of the sense of self. Subsequently, disturbing memories of the dissociated event(s) are deflected from consciousness and become accessible only under certain conditions.

36.2 THE DOMAIN OF DISSOCIATION

Originally, Janet (1911) used the term *dissociation* (*désagrégation*) to refer to the removal of disturbing memories of a psychologically traumatic event from consciousness in the form of subconscious fixed ideas. Though removed from awareness, subconscious fixed ideas are not liquidated but may continue to influence behavior in the form of trances, reenactments of traumatic events, paralysis of the will, or physical symptoms. Janet hypothesized that the tendency to dissociate derives from inborn temperament, prior experience, and the intensity of the emotions generated at the time of the traumatic event. Breuer and Freud (1955) associated "hysterical splitting" (i.e., dissociation) of the mind with autohypnoid states generated by psychologically traumatic events. As a result of splitting, large complexes of ideas are rendered inadmissible to consciousness. Breuer and Freud conceived of splitting as an active psychic process that deflects consciousness from distressing ideas, which are driven to an unconscious mental region created by autohypnosis. From this concept, the notion of unconscious ego defense evolved. Subsequently, the concept of dissociation was absorbed by the psychoanalytic concepts of repression and isolation (Fenichel, 1955). After 1970, the revival of interest in Janet, and the rediscovery of dissociation as a psychopathological mechanism have stretched the boundaries of its definition. The term is now used to apply to the following phenomena:

- The capacity of some people to behave with preternatural emotional control at times of great emotional stress.
- A narrowing of perceptual awareness associated with fearful experiences.
- The feeling of emotional "numbness" experienced by some during or after a psychologically traumatic experience.
- The "freezing" of volition experienced by some during a psychologically traumatic experience.
- Alterations in the perception of time, self, and identity during and after psychological trauma.
- The purposive forgetting of memories or parts of memories, or the fragmentation of memory, or the filling of gaps in memory with

confabulations, following a psychologically traumatic event.
- The stripping of emotion from the memory of a psychologically traumatic event.

All these phenomena are within the bounds of normality, and can be seen as adaptive in purpose. However, other phenomena have become associated with the term *dissociation*. In that they cause psychological distress and impairment, these phenomena can be regarded as psychopathological. Pathological dissociation disrupts or impairs the following mental functions:

- Autobiographical memory
- The sense of self-awareness, time, and identity
- Emotional regulation and the control of impulse
- Self-monitoring and executive functions
- Concentration, the continuity of thought, and learning
- Attachment, social competence, and the capacity to sustain personal relationships

The symptoms of pathological dissociation are as follows:

- Forgetfulness, fragmentation of memory, or dense amnesia for periods of time associated with psychological trauma
- The intrusion of dissociated memories in the form of unbidden, frightening, waking imagery, "flashbacks," nightmares, auditory hallucinations, or the reenactment of trauma in play or action
- Distortion of the perception of self and identity with emotional distancing from the self, depersonalization, the sense of being a spectator of the self, the sense of being controlled or influenced by external forces, or the fragmentation of identity into alter personalities
- Episodes of emotional dyscontrol and impulsivity characterized by restricted awareness, emotional turmoil, autonomic hyperarousal, assaultiveness, self-injury, and suicidal behavior, often in association with command hallucinations
- The sense that time is decelerated, accelerated, discontinuous, or "lost"
- Disorganized, poorly planned, self-defeating, impulsive behavior
- Inconsistent academic, technical, artistic, or sporting skills and varying habits and interests
- Failure to recognize friends or family members
- Loss of autobiographical memory for personal information (e.g., name, address, personal history)
- Episodes of fugue: traveling distances but not knowing why or how one got there
- Episodes of absences, vagueness, daydreaming, "blacking out," and trances, sometimes with regression to an infantile state

Associated with these pathological dissociative symptoms, the following secondary or tertiary posttraumatic phenomena may be manifest:

- The avoidance of situations, places, people, or conversations that remind the subject of trauma, with emotional arousal when such cues are encountered
- The use of fantasy to anticipate fearful situations, bolster defenses against anxiety, or repair dissociative gaps in autobiographical memory.
- Depression, anxiety, phobias, hypervigilance, excessive startle response
- Impairment of learning
- Sexual dysfunction
- Reckless or risky sexual behavior, with poor choice of partner and potential revictimization
- Somatic symptoms (e.g., headaches)
- Conversion symptoms (e.g., pseudoseizures)
- Suicidal behavior
- Repeated self-injury
- Substance abuse
- Antisocial behavior

The breadth of these behavior patterns suggests that the concept of dissociation has stretched to the extent that it has absorbed a number of related but arguably distinct phenomena. If the definition of dissociation is limited to *the deflection from conscious awareness of distressing traumatic memories and their retention in a manner from which they cannot be voluntarily accessed*, then the phenomena associated with (but not necessarily synonymous with) normal dissociation can be classified as follows:

- *Isolation*. Emotional control during a traumatic event, the subsequent affectless recall of traumatic events, and the emotional numbing that may occur in the aftermath of psychological trauma.
- *Freezing*. Paralysis of will and action experienced during and after a traumatic experience.
- *Restriction of awareness*. The narrowing of perception experienced during a traumatic event, with alteration of the perception of time, self,

and identity, and the concentration of the mind on threat location, self-defense, or flight.

The following classification is suggested for phenomena that have been included under the umbrella of pathological dissociation:

- *Dissociative amnesia.* The fragmentation of or inaccessibility of autobiographical memory for periods of time associated with psychological trauma, associated with the loss or absence of autobiographical memory for personal information, and (rarely) fugue states.
- *Distortion of the sense of self.* Depersonalization, derealization, passivity experiences.
- *Fragmentation of personal identity.* The sense of being "in pieces," unintegrated, and lacking in a core identity.
- *Failure or decompensation of dissociation.* Manifest as intrusive imagery, nightmares, "flashbacks," reenactment, emotional dyscontrol, and audiovisual hallucinosis.
- *Distortion of the working model of attachment.* Avoidance of or distrust of close personal relationships, combined with neediness, and alternating with the tendency to enter into intense, impulsive, poorly chosen liaisons.

If the individual is unable to resolve the psychological conflict associated with psychological trauma, assimilate its memory, and accommodate the self to its implications, a number of secondary phenomena may emerge, as follows:

- *Somatization.* The manifestation of chronic anxiety in the form of physical symptoms (e.g., dyspareunia, sexual frigidity, Somatization Disorder).
- *Conversion.* The reemergence of dissociated somatic memories in the form of bodily symptoms (e.g., pseudoseizures).
- *Repetition-compulsion.* The tendency to repeat or reenact traumatic experience, while being unaware that one is doing so (e.g., by sexual risk-taking, sexual perpetration, impulsive aggressive behavior).
- *Self-sedation.* The use of alcohol or drugs to moderate traumatic anxiety, anguish, depression, and self-hatred.
- *Diversion.* Engaging in activities that temporarily distract the mind from emotionally distressing thoughts or memories (e.g., running away, antisocial behavior).
- *Fantasy.* The use of imagination to disguise, ward off, or resolve traumatic anxiety (e.g., the enlistment of fantasy companions to deal with traumatic experiences).

Long-standing, unresolved conflict concerning psychological trauma, in association with familial and social facilitants, can lead to maladaptive lifestyles in which the personality incorporates pathological dissociation and pervasive secondary phenomena, for example:

- Borderline personality disorder
- Briquet's syndrome
- Intermittent explosive disorder
- Dissociative identity disorder
- Sexual perpetration
- Prostitution

In sexual perpetration, for example, the perpetrator copes with the threatened reemergence of dissociated memories of abuse by reversal and counterphobic action, converting a fear of passive victimization into its opposite.

The nature and outcome of psychological trauma is shaped by its context, frequency, duration, and meaning. The terror induced by a single motor vehicle accident differs from the fear associated with war, the shame and self-disgust of repeated sexual abuse, and the resentment engendered by chronic physical maltreatment. Whereas dissociation may be the primary ego defense, associated defenses and secondary and tertiary coping techniques mold the personality.

36.3 EXPLANATORY MECHANISMS

The primary, secondary, and tertiary mechanisms associated with dissociation require explanation at biological, psychological, and social levels. Unfortunately, insufficient evidence is available to do so.

Dissociation is a primitive coping mechanism that may be related to disruption of the processing of hippocampal working memory after activation of the amygdaloid alarm system. As a result, traumatic memories either fail to be transferred to long-term memory or, if they are transferred, are blocked from assimilation and access by inhibitory processes. The failure to assimilate such important data is reflected in *intrusive experiences* such as flashbacks, nightmares, hallucinations, reenactments, and traumatic play. When intrusive imagery emerges, it may be experienced in vivid form, as though pristine and unaffected by the accommodatory processing of long-term memory. Although intrusive imagery can convey great conviction, its veridicality is uncertain. Genuine memories may be colored or adulterated by *fantasy* (e.g., in order to heighten symbolic meaning, or as a form of wish-fulfilment, or to patch temporal gaps with confabulation).

Intrusive phenomena result from a *failure of dissociation*: deflected traumatic material is represented to working memory for transfer to long-term memory, with assimilation and accommodation. If the material being represented is psychologically disruptive, however, the subject is flooded with anxiety, activating secondary defenses (e.g., distancing, depersonalization, conversion, self-inflicted injury, or massive dissociation with trance or fugue). The purpose of the different forms of psychotherapy (e.g., cognitive behavior therapy, eye movement desensitization and reprocessing, and psychodynamic psychotherapy) is to promote the assimilation of traumatic memories in a controlled, supportive environment. Thus, what was once unthinkable and unspeakable becomes merely an unpleasant memory that is now potentially available for learning.

If large chunks of experience associated with psychological trauma are unassimilable, the individual will have *dissociative amnesia* for those periods of time. In extreme cases, whole epochs of development are dissociated, with the effect that the individual's entire childhood, or large chunks of it, become a blank. Since personal identity is constructed from memories and shared family narratives, the individual with no memories of childhood feels empty, isolated, and bereft of a sense of temporal continuity.

The dissociation of unassimilated memory is a highly unstable defense. Apart from the return of dissociated memories as formed imagery, the fragile quality of dissociation is revealed by *microdissociative intrusions* that interrupt the stream of thought, disrupting concentration and learning. Microdissociative intrusions are sometimes evident on projective testing, and may be misinterpreted by the unwary as evidence of schizophrenic thought disorder.

The *numbing of affect* commonly experienced by people who have come through a terrifying experience is often associated theoretically with dissociation. However, "numbing" may be the subjective experience associated with the exhaustion of noradrenergic, threat-recognition brain systems (e.g., associated with the locus cœruleus).

The *fragmentation of identity* associated with repeated trauma, particularly physical, sexual, and emotional abuse, stems from the depletion of autobiographical memory by massive dissociation and the distortion of the working model of attachment caused by maltreatment at the hands of attachment figures or their failure to protect the child from harm. Fantasy compounds fragmentation and attachment disruption, particularly when imaginary companions (some protective, some malignant, some innocent victims) proliferate and are used to contend with, avoid, escape, or represent traumatic experiences and their memories. Multiple personality disorder may evolve from a combination of internalized imaginary companions and intrusive auditory hallucinations, in some cases augmented by *role-playing* in the context of iatrogenic facilitation.

Somatization refers to the subjective experience of anxiety in the form of its physiological concomitants (e.g., muscle tension, headache, palpitations, diarrhea, urinary frequency).

Conversion *is associated with the reemergence of dissociated material in the form of somatic sensations previously experienced during trauma (e.g., globus hystericus, vomiting, pseudoseizures, vaginismus).*

Repeated self-injury (e.g., wrist, abdomen, or thigh cutting, genital mutilation, the swallowing of foreign objects, wall-punching, self-burning) generally occurs in an emotional setting of trauma-related anguish and self-disgust. Typically, the individual reports an immediate dampening of painful affect following skin damage, possibly due to the release of endogenous opiates. Less often, self-laceration is described by the individual as an attempt to revitalize an emotionally benumbed self.

Repetition-compulsion has defied explanation. The return of the traumatized person to the traumatic situation (e.g., in risk-taking or repeatedly exposing oneself to dangerous situations) may represent a distorted attempt to master traumatic anxiety. When repetition compulsion is combined with *reversal*, sexual perpetration may arise.

Emotional dyscontrol is manifest in the form of *dissociative hallucinosis* (the primary subject of this chapter) and *intermittent explosive disorder.* These conditions embody episodic emotional turmoil in association with impulsive, suicidal, or aggressive behavior, trance or altered consciousness, and audiovisual hallucinosis.

36.4 HALLUCINATIONS IN TRAUMA-SPECTRUM DISORDERS

Jaspers (1962) defined *hallucination* as "a false perception, which is not a sensory distortion or misinterpretation, but which occurs at the same time as real perceptions." There has been substantial debate concerning the differentiation of pseudohallucination from hallucination (Berrios & Denning, 1996). However, a lack of consensus about the definition of pseudohallucination has confused the issue. The term has been variably associated with perceptual disturbances lacking sensory vividness, hallucinations with intact insight and reality testing, and isolated phenomena that do not fit any known diagnostic category (Zwaard & Polak, 2001).

Hallucinations are generally regarded as indicating serious mental disorder (Honig et al., 1998). Hallucinations feature prominently in the formal diagnostic criteria for schizophrenia, mood disorder with psychotic features, and delirium (DSM-IV-TR, APA, 1994). Schneider (1959) contended that three types of auditory hallucination are strongly suggestive of schizophrenia: running commentaries, thought echoing, and third-person conversations. Many clinicians regard auditory hallucinations as prima facie evidence of major psychotic disorder, particularly schizophrenia. The recent interest in early intervention in schizophrenia (McGorry & Yung, 2003; Phillip, Yung, & McGorry, 2000) has led to the widespread treatment of hallucinatory states in adolescents and young adults with a combination of antipsychotic medication and psychosocial management, under the impression that these states are basically forms of schizophrenia.

Concurrently, there has been a surge of interest in trauma spectrum disorders such as posttraumatic stress disorder, dissociative identity disorder, and dissociative disorder not otherwise specified. According to DSM-IV (APA, 1994), hallucinations can occur as an element of the reexperiencing symptoms of posttraumatic stress disorder, implying that they reflect the traumatic experience. On those grounds, one would expect that the hallucinations associated with posttraumatic stress disorder should be distinguishable from those experienced by patients with schizophrenia. Berenson (1998) contends that the most common misdiagnosis in adolescent psychiatry occurs when trauma-related hallucinations are ascribed to schizophrenia. His contention is supported by several studies that have found an association between auditory hallucinations and posttraumatic stress disorder (Haviland, 1995; Famularo, 1996; and Lipschitz et al., 1999) and dissociative disorder (Coons, 1996; Dell & Eisenhower, 1990; Hornstein & Putnam, 1992; Nurcombe et al., 1996; Putnam et al., 1996). Children and adolescents with trauma-related disorders often report hallucinations similar to those associated with schizophrenia (Hornstein & Putnam, 1992). Patients who report hallucinations should be screened for posttraumatic stress disorder and dissociative disorder lest their symptoms be attributed to schizophrenia or bipolar disorder (Hornstein & Putnam, 1992). This question is more than a quibble: the treatment of posttraumatic stress disorder and dissociative disorder is arguably quite different from that of schizophrenia and bipolar disorder.

The phenomenology of hallucinations in trauma spectrum disorders in children and adolescents is unclear. Most studies have concentrated on dissociative identity disorder (Dell & Eisenhower, 1990; Hornstein & Putnam, 1992; Vincent & Pickering, 1988). For example, Hornstein and Putnam (1992) characterized the hallucinations occurring in this condition as internalized, perceived as distinctive voices with personal attributes, and likely to urge the child to commit aggressive or self-injurious acts. Coon (1996) reported "inner voices" in 77% of subjects who had dissociative disorder not otherwise specified and 100% of those with dissociative identity disorder. In a study of children and adolescents with dissociative disorder, the frequency of hallucinations increased between early childhood to early adolescence then dropped in late adolescence (Putnam, 1996). Hallucinations occurring in posttraumatic stress disorder have been reported as reflecting the traumatic event (Famularo, 1996). Hamner et al. (2000) found that, while some patients with posttraumatic stress disorder reported hallucinations reflecting the traumatic event, in others hallucinations were apparently unrelated to trauma.

Honig et al. (1998) compared the phenomenology of hallucinations in adult patients with schizophrenia, dissociative disorder, and nonpatients. Hallucinatory commentaries and dialogues occurred in all three groups. Auditory hallucinations were as often internal as external and, although hallucinations were predominantly negative in tone, neutral and helpful voices were also encountered. Steinberg et al. (1994) reported that, in dissociative identity disorder, auditory hallucinations are internalized, reflecting a dialogue between alters. Middleton (1998) reported that 95% of patients with dissociative identity disorder hear voices talking to each other.

Visual hallucinations have been reported in dissociative disorder not otherwise specified and dissociative identity disorder. Hornstein and Putnam (1992) recorded visions of ghosts or apparitions. Coons (1996) reported that 18% of adolescents with dissociative identity disorder had visual hallucinations. Visual hallucinations representing trauma have been reported in posttraumatic stress disorder (Famularo, 1992). Little is known about hallucinations in other modalities in association with trauma-spectrum disorders.

Most studies utilizing structured interviews have examined adult populations (e.g., The Dissociative Disorders Interview Schedule, DDIS, Ross et al., 1991,

Şar et al., 1996; and The Structured Clinical Interview for DSM III-R and -IV Dissociative Disorders, SCID-D, Tutkun et al., 1998, Boon & Draijer, 1991, Steinberg et al., 1994). In one study of incarcerated delinquent adolescents, according to the SCID-D, 28% of subjects met criteria for dissociative disorder (Carrion & Steiner, 2003). The prevalence of identity confusion, identity alteration, derealization, amnesia, and depersonalization was reported in this study but no mention was made of hallucinations.

Several studies of adolescent patients have used screening tools for dissociation such as the Dissociative Experiences Scale (DES) (Altman et al., 1997; Lipschitz et al., 1999), the Adolescent Version of the DES (A-DES) (Armstrong et al., 1997; Kisiel & Lyons, 2001). The DES screens for hallucinations but does not analyze them. These studies have confirmed a high prevalence of dissociative symptoms in traumatized children and adolescents. In adults, dissociative symptoms have been associated with self-reported physical, sexual abuse, psychological abuse, neglect, and adverse home atmosphere (Sanders & Golias, 1991). Draijer and Langeland (1999) found that the severity of dissociative symptoms was predicted by sexual abuse, physical abuse, and maternal dysfunction. While some studies of hallucinations occurring in posttraumatic stress disorder have found high levels of dissociation (e.g., Altman et al., 1997; Lipschitz, 1999), the nature of dissociated hallucinations has not been explored in detail.

Nurcombe et al. (1996) have described a condition in adolescent psychiatric inpatients that they refer to as dissociative hallucinosis. *Hallucinosis* is defined as a "disordered mental condition subject to the occurrence of hallucinations, without any other necessary impairment of consciousness" (Drever, 1952). The term *hallucinosis* has been used previously by Ey (1957) and Berrios (1985, 1996). According to Nurcombe et al. (1996), dissociative hallucinosis can be defined as follows. The onset is acute, dramatic, and usually precipitated by psychological threat or threatened abandonment. Recurrent episodes typically last for between 1 hour and 1 week and there is no psychological deterioration between episodes. The acute episodes are characterized by altered consciousness (e.g., trance-like states, autohypnosis), emotional turmoil (terror, rage, autonomic hyperarousal), impulsivity (self-injury, suicide attempts, assaultiveness, running away), abnormal perceptions (voiced thoughts, auditory hallucinations, and visual hallucinations) that often reflect traumatic experiences, amnesia, and disorganized thinking. The premorbid personality is typically borderline, histrionic, dependent, or needy and immature. This condition is more common in females than males. The families of these patients are commonly chaotic and neglectful, with parental discord, alcoholism, substance abuse, domestic violence, and sexual, physical, and emotional abuse. In a retrospective chart review, comparing cases diagnosed as having dissociative hallucinosis with those diagnosed as having posttraumatic stress disorder or schizophrenia, there were no differences between the first two conditions (except in regard to hallucinosis and impulsive sexual behavior). In contrast, dissociative hallucinosis differed from schizophrenia in regard to premorbid personality, the prevalence of histories of physical and sexual abuse, hyperarousal, intrusive symptoms, and phobic avoidance. In summary, dissociative hallucinosis and posttraumatic stress disorder were virtually identical except in respect of hallucinosis, whereas dissociative hallucinosis was distinct in most respects from schizophrenia. It can be hypothesized that dissociative hallucinosis evolves into the "transient psychotic episodes" that punctuate the life histories of some adult females with borderline personality disorder. It is possible that the male counterpart of dissociative hallucinosis is intermittent explosive disorder, a condition encountered in correctional settings more often than in the mental health system.

Scott et al. (2003) examined 66 adolescents consecutively admitted to an Australian adolescent inpatient unit, comparing the prevalence, form, and content of the hallucinations experienced by young people with psychotic disorder with the nature of hallucinations in adolescents who had posttraumatic stress disorder. For the purpose of this study, *psychotic disorder* was defined as schizophrenia, schizophreniform disorder, schizoaffective disorder, drug-induced psychotic disorder, mood disorder with psychotic features, or psychotic disorder due to a general medical condition. Hallucinations were highly prevalent in both adolescents with posttraumatic stress disorder and those with psychotic disorder. The hallucinations in these conditions could not be differentiated by modality, location, form, or content (including the experience of running commentaries, voices arguing, thought echoing, and command hallucinations, e.g.). Hallucinations clearly represented a traumatic experience in 25% of the adolescents with posttraumatic stress disorder and in none of those with psychotic disorder. Most hallucinations were in the form of derogatory or commanding voices. It was concluded that hallucinations were common in adolescent inpatients with a variety of psychotic disorders and posttraumatic stress disorder. The phenomenology of the hallucinations did not distinguish the two conditions. In posttraumatic stress disorder, the content of hallucinations directly related to a traumatic experience in a minority of cases; however, hallucinatory themes could often be understood in the context of trauma (e.g., derogatory comments referring to the subject's inadequacy, culpability, and need for punishment). Hallucinations occurred in all modalities in adolescents with psychotic disorder and posttraumatic stress disorder, but olfactory and gustatory hallucinations were rare in both conditions.

Jessop, Scott, and Nurcombe (2003) used a specially designed questionnaire to further analyze the nature of hallucinations in posttraumatic stress disorder compared to that in schizophrenia. Among 54 adolescents admitted to a psychiatric inpatient unit, hallucinations were prevalent in patients diagnosed as having posttraumatic stress disorder and schizophrenia. No differences were found between the two conditions in the form of the hallucinations; however, hallucinatory themes in posttraumatic stress disorder could often be interpreted in the context of psychological trauma.

36.5 NOSOLOGY

Existing nosological systems were designed for adult patients. The categories of dissociative disorder specifically designated in DSM-IV-TR (APA, 1994) (i.e., amnesia, fugue, identity disorder, depersonalization disorder) are uncommon in children and adolescents. As a consequence most dissociative children and adolescents are relegated to the default category (not otherwise specified) or diagnosed under separate headings (e.g., anxiety disorder, somatoform disorder, or mood disorder).

In childhood and adolescence, dissociative hallucinosis is much more common than dissociative identity disorder. Should it be classified as a separate category of dissociative disorder, or incorporated as a form of posttraumatic stress disorder (e.g., posttraumatic stress disorder with dissociative hallucinosis or complex posttraumatic stress disorder)? The advantage of classifying dissociative hallucinosis as a form of dissociative disorder is that it reminds the clinician not to relate hallucinosis automatically to schizophrenia. The advantage of classifying dissociative hallucinosis as a form of posttraumatic stress disorder is that the association with psychological trauma is emphasized. This matter requires debate.

Another unexamined question is the status of conversion disorder, a subcategory of somatoform disorder. Some forms of conversion disorder, particularly those associated with dramatic somatic symptoms (e.g., pseudoseizures), appear to be related to the reemergence of dissociated traumatic experiences in the form of unassimilated memories of body sensations. This kind of conversion is different in quality from those conversion phenomena derived from identification with an emulated or lost other person or from mimetic compromise solutions to psychic conflict. The diagnosis of chronic posttraumatic stress disorder with dissociation and conversion has implications for treatment that are not conveyed by the undifferentiated diagnosis of conversion disorder.

These considerations suggest that a broader category—trauma spectrum disorders—might be appropriate. This category could adumbrate acute stress disorder, noncomplex posttraumatic stress disorder, complex posttraumatic stress disorder with dissociation, complex posttraumatic stress disorder with somatoform symptoms, dissociative disorders (dissociative amnesia, fugue, identity disorder, depersonalization, and dissociative disorder not otherwise specified) and some forms of sexual dysfunction and paraphilia. Brief psychotic disorder and intermittent explosive disorder may turn out to be a form or forms of dissociative hallucinosis.

Against the concept of a superordinate diagnosis such as trauma spectrum disorder is the aim of DSM-III and -IV to be neutral with respect to theories of ætiology (a principle already breached in the criteria for posttraumatic stress disorder). Perhaps the time has come to advance the validity of DSM without sacrificing its reliability.

Many would recommend the inclusion of borderline and histrionic personality disorders under the trauma spectrum umbrella. This matter is unclear. Borderline and histrionic personality traits may be derived, fundamentally, from abnormal parent-infant attachment. The families in which attachment disorganization or distortion occurs are the same families that may fail subsequently to protect their children from sexual abuse or expose them to emotional or physical abuse. The superimposition of repeated psychological trauma onto a fundamentally flawed working model of attachment leads to a layering of psychopathology that contributes to its severity and chronicity.

36.6 RESEARCH

Should the concept of dissociation be restricted to the deflection of disturbing memories of events from consciousness? Or should it be extended to encompass other phenomena such as isolation of emotion, emotional numbness, the freezing of volition, alterations in the perception of self and time, trance-like states, confabulation, intrusive phenomena, and emotional dyscontrol that are the sequelae of psychological trauma? These questions cannot be resolved until the interactions between the basic amygaloid, limbic, hippocampal, and cortical mechanisms of alarm, working memory, and long-term memory are understood, along with the dysregulation of noradrenergic, glutamate, endogenous opiate, and glucocorticoid neurochemistry engendered by severe psychological trauma.

The polarized "recovered memories" battle between clinicians and cognitive psychologists will not be productive until the two sides collaborate to examine the effect on memory of emotionally overwhelming events. Until then, clinicians must depend on dated concepts of memory based on metaphor and 19th-century notions of neurophysiology. Why are some memories difficult to retrieve? Koutstaal and Schacter (1997) refer to a number of psychological phenomena as potentially related: for example, the mismatching of encoding and retrieval contexts, competition between retrieval cues, retroactive interference between new and old learning, intentional forgetting, and pathological distortion of memory. Unfortunately, none of these phenomena has been examined by cognitive scientists in the context of psychological trauma, with the result that the battle tends to collapse into competing anecdotes.

The genetics of dissociation should be further investigated. Little is known about the heritability of the capacity to dissociate and the interaction, if any, between genetic potential, early family environment, pathological dissociation, and pathological fantasy.

The continuity between exposure to early family pathology, disorganized or distorted attachment, later risk factors (e.g., child maltreatment), and the development of dissociative psychopathology will be understood only after longitudinal studies of cohorts of high-risk children have been conducted. Longitudinal studies could test other hypotheses of continuity: for example, between dissociative hallucinosis in adolescence and the transient psychotic episodes associated with borderline personality disorder in adulthood, and whether both dissociative hallucinosis in females and intermittent explosive disorder in males develop from similar backgrounds of physical, sexual, and emotional abuse. By this means, the conceptual hypothesis of a superordinate group of trauma spectrum disorders could be explored, and the role of fantasy (e.g., imaginary companions) in the development of dissociative identity disorder examined.

Finally, the effectiveness of treatment should be evaluated. At the present time, those who use medication or psychotherapy have no choice but to base their decisions on clinical experience and fashion, not empirical research. Which drugs (e.g., antidepressants, antianxiety agents, anticonvulsants, neuroleptics, or alpha-2-adrenergic agents) can alleviate the intrusive symptoms and hyperarousal of posttraumatic stress disorder with dissociative features? When is exploratory psychotherapy (e.g., cognitive behavior therapy or psychodynamic psychotherapy) appropriate and when is supportive therapy the better course of action? Of cognitive behavior therapy, psychodynamic psychotherapy, group therapy, and family therapy, which is preferable, for what kind of patient? How should patients be prepared for exploratory psychotherapy? Could language-stimulation intervention programs be of use in preparing for psychotherapy children with poor language development?

REFERENCES

Altman, H., Collins, M., & Mundy, P. (1997). Subclinical hallucinations and delusions in nonpsychotic adolescents. *Journal of Child Psychology & Psychiatry, 38*, 413–420.

American Psychiatric Association (1994). *DSM-IV – Diagnostic and Statistical Manual of Mental Disorders* (4th ed.). Washington, DC: Author.

Armstrong, J. G., Putnam, F. W., Carlson, E. B., Libero, D. Z., & Smith, S. R. (1997). Development and validation of a measure of adolescent dissociation: the Adolescent Dissociative Experiences Scale. *Journal of Nervous and Mental Disease, 185*, 491–497.

Berenson, C. K. (1998). Frequently missed diagnoses in adolescent psychiatry. *The Psychiatric Clinics of North America, 21*, 917–926.

Berrios, G. E. (1985). Hallucinosis. In J. Frederiks (Ed.), *Handbook of Clinical Neurology, Vol 46, Neurobehavioral Disorders.* Amsterdam: Elsevier.

Berrios, G. E. (1996). *The History of Mental Symptoms.* Cambridge UK: Cambridge.

Berrios, G. E., & Dening, T. R. (1996). Pseudohallucinations: a conceptual history. *Psychological Medicine, 26*, 753–763.

Boon, S., & Draijer, N. (1991). Diagnosing dissociative disorders in The Netherlands: A pilot study with the Structured Clinical Interview for DSM-III-R Dissociative Disorders. *American Journal of Psychiatry, 148*, 458–462.

Breuer, J., & Freud, S. (1955). Studies on hysteria (1893–1895). In J. Strachey (Ed.), *Standard Edition of the Complete Psychological Works of Sigmund Freud, Vol 2.* London: Hogarth.

Carrion, V., & Steiner, H. (2000). Trauma and dissociation in delinquent adolescents. *Journal of the American Academy of Child and Adolescent Psychiatry, 39*, 353–359.

Coons, P. M. (1996). Clinical phenomenology of 25 children and adolescents with dissociative disorders. *Child and Adolescent Psychiatric Clinics of North America, 5*, 361–372.

Dell, P. F., & Eisenhower, J. W. (1990). Adolescent multiple personality disorder: a preliminary study of eleven cases. *Journal of the American Academy of Child and Adolescent Psychiatry, 29*, 359–366.

Draijer, N., & Langeland, W. (1999). Childhood trauma and perceived parental dysfunction in the etiology of dissociative symptoms in psychiatric inpatients. *American Journal of Psychiatry, 156*, 379–385.

Ey, H. (1957). Les hallucinoses. *L'Encephale,* 46, 564–573.

Famularo, R., Kinscherff, R., & Fenton, T. (1996). Psychiatric diagnosis of maltreated children: preliminary findings. *Journal of the American Academy of Child and Adolescent Psychiatry, 31*, 863–867.

Fenichel, O. (1955). *The Psychoanalytic Theory of Neurosis.* London: Routledge & Kegan Paul.

Hamner, M. B., Fruech, B. C., Ulmer, H. G., Huber, M. G., Twomey, T. J., Tyson, C., & Arana, G. W. (2000). Psychotic features in chronic posttraumatic stress disorder and schizophrenia. *Journal of Nervous and Mental Diseases, 188*, 217–221.

Haviland, M. G., Sonne, J. L., & Woods, L. R. (1995). Beyond post traumatic stress disorder: object relations and reality testing disturbances in physically and sexually abused adolescents. *Journal of the American Academy of Child and Adolescent Psychiatry, 34*, 1054–1059.

Honig, A., Romme, M. A., Ensink, B. J., Escher, S. D., Pennings, M. H., & Devries, M. W. (1998). Auditory hallucinations: a comparison between patients and non-patients. *Journal of Nervous and Mental Diseases, 18*, 646–651.

Hornstein, N. L., & Putnam, F. W. (1992). Clinical phenomenology of child and adolescent dissociative disorders. *Journal of the American Academy of Child and Adolescent Psychiatry, 31*, 1077–1085.

Janet, P. (1911). *L'État mental des hysteriques* (2nd ed.). Paris: Alcan.

Jessop, M. E., Scott, J. G., & Nurcombe, B. (2003). The phenomenology of hallucinations in adolescents admitted to a psychiatric inpatient unit. Brisbane: The University of Queensland, unpublished paper.

Kisiel, C. L., & Lyons, J. S. (2002). Dissociation as a mediator of psychopathology among sexually abused children and adolescents. *American Journal of Psychiatry, 158*, 1034–1039.

Koutstaal, W., & Schacter, D. L. (1997). Inaccuracy and inaccessibility in memory retrieval: contributions from cognitive psychology and neuropsychology. In P. Applebaum, L. Uyehara & M. Elin (Eds.), *Trauma and Memory: Clinical and Legal Controversies.* New York: Oxford University Press.

Lipschitz, D. S., Winegar, R. K., Hartnick, E., Foote, B., & Southwick, S. M. (1999). Posttraumatic stress disorder in hospitalized adolescents: psychiatric comorbidity and clinical correlates. *Journal of the American Academy of Child and Adolescent Psychiatry, 38*, 385–392.

McGorry, P. D., & Yung, A. R. (2003). Early intervention in psychosis: an overdue reform. *Australian and New Zealand Journal of Psychiatry, 37*, 393–398.

Middleton, W., & Butler, J. (1998). Dissociative identity disorder: an Australian series. *Australian and New Zealand Journal of Psychiatry, 32*, 794–804.

Nurcombe, B., Mitchell, W., Begtrup, R., Tramontana, M., LaBarbera, J., & Pruitt, J. (1996). Dissociative hallucinosis and allied conditions. In F. R. Volkmar (Ed.), *Psychoses and Pervasive Developmental Disorders of Childhood and Adolescence.* Washington, DC: American Psychiatric Press.

Phillips, L. G., Yung, A. R., & McGorry, P. D. (2000). Identification of young people at risk of psychosis: validation of personal assessment and crisis evaluation clinic intake criteria. *Australian and New Zealand Journal of Psychiatry, 34* (suppl.), s164–s169.

Putnam, F. W. (1993). Dissociative disorders in children: behavioral profiles and problems. *Child Abuse and Neglect, 17*, 39–45.

Putnam, F. W., Hornstein, N. L., & Peterson, G. (1996). Clinical phenomenology of child and adolescent dissociative disorders. *Child and Adolescent Psychiatric Clinics of North America, 5*, 351–360.

Ross, C. A., Anderson, W., Fleisher, W. P., & Norton, G. R. (1991). The frequency of multiple personality disorder among psychiatric inpatients. *American Journal of Psychiatry, 148*, 1717–1720.

Sanders, B., & Giolas, M. (1991). Dissociation and childhood trauma in psychologically disturbed adolescents. *American Journal of Psychiatry, 148*, 50–54.

Şar, V., Yargıç, L. I., & Tutkun, H. (1996). Structured interview data on 35 cases of dissociative identity disorder in Turkey. *American Journal of Psychiatry, 153*, 1329–1333.

Schneider, K. (1959). *Clinical Psychopathology.* New York: Grune and Stratton.

Scott, J. G., Nurcombe, B., Sheridan, J., & McFarlane, M. (2003). Hospitalized adolescents who hallucinate: diagnostic implications. *British Journal of Psychiatry:* Submitted for publication.

Steinberg, M. (1994). *Structured Clinical Interview for DSM-IV Dissociative Disorders – Revised (SCID-D-R).* Washington, DC: American Psychiatric Press.

Steinberg, M., Cicchetti, D., Buchanan, J., Rakfeldt, J., & Rounaville, B. (1994). Distinguishing between multiple personality and schizophrenia using the Structured Clinical Interview for DSM-IV Dissociative Disorders. *Journal of Nervous and Mental Diseases, 182*, 495–502.

Tutkun, H., Şar, V., Yargıç, L. I., Özpulat, T., Yanık, M., & Kızıltan, E. (1998). Frequency of dissociative disorders among psychiatric inpatients in a Turkish university clinic. *American Journal of Psychiatry, 155*, 800–805.

Van der Zward, R., & Polak, M. A. (2001). Pseudohallucinations: a pseusoconcept? A review of the validity of the concept, related to associated symptomatology. *Comprehensive Psychiatry, 42*, 42–50.

Vincent, M., & Pickering, M. R. (1988). Multiple personality disorder in childhood. *Canadian Journal of Psychiatry, 33*, 524–529.

Zward, R., & Polak, M. (2001). Pseudohallucinations: a pseudoconcept? A review of the validity of the concept, related to associated symptomatology. *Comprehensive Psychiatry, 42*, 42–50.

37 The Theory of a Dissociative Subtype of Schizophrenia

Colin A. Ross, MD

OUTLINE

In 1980, two landmark papers addressed the relationship between multiple personality disorder (renamed dissociative identity disorder in DSM-IV) and schizophrenia; the authors proposed that multiple personality is often misdiagnosed as schizophrenia (Bliss, 1980; Rosenbaum, 1980). The relationship between schizophrenia and multiple personality has continued to be of interest in the dissociative disorders field (Fink & Golinkoff, 1990; Gainer, 1994; Kluft, 1987; Ross, Anderson, & Clark, 1994; Steingard, & Frankel, 1985; van der Hart, Witzum, & Friedman, 1993), but the schizophrenia field has shown relatively little interest.

Investigators of three large series of multiple personality cases found that 40% to 50% of these individuals had received prior diagnoses of schizophrenia (Putnam, Guroff, Silberman, Barban, & Post, 1986; Ross et al., 1990; Ross, Norton, & Wozney, 1989).

Following on this research, Ellason, Ross, and Fuchs (1996) found that two-thirds of patients with dissociative identity disorder met the criteria for either schizophrenia or schizoaffective disorder on the Structured Clinical Interview for DSM-III-R (SCID; Spitzer, Williams, Gibbon, & First, 1990). Conversely, when the Dissociative Disorders Interview Schedule (DDIS; Ross, 1997) was administered to 83 individuals who had stable clinical diagnoses of schizophrenia, one-quarter met the criteria for multiple personality disorder (Ross, Anderson, & Clark, 1994). These findings indicate that complex, pathological dissociation and psychosis are not easy to separate; perhaps, they are not completely discrete categories.

In my opinion, the relationship between dissociation and psychosis is a complex and subtle one. This relationship is an important problem for clinical treatment, research, epidemiology, etiology, and diagnostic classification. I believe that the problem of the relationship between dissociation and psychosis should be taken seriously by the schizophrenia field, the developers of DSM-V, and the mental health field as a whole.

I have hypothesized that there is a dissociative subtype of schizophrenia (Ross, 2004, 2007). This chapter summarizes the theory and the data that support this hypothesis.

37.1 DEFINITION OF DISSOCIATION

There are four meanings of the word *dissociation* (Ross, 1999, 2000). First, there is a general systems meaning of dissociation: *the opposite of association, a disconnection or lack of interaction between two variables.* For instance, there are dissociation constants in physical chemistry.

Second, dissociation is a technical term in experimental cognitive psychology. In cognitive psychology, dissociation is often *a normal property of cognitive functioning.* For example, countless studies have demonstrated the dissociation between procedural and declarative memory (Cohen & Eichenbaum, 1993). Such dissociation is normal; it does not entail any special operations or exceptional properties of the mind.

Third, dissociation is *a phenomenological term in clinical psychology and psychiatry that has been operationalized by various measures.* In this sense, dissociation is what is measured by the items of the Dissociative Experiences Scale (DES) (Bernstein & Putnam, 1986; Carlson et al., 1993), the Dissociative Disorders Interview Schedule (DDIS) (Ross, 1997), the Structured Clinical Interview for DSM-IV Dissociative Disorders (SCID-D) (Steinberg, 1995; Steinberg, Cicchetti, Buchanan, Rakfeldt, & Rounsaville, 1994; Steinberg, Rounsaville and Cicchetti, 1990), the Multidimensional Inventory of Dissociation (MID) (Dell, 2002), and so on.

Fourth, dissociation is an intrapsychic defense mechanism.

Confusion easily arises when these different meanings of the word *dissociation* have not been specified. For instance, a lack of experimental evidence for dissociation as an intrapsychic defense mechanism would not be relevant to (1) the scientific status of dissociation in cognitive psychology, or (2) the psychometric properties of measures of dissociation.

In this chapter I will deal primarily with the phenomena of dissociation as reflected by structured interviews and self-report measures of dissociation.

37.2 THE DOMAIN OF DISSOCIATION

Dissociative symptoms occur in both dissociative and nondissociative disorders in DSM-IV-TR. In fact, dissociative symptoms are included among the diagnostic criteria for acute stress disorder, posttraumatic stress disorder, somatization disorder, schizotypal personality disorder, and borderline personality disorder. As a comorbid symptom, depersonalization is common in depression, schizophrenia, substance abuse, panic disorder, and many other conditions.

Pathological dissociation can occur in one of two forms: (1) inherently pathological, and (2) normal, but pathologically frequent. Inherently pathological dissociative experiences are probably best exemplified by the dissociative taxon (Waller, Putnam, & Carlson, 1996; Waller & Ross, 1997). For instance, it is abnormal to look in a mirror and not recognize oneself. On the other hand, it is normal to occasionally stare off into space and miss part of a conversation. If this occurs 98% of the time, however, a psychiatric diagnosis might be made.

37.3 EXPLANATORY MECHANISMS OF DISSOCIATION

It has been suggested that there is no limit to the number of psychological, sociological, and biological mechanisms that could generate dissociative phenomena (Cardeña, 1994). My own view is that psychological trauma is the primary cause of dissociative phenomena. On this view, the psyche adapts to trauma by fragmenting itself into dissociated substates or part selves. The interactions of these modules or part selves generate dissociative symptoms. I believe that this psychobiological response to trauma underlies both dissociative identity disorder and the proposed dissociative type of schizophrenia.

37.4 NOSOLOGICAL PROPOSAL

I am proposing a new subtype of schizophrenia that would be added to DSM-V: *Schizophrenia, Dissociative Type.* DSM-IV-TR specifies six criteria for schizophrenia (A–F). Criterion B requires occupational and social deterioration, and Criterion C requires a duration of 6 months. Criteria D–F specify the relationship between schizophrenia and other disorders. Criterion A lists five symptoms: delusions, hallucinations, disorganized speech, disorganized behavior, and negative symptoms.

For the diagnosis of schizophrenia to be made, two Criterion A symptoms must be present. But there is an important exception to this diagnostic rule: only one symptom is necessary if (1) the delusions are bizarre or (2) the hallucinations consist of voices that talk to each other or that keep up a running commentary on the person.

In DSM-IV-TR, schizophrenia is divided into five subtypes, each of which is defined by its predominant symptoms: paranoid, disorganized, catatonic, undifferentiated, and residual. A proposed description of the sixth subtype, dissociative, would run as follows.

37.4.1 Schizophrenia, Dissociative Type

There are three essential features of the dissociative type of schizophrenia: childhood trauma, dissociative symptoms, and extensive comorbidity. Most individuals who manifest these three features will also meet the diagnostic criteria for numerous other Axis I and II diagnoses—especially dissociative disorders, depression, posttraumatic stress disorder, borderline personality disorder, obsessive compulsive disorder, panic disorder, and substance abuse. Most of these individuals will report severe, chronic childhood trauma that may include the following: sexual abuse, physical abuse, emotional and verbal abuse, family violence, extrafamilial violence, loss of primary caretakers, and exposure to war, famine, extreme poverty, starvation, natural disasters, serious illness, and disease. Prominent dissociative symptoms include auditory hallucinations, amnesia, depersonalization, and the existence of distinct identities or personality states. The voices often interact with each other and with the presenting part of the person. In addition, the voices often have specific names, ages, genders, and other characteristics. The voices often may be engaged in direct conversation by an outside person. There is usually an absence of severe cognitive disorganization or thought disorder.

37.4.2 Diagnostic Criteria for DSM-V: Schizophrenia, Dissociative Type

A type of schizophrenia in which the clinical picture is dominated by at least three of the following:

1. Dissociative amnesia
2. Depersonalization
3. The presence of two or more distinct identities or personality states
4. Auditory hallucinations
5. Extensive comorbidity
6. Severe childhood trauma

The concept of dissociative schizophrenia provides the schizophrenia field with (1) a testable hypothesis (i.e., that there is a dissociative subset of persons with schizophrenia) and (2) a testable model of dissociative schizophrenia (i.e., the hypothesized relationships among trauma, dissociation, and psychosis in this subset of persons with schizophrenia).

37.5 THE "BOUNDARIES" BETWEEN SCHIZOPHRENIA AND DISSOCIATIVE IDENTITY DISORDER

There is too much phenomenological overlap for there to be a simple, binary difference between schizophrenia and dissociative identity disorder. *The more positive symptoms of schizophrenia that one has, the less likely it is that one has DSM-IV-TR schizophrenia, and the more likely it is that one has DID* (see the following).

37.5.1 Description of Dissociative Schizophrenia by Bleuler

The Swiss psychiatrist, Eugen Bleuler (1911/1950), coined the term *schizophrenia*, which means *split mind*. In his classic text, translated into English in 1950, he described the phenomenology of schizophrenia and proposed that the fundamental process in schizophrenia is a splitting of mental contents. He said that his term *splitting* was synonymous with Pierre Janet's (1965, 1977) term *dissociation*:

> What Gross understands by his term, "fragmentation (or disintegration) of consciousness" corresponds to what we call "splitting". . . [T]he term, "dissociation," has already been in use for a long time to designate similar observations and findings. (p. 363)

Throughout his text, Bleuler stated that various mental contents (e.g., affect, identity, movement, sensation, memory, volition, arousal, and appetite) can be split or dissociated from the main body of consciousness in schizophrenia. He provided numerous clinical examples of such dissociative symptoms. These are consistent with the phenomenological meaning of *dissociation*; they also imply the activity of the defense mechanism of dissociation. Bleuler also described switches among personality states that have different names, genders, ages, voices, memories, and mannerisms. His description of this is clear and explicit. The following two quotations from Bleuler, which are typical of his description of schizophrenia, correspond exactly to the DSM-IV-TR diagnostic criteria and text for DID:

> Single emotionally charged ideas or drives attain a certain degree of autonomy so that the personality falls to pieces. These fragments can then exist side by side and alternately dominate the main part of the personality, the conscious part of the patient. *However, the patient may*

> *also become a definitely different person from a certain moment onwards.* (p. 143) [italics original]
>
> Naturally such patients must speak of themselves in one of their two versions or they may speak in the third person of the other two. This sort of reference is here not merely an unusual or awkward figure of speech such as we may find in mental defectives or in children, but is the expression of a real alteration in personality. But even when such a splitting cannot be demonstrated, a patient may speak of himself only in the third person. Usually he designates himself by one of his several names. (p. 144)

This suggests that, in many instances, Bleuler's schizophrenia and DSM-IV-TR's dissociative identity disorder are one and the same. Thus, it is not a semantic accident that Bleuler called his diagnosis *split mind*, a label that is as good a descriptor of multiple personality disorder as *dissociative identity disorder.*

Therefore, one of the two greatest early investigators of schizophrenia (the other being Kræpelin) actually described the core dissociative phenomena of DID. In describing these patients, Bleuler also noted the presence of a wide array of somatic symptoms, eating disorders, and other comorbidity that is typical of chronic, complex dissociative disorders. Many of his patients are indistinguishable from the "hysterical" patients of Pierre Janet (1965, 1977). In fact many of Bleuler's patients are typical of the present-day patients in my inpatient Trauma Programs. About 50% of these inpatients have DID; most of the rest have complex forms of dissociative disorder not otherwise specified (DDNOS). I have provided dozens of quotations from Bleuler that further illustrate these points (see Ross, 2004).

My point is that the phenomenological overlap between psychosis and dissociation is not a new finding. This overlap has been documented in the schizophrenia literature for almost 100 years. The schizophrenia field, however, seems to have considered this phenomenological overlap to be unimportant or irrelevant.

37.5.2 Case Histories of Dissociative Schizophrenia from the Schizophrenia Literature

If cases of apparent dissociative schizophrenia could be found only in the old literature, then we could dismiss such cases as being nothing but misclassified patients from another era. That is not the case, however. It is easy to find examples of dissociative schizophrenia in the contemporary literature on schizophrenia. Like Bleuler's accounts, the contemporary case histories are clear, explicit, and detailed; their phenomenology is compelling.

Over the years, *Schizophrenia Bulletin* has published many first-person accounts of people diagnosed with schizophrenia (e.g., Greenblat, 2000; Jordan, 1995; Ruocchio, 1989, 1991; Turner, 1993). These autobiographical accounts are published if they illustrate an important aspect of schizophrenia and are well-written. The authors of these first-person accounts have longstanding, stable diagnoses of schizophrenia. Their accounts are not regarded as atypical or rare variants of schizophrenia, but as representative of the disorder, and yet, the authors of these autobiographies often describe core phenomena of DID (e.g., dissociated personality states, conflicts between these states, competition for executive control, and command hallucinations originating from states that are specified by name and function). These autobiographical accounts often describe treatment plans that seek to suppress or eradicate the personality states from which dissociative intrusions originate. These dissociative intrusions take the form of classical Schneiderian first-rank symptoms of schizophrenia. These treatment plans usually do not work very well.

37.5.2.1 Case #1

> My name is Janice Jordan. I am a person with schizophrenia. I am also a college graduate with 27 hours toward a master's degree. I have published three articles in national journals and hold a full-time position as a technical editor for a major engineering/technical documentation corporation.
>
> I have suffered from this serious mental illness for over 25 years. In fact, I can't think of a time when I wasn't plagued with hallucinations, delusions, and paranoia. At times, I feel like the operator in my brain just doesn't get the message to the right people. *It can be very confusing to have to deal with different people in my head.* When I become fragmented in my thinking, I start to have my worst problems. I have been hospitalized because of this illness many times, sometimes for as long as 2 to 4 months.
>
> I guess the moment I started recovering was when I asked for help in coping with the schizophrenia. For so long, I refused to accept that I had a serious mental illness. During my adolescence, I thought I was just strange. I was afraid all the time. I had my own fantasy world and spent many days lost in it.
>
> *I had one particular friend. I called him the "Controller." He was my secret friend. He took on all of my bad feelings. He was the sum total of my negative feelings and*

my paranoia. I could see him and hear him, but no one else could.

The problems were compounded when I went off to college. Suddenly, *the Controller started demanding all my time and energy. He would punish me if I did something he didn't like.* He spent a lot of time yelling at me and making me feel wicked. I didn't know how to stop him from screaming at me and ruling my existence. It got to the point where I couldn't decipher reality from what the Controller was screaming. So I withdrew from society and reality. I couldn't tell anyone what was happening because I was so afraid of being labeled as "crazy." I didn't understand what was going on in my head. I really thought that other "normal" people had Controllers too.

While the Controller was most evident, I was desperately trying to make it in society and through college to earn my degree. The Controller was preventing me from coping with even everyday events. I tried to hide this illness from everyone, particularly my family. *How could I tell my family that I had this person inside my head, telling me what to do, think, and say?*

However, my secret was slowly killing me. It was becoming more and more difficult to attend classes and understand the subject matter. I spent most of my time listening to the Controller and his demands. I really don't know how I made it through college, much less how I graduated cum laude. I think I made it on a wing and a prayer. Then, as I started graduate school, my thinking became more and more fragmented. One of my psychology professors insisted that I see a counselor at the college. Well, it appeared that I was more than he could handle, so I quit seeing him.

Since my degree is in education, I got a job teaching third grade. This lasted about 3 months, and then I ended up in a psychiatric hospital for 4 months. I just wasn't functioning in the outside world. I was very delusional and paranoid, and I spent much of my time engrossed with my fantasy world and the Controller.

My first therapist tried to get me to open up, but I have to admit that I didn't trust her and couldn't tell her about the Controller. I was still so afraid of being labeled "crazy." I really thought that I had done something evil in my life and that was why I had craziness in my head. I was deathly afraid that I would end up like my three paternal uncles, all of whom committed suicide. I didn't trust anyone. I thought perhaps I had a special calling in life, something beyond normal. Even though the Controller spent most of the time yelling his demands, I think I felt blessed in some strange way. I felt above normal. I think I had the most difficulty accepting the fact that the Controller was only in my world and not in everyone else's world. (Jordan, 1995, pp. 501–503; italics added)

37.5.2.2 Case #2

Patricia Ruocchio (1989, 1991) wrote two accounts of her illness. If I included the following autobiographical description of her symptoms in a book about dissociative disorders, or read her account aloud in a workshop or lecture, it would easily pass as a typical case of DID. The disorder Patricia Ruocchio (1989) describes is one of conflict between dissociated personality states:

> I have never fought a fight harder than the fight my mind fights against itself. *I have two equally tenacious parts of my mind that are often at odds with one another.* I go back and forth endlessly, never able to resolve the struggle, because I do not know which part is true. It takes all my energy to keep vacillating and watch the battle being played out. I can almost see it visually. I see one side arguing with the other; the two are diametrically opposed and each side is equally strong. To me, each of these struggles is the fight of my life; to my therapist, it is something I suffer from called "ambivalence."
>
> *During these fights, I can be thinking one thing, but then when the antagonistic thought comes in, I can actually feel my brain split.* Sometimes it feels as though one part is the good part that punishes the bad part and causes me pain. Sometimes one part seems to censor what the other is allowed to feel. One part is a victim of The People in my head; the other part joins with my therapist in fighting them. What is similar about all these dichotomies is that they basically separate the part of me that is real from the part that is unreal: it is a battle between sanity and insanity.
>
> When my brain is pulled together I feel "solid." I can literally feel my feet on the ground, and I can feel that my thinking is clear. This state occurs rarely. When I am crazy, the insane part takes over. I am a victim of delusion, unreal thoughts, and severe disorganization. I have some sorts of hallucinations and many visual and auditory distortions. When I am in the former state, I feel good but tenuous, waiting for it all to fall apart any minute. The latter state may be terrifying or perhaps tolerable in a neutral kind of way, even if it is uncomfortable. The state that is most unbearable and causes me the most pain is the state in-between.
>
> I am in this state almost all the time, and usually it feels like a vague confusion, a swirling mass of thoughts and images going on in my head and clouding my thinking and functioning. When it speeds up and gets out of control, I get psychotic. When it slows down, I can see the two parts clearly, and it is almost as though I am in a clear phase except that I am at the mercy of my brain and I go tortuously back and forth, believing both parts and feeling torn apart. This causes great pain as my very self, all that I am inside, is rent in pieces.

> Usually I feel so torn because one part is a crazy ideation that makes perfect sense in my system of thought and the other part is my observing ego, connected with reality, trying to put a check on unreal thinking. It is as though I am trying to heal myself, but find the crazy side resistant to the intellectual side. Sometimes one side wins, and I begin to think clearly again. Sometimes the other wins, and I get psychotic—a system of delusion taking over all the reality that I once believed and filling it with false or disorganized thoughts.
>
> The part that is good and seems to punish the other part is the side of me that knows reality and knows I am crazy. I blame myself for not being able to let go of my crazy thinking and "get it right." The good part wants to get well and punishes the bad side for not wanting to get well and instead holding onto falsities. The bad or crazy part, not understanding that these are falsities, feels great pain at the hands of the good part. It is emotional pain, but the kind that is vague and inside, and feels almost physical in the misery it inflicts. Often I am doubled over in pain; usually it is because there is some conflict going on that I cannot resolve.
>
> There also exists another nuance to this self-division: when I have mixed feelings, the "right" side, the rational side, will censor what the other side is allowed to feel without being called bad or wrong. When my therapist goes away, I get furious, but I am not allowed to express my anger in words because the real part of me hears him saying that people do come and go and that he has his own life to lead. The result is that I cannot express my anger except by hurting myself. Though I have worked hard on this and no longer cut myself or burn myself, I fear that if I reveal how truly angry I am, he will stop being my therapist, and so I have self-destructive feelings again. Now, however, I am learning to talk about my feelings instead of acting on them—an example of the slow integration of the two parts.
>
> It was only recently that I recognized this censoring mechanism with regard to my therapist's vacations. I slowed down enough to see the two parts of myself and I heard one part saying that it was angry, while the other part rejoined with, "No, you can't feel that way; it's not allowed because it doesn't make sense." This process used to move so fast that it made me crazy, and I always ended up hurting myself or getting psychotic and ending up in the hospital. If I was not already in the hospital, I always went in while my therapist was gone or when he got back because my rage caused such intense turmoil.
>
> When I am working with my therapist, a part of me wants to work to dispel the delusions while a part of me is frightened and resists. This is particularly true with The People. When I first began talking about them, after I would tell my therapist something, I was afraid they would be waiting right outside his door to ambush me and beat me up. Inside his office I could resolve to be on his side, and together we would be stronger than they were; but when I was alone, I felt so vulnerable and often could not hold off their attack. The more I cooperated with my therapist, the more I put myself at risk. Medication helps sometimes with The People, and now by working with my therapist and my co-therapist whom I began seeing two years ago, I have more of a sense that the three of us are stronger than they are. I still believe they are there, but in working with two people grounded in reality, I can keep their pain away. (Ruocchio, 1989, pp. 163–164; italics added)

I have quoted these two autobiographical accounts of schizophrenia at length because case histories are a compelling form of data in support of my theory, even though they are uncontrolled and anecdotal.

37.5.3 Cases of Dissociative Schizophrenia in the Literature on Hysterical Psychosis

The literature on reactive and hysterical psychosis contains numerous case examples of "psychotic" individuals who have dissociative symptoms (Hirsch & Hollender, 1969; Hollender & Hirsch, 1964; Jauch & Carpenter, 1988a, 1988b; Kantor & Herron, 1966; Kind, 1966; Mallet & Gold, 1964; Martin, 1971; Richman & White, 1970; Siomopoulos, 1971; Spiegel & Fink, 1979). Like Bleuler's phenomenology of schizophrenia, the literature on hysterical psychosis is little remembered; nevertheless, this literature provides further evidence of a dissociative subtype of schizophrenia.

37.5.4 Posttraumatic Stress Disorder and Psychosis

There is a growing literature that attests to five interrelated facts:

1. *Psychotic symptoms may occur in posttraumatic stress disorder* (Butler, Mueser, Sprock, & Braff, 1996; Domash & Sparr, 1982; Hamner et al., 2000; Jeffries, 1977; Lundy, 1992; Mueser & Butler, 1987; Sautter et al., 1999; Sautter, Cornwall, Johnson, Wiley, & Faraone, 2002; Shaner & Eth, 1989; Waldfogel & Mueser, 1988; Wilcox, Briones, & Suess, 1991; Williams-Keeler, Milliken, & Jones, 1994).
2. *There are high rates of severe childhood trauma among individuals with schizophrenia and severe, chronic mental illness* (Beck & van der Kolk, 1987; Friedman & Harrison,

1984; Goff, Brotman, Kidlon, Waites, & Amico, 1991; Goodman et al., 1999; Heads, Taylor, & Leese, 1997; Heins, Gray, & Tennant, 1990; Lysaker, Meyer, Evans, Clements, & Marks, 2001; Muenzenmaier, Meyer, Struening, & Ferber, 1993; Read, 1997; Read, Agar, Argyle, & Aderhold, in press; Read & Argyle, 1999; Read, Perry, Moskowitz, & Connolly, 2001; Read & Ross, 2003; Rose, 1991; Rose, Peabody, & Stratigeas, 1991; Rosenberg et al., 2001; Rosenberg, Mueser, Jankowski, & Hamblen, 2002).

3. *Posttraumatic stress disorder can be caused by the experience of being psychotic and/or can occur in reaction to treatment for psychosis provided by the mental health system, especially arrest and other involuntary procedures* (Shaw, McFarlane, & Bookless, 1997; Shaw, McFarlane, Bookless, & Air, 2002).
4. *Posttraumatic stress disorder is common among individuals with severe mental illness* (McGorry et al., 1991; Meyer et al., 1999; Mueser et al., 1998; Sautter et al., 1999; Sautter, Cornwell, Johnson, Wiley, & Faraone, 2002).
5. *Psychological trauma can precipitate psychosis* (Bebbington et al., 1993; Norman & Malla, 1993a, 1993b).

This literature tends to support the relationship between psychological trauma and psychosis that is postulated by the theory of dissociative schizophrenia. Rather than being simple and unidirectional, the relationship between trauma and psychosis is multifaceted and multidirectional.

37.5.5 The Relationship Between DID and Schizophrenia

Putnam and colleagues (1986) reported that 50% of 100 patients with multiple personality disorder had received a prior diagnosis of schizophrenia from a psychiatrist. Similarly, Ross and colleagues (1989) reported that 41% of 236 patients with multiple personality disorder had received a prior diagnosis of schizophrenia. These patients' previous diagnoses of schizophrenia, and treatment with antipsychotic medications and electroconvulsive therapy (ECT) show that their previous therapists assessed them as suffering from severe mental illness with psychotic symptoms.

In another study (Ross et al., 1992, 1994), 166 patients with multiple personality disorder were compared to 83 patients with long-standing clinical diagnoses of schizophrenia. The multiple personality patients reported far higher rates of childhood physical and sexual abuse than schizophrenia patients. However, the base rate for physical and/or sexual abuse in the general population on the structured interview used in that study, The Dissociative Disorders Interview Schedule (DDIS), is 12.6% (Ross, 1991), which is much lower than the rate reported by the subjects with schizophrenia.

Recent reports by Janssen and colleagues (2004) and Bebbington and colleagues (2004) demonstrate a strong relationship between psychosis and childhood trauma in large general population samples. However, the Bebbington data demonstrate that this relationship is not specific for psychosis and also holds for other forms of psychiatric disorder. That is my point: childhood trauma is a risk factor for a broad range of comorbidity, and this includes psychotic symptoms and diagnoses. I am not arguing that the relationship between trauma and psychosis is specific; I am arguing that it is every bit as strong as the relationship between trauma and other forms of mental disorder.

According to Ross et al. (1994), schizophrenia is linked to childhood trauma, but the association is not as strong as it is for multiple personality disorder. In this study, 25.3% of patients in treatment for schizophrenia met DSM-III-R criteria for multiple personality disorder on the Dissociative Disorders Interview Schedule. When the sample from Ross et al. (1994) was compared to a second sample of 60 subjects with schizophrenia, similar findings emerged (Ross & Keyes, 2004).

Research has shown that 25% to 40% of persons in treatment for schizophrenia report chronic, complex dissociation and meet DSM-IV-TR criteria for complex dissociative disorders (Putnam et al., 1986; Ross et al., 1989, 1992, 1994; Ross & Keyes, 2004).

The Axis I and II comorbidity profiles of schizophrenia are less severe than those of multiple personality disorder, but the rates of comorbidity in schizophrenia are far higher than the base rates in the general population. It is an untested prediction of the theory that rates of childhood trauma are higher in patients with dissociative schizophrenia than in patients with other subtypes of schizophrenia.

Steinberg et al. (1994) administered the Structured Clinical Interview for DSM-IV Dissociative Disorders (SCID-D) (Steinberg, 1994; Steinberg, Rounsaville, & Cicchetti, 1990) to 19 patients with DID and 28 patients with stable clinical diagnoses of schizophrenia. Steinberg demonstrated that the patients with DID had significantly more dissociative symptoms than those with schizophrenia.

For my purposes, however, the opposite finding is of greater interest; that is, patients with schizophrenia scored far above general population norms on all the subscales of the SCID-D: 32% of schizophrenics reported moderate or severe identity alteration on the SCID-D, a figure close to the 25% who meet DDIS criteria for multiple personality disorder in Ross et al. (1994).

Haugen and Castillo (1999) administered the SCID-D to 50 psychotic outpatients (35 with schizophrenia and 15 with schizoaffective disorder). Haugen and Castillo's (1999) sample is especially interesting because it is so different racially and geographically from the samples of most studies done in the mainland United States (i.e., 27 Asian Americans, 19 Pacific Islanders, and 4 European Americans). On the SCID-D, 28% of these patients with psychosis met criteria for DID or DDNOS. This finding is consistent with DDIS data (Ross et al., 1992, 1994; Ross & Keyes, 2004). Even though each of Haugen and Castillo's psychotic subjects were diagnosed with either schizophrenia or schizoaffective disorder, the SCID-D also identified comorbid dissociative disorders other than DID or DDNOS, for example, depersonalization disorder (8%), dissociative amnesia (14%), and dissociative trance disorder (35%). This latter finding further supports the contention that persons diagnosed with schizophrenia often belong in the dissociative taxon (Waller et al., 1996; Waller & Ross, 1997). This, in turn, lends support to the hypothesis of a dissociative subtype of schizophrenia.

Kurt Schneider (1959) identified 11 first-rank symptoms of schizophrenia that he considered to be pathognomonic of schizophrenia. Although the pathognomonic specificity of first-rank symptoms has been abandoned, DSM-IV-TR still regards two of the first-rank symptoms (i.e., voices commenting and voices arguing) to be so characteristic of schizophrenia that the presence of either is sufficient to make a diagnosis of schizophrenia. Curiously, research has shown that the first-rank symptoms of schizophrenia have superior sensitivity and specificity as diagnostic criteria for DID.

The average number of Schneiderian symptoms is higher in DID than in schizophrenia (Ellason & Ross, 1995; Laddis, Dell, Ellason, Fridley, & Lamb, 2001). The relative weakness of the relationship between Schneiderian symptoms and schizophrenia is illustrated by the fact that only 55.5% of 2576 schizophrenic subjects in 12 series reported any Schneiderian symptoms at all (Ross & Joshi, 1992). Thus, paradoxically, research indicates that the more first-rank symptoms of schizophrenia you have, the less likely it is that you have schizophrenia. Conversely, the more first-rank symptoms of schizophrenia you have, the more likely it is that you have DID.

These well-replicated findings should lead to a revision of the DSM criteria for schizophrenia. Today, the first-rank symptoms are prominently included among the positive symptoms of schizophrenia (i.e., delusions, hallucinations; American Psychiatric Association, 2000; Andreasen, 1983, 1984; Kay, Opler, & Fizbein, 1994). Spitzer, Haug, and Freyberger (1997) used the Dissociative Experiences Scale (DES) and the Positive and Negative Syndrome Scale (PANSS) to compare dissociation in schizophrenic patients with predominantly positive symptoms and schizophrenic patients with predominantly negative symptoms. The mean DES score was 21.1 for the positive symptom group and 9.2 for the negative symptom group. DES scores for all 27 patients correlated 0.60 with the hallucinatory behavior scale of the PANSS. The mean SCL-90 score on the Psychoticism Scale was 1.55 for the positive symptom group and 0.74 for the negative symptom group. These data illustrate the close relationship between dissociation and psychotic symptoms, but especially positive psychotic symptoms.

Although additional replications are required, the findings to date are quite consistent. Trauma, dissociation, and the positive symptoms of schizophrenia are not only common in patients with schizophrenia, they are common in those with DID. In fact, the positive symptoms of schizophrenia are more characteristic of DID than they are of schizophrenia.

37.6 STRENGTHS AND WEAKNESSES OF THE THEORY OF A DISSOCIATIVE SUBTYPE OF SCHIZOPHRENIA

The proposal that there is a dissociative subtype of schizophrenia and the theory that it is trauma-induced are scientifically testable. The theory is operationalized and imbedded in the literatures on trauma, dissociation, and psychosis. The measures and procedures for testing the theory are specified, and the proposed diagnostic criteria are consistent with the format and rules of DSM-IV-TR. The theory can be tested at a reasonable cost. The potential impact of dissociative schizophrenia on theory, research, and treatment justifies the expenditure of the necessary time, energy, and resources.

37.7 NEEDED RESEARCH

The basic observation (i.e., that there are patients who manifest a dissociative form of schizophrenia) requires further replication. Some of these replication studies should be conducted by investigators who are not proponents of the trauma model of psychopathology.

This research should be based upon samples of patients who (1) have stable clinical diagnoses of schizophrenia that (2) have been confirmed by structured interviews. These latter research diagnoses of schizophrenia should, in turn, be subjected to reliability checks using independent interviewers.

These carefully diagnosed schizophrenia patients should be administered a battery of measures of trauma, dissociation, and psychosis. If possible, these patients' trauma histories should be independently verified. This methodology should identify two groups: (1) patients with a dissociative type of schizophrenia and (2) patients with nondissociative schizophrenia. Analysis of the data should be both categorical and dimensional in order to calculate correlations, determine the predictors of dissociation, and identify additional relationships between variables.

Having identified these two categories of schizophrenia (dissociative versus nondissociative; nondissociative schizophrenia groups the five subtypes described in DSM-IV-TR), the investigators should then explore the diagnostic reliability of these categories. The validity of dissociative schizophrenia should then be investigated via external validators such as additional phenomenology, patterns of comorbidity, treatment response, and family history.

Future studies should include placebo-controlled trials of medications, trials of psychotherapy, genetic studies, brain scan research, and biochemical studies.

REFERENCES

American Psychiatric Association (2000). *DSM-IV-TR—Diagnostic and statistical manual of mental disorders* (4th ed., text rev.). Washington, DC: Author.

Andreasen, N. C. (1983). *Scale for the assessment of negative symptoms (SANS)*. Iowa City: University of Iowa.

Andreasen, N. C. (1984). *Scale for the assessment of positive symptoms (SAPS)*. Iowa City: University of Iowa.

Bebbington, P. E., Bhugra, D., Brugha, T., Singleton, N., Farrell, M., Jenkins, R., Lewis, G., & Meltzer, H. (2004). Psychosis, victimization and childhood disadvantage. *British Journal of Psychiatry, 185*, 220–226.

Bebbington, P., Wilkins, S., Jones, P., Foerster, A., Murray, R., Toone, B., & Lewis, S. (1993). Life events and psychosis. Initial results from the Camberwell collaborative psychosis study. *British Journal of Psychiatry, 162*, 72–79.

Beck, J., & van der Kolk, B. (1987). Reports of childhood incest and current behavior of chronically hospitalized psychotic women. *American Journal of Psychiatry*, 144, 1474–1476.

Bernstein, E. M., & Putnam, F. W. (1986). Development, reliability, and validity of a dissociation scale. *Journal of Nervous and Mental Disease, 174*, 727–735.

Bleuler, E. (1911/1950). *Dementia præcox oder die Gruppe der Schizophrenien.* Leipzig: Deuticke. Trans. J. Zinkin, *Dementia præcox or the group of schizophrenias*. New York: International Universities Press.

Bliss, E. L. (1980). Multiple personalities. A report of 14 cases with implications for schizophrenia. *Archives of General Psychiatry, 37*, 1388–1397.

Butler, R. W., Mueser, K. T., Sprock, J., & Braff, D. L. (1996). Positive symptoms of psychosis in posttraumatic stress disorder. *Biological Psychiatry, 39*, 839–844.

Cardeña, E. (1994). The domain of dissociation. In S. J. Lynn & J. W. Rhue (Eds.), *Dissociation: Clinical and theoretical perspectives* (pp. 15–31). New York: Guilford.

Carlson, E. B., Putnam, F. W., Ross, C. A., Torem, M., Coons, P., Dill, D. L., Lœwenstein, R. J., & Braun, B. G. (1993). Validity of the Dissociative Experiences Scale in screening for multiple personality disorder: A multicenter study. *American Journal of Psychiatry, 150*, 1030–1036.

Cohen, N. J., & Eichenbaum, H. (1993). *Memory, amnesia, and the hippocampal system*. Cambridge: MIT Press.

Dell, P. F. (2002). Dissociative phenomenology of dissociative identity disorder. *Journal of Nervous & Mental Disease, 190*, 10–15.

Domash, M. D., & Sparr, L. F. (1982). Post-traumatic stress disorder masquerading as paranoid schizophrenia: A case report. *Military Medicine, 147*, 772–774.

Ellason, J. W., & Ross, C. A. (1995). Positive and negative symptoms in dissociative identity disorder and schizophrenia. *Journal of Nervous & Mental Disease, 183*, 236–241.

Ellason, J. W., Ross, C. A., & Fuchs, D. L. (1996). Lifetime Axis I and II comorbidity and childhood trauma history in dissociative identity disorder. *Psychiatry, 59*, 255–266.

Fink, D., & Golinkoff, M. (1990). MPD, borderline personality disorder and schizophrenia: A comparative study of clinical features. *Dissociation, 3*, 127–134.

Friedman, S., & Harrison, G. (1984), Sexual histories, attitudes and behavior of schizophrenic and normal women. *Archives of Sexual Behavior, 13*, 555–567.

Gainer, K. (1994). Dissociation and schizophrenia: An historical review of conceptual development and relevant treatment approaches. *Dissociation, 7*, 261–271.

Goff, D., Brotman, A., Kidlon, D., Waites, M., & Amico, E. (1991). Self-reports of childhood abuse in chronically psychotic patients. *Psychiatry Research, 37*, 73–80.

Goodman, L. A., Thompson, K. M., Weinfurt, K., Corl, S., Acker, P., Mueser, K. T., & Rosenberg, S. D. (1999). Reliability of reports of violent victimization and posttraumatic stress disorder among men and women with serious mental illness. *Journal of Traumatic Stress, 12*, 587–599.

Greenblat, L. (2000). First person account: Understanding health as a continuum. *Schizophrenia Bulletin, 26*, 243–245.

Hamner, M. B., Frueh, C., Ulmer, H. G., Huber, M. G., Twomey, T. J., Tyson, C., & Arana, G. W. (2000). Psychotic features in chronic posttraumatic stress disorder and schizophrenia. *Journal of Nervous & Mental Disease, 188*, 217–221.

Haugen, M. C., & Castillo, R. J. (1999). Unrecognized dissociation in psychotic outpatients and implications of ethnicity. *Journal of Nervous & Mental Disease*, *187*, 751–754.

Heads, T., Taylor, P., & Leese, M. (1997). Childhood experiences of patients with schizophrenia and a history of violence: A special hospital sample. *Criminal & Behavioral Mental Health*, *7*, 117–130.

Heins, T., Gray, A., & Tennant, M. (1990). Persisting hallucinations following childhood sexual abuse. *Australia & New Zealand Journal of Psychiatry*, *24*, 561–565.

Hirsch, S. J., & Hollender, M. H. (1969). Hysterical psychosis: Clarification of a concept. *American Journal of Psychiatry*, *125*, 909–915.

Hollender, M. H., & Hirsch, S. J. (1964). Hysterical psychosis. *American Journal of Psychiatry*, *120*, 1066–1074.

Janet, P. (1965). *The major symptoms of hysteria*. New York: Hafner. (Original work published in 1907.)

Janet, P. (1977). *The mental state of hystericals*. Washington, DC: University Publications of America. (Original work published in 1901.)

Janssen, I., Krabbendam, L., Bak, M., Hanssen, M., Vollebergh, W., de Graff, R., & van Os, J. (2004). Childhood abuse as a risk factor for psychotic experiences. *Acta Psychiatrica Scandinavica*, *109*, 38–45.

Jauch, D. A., & Carpenter, W. T. (1988a). Reactive psychosis I: Does the Pre-DSM-III-R concept define a third psychosis? *Journal of Nervous & Mental Disease*, *176*, 72–81.

Jauch, D. A., & Carpenter, W. T. (1988b). Reactive psychosis II: Does DSM-II-R define a third psychosis? *Journal of Nervous & Mental Disease*, *176*, 82–86.

Jeffries, J. J. (1977). The trauma of being psychotic: A neglected element in the management of chronic schizophrenia. *Canadian Psychiatric Association Journal*, *22*, 199–206.

Jordan, J. C. (1995). First person account: Schizophrenia—adrift in an anchorless reality. *Schizophrenia Bulletin*, *21*, 501–503.

Kantor, R. E., & Herron, W. G. (1966). *Reactive and process schizophrenia*. Palo Alto: California: Science and Behavior Books.

Kay, S. R., Opler, L. A., & Fiszbein, A. (1994). *Positive and negative syndrome scale manual*. North Tonawanda, NY: Multi-Health Systems.

Kluft, R. P. (1987). First-rank symptoms as a diagnostic clue to multiple personality disorder. *American Journal of Psychiatry*, *144*, 293–298.

Laddis, A., Dell, P. F., Ellason, J. W., Cotton, M., Fridley, D., & Lamb, T. (2001). A comparison of the dissociative experiences of patients with schizophrenia and patients with DID. Paper presented at the 18th International Fall Conference of the International Society for the Study of Dissociation, New Orleans, December 4.

Lundy, M. S. (1992). Psychosis-induced posttraumatic stress disorder. *American Journal of Psychotherapy*, *46*, 485–491.

Lysaker, P. H., Meyer, P. S., Evans, J. D., Clements, C. A., & Marks, K. A. (2001). Childhood sexual trauma and psychosocial functioning in adults with schizophrenia. *Psychiatric Services*, *52*, 1485–1488.

Mallett, B. L., & Gold, S. (1964). A pseudo-schizophrenic hysterical syndrome. *British Journal of Medical Psychology*, *37*, 59–70.

Martin, P. A. (1971). Dynamic considerations of the hysterical psychosis. *American Journal of Psychiatry*, *128*, 745–748.

McGorry, P. D., Chanen, A., McCarthy, E., Van Riel, R., McKenzie, D., & Singh, B. (1991). Posttraumatic stress disorder following recent-onset psychosis. *Journal of Nervous & Mental Disease*, *179*, 253–258.

Meyer, A., Jelliffe, S. E., & Hoch, A. (1911/1950). *Dementia praecox: A monograph*. Boston: Gorham Press.

Meyer, H., Taiminen, T., Vuori, T., Aijala, A., & Helenius, H. (1999). Posttraumatic stress disorder symptoms related to psychosis and acute involuntary hospitalization in schizophrenic and delusional patients. *Journal of Nervous & Mental Disease*, *187*, 343–352.

Muenzenmaier, K., Meyer, I., Struening, E., & Ferber, J. (1993). Childhood abuse and neglect among women outpatients with chronic mental illness. *Hospital & Community Psychiatry*, *44*, 666–670.

Mueser, K. T., & Berenbaum, H. (1990). Psychodynamic treatment of schizophrenia: Is there a future? *Psychological Medicine*, *20*, 253–262.

Mueser, K. T., & Butler, R. W. (1987). Auditory hallucinations in combat-related chronic posttraumatic stress disorder. *American Journal of Psychiatry*, *144*, 299–302.

Mueser, K. T., Trumbetta, S. L., Rosenberg, S. D., Vidaver, R., Goodman, L. B., Osher, F. C., Auciello, P., & Foy, D. W. (1998). Trauma and posttraumatic stress disorder in severe mental illness. *Journal of Consulting & Clinical Psychology*, *66*, 493–499.

Norman, R., & Malla, A. (1993a). Stressful life events and schizophrenia: I. A review of the research. *British Journal of Psychiatry*, *162*, 161–166.

Norman, R., & Malla, A. (1993b). Stressful life events and schizophrenia: II. Conceptual and methodological issues. *British Journal of Psychiatry*, *162*, 166–174.

Pincus, H. A., Rush, A. J., First, M. B., & McQueen, L. E. (2000). *Handbook of psychiatric measures*. Washington, DC: American Psychiatric Association.

Pinto, P. A., & Gregory, R. J. (1995). Posttraumatic stress disorder with psychotic features. *American Journal of Psychiatry*, *52*, 471–472.

Read, J. (1997). Child abuse and psychosis: A literature review and implications for professional practice. *Professional Psychology: Research & Practice*, *28*, 448–456.

Read, J., Agar, K., Argyle, N., & Aderhold, V. (in press). Sexual and physical abuse during childhood and adulthood as predictors of hallucinations, delusions and thought disorder. *Psychology & Psychotherapy: Theory Research & Practice*.

Read, J., & Argyle, N. (1999). Hallucinations, delusions, and thought disorder among adult psychiatric inpatients with a history of child abuse. *Psychiatric Services*, *50*, 1467–1472.

Read, J., & Argyle, N. (2000). A question of abuse. *Psychiatric Services*, *51*, 534–535.

Read, J., Perry, B. D., Moskowitz, A., & Connolly, J. (2001). The contribution of early traumatic events to schizophrenia in some patients: A traumagenic neurodevelopmental model. *Psychiatry: Interpersonal & Biological Processes, 64*, 319–345.

Read, J., & Ross, C. A. (2003). Psychological trauma and psychosis. *Journal of the American Academy of Psychoanalysis & Dynamic Psychiatry, 31*, 247–268.

Richman, J., & White, H. (1970). A family view of hysterical psychosis. *American Journal of Psychiatry, 127*, 280–285.

Rose, S. (1991). Acknowledging abuse backgrounds of intensive case management clients. *Community Mental Health Journal, 27*, 255–263.

Rose, S., Peabody, C., & Stratigeas, B. (1991). Undetected abuse among intensive case management clients. *Hospital & Community Psychiatry, 42*, 499–503.

Rosenbaum, M. (1980). The role of the term schizophrenia in the decline of diagnoses of multiple personality. *Archives of General Psychiatry, 37*, 1383–1385.

Rosenberg, S. I., Mueser, K. T., Friedman, M. J., Gorman, P. G., Drake, R. E., Vidaver, R. M., Torrey, W. C., & Jankowski, M. K. (2001). Developing effective treatments for post-traumatic disorders among people with severe mental illness. *Psychiatric Services*, 52, 1453–1661.

Rosenberg, S., Mueser, K., Jankowski, M. K., & Hamblen, J. (2002). Trauma exposure and PTSD in people with severe mental illness. *PTSD Research Quarterly, 13*, 1–4.

Ross, C. A. (1991). Epidemiology of multiple personality and dissociation. *Psychiatric Clinics of North America, 14*, 503–517.

Ross, C. A. (1997). *Dissociative identity disorder. Diagnosis, clinical features, and treatment of multiple personality.* (2 ed.). New York: John Wiley & Sons.

Ross, C. A. (1999). The dissociative disorders. In T. Million, P. Blaney, & R. Davis, (Eds.), *Oxford textbook of psychopathology* (pp. 466–481). New York: Oxford University Press.

Ross, C. A. (2000). *The trauma model: A solution to the problem of comorbidity in psychiatry*. Richardson, TX: Manitou Communications.

Ross, C. A. (2004). *Schizophrenia: Innovations in diagnosis and treatment*. New York: Haworth Press.

Ross, C. A. (2007). Dissociation and psychosis: The need for integration of theory and practice. In J. O. Johannessen & B. Martindale (Eds.), *Schizophrenia and other psychoses: Different stages, different treatment?* (pp. 238–254). New York: Brunner-Routledge.

Ross, C. A., Anderson, G., & Clark, P. (1994). Childhood abuse and positive symptoms of schizophrenia. *Hospital & Community Psychiatry, 45*, 489–491.

Ross, C. A., Duffy, C. M. M., & Ellason, J. W. (2002). Prevalence, reliability and validity of dissociative disorders in an inpatient setting. *Journal of Trauma & Dissociation, 3*, 7–17.

Ross, C. A., & Joshi, S. (1992). Schneiderian symptoms and childhood trauma in the general population. *Comprehensive Psychiatry, 33*, 269–273.

Ross, C. A., Joshi, S., & Currie, R. P. (1990). Dissociative experiences in the general population. *American Journal of Psychiatry, 147*, 1547–1552.

Ross, C. A., & Keyes, B. (2004). Dissociation and schizophrenia. *Journal of Trauma & Dissociation*, 5, 69–83.

Ross, C. A., Miller, S. D., Bjornson, L., Reagor, P., Fraser, G. A., & Anderson, G. (1990). Schneiderian symptoms in multiple personality disorder and schizophrenia. *Comprehensive Psychiatry, 31*, 111–118.

Ross, C. A., Norton, G. R., & Wozney, K. (1989). Multiple personality disorder: An analysis of 236 cases. *Canadian Journal of Psychiatry, 34*, 413–418.

Ruocchio, P. J. (1989). First person account: Fighting the fight – the schizophrenic's nightmare. *Schizophrenia Bulletin, 15*, 163–166.

Ruocchio, P. J. (1991). First person account: The schizophrenic inside. *Schizophrenia Bulletin, 17*, 357–360.

Sautter, F. J., Brailey, K., Uddo, M. M., Hamilton, M. F., Beard, M. G., & Borges, A. H. (1999). PTSD and comorbid psychotic disorder: Comparison with veterans diagnosed with PTSD or psychotic disorder. *Journal of Traumatic Stress, 12*, 73–88.

Sautter, F. J., Cornwell, J., Johnson, J. J., Wiley, J., & Faraone, S. V. (2002). Family history study of posttraumatic stress disorder with secondary psychotic features. *American Journal of Psychiatry, 159*, 1775–1777.

Shaner, A., & Eth, S. (1989). Can schizophrenia cause posttraumatic stress disorder? *American Journal of Psychotherapy, 43*, 588–597.

Shaw, K., McFarlane, A., & Bookless, C. (1997). The phenomenology of traumatic reactions to psychotic illness. *Journal of Nervous & Mental Disease, 185*, 434–441.

Shaw, K., McFarlane, A. C., Bookless, C., & Air, T. (2002). The aetiology of postpsychotic posttraumatic stress disorder following a psychotic episode. *Journal of Traumatic Stress, 15*, 39–47.

Siomopoulos, V. (1971). Hysterical psychosis: Psychopathological aspects. *British Journal of Medical Psychology, 44*, 95–100.

Spiegel, D., & Fink, R. (1979). Hysterical psychosis and hypnotizability. *American Journal of Psychiatry, 136*, 777–781.

Spitzer, C., Haug, H.-J., & Freyberger, H. J. (1997). Dissociative symptoms in schizophrenic patients with positive and negative symptoms. *Psychopathology, 30*, 67–75.

Spitzer, R. L., Williams, J. B. W., Gibbon, M., & First, M. B. (1990). *Users guide for the structured clinical interview for DSM-III-R*. Washington, DC: American Psychiatric Press.

Steinberg, M. (1995). *Handbook for the assessment of dissociation. A clinical guide*. Washington, DC: American Psychiatric Press.

Steinberg, M., Cicchetti, D., Buchanan, J., Rakfeldt, J., & Rounsaville, B. (1994). Distinguishing between multiple personality disorder (dissociative identity disorder) and schizophrenia using the structured clinical interview for DSM-IV dissociative disorders. *Journal of Nervous & Mental Disease, 182*, 495–502.

Steinberg, M., Rounsaville, B. J., & Cicchetti, D. V. (1990). The Structured Clinical Interview for DSM-III-R Dissociative Disorders: Preliminary report on a new diagnostic instrument. *American Journal of Psychiatry, 147*, 76–82.

Steingard, S., & Frankel, F. H. (1985). Dissociation and psychotic symptoms. *American Journal of Psychiatry, 142*, 953–955.

Turner, B. A. (1993). First person account: The children of madness. *Schizophrenia Bulletin, 19*, 649–650.

Van der Hart, O., Witztum, E., & Friedman, B. (1993). From hysterical psychosis to reactive dissociative psychosis. *Journal of Traumatic Stress, 6*, 43–64.

Waldfogel, S., & Mueser, K. T. (1988). Another case of chronic PTSD with auditory hallucinations. *American Journal of Psychiatry, 145*, 1314.

Walker, E., Cudbeck, R., Mednick, S., & Schlusinger, F. (1981). Effects of parental absence and institutionalization on the development of clinical symptoms in high-risk children. *Acta Psychiatrica Scandinavica, 63*, 95–109.

Waller, N. G., & Ross, C. A. (1997). The prevalence and biometric structure of pathological dissociation in the general population: Taxometric structure and behavior genetic findings. *Journal of Abnormal & Social Psychology, 106*, 499–510.

Waller, N. G., Putnam, F. W., & Carlson, E. B. (1996). The types of dissociation and dissociative types: A taxometric analysis of dissociative experiences. *Psychological Methods, 1*, 300–321.

Wilcox, J., Briones, D., & Suess, L. (1991). Auditory hallucinations, posttraumatic stress disorder, and ethnicity. *Comprehensive Psychiatry, 32*, 320–323.

Williams-Keeler, L., Milliken, H., & Jones, B. (1994). Psychosis as precipitating trauma for PTSD: A treatment strategy. *American Journal of Orthopsychiatry, 64*, 493–498.

Part XI

Assessment and Measurement of Dissociation

38 Dissociation and Dissociative Disorders: Clinical and Forensic Assessment With Adults

A. Steven Frankel, PhD, JD

OUTLINE

This chapter was originally construed as a review of psychodiagnostic instruments available to clinicians working with dissociative disorders. However, after considerable reflection and discussion with groups of practicing clinicians, I decided to construe the mission more broadly. I believe that a considerable majority of clinicians who provide services to dissociative patients are not professionals who have been trained in the principles of test construction, validation, administration, scoring, and interpretation. I would like this chapter to address their needs as well as those of professionals who are well-trained with psychological assessment instruments. Thus, I have structured the chapter in terms of the (overlapping) questions about which treating clinicians may be most concerned, the ways assessment relates to those questions, and which assessment approaches might be most productive.[1]

Table 38.1 is a list of assessment approaches, arranged in categories, including initial clinical assessment and screening instruments, ongoing clinical assessment, diagnostic instruments, and instruments designed to provide

[1] The decision to structure the chapter in terms of questions and approaches to their answers has also been made as a result of the recent publication of a helpful review of instruments for clinicians who treat dissociative disorders (Brand, Armstrong, & Loewenstein, 2006).

TABLE 38.1
Assessment Procedures and Protocols

I. Initial Interviewing
  A. Office Mental Status Examination
  B. Screening
    1. Adult Attachment Interview
    2. Dissociative Experiences Scale (DES)
    3. Gudjonsson Scale of Interrogative Suggestibility
    4. Hypnotic Induction Profile (HIPS)
    5. Millon Clinical Multiaxial Index (MCMI)
    6. Somatoform Dissociation Questionnaire (SDQ)
II. Diagnostic
  A. Dissociative Disorders Interview Schedule (DDIS)
  B. Multiscale Dissociation Inventory (MDI)
  C. Multidimensional Inventory of Dissociation (MID)
  D. Structured Clinical Interview for Dissociative Disorders-Revised (SCID-D-R)
III. Ongoing Screening
  A. Dimensions of Therapeutic Movement Inventory (DTMI)
  B. Structured Inventory of Malingered Symptomatology (SIMS)
  C. Structured Interview of Reported Symptoms (SIRS)
IV. Enriching Assessment Instruments
  A. Minnesota Multiphasic Personality Inventory–2 (MMPI-2)
  B. Rorschach Inkblot Test
  C. Thematic Apperception Test (TAT)
  D. Wechsler Adult Intelligence Scale–4th Edition (WAIS-IV)

For descriptions of these procedures and protocols, see 38.4, Appendix

enriched data about the ways in which patients think, feel, and function. The list is not intended to be exhaustive, as many assessment approaches have been developed over recent decades, only to be rarely utilized for any of a variety of reasons (e.g., their not being helpful, the tendency of practicing clinicians to refrain from formal assessment and rely on clinical interviewing to gather information,[2] etc.). Rather, the list includes assessment approaches that seem to have reached the criterion of general acceptance and use within the professional community (which, as it includes researchers and theoreticians, is broader than the practicing community) or which seem to me to show the greatest promise of general acceptance.[3] The table provides descriptive and evaluative (where possible) information about each approach as well as means of obtaining such materials as are available to employ the approach.

Table 38.2 is a list of assessment questions that I believe to be among the most critical questions to be addressed for purposes of treatment planning, implementation, and evaluation. These questions are discussed in the following.

38.1 ASSESSMENT QUESTIONS: WHAT CLINICIANS WANT AND NEED TO KNOW

38.1.1 Is Dissociation Involved in the Patient's Problems?

Since dissociation may be involved in a broad spectrum of clinical presentations, it is helpful and important to include questions about trauma history (including neglect) and dissociative symptoms as an integral part of the initial clinical assessment interview. Clinicians who are aware of the frequency of trauma and dissociation in the clinical population include, as a rule, questions about trauma history, modes of discipline in the family of origin, responses to trauma, and so on, as a part of the initial clinical assessment interview. Further, screening instruments such as the Dissociative Experiences Scale (DES) (Carlson & Putnam, 1993; Waller, Putnam, & Carlson, 1996), and the Somatoform Dissociation Questionnaire (SDQ) (Nijenhuis, Spinhoven, & Van Dyck, 1996) are "inexpensive," easily administered and scored, taking very little of the clinician's time and yielding potentially helpful information—not only in terms of actual scores,

TABLE 38.2
Ten Critical Assessment Questions

1. Is dissociation involved in the patient's problems?
2. Does the patient have a dissociative disorder, such as DID?
3. How much Axis-II involvement characterizes the patient?
4. How resilient is the patient?
5. How hypnotically capable is the patient?
6. How suggestible is the patient?
7. How does the patient's attachment style impact treatment?
8. What is the patient's preferred "treatment path"?
9. How can I assess whether a patient's symptoms are associated with factitious disorder or malingering?
10. Are there any other measures that can enhance the richness of my understanding and appreciation of the patient?

[2] Indeed, my own training as a psychologist taught me that formal assessment was a shortcut to information that would become available over time through clinical interviewing.

[3] Forensic practitioners in the United States will recognize "general acceptance" as the criterion for admissibility of expert testimony under *Frye* and one of the admissibility considerations for judges under *Daubert-Kumho*.

but also in terms of questions that might be followed up on interview.[4]

Should initial assessments such as those previously mentioned suggest that dissociation is present and/or indicate the presence of a history of trauma, a more structured clinical interview format is available (Loewenstein, 1991) that has stood the test of time as a thorough and thoughtful screening approach. While this office mental status examination is more "expensive" (in terms of clinician time and energy) than screening instruments like the DES and SDQ, it provides helpful and enriched information about known qualities of dissociative disorders.

38.1.2 Does the Patient Have a Dissociative Disorder, Such as DID?

Given a determination that dissociation plays a role in a patient's problems, the issue of whether a diagnosis is of a dissociative disorder (as opposed, e.g., to borderline personality disorder or posttraumatic stress disorder) is typically considered. While many patients with clear dissociative disorders make their dissociative symptoms known to clinicians who are willing to see them quite early in treatment, others do not. Fortunately, there are currently four diagnostic instruments available to assist in making the diagnosis of a dissociative disorder: in alphabetical order, these are the Dissociative Disorders Interview Schedule (DDIS) (Ross, Heber, & Anderson, 1999), the Multiscale Dissociation Inventory (MDI) (Briere, 2002), the Multidimensional Inventory of Dissociation (MID) (Dell, 2006), and the Structured Clinical Interview for Dissociative Dissociative Disorders–Revised (SCID-D-R) (Steinberg, 1995).

Each of these instruments has been systematically developed, published in peer-review journals, and yields information leading to making decisions about diagnosis. Each instrument differs from the others (see Table 38.1) in many respects, including how much of a clinician's time and energy are necessary for administration/scoring, how the diagnostic information relates to current diagnostic terminology (i.e., the Diagnostic and Statistical Manual of the American Psychiatric Association—DSM, and the International Classification of Diseases—ICD), how dissociative symptoms are understood and classified, how "treatment-friendly" the derived information might be (see the following), and so on. In the end, whether clinicians actually make the effort to employ one or more of these instruments (and will be richly rewarded for their efforts) will likely be some function of their own personal comfort/familiarity with the instruments, along with the growing attention to risk management principles, such as ISSTD's Treatment Guidelines (Chu et al., 2005).

38.1.3 How Much Axis II Involvement Characterizes the Patient?

Clinicians want and need to know the degree of Axis II involvement in their patients' problems. Axis II involvement has historically been associated with treatment that is longer in duration, more arduous in implementation, and more guarded in outcome than is treatment with little or no Axis II involvement.

One instrument that is available for the assessment of Axis II involvement is the Millon Multiaxial Clinical Inventory (MCMI) (Millon, 1987). Brand et al. (2006) report the results of MCMI II (now supplanted by the MCMI III) with persons diagnosed as DID, indicating that such patients score significantly higher than norms for borderlines on schizoid, avoidant, and schizotypal scales. However, there have been relatively few applications of the MCMI to dissociative patients and its helpfulness is not clear at the present time.

In addition to the helpfulness of assessment instruments such as the DDIS, MID, and SCID-D-R in evaluating for Axis II involvement, I have also found it clinically helpful to characterize Axis-II diagnoses as a variety of ways that people can be self-defeating. From this viewpoint, a very helpful way to characterize Axis II involvement lies in the degree to which patients are able to cooperate (both internally and externally) with treatment requests. Thus, in general, the greater the degree to which internal parts/alters can work cooperatively with each other and the greater the degree to which the patient as a whole person can work cooperatively with a clinician, the less the Axis II involvement. [However, extreme and absolutely faithful *apparent* cooperation may also reflect high degrees of suggestibility—a circumstance that has clear treatment as well as risk-management implications (see the following).] Consistent with this view is the idea that the presence of one or more "Inner Self Helpers" (ISH's) can be construed as an index of cooperation (Allison, 1996).

Finally, the idea that the "names" of the different Axis II disorders describe a variety of ways ("flavors," "colors," or whichever metaphor is appealing) that people can be self-defeating, leads to appreciating the difficulties in cooperation in such clinically appealing terms as "I hate you—don't leave me" (borderline), "get a load of this!" (histrionic), "how dare you suggest that I . . ." (narcissistic),

[4] Measures that take very little of the clinician's time and energy are often characterized as "cheap data"—where "cheap" refers to ease of accessibility rather than relative inferiority to other data forms.

"what do you intend by saying..." (paranoid), "huh?" (avoidant), etc. (Frankel & Fridley, 2001).

38.1.4 How Resilient Is the Patient?

Resilience (or resiliency) is a construct that concerns the degree to which people may "spring back" from traumatic experiences (Allen, 1998; Masten, 2001). It is invoked to account for how some people have horrendous life experiences and seem to (apparently) do quite well in life, while others do less well and still others have lifelong disabilities. While the study of resilience has historically been out of the mainstream of theory and research in the mental health professions (which are more concerned with psychopathology, while resilience is much more about health), the construct is increasingly important to those who provide professional care for the abused and neglected.

Resilience has many components (some of which are addressed individually in this paper, such as the degree of Axis II disorder, attachment style, etc.). However, research supports the view that the core contributing factors for high resilience are few and consistent:

> 1) Connections to competent and caring adults in the family and community; 2) cognitive and self-regulation skills; 3) positive views of self; and 4) motivation to be effective in the environment. (Masten, 2001)

Highly resilient people are therefore: (1) possessed of adequate personal boundaries and empathic capacities; (2) able to manage affective distress; (3) self-reflexive; (4) able to appreciate positive aspects of themselves and their functioning; and (5) "scrappy" or persistent in the service of achieving personal goals.

While research has resulted in some assessment measures (e.g., the Hardiness Scale), these have not been incorporated into the work with dissociative patients. However, Kluft (1994a, 1994b) has reported on the Dimensions of Clinical Movement Instrument (DTMI), which provides a framework for a clinician to assess the "treatment trajectory" followed by patients. Inspection of the qualities listed by Kluft as bases for these judgments reads as a "what's what" of resilience factors (therapeutic alliance, integration, capacity for adaptive change, management of life stressors, alters' responsibility for self-management, etc.).

The clinician's understanding and appreciation of resilience factors can be highly determinative of treatment strategy. Highly resilient patients may often manage their own treatment, with sessions devoted to evaluating progress and planning what the patient may do next, with rapid movement through treatment stages and establishment of relatively symptom-free lives. Moderately resilient patients may follow a more traditional course of psychotherapy as described in the ISSTD guidelines, while patients with significant resilience problems may fall into Kluft's lowest treatment trajectory, with treatment measured in decades rather than years.

38.1.5 How Hypnotically Capable Is the Patient?

Since hypnotic capacity and dissociative symptoms have some commonalities (e.g., degree of absorption), an assessment of a patient's hypnotic capacity can result in decisions about appropriate treatment methods. For example, a patient who has a dissociative disorder but who does not do well with visual imagery or may be low in fantasy-proneness, may respond more to somatically oriented approaches, energy therapies, EMDR, and the like, rather than hypnotically oriented treatment interventions.

At the current time, the most efficient means of assessing hypnotic capacity appears to be the use of the Hypnotic Induction Profile (HIPS, the "eye-roll technique," Speigel & Speigel, 2004)—an approach that, once mastered, is relatively easy to employ and is supported by empirical research.

38.1.6 How Suggestible Is the Patient?

Suggestibility and hypnotic capacity are not the same. While data support the view that, when in trance, we are more suggestible than we may be when not in trance, it is also clear that, even in trance, patients fall somewhere on a range of suggestibility.

The assessment of suggestibility is important for both treatment and risk management. For risk-management purposes, there are data consistent with the view that patients who may file lawsuits against clinicians are overrepresented with high suggestibility. Specifically, these may be patients who, posttreatment, come to believe (or have suggested to them by others) that their former clinicians "implanted" ideas or experiences that were not their own.

This risk-management problem relates directly to patient suggestibility. Most clinicians experienced with the treatment of dissociative disorders have seen patients who, when the clinician makes a suggestion about some hopefully helpful imagery, react by saying something like "that doesn't work for us. That image is something we can't work with, but we could do it this way...."

Most experienced clinicians are also likely to have seen patients who respond to any, every, and all clinician suggestions with absolute compliance—everything works in perfect accordance with the clinician's statements and recommendations.

These two reactions represent the polar ends of the continuum of suggestibility. The determination of where any particular patient falls along this continuum leads to differing treatment strategies. With less suggestible patients, clinicians may offer more direct recommendations for internal imagery, clinical interpretations of therapeutic phenomena, and so on. With more suggestible patients, clinicians should be less direct about imagery, interpretations, and the like, and support the patient's own efforts at developing his/her own imagery and interpretations. Thus, patient suggestibility relates quite directly to how directive a clinician might be.

At the present time, there is but one measure of suggestibility for adults: the Gudjonsson (1984) Scale of Interrogative Suggestibility. The Gudjonsson measure, in brief, involves the reading of a "story" and subsequent immediate and delayed posing of a series of questions about the story that imply content not included in the reading, to see if the test-taker will endorse such content. An example (not a part of the actual test itself) might be "Jack and Jill went up the hill to fetch a pail of water…." etc. followed by a question like: "were Jack's pants brown or black?" (when no mention of the color of Jack's pants were a part of the story). The endorsement of one color or the other would be consistent with suggestibility.

There is also a way to assess suggestibility clinically, over the course of treatment. This would be for the clinician to pay close attention to the way a patient adopts/doesn't adopt therapeutic suggestions. The more the patient adopts any and all suggestions wholesale, the greater the degree of caution that should be exercised by the clinician in terms of offering direct suggestions.

38.1.7 How Does the Patient's Attachment Style Impact Treatment?

Data increasingly point to the significant role of attachment in persons who dissociate. In addition to having a thorough grounding in the attachment literature, clinicians who work with dissociative patients are well-advised to be familiar with the Adult Attachment Interview (see, e.g., Crowell & Treboux, 1995), if not actually trained in its administration and scoring. The understanding and appreciation of attachment phenomena will greatly contribute to clinicians' capacities for helpful interpretations of patient behavior patterns as well as the assessment of their own countertransference reactions.

The "disorganized/disoriented" form of nonsecure attachment appears to be most descriptive of persons diagnosed with dissociative disorders (Lyons-Ruth, 2003; Liotti, 1999). This attachment form is characterized by parental figures who are both inconsistent in their approach to children's distress and, at times, frightening and/or harmful to their distressed children. Among the important contributions of attachment theory is the understanding that different parts or alters may represent differing ways of getting help with the management of overwhelming negative affect, especially shame. Mechanisms utilized by different parts may include: (1) codependent behavior—the soothing of caretakers in order to get the caretakers to soothe the children; (2) denial/suppression of painful affect such that the threatening caretaker is not aware of it and won't react unhelpfully; and (3) persistent coercive and intrusive demands that may result in a child being struck by the caregiver in order to make the child cease his/her demands.

Thus, self-examination and consultation regarding countertransference reactions may assist clinicians to understand and appreciate the ways in which intense distress is sought to be reduced by patients, resulting in intervention forms that more directly address the patient's affect management difficulties rather than contributing to those difficulties (also see Dalenberg, 2000).

38.1.8 What Is the Patient's Preferred "Treatment Path"?

It is increasingly clear that patients vary as to the pathways followed toward healing. For example, some may be able to work effectively as an internal system, with internal parts working together on problem-solutions via negotiation, cooperation, and mutual support. Others may be unable to work in this way, but may work well if each part engages directly with the clinician, as if each were in individual therapy.

Some may require that each and every aspect of a trauma history be "processed," "metabolized" and otherwise worked through, while others may be able to work on specific examples of types of trauma, and the other examples of each of those types will "heal" over time without direct therapeutic attention.

Some may work well if taught specific skill sets, like hypnotic techniques for the management of affect, while others may work well in the context of a therapeutic relationship in which the clinician's primary set of statements are limited to "what does that mean to you?"

Some may need to demonstrate (in gory detail) the trauma being worked on in treatment, while others may need to do their trauma work quite privately, reporting the process and outcome of their private work to the clinician rather than demonstrating it. Some may work more effectively if their clinician provides "bottom up" interventions, as with somatically oriented therapies, while others may flourish only with "top down" interventions (Ogden, Pain, & Fisher, 2006).

How does the clinician ascertain any given patient's particular healing path? First, the clinician must *pay attention* to what the patient teaches. While most patients (except the most resilient) do not have the self-reflexivity to tell us how we can be most helpful in a direct and thoughtful way, they do tell us indirectly, in their responses to interventions.[5]

Thus, for example, we may try to teach some self-regulation skills for patients in early stages of treatment. Some will try to use the skills; some may succeed, while others may not. Still others may tell us (directly or indirectly) that our acting as teachers of skills simply will not work for them, while we may notice that, over some period of weeks/months/years, they seem more distressed when we are away on vacation or at a conference and thus unable to meet with them consistently; or we may notice that they become more distressed at certain times of the day or month or year, or that they become less distressed when we seem to them to be more relaxed and comfortable. These observations may then lead to shared understandings of how they are.

In short, clinicians must be: (1) flexible in their approaches; (2) possessed of a significant armamentarium of observational frameworks and intervention skills; and (3) responsive to what and how patients teach.

And of the more formal assessment instruments currently available to us, the one that is most likely to provide us with the types of information relevant to these considerations is the MID, in that, more than any others, it addresses patients' subjective experience.

[5] A patient of mine taught me about ways to compensate for impaired self-reflexivity by sharing her appraisal of our work together in mid-January of each calendar year. As I scratched my head in wonder, she shared that, when preparing her taxes, she computed the number of workdays each year that were lost, due to her symptoms. Her reporting that our work was going well because her missed workdays were reduced each year were doubly encouraging, in that I saw that she was doing better (as did she), and I also saw how she was able to compensate for compromised self-reflexivity.

38.1.9 How Can I Assess Whether a Patient's Symptoms Are Associated With Factitious Disorder or Malingering?

While the issues of malingering and factitious disorder are always relevant to forensic evaluations, there are also times when such considerations are relevant to treatment. Dalenberg's (2000) data support the view that clinicians should expect that some elaboration of information and/or accompanying affect from trauma patients will be in part factitious (the conscious production of symptoms for the purpose of the benefits of the "sick" role). Our patients have histories in which relatively few people were interested in them for their own benefit, and it is thus not surprising that they might enhance, elaborate, or even fabricate. What is not clear is whether there is a clinician stylistic factor at play in these situations, such that clinicians who are more receptive to detailed descriptions of trauma may hear more elaborate reports (with attendant factitious features) than clinicians who are less receptive.

With malingering (the conscious production of symptoms to gain reward or avoid punishment) (Thomas, 2001; Welburn et al., 2003), however, clinicians are well advised to consider whether patients are engaged in personal injury lawsuits, workers compensation litigation and the like, as these are more likely to be associated with malingering than in clinical situations where there are no issues of financial gain or avoidance of punishment.

Additionally, research with the SCID-D-R (Draijer & Boon, 1987) and select assessment instruments developed to detect malingering (e.g., Structured Inventory of Malingered Symptomatology–SIMS and Structured Interview of Reported Symptoms–SIRS)[6] provides information that clinicians may find useful in the assessment of malingering in their patients.

38.1.10 Are There Any Other Measures That Can Enhance the Richness of My Understanding and Appreciation of the Patient?

Yes. In addition to the MID, which provides a unique insight into the subjective experiences of dissociative patients, Brand et al. (2006) report on the contributions of intelligence testing (as to cognitive capacities and deficits), objective testing (as with the MMPI-2), and

[6] For an online update on the assessment of malingering in general, please log on to http://www.kspope.com/assess/malinger.php

projective tests (including the Thematic Apperception Test–TAT, and Rorschach Inkblot Test). In particular, their presentation of Rorschach data obtained from 100 severely dissociative patients shows that, in competent hands, Rorschach responses may yield data bearing on the capacity of patients to form a therapeutic alliance, dissociative distancing in the face of threatening material, and cognitive disorganization.

38.2 CLINICAL VERSUS FORENSIC EVALUATIONS

There are fundamental differences between treating clinicians and forensic evaluators, and these differences translate into a set of "do's and don't's" for professionals. Greenberg and Shuman (1997) have analyzed these differences and have distilled them into a list of 10 (see Table 38.3).

The most fundamental differences between clinical and forensic roles lies in the nature of the questions to be addressed, to whom the answers are provided, and the nature of the relationship between the professional and the patient/evaluee. Clinical assessment for treatment purposes, on one hand, is devoted to the elucidation of factors that lead to treatment interventions which serve the goals of the patient—factors such as those listed in the clinical assessment portion of this chapter.

Forensic assessment, on the other hand, is devoted to the elucidation of facts that address psycholegal questions—questions that serve the interest of "triers of fact" (judges and juries). Psycholegal questions do not necessarily require facts bearing on diagnostic categories. In fact, there is a strong argument that diagnoses, as they exist in the world of psychiatric and psychological disorders, are misleading in the forensic context (Greenberg, Shuman, & Meyer, 2004). Rather, the questions to be addressed by forensic evaluation are more focused on a variety of issues, which may include (but are not limited to) mental state at the time of a crime (e.g., for criminal cases), parental fitness (e.g., in custody cases), fitness for duty (e.g., in workers compensation cases), nature and extent of damages (e.g., in personal injury cases), and so

TABLE 38.3
Ten Differences Between Therapeutic and Forensic Relationships

		Therapeutic Care	Forensic Examination
1	Whose client is the patient/litigant?	The mental health practitioner's	The attorney's
2	The relational privilege that governs disclosure in each relationship	Therapist-patient privilege	Attorney-client and attorney work-product privilege
3	The cognitive set and evaluative attitude of each expert	Supportive, accepting, empathic	Neutral, objective, detached
4	The nature and degree of alliance in each relationship	A helping relationship, allies; rarely adversarial	An evaluative relationship; frequently adversarial
5	The differing areas of competency of each expert	Therapy techniques for treatment of the impairment	Forensic examination techniques relevant to the legal claim
6	The nature of the hypotheses tested by each expert	Diagnostic criteria for the purpose of therapy	Psycholegal criteria for purpose of legal adjudication
7	The amount and control of structure in each relationship	Patient-structured and relatively less structure than forensic examination	Examiner-structured and relatively more structured than therapy
8	The scrutiny applied to the information used in the process, and the role of historical truth	Mostly based on information from the person being treated, with little external scrutiny of that information by the therapist	Litigant information supplemented with and verified by collateral sources and scrutinized by the examiner, adversaries, and the court
9	The goal of the professional in each relationship	Therapist attempts to benefit the patient by working within the therapeutic relationship	Examiner advocates for the results and implications of the evaluation for the benefit of the court
10	The impact on each relationship of critical judgment by the psychologist.	The basis of the relationship is the therapeutic alliance and critical judgment is likely to impair that alliance	The basis of the relationship is evaluative and critical judgment is less likely to cause serious emotional harm

Note: From Irreconcilable conflict between therapeutic and forensic roles, by S. Greenberg and D. Shuman, 1997, *Professional Psychology: Research and Practice; 1*, pp. 50–57. Copyright 1997 by American Psychiatric Association. Reprinted with permission.

forth. The critical issues here are less a matter of diagnosis and more a matter of the nexus (in legal language) or of the power of the correlation (in psychological terms) between characteristics of the evaluee and the question before the court.

The primary ethical obligation for the clinical evaluator and treater is to serve the goals of the patient (given that those goals are themselves ethically defensible) and to do no harm, while the primary ethical obligation of the forensic evaluator is to present evidence that is objective, without bias, beyond the ken of laypersons, and which is helpful to the trier of fact in addressing psycholegal questions.

The range of data available to forensic evaluators is much broader than that available to the clinical evaluator or treating clinician. While the primary source of data for clinicians is patient report (including patient responses to formal assessment tools), forensic evaluators access data from the evaluee, collateral sources (e.g., family, friends, workplace contacts, etc.) and formal assessment instruments.

Finally, clinical evaluators/treaters (quite properly) carry strong biases that support their patients' interests. Clinicians are in fiduciary relationships with their patients such that patient interests come first and foremost. Because of these biases, and because clinicians who testify in court are subject to vigorous cross-examination that may actually prove harmful to a therapeutic relationship, a group of leading forensic evaluators have raised the question of whether clinicians should, in fact, be barred from presenting testimony in courts (Shuman, Greenberg, Heilbrun, & Foote, 1998).

While this immodest proposal has not been adopted by the legal system, the concerns are worth considering. Consider the following scenario: a clinician provides individual psychotherapy for a dissociative patient who, late in treatment, is involved in an ugly divorce and custody fight. The patient has provided information about his/her soon-to-be former partner to the clinician over the course of treatment, all through the patient's eyes (the clinician has never met the partner). The patient requests that the clinician write a letter to the court, endorsing the patient's interest in having sole legal and physical custody of a child. In a moment of utter insanity, the clinician writes the letter, indicating that, based on the clinician's occasional observation of the patient and child in the waiting room and the patient's reports about the child and the other parent, the best interests of the child are served if sole legal and physical custody are in the patient.

The clinician's licensing board (or the other parent's lawyer) responds to the other parent's complaint by asking the clinician a series of questions:

1. Did you write this letter? (It would be great if the clinician said: "What letter? You mean someone stole my letterhead and forged my signature?") The answer is "yes."
2. Did you recommend custody in your patient? "Yes."
3. Did you do an assessment to arrive at this recommendation? The clinician cannot say "no," as no responsible professional would go on record making a recommendation without an assessment. "Yes."
4. To what degree did that assessment comport with the standards for custody evaluations done by court-appointed custody evaluators? What training and supervision experiences have you had as a custody evaluator? And how many custody evaluations have you done? And while you're thinking about how to answer those questions:
5. Did you get informed consent to perform a custody evaluation? "No, but I do have informed consent to treat my patient—won't that work? And is there any arsenic handy?"

In sum, the world of forensic assessment is very different from the world of clinical assessment and treatment.

As regards the conduct of forensic assessments, the following issues obtain.

First, the forensic evaluator's "client" is not the evaluee. The client is either the attorney who retained the evaluator or the court, depending on the circumstances of appointment (e.g., a forensic custody evaluator may be chosen from a list of candidates, with both parties approving the choice. The client is the judge). Understanding this issue provides immediate clarity to the related issue of whose interests the evaluator serves and how this impacts the relationship between the evaluator and evaluee: this is radically different from a "therapeutic relationship."

Second, when addressing how data obtained by the forensic evaluator apply to the psycholegal question(s) the evaluator should present the competing hypotheses about the question and then show why the evaluator's view is correct and the competing hypotheses are not. So, for example, an evaluation of a personal injury complaint by a dissociative plaintiff would be expected to provide data to show that the plaintiff was not malingering in order to win a monetary award, but was indeed injured. The evaluator would be expected to show which data were consistent/inconsistent with each hypothesis.

Third, the forensic evaluator should be familiar with the entire range of assessment modes and instruments relevant to the psycholegal questions to be addressed. Utilizing the biopsychosocial model that characterizes psychiatric training, Frankel and Dalenberg (2006) have described that range, starting with neurobiologic/neurophysiologic measures such as brain imaging studies, and moving through psychological measures such as indices of attachment, cognition and memory, suggestibility and malingering/deception, to social measures, including histories of exposure to dissociation literature, groups and treatment, corroboration of reports of abuse, past medical records, and litigation history, including depositions. "Evaluators should attempt to map the social context in which dissociative symptoms emerged, to make a determination of the role of suggestibility or social desirability (e.g., if the symptoms appear only with a therapist) and to chart the context-specific changes in clients' personality, knowledge and presentation" (p. 178).

Finally, the forensic evaluator should screen for alternative and comorbid diagnostic factors, including personality disorders, substance abuse, and Axis I disorders, with an eye toward evaluating alternative hypotheses to account for behavior and symptoms relevant to the psycholegal questions.

This section, dealing with differences between clinical and forensic assessment, is intentionally brief, as a more complete exposition of the problems confronted by forensic evaluators has recently been published, along with a review of specific assessment instruments (Frankel & Dalenberg, 2006).

38.3 SUMMARY

The assessment of dissociation and persons diagnosed with dissociative disorders is complex and demanding, both in clinical and forensic contexts. And the differences in assessment approaches between the clinical and forensic contexts are pronounced.

Clinical assessment serves the primary interest of developing, implementing, and evaluating treatment plans that serve the treatment goals of patients. The primary allegiance of the clinician is to the patient and his/her goals. The most fundamental questions for clinical assessment appear to include: (1) whether dissociation is involved in a patient's symptom picture; (2) whether the patient has a diagnosable dissociative disorder; (3) the role of Axis II involvement in the symptom picture; (4) how resilient the patient is; (5) how hypnotically capable the patient is; (6) how suggestible the patient is; (7) how the patient's attachment style impacts treatment; (8) how to discern the patient's preferred treatment path; (9) the degree to which factitious disorder and/or malingering play roles in the symptom picture; and (10) how to gather information that enhances the richness of the clinician's experience of the patient.

Forensic assessment serves the primary interest of gathering evidence to help a trier of fact reach decisions about psycholegal questions. The primary allegiance of the forensic evaluator is to the client, who may be a judge or an attorney, but is generally not the evaluee. To a great extent, psycholegal questions are confused by the psychiatric diagnostic system, such that the forensic evaluator's approach to assessment is much more focused on functions/deficits/qualities/abilities/competencies that are relevant to the particular psycholegal question(s) at hand. Finally, a forensic evaluation in a context where dissociative phenomena are relevant is best informed by awareness of the full range of approaches consistent with a biopsychosocial model.

38.4 APPENDIX

38.4.1 Descriptions of Procedures and Protocols

38.4.1.1 I. Initial Interviewing

A. The *Office Mental Status Examination* (Loewenstein, 1991) is a thorough and semi-structured interview protocol designed to tap known qualities of dissociative disorders. First published in 1991, it has become an oft-utilized protocol for clinicians who suspect that a patient may have a dissociative disorder.

B. Screening

1. *Adult Attachment Interview* (AAI)*: this is an interview protocol that has been implemented and validated worldwide and was developed by Mary Main (1998), one of the major figures in attachment theory and research. The actual adult attachment interview requires thorough training (which is quite available), but the items that make up the structured interview are helpful for clinicians to understand and appreciate. Sample questions from the AAI include:
    1. I'd like you to choose five adjectives that reflect your childhood relationship with your mother. This might take some time, and then I'm going to ask you why you chose them. (Repeated for father.)

* The AAI protocol is available at the Stony Brook Attachment Lab website at: www.psychology.sunysb.edu/attachment/measures/measures_index.html

2. To which parent did you feel closest and why? Why isn't there this feeling with the other parent?
3. When you were upset as a child, what would you do?
4. What is the first time you remember being separated from your parents? How did you and they respond?

2. *Dissociative Experiences Scale* (DES; Carlson & Putnam, 1994) is a screening instrument that yields a cut-off score that maximizes the likelihood that the test-taker has a dissociative disorder. Taxonomic analysis of the DES yields a "pathologic" versus a "nonpathologic taxon" (Waller, Putnam, & Carlson, 1995). The DES purports to screen for "psychoform" dissociation, whereas the DSQ purports to screen for "somatoform" dissociation (see the following). The DES has appeared in more than 1100 research studies and is a staple in the armamentarium of clinical and forensic evaluators. It is available without cost to ISSTD members through the Society's website.
3. The *Gudjonsson Scale of Interrogative Suggestibility* (1984) is described in the text of this chapter. It has been in use for over 20 years and forensic evaluators in particular should be aware that malingerers may be familiar with it.
4. *Hypnotic Induction Profile* (HIPS; Spiegel & Spiegel, 2004) is an easily administered (but requires training to administer) protocol that assesses for hypnotic capacity as a function of the amount of "white" of the eye that can be seen when evaluees or patients are asked to roll their eyes up into their heads and slowly open them without looking down. In general, the more "white" that is shown, the greater the hypnotic capacity.
5. *Millon Clinical Multiaxial Index* (MCMI; Millon, 1987) is an instrument that has emerged in concert with Millon's theories about personality disorders (Millon, 1996). A paper/pencil measure filled out by the patient/evaluee, the MCMI is currently in its third edition and has established some usefulness in forensic settings, but has yet to be used to study patients with DID. The Millon instruments are available at <www.millon.net/>.
6. *Somatoform Dissociation Questionnaire* (SDQ) comes in two varieties: a five-item scale and a 20-item scale. The SDQ (Nijenhuis, 1999) purports to screen for somatoform aspects of dissociative symptoms, like aches and pains that may not have a basis in biology but are consistent with childhood trauma histories. The SDQ is available, with norms, without cost to members of the ISSTD, through its website at <www.isst-d.org>.

38.4.1.2 II. Diagnostic Instruments

A. *Dissociative Disorders Interview Schedule* (DDIS; Ross, Heber, & Anderson, 1990) is a highly structured interview that makes DSM-IV diagnoses of somatization disorder, borderline personality disorder, and major depressive disorder, as well as all the dissociative disorders. It inquires about positive symptoms of schizophrenia, secondary features of DID, extrasensory experiences, substance abuse, and other items relevant to the dissociative disorders. The DDIS is available with instructions and scoring norms, without cost, at <www.rossinst.com/dddquest.htm>.

B. *Multiscale Dissociation Inventory* (MDI; Briere, 2002) explores six domains of dissociation in a 30-item self-report format and offers a profile of dissociative symptoms that can be compared to clinical and nonclinical samples. The MDI is a good choice for general dissociative phenomena and has published norms on a large standardization sample. It is available at *Psychological Assessment Resources* (PAR) with a published administration and interpretation manual available at <www3.parinc.com>.

C. *Multidimensional Inventory of Dissociation* (MID; Dell, 2006) is a 218-item, self-administered, multiscale instrument that assesses the dissociative disorders comprehensively. It measures 14 major facets of dissociation and has 23 dissociation diagnostic scales that operationalize
   1. The subjective and phenomenologic domain of dissociation and
   2. 23 hypothesized dissociative symptoms of DID

   The MID gives a more comprehensive profile of DID patients who actively report alters, and thus provides a highly enriched statement of what is happening inside DID patients. It is thus quite helpful for treatment planning purposes. It is available through Dr. Dell at <pfdell@aol.com>.

D. *Structured Clinical Interview for Dissociative Disorders–Revised* (SCID-D-R; Steinberg, 1995) has long held the première position as a structured diagnostic interview and is used routinely in both clinical and forensic evaluations. The instrument requires the examiner to cover common dissociative symptoms thoroughly and provides for a follow-up for each question, which often can lead to examples of the disorder emerging within the interview. It yields scores along five dimensions of dissociation, including amnesia, depersonalization, derealization, identity confusion, and identity alteration. It is available through the American Psychiatric Press at <www.appi.org>.

38.4.1.3 III. Ongoing Screening Instruments

A. *Dimensions of Clinical Movement Instrument* (DTMI) represents the results of reflections by Kluft on the characteristics of patients who progress through treatment along three "trajectories." While the DTMI has not received the research attention it deserves, the degree to which its components (the "dimensions") approximate the variables found to reflect differing levels of resilience and the fact that the research subjects whose data served to create the DTMI, all suggest that it may be a very helpful way for clinicians to consider treatment planning decisions. It is available without cost by searching for Kluft's two 1994 publications at the following website: <scholarsbank.uoregon.edu/dspace/handle/1794/1129>.

B. *Structured Inventory of Malingered Symptomatology* (SIMS): Kenneth Pope (<www.kspope.com/assess/malinger.php>) reports the following studies/results dealing with the SIMS:

1. "Detection of Feigned Psychosis with the Structured Inventory of Malingered Symptomatology (SIMS): A Study of Coached and Uncoached Simulators" by Jelicic, Hessels, & Merckelbach. Journal of Psychopathology and Behavioral Assessment March, 2006, vol. 28, #1, pages 19–22.

   Summary: Administered the SIMS and filler questionnaires to 60 undergraduates, asking some to complete the questionnaire honestly and others to fake psychosis as if they were standing trial facing a serious charge. "Before they completed the SIMS, instructed malingerers either received no further information (naïve malingerers; n = 15), some information about psychotic symptoms (informed malingerers; n = 15), or some information about psychosis and a warning not to exaggerate symptoms (coached malingerers; n = 15). Even in the group of coached malingerers, the SIMS had acceptable sensitivity and specificity rates."

2. "Diagnostic accuracy of the Structured Inventory of Malingered Symptomatology (SIMS) in detecting instructed malingering" by Harold Merckelbach & Glenn Smith. Archives of Clinical Neuropsychology, March, 2003, 18, pages 145–152.

   Summary: Examined the Dutch translation of the Structured Inventory of Malingered Symptomatology, finding "that undergraduate students instructed to simulate pathology display higher SIMS scores than either normal controls or psychiatric inpatients. Data pooled over several samples (n = 298) yielded sensitivity, specificity, and positive predictive power (PPP) rates that were all relatively high (> 0.90)."

3. "Screening for feigned psychiatric symptoms in a forensic sample by using the MMPI-2 and the Structured Inventory of Malingered Symptomatology" by Jason Lewis, Andrew Simcox, & David Berry. Psychological Assessment, June, 2002, pages 170–176.

   Summary: Report results of administering the Structured Interview of Reported Symptoms (SIRS), the Minnesota Multiphasic Personality Inventory-2 (MMPI-2), and the Structured Inventory of Malingered Symptomatology (SIMS) to 55 men in the midst of pretrial forensic assessments for criminal responsibility or competence to stand trial. "On the basis of results from the SIRS, 31 were classified as honest responders and 24 as feigning. Significant differences between the 2 groups were found on all SIMS scales as well as on all tested MMPI-2 fake bad validity scales. The SIMS total score and the MMPI-2 Backpage Infrequency (Fb) scale had relatively high negative predictive power (100% and 92%, respectively)." The SIMS is available at <www.parinc.com>.

C. *Structured Interview of Reported Symptoms* (SIRS): In addition to the Lewis et al. study, Dr. Pope Reports the following study using the SIRS: "What Tests Are Acceptable for Use in Forensic Evaluations? A Survey of Experts" by Stephen Lally. Professional Psychology: Research & Practice, October, 2003, vol. 34, #5, pages 491–498.

Summary: Surveyed diplomates in forensic psychology "regarding both the frequency with which they use and their opinions about the acceptability of a variety of psychological tests in 6 areas of forensic practice. The 6 areas were mental state at the offense, risk for violence, risk for sexual violence, competency to stand trial, competency to waive Miranda rights, and malingering." In regard to the forensic assessment of malingering, "the majority of the respondents rated as acceptable the Structured Interview of Reported Symptoms (SIRS), Test of Memory Malingering, Validity Indicator Profile, Rey Fifteen Item Visual Memory Test, MMPI-2, PAI, WAIS-III, and Halstead-Reitan. The SIRS and the MMPI-2 were recommended by the majority. The psychologists were divided between acceptable and unacceptable about using either version of the MCMI (II or III). They were also divided between acceptable and no opinion, for the WASI, KBIT, Luria-Nebraska, and Stanford-Binet-Revised. The diplomates viewed as unacceptable for evaluating malingering the Rorschach, 16PF, projective drawings, sentence completion, and TAT. The majority gave no opinion on the acceptability of the Malingering Probability Scale, M-Test, Victoria Symptom Validity Test, and Portland Digit Recognition Test." For the test materials and manual, see Rogers (1997).

38.4.1.4 IV. Enriching Assessment Instruments

A. *Minnesota Multiphasic Personality Inventory–2* (MMPI-2) is one of the most well-established psychological assessment instruments. It has many uses and has been the subject of a huge number of research studies. However, despite many attempts to apply it to dissociative disorders, it has not been found to be particularly helpful. The MMPI-2 is available through <www.pearsonassessments.com/tests/mmpi_2.htm>.

B. *Rorschach Inkblot Test:* Brand et al. (1996) have published the most recent article concerning their research on the use of the Rorschach with DID patients.

C. *Thematic Apperception Test* (TAT): Brand et al. (2006) also report on the use of the TAT to achieve greater insight into themes characterizing DID patients.

D. *Wechsler Adult Intelligence Scale* – 4th Edition (WAIS – IV): Brand et al. (2006) provide a helpful discussion of the role of intelligence testing in understanding cognitive functioning and impairments in DID patients.

REFERENCES

Allen, J. (1998). Of resilience, vulnerability and a woman who never lived. *Child & Adolescent Psychiatric Clinics of North America, 7(1).* Philadelphia: W. B. Saunders.

Allison, R. (1996). Essence memory: a preliminary hypothesis. *HYPNOS, 23(1)*, 6–13.

Brand, B., Armstrong, J., & Loewenstein, R. (2006). Psychological assessment of patients with dissociative identity disorder. *Psychiatric Clinics of North America, 29(1)*, 145–168.

Briere, J. (2002). *Multiscale Dissociation Inventory*. Odessa, FL: Psychological Assessment Resources.

Carlson, E., & Putnam, F. (1993). An update on the Dissociative Experiences Scale. *Dissociation, 6,* 16–27.

Chu, J. et al. (2005). *Guidelines for treating dissociative identity disorder in adults*. Northbrook, IL: International Society for the Study of Dissociation.

Crowell, J., & Treboux, D. (1995). A review of adult attachment measures: implications for theory and research. *Social Development, 4,* 294–327.

Dalenberg, C. (2000). *Countertransference and the treatment of trauma*. Washington, DC: American Psychological Association Press.

Daubert v. Merrill Dow Pharmaceuticals, Inc., 509 U. S. 579, 595 (1993).

Dell, P. (2006). The Multidimensional Inventory of Dissociation (MID): a comprehensive measure of pathological dissociation. *Journal of Trauma & Dissociation, 7(2),* 77–106.

Dell, P. (2006). A new model of dissociative identity disorder. *Psychiatric Clinics of North America, 29(1),* 1–26.

Draijer, N., & Boon, S. (1987). Validity of Dissociative Experiences Scale vs. Structured Clinical Interview for DSM-III-R Dissociative Disorders, differential diagnosis, psychiatric patients with vs. without dissociative disorders. *Dissociation, 6,* 432–458.

Frankel, A. S., & Dalenberg, C. (2006). The forensic evaluation of dissociation and persons diagnosed with dissociative identity disorder: searching for convergence. *Psychiatric Clinics of North America, 29(1),* 169–184.

Frankel, A. S., & Fridley, D. (2001) A cognitive and interpersonal approach to the treatment of DID and intercurrent Axis II disorders: a roadmap for clinicians. The 18th Annual Fall Conference of the International Society for the Study of Dissociation, New Orleans.

Frye v. United States, 293 F. 1013, 1014 (D. C. Circuit 1923).

Greenberg, S., & Shuman, D. (1997). Irreconcilable differences between therapeutic and forensic roles. *Professional Psychology, Research & Practice, 28(1),* 50–57.

Greenberg, S., Shuman, D., & Meyer, R. (2004). Unmasking forensic diagnosis. *International Journal of Law & Psychiatry, 1,* 1–15.

Gudjonsson, C. (1984). A new scale of interrogative suggestibility. *Personality and Individual Differences, 5,* 303–314.

Kluft, R. (1994a). Treatment trajectories in multiple personality disorder. *Dissociation, 7,* 63–76.

Kluft, R. P. (1994b). Clinical observations on the use of the CSDS dimensions of therapeutic movement instrument (DTMI). *Dissociation, 7(4),* 272–283.

Kumho Tire Company, Ltd., v. Patrick Carmichael (526 U. S. 137; 1999).

Liotti, G. (2004). Trauma, dissociation & disorganized attachment three strands of a single braid. *Psychotherapy: Theory, Research, Practice, Training, 41(4),* 472–486.

Loewenstein, R. (1991). An office mental status examination for complex chronic dissociative symptoms and multiple personality disorder. *Psychiatric Clinics of North America, 13,* 567–605.

Lyons-Ruth, K. (2003). Dissociation and the parent-infant dialogue: a longitudinal perspective from attachment research. *Journal of the American Psychoanalytic Association, 3,* 883–911.

Main, M., & Goldwyn, R. (1998). *Adult attachment classification system.* Unpublished manuscript. University of California: Berkeley, CA.

Masten, A. (2001). Ordinary magic: resilience processes in development. *American Psychologist, 56(3),* 227–238.

Millon, T. (1987) *Manual for the MCMI-II*, 2nd ed. Minneapolis: National Computer Systems.

Nijenhuis, E., Spinhoven, P., van Dyck, R., et al. (1996). The development and psychometric characteristics of the Somatoform Dissociation Questionnaire (SDQ-20). *Journal of Nervous and Mental Disease, 184,* 688–694.

Ogden, P., Pain, C., & Fisher, J. (2006). A sensorimotor approach to the treatment of dissociation. *Psychiatric Clinics of North America, 29,* 263–279.

Rogers, R. (Ed.) (1997). *Clinical assessment of malingering and deception*, 2nd ed. New York: Guilford Press.

Ross, C., Heber, S., & Anderson L. (1989). The Dissociative Disorders Interview Schedule. *American Journal of Psychiatry, 147,* 1698–1699.

Scheflin, A., & Brown, D. (1999). The false litigant syndrome: "nobody would say that unless it was the truth." *Journal of Psychiatry and Law, 27,* 649–705.

Shuman, D., Greenberg, S., Heilbrun, K., & Foote, W. (1998). An immodest proposal: should treating mental health professionals be barred from testifying about their patients? *Behavioral Sciences & the Law, 16,* 509–523.

Solomon, J., & George, C. (Eds.) (1999). *Attachment disorganization.* New York: Guilford Press.

Spiegel, H., & Spiegel, D. (2004). *Trance & treatment: clinical uses of hypnosis*, 2nd ed. Washington, DC: American Psychiatric Press.

Steinberg, M. (1995). *Handbook for the assessment of dissociation.* Washington, DC: American Psychiatric Press.

Thomas, A. (2001). Factitious and malingered dissociative identity disorder. *Journal of Trauma & Dissociation, 2,* 59–77.

Waller, N., Putnam, F., & Carlson, E. (1996). Types of dissociation and dissociative types: a taxonomic analysis of dissociative experiences. *Psychological Methods, 1,* 300–321.

Welburn, K., Fraser, G., Jordan, S., et al. (2003). Discriminating dissociative identity disorder from schizophrenia and feigned dissociation on psychological tests and structured interviews. *Journal of Trauma & Dissociation, 4,* 109–130.

39 True Drama or True Trauma? Forensic Trauma Assessment and the Challenge of Detecting Malingering

Laura S. Brown

OUTLINE

39.1 ASSESSING MALINGERING IN THE TRAUMA CONTEXT: THE NATURE OF THE CHALLENGE

Formal psychological assessment of persons with posttraumatic sequelæ occurs in three very different contexts: research, clinical, and forensic. In research settings, the goal of formal assessment is informed by the needs of the researchers. The possibility of malingering is rarely considered. The trauma assessment literature (e.g., Carlson, 1997, Briere, 2004) suggests that the primary goals of such research settings are refinement of an instrument's reliability and validity and enhancement of the instrument's other psychometric properties. There is frequently no question of whether the individuals being assessed have experienced an identifiable trauma; the secondary gain for the test-taker is assumed to be small.

Clinical assessment of posttraumatic sequelæ is somewhat less common than research assessments. Like researchers, clinicians rarely worry about malingering; testing is utilized to assist with diagnosis and treatment planning.

The third setting in which a trauma survivor may encounter formal psychological assessment is the forensic arena. Assessment of posttraumatic states routinely occurs in several common legal situations: personal injury cases, employment law cases, and criminal cases. In criminal cases, the defendant's trauma history may be central to defense strategy or post-sentencing determination. In any forensic setting, malingering is an ever-present concern. With money or freedom on the line, the stakes are high for the test-taker; the potential for secondary gain is magnified.

If malingering is always of concern to forensic psychological evaluators (see Rogers, 1997, for a complete discussion of these issues), why pay *special* attention to the question of malingering in trauma survivors (or in dissociative trauma survivors)? The answer to this question is both simple and complex. The simple answer is that forensic subjects frequently allege a history of trauma. In fact, in personal injury cases, trauma is often the immediate catalyst for the plaintiff's entry into the legal system. Persons with a history of childhood trauma are likely to be classic "eggshell plaintiffs," more than usually affected by an allegedly tortious action.

Despite its nearly ubiquitous presence in research, clinical, and forensic settings, traumatic sequelæ have rarely been taken into account in the development of psychological tests. Trauma has also rarely been a focus of the education or training of mental health professionals. For all of these reasons, it behooves us, in the spirit of practicing within our competency, to deepen our understanding of how trauma and the issue of malingering intersect in the forensic assessment process.

The complex answer (to the question of why pay special attention to the issue of malingering in trauma survivors) forms the basis for this chapter. Psychological trauma has been, and continues to be, a very controversial issue in some segments of the mental health field. It is a complicated topic that evokes powerful countertransferential responses from individual practitioners and from the mental health field as a whole. Posttraumatic dissociation has been even more controversial in some sectors; some scientists have spent their careers attempting to disprove the very existence of dissociative pathology (e.g., Spanos, 1997). As Herman (1992) has noted, the mental health disciplines have a lengthy history of ambivalence about trauma and its effects on human beings. Posttraumatic stress disorder (PTSD), the dissociative disorders, and other trauma-related disorders have been treated with suspicion and even hostility ever since "railway spine" was delineated to describe the victims of railroad disasters. Railway spine and other earlier diagnostic ancestors of PTSD (e.g., shell shock, hysteria) carry with them the not-always-faint whiff of disapproval. The shell-shocked were often considered to be cowards who were avoiding the battlefield. Hysterics were considered to be symptom-exaggerators who were not credible. Skeptics of DID insist that DID is an iatrogenic product of bad therapy. Victims of interpersonal violence, particularly gendered violence such as sexual assault and domestic abuse, were frequently believed to have brought the trauma on themselves. Thus, even when believed by legal or mental health authorities, they were considered to be culpable for the assaults that they endured.

Nearly 4 decades of research on trauma and dissociation have made a dent in these pejorative attitudes. But *only* a dent. Mental health training programs (e.g., psychiatry residencies, psychology doctoral programs, social work training programs) still provide little training in trauma and dissociation. This circumstance has fostered a pervasive lack of knowledge about trauma, which has also allowed erroneous ideas to flourish, such as the belief that serious reactions to trauma are uncommon. This misapprehension too often leads mental health professionals to believe that their patients' posttraumatic reactions are exaggerated. In the forensic arena, these misapprehensions are especially problematic. The normative suspicion that forensic examiners must bring to their practice is, I believe, invariably heightened by allegations of trauma—even when no one disputes that the trauma actually occurred.

39.1.1 Case Example

An individual who had practiced a physically risky occupation well and with honor for many years was accidentally injured on the job. No one disputed that the injury occurred, nor that it was life-threatening (as medical records verified). His experience met the definition of a Criterion A trauma as defined by the *DSM-IV-TR* (American Psychiatric Association, 2000). He experienced peritraumatic dissociation during the traumatic injury. The injury changed his physical and emotional capacities to perform his occupation, and undermined his well-developed adult identity in all spheres.

Yet, when he pursued compensation for the injuries and for the many losses attendant upon them, a tone of disbelief began to creep into professionals' descriptions of the experience. Blame for the injury began to be sought in the attitudes and motives of the injured person. His symptoms, which fell well within the biopsychosocial norms for persons who have experienced a DSM-IV Criterion A traumatic event, were woven into a forensic narrative of exaggeration and malingering. The subtext of this narrative was doubt that this person could possibly be so harmed.

To support the idea that his evinced degree of harm was exaggerated or malingered, the forensic narrative distorted the facts of his life prior to the trauma. It was as if the evaluator's suspicion about the posttraumatic compensation claim required that similar suspicion be cast on everything that was previously undisputed about the claimant's premorbid functioning. One of my earliest trauma survivor clients cried out to me in frustration after yet another evaluation in which she was alleged to have a long-standing characterological disorder, "I did so have a happy childhood!" Her trauma, service in the military during the Vietnam war, was well-documented and undisputed (Brown, 1986); nonetheless, her PTSD symptoms were for many years construed by VA evaluators as evidence of some underlying, undisclosed (and, in this instance, nonexistent) childhood trauma (an experience chillingly foreshadowing the current tendency to diagnose veterans of Iraq war service as suffering from personality disorders rather than PTSD).

Thus, the complex answer to "Why this chapter?" includes an intent to challenge some of these biases about trauma and dissociation. More generally, the purpose of this chapter is to discuss forensic evaluation strategies that both honor the reality of posttraumatic response and thoroughly assess the possibility of malingered responses—an approach that holds firmly in consciousness the view that this is rarely an "either-or" process. Instead, it is frequently a "both-and" process. A trauma survivor may malinger; a malingerer may have a history of trauma. What follows is not based on formal empirical research; it is heuristic and hypothetical in nature. The views expressed in this chapter reflect the author's experiences over a 25-year span as a forensic evaluator in close to 1000 cases where trauma was a central component of the legal process. This chapter also is enriched by my discussions with other trauma experts who work in forensic settings.

39.2 SIMILARITIES BETWEEN PRESENTATIONS OF TRAUMA AND MALINGERING

The malingering patient consciously and intentionally fabricates and/or exaggerates the nature and/or severity of symptoms (Rogers, 1997). This behavior is generally seen as motivated, consciously or otherwise, by secondary gains in the form of sympathy, attention, compensation, or being excused from responsibility. The malingering patient works hard to convince an evaluator of two things. First, the patient wishes the professional to believe that his or her reported symptoms are quite real. Thus, the patient may offer unusual or gratuitous information to the professional in an effort to provide a convincing picture of terrible distress.

Additionally, and particularly in the forensic arena, the malingerer's presentation will be marked by the message that these symptoms are quite intense and that they impair the person's functioning to an unusually severe degree. Superlatives such as "never" and "always" frequently pepper the discourse. When challenged, the malingering patient may feel insulted and state or imply that the evaluating professional is lacking in respect or empathy. Not surprisingly, these patients have their lives well-organized around the malingered presentation of distress. Their relationships with others are often predicated on others' willingness to endorse and validate the malingerer's claim of inability to work, inability to perform routine activities of daily living, or inability to remember his or her criminal activities.

The behavior of trauma survivors during assessment is often hauntingly similar to that of malingerers, but the motivational dynamics that drive that behavior are different. Being disbelieved is a common experience for many trauma survivors. Professional helpers and personal friends alike may explicitly or implicitly convey the message, "It wasn't that bad, was it?" or "You just need to put this out of your mind and you'll feel much better." The biopsychosocial realities of trauma, however, respond poorly to such clichés. Trauma exposure affects the brain; chronic trauma exposure affects both the structure and function of the brain and its stress response system. Although trauma is rarely put out of mind, either metaphorically or physically, many trauma survivors attempt to avoid posttraumatic memories and feelings via problematic coping strategies such as dissociation, substance abuse, and chronically self-injurious or suicidal behaviors.

Posttrauma responses are inherently unusual and dramatic. The reexperiencing symptoms (e.g., nightmares and flashbacks of the trauma) are florid. At times, their intensity may even seem to be exaggerated, a reflection of the exaggerated realities of trauma exposure. Dissociative symptoms are a common occurrence both during and after trauma. A "normal" response to severe trauma may include (1) feeling as if one had died; (2) feeling as if one were watching oneself as if in a movie; (3) hearing, seeing, and sometimes smelling or feeling frightening or disgusting events that occurred during the course of the trauma; and (4) dreams of mutilation and dismemberment. Posttraumatic dissociative symptoms may seem even more bizarre and dramatic, particularly those that entail frank identity disturbance, fugue states, and severe posttraumatic amnesias.

Many traumata are not public events. Sexual assault, domestic violence, workplace harassment, and other interpersonal traumata occur in private and in secrecy; such events often lead to questions about the victim's credibility. Consequently, in this author's experience, it is not uncommon for *these* survivors to unconsciously utilize the presence and severity of their symptoms as a strategy for proving that they truly experienced an event that no one aside from its perpetrator has witnessed. This dynamic has the "look and feel" of malingering; those in the presence of this dynamic may, in this author's experience, find themselves feeling as if the trauma survivor were attempting to control the shared reality so as to insure that no one would deny that something bad actually happened. At the same time, however, trauma survivors are frequently ashamed of what happened to them and/or of the symptoms that have arisen in the wake of the trauma. Thus, the trauma survivor may present to evaluation with a confusing mixture of apparently exaggerated symptoms and a conscious desire to minimize.

These dynamics and contradictory behaviors complicate a fundamental issue during assessment: Is it drama (i.e., malingering) or trauma? That is, the inner experience of the client that wishes to impress the evaluator with the veracity of symptoms, the claims of intense and unusual symptoms, and the presentation of extreme subjective distress can all be quite similar. The typical cautious evaluator will use formal psychometric instruments to confirm or refute clinical impressions. With trauma survivors, however, standardized assessment instruments such as the Minnesota Multiphasic Personality Inventory-2 (MMPI-2) may initially only muddy the waters.

39.3 PSYCHOLOGICAL TESTING AND THE TRAUMA RESPONSE: NOT IN THE COOKBOOK

The usual strategies for detecting malingering with standardized tests such as the MMPI-2 or Personality Assessment Inventory (PAI) may be problematic when the client presents with a history of trauma exposure. This problem is especially great if the MMPI-2 is used as the sole or primary source of test data. The MMPI-2 was not developed to take posttraumatic symptom pictures into account. This circumstance frequently (almost routinely in the past) has led to erroneous interpretations of the MMPI-2 profiles of persons who have serious posttraumatic symptoms. For example, an elevated Infrequency Scale (F), one of the benchmarks of suspicion for exaggeration or malingering, is common in the MMPI-2 profiles of trauma-exposed clients in clinical settings (Briere, 2004). Another benchmark of suspicion for exaggeration or malingering is the simultaneous elevation (above T = 65) of many MMPI-2 scales (Rogers, 1997). Research indicates, however, that simultaneous elevation of many scales is common in the MMPI-2 profiles of symptomatic trauma survivors (Briere, 2004).

A quick look at the nature of posttraumatic distress explains why trauma survivors often present in this way on the MMPI-2. The Infrequency Scale (F) and related scales, such as Back F Scale (F_b)[1] and Infrequency-Psychopathology Scale (F_p)[2] were constructed in order to assess the *number* of unusual symptoms that were endorsed. The reasoning behind these infrequency scales is that only exaggerators will endorse a large number of uncommon symptoms. In seriously symptomatic trauma survivors, however, symptoms that are unusual and even bizarre are routine. In these patients, elevated infrequency scales reflect their high levels of posttraumatic distress, rather than exaggeration. Even persons in the early stages of PTSD (i.e., those with Acute Stress Disorder) have very high levels of subjective distress and attendant high levels of unusual symptomatology. Much of the elevation of MMPI-2 scales is due to Criterion B reexperiencing symptoms and/or dissociative symptoms. Patients with reexperiencing symptoms and dissociative symptoms are genuinely plagued by a wide range of florid and dramatic symptoms, many of which (according to MMPI-2) are unusual and infrequent.

In this author's experience, the degree of elevation of the F Scale can indicate the chronicity of symptoms and the degree to which a client has habituated to distress. From this perspective, the degree of elevation of the F Scale is a sort of metaprocess indicator; that is, the F Scale reflects how much the symptoms are causing distress, and to what degree the client has developed coping strategies that effectively reduce reexperiencing symptoms and dissociative symptoms. For instance, if a client with long-standing PTSD and/or dissociative symptoms has learned to employ a variety of numbing strategies, the F Scale might be less elevated than it would be for a person who is still very frightened by symptoms and has yet to find a way to contain them. Ironically, in many forensic cases the trauma is relatively more recent, and numbing strategies have not yet been deployed. Or, the intrusive recollection of the trauma is very recent and old dissociative coping strategies are disintegrating in the face of environmental triggers or the psychotherapeutic process. Finally, the stress of the legal process, whether civil or criminal, should not be underestimated. Trauma survivors are particularly susceptible to the toxic aspects of the forensic arena. Accordingly, forensic evaluation of trauma survivors is likely to find them to be more floridly symptomatic and more subjectively distressed by the presence of the symptoms. Accordingly, their F Scales are likely to be more elevated during forensic evaluation

[1] Similar to the standard F Scale except that the items are restricted to the last half of the test. To test for lagging attention to test items and lapsing into random responding.

[2] Designed to detect malingered responses in clinical populations whose genuinely high level of psychopathology would reasonably lead to elevations on standard validity scales. To distinguish between exaggerated and accurate reports of psychopathology.

than they would be if the same clients were just being seen in clinical practice.

Severe posttraumatic symptoms can also mimic the copresence of multiple other diagnoses. Criterion B reexperiencing symptoms may resemble psychosis (e.g., dissociative flashbacks and other dissociative intrusive symptoms that mimic Schneiderian first-rank symptoms). Criterion C numbing and avoidance symptoms may mimic depression. Criterion D hyperarousal symptoms may be mistaken for other anxiety disorders. A person with PTSD is also likely to have a comorbid substance abuse diagnosis, interpersonal and vocational problems, and suicidality—symptoms that pertain to Cluster B personality disorders. Symptomatic posttraumatic clients may present so many intense symptoms that they may produce a test profile of questionable validity on the MMPI-2. Thus, a cookbook or actuarial approach to test interpretation will likely result in the wrong diagnosis at best (Buchanan, Mazzeo, Grzeborek, Ramos, & Fitzgerald, 1996; Rosewater, 1985a, 1985b), or, at worst, to the test being discarded as invalid and uninterpretable due to probable malingering.

Clinicians who work with trauma and dissociation are quite familiar with these phenomena because clients typically enter therapy when their numbing strategies cease to function. For example, persons who use extreme overwork as a numbing strategy will become overwhelmed with intrusive and dissociative symptoms if life events (e.g., being laid off, becoming a stay-at-home parent) prevent the overwork. In many other cases, clients will develop bizarre intrusive symptomatology if they are deprived of a numbing substance.

39.3.1 So What's an Evaluator to Do?

To paraphrase Buchanan and her coauthors, trauma assessment is a time for the evaluator to use the head instead of the formula (or perhaps, as Westen has suggested, to utilize both). In a forensic setting, however, it is unwise to use one's head without some sort of empirical foundation for that strategy. To do otherwise may lead to a Daubert challenge to testimony, an outcome devoutly not to wish for. This author, over many years of conducting forensic trauma assessments, has developed a series of decision algorithms that have helped increase confidence in the validity of the assessment process with trauma survivors. The remainder of this chapter will describe and discuss that decision tree and its accompanying rationales, with a special focus on objective psychological tests. At each point in the process the evaluator is looking for support or refutation for one of three hypotheses: (1) this is a valid posttraumatic picture; (2) this is a malingered picture; and (3) this is a combination of valid and malingered posttraumatic symptoms.

39.3.2 Validity and Posttrauma Responding

In attempting to determine whether a client is malingering on psychological testing, evaluators routinely look to F, F_b, and F_p Scales on the MMPI-2, or the Negative Impression Scale (NIM) on the PAI. Given that the MMPI-2 is the test of choice for almost all forensic psychologists, it will be discussed first.

On the MMPI-2, F Scale elevations above $T = 80$ are typically considered suspect, and elevations $\geq T = 90$ are considered evidence of a "fake bad" profile on the test. Friedman, Lewak, Nichols, and Webb (2001) have concluded that "the F scale was clearly the measure of choice for detecting 'faking bad'" (p. 35). Trauma survivors, however, may routinely achieve F elevations at or above $T = 90$. Research on F_b and PTSD suggests that scores in the $T = 85$ range are common for trauma survivors (Wetter, Baer, Berry, Robinson, & Sumpter, 1993).

Step 1. Accordingly, the first step of the decision process for forensic trauma assessment is to put the F Scale score aside while exploring other means of detecting malingering. With a symptomatic trauma survivor, an elevated F score simply indicates that the evaluator should deepen the strategies used to distinguish between malingering and normative posttraumatic responses.

Step 2. The evaluator must next examine scores on the F_p Scale and the F_{ptsd} Scale. Given a genuinely high level of psychopathology, F_p may elevate to $T = 100$ and still be indicative of a valid profile even when the F Scale has elevations that are solidly in the malingered range. The F_{ptsd} Scale was developed by Elhai et al. (2004) to detect possible malingering in a known trauma population of combat veterans; it has recently been renormed for use with civilian trauma populations. Because this scale was created with trauma in mind, it is highly sensitive to malingered PTSD; a score on the F_{ptsd} Scale of $T > 90$ should be considered a strong vote for a hypothesis of malingered presentation of symptoms in a trauma survivor client (Elhai et al., 2004). Although F_{ptsd} is relatively new and lacks the strong established literature that is available for the older F Scales, its specificity to the detection of malingered PTSD makes it an important component of malingering assessment in forensic trauma cases.

Like the MMPI-2, the PAI has both validity and clinical scales. It may be the test of choice when working with clients who are not members of the dominant culture; Morey's development of the PAI was exceptional in its attention to issues of culture in the wording of items and the development of norms and clinical cutoff scores. On the PAI, several scales and indices must be evaluated: NIM, RDF, and the Malingering Index. An elevated NIM Scale (Negative Impression Scale) indicates that the person is highly symptomatic. An evaluator coming to the PAI with an MMPI-2 mind-set might initially see value in interpreting extreme elevations on NIM as evidence of malingering, because the scale contains a number of face valid items that could easily be vulnerable to malingering by a person who is deliberately attempting to create an impression of severe psychopathology. However, research suggests that NIM elevations will be less probative of malingering than RDF scores. The Rogers Discriminant Function Index (RDF) has been empirically shown to be highly effective (at a comparable level of effectiveness to the MMPI-2 F Scale) in detecting directed fake-bad responses on the PAI in a nonclinical sample (Bagby, Nicholson, Bacchiochi, Ryder, & Bury, 2002). Ironically, the PAI's Malingering Index is weaker at detecting a malingered profile than the RDF.

39.3.3 Indicators of Antisocial Stance

Perhaps the analysis of the validity scales of the MMPI-2 and PAI leads to ambiguous or uncertain conclusions. Then, an evaluator should consider who malingers and why, and search for indices that would point toward the presence of cofactors. Sociopathy is one of the most likely factors to predict malingering (Roger, 1997) because the forensic situation is highly evocative for such individuals. The person who feels comfortable breaking the law or exploiting others for personal gain will likely also be comfortable exploiting a legal situation for money, freedom, or reduced sentencing. Because a history of trauma can elevate gross measures of antisocial functioning such as MMPI-2 Scale 4 (Dutton, 1991; Rosewater, 1985a, 1985b), care must be taken when one assigns meaning to scale elevations that appear to identify antisocial dynamics in a client alleging trauma. This author's decision process looks, rather, at Harris-Lingoes subscale elevations as richer sources of data about the potential to malinger test responses.

Several of the Harris-Lingoes subscales give clues to the interpersonal stance of an exploitative individual who may feel comfortable manipulating the evaluation process. Elevations on Pd3[lsbl] and MA3 (both imperturbability) suggest a self-centered, interpersonally insensitive stance, as does a very low score on Hy2 (need for affection); taken together, these three subscales paint a picture of a person who lacks concern about social disapproval and who is at home using others to more easily achieve desired goals or to avoid unpleasant outcomes. Elevations on Ma1 (amorality), as well as on several MMPI-2 content scales (e.g., ASP = antisocial practices; CYN = cynicism) may deepen the impression of an antisocial stance. When two or three of these scales are elevated, clients paint a sharper picture of themselves as people who are both willing and able to lie or distort.

On the PAI, the evaluator should carefully attend to elevations on the ANT Scale (antisocial) and its subscales, ANT-A (antisocial behaviors) and ANT-E (egocentricity). Using Hare's construct of psychopathy as the criterion measure, ANT and its subscales are superior to MMPI-2 Scale 4 in detecting psychopathy. PAI subscales have their own reliability and validity separate from their parent scale and may be interpreted independently even when the parent scale is not elevated; this cannot be done with MMPI-2 subscales. Additionally, if the evaluator's index of suspicion about malingering is beginning to rise, PAR-R (resentment) should be added to the analysis because the motive to malinger may be less purely antisocial and more a matter of revenge against the perceived source of the trauma.

It is important to note that the goal here is to detect the presence of a psychopathic stance, rather than to assess the person's history of antisocial behaviors *per se*. This distinction is particularly important when assessing persons with a childhood history of maltreatment and trauma. Many survivors of childhood maltreatment have an extensive history of criminality, including drug abuse, drug dealing, prostitution, and assault. In one study of the residents of a state women's correctional facility, 85% of the women admitted to a history of complex trauma (Washington State Department of Corrections, n.d.). It is very likely that persons with such histories will produce an elevated MMPI-2 Scale 4, thus requiring careful deconstruction of the meaning of this elevation via analysis of subscales.

39.4 DOES IT LOOK LIKE A DUCK? TRAUMA-CONSISTENT TEST RESPONSES ON NON-TRAUMA-SPECIFIC TESTS

Finally, one moves to the "duck test": is the profile of clinical scale scores consistent with published research on the profiles of symptomatic trauma survivors? Data exist on MMPI-2 profiles of several specific trauma survivor populations. A person who is malingering PTSD is more likely to know how to exaggerate symptoms in general, but much less likely to know how to construct a profile that reflects these research findings.

While Briere (2004) notes that combat trauma survivors frequently obtain 2/8 or 8/2 profiles, this information needs to be supplemented when the trauma alleged is interpersonal in nature. Rosewater (1985a, 1985b) and Dutton (1992) have each proposed common MMPI-2 profiles for battered women. The most frequent profile for recently battered women resembles a "V," with elevations on Scales 4 and 6 and a markedly lower score on Scale 5. Fitzgerald and Ormerod (1991) studied large numbers of sexually harassed women and reported that a 3/7 or 7/3 profile is most common in sexually harassed women who have not alleged any direct sexual or physical assault. These findings are consistent with other research on workplace harassment, which suggests that psychosomatic symptoms are the most common first-reported problems of harassed women.

Two scales were developed to measure combat PTSD on the MMPI-2, PK, and PS. While both of these scales do an adequate job of detecting combat-related PTSD, with an emphasis on the report of Criterion B reexperiencing symptoms, they are less sensitive to the presence of noncombat trauma. PK or PS scores lower than T = 80 may suggest general distress, but not PTSD. Conversely, very high elevations on this scale in the presence of allegations of civilian trauma exposure are likely to reflect the presence of PTSD, rather than exaggeration.

The PAI has one trauma-specific scale, ARD-T (Morey, 1996). Because of the very high rates of interpersonal trauma in the history of clinical populations, the average score on this scale is T = 64. Thus, as with PK and PS, only T scores above 75 can be considered to be a meaningful indication of posttraumatic functional impairment. An ARD-T score as high as T = 90 can be interpreted as a valid indicator of severe PTSD.

A thoughtful analysis of the nature of posttraumatic symptoms will suggest other factors to examine on objective tests. These include:

- *Indicators of dissociation.* Leavitt (2001) found that the mean MMPI-2 Scale 1 score for a group of patients previously diagnosed with a dissociative disorder was T > 80. Dissociative phenomena such as flashbacks can also lead to elevations on MMPI-2 subscale SC6 (bizarre sensory experiences). Many of the symptoms leading to this elevation will be those of somatoform dissociation, which is not well known to be a posttraumatic symptom outside of the community of dissociation professionals. As a consequence, when trauma is alleged, a test profile that includes posttraumatic somatoform symptoms is less likely to be produced by a malingerer and more likely to reflect the presence of genuine posttraumatic symptoms. On the PAI, persons with dissociative pathology may have extremely high scores on BOR-I, which measures identity confusion.
- *Reports of intrusive experiences.* Intrusive experiences are commonly indicated by elevations on Sc6, but content scale BIZ, which measures disordered thinking, should be within normal limits. Still, cultural issues may play an important part in BIZ elevations. Caution should be exercised when the client endorses belief in New Age or traditional Native American spiritualities, or is involved in a Christian faith that believes in "gifts of the Holy Spirit" (e.g., speaking in tongues, demonic possession); these beliefs can elevate BIZ even in high-functioning, nontraumatized individuals. On the PAI, moderate elevations (T = 75–85) on SCZ-P, which measures Schneiderian first-rank symptoms, may be present, but SCZ-T, which measures thought disorder, should be relatively normal. The malingerer will not make the fine distinction between these two factors and may tend to elevate both.
- *Evidence of impaired coping, containment, and self-soothing skills.* On the MMPI-2, impaired coping may be reflected by (1) low scores on K, Pd3, and Ma3; (2) extremely depressed scores (e.g., T ≤ 34) on the Ego Strength scale, which has been shown to occur in survivors of domestic violence (Rosewater, 1985a, 1985b; Dutton, 1991); and (3) supplementary scale A greater than supplementary scale R, indicating failure of higher level defenses to contain affect. Swanson (2007) has recently found similar results for battered women on the PAI.
- *Evidence of Criterion C–like social withdrawal and psychic numbing.* Indicators of social withdrawal and psychic numbing may include elevations on (1) MMPI-2 scales of self or emotional alienation such as Pd5 or Sc1, (2) scales measuring social alienation or discomfort, such as Pd4, Sc2, and Scale 0, and (3) content scale TRT, which taps the capacity to believe that one can be helped by therapists or other official helpers. On the PAI, the scale NON, which measures perceived quality and presence of social support, may be elevated.

The crucial question to be asked by the evaluator is whether the pattern of test responses, even if apparently exaggerated, is consistent with the subtleties of a genuine trauma presentation. Trauma does not produce general impairment of functioning; it impairs functioning in relatively specific ways that should be apparent in the test protocols of actually traumatized individuals. A malingerer is unlikely to know about the relationship between trauma and various physical ailments, but the genuinely traumatized person will likely suffer from several physical problems, whether or not the person is aware that there is a link between, for example, irritable bowel syndrome and trauma.

39.5 TRAUMA-SPECIFIC TESTS

Finally, whenever trauma is alleged, the evaluator should utilize tests that were specifically developed to assess posttraumatic reactions. A person who appears to be malingering or exaggerating on the MMPI-2 may respond well within the norms on a trauma-specific test because its validity norms have already taken into account the potentially exaggerated phenomenology of posttraumatic symptoms.

When trauma-specific tests are used as part of a determination of malingering, the evaluator is searching for convergent validity of either (1) a picture of general exaggeration, which would favor the malingering hypothesis, or (2) a portrait of trauma in all its complexities, which would include reports of intense and unusual symptoms. The validity indicators of trauma-specific tests play a particularly important role in assessing the issue of malingering versus genuine posttraumatic symptoms.

John Briere has developed several such trauma-specific tests (see Briere, 2004, for an in-depth discussion of these measures). Each was extensively normed on large groups of trauma survivors, and contains validity as well as clinical scales. Although each of the tests assists in answering slightly different questions, all of them allow an evaluator to compare perceptions of malingering on more general objective tests with the client's performance on trauma-normed tests.

The Trauma Symptom Inventory (TSI) is a 100-item Likert format test that contains three validity scales and 10 clinical scales, three of which measure long-term dysfunctional coping strategies of the sort seen in Complex PTSD (Briere, 1995) or the Cluster B personality disorders. The TSI's validity scales can illuminate the client's performance on the validity scales of the MMPI-2 or PAI. ATR (Atypical response) scores on the TSI provide an excellent check for F and NIM scores; if the latter are elevated, but the former is not, then the testing supports a hypothesis that the F or NIM elevations are not malingered exaggerations, but rather more typical of trauma response. Invalid ATR is usually a strong support for a malingering hypothesis. Care should be taken, however, when the client presents to evaluations with a diagnosis of DID, as some of these clients may elevate ATR even when not malingering (Dell, personal communication, 2004). Briere has developed separate African American and Hispanic norms for ATR after empirical research determined a risk of false positive assignment to the invalid category for those populations, nicely dealing with a problem that has been persistently present in personality testing with North American ethnic minority clients.

Until recently, evaluators who were interested in detecting the presence of dissociative symptoms commonly utilized the Dissociative Experiences Scale (DES; Bernstein & Putnam, 1986). The DES is extremely face-valid, making it very vulnerable to malingering. Since dissociative symptoms are well-known in popular culture via films and television depictions of "multiple personalities," the evaluator wishing to detect dissociative pathology in a more subtle manner may wish to utilize the Multiscale Dissociation Inventory (MDI), also developed by Briere (2002). The MDI is significantly less face-valid than the DES and is sensitive to malingering, as the test-taker cannot know how difficult it is to achieve a dissociative disorder diagnosis on this test. Extremely high T scores on the scale measuring identity confusion must be obtained for the test to diagnose a client as having DID. As Briere notes, while dissociative pathology is very common among trauma survivors, florid dissociative disorders are not. Also normed on trauma survivors, the MDI measures different types of dissociative pathology.

Finally, recent research on trauma presentations on projective assessment instruments may be a very helpful adjunct to assessment where questions of malingering arise (Armstrong, 2002). While questions about reliability and validity of projective techniques persist, the ambiguity of these instruments reduces the ability of an individual to overtly malinger distress in a trauma-specific manner.

39.6 NARRATIVE ANALYSIS

Finally we come to the question of the nature and quality of the client's trauma narrative. Trauma survivors generally have an ambivalent relationship with their experience and their impairments. Since shame is so frequently attached to the experience of trauma, particularly when the trauma is interpersonal in nature, trauma survivors will commonly give a narrative that appears confused and somewhat inconsistent. For instance, trauma survivors may initially avoid details about their nightmares, or they may be vague and general when asked how often the nightmares occur. When pressed for clarification, however, trauma survivors usually can and will give more specific information to the evaluator. Still, the effects of shame and ambivalence will usually be present and noticeable. These effects must be taken into account if the evaluation is to be accurate to any degree (Carlson, 1997).

In contrast, malingered narratives are frequently more forthright, more detailed, and less marked by ambivalence. The malingerer may, indeed, be a trauma survivor, as actual trauma is no protection against malingering. Thus, the general information about posttraumatic symptoms may be relatively truthful, for example, that the person experiences nightmares. The emotional flavor of the malingered narrative, however, is likely to be the clue to malingering. The malingered narrative may be precise in an exaggerated manner, for example, "I have nightmares every night," and the exaggerations will be defended in the face of mild challenge, such as an attempt by the evaluator to clarify whether the use of the term "every night" is hyperbole or an exact description. A nonmalingered response is likely to be along the lines of "Well, it feels like every night, but really, well, I have a lot of nightmares. More nights than not, but not really every night." The malingerer is more likely to hold fast to the original estimation.

Similarly, the malingerer, in attempting to impress upon the evaluator the seriousness of the problem, may manufacture details that are inconsistent with research on posttraumatic symptoms. A nonmalingered narrative of nightmares will likely include themes that speak to the dynamics, but not the specifics, of the trauma, for example, "In these dreams people are chasing me, always chasing me," when the trauma in question is repeated sexual harassment. A malingered narrative will insist that the nightmares reflect, in every detail, the waking experiences of the trauma, but will not report, as will be the case for severely dissociative trauma survivors, that the nightmare continues into waking life in the form of a flashback, or persists as a frightening hypnopompic hallucination upon awakening. Rather, the malingerer will offer the nightmare narrative, but then report waking into normal, nondissociative consciousness.

Genuine trauma narratives are marked by ambivalence. They usually contain mixed estimations of future functioning, flavored by fear, hopelessness, and the "sense of a foreshortened future"—but also hope for healing. Thus, the nonmalingered narrative may sound like this: "I have a really hard time doing anything right now. Everything is incredibly hard, and I'm scared that I'm never going to get better. But I really hope I do. I'm afraid of not ever getting better." A malingerer would like you to believe that she or he is terribly damaged and will never improve. Thus, the pessimism evident in the malingered narrative is more clear and nonambivalent; the combination of hopeless fear and hopeful willingness to heal will be absent. The malingered narrative tells the evaluator, "I've just had to come to terms with the fact that I will never be better. I'm permanently scarred by this." The trauma survivor fears to hope, but struggles in most cases to do so, making valiant, albeit small, attempts to act as if life will someday resume. The malingering individual hopes to remain impaired.

39.7 CULTURAL COMPETENCE IN ASSESSMENT

Cultural factors also play a role in the client's trauma narrative. Gender, age, and ethnicity are a determining factor in how a person experiences a Criterion A event (Brown, 2008; Marsella, Friedman, Gerrity, & Scurfield, 1996; Root, 1992, 1996). White women and African American men, for instance, are more likely to develop symptoms of PTSD following a trauma exposure than are White men. Age may inform the manner in which trauma is discussed, with older adults being more reluctant to disclose the depth and severity of their symptoms or impairment, and younger adults being more able to disclose their symptoms. When assessing for malingering, the evaluator must bring skills of multicultural competence to the process, or risk false positives due to unexamined bias.

These multicultural competencies include awareness of areas where gender, culture, or other roles may lead to (1) normative underreport or (2) apparent exaggeration or overreport of symptoms. For instance, White women, and both women and men from many Hispanic and Caribbean backgrounds risk being perceived as histrionic due to their normative styles of expressing affect (Ballou & Brown, 2002; Brown & Ballou, 1992). An evaluator will need to use caution in determining whether the apparent exaggeration of symptoms during evaluation is a characteristic style or an attempt to malinger. Asking the client to discuss emotionally laden but positive life events can serve as one source of information about this quandary; clients who are simply being their usual selves will bring the same apparently exaggerated strategy to the discussion of positive life experiences.

Similarly, many members of groups that have historically been targets of discrimination experience what Root (1992) calls "insidious traumatization." One of the effects of this process, in which a person has a lifetime exposure to lower-level stressors that do not rise to the level of Criterion A, is that the cumulative effects of this exposure can lead to an apparently innocuous or simply annoying event being experienced subjectively as traumatic by a member of one of these targeted groups. Root cautions against seeing such individuals as exaggerating their current response. She suggests that a careful inquiry be conducted into their lifetime exposure to such things as witnessing or hearing about racial harassment to others, experiencing non-life-threatening slights or experiences of discrimination, or having a family history of trauma related to membership in the targeted group.

Evaluators working with members of targeted groups must also factor in the normative hypervigilance used as a successful coping strategy by many such persons. Protective hypervigilance may appear to be a paranoid stance that could raise the evaluator's index of suspicion about possible malingering or distortion. Such clients may require time and care before they will deem an evaluator to be deserving of sufficient trust to be dealt with in a nondefensive manner. Of course, this same *caveat* applies to trauma survivors as well, particularly those who have been betrayed by others. Because it is not the job of the forensic evaluator to engender trust in those being assessed, a culturally competent stance during the evaluation process requires the examiner to take into account the absence of trust when analyzing and interpreting the test results (Brown, 2008).

Although some trauma survivors are characterologically invested in retaining the role of incapable victim, most trauma survivors strive to regain their premorbid functioning and are willing to work hard in therapy. Thus, in a forensic assessment setting, the nonmalingered trauma narrative will more closely resemble that of the usual trauma survivor in therapy—confused, ambivalent, frightened, and very interested in change, healing, and wholeness, even when there is little hopefulness that any of these might occur. Conversely, the malingered narrative in a forensic setting frequently springs from the same characterological dynamics that lead to treatment resistance in the clinical setting.

39.8 CAN WE BE SURE?

Ultimately, no evaluator can ever be certain about whether a client in a forensic setting has or has not malingered symptoms. In theory, a highly sophisticated client could carefully research the subtleties of the trauma response, memorize patterns of correct responses on tests, and present a coherent, apparently valid, albeit completely false picture on both testing and interview. In practice, however, it is far more common to encounter persons who have been severely traumatized that malinger the degree of their distress because of the problematic phenomenology of trauma and the fear that, if the less-dramatic truth were to be told, that he or she will be disbelieved. The bottom line is that forensic evaluators operate in a broader cultural context in which myths about trauma are pervasive, and undetected malingering will inevitably occur.

When an evaluator uses a complex multimethod strategy to arrive at a determination of malingering, he or she is less likely to make either false positive or false negative judgments. Overreliance on one data source (e.g., an MMPI-2 F scale score) should be replaced with a thoughtful consideration of the range of factors and data sources described in this chapter. In truth, the demand characteristics of the forensic setting call for higher degrees of certainty from evaluators than are actually possible. Nevertheless, greater precision of assessment may be achieved by not attempting to know some "truth" about the client's trauma and symptoms, but rather by offering a series of hypotheses and summarizing the data from the assessment process that would support those hypotheses. When the question is one of "true trauma or true drama," this cautious, hypothesis-based approach to the questions at hand will tend to preserve the integrity of the evaluation process and will help to create a norm of more complex and nuanced strategies for answering forensic assessment questions.

REFERENCES

Armstrong, J. G. (2002). Deciphering the broken narrative of trauma: Signs of traumatic dissociation on the Rorschach. In A. Andronikof (Ed.), Rorschachiana: *Yearbook of the International Rorschach Society*. Cambridge, MA: Hogrefe & Huber.

Bagby, R. M., Nicholson, R. A., Bacciochi, J. R., Ryder, A. G., & Bury, A. S. (2002). The predictive capacity of the MMPI-2 and PAI validity scales and indexes to detect coached and uncoached feigning. *Journal of Personality Assessment, 78*.

Ballou, M., & Brown, L. S. (Eds.) (2002). *Rethinking mental health and disorder: Feminist perspectives*. New York: Guilford.

Bernstein, E. M., & Putnam, F. W. (1986). Development, reliability, and validity of a dissociation scale. *Journal of Nervous and Mental Disease, 174*, 727–735.

Briere, J. (1995). *Trauma Symptom Inventory professional manual*. Odessa, FL: Psychological Assessment Resources.

Briere, J. (2002). *Multiscale Dissociation Inventory*. Odessa, FL: Psychological Assessment Resources.

Briere, J. (2004). *Psychological assessment of adult posttraumatic states* (2nd ed.). Washington, DC: American Psychological Association.

Brown, L. S. (1986). From alienation to connection: Feminist therapy with post-traumatic stress disorder. *Women and Therapy, 5,* 13–26.

Brown, L. S. (2008). *Cultural competence in trauma therapy: Beyond the flashback.* Washington, DC: American Psychological Association.

Brown, L. S., & Ballou, M. (Eds.) (1992). *Personality and psychopathology: Feminist reappraisals.* New York: Guilford Publications.

Buchanan, N. T., Mazzeo, S. E., Grzegorek, J., Ramos, A. M., & Fitzgerald, L. F. (1996, March). Use of the computerized MMPI-2 in sexual harassment litigation: Time to use your head instead of the formula. Paper presented at the Annual Conference of the Association for Women in Psychology, Portland, OR.

Carlson, E. B. (1997). *Trauma assessments: A clinician's guide.* New York: Guilford.

Dutton, M. A. (1991). *Empowering and healing the battered woman.* New York: Springer Publishing.

Elhai, J. D., Naifeh, J. A., Zucker, I. S., Gold, S. N., Deitsch, S. E., & Frueh, B. C. (2004). Discriminating malingered from genuine civilian posttraumatic stress disorder: A validation of three MMPI-2 infrequency scales (F, F_p, F_{ptsd}). *Assessment, 11,* 139–144.

Fitzgerald, L. F., & Ormerod, A. J. (1991). Breaking the silence: The sexual harassment of women in academia and workplace. In F. Denmark & M. Paludi (Eds.), *Handbook of the psychology of women.* New York: Greenwood Press.

Friedman, A. F., Lewak, R., Nichols, D. S., & Webb, J. T. (2001). *Psychological assessment with the MMPI-2.* Mahwah, NJ: Lawrence Erlbaum Associates.

Herman, J. L. (1992). *Trauma and recovery.* New York: Basic Books.

Liljequist, L., Kinder, B. N., & Schinka, J. A. (1998). An investigation of malingering Post traumatic stress disorder on the Personality Assessment Inventory. *Journal of Personality Assessment, 71,* 322–336.

Marsella, A. J., Friedman, M. J., Gerrity, E. T., & Scurfield, R. M. (1996). *Ethnocultural aspects of post traumatic stress disorder.* Washington, DC: American Psychological Association.

Morey, L. (1996). *An interpretive guide to the Personality Assessment Inventory.* Lutz, FL: Personality Assessment Resources.

Morey, L. (1991). *The Personality Assessment Inventory professional manual.* Odessa, FL: Psychological Assessment Resources.

Rogers, R. (Ed.) (1997). *Clinical assessment of malingering and deception* (2nd ed.). New York: Guilford.

Rosewater, L. B. (1985a). Schizophrenic, borderline, or battered? In L. E. A. Walker & L. B. Rosewater (Eds.), *Handbook of feminist therapy* (pp. 215–225). New York: Springer Publishing.

Rosewater, L. S. (1985b). Feminist interpretation of traditional testing. In L. E. A. Walker & L. B. Rosewater (Eds.), *Handbook of feminist therapy* (pp. 266–273). New York: Springer Publishing.

Swanson, L. K. (2007). A profile of domestic violence: The responding of female abuse survivors on the Personality Assessment Inventory (PAI). Unpublished doctoral dissertation, Argosy University, Seattle.

Wetter, M. W., Baer, R. A., Berry, D. T. R., Robinson, L. H., & Sumpter, J. (1993). MMPI-2 profiles of motivated fakers given specific symptom information: A comparison to matched patients. *Psychological Assessment, 5,* 317–323

Part XII

Treatment of Dissociation

40 A Clinician's Understanding of Dissociation: Fragments of an Acquaintance

Richard P. Kluft, MD

Mariska Kurtz (a pseudonym chosen by the patient) was an advanced postdoctoral fellow at a prestigious university in another major city along the Boston-Washington corridor when she called to request evaluation and consultation. Thirty-six years of age, divorced, fluent in several languages, and already well-published in her demanding scientific discipline, she told me that she would only see someone a good distance from where she worked and studied due to concerns about confidentiality. Initially she had seen a prestigious psychologist and a highly regarded psychopharmacologist at her own university, but she had misgivings about the correctness of their diagnoses and treatment recommendations. We scheduled double-length consultation sessions on two successive days some weeks in the future.

Mariska's evaluation and the early course of her treatment will be our texts for an exploration of dissociative symptoms and functioning from both her perspective and my own. Although I will convey some background material to orient the reader, for the most part I will try to demonstrate, with clinical vignettes, my own interventions and thinking, and Mariska's own words (from verbatim notes and journal entries) what it is like to have, to observe, and to intervene with dissociative processes and structures.

Mariska proved to be a striking dark-haired woman, tall, athletic, ready to smile, confident, and with a strong, firm handshake. She made good eye contact, and surveyed both me and my office with evident interest and curiosity. She spoke with a minimal accent I could not place. Once she had settled down on my couch, she continued much the same, but from time to time she appeared to feel brief waves of fright, and took furtive glances both at the door and toward the lower half of my body.

I asked Mariska to review what she hoped we could accomplish in our meetings together. She told me that she had sought treatment a few months previously for depression, panic attacks, increased anxiety, disrupted sleep, and nightmares about sexual violence directed at her or some unknown female. Anticipating my question, she told me that she had never experienced any mistreatment of this sort. Her psychologist had given her the diagnoses of major depression and generalized anxiety disorder. When she did not respond to initial interventions for depression and anxiety by the psychopharmacologist, she was rediagnosed as having bipolar II disorder, ruled out borderline personality disorder, and placed on mood stabilizers. When she complained as well of migraine headaches, difficulty concentrating, a sense that some things seemed unreal to her, and occasional lapses of memory, she was sent to a neurologist who ordered additional studies and started her on an anticonvulsant for suspected partial complex seizures.

She didn't feel helped, and ruminated on what impact her condition might have on her scientific career and personal life. With frightening efficiency she had reviewed the facts in her case and searched the medical literature and the Internet. She concluded that she was not sure she had what she was said to have, but, to her irritation and dismay, was becoming increasingly concerned that she might have a condition she was sure she could not have—a dissociative disorder. Her research had made her aware of my work. She laughed as she told me, "You are miles and miles away from my life." Inwardly, I translated, "Dissociated from my real world."

Mariska offered a complicated but essentially benign account of her past. Her parents were very affluent, from successful European manufacturing and banking families, and more played than worked at their occupations. They were more invested in their frenetic social lives and avocations. She and her younger sister were raised as much by a series of *au pair* girls and nannies as by their own parents, but she always felt loved by her mother and father. In her late teens and early twenties she became caught up with what she called "jet-set trash." She said,

"And I probably was as bad as the rest of them for a while; partying, and too much wine, drugs, and sex." Although her university grades were always excellent, she frequently discontinued her coursework or transferred universities to pursue various diversions or relationships until she decided she wanted to do something with her life.

Once she became determined, she focused on cutting-edge hard science, completed her degree, and won her doctorate rapidly. She had married a fellow graduate student, a German, only to find that he was more interested in her affluence than in creating a loving marriage. They divorced after 3 years, about the same time that she completed her doctorate. Much of the most creative research in her area was being done in the United States. Wanting a fresh start, she decided to take a research position in the United States.

She had made a wonderful initial adjustment, only to find herself becoming symptomatic, upset, and in need of help. When I tried to explore what was happening in her life immediately before and during the onset of her symptoms, she said she had no idea. As she did so, she looked downward, smiled, and shook her head. I remarked that it seemed that something had occurred to her, but she assured me that her mind was blank, and appeared puzzled by my line of inquiry.

Up to this point Mariska had pretty much directed the interview, presenting her story and concerns in a controlled and rational manner. I had already seen more than enough to suspect the possibility of a dissociative disorder, and now I felt ready to become more active in my inquiries. Although I conducted a full psychiatric evaluation, I will only discuss findings relevant to dissociation.

Dissociative identity disorder (DID) and allied forms of dissociative disorder not otherwise specified (DDNOS) are psychopathologies of hiddenness (Gutheil, quoted in Kluft, 1985). DID patients average 6.8 years in the mental health care delivery system before receiving an accurate diagnosis (Putnam et al., 1986). My own studies on the natural history of DID indicate only 20% of DID patients have an overt DID adaptation on a chronic basis, and 14% of them deliberately disguise their manifestations of DID. Only 6% make their DID obvious on an ongoing basis. Eighty percent have windows of diagnosability when stressed or when triggered by some significant event, interaction, situation, or date. Therefore, 94% of DID patients show only mild or suggestive evidence of their conditions most of the time. Yet DID patients often will acknowledge that their personality systems are actively switching and/or far more active than it would appear on the surface (Loewenstein et al., 1987).

What we usually see is the "dissociative surface" (Kluft, 2005), which takes effort to appreciate and decode. Alters need not assume executive control to influence the course of events. The dissociative surface reflects covert efforts of alters "behind the scenes" to influence behaviors, attitudes, feelings, and perceptions, or demonstrate the unintended leakage of other alters' feelings, issues, or intentions into others. Such intrusions are often subjectively experienced by the alter apparently in control as "made" passive-influence phenomena, like many Schneiderian first-rank symptoms of schizophrenia (Kluft, 1987; Ross & Joshi, 1992). Potential contributions/contributors to what is seen at the dissociative surface are listed in Table 40.1, and characteristic observations creating an index of suspicion for the activities in Table 40.1 are found in Table 40.2.

What had I noticed as I listened to Mariska? There were no admissions of severe memory problems, no unexplained out-of-character behaviors or possessions, and no history of overwhelming childhood events. Yet this brilliant woman, who had listed only minor derealization and some forgetfulness as possible indices of

TABLE 40.1
The Dissociative Surface

The host, or, the "usual patient"

The semblance of the host or "usual patient"

1. Passing for the host
2. Isomorphism
3. Tag-teaming

Copresence combinations

1. Mixed presentations
   a. Cooperations
   b. Clashes
   c. Vectors
   d. Temporary blendings
2. Fluctuating presentations
3. One-plus presentations
4. Shifting one-plus presentations

Instructed behavior

Intrusions

1. Simple
2. "Up the food chain"
3. From the "third reality"

Imposed or "made" behavior

1. Simple
2. "Up the food chain"

Switching, rapid switching, and shifting

Source: From Diagnosing dissociative identity disorder, by R.P. Kluft, 2005, *Psychiatric Annals, 35*, p. 636. Copyright 2005 by SLACK Inc. Reprinted with permission.

TABLE 40.2
Typical Manifestations of Dissociative Surface Processes at Work

1. Brief amnestic moments, apparent amnesia or forgetfulness about matters under discussion or subjects of ongoing concern within the treatment, or abrupt changes in the subject of discourse.
2. Derailing of an ongoing conversation by the patient's appearing spacey, perplexed, or surprised by what is coming out of his or her mouth.
3. Transient anxiety or distress.
4. Palpable but difficult to characterize alterations in the manifestations of an alter.
5. Changes in the attitude, emotions about, and stance taken toward matters under discussion.
6. Fluttering of eyelids or rolling of the eyes (suggesting an autohypnotic process).
7. Apparent distraction by attention to internal stimuli.
8. Appearances that often suggest a "double exposure" in which one alter's characteristic appearance seems superimposed upon or rapidly oscillating with the appearance of another, or gives the impression of blending two known alters' patterns of expression.
9. Certain aspects of facial expression being discordant with other aspects, such as smiling while the face otherwise expresses fear or sorrow, or one side of the face (or the ocular region compared to the oral region) expressing one affect while the other side (or region) expresses another.

Source: From Diagnosing dissociative identity disorder, by R.P. Kluft, 2005, *Psychiatric Annals, 35*, p. 637. Copyright 2005 by SLACK Inc. Reprinted with permission.

dissociation, had come to me because she suspected she might have a dissociative disorder. Two mutually incongruous realities were at play, with no apparent awareness of their incompatibilities. In the first, she had some mild to moderate symptoms and a benign background. In the second, she acknowledged sufficient distress to research her situation, suspected she had a dissociative disorder, sought out a specialist in dissociation and trauma, and made a number of nonverbal communications to indicate fright and apprehension of harm. I assumed that Mariska, as she gave her initial history, was in a state of mind reluctant to share, and/or may even have dissociated awareness of most of the symptoms that had prompted her concerns. That notwithstanding, here is a list of the phenomena to which I was reacting:

1. Strong suggestions of endorsing alternative realities, as noted previously. She has come for an evaluation for a condition she has researched and states she knows she could not have. A scientist of her caliber can be expected to have done an adequate literature search. It suggests that she both knows and cannot allow herself to know about a wider range of dissociative phenomena that she has both experienced and found in the literature; and that the knowledge may be in one or more alters able to handle the knowledge, while it is possible that the apparently well-functioning alter in apparent executive control thus far is unable and/or unwilling and/or not allowed to retain it. The hints of two alternate realities may also reflect trance logic, the tolerance and endorsement of mutually incongruous percepts by a highly hypnotizable subject. At this point I do not know about Mariska's hypnotizability, but I do know that patients with DID are highly hypnotizable (Frischholz et al., 1992), and that indicators of high hypnotizability constitute one of the six symptom-cluster areas in Loewenstein's (1991) special mental status examination for chronic complex dissociative disorders such as DID.
2. Brief waves of fright, with glances toward the door or toward the lower half of my body. These suggest the possible impact of apprehensive personalities' concerns that they are in a dangerous place with a potentially dangerous person whom they are checking for indices of sexual arousal.
3. She appears to be unaware that she, by smiling, looking down, and shaking her head and then denying there were any thoughts in her awareness about the onset of her symptoms, is demonstrating a possible brief amnestic moment and/or an intrusion or transient switch, a prevarication, or a deliberate withholding, or is indicating she is at least somewhat ashamed of something and planning not to speak of it (Kluft, 2006b; Nathanson, 1992).
4. She has a constellation of symptoms that are not uncommon in the aftermath of trauma, yet no trauma history has been given. Often trauma returns to awareness in a piecemeal fashion, with the recovery of narrative memory as a relatively late event.
5. She has not responded to medications appropriate to the conditions she was thought to have. This suggests that she may have a different condition. This is one of the classic suggestive diagnostic cues to DID (Kluft, 1987, 1991, 2005).
6. I take note of Mariska's major lifestyle changes and many relocations. At this point they may

be related to completely different factors. Such transitions are not infrequent in DID, and will be kept in mind.

No one of these findings is pathognomonic for DID, and numerous alternative explanations are possible for every one. Taken together, however, they offer food for thought and possible entryways into considering a dissociative disorder. I chose to return to point 3 to begin my inquiry.

Dr. K: Mariska, I am still in the very early stages of getting to know you and the way you express yourself. In order to better understand you, I will often ask questions that may seem unusual.

Mariska: OK.

Dr. K: When I asked you whether you were aware of something that might have been going on for you around the time your symptoms began, you told me that you were not, but then you lowered your head with a smile, which might indicate there was something you thought of, but might for some reason have been too embarrassed to say. Sometimes our shame or our misgivings cause us to hold back something that would be very important for our recovery. I couldn't help wondering if something like that was happening for you?

Mariska: Do I really have to say everything?

Dr. K: No, your privacy belongs to you. But when things are kept out of the therapy they often undermine it. They become secrets, and if we let them stay hidden, pretty soon more and more secrets are allowed to hide out, and treatment becomes a shot in the dark.

Mariska: That's Freud, isn't it?

Dr. K: It sure is.

Mariska: OK. It's about my name. When I came to the States and got into an apartment with some other girls, I was telling my roommates one night that I was glad they were willing to call me "Mariska," because it is such an unusual name here. They told me that they all knew the name because some actress named Mariska is on TV all the time. [*falls silent*]

Dr. K: Were you curious enough to watch some program she was on?

Mariska: Yes, I was. But what a horrible show! I mean, it's a great show, but all of that violence, all of those rapes. Have you ever seen it?

Dr. K: I'll respond to that question in a little while. I'd appreciate it if you could say more about your reactions to that actress Mariska and the show she is on before I do.

Mariska: Sure. At first I was just fascinated with her. I even flattered myself that I looked a little like her. But then I started getting nervous when I watched that show. It was as if I was enjoying the show on one level, but at another I was getting more and more terrified. When the cases on the show were about little girls who had been raped or bad things like that, I began to hear screaming inside my head as if so many little girls were screaming at once. And the dreams began.

Dr. K: The dreams?

Mariska: Yes. Sometimes I would have dreams about the cases on the show. But then sometimes I was the little girl being hurt, or the actress Mariska was being hurt. And sometimes what was happening was not where it was in the show. It was in my house, from when we lived in Zurich or Berlin.

Dr. K: Those dreams sound awful. What did your therapist say?

Mariska: She said I shouldn't watch "Law and Order SVU." But I was fascinated. Especially when I learned Mariska Hargitay's character had been raped. I was impressed that she could still be so strong. I had to watch her, [*voice drops*] … and learn.

In fact, this was an inaccurate memory, but I did not appreciate that it was erroneous until the treatment was in its follow-up stage. Part of the backstory for Hargitay's character is that she was conceived when her mother was raped, not that she was raped herself. I now think that my patient's attraction to the name "Mariska" refers to her seeing her dissociated selves as the product of rapes.

Dr. K: So as you watched this strong woman live in spite of what had happened to her, you took something very meaningful from each show.

Mariska: Yes, I did. [*becomes tearful*] I don't know what I'm crying about. It makes no sense.

Dr. K: I'm sure it makes sense in a way neither one of us can appreciate at this moment in time.

Mariska: So I must be experiencing that show, and God knows what else, in several different ways at the same time. If we could become aware of them all, I would probably know what is causing all this. I wonder if I really want to.

To clarify the reader's concern about the connection of a pseudonym to an actual person, there were a series of serendipitous events that caused the actual patient under discussion to identify with the actress Mariska Hargitay and to request that she be called "Mariska" when her material was used in publications. Hence, the identification is true to the dynamics of the case, but the way Mariska came to this identification has been altered in the interests of confidentiality.

In introducing Mariska to the power of shame to both mimic and reinforce dissociation (Kluft, 2006b; Nathanson, 1992), and to be a major determinant of withholding important information, I had offered Mariska a way to understand her conscious wish to withhold material that caused her discomfort and to take a new perspective on what was withheld from her own awareness as well. She "took the ball and ran with it"; that is, she began to appreciate the importance of sharing what she had planned to hold back. Furthermore, my observations appeared to have stirred the interest of other aspects of Mariska, one of which may have intruded to make a remark of its own ("and learn"). It no longer seemed to me or to Mariska that her symptoms had developed without any appreciable antecedent. Before the session had ended, Mariska was beginning to question whether her symptoms had been triggered by exposure to events on "Law and Order SVU" that bore some resemblance to events out of her awareness. Her initially benign view of her past was being augmented by a glimpse of darker possibilities.

I chose not to react to the apparent brief intrusion or switch ("and learn") for fear of overwhelming Mariska by prematurely confronting her about having alters, and out of concern that my being that intrusive that quickly might telegraph the message, "act out having alters—that's what he's really interested in." I did not want to risk destabilizing Mariska or confusing the situation, and did want to help her attain the goals of her visits to me. Therefore, I spent some time exploring areas remote from dissociation before I returned to begin some of the more structured and dissociation-focused aspects of her evaluation.

When I returned to the assessment of possible dissociative phenomena, I asked Mariska about the experiences of autohypnosis and spontaneous trance in Loewenstein's (1991) special mental status examination for dissociative disorder patients. Among other positive findings, I learned that she easily became absorbed in a good book, a movie, or music to the point that she either failed to respond to someone calling her name, or was actually startled when her focus of attention was disrupted. DID patients are characterized as a group by high hypnotizability (Frischholz et al., 1992). Bliss (1986) believed that DID was created and maintained by the involuntary abuse of autohypnosis.

There are many good reasons not to move directly to a standard test of hypnotizability. Under some circumstances and in some jurisdictions if a person has been hypnotized they are considered tainted, or even disqualified as witnesses to their own life experiences (ASCH Committee on Hypnosis and Memory, 1995; Brown, Scheflin, & Hammond, 1998). This is because hypnosis is held to have the potential to yield inaccurate information, and because it is thought that what emerges from work with hypnosis may be "concretized"; that is, believed in with such tenacity as to make cross-examination, a crucial aspect of the American legal system, unworkable (ASCH Committee on Hypnosis and Memory, 1995; Brown et al., 1998). I had no idea whether these concerns would prove relevant, so I did not do a formal test that would involve induction into trance.

However, it is feasible to test a phenomenon that co-occurs with high hypnotizability without inducing hypnosis. The eye roll sign, part of the Hypnotic Induction Profile (Spiegel & Spiegel, most recent edition 2004), co-occurs with high hypnotizability and can be tested without inducing hypnosis. The eye roll is scored from 0 to 4 based on how much of the iris, the colored part of the eye, is visible when a patient, having looked up as if looking through the top of his or her head, is asked to let his or her eyelids flutter down and close. For a score of 0, the iris is completely visible; for a score of 4, only sclera, the white part of the eye, is visible. If half the iris is visible, and half obscured, the score is 2, etc. If a person under evaluation for these types of dissociative disorder does not have indicators of high hypnotizability, it is probable that the condition is malingered (Kluft, 1987b).

Mariska scored the maximum 4, and remarked that doing the eye roll made her feel weird. Friends had noticed her rolling her eyes, usually when she was becoming upset. "That test—It gives me shivers. Shivers I have felt many times."

Dr. K: Can you say some more about the shivers?
Mariska: No. Just shivers.
Dr. K: Under what circumstances do you get the shivers?
Mariska: Stress.
Dr. K: Stress?
Mariska: I know I am being vague. I don't know. [*sighs, then in a flatter voice*] When sh- ... when I feel disliked, scared, rejected. And ...

Dr. K: It sounds like it costs you a lot of effort to answer, and that you might be reluctant to share part of the answer.

Mariska: I don't want to say this. Freud again?

Dr. K: Yeah. Talking about this stuff can be an exercise in titrated mortification.

Mariska: Well, I can answer if I tell myself I'll never have to see you again. [*silence, then a deep sigh*] Sex.

Dr. K: Is sex connected with feeling disliked, scared, or rejected?

Mariska: I don't think so, but it's funny.

Dr. K: Funny?

Mariska: Well, I like sex. I'm uninhibited. But ... I guess I get a little scared before I get into it, and when I get into it, I am so into it I never even remember it afterwards. So [*blushes*] what I said first is what men tell me.

Dr. K: Again, so difficult to talk about. Feel free to disregard my next question. Is there anything else your lovers have said that you found funny, interesting, or surprising?

Mariska: [*laughing, making bold eye contact, and tossing her hair*] I definitely will never come back here again. They say I tell them to call me Helga.

Dr. K: Helga?

Mariska: What?

Dr. K: You had just mentioned the name, Helga.

Mariska: [*confused*] Helga? In Berlin I had a nanny named Helga. [*fearful*] Was I talking about her?

In discussing Mariska's reaction to the eye roll we unexpectedly found several intriguing phenomena: (1) doing the eye roll unsettles her; (2) the eye roll, which can be used as part of an hypnotic induction (Spiegel & Spiegel, current edition, 2004), creates sensations she associated with psychosocial stress; (3) Mariska starts by claiming to like sex, reveals she is fearful as sex nears or begins, and then states she is amnestic for uninhibited sexual encounters; (4) Mariska lapses into talking about herself in the third person, a suggestive sign of DID (Kluft, 2005), but rapidly corrects herself, suggesting that a covert switch may have occurred to an alter who experiences Mariska as object rather than as subject, and that alter is trying to conceal its emergence; (5) there are suggestions that a number of alters are listening in and reacting, including an alter whose voice and demeanor is more saucy than subdued, perhaps the mysterious Helga; (6) we may have witnessed what is called a microamnestic event (Kluft, 1985), in which Mariska does not know what has just transpired, and is upset; (7) we put aside for future reference, making sure we do not use it in a manner that suggests a line of thought for the patient, that while in Berlin, in the care of Helga, she may have witnessed and/or experienced events that bear on her pattern of response to sexual matters.

After this conversation, I diverted Mariska from topics I thought might escalate her anxiety. Then I asked Mariska to fill out a Dissociative Experiences Scale (DES; Bernstein & Putnam, 1986). The DES is the instrument that is most widely utilized to screen patients for dissociative difficulties. It is not a diagnostic test, but is useful for identifying which patients should be considered likely to have a dissociative disorder. It consists of 28 questions, and is self-administered. The person taking the test is asked to make a vertical slash along a 100 mm horizontal line to indicate "the percentage of the time" that each experience applies to that individual. In other words, each mm is interpreted as 1% of the time. Although the DES is vulnerable to both malingering and dissimulation, it is nonetheless useful for making an initial inquiry about an individual's experiences of dissociative phenomena. The DES is scored by averaging all 28 items. It is typical for persons with dissociative identity disorder and allied forms of dissociative disorder not otherwise specified to endorse all items to some extent, and to have average scores of 30 or more across all items. In clinical practice, the score of 20 is often used to trigger further evaluation for a dissociative disorder.

I do not use the currently more popular DES-II because its form (circling numbers indicating 0%, 10%, in deciles up to 100% for an 11-point Likert scale) makes it hard for patients to admit a phenomenon is present without committing themselves to 10% at a minimum. There are also other considerations, noted in passing in a following discussion.

I was shocked to find that Mariska had a score of 15, which normally would not trigger further assessment for a dissociative disorder. Then I scrutinized the test more carefully, and noticed that every single question that would trigger suspicion of DID was rated as zero, or even had a slash mark to the left of zero. Furthermore, all eight questions that constitute the taxon for pathological dissociation (Waller, Putnam, & Carlson, 1996) were "zero or less."

Finally, I appreciated what was transpiring. Looking up from the DES sheets, I saw that Mariska was scrutinizing my face intently. We were involved in an intellectual chess match. I could expect Mariska to have done her research. She told me she did not want to have a dissociative disorder. On the DES she had disavowed the very sort of behavior she had just shown me.

I hypothesized that Mariska's desire to be understood and healed was balanced by her desire to deny and cover over the possibility of having both a dissociative disorder and an unwelcome history of trauma. At some level and/ or in some alters, there was an appreciation that she may already have let the cat out of the bag, giving rise to a strong compulsion to undo the revelations and once again lay claim to the dubious citadel of denial.

Mariska was more than my intellectual equal. I could assume she had digested several articles on the DES and some of my articles on diagnosis, and would be prepared to rebut any observations I might make to the effect that she might have a dissociative disorder.

Mariska: You sure studied those papers a long time. What do they tell you about me and my problems?

Dr. K: Your average score was 15, which is probably within normal limits for a European woman.

Mariska: That's good then?

Dr. K: I'm not sure. Let's come back to it when we complete the evaluation and can understand it in the context of everything else we find. (This was wishful thinking on my part.)

Mariska: You don't want to tell me what it means? Doctor, are you trying to protect me from something? Why wouldn't you answer me directly?

Dr. K: [*squirming a bit*] I'm not sure it would be helpful. [*Mariska stares stonily; Dr. K decides that trying to be evasive would be ineffective, countertherapeutic on a relational basis, and modeling the very sort of behavior he was trying to discourage*] OK. Let's discuss what it tells us about you and your diagnosis. The DES score is invalid, but the instrument tells me you are very gifted intellectually, have a great memory, and are very conflicted about coming to grips with your situation.

Mariska: Invalid? What do you mean?

Dr. K: You have been thoughtful. You have denied every symptom associated with DID or pathological dissociation. You acknowledge every symptom that would depict you as a high hypnotizable person who can get really absorbed in something, and who can get spacey from time to time.

Mariska: So?

Dr. K: And, for overkill, some items are scored as less than zero. I call that the "Methinks thou dost protest too much" sign. Usually I see it in mental health professionals who have hit the books to create a false negative diagnosis for some reason or other. You have really done your homework.

Mariska: I beg your pardon! [*changes facial expression, giggles delightedly, then abruptly sad and shakes her head*] I heard myself do that. I even watched it happen. My God!

Dr. K: I guess in your shoes I might feel strong temptations to convince myself that this couldn't be happening to me, that nothing traumatic had ever happened to me and I could never have a dissociative disorder.

Mariska: I really don't want this. I don't need this.

In the conversation that followed, I was able to convince Mariska that she should allow a full and candid exploration of her situation with a Structured Clinical Interview for the *Diagnosis of DSM-IV Dissociative Disorders – Revised* (SCID-D-R) (Steinberg, 1994). Then she could make a more reasonable decision about whether to address her problems or leave them untreated.

The SCID-D-R is considered 90% to 95% sensitive to populations of patients with dissociative disorders, and recent research allows for its use in the identification of malingerers. False positives are rare. The SCID-D-R obtains some background information and studies five core dissociative features: amnesia, depersonalization, derealization, identity confusion, and identity alteration, each of which is scored from 1 to 4, from absent to strongly present. The possible score range is thus 5 to 20. Five would indicate no dissociative phenomena whatsoever; 8 or less is characteristic of normal populations; 12 to 13 is found in mixed groups of psychiatric patients; 16 and above are characteristic of a severe and chronic or recurrent dissociative disorder; 20 would indicate maximal scores in all five core features. The SCID-D-R also elicits phenomena associated with DID and allied forms of DDNOS. Furthermore, the format of the SCID-D-R forces the closer observation of two of nine areas of inquiry in greater depth. The interviewer selects those two areas based on which of nine particular areas of inquiry have elicited answers that are most suggestive of the presence of alter personalities. The SCID-D-R also allows for the description of the clinician's observations of dissociative phenomena, and the tentative diagnosis of a dissociative disorder.

Mariska received maximal scores in all five symptom areas, for a total score of 20, acknowledged experiencing most of the associated symptoms. She also manifested several signs of dissociative processes. Typical examples of her responses were: (1) for amnesia, she had lost blocks of time since childhood, and could not remember most of her eighth and ninth years of life, and she had been told of angry outbursts she did not recall; (2) for depersonalization, she often saw herself going through life as if she were watching a movie of herself; (3) for derealization, she often was unsure if certain people and places were real; (4) for identity confusion, she had often been conflicted as to who she really was; (5) for identity alteration, she revealed that often, in private, she found herself acting as if she were a child. Under associated features, she often was aware of inner dialogues, and sometimes found herself enacting these dialogues out loud or having written both sides of a dialogue in her journal, in different handwritings. These dialogues sometimes involved her interacting with another aspect of herself, but usually involved her overhearing conversations between or among alters. Rarely, she overheard two conversations at once. What impressed her most during the SCID-D-R was that the answers to many questions came to her from voices within her head, and that these answers indicated that her dissociative symptoms were frequent and long-standing. She was both terrified and amused by answers, which indicated that being addressed by other names had been a recurrent feature of her life, but that all such incidents other than the "Helga" episodes were completely strange and unfamiliar to her. When I compiled all the names mentioned in either the SCID-D-R or the psychiatric interview, there were nine clearly-named and one unnamed but well-characterized potential alter in addition to Mariska.

The SCID-D-R diagnosis of DID was clear. I had not needed the SCID-D-R to make the diagnosis, but making the diagnosis with a reliable and valid instrument has many clinical, scientific, and self-protective virtues. In a litigious era during which the DID diagnosis has been challenged retroactively in lawsuits, along with accusations of iatrogenesis, there is much to be said for using a state-of-the-art instrument that is widely used and widely cited in the literature.

As a clinician, however, the wealth of information about the patient's subjective experience of his or her dissociation acquired during the administration of the SCID-D-R facilitates my understanding and my capacity to empathize with the patient in those crucial early sessions during which establishing a therapeutic alliance is a paramount goal. I have been impressed over and over again that the SCID-D-R interview pulls forth information that otherwise might not emerge until much later in the treatment.

Mariska and I discussed the SCID-D-R findings in depth. She acknowledged that, because she was forthright in answering its questions, she had to accept its conclusions, however reluctantly. We reviewed issues of diagnosis and treatment. Mariska both accepted and denied the diagnosis of DID. With perfect trance logic (characteristic of the highly hypnotizable), she entertained both alternatives despite their incompatibility. Such stances are far from unusual in treating DID patients, and may persist for an extended period of time, and even be renewed after a successful integration. We reviewed the treatment resources available to her in the city where she lived. Despite the presence of several exceptional DID therapists in her locale, she requested that I take her into treatment, and made no objection to the lengthy commute.

Mariska said she preferred to see me because of confidentiality concerns. She did not want to risk encountering her therapist outside of the office, or take the chance of being seen by those she knew entering the office of someone known to have special interest in trauma or dissociative disorders. She liked the fact that my office was one of the few medical offices in my building. I thought that while this might be true, we had both felt comfortable with one another and responded well to one another's sense of humor. She knew from her reading that I had reported the successful treatment of a large series of DID patients (Kluft, 1984, 1986, 1993a) and, scientist to the core, she would follow the evidence in the literature. Years later, I would learn that she had posed as a psychologist needing to find a therapist for a patient relocating to the Philadelphia area, and had read some of my forensic testimony on cases involving therapists' sexual exploitation via Internet searches.

Mariska and I discussed the treatment ahead. We agreed to meet for a double session once weekly, aware that we might have to change that arrangement, depending on what emerged in treatment. The first therapy session was scheduled 2 weeks in the future.

This evaluation of Mariska allows us to step back and list some of the phenomena that fall under the rubric of dissociation in Table 40.3. Some items on this list were appreciated only later in the course of treatment; those already apparent are asterisked. Many items are overlapping and redundant; some that appear under different headings reflect different approaches to conceptualizing and grouping dissociative phenomena. Most of them will be discussed in other chapters of this book. At this point we need note only that the phenomena alluded to in the *DSM-IV-TR* (2000) diagnostic criteria embrace only a small fraction of the manifestations of dissociation in DID (Dell, 2006; Kluft, 1985; Loewenstein, 1991), and attention to the wider range of these manifestations facilitates the more efficacious diagnosis and treatment of this disorder.

TABLE 40.3
Categories of Dissociative Phenomena Noted in Mariska

1. Alters, also known as personalities, identities, personality states, etc.*
2. Identity confusion*
3. Amnesia*
4. Compartmentalization/modularity phenomena
   a) Alters, as above*
   b) Segregation of some subsets of information from other subsets of information in a relatively rule-bound manner (Spiegel, 1986)
   c) BASK (Braun, 1988) dimensions (ablative expressions)
5. Detachment (as in depersonalization and derealization in the perception of self and/or others* and also in concerns over whether memories are real or unreal; also seen in alters' lacking senses of ownership or responsibility for the actions of other alters)
6. Absorption*
7. Altered states of consciousness (e.g., hypnotic/autohypnotic/spontaneous trance phenomena*)
8. Failures of compartmentalization* such as intrusion phenomena, including both alters, memories, and BASK (Braun, 1988) dimensions (intrusive expressions)
9. Simultaneous operation of separate self-aware processes or states of mind,* including parallel distributed processing, elsewhere thought known phenomena (Kluft, 1995), unconscious thought (Dijksterhuis et al., 2006), inner world activities, and creativity by alters not in apparent executive control
10. Simultaneous executive activity by separate self-aware processes or states of mind (copresence phenomena [Kluft, 1984])
11. Inner world and third reality phenomena (events within that inner world that are accorded historical reality) which sometimes intrude into ongoing experiences, and/or impact ongoing experiences from behind the scenes (Kluft, 1998)
12. Switching* and shifting*
13. Multiple reality disorder (Kluft, 1991), for which dissociative identity disorder, formerly called multiple personality disorder, is the delivery and maintenance system*

*Indicates phenomena already noted and observed during the evaluation period, before the psychotherapy actually got under way.

Mariska's journal entry the evening after our consultation meetings offered her own perspective. Several handwritings were evident. Some excerpts are:

> Before I began to write tonight I looked over the last several pages. I thought that I was writing my own journal, but for the first time I see I was not alone. Why couldn't I see all those other entries? Why can I see them now? Who made them? What does it all mean?
>
> I am amazed that I agreed to see that man! I'm not sure this is a good idea. I'm not sure I like him. What did I do? I didn't! I watched myself explain why I needed to see someone far away from my university, far away from where I live. What does that mean? Did some other part of me drag me into therapy, afraid that, left to myself, I'd just push the consultation out of my mind and limp along?
>
> You all will have to speak English, or let someone else tell your story for you. I know that this is offensive to me, and to many of you. He is intelligent, but he is a typical American. When I spoke to him in French he answered quickly, but with an accent that hurts my ears. He cannot communicate as a cultured European would. If you can forgive him this, you will find that he can speak to us about emotions, about feelings—the languages which all of us have failed to master.
>
> Every time he spoke I wanted to check my buttons, to cover myself because I felt completely naked. When he explained what he thought, I felt penetrated, painfully penetrated. Yes, he knows a lot, and that's supposed to be good, but I don't like it. Knowing that much gives him power. I don't want anyone to know me that well, to have that much power over me.
>
> I only wanted the best for you. I never hurt you. Those were just dreams. Bad dreams. Don't let him convince you that I did something to you that I did not.
>
> You never listen to us. You hear our screams and you try to block us out. If you won't let us talk to him, we'll scream louder.
>
> You are not to tell him about the forbidden things. Any transgressions will be punished severely.

Mariska's journal testifies to the complexity of her moment-to-moment experience of dissociation, and demonstrates many of the phenomena I listed. However, appreciating these phenomena in terms of the confusion, helplessness, terror, and conflict that they cause Mariska helps us to understand how difficult and potentially painful it is for the dissociative patient to commit herself to treatment. Mariska did experience a degree of relief and optimism because she felt I understood her and might be able to help her. But she was too sophisticated and knowledgeable to push aside her apprehensions for long. She leapt ahead to the consequences of being understood, and did not relish confronting painful material, accepting and addressing the existence and activities of alters who might prove very different from herself, grieving her previous more benevolent view of her past and of important people in her life, inner conflicts among the alters, and dealing with a man whose ability to understand her might be used to control and exploit her.

Mariska decided, with much misgiving, to share her journal entries with me. I was glad that she did so. I did not understand this gesture as an expression of trust or motivation, although I appreciated that those dimensions might play a role. Instead, I felt that at times her journal was written in a way that allowed her to probe and anticipate my reactions to feelings and experiences that she needed to talk about, but was apprehensive about addressing directly. She put subjects forward, and then waited, scrutinizing my reactions and remarks, to see if she could take the risk of discussing certain concerns, or whether it was too dangerous to do so.

As we began, I welcomed the full discussion and exploration of every topic, every misgiving, and every apprehension. Early work in building the therapeutic alliance with a DID patient involves, among many other things, a socialization to what the treatment will be like, and attention to issues of informed consent.

We went through the journal entry and discussed every concern that had been raised, even those that Mariska could not relate to herself. As we explored each area, I invited any other parts of the mind that might have concerns or reactions to share their remarks with Mariska so she could share them with me. Later in treatment I would ask them to either pass their remarks along or to speak to me directly, but at this early stage I thought Mariska might feel either very uncomfortable or treated dismissively if I did so.

This was Mariska's first experience with my working with both the whole patient and the alter system. Encouraging all of the alters to become involved in the treatment is a way of diminishing dissociative barriers, promoting a free flow of associations and information across alters, and diminishing the alters' "not me" (Chefetz, 2006; Kluft, 1995) attitudes toward one another. It involves a number of considerations. I welcome all of the alters to participate when their participation is neither problematic nor disruptive: the principle of invitational inclusionism. Elsewhere (Kluft, 2006a), I have discussed the many rationales for engaging the alters directly. In issuing this invitation, I insist on the alters' considerateness for one another, advocating for a "golden rule" mentality. I try to undermine pressures for irresponsible autonomy, insisting that "you are all in this together" and that "everybody wins, or everybody loses." I appreciate that in treating at once the whole person and the separate alters I often am doing double bookkeeping and making double appeals. Acknowledging and working within the alters' and the patient's subjective realities allows me to help them test and correct their misperceptions and misattributions. I move quickly to address issues of shame, narcissism, and masochism, which often govern alters' understandings of their situations and roles.

Two vignettes will illustrate these efforts. In the first, as we discussed the entries that questioned Mariska's safety with me, Mariska had started by apologizing for those remarks. I had normalized her misgivings, stating that it seemed reasonable for anyone who had been mistreated, or who wondered whether they had been mistreated, to proceed with caution in entering a relationship with a person with whom there appeared to be a power differential that might be used either in her service, or against her. I then invited Mariska to pass on to me any other observations or questions she might be hearing inwardly.

Mariska: I hear a few voices, but they are all talking at once.

Dr. K: Every observation is important, but if they are all said at once nothing except Mariska's distress and confusion will come through. One at a time, please.

Mariska: But there are so many! [*stares at me*] I've noticed you used that "A journey of a thousand miles starts with a single step" line a couple times already. This would be a good time not to say it again!

Dr. K: OK. But it's worth the effort.

Mariska: OK. I hear a little voice, speaking in German, saying, "Please don't hurt me."

Dr. K: How does that voice think I might hurt her?

Mariska: She won't talk. I feel myself wanting to roll up in a little ball and rock. I feel like crying.

Dr. K: If that part doesn't feel it's safe to talk further, that's fine for now.

Mariska: She asks, "Are you going to hit me?"

Dr. K: I will not hit you.

Mariska: "Are you going to hurt me down there?" I'm sorry. That's what she said.

Dr. K: No, I won't hurt you down there. You may feel hurt down there when you are worried or when you remember something bad, but I won't hurt you down there.

Dr. K [silently to himself]: I won't ask who, if anyone, has hurt her down there. The priority is to provide a safe environment for the therapy. If I ask her prematurely, she may start to relive a trauma or to experience a body memory. I will be seen by that part or by a protector part as having needlessly inflicted pain, fulfilling the fear that I will hurt her. Furthermore, she may hear me as encouraging her to speculate, or demanding that she offer an account of an event and identify her assailant. There would be a legitimate concern that an inaccurate account might be generated to please me and/or propitiate me.

Mariska: I hear a male voice, also speaking German, telling the little girl that grownups don't do that sort of thing to little children. She must have heard something bad in school and worried about it.

Dr. K: I wonder why this man would say something like that.

Mariska: It is saying that little girls who tell lies will be beaten. It says nothing bad has ever happened to her, that she should be ashamed to speak of such things.

Dr. K: I look forward to talking with that voice and better understanding why it says what it says.

Mariska: The short version is "Fuck you!"

Dr. K: Someday, hopefully someday soon, we can have a more serious discussion. For now, anything else?

Mariska: Another male voice says, "Doctor, I'll be watching you every minute."

Dr. K: To that voice: Good for you. That sounds wise.

Mariska: It says, "You can joke with the others, but not with me."

Dr. K: I appreciate that. You are on duty, and you take your duty seriously. You are welcome here, and I look forward to talking more with you.

Mariska: It says, "We'll see." There is one more. I really don't want this to be part of me.

Dr. K: Embarrassing?

Mariska: Very. I can't. I just can't. [*becomes very distressed*]

Dr. K: Let's back away from having you speak it out loud. Can you write it down?

Mariska: I'll try. She's calling me all sorts of names. [*Dr K hands her a clipboard and pen; she writes:*] "I can handle you. It might be fun, screwing my shrink. But I don't think you can handle me. Helga." I don't believe this. [*tears up the sheet of paper*] I really don't think I can do this treatment.

Dr. K: Helga upsets you. You don't want her to be there. Her being there mortifies you.

Mariska: That's for sure.

Dr. K: I'm not sure that I'm right, but it might be that Helga came out to reassure you, to say that if I misbehave she will protect you by bearing the brunt of what you fear I might do to you, that the most vulnerable parts of you will be shielded.

Mariska: But she comes out for sex! She loves sex!

Dr. K: That "loving sex" may be defensive, too.

Mariska: What do you mean?

Dr. K: Putting one's self in harm's way is difficult. One may have to distract one's self from what is really happening by focusing on a few aspects of what is going on, and convincing one's self that it is OK. I don't want to jump to any conclusions. I don't want to judge a book by its cover.

Mariska: Two things at once. I was thinking that your sayings and clichés are already driving me nuts [*laughs*] and Helga is saying that maybe you are not as dumb as you—as she thinks you look.

In this instance of invitational inclusionism, I am making an outreach to a number of alters and they are responding, beginning to build a relationship with me. I am impressed that the voices have responded as they have, bringing their dynamics with them. My experience is that the alters and their interactions with one another and with me express and/or enact crucial dynamics and subjectively experienced historical material, and I am allowing myself to hope that Mariska's personality system and, therefore, she, will be more readily accessible than in most DID patients.

Another example regards dreams. Mariska reported this dream in an early session:

> I am taking a walk with Helga. We meet Herr G, who was my father's business partner. They step away and begin an animated discussion. I am bored and walk toward a puppy someone has on a leash. There is a sudden noise and a tornado catches me up and whirls me around. Things from our house are whirling around me. I feel so bad that all my parents have is being destroyed. I feel dizzy and sick and I hurt all over. Then the wind

begins to die down and I see I'm going to hit the ground. I can't look down. I wake up screaming, with one of my roommates telling me loudly to wake up.

Mariska's associations were limited to her puzzlement that Herr G would be walking about during business hours, and that their conversation seemed so lively. Herr G was usually rather distant with those he considered below him. She thought that she "stole that dream from the Wizard of Oz." She could make no connection between her recent experiences and the dream.

Dr. K: OK, Mariska has shared her reactions to the dream. Are there other thoughts or points of view?

Mariska: It's very faint, but a little voice says, "He's a bad man."

Dr. K: Would that voice like to say anything more?

Mariska: I feel her fear, and I hear a man's voice, "She can't say any more. The little bitch has said too much already."

Dr. K: I want to remind that second voice that we have agreed that there are to be no reprisals for what is said in therapy.

Mariska: He says his usual, "Fuck you!"

Dr. K: Anything further?

Mariska: Someone is saying that that is no dream. The first part is a memory, and the tornado part says how bad it was.

Dr. K: How bad it was?

Mariska: It says, "The part no one is allowed to remember."

Dr. K: Anything further?

Mariska: And now Helga says, "It's true that Herr G usually had nothing to say to those below him. But I was below him so many times that we developed quite a relationship." No! Doctor, Herr G was my father's business partner, his best friend. He trusted him completely. In fact, when my parents went on long overseas trips, Herr G would visit the house every day to be sure that everything was being done correctly, and to be sure that we were alright. [*suddenly looks shocked*] Helga was in charge when my parents went abroad. Oh! I'm going to be sick. [*wretches, grabs a waste basket, bends over it, wretches repeatedly for about a minute; then voice and facial expressions change*] Doctor, she cannot be allowed to know about Herr G. She idolized him. She dreamed she'd grow up to marry him or someone just like him. This would kill her.

Dr. K: Can you say some more?

Mariska: [*switches back*] What are you talking about?

Dr. K: I think you may have lost a moment there.

Mariska: Helga is saying Herr G was a pig. I don't, I can't believe that. Helga says the day residue you were looking for was another episode of *Law and Order SVU*. I'd forgotten that. I can't remember the plot now. Just that it really upset me.

By inviting contributions from many parts, the exploration of the dream is enriched and deepened. Without making intrusive inquiries, the simultaneously active and engaged parts, some of which were restricted from knowing about any trauma, and some of which were not, have given ample food for thought. I could put aside for future consideration the possibility that Herr G had taken advantage of Mariska's parents' trust in him to debauch Mariska's nanny Helga, and expose Mariska to inappropriate activities, whether vicariously or directly experienced. I would not assume this represented historical accuracy, but I would regard it as a hypothesis to explore and reassess.

These vignettes are part of the first phase of DID treatment, *Establishing the Psychotherapy*. In a definitive DID treatment, the phase or stage of *Safety* in Herman's (1992) three-stage model of trauma treatment consists of *Establishing the Therapy*, *Preliminary Interventions*, and *History Gathering and Mapping* (Kluft, 1991, 1993a, 1993b, 1999). *History Gathering and Mapping* are included under *Safety* in a definitive treatment, because it may (and usually does) prove dangerous to proceed to trauma work without appropriate intelligence about what the therapist and patient are likely to encounter. In a supportive treatment, *Safety* would not include *History Gathering and Mapping*, because there would be no intention of exploring and addressing traumata systematically and exhaustively, and because this stage's efforts might destabilize a more compromised DID patient.

The major tasks of *Establishing the Psychotherapy* are listed in Table 40.4. Mariska is an ambivalently voluntary participant, and I am pleased to be working with her. Her affluence and flexible schedule and my availability mean that there will be no impediment to beginning and sustaining the treatment. Mariska comes to her appointments and talks about relevant concerns in treatment. That is as good as it gets in the treatment of patients whose capacity to trust has either not developed adequately, or has been shattered by betrayal.

Safety considerations apply to patient and therapist alike. I found no evidence that Mariska was suicidal or

TABLE 40.4
Establishing the Psychotherapy (Kluft, 1993a)

1. Mutual Voluntary Participation
2. Pragmatic Arrangements
3. A Facsimile of Trust
4. Aspects of Safety
5. The Treatment Frame
6. The Therapeutic Alliance
7. Self-Psychological Interventions
8. Demonstration of Expertise
9. Dealing with the Diagnosis
10. Dealing with Concerned Others

self-injurious, but I remained concerned that her self-destructiveness might take the form of sexual misadventures. She had already demonstrated that she felt safe enough to try to work with me, but brought with her preformed traumatic transferences that meant that parts of her mind had to struggle with fears that I might prove to be harmful. The material about Herr G alerted me to the possibilities that she would be scanning me carefully for signs I was transforming into a predator; that she was likely to try to block out signs I was bad in order to protect the relationship; and that she was at risk for developing a false positive submissive transference (Kluft, 2000), replaying a relationship with an abuser who insisted on being treated as if he were deeply loved.

For myself, I did not think Mariska was likely to endanger me, physically or psychologically. The first expressions of sexuality and seduction as defenses had been addressed adequately, and it appeared that Helga and I had formed the beginning of an alliance based on my recognition that she was far more a protector than a sexually driven identity.

We worked to clarify the treatment frame. We agreed that in the unlikely event that I had to communicate with some third party about her, Mariska would have the opportunity to review and suggest appropriate changes in any document I might send. We agreed that unless some issue made it relevant, she would not have access to my therapy notes.

Developing the therapeutic alliance was a major objective during the early sessions. Mariska and I were both confident that we could work well together, but it rapidly emerged that each of us entertained a very different notion about what was meant by "work well together." Mariska did comply with every reasonable expectation; in addition, she shared an ongoing series of "observations" about our work that at once praised me to the skies and deprecated my perception, intelligence, empathy, commitment to Mariska and her treatment, and my choice of interventions. When I asked her to consider the implications of what she was saying, she professed to be puzzled by my concern and occasional consternation, and distressed that I was unable to hear her remarks as objective observations that reflected both her dedication to her treatment and her intellectual curiosity as a hard science researcher who was bringing her observational skills to bear on a healing art derived from the softest of sciences. Much as I had to teach her, Mariska argued that she might have a great deal to teach me.

I found myself growing increasingly exasperated with Mariska's "objective observations." I wondered if I had let Mariska's attractiveness, intelligence, and wit blind me to some deeply rooted character pathology that would make our work together a painful ordeal. I could feel bursts of humiliation and mortification, and fought to contain my strong impulses to enact shame scripts (Nathanson, 1992); I wanted to withdraw, to deny the impact of her words or distract myself with some pleasurable reverie, to join Mariska by attacking myself, or to attack Mariska.

Fortunately, even while I was distressed and somewhat distracted by Mariska's incessant disingenuous attacks, I was asking myself what projective identifications had slipped past my attention, what enactments might be in the process of becoming, and what unrecognized transference paradigms I might be responding to. Therefore, after my initial efforts to bring Mariska's behavior to her attention "went down in flames," I empathized with her frustrations with me. These efforts enraged Mariska: "You are not empathic in the slightest. Your remarks are condescending and supercilious." Mariska wondered if she had overestimated my intelligence, sensitivity, integrity, and investment in helping her.

Despite our mutual misgivings, we continued to discuss Mariska's life and relationships. In a weird but wonderful way, the negativity with which we were struggling was not derailing the treatment, only declaring it derailed—an interesting dissociation in and of itself. We were apparently switching between two competing incompatible constructs of the nature of our relational interaction.

I took some verbatim notes from the times Mariska was critical of me, and studied them with Luborsky's (Luborsky & Crits-Cristoph, 1998) *Core Conflictual Relationship Theme* (CCRT) methodology. Oversimplified episodes of interaction are studied to find the components for the model, "X wants Y from Z, but X's failings and shortcomings (or strengths), and/or Z's failings and shortcomings (or strengths) prevent X from succeeding (or allow X to succeed) in getting Y from Z."

Again oversimplifying, what I found was that Mariska's dominant CCRT formulation was approximately: Mariska wants to be safe and taken care of by a powerful and helpful man, but Mariska is unworthy and uninteresting, and the men she looks to are inattentive and incompetent. A secondary formulation was: Mariska wants to be loved by a good man, but she is dirty and makes good men do bad things, and the men she looks to prove to be exploitive and hurtful.

I inferred that two patterns of transference and enactment might be at play when Mariska got after me. In the first, I was seen as a good man who failed to protect her because my attention was elsewhere and she could not get me to direct it toward her, and/or I just did not know what to do to help her. In the second, I was seen as a man who would pretend to be helpful or start to be helpful, but would hurt Mariska, because I was a bad man who recognized her as a dirty girl who deserved my mistreatment, or because I was a good man corrupted by Mariska's filth and seductive power.

These formulations were present, but did not emerge as predominant when I studied my notes from times when I was not being attacked. I hypothesized that although Mariska was not making overt switches very often, her verbalizations reflected several underlying configurations. Could those changes reflect the impact of various alters or groups of alters on the dissociative surface? Could those alters or groups of alters reflect experiences and expectations that colored the transference/enactments at particular moments in time? Could the two CCRT patterns be describing two of the common transferences of trauma victims observed by Davies and Frawley (1994), perceiving the therapist as a perpetrator in one formulation, and as a failed protector in the other? Was Mariska telling me that she had been victimized by one man whom she had initially seen as a good person, and had not been helped by another man whom she had relied upon to protect her (or that both of these patterns were characteristic of one particular important relationship)? My associations tentatively nominated Herr G as the man she had loved who betrayed her by molesting her, and her father as the man she had loved who betrayed her by not appreciating her distress and/or taking action to protect her. I decided to keep these ideas to myself. Sharing them would have been premature, and probably seen as manipulative blame-shifting.

As we progressed, Mariska began to take notice of the way her attitudes toward me were so different, so discrepant, and that the transitions among her attitudes generally occurred rapidly, and without apparent explanation. I told her that I had noticed these changes as well, and experienced them as surprising, even jarring at times. She handed me her journal. The previous day's entry included:

> Watch out for him! Yes, he's nice. Too nice. She still gets fooled so easily. Remember the last one!
>
> But we have to trust someone!
>
> Trust!! What an illusion! First impressions are deceiving. They almost always start out nice. The men who are strong enough to be worth anything will try to screw you. The men who stay nice are useless. They can't help you. They can't even let themselves see that they should be helping you.

Dr. K: So, your expectations are conflicted about how I'll betray you, but they all concur that I will betray you, sooner or later. [*Mariska nods vigorously*] I have asked you this before, but what you just said moves me to ask it again: I know that these dynamics come from your early years, but have you ever had an experience in which a health professional or a mental health professional behaved toward you in a way you experienced, or came to believe, was inappropriate?

Mariska: [*switching as I made my last remark and speaking in a deep harsh voice*] Leave this alone, Doctor. She can't handle this.

Dr. K: We have a problem. You all are behaving in ways and promoting ways of thinking that are likely to sidetrack or even undermine our work together. For reasons that I am sure are powerful and reasonable because of experiences we have yet to talk about, you all are reacting to me as if I may prove either unable or unwilling to help you, or as if you are certain I will come after you. That makes this office a difficult place to be in. I have no problem with your entertaining such notions about me as long as they are understood to be grist for the mill of therapy, but I am getting the impression that some parts of the mind feel, even if they know they don't rationally think so, that I will do you no good, and may do you harm. We should be in a position to discuss your misgivings and understand where they come from. And try to keep this in mind: once many things were too much for you and apparently there was no help to be had. Now you may remember your helplessness then not as part of your traumatic memories, but as an accurate appraisal of your vulnerability in the here and now. Addressing myself to the part or parts that have the misgivings: without getting feedback from any others, what year do you think this is?

Mariska: This is ridiculous. I hear three answers: one is this year, one is 15 years ago, and one is around 25 to 30 years ago.

Dr. K: Making me think that betrayal and mistreatment during childhood was followed by betrayal and mistreatment during your early 20s, perhaps by someone to whom you turned for help. Naturally, you are on your guard with me. Whenever you are ready to talk with me about those things, it will be important to do so. For the sake of our work together, I hope that will be soon.

Mariska: [*with the deeper voice*] She is not ready to know this, doctor, but I see you may need to in order to help her. [*startles, tears up, and continues in her usual voice*] How could I have forgotten this? This is too embarrassing. My first therapist screwed me. I went to him to figure out why I was so out of control and promiscuous … and he screwed me. [*holds her hands to the sides of her head*] Helga says she had to come out then … This is awful. [*switches*] It's like when she tried to tell her father that Herr G was getting after her. She didn't even know the right words to use, so maybe he didn't understand what she was saying. But that's nonsense. The truth is that her father chose to believe that his good friend and business partner could not have done anything to her. He was sure she had misunderstood some affectionate gesture or must have had a crazy dream. [*Dr. K shakes his head*] After a few times she gave up trying to convince him, and just convinced herself it couldn't be happening. [*back to the usual Mariska; cries*] I guess I have always known this stuff and not known it. Parts of it never left my mind, but it seemed so unreal, so surreal, that it had to be a nightmare or fantasy. [*sighs*] I can't recall them now, but there are a lot of weird thoughts I have that I convince myself can't be true, so I don't feel right in telling them to you. I worry—What if I am wrong? Isn't it awful to say horrible things about someone that may not be true?

Dr. K: So your sense of right and wrong reinforces the notion that you can't be sure whether you are reporting an injustice to yourself or committing an injustice against someone else. You wind up thinking that what you hold in your mind should be withheld from our conversations, yet the very patterns you feel you cannot share show up in your feelings about me, and we are drawn into patterns that, while you continue to deny such things occurred in the past, you experience as occurring in the here and now, between us, and it feels as real here as it feels unreal about the past.

Mariska: You should write that down. I can feel myself pushing your words away, losing them in some inner fog.

Dr. K: It is very painful to hold onto awareness that some of the people you have loved the most have betrayed you, hurt you, and condoned your being hurt.

Mariska: I don't know if I can live with this.

Dr. K: Some parts of your mind have been living with it for decades.

Mariska: They are saying inside, "She's not going to help us. We protected her for years and she's going to leave us with this shit."

Dr. K: They are afraid you will repeat your father's behavior—see it, know it, turn a blind eye to it, and convince yourself it was just fantasy, just dreams, just a little girl's imagination.

Mariska: I said I don't know if I can live with this knowledge. I am sure I can't live with just walking by them and their pain. [*sighs*] Watch me betray my good intentions in spite of myself. Please keep me on track. Inside they are saying, "If he doesn't, we will, and you won't like how we do it."

Dr. K: How about if those inside feel that anyone: I, Mariska, or any part of the mind, is messing up, you let me know in no uncertain terms rather than inflict anything on one another? There's been too much suffering already.

Mariska: They say they will think about it. But they are not sure I will listen.

In our exchange, Mariska and I are working on working together. Many components of what I recommend in building the alliance are demonstrated. Mariska comes expecting to be an active participant in the therapy. If she were taking a passive stance, I would have focused, with both dynamic and psychoeducational interventions, on making her a more proactive participant. The journaling was assigned. Assignments and patients' reaction to them and management of them often are instructive about the patient's degree of identification with the therapeutic process.

Exploring what transpired in prior psychotherapies is crucial; it is always a narcissistic error to assume that one can do a therapy that escapes all of the pitfalls encountered in previous work. Here we learn that Mariska was sexually exploited by her first therapist, and that Helga (and possibly other alters) played a role in coping with that. We learn that Mariska's dissociative capacities have remained vigorous in coping with contemporary adult trauma. I have to wonder how many alters are watching the therapeutic work without making themselves known, sizing up me and my reactions and the degree of risk I pose to them all, and preparing a variety of responses should they be perceived as necessary. I can infer that some alters may be prepared to take an active role in matters sexual, in order to control the situation and the risk of damage, and that Mariska can be expected to erase from her mind threatening material soon after it is discussed—the "magic slate" effect.

I am teaching Mariska how I expect her to behave in therapy, to explore rather than to avoid, to communicate rather than to act out, and initiating her into an early understanding of transference and enactment and their importance in our work. This is part of socializing the patient to psychotherapy. I am giving her some ground rules.

In this segment I am not dealing with informed consent, or giving her a map of what we may encounter (anticipatory socialization). There are some psychoeducational aspects to some of my remarks, but Mariska's aggressive literature searches preempted any deliberate psychoeducational efforts on my part. When she had asked for recommended reading, I had referred her to Jon Allen's (current edition, 2005) *Coping with Trauma* and Donald Nathanson's (1992) *Shame and Pride*. She had breezed through Allen's book, but bogged down in Nathanson's in a way that told me that she was so shame-bound that she was afraid of her own shame. Shame is a great instigator, maintainer, and enhancer of dissociation (Kluft, 2006b), and I correctly predicted it would be a central issue in her treatment.

Part of my effort to establish the therapeutic alliance is to address relational and intersubjective concerns. The previous dialogue was preceded by my sharing a reaction of my own. At this early point in the treatment, I felt it was premature to share my stronger reactions, lest they be disruptive and seen as criticism. Mariska and I had discussed how we would handle emerging questions about me and my reactions, and she had, for the moment, accepted my stance that while at times answering her questions might be helpful, at others it could be detrimental, so that if I had any concerns, I would share my misgivings about sharing particular information and, employing my own clinical judgment, reserve the right to withhold it if I had concerns.

Empathic observations were major interventions as we got underway, and Mariska seemed to find my empathy accurate most of the time, with some exceptions illustrated previously. It is important to help a patient deal with the DID diagnosis, and Mariska and I went back and forth over her simultaneously accepting and denying the diagnosis. As long as she was working on relevant topics, there was no need to debate the diagnostic issue.

Dealing with and helping the DID patient deal with concerned others is often a central concern, but I was not made aware of any such issues with Mariska. She had minimal but cordial relationships with her parents, whom she saw less than once a year, was not involved in any significant relationships, and was very absorbed in her work. She socialized primarily with colleagues in enjoyable but not very close relationships.

I find it important to demonstrate some degree of expertise in order to help the patient appreciate that therapy can "do something." At the outset of treatment of DID the achievement of major therapeutic goals is often well beyond any horizon the DID patient can envision. Demonstration of expertise here refers not to the therapist's wizardly skills, but to the therapist's skill in imparting useful strengths and coping strategies to the patient.

For example, as painful material began to emerge, and the foundations of Mariska's original understanding of her life and family began to erode, she had more and more moments of severe distress and somatoform symptoms which, by their nature, seemed likely to be body memories—that is, flashbacks or reenactments of the physical discomforts associated with traumatic experiences, the narratives of which remained cloaked from the awareness of Mariska and most of the alters. I taught Mariska autohypnosis, and two autohypnotic techniques in particular. The first was safe place imagery, and the second was glove anesthesia and its elaborations, which I use for trance ratification and to enhance mastery.

Dr. K: In order to create a safe place, we need to find either a place that feels right and safe for you all, or a series of places that will be envisioned simultaneously. A place or places where those of you who need rest, respite, or recharging can go.

Mariska: That's easy. The gardens at Mainau! Do you know them? Probably not.

Dr. K: Actually, I attended a professional meeting in Konstanz some years ago. I remember it well, especially the dahlia plantings.

Mariska: It is an amazing place. Some of my earliest childhood memories are from Mainau. From before things went bad … [*describes the gardens in detail*].

Dr. K: OK, great! If you are alone, you can use the Spiegel eye roll induction you've learned …

Mariska: Great? I'll look like a fool, rolling my eyes up and looking like a fool.

Dr. K: Well, if you are alone, it doesn't matter, and …

Mariska: Voices say, "You don't get it!" One or more of us is always watching the body.

Dr. K: Well, I have got to say I missed that. No one has ever told me that before. So, let me demonstrate two public methods. [*bows his head slightly; places his right hand in front of his eyes, as if fending off sun glare*] That is one way to hide it in public. Another is the "two hands for beginners" approach. Watch this. [*rubs his forehead with the fingers of both hands, obscuring the eyes with his palms as he does so*] Of course, the most protective would be to do either method, but to start with your eyes closed. It will look like you are fighting fatigue, or a headache.

Mariska: That will work. I'll just "remind" my colleagues about my migraines! Another iatrogenic artifact from the laboratories of that twisted charlatan, Dr. K!

I also taught Mariska to create numbness in either hand, and used (with her permission) a sterile pin to test the numbness. When she opened her eyes and saw a pin she had not felt stuck upright in her skin, she was impressed. Such demonstrations lead to trance ratification, the patient's conviction that he or she really is in trance, making the often vague and nebulous concept of hypnosis convincingly tangible.

Next, I taught Mariska to transfer the numbness to other parts of her body by rubbing the numb hand on those parts. Since that method has limited application in public settings, and since there may be drawbacks to its use in sexually traumatized areas, I also taught her to let the numbness travel through her bloodstream to the afflicted areas. A few sessions later, Mariska remarked on her use of these techniques:

Mariska: I don't know how to say this right, but I have this sense of being stronger, and an occasional little flash of glee. I don't know … I feel like I am becoming armed.

Dr. K: You are learning to use your dissociative and autohypnotic talents in the service of your recovery.

Mariska: Kind of like some martial arts, using the opponent's strength against them.

With these skills acquired, Mariska became more confident in herself, our relationship, and the treatment process. She was eager to learn still more.

As Mariska and I moved beyond evaluation and the tentative first sessions into the flow and process of the therapy, dissociation was no longer a set of phenomena to be noted, elicited, and understood, nor a series of abstract definitions. Instead, it was lived between us and within Mariska, infiltrating our relatedness and our experiences of ourselves and one another, becoming a new lens through which Mariska was becoming more able to unravel and comprehend the knotted skein of her life and her psyche.

We moved smoothly into the phase of preliminary interventions (Table 40.5). As more and more material emerged or was contributed by alters, Mariska was becoming more symptomatic. We were both aware that

TABLE 40.5
Preliminary Interventions

1. Alleviating punitive superego attitudes
2. Shame management
3. Gaining access to alters:
   –Dealing with "you can't get there from here."
4. Contracts
5. Fostering communication and cooperation and expanding the therapeutic alliance
6. Ego strengthening and system strengthening
7. Offering symptomatic relief:
   –Medication
   –Simplification
   –Exploring disruptive symptoms
   –Controlling spontaneous abreactions and flashbacks
8. Hypnosis with an emphasis on temporizing techniques
9. Ascertaining Core Conflictual Relationship Themes (CCRTS) (Luborsky & Crits-Cristoph, 1998)

Source: From The initial stages of psychotherapy in the treatment of multiple personality disorder by R.P. Kluft, 1993, *Dissociation, 6*, pp. 145–161. Copyright 1993 International Society for the Study of Dissociation. Reprinted with permission.

the symptoms of the moment were the tips of what might prove to be far more menacing icebergs.

Victims of childhood trauma usually are oppressed by guilt and shame, and DID patients often demonstrate these feelings by the actions of personalities against other personalities. Such terrible punitive actions often reenact punishment patterns from the patient's childhood and/or are understood to be protective. A prime example concerns sharing information that the patient, as a child, was instructed to keep secret. Abused children are often threatened with dire consequences to themselves and/or others if the information is revealed. Typically, an alter will begin to share some secret information only to be punished by being harmed in the inner world of the alters, or suffering a wound to the body inflicted by an alter that does not experience himself or herself as living in the body.

I did not want to see this pattern played out among Mariska's alters. As we discussed how we would proceed, I invited comments from all parts of the mind. Predictably, some comments passed on from within: (1) insisted nothing bad had ever befallen her; (2) told me Mariska had been a liar since she was a little girl; (3) warned "They know what will happen to them if they talk"; (4) told me to "Leave her alone! She belongs to me!"; and (5) insisted "Those people would never, never, never do anything to hurt you." In addition, Mariska heard crying and screaming in the background.

It was easy to hypothesize that there were parts that would oppose the treatment process and that alters based on abusers and those who had either colluded with the abusers and/or failed to defend Mariska (and alters closely attached to such alters) would have to be worked with before the treatment could proceed safely.

Dr. K: So, enthusiasm for pursuing this treatment is far from universal?

Mariska: Inside, voices are saying "Fuck you!"

Dr. K: Let me address this to those of you who are most concerned that this treatment is wrongheaded, or directed against them. You and all the others are all in this together, no matter how it feels to you at this moment. I don't expect you to believe what I am saying, because right now it is so important to many of you to be not-Mariska, to be anyone anywhere who was not ground zero for all of the bad stuff that was experienced. You've heard me tell you, "Either everybody wins, or everybody loses," because, at the core of it all, you are all one person. I don't want to see any of you trash the health, the body, the mind, the relationships, or the career that you will ultimately appreciate is yours, and then finally get the idea and realize that you've really screwed yourself. At this point this sounds either like nonsense or like a threat to many of you. But all of you, even those of you who make it your business to harm or sabotage one another, were created to defend one human being and to allow her to survive under intolerable circumstances, circumstances about which I still know very little. Therefore, at the deepest level, we are all on the same side, even though at the level you tend to experience, I just don't get what's going on and I may mess things up or seem to be your enemy. Some time down the road, we are going to be getting along much better, and laugh about how things are now.

Mariska: Just curses and laughter.

Dr. K: OK, in order to understand your concerns and elicit your advice, because you probably know a lot of important things I don't know, I am going to ask for a list of those who have misgivings about, or just plain oppose, the treatment. Then I will offer every one of you on that list a chance to come out, or to speak from within, and share your objections, concerns, and advice.

Mariska: They say, "You're full of shit. No one listens to us anyway."

Dr. K: I can promise to listen to you and treat you with respect. I can't promise to agree with you or collude with you in any way that might undermine the treatment or hurt you or any participants in the total human being, Mariska.

Mariska: [*in a masculine voice*] What do you want?

Dr. K: Cooperation with the treatment and a complete moratorium on anything whatsoever that would compromise the present or future of the woman known to others as Mariska, or cause internal pain and chaos.

Mariska: [*in the masculine voice*] You are asking a lot. A lot.

Dr. K: Hey, for you, nothing but the best!

Mariska: [*in her usual voice*] They are laughing. Some will give you their names and talk. Others are going to wait and see.

Dr. K: Are those whose names I will be given volunteers, or have they been shanghaied?

Mariska: They laughed again, and I heard, "To answer that would be to reveal classified material."

Mariska and I spent about 4 months primarily dealing with alters' misgivings and clarifying the role of shame in keeping information out of awareness. Mariska was reluctant to acknowledge or reveal awareness of alters who expressed anger or performed sexual functions. We discussed the pivotal role of shame in the trauma response, and the role shame plays in instigating, maintaining, and reinforcing dissociative adaptations.

Mariska: I can't deal with the idea that there are parts of me that reveled in being sluts, whores, I don't know what to call them. I am beginning to have vague memories of coming on to Herr G when I was just a little girl. How can I live with that? There are some doors I don't think I ever can open, and still live with myself.

Dr. K: What's your understanding of those behaviors?

Mariska: I'm a little piece of shit, and I got what was coming to me.

Dr. K: That offers you a perverse but straightforward explanation for everything. It's appealingly simple, not much strain to the brain.

Mariska: That's how it is. I'm waiting for you to throw me out of your office, or … [*silence*]

Dr. K: … or to finally appreciate your true nature and to respond accordingly?

Mariska: I hate you for saying that, and I hate me that you are right.

When Mariska had completed an extensive trashing of herself, during which she interrupted my every effort to intervene, I was able to get a word in edgewise.

Dr. K: The behaviors you are so ashamed of, and the alters that were involved in carrying them out, were created to manage unavoidable situations involving sexual demands upon you. Those who initiated sexual encounters probably had already learned one or more of four lessons: One, that if they resisted, they would be hurt in order to make them submit, and used anyway; Two, that some of the sexual options for victimizing them were more intolerable than others, so that initiating an option that was less intolerable might save them pain and difficulty, and offer them a modicum of control over what happened; Three, that their abuser insisted on being dealt with as if he or she was wanted, welcomed and desired, and efforts were made to provide that scenario—again, lest worse happen; or, Four, their own fear of abandonment by their abuser was so intense that they made every effort to demonstrate their love and devotion in the kind of encounter that their abuser clearly desired.

Mariska: I hear inside, "He understands us," and "Do we have to fuck you, too?" and "What do you like to do?"

Dr. K: My replies are, "I'm glad, and I look forward to working with you," "No, you don't have to," and "I like to see people like you get well, and get in control of their own lives."

Mariska: Some of them feel OK about you, and others say, "Wait and see. He's just like the others."

Dr. K: It's very hard to be in treatment after a previous therapist has exploited you. You have every right and reason to be skeptical about my intentions.

When the alters who initially objected to treatment became supportive of the treatment, it became safe to contact the alters associated with the experiences of abuse. My interactions with them were geared toward building a relationship in which they could feel safe. I did not ask for historical material, but noted the historical material that was freely offered. I came to understand that Mariska had been molested both by Herr G and by some of his friends and mistresses over the years, that Mariska's parents had an open marriage, and that several of Mariska's mother's lovers, a rogues' gallery that included Herr G, had abused Mariska. Herr G had seduced Helga, Mariska's nanny, and involved her in sexual encounters with Mariska.

We did encounter a mild version of the "you can't get there from here" problem.

Mariska: You will never reach the ones from before I learned English. They can't understand a word you say.

Dr. K: Well, let's not be so pessimistic. I would like to address myself to all of you who know English and know the languages of those who speak no English.

Mariska: Many of us.

Dr. K: Are there any among you who would be willing to help by telling those who don't know English what I am saying, and then translate their response for me?

Mariska: Hmm. I guess there will be no problem.

The previously narrated interventions give some indication of how I approached the matter of contracts. I was fortunate that Mariska was not inclined to hurt her body or attempt suicide, and further fortunate that she had eliminated substance abuse from her life prior to my work with her. However, we had to work very hard to contain Mariska's use of sexual encounters for tension release, self-punishment, and self-degradation.

Mariska loathed herself for these behaviors, but felt she was compelled to put herself in situations in which they were likely to occur. She also feared something awful would happen if she discontinued them. It was her idea to invite every alter to comment on this issue in her journal in between appointments.

Mariska: This is the most humiliating thing I've ever done!

Dr. K: To what are you referring?

Mariska: My most outlandish sexual behavior is less embarrassing to me than this journal. I almost burned it rather than bring it in. It was easier to believe I was nothing more than a slut. When you started to tell me about using sex as a defense, you scared me to the depths of my soul, but I wasn't convinced. Here are things that show that this whoring around is acting out things I don't want to remember. And it's acting like my mother, whose sex life I had completely blocked out of my mind. I find I have parts based on her. My God! And Herr G and the others inside—they get off on it! They pretend they are my partner and that once again, I belong to them. While one of them feels he's doing it to me, the others are watching, laughing, and sometimes taking pictures.

Dr. K: While they are believing they are doing this to you in your inner world, are others in your inner world experiencing themselves as being mistreated?

Mariska: Yes. But the others wouldn't let them write it down.

Dr. K: These are incredibly important insights, and incredibly painful and humiliating insights. We'll be spending a lot of time addressing them. But I've got to say that many of you are breaking your contract for safety. We have to talk about that.

Mariska: [*as Herr G*] The terms of the contract were clear. We have hurt no one!

Dr. K: I don't think those who experienced themselves as being raped by you and your buddies would agree, although you might coerce them to say they agree.

Mariska: [*as Herr G*] This is alright. I have been left in charge.

Dr. K: Let's spend as much time as we need to understand what drives you to think that I would accept such nonsense.

Mariska: [*as Herr G*] This is how it has always been, and how it always will be.

Dr. K: So you gave me your word, as you gave your word to Mariska's father, that you would take care of things, be in charge, keep her safe. And as you did to Mariska's father, you break your word to me, and still hope that I can be convinced that anything that seems wrong is quite all right.

Mariska: [*as Herr G*] It has to be this way!

Dr. K: I am beginning to wonder if you set the stage for these episodes when you feel threatened by what is happening and what is coming up, and need to reassure yourself that you still are powerful, the one dishing it out, the one who never has to take it. What has been happening in treatment that is scaring you and your friends?

Mariska: [*as Herr G*] Nothing. I have nothing more to say to you. [*switches to Helga*] The great Herr G is beginning to realize he has a vagina. Now that many of us are more connected, some of the men are feeling the pain of some of the abused girls.

Dr. K: So Herr G and others are wanting to show how grand and phallic they can be, and promoting these encounters to do so.

Mariska: [*as Helga*] I'm getting tired of this. I try to protect the little ones by stepping in for them, but I don't want to do this any more.

After a few more confrontations, during which I tried to empathize with the abuser alters' fear of coming to grips with the fact that they in fact had been abused, these alters settled down. The alters based on Mariska's mother proved very recalcitrant, determined at once to portray mother as a sexual adventuress without peer, and a good mother who had always been protective of Mariska. Mariska, of course, wanted to preserve mother as a good object, but found increasing reason to appreciate that her mother had abandoned and betrayed her repeatedly. This inner battle continued almost to the end of the treatment.

My efforts to bring Mariska symptomatic relief included numerous medication trials, none of which were satisfactory to either one of us. The personalities based on Mariska's mother resisted efforts to simplify Mariska's life by removing stressors and unnecessary burdens. My efforts were unavailing, but the majority of the alters confronted her and restricted her activities until she could be worked with therapeutically. Her various symptoms were explored by making inquiries, usually without hypnosis.

Mariska began to report severe headaches when she found herself to be the only woman in a group of men. As one of the few women in her field, such situations were commonplace.

Mariska: I have to do something about these headaches.

Dr. K: You have described the headaches very well, but for the sake of completeness, I want you to tell me about anything else you experience along with the headaches—ideas, images, feelings, sensations …

Mariska: [*interrupting*] No!

Dr. K: Well …

Mariska: [*interrupting*] No! Why don't you leave my headaches to the neurologist? Such questions you ask! No!

Dr. K: It seems from what you are saying that the headaches reflect both the intrusion of some uncomfortable material and your attempts to push that material away. Elements of the material succeed in pushing through as physical orphan symptoms, unconnected to the context in which they occurred.

Mariska: I'd rather have the headache. I'm not ready for this.

Dr. K: Well, that's a problem. Often I can get a symptom to subside, but that's usually associated with promising whatever parts are behind the symptom a chance to be heard.

Mariska: I really can't go there now. I have too much on my plate and a grant application that is due in 2 days.

Dr. K: OK, will you allow yourself to go to sleep while I talk with the others?

Mariska: I don't like this, but OK.

Dr. K: [*induces hypnosis, conducts all personalities other than those behind the headache to a safe place, suggests sleep*] It seems that there is something really important that you need today.

Mariska: Yes. But *she* needs to hear it. Not you.

Dr. K: You may be right, but let's start with me.

Mariska: Her mother sent her an e-mail.

Dr. K: An important e-mail?

Mariska: A terrible e-mail. Herr G is coming to the United States on business, and her mother gave him her e-mail and real address, and told her she had assured him that Mariska would be glad to put him up for a few days. Mariska is trying to push it out of her mind, and Helga says she is not going to take care of things. We have to do something. And we don't think we can say "No!" [*switch to Helga*] It's about time they stood up instead of saying "Helga! Helga! It's time to spread your legs." No more! No more!

Dr. K: Thanks. You can step back. Mariska, everybody, please listen. There is real danger here, and pushing it aside will put you all at risk. Mariska, this time I think you all need to listen.

Mariska: I hear it. I remember. What can I do? My parents don't know about Herr G. They will think I am horrible. [*switch*] We would like to see Herr G. [*switch*] Do you see why we tried to push through?

Dr. K: Mariska, is it true that your parents don't know about Herr G?

Mariska: [*cries*] I told my father over and over again, but he didn't believe me. My mother knows—she was in bed with Herr G and me. Why don't I just kill myself?

Dr. K: I think that when it seems easier to consider killing yourself than saying "No!" we have a lot to talk about.

Mariska: [*smiling weakly through her tears*] You think I have a problem? You think I need something like psychotherapy?

Dr. K: The thought had crossed my mind.

The crisis of Herr G's visit was averted. Mariska worked out a clever arrangement that allowed her both to decline Herr G access to her home, restricting her exposure to him, and hold a party in his honor at a restaurant. In this manner we approached and negotiated our way through myriad symptoms, which seemed to occur mostly when self-protective needs were in conflict with attachment needs. Mariska quickly mastered how to initiate inner dialogues in order to explore symptoms and how to get the alters involved to step back, and bring their issues to the next session. Often these alters left gargantuan telephone messages to assure themselves that I would be aware of their issues in case other alters "forgot" them, lest they not be addressed.

Mariska developed her own way of controlling spontaneous abreactions and flashbacks, based on techniques I had used in session. She relied on the basic psychodynamic question: "Why is this happening now?" Pursuing this through her inner world, she would find the alter or alters who had become upset, or whose issues were triggered, speak to them empathically, and persuade them to use a technique I had taught Mariska, hypnotically putting the upset alters to sleep between sessions, promising to call them and their issues to my attention. I rapidly found that I had to question Mariska about whether she had shut down anything to which we had to return, because she often "accidentally on purpose" gave herself what amounted to permissive amnesia instructions.

As we addressed the issues of this stage of treatment, many hypnotic techniques (or techniques derived from hypnotic techniques) proved useful. These included accessing alters, alter substitution (inherent in next example), reconfiguring the system (as I did when Mariska was put to sleep so I could converse with alters whose communications she wanted to avoid), provision of sanctuary, time-sense alteration (putting alters to sleep), and symptom relief (Kluft, 1993a, 1994). I also was gradually learning the key dynamics of each alter (CCRTs; Luborsky & Crits-Cristoph, 1998).

With a reasonably good therapeutic alliance that engaged almost all of the known alters (excepting parts based on Mariska's mother) and that had proven itself robust in handling a series of crises and difficult situations, it seemed safe to proceed to history-gathering and mapping. For reasons of confidentiality not much more of Mariska's history will be shared.

The history-gathering was done by asking each alter to tell its story, and then pursuing gaps and apparent and real discrepancies. If an alter became too emotional or disruptive, another alter that had witnessed the events in question, but was less prone to be upset, was asked to tell the story.

Only one additional piece of historical information will be shared. Near the end of the history-gathering a child alter said it missed "Heinrich." Another alter harshly told her to be quiet. Not a single alter could or would explain Heinrich. Thinking Mariska had given me honest answers, I wondered if Heinrich was an alter largely unknown to the others, and told Mariska I would try to see if there was an alter named Heinrich. Mariska gave no indication of distress.

When I induced hypnosis and tried to check for a Heinrich, an alter emerged and said, "I'm surprised I got out. They put me in prison and threw away the key. They pretend I don't exist." I was beginning to assure Heinrich that I would be glad to hear his story when the usual Mariska took over.

Mariska: There! We put him back in jail! Now forget about him. You will never hear about him again!

Dr. K: Forget about him? I'm pretty confused by all this.

Mariska: You understand Kaddish? The Mourners' Kaddish? I figure you are Jewish. You take off for the Jewish holidays.

Dr. K: Yes. I understand about the Mourners' Kaddish.

Mariska: When someone dies, you say the Kaddish. My brother is dead.

Dr. K: I'm sorry.

Mariska: Don't be. He is dead to me. I heard that Jews also say the Mourners' Kaddish when someone, even if they are alive, becomes dead to them. I learned about it in a class at university. He is dead to us. Just that one little brat wants to visit him in jail—the jail in my mind. My brother and I were inseparable. My parents always running here, running there, Herr G fucking our nannies, they were crazy for him, every stupid one hoping he'd leave his wife and marry her. Idiots! Herr G married into money. He'd never leave his wife. I told my brother about what Herr G was making me do, and he got all excited and tried to do the same things to me. It's complicated. I can't say any more now. [forcefully] I have said the Mourners' Kaddish for Heinrich. There is nothing more to say.

I was completely blindsided by these revelations. Mariska both took pleasure in how well she had hidden her secret and was ashamed that it had finally been revealed. Her understanding of "Why is this happening now?" was that, in spite of her conscious plan never to speak of her brother, at a deeper level her mind knew it had to reveal this material if she were ever to recover. In reflecting on this newly revealed brother, I was also shocked to realize that although I knew Mariska had a younger sister, she had never been mentioned after the initial sessions.

For mapping, I used Fine's technique (Fine, 1991, 1993). Mariska was asked to write her name in the center of a piece of paper, and all alters were invited to place their names or to instruct Mariska where to place their names, placing their names closest to those to whom they felt most close. I also ask those who have no name or who are not ready to share their names to make a mark, a circle, a check, a line, etc. Close to Mariska were half a dozen names: alters who proved to be very much like Mariska and able to pass for her or one another should the alter on the surface become tired, overwhelmed, or otherwise uncomfortable about remaining at the surface in apparent executive control. Just beyond them to the upper right was a cluster called "the smart kids," who inspired her scientific accomplishments and could fix anything. Beyond and to the upper left was a cluster of "good girls," who could always do the right thing with impeccable manners and social grace. They usually dealt with the parents and social situations. Below "Mariska" were two heavy dark lines, which I learned stood for two powerful figures of uncertain gender and age who kept another group of alters, whose names were just below the lines, from acting out sexually without permission from elsewhere in the mind. Those names included Helga, Helga 2, and Helga 3. In the lower left corner was a cluster of over two dozen names, which referred to a series of children and adolescents with encapsulated memories of particular experiences of abuse. At the lower right corner was the name Heinrich, covered over by vertical lines signifying the bars in his prison's window. Surrounding this corner was a fascinating series of German and Jewish names. These signified Teutonic Knights who guarded the prison and kept Heinrich in check. Assigned to each Teutonic Knight was an Orthodox Jewish Rabbi, perpetually chanting the Mourners' Kaddish for Heinrich. Closer to Mariska than these protectors was a teardrop, which stood for the alter that encapsulated the abuse from Heinrich. Between Mariska and the teardrop was a cluster of names with young ages, representing those alters based on the fantasy of preserving one's self from trauma. "They are untouched," Mariska said. Pointing to the teardrop, she added, "I can't let that happen to them." Across the top of the sheet, from left to right, were the names of alters based on her parents, Herr G, Herr G's friends (who were business associates of her father), and the names of two doctors. "I couldn't let myself tell you that it happened with a second therapist as well." I asked if the traumatization by the doctors had led to additional alters. Mariska became tearful. "I can't even write that down. I was no child or teenager then. I was an adult. No! Nothing more about that today!"

I asked if there were any parts that had not checked in, but which would now be willing to do so. Mariska took back the map, and made more entries. Now, scattered across the top among the abusers were several circles, filled in to be completely black. "Those are the parts that are what is evil in me. They make me my own worst abuser." I assumed, and later was able to confirm, that these included alters associated with her sexual exploitation by mental health professionals, and that more work would be needed for her to place these experiences in perspective.

I had no illusions that this mapping was definitive. For example, no alter admitted to knowledge of or connection to her sister. However, it did give Mariska and me an elementary road map, and an appreciation of her dissociative complexity. Without it, we might easily have moved on to the phase of what Herman (1992) calls "remembrance and mourning," and which I refer to as "the metabolism of trauma," without understanding what precautions might serve to better safeguard Mariska and her treatment from destabilization.

At this point, Mariska's treatment was well underway. From my perspective, and from hers as well, the early stages that form the foundation of the treatment had come to satisfactory conclusions. Mariska was well-equipped to explore and work through her experiences in relative safety and she had good prospects of preserving her functioning as she did.

We had become a team, both identified with the goals of the treatment and able to retain our connection with one another despite the vicissitudes of transference and countertransference. We were mutually accepting of the inevitability that intrusions from the past might become manifest in the present in myriad ways, and that they might test and try, but would not break, our alliance.

The way we organized our thinking about dissociation had undergone a series of transitions. We had begun by studying and appreciating dissociation from our different perspectives as a series of complex phenomena that we needed to observe and understand in order to determine the nature of Mariska's problems. From Mariska's perspective, they were a series of mortifying and confusing "not me" experiences and manifestations, not appreciated to be part of who she was. From my perspective, they were vital bits of information that might help me understand a patient in difficulty and pain. As we discussed them, and further explored them, we had begun to appreciate their patterns and the implications of those patterns.

As we continued, it became apparent that dissociation not only characterized Mariska's diagnosis, but that it also was a major determinant of the interpersonal field and the relational processes in which we were engaged. Dissociation was understood to underlie and play a role in determining how and who and what she was in relationship to me and among her many selves. As early interventions clarified and contained aspects of Mariska's dissociative disorder, it became possible to decode Mariska's dissociative phenomena and dissociative way of being and to make therapeutic interventions. Working with dissociation to cure dissociation became a characteristic aspect of the therapeutic process.

Mariska was able to build on the foundation we created together during these early stages of treatment. Although there would be many difficult moments in coming to grips with her mother's role in her traumatization, in dealing with those parts identified with mother, in learning about her sister's role in her life, and in addressing her brother's betrayal and mistreatment of her, she addressed and worked through her experiences and issues. After five additional (and seven and a half total) years of treatment, her psychotherapy was tapered gradually, and transitioned into periodic follow-up visits. During this period of follow-up visits, Mariska presented a paper at a symposium abroad, involving a number of colleagues whom she had never met before. One of these was a gentleman who responded as warmly to Mariska as she responded to him. A year and a half later Mariska and he married, and both relocated to share a life together. They were able to beat the biological clock and begin a family. Mariska is sufficiently prominent in her field that she is invited to speak in the United States quite frequently, and usually can squeeze in a follow-up session or two. Her life is good.

REFERENCES

Allen, J. (2005). *Coping with trauma,* 2nd ed. Washington, DC: American Psychiatric Press.

American Society of Clinical Hypnosis Committee on Hypnosis & Memory (1995). *Clinical hypnosis and memory: Guidelines for clinicians and for forensic hypnosis.* Chicago, IL: American Society of Clinical Hypnosis Press.

Bernstein, E. M., & Putnam, F. W. (1986). Development, reliability, and validity of a dissociation scale. *Journal of Nervous and Mental Disease, 174*, 727–735.

Bliss, E. L. (1986). *Multiple personality, allied disorders, and hypnosis*. New York: Oxford University Press.

Braun, B. (1988a). The BASK (behavior, affect, sensation, knowledge) model of dissociation. *Dissociation, 1*, 2–23.

Braun, B. (1989b). The BASK model of dissociation: Clinical applications. *Dissociation, 1*, 16–23.

Brown, D., Scheflin, A., & Hammond, D. C. (1998). *Memory, trauma treatment, and the law*. New York: Norton.

Chefetz, R., & Bromberg, P. (2004). Talking with "Me" and "Not-Me": A dialogue. *Contemporary Psychoanalysis, 40*, 409–464.

Davies, J. M., & Frawley, M. (1994). *Treating adult survivors of childhood sexual abuse: A psychoanalytic perspective.* New York: Basic Books.

Dell, P. (2006). A new model of dissociative identity disorder. *Psychiatric Clinics of North America, 29*, 1–26.

Fine, C. G. (1991). Treatment stabilization and crisis prevention: Pacing the treatment of the MPD patient. *Psychiatric Clinics of North America, 14*, 661–675.

Fine, C. G. (1993). A tactical integrationalist perspective on multiple personality disorder. In R. P. Kluft & C. G. Fine (Eds.), *Clinical perspectives on multiple personality disorder* (pp. 135–153). Washington, DC: American Psychiatric Press.

Frischholz, E., Lipman, L., Braun, B., & Sachs, R. (1992). Psychopathology, hypnotizability, and dissociation. *American Journal of Psychiatry, 149*, 1521–1525.

Herman, J. (1992). *Trauma and recovery*. New York: Basic Books.

Kluft, R. P. (1984a). An introduction to multiple personality disorder. *Psychiatric Annals, 14*, 19–24.

Kluft, R. P. (1984b). Treatment of multiple personality disorder. *Psychiatric Clinics of North America, 7*, 9–29.

Kluft, R. P. (1985). The natural history of multiple personality disorder. In R. P. Kluft (Ed.), *Childhood antecedents of multiple personality* (pp. 197–238). Washington, DC: American Psychiatric Press.

Kluft, R. P. (1986). Personality unification in multiple personality disorder. In B. G. Braun (Ed.), *Treatment of multiple personality disorder* (pp. 29–60). Washington, DC: American Psychiatric Press.

Kluft, R. P. (1987a). First-rank symptoms as a diagnostic clue to multiple personality disorder. *American Journal of Psychiatry, 144*, 293–298.

Kluft, R. P. (1987b). The simulation and dissimulation of multiple disorder. *American Journal of Clinical Hypnosis, 30*, 104–118.

Kluft, R. P. (1987c). An update on multiple personality disorder. *Hospital & Community Psychiatry, 38*, 363–373.

Kluft, R. P. (1991). Multiple personality disorder. In A. Tasman & S. Goldfinger (Eds.), *American Psychiatric Press annual review of psychiatry* (pp. 161–188). Washington, DC: American Psychiatric Press.

Kluft, R. P. (1993a). The initial stages of psychotherapy in the treatment of multiple personality disorder. *Dissociation, 6*, 145–161.

Kluft, R. P. (1993b). Treatment of multiple personality disorder: An overview of discoveries, successes, and failures. *Dissociation, 6*, 87–101.

Kluft, R. P. (1994). Applications of hypnotic interventions. *Hypnos, 21*, 205–223.

Kluft, R. P. (1995). Psychodynamic psychotherapy of multiple personality disorder and allied forms of dissociative disorder not otherwise specified. In J. Barber & P. Crits-Cristoph (Eds.), *Dynamic therapies for psychiatric disorders (Axis I)* (pp. 332–385). New York: Basic Books.

Kluft, R. P. (1998). Reflections on the traumatic memories of dissociative identity disorder patients. In S. Lynn & K. McConkey (Eds.), *Truth in memory* (pp. 304–322). New York: Guilford.

Kluft, R. P. (1999). Current issues in dissociative identity disorder. *Journal of Practical Psychiatry and Behavioral Health, 5*, 3–19.

Kluft, R. P. (2005). Diagnosing dissociative identity disorder. *Psychiatric Annals, 35*, 633–643.

Kluft, R. P. (2006a). Dealing with alters: A pragmatic clinical perspective. *Psychiatric Clinics of North America, 29*, 281–304.

Kluft, R. P. (2006b). Applications of innate affect theory to the understanding and treatment of dissociative identity disorder. In E. Vermetten, M. Dorahy, & R. Loewenstein (Eds.), *[title to be determined]*. Washington, DC: American Psychiatric Press.

Loewenstein, R. J., Hamilton, J., Alagna, S., Reid, N., & Devries, M. (1987). Experiential sampling in the study of multiple personality disorder. *American Journal of Psychiatry, 144*, 19–24.

Loewenstein, R. (1991). An office mental status examination for complex chronic dissociative symptoms and multiple personality disorder. *Psychiatric Clinics of North America, 14*, 567–604.

Luborsky, L., & Crits-Cristoph, P. (1998). *Understanding transference: The core conflictual relationship method*, 2nd ed. Washington, DC: American Psychological Association.

Nathanson, D. (1992). *Shame and pride*. New York: Norton.

Putnam, F. W., Guroff, J., Silberman, E. J., Barban, L., & Post, R. (1986). The clinical phenomenology of multiple personality disorder: Review of 100 recent cases. *Journal of Clinical Psychiatry, 47*, 285–293.

Ross, C., & Joshi, S. (1992). Schneiderian symptoms and childhood trauma in the general population. *Comprehensive Psychiatry, 33*, 269–273.

Spiegel, D. (1986). Dissociating damage. *American Journal of Clinical Hypnosis, 29*, 123–131.

Spiegel, H., & Spiegel, D. (2004). *Trance and treatment: Clinical uses of hypnosis*, 2nd ed. Washington, DC: American Psychiatric Press.

Steinberg, M. (1994). *Structured Clinical Interview for the Diagnosis of DSM-IV Dissociative Disorders – Revised.* Washington, DC: American Psychiatric Press.

Waller, N., Putnam, F., & Carlson, E. (1996). Types of dissociation and dissociative types: A taxometric analysis of dissociative experiences. *Psychological Methods, 1*, 300–321.

41 Treating Dissociation: A Contextual Approach

Steven N. Gold, PhD
Stacey L. Seibel, PhD, LP

OUTLINE

41.1 ABSTRACT

An approach to treating dissociation informed by multiple contexts—trauma history, family of origin environment, developmental trajectory, interpersonal influences, and sociocultural milieu—is described. A contextual perspective promotes a view of dissociation as a basic aspect of human functioning, rather than a rare, exotic phenomenon. Dissociation is construed as assuming a range of manifestations that can be adaptive as well as pathological. Consequently, one can learn to recognize, anticipate, decondition, and modulate dissociative responses as needed to reduce maladaptive functioning and enhance effective responding. An overview of how this model structures and guides treatment is provided.

Ultimately, the value of a diagnostic system of classification rests on its ability to guide treatment. Due to the process that led to its formulation, the proposed framework for diagnosis delineated throughout this volume represents an evolution and expansion of our understanding of the nature of dissociation. Wherever possible, diagnostic criteria were derived from the growing body of empirical findings on dissociation rather than solely from clinical observation and experience. When clinical findings were employed, this was based on consensus among a diverse group of specialists in dissociation who subscribed to a range of theoretical perspectives. In addition, there was an attempt to develop diagnostic criteria that relied less on reports of subjective experience than in the previous system and included more behavioral observation. As a result, the diagnostic system for dissociation arrived at constitutes an important departure from and advance beyond the one that appeared in the *Diagnostic and Statistical Manual of Mental Disorders,* fourth edition (DSM-IV; American Psychological Association [APA], 1994).

In analogous fashion, the reader should be aware that the conceptual perspective and corresponding approach to treatment described in this chapter are not representative of existing standard practice among experts in dissociation. In some important respects, the contextual model of dissociation and its treatment delineated in this chapter encompasses both an extension of and divergence from widely held assumptions and intervention strategies. It is our belief that these modifications are consistent with the diagnostic revisions proposed elsewhere in this volume. Contextual therapy cannot be readily categorized as squarely falling within one or another therapeutic orientation; it draws extensively on a wide range of treatment approaches ranging from psychodynamic to behavioral. Its intervention strategies attempt to avoid an exclusive reliance on the subjective, supplementing experiential description with behavioral observation. Although the conceptual framework and methodology of contextual therapy initially evolved from clinical experience, as is illustrated in the following, they are also grounded in empirical findings.

41.2 ORIGINS OF DISSOCIATION: TRAUMA AND IMPAIRED ATTACHMENT

The prevailing conceptualization of dissociation among clinicians, dating back to the models of Janet (1889) and Freud (1893/1959a; 1896/1959b) in the late 19th century, and widely subscribed to during the resurgence of interest in the dissociative disorders in the late 20th century (Briere & Runtz, 1988; Chu, Frey, Ganzel, & Matthews, 1999; Feeney, Zoellner, Fitzgibbons, & Foa, 2000; Irwin, 1996; Putnam, Guroff, Silberman, Barban, & Post, 1986), is that it is a response to trauma. Extensive evidence consistent with this contention exists in the empirical literature. The research supports the relationship among a variety of traumas (e.g., child abuse; physical abuse; sexual abuse; combat) and the development of dissociative symptomatology (Briere & Runtz, 1988; Chu et al., 1999; Irwin, 1996; Putnam, 1997; Putnam et al., 1986; Stein & Kendall, 2004).

Recently, however, more finely tuned studies have raised questions about whether the relationship of trauma to dissociation is as direct and causal as was previously believed (Briere, 2006; Ogawa, Sroufe, Weinfield, Carlson, & Egeland, 1997). Briere (2006) concluded that there is a complex relationship between trauma and dissociation. His findings confirmed that most individuals presenting with significant dissociative symptomatology reported a trauma history. Conversely, however, the majority of persons with trauma histories did not endorse appreciable dissociative presentations. Additional risk factors on the pathway between trauma and dissociation included reduced affect regulation capabilities and high posttraumatic stress responses[1] (Briere, 2006). Ogawa et al. (1997) also deduced that the relationship between trauma and dissociation is complex. They found that the following trauma characteristics were highly correlated with level of dissociation: chronicity, severity, and age of onset. An additional finding was that both disorganized and avoidant patterns of attachment were strong predictors of dissociative difficulties (Ogawa et al., 1997). Further support for an intricate relation between trauma and dissociation was provided by Waller, Putnam, and Carlson (1996), who found that while trauma is a necessary condition for the development of dissociation, it is not sufficient.

In conjunction with the trauma-based concept of dissociation, a growing consensus has emerged that attachment, or more precisely the failure to develop the resources for secure attachment, can contribute substantially to the formation of maladaptive dissociative patterns of response. First proposed independently by Barach (1991) in the United States and by Liotti (Liotti, Intreccialagli, & Cecere, 1991; Liotti, 1992) in Italy, the relationship between dissociation and attachment was initially recognized on the basis of the similarity in observable behavior between dissociative clients and infants with attachment difficulties. Barach stressed the concordance between what Bowlby referred to as "detachment" in neglected children and extensive signs of disordered attachment in dissociative therapy clients. He states, "My reading of Bowlby's work is that the detachment he describes is actually a type of dissociation" (Barach, 1991, p. 118). Liotti (1992) arrived at a similar, although more precise conclusion. He proposed that dissociation was specifically linked to a disorganized/disoriented attachment style, resulting not from parental detachment, but from an ongoing pattern in early childhood of frightened and/or frightening parental behavior.

In the intervening years, the initial conceptual work by Barach and Liotti has been supported and augmented by an expanding body of empirical literature. Carlson (1998), for example, found a correlation between a disorganized attachment style in infancy and dissociation at age 19. Hesse and van IJzendoorn (1999) reported that individuals who described unresolved trauma memories during the Adult Attachment Interview (AAI; Hesse, 1999; Hesse & van IJzendoorn, 1999) also scored high on a scale measuring dissociative phenomenon. The data point in particular to a link between attachment-related traumas and dissociation (Hesse, 1999). More recently, Calamari and Pini (2003) conducted a study examining the relationship(s) between dissociation, anger proneness, and attachment style in female adolescents. Results suggested that insecure females, especially those with

[1] The reader will note in our following discussion that difficulties controlling reactions to intense affect, which are compounded by the elevated chronic arousal associated with PTSD, play a key role in a contextual conception of and approach to treating dissociation.

ambivalent attachment styles, reported higher levels of dissociation as measured by the Dissociative Experiences Scale (DES) than respondents with other attachment orientations. In general, findings support the hypothesis proposing an inverse relationship between dissociation and secure attachment (Calamari & Pini, 2003).

41.3 A CONTEXTUAL MODEL OF DISSOCIATION

Our own conceptual framework subsumes and builds upon the trauma and attachment models of the origins of dissociation. Dissociative pathology, at least in its more extreme forms, has been widely documented among survivors of child abuse (Briere & Runtz, 1988; Chu & Dill, 1990; Irwin, 1996). This has led many theorists and clinicians to assume that dissociation is directly attributable to the impact of trauma. However, other forms of trauma, especially ones occurring later in life, are much less strongly associated with long-term dissociative symptomatology (Kirby, Chu, & Dill, 1993; Zlotnick et al., 1996). In addition, even among child abuse survivors, dissociative syndromes are most commonly seen among those whose maltreatment was prolonged and severe (Brand & Alexander, 2003; Briere, 2006; Lazarus & Folkman, 1984; Lipschitz, Kaplan, Sorkenn, Chorney, & Asnis, 1996). This suggests that rather than generically related to trauma, appreciable, chronic dissociative symptomatology is most commonly associated with trauma in the specific form of (1) abuse that (2) takes place in early childhood, (3) is relatively severe, and (4) persists over long periods of time.

An important clinical observation is that therapy clients with an extensive and ongoing child abuse history describe having grown up in families with high levels of chaos and conflict, high levels of control, and little consistent affection and emotional responsiveness (Gold, 2000). These accounts are consistent with a substantial body of empirical research showing these qualities are prevalent in the families of survivors of prolonged child abuse (PCA; Benedict & Zautra, 1993; Rudd & Herzberger, 2000; Seibel, 2004). Although one may assume that these are features of abusive and incestuous families, research indicates that they also characterize the families of survivors of abuse by perpetrators who were not family members (Benedict & Zautra, 1993; Gold, Hyman, & Andres-Hyman, 2004; Rudd & Herzberger, 2000). We therefore propose that growing up in this type of family atmosphere—with deficient levels of affection, consistency, predictability, or autonomy—renders children particularly vulnerable to victimization, because they are desperate for attention and interpersonal contact, inadequately equipped to assert themselves, and lack a strong sense of appropriate boundaries and personal rights (Gold, 2000).

In addition, growing up in families that fit this profile in all likelihood contributes to long-term problems in adjustment independently of the impact of overt abuse (Hill, 1999; Irwin, 1996; Seibel, 2004). For example, being reared in this type of atmosphere is consistent with the attachment difficulties observed in highly dissociative clients (Ogawa et al., 1997). However, we contend that it is not only attachment, but a much wider spectrum of aspects of psychological development that is affected by being reared in such an environment.

41.4 DIVERGENT MANIFESTATIONS OF DISSOCIATION

Originally a broad, central organizing concept in psychology (Cotsell, 2005), dissociation fell into relative obscurity for many decades. Unquestionably, the impetus for its reemergence in the late 20th century was interest in multiple personality disorder (now known as dissociative identity disorder [DID]). In fact, the original appellation of the International Society for the Study of Dissociation, founded in 1983, was the International Society for the Study of Multiple Personality. Many contemporary investigators of dissociation first became drawn to the topic of dissociation through clinical encounters with clients with DID. Growing attention to DID in the early 1980s was clearly related to the simultaneous increase in awareness of the prevalence of child abuse and other forms of trauma in clinical populations (Blizard, 1997; Boon, 1997; Ogawa et al., 1997).

DID is a disorder that often is characterized by dramatic features that challenge commonly held basic assumptions about the unity of the personality and about human nature itself. The descriptor one very commonly hears clinicians ascribe to the first cases of DID they encounter is "fascinating." Due to the extraordinary and compelling quality of DID, it is understandable that this extreme variant of dissociation was for a long time the central focus of investigation, almost completely eclipsing other aspects and manifestations of dissociation. Until relatively recently, the term DID was practically synonymous in the minds of many experts with dissociation; for numerous professionals without appreciable knowledge about dissociation, this continues to be the case. As a result, treatment for dissociation was until very recently focused almost exclusively on DID.

One unfortunate consequence of the overemphasis on DID was that less dramatic manifestations of dissociation were either overlooked or were assumed to be signs of DID. For example, when a client was identified as experiencing amnestic episodes, some therapists would infer the existence of an identify fragment or "alter" that was in executive control of the client's behavior during the period of amnesia. This type of perceptual bias tends to distract the practitioner from attending to the difficulty being presented (in this case, for example, amnesia) and to instead focus on a search for identity fragments that may not in actuality be part of the clinical picture.

To our way of thinking, another problem with the tendency to view DID as the quintessential exemplar of dissociation is that it encourages clinicians to conceptualize all manifestations of dissociation as reflecting the division of the personality or psyche. As we will explain presently, a contextual approach to conceptualization is not consistent with this assumption. Although DID is unquestionably the most extreme form of dissociative pathology, we do not see divisions of the mind as being the central defining feature of dissociation.

41.5 DISSOCIATION: A UNITARY SUBSTRATE FOR DIVERGENT MANIFESTATIONS

The conception that guides the intervention strategies we present here is grounded in an explicit recognition that dissociation assumes many guises beyond DID and that these various manifestations require corresponding modifications in conceptualization and treatment. From the vantage point of contextual theory, the diverse expressions of dissociation are not viewed as all being indicators of divided consciousness. Rather, they are understood to constitute reflections of the same fundamental psychological processes (e.g., attention, memory, awareness, attachment) that underlie adaptive as well as pathological responses. Dissociative symptoms—such as derealization, amnesia, and identity fragmentation—can be so disparate in appearance that many find it difficult to discern what it is they have in common that render them all instances of dissociation. Much of this ambiguity can be dispelled by remembering that the word *dissociation* literally means disconnection.

Conceptually, it is extremely useful to keep in mind that the progressive attainment of increasing capacities for connection—to other people, to one's own subjective experience, and to one's surroundings—reflected in increased complexity of interconnections between neuronal networks, is a fundamental aspect of human development[2] (Elman et al., 1997; Siegel, 1999). Contextual theory posits, therefore, that dissociation is inversely related to development. A major strand of development is comprised of increasing capacities for connection, although capacities for disconnection, which have adaptive uses, are not lost. Many aspects of development—secure attachment, immediate subjective awareness of emotions and sensations, emotional regulation, the capacity for critical thinking, perspective-taking, and the capacity for empathy—contribute to or are expressions of the general facility for connection. Therapy for dissociation, therefore, revolves around teaching and fostering the development of these capacities.

The relative absence of the capacity for connection, or a weakness in it that renders it hard to sustain under stress, results in various dissociative phenomena. For example, disconnection from one's surroundings may result in the experience of amnesia or derealization. Disconnection from inner experience can foster depersonalization. Disconnection from other people manifests as interpersonal detachment and a limited capacity for intimacy. Because much of development occurs through interpersonal interaction (Siegel, 1999), which is why attachment plays such a fundamental role in human development, interpersonal disconnection has a profound inhibiting effect on developmental progress. As we will see presently, this is why the therapeutic relationship plays an even more essential role in the treatment of dissociation than it does in interventions for other problems.

41.6 GENERAL PRINCIPLES OF TREATMENT

From the model of dissociation outlined in the previous discussion, follow three central principles of the contextual treatment of dissociation:

1. The primary objective of treatment is to improve adaptive functioning. This requires distinguishing means (e.g., processing trauma, exploring family background, identifying triggers of dissociative episodes) from ends (e.g., reducing the intensity and frequency of amnestic episodes, diminishing periods of "spacing out" and increasing the capacity to remain attentive to the immediate present). Ultimately it is not the interventions that guide treatment, but the objectives.

[2] It is important to appreciate that the increasing capacity for connection as development progresses does not mean that the ability to disconnect is lost, or that connection is always preferable to or more adaptive than disconnection. Intense concentration on an activity, for example, requires that one be able to disconnect from surrounding stimuli that could serve as potential distractions from the task at hand.

2. The main focus of treatment is on problems that find expression in the present rather than a search for hypothesized causes that may erroneously be assumed to all be traceable to the past. Exploration centers initially on identifying particulars such as: the nature of dissociative symptoms experienced by the client; how these symptoms affect daily functioning; factors that set off, exacerbate, or ameliorate levels of dissociative symptomatology, etc. If exploration of these dimensions leads spontaneously to historical material, such as experiences of childhood abuse, a chaotic family background, or problematic attachment relationships, then that information may be used to inform treatment, but it is not assumed that identifying factors such as these is essential to formulating effective interventions. This approach has the added advantage of priming the practitioner to be more open to recognize factors in the present that maintain or exacerbate dissociative symptoms.
3. Interventions are construed as means of teaching the client skills that can be applied to difficulties as they arise, rather than as being directed at solving difficulties for the client. The capacities that the client learns are aimed at the reduction of distress, the remediation of developmental warps and gaps, and the acquisition of adaptive living skills. Ideally, because in the course of treatment the client has acquired new adaptive capacities, substantial therapeutic progress will occur and continue well after termination has taken place.

41.7 TREATMENT STRATEGIES

41.7.1 The Triad of Affect, Cognition, and Behavior

Intense emotions potentiate dissociative reactions when they override cognitive processing. Dissociative clients often have poor capacities to recognize that they are experiencing affect, let alone to monitor the fluctuating intensity of feelings. When they are aware that they are experiencing emotion, it is often only dimly, because they frequently have difficulty identifying and labeling what type of feeling it is. For all these reasons, they are vulnerable to experiencing rapid escalation in affective levels without adequate ability to keep either their emotions or the expression of their feelings in check.

Consequently, it is not at all unusual for dissociative clients to be seized by strong affect that finds expression in relatively unrestrained and impulsive behaviors. It is not uncommon for an entire sequence of behavior to be executed without these clients even being aware that they are emotionally aroused. Note that awareness of the presence of affect, assessing the intensity of affect, and identifying the type of affect experienced are all cognitive functions. In the midst of the emotional intensity, cognitive processing may be so thoroughly derailed that the very awareness that they are acting may be obliterated, fostering dissociative amnesia for emotionally driven behavior. In effect, affective arousal is so intense and the capacities for cognitive processing of emotional experience so tenuous that the dissociative client goes directly from affect to behavior without cognitive processing—including, at times, without having awareness of either the affect or the overt behavior associated with it.

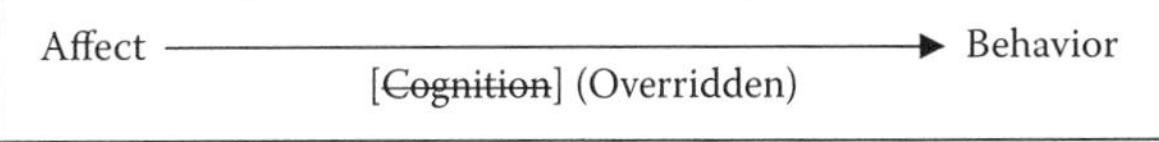

The experience of acting impulsively without recognizing the existence of the affect that prompted their actions, and often still not being aware of having experienced emotion even after having acted on it, impedes dissociative clients' ability to experience themselves as the agents of their own behavior. (It is not difficult to deduce that in clients with extreme dissociation in the form of dissociative identity disorder and ego-state disorder this phenomenon fosters a palpable sense that it was "someone else" and "not me" who executed the behavior.) It is this type of experience that led one dissociative client to remark, "My behavior is as much a mystery to me as it is to anybody." Baffled by their own conduct, experiencing themselves as out of control and unpredictable, saddled with the interpersonal consequences of repeatedly and unintentionally behaving in ways that invite condemnation, censure, and rejection, these clients are often riddled with shame. The shame and self-condemnation only serves to inhibit their ability to learn from experience; due to the discomfort aroused by thinking about these incidents, they avoid examining them, increasing the likelihood that the pattern will persist.

This formulation points to three goals for intervention that foster reduction in the frequency and intensity of dissociative episodes:

1. Reduce the potential for rapid and unchecked escalation of affect and foster the capacity for emotional de-escalation.
2. Increase the cognitive capacities for recognizing the presence of affect, for monitoring its intensity, and for labeling the type of affect experienced.

3. Increase the ability to refrain from executing behavior motivated by the emotional intensity of the moment.

From a contextual perspective, these affective, cognitive, and behavioral impairments frequently (although not always) have at least two major sources: (1) disruption of existing capacities due to the impact of traumatic events; and (2) gaps and warps in the development of these basic functional capacities due to having been reared in an interpersonal environment that did not provide sufficient resources to foster their attainment. To the extent that a client's dissociative reactions are attributable to capacities for affective regulation, cognitive processing, and behavioral control that were never adequately developed, processing traumatic material will not instill them. Therapy needs to explicitly concentrate on promoting the acquisition of these capacities. This means that the therapist has to be careful, for example, not to rely on finding ways to reduce the client's emotional arousal, but to help the client cultivate the capacity to do this, even after and beyond therapy.

41.7.2 Reducing the Propensity for Arousal

The limited capacity of many dissociative clients for awareness of affect, combined with the propensity, if they are trauma survivors, for the triggering of fight-flight reactions in response to trauma-related cues, leave them especially susceptible to developing chronically high levels of arousal. As delineated previously, elevated arousal levels, in turn, increase their vulnerability to dissociate. Teaching these clients how to reduce their habitual level of arousal, therefore, can be an important step toward reducing the frequency and intensity with which dissociative reactions occur.

To accomplish this goal, it is necessary for clients to master the use of relaxation techniques.[3] Using these exercises sporadically in response to particularly distressing situations, however, will accomplish little as an exclusive strategy. Only by practicing these exercises regularly and repeatedly over an extended period of time will the chronically elevated levels of arousal typical of clients with a history of prolonged childhood trauma subside. This objective is achieved in contextual therapy by providing clients with a log sheet recording their level of distress on a zero to 10 SUD (Subjective Units of Distress) scale before and after each instance practicing a relaxation technique in the morning, at midday, and just before retiring (Gold, 2000).

Teaching dissociative clients relaxation techniques and instructing them in their regular use is a relatively simple matter. Much more challenging is getting them to follow through and maintain a regular schedule of practice. Due to the lack of structure and consistency with which they grew up and which often continues to characterize their adult lives, it is difficult for these clients to appreciate the value of routine. It is similarly hard for them to recognize that activities that appear to yield little or no returns in the near term can have profound benefits in the long run with persistence repetition. Convincing these clients to maintain a schedule of practice long enough to find out firsthand how much can be gained from perseverance is where the greatest demands on the clinician's expertise lie. Strategies for accomplishing this are discussed in detail elsewhere (Gold, 2000).

41.7.3 Learning to Directly Counteract Dissociative Reactions

A constellation of strategies widely employed by therapists who are knowledgeable about dissociation to help clients counteract the propensity to dissociate are "grounding" or "anchoring" techniques (Dolan, 1991; Phillips & Frederick, 1995; Simonds, 1994). What this group of techniques has in common is that they all involve learning to direct one's attention to subjective experience and the surrounding environment in the immediate present. If dissociation is in effect a function of the inability to concentrate one's attention on what is occurring in the immediate subjective, interpersonal, and surrounding environment, grounding techniques are methods of developing this capacity by learning to direct and sustain one's focus on the here and now.

Probably the most powerful grounding technique is to engage in movement while purposefully concentrating one's attention on the corresponding tactile sensations of pressure and muscle tension. Walking while intentionally focusing on the sensations of one's feet alternately touching

[3] There are those who will wonder why we do not recommend the exposure therapies so commonly associated with trauma treatment. There are three major reasons for this. (1) Not all dissociative clients have a history of trauma. (2) Contextual therapy posits as a central tenet that many dissociative clients grew up in circumstances that did not adequately prepare them to cope with routine everyday stressors; in the face of exposure to traumatic stress, they are almost certain to experience an exacerbation rather than diminution of symptoms (Gold, 2000). (3) It is widely agreed upon by experts in trauma treatment that before processing of traumatic material occurs, there needs to be an initial phase of treatment that bolsters client safety and security (see, e.g., Herman, 1992).

the ground is an excellent way to bring one's attention to the immediate present. This is a particularly useful technique for someone who notices the ebbing of orientation to present time and place. In addition to the sensations of muscle movement involved in walking and the sensations of pressure on the soles of one's feet, one must tactilely and visually judge distance and timing to coordinate one's movements and navigate obstacles in the environment.

A less conspicuous method of anchoring oneself in the present is to direct one's attention to tactile sensations without moving. Gradually, clients can learn to detect increasingly subtle degrees and qualities of touch that are less intense and less readily detectable than the pressure of one's feet touching the ground while walking. These include the continuous pressure of one's feet on the floor while standing, of one's body making contact with the furniture while seated, or one's hands resting on one's lap, nestled in one's pockets, or touching each other.

Once a client has established awareness of tactile sensations that form a palpable connection with the immediate surroundings, she or he can move on to attend to visual stimulation. Often it is helpful to silently label salient features of the visual field and their qualities. For instance, clients may mentally make note of elements such as the "gray, textured carpeting," "beige walls," "dark brown wood desk," and other notable characteristics of the therapist's office to orient themselves during session.

To extend the depth of anchoring in the here and now even further, the client can also attend to sounds that for most of us routinely fade from awareness. Noises such as traffic sounds outside, the hum of a central air conditioning or heating unit, or voices in the next room often "disappear into the background" and slip outside our notice. Making a purposeful effort to focus on these sounds can help to solidify the client's sense of being firmly grounded in the present moment.

With practice, dissociative clients can extend their awareness of tactile sensations to more subtle, proprioceptive sensations. These might include sensations of the rib cage and diaphragm moving while breathing, sensory awareness with one's eyes closed of one's posture and one's orientation in space, and sensations of muscle tension in various parts of the body while immobile. Eventually, awareness of proprioceptive sensations can form the foundation of attaining the abilities to recognize, identify and label emotions which, because they were so tenuous, previously contributed to their propensity to dissociate.

41.8 THE ESSENTIAL ROLE OF THE THERAPEUTIC RELATIONSHIP IN CONTEXTUAL THERAPY FOR DISSOCIATION

We have already noted how essential early attachment in particular and relationships with other people in general are to human development. Numerous functional capacities evolve from the matrix of interactions and interconnections with other people that are a major contributor to the neurological and psychological development of the human organism (Siegel, 1999). In an analogous fashion, it is largely through the medium of the therapeutic relationship that the client attains developmental milestones that were not adequately achieved prior to treatment.

A major challenge and paradox of work with many dissociative clients, especially those at the relatively severe extreme of the dissociative spectrum, is that the therapeutic relationship is especially critical to the attainment of their treatment goals, yet their capacity to form a productive treatment alliance is usually significantly impaired. Due to a childhood history characterized by the unavailability of caretakers who could help instill secure attachment, inadequate guidance and preparation for adulthood, and repeated abuse, maltreatment and interpersonal violence, they often lack many of the capacities needed to ally themselves with another person and feel comfortable and connected to a therapist. Although these clients may be intensely desirous of contact with the therapist (Gold, 2000), the lack of reliably responsive figures in their formative years impeded the development of the ability to palpably experience interpersonal connectedness. (We view this weak capacity to experience connection with others as in itself representing an aspect of dissociative disconnectedness.) Despite a desire for a sense of relatedness that may in some reach intensely painful proportions, the relative absence of the ability to feel connected to others leads to frustration, despair, or becoming hopelessly resigned to perpetually feeling detached from others. For this reason, the therapist needs to be vigilant for opportunities to employ the therapeutic situation as an opportunity for the client to learn how to develop the capacity for interpersonal connectedness she or he is unlikely until now to have been able to consistently sustain.

Due to the urgency of their unmet interpersonal needs, however, some severely dissociative clients will be so preoccupied with spending time with the therapist that this will take precedence for them over working toward treatment goals. These clients may come to believe that solely being in the therapist's presence will somehow be "curative" in and of itself. While the therapeutic alliance is a key aspect of treatment, it is erroneous to believe that the relationship alone will lead to substantive change.

Although contextual theory emphasizes that the absence of reliable attachment resources are a major contributor to the client's difficulties, it also proposes that there are often numerous other types of deprivation in this client population that lead to crucial gaps in adaptive skills. It is imperative that the client understand that these abilities will not be remediated without commitment to persistently practicing these skills between meetings with the therapist. If this message is to be conveyed convincingly, it is necessary as much as possible to keep session time focused primarily on goal attainment rather than on simply allowing the client to "hang out' and "chat." We therefore believe that it is counterproductive in most cases to regularly schedule therapy sessions with these clients more than once a week (Gold, 2000); other authorities on treating dissociation have similarly come to recommend against routinely scheduling more often than this (International Society for the Study of Dissociation, 2005).

In essence, attempts to help severely dissociative clients develop a more secure attachment style need to rely primarily on the quality rather than the quantity of time spent with the therapist. To a degree that is difficult for practitioners who have not been specifically trained in working with dissociation to appreciate, these clients are so precariously oriented to the here and now that an inordinate amount of time can be spent in treatment without much being accomplished. Although they may not appear detached or disoriented in a way that would be readily detectable to an observer, careful questioning will reveal that much of what occurs in session is not noticed, registered, comprehended, or remembered.

In order for treatment to advance at a reasonable pace, therefore, it is absolutely essential that the therapist be watchful of, compensate for, and address the severely dissociative client's interpersonal detachment. To counteract the client's experiential distance from the therapeutic relationship, the practitioner needs to work that much harder to be emotionally engaged and present in an effort to make these qualities more readily discernable to the client. In addition, it is crucial to repeatedly and explicitly "check in" with the client to assess the degree to which she or he is tracking, registering, comprehending, and retaining what is transpiring in session. This not only spares the clinician from assuming that much more is "getting through" to the clients than actually is, but also helps the clients to recognize how much of what is going on is eluding them—not only in therapy, but also in daily life. It is obviously essential to guard against allowing these clients to slip into fruitless self-denigration in response to the realization of how much they are missing, which can only lead to a sense of hopelessness, distracting the client from learning how to stay more consistently focused. Particularly in the early phases of treatment with those who are highly dissociative, moment-to-moment monitoring of the degree to which the client is attending to and following what is transpiring, with repeated but diplomatic reorienting to the task at hand, may be required.

Readers without significant experience working with this population may understandably wonder how it is possible for someone to be actively participating in dialogue with someone else while minimally registering what is transpiring. A good example of this occurred in a therapy group in which a highly dissociative client would often provide lengthy accounts of events that had occurred to her the previous week. These descriptions, which were usually only tangentially relevant to the focus of the group, would ramble aimlessly from one topic to another, so that periodically the client herself would lose track of what she was saying. It gradually became evident to the cotherapists leading the group that this woman was speaking in an automatic fashion with minimal awareness of what she was saying.

Finally, one of the coleaders interrupted her and asked her to repeat what she had just said. When the client acknowledged that she was unable to do this, the therapist replied, "If you're not even listening to what you're saying, what reason is there to believe that you're taking in what anyone else in group is saying?" This interchange was pivotal for this client. After months in her current course of therapy, and years in a series of previous treatments, she realized for the first time how seldom she was cognizant of what was occurring in the present moment. In other words, it helped her to see how infrequently she was present—and how often she was instead dissociated from both herself and her surroundings.[4] This event engendered a radical shift in her orientation to both therapy and daily life, ending a long period of relative stagnation and initiating a much more productive phase of treatment.

[4] This incident also is an excellent illustration of contextual thinking about dissociation: at its core, it is not about the manifestation of symptoms such as depersonalization or amnesia, but about a general orientation to self, others, and one's surroundings characterized by experiential detachment.

41.9 DISRUPTING DISSOCIATIVE RESPONDING AND EXTINGUISHING DISSOCIATIVE CUES

Contextual theory proposes that emotional arousal indirectly contributes to the occurrence of dissociative episodes. Emotional arousal interferes with the ability to adequately sustain attention on the immediate present, which plays a more direct role in activating dissociative episodes by interrupting the experiential connection to the here and now. By practicing a relaxation technique with regularity over an extended period of time, dissociative clients can significantly reduce their vulnerability to the type of rapid, intense emotional arousal that fosters dissociative reactions. Similarly, habitually employing grounding techniques can diminish the client's propensity to lose touch with the immediate present and slip into dissociative experiencing.

While routinely practicing both of these strategies can appreciably decrease the instances of dissociation a client experiences, they can not be counted on to entirely eliminate them. There are, however, ways in which one can use these resources to progressively move toward the further reduction and eventual elimination of maladaptive dissociative reactions.[5] This is done by invoking relaxation and grounding techniques to disrupt a dissociative reaction once it is initiated or when its onset is imminent.

In order to achieve this, clients need to be able to anticipate when a dissociative episode is likely to occur. This can be accomplished by identifying cues that predictably trigger their dissociative episodes and the "early warning signs" of an incipient dissociative reaction. In contextual therapy, we employ the methodology of functional behavioral analysis to pinpoint the factors that set off dissociative response and are signs of the initial phases of dissociative reactions in a particular client (Gold, 2000; Gold & Seifer, 2002). To do this, it is essential to systematically examine a series of particular instances of dissociative reactions over a number of sessions. We ask the client to select a specific, discrete dissociative episode, preferably the most recent one, so that we can trace its course from the time the client first became aware of it.

This approach presents particular difficulties if the dissociative reaction is an amnestic one since usually it is only upon reorienting that the client becomes aware of having dissociated. In this case we ask the client to locate the last thing remembered before the onset of amnesia. Once we have tracked down the point at which the dissociative episode began, we then trace backward with the client what was occurring, what the client was thinking, and what the client was experiencing just prior to the amnestic period. By repeating this procedure with a number of dissociative incidents over several sessions, it is eventually possible in collaboration with the client to isolate the experiential indicators that commonly signal that a dissociative reaction is beginning, and to deduce the environmental or situational factors that predictably trigger these episodes.

Once the cues and signs of the onset of dissociation are detected, the client can use this information to invoke the use of relaxation and grounding techniques to disrupt the dissociative reaction. Usually at first it is only after the dissociative episode is over that the client is retrospectively aware that the dissociative cues and indicators were present. Gradually, however, the client is able to recognize their occurrence and intervene progressively earlier in the sequence of events. With regular practice, execution of the relaxation and grounding responses occurs increasingly more automatically over time. Eventually, the dissociative reaction is interrupted spontaneously, with little or no conscious effort. Ultimately, cues that previously triggered the dissociative response are extinguished.

One client, a middle-aged woman who experienced extensive periods of amnesia on a daily basis, was able in collaboration with her therapist to identify that it was events that took her by surprise that consistently set off periods of amnesia. She also came to recognize that one of the first reactions she had that led to amnestic episodes was heart palpitations. (As is typical of dissociative clients, before intervention she had not been able to detect what she later realized were relatively intense sensations of her heart pounding.) Armed with this information and having developed proficiency in the use of relaxation and grounding methods, she was able to interrupt the occurrence of amnestic reactions with increasing frequency. This is her spontaneous description in a follow-up interview 6 months after the termination of treatment of what happened in situations that previously would have culminated in an episode of amnesia:

> It really works for me. I can pop that [relaxation] imagery into my head, and—actually, I'm saying I can but

[5] Note the qualifier *maladaptive* here. Just as virtually everyone experiences instances of anxiety and depressed affect, contextual theory proposes that instances of dissociative responding are near-universal. Dissociative experiences are not assumed to be pathological *per se*. From a contextual perspective it is only when dissociative reactions become so habitual that they appreciably interfere with social, academic, and occupational functioning that they are considered pathological.

> it really goes very automatically. If something is coming to frighten me and my heart starts to pound, it's like very quickly after my heart starts to pound that I know... don't try to make any decisions, don't, you know, panic, just relax until I can get this emotional garbage out.... And that is so helpful to me because even if I just say to myself, you know in really bad moments I'll say to myself, 'Just do it, just do it and then deal with what's left,' and within a short period of time I'm clearer and better able to deal with whatever is confronting me.

41.10 SOME FINAL CONSIDERATIONS

Dissociation is a central problem area for the vast majority of clients with a history of PCA. However, for most of these clients, dissociation is just one of a wide range of symptoms patterns and problem areas that must be addressed if therapy is to be successful. Documentation for this can be found in the empirical literature on the prevalence of extensive comorbidity in dissociative clients (Gold & Seifer, 2002; Ross, Fast, Anderson, Auty, & Todd, 1990; Ross et al., 1992; Tezcan et al., 2003).

We have, obviously, concentrated here on interventions for dissociation because this volume is about the identification and treatment of dissociative disorders. It is important, however, to keep in mind that most survivors of PCA will exhibit a wide range of difficulties in addition to dissociation. In terms of symptoms, this will often include anxiety, depression, and a range of addictive and compulsive behaviors. Interpersonally, it will routinely encompass volatile interpersonal interactions, unassertiveness, deficient capacities for intimate relating, and problems sustaining friendships and social relationships. In terms of daily living, developmental gaps and warps result in an unimaginably wide and diverse spectrum of practical skills deficits that can be as concrete as not knowing how to file papers and as abstract as consistently misreading social cues (see Rabinovitch, 2003, for a detailed illustrative example).

Of necessity, therefore, contextual therapy for PCA survivors is designed to treat a complex network of interlocking difficulties. We have focused here on the particular topic of dissociation. While dissociation is a central difficulty for survivors of PCA, it can not be adequately addressed in isolation from the other problem areas often simultaneously faced by this population. To do so would be artificial and ineffective.

It is equally important to point out that because contextual therapy was originally devised for survivors of PCA, we have specifically focused here on treating dissociation in that spectrum of clients. However, we do not want to leave the reader with the mistaken impression that we believe that dissociative disorders occur exclusively in this population. Just as a contextual conceptualization helps to clarify that trauma is a contributing but not the sole cause of dissociation, it also highlights that dissociative disorders do not occur exclusively among PCA survivors, and that at times they are found in people who may have no trauma history whatsoever.

Depersonalization, for example, is one of the diagnostic criteria for panic disorder (American Psychiatric Association, 1994). Others have recognized that once someone has a panic attack the person may develop panic disorder because the anxious anticipation of further panic attacks actually promotes their recurrence (Barlow et al., 1984; Godemann, Schabowska, Naetebusch, Heinz, & Strohle, 2006). We have seen a number of cases of Depersonalization Disorder that had analogous origins. These clients had experienced a panic attack. Instead of dreading the possible repetition of the panic attack, however, it was the depersonalization that they found the most disturbing and which was therefore the focus of their anxious anticipation. Their fearful vigilance against depersonalization appeared to have paradoxically led to its recurrence. Sometimes the depersonalization was episodic, but in most of these clients it became chronic—fluctuating in its intensity, but almost always present to an appreciable degree. The source of the disorder did not appear to be traumatic; these clients denied a history of trauma. Rather, it seemed to have relatively recent onset (usually the chronic depersonalization was so unsettling that these clients did not wait long to seek out treatment) specifically in response to an episode of panic accompanied by depersonalization.

We would consider ourselves remiss if we did not make explicit an aspect of the contextual conceptualization of dissociation that we have thus far only mentioned in passing. From a contextual perspective, dissociation is not always symptomatic or pathological; it can and frequently does assume adaptive forms and functions. While both normal development and successful psychotherapy foster an increased capacity for experiential connection, this does not mean that the ability to disconnect is lost. Nor would this be desirable. There is nothing inherently maladaptive about dissociative disconnection; there are times when it is useful to be able to "turn off" awareness both for practical reasons and as a means of managing distress. Contextual therapy does not aim to eliminate dissociative disconnection, therefore. By bolstering the client's capacities for connection and anchoring in the present, it seeks to make dissociative disconnection less habitual, automatic, unwitting, and unintentional, not in order to take away the client's ability to dissociate, but to provide greater choice to connect or disconnect as the situation warrants.

REFERENCES

American Psychiatric Association (1994). *Diagnostic and statistical manual of mental disorders* (4th ed.). Washington, DC: Author.

Barach, P. M. (1991). Multiple personality as an attachment disorder. *Dissociation, 4(3),* 117–123.

Barlow, D. H., Cohen, A. S., Waddell, M., Vermilyea, J. A., Klosko, J. S., Blanchard, E., B., & Di Nardo, P. A. (1984). Panic and generalized anxiety disorders: Nature and treatment. *Behavior Therapy, 15,* 431–449.

Benedict, L. W., & Zautra, A. J. (1993). Family environmental characteristics as risk factors for childhood sexual abuse. *Journal of Clinical Child Psychology, 22(3),* 365–374.

Blizard, R. A. (1997). Therapeutic alliance with abuser alters in DID: The paradox of attachment to the abuser. *Dissociation, 10,* 246–254.

Boon, S. (1997). The treatment of traumatic memories in DID: Indications and contraindications. *Dissociation, 10,* 65–80.

Brand, B. L., & Alexander, P. C. (2003). Coping with incest: The relationship between recollections of childhood coping and adult functioning in female survivors of incest. *Journal of Traumatic Stress, 16(3),* 285–293.

Briere, J. (2006). Dissociative symptoms and trauma exposure: specificity, affect dysregulation, and posttraumatic stress. *Journal of Nervous and Mental Disease, 194(2),* 78–82.

Briere, J., & Runtz, M. (1988). Symptomatology associated with childhood sexual victimization in a nonclinical adult sample. *Child Abuse & Neglect, 12,* 51–59.

Calamari, E., & Pini, M. (2003). Dissociative experiences and anger proneness in late adolescent females with different attachment styles. *Adolescence, 38,* 287–303.

Carlson, E. A. (1998). A prospective longitudinal study of attachment disorganization/disorientation. *Child Development, 69,* 1107–1128.

Chu, J. A., & Dill, D. L. (1990). Dissociative symptoms in relations to childhood physical and sexual abuse. *American Journal of Psychiatry, 147,* 887–892.

Chu, J. A., Frey, L. M., Ganzel, B. L., & Matthews, J. A. (1999). Memories of childhood abuse: Dissociation, amnesia and corroboration. *American Journal of Psychiatry, 156,* 749–755.

Cotsell, M. (2005). *The theater of trauma: American modernist drama and the psychological struggle for the American mind,* 1900–1930. New York: Peter Lang.

Dolan, Y. M. (1991*). Resolving sexual abuse: Solution-focused therapy and Ericksonian hypnosis for survivors.* New York: W. W. Norton.

Elman, J. L., Bates, E. A., Johnson, M. H., Karmiloff-Smith, A., Parisi, D., & Plunkett, K. (1997). *Rethinking innateness: A connectionist perspective on development (neural networks and connectionist modeling).* Cambridge, MA: MIT Press.

Feeney, N. C., Zoellner, L. A., Fitzgibbons, L. A., & Foa, E. B. (2000). Exploring the roles of emotional numbing, depression and dissociation in PTSD. *Journal of Traumatic Stress, 13,* 489–498.

Freud, S. (1893/1959a). On the psychical mechanisms of hysterical phenomena. In J. Riviere (Trans.), *Sigmund Freud: Collected papers* (Vol. 1, pp. 24–41). New York: Basic Books.

Freud, S. (1896/1959b). The ætiology of hysteria. In J. Riviere (Trans.), *Sigmund Freud: Collected papers* (Vol. 1, pp. 183–219). New York: Basic Books.

Godemann, F., Schabowska, A., Naetebusch, B., Heinz, A., & Strohle, A. (2006). The impact of cognitions on the development of panic and somatoform disorders: A prospective study in patients with vestibular neuritis. *Psychological Medicine, 36(1),* 99–108.

Gold, S. N. (2000). *Not trauma alone: Therapy for child abuse survivors in family and social context.* Philadelphia, PA: Brunner-Routledge.

Gold, S. N., Hyman, S. M., & Andres-Hyman, R. C. (2004). Family of origin environments in two clinical samples of survivors of intrafamilial, extra-familial, and both types of sexual abuse. *Child Abuse & Neglect, 28,* 1199–1212.

Gold, S. N., & Seifer, R. E. (2002). Dissociation and sexual addiction/compulsivity: A contextual approach to conceptualization and treatment. *Journal of Trauma & Dissociation, 3(4),* 59–82.

Hesse, E. (1999). The Adult Attachment Interview: Historical and current perspective. In J. Cassidy & P. R. Shaver (Eds.), *Handbook of attachment* (pp. 395–433). New York: Guilford Press.

Hesse, E., & van IJendoorn, M. H. (1999). Propensities toward absorption are related to lapses in the monitoring of reasoning or discourse during the Adult Attachment Interview: A preliminary investigation. *Attachment and Human Development, 1,* 67–91.

Hill, E. L. (1999). *Interpersonal dependency among childhood sexual abuse survivors: Family environment and abuse characteristics.* Unpublished doctoral dissertation, Nova Southeastern University, Fort Lauderdale, FL.

International Society for the Study of Dissociation (2005). [Chu, J.A., Loewenstein, R., Dell, P.F., Barach, P.M., Somer, E., Kluft, R.P., Gelinas, D.J., Van der Hart, O., Dalenberg, C.J., Nijenhuis, E.R.S., Bowman, E.S., Boon, S., Goodwin, J., Jacobson, M., Ross, C.A., Sar, V, Fine, C.G., Frankel, A.S., Coons, P.M., Courtois, C.A., Gold, S.N., & Howell, E.] Guidelines for treating Dissociative Identity Disorder in adults. *Journal of Trauma & Dissociation, 6(4),* 69–149.

Irwin, H. J. (1996). Traumatic childhood events, perceived availability of emotional support, and the development of dissociative tendencies. *Child Abuse & Neglect, 20,* 701–707.

Janet, P. (1889/1973). *L'automatisme psychologique: essai de psychologie experimentale sure les formes inferieures de l'activite humaine.* [Psychological automatisms: Experimental psychology essay on the lower forms of human activity.] Paris: Société Pierre Janet/Payot.

Kirby, J. S., Chu, J. A., & Dill, D. L. (1993). Correlates of dissociative symptomatology in patients with physical and sexual abuse histories. *Comprehensive Psychiatry, 34(4),* 258–263.

Lazarus, R. S., & Folkman, S. (1984). *Stress, appraisal, and coping.* New York: Springer.

Liotti, G. (1992). Disorganized/disoriented attachment in the etiology of the dissociative disorders. *Dissociation, 5(4),* 196–204.

Liotti, G., Intreccialagli, B., & Cecere, F. (1991). Esperienzi di lutto nella madre e facilitazoine dello sviluppo di disturbi dissociatvi nella prole: uno studio caso con controllo [Unresolved mourning in mother and development of dissociative disorders in children: A case control study]. *Rivista di Psichiatria, 26(5),* 283–291.

Lipschitz, D. S., Kaplan, M. L., Sorkenn J., Chorney, P., & Asnis, G. M. (1996). Childhood abuse, adult assault and dissociation. *Comprehensive Psychiatry, 37,* 261–266.

Ogawa, J. R., Sroufe, L. A., Weinfield, N. S., Carlson, E. A., & Egeland, B. (1997). Development of the fragmented self: Longitudinal study of dissociative symptomatology in a nonclinical sample. *Development and Psychopathology, 9,* 855–879.

Phillips, M., & Frederick, C. (1995). *Healing the divided self: Clinical and Ericksonian hypnotherapy for post-traumatic and dissociative conditions.* New York: W. W. Norton.

Putnam, F. W. (1997). *Dissociation in children and adolescents: A developmental perspective.* New York: Guilford Press.

Putnam, F. W., Guroff, J. J., Silberman, E. K., Barban, L., & Post, R. M. (1986). The clinical phenomenology of multiple personality disorder: Review of 100 recent cases. *Journal of Clinical Psychiatry, 47,* 285–293.

Rabinovitch, J. (2003). PEERS: The prostitutes' empowerment, education and resource society. In M. Farley (Ed.), *Prostitution, trafficking, and traumatic stress* (pp. 239–253). Binghamton, NY: Haworth.

Ross, C. A., Fast, E., Anderson, G., Auty, A., & Todd, J. (1990). Somatic symptoms in multiple sclerosis and MPD. *Dissociation, 3,* 102–106.

Ross, C. A., Kronson, J., Koensgen, S., Barkman, K., Clark, P., & Rockman, G. (1992). Dissociative comorbidity in 100 chemical dependent patients. *Hospital and Community Psychiatry, 43,* 840–842.

Rudd, J. M., & Herzberger, S. D. (1999). Brother-sister incest–father-daughter incest: A comparison of characteristics and consequences. *Child Abuse & Neglect, 23*(9), 915–928.

Seibel, S. L. (2004). *Fear of intimacy and interpersonal dependency among survivors of childhood sexual abuse: Abuse characteristics and family environment.* Unpublished doctoral dissertation, Nova Southeastern University, Fort Lauderdale, FL.

Siegel, D. J. (1999). *The developing mind: How relationships and the brain interact to shape who we are.* New York: Guilford.

Simonds, S. L. (1994). *Bridging the silence: Nonverbal modalities in the treatment of adult survivors of childhood sexual abuse.* New York: W. W. Norton.

Stein, P. T., & Kendall, J. C. (2004). *Psychological trauma and the developing brain: Neurologically based interventions for troubled children.* Binghamton, NY: Haworth Press.

Tezcan, E., Atmaca, M., Kuloğlu, M., Geçici, O., Büyükbayram, A., & Tutkun, H. (2003). Dissociative disorders in turkish inpatients with conversion disorder. *Comprehensive Psychiatry, 44(4),* 324–330.

Waller, N., Putnam, F. W., & Carlson, E. B. (1996). Types of dissociation and dissociative types: A taxometric analysis of dissociative experiences. *Psychological Methods, 1(3),* 300–321.

Zlotnick, C., Shea, M. T., Pearlstein, T., Begin, A., Simpson, E., & Costello, E. (1996). Differences in dissociative experiences between survivors of childhood incest and survivors of assault in adulthood. *Journal of Nervous and Mental Disease, 184(1),* 52–54.

42 Multiple Self-States, the Relational Mind, and Dissociation: A Psychoanalytic Perspective

Philip M. Bromberg, PhD

OUTLINE

The human personality possesses the extraordinary capacity to negotiate stability and change simultaneously, and will do so under the right relational conditions. I believe that this attribute is what we rely on to make clinical psychoanalysis, or any form of psychodynamic psychotherapy, possible. How we understand this remarkable capability of the mind, and what we see as the optimal therapeutic environment for it to flourish, are, I suggest, the most fundamental questions that shape the theory and praxis of psychodynamic psychotherapy.

In discussing these issues I will explore the central role of dissociation in normal personality functioning, in psychopathology, and in the process of psychotherapy. I will try to show why psychotherapeutic personality growth is, at its core, an intersubjective-interpersonal engagement between human beings, each possessing a mind organized as a nonlinear configuration of multiple self-states. *I contend that the mind is inherently relational in both its normal process of developmental maturation and in its subsequent ability to usefully participate in a psychotherapeutic process.*

Beahrs (1982, pp. 65–66) said that "we are advised to ask when dissociation is useful and when it is not." I would add to this that in each *individual* treatment we are well advised to ask how dissociation is useful. We should assess the degree to which that usefulness has been enlisted in the formation of a dissociative mental organization that is so rigid that it defines its own pathology.

42.1 HYPNOID STATES, DISSOCIATION, AND PSYCHOANALYTIC HISTORY

The constraint on the inclusion of dissociation in the development of psychoanalytic theory began with Freud's break with Josef Breuer. Following the publication of *Studies on Hysteria* (Breuer & Freud, 1893–1895), Freud sharply disagreed with Breuer about hypnoid states and splitting of consciousness (see Bromberg, 1996b). Breuer essentially supported Charcot (1882, 1887), Binet (1892), and Janet (1889), by stating in his theoretical chapter in *Studies on Hysteria* (pp. 185–251), that "what lies at the centre of hysteria is a splitting off of a portion of psychical activity" (p. 227). Breuer then took this view still further by insisting that this was "a splitting not merely of psychical activity but of consciousness" (p. 229). In brief, Breuer claimed that traumatic hysteria is mediated by a process that can "be classed with autohypnosis" and that "it seems desirable to adopt the expression 'hypnoid,' which lays stress on this internal similarity" (p. 220).

But, while Breuer asserted that the basis of hysteria was the existence of hypnoid states that had the power to create an amnesia, Freud rejected Breuer's concept of self-hypnosis and later contended that he had never encountered a self-hypnotic hysteria, only defense neuroses (Bliss, 1988, p. 36). After *Studies on Hysteria*, Freud tended to be openly contemptuous about the theoretical usefulness of dissociation, hypnoid states, or alterations in consciousness (Loewenstein & Ross, 1992, pp. 31–32). Berman (1981) characterized Freud's position as a "one-sided anti-Janet stand" (p. 285) that led psychoanalysis, for the next century, toward an "emphasis on repression at the expense of dissociation" (p. 297).

Nevertheless, there has always been a small coterie of independent thinkers representing different schools of analytic thought who contended that the quality of the analytic relationship is necessarily shaped by dissociation because dissociation is a key aspect of mental functioning. Several major theorists (Ferenczi, 1928, 1930, 1931, 1933; M. Balint, 1935, 1937, 1952, 1968; Sullivan, 1940, 1953, 1954, 1956; Fairbairn, 1929, 1940, 1944, 1952; Bion, 1957, 1965; and Kohut, 1971, 1977) argued that severe dissociation was etiologically linked to an early history of psychological trauma. Each of these theorists was struggling, in his own way, with the question of how dissociation shapes the analytic relationship and its effectiveness.

The longevity of the term *dissociation* in psychoanalysis, however, is due largely to Sandor Ferenczi (1930, 1933), a debt that cannot be overestimated. In opposition to Freud, Ferenczi believed that dissociation is a normal aspect of routine human development, and because of this, the quality of the analytic relationship takes on special significance. Ferenczi saw the etiology of *defensive* dissociation as linked to an inevitable aspect of personality development designed to protect the mind, at almost any cost, against the reactivation of traumatizing affect. "To Ferenczi the dissociated state included more than a set of associatively isolated traumatic memories; he described the dissociated state as a whole person, a child, and the delirious quality of that child as a reactivation in the treatment setting of the traumatically overstimulating situation" (Davies & Frawley, 1992, p. 12). Ferenczi pioneered the contemporary analytic view that regressive reliving of early traumatic experience in the analytic transference is to some degree curative in itself because it encourages active mastery of the traumatic "past" through use of the here-and-now analytic relationship.

Today, increased attention is being paid to the normal multiplicity of states of consciousness. This is evoking a conceptual shift toward a view of the mind as a configuration of discontinuous, shifting states of consciousness. These states are understood to have varying degrees of access to perception and cognition because many domains of dissociated self-experience have only weak or nonexistent links to the experience of "I" as a communicable entity. It should be noted, by the way, that this is true not only of patients with a history of *massive* traumatization. Before these hypnoidally inaccessible self-states can be taken as objects of cognitive reflection, they must first become "thinkable" by becoming linguistically communicable through enactment in the therapeutic relationship. Until this happens, neither repression nor even the experience of intrapsychic conflict can take place because each state of consciousness holds its own experientially encapsulated "truth," which is repetitively enacted. The difficulty for psychoanalysts is that they have lacked a strong theoretical model that could deal with the implications of this. When Freud dismissed the phenomenon of dissociation, he formulated a belief system that posited that (except for the most seriously disturbed patients) his concepts of "repetition compulsion" and "interpretation of resistance to unconscious conflict" constituted sufficient foundation upon which to build a theory of clinical technique.

42.2 THE RELATIONAL MIND, MULTIPLE SELF-STATES, AND DISSOCIATION

42.2.1 The Relational Mind

Mitchell (1991), in developing his now seminal view of the mind as relationally organized, writes the following:

> The key transition to postclassical psychoanalytic views of the self occurred when theorists began thinking … of the repressed not as disorganized, impulsive fragments but as constellations of meanings organized around relationships, and they began to conceive of the id as

involving a way of being, a sense of self, a person in relation to other persons. M. Klein, Fairbairn, Jacobson, Loewald, and Kernberg, each in their own way and in their own language, portray the id as a person or collection of persons in passionate relationships to other persons or parts of persons. Fairbairn's ego and object units are … versions of the person himself, and they embody active patterns of experience and behavior, organized around a particular point of view, a sense of self, a way of being, which underlie the ordinary phenomenological sense we have of ourselves as integral. Because we learn to become a person through interactions with different others and through different interactions with the same other, our experience of self is discontinuous, composed of different configurations, *different selves with different others*.… [E]ach actual relationship may contain multiple self-organizations; and there may be many such relationships. (pp. 127–128, emphasis added)

The result is a plural or manifold organization of self, patterned around different self and object images or representations, derived from different relational contexts. We are all composites of overlapping, multiple organizations and perspectives, and our experience is smoothed out by an illusory sense of continuity.… Thus, the portrayal of self as multiple and discontinuous and the sense of self as separate, integral, and continuous are referring to different aspects of self. The former refers to the multiple configurations of self patterned variability in different relational contexts. The latter refers to the subjective experience of the pattern making itself … represented as having particular qualities or tones or content at different times; however, at every point, it is recognized as "mine," my particular way of processing and shaping experience. (p. 139)

42.2.2 The Relational Mind and Multiple Self-States: The Domain of Dissociation

Beahrs (1982) writes that "state of consciousness, schema, mood, role, system, ego state and alter personality all refer to some level of … mental unit. Separated by a boundary from others, each unit has characteristic features defining its identity and finite persistence over an extended period of time. Dissociation, then, is *the process of forming and maintaining the boundary of said unit*" (pp. 61–62, original italics). I believe that this definition would be considered by most researchers and clinicians to be empirically useful. The term *dissociation*, "first coined in psychology by William James, was developed to explain various phenomena of altered consciousness, such as somnambulism, fugue states, and conditions of double consciousness. Personality was considered a plurality of states ranging from pathological to transcendent, with waking consciousness being only one possible state among many" (Taylor, 2000, p. 1030). Slavin and Kriegman (1992) discussed this same issue in terms of evolutionary biology and the adaptive design of the human psyche:

> Multiple versions of the self exist within an overarching, synthetic structure of identity … [which] probably cannot possess the degree of internal cohesion or unity frequently implied by concepts such as the "self" in the self psychological tradition, the "consolidated character" in Blos's ego psychological model, or "identity" in Erikson's framework. … [T]he idea of an individual "identity" or a cohesive "self" serves as an extremely valuable metaphor for the vital experience of relative wholeness, continuity, and cohesion in self-experience. Yet, as has often been noted, when we look within the psyche of well-put-together individuals, we actually see a "multiplicity of selves" or versions of the self coexisting within certain contours and patterns that, in sum, produce a sense of individuality, "I-ness" or "me-ness." (p. 204)

As clinicians, we try to find within our patients a self we can talk to who can simultaneously talk to us: in the process, we find ourselves traversing states kept apart from one another by dissociation. This means that there are important ways in which the seemingly "unitary self" that we meet in our patients is incapable of true dialogic engagement and, in other important ways, incapable of the experience of intrapsychic conflict. When the acquired, developmentally adaptive illusion of being a unitary self is traumatically threatened with unavoidable, precipitous disruption, its very cohesiveness becomes a liability because that cohesiveness is in jeopardy of being overwhelmed by a trauma that it cannot process symbolically. In such situations, the mind, if able, will enlist its normal dissociative ability as a protective solution, to assure continuity and coherence of selfhood—its own survival.

In other words, when emotional experience is traumatic (more than the mind can bear), it remains unprocessed symbolically, leaving the person vulnerable to its *unanticipated* return if "triggered." To minimize the possibility of its *unexpected* repetition, a dissociative "early-warning system" develops—a self-curative dynamic that, in the long run is "worse than the disease" because the dynamic rigidifies into a dissociative mental *structure*. As an "early-warning system," this structure is designed to *anticipate* the triggering before it happens. It serves to gain some control over the shock of what cannot be regulated—the "triggering" of hypnoidally isolated emotion schemas that hold the affective memory of ungovernable hyperarousal.

In this context, the therapeutic goal of helping a patient to access and process unsymbolized experience is integral to any successful psychoanalytic process. It allows a patient's ongoing personality structure to safely accommodate new experience that leads to mutative growth. The traditional Freudian psychoanalytic focus on transference is based on two interrelated assumptions: (1) that the mind is organized by conflict and repression, and (2) that unconscious conflicts are objectively revealed when the patient transferentially "projects" his repressed unconscious conflicts onto the analyst. According to this Freudian model, the analyst's interventions should accurately interpret the patient's transference (and his resistance to the interpretation) in order to provide "insight" into the conflict being repressed. The problem with this formulation, however, is that it does not explain why interpretation of unconscious conflict and its "resistance" produces treatment failure or treatment impasse in such a large number of patients. It is now fairly clear that the dynamic conceptions of Freud participate in an ongoing dialectic with a complex latticework of psychic structure, one central organizing principle of which is dissociation.

42.2.3 Dissociation and Postclassical Psychoanalytic Thought

Dissociation was a pivotal concept in the birth and development of interpersonal psychoanalysis (Sullivan, 1940, 1953, 1954, 1956) and the "independent" school of British object relations theories (Fairbairn, 1929, 1940, 1944, 1952; Winnicott, 1945, 1949, 1960, 1971). Today, dissociation continues to receive its most active clinical and theoretical attention from contemporary analysts whose sensibilities represent one or both of these schools of thought (e.g., Bromberg, 1984, 1991, 1993b, 1994, 1998, 2000a, 2000b, 2001a, 2001b, 2003a, 2003b, 2003c, 2006; Chefetz, 1997, 2000, 2004; Chefetz & Bromberg, 2004; Davies & Frawley, 1992, 1994; Davies, 1996a, 1996b, 1998, 1999; Frankel, 2002; Grand, 1997, 2000; Harris, 1992, 1994, 1996; Howell, 1996, 2002, 2005; Mitchell, 1991, 1993; S. Pizer, 1998, 2002; Reis, 1993; Schwartz, 1994, 2000; B. L. Smith, 1989; D. B. Stern, 1983, 1996, 1997, 2003, 2004; S. Stern, 2002). Dissociation has also found its way into the work of analysts with a self-psychological orientation, particularly those interested in the phenomenology of self-states (e.g., Stolorow, Brandchaft, & Atwood, 1987; Ferguson, 1990).

Dissociation has begun to gain acceptance among postclassical Freudian analysts as well (e.g., I. Brenner, 1994, 1996, 2001; Faimberg, 1988; Gabbard, 1992; Goldberg, 1987; Lyon, 1992; Roth, 1992). Not insignificantly, some *classical* Freudian conflict theorists have begun to acknowledge dissociation as an intrinsic dimension of mental functioning, but they tend to minimize their conceptual departures from Freud by retaining his conceptual language (e.g., Gottlieb, 1997, 2003; Kernberg, 1991; Marmer, 1980, 1991; Shengold, 1989, 1992; H. F. Smith, 2000, 2001, 2003a, 2003b, 2003c, 2006; Waugaman, 2000).

All told, the shift within psychoanalysis toward recognition of dissociation is leading away from Freud's (1915) topographical stratification of unconscious-preconscious-conscious layering. The shift is leading toward a view of the mind as a configuration of discontinuous, shifting states of consciousness with varying degrees of access to perception and cognition. In this view, some self-states are hypnoidally unlinked from perception at any given moment of normal mental functioning—lending support to some of Freud's ideas in his *Project* (Freud, 1895) and *The Interpretation of Dreams* (Freud, 1900), while other self-states are virtually foreclosed from such access because they are either developmentally prelinguistic or unsymbolized as a response to trauma.

Freud believed that the "perceptual system" was circumvented or compromised during sleep and dreaming. More recent thinking about the mind argues that the perceptual system can also be circumvented by the mind's response to trauma. This is considered to be a normal developmental response to trauma and a basic defense against its recurrence. In broad terms, the older conception of psychodynamic therapy (i.e., that the therapist helps a patient to change a unified but unadaptive self-representation to a more adaptive one) is being replaced with a new understanding (i.e., that self-states of the therapist and patient relate to one another in a process that helps the boundaries between the patient's self-states to become more permeable).

Foundational to this view are two ideas: (1) every human being has a set of discrete, more or less overlapping schemata of who he is, and (2) each schema is organized around a core self-other configuration (Sullivan, 1953) that was shaped early in life. Wolff (1987), for example, sees the self as nonunitary in its very *origin*. Wolff's study of infants led him to see the self as (1) a structure that originated as a multiplicity of self-other configurations (i.e., "behavioral states"), (2) that developmentally attains coherence and continuity, and (3) that subjectively comes to be experienced as a cohesive sense of personal identity—an overarching feeling of "being a self."

According to Kihlstrom (1987) [quoted from LeDoux, 1989, p. 281], "in order for unprocessed subjective experience to become symbolized in conscious awareness, a link must be made between the mental representation of the event and a mental representation of the *self* as the agent or experiencer. These episodic representations … reside in short-term or working memory." Kihlstrom's identification of the need for this link focuses our attention on an essential question: What makes it so *difficult* to link the unsymbolized affective experience from the past with a mental representation of the self as the agent or experiencer of the event? In my view, the answer to this question is *dissociation*. The human self is a configuration of multiple states as well as a functional unit (Bromberg, 1996a; Mitchell, 1991); the more intense the unsymbolized affect, the more powerful the dissociative forces that prevent isolated islands of selfhood from becoming linked within working memory.

42.2.4 Current Research in Cognition, Neuroscience, and Attachment Theory

Wilma Bucci's cognitive research (2001, 2002, 2003, 2007a, 2007b), Joseph LeDoux's neuroscience research (1989, 1994, 1995, 1996, 2002), Allan Schore's research in Interpersonal Neurobiology (1994, 2003a, 2003b, 2007), and my interpersonal/relational view of psychoanalysis (Bromberg, 1994, 1996a, 1998, 1999, 2000a, 2000b, 2006) converge in their focus on the interface of dissociation, conflict, and self-state communication.

Bucci has studied the centrality of dissociation to normal human cognition and its relevance to the psychoanalytic process. She writes:

> The basic forms of emotional communication that operate in the analytic context also underlie all interpersonal interaction. In normal functioning as in pathology, we are constantly sending out and receiving subsymbolic signals; these often occur without accompanying verbal messages and are difficult to make explicit. A fundamental difference between normal and pathological functioning is that *in the former, the subsymbolic communication is connected, or readily connectable to the symbolic components … whereas in pathology the subsymbolic representations are largely dissociated from the symbolic modes that would provide meaning for them.* (Bucci, 2001, p. 68, emphasis added)

Bucci (2002) concludes that Freud's *repression-based* conception of the therapeutic action of psychoanalysis is in need of serious reconsideration and that "concepts such as regression and resistance need to be revised as well" (p. 788). Quite matter-of-factly, she offers the view that "the goal of psychoanalytic treatment is integration of dissociated schemas" (p. 766) and that *this requires activation of subsymbolic bodily experience in the session itself, in relation to present interpersonal experience and memories of the past.*

From different vantage points, both Bucci (2003) and I (Bromberg, 2003a) focus on Kihlstrom's (1987) crucial observation that in order for dissociated material to become symbolized and available to participate with other self-states in internal conflict resolution, a link must be made in the here-and-now between (1) the mental representation of that dissociated event and (2) a mental representation of the self as the agent or experiencer. In therapy, the more intense the fear of triggering unprocessed traumatic affect, (1) the more powerful are the dissociative forces, (2) the harder it is for working memory to cognitively represent the here-and-now event that (in the therapy itself) is triggering the affect, and (3) the harder it is to access long-term memories associated with it.

Similarly, LeDoux (2002) proposes in neurobiological terms that the enigma of brain processes is related to the enigma underlying multiplicity of self:

> Though [the self] is a unit, it is not unitary.… The fact that all aspects of the self are not usually manifest simultaneously, and that their different aspects can even be contradictory, may seem to present a complex problem. However, this simply means that different components of the self reflect the operation of different brain systems, which can be but are not always in sync. While explicit memory is mediated by a single system, there are a variety of different brain systems that store memory implicitly, allowing for many aspects of the self to coexist. As William James (1890) said, "Neither threats nor pleadings can move a man unless they touch some one of his potential or actual selves." Or as the painter Paul Klee (1957) expressed it, the self is a "dramatic ensemble." (LeDoux, 2002, p. 31)

This configuration of meaning develops early in life through reciprocal patterns of interaction with significant others that establish the internal templates for attachment behavior. These internal templates are core ways of being with an other that come to organize the self-meaning of "who one is." They provide the basis of self-continuity that assures stability and sometimes sanity in the face of psychological stress. Because continuity of self-meaning is the underpinning of mental stability, each human mind is dedicated to preserving its pattern of attachment at any cost. From this frame of reference, *psychological trauma can be defined as the precipitous disruption of self-continuity through the invalidation of these early attachment patterns of interaction that give meaning to "who one is."*

Attachment researchers are currently studying the relationship between disorganized/disoriented attachment and adult dissociative pathology (cf. Barach, 1991; Liotti, 1992, 1995; and Main & Morgan, 1996). Barach (1991, p. 118) contends that Bowlby's concept of detachment "is actually a type of dissociation." Although Bowlby described children's response to abandonment in terms of detachment, Barach insists that Bowlby was really describing a dissociative process.

42.3 WHAT CAUSES DISSOCIATION?

42.3.1 Nonlinear State Changes as a Developmental Paradigm

In a seminal paper discussing nonlinear state changes as a developmental paradigm, Putnam (1988) emphasizes the most central property of states—that they are discrete and discontinuous. Asserting that "states appear to be the fundamental unit of organization of consciousness and are detectable from the first moments following birth," Putnam says that states are

> self-organizing and self-stabilizing structures of behavior. When a transition (switch) from one state of consciousness to another state of consciousness occurs, the new state acts to impose a quantitatively and qualitatively different structure on the variables that define the state of consciousness. The new structure acts to reorganize behavior and resist changes to other states.... [S]witches between states are manifest by *non-linear changes* in a number of variables. These variables include: 1) affect; 2) access to memory, i.e., state-dependent memory; 3) attention and cognition; 4) regulatory physiology; and 5) sense of self.... *[C]hanges in affect and mood are, however, probably the single best marker of state switches in normal adults.* (p. 25, emphasis added)

Putnam's assertion, that nonlinear switching among discontinuous states of consciousness is a normal process, has profound implications. For one thing, it shows that dissociation is an essential part of the process through which human beings maintain personal continuity, coherence, and cohesiveness of the sense of self. But how can this be? How can the division of self-experience into relatively unlinked parts contribute to self-integrity? The most convincing answer to this question was previewed in the previous discussion: (1) self-experience originates in relatively unlinked self-states, *each coherent in its own right*, and (2) the experience of being a unitary self (cf. Hermans, Kempen, & van Loon, 1992, pp. 29–30; Mitchell, 1991, pp. 127–139) is an acquired, developmentally adaptive illusion. When threatened with unavoidable traumatic disruption, the illusion of unity becomes too dangerous to maintain; a defensive dissociative reaction will then occur that preserves continuity and coherence by abandoning the need for cohesiveness.

42.3.2 Normal Dissociation: The Capacity to Feel Like One Self While Being Many

A human being's ability to live a life that allows both authenticity and self-reflection requires an ongoing dialectic between the separateness and unity of one's self-states; crucially, this dialectic must allow each self to function optimally without foreclosing communication and negotiation between them. When all goes well, a person is only dimly or momentarily aware of the individual self-states and their respective realities because each functions as part of a healthy illusion of cohesive personal identity—an overarching cognitive and experiential state that is felt as "me." Each self-state is part of a functional whole, informed by a process of internal negotiation with the realities, values, affects, and perspectives of the others. Each aspect of self has its own degree of access to the various domains of psychic functioning (e.g., capacity to feel and tolerate the pressure of one's needs and wishes, capacity to judge what is adaptive social behavior, capacity to act from a sense of one's values as well as from a sense of purpose, capacity to maintain object constancy, and capacity to mentally bear the experience of intrapsychic conflict). Despite collisions and even enmity between aspects of self, it is unusual for any one self-state to function totally outside of the sense of "me-ness"—that is, without the participation of the other parts of self.

In a relatively coherent personality, dissociation is a healthy, adaptive function of the human mind. Dissociation is a basic process that allows individual self-states to function optimally (not simply defensively) when full immersion in a single reality, a single strong affect, and a suspension of one's self-reflective capacity is exactly what is called for or wished for. I am referring to times requiring concentration, single-mindedness, task orientation, or full surrender to a pleasurable experience. "Under normal conditions, dissociation enhances the integrating functions of the ego by screening out excessive or irrelevant stimuli" (Young, 1988, pp. 35–36). As a normal process, dissociation also includes the ability to defend against trauma by disconnecting the mind from its capacity to perceive that which is too much for selfhood and sometimes sanity to bear. It reduces what is in front of someone's eyes to a narrow band of perceptual reality that lacks emotional relevance to the self that is experiencing it ("whatever is going on is not happening to *me*").

42.3.3 Pathological Dissociation: The Transformation of a Flexible Dynamic to a Rigid Structure

When used defensively, dissociation is unlike any other defense; it bypasses cognitive modulating systems. As neuroscience research has shown, defensive dissociation is part of an evolutionary response whose survival priority is equivalent to certain genetically coded response patterns of lower animals to life-threatening attack by a predator. *Because of its survival priority, dissociation not only defends against immediate trauma, but it is then subverted into a nonrelational mental structure that is constantly anticipating a recurrence of that trauma. It is the non-negotiability of this mental structure that makes dissociation pathological. As I've described earlier, pathological dissociation is an inflexible "early-warning system" designed to proactively prevent mental destabilization associated with the unanticipated return of unprocessed traumatic affect.* I conceive of this structure as a conglomerate of discontinuous self-states that are vigilantly "on-alert" to preempt trauma by holding a perception of reality in which potentially unbearable psychic pain is always around the next corner.

Putnam (1992, p. 104) has called dissociation "the escape when there is no escape," to which I would add that dissociation then begins to take over as "an escape *before* there is no escape"; a dissociative structure with a life of its own. *The key quality of pathological dissociation is the state of readiness that is afforded by the hypnoid separateness of self-states, so that each can continue to play its own role, unimpeded by input from other self-states (or other people). The protective readiness of hypnoidally separated self-states is the difference between normal dissociation and pathological dissociation.*

42.3.4 Standing in the Spaces

I've written (Bromberg, 1993, p. 186) that "health is the ability to stand in the spaces between realities without losing any of them—the capacity to feel like one self while being many." *Standing in the spaces* is a shorthand way of describing a person's relative capacity to make room at any given moment for subjective reality that is not readily containable by the self that he experiences as "me" at that moment. This capacity is what distinguishes creative imagination from both fantasy and concreteness, and distinguishes playfulness from facetiousness.

Some people can't "stand in the spaces" at all. In these individuals we see a psyche that is organized more centrally by dissociation than by repression, so that each shifting "truth" can continue to play its own role without interference by the others, thus creating a personality structure that one of my patients described as "having a whim of iron."

But built into the personality of *every* human being are some dissociative areas of mental structure that were shaped by traumatic intrusions that were simply too disjunctive with ongoing selfhood to be held and processed as internal conflict. In those dissociated areas of mental structure, the illusion of unity (between the disjunctive aspects of self) was abandoned, and the tolerance for bearing intrapsychic conflict was either weakened or foreclosed. As a result, for all individuals, not only those who have suffered *pervasive* trauma, there are areas of the psyche in which discontinuous constellations of self are defensively kept apart by the autohypnotic process of dissociation.

The gaps between dissociated aspects of self must be linked by human relatedness in order for the experience of intrapsychic conflict to be possible. The hermeneutic process of interpretation in psychoanalysis *depends* upon this. Conversely, it should be understood that the ability to experience intrapsychic conflict does not always exist. When patients are unable to contain an experience of intrapsychic conflict, the immediate goal is to use the therapeutic relationship to help them turn self-experience into something more than islands of "truth." To utilize interpretation, a patient must be able to stand in the spaces between self-states so that reliance on the protection of dissociation is replaced by a capacity to feel internal conflict as bearable.

42.3.5 Dissociation, Nonlinear Dynamic Systems, and Growth of Self

In response to a major paradigm shift in psychoanalysis, most contemporary analytic theorists no longer consider the most relevant *clinical question* to be, What technique should be applied? but rather, What are the necessary and sufficient conditions to *support* an analytic process? The latter question is more rooted in gestalt field theory, chaos theory, and nonlinear dynamic systems theory than in the 19th-century positivism that shaped Freud's thinking. Barton (1994, p. 5) characterizes the new paradigm as a science without an implication of prescribed sequences. Barton postulates that complex systems (like the human mind) have an underlying order, but that simple systems (like a human interaction) can produce complex behavior. The old paradigm's conceptualization of personality growth (i.e., as being mediated by the lifting of repression and the uncovering of unconscious conflict) is being reexamined in light of a nonlinear understanding of the human mind. This new understanding emphasizes self-organization, states of consciousness, dissociation, and "multiple self states that can change suddenly from one to another when a parameter value crosses a critical threshold" (Barton, 1994, p. 8).

Data supporting this understanding have been provided by independent clinical and scientific domains. Particularly significant are Edelman's (1989, 1992) neurobiological research, Thelen and Smith's (1995) writings on nonlinear dynamics theory and cognition, and Piers's (1996, 1998, 2000, 2001) work on character as self-organizing complexity, including its relationship to multiplicity and wholeness.

Piers (2001), for example, in addressing the issue of "character" in terms of Self-Organizing Dynamic-Systems Theory, supports my conception of personality disorder as inherently dissociative (see Bromberg, 1993, 1995):

> When it comes to complex systems such as the human mind, self-organization arises naturally, resulting in *emergent structures* that are self-generating and draw the components into their functioning in order to sustain the whole. Some emergent structures are "*softly assembled'*" making them more sensitive to fluctuations, which in turn allow the system to remain responsive or adaptive. Other systems are more restrictive or "*firmly assembled,*" and result in *less responsiveness and adaptability of the system.* (Piers, 2001, presented paper)

Piers then addresses my thoughts about the link between personality *style* and personality *disorder* (Bromberg, 1993, 1995). Piers considers both personality style and personality disorder to be nonlinear, self-generating emergent structures; from this perspective, personality disorder may emerge from personality style in order to sustain coherence of self-organization:

> *[P]athology* is conceptualized [by Bromberg] as the proactively defensive use of normal dissociative processes.... [S]uch a defensive deployment of dissociation provides the individual with the protection afforded by the separateness and discontinuity of self-states, while minimizing the opportunity for the multiple self-states to inform or influence one another. (Piers, 2001, presented paper)

In this context, a personality *disorder* is an "emergent structure" that results from the *rigid* consolidation of certain character traits in the service of dissociative protection. Independent of type, a personality disorder (narcissistic, hysteric, schizoid, borderline, paranoid, etc.) constitutes a *personality style* organized as a proactive, dissociative solution to the potential repetition of childhood trauma. The centrally defining hallmark of a personality disorder is that the *interpersonal* threat that is presented by the "other" is foreclosed before it can become traumatic; the patient's mental processes are designed to create an interpersonal "impasse" in which neither person can reach the other intersubjectively, and spontaneity is preempted by predictability. The price is emotional deadness and relational stagnation.

42.4 PERSONALITY DISORDERS AND DISSOCIATIVE DISORDERS

I have suggested (Bromberg, 1993, 1995) that the psychoanalytic understanding of character pathology needs to be revamped to take into account the inherent dissociative structure of the mind. I also urge analysts to rethink their traditional understanding of what we mean by *unconscious* and their traditional ways of looking at character structure and character pathology (especially what we call *personality disorders*). I propose that personality *disorder* might usefully be defined as the characterological outcome of the inordinate use of dissociation in the schematization of self-other mental representation, and that independent of type (narcissistic, schizoid, borderline, paranoid, etc.) it reflects a mental structure organized in part as a proactive protection against the potential repetition of early trauma. Thus, the distinctive personality traits of each type of personality disorder are embodied within a mental structure that allows each trait to be always "on-call" for the trauma that is seen as inevitable.

All personality disorders therefore entail *ego-syntonic dissociation.* Each type of personality disorder is a dynamically on-alert configuration of dissociated states of consciousness that regulates psychological survival in terms of its own concretized blend of characteristics. Within each type of personality disorder, certain self-states hold the traumatic experience and the traumatic affect; other self-states hold the particular ego resources that (1) proved effective in dealing with the original trauma and (2) ensure that the pain will never recur (e.g., hypervigilance, acquiescence, paranoid suspiciousness, manipulativeness, deceptiveness, seductiveness, psychopathy, intimidation, guilt-induction, self-sufficiency, insularity, withdrawal into fantasy, pseudomaturity, conformity, amnesia, depersonalization, out-of-body experiences, trance states, compulsivity, substance abuse, etc.).

42.4.1 Dissociative Symptomatology and Dissociative Character Traits

When faced with a reminder of past trauma that threatens affective hyperarousal, the mental structure of a person with a *dissociative disorder* is usually not stable enough to successfully prevent *symptoms* from being triggered. This vulnerability to symptoms causes a person with a dissociative disorder to appear "sicker" than a person with a personality disorder (an individual whose dissociative mental organization is evidenced in the rigidity of ego-syntonic character pathology). But in *both* cases (dissociative disorders and personality disorders), mental functioning is mediated by the adaptive effort of a dissociative mental structure that is designed to prevent the intrusion of unbearable trauma. The dissociative structure is a bulwark against retraumatization, but it also creates an existential illness. It plunders both the present and the future on behalf of the past.

In a personality disorder, each personality configuration has its own characteristic pathologies of cognition, impulse control, affectivity, and interpersonal functioning. Each specific personality configuration represents a dissociative solution to trauma that has been preserved and perfected because it balanced safety and need satisfaction, characterologically, in a fashion that "worked" for that person. The subsequent cost of this solution, however, is always identical regardless of personality *type*—to one degree or another, an unlived life.

The dissociative disorders (i.e., Dissociative Identity Disorder, Dissociative Amnesia, Dissociative Fugue, or Depersonalization Disorder) are, from this vantage point, touchstones for understanding the personality disorders even though, paradoxically, dissociative disorders are defined by symptomatology rather than by personality style. *The symptoms of the dissociative disorders are direct manifestations of discontinuities between states of consciousness that the personality disorders are designed to mask.* In the personality disorders, discontinuities between states of consciousness are expressed only indirectly and "characterologically" as a relationally impaired but relatively "enduring pattern of inner experience and behavior that … is inflexible and pervasive across a broad range of social situations" (American Psychiatric Association, 1994, p. 275).

Each type of personality disorder has its own characterological configuration of dissociated self-states that are on-call to preempt the traumatic input of "otherness." For example, the obsessive-compulsive personality disorder neutralizes otherness by engaging in covert power operations that are designed to undo the impact of the therapist's words. The purpose of these power operations is to prevent the therapist's subjectivity from allying with dissociated "not-me" aspects of the patient's self, and thus risking the creation of mental confusion, if not chaos. In this dynamic, the therapist is always potentially dangerous because the therapist's subjectivity holds the potential to wipe out the patient's mind by trying to replace the patient's experience with something the therapist deems "better." Dangerous, "not-me" aspects of self become controllable *interpersonally* only when they are externalized as part of "the other." Thus, by pulling the therapist into covert power operations, an obsessive-compulsive patient helps keep the "not-me" aspects of self dissociated by making the therapist, at least temporarily, the sole proprietor of those unwanted aspects of self.

Ultimately, the ability of a patient to allow dissociated "self-truth" to be altered by the impact of the therapist depends on the development of a paradoxical relationship. By paradoxical, I mean a relationship in which the therapist can be experienced as someone who both accepts the validity of the patient's self-state "truths" and participates in the here-and-now act of constructing a negotiated reality broader than any of the individual truths. It should be added, however, that the ease or difficulty in the development of such a relationship is influenced by the history of a patient's attachment-based procedural memory and the *degree* to which its non-negotiability has been shaped by the dread of psychic trauma.

Just as the obsessive-compulsive patient uses words to magically make the potentially impinging other believe that the patient is "agreeing" while dissociating the here-and-now present from the ongoing interchange, the *hysteric* personality disorder uses affect and pain to keep the other at bay. "You won't let me be myself." "You don't understand what I am feeling." "No, that's not what I feel." The hysteric, by the way, is the only type of personality disorder that has already been acknowledged as "most likely" to be dissociative. Why? Probably because the hysteric has organized into the personality structure, the use of rapid switching of self-states as a proactive response to potential affective overload. This character trait, which we know as affective "lability," has more of the aroma of a dissociative disorder than do many of the character traits we find in other types of personality disorders.

I also have hypothesized (Bromberg, 1993, p. 179) that *paranoid* personalities are labeled "delusional" because the extreme dissociative isolation of the self-state that holds paranoid "truth" creates an immovably fixed self-narrative that is virtually *immune* to modification through relational negotiation. That is, paranoid personality disorders rely almost exclusively on a self-state that is designed to be *seamlessly* vigilant and to not only mistrust, but to actively *look* for reasons to mistrust.

There are different likelihoods that a dissociative personality structure will "fail." To some degree, the likelihood is determined by the type of personality style in which it is embedded. Sometimes the failure is seen in the development of *symptoms*; sometimes in a flooding of affect as in hysteria; sometimes in a bizarreness of obsessive thinking or compulsive behavior; sometimes in a loosening of a schizoid person's hold on reality; and sometimes in a paranoid person's "delusional" thinking. Some people with schizoid personality disorders have become so weakened by profound isolation that they risk loss of selfhood while trying to stay untouched by the annihilating presence of others. Others, whose dissociative structure is more "successful," simply "die before they have lived."

With personality-disordered patients, the therapist's overarching task is to facilitate a safe reorganization of self-structure into one that feels sturdy enough to withstand input from another person's mind without dissociating. This requires the gradual transformation of an ego-syntonic dissociative rigidity into something that feels ego-alien; the transformation of "This is who I *am*" into "This is what I *do*." The success of the process depends on whether the therapist does not *unreflectively* compromise the patient's here-and-now experience of selfhood by triggering a flood of shame and panic associated with early trauma that feels irreparable. When I say "not unreflectively," I am speaking about a process in which the unavoidable "collisions between subjectivities" are *negotiable*—what might be called the process of "negotiating otherness." Negotiating otherness is mediated in part by the therapist's ability to comprehend the particular personality style of a given patient. This requires that the therapist understand both the unique configuration of dissociated self-states that is distinctive of that personality type, as well as the uniqueness of the particular person that embodies it. The patient's capacity to open an internal negotiation between his hypnoidally isolated self-states depends on the therapist's ability to participate in a process of external negotiation through *enactment*—a process in which the patient's own otherness (his *not-me* self-states) is played out with the *actual* other (i.e., the therapist). In other words, the patient's affective safety is not something that is "delivered" to the patient through the analyst's unilateral judgment of what is "safe." A therapist cannot make the process feel "safe" by trying to minimize his presence and believing he can do so by avoiding active participation in the ongoing relationship. Allan Schore (2003b, 2007) in fact stresses the *dual role* of the therapist as *simultaneously* psychobiological regulator and co-participant, and that this simultaneity is especially vital during heightened affective moments in working with dissociated self-states. That is to say, the therapist's role is therapeutic *because* the analyst's regulating function is *not independent* of coparticipation, which means being a human being in a very human relationship.

42.5 MULTIPLE SELF-STATES, DISSOCIATION, AND ENACTMENT

I am not suggesting that addressing dissociation is all there is to psychoanalysis. What I *do* believe is that for some patients characterologically, and for all patients in certain areas of their personality, an analysis that is enduring and far-reaching is best achieved by working with dissociative processes as an intrinsic part of working with conflict. "Working in the transference" is inherently "working with dissociation" because *transference is inherently an enacted dissociative process that includes both patient and therapist.*

Transference and countertransference are simply aspects of enactment, a dyadic dissociative cocoon. Through enactment, patient and therapist play out together an externalization of the patient's communication with internal objects. The patients feel this dialogue *affectively*, and as they attempt to express respective "unformulated experiences" (Stern, 1983, 1997), they are given a chance, jointly, to arrive at language that gives this enacted dialogue relational meaning and intrapsychic meaning. But to do this, the analyst has to come to grips with the dissociated parts of *the therapist's* self that are contributing to the enactment. By using self-awareness as a source of therapeutic data, the therapist can make the patient's experience less shameful, less dissociated, more *real,* and thereby more accessible to an immediate sense of "me." The therapist's feelings and the patient's feelings, during an enactment, are part of a shared configuration of experience that must be processed linguistically within the immediacy of the therapeutic relationship in order for the multiple realities *within* the patient to become linked via cognitive symbolization by language. As this happens, the clinical process increasingly shifts from working with dissociation to working with conflict.

Every clinician knows that it is never a simple matter for a patient to confront dissociated self-experience, including memories. Even when an interpretation may seem to be successful, the resulting "awareness" of something from the past (or the present) does not in itself signify a personally relevant *experience* of what has been "confronted."

An experience that is available to self-reflection is often not created because the "awareness" is still organized around a dissociated structure that remains more powerful than the "interpreted" evidence of reason. Thus, what the therapist is *saying* often remains dissociated from the patient's here-and-now experience of the relational context that holds the personal impact of what is being said.

In other words, when self-states are islands of "truth" that are held in place by dissociative mental structure, they remain immune to the evidence of reason.

Under these conditions, dissociated experience is rigidly unyielding to cognitive processing and self-reflection. Apropos of this, Lyons-Ruth and the Boston Change Process Study Group (2001, pp. 13–17) have focused their attention on what arguably may be the next step in the growth of psychoanalysis—"a non-linear enactive theory of psychotherapeutic change," whereby "the process of psychodynamic therapy can usefully be thought of as the pursuit of more collaborative, inclusive, and coherent forms of dialogue between the two therapeutic partners."

> If clinical process is *affect-guided* rather than cognition-guided, [then] therapeutic change is a process that leads to the emergence of new forms of relational organization. New experiences emerge but they are not created by the therapist for the benefit of the patient. Instead, *they emerge somewhat unpredictably from the mutual searching of patient and therapist for new forms of recognition, or new forms of fitting together of initiatives in the interaction between them.* (Lyons-Ruth et al., 2001, p. 17, emphasis added)

Specifically, they argue that enlarging the domain and fluency of the dialogue is primary to enduring personality growth in treatment; it is this that leads to increasingly integrated and complex content. This does not mean that content is unimportant; rather, *it is in the relational process of exploring content that the change takes place, not in the discovery of new content per se.* The "content" is embedded in relational experience that embodies what they call "implicit relational knowing"—an ongoing *process* that is itself part of the content. This unsymbolized relational experience is relived by being enacted repeatedly between patient and therapist as an intrinsic part of their relationship.

Lyons-Ruth (2003, pp. 905–906) has emphasized the major contribution of relational theory to this new understanding of the source of therapeutic action. She urges that work continue toward developing "a language and structure that moves beyond a narrow focus on interpretation to encompass the broader domain of relational interchanges that contribute to change in psychoanalytic treatment." In my view, the concept of working with enactment and "not-me" experience provides the structure of which she speaks because it encompasses the essence of relational interchange—interpersonal and intersubjective—without losing the focus on the intrapsychic.

As an experiential process, enactment takes place *between* patient and therapist. As a concept, enactment is anchored in the view of a "relational mind." Moreover, it is more consistent with contemporary understanding of mental functioning than is the bifurcated conception of transference and countertransference.

From the perspective of the mind as relational, enactment does not take place *within* the patient. A relational concept of enactment considers both partners as an interpenetrating unit. Thus, enactment is a *dyadic* event in which therapist and patient are linked through a dissociated mode of relating, each in a "not-me" state that is affectively responsive to that of the other. In the language of enactment, this shared dissociative cocoon has its own imperative; it enmeshes and (at least for a time) traps the two partners within a "not-me" (Sullivan, 1953) communication field that is mediated by dissociation. In short, *enactment is an intrapsychic phenomenon that is played out interpersonally.*

42.5.1 Dissociation, Affective Safety, and Human Relationship

One might view the unconscious communication process of enactment as the patient's effort to negotiate unfinished business in those areas of selfhood where affective regulation of past traumatic experience has been insufficient to allow symbolic processing by thought and language. *In this light, a core goal of the therapeutic process is to increase competency in regulating affective states without pointlessly triggering the dread of retraumatization.* But this is not a simple matter. The problem is that the dissociated horror of the past fills the present with such powerful affective meaning that it often precludes any sense of safety. No matter how "obviously" safe the current situation may appear, patients cannot *perceive* themselves to be safe unless they allow themselves a moment of consciousness during which they can decrease their reliance on dissociative hypervigilance. But, often, that is simply too dangerous to the patient's felt stability of selfhood.

Even in routine analytic work, telling "about" oneself leads with surprising frequency to the dissociated reliving of an overwhelming experience that had been encapsulated as an unprocessed affective and somatic "memory." This experience cannot be therapeutically utilized unless the patient feels sufficient relational safety to have access to working memory during the reliving. I have proposed that safety and growth are part of the ongoing negotiation of the therapeutic relationship itself. The negotiation of safety and growth entails what a given patient and therapist do in an unanticipated way that is safe, but not *too* safe—namely, a replaying of the patient's past relational failures in the form of safe surprises. Patients are optimally released from the crippling effects of their traumatic past when they are simultaneously released from the grip of their own self-cure (i.e., *what they continue do to themselves and to others in order to cope with a past that continues to haunt them).* This is why the processing of enactments is so powerful. It simultaneously frees the patient from the nightmare of the past and the prison of the self-cure; it frees the patient from the grip of the dissociative personality structure that has been compulsively plundering both the present life and the capacity to imagine a pleasurable future.

42.5.2 Enactment and Shame

When unprocessed traumatic affect is relived with one's therapist, the reliving is almost always accompanied by a dissociated shame experience. The shame is, in part, shame that is relived from the past, but it is also *new* shame that is being evoked by the therapist-patient relationship *while* the reliving is taking place. As Lynd (1958, p. 42) puts it, "a double shame is involved"; the person is shamed by the original episode and shamed by the strong need to be understood about an event that the patient has come to believe is, in Lynd's words, "so slight that a sensible person would not pay any attention to it." As with the original trauma, the patient hungers for recognition of the pain from the person (in this case the therapist) who is least likely to offer it because he is also the person who is *causing* the pain (in this case, inadvertently). Consider this clinical vignette paraphrased from Fridley (2001, p. 5):

> After many years and much anger, your patient is finally able to tell you that the phone message they left two days ago was actually a request for you to call them back. While you have some patients whom you know *always* need a call back, this person's subtlety takes you by surprise. The alliance is wounded. They were distressed, they called, and you did not answer. Their cry for help, which would in infancy, lead to attachment behaviors, was ignored. You are able, eventually, to say: "When I didn't call you back I ignored you." You have then owned your contribution to the "negative transference." Now your patient says: "I sat by the phone for hours, hoping you would call, but nothing happened." You ask: *"What did you imagine I was doing while you were waiting?"*

Often, this question will lead to the creation of a "safe surprise" because it addresses a patient's unprocessed experience of what is in the mind of a person who does not take an interest in them. Sometimes, however, the question is, at that moment, too much for the patient to think about. If that happens, the therapist must be attuned to that occurrence and must acknowledge it to the patient. In other words, the therapist must not assume that the patient has a capacity for mentalization (i.e., the ability to represent a representation—to think about another person thinking about them). The question of what the patient thought the therapist was thinking is always valid to consider. But when actually asked, the question can be therapeutic *only* if the therapist is alert to the fact that this inquiry may be shame-inducing. Trying to think about what was in the mind of a needed "other" who failed to fulfill a need may flood the patient with shame, and trigger an automatic dissociative isolation of the shamed part of the self.

Put most simply, a patient's transition from "not-me" to "me" is not easy or neat. Typically, it is a process of messy, nonlinear spurts, closer to *lurching ahead* than the more euphemistic term *growth.* During this process, therapeutic action flows from the therapist's ability to do two things simultaneously: (1) to relate fully to whatever aspect of self the patient is experiencing and presenting as "the real me," and (2) to let the other, more dissociated parts, know that the therapist is aware they exist. As words are found and negotiated between them, the traumas of the past become "safe surprises" in the present that facilitate the patient's growing ability to symbolize and express in language what previously had not been voiced. The goal is for the patient to move, slowly and safely, from a mental structure in which self-narratives are dissociatively organized, to a mental structure that allows the patient to cognitively and emotionally hold the self-narratives as part of a coherent, self-experience that allows for finding new solutions that are more flexible, and though not totally satisfying to any *one* part of the self, are more *me* to the *total* personality.

REFERENCES

American Psychiatric Association (1994). *DSM-IV – Diagnostic and statistical manual of mental disorders* (4th ed.). Washington, DC: Author.

Balint, M. (1935/1965). Critical notes on the theory of the pregenital organizations of the libido. In: *Primary love and psychoanalytic technique*. New York: Liveright, pp. 37–58.

Balint, M. (1937/1965). Early developmental stages of the ego: Primary object love. In: *Primary love and psychoanalytic technique*. New York: Liveright, pp. 74–90.

Balint, M. (1952/1965). New beginning and the paranoid and the depressive syndromes. In: *Primary love and psychoanalytic technique*. New York: Liveright, pp. 230–249.

Balint, M. (1968). *The basic fault*. London: Tavistock Publications.

Barach, P. M. (1991). Multiple Personality Disorder as an attachment disorder. *Dissociation, 4*, 117–123.

Barton, S. (1994). Chaos, self-organization, and psychology. *American Psychologist, 49*, 5–14.

Beahrs, J. O. (1982). *Unity and multiplicity: Multilevel consciousness of self in hypnosis, psychiatric disorder and mental health*. New York: Brunner/Mazel.

Berman, E. (1981). Multiple personality: Psychoanalytic perspectives. *International Journal of Psychoanalysis, 62*, 283–300.

Binet, A. (1892/1896/1977). *Les altérations de la personnalité*. Paris: F. Alcan. English edition: *Alterations of personality*. New York: D. Appleton and Company, 1896. Reprint: University Publications of America/ Washington, DC, 1977.

Bion, W. (1957/1967). Differentiation of the psychotic from the non-psychotic personalities. In: *Second thoughts*. London: Maresfield Library, pp. 43–64.

Bion, W. (1965). *Transformations*. London: Heinemann.

Bliss, E. L. (1988). A reexamination of Freud's basic concepts from studies of multiple personality disorder. *Dissociation, 1*, 36–40.

Brenner, I. (1994). The dissociative character: A reconsideration of "multiple personality." *Journal of the American Psychoanalytic Association, 42*, 819–846.

Brenner, I. (1996). On trauma, perversion, and multiple personality. *Journal of the American Psychoanalytic Association, 4*, 785–814.

Brenner, I. (2001). *Dissociation of trauma: Theory, phenomenology, and technique*. Madison, CT: International Universities Press.

Breuer, J., & Freud, S. (1895/1955). Studies on hysteria. In J. Strachey (Ed.), *Standard Edition of the Complete Psychological Works of Sigmund Freud, 2*. London: Hogarth Press.

Bromberg, P. M. (1984/1998). On the occurrence of the Isakower phenomenon in a schizoid disorder. In: *Standing in the spaces: Essays on clinical process, trauma, and dissociation*. Hillsdale, NJ: The Analytic Press, pp. 97–118.

Bromberg, P. M. (1991/1998). On knowing one's patient inside out: The aesthetics of unconscious communication. In: *Standing in the spaces: Essays on clinical process, trauma, and dissociation*. Hillsdale, NJ: The Analytic Press, pp. 127–146.

Bromberg, P. M. (1993/1998). Shadow and substance: A relational perspective on clinical process. In: *Standing in the spaces: Essays on clinical process, trauma, and dissociation*. Hillsdale, NJ: The Analytic Press, pp. 165–187.

Bromberg, P. M. (1994/1998). "Speak!, that I may see you": Some reflections on dissociation, reality, and psychoanalytic listening. In: *Standing in the spaces: Essays on clinical process, trauma, and dissociation*. Hillsdale, NJ: The Analytic Press, pp. 241–266.

Bromberg, P. M. (1995/1998). Psychoanalysis, dissociation, and personality organization: In: *Standing in the spaces: Essays on clinical process, trauma, and dissociation*. Hillsdale, NJ: The Analytic Press, pp. 189–204.

Bromberg, P. M. (1996a/1998). Standing in the spaces: The multiplicity of self and the psychoanalytic relationship. In: *Standing in the spaces: Essays on clinical process, trauma, and dissociation*. Hillsdale, NJ: The Analytic Press, pp. 267–290.

Bromberg, P. M. (1996b/1998). Hysteria, dissociation, and cure: Emmy von N revisited. In: *Standing in the spaces: Essays on clinical process, trauma, and dissociation*. Hillsdale, NJ: The Analytic Press, pp. 223–237.

Bromberg, P. M. (1998). *Standing in the spaces: Essays on clinical process, trauma, and dissociation*. Hillsdale, NJ: The Analytic Press.

Bromberg, P. M. (1999). Playing with boundaries. *Contemporary Psychoanalysis, 35*, 54–66.

Bromberg, P. M. (2000a). Potholes on the royal road: Or is it an abyss? *Contemporary Psychoanalysis, 36*, 5–28.

Bromberg, P. M. (2000b). Bringing in the dreamer: Some reflections on dreamwork, surprise, and analytic process. *Contemporary Psychoanalysis, 36*, 685–705.

Bromberg, P. M. (2001a). The gorilla did it: Some thoughts on dissociation, the real, and the really real. *Psychoanalytic Dialogues, 11*, 385–404.

Bromberg, P. M. (2001b). Treating patients with symptoms, and symptoms with patience: Reflections on shame, dissociation, and eating disorders. *Psychoanalytic Dialogues, 11*, 891–912.

Bromberg, P. M. (2003a). "Something wicked this way comes": Trauma, dissociation and conflict; the space where psychoanalysis, cognitive science, and neuroscience overlap. *Psychoanalytic Psychology, 20*, 558–574.

Bromberg, P. M. (2003b). One need not be a house to be haunted. *Psychoanalytic Dialogues, 13*, 689–709.

Bromberg, P. M. (2003c). On being one's dream: Some reflections on Robert Bosnak's "Embodied Imagination." *Contemporary Psychoanalysis, 39*, 697–710.

Bromberg, P. M. (2006). *Awakening the dreamer: Clinical journeys*. Mahwah, NJ: The Analytic Press.

Bucci, W. (2001). Pathways of emotional communication. *Psychoanalytic Inquiry, 21*, 40–70.

Bucci, W. (2002). The referential process, consciousness, and sense of self. *Psychoanalytic Inquiry, 22*, 766–793.

Bucci, W. (2003). Varieties of dissociative experience: A multiple code account and a discussion of Bromberg's case of "William." *Psychoanalytic Psychology, 20*, 542–557.

Bucci, W. (2007a). Dissociation from the perspective of multiple code theory — Part I: Psychological roots and implications for psychoanalytic treatment. *Contemporary Psychoanalysis, 43*, 165–184.

Bucci, W. (2007b). Dissociation from the perspective of multiple code theory — Part II: The spectrum of dissociative processes in the psychoanalytic relationship. *Contemporary Psychoanalysis, 43*, 305–326.

Charcot, J.-M. (1882). Sur les divers états nerveux déterminés par l'hypnotisation chez les hystériques. *Comptes rendus hebdomadaires des séances de l'académie des sciences, 94*, 403–405.

Charcot, J.-M. (1887). Leçons sur les maladies du système nerveux faites à la Salpêtrière, III. In: *Œuvres complètes*. 9 vols. Paris: Progrès Médical.

Chefetz, R. A. (1997). Special case transferences and countertransferences in the treatment of dissociative disorders. *Dissociation, 10*, 255–265.

Chefetz, R. A. (2000). Disorder in the therapist's view of the self: Working with the person with dissociative identity disorder. *Psychoanalytic Inquiry, 20*, 305–329.

Chefetz, R. A. (2004). The paradox of "detachment disorders": Binding-disruptions of dissociative process. *Psychiatry: Interpersonal and biological processes, 67*, 246–255.

Chefetz, R. A., & Bromberg, P. M. (2004). Talking with "Me and Not-me": A dialogue. *Contemporary Psychoanalysis, 40*, 409–464.

Davies, J. M. (1996a). Dissociation, repression, and reality testing in the counter-transference: The controversy over memory and false memory in the psychoanalytic treatment of adult survivors of sexual abuse. *Psychoanalytic Dialogues, 6*, 189–218.

Davies, J. M. (1996b). Linking the "pre-analytic" and the postclassical: Integration, dissociation, and the multiplicity of unconscious process. *Contemporary Psychoanalysis, 32*, 553–576.

Davies, J. M. (1998). Multiple perspectives on multiplicity. *Psychoanalytic Dialogues, 8*, 195–206.

Davies, J. M. (1999). Getting cold feet, defining" safe-enough" boundaries: Dissociation, multiplicity, and integration in the analyst's experience. *Psychoanalytic Quarterly, 68*, 184–208.

Davies, J. M., & Frawley, M. G. (1992). Dissociation processes and transference-countertransference paradigms in the psychoanalytically oriented treatment of adult survivors of sexual abuse. *Psychoanalytic Dialogues, 2*, 5–36.

Davies, J. M., & Frawley, M. G. (1994). *Treating the adult survivor of childhood sexual abuse: A psychoanalytic perspective.* New York: Basic Books.

Edelman, G. M. (1989). *The remembered present: A biological theory of consciousness.* New York: Basic Books.

Edelman, G. M. (1992). *Bright air, brilliant fire*. New York: Basic Books.

Faimberg, H. (1988). The telescoping of generations. *Contemporary Psychoanalysis, 24*, 99–118.

Fairbairn, W. R. D. (1929/1994). Dissociation and repression. In E. F. Birtles & D. E. Scharff (Eds.), *From instinct to self: Selected papers of W. R. D. Fairbairn,* Vol. II. Northvale, NJ: Aronson, pp. 13–79.

Fairbairn, W. R. D. (1940/1952). Schizoid factors in the personality. In: *Psychoanalytic studies of the personality*. London: Routledge & Kegan Paul, pp. 3–27.

Fairbairn, W. R. D. (1944/1952). Endopsychic structure considered in terms of object-relationships. In: *Psychoanalytic studies of the personality*, pp. 82–132.

Fairbairn, W. R. D. (1952). *An object relations theory of the personality.* New York: Basic Books.

Ferenczi, S. (1928/1980). The elasticity of psychoanalytic technique. In: M. Balint (Ed.), *Final contributions to the problems and methods of psycho-analysis*. New York: Brunner/Mazel, pp. 87–101.

Ferenczi, S. (1930/1980). The principles of relaxation and neocatharsis. In: M. Balint (Ed.), *Final contributions to the problems and methods of psycho-analysis*. New York: Brunner/Mazel, pp. 108–125.

Ferenczi, S. (1931/1980). Child analysis in the analysis of adults. In: M. Balint (Ed.), *Final contributions to the problems and methods of psycho-analysis*. New York: Brunner/Mazel, pp. 126–142.

Ferenczi, S. (1933/1980). Confusion of tongues between adults and the child: The language of tenderness and passion. In: M. Balint (Ed.), *Final contributions to the problems and methods of psycho-analysis*. New York: Brunner/Mazel, pp. 156–167.

Ferguson, M. (1990). Mirroring processes, hypnotic processes, and multiple personality. *Psychoanalysis and Contemporary Thought, 13*, 417–50.

Frankel, J. B. (2002). Exploring Ferenczi's concept of identification with the aggressor: Its role in trauma, everyday life, and the therapeutic relationship. *Psychoanalytic Dialogues, 12*, 101–139.

Freud, S. (1895/1966). Project for a scientific psychology. *Standard Edition, 1*, 295–397.

Freud, S. (1900/1953). The interpretation of dreams. *Standard Edition, 4 & 5*.

Freud, S. (1915). The unconscious. *Standard Edition, 14*, 159–215.

Fridley, D. (2001). Critical Issues: attachment and dissociative disorders. *International Society for Study of Dissociation News, 19*, 4–5.

Gabbard, G. O. (1992). Commentary on "Dissociative processes and transference-countertransference paradigms…" by Davies and Frawley. *Psychoanalytic Dialogues, 2*, 37–47.

Goldberg, P. (1987). The role of distractions in the maintenance of dissociative mental states. *International Journal of Psycho-Analysis, 68*, 511–524.

Gottlieb, R. (1997). Does the mind fall apart in multiple personality disorder? Some proposals based on a psychoanalytic case. *Journal of the American Psychoanalytic Association, 45*, 907–932.

Gottlieb, R. (2003). Psychosomatic medicine: The divergent legacies of Freud and Janet. *Journal of the American Psychoanalytic Association, 51*, 857–881.

Grand, S. (1997). The paradox of innocence: Dissociative "adhesive" states in perpetrators of incest. *Psychoanalytic Dialogues, 7*, 465–490.

Grand, S. (2000). *The reproduction of evil: A clinical and cultural perspective.* Hillsdale, NJ: The Analytic Press.

Harris, A. (1992). Dialogues as transitional space: A rapprochement of psychoanalysis and developmental psycholinguistics. In N. J. Skolnick & S. C. Warshaw (Eds.), *Relational perspectives in psychoanalysis*. Hillsdale, NJ: The Analytic Press, pp. 119–145.

Harris, A. (1994). Gender practices and speech practices. Towards a model of dialogical and relational selves. Presented at the 1994 Spring Meeting of the Division of Psychoanalysis of the American Psychological Association, Washington, DC.

Harris, A. (1996). The conceptual power of multiplicity. *Contemporary Psychoanalysis, 32*, 537–552.

Hermans, H. J. M., Kempen, H. J. G., & van Loon, R. J. P. (1992). The dialogical self: Beyond individualism and rationalism. *American Psychologist, 47*, 23–33.

Howell, E. F. (1996). Dissociation in masochism and psychopathic sadism. *Contemporary Psychoanalysis, 32*, 427–453.

Howell, E. F. (2002). Back to the "states." *Psychoanalytic Dialogues, 12*, 921–957.

Howell, E. F. (2005). *The dissociative mind*. Hillsdale, NJ: The Analytic Press.

James, W. (1890). *Principles of psychology*. New York: Holt.

Janet, P. (1889). *L'automatisme psychologique*. Paris: Félix Alcan.

Kernberg, O. F. (1991). Transference regression and psychoanalytic technique with infantile personalities. *International Journal of Psycho-Analysis, 72*, 189–200.

Kihlstrom, J. (1987). The cognitive unconscious. *Science, 237*, 1445–1452.

Klee, P. (1957). *The diaries of Paul Klee 1898–1918*. Berkeley: U. of California Press.

Kohut, H. (1971). *The analysis of the self*. New York: International Universities Press.

Kohut, H. (1977). *The restoration of the self*. New York: International Universities Press.

LeDoux, J. E. (1989). Cognitive-emotional interactions in the brain. *Cognition & Emotion, 3*, 267–289.

LeDoux, J. E. (1994). Emotion, memory, and the brain. *Scientific American, 270*, 32–39.

LeDoux, J. E. (1995). Emotion: Clues from the brain. *Annual Review of Psychology, 46*, 209–235.

LeDoux, J. E. (1996). *The emotional brain*. New York: Touchstone.

LeDoux, J. E. (2002). *The synaptic self*. New York: Viking.

Liotti, G. (1992). Disorganized/disoriented attachment in the etiology of the dissociative disorders. *Dissociation, 5*, 196–204.

Liotti, G. (1995). Disorganized/disoriented attachment in the psychotherapy of the dissociative disorders. In: S. Goldberg, R. Muir, & J. Kerr (Eds.), *Attachment theory*. Hillsdale, NJ: The Analytic Press, pp. 343–363.

Lœwenstein, R. J., & Ross, D. R. (1992). Multiple personality and psychoanalysis: An introduction. *Psychoanalytic Inquiry, 12*, 3–48.

Lynd, H. M. (1958). *On shame and the search for identity*. New York: Harcourt Brace.

Lyon, K. A. (1992). Shattered mirror: A fragment of the treatment of a patient with multiple personality disorder. *Psychoanalytic Inquiry, 12*, 71–94.

Lyons-Ruth, K. (2003). Dissociation and the parent-infant dialogue: A longitudinal perspective from attachment research. *Journal of the American Psychoanalytic Association, 51*, 883–911.

Lyons-Ruth, K., & Boston Change Process Study Group (2001). The emergence of new experiences: Relational improvisation, recognition process, and non-linear change in psychoanalytic therapy. *Psychologist-Psychoanalyst, 21*, 13–17.

Main, M., & Morgan, H. (1996). Disorganization and disorientation in infant strange situation behavior: Phenotypic resemblance to dissociative states. In: L. Michelson & W. Ray (Eds.), *Handbook of dissociation: Theoretical, empirical, and clinical perspectives*. New York: Plenum.

Marmer, S. S. (1980). Psychoanalysis of multiple personality. *International Journal of Psycho-Analysis, 61*, 439–459.

Marmer, S. S. (1991). Multiple personality disorder: A psychoanalytic perspective. *Psychiatric Clinics of North America, 14*, 677–693.

Mitchell, S. A. (1991). Contemporary perspectives on self: Toward an integration. *Psychoanalytic Dialogues, 1*, 121–147.

Mitchell, S. A. (1993). *Hope and dread in psychoanalysis*. New York: Basic Books.

Piers, C. (1996). A return to the source: Rereading Freud in the midst of contemporary trauma theory. *Psychotherapy, 33*, 539–548.

Piers, C. (1998). Contemporary trauma theory and its relation to character. *Psychoanalytic Psychology, 15*, 14–33.

Piers, C. (2000). Character as self-organizing complexity. *Psychoanalysis and Contemporary Thought, 23*, 3–34.

Piers, C. (2001). Patterns of the mind: complexity theory and nonlinear dynamic systems. Presented to NYU Postdoctoral Program/Relational Orientation, January 27, New York City.

Pizer, S. A. (1998). *Building bridges: The negotiation of paradox in psychoanalysis*. Hillsdale, NJ: The Analytic Press.

Pizer, S. A. (2002). "There was a child went forth": Commentary on paper by Steven Stern. *Psychoanalytic Dialogues, 12*, 715–725.

Putnam, F. (1988). The switch process in multiple personality disorder and other state-change disorders. *Dissociation, 1*, 24–32.

Putnam, F. (1992). Discussion: Are alter personalities fragments or figments? *Psychoanalytic Inquiry, 12*, 95–111.

Reis, B. E. (1993). Toward a psychoanalytic understanding of multiple personality disorder. *Bulletin of the Menninger Clinic, 57*, 309–318.

Roth, S. (1992). Discussion: A psychoanalyst's perspective on multiple personality disorder. *Psychoanalytic Inquiry, 12*, 112–123.

Schore, A. N. (1994). *Affect regulation and the origin of the self*. Hillsdale, NJ: Erlbaum.

Schore, A. N. (2003a). *Affect dysregulation and disorders of the self*. New York: Norton.

Schore, A. N. (2003b). *Affect regulation and the repair of the self*. New York: Norton.

Schore, A. N. (2007). Review of "Awakening the Dreamer: Clinical Journeys," by Philip M. Bromberg. *Psychoanalytic Dialogues, 17*, 753–767.

Schwartz, H. L. (1994). From dissociation to negotiation: A relational psychoanalytic perspective on multiple personality disorder. *Psychoanalytic Psychology, 11*, 189–231.

Schwartz, H. L. (2000). *Dialogues with forgotten voices: Relational perspectives on child abuse, trauma, and treatment of dissociative disorders.* New York: Basic Books.

Shengold, L. (1989). *Soul murder.* New Haven, CT: Yale University Press.

Shengold, L. (1992). Commentary on "Dissociative processes and transference-countertransference paradigms" by Davies and Frawley. *Psychoanalytic Dialogues, 2,* 49–59.

Slavin, M. O., & Kriegman, D. (1992). *The adaptive design of the human psyche.* New York: Guilford.

Smith, B. L. (1989). Of many minds: A contribution on the dynamics of multiple personality. In: M. G. Fromm & B. L. Smith (Eds.), *The facilitating environment: Clinical applications of Winnicott's theories.* Madison, CT: International Universities Press, pp. 424–458.

Smith, H. F. (2000). Review essay: Conflict: *See under* dissociation. *Psychoanalytic Dialogues, 10,* 539–550.

Smith, H. F. (2001). Obstacles to integration: Another look at why we talk past each other. *Psychoanalytic Psychology, 18,* 485–514.

Smith, H. F. (2003a). Theory and practice: Intimate partnership or false connection? *Psychoanalytic Quarterly, 72,* 1–12.

Smith, H. F. (2003b). Conceptions of conflict in psychoanalytic theory and practice. *Psychoanalytic Quarterly, 72,* 49–96.

Smith, H. F. (2003c). Common and uncommon ground: A panel exchange. *Journal of the American Psychoanalytic Association, 51,* 1311–1335.

Smith, H. F. (2006). Analyzing disavowed action: The fundamental resistance of analysis. *Journal of the American Psychoanalytic Association, 54,* 713–737.

Stern, D. B. (1983). Unformulated experience. *Contemporary Psychoanalysis, 19,* 71–99.

Stern, D. B. (1996). Dissociation and constructivism. *Psychoanalytic Dialogues, 6,* 251–266.

Stern, D. B. (1997). *Unformulated experience: From dissociation to imagination in psychoanalysis.* Hillsdale, NJ: The Analytic Press.

Stern, D. B. (2003). The fusion of horizons: Dissociation, enactment, and understanding. *Psychoanalytic Dialogues, 13,* 843–873.

Stern, D. B. (2004). The eye sees itself: Dissociation, enactment, and the achievement of conflict. *Contemporary Psychoanalysis, 40,* 197–237.

Stern, S. (2002). The self as a relational structure: A dialogue with multiple-self theory. *Psychoanalytic Dialogues, 12,* 693–714.

Stolorow, R. D., Brandchaft, B., & Atwood, G. E. (1987). *Psychoanalytic treatment: An intersubjective approach.* Hillsdale, NJ: The Analytic Press.

Sullivan, H. S. (1940). *Conceptions of modern psychiatry.* New York: Norton.

Sullivan, H. S. (1953). *The interpersonal theory of psychiatry.* New York: Norton.

Sullivan, H. S. (1954). *The psychiatric interview.* New York: Norton.

Sullivan, H. S. (1956). *Clinical studies in psychiatry.* New York: Norton.

Taylor, E. (2000). Psychotherapeutics and the problematic origins of clinical psychology in America. *American Psychologist, 55,* 1029–1033.

Thelen, E., & Smith, L. B. (1995). *A dynamic systems approach to the development of cognition and action.* Cambridge, MA: MIT Press.

Waugaman, R. M. (2000). Multiple personality disorder and one analyst's paradigm shift. *Psychoanalytic Inquiry, 20,* 207–226.

Winnicott, D. W. (1945). Primitive emotional development. In: *Collected papers: Through pædiatrics to psycho-analysis.* London: Tavistock, 1958, pp. 145–156.

Winnicott, D. W. (1949). Mind and its relation to the psyche-soma. In: *Collected papers: Through pædiatrics to psycho-analysis.* London: Tavistock, 1958, pp. 243–254.

Winnicott, D. W. (1960). Ego distortion in terms of true and false self. In: *The maturational processes and the facilitating environment.* New York: International Universities Press, 1965, pp. 140–152.

Winnicott, D. W. (1971). Dreaming, fantasying, and living: A case-history describing a primary dissociation. In: *Playing and reality.* New York: Basic Books, pp. 26–37.

Wolff, P. H. (1987). *The development of behavioral states and the expression of emotion in early infancy.* Chicago: University of Chicago Press.

Young, W. (1988). Psychodynamics and dissociation. *Dissociation, 1,* 33–38.

43 Dissociation and Unformulated Experience: A Psychoanalytic Model of Mind

Donnel B. Stern, PhD

OUTLINE

While dissociation is conceived in many ways in the trauma literature, theories of dissociation tend to center around the idea of a self-protective process that takes place when the events of life are beyond tolerance. We leave ourselves, so to speak; psychically, we turn away.

In the particular way I use the term, these meanings are preserved, but expanded. Dissociation is not only a fall-back position. Instead, and in addition, dissociation is the core of a psychoanalytic understanding of the nature of experiencing, a means of understanding both the unconscious and the defensive processes, on the one hand, and consciousness on the other. Dissociation, that is, is the keystone of a psychoanalytic model of mind, a model that contrasts in significant respects with the theory of mind handed down in the psychoanalytic literature from Freud until now. The inspirations for my ideas about dissociation are both psychoanalytic (Levenson, 1972, 1983, 1991; Lionells et al., 1995; Schafer, 1976, 1983, 1992; Schachtel, 1959; Spence, 1982; Sullivan, 1940, 1954) and philosophical (Fingarette, 1969; Gadamer, 1975, 1976; James, 1890; Merleau-Ponty, 1964, 1968, 1973). I have sought to develop a relational perspective on mind that is at once clinically useful, hermeneutically grounded, and phenomenologically recognizable.

I came to dissociation via the influence of Harry Stack Sullivan (1940, 1953). Sullivan differed from the classical analysts of his day in seeing the origin of "problems in living" (a term he preferred to "psychopathology") not in the clash of drive and defense, but in what had actually happened in relationships with significant others. Relationships and the need for them replaced drive and defense as the stuff of life. For Sullivan, dissociation, not repression, was the primary defensive maneuver, because he understood the primary danger to be the revival of intolerable experience, not the breakthrough of primitive endogenous fantasy. From a modern perspective, we could say that, for Sullivan, the great threat was retraumatization. Eventually, Sullivan's views formed the basis for what became interpersonal psychoanalysis (see Lionells et al., 1995); and Sullivan and interpersonal thinking then became one of the primary springboards for relational psychoanalysis (e.g., Mitchell, 1988, 1993, 1997; Mitchell & Aron, 1999). For the most part, I will be able to credit in this short account only the most immediate sources of my views.[1]

The brevity of a summary chapter also precludes clinical illustrations. This is a necessity I particularly regret, because the ideas were originally developed in the attempt to make a clinical contribution. (For clinical illustrations, see Stern, 1992a, 1992b, 1997, 2002, 2003, 2004, 2008, in press a, b.) Most recently, I have written about dissociation and mutual enactment in the treatment

[1] For a detailed description of the views of Sullivan and others relevant to the issues discussed in this chapter, see Stern, 1994, 1995, 1997, 2002, 2003, 2004, in press b.

situation as the defensively motivated separation of self-states (2003, 2004, 2008, in press b), a view that, given space restrictions, I will only be able to mention briefly in this chapter.

In order to contextualize dissociation as a defensive process, I begin by outlining the ideas from which I depart. I start with certain assumptions underlying the repression-based classical psychoanalytic model of mind, and then contrast that perspective with a dissociation-based view. I do not intend my description of repression and the primary and secondary processes to be an authoritative account; rather, this description of the primary elements of the traditional psychoanalytic theory of mind serves as a foil against the background of which I clarify my own views and highlight major differences in emphasis of the two ways of thinking.

43.1 ASSUMPTIONS UNDERLYING THE REPRESSION MODEL

Mental representations due to be repressed, wrote Freud (1915a), are both repulsed by consciousness and attracted by previous repressed contents in the unconscious. Once repressed, representations can be cognized only via the primary process, Freud's (1895, 1900, 1915b) term for the means by which he believed the unconscious (or later in his work, the id) continuously sought to reinstate the perceptions associated with the original satisfactions of drive. The primary process seeks hallucinatory wish fulfillment. Except for certain nonlinguistic functions (such as the use of words as simple labels), language appears in the primary process only in a regressed and primitive form.[2]

But Freud also believed that, for those aspects of subjectivity that could be represented in language, consciousness was the natural state. These aspects of mental functioning, the secondary process, had been traditionally described in the psychology of the day: waking thought, attention, judgment, reasoning, and controlled (consciously chosen) action. On one hand, the secondary process regulates the primary process, inhibiting hallucinatory wish fulfillment (at least during waking life) and heedless observance of the pleasure principle (which would bring even greater unpleasure in its wake). It might also be said, though, that the secondary process is merely an *indirect* route to drive satisfaction, one shaped by a respect for the complexities of reality (Freud, 1895, 1900, 1915b).

In Freud's thinking, there is an insistent pressure for drive to be represented in awareness. All repressed representations, in the form of what Freud (1915a, b) called "derivatives" of the repressed or the unconscious, press for expression; derivatives "want" to be released, to be satisfied, just as drive itself does. And so we have the doctrine of the return of the repressed, the continuous pressure toward consciousness exerted by contents that have been repressed (Freud, 1915a). In turn, this urgent pressure is the origin of the necessity for the development by the ego of unconscious defenses: because the sudden appearance of certain drive-related material in consciousness would arouse intolerable anxiety (that is, in the end there would be more unpleasure than pleasure), there come to be processes in the mind that, when unconsciously deployed, prevent that kind of sudden eruption. Although the repressed does continuously come back in the form of "a *compromise* between the repressed ideas and the repressing ones" (Freud, 1896, p. 170; italics in the original), the ego turns out to be a worthy adversary.

Despite being the prize over which the battle between drive and defense is fought, however, that part of the ego which we know as consciousness is itself a fairly passive aspect of the mind in Freud's scheme.

The contents of consciousness are not specifically selected; rather, they are what can be tolerated by the defenses. They are what remains when the smoke of battle has cleared; they are the outcome, an epiphenomenon, a by-product of the clash of drive and defense. Consciousness is not the main event; it is what remains after the great events have taken place.[3] Just as symptoms or dreams are registrations of forces beyond themselves, and passive in that sense, consciousness, too, is a passive record in Freud's work. In Freud's terms, we can imagine consciousness as the most superficial layer of

[2] But see Loewald's (1978) brilliant reformulation of the theory of the primary and secondary processes, in which language can partake of the primary process without being schizophrenic, as in poetry or free association. In fact, for Loewald language is not really alive *unless* it is in contact with the primary process. Freud's account of the primary process and secondary process changed and developed over his lifetime. Gill (1967) feels, though, that in the end Freud offered "nothing like a comprehensive metapsychological treatment" (p. 265) of these ideas. Interested readers should consult Gill's (1967) careful study.

[3] This account might appear to leave out of consideration the work of Freudian ego psychologists, who followed Freud's lead in suggesting that the ego had a sphere of influence independent of the id (e.g., Bergman, 2000). One might say that I am especially ignoring the many ego psychological writings on the ego's integrative or synthetic functions. But keep in mind that while consciousness is part of the ego, consciousness and ego are hardly coterminous. Consciousness can be passive even if ego is not. Even the most sophisticated of ego psychologists did not question the assumptions about mind that I describe in the text.

an archeological dig—a fascinating record, an essential record, a record we must study if we want to appreciate the events that, in disguised fashion, are sedimented in it—but the record of a compromise nevertheless.

Like other writers of his day, Freud accepted without reservation the idea that the mind—and, therefore, the unconscious—is composed of fully formed contents. This unconsidered belief derives from the deep and culture-wide assumption, explicitly accepted by Freud (Schimek, 1975), that perception is a sensory given, and that experience is therefore rooted in mental elements that come to us already fully formed. Freud's era took place long before the development of the "New Look" in perception research (Bruner & Klein, 1960; Bruner & Postman, 1949), in which perception was reconceptualized in constructivist terms. Even today, and especially in everyday life, we are seldom aware that we construct our own experience. We are much more likely to feel as if everything we experience was already there, fully formed, merely awaiting our registration of it. The view I present later directly contradicts this view.

Following in the wake of the assumption that perception is merely a matter of registering fully formed sensory stimuli is an equally crucial corollary. This corollary is just as unconsidered and widely accepted in psychoanalysis today as the first point was in Freud's era: if we are unaware of some aspect of experience, it is because we have made ourselves unaware. That is, because the elements of thought are always already present in our minds, defense is necessarily a matter of unconsciously refusing to acknowledge fully formed and preexisting mental content. Lack of awareness is unconsciously purposeful. Most psychoanalysts still accept these postulates about consciousness and the unconscious in an unquestioning way—that is, without considering that they represent only one of the alternatives. Later in this chapter I will champion one of those neglected alternatives.

These points, of course, amount to Freud's hypothesis of repression, the model for virtually every model of unconscious defensive processes since Freud. In the terms of repression, to keep contents unconscious requires effort, what Laplanche and Pontalis (1973) call "a complex interplay of decathexes, recathexes and anticathexes [of] the instinctual representatives" (p. 394). These "instinctual representatives" are not "bound," as is the secondary process, and so it is their inclination to occupy the entire mind. In this "barbarians-at-the-gates" sense, consciousness is part of their "natural" domain, a land they would overrun immediately without the intervention of defense. (It would probably be more accurate, actually, to say that the id is continuously trying to convert the rest of subjectivity into a version of itself, a land run by the rules of the primary process.) In the imagery of a less military metaphor, it is as if the repressed were a beach ball we are trying to keep underwater by sitting on it. Unless we balance ourselves with the greatest care, expending a good deal of energy in the process (and even then we may be unsuccessful), the beach ball explodes out from under us and shoots up to the surface.

And so, in this view, unless defense interrupts the process, understanding ourselves and the world around us ought to be natural and effortless. For heuristic reasons, I ignore for the time being the fact that consciousness in Freud's scheme, being inconsistent with the primary process, would simply cease to exist if it were somehow overrun by the repressed. The point I want to make is that, in Freud's view, we already contain the knowing we need. It is there inside us, formed and ready: "*the essence of repression lies simply in turning something away, and keeping it at a distance, from the conscious*" (1915, p. 147, italics in the original). Except when we are genuinely ignorant, the thoughts and feelings we need in order to make sense of our lives would come into our minds if we would but allow them to do so.[4] It seems that understanding should arise by itself; the process of coming to understand does not seem to require any particular explanation. *Mis*understanding, on the other hand is an anomaly; *mis*understanding is the event we need to explain. We can misunderstand out of ignorance, of course. But with that single exception, misunderstanding is anomalous in the perspective associated with the repression hypothesis: when we do not understand, it can only be because the natural unfolding of comprehension has been interrupted by unconscious defensive processes.

Notice that this view implies yet another assumption. Although this assumption is much more open to question now than even 20 years ago, it is still taken for granted in many quarters. The assumption is this: if we accept that the truth impresses itself upon us, then we are (usually without realizing it) taking the position that truth is singular and objectively verifiable. On this view, the unconscious is made up of the truths we will not accept—fully formed feelings and thoughts and mental "objects" that have the kind of invisible, objective existence of a stage set behind a curtain. The goodness or fullness of our understanding is judged by reference to whether we

[4] Of course, the claim that certain novel formulations require effortful thought is perfectly consistent with Freud's theory. I am referring here not to extraordinary inventive moments (though they, too, often come unbidden [see D.B. Stern, 1997]), but to the everyday course of affairs.

accept the truth; and the truth, in turn, is defined as the mental representation of objective reality.

The question, then, is whether what we understand corresponds to objective reality. For this reason, the position I am describing often has been described as the "correspondence" view of truth: we judge that we have reached the truth when our understanding "matches" or "corresponds to" the supposedly objective reality that we are trying to grasp.

One might think that the respect for psychic reality (i.e., inner reality, the mind's own reality) in classical psychoanalytic views is inconsistent with the correspondence view. After all, in Freud's theory and the theories of those who followed him, psychic reality is the entirely *subjective* foundation of motivation, and therefore of psychic life. You cannot understand someone else's motives without first understanding the subjectively based intrapsychic fantasies that underlie them. In this sense, it is true that psychic reality is hardly an objective phenomenon. However, this subjectivity can still be *understood* in objective terms. As nonrational as it is, psychic reality can still be seen as a singular, predetermined phenomenon that allows only one objective understanding. In most cases, classical analysts do write, as a matter of fact, as if the proper psychoanalytic understanding of psychic reality is an objective understanding, as if the nature of subjectivity (psychic reality) is objectively verifiable. Nor does the existence of multiple subjective truths about the same mental contents necessarily contradict the correspondence view, because each of these multiple truths can still be understood to have an objective existence.

Note that the correspondence view implies that any influence on understanding, other than objective reality, must be misleading; this implication leads directly to our usual definition of bias or prejudice as a predisposition or preconception that distorts knowing by reducing our capacity to allow reality simply to register itself. (We shall find a different view in hermeneutics and the dissociation view associated with it.) From the correspondence perspective, understanding is absolute and noncontextual: the nature of truth in one circumstance is the same as it is in another. These points uniformly underscore the correspondence view's tendency to portray understanding as passive and unidirectional, a straightforward inscription of world on mind. The only effort required by the process of knowing is expended in the removal of impediments to a natural unfolding. Thus we understand by clearing away the obstacles that prevent mind from following its inclination to shape itself in reality's image.

43.2 UNFORMULATED EXPERIENCE: A DISSOCIATION-BASED PSYCHOANALYTIC MODEL OF MIND

But what if things are otherwise?

In point of fact, almost everyone these days agrees that things *are* otherwise. Almost no one accepts the correspondence view anymore—neither psychologists, psychoanalysts, philosophers, nor cognitive neuroscientists. Virtually no one would argue today, at least not in the most traditional way, that truth is defined simply by objective observation. Knowing and understanding are constructed, not merely registered.

And yet many classical psychoanalysts still accept a modified version of the older view. Lawrence Friedman (2000), for instance, one of the most influential of contemporary Freudian theorists, continues to champion objectivity as an ideal, describing objective observation as a construction built up from many small observations, each of which, in and of itself, may be subjective.

The particular dissociation-based view I am describing, rooted in the concept of unformulated experience, grew from the same soil that nurtured the move away from correspondence theory, and so it contradicts many of the assumptions underlying the repression-based view. I address these differences in the same order I presented the assumptions discussed previously.

Perception is *not* a sensory given in the dissociation model; instead, perception is constructed from a less fully formulated state: there is an ongoing process of emergence in perception, thought, and feeling, from vagueness to clarity. Mental contents, therefore, are not necessarily fully formed, especially unconscious contents. Instead, they are *unformulated*, less clearly actualized than they will be when they are formulated. The unconscious is composed of *potential* experience, contents that do not yet have an explicit, knowable shape, and that may take any one of several or many possible shapes when eventually they are formulated.

Until recently, my position was that the formulation of meaning takes place exclusively in language (Stern, 1983, 1997). I took that position because my purpose at that time was limited to charting the path of experience from its unformulated beginnings to the explicitly meaningful shape it takes in reflective awareness. I believed that only when experience is formulated in verbal language can it be consciously, explicitly reflected upon; and, of course, the creation of a capacity to reflect in areas of our lives in which we could not reflect before has always been a hallmark of psychoanalysis.

I have not changed my view about the nature or significance of explicit reflection. Recently, however, I have expanded the theory of unformulated experience to include formulated *nonverbal* meaning (Stern, in press b). In keeping with that expanded purpose, I now believe that we should recognize two varieties of unformulated experience. Some unformulated experience, when its potential is formulated, tends toward *articulation as verbal-reflective meaning*; this is the kind of formulation I have described before, the kind of formulation that allows explicit reflection. But a second kind of unformulated experience, when its potential is formulated, tends toward *realization as nonverbal meaning*. Some nonverbal meanings, once they are realized, can then be articulated as verbal-reflective meaning and enter explicit, reflective awareness. But many nonverbal meanings are not amenable to articulation in verbal language and, therefore, cannot be reflected on. These latter meanings participate in the creation of living only in their nonverbal form.

Let me offer a brief, simple example of what I mean by realized nonverbal meaning. Let us say that a particular (fictional) patient is highly anxious about sexual arousal, so anxious that he can allow himself only a very pale version of the sensory pleasure of sex. The unformulated experience of anyone's sexual encounter contains myriad possibilities, only some of which are realized in experience. In the case of our fictional patient, the possibilities that are realized—the nonverbal sensory and affective meanings that he derives from the sexual experience—are notably muted. Because language is not an adequate means of symbolizing the nuances of sensory experience, our patient can only reflect on a portion of even that part of his unformulated sexual experience that has been realized as nonverbal meaning. The realized nonverbal meanings that do not enter reflective awareness nevertheless help to shape the experience, and the nonverbal meanings that go unrealized, of course, contribute to the shape of the experience as well—by their very absence.

Perhaps the most significant role played by realized nonverbal meaning is its part in day-to-day, ongoing interpersonal relatedness. Imagine my fictional patient in a social situation in which flirtation is a possibility. Flirtation, we shall say, has been infected by the patient's anxiety about sexuality. My patient is therefore hobbled in such a context. He is unlikely to have access to the experience that he would need in order to make immediate, intuitive sense of the other person's flirting, or to participate in a natural way in the flirting himself. He is overcome with anxiety, both because of what he does grasp (again, nonverbally) about this kind of relatedness, and because of what his anxiety prevents him from comprehending.

Each of us enters each moment with an unformulated "way of being," and from that way of being we unconsciously select certain potentials and develop them into the meanings that become our verbal and nonverbal experience of the moments to come. The potentials that we cannot tolerate are neither selected nor constructed: we can say that these aspects of our unformulated ways of being, both verbal and nonverbal, are *dissociated*. The parts of our ways of being that we can tolerate, on the other hand, are either articulated (in verbal-reflective meaning) or realized (in nonverbal meaning). We are able to use the articulated and realized parts of experience in the ongoing negotiation of relatedness with others. But to the extent that we do not articulate or realize our way of being in any particular moment, our flexibility and freedom to relate to the other in that moment are compromised.

In the case of both verbal-reflective articulations and nonverbal realizations, then, consciousness is no longer a passive outcome, but a creation: an achievement that demands the expenditure of effort. We understand only what we formulate, and that process of construction requires mental work. If experience has a "natural" state, it is neither articulation nor realization, but lack of formulation. Without the application of attention and effort, unformulated experience stays just as it is. The contents of consciousness are therefore *not* merely what is left over after an internal battle. They are specifically and actively selected according to our (conscious and unconscious) interests and values, in interaction with the contexts in which the formulation of our experience takes place. The metaphor of the beach ball hurtling up from the depths as soon as it is no longer held down is replaced by a symbol of effort, perhaps something like a heavy adjustable lens that must be pointed in a particular direction and then wrested to a new setting in order to bring an unconsciously chosen view into clarity. Consciousness is an active creation—an accomplishment—not a leftover.[5]

[5] Loewald (1978) anticipated something like this view when he redescribed the new kind of meaning that can arise in Freud's theory of thinking when thing-presentations are linked to word-presentation by hypercathexis. Consistent with the view argued here, and emphasizing that language is not necessarily a pale form of unconscious meaning, but can be a richer form of cognitive organization, Loewald wrote, "the hypercathecting act, the linking of thing-presentations and word-presentations, brings about a presentation that differs from either in being a novel, more complexly organized psychical act" (p. 182). This view, however, is a creative reinterpretation of Freud and is not typical of the way the concepts of primary and secondary process have been used in the literature.

If unconscious mental contents are unformulated, it no longer makes sense to conceive of defense as a refusal to acknowledge a truth that already exists in parts of our minds to which we have no access. Instead, defense becomes the prevention of the formulation of unformulated experience—the prevention of the very existence of articulations and realizations. If we define dissociation as the inability or unconscious unwillingness to formulate experience in symbolic form (and most of us do define it that way), it follows that to prevent experience from being shaped into verbal-reflective or nonverbal meaning is to dissociate. The primary defense is therefore dissociation. In this way of thinking, it is not fully formed mental contents that must be controlled (because they are not "there" to *be* controlled). What must be controlled by defense is instead the effort that we would need to expend in order to formulate the unformulated. The willingness to make this effort, the willingness to try to open ourselves to what is questionable, and therefore to what it is possible to formulate, is what I refer to as "curiosity." In this frame of reference, defense, or dissociation, can be defined either as the unconscious refusal to formulate experience or as the unconsciously motivated refusal to be curious.

Remember that in the repression model, understanding is the natural state of affairs, interrupted only by the distortions of defense. It is probably clear by now that this cannot be true of the dissociation model I am presenting. If understanding always remains to be constructed, then it is not the *presence* of understanding, but its *absence* that is the natural state of affairs. Understanding does not happen "by itself": it is an outcome of some kind of effort. *Lack* of understanding is what happens "by itself." And, therefore, the mystery that surrounds not-knowing in the repression model is transferred to the process of understanding—that is, to the process by which meaning is formulated.

43.2.1 What Is Understanding?

I have already said that dissociation is the unconscious refusal to be curious; I have also said that curiosity is what makes understanding possible; and finally, I have said that understanding, not the absence of understanding, is now the mysterious event requiring explanation. And so, if we are to understand dissociation, we must understand the nature of understanding itself. What process is it that dissociation interrupts? How should we understand understanding?

According to hermeneutic philosopher Hans-Georg Gadamer (1975, 1976), we can never perceive reality itself; that is, we can never perceive reality in any absolute or unmediated sense.[6] Instead, we construct reality according to the various traditions sedimented in our languages and cultures. Reality is mediated to us by the meanings that have currency in our time and place. Language and culture are the lens through which our understanding of the world and ourselves comes into being. And so in Gadamer's work we have a view that is neither objectivist nor relativist, but that charts a course between the two (Bernstein, 1983; Sass, 1988). On the one hand, truth is constrained by reality; but on the other, each of our formulations is only one of the possibilities, potentiated by its context. Reality is manifold; truth is multiple.

Gadamer redefines "bias" and "prejudice," arguing that our "preconceptions," the meanings that our cultures predispose us to find, are what make it possible for us to make any meaning at all. We depend on bias and prejudice. They are crucial: "It is not so much our judgments as our prejudgments that constitute our being" (Gadamer, quoted by Linge, 1976, p. xvii). Elsewhere Gadamer (1966) says, "Prejudices are biases of our openness to the world. They are simply conditions whereby we experience something—whereby what we encounter says something to us" (p. 8). And yet, Gadamer (1975) also tells us that learning something new is a matter of transcending these prejudices: "Every experience worthy of the name runs counter to our expectation … Insight is more than the knowledge of this or that situation. It always involves an escape from something that had deceived us and held us captive" (pp. 319–320). Prejudices are both the ground on which we can experience anything at all and the blinders we must manage to reflect on and disconfirm if we are to experience anything new.

For hermeneuticists, including Gadamer, the process by which we bring our prejudices into play and then disconfirm them is the hermeneutic circle. The idea arises from a paradox. We can understand only those communications that we can locate in their proper contexts. Unless an utterance can be placed in the appropriate configuration of tradition, its meaning remains obscure. Imagine trying to understand certain passages in Freud without knowing that he was taking issue with Jung; or trying to understand a dream without knowing the events of the day preceding it, or the patient's associations to it; or trying

[6] In addition to Gadamer's (1975) magnum opus, *Truth and Method*, the reader interested in learning about Gadamer might consult a collection of his seminal papers (Gadamer, 1975), which is accompanied by a useful introduction to his work (Linge, 1976). Numerous secondary sources are also available (e.g., Bernstein, 1983; Warnke, 1987; Risser, 1997; Silverman, 1991; Weinsheimer, 1985; Scheibler, 2000).

to understand a patient's barely supportable characterization of a coworker as greedy without knowing that the patient himself is terribly afraid of being greedy.

We comprehend by means of continuously projecting complete understandings into communications from the other, communications we actually understand only partially. We extrapolate complete understandings on the basis of the partial understandings we already have. And where do the partial understandings come from? They are in turn stimulated by the complete understandings we project. Thus is the circle closed. But of course, something else must happen, or else comprehension would be nothing more than self-reference. All comprehension is a process of projecting partial understandings into fully rounded ones, and then modifying these projections on the basis of what we actually come into contact with in conversation with the other person.[7] In other words, when we have understood, we have been able to treat our projections like hypotheses; and when we have not understood, we have not managed to adopt this degree of uncertainty. The problem is clear: how do we avoid seeing nothing more than we expect to see? Under what circumstances can projections be hypotheses rather than givens?

Dissociation is the condition under which we see what we expect to see. Novelty does not speak to us; we are ruled by our preconceptions, which remain invisible to us. We are not able to be curious about what faces us and instead are satisfied, even insistent upon, limiting ourselves to what is familiar. Curiosity is the active attitude of openness that allows us to disconfirm our preconceptions and substitute new meanings for them.

In emphasizing curiosity as an active attitude of openness, I mean to be going far beyond the everyday meaning of the word. I intend to refer to an openness to what is unbidden in life, to what comes to us if we are able to allow ourselves to accept the uncertainty of the experience we will have in the next moment. Curiosity is *not* the asking of questions, or at least not merely the asking of questions. Because it is a kind of acceptance (to be differentiated from approval) of whatever arrives in one's mind, a surrender to one's own capacity to construct the unexpected, curiosity may, in fact, appear to be a passive state of being. But if it is passive, it is a very actively maintained kind of passivity. Unfettered curiosity is the polar opposite of dissociation.

[7] Gadamer applies his conception of understanding most often to the grasp of the meanings of cultural products such as art, drama, and literature. But he does also write about the kind of understanding that goes on between two people. I am limiting my discussion here to the attempt of two people to understand one another.

Perhaps the greatest divergence of Gadamer's hermeneutic view from correspondence theory is Gadamer's insistence that truth is always accomplished in dialogue. It can never be created in isolation. Uncertainty about preconceptions, and the consequent possibilities for the perception of novelty, can be created only when one's own projections are met by the attempt of the other to speak (or act) back, to converse. Truth is a mutual creation forged in dialogue.

In these points Gadamer unwittingly shares a view that has developed over many decades in interpersonal and relational psychoanalysis: the most important context in the creation of understanding or meaning is the interpersonal context, or the interpersonal field. Harry Stack Sullivan (1940) wrote that, "Situations call out motivations" (p. 191), reversing the usual polarity. He means that any particular moment's experience is heavily influenced by the people with whom we are relating at the time (by "people," I mean both real, flesh-and-blood beings in the outer world and the internal objects of the inner world). The contents of consciousness are a function of one's predispositions, in interaction with the nature of the interpersonal field.

And so we come to the conclusion, very different from the conclusion of early Freudian psychoanalysts, that what is true depends, within the significant constraints provided by reality, on the interpersonal situation in which that truth is formulated. The interpersonal field determines, to a large extent, the explicit shape taken by unformulated experience, or even whether it will take any shape at all. The interpersonal field is the single most significant of the contexts that continuously participate in the creation of experience and the decision about what is true.

To insist on keeping experience unformulated is to dissociate; to be open to formulating it, and to grasping the preconceptions that help give it shape, is to be curious. And so I hope it is also clear now that dissociation, too, exists relative to the interpersonal field. In fact, any particular interpersonal field can be said to be defined by the particular relationship of curiosity and dissociation within it. Think of it this way: the explicit experience it is possible to formulate (be curious about) in one field (that is, in the presence of one particular person, or a particular internal object) differs from the experience that can be formulated in another. And reciprocally, the experience that *cannot* be formulated (is dissociated, outside the range of curiosity) in one field also differs from the experience that cannot be formulated in another. Dissociation and curiosity define one another; each gains its meaning only in the context of the other. Curiosity is the absence of dissociation; dissociation is the absence of curiosity.

43.2.2 The Role of Language

The capacity to make new meaning, either linguistically or nonverbally, is one way to describe the process of effective curiosity, the absence of dissociation. Dissociation is an insistence on the creation of familiar experience, conventional forms that cannot contain novelty and that signify, as Mallarmé puts it, only as "the worn coin placed silently in my hand" (cited by Merleau-Ponty, 1964, p. 44). Conventionalization, of course, obscures novelty, which disappears into the familiar. We hardly notice what is being signified.

Gadamer's work is part of the linguistic turn in philosophy that began, in different ways, with Heidegger and Wittgenstein. Language is not a tool that we use as we please, as if words were clothing for meanings that exist independent of them. Instead, to the extent that we allow language to give us all it can, *it* controls *us*. In fact, it constitutes us. Language is the sum total of a culture's traditions; and tradition is the culture's collection of the prejudices and preconceptions that we must have if we are to make any meaning at all. Language does not simply label meanings, it creates their very possibility. Language has a life of its own, an unruly and generative life that Merleau-Ponty (e.g., 1964, 1968, 1973) has described particularly well.

Interestingly, the meanings made possible by language are not limited to those in the verbal-reflective mode. Among the possibilities created by language are the possibilities we have to realize *nonverbal* meaning—even the kind of nonverbal realizations that are not necessarily amenable to verbal-reflective articulation! This point is perfectly consistent with Gadamer's thought, because for Gadamer, as for his mentor Heidegger before him, it is language that creates the architecture of experience, and it is that architecture that makes *any* meaning possible. Therefore, and ironically enough, especially for those who think of the verbal and the nonverbal as independent modes of representation, the hermeneutic perspective holds that language plays a significant role in defining the possibilities for nonverbal meaning.[8]

If we give ourselves over to the "wild-flowering mind" (Merleau-Ponty, 1964, p. 181), we frequently experience ourselves as conduits for the meanings that arise in us. Despite feeling that meanings arrive in our minds unbidden at such times, we are liable to feel that it is just this experience that is most our own, and that it is in just such moments that we are most ourselves. We are at our best as conversational partners: it is at these times that we can most fully create in our own minds the world of the other, and thereby grasp what the other is conveying to us. It is at these times that novelty reveals itself to us. And because we give ourselves over to curiosity and the world of the other in the same instant that we give ourselves over to language, it is also at such moments that we are most fully imaginative and least dissociated.

43.3 TWO VARIETIES OF DISSOCIATION

Experience is a narrative process. We are attached to the stories we tell ourselves about our lives. We are so attached, as a matter of fact, that myriad possibilities in life remain unformulated simply because we experience in habitual ways, insistently telling and living our particular stories. We continuously burn bridges to meanings we might otherwise have formulated. These unconsidered alternatives are not necessarily meanings we would actively turn away from if we knew them: we miss the opportunity to actualize them only because of our focus elsewhere. This very common kind of dissociation I refer to as *passive dissociation*, or *dissociation in the weak sense* (Stern, 1997, Chapter 6; 2003, 2004). We can often be helped to see some of these meanings simply by having our attention drawn to their possibility.

But there are also meanings, of course, that we actively avoid, that we turn away from with unconscious purpose. This is experience that we maintain in an unformulated (unconscious) state for defensive reasons. The pain such experience would create in us is simply more than we will bear. The worst of such pain is caused when we are unable to avoid the formulation of experience that we cannot even acknowledge belongs to us; such experience is what Harry Stack Sullivan calls *not-me*, and it feels as if it exists outside the bounds of what we can accept as "self." Trauma, of course, falls in this category. If we are to maintain an acceptable degree of comfort and psychic equilibrium, *not-me* must be maintained as unformulated experience. We develop a quite specific unconscious refusal to articulate or realize these aspects of our subjectivity. This defensive process I refer to as *active dissociation* or *dissociation in the strong sense* (Stern, 1997, Chapter 7; 2003, 2004).

Now let me go back a step: remember that the contents of consciousness are heavily influenced by the nature of the interpersonal field. To make this claim, it turns out, is to arrive at the very same theory of dissociated self-states that has become highly influential in relational psychoanalysis in recent years (e.g., Bromberg, 1998, 2006;

[8] Space restrictions do not allow me to make this argument in the detail it deserves. Elsewhere (Stern, in press b) I have made a more complete presentation. The interested reader should also consult Taylor's (1985) cogent essay.

Davies & Frawley, 1994; Howell, 2005; Mitchell, 1993; Pizer, 1998; Stern, 1997, 2003, 2004, in press a, b). One merely has to reverse the lens and, instead of looking at the self-state (that is, the current configuration of the interpersonal field) as a significant part of the context that determines the shape of the experience to be formulated, look at the particular selection of experience that can be formulated as what defines a self-state. A self-state, if we think about it this way, is defined by the experience that can be formulated from within it. And therefore, dissociation in the strong sense (the unconscious refusal to formulate certain content) is synonymous with the dissociation of self-states from one another. Unconsciously refusing to formulate certain mental content, that is, is equivalent to unconsciously enforcing the defensive isolation of the self-state in which this content could be known (Stern, 2003, 2004, in press b).

43.3.1 From Dissociation to Imagination: The Question of Psychopathology

But I am not suggesting that dissociation in the strong sense is necessarily pathological. Every *me* is accompanied by a *not-me*, and all of us, therefore, dissociate in the strong sense, at least sometimes. The differentiation of "normal" and pathological dissociation is more complicated than that.

It is usually taken for granted that the aspects of psychic functioning most affected by dissociation are those we think of as the building blocks of experience: affect, thought, perception, and memory. In the largest sense, though, dissociation is not fully described as a failure of any of these functions. Dissociation is a failure to allow one's imagination free play. In many instances one can think of the failure of imagination as the collapse of transitional space (Winnicott, 1971) into deadness or literalness. Merleau-Ponty (1964, 1968, 1973), who has captured the sense of what I mean by imagination as well as anyone, writes that "speech takes flight from where it rolls in the wave of speechless communication." He tells us that creative speech, which is the domain of imagination, "tears out or tears apart meanings in the undivided whole of the nameable, as our gestures do in that of the perceptible" (1964, p. 17). Imagination is our capacity to allow meanings of both kinds, what Merleau-Ponty refers to as the nameable and the perceptible, and what I have described as the verbal and the nonverbal, to come to fruition within us as they will. Dissociation is our inhibition of that capacity. If we wish to do so, we can use Lacan's terms here: Imagination takes place in the realm of the Symbolic, dissociation in the Imaginary. Just as in the Imaginary, dissociation is the insistence on denying that life is in continuous, unpredictable flux. In order to prevent the eruption of *not-me*, the next moment must be completely (and falsely) predictable, at least in certain important respects. Experience must be forced into conventional, stereotyped shapes that are not necessarily the best fit for it.

The absence of dissociation, though, is not defined by the presence of some particular experience that had been prevented from existing. That way of thinking would be a simpleminded dualism, as if experience could be only present or absent, formulated or unformulated. I have already defined the absence of dissociation as (relatively) unfettered curiosity. I can now expand that point: experience ranges from highly imagined to highly dissociated, with all the implied variations in between.

It is by now a clinical truism that experience dissociated in the strong sense—dissociated with unconscious defensive purpose—does not simply disappear into some untended part of the mind, but is instead repetitively externalized, unconsciously enacted in relationship (Bromberg, 1998, 2006; Davies, 1996, 1997, 1998, 1999; Davies & Frawley, 1994; Stern, 1997, 2003, 2004, in press a, b; Pizer, 1998). Enactments are more or less stereotyped, rigid, constricted, and highly selective ways of behaving and experiencing. They require a dampening of curiosity and imagination. During an enactment, what one does not understand is precisely the dissociated meanings one is simultaneously bringing into play in the relationship. Of course, one does formulate meanings of some kind for any enactment in which one is unconsciously involved; it's just that the meanings formulated are tendentious, conventionalized, thin, bloodless, incomplete—that is, poorly or incompletely imagined. The most extreme form of unconscious enactment, of course, is the dissociated personality of dissociative identity disorder; but less extreme versions exist at all levels of pathology and normalcy.

There is no particular *variety* of dissociation, then, that we should define as pathological. We all dissociate in the same way for defensive purposes, and we all unconsciously enact the dissociated meanings. On the other hand, the degree of people's insistence on maintaining the enactment and the degree of their difficulty in thinking about (understanding, interpreting) the enactments in which they are involved varies considerably. The more pathological the dissociation, the more rigid and unyielding its enactment and the less accessible one's capacity to be curious about it. Pathological dissociation should be defined according to the frequency and thoroughness of impairment in the capacity for imagination.

The fact that pathological dissociation cannot be defined in qualitative terms means that, in this scheme, there can be no objective determination of abnormality. Selecting the point on the continuum between dissociation and imagination that separates normal and pathological dissociation is a personal and clinical matter.

The field of trauma and the field of psychoanalysis have grown closer in recent years (see especially Chefetz & Bromberg, 2004). In closing, I want to express my hope that the psychoanalytic model of mind I have described, in which dissociation plays such a central role, contributes to this *rapprochement.*

REFERENCES

Bergman, M. S., Ed. (2000). *The Hartmann era.* New York: Other Press.

Bernstein, R. J. (1983). *Beyond objectivism and relativism: Science, hermeneutics, and praxis.* Philadelphia: University of Pennsylvania Press.

Bromberg, P. M. (1998). *Standing in the spaces: Essays on clinical process, trauma, and dissociation.* Hillsdale, NJ: The Analytic Press.

Bromberg, P. M. (2006). *Awakening the dreamer: Clinical journeys.* Mahwah, NJ: The Analytic Press.

Bruner, J. S., & Klein, G. S. (1960). The function of perceiving: New Look retrospect. In S. Wapner & B. Kaplan (Eds.), *Perspectives in psychological theory.* New York: International Universities Press.

Bruner, J. S., & Postman, L. (1949). Perception, cognition, and personality. *Journal of Personality, 18,* 14–31.

Chefetz, R. A., & Bromberg, P. M. (2004). Talking with "me" and "not-me." *Contemporary Psychoanalysis, 40,* 409–464.

Davies, J. M. (1996). Linking the pre-analytic with the post-classical: Integration, dissociation, and the multiplicity of unconscious processes. *Contemporary Psychoanalysis, 32,* 553–576.

Davies, J. M. (1997). Dissociation and therapeutic enactment. *Gender and Psychoanalysis, 2,* 241–257.

Davies, J. M. (1998). The multiple aspects of multiplicity: Symposium on clinical choices in psychoanalysis. *Psychoanalytic Dialogues, 8,* 195–206.

Davies, J. M. (1999). Getting cold feet defining "safe- enough" borders: Dissociation, multiplicity, and integration in the analyst's experience. *Psychoanalytic Quarterly, 78,* 184–208.

Davies, J. M., & Frawley, M. G. (1994). *Treating the adult survivor of childhood sexual abuse: A psychoanalytic perspective.* New York: Basic Books.

Fingarette, H. (1969). *Self-deception.* London: Routledge and Kegan Paul.

Freud, S. (1895). Project for a scientific psychology. *Standard Edition, 1,* 295–387.

Freud, S. (1896). Further remarks on the neuro-psychoses of defence. *Standard Edition, 3,* 162–185.

Freud, S. (1900). The interpretation of dreams. *Standard Edition, 4–5.*

Freud, S. (1915a). Repression. *Standard Edition, 14,* 146–158.

Freud, S. (1915b). The unconscious. *Standard Edition, 14,* 166–204.

Friedman, L. (2000). Are minds objects or dramas? In D. K. Silverman & D. L. Wolitzky (Eds.), *Changing conceptions of psychoanalysis: The legacy of Merton Gill* (pp. 146–170). Hillsdale, NJ: The Analytic Press.

Gadamer, H.-G. (1966). The universality of the hermeneutical problem. In D. E. Linge (Trans. & Ed.), *Philosophical hermeneutics* (pp. 3–17). Berkeley, CA: University of California Press, 1976.

Gadamer, H.-G. (1967). On the scope and function of hermeneutical reflection, trans. G. B. Hess & R. E. Palmer. In D. E. Linge (Ed.), *Philosophical Hermeneutics* (pp. 18–43). Berkeley, CA: University of California Press.

Gadamer, H.-G. (1975). *Truth and method.* Translated and edited by G. Barden and J. Cumming from the 2nd edition. New York: Seabury Press.

Gadamer, H.-G. (1976) *Philosophical hermeneutics,* trans. & ed. D. E. Linge. Berkeley, CA: University of California Press.

Gill, M. M. (1967). The primary process. In R. R. Holt (Ed.), *Motives and thought: Psychoanalytic essays in honor of David Rapaport* (pp. 260–298). Psychological Issues, Vol. 18–19. New York: International Universities Press.

Hartman, H. (1939). *Ego psychology and the problem of adaptation.* New York: International Universities Press.

Howell, E. F. (2005). *The dissociative mind.* Hillsdale, NJ: The Analytic Press.

James, W. (1890). *Principles of Psychology.* New York: Henry Holt and Co., 1899.

Laplanche, J., & Pontalis, J.-P. (1973). *The Language of psychoanalysis.* Trans. D. Nicholson-Smith. New York: Norton.

Levenson, E. A. (1972). *The fallacy of understanding.* New York: Basic Books.

Levenson, E. A. (1983). *The ambiguity of change.* New York: Basic Books.

Levenson, E. A. (1991). *The purloined self.* New York: Contemporary Psychoanalysis Books.

Linge, D. E. (1976) Editor's Introduction. In D. E. Linge (Ed.), *Philosophical hermeneutics* (pp. xi–lviii). Berkeley, CA: University of California Press.

Linge, D. E. (1976). Editor's introduction. In D. E. Linge (Ed.), *Philosophical hermeneutics* (pp. xi–lviii). Berkeley, CA: University of California Press.

Lionells, M., Fiscalini, J., Mann, C. M., & Stern, D. B. (Eds.) (1995). *The handbook of interpersonal psychoanalysis.* Hillsdale, NJ: The Analytic Press.

Loewald, H. W. (1978). Primary process, secondary process, and language. In *Papers on psychoanalysis* (pp. 178–206). New Haven & London: Yale University Press, 1980,.

Merleau-Ponty, M. (1964). *Signs.* Trans. Richard McCleary. Evanston, IL: Northwestern University Press, pp. 3-35.

Merleau-Ponty, M. (1968). *The visible and the invisible*. Ed. C. Lefort, trans. A. Lingis. Evanston, IL: Northwestern University Press.

Merleau-Ponty, M. (1973). *The prose of the world*. Ed. C. Lefort, trans. J. O'Neill. Evanston, IL: Northwestern University Press.

Mitchell, S. A. (1988). *Relational concepts in psychoanalysis*. Cambridge, MA: Harvard University Press.

Mitchell, S. A. (1993). *Hope and dread in psychoanalysis*. New York: Basic Books.

Mitchell, S. A. (1997). *Influence and autonomy in psychoanalysis*. Hillsdale, NJ: The Analytic Press.

Mitchell, S. A., & Aron, L., Eds. (1999). *Relational psychoanalysis: The emergence of a tradition*. Hillsdale, NJ: The Analytic Press.

Pizer, S. (1998). *Building bridges: The negotiation of paradox in psychoanalysis*. Hillsdale, NJ: The Analytic Press.

Risser, J. (1997). *Hermeneutics and the voice of the other: Re-reading Gadamer's 'Philosophical Hermeneutics'*. Albany: State University of New York Press.

Sass, L. A. (1988). Humanism, hermeneutics, and humanistic psychoanalysis: Differing conceptions of subjectivity. *Psychoanalysis and Contemporary Thought, 12*, 433–504.

Schachtel, E. (1959). *Metamorphosis*. New York: Basic Books.

Schafer, R. (1976). *A new language for psychoanalysis*. New Haven: Yale University Press.

Schafer, R. (1983). *The analytic attitude*. New York: Basic Books.

Schafer, R. (1992). *Retelling a life*. New York: Basic Books.

Scheibler, I. (2000). *Gadamer: Between Heidegger and Habermas*. Lanham, MD: Rowman & Littlefield.

Schimek, J. G. (1975). A critical re-examination of Freud's concept of unconscious mental representations. *International Journal of Psycho-Analysis, 2*, 171–187.

Silverman, H. (Ed.) (1991). *Gadamer and hermeneutics: Science, culture, literature*. New York: Routledge.

Spence, D. P. (1982). *Narrative truth and historical truth: Meaning and interpretation in psychoanalysis*. New York: Norton.

Stern, D. B. (1983). Unformulated experience. *Contemporary Psychoanalysis, 19*, 71–99.

Stern, D. B. (1992a). What makes good questions? *Contemporary Psychoanalysis, 28*, 326–336.

Stern, D. B. (1992b). Commentary on constructivism in clinical psychoanalysis. *Psychoanalytic Dialogues, 2*, 331–363.

Stern, D. B. (1994). Conceptions of structure in interpersonal psychoanalysis: A reading of the literature. *Contemporary Psychoanalysis, 30*, 255–300.

Stern, D. B. (1995). Cognition and language. In M. L. Lionells, J. Fiscalini, C. Mann, & D. B. Stern (Eds.), *The handbook of interpersonal psychoanalysis* (pp. 79–138). Hillsdale, NJ: The Analytic Press.

Stern, D. B. (1997). *Unformulated experience: From dissociation to imagination in psychoanalysis*. Hillsdale, NJ: The Analytic Press.

Stern, D. B. (2000). The limits of social construction: Discussion of Dyess and Dean. *Psychoanalytic Dialogues, 10*, 757–769.

Stern, D. B. (2002). Words and wordlessness in the psychoanalytic situation. *Journal of the American Psychoanalytic Association, 50*, 221–247.

Stern, D. B. (2003). The fusion of horizons: Dissociation, enactment, and understanding. *Psychoanalytic Dialogues, 13*, 843–873.

Stern, D. B. (2004). The eye sees itself: Dissociation, enactment, and the achievement of conflict. *Contemporary Psychoanalysis, 40*, 197–237.

Stern, D. B. (2006). Opening what has been closed, relaxing what has been clenched: Dissociation and enactment over time in committed relationships. *Psychoanalytic Dialogues, 16*, 747–761.

Stern, D. B. (2008). On having to find what you don't know how to look for. In E. L. Jurist, A. Slade, & S. Bergner (Eds.), *Mind to mind: Infant research, neuroscience, and psychoanalysis* (pp. 398–413). New York: Other Press.

Stern, D. B. (2009). Shall the twain meet? Metaphor, dissociation, and co-occurrence. *Psychoanalytic Inquiry*.

Stern, D. B. (in press b). *Partners in thought: Working with unformulated experience, dissociation, and enactment.* Mahwah, NJ: Routledge.

Sullivan, H. S. (1950). The illusion of personal individuality. In *The fusion of psychiatry and social science* (pp. 198–226). New York: Norton, 1971.

Sullivan, H. S. (1940). *Conceptions of modern psychiatry*. New York: Norton, 1953.

Sullivan, H. S. (1954). *The interpersonal theory of psychiatry*, H.S. Perry & M.L. Gawel (Eds.). New York: Norton.

Taylor, C. (1985). Language and human nature. In *Human agency and language: Philosophical papers I* (pp. 215–247). Cambridge: Cambridge University Press.

Warnke, G. (1987). *Gadamer: Hermeutics, tradition and reason*. Stanford, CA: Stanford University Press.

Weinsheimer, J. C. (1985). *Gadamer's hermeneutics: A reading of truth and method*. New Haven, CT: Yale University Press.

Winnicott, D. W. (1971). *Playing and reality*. London: Tavistock.

Part XIII

Toward a Clarified Understanding of Dissociation

44 An Empirical Delineation of the Domain of Pathological Dissociation

Paul F. Dell, PhD
Douglas Lawson, DC, MSc

OUTLINE

44.1 THE PROBLEM: TO DELINEATE THE STRUCTURE OF THE DOMAIN OF PATHOLOGICAL DISSOCIATION

This chapter uses a large international data set (N = 2,696) of Multidimensional Inventory of Dissociation (MID) protocols to delineate the fundamental structure of the domain of pathological dissociation. Previous research on this topic has been handicapped because it was based on brief, screening instruments such as the 28-item Dissociative Experiences Scale (DES; Bernstein & Putnam, 1986). In contrast, the MID has 218 items, 168 of which assess pathological dissociation.[1]

The six most commonly used measures of dissociation—(1) Dissociative Experiences Scale (DES; Bernstein & Putnam, 1986), (2) the Structured Clinical Interview for DSM-IV Dissociative Disorders–Revised (SCID-D-R; Steinberg, 1994), (3) Dissociative Disorders Interview Schedule (DDIS; Ross, Norton, Anderson, Anderson, & Barchet, 1989), (4) Dissociation Questionnaire (DIS-Q; Vanderlinden, van Dyck, Vandereycken, Vertommen, & Verkes, 1993), (5) Somatoform Dissociation Questionnaire–20 (SDQ-20; Nijenhuis, Spinhoven, Van Dyck, Van der Hart, & Vanderlinden, 1996), and (6) Questionnaire of Experiences of Dissociation (QED; Riley, 1988)—have fair (i.e., QED) to excellent (i.e., DES, DDIS, SCID-D-R, SDQ-20) psychometric properties. None of these instruments were designed to comprehensively cover the phenomena of dissociation (Dell, 2006a, 2006b, 2009b).

At least 14 factor analyses have indicated that the DES is *multifactorial* (Amdur & Liberzon, 1996; Carlson & Putnam, 1993; Dunn, Ryan, & Paolo, 1993; Gleaves & Eberenz, 1995; Gleaves, Eberenz, Warner, & Fine, 1995; Goldberg, 1999; Ray & Faith, 1995; Ray, June, Turaj, & Lundy, 1992: Ross, Joshi, & Currie, 1991; Sanders & Green, 1994; Schwartz, Frischholz, Braun, & Sachs, 1991; Stockdale, Gridley, Balogh, & Holtgraves, 2002).

Similarly, at least five factor analyses have indicated that the QED is multifactorial (Gleaves & Eberenz, 1995; Gleaves, Eberenz, Warner, & Fine, 1995; Ray & Faith, 1995; Ray, June, Turaj, & Lundy, 1992; Wolfradt & Engelmann, 1999).

In addition, the authors of three other measures of dissociation, the Perceptual Alteration Scale (PAS; Sanders, 1986), the DIS-Q (Vanderlinden, van Dyck, Vandereycken, Vertommen, & Verkes, 1993), and the Multiscale Dissociation Inventory (MDI; Briere, 2002; Briere, Weathers, & Runtz, 2005) have reported that their instruments are multifactorial.

These multifactorial solutions have extracted two to seven factors that accounted for 29% to 65% of the variance.

Eight factor analyses have produced *one-factor* solutions of DES data (Bernstein, Ellason, Ross, & Vanderlinden, 2001; Fischer & Elnitsky, 1990; Holtgraves & Stockdale, 1997; Marmar et al., 1994; Waller, 1995; Wright & Loftus, 1999), PAS data (Fischer & Elnitsky, 1990), DIS-Q data (Bernstein et al., 2001), and data from the Adolescent Dissociative Experiences Scale (A-DES; Armstrong, Putnam, Carlson, Libero, & Smith, 1997; Farrington, Waller, Smerden, & Faupel, 2001).

The strongest case for the one-factor solution is found in two studies. Bernstein and Waller have argued that the multifactorial structures of the DES (Bernstein et al., 2001; Waller, 1995) and the DIS-Q (Bernstein et al., 2001) are artifactual difficulty factors[2] that reflect the difficulty of the items (see also Carlson & Putnam, 1993). This led Bernstein et al. to "translate" the three-factor solution of the DES (i.e., amnesia, depersonalization/derealization, and absorption) as "infrequently endorsed dissociative symptoms," "dissociative symptoms endorsed at an intermediate level," and "commonly endorsed dissociative symptoms" (p. 109), respectively. Bernstein's et al. unifactorial solutions of the DES and DIS-Q accounted for 35% to 41% of the variance; they concluded that the DES, the DIS-Q, and the trait of dissociation are unifactorial.

Briere and Stockdale have advanced the strongest arguments for the multifactorial view of dissociation. Based on a large exploratory factor analysis of the 30-item, six-scale MDI in a sample that was 93% nonclinical, Briere et al. (2005) argued that dissociation is a weakly coherent, multifactorial trait. They claimed that the five factors of dissociation (i.e., disengagement, identity dissociation, emotional constriction, memory disturbance, and depersonalization-derealization) are so weakly correlated with one another—the mean *r* of their factor scores was only 0.39—that the empirical coherence of the construct of dissociation is called into question.

To date, only one study of the factor structure of dissociation has used confirmatory factor analysis (CFA);

[1] The MID's other 50 items are validity items; they measure defensiveness, rare/bizarre symptoms, emotional suffering, attention-seeking behavior, and factitious behavior.

[2] "Factors produced by different distributions have been traditionally called *difficulty factors*. For example, in analyses of ability scales, it is commonly found that the least difficult items and the most difficult items form different factors. The factors result from the fact that easy items are positively skewed (and difficult items negatively skewed) and so correlate more highly than they do with difficult items not sharing that skew" (Gorsuch, 1997, p. 538).

all other studies of the factor structure of dissociation have used exploratory factor analysis (EFA). Stockdale et al. (2002) used CFA to compare one-, two-, three-, and four-factor models of the DES in two nonclinical university samples. Independent analyses of these nonclinical samples identified the three-factor model (i.e., absorption, depersonalization, and amnesia) as superior to the other models. The three factors had a mean intercorrelation of 0.55 and accounted for 46% of the variance of DES responses.

In summary, studies of the factor-structure of dissociation instruments have produced inconsistent results. EFA is data driven; it provides a weak test for theoretical models. None of the EFAs listed above has accounted for more than 65% of the variance in the data. CFA, on the other hand, compares a theoretical model to real-world data. A CFA of the three-factor model of the DES accounted for 87% of the variance in the data (Goodness-of-Fit Index: GFI = 0.87; Stockdale et al., 2002). Still, a GFI of 0.87 suggests substantial model misfit. We believe that the degree of misfit in all of the previously mentioned studies calls for a higher level of analysis with CFA. We also believe that any effort to investigate *the structure of dissociation itself* (as opposed to the factor-structure of a specific measure of dissociation) must use an instrument that provides comprehensive coverage of the domain of dissociative phenomena.

44.2 METHOD

44.2.1 Participants

The study is based on two heterogeneous combined samples (Ns = 1386 and 1310) of predominantly clinical research participants (63% and 74%, respectively). Each combined sample contained data from several studies.

Sample 1: 615 clinical adults and nonclinical adults from the United States, Canada, and Australia. Five hundred and ninety-five research participants (97%) were in active psychotherapy; 19 were nonclinical research participants (3%). Because the clinical research participants were recruited from the practices of therapists with an interest in dissociation, the sample is not random. Seventy-six percent (N = 464) of the entire sample had either (1) received a dissociative diagnosis by their therapists or (2) received a mean MID score of 15 or greater. Conversely, 24% of the sample (N = 149) were not dissociative (i.e., were neither diagnosed as dissociative by their therapist, nor obtained a MID score of greater than 15). Clinical participants included outpatients from all over the United States and Canada, and inpatients from California, Texas, Massachusetts, Canada, and Australia. Nonclinical participants were support staff and church members. Clinical participants were invited to participate by their therapists. Participants then completed the MID and other instruments at their therapist's office or at home between sessions. Nonclinical participants were invited to participate by the author; they completed their questionnaires at home.

The dissociative and nondissociative groups were demographically similar. The relevant demographic characteristics of the nondissociative group were: treatment setting: 31% inpatient; mean age = 40.4, SD = 13.6; mean years of education = 15.1, SD = 13.6; gender: 70% female; race: 86% Caucasian, 9% African American, 3% Hispanic, 1% Asian, 1% Pacific Islands. The relevant demographic characteristics of the dissociative group were: treatment setting: 29% inpatient; mean age = 39.3, SD = 9.9; mean years of education = 14.6, SD = 3.0; gender: 77% female; race: 92% Caucasian, 4% African American, 3% Hispanic, 0.5% Mixed, 0.2% Asian, 2% Pacific Islands).

Sample 2: 40 adults with schizophrenia from the United States. Forty schizophrenics from a community mental health center (CMHC) participated. Sixty-seven percent (N = 26) were male and 33% (N = 13) were female. The sample had a mean age of 42.2 years (SD = 10.1) and mean education of 12.3 years (SD = 1.5). Ninety percent (N = 35) of the sample was Caucasian; 8% (N = 3) was African American; and 3% (N =1) was Hispanic. Demographic data on one participant were unavailable. All research participants had been diagnosed with the Structured Clinical Interview for DSM-IV Axis I Disorders (SCID-I; First, Spitzer, Gibbon, & Williams, 1997). Participants completed the research packet at the CMHC while being monitored.

Sample 3: 142 clinical and nonclinical adults from Israel. One hundred and forty-two Israeli adults participated (74 university students and 68 nonstudents). The sample was 75% female, had a mean age of 28.1 (SD = 9.6), and mean of 14.1 (SD = 2.3) years of education. No information on race is available; almost all were Caucasian. This was a snowball sample in which students completed the questionnaires and obtained extra credit for enlisting a friend or family member to also complete the questionnaires. Participants completed the research packet at home.

Sample 4: 135 clinical and nonclinical adults from Israel. One hundred thirty Israeli adults participated. Ninety-six (71%) were nonclinical (65 women and 31 men; mean age = 33.8 years, SD = 12.7; mean years of education = 15.4, SD = 3.1). Thirty-nine (29%) were psychotherapy patients (31 women and 8 men; mean age = 33.8 years, SD = 11.5; mean years of education = 14.3, SD = 3.4). Nonclinical participants were graduate students, academics, and mental health professionals. Participants completed the research packet at home.

Sample 5: 100 adult psychiatric inpatients from Germany. One hundred German psychiatric inpatients participated (58 males and 42 females). Their mean age was 42.4 (SD = 12.7). The preponderance of patients (N = 44) had a primary diagnosis of substance abuse. Fourteen had primary diagnoses of psychosis. Most of the remaining patients had a primary diagnosis of mood disorder. Participants completed the research packet in their hospital room.

Sample 6: 172 college students from the United States. One hundred seventy-two students from a small southern college participated (62 males and 104 females, 6 unidentified; mean age = 20.7, SD = 4.6; mean years of education = 13.9, SD = 1.2). Research participants were members of a psychology class who participated in order to earn extra credit. Participants completed the research packet during a group administration in a classroom.

Sample 7: 67 college students from the United States. Sixty-seven students from a medium-sized Midwestern university participated (13 males and 55 females). All students were members of a psychology class who participated in order to obtain extra credit. Their mean age was 20.9 (SD = 3.7). Detailed information about race was not available; almost all participants were Caucasian. Participants were administered the research packet one by one while being monitored.

Sample 8: 50 male prison inmates from Canada. Fifty male offenders who were incarcerated in a medium-security federal penitentiary in British Columbia, Canada, participated. Their mean age was 35.0 (SD =9.16). Sixty-eight percent were Caucasian, 12% First Nation, and 2% Asian. The remainder of the sample was a mixture of Caucasian and First Nation. The predominant categories of their index offenses were physical violence (52%), sexual violence (30%), and property crimes (12%). Participants were recruited through posters and word of mouth. All participants received $5 for participating. Participants completed the research packet one by one while being monitored.

Sample 9: 10 persons with depersonalization disorder. This small sample of persons with depersonalization disorder was recruited via an advertisement in the newspaper for research participants who had symptoms of depersonalization. The 10 participants were administered the SCID-D and were diagnosed with depersonalization disorder. Subjects who participated in the research received a cash honorarium. Demographic information was not available for these research participants. Participants were individually interviewed and were individually administered the research packet (Simeon, Knutelska, & Dell, 2001).

Combined Sample 1 (i.e., Samples 1–9): The combined sample of 1386 was 74% female (N = 856) and 26% male (N = 299). Sixty-three percent of the sample were psychotherapy patients (N = 852); 37% were college students or members of the community (N = 508); and 3.7% (N = 50) were prison inmates. The mean age of the sample was 35.1 (range = 12–84; SD = 12.5) and the mean number of years of education was 14.0 (range = 5–26; SD = 2.9). Racial data were unavailable for 41% of the combined sample. The remainder of the sample was 82% Caucasian (N = 659), 12% African American (N = 95), 2.5% Hispanic (N=20), 1% other (N=9), 1% Asian (N=8), 1% Native American/Native Canadian (N = 8), and 0.2% Pacific Islands.

Sample 10: 522 research participants: 450 psychotherapy patients and 72 adults from the community. One hundred fifty-two (30%) were nondissociative (i.e., mean MID score < 15) and 370 (70%) were dissociative (i.e., mean MID score > 15). Twenty-two percent (N = 115) were males and 77% (N = 407) were females. The mean age of the research participants was 37.1 (SD = 11.4) and the mean years of education was 14.2 (SD = 3.1). The racial breakdown of the sample was 87% Caucasian (N = 379), 3% Hispanic (N = 14), 3% African American (N =13), 1% Native American/Native Canadian (N = 6), 0.2% Asian (N = 1), and 5% not known (N = 24). Eight percent of the research participants were performing artists who were taking a class. Ninety-two percent of the research participants were in active therapy and were asked to participate in the research by the clinician who was treating or evaluating them. Research participants came from all over the United States and Canada. A few participants came from Italy and The Netherlands. Most research participants were recruited by therapists with an interest in dissociation, so the sample was not random. One hundred and one participants (23%) were known to be psychiatric inpatients; 293 participants (74%) were known to be psychotherapy outpatients. The status of 12 participants (3%) was not known. Participants completed the research packet either at home or in their clinician's office.

Sample 11: 101 heroin detox patients and 46 general psychotherapy patients from Israel. The heroin detox patients were 87% male (N = 88) and 13% female (N = 13). Their mean age was 37.1 (SD = 9.1) and their mean years of education was 10.6 (SD = 2.5). The general psychotherapy patients were 37% male (N = 17) and 63% female

(N =29). Their mean age was 40.5 (SD = 15.3) and their mean years of education was 14.4 (SD = 2.9). Both the heroin detox patients and the general psychotherapy patients were asked to participate by their therapists. Participants completed the research packets at the treatment facility (i.e., heroin detox patients) or at home (i.e., general psychotherapy patients).

Sample 12: 120 clinical and 30 nonclinical adults from Germany. The 120 patients consisted of 66 severely dissociative patients (i.e., DID or DDNOS–1) and 54 patients with mixed psychiatric disorders. All participants had been administered the SCID-D. All participants were female. The mean age of the severely dissociative patients was 33.5 years (SD = 11.1). Thirty-three percent (N = 22) were outpatients; 67% (N =44) were inpatients. The mean age of the patients with mixed psychiatric disorders was 35.5 years (SD = 11.8). Eleven percent (N = 6) were outpatients; 89% (N = 48) were inpatients. The mean age of the nonclinical control group was 36.3 years (SD = 10.0). Patients were recruited by a member of the research team. Patients answered the questionnaires at home (outpatients) or in their hospital room (inpatients). Nonclinical participants were recruited via notices at universities, nursing homes, informational events, and via direct communication with potential participants. Questionnaires were answered at home. Nonclinical participants received 20 marks for their participation. Clinical participants did not receive money, but were given comprehensive evaluation about diagnoses, methods of treatment, and so on, if needed.

Sample 13: 150 nonclinical adults from Italy. Half of the subjects were male and half were female. Forty percent of the participants were ages 18–25; 40% were ages 26–45; and 20% were ages 46–60. Twenty-nine percent (N = 44) had at least some university education. This is very much a sample of convenience. All participants were nonclinical adults from three Italian cities; they were recruited by a psychology student from her friends, the friends of friends, friends of parents, and so on. Participants completed the research packet at home (Montesanto, 2004).

Sample 14: 136 nonclinical late adolescent college students from the Philippines.

Sample 15: 22 SCID-diagnosed patients with Bipolar Disorder from a community mental health center. Fourteen (64%) were female and eight (36%) were male. The mean age of these patients was 47.8 years.

Sample 16: 129 psychiatric inpatients from a trauma unit and a general psychiatric unit. Ten (8%) were male and 119 (92%) were female. The mean age of these inpatients was 38.7 (SD = 10.0). Fifty-two (40%) were diagnosed with a dissociative disorder. Forty-two (33%) patients were not dissociative patients, but did receive a diagnosis of PTSD. Most of the remaining patients in this sample received typical inpatient diagnoses such as Major Depressive Disorder, Bipolar Disorder, and substance abuse disorders.

Sample 17: 100 well-diagnosed patients with Borderline Personality Disorder from a community mental health center. Thirty-eight (38%) were male and 62 (62%) were female. The mean age of these patients was 33.8 (SD = 10.4).

Combined Sample 2 (i.e., Samples 10–17): The combined sample of 1310 was 72% female (N = 943) and 28% male (N = 367). Seventy-four percent of the sample were psychotherapy patients (N = 971); 10% were college students (N = 136); and 19% were members of the community (N = 388). The mean age of the sample was 33.91 (range = 16–72; SD = 12.1) and the mean number of years of education was 13.1 (range = 6–23; SD = 2.6). Racial data were unavailable for much of the combined sample. Given this sparse racial data, it is estimated that about 84% of the sample was Caucasian, 3% African American, 3% Hispanic, and 10% was Filipino.

44.2.2 Instruments

Multidimensional Inventory of Dissociation (MID). The MID is a 218-item self-report, multiscale measure of pathological dissociation (Dell, 2006a, 2006b, 2009b). The MID has an 11-point (0–10) Likert scale format that is anchored by *Never* and *Always*. Like the DES, MID instructions do not specify a time frame (e.g., the last 7 days, the past 30 days). The absence of a time frame is necessitated by the infrequent occurrence of amnesia, the most important indicator of severe dissociation. The MID has 168 dissociation items and 50 validity items. Unlike the DES, the MID assesses only pathological dissociation (Waller, Putnam, & Carlson, 1996).

The MID 6.0 has two different sets of dissociation scales: (1) 14 facet scales with 12 items in each and (2) 23 dissociation diagnostic scales that vary in length from 3 to 12 items. There is no item-overlap across the 14 facet scales. There is a very modest amount of item-overlap (i.e., eight items occur in more than one scale) across the 23 dissociation diagnostic scales. The two sets of scales are alternate apportionments of the MID's 168 dissociation items. The 23 dissociation diagnostic scales reflect the criteria for the diagnosis of DID that were proposed by Dell (2001a). The MID has five validity scales: Defensiveness, Rare Symptoms, Attention-Seeking Behavior, Factitious Behavior, and Emotional Suffering.

The 14 facet scales and 23 diagnostic scales achieved good-to-excellent Cronbach (1951) alpha values in a large clinical sample (range = 0.84 to 0.96; median alpha value = 0.91) and good-to-excellent temporal stabilities in a small clinical sample over a 4 to 8 week test-retest interval (range = 0.82 to 0.97; median temporal stability coefficient = 0.92). The overall mean MID score has a 3 to 4 week temporal stability of 0.98 (Somer & Dell, 2005) and a 4 to 8 week temporal stability of 0.97 (Dell, 2006a). The MID correlates highly with other measures of dissociation: DES (r = 0.90), DIS-Q (r = 0.83), SCID-D-R (r = 0.78), QED (r = 0.75), and SDQ-20 (r = 0.75). The MID has discriminated between different diagnostic groups in the United States, Israel, and Germany (Dell, 2006b; Gast et al., 2003; Somer & Dell, 2005).

Dissociative Experiences Scale (DES). The DES is a 28-item, self-report questionnaire that quantifies dissociative experiences (Bernstein & Putnam, 1986). The DES-II has an 11-point Likert scale (0–100), in increments of 10. The Cronbach alpha coefficient of the DES is 0.96 (Van IJzendoorn & Schuengel, 1996). DES scores of dissociative disorder patients (mean = 47.6) differ from those of nondissociative controls (mean = 12.0; van IJzendoorn & Schuengel, 1996). As of 1997, the DES had been used in over 250 published studies (Carlson, 1997).

Traumatic Experiences Questionnaire (TEQ). The TEQ (Nijenhuis et al., 1998) is a self-report questionnaire that assesses 25 potentially traumatic life events. When interpersonal violence items are endorsed, the TEQ asks about the source of the abuse (i.e., immediate family members, other relatives, or others), its duration, the developmental era in which it occurred, and its impact on the person. A slightly revised version of the TEQ, the Traumatic Experiences Checklist (TEC; Nijenhuis, Van der Hart, & Kruger, 2002), had good internal consistency (Cronbach α = 0.86 to 0.90). Test-retest reliability was 0.91 (Nijenhuis, 1999). The TEQ correlated moderately with both psychological dissociation and somatoform dissociation (Nijenhuis et al., 1999).

Structured Clinical Interview for DSM-IV Dissociative Disorders–Revised (SCID-D-R). The SCID-D-R (Steinberg, 1994) is a 277-item semi-structured interview that quantifies five dissociative symptoms: amnesia, depersonalization, derealization, identity confusion, and identity alteration. The SCID-D-R also diagnoses the five DSM-IV dissociative disorders. The SCID-D-R assesses not only the presence or absence of dissociative symptoms, but also their frequency and clinical severity. The SCID-D-R has good-to-excellent reliability and discriminant validity for each of the five dissociative symptoms and the five dissociative disorders. The total SCID-D-R score correlates 0.78 with the DES (Boon & Draijer, 1993).

Somatoform Dissociation Questionnaire-20 (SDQ-20). The SDQ-20 (Nijenhuis et al., 1996) is a 20-item, 5-point Likert scale instrument that measures somatoform manifestations of dissociation such as tunnel vision, auditory distancing, getting stiff, having trouble urinating, and pseudoseizures. The SDQ-20 has excellent internal consistency (Cronbach alpha coefficient = 0.95); strong convergent validity with measures of psychological dissociation: DIS-Q (r = 0.76), DES (r = 0.85; Nijenhuis et al., 1996, 1999); and construct validity as measured by its correlation with reported trauma (Nijenhuis, Spinhoven, Van Dyck, Van der Hart, & Vanderlinden, 1998).

Posttraumatic Stress Diagnostic Scale (PDS). The PDS is a 49-item self-report instrument that assesses the presence of PTSD (Foa, 1995). The PDS quantifies the 17 symptoms and three symptom clusters of PTSD. The internal consistency of the 17 symptoms was 0.92. The 10 to 22 day test-retest stability of the PDS Symptom Severity Score was 0.83. A 10 to 22 day test-retest study of diagnostic stability yielded a kappa of 0.74 (i.e., 87.3% agreement between diagnoses at Time 1 and Time 2). Using the PTSD module of the SCID as the "gold standard" for diagnosis of PTSD, a kappa of 0.59 was obtained, with a 79.4% agreement between the SCID and the PDS (Sensitivity = 82%; Specificity = 76.7%).

44.3 ANALYSIS

EFAs were conducted with SPSS 13.0 for Windows. CFAs were analyzed with AMOS 6.0. EFAs were conducted to determine (1) the number of factors in the item data and (2) the higher-order structure of these factors. CFAs were then conducted on the EFA-derived factor scales in order to test a model of a single, higher-order, latent variable: Pathological Dissociation. A Lagrange Multiplier (LM) Test was conducted to analyze the covariances in the model.

44.4 RESULTS

44.4.1 The Factor Structure of the MID's 168 Dissociation Items

44.4.1.1 Exploratory Factor Analysis

The Kaiser-Meyer-Olkin (KMO) measure of sampling adequacy was an extremely high 0.99, which indicates that the MID's 168 dissociation items are linearly related and are, according to Kaiser (1974), "marvelously" suited to factor analysis. Item analyses, however, present special

TABLE 44.1
Item Analysis: Exploratory Factors Analyses of the MID's 168 Dissociation Items in Two Independent Samples

	Combined Sample 1 N = 1386			Combined Sample 2 N = 1310		
	Eigenvalue	% of Variance	Cumulative %	Eigenvalue	% of Variance	Cumulative %
Self-confusion/dissociation	90.64	53.63	53.63	72.1	45.63	45.63
Amnesia	6.13	3.63	57.26	5.71	3.62	49.25
Subjective awareness of alters	3.55	2.10	59.36	4.01	2.54	51.79
Flashbacks	2.95	1.75	61.11	3.41	2.16	53.94
Body symptoms	2.77	1.64	62.75	2.41	1.52	55.47
Loss of remote autobiographical memory	2.07	1.22	63.97	1.88	1.19	56.65
Trance	1.88	1.11	65.08	1.75	1.11	57.76
Derealization/depersonalization	1.63	0.96	66.05	2.68	1.69	59.46
Dissociative disorientation	1.49	0.88	66.93			
Persecutory intrusions	1.38	0.82	67.75	1.97	1.25	60.70
Angry intrusions	1.23	0.73	68.47	1.31	0.83	61.54
Distress about memory problems	1.05	0.62	69.10	1.62	1.02	62.56
Self-alteration				1.41	0.89	63.45
Child part				1.07	0.67	64.12

Note: Self-Confusion/dissociation = self-confusion and dissociative loss of groundedness of self and world.

problems (Gorsuch, 1997): (1) items have lower reliabilities than scales; (2) items have a high level of confounding variance; and (3) a pool of items that measure the same construct may yield artifactual difficulty factors. Thus, in keeping with the recommendation of Gorsuch (1997), a common factor analysis was conducted.

Principal axis factor analysis of Combined Sample 1 (N = 1386) extracted 13 factors with eigenvalues greater than 1. Because the MID's 168 dissociation items were designed to measure a single construct, the items were expected to correlate well with one another; accordingly, an oblique rotation was used. Promax rotation yielded 12 coherent factors and one trivial factor (i.e., a factor where none of its variables had a pattern loading greater than 0.30). Twelve factors were retained (see Appendix for the five highest-loading items on each factor). These 12 factors accounted for 69% of the variance in MID item scores (Table 44.1).

Table 44.2 presents the correlation matrix of the 12 factor scores (mean $r = 0.55$; shared variance = 30.3%). Other extraction procedures and rotation strategies were applied in order to test the stability of this 12-factor solution: (1) a Direct Oblimin rotation of the principal axis factor solution, (2) a principal component analysis (PCA) with Varimax rotation, and (3) a PCA with Promax rotation. These additional analyses produced factor structures that were extremely similar to that of Table 44.1, thus supporting the stability of the 12-factor structure of the MID's 168 dissociation items.

The most important information about the stability of the 12-factor structure of the MID's 168 dissociation items was contributed by an EFA of MID data from a second sample of 1310 participants (i.e., Combined Sample 2; see Table 44.1). Like the data from Combined Sample 1, the KMO measure of sampling adequacy was an extremely high 0.99. Principal axis factor analysis with Promax rotation of these data extracted 16 factors with eigenvalues greater than 1. Thirteen factors were retained; three were trivial (i.e., each had only a single item with a pattern loading greater than 0.30). The 13 factors accounted for 64% of the variance in MID item scores.

Eleven of the 13 factors were virtually identical to those that had been extracted from the data of Combined Sample 1 (see Table 44.1). There were three notable differences between the factor solutions from the two samples. First, unlike Combined Sample 1, a Dissociative Disorientation Factor was not extracted from Combined Sample 2's data; instead, items that tapped dissociative

TABLE 44.2
Correlation Matrix of the 12 Factor Scores

	Amnesia	Alters	Flash	Body	LossAuto	Trance	Der/Dep	DisDis	Persec	Angry	Distress
Self-confusion/ dissociation	0.62	0.75	0.73	0.51	0.63	0.67	0.56	0.44	0.57	0.69	0.58
Amnesia	—	0.75	0.69	0.66	0.49	0.7	0.63	0.41	0.58	0.74	0.66
Subjective awareness of alters		—	0.70	0.59	0.56	0.63	0.64	0.40	0.56	0.72	0.55
Flashbacks			—	0.60	0.48	0.68	0.54	0.41	0.64	0.63	0.48
Body symptoms				—	0.32	0.54	0.64	0.26	0.47	0.65	0.52
Loss of remote autobiographical memory					—	0.46	0.41	0.44	0.39	0.40	0.49
Trance						—	0.62	0.38	0.53	0.67	0.67
Derealization/ depersonalization							—	0.32	0.41	0.62	0.64
Dissociative disorientation								—	0.25	0.31	0.28
Persecutory intrusions									—	0.61	0.37
Angry intrusions										—	0.68
Distress about memory problems											—

disorientation were split into two trivial factors. Despite this, the Cronbach alpha value was high ($\alpha = 0.93$) for the 12 Dissociative Disorientation items in Combined Sample 2's data. Second and third, the EFA extracted two factors from Combined Sample 2's item data that were not extracted from Combined Sample 1's item data: Self-Alteration and Child Parts. Despite this, the Cronbach alpha values in Combined Sample 1's data were good to excellent for the six Self-Alteration items and the five Child Parts items (α values = 0.85 and 0.92, respectively).

Finally, the stability of the *difference* between the factor solutions of Combined Sample 1 and Combined Sample 2 was evaluated. A principal axis factor analysis with Promax rotation was performed on All Data (N = 2696). That analysis perfectly replicated the 12-factor structure of Combined Sample 1; conversely, none of the *differences* between the factor structure of Combined Sample 1 and that of Combined Sample 2 were replicated by the All Data analysis. Accordingly, the 12-factor structure from Combined Sample 1 (and the All Data Sample) was accepted.

44.4.1.2 The 12 Factor Scales

The simplest factor scores are those that are routinely used in the factor analytic-driven construction of a scale (Gorsuch, 1983). That is, the scale is constructed from the items that had the highest loadings on that factor. When this method of scale construction is used, the items are being treated as equal factor scores of that factor or scale. In the present study, the highest loading items on each of the 12 factors were used to construct 12 factor scales. The data from Combined Sample 1 and Combined Sample 2 were then rescored to obtain scores for the 12 factor scales The Appendix lists the five highest-loading MID items for each of the 12 factor scales.

44.4.1.3 Psychometric Properties of the 12 Factor Scales

Our advocacy for the 12-factor structure of the MID's 168 dissociation items must demonstrate not only (1) that this 12-factor structure is stable across different samples, but (2) that the 12 factor scales are psychometrically robust, and (3) that these 12 factors have a meaningful pattern of external correlates (with other measures of dissociation and with other variables such as trauma history and the symptoms of PTSD).

44.4.1.4 Internal Consistency

The Cronbach alpha coefficients of the 12 factor scales (Table 44.3) are based on the data from Combined

TABLE 44.3
Factor Scale Analysis: Exploratory Factor Analyses of the 12 MID Factor Scales—Replications of the One-Factor Solution and Scale Reliabilities

		Analysis of Factor Scores				Analysis of Factor Scales					
		Combined Sample 1		Combined Sample 1		Combined Sample 1		Combined Sample 2			
				N = 1386				N = 1310			N = 34
		Principal Components		Principal Axis		Principal Components		Principal Components			
Scale	No. Of Items	Loading	Communality	Loading	Communality	Loading	Communality	Loading	Communality	Cronbach Alpha	Temporal Stability
Self-confusion/dissoc	50	0.84	0.71	0.83	0.69	–0.96	0.92	–0.96	0.91	0.98	0.97
Amnesia	29	0.87	0.75	0.86	0.74	–0.93	0.86	–0.91	0.83	0.97	0.93
Awareness of alters	36	0.86	0.74	0.84	0.72	–0.95	0.89	–0.93	0.86	0.98	0.96
Flashbacks	12	0.83	0.69	0.81	0.66	–0.86	0.74	–0.83	0.69	0.95	0.94
Body symptoms	14	0.74	0.55	0.71	0.50	–0.95	0.74	–0.84	0.70	0.88	0.86
Autobiographical memory	6	0.64	0.42	0.60	0.36	–0.79	0.62	–0.77	0.60	0.92	0.92
Trance	7	0.83	0.68	0.81	0.66	–0.87	0.76	–0.86	0.75	0.92	0.96
Dereal/deperson	16	0.77	0.59	0.74	0.55	–0.93	0.86	–0.91	0.83	0.95	0.93
Dissociative disorientation	12	0.50	0.25	0.46	0.21	–0.93	0.87	–0.93	0.86	0.93	0.95
Persecutory intrusions	11	0.69	0.48	0.66	0.43	–0.91	0.82	–0.87	0.76	0.95	0.89
Angry intrusions	18	0.85	0.72	0.84	0.70	–0.95	0.91	–0.94	0.89	0.95	0.97
Distress about memory problems	12	0.76	0.57	0.73	0.53	–0.93	0.87	–0.90	0.82	0.93	0.95
MID (12 factor scales)	12									.97	n/a
Mean MID Score	168									0.99	0.97
Eigenvalue		7.15		6.76		9.86		9.49			
Variance explained		59.58%		56.28%		82.14%		79.11%			

Note: Self-confusion/dissoc = self-confusion and dissociative loss of groundedness of self and world;
Awareness of alters = subjective awareness of the presence of alters or self-states;
Autobiographical memory = circumscribed loss of remote autobiographical memory;
Dereal/deperson = derealization/depersonalization.

Sample 2. These alpha values are unbiased because they do not capitalize on chance (as would alpha values that were calculated from the same sample that was used to derive the factor scales in the first place; i.e., Combined Sample 1). The 12 factor scales had excellent internal consistency (range of alpha values = 0.88 to 0.98; median alpha value = 0.94).

44.4.1.5 Temporal Stability of the 12 Factor Scales

Temporal stability of the 12 factor scales (Table 44.3) was assessed via a preexisting test-retest subsample of psychotherapy patients (N = 34) from Combined Sample 1. The 4 to 8 week temporal stability of the 12 factor scales was good to excellent (range of test-retest coefficients = 0.86 to 0.97; median 4 to 8 week test-retest coefficient = 0.94).

44.4.1.6 Convergent Validity of the 12 Factor Scores and 12 Factor Scales

DES. Five hundred and nineteen research participants from Combined Sample 1 completed the DES. Table 44.4 shows that the 12 factor scores/factor scales correlated highly with the DES (range of *r*s = .55/.68 to .81/.88; mean *r* = .71/.84).

SDQ-20. Thirty-seven research participants from Combined Sample 1 completed the SDQ-20. The SDQ-20 correlated most highly with the conceptually similar Body Symptoms Scale (*r*s = .82/.91; Table 44.6).

SCID-D-R. Ninety-eight research participants from Combined Sample 1 received a SCID-D-R interview. The SCID-D-R Total Score correlated most highly with the Self-Confusion Scale (*r*s = .77/.79; Table 44.6). Each

TABLE 44.4
Construct Validity and Convergent Validity of the 12 Factor Scores/Factor Scales

					SCID-D					
Factor Scale	**TEQ**	**PDS**	**DES**	**SDQ-20**	***Amnesia***	***Depersonal***	***Derealiz***	***Identity Confusion***	***Identity Alteration***	**Total Score**
	N=469	N=40	N=519	N=37	N=98	N=98	N=98	N=98	N=98	
Self-conf/ dissociation	.46/.46	**.69/.73**	**.81/.88**	.53/.71	.63/.65	**.66/.66**	.67/.72	**.68/.69**	.72/**.74**	**.77/.79**
Amnesia	.13/.24	.64/.69	.80/.86	.75/.81	.49/.56	.46/.52	.58/.63	.50/.55	.56/.62	.59/.66
Awareness of alters	.36/.37	.36/.65	.81/.87	.68/.74	.59/.62	.58/.60	**.71/.75**	.65/.67	**.73**/.73	.75/.77
Flashbacks	**.51/.51**	.51/**.75**	.76/.79	.69/.71	.40/.44	.40/.45	.51/.55	.38/.43	.48/.53	.49/.54
Body symptoms	.24/.28	.24/.57	.67/.80	**.82/.91**	.29/.42	.33/.44	.50/.57	.31/.45	.35/.46	.41/.53
Loss autobiog memory	.37/.43	.37/.50	.55/.68	.42/.52	**.70/.74**	.46/.56	.47/.61	.40/.51	.50/.61	.58/.69
Trance	.28/.34	.28/.72	.74/.82	.77/.83	.44/.47	.39/.44	.52/.56	.45/.50	.53/.57	.53/.58
Derealiz/deperson	.23/.36	.23/.64	.69/.87	.78/.83	.44/.58	.43/.58	.60/.72	.47/.62	.46/.65	.55/.72
Dissociative disorient	.16/.39	.16/.72	.58/.87	.47/.71	.44/.63	.41/.63	.43/.67	.37/.65	.50/.73	.49/.76
Persecutory intrusions	.18/.34	.18/.65	.63/.83	.40/.70	.34/.57	.27/.53	.45/.71	.37/.62	.35/.66	.41/.70
Angry intrusions	.29/.38	.29/.68	.79/.88	.76/.73	.45/.58	.43/.57	.58/.69	.50/.63	.56/.70	.58/.72
Distress about memory	.22/.37	.22/.69	.69/.87	.62/.74	.49/.65	.34/.57	.49/.64	.42/.61	.49/.69	.51/.72

Note. All coefficients are significant at $p < 0.005$. Boldface indicates the highest correlation in that column.
SCID-D = Structured Clinical Interview for DSM-IV Dissociative Disorders; TEQ = Traumatic Experiences Questionnaire; PDS = Posttraumatic Stress Diagnostic Scale; DES = Dissociative Experiences Scale; SDQ-20 = Somatoform Dissociation Questionnaire-20. Depersonal = depersonalization; Derealiz = derealization; Self-conf/dissociation = self-confusion and dissociative loss of groundedness in self and world; Awareness of alters = subjective awareness of the presence of alters or self-states; Loss autobiog memory = circumscribed loss of remote autobiographical memory; Derealiz/deperson = derealization/depersonalization; Dissociative disorient = dissociative disorientation; Distress about memory = distress about memory problems.

of the five SCID-D-R rating scales correlated highly with conceptually similar factor scales from the MID.

The MID's original scales. The MID has 14 nonoverlapping, facet scales and 23 minimally overlapping diagnostic scales. Tables 44.5 and 44.6 present the correlation matrices of these scales with the 12 factor scales. Each of the MID's original scales correlated most highly with a conceptually similar factor scale.

44.4.1.7 Construct Validity of the 12 Factor Scores and 12 Factor Scales

Table 44.4 shows the relationship of trauma history and current PTSD symptoms to the 12 factor scores and 12 factor scales.

TEQ. The number of endorsed traumas correlated significantly, albeit modestly, with the 12 factor scores/scales (Table 44.6). The TEQ Total Score correlated most highly with the Flashbacks factor scale (*rs* = .51/.51).

PDS. The Total PDS Score, a global measure of PTSD symptoms, correlated significantly with the factor scores/scales (Table 44.6). The PDS correlated most highly with the Self-Confusion factor score (r = 0.69) and the Flashbacks factor scale (r = 0.75).

44.4.1.8 Criterion-Related Validity of the 12 Factor Scales

Table 44.7 shows that three SCID-D-R-diagnosed groups (i.e., nondissociative, depersonalization disorder, and DID) differed significantly on a one-way ANOVA (*Wilks* = 0.15; $F(24, 146) = 9.64$, $p < 0.01$). Post-hoc Scheffé comparisons produced a clinically meaningful pattern of significant differences. Compared to DID patients, (1) nondissociative patients had lower scores on all 12 factor scales and (2) individuals with depersonalization disorder had significantly lower scores on all factor scales except Derealization/Depersonalization. Compared to nondissociative patients, individuals with depersonalization disorder had higher scores on four factor scales: Derealization/Depersonalization, Self-Confusion, Circumscribed Loss of Autobiographical Memory, and Dissociative Disorientation.

44.4.1.9 The Higher-Order Structure of the MID's 12 Factor Scales

The crucial question for *the concept of pathological dissociation* is whether the 12 factors that were extracted from the items are explained by a single higher-order factor (i.e., pathological dissociation). The crucial question for *the MID* is whether its scales—in this case, its factor scales—have a higher-order unifactorial structure. These questions were evaluated with both EFA and CFA.

44.4.1.10 Exploratory Factor Analysis

Factor scores. Both PCA and principal axis factor analysis extracted a single factor from the regression factor score coefficients of the 12 factors (Table 44.3).

Factor scales. Table 44.8 presents the correlation matrix for the 12 factor scales (mean $r = 0.84$; shared variance = 70.6%). A PCA of Combined Sample 1's scores for the 12 factor scales extracted a single factor, according to both Cattell's (1966) scree test and Kaiser's eigenvalue criterion (Kaiser, 1960). The most important information regarding the stability of the unifactorial structure of the MID's 12 factor scales was provided by an analysis of a second data set (i.e., Combined Sample 2). A PCA of scores on the 12 factor scales from Combined Sample 2 extracted only one factor that explained 79% of the variance (Table 44.3).

44.4.1.11 Confirmatory Factor Analysis of the One-Factor Model of the 12 Factor Scales

A maximum likelihood CFA was conducted on Combined Sample 1 (Table 44.9). An LM Test was conducted to analyze the covariances in the model. Based on the LM Test, four theoretically consistent (and clinically consistent) covariances were added, one at a time, to the one-factor model of the data from Combined Sample 1. That final model was then tested on a second data set (i.e., Combined Sample 2) and the All Data Sample (Table 44.9); CFAs produced a CFI of 0.96 and a RMSEA of 0.05 in each of the three data sets (i.e., Combined Sample 1, Combined Sample 2, and the All Data Sample).

44.5 DISCUSSION

The essential finding of this study is that pathological dissociation, as measured by the MID's 168 dissociation items, is a stable, second-order factor with 12 stable, first-order factors.

There are four essential differences between the present study and previous factor analytic investigations of dissociation. First, few prior investigations of the factor structure of dissociation were based on large, clinical samples. Pathological dissociation is not a normal phenomenon (Waller et al., 1996); research on pathological dissociation should be conducted on clinical samples.

TABLE 44.5
Correlation Matrix of the MID's 14 Facet Scales and the 12 Factor Scales

Primary Scales	Factor Scales											
	Self-Conf	Amnes	Alters	Flash	BodySx	AutobMem	Trance	Der/Dep	DisDis	Persec	Angry	Distress
Memory	.86	.79	.78	.69	.68	**.95**	.73	.77	.87	.74	.80	.93
Deperson	.94	.80	.87	.76	.80	.75	.80	**.96**	.86	.81	.87	.86
Derealiz	.92	.81	.82	.76	.82	.69	.80	**.95**	.86	.78	.85	.84
Flashback	.82	.78	.80	**1.00**	.72	.61	.75	.75	.78	.78	.79	.75
Somatic	.78	.83	.80	.75	**.97**	.62	.76	.83	.80	.76	.80	.78
Trance	.10	.83	.83	.79	.76	.70	**.96**	.85	.86	.79	.85	.86
Id Conf	**.97**	.76	.86	.78	.70	.75	.77	.84	.85	.82	.88	.85
Voices	.84	.83	.97	.78	.75	.66	.75	.82	.80	**.99**	.89	.78
Ego-Alien	.95	.85	.94	.81	.77	.72	.80	.87	.88	.90	**.97**	.86
S-Alter	.92	.89	.94	.79	.82	.71	.81	.92	.85	.87	**.95**	.86
S-States	.84	.83	**.97**	.76	.73	.67	.74	.82	.79	.89	.89	.78
TimeGap	.85	**.98**	.86	.78	.80	.70	.82	.83	.88	.82	.87	.88
Disremem	.80	**.98**	.85	.74	.80	.67	.76	.80	.83	.80	.87	.84
Ancillary	.92	.90	.90	.80	.82	.72	.81	.88	.88	.85	**.94**	.91

Note. Boldface indicates the highest correlation in each row.
Self-conf = self-confusion and dissociative loss of groundedness in self and world; Amnes = amnesia; Alters = subjective awareness of the presence of alters or self-states; Flash = flashbacks; BodySx = body symptoms; AutobMem = circumscribed loss of remote autobiographical memory; Der/Dep = derealization/depersonalization; Dis/Dis = dissociative disorientation; Persec = persecutory intrusions; Angry = angry intrusions; Distress = distress about memory problems; Memory = memory problems; Deperson = depersonalization; Derealiz = derealization; Flashback = flashbacks; Somatic = somatic symptoms; Id Conf = identity confusion; Ego-Alien = ego-alien experiences; S-Alter = disconcerting experiences of self-alteration; S-States = self-states and alters; Time Gap = discontinuities of time; Disremem = disremembered actions.

The two samples in the present study were 63% clinical and 74% clinical, respectively.

Second, previous studies of the factor structure of dissociation used screening measures of dissociation. Because the MID comprehensively covers the phenomena of pathological dissociation (Dell, 2006a, 2006b, 2009b), it is better-suited to investigating the phenomenological structure of pathological dissociation *per se*.

Third, with one exception, previous studies of dissociation have not conducted (or, at least, have not reported) a hierarchical factor analysis to determine whether multifactor solutions could be explained by a single, higher-order factor. In the only exception to this generalization, Stockdale et al. (2002) reported that two bifactor models did not improve the three-factor model of the DES.

Fourth, we performed a theoretically strong CFA on the data from the MID. Only Stockdale et al. have previously reported the results of CFA with a measure of dissociation.

44.5.1 First-Order Factors of Pathological Dissociation[3]

44.5.1.1 Self-Confusion

The strongest factor of pathological dissociation describes deep confusion about the self. Ten of the first 14 items on this factor come from the MID's 12-item Identity Confusion Facet Scale. The other items in this factor describe peculiar alterations of the person's experience that entail a profound and disorienting loss of groundedness in self and world. Such disruption of the expected functioning of self and world constitutes the experiential core of dissociative events; this is how it feels to undergo recurrent dissociative intrusions into one's conscious experience. Dissociative persons are chronically and deeply confused about themselves.

[3] The factors are listed in the order of their squared multiple correlations in the All Data CFA.

TABLE 44.6
Correlation Matrix of the MID's 23 Dissociation Scales and the 12 Factor Scales

MID	Factor Scales											
Scales	**S-Conf**	**Amnesia**	**Alters**	**Flash**	**BodySx**	**AutobMem**	**Trance**	**Der/Dep**	**DisDis**	**Persec**	**Angry**	**Distress**
Memory problem	.86	.79	.78	.69	.68	**.95**	.73	.77	.87	.74	.80	.93
Depersonalization	.94	.80	.87	.76	.80	.75	.80	**.96**	.86	.81	.87	.86
Derealization	.92	.81	.82	.76	.82	.69	.80	**.95**	.86	.78	.85	.84
Flashbacks	.82	.78	.80	**1.00**	.72	.61	.75	.75	.78	.78	.79	.75
Somatic Sx	.78	.83	.80	.75	**.97**	.62	.76	.83	.80	.76	.80	.78
Trance	.91	.83	.83	.79	.76	.70	**.96**	.85	.86	.79	.85	.86
Child voices	.79	.82	**.92**	.75	.72	.62	.70	.79	.78	.90	.84	.74
Struggle	.92	.83	**.96**	.80	.76	.70	.78	.86	.83	.95	.94	.83
Persecutory voice	.81	.80	.92	.76	.71	.63	.72	.78	.77	**.98**	.85	.76
Made speech	.83	.81	.84	.70	.72	.64	.73	.81	.83	.79	**.90**	.79
Made thoughts	**.94**	.77	.87	.79	.72	.72	.77	.83	.86	.84	.90	.83
Made emotion	**.93**	.75	.83	.78	.69	.71	.74	.79	.84	.80	.87	.82
Made impulses	.86	.80	**.93**	.74	.72	.66	.74	.81	.79	.90	.91	.78
Made actions	**.95**	.85	.93	.79	.77	.73	.81	.92	.88	.87	**.95**	.86
Loss knowledge	.81	.86	.79	.70	.78	.63	.74	.82	.78	.74	.82	**.88**
Self-alteration	.92	.89	.94	.79	.82	.71	.81	.92	.85	.87	**.95**	.86
Self-puzzlement	**.96**	.75	.83	.76	.68	.74	.76	.82	.85	.80	.86	.84
Time loss	.86	.75	.83	.76	.68	.75	.79	.80	**.90**	.77	.82	.87
Coming to	.78	**.94**	.82	.73	.75	.61	.76	.79	.80	.78	.83	.79
Fugues	.74	**.95**	.80	.74	.78	.59	.75	.77	.76	.76	.80	.79
Being told	.80	**.90**	.81	.72	.74	.67	.72	.75	.84	.77	.88	.83
Find objects	.72	**.93**	.79	.66	.75	.60	.69	.74	.75	.73	.79	.77
Find evidence	.73	**.94**	.79	.71	.78	.59	.73	.76	.74	.74	.80	.78

Note: Boldface indicates the highest correlation in each row. MID = Multidimensional Inventory of Dissociation.
Self-conf = self-confusion and dissociative loss of groundedness in self and world; Alters = subjective awareness of the presence of alters or self-states; Flash = flashbacks; BodySx = body symptoms; AutobMem = circumscribed loss of remote autobiographical memory; Der/Dep = derealization/depersonalization; Dis/Dis = dissociative disorientation; Persec = persecutory intrusions; Angry = angry intrusions; Distress = distress about memory problems; Memory problem = memory problems; Somatic Sx = somatic symptoms; Struggle = voices/internal struggle; Made speech = speech insertion; Made thoughts = thought insertion; Made emotions = made/intrusive emotions; Made impulses = made/intrusive impulses ; Made actions = made/intrusive actions; Loss knowledge = temporary loss of well-rehearsed knowledge; Self-alteration = disconcerting experiences of self-alteration; being told = being told about disremembered actions; Find objects = finding objects among one's possessions; Find evidence = finding evidence of disremembered actions.

44.5.1.2 Angry Intrusions

The existence and prominence of the Angry Intrusions Factor Scale is surprising for several reasons. First, this is a completely new empirical finding. None of the 30+ factor analytic studies of dissociation in the literature have reported such a finding. Of course, upon reflection, it is obvious that an Angry Intrusions factor cannot be extracted from the items of the DES, QED, DIS-Q, or SDQ-20; these instruments do not contain items that tap angry intrusive phenomena.

On the other hand, the clinical literature on dissociation is replete with accounts of "angry parts" or "angry alters" (e.g., Ross, 1997; Watkins & Watkins, 1997). And yet, the developer of the MID did not foresee that an Angry Intrusions factor would emerge from the MID. None of the MID's 14 facet scales and 23 diagnostic scales were conceptualized in terms of angry intrusions. This leads to an inevitable question: if the phenomena of *angry intrusions* were not built into the MID by design, whence comes the MID's ability to generate an Angry Intrusions Factor?

TABLE 44.7
Criterion-Related Validity of the 12 Factor Scales: Comparison of Three SCID-D-Diagnosed Groups

	Nondissociative (N = 24)		Depersonalization Disorder (N = 16)		Dissociative Identity Disorder (N = 47)		
	Mean	**SD**	**Mean**	**SD**	**Mean**	**SD**	***F******
Self-confusion/dissociation	12.2_a	10.6	37.6_b	17.7	61.4_c	20.7	60.86
Amnesia	1.3_a	2.3	9.2_a	11.0	35.7_b	24.2	31.62
Subjective awareness of alters	3.9_a	4.6	9.6_a	10.1	56.2_b	24.9	74.44
Flashbacks	10.8_a	15.0	20.1_a	18.4	50.9_b	28.8	25.49
Body symptoms	2.0_a	2.6	11.8_a	13.1	20.2_b	18.1	12.28
Loss of autobiographical memory	9.4_a	17.8	30.7_b	28.5	61.0_c	27.1	35.15
Trance	3.9_a	6.6	16.3_a	18.5	69.0_b	41.6	24.96
Derealization/depersonalization	3.8_a	4.4	33.3_b	17.4	42.7_b	23.3	34.07
Dissociative disorientation	8.2_a	8.3	28.9_b	20.8	56.4_c	22.9	50.25
Persecutory intrusions	3.1_a	4.8	6.6_a	11.4	56.1_b	29.9	55.34
Angry intrusions	5.6_a	7.0	17.4_a	14.2	53.7_b	26.2	49.45
Distress about memory problems	10.8_a	13.5	25.3_a	17.5	54.3_b	21.9	44.56

Note: Means in the same row that do not share subscripts differ at $p < 0.001$ in the Scheffé comparison.
SCID-D = Structured Clinical Interview for DSM-IV Dissociative Disorders.
Self-confusion/dissociation = self-confusion and dissociative loss of groundedness in self and world; Subjective awareness of alters = subjective awareness of the presence of alters or self-states; Loss of autobiographical memory = circumscribed loss of remote autobiographical memory.
*All F values are significant at $p < 0.001$; df = 2, 86.

TABLE 44.8
Correlation Matrix of the MID's 12 Factor Scales

	Amnesia	Alters	Flash	Body	LossAuto	Trance	Der/Dep	DisDis	Persec	Angry	Distress
Self-confusion/dissociation	0.83	0.89	0.82	0.77	0.77	0.83	0.91	0.92	0.85	0.92	0.90
Amnesia	—	0.87	0.78	0.83	0.68	0.80	0.84	0.85	0.82	0.88	0.88
Subjective awareness of alters		—	0.8	0.78	0.70	0.78	0.87	0.84	0.96	0.94	0.83
Flashbacks			—	0.72	0.61	0.75	0.75	0.78	0.78	0.79	0.75
Body symptoms				—	0.60	0.74	0.85	0.77	0.73	0.80	0.77
Loss of autobiographical memory					—	0.63	0.69	0.76	0.66	0.71	0.79
Trance						—	0.80	0.79	0.75	0.80	0.80
Derealization/depersonalization							—	0.84	0.81	0.88	0.84
Dissociative disorientation								—	0.80	0.87	0.90
Persecutory intrusions									—	0.89	0.79
Angry intrusions										—	0.86
Distress about memory problems											—

Note: N = 1,310. All coefficients are significant at $p < 0.001$. Self-confusion/dissociation = self-confusion and dissociative loss of groundedness of self and world; Subjective awareness of alters = subjective awareness of the presence of alters or self-states; Loss of autobiographical memory = circumscribed loss of remote autobiographical memory.

The answer to this question lies in Table 44.5 and the subjective nature of angry intrusions. Angry intrusions typically involve (1) sudden unexpected surges of anger into one's conscious mind and/or (2) *partially dissociated seizures of executive control* wherein the person has conscious awareness of being invaded and/or taken over by an autonomous *other*. This subjective experience is reflected in Table 44.6, which shows that Angry Intrusions correlated 0.95 with Subjective Experiences of Self-Alteration and 0.95 with "Made" Actions. Needless to say, these are bizarre, ego-alien experiences. In keeping with this, Table 44.5 shows that the Angry Intrusions factor correlated 0.97 with the MID's Ego-Alien Experiences Scale, 0.95 with the MID's Experiences of Self-Alteration Scale, and 0.94 with the MID's Ancillary Scale (which contains several items that tap ego-alien experiences). Thus, the MID's original scales explicitly acknowledge that ego-alien experiences such as made actions and a sudden sense of self-alteration are a prominent component of pathological dissociation, but the MID's original scales do *not* explicitly acknowledge the extent to which such ego-alien experiences may be synonymous with angry intrusions.

It is notable that Angry Intrusions was, statistically, the second strongest contributor to Pathological Dissociation in the All Data CFA.

TABLE 44.9
Confirmatory Factor Analyses: Three Tests of the One-Factor Model of the MID's 12 Factor Scales

	Combined Sample 1 N = 1386			Combined Sample 2 N = 1310			All Data Sample N = 2696		
Scale	**Path Coeffic**	**Residual**	**R^2**	**Path Coeffic**	**Residual**	**R^2**	**Path Coeffic**	**Residual**	**R^2**
Self-confusion/dissociation	0.98	0.22	0.95	0.98	0.2	0.96	0.98	0.20	0.96
Angry intrusions	0.95	0.32	0.9	0.94	0.35	0.88	0.94	0.33	0.89
Subjective awareness of alters	0.93	0.36	0.87	0.91	0.42	0.82	0.92	0.39	0.85
Derealization/depersonalization	0.92	0.39	0.85	0.90	0.45	0.8	0.91	0.41	0.83
Amnesia	0.94	0.36	0.87	0.92	0.4	0.84	0.93	0.37	0.86
Persecutory intrusions	0.88	0.48	0.77	0.83	0.56	0.69	0.85	0.52	0.73
Dissociative disorientation	0.93	0.36	0.87	0.93	0.36	0.87	0.93	0.36	0.87
Body symptoms	0.82	0.57	0.68	0.79	0.62	0.62	0.81	0.60	0.65
Distress about memory problems	0.93	0.36	0.87	0.91	0.42	0.82	0.92	0.39	0.85
Flashbacks	0.84	0.55	0.70	0.80	0.6	0.64	0.82	0.57	0.67
Trance	0.86	0.51	0.74	0.84	0.54	0.71	0.85	0.53	0.72
Loss of autobiographical memory	0.77	0.63	0.60	0.76	0.62	0.58	0.77	0.64	0.59
Correlations Among Independent Variables									
Amnesia + Self-confusion	−0.98			−0.99			−0.99		
Persecutory + Alters	0.77			0.72			0.75		
Angry intrusions + Persecutory	0.42			0.34			0.38		
Body symptoms + Dereal/ depersonalization	0.26			0.29			0.27		
χ^2	10,105			9,104			15,984		
Df	400			400			400		
χ^2/df	25.3			22.8			39.96		
NFI	.95			.95			.96		
CFI	.96			.96			.96		
RMSEA	.05			.05			.05		

Note: Self-confusion/dissociation = self-confusion and dissociative loss of groundedness of self and world; Subjective awareness of alters = subjective awareness of the presence of alters or self-states; Loss of autobiographical memory = circumscribed loss of remote autobiographical memory.

44.5.1.3 Dissociative Disorientation

The items on the Dissociative Disorientation Factor Scale portray a state of trancey, amnestic disorientation. The two atypical items in this scale (i.e., "difficulty swallowing" and inexplicable genital pain) may be due to statistical chance. Alternately, and more probably, there may be a meaningful relationship between trancey, amnestic disorientation and intrusive "body memories" of oral and genital rape. That is, highly dissociative individuals often respond to intrusive body memories of sexual abuse with a reactive, dissociative distancing that manifests as a trancey, amnestic disorientation. And, more generally, highly dissociative individuals may respond to all kinds of intrusive memories/flashbacks with an almost-automatic, reactive, defensive, dissociative distancing from those intrusions.

Three other research groups have reported such dissociative distancing. First, Lanius and colleagues have noted that about 30% of persons with PTSD manifest dissociative distancing (i.e., hypoarousal and depersonalization/derealization) when confronted with their own trauma script (Frewen & Lanius, 2006; Pain, Bluhm, & Lanius, 2009). Second, this trancey, amnestic disorientation may be the same phenomenon that Allen, Console, and Lewis (1999) have described as *pathological dissociative detachment.* Third, Briere (2002) found Dissociative Disorientation (he called it Disengagement) to be the first factor that emerged from factor analysis of the 30-item MDI in a small clinical sample.

44.5.1.4 Amnesia

The 29 items of the Amnesia Factor Scale describe the classic phenomena of amnesia (e.g., fugue, suddenly "coming to" in inexplicable circumstances, etc.). The Amnesia Factor Scale correlated 0.98 with the MID's two amnesia facet scales (Table 44.5). Like the items in the MID's amnesia facet scales, the items on the Amnesia Factor Scale describe recent, brief episodes of amnesia (which the person finds to be distinctly disturbing).

44.5.1.5 Distress about Severe Memory Problems

These items refer to certain problems with memory that are especially distressing, such as forgetting how to do one's job and forgetting how to execute well-rehearsed skills (e.g., how to drive, how to read), and so on.

44.5.1.6 Subjective Experience of the Presence of Alter Personalities and/or Self-States

This factor reflects the person's subjective experience of the presence and activities of other parts of the mind. These other parts of the mind are experienced as being autonomous—that is, outside his or her control (i.e., voices; intrusions into mind; intrusions into executive control; and the recurring sense that there is an *other* within). The 36 items of this factor provide the most detailed empirical portrayal to date of the subjective experience of having alter personalities.

44.5.1.7 Derealization/Depersonalization

The 16 items of this factor describe feelings of distance, disconnection, unfamiliarity, and unreality with regard to both self and world. This factor suggests that derealization and depersonalization are inseparably intertwined with one another. Previous factor analytic studies (e.g., Briere et al., 2005) have also reported that depersonalization items and derealization items load on the same factor. Simeon (2009), for example, has noted that research on Depersonalization Disorder indicates that depersonalization and derealization tend to co-occur, and that there is little difference between cases of Depersonalization Disorder that are marked by the presence of depersonalization, but not derealization (or vice versa).

44.5.1.8 Persecutory Intrusions

The items on the Persecutory Intrusions Factor Scale describe harsh, toxic, persecutory intrusions into consciousness—hateful voices that contemptuously degrade and abuse the person (e.g., "You're worthless," "You're a slut," "Die!"). In contrast to angry intrusions, persecutory intrusions were not statistically associated with seizure of executive control. Although persecutory voices in persons with DID is a clinical commonplace, the current study's extraction of a Persecutory Intrusions Factor is, nevertheless, a first. No previous factor analytic study of a dissociation instrument has shown that *persecutory intrusions are a significant, discrete component of pathological dissociation.*

Persecutory voices are not the sole province of psychosis. In fact, empirical evidence shows that no symptom of DID is better documented than voices (Dell, 2006b, 2009a), and clinical evidence shows that the most commonly reported form of voice in DID patients is an angry, persecutory one.

44.5.1.9 Trance

These seven items come from the MID's Trance Scale. Trance states are probably best characterized as episodes during which the person is (1) unresponsive to external stimuli, and (2) intensely absorbed by or involved with internal material (e.g., a flashback, a pleasant place, complete nothingness, etc.). The Trance Factor Scale taps not only the occurrence of such trance states, but also their duration, frequency, involuntary or habitual nature, and the person's accompanying subjective distress. Trance states have been reported to occur in dissociative adults and dissociative children since the mid-1800s (Kluft, 1985; Janet, 1889; Putnam, Helmers, & Trickett, 1993).

44.5.1.10 Flashbacks

This 12-item factor is identical to the MID's 12-item Flashbacks Scale. These items not only tap the presence of flashbacks, but also their frequency, psychological toxicity, and the extent to which they impair daily functioning. This factor is congruent with the high comorbidity between dissociative disorder and posttraumatic stress disorder (PTSD; Boon & Draijer, 1993; Coons, 1996; Middleton & Butler, 1998); it also implies that the prototypical symptom of PTSD (i.e., flashbacks) is integral to the construct of pathological dissociation.

44.5.1.11 Body Symptoms

The Body Symptoms Factor describes dissociative intrusions into one's body-self, such as classic conversion symptoms (e.g., blindness, deafness, paralysis, etc.) and weird bodily changes (e.g., alterations in vision, body parts that disappear, body parts that change size, etc.). These experiences constitute deeply disturbing "attacks" upon one's body-self. This factor replicates Nijenhuis' (1999, 2000) concept of *somatoform dissociation*.

44.5.1.12 Circumscribed Loss of Remote Autobiographical Memory

These six items come from the MID's Memory Problems Scale; they describe circumscribed remote amnesia—an inability to remember certain major life events or certain periods of time. None of these items, however, involves loss of personal identity. Loss of personal identity is part of the Amnesia Factor Scale.

Circumscribed loss of remote autobiographical memory appears to be identical to Loewenstein's concept of *nonclassic* Dissociative Amnesia (Loewenstein, 1991; Loewenstein & Putnam, 2004). Both Loewenstein and Dell (2009c) have noted that nonclassic amnesia patients are untroubled by their memory gaps. What troubles them, instead, is clinical inquiry *about* such memory gaps; these patients minimize their memory gaps and seek to change the subject. Loewenstein contrasts such ego-syntonic, nonclassic amnesias with *classic* Dissociative Amnesia in which the person is bewildered by losing his or her personal identity (i.e., generalized amnesia).

The distinction between generalized amnesia and circumscribed amnesia for certain autobiographical events is particularly interesting. It implies that *circumscribed forgetting of earlier autobiographical events—a remarkably common clinical phenomenon—is meaningfully different from generalized amnesia* (see also Dell, 2009c).

A somewhat different, and equally important, dichotomy of amnesias was anticipated during the development of the MID. That is, several MID scales measure *recent brief episodes of amnesia*, whereas a different MID scale measures *remote losses of autobiographical memory* (usually for a specific event or circumscribed period of time). It is notable in this regard that the one-factor model of the factor scales (see last column of Table 44.9) explained only 59% of the variance in scores on the Circumscribed Loss of Remote Autobiographic Memory Factor Scale, whereas it explained 86% of the variance in scores on the Amnesia Factor Scale. This suggests that there may be a meaningful clinical or theoretical difference between circumscribed remote amnesias and recent brief amnesias (see Dell, 2009c). The effects of this difference can also be seen in the correlations between the MID's factor scales and the SCID-D-R's Amnesia Score. The SCID-D Amnesia Score is based on items that assess *both* recent amnesia and circumscribed losses of remote autobiographical memory. The SCID-D-R Amnesia Score correlated more highly with the MID Circumscribed Loss of Remote Autobiographical Memory Scale ($r = 0.74$) than it did with the MID Amnesia Scale ($r = 0.56$; Table 44.6).

44.5.2 A Single, Coherent, Second-Order Factor of Pathological Dissociation

CFA showed that a single, higher-order factor, Pathological Dissociation, accounted for 96% of the variance in the first-order factors of the MID (Table 44.9). This CFA finding was replicated on a second data set. The heterogeneity of the 12 first-order factors emphasizes the robustness of this unitary second-order factor structure. Said differently, pathological dissociation has strikingly different clinical manifestations (i.e., Schneiderian-like intrusions into executive functioning and sense of self, hearing voices, general memory problems, episodes of frank amnesia, trances, self-confusion, depersonalization, derealization, etc.), and yet, these dramatically heterogeneous phenomena all stem from a single, coherent factor—pathological dissociation.

44.5.3 Limitations

The primary methodological shortcoming of the present study is its use of heterogeneous, combined samples. Relatedly, a significant proportion of both samples were recruited by clinicians who had an interest in dissociation. This led to a substantial oversampling of dissociative patients; 76% of the research participants in Combined Sample 1 obtained mean MID scores of 15 or higher. Thus, although heterogeneous, the combined samples were by no means random. These characteristics of the sample may introduce variance that could slant the results of the factor analyses in ways that are not completely predictable or identifiable. On the other hand, there are three reasons to believe that the sampling procedure did not unduly bias or skew the results. First, analysis of the two data sets produced nearly identical results. Second, the results are congruent with the clinical phenomena of severe dissociative disorder (e.g., Dell, 2001a, 2002, 2006b, 2009a). Finally, the results are congruent with previous findings and previous predictions about the factor structure of dissociation (Dell, 2002, 2006b; Somer & Dell, 2005).

44.6 A FINAL NOTE

The present findings provide a new kind of empirical validation for DID. The MID was developed from a rigorous effort to achieve comprehensive coverage of the domain of pathological dissociation. Factor analyses of the MID's 168 dissociation items suggest that pathological dissociation has (1) a stable, 12-factor, first-order structure and (2) a stable, unitary, second-order structure. *The 12 first-order factors of pathological dissociation unmistakably portray the phenomena of DID:* seizure of executive control by an angry self-state, subjective experiences of the presence and activities of alters, derealization/depersonalization, amnesia, persecutory voices, self-confusion, episodes of dissociative disorientation, weird body symptoms, chronic distress about memory problems, flashbacks, trance, and lacunae in autobiographical memory. In short, the factor analyses in this chapter provide a 'grass roots,' emergent validation of DID. Moreover, they imply that the symptoms of DID and the 12 factors of pathological dissociation are one and the same.

I am grateful to clinicians far and wide who helped me to collect these data, especially Marcia Cotton, Don Fridley, Jack Howley, Andreas Laddis, Richard Hicks, and Martin Dorahy. I am also indebted to several researchers who granted permission to include data from their own MID research in this large factor analytic study: Barry Cooper, Ursula Gast, Heather Davediuk Gingrich, Dean Lauterbach, Andreas Laddis, John Arnold, Francesca Montesanto, Eli Somer, Frauke Rodewald, and Daphne Simeon. Finally, I thank Eli Somer for his helpful critique of this chapter.

TABLE 44A.1
Principal Axis Factor Analysis (Promax Rotation) of the MID's 168 Dissociation Items (N = 1,359): Five Items With the Highest Pattern Matrix Loadings for Each Factor

MID Item	S-Con 1	Amn 2	Alt 3	Fla 4	Body 5	Mem 6	Tran 7	De real 8	Dis Dis 9	Pers 10	Ang 11	Distr 12
Factor 1: Self-Confusion (50 Items)												
107. Feeling very confused about who you really are.	**0.85**	0.10	−0.02	−0.01	−0.03	0.09	−0.04	0.12	−0.14	0.05	−0.10	0.01
54. Feeling very detached from your behavior as you "go through the motions" of daily life.	**0.80**	−0.04	0.00	−0.02	−0.02	−0.03	0.00	0.31	0.05	0.01	−0.14	−0.07
84. Feeling disconnected from everything around you.	**0.79**	0.00	−0.01	0.03	−0.01	0.05	−0.02	0.27	−0.01	0.02	−0.19	0.03
59. Feeling uncertain about who you really are.	**0.79**	0.09	0.05	0.03	0.01	0.05	−0.06	0.19	0.12	0.02	−0.12	−0.01
232. Being confused or puzzled by your emotions.	**0.77**	0.00	−0.02	0.14	−0.04	0.01	−0.06	−0.03	−0.01	0.01	0.09	−0.05
Factor 2: Amnesia (29 Items)												
208. Suddenly finding yourself somewhere (e.g., at the beach, at work, in a nightclub, in your car, etc.) with no memory of how you got there.	−0.04	**0.92**	−0.06	0.04	−0.07	0.03	0.01	0.09	0.04	0.02	−0.01	−0.04
193. Suddenly finding yourself somewhere odd at home (e.g., inside the closet, under a bed, curled up on the floor, etc.) with no knowledge of how you got there.	−0.05	**0.87**	−0.01	0.08	0.06	−0.07	0.05	0.03	−0.02	0.06	−0.1	−0.11
181. Discovering that you have changed your appearance (e.g., cut your hair, or changed your hairstyle, or changed what you are wearing, or put on cosmetics, etc.) with no memory of having done so.	−0.11	**0.83**	0.12	0.02	0.05	−0.02	−0.04	−0.04	−0.04	−0.09	0.04	−0.01
243. There were times when you "woke up" and found pills or a razor blade (or something else to hurt yourself with) in your hand.	−0.03	**0.83**	0.09	0.04	0.03	−0.01	−0.03	0.04	−0.07	0.12	−0.13	−0.20
215. "Coming to" and finding that you have done something you don't remember doing (e.g., smashed something, cut yourself, cleaned the whole house, etc.).	−0.01	**0.81**	−0.05	0.07	−0.12	0.01	0.07	0.05	0.00	0.02	0.14	−0.10

(Continued)

TABLE 44A.1 (continued)
Principal Axis Factor Analysis (Promax Rotation) of the MID's 168 Dissociation Items (N = 1,359): Five Items With the Highest Pattern Matrix Loadings for Each Factor

MID Item	S-Con 1	Amn 2	Alt 3	Fla 4	Body 5	Mem 6	Tran 7	De real 8	Dis Dis 9	Pers 10	Ang 11	Distr 12
Factor 3: Subjective Awareness of Alter personalities and Self-States (36 Items)												
180. Having other people (or parts) inside you who have their own names.	−0.14	0.22	**0.91**	−0.05	−0.09	0.02	0.06	−0.03	−0.02	0.00	−0.06	0.00
209. Feeling that there is another person inside who can come out and speak if it wants.	−0.03	0.13	**0.86**	0.00	−0.07	−0.02	0.05	−0.02	−0.09	−0.05	0.03	0.05
165. Feeling that you have multiple personalities.	−0.03	0.13	**0.86**	0.00	−0.07	−0.02	0.05	−0.02	−0.09	−0.05	0.03	0.05
7. Hearing the voice of a child in your head.	0.00	0.13	**0.76**	0.03	−0.06	−0.04	−0.08	0.07	0.18	0.11	−0.10	−0.06
241. Having another part inside that has different memories, behaviors, and feelings than you do.	−0.03	0.15	**0.76**	−0.02	−0.01	0.05	0.09	−0.07	−0.11	0.01	−0.01	0.07
Factor 4: Flashbacks (12 Items)												
176. Reliving a past trauma so vividly that you see it, hear it, smell it, etc.	0.04	0.09	0.06	**0.80**	−0.07	−0.01	−0.06	−0.04	0.02	−0.02	0.06	0.01
231. Being bothered by flashbacks for several days in a row.	−0.04	0.14	0.08	**0.77**	−0.02	−0.01	0.11	−0.05	−0.04	−0.04	−0.01	−0.02
81. Being so bothered by flashbacks that it was hard to get out of bed and face the day.	0.19	0.08	−0.02	**0.74**	0.05	−0.07	0.04	−0.09	−0.01	−0.07	0.00	0.08
137. Bad memories coming into your mind and you can't get rid of them.	0.32	−0.08	−0.1	**0.74**	−0.02	−0.01	−0.06	−0.04	0.00	−0.02	0.03	0.09
20. Reliving a traumatic event so vividly that you totally lose contact with where you *actually* are (that is, you think that you are "back there and then").												
Factor 5: Body Symptoms (14 Items)												
47. Not being able to see for a while.	−0.01	0.1	0.04	−0.12	**0.64**	0.03	−0.02	0.01	0.1	−0.04	−0.02	−0.08
86. Not being able to hear for a while (as if you are deaf) (for no known medical reason).	−0.1	0.2	0.04	−0.01	**0.58**	0.03	0.1	−0.05	−0.01	0.02	−0.19	0.03
99. Having difficulty walking (for no known medical reason).	0.02	−0.03	0.04	−0.02	**0.58**	0.02	0.1	0.00	0.04	0.07	−0.1	0.11

73. Being paralyzed or unable to move (for no known medical reason).	0.04	–0.03	0.06	0.16	**0.36**	0.00	0.12	0.00	0.09	0.08	–0.04	0.12
112. Having seizures for which your doctor can find no reason.	–0.03	0.1	–0.03	0.00	**0.32**	0.02	0.08	–0.14	0.04	0.05	0.00	0.08
Factor 6: Circumscribed Loss of Remote Autobiographical Memory (6 Items)												
147. Being able to remember very little of your past.	0.13	0.07	–0.07	–0.06	0.00	**0.74**	–0.03	0.00	–0.03	–0.03	0.15	0.08
82. Not remembering large parts of your childhood after age 5.	0.17	0.00	0.00	–0.03	0.01	**0.73**	–0.02	–0.02	0.03	–0.03	0.02	0.04
121. Feeling that there are large gaps in your memory.	0.16	0.00	0.02	0.06	–0.02	**0.70**	0.02	0.01	0.02	–0.01	0.07	0.09
95. Feeling that pieces of your past are missing.	0.28	–0.05	0.09	0.09	0.02	**0.62**	–0.05	0.00	0.02	–0.06	0.02	0.05
108. Feeling that important things happened to you earlier in your life, but you cannot remember them.	0.26	–0.06	0.06	–0.02	0.04	**0.58**	0.02	0.07	–0.04	–0.08	0.13	–0.01
Factor 7: Trance (7 Items)												
222. Having difficulty staying out of trance.	0.13	0.04	0.10	–0.09	–0.01	–0.02	**0.77**	0.08	–0.04	0.03	–0.06	–0.08
126. Going into trance for hours.	–0.01	0.13	0.04	0.01	0.14	–0.03	**0.76**	0.01	–0.03	–0.09	0.07	–0.09
113. Going into trance so much (or for so long) that it interferes with your daily activities and responsibilities.	0.09	–0.05	0.03	0.07	0.14	0.00	**0.70**	–0.08	0.03	–0.02	0.02	0.10
178. Going into trance several days in a row.	0.05	0.30	–0.03	–0.07	0.13	–0.01	**0.59**	0.02	–0.08	–0.07	0.02	–0.09
139. Drifting into trance without even realizing that it is happening.	0.15	–0.06	0.04	0.10	–0.05	0.04	**0.56**	0.03	0.13	0.00	0.10	0.03
Factor 8: Derealization/Depersonalization (16 Items)												
45. Things around you feeling unreal.	**0.59**	–0.01	–0.02	–0.08	–0.02	–0.04	–0.01	**0.62**	0.08	0.06	–0.10	–0.06
71. Feeling that other people, objects, or the world around you are not real.	**0.44**	0.01	0.02	–0.10	0.12	–0.08	0.02	**0.59**	–0.01	0.02	–0.03	–0.05
110. Feeling as if you were looking at the world through a fog so that people and objects felt far away or unclear.	**0.40**	0.05	0.00	0.06	–0.01	0.05	0.09	**0.52**	–0.05	0.00	–0.05	–0.10
4. Having an emotion (e.g., fear, sadness, anger, happiness) that doesn't feel like it is "yours."	**0.31**	–0.02	0.17	–0.10	0.11	0.03	–0.04	**0.50**	0.20	–0.04	–0.04	–0.15
230. Your body suddenly feeling as if it isn't really yours.	0.22	0.15	0.18	–0.01	0.03	–0.02	0.01	**0.39**	–0.11	–0.04	0.19	–0.08

(Continued)

TABLE 44A.1 (continued)
Principal Axis Factor Analysis (Promax Rotation) of the MID's 168 Dissociation Items (N = 1,359): Five Items With the Highest Pattern Matrix Loadings for Each Factor

MID Item	S-Con	Amn	Alt	Fla	Body	Mem	Tran	De real	Dis Dis	Pers	Ang	Distr
	1	2	3	4	5	6	7	8	9	10	11	12
Factor 9: Dissociative Disorientation (12 Items)												
30. Not remembering what you ate at your last meal—or even whether you ate.	0.29	0.29	−0.09	−0.05	0.03	−0.01	−0.06	−0.02	**0.41**	0.05	−0.05	0.27
22. Having trance-like episodes where you stare off into space and lose awareness of what is going on around you.	**0.43**	−0.06	−0.04	0.07	−0.01	−0.04	0.24	0.04	**0.37**	−0.03	0.07	−0.03
2. Forgetting what you did earlier in the day.	**0.41**	0.15	−0.01	−0.07	−0.07	0.01	−0.04	−0.02	**0.35**	0.05	−0.1	0.28
21. Having difficulty swallowing (for no known medical reason).	0.02	−0.10	0.07	0.17	**0.31**	0.05	0.00	0.09	**0.36**	0.01	−0.07	−0.01
25. Being told of things that you had recently done, but with absolutely no memory of having done those things.	0.18	**0.36**	0.03	−0.01	−0.02	0.08	−0.05	0.06	**0.34**	0.01	0.14	0.11
Factor 10: Persecutory Intrusions (11 Items)												
247. Hearing a voice that calls you no good, worthless, or a failure.	0.24	−0.06	**0.39**	0.02	−0.02	−0.06	−0.09	0.02	0.03	**0.56**	−0.11	0.13
167. Hearing a voice in your head that calls you names (e.g., wimp, stupid, whore, slut, bitch, etc.).	0.08	−0.01	**0.41**	−0.04	−0.03	−0.02	−0.02	0.01	0.10	**0.51**	0.04	0.09
192. Hearing a voice in your head that wants you to die.	0.09	0.01	0.24	−0.05	−0.06	−0.03	0.04	0.01	0.00	**0.50**	−0.06	0.03
238. Hearing a voice in your head that tells you to "shut up."	0.05	0.01	**0.41**	−0.02	0.00	−0.01	−0.01	0.03	0.00	**0.47**	0.08	0.09
102. Hearing a voice in your head that wants you to hurt yourself.	0.11	0.19	**0.46**	−0.01	−0.02	−0.02	−0.01	0.05	0.06	**0.42**	−0.15	−0.03
Factor 11: Angry Intrusions (18 Items)												
154. When you are angry, doing or saying things that you don't remember (after you calm down).	**0.3**	0.24	−0.07	−0.01	−0.01	0.10	−0.04	−0.16	0.08	−0.03	**0.52**	−0.07
117. Words just flowing from your mouth as if they were not in your control.	0.21	0.06	0.15	−0.01	−0.01	0.03	0.08	0.00	0.02	−0.08	**0.51**	−0.03

Item	S-Con	Amn	Alt	Fla	Body	Mem	Tran	Dereal	DisDis	Pers	Ang	Distr
140. Words come out of your mouth, but you didn't say them; you don't know where those words came from.	−0.07	0.28	0.29	−0.02	−0.05	0.02	0.06	0.04	0.03	−0.03	**0.45**	−0.05
248. Having a very angry part that "comes out" and says and does things that you would never do or say.	0.28	0.13	**0.33**	−0.03	0.03	0.01	0.01	−0.21	−0.08	0.08	**0.38**	−0.1
194. Feeling as if there is something inside you that takes control of your behavior and speech.	0.11	0.09	**0.32**	0.03	0.02	−0.03	0.05	0.01	−0.08	0.1	**0.38**	−0.01
Factor 12: Distress About Severe Memory Problems (12 Items)												
173. Poor memory causing serious difficulty for you.	0.29	0.01	−0.02	0.01	0.08	0.17	0.05	−0.16	0.11	0.08	−0.05	**0.53**
186. Being bothered or upset by how much you forget.	0.3	0	0.01	0.09	−0.03	0.13	−0.05	−0.12	0.14	0.08	−0.12	**0.51**
96. Immediately forgetting what other people tell you.	**0.52**	0.02	−0.01	−0.08	−0.01	0.07	0.01	−0.09	0.23	0.07	−0.09	**0.39**
228. Suddenly not knowing how to do your job.	0.29	0.26	0.04	0.01	0.1	−0.09	−0.04	−0.02	−0.08	0.01	0.02	**0.33**
195. Totally forgetting how to do something that you know very well how to do (e.g., how to drive, how to read, how to use the computer, how to play the piano, etc.).	0.13	**0.41**	0.06	0.06	0.09	−0.05	−0.13	−0.02	0.02	0.02	0.04	**0.33**

Note. S-Con = self-confusion and loss of groundedness in self and world;
Amn = amnesia;
Alt = subjective awareness of the presence of alters or self-states;
Fla = flashbacks;
Body = body symptoms;
Mem = circumscribed loss of remote autobiographical memory;
Tran = trance;
Dereal = derealization/depersonalization;
DisDis = dissociative disorientation;
Pers = persecutory intrusions;
Ang = angry intrusions;
Distr = distress about severe memory problems.

REFERENCES

Allen, J. G., Console, D. A., & Lewis, L. (1999). Dissociative detachment and memory impairment: Reversible amnesia or encoding failure? *Comprehensive Psychiatry, 40*, 160–171.

Amdur, R., & Liberzon, I. (1996). Dimensionality of dissociation in subjects with PTSD. *Dissociation, 9*, 118–124.

American Psychiatric Association (2000). *Diagnostic and statistical manual of mental disorders* (4th ed., text rev.). Washington, DC: Author.

Armstrong, J. G., Putnam, F. W., Carlson, E. B., Libero, D. Z., & Smith, S. R. (1997). Development and validation of a measure of adolescent dissociation: The Adolescent Dissociative Experiences Scale (A-DES). *Journal of Nervous and Mental Disease, 185*, 491–497.

Bernstein, E. M., & Putnam, F. W. (1986). Development, reliability, and validity of a dissociation scale. *Journal of Nervous and Mental Disease, 174*, 727–735.

Bernstein, I. H., Ellason, J. W., Ross, C. A., & Vanderlinden, J. (2001). On the dimensionality of the Dissociative Experiences Scale (DES) and the Dissociation Questionnaire (DIS-Q). *Journal of Trauma & Dissociation, 2(3)*, 103–123.

Boon, S., & Draijer, N. (1993). *Multiple personality disorder in the Netherlands: A study on reliability and validity of the diagnosis*. Amsterdam: Swets & Zeitlinger.

Braude, S. E. (1995). *First person plural: Multiple personality and the philosophy of mind* (rev. ed.). Lanham, MD: Rowman & Littlefield Publishers, Inc.

Braude, E. E. (2004). Memory: The nature and significance of dissociation. In J. Radden (Ed.), *The philosophy of psychiatry: A companion* (pp. 106–117). Oxford: Oxford University Press.

Briere, J. (2002). *Multiscale Dissociation Inventory: Professional manual*. Lutz, FL: Psychological Assessment Resources, Inc.

Briere, J., Weathers, F. W., & Runtz, M. (2005). Is dissociation a multidimensional construct? Data from the Multiscale Dissociation Inventory. *Journal of Traumatic Stress, 18*, 221–231.

Brunet, A., Holowka, D. W., & Laurence, J. R. (2002). Dissociation. In M. J. Aminoff & R. B. Daroff (Eds.), *Encyclopedia of the neurological* sciences (pp. 25–27). San Diego: Academic Press.

Cardeña, E. (1994). The domain of dissociation. In S. J. Lynn & J. W. Rhue (Eds.), *Dissociation: Clinical and theoretical perspectives* (pp. 15–31). New York: Guilford Press.

Carlson, E. B. (1997). *Trauma assessments: A clinician's guide*. New York: Guilford Press.

Carlson, E. B., & Putnam, F. W. (1993). An update on the Dissociative Experiences Scale. *Dissociation, 6*, 16–27.

Cattell, R. B. (1966). The scree test for the number of factors. *Multivariate Behavioral Research, 1*, 245–276.

Coons, P. M. (1996). Clinical phenomenology of 25 children and adolescents with dissociative disorders. *Child and Adolescent Psychiatric Clinics of North America, 5*, 361–373.

Cronbach, L. J. (1951). Coefficient alpha and the internal structure of tests. *Psychometrika, 16*, 297–334.

Dell, P. F. (2001a). Why the diagnostic criteria for dissociative identity disorder should be changed. *Journal of Trauma & Dissociation, 2(1)*, 7–37.

Dell, P. F. (2001b). Should the dissociative disorders field choose its own diagnostic criteria for dissociative identity disorder? Reply to Cardeña, Coons, Putnam, Spiegel, and Steinberg. *Journal of Trauma & Dissociation, 2(1)*, 65–72.

Dell, P. F. (2002). Dissociative phenomenology of dissociative identity disorder. *Journal of Nervous and Mental Disease, 190*, 10–15.

Dell, P.F. (2006a). Multidimensional Inventory of Dissociation (MID): A comprehensive measure of pathological dissociation. *Journal of Trauma & Dissociation, 7(2)*, 77–106.

Dell, P. F. (2006b). A new model of dissociative identity disorder. *Psychiatric Clinics of North America, 29*, 1–26.

Dell, P. F. (2009a). The long struggle to diagnose multiple personality disorder (MPD). I. MPD. In P. F. Dell & J. A. O'Neil (Eds.), *Dissociation and the dissociative disorders: DSM-V and beyond* (pp. 383–402). New York: Routledge.

Dell, P. F. (2009b). The phenomena of pathological dissociation. In P. F. Dell & J. A. O'Neil (Eds.), *Dissociation and the dissociative disorders: DSM-V and beyond* (pp. 225–238). New York: Routledge.

Dell, P. F. (2009c). Understanding dissociation. In P. F. Dell & J. A. O'Neil (Eds.), *Dissociation and the dissociative disorders: DSM-V and beyond* (pp. 709–825). New York: Routledge.

Dunn, G. E., Ryan, J. J., & Paolo, A. M., & Miller (1993). Screening for MPD: Clinical utility of the Questionnaire of Experiences of Dissociation. *Dissociation, 6*, 38–41.

Farrington, A., Waller, G., Smerden, J., & Faupel, A. W. (2001). The Adolescent Dissociative Experiences Scale: Psychometric properties and difference in scores across age groups. *Journal of Nervous and Mental Disease, 189*, 722–727.

First, M. B., Spitzer, R. L., Gibbon, M., & Williams, J. B. W. (1997). *Structured Clinical Interview for DSM-IV Axis I Disorders*. Washington, DC: American Psychiatric Press.

Fischer, D. G., & Elnitsky (1990). A factor analysis study of two scales of dissociation. *American Journal of Clinical Hypnosis, 32*, 201–207.

Foa, E. B. (1995). *Posttraumatic Stress Diagnostic Scale: Manual*. Minneapolis, MN: National Computer Systems.

Frankel, F. H. (1990). Hypnotizability and dissociation. *American Journal of Psychiatry, 147*, 823–829.

Frewen, P. A., & Lanius, R. A. (2006). Neurobiology of dissociation: Unity and disunity in mind-body-brain. *Psychiatric Clinics of North America, 29*, 113–128.

Gast, U., Rodewald, F., Dehner-Rau, C., Kowalewsky, E., Engl, V., Reddemann, L., & Emrich, H. M. (2003, November). *Validation of the German version of the Multidimensional Inventory of Dissociation (MID-d)*. Paper presented at annual meeting of the International Society for the Study of Dissociation. Chicago, IL.

Gingrich, H. D. (2004). *Dissociation in a student sample in the Philippines*. Doctoral dissertation. University of the Philippines.

Gleaves, D. H., & Eberenz, K. P. (1995). Assessing dissociative symptoms in eating disordered patients: Construct validation of two self-report measures. *International Journal of Eating Disorders, 18*, 99–102.

Gleaves, D. H., Eberenz, K. P., Warner, M. S., & Fine, C. G. (1995). Measuring clinical and nonclinical dissociation: A comparison of the DES and QED. *Dissociation, 8*, 24–31.

Goldberg, L. R. (1999). The Curious Experiences Survey, A revised version of the Dissociative Experiences Scale: Factor structure, reliability, and relations to demographic and personality variables. *Psychological Assessment, 11*, 134–145.

Gorsuch, R. L. (1983). *Factor analysis* (2nd ed.). Hillsdale, NJ: Lawrence Erlbaum.

Gorsuch, R. L. (1997). Exploratory factor analysis: Its role in item analysis. *Journal of Personality Assessment, 68*, 532–560.

Holtgraves, T., & Stockdale, G. (1997). The assessment of dissociative experiences in a nonclinical population: Reliability, validity, and factor structure of the Dissociative Experiences Scale. *Personality and Individual Differences, 22*, 699–706.

Janet, P. (1889). *L'automatisme psychologique: Essai de psychologie expérimentale sur les formes inférieures de l'activité humaine*. Paris: Félix Alcan.

Jaspers, K. (1963/1997). *General psychopathology* (7th ed.), Volume I (J. Hoenig & M. W. Hamilton, Trans.). Baltimore: Johns Hopkins University Press.

Jaspers, K. (1968). The phenomenological approach in psychopathology. *British Journal of Psychiatry, 114*, 1313–1323.

Kaiser, H. F. (1960). The application of electronic computers to factor analysis. *Educational and Psychological Measurement, 20*, 141–151.

Kaiser, H. F. (1974). An index of factorial simplicity. *Psychometrika, 39*, 31–36.

Kluft, R. P. (1985a). Childhood multiple personality disorder: Predictors, clinical findings, and treatment. In R. P. Kluft (Ed.), *Childhood antecedents of multiple personality* (pp. 168–196). Washington, DC: American Psychiatric Press.

Lilienfeld, S. O., Kirsch, I., Sarbin, T. R., Lynn, S. J., Chaves, J. F., Ganaway, G. K., & Powell, R. A. (1999). Dissociative identity disorder and the sociocognitive model: Recalling the lessons of the past. *Psychological Bulletin, 125*, 507–523.

Loewenstein, R. J. (1991). Psychogenic amnesia and psychogenic fugue: A comprehensive review. In A. Tasman & S. M. Goldfinger (Eds.), *American Psychiatric Press Review of Psychiatry*, Vol. 10 (pp. 189–221). Washington, DC: American Psychiatric Press.

Loewenstein, R. J., & Putnam, F. W. (2004). Dissociative disorders. In B. J. Sadock & V. A. Sadock (Eds.), *Comprehensive textbook of psychiatry* (8th ed., pp. 1844–1901). Baltimore, MD: Lippincott, Williams & Wilkins.

Marmar, C. R., Weiss, D. S., Schlenger, W.E., Fairbank, J. A., Jordon, B. K., Kulka, R. A., & Hough, R. L. (1994). Peritraumatic dissociation and posttraumatic stress in male Vietnam theater veterans. *American Journal of Psychiatry, 151*, 902–907.

McHugh, P. R. (1995). Resolved: Multiple personality disorder is an individually and socially created artifact. Affirmative. *Journal of the American Academy of Child and Adolescent Psychiatry, 34*, 957–959.

Merskey, H. (1992). The manufacture of personalities: The production of multiple personality disorder. *British Journal of Psychiatry, 160*, 327–340.

Montesanto, F. (2004). *Dissociation in an Italian sample*. Unpublished manuscript.

Middleton, W., & Butler, J. (1998). Dissociative identity disorder: An Australian series. *Australian and New Zealand Journal of Psychiatry, 32*, 794–804.

Nijenhuis, E. R. S. (1999). *Somatoform dissociation: Phenomena, measurement, and theoretical issues*. Assen, The Netherlands: Van Gorcum.

Nijenhuis, E. R. S. (2000). Somatoform dissociation: Major symptoms of dissociative disorders. *Journal of Trauma & Dissociation, 1(4)*, 7–29.

Nijenhuis, E. R. S., Spinhoven, P., Van Dyck, R., Van der Hart, O., & Vanderlinden, J. (1996). The development and the psychometric characteristics of the Somatoform Dissociation Questionnaire (SDQ-20). *Journal of Nervous and Mental Disease, 184*, 688–694.

Nijenhuis, E. R. S., Spinhoven, P., Van Dyck, R., Van der Hart, O., & Vanderlinden, J. (1998). Degree of somatoform and psychological dissociation in dissociative disorders is correlated with reported trauma. *Journal of Traumatic Stress, 11*, 711–730.

Nijenhuis, E. R. S., Van der Hart, O, & Kruger, K. (2002). The psychometric characteristics of the Traumatic Experiences Checklist (TEC): First findings among psychiatric patients. *Clinical Psychology and Psychotherapy, 9*, 200–210.

Pain, C., Bluhm, R. L., & Lanius, R. A. (2009). Dissociation in patients with chronic PTSD: Hyperactivation and hypoactivation patterns, clinical and neuroimaging perspectives. In P. F. Dell & J. A. O'Neil (Eds.), *Dissociation and the dissociative disorders: DSM-V and beyond* (pp. 373–382). New York: Routledge.

Putnam, F. W., Helmers, K., & Trickett, P. K. (1993). Development, reliability, and validity of a child dissociation scale. *Child Abuse & Neglect, 17*, 731–741.

Ray, W. J., & Faith, M. (1995). Dissociative experiences in a college age population: Follow-up with 1190 subjects. *Personality and Individual Differences, 18*, 223–230.

Ray, W. J., June, K., Turaj, K., & Lundy, R. (1992). Dissociative experiences in a college population: A factor analytic study of two dissociation scales. *Personality and Individual Differences, 13*, 417–424.

Reinders, A. A. T. S., Nijenhuis, E. R. S., Paans, A. M. J., Korf, J., Willemsen, A. T. M., & Den Boer, J. A. (2003). One brain, two selves. *NeuroImage, 20*, 2119–2125.

Riley, K. C. (1988). Measurement of dissociation. *Journal of Nervous and Mental Disease, 176,* 449–450.

Ross, C. A. (1997). *Dissociative identity disorder: Diagnosis, clinical features, and treatment of multiple personality.* New York: Wiley.

Ross, C. A., Heber, S., Norton, G. R., Anderson, D., Anderson, G., & Barchet, B. (1989b). The Dissociative Disorders Interview Schedule: A structured interview. *Dissociation, 2,* 169–189.

Ross, C. A., Joshi, S., & Currie, R. (1991). Dissociative experiences in the general population: A factor analysis. *Hospital and Community Psychiatry, 42,* 297–301.

Sanders, S. (1986). The perceptual alteration scale: A scale measuring dissociation. *American Journal of Clinical Hypnosis, 29,* 95–102.

Sanders, B., & Green, J. A. (1994). The factor structure of the Dissociative Experiences Scale in college students. *Dissociation, 7,* 23–27.

Schneider, K. (1959). *Clinical psychopathology.* New York: Grune & Stratton.

Schwartz, D. R., Frischholz, E. J., Braun, B. G., & Sachs, R. G. (1991, January). *A confirmatory factor analytic study of the Dissociative Experiences Scale (DES).* Paper presented at the Eighth International Conference on Multiple Personality/Dissociative States. Chicago, IL.

Simeon, D. (2009). Depersonalization Disorder. In P. F. Dell & J. A. O'Neil (Eds.), *Dissociation and the dissociative disorders: DSM-V and beyond* (pp. 435–446). New York: Routledge.

Simeon, D., Knutelska, M., & Dell, P. F. (2001, December). *A pilot study of the Multidimensional Inventory of Dissociation (MID) in depersonalization disorder.* Paper presented at the meeting of the International Society for the Study of Dissociation, New Orleans, LA.

Somer, E., & Dell, P.F. (2005). Development of the Hebrew Multidimensional Inventory of Dissociation (H-MID): A valid and reliable measure of pathological dissociation. *Journal of Trauma & Dissociation, 6(1),* 31–53.

Steinberg, M. (1994). Structured Clinical Interview for DSM-IV Dissociative Disorders *(SCID-D), Revised.* Washington, DC: American Psychiatric Press.

Stockdale, G. D., Gridley, B. E., Balogh, D. W., & Holtgraves, T. (2002). Confirmatory factor analysis of single- and multiple-factor competing models of the Dissociative Experiences Scale in a nonclinical sample. *Assessment, 9,* 94–106.

Vanderlinden, J., van Dyck, R., Vandereycken, W., Vertommen, H., & Verkes, R. J. (1993). The Dissociation Questionnaire (DIS-Q): Development and characteristics of a new self-report questionnaire. *Clinical Psychology & Psychotherapy, 1,* 21–27.

Van IJzendoorn, M., & Schuengel, C. (1996). The measurement of dissociation in normal and clinical populations: Meta-analytic validation of the Dissociative Experiences Scale (DES). *Clinical Psychology Review, 16,* 365–382.

Waller, N. G., Putnam, F. W., & Carlson, E. B. (1996). Types of dissociation and dissociative types: A taxometric analysis of dissociative experiences. *Psychological Methods, 1,* 300–321.

Waller, N. G. (1995). The Dissociative Experiences Scale. In *Twelfth mental measurements yearbook.* Lincoln, NE: Buros Institute of Mental Measurement.

Watkins, J.G., & Watkins, H.H. (1997). *Ego states: Theory and therapy.* New York: Norton.

Wolfradt, U., & Engelmann, S. (1999). Depersonalization, fantasies, and coping behavior. *Journal of Clinical Psychology, 55,* 225–232.

Wright, D. B., & Loftus, E. F. (1999). Measuring dissociation: Comparison of alternative forms of the Dissociative Experiences Scale. *American Journal of Psychology, 112,* 497–519.

Yung, Y., Thissen, D., & McLeod, L. (1999). On the relationship between the higher-order factor model and the hierarchical factor model. *Psychometrika, 64,* 113–128.

45 A Research Agenda for the Dissociative Disorders Field

Vedat Şar, MD
Colin A. Ross, MD

OUTLINE: (NB each section with a subsection entitled 'Recommended research')

Compared to previous decades, there was a marked increase in the quantity of research on Dissociative Disorders from 1984 to 2007. These publications also came from more countries and discussed a wider range of topics than previously (Pope, Barry, Bodkin, & Hudson, 2006; Ross, 1997; Şar, 2006a). A journal dedicated to the field, the *Journal of Trauma and Dissociation*, has been indexed by Medline and PubMed since 2005. A DSM-V Dissociative Disorders Research Planning Conference (RPC), sponsored by the International Society for the Study of Trauma and Dissociation, was held in 2005, 2006, and 2007. This conference, attended by 25 researchers in the field, focused on future research directions and potential input to the DSM-V by committee members. The RPC has prioritized three goals:

1. To critically evaluate the DSM-IV nosology of the Dissociative Disorders
2. To increase the congruence between the International Classification of Diseases (ICD) and the Diagnostic and Statistical Manual of Mental Disorders (DSM), especially concerning Conversion Disorder and Depersonalization Disorder
3. To reduce the DSM's Western cultural bias by integrating common non-Western dissociative presentations within a revised nosology of the Dissociative Disorders

In this chapter, we review several major issues in the Dissociative Disorders field. Based on the RPC's analysis and our own reading of the literature (as of 2008), we make specific recommendations for future research on dissociation and the Dissociative Disorders.

45.1 DID AND COMPLEX DISSOCIATIVE DISORDER

The DSM provides an NOS category for each disorder. The NOS category is designed to account for the small residuum of cases that do not fit any of the specific diagnostic categories. Epidemiological studies of both clinical (Şar, Tutkun, Alyanak, Bakım, & Baral, 2000; Tutkun et al., 1998) and nonclinical populations (Ross, 1991; Şar, Akyüz, & Doğan, 2007) have demonstrated that Dissociative Disorder Not Otherwise Specified (DDNOS) is the most prevalent Dissociative Disorder. Because these studies have consistently found that 40% of diagnosed Dissociative Disorders are DDNOS, it is evident that there is a problem with the DSM-IV nosology of the Dissociative Disorders (Cardeña & Spiegel, 1996; Dell, 2009b; Spiegel & Cardeña, 1991).

DSM-IV lists six examples of DDNOS. Careful analysis of the untoward surplus of DDNOS cases in the epidemiological literature reveals that the great majority of them are cases of DDNOS, example 1 (hereinafter DDNOS-1). DDNOS-1 describes forms of partial DID (Dell, 2009a, 2009b).

Given the dimensional nature of the relationship between DID and DDNOS-1, the RPC has considered two different nosological solutions to the current DSM-IV nosology that unacceptably labels far too many dissociative patients "NOS." First, DID and DDNOS-1 could be included as subtypes of a single diagnostic category—Complex Dissociative Disorder. By this option, Complex Dissociative Disorder would have two subtypes that are distinguished from one another on the basis of the presence or absence of switching between distinct self-states. Second, the RPC considered the nosological option of having two specific disorders at the severe end of the dissociative spectrum: DID and Complex Dissociative Disorder (i.e., DID without switching). It is hoped that future field studies will demonstrate which approach has greater clinical utility and is better supported by the data.

The RPC agreed that the diagnostic criteria for DID and the other Dissociative Disorders should be in greater accord with other sets of criteria in the DSM. Consequently, a monothetic-polythetic set of criteria was proposed for Complex Dissociative Disorder and DID. These criteria are based on four clusters of dissociative symptoms: consciously experienced intrusions, perceptual alterations, amnesia, and alterations of self-state (Dell, 2001, 2002, 2006, 2009a, 2009b). Because motor and sensory dissociative (conversion) symptoms have significant diagnostic discriminative power in many cultures (Nijenhuis et al., 1999; Şar, Akyüz, & Doğan, 2007; Şar, Kundakçı, Kızıltan, Bakım, & Bozkurt, 2000), these somatoform dissociative symptoms may yet be added to the four proposed diagnostic criteria for Complex Dissociative Disorder and DID.

45.1.1 Recommended Research

1. A field trial must now compare the diagnostic efficiency of the criteria of Complex Dissociative Disorder with the current diagnostic criteria for DID and the text description of DDNOS-1. The boundaries and relationships between DID and other complex Dissociative Disorders should be studied in this context.
2. Research must also assess the discriminative power of these new criteria *vis-à-vis* those of other psychiatric disorders—especially Schizophrenia.
3. Research should assess the nature of the relationship between somatoform dissociative symptoms and the four proposed symptom-clusters of Complex Dissociative Disorder and DID.

45.2 DISSOCIATIVE AMNESIA AND DISSOCIATIVE FUGUE

There is much that is uncertain or unknown about Dissociative Amnesia and Dissociative Fugue. Despite patient self-reports of amnesia, Huntjens, Peters, Postma, Woertman, Effting, and Van der Hart (2005) found evidence of intact memory-functioning and recall in DID (however, the material to be recalled in this research was not trauma-related). Markowitsch (1996), on the other hand, reported similarities between organic and psychogenic (i.e., dissociative) retrograde amnesia. He hypothesized that both psychogenic and organic amnesia may be caused by a desynchronization or blockade of trigger mechanisms or pathways. This leads him to propose an "mnestic block syndrome" (Markowitsch, 1999; Markowitsch et al., 1999) related to altered brain metabolism that might include changes in various transmitter and hormonal systems, such as GABA-agonists, glucocorticoids, and acetylcholine.

The main research problem for Dissociative Fugue is the small number of reported cases. Most studies clearly demonstrate that dissociative fugue is a relatively common symptom, but a rare freestanding disorder (Şar et al., 2007; Ross, 1991). When fugue occurs, it is almost invariably part of a Complex Dissociative Disorder such as DID or DDNOS-1. The RPC members considered the possibility of deleting Dissociative Fugue as a specific diagnosis, and subsuming it under Dissociative Amnesia in DSM-V, but came to no final conclusion.

45.2.1 Recommended Research

1. The nature and extent of amnesia in Dissociative Amnesia, DID, and other Dissociative Disorders need to be studied. Chronic and acute forms of amnesia should be differentiated in any such research.
2. New case series of Dissociative Amnesia and Dissociative Fugue must be investigated. Unlike most cases in the previous literature, these cases must be extensively assessed with modern instruments. Careful phenomenological and historical assessment of these cases is essential.

45.3 DEPERSONALIZATION DISORDER

The symptom of depersonalization is common among the Dissociative Disorders. Depersonalization connotes an impairment of a single faculty that Jaspers (1913) called personalization: the experience that all psychological faculties (perception, body sensation, memory retrieval, imagination, thought, feeling, etc.) belong to oneself. Matthias et al. (2007) demonstrated that the detached state of consciousness in Depersonalization Disorder contrasts with certain aspects of mindfulness, a state of consciousness characterized by being in touch with the present moment. It is worth noting that the ICD-10 remains faithful to the ICD-9 and DSM-II in declining to reclassify Depersonalization Disorder as a Dissociative Disorder. In ICD-10 (World Health Organization, 1992), Depersonalization Disorder remains *sui generis*, as one of the "other neurotic disorders."

Psychophysiological studies have provided evidence that Depersonalization Disorder is a distinct form of dissociative psychopathology. Persons with Depersonalization Disorder have a different pattern of hypothalamic-pituitary-adrenal axis dysregulation from patients with PTSD (Simeon, Guralnik, Knutelska, Hollander, & Schmeidler, 2001). Although dissociation accompanied by anxiety was associated with heightened noradrenergic tone, basal norepinephrine declined markedly as the severity of dissociation increased (Simeon, Guralnik, Knutelska, Yehuda, & Schmeidler, 2003); these findings are compatible with the hypothesis of autonomic blunting in Depersonalization Disorder.

A recent study (Guralnik, Giesbrecht, Knutelska, Sirroff, & Simeon, 2007) reports that individuals with Depersonalization Disorder manifest disruptions in early perceptual and attentional processes (compared to normal controls) independent of IQ, anxiety, or depression. Such distinct cognitive impairments lend support to the contention that Depersonalization Disorder is a distinct Dissociative Disorder.

In alcohol-dependent men, dissociation is related to alexithymia—difficulty in identifying feelings (Evren et al., 2008). An epidemiological study reported that no subjects with Somatization Disorder had Depersonalization Disorder (Şar, Akyüz, Doğan, & Öztürk, in press). The relationship between being out of touch with one's feelings (i.e., alexithymia) and being out of touch with one's body (i.e., depersonalization) requires further study (Matthias et al., 2007). In particular, the relationship between these two forms of psychic disconnection and somatization in general should be investigated because somatization can involve anesthesia, paralysis, blindness, deafness, and other symptoms of disconnection from normal bodily sensations and functions.

As is true for other Dissociative Disorders, Depersonalization Disorder is linked to childhood trauma (Matthias et al., 2007; Simeon et al., 2001), although the trauma tends to be less severe than that reported by individuals with DID.

45.3.1 Recommended Research

1. The status of Depersonalization Disorder as a separate dissociation disorder should be documented in studies focusing on neurobiology, long-term follow-up, and treatment outcomes.
2. Studies on interactions among alexithymia, somatization, and dissociation will shed new light on Depersonalization Disorder.
3. Phenomenological studies are needed to delineate qualitative similarities and differences between the dissociative symptoms of Depersonalization Disorder (especially, depersonalization and derealization) and those of complex Dissociative Disorders such as DID and DDNOS-1.

45.4 CONVERSION DISORDER

In an elegant critique of DSM-IV's Somatoform Disorders, Mayou, Kirmayer, Simon, Kroenke, and Sharpe (2005) recently proposed that this section of the manual be dissolved and that its disorders be redistributed to other sections of the DSM. Many clinicians and scholars, including Mayou et al. (2005), argue that Conversion Disorder should be classified with the Dissociative Disorders in DSM-V (Bowman, 2006; Bowman & Markand, 1996; Brown, Cardeña, Nijenhuis, Şar, & Van der Hart, 2007; Kihlstrom, 1994). This reclassification would be consistent with conversion's historical classification (with dissociation) as subtypes of Hysterical Neurosis in DSM-II and ICD-9, a precedent that ICD-10 continues to follow. The RPC unanimously agreed that Conversion Disorder ought to be classified as a Dissociative Disorder in DSM-V, bringing it back into line with the ICD.

Extensive research data support this recommendation. The precise relationship between dissociation and conversion needs to be clarified, however. At present, it is known that conversion is relatively common and that conversion and dissociation frequently co-occur. Among outpatients treated in a primary health care institution in Turkey, the 1-month prevalence of conversion symptoms was 27%; the lifetime prevalence was 48% (Sağduyu, Rezaki, Kaplan, Özgen, & Gürsoy-Rezaki, 1997).

Conversion Disorder is frequently accompanied by other chronic and complex psychiatric disorders (Şar, Akyüz, Kundakçı, Kızıltan, & Doğan, 2004). The overall psychiatric symptom scores of patients with Conversion Disorder are similar to those of general psychiatric patients, indicating high psychiatric comorbidity (Spitzer, Spelsberg, Grabe, Mundt, & Freyberger, 1999). Indeed, a 2-year follow-up showed that 90% of patients with conversion symptoms had at least one other psychiatric disorder in addition to their conversion disorder (Şar et al., 2004). Patients with a conversion symptom who also have a DSM-IV Dissociative Disorder have much higher rates of psychiatric comorbidity, including Somatization Disorder, Dysthymic Disorder, Major Depressive Disorder, Borderline Personality Disorder, self-destructive behavior, suicide attempts, and childhood trauma (Şar et al., 2004).

A high proportion of female primary-care patients report mental health problems and abusive experiences in childhood and adulthood (Coid et al., 2003). This fact makes somatoform presentations of interest for general medicine. For example, pseudoseizures have become a major area of study in neurology (Benbadis, 2005). Pseudoseizure patients report high rates of sexual abuse (Bowman & Markand, 1996), Somatization Disorder (Pribor, Yutzy, Dean, & Wetzel, 1993), other conversion symptoms (Şar et al., 2004) and, not uncommonly, the presence of true epileptic seizures as well (Barry, Atzman, & Morrell, 2000). Fibromyalgia patients have a higher prevalence of dissociation than have other rheumatic patients (Leavitt & Katz, 2003). Finally, 31% to 47% of patients with a conversion symptom have a DSM-IV Dissociative Disorder (Şar et al., 2004; Tezcan et al., 2003). Consistent with these data, a distinction between somatoform dissociation and psychoform dissociation has been proposed (Nijenhuis, Spinhoven, Van Dyck, Van der Hart, & Vanderlinden, 1998). Nijenhuis et al. (1998) contend that both somatoform dissociation and psychoform dissociation should be classified within a single diagnostic category. Such a classification would be congruent with DSM-II's Hysterical Neurosis and ICD-10's Dissociative (Conversion) Disorders.

Traditionally, somatization has been closely linked to culture (e.g., Somer, 2006). The general impression in the literature is that Conversion Disorder is more prevalent in less industrialized countries. This view, however, is not supported by a comparison of Dutch and Turkish patients with a Dissociative Disorder: both samples revealed similar scores for somatoform dissociation. The less industrialized Turkish sample had a higher prevalence only for pseudoseizures (Şar, Kundakçı, Kızıltan, & Doğan, 2000). German studies have reported the prevalence of Conversion Disorder in general medical settings, such as neurological clinics (Spitzer, Freyberger, Kessler, & Kömpf, 1994; Spitzer et al., 1999).

In an epidemiological study in Turkey, all subjects with Dissociative Identity Disorder also had at least one conversion symptom (Şar, Akyüz, & Doğan, 2007). In our view, "conversion" is simply a form of dissociation that affects motor and sensory functions (Nijenhuis, this volume). Accordingly, we think that the difference between conversion and dissociation is merely semantic. We recommend that the DSM-IV characterization of dissociation (i.e., disturbances of identity, consciousness, memory, and perception) be expanded in DSM-V to include dissociative disturbances of motor and sensory functions.

Despite the fascinating opportunity offered by Conversion Disorder to look at the interaction between body and psyche, studies on the biology of conversion symptoms are rather scarce. A case study of Conversion Disorder occurring in an individual with Dissociative Identity Disorder reported that a 15-year conversion blindness was successfully treated with psychotherapy. The authors showed that improvement was accompanied by changes in measures of visual evoked potential (VEP) on switching from one personality state to another, and on recovery from the conversion blindness (Waldvogel, Ullrich, & Strasburger, 2007). In two patients with a gait disturbance due to Conversion Disorder (Yazıcı, Demirci, Demir, & Ertğrul, 2004), a near total absence of sensory evoked potential (SEP) responses on the scalp was documented during the symptomatic periods; SEP normalized after recovery. One cerebral imaging study revealed a left temporal perfusion decrease in four of five patients with Conversion Disorder (Yazıcı & Kostakoğlu, 1998). A volumetric study revealed significantly smaller mean volumes in the left and right basal ganglia and right thalamus with a trend toward a smaller left thalamus volume compared to healthy controls (Atmaca et al., 2006).

45.4.1 Recommended Research

1. Research is needed to further clarify the relationship between conversion and dissociation.
2. Studies of the epidemiology, comorbidity, and long-term course of Conversion Disorder are needed.
3. Brain imaging and neurophysiological studies with Conversion Disorder patients are also needed.

45.5 PERITRAUMATIC DISSOCIATION, DISSOCIATIVE STATES, AND ACUTE DISSOCIATIVE SYNDROMES

Whereas European psychiatry and the ICD emphasize acute and reactive dissociative syndromes, North American psychiatry and the DSM emphasize chronic Dissociative Disorders. Accordingly, there is a need for DSM-V to more adequately address acute dissociative presentations, perhaps by including an acute Dissociative Disorder (with or without psychotic features). Studies in other cultures indicate that such a diagnostic category is warranted (Lewis-Fernandez, Martinez-Taboas, Şar, Patel, & Boatin, 2007).

Measures of *trait* dissociation such as the DES and the Multidimensional Inventory of Dissociation (MID; Dell, 2006) are well-suited to the study of chronic dissociation and treatment outcome research for chronic Dissociative Disorders (Ross, 2005). On the other hand, research on acute or time-limited dissociative episodes requires a measure of *state* dissociation, such as the Clinician-Administered Dissociative States Scale (CADSS; Bremner et al., 1998) or the State Scale of Dissociation (SSD; Kruger & Mace, 2002). Assessment of state dissociation may be especially important for neurophysiological research, treatment outcome studies of acute Dissociative Disorders, and the assessment of somatoform dissociative phenomena (e.g., pseudoseizures), which tend to be transient.

Acute Stress Disorder (ASD) emphasizes dissociative symptoms that occur in response to a recent traumatic experience. Initially called *Brief Reactive Stress Disorder*, ASD was originally proposed to the DSM as one of the Dissociative Disorders. The disorder was renamed, however, and classified as an anxiety disorder because it made little sense for a dissociative disorder to suddenly become an anxiety disorder (i.e., PTSD) when the symptoms lasted for more than 1 month. Peritraumatic dissociation has been proposed to be a marker of long-term psychopathology (Bremner & Brett, 1997).

A recent meta-analysis (Breh & Seidler, 2007) found a significant positive relation between peritraumatic dissociation and PTSD. However, one 4-year prospective study on victims of a fireworks disaster documented no independent predictive value of peritraumatic dissociation for intrusions, avoidance, and PTSD symptom severity (Van der Velden et al., 2006). Apparently, persistent rather than merely peritraumatic dissociation is associated with posttraumatic psychopathology including PTSD and Acute Stress Disorder (Panasetis & Bryant, 2003; Briere et al., 2005).

After reviewing a large set of empirical studies, Van der Hart et al. (2008) conclude that few methodologically sophisticated studies of peritraumatic dissociation have been conducted and that progress depends upon the refinement of the methodological quality of future studies. In addition, and perhaps more importantly, the literature is limited by inadequate and varied operationalizations of peritraumatic dissociation, which affect assessment and data interpretation. Future research should be guided by reevaluated definitions of peritraumatic dissociation (and by assessments that are based on these re-definitions).

45.5.1 Recommended Research

1. Studies of brief dissociative states are sorely needed. Such research should measure both state and trait dissociation.
2. Studies on the effectiveness of short-term interventions for acute dissociative conditions (somatoform, psychoform, and mixed type) should be conducted.
3. The relationship of acute dissociative conditions to underlying trait variables (such as Complex Dissociative Disorder and temperamental features) needs to be studied.

4. The distinctions, overlap, and comorbidity between Acute Stress Disorder, PTSD, and Dissociative Disorders should be studied in future research.
5. Peritraumatic dissociative symptoms do *not* always predict PTSD; accordingly, it is essential to identify the missing factors that explain this somewhat uncertain relationship (between peritraumatic dissociation and PTSD).

45.6 CHILDREN AND ADOLESCENTS

Escher, Romme, Buiks, Delespaul, and Van Os (2002) reported that, among children who hear voices, scores on the Dissociative Experiences Scale (DES; Bernstein & Putnam, 1986) were positively correlated with the likelihood that the voices would persist. These authors, however, misinterpreted the DES as being a measure of psychosis-proneness.

Among psychiatric inpatients under 18 years of age, the Dissociative Disorders rank among the most common clinical presentations—more common than Schizophrenia. Thus, hospitalization of adolescents for frequent impulsive behavior may be due to a Dissociative Disorder (Yargıç, Tutkun, Şar, & Zoroğlu, 1995).

As is true of adults, adolescents with a Dissociative Disorder have significant psychiatric comorbidity. A Finnish study reported that 50% of adolescent dissociative patients have a history of substance abuse (Lipsanen et al., 2004). This rate is higher than that of adult dissociative patients in Turkey, where substance abuse is found in 29% of dissociative inpatients and 22% of dissociative outpatients (Şar et al., 2000; Tutkun et al., 1998). Conversely, there was a 17% incidence of Dissociative Disorders in a large group of treatment-seeking inpatients with drug and/or alcohol abuse in Istanbul (Karadağ, Şar, Tamar-Gürol, Evren, Karagöz, & Erkıran, 2005); 68% of these dissociative patients reported that their dissociative symptoms predated their substance abuse by an average of 3.6 years (range = 1–11 years).

Although Dissociative Disorders may be mistaken for ADHD, or vice versa, the two disorders can be differentiated from each other (Zoroğlu, Şar, Tüzün, Tutkun, & Savaş, 2002; Zoroğlu, Tüzün, Öztürk, & Şar, 2002). A common tetrad of comorbidity includes ADHD, Dissociative Disorder, Bipolar Disorder, and Substance Abuse Disorder. In addition to possible genetic links between ADHD and mood disorders, environmental factors such as trauma may contribute to this pattern of comorbidity.

45.6.1 Recommended Research

1. Given a relatively high prevalence of Dissociative Disorder among child and adolescent psychiatric inpatients, screening studies for Dissociative Disorders in children and adolescents should be conducted.
2. Given high dissociative comorbidity among substance-abusing adolescents, screening studies for Dissociative Disorders in this population should be conducted.
3. Because the differential diagnosis of ADHD versus Dissociative Disorder is frequently difficult, it is important to study relationships among ADHD, trauma, and dissociation.

45.7 SCHIZOTYPY AND DISSOCIATION

Some studies indicate that childhood trauma and dissociation affect the clinical presentation of psychotic disorders. The relationship between dissociation and schizotypy is more contentious. Irwin (2001) finds that schizotypy predicts both pathological and nonpathological dissociation, even controlling for childhood trauma. In contrast, Simeon, Guralnik, Knutelska, and Nelson (2004) find that subjects with Depersonalization Disorder have higher schizotypy scores than healthy controls, but that this difference disappears in Depersonalization Disorder without Axis II comorbidity.

There are reports that many patients with Dissociative Disorders are mistakenly diagnosed as having Schizophrenia (Ross, 2004). Although Schneider (1939/1977) believed his first-rank symptoms to be highly characteristic of schizophrenia, Kluft (1987) and Dell (2006b; Laddis, Dell, Cotton, & Fridley, 2001) found most of them (8 of the 11) to be more common in Dissociative Disorders than in Schizophrenia. Dell (2002) also reported that most dissociative patients experience hallucinations.

Much additional research is required on the relationship between dissociation and schizophrenic psychosis. One study revealed that 57% of patients with Schizophrenia endorse dissociative symptoms sufficient for a DSM-IV Dissociative Disorder diagnosis on the Dissociative Disorders Interview Schedule (DDIS) (Şar et al., 2006). In this study, cluster analysis documented the presence of a subgroup of schizophrenics who have dissociative symptoms and a childhood history of trauma. This finding is compatible with the second author's proposal that there exists a dissociative subtype of schizophrenia (Ross, 2004). Various models have been proposed to explain this overlap between psychosis and dissociation: (1) a qualitative relationship between two categories that are often the same thing (Moskowitz & Corstens, 2007), (2) a syndromal relationship on a continuum (Ross, 2004), and (3) an interaction between two qualitatively distinct psychopathologies (i.e., comorbidity) (Şar & Öztürk, 2008). In some cases, the apparent confusion or overlap between dissociation and psychosis may be due simply to a false positive diagnosis of psychosis and a false negative diagnosis of a dissociative disorder.

45.7.1 Recommended Research

1. Phenomenological research should study similarities and differences between the hallucinations that occur in schizophrenia and the hallucinations that occur in DID.
2. Phenomenological research should study similarities and differences between the Schneiderian first-rank symptoms that occur in schizophrenia and those that occur in DID.
3. Research about the proposed dissociative subtype of schizophrenia should be conducted (e.g., differences between it and other subtypes of schizophrenia, its diagnostic criteria, its response to pharmacotherapy and psychotherapy, and its long-term treatment outcome).
4. Possible interactions between dissociation and psychosis should be investigated (e.g., which, if either, tends to occur first). Dissociation may be a risk factor for, a defense against, or a reaction to, schizophrenia, while being independently related to childhood trauma.

45.8 TRANCE, POSSESSION, AND DISSOCIATIVE PSYCHOSIS

Apart from DDNOS-1 (which we think should be reclassified as a subtype of Complex Dissociative Disorder), DDNOS-4 (i.e., Dissociative Trance Disorder) is probably the most important form of DDNOS. Dissociative Trance Disorder is the only DDNOS example that has its own name and its own DSM-IV research criteria (albeit relegated to the Appendix). This disorder encompasses trance (Ferracuti, Sacco, & Lazzarri, 1996), possession (Chiu, 2000), and dissociative psychosis (Şar & Öztürk, 2009; Van der Hart & Witztum, 2008). Although Dissociative Trance Disorder typically has unique cultural aspects, modern equivalents of this disorder are present in Western cultures as well. Şar et al. (2006) found that the dissociative subgroup of schizophrenics also reported trance and possession phenomena.

The structured interviews for the Dissociative Disorders (i.e., DDIS, SCID-D-R) inquire about trance states and possession experiences, but do not *diagnose* Dissociative Trance Disorder or dissociative psychosis. Research on cross-cultural dissociation, trance, possession, and dissociative psychosis awaits the development of new structured interviews and self-report measures.

In our opinion, the traditional category of hysterical psychosis (e.g., *bouffée délirante polymorphe aigüe*) is best classified as a dissociative psychosis; it is quite distinct from an acute schizophreniform psychosis in its course and treatment response (Tutkun, Yargıç, & Şar, 1996; Şar & Öztürk, 2009; Van der Hart, Witztum, & Friedman, 1992; Hirsch & Hollender, 1969; Hollender & Hirsch, 1964; Öztürk & Göğüş, 1973; Şar, 2006; Van der Hart & Witztum, 2008). To reduce confusion between hysterical psychosis and other psychotic disorders such as schizophrenia, a revised nosology might classify this condition as Acute Dissociative Disorder with psychotic features.

45.8.1 Recommended Research

1. Prevalence data on trance, possession, and dissociative psychosis in various cultures are needed.
2. Differences in the phenomenology of trance possession and dissociative psychosis in various cultures should be investigated.

45.9 SUICIDE AND SELF-DESTRUCTIVE BEHAVIOR

Almost all DID patients are suicidal at some time in their lives; many are chronically suicidal (Ross, 1997; Foote, Smolin, Neft, & Lipschitz, 2008). Although suicidology research has a long tradition, there is little awareness in the field of suicide studies that Dissociative Disorder is one of the leading correlates of suicide attempts.

Interest in self-injurious behavior, especially in adolescence, is growing in the mental health field (Izutsu et al., 2006; Tüzün, Şar, Tutkun, Savaş, & Öztürk, 2003). Interest in the Dissociative Disorders, however, lags far behind that of the general focus on suicide and self-harm. This is unfortunate because the risk for self-harm is quite high among children and adolescents with Dissociative Disorders (Alyanak & Tüzün, 1999; Zoroğlu et al., 2003). Similar observations have been reported among alcohol-dependent men (Evren, Şar, & Evren, 2008).

The field of suicidology needs to incorporate the study of dissociation.

45.9.1 Recommended Research

1. Given the strong link between suicidality and Dissociative Disorders, patients admitted to emergency medical and psychiatric units following a suicide attempt ought to be screened for the presence of a Dissociative Disorder as a basis for further research in this area (Şar et al., 2007).
2. More research is needed into clarifying the precise nature of suicidality and the frequency of acts of self-harm in patients with a Dissociative Disorder.
3. Research should be conducted on the relative contribution of Dissociative Disorders to suicide risk, and the efficacy of treatment for Dissociative Disorders on the reduction of suicidal behavior.

45.10 DEVELOPMENTAL TRAUMAS AND DISSOCIATION

The relationship between reported childhood trauma and dissociation has been documented in both retrospective and prospective studies (e.g., Lewis et al., 1997; Ogawa et al., 1997).The relationship between childhood trauma and dissociation has social and economic implications: for instance, violence (Fonagy, 2004), substance abuse (Karadağ et al., 2006), extreme psychiatric comorbidity, resistance to medical treatment (Ross, 2007), self-mutilation, and suicide all have socioeconomic impacts (Foote et al., 2008). These effects are important, not just for explaining human coping with extreme and/or chronic developmental stress, but also because they have implications for our understanding of and funding of psychotherapy for dissociative and other trauma-related disorders.

Research on the link between trauma and dissociation has been criticized for using uncorroborated and retrospective trauma reports in most studies. Other critics have voiced concern about possible bias in reports owing to the influence of current comorbid psychopathology. Counterbalancing these concerns, on the other hand, childhood trauma may be kept secret, minimized, or denied by some survivors; or, the perpetrator of an interpersonal trauma may be idealized by the victim, and the abuse therefore discounted or not reported. Childhood trauma occurs in a developmental context that makes an understanding of its role in subsequent psychopathology difficult to assess (Gold, 2000), thereby introducing further difficulty in establishing a causal link between childhood trauma and adult dissociation.

Different kinds of childhood trauma result in diverse psychopathological conditions. In one study, childhood abuse was related to a diagnosis of Borderline Personality Disorder (BPD) in early adulthood, whereas childhood neglect was related to a subsequent dissociative disorder (Şar, Akyüz, et al., 2006). It is not known whether these two overlapping syndromes (i.e., BPD and DD) represent two interconnected ways of responding to early traumatization or are qualitatively distinct forms of psychopathology.

Some researchers are now investigating the biological effects of childhood traumatization in relation to dissociation. For instance, brain volume was positively correlated with age of onset of trauma and was negatively correlated with the duration of abuse (DeBellis et al., 2002). However, because this study (like many others) did not assess dissociation, the findings shed no light on the relationship between trauma and dissociation.

45.10.1 Recommended Research

1. Prospective research on corroborated childhood trauma and dissociation should be conducted.
2. Factors leading to both acute and chronic dissociation in response to childhood trauma should be identified and studied.

45.11 ATTACHMENT DYSFUNCTIONS AND DISSOCIATION

Barach (1991) was one of the first theorists to connect dissociation with attachment theory. Liotti (1992) theorized that disorganized infant attachment behavior is a potential precursor to later dissociation. He defined three pathways to dissociation (that depend on various stressors that may occur in conjunction with the ongoing attachment problem). A prospective study documented that, in addition to abuse, both emotional unavailability of the mother (neglect) and disorganized attachment during the first 24 months of life predicted dissociation independently in later life (Ogawa et al., 1997).

After reviewing the literature, Lyons-Ruth et al. (2006) concluded that infant disorganization and disturbed parent-infant dialogue are not the only, or even the most, important factors in the development of dissociation.

Dissociation develops within a complex web of environmental, societal, familial, and genetic factors that interact in ways that are still not well-understood.

45.11.1 Recommended Research

1. Research on subtle traumas in apparently functional families should be conducted.
2. Interacting variables warranting research include family relations, individual vulnerabilities to trauma, and trauma-related processes.
3. Given the widely hypothesized relation between trauma and attachment, research on trauma-related processes in subjects with severe attachment problems in adult life should be conducted.

45.12 AFFECT DYSREGULATION AND DISSOCIATION

Mood disorder is probably the most frequent diagnosis in clinical psychiatry, but not all depressive or anxious clinical presentations are due to a primary mood disorder. We know, for example, that attenuated forms of depression and bipolar disorder in both children and adults may be due to another primary disorder such as Borderline Personality Disorder (McKinnon & Pies, 2006). This can also be the case with Dissociative Disorders and other trauma-related syndromes that cause affective dysregulation (Van der Kolk et al., 1996). Mood stabilizers and antidepressant medications may not be as effective in such cases.

45.12.1 Recommended Research

1. Complex Dissociative Disorders should be compared to nondissociative primary Mood Disorders using various assessment measures, including biological measures. This ought to clarify the distinct features of secondary depression and suicidality in complex Dissociative Disorders.
2. Mood disorders in dissociative patients ought to be studied over time. This would clarify differences between complex Dissociative Disorders and primary Mood Disorders.
3. All mood disorder research (child and adult) ought to include measures of trauma and dissociation. This would distinguish traumatized and dissociative subgroups from subjects with primary Mood Disorder.

45.13 DISSOCIOGENIC EFFECTS OF CULTURE, SOCIETY, AND THE FAMILY

Proponents of the "sociocognitive model" have routinely stated that Dissociative Disorders are iatrogenic or an artifact of contamination, demand characteristics, and/or suggestive influences (e.g., Spanos, 1994). Nevertheless, we insist that a sociocognitive contribution to the etiology of Dissociative Disorders does *not* necessarily imply iatrogenesis or contamination. Consider the following issues.

Aside from the diverse effects of local cultures on dissociation, does society, *qua* society, have a dissociogenic effect on its members? The dissociative disorders field could benefit from a greater emphasis on the causal role of social factors within the biopsychosocial model (Şar & Öztürk, 2007). Potentially dissociogenic social traumas include war, famine, poverty, cultural disintegration, and pervasive orphans (due to AIDS).

Years ago, family theories of schizophrenia produced several interesting (and controversial) concepts (e.g., pseudomutuality, the double-bind, marital schism, and the schizophrenogenic mother). These concepts may actually be more relevant to families of dissociative patients than to families of schizophrenic patients (Şar & Öztürk, 2005). A related area of interest is subtle dissociation in family members or in the family system as a whole. In contrast to previous reports of a high transgenerational incidence of Dissociative Disorders (Braun, 1985; Kluft, 1984), a recent family study on first-degree relatives of dissociative patients found that none of the family members had a Dissociative Disorder (Öztürk & Şar, 2005). It may be that some "apparently normal" families of dissociative patients are, in fact, characterized by denial, projection, disavowed dissociation, and similar dysfunctional defenses. Additional studies of the family members of Dissociative Disorder patients are needed.

45.13.1 Recommended Research

1. Research should investigate the individual and interactional psychopathology of dissociative patients' families of origin. Family rules and interactions leading to hidden or disavowed developmental traumas and consequent dissociative psychopathology should be investigated.
2. Cross-cultural research on the prevalence of different forms of childhood trauma—including social trauma such as war, famine, and poverty—should be conducted.

45.14 BIOLOGY OF DISSOCIATIVE DISORDERS

Biological research on the Dissociative Disorders is still in its infancy, but the frequency of such studies has increased recently. Brain imaging, neurochemistry, and genetic evaluation are among the areas of current study.

Brain imaging studies on Dissociative Disorders have focused on two issues: the brain imaging correlates of dissociation *per se*, and the brain imaging differences between dissociative patients and normal controls (or other psychiatric patients).

Significant brain imaging differences have been found between (1) different types of dissociative parts of the patient's personality in DID patients (Reinders et al., 2003, 2006; Nijenhuis & Den Boer, this volume); (2) dissociative responses and nondissociative responses to trauma-related scripts in PTSD patients' responses to triggers (Lanius et al., 2002); (3) perfusion before versus perfusion during switching in DID patients (Tsai, Condie, Wu, & Chang, 1999); and (4) the cerebral perfusion of dissociative patients versus that of normal controls (Şar, Ünal, Kızıltan, Kundakçı, & Öztürk, 2001; Şar, Ünal, & Öztürk, 2007).

Forrest (2001) proposed a neurodevelopmental model for understanding DID. The orbitofrontal lobe has been hypothesized to be affected by early trauma (Shore, 1996). Consistent with these hypotheses of Forrest and Shore, DID patients have exhibited orbitofrontal hypoperfusion in two studies (Şar et al., 2001, 2007). A recent study has demonstrated that impairment in the orbitofrontal cortex may also contribute to some core characteristics of Borderline Personality Disorder, especially impulsivity (Berlin, Rolls, & Iversen, 2005).

An initial MRI study has established that DID patients have smaller hippocampi and amygdalæ than normal controls, but replication of this finding is required (Vermetten, Schmal, Lindner, Loewenstein, & Bremner, 2006). Ehling, Nijenhuis, and Krikke (2008) also found reduced volumes in the parahippocampal gyrus of individuals with DID and strong correlations between reduction of parahippocampal volume and both psychoform and somatoform dissociation.

Studies on the possible genetic roots of Dissociative Disorders are rather scarce. One study showed no relationship between dissociation and temperamental or characterological features in a male alcohol dependency population (Evren, Şar, & Dalbudak, 2008). Grabe et al. (1999), in contrast, found a genetic contribution to character traits such as high transcendence and low self-directedness. In a study of patients with Obsessive Compulsive Disorder, Lochner et al. (2004) reported no significant difference between high- and low-dissociation groups in genetic polymorphisms involved in monoamine function. In a subsequent study, Lochner et al. (2007) found that physical neglect and the 5-HTT genotype jointly play a role in predicting dissociation in Obsessive Compulsive Disorder. The findings to date on the genetics of dissociation, then, are inconclusive.

45.14.1 Recommended Research

1. Comparisons of biological variables in dissociative patients and patients with other nondissociative psychiatric disorders (especially mood disorders and schizophrenia) would effectively test the validity of the Dissociative Disorders as a diagnostic grouping.
2. Studies of dissociation ought to include concurrent neuropsychological measures.
3. Brain imaging studies may document neural changes that accompany positive treatment responses in dissociative disordered patients.
4. Genetic studies of dissociation should take childhood trauma into account.

45.15 DISSOCIATIVE DISORDERS AS A CONFOUNDING FACTOR; COMORBIDITY

The lack of a Dissociative Disorders module in widely used psychiatric assessment instruments (e.g., SCID, CIDI) has generated a near-total neglect of dissociation for many decades. This neglect has inevitably affected, in unknown ways, research on samples of *other* disorders, whose comorbidity with Dissociative Disorder was not assessed (Şar & Ross, 2006). From the perspectives of both diagnosis and treatment, studies concerning childhood trauma need to assess dissociation. Comorbidity in psychiatry is especially related to certain risk factors, two of which are trauma and dissociation. A 12-month follow-up of mood, anxiety, and substance use disorders in the general population demonstrated that the odds ratios for parental psychiatric history and childhood trauma were higher for individuals with comorbid conditions than for those with only one disorder (De Graaf, Bijl, Simit, Vollebergh, & Spijker, 2002).

The presence of dissociation or a childhood history of trauma can compromise the effectiveness of pharmacological and behavioral treatment (even those that are considered to be the most effective for the disorder in question). This pattern has been observed in studies of Obsessive Compulsive Disorder (Rufer et al., 2006) and Major Depressive Episode (Nemeroff et al., 2003).

Dissociative Disorder comorbidity studies have been conducted for substance abuse (Karadağ et al., 2005), Borderline Personality Disorder (Ross, 2007; Şar, Akyüz, Kuğu, Öztürk, & Ertem-Vehid, 2006; Şar & Öztürk, 2003; Zanarini, Ruser, Frankenburg, & Hennen, 2000), Conversion Disorder (Şar et al., 2004), Obsessive Compulsive Disorder (Lochner et al., 2004), Social Phobia (Evren, Şar, Dalbudak, Öncü, & Çakmak, in press; Michal et al., 2005), and Schizophrenia (Holowka, King, Sahep, Pukall, & Brunet, 2003; Ross, 2004; Ross & Keyes, 2004; Şar & Öztürk, 2009; Şar et al., 2006).

45.15.1 Recommended Research

1. The phenomenological overlap between complex Dissociative Disorders and DSM-IV Borderline Personality Disorder requires further investigation. It would also be fruitful to study the degree of structural dissociation of the personality in both disorders, if this could be operationalized (Van Der Hart, Nijenhuis, & Steele, 2006).
2. Follow-up studies, family studies, treatment studies, and so on should assess for comorbid Dissociative Disorder.
3. Treatment strategies for common comorbidity patterns should be developed and tested in treatment outcome studies.

45.16 EPIDEMIOLOGICAL STUDIES AND FIELD TRIALS

Two large-scale epidemiological studies using the DDIS in Canada and Turkey have documented that the community prevalence of DSM-III-R and DSM-IV Dissociative Disorders is above 10% (Ross, 1991; Şar et al., 2007). A recent study on a U.S. population revealed a prevalence of 9.1% (Johnson, Cohen, Kasen, & Brook, 2006). Two Turkish epidemiological studies screened for conversion symptoms (somatoform dissociation) via different methods; they found lifetime prevalences of 5.6% (both genders) and 48.7% (women only) in the general population (Deveci et al., 2007; Şar, Akyüz, Doğan, & Öztürk, in press).

45.16.1 Recommended Research

1. Epidemiological studies in a wide range of countries are required in order to understand worldwide variations in the features and prevalence of Dissociative Disorders.
2. Major epidemiological studies, such as the Epidemiological Catchment Area (ECA) study and the National Comorbidity Surveys (NCS), have not assessed the presence of Dissociative Disorders. In the future, all such major epidemiological studies should include a module for diagnosing the Dissociative Disorders.
3. Major diagnostic instruments such as the Structured Clinical Interview for the DSM-IV Disorders (SCID) and the Composite International Diagnostic Interview (CIDI), do not include a Dissociative Disorders module. It is urgent that Dissociative Disorders researchers collaborate with the developers of these instruments so that future revisions of the SCID and the CIDI include a Dissociative Disorders module.

45.17 TREATMENT OUTCOME STUDIES

The ICD-10 (World Health Organization, 1992) and the DSM-IV have some important differences regarding the Dissociative Disorders. In general, ICD-10 assumes Dissociative Disorders to be acute and time-limited, whereas DSM-IV assumes them to be chronic. The *Treatment Guidelines for Dissociative Identity Disorder* of *The International Society for the Study of Trauma & Dissociation* are in keeping with the DSM-IV interpretation (Chu, 2006).

Prospective treatment outcome studies concerning the psychotherapy of Dissociative Disorders are rather scarce, and deal only with DID (Ellason & Ross, 1996, 1997; Ross, 2005; Ross & Burns, 2007; Ross & Dua, 1993; Ross & Ellason, 2001; Ross & Haley, 2004). These studies are based on the second author's Trauma Model Therapy (Ross, 2007). Current neurobiological theories of dissociation suggest a possible role of glutamate in at least some dissociative symptoms, warranting further pharmacological investigation (Loewenstein, 2005).

The existing prospective treatment outcome studies for DID demonstrate a significant reduction in a broad range of comorbid symptoms in response to acute hospitalization, with further improvement at 3-month and 2-year follow-ups (Ross, 2005). The primary methodological limitation of these studies is their lack of randomization and lack of a comparison treatment condition.

45.17.1 Recommended Research

1. A much larger body of treatment outcome research is needed, both for DID and for the other Dissociative Disorders. There is a need for both short-term replication of existing studies and for multicenter, randomized controlled studies of manualized therapies for the Dissociative Disorders.

45.18 SUMMARY AND CONCLUSIONS

The study of dissociation and its links to childhood trauma have implications for the stress-diathesis model of general psychiatry. These matters are central to the emerging subspecialty of psycho-traumatology. For reasons outlined in this chapter, dissociation should be an important consideration for clinicians and researchers of all professional backgrounds, including psychiatry, psychology, and social work. Dissociation and the Dissociative Disorders should be routinely measured in a wide range of future research studies, in general medicine, and in the mental health field.

REFERENCES

Alyanak, B., & Tüzün, Ü. (1999). İntihar girişimi olan çocuklarda dissosiyatif bozukluk: olgu sunumu (Dissociative disorders in children who attempted suicide: case presentations). *Journal of Istanbul Faculty of Medicine, 62*, 4.

Atmaca, M., Aydın, A., Tezcan, E., Poyraz, E. K., & Kara, B. (2006). Volumetric investigations of brain regions in patient with conversion disorder. *Progress in Neuropsychopharmacology & Biological Psychiatry, 30,* 708–713.

Barach, P. M. (1991). Multiple personality disorder as an attachment disorder. *Dissociation, 4*, 117–123.

Barry, J. J., Atzman, O., & Morrell, M. J. (2000). Discriminating between epileptic and nonepileptic events: The utility of hypnotic seizure induction. *Epilepsia, 41*, 81–84.

Benbadis, S.R. (2005). The problem of psychogenic symptoms: Is the psychiatric community in denial? *Epilepsy & Behavior, 6*, 9–14.

Berlin, H. A., Rolls, E. T., & Iversen, S. D. (2005). Borderline personality disorder, impulsivity, and the orbitofrontal cortex. *American Journal of Psychiatry, 162*, 1–14.

Bernstein, E. M., & Putnam, F. W. (1986). Development, reliability, and validity of a dissociation scale. *Journal of Nervous & Mental Disease, 174*, 727–735.

Bowman, E. S. (2006). Why conversion seizures should be classified as a dissociative disorder. *Psychiatric Clinics of North America, 29*, 185–211.

Bowman, E. S., & Markand, O. N. (1996). Psychodynamics and psychiatric diagnoses of pseudoseizure subjects. *American Journal of Psychiatry, 153*, 57–63.

Braun, B. G. (1985). The transgenerational incidence of dissociation and multiple personality disorder: A preliminary report. In R. Kluft (Ed.), *Childhood antecedents of multiple personality* (pp. 127–150). Washington, DC: American Psychiatric Press.

Breh, D. C., & Seidler, G. H. (2007). Is peritraumatic dissociation a risk factor for PTSD. *Journal of Trauma and Dissociation, 8(1)*, 53–69.

Bremner, J. D., & Brett, E. (1997). Trauma-related dissociative states in long-term psychopathology in posttraumatic stress disorder. *Journal of Traumatic Stress, 10,* 37–49.

Bremner, J. D., Krystal, J. H., Putnam, F. W., Southwick, S. M., Marmar, C., Charney, D. S., et al. (1998). Measurement of dissociative states with the Clinician-Administered Dissociative States Scale (CADSS). *Journal of Traumatic Stress, 11*, 125–136.

Briere, J., Scott, C., & Weathers, F. (2005). Peritraumatic and persistent dissociation in the presumed etiology of PTSD. *American Journal of Psychiatry, 162,* 2295–2301.

Brown, R. J., Cardeña, E., Nijenhuis, E. R. S., Şar, V., & Van der Hart, O. (2007). Should conversion disorder be reclassified in the DSM-V as a dissociative disorder. *Psychosomatics, 48*, 369–378.

Cardeña, E., & Spiegel, D. (1996). Diagnostic issues, criteria, and comorbidity of dissociative disorders. In L. K. Michelson & W. J. Ray (Eds.), *Handbook of dissociation: Theoretical, empirical, and clinical perspectives* (pp. 227–250). New York: Plenum Press.

Chiu, S. N. (2000). Historical, religious and medical perspectives of possession phenomenon. *Hong Kong Journal of Psychiatry, 10*, 14–18.

Chu, J., Loewenstein R., Dell, P. F., Barach, P. M., Somer, E., Kluft, R. P., Gelinas, D. J., Van der Hart, O., Dalenberg, C. J., Nijenhuis, E. R. S., Bowman, E. S., Boon, S., Goodwin, J., Jacobson, M., Ross, C. A., Şar, V., Fine, J. G., Frankel, A. S., Coons, P. M., Courtois, C. A., Gold, S. N., & Howell, E. (2005). Guidelines for treating dissociative identity disorder in adults. *Journal of Trauma & Dissociation, 6(4)*, 69–149.

Coid, J., Petruckevitch, A., Chung, W. S., Richardson, J., Moorey, S., & Feder, G. (2003). Abusive experiences and psychiatric morbidity in women primary care attenders. *British Journal of Psychiatry, 183*, 332–339.

De Bellis, M. D., Keshavan, M. S., Shifflett, H., Iyengar, S., Beers, S. R., Hall, J., et al. (2002). Brain structures in pediatric maltreatment-related posttraumatic stress disorder: a sociodemographically matched study. *Biological Psychiatry, 52,* 1066–1078.

De Graaf, R., Bijl, R. V., Simit, F., Vollebergh, W. A. M., & Spijker, J. (2002). Risk factors for 12-month comorbidity of mood, anxiety, and substance use disorders: findings from the Netherlands Mental Health Survey and Incidence Study. *American Journal of Psychiatry, 159*, 620–629.

Dell, P. F. (2001). Why the diagnostic criteria for dissociative identity disorder should be changed. *Journal of Trauma & Dissociation, 2(1),* 7–37.

Dell, P. F. (2002). Dissociative phenomenology of dissociative identity disorder. *Journal of Nervous & Mental Disease, 190,* 10–15.

Dell, P. F. (2006a). The Multidimensional Inventory of Dissociation (MID): A comprehensive measure of pathological dissociation. *Journal of Trauma & Dissociation, 7(2),* 77–106.

Dell, P. F. (2006b). A new model of dissociative identity disorder. *Psychiatric Clinics of North America, 29*, 1–26.

Dell, P. F. (2009a). The long struggle to diagnose multiple personality disorder (MPD): I. MPD. In P. F. Dell & J. A. O'Neil (Eds.), *Dissociation and the dissociative disorders: DSM-V and beyond* (pp. 383–402). New York: Routledge.

Dell, P. F. (2009b). The long struggle to diagnose multiple personality disorder: II. Partial forms. In P. F. Dell & J. A. O'Neil (Eds.), *Dissociation and the dissociative disorders: DSM-V and beyond* (pp. 403–428). New York: Routledge.

Deveci, A., Taşkın, O., Dinç, G., Yılmaz, H., Demet, M. M., Erbay-Dündar, et al. (2007). Prevalence of pseudoneurologic conversion disorder in an urban community in Manisa, Turkey. *Social Psychiatry & Psychiatric Epidemiology, 42,* 857–864.

Ehling, T., Nijenhuis, E. R., & Krikke, A. P. (2008). Volume of discrete brain structures in complex dissociative disorders: preliminary findings. *Progress in Brain Research,* 167, 307–310.

Ellason, J. W., & Ross, C. A. (1996). Millon Clinical Multiaxial Inventory-II follow-up of patients with dissociative identity disorder. *Psychological Reports, 78*, 707–716.

Ellason, J. W., & Ross, C. A. (1997). Two-year follow-up of inpatients with dissociative identity disorder. *American Journal of Psychiatry, 154*, 832–839.

Escher, S., Romme, M., Buiks, A., Delespaul, P., & Van Os, J. (2002). Independent course of childhood auditory hallucinations: a sequential 3-year follow-up study. *British Journal of Psychiatry, 181 (suppl. 43),* 10–18.

Evren, C., Şar, V., & Dalbudak, E. (2008). Temperament, character, and dissociation among detoxified male inpatients with alcohol dependency. *Journal of Clinical Psychology, 64,* 717–727.

Evren, C., Şar, V., Dalbudak, E., Öncü, F., & Çakmak, D. (in press). Social anxiety and dissociation among male patients with alcohol dependency. *Psychiatry Research.*

Evren, C., Şar, V., Evren, B. (2008). Self-mutilation among male patients with alcohol dependency: the role of dissociation. *Comprehensive Psychiatry, 49(5),* 489–495.

Evren, C., Şar, V., Evren, B., Semiz, U., Dalbudak, E., & Çakmak, D. (2008). Dissociation and alexithymia among men with alcoholism. *Psychiatry and Clinical Neurosciences, 62*, 40–47.

Ferracuti, S., Sacco, R., & Lazzari, R. (1996). Dissociative trance disorder. Clinical and Rorschach findings in ten persons reporting demon possession and treated by exorcism. *Journal of Personality Assessment, 66*, 525–539.

Fonagy, P. (2004). Early-life trauma and the psychogenesis and prevention of violence. *Annals of New York Academy of Sciences, 1036,* 181–200.

Foote, B., Smolin, Y., Neft, D. I., & Lipschitz, D. (2008). Dissociative disorders and suicidality in psychiatric outpatients. *Journal of Nervous & Mental Disease, 196*, 29–36.

Forrest, K. A. (2001). Toward an etiology of dissociative identity disorder – A neurodevelopmental approach. *Consciousness & Cognition, 10*, 259–293.

Gold, S. (2000). *Not trauma alone: Therapy for child abuse survivors in family and social context.* Philadelphia, PA: Brunner Routledge.

Grabe, H. J., Spitzer, C., & Freyberger, H. J. (1999). Relationship of dissociation to temperament and character in men and women. *American Journal Psychiatry, 156,* 1811–1813.

Guralnick, O., Giesbrecht, T., Knutelska, M., Sirroff, B., & Simeon, D. (2007). Cognitive functioning in depersonalization disorder. *Journal of Nervous and Mental Disease, 195*, 983–988.

Hirsch, S. J., & Hollender, M. H. (1969). Hysterical psychosis: clarification of the concept. *American Journal of Psychiatry, 125*, 909–915.

Hollender, M. H., & Hirsch, S. J. (1964). Hysterical psychosis. *American Journal of Psychiatry, 120*, 1066–1074.

Holowka, D. V., King, S., Sahep, D., Pukall, M., & Brunet, A. (2003). Childhood abuse and dissociative symptoms in adult schizophrenia. *Schizophrenia Research, 60*, 87–90.

Huntjens, R. J. C., Peters, M. L., Postma, A., Woertman, L., Effting, M., & Van der Hart, O. (2005). Transfer of newly acquired stimulus valence between identities in dissociative identity disorder. *Behaviour Research & Therapy, 43*, 243–255.

Irwin, H. J. (2001). The relationship between dissociative tendencies and schizotypy: An artifact of childhood trauma? *Journal of Clinical Psychology, 57*, 331–342.

Izutsu, T., Shimotsu, S., Matsumoto, T., Okada, T., Kikuchi, A., Kojimoto, M., et al. (2006). Deliberate self-harm and childhood hyperactivity in junior high school students. *European Journal of Child & Adolescent Psychiatry, 15,* 172–176.

Jaspers, K. (1913). *Allgemeine Psychopathologie* [General Psychopathology]. Berlin: Springer/Verlag.

Johnson, J. G., Cohen, P., Kasen, S., & Brook, J. S. (2006). Dissociative disorders among adults in the community, impaired functioning, and axis I and II comorbidity. *Journal of Psychiatry Research, 40*, 131–140.

Karadağ, F., Şar, V., Tamar-Gürol, D., Evren, C., Karagöz, M., & Erkıran, M. (2005). Dissociative disorders among inpatients with drug or alcohol dependency. *Journal of Clinical Psychiatry, 66,* 1247–1253.

Kihlstrom, J. F. (1994). One hundred years of hysteria. In S. J. Lynn & J. W. Rhue (Eds.), *Dissociation: Clinical and theoretical perspectives* (pp. 365–394). New York Guilford Press.

Kluft, R. P. (1984). Multiple personality in childhood. *Psychiatric Clinics of North America, 7*, 121–134.

Kluft, R. P. (1987). First rank symptoms as a diagnostic clue to multiple personality disorder. *American Journal of Psychiatry, 144*, 293–298.

Kruger, C., & Mace, C. J. (2002). Psychometric validation of the State Scale of Dissociation (SSD). *Psychology & Psychotherapy, 75*, 33–51.

Laddis, A., Dell, P.F., Cotton, M., & Fridley, D.A. (December, 2001). *A comparison of the dissociative experiences of patients with schizophrenia and patients with DID*. Paper presented at the 18th International Fall Conference of the International Society for the Study of Dissociation, New Orleans, Louisiana.

Lanius, R. A., Williamson, P. C., Boksman, K., Densmore, M., Gupta, M., Neufeld, R. W. J., et al. (2002). Brain activation during script-driven imagery induced dissociative responses in PTSD: A functional magnetic imaging investigation. *Biological Psychiatry, 52,* 305–311.

Leavitt, F., & Katz, R. S. (2003). The dissociative factor in symptom reports of rheumatic patients with and without fibromyalgia. *Journal of Clinical Psychology in Medical Settings, 10,* 259–266.

Lewis, D.O., Yeager, C.A., Swica, Y., Pincus, J.H., Lewis, M. (1997). Objective documentation of child abuse and dissociation in 12 murderers with dissociative identity disorder. *American Journal of Psychiatry, 154,* 1703–1710.

Lewis-Fernandez, R., Martinez-Taboas, A., Şar, V., Patel, S., Boatin, A. (2007). The cross-cultural assessment of dissociation. In: J. P. Wilson & C. So-kum Tang (Eds.), *Cross-cultural assessment of psychological trauma and PTSD*, (pp. 279–318). New York: Springer Publications.

Liotti, G. (1992). Disorganized/disoriented attachment in the etiology of the dissociative disorders. *Dissociation, 5,* 196–204.

Lipsanen, T., Korkeila, J., Peltola, P., Järvinen, J., Langen, K., & Lauerma, H. (2004). Dissociative disorders among psychiatric patients: comparison with a nonclinical sample. *European Psychiatry, 19*, 53–55.

Lochner, C., Seedat, S., Hemmings, S. M. J., Kinnear, C. J., Corfield, V. A., Niehaus, D. J. H., et al. (2004). Dissociative experiences in obsessive-compulsive disorder and trichotillomania: clinical and genetic findings. *Comprehensive Psychiatry, 45*, 384–391.

Lochner, C., Sedat, S., Hemmings, S.M., Moolman-Smook, S.C., Kidd, M., Stein, D.J. (2007). Investigating the possible effects of trauma experiences and 5-HTT on the dissociative experiences of patients with OCD using path analysis and multiple regression. *Neuropsychobiology, 56,* 6–13.

Loewenstein, R. J. (2005). Pharmacologic treatments for dissociative identity disorder. *Psychiatric Annals, 35,* 666–673.

Lyons-Ruth, K., Dutra, L., Schuder, M.R., Bianchi, I. (2006). From infant attachment disorganization to adult dissociation: Relational adaptations or traumatic experiences? *Psychiatric Clinics of North America , 29,* 63–86.

Markowitsch, H. J. (1996). Retrograde amnesia: Similarities between organic and psychogenic forms. *Neurology, Psychiatry & Brain Research, 4*, 1–8.

Markowitsch, H. J. (1999). Functional neuroimaging correlates of functional amnesia. *Memory, 7*, 561–583.

Markowitsch, H. J., Kessler, J., Russ, M. O., Frölich, L., Schneider, B., & Maurer, K. (1999). Mnestic block syndrome. *Cortex, 35*, 219–230.

Matthias, M., Beutel, M. E., Jordan, J., Zimmermann, M., Wolters, S., & Heidenreich, T. (2007). Depersonalization, mindfulness, and childhood trauma. *Journal of Nervous and Mental Disease, 195*, 693–696.

Mayou, R., Kirmayer, L. J., Simon, G., Koenke, K., & Sharpe, M. (2005). Somatoform disorders: Time for a new approach in DSM-V. *American Journal of Psychiatry, 167*, 847–855.

McKinnon, D. F., & Pies, R. (2006). Affective instability as rapid cycling: Theoretical and clinical implications for borderline personality and bipolar spectrum disorders. *Bipolar Disorders, 8,* 1–14.

Michal, M., Kaufhold, J., Grabhorn, R., Krakow, K., Overbeck, G., & Heidenreich, T. (2005). Depersonalization and social anxiety. *Journal of Nervous & Mental Disease, 193*, 629–632.

Moskowitz, A., & Corstens, D. (2007). Auditory hallucinations: Psychotic symptom or dissociative experience. *Psychological Trauma, 6,* 35–63.

Nemeroff, C. B., Heim, C. M., Thase, M. E., Klein, D. N., Rush, A. J., Schatzberg, A. F., et al. (2003). Differential responses to psychotherapy versus pharmacotherapy in patients with chronic forms of major depression and childhood trauma. *Proceedings of the National Academy of Sciences (USA), 100*, 14, 293–296.

Nijenhuis, E. R. S. (2009). Somatoform dissociation and somatoform dissociative disorders. In P. F. Dell & J. A. O'Neil (Eds.), *Dissociation and the dissociative disorders: DSM-V and beyond* (pp. 259–275). New York: Routledge.

Nijenhuis, E. R. S., & Den Boer, J. A. (2009). Psychobiology of traumatization and trauma-related structural dissociation of the personality. In P. F. Dell & J. A. O'Neil (Eds.), *Dissociation and the dissociative disorders: DSM-V and beyond* (pp. 337–365). New York: Routledge.

Nijenhuis, E. R. S., Spinhoven, P., Van Dyck, R., Van der Hart, O., & Vanderlinden J. (1998). Degree of somatoform and psychological dissociation in dissociative disorder is correlated with reported trauma. *Journal of Traumatic Stress, 11*, 711–730.

Nijenhuis, E. R. S., Van Dyck, R., Spinhoven, P., Van der Hart, O., Chatrou, M., Vanderlinden, J., et al. (1999). Somatoform dissociation discriminates among diagnostic categories over and above general psychopathology. *Australian & New Zealand Journal of Psychiatry, 33,* 511–520.

Ogawa, J. R., Sroufe, L. A., Weinfield, N. S., Carlson, E. A., & Egeland, B. (1997). Development and the fragmented self: Longitudinal study of dissociative symptomatology in a nonclinical sample. *Development and Psychopathology, 9,* 855–879.

Öztürk, E., & Şar, V. (2006). Apparently normal family. A contemporary agent of transgenerational trauma and dissociation. *Journal of Trauma Practice, 4(3–4)*, 287–303.

Öztürk, O. M., & Göğüş, A. (1973). Ağir regressif belirtiler gösteren histerik psikozlar [Hysterical psychoses presenting with severe regressive symptoms]. *Proceedings of the 9th National Conference of Psychiatry & Neurology* (pp. 155–164). Ankara, Turkey.

Panasetis, P., & Bryant, R. A. (2003). Peritraumatic versus persistent dissociation in acute stress disorder. *Journal of Traumatic Stress, 16*, 563–566.

Pope, H. G., Jr., Barry, S., Bodkin, A., & Hudson, J. I. (2006). Tracking scientific interest in the dissociative disorders: A study of scientific publication output 1984–2003. *Psychotherapy & Psychosomatics, 75*, 19–24.

Pribor, E. F., Yutzy, S. H., Dean, J. T., & Wetzel, R. D. (1993). Briquet's syndrome, dissociation, and abuse. *American Journal of Psychiatry, 150*, 1507–1511.

Reinders, A. A. T. S., Nijenhuis, E. R. S., Paans, A. M. J., Korf, J., Willemsen, A. T. M., & Den Boer, J. A. (2003). One brain, two selves. *NeuroImage, 20*, 2119–2125.

Ross, C. A. (1991). Epidemiology of multiple personality disorder and dissociation. *Psychiatric Clinics of North America, 14*, 503–517.

Ross, C.A. (1997). *Dissociative identity disorder: Diagnosis, clinical features, and treatment of multiple personality* (2nd ed.). New York: John Wiley & Sons.

Ross, C. A. (2004). *Schizophrenia – Innovations in diagnosis and treatment.* New York: The Haworth Press.

Ross, C. A. (2005). A proposed trial of dialectical behavior therapy and trauma model therapy. *Psychological Reports, 96*, 901–911.

Ross, C. A. (2007). *The trauma model. A solution to the problem of comorbidity in psychiatry.* Richardson, TX: Manitou Communications.

Ross, C. A., & Burns, S. (2007). Acute stabilization in a trauma program: A pilot study. *Journal of Psychological Trauma, 6*, 20–28.

Ross, C. A., & Dua, V. (1993). Psychiatric health care costs of multiple personality disorder. *American Journal of Psychotherapy, 47*, 103–112.

Ross, C. A., & Ellason, J. W. (2001). Acute stabilization in an inpatient trauma program. *Journal of Trauma & Dissociation, 2(2)*, 83–87.

Ross, C. A., & Haley, C. (2004). Acute stabilization and three-month follow-up in a trauma program. *Journal of Trauma & Dissociation, 5(1)*, 103–112.

Ross, C. A., & Keyes, B. (2004). Dissociation and schizophrenia. *Journal of Trauma & Dissociation, 5(3)*, 69–83.

Rufer, M., Held, D., Cremer, J., Fricke, S., Moritz, S., Peter, H., & Hand, I. (2006). Dissociation as a predictor of cognitive behavior therapy outcome in patients with obsessive-compulsive disorder. *Psychotherapy & Psychosomatics, 75*, 40–46.

Sagduyu, A., Rezaki, M., Kaplan, İ., Özgen, G., & Gürsoy-Rezaki, B. (1997). Sağlık ocağına başvuran hastalarda dissosiyatif (konversiyon) belirtiler [Prevalence of conversion symptoms in a primary health care center]. *Turkish Journal of Psychiatry, 8*, 161–169.

Şar, V. (2006a). The scope of dissociative disorders: An international perspective. *Psychiatric Clinics of North America, 29*, 227–244.

Şar, V. (2006b). Schizophrenia: Innovations in diagnosis and treatment. Book Review. *Journal of Trauma & Dissociation, 7(1)*, 97–102.

Şar, V., Akyüz, G., & Doğan, O. (2007) Prevalence of dissociative disorders among women in the general population. *Psychiatry Research, 149*, 169–176.

Şar, V., Akyüz, G., Doğan, O., & Öztürk, E. (in press). The prevalence of conversion disorder in women from a Turkish general population. *Psychosomatics.*

Şar, V., Akyüz, G., Kuğu, N., Öztürk, E., & Ertem-Vehid, H. (2006) Axis-I dissociative disorder comorbidity of borderline personality disorder. *Journal of Clinical Psychiatry, 67*, 1583–1590.

Şar, V., Akyüz, G., Kundakçı, T., Kızıltan, E., & Doğan, O. (2004). Childhood trauma, dissociation and psychiatric comorbidity in patients with Conversion Disorder. *American Journal of Psychiatry, 161*, 2271–2276.

Şar, V., Koyuncu, A., Öztürk, E., Yargıç, L. I., Kundakçı, T., Yazıcı, A., et al. (2007). Dissociative disorders in the psychiatric emergency ward. *General Hospital Psychiatry, 29*, 45–50.

Şar, V., Kundakçı, T., Kızıltan, E., Bakım, B., & Bozkurt, O. (2000). Differentiating dissociative disorders from other diagnostic groups through somatoform dissociation in Turkey. *Journal of Trauma & Dissociation, 1(4)*, 67–80.

Şar, V., & Öztürk, E. (2007). The functional dissociation of the self: A sociocognitive approach to trauma and dissociation. *Journal of Trauma & Dissociation, 8(4)*, 69–89.

Şar, V., & Öztürk, E. (2008). Psychotic symptoms in dissociative disorders. In A. Moskowitz, I. Schaefer, & M. Dorahy (Eds.), *Psychosis, trauma, and dissociation: Emerging perspectives on severe psychopathology,* (pp. 166–175). London: Wiley Press.

Şar, V., & Öztürk, E. (2009). Psychotic presentations of dissociative identity disorder. In P. Dell & J. O'Neil (Eds.), *Dissociation and the dissociative disorders: DSM-V and beyond* (pp. 535–545). New York: Routledge.

Şar, V., & Ross, C. (2006). Dissociative disorders as a confounding factor in psychiatric research. *Psychiatric Clinics of North America, 29*, 129–144.

Şar, V., Taycan, O., Bolat, N., Özmen, M., Duran, A., & Öztürk, E. (2006). Dissociative disorder comorbidity of schizophrenic disorder. *Paper presented at the 23rd Annual Conference of the International Society for the Study of Trauma & Dissociation.*

Şar, V., Tutkun, H., Alyanak, B., Bakım, B., & Baral, I. (2000). Frequency of dissociative disorders among psychiatric outpatients in Turkey. *Comprehensive Psychiatry, 41*, 216–222.

Şar, V., Ünal, S. N., Kızıltan, E., Kundakçı, T., & Öztürk, E. (2001). HMPAO SPECT study of cerebral perfusion in dissociative identity disorder. *Journal of Trauma & Dissociation, 2(2)*, 5–25.

Şar, V., Ünal, S. N., & Öztürk, E. (2007) Frontal and occipital perfusion changes in dissociative identity disorder. *Psychiatry Research-Neuroimaging, 156*, 217–223.

Schneider, K. (1939/1977). *Klinische Psychopathologie* (Clinical Psychopathology). Stuttgart: Georg Thieme Verlag.

Shore, A. N. (1996). The experience-dependent maturation of a regulatory system in the orbital prefrontal cortex and the origin of developmental psychopathology. *Development & Psychopathology, 8*, 59–87.

Simeon, D., Guralnik, O., Knutelska, M., Hollander, E., & Schmeidler, J. (2001). Hypothalamic-pituitary-adrenal axis dysregulation in depersonalization disorder. *Neuropsychopharmacology, 25*, 793–795.

Simeon, D., Guralnik, O., Knutelska, M., & Nelson, D. (2004). Dissection of schizotypy and dissociation in depersonalization disorder. *Journal of Trauma & Dissociation, 5(4)*, 111–119.

Simeon, D., Guralnik, O., Knutelska, M., Yehuda, R., & Schmeidler, J. (2003). Basal norepinephrine in depersonalization disorder. *Psychiatry Research, 121*, 93–97.

Simeon, D., Guralnik, O., Schmeidler, J., Sirof, B., & Knutelska, M. (2001). The role of childhood interpersonal trauma in depersonalization disorder. *American Journal of Psychiatry, 158*, 1027–1033.

Somer, E. (2006). Culture-bound dissociation: A comparative analysis. *Psychiatric Clinics of North America, 29*, 213–226.

Spanos, N. P. (1994). Multiple identity enactments and multiple personality. A sociocognitive perspective. *Psychological Bulletin, 116*, 143–165.

Spiegel, D., & Cardeña, E. (1991). Disintegrated experience: The dissociative disorders revisited. *Journal of Abnormal Psychology, 100*, 366–378.

Spitzer, C., Freyberger, H. J., Kessler, C., & Kömpf, D. (1994). Psychiatrische Komorbidität dissoziativer Störungen in der Neurologie [Psychiatric comorbidity of dissociative disorders in a neurological clinic]. *Nervenarzt, 65*, 680–688.

Spitzer, C., Spelsberg, B., Grabe, H. J., Mundt, B., & Freyberger, H. J. (1999). Dissociative experiences and psychopathology in Conversion Disorders. *Journal of Psychosomatic Research, 46*, 291–294.

Tezcan, E., Atmaca, M., Kuloğlu, M., Geçici, O., Büyükbayram, A., & Tutkun, H. (2003). Dissociative disorders in Turkish inpatients with Conversion Disorder. *Comprehensive Psychiatry, 44*, 324–330.

Tsai, G. E., Condie, D., Wu, M. T., & Chang, I. W. (1999). Functional magnetic resonance imaging of personality switches in a woman with dissociative identity disorder. *Harvard Review of Psychiatry, 7*, 119–122.

Tutkun, H., Şar, V., Yargıç, L. I., Özpulat, T., Kızıltan, E., & Yanık, M. (1998). Frequency of dissociative disorders among psychiatric inpatients in a Turkish university clinic. *American Journal of Psychiatry, 155*, 800–805.

Tutkun, H., Yargıç, L. I., & Şar, V. (1996). Dissociative identity disorder presenting as hysterical psychosis. *Dissociation, 9*, 241–249.

Van der Hart, O., Nijenhuis, E.R.S., & Steele, K. (2006). *The haunted self: Structural dissociation and the treatment of chronic traumatization.* New York: Norton.

Van der Hart, O., Van Ochten, J. M., Van Son, M. J. M., Steele, K., & Lensvelt-Mulders, G. (2008). Relationships among peritraumatic dissociation and posttraumatic stress: A critical review. *Journal of Trauma & Dissociation, 9*, 481–505.

Van der Hart, O., & Witztum, E. (2008). Dissociative psychosis: Clinical and theoretical aspects. In A. Moskowitz, I. Schäfer, & M. Dorahy (Eds.), *Trauma, psychosis, and dissociation: Emerging perspectives on severe psychopathology*. London: Wiley.

Van der Hart, O., Witztum, E., & Friedman, B. (1992). From hysterical psychosis to reactive dissociative psychosis. *Journal of Traumatic Stress, 6*, 43–64.

Van der Kolk, B. A., Pelcovitz, D., Roth, S., Mandel, F. S., McFarlane, A., Herman, J. L. (1996). Dissociation, somatization, and affect dysregulation: The complexity of adaptation to trauma. *American Journal of Psychiatry, 153 (Suppl.)*, 83–93.

Van der Velden, P. G., Kleber, R. J., Christiaanse, B., Gersons, B. P. R., Marcelissen, F. G. H., Drogendijk, A. N., et al. (2006). The independent predictive value of peritraumatic dissociation for post-disaster intrusions, avoidance reactions, and PTSD symptom severity: A 4-year prospective study. *Journal of Traumatic Stress, 19*, 493–506.

Vermetten, E., Schmal, C., Lindner, S., Loewenstein, R. J., & Bremner, J. D. (2006). Hippocampal and amygdalar volumes in dissociative identity disorder. *American Journal of Psychiatry, 163*, 630–636.

Waldvogel, B., Ulrich, A., & Strasburger, H. (2007). Sighted and blind in one person. *Nervenarzt, 78*, 1303–1309.

World Health Organization (1992). *International Classification of Diseases, 10th Edition (ICD-10)*. Geneva: World Health Organization.

Yargıç, H., Tutkun, H., Şar, V., & Zoroğlu, S. S. (1995). Comparison of dissociative identity disorder between adolescents and adults. *Paper presented in the Spring Conference of the International Society for the Study of Dissociation,* Amsterdam.

Yazıcı, K. M., Demirci, M., Demir, B., & Ertuğrul, A. (2004). Abnormal somatosensory evoked potentials in two patients with conversion disorder. *Psychiatry and Clinical Neurosciences, 58*, 222–225.

Yazıcı, K. M., & Kostakoğlu, L. (1998). Cerebral blood flow changes in patients with conversion disorder. *Psychiatry Research, 83(3)*, 163–168.

Zanarini, M. C., Ruser, T., Frankenburg, F. R., & Hennen, J. (2000). The dissociative experiences of borderline patients. *Comprehensive Psychiatry*, 41, 223–227.

Zoroğlu, S. S., Şar, V., Tüzün, Ü., Tutkun, H., & Savaş, H. A. (2002). Reliability and validity of the Turkish version of the Adolescent Dissociative Experiences Scale. *Psychiatry & Clinical Neurosciences*, 56, 551–556.

Zoroğlu, S. S., Tüzün, Ü., Öztürk, M., & Şar, V. (2002). Reliability and validity of the Turkish version of the Child Dissociation Checklist. *Journal of Trauma & Dissociation, 3(1)*, 37–49.

Zoroğlu, S. S., Tüzün, Ü., Şar, V., Tutkun, H., Savaş, H. A., Öztürk, M., et al. (2003). Suicide attempts and self-mutilation among Turkish high-school students in relation to abuse, neglect and dissociation. *Psychiatry & Clinical Neurosciences, 57*, 119–126.

46 Understanding Dissociation

Paul F. Dell, PhD

OUTLINE

The goal of this book is to explicate the meaning(s) of the concept of dissociation. This goal is an important one because *dissociation* has never suffered from an excess of clarity. Indeed, several scholars have bluntly stated that the concept of dissociation is quite vague, in large part because it has been promiscuously applied to disparate phenomena (Brunet, Holowka, & Laurence, 2001; Cardeña, 1994; Frankel, 1990, 1994).

In Chapter 1, Van der Hart and Dorahy demonstrate that our current meanings of *dissociation* diverge from that of Janet who defined the term in the late 1880s. Van der Hart and Dorahy contend that the dissociative disorders field should return to the original Janetian meaning of dissociation. Here, however, I will begin my explication of dissociation by focusing not on the "correct" meaning of dissociation (Janetian or otherwise), but simply by examining today's *de facto* meanings of dissociation. Specifically, I will begin by examining the meanings that seem to be implicit in clinicians' daily use of the word *dissociation* and its cognates: *dissociative, dissociate, dissociated,* and *dissociating.*

46.1 CLINICIANS' COLLOQUIAL USE OF THE TERM *DISSOCIATION*

46.1.1 Dissociation (Noun)

Clinicians use the word *dissociation* primarily in academic/instructional contexts: "I read a good article on dissociation last week"; "I'm going to a conference on dissociation next month"; "Where can I learn more about dissociation?" Clinicians also use the word *dissociation* when they explain dissociation to someone else—a friend, a patient, a room full of students. I am not certain, but I suspect that clinicians' verbal explanations of dissociation are often rather homespun and substantially assisted by the use of examples that are already familiar to the listener (e.g., amnesia, multiple personalities, etc.). I think that clinicians use the word *dissociation* less frequently than any of its cognates.

46.1.2 Dissociative (Adjective)

Clinicians use the term *dissociative* to refer to patients who manifest certain symptoms: "I think your patient is dissociative"; "She has a dissociative disorder"; "He is dissociative." Most commonly, clinicians seem to call patients dissociative when they manifest amnestic symptoms (or look "trancey" during a therapy session). Clinicians seem to use the adjective *dissociative* more frequently than any of its cognates.

46.1.3 Dissociate (Verb, Intransitive)

Clinicians' use of the terms *dissociation* and *dissociative* is reasonably straightforward; matters become more complex, however, when they use the verb *dissociate.*

Clinicians routinely use verb forms of dissociate (i.e., dissociate, dissociated, and dissociating): "She would dissociate during the sexual abuse"; "He dissociated during the therapy session"; and "I think she is dissociating." Such statements typically refer to specific dissociative phenomena. For example, "She would dissociate during the sexual abuse." Translation: when molested as a child, the patient would "go away" or go "out of body" during the incest. "He dissociated during the therapy session." Translation: the patient "switched" to another personality during the session. Or, the patient went into trance during the session (i.e., manifested a blank stare while simultaneously being unresponsive). And so on.

In short, when clinicians use *dissociate* as an intransitive verb, they are attributing an act to the patient: "She dissociated." This is striking because clinicians rarely describe an Axis I symptom as an act. Clinicians do not say, "He depresses," or "She panic-attacked," or "He psychosed." Instead, they say, "He is depressed"; "She had a panic attack"; and "He became psychotic." So, when clinicians use *dissociate* as an intransitive verb, they appear to be claiming that the patient has actively done something (as opposed to being the passive recipient of a symptom—i.e., becoming psychotic, having a panic attack, etc.).

46.1.4 Dissociate (Verb, Transitive)

The preceding section discussed the word *dissociate* as an intransitive verb; intransitive verbs do *not* require a direct object. Transitive verbs, however, may have a direct object. Clinicians frequently use the verb *dissociate* as a transitive verb: "He dissociated the memory"; "She has dissociated most of her childhood"; "He dissociated the pain"; "She dissociates her feelings." When used in this fashion, the transitive verb, *dissociate*, denotes an act of doing something to another object (e.g., memory, body sensation, emotions, etc.). This transitive use of the verb *dissociate* entails a stronger sense of active enactment than the intransitive use of the verb. Both uses of dissociate, but especially the transitive form, are consistent with the idea of dissociation as a defensive, self-protective action: "He split off the memory"; "She has blocked out most of her childhood"; "He blocked the pain"; and "She pushes away her feelings."

As noted, it is uncommon for clinicians to use a verb when they discuss Axis I symptoms. Still, there are exceptions to this generalization. Clinicians use verbs when they discuss Axis I symptoms that they consider to be *behaviors* (as opposed to subjective experiences). For example, clinicians routinely use verbs to discuss substance abuse ("He drank," "She did drugs," "He lapsed"), obsessive-compulsive symptoms ("He checks the locks seven times every night," "She counts her steps"), and eating disorders ("She binged," "He purged," "She is restricting her food intake"). Thus, when clinicians use the verb *dissociate*, they are saying that these patients are *doing* something—they are avoiding or defending against something.

I will return to clinicians' colloquial meanings of dissociation. In the following, I will argue that, whenever clinicians use dissociation as a verb (i.e., dissociate, dissociated, dissociating), they are giving a distinctly Freudian slant to Janet's concept of dissociation.

46.2 THE HISTORICAL CONTEXT OF THE "BIRTH" OF DISSOCIATION

It is important for modern readers to know an important historical fact: the field of dissociation did not begin with trauma. It began with hypnosis. From the time of Mesmer (circa 1778) until the turn of the century in 1900, Western Europe experienced recurring waves of fascination with animal magnetism or hypnosis. Each wave of fascination was, in turn, undercut by periods during which hypnosis was widely discredited. The fact that each discrediting was supplanted by yet another surge of interest testifies to the inherently fascinating nature of hypnotic phenomena.

The absolute peak of interest in, and fascination with, hypnosis—in the general population, in medicine, and in the professions—occurred in the 1880s, especially (but by no means, exclusively) in France. Ellenberger insists that:

> We can hardly realize today to what extent hypnotism and suggestion were invoked in the 1880s to explain countless historical, anthropological, and sociological facts such as the genesis of religions, miracles, and wars.... Entire educational systems were based on the concept of suggestion. (Ellenberger, 1970, pp. 164–165)

This fever of interest in hypnosis and hypnotic phenomena was probably due to the confluence of at least three factors: (1) the testimony of great men (e.g., Richet and Charcot), (2) widespread discussion of the phenomenon of dual consciousness, and (3) the *Zeitgeist* of fascination with the miraculous.

46.2.1 The Testimony of Great Men

Charles Richet was a leading physiologist who won the Nobel Prize for Physiology and Medicine for his research on anaphylaxis. A man of wide interests, Richet studied many areas, including hypnosis. He published a series of articles on hypnosis (between 1875 and 1883), in which he successfully debunked the widely held belief that hypnotic phenomena were nothing but fraudulent performances by deceitful, attention-seeking subjects. In particular, Richet's 1875 article, *Du somnambulisme provoqué* "exerted a major influence in legitimatizing the investigation of hypnosis and artificial somnambulism for the French scientific establishment" (Crabtree, 1988, p. 235). The legitimizing of hypnosis was completed in 1882 by Jean-Martin Charcot, the greatest neurologist of that era, who presented a scientific analysis of hypnosis to the French Academy of Science. After Charcot's triumphant presentation, there was a deluge of investigations and publications about hypnosis. As Hack Tuke in London announced, "Everywhere *hypnosis redivivus*!"

46.2.2 The Phenomenon of Dual Consciousness

The seeds for the 1880s' excitement about hypnosis were actually sown a century before. In 1784, Amand-Marie-Jacques de Chastenet, Marquis de Puységur (hereinafter, simply Puységur), a disciple of Mesmer and a practitioner of animal magnetism, magnetized a peasant on his estate, Victor Race, and discovered a new phenomenon—artificial somnambulism (*somnambulisme provoqué*). Prior to this event, the defining phenomenon of Mesmer's animal magnetism was the "crisis" that often concluded a session of magnetic healing. During Mesmer's sessions, fully conscious and alert patients were "magnetized" by the animal magnetist (who either made magnetic "passes" of his hands or requested that the subject hold an object that he had already magnetized). Many subjects would then undergo a "crisis"—a sort of hysterical fit—during which they fell down, writhed, thrashed, and generally created a commotion. Many of Mesmer's patients experienced a subsequent improvement of their symptoms—magnetic healing. In contrast, when magnetized, Victor did not fall down and thrash; instead, he went into a deep magnetic "sleep" during which he spoke with considerable intelligence and was profoundly responsive to Puységur's suggestions. When Victor awoke, he had amnesia for all that had transpired during his sleep. Modeled on sleepwalking (somnambulism), which is followed by amnesia when the sleepwalker awakens, Victor's sleep became known as artificial or induced somnambulism (*somnambulisme provoqué*). Amnesia upon awakening was considered to be the defining characteristic of artificial somnambulism.

It was quickly found, however, that artificial somnambulism had other, even more mysterious, characteristics. Somnambulists (i.e., those persons who are capable of somnambulistic sleep and amnesia) remembered everything that happened during any *previous* episode of somnambulistic sleep when they were again put into a state of artificial somnambulism. Moreover, during sleep, somnambulists not only had complete memory for all of their episodes of somnambulism, but they also had complete memory for all that occurred during normal consciousness (i.e., when they were "awake"). Finally, it was soon discovered that, when an awakened somnambulist carried out a posthypnotic suggestion, he or she immediately forgot the posthypnotic action. The person did not know or remember what he or she had just done.

This striking pattern of memory and amnesia became a topic of enduring discussion and speculation. Speculation led, almost effortlessly, to the idea of a divided mind or a divided consciousness:

> The first magnetizers were immensely struck by the fact that, when they induced magnetic sleep in a person, a new life manifested itself of which the subject was unaware, and that a new and often more brilliant personality emerged with a continuous life of its own. *The entire nineteenth century was preoccupied with the problem of the coexistence of these two minds and of their relationship to each other.* (Ellenberger, 1970, p. 145, italics added)

Extended accounts of this 19th-century fascination with double minds, double consciousnesses, and double personalities are to be found in Crabtree (1993), Ellenberger (1970), and Van der Hart and Dorahy (2009).

46.2.3 Fascination With the Miraculous

Late 19th-century France was fascinated with phenomena that appeared to be miraculous. Hypnotic phenomena, somnambulists who seemed to have two different lives, and cases of double personality (and multiple personality) were the topic of newspaper accounts, drawing room discussions, and great public interest (to say nothing of scientific publications and presentations at international congresses).

Thus, when Pierre Janet began his research in 1882, he did so within a cultural-historical context of fascination with somnambulism and double consciousness. Given that context, one can see that Janet's studies of somnambulism and hysteria would require but a relatively small step to reach the concept of dissociation.

46.2.4 Science in 19th-century France

In seeking to understand Janet's thoughts about the phenomena of hypnosis and hysteria, the reader will be helped by knowing one thing about 19th-century science: French scientists of this period were quite hostile to theorizing. Janet, like his teachers and intellectual precursors in French psychology, Hippolyte Taine and Théodule Ribot, was a follower of August Comte's school of positivism. Put simply, positivism insisted that scientists employ rigorous empiricism—rather than the unfettered, theoretical speculation of armchair metaphysicians. Practically, positivism meant that theory should be eschewed in favor of inescapable generalizations that were closely tied to repeated observations of the phenomena in question:

> In France, the authority of Comte was felt everywhere within the scientific community, and the commitment to "positive" knowledge was made with religious zeal.... The positivist message was clear: Errant theorizing is merely metaphysics in disguise; concepts not grounded in experimental findings are empty.... Men such as Charcot and Janet struggled to refine their lectures and essays; to distill their thoughts over and over again until only confirmable facts remained, and until "theory" was no more than the sort of generalization a clever child would make in the face of the same evidence. (Robinson, 1977, pp. xxxiii–xxxiv)

The bottom line is that Janet was extremely reluctant to engage in theorizing (see also Janet, 1907/1910). As a proper French scientist of his era, Janet valued, above all else, careful and repeated observation. Only after a lengthy period of observation would Janet advance some cautious generalizations about the phenomena in question. Janet's attitude toward theory was profoundly different from that of Freud, who was a bold and daring theorist.

46.3 PIERRE JANET'S CONCEPT OF DISSOCIATION

The research that led to Janet's identification of the phenomena of dissociation was conducted at Le Havre Hospital from February 1883 to July 1889. During these six and one-half years, Janet studied 19 hysterics (Ellenberger, 1970). Most of this research was based on extensive study of four hysterics, three of whom (Léonie, Lucie, and Marie) manifested multiple personalities. The essence of his studies on somnambulism and hysteria were reported in three landmark articles in *Revue Philosophique* (1886, 1887, 1888)[1] and in his doctoral thesis, *L'automatisme psychologique* (1889).

[1] An excellent account of Janet's three *Revue Philosophique* articles can be found in Crabtree (1993).

46.3.1 Janet (1886)—Somnambulistic Amnesia Is an Illusion

Janet's first *Revue Philosophique* article (Janet, 1886), "Unconscious acts and the doubling of the personality during artificial somnambulism," was based on months of hypnotic experimentation with a 19-year-old subject, *Lucie*. Although Lucie had a long-standing history of severe hysteria—she had hysterical attacks that could last for hours—Janet described his observations of Lucie as *phenomena of hypnosis* (rather than phenomena of hysteria). In particular, he reported that (1) Lucie had no memory for the events that occurred while she was hypnotized, and (2) Lucie unknowingly executed posthypnotic suggestions upon awakening (i.e., she would carry out the posthypnotic suggestion, but, immediately afterwards, she would not remember having done so).

In this article, Janet reported that Lucie had a second "hypnotic personality" (whose name was Adrienne). The presence of an apparent second personality was not unexpected. Magnetizers and hypnotists had been describing such phenomena for the previous century (Crabtree, 1993; Ellenberger, 1970; Gauld, 1992). In keeping with these prior observations, Adrienne remembered all that occurred when Lucie was hypnotized, but Lucie remembered none of it. Moreover, Adrienne claimed that she, not Lucie, had carried out the posthypnotic suggestions. These observations led Janet to a startling realization: Lucie did not *forget* the posthypnotic hypnotic suggestions. In fact, she neither knew about the suggestion when it was given to "her" during hypnosis, nor did she know about the suggestion when "she" carried it out. Thus, Lucie could not forget what she never knew in the first place. It followed, therefore, that Lucie's amnesia for her hypnotic sessions and for carrying out the posthypnotic suggestions was an illusion. In fact, nothing whatsoever had been forgotten; Adrienne never forgot and Lucie never knew (in the first place).

As a result of these findings, Janet concluded that hypnosis led to a doubling of consciousness (see Crabtree, 2003). As noted previously, this conclusion was very much in keeping with the observations and speculations of the magnetizers and hypnotists of the previous 100 years. Janet, however, would abandon this conclusion within a matter of months.

46.3.2 Janet (1887)—Parts of the Personality Are Not Split Off

Janet quickly realized that the doubling of consciousness (and the doubling of personality) was a phenomenon of *hysteria* (rather than a phenomenon of hypnosis).[2] Thus, in his second *Revue Philosophique* article (Janet, 1887), "Systematized anesthesia and the dissociation of psychological phenomena," Janet reported and justified his new conclusion—that Adrienne was not a product of inadvertent hypnotic suggestion. The evidence showed that Adrienne had existed prior to Janet's hypnotic sessions with Lucie. Janet now asserted that *second personalities such as Adrienne are a core feature of hysteria.*

This 1887 article arguably marks the decisive breakthrough in Janet's thinking about dissociation. Prior to this article, Janet was studying hypnosis and hypnotic phenomena. Now, in this article, Janet has begun to study hysteria, second consciousnesses, and the phenomena that distinguish between usual consciousness and the second consciousness. In this article, Janet used the word *dissociation* for the first time. He even proposed two "laws of dissociation."

Janet reported that when he gave Lucie a hypnotic suggestion for negative hallucination (e.g., that she would not be able to see, or that she would not be able to feel), Adrienne was unaffected. She saw and felt what Lucie could not. Moreover, Adrienne knew some traumatic life events that Lucie did not. This situation led Janet to conclude that the unconscious psychological functions of somnambulists and hysterics (e.g., hysterical or hypnotic blindness, anesthesia, paralysis, amnesia, and so on) are not really unconscious at all. He called this "the first law of dissociation": ideas and psychological functions can be conscious, but not be associated with "the 'I' " of the primary personality. As Janet put it, "a psychological phenomenon can be conscious and yet not attached by association to the group of sensations and memories that constitute the idea of the 'I' " (Janet, 1887, p. 462). Instead, these conscious phenomena are associated with the group of ideas and sensations that constitute the second consciousness (which has its own idea of the "I," its own sense of self). This perspective directly implies that *hysterical sensory and motor symptoms are not deficits of sensation or of movement; they are problems of association.* In hysteria, such sensory and motor functions are associated with the "I" of the second consciousness, but they are not associated with the "I" of the primary personality. And, Hilgard might later say, that hypnotically blocked pain is not associated with the person's conscious mind, but with that of "the hidden observer" (Hilgard, 1986).

Janet's "second law of dissociation" may come as a surprise to some readers. According to Janet, dissociation does *not* split off memories from the primary personality. According to Janet, the unity of the primary personality remains unchanged; nothing breaks away, nothing is split off. Instead, dissociated experiences (and the memory of those experiences) were always, from the instant of their occurrence, assigned to, and associated with, the second system within. Those experiences and the memories of those experiences were never part of the primary personality.

As jarring as the second law of dissociation may be for some readers, I urge the reader to take a moment to absorb what Janet is saying here. I will argue in the following that the second law of dissociation explains much of Janet's discomfort with the Freudian concept of defense (and, especially, repression).

The second law of dissociation is an elaboration of the same insight that Janet had reached the year before when he claimed that amnesia is an illusion (because Lucie never knew what happened in the first place). Only Adrienne, the second personality, knew what happened. As Crabtree (1993) put it, "Forgetting is not involved" (p. 313). And, because the primary personality never knew what happened in the first place, breaking away or splitting off is not involved either. At the instant that the event occurred, the experience was assigned to (i.e., associated with) the second personality.

46.3.3 Janet (1888)—Second Personalities Are Subconscious

Janet continued to develop his ideas about the second personality in his third *Revue Philosophique* article (Janet, 1888), "Unconscious acts and memory during somnambulism." Because the second personality was conscious, Janet insisted that, even with respect to the primary personality, the second personality was not unconscious, but *subconscious*. Thus, when Janet uses the term *subconscious*, he is always referring to one or more other consciousnesses that are unknown to the primary consciousness. Conversely, because Janet believes that all psychological acts require consciousness, he rejects the notion of a Freudian unconscious, where psychological acts can occur "unconsciously," and into which urges and memories can supposedly be "repressed."

[2] There are some subtleties in this matter, however, because Janet came to hold two important beliefs about hypnosis. First, like many others of his time (e.g., Binet, Charcot), Janet believed that somnambulism (hypnosis) was inherently pathological. Second, Janet would soon come to believe that hypnotizability was the pathogen, rather than hysteria. He believed that hysteria was a (frequent) symptom of the ability to be hypnotized (Janet, 1889); but he vacillated about this issue. Throughout his life, Janet implicitly claimed that successful treatment for hysteria was also a successful treatment for hypnotizability; that is, he repeatedly asserted that a successfully treated hysteric could no longer be hypnotized.

In this same vein, Janet redefined unconscious acts as "subconscious acts." By this, he meant that these acts stem from a subconscious personality. Specifically, Janet asserted that subconscious acts are intelligent and psychologically informed (as contrasted with reflex actions or the enactment of procedural knowledge routines); moreover, subconscious acts are executed totally without the knowledge of the person. Examples of subconscious acts include automatic writing and the execution of posthypnotic suggestions. Finally, Janet claimed that a person can have any number of subconscious personalities.

46.3.4 Janet (1889)—Automatisms Are the Primary Indicator of Mental Disaggregation

46.3.4.1 Psychological Automatism

In 1889, Janet completed and published his doctoral thesis, *L'automatisme psychologique*—a book that William James (1890) said "made quite a commotion in the world to which such things pertain" (p. 363). In this volume, under the organizing rubric of "automatism," Janet presented his six years of research on hysteria, somnambulism, and dissociation.[3] The focus on automatism in this book constituted a distinctly new synthesis of Janet's ideas about dissociation:

> One of the striking things about this book ... was the sudden appearance of a new organizing framework for the research he had conducted up to that point. Although "automatism" was mentioned only a few times in the three articles [i.e., Janet, 1886, 1887, and 1888], in the book "psychological automatism" became the central unifying principle for his data. (Crabtree, 2003, p. 65)[4]

Janet's new synthesis of his research findings accomplished at least two things—one analytical and the other historical (Crabtree, 2003). Analytically, *L'automatisme psychologique* asserted not only that automatism is the most elemental form of psychological functioning, but also that *automatism is the central phenomenon that characterizes all dissociated functioning*. Historically, Janet linked his research on dissociation to a preexisting literature on automatic functioning (Laycock, 1845, 1876; Luys, 1876), automatism (Despine, 1868, 1880; Huxley, 1874; Myers, 1888, 1889), and unconscious cerebration (Carpenter, 1855, 1874).

So, what are automatisms? *Automatisms* are behaviors that occur automatically, "on their own," without being directed by the conscious mind. There appears to be a continuum of automatisms—from simple and mindless ones to those that are increasingly complex and intelligent. At that time, it was generally agreed that spinal reflexes were the simplest form of automatism. Discussants of automatism disagreed, however, about the nature of complex automatisms. The most extreme position in this debate was staked out by Thomas Huxley (1874), who claimed that *all* human behaviors were automatisms because humans are nothing more than "conscious automata." Huxley drove home this point by asserting that consciousness is just a collateral product of our functioning. Consciousness, said Huxley, had no more effect on our behavior than does the steam-whistle on a locomotive have an effect on the machinery of the locomotive.

Janet had his own local Huxley, Prosper Despine (1868, 1880), with whom he argued throughout *L'automatisme psychologique*. Unlike Huxley, Despine believed that the human mind had a guiding consciousness. Despine insisted, however, that complex human automatisms (e.g., somnambulism) operated without any consciousness at all. Thus, he defined psychological automatisms as:

> [V]ery complex and intelligent acts reaching a goal which is perfectly specific and adjusted to circumstances; acts exactly similar to those which the [conscious] ego commands in other occasions through the same apparatus. (Despine, 1968, I, pp. 490–491)

In this definition, despite his use of the term *psychological automatism*, Despine is really saying that automatisms are completely *physiological:* although these automatisms may be complex and intelligent, they have no consciousness. In contrast, Janet (1889) insisted that many automatisms are *psychological*; they have their own conscious intelligence (which is utterly dissociated from the ordinary consciousness of the person). These psychological automatisms, then, are the topic of Janet's *L'automatisme psychologique*:

> We believe that one can accept simultaneously both automatism and consciousness.... [O]ur goal is to not only demonstrate that there is a human activity that merits the name of automatic, but also that it is legitimate to call it a psychological automatism. (Janet, 1889, pp. 2–3)

[3] The best accounts in English of *L'automatisme psychologique* can be found in Crabtree (1993 and 2003).

[4] Crabtree (2003, 2007) argues persuasively that Janet's adoption of the term *automatism* stemmed from his familiarity with Myers's writings about automatism. In particular, Crabtree contends that Janet was influenced by Myers's (1888) paper, "French Experiments in the Strata of Personality," in which Myers examined in detail Janet's (1888) article on unconscious acts.

The alert reader may have noticed something familiar about Janet's definition of psychological automatism—*intelligent acts, with their own consciousness, that operate outside the conscious awareness of the person.* Janet had previously referred to such phenomena as "unconscious acts" (*les actes inconscients*) or, as he preferred, subconscious acts (see my previous discussion of Janet, 1888). Janet said that *subconscious acts are intelligent and psychologically informed actions that are executed totally without the knowledge of the person.* Janet believed that all subconscious acts (i.e., all automatisms) are the actions of a second psychological system that possesses at least a rudimentary consciousness. Some secondary psychological systems have their own sense of self and are called "personalities" by Janet:

> When a certain number of psychological phenomena are united, ordinarily there is produced in the mind a new, very important reality; their unity, noted and understood, gives birth to a particular judgment that one calls the ideas of the "I." ... Judgment ... synthesizes different acts, establishes their unity and ... forms a new idea: that of personality. (Janet, 1889, p. 117)

At this juncture, it is finally possible to give a thumbnail description of Janet's 500-page volume. *L'automatisme psychologique* is an extended explication of subconscious psychological systems and the automatisms that they produce. Janet's explication of these topics revolved around three concepts: total automatism, partial automatism, and psychological misery.

46.3.4.2 Total Automatism

Total automatism occurs when the activity of the subconscious psychological system affects (takes over?) the entire functioning of the person. Examples of total automatism include catalepsy, artificial somnambulism (i.e., hypnosis), multiple personalities, and some flashbacks (i.e., those accompanied by a "reliving" that is so intense that the person is completely "back there and then"). In each of these examples, Janet claimed, the functioning of the person is totally supplanted by the activity of the underlying subconscious system.

In 1889, the manifestations of what Janet called "total automatism" were already well-known to the scientific community under the heading *successive existences.* This term and its variations (e.g., second states, second condition, successive states of consciousness, successive personalities, alternating personalities) had repeatedly been employed to describe cases of dual and multiple personality (e.g., Azam, 1876, 1877; Bourru & Burot, 1885, 1888). These slightly odd terms were used for a very good reason—to avoid the implication that multiple personalities had a "simultaneous existence." In other words, in the 1870s and early 1880s, multiple personalities were understood to operate via a mysterious process that 'turned off' one personality and "turned on" another one. Hence, *successive* existences. Not simultaneous existences.

The on/off model of successive existences is based on artificial somnambulism. Somnambulists have two successive states (awake and "asleep") that are separated by amnesia. In modern language, a total automatism has occurred whenever a person with dissociative identity disorder (DID) (1) switches from one personality to another, and (2) the first personality has "amnesia" for the subsequent activities of the second personality. Said differently, total automatism neatly encapsulates the DSM-IV diagnostic criteria for DID (i.e., one personality totally supplants the functioning of another personality and amnesia occurs).

With the concept of *partial* automatism, Janet finally transcended the on/off metaphor of successive existences: partial automatisms reveal the activity of *simultaneous* existences. This is a critically important clinical and conceptual advance.

46.3.4.3 Partial Automatism

Partial automatisms occur when both the person and a subconscious psychological system are *active at the same time.* In partial automatism, the internal activity of the subconscious system intrudes into one or more aspects of the person's conscious experience (in ways that the person finds to be inexplicable):

> Psychological automatism, instead of being complete and regulating *all* conscious thought, can be *partial* and regulate a small group of phenomena [e.g., actions, or feelings, or thoughts, or impulses, or bodily functioning, or sensations]. (Janet, 1889, p. 224, italics added)

Partial "regulation" of functioning is exactly what Janet originally meant by the term *unconscious act*—an automatic action over which the person is powerless. Examples of partial automatism include partial catalepsy, some posthypnotic suggestions, automatic writing, auditory hallucinations, and some flashbacks (i.e., those that do *not* vitiate the person's orientation to "here and now").

Janet was inconsistent about the relationship between partial automatism and amnesia. Sometimes, he insisted that amnesia always accompanied partial automatism. At other times, he described examples of partial automatism where amnesia was clearly absent. For example, Janet defined an unconscious act (the paradigmatic example of partial automatism) as "an action having all the characteristics of a psychological act, save one: that *it is always unknown by the person himself who executes it at the moment of its execution*" (Janet, 1889, p. 225, italics added). Elsewhere in the book, however, he described partial automatisms of emotion, sensation, ideas, and urges. These partial automatisms are consciously experienced by the person; they are *not* accompanied by amnesia.

One is tempted to conclude that amnesia accompanies partial automatisms of movement, but not partial automatisms of emotion, sensation, ideas, urges, and so on. In fact, Janet drew precisely this distinction four years later. In speaking of subconscious acts (i.e., automatisms), Janet said:

> It presents itself in two different ways: at one time it is ... subconscious phenomena manifested solely by *movement of which the subject is ignorant*; at another time ... it is subconscious phenomena ... which ... *call forth in the conscious mind* emotions, varied images springing up in an unexpected manner." (Janet, 1893/1901/1977, p. 261, italics added)

But, the matter is not so simple: partial automatisms of movement can (and often do) occur *without* amnesia. And Janet (1893/1901/1977) conceded as much (see p. 262).

Janet's account of unconscious acts was based on his observation that the typical person of his era was amnesic for executing a posthypnotic suggestion. Such amnesia, however, does not always occur. The person carrying out a posthypnotic suggestion may be quite aware of what he is doing (but have no idea why he feels so compelled to do it). A similar situation occurs in multiple personality when one personality (who remains "inside") "causes" the person to do something. When that happens, persons with multiple personality do things they did not choose to do (and which they cannot stop themselves from doing).

46.3.5 Understanding Automatisms

I have dwelt, at some length, on Janet's contradictory accounts of partial automatism. I assure the reader that this is not just an academic obsession of mine. I am paying very close attention to what Janet said about this issue because I believe that partial automatism is *the* fundamental phenomenon of dissociation (I see total automatism as being just a subtype of it). Moreover, I believe that, for over a century, our understanding of dissociation has been hindered by lack of clarity about partial automatism.

Interest in dissociation underwent a great decline shortly after the turn of the 20th century (Ellenberger, 1970; Hilgard, 1986; Rosenbaum, 1980). When this happened, the concept of automatism "got lost." The concept of dissociation (vague though it may be) was carried forward and is much discussed today. Automatism, however, is no longer mentioned.[5] This is a curious occurrence because turn-of-the-century scholars of dissociation used the word *automatism* at least as often as they used the word *dissociation*.

There can be little doubt that Janet's thinking in *L'automatisme psychologique* was deeply influenced by his reading of then-contemporary authorities on automatism—Prosper Despine, Edmund Gurney, Frederick Myers, and Charles Richet. Both Myers and Richet traveled to Le Havre in 1886 to witness some of Janet's research with Léonie. Janet conducted a running argument with Despine (1868, 1880) throughout *L'automatisme psychologique*. Crabtree (2003, 2007) has made a persuasive case that the organizational framework of the book (i.e., automatism) is directly due to Janet's reading of Myers (see footnote 4). Finally, Janet's use of the term *subconscious* probably comes from Myers as well (see Myers, 1884, p. 234).

Prior to *L'automatisme psychologique,* debate about automatism[6] centered around four interrelated issues: (1) whether automatic actions were conscious or unconscious, (2) whether or not the person was aware of the automatic action, (3) whether the automatic actions stemmed from autonomous centers of action, and (4) whether the automatic actions were experienced as involuntary.

46.3.5.1 Are Automatisms Conscious or Unconscious Actions?

Physiologists insisted that automatisms are unconscious actions of the spine or the brain (Carpenter, 1855, 1874; Despine, 1868, 1880; Huxley, 1874; Laycock, 1845, 1876; Luys, 1876). Carpenter (1855), for example, famously claimed that automatisms were the product of "unconscious cerebration." Some even claimed that the complex, intelligent actions of somnambulists (Despine), and even Mozart (Carpenter), were just unconscious brain reflex activity. In contrast, nonphysiological scholars adopted a psychological perspective and claimed that automatisms are conscious actions of a second consciousness to which the ordinary consciousness does not have access (Gurney,

[5] Except by historians such as Crabtree (1993, 2003, 2007) and Ellenberger (1970).

[6] For a superb analysis of the issues surrounding automatism, see Crabtree (2003).

1884; Myers, 1885, 1888). Janet's (1889) view of automatism places him in this latter group. Janet believed that automatisms are the intelligent actions of another consciousness to which the person's ordinary (Janet used the word *personal*) consciousness does not have access.

46.3.5.2 Is the Person Aware of the Automatism While It Is Happening?

Most physiologists of that time comfortably asserted that a person was quite aware of the automatism while it was happening. Because their physiological thinking was modeled on spinal reflexes, this was a sensible position for them to take. If your doctor whacks your knee with a rubber hammer, you are quite aware of the reflexive kick of your leg. One physiologist, however—Prosper Despine (1880)—simply could not accept the idea that a person was aware of the automatism while it was happening. And, because his thinking was modeled on the behavior of somnambulists, his position also made sense. After all, Despine might say, the person knows nothing of the actions performed during somnambulistic "sleep," nor does the person know anything of posthypnotic suggestions that are carried out later.

Janet certainly agreed with Despine that the person had amnesia for what happened during the somnambulistic state,[7] but Janet also knew, from observation, that hysterics suffering from partial automatisms were quite *aware* of the emotions, images, ideas, and urges that intruded into their conscious mind (from the subconscious). Moreover, he knew that hysterics could be uncomfortably aware even of *automatisms of movement*. For example, Janet described one hysterical patient's disconcerting, conscious experience of automatisms:

> It is not I that walk; it is my legs which walk quite alone.... When I think of some object, it seems as if someone took me by the hand to look for it; I go to it without knowing why; I ask myself who is this person.... He robs me of my thought, he writes what I think. (Janet, 1893/1901/1977, p. 262)[8]

This quotation begins to reveal an essential phenomenological fact about persons with a severe dissociative disorder; namely, *partial automatisms comprise the core of dissociative experience* (see the following).

46.3.5.3 Are Automatisms Generated by Autonomous Centers of Action?

This issue was not comprehensively resolved until Morton Prince advanced the concept of *co-consciousness* in 1907. The physiologists certainly did not believe that automatisms originated in some previously unknown center of autonomous action. They insisted that automatisms were just unconscious brain reflex actions. Gurney, Janet, and Myers, however, believed that automatisms were manifestations of the activity of a previously unknown conscious center of intelligent activity. They believed that these centers of activity were "subconscious"—separate, independent centers of consciousness to which the usual personal consciousness of the individual has no access.

At a 1906 symposium on subconsciousness in Boston, Prince argued, correctly I think, that Janet's descriptions of automatisms and the subconscious had been chronically skewed by Janet's overemphasis of amnesia[9]:

> As I view this question of the subconscious, far too much weight is given to the point of awareness or not awareness of our conscious processes. As a matter of fact we find entirely identical phenomena, that is identical in every respect but one—that of awareness—in which sometimes we are aware of these conscious phenomena [of the subconscious] and sometimes not; but the one essential and fundamental quality in them is automaticity or independence of the personal consciousness.... Dissociation, with activity, independent of the main focus of consciousness, does not necessarily imply or require absence of awareness on the part of the latter.... *I believe it important to insist that lack of awareness is not an essential fact or [essential] in the development of the subconscious.* (Prince, 1907/1910, pp. 87–97, italics added)

Unlike many participants in the debates about automatism, Prince based his views on extensive observation of patients with multiple personality (e.g., Prince, 1905/1908, 1906). His (1905/1908) detailed account of Miss Beauchamp's verbal reports of her subjective experience provided Prince with clear evidence that autonomous activity, rather than amnesia, is the primary phenomenon of the subconscious. As a consequence, Prince opted for a concept of co-consciousness (and co-activity):

[7] Janet disagreed vehemently, however, with Despine's understanding of hypnotic sleep and posthypnotic amnesia—namely, that all actions during the somnambulistic state are just automatic reflex brain activity.

[8] For readers with limited experience of severely dissociative patients, it may be helpful to know that this is not a psychotic patient. In fact, modern literature shows that these are the typical experiences of a person with a severe dissociative disorder (e.g., Dell, 2002, 2006c; Dell & Lawson, 2009).

[9] Interestingly, some 80 years later, Bowers (1992) advanced precisely the same criticism of neodissociation theory—that, like Janet, Hilgard (1986) had overemphasized the phenomenon of amnesia.

> I prefer ... the term co-conscious to subconscious, partly to express the notion of *co-activity of a second co-consciousness* [italics added], partly to avoid the ambiguity of the conventional term due to its many meanings, and partly because such ideas are not necessarily *sub*-conscious at all; that is, there may be no lack of awareness of them. (1907/1910, p. 72)

Prince summarized his position by saying that, "The one fundamental principle and criterion of the subconscious is dissociation and co-activity (automatism)" (p. 96). Prince's conclusion, I think, decisively resolved the first three issues in the debates on automatism: are automatisms conscious or unconscious actions? (they are conscious); (2) is the person aware of the automatism while it is happening? (the person is usually, but not always, aware); and (3) do automatisms derive from truly autonomous centers of action? (they do). In my opinion, Prince's lucid conceptualization of automatisms, dissociation, and the subconscious has not received the attention that it deserves.

Putting together the ideas of Prince and Janet, we can now approximate a fundamental statement regarding the structure, dynamics, and phenomena of mental disaggregation (i.e., dissociation).

> **Understanding Dissociation #1:** In persons with a severe dissociative disorder, the essential fact is not that amnesia may occur, but that a second, *co-active* center of autonomy (with at least a rudimentary sense of consciousness and self) recurrently intrudes upon the person's conscious mind.

The involuntary nature of these intrusions, however, requires further amplification.

46.3.5.4 Are Automatisms Involuntary?

Involuntariness is a subjective experience: do we experience automatisms as happening involuntarily? Do they just "happen on their own?" I think that the answer to these questions is inescapably, and importantly, "yes." All of the physiologists, except Despine, answered this question with an unqualified "yes." Despine (1880) gave a highly qualified "yes." He agreed that automatisms occur involuntarily, but he insisted that so many brain activities are involuntary that it would be unhelpful to define automatisms in terms of involuntariness.

Janet was certainly aware that many automatisms were experienced as being involuntary. He mentioned this point repeatedly, both directly and indirectly,[10] but he never emphasized how important the experience of involuntariness really is. Janet almost always alluded to involuntariness *en passant*.

Subsequent scholars made involuntariness somewhat more salient in their discussions of automatism. Prince (1907/1910), for example, said that "the one essential and fundamental quality [of automatisms] ... is automaticity or *independence of the personal consciousness*" (italics added, p. 87). This assertion points directly to involuntariness, but Prince's emphasis remains mostly at the level of explanation (of the independent functioning of the subconscious) rather than at the level of subjective experience. Crabtree's (2003) discussion of a DID person's experience increased the salience of involuntariness beyond that expressed by Prince:

> These [dissociated] personalities are not known to ordinary consciousness and carry on with a life of their own. Yet they can affect ordinary life by producing behavior, causing emotions, and creating sensations that are not within the control of the everyday conscious self. To that ordinary self these effects are experienced as psychological automatisms [i.e., experienced as involuntary]. (Crabtree, 2003, p. 67)

Despite its incisive clarity, this quotation from Crabtree still does not highlight the importance of the involuntariness of automatisms. Contrast these quotations about involuntariness from Prince and Crabtree with (1) a recent phenomenological definition of chronic pathological dissociation and (2) a recent description of the subjective experience of persons with DID:

> The phenomena of pathological dissociation [i.e., the phenomena of automatisms] are recurrent, jarring, involuntary intrusions into executive functioning and sense of self. Thus, dissociative symptoms are startling, alien invasions of one's mind and one's experience. (Dell, 2009c, p. 226)
>
> [According to well-replicated research on DID with the Dissociative Experiences Scale (DES)] about 40–50% of the time [DID patients] are undergoing ... dissociative ... invasions of their executive functioning and ... their sense of self. These constant intrusions leave them with two unappetizing alternatives: (1) "I must not be who I think I am," or (2) "I do not make any sense (to me); I must be going crazy." (Dell, 2009c, p. 227)

These quotations highlight the subjective experience of involuntariness. Moreover, they implicitly reveal why *partial* automatisms (as opposed to total automatisms) are so important. Partial automatisms *intrude* into the conscious mind, whereas total automatisms do not. Total

---

[10] See the previous quotation from one of Janet's patients: "It is not I that walk; it is my legs which walk quite alone ..."

automatisms *supplant* the conscious mind and are "hidden" behind a veil of amnesia. Because the person did not directly experience the (total) automatism, he or she is left, haphazardly, to discover (or not) its aftereffects (e.g., time loss, personal effects that have been moved or changed, acquaintances who allude to his/her unremembered behavior) (see also Dell, 2006c, 2009b).

The point that I want to emphasize is that involuntary, consciously experienced intrusions (i.e., partial automatisms) are a central aspect of the daily experience of severely dissociative individuals. They are probably *the* major source of dissociative patients' pervasive sense of self-confusion (see Dell & Lawson, 2009).

This information about the experiential impact of automatisms allows us to now revise our description of the structure, dynamics, and phenomena of mental disaggregation (i.e., dissociation).

> **Understanding Dissociation #2:** The occurrence of automatisms indicates the presence of mental disaggregation. Mental disaggregation entails the existence of a second, co-active center of autonomy. This second center has at least a rudimentary sense of consciousness and self. The second center affects the person's functioning in two ways. In *total* automatisms, the functioning of the person is totally supplanted such that the person is unaware of the event, both during and after the intrusion. That is, total automatisms are hidden from the person by "amnesia." *Partial* automatisms only affect part of the person's functioning. As a consequence, the person is fully aware of what is happening, involuntarily, to an aspect of his or her functioning. These intrusions, which are unexpected, unbidden, and uncontrollable, provoke a variety of secondary reactions (i.e., confusion, surprise, frustration, shame, fear, etc.).

Although this revised account of the structure, dynamics, and subjective phenomena of dissociation is an improvement over our first account (i.e., Understanding Dissociation #1), it still does not explain the *cause* of mental disaggregation.

46.3.6 Janet: What Causes Dissociation?

Janet's discussion of the fundamental, necessary cause of mental disaggregation is probably the least understood and, for many, the least satisfying aspect of Janet's account of dissociation. To be fair, however, Janet is hardly alone in this regard. We will see (in the following) that almost all portrayals of dissociation are quite vague about what causes it.

It is important to know two things about Janet's approach to the cause of dissociation. First, for Janet, mental disaggregation was synonymous with hysteria. Accordingly, his questions about the cause of mental disaggregation were questions about the cause of hysteria. Second, Janet was *not* a theorist. By both training and disposition, he disliked theory; he pejoratively called it "metaphysics" or "speculating").[11] He considered theorizing to be a fruitless and premature endeavor, if not a narcissistic indulgence. Needless to say, this outlook did not bode well for Janet's encounter with the writings of Freud, theoretician and metapsychologist extraordinaire.

Unlike Freud, Janet's writings about dissociation and hysteria were based on observation—not theory (Ellenberger, 1970; Hart, 1910, Robinson, 1977).[12] He did not theorize about the causes of mental disaggregation so much as he offered descriptive generalizations (of the phenomena that he had repeatedly observed).[13]

In 1907, Janet published 15 lectures on hysteria that he had given at Harvard the previous year. In Lecture 13, Janet defined two kinds of "stigma" that characterize hysteria: (1) frequent signs and symptoms that enable diagnosis, and (2) stigma that are "fundamental" to hysteria. By fundamental stigma, Janet meant the necessary cause of hysteria. This stigma, said Janet:

---

[11] During the 1906 Boston symposium on the subconscious, for example, Janet (1907/1910) repeatedly frustrated his interlocutors, who wanted him to explicate his theory of the subconscious: "I intentionally avoid discussing theories so consoling and perhaps true withal; I simply remind myself that I have something quite different to do" (p. 62); "Certainly it ought not to be with regard to half understood symptoms of mental disease that we should try to resolve these great problems of metaphysics. In my opinion, we have got other psychologic and clinical problems to resolve concerning the subconscious without embarrassing ourselves with these speculations" (p. 65); and "There are many other clinical problems of great importance which it seems to me must be studied. None of these researches can be made without exact and long continued observations carried on under good conditions, and the very least of them is to my mind more important than all the huge tomes full of speculations put together" (p. 66).

[12] Which is not to say that Janet did not have theoretical biases; he did. Probably his most repeatedly asserted bias was that only hysterics were hypnotizable. Somehow Janet never observed a normal person with high hypnotizability, a situation that flies in the face of decades of modern hypnosis research, and, indeed, the vocal protests of his colleagues at professional meetings.

[13] My coeditor, John O'Neil, the true philosopher of the two of us, reminds me that it is simply impossible to make observations from an atheoretical perspective. I agree that this is, epistemologically, a flawless assertion. My point about Janet, however, is that he was a vocal critic of theoretical endeavors and liked to think that he refrained from constructing any (explicit) theories. He would also, for the same reason, be put off by Freud's penchant for unrestrained theorizing.

> has a theoretical meaning, it indicates the fundamental character, the causal character from which the rest of the disease springs. For instance, if you consider a tuberculous lesion, the real stigma will be the bacillus of Koch, because we consider it, at least at the present day, as the cause of all the innumerable lesions.... It will be the same with the existence of the pale spirochaete [*Treponema pallidum pallidum*] of Schaudin in syphilis. (p. 275)

Curiously, despite this introduction, Janet did not provide, nor even discuss, the necessary cause of hysteria. Instead, in Lecture 14, he defined two kinds of stigmata: common and proper. The common stigmata occurred in both hysteria and other disorders, whereas the proper stigmata were unique to hysteria ("the phenomena that exist in hysteria, but scarcely exist in any other disease," p. 294). Thus, proper stigmata are pathognomonic to hysteria (and to mental disaggregation).

Janet proposed (and discussed in some detail) three pathognomonic symptoms of hysteria: (1) high susceptibility to suggestion, (2) absentmindedness (the modern concept of absorption), and (3) alternation (i.e., the annoying regularity with which hysterics substitute one symptom for another). He then asked whether the three proper stigmata of hysteria had anything in common. According to Janet they do: all three entail a "retraction of the field of consciousness."

"Retraction of the field of consciousness" is inseparable from Janet's decades-long effort to describe a person's daily functioning in terms of "ego strength" (Janet would never use the term) and levels of mental efficiency. The following paragraph sketches hundreds of pages of Janet's later writing that delineate his model of mental functioning. It will help the reader to know that Janet always discussed mental and psychological functioning in terms of levels. Thus, he discussed decreased functioning in terms of a "lowering of the mental level" (*abaissement du niveau mental*) and "depressed" functioning (which did *not* mean affectively depressed, but a depressed level of mental efficiency).

The central concept in Janet's writings is *personality*, but he used the term differently from current usage. When Janet said *personality*, he meant something like "the conscious functioning of the ego or self." As noted previously, he discussed the conscious functioning of the ego, self, or personality in terms of its level of mental efficiency.

According to Janet, the task of the personality is to deal with daily life by consciously perceiving the relevant aspects of the environment, thinking about them, taking well-considered actions in response to those stimuli, and, ultimately, understanding their meaning for oneself. Personalities that operate at lower levels of mental efficiency (1) are impaired in their *capacity to consciously perceive* the relevant aspects of the environment (they might be able to perceive only a few elements of the environment); (2) are impaired in their *ability to think about* those conscious perceptions (their mind might be empty of all associations to those perceptions so that those conscious perceptions could not be judged or compared by reference to past experiences); (3) impaired in their *capacity to take well-considered actions* in response to those perceptions (their ego strength might be too weak to reflect on the matter and, as a result, they react impulsively); and (4) impaired in their *capacity to understand the personal meaning* of those perceptions (they might be too weak to do the internal psychological "work" of truly assimilating those perceptions and accommodating their sense of self to those new understandings).[14]

With this too-brief introduction to the later Janet, we can now return to Janet's effort to specify the fundamental cause of hysteria. Janet identified three pathognomonic symptoms of hysteria (high susceptibility to suggestion, absentmindedness, and alteration), which he said could be summarized in terms of a single feature of hysterical functioning: retraction of the field of consciousness. Retraction of the field of consciousness is a narrowing of attention. Narrowing of attention can impair the first two functions of the personality (see preceding paragraph). In other words, a retracted field of consciousness (1) reduces the number of elements of the environment that can be consciously perceived, and (2) reduces the number of associations that are evoked by what is consciously perceived.

Janet claimed that hysterics routinely suffer from a restricted field of consciousness. A restricted field of consciousness is, he said, the characteristic form of (lowered) mental functioning in hysteria. Moreover, Janet insisted that a restricted field of consciousness was hereditary (Janet, 1889, 1893, 1919, 1920). Janet reported that the inherently impaired mental functioning of a hysteric could be (and frequently was) further impaired by incidents of illness, fatigue, stress, or exhaustion. At such times of illness or stress, the hysteric's mental functioning became so inefficient that he or she entered a state of "psychological misery" in which hysterical symptoms flourished.

---

[14] The most accessible explication in English of Janet's model of the personality and its levels of mental efficiency can be found in *The Haunted Self* (Van der Hart, Nijenhuis, & Steele, 2006, especially Chapters 7–9).

At this juncture, the relevant question becomes, "Is retraction of the field of consciousness the fundamental cause of hysteria, the fundamental cause of *désagrégation mentale*?" And the answer is "No," but Janet often seemed to imply that the answer is "Yes." The picture of hysteria that emerged from *L'automatisme psychologique* is that hysterics suffer from a mental/psychological weakness that severely limits their capacity to hold in mind many thoughts at one time. As a consequence of this weakness, important elements of perception escape the impaired conscious mind and drop into a separate area of the mind where they form a second psychological system, a second consciousness, a subconscious. Janet never really explained how or why this happened. He simply claimed that this occurred in hysteria, but that it did not occur in other disorders (Janet, 1920). Again, he did not explain why this was the case—other than to imply that it was innate.

In truth, explanation was not Janet's *forte*. In 1910, Freud famously mocked Janet's "explanation" of mental disaggregation:

> According to [Janet], hysteria is a form of degenerate modification of the nervous system, which shows itself in an innate weakness in the power of psychical synthesis. Hysterical patients, he believes, are inherently incapable of holding together the multiplicity of mental processes into a unity, and hence arises the tendency to mental dissociation. If I may be allowed to draw a homely but clear analogy, Janet's hysterical patient reminds one of a feeble woman who has gone out shopping and is now returning home laden with a multitude of parcels and boxes. She cannot contain the whole heap of them with her two arms and ten fingers. So first of all one object slips from her grasp; and when she stoops to pick it up, another one escapes her in its place, and so on. (pp. 21–22)

In 1920, Janet implicitly conceded that retraction of the field of consciousness was *not* the fundamental cause of hysteria. He did say, however, that retraction of the field of consciousness was the primary pathognomonic symptom of hysteria:

> [T]his notion of the retraction of the field of consciousness summarizes the preceding stigmata [i.e., suggestibility, absent-mindedness, and alternation], and we may say that their fundamental mental state is characterized by a special [psychological] weakness, consisting in the lack of power, on the part of the feeble subject, to gather, to condense his psychological phenomena, and assimilate them to his personality. (Janet, 1920, p. 311)

Unfortunately, even this statement is inaccurate. Simply said, retraction of the field of consciousness is an alteration of consciousness that is *not* specific to hysteria and mental disaggregation (Steele, Dorahy, Van der Hart, & Nijenhuis, 2009). So, retraction of the field of consciousness is not even pathognomonic of the disorder.

So, what *is* the fundamental cause of dissociation? Janet did not really answer this question, but he did drop a hint in his final definition of hysteria:

> Hysteria is a form of mental depression characterized by the retraction of the field of consciousness and *a tendency to the dissociation and emancipation of ideas and functions* that constitute personality. (Janet, 1920, p. 332, italics added)

"A tendency to dissociation," aha! Now what is that? Of all things, Janet gives us another hint by quoting Breuer and Freud (1893)!

> Many authors, Gurney, Myers, Laurent, Breuer and Freud, Benedict, Oppenheim, Jolly, Pick, Morton Prince, have thought like me that a place should be made for the *disposition to somnambulism*. Was not the somnambulistic attack for us the type of hysterical accidents in 1889? "The disposition to this dissociation and, at the same time, the formation of states of consciousness, which we propose to collect under the name of hypnoid states, constitute the fundamental phenomenon of this neurosis," said MM.[15] Breuer and Freud, of Vienna, in 1893. (Janet, 1920, pp. 331–332, italics added)

"The disposition to somnambulism," aha! In modern language, the disposition to somnambulism is high hypnotizability. This, of course, makes perfect sense to any clinician who has encountered severely dissociative patients. Unfortunately, high hypnotizability could only be a dead end for Janet. High hypnotizability was a road that his theoretic biases forbade him to travel. Janet believed that hysteria and the disposition to somnambulism were one and the same—all somnambulists were hysterical and all hysterics were somnambulists. Indeed, for Janet, hypnotizability was a *symptom* of hysteria. Because he continued to believe that high hypnotizability could not be studied apart from hysteria, Janet could never pursue what just might be *the* fundamental cause of hysteria, *the* fundamental cause of mental disaggregation, *the* fundamental cause of dissociation—high hypnotizability.

Occasionally, Janet allowed himself to wrestle with the question: which came first, high hypnotizability or hysteria? Still, his prejudice (that they were isomorphic)

[15] "M." is short for "Monsieur"; "MM." is short for the plural, "Messieurs."

would not allow him to settle upon an answer. His views wavered and vacillated from year to year. My favorite quotation from Janet regarding hysteria and hypnotizability can be found in *L'automatisme psychologique.* I think he had it right in 1889 when he said:

> It is not hysteria which constitutes terrain favorable to hypnotism, but it is hypnotic sensibility that constitutes favorable terrain for hysteria and other illnesses. (Janet, 1889, pp. 451–452)

This view—that high hypnotizability can cause hysteria—is quite congruent with contemporary thinking about high hypnotizability. In the following we will examine closely the relationships between high hypnotizability and dissociation. First, however, we must understand Freud's concept of repression. We will see that our modern *de facto* understanding of dissociation is an undifferentiated tangle of Freudian repression and the Janetian subconscious.

46.4 SIGMUND FREUD'S CONCEPT OF REPRESSION

46.4.1 Jean-Martín Charcot and Traumatic Hysteria

A few words about Charcot are necessary at this point. Unlike Janet,[16] Freud's story *does* begin with Charcot. Freud was a neurologist and Charcot was the greatest neurologist of his era. In the fall of 1885, Freud was awarded a travel bursary to go to Paris and study the work of Charcot at the Salpêtrière.[17] At that time, Freud idealized Charcot; he named his son "Martin" after Charcot, translated two of Charcot's books into German (Charcot, 1886, 1887/1888), and repeatedly declared himself to be a pupil of Charcot (Andersson, 1962).

Much of Charcot's important work on hysteria has been forgotten. The professional world's awareness of Charcot's suggestion-driven misadventures with the grand hysterics at the Salpêtrière apparently did not allow his insights into hysteria to be retained following his death in 1893 (Ellenberger, 1970; Harris, 1991; Owens, 1971). To the extent that some of Charcot's insights about hysteria have been retained, they are seldom remembered as being *his* ideas.[18]

When Charcot began his study of hysteria, he accepted the received truth of his era: hysteria was caused by poor heredity. In the mid-1880s, however, Charcot participated in an important debate about traumatic causes (e.g., railroad accidents, injuries in the workplace, etc.) of hysteria. It is important for the reader to understand that *the idea of traumatic hysteria was new at that time (and highly controversial).* Yes, Briquet (1859) had written that there was much violence and alcoholism in the families of his hysterical patients, but his *Treatise* in no way undermined the widely held conviction that hysteria was due to degenerate heredity—a conviction that was held by both Charcot[19] and Janet.

Traumatic hysterical symptoms were thrust into bold relief when railroad crashes provoked passengers to seek compensation for their nonorganic disabilities. Oppenheim called these symptoms a "traumatic neurosis" and denied that they were hysterical in nature (Thomsen & Oppenheim, 1884). Page (1883), on the other hand, persuasively argued that these symptoms were, indeed, hysterical. Hysterical symptoms, said Page, could be caused by "nervous shock."[20] Charcot (1889/1991) sided with Page.[21]

---

[16] Upon completion of *L'automatisme psychologique* in Le Havre, Janet moved to Paris to teach at Lycée Louis-le-Grand and to begin his studies for an MD. Charcot soon appointed him as the Director of the Laboratory of Pathological Psychology at the Salpêtrière. This sequence of events is important: Janet's foundational work on hypnosis, hysteria, and dissociation predated his professional association with Charcot. The four publications (1886, 1887, 1888, and 1889) reviewed previously had established Janet as an important voice in the new field of psychology. These publications and Janet's presentations at congresses in Paris prompted Charcot to recruit Janet. Thus, it is not true, despite oft-repeated statements to the contrary, that Janet was a student of Charcot. Janet was Charcot's brilliant young colleague.

[17] Freud's contact with Charcot extended from October 20, 1885, to February 23, 1886.

[18] Shakespeare's Mark Antony could equally well have been speaking of the "Caesar of the Salpêtrière" (Owen, 1971) (as opposed to Julius Caesar) when he said, "The evil that men do lives after them, the good is oft interred with their bones."

[19] "Charcot shared the pervasive late-nineteenth century preoccupation with the theory of degeneration which marked many branches of medicine and particularly psychiatry.... So convinced was he by the theory of degeneration that Charcot seemed frustrated when hereditary antecedents could not be rooted out" (Harris, 1991, p. xxv).

[20] An excellent account of the debates about traumatic hysteria can be found in Trimble's (1981) *Post-Traumatic Neurosis: From Railway Spine to Whiplash.*

[21] "[I]n consequence of traumatism, we may observe in one individual, narrowing of the visual field, paralysis, or contracture with special symptoms and alterations of sensibility and of localization of anaesthesia; different marks of hysteria, as micropsy and monocular polyopia; the hysterogenic zones, glosso-labial hemo-spasm, &c.; frequently even convulsive attacks identical with those of genuine hysteria. In one word, we may see the complete clinical picture of hysteria. Why then should this ensemble of phenomena receive another name than that due to it—hysteria?" (Charcot & Marie, 1892, p. 639–640).

Earlier, I called the reader's attention to the fact that the field of dissociation began with hypnosis, not trauma. Now, I call the reader's attention to the fact that it was Charcot who decisively brought trauma into the field of dissociation. In his last major book (Vol. III of *Clinical Diseases of the Nervous System*), Charcot (1889) discussed the cases of several men who became contractured or paralyzed following an accident in the workplace, at home, or on the highway. Building upon Page's concept of nervous shock, Charcot proposed the first, well-organized, psychological theory of hysteria: a sudden, terrifying accident could provoke a hypnotic-like state during which the person was highly suggestible to hysterogenic ideas. Thus, for example, in discussing the cases of "Porcz– and Pin–," Charcot asked a question:

> [I]t may be inquired whether the mental condition occasioned by the Nervous Shock experienced at the moment of the accident and for some time after, is not equivalent in a certain measure, in subjects predisposed as Porcz– and Pin– were, to the cerebral condition which is determined in "hysterics" by hypnotism. (Charcot, 1889/1991, p. 305)

Like many others of that time, Charcot considered hypnosis to be pathological—a symptom of hysteria. He understood hypnosis to be a state during which the ego was neutralized such that suggestions could gain a powerful purchase on the mind. Thus, the person's terrified thoughts (of death, loss of limb, paralysis, etc.) at the instant of trauma, or even the painful physical sensation itself, might act as a hypnotic autosuggestion:

> [B]ecause of the annihilation of the *ego* produced by the hypnotism in the one case, and, as one may suppose, by the nervous shock in the other, that idea once installed in the brain takes sole possession and acquires sufficient domination to realize itself objectively in the form of paralysis. The sensation, in question, therefore … plays the part of a veritable suggestion. (Charcot, 1889/1991, p. 305)

Charcot stated that, after a brief period of incubation, such suggestions could become fixed ideas that produced hysterical symptoms:

> [A]n idea, a coherent group of associated ideas settle themselves in the mind in the fashion of parasites, remaining isolated from the rest of the mind and expressing themselves outwardly through corresponding motor phenomena. (Charcot, 1889/1991, p. 290)
>
> The paralysis was not produced at the very moment of the accident, but it was only after an interval of several days, after a sort of incubation stage of mental elaboration.… We have here a phenomenon of unconscious or sub-conscious cerebration, mentation or ideation.… By reason of the easy dissociation of the mental unity of the *ego* in cases of this kind, these centres can be set in operation without any other region of the psychic organ being interfered with or forming part of the process. (Charcot, 1889/1991, p. 387)

Although he was strongly convinced that degenerate heredity provided the underlying vulnerability to hysteria,[22] Charcot articulated a traumatogenic model[23] of hysterical symptoms in this book (Charcot, 1889/1991). Thus, according to Charcot, a sudden trauma sometimes evoked a spontaneous hypnotic-like state, during which autosuggestion occurred.[24] The autosuggestion became a fixed unconscious idea whose activity bypassed the ego. Following a period of incubation, these unconscious ideas produced hysterical symptoms.

Freud translated this book (Charcot, 1889/1991) into German upon his return to Vienna from Paris in early 1886. Due to Freud's alacrity in completing the translation, Charcot's book was published in German (Charcot, 1886) later that year, three years before it was published in French. The extent to which Freud and Breuer subsequently drew upon Charcot's ideas in this book is unmistakable (Breuer & Freud, 1893, 1895; Freud, 1896)—a fact that Freud freely admitted.[25]

---

[22] Harris (1991) emphasized that "Charcot was also keen to demonstrate that some victims were more susceptible than others to nervous symptoms. Although they might have had the appearance of robust working-class health, deeper investigation could well uncover a wealth of irregularities, especially tendencies to shyness, terror, and rage" (Harris, 1991, p. xxix). Even several years later, Charcot continued to insist that heredity is the fundamental cause of hysteria: "The dominant idea for us in the aetiology of hysteria is, therefore (in the widest sense), that of hereditary predisposition" (Charcot & Marie, 1992, p. 628).

[23] "Most of the sufferers had both unfortunate heredity and bad habits of some kind, but it was the series of accidents, and the extreme fright associated with them, which brought on the hysterical symptoms" (Harris, 1991).

[24] Charcot insisted that "autosuggestion plays the principal part" [in the] "mechanism of the development of hystero-traumatic paralyses" (Charcot, 1889/1991, p. 384).

[25] "[W]hen Breuer and I published our 'Preliminary Communication' on the psychical mechanism of hysterical phenomena [1893a], we were completely under the spell of Charcot's researches. We regarded the pathogenic experiences of our patients as psychical traumas, and equated them with the somatic traumas whose influence on hysterical paralyses had been established by Charcot; and Breuer's hypothesis of hypnoid states was itself nothing but a reflection of the fact that Charcot had reproduced those traumatic paralyses artificially under hypnosis" (Freud, 1910, p. 21). See Andersson (1962) for a more complete explication of Freud's early proclamations that he was a pupil of Charcot, and his advocacy of Charcot's views regarding hysteria.

46.4.2 Breuer and Freud's Traumatic Hysteria

In early 1893, Breuer and Freud published their "Preliminary Communication" about the psychical[26] mechanism of hysterical phenomena. This paper was a bold generalization of Charcot's explanation of traumatic hysteria. Whereas Charcot claimed that *some* cases of hysteria were evoked by psychological trauma, Breuer and Freud now claimed that almost all hysteria was caused by psychical (i.e., psychological) trauma[27]:

> In traumatic neuroses the operative cause of the illness is not the trifling physical injury but the affect of fright—the psychical trauma. In an analogous manner, our investigations reveal, for many, if not for most, hysterical symptoms, precipitating causes which can only be described as psychical traumas. Any experience which calls up distressing affects—such as those of fright, anxiety, shame, or physical pain—may operate as a trauma of this kind; and whether it does so depends naturally enough on the susceptibility of the person affected (as well as on another condition [hypnoid states] which will be mentioned later). (p. 6)

Like Charcot, Breuer and Freud emphasized the role of hypnoid (i.e., spontaneous hypnotic-like) states in creating hysterical symptoms. They did *not*, however, claim that autosuggestion was responsible for those symptoms. Instead, Breuer and Freud reasoned that, because the psychological trauma was experienced during a hypnoid state, it became cut off from the ordinary conscious mind. By virtue of being cut off from consciousness, the traumatic experience could not be metabolized:

> [T]he basis and *sine qua non* of hysteria is the existence of hypnoid states. These hypnoid states share with one another and with hypnosis … one common features: the ideas which emerge in them are very intense but are cut off from associative communication with the rest of the content of consciousness. (p. 12)

When they shed Charcot's autosuggestion theory of hysterical symptoms, Breuer and Freud freed themselves to posit a much more credible, and rather Janetian, mechanism of hysterical symptoms. Specifically, Breuer and Freud claimed that hysterical symptoms were an intrusion into the mind and body by undigested, split-off traumatic memories:

> It is of course obvious that in cases of "traumatic" hysteria what provokes the symptoms is the [terrifying] accident. The causal connection is equally evident in hysterical attacks when it is possible to gather from the patient's utterances that in each attack he is hallucinating the same event which provoked the first one. (p. 4)
>
> [T]he psychical trauma—or more precisely the memory of the trauma—acts like a foreign body which long after its entry must continue to be regarded as an agent that is still at work. (p. 6)
>
> Hysterics suffer mainly from reminiscences. (p. 7)

Finally, Breuer and Freud (1893) espoused a frankly Janetian view of the underlying structure of hysteria—splitting of consciousness:

> The longer we have been occupied with these phenomena the more we have become convinced that *the splitting of consciousness which is so striking in the well-known classical cases of* "double conscience" [dual consciousness] *is present to a rudimentary degree in every hysteria, and that a tendency to such dissociation, and with it the emergence of abnormal states of consciousness (which we shall bring together under the term "hypnoid") is the basic phenomenon of this neurosis.* In these views we concur with Binet and the two Janets. (p. 12)[28]

46.4.3 Repression

Freud would not remain long in intellectual debt to Janet. Within a year, he insisted that "Janet … assigns too great an importance to the splitting of consciousness in his characterization of hysteria" (Freud, 1894, p. 51).[29] Freud now (1894) explained hysteria in terms of repression and conversion (Breuer & Freud, 1895; Freud, 1894). The crucial

[26] At this time, psychological explanations (as opposed to physical/somatic explanations) of psychiatric symptoms were just beginning to emerge. Freud used the term *psychical* to mean psychological or mental.

[27] Three years later, Freud (1896) claimed that all cases of hysteria were caused by childhood sexual abuse ("seduction"). And a year after that, he decided that his patients' reports of sexual abuse were merely fantasies (Freud, 1897)!

[28] Breuer and Freud acknowledged that Charcot, too, had "suggested that hysterical attacks are a rudimentary form of condition seconde" [second consciousness]. (p. 16)

[29] Even Breuer, whose contribution to Studies on Hysteria was an unmistakable case of multiple personality (Anna O.), went along with Freud. Breuer described hysterical patients as follows: "Their psychical ideational activity is divided into a conscious and an unconscious part, and their ideas are divided into some that are admissible and some that are inadmissible to consciousness. We cannot, therefore, speak of a splitting of consciousness, though we can of a splitting of the mind" (p. 225). This is Freud's view—to which he adhered for the remainder of his life. This view is of major importance because, in Freud's hands, it entailed a total rejection of the multiple-centers-of-consciousness model of multiple personality that had been proposed by Janet, Prince, and others.

point for the reader is that Freud's agreement with Janet's description of dissociation was fleeting at best. Even in Breuer and Freud's (1893) "Preliminary Communication," Freud was already suggesting that hysterical amnesia was *a defensive maneuver of the mind—an intentional fending off of uncomfortable ideas and urges.*

Repression (*Verdrängt*) made its debut in the "Preliminary Communication" when Freud argued that some cases of hysteria did not involve hypnoid states. Despite that article's assertion that "the basis and *sine qua non* of hysteria is the existence of hypnoid states" (p. 12), Freud insisted upon the existence of *non*-hypnoid cases of hysteria that were caused by "repression" (rather than hypnoid states). According to Freud, in nonhypnoid hysteria, "it was a question of things which the patient wished to forget, and therefore intentionally repressed from his conscious thought and inhibited and suppressed" (Breuer & Freud, 1893, p. 10).

By the time that Freud and Breuer finished writing their book (Breuer & Freud, 1895) 2 years later, Freud was saying that he had never encountered a genuine case of hypnoid hysteria (such as Breuer's Anna O.).[30] Freud, as we will see in the following, not only rejected Janet's (and Breuer's 1893) idea of split consciousness, but he claimed that hypnoid states [i.e., dissociative alterations of consciousness] were preceded by, and based upon, defensive acts of repression (Breuer & Freud, 1895). Freud would eventually proclaim that "the theory of repression is the cornerstone on which the whole structure of psycho-analysis rests" (Freud, 1914a, p. 16).

The bottom line here is that Freud's insistence upon the causal and temporal primacy of repression meant that, for him (and for psychoanalytic theory), dissociative phenomena were permanently consigned to a secondary status. Defense was primary; everything else was (very) secondary. For example:

> I was repeatedly able to show that the splitting of the content of consciousness is the result of an act of will on the part of the patient [i.e., repression]; that is to say, it is initiated by an effort of will whose motive can be specified. By this I do not, of course, mean that the patient intends to bring about a splitting of consciousness. His intention is a different one; but, instead of attaining its aim, it produces a splitting of consciousness.... I shall call this ... "*defence hysteria.*" (Freud, 1894, pp. 46–47)

> The psycho-analyst has a line of approach altogether different from that followed by the investigators of multiple personality. The focus of his interest is not on the manifestations observed on the phenomenal plane, but on the dynamic factors conceived to lie behind them. The conflicting forces on the latter plane are the things that matter, and whether they manifest themselves on the phenomenal plane as one or other of various possible symptoms, or whether they lead to the complete splitting of double personality is of comparatively minor importance. (Hart, 1926, p. 255)

So, what is repression, exactly? Although Freud said a great deal about repression, I think it is fair to say that his explanations of repression were always more metaphorical and intuitive than they were concrete or precise. In four decades of articles and books that touched on repression, Freud only reiterated various versions of his original 1893 definition (Breuer & Freud, 1893, p. 10)—motivated forgetting of unpleasant realities:

> [A] psychical force, aversion on the part of the ego had originally driven the pathogenic idea out of association and was now opposing its return to memory. The hysterical patient's "not knowing" was in fact a "not wanting to know"—a not wanting which might be to a greater or less extent conscious. (Breuer & Freud, 1895, pp. 269–270)

> [T]he *essence of repression lies simply in turning something away, and keeping it at a distance, from the conscious.* (Freud, 1914b, p. 147, Freud's italics)

> [T]he motive and the purpose of repression [is] nothing else than the avoidance of unpleasure. (Freud, 1914b, p. 153)

> The psychical apparatus is intolerant of unpleasure; it has to fend it off at all costs, and if the perception of reality entails unpleasure, that perception—that is, the truth—must be sacrificed. (Freud, 1937, p. 237)

Freud simultaneously saw repression as a biological universal (a mental defense by which humans do what all organisms do—avoid unpleasure and pain) and as a mechanism that generated symptoms when it failed—for instance, "the return of the repressed" (Freud, 1914b, 1939).

Freud repeatedly insisted that repression is not a one-time event. It is a continuing, energy-intensive operation:

[30] Freud said, "Strangely enough, I have never in my own experience met with a genuine hypnoid hysteria. Any that I took in hand has turned into a defence hysteria [i.e., a hysteria based on repression]. It is not, indeed, that I have never had to do with symptoms which demonstrably arose during dissociated states of consciousness and were obliged for that reason to remain excluded from the ego. This was sometimes so in my cases as well; but I was able to show afterwards that the so-called hypnoid state owed its separation to the fact that in it a psychical group had come into effect which had previously been split off by defence. In short, I am unable to suppress a suspicion that somewhere or other the roots of hypnoid and defence hysteria come together, and that there the primary factor is defence" (p. 286)

> The process of repression is not to be regarded as an event which takes place *once*, the results of which are permanent …; repression demands a persistent expenditure of force, and if this were to cease the success of the repression would be jeopardized, so that a fresh act of repression would be necessary. We may suppose that the repressed exercises a continuous pressure in the direction of the conscious, so that this pressure must be balanced by an unceasing counter-pressure. Thus the maintenance of a repression involves an uninterrupted expenditure of force. (Freud, 1914b, p. 151)

What is this "unceasing counter-pressure" that keeps repressed material unconscious? Freud's answer is "anticathexis":

> This other process [i.e., the unceasing counter-pressure] can only be found in the assumption of an anticathexis, by means of which the system *Pcs* [preconscious] protects itself from the pressure upon it of the [repressed] unconscious idea.… It is this which represents the permanent expenditure [of energy] of a primal repression, and which also guarantees the permanence of that repression. Anticathexis is the sole mechanism of primal repression. (Freud, 1915, p. 181)

Cathexis and anticathexis are obscure Freudian theoretical concepts that I will not try to explain (see Freud, 1950). Freud's most transparent illustration of repression and anticathexis is a metaphor whereby students eject an unruly class member and blockade the door so that he cannot burst back into the room:

> Let us suppose that in this lecture-room … there is … someone who is causing a disturbance and whose ill-mannered laughter, chattering and shuffling with his feet are distracting my attention from my task. I have to announce that I cannot proceed with my lecture; and thereupon three or four of you who are strong men stand up and, after a short struggle, put the interrupter outside the door. So now he is "repressed," and I can continue my lecture. But in order that the interruption shall not be repeated, in case the individual who has been expelled should try to enter the room once more, the gentlemen who have put my will into effect place their chairs up against the door and thus establish a "resistance" after the repression has been accomplished. If you will now translate the two localities concerned into psychical terms as the "conscious" and the "unconscious," you will have before you a fairly good picture of the process of repression. (p. 25)

Perhaps what is most important here is that, in modern terms, repression is an effortful cognitive strategy whose implementation requires continuing mental work.

Understanding dissociation #3: Repression is an intentional, motivated, cognitive defense (*abwehr*) against unpleasant ideas and realities that the person does not wish to know about. This defense is an energy-intensive process that must be constantly sustained in order to be effective. When repression periodically fails, as Freud says all defenses do at some point (Freud, 1940), the "return of the repressed" causes symptoms.

46.4.4 Freud: What Causes Repression?

There is, I think, a significant lacuna in Freud's explication of repression. He never really tells us what *causes* repression. True, he says that repression is driven by The Pleasure Principle, the universal biological drive to avoid pain. Similarly, Freud says that the person intentionally represses that which he or she does not want to know. These explanations are Aristotelian final causes; they tell us *why* repression occurs, they tell us the purpose that it serves. The problem is that Freud does not tell us *how* repression occurs or why it occurs for some people (in given circumstances) and not for others. Similarly, Freud does not tell us why the consequences of repression are so different for some people than for others. Nor does he tell us why "the return of the repressed" produces very different symptoms in some people compared to others.

Admittedly, Freud tried to identify the specific (sexual) causes of each neurosis. Freud claimed that neurasthenia was caused by too much masturbation, that anxiety neurosis was caused by too many unsatisfactory sexual experiences, and that hysteria was caused by childhood sexual abuse (Freud, 1895, 1896b). Unfortunately (and somewhat oddly), Freud explicitly refused to deal with the fact that these specific necessary causes were not sufficient to cause the neuroses in question. That is, Freud acknowledged that there existed non-neurasthenic individuals who masturbated too much, and nonanxious persons with many unsatisfactory sexual experiences—but he insisted that such cases were irrelevant (Freud, 1895, 1896b; Macmillan, 1986)!

Freud pursued this same scientifically invalid strategy with regard to repression and hysteria. He explicitly refused to deal with two inconvenient facts: (1) only some sexually abused children repress their experiences, and (2) only some sexually abused children became hysterical:

> It does not matter if many people experience infantile sexual experiences without becoming hysterics, provided only that all the people who become hysterics have experienced scenes of that kind. (Freud, 1896a, p. 209)

This claim is scientifically unacceptable.[31] One cannot prove that X causes Y solely by gathering data from a group of cases with Y and finding X in all of those cases. Other cases of Y may not have X, or X may just be a noncausal correlate of some third (genuine) cause, Z.

Freud had adapted (incorrectly) Koch's postulates for determining whether a particular bacterium was the cause of a given disease (Macmillan, 1997). Koch's third postulate requires that inoculation with the bacterium must produce the disease. Obviously, Freud could not experimentally inflict infantile sexual experiences on healthy subjects to see if they would then suffer hysteria. However, there existed a naturalistic substitute for experimental inoculation—namely, to search for the possible existence of cases where infantile sexual experiences had *not* caused hysteria. Freud was well aware that such cases existed, but dismissed them as scientifically irrelevant (see the following). This is poor science.[32]

The obvious implication of sexually abused children who do not become hysterical is that sexual abuse is not sufficient to cause hysteria. What does Freud say about this?

> What can the other factors be which the "specific ætiology" of hysteria still needs in order actually to produce the neurosis? *That, Gentlemen, is a theme in itself, which I do not propose to enter upon.* (Freud, 1896a, p. 210, italics added)

Similarly, Freud admitted that some sexually abused children repress these events, whereas others do not. Despite the fact that, according to Freud, repression of these events is a necessary condition for hysteria, he openly refused to discuss this issue:

> From this you will perceive that the matter is not merely one of the existence of the sexual experiences, but that a psychological condition enters in as well. The scenes must be present as unconscious memories; only so long as, and in so far as, they are unconscious are they able to create and maintain hysterical symptoms. *But what decides whether those experiences produce conscious or unconscious memories*—whether that is conditioned by the content of the experiences, or by the time at which they occur, or by later influences—*that is a fresh problem, which we shall prudently avoid.* (Freud, 1896a, p. 211, italics added)

I suspect that a significant determinant of Freud's obstinacy in these matters is that these inconvenient facts might point in a direction that Freud does not like—toward an underlying, perhaps innate, disposition to repression and hysteria.[33] Freud does not want to "go there" for at least two reasons. First, Freud would not want to give repression a special or privileged role in hysteria because he considered repression to be a universal aspect of human psychological functioning. Freud sought to make repression a cornerstone of his model of the dynamic functioning of the human mind (see especially Freud, 1900, 1912, 1914, and 1915). Secondly, a major purpose of Freud's focus on the "specific ætiologies" of the neuroses (Freud, 1895, 1896a, 1896b) was to refute the importance that Charcot (and Janet) had accorded to heredity in general (see especially Freud, 1896b) and the heredity of hysteria in particular.

The reader may recall that I urged leniency for Janet's vagueness about the fundamental causes of dissociation—on the ground that most scholars in the field have been incredibly vague about what causes dissociation. At this juncture, we can see that Freud, too, was startlingly (and intentionally) vague about the fundamental causes of repression and hysteria. Janet, at least, gave us some hints about where to look for an answer (i.e., a tendency toward dissociation and the disposition to somnambulism[34]). Freud gave us no hints; he certainly did not want to look for a tendency toward dissociation or a disposition to somnambulism. But his erstwhile colleague, Josef Breuer, did.

Breuer's theoretical chapter in *Studies on Hysteria* is a scholarly and well-argued analysis of hysteria and its causes. In fact, I find Breuer's analysis and argumentation to be superior to Freud's. Breuer advanced several propositions, admitted what he did not know, employed careful reasoning, and did not avoid logically dictated paths that he disliked. Freud, on the other hand, avoided some logically dictated paths that he disliked and was quite

[31] See Macmillan (1986, 1997) for excellent discussions of Freud's defective causal analysis and his inadequate implementation of the causal postulates of Koch's germ theory.

[32] Yes, an inadequate scientific method such as Freud's will sometimes correctly identify the specific cause of a disorder. More often, however, such methodology will incorrectly identify the cause of the disorder. Note, for example, that Freud incorrectly identified the specific causes of neurasthenia and anxiety neurosis, and that he rejected his own "scientific" evidence for the cause of hysteria 2 years after publishing them.

[33] Mitchell (1921) was certainly thinking along these lines when he noted that "The possibility of conversion seems to depend on some native peculiarity which is not always present" (p. 47).

[34] The reader is reminded that Janet (diabolically?) advanced his hint about the disposition to somnambulism via a quotation from Breuer and Freud (1893)!

willing to substitute rhetoric for logic when it served his purposes.[35]

Studies on Hysteria contains a polite, but irreconcilable, argument between Freud and Breuer. Freud consistently undermined Breuer's concepts (i.e., hypnoid states and hypnoid hysteria) and sought to replace them with his own concepts (i.e., repression and defense hysteria). In addition, by the time that *Studies on Hysteria* was published, Freud had left hypnosis behind. Breuer, on the other hand, remained convinced that hypnosis was fundamental to hysteria. In a remarkable echo of Janet's (1889) statement that "hypnotic sensibility constitutes favourable terrain for hysteria," Breuer asserted that

> What we should be doing would be first to assign the phenomena of hysteria to hypnosis, and then to assert that hypnosis is the cause of those phenomena. (Breuer & Freud, 1895, p. 248)

Despite their respectful politeness, it is clear that Freud and Breuer were at loggerheads over hypnosis and its relationship to hysteria. In a kind of counterpoint to Freud's undermining of his ideas, Breuer quietly and repeatedly stated that his ideas applied to cases of hysteria that were "severe," "major," "complicated," and so forth. Moreover, in sharp contrast to Freud, Breuer was a great believer in the disposition to hysteria. Breuer proposed that the disposition to hysteria had three components: a disposition to conversion of affect (into somatic phenomena), a disposition to suggestibility, and a disposition to hypnoid states. Breuer believed that a strong disposition to hypnoid states characterized the difference between major hysteria and minor hysteria:

> The third constituent of the hysterical disposition, which appears in some cases … is the hypnoid state, the tendency to auto-hypnosis. This state favours and facilitates in the greatest degree both conversion and suggestion; and in this way it erects, as we might say, on the top of the minor hysterias, the higher storey of major hysteria. (Breuer & Freud, pp. 215–216)

In a prescient anticipation of some very recent thinking about dissociation (Dorahy, 2006), Breuer also suggested that hysterics had a premorbid tendency toward dual thinking:

> I believe that in a great many cases what underlies dissociation is an excess of efficiency, the habitual co-existence of two heterogeneous trains of ideas.… I suspect that the duplication of psychical functioning, whether this is habitual or caused by emotional situations in life, acts as a substantial *predisposition* to a genuine pathological splitting of the mind. (pp. 233–234)

Finally, Breuer was the first to suggest, in effect, that high hypnotizability facilitates repression:

> Freud's observations and analyses show that the splitting of the mind can also be caused by "defence," by the deliberate deflection of consciousness from the distressing ideas.… I only venture to suggest that the assistance of the hypnoid state is necessary if defence is to result not merely in single converted ideas being made into unconscious ones, but in a genuine splitting of the mind. Auto-hypnosis has, so to speak, created the space or region of unconscious psychical activity into which the ideas which are fended off are driven. (pp. 235–236)

This is actually a stronger theoretical proposal than that of Janet (1914, 1919) and McDougall (1938), both of whom would later assert that repression was one route to dissociation.

So, what can we say at this point about the cause of repression? Surprisingly little. Freud extensively described the *function* of repression—suppression of memories of unpleasant realities—but he gave us little beyond this, except for his metapsychology.[36] According to Freud's metapsychology, (1) repression was implemented by the ego, (2) the repressed material resided in the structural unconscious (the id), and (3) repression had to be continuously maintained via an ongoing expenditure of energy. Freud considered repression to operate in accord with a biologically universal Pleasure Principle. But when he was confronted with trauma-driven repetitions that apparently contradicted the Pleasure Principle (i.e., posttraumatic nightmares, traumatic play in children, and other manifestations of "the repetition compulsion"), Freud retreated still deeper into his metapsychology. He explained these phenomena on the basis of a newly postulated Death Instinct (Freud, 1920). In short, Freud may have been a creative theoretician and metapsychologist, but he faltered in his efforts to forge a comprehensive explanation of repression.

---

[35] The best example of Freud's too-easy resort to rhetoric is the facility with which he first argued that memories of sexual abuse were absolutely valid and true and, subsequently, argued that they were just oedipal fantasies. Little of Freud's argumentation in either case is adequately buttressed by logic or evidence.

[36] "I propose that when we have succeeded in describing a psychical process in its dynamic, topographical, and economic aspects, we should speak of it as a metapsychological presentation" (Freud, 1915, p. 181).

46.5 WHAT IS THE RELATIONSHIP BETWEEN DISSOCIATION AND REPRESSION?

46.5.1 Pierre Janet and Sigmund Freud

Janet and Freud did not "play well together." They were towering intellects of rival nations whose distinctly different dispositions doomed their relationship. Janet was a cautious and obsessive observer who eschewed theory and did not even like to generalize (Perry & Laurence, 1984). He preferred facts and the particulars of things. Freud, on the other hand, was a daring and creative theoretician. An inveterate conceptualizer, Freud sought to identify universals. He preferred theory to facts and often used rhetoric and conceptual leaps to bypass annoying data. Freud was an empire-builder and a proselytizer. Janet, by contrast, was not—nor did he found his own school of thought or attract a coterie of followers (as Freud did). But, worst of all, Janet and Freud began their careers on the same terrain—hysteria and psychotherapy. Although they dealt with the same clinical phenomena, their respective theories were quite different. Despite this, they accused one another of making false claims of priority and even of intellectual theft. Feeling disrespected and ill-treated, neither made room for mutual dialogue.[37]

46.5.2 Defense versus Deficit

Freud's repression is a defense; Janet's dissociation is not. The purpose of repression is to protect the person from discomfort or pain by thrusting the undesirable memory into the depths of the unconscious, and keeping it there. In contrast, Janet's dissociation does not have an adaptive purpose, nor is it a skill or a talent (as some contemporary clinicians would have it). Janet's dissociation is a cognitive deficit of the capacity to synthesize; the hysteric has a severe restriction of the field of consciousness during which mental functioning is so inefficient that many stimuli bypass the ego and "fall into" another part of the mind (and thereby create or add to a second consciousness—the subconscious). The more that this happens, the more that hysterical/dissociative symptoms proliferate.

Freud offered his own description of repression versus dissociation:

> You will now see in what the difference lies between our view and Janet's. We do not derive the psychical splitting from an innate incapacity for synthesis on the part of the mental apparatus, we explain it dynamically, from the conflict of opposing mental forces and recognize it as the outcome of an active struggling on the part of the two psychical groupings against each another. (Freud, 1910, pp. 25–26)

The bottom line here is that Janet never suggested that dissociation had a positive or adaptive purpose; for him, dissociation was irretrievably pathological.

This jarring collision between repression-as-defense and dissociation-as-deficit should immediately reveal to the reader that our contemporary understanding of dissociation is deeply "infected" by the concept of repression.

The reader may recall that I began this chapter by describing clinicians' colloquial use of the term *dissociation* (and its cognates). Our everyday speech about dissociation contains our implicit understanding of the phenomena and dynamics of dissociation. It should now be readily apparent that, whenever we use *dissociation* as a verb (especially as a transitive verb; see previous discussion), we are viewing dissociation through the lens of repression. When we do that, we are describing dissociation as an active, motivated, self-protective course of action.[38] We are describing dissociation as a defense. And, of course, we do this routinely.[39]

46.5.3 Active Splitting versus Passive Disaggregation

Repression is an active process of splitting off whereby certain contents of the mind are pushed into the unconscious and forcibly confined there. Janet, on the other

[37] Janet and Freud never met. At age 78, Janet came to Vienna and sought to visit Freud. When Janet rang the doorbell at Bergasse 19, a servant told him that Freud refused to receive him. Knowing that Janet was coming to see him, Freud had decided in advance to spurn him, but did not tell Janet not to come! "No I will not see him. I thought at first of sparing him the impoliteness by the excuse that I am not well or that I can no longer talk French, and he certainly can't understand a word of German. But I have decided against that. There is no reason for making any sacrifice for him. Honesty the only possible thing; rudeness quite in order" (Jones, 1980, pp. 228–229).

[38] Way (2006) has emphasized the importance of metaphors that portray dissociation with a verb rather than a noun (e.g., division, parts). She acknowledges, but says little about the active, repression-driven idea of dissociation that is presented in this chapter.

[39] There are several ironies here. A Janetian might curse the darkness and complain bitterly that the Freudians have hijacked the Janetian concept of dissociation. Frankel (1990, 1994), on the other hand, who spoke for the Freudians, complained in essence, that advocates of today's (defensive) concept of dissociation had hijacked the concept of repression. Ironically, both accusations are true. Perhaps, after more than a century, Janet and Freud are still stealing each other's ideas!

hand, never portrayed dissociation as an active splitting of the mind (or an active splitting of consciousness). He explicitly denied that any part of the personal consciousness was split off and pushed into the subconscious. Janet's second law of dissociation (Janet, 1888) stated this position quite clearly.

Janet's denial (that parts of the primary consciousness are split off) follows logically from his deficit model of dissociation. Put simply, *the material that "falls" into the subconscious never entered the primary (personal) consciousness in the first place.* Mental disaggregation occurs because the person's field of consciousness is so severely restricted that it takes in (or synthesizes) very little of the stimulus field. The material that cannot be "taken in" then "drops" into the subconscious. This new subconscious material was never part of the primary consciousness, nor was it actively split off.

Clinical data occasionally confronted Janet with evidence that he was wrong about this. In some cases, parts of the personal conscious were definitely split off. For example, it was not uncommon for a dissociated traumatic event to "carry away" some closely related events that had unquestionably been experienced by, and known to, the person. Such occurrences puzzled Janet and he sought, unsuccessfully, to explain them in terms of his deficit model of dissociation.

Not surprisingly, some of Janet's contemporaries, even those who strongly endorsed Janet's *description* of dissociation, preferred Freud's *explanation* (i.e., repression) of it. For example, one strong proponent of dissociation said that:

> [Janet] seems to emphasize unduly the purely cognitive aspect of consciousness and to neglect the part played by the emotions and the will. Dissociation is for Janet *a curtailment of capacity*, passively submitted to by an enfeebled consciousness—a catastrophe in which the emotions and the will take no active part.... Instead of regarding dissociation as a merely mechanical splitting consequent upon *misère psychologique*, a letting go of certain functions because the personality is too feeble to hold on to them, Freud puts in the first line, *as a determining factor of dissociation*, the mental conflict that ensues when incompatible wishes or desires arise in the mind. The splitting of consciousness is explained dynamically as being due to [repression]. (Mitchell, 1921, pp. 40–41, italics added)

In summary, it would seem that Freud was right about splitting off (and Janet was not). Similarly, today's clinicians who allude to dissociation as an active process are probably also right (whereas Janet was not).

> **Understanding Dissociation #4:** DSM-IV presents a neutral description of dissociation—lack of integration among processes that are normally integrated. Janet gave us a structural description of dissociation: hysterics are unable to integrate (i.e., synthesize) all of their processes, which culminates in a mental disaggregation between two structures (i.e., the personal consciousness and a newly developed subconscious). When subconscious activity intrudes into the personal consciousness, the person experiences automatisms (i.e., dissociative symptoms). Freud was uninterested in dissociation; he focused on those times when a person refused to contemplate (integrate?) certain unpleasant realities and pushed them out of his or her conscious mind. Between them, Janet and Freud described three of today's major meanings of dissociation: (1) active dissociation (i.e., the motivated, active, pushing away, dissociating, and compartmentalizing of unwanted information); (2) structural dissociation (i.e., the resulting cluster of dissociated material and dissociated mental activity); and (3) automatisms (i.e., the dissociative symptoms that intrude into a person's normal functioning). In short, there are dissociating forces or processes, dissociated contents or structures, and dissociative intrusions into consciousness.

46.5.4 Normal and Universal versus Pathological and Limited to Hysterics

When Freud called repression "the cornerstone of psychoanalytic theory" (Freud, 1914a, p. 16), he meant, among other things, that repression is a universal aspect of the human mind. We humans, he said, have a biologically inherent tendency to avoid or escape displeasure by pushing unpleasant realities out of our conscious thoughts. We seek to repress them. Janet, on the other hand, insisted that dissociation was neither universal nor normal. He characterized dissociation as an inherently pathological cognitive deficit that occurred only in hysterics. Janet and Freud are clearly describing very different phenomena (i.e., a universal and normal process of the human mind vs. a pathological phenomenon that is limited to hysterics). Freud and Janet are *not* just using different theoretical terms to describe the same thing.

At this point, a devil's advocate might say, "but they both produce forgetting, so repression and dissociation *do* describe the same thing." My answer to this (see the following) is that these two "forgettings" are different (and that they are accompanied by different phenomena and different *sequellae*).

46.5.5 When Dissociation and Repression Interact

Repression is universal, whereas dissociation occurs only in hysterics. This would mean that *both repression and dissociation occur in hysterics*, but only repression occurs in nonhysterics. I think that this seemingly trivial inference has weighty implications—implications that can significantly advance our efforts to produce an elucidated view of dissociation.

Is there a difference between hysterical repression and nonhysterical repression? I think not. Repression is repression. Still, the *nature* of the forgetting that occurs in hysteria is certainly different from the forgetting that occurs in nonhysterical individuals. That is, dissociative amnesia is typically both stark and reversible (Loewenstein, 1991; Nace, Orne, & Hammer, 1974; Nemiah, 1979). Posthypnotic amnesia and dissociative amnesia often have a striking "in-your-face" quality, and typically, both can be suddenly and dramatically reversed.[40] Hilgard (1986) summarized the difference between repressive forgetting and dissociative forgetting by noting that unconscious, repressed material could only be accessed indirectly via its derivatives (e.g., dreams and symptoms), whereas the dissociated subconscious could often be accessed directly and conversed with (usually via hypnosis).[41]

What happens when a hysteric or a dissociative patient defensively tries to push something unpleasant out of consciousness? Might not this repressive process activate a second (dissociative) process that produces a qualitatively different kind of forgetting? Breuer thought so:

> [T]he assistance of the hypnoid state is necessary if defence is to result not merely in single converted ideas being made into unconscious ones, but in a genuine splitting of the mind. (Breuer & Freud, 1895, pp. 235–236)

Even Janet (1914, 1919), Mitchell (1921), and McDougall (1938) agreed that repression was one possible route to dissociation. In short, it seems likely that the effort to push uncomfortable realities out of consciousness may activate a second (dissociative) process in certain individuals. This conclusion, of course, returns us to our central question. What *is* this second process?

46.5.6 Once Again—What Is Dissociation?

Janet said that dissociation entailed a restricted field of consciousness wherein an insufficient capacity to synthesize ongoing events led to mental disaggregation. Similarly, he said that somnambulism entailed a restricted field of consciousness wherein the person monoideistically dwelt solely upon the words and suggestions of the hypnotist. Janet repeatedly insisted that both mental disaggregation and its close cousin, somnambulism, occurred only in hysterics. When we "pushed" the later Janet (1919, 1920) to specify the cause of mental disaggregation (see "Janet: What Causes Dissociation?" above), Janet, perhaps unsurprisingly, hinted that dissociation might involve a "tendency to dissociation" and a "disposition to somnambulism."

We seem to keep returning to high hypnotizability.[42] I agree with Janet's intuitions about a tendency to dissociation and a disposition to somnambulism. As already noted, so did Breuer (Breuer & Freud, 1895). Taken as a whole, these intuitions suggest that high hypnotizability has a vital and necessary role in the process of dissociation.[43]

So, is high hypnotizability a *sine qua non* of dissociation? Is high hypnotizability a necessary precondition

[40] Reversal of dissociative amnesia is typically slower than reversal of posthypnotic amnesia (due to the patient's motivation to maintain the amnesia).

[41] Kenneth Bowers has reported data that may be related to the contrast between repression and dissociation. In a series of rigorous experimental studies, Bowers and colleagues report that hypnotic suggestions to block pain or to push certain thoughts out of the conscious mind produce different results than do conscious efforts to accomplish the same (Bowers & Woody, 1996; Hargadon, Bowers, & Woody, 1995; Miller & Bowers, 1993). Specifically, hypnotic suggestion was experienced as effortlessly producing results that were often superior to those that were obtained from effortful cognitive strategies.

[42] Janet, following Breuer, hinted that dissociation might involve "a tendency to dissociation" and "a tendency to somnambulism." In the remainder of this chapter, I will focus on high hypnotizability (i.e., "a disposition to somnambulism") as the underlying mechanism of dissociation. However, the "tendency to dissociation" may not be isomorphic with high hypnotizability. There are, in fact, two other plausible possibilities. First, the "tendency to dissociation" may be a special capacity/ability that is possessed by only a subset of high hypnotizables. Second, the "tendency to dissociation" may be completely independent of high hypnotizability, but may be enormously augmented when high hypnotizability is also present (i.e., Putnam's "double dissociators"; see the following). I ask the reader to keep these latter two possibilities in mind whenever I speak of high hypnotizability and dissociation during the remainder of this chapter.

[43] The earliest unambiguous statement (albeit implicit) of the high hypnotizability hypothesis is probably that of Mitchell (1921): "We may suppose that *some special capacity for dissociation is the one qualification necessary for both the occurrence of hysterical symptoms and for the induction of hypnosis.* A person who can be hypnotized is a person who may under appropriate circumstances, become an hysteric, but who need not already have suffered from any manifest hysterical ability" [i.e., in contrast to what Janet insisted was always the case]. (p. 32, italics added)

for the occurrence of pathological dissociation?[44] We will examine, in considerable detail, the relationship between hypnotizability and dissociation (in the following). For the time being, I will tentatively propose that high hypnotizability is, indeed, a *sine qua non* of pathological dissociation, a *sine qua non* of mental disaggregation, a *sine qua non* of severe hysteria. We will eventually see, however, that this hypothesis requires at least one important qualification.

Understanding Dissociation #5: Freud defined repression as a motivated defense whose purpose was to push unpleasant realities out of conscious awareness. He never considered the possibility of qualitatively different forms of repression. Janet insisted that only hysterics could dissociate. For Janet, hysteria, dissociation, and high hypnotizability were inseparably entangled. Evidence suggests that highly hypnotizable persons manifest a qualitatively different form of repression (i.e., dissociation) from persons with low-to-moderate hypnotizability. Thus, high hypnotizables' normal defensive efforts to escape pain and unpleasure (i.e., repression) may, at times, evoke dissociation.

46.5.7 Continuing Effort versus Effortlessness

Freud's accounts of repression are unambiguous in their insistence that repression is an effortful process whose maintenance requires an ongoing expenditure of energy. In contrast, Janet's accounts of dissociation describe mental disaggregation as a deficit that "just happens." Moreover, once mental disaggregation has occurred, it requires no energy to "maintain" it. If anything, Janet says that it takes energy to undo or to heal the disaggregation (Janet, 1919).

The modern hypnosis field contains a remarkable reprisal of this contrast between the effortfulness of Freud's repression and the effortlessness of Janet's dissociation. For the last 30 years or so, the hypnosis literature has been dominated by a debate about the nature of hypnosis (i.e., state vs. nonstate). Advocates of a social-psychological view of hypnosis contend that (1) there is no such thing as a special hypnotic state and (2) hypnotic behavior is not qualitatively different from nonhypnotic behavior. Conversely, advocates of a special process or state view of hypnosis insist that hypnotic behavior (1) is qualitatively different from nonhypnotic behavior and (2) often entails a special hypnotic state or process. This debate in the hypnosis field is directly relevant to our analysis of repression and dissociation: the social-psychological view of hypnosis portrays hypnotic behavior as *an effortful cognitive strategy*, whereas the special process view of hypnosis portrays hypnotic behavior as being *effortless*.

At the present time, this debate has substantially ebbed due to the emergence of a loose consensus in much of the hypnosis field that persons with low-to-moderate hypnotizability are better described by the social-psychological perspective, whereas persons with high hypnotizability are better described by the special process perspective.

I suggested (in the previous discussion) that repression often drives the dissociation of memory in highly hypnotizable persons. This conjecture, in turn, generates three useful inferences. First, the dissociation of painful material may begin with *efforts* (i.e., repression) to drive the unpleasant material out of consciousness. Second, in highly hypnotizable persons, the effort to repress unpleasant material may spontaneously activate a successful hypnotic forgetting of that material (i.e., dissociation). Unlike classic repression, however, dissociation may not require continuing work or expenditure of energy to maintain. Left undisturbed (i.e., if the person is not subjected to continuing stress, loss, and trauma), the dissociated material may *effortlessly* "rest quietly" in isolation for years.

Third, encounters with stressful stimuli that "remind" the person of the dissociated material may evoke intrusions and flashbacks (i.e., what the Freudians call "the return of the repressed"). Such intrusions (or "de-repressions" or failures of dissociation) immediately evoke renewed *efforts* to (re)repress the material. For persons with a severe dissociative disorder, this is a time of clinical crisis. The intruding material is often so destabilizing that dissociative individuals become incapable of accessing the hypnotic processes that previously allowed them to dissociate the painful material. When dissociative individuals find themselves unable to successfully (re)dissociate the material, they frantically and repeatedly attempt to push away the intruding material. In that effort, they seize upon any and every defense that comes to mind—repressive pushing away, distraction via compulsive busyness, alcohol and other drugs, self-injury, and so on.

This account of repression and dissociation implies that the first priority of clinicians at a time of de-repression (or de-dissociation) is to enable the person to restore order by re-dissociating the destabilizing material. The account also makes clear that these particular dissociative symptoms (i.e., intrusions of traumatic material) occur when dissociation begins to fail or frankly collapses.

[44] I want the reader to remember that we (and Janet and Breuer) are talking about severe and recurrent dissociative symptoms, not fleeting, probably normal, alterations of consciousness that may have causes that differ from those of pathological dissociation.

Understanding Dissociation #6: Repression is the normal, biologically and evolutionarily based instinct to avoid and escape discomfort and pain. Dissociation is, among other things, a normal, biologically and evolutionarily based mechanism (rooted in high hypnotizability), for avoiding and escaping discomfort and pain by protecting us from conscious awareness of painful realities. Repression is a universal response of all humans. Hypnotically supported dissociation of memory, however, is not a universal human response. The capacity for stark dissociation is possessed by only a small minority of humans. When this capacity is present in an individual, it may be activated in the service of repressing uncomfortable realities. Successful dissociation of painful material brings an end to repressive efforts.[45] Conversely, both unsuccessful repression and the collapse of previously successful dissociation (as indicated by flashbacks, intrusive memories, revivifications of traumatic events, etc.) guarantee that efforts to repress (or re-repress) the painful material will continue. Thus, successful dissociation is always temporally bracketed by ongoing efforts to repress (i.e., both before the dissociation has occurred and after it begins to fail).

46.5.8 Heredity: Hysteria, Repression, and Dissociation

The putative hereditary etiology of hysteria began with the theory of *dégénérescence*—degeneration. Degeneration was the 19th century's rough equivalent of today's "bad genes" or "poor protoplasm." Degenerate families produced offspring who were at high risk for all manner of medical, neurological, and psychiatric problems. According to the theory of degeneration, one did not specifically inherit hysteria; instead, one inherited an undifferentiated susceptibility to all manner of diseases and disorders. This, by the way, is an important difference between Charcot and Janet. Charcot accepted the theory of degeneration, whereas Janet ultimately did not. Thus, Janet's conviction that hysteria was hereditary entailed a specific inheritance of hysteria (rather than a general inheritance of an undifferentiated morass of diseases and disorders).

Freud's attitude toward the heredity of the neuroses was almost one of annoyance. He strongly wished to "demote" heredity from the prominent position which his "teacher," Charcot, had given it (see especially Andersson [1962] and Freud [1896b]). Freud's position about the heredity of the neuroses had at least five components. First, Freud argued that each neurosis had a specific sexual experience that was necessary for the neurosis to occur. Second, Freud admitted that heredity was also necessary, but that the importance of heredity had been overemphasized:

> [H]ereditary disposition and the specific sexual factor ... support and supplement each other. The sexual factor is usually only operative in those who have an innate hereditary taint as well; heredity alone is usually not able to produce an anxiety neurosis, but waits for the occurrence of a sufficient amount of the specific sexual noxa. The discovery of the hereditary element does not, therefore, exempt us from searching for a specific factor.... [T]aken by itself, [heredity] cannot help us to understand either the episodic onset of a neurosis or the cessation of a neurosis as a result of treatment. [Heredity] is nothing but a precondition of the neurosis—an inexpressibly important precondition, it is true, but nevertheless one which has been over-estimated, to the detriment of therapy and theoretical comprehension. (Freud, 1985, p. 138)

Third, Freud almost conflated pathognomonic cause (i.e., the "specific sexual ætiology") with necessary and sufficient cause:

> The specific cause is the one which is never missing in any case in which the effect takes place, and which moreover suffices, if present in the required quantity or intensity, to achieve the effect, *provided only that the preconditions are also fulfilled.* (Freud, 1895, p. 136, italics added)

Notice that the italicized phrase at the end of this quotation essentially "smuggles heredity back in under cover of darkness," so to speak. Fourth, Freud brushed aside the fact that specific sexual causes sometimes failed to cause neurosis: "It does not matter," said Freud, that this occurs (Freud, 1896a, p. 209, see previous discussion).

Fifth, Freud stated with a certain amount of asperity that heredity was useless in any case because it could not be treated with analysis (Freud, 1895, 1896b). This is a nice rhetorical point, but it ignores the possibility that heredity (of hysteria, for example) might be accompanied by specific factors (high hypnotizability, for example) that have potent therapeutic implications.

So much for Freud's views regarding the heredity of the neuroses. What did Freud say about the heredity of repression? As Erdelyi (1990) noted, individual differences

[45] As McDougall noted over 80 years ago: "Unless dissociation results, the conflict continues subconsciously; the repressed motives continue to be active with varying degrees of intensity; the energy of the organism continues to be wastefully consumed in the work of repression" (McDougall, 1926, p. 226).

in a person's propensity or ability to exercise repression underlie the repressor-sensitizer dimension in personality (e.g., Bonanno & Singer, 1990; Weinberger, Schwartz, & Davidson, 1979). Perhaps because he saw repression as a universal feature of the human mind, Freud had little to say about individual differences in repression, whether inherited or acquired.[46] To my knowledge, there is no extant research on the heredity of repression.

There are no modern studies of the heredity of hysteria, and only methodologically questionable studies of the familial prevalence of the dissociative disorders (Braun, 1985; Kluft, 1984) and studies with negative findings (Öztürk & Şar, 2005). On the other hand, two methodologically sound twin and adoption studies have documented that dissociation has a hereditary component (Becker-Blease et al., 2004; Jang, Paris, Zweig-Frank, & Livesley, 1998). Jang et al. reported that dissociation in adults has a heritability index of 0.48 and 0.55. Similarly, Becker-Blease et al. reported that dissociation in children and adolescents has a heritability index of 0.58, and 0.59.

Studies of hypnotizability have consistently reported heritability indices that range from 0.52 to 0.63 (Bauman & Bul, 1981; Morgan, 1973; Morgan, Hilgard, & Davert, 1970; Rawlings, 1978). Finally, absorption (see following discussion), a trait that has been associated with both hypnotizability (Tellegen & Atkinson, 1974) and dissociativity (Bernstein & Putnam, 1986; Butler, 2004; Dalenberg & Paulson, 2009), has a heritability index of 0.50 (Tellegen et al., 1998).

In short, methodologically sound research has repeatedly documented the existence of a significant hereditary component of dissociation and hypnotizability.[47]

Studies of the heritability of repression are yet to be conducted.

Understanding Dissociation #7: There is absolutely nothing special about repression. Repression is merely the effort not to think about something that is painful. As such, Freud was right: we all repress things. Dissociation, however, is different. When enlisted in the service of repression, dissociation supercharges repression; it brings about a quantum leap in the effectiveness of the effort to put something painful out of mind. Because the ability to bring about this kind of dissociation is only possessed by a relative few, we do not all dissociate things. Repression was Freud's (mutually exclusive) alternative to Breuer's hypnoid states and Janet's dissociation. Because Freud totally rejected hypnoid states and dissociation, he attributed all forgetting solely to repression (i.e., both the forgetting that followed repression alone and the qualitatively different forgetting-dissociative amnesia that occurred when the effort to forget was supercharged by high hypnotizability). In this sense, it is necessarily the case that all defensive forgetting is driven by repression.

46.5.9 Freud's Unconscious versus Janet's Subconscious

Freud flatly denied the possibility of Janetian dissociation. He insisted that a subconscious could not exist! As early as 1895, Freud claimed that multiple personality was nothing but an illusion:

> The pathogenic psychical material appears to be the property of an intelligence which is not necessarily inferior to that of the normal ego. *The appearance of a second personality is often presented in the most deceptive manner.* (Breuer & Freud, 1895, p. 287, italics added)

In subsequent comments on multiple personality, Freud mocked the idea of "an unconscious consciousness" (i.e., a second consciousness of which the conscious mind is unconscious; see Freud, 1912, 1915). Instead, he argued that the appearance of multiple personalities was due to the sequential activation of different psychical complexes (Freud, 1912, 1915):

> The cases described as splitting of consciousness, like Dr. Azam's, might better be denoted as shifting of consciousness—that function—or whatever it be—oscillating between two different psychical complexes which become conscious and unconscious in alteration. (Freud, 1912, p. 263)

> We shall ... be right in rejecting the term "subconscious" as incorrect and misleading. The well-known cases of "double conscience" (splitting of consciousness) prove nothing against our view. We may most aptly describe them as cases of a splitting of the mental activities into two groups, and say that the same consciousness turns to one or other of these groups alternately. In psychoanalysis there is no choice for us but to assert that mental processes are in themselves unconscious, and to liken the perception of them by means of consciousness to the perception of the external world by means of the sense organs (Freud, 1915, pp. 170–171)

[46] Freud seemed to be more interested in the patterns and contents of repression than in repression as a trait or an individual difference. He did, however, acknowledge that such differences existed: "The tendency to forget what is disagreeable seems to me to be a quite universal one; the capacity to do so is doubtless developed with different degrees of strength in different people" (Freud, 1901, p. 144).

[47] For an anomalous heritability finding, see Waller & Ross (1997).

In a similar vein, Freud later suggested that the appearance of multiple personalities occurred when "different identifications seize hold of consciousness in turn" (Freud, 1923, p. 31). The bottom line is that Freud flatly denied that a second consciousness could exist (Freud, 1915, 1925):

> Thus for Freud dissociated systems are simply separate groups of mental but unconscious elements. As our consciousness turns now to one group, now to another, as a searchlight shines now on one object and now on another, the dissociated groups manifest in conscious life. Of themselves the dissociated systems are mental in character, but not conscious. There exists no doubling of consciousness, no second consciousness. (Crabtree, 1986, p. 102)

Freud believed that consciousness is always unitary; whereas Janet believed, as did his teachers,[48] that the unity of consciousness is far from absolute.

Freud's view of multiple personalities constituted a return to a very conservative version of the on/off model of successive existences[49] that was in vogue prior to Janet's important publications of the late 1880s (see the previous section on "Total Automatism").

Finally, because Freud rejected the possibility of Janetian dissociation, and because he had little interest in dissociative phenomena, Freud never advanced a psychoanalytic explanation of dissociation or dissociative disorders—a shortcoming for which he has been criticized (Bliss, 1986; Crabtree, 1993, 2007; Hart, 1927). Mitchell (1925) argued that "psychoanalysis as a method is ill-suited to bring into prominence the characteristic features of this condition [i.e., multiple personality]" (p. 200). And McDougall (1926) implied that Freud's scorn and rhetoric were an insufficient basis for denying the existence of the subconscious: "Freud offers no good reason for rejecting the very strong evidence of coconscious activity" (p. 523). And again, "But [Freud's] explanation [of double personality as "oscillating between two different psychical complexes which become conscious and unconscious in alternation"] is not applicable to such a case as Doris Fischer, for here we seem to have good evidence of *two or more psychical complexes being simultaneously conscious*" (Mitchell, 1923, p. 182, italics added).[50]

The following sections propose a comprehensive autohypnotic model of clinical dissociation.[51] The apex of this model is the phenomenon whose existence Freud denied—personalities that are simultaneously co-conscious and co-active.

46.6 REVISITING THE AUTOHYPNOTIC MODEL OF DISSOCIATION

The preceding analysis of repression and dissociation contains important elements of a comprehensive model of clinical dissociation, but it lacks a developmental framework. Without doubt, Frank Putnam (1997) has provided the most robust analysis of the developmental etiology of dissociation and the dissociative disorders. The following account is heavily indebted to Putnam's discrete behavioral states model, but it departs from Putnam's analysis in one essential respect—it seeks to forge an accommodation between (1) the discrete behavioral states model of dissociation and (2) the autohypnotic model of dissociation.

---

[48] For example, in *The Diseases of the Personality* (1885), Ribot wrote: "The unity of the ego, in the psychological sense of the word, is the cohesion for a given time of a certain number of states of clear consciousness, accompanied by others less clear, and by a multitude of physiological states which, although not themselves conscious like the others, yet operate as much as they. Unity means co-ordination" (p. 46). As Perry and Laurence (1984) noted: "In this passage the foundations of Janet's concept of psychological disaggregation can already be seen" (p. 19).

[49] I think that a close reading of Freud's comments on multiple personality (Freud, 1912, 1915, 1923) reveal that he was primarily interested, to the extent that he was interested in this topic at all, in explaining the mechanism and dynamics of switching (from one part being dominant to another part being dominant). On the other hand, Freud offered no thoughts whatsoever about the mechanism or dynamics of the remarkable amnesias that kept pace with these switches. Because Freud's curiosity was usually boundless, his repeated lack of curiosity about these dramatic amnesias is striking. I suspect that the difference between the amnesia of dissociation and the forgetting of repression was another inconvenient fact that he avoided contemplating.

[50] In fairness to Freud, however, it should be noted that at the end of his life, he began to wrestle with "splitting of the ego" (Freud, 1940). Moreover, Freud's most compelling description of starkly dissociative phenomena occurs in *Moses and Monotheism*: "All these phenomena [i.e., posttraumatic symptoms] ... have a compulsive quality: that is to say that they have great psychical intensity and at the same time exhibit a far-reaching independence of the organization of the other mental processes, which are adjusted to the demands of the real external world and obey the laws of logical thinking. They [i.e., the posttraumatic symptoms] are insufficiently or not at all influenced by external reality.... They are, one might say, a State within a State, an inaccessible party, with which cooperation is impossible, but which may succeed in overcoming what is known as the normal party and forcing it into its service" (Freud, 1939, p. 76). Although Freud did not use the term *automatism*, this quotation from Moses and Monotheism is the strongest acknowledgement of automatism in the entire body of Freud's work.

[51] According to the autohypnotic model, "dissociation can be viewed as a mobilization of spontaneous hypnotic ability in the service of defending against extreme environmental stress" (Spiegel, 1990, p. 128).

46.6.1 Discrete Behavioral States and Dissociation

The infant researcher, Peter Wolff (1987), demonstrated that infants begin life with a very finite set of states of functioning: (1) non-REM sleep, (2) REM sleep, (3) alert inactivity "with bright and shiny eyes," (4) fussy waking activity (pre-crying), and (5) crying. The neonate's transitions from one state to another are discontinuous and often distressingly bumpy. Unable to regulate its own state transitions, the infant is dependent upon its mother to provide the support and emotional scaffolding that enables (increasingly) nondistressing switches (from, for example, fussy waking activity to non-REM sleep).

From this perspective, it is readily apparent that infant and mother have a conjoint developmental task. Together, they must enable the child to develop a rich, integrated set of states of functioning, of which the child becomes more and more the master.

Healthy development produces a child with (1) an increasing number of states that are increasingly well-integrated with one another, and (2) an increasing ability to regulate those states. Such self-regulation has at least two important components. First and foremost, self-regulation includes the ability to make soothing or distress-reducing transitions from uncomfortable states to more comfortable states. Second, self-regulation also includes the emotional resilience or ego strength that enables the child to tolerate the tension of maintaining certain states long enough to accomplish a desired or necessary task. In short, self-regulation lies at the heart of both emotional and practical coping.

So what does self-regulation have to do with dissociation? Everything. From a psychodynamic perspective, repression and dissociation are mechanisms of defense. From a behavioral states perspective, however, repression and dissociation are mechanisms of self-regulation. Repression and dissociation enable a person to make a transition from a state that is uncomfortable and undesirable to another state that is more comfortable. Moreover, with repeated use, repression and dissociation may become self-regulatory skills whose exercise is increasingly automatic and less and less a matter of conscious awareness (e.g., Hermans, Nijenhuis, Van Honk, Huntjens, & Van der Hart, 2006).

Because it is a universal aspect of human mental functioning, repression is an inevitable participant in each person's self-regulatory activities. On the other hand, dissociation is not inevitable. It occurs only in children who meet three conditions: (1) children who possess high hypnotizability and (2) who are exposed to emotionally painful situations that motivate them to escape the pain by any means possible and (3) who spontaneously manage to activate their hypnotic/dissociative ability to "escape."

There is not enough space in this chapter for a detailed description of the vicissitudes of repression and dissociation in child development. Instead, I will try to illustrate these vicissitudes by briefly sketching three developmental trajectories—one of healthy development and two of unhealthy development. In the process of doing so, I will review Putnam's definition of dissociation and I will describe some ways in which his discrete behavioral states model and an autohypnotic model might accommodate one another.

46.6.1.1 Healthy Development

I fully endorse both Putnam's (1997) *Discrete Behavioral States (DBS) Model* and his analysis of healthy development and normal childhood dissociation. As noted previously, healthy development entails the acquisition of a rich set of behavioral states that are well-integrated and able to be (more or less) effectively self-regulated. A healthy child also develops "state-bridging metacognitive capacities" (Putnam, 1997, p. 163) that integrate information and behavior across different states. In other words, the child develops a sense of self that encompasses all of his or her behavioral states.

46.6.1.2 The DBS Concept of Pathological Dissociation

This sketchy and abstract description of healthy development is quickly enriched when contrasted with Putnam's DBS portrayal of pathological dissociation:

> In the DBS model, "pathological dissociation" is defined as a category of trauma-induced discrete behavioral states that are widely separated in multidimensional state space from normal states of consciousness. (Putnam, 1997, p. 173)

Thus, from the DBS perspective, pathological dissociation consists of "trauma-induced behavioral states" that lie far from normal consciousness. Although a bit abstract, this DBS portrayal of pathological dissociation makes sense to anyone with even a modicum of experience with dissociative patients. Unlike the well-integrated "state-space" (i.e., the entire domain of behavioral states) of a healthy child, the state-space of a dissociative child contains one or more states that are substantially cut off from (or very poorly integrated with) the remainder of the child's state-space. Transitions to and from these trauma-induced states (i.e., "switches") are substantially discontinuous, typically quite uncontrolled, and marked by a disrupted sense of self (which, in extreme cases, includes a shift in identity).

46.6.1.3 Normal and Pathological Dissociation

Putnam considers absorption to be a form of *normal* dissociation (Putnam, 1997; Waller, Putnam, & Carlson, 1996):

> Normal dissociation is expressed primarily in the form of intense absorption with internal stimuli (e.g., daydreams) or external stimuli (e.g., a fascinating book or television program). Normal dissociation consists of a set of discrete states of consciousness that are characterized by a narrowing of perceptual and attentional focus, but without significant state-dependency for memory or identity (i.e., no wide separation from normal states of consciousness). (Putnam, 1997, p. 177)

For allied but somewhat different reasons, Van der Hart and colleagues have drawn a very similar distinction between altered states of consciousness such as absorption and the phenomena of structural dissociation (Steele, Dorahy, Van der Hart, & Nijenhuis, 2009; Van der Hart, Nijenhuis, Steele, & Brown, 1994).

I agree with Putnam and with Van der Hart and colleagues that absorption, although phenomenologically similar to many dissociative phenomena, is certainly not a form of *pathological* dissociation. In fact, I (along with Van der Hart and colleagues) question whether absorption is any kind of dissociation at all. Even Putnam (1997) notes that such altered states of consciousness "are not dissociative *per se*" (p. 199). In any case, I place myself with Putnam and with Van der Hart and colleagues as a firm proponent of the typological or taxon model of dissociation.

Using his 1996 terminology of "normal dissociation," Putnam (1997) described the taxon model:

> A taxonic model or typological model basically returns to Janet's 19th-century clinical formulation that certain people experience certain dissociative states that are, by and large, not encountered by the majority of the general population. It postulates that there are at least two distinct types of dissociation, normal and pathological. There is a discrete group of people—whom we label "pathological dissociators—who are profoundly different from the rest of the population. (Putnam, 1997, p. 66)

It should be noted that proponents of the typological model of dissociation reject the continuum model that has dominated the dissociation field for the past 3 decades (Braun, 1993; Hilgard, 1986; Vermetten, Bremner, & Spiegel, 1998; Waller et al., 1996). According to the continuum model, dissociative phenomena are pervasive in human experience and extend from the normal (e.g., daydreaming, absorption) to the frankly pathological (e.g., dissociative amnesia, chronic depersonalization, MPD). According to the typological model, dissociative phenomena are restricted to a small subset of persons (i.e., pathological dissociators) who undergo dissociative experiences that are "profoundly different from the rest of the population." Finally, it should be noted that those who insist that absorption is an important aspect of dissociation are strong advocates of the continuum model of dissociation (Butler, 2004, 2006; Dalenberg & Paulson, 2009; Gold, 2004).

So does normal dissociation exist at all? Yes, I think so. I will discuss this issue in greater detail in the following. For the moment, let us examine developmentally normative dissociation.

46.6.1.4 Developmental Trajectory #1: Healthy

Young children are normatively much more dissociative than adults. From the DBS perspective, the dissociation of young children is a natural consequence of their still-developing integration of their behavioral states and the pathways of transition among them. Remember, infants begin life with only five behavioral states that are poorly integrated with one another. Some of these states are substantially dissociated from one another; they are relatively distant from one another in state space. As children develop, they acquire more and more behavioral states, all of which need to become more or less integrated with one another. To the extent that such integration is slow in developing or, worse, is frankly impaired, the child is dissociative in his or her functioning. Research with the Child Dissociative Checklist has shown that children are, indeed, more dissociative than adults and that their dissociation declines with age (Putnam, 1996; Putnam, Helmers, & Trickett, 1993). These developmentally normal children grow into adults with low levels of dissociation.

The next two sections discuss unhealthy developmental trajectories in children with and without high hypnotizability.

46.6.1.5 Developmental Trajectory #2: Unhealthy (With Only Low-to-Moderate Hypnotizability)

To the extent that children achieve self-modulation or self-regulation, their level of dissociation decreases. But the converse is also true. To the extent that children poorly achieve this core developmental task, their dissociation does not decrease, and, in some cases, their dissociation even increases (due to neglect, maltreatment, severe parent-child misattunement, etc.). Behaviorally, such children often appear to be oppositional, defiant, hyperactive, or conduct-disordered.

As a group, the members of this Unhealthy Developmental Trajectory have poor impulse control and inadequate self-regulatory skills. In turn, their poorly integrated behavioral states are reflected in their elevated dissociative functioning. This elevation, however, is at best only moderate because it is not amplified by high hypnotizability. Because the members of this group have only low-to-moderate hypnotizability, they do not manifest high dissociation, even if they have experienced chronic and severe maltreatment! Instead, as they grow older, some will develop a nondissociative kind of PTSD and/or a largely nondissociative kind of borderline personality disorder (BPD). These adults have low-to-moderate levels of dissociation.

46.6.1.6 Developmental Trajectory #3: Unhealthy (With High Hypnotizability)

What happens when a child with high hypnotizability encounters trauma and maltreatment? The answer is, "It depends." There are at least three possible outcomes. First, if the maltreatment is not chronic, the child may not spontaneously activate his or her hypnotic capabilities to deal with it. In fact, if the child received parenting that was otherwise sound, the child may develop a low level of dissociation. Such children may (or may not) develop PTSD, but they will not develop a dissociative disorder.

Second, if the child is chronically or severely abused (especially by multiple perpetrators when the child is quite young), then native hypnotic capacities will almost certainly be spontaneously activated in order to escape the pain. These children develop a major dissociative disorder and/or a dissociative kind of PTSD.

Third, if the child suffers chronic abuse and if their parents were emotionally unavailable or, worse, emotionally abusive as well, then the child may develop an additional diagnosis—a dissociative kind of BPD. Dissociative forms of BPD are often, but not always, accompanied by MPD and a dissociative form of PTSD.

46.6.1.7 Integrating Autohypnosis with the DBS Model of Dissociation

Putnam portrays MPD as an almost-expectable outcome when repeated trauma occurs during a critical developmental period (0–6 years of age). According to Putnam, trauma produces "traumatic states" that are so different from other states that they are quite "distant" from them in state-space. When repeatedly activated due to continuing trauma, these traumatic states become hardwired into the brain (Perry et al., 1995). As time goes by, traumatic states become increasingly elaborated, increasingly self-organized, increasingly isolated from normal states of consciousness, and MPD may arise.

Putnam emphasizes that MPD is a developmental failure to integrate traumatic states with other states of consciousness. In particular, he insists that MPD alters are not split off (i.e., subtracted) from the self:

> The DBS model implies that the identity fragmentation seen in MPD and other disorders associated with childhood trauma is not a "shattering" of a previously intact identity, but rather a developmental failure of consolidation and integration of discrete states of consciousness. In particular, it is a profound developmental failure to coherently bind together the state-dependent aspects of self experienced by all young children that leads to the MPD patient's experience of multiple "selves." (Putnam, 1997, p. 176)

This is the point of disagreement between the autohypnosis model and Putnam's DBS model. Putnam explicitly rejects the autohypnosis model (see Putnam, 1997, pp. 141–144; Putnam & Carlson, 1998, pp. 29–32). On the other hand, the autohypnosis that I am proposing does not reject the DBS model.

To put the matter simply, I think that high hypnotizability is a *sine qua non* of MPD. I believe that when high hypnotizability is absent, poor parenting and chronic abuse can produce a pervasive general psychopathology that may include mood disorder, anxiety disorder (especially PTSD), and personality disorders (especially BPD), but it cannot produce MPD. Conversely, only high-level hypnotic processes can produce the degree of separation and compartmentalization that characterizes MPD. Finally, although it seems certain that "a profound developmental failure to coherently bind together the state-dependent aspects of self" facilitates the production of MPD, it is not yet clear whether MPD can occur in the absence of maltreatment-induced developmental failure.

> **Understanding Dissociation #8:** High hypnotizability is both a *sine qua non* of MPD and the fundamental mechanism of clinical dissociation. When sufficiently motivated by recurrent trauma and pain, children with high hypnotizability will eventually utilize their hypnotic capacities in order to escape from, and to encapsulate or compartmentalize, the traumatic material. On the other hand, no amount of trauma can produce MPD unless the child is highly hypnotizable. It remains to be seen whether high

> hypnotizability alone is sufficient, in the absence of trauma and/or profound developmental failure, to produce high levels of dissociation (Marmar, Weiss, & Metzler, 1998) or full-blown MPD (see Ross [1991] for MPD cases without a history of trauma).

Although intuitively attractive, the autohypnosis model of MPD has been in decline for the past decade. This decline is probably best marked by the publication of two reviews of 15 correlational studies of hypnotizability and dissociativity (Putnam & Carlson, 1998; Whalen & Nash, 1996). These 15 studies collectively reported an abysmally small sample-size-weighted mean correlation of 0.12 between the DES and various measures of hypnotizability. Whalen and Nash concluded:

> In sum, there is no compelling evidence to support the proposition that hypnotizability and dissociativity are overlapping traits.... Sharing little variance, hypnotizability and dissociativity, in fact, seem to exist fairly independently of one another. (Whalen & Nash, 1996, p. 197)

This near-total lack of relationship between hypnotizability and dissociative experiences seemed to be the death knell for the autohypnosis model's claim that high hypnotizability drives dissociation. Since the definitive explication of the autohypnotic model of dissociation by Spiegel's research team in 1996 (Butler, Duran, Jasiukaitis, Koopman, & Spiegel, 1996), no subsequent publication on dissociation has made autohypnosis its central concern.[52]

46.7 HYPNOSIS AND DISSOCIATION

In this section, I will describe the history of the encounters between hypnosis and dissociation and I will argue that there are good empirical reasons to assert that the interment of the autohypnosis model of dissociation may be premature.

I will prefigure my line of argument by saying that a clear understanding of the relationship between hypnotizability and dissociation has been hindered by two major factors: (1) debates about the nature of hypnosis and dissociation, and (2) problems with the scales that measure hypnotizability and dissociativity. Note, by the way, that Putnam and Carlson are well aware that the ultimate viability of their theoretical conclusion (i.e., that hypnotizability does not drive dissociation) rests solely on the adequacy of the "current instruments" that measure hypnotizability and dissociation:

> Standard measures of hypnotizability and dissociation are only weakly related, even in samples that include identified victims of trauma. Hypnotizability and dissociativity, *as measured by current instruments*, are clearly not synonymous processes. In fact, they are largely independent, and changes in one account for little of the variance in the other. (Putnam & Carlson, 1998, p. 36, italics added)

46.7.1 Hypnosis: The Historical Root of Dissociation

During the late 18th century and the early 19th century, the concept of dissociation arose from hypnosis.[53] Although dissociation awaited its christening and detailed description by Janet in the 1880s, dissociative phenomena had been on conspicuous display ever since Puységur's discovery of "magnetic sleep" (i.e., artificial somnambulism). The defining characteristic of magnetic sleep was the amnesia that inevitably ensued upon "awakening." Curiously, however, the events during "sleep" that had been forgotten by the awakened "sleeper" were promptly recalled as soon as he or she was returned to a state of magnetic "sleep."

The demarcation between the "waking" and the "sleeping" *somnambule*[54] was so great that the Comte de Puységur (the Marquis's younger brother) concluded that "the demarcation is so great that one must regard these two states as two different existences" (Puységur, 1784, p. 90, reported in Crabtree, 1993, p. 42). This idea, of two separate (dissociated) existences, immediately took hold in the field of animal magnetism and, subsequently, the field of hypnosis. This same notion of two-existences-separated-by-a-boundary-of-amnesia is

[52] The chief exception to this generalization is the work of Cardeña, a close colleague of Spiegel, who continues to be a strong advocate of the autohypnosis model of hypnosis (e.g., Cardeña, 1996; Cardeña, van Duijl, Weiner, & Terhune, 2009). Also, although he has not claimed to be an advocate of the autohypnosis model of dissociation, Loewenstein (1991a; Loewenstein & Putnam, 2004) contends that persons with DID routinely display a cluster of autohypnotic symptoms (i.e., spontaneous trance, spontaneous age regression, negative hallucinations, hidden observer phenomena, trance logic, and voluntary analgesia/anesthesia).

[53] MPD cases were also reported during this period, but even the first of these (i.e., Gmelin's report of "exchanged personality" in 1791) occurred subsequent to the discovery of magnetic sleep in 1784. This means that animal magnetism and hypnosis had already provided the template for describing and understanding MPD (i.e., as separate existences that were separated by amnesia).

[54] *Somnambules* are those who are capable of magnetic sleep (i.e., sleep followed by spontaneous posthypnotic amnesia). Inasmuch as most people were not *somnambules*, the reader can see that individual differences in hypnotizability were already apparent over 200 years ago.

readily apparent in Braid's 1855 treatise that sharpened his definition of "hypnotism" (i.e., nervous sleep):

> Let the term hypnotism be restricted to those cases alone in which, by certain artificial procedures, oblivious sleep takes place, in which the subject has no remembrance on awaking of what occurred during his sleep, but of which he shall have the most perfect recollection on passing into a similar stage of hypnosis thereafter. In this mode, hypnotism will comprise only those cases in which what has hitherto been called the double-conscious state occurs. (Braid, 1855/1970, pp. 370–371)

Thus, long before Janet's researches in the 1880s, hypnosis was already understood in terms of two defining dissociative characteristics: (1) two separate consciousnesses (2) that were separated by amnesia. Today's reader knows, of course, that these are long-outdated views of hypnosis. My point, however, is that this understanding of hypnosis is the historical root of dissociation. Janet's research on hysteria was directly founded on his deep reading of the continental literature on animal magnetism and hypnosis (Janet, 1930). And that literature, for almost a century, had already described MPD in terms of somnambulism's two streams of consciousness. Crabtree underlined the remarkable fit between somnambulism and MPD:

> Multiple personality seems to be the perfect spontaneously occurring illustration of the reality of the artificially induced double consciousness that magnetizers were so diligently probing.... It is as though the victim of multiple personality alternates between normal consciousness and the consciousness of somnambulism, in the latter state manifesting a new personality that is the personification of that somnambulistic consciousness. (Crabtree, 1993, p. 289)

As we showed earlier in this chapter, Janet used hypnosis to study amnesia and separate streams of consciousness in somnambules. These studies, in turn, led Janet to conceptualize hysteria in terms of mental disaggregation, the subconscious, and, what Prince (1907/1910) later called "co-consciousness." The next important event in the story of hypnosis and dissociation is the unfortunate fate of Prince's concept of co-consciousness.

46.7.2 Co-consciousness and Interference

The Janetian subconscious is unmistakably co-conscious and co-active with the primary (personal) consciousness. This central fact about the subconscious tended to be somewhat obscured, however, by Janet's overemphasis of the phenomenon of amnesia. Prince (1906, 1907/1910) finally pared away Janet's distorting overemphasis of amnesia. Using clinical data from cases of multiple personality, Prince (1907/1910, 1905/1908) argued convincingly that the subconscious and multiple personality are based upon multiple centers of consciousness that are simultaneously co-conscious and co-active with the personality that is dealing with everyday life.

With the passing of the 19th century, the concept of dissociation faded from popularity in Europe.[55] Interest in dissociation then moved to Boston, as reflected in the writings of William James, Boris Sidis, Morton Prince, and William McDougall. Each of these scholars was a vocal advocate of co-consciousness. James provided the first detailed and unambiguous clinical description of co-consciousness ("Old Stump"; James, 1889). Prince coined the term (i.e., co-conscious), defined the concept, redefined hysteria, wrote case histories of co-conscious multiple personalities, and conducted empirical research on co-consciousness (Prince, 1901, 1905/1908, 1906, 1907/1910, 1908; Prince & Peterson, 1909). Case studies of multiple personality that featured co-consciousness were published in Prince's new *Journal of Abnormal Psychology* (B. C. A., 1908, 1908–1909; Cory, 1919; Fox & Culp, 1909; Prince, 1919). McDougall at Harvard recognized that co-consciousness was dissociation's single most controversial aspect (McDougall, 1926). Much later, Nemiah, yet another Bostonian, suggested that the co-consciousness of alter personalities was one of dissociation's least-understood phenomena (Nemiah, 1979). Nemiah was absolutely correct about this. And Prince certainly agreed with him:

> Although a large and still accumulating mass of evidence has shown, under certain pathological and other conditions, the presence of co-conscious (subconscious) processes of which the subject is unaware and yet which manifest themselves through intelligent actions, still all writers are not in accord as to the interpretation which shall be put on these manifestations. (Prince, 1908, p. 33)

Prince (1908) investigated co-conscious functioning by asking MPD patients to perform two tasks at once (under

[55] Ellenberger suggests that the decline of hypnosis and dissociation can be understood as a fad that had burned itself out: "The history of the first dynamic psychiatry shows a paradox: for an entire century (1784 to 1882), new discoveries struggled for recognition, and, after they were at long last acknowledged by 'official medicine' with Charcot and Bernheim, they enjoyed a brilliant phase of success of less than twenty years, to be followed by a swift decline. The problem of these ups and downs puzzled many minds. Janet suggested that there are trends, not only in the style of life, but in medicine. After 1882 the medical world became infatuated with hypnotism; publications on it reached the hundreds until a point of saturation was reached and the trend abandoned" (Ellenberger, 1970, p. 171).

conditions where the "waking" personality did not know that another personality was simultaneously performing another task "inside"). In six experiments, Prince found that his MPD patients were quite successful in such simultaneous performances. Prince also noted that there appeared to be little interference between the two personality's simultaneous task-performance:

> Once only (the first experiment) she stumbled a bit while writing, as if there was a momentary inhibition of her thoughts by the subconscious process [i.e., the second personality's simultaneous task performance "inside"]. (p. 37)

This brief comment by Prince about interference would become the pivot upon which the scientific fate of the concept of dissociation would turn for over 80 years.

From about 1910 to 1925, interest in dissociation was largely swamped by the widespread attention given to Freud and psychoanalytic theory. In the mid-1920s, researchers began to study dissociation again. The concept of co-consciousness, however, was suddenly (and incorrectly) reinterpreted. Noninterference was now considered to be the defining feature of co-conscious dissociation. According to this reinterpretation, if interference occurred, then the concept of dissociation was effectively disproved!

Both Prince and Janet (1889) had noted that the simultaneous performance of two dissociated tasks occasioned relatively little mutual interference, but neither had claimed that noninterference was a necessary feature of dissociation. Quite the contrary. Both knew full well that subconscious actions could intrude into conscious functioning; both had described instance upon instance of subconscious activity interfering with conscious thought, emotions, and activities. In fact, Dell's modern phenomenological definition of dissociation emphasizes these very intrusions: "The phenomena of pathological dissociation are recurrent, jarring, involuntary intrusions into executive functioning and sense of self" (Dell, 2009c, p. 226). Yet, somehow, dissociation was reinterpreted in the 1920s to require a total absence of interference between dissociated activity and conscious functioning (Barry, Mackinnon, & Murray, 1929; Burnett, 1925; Hull, 1933; Messerschmidt, 1927–1928; Mitchell, 1932). This fateful redefinition of dissociation crystallized during the research of Ramona Messerschmidt, one of Clark Hull's doctoral students:

> What was the degree of interference? This is the real question at issue.… If the two activities are found to go on simultaneously without any interference whatever, they may be supposed to constitute distinct intellectual processes, and to be truly co-conscious. On the other hand, the amount of interference, if any, will be assumed to represent a lack of separation or discreteness of the two processes. (Messerschmidt, 1927–1928, pp. 328–329)

Several factors probably played a role in this reinterpretation of dissociation. First, Janet's and Prince's original research on the simultaneous performance of two dissociated tasks was conducted with MPD patients; the new research that began in the 1920s studied normal adults. Second, the new generation of researchers did not study clinical dissociation; they studied hypnosis. They used hypnosis to suggest dissociated task performance and amnesia. Third, the new researchers picked up a very minor thread of Janet's and Prince's thinking. Janet was focused on the amnesia of the "waking" personality (for the actions of the subconscious personality). Prince was focused on the evidence for simultaneous co-conscious activity. Neither was focally interested in the degree of interference during dissociated functioning, but each noted that it was minimal. The new hypnosis researchers would now follow this underdeveloped thread of the thinking of Janet and Prince.

I contend that Hull's noninterference doctrine of dissociation was a straw man that was easily and incorrectly used to discredit the phenomenon of dissociation. Ever since the days of Mesmer and Puységur, credulous views of hypnosis had asserted that somnambules were clairvoyant, had superhuman sensory acuity, superhuman strength, could diagnose the sick, predict the future, and so on (Gauld, 1992). All of these claims, of course, are fantastic and were eventually disproved. Hull's noninterference doctrine of dissociation is yet another of these fantastic claims:

> Now if dissociation is complete in the sense of a functional independence such as might be expected in the minds of two different persons or in the completely separated portions of a disembodied consciousness such as is contemplated by metaphysical idealism, task A and task B should each be executed as rapidly when performed simultaneously as when each is performed at a different time. (Hull, 1933, p. 177)

This fantastic conception stacked the deck against dissociation. Not surprisingly, studies repeatedly found interference, and the concept of dissociation was (supposedly) empirically refuted.

A decade later, White and Shevach (1942) reviewed the interference studies and conducted one of their own. They reiterated Hull's conclusions when they pronounced dissociation to be (1) prone to interference phenomena and (2) a poor explanation of hypnotic phenomena.

The bottom line here is that the publications of Hull, White, and Shevach effectively discredited dissociation theory for almost half a century—until Hilgard proposed his neodissociation theory in the 1970s (Hilgard, 1977/1986). Even then, Hilgard did not refute the noninterference doctrine. He simply asserted that his neodissociation theory did not require noninterference.

The noninterference doctrine of dissociation was not effectively confronted until 1992 when Kihlstrom pointed out that human cognitive functioning had the same limitations both in and out of hypnosis:

> Janet's views aside, our contemporary understanding of cognitive processes gives plenty of reasons to expect that interference will occur between simultaneous streams of information processing, even if one of these streams is dissociated from conscious awareness.... [The two streams of information processing] still draw on a common fund of attentional resource capacity. Thus ... if two tasks consume attentional resources, then performance of one may very well interfere with performance of the other. Interference will occur if the total requirements of the two tasks exceed available capacity; interference will not occur if the total requirements leave a surplus of capacity.... These are facts about the human information-processing system, and there is no reason to believe that hypnosis *per se* alters these facts in any way. (Kihlstrom, 1992, pp. 307–308)

In short, the noninterference doctrine of dissociation was just one more fantastic attribution of extraordinary or supernormal capacities to hypnosis (and dissociation). As Kihlstrom (1998) wryly noted, "Nothing about hypnosis changes the way the mind works" (p. 189).

46.7.3 Measuring Hypnosis

Now let us consider the polar opposite of fantastic conceptions of hypnosis—namely, the modern scientific instruments that measure hypnotic responding (e.g., the Stanford Scale of Hypnotic Susceptibility, Form C [SHSS:C; Weitzenhoffer & Hilgard, 1962] and the Harvard Group Scale of Hypnotic Susceptibility, Form A [HGSHS:A; Shor & Orne, 1962]). These instruments (and more recent ones) are the foundation upon which all modern empirical hypnosis research is based. Consequently, the validity of the conclusions that have been drawn from modern scale-based research depends on the degree of verisimilitude between (1) the domain of hypnosis and (2) what these scales measure.

This issue is by no means settled. The hypnosis field still argues about what the scales measure. This chapter is not the place for a lengthy disquisition on hypnosis scales. On the other hand, it is critical that we understand the scale-related issues that bear upon the validity of Whalen and Nash's (1996) and Putnam and Carlson's (1998) conclusion that hypnosis and dissociation are largely unrelated.

46.7.3.1 Hypnosis Scales Measure More Than One Thing

The central measurement issue in the hypnosis field is the question of whether hypnotic responsiveness is or is not a unitary phenomenon, and, concomitantly, whether hypnosis scales measure one thing or more than one thing. Ernest Hilgard, the scientific father of the modern hypnosis field, was of two minds about this question. On the one hand, he believed that the Stanford Scales measured one general factor. He said that "Hypnosis is sufficiently one thing to permit the high common factor or general factor to emerge [from the data]" (Hilgard, 1965, p. 281). On the other hand, after several years of repeatedly encountering what he called "the haunting problem of bimodality" (p. 260) (i.e., bimodal distributions of hypnotizability scores) he stopped insisting that bimodality was just a statistical artifact (Hilgard, Weitzenhoffer, & Gough, 1958; Hilgard, Weitzenhoffer, Landes, & Moore, 1961). In 1965, Hilgard finally concluded that "there is some genuine bimodality within our data" (p. 227).

One contingent of the hypnosis field disagrees with Hilgard and insists that hypnosis scales measure only one thing—the effects of suggestion and expectancies (e.g., Kirsch, 1991):

> The effectiveness of a hypnotic induction appears to depend entirely on people's belief about its effectiveness.... In other words, response expectancy may be the sole determinant of the situations in which hypnotic responses occur, and also of the nature of the responses that occur in those situations.... Once expectancy effects are eliminated, there may be nothing left. (Kirsch, 1991, p. 460–461)

Another contingent of the hypnosis field advocates a two-component model of hypnotic responding that is congruent with Hilgard's thinking about bimodality (Balthazard, 1973; Balthazard & Woody, 1985, 1992; Bowers, 1976, 1992; Kihlstrom, 1985; Shor, Orne, & O'Connell, 1962; Spanos, Mah, Pawlak, D'Eon, & Ritchie, 1980; Tellegen, 1978–1979). On this view, responses to easy hypnotic suggestions are mostly determined by expectancies, whereas responses to difficult suggestions are mostly due to true hypnotic ability.

Empirical research during the past decade tends to support the two-component model of hypnosis (e.g., Benham, Woody, Wilson, & Nash, 2006; Oakman & Woody, 1996; Woody, Drugovic, & Oakman, 1997). Moreover, a recent highly sophisticated study indicates that true hypnotic ability is a larger contributor to hypnotizability scores than are subjects' beliefs and expectancies (Benham et al., 2006).

The take-home message about measurement is that the hypnosis scales measure more than one thing. At a minimum, hypnosis scales simultaneously and indiscriminately measure both expectancy and true hypnotic ability. This, in turn, has immediate implications for correlational studies of hypnotizability and dissociation. Because hypnotizability scores simultaneously represent more than one underlying process, the possible size of a hypnotizability scale's correlation with any other variable (including, of course, the DES) is necessarily reduced. Balthazard and Woody, the most sophisticated commentators on the scales' psychometric complexities, have concluded that hypnotizability scales are fated to have only modest correlations with other variables:

> [G]iven the factorial complexity of the hypnosis scales, and attenuation due to unreliability, a correlation of about 0.35 between the total hypnosis score and a given questionnaire measure is about all that can be expected. (Balthazard & Woody, 1992, p. 37)

Clearly, when drawing conclusions from their modest correlations, investigators of the relationship between hypnosis and dissociation ignore such psychometric issues at their peril.

46.7.3.2 Highly Hypnotizable Individuals Are Not All the Same

And yet, there is more. The measurement issues regarding hypnosis are even more complicated than is revealed by the above analysis. Highly hypnotizable individuals are not all the same. Some highly hypnotizable individuals experience the hidden observer phenomenon and some do not (e.g., Nogrady, McConkey, Laurence, & Perry, 1983). Some experience duality during age regression and some do not (e.g., Nogrady et al., 1983). Some experience extensive imagery and some do not (Cardeña, 1996; Pekala, 1991a; Pekala & Forbes, 1997). Some must employ imagery in order to effectively block pain, whereas others can block pain without using any imagery whatsoever (Hargadon et al., 1995). Some can experience vivid auditory hallucinations and others cannot (Szechtman, Woody, Bowers, & Nahmias, 1998). Some can experience posthypnotic amnesia and others cannot (Barrett, 1996; Cardeña, 1996; Woody, Barnier, & McConkey, 2005). Some are fantasy-prone and others are not (Barrett, 1996; Wilson & Barber, 1982). And so on. Such individual differences can produce surprising gaps in the performance of otherwise highly hypnotizable persons. Such gaps led Hilgard and Weitzenhoffer to develop the Stanford Profile Scales so that the pattern of a subject's hypnotic abilities could be rigorously assessed (Weitzenhoffer & Hilgard, 1967).

These differences among the highly hypnotizable are particularly germane to the nature of the relationship between hypnotizability and dissociation. Why? Because both research and clinical experience tell us that persons with a dissociative disorder are highly hypnotizable (e.g., Bliss, 1984, 1986; Frischholz, Lipman, Braun, & Sachs, 1992). The conjunction of these two findings requires us to ask: which kinds of highly hypnotizable persons are susceptible to acquiring a dissociative disorder? Some? All? Just one kind? The remarkable heterogeneity among the highly hypnotizable (McConkey, Glisky, & Kihlstrom, 1989) can only serve to further reduce the correlations between the DES and measures of hypnotizability.

There is an urgent need for greater understanding of the differences among highly hypnotizable individuals (McConkey & Barnier, 2004). Few researchers have conducted in-depth studies of the highly hypnotizable. One of the few in-depth investigations led to the discovery of the concept of fantasy proneness (Wilson & Barber, 1982). Wilson and Barber conducted in-depth interviews with 27 very highly hypnotizable women and a comparison group of 25 women with lower levels of hypnotic ability. All but one of their highly hypnotizable women had a profound fantasy life. As children, they had "lived in a make-believe world much or most of the time" (p. 345). As adults, "they typically spent a large part of their time fantasizing" (p. 350). According to Wilson and Barber, each of these fantasy-prone subjects had "a secret fantasy life that she [had] typically revealed to no one" (p. 350). Moreover, their fantasies were of hallucinatory intensity and often had "an involuntary, automatic, self-propelled quality" (p. 353) to them. Most said that they could not imagine life without fantasizing.

This is a stunning finding—26 of 27 very highly hypnotizable women are fantasy-prone! This result can only imply that there is something about extreme hypnotizability that naturally (almost inevitably?) breeds a pervasive fantasy life that consumes, according to Wilson and Barber, 50% of the person's adult waking life. Moreover, Wilson and Barber were at some pains to emphasize that these women were not psychologically ill. Wilson and Barber insisted that these fantasy-prone women were psychologically healthy, led full and productive lives, and used fantasy adaptively.

Oddly, the implications of the relationship between extreme hypnotizability and fantasy proneness have attracted remarkably little interest.[56] In one of the few efforts to continue this line of investigation, Deirdre Barrett (1992, 1996) replicated Wilson and Barber's (1981) study. Barrett studied 34 very highly hypnotizable college students (each had obtained a score of 11 or 12 on both the HGSHS:A and the SHSS:C). In contrast to the findings of Wilson and Barber, however, Barrett found that only 56% of her subjects were fantasizers; the remaining 44% were dissociators!

Barrett's fantasizers closely resembled Wilson and Barber's fantasy-prone women. Barrett's fantasizers easily passed Stanford items without an induction, entered deep trance rapidly, had vivid and realistic imagery, and fantasized during most of their waking hours. All scored high on the Tellegen Absorption Scale (TAS mean = 34). Thirty-seven percent reported daymares (frightening fantasies that seemed to be out of their control), and all awoke immediately from trance, usually with a big smile. They experienced no spontaneous amnesias; in fact, a third of them failed the amnesia item on the HGSHS:A. None reported a history of frank abuse.

Barrett's highly hypnotizable dissociators were quite different from her highly hypnotizable fantasizers. Barrett's dissociators were unable to enter trance quickly and none experienced their waking imagery as entirely realistic. When they became deeply absorbed in something (either internal or external), their absorption was often intertwined with amnestic phenomena. Their TAS scores were noticeably lower than those of the fantasizers (TAS means = 26 vs. 34, respectively). During hypnosis, dissociators experienced persistent and total amnesias that often persisted after removal cues had been given. Half of Barrett's dissociators experienced some degree of spontaneous amnesia for trance events, even when it had not been suggested. When they awoke from trance, they typically blinked their eyes and looked confused. Almost all (93%) reported either frank abuse that they remembered (27%), had been told they were abused (13%), had a history of multiple burns and fractures for which parents presented improbable explanations (7%), or had recurrent nightmares and an absence of any memory before age 7 or 8 (40%). Twenty-seven percent met criteria for a dissociative disorder (4 = DDNOS, 1 with features of MPD; 1 = Dissociative Amnesia). Despite their dissociative diagnoses, these subjects had only mild levels of impairment.

Barrett concluded that the remarkable difference between highly hypnotizable fantasizers and highly hypnotizable dissociators originated with their life experiences:

> On the basis of this research, it seems most accurate to think of high hypnotizables as composed of two groups whose life histories have specialized them primarily toward one of the major hypnotic phenomena: hallucinatory imagery or dissociative abilities. (Barrett, 1996, p. 134)

Barrett's conclusion, of course, parallels that of Josephine Hilgard (1970) who proposed two routes to high hypnotizability-imaginative involvement in fantasy and avoidance of the pain of parental mistreatment.

A crucial question arises at this point: what exactly is the relationship between life experience and Barrett's two kinds of highly hypnotizable persons? Do life experiences, which encourage enjoyable fantasizing or escape from pain, directly breed high hypnotizability? That was J. Hilgard's hypothesis. Or do life experiences shape the expression of an already existing capacity for high hypnotizability? If life experiences such as abuse directly breed high hypnotizability, then a history of abuse should be significantly correlated with hypnotizability. Modern research shows that this is not the case (Nash & Lynn, 1985; Nash, Lynn, & Givens, 1984). Accordingly, it would seem that Barrett is probably correct: life experiences shape the expression of an already existing capacity for high hypnotizability.

Nevertheless, there remains a third possibility. Fantasy proneness may require a preexisting superior capacity for imagery. Similarly, pervasive dissociative functioning may require a preexisting superior capacity for

[56] Subsequent research on fantasy proneness has not been guided by issues related to hypnotizability, but by a self-report measure of fantasy proneness (Inventory of Childhood Memories and Imaginings; ICMI) that was derived from Wilson and Barber's (1981) original interview schedule. Fantasy proneness has now been completely shorn of its connection to very high hypnotizability: "it is not the case that there is a close association between hypnotic suggestibility and fantasy proneness in general. Indeed, there is generally a small relationship (0.24–0.26)" (Lynn, Meyer, & Shindler, 2004, p. 189). Recent literature focuses mostly on the maladaptive nature of fantasy proneness. Fantasy proneness is now considered to be (1) significantly related to psychopathology (Lynn & Rhue, 1988; Rauschenberger & Lynn, 1995; Rhue & Lynn, 1987), (2) a putative cause of false memories (Bryant, 1995), and (3) a hypothesized cause of dissociation in general (Kihlstrom, Glisky, & Angiulo, 1994; Rauschenberger & Lynn, 1995) and MPD in particular (Bowers, 1991; Halleck, 1989; Lynn, Rhue, & Green, 1988).

dissociation. The results of Pekala's three cluster analytic studies of phenomenal experience during hypnosis tend to support this third possibility.

Pekala administered the HGSHS:A and the Phenomenology of Consciousness Inventory (PCI: Pekala, 1991b) to college students. In four studies, analyses of the 12 major PCI dimensions repeatedly identified two clusters of highly hypnotizable subjects (and several clusters of "lows" and mediums" as well; Pekala, 1991a; Pekala & Forbes, 1996, 1997; Pekala, Kumar, & Marcano, 1995). "Classic highs" were the most highly hypnotizable cluster (HGSHS:A mean = 7.85; SD = 2.28); they reported more loss of memory and less imagery than any of the other eight clusters (Pekala & Forbes, 1997). "Fantasy highs" were the second most hypnotizable cluster (HGSHS:A mean = 7.85; SD = 2.62); they reported extensive imagery and much less loss of memory than "classic highs."

Pekala's "classic highs" resemble Barrett's highly hypnotizable dissociators, and Pekala's "fantasy highs" resemble Barrett's highly hypnotizable fantasizers and Wilson and Barber's fantasy-prone women. Barber (1999) has likened them to one another—but there is a huge difference in their hypnotizability scores. Pekala's "classic highs" and "fantasy highs" are not restricted to those who are extremely hypnotizable. Unlike Barrett (1996) or Wilson and Barber (1981), Forbes and Pekala (1996) and Pekala and Forbes (1997) did not study a selected sample of extremely hypnotizable subjects. Instead, they studied large unselected samples of college students. Their cluster analyses in these studies were not based on HGSHS:A scores; they were based on the phenomenal-experiential data of the PCI. They then determined the mean HGSHS:A score for each cluster. So, whereas Barrett's fantasizers and dissociators had mean SHSS:C scores of 11+, Pekala's "classic highs" and "fantasy highs" had mean HGSHS:A scores of 7.85 (Pekala & Forbes, 1997)! This is a huge difference in hypnotizability.

Barrett's fantasizers' and dissociators' mean SHSS:C scores of 11+ easily invite an explanation of fantasizing and dissociating in terms of a potent interaction between life events and extreme hypnotizability. Pekala's findings, on the other hand, certainly do not invite an explanation in terms of extreme hypnotizability. Instead, Pekala's clusters invite an explanation in terms of individual differences in multiple dimensions of conscious experience (e.g., imagery, memory, altered state, volitional control, etc.).

Finally, because Pekala's dimensions of conscious experience have only a moderate relationship to hypnotizability, they invite me to ask a related question: to what extent might fantasizing and dissociating be independent of hypnotizability?

We shall return to this question after we discuss the measurement issues that relate to dissociativity (in the following). But, in order to understand the measurement issues that pertain to dissociation, we must first discuss absorption.

46.7.4 Absorption

The districts of Alsace and Lorraine became alternately part of Germany and part of France as a result of successive wars between the two countries. In 1986, the DES annexed absorption to dissociation. There has not been a "war" between the dissociation field and the hypnosis field for possession of absorption, but perhaps there should be. Absorption is not a dissociative phenomenon; it is a hypnotic phenomenon.

46.7.4.1 Some History: How Did Absorption Enter the Picture?

In the 1960s, several researchers sought to develop a paper-and-pencil measure of hypnotizability that was based on hypnotic-like experiences in daily life: the Personal Experiences Questionnaire (Shor, 1960; Shor, Orne, & O'Connell, 1962), the Experience Inventory (Ås, 1963; Ås & Lauer, 1962; Ås, O'Hara, & Munger, 1962), and the Hypnotic Characteristics Inventory (Lee-Teng, 1965).

These three scales were a cumulative effort. Each borrowed items from its predecessors and each added new items in the effort to develop a successful paper-and-pencil instrument that would measure hypnotizability on the basis of spontaneous daily experiences (rather than the "work sample" approach that is used by formal hypnotizability scales). In the early 1970s, Auke Tellegen, quantitative psychologist and psychometrician extraordinaire, joined the effort (Tellegen & Atkinson, 1974).

Tellegen assembled a 71-item research questionnaire, "Q3," which was composed of 48 items from predecessor instruments and 23 new items. Factor analysis of Q3 data from 481 subjects produced 11 factors, which now became Q3 subscales. Two subsamples (of 142 and 171) were also administered measures of stability-neuroticism and introversion. The data on these 13 variables (i.e., the 11 Q3 subscales, stability, and introversion) were factor analyzed for each sample. Both of these factor analyses yielded three factors: Q3 subscales, stability, and introversion. In both of the factor analyses, only six of the Q3 scales loaded substantially on the Q3 factor: reality absorption, fantasy absorption, dissociation, openness to experience, devotion-trust, and autonomy-criticality.

At this point in the analyses, Tellegen renamed the Q3 factor: "We labeled this factor 'Openness to Absorbing and Self-Altering Experiences' or 'Absorption' " (p. 271). Tellegen characterized absorption as a special kind of attention:

> We suggest ... that the attention described in Absorption items is a "total" attention, involving a full commitment of available perceptual, motoric, imaginative and ideational resources to a unified representation of the attentional object. (Tellegen & Atkinson, p. 274)

Subjects' scores on the absorption scale were then correlated with their scores on indicators of hypnotizability (i.e., Field's [1965] Hypnotic Depth Inventory and a modified version of the HGSHS), yielding positive correlations of 0.27, 0.42, and 0.43. In terms very similar to those of Balthazard and Woody (1992, see previous discussion), Tellegen argued that the modest size of the correlations between the absorption scale and measures of hypnotizability was to be expected because artifacts unrelated to true hypnotic ability would necessarily attenuate the relationship between the scales. Finally, Tellegen concluded that absorption was a core component of hypnotizability:

> [W]e conclude that Absorption, interpreted as a capacity for absorbed and self-altering attention, represents an essential component of hypnotic susceptibility. (Tellegen & Atkinson, p. 276)

Spiegel agrees with Tellegen, calling absorption one of the three basic components of hypnotizability (along with suggestion and dissociation; Cardeña & Spiegel, 1989; Spiegel, 1990).

46.7.4.2 The Hypnosis Literature on Absorption

The much-studied relationship between absorption and hypnotizability has typically been reported to be a correlation of about 0.22. As noted previously, this low correlation has been attributed to nonhypnotic artifacts and to the hetereogeneity of what is measured by the scales of hypnotizability (Balthazard & Woody, 1992; Glisky, Tartaryn, McConkey, Tobias, & Kihlstrom, 1991; Tellegen & Atkinson, 1974). Efforts to gain a more accurate estimate of the relationship between absorption and hypnotizability rapidly ensued.

It is notable that the TAS and its predecessors were developed by investigators who advocated a two-component theory of hypnotizability: Shor (see Shor et al., 1962), Ås (developed his scale in Hilgard's laboratory; see Hilgard, 1965), Lee-Teng (developed her scale in Hilgard's laboratory), and Tellegen (see Tellegen, 1978–1979). This historical fact is of interest because several of these scale-developers (and others) subsequently argued that absorption was more highly related to one component of hypnotizability (i.e., true hypnotic ability) that is (supposedly) best measured by the cognitive or difficult hypnotic items. Conversely, they argued that absorption is much less related to the other component of hypnotizability (i.e., expectancy) that is (supposedly) best measured by the easy ideomotor items.

The statistical term for this phenomenon is *heteroscedasticity.* A scale is heteroscedastic when, for example, lower scores on the scale have a markedly smaller correlation with another variable than do higher scores on the scale. Many investigators have claimed that the hypnotizability scales are heteroscedastic with regard to absorption (Balthazard, 1993; Balthazard & Woody, 1985, 1992; Farthing, Venturino, & Brown, 1983; Glisky et al., 1991; Roche & McConkey, 1990; Shor et al., 1962; Tellegen, 1978–1979; Woody, Bowers, & Oakman, 1992).

Reports of heteroscedastic performance of the hypnotizability scales vis-a-vis "absorption" began with Shor and colleagues in 1962 when they developed the first precursor to the TAS. Shor et al. reported that their sample as a whole obtained a 0.44 correlation between Personal Experiences Questionnaire scores and Overall Depth Ratings. That same correlation increased to 0.84, however, when the data were restricted to the sample's eight deeply hypnotic subjects. Conversely, that same correlation decreased to 0.17 when the eight deeply hypnotic subjects were subtracted from the whole sample.

In 1971, Bowers reported heteroscedastic correlations between the Personal Experiences Scale and the HGSHS:A. These correlations increased from less than zero for women with low hypnotizability, to about 0.40 for women with moderate hypnotizability, to 0.63 for women with high hypnotizability.

In 1983, Farthing and colleagues reported that absorption correlated more strongly with the difficult cognitive items than with easier ideomotor and challenge items.

In 1992, Balthazard and Woody examined the relationship between the TAS and specific items on the hypnotizability scales. They reported that correlations increased as item-difficulty increased. For example, the easiest item (hand lowering) had a point biserial correlation of 0.23 with the TAS, whereas the most difficult item (music hallucination) had a point biserial correlation of 0.53 with the TAS.

When correlations are calculated for a restricted range of scores on a scale, the usual outcome is that the correlation is much smaller than the correlation for the entire range of scores on that scale. And yet, when correlations between absorption and hypnotizability scores are calculated for a restricted range of hypnotizability scores (i.e., high scores on the scale), the correlation becomes larger. This is a striking outcome that has led some investigators to wonder whether the TAS is a better measure of hypnotizability than are the hypnosis scales themselves: "is it possible that the Absorption Scale, despite its label, taps the core or essence of hypnotic performance less ambiguously than the hypnosis scales themselves?" (Balthazard, 1993, p. 68).

In short, members of the hypnosis field have no doubt that absorption is a very important component of hypnosis. On the other hand, researchers outside the hypnosis field often treat absorption as "just another interesting psychological variable." They seldom evidence any awareness that absorption is a central component of hypnosis and that Tellegen developed the TAS in order to measure everyday hypnotic experiences. This situation led Frankel to complain 2 decades ago that members of the dissociation field were oblivious to hypnotic phenomena:

> Hypnotizability, even when ratings are moderate, has been virtually equated with dissociative capacity. This approach gives short-shrift, in my view, to the other mechanisms involved in hypnosis and should be reconsidered. (Frankel, 1989, p. 13)

46.7.4.3 The Dissociation Literature on Absorption

At the time that Bernstein and Putnam constructed the DES, the continuum model of dissociation was widely accepted. As previously noted, the continuum model posits that dissociative phenomena extend from the normal (e.g., daydreaming, absorption) to the pathological (e.g., dissociative amnesia, chronic depersonalization, MPD). Explicitly relying upon the continuum model, Bernstein and Putnam (1986) devised three types of items for the DES: amnesia, depersonalization/derealization, and absorption. In doing this, they transformed a loose understanding in the dissociation field—that absorption was probably a dissociative phenomenon—into orthodoxy. Due to its briefness and user-friendliness, the DES rapidly became the most widely used measure of dissociation, especially in empirical research. Although some studies reported differing results, most factor analyses of DES data extracted three factors: amnesia, depersonalization/derealization, and absorption (see Dell & Lawson [2009] for a review of the factor analysis literature on measures of dissociation). As a consequence of these factor analyses, the DES (and even dissociation itself) was soon understood to be composed of three factors.

Subsequent experimental research on dissociation used the results of these factor analyses to divide the DES into three subscales: amnesia, depersonalization/derealization, and absorption. These subscales, in turn, correlated strongly with one another. All seemed in order until 1996 when the matter suddenly became more complicated.

Using taxometric analyses, Waller et al. (1996) demonstrated that there was an important difference among certain DES items. Namely, taxometric analyses repeatedly showed that there was a typological difference between amnesia and depersonalization/derealization on the one hand, and absorption on the other. According to this typological difference, the general population is divided into two types of people: those that experience dissociative amnesia and/or recurrent depersonalization/derealization and those that do not. Absorption is a different matter, however. As measured by the DES, absorption is a dimensional trait; everyone exhibits some absorption, and some people exhibit a great deal of absorption. Consequently, the world is not divided into the absorbed and the unabsorbed; whereas, according to Waller and colleagues, the world is composed of dissociators and nondissociators.

These taxometric findings have evoked a debate in the dissociation field between what might be called "typology advocates" and "continuum advocates." Typology advocates generally insist that absorption is not a dissociative phenomenon (Dell, 2006b; Putnam, 1997; Steele, Dorahy, Van der Hart, & Nijenhuis, 2009; Van der Hart, Nijenhuis, Steele, & Brown, 1994; Waller et al., 1996). Continuum advocates insist that there are many normal forms of dissociation, chief among them being absorption (Butler, 2004, 2006; Dalenberg & Paulson, 2009; Gold, 2004): "The essence of the normative dissociative process, as I see it, is absorption" (Butler, 2004, p. 5).

Continuum advocates such as Butler might well ask, "If absorption is not a component of dissociation, then why does the TAS correlate 0.70 (Nadon, Hoyt, Register, & Kihlstrom, 1991) with the DES?" Kihlstrom shed some light on this question when he examined the full array of correlations between the TAS and the DES for two nonclinical samples: TAS × DES = 0.70 and 0.70; TAS × DES-Absorption subscale = 0.80 and 0.82; TAS × DES-Depersonalization/derealization subscale = 0.64 and 0.67; and TAS x DES-Amnesia subscale = 0.40 and 0.42 (Kihlstrom, Glisky, & Angiulo, 1994). These correlations show that absorption and depersonalization/derealization share 43% of their variance, and that absorption and amnesia share only 17% of their variance. Given that (a) there is a paucity of theory that connects absorption to dissociation, and (b) theory and strong empirical evidence do connect absorption to hypnotizability, and (c) there is strong empirical evidence that absorption is not a component of pathological dissociation (Waller et al., 1996), one must conclude that Kihlstrom's data do not indicate that absorption is a component of dissociation. Instead, Kihlstrom's data indicate that absorption is a meaningful correlate of dissociation. In short, absorption is part of dissociation's nomological net[57] (Kihlstrom et al., 1994; Nadon, 1997), but not part of dissociation itself.

46.7.4.4 Is Defensive Absorption a Kind of Dissociation?

So far, I have treated absorption as a normal psychological trait. And, indeed, absorption is normal. Openness to Experience, the Big Five counterpart of absorption, is considered to be one of the five core dimensions of human personality (McCrae & Costa, 1997). But—like any other trait, ability, or behavior—absorption can be used for defensive purposes.

In elaborating her thesis that absorption is a normal form of dissociation, Butler (2004, 2006) listed three forms of normal, dissociative absorption: daydreaming, escape, and immersion in flow or peak experiences. When used as an escape, absorption enables

> actively sought experiences [to] fill up conscious awareness, thereby temporarily supplanting personal concerns or preoccupations or dissociating them to the periphery of awareness.... [These actively sought experiences such as]... listening to music, watching films, reading fiction... contemplative religious trance or meditative states ... may serve as diversions, distractions, escapes from life stresses, preoccupations, and perhaps dysphoria. (Butler, 2004, p. 6–7)

Butler is certainly correct about this. One can easily use immersion in other experiences to distract from, and to ameliorate, discomfort. This strategy is well-known to parents who use distraction to soothe a child and to hypnotists who use imaginative involvement in imagery to alleviate pain. On the other hand, whether such absorptive strategies constitute "dissociation" is open to question.

In my opinion, the most interesting ideas about defensive absorption have been advanced by Jon Allen. In a compelling series of studies that have received too little attention, Allen and colleagues showed that high levels of absorption are closely related to psychotic symptoms and to dissociation (Allen, Console, & Lewis, 1999; Allen & Coyne, 1995; Allen, Coyne, & Console, 1996, 1997; Allen, Fultz, Huntoon, & Brethour, 2002).

While Allen agrees with continuum advocates who argue that absorption is an essential aspect of "normal" dissociation, Allen and colleagues have radically extended this perspective by insisting that absorption is an essential aspect of pathological dissociation. Extreme absorption, Allen contends, amounts to dissociative detachment:

> In the context of severe dissociation and other psychopathology, the benign term "absorption" is misleading.... In effect, to be absorbed in any one facet of experience is to be detached from every other.... [I]t is not so much absorption as the detachment that impairs adaptation.... At mild levels, transient detachment from the outer world is benign. However, in the context of pathological dissociation, detachment entails depersonalization and derealization—at worst, detachment from one's actions, body, and sense of self, as well as other persons and outer world more generally. (Allen et al., 1997, p. 332)

Allen emphasizes three points about severe absorptive detachment. First, unlike absorption in a book or a movie, the absorption of severe detachment is content-less. These severely detached persons are deeply absorbed in nothing; they are absorbed in the void. Allen notes that these patients complain about feeling spacey, foggy, unreal, or, worse, being blank, gone, "in the blackness." These patients may be found sitting with a blank stare. Allen calls this the "dissociative void." Second, he contends that frequent use of absorptive detachment can become unconscious or automatic; when this happens, these patients feel that absorptive detachment just happens (to them). Third, Allen insists that absorptive detachment produces memory gaps that are not reversible:

> [W]e propose that evidence of complex actions in dissociative states is not necessarily diagnostic of dissociative identity disorder and that memory gaps are not necessarily reversible by various memory retrieval techniques. (Allen et al., 1999, p. 160)

According to Allen, these nonreversible memory gaps come about because severe detachment entails a

---

[57] Cronbach and Meehl coined the term *nomological network*: "Scientifically speaking, to 'make clear what something is' means to set forth the laws in which it occurs. We shall refer to the interlocking system of laws which constitute a theory as a nomological network" (Cronbach & Meehl, 1955, p. 290). In practice, a construct's nomological net consists of those other constructs to which it is both theoretically and empirically (i.e., lawfully) related. Although much remains to be worked out, and many details are still wanting, the nomological net of dissociation seems to include trauma, hypnotizability, and absorption. Kihlstrom et al. (1994), on the other hand, has suggested that dissociation's nomological net includes hypnotizability, absorption, imaginative involvement, and fantasy proneness. Kihlstrom further suggested that these latter constructs may "constitute risk factors or diatheses, for dissociation" (Kihlstrom et al., 1994, p. 121).

"dissociation of context" (Butler, Duran, Jasiukaitis, Koopman, & Spiegel, 1996) that hinders memory storage by undermining elaborative encoding:

> We propose that, to the extent that the individual is detached, the dissociation of context interferes with the process of elaborative encoding that Schacter (1996) considers requisite for constructing declarative memories.... [I]n a state of dissociative detachment there is liable to be a more diffuse and pervasive impairment of the elaborative encoding of episodic memory that would support autobiographical narrative. (Allen et al., 1999, p. 165)

Perhaps Allen's most radical claim is that even complex actions may fall victim to detachment-related memory gaps:

> Many dissociative patients report no memory, for example, of putting on clothes, holding a conversation, writing a list, driving around town, or buying articles at a store. They may be chagrined when they find evidence of having engaged in such unremembered actions. They have "lost time." (Allen et al., 1999, p. 164)

Allen claimed that such memory gaps occur in two kinds of patients: dissociative patients with DID and dissociative patients without DID. According to Allen, the unremembered actions of some non-DID patients "are relatively consistent with their ordinary behavior and sense of identity" (Allen et al., 1999, p. 165).

When I first read Allen's article in 1999, I discounted his diagnostic judgment about these non-DID dissociative patients with memory gaps. I was certain that these patients had covert, difficult-to-diagnose forms of DID. Although this may certainly be true in some cases, I now think that my initial reaction was precipitous and one-sided. I still do not accept Allen's entire explanation of these severely absorptive patients, but I believe that Allen has put his finger on a phenomenon of considerable significance. He has pointed to a difference between classic dissociative symptoms on the one hand, and the dissociative-like symptoms of severe absorptive detachment on the other. Despite having different mechanisms, these symptoms are phenotypically similar and, importantly, I do not think that the DES (or the MID) can tell them apart.

Allen claims that severe defensive absorption (which he calls "dissociative detachment") is inseparably intertwined with the classic dissociative symptoms of amnesia and depersonalization/derealization. He supports this position via clinical observation and at least two strong empirical findings. First, factor analysis is unable to separate severe absorption from classic dissociative symptoms. Whereas most factor analyses of DES data have produced three factors (i.e., amnesia, depersonalization/derealization, and absorption), factor analysis of DES data from Allen's inpatient trauma population produced an atypical factor structure: Factor I: some absorption items and some depersonalization items; Factor II: amnesia items; and Factor III: an admixture of absorption, amnesia, and depersonalization items (Allen et al., 1997). In short, even factor analysis shows severe absorption to be inseparably intertwined with depersonalization and amnesia. Second, Allen notes that the DES-Taxon (DES-T) scale (Waller et al., 1996) correlates 0.83 with DES-Absorption (which supposedly measures "normal" dissociation; Waller et al., 1996). This is indeed impressive. The sheer size of this relationship can be appreciated by comparing it with similar data from a nonclinical population. Kihlstrom, for example, found that the TAS shared an estimated 30% of its variance with the DES-T[58] (Kihlstrom et al., 1994). In contrast, Allen's 0.83 correlation means that DES-Absorption shares a full 69% of its variance with the DES-T! Allen thus seems to be quite justified in his claim that (in his inpatient trauma population) severe absorption and pathological dissociation are inseparably intertwined.

My primary point of disagreement with Allen is his implication that there is no real difference between severe absorption and pathological dissociation.

Allen even suggests that absorption is the "g factor" of dissociation (Allen & Coyne, 1995). I think it is unhelpful to equate (or conflate) severe defensive absorption with pathological dissociation. These phenomena are, in some ways, phenotypically similar, but they have very different genotypes. They resemble each other, but they have different mechanisms (Steele et al., 2009; Van der Hart et al., 2004).

Earlier in this chapter we examined the defensive use of repression, hypnotizability, and dissociation. Now it is time to examine the defensive use of absorption. In doing so, it may be helpful to remember that it took Freud many years to clearly articulate that repression is but one of many defense mechanisms. The same is true of dissociation; it is just one of many defense mechanisms. Or, said differently, people resort to many different defensive behaviors and strategies in the face of psychological discomfort—avoidance, acting out, procrastinating, drugs, sex, dissociation, distraction via absorptive immersion

[58] This is my estimate based on the fact that the TAS shared 17% of its variance with DES-Amnesia and 43% of its variance with DES-Depersonalization/derealization (Kihlstrom et al., 1994).

in television, music, fantasies, and so on. Each person develops his or her own set of defensive behaviors and strategies.

Like individual differences in hypnotizability, people differ in their ability to use absorption. Those with lower levels of absorption can probably use only "content-ful" forms of absorption to deal with psychological discomfort (e.g., music, television, work, and other physical activities). Only those with greater native ability to become deeply absorbed can use "content-less" absorption (i.e., absorption in nothing, absorption in the void) to escape psychological pain. Individuals who possess a superior capacity for absorption will almost certainly use that capacity to escape pain.

When PTSD symptoms are so intense that they necessitate inpatient care, they make an especially urgent demand on the person's defenses. At such a time, whatever other defenses the person may use, he or she will use "content-ful" absorption and, if possible, "content-less" absorption to escape the pain. Similarly, truly dissociative patients will use dissociation to try to escape their pain. In fact, truly dissociative patients will do both of these things; they will use both absorptive and dissociative defenses. Interestingly, Allen claims that patients with a dissociative disorder may use more absorptive defenses than dissociative defenses:

> Even in the presence of other pathological forms of dissociation [i.e., amnesia, depersonalization, and derealization], detachment may constitute the most pervasive form of "dissociativity." (Allen et al., 2002, p. 105)

Most dissociative inpatients have structural dissociation (Van der Hart et al., 2006); that is, they have "internal" parts or alters that intrude into the executive functioning and sense of self of the person, thereby producing dissociative symptoms (i.e., recurrent incidents of depersonalization, derealization, and amnesia). On the other hand, there are many inpatients who do not have structural dissociation, but who manifest a variety of dissociative-like symptoms whose occurrence is a consequence of their absorptive detachment. As Allen has noted, severe absorptive detachment produces nonreversible (dare I say "nondissociative") memory gaps because absorptive detachment impairs elaborative encoding (Allen et al., 1999). Similarly, Allen notes that "Patients report that they are 'tuned out,' and they may not be aware of anything to which they are not 'tuned in' (Allen et al., 1999, p. 164). Being absorbed in nothingness also generates experiences of depersonalization and derealization: "detachment from one's actions, body, and sense of self, as well as other persons and outer world more generally" (Allen et al., 1997, p. 332).

The important point here is that there is a meaningful difference between the dissociative symptoms of structural dissociation and the "dissociative" symptoms of severe absorptive detachment (see the following).

46.7.5 Measuring Dissociation

Because science requires valid and reliable measurement, modern research on dissociation can be dated to the development of reliable and valid measures of dissociation, especially the DES (Bernstein & Putnam, 1986), the Dissociative Disorders Interview Schedule (DDIS; Ross et al., 1989), and the Structured Clinical Interview for DSM-III-R Dissociative Disorders (SCID-D; Steinberg, Rounsaville, & Cicchetti, 1990).

The following discussion will focus almost entirely on the DES—and deservedly so. It is only a slight exaggeration to assert that the DES has been the empirical core of almost every study of dissociation that has been conducted in the last 2 decades. The likelihood that the DES and other dissociation instruments measure several different things (see the following) places important limitations on our efforts to interpret the dissociation scores of past and future research.

46.7.5.1 Do Dissociation Instruments Measure More Than One Thing?

There has been increasing interest, and growing debate, about the question of whether dissociation instruments measure more than one thing. The initial manifestation of this interest was the large number of factor analytic studies of the DES and other self-administered measures of dissociation. Whether the authors of these studies acknowledged it or not, these factor analytic studies always had implications for two questions. First: do the items of this particular instrument measure one thing or several things? And second: does the construct of dissociation have a unitary structure or does it have multiple components? Briere, for example, used a factor analytic study of the Multiscale Dissociation Inventory (MDI) to claim that the MDI has five factors that are so weakly correlated with another that they call into question the empirical coherence of the construct of dissociation (Briere, Weathers, & Runtz, 2005).

Many factor analytic studies produced unifactorial solutions; many others produced multifactorial solutions (see Dell & Lawson, 2009, for a brief review). The factor structure of the domain of dissociation may have been finally settled by a cross-validated confirmatory factor analysis of MID data from two very large samples. The MID is a highly comprehensive measure of pathological dissociation that contains no absorption items (Dell, 2006b). The MID's 168 dissociation items were found to have 12 first-order factors and a single second-order factor (Dell & Lawson, 2009). The implication of this finding is that pathological dissociation is phenomenologically complex (i.e., it has 12 components), but structurally unitary.

The second major arena for questioning what is measured by dissociation instruments arose with the taxometric findings of Waller and colleagues (1996) and the complementary nontaxometric findings of Putnam and colleagues (1996). Both of these studies provided strong evidence for a typological view of dissociation. The first study clearly indicated that there was a qualitative difference between pathological dissociation (i.e., depersonalization/derealization and amnesia) and "normal" dissociation (i.e., absorption). Because the DES taps both absorption and pathological dissociation, and because the DES has been the foundation of empirical research on dissociation, one is led to ask whether absorption might have some important hidden effects on DES scores.

A third major challenge to dissociation instruments has come from the work of Van der Hart and colleagues. They contend that a wide variety of alterations of consciousness produce dissociative-like symptoms, but that only a subset of those dissociative-like symptoms properly deserve the label *dissociative* (Steele et al., 2009; Van der Hart et al., 2004, 2006). Specifically, they claim that only the phenomenological manifestations of structural dissociation should be called *dissociative*. Steele et al. (2009) readily concede that the unique phenomenological features that distinguish the symptoms of structural dissociation from the symptoms of other alterations of consciousness have yet to be identified. They urge that the identification of such features should be a major priority for future research.

Most relevant to our current focus on measurement is the firm assertion of Steele and colleagues that only a minority of depersonalization symptoms and a minority of derealization symptoms stem from structural dissociation. This, of course, directly implies that the depersonalization items and derealization items of the DES (and other dissociation instruments) measure at least two different things: (1) structural dissociation, and (2) miscellaneous, "nondissociative" alterations of consciousness.

Allen's absorptive detachment studies constitute a fourth major challenge to the view that dissociation instruments measure only one thing. As previously noted, I contend, as do Steele and colleagues (2009), that there is a meaningful difference between the dissociative symptoms of structural dissociation and the dissociative-like symptoms of absorptive detachment. Moreover, I believe that the DES, the MID, and most clinicians cannot (yet) distinguish between the symptoms of structural dissociation and other dissociative-like symptoms.[59] This can be problematic because, to the best of our current knowledge, patients with structural dissociation have a DSM dissociative disorder, but patients with only absorptive detachment do not.

A fifth challenge to the view that dissociation instruments measure only one thing comes from the work of Holmes and Brown (Brown, 2006; Holmes et al., 2005). Holmes and Brown contend that "commonly cited definitions of dissociation are arguably too all-encompassing" (Holmes et al., 2005, p. 2) and that there are really two kinds of dissociation—detachment and compartmentalization—each with a different mechanism. Although the grounds that Holmes and Brown cite for drawing this distinction are different from the grounds cited by Van der Hart et al. (2004) and Steele et al. (2009) for distinguishing between structural dissociation and alterations of consciousness, the outcome is quite similar (but not identical).

There appears to be little practical difference between Van der Hart and colleagues' (2006) concept of structural dissociation and Holmes and Brown's concept of compartmentalization. But there are several important differences between Holmes' and Brown's detachment and Van der Hart and colleagues' miscellaneous alterations of consciousness. Van der Hart and colleagues' explication of alterations of consciousness is a definition-by-exclusion. For them, alterations in consciousness are completely nonspecific; they consist of all alterations of consciousness that are not caused by structural dissociation. Holmes and Brown's detachment, on the other hand, specifically refers to depersonalization and derealization:

> [T]he subject experiences an altered state of consciousness characterized by a sense of separation (or "detachment") from certain aspects of everyday experience, be it their body (as in out-of-body experiences), their sense of self (as in depersonalization), or the external world (as in derealization). (Holmes et al., 2005, p. 5)

[59] Yes, the DES measures absorption. The problem lies in the fact that severe absorption seems to generate both depersonalization/derealization and memory gaps that are phenotypically similar to those of structural dissociation—and that the DES cannot distinguish between them.

In a revised treatment of detachment, Brown (2006) stated that the phenomenon of "made" actions, ostensibly a form of depersonalization, has been reassigned by him to the construct of compartmentalization. This is a very interesting decision for several reasons. First, Brown offers no explanation for this decision. Second, the decision cannot be justified on the basis of his preferred definition of detachment: "an altered state of consciousness characterized by a sense of separation (or detachment) from aspects of everyday experience" (Brown, 2006, p. 12). Third, by assigning made actions to the mechanism of compartmentalization, he has (1) rejected the Holmes et al. (2005) model of detachment in which "all depersonalization phenomena were regarded as examples of detachment" (Brown, 2006, p. 13), (2) repositioned his revised model much closer to that of Van der Hart and colleagues (who assign a subset of depersonalization phenomena, including made actions, to structural dissociation), and (3) increased the congruence of his revised model with the empirical evidence that made actions routinely occur in the clinical prototype of compartmentalization—DID (see, for example, Dell, 2006c).

With regard to current instruments of dissociation, however, the precise location of the boundary between detachment and compartmentalization is, in one sense, inconsequential. The verdict for these instruments remains the same: "total scores on the DES may not be the most useful way of describing the 'dissociative' tendencies of subject groups" (Brown, 2006, p. 24) because the DES indiscriminately measures more than one thing (and even the DES depersonalization/derealization subscale does not "carve Nature at her joints").

At a minimum, then, the distinctions drawn by the authors discussed in this section imply that there are two crucial distinctions that existing instruments of dissociation are unable to detect. First, there is a difference between (1) the symptoms of structural dissociation (i.e., compartmentalization) and (2) the symptoms of other miscellaneous alterations of consciousness (i.e., severe absorptive detachment, some forms of depersonalization, and some forms of derealization). Second, structural dissociation and certain kinds of alteration of consciousness (i.e., Allen's severe absorptive detachment and at least some forms of Holmes/Brown detachment) produce two different kinds of memory problems: (1) reversible dissociative amnesia and (2) nonreversible memory gaps due to impaired storage and impaired elaboration.

Again, existing measures of dissociation are, as yet, unable to distinguish between (1) these two kinds of "dissociation" and (2) these two kinds of memory gap.

46.7.5.2 Is There More Than One Kind of High Dissociator?

Like the preceding section, the present section examines the heterogeneity of "dissociative" phenomena. The present section asks: "are high dissociators all the same, or are there different kinds of high dissociators?"

In one sense, there has been no research on this question. When we consider the in-depth studies of very highly hypnotizable subjects that were conducted by Wilson and Barber (1982) and Barrett (1992, 1996), we can immediately see that there have been no comparable in-depth studies of high dissociators. In-depth studies of high dissociators are sorely needed. There are, however, a variety of empirical findings and theoretical propositions that do, indeed, imply the existence of different kinds of high dissociators.

Perhaps the natural starting point in discussing high dissociators is the difference between DID and Depersonalization Disorder—or, to put the contrast more precisely, the contrast between (1) chronic complex dissociative disorders of structural dissociation such as DID and the almost-DID forms of Dissociative Disorder Not Otherwise Specified (i.e., DDNOS-1; see Dell, 2009a), and (2) Depersonalization Disorder (DPD). The symptoms of DID and DDNOS-1 are understood to derive from the activities of one or more compartmentalized dissociative structures. The proposed mechanisms of DPD, although still a matter of debate, certainly do not include structural dissociation.[60] DID and DPD have at least two notable differences in their respective symptom-pictures: amnesia and the periodicity or time scale of their symptomatic manifestations. Structural dissociation generates reversible amnesia, but DPD does not. Because amnesia is absent, DPD patients obtain somewhat lower dissociation scores than do DID patients. Second, structural dissociation generates dissociative symptoms that are episodic and recurrent, whereas DPD generates symptoms of depersonalization and derealization that are fixed and unyielding for very long periods of time.

[60] The closest thing to a structural explanation of chronic DPD was proposed by Mitchell early in the 20th century: "Dissociation is revealed by gaps or disabilities in the normal self, rather than by the appearance of any new form of activity simulating a second self. But if the dissociated portions of consciousness should suddenly become reinstated so as to lead to the formation once more of the normal personality, and if again they should gradually or suddenly drop out of consciousness so as again to leave the normal self crippled and constricted by their disappearance [in a state of chronic depersonalization?], we should have an alternation of two selves, whose relation to each other might not be readily recognized" (Mitchell, 1923, p. 115). Mitchell's formulation could explain DPD if only affective aspects of the self were dissociated (and memorial aspects of the self were not dissociated).

Second, Allen's articles invite the question of whether patients with only severe absorptive detachment (i.e., persons who do not have structural dissociation) can obtain high scores on measures of dissociation such as the DES, MID, and so on. If so, they would seem to constitute a third kind of high dissociator (in addition to DID/DDNOS-1 and DPD).

Third, Pekala and Kumar (2000) have presented evidence of two kinds of high dissociators: those with and those without high hypnotizability. In a graph (fig. 46.1) of unpublished data from Kumar et al. (1996), Kumar and Pekala show that one cluster of students with high DES scores have high HGSHS:A scores, whereas another cluster of students with high DES scores have low HGSHS:A scores. Interestingly, both the high-hypnotizable/high-dissociators and the low-hypnotizable/high-dissociators have high Hypnoidal Scores (i.e., Pekala's phenomenological measure of subjective hypnotizability that correlates 0.60 with the HGSHS:A). Thus, all of Kumar and Pekala's high dissociators report high levels of phenomenological experiences that are associated with deep trance, but one cluster of these high dissociators nevertheless performs poorly on the HGSHS:A. It is difficult to know how to interpret this pattern of scores because there are so many sources of variance in these data (i.e., the DES, the HGSHS:A, dissociation taxon membership, severe absorption, late adolescents, etc.). Putnam, too, has identified a group of "double dissociators"—persons with both high hypnotizability and high dissociation scores (Putnam et al., 1995). If single dissociators really exist, that is, if high dissociators with low hypnotizability really exist, then it is essential that they be investigated and be thoroughly compared with double dissociators and other groups of high dissociators.

Fourth, what is the relationship between fantasy proneness and high levels of dissociation? Do high dissociators differ as a function of fantasy proneness? Is fantasy proneness a major risk factor for DID as several authors have suggested (Bowers, 1991; Halleck, 1989; Lynn, Rhue, & Green, 1988)? Despite these forceful claims about fantasy proneness and DID, relatively little is known about the relationship between fantasy proneness and severe dissociation. There is little evidence, however, that DID patients are fantasy prone. Whereas the incidence of fantasy proneness in the general population is about 4%, the incidence of fantasy proneness in a private practice sample and consulation sample of 100 DID patients was 11% (Dell, unpublished data). Accordingly, fantasy proneness does not seem to be a major risk factor for DID. It remains to be seen whether there are important differences between fantasy-prone DID patients and DID patients who are not fantasy prone.

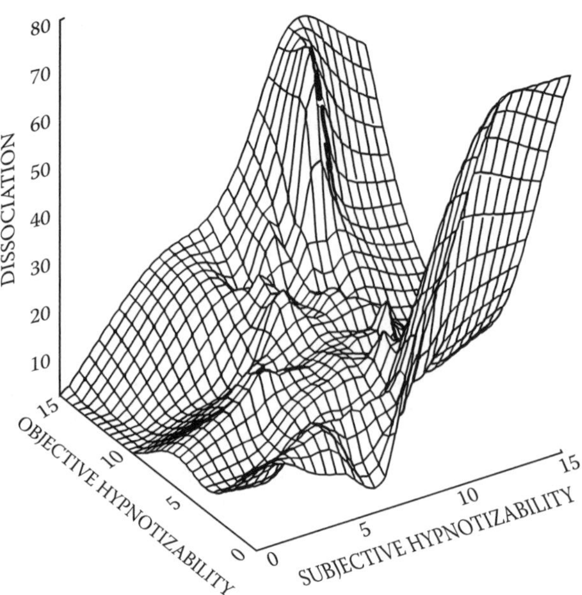

FIGURE 46.1 This graph shows that there are two groups of subjects with high DES scores—those with low hypnotizability and those with high hypnotizability. From Operationalizing trance. I: Rationale and research using a psychophenomenological approach, by R. J. Pekala and V. K. Kumar, 2000, American Journal of Clinical Hypnosis, 2000, 43(2), p. 114. Copyright 2000 by American Society of Clinical Hypnosis. Reprinted with permission.

By the way, in considering these issues it is helpful to recall that absorption is a normal psychological trait that can be used in a maladaptive, pathological fashion. Fantasy proneness is a particular manifestation of absorption. Like absorption, fantasy proneness is a normal psychological behavior (Wilson & Barber, 1982), which can be used in a maladaptive, pathological fashion. I believe that our thinking about fantasy proneness will be enriched if we retrieve the fact that fantasizing is a normal phenomenon. Even full-blown fantasy proneness is not inherently pathological. This is important to recall because the past decade's research on fantasy proneness has left the impression that fantasy proneness is, *per se*, pathological. It is not. Some fantasy-prone persons are maladjusted, but most are not (Barrett, 1992, 1996; Wilson & Barber, 1982).

Fifth, Colin Ross's epidemiological data from Winnipeg produced evidence of persons with DID who lacked a history of trauma and abuse (Ross, 1991). This is another phenomenon that requires further investigation. If nontraumatized persons with DID actually occur, a not unlikely mechanism of the phenomenon would be healthy fantasy proneness. In any case, nontraumatized persons with DID, should they exist, must be thoroughly compared with the typical traumatized cases of DID that are so well known.

Sixth, there is recurrent evidence that the DES scores of late adolescent samples differ from those of adult samples. The atypical nature of these scores, however, is usually reported in an almost euphemistic fashion: it is simply said that dissociation scores decrease with age (e.g., Van IJzendoorn & Schuengel, 1996). The important issue here is why. Why do late adolescents consistently have higher DES scores than adults? What is going on? Are all adolescents more dissociative than adults? Only some? Do late adolescents have a higher incidence of structural dissociation than adults? Does their structural dissociation spontaneously heal in early adulthood? These, of course, are provocative rhetorical questions whose purpose is to provoke us to think about this phenomenon. I believe that the dissociation field has not been well-served by its unthinking acceptance of late adolescents' atypical high-dissociation scores.

Consider the following. The percentage of high dissociators (DES > 30) in an adult nonclinical sample (mean age = 40.5) is 4.4%, whereas the percentage of high dissociators in a sample of late adolescents (mean age = 20.9) is 11.1%—a 250% difference in the incidence of high dissociators (Putnam et al., 1996). What is going on here? The truth is that we have no idea. We don't know whether these apparently dissociating late adolescents are detached, absorbed, fantasy-prone, members of the dissociative taxon (Watson, 2003), or whatever. Again, there is an urgent need for in-depth studies of various groups of high dissociators, including late adolescent high dissociators. It is not acceptable to unthinkingly state the obvious—that adolescents are more dissociative than adults—and to consider that to be an adequate explanation. It is even less acceptable to conduct dissociation research on this population while simultaneously displaying neither concern for, nor apparent interest in, the fact that the DES scores of college students are atypical. The fact that the variance of DES scores in late adolescent students is significantly larger than that of adults (Näring & Nijenhuis, 2005) clearly indicates that these two populations cannot be equated with one another.

46.7.5.3 Additional Implications of "Dissociative" Heterogeneity

The distinction between the dissociative symptoms of structural dissociation and the dissociative-like symptoms of severe absorption would seem to have several likely implications. First, truly dissociative patients almost certainly have both dissociative and dissociative-like symptoms (Allen et al., 2002; Steele et al., 2009). Persons with structural dissociation use defensive absorption, too, especially at times of unremitting psychological discomfort. Conversely, when treatment stabilizes the functioning of a dissociative patient, that treatment almost certainly reduces both dissociative functioning and absorptive detachment (Allen et al., 2002). Because our current dissociation instruments do not distinguish between structural dissociation and absorptive detachment, we do not know their relative proportion in dissociative patients. Do the relative proportions of the symptoms of absorptive detachment and the symptoms of structural dissociation differ when the patient is stable versus when the patient is destabilized and flooded with "dissociative" symptoms? Allen appears to imply that the proportion of symptoms due to absorptive detachment increases when a patient is destabilized (e.g., during an inpatient stay).

Second, the intrusive symptoms of PTSD would seem to be an especially strong motivator of absorptive detachment. Putnam et al. (1996) have shown that there are two clusters of persons with PTSD: those with severe dissociative symptoms (mean DES = 48) and those with moderate dissociative symptoms (mean DES = 17). Similarly, Waelde, Silvern, and Fairbank (2005) have shown that there are two groups of patients with PTSD, those who are members of a dissociative taxon (mean DES = 34.8) and those who are not (mean DES = 6.1). Are the moderately elevated DES scores of Putnam's first PTSD cluster an index of absorptive detachment rather than structural dissociation?

Third, research has repeatedly reported a global elevation of DES scores in certain settings, such as state hospitals and community mental health centers. Two sources of that global elevation are already understood: (1) the well-known tendency of many chronic patients to overendorse items on psychological tests; and (2) the increased incidence of dissociative patients in those highly symptomatic populations. We now may ask whether a portion of that global elevation of DES scores is due to severe absorptive detachment.

Fourth, despite the inability of dissociation instruments (including the MID) to distinguish between different kinds of dissociative symptoms (i.e., phenotypically similar, dissociative-like symptoms that are produced by different mechanisms), Dell and Lawson (2009) have shown that pathological dissociation, as measured by the MID, has a robust, replicable factor-structure, even when submitted to confirmatory factor analysis (CFA). If dissociative symptoms are as heterogeneous as the previous discussion implies, and are indiscriminately swept together by current instruments, then why are the replicated MID CFAs so robust?

The MID was explicitly designed to be a measure of pathological dissociation. Pathological dissociation is an index of membership in the dissociation taxon, an index of major structural dissociation. And yet, the MID inevitably detects, indiscriminately, other dissociative-like symptoms. Accordingly, there would seem to be two possible interpretations of Dell and Lawson's impressive cross-validated CFAs. First, the variance in the data due to pathological dissociation may be so great that it swamps the "noise" variance of other forms of dissociation. Second, perhaps the MID actually measures a broader construct than pathological dissociation; that is, perhaps the MID functions as a measure of motivated, quasi-automatic, defensive alterations of cognitive functioning. Such a broad construct of cognitive defense would encompass at least pathological dissociation, absorptive detachment, various forms of depersonalization and derealization, as well as evolution-prepared spontaneous peritraumatic dissociation.

46.7.6 Once Again—Dissociation and Hypnotizability

46.7.6.1 Deferring Judgment on the Autohypnotic Model of Dissociation

We embarked upon the previous analysis of hypnotizability, dissociation, and their respective instruments of measurement in order to more carefully assess the status of the autohypnotic model of dissociation. As previously noted, the autohypnotic model of dissociation has been in a period of near-fatal decline since the reviews of Whalen and Nash (1996) and Putnam and Carlson (1998) showed that the correlation between standard measures of dissociation and standard measures of hypnotizability was a feeble 0.12.

As a consequence of our analysis in the previous 16 pages, it should now be apparent that our measures, and indeed our understanding of the concepts, of hypnotizability and dissociation are not as firmly grounded as we might hope. This, of course, has important implications for the 0.12 correlation between measures of dissociation and measures of hypnotizability and for the fate of the autohypnotic model of dissociation. I think that we should defer our judgment on the autohypnosis model until we know more. Our analysis has shown that far too many irrelevant variables play a role in generating that small correlation.

Finally, it is worth remembering that both Whalen and Nash (1996) and Putnam and Carlson (1998) were quite aware of the extent to which the validity of the 0.12 correlation rested upon the less-than-foundational status of our current measures of dissociation and hypnotizability. Whalen and Nash were certainly correct when they insisted that "the time for unrefined examination of correlations between hypnotizability and dissociativity scales has passed" (Whalen & Nash, 1996, p. 202).

46.7.6.2 A Plea for More Investigation of Hypnotizability and Dissociation

Putnam and Carlson, the dissociation field's most persistent investigators of the relationship between dissociation and hypnotizability (Carlson & Putnam, 1989; Carlson, 1994; Putnam & Carlson, 1998; Putnam et al., 1995) began their investigation by concluding that hypnotizability and dissociation are "two overlapping phenomena" (Carlson & Putnam, 1989, p. 34). They ended by concluding that "Hypnotizability and dissociativity, as measured by current instruments, are clearly not synonymous processes" (Putnam & Carlson, 1998, p. 46).

Since that time, there has been almost no research on the relationship between dissociation and hypnosis. I urge that this dormant strand of research be taken up anew by the field of dissociation.

As a starting point, I would recommend that careful attention be given to the research of Pekala and Kumar (especially Kumar et al., 1996 and Pekala & Kumar, 2000). As briefly noted in the previous discussions, in a sample of 435 college students, Kumar et al. (1996) reported that they found 10 high dissociators (mean DES = 36.5) who had very low scores on the HGSHS:A (mean = 1.90)! This is a very unexpected finding. Its unexpectedness is only exceeded by the surprising fact that no researcher has yet sought to replicate, or even understand, this unexpected juxtaposition of high dissociativity and low hypnotizability. As I implied above, this curious finding may be just an artifact (of atypical late adolescents, the limitations of the HGSHS:A, the heterogeneity of what is measured by the DES, Pekala's category of Pseudo-Low hypnotic subjects, etc.). Nevertheless, this finding warrants prompt investigation.

Kumar et al. (1996) also reported that both high- and low-hypnotizable high-dissociators had high scores on Pekala's Hypnoidal Score. The Hypnoidal Score is derived from an algorithm of scale scores from Pekala's (1991b) Phenomenology of Consciousness Inventory. The Hypnoidal Score rates the degree to which the person, after responding to the HGSHS:A, reported having phenomenological experiences that are typical of deep trance (Pekala & Nagler, 1989; Pekala & Kumar, 2000).

More remarkable still is Kumar's et al. 3x3 table of hypnoidal scores (see Table 46.1). When hypnoidal scores were laid out in a 3x3 table of level of hypnotizability (low, medium, and high) and level of dissociativity (low, medium, and high), they form a perfectly monotonic, nine-point ordinal scale of hypnoidal scores! And yet, despite the perfect ordinality of the hypnoidal scores, the overall correlations of the hypnoidal scores with the HGSHS:A and the DES were quite different: Hypnoidal Score x HGSHS:A = 0.60;

TABLE 46.1
Hypnoidal Scores as a Function of Level of Hypnotizability and Level of Dissociativity

	Dissociativity			
Susceptibility	**Low**	**Medium**	**High**	**Total**
Low	1.78	2.18	2.54	2.06
Medium	3.85	4.43	5.02	4.40
High	5.40	6.20	7.26	6.31
Total	3.16	3.97	5.06	

This table is adapted from Hypnotizability, dissociativity, and phenomenological experience, by V. K. Kumar, R. J. Pekala, and G. Marcano, 1996, Dissociation, 9, p. 149. Copyright 1996 by Dissociative Disorders Research Publications, Limited. Reprinted with permission.

Hypnoidal Score x DES = 0.27. These correlations suggest that hypnotic performance may be a major determinant of trance-like experience (i.e., Hypnoidal Score), but that everyday dissociativity (i.e., DES score) is, at best, a minor determinant of trance-like experience during hypnosis—except that, as previously noted, 10 high-dissociators, who performed poorly on the HGSHS:A, had high hypnoid scores. Inspection of figure 46.1 suggests that the DES is, in fact, heteroscedastic *vis-à-vis* hypnoid scores. That is, high DES scores appear to correlate better with hypnoid scores than do lower DES scores.

Differences in trance-like experience are quite apparent in contrasts between subjects with low and high hypnotizability, but not in contrasts between subjects with low and high dissociativity. That is, compared to low-hypnotizable subjects, the phenomenological experience during the HGSHS:A of subjects with high hypnotizability reflected the classic suggestion effect[61] (i.e., decreased volitional control, decreased rationality, and increased absorption and inward attention). In contrast, compared to low-dissociativity subjects, the phenomenological experience during hypnosis of subjects with high dissociativity did not show signs of the classic suggestion effect, or even of dissociation! That is, low- versus high-dissociators did not differ in their experience of volitional control, self-awareness, absorption, or memory.

Finally, compared to low-hypnotizable subjects, highly hypnotizable subjects reported more experiences of joy and love (i.e., positive affect) during the HGSHS:A. Joy and love are not unlike the posture of trust and the incredible ability to affiliate that characterizes Spiegel's (1974) Grade 5 syndrome. In contrast, compared to low-dissociativity subjects, high dissociators reported more experiences of sadness and anger (i.e., negative affect) during the HGSHS:A. These increased levels of sadness and anger replicate earlier findings that DES scores are positively correlated with negative affect (e.g., Groth-Marnat & Jeffs, 2002).

The bottom line here is that the data of Kumar et al. (1996) have three implications for high dissociators. First, although there is little relationship between DES scores and either hypnotizability or phenomenological experience during hypnosis, high DES scores do appear to be preferentially associated with high hypnoidal scores (i.e., the DES seems to be heteroscedastic with respect to trance-like experiences). Second, the subjective experiences that characterize elevated levels of everyday dissociativity do not manifest themselves during a 2-minute resting period in hypnosis. Third, despite this disjunction between everyday dissociative experiences and resting hypnotic experience, the negative affectivity of high dissociators does manifest itself during resting hypnosis. This suggests that ostensibly healthy students with elevated DES scores are, nevertheless, emotionally distressed.

46.7.7 The Heterogeneity of "Dissociation"

It should now be apparent that dissociation is notable for nothing, if not its heterogeneity. The word *dissociative* can be, and has been, applied to a bewildering variety of very similar cognitive/phenomenological phenotypes, which almost certainly derive from different mechanisms. The next several sections of the chapter seek to draw distinctions among several kinds of dissociation.

We will begin at the beginning—evolution and natural selection. Dissociation is a product of evolution, and the first kind of dissociation—automatic peritraumatic dissociation—is part of an evolution-prepared, biological effort to survive.

46.8 PERITRAUMATIC DISSOCIATION IS PART OF AN EVOLUTION-PREPARED SET OF RESPONSES TO SUDDEN LIFE-THREAT

During the course of evolution, natural selection has ensured that organisms perceive and respond to stimuli in terms of their biological significance (for survival and

[61] The classic suggestion effect occurs when a suggestion is transformed into an action or response that the person experiences as happening involuntarily (Weitzenhoffer, 1978).

reproduction). In particular, organisms have been shaped to react rapidly and decisively to stimuli that have been associated with a fatal outcome during their evolutionary history. These defensive responses to dangerous stimuli are both physiological and behavioral in nature.

46.8.1 General Features of Evolution-Prepared Defenses

46.8.1.1 Danger, Threat, and Survival

Evolution-prepared defenses foster survival. They are rooted in the fear system (Fanselow, 1994; Fendt & Fanselow, 1999; Gallup, 1977; LeDoux, 1996; Öhman & Mineka, 2001; Panksepp, 1998, 2004). They have been selected to cope with dangers that have been recurrently encountered during the course of the organism's evolution.

46.8.1.2 Rapid, Automatic, Without Decision, and Often Without Awareness

Many biological defenses operate almost instantaneously—out of necessity. In fact, the more urgent the danger, the shorter is the time-scale upon which evolution-prepared defenses operate (Williams, 2006). When one is about to step on a snake or when one begins to fall off a cliff, there is literally no time to think. In such circumstances, the response time for a reaction that enables survival is measured in milliseconds. This near-instantaneous defensive response can only occur if it has been prewired by evolution. The behaviors and physiological adjustments that evolution has shown to be most effective in this circumstance are enacted automatically (i.e., without conscious thought). The neural substrates of automatic biological defenses are subcortical; they lie in the midbrain and the brainstem (Bandler & Depaulis, 1991; LeDoux, 1996; Williams, 2006).

46.8.1.3 Organized Defensive Behavioral Systems

An evolution-prepared defense does not consist of a single behavior; instead, it is an organized behavioral system (Timberlake & Lucas, 1989). "A behavior system is a complex control structure related to a particular function or need of the organism, such as feeding, reproduction, defense, or body care" (Timberlake & Lucas, 1989, p. 244). As such, an evolution-prepared defense is a prewired control structure of physiological responses, neural circuits, and integrated subsystems. When an evolution-prepared defense is activated, perception is immediately adjusted and instantly tuned to the most survival-relevant aspects of the environment. Similarly, perceptual-motor modules are primed to respond instantaneously to survival-relevant stimuli with action patterns that the evolutionary history of the organism has shown to be most protective. These defensive behavioral systems are species-specific defense reactions (Bolles, 1970) that are specific to the survival problem at hand, diverse (in order to handle different problems, which are often a function of the changing gradient of danger), and predictable (Sigmundi, 1997).

46.8.2 Six Inferences About Peritraumatic Dissociation as an Evolution-Prepared Survival-Response

46.8.2.1 Peritraumatic Dissociation Is About Danger, Threat, and Survival

If dissociation is an evolution-prepared biological defense against immediate danger, then it necessarily follows that dissociation is fundamentally about danger and survival. Conversely, it also follows that dissociation is fundamentally not about trauma, distress, and pain. Only secondarily is dissociation about these things. Said differently, survival is the goal, whereas dissociation is one of the organism's methods (of facilitating survival).

46.8.2.2 Peritraumatic Dissociation Is Automatic and Instantaneous

Evolution-prepared dissociation is an implicit, procedural skill. There is no more conscious awareness of doing it (or of how we do it) than there is conscious awareness of throwing our arms forward if we are pushed down from behind. Like most evolution-prepared biological defenses against immediate danger, this kind of dissociation is automatic, near-instantaneous, and implemented without conscious awareness or decision.

46.8.2.3 Peritraumatic Dissociation Is Always Just One Component of an Organized Defensive Response

Dissociation, itself, is almost certainly not a behavioral system. It is much more likely that dissociation is a neurophysiological module that is integrated in different ways into different defensive behavior systems. Consequently, it is proposed that a dissociative reaction to a particular danger is an integral component of an organized defensive response to that danger. That particular organized defensive response exists because it has recurrently increased the likelihood of surviving that danger (during the evolutionary history of that organism and its phylogenetic progenitors).

46.8.2.4 The Manifestations of Peritraumatic Dissociation Are Determined by the Particular Danger

Dissociative reactions can take many different forms. For any given danger, the form of the dissociative reaction will vary depending on the particular organized defensive response that has been activated. Different dangers evoke different defensive responses and different manifestations of dissociation.

46.8.2.5 Peritraumatic Dissociation Is a Brief, Time-Limited Phenomenon

Evolution-prepared biological defenses are situation-specific coping responses that are triggered by the organism's encounter with particular life-threatening situations. As such, a dissociative reaction to danger is situation-specific, "task-oriented," and time-limited. The dissociative response lasts only as long as it is helpful, only as long as that life-threatening situation lasts. When the person survives and escapes with his or her life, the dissociation ceases.

46.8.2.6 Peritraumatic Dissociation Is a Subcortical Phenomenon

Like other defensive responses such as fear, freezing, the startle response, flight, fighting, and tonic immobility, the neural substrates of peritraumatic dissociation are almost certainly subcortical. Nijenhuis et al. (1998) came to a similar conclusion:

> Finally, taking into consideration the evolutionary importance of rapid responding to major threat, it would seem odd if dissociative defense were strongly dependent upon the relatively slow cognitive hippocampal-neocortical information processing system (LeDoux, 1989). The present model postulates that dissociative defensive reactions are elicited almost instantaneously. (pp. 118–119)

Peritraumatic dissociation must be rooted in the fear/defensive system of the midbrain and brainstem. The degree of cortical participation remains to be determined, and probably varies across different threats to life and different manifestations of dissociation.

46.8.3 Life-Threatening Situations

Life-threatening situations can trigger peritraumatic dissociation—falls, natural disasters, near-drownings, automobile accidents, and so on. Of these, dangerous falls probably have the longest phylogenetic history. That is, falls have probably provided natural selection with the longest opportunity to "shape" the defensive responding not only of humans, but of our phylogenetic ancestors as well. Thus, life-threatening falls may be taken to represent the prototypical dangerous encounter between humans and the physical world.

Does dissociation really occur during falls? Yes, routinely. In 1892, Albert Heim, an avid mountain climber and university professor of geology from Zurich, published an article in the *Jahrbuch des Schweizer Alpenclub* (Yearbook of the Swiss Alpine Club). He described and summarized the accounts of dozens of mountain climbers who had suffered potentially fatal falls, but had survived:

> [N]o grief was felt, nor was there paralyzing fright of the sort that can happen in instances of lesser danger (e.g., outbreak of fire). There was no anxiety, no trace of despair, no pain; but rather calm seriousness, profound acceptance, and a dominant mental quickness and sense of surety. Mental activity became enormous, rising to a hundred-fold velocity or intensity. The relationships of events and their probable outcomes were overviewed with objective clarity. No confusion entered at all. Time became greatly expanded. The individual acted with lightning-quickness in accord with accurate judgment of his situation.... Men who had fallen from great heights were unaware that their limbs had been broken until they attempted to stand. (Heim, 1892/1980, p. 130–131)

Heim reported that "nearly 95 percent of the victims ... experienced ... a similar mental state" (p. 130). Moreover, he reported that this mental state "ensues in clear consciousness, in heightened sensory and ideational activity, and without anxiety or pain" (p. 135). Thus, it would seem that dissociation does, indeed, occur during the overwhelming majority of potentially fatal falls.

But what about falls that almost happen, but do not? Does dissociation occur then? Adams (1988) provides a first-person account of a very experienced climber who was certain that he would fall, but did not:

> After gaining a point about halfway to the top, I was suddenly brought to a dead stop, with arms outspread, clinging to the face of the rock, unable to move hand or foot either up or down. My doom appeared fixed. I must fall. There would be a moment of bewilderment, and then a lifeless tumble down the one general precipice to the glacier below. When this final danger flashed upon me, I became nerve-shaken for the first time since setting foot on the mountains, and my mind seemed to fill with a stifling smoke. But this terrible eclipse lasted only a moment, when life blazed forth again with preternatural clearness. I seemed suddenly to become possessed of

> a new sense. The other self, bygone experiences, instinct, or Guardian Angel—call it what you will—came forward and assumed control. Then my trembling muscles became firm again, every rift and flaw in the rock was seen as through a microscope, and my limbs moved with a positiveness and precision with which I seemed to have nothing at all to do. (p. 33)

The dissociative aspects of this experience are unmistakable. Finally, here is yet one more example of a potentially fatal fall. Unlike the previous examples, which come from outside the dissociation literature, the following example is especially interesting because it comes from the first scientific article to clearly identify and delineate the concept of peritraumatic dissociation (Spiegel, 1991). This quotation describes the prototypical case example that Spiegel used to exemplify peritraumatic dissociation in that landmark publication:

> A petite young woman, who experienced an accidental fall from a third story balcony which resulted in a broken pelvis, described the event in the following manner. She was at a party talking to a friend when a large man standing next to her turned around suddenly, knocking her over the railing. When asked how terrifying she had found the experience, she responded that it was "quite pleasant." This surprising statement led to further inquiry which revealed that she had experienced the fall as though she had been standing on a nearby balcony watching "a pink cloud float down to the ground. I felt no pain and tried to walk back upstairs." (Spiegel, 1991, p. 262)

These examples of potentially fatal falls emphasize an absence of pain, absence of fear, a calm state of mind, a slowing of time, accelerated thought, clear thinking, heightened sensory perception, and a heightened ability to execute motor skills with precision and confidence. The latter two aspects (heightened sensory perception and heightened motor skills) are more apparent in the climber who did not fall but who had the opportunity to take effective, lifesaving action. Those who fell emphasized a calm, unafraid mind that was able to think rapidly and very clearly. Russell Noyes, a near-death researcher, reported these same phenomena in his articles on depersonalization during falls, accidents, near-drownings, and so on (Noyes, Hoenk, Kuperman, & Slymen, 1977; Noyes & Kletti, 1976, 1977; Noyes & Slymen, 1978–1979). For example, Noyes and Kletti (1977) provided a first-person account of a car accident during which the steering failed at 60 miles per hour:

> My mind speeded up. Time seemed drawn out. It seemed like five minutes before the car came to a stop when, in reality, it was only a matter of seconds. I remember that my sense of touch and hearing became more acute. I was actually aware of my grip on the steering wheel and of my body touching the seat behind me. The grass brushing the door was unusually loud. On the other hand, my vision was blurred except for an instant when my attention became focused on the abutment ahead.... My mind was working rapidly and reviewed information from driver's education that might bear on what I should do to save myself.... While all this was taking place I felt calm, even detached. (Noyes & Kletti, 1977, p. 376)

46.8.4 The Scientific "Birth" of Peritraumatic Dissociation

The previous examples emphasize that peritraumatic dissociation is merely one component of an array of instantaneous, adaptive changes of affect, sensation, information processing, and behavior that facilitate survival in a life-threatening situation. I hope that this emphasis on survival-oriented adaptation can serve as a corrective to the scientific literature on peritraumatic dissociation that has typically underemphasized, if not entirely omitted, the evolution-prepared essence of peritraumatic response.

The scientific literature on peritraumatic dissociation began with Spiegel's seminal article in 1991, which firmly established the idea that dissociation was a frequent defensive concomitant of trauma:

> Dissociation has another unusual feature. It serves as a defense not only against warded-off memories, fears, and wishes, but against trauma while it is occurring. It is quite common for victims to report dissociative experiences during traumatic experiences (Rose, 1986; Spiegel et al., 1988). These spontaneous experiences are often extremely helpful in allowing the person to defend against overwhelming fear, pain, and helplessness. Many rape victims report that they experienced the rape as if they were floating above their own body, feeling sorry for the person undergoing the sexual assault.... *The immediate response to trauma involves an experience of unreality with distortions of perception, memory, temporal processing, and relating to the environment.* Alterations of mental state are the rule rather than the exception during and after trauma. (pp. 261–262; italics added)

Subsequent research on peritraumatic dissociation has seldom (except in passing) dwelt on its contribution to survival. Instead, research on peritraumatic dissociation had sought to document its occurrence, its frequency, and its relationship to the development of PTSD. Due to this latter issue, especially, peritraumatic dissociation has generally been of greater interest to the trauma field than the dissociation field. Both fields, however, underemphasize the fact that peritraumatic dissociation is part of an evolution-prepared set of responses that maximize survival. This stance, in turn, has made it difficult for either field to understand the mixed findings about the relationship between peritraumatic dissociation and PTSD.

46.8.5 There Are Two Kinds of Peritraumatic Dissociation

Earlier in this chapter, we established that *dissociation* is heterogeneous. This heterogeneity, I believe, must be extended to peritraumatic dissociation. There are two kinds of peritraumatic dissociative-like responses: (1) an automatic, time-limited, set of evolution-prepared survival responses that typically include dissociative alterations of experience and information processing; and (2) secondary efforts to manage the intrusive memories that always follow any truly major life event—whether positive or negative (Horowitz, 1986/2001). Some individuals attempt to manage intrusive memories via avoidance and suppression. And some of these avoiders/suppressors use dissociation to defend themselves from the memories. Such secondary, motivated, defensive dissociation is different from the automatic, evolution-prepared survival response that occurred at the instant of the sudden life-threat.

The crucial point here is that an immediate dissociative reaction to a life-threatening event is normal—it is not a sign of psychopathology (Bryant, 2009; Horowitz, 1986/2001; Panasetis & Bryant, 2003). In fact, Shilony and Grossman (1993) demonstrated that those who failed to experience depersonalization during trauma reported significantly greater psychopathology on eight scales of the SCL-90-R than did those who did experience depersonalization. On the other hand, persistent posttraumatic dissociative symptoms are not normal. Persistent posttraumatic dissociative symptoms almost certainly have a mechanism different from the evolution-prepared dissociation that occurs at the instant of trauma.

Some research has reported that peritraumatic dissociation predicts the subsequent development of PTSD (e.g., Tichenor, Marmar, Weiss, Metzler, & Ronfeldt, 1996), whereas other research has reported that it does not (e.g., Dancu, Riggs, Hearst-Ikeda, Shoyer, & Foa, 1996). Subsequent studies produced the same mixed findings. Nevertheless, a meta-analysis of these investigations reported that peritraumatic dissociation is the single strongest predictor ($r = 0.35$) of PTSD (Ozer, Best, Lipsey, & Weiss, 2003). I contend that the weakness of this correlation (it accounts for only 12% of the variance) and the inconsistent results of many studies are due to the use of experimental methodologies that do not distinguish between (1) immediate evolution-prepared dissociative survival responses and (2) persisting posttraumatic dissociation (that may reflect a cognitive defense against intrusive memories and a resultant failure to assimilate the traumatic experience; Foa & Hearst-Ikeda, 1996; Horowitz, 1986/2001).

Recent research, which distinguishes between immediate and persisting peritraumatic dissociation, supports this contention (Briere, Scott, & Weathers, 2005; Panasetis & Bryant, 2003). In a small sample of traumatized persons, Panasetis and Bryant (2003) reported that acute peritraumatic dissociation correlates 0.38 with scores on the Acute Stress Disorder Interview (ASDI), whereas persistent dissociation correlated 0.77 with the ASDI.

Briere and colleagues reported analogous findings—namely, that acute posttraumatic dissociation does not correlate significantly with PTSD, whereas persisting posttraumatic dissociation does:

> Overall, the findings of studies 1 and 2 suggest that the primary risk for PTSD is less whether one dissociates during (or soon after) a traumatic event than whether such dissociation persists over time. Although it is possible that peritraumatic and persistent dissociation reflect the same underlying phenomenology and function, the temporal component of this response appears to be critical. (Briere et al., 2005, p. 2299)

In short, when acute, time-limited, evolution-prepared dissociative responses to a life threat are distinguished from persisting posttraumatic dissociative symptoms, the mixed findings about the relationship between peritraumatic dissociation and PTSD are explained, and the small correlation (0.35) between the two (Ozer et al., 2003) is understood to be a contaminated underestimate of the true correlation between persisting posttraumatic dissociation and PTSD.[62]

46.9 NORMAL DISSOCIATION REVISITED

If we were to accept that Janetian mental disaggregation is the only true form of dissociation—as Van der Hart and colleagues would have us do (Steele et al., 2009; Van der Hart et al., 2004, 2009)—then normal dissociation simply does not exist. This point of view is internally coherent and is defensible up to a point. Structural dissociation also has the advantage of providing an excellent model of half or

---

[62] And yet, as Briere et al. (2005) noted, the persistence of posttraumatic dissociation is by no means the sole determinant of PTSD; nearly half of the PTSD cases in Briere's et al. second study did not have elevated levels of posttraumatic dissociation.

more of the dissociative disorders (i.e., DID, Dissociative Fugue, and DID-like forms of DDNOS; see Dell, 2009b).

Structural dissociation also has an important corollary that is congruent with the previous discussion of the heterogeneity of dissociation. As noted, Van der Hart and colleagues aver that a wide variety of alterations of consciousness produce dissociative-like phenomena. These many alterations of consciousness (and their accompanying dissociative-like manifestations) are produced by miscellaneous mechanisms. According to Van der Hart and colleagues, however, only those dissociative-like phenomena that are produced by the mechanism of structural dissociation are truly dissociative in nature. On this view, it is irrelevant that these other dissociative-like phenomena are phenotypically similar to the manifestations of structural dissociation: these other dissociative-like phenomena are not produced by "internal" dissociative structures—so, according to Van der Hart and colleagues, they are not dissociative in nature.

Although I have substantial sympathy for the concept of structural dissociation, I am not sure that the dissociation field would be helped by discontinuing our discussion of other dissociative-like phenomena. Van der Hart and colleagues make their most compelling case with regard to absorption, but there are many other dissociative-like phenomena that, I think, deserve to be studied by dissociation researchers. Most of these nonstructural, dissociative-like phenomena have both normal and pathological forms. In the following, I discuss five kinds of normal dissociative-like phenomena that, I think, warrant our attention.

46.9.1 Evolution-Prepared, Survival-Oriented Dissociation

If any dissociative-like phenomenon deserves the label of normal dissociation, this is it. Evolution-prepared dissociation has ancient phylogenetic roots (Öhman, Hamm, & Hugdahl, 2000; Ratner, 1967, 1977). It is a species-specific defense reaction (Bolles, 1970) that is certainly related to other well-known animal defenses such as freezing, predator-related spontaneous analgesia, and tonic immobility (see also Galliano, Noble, Travis, & Puechl, 1993; Suarez & Gallup, 1979; Marx, Forsyth, Gallup, Fusé, & Lexington, 2008; Nijenhuis et al., 1998). Moreover, it is an utterly normal (albeit situation-specific), time-limited response. And, as noted, such automatic evolution-prepared dissociation is part of a larger "package" of survival-facilitating changes of information processing (which often includes accelerated, ultra-clear thinking; Heim, 1892/1980; Noyes & Kletti, 1976, 1977). It is also important to emphasize that, unlike the symptoms of dissociative patients, evolution-prepared survival-oriented dissociation is not personally motivated, either consciously or unconsciously. At times of serious life threat, evolution-prepared dissociation just happens. Such responses are usefully thought of as approximating a fixed action pattern that is released by the appropriate stimuli (Tinbergen, 1951).

Although evolution-prepared dissociation is a product of natural selection (Ludwig, 1983; Öhman, Dimberg, & Öst, 1985; Perry, Pollard, Blakley, Baker, & Vigilante, 1995; Porges, 2004), both inheritance and prior life experience produce individual differences in the readiness and the strength of this evolution-prepared response. For example, individual differences in tonic immobility have been found to be related to previous experiences (Gallup & Rager, 1996; Moore & Amstey, 1962) and to selective breeding (Gallup, 1974). Similarly, individual differences in training and maturity (and probably temperament) are related to the incidence of peritraumatic dissociation in both emergency personnel (Marmar, Weiss, Metzler, & Delucchi, 1996) and military forces (Morgan et al., 2001).

Finally, as previously noted, evolution-prepared survival-facilitating dissociation is probably a subcortical phenomenon. Specifically, this evolution-prepared dissociation, like other animal defenses, probably originates with activity of the periaqueductal gray (PAG) in the mesencephalon (Williams, 2006). PAG activity has various consequences. In the case of evolution-prepared dissociation, these consequences probably include inhibiting the amygdala (Bolles & Fanselow, 1980; Campbell, Wood, & McBride, 1997; Fendt & Fanselow, 1999). The endangered person cannot think clearly and take protective action if the powerful fear system is allowed to react freely and produce a frozen "deer in the headlights" paralysis. Inhibition of fear is an important and little-studied aspect of dissociation. As Fendt and Fanselow have noted, "analysis of the neural mechanisms that inhibit fear lags far behind that of the mechanisms that produce fear" (p. 754).

46.9.2 Hypnotic Performance

Without doubt, the most striking examples of normal dissociation are the responses of highly hypnotizable persons to hypnotic suggestions. The distinctly dissociative nature of these hypnotic responses was highlighted by Kirsch and Lynn (1998) when they accurately noted that "hypnotic responsiveness [as measured by the SHSS:C, for example] is measured as the number of dissociative and conversion symptoms that a person produces in response to suggestion" (p. 100). Typical hypnotic "symptoms" include the inability to lift one's arm, auditory hallucinations, deafness, negative visual hallucinations, amnesia, automatic writing, and other dissociated actions, such as execution of a posthypnotic suggestion. Unlike the clinical versions of these symptoms, however, hypnotically induced symptoms are readily undone or reversed.

Shortly prior to Janet's research on hysteria, Charles Richet (1883), under the influence of Ribot's (1885) views about the relationship between memory and personality, used hypnosis to investigate what he called "the objectification of types." Specifically, Richet did two things: (1) he suggested amnesia for the subject's identity, and (2) he suggested that the subject was someone else—a farmer, a soldier, etc. When these two suggestions were given to highly hypnotizable subjects (i.e., somnambulists):

> each could give various different forms to her self, believe herself to be a soldier, a priest, a little girl, a rabbit, and so forth. These characterizations were what Richet calls, "the objectification of types"—amnesia for the real personality combined with a new and assumed personality. (Gauld, 1992, p. 300)

Over the years, Richet's *objectification of types* has been replicated in a variety of ways (e.g., Estabrooks, 1971; Harriman, 1942a, 1942b, 1943; Kampman, 1976; Leavitt, 1947) and these later findings have led some of these authors, as well as others (e.g., Spanos, 1996; Spanos, Weekes, & Bertrand, 1985; Spanos, Weekes, Menary, & Bertrand, 1986), to argue that DID is merely an artifact of suggestive interactions between therapists and highly hypnotizable patients. This contention has been countered by clinician-researchers who, unlike the latter authors, possessed extensive experience with DID. They pointed out that the experimental production of new identities is a normal, time-limited (hypnotic) phenomenon that has little resemblance to the pervasive, unremitting, and intensely symptomatic phenomena of clinical DID (e.g., Braun, 1984; Kluft, 1995; Ross, 1997).

Today, dramatic hypnotic suggestions for a changed identity are largely the province of stage hypnotists. There are, however, a variety of normal, spontaneous, dissociative-like phenomena that bear a startling resemblance to Richet's hypnotic production of other personalities.

46.9.3 Psychologically Healthy Forms of Possession

It sounds odd and bizarre in our Western culture to speak of normal forms of possession. And yet, there are, indeed, normal, psychologically healthy forms of possession in Western culture (and in many other cultures): shamans, healers, mediums, chanellers, glossolalists, and so on. The perceived oddness of these normal forms of possession comes from the fact that, for most of us, these practices lie far outside our worldview. Conversely, as Cardeña (1996) has perceptively noted, the members of many other cultures are better "supported" when they undergo possession (or other highly unusual experiences) than are his Western subjects when they encounter unusual experiences during very deep hypnosis:

> Whereas shamanic traditions have shared cultural interpretations and even "cartographies" for these experiences, my participants did not have a framework for their experience other than the vague notion of being in an undefined state of deep hypnosis. A more overarching difference is the lack of cultural acknowledgement and validation of the experiences manifested during hypnosis. (Cardeña, 1996, p. 94)

For exactly these reasons, it is easier for Westerners to imagine that members of other, supposedly primitive, cultures could experience and believe in spirit possession or mediumistic communication with spirits. And yet, given our cultural biases, it may still be difficult for us to grasp the fact that those who undergo such experiences can be decidedly normal. Nevertheless, this is the case. Shamans, healers, and mediums in traditional cultures, who undergo possession and/or through whom spirits speak, are usually psychologically normal individuals (Cardeña, 1991; Cardeña et al., 2008; Negro, 2002). Yes, there are also psychologically abnormal forms of possession in those cultures (see the following), but in this section of the chapter we are discussing only normal dissociation, normal forms of possession.

Let's tackle this cross-cultural feeling of oddness head-on by discussing some normal forms of possession that occur in Western culture. We will begin with a bit of history. It tends to be forgotten (or even intentionally "repressed") that the field of dissociation was richly connected to Spiritualism[63] at the end of the 19th century (Alvarado, 2002; Taylor, 1996). Many authorities on dissociation belonged to the Society for Psychic Research (SPR); they presented papers at SPR meetings, and published articles in the *Proceedings of the SPR*.[64]

[63] *Spiritualism* was the name adopted by a movement at that time in history.

[64] Those who presented at SPR meetings or published in the *Proceedings of the Society for Psychical Research* included Sigmund Freud, William James, Carl Jung, William McDougall, T. W. Mitchell, and Morton Prince. James, McDougall, and Mitchell each served as president of the SPR.

At that time, mediums were common. They held séances, entered trances, communicated with the dead, were "possessed" by spirits, and often had amnesia after the séance was over. Major authorities on dissociation studied these mediums and their peculiar dissociative experiences: Theodore Flournoy (1900/1994), William James (Taylor, 1996), Carl Jung (1902). All three of these authorities approached the matter psychologically, but James clearly wished that more than just psychology were involved. In any case, there can be no doubt that many turn-of-the-century mediums truly believed in spirits and genuinely underwent a variety of involuntary (albeit invited) dissociative experiences (Alvarado, 2002; Taylor, 1996).

The widespread belief in spiritualism at that time provided a supportive sociocultural context within which mediums could flourish and manifest a plethora of dissociative phenomena. The situation is no different today.

The members of charismatic churches often "speak in tongues" as they are taken over by the Holy Spirit and "receive the gift" of languages (Garrett, 1987). Such glossolalia is an involuntary (albeit invited and welcomed) possession experience that has meaning and great value as a part of that community's religious beliefs and rituals. Research has shown that glossolalists are psychologically healthy individuals (e.g., Francis & Robbins, 2003; Newberg, Wintering, Morgan, & Waldman, 2006; Samarin, 1972).

Similarly, the New Age community has its own set of beliefs and practices that, in some cases, includes mediumship, or, as it is better known today, channeling. Although the trappings are different—it no longer takes place in darkened rooms—today's channeling is clearly the modern form of mediumship and spiritualism. Although there is some variety, channelers typically undergo either a change of consciousness or a transformation wherein they channel (are possessed by?) a wise spirit or entity, and subsequently experience varying degrees of amnesia for what the entity said. And, like glossolalists, channelers have been found to be psychologically healthy (e.g., Hastings, 1991).

Finally, it should be noted that mediumship or channeling has also been a mainstay of some of the world's major religions: seminal religious figures have reported "receiving" (via channeling or mediumship?) important religious texts, which they typically consider to be divinely revealed (Goodman, 1988; James, 1902/2003).

These nonpathological forms of possession, whether they occur in traditional cultures or in today's Western culture, have been understood by Cardeña et al. (2008) in terms of Lewis's (2003) concept of "central possession." Lewis (2003) conceptualized healthy possession and unhealthy possession as "central possession" and "peripheral possession,"[65] respectively. Central possession is culturally sanctioned. The culture prescribes when, where, and for how long such possession experiences should occur. Cardeña et al. propose that central possession is based upon the interaction of two factors: (1) a person's innate dissociative ability and (2) the culture's prescriptions regarding possession:

> Central possession might be explained by a predisposition, probably biological, to dissociate/be suggestible/have unusual experiences. These predispositions, in turn, are interpreted and shaped by sociocultural factors into the experience of controlled ritual possession and mediumship. (Cardeña et al., 2009, p. 177)

In summary, then, normal possession experiences are culturally sanctioned; they are a valued and meaningful aspect of the culture and/or religious community. The community or culture prescribes the appropriate context, place, and time for possession to occur. As such, possession is invited, sought after, and welcomed by members of the community. It is a time-limited event that is experienced as involuntary. Its occurrence is organized within (and hence, controlled by) the communal or religious context of ritual, personal/spiritual acceptance, insight, and so on. Such possession does not cause either distress or dysfunction.

46.9.4 Creative/Productive Automatisms

Some of Wilson and Barber's (1983) highly hypnotizable, fantasy-prone women reported fantasies that had "a life of their own." These fantasies unfurled and developed in a completely autonomous fashion, with absolutely no input from the fantasizer (who was reduced to the role of passive observer). There also are negative fantasizers (e.g., guilty-dysphoric daydreamers) who engage in unpleasant daydreams (Huba, Aneshensel, & Singer, 1981). Like Wilson and Barber's positive fantasizers, the fantasies of some negative fantasizers can acquire "a life of their own" such that the fantasies become daymares (Barrett, 1996) and develop autonomously (to the distress and even terror of the individual). Such autonomous fantasies are distinctly similar to the experience of Robert Louis Stevenson and other authors who have reported that some of their writing was undirected, autonomous, and seemed to come from some place or person other than the self (Stevenson, 2005). When episodes of automatic composition are

[65] Unhealthy, peripheral possession will be discussed under the heading of "Pathological Dissociation."

recurrent or semi-routine (especially compositions of a religious or spiritual nature), they become indistinguishable from mediumship or channeling.

46.9.5 Transcendent Experiences

Transcendent experiences often consist of sudden, inbreaking surges of joy and love that are intertwined with a profoundly altered sense of relationship to God or the universe. Such experiences often have a lasting transformative impact on the individual. From one perspective, transcendent experiences are spiritual or religious; from another perspective, they are psychological and, specifically, dissociative (James, 1902/2003).

Although many had previously described the remarkable personal experiences that often attend religious conversion (or "being saved"), James brought cutting-edge psychology to bear on these transformative moments. In doing so, he was quite explicit that sudden conversions were the sole province of highly hypnotizable persons who were innately prone to dissociation. In *Varieties of Religious Experience*, James discussed dissociation in terms of Myers's concept of the subliminal self:

> I do indeed believe that if the Subject have no liability to such subconscious activity, or if his conscious fields have a hard rind of a margin that resists incursions from beyond it, his conversion must be *gradual* if it occur, and must resemble any simple growth into new habits. His possession of a developed subliminal self, and of a leaky or pervious margin, is thus a *conditio sine qua non* of the Subject's becoming converted in the *instantaneous* way. (James, 1902/2003, p. 190, italics added)

At the core of these experiences of instantaneous conversion lie "the immediate and intuitive … assurance … that I, this individual I, just as I stand, without one plea, etc., am saved now and forever" (James, 1902/2003, p. 193). James identified five typical accompaniments of the assurance of being saved: (1) the loss of all worry wherein one absolutely knows that "all is well," (2) a deep experiential sense of receiving or perceiving previously unknown truths, (3) the world appears clean, beautiful, and new, (4) automatisms occur, and (5) ecstatic joy.

Many traditional cultures have their own institutionalized transcendent experiences. In particular, there are notable parallels between Western conversion experiences and the spirit journeys of traditional cultures (e.g., Goodman, 1990).

As noted, James insisted that sudden conversion experiences occurred only in those with high hypnotizability or dissociativity. Others have reported findings that support this. Coe (1900), for example, studied the hypnotic responsiveness of persons who attended a revival meeting. He found that those who had been deeply affected by the revival meeting were distinctly more hypnotically responsive than those who had experienced nothing striking. Similarly, Gibbons and De Jarnette (1972) assessed the hypnotizability of students at a conservative Georgia college and collected the personal accounts of those students who professed to have been "saved." Gibbons and De Jarnette found that all of the highly hypnotizable students reported "profound experiential changes" (p. 152) when they were saved, whereas none of the low hypnotizable students reported such phenomena. Here are excerpts from Gibbons and De Jarnette's interviews of three "highs" (HGSHS:A = 10, 11, and 12) and three "lows" (HGSHS:A = 2, 3, and 4) who were saved:

> *High Hypnotizability:*
>
> It was like I could feel Christ's presence right there beside me … just like He was standing there; and He spoke to me, and He told me he wanted me to do His work.
>
> Everything seemed so different and so unreal.… It was like I'd been hit by a bolt of lightning.
>
> It was like the Hand of God came down and touched me. I felt so happy; I never felt joy like I felt it that day. (p. 154)
>
> *Low Hypnotizability:*
>
> I had been going to that church for about six months, mainly because my girlfriend went there, but I never "went forward." Then one day the preacher asked all those who had accepted the Lord to put up their hands, and we both put our hands up and that was it.
>
> I never felt much in the way of emotion, I guess, but if that's the way you've been brought up and your parents are standing there every Sunday looking at you, you're going to go forward sooner or later.
>
> No, I never felt too much emotion about it, but one day I just went forward and accepted the Lord. (Gibbons & De Jarnette, 1972, p. 155)

The difference between these accounts of high- and low-hypnotizables is, indeed, impressive. Moreover, this difference is reminiscent of James's contention that conversion experiences are gradual (if they occur at all) for nondissociative individuals, but instantaneous for dissociative persons. Accordingly, I will close this section on transcendent experience with a final quotation from James that, I think, points the way toward a general understanding of "normal dissociation":

> Instantaneous conversions ... abound, some with and some without luminous visions, all with a sense of astonished happiness, and of being wrought on by a higher control. If ... we take them on their psychological side exclusively, so many peculiarities in them remind us of what we find outside of [religious] conversion that we are tempted to class them along with other automatisms. (James, 1902/2003, p. 186)

46.9.6 One Final Time—What Is Normal Dissociation?

The preceding discussion invites a simplifying conclusion: there are two fundamentally different types of "normal dissociation." Type I Normal Dissociation is a universal, evolution-prepared capacity for dissociative alterations of functioning that facilitate survival. Type II Normal Dissociation is a special ability, which is only possessed by some, for culturally meaningful dissociative performances and/or experiences. Both Type I and Type II Normal Dissociation have positive consequences. Neither causes distress; neither brings dysfunction in its wake.

46.9.6.1 Type I Normal Dissociation

Type I Normal Dissociation is well described in the previous discussion. Virtually all humans possess a built-in capacity for automatic activation of an evolution-prepared dissociative process (which is but one component of a "package" of instantaneous changes of functioning) that facilitates survival in a life-threatening situation.

Whether evolution-prepared dissociation has a pathological form is unknown, but there is at least one intriguing possibility. Perhaps evolution-prepared dissociation "gone haywire" causes the tonic depersonalization and derealization of Depersonalization Disorder and the dissociative reaction to reminders of trauma (which occur in about 30% of persons with PTSD). See the following discussion.

46.9.6.2 Type II Normal Dissociation

Type II Normal Dissociation is a special dissociative ability that is possessed by only a minority of individuals. This special ability can produce sudden automatisms that are (1) personally motivated (consciously or unconsciously), and (2) socioculturally meaningful, and (3) socioculturally valued. In other words, the individual's local community and culture shape the expression of that dissociative ability and, importantly, help to generate the values that motivate the occurrence of these personally and socially valuable automatisms (James, 1902/2003). As Martinez-Taboas noted, "dissociation is a mechanism that is exquisitely and always mediated by cultural expectations" (Martinez-Taboas, 1991, p. 131; see also Cardeña, 1996; Cardeña et al., 2008; Kirmayer, 1994; Krippner, 1997; and Lewis-Fernández, 1994).

The relationship of Type II Normal Dissociation to the dissociative disorders remains to be determined. Given the present evidence regarding pathological dissociation, however, it seems likely that the mechanisms that underlie Type II Normal Dissociation are also present in "Conversion" Disorder (see the following).

Type II Normal Dissociation includes both partial and total automatisms. When Type II Normal Dissociation involves only partial automatisms (i.e., hypnotic responses, automatic fantasizing, automatic literary composition, lucid mediumistic experiences, transcendent experiences), the person has contemporary conscious awareness of what happens during the automatism, as well as comprehensive subsequent memory of it (see Dell, 2009c). When Type II Normal Dissociation involves total automatism (i.e., possession experiences), the possession may be either lucid or somnambulistic (Oesterreich, 1921/1966). When lucid possession occurs, the person has full contemporary awareness of the possession and comprehensive subsequent memory of it. In contrast, when somnambulistic possession occurs, the person has neither contemporary awareness nor subsequent memory of the possession.

Dissociative ability and cultural framework. The automatisms of Type II Normal Dissociation have two underlying causes: (1) an ability to dissociate that is probably biological and genetic, and (2) the dissociator's local culture or community (see Cardeña, 2008; Lewis, 2003). The cultural context is crucial: it allows, invites, shapes, organizes, controls, normalizes, motivates, and gives meaning and value to the automatism. Some cultures, however, do not provide an adequate framework for the phenomena of normal dissociation. As mentioned previously, Cardeña has charged (correctly) that Western culture is notable for its "lack of cultural acknowledgement and validation of the experiences manifested during hypnosis" (Cardeña, 1996, p. 94). This is even more true of other forms of Type II Normal Dissociation.

The importance of motivation. Whereas motivation plays no role in Type I Normal Dissociation, Type II Normal Dissociation is imbued with, and surrounded by, both personal and community motivation. Each Type II normal dissociator is guided, to a greater or lesser degree, by his or her culture to desire, invite, seek after, accept, and welcome particular automatisms and/or their product or outcome. When Type II normal automatisms occur, the culture or community endorses and confirms the normal dissociator as a valued member because, to a greater or lesser degree, the dissociative person's automatism (and/or its product or outcome) is always a validation of that community. Conversely, to the extent that the local community does not validate a person's Type II Normal Dissociation, that person risks being labeled as mad or insane, despite being otherwise quite functional (e.g., Jones & Fernyhough, 2008).

Type II Normal Dissociation is involuntary. Although these automatisms may be sought after, they are, nevertheless, experienced as being spontaneous, uncontrollable, and involuntary. Thus, Type II Normal Dissociation is routinely characterized by Weitzenhoffer's (1978) "classic suggestion effect."

46.9.7 What Is Not Normal Dissociation?

As previously discussed, the debate about normal dissociation (Butler, 2004, 2006; Dalenberg & Paulson, 2009; Steele et al., 2009; Van der Hart et al., 2004; Waller et al., 1996) has centered on absorption: "The heart of the normative dissociative process would seem to be *absorption*—intense focal concentration and cognitive involvement in one or more aspects of conscious awareness" (Butler, 2006, p. 46). Butler asserts that absorption is inherently dissociative:

> In most cases the normative dissociative experience is an admixture of absorption and its object, with intense focal concentration and suspension of contextual features—such as self-awareness and reflection, feelings of relatedness to self or the world, constraints of normal thinking, or awareness of volition—which allow for the conditions necessary to the achievement of its benefits. The fact of the pervasiveness of such experiences does not disqualify their essentially dissociative nature. (Butler, 2006, p. 59)

I believe that Butler is describing a very important kind of everyday conscious functioning, but, like Van der Hart and colleagues, I see no reason to consider this alteration of consciousness to be a form of dissociation.

Although there is evidence that high levels of absorption can be dissociation-like (e.g., Allen et al., 2002), there is no convincing evidence that healthy levels of absorption are, by nature, dissociative. Butler (2004, 2006) said that one can escape from emotional discomfort by becoming absorbed in music, television, reading, and so on. True enough. Absorption can be used defensively, but normal defensive absorption is not a *dissociative* defense.

It has also been proposed that fantasy proneness, an extreme form of absorption (in fantasy), is a dissociative phenomenon (or that it underlies dissociation). These contentions are not proved by the two findings that are usually advanced by the proponents of this point of view: (1) that ICMI scores correlate moderately with DES scores, and (2) that a significant minority of fantasy-prone individuals are psychologically maladjusted. Extensive daily fantasizing can be done either for pleasure or for defensive purposes (Somer, 2002). In neither case, however, is fantasy proneness, in itself, dissociative. Remember, only 11% of DID patients are fantasy-prone (Dell, unpublished data). This incidence is higher than that of the general population (i.e., 4%), but commensurate with the 9% to 14% incidence of fantasy proneness that occurs among individuals with a history of child abuse (Rhue, Lynn, Henry, Buhk, & Boyd, 1990–1991). The bottom line is that the 11% incidence of fantasy proneness in DID speaks against the contention that fantasy proneness underlies dissociation.

And yet, there *is* a point of intersection between absorption or fantasy proneness on the one hand, and genuine normal dissociation on the other hand. Type II normal automatisms occur at that intersection (i.e., automatic fantasies, automatic literary composition, possession experiences, transcendent experiences, etc.). Short of that intersection, however, there is no dissociation in either absorption[66] or fantasy proneness. The situation is the same with regard to repression. That is, repression is not a dissociative phenomenon. And yet, there *is* a point of intersection between repression and genuine dissociation—in this case, *pathological* dissociation. Repression intersects with dissociation at the moment in time when, suddenly, dissociative amnesia occurs. Short of that point, there is only repression (and no dissociation).[67]

Finally, those who propose that absorption is a normal form of dissociation also contend that dissociation is a ubiquitous aspect of daily human life (Butler, 2004, 2006; Hilgard, 1977/1986). This chapter's analysis of normal dissociation, however, implies that while absorption

---

[66] Butler (2006) is well aware that a discontinuous change occurs when normal forms of absorption suddenly "become" pathological forms of dissociation. She attributes this sudden change to trauma and borrows Steve Gold's idea that the discontinuous shift can be likened to the phase-change that occurs when water freezes or turns to steam. I disagree that absorption undergoes a phase-change; I see Butler's phase-change as the initial occurrence or onset of dissociation. Moreover, as the previous discussion reveals, the sudden change can mark the genuine occurrence of normal dissociation. Absorption is an invaluable human cognitive ability, but it is not a form of dissociation, normal or otherwise.

[67] This is admittedly only a conceptual distinction. We have no way at present to empirically distinguish when dissociative amnesia is added to repression.

and repression may, indeed, be ubiquitous, dissociation is not. We already knew that *pathological* dissociation is not ubiquitous. If this chapter's analysis of normal dissociation is correct, we now know that normal dissociation cannot be ubiquitous either.

46.10 PATHOLOGICAL DISSOCIATION

46.10.1 What Is the Essence of Pathological Dissociation?

Automatisms. A *sine qua non* of dissociative functioning is, as Janet asserted in 1889, the occurrence of automatisms—behaviors and reactions that occur automatically, "on their own," without being directed by the conscious mind or by the stimuli of the environment. As previously noted, the term has fallen out of use, but *automatism* is the word that the dissociation field originally used to describe a dissociative event. The concept of automatism also points to the lack of integration that characterizes the dissociative disorders (APA, 2000). According to DSM-IV, the dissociative disorders are characterized by "a disruption in the usually integrated functions of consciousness, memory, identity, or perception" (APA, 2000). Dell (2009b) has proposed a phenomenological definition of pathological dissociation that hews closely to the idea of automatism; he described pathological dissociation as "recurrent, jarring, involuntary intrusions into executive functioning and sense of self."

Note that DSM-IV limits dissociation to consciousness, memory, identity, and perception, whereas Dell sets no limits on the functions that can be disrupted by a dissociative event. He insists that dissociation can invade and disrupt all areas of conscious human functioning (Dell, 2006c, 2009b). Thus, there is no aspect of conscious human functioning that is immune to dissociative intrusions. Others have reached a similar conclusion (Butler et al., 2004; Gleaves, May, & Cardeña, 2001). Thus, the domain of dissociation and automatisms is the entirety of human conscious functioning.

In the preceding section of this chapter, we saw that Type II Normal Dissociation is characterized by both partial and total automatisms and that Type I Normal Dissociation is characterized by only partial automatisms—that is, sudden, involuntary alterations of information processing, sensation, and affect.

In short, automatisms lie at the heart of both normal and pathological dissociation.

The automatisms are sustained, or brief and recurrent. The second major feature of pathological dissociation is that its symptoms (i.e., automatisms) are either sustained (e.g., Depersonalization Disorder) or chronically recurrent, often for many years (e.g., the depersonalization and amnesia of DID). This feature distinguishes pathological dissociation from Type I Normal Dissociation because such evolution-prepared dissociation is brief and limited to the life-threatening situation.

The automatisms cause distress and/or dysfunction. Although almost every mental disorder in the DSM requires the presence of distress and/or dysfunction, DID does not. Nevertheless, distress about dissociative automatisms *is* important. This feature (of some dissociation) is truly important because it distinguishes pathological dissociation from Type II Normal Dissociation (which, by definition, occurs in healthy contexts such as hypnosis, mediumship, shamanistic healing, religious rituals, and transcendent experiences).

The person knows that the automatisms are abnormal. Dell (2006c, 2009b) has emphasized that the overwhelming majority of dissociative symptoms (99%?) are subjective and, hence, invisible to an observer. Conversely, these subjective symptoms are exceedingly "visible" to the person who is experiencing them. As Dell (2009b) noted, these symptoms are "jarring, involuntary intrusions" into the person's functioning. Said differently, the person knows very well that these intrusions are *not normal.* These symptoms occur with the metaphorical impact of a flashing neon sign in a darkened room. Dissociators are not psychotic; they know very well that what is happening should not be happening. They know that certain aspects of their functioning are abnormal, they fear that they are "going crazy," and they have very high levels of self-confusion (Dell, 2002, 2006b, 2006c; Dell & Lawson, 2009). In fact, persons with a severe dissociative disorder have higher levels of self-confusion than do persons with Borderline Personality Disorder (Laddis & Dell, 2002)!

Drawing upon his cross-cultural studies of dissociation, Krippner (1994, 1997) has proposed a definition of dissociation that complements Dell's emphasis on the person's jarring sense that his or her functioning has suddenly gone strangely awry:

> For me, "dissociative" is an English-language adjective that attempts to describe reported experiences and observed behaviors that seem to exist apart from, or appear to have been disconnected from, the mainstream, or flow, of one's conscious awareness, behavioral repertoire, and/or self identity. (Krippner, 1997, p. 8)

Although this is rather abstract, Krippner's definition is, to my knowledge, the only other portrayal of dissociation that directly ties dissociation to *the person's deep implicit knowledge of how he or she functions*. It is unclear whether Kirmayer (1994) was implying the same thing when he spoke of dissociation as "ruptures in the normally expected integration of psychological functions" (p. 92).

I cannot overemphasize the importance (or the impact) of our deep implicit knowledge of how we function. That implicit knowledge generates a reflexive hyperawareness of deviations from our implicitly expected functioning. We instantly realize that something has gone amiss. These jarring instant realizations pervade the daily life of severely dissociative persons; they live with the moment-to-moment experience of something going wrong with their mind and their body.

The automatisms are not *given a delusional explanation*. Here lies a crucial distinction between dissociation and psychosis. Automatisms have much in common with 8 of Schneider's 11 first-rank symptoms of schizophrenia. Both psychotics and dissociators undergo "passive-influence" symptoms: voices arguing, voices commenting, "made" feelings, "made" impulses, "made" actions, influences on the body, thought withdrawal, and thought insertion (Dell, 2006c; Kluft, 1987; Ross, Miller, & Reagor, 1990). The difference, of course, is that psychotics immediately give these intrusions a delusional explanation (e.g., "The CIA has implanted a computer chip in my brain."). Dissociators are deeply puzzled and unnerved by their dissociative intrusions, but they do not claim that the CIA is speaking to them or that their neighbor is pointing an "influencing machine" at their house. Persons with Depersonalization Disorder do not offer delusional explanations of their depersonalization and derealization. Similarly, DID patients experience time loss, fugues, and a flood of other intrusive automatisms, but they do not claim that the FBI is doing these things to them. They try to ignore and minimize what is happening, but they do not provide delusional explanations of these happenings.[68]

The bottom line here is that psychotics have delusional automatisms (i.e., Schneider's first-rank symptoms) and dissociators have nondelusional automatisms (i.e., Kluft's passive influence symptoms).

Automatisms are motivated. With the exception of (1) the automatic intrusive memories that follow any major life event (Horowitz, 1986/2001), (2) the chronic intrusions that accompany PTSD, and (3) the tonic detachment of Depersonalization Disorder, psychological automatisms are personally motivated.[69] In particular, pathological dissociation is driven by motives of avoidance and defense of the self.[70] These motivations are typically not known, denied, or minimized by the dissociator. Nevertheless, these motives are always present and they are persistently operative.

As previously noted, psychotics often have delusional automatisms, whereas dissociators have nondelusional automatisms. It is probable that psychotic automatisms (i.e., the eight passive-influence first-rank symptoms) and dissociative automatisms also differ in their motivation. That is, whereas dissociative automatisms are personally motivated, the first-rank symptoms of psychotics are probably caused by neurological dysfunction (rather than by personal motivations). If so, this would mean that psychotic first-rank symptoms are *neurological (or neurobiological)* automatisms, whereas dissociative symptoms are *psychological* automatisms.[71]

46.10.2 Three Classes of Dissociative Disorders

The dissociative disorders can be meaningfully sorted into three classes: (1) dissociated structures that produce widespread positive dissociative symptoms,

[68] There are exceptional DID patients who are truly psychotic as well. Also, some DID patients defensively resort to a claim of possession to explain their symptoms (if such a claim is congruent with their religious/cultural background).

[69] The automatic intrusions that follow major life events (i.e., intrusive memories, flashbacks, etc.), especially life events that involved pain and danger, are not personally motivated. Instead, these intrusions reflect the operation of an evolution-prepared mechanism whose function is to ensure that the organism assimilates information that is critically important: "Stress-related information is, by definition, very important and hence is not terminated until it is assimilated" (Horowitz, 1986/2001, p. 121). Or, as Chris Brewin (2007) recently said, "We are wired this way so that we have an extended opportunity to extract and take in all of the relevant or needed information" [from the potentially dangerous event].

[70] The only likely exception to this generalization about pathological dissociation might be Depersonalization Disorder—if it is caused by neurological dysfunction (see the following). Nevertheless, some experts on Depersonalization Disorder insist that it is grounded in (or, at least, accompanied by) a motivated cognitive strategy to avoid aversive emotional experience (Medford et al., 2006).

[71] It is crucial that the reader understand the difference between my account of motivation and the sociocognitive hypothesis that dissociative "performances" are nothing but intentional role-playing that is accompanied by self-deceptive experiences of involuntariness (e.g., Coe & Sarbin, 1991; Sarbin, 1995; see also Segall, 1996). Neither the cultural/personal motivations for normal psychological automatisms nor the personal motivations for pathological psychological automatisms (i.e., avoidance and defense of the self) involve the intention—conscious or unconscious—to produce alter personalities, act like a child alter, and so on. In pathological dissociation, the motivations are global (i.e., to avoid, forget, protect the self); these motivations never include the intent to enact certain behaviors or to deceive themselves about their experience of involuntariness.

(2) pseudoneurological dissociative disorders that typically manifest a single negative dissociative symptom, and (3) Depersonalization Disorder.

46.10.2.1 Dissociated Structures

As discussed previously, the continuum model has been the received truth about dissociation since at least the early 1980s. According to the continuum model, dissociation stretches from normal phenomena (e.g., absorption, hypnotizability, fantasizing) to frankly pathological phenomena (e.g., amnesia, fugues, Depersonalization Disorder, and DID). Some scholars have now rejected this model because the phenomena that anchor the normal end of the continuum do not seem to be truly dissociative. For example, neither absorption nor fantasizing seem to be truly dissociative: neither is characterized by the occurrence of automatisms.

I now propose a different continuum model that applies solely to a subset of the dissociative disorders (see also Dell, 2009a; Myers, 1903; and Watkins & Watkins, 1997). Specifically, I propose that most (but not all) dissociative disorders can be meaningfully ordered along *a continuum of dissociated structures*. Table 46.2 illustrates this continuum by listing six dissociative disorders in descending order of structural complexity and elaboration. The defining feature of these six disorders is a more-or-less encapsulated, "internal" structure that is experienced as operating with considerable autonomy *vis-à-vis* the person's daily conscious mind—thereby generating recurrent automatisms. These dissociated structures "contain" unaccepted or disowned aspects of life, the self, and significant others.

TABLE 46.2
Three Classes of Dissociative Disorder

1. *The continuum of dissociated structures*
   - Dissociative Identity Disorder (DID)
   - DID-like presentations (DDNOS-1)
   - Possession Disorders (DDNOS-4)*
   - Dissociative Fugue
   - Ego-State Disorders
   - Remote, localized amnesia
2. *Simple 'conversion' symptoms*
   - Sensory/motor dissociation
   - Generalized amnesia
3. *Depersonalization Disorder*

*I do not know whether the continuum of dissociated structures should list possession disorders before or after DDNOS-1. The issue can be argued either way.

Such dissociated structures are the defining feature of the *Theory of the Structural Dissociation of the Personality*, which has been proposed by Onno van der Hart, Ellert Nijenhuis, and Kathy Steele (2006). Van der Hart and colleagues have proposed two continua of structural dissociation—a three-level model of structural dissociation and a spectrum of trauma-related disorders (see Van der Hart et al., 2006). Unlike these continua of Van der Hart and colleagues, the continuum that I am proposing is not founded upon the distinction between the Apparently Normal [part of the] Personality (ANP) and the Emotional [part of the] Personality (EP)—nor is my model founded on the psychobiological action systems that underlie ANPs and EPs (Van der Hart et al., 2006). The continuum in Table 46.2 also does not classify PTSD as a form of structural dissociation, whereas Van der Hart and colleagues' three-level model of structural dissociation does.

I have proposed (previously) that a *sine qua non* of all pathological dissociation is the presence of psychological automatisms. As noted, pathological psychological automatisms have five features; they are personally motivated; recurrent or persisting; a source of distress or dysfunction; considered by the dissociator to be abnormal; and are not given a delusional explanation (by the dissociator). In addition to these five general features of psychological automatism, *dissociated structures* have five additional characteristics: (1) recurrent positive dissociative symptoms (i.e., passive influence experiences: "made" feelings, "made" impulses, "made" actions, thought insertion, etc.), (2) loss or alteration of identity or sense of self, and, in most cases (3) recurrent incidents of amnesia, (4) chronicity, and (5) a plethora of accompanying dissociative symptoms.

Dissociated structures are frequently characterized by a defining triad of symptoms: (1) passive influence experiences, (2) recurrent amnesia, and (3) loss/alteration of identity/self. This triad of symptoms is pathognomonic of the presence (and activity) of one or more dissociated structures. Not all persons with a dissociated structure manifest this triad. But when the triad is present, it is an unfailing sign that a dissociated structure is at work.

Dissociative Identity Disorder. Persons with DID usually have one or more dissociated structures; they invariably generate the pathognomonic symptom-triad. In addition, DID is marked by great chronicity and a wide range of other dissociative symptoms (Dell, 2006c). Persons with DID can also switch from one personality to another, but only 15% switch visibly with any frequency. The remainder of DID cases (1) switch infrequently, (2) switch in a deliberately hidden manner, (3) switch in privacy, and (4) only switch visibly during a time of great stress or decompensation (Dell, 2009a, 2009b; Kluft, 1985a, 1985b). Thus, despite the diagnostic criteria set forth in DSM-IV, the visible presence of distinct personalities is too infrequent for dependable use as a diagnostic sign (Dell, 2009a, 2009b, 2009c). In contrast, the pathognomonic symptom triad of passive influences, amnesia, and subjective experiences of self alteration is a routine occurrence and, hence, an excellent diagnostic indicator of DID.

DID-like presentations. DDNOS-1 (i.e., DID-like presentations that do not meet the DSM-IV criteria for DID) is quite similar to DID. The primary difference is that persons with DDNOS-1 switch less frequently and/or more privately than do persons with DID. Overall, persons with DDNOS-1 exhibit the same pattern of dissociative symptoms as do persons with DID (Dell, 2009b, 2009c). They also exhibit the five characteristics of a dissociated structure: intrusive passive-influence experiences, alteration of identity or sense of self, amnesia, chronicity, and a variety of other dissociative symptoms.

Possession Disorders. Indigenous dissociative disorders are found in most non-Western cultures (Bourguignon, 1970, 1973; Saxena & Prasad, 1989). It is admittedly perilous to subject indigenous disorders to the etic, universalizing conceptions of a Western mind (Lewis-Fernández, 1992/1998; Somer, 2006), but there is an urgent need for analyses of the dissociative disorders to address both Western and non-Western dissociative presentations (Adityanjee, 1990; Alexander, Joseph, & Das, 1997; Cardeña, 1996; Das & Saxena, 1991; Lewis-Fernández, 1992/1998; Martinez-Taboas, 1991; Somer, 2006). Moreover, if done with caution, I believe that there is much to be gained. For example, DID and possession disorder can shed light on one another (Krippner, 1994, 1997; Lewis-Fernández, 1994).

Although nondelusional possession-form DID occurs in the West (e.g., Goodman, 1981), possession disorder typically occurs in non-Western cultures where *normal* possession is a routine part of religious or healing rituals. In these cultures, possession *per se* is not pathological, but its uncontrolled occurrence at unacceptable times and places is deemed to be pathological. In Haiti, for example:

> People assemble at a certain spot; external preparations have to be completed; the appropriate point in time for possession to start is marked by certain unmistakable signals in the ceremony. (Goodman, 1988, p. 17)

In short, "Possession occurs according to well-defined rules and under specific circumstances" (Herskovits, 1971, p. 143). When possession violates these cultural prescriptions and proscriptions, it is considered to be pathological (Cardeña et al., 2008; Lewis, 2003).

Ethnopsychiatric portrayals of possession disorder vary significantly from culture to culture. Although these portrayals lack a certain amount of rigor, they indicate certain commonalities (Goodman, 1988). The onset of pathological possession phenomena is typically spontaneous, sudden, and uncontrolled (Cardeña et al., 2008; Lewis, 2003). It is routinely described as being very much against the will of the person. The manifestations of possession are quite overt. Possessing spirits are highly visible, confronting, challenging, demanding, and even threatening. These full-blown appearances of the possessing spirit, ghost, or demon may be preceded by a period of dramatic, passive-influence phenomena (especially "made" actions) that would normally be ego-alien for the person and that tend to be culturally proscribed: aggression, destructive acts, public sexuality, trance-like episodes, antireligious behavior, and so on. The possessed person typically has amnesia after each episode of possession, but modern examples of lucid possession have been reported (e.g., Goodman, 1981). Possession disorder tends to be chronic and recurrent.

Perhaps the most striking difference between Western DID and non-Western possession disorder is *the visibility to others of the possessing entity.* As already noted, in DID, switches from one personality to another are infrequent, hidden, and tend to occur in privacy. Thomas Gutheil has aptly characterized DID as "a disorder of hiddenness" (quoted in Kluft, 1985a). Non-Western possession disorder, however, is the antithesis of hiddenness. It is marked by highly visible, "in your face" possessing spirits that act out and disrupt both the family and the local community. As such, the role of possession disorder in family and social conflict is much more apparent (Bourguignon, 1976; Gaw, Ding, Levine, & Gaw, 1998; Somer, 2006) than is the case with Western DID.

In summary, although its familial and social dynamics would appear to be quite different from that of Western DID, possession disorder manifests the typical signs of a dissociated structure: intrusive passive-influence experiences, alteration of identity, amnesia, chronicity, and a variety of other dissociative symptoms.

Dissociative Fugue. Fugues are common in dissociative patients, but cases of "pure" Dissociative Fugue are quite rare (Coons, 1999, 2000; Loewenstein, 1991; Ross, 2009). This difference is explained by the fact that fugues occur in almost all cases of DID and in many cases of DDNOS-1, but fugues rarely occur in isolation from other dissociative symptoms (remember that "isolated fugue" is necessary for a DSM-IV diagnosis of Dissociative

Fugue). In short, a fugue almost invariably indicates the presence of a complex dissociative disorder (i.e., DID or almost-DID). Pure Dissociative Fugue, on the other hand, is truly rare.

Clinically, most fugues manifest all five characteristics of a dissociated structure (because most cases actually have DID or DDNOS-1, rather than "pure" or "isolated" Dissociative Fugue). Pure cases of Dissociative Fugue manifest only three features of a dissociated structure: amnesia, loss or alteration of identity, and chronicity. The overall low level of dissociative symptoms in pure cases of Dissociative Fugue is readily seen in their remarkably low scores on the DES (7.3–12.0; Coons, 1999) and the MID (12.2–14.7; Howley & Ross, 2003). In contrast, most patients who report an incident of fugue also report a pervasive set of accompanying dissociative symptoms (and they usually obtain DES and MID scores in excess of 35).

The chronicity of cases of Dissociative Fugue is reflected in their residual amnesia. That is, although they may recover from their generalized amnesia in relatively short order, they continue to manifest a dense amnesia for the events that occurred during the period of loss/alteration of identity. In some cases, even the generalized amnesia is stubbornly persistent (e.g., Kritchevsky, Chang, & Squire, 2004; Markowitsch, Fink, Thöne, Kessler, & Heiss, 1997).

Ego-state disorders.[72] Ego-state disorders are substantially equivalent to what I am calling *dissociated structures* and what Van der Hart and colleagues call *structural dissociation.* All three of these concepts (i.e., ego-state disorders, dissociated structures, and structural dissociation) embrace DID, DDNOS-1, and Dissociative Fugue. Here, however, I use the term *ego-state disorder* in a much narrower sense, one that is commonly used by dissociation-savvy clinicians. Clinicians often apply the term *ego-state disorder* to a clinical presentation that stems from a relatively simple dissociated structure—a structure that falls far short of DID, DDNOS-1, or Dissociative Fugue. Such cases fall at the lower end of the continuum of dissociated structures (and the lower end of the continuum of structural dissociation, and the lower end of the continuum of ego-state disorders). For a detailed account of the entire continuum of ego-state disorders, see Dell (2009c).

In contrast to the ego-states of DID, DDNOS-1, and Dissociative Fugue (i.e., alters or dissociated structures), the ego-states of persons with a minor ego-state disorder never assume executive control of the person (i.e., switches do not occur). These ego-states can, however, be "called out" during hypnosis (Watkins & Watkins, 1997). During ego-state therapy, their concerns can be empathically listened-to and ego-states can often be persuaded to cease their hitherto maladaptive solutions and to adopt a new solution that is less counterproductive and more acceptable to the person as a whole.

Ego-states influence the person via "intrusions from within" (Dell, 2009b). Intrusions from within manifest themselves as psychological automatisms—intrusions into the person's executive functioning and sense of self. In minor ego-state disorders, the person does not disown these intrusions or even experience them as alien. Instead, the person experiences the intrusions in the form of psychophysiologic symptoms such as headaches, or as a *compulsion* to surrender to an unfortunate, but ego-syntonic, urge for maladaptive behavior (Watkins & Watkins, 1997).

All ego-state disorders (i.e., DID, DDNOS-1, Dissociative Fugue, and minor ego-state disorders) tend to be characterized by the presence of fixed ideas (about the past, the nature of reality, and what must be done to ameliorate present circumstances or to prevent the past from recurring). These (often unknown) fixed ideas drive symptoms and symptomatic behavior until they are unearthed and addressed in therapy.

Minor ego-state disorders manifest only two of the symptoms of dissociated structures: (1) compulsions (a form of passive-influence intrusion) and (2) chronicity. Patients with a minor ego-state disorder do not look dissociative at all. They do not have amnesias; they do not have other dissociative symptoms. They have no alterations in their sense of identity.

Dissociative Amnesia. In some ways, less is known about Dissociative Amnesia than the other three specific DSM-IV dissociative disorders (i.e., DID, Dissociative Fugue, and Depersonalization Disorder). The reason for this is that amnesia occurs in most dissociative disorders and, failing to recognize the presence of DID or almost-DID in a patient with amnesia, the average clinician may render an oversimplifying (and inaccurate) diagnosis of Dissociative Amnesia. Thus, clinical and research data about Dissociative Amnesia may be substantially contaminated by data from cases that actually have a different (and more complex) dissociative disorder. Loewenstein and Putnam (2004), for example, show how easily a complex dissociative disorder (i.e., DDNOS-1) can be (mis)diagnosed as Dissociative Amnesia.

DSM-IV-TR has not been of great assistance to clinicians in this matter. Its discussions of amnesia and dissociative amnesia miss an opportunity to provide critical

[72] I am using the historical term, *ego-state disorder.* A more modern, and probably more accurate, term would be *self-state disorder.*

diagnostic guidance to clinicians. To begin with, DSM-IV-TR does not really define amnesia. Clinicians are left to extract a definition of amnesia from the diagnostic criteria of DDNOS-1—"amnesia for personal information" (p. 532); Dissociative Fugue—"inability to recall one's past" (p. 526); DID—"inability to recall personal information that is too extensive to be explained by ordinary forgetfulness" (p. 529); and Dissociative Amnesia—"inability to recall important personal information, usually of a traumatic or stressful nature, that is too extensive to be explained by ordinary forgetfulness" (p. 523). In fact, these definitions of dissociative amnesia contain a troubling number of inaccuracies and inadequacies. These so-called definitions of amnesia are overly abstract, vague, nonspecific, incomplete, partly inaccurate, and easily misleading.

The DSM-IV definition of amnesia is *abstract* because it gives clinicians nothing but a terse, conceptual definition that is underspecified: inability to recall important personal information that is too extensive to be explained by ordinary forgetting.

The DSM-IV definition of amnesia is *vague* because it gives clinicians no concrete signs or symptoms with which to determine the presence of amnesia.

The DSM-IV definition of amnesia is *nonspecific* because it does not adequately exemplify the different kinds of "inability to recall" that can occur (or the relationship of particular kinds of "inability to recall" to specific dissociative disorders). In my opinion the DSM's introductory text on the dissociative disorders should contain (1) a comprehensive definition of dissociative amnesia, (2) a clinical explication of the different kinds of dissociative amnesia (i.e., localized, selective, generalized, systematized, and continuous), and (3) a preliminary discussion of the diagnostic implications of each kind of dissociative amnesia. DSM-IV-TR places the latter material in the text that pertains solely to Dissociative Amnesia. This misplacement easily confuses the reader who is trying to learn about Dissociative Amnesia. Why? Because generalized, systematized, and continuous amnesia do not occur in Dissociative Amnesia.

The DSM-IV-TR definition of amnesia is also *incomplete;* it omits any mention of the essential feature of dissociative amnesia—its reversibility. Compared to other kinds of forgetting, dissociative forgetting is inherently reversible; the amnesia can be undone and the person can remember what was forgotten. Temporary inaccessibility of a successfully stored memory (i.e., reversibility) is an inherent aspect of dissociative amnesia—unlike so many other kinds of amnesia that are based on inadequate storage of the memory in the first place.

The DSM-IV definition of amnesia is also *inaccurate* because it requires a forgetting "that is *too extensive* to be explained by ordinary forgetfulness (italics added)." An inability to recall the first 16 years of one's life is certainly "too extensive" to be explained by ordinary forgetfulness, but is an inability to recall a recent act of violence *too extensive*? Is an inability to recall an unacceptable one-night stand *too extensive*? The brief periods of time in these examples are not well-described with the words *too extensive.* Such brief amnesias are highly unlikely, but they are not "too extensive."[73] The brevity of amnestic episodes becomes even more problematic with DID patients. Very brief amnestic incidents (of 60 seconds or less) are pervasive in DID. Kluft (1985b) refers to these as "microamnestic behaviors" and Loewenstein (1991a) refers to these as "micro-dissociations."

I also suspect that DSM-IV-TR's Criterion C for DID is at best, less helpful than it might be, and, at worst, potentially *misleading.* As I see it, the problem is two-fold: (1) as a whole, the Dissociative Disorders Section of DSM-IV-TR provides only a vague and underdeveloped explication of amnesia, and (2) Criterion C for DID provides a vague and underdeveloped explication of the kinds of amnesia that occur in DID: "Inability to recall personal information that is too extensive to be explained by ordinary forgetfulness" (p. 529).

Putting aside the problem with the words *too extensive*, Criterion C is correct as far as it goes, but it is so underdeveloped that it leaves the average clinician in a (dissociative?) fog; Criterion C misses a crucial opportunity to give the clinician some potent diagnostic guidelines. For example, most amnestic episodes in DID do *not* involve trauma or traumatic information. Instead, they involve time loss and inability to recall apparently mundane actions such as buying something, writing something, completing a task at work, cleaning the kitchen, going to the store, and so on. Recurrent amnestic episodes that involve mundane activities almost always indicate the presence of DID. Such amnesias may even be pathognomonic of DID. The diagnostic power of Criterion C would be vastly increased by mentioning that it includes both amnesia for traumatic material and recurrent amnesias for mundane material—and that the latter is nearly pathognomonic for DID.[74]

---

[73] Perhaps the DSM definition of amnesia should be "an inability to recall personal information that is so unlikely or so extensive that it cannot be explained by ordinary forgetfulness."

[74] A person with DDNOS-1, a close nosological "relative" of DID, may also experience recurrent amnesias for mundane events, especially events that occur at home.

Different dissociative structures have different amnesias. With the preceding considerations in mind, I propose that different dissociative disorders are characterized by different kinds of amnesia. If true, this proposition will clarify our understanding of Dissociative Amnesia. Our thinking about this may be helped if we keep in mind that DSM-IV-TR implicitly defines Dissociative Amnesia as a "residual amnestic disorder." That is, if we take the entire population of persons that report amnesia, and then subtract from that population all cases of DID, Dissociative Fugue, and DDNOS-1, then most of the remaining cases will meet the DSM-IV-TR criteria for Dissociative Amnesia—cases with amnesia that do not meet the criteria for another dissociative disorder.

Janet (1893/1901/1977) distinguished four kinds of amnesia: localized, generalized, systematized, and continuous. In *localized* amnesia, the person forgets all that happened during a specific period of time. For example, a patient may report having no memory for anything before age 12, or for ages 7 to 10, and so on. In *generalized* amnesia, the person forgets his or her entire life—"I don't know who I am." In *systematized* amnesia, a person forgets all events that pertain to a particular theme or place. For example, a sexually abused person might remember their childhood well, but have no recall of the sexual abuse that occurred for 6 years. Or the person might remember their childhood at school and in the neighborhood, but have no memories for what occurred inside their home. *Continuous* dissociative amnesia is rare. It entails continuous anterograde forgetting of all new events. A fifth kind of amnesia has been added to Janet's four—selective amnesia. In *selective* amnesia, a person remembers most, but not all, of what happened during a specific event—usually a trauma. For example, a rape victim might remember being raped, but may not recall the most distressing event that occurred during the assault.

In addition to these five kinds of amnesia, other diagnostically relevant features of amnesia include (1) whether the amnesia is recent or remote, (2) whether the amnesia is recurrent, (3) the nature of the forgotten material (e.g., trauma-related vs. mundane), (4) the length of the amnestic period, and (5) whether other dissociative experiences (e.g., passive-influence experiences, depersonalization, derealization, etc.) are present.

A person with *DID* can potentially experience all five kinds of amnesia, but will typically experience only localized, selective, and systematized amnesia. Persons with DID frequently have a remote localized amnesia (for a chunk of childhood) and they almost universally undergo recurrent recent episodes of amnesia. Persons with DID may have amnesias of all lengths, from microamnesias to lack of memory for a period of several years. They have amnesia for both traumatic and mundane material. Finally, in DID, amnesia does not occur in isolation; the person also experiences a wide variety of nonamnestic dissociative experiences. *The most robust amnesia-related diagnostic indicators of DID are (1) recurrent recent amnesias and (2) amnesia for mundane actions.* An amnestic patient that reports (1) recurrent recent amnesias for mundane actions and (2) the other two components of the pathognomonic symptom-triad for dissociated structures (i.e., passive-influence and odd changes of self) is certainly *not* a case of Dissociative Amnesia.

Persons with *DDNOS-1* manifest the same kinds of amnesia as do persons with DID, but they typically do so with decreased frequency and with decreased intensity. Remember, we are describing a continuum of dissociative structures. DID occupies the high end of the continuum, and DDNOS-1 is DID's closest neighbor. Thus, persons with DDNOS-1 are quite similar to persons with DID (see Dell, 2009c). Like DID, the best amnesia-related diagnostic indicators of DDNOS-1 are (1) recurrent recent amnesias and (2) recurrent amnesias for mundane actions. These phenomena are pathognomonic of the functioning of one or more complex dissociated structures.

A person with Dissociative Fugue usually undergoes two forms of amnesia. With the onset of the fugue episode, the person undergoes a generalized amnesia and travels in an apparently purposeful manner. Fugue-ing individuals usually do not attract attention to themselves; hence, little is known about their functioning and behavior during the fugue. At some point (usually hours to days later), the fugue ends and may be marked by the offset of the generalized amnesia. Most post-fugue individuals then manifest a refractory localized amnesia (for all that occurred during the fugue). *This characteristic pattern of generalized amnesia/travel/localized amnesia makes it easy to distinguish cases of Dissociative Fugue from cases of Dissociative Amnesia.* The more difficult differential diagnosis is between Dissociative Fugue and complex dissociative disorder (i.e., DID and DDNOS-1). That is, in the aftermath of a fugue episode, it is easy for clinicians to mistake a case of full-blown DID (or DDNOS-1) for "mere" Dissociative Fugue (Loewenstein, 1991b; Loewenstein & Putnam, 2004).

As Loewenstein has noted, there are two very different kinds of Dissociative Amnesia (Loewenstein, 1991b; Loewenstein & Putnam, 2004), which he calls "classic" and "nonclassic." These two kinds of Dissociative Amnesia manifest different forms of amnesia.

Classic Dissociative Amnesia is well known to the entire culture; these cases have generalized amnesia and present themselves to police and hospital emergency rooms: "I don't know who I am; I can't remember anything." Classic cases of Dissociative Amnesia do not travel purposefully. They wander in perplexity and attract attention to themselves (Loewenstein, 1991b; Loewenstein & Putnam, 2004). These individuals are usually fleeing from current life stresses. Classic Dissociative Amnesia is said to resolve in hours to months but more recent evidence indicates that the generalized amnesia may be persistent (Kritchevsky et al., 2004).

Nonclassic Dissociative Amnesia is far more prevalent than classic Dissociative Amnesia. Its phenomena are widely known to clinicians, but, oddly, nonclassic Dissociative Amnesia is seldom diagnosed—even when patients disclose their amnesia to the clinician.[75] These patients have a remote localized amnesia (which is typically related to one or more traumatic incidents). In contrast to classic cases, which may worry plaintively about their memory loss, nonclassic cases do not complain. In fact, they are almost secretive about their amnesia. They reveal its presence only if asked and they are quick to minimize its significance (and to change the topic of conversation if they can). Such behavior usually points to the existence of sequestered traumatic material, which they have successfully avoided for years. Thus, unlike the time-limited nature of classic cases, nonclassic Dissociative Amnesia is a chronic disorder.

Such generalized and localized amnesias also occur in DID and DDNOS-1. Accordingly, any person who reports a generalized or a localized amnesia should be carefully evaluated for the presence of other forms of amnesia (especially recurrent recent amnesias for mundane activities), other dissociative symptoms (especially passive-influence experiences), and evidence of internal parts or odd changes in the patient's sense of self. Repeated assessments are important because these additional dissociative symptoms may be denied, despite being present, during early stages of the patient-clinician relationship.

There is an empirical mystery, however, about Dissociative Amnesia. According to the DSM, Dissociative Amnesia is a simple amnestic disorder. That is, the DSM specifies that a person with Dissociative Amnesia must not meet the criteria for any other dissociative disorder with amnestic symptoms (i.e., DID or Dissociative Fugue). As such, a person with (only) Dissociative Amnesia should obtain a low score on the DES. And thus arises the empirical mystery of Dissociative Amnesia.

There have been only two published case series of Dissociative Amnesia in the last 40 years. One series examined 25 cases of "dissociative amnesia" from a modern dissociative point of view (Coons & Milstein, 1992); the other series examined 10 cases of "functional retrograde amnesia" from a modern neuropsychiatric perspective (Kritchevsky, Chang, and Squire (2004). Unlike all earlier studies of amnesia patients, Coons and Milstein used a modern instrument of dissociation—the DES—during their comprehensive assessments. The amnesia cases of Coons and Milstein obtained a mean DES score of 39.5 (range = 26–56)! These are very high scores. DES scores of this magnitude usually indicate the presence of a complex dissociative disorder such as DID. Coons, however, reports that his Dissociative Amnesia sample did not present "any significant depersonalization or derealization or identity alteration" (personal communication, 19 June 2006). How this can be the case, in light of their very high DES scores, is a mystery. In the absence of Coons and Milstein's (1992) original DES data, which are no longer available, these very high DES scores are difficult to explain. In this instance, it is certainly not a cliché to assert that "more research is necessary."

Finally, the difference between classic and nonclassic Dissociative Amnesia may be conceptually important. The chronic localized amnesias (probably for traumatic material) of nonclassic Dissociative Amnesia are readily understood in terms of dissociated structures. In contrast, the time-limited, generalized amnesia of classic Dissociative Amnesia has a very different "feel." These generalized amnesias without travel seem to represent a dissociative flight from current life stresses, but not from frank trauma. Perhaps classic Dissociative Amnesia is better understood to be a simple conversion disorder such as paralysis, blindness, deafness, and so on.

Pope has argued that localized amnesia for trauma is just a modern, culture-bound conversion symptom (Pope, Hudson, Bodkin, & Oliva, 1998; Pope, Poliakoff, Parker, Boynes, & Hudson, 2007). I disagree—in part, because I think that sequestered traumatic material operates as a dissociated structure that, sooner or later, generates positive dissociative intrusions. On the other hand, the generalized amnesia of classic Dissociative Amnesia is not about trauma and it *does* seem to operate in a fashion that is similar to that of simple negative conversion symptoms.

46.10.2.2 Simple "Conversion" Symptoms

The intrusion of a dissociated structure. I think that two very different mechanisms can (and do) produce

[75] Perhaps the primary reason that clinicians do not diagnose nonclassic Dissociative Amnesia is twofold: (1) the patient denies being troubled by the amnesia, and (2) the DSM does not clearly state that a person with a remote, localized amnesia, despite seeming otherwise asymptomatic, should receive a diagnosis of Dissociative Amnesia.

somatoform dissociative symptoms (i.e., conversion symptoms). The first mechanism of somatoform dissociation is the intrusion of a traumatized, dissociated structure (which already embodies one or more trauma-related, somatoform dissociative symptoms). When this dissociated structure intrudes into the person's functioning, it "imposes" its somatoform dissociative symptoms upon the person. Under these circumstances, the somatoform dissociative symptoms have no underlying motivation. They have neither a function nor a purpose. Their occurrence is merely incidental to the intrusion of the traumatized dissociated structure. Dynamically, these somatoform dissociative symptoms are *positive dissociative intrusions* (into the person's bodily functioning).

Self-hypnotic negation of a psychological function. The second mechanism of somatoform dissociation is unconscious self-hypnotic suggestion. These somatoform dissociative symptoms give the appearance of being due to a simple disconnection from conscious awareness of one or more bodily or psychological functions (e.g., vision, hearing, sensation, memory, etc.). Research, however, suggests that amnesia and conversion are not caused by disconnecting a psychological function (or certain information) from conscious awareness. Rather, the apparent amnesia or negative dissociative symptom is brought about by denial, negation, or disowning of the (supposedly amnestic) information or the (supposedly disconnected) psychological function (see, for example, Dorahy & Huntjens, 2007; Sackeim, Nordlie, & Gur, 1979; Kuyk, van Dyck, & Spinhoven, 1996). I believe that such negation or disowning is potentiated by hypnotic ability (Bliss, 1986; Kuyk et al., 1996).

In contrast to the symptoms of somatoform dissociation that are caused by the first mechanism (i.e., the intrusion of dissociated structures), symptoms of somatoform dissociation that are caused by self-hypnotic negation do have a motivation or purpose. They represent the implementation of a wish to avoid something unpleasant in the person's current life situation. Neither frank trauma nor a dissociated structure is at work in simple conversion symptoms. Finally, it might be noted that avoidance of unpleasantness strongly suggests that something akin to repression (i.e., motivated pushing-away or avoidance of unpleasant material) is operative here. These somatoform dissociative symptoms should be understood to be *simple negative dissociations* (or disowning) of specific psychological functions.

Non-Western dissociative syndromes and negation of sensory/motor function. There is an important similarity between simple sensory/motor conversion symptoms and non-Western dissociative syndromes. Specifically, unlike the Western disorders (which involve dissociated structures; see Table 46.2), simple sensory/motor conversion symptoms and non-Western dissociative syndromes are *highly visible to the family and/or local community.* In fact, clinical researchers have emphasized the intrafamilial and intracommunity functions of Western conversion symptoms (e.g., Frankel, 1994) and non-Western dissociative symptoms (Bourguignon, 1976; Gaw, Ding, Levine, & Gaw, 1998; Somer, 2006). The "in your face" quality of these symptoms is used by these dissociative persons to renegotiate the power relations between them and their family or community. As such, the extent to which a dissociative disorder is publicly visible (and interpersonally intrusive) is a major factor in understanding (and treating) that disorder. Most Western dissociative disorders are invisible and hidden—with the exception of generalized amnesia and major conversion symptoms, which are quite visible to others.

Do somatoform dissociative symptoms have more than one mechanism? Complex dissociative disorders (i.e., DID and DDNOS-1) can (and do) produce *both* positive somatoform dissociative intrusions and simple negative somatoform dissociations. This, in turn, raises an interesting question: are *both* positive and negative somatoform dissociation (as defined here) subsumed under Nijenhuis's (2009) concept of somatoform dissociation? Or, does somatoform dissociation include *only* those somatoform dissociative symptoms that are generated by structural dissociation (i.e., the intrusion of dissociated structures)? I would think that Nijenhuis's somatoform dissociation refers only to the somatoform symptoms that are caused by the intrusion of a dissociated structure.

Holmes and Brown, on the other hand, have implicitly subsumed both forms of somatoform dissociation under the single rubric of "compartmentalization" (Brown, 2006; Holmes et al., 2005). Because I believe that positive dissociative intrusions and simple negative dissociations are caused by different mechanisms, I think that the concept of "compartmentalization" probably obscures as much as it reveals (via its contrast with Holmes and Brown's complementary concept of "detachment").

46.10.2.3 Depersonalization Disorder

Holmes and Brown have proposed a continuum of detachment to organize the dissociative symptoms of depersonalization, derealization, and related phenomena (Brown, 2006; Holmes et al., 2005). Although they have discussed possible mechanisms of detachment, Holmes's and Brown's concept of detachment is inherently phenomenological:

> [T]he subject *experiences an altered state of consciousness* characterized by a sense of separation (or "detachment") from certain aspects of everyday experience, be it their body (as in out-of-body experiences), their sense of self (as in depersonalization), or the external world (as in derealization). (Holmes et al., 2005, p. 5, italics added)

> [D]etachment refers to *an experienced state of disconnection* from the self or environment. (Holmes et al., 2005, p. 13, italics added)

In summary, then, detachment is the peculiar subjective experience of being disconnected from one's body, self, or world.

I believe that the subjective experience of dissociation (including the experience of detachment) is a major key to diagnosis (Dell, 2006b, 2006c, 2009c), but I am also convinced that there exists such a plethora of genuine and *faux* dissociative phenomena that clarity and order can only come from identifying the underlying mechanisms (e.g., dissociated structures, self-hypnotic negation of psychological functions, etc.) of these various phenomena. And, like Van der Hart and colleagues, I believe that there is more than one mechanism of detachment (Steele et al., 2009; Van der Hart et al., 2004). In fact, evidence suggests that many phenotypically similar symptoms of detachment are actually quite different from one another (because they are produced by different mechanisms—fever, toxicity, drug abuse, epilepsy, neurological conditions, certain brain lesions, dissociated structures, major life change, severe defensive absorption, evolution-prepared dissociation, etc.).

In this section, I will focus solely on the "800-pound gorilla" of detachment—Depersonalization Disorder.

Depersonalization Disorder is notably different from the other dissociative disorders. Other dissociative disorders exhibit amnesia and are readily described in terms of dissociated structures and sequestered traumatic material. This is not the case with Depersonalization Disorder. Depersonalization Disorder seems to be best described as a disorder of detachment that entails an exaggerated and often unpleasant hyperawareness of the self (Simeon & Abugel, 2006).

Whereas the dissociative symptoms of DID and DDNOS-1 are episodic (if not spasmodic) and brief in length, the symptoms of Depersonalization tend to be fixed and lasting. Simeon describes Depersonalization Disorder as "a stable alteration of consciousness" (Simeon & Abugel, 2006, p. 67) that is marked by a set of "nonchanging core symptoms [which] include visual derealization, altered body experience, emotional numbness, loss of agency feelings, and changes in subjective experiencing of memory" (p. 79).

Unlike some dissociative disorders (especially DID and DDNOS-1), Depersonalization Disorder does not appear to be posttraumatic in nature. Only emotional abuse has been shown to be significantly related to Depersonalization Disorder (Simeon, Guralnik, Schmeidler, Sirof, & Knutelska, 2001). Moreover, unlike DID, which is highly comorbid with PTSD, only 3% of Depersonalization Disorder patients have PTSD (Simeon, Knutelska, Nelson, & Guralnik, 2003). The onset of Depersonalization Disorder is sometimes precipitated by drug abuse (especially marijuana, ketamine, and MDMA [methylenedioxymethamphetamine or "Ecstasy"]) or psychological stress (but rarely frank abuse).

Finally, although psychological factors play a role in some cases (Simeon & Abugel, 2006), the phenomena of Depersonalization Disorder more closely resemble a biological survival response than a psychological defense mechanism. Mayer-Gross (1935), for example, considered Depersonalization Disorder to be a physiological disorder: "a non-specific pre-formed functional response of the brain" (p. 118). In keeping with that idea, many researchers have interpreted depersonalization and related phenomena in terms of evolution-prepared survival mechanisms: Depersonalization Disorder (Roth & Argyle, 1988; Sierra & Berrios, 1998; Sierra et al., 2002; Simeon, 2006), secondary dissociation (Frewen & Lanius, 2006), acute peritraumatic dissociation (Dell, 2006a; Noyes, Kletti, & Kupperman, 1977; Perry, 1999; Perry et al., 1995), and dissociation in general (Nijenhuis et al., 1998; Schore, 2009). For example:

> The data presented suggest that depersonalization is, like fear, an almost universal response to life-threatening danger. It develops instantly upon the recognition of danger and vanishes just as quickly when the threat to life is past. Depersonalization appears to be an adaptive mechanism that combines opposing reaction tendencies, the one serving to intensify alertness and the other to dampen potentially disorganizing emotion. (Noyes, Kletti, & Kupperman, 1977, pp. 381–382)

> [W]e endorse the view that depersonalization is a "hard-wired" vestigial response for dealing with extreme anxiety combining a state of increased alertness with a profound inhibition of the emotional response system. (Sierra & Berrios, 1998, p. 193)

> From an evolutionary perspective, acute transient depersonalization, typically precipitated by severe or life-threatening stress, must be viewed as adaptive in the short term, allowing the individual emotional distance and detachment from circumstances that might other wise be overwhelming, so that steps appropriate to survival can be taken. (Simeon & Abugel, 2006, p. 112)

Here, of course, is our old friend—evolution-prepared, survival-related dissociation (see previous discussion). But, as Noyes et al. (1977) correctly state: survival-related dissociation "develops instantly upon recognition of danger and vanishes just as quickly when the threat to life is past." Depersonalization Disorder, of course, does not vanish quickly; it perversely persists in the absence of danger. Accordingly, Depersonalization Disorder feels more like a neurological disorder than a psychological or psychiatric disorder. Even Simeon has noted that a "depersonalization that becomes chronic and autonomous from its stressful origins is clearly maladaptive, suggesting *dysregulated brain function that has failed to repair*" (Simeon & Abugel, 2006, p. 112, italics added). Indeed, Simeon has even likened Depersonalization Disorder to the parietal-lesion neglect syndromes:

> We speculate that body schema distortions characteristic of depersonalization might be more subtle, functionally based, less neurologically damaged versions of well-known parietal lobe neurological syndromes such as neglect, finger agnosia, and hemidepersonalization. The psychiatric version might be characterized by an "as if" quality to the experience of bodily detachment, whereas in the neurological version, entire body parts or sides are treated as truly absent or not part of the self. (Simeon et al,, 2000, p. 1786)

Simeon and colleagues (2000) attributed these patients' pervasive experience of unreality to a widespread metabolic dysfunction (i.e., hyperactivation) of the sensory-association cortex.

An important issue hangs in the balance here. To the extent that Depersonalization Disorder is more neurological than psychological, more an evolution-prepared, survival related response that has gone haywire than a psychological defense mechanism, then the symptoms of Depersonalization Disorder are *not* motivated (either consciously or unconsciously); they are, instead, an autonomous, unstoppable brain response that is fully disconnected from the self (as Dugas, 1898, asserted over a century ago). In fact, to the extent that this is true, it means that Depersonalization Disorder is not only without motivation, but without any "purpose" at all. That is, as a form of brain dysfunction, Depersonalization Disorder would lack not only the proximal final causation of personal motivation, but the distal final causation of natural selection as well.

This neurological interpretation of Depersonalization Disorder has one last implication. I have proposed previously that psychological automatisms are a *sine qua non* of all pathological dissociation. If Depersonalization Disorder is more neurological than psychological, then its tonic automatism (of profound detachment from self, body, and world) is a *neurological (or neurobiological) automatism*. Such a neurological automatism would differ from psychological automatisms in one crucial respect—motivation. We noted previously that pathological psychological automatisms have five features: they are personally motivated, recurrent or persisting, a source of distress or dysfunction, considered by the dissociator to be abnormal, and are not given a delusional explanation (by the dissociator). The tonic neurological automatism of Depersonalization Disorder is correctly described by all of these features—except motivation. Neurological automatisms have no personal motivation (nor do evolution-prepared biological automatisms such as spontaneous, survival-related dissociation).

Understanding Dissociation #9: There are three classes of dissociative disorder: (1) dissociated structures, (2) self-hypnotic negations of a psychological function, and (3) Depersonalization Disorder (see Table 46.2). Each involves a different mechanism. Dissociated structures underlie most Western dissociative disorders. Dissociated structures are almost exclusively subjective in nature and are hidden from public view. Self-hypnotic negations of psychological function (i.e., conversion symptoms) (1) tend to be simple, (2) can occur in the absence of any dissociated structures, (3) are highly visible to family and community, and (4) are similar to non-Western dissociative syndromes in that they can alter the person's position in the local power structure. Depersonalization Disorder is so different from other dissociative disorders that it may be a neurological disorder, rather than a psychiatric disorder. A *sine qua non* of pathological dissociation is the presence of psychological automatisms—recurring autonomous intrusions into the person's psychological functioning and sense of self that (1) cause distress or dysfunction, (2) are recognized by the person to be abnormal, and (3) are not given a delusional explanation (by the person). In addition, psychological automatisms are always, at some level, motivated. If Depersonalization Disorder should prove to be a neurological disorder, then it would follow that its primary symptom—tonic detachment—is a purposeless, tonic neurological automatism that has no motivation whatsoever.

46.11 AGAIN, WHAT IS DISSOCIATION?

Dissociation has been notoriously difficult to define. As Cardeña (1994) noted, the term *dissociation* has been applied to phenomena that are so different from one another that it makes little sense to subsume them under the same label (Cardeña, 1994). Despite a careful and rigorous effort, my analysis, too, has failed to free dissociation from its unrepentant heterogeneity.

And yet, perhaps this is the correct answer—namely, that there is more than one kind of dissociation. My analysis of repression, hypnotizability, normal dissociation, and pathological dissociation seems to yield five kinds of phenomena that are strongly *dissociative*: (1) dissociation-potentiated repression, (2) intrusions from dissociated structures, (3) evolution-prepared dissociation, (4) Depersonalization Disorder, and (5) Conversion Disorder (and Type II Normal Dissociation). Although they share many similarities—enough to call them all dissociative—it is unlikely that they have identical mechanisms or identical etiologies. On the other hand, if they do have different mechanisms, then it is probably unhelpful to call these phenotypically similar phenomena by the same name. After all, they have several different "genotypes."

In any case, I offer definitions and descriptions of five forms of dissociation, some of which may deserve a name different from *dissociation*.

46.11.1 Dissociation-Potentiated Repression

The most common form of dissociation is rooted in repression. As defined by Freud, repression is the normal, motivated, consciously intended, mental effort to escape current (and avoid future) discomfort and pain by pushing uncomfortable realities out of conscious awareness. Repression is an energy-intensive mental effort that must be constantly sustained (in order to keep the uncomfortable realities out of awareness). All humans repress, but only some can successfully dissociate their memory of uncomfortable realities. *Dissociation* occurs when (1) the uncomfortable reality disappears from conscious awareness, and (2) the person is apparently unable to retrieve a memory of that unaccepted reality, and (3) no effort is required to maintain that situation (or any such effort occurs preattentively and outside of conscious awareness), and (4) the now-disowned material retains an ability to influence the person's functioning.

Dissociation-potentiated repression of uncomfortable realities produces what I (and others) have called *dissociated structures* (see also Spiegel, 1990); these "hold" unaccepted or disowned aspects of life, the self, and significant others. Clinical manifestations of dissociated structures include fixed ideas, localized amnesia for past trauma, ego-state disorders, Dissociative Fugue, possessions disorders, DID, and DID-like clinical presentations.

46.11.2 Intrusions from Dissociated Structures

Dissociated structures are (1) experienced by the person as operating with considerable autonomy, thereby generating (2) recurrent automatisms, which are (3) personally motivated (but disowned), (4) usually of sudden onset, (5) phasic, (6) chronically recurrent, (7) a source of distress or dysfunction, (8) considered by the dissociator to be abnormal, and (9) are not given a delusional explanation (by the dissociator). Intrusions from dissociated structures can cause (10) passive-influence experiences such as "made" feelings, "made" impulses, "made" actions, thought insertion, and so on; (11) loss or alteration of identity or sense of self; (12) incidents of amnesia; and (13) various other dissociative symptoms, including depersonalization, derealization, trance, somatoform dissociative symptoms, and dissociative flashbacks.

The intrusions of dissociated structures produce a characteristic set of experiences and reactions in dissociative persons—namely, a *private conscious experience* of recurrent, inexplicable intrusions into, and alterations of, their typical reactions, their intended actions, and their sense of who they are. These peculiar intrusions are typically accompanied by a subjective sense of unexpectedness, involuntariness, uncontrollability, "not-mineness," and a deeply disturbing sense that "something is very wrong with me."

Many (most?) of the dissociative symptoms that are reported upon inquiry in psychiatric settings will prove to be intrusions from a dissociated structure.

46.11.3 Evolution-Prepared Dissociation

Evolution-prepared dissociation is (1) the sudden and automatic onset, (2) at a moment of life-threat, (3) of an altered state of consciousness that is characterized by (4) altered information processing, and (5) the immediate execution of nonreflective actions that facilitate survival, (6) all of which automatically ceases when the danger is past.

46.11.4 Depersonalization Disorder

Depersonalization Disorder is (1) an altered state of consciousness (2) involving an unyielding experiential alteration of the quality of one's conscious awareness of body, self, and surrounding world, such that (3) *every aspect of experience has been drained of its personal emotional immediacy*. This unyielding state of detachment from body, self, and world has (4) no motivation, no "purpose," and no adaptive function.

46.11.5 Type II Normal Dissociation and Conversion Disorder

Type II Normal Dissociation is the product of a special dissociative ability that is possessed by only a minority of individuals. This special ability can produce sudden automatisms that are (1) personally motivated (consciously or unconsciously), and (2) socioculturally meaningful, and (3) socioculturally valued. As noted previously, Type II Normal Dissociation includes hypnotic performance, psychologically healthy forms of possession, creative/productive automatisms, and transcendent experiences. The automatisms of Type II Normal Dissociation are highly valued; they produce neither distress nor dysfunction.

Conversion Disorder is the pathological form of Type II Normal Dissociation. Conversion Disorder is (1) a persistent (tonic) publicly-visible impairment of sensory-motor or memorial functioning, (2) associated with a relatively untroubled realization that "something is wrong with me," (3) that often affords an alteration or renegotiation of the power relations between the symptomatic person and his or her family and/or local community.

46.12 ONE LAST TIME—WHAT, EXACTLY, IS DISSOCIATIVE AMNESIA?

Almost all research on dissociation has addressed itself solely to *failing* dissociation. When dissociation begins to fail, dissociative symptoms intrude into conscious awareness. Relatively little research has addressed itself to *successful* dissociation. When dissociation is completely successful, it is marked by a sustained amnesia. There are three obvious reasons for the relative lack of research on successful dissociation. First, the presence of amnesia is difficult to detect (because patients are often unaware of their amnesia, and avoid mentioning it even when they are aware of it). Second, experimental analogues of clinical amnesia are difficult to construct and have questionable ecological validity. Third, in contrast to *successful* dissociation, the symptoms of *failing* dissociation are highly prevalent, easy to detect (Dell, 2006c, 2009c), and attract the bulk of research on dissociation. These three considerations may be dwarfed, however, by the discouraging effect on researchers of consistently inconsistent findings about dissociative amnesia.

Thankfully, these inconsistent findings about amnesia increasingly appear to be explained by a new understanding of the paradox that lies at the heart of dissociative amnesia. Namely, dissociative amnesia may *never* be truly successful!

To put the matter less provocatively, the best current evidence shows that amnesia is *subjectively successful* (i.e., the person has the experience of not being able to remember), but *objectively unsuccessful*—the supposedly amnestic material routinely "flows" into the person's mind and affects his or her behavior (Elzinga, Phaf, Ardon, & van Dyck, 2003; Huntjens et al., 2002, Huntjens, Postma, Peters, Woertman, & van der Hart, 2003; Huntjens, 2003; Kindt & van den Hout, 2003).

In one sense, the subjective success and objective failure of amnesia have been known for almost two centuries; 19th-century investigators were well aware of the contrast between the subjective experience of amnesia and the objective behavioral effects of posthypnotic suggestion, subconscious acts, and fixed ideas. Nevertheless, the full implications of dissociative amnesia's dichotomous phenomena (i.e., subjective amnesia vs. objective behavioral performance) were not realized until quite recently.

As noted, until recently, experimental research on dissociative amnesia produced inconsistent findings. Then, new research methods were introduced. These new methods allowed investigators to draw a clear distinction between (1) their subjects' subjective experience of amnesia, and (2) their subjects' objective performance on memory tests. These methods, in turn, produced new research data that consistently have shown that the memory of dissociative subjects is as good as that of normal subjects—but that dissociative subjects still have a deeply convincing *experience* of amnesia (Elzinga, Phaf, Ardon, & van Dyck, 2003; Huntjens et al., 2002; Huntjens, Postma, Peters, Woertman, & van der Hart, 2003; Huntjens, 2003; Kindt & van den Hout, 2003).

The importance of this finding cannot be overemphasized; it radically revises many of our conventional notions about dissociative amnesia. In order to help the reader to accommodate to this new understanding of dissociative amnesia, I provide quotations from three recent experimental studies of dissociative amnesia and dissociated memory recall:

> [DID] patients' subjective reports of interidentity amnesia may reflect their *genuine phenomenological experiences*, but their intact memory traces for an event may [exist] without their being aware of … that memory. … Dissociative amnesia may thus not be the correct term to describe perceived memory problems in DID (e.g., Read & Lindsay, 2000). Instead, *the presence of intact memory performance combined with the absence of memory meta-awareness may be at the core of dissociative amnesia.* (Huntjens et al., 2002, p. 82, italics added)

> Dissociative amnesia in DID may more adequately be described as *an experiential disturbance in memory functioning.* Central to the disorder seems to be the patients' belief of the inability to recall information instead of an actual objective inability to recall. Patients seem to lack the acknowledgement of remembered memories of other identities as belonging to themselves.... *Objectively, however, there is transfer of memories across identities in DID.* (Huntjens, 2003, p. 120, italics added)

> The main finding in the present study was that dissociation ... was not related to fragmentation in actual memory performance, but it was related to the subjective experience of memory being fragmented.... No effect of dissociation on fragmentation in actual memory performance was observed.... [In short, the data suggest] that dissociation-induced memory fragmentation is confined to the realm of subjective experience and that *dissociation may leave actual memory performance unaffected.* (Kindt & Van den Hout, 2003, p. 176, italics added to final sentence)

Thus, there is robust evidence for the subjective experience of amnesia, but there is no evidence that the amnesia prevents the "forgotten" material from affecting the person's behavior and reactions. This does *not* mean that reports of dissociative amnesia are phony or factitious—far from it. Patients' reports of subjectively experienced amnesia reflect their "genuine phenomenological experiences" (Huntjens et al., 2002, p. 82). Nevertheless, the dissociated material is simultaneously out of conscious awareness—and yet fully operative.

The bottom line is that dissociative amnesia is a typical conversion symptom, despite its not being somatoform, and its not being so recognized by the DSM or the ICD. Like other conversion symptoms such as hysterical blindness or hysterical deafness, *dissociative amnesia is a subjective inability to perform a psychological function (in this case, remembering), despite an unimpaired nervous system.* And, like hysterical blindness and hysterical deafness, one can always find convincing evidence that the person does see (e.g., Sackeim et al., 1979), does hear (e.g., Pincus & Tucker, 1985), does remember (e.g., Huntjens et al., 2002), and so on.[76] And yet, the person claims—and, more importantly, *experiences*—a truthfully perceived inability to see, hear, or remember. Few symptoms show so clearly the paradoxes that are inherent in human consciousness.

Perhaps the final evidence that dissociative amnesia is a conversion symptom is that, just as Janet long ago showed that dissociative anesthesias conform to patients' lay ideas of anatomy (e.g., glove anesthesia or stocking anesthesia) and not the actual nerve tracts of the body, so, too, have Kritchevsky et al. (2004) shown that dissociative amnesia patients' patterns of memory loss conform to their "commonsense concept of memory" (p. 213) rather than to the neurological structures of the brain. In this chapter, I cannot delve into the complexities of human consciousness, but I must mention one crucial point: dissociation and dissociative phenomena are inseparable from the peculiarities of human consciousness. Human consciousness is necessary for dissociation. No consciousness, no dissociation (see also Oakley, 1999a).

I will now try to explicate a few key aspects of the relationship between dissociation and human consciousness. In doing so, I will focus mostly, but not exclusively, on *the fate of dissociated memories.* What happens to dissociated memories? Where do they go? What do they do while they are "there"? What happens when dissociation fails and dissociated memories intrude into consciousness?

46.13. INTRUSIONS INTO CONSCIOUSNESS

There are several kinds of intrusive thoughts (and other intrusive phenomena, such as affect and movement), only a few of which deserve the label *dissociative*. Let us begin with *normal intrusive thoughts*: they signal a need to revise our conscious "map" of ourselves and the world.

46.13.1 Normal Intrusive Thoughts

Mardi Horowitz (1986/2001) demonstrated that *any* important event generates a series of intrusive thoughts. According to Horowitz, these thoughts intrude into conscious awareness until the person has cognitively (and emotionally) assimilated the event and, ideally, accommodated to its personal implications. Horowitz called this process of "intrusion-until-accommodation-is-finished" the *completion principle.* These intrusive thoughts are a *normal psychological process.* They facilitate mental processing of important events, regardless of whether the person considers the important event to be positive or negative.

It makes excellent evolutionary sense that natural selection has produced human minds that repetitively process important events until we have extracted as much information as possible from the event (and used that information to update our conscious map of ourselves and the world). It is obviously adaptive for us to thoroughly accommodate to any important changes in our world; such accommodation may even be life-saving.

---

[76] Or, as Oakley (1999b) provocatively stated, "the individual's performance may display characteristics which could only be present if the symptoms did not exist" (p. 246).

At this point, it is easy to see that *posttraumatic intrusive thoughts are normal.* Intrusive thoughts only count as a symptom of PTSD when they are still occurring 30 days after the trauma (American Psychiatric Association, 2000). Research has consistently shown that only about a quarter of trauma survivors develop PTSD. The other 75% of trauma survivors go through a normal process of intrusive thoughts and mental/emotional processing that rapidly subsides. In short, intrusive thoughts are not inherently pathological; they are, in fact, inherently normal and healthy. It is only *persisting* intrusive thoughts that are pathological.

Are normal intrusive thoughts dissociative? No. Normal, time-limited, intrusive thoughts are automatic, but they are not dissociative. Intrusive thoughts are a *normal psychological automatism.* They are normal because the brain and the mind are functioning according to their evolutionary "design." Intrusive thoughts have an adaptive purpose.

46.13.2 Abnormal (i.e., Persisting) Intrusive Thoughts—PTSD

In most cases, the persisting intrusive thoughts about trauma (which typify PTSD) are *not* dissociative. Most of these persistent thoughts are sustained by an overactive amygdalar fear system, which is generally thought to be purely neurobiological in nature, and/or by an overused cognitive strategy of thought suppression (e.g., Vázquez, Hervás, & Pérez-Sales, 2008) which secondarily generates abnormal neurobiological functioning. *In most PTSD patients, nothing was dissociated*; their intrusions do not come from dissociated memory (or dissociated experience). In PTSD, intrusive thoughts are intertwined with a phobia of the trauma (and reminders of the trauma). Their trauma-related thoughts are, indeed, intrusive. But unless these thoughts come from a "pocket" of dissociated memory (which they do in some cases of PTSD), these intrusive thoughts are not usefully considered to be "dissociative."

The persisting intrusive phenomena of PTSD are *abnormal neurobiological automatisms* that do not have an adaptive purpose.

46.13.3 Dissociative Flashbacks

But what about *dissociative flashbacks* (where the person relives a trauma with full sensory revivification)? Are these relivings dissociative? Yes, but they are an unexpected kind of dissociation.

The crucial issue is: why do some persons with PTSD suffer from full-blown revivifications (i.e., dissociative flashbacks), whereas other persons with PTSD do not? Are full-blown revivifications a sign that a previously "blocked" aspect of trauma is now "leaking" back into conscious experience? No. Dissociative flashbacks definitely occur in cases of PTSD that lack dissociation of the trauma (or any part of the trauma). Thus, *dissociative flashbacks are not a valid indicator of blocked or dissociated trauma.*

On the other hand, it is also true that PTSD-patients-*with*-dissociated-trauma manifest dissociative flashbacks more often than do PTSD-patients-*without*-dissociated-trauma.

So what is going on here? What causes dissociative flashbacks? I think that dissociative flashbacks require a certain kind of brain, a kind that is found in a subset of highly hypnotizable individuals with, for example, highly responsive sensory cortices and a highly responsive anterior cingulate cortex.

Dissociative flashbacks are basically a form of hallucination. Szechtman and Woody studied two groups of high hypnotizables in a PET study: (1) those that could experience vivid, hypnotically suggested, auditory hallucinations of a voice; and (2) those that could not (Szechtman et al., 1998; Woody & Szechtman, 2000). The highly hypnotizable hallucinators showed significantly greater activation of the right anterior cingulate cortex (ACC) during both waking hearing and hypnotic auditory hallucination (than did nonhallucinating high hypnotizables). The most startling finding, however, is that *during normal, waking hearing, the hallucination-capable high-hypnotizable subjects activated 7 to 8 times more of their temporal cortex* (2700 voxels vs. 350 voxels) than did the nonhallucinating high hypnotizables! This suggests that hypnotic hallucinations may occur in persons who have highly sensitive (i.e., highly responsive) sensory cortices.

It seems quite possible that dissociative flashbacks, a form of hallucination, may occur spontaneously when certain highly hypnotizable individuals (i.e., those who have highly responsive sensory cortices and a highly responsive right rostral ACC) experience the typical amygdala-amplified intrusive memories of PTSD. For this subset of highly hypnotizable individuals, intrusive memories may function as implicit suggestions to hallucinate (i.e., to remember with full sensory revivification). This would mean that *a subset of highly hypnotizable PTSD patients are routinely at risk for dissociative flashbacks*—regardless of whether their intrusive memories come solely from a typical PTSD-sensitized amygdalar fear system, or whether their intrusive memories (also) come from a pocket of dissociated trauma.

If this line of reasoning is correct, then dissociative flashbacks are never caused by dissociated trauma *per se*. Instead, dissociative flashbacks are caused by a certain type of highly hypnotizable brain (which may be a common causal factor for both dissociative flashbacks and dissociative amnesia). Or, said differently, so-called dissociative flashbacks are a secondary (and independent) phenomenon, which can be triggered either by the typical intrusions of PTSD or by intrusions from a pocket of dissociated traumatic material.

This explanation of dissociative flashbacks has an ironic consequence. If a "hypnotic brain" can spontaneously transform PTSD intrusions into dissociative flashbacks, then this phenomenon would validate a variant of the autohypnosis model of dissociation. And therein lies the irony; these dissociative flashbacks do not involve the prototypical defensive activity of dissociation (i.e., splitting off or defending against traumatic material)—which the autohypnotic model of dissociation was devised to explain in the first place (Bliss, 1986; Spiegel, 1990).

If this explanation of dissociative flashbacks is correct, then dissociative flashbacks are a binary phenomenon in which a neurobiological automatism (i.e., a PTSD intrusion) drives or causes the occurrence of a (usually) normal form of dissociation (i.e., "hypnotic" performance—in this case, a hallucinatory reliving of trauma).[77]

The idea that affect-laden PTSD intrusions can evoke dissociative flashbacks in a subset of high hypnotizables is in keeping with Szechtman and colleagues' (1998) interpretation of their PET findings—namely, that "the attention of hallucinators is more affect-laden than that of non-hallucinators" and that "when attention is more affect-laden, self-generation of [a hallucinatory event] is more likely to occur" (p. 1959). Woody and Szechtman (2000) drew a parallel between their hypnotic hallucinators and fantasy-prone personalities, who, they said, "seem to be acutely sensitive to sensory stimuli" (p. 7).

The important remaining questions at this point are, What kind of dissociation is this? What kind of dissociation occurs in binary dissociative flashbacks? Is it dissociation-potentiated repression? Is a dissociative flashback an intrusion from a dissociated structure? Are dissociative flashbacks an evolution-prepared form of dissociation? Depersonalization Disorder? Conversion Disorder?

[77] Such binary dissociative flashbacks would be an excellent example of why Wickramasekera (1988) insists that high hypnotizability is a risk factor for psychopathology.

I think that the binary mechanism of dissociative flashbacks is an atypical one. It most closely resembles the mechanism of conversion symptoms, but, unlike typical conversion symptoms (which are unconsciously purposeful and motivated), dissociative flashbacks lack both motivation and purpose. Dissociative flashbacks lack purpose and motivation because their normal mechanism (i.e., the "hypnotic brain") has been "hijacked" by an abnormal neurobiological automatism (which has neither motivation nor purpose).

This analysis of dissociative flashbacks leads naturally to a clarification of the relationship(s) between dissociation and PTSD. Persons with dissociative flashbacks have dissociative PTSD, but of a kind that is different from two other forms of dissociative PTSD: (1) dissociative PTSD that involves an overuse of evolution-prepared dissociation (Frewen & Lanius, 2006), and (2) dissociative PTSD that involves defensive compartmentalization of trauma (Spiegel, 1984, 1986).

In short, there are not only dissociative and nondissociative forms of PTSD, as Bremner (1999) proposed, but there would seem to be at least three kinds of dissociative PTSD. In fact, there may be a fourth kind; thus we might ask, "Is the chronic numbing of some PTSD patients actually a chronic depersonalization (perhaps even full-blown Depersonalization Disorder, or some variant thereof)?"

Before proceeding to the next section, it is worthwhile to note that, thus far, we have discussed three kinds of intrusion onto consciousness—normal intrusive thoughts, abnormal intrusive thoughts, and dissociative flashbacks—and none of them are prototypical dissociative intrusions. We have not yet discussed intrusions of painful material that the individual previously dissociated or split off—nor will we in the next section on successful dissociation.

46.13.4 Activated Thoughts That Do Not Intrude (Successful Dissociation)

"Activated thoughts that do not intrude" might seem to be a contradiction in terms. And yet, it is impossible to understand prototypical *dissociative* intrusions without also understanding the obverse side of the dissociative coin—namely, successful dissociation.

When dissociation is successful, dissociated material does *not* intrude upon consciousness. What goes on there? Is the dissociated material quiescent? Is the material so compartmentalized that it cannot intrude upon consciousness? Does this material begin to intrude upon consciousness, but is somehow neutralized or warded off via subliminal or preconscious defenses? These questions are largely *terra incognita* in the dissociation literature, but a variety of findings, mostly in other areas of literature, are quite illuminating.

Research has shown that amnesia (even organic amnesia) usually leaves implicit memory intact. More impressive, however, are the studies (discussed previously) that show dissociative amnesia is a compelling subjective experience that is not borne out by the person's objective performance. As we noted, the behavior of persons with dissociative amnesia is often guided by the very information that they report to be absent (i.e., dissociated). This means that dissociated information is readily *available* (i.e., has been successfully stored) and easily activated by appropriate circumstances, but it is not *accessible* to conscious awareness (Tulving & Pearlstone, 1966). When memory of dissociated information is activated by appropriate cues, but still does not intrude into conscious awareness, then there are "activated ideas that do not intrude."

This analysis clarifies one point, but it confronts us with a mystery. On the one hand, this analysis suggests that dissociated material can be quiescent when it is *not* activated by circumstances—just as any other kind of memory can be quiescent (i.e., preconscious) until it is activated (into consciousness) by the appropriate circumstances or cues. Thus, when dissociated information is quiescent, its dissociative status needs no explanation; at that moment, the person cannot be aware of the information because it is inactive (i.e., no cues are currently activating it).

On the other hand, we are now unavoidably confronted with the essential mystery of dissociative amnesia: When the dissociated information is activated (by appropriate cues), why does the person remain unaware of it? Or, as Tulving would put the question, Why does ecphory[78] not occur? *This* is what needs to be explained: what stops dissociated information from intruding into consciousness?

Much research will be necessary before the dissociative disorders field can adequately delineate the psychological and neuroanatomical mechanisms that sustain dissociative amnesia. At present, I can only sketch the outline of one possible explanation.

First of all, it is almost certain that *dissociative amnesia is an active psychological and neural process* (both at the onset of the amnesia and throughout the period of its continuation). Contrary to Janet's model of passive mental disaggregation, dissociation-potentiated repression splits off memory via an active, defensive process. Similarly, in contrast to Janet's deficit model of disaggregation, such split off (i.e., dissociated) material is almost certainly kept separate from consciousness via an active process of control. This means that so-called compartmentalization is an ongoing, active process; the mind does not possess an internal compartment that passively contains dissociated material. Although compartmentalization is a useful metaphor for dissociation, the reader is urged to keep in mind that this metaphor is also somewhat misleading (because it tends to veil the active process that almost certainly sustains dissociative amnesia).

Second, it is quite likely that *dissociative amnesia is the product of inhibitory control processes* (e.g., Anderson & Green, 2001; Anderson et al., 2004; Depue, Curran, & Branch, 2007; Elzinga et al., 2007; Schnider, 2003). Natural selection has shaped the human brain to respond efficiently (with speed and accuracy) to environmental stimuli. Natural selection has also shaped the human brain to exercise speedy and efficient control of mental processing. As noted previously, appropriate cues will readily activate internal representations of dissociated information. Because dissociated information will become conscious when it is activated, it seems logical that dissociation can only be maintained if inhibitory control processes intervene and prevent that from happening.

Third, *dissociative amnesia is almost certainly maintained by preattentive processes of the prefrontal cortex.* A truly effective mechanism for controlling dissociated information would suppress dissociated information (whenever it is activated) before it reaches conscious awareness. In other words, dissociative control-processes should be faster than the processes of conscious attention. Is there any evidence that such high-speed dissociative control processes actually exist? Yes. Schnider and colleagues have shown that if activated memories are *deemed irrelevant to current reality* they can be "silenced" and deleted from further processing within 300 ms or less (Schnider, 2003; Schnider, Valenza, Morand, & Michel, 2002):

> [T]he stimuli evoking a currently irrelevant memory … specifically failed to induce the negative deflection of the frontal potential after 200–300 ms which was induced by the other [i.e., relevant] stimuli. In terms of cortical network activity, … the processing of these "currently irrelevant" memories … induced *absence of a particular cortical map configuration after 220–300 ms … indicating that these stimuli induce suppression of a processing stage….* These results show that before memories enter the stage of … recognition, their cortical representation is specifically adapted according to whether they relate to ongoing reality or not…. [This] suggests *that the*

[78] Ecphory is the process by which retrieval cues interact with stored information so that an image or a representation of the target information appears to the conscious mind (Tulving, 1983).

> *suppression of memories that do not pertain to ongoing reality is a preconscious process.* (Schnider et al., 2002, p. 58–59, italics added)

Schnider's research on irrelevant activated memories does not pertain to dissociative amnesia. Instead, his research project focuses on the neural processing in the orbitofrontal cortex, which, when impaired, causes the neurological symptom of confabulation. Because Schnider's research project is rooted in an entirely different research tradition, its applicability to, and validity for, dissociative amnesia may be that much the greater.

Redgrave has proposed an even faster defensive process, which is rooted in the short-latency dopamine signal's <100 ms response to biologically significant stimuli (Redgrave & Gurney, 2006). Like other short-latency neural responses, the short-latency dopamine signal has evolutionary survival value (Williams, 2006):

> From the perspective of survival, whenever some aspect of an animal's behaviour causes an unpredicted noxious or disadvantageous event … the evolutionary imperative would be to immediately terminate and then suppress any tendency to repeat immediately preceding actions, and avoid the context(s) in which they occurred. (Redgrave & Gurney, 2006, p. 972)

Recent research has, in fact, reported that noxious stimuli elicit a short-latency (<100 ms) phasic *suppression* of dopamine activity that lasts at least as long as does the noxious event (Coizet, Dommett, Redgrave, & Overton, 2006; Ungless, Magill, & Bolam, 2004). Redgrave suggests that "this negative [dopamine] signal could act to reduce the likelihood of reselecting the contexts and actions associated with the unpredicted detrimental event" (Redgrave & Gurney, 2006, p. 972). I suggest that, for some individuals, this short-latency suppression of immediately preceding actions (which are associated with noxious consequences) might also serve to suppress immediately preceding thoughts.

Defensive, high-speed preattentive processing of undesired stimuli has also been demonstrated in dissociative patients (Hermans, Nijenhuis, van Honk, Huntjens, & van der Hart, 2006). Similarly, Elzinga and colleagues (2007) conducted an fMRI study on dissociative individuals that supported the hypothesis that "dissociative patients may be characterized by strong executive control capacities, thereby inhibiting the processing of trauma-related memories" (p. 243).

Fourth, *dissociative amnesia is probably based upon a learning process that improves with practice* (i.e., repeated and sustained efforts to prevent conscious awareness of the dissociated memories). Research has shown that suppression of memory improves with sustained practice (Anderson & Green, 2001; Depue et al., 2007). This is a particularly important finding because it suggests that a closely related but shorter-term body of research—i.e., thought-suppression—may not be applicable to dissociative amnesia. That is, short-term studies of thought suppression have consistently shown that thought suppression is subsequently followed by a rebound of increased intrusions. If amnesia-like suppression of memory is actually a longitudinal learning process, then short-term thought-suppression studies may not be germane to the mechanisms and dynamics of a long-practiced amnesia.

Fifth, *there are robust individual differences in the ability to achieve dissociative amnesia.* Both the hypnosis literature (e.g., Hilgard, 1965) and the dissociation literature have repeatedly documented the existence of such individual differences.

The preceding five points outline only one model of dissociative amnesia—preattentive neural censorship. Other potential mechanisms of dissociative amnesia do not prevent conscious awareness of the dissociated memories. Instead, these alternative mechanisms of dissociative amnesia may alter the memory by stripping it of a "feeling of rightness" (Gilboa, 2004), a "feeling of mineness" (Reinders et al., 2003; Reinders et al., 2006; Ruby & Legrand, 2007), "feelings of knowing" (Woody & Szechtman, 2000), or by a deliberate avoidance of the retrievable memory (Erdelyi, 1990). Preattentive neural censorship is an early-stage model of dissociation, whereas the other possible mechanisms of dissociation are late-stage models of dissociation. Oakley (1999a), however, has asserted that neural censorship is a late-stage mechanism.

In any case, each of these mechanisms seeks to explain how dissociated thoughts or memories can be activated, but fail to intrude (in a recognizable form) into consciousness. These mechanisms describe *successful dissociation.*

Dissociation, of course, is not always successful. In many instances, dissociated memories become activated and then intrude, with considerable impact, into conscious awareness. The following section discusses the intrusive thoughts that characterize *unsuccessful dissociation.*

46.13.5 The Intrusion of Dissociated Memories (Unsuccessful Dissociation)

We have relatively little understanding of why dissociated memories, often of long standing, suddenly begin to intrude into consciousness. Similarly, little is known about the phenomenology of these *memorial intrusions*. I distinguish between two major classes of dissociative intrusion (memorial and nonmemorial). Here, I will discuss only memorial intrusions. The much larger class of nonmemorial intrusions is discussed in the following under "Intrusions of Autonomous Structures."

As noted previously, current stimuli or cues routinely activate various associations. In successful dissociation, however, activation of dissociated memories is neutralized by either preattentive "silencing" (e.g., Schnider et al., 2002) or preattentive alteration such that the memories enter consciousness in an unrecognizable form[79] (i.e., unaccompanied by the usual feeling of knowing, feeling of mineness, or feeling of rightness). On the other hand, when dissociated memories *do* intrude into consciousness and *are* accompanied by their usual feelings (of knowing, rightness, and/or mineness), they are typically met with renewed defensive efforts.

There then ensues a period of time during which the person fends off the intruding memory via denial, avoidance, or successful re-repression. During therapy, after the patient has achieved relative stability, the treatment strategy often consists of simply convincing the patient to "sit still" and allow him- or herself to examine introspectively the memory(ies) that he or she has been reflexively denying and avoiding.

The intrusion of memories, however, is but a small aspect of dissociative intrusions. Most dissociative intrusions do not involve memory *per se*. There are a wide variety of nonmemorial dissociative intrusions that impinge on every aspect of human experience and functioning (Dell, 2009c).

46.13.6 The Intrusion of Unintegrated Parts or Behavioral States

As Putnam's (1997) theory of discrete behavioral states makes clear, behavioral states vary in how well-integrated they are with one another. Relatively unintegrated behavioral states have received many names. A partial list of names for unintegrated behavioral states includes "mental disaggregation" (Janet), "alter personalities" (many authors), "hypnoid states" (Breuer), "a second psychical group" (Freud), "complexes" (Jung), "the apparently normal personality" and "the emotional personality" (C. S. Myers, 1940; Van der Hart, Nijenhuis, & Steele), "ego states" (Watkins), and "defensively unlinked islands of self-experience" (Bromberg, 1998), and "dissociated structures" (Dell, this chapter). See Dell (2009c) for a longer historical discussion of unintegrated states (or "parts").

Unintegrated states or parts differ in complexity or degree of elaboration. The more that the part is complex and elaborated, and the more that it is not integrated with other parts of the mind, the more these other parts will experience the first part's activity as an automatism—that is, as an automatic, involuntary, and unexpected intrusion into his or her conscious functioning (see Dell 2006c, 2009c). Unintegrated parts or behavioral states produce, by far, the vast majority of the dissociative intrusions to which humans are subject.

I draw a sharp distinction between the intrusion of an unintegrated part and the intrusion of a dissociated memory because they seem to have different mechanisms and different phenomena. With some exceptions,[80] the intrusion of dissociated memories seems to be *a passive process* (in which repression collapses and the activated memory intrudes into consciousness).[81] In contrast, nonmemorial intrusions (by an unintegrated part or behavioral state) seem to be *an active psychological process* (in which a more or less autonomous part of the mind is activated by its own concerns). These autonomous responses and actions then intrude, utterly unexpectedly, into the person's conscious functioning.

As I have described elsewhere (Dell, 2006c, 2009c), unintegrated behavioral states and parts can and do intrude upon every aspect of human conscious functioning—behavior, perception, affect, ideation, bodily experience, and so on. In turn, these intrusions can be described in terms of several dimensions of subjective intrusiveness. For example, almost all of these intrusions are unexpected, involuntary, and uncontrollable, but they vary along dimensions of subjective explicability-inexplicability, the person's equanimity-surprise, and the person's degree of self-confusion. Perhaps most important is the dimension of "mineness." At the lower end of this dimension of subjective experience, the intrusions are felt to be involuntary, uncontrollable, and probably somewhat confusing, but they are still very much considered by the person to be "mine." At the higher end of this dimension, dissociative intrusions are increasingly felt to be inexplicable and "not mine" (see also, Dell, 2009c).

[79] Note that, unlike the distorted memories of repressive derivatives (as discussed by psychoanalytic theory), the content of these memories is neither changed nor distorted. In my proposed framework, only the memories' *experiential quality* is changed.

[80] Alter personalities and ego states sometimes report that they deliberately thrust into consciousness a memory, idea, or image that they want the person to face.

[81] Memorial intrusions may also be (actively) driven by a neurobiological automatism (i.e., by an eruption of the amygdalar fear system).

Unlike psychotic patients, however, dissociative patients have intact reality testing. Thus, despite their bewildering sense that some of their reactions and behaviors are "not mine," dissociative persons usually do not explain their intrusions via delusional attributions of external control; they know that these intrusions come from within. At most, they have the experience (and the idea) that the intrusions come from another part inside.

46.13.7 Psychotic Intrusions (Some Schneiderian First-Rank Symptoms)

At this point, it should be readily apparent to the reader that many of Kurt Schneider's (1959) first-rank symptoms of schizophrenia include perceived intrusions into the conscious functioning of the person: "made" actions, "made" impulses, "made" emotions, influences playing on the body, thought insertion, thought withdrawal, voices commenting, and voices arguing (see Dell, 2006c; Kluft, 1987; Ross et al., 1990). Despite their similarities to dissociative intrusions, however, Schneider's intrusions appear to have a different mechanism. Whereas the mechanism of dissociative intrusions seems to be psychological, the mechanism of psychotic delusions of control appears to be neurobiological.

46.13.8 Intrusions Are Automatisms

In summary, then, we can assert that intrusions are automatisms—unexpected, involuntary, and largely uncontrollable invasions of conscious functioning.[82] In the late 19th century and the early 20th century, the term *automatism* was used as a synonym for dissociation. The preceding sections on intrusions, however, show that there are many kinds of intrusion, only some of which are dissociative. Thus, it would be incorrect to assert that all automatisms are "dissociative."

Earlier in this chapter, we reviewed Janet's participation in the 19th-century debate about automatisms. For Janet (and others such as F. W. H. Myers), the question was: Are all automatisms purely physiological, or are some automatisms psychological? Both my analysis of intrusions and the writings of Janet and F. W. H. Myers argue that automatisms are, indeed, heterogeneous; some automatisms (i.e., some intrusions) are dissociative, but others are not. In fact, I contend that automatisms can be meaningfully sorted into three classes: (1) normal, evolution-prepared, biological automatisms; (2) abnormal neurobiological and neurological automatisms; and (3) psychological automatisms.

A proper clarification of dissociative phenomena requires that we specify the relationship between dissociative intrusions and these different classes of automatism. I will argue that different automatisms (and different intrusions) have different mechanisms, and that one or more different kinds of dissociative intrusion are generated by each of these three classes of automatisms.

46.14 AUTOMATISMS AND DISSOCIATION

46.14.1 Evolution-Prepared Biological Automatisms

Automatisms that emanate from an intact or normally functioning neural system are normal, evolution-prepared biological automatisms.

Evolutionary pressures and natural selection have provided humans (and other animals) with preset physiological and behavioral reaction patterns (i.e., automatisms) that facilitate survival. Various bodies of literature have conceptualized these evolution-prepared automatisms in terms of instincts, fixed behavior patterns, animal defenses, and so on. We have already discussed one such biological automatism—the evolution-prepared, survival-related dissociative responses that spontaneously occur at moments of life-threat. As already noted, evolution-prepared dissociative responses are normal, time-limited, and highly adaptive.

Frewen and Lanius (2006) have noted that 30% of persons with PTSD respond to trauma scripts with hypoarousal and dissociative distancing; they suggest that this dissociative response is an evolution-prepared, animal defense reaction. Thus, they argue that about 30% of PTSD patients react to reminders of their trauma with the same evolution-prepared dissociative survival response that Nature "meant" to assist us with an actual threat to life. If Frewen and Lanius are correct, in about 30% of PTSD patients an evolution-prepared dissociative response inhibits the near-instantaneous subcortical eruption from the amygdalar fear system (that is triggered by trauma scripts in the other 70% of PTSD patients). As noted earlier, one of the crucial "purposes" of evolution-prepared dissociation is to inhibit the fear system so that the person can cope with the emergency (rather than being paralyzed with terror).

Lanius et al. (2007) have reported that some of their PTSD subjects simultaneously had *both* a flashback and

[82] But not all automatisms breed conscious intrusions. Some automatisms are purely physiological; their occurrence does not require the presence of consciousness. In this chapter, intrusions are defined as a *subjective conscious phenomenon*.

dissociative distancing. Lanius also reported that some of their PTSD subjects had hyperarousal and a flashback on one occasion and hypoarousal and dissociative distancing on another. Taken as a whole, these findings present a compelling picture of incipient flashbacks (in about 30% of persons with PTSD) that reflexively trigger a normal, evolution-prepared survival response. When this sequence (i.e., incipient flashback followed by dissociative distancing) repeatedly occurs, it constitutes a perverse neural dynamic that can only lead to a variety of use-dependent changes in neurochemistry and neuroanatomy (Perry et al., 1995).[83] Thus, dissociation-related, neurobiological changes would seem to be inevitable in this 30% of persons with PTSD.

The bottom line here is that this normal biological automatism (i.e., evolution-prepared dissociation) can be triggered under two sets of circumstances: (1) imminent threat to life, and (2) stimuli that remind the person of imminent threat to life. In the latter case, some aspect of the person's neurophysiology would appear to be *hypersensitive* (e.g., the periaqueductal gray animal defense system, the amygdalar fear system, or the glucocorticoid system; Koenen et al., 2005) and/or *impaired* (e.g., frontal cortical inhibition mechanisms). Hyperreactive evolution-prepared dissociation is probably best considered to be an abnormal neurobiological automatism. In this sense, hyperreactive evolution-prepared dissociation is similar to dissociative flashbacks; in both cases, a normal biological capacity has been "hijacked" by an abnormal neurobiological automatism.

46.14.2 Abnormal Neurological and Neurobiological Automatisms

Although *all* automatisms necessarily have a neurobiological or neurological foundation, I prefer to limit the class of neurological and neurobiological automatisms to *automatic manifestations of a damaged or abnormally functioning nervous system.* The prototype of the abnormal neurological automatism is the anarchic or alien hand. Anarchic hand occurs in some persons who suffer from a damaged frontal lobe (Marchetti & Della Sala, 1998). In these persons, the contralateral hand autonomously and uncontrollably grasps and turns doorknobs, seizes writing utensils and begins to scribble, and so on. These anarchic behaviors often provoke the person to try to restrain the errant hand (as did Peter Sellers in *Dr. Strangelove* when his anarchic hand would suddenly make a Nazi salute).

PTSD includes at least two major forms of abnormal neurobiological automatism—PTSD intrusive symptoms (including hypersensitive amygdalar fear reactions) and hypersensitive startle reactions. I have suggested that these abnormal automatisms of PTSD sometimes "hijack" normal biological functioning, thereby producing two different forms of dissociation: (1) dissociative flashbacks, and (2) reflexive dissociative distancing (i.e., evolution-prepared dissociation). I have also suggested previously that the tonic dissociative distancing of Depersonalization Disorder (and its accompanying phasic suppression of aversive emotions) is a neurological or neurobiological disorder, rather than a psychological disorder.

If these speculations are correct, then at least three forms of dissociation are manifestations of a neurological or neurobiological disorder: (1) dissociative flashbacks in PTSD, (2) reflexive dissociative distancing (i.e., hyperreactive evolution-prepared dissociation in persons with PTSD), and (3) chronic dissociative distancing (i.e., Depersonalization Disorder).

Some researchers consider PTSD to be a dissociative disorder (e.g., Van der Hart et al., 2006; Van der Kolk, van der Hart, & Marmar, 1996). As a group, PTSD patients have a moderately high level of dissociation (Spiegel, Hunt, & Dondershine, 1988). Elevated dissociation, however, is by no means universal in PTSD. Research and clinical experience has consistently shown that some PTSD patients have elevated levels of dissociation, whereas others do not (e.g., Bremner, 1999; Lanius et al., 2002; Putnam et al., 1996; Waelde, Silvern, & Fairbank, 2005).

My point here is that this evidence fails to support the contention that PTSD is a dissociative disorder. True, many persons with PTSD are dissociative, but most are not. This pattern (of elevated dissociation in a significant minority of persons with PTSD) is typical of what occurs when two disorders (in this case, PTSD and a dissociative disorder) share a common etiological factor (in this case, trauma). Thus, PTSD and, for example, DID are both *posttraumatic* conditions, but they are not both *dissociative* conditions. The bottom line is that PTSD is a posttraumatic condition, which is often comorbid with a second posttraumatic condition (i.e., dissociative disorder), but PTSD itself is not a dissociative disorder.

This conclusion, in turn, invites the question, If this is so, then why do some authorities insist that PTSD is a dissociative disorder? I think that the crux of the matter is the intrusive symptoms of PTSD, especially flashbacks.

[83] Of course, repeated flashbacks that are not accompanied (or parried) by dissociative episodes generate their own pattern of use-dependent neurological changes.

Flashbacks are automatisms—spontaneous, uncontrollable intrusions into the person's consciousness and executive functioning. As automatisms, they have a marked dissociative quality. The crucial question, however, is, What kind of automatisms are they? Are they unmotivated *neurological* automatisms like a reflexive knee-jerk? Are they *evolution-prepared* automatisms like the automatic depersonalization and derealization that is triggered by life-threat? Or are they motivated *psychological* automatisms like the intrusions of a dissociated structure or the unconsciously motivated intrusions from sensory/motor conversion symptoms? Despite their automatic dissociative quality, I think that the intrusive symptoms of PTSD are best understood to be abnormal neurological automatisms.

Finally, before discussing psychological automatisms, it bears mentioning that, unlike psychological automatisms, neither normal evolution-prepared biological automatisms nor abnormal neurological or neurobiological automatisms have a personal motivation or a connection to the conscious self. They are simply spontaneous and uncontrollable patterns of neurophysiologic reaction.

46.14.3 Psychological Automatisms

Table 46.2 delineates three classes of dissociative disorder. Two of these are *psychological* automatisms (i.e., dissociated structures and self-hypnotic negations of psychological function [i.e., sensory/motor conversion symptoms and generalized amnesia]). Thus, the bottom line about dissociative disorders is that *the vast majority of dissociative symptoms are psychological automatisms.*

As discussed earlier in this chapter, the essential features of psychological dissociative symptoms are three. First, these psychological automatisms emerge from a normal, intact nervous system. Second, these psychological automatisms are, at some level, personally motivated. Third, dissociative persons realize that their dissociative automatisms are abnormal. These facts, I think, are relatively straightforward. I suspect, however, that it has been difficult to "see" this simple account of psychological automatisms because its simplicity has been obscured by the extensive heterogeneity of automatisms, intrusions, and other dissociative-like phenomena.

For example, the dissociative disorders field is confronted with at least five kinds of dissociative intrusion: (1) peritraumatic dissociation, (2) Depersonalization Disorder, (3) the intrusive symptoms of PTSD, (4) the dissociative intrusions of DID and DDNOS-1, and (5) conversion symptoms. These different kinds of dissociative intrusion resemble one another, but they are not the same. They have different underlying mechanisms—and only two of them (4 and 5) are predominantly psychological in nature. This problem of heterogeneous dissociative intrusions is further complicated by the fact that instruments that measure dissociation do not distinguish among these five kinds of dissociation. Dissociation instruments simply assess the overall frequency of automatisms (Dell, 2008), but they do not specify the *kinds* of automatisms that are being experienced.

46.15 THE CAUSES OF DISSOCIATION

Many clinicians and researchers have discussed the *causes* of dissociation. They have variously ascribed dissociation to a cognitive deficit that causes mental disaggregation (Janet, Nijenhuis, Van der Hart, Steele), high hypnotizability (Breuer, Bliss, Spiegel, Cardeña, Butler), trauma (Putnam, Kluft, Braun, Ross), suggestion and social role (Orne, Spanos, Bowers, Spanos, Kirsch, Lynn), high dissociativity (Breuer, Carlson, Putnam), compartmentalization (Cardeña, van der Kolk, Van der Hart, Marmar, Holmes, Brown), detachment (Cardeña, Holmes, Brown, van der Kolk), animal defenses (Nijenhuis, Frewen, Lanius), and discrete behavioral states (Putnam). The best discussion to date of the causes of dissociation is probably that of Putnam (1997).

For the most part, however, these etiological accounts have tended to be piecemeal and underdeveloped. The fragmentary nature of these accounts is largely due to the fact that the field of dissociation still lacks consensus about the definition of dissociation. In the following sections, I will attempt to sketch the causes of the five kinds of dissociation which I defined in section 46.11.

Aristotle divided explanation into four components that have generally been referred to as Aristotle's four causes, or Aristotle's four "becauses" (Hocutt, 1974): efficient causes, material causes, formal causes, and final causes. In most cases, an adequate explanation of a phenomenon requires an understanding of all four causes. I will use Aristotle's four aspects of explanation to explain the five kinds of dissociation (i.e., dissociation-potentiated repression, intrusions of dissociated structures, evolution-prepared dissociation, Depersonalization Disorder, and Conversion Disorder).[84]

[84] This etiological analysis of dissociation was inspired, and substantially enabled, by Killeen and Nash's (2003) Aristotelian explication of hypnosis.

46.15.1 Efficient Causes of Dissociation

Efficient causality refers to the collection of traits, circumstances, and events that are jointly necessary for (i.e., which can trigger) the occurrence of the phenomenon in question. Note that the efficient causes of a phenomenon are always plural; there is never a single efficient cause.

If all of the necessary causes of a phenomenon, but one, are present, then that phenomenon will be triggered when the missing cause is added. The introduction of that missing cause becomes "the straw that breaks the camel's back," so to speak. Under these circumstances (i.e., the presence of all necessary causes, but one), adding the missing cause is sufficient to trigger the phenomenon in question. Under those circumstances, that missing cause is called a *necessary and sufficient cause*. Conversely, the totality of circumstances that make it possible for that "last straw" to trigger the phenomenon are *necessary but not sufficient causes*. If all of the necessary causes are not present, a (supposedly) sufficient cause will not trigger the phenomenon.

For example, we speak of PTSD as being caused by trauma—but trauma does not always cause PTSD. The research literature is very clear on this point; only about 25% of persons who are exposed to serious trauma develop PTSD. Said differently, trauma is *necessary but not sufficient* to cause PTSD. Trauma can only be sufficient to trigger the development of PTSD when the other necessary causes of PTSD are present (e.g., certain hereditary, biological, psychological, and neuroanatomical factors). Thus, the efficient cause of PTSD is the simultaneous presence of all of its necessary causal factors—trauma, heredity, psychology, biology, neuroanatomy, and so on. Properly, research on the etiology of PTSD seeks to identify *all* of its necessary causes. Such research is not solely concerned with the traumas that are sufficient (when all of the other necessary causes are *also* present) to trigger the development of PTSD. To the extent that research on PTSD has overemphasized trauma (and I think that it has), then PTSD research has underemphasized the other necessary causes of PTSD (which collectively explain why only 25% of traumatized persons develop PTSD).

Similarly, we often say that dissociation is caused by trauma, but all traumas do not cause dissociation. Most victims of natural disasters or interpersonal violence (including child abuse) do not develop a dissociative disorder. If trauma is truly a major causal factor of dissociation—and I believe that it is—then it is clear that *trauma is a necessary but not sufficient cause of dissociative disorder.* Trauma can only be sufficient to cause a dissociative disorder when the other necessary causes of pathological dissociation are also present (e.g., hereditary factors, hypnotic ability, dissociative ability, psychological factors, neuroanatomical factors, etc.). Research on the etiology of pathological dissociation must identify all of its necessary causes—not just the traumas that are sufficient (when all of the other necessary causes are present) to trigger the development of a dissociative disorder.

46.15.1.1 Dissociation-Potentiated Repression

The efficient cause of dissociation-potentiated repression is the simultaneous presence of its jointly necessary causes. Although there are likely to be some complexities involved, there are probably only two necessary causes of this phenomenon—motivation and ability. Thus, the necessary causes of dissociation-potentiated repression are (1) a motivated mental effort to escape discomfort by pushing uncomfortable realities out of conscious awareness; and (2) a high level of dissociative ability.

All of us (at times) seek to avoid thinking about unpleasant matters, but only those of us who possess substantial dissociative ability can successfully *dissociate* the memories of important, but unpleasant realities. When a person possesses that ability, then a strongly motivated mental effort to escape that unpleasantness may be sufficient to cause dissociation.

46.15.1.2 Intrusions from Dissociated Structures

The efficient cause of intrusions from dissociated structures is the simultaneous presence of its jointly necessary causes: (1) the existence of a dissociated structure—which, itself, already required (a) the existence of substantial dissociative ability and (b) a previous motivated effort to escape conscious awareness of unpleasant realities (see preceding discussion); and (2) circumstances that activate the dissociated structure. When a person has a dissociated structure, the presence of a yet-to-be-delineated set of activating circumstances is sufficient to cause dissociative intrusions.

Each dissociated structure, and the particular brain that embodies it, specify the circumstances that can activate that particular dissociated structure (Maturana, 1978). If the dissociated structure contains memories of sexual abuse, then the appropriate set of activating circumstances will activate those memories. Whether those memories then become conscious will depend on a variety of yet-to-be-delineated aspects of that person's neural functioning (see previous section on "Intrusions into Consciousness"). If the dissociated structure is an alter personality that has developed substantial functional autonomy (from its original traumatic events), then the alter personality may be activated by circumstances that pertain to its *non*-trauma-related interests (see, for example, Prince, 1921).

46.15.1.3 Evolution-Prepared Dissociation

The efficient cause of evolution-prepared dissociation is the simultaneous presence of (1) an evolution-prepared mechanism for effective and near-instantaneous responses to a threat to life; and (2) life-threatening circumstances. Because all humans possess these evolution-prepared mechanisms for dissociation, an imminent threat to life is usually a sufficient cause for dissociation (e.g., Heim, 1892/1990; Noyes & Kletti, 1976). On the other hand, there are almost certainly individual differences in the sensitivity and readiness-to-activate of these evolution-prepared mechanisms.

Many (most?) PTSD patients do not report much dissociation, but a significant minority do (e.g., Bremner, 1999; Lanius et al., 2002; Putnam et al., 1996; Waelde, Silvern, & Fairbank, 2005). The presence or absence of dissociation in persons with PTSD may, in many instances, be caused by individual differences in the sensitivity of evolution-prepared mechanisms of dissociation (see Frewen & Lanius, 2006).

For example, laboratory research on PTSD has consistently found that about 30% of persons with chronic PTSD respond to trauma scripts with a dissociative episode (i.e., hypoarousal and dissociative distancing):

> [H]ypoaroused subjects did not have an increase in heart rate while remembering their traumatic memory. Instead, they reported feeling distanced from their experience of the memory; some said that they were "zoned out," or "out of their body." (Pain et al., 2009, p. 378)[85]

Conversely, 70% of PTSD subjects respond to trauma scripts with hyperarousal and/or flashbacks (e.g., Frewen & Lanius, 2006; Lanius, Bluhm, & Lanius, 2007; Pain, Bluhm, & Lanius, 2009).

The point here is that hyperarousal/flashback versus hypoarousal/dissociation is a major individual difference among persons with PTSD. And, if Frewen and Lanius (2006) are correct, hyperarousal versus hypoarousal is, specifically, an individual difference in the sensitivity or readiness-to-activate of evolution-prepared dissociative mechanisms. If so, this would mean that about 30% of persons with PTSD have overly sensitive evolution-prepared mechanisms of dissociation. Such overly sensitive mechanisms activate when the person encounters a mere reminder of life-threat.

46.15.1.4 Depersonalization Disorder

Considerably less is known about the efficient causes of Depersonalization Disorder (Simeon & Abugel, 2006). Whereas the preceding three kinds of dissociation are typically triggered by emotional pain and/or threat to life, this is not always the case with Depersonalization Disorder. Although the onset of Depersonalization Disorder is sometimes related to stress, it is rarely related to frank trauma or abuse (with the possible exception of emotional abuse; Simeon et al., 2001). Finally, Medford and colleagues (2006) suggest that persons with depersonalization employ a cognitive strategy that successfully protects them from aversive emotions.

The bottom line, however, is that the necessary causes of Depersonalization Disorder are largely unknown. The onset of the disorder is related to severe stress (about 25%), episodes of (another) mental illness (about 20%), and drugs—especially marijuana and hallucinogens (about 20%). Onset may also occur without any known trigger. An as-yet-unknown diathesis is hypothesized. Simeon, for example, suggests that relatively ordinary (albeit strong) sources of stress can trigger Depersonalization Disorder in "a vulnerable individual presumably prone to dissociating" (Simeon & Abugel, 2006, p. 37). This proneness to dissociating is due to "some underlying neurochemical vulnerability" (Simeon & Abugel, 2006, p. 22).

46.15.1.5 Type II Normal Dissociation and Conversion Disorder

The efficient cause of Type II Normal Dissociation (and uncomplicated Conversion Disorder) is the simultaneous presence of its jointly necessary causes. Similar to dissociation-potentiated repression, there are probably two necessary causes of Conversion Disorder—motivation and ability (see also Killeen & Nash, 2003). Thus, the necessary causes of simple Conversion Disorder are (1) a strong wish to escape or to alter a chronically unpleasant set of interpersonal circumstances; and (2) a moderate-to-high level of hypnotizability or dissociativity. The mental effort to escape an unpleasant interpersonal reality suggests that something akin to repression (i.e., mental escape from an unpleasant reality) is operative in Conversion Disorder.

[85] Van der Kolk, van der Hart, and Marmar (1996) have referred to such dissociative distancing as "secondary dissociation." According to them, primary dissociation consists of unintegrated traumatic experience that generates fragmentary flashbacks (e.g., Van der Kolk & Fisler, 1995). Tertiary dissociation entails the development of "ego states that contain the traumatic experience, consisting of complex identities with distinctive, cognitive, affective, and behavioral patterns" (p. 308).

46.15.2 Material Causes of Dissociation

Material causes are the "hard science" of explanation. In psychiatry and psychology, material cause refers to the neuroanatomical, neurobiological, and genetic substrates of a phenomenon. The neuroscience and genetics of dissociation are still in their infancy, but there are already a few intriguing findings, mostly from neuroimaging studies.

46.15.2.1 Dissociation-Potentiated Repression

Nothing is yet known about the genetics of dissociation-potentiated repression. Similarly, little is known about its neurobiological or neuroanatomical underpinnings. If, as hypothesized, dissociation-potentiated repression is enabled by high hypnotizability, then neuroscientific and genetic studies of hypnotic phenomena may shed some light on the matter.

Kihlstrom (2003) has cautioned that there may be no specific or unique neural correlates of hypnosis or hypnotizability. For some tasks, this is certainly true (e.g., Haggard, Cartledge, Daffyd, & Oakley, 2004), but recent findings increasingly suggest that there are important hypnosis-related differences in neuroanatomy, neural activation, and genetics. For example, Horton, Crawford, Harrington, and Downs (2004) have reported a neuroanatomical difference in highly hypnotizable persons who possess the ability to block pain in response to hypnotic suggestion. These subjects were found to have a significantly larger rostrum (i.e., an area of the corpus callosum, which facilitates the transfer of information between the left and right prefrontal cortices).

Hoeft, Reiss, Whitfield-Gabrieli, Gabrieli, Greicius, Menon, and Spiegel (2008) examined the functional coherence of regions of brain activation in high and low hypnotizables during a resting state. The results indicated a clear difference in the functional connectivity of high and low hypnotizable subjects. Specifically, the dorsal ACC (BA 32) drove the resting state network (see Gusnard & Raichle, 2001) more in high hypnotizables than in low hypnotizables. Conversely, the ventrolateral prefrontal cortex (BA 47, 45) drove the resting state network more in low hypnotizables than in high hypnotizables.

Szechtman et al. (1998) found a difference in the neural activation of those highly hypnotizable subjects who could produce realistic auditory hallucinations in response to hypnotic suggestion. Specifically, these subjects showed a wider activation of the auditory cortex (by a factor of 7 to 8 times) *during ordinary (nonhypnotic) hearing.*

Interestingly, a recent MRI study reported that BPD patients with a comorbid diagnosis of DID or Dissociative Amnesia had larger left postcentral gyri (i.e., left primary somatosensory cortex; BA 1,2, and 3) than did BPD patients and healthy controls without such dissociative diagnoses (Irle, Lange, Weniger, & Sachsse, 2007).

Genetic research on hypnotizability is just beginning. To date, only "the dopamine hypothesis" of hypnotizability has received some empirical support. Lichtenberg has twice reported that polymorphisms of catechol-*O*-methyltransferase (COMT), an enzyme associated with dopamine metabolism, is significantly associated with hypnotizability as measured by the SHSS:C (Lichtenberg, Bachner-Melman, Gritsenko, & Ebstein, 2000; Lichtenberg, Bachner-Melman, Ebstein, & Crawford, 2004). Specifically, the heterozygous valine/methionine allele of COMT was significantly associated with higher hypnotizability in the whole sample ($r = 0.30$), in women ($r = 0.38$), but not in men ($r = 0.21$). Raz, Fan, and Posner (2006) also reported that the COMT valine/methionine allele was associated with higher hypnotizability. Relatedly, Spiegel and King (1992) found that cerebrospinal fluid levels of homovanillic acid (HVA), a metabolite of dopamine, was significantly correlated with hypnotizability.

Subsequent research by Lichtenberg has produced mixed support for the dopamine hypothesis. On the one hand, a study of the relationship between hypnotizability and prepulse inhibition (PPI), a technique for assessing primary unconscious information processing, showed that, as predicted, low hypnotizables showed a significantly greater PPI than medium and high hypnotizables (Lichtenberg et al., 2007). This finding supports the hypothesis that reduced dopaminergic tone is associated with both lower hypnotizability and increased PPI. On the other, the dopamine hypothesis is not supported by a study of hypnotizability and the blink rate (Lichtenberg et al., 2008). Although the blink rate is known to increase as a function of increased central dopaminergic tone, increased blink rate was not associated with high hypnotizability (as the dopamine hypothesis would require).

Dissociation-potentiated repression removes an unpleasant reality from conscious awareness. As such, amnesia is the defining phenomenon of dissociation-potentiated repression. As long as the amnesia is sustained, the repression or dissociation is successful. There is, however, no research on the material substrates of remote localized amnesia (i.e., the primary symptom of repression) in persons who do not suffer from a major dissociative disorder. On the other hand, there are some very interesting neuroimaging studies of amnesia in persons with DID.

In PET studies of DID patients (which contrasted host personalities with traumacentric personalities under two memory script conditions [i.e., neutral and trauma-related]), Reinders et al. (2003, 2006) reported that patterns of neural activation of host personalities and traumacentric personalities did not differ during *neutral* memory scripts, but differed profoundly during *trauma-related* memory scripts. Interestingly, the neural activation of *host personalities* (who disown memory of trauma) did not differ as a function of neutral versus trauma-related memory scripts, but the neural activation of traumacentric personalities (who do own memories of trauma) did differ as a function of neutral versus trauma-related memory scripts.

Specifically, during trauma-related memory scripts, *traumacentric personalities* manifested a significantly increased activation of the left parietal operculum and insula. These areas of the brain play a role in regulating emotional and behavioral reactions to pain (Sawamoto et al., 2000) and other distressing somatosensory cues (Reiman, 1997). In addition to the increased activation of the left parietal operculum/insula, *traumacentric* personalities manifested a pervasive *deactivation* of the right superior frontal gyrus (Brodmann Area [BA] 10), right and left frontal gyrus (BA 6), right and left intraparietal sulcus (BA 7/40), right and left parieto-occipital sulcus (BA 18/precuneus), and the left middle occipital gyrus (BA 19). These areas collectively pertain to the conscious processing and integration of somatosensory experience. The deactivation of these areas during trauma-related memory scripts allows traumacentric personalities to vividly (re)experience the traumas. Conversely, the unchanged activation of these areas in *host personalities* indicates that they processed traumatic material in the same way that they processed neutral material. This unusual performance is strongly reminiscent of persons with Depersonalization Disorder, who process aversive stimuli in the same way that they process neutral stimuli (Medford et al., 2006). Reinders et al. consider the host personalities' unchanged activation of these areas in the face of a trauma script to be a defensive response that *prevents* the host personality (ANP) from (re)experiencing the trauma. According to Reinders and colleagues, the host personality

> seems to apply a censor mechanism to avoid access to or subsequent processing of at least a part of the painful memories.... [W]hen listening to the trauma-related memory script, compared to [traumacentric personalities], [host personalities] display ... perfusion differences in brain areas associated with inhibition of emotional responses to trauma-related information and with depersonalization. (Reinders et al., 2006, p. 730–731)

This view of neural defensiveness in host personalities is also supported by the results of Hermans's et al. (2006) study of DID host personalities, DID traumacentric personalities, and healthy simulators of these personalities. Using a pictorial emotional Stroop test, Hermans et al. exposed subjects to angry or neutral faces for 30 ms, followed by backward masking with color-congruent stimuli. The dependent variable was the latency of subjects' verbal identification of the color of the masking picture. Compared to simulators, host personalities had significantly shorter response latencies to masked angry faces than to masked neutral faces, whereas traumacentric personalities had significantly longer response latencies to masked angry faces than to masked neutral faces. Hermans and colleagues interpreted these results to reflect an adaptive defensiveness in host personalities (and an adaptive focus on threat by traumacentric personalities):

> We interpret these shorter color-naming latencies in [DID host personalities] as an adaptive response ... preventing uncontrollable fear, which helps to cope with social threat cues in a way that enables them to function in daily life. (p. 235)

These studies, which support a role for preattentive defensiveness in dissociative amnesia, are consistent with the hypothesized neurobiological mechanisms of dissociative amnesia that were previously proposed (in the section entitled "Activated Thoughts That Do Not Intrude").

46.15.2.2 Intrusions from Dissociated Structures

There are, as yet, no publications in the dissociation literature that investigate the neurobiological or neuroanatomical underpinnings of intrusions from dissociated structures. Studies of other kinds of intrusions, however, have been conducted by investigators of (1) the neural underpinnings of the first-rank symptoms of schizophrenia (Schneider, 1959) and (2) the neural correlates of the experience of agency. These two bodies of research are relevant to intrusions from dissociated structures because dissociative intrusions are phenomenologically similar to (1) psychotic intrusions (i.e., certain first-rank symptoms) and (2) nonagentic experiences (i.e., the experience of not being the agent of one's "own" actions). In particular, both dissociative patients and psychotic patients undergo involuntary intrusions into their executive functioning and sense of self (Dell, 2009c). Although it is probable that different mechanisms underlie the intrusions of schizophrenia and the intrusions of dissociated structures, it is also likely that these two kinds of intrusions have some common neuroanatomical underpinnings.

Studies of the neural correlates of first-rank symptoms in persons with schizophrenia have consistently reported the presence of right parietal hyperactivation (BA 40/7; Franck, O'Leary, Flaum, Hichwa, & Andreasen, 2002; Ganesan, Hunter, & Spence, 2005; Spence et al., 1997). Impressively, schizophrenics *without* first-rank symptoms did not manifest parietal hyperactivation (Ganesan et al., 2005; Spence et al., 1997). Even more impressively, the parietal hyperactivation of schizophrenics *with* first-rank symptoms was no longer present after the first-rank symptoms had remitted (Spence et al., 1997).

Closely related to these neuroimaging studies of first-rank symptoms in schizophrenia are investigations of healthy research participants under experimental conditions that (1) simulate first-rank symptoms (e.g., passive movement of the person's arm), (2) compare self-produced stimuli with externally produced stimuli, or (3) compare the person's sense of agency or control to experiences of noncontrol. The experimental literature on these topics is growing rapidly. Fortunately, the core findings of that literature are easily summarized. Namely, experiences of self-control, agency, and body ownership are consistently correlated with activation of the anterior insula. Conversely, experiences of external control, lack of agency, and lack of body ownership are consistently correlated with activation of the inferior parietal lobe (e.g., Blakemore, Wolpert, & Frith, 2000; Farrer & Frith, 2002; Farrer et al., 2007; Tsakiris, Hesse, Boy, Haggard, & Fink, 2007). This latter finding (in healthy research participants) is, of course, striking because it precisely mirrors the parietal hyperactivation of schizophrenics with first-rank symptoms.

As noted previously, there are no extant studies of the neural correlates of dissociative intrusion. The closest approximation to such research can be found in a neuroimaging study with highly hypnotic, healthy subjects who received a suggestion to experience their arm movements as being caused by a pulley (Blakemore, Oakley, & Frith, 2002). Compared to normal arm movements, the hypnotic pulley-movements of the arm produced significantly greater activation of six areas of the brain: right and left cerebellum, left inferior parietal cortex, right parietal operculum, left putamen (extending to the insula), and left prefrontal cortex. Again, we see the parietal hyperactivation. Blakemore and Frith (2003) attribute this recurrent finding to "overactivation of the cerebellar-parietal network" (p. 223).

These hypnotic neuroimaging findings are almost astounding. At the most general level, they show that hypnotic suggestion can have profound effects on neural functioning. More importantly, however, these findings specifically show that hypnotic suggestion (of one's arm being raised and lowered by a pulley) can produce brain responses that have repeatedly been shown to be associated with passivity and other nonself experiences. In short, *hypnosis can produce neural patterns that have been shown (in other research) to be correlates of the subjective experience that one's body and one's behavior belong to another.* Such experiences, of course, are routine occurrences in persons with DID (Dell, 2006c; Kluft, 1987; Ross et al., 1990). Blakemore's et al. (2002) findings raise, in an entirely new way, the importance of the experience of involuntariness in hypnotic performance and the role of hypnotizability in DID (Dell, 2008).

46.15.2.3 Evolution-Prepared Dissociation

There are no extant neuroimaging studies of evolution-prepared, peritraumatic dissociation in humans. Because of its early phylogenetic origins, evolution-prepared dissociation, like other animal defense mechanisms, is probably a bottom-up phenomenon that is rooted in the periaqueductal gray (PAG) of the midbrain. Recent research, for example, has shown that predominant neural functioning in humans shifts from the prefrontal cortex to the PAG as threat increases or as a predator comes close enough to strike (Butler et al., 2007; Mobbs et al., 2007). Recent research has also shown that increased peritraumatic dissociation is associated with two polymorphisms of the FKBP5 gene, a glucocorticoid receptor-regulating cochaperone of stress proteins, which may result in "more rapid onset of stress hormone hyperactivity after stressful life events" (Koenen et al., 2005, p. 1323).

As discussed earlier, Frewen and Lanius (2006) have proposed that the dissociative response to trauma scripts, which occurs in 30% of persons with PTSD, is an evolution-prepared defensive response. Neuroimaging has shown that this dissociative response is marked by significant activations of seven areas of the brain: superior and middle temporal gyri (BA 38), inferior frontal lobe (BA 47), occipital lobe (BA 19), parietal lobe (BA 7), medial frontal lobe (BA 10), medial prefrontal lobe (BA 9), and ACC (BA 24 and 32). Functional connectivity during this dissociative reaction showed that activation in the right insula correlated with activity in the left ventrolateral thalamus. Noting that significant activations of the occipital area (BA 19) and the parietal area (BA 7) also occurred in persons with Depersonalization Disorder (Simeon et al., 2000), Lanius et al. (2007) suggested that these activations of sensory cortices "may underlie the lack of integration of sensory experience that is characteristic of dissociative symptoms" (p. 209).

Clearly the neural correlates of this trauma-script-provoked dissociative reaction in (some) persons with PTSD is more complex than the non-trauma-related pattern of neural activity in (1) schizophrenics and (2) healthy subjects whose experiences of agency were experimentally manipulated (see preceding section). The neural correlates of this dissociative reaction (in some persons with PTSD) to a trauma script is also decidedly more complex than the neural correlates of the "nonreaction" to trauma scripts of host personalities in DID (whose pattern of neural activation to trauma scripts did not differ from their pattern of neural activation to neutral memory scripts; Reinders et al., 2006).

Finally, it may be worth recalling that several authorities on Depersonalization Disorder have suggested that it may be a vestigial biological defense mechanism (e.g., Sierra & Berrios, 1998; Simeon & Abugel, 2006).

46.15.2.4 Depersonalization Disorder

Two neural correlates of Depersonalization Disorder are very strongly related to the subjective experience of Depersonalization Disorder (Simeon et al., 2000): (1) persons with Depersonalization Disorder report a chronic sense of detachment and emotional alienation from themselves and the world around them, and (2) these persons manifest hyperactivation in areas BA 7B and BA 39 of their parietal lobes (Simeon et al., 2000). Moreover, self-report measures of the experience of depersonalization correlate 0.84 with the level of activation in BA 7B (a parietal somatosensory association area) and 0.74 with the level of activation of BA 39 (a parietal multimodal association area; Simeon et al., 2000)! Given the inevitable presence of measurement error and the use of two completely different methods of assessment (i.e., neurophysiological imaging and self-report), the size of these correlations is nothing short of stunning. These correlations essentially indicate that there is a 1:1 relationship between parietal hyperactivation and the symptoms of Depersonalization Disorder.

Alienation from the experience of body, self, and world in Depersonalization Disorder obviously has some similarity to the alienated sense of agency that occurs in the first-rank symptoms of schizophrenia and the "disowned" agency that attends certain hypnotic performances (Blakemore et al., 2002). These different forms of alienated experience (in schizophrenics, depersonalized persons, and hypnotized persons) are all accompanied by parietal hyperactivation. This congruence of findings is quite compelling; it strongly suggests that the parietal lobe causes experiences of depersonalization, derealization, bodily and affective alienation, and distortions of sense of agency. In keeping with this conclusion, Simeon et al. (2000) have also noted that disturbances of body schema are primarily associated with the parieto-occipital junction around the angular gyrus (BA 39), where visual and somatosensory information is integrated to provide an intact well-integrated body image (Benton & Sivan, 1993).

Other neural correlates of Depersonalization Disorder include activation of the left occipital area BA 19 (a visual association area) and deactivation of the right temporal lobe (BA 22; an auditory association area).

Persons with Depersonalization Disorder respond in distinctive ways to experimental tasks that confront them with emotional material. For example, persons with Depersonalization Disorder rated disgusting scenes as less emotional than did healthy controls; they also showed reduced activation of brain regions that have been shown to be related to the perception of disgust (i.e., left insula, middle and superior temporal gyri, inferior parietal lobe, bilateral ACC, and posterior cingulate gyrus). Conversely, they activated the right ventral prefrontal cortex. Overall, this pattern of neural activation indicates reduced neural response in emotion-sensitive regions of the brain and increased neural activation in brain areas associated with the control of emotions (Phillips et al., 2001).

In a study with similar implications, Medford et al. (2006) reported that neuroimaging data showed no differences when persons with Depersonalization Disorder learned emotional words versus when they learned neutral words. Thus, their neural responses to emotional and to neutral stimuli were equivalent. Curiously, they showed significantly enhanced recognition memory for words that were overtly emotional, but did not show enhanced recognition memory for neutral words that had been learned in an emotional context. Because this difference in memory performance was not reflected in patterns of neural activation, Medford and colleagues proposed that persons with Depersonalization Disorder use a cognitive strategy (whereby they process aversive emotional stimuli with the region of the brain that usually processes neutral stimuli).

In keeping with these findings (of reduced neural response to emotional stimuli), Sierra et al. (2002) reported that persons with Depersonalization Disorder manifested reduced skin conductance responses, with longer response latencies, to unpleasant pictures.

Finally, there is some evidence that Depersonalization Disorder may be associated with blunted cortisol stress reactivity, but the stronger evidence suggests that such blunting is more highly associated with severity of dissociation than with Depersonalization Disorder *per se*

(Simeon, Guralnik, Knutelska, Yehuda, & Schmeidler, 2003; Simeon et al., 2007).

46.15.2.5 Type II Normal Dissociation[86] and Conversion Disorder

The neuroimaging literature on hysterical sensorimotor conversion is a maze of inconsistency, both between (Black, Seritan, Taber, & Hurley, 2004) and even within (Ghaffar, Staines, & Feinstein, 2006) studies. The most commonly reported neural correlates of hysterical and hypnotic conversion symptoms are activation of the *orbitofrontal cortex* (Ghaffar et al., 2006; Halligan, Athwal, Oakley, & Frackowiak, 2000; Mailis-Gagnon et al., 2003; Marshall, Halligan, Fink, Wade, & Frackowiak, 1997; Ward, Oakley, Frackowiak, & Halligan, 2003), and activation of the *ACC* (Ghaffar et al., 2006; Halligan et al., 2000; Marshall et al., 1997).

Less consistently, other studies have reported the presence of activation or hypoactivation of the *thalamus* (Ghaffar et al., 2006; Mailis-Gagnon et al., 2003; Vuilleumier et al., 2001; Ward et al., 2003), and activation (Ward et al., 2003) or hypoactivation of the *basal ganglia,* especially the caudate (Vuilleumier et al., 2001).

Several investigators have concluded that hysterical symptoms are caused by ACC and frontal inhibition of normal functioning (Halligan et al., 2000; Marshall et al., 1997; Oakley, 1999b) or by a phasic frontal deactivation that prevents normal execution of movement of the paralyzed limb (Spence, Crimlisk, Cope, Ron, & Grasby, 2000). Vuilleumier, on the other hand, proposes that "attentional or motivational mechanisms might operate at the level of thalamus or basal ganglia to influence sensorimotor processes in hysterical conversion" (Vuilleumier et al., 2001, p. 1086).

Overall, it seems that investigation of hysterical and hypnotic conversion has been substantially hindered by an excess of heterogeneity—of methodologies and kinds of conversion symptom.

In keeping with my conclusion (in the previous discussion) that generalized amnesia is best understood as a conversion symptom, I will discuss generalized amnesia here. The earliest important empirical and conceptual research regarding the neuroanatomy and neurobiology of generalized amnesia was conducted by Hans Markowitsch.

Retrieval of autobiographic/episodic memory involves the right hemisphere, whereas retrieval of semantic memory involves the left hemisphere (Fink et al., 1996; Markowitsch, Fink, Thöne, Kessler, & Heiss, 1997; Tulving et al., 1994b). Markowitsch has noted that organic amnesia for autobiographical memory is accompanied by damage to the right hemisphere (Calabrese et al., 1996; Kapur, Ellison, Smith, McLellan, & Burrows, 1992; Markowitsch et al., 1993) and that dissociative amnesia for autobiographical material is accompanied by activation of the left hemisphere and a corresponding deactivation of the right hemisphere (Markowitsch, 1999, 2003; Markowitsch et al., 1997; Yasuno, Nishikawa, Nakagawa, Ikejiri, Tokunaga, Mizuta, et al., 2000). Markowitsch (1998) has proposed that dissociative amnesia is caused by "mnestic block syndrome," a trauma-related alteration of brain metabolism (which includes changes in various transmitter and hormonal systems such as GABA-agonists, glucocorticoids, and acetylcholine). According to Markowitsch, this syndrome blocks the connection between the structures that trigger retrieval and the structures in which the memory is stored.

A recent neuroimaging case study of functional retrograde amnesia reported that "the temporo-occipital part of the network known to be related to autobiographical memory was not activated" (Hennig-Fast et al., 2008, p. 3001). One year later, the patient's amnesia for autobiographical memories continued unabated, but there was moderate improvement in the activation of this network. Most notably, however, the patient's anterograde visual memory had further deteriorated, leading Hennig-Fast and colleagues to conclude that "anterograde visual memory impairment may be crucial for the perpetuation of RA [retrograde amnesia]" (p. 3002). This conclusion receives strong support from studies which show that visual memory is highly correlated with successful retrieval of autobiographical memories (Cabeza, Prince, Daselaar, Greenberg, Budde, Dolcos, LaBar, & Rubin, 2004; Greenberg & Rubin, 2003; Johnson, Foley, Suengas, & Raye, 1988; Rubin, 2005).

46.15.3 Formal Causes of Dissociation

Formal causes explain a phenomenon in terms of familiar analogies, metaphors, or models. This explanatory strategy transforms an unfamiliar phenomenon into a phenomenon that feels familiar and understandable. History shows that recent technological developments have frequently been used as explanatory metaphors. Thus, many psychological phenomena have been explained in terms of hydraulic pressure, electricity, machines, computers, and so on.

The three great explanatory metaphors of dissociation are *dividedness (and separate parts of the mind or*

[86] Some of the neuroscience literature on hypnosis and hypnotizability has already been discussed (see the section on material causes of dissociation-potentiated repression).

self), automatism, and *splitting* or *splitting-off.* These explanatory metaphors arose in the 18th and 19th century and they are still with us today (though less so for automatism).

The metaphor of dividedness is actually *older* than the field of dissociation (which began in the late 1800s) because the problem of dissociative dividedness originated with two discoveries in the late 1700s: (1) Puységur's discovery of "magnetic sleep" (i.e., artificial somnambulism) which is separated from waking consciousness by a barrier of amnesia, and (2) the initial reports of alternating or dual personalities.

Beginning with Puységur, one researcher after another has considered divided functioning to be the core of dissociation: "two different existences" (Puységur, 1784), "the double-conscious state" (Braid, 1855), "doubling of the personality" (Azam, 1876b), "second condition" (Charcot, 1889/1991), "subliminal self" and "supraliminal self" (Myers, 1888, 1889), "mental disaggregation" (Janet, 1889), simultaneous existences (Janet, 1889), "the hidden self" (James, 1890), "double consciousness" (Binet, 1890), alterations of personality (Binet, 1991), "second consciousness" (Breuer & Freud, 1893), "the waking self" and "the subwaking self" (Sidis, 1898), "disintegrated personality" (Myers, 1903), "complexes" (Jung, 1907), "co-consciousness" (Prince, 1907), "a division of consciousness" (Mitchell, 1921), "independently acting functional units" (Hart, 1927), "divided consciousness" (Hilgard, 1977), "dissociated control" (Bowers, 1992a), "structural dissociation of the personality" (Van der Hart et al., 2006), compartmentalization (Holmes et al., 2005), and so on. Thus, dividedness (and its structural consequents—i.e., separate parts of the mind or self) has been dissociation's root metaphor since the 18th century.

During the 19th century, there was much debate about "automatisms" (i.e., autonomous, involuntary intrusions into a person's conscious mental or bodily functioning). Physiologists insisted that all automatisms were "unconscious" physiological phenomena. Janet and F. W. H. Myers disagreed. They claimed that some automatisms were psychological phenomena that possessed consciousness. Indeed, Janet's (1889) foundational volume on dissociation was entitled *Psychological Automatisms*. Thus, although Janet initially explained dissociation in terms of "dividedness" and "separate parts of the mind" (i.e., mental disaggregation), "automatism" became his foundational metaphor for dissociation. This model of dissociation was taken quite seriously by others; until about 1920, scholars and investigators referred to dissociative phenomena as "automatisms" more frequently than as "dissociation."

Janet used the term *splitting* as a synonym for *division*. He proposed that the constitutional mental weakness of hysterics led to a "splitting of consciousness." Breuer and Freud (1893) adopted both Janet's idea and his phrase when they asserted that all hysteria was characterized by a "splitting of consciousness." By the time Breuer and Freud (1895) published *Studies on Hysteria*, however, Freud was insisting that hysteria involved a "splitting of the mind" (instead of consciousness) and that the split was caused by a defensive effort to push uncomfortable information out of conscious awareness (i.e., repression). This new idea—that the split in the mind was caused by an active defensive effort—rapidly led to an action metaphor: the now unconscious material had been "split off." This transformation of a structural metaphor (a split mind) into an action metaphor ("splitting off") has bedeviled discussions of dissociation ever since because this change of metaphor completely undermines the Janetian account of dissociation.

The changing popularity of these metaphors for dissociation has, I think, greatly influenced (not always for the good) our efforts to understand dissociation. For example, I would argue that discussions of dissociation are fraught with an often-unrecognized tension between structural metaphors (parts, systems, subsystems) and action metaphors (splitting-off, dissociating, etc.). Theorists seem to prefer structural metaphors, whereas clinicians often seem to prefer action metaphors. This tension replicates the century-old conflict between Janet and Freud, between dissociation and repression. I have tried to resolve this conflict via my proposed concept of dissociation-potentiated repression. Finally, the loss of the metaphor of automatism (since 1920) has, I believe, led the field to underemphasize the centrality of autonomous intrusions in dissociative phenomena. I have tried to remedy this problem by reemphasizing the intrusions of dissociated structures.

The following paragraphs examine the analogies, metaphors, and models that can help to explain each of the five kinds of dissociation that I have proposed.

46.15.3.1 Dissociation-Potentiated Repression

The motivational impetus for dissociation-potentiated repression is best portrayed via action metaphors of defense and suppression: fended off, pushed away, split off, dissociated. The best metaphor for mere repression is probably Freud's analogy of lecture-attendees who eject a disruptive audience-member from the room and then bar the door against his reentry.

These action metaphors, however, seem to refer indistinguishably to *both* mere repression and dissociation-potentiated repression (because both phenomena derive from the same motivated effort to extrude undesired information from consciousness). The difference between the two lies in the fact that, in some cases (when the individual possesses a high level of hypnotizability or dissociativity), the effort to repress may spontaneously and unexpectedly activate a second mechanism (of dissociation) that produces a qualitatively different kind of forgetting (i.e., localized, dissociative amnesia). On the other hand, if we do, indeed, contend that the two mechanisms produce different kinds of forgetting, then perhaps we might assert that *fended off* and *pushed away* are apt actions metaphors for mere repression, whereas *split off* and *dissociated* are apt action metaphors for the frank amnesia that occurs when a dissociative mechanisms is activated.

46.15.3.2 Intrusions from Dissociated Structures

There is another, even more important, difference between mere repression and dissociation-potentiated repression. Namely, dissociation-potentiated repression produces *dissociated structures* (see also Spiegel, 1990); these "hold" the unaccepted or disowned aspects of life, the self, and significant others which have been split-off. Clinicians encounter dissociated structures in the form of DID, partial DID (DDNOS-1), Possession Disorder (DDNOS-4), Dissociative Fugue, localized amnesia for past trauma, ego-state disorders, and fixed ideas.

Structural metaphors for dissociated structures have dominated theoretical discourse about dissociation for the last 3 decades: ego-states (Watkins and Watkins), systems and subsystems (Hilgard, Bowers, Woody), modularity and modules (Erdelyi, Kirmayer, Woody, Bowers), identities (DSM-IV), discrete behavioral states (Putnam), structural dissociation of the personality (Van der Hart, Nijenhuis, Steele), compartments (Holmes, Brown), and, of course, alter personalities (many).

The dominance of structural metaphors in theoretical discourse about dissociation has, unfortunately, been accompanied by a near-total absence of the metaphor of automatism. On the other hand, clinical discourse has included the concept of "passive-influence phenomena" (Kluft), which are clearly automatisms. The most penetrating recent conceptual analysis of dissociation (Holmes et al., 2005) posited two quite different kinds of dissociation: (1) compartmentalization (a structural metaphor), and (2) detachment (a phenomenological or experiential metaphor). This classification, however, omits the most common experience of dissociation—intrusions into conscious functioning (i.e., automatisms).

The second kind of dissociation that I have identified (i.e., intrusions from dissociated structures) proposes that *intrusions are the primary phenomenon of dissociated structures.* Thus, the concept of "intrusions from dissociated structures" rebalances the last century's underemphasis of automatisms (and its corresponding overemphasis of divided structures).

As noted previously, dissociated structures are experienced by the person as operating with considerable autonomy, thereby generating a wide range of recurrent automatisms such as passive-influence experiences (i.e., "made" feelings, "made" impulses, "made" actions, thought insertion, etc.), loss/alteration of identity or sense of self; incidents of amnesia; and various other dissociative symptoms. These intrusions are experienced as being involuntary, unexpected, uncontrollable, and to a greater or lesser degree "not-mine." The best metaphor for these dissociative experiences is *intrusions.* At the cultural level, however, the best known metaphor for "intrusions from dissociated structures" is undoubtedly *multiple personalities.*

46.15.3.3 Evolution-Prepared Dissociation

To the extent that a phenomenon is unfamiliar, metaphors can help to explain it. On the other hand, a familiar phenomenon often needs no metaphor. Multiple personality disorder, for example, needs no metaphor to explain it. It is its own metaphor. Somewhat similarly, evolution-prepared dissociation is familiar to the culture. Novelists and film directors routinely portray evolution-prepared dissociation. They seem to know that a severe threat to life can automatically cause derealization (which they portray via altered visual perception, altered auditory perception, and time slowing down). Accordingly, there are no ready metaphors for evolution-prepared (or peritraumatic) dissociation.

46.15.3.4 Depersonalization Disorder

As I facetiously noted previously, Depersonalization Disorder is the 800-pound gorilla of detachment. Unquestionably, as Holmes and colleagues (2005) have asserted, the best metaphor for Depersonalization Disorder is *detachment* (from the self and from the world).

46.15.3.5 Type II Normal Dissociation and Conversion Disorder

One of the central purposes of a metaphor is to render the unfamiliar familiar. Conversely, only the familiar can serve as a metaphor. The importance of this latter point is illustrated by the metaphors for the four kinds of Type II Normal Dissociation (i.e., hypnotic performance, healthy possession, creative automatisms, and transcendent experiences). Here, we find that, over and over again, *the phenomena and the metaphors are one and the same.* In fact, the phenomena of Type II Normal Dissociation are so familiar that they even serve as metaphorical explanations for *other* unfamiliar phenomena.

Thus, the primary metaphors for hypnotic performances include *hypnosis*, *hypnotized*, and *hypnotic trance*. The primary metaphors for healthy possession include *possessed*, *mediums* and *séances* (terms which are now dated), *speaking in tongues*, *channeling*, and *trance*. There are no ready metaphors for the less-familiar phenomenon of creative/productive automatisms (although *dreams* are often invoked as a partially explanatory metaphor). When creative/productive automatisms are regularly recurrent, then this phenomenon becomes indistinguishable from mediumship, channeling, or even divine inspiration. Finally, transcendent experiences seem to be well known to all cultures. In the West, the primary metaphors for transcendent experience are *religious conversion*, being saved, visitations, and spiritual experiences.

In contrast to Normal Type II Dissociation, Conversion Disorder has few metaphors. The primary metaphor for Conversion Disorder is hysteria, but hysteria is no longer understood by the culture (if it ever was). Currently, *hysterical* has become a colloquial referent for exhibiting a florid loss of emotional control. Only one form of Conversion Disorder is well-recognized by the culture—generalized amnesia. Amnesia has become its own metaphor.

46.15.4 Final Causes of Dissociation

Final causes explain *why* something happened or why something exists. For example, the final cause of a biological phenomenon describes what the phenomenon does—its function or its "purpose."

There are two classes of final explanation: (1) proximate causes, and (2) ultimate causes. *Proximate causes* explain why something happened in terms of reinforcement, intentions, and personal motivations. Proximate causes will not be discussed here; their role in causing dissociation has already been discussed under the heading of "Efficient Causes of Dissociation." *Ultimate causes* explain biological phenomena in terms of evolutionary advantage. In the present case, ultimate causes describe how dissociation facilitated survival (and reproduction) during the phylogeny of *Homo sapiens*.

46.15.4.1 Phylogenetically-Early Forms of Dissociation

The evolution of dissociation took place in at least two stages. The first stage of the evolution of dissociation actually took place prior to the emergence of hominids. Lizards and prehominid mammals had already developed a set of animal defenses that substantially increased their ability to survive predation. These defenses allowed the animal to react reflexively to stimuli that had been associated with a fatal outcome during their evolutionary history. As Perry (1999) has noted:

> The prime directive of the human brain is to promote survival and procreation. Therefore, the brain is "overdetermined" to sense, process, store, perceive and mobilize in response to threatening information from the external and internal environments. (Perry, 1999, pp. 13–14)

These overdetermined responses of the brain have been referred to as *animal defenses*. Animal defenses are attuned to specific dangers. Thus, different packages or "organized behavioral systems" (Timberlake & Lucas, 1989) are activated in response to different dangers. When an evolution-prepared defense is activated, perception is immediately adjusted and instantly tuned to the most survival-relevant aspects of the environment. Similarly, perceptual-motor modules are primed to respond instantaneously to survival-relevant stimuli with action patterns that the evolutionary history of the organism has shown to be most protective. As a component of these different evolution-prepared defense packages, different patterns of dissociation are evoked by different kinds of danger. These various dissociative defensive reactions include suppression of physical pain, suppression of emotion (especially fear), and tonic immobility.

In keeping with their early phylogenetic origin (and their need to operate with reflexive speed), these dissociative reactions are subcortical. They are located primarily in the PAG and limbic system. On the other hand, with the emergence of hominids and larger, more complex brains, subcortical animal defenses became integrated, to some degree, with the cortex. This integration allows evaluation and planning for survival to take place during the activation of dissociative survival responses (see especially the descriptions of Heim, 1892). For example:

> There was no anxiety, no trace of despair, no pain; but rather calm seriousness, profound acceptance, and a dominant mental quickness and sense of surety. Mental activity became enormous, rising to a hundred-fold velocity or intensity. The relationships of events and their probable outcomes were overviewed with objective clarity. No confusion entered at all. Time became greatly expanded. The individual acted with lightning-quickness in accord with accurate judgment of his situation. (p. 130)

Perry was among the first to link animal defenses to the known history of early humans. Specifically, Perry argued that dissociative compliance was especially important for the survival of women and children:

> As described extensively in anthropological literature, it was likely a common practice for clans of hominids to raid a competing clan's camp, drive away or kill the males and take the females and young children as property (not unlike the recent history of Western "civilization"). It promoted survival of the species if young children and females survived these raids. It was more adaptive for children to dissociate and surrender than to be hyperaroused and try a fight or flight response. In the face of threat, it was self-protective to become numb, nonhysterical, compliant, obedient, and not combative. Running would result in isolation and sure death. Fighting would be futile. (Perry et al., 1995, p. 282)

The reader should note at this juncture that some particularly important dissociative symptoms—amnesia and intrusions from dissociated structures—are *not* aspects of our PAG-driven animal defenses. Amnesia would be counterproductive for surviving predators and potential falls. *The dissociative components of animal defenses modulate sensation, affect, and movement.* Amnesia, dissociated structures, and intrusions from dissociated structures did not arise until dissociation's second stage of evolution.

I will not discuss here the evolutionary underpinnings of Depersonalization Disorder, because I believe that Depersonalization Disorder is a neurological or neurobiological dysfunction (which almost certainly lacks any evolutionary advantage). Nevertheless, Depersonalization Disorder should probably be acknowledged here because it may owe its existence to the evolution-prepared animal defenses (which, gone awry, may produce unyielding detachment).

Finally, as noted earlier in the chapter, there are no proximate final causes (i.e., personal motivations or intentions) of phylogenetically-early, evolution-prepared dissociation. On the other hand, there are always personal motivations for the phylogenetically-*recent* forms of dissociation.

46.15.4.2 Phylogenetically-Recent Forms of Dissociation

With the exception of the phylogenetically-early forms of dissociation that we have just discussed, the dissociation literature has seldom discussed the evolutionary origins of dissociation. After careful and repeated efforts to analyze the relationship between natural selection and dissociation, perhaps I have discovered why there are so few evolutionary accounts of the phylogenetically-*recent* forms of dissociation (i.e., amnesia, dissociated structures, dissociative intrusions, and Type II Normal Dissociation).

Put simply, after much thought, I have concluded that phylogenetically-recent manifestations of dissociation are *not* a direct product of evolutionary pressures. There is simply too much individual variation in dissociative abilities for this to be the case. Accordingly, I think that *individual differences in dissociative ability should be understood to be part of the variation upon which natural selection can act* (Darwin, 1859/1968). Acute selective pressures may vary from locality to locality and from time to time (perhaps thereby shifting the local population's prevalence of high dissociative ability), but, overall, the selective pressures (to which humans have been exposed over the course of evolution) have not eliminated the extensive variation of dissociative capacities that exists in the human population. Said differently, if high dissociative ability were critical to human survival, then natural selection would have ensured that we all have high levels of dissociative ability. In fact, of course, only a small minority of us have superior dissociative ability. In short, the bottom line is that *phylogenetically-recent forms of dissociation have not played a significant role in human survival.*

This conclusion burdens me with the uncomfortable task of attempting to reconcile my point of view with the evolutionary accounts of two scholars of dissociation whom I respect: Arnold Ludwig and Jennifer Freyd.

Arnold Ludwig. Ludwig's (1983) article, "The Psychobiological Functions of Dissociation," is the foundational statement in the literature about the evolutionary underpinnings of dissociation. Noting that dissociation is a remarkably widespread phenomenon, Ludwig (1983) argued that this fact alone shows that dissociation must have great evolutionary value:

> The widespread prevalence of dissociative reactions and their many forms and guises argues for their serving important functions for man and their possessing great survival value. (Ludwig, 1983, p. 95)

Certainly Ludwig is correct about most of this: dissociative reactions are widespread, they assume many forms, and they serve many important functions. But do these facts really indicate that dissociation "possesses great survival value"? Art and literature are widespread. Art and literature assume many forms. And art and literature serve many important functions. These facts, however, certainly do not prove that art and literature have great survival value. Darwinian proof of the survival value of dissociative ability would require evidence that selective pressures have produced a human population in which most or all possess high dissociative ability. There simply is no such evidence.

Take, for example, Type II Normal Dissociation. It is a special ability that is possessed by only a minority of individuals. This fact indicates that its evolutionary advantage is not great. Dissociation is obviously not a trait that kills those who lack it. Otherwise, all humans would possess a strong capacity for hypnotic performance, possession phenomena, creative automatisms, and transcendent experiences. This obviously is not the case. Thus, Type II normal dissociative ability would seem to be an individual difference that has *not* been subject to strong selection pressures. The bottom line is that, at the level of the population or species, there is no evidence that high dissociative ability increases survival.

Jennifer Freyd. In her book, *Betrayal Trauma,* Freyd (1996) has advanced a compelling hypothesis about the survival value of dissociative amnesia for children. Noting children's lengthy period of absolute dependency on their parents, Freyd contends that the ability to manifest amnesia is an essential adjunct of the attachment system. That is, children must be capable of amnesia if they are to survive abusive parents. She says:

> If a child experiencing sexual abuse were to process the betrayal in the normal way, he or she would recognize the betrayal and be motivated to stop interacting with the betrayer. Instead, the child must ignore the betrayal. If the betrayer is a primary caregiver, it is essential that the child not stop behaving in a way that inspires attachment. For the child to withdraw from a caregiver he or she is dependent on could be life-threatening. Thus, the trauma of childhood sexual abuse, by its very nature, requires that information about the abuse be blocked from the mental mechanisms that control attachment and attachment behavior. (Freyd, 1996, p. 75)

I have several thoughts about this. First, Freyd is certainly correct about the life-threatening dilemma of children with parents who are chronically abusive. Such children simply cannot afford to consciously recognize that their parents are bad and abusive. Any child in such circumstances will avoid knowing the crushing facts about his or her parents by any means available. But, dissociation is not the only means available. All children have the ability to reframe what is going on. Thus, mistreated children routinely blame themselves: "I'm bad. I ask for too much. If I weren't so bad, Mommy and Daddy would love me." And so on. Repression is another means that is available to all children; all children will consciously (and unconsciously) do their best to push out of their conscious mind the worst facts about their parents. Finally, those children who possess significant dissociative ability will probably amplify their repression with dissociation. So, my second thought about Freyd's account is that dissociative amnesia is not the only means that children use to cope with abuse. I think that she is aware of this because she prefers to lump together both repression and dissociation as means of producing forgetting.

Third, my argument against an evolutionary explanation of dissociative amnesia still holds, at least at the level of the population or species. If dissociation were critical to survival, then natural selection would have created (i.e., selected) a planet full of humans with high dissociative ability. That simply is not the case. On the other hand, the process of natural selection is driven by the environment. If *all* parents were abusive, then those selective pressures might, indeed, select a human species that is universally marked by high dissociative ability. In the absence of universally abusive parents, however, we don't know dissociation's true survival value. Still, it seems likely that dissociation would facilitate survival in a situation that is chronically dangerous. The field of dissociation generally assumes this to be the case.

Fourth, my analysis of Freyd's betrayal theory does not change its empirical implications. Betrayal trauma *is* more dangerous than other kinds of trauma; accordingly, betrayed persons will be very highly motivated to dissociate their knowledge of the betrayal (if they can). This directly implies that the incidence of amnesia in those who experience betrayal trauma will be higher than the incidence of amnesia in those who experience (only) nonbetrayal trauma.

46.15.4.3 Understanding the Difference Between Trauma and Natural Selection

Natural selection definitely "produced" our phylogenetically-*early,* evolution-prepared forms of dissociation. On the other hand, the role of natural selection in producing our phylogenetically-*recent* forms of dissociation is, at best, yet to be demonstrated. In both forms of dissociation, however, it is important for the reader to appreciate that an evolutionary perspective changes how we talk (and think) about dissociation.

Clinicians talk about dissociation as a way to reduce or block pain; this is correct, but it misses the biological "reason" for dissociation. We do not possess the capacity to dissociate so that we can ameliorate pain; rather, we possess the ability to dissociate so that we can survive

(Freyd, 1996; Dell, 2006a). In short, an evolutionary perspective shifts our understanding of dissociation away from trauma, to survival, and away from pain, to the danger of death. As Freyd (1996) put it, "Forgetting occurs not for the reduction of suffering but to stay alive" (p. 165).

But, once natural selection has produced a mechanism (that directly or indirectly serves survival), that mechanism then becomes available for purposes other than survival. Accordingly, dissociative abilities are also used (just) to minimize pain or discomfort, and to manipulate one's immediate familial/community power structure. Indeed, some people so overutilize their dissociative ability that they can be said to have a "dissociative personality disorder."

46.15.4.4 Why Do Some of Us Possess High Dissociative Ability?

If there is no evidence that evolutionary pressures have selected for high dissociative ability, then why do a minority of the population possess superior dissociative ability? The most likely answer to this question is that *high dissociative ability arises from a normal variation of other brain mechanisms that were selected by natural selection.* Thus, I propose that dissociative amnesia, dissociated structures, intrusions from dissociated structures, and Type II Normal Dissociation arise from normal variations of one or more essential structures and capacities of the human brain. It is beyond the scope of this chapter to identify these essential structures and capacities (and, indeed, I know relatively little about these matters), but I can sketch a few ideas.

1. Dissociation-potentiated repression. Amnesia is the central dissociative phenomenon of dissociation-potentiated repression. The human brain possesses a great many highly efficient mechanisms for monitoring, controlling, and manipulating information. Dissociative amnesia entails the monitoring and control of information that has already been successfully stored. Information is controlled and manipulated by many different regions or structures of the brain. Any and all of these many regions of the brain might play a role in creating and maintaining dissociative amnesia.

But, of course, only a small minority of us are capable of dissociative amnesia. This is where the normal variation comes in. All of us have coordinated movement, but only some of us have truly superior coordination. All of us have some degree of musical ability, but only some of us have truly superior musical ability. And so on. Where, exactly, do these differences lie in the brain? We don't know, but it is quite likely that normal variations of certain regions or structures of the brain produce these individual differences in ability. I propose that such normal variations also account for individual differences in dissociative ability.

2. Intrusions from dissociated structures. Those same normal variations of brain regions and structures also probably enable the creation of "dissociated structures."

Our *awareness* of the "intrusions" from dissociated structures is another matter. I think that the capacity for awareness of intrusions is universal (rather than a normal variation that occurs only in a minority of persons). On the other hand, I do not think that Nature directly selected for conscious awareness of dissociative intrusions. I think the matter is much broader than that—but deeply survival-related nevertheless.

Dissociative intrusions are automatisms—involuntary, unexpected intrusions into our functioning. Automatisms derive from neural systems, and *we are hardwired to take notice of certain automatisms.*

Neural systems are learning systems. The ability to learn is not just a new set of inconsequential evolutionary bells and whistles; the ability to learn is a huge step forward in the organism's capacity for survival. The plasticity of neural systems (i.e., their capacity to learn) allows them to form a model of their environment on the basis of past events (Sokolov, 1963). This model increases the organism's ability to respond adaptively to its environment.

Biological learning systems are *de facto* prediction-machines; they predict the events of the causal world around them. This ability to predict is their evolutionary *raison d'être;* a neural system increases an organism's ability to "fit" its environment (i.e., to behave in ways that enable it to survive). The more sophisticated an organism's neural system, the more that neural system will contain multiple neural mechanisms for (1) predicting the future responses of both the body and the environment, (2) recognizing familiar stimuli and expected outcomes, and (3) noticing stimuli or outcomes that are unexpected or novel. Stimuli that are novel or unexpected (especially unexpected stimuli that are correlated with the organism's own behavior) are often *prediction-errors* that call for immediate *attention* (and *new learning* that will update the organism's implicit map of the environment).[87]

[87] Increasingly, both learning theory and research on neural processing have focused on prediction errors (e.g., Rescorla & Wagner, 1972; Schultz & Dickinson, 2000) and the allocation of attention to unexpected stimuli and unexpected outcomes of the organism's behavior (e.g., Lisman, & Otmakhova, 2001; Mackintosh, 1975; Pearce & Hall, 1980).

Any stimulus that deviates from the expected will evoke neural reactions that immediately (re)allocate attention to that stimulus so that new learning can take place. At such moments, the novel or unexpected stimulus is highly *salient* to the organism.[88] Although human reactions to unexpected stimuli involve the cortex, the more that the unexpected stimuli point toward danger, the more that subcortical functioning will predominate over cortical functioning (e.g., Butler et al., 2007; Mobbs et al., 2007).

Phylogenetically, neural responses to unexpected stimuli (i.e., orienting and alerting) arose long before the development of human consciousness. This means that our *consciousness* of intruding automatisms is phylogenetically young; such sophisticated awareness of certain stimuli only became possible with the development of human consciousness.

The bottom line about intrusions from dissociated structures is that they are unexpected and unpredicted stimuli, which humans are "designed" to notice immediately. Nature did not specifically "intend" for us to be aware of dissociative intrusions, but Nature did very much intend for us to be consciously aware of any and all unexpected stimuli, especially unpredicted variations and outcomes of our own functioning. Thus, humans orient or alert when their dissociated structures unexpectedly intrude into their functioning.

3. Type II Normal Dissociation. I certainly do not think that Nature selected for a human capacity to have dissociative disorders. In fact, as the preceding paragraphs indicate, I doubt that Nature selected for Type II Normal Dissociation, either. Again, I strongly suspect that a superior capacity for Type II Normal Dissociation (i.e., hypnotic performance, possession phenomena, creative automatisms, and transcendent experiences) is the result of normal variations of various regions and structures of the brain. I have already mentioned my favorite example of normal variations—the Szechtman study of hypnotic auditory hallucinations (Szechtman et al., 1998; Woody & Szechtman, 2000).

This study compared high hypnotizables who could *not* experience realistic auditory hallucinations with high hypnotizables who *could* experience realistic auditory hallucinations. The hallucination-capable subjects activated more of their auditory cortex and their right rostral ACC *during nonhypnotic waking hearing.* As Szechtman et al. noted, this suggests that: "these individuals are distinct from the general population in a number of ways" (p. 1958). They then cited Wilson and Barber's (1983) findings, noting that Wilson and Barber's subjects, who could hallucinate under hypnosis, were "acutely sensitive to sensory stimuli" (p. 1958).

I believe that the findings of Szechtman and colleagues reflect normal variations in the nature and operation of the sensory cortices and the ACC. This would mean that these variations are not a product of evolutionary pressures. In short, I contend that neither superior hypnotic ability nor superior dissociative ability is the product of natural selection. They are nothing more than normal structural and functional variations of the brain, which are, nevertheless, inheritable.

[88] Heightened salience is also accorded to stimuli that the organism associates with major positive reinforcers (e.g., food, sex) or major punishing reinforcers (e.g., pain, fear).

46.16 UNDERSTANDING DISSOCIATION: PUTTING IT ALL TOGETHER

Our understanding of dissociation has long been hindered by the untoward scope of its applicability. Accordingly, much of this chapter has sought to determine what is (and what is not) dissociation. This was a helpful exercise, but it did not yield a unitary concept of dissociation. Despite eliminating a variety of *faux* dissociative phenomena (e.g., absorption and PTSD), I have been forced to conclude that the legitimate aegis of the concept of dissociation remains a broad one. Thankfully, however, the various forms of dissociation seem to share a single defining feature—the occurrence of automatisms (i.e., involuntary intrusions into conscious functioning). The following paragraphs briefly summarize this chapter's analysis of dissociation.

46.16.1 Dissociation and Repression

The relationship between dissociation and repression has been a perplexing one ever since Freud began to speak of "defense hysteria" in the 1890s. Neither the principals (i.e., Janet and Freud) nor their adherents have been able to forge a rapprochement (or even a mutually convincing analysis that distinguished the two concepts). Today, repression is rarely mentioned by members of the dissociative disorders field.

Janet defined dissociation as a deficient mode of what we would today call "information-processing," which occurred only in hysteria. In his view, hysterics are constitutionally unable to process very many stimuli at once. Under stress or illness (or trauma), their already weak capacity for integration of their experience becomes further impaired. At this point, many aspects of their ongoing experience "fall" to the side and create, or become part of, a separate region of the mind. He called this separate region of the mind "the subconscious." He called the process as a whole "mental disaggregation."

Freud defined repression in a very straightforward fashion. Repression, he said, is a motivated (and sustained) effort to push unpleasant information out of consciousness. Unlike Janet, who limited dissociation to hysterics, Freud firmly insisted that repression is a universal process that occurs in all humans.

I have argued that the primary shortcoming of Freud's concept of repression is that he never distinguished between *mere repression* and *dissociative amnesia*. To him, they were the same. He considered all motivated forgetting to be repression. Freud's indifference to the distinction between repression and dissociation meant that he was largely uninterested in individual differences in the ability to repress. I contend that those who possess substantial dissociative ability also possess superior "forgetting abilities" (compared to those who cannot dissociate, but can only repress). I concluded that a motivated effort to forget underlies both mere repression and dissociation-potentiated repression. Dissociation-potentiated repression, however, involves a second mechanism (i.e., dissociation), which produces a qualitatively different kind of forgetting. This second mechanism is not available to those who are only capable of mere repression.

46.16.2 Automatisms

Automatisms are unexpected, involuntary intrusions into one's conscious functioning. Prior to 1920, *automatisms* was the primary term for dissociative phenomena; Janet's seminal work on dissociation was *Psychological Automatisms*. I propose that all dissociative experiences are automatisms. On the other hand, there are many purely physiological or reflexive automatisms that are not usefully called "dissociative."

I described three kinds of automatism (i.e., biological/evolutionary, neurological/neurobiological, and psychological), each of which subsumes at least one of the five kinds of dissociation.

46.16.2.1 Normal Biological/Evolutionary Automatisms

Automatisms that emanate from an intact or normally functioning neural system are normal biological automatisms. Evolutionary pressures and natural selection have provided humans (and other animals) with preset physiological and behavioral reaction-patterns (i.e., automatisms) that facilitate survival. Evolution-prepared dissociation is one such biological automatism—a survival-related set of dissociative responses that spontaneously occur at moments of life-threat.

46.16.2.2 Abnormal Neurological and Neurobiological Automatisms

I limit the class of neurological and neurobiological automatisms to *automatic, intrusive manifestations of a damaged or abnormally functioning nervous system.* PTSD includes at least two major forms of abnormal neurobiological automatism—PTSD intrusive symptoms (including hypersensitive amygdalar fear reactions) and hypersensitive startle reactions. I have suggested that these abnormal automatisms of PTSD sometimes hijack normal biological functioning, thereby producing two different forms of dissociation: (1) dissociative flashbacks that hijack normal high hypnotizability, and (2) reflexive dissociative distancing, a recurrent hijacking of normal evolution-prepared dissociation (in the absence of any true threat to life). I have also proposed that the tonic dissociative distancing of Depersonalization Disorder is a neurological or neurobiological disorder, rather than a psychological disorder. In short, I have proposed that three forms of dissociation are manifestations of a neurological or neurobiological disorder: (1) dissociative flashbacks in PTSD, (2) reflexive dissociative distancing (i.e., hyperreactive evolution-prepared dissociation in persons with PTSD), and (3) chronic dissociative distancing (i.e., Depersonalization Disorder).

46.16.2.3 Psychological Automatisms

I discussed two kinds of psychological automatisms—normal ones such as normative intrusive thoughts after a major life event, and abnormal ones such as dissociative symptoms. Abnormal psychological automatisms have three essential features. First, they are produced by a normal, intact nervous system. Second, they are, at some level, personally motivated. Third, their recipients (i.e., dissociative individuals) are well-aware that their dissociative automatisms are not normal.

Because two of the three classes of dissociative disorder entail psychological automatisms (i.e., dissociated structures and Conversion Disorder), the vast majority of dissociative symptoms in any clinical population are *psychological* automatisms.

46.16.2.4 The Clinical Heterogeneity of Automatisms and Intrusions

Clinicians who treat dissociative-disordered patients are routinely confronted with a plethora of automatisms (i.e., intrusive phenomena): (1) peritraumatic dissociation,

(2) Depersonalization Disorder, (3) the intrusive symptoms of PTSD, (4) the dissociative intrusions of DID and DDNOS-1, and (5) conversion symptoms. These different kinds of dissociative intrusion resemble one another, but they are not the same. They have different underlying mechanisms. Some are normal, biological automatisms (peritraumatic dissociation); some are abnormal neurological or neurobiological automatisms (PTSD, Depersonalization Disorder); and some are abnormal psychological automatisms (conversion symptoms and intrusions from dissociated structures). This chapter is an extended effort to draw some meaningful distinctions among these phenotypically-similar (but genotypically-different) phenomena.

46.16.3 Normal Dissociation

I identified five kinds of normal dissociation: (1) evolution-prepared, survival-oriented dissociation, (2) hypnotic performance, (3) psychologically healthy forms of possession (mostly limited to non-Western indigenous cultures), (4) creative/productive automatisms, and (5) transcendent experiences. Evolution-prepared dissociation is a hardwired survival-response to imminent threat of death; it has no personal motivation. In contrast, the other four kinds of normal dissociation (which I have called Type II Normal Dissociation) are rooted in culture and have both personal and cultural motivations.

The essential feature of all dissociation (both normal and pathological) is the occurrence of automatisms—behaviors and reactions that occur automatically, on their own, without being directed by the conscious mind. The healthy automatisms of normal dissociation are culturally syntonic and personally syntonic. They are positively valued by the culture and by the individual who experiences them.

46.16.4 Pathological Dissociation

In contradistinction to healthy automatisms, pathological automatisms cause distress and/or dysfunction. Moreover, they are neither personally syntonic nor culturally syntonic. The individual in question knows quite well that his or her automatisms are abnormal (as does the local community if the automatisms should be publicly visible).

I divided pathological dissociation into three classes of dissociative disorder: (1) dissociated structures, (2) Depersonalization Disorder, and (3) simple conversion symptoms.

46.16.4.1 Dissociated Structures

Dissociated structures are the most common form of dissociative disorder; they include DID, partial DID (DDNOS-1), Possession Disorder (DDNOS-4), Dissociative Fugue, minor ego-state disorders, and remote, localized amnesia (i.e., Loewenstein's [1991b] nonclassic Dissociative Amnesia). Most dissociated structures have five characteristics: (1) recurrent positive dissociative symptoms (i.e., passive-influence experiences: "made" feelings, "made" impulses, "made" actions, thought insertion, etc.), (2) loss or alteration of identity or sense of self, and, in most cases (3) recurrent incidents of amnesia, (4) chronicity, and (5) a plethora of accompanying dissociative symptoms.

46.16.4.2 Depersonalization Disorder

I believe that Depersonalization Disorder is meaningfully different from the other two classes of dissociative disorder. Specifically, Depersonalization Disorder has more of a neurological "feel" to it. Moreover, unlike the phasic or episodic nature of almost all other dissociative symptoms, the detachment of Depersonalization Disorder tends to be tonic and unyielding. Avoidant motivations may be present in some persons with Depersonalization Disorder, but the persistent, unyielding detachment appears to be quite independent of any such personal motivations. Accordingly, I have tentatively concluded that Depersonalization Disorder is a tonic, neurological (or neurobiological) automatism.

46.16.4.3 Conversion Disorder

I have proposed that conversion symptoms are *unconscious self-hypnotic negations of bodily or mental functions.* I have emphasized that generalized amnesia is a typical conversion symptom. Conversion symptoms seem to implement a wish to avoid something unpleasant in the person's current life situation. Moreover, unlike the private subjective symptoms of Depersonalization Disorder and dissociated structures, conversion symptoms are *highly visible to the family and/or local community.* I agree with many other authorities that these symptoms often allow conversion-disordered persons to renegotiate the power relations between them and their family or community.

46.16.5 Five Kinds of Dissociation

My analysis of repression, normal dissociation, and pathological dissociation led me to conclude that there are five kinds of dissociation: (1) dissociation-potentiated repression, (2) intrusions from dissociated structures,

(3) evolution-prepared dissociation, (4) Depersonalization Disorder, and (5) Type II Normal Dissociation and Conversion Disorder. Each is accompanied by automatisms.

46.16.5.1 Dissociation-Potentiated Repression

Dissociation-potentiated repression may occur when the desire to push uncomfortable information out of awareness occurs in a person who possesses substantial hypnotic and/or dissociative ability. Under such circumstances, the person's conscious effort to forget may be suddenly implemented (via the spontaneous activation of an entirely different mechanism).

The necessary causes of dissociation-potentiated repression appear to be twofold: (1) a motivated mental effort to escape discomfort by pushing uncomfortable realities out of conscious awareness; and (2) a high level of dissociative ability. When these two causes are present, a routine effort to "fend off" or "push away" undesirable information may be transformed by the mechanism of dissociation into a full-blown splitting off. The neural mechanisms that implement this dissociation are not yet known, but various findings suggest that remote localized amnesia may involve activation of the right medial prefrontal cortex and orbitofrontal lobe (BA 10), activation of the dorsal ACC (especially BA 32), and hyperactivation of the parietal lobe (especially BA 7, 39, and 40). These neural structures seem to participate in one or more preattentive defenses that sustain the dissociative amnesia.

Evolution has selected for an efficient neural capacity to monitor, evaluate, manipulate, and control information. On the other hand, however, there is no evidence that a superior ability to dissociate information has been directly subjected to selective pressures. Instead, high dissociative ability appears to be a normal variation of human brain structures and processes.

46.16.5.2 Intrusions from Dissociated Structures

Dissociation-potentiated repression produces what I (and others) have called *dissociated structures.* Dissociated structures hold unaccepted or disowned aspects of life, the self, and significant others. Examples of dissociated structures include DID, partial DID (DDNOS-1), Possession Disorder (DDNOS-4), Dissociative Fugue, localized amnesia for past traumas, ego-state disorders, and fixed ideas.

Dissociated structures are experienced by the person as operating with considerable autonomy. Dissociated structures produce a characteristic set of experiences and reactions in dissociative persons—namely, a *private conscious experience* of recurrent, inexplicable intrusions into, and alterations of, their typical reactions, their intended actions, and their sense of who they are. These dissociative intrusions include (1) passive-influence experiences such as "made" feelings, impulses, and actions, thought insertion, etc., (2) loss or alteration of identity or sense of self, (3) incidents of amnesia, and (4) various other dissociative symptoms, including depersonalization, derealization, trance, and somatoform dissociative symptoms.

Intrusions from dissociated structures are typically accompanied by a subjective sense of unexpectedness, involuntariness, uncontrollability, a greater or lesser degree of "not-mineness," and a disturbing sense that "something is wrong with me." Intrusions are what the DES, MID, and other dissociation instruments actually measure. A high score on any measure of dissociation indicates the presence of one or more dissociated structures that are quite active.

These dissociative intrusions are evoked by the simultaneous presence of two necessary causes: (1) the existence of a dissociated structure—which, itself, already required (a) the existence of substantial dissociative ability and (b) a previous motivated effort to escape conscious awareness of unpleasant realities (see previous discussion); and (2) circumstances that activate that dissociated structure.

Broadly, these dissociative intrusions are of two kinds: those that are trauma-related and those that are not. Intrusions that are trauma-related can be produced by any dissociated structure. Intrusions that are not trauma-related can only be produced by dissociated structures that have attained some degree of autonomy from their original traumatic concerns (and that have developed a domain of interests and concerns that are unrelated to trauma).

Although neuroimaging research has not yet directly addressed intrusions from dissociated structures, four areas of neuroimaging research are relevant to dissociative intrusions: research on (1) schizophrenics with first-rank symptoms (i.e., psychotic intrusions), (2) healthy research participants who undergo experimentally altered experiences of agency (passivity experiences), (3) highly hypnotizable subjects who are told that a pulley is moving their arm up and down (passivity experiences), and (4) DID host personalities who listened to their (disowned) trauma scripts (i.e., potential intrusions that were successfully blocked). In all four instances, neuroimaging showed activation or even hyperactivation of the inferior parietal lobule (BA 40) and/or the superior parietal lobule (BA 7). These areas of the brain integrate sensory information from the rest of the body and help to generate an integrated body schema. These studies suggest that activation of these parietal areas is directly related to experiences of passive external control, experiences of the body not being one's own, and experiences of one's life history not being one's own.

These experiences, in turn, give new meaning to what is split-off and to potential intrusions from that which is split-off. Namely, *split-off material is experienced as being odd, unfamiliar, not mine, belonging to an other, and so on.*

That which is split-off is often conceptualized as a dissociated structure, and is generally described as another part of the self or mind. When the activities of a split-off or dissociated structure intrude into conscious awareness, those activities are usually conceptualized as some kind of automatism. For example, Kluft and others have long called the intrusions of DID "passive-influence experiences."

Nature has "designed" humans to be exquisitely sensitive to unexpected stimuli, especially unexpected outcomes of their own movement or functioning. This reflexive conscious awareness of the unexpected (i.e., orienting and alerting) is "built-in." Our conscious awareness of *dissociative* intrusions piggybacks on this more general capacity for noticing the unexpected.

46.16.5.3 Evolution-Prepared Dissociation

Evolution-prepared dissociation occurs automatically at a moment of life-threat; it is characterized by (1) immediate suppression of fear and other emotions, (2) altered information processing, and (3) immediate execution of nonreflective actions that facilitate survival. Evolution-prepared dissociation is time-limited; it promptly ceases when the danger is past.

Evolution-prepared dissociation is triggered by the simultaneous presence of its two necessary causes: (1) an evolution-prepared mechanism for effective and near-instantaneous response to a threat to life; and (2) life-threatening circumstances. Because all humans possess these evolution-prepared mechanisms for dissociation, an imminent threat to life is usually a sufficient cause for dissociation. Evolution-prepared dissociation primarily modulates sensation, affect, and movement.

In keeping with their early phylogenetic origin (and their need to operate with reflexive speed), these dissociative reactions are subcortical. They are located primarily in the PAG and limbic system. These animal defenses have existed since the phylogenetic time of the lizard. On the other hand, with the emergence of hominids and larger, more complex brains, our subcortical animal defenses have become integrated with the cortex. Among other things, this integration allows evaluation and planning for survival to take place during the activation of dissociative survival responses. It is important for the reader to note that, unlike all other kinds of dissociation, *only* evolution-prepared dissociation was directly selected for by natural selection.

Because all humans possess this ability for spontaneous evolution-prepared dissociation, the culture is loosely familiar with the phenomenon. For example, novelists and film directors (accurately) portray evolution-prepared dissociation as altered visual perception, altered auditory perception, and time slowing down during a time of extreme danger.

For obvious reasons, there has been no neuroscientific research on deliberately provoked incidents of evolution-prepared dissociation. Animal research and recent virtual predator research on humans (Mobbs et al., 2007) strongly suggests that evolution-prepared dissociation, like the other components of animal defensive responding, is primarily located in the PAG. There is, however, some neuroimaging research that may (or may not) portray incidents of evolution-prepared dissociation.

Lanius has long emphasized the interesting fact that not all persons with PTSD are the same. In particular, she has repeatedly shown that exposure to scripts of their trauma provokes hyperarousal and flashbacks in about 70% of persons with PTSD, and hypoarousal and dissociative distancing in about 30% of persons with PTSD. Frewen and Lanius (2006) have suggested that such dissociative responses are, in fact, incidents of evolution-prepared dissociation.

Lanius and colleagues report that this dissociative response is marked by significant activations of the superior and middle temporal gyri (BA 38), inferior frontal lobe (BA 47), occipital lobe (BA 19), inferior parietal lobule (BA 7), medial frontal lobe (BA 10), medial prefrontal lobe (BA 9), and ACC (BA 24 and 32). Functional connectivity during this dissociative reaction showed that activation in the right insula correlated with activity in the left ventrolateral thalamus.

Noting that significant activations of the occipital area (BA 19) and the parietal area (BA 7) also occurred in persons with Depersonalization Disorder (Simeon et al., 2000), Lanius et al. (2007) suggested that these activations of sensory cortices "may underlie the lack of integration of sensory experience that is characteristic of dissociative symptoms" (p. 209).

46.16.5.4 Depersonalization Disorder

Depersonalization Disorder is usually marked by a chronic and unyielding emotional detachment from self and world. Its cause is largely unknown. The disorder is loosely attributed to stress and an underlying neurochemical diathesis. These patients' scores on self-report measures of depersonalization are positively correlated ($rs = 0.74$ and 0.84) with the activation of their inferior and superior parietal lobules (BA 39 and 7B), respectively. These patients also have activated occipital lobes (BA 19).

Persons with Depersonalization Disorder routinely respond to emotional stimuli, especially aversive ones, with a distinctive muted, or even absent, emotional response. According to neuroimaging studies, their overall pattern of neural response is one of reduced neural activation in emotion-sensitive regions of the brain and increased neural activation in brain areas associated with the control of emotions. This pattern of subdued or absent emotional response is also present in their autonomic and hormonal functioning.

Remembering Frewen and Lanius's (2006) hypothesis (that a dissociative response to trauma scripts in PTSD patients may be an evolution-prepared dissociative reaction), it is also worth recalling that several experts have suggested that Depersonalization Disorder may be a vestigial biological defense mechanism (e.g., Sierra & Berrios, 1998; Simeon & Abugel, 2006). In short, Depersonalization Disorder seems to be deeply biological in nature—so much so that I consider it to be a neurobiological dysfunction that is quite different from all other kinds of dissociation.

I do not believe that Depersonalization Disorder entails any evolutionary advantage. Perhaps it owes its existence to the evolution-prepared, animal defenses (which, gone awry, may produce unyielding detachment).

46.16.5.5 Type II Normal Dissociation and Conversion Disorder

Type II Normal Dissociation is the product of a special dissociative ability that is possessed by only a minority of individuals. This special ability produces automatisms that are positively valued by both the person and his or her culture (such as hypnotic performance, psychologically healthy forms of possession, creative/productive automatisms, and transcendent experiences). Type II Normal Dissociation produces neither distress nor dysfunction. Conversion Disorder is the pathological form of Type II Normal Dissociation (see previous discussion).

Both Type II Normal Dissociation and uncomplicated Conversion Disorder require the joint presence of two necessary causes—motivation and ability. In the case of Conversion Disorder, the two necessary causes are (1) a strong wish to escape or to alter a chronically unpleasant set of interpersonal circumstances; and (2) a moderate-to-high level of hypnotizability or dissociativity.

The best current evidence suggests that the neural underpinnings of hypnotizability lie in the corpus callosum, the dorsal ACC (BA 32), and highly responsive sensory cortices. The neuroimaging literature on hysterical conversion, however, is a maze of inconsistency. The two most consistent findings involve activation of the orbitofrontal cortex and the ACC. Several investigators have concluded that hysterical symptoms are caused by ACC and frontal inhibition of normal functioning or by a phasic frontal deactivation that prevents normal execution of movement (of the paralyzed limb).

Despite usually being classified otherwise, generalized amnesia resembles a classic conversion symptom. Neuroimaging studies have suggested that such amnesia is accompanied by activation of the left hemisphere and a corresponding deactivation of the right hemisphere.

Many forms of Type II Dissociation (e.g., hypnosis, possession, transcendent experiences) are so well-known in Western culture that they serve as metaphors for *other* phenomena. Conversion Disorder, however, is little known by the members of modern Western culture. Its primary metaphor, *hysteria*, is no longer understood by the culture (if it ever was). Only one form of Conversion Disorder is well-recognized by the culture—generalized amnesia. Amnesia has become its own metaphor.

Although many have speculated that hypnotizability is the product of natural selection, I disagree. There is no convincing evidence that either high hypnotic ability or high dissociative ability were produced by natural selection. Instead, high hypnotizability and high dissociativity seem to be normal (and inheritable) variations of the structures and functions of the human brain. Of course, that said, it will still be most interesting to identify *which* variations of the brain are responsible for these truly remarkable abilities.

REFERENCES

Adams, J. A. (1988). *Dangling from the Golden Gate Bridge and other narrow escapes*. New York: Ballantine Books.

Adityanjee, G. S. (1990). Multiple personality in India: Dr. Adityanjee replies. *American Journal of Psychiatry, 147*, 1260–1261.

Alexander, P. J., Joseph, S., & Das, A. (1997). Limited utility of ICD-10 and DSM-IV classification of dissociative and conversion disorders in India. *Acta Psychiatrica Scandinavica, 95*, 177–182.

Allen, J. G., Console, D. A., & Lewis, L. (1999). Dissociative detachment and memory impairment: Reversible amnesia or encoding failure? *Comprehensive Psychiatry, 40,* 160–171.

Allen, J. G., & Coyne, L. (1995). Dissociation and vulnerability to psychotic experience: The Dissociative Experiences

Scale and the MMPI-2. *Journal of Nervous and Mental Disease, 183*, 615–622.

Allen, J. G., Coyne, L., & Console, D. A. (1996). Dissociation contributes to anxiety and psychoticism on the Brief Symptom Inventory. *Journal of Nervous and Mental Disease, 184*, 639–641.

Allen, J. G., Coyne, L., & Console, D. A. (1997). Dissociative detachment relates to psychotic symptoms and personality decompensation. *Comprehensive Psychiatry, 38*, 327–334.

Allen, J. G., Fultz, J., Huntoon, J., & Brethour, J. R. (2002). Pathological dissociative taxon membership, absorption, and reported childhood trauma in women with trauma-related disorders. *Journal of Trauma & Dissociation, 3(1)*, 89–110.

Alvarado, C. S. (2002). Dissociation in Britain during the late nineteenth century: The Society for Psychical Research, 1882–1900. *Journal of Trauma & Dissociation, 3(2)*, 9–33.

American Psychiatric Association (2000). *DSM-IV-TR – Diagnostic and statistical manual of mental disorders* (4th ed., text rev.). Washington, DC: Author.

Anderson, M. C., & Green, C. (2001). Suppressing unwanted memories by executive control. *Nature, 410*, 366–369.

Anderson, M. C., Ochsner, K. N., Kuhl, B., Cooper, J., Robertson, E., Gabrieli, S. W., Glover, G. H., & Gabrieli, J. D. E. (2004). Neural systems underlying the suppression of unwanted memories. *Science, 303*, 232–235.

Andersson, O. (1962). *Studies in the prehistory of psychoanalysis: The etiology of psychoneuroses and some related themes in Sigmund Freud's scientific writings and letters 1886–1896*. Norstedts, Sweden: Svenska Bokförlaget.

Ås, A. (1962). Non-hypnotic experiences related to hypnotizability in male and female college students. *Scandinavian Journal of Psychology, 3*, 112–121.

Ås, A., & Lauer, L. W. (1962). A factor analytic study of hypnotizability and related personal experiences. *International Journal of Clinical and Experimental Hypnosis, 10*, 169–181.

Ås, A., O'Hara, J. W., & Munger, M. P. (1962). The measurement of subjective experiences presumably related to hypnotic susceptibility. *Scandinavian Journal of Psychology, 3*, 47–64.

Azam, E. (1876a). Amnésie périodique ou dédoublement de la vie. *Revue Scientifique, 16*, 481–489.

Azam, E. (1876b). Le dédoublement de la personnalité: Suite de l'histoire de Félida X. *Revue Scientifique, 18*, 265–269.

Azam, E. (1877). Le dédoublement de la personnalité et l'amnésie périodique. *Revue Scientifique, 20*, 577–581.

B. C. A. (1908). My life as a dissociated personality. *Journal of Abnormal Psychology, 3*, 240–260.

B. C. A. (1908–1909). An introspective analysis of co-conscious life, by a personality (B) claiming to be co-conscious. *Journal of Abnormal Psychology, 3*, 311–334.

Balthazard, C. G. (1993). The hypnosis scales at their centenary: Some fundamental issues still unresolved. *Journal of Clinical and Experimental Hypnosis, 41*, 47–53.

Balthazard, C. G., & Woody, E. Z. (1985). The "stuff" of hypnotic performance: A review of psychometric approaches. *Psychological Bulletin, 98*, 283–296.

Balthazard, C. G., & Woody, E. Z. (1992). The spectral analysis of hypnotic performance with respect to "absorption." *International Journal of Clinical and Experimental Hypnosis, 40*, 21–43.

Bandler, R., & Depaulis, A. (1991). Midbrain periaqueductal gray control of defensive behavior in the cat and the rat. In A. Depaulis & R. Bandler (Eds.), *The midbrain periaqueductal gray matter: Functional, anatomical, and neurochemical organization*. NATO ASI Series A: Life Sciences, Vol. 213 (pp. 175–198). New York: Plenum Press.

Barber, T. X. (1999). A comprehensive three-dimensional theory of hypnosis. In I. Kirsch, A. Capafons, E. Cardeña-Buelna, & S. Amigo (Eds.), *Clinical hypnosis and self-regulation: Cognitive-behavioral perspectives* (pp. 21–48). Washington, DC: American Psychological Association.

Barrett, D. (1992). Fantasizers and dissociators: Data on two distinct subgroups of deep trance subjects. *Psychological Reports, 71*, 1011–1014.

Barrett, D. (1996). Fantasizers and dissociators: Two types of high hypnotizables, two different imagery styles. In R. G. Kunzendorf, N. P. Spanos, & B. Wallace (Eds.), *Hypnosis and imagination* (pp. 123–135). Amityville, NY: Baywood Publishing Company.

Barry, H., Jr., Mackinnon, D. W., & Murray, H. A., Jr. (1931). Studies in personality: A hypnotizability as a personality trait and its typological relations. *Human Biology, 3*, 1–36.

Bauman, D. E., & Bul, P. I. (1981). Human inheritability of hypnotizability. *Genetika, 17*, 352–356.

Becker-Blease, K. A., Deater-Deckard, K., Eley, T., Freyd, J. J., Stevenson, J., & Plomin, R. (2004). A genetic analysis of individual differences in dissociative behaviors in childhood and adolescence. *Journal of Child Psychology and Psychiatry, 45*, 522–532.

Benham, G., Woody, E. Z., Wilson, K. S., & Nash, M. R. (2006). Expect the unexpected: Ability, attitude, and responsiveness to hypnosis. *Journal of Personality and Social Psychology, 91*, 342–350.

Benton, A. L., & Sivan, A. B. (1993). Disturbances of the body schema. In K. M. Heilman & E. Valenstein (Eds.), *Clinical neuropsychology* (pp. 123–140). New York: Oxford University Press.

Bernstein, E. M., & Putnam, F. W. (1986). Development, reliability, and validity of a dissociation scale. *Journal of Nervous and Mental Disease, 174*, 727–735.

Binet, A. (1890/1977). On double consciousness. In P. Binet, *Alterations of personality*, and *On double consciousness*. Washington, DC: University Publications of America, 1977.

Binet, A. (1891/1896/1977). Alterations of personality. In P. Binet, *Alterations of personality*, and *On double consciousness*. Washington, DC: University Publications of America, 1977.

Black, D. N., Seritan, A. L., Taber, K. H., & Hurley, R. A. (2004). Conversion hysteria: Lessons from functional neuroimaging. *Journal of Neuropsychiatry and Clinical Neuroscience, 16*, 245–251.

Blakemore, S.-J., & Frith, C. D. (2003). Self-awareness and action. *Current Opinion in Neurobiology, 13*, 219–224.

Blakemore, S.-J., Oakley, D. A., & Frith, C. D. (2003). Delusions of alien control in the normal brain. *Neuropsychologia, 41*, 1058–1067.

Blakemore, S.-J., Wolpert, D., & Frith, C. (2000). Why can't you tickle yourself? *Neuroreport, 11(11)*, R11–R16.

Bliss, E. L. (1984). Spontaneous self-hypnosis in multiple personality. *Psychiatric Clinics of North America, 7*, 135–148.

Bliss, E. L. (1986). *Multiple personality, allied disorders and hypnosis*. New York and Oxford: Oxford University Press.

Bolles, R. C. (1970). Species-specific defense reactions and avoidance learning. *Psychological Review, 77*, 32–48.

Bolles, R. C., & Fanselow, M. S. (1980). A perceptual-defensive-recuperative model of fear and pain. *Behavioral and Brain Sciences, 3*, 291–323.

Bonanno, G. A., & Singer, J. L. (1990). Repressive personality style: Theoretical and methodological implications for health and pathology. In J. L. Singer (Ed.), *Repression and dissociation: Implications for personality theory, psychopathology, and health* (pp. 435–470). Chicago: University of Chicago Press.

Bourguignon, E. (1970). *Possession*. San Francisco: Chandler & Sharp.

Bourguignon, E. (Ed.) (1973). *Religion, altered states of consciousness, and social change*. Columbus, OH: Ohio State University Press.

Bourguignon, E. (1976). *Possession*. San Francisco: Chandler & Sharp.

Bourru, H., & Burot, P. (1885). Observations and documents de la multiplicité des états de conscience chez un hystéro-épileptique. *Revue Philosophique, 20*, 411–416.

Bourru, H., & Burot, P. (1886). Sur les variations de la personnalité. *Revue Philosophique,* 21, 73–74.

Bowers, K. S. (1971). Sex and susceptibility as moderator variables in the relationship of creativity and hypnotic susceptibility. *Journal of Abnormal Psychology, 78*, 93–100.

Bowers, K. S. (1976). *Hypnosis for the seriously curious*. Monterey, CA: Brooks/Cole.

Bowers, K. S. (1991). Dissociation in hypnosis and multiple personality disorder. *International Journal of Clinical and Experimental Hypnosis, 39*, 155–176.

Bowers, K. S. (1992a). Dissociated control and the limits of hypnotic responsiveness. *Consciousness and Cognition, 1*, 32–39.

Bowers, K. S. (1992b). Imagination and dissociation in hypnotic responding. *International Journal of Clinical and Experimental Hypnosis, 60*, 253–275.

Bowers, K. S., & Woody, E. Z. (1996). Hypnotic amnesia and the paradox of intentional forgetting. *Journal of Abnormal Psychology, 105*, 381–390.

Braid, J. (1855/1970). The physiology of fascination and the critics criticized. In M. M. Tinterow (Ed.), *Foundations of hypnosis: From Mesmer to Freud* (pp. 365–389). Springfield, IL: Charles C. Thomas.

Braun, B. G. (1984). Hypnosis creates multiple personality: Myth or reality? *International Journal of Clinical and Experimental Hypnosis, 32*, 191–197.

Braun, B. G. (1985). The transgenerational incidence of dissociation and multiple personality disorder: A preliminary report. In R. P. Kluft (Ed.), *Childhood antecedents of multiple personality* (pp. 127–150). Washington, DC: American Psychiatric Press.

Braun, B. G. (1993). Multiple personality disorder and post-traumatic stress disorder: Similarities and differences. In J. P. Wilson & B. Raphael (Eds.), *International handbook of traumatic stress syndromes* (pp. 35–47). New York: Plenum Press.

Bremner, J. D. (1999). Acute and chronic responses to psychological trauma: Where do we go from here? *American Journal of Psychiatry, 156*, 349–351.

Breuer, J., & Freud, S. (1893). On the psychical mechanism of hysterical phenomena: Preliminary communication. *Standard Edition, 1*, 3–17.

Breuer, J., & Freud, S. (1893–1995). Studies on hysteria. *Standard Edition, 1.*

Brewin, C. (2007, November). *Dissociative and identity processes in PTSD*. Plenary lecture, Annual conference of the International Society for the Study of Trauma and Dissociation, Philadelphia, PA.

Briere, J., Scott, C., & Weathers, F. (2005). Peritraumatic and persistent dissociation in the presumed etiology of PTSD. *American Journal of Psychiatry, 162*, 2295–2301.

Briere, J., Weathers, F. W., & Runtz, M. (2005). Is dissociation a multidimensional construct? Data from the Multiscale Dissociation Inventory. *Journal of Traumatic Stress, 18*, 221–231.

Briquet, P. (1859). *Traité clinique et thérapeutique de l'hystérie*. Paris: J.-P. Baillière & Fils.

Bromberg, P. M. (1998). *Standing in the spaces: Essays on clinical process, trauma, and dissociation*. Hillsdale, NJ: Analytic Press.

Brown, R. J. (2006). Different types of "dissociation" have different mechanisms. *Journal of Trauma & Dissociation, 7(4)*, 7–28.

Brunet, A., Holowka D., & Laurence, J. R. (2002). Dissociative phenomena. In M. J. Aminoff & R. B. Daroff (Eds.), *Encyclopedia of the neurological sciences* (pp. 25-27). San Diego, CA: Academic Press.

Bryant, R. A. (1995). Fantasy proneness, reported childhood abuse, and the relevance of reported abuse onset. *International Journal of Clinical and Experimental Hypnosis, 43*, 184–193.

Bryant, R. A. (2009). Is peritraumatic dissociation always pathological? In P. F. Dell & J. A. O'Neil (Eds.), *Dissociation and the dissociative disorders: DSM-V and beyond* (pp. 185–196). New York: Routledge.

Burnett, C. T. (1925). Splitting the mind: An experimental study of normal men. *Psychological Monographs, 34*, No. 2.

Butler, L. D. (2004). The dissociations of everyday life. *Journal of Trauma & Dissociation, 5(2),* 1–12.

Butler, L. D. (2006). Normative dissociation. *Psychiatric Clinics of North America, 29*, 45–62.

Butler, L. D., Duran, R. E. F., Jasiukaitis, P., Koopman, C., & Spiegel, D. (1996). Hypnotizability and traumatic experience: A diathesis-stress model of dissociative symptoms. *American Journal of Psychiatry, 153*, Festchrift Supplement, 42–63.

Butler, T., Pan, H., Tuescher, O., Engelien, A., Goldstein, J., Weisholtz, D., Root, J. C., Protopescu, X., Cunningham-Bussel, A. C., Chang, L., Xie, X.-H., Chen, Q., Phelps, E. A., LeDoux, J. E., Stern, E., & Silbersweig, D. A. (2007) Human fear-related motor neurocircuitry. *Neuroscience, 150*(1), 1-7.

Cabeza, R., Prince, S. E., Daselaar, S. M., Greenberg, D. L., Budde, M., Dolcos, F., LaBar, K. S., & Rubin, D. C. (2004). Brain activity during episodic retrieval of autobiographical and laboratory events: an fMRI study using a novel photo paradigm. *Journal of Cognitive Neuroscience, 16*, 1583–1594.

Calabrese, P., Markowitsch, H. J., Durwen, H. F., Widlitzek, B., Haupts, M., Holinka, B., & Gehlen, W. (1996). Right temporo-frontal cortex as critical locus for the ecphory of old episodic memories. *Journal of Neurology, Neurosurgery, and Psychiatry, 61*, 304–310.

Campbell, B. A., Wood, G., & McBride, T. (1997). Origins of orienting and defensive responses: An evolutionary perspective. In P. J. Lang, R. F. Simons, & M. T. Balaban (Eds.), *Attention and orienting: Sensory and motivational processes* (pp. 41–67). Mahwah, NJ: Lawrence Erlbaum Associates.

Cardeña, E. (1991). Max Beauvoir: An island in an ocean of spirits. In R.-I. Heinze, *Shamans of the 20th century* (pp. 27–32). New York: Irvington.

Cardeña, E. (1994). The domain of dissociation. In S. J. Lynn & J. W. Rhue (Eds.), *Dissociation: Clinical and theoretical perspectives* (pp. 15–31). New York: Guilford Press.

Cardeña, E. (1996). "Just floating on the sky": A comparison of hypnotic and shamanic phenomena. In R. Van Quekelberghe & D. Eigner (Eds.), *Jahrbuch für transkulturelle medizin und psychotherapie 1994* [*Yearbook of cross-cultural medicine and psychotherapy 1994*] (pp. 85–98). Berlin: Verlag für Wissenschaft und Bildung.

Cardeña, E., van Duijl, M., Weiner, L. A., Terhune, D. B. (2009). Possession/trance phenomena. In P. F. Dell & J. A. O'Neil (Eds.), Dissociation and the dissociative disorders: DSM-V and beyond (pp. 171–184). New York: Routledge.

Cardeña, E., & Spiegel, D. (1991). Suggestibility, absorption, and dissociation: An integrative model of hypnosis. In J. F. Schumaker (Ed.), *Human suggestibility: Advances in theory, research, and application* (pp. 93–107). New York: Routledge.

Carlson, E. B. (1994). Studying the interaction between physical and psychological states with the Dissociative Experiences Scale. In D. Spiegel (Ed.), *Dissociation, culture, mind, and body* (pp. 41–58). Washington, DC: American Psychiatric Press.

Carlson, E. B., & Putnam, F. W. (1989). Integrating research on dissociation and hypnotizability: Are there two pathways to hypnotizability? *Dissociation, 2*, 32–38.

Carpenter, W. (1855). *Principles of human physiology*, fifth edition. London: John Churchill.

Carpenter, W. (1874/1877). *Principles of mental physiology*, fourth edition. New York: D. Appleton & Company.

Charcot, J.-M. (1882). Physiologie pathologique: Sur les divers états nerveux déterminés par l'hypnotization chez les hystériques. *CR Academie des Sciences, Paris, 94*, 403–405.

Charcot, J.-M. (1886). *Neue Vorlesungen über die Krankenheiten des Nervensystems insbesondere über Hysterie*. S. Freud (Trans.), Leipzig and Vienna: Toeplitz and Deuticke. [*New studies on the diseases of the nervous system, especially with regard to hysteria.*]

Charcot, J.-M. (1889/1991). *Clinical lectures on diseases of the nervous system*, Volume III. London: Tavistock/Routledge.

Charcot, J.-M. (1887/1888). *Poliklinische vortrage*, I Band. S. Freud (Trans.), Leipzig: Franz Deuticke. [Clinical lectures.]

Charcot, J.-M., & Marie, P. (1892/1976). Hysteria, mainly hystero-epilepsy. In D. H. Tuke (Ed.), *A dictionary of psychological medicine* (pp. 627–641). New York: Arno Press.

Coe, G. A. (1900). *The spiritual life: Studies in the science of religion*. New York: Eaton & Mains.

Coe, W. C., & Sarbin, T. R. (1991). Role theory: Hypnosis from a dramaturgical and narration perspective. In S. J. Lynn & J. W. Rhue (Eds.), *Theories of hypnosis: Current models and perspectives* (pp. 303–323). New York: Guilford Press.

Coizet, V., Dommett, E. J., Redgrave, P., & Overton, P. G. (2006). Nociceptive responses of midbrain dopaminergic neurons are modulated by the superior colliculus in the rat. *Neuroscience, 139*, 1479–1493.

Coons, P. M. (1999). Psychogenic or dissociative fugue: A clinical investigation of five cases. *Psychological Reports, 84*, 881–886.

Coons, P. M. (2000). Dissociative fugue. In B. J. Sadock & V. Sadock (Eds.), *Comprehensive textbook of psychiatry* (pp. 1549–1552). New York: Lippincott, Williams & Wilkins.

Coons, P. M., & Milstein, V. (1992) Psychogenic amnesia: A clinical investigation of 25 cases. *Dissociation, 5*, 73–79.

Cory, C. E. (1919). A divided self. *Journal of Abnormal Psychology, 14*, 281–291.

Crabtree, A. (1986). Explanations of dissociation in the first half of the twentieth century. In J. M. Quen (Ed.), *Split minds/split brains: Historical and current perspectives* (pp. 85–107). New York: New York University Press.

Crabtree, A. (1988). *Animal magnetism, early hypnotism, and psychical research, 1766–1925: An annotated bibliography*. White Plains, NY: Kraus International Publications.

Crabtree, A. (1993). *From Mesmer to Freud: Magnetic sleep and the roots of psychological healing*. New Haven, CT: Yale University Press.

Crabtree, A. (2003). "Automatism" and the emergence of dynamic psychiatry. *Journal of History of the Behavioral Sciences, 39*, 51–70.

Crabtree, A. (2007). Automatism and secondary centers. In E. F. Kelly, E. W. Kelly, A. Crabtree, A. Gauld, M. Grosso, & B. Greyson, *Irreducible mind: Toward a psychology for the 21st century* (pp. 301–365). New York: Rowman & Littlefield Publishers.

Cronbach, L. J., & Meehl, P. E. (1955). Construct validity in psychological tests. *Psychological Bulletin, 52*, 281–302.

Dalenberg, C. J., & Paulson, K. (2009). The case for the study of "normal" dissociation processes. In P. F. Dell & J. A. O'Neil (Eds.), *Dissociation and the dissociative disorders: DSM-V and beyond* (pp. 145–154). New York: Routledge.

Dancu, C. V., Riggs, D. S., Hearst-Ikeda, D., Shoyer, B. G., & Foa, E. B. (1996). Dissociative experiences and posttraumatic stress disorder among female victims of criminal assault and rape. *Journal of Traumatic Stress, 9*, 253–267.

Darwin, C. (1859/1968). *The origin of species*. Baltimore: Penguin.

Dell, P. F. (2002). Dissociative phenomenology of dissociative identity disorder. *Journal of Nervous and Mental Disease, 190*, 10–15.

Dell, P. F. (2006a, November). *Evolutionary foundations of dissociation*. Paper presented at the 23rd International Fall Conference of the International Society for the Study of Dissociation, Los Angeles, CA.

Dell, P. F. (2006b). The Multidimensional Inventory of Dissociation (MID): A comprehensive measure of pathological dissociation. *Journal of Trauma & Dissociation, 7(2)*, 77–106.

Dell, P. F. (2006c). A new model of dissociative identity disorder. *Psychiatric Clinics of North America, 29*, 1–26.

Dell, P. F. (2008, October). *The experience of involuntariness: Reconnecting hypnotic response to clinical dissociation*. Paper presented at the annual meeting of the Society for Clinical and Experimental Hypnosis, Philadelphia, PA.

Dell, P. F. (2009a). The long struggle to diagnose multiple personality disorder (MPD). I. MPD. In P. F. Dell & J. A. O'Neil (Eds.), *Dissociation and the dissociative disorders: DSM-V and beyond* (pp. 383–402). New York: Routledge.

Dell, P. F. (2009b). The long struggle to diagnose multiple personality disorder (MPD). II. Partial MPD. In P. F. Dell & J. A. O'Neil (Eds.), *Dissociation and the dissociative disorders: DSM-V and beyond* (pp. 403–428). New York: Routledge.

Dell, P. F. (2009c). The phenomena of pathological dissociation. In P. F. Dell & J. A. O'Neil (Eds.), *Dissociation and the dissociative disorders: DSM-V and beyond* (pp. 225–238). New York: Routledge.

Dell, P. F., & Lawson, D. (2009). Empirically delineating the domain of pathological dissociation. In P. F. Dell & J. A. O'Neil (Eds.), *Dissociation and the dissociative disorders: DSM-V and beyond* (pp. 667–692). New York: Routledge.

Depue, B. E., Curran, T., & Banich, M. T. (2007). Prefrontal regions orchestrate suppression of emotional memories via a two-phase process. *Science, 317*, 215–219.

Despine, P. (1868). Psychologie naturelle. *Études sur les facultés intellectuelles et morales dans leur état normal et dans leurs manifestations anomales chez les aliénés et chez les criminels*. Tome premier. Paris: F. Savy.

Despine, P. (1880). *Étude scientifique sur le somnambulisme, sur les phénomènes qu'il présente et sur son action thérapeutique*. Paris: F. Savy.

Dorahy, M. (2006). The dissociative processing style: A cognitive organization activated by perceived or actual threat in clinical dissociators. *Journal of Trauma & Dissociation, 7(4)*, 29–53.

Dorahy, M. J., & Huntjens, R. J. C. (2007). Memory and attentional processes in dissociative identity disorder: A review of the empirical literature. In E. Vermetten, M. J. Dorahy, & D. Spiegel (Eds.), *Traumatic dissociation: Neurobiology and treatment* (pp. 55–75). Washington, DC: American Psychiatric Press.

Dugas, L. (1898). Un cas de depersonnalisation. *Revue Philosophique, 45*, 500–507.

Ellenberger, H. (1970). *The discovery of the unconscious*. New York: Basic Books.

Elzinga, B. M., Ardon, A. M., Heijnis, M. K., De Ruiter, M. B., van Dyck, R., & Veltman, D. J. (2007). Neural correlates of enhanced working-memory performance in dissociative disorder: A functional MRI study. *Psychological Medicine, 37*, 235–245.

Elzinga, B. M., Phaf, R. H., Ardon, A. M., & van Dyck, R. (2003). Directed forgetting between, but not within, dissociative personality states. *Journal of Abnormal Psychology, 112*, 237–243.

Erdelyi, M. H. (1990). Repression, reconstruction, and defense: History and integration of the psychoanalytic and experimental frameworks. In J. L. Singer (Ed.), *Repression and dissociation: Implications for personality theory, psychopathology, and health* (pp. 1–31). Chicago: University of Chicago Press.

Erdelyi, M. H. (1994). Dissociation, defense, and the unconscious. In D. Spiegel (Ed.), *Dissociation: Culture, mind, and body* (pp. 3–20). Washington, DC: American Psychiatric Press.

Estabrooks, G. H. (1971, April). Hypnosis comes of age. *Science Digest*, 44–50.

Fanselow, M. S. (1994). Neural organization of the defensive system responsible for fear. *Psychonomic Bulletin & Review, 1*, 429–438.

Farrer, C., Frey, S. H., Van Horn, J. D., Tunik, E., Turk, D., Inati, S., & Grafton, S. T. (2008). The angular gyrus computes action awareness representations. *Cerebral Cortex, 18*, 254–261.

Farrer, C., & Frith, C. D. (2002). Experiencing oneself vs experiencing another person as the cause of an action: The neural correlates of the experience of agency. *NeuroImage, 15*, 596–603.

Farthing, G. W., Venturino, M., & Brown, S. W. (1983). Relationships between two different types of imagery vividness questionnaire items and three hypnotic susceptibility scale factors: A brief communication. *International Journal of Clinical and Experimental Hypnosis, 31*, 8–13.

Fendt, M., & Fanselow, M. S. (1999). The neuroanatomical and neurochemical basis of conditioned fear. *Neuroscience and Biobehavioral Reviews, 23*, 743–760.

Field, P. B. (1965). An inventory scale of hypnotic depth. *International Journal of Clinical and Experimental Hypnosis, 132*, 238–249.

Fink, G. R., Markowitsch, H. J., Reinkemeier, M., Bruckbrauer, T., Kessler, J., & Heiss, W.-D. (1996). Cerebral representation of one's own past: Neural networks involved in autobiographical memory. *Journal of Neuroscience, 16*, 4275–4282.

Flournoy, T. (1900/1994). *From India to the planet Mars: A case of multiple personality with imaginary languages*. Princeton, NJ: Princeton University Press.

Foa, E. B., & Hearst-Ikeda, D. (1996). Emotional dissociation in response to trauma: An information-processing approach. In L. K. Michelson & R. J. Ray (Eds.), *Handbook of dissociation: Theoretical, empirical, and clinical perspectives* (pp. 207–224). New York: Plenum Press.

Forbes, E. J., & Pekala, R. J. (1996). Types of hypnotically (un) susceptible individuals as a function of phenomenological experience: A partial replication. *American Journal of Clinical Hypnosis, 24*, 92–109.

Fox, C. D., & Kulp, H. L. (1909). Report of a case of dissociated personality, characterized by the presence of somnambulistic states and ambulatory automatism, which recovered, following the employment of hypnotic suggestion. *Journal of Abnormal Psychology, 4*, 201–217.

Francis, L. J., & Robbins, M. Personality and glossolalia: A study among male evangelical clergy. *Pastoral Psychology, 51*, 391–396.

Franck, N., O'Leary, D. S., Flaum, M., Hichwa, R. D., & Andreasen, N. C. (2002). Cerebral blood flow changes associated with Schneiderian first-rank symptoms in schizophrenia. *Journal of Neuropsychiatry and Clinical Neuroscience, 14*, 277–282.

Frankel, F. H. (1989). Hypnosis is a multi-dimensional event. *American Journal of Clinical Hypnosis, 32*, 13–14.

Frankel, F. H. (1990). Hypnotizability and dissociation. *American Journal of Psychiatry, 147*, 823–829.

Frankel, F. H. (1994). Dissociation in hysteria and hypnosis: A concept aggrandized. In S. J. Lynn & J. W. Rhue (Eds.), *Dissociation: Clinical and theoretical perspectives* (pp. 80–93). New York: Guilford Press.

Freud, S. (1894). Neuro-psychoses of defence. *Standard Edition, 3*, 45–61.

Freud, S. (1895). A reply to criticisms of my paper on anxiety neurosis. *Standard Edition, 3*, 123–139.

Freud, S. (1896a). The aetiology of hysteria. *Standard Edition, 3*, 191–221.

Freud, S. (1896b). Heredity and the aetiology of the neuroses. *Standard Edition, 3*, 143–156.

Freud, S. (1897/1986). Letter from Freud to Fliess, September 21, 1897. In J. M. Masson (Ed.), *The complete letters of Sigmund Freud to Wilhelm Fliess 1887–1904* (pp. 264–267). London: Belknap Press.

Freud, S. (1900). The interpretation of dreams. *Standard Edition, 4 and 5*.

Freud, S. (1901). The psychopathology of everyday life. *Standard Edition, 6*.

Freud, S. (1910). Five lectures on psycho-analysis. *Standard Edition, 11*, 9–55.

Freud, S. (1912). A note on the unconscious in psycho-analysis. *Standard Edition, 12*, 260–266.

Freud, S. (1914a). On the history of the psycho-analytic movement. *Standard Edition, 14*, 7–66.

Freud, S. (1914b). Repression. *Standard Edition, 12*, 146–158.

Freud, S. (1915). The unconscious. *Standard Edition, 12*, 166–215.

Freud, S. (1923). The ego and the id. *Standard Edition, 19*, 12–66.

Freud, S. (1925). An autobiographical study. *Standard Edition, 20*, 7–74.

Freud, S. (1939). Moses and monotheism: Three essays. *Standard Edition, 23*, 7–137.

Freud, S. (1940a). An outline of psychoanalysis. *Standard Edition, 23*, 144–207.

Freud, S. (1940b). Splitting of the ego in the process of defence. *Standard Edition, 23*, 275–278.

Freud, S. (1950). Project for a scientific psychology. *Standard Edition, 1*, 295–397.

Frewen, P. A., & Lanius, R. A. (2006). Neurobiology of dissociation: Unity and disunity in mind-body-brain. *Psychiatric Clinics of North America, 29*, 113–128.

Freyd, J. J. (1996). *Betrayal trauma: The logic of forgetting childhood abuse.* Cambridge, MA: Harvard University Press.

Frischholz, E. J., Lipman, L. S., Braun, B. G., & Sachs, R. G. (1992). Psychopathology, hypnotizability, and dissociation. *American Journal of Psychiatry, 149*, 1521–1525.

Galliano, G., Noble, I. M., Travis, L. A., & Puechl, C. (1993). Victim reactions during rape/sexual assault: A preliminary study of the immobility response and its correlates. *Journal of Interpersonal Violence, 8*, 107–114.

Gallup, G. G. (1974). Animal hypnosis: Factual status of a fictional concept. *Psychological Bulletin, 81*, 836–853.

Gallup, G. G. (1977). Tonic immobility: The role of fear and predation. *Psychological Record, 27*, 41–61.

Gallup, G. G., & Rager, D. R. (1996). Tonic immobility as a model of extreme states of behavioral inhibition: Issues of methodology and measurement. In P. R. Sanberg, K.-P. Ossenkopp & M. Kavaliers (Eds.), *Motor activity and movement disorders: Research issues and applications* (pp. 57–80). Totowa, NJ: Humana Press.

Ganesan, V., Hunter, M. D., & Spence, S. A. (2005). Schneiderian first-rank symptoms and right parietal hyperactivation: A replication using fMRI. *American Journal of Psychiatry, 162*, 1545.

Garrett, C. (1987). *Spirit possession and popular religion.* Baltimore, MD: Johns Hopkins University Press.

Gauld, A. (1992). *A history of hypnotism.* Cambridge: Cambridge University Press.

Gaw, A. C., Ding, Q., Levine, R. E., & Gaw, H. (1998). The clinical characteristics of possession disorder among 20 Chinese patients in the Hebei Province of China. *Psychiatric Services, 49*, 360–365.

Ghaffar, O., Staines, W. R., & Feinstein, A. (2006). Unexplained neurological symptoms: An fMRI study of sensory conversion disorder. *Neurology, 67*, 2036–2038.

Gibbons, D., & De Jarnette, J. (1972). Hypnotic susceptibility and religious experience. *Journal for the Scientific Study of Religion, 11*, 152–156.

Gilboa, A. 92204). Autobiographical and episodic memory—one and the same? Evidence from prefrontal activation in neuroimaging studies. *Neuropsychologia, 42*, 1336–1349.

Gleaves, D. H., May, M. C., & Cardeña, E. (2001). An examination of the diagnostic validity of dissociative identity disorder. *Clinical Psychology Review, 21*, 577–608.

Glisky, M. L., Tartaryn, D. J., McConkey, K. M., Tobias, B. A., & Kihlstrom, J. F. (1991). Absorption, openness to experience, and hypnotizability. *Journal of Personality and Social Psychology, 60*, 263–272.

Gold, S. N. (2004). Fight Club: A depiction of contemporary society as dissociogenic. *Journal of Trauma & Dissociation, 5(2)*, 13–34.

Goodman, F. D. (1981). *The exorcism of Anneliese Michel.* New York: Doubleday.

Goodman, F. D. (1988). *How about demons? Possession and exorcism in the modern world.* Bloomington, IN: Indiana University Press.

Goodman, F. D. (1990). *Where the spirits ride the wind: Trance journeys and other ecstatic experiences.* Bloomington, IN: Indiana University Press.

Greenberg, D. L., & Rubin, D. C. (2003). The neuropsychology of autobiographical memory. *Cortex, 39*, 687–728.

Groth-Marnat, G., & Jeffs, M. (2002). Personality factors from the five-factor model of personality that predict dissociative tendencies in a clinical population. *Personality and Individual Differences, 32*, 969–976.

Gurney, E. (1884a). The problem of hypnotism. *Society for Psychical Research Proceedings, 2*, 265–292.

Gusnard, D. A., & Raichle, M. E. (2001). Searching for a baseline: Functional imaging and the resting human brain. *Nature Reviews Neuroscience, 2*, 685–694.

Haggard, P., Cartledge, P., Dafydd, M., & Oakley, D. A. (2004). Anomalous control: When "free-will" is not conscious. *Consciousness and Cognition, 13*, 646–654.

Halleck, S. (1989, October). Dissociative phenomena and the question of responsibility. Presidential address. Society for Clinical and Experimental Hypnosis. Revised version published in the *International Journal of Clinical and Experimental Hypnosis, 38*, 298–314.

Halligan, P. W., Athwal, B. S., Oakley, D. A., & Frackowiak, R. S. J. (2000). Imaging hypnotic paralysis: Implications for conversion hysteria. *Lancet, 355*, 986–987.

Hargadon, R., Bowers, K. S., & Woody, E. Z. (1995). Does counterpain imagery mediate hypnotic analgesia? *Journal of Abnormal Psychology, 104*, 508–516.

Harriman, P. L. (1942a). The experimental induction of multiple personality. *Psychiatry, 5*, 179–186.

Harriman, P. L. (1942b). The experimental production of some phenomena related to multiple personality. *Journal of Abnormal and Social Psychology, 37*, 244–255.

Harriman, P. L. (1943). A new approach to multiple personalities. *American Journal of Orthopsychiatry, 13*, 638–643.

Harris, R. (1991). Introduction. In J.-M. Charcot (1889/1991), *Clinical lectures on diseases of the nervous system*, Volume III (pp. ix–lxviii). London: Tavistock/Routledge.

Hart, B. (1910). The conception of the subconscious. *Journal of Abnormal Psychology, 4*, 351–371.

Hart, B. (1927). The conception of dissociation. *British Journal of Medical Psychology, 6*, 241–263.

Hastings, A. (1991). *With the tongues of men and angels. A study of channeling.* Fort Worth, TX: Holt, Rinehart and Winston.

Heim, A. (1892). Notizen über den Tod durch absturz (Remarks on fatal falls). *Jahrbuch des Schweizer Alpenclub, 27*, 327–337. Translated and reprinted in English as R. Noyes & R. Kletti (1980). The experience of dying from falls. In R. A. Kalish (Ed.), *Death, dying, transcending* (pp. 129–136). Farmingdale, NY: Baywood Publishing Company.

Hennig-Fast, K., Meister, F., Frodl, T., Beraldi, A., Padberg, F., Engel, R. R., Reiser, M., Möller, H.-J., & Meindl, T. (2008). A case of persistent retrograde amnesia following a dissociative fugue: neuropsychological and neurofunctional underpinnings of loss of autobiographical memory and self-awareness. *Neuropsychologia, 46*, 2993–3005.

Hermans, E. J., Nijenhuis, E. R. S., van Honk, J., Huntjens, R. J. C., & van der Hart, O. (2006). Identity state-dependent attentional bias for facial threat in dissociative identity disorder. *Psychiatry Research, 141*, 233–236.

Herskovits, M. J. (1971). *Life in a Haitian valley.* Garden City, NJ: Doubleday.

Hilgard, E. R. (1965). *Hypnotic susceptibility.* New York: Harcourt, Brace, and World, Inc.

Hilgard, E. R. (1977/1986). *Divided consciousness: Multiple controls in human thought and action.* New York: John Wiley & Sons.

Hilgard, E. R., Weitzenhoffer, A. M., & Gough, P. (1958). Individual differences in susceptibility to hypnosis. *Proceedings of the National Academy of Science, 44*, 1255–1259.

Hilgard, E. R., Weitzenhoffer, A. M., Landes, J., & Moore, R. K. (1961). The distribution of susceptibility to hypnosis in a student population: A study using the Stanford Hypnotic Susceptibility Scale. *Psychological Monographs: General and Applied, 75(8)*, 1–22.

Hilgard, J. (1970). *Personality and hypnosis: A study of imaginative involvement.* Chicago: University of Chicago Press.

Hocutt, M. (1974). Aristotle's four becauses. *Philosophy, 49*, 385–399.

Hoeft, F., Reiss, A., Whitfield-Gabrieli, S., Gabrieli, J., Greicius, M., Menon, V., & Spiegel, D. (2008, May). *Neural basis of hypnotizability.* Paper presented at the American Psychiatric Association, Washington, DC.

Holmes, E. A., Brown, R. J., Mansell, W., Fearon, R. P., Hunter, E. C. M., Frasquilho, F., & Oakley, D. A. (2005). Are there two qualitatively different forms of dissociation? A review and some clinical implications. *Clinical Psychology Review, 25*, 1–23.

Horowitz, M. J. (1986/2001). *Stress response syndromes*, fourth edition. Northvale, NJ: Jason Aronson Inc.

Horton, J. E., Crawford, H. J., Harrington, G., & Downs, J. H. III (2004). Increased anterior corpus callosum size associated positively with hypnotizability and the ability to control pain. *Brain, 127*, 1741–1747.

Howley, J., & Ross, C. A. (2003). The structure of dissociative fugue: A case report. *Journal of Trauma & Dissociation, 4(4),* 109–124.

Huba, G. J., Aneshensel, C. S., & Singer, J. L. (1981). Development of scales for three second-order factors of inner experience. *Multivariate Behavior Research, 16*, 181–206.

Hull, C. L. (1933). *Hypnosis and suggestibility: An experimental approach*. New York: Appleton-Century-Crofts.

Huntjens, R. J. C. (2003). *Apparent amnesia: Interidentity memory functioning in dissociative identity disorder*. Ridderkirk, The Netherlands: Ridderprint offsetdrukkerij.

Huntjens, R. J. C., Postma, A., Hamaker, E. L., Woertman, L., Van der Hart, O., & Peters, M. (2002). Perceptual and conceptual priming in patients with dissociative identity disorder. *Memory & Cognition, 30*, 1033–1043.

Huntjens, R. J. C., Postma, A., Peters, M. L., Woertman, L., & van der Hart, O. (2003). Interidentity amnesia for neutral, episodic information in dissociative identity disorder. *Journal of Abnormal Psychology, 112*, 290–297.

Huxley, T. (1874). On the hypothesis that animals are automata, and its history. *Nature, 19*, 362–366.

Irle, E., Lange, C., Weniger, G., & Sachsse, U. (2007). Size abnormalities of the superior parietal cortices are related to dissociation in borderline personality disorder. *Psychiatry Research Neuroimaging, 156*, 139-149.

James, W. (1889). Notes on automatic writing. *Proceedings of the [Old] American Society for Psychical Research*, 1, 548–564.

James, W. (1890). The hidden self. *Scribner's Magazine, 7(3),* 361–373.

James, W. (1902/2003). *The varieties of religious experience: A study in human nature*. New York: Routledge.

Janet, P. (1886). Les actes inconscients et le dédoublement de la personnalité pendant somnambulisme provoqué. *Revue Philosophique, 22*, 577–592. [Reprinted in (1928) *American Journal of Psychiatry, 8*, 209–234]

Janet, P. (1887). L'anesthésie sytématisée et la dissociation des phénomènes psychologiques. *Revue Philosophique, 23*, 449–472.

Janet, P. (1888). Les actes inconscients et la mémoire pendant le somnambulisme. *Revue Philosophique, 25*, 238–279.

Janet, P. (1889). *L'automatisme psychologique: essai de psychologie expérimentale sur les formes inférieures de l'activité humaine* [Psychological automatism: Experimental-psychological essay on the inferior forms of human activity]. Paris: Félix Alcan.

Janet, P. (1893/1901/1977). *The mental state of hystericals: A study of mental stigmata and mental accidents*. Washington, DC: University Publications of America, 1977.

Janet, P. (1907/1910). The subconscious. In M. Prince (Ed.), *Subconscious phenomena* (pp. 53–70). Boston: Richard G. Badger, The Gorham Press.

Janet, P. (1914). Psychoanalysis. *Journal of Abnormal Psychology, 9*, 1–35.

Janet, P. (1919/1925/1976). *Psychological healing: A historical and clinical study*. New York: Arno Press.

Janet, P. (1920/1929/1965). *The major symptoms of hysteria*. New York: Hafner Publishing Company.

Janet, P. (1930). Autobiography of Pierre Janet. In C. Murchison (Ed.), *History of psychology in autobiography*, Vol. 1 (pp. 123–133). Worcester MA: Clark University Press.

Jang, K. L., Paris, J., Zweig-Frank, H., & Livesley, W. J. (1998). Twin study of dissociative experience. *Journal of Nervous and Mental Disease, 186*, 345–351.

Johnson, M. K., Foley, M. A., Suengas, A. G., & Raye, C. L. (1988). Phenomenal characteristics of memories for perceived and imagined autobiographical events. *Journal of Experimental Psychology: General, 117,* 371–376.

Jones, E. (1961). *The life and work of Sigmund Freud*. New York: Basic Books.

Jones, S. R., & Fernyhough, C. (2008). Talking back to the spirits: the voices and visions of Emanuel Swedenborg. *History of the Human Sciences, 21*, 1–31.

Jung, C. G. (1902/1978). On the psychology and pathology of so-called occult phenomena. *Collected works of C. G. Jung*, Vol. 1 (pp. 3–88). Princeton, NJ: Princeton University Press.

Kampman, R. (1976). Hypnotically induced multiple personality: An experimental study. *International Journal of Clinical and Experimental Hypnosis, 24*, 215–227.

Kapur, N., Ellison, D., Smith, M. P., McLellan, D. L., & Burrows, E. H. (1992). Focal retrograde amnesia following bilateral temporal lobe pathology. *Brain, 115*, 73–85.

Kihlstrom, J. F. (1985). Hypnosis. *Annual Review of Psychology, 36*, 385–418.

Kihlstrom, J. F. (1992). Hypnosis: A sesquicentennial essay. *International Journal of Clinical and Experimental Hypnosis, 40*, 301–314.

Kihlstrom, J. F. (1998). Dissociations and dissociation theory in hypnosis: Comment on Kirsch and Lynn (1998). *Psychological Bulletin, 123*, 186–191.

Kihlstrom, J. F., Glisky, M. L., & Angiulo, M. J. (1994). Dissociative tendencies and dissociative disorders. *Journal of Abnormal Psychology, 103*, 117–124.

Kindt, M., & Van den Hout, M. (2003). Dissociation and memory fragmentation: Experimental effects on meta-memory but not on actual memory performance. *Behaviour Research and Therapy, 41*, 167–178.

Kirmayer, L. J. (1994). Pacing the void: Social and cultural dimensions of dissociation. In D. Spiegel (Ed.), *Dissociation: Culture, mind, and body* (pp. 91–122). Washington, DC: American Psychiatric Press.

Kirsch, I. (1991). The social learning theory of hypnosis. In S. J. Lynn & J. W. Rhue (Eds.), *Theories of hypnosis: Current models and perspectives* (pp. 439–465). New York: Guilford Press.

Kirsch, I., & Lynn, S. J. (1998). Dissociation theories of hypnosis. *Psychological Bulletin, 123*, 100–115.

Kluft, R. P. (1984). Multiple personality in childhood. *Psychiatric Clinics of North America, 7*, 121–134.

Kluft, R. P. (1985a). Making the diagnosis of multiple personality disorder (MPD). In F. F. Flach (Ed.), *Directions in psychiatry, 5(23)*, 1–10.

Kluft, R. P. (1985b). The natural history of multiple personality disorder. In R. P. Kluft (Ed.), *Childhood antecedents of multiple personality* (pp. 197–238). Washington, DC: American Psychiatric Press.

Kluft, R. P. (1987). First-rank symptoms as a diagnostic clue to multiple personality disorder. *American Journal of Psychiatry, 144*, 293–298.

Kluft, R. P. (1995). Current controversies surrounding dissociative identity disorder. In L. Cohen, J. Berzoff, & M. Elin (Eds.), *Dissociative identity disorder: Theoretical and treatment controversies* (pp. 347–377). Northvale, NJ: Jason Aronson.

Koenen, K. C., Saxe, G., Purcell, S., Smoller, J. W., Bartholomew, D., Miller, A., Hall, E., Kaplow, J., Bosquet, M., Moulton, S., & Baldwin, C. (2005). Polymorphisms in FKBP5 are associated with peritraumatic dissociation in medically injured children. *Molecular Psychiatry, 10*, 1058–1059.

Krippner, S. (1994). Cross-cultural perspectives on dissociative disorders. In S. J. Lynn & J. W. Rhue (Eds.), *Dissociation: Clinical and theoretical perspectives* (pp. 338–361). New York: Guilford Press.

Krippner, S. (1997). Dissociation in many times and places. In S. Krippner & S. M. Powers (Eds.), *Broken images, broken selves: Dissociative narratives in clinical practice* (pp. 3–40). Washington, DC: Brunner/Mazel.

Kritchevsky, M., Chang, J., & Squire, L. R. (2004). Functional amnesia: Clinical description and neuropsychological profile of 10 cases. *Learning & Memory, 11*, 213–226.

Kumar, V. K., Pekala, R. J., & Marcano, G. (1996). Hypnotizability, dissociativity, and phenomenological experience. *Dissociation, 9*, 143–153.

Kuyk, J., van Dyck, R., & Spinhoven, P. (1996). A case for a dissociative interpretation of pseudoepileptic seizures. *Journal of Nervous and Mental Disease, 184*, 468–474.

Laddis, A., & Dell, P. F. (2002, November). A comparison of borderline personality disorder and dissociative identity disorder with the Multidimensional Inventory of Dissociation. Paper presented at the conference of the International Society for the Study of Dissociation, Baltimore, MD.

Lanius, R. A., Williamson, K., Boksman, M., Densmore, M., Gupta, J. W. J., Gati, J. S., & Menon, R. (2002). Brain activation during script-driven imagery induced dissociative responses in PTSD: A functional MRI investigation. *Biological Psychiatry, 52*, 305–311.

Lanius, R. A., Bluhm, R., & Lanius, U. (2007). Posttraumatic stress disorder symptom provocation and neuroimaging. In E. Vermetten, M. J. Dorahy, & D. Spiegel (Eds.), *Traumatic dissociation: Neurobiology and treatment* (pp. 191–217). Washington, DC: American Psychiatric Press.

Laycock, T. (1845). On the reflex function of the brain. *British and Foreign Medical Review, 19*, 298–311.

Laycock, T. (1876). Reflex, automatism, and unconscious cerebration. *Journal of Mental Science, 21*, 477–498 and *22*, 1–17.

Leavitt, H. C. (1947). A case of hypnotically produced secondary and tertiary personalities. *Psychoanalytic Review, 34*, 274–295.

LeDoux, J. (1996). *The emotional brain: The mysterious underpinnings of emotional life*. New York: Simon & Schuster.

Lee-Teng, E. (1965). Trance-susceptibility, induction-susceptibility, and acquiescence as factors in hypnotic performance. *Journal of Abnormal Psychology, 70*, 383–389.

Lewis, I. M. (2003). *Ecstatic religion: A study of shamanism and spirit possession*, third edition. New York: Routledge.

Lewis-Fernández, R. (1994). Culture and dissociation: A comparison of *ataque de nervios* among Puerto Ricans and possession syndrome in India. In D. Spiegel (Ed.), *Dissociation: Culture, mind, and body* (pp. 123–167). Washington, DC: American Psychiatric Press.

Lewis-Fernández, R. (1992/1998). The proposed DSM-IV Trance and Possession Disorder category. *Transcultural Psychiatric Research Review, 29(4)*, 301–317. Reprinted in R. J. Castillo (Ed.), *Meanings of madness* (pp. 234–240). Boston: Brooks/Cole Publishing Company.

Lichtenberg, P., Bachner-Melman, R., Ebstein, R. P., & Crawford, H. J. (2004). Hypnotic susceptibility: Multidimensional relationships with Cloninger's Tridimensional Personality Questionnaire, COMT polymorphisms, absorption, and attentional characteristics. *International Journal of Clinical and Experimental Hypnosis, 52*, 47–72.

Lichtenberg, P., Bachner-Melman, R., Gritsenko, I., & Ebstein, R. P. (2000). Exploratory association study between catechol-*O*-methyltransferase (COMT) high/low enzyme activity polymorphism and hypnotizability. *American Journal of Medical Genetics, 96*, 771–774.

Lichtenberg, P., Even-Or, E., Bachner-Melman, R., Levin, R., Brin, A., & Heresco-Levy, U. (2008). Hypnotizability and blink rate: A test of the dopamine hypothesis. *International Journal of Clinical and Experimental Hypnosis, 56*(3), 243–254.

Lichtenberg, P., Even-Or, E., Bar, G., Levin, E., Brin, A., & Heresco-Levy, U. (2007). Reduced prepulse inhibition is associated with increased hypnotizability. *International Journal of Neuropsychopharmacology, 11*, 541–545.

Lisman, J. E., & Otmakhova, N. A. (2001). Storage, recall, and novelty detection of sequences by the hippocampus: Elaborating on the SOCRATIC model to account for normal and aberrant effects of dopamine. *Hippocampus, 11*, 551–568.

Loewenstein, R. J. (1991a). An office mental status examination for chronic complex dissociative symptoms and multiple personality disorder. *Psychiatric Clinics of North America, 14*, 567–604.

Loewenstein, R. J. (1991b). Psychogenic amnesia and psychogenic fugue: A comprehensive review. In A. Tasman & S. M. Goldfinger (Eds.), *American Psychiatric Press Review of Psychiatry*, Vol. 10 (pp. 189–221). Washington, DC: American Psychiatric Press.

Loewenstein, R. J., & Putnam, F. W. (2004). Dissociative disorders. In B. J. Sadock & V. A. Sadock (Eds.), *Comprehensive textbook of psychiatry*, eighth edition (pp. 1844–1901). Baltimore, MD: Lippincott, Williams & Wilkins.

Ludwig, A. M. (1983). The psychobiological functions of dissociation. *American Journal of Clinical Hypnosis, 26*, 93–99.

Luys, J. (1876/1887). *The brain and its functions*. New York: Appleton.

Lynn, S. J., Meyer, E., & Shindler, K. (2004). Clinical correlates of high hypnotizability. In M. Heap, R. J. Brown, & D. A. Oakley (Eds.), *The highly hypnotizable person: Theoretical, experimental and clinical issues* (pp. 187–212). London and New York: Routledge.

Lynn, S. J., & Rhue, J. W. (1988). Fantasy proneness: Hypnosis, developmental antecedents, and psychopathology. *American Psychologist, 43*, 35–44.

Lynn, S. J., Rhue, J. W., & Green, J. P. (1988). Multiple personality and fantasy proneness: Is there an association or dissociation? *British Journal of Experimental and Clinical Hypnosis, 5*, 138–142.

Mackintosh, N. J. (1975). A theory of attention: Variations in the associability of stimulus with reinforcement. *Psychological Review, 82*, 276–298.

Macmillan, M. (1986). Souvenir de la Salpêtrière: M. le Dr. Freud à Paris, 1885. *Australian Psychologist, 21*, 3–29.

Macmillan, M. (1997). *Freud evaluated: The completed arc*. Cambridge, MA: MIT Press.

Mailis-Gagnon, A., Giannoylis, I., Downar, J., Kwan, C. L., Mikulis, D. J., Crawley, A. P., Nicholson, K., & Davis, K. D. (2003). Altered central somatosensory processing in chronic pain patients with "hysterical" anesthesia. *Neurology, 60*, 1501–1507.

Marchetti, C., & Della Sala, S. (1998). Disentangling the alien and anarchic hand. *Cognitive Neuropsychiatry, 3*, 191–207.

Markowitsch, H. J. (1998). The mnestic block syndrome: Environmentally induced amnesia. *Neurology, Psychiatry and Brain Research, 6*, 73–80.

Markowitsch, H. J. (1999). Functional neuroimaging correlates of functional amnesia. *Memory, 7*, 561–583.

Markowitsch, H. J., Calabrese, P., Haupts, M., Durwen, H. F., Liess, J., & Gehlen, W. (1993). Searching for the anatomical basis of retrograde amnesia. *Journal of Clinical and Experimental Neuropsychology, 15*, 947–967.

Markowitsch, H. J., Fink, G. R., Thöne, A., Kessler, J., & Heiss, W.-D. (1997). A PET study of persistent psychogenic amnesia covering the whole life span. *Cognitive Neuropsychiatry, 2*, 135–158.

Marmar, C. R., Weiss, D. S., & Metzler, T. (1998). Peritraumatic dissociation and posttraumatic stress disorder. In J. D. Bremner & C. R. Marmar (Eds.), *Trauma, memory, and dissociation* (pp. 229–247). Washington, DC: American Psychiatric Press.

Marmar, C. R., Weiss, D. S., Metzler, T. J., & Delucchi, K. (1996). Characteristics of emergency services personnel related to peritraumatic dissociation during critical incident exposure. *American Journal of Psychiatry, 153(7)*, July 1996 Festschrift Supplement, 94–102.

Marmar, C. R., Weiss, D. S., Schlenger, W. E., Fairbank, J. A., Jordan, B. K.., Kulka, R. A., & Hough, R. L. (1994). Peritraumatic dissociation and posttraumatic stress in male Vietnam theater veterans. *American Journal of Psychiatry, 151*, 902–907.

Marshall, J. C., Halligan, P. W., Fink, G. R., Wade, D. T., & Frackowiak, R. S. J. (1997). The functional anatomy of hysterical paralysis. *Cognition, 64*, B1–B8.

Martínez-Taboas, A. (1991). Multiple personality disorder as seen from a social constructionist viewpoint. *Dissociation, 4*, 129–133.

Marx, B. P., Forsyth, J. P., Gallup, G. G., Fusé, T., & Lexington, J. M. (2008). Tonic immobility as an evolved predator defense: Implications for sexual assault survivors. *Clinical Psychology: Science and Practice, 15(1)*, 74–90.

Maturana, H. R. (1978). Biology of language: The epistemology of reality. In G. Miller & E. Lenneberg (Eds.), *Psychology and biology of language and thought: Essays in honor of Eric Lenneberg* (pp. 27–63). New York: Academic Press.

Mayer-Gross, W. (1935). On depersonalization. *British Journal of Medical Psychology, 15*, 103–126.

McConkey, K. M., & Barnier, A. J. (2004). High hypnotizability: Unity and diversity in behaviour and experience. In M. Heap, R. J. Brown, & D. A. Oakley (Eds.), *The highly hypnotizable person: Theoretical, experimental and clinical issues* (pp. 61–84). London and New York: Routledge.

McConkey, K. M., Glisky, M. L., & Kihlstrom, J. F. (1989). Individual differences among hypnotic virtuosos. *Australian Journal of Clinical and Experimental Hypnosis, 17*, 131–140.

McCrae, R. R., & Costa, P. T. (1997). Conceptions and correlates of openness to experience. In R. Hogan, J. A. Johnson, & S. R. Briggs (Eds.), *Handbook of personality* (pp. 825–847). London: Academic Press.

McDougall, W. (1926). *Outline of abnormal psychology*. New York: Charles Scribner's Sons.

McDougall, W. (1938). The relation between dissociation and repression. *British Journal of Medical Psychology, 17*, 141–157.

Medford, N., Brierley, B., Brammer, M., Bullmore, E. T., David, A. S., & Phillips, M. L. (2006). Emotional memory in depersonalization disorder. *Psychiatry Research: Neuroimaging, 148*, 93–102.

Messerschmidt, R. (1927–1928). A quantitative investigation of the alleged independent operation of conscious and subconscious processes. *Journal of Abnormal and Social Psychology, 22*, 325–340.

Miller, M. E., & Bowers, K. S. (1993). Hypnotic analgesia: Dissociated experience or dissociated control? *Journal of Abnormal Psychology, 102*, 29–38.

Mitchell, M. B. (1932). Retroactive inhibition and hypnosis. *Journal of General Psychology, 7*, 343–358.

Mitchell, T. W. (1912). Some types of multiple personality. *Proceedings of the Society for Psychical Research, 26*, 257–285.

Mitchell, T. W. (1921). *The psychology of medicine*. London: Methuen & Co.

Mitchell, T. W. (1923). *Medical psychology and psychical research*. New York: E. P. Dutton and Company.

Mitchell, T. W. (1925). Divisions of the self and co-consciousness. In C. M. Campbell, H. S. Langfeld, W. McDougall, A. A. Roback, & E. W. Taylor (Eds.), *Problems of personality: Studies presented to Dr. Morton Prince, pioneer in American psychopathology* (pp. 189–203). London: Kegan Paul, Trench, Trubner, & Co.

Mobbs, D., Petrovic, P., Marchant, J. L., Hassabis, D., Weiskopf, N., Seymour, B., Dolan, R. J., & Frith, C. D. (2007). When fear is near: Threat imminence elicits prefrontal-periaqueductal gray shifts in humans. *Science, 317*, 1079–1083.

Moore, A. U., & Amstey, M. S. (1962). Tonic immobility: differences in susceptibility of experimental and normal sheep and goats. *Science, 135*, 729–730.

Morgan, A. H. (1973). The heritability of hypnotic susceptibility of twins. *Journal of Abnormal Psychology, 82*, 55–61.

Morgan, A. H., Hilgard, E. R., & Davert, E. C. (1970). The heritability of the hypnotic susceptibility of twins: A preliminary report. *Behavior Genetics, 1,* 213–224.

Morgan, C. A., Hazlett, G., Wang, S., Richardson, E. G., Jr., Schnurr, P., & Southwick, S. M. (2001). Symptoms of dissociation in humans experiencing acute, uncontrollable stress: A prospective investigation. *American Journal of Psychiatry, 158*, 1239–1247.

Myers, C. S. (1940). *Shell shock in France 1914–1918*. Cambridge: Cambridge University Press.

Myers, F. W. H. (1884). A telepathic explanation of some co-called spiritualistic phenomena. *Society for Psychical Research Proceedings, 2*, 217–237.

Myers, F. W. H. (1885b). Automatic writing II. *Society for Psychical Research Proceedings, 3*, 1–63.

Myers, F. W. H. (1888). French experiments in the strata of personality. *Proceedings of the Society for Psychical Research, 5*, 374–397.

Myers, F. W. H. (1889). Automatic writing. IV. The daemon of Socrates. *Proceedings of the Society of Psychical Research, 5*, 522–547.

Myers, F. W. H. (1903). *Human personality and its survival of bodily death*. London: Longmans, Green and Company.

Nace, E. P., Orne, M. T., & Hammer, A. G. (1974): Posthypnotic amnesia as an active psychic process: The reversibility of amnesia. *Archives of General Psychiatry, 31*, 257–260.

Nadon, R. (1997). What this field needs is a good nomological network. *International Journal of Clinical and Experimental Hypnosis, 45,* 314–323.

Nadon, R., Hoyt, I. P., Register, P. A., & Kihlstrom, J. F. (1991). Absorption and hypnotizability: Context effects reexamined. *Journal of Personality and Social Psychology, 60*, 144–153.

Näring, G., & Nijenhuis, E. R. S. (2005). Relationships between self-reported potentially traumatizing events, psychoform and somatoform dissociation, and absorption, in two non-clinical populations. *Australia and New Zealand Journal of Psychiatry, 39*, 982–988.

Nash, M. R., & Lynn, S. J. (1985). Child abuse and hypnotic ability. *Imagination, Cognition, and Personality, 5*, 211–218.

Nash, M. R., Lynn, S. J., & Givens, D. L. (1984). Adult hypnotic susceptibility, childhood punishment, and child abuse: A brief communication. *International Journal of Clinical and Experimental Hypnosis, 32*, 6–11.

Negro, P. J. (2002). Do religious mediumship dissociative experiences conform to the sociocognitive theory of dissociation? *Journal of Trauma and Dissociation, 3(1)*, 51–73.

Nemiah, J. C. (1979). Dissociative amnesia: A clinical and theoretical reconsideration. In J. F. Kihlstrom & F. J. Evans (Eds.), *Functional disorders of memory* (pp. 303–324). Hillsdale, NJ: Erlbaum.

Newberg, A. B., Wintering, N. A., Morgan, D., & Waldman, M. R. (2006). The measurement of regional cerebral blood flow during glossolalia: A preliminary SPECT study. *Psychiatry Research: Neuroimaging, 148*, 67–71.

Nijenhuis, E. R. S. (2009). Somatoform dissociation and somatoform dissociative disorders. In P. F. Dell & J. A. O'Neil (Eds.), *Dissociation and the dissociative disorders: DSM-V and beyond* (pp. 259–276). New York: Routledge.

Nijenhuis, E. R. S., Vanderlinden, J., & Spinhoven, P. (1998). Animal defense reactions as a model for dissociative reactions. *Journal of Traumatic Stress, 11,* 243–260. Reprinted in E. R. S. Nijenhuis (1999). *Somatoform dissociation: Phenomena, measurement, and theoretical issues* (pp. 108–124). Assen, The Netherlands: Gorcum.

Nogrady, H., McConkey, K. M., Laurence, J.-R., Perry, C. (1983). Dissociation, duality, and demand characteristics in hypnosis. *Journal of Abnormal Psychology, 92*, 223–235.

Noyes, R., Hoenk, P. R., Kuperman, S., & Slymen, D. J. (1977). Depersonalization in accident victims and psychiatric patients. *Journal of Nervous and Mental Disease, 164*, 401–407.

Noyes, R., & Kletti, R. (1976). Depersonalization in the face of life-threatening danger: A description. *Psychiatry, 39*, 19–27.

Noyes, R., Kletti, R., & Kupperman, S. (1977). Depersonalization in response to life-threatening danger. *Comprehensive Psychiatry, 18,* 375–384.

Noyes, R., & Slymen, D. J. (1978–1979). The subjective response to life-threatening danger. *Omega, 9,* 313–321.

Oakley, D. A. (1999a). Hypnosis and consciousness: A structural model. *Contemporary Hypnosis, 16*, 215–223.

Oakley, D. A. (1999b). Hypnosis and conversion hysteria: A unifying model. *Cognitive Neuropsychiatry, 4*, 243–265.

Oakman, J. M., & Woody, E. Z. (1996). A taxometric analysis of hypnotic susceptibility. *Journal of Personality and Social Psychology, 71,* 980–991.

Oesterreich, T. K. (1921/1966). *Possession demoniacal and other among primitive races, in antiquity, the middle ages, and modern times*. New Hyde Park, NY: University Books.

Öhman, A., Dimberg, U., & Öst, L.-G. (1985). Animal and social phobias: Biological constraints on learned fear responses. In S. Reiss & R. R. Bootzin (Eds.), *Theoretical issues in behavioral therapy* (pp. 123–175). New York: Academic Press.

Öhman, A., Hamm, A., & Hugdahl, K. (2000). Cognition and the autonomic nervous system: Orienting, anticipation, and conditioning. In J. T. Cacioppo, L. G. Tassinary, & G. G. Berntson (Eds.), *Handbook of psychophysiology*, second edition (pp. 533–575). Cambridge: Cambridge University Press.

Öhman, A., & Mineka, S. (2001). Fears, phobias, and preparedness: Toward an evolved module of fear and fear learning. *Psychological Review, 108*, 483–522.

Owen, A. R. G. (1971). *Hysteria, hypnosis and healing: The work of J.-M. Charcot*. New York: Garrett Publications.

Ozer, E. J., Best, S. R., Lipsey, T. L., & Weiss, D. S. (2003). Predictors of posttraumatic stress disorder and symptoms in adults: A meta-analysis. *Psychological Bulletin, 129*, 52–73.

Öztürk, E., & Şar, V. (2006). Apparently normal family. A contemporary agent of transgenerational trauma and dissociation. *Journal of Trauma Practice, 4,* 287–303.

Page, H. (1883). *Injuries of the spine and spinal cord without apparent mechanical lesions, and nervous shock, in their surgical and medico-legal aspects*. London: Churchill.

Pain, C., Bluhm, R. L., & Lanius, R. A. (2009). Dissociation in patients with chronic PTSD: Hyperactivation and hypoactivation patterns, clinical and neuroimaging perspectives. In P. F. Dell & J. A. O'Neil (Eds.), *Dissociation and the dissociative disorders: DSM-V and beyond* (pp. 373–382). New York: Routledge.

Panasetis, P., & Bryant, R. A. (2003). Peritraumatic versus persistent dissociation in acute stress disorder. *Journal of Traumatic Stress, 16*, 563–566.

Panksepp, J. (1998). *Affective neuroscience: The foundations of human and animal emotions*. New York: Oxford University Press.

Panksepp, J. (2004). Emerging neuroscience of fear and anxiety: Therapeutic practice and clinical implications. In J. Panksepp (Ed.), *Textbook of biological psychiatry* (pp. 489–519). Hoboken, NJ: Wiley-Liss.

Pearce, J. M., & Hall, G. (1980). A model for Pavlovian conditioning: Variations in the effectiveness of conditioned but not of unconditioned stimuli. *Psychological Review, 87*, 532–552.

Pekala, R. J. (1991a). Hypnotic types: Evidence from a cluster analysis of phenomenal experience. *Contemporary Hypnosis, 8*, 95–104.

Pekala, R. J. (1991b). *The phenomenology of consciousness inventory*. West Chester, PA: The Mid-Atlantic Educational Institute.

Pekala, R. J., & Forbes, E. J. (1997). Types of hypnotically (un) susceptible individuals as a function of phenomenological experience: Towards a typology of hypnotic types. *American Journal of Clinical Hypnosis, 39,* 212–224.

Pekala, R. J., & Kumar, V. K. (2000). Operationalizing "trance" I: rationale and research using a psychophenomenological approach. *American Journal of Clinical Hypnosis, 43,* 107–135.

Pekala, R. J., Kumar, V. K., & Marcano, G. (1995). Hypnotic types: A partial replication concerning phenomenal experience. *Contemporary Hypnosis, 12*, 194–206.

Pekala, R. J., & Nagler, R. (1989). The assessment of hypnoidal states: Rationale and clinical application. *American Journal of Clinical Hypnosis, 31*, 231–236.

Perry, B. D. (1999). The memories of states: How the brain stores and retrieves traumatic experience. In J. Goodwin & R. Attias (1999), *Splintered reflections: Images of the body in trauma* (pp. 9–38). New York: Basic Books.

Perry, B. D., Pollard, R. A., Blakley, T. L., Baker, W. I., & Vigilante, D. (1995). Childhood trauma, the neurobiology of adaptation, and "use-dependent" development of the brain: How "states" become "traits." *Infant Mental Health Journal, 16,* 271–291.

Perry, C., & Laurence, J.-R. (1984). Mental processing outside of awareness: The contributions of Freud and Janet. In K. S. Bowers & D. Meichenbaum (Eds.), *The unconscious reconsidered* (pp. 9–48). New York: John Wiley and Sons.

Phillips, M. L., Medford, N., Senior, C., Bullmore, E. T., Suckling, J., Brammer, M. J., Andrew, C., Sierra, M., Williams, S. C., & David, A. S. (2001) Depersonalization disorder: thinking without feeling. *Psychiatry Research: Neuroimaging, 108*, 145–160.

Pincus, J. H., & Tucker, G. J. (1985). *Behavioral neurology*, third edition. New York: Oxford University Press.

Pope, H. G., Hudson, J. I., Bodkin, J. A., & Oliva, P. (1998). Questionable validity of "dissociative amnesia" in trauma victims: evidence from prospective studies. *British Journal of Psychiatry, 172,* 210–215.

Pope, H. G., Poliakoff, M. B., Parker, M. P., Boynes, M., & Hudson, J. I. (2007). Is dissociative amnesia a culture-bound syndrome? Findings from a survey of historical literature. *Psychological Medicine, 37,* 225–233.

Porges, S. W. (2004). Neuroception: A subconscious system for detecting threats and safety. *Zero to Three*, May, 19–24.

Prince, M. (1901). The development and the genealogy of the Misses Beauchamp: A preliminary report on a case of multiple personality. *Proceedings of the Society for Psychical Research, 15*, 466–483.

Prince, M. (1905/1908). *The dissociation of a personality: A biographical study in abnormal psychology*. London: Longmans, Green.

Prince, M. (1906). Hysteria from the point of view of dissociated personality. *Journal of Abnormal Psychology, 1(4),* 170–187.

Prince, M. (1907/1910). The subconscious. In M. Prince (Ed.), *Subconscious phenomena* (pp. 71–101). Boston: Richard G. Badger, The Gorham Press.

Prince, M. (1908). Experiments to determine co-conscious (subconscious) ideation. *Journal of Abnormal Psychology, 3(1)*, 33–42.

Prince, M. (1919). The psychogenesis of multiple personality. *Journal of Abnormal Psychology, 14(4)*, 225–280.

Prince, M. (1921). *The unconscious, second edition revised.* New York: Macmillan Company.

Prince, M., & Peterson, F. (1909). Experiments in psycho-galvanic reactions from co-conscious (subconscious) ideas in a case of multiple personality. *Journal of Abnormal Psychology, 3(2),* 114–131.

Putnam, F. W. (1996). Child development and dissociation. *Child and Adolescent Psychiatric Clinics of North America, 5,* 285–302.

Putnam, F. W. (1997). *Dissociation in children and adolescents: A developmental perspective*. New York: Guilford Press.

Putnam, F. K., & Carlson, E. B. (1998). Hypnosis, dissociation, and trauma: Myths, metaphors, and mechanisms. In J. D. Bremner & C. R. Marmar (Eds.), *Trauma, memory, and dissociation* (pp. 27–55). Washington, DC: American Psychiatric Press.

Putnam, F. W., Carlson, E. B., Ross, C. A., Anderson, G., Clark, P., Torem, M., Bowman, E., Coons, P., Chu, J., Dill, D., Loewenstein, R. J., & Braun, B. G. (1996). Patterns of dissociation in clinical and non-clinical samples. *Journal of Nervous and Mental Disease, 184*, 673–679.

Putnam, F. W., Helmers, L. A., & Trickett, P. P. K. (1993). Development, reliability, and validity of a child dissociation scale. *Child Abuse and Neglect, 17*, 731–741.

Puységur, J. M. P. de Chastenet, comte de– (1784). *Rapport des cures opérées à Bayonne par le magnétisme animal, adressé à M. l'abbé de Poulouzat, conseiller clerc au Parlement de Bourdeaux*, par le comte de Puységur, avec notes de M. Duval d'Eprémesnil, conseiller au Parlement de Paris. Bayonne and Paris: Prault.

Ratner, S. C. (1967). Comparative aspects of hypnosis. In J. E. Gordon (Ed.), *Handbook of clinical and experimental hypnosis* (pp. 550–587). New York: Macmillan Company.

Ratner, S. C. (1977). Immobility of invertebrates: What can we learn? *Psychological Record, 27*, 1–13.

Rauschenberger, S. L., & Lynn, S. J. (1995). Fantasy proneness, DSM-III-R Axis I psychopathology, and dissociation. *Journal of Abnormal Psychology, 104*, 373–380.

Rawlings, R. M. (1978). *The genetics of hypnotizability*. Dissertation. University of New South Wales.

Raz, A., Fan, J., & Posner, M. I. (2006). Neuroimaging and genetic associations of attentional an hypnotic processes. *Journal of Physiology-Paris, 99*, 483–491.

Redgrave, P., & Gurney, K. (2006). The short-latency dopamine signal: A role in discovering novel actions? *Nature Reviews Neuroscience, 7*, 967–975.

Reiman, E. M. (1997). The application of positron emission tomography to the study of normal and pathologic emotions. *Journal of Clinical Psychiatry, 58 (Suppl.16)*, 4–12.

Reinders, A. A. T. S., Nijenhuis, E. R. S., Paans, A. M. J., Korf, J., Willemson, A. T. M., & den Boer, J. A. (2003). One brain, two selves. *NeuroImage, 20*, 2119–2125.

Reinders, A. A. T. S., Nijenhuis, E. R. S., Quak, J., Korf, J., Haaksma, J., Paans, A. M. J., Willemson, A. T. M., & den Boer, J. A. (2006). Psychobiological characteristics of dissociative identity disorder: A symptom provocation study. *Biological Psychiatry, 60*, 730–740.

Rescorla, R. A., & Wagner, A. R. (1972). A theory of Pavlovian conditioning: variations in the effectiveness of reinforcement and nonreinforcement. In A. H. Black & W. F. Prokasy (Ed.), *Classical conditioning II: Current research and theory* (pp. 64–99). New York: Applegate-Century-Crofts.

Rhue, J. W., & Lynn, S. J. (1987). Fantasy proneness and psychopathology. *Journal of Personality and Social Psychology, 53*, 327–336.

Rhue, J. W., Lynn, S. J., Henry, S., Buhk, K., & Boyd, P. (1990–1991). Child abuse, imagination, and hypnotizability. *Imagination, Cognition and Personality, 10*, 53–63.

Ribot, T. (1885/1910). *The diseases of the personality*, fourth, revised edition. Chicago: Open Court.

Richet, C. R. (1883). La personnalité et la mémoire dans le somnambulisme. *Revue Philosophique, 15*, 225–242.

Richet, C. R. (1875). Du somnambulisme provoqué. *Journal de l'anatomie et de la physiologie normales et pathologiques de l'homme et des animaux, 11*, 348–378.

Robinson, D. N. (1977). Preface. In P. Janet (1977), *The mental state of hystericals: A study of mental stigmata and mental accidents* (pp. xxi–xxxvii). Washington, DC: University Publications of America.

Roche, S. M., & McConkey, K. M. (1990). Absorption: Nature, assessment, and correlates. *Journal of Personality and Social Psychology, 59*, 91–101.

Rosenbaum, M. (1980). The role of the term schizophrenia in the decline of multiple personality. *Archives of General Psychiatry, 37*, 1383–1385.

Ross, C. A. (1991). Epidemiology of multiple personality disorder and dissociation. *Psychiatric Clinics of North America, 14*, 503–517.

Ross, C. A. (1997). *Dissociative identity disorder: Diagnosis, clinical features, and treatment of multiple personality*, second edition. New York: John Wiley & Sons.

Ross, C. A. (2009). Dissociative amnesia and dissociative fugue. In P. F. Dell & J. A. O'Neil (Eds.), *Dissociation and the dissociative disorders: DSM-V and beyond* (pp. 429–434). New York: Routledge.

Ross, C. A., Heber, S., Norton, G. R., Anderson, D., Anderson, G., & Barchet, P. (1989). The Dissociative Disorders Interview Schedule: A structured clinical interview. *Dissociation, 2*, 169–189.

Ross, C. A., Miller, S. D., & Reagor, P., Bjornson, L., Fraser, G. A., & Anderson, G. (1990). Schneiderian symptoms in multiple personality disorder and schizophrenia. *Comprehensive Psychiatry, 31*, 111–118.

Roth, M., & Argyle, M. (1988). Anxiety, panic, and phobic disorders. *Journal of Psychiatric Research, 22*, 33–54.

Rubin, D. C. (2005). A basic-systems approach to autobiographical memory. *Current Directions in Psychological Science, 14*, 79–83.

Ruby, P., & Legrand, D. (2007). Neuroimaging the self? In Y. Rossetti, P. Haggard, & M. Kawato (Eds.), *Sensorimotor foundations of higher cognition* (pp. 293–318). Oxford: Oxford University Press.

Sackeim, H. A., Nordlie, J. W., & Gur, R. C. (1979). A model of hysterical and hypnotic blindness: Cognition, motivation, and awareness. *Journal of Abnormal Psychology, 88*, 474–489.

Samarin, W. J. (1972). *Tongues of men and angels*. New York: Macmillan.

Sarbin, T. R. (1995). On the belief that one body may be host to two or more personalities. *International Journal of Clinical and Experimental Hypnosis, 13*, 165–183.

Sawamoto, N., Honda, M., Okada, T., Hanakawa, T., Kanda, M., Fukuyama, H., Konishi, J., & Shibasaki, H. (2000).

Expectation of pain enhances responses to nonpainful somatosensory stimulation in the anterior cingulate cortex and parietal operculum/posterior insula: an event-related functional magnetic resonance imaging study. *Journal of Neuroscience, 20*, 7438–7445.

Saxena, S., & Prasad, K. V. S. R. (1989). DSM-III subclassification of dissociative disorders applied to psychiatric outpatients in India. *American Journal of Psychiatry, 146*, 261–262.

Schacter, S. (1996). *Searching for memory: The brain, the mind, and the past*. New York: Basic Books.

Schneider, K. (1959). *Clinical psychopathology*. New York: Grune & Stratton.

Schnider, A. (2003). Spontaneous confabulation and the adaptation of thought to ongoing reality. *Nature Reviews Neuroscience, 4*, 662–671.

Schnider, A., Valenza, N., Morand, S., & Michel, C. M. Early cortical distinction between memories that pertain to ongoing reality and memories that don't. *Cerebral Cortex, 12*, 54–61.

Schore, A. N. (2009). Attachment and the developing right brain: Origins of pathological dissociation. In P. F. Dell & J. A. O'Neil (Eds.), *Dissociation and the dissociative disorders: DSM-V and beyond* (pp. 107–144). New York: Routledge.

Schultz, W., & Dickinson, A. (2000). Neural coding of prediction errors. *Annual Review of Neuroscience, 23*, 473–500.

Segall, S. R. (1996). Metaphors of agency and mechanism in dissociation. *Dissociation, 9*, 154–159.

Shilony, E., & Grossman, F. K. (1993). Depersonalization as a defense mechanism in survivors of trauma. *Journal of Traumatic Stress, 6*, 119–128.

Shor, R. E. (1960). The frequency of naturally occurring "hypnotic-like" experiences in the normal college population. *International Journal of Clinical and Experimental Hypnosis, 8*, 151–163.

Shor, R. E., & Orne, M. T. (1962). *The Harvard Group Scale of Hypnotic Susceptibility*, Form A. Palo Alto, CA: Consulting Psychologists Press.

Shor, R. E., Orne, M. T., & O'Connell, D. N. (1962). Validation and cross-validation of a scale of self-reported personal experiences which predicts hypnotizability. *Journal of Psychology, 53*, 55–75.

Sidis, B. (1898). *The psychology of suggestion*. New York: Appleton.

Sierra, M., & Berrios, G. E. (1998). Depersonalization: Neurobiological perspectives. *Biological Psychiatry, 44*, 898–908.

Sierra, M., Senior, C., Dalton, J., McDonough, M., Bond, A., Phillips, M. L., O'Dwyer, A. M., & David, A. S. (2002). Autonomic response in depersonalization disorder. *Archives of General Psychiatry, 59*, 833–838.

Sigmundi, R. A. (1997). Performance rules for problem-specific defense reactions. In M. E. Bouton & M. S. Fanselow (Eds.), *Learning, motivation, and cognition: The functional behaviorism of Robert C. Bolles* (pp. 305–319). Washington, DC: American Psychological Association.

Simeon, D., & Abugel, J. (2006). *Feeling unreal: Depersonalization disorder and the loss of the self*. Oxford: Oxford University Press.

Simeon, D., Guralnik, O., Hazlett, E. A., Spiegel-Cohen, J., Hollander, E., & Buchsbaum, M. S. (2000). Feeling unreal: A PET study of depersonalization disorder. *American Journal of Psychiatry, 157*, 1782–1788.

Simeon, D., Guralnik, O., Knutelska, M., Yehuda, R., & Schmeidler, J. (2003). Basal norepinephrine in depersonalization disorder. *Psychiatry Research, 121*, 93–97.

Simeon, D., Guralnik, O., Schmeidler, J., Sirof, B., & Knutelska, M. (2001). The role of interpersonal trauma in depersonalization disorder. *American Journal of Psychiatry, 158*, 1027–1033.

Simeon, D., Knutelska, M., Nelson, D., & Guralnik, O. (2003). Feeling unreal: A depersonalization disorder update of 117 cases. *Journal of Clinical Psychiatry, 64*, 990–997.

Simeon, D., Knutelska, M., Yehuda, R., Putnam, F., Schmeidler, J, & Smith, L. M. (2007). Hypothalamic-pituitary-adrenal axis function in dissociative disorders, post-traumatic stress disorder, and healthy volunteers. *Biological Psychiatry, 61*, 966–973.

Sokolov, E. N. (1963). *Perception and the conditioned reflex*. Oxford: Pergamon Press.

Somer, E. (2002). Maladaptive daydreaming: A quantitative study. *Journal of Contemporary Psychotherapy, 32*, 197–212.

Somer, E. (2006). Culture-bound dissociation: A comparative analysis. *Psychiatric Clinics of North America, 29*, 213–226.

Spanos, N. P. (1996). *Multiple identities & false memories: A sociocognitive perspective*. Washington, DC: American Psychological Association.

Spanos, N. P., Mah, C. D., Pawlak, A. E., D'Eon, J. L., & Ritchie, G. (1980). *A multivariate and factor analytic study of hypnotic susceptibility*. Unpublished manuscript, Carleton University, Ottawa, Ontario, Canada.

Spanos, N. P., Weekes, J. R., & Bertrand, L. D. (1985). Multiple personality: A social psychological perspective. *Journal of Abnormal Psychology, 94*, 362–376.

Spanos, N. P., Weekes, J. R., Menary, E., & Bertrand, L. D. (1986). Hypnotic interview and age regression procedures in elicitation of multiple personality symptoms: A simulation study. *Psychiatry, 49*, 298–311.

Spence, S. A., Brooks, D. J., Hirsch, S. R., Liddle, P. F., Meehan, J., & Grasby, P. M. (1997). A PET study of voluntary movement in schizophrenic patients experiencing passivity phenomena (delusions of alien control). *Brain, 120*, 1997–2011.

Spence, S. A., Crimlisk, H. L., Cope, H., Ron, M. A., & Grasby, P. M. (2000). Discrete neurophysiological correlates in prefrontal cortex during hysterical and feigned disorder of movement. *Lancet, 355*, 1243–1244.

Spiegel, D. (1984). Multiple personality as a posttraumatic stress disorder. *Psychiatric Clinics of North America, 7*, 101–110.

Spiegel, D. (1986). Dissociating damage. *American Journal of Clinical Hypnosis, 29*, 123–131.

Spiegel, D. (1990). Hypnosis, dissociation, and trauma: Hidden and overt observers. In J. L. Singer (Ed.), *Repression and dissociation: Implications for personality theory, psychopathology, and health* (pp. 121–142). Chicago: University of Chicago Press.

Spiegel, D. (1991). Dissociation and trauma. In A. Tasman & S. M. Goldfinger (Eds.), *American Psychiatric Press Review of Psychiatry*, Vol. 10 (pp. 261–275). Washington, DC: American Psychiatric Press.

Spiegel, D., Hunt, T., & Dondershine, H. E. (1988). Dissociation and hypnotizability in posttraumatic stress disorder. *American Journal of Psychiatry, 145*, 301–305.

Spiegel, D., & King, R. (1992). Hypnotizability and CSF HVA levels among psychiatric patients. *Biological Psychiatry, 31*, 95–98.

Spiegel, H. (1974). The Grade 5 syndrome: The highly hypnotizable person. *International Journal of Clinical and Experimental Hypnosis, 22*, 303–319.

Steele, K. S., Dorahy, M. J., Van der Hart, O., & Nijenhuis, E. R. S. (2009). Dissociation versus alterations in consciousness: Real but different concepts. In P. F. Dell & J. A. O'Neil (Eds.), *Dissociation and the dissociative disorders: DSM-V and beyond* (pp. 155–170). New York: Routledge.

Stevenson, R. L. (2005). *Across the plains: With other memories and essays*. New York: Cosimo Classics.

Szechtman, H., Woody, E., Bowers, K. S., & Nahmias, C. (1998). Where the imaginal appears real: A positron emission tomography study of auditory hallucinations. *Proceedings of the National Academy of Science of USA, 95*, 1956–1960.

Steinberg, M., Rounsaville, B. J., & Cicchetti, D. V. (1990). The Structured Clinical Interview for DSM-III-R Dissociative Disorders: Preliminary report on a new diagnostic instrument. *American Journal of Psychiatry, 147*, 76–82.

Suarez, S. D., & Gallup, G. G. (1979). Tonic immobility as a response to rape in humans: A theoretical note. *Psychological Record, 29*, 315–320.

Taylor, E. (1996). *William James on consciousness beyond the margin*. Princeton, NJ: Princeton University Press.

Tellegen, A. (1978–1979). On measures and conceptions of hypnosis. *American Journal of Clinical Hypnosis, 21*, 219–236.

Tellegen, A., & Atkinson, G. (1974). Openness to absorbing and self-altering experiences ("absorption"), a trait related to hypnotic susceptibility. *Journal of Abnormal Psychology, 83*, 268–277.

Tellegen, A., Lykken, D. T., Bouchard, T. J., Wilcox, W. J., Segal, N. L., & Rich, S. (1998). Personality similarity in twins reared apart and together. *Journal of Personality and Social Psychology, 54*, 1031–1088.

Thomsen, R., & Oppenheim, H. (1884). Über das Vorkommen und die Bedeutung der Sensorischen Anästhesie bei Erkrankungen des Zentralen Nervensystems. *Archiv für Psychiatrie, 15*, 559–583; 633–680; 656–667.

Tichenor, V., Marmar, C. R., Weiss, D. S., Metzler, T. J., & Ronfeldt, H. M. (1996). The relationship of peritraumatic dissociation and posttraumatic stress: Findings in female Vietnam theater veterans. *Journal of Consulting and Clinical Psychology, 64*, 1054–1059.

Timberlake, W., & Lucas, G. A. (1989). Behavior systems and learning: From misbehavior to general principles. In S. B. Klein & E. R. Mowrer (Eds.), *Contemporary learning theories: Instrumental conditioning theory and the impact of biological constraints on learning* (pp. 237–275). Hillsdale, NJ: Lawrence Erlbaum Associates.

Tinbergen, N. (1951). *The study of instinct*. New York: Oxford University Press.

Trimble, M. (1981) *Post-Traumatic neurosis: From railway spine to whiplash*. NY: John Wiley & Sons.

Tsakiris, M., Hesse, M. D., Boy, C., Haggard, P., & Fink, G. R. (2007). Neural signatures of body ownership: A sensory network for bodily self-consciousness. *Cerebral Cortex, 17*, 2235–2244.

Tulving, E. (1983). *Elements of episodic memory*. Oxford: Oxford University Press.

Tulving, E., Kapur, S., Markowitsch, H. J., Craik, G., Habib, R., & Houle, S. (1994). Neuroanatomical correlates of retrieval in episodic memory: Auditory sentence recognition. *Proceedings of the National Academy of Sciences of the USA, 91*, 2012–2015.

Tulving, E., & Pearlstone, Z. (1966). Availability versus accessibility of information in memory for words. *Journal of Verbal Learning and Behavior, 5*, 381–391.

Ungless, M. A., Magill, P. J., & Bolam, J. P. (2004) Uniform inhibition of dopamine neurons in the ventral tegmental area by aversive stimuli. *Science, 303*, 2040–2042.

Van der Hart, O., & Dorahy, M. (2009). Dissociation: History of a concept. In P. F. Dell & J. A. O'Neil (Eds.), *Dissociation and the dissociative disorders: DSM-V and beyond* (pp. 3–26). New York: Routledge.

Van der Hart, O., Nijenhuis, E., & Steele, K. (2006). *The haunted self: Structural dissociation and the treatment of chronic traumatization*. New York: W. W. Norton & Company.

Van der Hart, O., Nijenhuis, E., Steele, K., & Brown, D. (2004). Trauma-related dissociation: conceptual clarity lost and found. Australian and New Zealand *Journal of Psychiatry, 38*, 906–914.

Van der Kolk, B. A., & Fisler, R. (1995). Dissociation and the fragmentary nature of traumatic memories: Review and experimental confirmation. *Journal of Traumatic Stress, 8*, 505–525.

Van der Kolk, B. A., Van der Hart, O., & Marmar, C. R. (1996). Dissociation and information processing in posttraumatic stress disorder. In B. A. Van der Kolk, A. C. McFarlane, & L. Weisaeth (Eds.), *Traumatic stress: The effects of overwhelming experience on mind, body, and society* (pp. 303–327). New York: Guilford Press.

Van IJzendoorn, M. H., & Schuengel, C. (1996). The measurement of dissociation in normal and clinical populations: Meta-analytic validation of the Dissociative Experiences Scale (DES). *Clinical Psychology Review, 16*, 365–382.

Vázquez, C., Hervás, G., & Pèrez-Sales, P. (2008). Chronic thought suppression and posttraumatic symptoms: Data from the Madrid March 11, 2004 terrorist attack. *Journal of Anxiety Disorders, 22,* 1326–1336.

Vermetten, E., Bremner, J. D., & Spiegel, D. (1998). Dissociation and hypnotizability: A conceptual and methodological perspective on two distinct concepts. In J. D. Bremner & C. R. Marmar (Eds.), *Trauma, memory, and dissociation* (pp. 107–159). Washington, DC: American Psychiatric Press.

Vuilleumier, P., Chicherio, C., Assal, F., Schwartz, S., Slosman, D., & Landis, T. (2001). Functional neuroanatomical correlates of hysterical sensorimotor loss. *Brain, 124*, 1077–1090.

Waelde, L. C., Silvern, L., & Fairbank, J. A. (2005). A taxometric investigation of dissociation in Vietnam veterans. *Journal of Traumatic Stress, 18*, 359–369.

Waller, N. G., Putnam, F. K., & Carlson, E. (1996). Types of dissociation and dissociative types. *Psychological Methods, 1*, 300–321.

Waller, N. G., & Ross, C. A. (1997). The prevalence and biometric structure of pathological dissociation in the general population: Taxometric and behavior genetic findings. *Journal of Abnormal Psychology, 106*, 499–510.

Ward, N. S., Oakley, D. A., Frackowiak, R. S. J., & Halligan, P. W. (2003). Differential brain activations during intentionally simulated and subjectively experienced paralysis. *Cognitive Neuropsychiatry, 8*, 295–312.

Watkins, J. G., & Watkins, H. H. (1997). *Ego states: Theory and therapy*. New York: W. W. Norton and Company.

Watson, D. (2003). Investigating the construct validity of the dissociative taxon: Stability analyses of normal and pathological dissociation. *Journal of Abnormal Psychology, 112*, 298–305.

Way, K. G. (2006). How metaphors shape the concept and treatment of dissociation. *Psychiatric Clinics of North America, 29*, 27–43.

Weinberger, D., Schwartz, G., & Davidson, R. (1979). Low-anxious, high anxious and repressive coping styles: Psychometric patters and behavioral and psychophysiological responses to stress. *Journal of Abnormal Psychology, 88*, 369–380.

Weitzenhoffer, A. M. (1978). Hypnotism and altered states. In A. A. Sugerman & R. E. Shor (Eds.), *Expanding dimensions of consciousness* (pp. 183–225). New York: Springer.

Weitzenhoffer, A. M., & Hilgard, E. R. (1967). *Revised Stanford profile Scales of Hypnotic Susceptibility, Forms I and II*. Palo Alto, CA: Consulting Psychologists Press.

Whalen, J. E., & Nash, M. R. (1996). Hypnosis and dissociation: Theoretical, empirical, and clinical perspectives. In L. K. Michelson & W. J. Ray (Eds.), *Handbook of dissociation: Theoretical, empirical, and clinical perspectives* (pp. 191–206). New York and London: Plenum.

White, R. W., & Shevach, B. J. (1942). Hypnosis and the concept of dissociation. *Journal of Abnormal and Social Psychology, 37*, 309–328.

Wickramasekera, I. E. (1988). *Clinical behavioral medicine: Some concepts and procedures*. New York: Plenum.

Williams, L. M. (2006). An integrative neuroscience model of "significance" processing. *Journal of Integrative Neuroscience, 5*, 1–47.

Wilson, S. C., & Barber, T. X. (1982). The fantasy-prone personality: Implications for understanding imagery, hypnosis, and parapsychological phenomena. In A. A. Sheikh (Ed.), *Imagery: Current theory, research, and application* (pp. 340–387). New York: John Wiley & Sons.

Wolff, P. H. (1987). *The development of behavioral states and the expression of emotions in early infancy*. Chicago: University of Chicago Press.

Woody, E. Z., Barnier, A. J., & McConkey, K. M. (2005). Multiple hypnotizabilities: Differentiating the building blocks of hypnotic response. *Psychological Assessment, 17*, 200–211.

Woody, E. Z., Bowers, K. S., & Oakman, J. M. (1992). A conceptual analysis of hypnotic responsiveness: Experience, individual differences, and context. In E. Fromm & M. R. Nash (Eds.), *Contemporary hypnosis research* (pp. 3–33). New York: Guilford.

Woody, E. Z., Drugovic, & Oakman, J. M. (1997). A reexamination of the role of nonhypnotic suggestibility in hypnotic responding. *Journal of Personality and Social Psychology, 72*, 399–407.

Woody, E., & Szechtman, H. (2000). Hypnotic hallucinations: Towards a biology of epistemology. *Contemporary Hypnosis, 17*, 4–14.

World Health Organization (1992). *The ICD-10 classification of mental and behavioural disorders: Clinical descriptions and diagnostic guidelines*. Geneva: Author.

Yasuno, F., Nishikawa, T., Nakagawa, Y., Ikejiri, Y., Tokunaga, H., Mizuta, I., Shinozaki, K., Hashikawa, K., Sugita, Y., Nishimura, T., & Takeda, M. (2000). Functional anatomical study of psychogenic amnesia. *Psychiatry Research, Neuroimaging Section, 99*, 33–57.

Author Index

C

D

H

M

N

O

P

S

X

Y

Z

Subject Index

Page numbers followed by f indicate figures; those followed by t indicate tables.

Q

R

T

U

V

W